VOLUME 2   Ankara to Azusa

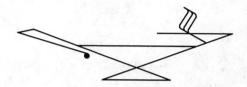

THE ENCYCLOPEDIA
AMERICANA
INTERNATIONAL EDITION

COMPLETE IN THIRTY VOLUMES   FIRST PUBLISHED IN 1829

AMERICANA CORPORATION   International Headquarters: 575 Lexington Avenue, New York, New York 10022

Library of Congress Cataloging in Publication Data
Main entry under title:

THE ENCYCLOPEDIA AMERICANA.

    Published 1828–1858 under title:
Encyclopaedia Americana; 1907–1912: The Americana.
    Includes bibliographical references.
    1. Encyclopedias and dictionaries.
AE5.E333   1974   031   73–8981
ISBN 0–7172–0105–8

ANKARA is the site of the mausoleum of Kemal Atatürk, founder and first president of the Turkish Republic. The mausoleum, which took 19 years to build, was dedicated on Nov. 10, 1953, the 15th anniversary of Atatürk's death.

ANKARA, äng'kə-rə, is the capital of Turkey and the country's second-largest city. It was formerly called *Angora*. The city is situated on the Ankara River, a tributary of the Sakarya, in the heart of the central Anatolian plateau, 220 miles southeast of Istanbul. It is spread out at the foot and along the slope of a mountain that rises to 3,208 feet (978 meters) above sea level.

Ankara is a cosmopolitan city with impressive public buildings, wide avenues, parks, an opera, and an international airport. The city is the site of the University of Ankara, founded in 1946, and of the British Institute of Archaeology, opened in 1948.

Because of its location in central Turkey, Ankara is an important commercial city. It is the processing and marketing center for the surrounding agricultural area, which has long been celebrated for the breeding of long-haired goats and for the production of Angora wool (mohair). Textiles, vaccines, cement, tiles, leather goods, and beer are manufactured there.

History. Known to the ancients as *Ancyra*, the city was from the 200's B.C. the capital of Galatia, which, after 25 B.C., was a Roman province. The city was occupied successively by the Persians, Arabs, Seljuk Turks, and Crusaders. In the 1360's it was captured by the Ottoman Turks. Sultan Bajazet I was defeated in the area in 1402 by Tamerlane, the Mongol conqueror. Recovered by the Turks in 1431, the city remained part of the Ottoman empire until the empire's collapse after World War I.

Ankara was chosen as the site of a provisional government set up by Kemal Atatürk and the Turkish Nationalists in 1920. The choice was made partly as a break with tradition and partly because of Ankara's central location. In 1923 the seat of government was officially transferred to Ankara from the former capital, Istanbul (Constantinople). The name was officially changed from Angora to Ankara in 1930. Population: (1960) 129,934.

ANKING, än'king', is a port in east central China, in Anhwei province, of which it was formerly the capital. The name is also spelled *An-ch'ing*. The city is situated on the north bank of the Yangtze River, midway between Wuhan and Nanking. It is a major tea-trading center, but recurrent floods, and poor connections with other parts of the province have limited its growth.

During the T'ai-p'ing Rebellion insurgents marched through Anking in 1852 and caused considerable damage. By treaty with Britain in 1902, the city was made an open port. From 1912 to 1949 it was known as *Hwaining*. Hofei replaced it as the capital of Anhwei province after World War II. Population: (1958) 129,000.

KUEI-SHENG CHANG, *Wayne State University*

ANKRAH, ang-krä', **Joseph Arthur** (1915–   ), Ghanaian general, who took control of the government after the overthrow of President Nkrumah in 1966. Ankrah was born in Accra on Aug. 18, 1915. He joined the British army in World War II and saw action in Burma. One of the first Ghanaians to receive officer training in Britain, he rose rapidly in the Ghanaian army. During the Congo crisis of 1960–1961, Ankrah commanded the Ghanaian battalion of the UN force in the Congo. He was promoted to major general and chief of defense staff of the Ghanaian army in 1961 but was dismissed in July 1965 by Nkrumah. After the coup of Feb. 24, 1966, he was chosen chairman of the governing National Liberation Council.

L. GRAY COWAN, *Columbia University*

ANN ARBOR, an är'bər, a city in Michigan, is the seat of Washtenaw County and the site of the University of Michigan. It is located on the Huron River, 36 miles west of Detroit, and is served by the Michigan Central and Ann Arbor railroads and by a municipal airport.

Ann Arbor is the trading center for a rich agricultural section. The city's manufacturers in-

1

clude steel ball bearings, machinery and tools, scientific instruments, doors and blinds, cameras, and coil springs. The University of Michigan, established here in 1837, has one of America's greatest libraries, and its colleges of engineering, medicine, and music are outstanding. The hill region surrounding the city has many beautiful lakes and is popular as a vacation resort

Ann Arbor was settled in 1823 by John and Ann Allen, from Virginia, and Elisha and Ann Rumsey, from New York. Allen and Rumsey named the settlement after their wives' first name. It became the county seat in 1824 and was incorporated as a village in 1833. In 1851 it was chartered as a city. Government is by council-manager. Population: 99,797.

ANNA IVANOVNA (1693–1740), an'ə i-vän'ôv-nə, was empress of Russia from 1730 to 1740. Born in Moscow on Jan. 25, 1693, she was the second daughter of Czar Ivan V and was a niece of Peter the Great. In 1710 she was married to Frederick William, duke of Courland, who died almost immediately after the wedding.

After Emperor Peter II died in 1730, the supreme privy council elected Anna to the throne because its members believed she would reign under conditions that would greatly restrict her authority. Anna, however, overthrew the council with the aid of some friends, and appointed a three-man cabinet to help her rule. Her favorite, Ernst Johann Biron, who had no official position in the government, held the real power. Under his influence, Anna's administration of Russia was cruel. Thousands of people were exiled to Siberia, and hundreds of others were executed. She died in St. Petersburg on Oct. 17, 1740.

During Anna's reign, Russia participated successfully in the War of the Polish Succession (1733–1735), which resulted in the accession of August III, the Russian-sponsored candidate, as king of Poland. She also joined Austria in a war against Turkey in the Crimea (1736 and 1739).

ANNA KARENINA, än'nə kä-rā'nyi-na, is a novel by the Russian author Leo Tolstoy (q.v.). It is considered to be one of the masterpieces of world literature. It was first published from 1875 to 1877 as a serial in the *Russki Vestnik* (*Russian Messenger*). The first complete English translation appeared in 1899.

Anna Karenina contains two main narrative lines. The major story deals with the unhappy marriage of Anna and Aleksei Karenin and with Anna's tragic affair with Count Vronsky. The unhappy domestic life of Anna's brother, Prince Stepan Oblonsky, serves to echo Anna's predicament. In contrast, Tolstoy presents the second plot, dealing with the relationship between Kitty Shcherbatskaya and Konstantin Levin, who marry and pursue lives of homely "family happiness." In his examination of these two different stories, Tolstoy creates a multitude of episodes of high life in Moscow and St. Petersburg (now Leningrad) and of country life in the district of Korazinsky. Tolstoy also contrasts the shallowness of Karenin, a public official who moves in a corrupt society, and the serious dedication of the idealistic landowner Levin.

Tolstoy undoubtedly depicted his own nature in the personality of Levin, using this character to voice his observations on philosophy, agronomy, and religion. There is no doubt that Tolstoy drew many of the details of the novel from his own experiences, and the characterizations from his keen study of his relatives and friends. Thus he painted from real life the gambling scenes, the horse racing, the death of Levin's disreputable brother, the hunting episodes, and the quaint naïveté of the peasantry.

Although the novel is distinguished for its fine evocation of the old order in Russia, its greatest strength lies in its brilliant characterizations. In his heroine Anna—a woman of sensitivity and honesty, who also possesses fears and weaknesses—Tolstoy has drawn one of the most unforgettable characters in all fiction. All of the major characters, as well as many of lesser importance, are delineated with equal precision. Despite some carelessness in style and occasional incongruities, *Anna Karenina* is a masterwork of both social history and fiction.

ANNA LEOPOLDOVNA (1718–1746), an'ə lē-ō-pôld'ôv-nə, was regent of Russia for her son, Emperor Ivan VI, who reigned in 1740–1741. Born in Rostock, Germany, on Dec. 18, 1718, she was a niece of Anna Ivanovna, empress of Russia from 1730 to 1740. Anna Leopoldovna married Prince Anthony Ulrich of Brunswick, a nephew of Emperor Charles VI of the Holy Roman Empire. Their first child, Ivan, was born in August 1740. In October 1740, just before her death, the childless Empress Anna Ivanovna named Ivan as her successor and designated Ernst Johann Biron as regent for the child. In November 1740, after Anna Ivanovna's death, Biron was deposed, and Anna Leopoldovna was appointed regent.

Anna's regency was characterized chiefly by indecision. The court was ruled by a clique of German aristocrats who cared nothing for domestic affairs and counseled a ruinous foreign policy. Anna was overthrown on Dec. 6, 1741, and her son was deposed. Elizabeth I, daughter of Peter the Great, was then proclaimed empress, and Anna was exiled to Siberia, where she died in childbirth on March 18, 1746.

ANNABA is the official name (since 1962) of the Algerian city that has been known historically as Bône. See Bône.

ANNAM, a-nam', was the name for Vietnam that was in use until the end of World War II. The region consists of a long, narrow coastal strip in Southeast Asia, stretching for nearly 800 miles between the South China Sea to the east and the kingdoms of Laos and Cambodia to the west. The name *Annam*, meaning "Pacified South," originated in 264 A.D. in the title of a Chinese marshal who was known as the "Pacifier of the South"; the "south" here refers to the regions south of China inhabited by the Vietnamese, then under Chinese domination. The Chinese gradually transferred the name Annam to the country itself. To the Chinese, Vietnam was always Annam, but when the Vietnamese became independent of China in 939 A.D., they rejected this name in favor of *Dai Viet,* meaning "great country of the Viets."

In the West, Vietnam became known as Annam only during the 19th century. During the 17th and 18th centuries, the name usually given to Vietnam by Western authors was *Cochinchina,* with the subsidiary appellation Tongking (Tonkin) for the north of Vietnam, which Westerners then erroneously regarded as a separate country. When the name Annam was first introduced in the West, it designated the country as a whole. This changed after the conquests made by the French in Indochina between 1859 and 1883. Then the term took on a double meaning: in the older and broader sense, it remained synonymous with Vietnam, but in a new and narrower sense it denoted only the central provinces of Vietnam. This change came about because the French, in their conquest of Vietnam in several stages, found it useful to divide the country into three parts. Annam, although it still stood for Vietnam, became also the name of one of the five separate administrative units, or "states," of French Indochina. The other four were Cochinchina (southern Vietnam), Tongking (northern Vietnam), and the kingdoms of Cambodia and Laos.

The partition of Vietnam into the three components, Cochinchina, Annam, and Tongking, conflicted increasingly with the growing national sentiment and the political aspirations of the Vietnamese. For them, this partition came to an end in 1945, when both the government constituted by Bao Dai, the last emperor of Annam, and the one set up by the Communist Ho Chi Minh proclaimed Vietnam to be independent and its three parts united under one national administration. The Vietnamese call the southern section Nam Bo, the northern section Bac Bo, and the central section Trung Bo. After 1945, even the French dropped the name Annam for the country as a whole in favor of Vietnam. As a name for central Vietnam, Annam was given up soon afterward, together with the fiction that Vietnam consisted of three different countries. This happened in 1949, when the French, five years before Vietnam obtained full independence, agreed that Cochinchina be united with the rest of Vietnam. See VIETNAM.

JOSEPH BUTTINGER, *Author of "Vietnam: A Dragon Embattled"*

ANNAPOLIS, ə-nap'ə-lĭs, a city in central Maryland, is the capital of the state and the seat of Anne Arundel County. It is 30 miles (48 km) east of Washington, D.C., on the south bank of the Severn River near its mouth on Chesapeake Bay. Since 1845, Annapolis has been the home of the United States Naval Academy. The city has few industries, but research and development firms have located here because it is near the nation's capital. The Chesapeake Bay Bridge to Maryland's Eastern Shore is just north of Annapolis. Residential developments are replacing tobacco and truck farms in the area.

Many tourists are attracted to Annapolis by its authentically colonial character and by the Naval Academy. More than 80 of the city's buildings have been documented as pre-Revolutionary. In July 1965 the secretary of the Interior declared the "old city" a national historic district. It was laid out in 1696 by the colonial governor, Sir Francis Nicholson, when the capital of Maryland colony was moved from St. Mary's. Its plan of radiating streets and interconnecting circles is remarkably similar to the plans of Sir Christopher Wren and John Evelyn for rebuilding London after the fire of 1666. At the center of the "old city" is the State House (1772–1790), the third on that site and the oldest in the nation still in legislative use.

The spacious grounds of the Naval Academy are along the Severn River, as is St. John's College, which was established in 1784 as a successor to King William's School (1696). A particular

M. E. WARREN, ANNAPOLIS, MD.

ANNAPOLIS' city plan features circles. St. Anne's Episcopal Church (lower left) stands in Church Circle. The State House (upper right) dominates State Circle.

attraction at the academy is its collection of naval memorabilia and the ship models donated by Henry Huddleston Rogers. Other notable buildings in Annapolis open to the public are St. Anne's Episcopal Church and three late 18th century houses—Paca, Chase-Lloyd, and Hammond-Harwood. In the Paca House are the headquarters of Historic Annapolis, Inc., the city and county preservation society that provides tour guides for visitors. Libraries in the city include the state library, the main county library, and libraries at the Naval Academy and St. John's College.

Annapolis was settled in 1649 by 10 Puritan families from Virginia who were offered asylum from religious persecution. Their first settlement on the north bank of the Severn was called the Town at Greenbury. The first recorded activity on the south side of the river—variously known as Providence, the Townland at Proctor's, Town at Severn, Town and Port of Anne Arundel, and finally Annapolis (since 1695)—was the establishment of a boatyard by Thomas Todd in 1650. Annapolis became a port of entry in 1668 and the capital of the crown colony in 1694. It was chartered by Queen Anne in 1708 and incorporated as a city in 1796.

Annapolis became the temporary national capital when the Continental Congress met here from Nov. 26, 1783, to Aug. 13, 1784. In the old Senate Chamber of the State House, on Dec. 23, 1783, George Washington resigned his commission as commander in chief of the Continental Army. There, too, on Jan. 14, 1784, the peace treaty with England was ratified, ending the Revolutionary War. The Annapolis Convention of 1786 was a precursor of the Constitutional Convention of the next year. Annapolis has a mayor-council government. Population: 29,592.

RUTH KING KEITH, *Historic Annapolis, Inc.*

Further Reading: Hopkins, Henry, *Colonial Houses of Annapolis, Md., and Their Architectural Details* (Annapolis 1959); Norris, Walter, *Annapolis: Its Colonial and Naval Story* (New York 1925); Sturdy, Henry, and Trader, A., *Seeing Annapolis and the Naval Academy* (Annapolis 1949).

ANNAPOLIS CONVENTION, ə-nap′ə-ləs kən-ven′-shən, in United States history, a meeting of state delegates in 1786 at Annapolis, Md., which served as a forerunner to the Constitutional Convention of 1787. The Annapolis Convention had its origin in disputes between Virginia and Maryland concerning navigation rights on the Potomac River. Following a meeting of commissioners of the two states at Mount Vernon in 1785, Virginia issued an invitation to the states to attend a conference on interstate commerce. Nine of the states accepted (Maryland was one that did not), but when the meeting convened on Sept. 11, 1786, only New York, New Jersey, Pennsylvania, Delaware, and Virginia were represented. The 12 commissioners present included John Dickinson, chairman, Alexander Hamilton, and James Madison.

Because of the poor attendance, the delegates had to abandon their original purpose of considering a system of uniform commercial regulations for all the states. Before adjourning, however, they agreed that not only commerce but other operations of government under the Articles of Confederation needed revision. A resolution, drafted by Hamilton, was adopted. It called upon the states to meet in Philadelphia the next spring for the purpose of taking steps "to render the constitution of the Federal Government adequate to the exigencies of the Union." The proposal was approved by Congress on Feb. 21, 1787, and the Constitutional Convention met in May.

ANNAPOLIS ROYAL, ə-nap′ə-ləs roi′əl, is a historic town in southwestern Nova Scotia, Canada. The seat of Annapolis County, it lies 95 miles due west of Halifax on the south bank of the Annapolis River where the river empties into Annapolis Basin. Although the town once had busy shipyards and lumber mills, it is now principally a tourist attraction and the commercial center for an apple-growing region.

Annapolis Royal was one of the earliest European settlements in North America north of the Gulf of Mexico. It was established originally as *Port Royal* on the north shore of Annapolis Basin in 1605 by an expedition led by Samuel de Champlain and the Sieur de Monts. In 1613, Capt. Samuel Argall destroyed the settlement and claimed the territory for England. The Treaty of St. Germain (1632) restored Port Royal to the French, and three years later the Sieur d'Aulnay Charnisay erected a fort and settlement on the town's present site.

Captured by Robert Sedgwick of New England in 1654, the town was formally returned to France by the Treaty of Breda (1667) and subsequently became the seat of French government in Acadia (Nova Scotia). It finally was taken by the British under Brig. Gen. Francis Nicholson in 1710, and its name was changed to Annapolis Royal in honor of Queen Anne. It remained the capital of Nova Scotia until 1749.

The original site of Port Royal—Champlain's 1605 "Habitation"—was taken over by the Canadian government and preserved as Port Royal National Historic Park, established in 1940. The 20.5-acre park, a popular tourist attraction, contains an exact replica of the original fortification. At Annapolis Royal proper is 31-acre Fort Anne National Historic Park, established in 1917. It includes a restoration of the old officers' quarters built in 1797–1798. Population: 800.

ANNAPURNA, un-ə-poor′nə, is a mountain range in the Himalaya in central Nepal, northwest of Katmandu. It rises to a height of 26,502 feet at Annapurna I, the 11th highest peak in the world. Annapurna I was scaled for the first time in 1950 by a French expedition led by Maurice Herzog. It was the highest peak ever reached until Mount Everest was conquered in 1953. To the east is Annapurna II (26,041 ft.).

ANNAS, an′əs, in the New Testament, was a Jewish high priest. After Jesus was arrested, he was taken before Annas for a preliminary hearing. Jesus was then sent to Caiaphas, another high priest and the son-in-law of Annas, for a further hearing. Annas is mentioned in Luke 3:2; John 18: 13, 24; and Acts 4: 6. He was a member of an important family, and five of his sons were high priests.

ANNATTO, ə-nät′ō, is a nonpermanent yellow to orange-red dye, or the tree from which it is obtained. The name is also spelled *anatto, arnatto,* or *arnotto.* Native to tropical America, the tree is now widely distributed in the tropics in both wild and cultivated forms. It is a small tree, with heart-shaped leaves. The flowers are clustered, conspicuous, and rose-colored, and the capsules are spiny with numerous seeds. The dye is derived from the outer seed coat. The seeds are stirred in water, and the liquid, when separated from the seeds, yields a paste that is shipped in "rolls" or "cakes." The tree, *Bixa orellana,* is the only member of its genus in the family Bixaceae.

ANNE, an′, **Saint,** traditional name of the mother of the Blessed Virgin Mary. The Hebrew form of her name is *Hannah,* meaning "grace." Knowledge of St. Anne is derived chiefly from the *Protoevangelium,* or apocryphal gospel, of James, dating from the mid-2d century. Anne and her husband Joachim, still childless at an advanced age, prayed for divine aid. In answer, an angel appeared to Anne, saying: "The Lord has looked upon thy tears; thou shalt conceive and give birth, and the fruit of thy womb shall be blessed by all the world." Anne later bore a daughter, whom she called Miriam (Mary). St. Anne's feast is celebrated on July 26. Major shrines in her honor are Ste. Anne d'Auray, Brittany, and Ste. Anne de Beaupré, Quebec.

ANNE (1665–1714), an′, was queen of England, Scotland, and Ireland who became, after the union of England and Scotland in 1707, the first monarch of Great Britain and Ireland. Her conservative rule brought to a close more than 75 years of political instability in Britain.

She was born in St. James's Palace, London, on Feb. 6, 1665, the second daughter of James, duke of York (later King James II) and his first wife, Anne Hyde. Although her mother was a Roman Catholic, Anne was educated as a Protestant and became a loyal member of the Church of England. The most important fact of her childhood was the beginning of her intimate and longstanding friendship with Sarah Jennings, the future duchess of Marlborough.

In 1683, Anne married George, prince of Denmark. Two years later her father became king, but his Roman Catholic faith produced a movement to depose him. When William of Orange landed in England in 1688 to accept the crown

QUEEN ANNE of Great Britain and Ireland. (Painting by John Closterman, National Portrait Gallery, London.)

jointly with Anne's sister Mary, Anne deserted the cause of her father and joined the side of her Dutch brother-in-law. She took this step, essential to her hope of becoming queen, on the advice of Sarah Jennings, who was generously rewarded when Anne ascended the throne.

By the Declaration of Rights (1689) Anne was recognized as the heir to the throne in case William and Mary left no children. During the early part of William and Mary's reign Anne was in disfavor, but soon after Mary's death in 1694, Anne was reconciled with William and resumed her place in court circles.

When William died in 1702, Anne succeeded him as monarch. Her reign did not begin auspiciously. Her right to the throne was challenged from exile by her brother James, the "Old Pretender"; she herself had few attainments, and she was afflicted by constant illness. Yet Britain prospered under her rule. Her devotion to church and state in a nation recently divided proved extremely popular; and although she appointed Tory ministers even when there was a Whig majority in Parliament, she accepted the growth of parliamentary power.

The Tory ministers she chose in 1702 avoided partisan politics. They concentrated on prosecuting the War of the Spanish Succession and maintaining harmony at home. Although a Whig majority did force Anne to choose Whig ministers in 1708, her wishes always had to be taken into account.

In spite of her personal leaning toward a Stuart succession, Anne recognized, tacitly at least, the succession of the elector of Hanover (who followed her on the throne as George I). Toward the end of her life, Viscount Bolingbroke, her secretary of state, determined to effect the succession of her brother. In her last days, Anne refused his assistance. The last Stuart ruler, she died at London on Aug. 1, 1714.

Of Anne's many children only one survived infancy. The one, William, duke of Gloucester, died in 1700 at 10 years of age. Her husband died in 1708, in the middle of her reign.

Further Reading: Kenyon, John P., *The Stuarts* (New York 1959); Trevelyan, George M., *England Under Queen Anne*, 3 vols. (London 1930–34).

ANNE OF AUSTRIA (1601–1666) was queen and regent of France. She was born at Vallodolid, Spain, on Sept. 22, 1601, the daughter of Philip III of Spain and Marguerite of Austria. Her marriage to Louis XIII of France in 1615 proved to be an unhappy one, in great part because Cardinal Richelieu, Louis' adviser, dominated the king and was hostile to the Austrian influence brought to the court by the new queen.

Virtually separated from her husband after 1620, Anne became regent for their son, Louis XIV, when Louis XIII died in 1643. She ruled for Louis in conjunction with Cardinal Mazarin, her chief minister, whom she may have married. The most serious threat to their rule came from the Fronde. The first Fronde rebellion in 1648–1649 principally involved the bourgeois legislators of the Parlement; the nobility was responsible for the second outbreak of 1649–1653. Although forced at one time by the Fronde to leave Paris, Anne and Mazarin eventually subdued the nobles. After the death of Mazarin and the assumption of power by Louis XIV in 1661, Anne lived in retirement at a convent in Val-de-Grâce until her death on Jan. 20, 1666.

ANNE OF BOHEMIA (1366–1394), an', bō-hē′-mē-ə, was the wife of Richard II of England. Her gentleness as queen tempered widespread resentment in England toward her marriage to Richard. She was born at Prague, Bohemia, on May 11, 1366, the daughter of Emperor Charles IV (who was also king of Bohemia) and Elizabeth of Pomerania. Her father had little wealth and less power, and her arranged marriage to Richard II, the 15-year-old king of England, was regarded in England as disadvantageous.

They were married at Westminster on Jan. 14, 1382, after a delay occasioned by Wat Tyler's rebellion. From then on she lived in the eye of a political storm that ended in the deposition and imprisonment of her husband after her death. Although she failed generally to restrain the excesses of Richard, she intervened in 1392 to make him restore privileges he had withdrawn from the City of London. She died of the plague, childless, at Shene on June 7, 1394.

ANNE OF BRITTANY (1476–1514) was queen of France. She was born at Nantes on Jan. 26, 1477, the daughter of Duke Francis II of Brittany and Marguerite de Foix. When her father died in 1488 without a male heir, both France, to whom Brittany had feudal obligations, and Austria sought closer ties with the duchy. France hoped to increase its territory, while Austria wanted to encircle France.

Anne first married Maximilian of Austria (later emperor) by proxy in 1490, but France was able to have the marriage annulled in 1491. Later in the year she married Charles VIII of France after the French regent, Anne of France, invaded Brittany and forced Anne of Brittany to surrender.

The year following Charles' death in 1498, Anne married his distant cousin and successor, Louis XII. The marriage of their eldest daughter, Claude of France, to Francis, duke of Angoulême, who became king of France as Francis I in 1515, further strengthened the ties between Brittany and France. Although Brittany did not formally become a part of France until 1532, Anne's marriages had tied her province to France before her death at Blois on Jan. 9, 1514.

ANNE OF CLEVES (1515–1557), klēvz, was the fourth wife of Henry VIII of England. The king sought and got a separation from her six months after their marriage. She was born in the duchy of Cleves, Germany, on Sept. 22, 1515, the daughter of John, duke of Cleves.

Before her betrothal to Henry, the king had never seen her. He arranged the marriage for political reasons, to strengthen his position against an alliance of Catholic France and the Holy Roman Empire by reaching an understanding with Protestant Cleves. The plan turned out to be unnecessary, and Henry, who first met his betrothed on Jan. 1, 1540, found her plain and graceless. He reluctantly married her five days later but obtained an annulment from Parliament the following July. Thomas Cromwell, his principal adviser in arranging the marriage, was beheaded on July 28—the day Henry secretly married his fifth wife, Catherine Howard. Anne remained in England, supported by the crown, until her death in London on July 16, 1557.

ANNE OF DENMARK (1574–1619), wife of James I of England, was noted for her gaiety and love of extravagant finery. She was born at Skanderborg, Jutland, on Dec. 12, 1574, the daughter of Frederick II, king of Norway and Denmark.

Anne was married to James by proxy on Aug. 20, 1589, when he was James VI of Scotland but not yet king of England, and she was crowned at Edinburgh on May 17, 1590. When her husband succeeded to the English throne as James I in 1603, she was crowned with him at Windsor Castle on July 24. Though she showed occasional concern for affairs of state, her activities as queen were largely social and domestic. She and the king had few common interests, and they lived separately after about 1606. Anne died at Hampton Court on March 2, 1619.

ANNE OF FRANCE (1461–1522), regent of France. The eldest daughter of Louis XI of France and Charlotte de Savoie, she married Pierre de Beaujeu, who became duke of Bourbon in 1488 following the death of his elder brother. She is also known as *Anne de Beaujeu*.

After her father's death in 1483, Anne was made regent for her younger brother, Charles VIII. She and her husband ably governed France during the regency, defeating rebellious nobles in the "Silly War" (*La guerre folle*) of 1485 and suppressing an insurrection in Brittany in 1487. She was instrumental in compelling Anne of Brittany to marry Charles VIII. The marriage was a vital factor in the eventual subjection of Brittany to the French crown. Although less powerful at court after Charles took full control in 1491, Anne remained politically active until her death.

ANNEALING, ə-nēl′ing, is a heat-treating process that is applied to glass, metals, and alloys to obtain desirable properties in the material.

Glass. Strains arise in glass during processing because there are temperature inequalities in the molds and nonuniform cooling rates in the unequal thicknesses of glass sections. When room temperature is reached, the last portions to cool are in tension and the first portions to cool are in compression. Because the strains may adversely affect the glass properties, they are eliminated by heating the glass to a temperature of about 1000° F (538° C), followed by controlled cooling

until a temperature of about 100° F (38° C) is reached. When the glass is at high temperatures, its viscosity is lowered, and its atoms can move freely to assume strain-free positions. Slow cooling from the maximum temperature prevents the reintroduction of strains.

Metals. When most metallic substances are deformed at room temperature, they become harder and stronger and tend to get brittle. This behavior can be demonstrated by bending a piece of coat-hanger wire. As it is bent back and forth, each bend becomes a little more difficult, and eventually the wire breaks. The properties existing before bending can be restored by heating the wire to a suitable temperature for a suitable time. In the case of the coat hanger, heating for a few minutes in a soldering-torch flame will accomplish the result. The bending operation is an example of cold working, and the heating operation is called annealing. Annealing of cold-worked materials tends to undo the effects of cold work by restoring softness and ductility.

Annealing is important where the shape of the material must be radically changed, as in forming cups from sheet brass. The partially formed cup is annealed periodically so that additional shaping can be accomplished without tearing the brass. In addition, annealing of cold-worked metal brings about recrystallization of the deformed grains and relieves internal stresses and strains. These changes bring an improvement in the electrical conductivity of the metal.

Annealing also is used for cast metals to homogenize the mass and relieve solidification and cooling strains. The distribution of alloying elements in casting often is not uniform. Annealing increases atom mobility and permits redistribution of the various kinds of atoms in an alloy so that homogeneity is attained. At the same time, internal strains are relieved.

Full annealing of steel involves heating the steel to a high enough temperature so that a face-centered-cubic (FCC) structure is attained. The alloy then is cooled slowly to permit maximum development of the body-centered-cubic (BCC) structure. This achieves maximum softness in the steel.

Annealing also is used for age-hardenable alloys to prepare the alloy for subsequent hardening treatments. It is used for zinc die castings to stabilize the dimensions of the casting. White cast iron is converted to malleable cast iron by an annealing treatment. See also ALLOYS.

The easiest way to follow the progress of annealing is to check the hardness of the material. The temperatures and times used for annealing are inversely related. In general, the higher the melting temperature of the metal or alloy, the higher is the annealing temperature.

CARL A. KEYSER, *University of Massachusetts*

ANNECY, àn-sē′, is a town in southeastern France, 63 miles northeast of Lyon. The capital of the department of Haute-Savoie, it has a 12th–14th century castle and a 16th century cathedral. The area's chief manufactures are linens, silk, paper, and aluminum.

Known as *Anneciacum Vetus* in ancient times, the town became the seat of the counts of Geneva in the 10th century. It was under the control of the house of Savoy from the 15th century until France acquired Savoy in 1860. The French philosopher Jean Jacques Rousseau lived here in 1728–1729. Population: (1962) 42,304.

ANNELIDA, ə-nel'ə-də, is a phylum of inverte-brates that contains the segmented worms. In-cluded among these are the marine bristle worms, earthworms, and leeches. Found in areas all over the world, from the highest mountains to the greatest ocean depths, annelids are characterized by long, segmented bodies with two-sided (bi-lateral) symmetry.

Anatomy of the Annelids. The typical annelid exterior is divided into three main sections: an anterior head, or prostomium; a trunk of few to many segments, or metameres; and a posterior terminal region, or pygidium. Each segment may be a simple, smooth ring or may consist of two or many rings. Also, each segment may have a pair of lateral, fleshy extensions of the body wall; these are called parapodia. The parapodia are armed with horny (chitinized) rods called setae. When present, they are highly diversified for various functional purposes and also are useful in classifying the types of Annelida.

The body surface of the annelids may be con-cealed by spines, respiratory processes, or other structures that obscure the segmental pattern. The skin may be drab or highly colored and patterned, and it is enhanced by the color of the blood, which may be yellow, red, or green, or by chromatophores (pigment-bearing cells).

The general plan of the annelid body is a double tube with a mouth located behind the prostomium and an anal pore at the posterior pygidium. The outer body tube is epithelial, and it may be cylindrical, or it may be modified as a complex system with accessory processes that show little relation to the primitive annelid form, except that they retain metamerism (segmenta-tion). The inner tube, or alimentary tract, in-cludes an anterior mouth, buccal (mouth) cavity, esophagus (pharynx), stomach region, digestive tract, rectum, and anus.

The length of the body varies from a fraction of an inch to several yards (fraction of a centi-meter to several meters). The smallest annelids are found among the aquatic and marine forms; the largest are terrestrial and intertidal forms.

The alternate push and pull movements of creeping, looping, and crawling and the undula-tory movements used for rapid swimming require a well-developed musculature in annelids. Their muscular system consists of an inner longitudi-nal layer, an oblique layer, and an outer longi-tudinal layer. The muscle cells are either striated or smooth. Muscles are well-developed in many atypical forms and are comparatively weak in sedentary types. The proboscis is muscular and may be turned outward to aid in the capture of food and in locomotion.

The circulatory system is either closed (blood circulates in a system of vessels) or is partly to entirely open (blood and body cavity fluids mix in a cavity called the haemocoel). One or more pulsating vessels, or hearts, may occur in the anterior segments; they propel the blood forward in the dorsal vessel and backward in the ventral longitudinal vessel. A muscular cardiac body may be fused with the dorsal vessel in many annelid forms, but its functions are related to other processes. The dorsal and ventral longitudinal vessels are connected in each segment by a series of transverse segmental vessels; there also is a system of capillaries.

The excretory system is nephridial and con-sists of a pair of tubular excretory organs (ne-phridia) located in each body segment. In some annelids the nephridia are limited to one or a few pairs in the anterior segments, or they are dispersed throughout the body. Their function is to collect wastes from the coelom (body cavity) at the ciliated inner collecting end, or nephro-stome, and transfer them to the exterior through small pores called nephridiopores.

The nervous system in annelids consists of an anterior ganglionic mass, or brain, and a ring of nerves surrounding the esophagus and connecting to the ventrally located nerve cord. This nerve ring may be single or multiple and may have lad-derlike cross connections and segmental branches. In some annelids the adult brain is derived from the larval brain; in other annelids it is derived from an anterior body segment. Giant nerve fibers, or nerve centers, that permit abrupt re-sponses to stimuli occur in some annelids.

Annelid Reproduction and Development. Annelids display many kinds of reproduction, which are both asexual (vegetative) and sexual. Asexual reproduction by fragmentation is common in some annelid forms. Budding from a posterior end is highly evolved in others, and transverse fission, resulting in a chain of successively older individuals, also occurs.

The sexes are separate in most of the bristle-worms, with males and females about equal in number and size. Hermaphroditism, in which both male and female elements are present in all in-dividuals, occurs in all the earthworms and their relatives and in some of the bristleworms; fertili-zation here is reciprocal. Protandry, with both sexes present but at different time intervals, is found in some bristleworms.

Development frequently is from a fertilized ovum. The single fertilized egg cell divides by spiral cleavage to a ciliated, almost spherical larva called a trochophore.

Bilateral symmetry is established at the onset of segmentation, when the larva is called a polytroch. Earthworms and leeches, which lack a larval stage, hatch from a fertilized egg in a stage resembling a young adult. Future growth results in replication of segments and diversifi-cation of body parts.

The life span of annelids has been studied best in a few species. The medicinal leech is said to live as long as 27 years; the common earthworm lives about 6 years, and some bristle-worms live to 3 years.

Feeding Habits. The mouth structures of the various groups of annelids are related to their methods of feeding. Members of the earthworm group have a soft pharyngeal pouch because they are primarily scavengers in mud or earth. The leeches, which are parasitic predators or scaven-gers, have mouth parts adapted to sucking.

The bristleworms are diversified—many are grazers, scraping off surface crops; others are scavengers, selecting food particles with the aid of sense organs. Detritus feeders indiscriminately scoop up food together with large amounts of inert sediments, which are defecated in charac-teristic fecal pellets through the alimentary tract. Feeders that capture living animals have captur-ing mouth parts and special jaws, mandibles, or paragnaths (small, horny, toothlike jaws). Some bristleworms with long, ciliated structures entrap small animals in a ciliated groove and transfer them to the oral cavity. Others enmesh the food in mucous balls before placing it in the oral cavity. Bristleworms found in the open sea capture prey through a wide-open mouth. Some commensals,

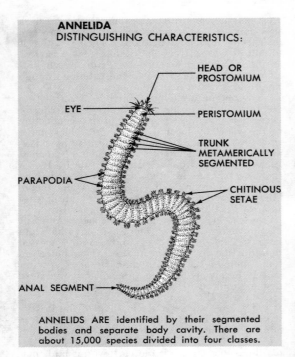

ANNELIDA
DISTINGUISHING CHARACTERISTICS:

HEAD OR PROSTOMIUM

EYE

PERISTOMIUM

TRUNK METAMERICALLY SEGMENTED

PARAPODIA

CHITINOUS SETAE

ANAL SEGMENT

ANNELIDS ARE identified by their segmented bodies and separate body cavity. There are about 15,000 species divided into four classes.

HUGH SPENCER

AMERICAN MUSEUM OF NATURAL HISTORY

MAIN CLASSES OF ANNELIDS AND A CLOSELY ALLIED PHYLUM: *1.* Hirudinea (leech), with terminal suckers and no parapodia or setae. *2.* Oligochaeta (earthworm), terrestrial with clitellum and reduced head.

which live in tubes or burrows of other animals, subsist on the offal of their hosts; still others are parasites and either attach themselves externally or invade the tissues of the host.

Habitats of Annelids. Because of their soft, unprotected bodies, annelids generally inhabit concealed places and thus escape detection. They frequently are found in surface deposits of sand, mud, rocky crevices, and in clustered biotic associations, such as kelp, sponge, bryozoan, and other masses. They often live in tubes specially constructed with bodily secretions. The habitat of the annelid is as closely adapted to the species as the feeding mechanism is to the requirement of nutrition.

The range of physiological tolerances is exceptionally wide. Some annelids are found in thermal springs; others are found in deep marine sediments at or near freezing temperatures. Some occur in saline lakes, while others are found in variable brackish estuaries. Anaerobic (absence of free oxygen) to highly oxygenated aquatic conditions are tolerated by some species.

Terrestrial and freshwater annelids, especially the wandering species, such as the earthworm, in temperate zones are more cosmopolitan than others. Marine species are not transplanted readily and show a higher degree of endemism (being restricted to a particular area), as well as a greater diversity.

Classification of Annelids. The phylum Annelida (also called Polymera) is characterized by the presence of many segments in linear arrangement. The phylum includes the classes Polychaeta, marine bristleworms; Oligochaeta, earthworms and freshwater worms; and Hirudinea, leeches.

Polychaeta. Sometimes called Chaetopoda,

these are largely free-living annelids found in coastal waters up to depths of 150 fathoms (900 feet, or 274.5 meters). They occur in smaller numbers and more numerous kinds in all oceanic depths from polar to tropical seas. Polychaetes are classified into 64 families, with about 1,600 genera and more than 8,000 species.

The most convenient breakdown of the class Polychaeta is into Errantia, or freely moving species, and Sedentaria, or tube-dwelling species. The separation is not entirely applicable, since many Errantia are tube-dwellers, and some Sedentaria are not sedentary. However, this system groups morphologically similar species into workable units. A few lesser families with atypical characteristics are known as Archiannelids, meaning primitive annelids; however, this is a mixed group, and it is uncertain whether or not they are primitive or specialized forms.

The polychaetes vary in size from a fraction of an inch to several yards (a fraction of a millimeter to several meters) long. They may have 6 to 800 segments. The largest polychaetes are in the superfamily Eunicea, where lengths of 2.2 yards (2 meters) have been reported for *Onuphis teres,* a species found in southern Australia. Some common genera are *Aphrodita, Polynoe, Nereis, Glycera, Cirratulus,* and *Terebella.*

Oligochaeta and Hirudinea. Oligochaeta and Hirudinea sometimes are called collectively Clitellata, in reference to the presence of the clitellum, a swollen ring of glandular cells, present in most larger forms. The class Oligochaeta includes about 2,400 species in four major groups or suborders and about 211 genera. They are mainly free-living, freshwater and terrestrial dwellers. Common aquatic genera are *Dero, Nais,* and

ANNAN PHOTO FEATURES

3. and 4. Polychaeta (clamworm, or Nereis, and tubeworm), largely marine with parapodia and numerous setae. 5. Echiuroida (spoonworm), a closely related phylum representing a post-annelid stage of development; only the larvae are segmented.

WALTER DAWN

AMERICAN MUSEUM OF NATURAL HISTORY

Tubifex, and common terrestrial genera of larger species are *Lumbricus, Pheretima,* and *Eisenia.* The largest of known oligochaetes are *Rhinodrilus fafner,* which reach a length of 2.2 yards (2 meters), and *Megascolides australis,* which is nearly as long.

The oligochaetes have distinct segmentation, and segment numbers vary from 7 to 500 or 600. They lack parapodia but have setae in double-branching bundles. The clitellum, or glandular area, secretes mucus, aiding in copulation and cocoon formation in the larger oligochaetes. Calciferous glands, limited to oligochaetes, are derived from the esophageal wall and function to control the level of calcium and carbonate ions in the blood.

Respiration is usually through the epithelium or through special gills in some aquatic species. Choragen tissue, which surrounds the dorsal vessel, is the center of glycogen and fat synthesis and may store silicate excesses, which then are excreted as waste.

Oligochaetes are believed to be derived either from small, primitive, now-extinct polychaetes or from a medium-sized nereidlike polychaete.

The class Hirudinea, which contains the leeches, has more than 400 species; they are marine, freshwater, and terrestrial. The best-known are the bloodsuckers. Sizes range from a fraction of an inch to more than 20 inches (a fraction of a centimeter to 50.8 cm). The bodies of leeches are long and depressed and terminate in a sucker at either end. The number of segments is constant at either 34 or 33, and each segment has several rings. The body is divided into five main regions. Some common genera are *Hirudo, Glossiphonia,* and *Pisciola.*

Paleontological Evidence of Annelids. Annelids have left little evidence of past life, except for the remains of jaw and opercular (flaplike) parts, tubes, trails, or castings. They evolved in Precambrian times (500 million or more years ago) and left remains known as scolecodonts, which can be related to present-day eunicid and nereid (two polychaete types) jaws. The well preserved series of middle Cambrian (about 450 million years ago) fossils indicates their diversification at that level of time.

Annelids are related to other phyla by their segmentation and trochophore larva. Metamerism, or segmentation of the body, into a bilateral (two-sided) linear form, is a feature shared with the phylum Arthropoda. However, the arthropods have an exoskeleton (horny outer skeleton), which is lacking in the Annelida. The more closely related phyla, Echiuroida and Sipunculida, differ in that they lack external segmentation. A larval trochophore is present in these forms and also in mollusks and some animals with few or obscure segments, such as Bryozoa and Brachiopoda. The presence of setae is unique to polychaetes and oligochaetes and a few echiurids.

OLGA HARTMAN, *Allan Hancock Foundation University of Southern California*

Bibliography

Borradaile, L.A., and Potts, F.A., and others, *The Invertebratae* (London 1961).

Buchsbaum, Ralph, *Animals Without Backbones* (Chicago 1948).

Hartman, Olga, *Literature and Catalogue of the Polychaetous Annelids of the World* (Los Angeles 1951–65).

Hogner, Dorothy C., *Earthworms* (New York 1953).

Laverack, Michael S., *Physiology of Earthworms* (Oxford 1962).

Mann, Kenneth H., *Leeches (Hirudinea), Their Structure, Physiology, Ecology, Embryology* (Oxford 1962).

ANNEXATION, an-ek-sā′shən, in international law, is the formal act by which a state declares its title to a territory. It differs from acquisition in that a state may acquire territory, without formal annexation, by means of *prescription,* or uncontested occupation of territory of another state over a long period of time; by *accretion,* or adding to its territory on a river or maritime frontier through the operation of natural forces; or by discovery and occupation of *territorium nullius* (unclaimed territory).

International law permits the annexation of territory that has been ceded by a valid treaty with the former sovereign. Formerly it permitted the annexation of territory conquered from an enemy if the conquest had been "completed" by the defeat and surrender of the enemy. However, treaty obligations to refrain from the use of force as an instrument of national policy, as in the Kellogg-Briand Pact (1928) and the United Nations Charter, have been held to invalidate annexations effected by the use of armed force, even if such annexations are supported by a treaty with the defeated state. Such nonrecognition of the fruits of aggression has been the practice of the United States and the U.N.

International jurists have related this principle to the legal doctrine *jus ex injuria non oritur* (rights do not arise from wrongs), though they consider it qualified by the opposing doctrine *ex factis jus oritur* (rights arise from facts). Thus it is suggested that collective recognition may give good title to annexations that originated in force but have been retained for a long time and have conformed to the general interests of the parties concerned.

QUINCY WRIGHT, *University of Virginia*

ANNISTON, an′əs-tən, is a city in northeastern Alabama, in the foothills of the Appalachian Mountains, 65 miles (105 km) by road east of Birmingham. It is the seat of Calhoun County, in an iron-mining and cotton-growing area. Anniston is an industrial center that makes cast-iron soil pipe and pipe fittings, industrial castings and machine parts, chemicals, cotton yarn, and clothing. The city is the home of the Regar Memorial Museum of Natural History. Anniston Army Depot is 10 miles west of the town.

The city was settled in 1863, when its first blast furnace was built to supply the Confederate Army. Destroyed by Union cavalry in 1865, the community was rebuilt, beginning in 1872, as a model industrial center. At first called Woodstock, it was renamed for Anne Scott Tyler, the wife of Alfred Tyler, president of the Woodstock Iron Company. Anniston was incorporated as a city in 1879 and has a commission form of government. Population: 31,533.

ANNONACEAE, an-ə nā′sē-ē, a family of plants found in the Old and New World tropics. It is commonly known as the *custard apple* family. It contains some 80 genera and about 850 species of trees, shrubs, and vines with aromatic wood and foliage. Most of the genera are grown for fruit, ornament, or perfume.

The family is characterized by flowers that have spirally arranged stamens and numerous pistils that show various degrees of fusion. In most genera, for example *Asimina,* the pistils remain separate and develop into fleshy, many-seeded berries. In some genera, such as *Annona,* the numerous spirally arranged pistils and the floral axis form a fleshy structure in which the seeds are embedded. The flowers themselves are large, although not showy; they are regular and often solitary. They consist of 3 sepals and 6 petals and range in color from brown to tawny yellow. The leaves are aternate and simple.

The most valuable of the Annonaceae genera is *Annona,* the custard apple, which contains 90 or so species of shrubs and trees with large edible fruits. It is found in tropical America and Africa. *Uvaria,* with 100 species, is the largest genus. It is found in the Old World, and most of its species are lianas (tropical, woody, climbing plants). About 8 species of the genus *Asimina* are grown in North America; the best-known species is *A. triloba,* the papaw. The genus *Cananga,* which is found in southern India, Java, and the Philippines, is prized for its fragrant extract. *C. odorata* is the source of Cananga oil, a perfume of the Pacific islands. *Artabotrys,* the tail grape, is a genus containing many of the tropical woody climbers, including *A. odoratissimus,* the clinging ylang-ylang.

ANNUAL, an′ū-əl, a plant that completes its entire life cycle in one growing season. In colder climates, the season is from spring to autumn, while in warmer regions it may be from autumn to spring. Annuals are particularly suited to regions in which there is a short growing season followed by an unfavorable cold or dry season. Examples of annual plants are corn (maize), wheat, bean, cucumber, pumpkin, calendula, aster, California poppy, morning glory, nasturtium, zinnia, and petunia.

ANNUALS, an′ū-əlz, are reference books that are published each year and summarize current political events, scientific developments, and cultural trends. Most annuals are issued by publishers of reference works to update their encyclopedias. They contain articles written by authorities on a wide variety of subjects, usually presented in alphabetical order.

The annual with the longest record of continuous publication is the *Annual Register,* founded in England in 1759 by Robert Dodsley, with Edmund Burke as editor. In the United States the *International Year Book* was published annually from 1899 to 1903 and resumed publication in 1907 as *The New International Year Book. The Americana Annual,* yearbook of the ENCYCLOPEDIA AMERICANA, began continuous publication in 1923. Other encyclopedia annuals include *The Book of Knowledge Annual* (1939–), *Britannica Book of the Year* (1938–), *Collier's Year Book* (1939–), and *Encyclopedia Year Book* (1956–).

Another type of annual containing tales, essays, and poems was popular in the 19th century. These annuals were illustrated with engravings or color plates and were often given as Christmas presents. The first literary annual, *Forget-me-not,* appeared in England in 1823; the first in the United States, *Atlantic Souvenir,* was published in Philadelphia in 1826. By 1832, 63 annuals and gift books were published in England, and about 60 annuals appeared in the United States in 1851. Among the famous writers who contributed to the books were Byron, Scott, Wordsworth, Hawthorne, Poe, Emerson, and Longfellow. Most annuals were published only once, but *Keepsake,* last of the literary annuals, appeared for 30 years, until 1857.

ANNUITY, ə-nū′ə-tē, strictly speaking, an annual payment. More broadly, an annuity has been defined as "a periodical payment to continue during a given status." In this sense of the term, payments may be made monthly, quarterly, annually, or at other intervals. They may continue for a fixed number of years, for life, or in perpetuity.

An annuity is life insurance in reverse. Life insurance is concerned with the creation of estates. It represents a pooling arrangement whereby the many contribute so that substantial funds may be paid on behalf of those who die in any given year. The annuity embodies a pooling arrangement whereby those who live long benefit at the expense of those who die early. In life insurance, protection is obtained against dying too soon; in annuities, protection is purchased against the hazard of living too long (outliving one's income). In contrast with life insurance, which emphasizes estate creation, the annuity emphasizes estate liquidation.

Most annuities are *conventional annuities,* which provide a fixed dollar income. A newer form, the *variable annuity,* yields income on the basis of investment results.

Conventional Annuity. Essentially, an annuity provides for payment of money by a life insurance company in installments over a time period. Each payment represents part interest and part principal, and payments generally are made for the annuitant's lifetime. The annuitant under a conventional annuity is assured a fixed income that cannot be outlived. Such income is more than is obtainable from other gilt-edged investments because payments combine principal with interest.

Religious and charitable institutions have developed an annuity for an individual donor, who receives payments until his death. At his death the residue of the principal reverts to the institution.

The conventional (standard) forms of annuities may be classified in several ways. One classification pertains to the plan of distribution (pure versus refund); another distinguishes between the time when payments begin (immediate versus deferred). Annuities may also be classified according to the method of purchase (single premium versus periodic premiums). A fourth classification involves the number of life contingencies in the annuity arrangement (single life versus annuities involving more than one life).

Plan of Distribution. According to this classification, annuities fall into two classes—the *straight life* or *pure annuity,* and the *refund annuity.*

The pure annuity provides an income to the annuitant as long as he lives. Payments cease at his death. No matter how many or how few payments have been made—it may even happen that no payment has been made—death ends the obligation of the insurance company. A pure annuity pays the largest income for a given premium outlay. Maximum income is guaranteed the annuitant for life.

Besides pure annuities, companies sell varieties of refund annuities. These are sold much more frequently than pure annuities. Refund annuities have provisions that apply (1) in case the annuitant dies before the income has commenced and (2) in case the annuitant dies after the income has commenced.

In case the annuitant dies before the income has commenced, refund annuities usually provide for the return of premiums paid. Some companies

will return premiums plus interest. If the annuitant dies after the income has commenced, several refund arrangements are available. There are annuities guaranteeing a minimum number of payments, annuities with an installment refund feature, and annuities with a cash (lump sum) refund feature.

Annuities with a guaranteed number of installments provide that a certain minimum number of payments will be made whether or not the annuitant dies before receiving them. A person 65 years of age buys a life annuity guaranteeing 120 monthly payments. As long as he lives he will receive a monthly income. If he should die after 60 payments have been made, payments will continue to his named beneficiary for five additional years. If the annuitant dies any time after receiving 120 payments, the insurance company has no further obligation.

Installment refund life annuities provide for payments to continue until they equal the consideration paid for the annuity, if the annuitant dies before receiving this amount. Assume the purchase of an annuity of this type for a consideration of $10,000. The periodic income payable is $50 a month. If the annuitant should die after 10 years (120 months), payments will continue to the named beneficiary for another 80 months until the full purchase price has been returned. If the annuitant should outlive the 200-month period, he will continue to receive benefits for life, and his death ends the annuity arrangement. Some companies sell a 50 percent installment refund life annuity as well as the above-described 100 percent installment refund life annuity. For the same premium, a 100 percent refund life annuity will pay a smaller periodic income than the 50 percent refund annuity.

Cash refund life annuities provide for a single payment at the death of the annuitant equal to the difference between the purchase price of the annuity and the annuity payments received before death. Thus if $7,000 has been received by an annuitant on an annuity costing $10,000, the balance of $3,000 is paid in a lump sum to the beneficiary.

When annuities are sold with refund arrangements, periodic income for the same premium will be less than under the pure form of annuity. Many annuitants are willing to sacrifice higher periodic income for a refund feature. At younger ages the difference in income between pure and refund arrangements is very slight, but it becomes greater for older annuity purchasers.

Time When Payments Begin. Under this classification, annuities can be categorized as *immediate annuities* or *deferred annuities.*

An immediate annuity begins payments to the annuitant one time interval from the date of purchase. Thus, if the payments are annual, the first payment is one year from date of purchase; if monthly payments are called for, the first payment is one month from date of purchase; if the payment is semiannual, the first check will come six months from date of purchase.

Deferred annuities are those under which payments to the annuitant begin later than one time interval after purchase. Thus, a person 35 might purchase an annuity that starts payment at age 65. The payments here are deferred until normal retirement age.

Most immediate annuities are whole life annuities with or without a refund feature. Some companies sell temporary life annuities. The latter

provide payments for a temporary period or until
death, if death occurs before the end of the
period. Income payments end if the annuitant is
alive at the end of the period. Temporary annuities furnish protection for a specified period,
at the end of which it is expected that income
from another source will be available. Such annuities are issued very infrequently.

Premium rates in annuity contracts are different for men and women. Because of the significantly greater longevity of women, the cost of
annuities for them is greater than for men. One
company quoted a rate of $15,920 at age 65 for
a male for an immediate annuity (pure) paying
$100 a month. The same contract for a female
cost $18,750. The same premium will, of course,
pay a female annuitant a smaller income than the
male annuitant.

Method of Purchase. By definition, immediate
annuities are purchased by one lump sum payment—by a single premium. Many annuities, however, are purchased by the payment of periodic
premiums. Most deferred annuities are purchased
in this manner, the annuitant paying periodic
premiums during the entire deferred period. The
periodic premium may be paid annually, semiannually, quarterly, or monthly. It also is possible
to pay for deferred annuities with a single payment or with payments limited to a portion of the
deferred period.

Number of Lives Involved. Most standard annuities sold are on the basis of one life contingency. Such single life annuities are contingent
on the continuation of one life although they may
include a refund provision. But annuities also
can be purchased where more than one life contingency is involved—usually two lives. These
contracts may be in the form either of joint annuities or of joint and last survivorship annuities.

A joint annuity on two lives provides for payments while both annuitants are alive. Payments
cease upon the first death. Thus a husband and
wife might have a source of income sufficient for
one but not for both. The income from the joint
annuity will augment the outside income while
both are living.

The joint and last survivorship annuity is the
more common annuity where more than one life
is involved. This type of annuity calls for payments to be made as long as any one of the annuitants is alive. Thus a husband and wife are
assured an income while both are alive with payments continuing to the survivor upon the death
of the first annuitant. The income to the survivor
may be the same amount as when both were
alive or it may be reduced by one third or one
half. When payments are reduced for the survivor, a larger income can be provided while both
annuitants are alive, assuming the same purchase
price.

Variable Annuity. The central objective behind
the variable annuity is to offer the annuitant some
protection against rising price levels. Inflation
has been one of the major economic problems in
the United States and other countries, since the
1950's. Many economists are of the opinion that
the long-run inflationary trend will continue in
the future.

Conventional annuities provide for periodic
payments on a fixed dollar basis. The guaranteed
dollars do not fluctuate with price levels but stay
the same whether prices are depressed or inflated.
It is clear, however, that the purchasing power
of these fixed dollars decreases as the price level

increases. Since 1952, when the College Retirement Equities Fund began issuing variable annuity contracts in the limited field (higher education) in which it operates, a great deal of
interest and controversy has arisen concerning
this subject.

The variable annuity does not offer guaranteed fixed dollar payments. The dollars payable
under this form of annuity fluctuate according to
investment results. The premium dollars for variable annuities are invested primarily in fluctuating dollar investments such as common stocks
and other equity investments. In contrast, the
investments behind conventional annuities are
chiefly in bonds and mortgages. Both the conventional annuity and the variable annuity stress
the feature of liquidation of principal over the
lifetime of the annuitant. However, one pays
fixed dollars; the other pays variable dollars.

A simple illustration of the variable annuity
may be helpful. A person buys a variable annuity on a deferred basis paying a fixed annual
premium. This premium purchases the "units,"
the number of units depending upon their current value in dollars. The premium in year A
might buy 6 units; in year B, 5 units; in year C,
8 units. At retirement age, a certain number of
units have been accumulated. These units will
then be liquidated on the annuity principle involving life contingencies. The annuitant will
receive an annuity of a certain number of units
yearly. The dollar value of the units will depend
on the performance of the investments behind
these annuities and will normally fluctuate period
by period.

It has been the general rule for stock prices
and the cost of living to move in the same direction. Thus the annuitant anticipates receiving a
higher dollar income in times of higher prices,
maintaining some degree of stability in purchasing power. This stability cannot be accomplished
through a fixed dollar annuity.

On the other hand, changes in cost of living
and changes in common stock prices show significant variance. The stock market traditionally has
been more volatile than price levels. This characteristic points to the need for sensible financial
planning involving balance, where possible, between fixed dollar and variable dollar investments.

The variable annuity has stirred a great deal
of controversy within the life insurance business
and in the general investment field. The pro-
priety of life insurance companies selling variable
annuities has been questioned—indeed the legality
of such an activity has been a matter of dispute.
Within the life insurance industry itself, there is
no unanimity. Some companies are opposed to
the concept while others support it. The variable
annuity involves many legal and related questions. In the case of *Securities and Exchange
Commission* v. *Variable Annuity Life Insurance
Co.*, the Supreme Court ruled in 1959 that variable annuities are not insurance and are subject
to federal regulation as securities. Nevertheless,
a few small insurance companies are offering
variable annuities to individuals, and several
large companies have made them available under
group pensions.

History. Annuities are probably as old as the
Babylonian empire of Nebuchadnezzar II in the
7th and 6th centuries B.C. In this era, banking
houses and other commercial and mercantile
facilities were well developed. But the first

positive mention of annuities is found in the Falcidian Law (*Lex Falcidia*) of Rome in 40 B.C., which held that not more than three fourths of a property should be willed away in specific legacies. For this to be followed, some method of valuing annuity legacies had to be devised. The following rough estimate was accepted: up to age 30, 30 years more of life; up to age 60, as many years as were wanting to make a total of 60. This crude approach was replaced and improved by the Roman jurist Ulpian about 200 A.D.

Great actuarial strides were made in the 18th century. Particularly significant was the publication in 1771 of the "Northampton Table of Mortality" by Richard Price. This work has been termed the foundation of modern life insurance and of scientific annuities. Within the last two centuries there have been great advances in actuarial science.

The annuity has long been a popular investment in England and on the European continent, but it did not rise to general popularity in the United States until the Great Depression of the 1930's. During this period of economic disaster, people realized the need for a secure investment that would yield an unfailing and fixed dollar income involving systematic liquidation of principal. In the 1950's and the 1960's, the general inflation led to the development of the variable annuity.

DAVID A. IVRY, *University of Connecticut*

Further Reading: Donald, D.W.A., *Compound Interest and Annuities Certain* (New York 1953); Fricke, Cedric, *Variable Annuity: Its Impact on the Savings-Investment Market* (Ann Arbor, Mich., 1960); Hart, William L., *Mathematics of Investment* (Boston 1958).

ANNULMENT OF MARRIAGE, ə-nul'mənt, mar'ij,

is a device for terminating marriage without divorce. It is a legal declaration that the marriage was void from the beginning because of some violation of the marriage code. Fraudulent intent alone in some states of the United States is grounds for making the marriage void. For example, in New York State, when either mate can convince the court that the other mate had determined prior to marriage never to have children, ground for annulment is established. The most common grounds for annulment, and the least abused, are being under age and bigamy. Other grounds are impotence, illegal marriage, failure to wait out a legally established waiting period, unsound mind, and fraud.

Although annulment is usually thought of as a device used very soon after marriage, census data show that it has been used as late as 30 years after marriage. Most annulments, however, come during the first year.

PAUL H. LANDIS, *Washington State University*

ANNUNCIATION, ə-nun-sē-ā'shən, the announce-

ment to the Virgin Mary that she was to be the mother of Jesus Christ. The story is found in the New Testament in the Gospel According to St. Luke (1:26–38), and is told in the highly poetic language of the Jewish messianic hope. It is because of the "overshadowing" by the Holy Spirit that Mary's Son is to be "the Son of the Most High" and "reign for ever over the house of Jacob."

In the church calendar, the festival of the Annunciation (or "Lady Day") comes on March 25. For a time it was shifted, in Spain and elsewhere, to December 18 in order to remove it from Lent. But since the birth of Christ (Christmas) is celebrated on December 25, the Annunciation inevitably became fixed at nine months earlier.

Protestants as a rule do not observe the festival (the Anglican Church is an exception). The Roman Catholic, Anglican, Orthodox, and some other churches give the Annunciation an important theological significance as the announcement of the incarnation, and accompany it with other doctrines and observances that round out or stress the dogma more fully. Other religions (for example Buddhism) possess legends of the announcement of the coming birth of kings, prophets, teachers, and saviors. Rarely, however, is there such emphasis upon the character or position of the mother as in the Christian church.

The Annunciation has been a favorite subject with artists for centuries, especially since the early Italian Renaissance. Some artists have

THE ANNUNCIATION portrayed by Robert Campin, a Flemish painter (died 1444). The center panel of this altarpiece shows the angel Gabriel and The Virgin Mary. At the left, the donors of the painting; at the right, St. Joseph.

pictured the scene with great imagination and insight, using a rich background and picturing the Virgin engaged in prayer or meditation or reading the Bible when the angel Gabriel appears to her with the divine message.

FREDERICK C. GRANT
Union Theological Seminary

ANNUNZIO, Gabriele d'. See D'ANNUNZIO, GABRIELE.

ANOA, ə-nō′ə, is a small dark-brown buffalo about 3½ feet (1 meter) high that inhabits the forests of Celebes. It is commonly called *dwarf water buffalo* or *tamarau*. The anoa has a thick hide, short limbs, plump body, and sharp, short, almost straight horns. It is hunted for its hide, horns, and meat.

The genus *Anoa* belongs to the Bovidae family, and anoas are regarded as true oxen. Of the three species, *A. depressicornis* is the most common. The anoa is related to the American bison.

ANODE. See ELECTRODE.

ANODIZING, an′ə-dīz-ing, is the production of a porous oxide coating on a metallic object in an electrolytic cell. The electrolyte liberates oxygen at the surface of the object, which serves as the cell anode. Anodizing is restricted to metallic substances, usually aluminum and its alloys. The most commonly used electrolytes are sulfuric and chromic acids.

Aluminum-oxide coatings vary from transparent to opaque, depending on the film thickness. Film thickness, in the range from 0.00005 to 0.001 inch, depends on the quantity of electricity and the choice of electrolyte. Alloying elements may tint the film gray or brown, but otherwise it is colorless as formed. Colored finishes are produced by organic dyes. Film porosity is eliminated by using boiling water, which changes the oxide to a monohydrate of aluminum. Hot solutions of nickel acetate, waxes, and oils also are used as sealants.

Anodic-oxide coatings provide transparent protective films over the polished surfaces of aluminum reflectors or brightwork. The coating is used on architectural trim because it minimizes corrosion, streaking, and discoloration in the atmosphere. The coating also serves as an electrical insulating material.

CARL A. KEYSER
University of Massachusetts

ANOINTING is a custom, observed since ancient times, of applying oil to the head or body. The Bible mentions anointing the head as a preparation for social festivities or formal appearances (Psalm 23:5, Luke 7:46) and general anointing for medical purposes (Mark 6:13, Luke 10:34, James 5:14).

The use of oil for ceremonial purposes is also ancient. Under Mosaic law, anointing the priestly garments gave them a sacred character. Jewish priests and kings were anointed when inducted into office. The custom of anointing is still used in various churches and in coronation ceremonies. See also ANOINTING OF THE SICK; HOLY OILS.

ANOINTING OF THE SICK, in the Roman Catholic and some other Christian churches, is a sacrament that, through anointing and prayer by a priest, bestows spiritual good and sometimes bodily health on a person who is seriously ill. The sacrament of anointing with Holy Oils is sometimes called Extreme Unction. It is intended for all who are seriously ill, not as a sacrament for the dying.

References to this rite in the Bible and in early church documents are rare as compared with the mention of other sacraments such as Baptism and the Eucharist. The principal biblical source is the Epistle of James (5:14–16), which gives an indication of an anointing of the seriously ill by the presbyters (priests or elders).

In Roman Catholic theology, the primary effect of this sacrament is held to be a spiritual or religious victory over sickness. The victory involves both a spiritual effect—a grace that is in some sense a complement of the sacrament of Penance, or reconciliation—and a physical or bodily effect.

The Eastern Orthodox and some of the other Eastern churches accept Anointing as a true sacrament. However, the rite of administration differs among the various Eastern churches and in all cases is markedly different from the ceremonies used by the Western church.

The leaders of the Reformation, especially Luther and Calvin, rejected the sacramental character of the Anointing of the Sick, and Protestants generally have denied the utility of the rite. In the Anglican Communion, many consider anointing a ceremony developed by the church rather than a sacrament instituted by Christ. Others hold it to be a true but "lesser" sacrament —lesser than the "Sacraments of the Gospel," Baptism and the Lord's Supper, which alone are considered necessary for salvation.

ROBERT J. HENNESSEY, O. P.
Albertus Magnus College

ANOKA, ə-nō′kə, is a city in eastern Minnesota, situated on the Mississippi and the Rum rivers, 17 miles (27 km) northwest of Minneapolis. It is the seat of Anoka County, in a dairy and poultry, suburban, and industrial area. Its manufactures include ammunition and machine parts. Anoka was settled in the 1840's and incorporated as a city in 1878. It is governed under a city manager plan, adopted in 1914. Population: 13,489.

ANOLE, ə-nō′lē, an iguanid lizard of the genus *Anolis,* found in the Western Hemisphere. Anoles are sometimes called "chameleons" because some species, but by no means all, have the ability to change color, generally from green to brown. The true chameleons of Africa and India belong to a different family (Chamaeleonidae) and are only distantly related. See also CHAMELEON.

Anoles, of which there are hundreds of species, occur in southern Mexico, Central America, northern South America, and the West Indies. *Anolis carolinensis* is found over much of the southeastern United States. *A. sagrei* is common in the West Indies, but in the United States it occurs only at the southern tip of Florida.

Anoles are specialized climbers, with dilated friction pads on the toes and fingers. They also are good swimmers. Males establish "territories," which they guard against other males, advertising their ownership from some prominent point by expanding a brightly colored fan of skin beneath the throat to intimidate other males.

SAM B. McDOWELL, JR.
American Museum of Natural History

ANOMALY, ə-nom′ə-lē, in astronomy, is the distance that a planet has moved in its orbit away from perihelion (the point in the planet's orbit at which it is closest to the sun). This distance is expressed as the angle formed by lines extended from the sun to the planet's perihelion and to the planet's actual position.

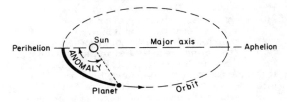

The time it takes the earth to travel from perihelion back to perihelion is known as the *anomalistic year,* a unit of time measurement that is seldom used. The anomalistic year is 365 days 6 hours 13 minutes 53 seconds long, or 25 minutes 7 seconds longer than the ordinary or tropical year. This difference results from the slow but steady shifting of the earth's perihelion in the direction of the planet's motion, so that the earth takes a little longer than an ordinary year to return to this point in its orbit. See also YEAR.

ANOPHELES. See MOSQUITO; FLIES—*Flies and Disease.*

ANORTHITE. See FELDSPAR.

ANORTHOSITE, ə-nôr′thə-sīt, is an igneous rock, a kind of gabbro that consists almost entirely of labradorite, a soda-lime feldspar. The rock is not very abundant. Because dark minerals such as pyroxene are not present in anorthosite in any great quantity, it may be light in color. See also FELDSPAR; GABBRO.

Anorthosite is plutonic—that is, it formed deep within the earth from molten rock material known as magma. Such molten material could cool very slowly beneath the earth's surface when not extruded as lava. Thus the crystals making up anorthosite and other plutonic rocks could grow large enough to be recognized by the naked eye, giving the rocks a coarse texture. Important examples of anorthosite are found in Labrador, the Adirondack Mountains of New York, and the Laramie Range of Wyoming.

ANOUILH, a-nōō′ē, **Jean** (1910–   ), French dramatist, whose plays range from austere tragedy in the classic tradition to witty comedy in the most sophisticated manner of the 20th century. A master of dialogue and dramatic technique, Anouilh cannot be classified with any particular school of dramatic writing, although he generally is associated with the avant-garde element of the modern theater.

He was born in Bordeaux on June 23, 1910. In his youth he acquired theatrical experience as secretary to Louis Jouvet, the great French actor and producer. Anouilh's first play, *L'hermine* (1932), was forceful but uneven and melodramatic. This work, influenced like many of his dramas by the contemporary playwright Jean Giraudoux, was followed by *Le bal des voleurs* (1932), *Le voyageur sans bagages* (1937), and *La sauvage* (1938).

During World War II, when the German occupation of France and the Vichy regime made it impossible to treat political problems directly, Anouilh turned to classical mythology for his themes. His best play of this period was *Antigone* (1942), which expresses the spirit of individual resistance against oppression. The production of *Antigone,* because of its use of modern evening dress rather than period costumes, was a novel theatrical experiment.

Anouilh categorized his plays by types. The *pièces noires* (black plays), including *Antigone* and *L'alouette* (1953), are characterized by a deep conviction that human happiness is always achieved at the cost of personal integrity. The *pièces roses* (pink plays), while no less pessimistic or contemptuous of social conventions, have a mood of bitter irony that sometimes develops into buffoonery, as in *Le bal des voleurs* and *Ardèle ou la marguerite* (1949). The *pièces brillantes* (glittering plays), such as *L'invitation au château* (1947) and *La répétition ou l'amour puni* (1950), are playful modern imitations of the witty works of the 18th century dramatist Pierre Marivaux. The *pièces grinçantes* (jarring plays)—an epithet that might be applied to most of Anouilh's work—include *La valse des toréadors* (1952).

Many of Anouilh's dramas have been translated into English. Although his plays command serious critical attention in the United States, few of them have enjoyed commercial success on Broadway. Notable exceptions were *L'alouette,* produced on Broadway as *The Lark* in 1955; *The Waltz of the Toreadors,* staged in New York in 1958; and *Becket,* which was a popular and critical success in both its Broadway production in 1960 and its film adaptation in 1964. Anouilh's other plays produced on the New York stage include *The Fighting Cock* (1959), *The Rehearsal* (1963), and *Poor Bitos* (1965).

Further Reading: Didier, J., *A la rencontre de Jean Anouilh* (Brussels 1946); Gignoux, Hubert, *Jean Anouilh* (Paris 1946); Harvey, John, *Anouilh: A Study in Theatrics* (New Haven, Conn., 1964); Pronko, Leonard C., *The World of Jean Anouilh* (Berkeley, Calif., 1961).

ANOXIA, a-nok′sē-ə, is a shortage of oxygen in an animal's body cells. In its narrowest sense, anoxia denotes the complete absence of oxygen, but in common usage the term is interchangeable with *hypoxia,* a condition in which an animal's body cells do not receive, or cannot use, enough oxygen to carry on their normal activities. Anoxia is sometimes confused with asphyxia, a condition in which anoxia occurs but which is also characterized by the accumulation of excess carbon dioxide. Strangulation is a form of asphyxia due to an obstruction of the air passages that prevents the normal exchange of oxygen and carbon dioxide in the lungs.

Types. Anoxia is usually divided into four basic types, depending on its cause. *Hypoxic anoxia* is primarily due to an inadequate concentration of oxygen in the air. This form of anoxia occurs at high altitudes and sometimes affects mountain climbers and pilots.

Anemic anoxia results when there is a reduction in the oxygen-carrying capacity of the blood. This is sometimes due to decreased amounts of hemoglobin in the blood, resulting from a hemorrhage or a blood disease. Anemic anoxia may also result when the hemoglobin has been modified so that it cannot transport oxygen, as in carbon monoxide poisoning.

Histotoxic anoxia occurs when the body cells are unable to utilize oxygen. This condition occurs most commonly in certain types of poisoning, such as cyanide poisoning. The supply of oxygen to the cells is normal, but the cells are unable to metabolize the delivered oxygen.

In *stagnant anoxia* there is a reduced flow of blood through the body tissues. This condition may be generalized, as in many forms of advanced heart disease, or it may be localized, due to a disease of a blood vessel, the application of a tourniquet, or an arterial spasm. The "blackout" of an aviator during aerial maneuvers is the result of insufficient blood reaching the eyes and brain because of the heart's inability to pump enough blood to these regions against the high centrifugal force.

Symptoms. One of the body's responses to anoxia is an increase in the rate and depth of breathing. At an altitude of 15,000 feet (4,575 meters), where the oxygen pressure of the air is 90 mm (3.5 inches) of mercury, as compared with approximately 160 mm (6.2 inches) of mercury at sea level, pulmonary ventilation is increased by about 15 percent.

The pulse rate begins to increase when the oxygen pressure drops to or below 110 mm (4.2 inches) of mercury, at an altitude of about 10,-000 feet (3,050 meters). As the pulse rate increases, the volume of blood pumped from the heart also increases. During prolonged exposure to low oxygen pressure, the pulse rate may return to normal, but the output of the heart will remain elevated because of the increased volume of blood pumped from the heart with each beat.

Even when anoxia is severe, both the heart and the brain are able to function because of the dilation of the blood vessels within these organs. Functioning may also be aided by the increased extraction of oxygen from the blood. Of the special senses, night vision is the first to show impairment, while hearing is the last sense to fail. It has frequently happened that an individual suffering from anoxia was able to hear while unable to move his body.

The onset of anoxia symptoms is usually very slow, and generally is first marked by an impairment of judgment. Aviators are taught that unstable emotions and a loss of judgment, accompanied by a false sense of well-being, may be the first signs of mild or moderate anoxia. In severe anoxia, unconsciousness, often accompanied by convulsions, occurs rapidly. Symptoms of heart failure may begin just before, with, or shortly after collapse. When death occurs, it is due to heart failure.

Anoxia of long duration may be symptomless if it is not severe. This is because the body undergoes various changes that compensate for the low oxygen supply. One of the most significant changes that occurs in the process of adjusting to high altitudes is a growth in the number of red blood cells, thus increasing the body's ability to pick up and transport the available oxygen. A fully acclimated person who is in good physical condition can get along surprisingly well at altitudes up to 19,000 feet (5,800 meters). Above 20,000 feet (6,100 meters), however, mountain climbers who undertake strenuous exercise are often on the verge of physical collapse.

MAJ. GEN. OTIS O. BENSON, JR., M.D.
Southwest Research Institute,
San Antonio, Texas

ANQUETIL-DUPERRON, änk-tēl' dü-pe-rôn', **Abraham Hyacinthe** (1731–1805), French Orientalist. He was born in Paris. Abandoning studies for the priesthood, he devoted himself to Oriental languages and religions, particularly to a search for the works of Zoroaster. At Pondicherry, India, where he arrived aboard a troop ship in 1755, he studied modern Persian. From there he went to Chandernagore to study Sanskrit. However, the English conquest of Chandernagore forced him to return to Pondicherry.

Accompanied by one of his brothers, he embarked for Surat, where he acquired sufficient knowledge of the Zend and Pahlevi languages from Parsee priests (one of whom revealed to him the mysteries of their fire-worship cult) to enable him to translate the *Vendidad Sade* and other works. His hope of proceeding to Benares (now Varanasi) to study the Hindu language, literature, and sacred laws was dashed by the British capture of Pondicherry, which forced him to leave India. Returning to Paris in 1762, he took with him 180 Oriental manuscripts, which he deposited in the Royal Library.

His major work, the text and translation of the *Avesta,* appeared in 1771. His other works include *Législation orientale* (1778), *Recherches historiques et géographiques de l'Inde* (1786), and *Oupanichads* (1804).

ANSBACH, äns'bäкн, a town in West Germany, is in Bavaria, 25 miles (40 km) southwest of Nuremberg. It has manufactures of motors and electrical equipment, linen and clothing, plastics, and printing materials.

Originally called *Onoldsbach,* the town grew up around the 8th-century Benedictine abbey of St. Gumbertus. It later became the capital of the principality of Ansbach. It was the seat of the Franconian branch of the Hohenzollern family from 1331 to 1791, when the last margrave deeded the territory to Prussia. In 1806 Prussia ceded it to Bavaria. Population: (1961) 32,948.

ANSELM, an'selm, **Saint** (c. 1033–1109), Italian-born archbishop of Canterbury and doctor of the church. He was born of noble parentage at Aosta, Italy. Prevented as a boy from entering a monastery, he for a time lived a careless life. After his mother's death he left home and went to Burgundy to study. In 1060 he joined the Benedictine monastery at Bec, Normandy, and became its prior in 1063. In 1078, Anselm became abbot, succeeding Lanfranc, who later became archbishop of Canterbury in England.

After Lanfranc's death in 1089, King William Rufus prevented a new appointment to the see of Canterbury until 1092. In that year Anselm, who was known in England because of official visits as abbot of Bec, became archbishop and primate of England. In this post he defended the rights of the church against royal aggression. In 1097 he went to Rome to appeal to Pope Urban II for help in his struggle with the king. Anselm was unable to return to England until after the king's death in 1100. Problems continued under Henry I, the new king, but peace was finally made, and Anselm served for some months as regent during the king's absence. Anselm died at Canterbury in 1109. His feast day is April 21.

Theology and Philosophy. Anselm is one of the most important of medieval philosophers and theologians. His most famous theological work is *Cur Deus Homo* (*Why God Became Man*), which answers various objections against Christian beliefs. The book then treats the doctrines of the Incarnation and Redemption, expounding the doctrine that Christ, the Saviour of mankind, is both God and man. In philosophy his chief works are on theodicy. The *Monologium* is a discussion of the divine essence. The *Proslogium*—which contains the famous *ratio Anselmi,* or Anselmian argument, usually but improperly called the ontological argument—discusses the existence and nature of God. Anselm hoped to add a new proof to the traditional arguments from reason that God exists. The proof is to be found, he holds, in the idea of God as the greatest of conceivable beings. This must be the idea of a really existent, not merely of an imaginary, being. The atheist contradicts himself, since he claims to think of the greatest of conceivable beings and yet says that it is not even the least of beings, but nothing at all. Immediately challenged, the Anselmian argument has been debated ever since. St. Thomas Aquinas and Kant, for instance, reject it, while Descartes and Spinoza accept it.

Anselm also contributes to epistemology: he distinguishes between sensuous and intellectual knowledge, helps clarify the important subject of universal ideas, discusses the nature and kinds of truth, and takes up the problem of meaning. In psychology he investigates free will and the immortality of the soul. Much concerned with the problem of the relation between faith and reason, he subscribes to the formula "I believe so that I may understand" and to its correlative, "I understand so that I may believe." That is, faith enlightens reason, while reason and philosophy aid faith by answering objections, defining terms, and providing proofs. Anselm also stresses the need for love in relation to both faith and understanding. His doctrine is strongly influenced by St. Augustine. Anselm is an effective and even brilliant writer as well as a profound and original thinker.

JOHN K. RYAN, *The Catholic University of America*

Further Reading: Anselm, St., *Opera omnia*, ed. by F.S. Schmitt, 4 vols. (Edinburgh 1946–49); id., *Proslogium, Monologium, and Cur Deus Homo,* tr. by S.N. Deane (La Salle, Ill., 1939); Clayton, Joseph, *Saint Anselm, a Critical Biography* (Milwaukee 1933); Gilson, Étienne, *History of Christian Philosophy in the Middle Ages* (New York 1955).

ANSELM OF LAON (died 1117), an'selm, län, French theologian known as *The Scholastic,* who systematized the teaching of theology. He was born in Laon, France. He studied under St. Anselm of Canterbury at the abbey of Bec and later taught in Paris. About 1100 he founded a school of theology in Laon which attracted such scholars as William Champeaux and Peter Abelard. Anselm wrote *Glossa interlinearis,* a widely used commentary on the Latin Bible.

ANSELM OF LUCCA, an'selm, lōō'kä, **Saint** (c. 1036–1086), Italian churchman noted for his crusade against lay investiture. Born in Mantua, Italy, Anselm was named bishop of Lucca by his uncle Pope Alexander II (also called Anselm of Lucca) in 1071. Because installation as bishop required lay investiture by Emperor Henry IV, Anselm at first refused the honor, but in 1073 he accepted it from Pope Gregory VII. Anselm soon regretted his decision and resigned, but was ordered by the pope to return to Lucca.

His efforts to reform the clergy led to his expulsion by Henry IV and antipope Clement III (Guibert of Ravenna) in 1081. Subsequently, Anselm became spiritual adviser to Countess Mathilda of Tuscany and papal legate in Lombardy. He wrote many treatises against lay investiture and a noted collection of canons. Anselm is patron of Mantua, where he died on March 18, 1086. His feast is March 18.

ANSERIFORMES, an-sə-rə-fôr'mēz, is a group of birds that contains the screamers, geese, swans, and ducks. They are all aquatic and are found all over the world, except in Antarctica. Many members of the group are important sources of meat or eider; others are important as game birds. There are about 45 genera and 150 species.

The order Anseriformes is divided into two living families—the screamers or Anhimidae, found in South America; and the ducks, geese, and swans (cosmopolitan waterfowl), or Anatidae. (A third family has been established to include a fossil form.) Characteristics of the Anhimidae are unwebbed toes, long legs, horny spurs at the bend of each wing, and chickenlike bills. The Anatidae have webbed toes and relatively long necks. Their bills are covered by a thin layer of skin and tipped with a horny nail.

ANSHAN, än'shän', a municipality in China, is the leading iron and steel center of the country. It is located in Liaoning province, in the northeastern region of China known as Manchuria. The city lies on the Shenyang-Lüta section of the South Manchurian Railway, 55 miles (89 km) southwest of Shenyang (Mukden).

Within an 8½-mile (14 km) radius of Anshan are 11 large iron-ore mines. Large-scale mining operations began soon after mining rights were granted to Japan in 1915. The Japanese built the first blast furnaces in 1919. After Japan's creation of the Manchukuo regime in Manchuria in 1932, the Showa Iron and Steel Works was organized and began manufacturing steel a year later.

Continued expansion during World War II made Anshan the second-largest iron-and-steel-producing center in Asia. During the height of production in 1943–1944, annual output reached 2,756,026 tons (2,500,250 metric tons) of pig iron and 922,625 tons (837,000 metric tons) of steel. In the summer of 1944, U.S. planes made several raids on Anshan, destroying much of its production capacity.

Soviet troops entered Anshan on Sept. 20, 1945, and during a 53-day occupation they dismantled and carried away about two thirds of the industrial equipment. In February 1946, Anshan was transferred to the Chinese Communists, who destroyed much of the remaining facilities shortly before the Nationalist government gained control of the area. The city again fell to the Communists on Nov. 3, 1948. The following years witnessed the rapid reconstruction of Anshan, and by the early 1960's the city's plants had achieved an operating capacity of 4,170,000 tons (3,782,900 metric tons) of pig iron and 3,300,000 tons (2,993,700 metric tons) of steel. Population: (1958) 833,000.

KUEI-SHENG CHANG, *Wayne State University*

ANSHUN, än-shoon', a city in China, is in the west central part of Kweichow province, about 50 miles southwest of Kweiyang. Anshun is located in an area rich in coal deposits. It was made a city in 1958. Population: (1953) 40,000.

ANSKY, an'skē, **Shloime** (1863–1920), Russian-Jewish folklorist and author of *The Dybbuk*, one of the most important plays of the modern Jewish theater. Ansky (also spelled *An-Ski*), whose real name was *Solomon Seinwil Rapoport*, was born in Vitebsk, Russia. He was active in the Jewish Socialist party in Russia, which adopted his poem *Die Shvueh* for its anthem. During World War I he traveled to various European communities collecting material for his three-volume *Der Yidisher Khurbn*, which describes the destruction of the Jews of Poland, Galicia, and Bukovina. Ansky left Russia after the revolution of 1917. He died in Warsaw, Poland, on Nov. 8, 1920.

The Dybbuk, Ansky's masterpiece, is a tragedy based on the Hassidic folk belief in predestined human relationships. A young girl, who had been promised in marriage, from birth, to a poor student, is given by her father to a wealthier man. The student dies, and his soul—the dybbuk—enters the girl's body and finally summons her to death. The play was first produced in Yiddish in Vilna, Lithuania, in 1920.

ANSON, an'sən, **Cap** (1851–1922), American baseball player, who was elected to baseball's Hall of Fame in 1939 as "the greatest hitter and greatest National League player-manager of the 19th century."

Adrian Constantine Anson was born in Marshalltown, Iowa, on April 11, 1851. At the age of 19 he left Notre Dame University to play ball with Rockford, Ill. He became an infielder and catcher for the Athletics in the National Association (1872–1875) and then a third baseman for the new National League Chicago White Stockings in 1876. He played first base and managed Chicago from 1879 through 1897, winning five National League pennants. Anson batted .339 in his 22 years with the league, hitting .421 in 1887. He made 3,081 hits in his National League career. He died in Chicago on April 14, 1922.

BILL BRADDOCK
New York "World Journal Tribune"

ANSON, an'sən, **Lord** (1697–1762), British admiral. He was born George Anson in Shugborough, Staffordshire, England, on April 23, 1697. The account of his four-year voyage round the world, compiled from his records and published as *Voyage round the World*, remains an 18th century maritime classic.

Anson entered the British Navy at the age of 14. Promoted to captain in 1724, he was sent to protect the Carolina coast from pirates and Spanish raiders. In 1740, he was ordered to harass Spanish shipping in the Pacific with a squadron of six ships. Only his flagship reached the mid-Pacific, but with it he captured a Spanish galleon carrying £500,000 in treasure from the Philippines to Mexico. Completing a round-the-world voyage, Anson returned to London in triumph in 1744. Two years later he defeated a French fleet in the Atlantic, off Cape Finisterre, Spain, and was created Baron Anson of Soberton. Anson County, North Carolina, was named for him in 1750.

Lord Anson was active in reorganizing the British Navy. He twice served as first lord of the admiralty, in 1751–1756 and 1757–1762. He died at Moor Park, Hertfordshire, on June 6, 1762.

ANSON, an'sən, **Sir William Reynell** (1834–1914), British legal scholar. He established an enduring reputation by his great work, *Law and Custom of the Constitution* (part 1, 1886; part 2, 1892), a monument of learning and lucid exposition and a guide to the complex machinery of British government. It is the textbook from which British statesmen learn their business. His other chief work, *The Principles of the English Law of Contract* (1879), is also a classic.

Anson was born in Walberton, Sussex, England, on Nov. 14, 1843. Educated at Eton and Oxford, he won some of the highest academic distinctions. He practiced law until 1873. In 1874 he was appointed Vinerian reader in English law at Oxford, where he took an active part in promoting the foundation of a school of law.

In 1899, Anson was elected to Parliament from Oxford University as a Unionist. He remained a member of Parliament until the time of his death. In 1902 he was made parliamentary secretary of the Board of Education, and, as the representative of the Education Department in the House of Commons, he had much to do with the defense and passage of the Education Act of 1903. Anson died at Oxford on June 4, 1914.

ANSON, an'sən, is a city in western Texas, 25 miles (40 km) by road northwest of Abilene. It is the administrative seat and commercial center of Jones County, which is an agricultural and oil-producing area. The city has an oil refinery and cotton gins.

Settled in 1880 and incorporated in 1904, it was named for Anson Jones, the last president of the Republic of Texas. Since 1885, the Cowboys' Christmas Ball has been held in Anson each year. The community has the mayor-council form of municipal government. Population: 2,615.

ANSONIA, an-sō'nē-ə, is an industrial city in southwestern Connecticut, in New Haven County. It is situated on the Naugatuck River, 16 miles (25.8 km) northeast of Bridgeport. The city's principal manufactures are brass and copper products, iron castings, foundry products, automatic screw machine products, and novelties.

Ansonia was named for its founder, Anson G. Phelps, a merchant and philanthropist. It was settled in 1651 and was a part of Derby until 1845, when it was organized independently. It became a borough in 1864, a township in 1889, and a city in 1893. Government is by a mayor and council. Population: 21,160.

ANSTEY, an'stē, **F.** (1856–1934), English writer of humorous tales, plays, and poems, many of which first appeared in *Punch* magazine. His real name was *Thomas Anstey Guthrie*. He was born in London on Aug. 8, 1856, and graduated from Trinity Hall, Cambridge, in 1875. He was called to the bar in 1881, but the great success of his first novel, *Vice Versa, or a Lesson to Fathers* (1882), turned his interest from law to writing. The novel, which relates the adventures of a British businessman who magically exchanges bodies with his schoolboy son, attained such popularity that pirated editions were widely sold in the United States. Anstey joined *Punch* in 1887 and contributed to that magazine until 1930. He died at London on March 10, 1934.

Anstey's other books include *Voces Populi* (1890), *The Man from Blankley's* (1893), *Mr. Punch's Pocket Ibsen* (1893), and *The Brass Bottle* (1900). His memoirs, *A Long Retrospect*, were published posthumously in 1936.

ANT. Ants have been living on the earth for more than 100 million years. During this span many other kinds of animals came into existence and then lost out in the struggle for survival. Man became the world's master, making vast changes in its natural state. But in spite of keen competition for survival and changing living conditions, ants have continued to thrive. Today they are found everywhere—from the Arctic to the tropics, from damp forests to deserts, from seashore to the timberline of mountains, from under city pavements to the pantries of suburban kitchens.

Ants have an elaborate social structure, and they enjoy a longevity far greater than that of most insects. Queen ants have lived in captivity for as long as 20 years; workers, for nearly 10 years. The thousands of ant species that have been described by scientists far exceed the total number of all other existing social insects combined, and the number of individual ants is greater than the total number of all other terrestrial animals.

Body Structure. An ant's small body does not suggest great durability. However, it is encased in chitin, a tough, rigid substance, forming an "outside skeleton." Its body has three distinct parts: head, thorax, and abdomen.

The head contains a brain, which is sometimes no more than a fraction of a millimeter in size, and supports long, flexible antennae. The antennae are so efficient as sense organs that eyes are not of great importance. In certain species the workers either are blind or have only enough sight to distinguish light from darkness. Other species, however, have two well-developed compound eyes (each visual unit has its own lens), with three simple eyes (there is only one lens for all the sensory cells) between.

The mouth is composed of two sets of jaws, and each can open and close independently of the other. The outer jaws are the mandibles and are used for excavating soil or wood, for cutting up food, for carving, and for fighting. The inner jaws bear rows of bristles, which serve in cleaning legs and antennae. The tongue is a small pad covered with fine ridges. Three pairs of jointed legs are attached to the thorax, as are the wings of queens and males during the flight season.

The distinctive waist of the ant—the petiole, or pedicel—is considered a part of the abdomen and may have either one or two segments, depending on the species. The large part of the abdomen is called the gaster. In this portion of the abdomen are the heart and digestive organs.

Like other insects, ants do not have lungs but take in oxygen through small breathing tubes called tracheal tubes, which branch throughout the body. Colorless blood fills the body cavity, and in most species it is kept circulating by small hollow tubes that contract in waves from one end to the other. The ant has two stomachs, a true stomach and a "social" stomach, or crop. Food, in liquid form, goes into the social crop first. The food can be regurgitated from it to feed other ants. Connecting the crop and the true stomach is a "pumping" stomach. Its action helps to draw food into the crop and also makes some food pass from the crop into the true stomach, where digestion takes place.

Not all ants have stings, but in the species that do, the weapon is the ovipositor (the egg-laying organ), which is located at the end of the abdomen, and through it poison is discharged

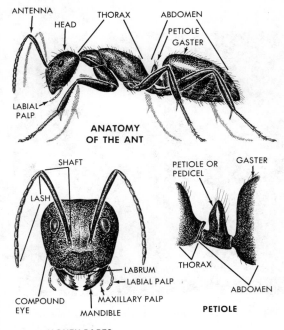

ANATOMY OF THE ANT

MOUTH PARTS AND HEAD

PETIOLE

from muscular sacs. Only females are able to sting. Some ants inflict severe bites with their jaws and inject poison into the bite. Others eject a spray of formic acid at their victims.

The Life of an Ant Colony. There is great variety in the activities of different kinds of ants —so great that it is not possible to describe here all their living habits beyond saying that every kind of ant is social. All are organized in groups, or castes, consisting, fundamentally, of a queen mother and her offspring—the workers and males. However, the males exist only for short reproductive seasons and are not really a part of colony life. Sometimes there may be more than one queen in a colony.

There may be several kinds of workers, such as supersoldiers, pigmy soldiers, and "nurse" workers. The name "soldier" suggests an unusually aggressive type, but this is not always a true picture. A soldier often devotes itself exclusively to defending the colony. One kind, which lives in plant stems, thrusts its head against the nest's entrance to keep out intruders. Soldiers usually do not take part in gathering food, but among certain species they perform domestic chores, such as licking the larvae clean and carrying them from one part of the nest to another. A soldier has an unusually large head, protected by a hard, armorlike covering. Its jaws are larger and stronger than those of an ordinary worker. (The workers have several tasks, which are described later in this article.)

The species *Lasius niger* provides an interesting colony to observe. It lives in many areas throughout the Northern Hemisphere. In North America its popular name is the *garden* or *cornfield ant.* In Europe it commonly is called the *dark brown ant.*

Establishing a New Colony. A new colony of the species *Lasius niger* is established in the spring when young winged females, the queens, and males fly out of their old home. This great exodus is a means of dispersal and is also a marriage flight, for mating takes place in the air.

THE QUEEN ANT, a winged female, establishes a new
colony in the spring by choosing a site and laying eggs.

LARVAE (foreground) and then pupae (left) develop
from the eggs and are cared for at first by the queen.

The ants drift or fly to a scattered number of
landing places. Many of them fall prey to birds
and other insect-eating creatures. The males that
escape this fate soon die anyway, for their purpose is only reproductive, and they do not have
the ability to hunt for food. The future of the
species depends on the females that survive this
flight.

A young queen's first task is to remove her
wings. She may pull at them with her legs or
bend sideways to press them against stones or
blades of grass. If they are not pulled off,
eventually they begin to shrink and soon are shed
as a natural process.

The wingless queen examines the area in
which she has landed until she finds a suitable
location for a nest. Then she begins to excavate
in the earth with her mandibles. When she has
dug a small burrow, she shuts herself into it,
completely closing the opening, and begins a
lonely exile from the active world. For many
weeks she remains there, while the eggs mature
inside her. She is sustained only by nourishment
from the muscles that once supported her wings.
From time to time she may make slight improvements in her burrow, but otherwise she is inactive.

When her first eggs are laid, the queen does
a surprising thing—she eats them. But this gives
her strength for the new work that soon will be
necessary. Other eggs are produced that are not
eaten, and before long these develop into wormlike larvae. They are active, growing insects
that must be fed promptly and often, and the
young queen feeds them with her saliva. She
concentrates her feeding program, giving most
food to one particular larva; then a second receives preference, then a third, and so on. As a
result, a few of the brood grow very quickly. As
they grow, they periodically burst their skins and
shed them. When they have reached almost full
growth, each larva spins a cocoon about itself
and enters a pupal stage. Now it needs no food
or special care. For several weeks it remains inside the cocoon, metamorphosing into an adult.

As the young ants are ready to emerge from
their cocoons, the queen mother helps them
break free by biting at their wrappings. Then
she cleans and feeds them. These first workers
usually are smaller than those born later. They
begin work by enlarging the original chamber,
making an opening to the outside world, and then
setting out to hunt for food and carrying back
to the nest whatever they find.

Expanding the Colony. Once there is a working group, the colony becomes thoroughly organized; and from this point on the colony develops rapidly. The queen no longer has to carry
all the responsibilities; and her sole activity is egg
laying. She is fed and tended by the workers,
which also take over the job of feeding the larvae. As new eggs are laid, workers take immediate charge of them, grouping them together in
compact bundles. When the eggs hatch into
larvae, the workers feed them partially digested
food. Later, the larvae are fed pieces of captured
insects and other edible matter.

After the larvae reach their pupal stage, the
workers are concerned with providing proper temperatures for them. During the heat of the day
the worker "nurses" move the pupae deeper into
the ground; with the coolness of evening they
carry them up again nearer the warmth of the
earth's surface. The nurse workers also keep the
pupae clean and protect them if the nest is
attacked.

The pupae complete their development in approximately three weeks, and the young adult
ants then are ready to emerge. This time they
receive help from workers rather than from the
queen. The nurses help them break out of their
cocoons and may assist in straightening out their
legs and antennae. Then they may drag or pull
them into the most desirable position in the nest.
The newly hatched adults, known as callows, are
pale, and their eyes are very dark.

The length of time required for the development of a colony's first workers varies with the
species. With some it is as long as 10 months
before the queen first receives assistance from

MOUND NESTS, or hill nests, are built of earth, twigs, and straw carried to the site by worker ants.

INSIDE THE MOUND are many storage galleries and tunnels. The ants shown here are harvester ants.

the workers. In perhaps four or five years a colony is large and strong enough to send out a batch of winged males and females on a marriage and dispersal flight.

The eventual population of a colony depends on several factors: the type of ant, the nature of food that is available and its abundance, and the fertility of the queen. Some species, under the best of circumstances, do not have more than several hundred members in a well-established colony. Other colonies may have many thousands of individuals.

As the population of the colony continues to grow, the size of the nest also increases. The first small burrow made by the young queen is expanded by the workers into an intricate network of chambers, or galleries, and connecting tunnels. Some of the galleries are used for storing eggs, others for larvae and pupae. Still others are for food storage.

Nest Construction. The most favorable time for nest construction is after a shower, when the soil is damp and easy to handle. The workers scoop up pellets of the soil in their mandibles. Some of the soil is carried outside the nest; the soil is molded into bricklike form and used to build walls and ceilings for a tunnel or gallery. A successful colony grows year after year, and along with new building the workers also maintain older parts.

There are many kinds of ants besides *Lasius niger* that make their nests in the soil. In some cases, the pellets of soil cleared out to make tunnels and galleries are carried away from the nest's entrance and are scattered. The entrance itself may be concealed among grass or leaves or kept closed with a few pebbles. In the colonies of some other kinds of ants the workers dump all the excavated soil in a heap near the entrance to the nest, forming a small crater. As the colony grows older, the crater is enlarged. Should it be destroyed by rain or wind, the ants rebuild it. Such craters may be only a few inches in diameter or several feet, depending on the species of ants.

In addition to craters made up entirely of excavated soil, there are mounds that actually are hill nests. These are composed not only of pieces of earth that have been brought up from below the surface, but also of such materials as pebbles, twigs, leaves, and straw. In mound nests, galleries and tunnels occupy much of the mound. There may be many openings in the mound for entrances and exits, or there may be only one.

Some ants do not live in the ground, but in cavities in plants, such as hollow stems or thorns. Also, they may excavate in twigs and tree trunks.

TREE TRUNKS are used as nesting sites by carpenter ants. Larvae are stored in hollowed-out chambers.

ROSS E. HUTCHINS

THE ANTENNAE are the ant's sense organs. The ants above are communicating by rubbing their antennae.

In the tropics some species construct nests of earth or silk and suspend them from tree branches. Ants that leave their natural backgrounds in favor of human habitats adapt their way of life to the limitations of crevices in walls and woodwork. Added to these varied types are the nomad-army ants and driver ants, which make no nests at all.

Communication. Smell, taste, and touch are an ant's most important senses. The principal sense organs are the antennae, although on the ant's body there are short hairs, with nerve endings at their bases, that also aid in the sense of touch. Such hairs are particularly abundant on the antennae.

Each antenna consists of a long, single joint (the shaft) and a section made up of anywhere from 9 to 13 joints (the lash). Organs of smell as well as touch are located in these segments. If any of them are broken, the ant's ability to take part in colony activities is greatly reduced. It is quite possible to observe an ant, either in a man-made nest or out-of-doors, using her antennae for explorations. It also may appear to "talk" to another ant, as she and another individual meet and stand together with antennae fluttering. Sometimes two ants cross their antennae, and at other times they touch each other with them.

An ant cleans her antennae regularly and often with a brushlike structure located on each front leg. Usually she begins by lifting a leg over one antenna, pulling the antenna through the brush. She cleans the brush with her mouth and then cleans the second antenna. An ant does not groom only herself. There is an almost constant grooming and stroking of one ant by another in a colony. Much of this is done by the antennae, some of it by the tongue.

Each ant colony has its own characteristic odor. Thus, each ant can recognize the members of her own nest, even if the two meet a considerable distance from the nest. If an ant from one colony strays into another, even though they

are of the same species, she is attacked and killed or driven away.

Wherever ants live, the care of the nest is of vital importance. Good housekeeping is necessary not only for convenience but also for sanitary reasons. With all species, bits of unused food, bodies of dead members of the colony, remains of pupal wrappings, and all other types of refuse are carried a distance away from the living quarters.

New Nest Locations. The members of a colony do not always live in complete harmony. In a well-established group there are times when certain members take the initiative of moving to a new location. The enterprising ones work together to start a second nest, then return to their original home, seize the queen and young, and carry them to the new quarters. However, the ants that were not part of the moving program may choose to live in the first nest. Their resistance is overcome to a certain extent when they, too, are carried to the new home. But once released, they are likely to pick up some larvae and pupae and carry them back to the original home. For a second time the pioneers move them to the new site, and again they may return to the first. This back-and-forth shuttle may go on for weeks and months until one side—usually the side that has resisted a change—becomes discouraged and gives up. No fighting is involved.

Types of Ants. There is no "typical" ant. The types of ants vary so that one can name only a typical primitive ant, a typical army ant, a typical "harvester," or a representative of one of the other distinctive groups.

Ponerines. The primitives are known as the ponerines (subfamily Ponerinae). They are so different in behavior from more highly developed types that the queens sometimes must seek their own food. Among some of the primitive species, workers as well as queens lay eggs. These ants hunt a variety of insects for food, particularly termites and sowbugs. The distribution of the ponerines is worldwide, but they are especially numerous in Australia. On that continent and in Tasmania and New Caledonia they are notably large and fierce and are called *bulldog* or *jumper ants.* The bulldog ants may grow to an inch (2.54 cm) or more in length. When they defend their nest, they rush out in a series of leaps, each about a foot high. They have extremely powerful stings that can prove quite dangerous to humans. Some species of bulldog ants make simple mound nests. With others, the individuals may use simply a stone as a shelter. Usually they hunt alone, but sometimes, working in groups, they carry out devastating raids against such targets as termite nests.

Army Ants. The notorious army ants (subfamily Dorylinae) form another distinctive ant group. Many legends have been woven about these nomadic insects, and erroneous popular notions about them are hard to dispel. Yet the facts are interesting enough. The "armies" wander in gypsy fashion about the countryside, perhaps 150,000 strong, never building nests but occupying temporary bivouacs. They live in tropical regions of Africa, Asia, and South America. They are found in limited numbers in some southern parts of the United States.

The dorylines of Africa are commonly called *driver ants.* They travel in enormous swarms, and the front of a raiding party, made up of "scouts" and "raiders," may be several yards wide. The

ANTS

ANT NESTS

LEAF CUTTER ANTS (right), also called parasol ants, sometimes form long processions as they carry bits of leaves to their underground nest. The ants use their sharp mouthparts to cut the leaves (lower right), and large colonies have been known to defoliate entire trees and shrubs.

E. S. ROSS

A TAILOR ANT NEST (below) consists of leaves fastened by a type of silk secreted by the ant larvae. Such nests are often built high in trees, sometimes 100 feet or more above the forest floor.

E. S. ROSS

E. S. ROSS

AN ARMY ANT BIVOUAC (below) is made up of workers who interlock their legs to form a living curtain surrounding the queen and her brood.

PONERINES (below), the most primitive ants, build simple nests in the ground. Unlike other ants, the worker ponerines, as well as the queen, sometimes lay eggs.

E. S. ROSS

CARPENTER ANTS (below) usually nest in rotting tree stumps and logs, chewing tunnels through the wood. Sometimes they invade a healthy tree or the wooden framework of a house.

E. S. ROSS

RUDOLF FREUND

LIFE IN A *FORMICA* ANT NEST

slave raiders carrying off young

tending pupae

guest fly larvae

mutual feeding

tending larvae

a beetle guest

tending a queen

nest of thief ants

This illustration shows some of the important activities that go on inside the underground nest of a common widespread ant, *Formica pallidefulva*. The nests of these ants sometimes have tunnels that are 10 feet long. The life of the ant colony centers around the queen, or queens, which lay the eggs that develop into males, females, and worker ants. Each queen is constantly fed and groomed by the workers, and the eggs that she lays are carried off to chambers where they hatch into the tiny larvae. The larvae, too, are carefully cleaned and fed, and the pupae into which they develop are also continually groomed. Sometimes, the larvae and pupae are captured and carried away by slave-making ants, such as *F. sanguinea*, who often raid the ant nest. Within the nest there may also be "guest" insects, such as fly larvae and beetles.

PLATES 2 AND 3

actual size of F. pallidefulva

gathering honeydew from aphids

bringing in food

digging new tunnels

resting and grooming

The workers spend much of their time in housekeeping activities. Old tunnels must be maintained and new ones must be dug. Wastes must be removed along with any trace of mold or decay. The workers also clean and groom each other, and a worker with a crop full of liquid food feeds drops of it to many others. Foraging ants are constantly bringing food into the nest and these ants feed chiefly on insects and other invertebrate animals. However, the sweet honeydew secreted by many types of insects, including aphids, scale insects, and even some butterfly larvae, is also a highly relished food. Sometimes, workers climb high in trees and shrubs to find honeydew producers. The workers are also always ready to defend the colony against intruders, and if the colony is disturbed, they move the young to the safety of deeper tunnels.

ILLUSTRATION BY ARABELLE WHEATLEY

OTHER FORMICINE ANTS

A *Formica fusca* ant (*right*) feeds an obligatory slave-maker, *Polyergus,* who can no longer feed herself.

An allegheny mound ant, *F. exsectoides,* helps a callow emerge from its cocoon. Only some formicine ants build cocoons.

A queen carpenter ant, *Camponotus,* tends her first brood inside a cavity she has made in a tree.

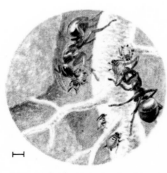

The cornfield ant, *Lasius,* tends root aphids for their sweet honeydew.

PLATE 4

GATHERING AND STORING FOOD

HONEY ANT REPLETES *(left)* are workers whose swollen abdomens store honeydew. Repletes cannot walk but must remain suspended from the ceiling of their underground nest.

DR. THOMAS EISNER

E. S. ROSS

THE HARVESTER ANT *(above)* gathers seeds and stores them in its underground nest. If the seeds get wet and start to sprout, they are promptly discarded.

E. S. ROSS

E. S. ROSS

CARNIVOROUS ANTS feed on many animals, even other ants. *(Above)* Army ants attack a leaf cutter soldier. *(Below)* Formicine ants work together to drag a dead worm snake into their underground nest.

CATTLE-TENDING ANTS obtain honeydew by cultivating aphids *(above)*, leaf-hoppers *(below)*, and other insects that secrete the sweet liquid. .

E. S. ROSS

E. S. ROSS

ROSS E. HUTCHINS

ROSS E. HUTCHINS

(*Above*) ARMY ANTS (*Eciton*) are a nomadic variety. The soldiers have tiny eyes and large pincer-like jaws.

(*Left*) PONERINES are primitive ants found especially in Australia. They often reach an inch or more in length.

raiding mass narrows down to a single column in the rear, or a few columns. Those in the front make short advances, then turn back, to be followed immediately by individuals that had been behind them. Thus each successive group progresses a little farther forward in a huge relay process. They not only cover the ground, but they also swarm over trees and shrubs. These ants eat only meat; snakes, mice, rats, birds, and insects are devoured regularly. Larger victims may be any creature, from deer to crocodile, that is injured or trapped so that it cannot escape.

The activities of the driver ants seem the more remarkable when it is realized that workers and queens are blind. Only the males have eyes. Also, they are allergic to bright light; direct sunshine kills them in a short time. They resolve this problem by being active at night and on dull days. If they must move while the sun shines, they travel through thick grass or heavy foliage, or they may construct covered archways of earth. The genus *Eciton,* the army ants of the New World, is not so devastating as the driver ants. In some villages of South America, the people actually welcome the approach of these ants, as they clean out such pests as cockroaches and bedbugs while passing through.

The nomads are not constantly on the move. Each group has two succeeding phases, repeated over and over again. There is a statary period during which eggs are laid and larvae, which the workers have been carrying develop into adults. In less than a week a single queen may lay 25,000 eggs. They hatch into larvae in a few days and are ready to be moved along. This pause for developing a new generation is followed by a nomadic phase in which the group travels almost constantly. A bivouac is made for a daily nest.

Migrants from South America. The *Argentine ant* (*Iridomyrmex humilis*) is a type of nomad, for it makes a nest but does not stay there permanently, moving frequently to wherever food is abundant. Despite its popular name, its origin apparently was in Brazil and Bolivia. After invading Argentina, it was carried on ships to many parts of the globe, including the United States, Africa, and Europe. Wherever Argentine ants go, the native ants begin to disappear as the newcomers aggressively attack colonies and take over territory. They multiply at a fantastic rate. In regions where there is no cold weather they live outdoors the year round. Otherwise they become dreaded pests, for during the winter they swarm into houses, invading food, clothing, and furniture.

Another unpopular migrant to other lands from South America is the *fire ant* (*Solenopsis geminata*), which is somewhat different from the fire ants native to the United States. The imported variety has become a major pest, especially to farmers. They destroy growing plants, by chewing the plant tissues and sucking the juices. They eat cultivated as well as wild seeds. They also attack hatching birds and other newborn animals. The large mounds that they build in hayfields often break the blades of harvesting machines. The mounds also can be damaging to mowing equipment along roads and highways.

Leaf Cutters and Leaf Sewers. A troublesome species confined to Central and South America is the leaf cutter, or *parasol,* ant. This kind marches in large numbers to a tree, and each individual cuts a sizable circular piece of leaf. When they leave for their nest, the tree may be completely stripped of its foliage; whole plantations may be ruined in a short time where parasol ants are unchecked.

For many years observers had wondered about the use for these pieces of leaves; it seemed obvious that they were not meant to be eaten. Finally, it was discovered that the leaf cutters are gardeners. Inside their nest they chew the leaf sections into spongelike masses, which they store in a special chamber far under the earth's surface. This becomes a fungus garden in which mushrooms grow, and it is the mushrooms that are eaten. The success of the crops is not left

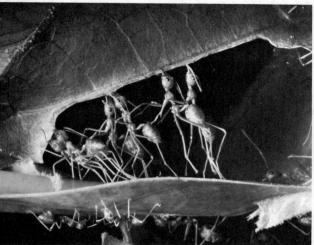

(*Above*) WEAVER ANTS (*Oecophylla*) build nests by sewing leaves together with silk produced by the larvae.

(*Right*) LEAF CUTTERS, or parasol ants, cut leaf sections and carry them to their nests for growing mushrooms.

to chance. If the pieces of leaves brought to the nest are very dry, they are put outside overnight so that they absorb moisture. If they are too damp when collected, they are left above ground for a while on a clear day. Should a sudden rain soak them thoroughly, they are ignored and a new supply is gathered. As the workers store their chewed leaves underground, they arrange hollow areas and passages in the masses through which they can regulate ventilation and temperature.

While the true fungus growers, the Attii tribe, are native to the tropics, some of the species have spread into the southern portions of the United States. Parasol ant workers have extremely powerful jaws, and they can give a nasty bite, even to humans.

In southern Asia and on some of the Pacific islands are ants named *Oecophylla*, which have the extraordinary habit of "sewing" leaves together for the construction of their nests. A worker stations itself along the border of a leaf and, with its jaws embedded in the edge of the next leaf, pulls the two close together. At this point another worker carries a larva equipped with silk-producing glands to the leaf edge and squeezes the larva to stimulate its silk glands. The silk is pressed against the edge of one leaf, and the ant then moves the larva to the edge of the next leaf and anchors the silk thread there. The process is repeated over and over until the two leaves are joined. This work may be accomplished by two ants working as a team or, if the leaves are far apart, by two groups.

Oecophylla are colorful ants. The queen and some workers are green, other workers are reddish, and the males are black. They are extremely aggressive, and no other insect can survive in a tree that they adopt for their own.

Black Carpenters and Honey Ants. The black carpenter (*Camponotus pennsylvanicus*) is one of the largest ants native to North America and one of the most destructive. A queen measures nearly an inch (2.54 cm) in length, and workers may

be ½ inch (1.3 cm) long. In a natural setting these wood-chewing insects are not especially destructive because, for the most part, they seek out old logs and stumps in which to tunnel. However, as forests have been disappearing, the carpenters have been adapting their lives to those of people, and they invade frameworks of houses, pantries, and food supplies of all kinds. They may destroy good, sound trees as well as those that are rotting.

Because carpenter ants chew wood, they often are compared with termites. But termites actually eat wood; the carpenters merely chew it in order to make living quarters. They often take over a location originally inhabited by termites and use it for nesting. Many American carpenter ants are carried to Europe on timber, but they do not settle in and around homes in Europe as they do in America.

A notable relative of the carpenter is a yellow-brown honey ant (*Myrmecocystus*). Its name is not concerned with its diet of a kind of natural "honeydew" but with its unique manner of storing honey. The honeydew is either the sweet sap of plants or a liquid that the ants lick from the bodies of tiny "plant lice" called aphids. In dry areas where fresh supplies are not always available, this storage prevents any season of famine. Below the regular living quarters, several feet under the surface of the ground, the ants construct storage rooms. In them hang strange potbellied creatures; they are worker ants, but they are special workers that have been turned into living storage tanks known as repletes. The repletes are chosen when the workers are young enough for their skin to stretch. Normal workers collect honeydew and pump it into the repletes until their abdomens are distended to many times the normal diameter. The repletes are unable to walk. They spend their lives hanging from the ceiling, receiving honey and giving it out as it is needed.

A number of related species of ants have developed this storage habit, and they are found in

(*Above*) CARPENTER ANTS are wood-chewers that live in logs and stumps. The ant here has captured a robberfly.

(*Left*) HONEY ANTS feed on honeydew that they store in the bodies of worker ants (shown here) called repletes.

various parts of the world. They are well known in the southwestern United States and in Mexico. In fact, the "honeypots" are collected by Mexicans to be served as a gourmet's delicacy.

Ant "Cows." Taking honeydew from aphids is a habit practiced by many ants. However, some ants go beyond the simple procedure of licking the sweet liquid from the aphids they encounter by chance; they capture a number of the tiny insects, care for them, and "put them out to pasture," having them ready to "milk" at will. Such aphids are known as ant "cows"; the ants that tend them are "cattle-tending" species.

In North America the most widespread of the cattle-tenders are the *cornfield ants* (*Lasius niger americanus*), which often are a great pest to farmers. The aphids have long sucking tubes, which they use to drill into plants and draw out juices. Any surplus liquid drops out from the end of their abdomen, thus being made available to their insect keepers. Some aphids, especially those used by the cornfield ants, specialize in attacking corn plants. During the winter, cornfield ants store the aphid eggs in their nest while adult aphids stay nearby on the roots of grasses. The ants construct communicating tunnels to the aphids' resting places. As soon as a new crop of corn has been started in the spring,

CATTLE-TENDING ant species capture and care for aphids to maintain a supply of honeydew for food.

HARVESTER ANTS collect seeds and store them in underground "bins." The species shown is *Pogonomyrmex*.

the ants carry the aphids to the roots of the plants. The aphids reproduce rapidly, producing 16 generations between mid-spring and late fall.

Not all ants that use aphids have this elaborate procedure. Some species simply carry their "cows" with them, transferring them from one leaf to another. They may cut off the wings of winged aphids to prevent them from flying away. Or the ants may construct shelters of wood, mud, or bark on a tree or bush a little distance from their nest in which to keep herds of aphids. Still another system is to construct underground galleries about roots and stock them with aphids.

Harvesters. Another group of ants are known as harvesters. The harvest ant workers collect great quantities of seeds, carry them to the nest, and then husk and store them. During rainy seasons, when the underground granaries become moist, the workers keep the seeds dry so that they do not sprout or get moldy. On the first clear day they take all the seeds out in the open to dry and carry them back again to storage before evening. Another method the workers use to prevent the seeds from sprouting is to bite out the growing point of each seed. Sometimes they do this as soon as the seeds have been gathered, and sometimes not until they begin to sprout.

Slave Keepers. Strange as it may seem for ants to keep "cows," this is no more startling than the fact that some species have slaves, which are obtained when a weaker species is overcome and captured. More than one type is a slave keeper. Probably best known for the practice is the large brownish-red *amazon* (*Polyergus rufescens*), widespread over temperate regions of the Northern Hemisphere.

A slave raid starts with an assembly of the amazon warriors outside their own nest. Then, almost as if at a given signal, the group begins to march toward the colony to be raided. Very likely this is a colony of *black ants* (*Formica fusca*), which are used very often as slaves by the amazons and by *sanguinary ants* (*F. sanguinea*) as well. When the amazons reach the nest of their intended victims, a fierce battle may take place. The amazons use their sharp, sickle-shaped jaws to pierce the heads and bodies of the black ants. The black ants gnaw at the legs of their attackers in defense, but the amazons fight on until they can seize the pupae of the raided nest. They carry these back home and stow them away carefully. In time the pupae develop into adults and spend their lives working for the amazons by finding food and feeding them. The amazons are completely dependent on their slaves because their sharp jaws, so well suited for fighting, are useless in taking care of larvae or for digging. Also, their tongues have become shortened to such an extent that they cannot feed themselves without help. The sanguinary ants can, and often do, take care of themselves.

Some ants let others do their work for them without pressing them into "slavery." These are the various tiny species that creep into the nests of big ants and steal their food or even eat the larvae. Such parasitic ants sometimes are tolerated by the nest's owners, which seem to have no objection to having the tiny ants crawling over them. They even may feed them droplets of honey and lick and stroke them. When they no longer are welcome, they escape into passages too small for the big ants to enter.

The guests in an ant colony are not always other ants. Several thousands of other kinds of insects, including small beetles, crickets, and roaches, take advantage of the efficient homes constructed by the ants. Some of them do no harm, but others prove quite disastrous, in time causing the disintegration of a colony.

Although some ants create problems, there are some ways in which they are helpful. They kill vast numbers of other insects that are harmful to crops, and their burrowing in the soil helps to make it loose and absorbent so that rainwater can soak into it rather than run off.

Classification. Ants are a part of the order Hymenoptera, which also includes bees, wasps, and all the truly social insects except termites. Hymenoptera, in turn, belongs to the class Insecta, and Insecta is a part of the phylum Arthropoda. The members of the Hymenoptera order are divided into two groups, or suborders: those with a constricted abdomen and those without the constriction, such as the sawfly. The former group, Clistogastra, is composed of the wasps and bees and the family Formicidae—the ants.

DOROTHY SHUTTLESWORTH
Author of "The Story of Ants"

Bibliography
Barker, Will, *Familiar Insects of America* (New York 1960).
Haskins, Caryl P., *Of Ants and Men* (San Francisco 1939).
Klots, Alexander B., and Klots, Elsie B., *Living Insects of the World* (New York 1959).
Lanham, Url, *The Insects* (New York 1964).
Maeterlinck, Maurice, *Life of the Ant* (New York 1930).
Michener, Charles D., and Michener, Mary, *American Social Insects* (New York 1951).
Shuttlesworth, Dorothy, *The Story of Ants* (New York 1964).
Wheeler, William Morton, *Ants* (New York 1960).

ANT LION, a highly predacious insect larva. Also known as *lacewing fly* (in the adult form) and *doodlebug*, this insect is widely distributed throughout the world, particularly where dry, sandy, or dusty soil occurs. The larva is especially adapted in structure and behavior for obtaining its food. It is usually ⅖ inch (10 to 12 mm) long. The body is oval, the head distinct, the eyes well developed, the jaws elongated and curved, and the skin covered with stiff bristles. It digs rapidly into crumbly soil and excavates a circular pit, at the bottom of which it lies concealed awaiting some prey, such as an ant or other insect. The ant lion seizes its prey between long, sharply toothed jaws and sucks its blood. Ant lions comprise many species in the family Myrmeleontidae of the Order Neuroptera.

ROBERT E. GREGG, *University of Colorado*

Ant lion

HUGH SPENCER

ANTA. See AMERICAN NATIONAL THEATRE AND ACADEMY.

ANTABUSE. See ALCOHOLISM.

ANTACID, ant-as'əd, a drug that, on ingestion, neutralizes the hydrochloric acid present in the stomach fluids. The most common antacid is sodium bicarbonate (baking soda), which is used for simple indigestion and "heartburn." Sodium bicarbonate may cause stomach (gastric) distension, however, because it releases carbon dioxide. Calcium carbonate (precipitated chalk) provides more neutralizing power than any other inorganic salt, but it also causes constipation. Magnesium hydroxide (milk of magnesia) is an effective antacid, but it acts as a laxative in larger doses. Aluminum hydroxide, either alone or in combination with various magnesium compounds, is the most popular antacid used.

Commercial antacids vary in their effectiveness and speed of action. The ideal antacid would effectively neutralize hydrochloric acid and have a prolonged effect. It would not cause the blood to become too basic, interfere with digestion, be an irritant to the stomach, release carbon dioxide, or cause constipation, diarrhea, or overstimulation of acid secretion.

GEORGE GRIFFENHAGEN
American Pharmaceutical Association

ANTAEUS, an-tē'əs, in Greek mythology, was a king of Libya, a giant of prodigious strength and an invincible wrestler. The son of the sea god Poseidon (Neptune) and Gaea (Terra), the Earth, he derived his great strength from contact with the earth. Thus, with each fall in a wrestling bout he revitalized his strength and, in this way, could wear down any opponent. He challenged strangers to wrestle with him, and with the skulls of those he had slain he built a temple to Poseidon.

When Heracles (Hercules), in quest of the golden apples of Hesperides, stopped in Libya, he discovered Antaeus' secret. Lifting the giant off the ground, Heracles crushed him to death in mid-air. The bout between Antaeus and Hercules was a favorite subject in ancient art.

ANTÂKYA. See ANTIOCH.

ANTALYA, än-täl'yä, is a port city on the Mediterranean coast of Turkey. It is the capital of Antalya province. It was formerly known as *Adalya* and to medieval Europe as *Satalia*. Picturesquely situated on steep cliffs overlooking the Gulf of Antalya, the city is third in importance of Turkey's Mediterranean ports, after Mersin and İskenderun. The harbor is not deep, however, and only ships of very shallow draft can put into the port. All others must anchor in the roads and be served by tender.

This commercial disadvantage is further aggravated by the city's isolation from central Anatolia by the high range of the western Toros Mountains that encircles the region. The road connecting Antalya with Burdur and İsparta through the Çubuk Pass is inadequate for a large volume of traffic, and the city has only a small airport. Plans for a railway through the mountains have been economically infeasible. Trade is, therefore, confined to exporting the fruits (oranges, lemons, bananas, and olives) grown on the fertile plains in the area, and small amounts of chrome, timber, and animal products.

In recent years the growth of tourism has opened new avenues of development. Except for the excessive heat of July and August, the climate is mild and sunny throughout the year. The city's seclusion from industry, its miles of uncrowded beaches, its palm-shaded streets and parks, and the great wealth of relics of classical antiquity in its vicinity have accelerated its conversion into a Turkish "Riviera."

The city was founded by King Attalus II of Pergamum (reigned 159–138 B.C.) and called *Attaleia*. Until taken by the Romans in 79 B.C., it was a notorious pirate haven. It became a senatorial province of the Roman empire about 43 A.D., and because of the great increase in maritime activity it replaced in importance the older neighboring cities of the Pamphylian plain, Perge, Aspendos (Belkis), and Side. In 1207 it was taken from the Byzantines by the Anatolian Seljuks. About the beginning of the 14th century, Antalya passed to the Teke Beğleri, a branch of the Turkman dynasty of the Hamidoğlu, who lost it to the Ottomans in 1423. Population: (1965) 71,600.

JOHN R. WALSH, *University of Edinburgh*

ANTARCTIC PENINSULA, ant-ärk'tik pə-nin'sə-lə, an arm of land about 1,000 miles (1,660 km) long reaching from the continent of Antarctica toward South America. It has been known by various names. The United States formerly called it *Palmer Peninsula* after Nathaniel Brown Palmer, American explorer, who sighted it on Nov. 18, 1820. The British claimed that Edward Bransfield of the Royal Navy had discovered the peninsula on Jan. 30, 1820, and they called it *Graham Land* in honor of Sir James R.G. Graham, first lord of the admiralty at the time of the voyage. Argentina called the same peninsula *San Martin Land;* Chile called it *O'Higgins Land.*

In 1964, the name "Antarctic Peninsula" was agreed upon as a designation for the whole area. The northern part was called Graham Land and the southern part Palmer Land. The peninsula is claimed by Britain, which administers it under the British Antarctic Survey, and by Argentina and Chile. Continuously since World War II each of these three countries has maintained several bases there. In 1965, the United States established Palmer Station on Anvers Island as a permanent research base.

The first man to land on the peninsula (and on the Antarctic continent) was the American sealer Capt. John Davis, on Feb. 7, 1821. Since 1900 many notable explorations have been made. Sir Hubert Wilkins flew down the east coast to beyond latitude 69° south in 1928 and believed that the peninsula was separated from the mainland by an ice-locked strait. John Rymill's British Graham Land expedition (1934–1937) and the U.S. Antarctic Service Expedition (1939–1941) both suspected that it was part of the mainland. Finn Ronne's Antarctic Research Expedition (1946–1948) photographed 750,000 square miles (1,943,000 sq km) of the area and proved that high land existed at the site of Wilkins' assumed ice-locked strait and continued on to the south. In the early 1960's, seismic surveys suggested that the Antarctic Peninsula might be part of a huge island, one of an archipelago comprising West Antarctica, all of which is covered by the permanent continental ice cap.

EDITH M. RONNE, *Specialist in Antarctic Affairs*

THE ANTARCTIC SUN illuminates an ice formation on the Ross Sea near Little America.

ANTARCTICA

ANTARCTICA, ant-ark′ti-kə, the snow-covered landmass around the South Pole, is the world's fifth-largest continent. It is surrounded by an often stormy, ice-dotted sea known as the Antarctic Ocean—which is, in fact, merely a continuation of the Atlantic, Pacific, and Indian oceans. Antarctica is nearly circular in outline, except for the indentations of the Ross and Weddell seas and the projection of Antarctic Peninsula. The continent's 5,100,000 square miles (13,209,000 sq km), equaling about one tenth of the earth's land surface, lie almost entirely within the Antarctic Circle (66° 36′ S).

The average altitude of the Antarctic continent—without its covering of snow and ice—is 6,000 feet (1,830 meters), which is almost twice that of any other continent. The dome-shaped mantle of snow and ice on top of the landmass has an average thickness of about 8,000 feet (2,440 meters), making the total average altitude about 14,000 feet (4,270 meters). The icy dome reaches a thickness of about 10,500 feet (3,200 meters) in the interior of the continent and terminates at the coastline in towering cliffs 100 feet (30 meters) or more above the green-gray sea. In the waters around the 18,648 miles (30,010 km) of coastline, icebergs and floating glacier ice mingle with floes of pack ice to create hazardous conditions for shipping.

Climate. Mean temperatures are generally about 20° F (11° C) colder than those in an equivalent latitude of the Arctic, thus making the Antarctic the coldest region in the world. The coastal fringes of the continent, where most wintering expeditions have encamped, are not so cold as the higher elevations of the interior. During the International Geophysical Year (IGY), 1957–1958, when the average temperature in the coldest month at a coastal station was only − 0.6° F (− 18° C), at the South Pole station the average temperature for the same month was − 80.1° F (− 62.3° C). On Aug. 24, 1960, the Russians reported a world-record low reading of

− 126.9° F (− 88.3° C) at their Vostok station, 13,000 feet (3,962 meters) above sea level.

Wind conditions vary in Antarctica. In general winds are strongest near the coasts. Sir Douglas Mawson named Cape Denison, on Commonwealth Bay, south of Australia, the "Home of the Blizzard" because of the almost continual gales pouring down the passes from the interior. It is the windiest place in the world; gales from the ice plateau sometimes hit 200 miles per hour (322 kph). At the Bay of Whales the average wind speed during four years of observations was only 11 mph (17.6 kph), less than at Springfield, Ill., or Wichita, Kans., and the strongest wind was only 60 mph (96.5 kph).

Except for near-frost deposits and occasional rain and drizzle at the northern tip of Antarctic Peninsula, precipitation consists almost entirely of snow. It totals 10 to 20 inches (25 to 50 cm) of water (when melted) along the coasts, more in the coastal mountains, and much less in the interior. (Depth of snowfall equals about three times its depth in water when melted.) At the South Pole the snowfall has been found to be equivalent to only 1 to 2 inches (2.5 to 5 cm) of water, and the average for the continent is presumed to be somewhere between 2 and 4 inches (5 to 10 cm).

Territorial Claims. Argentina set up the first weather station on Laurie Island in the South Orkney Islands in 1904. In 1908 the pie-shaped sector between 25° and 68° west longitude, toward the South Pole and including Antarctic Peninsula, was claimed for Argentina and declared a part of its mainland. Other nations followed suit and divided the continent into similar sectors of various widths. These claims were based partly on sporadic explorations by certain nationals and some, because of their proximity to other claims, caused tension among the claimant nations. Specifically, this was true in the Antarctic Peninsula sector, where claims made by Argentina, Chile, and Britain overlapped. Although American explorers have discovered and mapped larger areas of the continent than all the other nations together, the United States has never claimed nor recognized any other nation's claim to any Antarctic territory. The Russians, until the IGY, had not been involved in Antarctic affairs since the Russian explorer von Bellingshausen circumnavigated the continent in 1819–1821, but they took a stand on Antarctic claims similar to that of the United States.

On May 3, 1958, the United States proposed to the 11 other nations in the IGY program that a treaty be formulated to preserve the present legal and political status of the continent. In Washington, D.C., on Dec. 1, 1959, delegates of the 12 original nations signed a treaty that prohibits (1) the use of Antarctica for warlike purposes; (2) permits free scientific use of the continent; (3) freezes existing territorial claims there; (4) promotes international cooperation for scientific purposes; and (5) sets up an inspection system to make sure its provisions are not violated. The fifth article bans all nuclear explosions and disposals of atomic wastes in Antarctica. Within two years the various governments had ratified the treaty and it was to remain in effect for 30 years.

Geography and Geology. By September 1966 more than nine tenths of the earth's highest continent had been seen either by eye or by camera. Large areas, about 10 percent of the total, have been mapped from the air, especially those containing distinguishing features, such as rock outcrops, peaks, and mountain ranges, some of which are as high as 17,000 feet (5,181 meters) above sea level.

Studies made during the IGY indicate that the continent contains about 40 percent more ice than had previously been believed. This enormous ice cap represents 90 percent of the world's ice surface. The ice dome's highest elevation of about 14,000 feet (4,267 meters) is found along the 60th meridian of east longitude in the vicinity of the Pole of Inaccessibility, the point farthest from any coast. The geographical South Pole is at an elevation of 9,200 feet (2,804 meters), of which approximately 900 feet (274 meters) is bedrock and the remainder ice cover. The minimum age of Antarctic glaciation is estimated at 170,000 years. Less than 10 percent of the continent's area consists of rock outcrops. Intensive geological investigations, coupled with seismic soundings throughout strategic areas, have produced a fairly accurate record of the Antarctic's long and varied geological history. Antarctica once had a temperate climate, with forests and swamps, but that changed radically about 170,000 years ago.

Evidence suggests that two separate ice sheets, beginning in two structurally different mountain areas, gradually expanded until they bridged and covered an important subsurface trough. This trough separates three areas of entirely different geological periods. East Antarctica, the portion south of the Indian Ocean, is a single landmass, composed mostly of igneous rock formed in the Precambrian era about a billion years ago. It is separated from West Antarctica by an extensive mountain range, called the Great Antarctic Horst (or Transantarctic Mountains) which has the deep subsurface trough running alongside it. This trough, now filled with ice two miles (3.2 km) thick, of which as much as one mile (1.6 km) is below

sea level, continues on into West Antarctica. There it again marks the line between two different time periods, an ancient one and a newer, volcanic era.

West Antarctica is an archipelago of islands, some of which are below sea level but all of which are covered by the continental ice cap. The older part has a mountain system composed of ancient granites and sedimentary rock extending down the middle of the northward-protruding Antarctic Peninsula. And it can be traced beneath the ocean, along the Scotia Arc, as an extension of the Andes Mountains of South America. This older sector of West Antarctica includes the southern portion of Byrd Land, Ellsworth Land, the Ronne Ice Shelf, and Queen Maud Land. The northern portion of Byrd Land is separated from the older part by the subsurface trough as it turns from the Great Antarctic Horst and runs from the Ross Sea to the Bellingshausen Sea. The northern, or newer, portion of West Antarctica was formed by fairly recent volcanic action in Antarctica's third period of geological time.

The Beardmore Glacier, largest discovered in the Antarctic, originates at the South Polar Plateau and flows onto the huge Ross Ice Shelf, which is about the size of France. The ice shelf forms the southernmost boundary of the Ross Sea. On the other side of the continent the Weddell Sea, another deep indentation, terminates in the Filchner Ice Shelf. The Filchner Ice Shelf stretches southward to meet the higher elevation of the Ronne Ice Shelf in front of the polar plateau.

The Antarctic Ocean. The body of water known as the Antarctic Ocean is characterized by an abundance of plankton and crustacean forms of life. Ocean currents, running deep along the bottom of the sea from the Northern Hemisphere to the Antarctic Ocean, scoop up minute sediments along their path. These sediments, extremely rich in food value, are carried by the current until they emerge in the upper layers of the cold Antarctic waters, generally between 50° and 60° south latitude. The warm-water currents rise and become the main source of heat for Antarctic waters. The cold Antarctic water sinks and continues as a cold, deep-sea current at a steady pace of about 8 miles (12.8 km) per year. The demarcation line between warm water and cold is called the Antarctic Convergence. It forms an irregular line around the entire Antarctic continent and can be traced by a marked drop of about 5° F (2.8° C) in surface temperature, and a noticeable drop in the water's salt content. The greater turbulence of the Antarctic Ocean is caused by strong, constant west winds moving the surface water from west to east around the continent. There the color of the water changes from the blue of tropical oceans to the murky, greenish-gray of the Antarctic seas. Much of this color change is caused by the abundance of microscopic organisms that make these waters so rich in nutritional matter.

Natural Resources. In natural resources, Antarctica is considered by scientists to be the most worthless of all the continents. Traces of minerals, such as nickel, copper, molybdenum, iron, gold, and silver have been found in rock outcrops in the more massive mountain ranges, and there are large coal deposits in some sedimentary rocks. But none has been found in sufficient quantity to justify the financial investment required to

ICEBERG in the Ross Sea is surrounded by numerous ice floes through which ships must crunch their way.

U.S. NAVY

exploit it under such difficult climatic conditions.

Wealth derived thus far from the Antarctic regions has been realized principally by the whaling industry of several nations since the Norwegian Christen Christensen sent the first whaling expedition into Antarctic waters in 1892. But this industry is rapidly dying out because some nations have failed to adhere to international quota agreements. This has led to indiscriminate slaughter and the near-extinction of the whales.

Plants and Animals. Since the temperatures rarely rise above the freezing point, Antarctica is virtually a botanical and zoological desert. Only the lowest forms of vegetation can be found on rocks and slopes facing north toward the sun. Botanists have found almost 400 different species of mosses along the continent's rim and on nearby islands. Two types of pink flowering plants are found on the islands in the South Shetland group and on the northern part of Antarctic Peninsula, the mildest areas of the continent. Here also are found some 200 species of freshwater algae in summer melt-pools, as well as terrestrial algae, which live on the snow.

Whales, seals, and penguins found along the coastal fringes derive their food from the waters surrounding the continent. Marine animals, particularly whales and seals, abound in Antarctic seas. Some of the species are peculiar to Antarctica; others, especially the larger whales, are related to those in the Arctic seas. Blue whales and finbacks outnumbered all other species until about 1955, when attempts at international control failed to halt the whaling industry's mass assaults. The biggest blue whale ever caught measured 124 feet (37.8 meters) in length and was estimated to weigh about 1 ton per foot (3 metric tons per meter). It was the largest animal known to have existed in the world.

Fur-bearing seals were exterminated in Antarctic waters by commercial hunters in the 1850's. Only five species of hair-seals are now found along the coastal rim.

Of the 17 species of penguins found in the Southern Hemisphere, only three—the emperor, Adélie, and chinstrap—are confined strictly to the Antarctic. The chinstrap is found mostly on Antarctic Peninsula. The emperor penguin, about 38 inches (97 cm) in height and weighing up to 80 pounds (36 kg), is the largest; the king penguin, weighing about 40 pounds (18 kg), is second; while the comical Adélie penguin, the most common of all the birds in the Antarctic, is about 18 inches (48 cm) in height and weighs

about 11 pounds (5 kg). Numerous other species of birds, including petrels, albatrosses, gulls, skuas, and terns, breed on many of the islands.

A few species of wingless insects were found by the explorers Borchgrevink and Arctowski in the late 1890's and Wilkins in 1929. Originally, these could have been brought from other continents by birds or gale-force winds. They are found in freshwater melt-pools, on mosses, and on lichens, and are active only in the short summer season. During the IGY a few insects were found living as parasites on other animals. These were mostly biting lice, which live on seabirds. Sucking lice were also found on seals, and ticks on seabirds. Flies were discovered living in coastal waters, and a pink mite was found within 300 miles (483 km) of the South Pole.

EXPLORATION

Early Expeditions. The earliest explorations of the south polar seas were made in 1772–1775 by a British expedition commanded by Capt. James Cook. No land was seen on these voyages. In October 1819, Capt. William Smith of Britain sighted the South Shetland Islands. Then, on Nov. 18, 1820, the American Nathaniel Brown Palmer, in the sloop *Hero,* discovered Orléans Strait and the northwest coast of what later proved to be a peninsula extending from the Antarctic continent. American map makers called this Palmer Peninsula. The British, however, claimed that Edward Bransfield of the Royal Navy had sighted it on Jan. 30, 1820, and they called it Graham Land. In 1964 the English-speaking countries agreed on the name Antarctic Peninsula (q.v.), the northern part to be called Graham Land and the southern part Palmer Land.

Exploration of the Antarctic intensified in the 1820's and 1830's. Adm. Fabian von Bellingshausen, a Russian explorer, circumnavigated the continent and discovered Alexander Island and Peter I Island in January 1821. When the log of the American sealer *Huron* was discovered in 1955, it revealed that the *Huron's* captain, John Davis, had been the first person to set foot on the Antarctic continent, having landed on Antarctic Peninsula on Feb. 7, 1821, from the auxiliary schooner *Cecilia.* In 1823 the English navigator James Weddell found the sea that bears his name. John Biscoe, an English whaling captain, discovered Enderby Land in 1821, and Capt. John Balleny, an English sealer, discovered the Balleny Islands in 1839. The French explorer Dumont d'Urville in 1840 charted Adélie Coast. The existence of Antarctica as a continent was finally established by the expedition of Lt. Charles Wilkes of the U.S. Navy in 1838–1842. The land that he sighted, on the Indian Ocean coast, was called Wilkes Land in his honor.

Sir James Clark Ross, in 1839–1843, found an ice-free body of water, now named the Ross Sea. Thinking the door to the South Pole was open, he continued southward. A steep, rocky coastline loomed over the horizon in latitude 70° 41′ S, longitude 172° 30′ E, later named Cape Adare. Farther south a huge ice barrier blocked advance in latitude 77° 32′ S, and an active volcano, which Ross named Mount Erebus, was sighted rising 13,200 feet (4,023 meters) above the sea. A nearby inactive volcano he called Mount Terror. For 450 miles (724 km) he sailed eastward along an ice barrier that averaged 150 feet (45 meters) above the water. Ross made no landing on the continent.

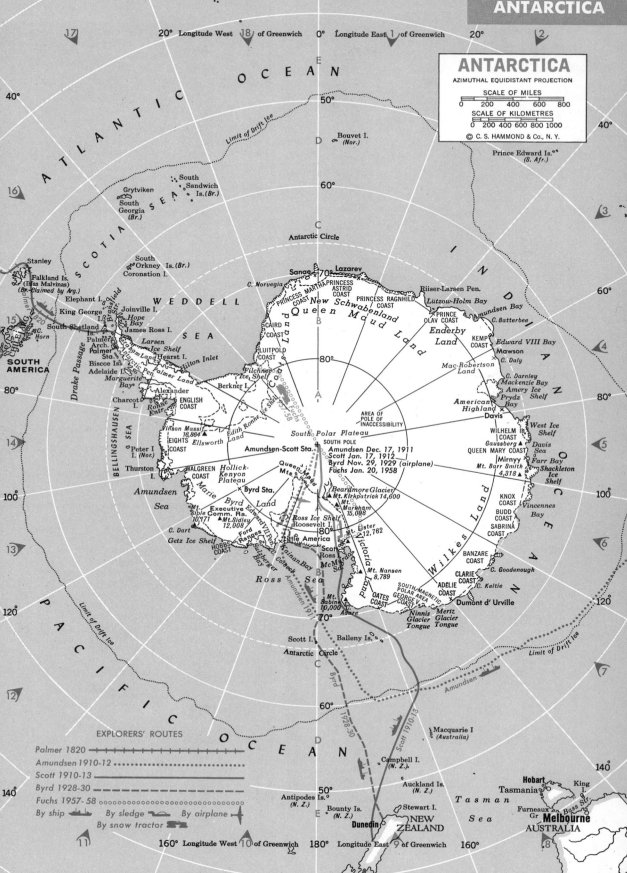

ANTARCTICA

OCEAN

ATLANTIC

ANTARCTIC

PACIFIC OCEAN

INDIAN OCEAN

ANTARCTICA
AZIMUTHAL EQUIDISTANT PROJECTION
SCALE OF MILES
0   200   400   600   800
SCALE OF KILOMETRES
0   200 400 600 800 1000
© C. S. HAMMOND & Co., N. Y.

20° Longitude West 18 of Greenwich 0° Longitude East 1 of Greenwich 20°

Limit of Drift Ice

Bouvet I.
(Nor.)

Prince Edward Is.
(S. Afr.)

South
Sandwich
Is. (Br.)

Grytviken
South
Georgia
(Br.)

SCOTIA SEA

Antarctic Circle

Sanae   Lazarev
C. Norvegia   PRINCESS MARTHA COAST
PRINCESS ASTRID COAST
PRINCESS RAGNHILD COAST
Riiser-Larsen Pen.
Lützow-Holm Bay
Amundsen Bay
C. Batterbee

Stanley
Falkland Is.
(Islas Malvinas)
Br.-Claimed by Arg.)
Elephant I.
King George I.
Joinville I.
Hope Bay
James Ross I.
South Shetland Is.
Cape Horn

WEDDELL SEA

New Schwabenland
Queen Maud Land
CAIRD COAST
LUITPOLD COAST
Filchner Ice Shelf
Berkner I.

PRINCE OLAV COAST
Enderby Land
KEMP COAST
Edward VIII Bay
Mawson
C. Daly
Mac-Robertson Land
C. Darnley
Mackenzie Bay
Amery Ice Shelf
Prydz Bay

Larsen
Ice Shelf
Land
Hearst I.
Hilton Inlet
Palmer Land
Alexander I.
Charcot I.
ENGLISH COAST
Ronne Entr.

American Highland
Davis
WILHELM II COAST
QUEEN MARY COAST
Gaussberg
West Ice Shelf
Davis Sea
Mirnyy
Mt. Barr Smith
4,318
Farr Bay
Shackleton Ice Shelf

SOUTH AMERICA

Drake Passage

Adelaide I.
Marguerite Bay

Vinson Massif
16,864
EIGHTS COAST
Ellsworth Land
Edith Ronne Ice Shelf
South Polar Plateau
AREA OF POLE OF INACCESSIBILITY
SOUTH POLE
Amundsen-Scott Sta.
Amundsen Dec. 17, 1911
Scott Jan. 17, 1912
Byrd Nov. 29, 1929 (airplane)
Fuchs Jan. 20, 1958

Peter I I.
(Nor.)
Thurston I.
Amundsen Sea
WALGREEN COAST
Hollick-Kenyon Plateau
Byrd Sta.
Marie Byrd Land
Mt. Executive Comm. Ra.
Siple 10,171
Mt. Sidley 12,008
C. Dart
Getz Ice Shelf
Ford Ranges
HOBBS COAST
Mts. Queen Maud
Beardmore Glacier
Mt. Kirkpatrick 14,600
Mt. Markham 15,088
Ross Ice Shelf
Roosevelt I.
Little America
Kainan Bay
Amundsen 1911

KNOX COAST
BUDD COAST
SABRINA COAST
Vincennes Bay
Mt. Lister 12,762
BANZARE COAST
CLARIE COAST
C. Goodenough
C. Keltie
Mt. Nansen 8,789
SOUTH MAGNETIC POLAR AREA
GEORGE V COAST
OATES COAST
ADELIE COAST
Dumont d'Urville

Wilkes Land
Victoria Land
Scott
Ross
McMurdo Sd.
Mt. Sabine 10,000
C. Adare

Bellingshausen Sea

Kainan Bay
Prestrud Inlet
Colbeck
Biscoe Bay

Ross Sea

Ninnis Glacier Tongue
Mertz Glacier Tongue

Limit of Drift Ice

Scott I.   Balleny Is.
Antarctic Circle
Byrd
Scott 1910-13
Amundsen
Macquarie I
(Australia)

Byrd 1928-30

Campbell I.
(N. Z.)
Auckland Is.
(N. Z.)

Antipodes Is.
(N. Z.)
Bounty Is.
(N. Z.)
Stewart I.
Dunedin
NEW ZEALAND

Tasman Sea

Hobart
Tasmania
King I.
Furneaux Gr
Melbourne
AUSTRALIA

EXPLORERS' ROUTES
Palmer 1820
Amundsen 1910-12
Scott 1910-13
Byrd 1928-30
Fuchs 1957-58
By ship   By sledge   By airplane
By snow tractor

160° Longitude West 10 of Greenwich 180° Longitude East 9 of Greenwich 160°

ANTARCTICA

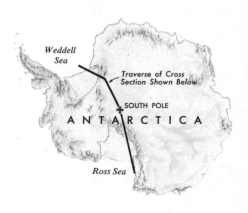

Weddell
Sea

Traverse of Cross
Section Shown Below

SOUTH POLE

A N T A R C T I C A

Ross Sea

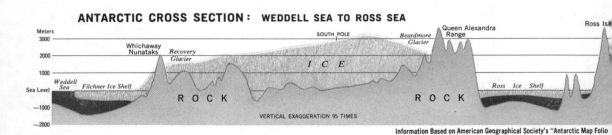

ANTARCTIC CROSS SECTION: WEDDELL SEA TO ROSS SEA

Meters

SOUTH POLE

Beardmore
Glacier

Queen Alexandra
Range

Ross Isl

3000

Whichaway
Nunataks

Recovery
Glacier

I C E

2000

1000

Weddell
Sea

Filchner Ice Shelf

Ross Ice Shelf

Sea Level

R O C K

R O C K

−1000

VERTICAL EXAGGERATION 95 TIMES

−2000

Information Based on American Geographical Society's "Antarctic Map Folio"

EMPEROR PENGUINS crowd an Antarctic rookery. Zoologist uses bag (center) to catch a bird for study.

After the landing by Captain Davis in 1821 the next to land on the Antarctic continent was Capt. Leonard Kristensen of the Norwegian whaler *Antarctic*. He put a party ashore at Cape Adare in January 1895. A member of that party, Carsten E. Borchgrevink, also a Norwegian, returned in 1899 as the leader of a British expedition that was the first to spend a winter on the Antarctic continent. He was also the first to sledge into the interior, reaching latitude 78° 50′ S, the farthest south then attained. In 1898, Lt. Adrien de Gerlache in the *Belgica* led a Belgian expedition that penetrated the pack ice to latitude 71° 30′ S, was frozen in, wintered on the ship, and under Henryk Arctowski produced noteworthy scientific results.

From 1901 to 1916, Antarctic exploration was very active. One expedition, under Capt. Robert Falcon Scott, in 1901 sledged to latitude 82° 17′ S, longitude 163° 30′ E. A vast amount of scientific work was also achieved. The Swedish expedition under Nils Otto Gustaf Nordenskjöld in 1901–1904 made geographical discoveries on the east coast of Antarctic Peninsula and brought back much scientific data. His ship, the *Antarctic*, was lost in the ice; the crew was rescued the next season. An important expedition was led by Ernest Henry Shackleton (1907–1909). He wintered at Ross Island in the Ross Sea with easy access to the Ross Ice Shelf. With three companions he started south in early spring, using Siberian ponies. These were soon lost, forcing the party to man-haul their supplies. Their turning point at latitude 88° 23′ S, longitude 162° E, within 97 nautical miles (179.7 km) of the South Pole, was reached on Jan. 9, 1909, passing all previous records by 366 miles (589 km). This feat resulted in Shackleton's being knighted in 1909. A second party under Sir T.W. Edgeworth David sledged along the coast of Victoria Land and reached the vicinity of the south magnetic pole. In 1909–1910, Jean Charcot in his vessel *Pourquoi Pas?* successfully explored the west coast of Antarctic Peninsula and discovered Charcot Island.

The South Pole Reached. In 1911 five expeditions—Norwegian, Roald Amundsen; German, Wilhelm Filchner; British, Robert Scott; Australian, Douglas Mawson; and Japanese, Lt. Nobu Shirase—were in the field. All had the South Pole as their goal. Amundsen was the first to reach the Pole. He left Norway aboard the *Fram* in July 1910, having announced that he was headed for the North Pole via Cape Horn and Bering Strait. Meanwhile, Robert E. Peary's attainment of the North Pole (April 6, 1909) had electrified the world, and Amundsen altered the goal of his expedition to the South Pole. Scott, who was ready to sail on the *Terra Nova* from New Zealand for an intended wintering base on McMurdo Sound, received a cablegram from Amundsen regarding his change in plans. Scott arrived at the sound on Jan. 3, 1911. Amundsen reached the Bay of Whales, an inlet in the Ross Ice Shelf, 400 miles (844 km) farther east and 60 miles (96 km) farther south, on Jan. 14, 1911, and set up his base, Framheim. There he was visited by the *Terra Nova*, which had deposited Scott's wintering party and was now on a survey trip to King Edward VII Land (now Edward VII Peninsula).

Before the Antarctic winter set in, Amundsen built caches of food to latitude 82° S. He started for the pole on Oct. 20, 1911, with four companions, 52 dogs, four sledges, and a four months' food supply. At 85° S, where the Ross Ice Shelf joins land, the party had to climb glaciers to an elevation of 10,600 feet (3,231 meters). The highest altitude, 10,750 feet (3,276 meters), was reached on December 6, at 87° 40′ S, in the Queen Maud Mountains, discovered by Amundsen. On Dec. 14, 1911, the South Pole was located by celestial observation on the smooth South Polar Plateau (at first named after King Haakon VII). The Norwegian flag was unfurled, and the party remained at the pole until December 17. All five men reached their wintering base, Framheim, on Jan. 25, 1912.

The most dramatic story in Antarctic polar exploration began when Scott's party of five, accompanied by supporting groups, left McMurdo Sound on Nov. 1, 1911. Their Siberian ponies proved ill-adapted to the snowy surface, and they had to man-haul their supplies on sledges. Exhausted, they reached the pole 35 days after Amundsen and were disheartened to find Amundsen's caches. Scott determined the pole to be less than ½ mile (0.8 km) from Amundsen's tent. On their return journey, weakened by shortage of food, man-hauling, and low temperatures, Scott's party was beset by mishaps, with the result that the entire group perished. The last entry in Scott's journal was dated March 29, 1912. Not until the following Antarctic spring, on Nov. 12, 1912, did a rescue party succeed in reaching the tent of the dead. A cairn with a cross above it was built over the spot.

Further Explorations. In 1911, Wilhelm Filchner's ship, the *Deutschland*, was the first to reach the head of the Weddell Sea by an approach from its eastern side. The expedition was erecting its base huts on the ice in Vahsel Bay when the ice shelf suddenly broke loose and drifted northward, in March 1912. The men were rescued. Shirase visited the Bay of Whales in 1912 and made a short sledge trip on the Ross Ice Shelf. From 1911 to 1914, Mawson commanded an expedition to the Australian sector, made geographical discoveries, and gathered extensive scientific data. In recognition of his work he was knighted in 1914.

Shackleton, in August 1914, launched a daring Antarctic project, to sledge across the continent from Coats Land at the Weddell Sea to McMurdo Sound in the Ross Sea. He employed two ships: one for a party headed by himself to make the transpolar sledge trip with dogs, the other to meet him at the Ross Sea side of the continent. Shackleton's ship, the *Endurance*, was within a few miles of its destination, Vahsel Bay, when it was beset in the heavy pack ice and began a drift northward in the Weddell Sea. It eventually sank near latitude 69° S, longitude 52° W. The men, after a perilous journey drifting on the ice floes, reached Elephant Island. There 22 of them remained behind while Shackleton, with five companions in a small whaleboat, made a hazardous crossing of treacherous waters to South Georgia Island, 800 miles northeast. All the men were rescued by the end of 1916. In 1921, Shackleton again sailed south, this time aboard the *Quest* to explore the Enderby Land quadrant. In 1922 he died aboard his ship at South Georgia, where he was buried.

Explorations by Air. The use of airplanes opened a new era in Arctic and Antarctic exploration. Sir Hubert Wilkins was knighted in 1928 after a remarkable flight across the Arctic. Later the same year he became the first man to use an airplane in Antarctica. His daring flight from Deception Island in the South Shetlands, along the east coast of Antarctic Peninsula to latitude 70° S, added thousands of square miles to the known Antarctic. Wilkins led a second expedition in 1929, established the outlines of Charcot Island, and flew southward over the pack ice to the west. In 1928–1930, Comdr. Richard E. Byrd, U.S.N. (Ret.), established Little America I, close to Amundsen's old base, Framheim, in the Bay of Whales. On Nov. 28–29, 1929, with pilot Bernt Balchen, air photo reconnaissance mapping was performed by the first flight to penetrate the interior, when the South Polar Plateau was attained and the South Pole encircled. Many fields of science were pursued under Laurence M. Gould. Byrd returned to the same base in 1934, and from here set up the southernmost outpost 120 miles (193 km) south, where he wintered alone. His scientists discovered and explored much of Byrd Land to the east. At various times from 1926 to 1937 the Norwegian Lars Christensen, in conjunction with his whaling operations, conducted exploratory mapping flights in the Norwegian- and Australian-claimed sectors. During his expedition in 1929–1930 he laid formal claim to Queen Maud Land, Lars Christensen Coast, Ingrid Christensen Coast, Princess Astrid Coast, and Crown Princess Martha Coast. Detailed mapping was done of Queen Maud Land, and ice-free lakes were found along the rocky coastline. (These lakes are caused by melting snow running into depressions along the coast, where the summer sun is strong enough to keep them free of ice.) Lincoln Ellsworth's four American expeditions (organized with the aid of Sir Hubert Wilkins), from 1933 to 1939, discovered large areas of new land. His transantarctic flight in 1935 from Dundee Island, off the east coast of Antarctic Peninsula, to the Bay of Whales, was a feat of daring. It was done in a single-engine plane, with four landings enroute, and took 22 days. The newly discovered area he named Ellsworth Land. In 1938–1939 he penetrated 300 miles (483 km) in longitude 80° E, in an area now called American Highland. Capt. Alfred Ritscher's German expedition to the Queen Maud Land sector in 1939 mapped new land between longitudes 21° E and 12° W.

The British Graham Land Expedition 1934–1937, led by John Rymill, was based on the Debenham Islands in Marguerite Bay. The expedition found that Antarctic Peninsula is connected with the mainland of Antarctica, and it explored and named George VI Sound, between Antarctic Peninsula and Alexander Island.

The United States Antarctic Service Expedition 1939–1941, organized by the Department of the Interior and headed by Admiral Byrd, established West Base at the Bay of Whales, and East Base in Marguerite Bay on Stonington Island. The expedition conducted aerial reconnaissance and continued earlier scientific programs. The Weddell Sea coastline was extended 250 miles (402 km) beyond the southern limit of Wilkins' flight in 1928. A party under Finn Ronne sledged 1,260 miles (2,027 km) in 84 days and while surveying 500 miles (804.6 km) of new continental coastline followed the extension of George VI Sound to where it ends in the open water of Ronne Entrance. This discovery proved that Alexander Land actually was an island.

Post-World War II Explorations. Because of World War II, Antarctic exploration was at a standstill until 1946, when the U.S. Antarctic Development Project under Admiral Byrd with U.S. Navy Task Force 68, Operation Highjump, under Rear Adm. Richard H. Cruzen sailed south with 13 ships, 21 aircraft, and 4,000 men to train navy personnel in cold-climate operations. During its five-week stay in Antarctic waters, when Little America was reoccupied, flights were made south and east from the base in the Bay of Whales. Aerial mapping flights, from two seaplane tenders operating along the periphery of the continent, covered virtually all the Antarctic coasts except those of Antarctic Peninsula and the Weddell Sea area.

The Ronne Antarctic Research Expedition (1946–1948) wintered on Antarctic Peninsula at Marguerite Bay, where its ship was intentionally frozen into the ice near the base camp. To explore the world's last unknown coastline and prove that the Antarctic was one continent, its three airplanes flew 346 hours and made 86 landings in the field. This program obtained 14,000 trimetrogon aerial photographs, supplemented by surface geodetic control points over an area of more than 700,000 square miles (1,913,-000 sq km). One third of this area was newly discovered and named Edith Ronne Land (now Ronne Ice Shelf) for the wife of the leader, who was one of the first two women to spend a year in the Antarctic. Ronne's discoveries of high land south of the Weddell Sea eliminated the possibility of a strait dividing the continent at this point. Studies in 11 branches of science had valuable results.

A joint Norwegian-Swedish-British expedition (1949–1952) under John Giæver wintered on Queen Maud Land in longitude 10° W, doing scientific research. Seismic soundings made from their base, Maudheim, for a distance of 300 miles (483 km) southward determined the icecap to vary from 900 to 7,450 feet (274–2,271 meters) in thickness, and their aircraft delineated 500 miles (804 km) of coastline. The expedition was directed by the Swedish glaciologist Hans Wilson Ahlmann and the Norwegian geophysicist Harald Ulrik Sverdrup. In January 1950 the French, under Paul Émile Victor, set up Port Martin Base on Adélie Coast for meteorological and other studies. Abandoned in 1952, the base was reoccupied in 1956 to continue science studies as part of the IGY in 1957–1958. The Australian government early in 1954 set up its first permanent base, Mawson Base, at latitude 67° 36' S, longitude 62° 55' E, on Mac-Robertson Land, so as to

AMUNDSEN takes a sighting at the South Pole on his trip in 1911. Flag is that of his native Norway.

FIRST HELICOPTERS land at the South Pole in 1963. They are part of a U.S. Army transport unit.

"establish beyond dispute" its territorial claims. There the Australians have explored unknown land and made meteorological and other studies. The Argentine icebreaker *General San Martín* penetrated the Weddell Sea pack ice in January 1955 and set up a base less than 800 miles (1,287 km) from the South Pole. In the same month the American icebreaker *Atka* reconnoitered the Ross Sea area to select a base for United States participation in the IGY. A huge segment of the Ross Ice Shelf had sloughed off at the Bay of Whales, making it no longer suitable for a landing.

International Geophysical Year. Sixty-six nations participated in the IGY. Twelve nations set up bases on the Antarctic continent and offshore islands. The United States scientific program was directed by the National Research Council, under Joseph Kaplan while the U.S. Navy under Adm. George J. Dufek provided logistic support. Navy Task Force 43 left the United States in November 1955 to set up facilities at McMurdo Sound in the Ross Sea and a scientific base at the Bay of Whales. Operation Deep Freeze II, consisting of 12 ships, 3,525 men, and 40 aircraft, established five additional stations: Byrd, 5,000 feet (1,524 meters) above sea level in Byrd Land; Ellsworth, on Ronne Ice Shelf; Wilkes, on Budd Coast; Amundsen-Scott South Pole, set up entirely by air; and Hallet, in Victoria Land, operated jointly with New Zealand. In addition, Little America V was manned in the winter of 1957 by a party of 88 men.

Belgrano Base was established by the Argentines on the Filchner Ice Shelf in the 1954–1955 season. In October 1955 the Argentines made their first flights south in this unknown area. The French set up a base on Adélie Coast, and the Japanese, using their icebreaker *Soya*, established a base on Prince Olav Coast. The Belgians, under Baron Gaston de Gerlache, son of the explorer Adrien de Gerlache, set up an IGY station in the Queen Maud Land sector while the Norwegians established their station about 40 miles (64 km) inland from Princess Martha Coast.

New Zealand's Scott Station was established at Pram Point, Ross Island, in January 1957. Led by Sir Edmund Hillary, 17 men laid supply depots for Dr. Vivian Fuchs' party, which was scheduled to cross the continent via the South Pole, from the Weddell Sea to the Ross Sea, in late 1957. In addition, the British maintained 12 bases; the Chileans six; and the Argentines eight.

The Russians renewed their interest in the Antarctic by sending two ships to their Mirnyy base on Queen Mary Coast and establishing Pionerskaya, an advance base 230 miles (370 km) inland. In February 1956 the Australians re-equipped Mawson Base on Mac-Robertson Land. A field party extended geological and geographical discoveries 300 miles (483 km) inland.

The main contingent of Dr. Fuchs' party arrived at the Shackleton base on the Filchner Ice Shelf in January 1957. On Nov. 24, 1957, using sno-cats, weasels, and dog teams, they set off across the continent to the Ross Sea, which they reached on March 2, 1958. A U.S. Navy unit, under Captain Ronne at Ellsworth Station, flew fuel supplies to the British party's South Ice Station, 250 miles (403 km) south of Shackleton. Additional support was given the party at the South Pole station by the U.S. Navy. Continuous seismic soundings revealed that the main portion of Antarctica is a single body of land.

In January 1957 the U.S. Navy icebreaker *Staten Island* and cargo ship *Wyandot* reached Gould Bay on the Filchner Ice Shelf where Ellsworth station was built. There 30 military personnel and 9 scientists, under Captain Ronne, wintered. A traverse party led by Dr. Edward Thiel covered 816 miles (1,313 km) in 80 days and located a narrow ditch about 3,500 feet (1,067 meters) below sea level extending from Gould Bay almost to Byrd Station. Ronne made many exploration flights inland. He discovered some new mountains and delineated a huge new island, about 200 miles (322 km) long and 200 miles wide, with three embayments on its east side and rising in the center to 3,200 feet (975 meters). This major geographical feature proved to be high land noted by Ronne in 1947.

After the termination of the remarkably successful IGY program on Dec. 31, 1958, an international group, the Special Committee on Antarctic Research (SCAR), was formed to continue certain aspects of the scientific research. Some nations reduced their activities, and a few dropped out, while others increased their efforts. By the end of 1966, the United States, working from its large logistic facility at McMurdo Sound, supported the following stations: South Pole, Byrd, Eights, Plateau (near the Pole of Inaccessibility), and Palmer (for oceanographical and biological studies), on Anvers Island off Antarctic Peninsula. Since 1962 the National Science Foundation has carried on oceanographic and ionospheric research from a floating scientific laboratory, the USNS *Eltanin*. See also POLAR EXPLORATION, SOUTH.

FINN RONNE, *Captain, USNR (Ret.)*, *Antarctic Explorer*

Bibliography

Amundsen, Roald, *The South Pole*, 2 vols. (New York 1913).

Billing, Graham J., *South; Man and Nature in Antarctica* (Seattle 1965).

Borchgrevink, Carsten E., *First on the Antarctic Continent* (London 1901).

Byrd, Richard E., *Discovery* (New York 1935).

Byrd, Richard E., *Little America* (New York 1930).

Caras, Roger A., *Antarctica: Land of Frozen Time* (Philadelphia 1962).

Clift, A. Denis, *Our World in Antarctica* (Chicago 1962).

Cook, James, *A Voyage Towards the South Pole and Round the World*, 3 vols. (London 1777).

Dufek, George J., *Operation Deepfreeze* (New York 1957).

Dukert, Joseph M., *This Is Antarctica* (New York 1965).

Eklund, Carl Robert, and Beckman, Joan, *Antarctica* (New York 1963).

Ellsworth, Lincoln, *Beyond Horizons* (New York 1938).

Fraser, Ronald G.J., *Once Round the Sun; the Story of the International Geophysical Year*, pp. 109–288 (New York 1958).

Fuchs, Vivian, and Hillary, Edmund, *The Crossing of Antarctica* (New York 1959).

Giaever, John, *The White Desert*, tr. from the Norwegian by E.M. Huggard (New York 1955).

Hobbs, William Herbert, *Explorers of the Antarctic* (New York 1941).

Lewis, Richard D., *A Continent for Science: The Antarctic Adventure* (New York 1965).

Marret, Mario, *Seven Men Among the Penguins; an Antarctic Venture* (New York 1955).

Mawson, Douglas, *The Home of the Blizzard* (London 1915).

Nordenskjöld, Otto, and Andersson, Johan G., *Antarctica* (London 1905).

Owen, Russell, *The Antarctic Ocean* (New York 1941).

Priestley, Raymond E., and others, eds., *Antarctic Research* (London 1964).

Ronne, Finn, *Antarctic Command* (Indianapolis 1961).

Ronne, Finn, *Antarctic Conquest* (New York 1949).

Schulthess, Emil, *Antarctica* (New York 1960).

Scientific American, Inc., *Scientific American*, vol. 207, no. 3 (New York 1962).

Scott, Robert F., *Scott's Last Expedition*, ed. by Leonard Huxley, 2 vols. (London 1913).

Scott, Robert F., *The Voyage of the "Discovery,"* 2 vols. (London 1929).

Shackleton, Ernest H., *The Heart of the Antarctic*, 2 vols. (London 1932).

Speras, Jon R., *Captain Nathaniel Brown Palmer* (New York 1922).

Stackpole, Edouard A., *The Voyage of the Huron and the Huntress* (Hartford, Conn., 1955).

Sullivan, Walter, *Quest for a Continent* (New York 1957).

Wilkes, Charles, *Narrative of the Exploring Expedition During 1838–1842*, 6 vols. (Philadelphia 1945).

Wilkins, Hubert, "The Wilkins-Hearst Antarctic Expedition, 1928–1929," *Geographical Review*, vol. 19, no. 3, pp. 353–376 (New York 1929).

Wilkins, Hubert, "Further Antarctic Explorations," *Geographical Review*, vol. 20, no. 3, pp. 357–388 (New York 1930).

For Specialized Study

Mitterling, Philip I., *America in the Antarctic to 1840* (Urbana, Ill., 1959).

Ritscher, A., *Deutsche Antarktische Expedition (1938–1939)* (Leipzig 1942).

American Elsevier Publishing Co., *Soviet Antarctic Expedition, 1955*, 3 vols. (New York 1964).

ANTARES, an-târ′ēz, is a star of the first magnitude in the constellation Scorpius. It is a red giant. If it occupied the sun's place in the solar system it would envelop the orbit of Mars. It is actually a double star. It has a small green companion, which can be seen only through powerful telescopes. Navigators use Antares in ascertaining longitude. The star was important in several ancient religions, and temples were oriented toward its rising or setting.

ANTEATER, ant′ēt-ər, an insect-eating mammal that is found from southern Mexico to Central America and as far south as Paraguay. An inhabitant of tropical forests, it has an elongated skull with short ears, a tapered snout, and a tubular mouth. It has no teeth, and its long tongue is covered with a sticky salivary secretion.

Collared anteater (*Tamandua tetradactyla*)

The fingers and toes have long claws used for opening ant and termite nests. The anteater has a good sense of smell, but its sight and hearing are not well developed. Most anteaters are nocturnal. They live in burrows of other animals or in trees and hollow logs.

The anteater belongs to the order Edentata, family Myrmecophagidae. There are three genera. *Myrmecophaga*, the giant anteater, is over five feet long (1½ meters) and has coarse gray hair. It has a diagonal black stripe with white borders along its shoulders. *Tamandua*, the collared anteater, is almost four feet (1.2 meters) long and is tan with a black band between its front and hind legs. *Cyclopes*, the least anteater, is about seven inches (17½ centimeters) long and is covered with silky, grayish yellow hair.

ANTELAMI, än-tä-lä′mē, **Benedetto** (c. 1150–c. 1230), Italian sculptor, who was one of the most important North Italian artists of the Romanesque period. His work is strongly influenced by Provençal style, and he may have lived for a time in Provence. However, he probably spent most of his life in the Valle d'Intelvi on Lake Como.

Antelami's earliest known work is a relief of the *Deposition* (1178) in the Cathedral of Parma. Here, Provençal influence can be seen in such features as the rigid structure of the figures, the flow of the drapery folds, and the quatrefoil and triangular motifs on the garments. Between the Parma *Deposition* and his sculpture for the Parma Baptistery (1196), Gothic influences entered his work. The Baptistery, of which he may also have been the architect, is an artistic triumph in its combination of Romanesque with Gothic dynamism. Later he worked on the Cathedral of Borgo San Donnino (now Fidenza), completed in 1218, and on the Abbey of San Andrea at Vercelli, completed in 1227. Antelami's *Martyrdom of St. Andrew* stands above the abbey's great portal.

To Antelami's last period of activity may be ascribed the pulpit (1226) of the Cathedral of Vercelli. His influence on other artists is seen in such diverse works as the equestrian relief of Orlando da Tresseno in Milan and the arch above the main portal of San Marco in Venice.

ANTELOPE, an'tə-lōp, any of a large number of cud-chewing, hoofed mammals that live throughout Africa and Asia. To many, the name "antelope" suggests a slender agile animal about the size of a small deer, with two slender horns gracefully sweeping back. However, there is a remarkable degree of variation in appearance and habits among different species. There is also a great variation in their habitats. The majority of antelopes are found in the grasslands, the steppe country, the savannas, and the forests. Others, however, inhabit hot deserts, swamplands, and high mountain elevations.

Size. The royal antelope (*Neotragus pygmaeus*), which lives in western coastal regions of Africa, stands only about 10 inches (25.4 cm) tall at the shoulders and has horns less than an inch (25 mm) long. It is probably the smallest of all hoofed mammals. The suni *Neotragus moschatus*), a native of eastern Africa's forests, and the dik-dik (*Madoqua*), which lives in semi-arid brushlands, are only slightly larger. At the other extreme is the giant eland (*Taurotragus derbianus*), which is native to western Africa. A fully grown male may measure over 6 feet (1.8 meters) tall at the shoulders and weigh more than 1,200 pounds (545 kg).

Horns. Horns are present in all species, and they usually occur in the females as well as the males. In general, the horns rise from the top of the head and gently sweep backward, as do those of the sable antelope (*Hippotragus niger*); but there is also a wide variety of horn shapes and sizes. For example, the horns of the kudu (*Tragelaphus strepsiceros*) are corkscrew-shaped and sometimes reach a length of 5 feet (1.5 meters). The gemsbok (*Oryx gazella*) has rather straight rapierlike horns that often reach a length of 4 feet (1.2 meters), the females having longer horns than the males. In some species, such as the addax (*Addax nasomaculatus*), the horns are spiral-shaped, while in others, such as the waterbuck (*Kobus*) and the hartebeest (*Alcelaphus buselaphus*), the horns are shaped like a lyre. Generally only one pair of horns is present, but in one species, the four-horned antelope (*Tetracerus quadricornis*), the male has two pairs—one pair about 5 inches (127 mm) long on the top of the head and another pair, about 2 inches (50 mm) long, on the forehead.

Habits. Generally, antelopes are gregarious animals, traveling in herds that range in number from a few to several thousand. By traveling in groups, rather than singly, they are much less subject to predation. Members of a herd are able to warn others of approaching danger, and consequently it is often difficult for a predator to come within striking range. Some species, however, prefer solitude to the company of others. One such species is the bushbuck (*Tragelaphus scriptus*), a shy, elusive animal that is active only at night and associates with other members of the species only during the breeding season. Another elusive species is the bongo (*Boocercus eurycerus*), which may be found in small groups or, especially the older males, as solitary individuals.

Most often, antelopes travel slowly, browsing on twigs, leaves, and grasses as they go. When chased, however, they may attain speeds as fast as 40 mph (64 kph). Their long slender limbs, combined with their enlarged nails (hooves) and comparatively rigid backs, contribute to their rapid movement and also enable them to maintain these speeds for long distances. Speed is the

Antelope (lechwe antelope or waterbuck).

antelope's most important means of escaping hungry predators, and although some of their predators, such as the cheetah, can reach greater speeds, they cannot maintain these speeds for long distances. Many antelopes are also capable of making long leaps, often in rapid succession. The impala (*Aepyceros melampus*) has been known to leap as high as 8 feet (2.4 meters) and cover a distance of 30 feet (9 meters) in a single leap.

Breeding and Life Span. The breeding season for different species varies from the early spring to the middle of the winter, and for some antelopes there is no fixed breeding season at all. Generally the female antelope gives birth to a single young, called a calf, about 8 or 10 months after mating. In some species, however, such as the duiker (*Sylvicapra grimmia*), twins are not uncommon. Sometimes, while the young antelope is growing, it is hidden in the grass or underbrush for one or two months until it is strong enough to join the herd. In a few species the young calf is marked with white spots and stripes; but these markings fade with age, and as the calf matures, it becomes the same color as the adults.

The average life span for an antelope ranges from about 15 to 20 years. Like many other forms of African wildlife, however, the antelope is not well protected, and many species are slowly diminishing in number. Some, such as the bontebok (*Damaliscus pygargus*), are found only on protected reservations.

Classification. Antelopes belong to the family Bovidae of the order Artiodactyla. They are closely related to the gazelles. Contrary to popular belief, the pronghorn antelope (*Antilocapra americana*) of North America is not a true antelope but belongs to the family Antilocapridae, and is the only living member of that family. The closest North American relative of the true antelopes is the Rocky Mountain goat (*Oreamnos americanus*), which belongs to the family Bovidae.

CHARLES LAUN, *Stephens College*

ANTENNA, an-ten′ə, a structure that is designed to transmit or receive radio waves. Television and radio antennas usually consist of wires, rods, or towers; in transistor radios they may be small coils of wire wound on ferrite rods. In directive microwave communication links or radio telescopes, they may be metal horns or dielectric rods, with or without large metal reflectors.

A transmitting antenna usually is connected by a transmission line to a power oscillator in which large currents oscillate at a controlled frequency. These currents induce currents in the line which, in turn, induce currents in the antenna. A small part of the power supplied to an efficient antenna is dissipated as heat, but most of the power is radiated into space in the form of electromagnetic radiation.

Characteristics of Electromagnetic Radiation. Three significant characteristics of electromagnetic radiation that affect the operation of antennas are illustrated by the transmission of radio signals from a spacecraft. (1) Energy is transferred from the spacecraft's transmitting antenna across millions of miles of empty space to a receiver on earth. (2) As the spacecraft recedes, the power in the receiver decreases inversely as the square of the distance, r, between the receiving and transmitting antennas. (3) Regardless of the relative velocities of the antennas, a signal (such as a change, or modulation, in the current in the transmitting antenna) is received r/c seconds after the change occurred, c being the velocity of light: 186,000 miles (3×10^8 meters) per second.

The absence of a material medium and the existence of a velocity of propagation that is a universal constant are unique to electromagnetic interaction. There is no counterpart in the transmission of signals by other means, such as pressure waves in a gas or liquid or vibrations in an elastic solid. Thus the transmission of signals electromagnetically from one antenna to another cannot be described in the physically tangible manner familiar in the transmission of

ANTENNA RADIATION PATTERNS

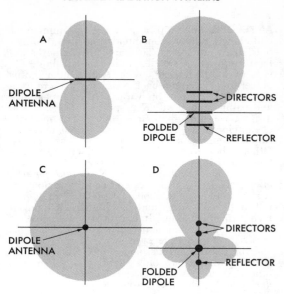

Fig. 2 Electromagnetic field patterns that are typical for antenna A are shown in A and C. Patterns that are typical for antenna array B are shown in B and D.

Fig. 1 Antenna A can be used to receive TV and FM programs, but antenna array B gives better reception.

ANTENNA CONFIGURATIONS

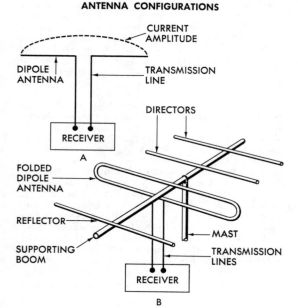

sound. Nevertheless, a complete and highly successful mathematical theory has been developed. It introduces the abstract concept of an electromagnetic field that pervades all space and is determined by the relative locations and motions of electric charges. In the mathematical formulation, this field serves as a substitute for a medium. It can exert forces and carry energy and momentum by means of wavelike disturbances that travel with the velocity of light. In this model, accelerated charges in an antenna generate a unique, time-varying electromagnetic field that travels outward from each element of alternating current as a spherical wavelet. By proper shaping and sizing of a transmitting antenna, the many wavelets emanating from its elements of current reinforce one another in a desired direction and thereby maintain a significant electromagnetic field on the surface of a distant receiving antenna. In each element of the antenna, this field induces currents that are proportional to the strength of the incident field at each instant.

The transmitting and receiving properties of antennas depend critically on a characteristic length, the wavelength λ defined by $\lambda = c/f$, where f is the frequency of oscillation of the currents. (The unit of frequency is the cycle per second or the hertz [hz]; the kilohertz [khz] is a thousand cycles per second; the megahertz [Mhz] is a million cycles per second.) In the electromagnetic-wave picture, the wavelength is the distance between successive crests or the distance traveled by a crest in the time of one complete oscillation. When the antenna dimensions are not too small compared with the wavelength, power is more easily and efficiently supplied to and radiated from a transmitting antenna or absorbed by a receiving antenna and transferred to a radio or television set.

Types of Antennas. A simple wire or rod antenna useful in UHF television (174 to 216 Mhz), FM radio (88 to 108 Mhz), and television (44 to 88 Mhz) is a half-wavelength long (Fig.

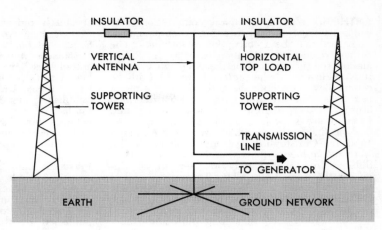

Fig. 3 Installation for transmitting home radio programs uses a vertical antenna and tower support. This type of antenna also is used to transmit other lower frequency waves that travel near the ground.

1A). Its directional properties are enhanced by one or more correctly sized and spaced conductors that serve as directors and reflectors (Fig. 1B). The same antenna can be used for transmission when the receiver is replaced by a transmitter. Typical field patterns for a single dipole antenna (Fig. 1A) and for the array (Fig. 1B) are shown in Fig. 2. The field pattern of an antenna is the same for transmission as for reception.

Short-wave radio uses lower frequencies (9 to 21 Mhz) than television and FM radio; broadcast AM radio frequencies are much lower (550 to 1,600 khz), and the VLF (very low frequency) band for long-wave communication systems includes still lower frequencies (10 to 30 khz). Broadcast and VLF antennas are usually placed vertically on the earth instead of horizontally over it as for television and FM radio (in the U.S.). The conducting earth then serves effectively as the lower half of the antenna when a ground connection of buried wires is provided. At these frequencies, vertical antennas one-quarter wavelength long are difficult to provide. Therefore, a part of the antenna is often horizontal in the form of an inverted L or a T (Fig. 3). For receiving, small loop antennas may be used if sufficient amplification is available.

A radar antenna is connected alternately to a high-power transmitter and a sensitive receiver. It is excited by series of pulses, each consisting of a succession of oscillating currents. These currents induce similar but much feebler oscillations in distant objects, such as aircraft and ships, which then reradiate as very low-power antennas. The signals from them are received by the same radar antenna in the intervals between transmitted pulses and are transferred to special receivers that display the distance and direction of an obstacle as a bright spot on a screen (cathode-ray tube). Frequencies in the microwave range (600 to 10,000 Mhz) are used because adequate resolution requires the wavelength to be short compared with the obstacles to be detected. For these frequencies, a half-wave antenna is so short that radiation of sufficient power would require hundreds of coupled antennas. For this reason, large metal surfaces are used instead of coupled antennas. One example is the horn that is obtained by flaring the output end of a hollow wave guide. Horns also may be arranged to excite sheets of current on large metal reflectors that have highly directional field patterns. Reflectors similar to those used for radar have important applications in micro-

wave links for telephone transmission and for receiving microwave radiation from radio stars.

See also RADAR; RADIO; TELEVISION.

RONOLD W.P. KING, *Harvard University*

Bibliography

Flugge, S., ed., *Encyclopedia of Physics*, vol. 16 (Berlin 1958).
Fradin, A.Z., *Microwave Antennas* (New York 1961).
Jordan, Edward C., *Electromagnetic Waves and Radiating Systems* (New York 1950).
King, Ronold W.P., *Theory of Linear Antennas* (Cambridge, Mass., 1956).
King, Ronold W.P., and others, *Transmission Lines, Antennas, and Wave Guides* (New York 1965).

ANTERUS, an'tǝr-ǝs, **Saint,** pope from Nov. 21, 235, to Jan. 3, 236. He is thought to be of Greek origin, and his name is sometimes spelled *Anteros.* He is noted in the Book of the Popes (*Liber Pontificalis*) as having suffered martyrdom for authorizing notaries to collect records of the acts of the martyrs and depositing them in the church archives. He is buried in the papal crypt of the catacomb of St. Calistus, and his feast day is January 3.

ANTHEIL, an'tīl, **George** (1900–1959), American composer, who shocked audiences of the 1920's with his use of jazz rhythms and mechanical devices in symphonic music. He was born at Trenton, N.J., on June 8, 1900. He began piano lessons when he was six and later studied composition with Ernest Bloch. In 1922 while he was on a European tour, his First Symphony was given its premiere performance by the Berlin Philharmonic. Taking up residence in Paris, he then turned to full-time composing.

Antheil's most spectacular composition is *Ballet mécanique* (1926), which he scored for mechanical pianos, the sound of whirling airplane propellers, and electric bells. At its first performance, in Paris in 1926, it was nearly hissed off the stage. However, because of the change in musical tastes, when it was performed in 1954 in New York City the audience considered it merely ebullient.

Antheil returned to the United States in 1933 and began to compose for motion pictures, writing the scores for films that included *The Plainsman* (1936) and *The Spectre of the Rose* (1946). His film scores and most of his symphonic and operatic music written after the 1920's were in a style that had elements of classicism, romanticism, and impressionism, and were only moderately advanced harmonically. He died at New York City on Feb. 12, 1959.

ANTHEM, an′thəm, a choral composition with English words, often with organ accompaniment. The word may be a corruption of *antiphon.* The anthem developed in Britain early in the Reformation for the services of the Anglican Church. It is analogous to the *motet* of Roman Catholic ceremonies, since both the anthem and the motet use texts that are not part of the prescribed liturgy. Excerpts from oratorios, masses, and Passions are sometimes used as anthems.

The first anthems, which were written about 1560 by Christopher Tye and Thomas Tallis, were *full anthems*—that is, entirely choral. They differed from motets only in their use of English rather than Latin texts. Toward the end of the 16th century, William Byrd and Orlando Gibbons developed the *verse anthem,* in which chorus sections alternate with solo sections.

Restoration composers John Blow and Henry Purcell developed an elaborate type of anthem with solo recitatives, instrumental interludes, and choruses, but later 18th century composers, such as Maurice Greene and William Boyce, returned to a simpler style of anthem writing. The anthems of the 19th century were serviceable but undistinguished. A number of composers in the 20th century, led by Sir Charles Parry and Sir Charles Stanford, and including Martin Shaw, Gustav Holst, Ralph Vaughan Williams, and Benjamin Britten, revived anthem writing.

CHARLES N. HENDERSON
St. George's Church, New York

ANTHEMIUS OF TRALLES, an-thē′mē-əs, tral′ēz, Greek architect and mathematician of the 6th century A.D. With Isidorus of Miletus he designed the great domed basilica of Hagia Sophia in Constantinople, commissioned by Emperor Justinian and built between 532 and 537. Anthemius was also the author of *Concerning Remarkable Mechanical Devices,* a treatise on burning glasses that recorded the mathematical function of the directrix (q.v.).

ANTHOLOGY, an-thol′ə-jē, a collection of selected materials of many kinds. The word derives from the Greek *anthologia,* meaning a collection of flowers, and was originally applied to *The Greek Anthology* (q.v.), a 10th century collection of short poems and other writings.

History. Many medieval scholars copied out in one manuscript the most striking passages in the works they studied. Satirical invective, anecdotes, witty sayings, and folk tales made up the entertaining *De Nugis Curialium (Courtier's Trifles)* of Walter Map, who was in the service of King Henry II of England. The *Carmina Burana* of the 13th century assembled rhymed Latin poems by the wandering scholars known as goliards. Such manuscripts as the *Friar Miscellanies* and the *Aureate Collections* preserve poems of the Middle English period.

The invention of printing led to more anthologies. The most celebrated of 16th century anthologies is the *Book of Songs and Sonnets (Tottel's Miscellany;* 1557). *The Passionate Pilgrim* (1599), a collection of 20 poems, deceitfully claimed Shakespeare as the compiler. *England's Helicon* (1600) included poems by Shakespeare, Sidney, and Spenser.

Thomas Percy's *Reliques of Ancient English Poetry* (1765) may be unrivaled for its influence on later literature. "The poetry of the age," wrote Wordsworth in 1815, "has been absolutely redeemed by it." For popularity, Sir Francis Palgrave's *Golden Treasury of English Songs and Lyrics* (1861) is unchallenged.

Modern Anthologies. In the 20th century, anthologies have proliferated, both in the number of titles published and in the variety of content. Louis Untermeyer and Oscar Williams established themselves as professional compilers. Publishers, not content with successful single volumes, now issue series of related works. One such series is *Twentieth Century Views,* in which each volume reprints critical essays dealing with a single writer. *The Oxford Book of English Verse* has many companion volumes dealing with specific periods and types of English poetry. Other anthologies give the original text and an English translation of foreign-language poems.

Anthologies of individual authors have been published by the Viking Portable Library. *A Subtreasury of American Humor* (1941), edited by E.B. and Katharine S. White, anthologized works by foremost humorists. Annual collections include the *Best Plays* series (1919–   ) and *Prize Stories: The O. Henry Awards* (1947–   ).

Inevitable differences in taste and differences in readership and the purposes of anthologies preclude agreement on what is "the best anthology" in a given field. Some flaws of inclusion or omission may be due to obstacles, such as copyright laws, that the compiler met but could not overcome. In anthologies intended for purchase by school systems, certain social and moral taboos restrict the anthologist's choice.

Anthologies are no longer limited to literature. There are many published collections of art and cartoons that serve as anthologies. Series of phonograph records have become musical anthologies. Portions of motion pictures have been spliced together to form anthologies of film artistry, such as the performances of comedians like Charlie Chaplin and Ben Turpin.

KENNETH DOUGLAS
Editor of School Dept., Harcourt, Brace & World

ANTHONY, an′thə-nē, **Saint** (c. 250–356), Christian ascetic, who is called the "father of monks," or founder of Christian monasticism. He is often called St. Anthony (or Antony) of Egypt. He was born of an affluent Christian family, probably in Qeman, Egypt. At about the age of 18, Anthony disposed of his possessions and, under the direction of a noted ascetic, devoted himself to manual labor, prayer, fasting, and meditation on the Scriptures. Later he retired to an abandoned fortress at Pispir where other Christians joined him. During the persecution of Maximinus, Anthony and some of his followers went to Alexandria to encourage their fellow Christians. Later, Anthony sought new seclusion in a monastery he founded at Dêr Mar Antonios. From this retreat he made frequent trips to counsel his numerous monks in the Egyptian desert and to combat the Arians in Alexandria. According to tradition, he died on Jan. 17, 356.

The Life of St. Anthony, written by St. Athanasius, is essentially an accurate account of Anthony and had profound influence on subsequent hagiography. Anthony wrote no rule for the monastic life; his life and examples served that purpose for his followers. Of the 20 letters attributed to him, only the first 7 are now considered authentic.

HERMIGILD DRESSLER, O.F.M.
The Catholic University of America

ANTHONY, an′thə-nē, **Susan Brownell** (1820–1906), American reformer and advocate of woman's rights. She was an effective speaker and writer, but her greatest assistance to the cause of woman's rights was as an organizer and initiator of action. For more than 50 years she made major contributions, in the face of continuous opposition, to the struggle for equality of women.

Miss Anthony was born in Adams, Mass., on Feb. 15, 1820. Brought up by Quaker parents in western New York, she early developed a sense of independence and moral zeal. Because it was the only profession open to women, she became a teacher. Susan's views were influenced by the reformers who gathered in the family home near Rochester, N.Y., and especially by her acquaintance with Elizabeth Cady Stanton. By the time she was in her early thirties she was convinced that until women were granted equal rights with men, there was no hope for social betterment in America.

Miss Anthony, who never married, first crusaded publicly in behalf of temperance. Rebuffed by male temperance workers in 1852, she and others then formed the Woman's State Temperance Society of New York, unique in its time. She was also an ardent abolitionist.

Miss Anthony campaigned, first in New York, then across the country, for the right of women to control their own property, to have guardianship of children in case of divorce, and to vote. She developed the technique of showering elected officials with thousands of petitions demanding action. The results were often discouraging, but gradually many states began to give women some legal status—the right to control property and to get an education—though they were never considered the equal of men in her day.

When the 14th Amendment to the Constitution granted the vote to all "male inhabitants," Miss Anthony fought unsuccessfully to have women included. In 1872 she registered and voted in Rochester in order to test the legality of the amendment. She was arrested, tried, and fined for violating the law, but she refused to pay on the grounds that the law was wrong.

When the woman's rights movement split into two groups in 1869, Miss Anthony became, along with Mrs. Stanton, a leading member of the faction that advocated woman suffrage by an amendment to the Constitution rather than through state action. Years later (1892–1900) she served as president of the National American Woman Suffrage Association, which represented the reunited movement. She died in Rochester on March 13, 1906. Fourteen years after her death, the "Anthony Amendment," providing for full woman suffrage, became the 19th Amendment to the Constitution.

In appearance, Miss Anthony was rather austere, and she sometimes seemed aggressive and bold, but she had great physical vigor and an ability to inspire.

Miss Anthony helped to compile the first four volumes (1881–1900) of the *History of Woman Suffrage*. See also WOMAN SUFFRAGE.

ALLEN F. DAVIS, *University of Missouri*

Further Reading: Flexner, Eleanor, *Century of Struggle: The Woman's Rights Movement in the United States* (Cambridge, Mass., 1959); Harper, Ida Husted, *The Life and Work of Susan B. Anthony*, 3 vols. (Indianapolis 1899–1908); Lutz, Alma, *Susan B. Anthony: Rebel, Crusader, Humanitarian* (Boston 1959).

THE GRANGER COLLECTION

Susan B. Anthony (1820–1906)

ANTHONY ADVERSE, an′thə-nē ad′vərs, is a historical novel by the American author Hervey Allen (q.v.), published in 1933. Incorporating almost every device associated with costume romances, the novel wanders, in pursuit of its picaresque hero's affairs, from Spain to Africa to New Orleans.

The story tells of the adventures and misadventures of Anthony Adverse, a bastard child who inherits a shipping fortune from his maternal grandfather. Anthony's mother's husband, Don Luis, the arrogant Marquis da Vincitata, is the principal antagonist of the plot. Having killed his wife's lover, Anthony's father, at the beginning of the book, Don Luis attempts, throughout the rest of the tale, to do away with Anthony. Other prominent characters are Faith Paleologus, a scheming lady who starts as Anthony's housekeeper and seductress and ends as Don Luis' second wife (Anthony's mother died in childbirth); Vincent Nolte, Anthony's longtime friend and business associate; Father François, a monk who meets Anthony on a slave-trading venture and is eventually captured by a witch doctor and crucified; and John Bonnyfeather, from whom Anthony inherits his fortune. Historical personages dotting the pages of the novel include Napoleon Bonaparte, King Charles IV of Spain, and Aaron Burr.

Anthony Adverse is notable for its episodic sweep and historical veracity rather than for its depth of characterization. However, in spite of the shallowness and somewhat wooden quality of its characters, it gained enormous popularity, paving the way for a succession of lusty costume romances, spiced at intervals with erotic episodes.

ANTHONY OF PADUA, an′thə-nē paj′ə-wə, **Saint** (1195–1231), doctor of the church, preacher, and teacher. Baptized *Ferdinand* at his birth in Lisbon, Portugal, on Aug. 15, 1195, he began his religious life as an Augustinian canon at the age of 15. While on retreat at Coimbra he was inspired with missionary zeal by the sight of Franciscan missionary martyrs who had been slain in Morocco. He requested permission to leave the Augustinians and in 1220 joined the Franciscan Friars Minor, adopting the name of Anthony. But when he reached the Moroccan missions, illness forced his return, and a storm drove his ship to Sicily.

At the Franciscan assembly in Assisi in 1221, Anthony was assigned to the hermitage at Monte-

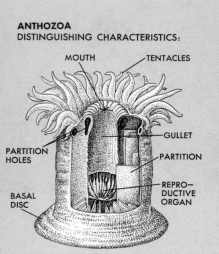
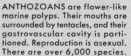

T. PARKINSON, FROM NATIONAL AUDUBON SOCIETY

DOUGLAS P. WILSON

WOODBRIDGE L. WILLIAMS, FROM ANNAN PHOTOS

The main orders of anthozoans are: 1. Pennatulacea, or sea pens, bearing polyps along a single stalk. 2. Gorgonacea, which includes the sea fans. 3. Actiniaria, the sea anemones, which have no skeletons. 4. Corals (solitary cup corals shown here), comprising many orders.

DOUGLAS P. WILSON

paolo. Here his ability as a preacher was noted and he was delegated by St. Francis to preach and to teach. Anthony was sent to France where, in 1226, he became provincial of the order in Limousin. After St. Francis' death, also in 1226, Anthony returned to Italy as provincial in Emilia, where he became renowned for the eloquence of his preaching. Fatigue caused his retirement to Padua in 1231, and a serious illness contracted while at a nearby mission resulted in his death at Arcella, near Padua, on June 13.

Anthony was canonized in 1232 and declared an evangelical doctor in 1946. His feast day is June 13. Padua and Portugal claim him as their patron, and his favor is sought by travelers and as a finder of lost articles.

ANTHOZOA, an-thə-zō′ə, is the scientific name for the large class of invertebrate animals that includes sea anemones, sea fans, and corals. Anthozoans, sometimes called actinozoans, inhabit salt waters throughout the world. Although some species are found in cold polar seas, most anthozoans inhabit warm temperate or tropical regions, living in shallow waters as well as at great depths.

Anthozoans vary greatly in appearance. Many species are various shades of red, pink, and purple, while others may be blue, yellow, white, or orange. In size, they range from tiny solitary individuals measuring less than half an inch (12.7 mm) long to large colonial sea pens that may grow to a length of more than 2 feet (60 cm). Many anthozoans, such as sea anemones, live singly, while others, including most of the corals, live in colonies.

Body Structure. The basic anthozoan body plan is a modified cylinder. In some, such as sea anemones, the body is stout and muscular, but in others, such as sea pansies, sea fans, and corals, the body is thin and only slightly muscular. Most anthozoans secrete some nonliving substance around the outside of the body. This substance, which may be calcium carbonate or a much softer material, serves to support and protect the soft body tissues.

At the basal end of the body is a smooth, sometimes slimy disc, called the basal disc. Some anthozoans, such as the sea anemone, use this disc for slowly sliding about during periods of migration. Other anthozoans are sessile, or attached, and use this disc for adhering to the ocean floor or to a rock or other object.

At its upper end the anthozoan's body is expanded to form a flattened disc, called the oral disc, which contains a central mouth opening surrounded by one or more rows of hollow tentacles. These tentacles are armed with special stinging cells, called nematocysts, which are used for paralyzing enemies and prey. Once paralyzed by the nematocysts, the victim is passed by the tentacles into the mouth opening.

From the mouth, a muscular gullet, called the stomodaeum, hangs down into the body cavity and is connected with the body wall by a series of partitions called mesenteries. Between these mesenteries are sets of incomplete mesenteries that extend only part way between the body wall and the stomodaeum. These mesenteries are referred to as primary, secondary, tertiary, or quaternary mesenteries, depending on how far they extend from the body wall toward the stomodaeum. The chambers formed by the mesenteries are known as perivisceral chambers.

Below the gullet they form one large chamber, but above the point where they attach to the gullet, they connect with each other through one or more small holes in the mesenteries.

Located at the free ends of the mesenteries are special gland cells that secrete digestive fluids. In addition, the mesenteries contain many cells that are specialized for digesting food particles. These cells are also scattered throughout the inner wall of the body cavity, but it is the presence of these cells on the mesenteries that allows anthozoans to digest larger organisms than would otherwise be possible. Some sea anemones have been known to digest extremely large fish.

In many anthozoans, the stomodaeum is lined with many whiplike projections, called flagella, which lash back and forth creating water currents in the body cavity. These water currents help bring food particles and oxygen to the body cells, while also removing their wastes.

Anthozoans do not possess a well-developed nervous system. Their nerve tissue usually consists of a network of ganglionic nerve cells connected by large nerve fibers.

The development of muscle tissue varies greatly in different anthozoans. Sea anemones, for example, have rather well-developed muscles that run lengthwise along the mesenteries, as well as bands of muscles that encircle the body. Other anthozoans have only a few, rather poorly developed muscle fibers.

Reproduction. The anthozoan's reproductive tissues are usually located along the free edges of the mesenteries. In some species, the sexes are separate; each individual produces either egg or sperm cells. Other species are hermaphroditic, with each individual producing both eggs and sperm.

In sexual reproduction, the sex cells may be expelled through the mouth opening to the outside, where fertilization occurs. After passing through several early stages of embryonic development, the new individual usually settles to the bottom. However, in some anthozoans the new individual becomes a free-swimming larva, called a planula, which swims about for a while before settling.

In addition to reproducing sexually, anthozoans reproduce asexually, either by splitting in half or by budding. In splitting, the anthozoan simply forms two separate individuals. In budding, a new individual forms as a small bud extending from the body wall. After a period of growth, the bud may either break off from the parent or remain attached to it. In many corals the process of budding is responsible for the formation of colonies, some of which form gigantic coral reefs.

Evolution. Anthozoans first appeared during the middle of the Ordovician period, about 400 million years ago. In their evolutionary development they represent an advance over one-celled organisms and the sponges by having distinct body tissues and a division of labor among the different cell types.

Because of their abundance during past geologic times, the reef-building anthozoans have been valuable to scientists in learning about the past climates of certain regions. Since most of these anthozoans live in shallow, well-lighted marine waters where the temperature ranges between 77° F and 84° F (25° C to 29° C), it is inferred that ancient reef-building corals lived in similar habitats. Therefore, when ancient coral reefs are discovered in rock formations of inland areas, scientists may assume that those particular areas were once covered by bodies of clear, warm, shallow marine water.

Classification. Anthozoans make up the class Anthozoa of the phylum Coelenterata. They are usually divided into two subclasses, the Alcyonaria and the Zoantharia. The Alcyonaria are characterized by eight mesenteries and branching tentacles, while the Zoantharia have mesenteries in multiples of six and unbranching tentacles.

There are 15 orders of anthozoans. Eleven of the 15 are represented by living members. The remaining four orders are known only through their fossil remains.

DAVID A. OTTO, *Stephens College*

ANTHRACENE. See AROMATIC COMPOUNDS.

ANTHRACITE. See COAL.

ANTHRACNOSE, an-thrak'nos, is a name applied to any of a group of fungus diseases of crop plants, particularly to one that attacks bean plants. Also called *bitter rot*, the disease causes blisters, lesions, or cankers on leaves, stems, or fruit. Infected spots may have dark sunken centers or gray or white centers with reddish brown edges. The fungus spores are carried chiefly by rain, infected seeds, and insects.

Anthracnose is caused by parasitic imperfect fungi of the order Melanconiales, especially of the genera *Gloeosporium* and ·*Colletotrichum*. The condition can be prevented by plant rotation, sanitation, and use of disease-free seed.

ANTHRAQUINONE, an-thrə-kwē-nōn', is an important intermediate material used in manufacturing many dyes. The dyestuff industry in the United States annually uses more than 2,500,000 pounds of anthraquinone.

Development. The beginning of anthraquinone chemistry can be dated to 1868, when the German chemists K. Graebe and K. Liebermann found that alizarin, one of the oldest natural dyes, was a derivative of anthracene. This discovery soon was followed by the synthesis of alizarin by H. Caro, Graebe, and Liebermann. From then on, the dyestuff industries devoted enormous efforts and brilliant skills to developing many anthraquinone dyes.

For many decades, anthraquinone ($C_6H_4 - (CO)_2 - C_6H_4$) was manufactured by oxidizing anthracene ($C_6H_4 - (CH)_2 - C_6H_4$), a coal-tar product. Anthraquinone now is usually manufactured from phthalic anhydride and benzene, using aluminum chloride and sulfuric acid as condensing agents. Through many varied chemical reactions, anthraquinone is converted into other intermediates and finally into thousands of varied anthraquinone dyes. These dyes excel other types of dyes, such as azo dyes and triphenylmethane dyes, by providing both brightness of color and good to excellent fastness properties.

Uses. Anthraquinone dyes and pigments have been used for dyeing or coloring all kinds of materials—wool, silk, cotton (vat dyes), synthetic textile fibers, and plastics. As new materials, such as synthetic fibers, appeared on the market, anthraquinone chemists developed new dyes and variations of old dyes specifically for use with the new materials. See also DYES AND DYEING.

CURT BAMBERGER, *Patent Chems Inc.*

ANTHRAX, an'thraks, is one of the most dreaded infectious diseases of animals. It is caused by the bacterium *Bacillus anthracis* and is transmissible to man. Cattle, sheep (except Algerian), goats, horses, mules, and wild herbivores are very susceptible; man, swine, and carnivores are somewhat resistant. The disease is also called *splenic fever, black bain, charbon, malignant pustule,* and *murrain.*

The disease has been known since early times. Hippocrates, Virgil, Pliny, and Galen described lesions that were probably those of anthrax. In 1613 some 60,000 persons died of anthrax in southern Europe. Robert Koch, in 1876, demonstrated conclusively that a rod-shaped bacterium, *Bacillus anthracis,* was the cause of anthrax, and on June 2, 1881, Louis Pasteur produced a vaccine that successfully prevented infection. These two events were milestones in medical history, for the anthrax bacillus was the first microorganism that was proved to be the cause of a disease, and anthrax was the first disease to be prevented by a vaccine.

Anthrax occurs throughout the world. The incidence is low in countries where restrictive and preventive measures are in use, but it is still very high among animals in Asia and Africa. The disease has been recognized in America since colonial days. The first human case recorded in the United States occurred in 1834 at Philadelphia.

Infection. In the spore stage, which it forms when exposed to conditions unfavorable for existence and growth, *Bacillus anthracis* is very resistant. Spores protected by contact with soil, hides, hair, wool, bone meal, or dried blood may live for many years, still capable of causing the disease.

Sources of infection may be either agricultural or industrial. The important agricultural source is the soil, which, once contaminated, may harbor the spores for years. If anthrax spores are brought to the surface by cultivation or burrowing animals, any susceptible animal may become infected through a scratch, even though minute, on the feet or legs. People who walk barefoot may contract the infection in the same way. Herbivores may get anthrax by eating contaminated food; carnivores and swine acquire the disease from consuming infected meat. Most human infection arises from contact with products from diseased animals.

Contaminated hair, wool, and hides are the most common industrial sources of infection. Thus, brushmakers, woolsorters, carpetmakers, and tanners most often develop anthrax, and the incidence is highest where these industries are concentrated. Widespread human infection approaching epidemic proportions, which occurred in England and the United States during and just after World War I, was traced to contaminated horsehair imported from Siberia and China for making shaving brushes. More stringent regulations now prevent the importation of infected materials, and more efficient methods of sterilizing hair, wool, and hides are being developed as preventive measures.

Description and Diagnosis. Animals suffering from an extremely acute form of anthrax are either found dead or die from overwhelming blood poisoning within 12 hours after the first sign of disease. The infection may be classed as acute when death occurs in 12 to 24 hours. A few animals recover from the less acute form, though most die within three to five days. A chronic form occurs in swine, seldom in other species. Animals affected with any general form of anthrax show fever, increase in breathing and heart rates, progressive weakness, and convulsions, followed by death. Other more significant symptoms are rapidly developing swellings in various parts of the body, and hemorrhages from the natural body openings.

Human anthrax is classified as internal or external. The internal form, while not so rapidly progressive as in animals, is nearly always fatal unless treated promptly and effectively. This form of the disease tends to localize in certain organs before the bacillus gains access to the blood stream; thus, "woolsorter's disease" is a massive pneumonia, the bacillus being taken into the lungs by breathing contaminated dust from the wool. Intestinal injuries may develop when the bacillus is ingested with inadequately cooked meat. In man, anthrax also may be manifested as a meningitis.

The external form is characterized by the anthrax carbuncle, which typically develops a black center, and this has given the disease its name (Greek *anthrax,* coal, ulcer). If treatment is not adequate during this stage of development, the bacillus may spread from the carbuncle to the lymphatics and the blood stream, and will result in fatal bacteremia (bacteria in the blood stream).

Diagnosis in cases of suspected anthrax is confirmed by finding the bacillus, which may be recovered from the carbuncle in man or from the blood stream of either man or animal during the blood poisoning stage. Because of the danger of contracting infection, autopsies of suspected animals are usually avoided. It is customary procedure to remove an ear from the animal and to examine microscopically the blood it contains to determine whether the bacillus is present.

Prevention and Treatment. Since Pasteur's epoch-making demonstration of the value of his vaccine in preventing anthrax, still further improvements have been made in prevention and treatment. Pasteur's was a live vaccine made from bacilli with reduced disease-causing ability. The use of a weakened spore vaccine combined with potent hyperimmune anthrax serum (that is, one that contains a large amount of antibodies) produces a high degree of immunity. Anthrax bacterins (killed vaccines) are also very useful under certain conditions, but the antibody level (and therefore the degree of immunity) produced is not so high as that provided by living cultures. Antianthrax serums give immediate though short-lived immunity, and are useful both for prompt protection and for treatment.

For many years carbuncles were treated by excision and cauterization; later it was found that a combination of injections of serum and arsenicals was better. Sulfonamides and antibiotics, such as penicillin and tetracyclines, have replaced these agents because of their greater effectiveness and the fewer undesirable side reactions they produce. In some cases, corticosteroids are used as supplementary therapy.

WALTER E. LA GRANGE, D.V.M.
University of Pennsylvania
ELIZABETH BURBANK ATWOOD, V.M.D.

Further Reading: Roueché, Berton, *A Man Named Hoffman* (Boston 1965); Stein, C.D., "Anthrax," in Thomas G. Hull, *Diseases Transmitted from Animals to Man,* 4th ed., pp. 65–108 (Springfield, Ill.; 1954).

ILLINOIS STATE MUSEUM

KEN HEYMAN

Anthropology includes the study of man as a physical being and the study of man's culture, or his whole way of life. (*Left*) A physical anthropologist measures an ancient skull. (*Right*) Cultural anthropologist Margaret Mead in Bali.

ANTHROPOLOGY

ANTHROPOLOGY, an-thrə-pol′ə-jē, is the study of man from both a biological and a cultural perspective. That part of anthropology concerned with man as an animal species is called *physical anthropology*. The portion concerned with the ways of life devised by human beings living in societies is called *cultural anthropology*. No single anthropologist can possibly cover all the ground marked out by this definition; however, man in his entirety is the central focus of all anthropological research.

THE SCOPE OF ANTHROPOLOGY

The humanities and the social sciences also deal either with human beings living in societies or with the cultural products of such societies; hence there must be a division of labor between anthropology and these other disciplines. The division is based on mutual exchange and borrowing of ideas and theories. Anthropologists feel free to move over the entire territory of man's creations, and other disciplines borrow freely from the findings of anthropologists.

The breadth of the field of anthropology is primarily the product of its historical development. Anthropologists first studied those portions of the world's cultures outside western Europe. When a man worked in a society away from his own culture, he had to be a jack-of-all-trades, or at least he attempted to be. He was usually alone in the field, and he made his study of such diverse cultural material as art, music, literature, and economics without the assistance of specialists in these areas.

An anthropologist who studied the Eskimo, for example, was expected to know enough about physical anthropology to measure the living people or at least to describe their physical characteristics. He also had to be able to recognize archaeological remains and to try to trace their relationship to the living culture. He learned to speak the language and write down native texts, here specializing in linguistics. He then moved

into political science to describe how the village was controlled. When he observed how hunting and food gathering were carried out and how food items were distributed and furs traded or sold at the trading post, he was concerned with economics. He might then map the village and record the social interaction of people within the village, here practicing social anthropology or, in more complex societies, sociology. To collect songs, chants, and myths, he would need some knowledge of literature, folklore, and music. When he observed midwinter ceremonials and shamanistic practices, he had turned to the study of religion. If he collected life histories and charted genealogical connections of individuals and recorded their disease theories and curative practices, the anthropologist was working in the areas of clinical and social psychology and medicine.

Divisions of Anthropology. The modern anthropologist is less a jack-of-all-trades and more a specialist. Nevertheless, the scope of the field remains broad, particularly as the discipline is defined in the United States. In graduate schools in the United States a student of anthropology is expected to acquire an understanding of physical anthropology and of cultural anthropology.

Broadly defined, cultural anthropology includes linguistics and archaeology. But because of the growing size and complexity of anthropological studies, there is a tendency for modern American anthropologists to specialize in one division. Interconnections among the divisions, however, remain essential to the meaning of anthropology as an integrating science of man.

In Europe, anthropology is defined differently. The term "anthropology" usually means physical anthropology. The other studies that make up the comprehensive field in the United States are separated from one another and from physical anthropology. Thus in Europe a man would specialize in anthropology (that is, the biological branch), in archaeology, in linguistics, or in ethnography (the study of individual cultures). The present article deals with anthropology in the broad sense, embracing the physical and cultural study of man.

Widening Focus of Anthropology. The scope of anthropology has broadened as the discipline has evolved. From the 15th through the 18th century the forerunners of modern anthropologists were men who wrote treatises trying to explain the origin and distribution of the races, languages, and cultures that were brought into European consciousness by world exploration. By the 18th century some philosophers were viewing groups like the American Indians as living in a state of nature, uncorrupted by civilization, while another school viewed native peoples as the remnants of people who had fallen from a state of civilization into savagery.

In the 19th century speculation continued to center around the historical relationship of native peoples and cultures to the Graeco-Roman and Hebrew roots of European civilization. Darwin's theory of biological evolution, however, produced an impetus to see native peoples and cultures as fossilized remnants of man's racial and cultural development. In the 20th century, in addition to these attempts to explain the origin and evolution of other cultures, anthropologists began to concentrate on the day-to-day functioning of native cultures in their own day. There has been a continuous shift in emphasis from the historical reconstruction of cultural development—now left largely to the archaeologists, and certain synthesizing theorists—to an understanding of the more or less contemporary scene.

The earlier anthropologists looked at native peoples and asked questions different from those being asked today. The first group asked, Where did you come from and how are you related to the Christian cosmology? The answers were equivocal. Some held that natives were noble savages living outside the Biblical fall of man, while others concluded that natives were renegades from higher civilizations. Scholars argued whether all races of mankind had had a single origin or multiple origins.

In the 19th century the attempt was to determine evolutionary stages of cultural development and to classify living cultures in terms of those stages. In the 20th century, anthropologists have been asking how a particular culture works and how it satisfies basic human needs. Many anthropological inquiries center on how people change their cultures when their institutions no longer satisfy their psychological and other needs.

Ties with Other Disciplines. In subject matter and research methods, anthropology has ties not only with psychology and other social sciences but with the natural sciences as well. For example, anthropology uses techniques of research borrowed from biology and geology. The study of other cultures is related equally to the humanities in that the anthropologist studies the philosophies and cosmologies of native peoples, as well as their music, dance, and plastic and graphic arts. This confluence of the arts, sciences, and social sciences within its sphere of activity puts anthropology in a unique position to provide an integrated approach to the various dimensions of human behavior.

Thus anthropology forms a bridge between the three cultures of the academic world: the natural sciences, the humanities, and the social sciences. In the final analysis, the anthropologist is as much concerned with the broadest possible perspective on man as a culture-building, values-oriented animal as he is in exploring man's day-to-day existence in a particular culture.

Anthropology tends to attract individuals who wish to live beyond the boundaries of their own culture, place, and time. While the historian has been traditionally concerned with past times, his interests have tended to focus almost exclusively on the development of civilizations, that is, on peoples whose history is documented with a written record. Such social sciences as sociology, psychology, economics, and political science also have tended to focus on western European culture. Partly through the stimulus of anthropology, many of these fields have broadened their inquiries to give them a cross-cultural, comparative scope.

As other social scientists have looked into the findings of anthropologists, they have enriched their own disciplines. Conversely, psychology, sociology, political science, and economics have become fertile borrowing places where the anthropologist can find new questions and techniques to employ in his study of non-European cultures. These cultures outside the European tradition have provided the closest available approximation to a living laboratory for checking the theories of other social scientists who work primarily within their own cultural borders.

The anthropologist who works in the field and lives within a smaller cultural group operates by direct observation. He is forced to see the interconnection between the institutions in the society he is studying. His field studies make him aware of the false boundaries between the disciplines in Western academic circles—boundaries that have arisen mostly through the accidents of history. He sees clearly that the economic, political, religious, and artistic spheres of life are not independent entities but are in fact interdependent parts of a unified design for living.

CULTURAL ANTHROPOLOGY

There is considerable variation in the way in which scholars divide the field of cultural anthropology. Historically its major divisions were archaeology and ethnology, with ethnology being subdivided into ethnography, linguistics, and social anthropology. Ethnography is the study of the way of life within a single tribe or group, while ethnology is the comparative study of two or more cultures or parts of cultures. Archaeology may be viewed as the ethnography and ethnology of extinct cultures.

In the United States there is a trend toward organizing cultural anthropology by subdivisions dealing with the institutions within primitive societies. For example, some specialists devote their time to the comparative study of religious, political, economic, or social institutions. Other specialists concentrate on such processes as culture change and acculturation. Some specialists deal with such products of culture systems as dance, music, art, and oral literature, while others bridge the fields of ethnology and history or ethnology and psychology.

Ethnography. Ethnography—the study of the culture of single groups—is at the heart of anthropology. Fieldwork is basic to the training of a cultural anthropologist, and the written accounts of fieldwork form the central focus of cultural anthropology. Native cultures of the world may be viewed as the living laboratory in which the cultural anthropologist finds his experiments always in progress when he arrives. In his reports he must construct a model of the native culture in order to understand its working parts, and he must also translate this model into the common language of other anthropological theorists. Thus in anthropology the study of any tribal culture that focuses on an experimental premise requires both observation and hypothesis. This alternation between the deductive and the empirical gives cultural anthropology a special character as a study of man.

Leaving his own culture behind, the field observer must become as totally immersed as possible in the culture he is observing (avoiding the danger of becoming completely involved and thus psychologically unable to disassociate himself). He must come to see the culture as the native sees it. Beyond that, he must construct a picture of its workings, of which even a native is not necessarily aware, just as a person may speak a language without knowing its underlying grammar. The anthropologist has normally had to be both judge of what is important in the culture and his own critic of the final analysis. In some instances, restudies by another ethnographer have revealed the degree to which the personality and perceptions of the fieldworker color his report on the culture.

Since the time of William L. Warner's *Yankee City* studies (publication of which began in 1941), small-society field techniques have been used by anthropologists to examine parts of the society of the United States. The approach Warner brought from his Australian field work—stressing face-to-face, participant-observer method—was a departure from the massive survey and questionnaire methods traditionally used by sociologists to study Western societies.

Until relatively recently much of the work of ethnographers was concentrated on descriptions in an effort to record data on tribes and groups before their cultures disappeared in a changing world. Some urgent salvage ethnology of this character is still in progress, but ethnographers now are more likely to go into the field of restudy some previously worked society or test out a limited hypothesis about culture or culture change. The modern field anthropologist is much more aware of his theoretical underpinnings than was his predecessor some years ago.

Ethnology. Ethnology is the arena for the confrontation of the historical and structural views of human cultures. The comparative study of institutions began with the characteristic 19th century search for origins and developmental stages; marriage, kinship, and religious institutions were the major concerns. This movement represented attempts to interpret the past by the analysis of current data, or in other words, to understand the course of cultural evolution on the basis of indirect evidence, much as Darwin and Wallace had come to the concept of biological evolution primarily on the basis of current phenomena.

Data from archaeology have largely replaced these speculations about past cultural origins. The historical particularists who developed later in opposition to the evolutionistic approach were trying to reconstruct the history not of culture but of individual cultures, and they were also looking for the principles of culture formation and change.

The modern structural-functionalists are still

THE TIMES, LONDON, FROM PICTORIAL PARADE

FIELD STUDY of peoples and customs is speeded by the use of modern devices such as the tape recorder. Here the speech of Easter Islanders is being recorded.

interested in the description of, and principles inherent in, culture change, but they work more intensively in the immediate present. Modern functional analysis tends to view societies as having a hidden structure that must be discovered or rendered explicit by the cultural anthropologist. The people within the culture are assumed to be as completely unaware of this underlying structure as native speakers of English are unaware of its unconsciously patterned phonemic system.

By convention and historical development the anthropologist tends to view human activities as systems of symbolic interactions along lines that facilitate comparison with other cultures. The breakdown usually consists of the kinship and social, economic, magic and religious, military, and legal and political institutions. It must be stressed, however, that these subdivisions are arbitrary and that the functional separation will be the work of the ethnographer and ethnologist and are not necessarily obvious within a specific culture. The natives of a New Guinea tribe who send out invitations to neighboring kindred and prepare with magic and religious ritual for warfare—which may have been stimulated by a surplus of pigs or ripe fruits—do not divide the world up into the usual categories of ethnography. Furthermore, the outward, or manifest, function of such warfare may be different from the covert, latent functions it performs in the ecological balance of the tribe within its environment.

Kinship. One of the first problems that impressed the European cultural anthropologist with the need for new descriptive tools was the problem of dealing with family and clan organizations that had little similarity to those of Europe. These bizarre kinship systems were at first thought to be survivals of earlier marriage-family relationships, but ethnologists now view them as symbolic maps of existing social relationships. Kinship systems provide cues to the attitudes and behavior that may be expected between people who use a particular term to address or refer to one another. G.P. Murdock in *Social Structure* (1949) not only classified kinship systems but also indicated their tendency to change in a predictable direction. He noted that new descent and lineage groups tend to form as a response to new residence rules. More recent research has centered on nonlinear kin groups and the analysis of kinship terms.

Religion. The study of religion as an institution within primitive cultures has changed materially in the 20th century. Many 19th century anthropologists thought of the evolution of religion as a linear progression, usually from animism (a belief in spirits) to monotheism. The culture-sphere theorists had a different view, postulating an original monotheism initially revealed to man, followed by decay and falling away from this original religion. Another evolutionary scheme, proposed by Sir James Frazer, envisioned a development from magic to religion to science. R.R. Marrett extended the conceptualization of religious feeling by his discussion of the Polynesian concept of *mana*—a lifeless, impersonal force that seemed to be the most basic element in the Polynesian religious system.

Emil Durkeim systematized the concepts within religious institutions, basing his analysis on the Arunta of Australia. Max Weber probed the relationship between the religious and economic institutions of western Europe but also extended his comparative analysis to the religions of India and China. The modern concern, as expressed by Claude Lévi-Strauss, is with the analysis of the elementary structural bases of religious systems. He attempts to apply a linguistic-structural model to the study of religious and mythical systems.

The study of ecological systems and adjustments as expressed in religious systems was represented by Marvin Harris' 1965 study of the sacred cow in India. The treatment of the cow has been frequently cited as a wasteful system, but Harris demonstrated that it is a functional system for maximum exploitation of marginal wastelands and of the cow as well. Another modern interest is the religious component in culture change. The study of new religions as revitalization movements is exemplified by A.F.C. Wallace's analysis of the Handsome Lake religion among the Iroquois. In this view, religion serves as a summation of the value system and world view as well as the moral order for the behavioral world in which the individual personality must function.

Economic Anthropology. The breakthrough in economic anthropology came in the 1940's with Karl Polanyi's recognition of the ethnocentric basis of the classical economic analysis of money, markets, and the rationalization of work and production. This awareness of the culture-bound nature of economic analysis made it obvious that the market mentality did not apply to the economies of most of the societies studied by anthropologists. Their economic life was embedded in their total culture. Polanyi, with George Dalton and others, has developed explanations of non-Western economic systems in terms of gift-giving, reciprocity, and a functional analysis of monetary and market systems on a truly comparative basis. Through acculturation, Western-type markets and money and the Western economic rationale for work are being introduced into wider areas of the world. As this happens, Western concepts may be more appropriately used in the analysis of these economic systems.

Personality and Culture. The rapid growth of personality and culture studies has resulted from the cross-stimulation between clinical psychology, psychoanalytic theory, and anthropological fieldwork. The testing of hypotheses from academic and medical psychology has led to important new ideas in the cultural anthropologist's understanding of the relationship between the individual and his culture. Some of the pioneer work in this area was the examination of Freudian theory by Bronislaw Malinowski in the light of his Trobriand Island field work. Two important early works that viewed individual Indians psychologically were Paul Radin's *Crashing Thunder* (1926), the biography of a Winnebago Indian, and Walter Dyk's *Son of Old Man Hat* (1938), a Navajo autobiography.

An illustration of how one discipline stimulates another is John W. Whiting and Irvin L. Child's *Child Training and Personality* (1953). Whiting and Child defined the Freudian theory of fixation operationally in terms of learning theory and then tested the theory by applying it to a number of cultures on which data were available in the cross-cultural survey known as the Human Relations Area Files (HRAF). On the basis of this study, concepts of the relationship between child training and personality were reformulated. Later, six research teams were sent into the field to study further the interaction of socialization and personality formation.

The use of the Rorschach and other projective techniques derived from clinical psychology has enabled the ethnographer to quantify some of his subjective opinions on the nature of personality characteristics shared by members of a tribe. It is also possible to make quantitative studies of changes in personality through time. This can be done by restudying one group or by studying groups at different degrees of assimilation into Western culture. From the 1930's to the 1960's, A.I. Hallowell and his students documented both the degree of change at varying levels of acculturation and the concomitant levels of healthy personality functioning among the Ojibwa of Canada and the Chippewa of the United States. More recently, George and Louise Spindler, in their studies of Menomini males and females, found significant differences between the most representative personality types of males and females. The psychological "center of gravity" in the two sexes seemed to be pulling in opposite directions—the males toward Westernization and the females toward a conservative position. When statistically compared with the men, the women showed better health. This conclusion was similar to Hallowell's findings among the Ojibwa.

Studies of Art, Music, Dance, and Oral Literature. The plastic and graphic arts have received the longest and most intense scrutiny of any of man's symbolic cultural products. Many artifacts collected in the 19th century—specimens of pottery and basketry, for example—came to be redefined as art when Western artists began to use the productions of native peoples as a basis for modern art. The American anthropologist Franz Boas did not make a sharp distinction between art, artifacts as aesthetic objects, and artifacts as useful objects. Boas' examination of art in its social context dispelled 19th century theories that arranged primitive arts according to some evolutionary scale.

The anthropological study of dance and music lagged behind the study of plastic and graphic arts. The early field collector lacked equipment for recording and coding the dance and music of native peoples. Annotations designed for Western dance and music were inadequate for representing the richness and variation of the ethnographic material. Only with the development of annotation systems designed for cross-cultural analysis and the even more revolutionary use of tapes, records, and films did the direct recording of these cultural productions become possible.

Much early folklore collecting served as a means for obtaining linguistic texts, and there was also, of course, collecting for the sake of collecting. Art, music, and folklore attracted ethnographers with the same type of interest. Possibly because music and folklore are readily transportable from one culture to an adjoining one, they formed the basis of diffusion studies that stressed the spread of plots in folklore and of songs and melodies in music. In the field of folklore the early diffusion studies concentrated on the spread of tales from high cultures, such as those of India or the Mediterranean. Later studies were more detailed and specific in terms of geographic spread to contiguous areas. There were also theories that folklore represented an evolution from ritual to myth. Franz Boas saw folklore as holding up a mirror to technology and other aspects of culture. Modern structural analysis attempts to follow the linguistic model, breaking down oral literature into component parts and analyzing how they are assembled. The relationship between ideal personality and oral literature is another area of modern research. Studying culture heroes may reveal the character traits that members of a society consider ideal. Thus folklore may be seen as a projective system built within the culture.

The collection of texts of chants, myth, folklore, and all the verbal arts led to the need to delineate the relationship between the cultural literary style and the individual variations within it. Anthropologists also collect oral histories within their own cultures in an attempt to get at the individual's personal expression of his cultural impressions. The possible relationship between the structure of a language and the verbal arts that develop within it is another area of current research. A folk science, narrative style, and perception of the world may be influenced by the way in which a specific language orders reality. The relationship between a specific language and the world view and habitual thought of those who use it is a primary concern of students of communication.

Modern anthropological research in the arts centers on the context of the arts within societies. The anthropologist asks: Who practices them and under whose auspices? How are critics and aesthetic standards involved? What is the actual structure of music, art, and dance, not only as it is known to the practitioners, but also the unconscious patterning, which comparative analysis reveals? What is the relationship of the particular art under examination to other activities of life? Where does the art fit into the pattern of work and play? What are the manifest and latent functions of art, for creator, and audience?

Linguistics. The study of linguistics in ethnography and ethnology grew out of necessity. The anthropologist in the field often was confronted with the task of writing down texts and folklore in a strange language. Indo-European languages offered little or no help in understanding its sound system or its structure or grammar. Analyzing the language and working out a system for transcribing texts often became the first field task of the anthropologist working with an unknown language. Ethnologists also found that the study of the distribution of related languages could be used to help establish degrees of relationship between cultures and to supply evidence for culture history.

Anthropologists used the comparative method of language study, which had established the relationship between such languages as German, Latin, Hindi, and Sanskrit languages and placed them all in the Aryan or Indo-European language family. The same method was applied to American Indian languages, such as those of the Algonkian and Iroquois. Ethnologists were then able to construct classifications of the world's languages based on dialect, language, family, branch, and stock. Modern techniques called lexicostatistics and glottochronology are used as a means of approximating the time of separation of two historically related languages. Both techniques are based on the degree or rate of sound shifts in a selected vocabulary that is thought to be relatively consistent in its rate of change and impervious to borrowing.

Archaeology. The ultimate aims of archaeological research are the same as those of ethnology: to understand man and his works. Archaeologists use the remains of past cultures and civilizations to reconstruct their culture history. The archaeologist has to concentrate on the material available to him; thus he emphasizes material culture and technology. The hard facts culled from excavations have replaced many older assumptions about how people lived.

Archaeology can be subdivided as follows: *Prehistoric archaeology* deals with cultures that had no written languages and of which there are no written descriptions. All the archaeology of the American Indians north of Mexico before Columbus falls in this category. *Protohistoric archaeology* deals with such peoples as the Scythians, who are documented to some extent in Greek historical writings. *Historic archaeology* is represented by such excavations as those at Williamsburg, Va., which aid in the reconstruction of these historic sites by supplementing written sources.

Archaeologists have developed special techniques for working in the field. Mapping and surveying have some similarities to the field techniques of the ethnographer, but the actual excavation procedures have become specialized, and the archaeologist finds his closest counterpart in the geologist. The need to retrieve a maximum of information from excavations has led archaeologists to enlist the aid of the biologists—the zoologist to analyze the animal remains, the botanist for plant and pollen analysis. Biological information of this nature aids the excavator in reconstructing the climate and ecological setting of the culture. New dating techniques using radioactive materials necessitate closer relations between the archaeologist and the physicist.

In processing and publishing his information, the archaeologist must also work in the manner of

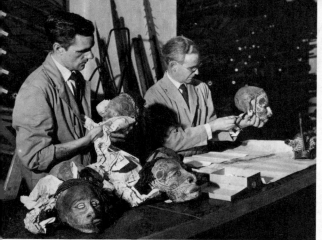

MUSEUMS are centers for anthropological research. Here curators in the British Museum inspect decorated skulls brought from New Guinea by a field expedition.

a skilled ethnologist. He must take into consideration the ethnography of related peoples through time in the same geographic area and of those contemporary peoples who are living in a comparatively similar setting and at a similar technological level. Pottery, stone and bone tools, metalwork, and house types vary from period to period and place to place. Studies of things people made and used throw light on the spread and development of culture and make it possible to trace trade and intermarriage between peoples and migrations of groups.

The final task of the archaeologist is to give as full and accurate a picture of the culture as he can uncover and as full and accurate a picture of the history and relationships of the people as it is possible for him to reconstruct. Excavation usually yields very uneven information on a culture. There is strong evidence on economic pursuits and technology, somewhat weaker information on politics and religion, and usually no reliable data on any area of social organization, such as kinship, dance, music, or oral literature. The success of the final report of an excavation measures equally the archaeologist's skill as an excavator, how well he uses scientific apparatus and procedures to produce a maximum of information from a site, and his ability to apply the most appropriate historical, ethnographic, and ethnological analogies to reconstruct a picture of the culture. See also ARCHAEOLOGY.

Applications of Cultural Anthropology. The major significance of cultural anthropology to the contemporary world has probably been its contribution to the understanding that most tensions between human groups result from cultural rather than biological factors. Anthropologists have thus played an important role in the quest for better intergroup relations, in reducing the effects of cultural shock, and in improving the adjustment of social groups to changing conditions. Anthropologists worked for these ends in Japanese relocation camps during World War II. They have participated in directed culture change, as in the Vico Valley project in Peru. They have applied what they have learned in simpler societies to aspects of modern industrial life, such as the cultural systems in factories and hospitals.

Anthropologists also have advised on the administration of trust territories for which the United States has been responsible since World War II. In employing anthropologists in this capacity, the United States is following the example of the English, Germans, and Dutch. All these countries used anthropologists as advisers to their cultural administrators. As Claude Levi-Strauss noted, anthropology is to a considerable extent the child of European colonial expansion. It has been the job of anthropology to make the European see the former colonial world as one of human beings living in cultures, not as a group of objects for exploitation.

PHYSICAL ANTHROPOLOGY

Physical anthropology is concerned with the study of man as a biological species. This study began in Europe long before there was any hypothesis that man was a species that had evolved from an earlier animal form. Much of the earliest work in this field was based on the assumption that human varieties were inherent and unchanging, just as species of plants and animals were thought to be immutable. The first physical anthropologists tried to describe the varieties of the human species in anatomical terms.

Anthropometry—the measurement of the parts of the body—is one of the descriptive techniques that developed in physical anthropology. Except in special cases, single measurements are not of much importance. The relationship of measurements gives indices or proportions, and these are descriptive of form. Measurements taken in a standardized manner make it possible to compare one individual with another and one group with another and to compare the descriptions by one investigator with those by another. Statistical summary treatment of data makes it possible to interpret large series of measurements, to check on the probability of observable differences being valid and not just the result of insufficient sampling, and to analyze the degree of variations of a physical characteristic.

Human Evolution. With the coming of the theory of evolution, the hypothesis that the human physical form was the result of descent with modification greatly influenced the field of physical anthropology. The course of man's evolutionary development was charted in the light of comparative anatomy and embryology, and finally documented with direct evidence from fossil human remains.

Today human variation in all its dimensions is the principal concern of the physical anthropologist. Racial differences are seen in their evolutionary context as the result of inbreeding due to geographical isolation and cultural barriers, natural selection to fit different environments, genetic drift, and susceptibilities and immunities to disease. Genetic studies now supplement and extend comparative studies in physiology and pathology. Recent research has centered on the description of body build, or somatotype. Current workers are investigating the relationship between body build and physiological processes that seem to underlie disease susceptibility. Growth studies include not only anthropometric measures of height, weight, and girth but also photographic assessment of somatotype and X-ray determination of the rate of skeletal maturation, or bone aging. The modern physical anthropologist studies the growth of the individual as seen in relationship to the growth and evolution of the human species.

Fossil primates and fossil human material provide the physical anthropologists with direct evidence of human evolution. Their association with animal remains of known antiquity that mark placement in time is derived from their geological time periods. Associated cultural remains also provide the anthropologists with the only direct evidence for the growth and development of culture. Much of the key fossil evidence that will unravel the precise time and place of the origin of man has not yet come to light. We must await more discoveries from the Pliocene, during which the major transition from an ape form to an apeman took place.

The more recent million-year period of the Pleistocene contains most of the known fossils related to man's evolution. The remains of upright bipedal man-apes dating from about 1,750,000 years ago, or before the start of the Pleistocene, have been found in East and South Africa. These Australopithecines show considerable physical variability, ranging from large- to small-jawed types and also differing in adaptations to wet and dry areas. These man-apes seem to have lived on the ground and to have used tools, although the associated *Homo habilis* may actually have been the maker of these tools. The archaeological as well as the physical beginnings of man can thus be traced back to the earliest part of the Pleistocene, but no further at present.

During the course of the four glacial advances in the Pleistocene, man underwent a rapid advance in brain size, accompanied by an increase in the number and variety of his tools. The mid-Pleistocene record shows the evolution to *Homo erectus*, who, in China at least, had learned to make controlled use of fire. By the time of the fourth glacial advance, man had developed biologically into the modern species. He had increased his cultural equipment to a degree that enabled him to live in Europe under arctic-type conditions comparable to those faced by the Eskimo today.

The modern physical anthropologist sees contemporary man as representing the current phase of human evolutionary development. He is concerned with tracing the record of man's descent and also with man as a biological phenomenon of today. Furthermore, he is aware that evolution is an ongoing process, and he thus also investigates the mechanisms of modification that are now operative and hopes to predict the direction that future changes may take.

Primatology. Comparative anatomists have long recognized that man resembles the apes and monkeys. This group is called the prime order of animals, or primates, because of their illustrious relation, man. The early phase of primate studies was based on specimens brought back and dissected in the laboratory, and these forms were studied carefully in the 19th century by men who were for or against Darwin's theory of evolution. In the 20th century the study has been expanded to include detailed studies of physiology, growth, and blood groups, as well as other genetic factors. These studies continue to show what T.H. Huxley demonstrated in the 19th century, that man is closest in his natural relations to the chimpanzee and gorilla, followed by the orangutan and gibbon, and that he is further removed from the Old and New World monkeys and is furthest from the lemurs, tarsiers, and tree shrews.

The study of primate behavior and societies began with travelers' anecdotes and folklore and continued in zoological gardens in the 19th century. In the 20th century detailed studies of the primates in their native habitat began with C.R. Carpenter's field studies of the gibbon and of New and Old World monkeys. More recently, George Schaller studied the mountain gorilla, and Jane Goodall reported on the chimpanzee. These studies, along with laboratory studies of primate behavior by psychologists, provide a base line for the understanding of human behavior.

Race. The geographical patterning of human variation was long studied before Darwin stated his evolutionary hypotheses. One of the earliest preevolutionary controversies in ethnology centered on single versus multiple origins of the human species. Today racial variations are recognized as the result of the evolutionary process. That is, mutations that are inheritable are acted upon by natural selection in conjunction with degrees of isolation, population size, and mechanisms of population genetics, such as genetic drift, to produce observable differences in human populations. These subtypes within the human species consist of different combinations of inheritable traits; they are the result of the relative isolation of our human ancestors during the ice ages and the adaptation of each population to the selective pressures of the very diverse environments in which men lived. During these ice advances, man did not have the tools and other facilities to protect himself from the forces of nature that modern man possesses.

The physical anthropologist thus looks at gross climatic factors to which human populations adjusted—variations in heat and cold, high and low humidity, altitude, insect pests, and diseases associated with particular environments—as screening devices that have contributed to human diversity through natural selection. An element in the blood, hemoglobin S, produces sickle-cell anemia in some people but in others gives some immunity to malaria. Anthropologists have found large numbers of people with this immunity in regions where the *Anopheles* mosquito, which transmits malaria, is found. A cultural factor, the spread of slash-and-burn horticulture, greatly increased the environments in which the *Anopheles* mosquito could breed.

Racial differences thus reflect current environmental pressures, genetic drift, the nonselected shift in variability in a small population by accidental loss, past and present hybridization between geographically distinct subspecies or types, and the present selective adaptation of human varieties to their environment, whether that be arctic or temperate, rural or urban. Each such environment would have its own selective advantage and disadvantage for the physical types (genetically based) living within it.

Genetics. The last area to develop in the modern evolutionary theory is genetics, and it is the last to reach maturity in physical anthropology. We still know relatively little about human genetics, primarily because man is a slow-breeding animal, and this breeding is not deliberately controlled to produce pure lines of descent for specific characteristics. Human genetic analysis is forced to rely on observational data, often derived from the association of genetic factors with pathological conditions. Examples were the discovery of the incompatibility of different blood types in transfusions and the later discovery of the Rh factor.

In the 20th century there has been a great increase in the number of human genetic factors that have been analyzed. These factors are used along with older anthropometric techniques to determine the degree of racial admixture in populations—for example, to study the relative proportion of Negroid, Caucasoid, and American Indian in the populations of Brazil. Population genetics is taking its place as an increasingly important analytic tool in the hands of the physical anthropologist. The current view of biological evolutionary change is that it begins with mutations that survive and become fixed within the hereditary patterns of groups through patterns of Mendelian inheritance. Mutations survive or disappear according to the principles of natural selection as they apply to both internal and population genetic processes.

Applications of Physical Anthropology. The studies of physical anthropologists have provided precise descriptions of the human body and knowledge of the fact that people vary greatly, even in one population. This information has been put to practical use in the design of army equipment, such as gas masks, and in improving shoes, clothing, and furniture. The form of these items had been determined historically by custom, not by a scientific knowledge of human form and the needs of the organism. The application of knowledge of the range of human variability has contributed greatly to the design of many industrial products, ranging from sun glasses and railroad seats to airplane cabins and equipment for space exploration.

Many of the genetic complexes discovered in man are related to disease. Hence there continues to be a bridge between medicine and physical anthropology. Growth studies are also useful, as for example in detecting disease conditions associated with abnormal deviances from growth norms. A knowledge of the stages of bone aging and facial growth is important to the orthodontist, the dental specialist who is concerned with correcting irregularities of the teeth. The statistics that physical anthropologists have accumulated on racial, sexual, age, and pathological differences in people can be useful in identifying human remains after accidents and during wars. In legal cases involving identification of a body, an anthropologist's testimony may be crucial.

HISTORY OF ANTHROPOLOGY

Herodotus had the eye of a cultural anthropologist as well as that of a historian when he reported on the peoples bordering the Greek world. His ethnological interests, however, were exceptional in the ancient world. The Roman historian Tacitus described the Germans, and Caesar the Gauls, but there was no continuity of anthropological studies. Sustained interest in anthropological subjects began with capitalist expansion in the early days of the Renaissance. Intensive exploration and trade in the 14th and 15th centuries made Europeans notice peoples of other lands and stimulated speculations on the origins and relationships of newly discovered societies. The attempt to fit them into the western European view of the world produced the first ethnological theories.

In the 18th century, private collections of artifacts brought back by world travelers were arranged in curio cabinets by their proud owners. As these collections outgrew their private housings, they were often donated to governments and became the basis of the great national natural history and anthropological museums of today. The British Museum, founded on the collection of Sir Hans Sloane, is an example of a collection of all manner of objects—animal, vegetable, and mineral—as well as books and manuscripts. Throughout the history of modern anthropology the major training institutions for anthropologists have been associated with natural history museums. The field approach that characterizes anthropology is basically derived from the work of naturalists. The anthropologist applies to the study of the human species and its cultures techniques that were originally devised for the study of the animal and plant world.

Origins of Cultural Anthropology. In the 19th century, Darwin's theory of evolution provided the focus for the founding of the field of cultural anthropology. If biological life had developed from the simple to the complex, it was possible to apply this same developmental hypothesis to human culture. The early cultural anthropologists were largely amateurs in the study of man; many of them were active in such professions as

UPI

SKULLS provide evidence for physical anthropologists in the study of the ancestry of man. Here a skull of a modern man (*upper left*) is compared with fossil skulls from Africa (*upper right and lower left*) and skulls of Java Man (*lower center*) and Peking Man (*lower right*).

law. They started with inquiries into the history of particular human institutions, such as religion, art, or marriage. These were "armchair anthropologists" who did not go out to study natives. They concerned themselves with the evolution of all human culture, not with particular cultures. They looked into travelers' and missionaries' accounts for evidence to support the general theory of cultural evolution.

In Sir Edward Tylor's view, non-Western cultures were survivals. Isolated peoples were thought to retain earlier patterns, just as the zoologists saw the Australian continent as a refuge area for archaic fauna. Archaic survivals within Western culture became the foundation for reconstruction of the cultural history of mankind. The early anthropologists tried to unravel the growth and development of all human culture from the simple to the complex, and they believed that the growth of culture had proceeded in uniform stages. These beliefs were most carefully detailed in Lewis H. Morgan's *Ancient Society* (*1877*), which summarized his view of the inevitable onward and upward sweep of human culture and institutions as they were correlated with developments in technology. The field experience of 20th century anthropologists, both ethnologists and archaeologists, destroyed the grand evolutionary scheme of 19th century cultural anthropology. The modern discipline, however, owes many of its concepts and much of its working vocabulary to these 19th century theories.

Modern Anthropology. During the closing decades of the 19th century the emphasis in all disciplines shifted away from the building of grand systems and reasoning from the general to the particular. The shift was to empiricism—the pursuit of knowledge by observation and experimentation. The new direction in all fields of scientific endeavor was toward exact laboratory research and intensive field work, which would yield data, not theory. The shift in anthropology was particularly marked because America's leading professor, Franz Boas, had come to anthropology after training in physics. Boas and his students stressed fieldwork in depth, with emphasis on understanding the native language. Their first aim was to capture the ethnographic riches among the American Indians before the evidence vanished. These investigators were interested in limited historical reconstructions and in cultural processes; for example, they studied the spread of such culture elements as folktales to contiguous groups and their incorporation into existing patterns of folklore.

Functionalism. To the Boasian tradition in American anthropology was then added functionalism, as championed and developed by Reginald Radcliffe-Brown and Bronislaw Malinowski. These men abandoned the search for even limited historical reconstructions. They insisted instead that the primary task of the anthropological fieldworker is to understand the ongoing culture as it functions while he is there as participant-observer. In their view this approach removed the last shred of antiquarian orientation from anthropology. The fieldworker would no longer encourage old men to describe how the way of life used to be. Instead, the functional ethnographer was to observe, record, and participate in the culture and its interdependent institutions. One criticism leveled at this functional approach is that in its emphasis on structure it tends to overlook culture change.

THE NEW YORK TIMES

L.S.B. LEAKEY, British anthropologist noted for finds of fossil man-apes in Africa, compares cast of African skull with larger skull of Peking Man, at left.

Culture Change. Concern with culture change and personality change, and the interrelations of culture and personality, is central to much modern research and theory. The indirect study of the processes of cultural evolution by analysis of cultural innovations, such as new cults and religious movements, and the examination of culture stress, breakdown, and reintegration represent developments beyond functionalism. Since functional analyses represent inquiries at specific points in time, there is now a trend toward restudying the same groups in order to ascertain what has been happening to them during the interval between the original ethnographic description and the present one.

This interest in the process of growth and development may seem like a return to the growth models that were popular in the 19th century, but the modern ethnographer is studying a particular culture at the very location of change, collecting projective materials and personal histories of individuals involved in cultural innovation. It is obvious, of course, that in order to understand changes that are or have been taking place, a base line of "the way things used to be" is essential. Thus historical data based on memories of the aged or on circumstantial reconstruction of the past become critical. The anthropologist is still interested in understanding the full sweep of man and cultures, but his techniques of observation and recording have moved from the study of man at a distance to include studies of the intimate details of life within a specific cultural setting.

ANTHROPOLOGY AS A CAREER

There are few jobs for an anthropologist who does not have a doctor of philosophy degree in anthropology. Training for the Ph.D. includes study of the major subfields: physical anthropology, ethnology and ethnography, archaeology, and anthropological linguistics. The candidate should include in his college plan as many courses as possible from related fields, such as biology, psychology, and history. Cultural anthropology generally requires fieldwork in a non-Western society as part of the graduate course. The American Anthropological Association annually publishes the *Guide to Departmental Offerings in the Field of Anthropology*, which lists teaching staff, special courses or areas of concentration, and unique training facilities at the approximately 90 schools in the United States, Canada, and Mexico that offer graduate work.

Teaching and Museum Work.—Many anthropologists spend the majority of their productive years teaching at one of three levels: (1) training future anthropologists on the graduate level; (2) teaching anthropology to college students as a part of a liberal arts education; and (3) introducing anthropology into secondary schools. Anthropology is introduced into high schools in several ways. First, anthropologists teach the discipline to future teachers to help them understand the school as a cultural system and to understand something of the meaning of the cultural context from which their pupils come. Anthropologists also teach linguistics to those who will be teaching students for whom English is a second language. Moreover, anthropology courses are introduced into the secondary school curriculum itself. Study of the history and structure of human cultures can help the young to extend their view of the world and stimulate their intellectual awakening. Teaching anthropologists frequently spend their summers and sabbatical years in fieldwork.

The historical ties between anthropology and museums have been noted, and many anthropologists prefer museum work. Both fieldwork and research are involved in being a curator of museum collections, and some curators also teach.

Other Careers. Beyond the two major jobs of college or high school teaching and museum work, there are other career possibilities. These include teaching trainees for the Peace Corps, advising the government in its trust territory administration, or even training native peoples to record their own cultural systems. New areas opening up in developed societies include staff positions in hospitals, mental institutions, schools, or factories, where anthropologists are increasingly used to analyze doctor-patient, teacher-student, and other areas of intimate face-to-face contact. William Sturtevant has published a summary of careers available to anthropologists.

Many professional anthropologists believe that their discipline can help students break out of the narrow confines of ethnocentrism and take a wider view of the world at large. For the average student, anthropology has the broadening role in a liberal arts education that was formerly held almost totally by classical studies. Anthropology makes a student experience a cultural system other than his own and enables him to see other cultures as symbolic systems with all the parts integrated into a whole. Seeing the integration and interdependence in another culture may aid in reintegrating his own complex cultural system.

GERALD M. HENDERSON
Brooklyn College
The City University of New York

Related articles elsewhere in the *Americana* can be grouped under two main headings. (See also the Index entry *Anthropology*.)

Cultural Anthropology. See ARCHAEOLOGY; ETHNOGRAPHY; ETHNOLOGY; also articles on aspects of culture, such as AGRICULTURE, HISTORY OF; ANIMALS, DOMESTICATION OF; ANIMALS, SACRED; ANIMISM; AX; BARTER; BASKET; FOLKLORE; and MYTHOLOGY. Peoples and their cultures are covered in articles on countries and continents; for example, AFRICA—*1. African Peoples.* See also INDIANS, AMERICAN.

Physical Anthropology. See ANTHROPOMETRY; MAN, PREHISTORIC TYPES OF; RACES, NATURE AND ORIGINS OF; EVOLUTION; and articles on specific topics such as ABORIGINES and NEGRITOS.

Bibliography

Beals, Ralph L., and Hoijer, Harry, *An Introduction to Anthropology*, 3d ed. (New York 1965).
Beattie, John, *Other Cultures* (New York 1964).
Childe, V. Gordon, *A Short Introduction to Archaeology* (New York 1962).
Coon, Carleton S., *The Story of Man*, 2d ed. (New York 1962).
Coon, Carleton S., ed., *A Reader in General Anthropology* (New York 1948).
Daniel, Glyn, *A Hundred Years of Archaeology* (London 1950).
Herskovits, Melville J., *Cultural Anthropology* (New York 1955).
Kluckhohn, Clyde, *Mirror for Man* (New York 1949).
Kroeber, Alfred L., *Anthropology*, rev. ed. (New York 1948).
Kroeber, Alfred L., and others, *Anthropology Today* (Chicago 1953).
Linton, Ralph, *The Tree of Culture* (New York 1955).
Lowie, Robert H., *The History of Ethnological Theory* (New York 1937).
Montagu, M.F. Ashley, *An Introduction to Physical Anthropology*, 3d ed. (Springfield, Ill., 1960).
Service, Elman R., *Profiles in Ethnology* (New York 1963).
Tax, Sol, ed., *Horizons of Anthropology* (Chicago 1964).

For Specialized Study

American Anthropological Association, *Guide to Departmental Offerings in the Field of Anthropology* (Washington, annually).
Bloomfield, Leonard, *Language* (New York 1961).
Boas, Franz, *Primitive Art*, new ed. (Gloucester, Mass., 1962).
Dundes, Alan, *The Study of Folklore* (Englewood, N.J., 1965).
Eiseley, Loren C., *Darwin's Century* (New York 1958).
Evans-Pritchard, Edward, *Essays in Social Anthropology* (New York 1963).
Firth, Raymond, *Human Types* (New York 1938).
Garn, Stanley, *Human Races*, 2d ed. (Springfield, Ill., 1965).
Hallowell, A. Irving, *Culture and Experience* (Philadelphia 1957).
Hulse, Frederick S., *The Human Species* (New York 1963).
Lévi-Strauss, Claude, *Structural Anthropology* (New York 1963).
Merriam, Alan P., *The Anthropology of Music* (Chicago 1964).
Sapir, Edward, *Language: An Introduction to the Study of Speech* (New York 1921).
Sturtevant, William C., *Anthropology as a Career*, Smithsonian Publication No. 4343 (Washington 1958).
Wallace, Anthony F.C., *Culture and Personality* (New York 1961).
Wallace, Anthony F.C., *Religion, an Anthropological View* (New York 1966).
Whorf, Benjamin L., *Language, Thought and Reality*, ed. by John Carroll (Cambridge, Mass., 1956).

Periodicals

American Anthropological Association, *American Anthropologist* (Washington, bimonthly).
Archaeological Institute of America, *Archaeology* (New York, quarterly).
Linguistic Society of America, *Language* (Austin, Texas, quarterly).
University of New Mexico, *Southwestern Journal of Anthropology* (Albuquerque, N.Mex., quarterly).
Wistar Institute of Anatomy and Biology, *American Journal of Physical Anthropology* (Philadelphia, quarterly).

ANTHROPOMETRY, an-thrə-pom'ə-trē, is the branch of physical anthropology concerned with measuring the human body. In the early days of physical anthropology great interest centered in the measurement of certain portions of the body. It appeared, for example, that central Europeans, on the average, had short, broad heads, narrow noses, and nonprojecting faces. Their features seemed observably different from those of the Caucasoid peoples along the Mediterranean Sea and the peoples of northern Europe.

Classifications of peoples by this method recognized assemblages of inheritable physical characteristics. It was assumed that head and nasal form, proportions of arm and leg, and other features showed great stability. Thus it was shown that the head form of the modern Egyptian peasant differed little from that of the skeletons of Egyptians 6,000 years earlier.

In the description of races the human taxonomist made use of stature, color of skin and eye, hair form, and many other features. To these he was able to add measurements that could be treated mathematically to secure the average of any group and also the variants from the standard type. To be of value, the measurements had to be taken from well-defined points on the body by specially trained observers. International conferences were held, and peoples were classified on the basis of selected traits. The result was the recognition of a special branch of physical anthropology known as anthropometry.

From the measurements obtained it was possible to work out ratios or indices that facilitated description. Thus the ratio of the breadth to the length of the skull was known as the *cephalic index.* Skulls with an index up to 75 were called *dolichocephalic,* or long-headed. Those between 75 and 80 were *mesocephalic,* and all above 80 were *brachycephalic,* or broadheaded. In the same manner, nasal indices were computed, while other indices dealt with such features as proportions of upper arm to lower arm, or upper leg to lower, and so on.

The system was also applied to individuals, on the theory that each is unique in bodily proportions. This developed into a police identification system named after the French criminologist Alphonse Bertillon. (See BERTILLON SYSTEM.) The system was effective when carried out by expert operators, but it was so cumbersome that it was eventually replaced by the simpler fingerprinting method now in use.

It was early recognized that abnormalities such as gigantism might occur, and that malnutrition or unfavorable environment could affect the stature of growing individuals. However, it was assumed that barring race mixture, the indices —such as the cephalic and nasal—remained relatively unchanged over many generations.

Then in 1911 appeared the results of Franz Boas' study of the descendants of immigrants to the United States. This proved that measurable changes were taking place. Further substantiation was furnished by a study of the Japanese in Hawaii. Moreover, records of Harvard students over three generations showed a progressive increase in size and changes in bodily proportions. It thus became evident that there was considerable plasticity in ethnic groups due to the effects of environment and perhaps other factors.

Anthropometry has helped in the classification of racial groups and in the study of growth changes. However, the emphasis has shifted from the measurements themselves to the problems they present. Like other taxonomic features, they describe and set the stage for studies that seek to answer the question "why." See also ANTHROPOLOGY—*Physical Anthropology.*

FAY-COOPER COLE
Author of "Peoples of Malaysia"

ANTHROPOMORPHISM, an-thrə-pə-môr'fiz-əm, is the attribution of human qualities to beings that are not human or to objects or phenomena in nature. Anthropomorphism is an important term in theology and mythology because people often speak of gods as having human traits. Anthropomorphism is also common in other areas, as when people speak of "wise old owls," "dancing flowers," or "furious storms." It is used as a technical term in anthropology, psychology, and the study of literature.

Some of the best-known examples of anthropomorphism are found in Greek and Roman religion. The ancient Greeks and Romans described their gods and goddesses as having human form and carrying on many human activities, including feasting, feuding with one another, and intervening in wars. The characteristics of gods often reflected human interests and needs. For example, the Greek goddess Demeter (often portrayed as a matronly woman) was associated with the cycle of the seasons and the growth of crops that the people needed for food. Such anthropomorphisms are held to be a response to man's need to explain mysterious forces and events in human terms and to feel close to the sources of life.

Many passages in the Old Testament appear to give God human attributes. There are many references to the hand and the voice of God. A portion of Psalm 77 reads: "Thy way is in the sea, and thy paths in the great waters, and thy footsteps are not known." Philosophical theologians believe that such passages are to be interpreted as poetic and symbolic.

Anthropomorphic symbols are frequently found in secular literature, as when a poet speaks of "rosy-fingered dawn" or "the wrathful sea." Animals with human qualities have been the main characters in fables and fairy tales for thousands of years, from the fables of Aesop through the medieval stories of Reynard the Fox or down to Brer Rabbit and Mickey Mouse. The popularity of animated cartoons shows the willingness of the public to accept anthropomorphic figures.

Anthropomorphism is of interest to psychologists as an example of the way humans view their world. The tendency to see animal behavior in human terms is sometimes a problem in interpreting psychological experiments in which animals are the subjects.

ANTIAIRCRAFT DEFENSE. See AIR DEFENSE; ARTILLERY; CIVIL DEFENSE; FUSE; GUIDED MISSILES; GUNNERY.

ANTIBES, äN-tēb', is a town in France in Alpes-Maritimes department. It is on the Mediterranean's Riviera, about 11 miles (18 km) southwest of Nice. Oranges and olives are among its agricultural exports.

Greek colonists founded the town about 340 B.C., naming it *Antipolis.* Ruins of a later Roman settlement can be seen, and 16th-17th century fortifications are still standing. The adjacent southern promontory of Cap d'Antibes is a fashionable resort. Population: (1962) 24,730.

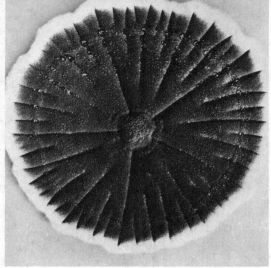

THE PENICILLIN MOLD *Penicillium chrysogenum* produces almost all of the world's commercial penicillin. The symmetrical growth of its colony is shown above.

ANTIBIOTICS, an-ti-bī-ŏt′iks, are chemical substances that are produced by microorganisms and that are capable, in dilute solutions, of inhibiting the growth of—and even destroying—bacteria and other microorganisms. They vary greatly in their chemical structure, comprising saccharides, polypeptides, and sulfur and iron compounds. Some antibiotics have remarkable chemotherapeutic potentialities and can be used for the control of infectious diseases in man and animals.

The introduction of antibiotics has had a tremendous impact upon medical science and clinical practice, veterinary science, animal nutrition, and preservation of certain foodstuffs and biological fluids. More than 80 antibiotics are used now as chemotherapeutic agents. Diseases that only a century ago were thought to be incurable have been treated successfully with antibiotics. This is true of diseases of childhood, pneumonia, dysentery, typhoid and typhus fevers, plague and cholera, tuberculosis, and various other infectious diseases caused by bacteria, fungi, and protozoa.

Characteristics of Antibiotics. The antimicrobial action of antibiotics is selective; some organisms are affected by antibiotics and others are not affected at all or only to a limited degree. Each antibiotic is characterized by a specific antimicrobial spectrum, or range, of activity against different microorganisms. Some have a broad spectrum and are active against various bacteria belonging to both gram-positive and gram-negative types (these are bacteria classified according to their reaction to a differential stain known as the Gram stain); or against bacteria and fungi; or against bacteria, rickettsias, and the psittacosis-lymphogranuloma group of intracellular organisms. Others have a narrow spectrum and are active largely upon members of a specific group of microbes, such as gram-positive bacteria, gram-negative bacteria, acid-fast bacteria, or yeastlike organisms. Since antibiotics are characterized by their selective action upon bacteria, none can be used as a general disinfectant against all infections.

Microbes vary in their sensitivity to antibiotics. A microbe may become resistant to one antibiotic and yet still be sensitive to others.

Different antibiotics vary greatly in their toxicity to animals and in their effect upon blood and other body fluids. Some are highly toxic to animal tissues, while others either are nontoxic or possess only limited toxicity. They also vary in their physical and chemical properties and in their mode of action upon microorganisms.

Production of Antibiotics. The capacity to produce antibiotics is not characteristic of any special genus or of any given species of microorganisms, but rather of certain strains, or variants, within a given species. Thus, the ability to produce penicillin, streptomycin, or other antibiotics is due to the capacity of certain strains of *Penicillium notatum* and *P. chrysogenum*, of *Streptomyces griseus* and strains of other species, to form metabolic products that possess antimicrobial properties. Other strains of the same species either may produce no antibiotic at all or a totally different kind of antibiotic.

There also are quantitative, as well as qualitative differences, between various antibiotic-producing strains. Greater yields of a given antibiotic may be produced by one strain as compared to another under the same conditions of culture. Some microorganisms are capable of producing more than one antibiotic. For example, *Penicillium notatum* produces penicillin and penatin; and *Streptomyces griseus* forms streptomycin, mannosidostreptomycin, actidione, and streptocin. Also, different organisms are able to produce different chemical modifications of the same antibiotic, as in the case of the several penicillins, the neomycins, the tetracylines, and the erythromycins.

Mode of Action of Antibiotics. Antibiotics are largely bacteriostatic agents, inhibiting the growth of sensitive organisms without destroying them. Some also have marked bactericidal (bacteria-killing) or bacteriolytic (bacteria-dissolving) properties. They act upon bacteria by interfering with their capacity to absorb and assimilate nutrients and to synthesize cell substances; they also affect various enzyme systems and bacterial cell division.

The specific mode of action of antibiotics on the microbial cell and the cells of the host varies greatly. Some antibiotics behave as generalized protoplasmic poisons and make little distinction in attacking bacterial or animal cells, while others of limited toxicity are characterized by their specific action upon different pathogenic microorganisms.

Many of the nontoxic antibiotics, such as penicillin and bacitracin, specifically block the cell wall formation of the microorganisms that they attack. Such antibiotics are clinically useful against bacterial infections.

Some antibiotics (polymyxin and novobiocin) combine with the cell membrane to block its metabolism. (The bacterial cell membrane, which lies immediately under the cell wall, is of great importance to the cell, serving as a semipermeable barrier and controlling passage of nutrients and excretory products of the cell. It also is the site of many enzymatic processes in the cell.) One antibiotic, tyrocidin, destroys the bacterial membrane.

Another mode of action of an antibiotic is blocking protein synthesis in the bacterial cell. Antibiotics that act in this way are the tetracyclines, puromycin, and erythromycin. More specifically, nucleic acid metabolism is affected by actinomycins, mitomycin C, and cycloheximide, while streptomycin interferes with certain enzyme systems, imparing oxidation in the bacterial cell.

Antibiotics also may influence the binding of vital cellular components and thus cause their loss from the cell. For example, tetracycline influences the binding of calcium, magnesium, and manganese to the cell, and nystatin is bound to the membranes of various yeasts and molds and causes loss of potassium from the cell. Also, certain antibiotics cause a bleaching effect upon the chlorophyll in cells of algae and other green plants; this is true of streptomycin and the nonpolyenic macrolides.

Bacterial Resistance to Antibiotics. Many bacteria adapt themselves to the effect of antibiotics upon continued contact with them, leading to the development of resistance. There are two possible explanations for the development of bacterial resistance: either there is a spontaneous mutation of the bacterial culture or there is a gradual killing of the sensitive cells within a culture by the antibiotic, thus leaving the resistant cells to develop into a new strain resistant to the antibiotic.

The degree to which the resistance develops varies with each antibiotic. Fortunately, a culture of an organism that has become resistant to one antibiotic still may remain sensitive to others. In the case of some antibiotics, as in streptomycin, sensitive bacteria may give rise to mutants that become dependent on the antibiotic for their further growth.

In order to prevent the development of resistance, combinations of antibiotics, such as penicillin and streptomycin, often are used. Antibiotics also may be combined with synthetic compounds, as in the treatment of tuberculosis.

Antibiotics and Their Uses. Antibiotics have revolutionized medical practice. Among the various antibiotics that have found extensive application as chemotherapeutic agents, the penicillins, streptomycins, tetracyclines, chloramphenicol, erythromycin, and certain others are used in greatest quantities. Tyrothricin, bacitracin, polymyxin, neomycin, kanamycin, novobiocin, oleandomycin, lincomycin, ristocetin, nystatin, amphotericin B, perimycin, candicidin, and griseofulvin also have found important clinical applications.

Antimicrobial Antibiotics. Penicillins—Effective Against: Staphylococci-caused infections including osteomyelitis, suppurative arthritis, bronchitis, empyema, endocarditis, furuncles, laryngotracheitis, mastitis, otitis media, peritonitis, suppurative pneumonia, burns, septicemia, sinusitis, tonsillitis, wounds; rheumatic fever; hemolytic and anaerobic streptococci; pneumococci; gonococci; meningococci; anaerobic clostridia (gas gangrene); diphtheria; anthrax; syphilis; actinomycetic diseases. *Not Effective Against:* mixed infections caused by gram-negative bacteria; malaria; tuberculosis; virus infections; fungus diseases; and others. *Possible Toxic Effects:* conditions of allergy from minor reactions, such as hives, to anaphylactic shocks, which may be fatal.

Streptomycins—Effective Against: gram-negative bacteria; certain gram-positive cocci; tuberculosis bacillus; meningitis, endocarditis, laryngotracheitis, urinary tract and pulmonary infection due to Pfeiffer's bacillus, bacteremia, other urinary tract infections (due to *Escherichia coli, Proteus vulgaris, Aerobacter aerogenes, Pseudomonas aeruginosa*), meningitis due to *Salmonella*, tularemia, peritonitis, liver abscesses, bile duct infections, empyema, tuberculosis, chronic lung infections due to gram-negative bacteria, endocarditis due to penicillin-resistant but streptomycin-sensitive pathogens; pneumonia due to *Klebsiella pneumoniae*; bacterial and fungal diseases of plants. *Possible Toxic Effects:* dizziness, loss of balance, loss of hearing. There is a rapid development of resistance to the streptomycins among the sensitive bacteria.

MUTATIONS of microorganisms often yield promising antibiotics. The cultures in the sealed flasks above will be tested for mutations and new antimicrobial activity.

CHAS. PFIZER & CO. INC.

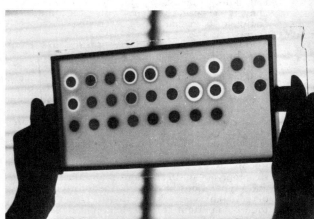

PARKE, DAVIS AND COMPANY

FINDING NEW ANTIBIOTICS involves the testing of thousands of soil cultures. Each dark dot above is a soil culture liquid placed on a bacteria-saturated plate. The clear circles indicate antibacterial activity and possible antibiotic potential for some of the cultures.

Chloramphenicol, Tetracyclines—Effective Against: bacterial and rickettsial infections including typhoid fever, forms of typhus fever, spotted fever, gonorrheal infections, syphilis, brucellosis, urinary tract infections, trachoma, psittacosis, lymphogranuloma; also most diseases that respond to penicillin. *Possible Toxic Effects:* secondary infections or disturbances of the gastrointestinal tract; nausea, diarrhea, and overgrowth of fungi; depression in the blood-forming tissues (chloramphenicol).

*Erythromycin, Spiramycin, Oleandomycin, Novobiocin, Lincomycin—*the range of these antibiotics is similar to that of penicillin; it also extends to some gram-negative infections.

Other Applications. Antibiotics also are used in the treatment of tumors (actinomycins, puromycin, chromomycin); veterinary practice and treatment of plant diseases; and fundamental science research such as in genetics, protein synthesis, nucleic acid formation, and in microbial metabolism.

Manufacture of Antibiotics. The manufacture of antibiotics has led to the establishment of an important pharmaceutical industry and the development of special methods of sterilization, inoculation, aeration, temperature control, and incubation.

Industrial Procedure. Potent antibiotic-producing cultures first have to be selected for the production of the desirable antibiotics. The cultures are treated with radiation and other mutation-producing agents. The different strains produced by this process are isolated and evaluated until a highly potent strain is obtained. The active culture then is transferred, through a series of stages, from test tubes to flasks to fermentation tanks. Proper conditions of temperature and aeration are observed, and at the end of the incubation period the culture broth is removed and the antibiotic isolated. Special culture media have to be developed for each antibiotic and even for each strain of antibiotic-producing organisms.

Since each antibiotic represents a distinct chemical entity, or a group of closely related entities, methods have to be developed for the removal and separation of each antibiotic from the culture broth. The further purification, crystallization, and identification of the chemical structure of the antibiotic requires special chemical skills. Finally, pharmacological testing and clinical experimentation with the antibiotic complete its evaluation as a potential therapeutic agent.

Many of the antibiotics are formed in the culture broth, not as single chemical entities, but as mixtures of compounds, which differ from one another not only in chemical structure, but also in antimicrobial potency and therapeutic effectiveness. They have to be separated from one another and individually tested.

Antibiotic-Producing Organisms. The actinomycetes, a group of filamentous bacteria, must be considered at the present time as the leading antibiotic organisms. Since the discovery of actinomycin in 1940, streptothricin in 1942, and streptomycin in 1943, more than 500 compounds and preparations have been isolated from cultures of actinomycetes. More than 50 of these have found important practical applications in the treatment of human, animal, and plant diseases; in animal feeding; and in food preservation. The bacteria and fungi also have contributed several important antibiotics, notably the penicillins.

Drug Standards. In view of their great importance for the treatment of human diseases, the U.S. Food and Drug Administration (Antibiotics Control Division) has established standards for each antibiotic which the drug manufacturers must meet. These standards are expressed in terms of the antibiotic's effectiveness (units) upon a selected bacterial culture, or on a weight basis (micrograms or milligrams). The antibiotics manufacturers must provide information not only of the effectiveness of the antibiotics produced but also of their potential toxicity.

History of Antibiotics. Although it has been recognized since the latter part of the 19th century that various bacteria and fungi have the capacity to inhibit the growth of other microbes, and although attempts have been made to utilize organisms in the treatment of various infectious diseases, no systematic study of the antibiotic phenomenon has been undertaken; thus antibiotic studies remained uncoordinated and sporadic.

In 1877, Louis Pasteur observed a repressive effect of saprophytic (non-parasitic) bacteria on the pathogenic anthrax organism. (When microbes are grown in mixed culture, various interrelationships take place, some of which are associative and others antagonistic.) He suggested that therapeutic methods might be developed based on this type of growth inhibition. Later, antagonistic microorganisms were found capable of producing, under certain conditions of culture, metabolic substances responsible for this inhibition; and the concept of antibiosis (the inhibition of growth of one organism by another) was described by P. Vuillemin in 1891. The word "antibiotic," in its presently accepted meaning, was coined only in 1942. Prior to that time, these substances were known as lysins, toxins, antibacterial agents, bacteriostatic and bactericidal agents, and lethal or staling principles.

The first chemical compounds possessing antibiotic properties were isolated (pyocyanin in 1860, mycophenolic acid in 1896, gliotoxin in 1936) from cultures of microorganisms long before their growth-inhibiting properties were recognized.

The British bacteriologist Alexander Fleming observed in 1928 the inhibition of bacterial growth by a culture of green mold, later identified as *Penicillium notatum*. He designated the active substance present in the culture-broth as penicillin, and suggested its therapeutic potentialities. Several attempts to isolate this substance in pure form failed; and it was not until 1940 that Howard W. Florey and Ernst B. Chain succeeded in isolating penicillin from the broth and in demonstrating its actual therapeutic value in the treatment of certain bacterial infections.

In 1939, René Dubos found that certain aerobic soil bacteria are capable of producing antibacterial substances, which he designated as gramicidin and tyrocidin, the mixture later being called tyrothricin. These antibiotics were isolated in a purified state and their use in the therapy of animal and human infectious diseases was established. The work was soon followed by the systematic studies of Selman A. Waksman and his associates on the production of antibiotics by actinomycetes. Other investigators were encouraged to pursue these studies, and a number of antibiotics were isloated with even greater clinical potential.

The isolation of tyrothricin from a bacterial culture, the reisolation of penicillin from a mold culture, and the isolation of actinomycin from a culture of an actinomycete, all occurring in 1939–1940, launched a new era in medical science—that of antibiotics.

Streptomycin, isolated from a culture of S. *griseus* in 1943, proved to be highly useful in the treatment of numerous infectious diseases caused by gram-negative bacteria, gram-positive organisms that became resistant to penicillin, and most important, it proved effective against the tuberculosis organism. Frank L. Meleney and Balbina A. Johnson at Columbia University discovered bacitracin, a product of spore-forming bacteria, which proved of value in treating certain infections. These studies were followed by those of Paul Burkholder who isolated from Venezuela soil a culture of *Streptomyces* (S *venezuelae*) yielding chloramphenicol. Benjamin M. Duggar soon isolated another culture, S. *aureofaciens*, which produced chlortetracycline. The related antibiotics, oxytetracycline and tetracycline, were obtained later in other laboratories. Numerous other important antibiotics were isolated in rapid succession, especially from cultures of actinomycetes.

Present Antibiotic Research. Extensive screening programs now have been initiated in numerous laboratories throughout the world for the discovery of new antibiotics. Several thousand antibiotics have been isolated during the past few years from cultures of bacteria, actinomycetes, filamentous fungi, and other microorganisms. Many of these antibiotics have found application in the treatment of numerous infectious diseases of man, plants, and animals. Although a few antibiotics have been found to be effective against certain viruses and tumors, none as yet can be considered a cure in the sense that penicillin and streptomycin are in the treatment of bacterial infections.

SELMAN A. WAKSMAN, *Rutgers University*
Nobel Prize Winner,
Medicine and Physiology, 1952

Bibliography
Barber, Mary, and Garrod, Lawrence P., *Antibiotics and Chemotherapy* (Edinburgh 1963).
Florey, Howard Walter, and others, *Antibiotics,* 2 vols. (London 1949).
Florey, Mary E., *The Clinical Application of Antibiotics,* 4 vols. (London 1952–1960).
Goldberg, Herbert S., ed., *Antibiotics: Their Chemistry and Non-Medical Uses* (New York 1959).
Karel, Leonard, and Roach, Elizabeth S., comp., *A Dictionary of Antibiosis* (New York 1951).
Kavanaugh, Frederick, *Analytical Microbiology* (New York 1963).
Miller, Max W., *The Pfizer Handbook of Microbial Metabolites* (New York 1961).
Stock, J.A., "Antitumor Antibiotics" in *Experimental Chemotherapy* by R.J. Schnitzer and F. Hawking (New York 1966).
Umezawa, H., *Recent Advances in Chemistry and Biochemistry of Antibiotics* (Tokyo 1964).
Waksman, Selman A., *The Conquest of Tuberculosis* (Berkeley, Calif., 1965).
Waksman, Selman A., *Microbial Antagonisms and Antibiotic Substances,* 2d ed. (New York 1947).
Waksman, Selman A., *Streptomycin—Its Nature and Practical Application* (Baltimore 1949).
Waksman, Selman A., "What is an Antibiotic or an Antibiotic Substance?" *Mycologia,* vol. 39, pp. 565–569 (New York 1947).
Waksman, Selman A., and Lechevalier, Hubert A., *The Actinomycetes,* vol. 3 (Baltimore 1962).
Woodbine, M., ed., *Antibiotics in Agriculture,* Proceedings of the University of Nottingham Ninth Easter School, in Agricultural Science, 1962 (London 1962).

ANTIBODIES AND ANTIGENS, an′ti-bod′ēz, an′-ti-jənz. Antibodies are complex molecules manufactured in the body of an organism as a reaction to the presence of other complex molecules, called antigens. The role of antibodies is primarily defensive; they combine with antigens that enter an organism, and they thus may neutralize possible harmful effects of the antigens.

Properties and Actions. Antigens generally are large molecules, usually protein or polysaccharide in nature, with molecular weights over 10,000. The antibodies produced by the body are proteins of the blood plasma and are classified as gamma globulins (q.v.).

When an antibody is manufactured, it is formed for a specific invading antigen. For example, antibodies against bacteria and viruses tend to inhibit their activity by combining with specific molecules in the outer coatings of the microorganisms, thus blocking their effects. Also, neutralizing antibodies, called antitoxins, may be formed in response to the poisonous proteins, or toxins, released by certain invading bacteria.

Antibodies formed in one organism against a particular disease will confer temporary immunity against the disease if injected into another organism. Also, a harmless strain of a particular microorganism, as in a vaccine, may stimulate the formation of antibodies that are effective not only against that harmless strain but also against very virulent strains of the same microorganism.

Antibody Formation. At birth, the ability to form antibody is concentrated in the thymus gland, which forms lymphocytes—a variety of white blood cell that is carried to the lymph nodes. When thymus glands are removed from mice immediately after birth—before the lymphocyte machinery can be set up—the mice soon die of simple infections that ordinarily would not be dangerous.

As the organism matures, antibodies are manufactured in lymphatic tissue centers, such as lymph nodes, spleen, and bone marrow, by large lymphocytes called plasma cells. It is believed that the presence of an antigen stimulates these lymphatic centers to manufacture antibody-producing plasma cells. Initially, the spleen is most active in production; its activity decreases as the bone marrow and other lymphoid tissue become active. As for the actual structure of the antibody, evidence seems to indicate that it is controlled genetically rather than being molded in template fashion on the antigen.

Occasionally, human beings are born without the capacity to form the antibody-containing gamma globulins. Those suffering from such agammaglobulinemia die soon of infection unless massive antibiotic therapy is used.

Antibody Reactions. Antibodies are highly specific, and they will react only with the antigen that stimulated their formation or with very similar antigens. For instance, an antibody that is sensitive to human blood will not react with chicken blood.

Virus Invasion Response. Antibodies formed in response to a virus invasion will persist in the blood stream for long periods. Even if they are declining in concentration, the antibodies can build up to high levels as soon as contact with virus is renewed. It is for this reason that after a single attack of measles, chickenpox, or mumps, the patient is permanently immune to those diseases. However, in the flu or the common cold, viruses frequently develop new strains that must be countered by new antibodies; immunity in such cases is only temporary.

Allergic Reaction. The machinery of antibody formation sometimes is set in motion by proteins that are essentially harmless. This is an allergic reaction, and the body is said to suffer from an allergy. An allergy can be merely inconvenient, as when a sufferer must avoid certain foods (food sensitivity) or take precaution against some kinds of plant pollen (hay fever). It also can be a matter of life or death, as when a patient develops a sensitivity against a drug that might, under normal conditions, save his life. In hypersensitive persons an allergic reaction to a foreign antigen can be strong enough to kill; this is called anaphylactic shock. See ALLERGY: ANAPHYLAXIS.

Reactions Within and Between Species. Individuals within a species possess molecules sufficiently different to allow one member of the species to develop antibodies against the corresponding molecules of the other. This is most notably true in the case of blood where, for instance, a person with blood type A will develop antibodies against the substances in the red cells of blood type B, and vice versa. It was not until this mechanism was understood that blood transfusions were carried out only among compatible blood types and thus could be relied on to save rather than kill.

The formation of antibodies by one person against the tissue components of another person makes tissue transplantation difficult. An organ or piece of tissue from one individual usually will not "take" in another individual because of antibody formation and consequent rejection of the foreign tissue. Transplants are most successful when made between identical twins for such twins have the same tissue components and thus antibodies are not formed.

Relationships among species can be detected by antibody reactions. Antibody reacting to human blood will respond weakly to chimpanzee blood; while antibody reacting with chicken blood will respond weakly to duck blood. The stronger the reaction, the closer the relationship of the species being tested.

Autoimmunity. There is even the possibility that under certain abnormal conditions the body may form antibodies against some of its own components. It forms an immunity against itself, so to speak, producing a variety of disorders that are classified as autoimmune diseases.

ISAAC ASIMOV
Boston University School of Medicine

Further Reading: Nossal, G.J.V., "How Cells Make Antibodies," *Scientific American,* vol. 211, no. 6, pp. 106–115 (New York 1964).

ANTICHRIST, an'ti-krīst, a term used in the Bible to refer to an evil person or power expected to appear at the end of the world and oppress the Jews or the Christians or all mankind just before the final judgment. The term is found in the Epistles of John (I John 2:18, 22; 4:3; II John 7) where it is obviously given a special interpretation: the antichrist has arrived and is present in the persons of those who deny that Christ has "come in the flesh" (that is, the Docetic Gnostics, who insisted that Jesus was wholly divine, his human nature being only an apparition), and who are now deserting the church (which insists upon the reality of Jesus' human personality and physical body). Other New Testament texts refer to false Christs and false prophets, evil powers arrayed against God and His Christ, the false leader or invading army in the temple (Matthew 24:15, 24) and the "man of sin" (or of lawlessness), the "son of perdition, who opposes and exalts himself against every so-called god or object of worship, so that he takes his seat in the temple of God, proclaiming himself to be God" (II Thessalonians 2:3–5). All these obscure, cryptic references have usually been thought to refer to the expected antichrist.

The antecedents of the conception are found in the Book of Daniel (written about 165 B.C.). Here the oppressor is Antiochus IV Epiphanes, the Seleucid king who tried to do away with the Jewish religion. Among other things, he ordered a small pagan altar set up on top of the great altar outside the temple in Jerusalem and a pagan sacrifice (a pig, to Jews an unclean animal) to be offered to Zeus Ouranios (the heavenly Zeus, identified with Baal Shamayim, the "Lord of the Heavens," with whom the Jewish God was henceforth to be identified). This terrible outrage (the abomination that "makes desolate" in Daniel 9:27) led to the Maccabean war of independence and was never forgotten by the Jewish people.

In later apocalyptic books, the figure of the evil oppressor is retained though the features are somewhat altered. In Daniel, as noted, he is recognizably Antiochus IV, who destroys three rulers (Daniel 7:8, 24), persecutes the saints—that is, the holy or sacred people of God (Daniel 7:25), rules 3½ years, and is eventually overthrown. He is the last of the wicked world rulers, and after him the series of pagan world empires comes to an end, supplanted by the world empire of the Jews (Daniel 7:27). But the end did not come, and in later works the figure takes on the features of other persecutors, for example, Pompey the Great (Psalms of Solomon 2:26, a work written about 50 B.C.). In the Ascension (or Assumption) of Moses, written about 30 A.D., he has the features of Herod the Great. In the "Little Apocalypse" underlying Mark 13, he is thought to be the Emperor Gaius (Caligula), who ordered his own statue set up in the temple at Jerusalem. Later writings identify the figure with Nero, who persecuted the Roman Christians (the Syriac II Baruch, 36–40), or with some other emperor, possibly Domitian who persecuted Christians and also philosophers: "the one they did not expect will reign" (II Esdras 5:6). All this is typical of ancient Jewish and early Christian apocalyptic literature: old prophecies are retained and reinterpreted, unfulfilled predictions are applied to new conditions and persons, and the anticipated course of events is like the changing pattern in a kaleidoscope.

Two facts of importance emerge from a study of the history of the antichrist idea. First, its ultimate origin is older than Jewish apocalyptic writings and may go back to ancient Persian or Babylonian mythology, according to which the rebellious forces of evil will some day undertake to seize the universe and wrest it from the divine control. The first appearance of this type of apocalyptic expectation in Jewish literature is probably Ezekiel 38–39, where it is said that Gog and Magog (possibly meaning the Scythians or the Kingdom of Lydia) will sweep down upon the Jews and try to crush them, but will be utterly defeated, and it will take months to gather up their whitened bones and bury them. The principle of a final onslaught of the forces of evil against those of good is thus lodged deep within the whole apocalyptic speculation of later Jewish and Christian writers.

The second important fact is that the explicit term "antichrist" is Christian, not Jewish, and belongs to the specific development of apocalyptic ideas found among the early Christians and thence reflected in the New Testament. What we find in the Johannine Epistles, therefore, is a further interpretation of an idea already taken over from Judaism and both reinterpreted and renamed: Antichrist is now the last earthly opponent of the Christian Messiah, Jesus. who is to come at the end of the age and hold the final judgment.

FREDERICK C. GRANT
Union Theological Seminary

Bibliography
Bousset, Wilhelm, *The Antichrist Legend* (London 1896).
Charles, Robert Henry, *Eschatology: A Critical History of the Doctrine of a Future Life in Israel, in Judaism, and in Christianity,* 2d ed. (London 1913).
Grant, Frederick G., *How to Read the Bible* (New York 1956).
Klausner, Joseph, *The Messianic Idea in Israel* (New York, 1956).

ANTICLERICALISM, an-ti-kler′i-kəl-iz-əm, is an ambiguous term susceptible of several overlapping interpretations. In the 19th century, when the word became current, it meant opposition to "clericalism"—itself an emotionally loaded term implying undue influence of the clergy in society and politics. Since "clericalism" became a polemical issue, especially in predominantly Roman Catholic countries, anticlericalism often came to mean opposition to the Roman Catholic Church. Taken in a broader sense, as it often is today, anticlericalism denotes an attitude of resentment against the prerogatives of clerics and their presumed or real influence.

Opposition to a clerical or priestly class is no new phenomenon, nor one restricted to institutional Christian churches. In the early Christian church, when the statuses of clergy and laity were less sharply differentiated than they later became, there were few traces of anticlericalism. Once Christianity became the official religion of the Roman empire, however, and the higher clerics were endowed with privileges and some of the insignia of state officials, anticlerical resentment began to appear.

Middle Ages. During the Middle Ages anticlericalism often took the form of popular opposition to the riches and abuses of some of the clergy. The loftier the role of priests and bishops, the more offensive became any apparent discrepancy between the role and the actual performance. Thus medieval anticlericalism often appeared as a current of protest and reform similar to that of the later Puritans and Quakers. The Waldensian group, for example, rejected worldly advantages and attacked the clergy for not doing so. Leaders of such protests were frequently monks and friars, like Joachim de Floris and Peter Olivi (see SPIRITUALS), or political reformers like Arnold of Brescia.

Medieval anticlericalism was also sometimes allied to heretical movements, which were frequently linked with some popular political cause. The Albigensian movement, for example, was strongly identified with Count Raymond of Toulouse's struggle to keep his holdings independent of Louis VIII of France. When his area of Languedoc was incorporated into France, the movement rapidly died out. Later, the Hussite movement was associated with Bohemian national reaction against German hegemony and German bishops. The medieval conflict between the papacy and the empire and between princes and bishops often exhibited an anticlerical tone. This is suggested by the encounters between Pope Gregory VII (Hildebrand) and Emperor Henry IV at Canossa in 1077 and the physical attack on Boniface VIII in 1303, by representatives of Philip IV of France at Anagni. See also CHURCH AND STATE.

Modern Period. Anticlericalism, again in the broad sense, proved a vigorous element in the Reformation, when the Protestants stressed the priesthood of all Christians and the diminished role of ordained clerics. During the Enlightenment, too, and with the rise of the modern secular state, anticlerical sentiment grew. Because of the traditional alliance of "throne and altar" and the association of higher clergy with the *ancien régime,* particularly in Roman Catholic countries, most 19th-century liberals were more or less anticlerical. This was especially the case in France, where anticlerical laws were enacted as recently as 1905, and in Italy, where the *Risorgimento*

brought about a gulf between "clericals" favoring the Papal States and partisans of total Italian unification. In Spain and Portugal several governments passed anticlerical laws, and after independence was achieved in Latin America, anticlericalism frequently developed there. In Germany the *Kulturkampf* (q.v.), with its strong nationalism, was antipapal if not anticlerical.

In the 20th century, anticlericalism has been, together with explicit irreligion, characteristic of totalitarian systems such as communism and nazism. But Italian fascism worked out a *modus vivendi* with the papacy with the signing of the Lateran Concordat in 1929, and the Franco regime in Spain restored the clergy to its traditional position of privilege. In predominantly Protestant countries, even where established churches still exist, little anticlericalism is noted, while in religiously pluralistic countries neither clericalism nor anticlericalism seems very significant. In the United States, where clergy and laity have been closely identified, anticlericalism has seldom been noteworthy. Immigrant Roman Catholics, for example, were generally proclerical. In recent years, however, a strong reaction in favor of full lay participation, sometimes loosely called "anticlericalism," has set in, especially since the second Vatican Council.

C.J. McNASPY, S.J., *"America" Magazine*

Further Reading: Hughes, Philip, *History of the Church* (London 1948); Moody, Joseph N., *Anticlericalism* (Washington 1966).

ANTICLINE, ant′i-klīn, is an archlike upfold of layered rock. See also FOLDS.

ANTICOSTI ISLAND, an-tə-kôs′tē, is in Quebec, Canada, in the Gulf of St. Lawrence, at the mouth of the St. Lawrence River, 50 miles (80 km) northeast of the Gaspé Peninsula. It is separated from the mainland on the north by Mingan Passage, 30 miles (48 km) wide. The island is about 140 miles (225 km) long and 30 miles (48 km) wide, with an area of 3,043 square miles (7,881 sq km). Its highest point is 625 feet (191 meters). It is extensively forested with spruce and pine, and lumbering is the chief industry. There is some fishing and fur farming. Port Menier, a village at the southwestern end, is the largest settlement.

Jacques Cartier discovered the island in 1534. The French king Louis XIV awarded it to the explorer Louis Jolliet in 1673. Jolliet's heirs ceded it to Britain in 1763, and in 1774 it became part of Canada. Henri Menier, French chocolate manufacturer, bought it in 1895. His heirs sold it in 1926 to a Canadian paper company, which administers it. Population: 494.

ANTICYCLONE. See METEOROLOGY—*The Weather Map.*

ANTI-DEFAMATION LEAGUE OF B'NAI B'RITH, an′tī-def-ə-mā′shən lēg, bə-nā′ brith, a civil rights organization. It was founded in 1913 by Sigmund Livingston, an Illinois lawyer, to stop the defamation of Jews. It now acts to secure justice and fair treatment for all Americans alike. ADL operates through a national office in New York City and 28 regional offices. It publishes the *ADL Bulletin* and many works on contemporary problems.

ANTIDOTES. See TOXICOLOGY—*Treatment.*

ANTIETAM, Battle of, an-tē'təm, one of the decisive battles of the American Civil War, fought on Sept. 17, 1862, in Maryland. It was at once the climax and the end of the first Confederate invasion of the North. As was often true in the War Between the States (as the conflict is usually called in the South), the battle is known by two different names. Union leaders selected the name of the creek that flows across the battlefield. The Confederates called it the Battle of Sharpsburg, after the nearest village.

Events Preceding the Battle. The campaign, although lasting only two weeks, is full of human and military interest. After winning the Second Battle of Manassas (Bull Run) and driving the Union Army into the defenses of Washington, Gen. Robert E. Lee decided to march northward into Maryland. On September 4 the Confederate Army of Northern Virginia, numbering about 55,-000 men, started crossing the Potomac 30 miles northwest of Washington and, moving due north, concentrated at Frederick, Md.

Although the Union cavalry kept in close contact with the Confederate cavalry covering Lee's advance, the authorities in Washington were in doubt as to what action they should take. They were confused by the sudden turn of events and feared for the safety of the capital. Maj. Gen. Henry W. Halleck, acting as commander of all the Union armies, and Maj. Gen. George B. McClellan, commander of the Army of the Potomac, agreed that it was essential to keep the Union forces between the Confederates and Washington. So, although they greatly outnumbered their enemy, the Union troops were restricted to slow and cautious marches in the direction of Frederick, always making sure that the approaches to Washington were kept well guarded. For all practical purposes the Confederates were free to roam at will through western Maryland.

At this point in the campaign Lee made a decision that was to affect the outcome vitally. He decided to shift his line of supply farther to the west beyond the mountains, where it would not be so vulnerable to attack. To do so, it would be necessary to capture Harpers Ferry, held by a strong Union garrison. This was a post that McClellan had wanted to abandon, but Halleck refused to permit it. There is no doubt that the troops should have been withdrawn. In their position they were of no value to McClellan, and the place was indefensible.

On September 9, Lee issued probably the most famous written order of the Civil War. Special Orders No. 191 divided the Confederate command into four parts. One column under Lee's command was to march westward across South Mountain, while the other three were to converge upon Harpers Ferry from different directions. To split his inferior force into so many different parts in the face of a Union army of 90,000 men was risky. But Lee believed that there was sufficient time to accomplish the task and again concentrate his army. McClellan was still inching his way forward with excessive caution and did not appear likely to intervene.

Four days later, on September 13, a Union soldier found a copy of Lee's order at an abandoned camp site near Frederick, wrapped around three cigars. Here was an army commander's dream come true. McClellan now knew that Lee's army was split into four parts, and he also knew almost exactly where each element

should be and its mission. Yet he waited until the next morning before moving to attack.

That night Lee learned that a copy of his order had been captured. He immediately turned back to South Mountain. If he could hold the passes until the rest of the army could rejoin him, the campaign might yet be saved. The battles in the mountains lasted until after dark on the 14th, but in the end the Union troops forced their way through. Lee had gained a day, but it was not enough. His portion of the army numbered only 19,000 men, and he had received no word from Harpers Ferry. Faced with possible annihilation or capture, he had to retreat as rapidly as possible and reunite his divided army before McClellan destroyed each part separately.

Marching toward the Potomac about noon of the next day (September 15), Lee had just reached the village of Sharpsburg when he received a message from Maj. Gen. Thomas J. (Stonewall) Jackson. Harpers Ferry with its garrison of 11,000 men had surrendered, and Jackson was hurring to rejoin. It is 17 miles from Harpers Ferry to Sharpsburg and scarcely 10 miles to South Mountain. McClellan should have been pursuing closely on the heels of Lee's small force, yet Lee unhesitatingly turned to form a line of battle. The Battle of Antietam could have been fought that same day and should have been fought by the 16th at the latest. One Union corps commanded by Maj. Gen. Joseph Hooker did push forward to locate the Confederate left flank, but only skirmishing resulted; McClellan did not attack until the following day. Three Confederate divisions reached the field on the 16th, but as the day of battle dawned, three more were still en route.

Course of the Battle. The position in which the Confederate Army of Northern Virginia found itself when Lee turned to offer battle was not a strong one. It was a region of low hills with numerous small farms and a few scattered woods. The left flank was in one of these wooded areas, north of Sharpsburg on the Hagerstown Turnpike. From there the line curved along the ridges and southward to Antietam Creek, a small stream easily forded. There were many rail fences and occasionally a stone wall, but no really strong obstacles to troop movements. Furthermore, the hills to the east to be occupied by the Union artillery dominated the battlefield, and in case of defeat there was the Potomac River to Lee's rear.

The battle began early in the morning of September 17 and lasted throughout the day. There is no general plan of attack to describe because McClellan had none. The battle resolved itself into five separate, practically unrelated assaults conducted by the Union forces, from right to left. The first was made at dawn by Hooker's 1st Corps of three divisions against the Confederate left under Jackson. The attack was valiantly executed and as bravely met. The battle raged for over an hour in the east and west woods and the cornfield between; casualties were terrible on both sides. The Confederates were pushed back, but finally Hooker's men were repulsed.

The Confederate divisions of Brig. Gen. John B. Hood and Brig. Gen. Jubal A. Early had taken the hardest blows, but before they or their comrades could rest, they were struck again from a different direction. This time it was the Union 12th Corps of two divisions led by Maj. Gen. Joseph K. Mansfield. He was killed, but his

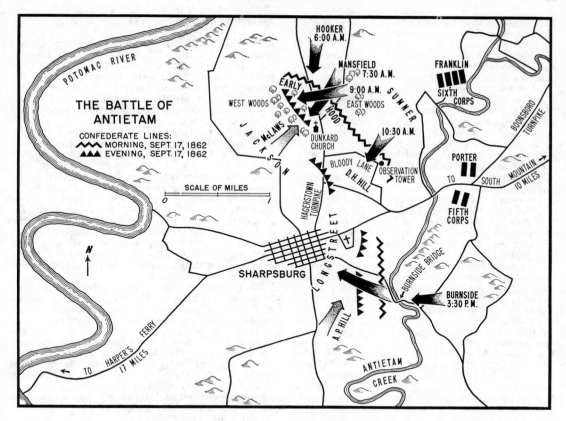

THE BATTLE OF
ANTIETAM

CONFEDERATE LINES:
⩕⩕ MORNING, SEPT. 17, 1862
▲▲▲ EVENING, SEPT. 17, 1862

SCALE OF MILES

0   1   2

SHARPSBURG

attack penetrated the Confederate lines to capture the Dunkard church. It was now about 9 o'clock in the morning, and the battle had been raging almost three hours. The situation on both sides in this sector was critical. The attacking Union forces had suffered heavy losses, but so had the Confederates, who had been pounded by the Union artillery firing from the hills and ridges to the east.

Then came the third Union attack of the day. Maj. Gen. Edwin V. Sumner's 2d Corps had arrived on the battlefield. Without waiting for his other two divisions, Sumner plunged into the fray with his leading division. Meanwhile Confederate reinforcements had arrived. By hard marching night and day they had come from Harpers Ferry, were allowed to rest for one hour, and then were rushed into battle. The division commanded by Maj Gen. Lafayette McLaws had been sent to the exact location where it could strike Sumner's advancing troops on the left flank. Trapped in a pocket, over 2,000 Union soldiers fell in just a few minutes. The attack on the Confederate left ceased.

The scene now shifted to the center of the battleline, held by Maj. Gen. James Longstreet. Here the other two divisions of Sumner's corps were assaulting Maj. Gen. Daniel H. Hill's division. The fighting, centering around a sunken road, was probably the most bitter and desperate of the entire war. This road has since been known to hstory as The Bloody Lane. Facing intense rifle and cannon fire, the Union troops pushed forward until at last they reached a position (near where the observation tower is now situated) from which they could shoot down the length of The Bloody Lane. At this moment

a Confederate officer gave an unfortunate command which could have lost the battle and might have meant the destruction of Lee's entire army. With his colonel wounded and unconscious, the second-in-command of the nearest regiment, intending to fall back from the road and face the threat to his right flank, gave the command, "About face, forward march." The effect of this command spread to the whole brigade, which fled in confusion. The Confederate line was broken. One vigorous Union charge with nothing to stop it would have meant victory, yet it never came.

The fifth and final Union attack was to have been made by Maj. Gen. Ambrose E. Burnside with the 9th Corps of four divisions. About 7 A.M. he had received orders to prepare to attack on the Confederate right flank. Two or three hours later he was told to attack, but he was slow to carry out his task. Apparently he considered Antietam Creek, which he must cross to reach the Confederates in his front, a much more serious obstacle than it actually was. It could be easily forded at almost any point, but the bridge that has ever since borne his name attracted him like a magnet. During the morning several unsuccessful attempts were made to storm across. Other forces were sent to wade the creek at other points, but the main effort was still to be made at the bridge. Finally about 1 P.M. his men succeeded in rushing the bridge, to find very few defenders at the site. The bulk of them had been withdrawn nearer the village of Sharpsburg, on the hills above, or had been taken away to engage in the fighting on other parts of the field. Slowly forming for the attack, the Union leaders waited for more than two hours before charging the thin line in front of them. When they finally did move forward, the Union soldiers easily pushed the Confederates in front of them and in an hour had reached the outskirts of Sharpsburg. Again it appeared as if a Northern victory were certain. There were no Confederate reserves remaining to oppose the advance.

But too much time had been wasted. The last Confederate division, which had been left at Harpers Ferry to supervise the surrender of the garrison, was approaching the battlefield. Led by Maj. Gen. Ambrose P. Hill, the famous Light Division had marched 17 miles that day, with colors flying, urged forward by their commander with drawn sword. They burst upon the flank of the Union forces and drove them back toward Antietam Creek.

Outcome. The Battle of Antietam was one of the most decisive battles of the war, ending Lee's first invasion of the North; it is also known as the day on which more men were killed and wounded than on any other day of the entire Civil War. In this battle Lee had a force of nearly 40,000 men. All were actively employed. They suffered about 10,000 casualties—killed, wounded, captured, and missing. Of the more than 70,000 Union troops present, only about 46,000 were engaged. Their losses were over 12,000.

Throughout the battle Maj. Gen. Fitz-John Porter's Union 5th Corps had been present. In the morning Maj. Gen. William B. Franklin's 6th Corps had also arrived on the scene. Neither of these entered the battle; McClellan let them stand idly by while opportunities to use them to grasp the victory slipped through his fingers. Surely, if Lee remained where he was on the morrow, McClellan would use these fresh troops and with his entire force crush the Confederates. The men of the Army of the Potomac had fought well and inflicted heavy losses on their enemy. If their commander had not permitted them to deliver so many separate, uncoordinated attacks, they might have already won the battle. The next day would surely bring victory.

Fearing this disaster, the Confederate generals urged Lee to retreat, but he refused. At dawn the army was still there, inviting attack. Although more than 10,000 additional Union troops reached the battlefield, McClellan made no move. Lee had correctly read his opponent's mind. He also knew his own men. He knew that his soldiers' morale and prestige would be strengthened if they believed that the Army of Northern Virginia could never be driven from a battlefield. It certainly was not driven at Antietam. Not until the night of the 18th did the retreat begin, and by morning the army was safely across the Potomac. The first campaign to invade the North had ended in failure.

JOSEPH B. MITCHELL
Author of "Decisive Battles of the Civil War"

Bibliography

Alexander, Brig. Gen. E. Porter, *Military Memoirs of a Confederate* (New York 1907).
Catton, Bruce, *Mr. Lincoln's Army* (New York 1951).
Fiebeger, Col. Gustave J., *Campaigns of the American Civil War* (West Point 1914).
Freeman, Douglas S., *Lee's Lieutenants* (New York 1942–44).
Freeman, Douglas S., *R. E. Lee: A Biography* (New York 1934–35).
Henderson, Col. George F.R., *Stonewall Jackson and the American Civil War* (New York 1936).
Johnson, Robert U., and Buel, Clarence C., eds., *Battles and Leaders of the Civil War* (New York 1884–87).
Ropes, John C., *The Story of the Civil War*, completed by Col. William R. Livermore (New York 1933).
Williams, Kenneth P., *Lincoln Finds a General* (New York 1949–52).

ANTIFEBRIN. See ACETANILIDE.

ANTIFEDERALISTS, an-tī-fed′rə-ləsts, in United States history, those who opposed ratification of the federal Constitution in 1787–1788. They feared that a strong federal government would infringe on individual freedom and states' rights. It was largely to satisfy their demands that the first 10 amendments (Bill of Rights) were added to the Constitution.

When the Constitution was ratified and the new federal government began to function in 1789, the Antifederalists became the opposition party in Congress. They opposed the centralizing measures of Alexander Hamilton, secretary of the treasury, and advocated a strict interpretation of the Constitution. They fought Hamilton's plans for clearing up the public debt, especially his proposal that the federal government assume the state debts; opposed his national bank plan and his tariff and excise proposals; and in general were against any attempts to extend the scope of the Constitution beyond a literal interpretation of its terms.

Secretary of State Thomas Jefferson, James Madison, and Edmund Randolph were the party's leaders in office. But Jefferson disclaimed being an Antifederalist. He based his policy on attachment to "republicanism," in sympathy with the French Revolution, and called the Hamiltonians "monarchists." The Republicans and the Antifederalists included the same elements and were based on the same natural division, however. Washington's proclamation of neutrality in the European conflict in 1793 fused them into one as the Republican (later known as the Democratic-Republican) party.

ANTIFREEZE, an′ti-frēz, is a substance that is added to the water in the cooling system of an automobile engine. The antifreeze lowers the freezing temperature of the water and thereby prevents engine damage in cold weather. Sometimes the term "antifreeze" is used to denote an agent that lowers the freezing temperature of other liquids.

Water expands as it approaches its freezing temperature. The radiator, cylinder block, or other parts of the engine can be cracked by the pressure exerted by the expanding liquid, which becomes trapped in the engine by ice already formed. Liquid antifreeze—ethanol, methanol, or ethylene glycol—is added to the cooling water in the engine to prevent damage from freezing. A sufficient amount of antifreeze is added to the water in winter to protect against freezing at the lowest temperatures expected. Increasing the amount of antifreeze in the water further lowers the freezing temperature. See also AUTOMOBILE.

Ethanol and methanol provide antifreeze protection, but they evaporate from a water solution. "Permanent" ethylene-glycol antifreezes are more effective but more expensive. A rust inhibitor and a water-pump lubricant usually are added to the commercial antifreezes.

Some evidence indicates that certain insects provide their own antifreeze protection by secreting increased amounts of glycerol as winter approaches. Glycerol lowers the freezing temperature of fluids in the organism, but damage from freezing results from a more complicated process than simple expansion.

MICHAEL McCLINTOCK
University of Colorado

ANTIFRICTION METALS, an-ti-frik'shən met'əlz, are a group of metals and alloys used in the manufacture of bearings, which are machine elements designed to permit free movement between fixed and moving parts. The bearings carry the loads transmitted by the moving parts. A thin film of lubricant usually separates the bearing from the shaft. The metal or alloy selected for any bearing application represents a compromise because no single material can meet all requirements for excellent properties. Some significant factors are corrosion resistance, deformability, fatigue strength, cost, wear, and antiseizure characteristics.

There are many different bearing materials. A large group of nonferrous bearing alloys has a soft, plastic matrix in which wear-resistant particles are embedded. Babbitt metals (q.v.) are in this group. Copper alloys form another large group and include copper-lead, lead-bronze, tin-bronze, and aluminum-bronze alloys. Aluminum alloys with special bearing qualities have found increased use. Other bearing materials include cadmium, silver, cast iron, porous bronze, porous iron, ceramics, cermets (alloys of ceramic and metal materials), and some very hard metals.

Tin-base babbitts generally contain 80 to 90 percent tin, 4 to 12 percent antimony, and 4 to 7 percent copper. Lead can be added to lower the cost, but it decreases strength as temperatures rise. Tin-base babbitts, which have excellent antifriction properties, are useful where speeds, loads, and stresses are low. Lead-base babbitts usually contain 75 to 90 percent lead, 10 to 15 percent antimony, and up to 10 percent tin. The addition of small amounts of arsenic, nickel, or silver increases their hardness. Lead-base babbitts are cheaper and more widely used than tin-base babbitts. Where greater bearing strength is required, an intermediate layer of copper, bronze, aluminum, or silver is applied between a steel backing and layer of babbitt metal. Babbitt bearings are widely used in household appliances, automobile and diesel engines, electrical motors and generators, and steam and gas turbines.

Copper-lead alloys are used extensively in trucks, aircraft, and other applications where loads are greater than the babbitts can carry. The composition is generally about 70 percent copper and 30 percent lead, but silver and tin can be substituted for part of the copper to increase fatigue resistance. Where necessary, a steel backing is used to increase strength.

Lead-bronze alloys generally contain 4 to 25 percent lead and 4 to 10 percent tin, the balance being copper. Zinc can be used instead of tin, and corrosion resistance can be increased by adding nickel. Lead-bronze alloys are used in machine tools, farm machinery, and pumps. Lead-bearing tin-bronze alloys are used in heavy-duty aircraft engine bearings. They usually contain 8 to 20 percent tin, small amounts of lead, and the balance copper.

Aluminum alloys contain about 6.5 percent tin, 1 percent nickel, 1 percent copper, and the balance aluminum. They have all the properties of a superior bearing at high pressures, speeds, and temperatures. They are used in internal-combustion engines and aircraft. The addition of silicon or cadmium improves their properties.

Cadmium-base alloys contain 98 percent cadmium, 1 to 1.6 percent nickel or 0.4 to 0.75 percent copper, and 0.5 to 2 percent silver. Although expensive, they are suitable for use in aircraft engines and truck engines.

Silver of very high purity is an excellent bearing material for severe service at temperatures encountered in aircraft or diesel engines. Cast-iron bearings, which are inexpensive, are used for light loads.

Porous bronze bearings of powdered metal, containing 90 percent copper and 10 percent tin, are impregnated with oil. These so-called oilless bearings, which require no additional lubrication in service, are used in enclosed equipment or small equipment, such as fractional-horsepower motors. Porous iron bearings, which are low in cost, are used for machine tools and farm equipment.

Very hard materials provide good bearing properties for applications in space vehicles, atomic reactors, and power-generating equipment. High-alloy steel, stainless steel, tungsten carbide, titanium carbide, Stellites, and Hastelloys are used for bearing materials to meet the demands imposed by such applications, where very high speeds, heavy loads, and extremely high and low temperatures are encountered.

Nonmetallics, such as ceramics, plastics, rubber, and wood, also have found increased use as bearing materials. See also BEARINGS.

ALVIN S. COHAN, *Scientific Design Company, Inc.*

ANTIGEN. See ANTIBODIES AND ANTIGENS.

ANTIGO, an'ti-gō, a city in northern Wisconsin, is the seat of Langlade County. It is situated on the Spring River, 143 miles (230.1 km) north of Madison. The city lies in a fertile area known as the Antigo Flats, which is used largely for potato growing, dairying, and fur farming. Antigo is also an industrial community, with factories producing lumber and wood products, furniture, aluminum windows and other metal products, dairy products, beverages, flour and feed, fishing tackle, shoes, and sporting goods.

Langlade County Teachers College is in the city. The public library houses the county's historical society and museum, which has pioneer and Indian relics among its collections.

The site of the city was chosen by Francis A. Deleglise in 1876, and its name was derived from the Indian name of the river that flows through it. Incorporated in 1885, Antigo is governed by a mayor and council. Population: 9,005.

ANTIGONE, an-tig'ə nē, in Greek legend, was a daughter of Oedipus and Jocasta, king and queen of Thebes. She had two brothers, Eteocles and Polynices, and a sister, Ismene. She was engaged to Haemon, son of her uncle Creon, king of Thebes. Though not prominent in literature before the 5th century B.C., Antigone became one of antiquity's most eminent legendary heroines—thanks to the tragedies of Sophocles and Euripides and to numerous references by later ancient authors, who imported variations into Sophocles' account of her. Since her story is told more fully in the article on the play *Antigone*, it suffices here to state that Antigone accompanied the abdicated Oedipus until his death, tried to prevent Polynices from attacking Thebes (see ETEOCLES AND POLYNICES), and committed suicide after she was condemned by Creon to a living death for having defied his prohibition against burying Polynices.

P.R. COLEMAN-NORTON, *Princeton University*

ANTIGONE, an-tig′ə-nē, is a Greek tragedy by Sophocles (q.v.), first produced at Athens about 440 B.C. Its subject is the heroic devotion of the maid Antigone to her brother's honor. Prior to the action of the play, Polynices, Antigone's brother, had led an army against Thebes to dethrone another brother, Eteocles. After each brother had died by the other's hand, Creon, Eteocles' successor as ruler of Thebes, proclaimed that Eteocles was to be interred with honor, but that Polynices was to be left unburied and unmourned.

At this point, the play begins. Antigone and her sister Ismene emerge at dawn from the royal palace, discussing Creon's decree. Antigone tries to persuade Ismene to aid in the burial of Polynices, believing that the religious duty to bury the dead transcends any political command. Ismene refuses, but promises not to betray her sister, and Antigone proceeds alone. She succeeds in burying Polynices, but word of her deed reaches Creon, who has the body disinterred and condemns Antigone to death. Ismene pleads for her, as does Creon's son Haemon, who is betrothed to Antigone. Haemon's argument with Creon only further angers his father, and Antigone is condemned to an even more severe punishment; she is to be sealed alive in a cave outside Thebes.

The prophet Tiresias warns Creon that the gods are offended and that the dead must be buried. He prophesies that Haemon will die if Polynices is not buried and Antigone is not released. Thus warned, Creon repents, but too late to have prevented Antigone from hanging herself. In his grief at her death, Haemon commits suicide, and Eurydice, Creon's wife, hearing of these tragedies, also kills herself. The play ends as Creon, stricken with remorse, begs for his own death and calls for the guards to lead him out of sight, "more crushed to nothing than the dead unborn."

Antigone supports neither Creon's nor Antigone's point of view exclusively. The crux of the drama is the conflict between the laws of the gods and the laws of the state—religious duty versus civil duty. Creon's fault lies in issuing an impious interdiction; Antigone's in refusing to obey it. Although neither is guiltless, Antigone is the protagonist who wins the audience's sympathy, and the beauty of the tragedy stems principally from the playwright's portrayal of her character. Some critics consider Sophocles' use of sententious and moral maxims excessive, but the nobility of Antigone's words and the poignancy of her martyrdom transcend such objections.

Further Reading: *Antigone*, ed. and tr. by Gilbert Murray (Toronto 1941).

ANTIGONISH, an-ti-gō-nish′, is a town in north central Nova Scotia, Canada, at the head of Antigonish Bay, 110 miles (177 km) northeast of Halifax. It is the administrative seat of Antigonish County and a shopping and service center for a farming and lumbering region. Antigonish is also the seat of a Roman Catholic diocese and the site of St. Francis Xavier University (see ANTIGONISH MOVEMENT). Mount St. Bernard, on the same campus, is an undergraduate college for women, affiliated with St. Francis Xavier.

The name Antigonish comes from a Micmac Indian word meaning "the place where branches were broken off the trees by bears gathering beechnuts." The first British settlement was made in 1784 by disbanded officers and men of a Nova Scotia regiment. Later immigrants came from the Highlands of Scotland. The Scottish flavor has been preserved, and there are annual Highland games. Population: 5,489.

HAROLD D. SMITH
Nova Scotia Research Foundation

ANTIGONISH MOVEMENT, an-ti-gō-nish′, a Canadian program combining adult education with the organization of cooperative enterprises for the improvement of the economic status of primary producers and industrial workers. It originated in 1928 in the work of the Extension Department of St. Francis Xavier University at Antigonish, Nova Scotia. As a consequence of the deflation that followed World War I, the economy of the Maritime Provinces had sunk to a low ebb. Acting on a recommendation from a royal commission that had examined the problem, the Department of Fisheries at Ottawa commissioned the Rev Dr. Moses M. Coady of the university to undertake the rehabilitation of the fishing industry. He traveled from one community to another, preaching a gospel of self-help through the establishment of local cooperatives, and in 1930 the fishermen were organized into the United Maritime Fishermen, at Halifax. The method of group study and action was extended to the rural and urban areas of the Maritimes and brought the formation of credit unions, consumer and producer cooperatives, and cooperative housing groups. Although the immediate objective of this program is to give a greater degree of ownership and wealth to the people, the ultimate objective is to raise them spiritually as well. Since 1950 students have been trained by world agencies and foreign governments in the techniques of the movement for work in Asia, Africa, the Caribbean area, and Latin America, and in 1959 the Coady International Institute was founded at the university to advance this purpose.

HAROLD D. SMITH
Nova Scotia Research Foundation

ANTIGONUS, an-tig′ə-nəs, was the name of three Macedonian kings.

ANTIGONUS I (382–301 B.C.) was the greatest of the successors of Alexander the Great. He was the father of Demetrius I Poliorcetes. He served as satrap of Phrygia under Alexander. In 321, two years after the latter's death, he received command of the royal army in Asia with orders to crush the "rebel" Eumenes. The defeat of Eumenes near Susa (316) gave Antigonus control of the upper satrapies and encouraged him to try to bring all of Alexander's empire under his rule. War followed (315–311) with the "separatists": Ptolemy in Egypt, Cassander in Macedonia, and Lysimachus in Thrace. The victory of Ptolemy and Seleucus over Demetrius at Gaza (312) and Seleucus' subsequent recovery of Babylon and winning of the east were to prove disastrous to Antigonus' ultimate aims. After a brief peace, Antigonus failed to expel Seleucus, but through Demetrius and a policy of freedom for the Greeks, he weakened Cassander's hold over Greece, and in 306 Demetrius crushed Ptolemy's fleet off Salamis in Cyprus; Antigonus and Demetrius assumed the title of kings. Cassander, Ptolemy, Lysimachus, and Seleucus combined against them. In 301, at Ipsus in Phrygia, Antigonus was defeated and killed fighting against Seleucus and Lysimachus. This outcome ended any real chance of uniting Alexander's empire under one ruler.

ANTIGONUS II GONATAS (320–239 B.C.) was the son of Demetrius I Poliorcetes. When his father sailed to Asia against Lysimachus (286), Antigonus remained in charge of their Greek holdings. On Demetrius' death (283), he took the title of king but, surrounded by enemies, had no kingdom until 277. Then, after defeating the Gauls near Lysimachia, he was proclaimed king of the Macedonians. His marriage to Phila, sister of Antiochus I Soter (276) had important political consequences. In 265(?) Athens and Sparta, instigated by Ptolemy II, began the Chremonidean War, hoping to eradicate Macedonian influence in Greece, but Antigonus was victorious (261); in this period he defeated Ptolemy's fleet off Cos. As a protection against further Egyptian interference, Antigonus maintained garrisons at Demetrias, Chalcis, Corinth, and Piraeus; in 243 Aratus of Sicyon, general of the Achaean League, expelled the garrison from Corinth. Throughout his life Antigonus was influenced by his early teachers Menedemus and Zeno, and he gathered a circle of intellectuals at his court. Unlike his father and grandfather, he was a national king; he established a dynasty to which the Macedonians remained devoted until the Roman conquest (168).

ANTIGONUS III DOSON (d. 221 B.C.) was the son of Demetrius the Fair (half brother of Antigonus II). In 229 he became the guardian of the son of Demetrius II, the future Philip V. After expelling the invading Dardanians and recovering much of rebellious Thessaly, he was proclaimed king in 227. The Macedonian naval victory over Egypt off Andros probably occurred in that year. When promised Acrocorinth, Antigonus aided the Achaean League against Cleomenes III of Sparta. In this war he established the Hellenic League, and in 222 he defeated Cleomenes at Sellasia. Returning home immediately, he died after routing the Illyrian invaders. Antigonus' ability and integrity were admitted even by the anti-Macedonian Polybius.
JOHN V.A. FINE, *Princeton University*
Further Reading: *Cambridge Ancient History,* vol. 6, chap. 15; vol. 7, chaps. 3, 6, 22, and 23 (Cambridge, England, 1927–28); Tarn, William W., *Antigonos Gonatas* (Oxford 1913).

ANTIGUA, än-tē′gwä, a city in Guatemala, attracts tourists by its fine examples of Spanish colonial architecture. It is situated about 15 miles (24.1 km) southwest of Guatemala City and is the capital of Sacatepequez department. It is a commercial center in an agricultural area that raises coffee, sugarcane, and grain. The city's few industries include pottery making, ironworking, and weaving.

Around the Plaza de Armas are grouped the University of San Carlos Borromeo, founded in 1678 and now a museum of colonial art; the municipal palace; the Palace of the Captains General; and the cathedral, begun in 1543. Many colonial buildings now stand in ruins.

Antigua was founded by the Spaniards in 1542 and became the capital of the province of Guatemala. In the 17th century it was a center of culture and learning and had a population of about 80,000. An earthquake in 1773 almost destroyed the city, and the capital was moved to Guatemala City. Population: (1964) 13,576.

ANTIGUA, an-tē′gə, is one of the islands of the West Indies. Its pleasant climate and attractive scenery have made it a popular resort, and expanded facilities for tourists are being developed. Antigua lies at the northeastern edge of the Caribbean Sea, in the Leeward Islands group. The island has an area of 108 square miles (279.7 sq km). With dependent Barbuda (62 square miles, or 160.6 sq km) and Redonda (1 square mile, or 2.6 sq km), it constitutes a British colony. The capital is St. John's.

Antigua's varied landscape includes small, scrub-covered hills in the north, a fertile central plain, and, in the southwest, eroded remains of volcanoes, with valleys that support tropical vegetation. Overdependence on revenue from agricultural products, chiefly sugar and cotton, is lessening as the tourist industry grows. Resort hotels dot the deeply indented shoreline. Barbuda is noted for game—fowl, deer, and boar.

Antigua was discovered by Christopher Columbus in 1493 and was settled by the English from St. Kitts island in 1632. After a short period of French control, it passed permanently to England in 1667. During the 1780's the dockyard at English Harbor served as headquarters of the British admiral Horatio Nelson. Population: (1960) of Antigua, 53,209; of the colony, 54,304.

See also WEST INDIES; LEEWARD ISLANDS.

ANTIHISTAMINE, an-ti-his′tə-mēn, any chemical that counteracts, blocks, or otherwise prevents the manifestations of histamine. Histamine is a natural substance, present in many animal tissues, that functions in allergic reactions. It is released by injuries or by antigens. An example of an antigen is ragweed pollen, which causes a histamine reaction known as hay fever. Histamine, when released, causes burning eyes, running nose, and sneezing—characteristic symptoms of an allergy. It also causes hives and spasms of the bronchial tubes (as in asthma).

Some common antihistamines are chlorpheniramine, methapyrilene, and pyrilamine. These drugs and the other antihistamines act by combining with the receptors on which histamine acts. By blocking these receptors, they prevent the harmful effects of histamine on the body. Some antihistamines have also been found to be effective in the treatment of motion sickness and as mild nonnarcotic sedatives.

The first antihistamines, antergan and neoantergan, were discovered by the French in 1938. Two others, diphenhydramine and tripelennamine, were introduced by the Americans in 1945. Since then, many antihistaminic drugs have been studied, and more than 20 are now in use.
GEORGE GRIFFENHAGEN
American Pharmaceutical Association

ANTI-LEBANON. See LEBANON (mountain range).

ANTILLES, an-til′ēz, an island chain between North America and South America and east of Central America. They include most of the West Indies. The two chief groups of islands form the boundary between the Atlantic Ocean to the north and east and the Caribbean Sea to the south and west. The larger group is the Greater Antilles, including Cuba, Jamaica, Hispaniola, and Puerto Rico; the smaller is the Lesser Antilles, which curve south from Puerto Rico to Trinidad and then west along the coast of Venezuela. See WEST INDIES.

ANTIMACHUS, an-tim′ə-kəs, Greek poet who lived in the 5th century B.C. He was probably born in Claros, which then was controlled by the city of Colophon, and hence was known as *Antimachus of Colophon,* or *of Claros.* His best-known work, *Lyde,* a narrative elegy on the death of his mistress, incorporates his vast knowledge of mythology and antiquarian information. So many poets imitated this type of poetry that Antimachus is considered to be the founder of narrative elegy and the forerunner of the scholarly poets of the Alexandrian school, located in Alexandria, Egypt, from the 4th century B.C. through the 5th century A.D. Antimachus wrote the epic *Thebais,* which treated the tale of the Seven against Thebes. His extant works were published in Bernhard Wyss' *Antimachi Colophonii reliquiae* (1936).

P.R. COLEMAN-NORTON, *Princeton University*

ANTI-MASONIC PARTY, ant-i-mə-son′ik, the first "third party" on the American national political scene. It was a reaction to the supposed Masonic threat to public institutions. Although secret societies in general were frowned upon by early 19th century Americans, the Freemasons long continued exempt from criticism—perhaps because George Washington and other statesmen and soldiers of the Revolutionary period had been Masons. Indeed, in the first quarter of the 19th century membership in a Masonic lodge was almost a necessity for political preferment.

In 1826, general approval of Masonry suffered a sudden, dramatic reversal as a result of the mysterious disappearance in western New York of William Morgan (q.v.), a Mason known to be on the point of publishing an exposé of his order's secrets. It was popularly believed, although never proved, that fellow Masons had murdered Morgan. Masonry in New York received a nearly mortal blow, membership dwindling in the decade 1826–1836 from 20,-000 to 3,000.

The Anti-Masonic Party, formed in New York in 1828, reflected the widespread hostility toward Masons holding public office. Thurlow Weed in 1828 established in Rochester, N.Y., his *Anti-Masonic Enquirer* and two years later obtained financial backing for his Albany *Evening Journal,* which became the chief party organ. There was a rapid proliferation of anti-Masonic papers, especially in the Eastern states. By 1832 there were 46 in New York and 55 in Pennsylvania.

The Anti-Masonic Party was the first party to hold a nominating convention and the first to announce a platform. On Sept. 26, 1831, convening in Baltimore, it nominated William Wirt of Maryland for the presidency and Amos Ellmaker of Pennsylvania for the vice presidency. The political effect of the entrance, for the first time, of a third party into a United States presidential election was to draw support from Henry Clay and to help President Andrew Jackson (who was a Mason) win reelection by a wide margin. Vermont gave the party seven electoral votes and elected an Anti-Masonic governor, William A. Palmer. The party also gained members in Pennsylvania, Massachusetts, Connecticut, Rhode Island, New Jersey, and Ohio.

After the elections of 1836, however, the Anti-Masonic party declined. Together with the National Republican Party, it eventually was absorbed into the new Whig Party.

ANTIMATTER, an-ti-mat′ər, is the name for material consisting of antiparticles. The importance of antimatter has resulted from the discovery that antiparticles exist and from the possibility, at least in principle, that there are atoms made up of antiparticles.

Ordinary matter has an atomic structure composed of light negative electrons surrounding a heavy nucleus containing positive protons and neutrons, which have zero charge. For each of these particles there is an antiparticle. Antimatter would have positive electrons surrounding nuclei containing antineutrons and negatively charged antiprotons.

Dirac's Theory. The discovery that the ordinary atomic structure is not the only one possible did not stem from a search for symmetry of electric charges. It stemmed from an attempt to make the quantum theory consistent with the theory of relativity. In 1928, P.A.M. Dirac reconciled the two theories under certain conditions. However, he found that his equations called for an electron with negative energy. His ingenious interpretation was to picture a whole range of positive and negative energy states that are available to electrons. In this model there is a forbidden zone that extends from minus the rest-mass energy to plus the rest-mass energy. Dirac considered the total energy of the electron, including both the rest-mass energy and the kinetic energy. Since an electron tends to fall to the lowest energy state possible, it might be expected that all electrons would fall to negative energy states. Nevertheless, there are electrons in the positive energy state. Therefore, Dirac suggested that the negative energy states were all filled with electrons. If sufficient energy were supplied to one of these negative-energy electrons to get it over the forbidden zone, it would be free to move about as an ordinary negatively charged electron with positive kinetic energy. However, a hole would be left among the electrons in the negative energy states. As other negative-energy electrons moved to fill the hole, the hole would move and have all the characteristics of an electron with a positive charge.

Antiparticles. In 1932, Dirac's positron (coined from "positive electron") was observed by C.D. Anderson, who found this antiparticle in a cloud chamber exposed to cosmic rays. Whether antiprotons and antineutrons could exist was not so clear from Dirac's theory. This issue was settled in 1955 when Owen Chamberlain, Emilio Segrè, Clyde Wiegand, and Thomas Ypsilantis detected antiprotons that had been produced in the Berkeley Bevatron accelerator. Antineutrons also were produced in the Bevatron.

The Bevatron can accelerate protons to an energy value about three and one-half times greater than that of the rest-mass energy of the proton-antiproton pair that is produced. In the standard energy units used in particle physics the rest mass of an electron-positron pair is 1 Mev (million electron volts), and the rest mass of a proton-antiproton pair or a neutron-antineutron pair is almost 2,000 Mev. High-energy accelerators can provide sufficient energy for the formation of antiparticles of all the known subatomic particles, including the proton, the neutron, the electron, the mesons, and the hyperons (particles heavier than the neutron).

Virtual State. The present view of subatomic particles does not require the use of Dirac's concept of filled negative energy states. Instead, we can picture any particle as existing part of the time as a combination of other particles that it might become if it had sufficient energy. This partial existence of a particle, called a virtual state, is quite real and is consistent with the other laws of physics.

According to Heisenberg's uncertainty principle, the uncertainty in the energy of a system (ΔE) multiplied by the uncertainty in the time during which we know that energy (Δt) cannot be smaller than Planck's constant h (6.624 $\times$ 10^{-27} erg-second) divided by 2π. In the large-scale world this uncertainty principle has no effect on our limits of measurement. In the subatomic world the effects of the uncertainty principle can be dominant. For instance, during 10^{-21} second, the uncertainty in the energy of a photon (a packet of light energy) is sufficiently great to provide the rest-mass energy of an electron-positron pair, even though the photon may have only one millionth that much energy. During the 10^{-21} second, the photon must be considered to be an electron-positron pair. For instance, within the atom the electrons are bound to the nucleus by electromagnetic fields, and photons are exchanged among these electrons. Each of these photons acts as an electron-positron pair for a brief fraction of the time. This small disturbance, which slightly affects the energy levels of the atomic system, has been observed experimentally.

In the virtual state the particle-antiparticle pair must rapidly turn back into the particle from which they came and of which they are a part. All that is needed to give them an existence of their own is sufficient outside energy to provide their rest mass. This picture of virtual particle pairs waiting to be liberated predicts the same experimental results as the older model of Dirac but corresponds more closely to the present mathematical formulation.

Particle-Antiparticle Annihilation. A union of a particle and its antiparticle results in their mutual annihilation. Their rest-mass energy is converted to the rest-mass energy of other particles or to kinetic energy. For instance, when a positron forms a brief union with an electron, the two of them disappear and two X rays normally shoot out in opposite directions. These X rays share the total rest-mass energy of the electron-positron pair. When a proton-antiproton pair is annihilated, mesons are emitted. These mesons rapidly decay to electrons, massless neutrinos, and X rays.

Other Differences Between Particles and Antiparticles. So far, only the charge difference between particles and antiparticles has been mentioned. Other parameters, or attributes, also are different.

Although both neutron and antineutron have zero electric charge, the magnetic moment, or magnetic effect, of the antineutron, associated with its spin, is oriented opposite to that of the neutron. Some other particles (as, for example, mesons and hyperons) have other parameters that are reversed in the case of their antiparticles. Except for the reversal of certain parameters such as electric charge, antiparticles are identical with their corresponding particles in terms of such properties as mass, spin, and strength of interactions with other particles.

Antimatter Structures. Antiprotons and positrons, which are annihilated with appropriate partners, are not usually present in our section of the universe. It might seem that they are unstable en-

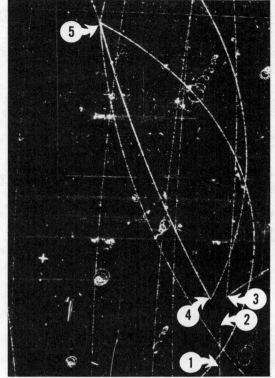

ANTIPARTICLE and particle tracks in this photograph provide the first complete record of the creation and decay of an antilambda particle. Antiproton on the straight track (1) decays (2) into a lambda particle and an antilambda particle, which leave no tracks because they have no electric charge. The lambda particle decays (3) into a proton and a negative pi meson. The antilambda particle decays (4) into a positive pi meson and an antiproton. This antiproton also decays (5).

tities and not quite real. However, they are indeed as stable and as real as protons and electrons. The antiparticles of the other particles, most of which are unstable and decay in brief times, have exactly the same lifetimes as their counterparts. We do not know why our galaxy has a predominance of matter, and it is quite possible that there are other galaxies made of antimatter. In a galaxy of antimatter, protons would be as rare as antiprotons are in our galaxy. Antimatter would have negatively charged atomic nuclei with positively charged electrons (positrons) in the same energy configurations about the nucleus as the electrons in our world. With the exception of a few very special experiments that would interchange left for right, all the physical and chemical rules would be the same as those we know.

Besides the individual antiparticles that have been produced, two structures involving antimatter have been produced and studied. One of these is a short-lived atom, called positronium, that is composed of a positron and an electron. Although this atom contains one positive and one negative particle, positronium is quite different from hydrogen because in positronium both particles have the same mass. An antideuterium nucleus also has been produced in a high-energy experiment. This nucleus consisted of an antineutron and an antiproton.

C.E. SWARTZ
State University, Stony Brook, N.Y.

ANTIMETABOLITES, an-ti-mə-tab′ə-līts, are substances that resemble essential metabolites in molecular structure. They compete with metabolites for incorporation into enzyme molecules involved in metabolism and thus block proper metabolism.

Normal Metabolism. Metabolism consists of the chemical reactions that take place in living tissue; metabolites are the individual substances involved in these reactions. Each individual reaction in the vast metabolic scheme is made to take place with the necessary speed by a complex protein molecule called an enzyme. In general, there is a specific enzyme for each different reaction, and one enzyme cannot substitute for another. Any interference with the working of a particular enzyme will slow one of the reactions of the metabolic scheme. This will affect other related reactions, and these, in turn, will affect still others. A single point of interference can therefore produce a serious disturbance of the organism—a metabolic disease.

Most metabolites can be built up by living tissue out of simpler substances in the course of metabolism. A few, however, cannot be built up in the body but must be ingested, ready-made, with food. These are the essential metabolites (essential, that is, in the diet), and the most prominent ones are the various vitamins. When vitamins are in short supply, the enzymes with which they are associated cannot fulfill their functions, and the various vitamin-deficiency diseases result.

Antimetabolic Interference. Vitamins, generally, are incorporated into the structures of their associated enzymes. However, an enzyme molecule may incorporate an antimetabolite into its own structure in place of a vitamin, since the shape of the antimetabolite is similar to that of the vitamin. Its structural similarity allows the antimetabolite to fit into the enzyme's molecular surface in a specifically shaped "hole," which normally holds the vitamin. An enzyme incorporating such an antimetabolite cannot, however, perform its function in the metabolic scheme. It is as though a nearly correct key, which can be fitted into a lock, cannot be made to turn and open the door. Worse still, this key may break off in the lock, making it inoperable—as an antimetabolite may remain combined with an enzyme molecule over a long period of time.

Bacteria and other parasites can be damaged by antimetabolites. The drug sulfanilamide, for instance, is similar in structure to a substance called para-aminobenzoic acid, which forms a part of folic acid, a vitamin. If the sulfanilamide is administered as an antimetabolite, the bacterial cell uses it in place of para-aminobenzoic acid, producing a mock folic acid. Since this product does not fit into the bacterial metabolism, bacterial growth stops. The body's natural defenses can then easily handle the stymied bacteria, and an infection is conquered.

Isaac Asimov
Boston University Medical School

ANTI-MONOPOLY PARTY, ant-i-mə-nop′ə-lē, a minor American political party of the late 19th century. In 1884 it nominated Benjamin Franklin Butler (q.v.) for the presidency. The party platform advocated popular election of U.S. senators, a graduated income tax, and repeal of all tariffs. It also called for the prohibition of land grants to corporations.

ANTIMONY, an′tə-mō-nē, is a chemical element that is found in mineral deposits. The element has been known to man since the days of ancient Egypt and Rome. Its chemical symbol is Sb, its atomic number is 51, and its atomic weight is 121.75. The element is a member of Group Va of the periodic table. Other members are nitrogen, phosphorus, arsenic, and bismuth.

Antimony is predominantly metallic in chemical character, but it exhibits some degree of nonmetallic behavior. Four allotropic forms of antimony are known. The ordinary, stable allotrope is a crystalline, brittle, silver-white metal with a melting point of 630.5° C (1167° F), a boiling point of 1380° C (2516° F), and a specific gravity of 6.7. An explosive allotrope changes violently to the ordinary form. A yellow antimony allotrope consists of Sb_4 molecules and behaves much like white phosphorus. Above −130° F (−90° C), it decomposes into a black antimony allotrope.

Occurrence. Antimony ores are widely distributed in the world. China, South Africa, Bolivia, Mexico, Yugoslavia, Czechoslovakia, Australia, Algeria, Turkey, Peru, the United States, Austria, and Canada are producers of antimony. Stibnite (antimony sulfide, Sb_2S_3) is the most important mineral source. Antimony also occurs in minerals as antimony oxide, antimony oxysulfide, and as a double sulfide. It forms double sulfides with lead, copper, or silver; for example, Ag_3SbS_3.

Preparation. Antimony is prepared industrially by smelting the sulfide with iron or by roasting the sulfide to form Sb_2O_3, which is then reduced to antimony. High-purity antimony is produced by electrolysis.

Compounds. Antimony is oxidized to trivalent (Sb^{+3}) and pentavalent (Sb^{+5}) states by nitric acid, chlorine, bromine, and other strong oxidizing agents. When the metal is burned in air, the trioxide, Sb_2O_3, and some tetroxide, Sb_2O_4, are formed. The trioxide is amphoteric and dissolves in both acids and alkalis. The tetroxide is acidic; it dissolves only in basic solutions. The pentoxide, Sb_2O_5, is only slightly soluble in water but readily soluble in alkali. Antimony also forms antimonite, $Sb(OH)_4$, and antimonate, $Sb(OH)_6^-$.

Antimony trifluoride, SbF_3, is useful in the laboratory as a moderately active fluorinating agent. The trihalides are colorless solids, except SbI_3, which is yellow. SbF_5 and $SbCl_5$ are colorless and yellow liquids, respectively.

In common with the other Group V elements, antimony forms a hydride. The antimony hydride, stibine (SbH_3), is a colorless, poisonous gas that is used in analytical separations of antimony.

Uses. Antimony is used in alloys because it hardens soft metals such as tin and lead. Its major use is in the alloy used for the grids in lead storage batteries. Antimony is also used in type metal (15 to 25 percent antimony) because of its unusual tendency to expand on solidification, resulting in very complete filling of even the sharp corners of the molds. In britannia metal and pewter, up to 8 percent antimony is added to form a harder, tougher tin alloy. Some organic compounds of antimony are used as remedies for certain tropical diseases.

Gregory Choppin, *Florida State University*

ANTINEUTRINO. See Antimatter.

ANTINEUTRON. See Antimatter.

ANTINOMIANISM, an-ti-nō′mē-ə-niz-əm, is a theological term used to mean lawlessness in general but correctly meaning opposition to legalism or to ethics based on law. The theory on which antinomianism is based is derived chiefly from St. Paul's teaching that Christians are no longer under the religious law but under grace and are led by the Holy Spirit (Galatians 3 to 4). But Paul was deeply concerned with moral behavior (Galatians 5 to 6), and it was mainly the 2d and 3d century Gnostic sects that were responsible for misinterpreting his views in order to justify their own extreme aversion to rules of behavior. Later sects did likewise, sometimes with dire social consequences. Paul's chief concern was to substitute real religious ethics for the superficial observance of regulations imposed by ritualistic piety, whether Jewish, pagan, or Christian. (See also GNOSTICISM.)

The danger of a one-sided misinterpretation of religious teachers who attack external observances may be seen in the case of some of Martin Luther's followers. They exaggerated his principle, based on Paul, of justification by faith only, apart from works of the law (that is, Old Testament legislation), and made this principle an excuse for moral irresponsibility. It is still a danger in some interpretations of religion—for example, in the popular saying, "Love, and do what you will."

In England there were Antinomians in the 16th and 17th centuries. Some of them claimed that, since the elect cannot fall from grace, any act performed by them, however sinful it may seem to men, is not in reality a sin. Theologians consider this theory self-contradictory.

FREDERICK C. GRANT, *Union Theological Seminary*

ANTINOÜS, an-tin′ō-əs (c. 110–130 A.D.), was a Greek page whose beauty and grace made him the favorite of the Roman emperor Hadrian. He was born about 110 A.D. in Bithynium in Asia Minor. Accompanying Hadrian up the Nile River in 130 A.D., Antinoüs was drowned, perhaps accidentally, to the emperor's bitter grief. Hadrian founded the city of Antinoöpolis on the Nile in his memory and established a cult to deify him. Temples were erected in his honor, and festivals were instituted in many lands. The statues of Antinoüs, many of which still exist, portray him as an ideal of youthful beauty.

P.R. COLEMAN-NORTON, *Princeton University*

ANTIOCH, an′tē-ok, an ancient Phrygian city was situated in southwestern Anatolia (now Turkey). It lay so near the border with Pisidia that the Greeks called it *Antioch toward Pisidia* to distinguish it from another Antioch in Phrygia located on the Maeander River. It was settled by colonists from Magnesia ad Maeandrum sent by Antiochus I Soter, king of Syria (reigned 280–c. 260 B.C.), to control the region. In 189 B.C., after the defeat of Antiochus III Megas by the Romans, Antioch became a free city. About 25 B.C., however, a group of Roman veterans settled there and it was made a Roman colony with the name *Caesarea Antiochia*. Saint Paul is known to have preached there (Acts 13:14–51). When the Roman emperor Diocletian (reigned 284–305 A.D.) reorganized the Empire, Antioch was assigned to the province of Pisidia.

The modern Turkish village of *Uluborlu* is near the ancient site.

P.R. COLEMAN-NORTON, *Princeton University*

ANTIOCH, an′tē-ok, is a city in California, in Contra Costa County, on the San Joaquin River, 40 miles (64 km) northeast of Oakland by road. An industrial and commercial center, it manufactures paper products, gypsum board, chemicals, and glass containers. It is a packing and shipping point for the agricultural produce of the Delta region between the San Joaquin and Sacramento rivers, which join near Antioch. This region, sometimes called the Everglades of the West, is crisscrossed by 4,000 miles of waterways forming fertile islands protected by levees.

Twin brothers, Joseph H. and W.W. Smith, settled in 1849 on land now occupied by the city. Other homesteaders arrived from New England the next year, and the community was named for Biblical Antioch, where the followers of Christ were first called Christians. Antioch was incorporated in 1872 and adopted city manager government in 1948. Population: 28,060.

ANTIOCH, an′tē-ok, is a city in Turkey, on the Orontes River, about 20 miles east of the Mediterranean Sea. Its name in Turkish is *Antâkya.* The city is the capital of Hatay province and a trade and manufacturing center. In ancient times it was a major Roman capital in Asia and a center of early Christian culture. The ancient Greeks called it *Antiocheia;* the Romans, *Antiochia.*

Ancient Grandeur. Antioch was founded about 300 B.C. by Seleucus I Nicator, one of Alexander the Great's generals, and was named for Seleucus' father, Antiochus. Colonized by Macedonians, Greeks, and Syrians, the city grew quickly. It commanded the roads of northwestern Syria and controlled the caravan routes between the Euphrates River and the Mediterranean Sea. Its thriving commerce and manufacture of luxury goods soon brought it great prosperity.

When the Romans occupied Syria in 64 B.C., Antioch became the capital of the new province of Syria and the most important Roman city in Asia. Its cosmopolitan character and its importance as a communications center made it an ideal place for the early Christian mission to the Greeks, and it was in Antioch that the disciples were first called Christians (Acts 11:26).

In the early 300's A.D., Antioch became an important center of Christian scholarship. It reached the zenith of its prosperity in the late 300's, when it also was distinguished as the residence of the celebrated pagan teacher and orator Libanius and of the famous Greek Christian preacher St. John Chrysostom. It was the headquarters of Roman Emperor Julian (reigned 361–363) during his campaign to revive Hellenism.

Antioch had been beautified by its Seleucid kings (descendants of Seleucus I) and it was embellished further by the Romans. It was noted for its beautiful architecture and for its colonnaded main street, flanked with porticoes, one of the earliest such streets in the ancient world.

Decline and Revival. Under Emperor Justinian I (reigned 527–565) the city suffered from two earthquakes, a fire, and a plague, and it was sacked by the Persians. It never fully recovered. Taken by the Arabs in about 638, Antioch sank into obscurity. The Byzantines recaptured it in 969 and made it an important frontier post. It was captured by the Seljuk Turks in 1084 and by the Crusaders in 1098.

In 1137, Antioch returned to Byzantine control and entered a new period of prosperity as a center for the manufacture of silk, glass, and soap, which were exported to western Europe. In 1268 the city was taken by the Egyptian Mamluks, and in 1516 it fell to the Ottoman Turks, under whose control it remained until after World War I. In 1920 it was attached to the autonomous Sanjak of Alexandretta, administered by the French high commissioner in Syria. In 1939, after a plebiscite, it passed to Turkey.

Modern Antioch is a provincial administrative center and the market for the surrounding agricultural region. The chief farm products of the area are cotton, olives, and grain. Sheep, goats, and camels are also raised. The city itself has plants manufacturing soap and processing food and cotton. Other industries include tanning and leather working and various types of handicrafts. Population: (1960) 45,674.

GLANVILLE DOWNEY
Dumbarton Oaks Research Library and Collection of Harvard University, Washington, D.C.
Further Reading: Bouchier, Edmund S., *A Short History of Antioch* (Oxford 1921); Downey, Glanville, *A History of Antioch in Syria from Seleucus to the Arab Conquest* (Princeton 1961).

ANTIOCH COLLEGE, ant'ē-ok, is a private, coeducational, liberal arts college in Yellow Springs, Ohio. Chartered in 1852, it opened a year later with Horace Mann as its president.

The college is noted for its work-study curriculum, instituted in 1921. Under this program, the school year is divided into quarter sessions, each 11 weeks in length. Study sessions alternated with work projects in business and industry throughout the United States and about 25 foreign countries. Work experiences are analyzed in relation to the curriculum, and this analysis provides a basis for career selection as well as for the adjusting of teaching to meet vocational needs. Students may also spend one full year in foreign study and work. There is an extensive visiting faculty program. The student body and the faculty share responsibility for college government and management.

Constant experimentation in projects to widen academic experience has attracted increasing numbers of students. Enrollment rose from about 700 in 1940 to over 1,600 in the mid-1960's.

ANTIOCHUS, an-tī'ə-kəs, was the name of 13 kings of Syria who belonged to the Seleucid dynasty (see SELEUCIDS). From their capital at Antioch they ruled gradually diminishing dominions in western Asia Minor from the early 3d century B.C. until the middle of the 1st century B.C. The most important were the following:

ANTIOCHUS I SOTER (324–c.261 B.C.) was the son of Seleucus I Nicator, one of the generals of Alexander the Great and founder of the Seleucid dynasty. Antiochus ruled the eastern Seleucid territories from about 293 B.C. as coregent with his father. Perhaps for political reasons, he married his stepmother in his father's lifetime. He succeeded to the throne at Seleucus' death in 280 B.C. Antiochus' chief exploit was the defeat of Gallic invaders in 276 B.C. In wars during the periods 276–272 and 266–261 he lost much of the Palestine region of Asia Minor, mostly to Egypt. He founded many cities throughout the empire.

ANTIOCHUS II THEOS (c.287–247 B.C.), second son of Antiochus I, succeeded his father, probably in 261 B.C. From 260 to 255, in alliance with Macedonia, he recovered from Egypt most of the coast of Asia Minor lost by his father.

ANTIOCHUS III MEGAS (241–187 B.C.) was the grandson of Antiochus II. His reign—from 223 to 187 B.C.—was the longest in the dynasty. He earned his epithet *Megas* (*the Great*) because of the magnitude of his enterprises. He failed, at first, to conquer Egyptian Syria and Palestine, but in his eastern campaign (212–206 B.C.) he acquired Armenia and won back Parthia and Bactria. When he invaded India, he acquired so many elephants for use in future wars that the elephant became a symbol appearing on Seleucid coins.

In 202 B.C., Antiochus secretly negotiated with Philip V of Macedon to partition the coastal possessions of Egypt. After conquering Egyptian Syria and Palestine (202–198 B.C.), he invaded Thrace in 196 B.C., arousing Roman fears of Seleucid expansion in Europe. Negotiations with Rome proved inconclusive, and at the invitation of the Aetolian League he invaded Greece in 192 B.C. He was defeated by the Romans at Thermopylae in 191 B.C. and again, disastrously, a year later at Magnesia. By a peace treaty in 188 B.C. he was deprived of all dominions in Asia Minor west of the Taurus Mountains. The Seleucids thereafter ceased to be a major influence in the lands surrounding the Mediterranean Sea.

ANTIOCHUS IV EPIPHANES (c.215–163 B.C.), third son of Antiochus III, became king in 175 B.C. He was forced by Rome to give up a campaign against Egypt (169–168 B.C.). His intolerance of the Jews, whom he sought to Hellenize, led to the Wars of the Maccabees (167–160 B.C.) in Judea.

ANTIOCHUS VII SIDETES or EUERGETES (c.159–129 B.C.) was the son of Demetrius I Soter. He succeeded his brother, Demetrius II Nicator, in 139 B.C. He destroyed Jerusalem when he reconquered Palestine (135–134 B.C.). His defeat (and death in battle) against the Parthians caused the loss of the Seleucid provinces in the east.

ANTIOCHUS VIII GRYPUS (died 96 B.C.) was the son of Demetrius II Nicator and Cleopatra Thea. He ruled jointly with his mother from 125 to 120 B.C. and was sole ruler from 120 to 115 B.C. As the result of civil war, he was forced to rule jointly with his half brother, Antiochus IX Cyzicenus, from 115 to 96 B.C.

ANTIOCHUS IX CYZICENUS (died 95 B.C.) was the son of Antiochus VII. At the death in 96 B.C. of his half brother Antiochus VIII, with whom he had been joint sovereign, he attempted to rule over all of Syria, but he was slain in battle by his nephew Seleucus, his half brother's son.

ANTIOCHUS XIII ASIATICUS (died after 64 B.C.), last of the Seleucids, was the son of Antiochus X. He lived in Rome while the Armenian king, Tigranes, ruled Syria. He was installed as king by the Romans upon Tigranes' defeat in 69 B.C., but was deposed in 64 B.C. when Pompey made Syria a Roman province.

P.R. COLEMAN-NORTON, *Princeton University*

ANTIPHANES (c.388–c.311 B.C.) an-tif'ə-nēz, was a Greek comic poet. Probably a native of Asia Minor, he became a citizen of Athens. He composed between 260 and 365 comedies, though only about 120 titles are known and some 330 fragments are identified. His plays, which won 30 prizes, belong to the Middle Comedy, which realistically depicted daily life, burlesqued mythological personages, and emphasized love. Fragments of Antiphanes' works survive in Theodor Kock's *Comicorum Atticorum fragmenta*.

P.R. COLEMAN-NORTON, *Princeton University*

ANTIPHON, an'tə-fən, in the Christian church, a verse from a psalm or other quotation from Holy Scripture that is recited or sung before and after a Psalm or canticle during Mass or Vespers. Its content sets the mood for the feast being celebrated. Antiphons were introduced in the early church by patriarchs of the Eastern sees as hymns of praise. They were first used in the Western church in the 5th century at the Introit, or beginning, of the Mass, alternating with verses from the Psalms. By the 16th century the Introit had been shortened to a recitation of a single verse from a Psalm, although the introductory and subsequent antiphons were retained. Most antiphonal chants follow an extremely simple melodic line.

ANTIPODES, an-tip'ə-dēz, the parts of the globe diametrically opposite each other. The term frequently is used by writers in the Northern Hemisphere to characterize the regions of the Southern Hemisphere, especially Australia and New Zealand. The word is derived from the Greek *antipous* (with opposite foot).

ANTIPODES ISLANDS, an-tip'ə-dēz, an island group in the South Pacific Ocean, situated about 450 miles southeast of New Zealand, to which they belong. Their name is derived from their location at 49° 41' south latitude and 178° 43' east longitude, roughly antipodal to Greenwich, England. The islands, which extend for about 5 miles from north to south and cover an aggregate area of approximately 24 square miles, are rocky and uninhabited. They were discovered in 1800 by Capt. Henry Waterhouse on a voyage of the H.M.S. *Reliance.*

ANTIPOPE, an'ti-pōp, one who falsely claims, or is claimed, to be pope, either during a vacancy in the Holy See or in opposition to a validly elected pope. Antipopes have appeared in church history at irregular intervals since the 3d century. There were only two before the reign of Constantine the Great (306–337), and none has appeared since the 15th century. Only three—Hippolytus, Novatian, and Felix V—based their claims, even in part, on theological or canonical issues. The rest arose as a result of factional disputes in Rome, conflict between the church and lay authority, or, in the case of the Avignon popes, a power struggle on a wider scale (see PAPACY). Their reigns lasted from a minimum of one day (Philip) to a maximum of 29 years (Benedict XIII). Most submitted in time to the authority of the real popes. The *Annuario Pontificio* (Vatican Yearbook) lists 39 antipopes.

MSGR. FLORENCE D. COHALAN
Cathedral College, New York

ANTIPROTON. See ANTIMATTER.

ANTIPYRETICS, an-ti-pī-ret'iks, are agents used to reduce the body temperature if it rises above normal, as in fever. Some of the antipyretics have pain-killing properties and are sometimes used in minor fever reactions to give relief and comfort.

Antipyretics reduce fever by depressing the heat-regulating centers in the mid-brain, by reducing the metabolic rate of the body, and by increasing heat loss. Antipyretics do not, however, affect the infectious cause of a fever. Therefore, their use has been replaced considerably by drugs such as sulfa drugs, antibiotics, and antimalarial agents that reduce fever and also attack its infectious cause.

The oldest antipyretic method, and one that is still valuable and efficient, is the application of cold in the form of cool baths, cold wrappings, and ice packs. The most common antipyretics and analgesics are acetylsalicylic acid (aspirin) and salicylic acid itself. Both are comparatively nontoxic, but ingestion of large doses, especially by children, may lead to severe poisoning. In hypersensitive people, these drugs may produce allergic reactions, such as asthma, skin eruption, and deficiency of prothrombin (a blood-clotting factor), which may lead to hemorrhages.

Many antipyretic agents are derivatives of acetanilid (Antifebrin). This and its commonest derivative, acetophenetidin (Phenacetin), have been used in pure form and still are used extensively as constituents in patented preparations with other drugs. Their indiscriminate use is not without danger, however, for they may produce changes of the blood pigment (methemoglobinemia) that may lead to oxygen-lack in the arterial blood and circulatory disturbances. Prolonged, uncontrolled medication with acetophenetidin preparations has led to habituation, anemia, and injury of the kidneys. Other antipyretics are phenazone (Antipyrine), aminopyrine (Pyramidon), and phenylbutazone (Butazolidin). Though effective as antipyretics, analgesics, and sedatives, their indiscriminate use may result in eruptions of the skin; in hypersensitive persons, aminopyrine and phenylbutazone may also cause damage to the blood (agranulocytosis).

W.F. VON OETTINGEN, M.D.
National Institutes of Health

THE THIRTY-NINE ANTIPOPES

Antipope	Reign	Nationality	Antipope	Reign	Nationality
St. Hippolytus	217–235	Roman	Theodoric	1100–c. 1102	Roman
Novatian	251	Roman	Albert	1102	Roman
Felix II*	355–365	Roman	Sylvester IV	1105–1111	Roman
Ursinus	366–367	Roman	Gregory VIII*	1118–1121	French
Eulalius	418–419	Roman	Celestine II*	1124	Roman
Lawrence	498–501/505	Roman	Anacletus II	1130–1138	Roman
Dioscorus	530	Egyptian	Victor IV	1138	Roman
Theodore	687	Roman	Victor IV	1159–1164	Roman
Paschal	687	Roman	Paschal III	1164–1168	Italian
Constantine II*	767–769	Roman	Calixtus III*	1168–1178	Roman
Philip	768	Roman	Innocent III*	1179–1180	Roman
John	844	Roman	Nicholas V*	1328–1330/1333	Roman
Anastasius	855–c. 880	Greek	Clement VII*	1378–1394	French
Christopher	903–904	Roman	Benedict XIII*	1394–1423	Spanish
Boniface VII*	974, 984–985	Roman	Alexander V	1409–1410	Cretan
John XVI	997–998	Greek	John XXIII*	1423–1429	Spanish
Gregory VI*	1012	Roman	Clement VIII*	1423–1429	Spanish
Benedict X	1058–1059	Roman	Benedict XIV*	1425–1430/1436	French
Honorius II*	1061–1072	Italian	Felix V*	1439/1440–1449	Italian
Clement III	1080–1100	Italian			

* Name used by a legitimate pope. / Date in dispute.

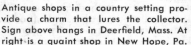

Antique shops in a country setting provide a charm that lures the collector. Sign above hangs in Deerfield, Mass. At right is a quaint shop in New Hope, Pa.

ANTIQUE COLLECTING, an-tēk′ kə-lekt′ing. "Antique"—a term primarily meaning "old," but also carrying implications of artistic, historic, and monetary value—originally referred only to the classical cultures of Greece and Rome. In modern times the term has been applied to the decorative arts of all past eras and cultures. In the 20th century, interest in antiques has increased and diversified to the point that such recently made items as bentwood chairs and wall telephones may be sold as "antiques."

What Is an Antique? The tariff regulations of various countries use the date of production or manufacture in stipulating what items can be imported duty-free as antiques or works of art. In the United States the Educational, Scientific, and Cultural Materials Importation Act of 1966 placed on the duty free list "antiques made prior to 100 years before their date of entry." The Canadian customs tariff act of 1948 exempts from import duty objects of artistic interest that were produced before Jan. 1, 1847.

Britain's customs and excise tariff law of 1959 specifies that articles to be exempt must have been produced more than 100 years before the date of importation. Most European countries now have similar regulations. In most cases, two generations, or 60 years, rather than 100 years or more, is the period required to make an artifact an antique.

Early Collections. The collecting of antiques in the United States dates back almost to the start of the nation's history. Not until the Centennial Exposition of 1876 in Philadelphia, however, did the acquisition of antiques become a serious endeavor. The exposition coincided with a reawakening interest in the country's past, and with it came a veneration for the art objects and articles of the everyday life of the people.

Collecting, in the proper sense of the term, scarcely existed in early colonial times in America. The pre-Revolutionary generations built comfortable houses for themselves and filled them with handsome furniture, silverware, porcelain, glass, and fabrics. Some of the furnishings were made locally; others were imported from Europe as works of art or as historical material. Such objects were acquired for everyday use, however, and not as collectors' trophies.

The collecting of antiques in America really began in the 18th century. Collectors were mainly interested in antiquities: old manuscripts and rare books, paintings and sculpture of the classical past, and ancient relics and curiosities. Some of the 18th century collections are virtually intact today. For example, Thomas Prince (1687–1758) collected civil and religious books and other writings about the history of New England. His accumulations are preserved in the Boston Public Library. Thomas Jefferson assembled about 10,000 books over a period of 50 years. Many of these were rare, old, or first editions. Jefferson's volumes are preserved in the Library of Congress in Washington, D.C.

A variety of glassware is featured in an attractive window setting in an antique shop at Silvermine, Conn.

By 1838 every state in New England had a historical society interested in preserving documents and memorabilia. The early 19th century also witnessed the birth of numerous local art associations, which led to increased patronage and a broadening ownership of art. There developed a growing interest in painting and sculpture, but few at this time realized that furniture and utensils of colonial days possessed interest and beauty of their own.

The possessions of important figures, such as George Washington and John Hancock, were held in great esteem. In 1857 the Mount Vernon Ladies' Association was formed to preserve the house and possessions of the first president, including whatever original furnishings could be reclaimed. The Mount Vernon restoration was the first of the house museums.

The Centennial Exposition. New interest in 18th century American arts and crafts blossomed on the 100th anniversary of the Declaration of Independence. At the Centennial Exposition of 1876 in Philadelphia, exhibits of period rooms and early paintings were shown in order to recreate an image of everyday life in the new republic. Collectors' interest grew when they perceived the beauty of the functional objects of their forefathers. The vogue for American antiques became widespread by the early 1880's, as the comfortably ornate citizens of the Victorian era began to discover the charm of such items as native pewter, quaint old furniture, and even rude and primitively fashioned hardware.

Between the Centennial and the turn of the century, Charles Henry Hart, director of the Pennsylvania Academy of Fine Arts in Philadelphia, emerged as the leading authority on early American portraiture, and Irving W. Lyon, author of *Colonial Furniture of New England* (1891), was the leading expert on furniture.

Major Private Collections. Little interest was shown by museums in American fine and decorative arts until the Hudson-Fulton Celebration of 1909 in New York City. Private collections of American-made furniture on display at the Metropolitan Museum of Art as part of the Hudson-Fulton festivities aroused public interest in American-made art objects. A direct result of the 1909 exhibit was the planning and building of the American Wing in the Metropolitan Museum of Art in 1924.

Other private collections and privately financed restorations soon were large enough to be opened to the public. These included the 18th and 19th century paintings in the M. and M. Karolik Collection (Museum of Fine Arts in Boston); the early American objets d'art in the Mabel Brady Garvan Collection (Yale University Art Gallery in New Haven, Conn.); Henry Francis du Pont's assemblage of early American decorative arts and exhibits of period rooms (Winterthur Museum in Winterthur, Del.); Henry Ford's exhibits of Americana and restorations of historic English and American buildings (Henry Ford Museum and Greenfield Village in Dearborn, Mich.); and John D. Rockefeller, Jr.'s restoration of Williamsburg, Va.

The Boom Market. In the decade 1955–1965 the number of antiques dealers in the United States doubled, reaching a total of about 20,000. By the mid-1960's the sales of antiques had climbed to a gross value of about $650 million a year. The current boom in the market for fine and decorative American antiques can be attributed to several causes. Rising educational and cultural levels have spurred collecting by museums and individuals. And mounting personal income has prompted many to acquire and satisfy a taste for the finer things.

Between 1959 and 1966 the average prices for paintings by the so-called masters rose 50 to 100 percent. Many smaller items—such as etchings, engravings, silverware, furniture, and fine porcelain—more than doubled in price. At the same time, many of these items remain within the reach of thousands of aspiring collectors of modest means. But the supply of objets d'art is limited, and it may be said that the recent changes in their value reflect no more than the extreme scarcity of adequate examples of the types of antiques most in demand.

Collectors' Specialties. Furniture collecting ranges from the rare, often crude items of colonial days to the heavily upholstered pieces of the Victorian period. What the settlers and cabinetmakers built not only differed distinctly in workmanship from furniture imported from abroad but also possessed regional characteristics and deco-

Furnishings and crafts of the 18th century are shown in the kitchen of the Van Cortlandt Manor House. This restoration at Croton-on-Hudson, N.Y., is typical of the many house museums open to the public.

Chinese Chippendale woodwork and lovely antiques are on exhibit in the dining room of Gunston Hall, George Mason's restored Georgian Colonial home in Lorton, Va.

rative details that are clearly recognizable today, such as shell carvings (the work of craftsmen from Newport, R.I.), gadroons (New York), and cartouches (Philadelphia). Antique furniture pieces valued by collectors include secretaries, chests, chests of drawers, candlestands, highboys, linen presses, sideboards, beds, card tables, tea tables, arm and side chairs, and mirror frames.

Because of its fragility, few pieces of American-made glass dating before 1800 have survived. However, glass was made in many regions after 1830, and examples are relatively plentiful.

Of special value to collectors are the rare works from the glasshouses of Henry William Stiegel (1729–1785) and Richard Wistar (1727–1781), producers of bottles, flasks, flip glasses, vases, and other small South Jersey glass items. Also prized are the Lacy Sandwich glass pieces of Deming Jarves (1790–1869)—such as salt cellars, relish dishes, compotes, candlesticks, and drawer knobs—made before 1830 at Sandwich, Mass. Many patterns of pressed glass fashioned as late as 1880 are sought by collectors.

China was not made extensively in the United States until well into the 19th century, except for a few pottery products, such as earthenware jugs, crocks, and jars. The fine old china and porcelain tea sets and dinner services treasured today are American only by virtue of having been in the country for generations. These pieces were probably imported from Europe or the Orient. English ceramics ranged from the long-proved redwares, stonewares, creamwares, and lustrous brown Rockingham to the refinements of porcelain and bone china. Chinese export porcelain for the American market consisted of pieces handpainted in several colors and decorated with eagles, monograms, ciphers, ships, Biblical scenes, and floral designs.

Silversmiths in America have plied their craft since the early days of colonization. Although examples of antique articles made in the 17th and 18th centuries are relatively scarce now, silver pieces made during the first half of the 19th century are not difficult to come upon.

Silversmiths catered to the demands and tastes of their patrons; thus, many different items were made, ranging from simple teaspoons, salt cellars, and candlesticks to elaborate tea services, goblets, trays, tankards, and coffee urns. Most pieces of silverware have a touchmark (name or initials of the maker), and it is quite easy to determine the age of the item and its maker.

Pewtermaking flourished between 1750 and 1850. Spoons, saltcellars, candlesticks, plates, mugs, and coffeepots are common collectors' items. Metalcraftsmen also fashioned household objects from other metals and alloys, such as copper, brass, iron, tin, and bell metal. Aside from tools and cabinet hardware, the most plentiful old metal articles in existence are fireplace equipment and devices for lighting.

Colored lithographs published in the second half of the 19th century are popular collectors' items. The subjects of these old prints depict American life of that time: prints of horse racing, ice skating, clipper ships, political characters, Indian and country scenes, and advertisements, to mention a few. The imprint of Currier & Ives, the most outstanding of the various firms that worked in this branch of the graphic arts, is on many of these pictorial delineations. Even though many prints date from the 1860's and 1870's, they now rank as antiques and represent one aspect of collecting Americana.

American women have practiced the techniques of art needlework since colonial times. "Homespun" and "handwoven" are terms that describe the majority of the fabrics used in colonial America. Brocades and velvets, satins and damasks were imported. Collectibles of embroidery, quilting, patchwork, and appliqué work are mainly from the 19th century, others having disappeared through usage. Also of particular interest are embroidered samplers, such as the row-type door panel made by the Pennsylvania Germans and the frame-style proverb or alphabet decoration, colorful crazy quilts and elaborate patchwork coverlets, and hooked rugs.

Collectibles vary from such objects as clocks, buttons, dolls, toys and mechanical banks, and Indian relics to heirlooms, such as firearms and powder horns, carved whalebone, carved molds for butter making, cigar-store Indians, paper hatboxes, and brass tobacco boxes. Whether the objects are collected for sentimental, artistic, or monetary reasons, the main criterion of their value is that they delight their owner.

See also ART COLLECTING; DECORATIVE ART; FURNITURE, AMERICAN; GLASS; PEWTER; PORCELAIN; POTTERY; SILVERWARE.

WENDELL D. GARRETT, *"Antiques" Magazine*

Bibliography

Constable, W.G., *Art Collecting in the United States of America* (New York 1964).

Horn, Jeanne, *Hidden Treasure: How and Where to Find It* (New York 1962).

Lewis, Wilmarth, *Collector's Progress* (New York 1951).

McClinton, Katharine M., *The Complete Book of Small Antiques Collecting* (New York 1965).

Ormsbee, Thomas H., *Collecting Antiques in America*, 3d ed. (New York 1962).

Reitlinger, Gerald, *The Economics of Taste* (New York 1964).

Reitlinger, Gerald, *The Economics of Taste: The Rise and Fall of the Objets d'Art Market Since 1750* (New York 1965).

Saarinen, Aline B., *The Proud Possessors* (New York 1958).

Singleton, Esther, *The Collecting of Antiques* (New York 1937).

Taylor, Francis H., *The Taste of Angels: A History of Art Collecting from Rameses to Napoleon* (Boston 1948).

Winchester, Alice, *How to Know American Antiques* (New York 1951).

Wilson, Philip, ed., *The International Antiques Yearbook* (New York, revised annually).

ANTIRENT MOVEMENT, ant-i-rent', a political protest against the semimanorial system of land tenures in New York State. It began in Albany County in 1839 and spread throughout the central part of the state.

In the 17th century the Dutch and the English had granted large tracts of public land to the Van Rensselaer, Livingston, and other families. The land had then been leased to tenant farmers, who paid annual rents and taxes, owed feudal obligations, and had no rights to mines or millsites. This system continued well into the 19th century, but, by the 1830's, Hudson Valley farmers believed that the leaseholds were a direct violation of the Declaration of Independence. It was time, they felt, to abolish slavery, promote temperance, and end an economic system that relegated them to the status of semiserfs.

The event that catalyzed the antirent agitation was the death of Stephen Van Rensselaer, the landlord of a large estate in Albany and Rensselaer counties. His will instructed his two heirs to collect $400,000 in back rent in order to balance outstanding debts, but their attempts to obey the injunction met with resistance and promoted similar demonstrations on neighboring estates. The antirenters, dressed as Indians, resisted state militia units and tarred and feathered hostile sheriffs. A high pitch of violence was reached on Aug. 7, 1845, when Deputy Sheriff Osman Steele was killed in Delaware County. Governor Silas Wright declared a state of insurrection. More than 50 men were tried and convicted, and two received life sentences.

The campaign of violence had failed, but the antirent movement was not ended. Both the Whigs and the Democrats recognized the value of farmer support. In June 1846, the state constitutional convention, meeting in Albany, abolished manorial obligations and limited leases to 12 years. In the subsequent gubernatorial election, Whig candidate John Young, with antirent endorsements, defeated incumbent Wright. Young redeemed his campaign promises, pardoning the participants in the Steele murder and directing his attorney general to institute proceedings against defective titles. The great estates were being gradually divided, and the ballot box, not tar and feathers, led to the antirent victory.

James Fenimore Cooper described incidents in the antirent movement from a conservative position in *The Littlepage Manuscripts*, a trilogy consisting of the novels *Satanstoe* (1845), *The Chainbearer* (1845), and *The Redskins* (1846).

DAVID L. STERLING, *Ohio State University*

Further Reading: Christman, Henry, *Tin Horns and Calico* (New York 1945); Ellis, David, *Landlords and Farmers in the Hudson-Mohawk Valley* (Ithaca, N.Y., 1946).

ANTI-SALOON LEAGUE OF AMERICA, ant-i-sə-lōōn' lēg, a U.S. organization that sought the prohibition of the liquor traffic. Founded in 1895 at Washington, D.C., two years after the establishment of the influential Ohio Anti-Saloon League, it worked in partnership with the Prohibition Party (q.v.). Prior to the passage of the 18th (or Prohibition) Amendment, the politically effective Anti-Saloon League of America worked to obtain local option, county option, state prohibition, and finally national prohibition. James Cannon, Jr., a Methodist bishop, vigorously directed the league for 40 years. Since 1950 it has been part of the National Temperance League. See also PROHIBITION.

ANTI-SEMITISM. See JEWISH HISTORY AND SOCIETY—15. *Anti-Semitism.*

ANTISEPTICS, ant-ə-sep'tiks, are substances used for the destruction of disease-causing and other organisms on the surface of the human body or in body cavities accessible from the outside. Antiseptics are in contrast to such agents as the sulfonamides and antibiotics, which exert their bacteria-killing action within the human and animal organism.

Most antiseptics are highly toxic for human beings when ingested and may cause serious and even fatal poisonings if taken internally. Moreover, in many instances the use of strong solutions of antiseptics on the skin may lead to irritation, which may be followed by inflammation of the skin and sometimes by ulceration and tissue death. For these reasons, antiseptics should be stored out of the reach of children and always be labeled properly and legibly.

History. The term "antiseptics" was applied originally to agents that inhibit the action of bacteria and molds involved in fermentation, putrefaction, and infections. Early antiseptic methods, which date back to prehistoric times, were the preservation of food by salting, smoking, and spicing. The ancient Egyptians used ethereal oils, gums, and spices for the preservation of mummies, and the Greeks used wine and vinegar for the dressing of wounds. Sulfur dioxide has long been used for fumigation.

Use of antiseptics in the modern sense began in 1847 when Ignaz Philipp Semmelweis employed chlorinated lime to combat childbirth infections. In 1867, Joseph Lister used phenol (carbolic acid) for the prevention of infections during surgery. With the advent of bacteriology and the great discoveries of Louis Pasteur and Robert Koch, the importance of antiseptics was fully recognized for the preservation of food and the prevention of disease.

Types of Antiseptics. Among the numerous antiseptics available, alcohols, especially ethyl alcohol, are widely used. The optimal bactericidal concentration of ethyl alcohol is 70 percent by weight, concentrations below 60 percent and above 90 percent being unreliable in their antiseptic action.

Phenol is also used quite extensively, and its effectiveness against *Salmonella typhi* (typhoid fever bacteria) serves as the basis for the evaluation of other germicides (the phenol coefficient). Phenol concentrations above 1 percent kill common bacteria, but higher concentrations are required to kill spores and viruses. Among phenol derivatives, the alkyl phenols are very effective. Creosote, a mixture of phenols from wood tar, is two to three times as effective as phenol itself. Other antiseptics of the alkyl phenol group are guaiacol and resorcinol. The latter is a third as active as phenol, but its derivative, hexyl resorcinol, is much more effective. Among other phenolic antiseptics are pyrogallol, thymol, thymol iodide, and picric acid. Of the chlorinate phenols, hexachlorophene is widely used for surgical scrubs.

Of the aldehydes, only formaldehyde is extensively used. It is used to disinfect nonliving matter. Among the acids, acetic, benzoic, and salicylic acid are relatively weak antiseptics, but undecylenic acid is valued as a fungicide in dermatomycoses, fungal skin diseases.

Chlorine and iodine are powerful antiseptics.

Chlorine is used extensively for the sterilization of drinking water, and iodine for that of the skin. Iodoform, which acts by the gradual release of iodine, has been used for the disinfection of wounds. Of the derivatives of chlorine, hypochlorite solutions, such as Dakin's solution, the Carrel-Dakin solution, and Labarraque's solution, are used in adequate concentration for sterilization in surgery. They are relatively unstable, however, and must be prepared freshly before use. Chlorinated lime is used extensively as a disinfectant for inanimate objects. Other chlorine derivates of this type are the chloramines, chloramine-T, and chloroazodin, which in proper dilutions are used for surgical dressings; and halazone, which is used for the sterilization of drinking water.

Antiseptic action is also exerted by certain oxidizing agents, such as hydrogen peroxide, sodium peroxide, calcium peroxide, zinc peroxide, sodium perborate, and potassium permanganate. Hydrogen peroxide is a relatively weak antiseptic, whereas zinc peroxide and sodium perborate are of value in oral infections. Potassium permanganate is a potent antiseptic, but its effectiveness varies with different organisms and is greatly reduced by the presence of organic matter. Moreover, potassium permanganate causes marked irritation and should be used only in proper dilutions.

Among the earliest antiseptics are the salts of mercury, but they inhibit the growth of bacteria instead of killing them. Because of its great toxicity, mercuric chloride should be used only for nonliving materials or in dilute solutions on the intact skin. Organic mercurials, such as merbromin (Mercurochrome), nitromersol (Metaphen), phenylmercuric nitrate (Merphenyl nitrate), acetomeroctol (Merbak), and thimerosal (Merzonin), are considered to be more active and less irritating than inorganic mercurials, but they are relatively ineffective in killing spores. On the other hand, ionizable silver salts form highly germicidal solutions, although they are irritating to mucous membranes. Colloidal silver compounds only inhibit the growth of bacteria. Zinc salts have only moderate antiseptic properties, but the most ionizable ones are quite irritating.

Chemicals used as antiseptics include benzalkonium chloride (Zephiran Chloride), benzethonium chloride (Phemerol Chloride), and cetylpyridinium chloride (Ceepryn Chloride). They are used for the disinfection of the skin, mucuous membranes, and tissues, and are relatively nonirritant in effective concentrations.

In addition, certain acridine dyes, such as acriflavine and proflavine hydrochloride, are used as antiseptics in the treatment of wounds and applications to mucuous membranes. Also there are some triphenylmethane (rosaniline) dyes (gentian violet, methyl violet, crystal violet) that are effective antiseptics against certain bacteria. These are applied to infected wounds and mucuous membranes.

See also DISINFECTION; SURGERY.

W.F. VON OETTINGEN, M.D.
Consultant, National Institutes of Health

Further Reading: Reddish, George F., ed., *Antiseptics, Disinfectants, Fungicides, and Chemical and Physical Sterilization,* 2d ed., rev. (Philadelphia 1957).

ANTISLAVERY MOVEMENT. See ABOLITIONISTS; NEGRO IN AMERICA.

ANTISPASMODICS, an-ti-spaz-mod'iks, are agents used for the control of spasms and convulsions (anticonvulsants). They exert a depressing action on the brain, the spinal cord, certain nerves that exert involuntary control, or smooth muscle structures. Convulsions arising from the brain and the spinal cord are controlled by narcotics (chloroform and ether), by sedatives (barbiturates and bromides), and, if of an epileptic type, by hydantoin derivatives. Bronchial and intestinal spasms may be relieved by atropine alkaloids and similar compounds, and those of the blood vessels may be eased by nitrous and nitric acid esters.

Although antispasmodics control spasms and convulsions, they do not necessarily affect the underlying causes, which may require additional measures. If they are not used properly, they may produce acute toxic effects; and if they are used over prolonged periods, they may cause chronic poisoning. Among possible toxic effects are serious disturbances of the circulation (nitric acid esters), psychoses (atropine alkaloids), and death (chloroform). Chronic effects (addiction) may result from the continued use of barbiturates and bromides.

W.F. VON OETTINGEN, M.D.
Consultant, National Institutes of Health

ANTISTHENES, an-tis'thə-nēz (c.455–360 B.C.), was a Greek philosopher who established his own school of philosophy, from which the semi-Socratic sect of the Cynics evolved.

Born in Athens, he was a pupil of Socrates. After Socrates' death in 399 B.C., Antisthenes developed the Socratic teaching that happiness results from virtue alone, and that virtue, arising from the knowledge of what is good, is the sole end of life. He one-sidedly insisted that the virtuous man must practice rigid self-control, maintain complete independence of all external things, and live with ascetic simplicity by despising all desires and by eschewing all erudition. The virtuous man, therefore, is the only wise man.

Antisthenes composed dialogues in which he expounded his philosophy. He also wrote fictitious orations, and commentaries on Homer's *Iliad* and *Odyssey.* Only fragments of his literary works remain.

Further Reading: Sayre, Farrand, *The Greek Cynics* (Baltimore 1948); Winckelmann, August W., *Antisthenis fragmenta* (Zurich 1842).

ANTITOXIN, an-ti-tok'sən, an antibody that is formed in the blood plasma in response to the presence of a bacterial toxin (poison). Each kind of bacterial toxin stimulates the formation of a different antitoxin, and once the antitoxin is produced, it combines with the toxin and neutralizes it.

Because of their ability to neutralize toxins, antitoxins have become an important means of treating and preventing many bacterial diseases, especially diphtheria, botulism, and tetanus. Large quantities of antitoxins are produced by injecting solutions of weakened bacteria into laboratory animals, usually horses, and later drawing off some of their blood plasma. This blood plasma, containing the antitoxin, may then be injected into a person who has the related disease or has been exposed to it.

Further Reading: Parish, Henry James, *History of Immunization* (Baltimore 1965).

ANTITRUST LAWS are laws designed to combat business monopoly and unfair commercial practices and to preserve or restore competition.

During the 20th century the very large firm has become a common type of business enterprise in the United States and other economically developed nations. Big business has become the dominant form in many industries. At the same time geographical barriers have crumbled, reducing both the isolation and the degree of self-sufficiency of the farm and frontier while permitting the markets served by indvidual firms to broaden.

In the United States one basic set of responses to the problems raised by big business and the growing role of interstate and national markets has been the passage of laws labeled, unduly narrowly, *antitrust laws*.

Need for Antitrust Legislation. Economists and other students of business long have recognized that firms with the power to control or influence the output of an industry will commonly be able to raise prices and thereby profits by restricting production below the level that would prevail with more intense competition. According to one widely accepted economic theory, restrictions on output in industries dominated by a few firms often will approximate those of pure monopoly, even without any collusion. This is because each firm knows that its rivals have the power to retaliate if it increases output or lowers price.

Big business and even monopoly power have been defended and certain aspects of the antitrust laws have been severely criticized on the grounds that giant firms are necessary to gain the full benefits of modern technology and science. About 1900, supporters of the trust movement argued that, in many branches of industry, only very large firms could produce at the lowest possible cost per unit of output. By 1950, the emphasis in argument had shifted somewhat to the role of big business in research and development. Large firms are needed, it was claimed, to maintain efficient corporate laboratories and engineering staffs. In rebuttal, it was argued that there is no persuasive evidence to suggest that the giants are generally any more efficient or progressive than medium-sized firms.

Early Legislation. Constitutions of several states of the United States contain strongly worded prohibitions against monopoly. But these provisions are directed against special grants of monopoly by government and not against monopoly achieved by private business without the benefit of exclusive privileges awarded by the state.

In the 1880's several states enacted antitrust laws designed to combat business combinations. But these laws were ineffective in the absence of unanimity among the states, since the principle of interstate comity required each state to permit corporations duly chartered by other states to do business within its borders.

Sherman Antitrust Act. In 1890, Congress, relying on its constitutional power to regulate interstate commerce, passed the Sherman Antitrust Act. Section 1 of the Sherman Act states: "Every contract, combination in the form of trust or otherwise, or conspiracy, in restraint of trade or commerce among the several States, or with foreign nations, is hereby declared to be illegal." Section 2 declares: "Every person who shall monopolize, or attempt to monopolize . . . any part of the trade or commerce among the several States, or with foreign nations, shall be deemed guilty of a misdemeanor."

The act provides both for civil remedies (such as dissolution or cease and desist orders) and for criminal penalties of up to one year's imprisonment, or fine of up to $5,000, or both. In 1955 the act was amended to increase the fine to a maximum of $50,000. A person injured by a restraint of trade or monopolization in violation of the law may sue for threefold damages.

Under the Sherman Act many individuals and firms have been punished for such offenses as price fixing or agreeing to share markets. In addition, divestiture orders have been entered against such firms as the old American Tobacco Company, Standard Oil, du Pont, Alcoa, and major motion picture companies that both produced films and owned first-run theaters. See also SHERMAN ANTITRUST ACT.

The 1914 Legislation. In the presidential campaign of 1912 both Woodrow Wilson and Theodore Roosevelt stated the need for further legislation of a preventive nature to prohibit certain actions that would, if unchecked, lead to violations of the Sherman Act and then require painful remedial action. To meet this need, the Federal Trade Commission Act and the Clayton Antitrust Act were enacted in 1914.

The Federal Trade Commission Act created the Federal Trade Commission (FTC) as a regulatory agency. The FTC was granted powers to investigate suspected violations of the law, hear evidence, and issue cease and desist orders. Section 5 of the act declares "that unfair methods of competition in commerce are hereby declared unlawful." A 1938 amendment extends the prohibition to include "unfair or deceptive acts or practices in commerce," whether or not in competition. See also FEDERAL TRADE COMMISSION.

The Clayton Act, including later amendments, contains four substantive provisions. It prohibits, under certain conditions, price discrimination, exclusive dealing contracts and tying arrangements, mergers, and interlocking corporate directorships. Exclusive dealing contracts, tying arrangements, and mergers are forbidden where their effect may be substantially to lessen competition or where they tend to create a monopoly.

Since amendment of the Clayton Act by the Robinson-Patman Act of 1936, price discrimination is illegal under the same circumstances and also where competition with any person is injured, destroyed, or prevented. No one person may sit on the boards of two or more corporations of a certain size if the elimination of competition by agreement between the companies would violate any of the antitrust laws. See also CLAYTON ANTITRUST ACT.

Enforcement Agencies. Both the Federal Trade Commission and the antitrust division of the Department of Justice enforce the Clayton Act. The FTC has sole jurisdiction over Section 5 of the Federal Trade Commission Act, and the antitrust division alone has responsibility for enforcing the Sherman Act.

Several full or partial exemptions are permitted from the provisions of the antitrust laws. Exempted organizations include agricultural marketing cooperatives, export associations, labor unions as long as they do not collude with employers, insurance firms, and professional baseball clubs. Also exempted are resale price maintenance agreements if they are legal in the state in which the resale occurs.

Some confusion still surrounds the authority of the antitrust agencies over firms in industries regulated by other government agencies (such as the Federal Communications Commission, Securities and Exchange Commission, Interstate Commerce Commission, and Federal Reserve Board). The courts have held that the antitrust laws are fully applicable to regulated industries unless there are specific exemptions by statute. In some cases, however, there is not yet full agreement on the scope of statutory exemptions.

As interpreted by the courts, intent or purpose to restrain or monopolize trade is essential to a conviction under the Sherman Act. But the courts have held that illegal intent may be inferred from a course of action or established by circumstantial evidence. Further, certain practices have been declared in and of themselves, or *per se*, illegal under the Sherman Act. These practices, which may not be justified by a claim of proper intent, include price-fixing and market-sharing agreements, collusive action in submission of bids, and collusive refusals to deal.

The basic test of illegality under the Clayton Act is effect, not intent. Thus the main problem facing a court in a Clayton Act case is determining whether or not there is a reasonable probability that the proscribed effects will occur.

Regulation in Other Countries. Until World War II, the major European governments were either indifferent toward or in favor of collective action by firms in a given industry. Such collective action often took the form of cartel agreements. The typical cartel was a loose-knit association in which members agreed to share markets, restrict output, and fix prices.

Governmental support of cartels in Europe took many forms. Cartel agreements usually were treated as legally enforceable contracts. Some nations set up special trade courts to adjudicate disputes among cartel members. Laws were passed from time to time compelling firms to join cartels or to submit to their discipline in matters of price, output, and market share. Occasionally, governmental bodies joined cartels or were instrumental in their establishment.

The European Economic Community (Common Market) is both a symbol and an effect of the change in attitudes in Europe since World War II. The 1957 Treaty of Rome, which established the EEC, contains two articles promulgating antitrust rules that became effective in March 1962.

Europeans have come to reject the so-called "monopoly capitalism" of their prewar years. Many who also oppose the idea of government ownership or guidance of major industries have come to accept "competitive capitalism," maintained by antitrust legislation, as the best available form of economic organization. Thus Britain created a Monopolies and Restrictive Practices Commission in 1948, and Parliament passed a Restrictive Trade Practices Act in 1956.

Countries that passed some type of antitrust law after 1945 include Germany, France, Austria, Norway (which alone in Europe had a trust act before the war), Denmark, Sweden, the Netherlands, and Ireland.

In Japan, the major non-Western industrial nation, a high concentration of business activity developed somewhat differently. A small number of highly diversified and family-dominated combines, called *zaibatsus*, virtually controlled industry, trade, banking, and national economic policy. In any one industry there was likely to be more than one *zaibatsu*, but each competed with the other in only the most restrained fashion. An attempt was made at deconcentration after World War II; but by the late 1950's and early 1960's old patterns of noncompetitive behavior seemed to be reasserting themselves.

On the basis of the experiences of Europe and Japan, it would appear that concentration of business activity and a decline in competition are among the most likely consequences of industrialization in a private-enterprise economy, unless these trends are deliberately combatted by some form of antitrust legislation.

See also CARTEL; COMBINATIONS AND MERGERS; MONOPOLY; TRUSTS.

WILLIAM L. BALDWIN, *Dartmouth College*
Author of "Antitrust and the Changing Corporation"

Bibliography

Berle, Adolf A., *The 20th Century Capitalist Revolution* (New York 1954).
Dirlam, Joel B., and Kahn, A.E., *Fair Competition: The Law and Economics of Antitrust Policy* (Ithaca, N.Y., 1954).
Edwards, Corwin D., *Big Business and the Policy of Competition* (Cleveland 1956).
Kintner, Earl W., *An Antitrust Primer* (New York 1964).
Lindahl, Martin L., and Carter, William A., *Corporate Concentration and Public Policy*, 3d ed. (Englewood Cliffs, N.J., 1959).
Miller, John P., ed., *Competition, Cartels, and Their Regulation* (Amsterdam, Netherlands, 1962).
Neale, A.D., *The Antitrust Laws of the United States of America* (London 1960).
Stocking, George W., *Workable Competition and Antitrust Policy* (Nashville, Tenn., 1961).
U.S. Government Printing Office, *Antitrust Laws with Amendments, 1890–1964* (Washington 1964).
Wilcox, Clair, *Public Policies Toward Business*, 3d ed. (Homewood, Ill., 1966).

ANTIUM, an'shi-əm, an ancient city in Latium, Italy, was located on the Tyrrhenian Sea about 30 miles (48.2 km) south of Rome. Latins occupied the site in the 6th century B.C., but shortly thereafter the Volsci captured it and made Antium the chief Volscian city for the next 200 years. In the 4th century B.C. the city rose with Latium against Rome but was defeated and was made a Roman maritime colony in 338.

By the time of Augustus (27 B.C.), Antium had become one of the most fashionable summer resorts of the empire, with many villas and celebrated temples. It was the birthplace of the emperors Nero and Caligula, both of whom later patronized the city. Antium gradually declined, however, when resorts near Naples became more popular after the mid-1st century A.D. The sculptures *Apollo Belvedere* and *Maid of Antium* and other art objects have been found in the city's ruins. The modern city of *Anzio* is on the site.

P.R. COLEMAN-NORTON, *Princeton University*

ANTLERS, ant'lərz, are outgrowths of the skull of most male members of the deer family, including deer, elk, and moose, and both sexes of reindeer and caribou. They grow anew annually in most species and serve as sexual ornaments and as weapons during the mating season.

Antlers begin their growth in the early summer. They grow on a base, or pedicel, of the frontal bone of the skull, beginning as a small nubbin that gradually increases in length. They are covered with a thin, hair-covered skin called velvet, containing a rich blood supply that brings nourishment for the growth of the antlers. The antlers are composed of dense connective tissue at first; this later calcifies to form a solid bony core.

The antlers reach their maximum size in late summer. At that time, a wreathlike burr grows around the base of the antler and cuts off the blood supply to the skin covering. The velvet dries and loosens, and is rubbed off by the animal. The antlers are shed between January and April following the mating season.

The first growth of antlers occurs when the animal is one to two years old. In young animals, antlers are spikelike. As the animal grows older, the antlers branch into prongs or points that increase in number with age.

The growth of antlers is regulated by hormone secretions from the pituitary gland and the reproductive glands (testes). Growth begins when the reproductive glands are inactive. When the testes begin production of the hormone androgen, calcification of the antler connective tissue is induced along with loss of the skin covering. The decrease of androgen secretion in the winter causes the shedding of the antlers.

ANTOFAGASTA, än-tō-fä-gäs'tä, is the largest and most important city in northern Chile. It is situated on the Pacific Ocean, 576 miles (926.9 km) north of Valparaiso, and is an industrial and commercial center and a major seaport. Surrounded by desert country, the city receives its limited water supply by aqueduct from the Andes more than 150 miles (241.3 km) away. It is the capital of Antofagasta province, which has rich deposits of copper, nitrate, borax, iron, silver, and gold.

Most of the copper from the famous mines at Chuquicamata, 140 miles (225.2 km) by rail to the northeast, is shipped from Antofagasta. Ni-

trates also are shipped. The city has shipyards, fish canneries, a meat-packing plant, and breweries. Manufactures include chemicals, paints, furniture, shoes, and paving tiles. There is an international airport. The University of the North and branches of the University of Chile and of the State Technical University are in Antofagasta.

The city was founded by Chileans in 1870 as a center to exploit nitrates in the Atacama Desert. The area was then under Bolivian control. Occupation of the city by Chilean troops in 1879 began the War of the Pacific (q.v.) After the war the city and province of Antofagasta were ceded to Chile by Bolivia. Population: (1960) 87,860.

ANTOINE, än-twản', **André** (1858–1943), French actor, producer, and theatrical manager, who introduced naturalism into the French theater. He was born in Limoges, France, on Jan. 31, 1858. For a time, Antoine did part-time acting while working as a clerk in Paris. In 1887, with funds saved from his modest salary, he founded the experimental Théâtre Libre, which departed from the stylized formality of conventional French theater by producing the naturalistic plays of Ibsen, Strindberg, and Brieux. Ten years later he founded the Théâtre Antoine, which became a rallying place for aspiring dramatists. From 1906 to 1913 he managed the Paris Odéon. *Mes souvenirs sur le Théâtre Libre,* his memoirs, was published in 1921. Antoine died in Le Pouliguen, Brittany, on Oct. 19, 1943.

ANTOMMARCHI, än-tōm-mär'kē, **Francesco** (1780?–1838), French physician who attended Napoleon Bonaparte during the last years of the former emperor's life. A Corsican by birth, he was a professor of anatomy in Florence when he volunteered in 1818 to become Napoleon's physician on St. Helena Island, Bonaparte's place of exile. Napoleon at first received him with reserve, but soon admitted him to his confidence and left him 100,000 francs when he died in 1821. The next year, Antommarchi exhibited in Europe what he asserted to be a death mask of Napoleon. In 1824 he published *Les derniers moments de Napoléon.* He also wrote the text for a folio series of anatomical plates published in 1823–1826. In 1836 he went to New Orleans, La., where he practiced homeopathy. He died in San Antonio, Cuba, on April 3, 1838.

ANTONELLI, än-tō-nel'lē, **Giacomo** (1806–1876), Italian cardinal who headed the first constitutional ministry of the papal states and later served as papal secretary of state. Born in Sonnino, Italy, on April 2, 1806. Antonelli attended a seminary in Rome and then studied law. After obtaining a doctrate in law, he entered the Vatican diplomatic service and attracted the favorable attention of Pope Gregory XVI.

Although not an ordained priest, Antonelli was created cardinal in 1846 by Pope Pius IX. Two years later Antonelli helped to draft a democratic constitution for the papal states and became premier of the first constitutional papal cabinet. He arranged Pius' escape from Roman revolutionaries to Gaeta, where Pius named him papal secretary of state in 1850. In that post, Antonelli tried unsuccessfully to preserve the pope's position as political ruler of territories outside the Vatican. He served as secretary of state until his death in Rome on Nov. 6, 1876.

ANTONELLO DA MESSINA (1430?–1479), än-tō-nel′ō dä mäs-sē′nä, was one of the most important Renaissance painters of southern Italy in the 15th century. His strong influence on the Venetian school is apparent in the portraits painted by his contemporary, Giovanni Bellini. Antonello was among the first Italians to master oil painting, a technique developed in Flanders early in the 15th century. In his mature work he combined a typically Italian grace of line and breadth of form with an attention to detail that is characteristic of Flemish painting. Where Antonello came into contact with Flemish painting is a mystery, because there is no evidence that he was ever in Flanders. Perhaps he saw examples of it in Naples, where he may have been apprenticed to the painter Colantonio.

Life. An account of Antonello's life, not entirely accurate, is included in Giorgio Vasari's *Lives of the Painters, Sculptors, and Architects* (1550). He was born in Messina, Sicily, in 1430 (if Vasari is correct in stating that he died at the age of 49). His father was a marble worker; a brother, Giordano, was a painter. By 1456 Antonello had a workshop in Messina and had hired an apprentice. There is evidence that he traveled sometime before 1460, and documents indicate that he was in Messina between 1460 and 1465. The voyages to which Vasari vaguely refers may have taken place between 1465 and 1473, when there is little evidence that he was in Messina. He may have traveled to Rome, where he would have seen the work of Piero della Francesca, whose paintings also show Flemish influence.

In 1473 and 1474, Antonello was again in Messina, where he did some of his most famous work, including the *Polyptych of St. Gregory* (1473; Museo Nazionale, Messina); *A Young Man* (1474; Dahlem Museum, Berlin), which is often considered to be his greatest extant painting; *Ecce Homo* (1474; Metropolitan Museum, New York); and *The Annunciation* (1474; Galeria Nazionale, Palermo). In 1475 and 1476 he was in Venice—another very fruitful period, during which he produced a *Crucifixion* (1475; Musée Royal des Beaux-Arts, Antwerp); the *Altarpiece of S. Cassiano* (1475–76; Kunsthistorisches Museum, Vienna), one of the first paintings to treat pictorial space as a continuation of the real space from which the spectator views the painting; *Portrait of a Man*, also called *Il Condottiere* (1475; Louvre, Paris); and another *Crucifixion* (1475?; National Gallery, London).

Sometime during 1476, Antonello was briefly in Milan, where he was called to serve as portrait painter to Galeazzo Maria Sforza, duke of Milan. By September of that year, however, he had returned to Messina where he worked intently until his death, which occurred between Feb. 14 and 25, 1479.

Attributed Works. Other paintings attributed with some certainty to Antonello are *Madonna and Child* (National Gallery, London); *St. Jerome in His Study* (National Gallery, London); *Virgin Annunciate* (Alte Pinakothek, Munich); *Madonna and Child* (National Gallery, Washington); *Portrait of a Man* (Metropolitan Museum, New York); a presumed *Self-Portrait* (National Gallery, London); *Portrait of a Man* (Philadelphia Museum); *Pietà* (Museo Correr, Venice); and *St. Sebastian* (Gemäldegalerie, Dresden).

Further Reading: Bottari, Stefano, *Antonello da Messina* (Greenwich, Conn., 1956); Vigni, Giorgi, ed., *All the Paintings of Antonello da Messina* (New York 1963).

ANTONESCU, än′to-ne-skōō, **Ion** (1882–1946), dictator of Rumania in 1941–1944. Born at Piteşti, Rumania, in June 1882, Antonescu was educated at military academies in France. He served with the Rumanian Army in World War I and later became a military attaché in Rome and London. In 1937 he was appointed chief of staff, but in 1938 he was suspended from the army for condemning King Carol's suppression of the pro-Fascist Iron Guard, and was subsequently arrested as one of the leaders of an abortive revolt against the king. Released from prison shortly afterwards, he was appointed minister of war. He was forced to resign the post in 1940, and was once again arrested, this time for opposing the cession of Bessarabia and northern Bucovina to the USSR. This stand won him the support of both the Iron Guard and Iuliu Maniu's Peasant party, and on Sept. 5, 1940, three days after his release from prison, he became premier.

As soon as he had taken office, Antonescu forced King Carol to abdicate in favor of Crown Prince Michael. On Jan. 27, 1941, he set up a military dictatorship. German troops were invited to reorganize the Rumanian Army, and Rumania joined Germany in declaring war on Russia on June 22, 1941. As the Russian armies advanced to the Rumanian border in 1944 and presented their peace terms, King Michael staged a coup d'état on Aug. 23, 1944, invited Antonescu to his palace, and had him arrested and imprisoned. The new premier, Gen. Constantine Sanatescu, accepted the Russian terms, and Rumania declared war on Germany two days later. Antonescu was convicted as a war criminal, and was sentenced to death by a Rumanian military tribunal on May 17, 1946. He was executed by a firing squad in Bucharest on June 1, 1946.

ANTONINUS, Marcus Aurelius. See MARCUS AURELIUS ANTONINUS.

ANTONINUS PIUS (86–161 A.D.) an-tō-nī′nəs pī′əs, was emperor of Rome from 138 to 161 A.D. His full name was *Titus Aurelius Fulvus Boionius Arrius Antoninus.* He was born at Lanuvium, in Latium, the son and grandson of consuls. Embarking on a political career, he served as quaestor and praetor, and attained the consulship in 120 A.D. After serving in a legal capacity in Etruria and Umbria, he held the office of proconsul in the province of Asia from 133 to 136 A.D. As a member of the *consilium,* the chief advisory body to the emperor, he won the respect of the emperor Hadrian by his integrity and loyalty. After the death of Lucius Aelius, Hadrian's choice for the succession, Antoninus was adopted by Hadrian as heir to the throne, and succeeded him when he died in 138 A.D.

It had been Hadrian's wish that Antoninus should adopt Lucius Verus, the son of Lucius Aelius. He did so, but also adopted Marcus Aurelius, his nephew by marriage. In 139 A.D., Marcus Aurelius was made heir to the throne. He later married Antoninus' daughter, Faustina.

The 23-year reign of Antoninus was a relatively peaceful period during which trade and communications advanced and literature was encouraged. Disorders in Numidia, Mauretania, and Egypt were settled, and a revolt in Dacia was put down. In Britain, the turf wall known as the wall of Antoninus was built across Scotland from the Firth of Forth to the Firth of Clyde. On the continent, Roman defenses were strengthened between the Rhine and the Danube. Unlike Hadrian, Antoninus does not seem to have traveled throughout the empire after his accession. He maintained good relations with the Senate, consulted his advisory *consilium* on all matters, and managed the fiscal affairs of the state soundly.

Antoninus died at Lorium in March 161 A.D. He received the title of Pius upon his accession, probably because of his unusual reverence for the gods. Marcus Aurelius, in his *Meditations,* described him as mild, even-tempered, judicious, and resolute.

TOM B. JONES, *University of Minnesota*

ANTONIONI, än-tō-nyō′nē, **Michelangelo** (1912–), Italian film director, who, along with Federico Fellini and Roberto Rossellini, became one of the most influential Italian film makers after World War II. Antonioni was born at Ferrara on Sept. 29, 1912, and educated at the Technical Institute of the University of Bologna. Before and during World War II he experimented with making documentary films. After the Allied liberation of Italy in 1944, he wrote film criticism for several Italian magazines.

After the war, Antonioni returned to documentaries, using the techniques that dominated Italian films in the postwar era—the "new realism," in which action and dialogue are subordinated to setting and atmosphere. He later applied these techniques to full-length dramatic films.

Antonioni's first film to gain international recognition was *L'avventura* (1960; *The Adventure*), an exposé of the bored, useless lives of a group of wealthy young people who seek escape in loveless eroticism. The barren rocks of the film's island setting symbolize the barren lives of the film's characters. *La notte* (1960; *The Night*) was another study of sexuality without love, and *L'eclisse* (1961; *The Eclipse*) was a pitiless investigation of the ways in which human beings become estranged. In 1964 he directed his first color film, *Il deserto rosso* (*The Red Desert*), a comment on the barrenness of machine civilization. In 1964 it won the Golden Lion, the highest prize at the Venice Film Festival.

ANTONIUS, an-tō′nē-əs, **Marcus** (143–87 B.C.), Roman statesman and orator. A member of an aristocratic family, he was praetor in 102 B.C. when he destroyed pirate strongholds in Cilicia. Subsequently he was consul (99 B.C.) and censor (97 B.C.). Politically he supported the senatorial nobility and was executed in 87 B.C. when Gaius Marius seized Rome. Antonius was noted for his sharp reasoning and was one of the interlocutors in Cicero's treatise on oratory, *De oratore.* Mark Antony, the Roman triumvir, was his grandson.

ANTONY, an′tə-nē, **Mark** (c. 82–30 B.C.), Roman triumvir and general. The latin form of his name is *Marcus Antonius.* Because of his relationship with Cleopatra, his life has been romanticized by ancient biographers, by Shakespeare, and frequently by modern historians.

Antony, wild in his youth, was descended from a distinguished senatorial family. He early served as a cavalry commander with Gabinius, the governor of Syria, but he soon found a more suitable outlet for his energies with Julius Caesar and rapidly became a talented military commander. Several times he was placed in control of Italy while Caesar was busy elsewhere.

Antony was promoted to the highest ranks. At the time of Caesar's assassination in 44 B.C., Antony was consul and found himself in control of the machinery of government. Thereafter he became involved in a quarrel with the senatorial faction led by Cicero and with Octavian, who had been adopted by Caesar, much to Antony's dismay.

The Triumvirate. The result of this struggle was a victory for the senatorial armies. After Antony's defeat at Mutina in 43 B.C., Octavian fell out with Cicero and allied with Antony who had, in the meantime, united his armies with those of Lepidus in Gaul. Late in 43 B.C. the three men marched on Rome and forced passage of a law naming them triumvirs for the purpose of reorganizing the state. In the proscription that followed, Cicero and many other leading men in Rome were executed.

Sharing the command, Antony and Octavian went to Greece in pursuit of Brutus and Cassius, Caesar's assassins, whom they defeated at the Battle of Philippi in 42 B.C. Antony remained in the East to settle troubled conditions and to prepare for an invasion of Parthia, a kingdom east of the Euphrates River. Needing Egyptian support for this campaign, he summoned Cleopatra, Egypt's queen, to Tarsus. She became his mistress, and he spent the winter of 41 B.C. with her in Egypt. He soon left her, however, and they were not to see each other again for four years.

Alienation from Octavian. Relations between Antony and Octavian had meanwhile become so strained that they decided to meet at Brundisium in Italy in 40 B.C. There Antony took the Eastern provinces and gave the Western ones to Octavian and Lepidus. Antony also agreed to marry Octavia, Octavian's sister.

Antony then returned to the East. After settling various frontier problems, he went to Syria in 37 B.C., intent on the invasion of Parthia in the following year. Again he summoned Cleopatra and made Egypt stronger by his famous "Donation" of portions of Syria, the Phoenician coast, and Cyprus to Cleopatra. Perhaps in 36 B.C. (the date is disputed) he married her, although he had not divorced Octavia, who was still his legal wife in Roman eyes.

The invasion of Parthia, which Cleopatra opposed, was unsuccessful, and Antony had to employ all his military genius to withdraw his army. In Italy, Octavian circulated false rumors, claiming that Antony was dominated by an Oriental queen whom he intended to make queen of Rome. Octavian became so aggressive that, in 33 B.C., Antony publicly divorced Octavia, and the Romans prepared for a showdown.

In 31 B.C. the forces of Antony and Cleopatra met those of Octavian in the naval Battle of Actium. During the course of the battle Cleopatra fled to Egypt, followed by Antony. There, in the following year, they both committed suicide.

Although it seems clear that Antony had some affection for Cleopatra, he did not throw away his career and his life out of blind love for his mistress. Political factors conditioned their relationship. To control the Eastern province, Antony needed the support of Egypt. To make Egypt strong again, Cleopatra needed the support of Antony. But neither of them was a match for Octavian.

ARTHER FERRILL, *University of Washington*

ANTONY, Saint. See ANTHONY, SAINT.

ANTONY AND CLEOPATRA, an'tə-nē, klē-ə-pa'-trə, is one of Shakespeare's most magnificent tragedies. Probably written and presented in 1606–1607, it was entered in the Stationers' Register on May 20, 1608, but was not published until the Folio of 1623. The Folio text, based on Shakespeare's manuscript or a transcript of it, is sound, except for mislineation and misprints, and is the sole authority for later editions.

Shakespeare's source was Plutarch's life of Mark Antony, in the English version by Sir Thomas North. Shakespeare's masterly adaptation condenses 10 years into a timeless but relatively brief period, omits the irrelevant, and creates Enobarbus as both participant in and commentator on the action. Even when it is closest to North's diction—the classic example is the barge speech (Act II, scene 2)—it transforms North's vivid prose, through imagery and sweep of rhythm, into poetry of the widest diversity of expression that is most memorable in its evocation of passion and sensuous atmosphere. Through this poetry and his skill in characterization, Shakespeare heightens and changes the protagonists into figures of tremendous dimensions—Antony, the triple pillar of the world, and Cleopatra, a woman of infinite variety.

The Story. At the beginning of the play Antony is in Egypt under the spell of Cleopatra's fascination. The lovers separate when Antony is recalled to Rome by the death of his wife, Fulvia, and the uprising of Pompey against the triumvirs. The estrangement between Antony and Octavius Caesar is healed temporarily by Antony's marriage to Caesar's sister, and the war ends in a truce, but Antony soon leaves Octavia for the enticements of Cleopatra, and Caesar, coming into full power, pursues Antony. At the Battle of Actium, Cleopatra's fleet withdraws, and Antony is finally overwhelmed. Hearing a false report of Cleopatra's death, he falls on his sword. He learns the truth, is borne to the monument where Cleopatra has taken refuge, and dies in her embrace. Cleopatra, unwilling to outlive Antony and fearing disgrace as a captive, commits suicide by the bite of an asp.

The plot of the play, however, indicates little of its quality. Against the background of coolly efficient Rome and the luxurious warmth of Alexandria, Shakespeare dramatizes the story of the lovers: a gray-haired general and an erotically experienced queen, no longer in her salad days. That neither is wise nor governed by conventional ethical standards is less important than that, despite the emotional torture to which each subjects the other, they are in love. They lose the world, but their love is glorified both by its excess and the greatness of the lovers. In a sense their defeat is their triumph.

The Characters. *Antony and Cleopatra* is somewhat different from Shakespeare's other tragedies. The protagonists are not wholly sympathetic, but alternately base and noble, mixed in their motivations—and very human, though on a grand scale. Antony is a great conqueror of heroic proportions who wins a captivating woman and gives up all for her; Cleopatra is a queen, calculating but defying calculation, whose being calls for Antony, and who forfeits throne and life itself to have and hold him. The conflict in the soul between good and evil is less apparent than the conflict between responsibility and passion. There is less inner struggle, but there is also less isolation. Though the characters depart from virtue, the spectator does not necessarily think of them in moral terms; moral ideas are included, but they are not the source of tragic residue. The personalities are so real that though the viewer may not identify with them, their individuality makes him suffer with them and understand them and himself.

For this different kind of tragedy, Shakespeare used a host of vividly different characters: Caesar, right and able but stiff and unattractive; the wanton but loyal attendants of Cleopatra, Iras and Charmian; the feeble Lepidus; Ventidius, who conquers in Antony's name but stops lest he become the general's rival; the pale and virtuous Octavia; Eros, who kills himself rather than kill Antony; the eunuch, Alexis; the bluff Scadrus; the realist Enobarbus, devoted to Antony but deserting him and dying in remorse.

Construction. For this wide expanse of action, Shakespeare uses an almost panoramic technique. The play has been criticized on the grounds of its 42 scenes and "looseness" of construction. But the Folio text is not divided into acts or scenes—this is the work of later editors—and the stage is left bare only momentarily during performance. The swift shifts of place and characters, entirely suitable for the Elizabethan theater, heighten the bustle of battle and contrast the participants and their varied actions, all thematic in the great symphony of politics and love—a symphony whose music Edith Sitwell well describes as "one of the greatest miracles of sound that has ever come into this world."

Stage History. The play's construction has resulted in a curious stage history for *Antony and Cleopatra*. It was not intended for the picture-frame stage. John Dryden's *All for Love* (1678), less powerful but more regularly built, drove it off the boards for almost 100 years. David Garrick, himself in the part of Antony, brought the play back to the stage in 1759. Not until the 19th century is there anything resembling a continuous stage history of the play. Some 19th century adaptations, like that of John P. Kemble, mingled Shakespeare's and Dryden's works. Most of the productions in the 1800's made the mistake of substituting stage spectacle for the more compelling imaginative pageantry created by Shakespeare's poetry. E.H. Sothern and Julia Marlowe chose *Antony and Cleopatra* to open the New Theatre in New York in 1908. The title roles were later played by Godfrey Tearle and Katharine Cornell in New York and by Robert Ryan and Katharine Hepburn at Stratford, Conn.; and by Sir Laurence Olivier and Vivien Leigh and by Sir Michael Redgrave and Dame Peggy Ashcroft in English productions.

ROBERT HAMILTON BALL
Queens College of the City University of New York

Bibliography

Texts of *Antony and Cleopatra* were edited by Robert H. Case (London 1930) and by J. Dover Wilson, with a stage history by Charles B. Young (Cambridge, Eng., 1950).

Bradley, Andrew C., *Oxford Lectures on Poetry* (London 1909).

Dickey, Franklin, *Not Wisely but Too Well: Shakespeare's Love Tragedies* (New York 1957).

Granville-Barker, Harley, *Prefaces to Shakespeare,* vol. 3 (Princeton 1946).

MacCallum, Mungo W., *Shakespeare's Roman Plays and Their Background,* 2d ed. (New York 1964).

Mills, Laurens J., *Tragedies of Shakespeare's Antony and Cleopatra* (Bloomington, Ind., 1964).

Sitwell, Edith, *A Notebook on William Shakespeare* (London 1948).

Stoll, Elmer E., *Poets and Playwrights* (Minneapolis, Minn., 1930).

ANTWERP'S GUILDHOUSES in the Groote Markt, dating from the 1500's, face the plaza's Brabo Fountain.

ANTRIM, an'trəm, is a county of Northern Ireland, bounded on the north and east by the Atlantic Ocean and the North Channel, on the south by County Down, and on the west by County Londonderry. The land is mostly a low plateau; its area is 1,176 square miles (3,406 sq km). The Giant's Causeway (q.v.), a notable basaltic rock formation, extends along the northern coast.

Belfast—the capital, chief port, and largest city of Northern Ireland—is the county town. Other industrial centers include Ballymena, Carrickfergus, Larne, and Lisburn. Fishing, textile milling, shipbuilding, and production of rock salt and bauxite are important industries. Farm products include potatoes, flax, and livestock. Population: (1961) 273,905, excluding Belfast.

ANTUNG, än'dŏong', a city in China, is in Liaoning province, near the mouth of the Yalu River, on the North Korean border. Most overland traffic between China and North Korea passes through the city, which is linked by a half-mile-long railroad bridge with Sinuiju, Korea, directly across the Yalu River. Small ships dock in Antung's harbor, but most oceangoing vessels anchor off the outer port at Tatungkow on Korea Bay.

The city lies in a lumber area. Its major industries, powered by the Shuifeng hydroelectric station on the Yalu, include sawmilling and match manufacturing, as well as silk milling. Population: (1958 est.) 370,000.

ANTWERP, ant'wûrp, is the largest city in Belgium and one of the principal ports of Europe. It is situated on both banks of the Scheldt River, about 55 miles (88.4 km) from the sea, in the center of a wide alluvial plain, about 25 miles (40.2 km) north of Brussels. It is the capital of Antwerp province. The name of the city in French is *Anvers* and in Dutch *Antwerpen*. The official language of the city is Dutch.

Economy. Antwerp, noted for its skilled gem cutting, is famous as the diamond center of the world. Its main commercial activity, however, is shipping. The processing of foods, oil refining, and automobile assembly are also important.

More than 30 million tons of cargo are handled each year by the port of Antwerp, through which 90 percent of Belgium's total tonnage passes. About 250 shipping lines connect the port with the rest of the world, while 170 lines are occupied with land-waterway shipping. Britain, the Netherlands, Norway, Germany, and Sweden are the principal foreign traders in the port. The port, with about 31 miles of quays along the river and docks, is exceptionally well equipped. The name Antwerp literally means "at the wharf" (*aan het werf*), although a legend ascribes the origin of the name to the severed hands (*hand*) of mariners thrown (*werpen*) into the Scheldt by the mythological giant Antigonus as the price exacted when the mariners could not pay his toll on the river. (Two severed hands make up part of Antwerp's armorial bearings.)

The two halves of Antwerp are joined by two tunnels under the Scheldt—one for pedestrians and one for vehicles. The city is well connected by rail with other major centers in Europe, and several canals connect it with the interior of Belgium. The most important, the Albert Canal, was completed in 1939 and links the port of Antwerp with Liège and the Meuse River industrial area. Its location and high retaining walls made it part of Belgium's first line of defense against the Germans in 1940. Antwerp's airport is at Deurne, an eastern suburb.

Points of Interest. The atmosphere in Antwerp is cosmopolitan, and intellectual and artistic life flourishes. The city is the home of the Royal Academy of Fine Arts and the Prince Leopold School of Tropical Medicine, as well as of schools of engineering, business, navigation, and architecture. Antwerp's towering architectural monument is the Gothic Cathedral of Notre Dame, with a spire 400 feet high. It was begun in 1352 and completed nearly 200 years later. The largest cathedral in Belgium, it contains two of the finest works of Peter Paul Rubens (1577–1640), *The Raising of the Cross* and *The Descent from the Cross*. The Church of St. James (15th–16th centuries), where Rubens is buried, and the churches of St. Paul (16th century) and St. Augustine (17th century) are decorated in baroque style.

The city has restored to their former baroque splendors the house and workshop of Rubens and the printing house of the 16th century printer Christophe Plantin, publisher of the Polyglot Bible. Other notable 16th century buildings are the Town Hall and Butchers Hall, now a museum of industrial art. In addition, many fine old guild houses line the two squares, the Groote Markt and the Groen Plaats.

Among the numerous museums in Antwerp are the Royal Museum of Fine Arts, housing more than 1,000 Flemish and Dutch masterpieces, and the Mayer van der Bergh Museum, noted for its collection of furniture and sculpture and for its paintings by the elder Brueghel. The National Museum of shipping is housed in the Steen, a part of the old castle of Antwerp, which dates from the 16th century. Antwerp's zoological gardens are well stocked and contain an aquarium.

History. Although Antwerp is mentioned in 7th century documents, it did not gain renown as an international port until the decline of Bruges and Ghent in the second half of the 1400's. Excellently connected with inland trade routes, the city rapidly developed into the greatest commercial and financial center of Europe and attracted the establishment (1460) at Antwerp of Europe's first stock exchange. As the century ended, the population neared 200,000, and more than 500 vessels were entering the port every day. Antwerp's prosperity was aided by favorable city policies concerning taxes and religion. The city's diamond industry expanded greatly when Jewish craftsmen, expelled from Portugal, settled in Antwerp.

Further growth was checked, however, during the late 1500's. Philip II of Spain, who then ruled the Low Countries, initiated a repressive policy against the Protestants. Antwerp, a citadel of resistance, was sacked by Spanish troops (the so-called "Spanish Fury") in 1576 and finally surrendered in 1585. The Dutch provinces to the north had meanwhile declared their independence (1581). By recognizing Dutch independence, the Peace of Westphalia (1648) sealed Antwerp's decline for centuries. The Dutch had full control of the estuary of the Scheldt, and at the behest of merchants in Amsterdam the river was closed to navigation. Antwerp was to languish in economic isolation until the 1800's.

Following the Belgian revolution in 1830 and a cash payment to the Dutch in 1863, the Scheldt was again opened to international trade. Antwerp steadily developed to become the world's third- or fourth-greatest port. In 1914 it fell to the Germans after a short but intensive siege. In World War II it suffered heavily after liberation by the Allies in 1944, when it became a constant target for German rocket attacks. The city soon regained and even surpassed its prewar prosperity. Population: (1961) 253,295.

JAN-ALBERT GORIS, *Belgian Government Information Center, New York*

ANUBIS, ə'nyo͞o-bəs, was an ancient Egyptian god of the dead. Originally represented as a jackal, he was later depicted with a human body and a jackal's head. He was the god of embalming and the guardian of tombs. The Egyptians believed that during the ceremony before Anubis' father, Osiris, by which a dead man was admitted to the underworld, Anubis weighed the heart of the dead against the feather of truth. Therefore he was a judge of the dead as well as their protector.

ANURADHAPURA, ə-no͞o-rä′da-po͞o′rə, a city in Ceylon, is the capital of North Central province. It is situated on the Aruvi River, 106 miles (170.6 km) northeast of Colombo. Founded in 437 B.C., it was the capital of the ancient Sinhalese kings of Ceylon for four centuries.

Anuradhapura is one of the leading Buddhist centers of the world. Ruins of a rock-hewn temple, a palace, large stupas, and other relics remain. An ancient pipal tree is believed to have grown from a slip of the Bo Tree at Buddh Gaya (in India), under which Gautama Buddha attained enlightenment. Population (1963): 29,397.

ANUS, ā′nəs, the terminal opening of the intestinal tract through which body wastes are expelled. The overlying skin is richer in pigment and presents a much darker appearance than the skin of adjacent areas. In repose the anus is slitlike and puckered, because of the action of an underlying corrugator or puckering muscle.

The anal area is subject to injury from abrasions, pressure, and forcible stretching. It is of importance surgically in congenital malformations, perianal blood clots, abscess formation, and tumors. Medically one encounters the same skin problems in the anus as elsewhere, such as itching, allergies, eczema, and complications involving hair follicles, sweat, and oil glands.

The *anal canal,* varying in length from 1 to 1½ inches, is interposed between the anus and rectum. The lining is composed of a membrane whose texture is between that of external skin and that of the soft mucous coat of the bowel. The anal canal is surrounded by superficial and deep external and internal sphincter muscles, which are the control muscles of the outlet. These muscles, working together with the elevator muscle of the pelvis, control the action of emptying the rectum. The nerve supply and its pattern of arrangement are responsible for great sensitivity in this area, and when it is irritated, muscle spasm ensues, causing considerable pain. Common causes of anal canal pain are acute fissures, ulcers, and tumors. Interference with the nerve or muscle supply of the anal canal frequently causes loss of control and leakage of intestinal contents. The reverse condition, stricturing, occurs when excess scarring follows injury or extensive surgery.

JOHN U. SCHWARZMAN, M.D.

ANVILLE, äN-vēl′, **Jean Baptiste Bourguignon d'** (1697–1782), French geographer. He was born at Paris on July 11, 1697. Appointed royal geographer in 1718, he published his earliest maps the following year. In all he issued 200 maps of continents and countries. By continually correcting and revising them in the light of new discoveries he established high standards of accuracy that revolutionized map making. His maps of China, first published in 1735, remained standard until the 19th century. D'Anville was one of those who disagreed with Sir Isaac Newton as to the shape of the earth, maintaining that it was egg-shaped, with greater polar than equatorial diameter.

From 1737 d'Anville published collections of maps under the title *Atlas général.* The French government bought his entire collection in 1779. He was elected to the Académie des Inscriptions in 1754 and to the Académie des Sciences in 1773. He died at Paris on Jan. 28, 1782.

ANXIETY, ang-zī-ət-ē, is a state of emotional and physical disturbance induced in a person by a real or imagined threat. In psychiatry the term refers to disturbances caused by threats that are only apparent to the patient and cause him to behave in a way that is not relevant to the true situation. Many psychiatric schools define anxiety more narrowly, based on the theories of its cause.

Anxiety may arise in a specific situation that the person seeks to avoid. Such a state is called a *phobia*. More often, however, the person experiences a persistent feeling of dread and is said to suffer from *free-floating anxiety*. A phobia is often an exaggerated form of free-floating anxiety.

Causes. Sigmund Freud developed the theory that anxiety arises when the memory of certain childhood experiences or emotions is so intolerable that it is repressed, or forced from the person's consciousness. The memory is kept in his unconscious by defense reactions—attitudes that are developed to continue repressing the anxiety-provoking thought. According to Freud, the unconscious memory, along with the resulting defense reactions, forms a *complex*, which can only be unraveled by psychoanalysis.

In contrast to Freud's theory, the behaviorist's theory states that anxiety is a learned reaction that develops when the emotion evoked by a frightening event is generalized, or attached to surrounding circumstances. Sometimes generalization includes even remotely related circumstances. For example, a child bitten by a dog in a flower bed may thereafter be afraid of any flower bed.

Symptoms. One of the commonest emotional symptoms of anxiety is a feeling of constriction. The person may also feel far away from reality or other people, and he may become depressed, agitated, or unable to concentrate. Physiological symptoms include palpitations, pounding in the head, profuse sweating, and tightness of the chest. In addition, anxiety is almost always accompanied by increased muscle tension, which may cause headache, tiredness, overbreathing (hyperventilation), and various aches and pains.

Treatment. Anxiety may be cured spontaneously or by a change in the person's life circumstances. (It may be temporarily allayed by the excessive consumption of food, cigarettes, or alcohol.) Psychiatrists treat anxiety by physical or chemical means, such as tranquilizers or muscular relaxation, or through one of the many forms of psychotherapy.

HANNAH FRENCH, M.D.

ANZA, än'sä, **Juan Bautista de** (1735–1788), Spanish explorer in North America, who was the founder of San Francisco. He was born in Fronteras, Sonora, Mexico. Anza was captain of the presidio of Tubac in 1774 when, with a few soldiers, he opened an overland route from Sonora through what is now Arizona to the San Gabriel and Monterey missions in California. In 1776, under orders from the viceroy, he established a settlement at San Francisco to thwart possible occupation of the region by the Russians or the English. As governor of New Mexico from 1777 to 1788 he strengthened Spanish frontier defenses, notably through skillful negotiations with the Indians.

Further Reading: Bolton, Herbert E., ed., *Anza's California Expeditions*, 5 vols., reprint (New York 1965); Thomas, Alfred B., ed. and tr., *Forgotten Frontiers* (Norman, Okla., 1932).

ANZACS, an'zaks, are the troops of Australia and New Zealand. The name was coined by army clerks in World War I from the initials of *Australian-New Zealand Army Corps*. The corps, commanded by Gen. William R. Birdwood, was part of the Allied force that landed on April 25, 1915, on the Gallipoli Peninsula in Turkey, north of the Dardanelles, to begin a campaign designed to knock Turkey out of the war. The severe fighting resulted in a stalemate. After heavy losses, including many deaths from disease, the Allied troops were evacuated in January 1916. Anzac Day is observed on April 25 as a public holiday in Australia and New Zealand.

In World War II, Australian and New Zealand soldiers were again called Anzacs, and the name has persisted.

ANZENGRUBER, än'tsən-grōō-bər, **Ludwig** (1839–1889), Austrian dramatist, who was one of the early exponents of realism in the German theater. He was born in Vienna on Nov. 29, 1839. After the success of his play *Der Pfarrer von Kirchfeld* (1870), he quit his job as clerk in the Vienna police department and devoted all his time to writing.

Anzengruber's plays, written in popular speech and peasant dialect, present a realistic view of common people. For example, in *Der Meineidbauer* (1871) and *Der Doppelselbstmord* (1875), he attempted to show that true tragedy—treated by other dramatists as almost exclusively a characteristic of the aristocracy—is found in peasant life. His best-known play, *Das vierte Gebot* (1877), was the first German play produced at Otto Brahm's experimental Freie Bühne (Free Stage), established in Berlin in 1889. Anzengruber died at Vienna on Dec. 10, 1889.

ANZHERO-SUDZHENSK, ən-zhe'rə sōōd-zhensk', a city in the USSR, is in Kemerovo oblast in southern Siberia, 150 miles northeast of Novosibirsk. A coal mining center on the Trans-Siberian Railroad, Anzhero-Sudzhensk produces mainly steam coal for locomotives. The city's diversified industries manufacture mining equipment, glass, and pharmaceuticals.

Anzhero-Sudzhensk was established in 1897, at the time of the construction of the Trans-Siberian Railroad, by a merger of Anzherka and Sudzhenka, two small mining settlements. The city still consists of scattered settlements clustered around mines. Population: (1965) 119,000.

THEODORE SHABAD
Author of "Geography of the USSR"

ANZIO, än'tsyō, a commune and town in Italy, is in Roma province, 33 miles (53 km) south of Rome, on a small bay of the Tyrrhenian Sea. It stands on the site of ancient Antium (q.v.), a resort and fishing center in Roman times. Antium was the birthplace of the Roman emperors Caligula and Nero, and the ruins of a villa in which Nero once lived can be viewed in the park of Villa Sarsina.

The town fell into decay in the Middle Ages, but was revived in the 18th century. The town has regained its popularity as a seaside resort and fishing center. Fine new villas have been constructed, especially along the road leading to Nettuno.

During World War II, British and American forces landed at Anzio on Jan. 22, 1944, to divert German forces from the Cassino area, where the Allied advance on Rome had been halted. Despite fierce German attacks, the beachhead was held until May 25, when contact was made with the United States Fifth Army. Population: (1961) of the town, 12,102.

ANZUS COUNCIL. See PACIFIC COUNCIL.

AOMORI, ä-ō-mō-rē, a seaport in northern Japan, is the capital and largest city of Aomori prefecture. It is situated on Aomori Bay, at the northern end of Honshu Island.

The city of Aomori is an important transportation center. The Honshu railroads end at Aomori, but railroad ferry service continues northward from there to Hokkaido Island. Lumber, fish, rice, and textiles, the chief commercial products of the Aomori region, are shipped from the port, mainly to Hokkiado. Population: (1960): 202,211.

AORTA, ä-ôr′tə, the largest artery of the body. The primary function of the aorta is to carry oxygenated blood from the heart to the cells of the body. In shape the artery resembles a walking cane, with the tip of its curved end arising from the aortic valve in the left ventricle of the heart. The arch of the aorta, the part corresponding to the handle of the cane, is located above the heart in the upper middle portion of the chest. The long part of the aorta extends down along the left side of the spine and ends in the lower portion of the abdomen, where it divides into the two common iliac arteries. At its very beginning, the aorta gives rise to the coronary arteries, and as it curves upward and then downward, it gives rise to many other arteries, which carry blood to all parts of the body, including the brain and intestines.

Diseases. Diseases of the aorta are sometimes classified into two major groups: congenital defects, and disorders caused by diseases also affecting other parts of the body. In one kind of congenital disorder, the portion of the aorta just above the aortic valve may be weak and enlarged, impairing the function of the aorta or causing it to rupture into one of the chambers of the heart. Sometimes a baby is born with an atretic, or very small, aortic arch. This condition may lead to heart failure and death during the first few days of life. The aorta may also be abnormally small in a narrow segment just beyond the left subclavian artery. This condition causes high blood pressure in the arms and low blood pressure in the lower limbs. Generally, most congenital defects of the aorta can be corrected surgically.

Among the most serious diseases that may affect the aorta are syphilis and atherosclerosis. In syphilis, the disease-causing organisms may invade the first portion of the aorta and the aortic arch, causing them to become dilated. Sometimes the infection may damage the aorta wall to such a degree that it thins out and balloons up to form an aneurysm. The syphilis itself can often be treated with penicillin, and the abnormalities it produces in the aorta can usually be corrected through surgery.

Atherosclerosis of the aorta is a common disease of adults. It is characterized by fatty deposits in the inner lining of the aorta and its branches. This disease can cause gradual narrowing of the end portion of the aorta and lead to pain in the thigh muscle and around the hip during exercise. If atherosclerosis affects the

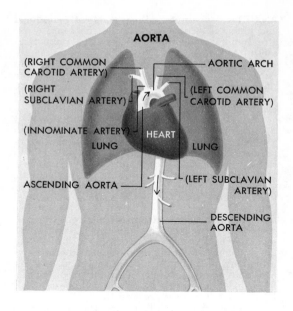

AORTA

(RIGHT COMMON CAROTID ARTERY)
AORTIC ARCH
(RIGHT SUBCLAVIAN ARTERY)
(LEFT COMMON CAROTID ARTERY)
(INNOMINATE ARTERY)
HEART
LUNG
LUNG
(LEFT SUBCLAVIAN ARTERY)
ASCENDING AORTA
DESCENDING AORTA

coronary arteries, the vessels supplying the heart tissue, a heart attack may result. If it affects the arteries of the brain, a stroke may occur. Although the obstructed portion of the artery can sometimes be removed through surgery, this is not always necessary.

J. WILLIS HURST, M.D.
Emory University School of Medicine

AOSTA, ä-ô′stä, a city in northwestern Italy, is the capital of Valle d'Aosta Autonomous Region. It is situated on the Dora Baltea River about 50 miles (80 km) northwest of the city of Turin. Aosta lies at the junction of roads through the Alps to Switzerland (by way of the Great St. Bernard Tunnel) and to France (one branch via the Mont Blanc Tunnel and one over the Little St. Bernard Pass). Aosta is an Alpine tourist center, but has important iron and steel industries. There is a hydroelectric station nearby.

The Romans founded the town about 24 B.C. and named it *Praetoria Augusta*. Notable Roman remains include the Porta Praetoria, the Arch of Augustus, a theater, an amphitheater, and the well-preserved city walls. The city has been a Roman Catholic bishopric since 1451. It was the birthplace of St. Anselm. Next to the 12th century Church of Sant'Orso are a 12th century cloister and a 15th century priory.

The *Valley d'Aosta Autonomous Region*, established by the Italian constitution of 1948, has an area of 1,260 square miles (3,263 sq km). The people are chiefly French-speaking. It is bounded by Switzerland on the north, France on the west, and the Piedmont region of Italy on the east and south. It includes the valleys of the upper Dora Baltea and tributary rivers. The Pennine Alps rise to the north, and the Graian Alps to the west and south. Among the peaks along the region's borders are Mont Blanc, the Matterhorn, Monte Rosa, and Gran Paradiso.

Cereals, grapes, and potatoes are raised in the valleys, and cattle and goats on the uplands. Iron, coal, copper, and gold are mined. Its metallurgical, chemical, and textile industries are important. Population: (1961) of the city, 28,637; of the region, 100,959.

AOUDAD

AOUDAD, ä′ōō-dad, a large wild sheep found in the isolated areas of the Atlas and Aurès mountains in northwestern Africa. It is also sometimes seen on rocky outcroppings in the desert.

The aoudad stands three feet (90 cm) high at the shoulder, and its short, tawny coat gives it protective coloration. The ram has a thick mane and long, whitish hair hanging from the throat, chest, and upper forelegs. The heavy, sharp-tipped, backward-curving horns are from 20 to 30 inches (50 to 75 cm) long. The ewes live in small groups, but the rams are mostly solitary except in the breeding season. Other names for this sheep include *arui, Barbary sheep,* and *maned sheep.* Its biological classification is *Ammotragus lervia.*

APACHE INDIANS, ə-pach′ē, the generic name for Indians of the Athabascan (or Athapaskan) linguistic stock. When first encountered by white men, they were scattered from western Arizona to central Texas and western Kansas. Tribal organization among these Indians was loose, and accurate identification of the early divisions is difficult. In the 18th century, the tribes in the eastern part of the Apache region were probably the Lipan, Jicarilla, Mescalero, and Kiowa Apache. They were strongly influenced by Plains culture. In the western part of the region, the chief tribes were the Chiricahua, Tonto, Pinal, Coyotero, Arivaipa, and White Mountain Apache.

The Jicarilla farmed and made pottery. In this respect and in others they showed a closer relation to the Navajo and evidenced Pueblo influence. All Apache except the Kiowa were fine basketmakers. The eastern group lived in tepees or brush dwellings erected on a tepee-like frame; the western group lived in brush wickiups built on a domed frame of poles bent over and tied together at the top. When first known to white men, the Kiowa Apache had annexed themselves to the Kiowa, a powerful Plains tribe.

Athabascans probably began infiltrating the Southwest in the 10th century A.D. and continued to do so until the end of the 17th century, when modern Plains tribes drove the rear guard out of Kansas and eastern Colorado. In that century the Apache developed into remorseless raiders and expert guerrilla fighters against the Spanish and the peaceful farming tribes of the region. Neither the Spanish nor the Mexicans could suppress them, and, in the first 20 years after 1846, when the United States annexed the region that became the Territory of New Mexico, its army did little better. During the 1850's the powerful Chiricahua kept peace with the Americans, but in 1861, their chief, Cochise, was treacherously seized while under a flag truce and the Chiricahua were driven to war. Shortly thereafter the outbreak of the Civil War diverted the troops, leaving Arizona and New Mexico nearly helpless for a time.

Wars between Apache and whites were characterized by extreme atrocities on both sides. Many tribes, such as the Coyotero and Lipan, were subdued by a process of attrition which, in many cases, all but exterminated them. The Mescalero surrendered in 1863 and the Jicarilla in 1868. Cochise and the main body of Chiricahua made peace in 1872. A number of Chiricahua, led by Geronimo, rejected Cochise's peace and split off, and other Apache groups from time to time broke out of their reservations to raid. Resistance of this kind ended with the surrender of Geronimo and his band in 1886, brought about by the use against them of Chiricahua scouts. The "hostiles" were imprisoned in Florida and then removed to Fort Sill, Okla., where some of their descendants still live.

Apache are now found on the Camp Verde, Fort Apache, and San Carlos reservations in Arizona, the Jicarilla and Mescalero reservations in New Mexico, and at Fort Sill and Anadarko in Oklahoma. They number approximately 10,000 in all. The San Carlos, Mescalero, and Jicarilla groups are rated among the most progressive and energetic of American Indians.

OLIVER LA FARGE, *Author of "A Pictorial History of the American Indian"*

Further Reading: Atkinson, Mary Jourdan, *Indians of the Southwest,* rev. ed. (San Antonio 1963); Lockwood, Francis C., *The Apache Indians* (New York 1963).

APALACHEE INDIANS, ap-ə-lach′ē, a tribe of North American Indians of Muskhogean linguistic stock, who occupied the territory near Apalachee Bay in northwestern Florida. They were an industrious agricultural people, and able warriors. Near the end of the 16th century, they were Christianized by the Spanish.

In 1702 the Apalachees joined the Spanish in an attempted invasion of British-held Carolina. While crossing Creek territory in Georgia, the Apalachees were ambushed and many were slaughtered by the Creeks. In a raid organized by Gov. James Moore of Georgia in 1703, a band of whites and Creeks destroyed several Apalachee villages and Spanish forts, and captured some 1,400 Apalachees. Subsequent raids further reduced their numbers. Finally, they were assimilated among the Creeks and other southeastern Indian tribes and lost their tribal identity.

APALACHICOLA RIVER, ap-ə-lach-i-kō′lə, is a stream in northwestern Florida. It is formed by the junction of the Chattahoochee and Flint rivers at Jim Woodruff Dam, on the Georgia border. The river flows south for about 110 miles (177 km) and enters the Gulf of Mexico through Apalachicola Bay. It has a dredged channel and is navigable for small boats. The bay, sheltered from the gulf by St. George and St. Vincent islands, forms an excellent landlocked harbor.

APAMEA, ap-ə-mē′ə, was an ancient city in western Syria and a favored residence of the kings of the Seleucid dynasty (312–64 B.C.). Situated in the valley of the middle Orontes River about 50 miles (80.4 km) southeast of Antioch, it was frequently called *Apamea ad Orontem* (Apamea-on-the-Orontes). The modern site is called *Afamiyah* or *Qalaat al-Madiq*.

The city was founded by the first Seleucid king, Seleucus I (reigned 312–280 B.C.), who was the successor to a large part of the divided empire of Alexander the Great. During most of the Seleucid era, Apamea was a depository of royal treasures. Antiochus the Great (reigned 223–187 B.C.), the ablest of the Seleucid kings, bred and trained his war elephants here. The city was destroyed by Khosrau II of Persia in the early 600's A.D. Rebuilt shortly afterwards, it was devastated by an earthquake in 1152 and abandoned thereafter. Excavations have revealed remains of buildings of the Seleucid period.

APARRI, ə-pär′rē, is a seaport town in the northern Philippines, in Cagayan province, on Luzon Island. It is at the mouth of the Cagayan River, on Babuyan Channel. Located in an agricultural area important for its tobacco, rice, and corn, Aparri is Luzon's chief port of export for tobacco. Other economic activities include lumbering and fishing. During World War II, the Japanese launched their invasion of the Philippines at Aparri, on Dec. 10, 1941. It was temporarily the site of a U.S. Navy air base following World War II. Population: (1960) 33,528.

APARTHEID, ə-pär′tāt, an Afrikaans word meaning "apart-ness," is the official designation for the racial policies of the government of the Republic of South Africa. The term was coined as a political slogan of the Afrikaner National party in the early 1940's, but the policies themselves have roots going back to the beginnings of white settlement in South Africa in 1652. Since 1948, when the Nationalists came to power, apartheid has become intensified and systematized. More recently the government has tended to substitute the slogan "separate development" for "apartheid."

Racial Separation. Apartheid is, firstly, a policy of racial separation. Such segregation rests on sociological and theological assumptions that races are the fundamental divisions of mankind and that each race has its own peculiar culture and destiny, which cannot be fulfilled if races intermingle in a common society. From these premises it is argued that a country like South Africa —where whites form 19 percent of the population, Africans 68 percent, Asians 3 percent, and Coloureds (people of mixed descent) 10 percent —should separate its races into distinct territories, each of which ultimately should become an autonomous, uniracial state.

In South Africa the separative aspect of apartheid is expressed in law as well as in custom. Every resident is classified officially by race. Miscegenation, in or out of wedlock, is unlawful. There are separate educational facilities for each race. Only Africans may own land in the "Bantu areas," but they may not own land in the "white areas." Local administration in white areas is in the hands of white provincial and municipal councils; in Bantu areas, in the hands of traditional chiefs. In one Bantu area, the Transkei, there is an African legislature, consisting of a majority of chiefs and a minority of elected members.

However, racial separation is not applied in a pure form. The Bantu areas constitute only 12 percent of the land. Over 63 percent of the Africans and virtually all of the Asian and Coloured inhabitants reside in white areas, where the economy depends upon their labor.

White Supremacy. Apartheid involves more than separation. The white population in South Africa occupies a position of supremacy, based on history and custom and buttressed by law. The central government has sovereign powers over the entire country, including the Transkei. Only whites may be members of Parliament and the cabinet. Members of Parliament are elected by white voters or appointed by the government —except four, who are elected by Coloured voters. African chiefs are paid by the government and may be dismissed by the government. The major organizations opposed to apartheid are banned; many individual opponents of the doctrine are imprisoned or otherwise silenced. African trade unions are not recognized in industrial bargaining. Only whites may possess firearms or be arms-carrying members of the military and police forces.

LEONARD M. THOMPSON
University of California, Los Angeles

APATITE, ap′ə-tīt, is the name of a series of calcium phosphate minerals that are common minor constituents of all classes of rocks. Apatite is the most abundant of the phosphate-bearing minerals. Fluorapatite, containing fluorine, is the most widespread variety of the mineral. Either chlorine or the hydroxyl (OH) group may be found in place of the fluorine in less common varieties. The calcium in apatite may also be replaced in part by manganese or other metals. In the massive form making up the bulk of phosphate rock and fossil bone, apatite is referred to as *collophane* (or *collophanite*).

Apatite crystals are brittle, have a glassy luster, and may be transparent or translucent. They are usually green or brown but are sometimes blue, red, or colorless. Clear, violet crystals are occasionally used as gems. Canadian apatite, which occurs in large crystals or in massive form, was formerly mined as a fertilizer. Its use has been almost entirely supplanted by the rock phosphate of Florida, South Carolina, and Tennessee.

Composition: general formula, $Ca_5(PO_4)_3$-(F,Cl,OH); hardness, 5; specific gravity, 3.15 to 3.20; crystal system, hexagonal.

APATURIA, ap-ə-chōō′rē-ə, an annual meeting of phratries—family brotherhoods or clans—in the Ionian cities of ancient Greece. In Athens the apaturia was held in the Greek month of Pyanepsion (October-November) and lasted for three days. Toward evening of the first day, each phratry discussed matters of common interest at a banquet. Sacrifices to Zeus and Athena were offered on the second day. On the last day the infants born since the preceding apaturia were presented to their respective phratries. After swearing an oath to their legitimacy, their fathers or guardians inscribed their names in the phratry registers. This assignment precluded many from holding certain offices in the state and priesthood, since these offices were reserved for members of particular phratries.

APE, any of the primates most closely related to man: the chimpanzees, gorillas, orangutans, and gibbons. The term is short for "anthropoid ape." "Ape" also refers to two species of monkeys.

Apes are rather manlike in general appearance. They are distinguished from the other higher primates, the monkeys, by their complete absence of an external tail and by their more complex brains. They have well-developed senses of hearing and vision, including color perception. Typically, apes swing from branch to branch hanging by their arms—a mode of progression called brachiation. They also show a tendency to stand erect. The arms are longer than the legs, and the big toe is opposed to the other toes. The coarse hairy coat may range from black to an almost creamy color. The apes' diet consists of fruits, nuts, buds, and, in some species, some animal food. Apes constitute the family Pongidae.

Types of Apes. Gibbons are slender, long-limbed apes confined to the tropical forests of Southeast Asia, including the islands of Java, Borneo, and Sumatra. They have very long arms and are extremely agile in leaping between trees. Gibbons are usually monogamous, living in family units consisting of a male, a female, and their offspring. The largest and most unusual gibbon is the siamang gibbon (*Hylobates syndactylus*), found in mountainous regions of the Malay Peninsula and Sumatra. It has a large red inflatable throat sac of naked skin that is filled with air when the gibbon utters its loud whooping cries. There are several other species of gibbons, including the white-handed, or lar, gibbon (*H. lar*), the dark-handed gibbon (*H. agilis*), the hoolock gibbon (*H. hoolock*), the black gibbon (*H. concolor*), the gray gibbon (*H. moloch*), and the rare dwarf gibbon (*H. klossi*).

The large, heavy-bodied, reddish orange orangutans (*Pongo pygmaeus*) are confined entirely to the dense forests of Sumatra and Borneo. They are generally slower-moving than the other apes. They are active during the day. At night they sleep on stick and vine platforms that they have built in the trees. The adult male orangutan frequently develops huge fleshy cheek pads and also large throat pouches. Hunting has reduced the world's orangutans to a few thousand.

The chimpanzee is a black-haired ape con-

R. VAN NOSTRAND, FROM NATIONAL AUDUBON SOCIETY

Gorilla, found in the forests of equatorial Africa.

fined to the forests of tropical West Africa. Like the orangutan, it constructs sleeping nests in the trees. It is probably the most intelligent of the apes. There are two species of chimpanzees: the white-faced chimpanzee (*Pan troglodytes*) and the pygmy chimpanzee (*Pan paniscus*), a black-faced, slender ape.

The gorilla (*Gorilla gorilla*) is also a black-haired ape confined to the tropical forests of Africa. It is the largest of all living primates; outstanding specimens have reached as much as 600 pounds (272 kg). They are shy and retiring creatures and live in more or less nomadic family parties consisting of a number of adult males and females and their offspring.

The two species of monkeys sometimes referred to as "apes" are the Barbary ape (*Macaca sylvana*) of North Africa and the black ape (*Cynopithecus niger*) of Celebes, an island in the Malay Archipelago. Both these species are virtually tailless, but in other respects they are typical monkeys and are not closely related to the true apes.

DESMOND MORRIS, *Zoological Society of London*

Gibbon (*left*), native to Southeast Asia, and orangutan (*right*), from Borneo and Sumatra.

A.W. AMBLER, FROM NATIONAL AUDUBON SOCIETY

JEANNE WHITE, FROM NATIONAL AUDUBON SOCIETY

APELDOORN, ä'pəl-dōrn, is a summer resort in the east Netherlands, located north of Arnhem in Gelderland province. On the outskirts is Het Loo, the royal summer palace. Apeldoorn manufactures drugs and paper. Population: (1960) 78,961.

APELLES, ə-pel'ēz, Greek painter of the second half of the 4th century B.C., who was the most famous painter of antiquity. All of his works are lost and are known only through descriptions found in the works of such writers as Pliny, Lucian, and Ovid.

It is likely that Apelles was born at Colophon, in Lydia, near the Aegean coast of Asia Minor. Some early sources cite the nearby city of Ephesus or the island of Kos in the Aegean as the place of his birth, probably because he lived in these places. In the reign of Philip II, Apelles went to Macedonia, where he became court portrait painter to Philip's son, Alexander the Great. He apparently returned to Asia after Alexander's conquest.

The many references in ancient writings indicate that Apelles' most famous work was the *Aphrodite Anadyomene,* painted for the Asklepieion at Kos. The painting was later transported to Rome by Augustus, who paid the city of Kos 100 talents for its loss. It represented Aphrodite rising from the sea, wringing the water from her hair. Apelles also painted an allegory titled *Calumny,* of which Botticelli's famous painting is a reconstruction based on a description in Lucian. Among Apelles' portraits of Alexander were paintings showing Alexander holding the thunderbolts of Zeus, Alexander in triumph, and Alexander on horseback. He also painted portraits of Menander, king of Caria, in Rhodes; Pankaspe, concubine of Alexander; and many of Alexander's officers and officials.

Apelles painted in the four traditional colors of ancient Greek painters—white, black, yellow, and red. He was, however, the first to blend these colors to achieve different effects.

APENNINES, ap'ə-nīnz, a mountain system that forms the backbone of the Italian peninsula. It extends in a wide curve from the Maritime Alps in the northwest to the toe of the Italian boot and the Strait of Messina in the southwest. The system, called *Appennino* or *Appennini* in Italian, is about 840 miles (1,352 km) long and between 25 and 85 miles (40–137 km) wide. It continues in the mountains of Sicily. Although the Apennines are a prolongation of the Alps, the difference between the two systems is striking. The Apennines lack the variety of landscape and picturesque grandeur of the Alps, and their peaks often present a rounded profile.

The Apennines constitute the watershed of the Italian peninsula. Rivers flowing from the western slopes into the Tyrrhenian Sea—except those running into the Gulf of Genoa in the north and descending from the Calabrian chain in the south—are fairly long and carry some water the year round. From the eastern slopes rise tributaries of the Po in the north and streams flowing into the Adriatic and Ionian seas.

The name "Apennines," probably derived from the Celtic word *pen,* meaning "mountain top," was originally limited to the northern section. The historian Polybius (205?–125 B.C.) and the geographer Strabo (63 B.C.–?24 A.D.) applied it to the whole chain.

Geology. The Apennine system, a contemporary of the Alps and the Himalayas, is a young geological formation. It has generally a folded structure, although much fragmentation has occurred in parts of the central section and in the south. There is a great variety of rock formations. While the mountains in the north consist mostly of weak sandstones and clays, the main peaks of the central Apennines are rugged limestone. In the south the mountains are limestone, sand, and clay until their formations change drastically in the Calabrian Apennines, the oldest part of the system, where crystalline schists, gneiss, and granite prevail. The reliefs of Latium and Campania are volcanic rock formations.

Regions. Divisions of the Apennines are arbitrary because there are no pronounced geological or geographical characteristics to distinguish one section from the other. However, the division into northern, central, and southern Apennines has been widely accepted since the 19th century. While the northern and most of the central Apennines consist of longitudinal chains separated by valleys and depressions and are cut by relatively few passes, the southern and some central Apennines are formed by mountain blocks and high plateaus interrupted by valleys, basins, and gorges with easier transverse routes.

Northern Apennines. The northern ranges extend from Cadibona Pass, separating the Apennines from the Alps, to Bocca Serriola, near the sources of the Metauro River. They are divided into the Ligurian and Tuscan-Emilian Apennines.

The Ligurian group, of moderate height, skirts the Gulf of Genoa and drops into the sea, forming a highly indented coast, the Italian Riviera, which is noted for its mild climate and resorts. Flowers, grapes, olives, and figs are grown. The Giovi Pass connects Genoa with Milan.

The Tuscan-Emilian Apennines swing eastward toward the Adriatic and are higher than the Ligurian chains; Monte Cimone reaches 7,096 feet. Wheat is grown in the northern foothills, and grapes, olives, and maize flourish on the Tyrrhenian side. Several tributaries of the Po—

THE APENNINES

THE APENNINES form the spine of the Italian peninsula. Because of seasonal floods, farms are often situated on the slopes. The scene shown here is in the Ligurian Apennines, near Genoa.

the Reno and Metauro flowing into the Adriatic, and the Serchio, Arno, and Tiber descending into the Tyrrhenian—have their headwaters here. The most important are the Abetone, Cisa, Porretta, and Futa passes. The Apuanian Alps, with their dazzling white, jagged peaks, rise steeply near the Tyrrhenian coast; their famous marble quarries near Massa and Carrara are centuries old.

Central Apennines. The central ranges, extending from Bocca Serriola to the Sangro River, are divided into the Umbrian-Marches (sometimes called Roman) Apennines and the Abruzzi Apennines.

The Umbrian-Marches Apennines are drained by the Tiber River and its tributaries, and by short streams flowing into the Adriatic. Monte Vettore (8,130 feet) is the highest peak. The ancient Via Flaminia, which crosses near the Scheggia Pass, is still an important travel route.

The Abruzzi Apennines are the highest and most rugged of the system. The loftiest peak is Monte Corno (9,560 feet), in the imposing Gran Sasso d'Italia massif; next in height is Monte Amaro (9,170 feet), in the Maiella group. Here the mountains present a more alpine character; there is a small glacier, the only one in the system, near the Gran Sasso. Long winters and heavy snowfall favor ski resorts.

To the west of the central Apennines proper are various hills known as Antiapennines. In Tuscany they include ranges of hills covered with vineyards and olive groves; the Colline Metallifere, where some iron and copper is mined; and Monte Amiata, which yields tin and mercury. There are also thermal springs, soffioni (hot jets), and other volcanic phenomena, which are exploited for producing borax and thermoelectric power. In Latium there is a volcanic area of low mountains, hills, and crater lakes.

Southern Apennines. South of the Sangro River the system swings back to the Tyrrhenian Sea and is divided into the Neapolitan, Lucanian, and Calabrian Apennines.

The highest summit of the Neapolitan Apennines is Monte Miletto (6,660 feet), in the Matese group. The Volturno and Sele rivers, which have their sources on these slopes, water the plains of Campania. Volcanic phenomena are evident around Naples in Mount Vesuvius, the Phlegraeán Fields, and Lake Averno, which occupies the crater of a volcano.

The Lucanian Apennines rise from the surrounding hill country and reach their highest point in Monte Pollino (7,450 feet). The rivers that rise on these slopes flow erratically into the Tyrrhenian and Ionian seas.

In the narrow Calabrian Peninsula the mountains have a different geologic structure. In the north the Sila, an erosion plateau rising to 6,600 feet in Botte Donato, has rounded summits and wide valleys. From there the rivers and torrents plunge into the sea through impressive gorges and cause seasonal floods and erosion.

Climate and Vegetation. The climate of the Apennines presents great contrasts and varies with latitude and altitude. Rainfall is heavier in the north and in the higher ranges of the central Apennines. The eastern slopes throughout the range are drier than the western.

Most of the Mediterranean flora thrives in the Apennines. Olives and grapes (up to a maximum altitude of 2,400 feet in the sheltered areas of the south), various types of fruit, cereals, and nuts are grown. Forests consist of chestnut, oak, beech, birch, and occasional pines.

Economy. Compared with the rest of Italy, the Apennine regions are sparsely populated. People live in small towns rather than on isolated farms. The towns are mostly built on hills to escape floods and, in the past, military attack. The gray houses and narrow streets appear grim, but tourists are attracted by their artistic interest and medieval atmosphere. The only industrial complex (steel mills and arms factories) is at Terni in the central Apennines. There are practically no minerals, although some lignite is mined in the central Apennines.

Extensive tree cutting has been practiced through the centuries. Indiscriminate deforestation, with consequent soil erosion and landslides, has reduced large areas to barren, rocky regions.

After World War II much attention was devoted to conservation and other land-improvement projects. Dams and hydroelectric power plants were built, new trees were planted, and agriculture was modernized with funds provided by the Cassa del Mezzogiorno, a state development fund. Pastures are generally too poor to support cattle, but sheep and goats are raised in great numbers.

Modern highways and railroads traversing the Apennines often follow the old Roman routes.

APHASIA, ə-fā′zhə, is the loss or impairment of the ability to convey ideas by use of words. It is a symptom-complex in which an inability (partial or total) to express thoughts or a failure to understand the spoken word occurs. Aphasia is an organic disease, since its underlying pathology is an injury of the brain cortex and the association paths of the dominant hemisphere (left or right).

Among physiologists and neurologists, there has been much difference of opinion as to localization of the brain areas affected in different types of aphasia.

Since 1945 most scientists have rejected the doctrine of exact localization and assignment of sharply limited brain areas for motor and auditory speech and other functions, and have accepted a simple division of speech into voluntary, emotional, and "common." There are two important schools of thought: one maintains that speech function is strictly localized in definite areas of the brain, injury to which causes marked speech disorder; the other minimizes the function of speech localization and emphasizes the psychological aspects of speech.

In general, speech disorders are grouped in two classes: *motor aphasia* and *sensory aphasia*. Motor aphasia is characterized by inability of the person affected to express himself in words, where no mechanical defect of the articulatory mechanism exists. The patient understands what is said to him but can reply only by gestures and motions. He may occasionally be entirely mute, but at times single words, often unintelligible, may be uttered. There are many varieties of motor aphasia, and some persons can repeat what they are told but cannot write unaided.

Sensory aphasia is caused by inability of the person affected to comprehend what he can see or hear. This is actually word deafness, which may be either word-hearing deafness or word-meaning deafness. In word deafness, the person cannot differentiate between the sounds of words and other sounds, although he has no defect in the hearing apparatus. In the word-hearing deafness, the person recognizes words for what they are, but they convey no meaning to him. Such persons can write from dictation, can copy, and even can read aloud, but they are ignorant of any meaning in what they read or write.

Other varieties of aphasia have been described, such as *amnesic aphasia*, in which there is loss of memory for specific words, with hesitant and fragmentary speech; *paraphasia*, where a torrent of words is uttered fluently but inappropriately; *acalculia*, manifested by loss of ability to do arithmetical reckoning; and *nominal aphasia*, where the ability to remember names is lost.

The cause of aphasia is not always apparent and it may be caused by a variety of conditions. The most frequent causes are cerebral thrombosis and embolism and hemorrhage from the middle cerebral artery. Hemiplegia (paralysis of one lateral half of the body) may be present. Other causes are trauma to the brain, encephalitis, meningitis, and the presence of tumors near the speech centers. The treatment depends on recognition of the cause and the ability to remove it. In some cases of cerebral hemorrhage the removal of a blood clot gives relief. In cases of brain tumor the removal of the growth may result in the disappearance of the aphasia.

HAROLD WELLINGTON JONES, M.D., *Former Editor "Blakiston's New Gould Medical Dictionary"*

APHELION, ā-fēl′yən, that point in the orbit of a body revolving around the sun at which the body is farthest from the sun. (The opposite point in the orbit is *perihelion*.) A circular orbit centered on the sun would have no aphelion or perihelion; however, most bodies orbiting the sun move in elliptical orbits. The sun is at one focus of such an ellipse; aphelion is the point of closest approach to the other focus. See also APSIDES.

APHID, ā′fəd, a member of a group of softbodied insects that suck sap from the leaves or stems of plants. Also known as *plant lice,* these insects are serious pests to cultivated plants and transmit several virus plant diseases.

Aphid Life Cycle. The life histories of aphids are exceedingly varied. Some aphids live upon a single host plant and have only two or three generations a year, but the vast majority have three or more generations. Sexual forms usually develop in the autumn and lay eggs on the twigs of shrubs or trees from which "stem mothers" hatch in the spring of the year. The stem mothers produce sufficient offspring to start flourishing colonies as a result of parthenogenetic reproduction (that is, the egg cells develop without fertilization by the male) during one to several generations on the same plant. In those species that feed upon a single host the number of generations is usually small, but there are many exceptions, and more than 15 generations may develop in a single year, depending in part upon temperature. In some cases winged forms develop and migrate to new hosts.

A great many aphids have more than one host. Aphids pass the winter as eggs on woody plants. In the spring, these eggs hatch into parthenogenetic females. After one or two generations, winged forms develop and migrate to grasses and other herbaceous plants, which are the summer host plants. One or more wingless generations develop on the summer host, and then winged forms are developed, which return to the winter host plant. The winged forms produce one or more wingless generations, which give rise to a sexual (male and female) generation. They mate, and the females lay the eggs which overwinter.

The life history of a single species of aphid may be much more complicated, as in the peach aphid, *Myzus persicae*. In the cold parts of its range it has a normal development, with only about six generations a year, but in warm climates there are twice as many generations, and sexual forms may occur only occasionally, although winged forms develop whenever a colony becomes overcrowded. However, in South Africa both winged and sexual forms are unknown, the insects crawling over the ground from one host to another. Many other kinds do not produce sexual forms in the warm part of their range.

Classification. Aphids belong to the superfamily Aphidoidea in the order Homoptera. Aphidoidea is divided into four families: Aphididae, Adelgidae, Phylloxeridae, and Eriosomatidae.

Aphididae. Aphididae is by far the largest and most important family in the group. It contains a great number of serious pests of cultivated crops, although many species attack weeds, which may be killed or prevented from producing seeds as a result of infestations by the aphids. Like other members of the superfamily, Aphididae live on the juices of plants, and their uniformly membranous wings are held rooflike over

APHIDS, shown at left in various stages of development, cover the stems of plants in great numbers and suck the sap. Aphids are identified by their pear-shaped body (above) and two posterior wax-secreting tubes.

the abdomen. Wax-secreting organs may be present or absent. The same is true of the cornicles, a pair of tubes arising toward the end of the abdomen, through which honeydew is secreted.

Honeydew, a byproduct of digestion in the aphids, is extremely rich in sugar and is highly valued as a food by many kinds of ants and other insects. Some ants are so fond of it that they not only fight off potential aphid enemies but actually carry the plant lice to underground cells where the aphids feed on the roots of plants while the ants obtain the honeydew. The ant strokes the aphid with its antennae, and a droplet of honeydew is ejected from each of the aphid's cornicles and is immediately ingested by the ant. The name "ant cows" has therefore been applied to aphids that secrete honeydew.

Adelgidae. The Adelgidae, or adelgids, are a small family that occurs chiefly in evergreen forests of Eurasia and North America. There are about 20 species in North America. The adelgids are characterized by weakly segmented abdomen. Like other aphids they have a complicated life cycle, consisting of several forms, and many of them have alternate hosts.

Phylloxeridae. Phylloxeridae, or phylloxeras, have oval, somewhat tapering bodies and may be naked or covered with a secretion of wax. Their life cycle is also complicated, and various forms are produced. The most important member of the family is the grape phylloxera, *Dactylosphaera vitifoliae*. It is a native of America where it originally fed on the roots, stems, and foliage of wild grapes, but it has been introduced into many of the cultivated grape-growing regions of the world.

In some parts of the world (especially in Europe) only wingless, parthenogenetic root-feeding forms occur. These spread to uninfested

vines by crawling over the ground. In America there are at least five forms, two of which, parthenogenetic females and sexual forms, are winged. Two of the forms make galls (swellings of the plant tissue) on the leaves or roots. In the sexual forms the females lay only a single egg on a grape vine, which overwinters and hatches into a stem mother that starts a new colony in the spring. Control in Europe, where it has been a serious pest, is attained by grafting European varieties of grapes upon the most resistant American varieties.

Eriosomatidae. Eriosomatidae are woolly gall-making aphids that include a number of pests of trees and cultivated plants. The cornicles are poorly developed or absent. All have well-developed wax-secreting organs, the wing venation is reduced, and in the sexual forms the mouth parts are atrophied (decreased in size) so that they are unable to feed. Apparently all of the forms have an alternation of hosts: some produce galls on woody plants, form pseudogalls, roll leaves, or cause other malformations, but no malformations are caused on secondary hosts, such as grasses and other plants.

The pear root aphid (*Eriosoma lanuginosum*) may exist indefinitely on the roots of pear trees in parts of California, while *Pemphigus populitransversus* forms conspicuous galls on the poplar but may live indefinitely on the roots of sugar beets and lettuce, if other plants are present to provide overwintering on their roots.

The most notorious member of the family is the apple or elm woolly aphid, *Eriosoma lanigerum.* This is an American species that has become almost cosmopolitan as a result of transportation of nursery stock. In the colder parts of its range, winged sexual forms are produced that lay eggs on the bark of the host, but in warmer regions sexual forms are unknown. The insect attacks elms and apple and related trees, where it feeds upon the roots, bark, or young branches. In Europe it is known as *American blight*. It was introduced to England on American elms in the late 1800's and has become a serious pest of apple trees, whose branches it causes to become knotty and gnarled. The larvae of several kinds of flowerflies of the genus *Pipiza* and related genera are predaceous upon this and other woolly aphids.

Aphids as Plant Pests. Among the most serious agricultural pests are the peach aphid (*Myzus persicae*), the potato aphid (*Macrosiphum euphorbiae*), and the cotton aphid (*Aphis gossypii*). These are rather general feeders and do not require specific hosts. The tulip aphid (*A. tulipae*) attacks the bulbs, roots, and stems of tulips, lilies, irises, and other bulbous plants. The water lily aphid (*Rhopalosiphum nymphaeae*) feeds on various kinds of water plants during the summer, but the primary hosts are apricot, almond, and plum; it is fairly large and dark green or maroon in color. It also occurs in greenhouses where it reproduces parthenogenetically the year round. The cabbage aphid (*Brevicoryne brassicae*) is a cosmopolitan species that feeds on crucifers and is a serious pest of cabbages and related crops. The genus *Macrosiphum* contains such well-known cosmopolitan pests as the rose aphid (*M. rosae*), which may be green or pinkish in color and infests the young shoots and flowers; the pea aphid (*M. pisi*), which attacks various legumes; the cereal aphid (*M. granarium*), which attacks grasses and cereal crops; and the notorious potato aphid.

Control of Aphids. Fortunately aphids have a great many enemies, including tiny, parasitic hymenoptera, which lay their eggs in the bodies of growing aphids. More conspicuous are the usually wedge-shaped larvae of the Syrphidae, with a great many genera, which are voracious feeders, some kinds destroying more than 1,000 aphids during their larval development. Three or four of these larvae may decimate an entire aphid colony.

The Coccinellidae, or lady beetles, are a familiar sight among aphid colonies, both the adults and larvae feeding upon the pests. Aphis lions, the larvae of members of the Neuropterous family Chrysopidae, and aphis wolves, of the closely related family Hemerobiidae, are actively crawling creatures that feed largely on aphids.

Much less conspicuous, but very efficient in reducing the number of aphids, are the small subtriangular larvae belonging to the genus *Leucopis*, the adults of which are small, grayish white, two-winged flies belonging to the family Chamaeyiidae. The larvae of butterflies belonging to several genera of the family Lycaenidae are predacious upon woolly aphids. The caterpillar of the American *Feniseca tarquinius*, "the wanderer," feeds chiefly upon the alder aphid (*Prociphilus tessellatus*), a large, woolly species, in the colony of which the larvae live and feed. Some small birds feed upon aphids, but they are not important in their control.

Aphids are chemically controlled by spraying with a contact insecticide, such as nicotine sulfate, to which a wetting agent has been added, or with a soap solution. Some of the newer insecticides are especially effective against aphids.

CHARLES H. CURRAN
The American Museum of Natural History

APHRODISIAC, af-rə-diz′ē-ak, any agent that excites erotic desire or stimulates the sexual instinct. Among the agents once thought—with little or no justification—to be aphrodisiacs were mandrake root (*Mandragora autumnalis*); damiana, obtained from the Brazilian plant *Turnera diffusa;* santonin, the active ingredient extracted from the flowering heads of several species of the plant *Artemisia;* absinthe, obtained from *Artemisia absinthium;* ginseng (*Panax*); marijuana (*Cannabis sativa*); and arsenic.

Perhaps the most dangerous drug employed as an aphrodisiac was cantharides (Spanish flies), consisting of dried beetles of the species *Cantharis vesicatoria*. This substance is extremely irritating when applied to the skin; taken internally, it acts as a powerful irritant on the genitourinary tract, causing difficulty in urinating, excruciating pain, and bloody urine. As little as 1.5 grams have proved fatal.

Yohimbine, an alkaloid obtained from an African tree (*Corynanthe yohimbi*), has been used as a male sexual stimulant, particularly in veterinary medicine to incite heat in bulls and stallions; it also has been tried on humans to overcome sexual impotence, but it is of no value when the impotence is caused by an organic disease, and it may even be harmful when the impotence is caused by an inflammatory disease of the sexual organs.

But today the notion that there are effective aphrodisiacs is not so commonly held. When treatment for any sexual disorder is required, the sexual hormones generally are used.

GEORGE GRIFFENHAGEN
American Pharmaceutical Association

APHRODITE, af-rə-dī′tē, in Greek mythology, was the goddess of love, beauty, and fruitfulness, identified by the Romans as *Venus*. According to Homer, she was the daughter of Zeus (Jupiter) and Dione, a female Titan. In Hesiod's account, she arose from the sea as a result of the mingling of foam with the blood Uranus shed when he was mutilated by his son Cronus (Saturn). Some scholars derive her name from the Greek word *aphros*, meaning foam.

Worship of this goddess is believed to have originated with a Semitic deity known as *Ishtar* by the Assyrians, *Astarte* by the Phoenicians, and *Mylitta* by the Babylonians. Her cult was introduced by Phoenician colonists into Cyprus, Cythera, and Crete, and from these islands it spread through the whole of Greece and as far west as Italy.

In her dual aspect she was known as *Aphrodite Urania*, goddess of the heavens and patroness of pure and heavenly love, and as *Aphrodite Pandemos* (of all the people), goddess of earthly and carnal love.

Most accounts designate Hephaestus (Vulcan) as her husband, although she loved a number of other gods and legendary mortals. Notable among these were Ares (Mars), by whom she was the mother of Eros and Harmonia; Adonis, whose death left her brokenhearted; and Anchises, who was the father of Aeneas.

The dove, swan, and sparrow were sacred to Aphrodite. Her favorite plants were the rose, myrtle, and apple. Representations of her in art include two famous statues: Aphrodite of Cnidus (now in Rome), and Aphrodite of Melos, better known as Venus de Milo (in the Louvre). See also VENUS.

APIA, ä-pē′ä, is the capital and chief port of Western Samoa. It stretches along an open harbor on the northern coast of the island of Upolu. The open harbor, which provides little protection against northerly gales, is lined with coral reefs, and oceangoing vessels must be loaded offshore from smaller ships. Apia extends into the foothills of the volcanic peaks that dominate the center of Upolu Island. The climate is tropical, with a rainy season from November to April.

Apia's population is almost entirely Samoan and Christian. The major religious denominations are Congregational, Roman Catholic, and Methodist.

European-style buildings of the business district line the shore. Samoan dwellings are further inland. They are usually surrounded by a plot of land where families raise their own food. Industries in Apia include lumber milling, handicrafting, and the processing of cacao, coffee, and copra. The chief exports are bananas, copra, and cocoa.

Apia has a government hospital, a teachers training school, an agricultural college, and a radio station. At the northeast end of the city, on Malinu′u Peninsula, is the Apia geophysical observatory, built by German scientists in 1902. On Mount Vaea, south of the city, is the grave of Robert Louis Stevenson, who lived near Apia for the last five years of his life. Western Samoa's only airport is about 23 miles (37 km) from Apia, at the eastern end of Upolu.

Apia was the site of a Samoan village when the first European missionaries and traders arrived in the 1830's. Its harbor made Apia a center for Pacific Islands trade, and, in 1879, Britain declared it an international settlement. Apia was governed by a six-member board representing Britain, Germany, and the United States until 1899, when Germany made Western Samoa a colony, with Apia as its capital. New Zealand occupied Western Samoa during World War I, and then governed it from Apia, first under a League of Nations mandate (1920–1946) and later as a United Nations trust territory (1946–1962). The city has been the national capital since Western Samoa became an independent country in 1962. Population: (1961) 21,699.

APIS, a′pəs, was a bull sacred to the ancient Egyptians, who regarded him as the representative of the god Osiris. The bull had to be black, with a triangle of white on the forehead, a white spot in the form of a crescent on the right side, and a sort of knot like a beetle under his tongue. When a specimen of this description was found, he was fed for four months in a building facing the east. At the new moon he was led with great solemnity to a splendid ship and conveyed to Heliopolis, where he was fed 40 days more by the priests. He was then conducted to Memphis, where he had a temple, two chambers to dwell in, and a large court for exercise. His actions were thought to have prophetic significance. His birthday was celebrated every year when the Nile began to rise.

Notwithstanding all this veneration, Apis was not allowed to live beyond 25 years. The reason for this was probably to save him from the weakness and frailty of age. His body was embalmed and entombed, and the country was searched, sometimes for years, to find a successor with the required sacred markings.

APOCALYPSE, ə-pok′ə-lips, is a term derived from the Greek word *apokalypsis,* meaning "uncovering" or "revealing." As a general term, it designates a type of Jewish and Christian literature purporting to reveal divine secrets about future events (see APOCALYPTIC LITERATURE). Specifically, it designates the last book in the New Testament, the Revelation of St. John the Divine.

The Apocalypse of John claims to be a revelation of Jesus Christ "to shew unto his servants things which must shortly come to pass." Its first three chapters take the form of letters to the seven churches in Asia Minor warning against failure to withstand evil and encouraging them to endure persecution. In the balance of the book, visions describe the terrible events surrounding the opening of the seven seals of the great scroll, the warfare between good and evil, and the final triumph of the new heaven and earth with the new Jerusalem.

The author was apparently an early Christian who had been banished to the island of Patmos off the coast of Asia Minor during the Domitian persecution in 95–96 A.D. Whether or not he was John the disciple of Jesus or another person with this common name is much debated.

Apocalyptic writing was well understood in early Christian circles. Its images, which would have been incomprehensible to Roman censors, made the Christian feel that the Roman empire, like Babylon of old, was doomed to destruction and that the victory of Christ was near at hand. Yet, because of its unusual language this book has been explained differently by almost every generation of interpreters, and it has furnished religious sects and fanatics with support for their creeds or pretensions. For example, the beast with the number 666 (or 616) has been seen in successive eras as various Roman emperors, Napoleon, Kaiser William II of Germany, and Hitler. Actually, the beast is a typical apocalyptic symbol, whose numbers most likely refer to the letters for "Nero Caesar" (or "Neron Caesar") and stand for the emperor Domitian. During the persecution of 95–96 A.D., Domitian seemed a Nero come to life again, an Antichrist.

For further details concerning the meaning of this book and the history of its interpretation, see REVELATION, BOOK OF.

APOCALYPTIC LITERATURE, ə-pok-ə-lip′tik, is a distinct type of religious literature that gets its name from the Greek word *apokalypsis* meaning "an unveiling, uncovering, revealing." Its formative period in Judaism runs from about 200 B.C. to 100 A.D., and in Christianity from about 50 to 350 A.D. This type of writing began as an outgrowth of prophetic literature. The occasion for its appearance among the Jews was the severe reaction against Hellenism's threatened domination of Jewish life and thought which produced the Maccabean revolt. The clash between Hellenism and Judaism—almost mutually exclusive nationalities and religions—required the encouragement that this literature, produced as "tracts for bad times," brought. Attempts have been made to find sources for this distinctive literature in the Persian dualism of angelology and demonology or even in Hellenistic ideas, but it seems clear that the origin of this literature is peculiarly Jewish and Palestinian. Definitely, however, the Jewish and Christian apocalyptists made use of thought forms and imagery drawn from current mythology, the nature of which may sometimes be misunderstood by the modern reader.

The most obvious characteristic of this literature is its use of visions, which are frequently elaborate. Through these visions the secrets of events that will take place in the future are "disclosed" or "revealed" to the knowing reader. In these visions symbolic representations of persons and nations appear. For example, the "horn" of an animal generally represents a king, as the "little horn" of Daniel signifies Antiochus Epiphanes. The patriarchs are portrayed as white bulls, and the righteous Israelites as sheep or lambs. Foreign nations or emperors are pictured as ravenous beasts.

Most of this literature is pseudepigraphic; that is, it is written under the assumed name of some ancient worthy such as Enoch or Daniel. Into the mouth of this inspired person of ancient times are put elaborate details of what he reveals to be the course of future events. The reason for this assumption of an earlier name as the medium of revelation is that, by the time these apocalypses were written, the canon of sacred scripture was practically closed. The time of revelation had passed. Hence the writer could reach the people with a new message for the crisis of his day only through such means.

The relationship between the Old Testament prophetic literature and the rise of this apocalyptic type of writing is of the utmost importance. The apocalyptic writers were the best successors of the great prophets. They made the same high ethical demands upon man's conduct, even though the apocalyptists were more inclined than the prophets to assume allegiance to the law and to be loyal to temple worship. Both prophets and apocalyptists believed in the direct inspiration of the divine. Both were convinced of the ultimate reign of God. The prophets preached repentance and righteousness as the condition of future bliss for a nation or an individual. The apocalyptists were faced by the awful persecution of the righteous in this world—the delay of their expected just reward. Thus apocalyptic literature grew out of the despairing sense that in this present human scene God's goodness and truth would not be vindicated. That would take place in an otherworldly scene soon to be ushered in. Then would the just and righteous nation, or, more frequently, individual, now suffering terribly, receive his promised reward. Thus an eternal or at least temporal Messianic kingdom, a definite future life, frequently a new heaven and a new earth, were the expected outcomes of God's dealings with men and history.

The end of this present age of crisis and the imminent coming of God's kingdom were thought to have been revealed, perhaps ages ago, in vision to a seer. This seer was guided, perhaps by an angel, through remote parts of the universe, even through the seven heavens. The problem for the interpreter of this literature is to determine where actual history, written as predictive vision of ages ago, leaves off, and where real prediction of events beyond the author's time begins. Usually, the point at which the author ceases to be historically precise and accurate and becomes vague, fanciful, or even historically wrong, is the point at which the work was probably written. This is the crisis point for which this "tract for bad times" was written. Evidence of this type is chiefly the basis for determining the writing of Daniel, as having taken place about 165 B.C.

OLD TESTAMENT APOCALYPTIC LITERATURE

The transition from prophetic to apocalyptic literature appeared in the prophetic books of the Old Testament. These apocalyptic passages include Isaiah 24–27, Ezekiel 38–39, Joel 2–3 (in part), and Zechariah 12–14. The Book of Daniel, produced in the Maccabean crisis, is one of the best apocalypses. (See DANIEL, BOOK OF.) In the Old Testament Apocrypha, II Esdras is a primarily Jewish apocalypse with certain Christian additions, and there are apocalyptic sections in several apocryphal books. (See APOCRYPHA.)

A brief description of the principal noncanonical Jewish apocalypses arranged in chronological order follows:

I Enoch. Ascribed to this famous ancestor of Noah, who, after 365 years of walking with God, "was not; for God took him" (Genesis 5:21–24), this work is really a series of books written during the 2d and 1st centuries B.C. The oldest section, chapters 83–90, is typically and completely apocalyptic. It consists of dream visions of history from the beginning to the end of time. Chapters 1–36 have been called the work of a "Jewish Dante," for they narrate Enoch's journeys through earth, the underworld, and the heavenly places. Chapters 37–71, written the 1st century B.C., are called the "Parables or Similitudes of Enoch." They are three pictures of, respectively, the judgment of the wicked, the fate of the unbelievers, and the blessedness of the saints. Chapters 72–82 are a description of astronomy, and chapters 91–108 are primarily a series of exhortations. For the history of religious thought this Book of Enoch is the most important of all the noncanonical writings.

Assumption of Moses. This book, written in Aramaic in Palestine during the lifetime of Jesus, is supposedly Moses' farewell instructions before his bodily assumption to heaven. It predicts the history of Israel in the world from the days of Moses until God establishes His kingdom on earth. Apparently its author was a Pharisee who was protesting against the secularization of the Pharisaic party through the adoption of popular political ideals. This work is now known only in a Latin fragment and through allusions in the New Testament books of Jude and II Peter.

II Enoch. Also called the Book of the Secrets of Enoch, or Slavonic Enoch because it is known only in Slavic versions, this work was written by an Alexandrian Jew in the first half of the 1st century A.D. As in I Enoch, this famous patriarch ascended to the heavens—here ten heavens—and left admonitions to his sons from these celestial experiences. One notable point of this book is its doctrine of the preexistence of man.

II Baruch. This work, although originally in Greek, is often called the Syriac Apocalypse of Baruch, because of the discovery in 1866 of a very fine copy in the Syriac language. Its conflicting views on various subjects indicate composite authorship. It was completed in its present form soon after the destruction of Jerusalem in 70 A.D. Purporting to be the work of Jeremiah's secretary, Baruch, at the time of Jerusalem's earlier fall in 586 B.C., the book concerns Israel's misery, the problems of man's original sin and God's justice, and the coming Messiah and Messianic kingdom. This book seems to have been influenced by some of Paul's letters.

III Baruch. This work, also called the Greek Apocalypse of Baruch, was written early in the

2d century A.D. The author was apparently acquainted with II Enoch and II Baruch. Here Jeremiah's secretary records his ascent through five heavens. Of particular interest for the development of certain Christian doctrines are the mediation of angels bringing human merits to the archangel Michael, and some interesting views concerning Adam's fall.

NEW TESTAMENT APOCALYPTIC LITERATURE

Early Christianity found the Jewish apocalyptic literature very congenial to its own spirit. In the New Testament itself, apocalyptic literature was not written under assumed names, a fact which may be due largely to the new emphasis upon personality in Christianity. Clearly apocalyptic passages are Mark 13 and II Thessalonians 2, which are concerned with the second coming of Christ. The New Testament Book of the Revelation of St. John the Divine, sometimes called the "Apocalypse of John," was the fullest expression of this type of literature in Christianity. (See APOCALYPSE.)

The noncanonical Christian apocalyptic literature, like the Jewish, took the literary form of pseudonymous writings. The following are the chief noncanonical Christian apocalypses:

Apocalypse of Peter.—Visions in which Christ shows the Apostle Peter the righteous in heaven and the different grades of sinners in various torments of hell.

Testament of Abraham.—When the archangel Michael shows Abraham the realm of the departed, the patriarch gains a pardon for the wicked through his intercessory prayer—an obvious reflection of the story in Genesis 18:22–33.

Shepherd of Hermas.—A work containing visions concerning the church, commands for Christians, and parables of the end of the age—giving an important view of the early Christian church.

Christian Sibylline Oracles.—Similar to the Jewish Sibyllines.

Apocalypse of Paul.—Description of what this great apostle saw in heaven and hell.

Apocalypse of John.—A 5th century A.D. imitation of the canonical Revelation of John describing the resurrection and punishment of the wicked and reward of the righteous, and referring to the "venerable and holy images" and "the glorious and precious crosses and sacred things of the churches."

Revelations of Bartholomew.—Bartholomew and the other apostles receive consecration from the Father, Son, and Holy Spirit, and Peter is made archbishop of the universe.

For further material on apocalyptic literature and the Book of Revelation see REVELATION, THE BOOK OF.

LESLIE E. FULLER
Revised by CHARLES F. KRAFT
Garrett Biblical Institute

Bibliography

Charles, Robert H., *The Apocrypha and Pseudepigrapha of the Old Testament in English* (Oxford 1913).
Charles, Robert H., *Religious Development Between the Old and New Testaments* (New York 1914).
Pfeiffer, Robert H., *History of New Testament Times* (New York 1949).
Rowley, Harold H., *Jewish Apocalyptic and the Dead Sea Scrolls* (New York 1957).
Rowley, Harold H., *The Relevance of Apocalyptic*, 2d rev. ed. (Naperville, Ill., 1961).
Russell, D.S., *Between the Testaments* (Philadelphia 1960).
Russell, D.S., *Method and Message of Jewish Apocalyptic* (Philadelphia 1964).
Weintraub, W., *Literature as Prophecy* (New York 1959).

APOCRYPHA, ə-pok′rə-fə, is the term usually applied in the English-speaking world to those 14 Old Testament books or parts of books that are found in the English Bible, in the Greek Bible, or in the Latin, but not in the Hebrew. The term is derived from the Greek word *apokryphos* (hidden). By an extension of usage, the word is applied to the New Testament Apocrypha, although these books are on a very different level from the apocryphal books of the Old Testament and never were included in lists of canonical (authoritative) or inspired writings.

In English Bibles the Apocrypha (the term is used both as a plural and as a singular) usually is printed between the Old and New Testaments as a supplement to the Old Testament and includes, for the most part, books written later than the latest books of the Old Testament. They are the following: I Esdras; II Esdras; Tobit; Judith; Additions to Esther (passages found in the Greek but not in the Hebrew of that book); The Wisdom of Solomon; Ecclesiasticus (or The Wisdom of Jesus, the Son of Sirach); Baruch; The Letter of Jeremiah (sometimes called chapter 6 of Baruch); The Prayer of Azariah, and the Song of the Three Young Men (or, sometimes, the Three Holy Children); Susanna; Bel and the Dragon; The Prayer of Manasseh; I Maccabees; II Maccabees. See also BIBLE: table of books of the Bible accompanying section 1. *Canon of the Old Testament.*

The term "Apocrypha" is unfortunate and rests on a misunderstanding. Its earliest use with reference to books of the Old Testament was by Jerome (died 420 A.D.), who made the Vulgate translation of the Bible. He used it to designate books in the Greek or Latin Old Testament not found in the Hebrew, thus implying that they were of less importance for general use. This view came to be identified with the one set forth in II Esdras (Latin: IV Esdras) 14:45–48.

When the forty days were ended, the Most High spoke to me [to Ezra], saying, "Make public the twenty-four books that you wrote first [the Hebrew Old Testament] and let the worthy and the unworthy read them; but keep the seventy that were written last, in order to give them to the wise among your people. For in them is the spring of understanding, the fountain of wisdom and the river of knowledge." And I did so.

The identification of the non-Hebrew books in the Greek Bible with these 70 esoteric writings was most unfortunate and really groundless; for the 14 books listed above are all, with the exception of II (IV) Esdras, books meant for general reading and not in the least secret, hidden, or esoteric in character or purpose.

Catholic, Orthodox, and Protestant Views. In both the Roman Catholic and the Eastern Orthodox churches the term "Apocrypha" is used only of heretical or noncanonical books, especially of the so-called Pseudepigrapha. Nevertheless, they distinguish between these 14 books and the rest of the Old Testament. The Roman Catholic Church refers to them as *deuterocanonical* (added later to the canon as a second collection). The Eastern Orthodox Church calls them *anagignoskomena*, or "to be read" (that is, suitable for reading at public worship and valuable for edification, but not for the establishment of doctrine). Thus both in the East and in the West they are recognized as canonical or inspired. The Council of Trent recognized most of them at Session IV (April 8, 1546), reaffirming the view that had been traditional in the West. The Greek Orthodox Church affirmed most of them to be canonical at the Second Trullan Council (692 A.D.), thus reaffirming the view that had prevailed in the East from early times.

Most Protestants have viewed the Apocrypha as uninspired, although some have accepted them as useful for historical information or for "example of life and instruction of manners," but not "to establish any doctrine" (Article 6 of the Anglican Thirty-nine Articles, 1563 A.D.). Martin Luther viewed them as uninspired yet "useful and good to read." Calvinists rejected them completely as "of no authority in the Church of God" (Westminster Confession, Article 3). Nevertheless, some groups held them, at least in part, to be edifying and valuable and therefore to be retained, and it was not until 1827 that the British and American Bible societies ceased printing the Apocrypha.

The rejection of these books by Protestants was due chiefly to the fact that they often were cited in support of prayers for the departed, of the meritorious value of good works (for example, almsgiving), and of other "Jewish" or "Romish" doctrines that the 16th century reformers repudiated. Nevertheless, by the middle of the 20th century, the Protestant world was tending to view these books somewhat more favorably, especially on account of their great value as sources for the history of Jewish religious life and thought during the period between the Old and New Testaments, which is the immediate background of the life of Jesus and the rise of the Christian church. Along with these works a whole group of noncanonical books (chiefly the Pseudepigrapha) have been studied intensively during the past century.

Order of Books. The order of the Old Testament books (including the Apocrypha, as we call them) varies considerably in the Greek, Latin, and English Bibles. As a whole, the Latin Vulgate and the standard English version (the King James or Authorized Version, followed by the Revised Version and the Revised Standard Version) are in agreement, except that the English version segregates the Apocrypha at the end of the Old Testament, while the Vulgate keeps them in their traditional locations. Thus, following II Chronicles (Latin: II Paralipomena) the Latin Bible has I Esdras (English: Ezra), II Esdras (English: Nehemiah), Tobias (English: Tobit), and Judith; after the Song of Songs (or Song of Solomon) come Wisdom (The Wisdom of Solomon) and Ecclesiasticus (Greek: Sirach); after Jeremiah (including Lamentations) comes Baruch (including, as chapter 6, the Letter of Jeremiah); following Malachi come I and II Maccabees; then following the New Testament, as an appendix of *Libri apocryphi*, come the Prayer of Manasseh, III Esdras (Greek and English: I Esdras), and IV Esdras (English: II Esdras, extant in Latin and Eastern versions, not Greek).

The Vulgate includes the remainder of the 14 English Apocrypha as parts of other books: the Additions to Esther from deuterocanonical appendices to the Book of Esther (10:4 to 16:24); the Song of the Three Youths appears in Daniel 3; the History of Susanna forms an appendix to Daniel (13:1–64), while the stories of Bel and the Dragon form a second appendix (13:65 to 14:42).

In the Eastern churches (as in the Greek and Russian Orthodox churches), the order is the same through II Chronicles (Latin: Paralipomena), although I-II Samuel and I-II Kings are called I-IV Kingdoms; then follows I Esdras (the Apocryphal book based on II Chronicles, Ezra, and Nehemiah); II Esdras (English: Ezra), Nehemiah, Tobit, Judith, Esther, I-III Maccabees (III Maccabees is not in the Vulgate or the English Bible); Psalms, Job, Proverbs, Ecclesiastes, Song of Solomon, The Wisdom of Solomon, the Wisdom of Sirach, the Twelve "Minor" (that is, shorter) Prophets (the order of the first three is Hosea, Amos, Micah); Isaiah, Jeremiah, Baruch, Lamentations, Letter of Jeremiah, Ezekiel, Daniel (with the additions: Susanna, the Prayer of Azariah, Song of the Three Youths, Bel and the Dragon); and the Additions to Esther.

The nomenclature of the various texts and versions is somewhat confusing with reference to the books of Esdras. It is as follows:

HEBREW	GREEK	LATIN	ENGLISH
Ezra	II Esdras 1–10	I Esdras	Ezra
Nehemiah	II Esdras 11–23	II Esdras (or Nehemiah)	Nehemiah
	I Esdras	III Esdras	I Esdras
		IV Esdras	II Esdras

Prior to the King James Version of 1611 the titles used, for example, in the Thirty-nine Articles, were those of the Latin Vulgate.

Content of the Apocrypha. The following paragraphs summarize the 14 apocryphal books of the Old Testament.

I Esdras (III Esdras in the Vulgate) begins with an account of the great Passover held by King Josiah, the fall of Jerusalem, and the Exile; the Return and the rebuilding of the Temple and, finally, Ezra's reform—the dismissal of foreign wives and children. The work is based on II Chronicles, Ezra, and Nehemiah but is sketchy and incomplete, although in better Greek than the Septuagint (LXX) translation of the underlying passages; it is thought to be a separate recension, independent of the LXX. Included in it is the story of the three pages at the court of Darius I (chapters 3:1 to 4:42). The book was written probably between 150 and 50 B.C.

II Esdras (IV Esdras in the Vulgate) was written in Aramaic, about 90 A.D., then translated into Greek; but both the original and the Greek translation have disappeared—all ancient versions (Latin, Syriac, Ethiopic, others) were made from the Greek. (Some scholars hold that the Syriac translation was made directly from the Aramaic original). Only the Latin contains the Christian additions, chapters 1 and 2 (about 150 A.D.) and chapters 15 and 16 (about 250 A.D.). The original Apocalypse of Ezra (chapters 3 to 14) consisted of six visions dealing with the problem of evil and especially with the sufferings of the Jews following the destruction of Jerusalem—not in 586 B.C., but quite obviously in 70 A.D. The coming of the Messiah is to bring this age of defeat and discouragement to a close.

Tobit is a short story from about 190–170 B.C. It combines a dozen or more popular motifs, such as a tale of travel to distant lands, a fishing expedition, a wonder drug, a love story, the rescue of a maiden in distress, a family quarrel, the recovery of treasure, an angel in disguise, and a demon and its banishment; and it stresses such pious themes as the burial of the dead (especially paupers and strangers), prayer, and God's care for the devout and obedient. The work gives a remarkable picture of ancient Jewish piety in the early 2d century B.C. The Greek version is a translation of the Aramaic original.

Judith is another short story, from about 150 B.C., the period of the Maccabean War. The heroine is an idealization of courageous, devout Jewish womanhood in that heroic era. The teaching emphasizes complete obedience to the will of God and loyalty to His Law, regardless of personal sacrifices and even the threat of death. The rulers of Bethulia must not lay down terms to God or agree to surrender the city if divine help fails to arrive within five days.

Additions to Esther are passages supplementing the secular tale of the Book of Esther, which was read at the Feast of Purim, and emphasizing the religious meaning of the original story. The translation was made in Alexandria about 114 (or perhaps 78) B.C. The Vulgate and the English version gather these additions into an appendix, thus producing confusion. The Revised Standard Version (1957) preserves the order of the Greek, making them intelligible.

The Wisdom of Solomon was written in Greek at Alexandria about 100–50 B.C. It sets forth the praise of wisdom—which is righteousness and also a divine hypostasis, almost a divine being—and the folly of idolatry, especially of Egyptian animal worship. Chapter 3 sets forth a sublime statement of the doctrine of the immortality of the soul. This differs radically from the conception of the resurrection (seen in the Palestinian Hebrew Book of Daniel) and probably reflects the influence of Greek philosophy (especially Platonic and Stoic) upon the Alexandrian Jewish teachers.

Ecclesiasticus or the Wisdom of Jesus the Son of Sirach is by far the longest book in the Apocrypha. Sirach was a religious teacher in Jerusalem, a scribe or expounder of the Scriptures. He wrote this collection of aphorisms, brief paragraphs, and tiny essays on religion and morals about 185 B.C. The book was in two volumes (Part II begins with chapter 24). About two thirds of the work is still extant in Hebrew. The encomiums on the scribe (chapters 38:24 to 39:11) and the physician (chapter 38:1–23) and the Praise of Famous Men (chapters 44 to 50) conclude with praise of the great high priest Simon, who lived at the beginning of the 2d century B.C. The "Prologue Made by an Uncertain Author," given in the Authorized Version, is a very late Christian synopsis and should be disregarded.

Baruch is a composite work originally in Hebrew, but extant now in Greek. It probably was written about 150–100 B.C. in order to supply information about the scribe or secretary of the prophet Jeremiah, known only from the Old Testament. The work combines a confession of Israel's sins, which led to the destruction of Jerusalem in 586 B.C.; a section in praise of wisdom; and one on the future salvation of Israel.

The Letter of Jeremiah, which follows Baruch, often is included (as chapter 6) in Baruch; it was written in Aramaic about 150 B.C. and is a scathing attack on idolatry and reflects the teaching of loyal Jews surrounded by pagans.

The Prayer of Azariah, the Song of the Three Young Men, and *The Story of Susanna* are all additions to Daniel in the Greek and Latin Bibles. The Prayer, including the Song, follows Daniel 3:23. Susanna precedes the beginning of Daniel in the Greek Bible but is chapter 13 in the Latin Vulgate. *Bel and the Dragon* is at the end of Daniel in the Greek but is chapter 14 in the Vulgate. The Prayer and the Song are wonderful examples of Jewish liturgical poetry; the Song still is used in Christian worship (as the Benedicite, in two parts in the Prayer Book). The date of these additions to Daniel is probably 2d century B.C., and they were added to the canonical book before 100 B.C. Susanna is a short story that emphasizes God's protection of those who serve Him faithfully; it also proves the necessity of separate examination of the two witnesses required by Jewish law. *Bel and the Dragon* is a story showing how the trickery of Babylonian idolaters was unmasked.

The Prayer of Manasseh is a typical Jewish penitential psalm appropriately assigned to King Manasseh (II Chronicles 33:11–13) but probably written in the 1st century B.C. The Apocryphal books are full of religious poetry and prayers, not only public and liturgical, but also private and personal. Hence the great value of these works for the historical study of pre-Christian Judaism and as classics of devotion.

I Maccabees is an account of the Maccabean War of Independence from its beginning, in the days of Antiochus IV Epiphanes (reigned 175–164 B.C.) to the reign of John Hyrcanus (135–104 B.C.) who became high priest and ruler of the Jews. The book originally was written in Hebrew, probably soon after 104 B.C., when Hyrcanus died. It probably was translated into Greek soon after its appearance in Hebrew. The narrative is objective, obviously based on records and observations.

II Maccabees is a summary of the work of Jason of Cyrene (about 100 B.C.), which was in five books, but deals with a far briefer period than I Maccabees (15 years instead of 40). I Maccabees 1 and 2 are parallel to II Maccabees 4 to 7; I Maccabees 3 to 5 are parallel to II Maccabees 8 to 10; I Maccabees 6 and 7 are parallel to II Maccabees 11 to 15. Jason's work probably was written in Greek, and so was II Maccabees. It makes far more use of supernatural intervention than I Maccabees. Like the Chronicler in the Old Testament, the author is greatly interested in God's concern for His temple in Jerusalem. The work abounds in miracles and sacred legends, such as the martyrdom of the seven brothers, and sets forth doctrines that the Protestant reformers rejected—and with them the whole Apocrypha.

III Maccabees, found in the canon of the Eastern churches, sometimes was called the Ptolemaica. It is a story from the reign of Ptolemy Philopator (reigned 222–205 B.C.), who, according to the tale, was angered by the refusal of the Jews to admit him to the Holy of Holies in the temple at Jerusalem and returned to Alexandria intent upon avenging himself upon the Jews there. But, as in other stories of this kind, divine intervention frustrated his purposes. The style is very rhetorical. The book probably dates from the 1st century B.C. or A.D.

IV Maccabees, found in some ancient manuscripts and canonical lists, is a philosophical work on the question of whether or not devout reason is master of itself. Its contents are chiefly a panegyric on the Jewish martyrs—Eleazar, the seven brothers, and their mother—obviously based on II Maccabees 6:18 to 7:42, which it amplifies with vivid realism. The style is rhetorical and the philosophy is basically Stoic. The book probably comes from the 1st century A.D.

Other Books. There were many other books written during the three centuries from 200 B.C. to 100 A.D. that belong to the religious literature of ancient Judaism. Some of these also were read in the early church and appear in manuscripts or canonical lists but did not become part of the official canon. Several of them were apocalypses (see APOCALYPTIC LITERATURE); others contained legends or fictitious lives of Old Testament characters or additions to the Old Testament Psalter. The following are some of the most important of these books:

The Book of Jubilees was a rewriting of Genesis and Exodus 1 to 12 by a Pharisee late in the 2d century B.C. who arranged the patriarchal history in a series of jubilees (periods of 49 years) and read back into ancient times the institutions and customs of 2d century Judaism. His theory was the eternal validity of the Law. There is a strongly messianic strain in the book.

The Testaments of the Twelve Patriarchs also was inspired by the Book of Genesis, chapter 49. It contains the last will and testament of each of the 12 sons of Jacob; but they are more like the later Jewish ethical wills than testamentary bequests of property. Each patriarch gives a sketch of his own life (based on Genesis) and then exhorts his descendants to practice virtue and avoid sin and vice, concluding with a prediction of the future. The ethical teaching of the work had a profound influence upon both Jews and Christians. Its date is probably late 2d century B.C. or early 1st century A.D.

The Martyrdom of Isaiah comes from the 1st century B.C. and records the tradition that Isaiah was sawn asunder by order of King Manasseh (compare Hebrews 11:37).

The Psalms of Solomon is a collection of psalms written about 50 B.C., strongly Pharisaic in tone and messianic (especially Psalm 17).

The manuscripts discovered in 1947 at Khirbet Qumrân (the so-called Dead Sea Scrolls) include works written during this period (200 B.C.– 100 A.D.) or earlier, but they cannot be included among the deuterocanonical Biblical books or Apocrypha. Neither can the so-called New Testament Apocrypha, which are works written in the 2d century A.D. or later: for example, the Gospel of the Egyptians, the Gospel of Peter, the Gospel of Thomas, which represent Gnostic or Encratite or mythological versions of the gospel story; the Acts of Andrew, James, Peter, Thomas, and Paul are similar elaborations of the story of the apostles in the New Testament Book of Acts. Only one of these writings, the Gospel according to the Hebrews, contains apparently authentic material, but it is based on the canonical Gospel according to Matthew. See also GOSPELS, APOCRYPHAL.

FREDERICK C. GRANT
Union Theological Seminary

Bibliography

English translations of the Apocrypha appear in the Bible, in the Revised Standard Version (New York 1957).

Charles, Robert H., ed., *The Apocrypha and Pseudepigrapha of the Old Testament in English*, 2 vols. (Oxford 1913).

Charles, Robert H., *Religious Development Between the Old and New Testaments* (New York 1914).

Goodspeed, Edgar J., *The Story of the Apocrypha* (Chicago 1939).

James, Montague R., *Lost Apocrypha of the Old Testament* (London 1920).

Metzger, Bruce M., *An Introduction to the Apocrypha* (New York 1957).

Oesterley, William O.E., *An Introduction to the Books of the Apocrypha* (New York 1935).

Pfeiffer, Robert H., *History of New Testament Times, with an Introduction to the Apocrypha* (New York 1949).

Schürer, Emil, *A History of the Jewish People in the Time of Jesus,* (New York 1891).

APOCYNACEAE, ə-pos-i-nā′sē-ē, is a family of mostly tropical herbs, shrubs, and trees, including many twining vines. It has opposite, simple leaves and a milky juice. The flowers have a tubular or funnel-shaped flower tube of 4 or 5 fused petals twisted in the bud, and 4 or 5 arrow-shaped stamens.

Also known as the dogbane family, Apocynaceae is related to the milkweeds. The dogbanes comprise nearly 200 genera and 1,500 species. Temperate representatives include the dogbane and Indian hemp (*Apocynum*) of North America, the latter used by the Indians for fiber; the bluestar (*Amsonia*) of North America and Japan; the common periwinkle (*Vinca minor*), a native of Europe but widely dispersed and cultivated; and the oleander (*Nerium oleander*) of the Mediterranean region, abundant also in southern United States and often grown as a house plant. Oleander is toxic if eaten, and its bark has served as rat poison.

Several tropical genera yield rubber: *Kickxia elastica*, *Landolphia*, and *Clitandra* of Africa, and *Willoughbya* and *Urceola* of Indo-Malaya. Although a few genera, including *Willoughbya edulis* and *Arduina carandas*, have edible fruits, others are highly poisonous, such as the seeds of the "ordeal-tree" of Madagascar (*Tanghinia venenifera*) and species of *Adenium* and *Strophanthus,* which furnish African arrow poisons. The seeds of several species of *Strophanthus* contain drugs used as heart stimulants. A glucoside (sugar derivative) that can be changed into cortisone has been extracted from *Strophanthus.*

EDWIN B. MATZKE, *Columbia University*

APOGEE, ap′ə-jē, that point in the orbit of a body revolving around the earth at which the body is farthest from the earth. The opposite point in the orbit of the body, the point at which it is nearest the earth, is called its perigee. Thus, the moon at apogee is 252,710 miles from the earth, but at perigee the moon is only 221,463 miles away. The moon has an elliptical orbit. A body which followed a perfectly circular path around the earth would have no apogee or perigee. The many artificial earth satellites that have been launched, however, usually have elliptical orbits. Such an orbit may carry a satellite thousands of miles above the earth at apogee and little more than one hundred miles above the earth at perigee. See also APSIDES; ELLIPSE.

APOGEE AND PERIGEE

The moon and most artificial satellites move around the earth in elliptical paths which have points of apogee and perigee.

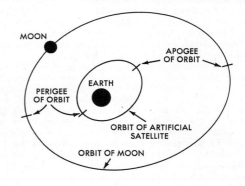

APOLLINAIRE, à-pô-lē-nâr', **Guillaume** (1880–1918), French poet, who was one of the major modernists of the first two decades of the 20th century. Apollinaire's pan-European background, experimental bent, and keen interest in the plastic arts gave him an influential role at a time when symbolism and impressionism were yielding to more extreme breaks with tradition.

Career. He was born *Guillaume Albert Dulcigni* (later, *de Kostrowitzky*), in Rome, on Aug. 26, 1880. The illegitimate son of an Italian father and a Polish mother, he liked to keep his birth a mystery. He was educated on the French

FRENCH CULTURAL SERVICES, NEW YORK

GUILLAUME APOLLINAIRE (1880–1918), as sketched by the artist Henri Matisse.

Riviera and later traveled widely in Germany and eastern Europe. He finally settled in Paris in 1902 and frequented literary circles while earning a scanty living. Gradually, publication of his poems, and his friendship with young poets and painters, brought him recognition, tinged with scandal when he was arrested in 1911 on suspicion of theft of the *Mona Lisa*, which had been stolen from the Louvre by Vincenzo Perugia, an Italian. The peak years of his career lie between 1908 and 1914, when he was active in all the arts.

Though not a naturalized French citizen, Apollinaire volunteered for military service in 1914. He trained first with the artillery and then saw frontline service as a lieutenant in the infantry. A serious head wound in 1916 caused him to return to Paris for two operations and a non-combatant assignment. Although he seemed to recover, he was unable to resist the influenza that took his life, in Paris, on Nov. 9, 1918. He had married only six months earlier.

Poems and Fiction. Two collections of poetry, *Alcools* (1913) and *Calligrammes* (1918), constitute the most significant part of Apollinaire's literary work. *Alcools*, though printed without punctuation and containing a number of modernist poems (for example, *Zone*), is essentially traditional and lyric in character. It contains the long love poem *La chanson du mal-aimé*, often considered his masterpiece. This poem celebrates his love for Annie Pleyden, an English governess, who had resisted his advances in Germany in 1901. *Calligrammes* is more deliberately modern in spirit and technique and contains some

inspired war poems as well as calligraphic works whose visual shape corresponds to their subject. He also published a volume of stories and two conglomerate novels.

Criticism. Apollinaire wrote a large mass of critical and journalistic material. He also brought out semischolarly editions of licentious classics like the works of marquis de Sade and Aretino, and also edited several literary-artistic reviews. The most important of these was *Les soirées de Paris* (1911–1914), in which he fulfilled his role of champion and impresario of the new artistic schools, cubism, orphism, *simultanéisme*, and others. Despite a somewhat naïvely enthusiastic point of view, he had a flair for singling out many of the greatest painters of the century long before their names were known, including Picasso, Matisse, Braque, Henri Rousseau, Delaunay, Chagall, and Chirico. His volume *The Cubist Painters* (1913) is still considered a revealing document. By coining the word "surrealist" in 1917 for the Picasso-Satie-Cocteau ballet *Parade,* he provided the name for a major artistic movement.

General Characteristics. Apollinaire's work has a marked double orientation toward an unshakable sense of tradition and an arrogant modernism—toward "Order and Adventure" as he himself said in one of his last poems. He remains one of the heroes of the avant-garde in all countries and a lyric poet of beauty and profound significance.

ROGER SHATTUCK, *Author of "The Banquet Years"*

Bibliography
Alcools has been translated under that title by Anne Hyde Greet (Berkeley, Calif., 1965), and by William Meredith in *Poems, 1898–1913* (New York 1964). *Selected Writings of Guillaume Apollinaire* was translated by Roger Shattuck (New York 1950).
Adema, Marcel, *Apollinaire,* tr. by Denise Folliot (New York 1955).
Davies, Margaret, *Apollinaire* (New York 1964).
Shattuck, Roger, *The Banquet Years* (New York 1959).
Steegmuller, Francis, *Apollinaire, Poet Among the Painters* (New York 1963).

APOLLINARIANISM, ə-pol-ə-nâr'ē-ən-iz-əm, a Christian heresy of the 4th century that developed as a result of another heresy, Arianism. One of the most respected defenders of the orthodox view of Christ's divinity was a bishop of Laodicea, Apollinarius the Younger (about 326–392). In attempting to reconcile the divinity of Christ, which the Arians denied, with the humanity of Christ, he lapsed into the theological error that came to be called Apollinarianism.

Although Apollinarius subscribed to the church's teaching that God himself became man in Christ, he repudiated the belief that the whole divine nature of God, or Logos, could become an integral part of a complete human nature. Apollinarius reasoned that Christ was a "natural" man who possessed a body and a soul, but in Him the whole divinity—the Logos—replaced the human mind.

In effect, this teaching denied Christ's total humanity. The fathers of the church, therefore, condemned both the doctrine and its many adherents, who were known as Apollinarists. The synods of Rome (374-380) and in particular the Council of Constantinople (381) took strong actions against the heresy. In 383, Emperor Theodosius the Great outlawed all followers of Apollinarius. The heresy persisted nevertheless and survived Apollinarius' death. Eventually, most of the Apollinarists became Monophysites. See also ARIANISM; CHRISTOLOGY; MONOPHYSITES.

APOLLO BELVEDERE, most famous of Apollos, in the Vatican Museum, is a Roman copy of the original by Leochares, Athenian sculptor of the 4th century B.C.

APOLLO, ə-pol′ō, in Greek mythology, was the greatest of the gods after Zeus (Jupiter). He was, at the same or various times, the god of the sun or of light; the god of archery; the god of agriculture and animal husbandry, and the patron of farmers and shepherds; the god of poetry and song, and the leader of the Muses; the god of healing, or medicine, and the patron of physicians; the god of prophecy and of morality and ethics; and the founder of cities and the giver of laws. He originated as a sun god, identified with Helios and known as *Phoebus Apollo*—a primitive energizing force, the guardian of crops, cattle, and sheep. In time he became an all-pervasive spiritual influence whose oracle was consulted in temples throughout Greece and Asia Minor.

Apollo was the son of Zeus and Leto (Latona) and the twin brother of Artemis (Diana). He and Artemis were born on the island of Delos, and one of his many names was *Delios*. As a newborn infant he was fed nectar and ambrosia, and he at once sprang into full maturity. While searching for a place in which to establish his temple, he came to a gorge in Parnassus where he killed the serpent Python with bow and arrows. On that site he founded Delphi (originally called Pytho), which became the seat of his chief temple and oracle. Commemorating this event, the Pythian Games were held in the third year of each Olympiad, beginning in 776 B.C. Another festival held at Delphi in his honor was known as Delphinia, for which Apollo was surnamed *Delphinios*.

As the leader of the Muses, Apollo was surnamed *Musagetes*. In festivals he played the lyre and sang while the Muses danced around

him. At one contest King Midas judged Apollo's playing of the lyre to be inferior to Pan's playing of the pipes. For this judgment Apollo bestowed on Midas the ears of an ass.

In time Apollo became identified as the god of healing and as the father by Coronis of Aesculapius (Asclepius), the god of medicine. When Zeus had Aesculapius killed by thunderbolts for restoring certain dead men to life, Apollo in retaliation killed the Cyclopes for forging the thunderbolts. Zeus then banished Apollo from Olympus and compelled him to spend a year on earth as a mortal. He spent the year as a keeper of cattle and horses for Admetus, king of Pherae in Thessaly.

In the Trojan War, Apollo sided with Troy. He sent a great plague against the Greeks when Agamemnon refused to return the captive girl Chryseis to her father, a priest of Apollo.

Most important, however, Apollo came to be revered by the Greeks, and later by the Romans, for his spiritual powers. In this aspect he could be both severe and lenient. He punished those who were guilty of overweening pride and presumption. He purified wrongdoers who were contrite and sought his oracle.

In another light, Apollo was the personification of eternal youth and beauty—stalwart, athletic, and beardless. In art and sculpture, he is represented as a partially draped figure with a bow and quiver, a shepherd's crook, or a laurel crown, sometimes accompanied by an animal sacred to him.

See also ARTEMIS; LETO; DELPHI.

APOLLO, PROJECT. See SPACE VEHICLES.

APOLLODORUS, ə-pol-ə-dôr′əs, was a Greek painter of the 5th century B.C. He was one of the first artists to experiment with the use of shadows to make his figures appear three-dimensional. Because of his work with this technique, he earned the epithet *Shadowpainter*. No Greek paintings of his time have survived, and his work, such as *Ajax Struck by Lightning* and *Priests in the Act of Devotion*, is known only from literary evidence.

APOLLODORUS OF DAMASCUS, ə-pol-ə-dôr′əs, də-mas′kəs, was a Greek architect and engineer of the 2d century A.D. He was born in Damascus, Syria, but he lived and worked in Rome, where he was official architect to Emperor Trajan. His masterpiece was the Forum of Trajan built in 113–117 A.D. He also planned the markets at the end of the Quirinal Hill in the Forum. His designs of the markets were completely functional and blended in harmoniously with the surroundings. As an engineer, he designed a bridge over the Danube River, near Dobreta, in 104 A.D. Apollodorus was banished from Rome for criticizing some of Emperor Hadrian's architectural plans and was later put to death.

APOLLONIUS OF ALEXANDRIA, ap-ə-lō′nē-əs, was a Greek grammarian of Alexandria, Egypt, who lived in the 2d century A.D. Nicknamed *Dyscolus* (the crabbed), he is ranked among the greatest Greek grammarians. He composed almost 30 treatises, mostly on syntax, of which *On Syntax of Parts of Speech, On the Pronoun, On Conjunctions,* and *On Adverbs* survive. His systematic studies, based on critical method, greatly influenced later Greek and Latin grammarians.

APOLLONIUS OF PERGA (c. 262–190 B.C.), ap-ə-lō′nē-əs, pûr′gə, was a Greek geometer and mathematician who improved the theory on conic sections and made original contributions on geometrical properties related to conic sections. He was born in Perga (now Murtana, Turkey) and studied in Alexandria. Of his 13 known treatises, the extant ones are *On Conic Sections* (eight books) and *On Section of a Ratio*. He introduced the names "ellipse," "parabola," and "hyperbola" for the three types of conic sections, and he invented or perfected the theory of epicycles and the theory of eccentrics to account for the motion of the planets. See also CONIC SECTIONS.

APOLLONIUS OF RHODES (c. 295–215 B.C.), ap-ə-lō′nē-əs, rōdz, was a Greek epic poet, whose best-known work was the *Argonautica*. He was born in Alexandria, Egypt, and was a pupil of the grammarian Callimachus. He was director of the Alexandrian Library from about 260 B.C. to 247 B.C. In his *Argonautica*, an epic in four books relating the legend of the Argonauts, he turned from the artificial style preferred by Callimachus and strove for the simplicity of Homer's style. This caused a quarrel with Callimachus, and Apollonius went to Rhodes, where he was well-received and was granted citizenship, hence his surname.

APOLLONIUS OF TRALLES, ap-ə-lō′nē-əs, tral′ēz, was a Greek sculptor of the 1st century B.C. He was born in Tralles, Asia Minor (now Aydin, Turkey). With his brother Tauriscus, he carved the marble group called the *Farnese Bull*, of which an enlarged copy was in the Farnese Palace, Rome, from 1540 to 1786, and is now in the National Museum, Naples.

APOLLONIUS OF TYANA, ap-ə-lō′nē-əs, tī′ə-nə, was a Greek philosopher of the 1st century A.D. He was born in Tyana, Asia Minor. The chief professor of Neo-Pythagoreanism, he traveled widely within and outside the Roman Empire as an ascetic teacher and thaumaturgist. Flavius Philostratus (170?–?245 A.D.) preserved 97 of his letters in an eight-book biography.

APOLLOS, ə-pol′əs, was a Christian missionary of the 1st century. Born a Jew in Alexandria, Egypt, he first was converted to the movement of John the Baptist and was instructed in the teachings concerning Jesus by Priscilla and Aquila at Ephesus (Acts 18:24–28; 19:1–7). He won a considerable following at Corinth. His success is demonstrated by the fact that Paul found it necessary to rebuke the partisans of Apollos there (I Corinthians 1:10–12; 3:4–6; 16:12). Apollos probably represented a fairly large group of Christians in the 1st century who combined a Jewish religious inheritance and knowledge of the Scriptures with the new faith in Christ, and who contributed greatly to the growth of the church.

FREDERICK C. GRANT, *Union Theological Seminary*

APOLLYON, ə-pol′yən, in the New Testament, is a Greek equivalent for the Hebrew word *Abaddon* (destroyer), the name of the angel who serves as keeper of the bottomless pit (Revelation 9:11). In John Bunyan's *Pilgrim's Progress*, Christian's fight against his sins is depicted as a battle against Apollyon in the Valley of Humiliation. See also PILGRIM'S PROGRESS.

APOLOGETICS, ə-pol-ə-jet′iks, is the branch of Christian theology that has the twofold task of defending the Christian faith against its critics and of discovering the common ground in reason and experience that may offer the basis for leading non-Christians toward Christian belief. Apologetics thus is distinguished from *dogmatics*, which is the setting forth of the faith of the Christian church and is addressed to those who already believe.

In the work of apologetics the theologian speaks to those outside the Christian faith, or he is doing the intellectual work necessary to prepare for such conversation. The first apologists, such as Justin Martyr (about 100–165) and Tertullian (about 160–230), answered charges against the Christians and sought to convince the emperors that the beliefs and behavior of Christians contributed to the good of society. Justin Martyr tried to convince Greek philosophers of the reasonableness and truth of Christian beliefs. So also St. Augustine (354–430) in *The City of God* refuted the charge that Christianity was the cause of the decline of the empire; and he discussed the extent to which Christian belief is in harmony with Platonist philosophy and to what extent there remained irreconcilable differences.

Faith and Reason. When Arabian versions of Greek philosophy were introduced into western Europe in the Middle Ages, Christian theologians had to interpret their faith in relation to these new versions of Greek philosophy and to reconsider the relation of Christian faith to the major concepts in the philosophical tradition. St. Thomas Aquinas (died 1274) entitled one of his chief works *Summa contra Gentiles*, since it was a treatise written to help missionaries interpret Christian truth to nonbelievers. All of St. Thomas' work has an apologetic element, the foundation for which was laid in a distinction of four kinds of propositions that had been made earlier by Hugh of St. Victor (died 1141). There are, first, propositions contrary to reason that have no standing in Christian faith. There are, second, propositions that can be demonstrated by reason, such as the existence of God, the freedom of the human will, and the immortality of the soul. Third, there are propositions above reason, such as the doctrines of the Trinity and the Incarnation, that are revealed truths known only by faith, not proved by reason. There is also a fourth class of propositions "according to reason" that occupy a somewhat ambiguous position. The creation of the world in time is an idea belonging to this class.

Apologetics in the Thomist manner makes use of this analysis in arguing for the existence of God, freedom, and immortality on the basis of an appeal to man's reason apart from any claim to special revelation.

A further step is necessary if the nonbeliever is to become a Christian. The nonbeliever must recognize the reasonableness of the act of faith in accepting the teaching of the church. Here apologetics must establish the credibility of Christian teaching about God's special revelation. Arguments are drawn from prophecy and miracles to show the plausibility of the belief that God has revealed Himself in the special ways attested in the Bible.

Not all Roman Catholic apologetics has been based upon the Thomist type of confidence in reason. Blaise Pascal (1623–1662) followed the

Augustinian tradition when he emphasized the necessity of faith for belief in God. Yet Pascal's thought also has an apologetic aspect as he introduces arguments to show the futility of cynicism and atheism.

Christianity and Science. The tradition of apologetics in Anglican and Protestant theology has been closely related historically to the rationalistic thought of the 18th century. Theologians of that period tried to adjust theological beliefs to the scientific theories of Copernican astronomy and Newtonian physics. An important method in this adjustment was the development of the arguments of natural theology for the existence of God and for belief in a universal moral order culminating in eternal life with its just rewards and punishments. The arguments were revised versions of St. Thomas' proofs. They asserted the necessity of a First Cause to explain the world of finite things and the necessity of a Supreme Intelligent Designer to explain the adjustment of means to ends in the world. William Paley's *Natural Theology* (1802) is a classic of this type of apologetics.

A vital problem for 18th century apologists was the adjustment of the supernatural elements in the Christian tradition, such as belief in miracles, to the concept of a natural order obeying mathematical laws. Some thinkers, like John Locke in the latter part of the 17th century, adopted the arguments of natural theology but held also to the validity of belief in the supernatural. Radical deists discarded the supernatural element entirely.

Because of the impact of modern scientific method and knowledge on religious beliefs, apologetics in the modern period often has sought to draw a boundary line between scientific and religious beliefs so that conflict between the two is avoided. One of the classic 18th century works in this spirit is Joseph Butler's *Analogy of Religion, Natural and Revealed, to the Constitution and Course of Nature* (1736). Butler argued that all human knowledge depends on judgments of probability and that the same difficulties that are urged against natural religion and against Christian beliefs are found also in our knowledge of nature. He argues for the reasonableness of belief in miracles, for example, by saying that much of nature remains inexplicable and displays extraordinary happenings.

Many theologians have felt the insufficiency of the rational arguments for belief in God. David Hume and Immanuel Kant attacked the traditional arguments during the latter part of the 18th century, and their criticism increased the need for another interpretation of the grounds of Christian belief. Friedrich Schleiermacher's *Reden über die Religion an die Gebildeten unter ihren Verächtern* (1799; *Speeches on Religion to Its Cultured Despisers*), was an essay in apologetics that appealed to intuition and feeling rather than to abstract reason for the clue to the nature of God and the world. Such an appeal to religious experience has been a primary mode of apologetics in the 19th and 20th centuries. As scientific developments became more influential with the rise of evolutionary theory, increasing attention was given to the distinctive nature of religion, and the attempt was made to show how religious belief complements and does not contradict science.

Among the powerful attacks upon Christian faith in the late 19th and early 20th centuries were those of Friedrich Wilhelm Nietzsche, Karl Marx, and Sigmund Freud. Nietzsche sought to show that Christianity exploits human weakness by turning it into a morality of subservience. Karl Marx classified all religious belief as ideology, that is, a false projection resulting from the class divisions in society. Sigmund Freud taught that religious belief is the illusory projection of unfulfilled human wishes. Christian apologetics has had to face these criticisms; to ask whether or not they may be perversions of some valid insights; and finally to show that Christian faith rests on firm ground that cannot be undermined by such criticisms.

The 20th Century. The complex intellectual situation of Christianity in the 20th century, coupled with the rise of such violently anti-Christian movements as national socialism in Germany, has produced two developments in the theory of apologetics.

One development is the assertion, by the Swiss theologian Karl Barth and his followers, of the confessional character of all Christian theology. All natural theology is rejected, along with any appeal to human experience and reason as giving preliminary grounds for faith. The truth that Christianity proclaims, this group asserts, can be accepted only by personal faith. All attempts to find any common ground between Christians and non-Christians break down on the point that man's mind and spirit are corrupted by sin; and, therefore, all attempts to understand God apart from faith result in false and idolatrous beliefs.

A second group of theologians believes that the confessional theology goes too far in rejecting all apologetics. This group holds that theologians must discover the relevant way to communicate the Christian faith to those whose lives are shaped by contemporary culture outside the Christian faith. The apologist is not so much concerned with proving by argument the existence of God as he is with interpreting the meaning of such terms as God, grace, creation, and forgiveness to people for whom this language has lost its meaning. The task of apologetics, viewed from this standpoint, is to interpret the relation between Christian beliefs and man's fundamental questions about his existence without compromising the distinctive character of the Christian revelation. In this way apologetics becomes one of the modes in which Christian truth is clarified and interpreted.

Any theology that seeks to enter into a serious conversation with questioning minds will have an apologetic element. The term "apologetics" has nothing to do with "apologizing" in the ordinary use of that term. It is the entry of the theologian into the intellectual arena, where questions are asked about the meaning of human life, and his grappling with those questions from the standpoint of Christian faith.

DANIEL D. WILLIAMS, *Union Theologial Seminary*

Bibliography

Barth, Karl, *Knowledge of God and the Service of God* (Naperville, Ill., 1955).
Fenton, Joseph C., *We Stand with Christ: An Essay in Catholic Apologetics* (St. Paul, Minn., 1942).
Illingworth, John Richardson, *Reason and Revelation, an Essay in Christian Apology* (London 1902).
Richardson, Alan, *Christian Apologetics* (New York 1947).
Temple, William, *Nature, Man and God* (New York 1934).
Tillich, Paul Johannes, *Systematic Theology*, 3 vols. (Chicago 1951–63).

APOLOGIA PRO VITA SUA, ap-ə-lō′jē-ə prō vītə sū′ə, is an autobiographical work by John Henry, later Cardinal, Newman, published in 1864. Literally the title means "A Defense of His Life." The work is best characterized by its subtitle, *Being a History of His Religious Opinions.*

Writing and Publication. In the years following his conversion to the Roman Catholic Church in 1845, Newman's great reputation had undergone various changes, and at the end of 1863 he was living, not in retirement or inactivity, but, as he put it, "out of the world," and not "in active controversy with the Anglican body, or any portion of it." It was then that an anonymous correspondent called his attention to an attack upon him in *Macmillan's Magazine* of January 1864. The attack was part of a book review, signed "C.K.," in which it was stated: "Truth, for its own sake, had never been a virtue with the Roman clergy. Father Newman informs us that it need not, and on the whole ought not to be."

Not knowing who the author was, Newman wrote to Macmillan & Co., calling their attention to this "grave and gratuitous slander," but not asking for an answer or apology. The publishers referred his letter to the author of the review, Charles Kingsley, the popular clergyman and novelist, who informed Newman that the basis for the charge was a sermon entitled *Wisdom and Innocence.* In answer Newman showed that the sermon contained nothing to substantiate the charge, and that it had been preached and published while he was still a Protestant. In the ensuing correspondence Kingsley's position became increasingly difficult and untenable as he added mistake after mistake to the original error. Few passages in literature contain finer or more justified satire than Newman's analysis of Kingsley's attitude, reasoning, and methods of debate.

This incident led to the writing of the *Apologia* proper. The complete work was written over a period of about 10 weeks and consisted of seven parts, published as pamphlets on consecutive Thursdays between April 21 and June 2, 1864, together with an appendix, issued on June 16. When he put these pamphlets into book form, Newman condensed the controversy between himself and Kingsley into a preface and added notes and other supplementary matter.

Content and Reputation. The body of the book consists of five chapters, the first giving the history of his religious opinions up to 1833, the next three his account of the changes that took place between 1833 and 1845, and the last describing the position of his mind since 1845. Newman tells how he "was brought up from a child to take great delight in reading the Bible," and was subjected to various religious influences in his childhood, youth, and years at Oxford. However, the movement of his thought was consistently in the direction of traditional Anglican doctrine. He describes his voyage to the Mediterranean in 1832–1833 and his return to England, where he had "a work to do," although he did not then know that it was to be the Oxford, or Tractarian, movement, which was to have such momentous consequences.

Events of that great activity are described in chapters 2 and 3. "From the end of 1841," Newman writes, "I was on my death-bed as regards my membership with the Anglican Church, though at the time I became aware of it only by degrees." During the next four years he moved gradually closer to the Roman Catholic Church, into which he was received on Oct. 9, 1845. Since that date, he writes, "I have had no variations to record, and have had no anxiety of heart whatever. I have been in perfect peace and contentment; I have never had one doubt. . . . it was like coming into port after a rough sea; and my happiness on that score remains to this day without interruption."

The *Apologia pro Vita Sua* was recognized as a masterpiece of spiritual and intellectual self-analysis and self-revelation upon its first appearance, and that verdict has never been challenged. Although written with the utmost clarity, it is not an easy book for the ordinary reader. The subject matter requires a knowledge of theology and an appreciation of the profound issues involved. Such knowledge and appreciation were possessed more widely by the educated public in Victorian England than by the educated public today. Yet the *Apologia* remains a unique work in English, and world, literature and an indispensable document for understanding Newman and the period in which he lived.

JOHN K. RYAN
The Catholic University of America

Bibliography

Editions of *Apologia pro Vita Sua* include the one in Charles F. Harrold's edition of Newman's works (New York 1947), and one with an introduction by Basil Willey (New York 1964).
Blehl, Vincent F., and Connolly, Francis X., eds., *Newman's Apologia: A Classic Reconsidered* (New York 1964).
Harrold, Charles F., *John Henry Newman* (New York 1945).
Houghton, Walter E., *The Art of Newman's Apologia* (New Haven 1945).

APOLOGY, ə-pol′ə-jē, a short work by the Greek philosopher Plato, probably written in the 390's B.C. It purports to be the speech delivered by Socrates, Plato's mentor, in his own defense at his trial in 399 B.C.

The Apology falls into three parts. The first and longest section contains Socrates' arguments against the official charge that he made innovations in religion and corrupted the young. It also answers the real and unspoken charges that he represented the new instruction of the Sophists, regarded as immoral, and that he had been in league with the Thirty Tyrants, who ruled Athens after its defeat in the Peloponnesian War. Socrates dissociates himself from the Sophists, saying that, unlike them, he neither taught for pay nor professed to teach wisdom.

Socrates, in his role as the "gadfly" of society, had made many enemies by exposing their pretension to possess wisdom. He had assumed this role because of the Delphic oracle's statement that no man was wiser than Socrates. In order to discover the meaning of the oracle's words, Socrates went among his fellow Athenians, asking questions of politicians, poets, and laborers alike. He found that although they used philosophical concepts, they had no firm understanding of them. Socrates, therefore, interpreted the oracle's pronouncement to mean that he was the only Greek who realized that he knew nothing.

The last two parts of *The Apology* deal with Socrates' condemnation to death. He takes leave of the jurors without fear: "No evil can happen to a good man, either in life or after death."

RICHMOND Y. HATHORN
Author of "Tragedy, Myth, and Mystery"

APOMORPHINE, ap-ə-môr′fēn, is a colorless, crystalline compound made from morphine and used in medicine to induce vomiting. Injected hypodermically, it has almost no morphinelike action.

Apomorphine is formed by the action of acidic agents on morphine. The change involves a complex structural rearrangement of the molecules and the loss of a molecule of water. The molecular formula of apomorphine is $C_{17}H_{17}NO_2$; its structure is well known and has been confirmed by synthesis.

Apomorphine is soluble in alcohol, acetone, and chloroform; it is slightly soluble in water, benzene, and ether. In air, it oxidizes rapidly and turns green.

APOPHYLLITE, ap-ə-fil′īt, is a hydrated, or water-containing, silicate mineral. In its molecular structure it is related to the clay minerals such as kaolin and mica. Apophyllite almost always occurs as crystals in ore veins or lining the cavities in basalt. The crystals are squarish prisms, transparent to translucent, that are easily identified because the base of the crystal has a pearly luster while the other sides are glassy in appearance. The crystal is usually colorless or whitish but may be tinted pink or green. It cleaves readily along planes parallel to the base.

Beautiful apophyllite crystals have been found in India, Mexico, and Nova Scotia. In the United States they are found in New Jersey and around Lake Superior.

Composition: $Ca_4K(Si_4O_{10})_2F\cdot8H_2O$; hardness, 4.5 to 5; specific gravity, 2.3 to 2.4; crystal system, tetragonal.

APOPLEXY, ap′ə-plek-sē, is a term, no longer in common use, for the group of symptoms indicating hemorrhage into the interior of the brain or upon its surface. Apoplexy was described clinically as early as the mid-17th century, but the term now has been superseded by the designation, cerebral hemorrhage.

Apoplexy occurs suddenly and is the immediate result of a blockage or a blood clot in blood vessels of the brain. The obstruction or blood clot may develop in the vessels of the brain or it may develop elsewhere and be brought to the vessels of the brain by the blood current. A typical apoplectic seizure or "stroke" is recognized by hemiplegia (paralysis of one lateral half of the body) accompanied by the loss of consciousness, prolonged coma, and often by death within a few hours or days. Partial recovery may take place and the patient may survive for many years. In a certain percentage of cases, the speech center of the brain is involved and blindness in one eye is common.

Hemiplegia is caused by bleeding into the internal cavities of the brain. The result is a paralysis of the facial muscles or one side of the tongue, with palsy of the extremities on the opposite side. Patients who recover walk with a spastic gait, and the reflexes on the paralyzed side are exaggerated. Hemiplegia also may be caused by a degenerative arteriosclerosis of the cerebral vessels. The prognosis for recovery is variable, and some disability is inevitable. Mental impairment is common.

The term "apoplexy" also may be applied to massive bleeding into an internal organ such as the lung, spleen, or eye.

HAROLD WELLINGTON JONES, M.D., *Former Editor*
"Blakiston's New Gould Medical Dictionary"

APOSTASY, ə-pos′tə-sē, is rejection of faith, usually of the Christian religion. An apostate is one who, having accepted the faith, consciously abandons it. An individual who has been baptized but who has not been brought up in the church cannot be called an apostate if he does not adhere to the church. Another essential element in apostasy is total rejection of faith. But neither laxity in practice of religion nor heresy is apostasy. Heresy often means questioning or rejecting some part of religious doctrine but not abandoning all the beliefs of the church.

In earlier times apostasy could be punished by the church and by the civil government. For example, English laws of the time of King William III provided that a person who rejected the Christian religion should be barred from holding office and be liable to imprisonment.

Apostasy is no longer treated as a civil crime but remains a concern of the church. In the Roman Catholic Church the term is used to mean the abandonment of Christianity. It is also applied when a monk or nun unlawfully leaves the religious life.

APOSTLE, ə-pos′əl, a term applied chiefly to the original disciples of Jesus who became the leading missionaries and heads of the Christian church after the Resurrection. The word comes from the Greek *apostellein* (to send away) and literally means "one sent," as on a mission. The names of the original Twelve Apostles are given in the New Testament (Mark 3:14–19, Matthew 10:1–4, Luke 6:12–16, and Acts 1:13) as follows: Simon (called Peter), James (or Jacob), John (James' brother), Andrew (Peter's brother), Philip, Bartholomew, Matthew, Thomas, James (or Jacob, the son of Alphaeus), Thaddaeus (called Lebbaeus in some manuscripts), Simon "the Cananaean," and Judas "Iscariot," who betrayed the master. Judas' place was later taken by Matthias (Acts 1:15–26). In Mark 2:14, "Levi the son of Alphaeus" was called to be a disciple; in Matthew 9:9, he is said to have been called Matthew, though Luke 5:27 retains the name Levi. In Luke 6:15, Simon the Cananaean is called "the Zealot," and in the following verse Judas, the son (or brother) of James, is mentioned.

In addition to the original Twelve, other missionaries and leaders, such as Barnabas (Acts 14:14) and Paul, were given the title "apostle." Paul laid great stress upon his apostleship, describing himself as an "apostle to the gentiles" (Romans 11:13) and claiming both to have seen the Lord in a vision (I Corinthians 9:1, 15:8) and to have worked miracles (II Corinthians 12:12). It is probable that the apostles had wives (I Corinthians 9:5), though the later account of Peter's daughter, Petronilla, has no New Testament support. The reference in Romans 16:7 to Andronicus and Junias is often taken to mean that they were apostles, but the sounder interpretation of the phrase "of note among the apostles" is that they were well known to the apostles as leaders in the church.

In later history, the name "apostle" was used of great missionaries such as Augustine, the apostle of the English; Patrick of Ireland; Ulfilas of the Goths; Boniface of the Germans; Denis of the French; and John Eliot of the American Indians.

FREDERICK C. GRANT
Union Theological Seminary

APOSTLE ISLANDS, ə-pos'əl, in Wisconsin, are a group of about 20 islands in southwest Lake Superior, belonging to Ashland and Bayfield counties. The largest, Madeline, about 13 miles long, has the only settlement, La Pointe. Other important islands are Stockton, Bear, Raspberry, Oak, Outer, and Sand. Picturesque cliffs have been worn into strange shapes by the action of the waves. The islands are covered with a rich growth of timber, and attract many tourists as well as duck and deer hunters.

APOSTLES' CREED, ə-pos'elz krēd, the creed used in services of worship by Roman Catholics and by most Protestants as the principal traditional affirmation of the Christian faith. In the Anglican Book of Common Prayer it reads:

> I believe in God the Father Almighty, Maker of heaven and earth:
> And in Jesus Christ his only Son our Lord, Who was conceived by the Holy Ghost, born of the Virgin Mary, Suffered under Pontius Pilate, Was crucified, dead and buried. He descended into hell; The third day he rose again from the dead, He ascended into heaven, And sitteth on the right hand of God the Father Almighty; From thence he shall come to judge the quick and the dead.
> I believe in the Holy Ghost; The holy Catholic Church; The Communion of Saints; The Forgiveness of sins; The Resurrection of the body; And the Life everlasting. Amen.

This form of the creed is a local elaboration of the old Roman creed and was used in southwestern France in the 7th century. The Roman creed itself, says Tyrannius Rufinus (who wrote a commentary on it early in the 5th century), was composed by the apostles, inspired by the Holy Spirit, shortly after Pentecost. It was handed down in the Roman church without alteration, he says, because no heresy ever originated at Rome and because it was used publicly at baptism. These statements contain elements of legend, but they point to the apostolic origin of the creed, in the sense of its harmony with the faith of the New Testament, and so to its development out of earlier, simpler confessions of faith.

In the *Apostolic Tradition* of Hippolytus, there is a Roman question-and-answer creed dating from the beginning of the 3d century. It is divided into three parts:

> Do you believe in God the Father Almighty?
> Do you believe in Christ Jesus, the Son of God, who was born by the Holy Spirit of the Virgin Mary, died and was buried, was raised living from the dead on the third day, ascended into heaven, and sits on the right hand of the Father, and will come to judge the living and the dead?
> Do you believe in the Holy Spirit and the Holy Church and the resurrection of the flesh?

The phrase "was crucified under Pontius Pilate," should probably be added after the reference to the Virgin Mary; it is in the Latin version.

The three main headings of this confession can be traced back at Rome to the middle of the 2d century, when Justin Martyr (*Apology* i, 61, 3) speaks of baptism "in the name of God the Father of the universe and sovereign, and of our Savior Jesus Christ, and of the Holy Spirit," and, even earlier, to the commandment of Christ in the Gospel of Matthew (28:19): "Go make disciples of all nations, baptizing them in the name of the Father and the Son and the Holy Spirit."

The prototypes of baptismal confessions are thus to be found in the New Testament itself, as in such verses as I Corinthians 8:6 ("For us there is one God the Father . . . and one Lord Jesus Christ") and in the whole apostolic preaching of God (I Thessalonians 1:9) and of Christ (I Thessalonians 1:10; I Corinthians 15:1–11). Fairly soon such confessions were expanded, by use of the New Testament books, to include the Virgin Birth, the Ascension, and Christ's sitting at the right hand of God (Psalm 110:1, interpreted Christologically in the New Testament). The last of the three articles was the slowest to be developed, though the expression "holy church" is found among Christian writers in the middle of the 2d century, and the resurrection of the flesh (translated "body" at the time of the Reformation) is defended vigorously as early as Ignatius (early 2d century). The forgiveness of sins was also part of the baptismal confessions current at the end of the 2d century.

The last items to be added were (1) a statement about Christ's descent into hell, based on I Peter 3:19–20 and 4:6 (and possibly Ephesians 4.9), and appearing first in a creed of 359 at Sirmium; (2) "Life everlasting," taken from various Eastern creeds (more literally, "eternal life"); and (3) "The Communion of Saints," first in Nicetas of Remesiana (end of the 4th century), which probably means "the fellowship of the saints" and is thus correlate with "the holy Catholic Church."

The Apostles' Creed is a summary of the faith of the church and sets forth its belief in the significance of the principal "saving events" of the Biblical revelation. It is not a technical theological document, since it contains no analysis of the doctrines of the Trinity and the Incarnation and no explanation of the function of the Holy Spirit. Scholars have sometimes argued that its forerunners were composed for the negative purpose of combatting heresies, such as the denial of the humanity of Jesus, but the positive purpose of proclaiming a common faith is more evident. On the other hand, Rufinus rightly points out that in his time a distinction was made between the primary faith in Father, Son, and Holy Spirit and the secondary faith in "created beings and saving mysteries," church, forgiveness, and resurrection.

ROBERT M. GRANT
The Divinity School, The University of Chicago

Further Reading: Cullmann, Oscar, *The Earliest Christian Confessions*, tr. by J.K.S. Reid (London 1949); Dix, Gregory, ed., *Treatise on the Apostolic Tradition of St. Hippolytus of Rome*, vol. 1 (New York 1937); Kelly, John N.D., *Early Christian Creeds* (New York 1950); Rufinus Tyrannius, *A Commentary on the Apostles' Creed*, tr. by John N.D. Kelly (Westminster, Md., 1955).

APOSTLESHIP OF PRAYER, ə-pos'əl-ship, prā'er, a Roman Catholic association whose purpose is the sanctification of its members and the development of an awareness of their vocation to help in saving souls through a special devotion to the Sacred Heart of Jesus. Members observe three practices; the first is essential, the others are recommended: (1) daily recitation of the morning offering and dedication to its promises throughout the day; (2) regular attendance at Mass and communion of reparation, especially on First Fridays of the month; (3) daily recitation of all, or at least a decade, of the rosary. The purpose of these practices is to form a true rule of Christian life.

Founded in France in 1844, the organization has a worldwide membership of over 40 million, with general headquarters in Rome. In the United States, membership exceeds 2 million. See also SACRED HEART OF JESUS.

APOSTOLIC CONSTITUTIONS AND CANONS, a collection, in eight books, of ecclesiastical rules attributed to Pope Clement I (late 1st century A.D.). The compilation dates from the late 4th century but contains much earlier material. Book 8 includes the so-called Egyptian Church Order, really by Hippolytus of Rome (3d century), and the famous Clementine Liturgy, along with a homily on the gifts of grace. Book 7 contains a collection of Jewish prayers. The 85 Canons, a supplement to the work, are based on the decisions of older Oriental church synods. The author or compiler of the work is unknown, but was probably a monk in Syria. There is a modern edition by Franz X. Funk, *Didascalia et Constitutiones Apostolorum* (2 vols., 1905).

FREDERICK C. GRANT
Union Theological Seminary

Further Reading: Hippolytus, St., *Apostolic Tradition,* tr. and ed. by Burton S. Easton (New York 1934); *Liturgy of the Eighth Book of "The Apostolic Constitutions,"* tr. by Richard H. Cresswell (London 1900); Srawley, James H., *Early History of the Liturgy,* 2d ed. (New York 1947).

APOSTOLIC FATHERS, a collection of Christian writings dating from the end of the 1st century and the middle of the 2d century. The authors were mostly Gentiles, perhaps disciples of apostles or of those in apostolic circles. The writings are characterized by literary simplicity, sincere religious conviction, and independence of thought and expression. They are not part of the Bible, but they reveal great concern for the New Testament's basic message and for church order in the face of the threat of schism and heresy.

The writings include I Clement, a letter written from Rome to Corinth (about 96); II Clement, a sermon formerly believed to have been written at Alexandria about 150, but no longer considered authentic; the seven letters of Ignatius of Antioch, written on his way to martyrdom at Rome during Trajan's reign (98–117); the letter of Polycarp to the Philippians (about 135); the Didache, or Teaching of the Twelve Apostles, a composite (no agreed date); the letter of Barnabas (about 130); the Shepherd of Hermas (100–150); the Martyrdom of Polycarp (155 or later); and the letter of Diognetus (about 129).

Further Reading: Richardson, Cyril C., and others, eds., *Early Christian Fathers* (Philadelphia 1953).

APOSTOLIC SUCCESSION, the succession of the bishops in the Christian church. The *doctrine* of Apostolic Succession holds that the church's ministry is handed down by the laying on of hands, and has come from the apostles through the bishops. Only such ordination is considered valid; the sacraments and other ministrations likewise depend on this succession for their validity. This doctrine is held by the Roman Catholic, Eastern Orthodox, and Anglican churches, and by a few others. Most Protestants reject it, not recognizing the exclusive authority of bishops, or the sole validity of one mode of ordination or consecration, or the limitation of divine grace to this channel.

Originally, the term was not limited to sacramental validity or administrative authority, but guaranteed authentic or authoritative teaching. The succession of the church's teachers was found in the bishops, especially in the great sees, Jerusalem, Antioch, Ephesus, Alexandria, and Rome. In the conflict with Gnosticism in the 2d and 3d centuries, the appeal to tradition was inevitable

and cogent (see GNOSTICISM). As against such new teachings as those of Marcion (who wished to break all connection with Judaism and the Old Testament) and Valentinus (who elaborated a system of *aeons* between the supreme God and the world of men), the orthodox appealed to what had been taught by the predecessors of the bishops in the major sees, and by those preceding them, all the way back to the apostles.

FREDERICK C. GRANT
Union Theological Seminary

APOSTROPHE. See PUNCTUATION.

APOTHEOSIS, ə-poth-e-o′səs, is the act of deifying a human being. The term does not apply to individuals like the Egyptian pharaohs, who were regarded as sons of a god. Apotheosis is illustrated by the ancient Greek practice of elevating the founders of cities and colonies to the status of gods after their deaths. The Romans likewise deified their founder, Romulus. No other Roman was deified until the time of Julius Caesar. Both he and Augustus were worshiped after their deaths. Following the reign of Claudius, apotheosis of the emperor was certain unless he had been corrupt. Domitian was the first emperor to be deified before his death, and Aurelian was the first to claim divinity for himself, using the title *dominus et deus.*

After Christianity became the official religion of the Roman empire, emperors could not be deified. As late as the rule of Valerian, however, emperors were consecrated at their deaths; and *divus,* indicating divinity, was used for centuries as an imperial title.

APPALACHIA, ap-ə-lā′chē-ə, is a region of the eastern United States, mainly in the Appalachian Mountains. The name was coined in 1960 at the Appalachian Governors Conference on unemployment. The states represented were Alabama, Georgia, Kentucky, Maryland, North Carolina, Pennsylvania, South Carolina, Tennessee, Virginia, and West Virginia. Five years later, Congress voted aid to Appalachia, including these 10 states plus Indiana, Ohio, and New York.

The name Appalachia was applied, not to all parts of the states named, but to those poverty-stricken mountainous areas where health, housing, education, and roads were substandard, unemployment was high, and much land was devastated by surface mining. This impoverished area was about the size of Great Britain, with a population of some 15 million. Many of the people were living on welfare payments or government-distributed surplus food. A reduced market for coal, the closing of many mines, and the automation of others had left most of the miners without hope of employment. Poverty was most extreme in isolated hamlets strung out along creeks in the mountains, where even rudimentary roads were costly. Much of the water was polluted by sewage and by sulfuric acid draining from abandoned coal mines.

In 1965, Congress passed the Appalachian Regional Development Act, with planned expenditures of $1.2 billion. About 80 percent of the funds was for a five-year roadbuilding program, and the rest was for hospitals, schools, sewage treatment plants, and land rehabilitation.

Further Reading: Caudill, Harry M., *Night Comes to the Cumberlands* (Boston 1963); Weller, Jack E., *Yesterday's People* (Lexington, Ky., 1965).

PARALLEL RIDGES pierced by rivers like the Susquehanna in Pennsylvania typify sections of the long Appalachian system.

GRANT HEILMAN

APPALACHIAN MOUNTAINS, ap-ə-lā'chən, the principal mountain system of the eastern United States and Canada. Roughly paralleling the Atlantic coast from the island of Newfoundland to central Alabama, the Appalachians are a nearly continuous chain of mountain ranges. Prominent among them are the Newfoundland Long Range Mountains; the Notre Dame and Shickshock mountains on the Gaspé Peninsula, Quebec; the Green, White, and Taconic mountains of New England; the Catskills in New York; the Lehigh and South mountains in Pennsylvania; the Blue Ridge, extending from southern Pennsylvania to Tennessee; and the Great Smoky Mountains on the North Carolina-Tennessee border.

Despite their great length from northeast to southwest, the Appalachian Mountains are a relatively narrow mountain system, rarely exceeding a width of 100 miles (160 km). Nearly parallel to them on the west, from Pennsylvania southwestward, are the even-crested ridges of the Allegheny and Cumberland mountains.

Few areas in the world have such extensive forests of mixed hardwoods and softwoods as the Appalachians. The most colorful of their flowering plants and shrubs are the mountain laurel, flame azalea, and rhododendron. The U.S. government has done much to preserve the natural beauty and wildlife of the Appalachians. Two great national parks are located on Appalachian slopes—Shenandoah, in Virginia, and Great Smoky Mountains. There are also a number of national forests, including those in the White, Green, Allegheny, and Cumberland mountains; Pisgah and Nantahala in North Carolina; and Cherokee in Tennessee and North Carolina. The Appalachian Trail for hikers and campers extends more than 2,000 miles (3,200 km) from Maine to Georgia.

Natural Resources. The Appalachians have the world's largest deposits of asbestos, in Quebec; of anthracite coal, in Pennsylvania; and of bituminous coal, in West Virginia, Pennsylvania, and Kentucky. Asbestos deposits in Vermont make that state the leading United States producer of asbestos. Iron ore is mined extensively in the Appalachian region of New Jersey and Pennsylvania. The best United States marble is quarried in Vermont, Georgia, and Tennessee, and Vermont and Georgia lead in granite production. Semiprecious stones are found in the neighborhood of Asheville and Spruce Pine, in North

Carolina. There are also small deposits of gold, silver, copper, and lead in the Appalachians.

Northern Appalachians. East of the upper Connecticut River valley are the White Mountains of New Hampshire. In Massachusetts and Connecticut this same range has been so subdued by stream erosion and glaciation that the region appears to be an upland. In New Hampshire, for example, Mount Monadnock rises 3,165 feet (965 meters) above sea level, while in Massachusetts, Mount Watatic and Mount Wachusett, true monadnocks (mountains of resistant rocks standing above a plain), with altitudes of about 2,000 feet (610 meters), rise only a few hundred feet above the upland surface. In the Presidential Range in central New Hampshire, the highest mountain is Mount Washington (6,288 feet; 1,920 meters), while Mount Adams, Mount Jefferson, Mount Madison, and Mount Monroe have peaks above 5,000 feet (1,520 meters).

West of the Connecticut Valley in Vermont, Massachusetts, and Connecticut are the old worn-

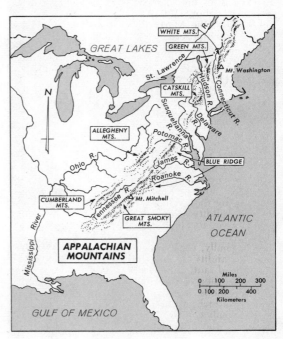

APPALACHIAN MOUNTAINS

109

MT. WASHINGTON, in New Hampshire's White Mountains, is the highest peak in the northern Appalachians.

APPALACHIAN TRAIL in the Great Smokies takes hikers to the heart of the southern Appalachian wilderness.

down mountain ranges known in Vermont as the Green Mountains, a counterpart of the Blue Ridge in the South. In Massachusetts and Connecticut they are called the Berkshire Hills. The general elevation in Vermont ranges from 3,500 to 3,800 feet (1,070–1,160 meters), although Mount Mansfield is 4,393 feet (1,340 meters) high. Mount Greylock in the Berkshire Hills of western Massachusetts has an elevation of 3,491 feet (1,064 meters), although 1,500 to 2,300 feet (460–700 meters) is the general range of elevation for the Berkshires. West of the Berkshires and the Green Mountains and north to Brandon, Vt., are the Taconic Mountains, with heights of 1,800–2,000 feet (550–610 meters).

Southern Appalachians. The Blue Ridge is divided into two parts by the Roanoke River. North of the Roanoke the term "ridge" is descriptive, because at numerous places there is a central ridge with subordinate ridges grouped about it. South of Roanoke, Va., to near Gainesville, Ga., is a prominent scarp called the Blue Ridge Front or Scarp. The crest, with an altitude of 2,500 feet (760 meters) near Roanoke, increases until it is 4,000 feet (1,220 meters) at Blowing Rock, N.C. It then decreases until it is almost 1,000 feet (305 meters) less at Mount Oglethorpe, near Gainesville. Massive mountains and high peaks in Tennessee and North Carolina contrast strongly with the northern Blue Ridge. Mount Mitchell, in North Carolina, is the highest peak in the eastern United States, with an elevation of 6,684 feet (2,040 meters).

The western front of the Blue Ridge province is known as the Unaka Mountains. Included in this group are the Tennessee mountains known as Chilhowee, Stone, Bald, Holston, and Iron. Best known of all are the Great Smoky Mountains on the North Carolina-Tennessee border. Some of the peaks in Tennessee, with their elevations, are Clingmans Dome (6,642 feet; 2,024 meters), Mount Le Conte (6,593 feet; 2,010 meters), and Mount Guyot (6,621 feet; 2,018 meters).

Geology of the Appalachians. Geologic study has shown that the differences in the ages of the rocks of the Appalachians are not as fundamental as was once thought. Rocks previously called Precambrian are now known to be Paleozoic in age. It is more important to divide the rocks into areas of sedimentary and crystalline rock. In the Blue Ridge are found Precambrian metamorphic and igneous rocks and early Paleozoic rocks that are strongly folded, faulted, and metamorphosed. In the Allegheny and Cumberland mountains rocks are sedimentary. They range in age from Lower to Upper Paleozoic. Here carbonate rocks are plentiful, and certain sandstone formations are prominent. In northern West Virginia and adjacent Pennsylvania is an area of Permian rocks.

Wind gaps, formerly water gaps, are important in explaining the geology of the Appalachian ranges. Their depth and distribution may be interpreted as indicating former peneplanation. Examples are Snickers, Ashby, and Manassas gaps south of the Potomac and Cumberland Gap at the juncture of Kentucky, Virginia, and Tennessee.

HAROLD C. AMICK, *University of Tennessee*

Further Reading: Atwood, Wallace W., *Physiographic Provinces of North America* (New York 1940); Brooks, Maurice, *The Appalachians* (New York 1964); Fenneman, Nevin, *Physiography of the Eastern United States* (New York 1948); Thornbury, William D., *Regional Geomorphology of the United States* (New York 1965).

APPALACHIAN TRAIL, ap-ə-lā′chən, in the eastern United States, is a marked footpath for public recreation. It is 2,000 miles (3,200 km) long, crosses 14 states, and stretches from Mount Katahdin, Me., to Springer Mountain, Ga. Designed as a wilderness route, the trail generally follows the crestline of the Appalachian Mountain system. Much of it is on public land; private land is used with consent. In crossing valleys, the trail follows short stretches of roads.

The Appalachian trail is marked by steel plates and white paint on trees and rocks. Side trails provide approaches. Shelters for public use stand at frequent intervals.

The trail was built by volunteers between 1922 and 1937. Maintenance is by groups and individuals. The Appalachian Trail Conference, of Washington, D.C., coordinates the work and publishes guide books and other material.

APPEAL, ə-pēl′, in law, is a complaint to a higher court of an injustice done by a lower one. In English law the earliest meaning of "appeal" was "to accuse." Not until the late 13th century was the term applied to a proceeding to transfer a case to a higher court, there to be tried and decided *de novo* (anew) on newly introduced evidence, without reference to the inferior court's decision.

In modern legal procedure, however, an appeal brings judgments of lower courts or of administrative and other tribunals to a higher court for a review of their correctness. Appellate courts may reverse, modify, or sustain the challenged determination after examining the whole or pertinent parts of the record. The U.S. Supreme Court and other courts of last resort deal primarily with legal, not factual, questions.

Appeal is not an inherent or constitutional right in the United States. An appellate court comes into existence only through constitutional or statutory enactment. Although no state is required by the U.S. Constitution to provide appellate remedies, such remedies are traditional in the Anglo-American legal system.

In the federal judicial system there are intermediate appellate courts and the court of last resort—the U.S. Supreme Court. Although the Constitution vests the Supreme Court with both original and appellate jurisdiction, the former type is rare. The Supreme Court's appellate jurisdiction is under the unlimited discretionary control of the U.S. Congress. Without a federal statute affording review in any specified area, jurisdiction is lacking.

In 1925, with a progressively increasing caseload, the Supreme Court was given discretionary power by Congress to control its appellate functions. Review is by permission only, except for a state statute repugnant to the Constitution, treaties, or laws of the United States, or for an act of Congress held unconstitutional and so reviewable as of right. Neither error nor correctness of decision determines reviewability. The court accepts a case for review "in the interest of the law, its appropriate exposition and enforcement; not in the mere interest of the litigants" (Supreme Court Justice John M. Harlan in *Manning the Dikes*, 1958).

Review by the Supreme Court of a death sentence for a federal offense was a matter of right until abolished by Congress in 1911. The court's present discretionary power was strikingly illustrated in an espionage case, involving the atomic bomb, in which a death sentence was imposed. In *Rosenberg* v. *United States* (1952), the court held that a "sentence imposed by the United States District Court, even though it be a death sentence, is not within the power of this Court to revise."

Yet when a state, though not so required, does create an appellate remedy, the Supreme Court has held that "destitute defendants must be afforded as adequate appellate review as defendants who have money enough to buy transcripts"; to do otherwise would be a denial of "a constitutional right guaranteed by the Fourteenth Amendment" (*Draper* v. *Washington*, 1963).

State appellate court organization and jurisdiction are similar to those of the federal courts, with local variations. The same is generally true of Canada, whose Supreme Court hears appeals from final judgments of the court of last resort in each province.

Appellate courts in the United States are the source of much "judicial legislation," as sweeping and effective in its impact, and often more so, than legislative enactment. Although this judge-made law embodied in precedent is binding and respected, it may be overruled by later judicial decision.

Britain's highest court, the House of Lords, announced in 1966 that it will "depart from a previous decision when it appears right to do so." Until then, judicial precedent was the law of the land and, if wrong, could be remedied only by an act of Parliament.

Britain has no written constitution; the law lords, appointed like other high judges, are entitled to sit in legislative capacity in the House of Lords. When acting as a court they comprise a banc of nine and hear appeals just as does the U.S. Supreme Court.

SAMUEL GOTTLIEB
Member of the New York Bar

Further Reading: Breitel, Charles D., *The Lawmakers*, Benjamin N. Cardozo Lectures (New York 1965); Douglas, William O., *Stare Decisis*, Benjamin N. Cardozo Lectures (New York 1949); Klein, Fannie J., *Judicial Administration and the Legal Profession* (Dobbs Ferry, N.Y., 1963).

APPEL, ap′el, **Karel** (1921–   ), Dutch painter, whose explosive, wildly colorful paintings are in the tradition of American abstract expressionism. He was born in Amsterdam, the Netherlands, on April 25, 1921, and studied there at the Royal Academy of Fine Arts from 1940 to 1943. In 1948 he helped to found the Cobra group of young avant-garde painters from the Low Countries. The group, which included Pierre Alechinsky, "Corneille" (Cornelis Van Beverloo), and Asger Jorn, held exhibitions and published the *Cobra Review*. Appel's work at that time (for example, *Cry of Liberty*, 1948) was already boldly expressionistic but utilized contained forms and representational elements more than did his later work.

After 1950, Appel lived in Paris and exhibited internationally with the School of Paris painters. His work was first seen in the United States in 1954, in an exhibition of younger European artists at New York City's Solomon R. Guggenheim Museum. Appel was awarded the Guggenheim International Award of $10,000 in 1960 for his *Woman with Ostrich* (1957). He painted several important murals, including one in 1958 for UNESCO headquarters in Paris.

APPENDICITIS, ə-pen-də-sīt′əs, is the inflammation of the vermiform appendix, a small pencil-like structure connected with the cecum, the first part of the large intestine. Appendicitis is caused by an obstruction and infection in the appendix and interference with the blood supply there.

As in most types of inflammation, appendicitis occurs in either an acute, subacute, or chronic form. In most instances, appendicitis is acute, developing suddenly and rapidly in a previously undiseased appendix and running a relatively brief course. In subacute appendicitis, the onset is less abrupt and violent, or, after an initial onset of the acute type, the process partially subsides. Chronic inflammation of the appendix is the residual disease following in the wake of untreated but self-controlled acute or subacute appendicitis. The changes in this form of the disease usually are so mild that the individual is not aware of the condition.

Cause. The appendix is a sac four to five inches (10 to 12.7 cm) long and open only at one end. It is made up of the same tissue layers as the large intestine. Its function is not known.

In most cases of appendicitis, the cause of the inflammation is interference with free drainage from the appendix. Inflammation usually develops when the opening through which the appendix communicates with the intestine is obstructed or narrowed. The obstruction causes the pressure to rise in the appendix since more material is being secreted into the appendix (from its lining) than is being absorbed from it. As a result, the increased pressure sets the stage for inflammation. A common obstruction found in cases of acute appendicitis is a small piece of hardened fecal residue. Also, accumulations of lymphoid tissue, which are found in the appendix as in other areas of the intestinal tract, may swell up under certain conditions and obstruct the opening of the appendix. Whatever the basic factors that lead to appendicitis, the inflammation itself is provoked by bacteria that are permitted to invade the wall of the organ.

Symptoms and Nature of Appendicitis. The signs and symptoms of appendicitis are determined by two factors—the type of inflammation (acute, subacute, or chronic) and the location of the appendix.

Type of Inflammation. In acute appendicitis, the victim develops a characteristic stomach ache, followed, shortly after, by nausea and frequently by vomiting. After a variable period of 1 to 12 hours, the diffuse abdominal discomfort changes to a pain localized to a restricted area on the right side of the lower abdomen. At this point, the individual is aware of the localized discomfort if he moves or coughs. A slight elevation of one or two degrees of temperature then may appear. These symptoms may progress to the stage that is described as peritonitis (see *Complications,* below), or improvement will take place with partial or complete recovery.

In the very early stages of acute appendicitis, the appendix, which usually has a pearly white appearance, becomes thickened and reddened. The fatty tissue through which its blood vessels run becomes markedly swollen. As the acute process progresses, the organ becomes more enlarged, and eventually one area becomes dark, indicating the point at which perforation will take place. This rupture leads to the peritonitis.

If these symptoms abate only partially and there is continued but less severe pain, the condition is subacute appendicitis. In this condition, the appendix is walled off from the rest of the peritoneal cavity by the swelling of the adjacent abdominal organs.

Finally, complete recovery may seem to take place; however, the appendix usually does not return to a normal state, and it remains chronically infected in most cases. The symptoms of this chronic type of infection are characteristically ill-defined and difficult to interpret. Commonly, there is mild intermittent pain in the lower abdomen. The appendix itself is scarred and chronically inflamed.

Location of the Appendix. In most people, the appendix is situated normally. Thus when it becomes inflamed, the maximal tenderness is found at a point between the umbilicus and the sharp front edge of the right hip bone. This is known as *McBurney's point,* and localized tenderness in this area usually is characteristic of acute appendicitis.

However, in a considerable number of people, the appendix is located in an abnormal position, and as a result the physical findings as well as the subjective complaints may be altered, making the diagnosis difficult and often confusing. The so-called *retrocecal appendix* is one located behind the cecum. In this position, very pronounced acute inflammation of the appendix may develop with little or no perceptible abdominal tenderness. In fact, the maximum tenderness in these instances may be found in the flank on the right side of the body. In other cases, the appendix is located toward the midline of the abdomen and may rest on the urinary bladder. In this instance, inflammation commonly will be associated with a frequent and urgent desire to urinate, and on urinalysis, pus cells may be discovered in the urine.

Diagnosis. The diagnosis of appendicitis rests principally on physical findings instead of laboratory aids. Although many believe that an elevated white blood cell count is necessary for a diagnosis of appendicitis, this is not true. While the white blood count usually is elevated in appendicitis, an identical elevation may occur in other acute inflammatory conditions within the abdomen. Therefore, the white blood count is significant only when it is correlated with the physical findings as determined by the physician.

In acute appendicitis, the total white blood cell count is elevated to the range of 15,000 to 25,000 per cubic millimeter of blood (7,000 to 8,000 per cu mm is normal). But an increase of

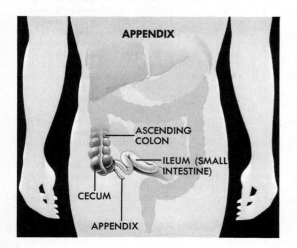

APPENDIX

ASCENDING COLON

ILEUM (SMALL INTESTINE)

CECUM

APPENDIX

immature forms of white cells, better known as "a shift to the left," gives the physician a good index of the severity of the inflammation in appendicitis.

An X-ray of the abdomen is helpful in certain circumstances because it reveals significant changes. In chronic appendicitis, examination of the colon by means of a barium enema often indicates localized tenderness in the region of the appendix.

After a careful diagnostic survey is completed, the diagnosis may remain in doubt in a small percentage of cases. In these instances, the astute physician may withhold a final diagnosis during an observation period of 8 to 24 hours in the hope that further developments may clarify the problem.

In the great majority of cases, the diagnosis of appendicitis is a relatively simple one based on the symptoms described. However, the characteristic symptoms do not develop in about one third of appendicitis cases. For example, diagnosis is difficult in individuals whose appendix is in an abnormal position. Also, there are many acute inflammatory conditions of other organs that may simulate appendicitis. Inflammation of the lymph glands of the mesentery of the small intestine (acute mesenteric adenitis) in young patients is almost indistinguishable from appendicitis because the lymph glands in a child are conspicuous in the region of the intestine where the appendix is located. Disease of the right uterine tube or ovary in the female may be extremely difficult to differentiate from appendicitis because these organs are near the appendix. Inflammatory disease of the end portion of the small intestine (regional enteritis) sometimes is identified for the first time when the patient is operated on with a preoperative diagnosis of acute appendicitis. In the older patient, cancer of the cecum may simulate acute appendicitis. In addition, it may cause appendicitis if the tumor obstructs the intestine where the appendix branches off.

Treatment. The treatment of appendicitis primarily and basically is surgery in which the diseased organ is removed. This operation is called an *appendectomy*.

An appendectomy usually is carried out under general anesthesia. Spinal anesthesia may be preferable under certain circumstances, and there are clinical situations in which local anesthesia using novocaine or a similar agent is employed after appropriate preoperative medication.

When the diagnosis of appendicitis is clear, a small two- to three-inch oblique, muscle-splitting incision is used in the male patients. However, in the female and in instances where the diagnosis is not definite, a larger vertical incision permittng exploration is made. The operation itself consists of tying off the blood vessels that supply the appendix and then removing the appendix.

The operative procedure commonly requires 30 to 45 minutes. The patient has relatively little postoperative discomfort for a period of one to two days and, barring complications, leaves the hospital on the fifth to seventh day.

There are a few instances in which this standard surgical treatment is inadvisable. For example, if appendicitis occurs in a hemophiliac, the danger of uncontrolled bleeding must be weighed against the likelihood that the appendicitis will progress to a fatal stage. An extremely

debilitated, aged person may be such a poor operative risk that treatment with antibiotics is substituted for surgery. In those unusual circumstances in which a surgeon is not available, the patient with acute appendicitis should be treated with antibiotics and other conservative measures rather than undergo surgery by untrained and inexperienced personnel.

When the diagnosis of appendicitis is in doubt, surgery usually is delayed temporarily. While this practice involves the danger that an acute appendicitis will progress to an advanced stage, it ordinarily can be used safely if the individual is under continual medical observation. In such instances, it is a common procedure to place the patient in the hospital where repeated examinations and laboratory tests during a period of 8 to 24 hours may clarify the diagnosis of appendicitis or one of the other conditions mentioned. Under such circumstances, prompt and alert surgical intervention must be undertaken once the diagnosis becomes clear. After a reasonable period of observation, surgery occasionally is undertaken in spite of the fact that the diagnosis remains somewhat clouded.

Removal of the inflamed appendix is as clearly recommended in the case of subacute appendicitis as in acute appendicitis. Also, removal of a chronically diseased appendix ordinarily is indicated. However, this diagnosis must be based on a clear history of one or more previous acute attacks, and the complaints of the individual must be persistent or recurrent.

Complications. The complications of appendicitis may be fatal in neglected cases. These are avoided by prompt removal of the appendix early in the course of the disease. The most feared and lethal complication is perforation of the appendix leading to contamination of the peritoneal cavity and the development of *peritonitis*. Peritonitis is identified by the spreading of the tenderness from a localized area to the entire abdomen. The abdomen becomes distended, the fever becomes more elevated, and the patient appears extremely ill. In the "preantibiotic" days, the majority of these victims died. However, at the present time, the use of antibiotics, even in the far-advanced cases, has reduced this mortality to an extremely small figure. Thus the surgeon can remove the appendix even after it has ruptured, in order to prevent continued contamination of the peritoneal cavity.

Another serious complication is the development of an intraperitoneal abscess. This is the body's method of localizing the products of perforation into a confined area, thereby avoiding infection of the entire peritoneum (peritonitis). Such an abscess develops most commonly in the region near the appendix and is known as a *periappendiceal abscess*. If this abscess does not respond to intensive antibiotic treatment, an operation must be performed to drain it.

A final but extremely lethal complication is that resulting from the spread of the infection of the appendix to the veins that drain the organ. Known as *septic pyelophlebitis*, this infection results in abscesses of the liver. These abscesses often do not respond to specific antibiotic therapy and in many cases terminate fatally.

ROBERT J. COFFEY, M.D.
Georgetown University Hospital

Further Reading: Apley, John, *Child With Abdominal Pains* (Philadelphia 1964); Maingot, Rodney, *Abdominal Operations* (New York 1961).

APPENZELL, ap'ən-zel, is a canton in the northeastern part of Switzerland. Situated in the mountainous, pine-covered country south of Lake Constance, it is surrounded by St. Gallen Canton. Its area is 161 square miles. The first rulers of the region were the abbots of St. Gallen. Later, Appenzell came under the domination of the Habsburgs. The canton fought sporadically for its independence from the 13th century until 1513, when it finally achieved full membership in the Swiss Confederation.

Since 1597, Appenzell has been divided into two portions, or demicantons: Appenzell Ausser Rhoden and Appenzell Inner Rhoden. The more populous and larger Ausser Rhoden is predominantly Protestant; Inner Rhoden is almost entirely Catholic. Although farming remains the basic occupation, textile manufacturing has increased. Inner Rhoden depends on cattle raising. German is the principal language of both areas. Each demicanton is represented in the Federal Assembly, and each has an independent local government, a feature of which is the traditional *Landsgemeinde,* an assembly attended by all male citizens over the age of 20.

The capital of Inner Rhoden is the town of Appenzell which is situated on the Sitter River, seven miles south of St. Gallen. Its famous embroidery and delicate lace work are exhibited at the College of St. Anton. The town has a cobbled main street, a great many timbered houses, and a picturesque central square where the annual meeting of the *Landsgemeinde* of Inner Rhoden is held. Herisau, a textile center and the largest town in Appenzell, is the capital of Ausser Rhoden. Population: (1960) of Ausser Rhoden, 48,920; of Inner Rhoden, 12,943.

APPERT, à-pâr', **Nicolas** (1749–1841), French confectioner and inventor. He was born in Châlons-sur-Marne, France, on Nov. 17, 1749. He is sometimes erroneously called *François Appert.* Appert is renowned as the originator of the modern process of thermal sterilization of foods in sealed containers, which led to the development of the canning industry. He served his apprenticeship as a cook at the Palais Royal Hotel in Châlons and was later employed by the duke and duchess of Deux-Ponts. By about 1780, however, he was settled in Paris and became widely known as the "confectioner of Paris located at Lombard Street."

He soon began to experiment in the preservation of foods of various sorts and eventually obtained from the ministry of the navy authorization to ship the products of his manufacture on board vessels. The certificates of commendation resulting from these experiences attracted official notice with the result that, in 1809, Napoleon I gave Appert a grant of 12,000 francs with the sole stipulation that he make public his invention. In 1810, Appert published *A Book for All Housekeepers, or the Art of Preserving All Kinds of Animal and Vegetable Substances for Several Years.* He was honored as a "benefactor of humanity" and presented with a gold medal by the Société d'Encouragement pour l'Industrie Nationale in 1812. Appert erected a factory at Massy, south of Paris, to exploit his process, but he was ruined during the invasion of France by the armies of the Allies in 1814. The government failed to restore his wrecked properties, and he was virtually a pauper when he died, at Massy, on June 2, 1841. In his declining years he saw the process he invented undergo extensive exploitation in England.

MILTON E. PARKER
Illinois Institute of Technology

APPIAN, ap'ē-ən, was a Greek historian of the 2d century A.D. who compiled a history of the conquests of Rome. His Greek name was *Appianos.* He left Alexandria, his birthplace, after gaining Roman citizenship, and went to Rome where he practiced law.

He may have performed official duties there under the emperors Hadrian (reigned 117–138) and Antoninus Pius (reigned 138–161). Late in life Appian became a procurator, although it may have been only in an honorary capacity.

His history of Rome, *Romaïca,* was written in Greek and covered the various Roman wars from the earliest times to about 70 A.D. Only 10 books of the original 24 survive. The work is chiefly a compilation from earlier writers, but it is nevertheless a valuable source, especially the books dealing with the civil wars (from about 88 to 34 B.C.).

APPIAN WAY, ap'ē-ən, the earliest and best-known of the great military roads of ancient Rome. Publius Papinius Statius, a Roman poet of the 1st century A.D., referred to it as the *longarum regina viarum,* "queen of long-distance roads." Its Latin name was *Via Appia.*

The first portion of the road—132 miles (212 km) from Rome to Capua—was built by the censor Appius Claudius Caecus in 312 B.C. Its initial course was practically straight, cutting southeast across Latium to Tarracina (modern Terracina) on the Tyrrhenian Sea. From there it mostly followed the coast until, on entering Campania, it bore inland to Capua.

By about 240 B.C. the highway had been extended an additional 230 miles (370 km) across the country to Brundisium (modern Brindisi) on the Adriatic Sea. From Capua it ran east to Beneventium (modern Benevento). It then resumed its generally southeasterly course, crossing the provinces of Samnium and Apulia to Tarentum (modern Taranto). There it again veered eastward across the "heel" of Italy to Brundisium. With the completion of branch roads to the major seaports, the Appian Way became the major highway to Greece and the eastern Mediterranean.

So important was the Appian Way to Rome that, under the empire, its repair was administered by a curator of praetorian rank. Excavation indicates that the road had an average width of at least 20 feet (6 meters). The original base consisted of heavy stone blocks, cemented with a lime mortar and laid in such a way as to form a convex surface, in order to insure good drainage. It may, at first, have been covered with gravel, but later it was overlaid with polygonal blocks of lava, expertly fitted together, providing a surface of extraordinary durability. Most of the road was still passable as late as the middle of the 6th century A.D.

In ancient times the northern section of the Appian Way, near Rome, was a select cemetery area with many tombs and monuments and the extensive catacombs the early Christians subsequently used as places of refuge. The principal ruins are the Casale Rotondo, the tomb of Caecilia Metella, and the remains of the villa of the Quintilii.

APPLE BLOSSOMS range in color from pinkish-white to red. They emerge in clusters in late spring.

J.C. ALLEN & SON

APPLE FRUIT is most frequently spherical or ovoid in shape, and ripens in shades of red, yellow, or green.

A. DEVANEY, INC.

APPLE, ap'əl, an edible fruit and the tree on which it grows. Found in the northern temperate zone in both hemispheres, apple trees belong to the rose family, Rosaceae. Their genus is *Malus,* although some botanists consider the apple a subgenus of *Pyrus,* the pear genus. There are about 25 existing species of apple, all of which are descendants of two original forms, *Pyrus malus* and *Pyrus baccata.*

As a rule, the common apple tree is not more than 30 feet (9 meters) tall. Its trunk and branches are crooked and gnarled. Its leaves are short-stemmed. The blossoms emerge in clusters and have permanent calyxes, or sepals. When in leaf, the tree has a symmetrical outline that suggests long domestication. The fruit is usually round, or sometimes oblate or ovoid, and depressed at both ends. It varies in size from two to six inches (5 to 15 cm) in diameter. The pulp is white, crisp, watery, and sweet or sour; its core contains several small brown seeds. The fruit is covered by a thin, glossy (sometimes russet) skin, which, when cut open, yields an agreeable odor. In some varieties this becomes quite pungent.

CULTIVATION

Propagation. New varieties of apples are propagated from seeds, but since seeds rarely improve upon the parent, seedlings are used chiefly to produce stocks for grafting or budding. Standard (that is, natural-sized) trees are so propagated. Dwarf trees result from grafting or budding the standard varieties upon the small-growing, almost bushlike varieties.

Much discussion has arisen concerning the relative advantages of grafting over budding, and also concerning methods of grafting. Opinions in the first case are very conflicting. In the latter they seem to favor the use of a small piece of apple root as stock (that is, the underground part of the graft) and a rather long scion (the shoot or twig that supplies the aerial parts of the graft), which should be set deeply in the soil of nursery or orchard. This procedure ensures the rooting of the scion and produces a tree that draws its nourishment from its own roots instead of from the nondescript roots of the seedling stock. In rigorous climates, hardy va-

rieties are selected upon which to topwork less robust varieties and to increase their hardiness.

When the trees are set out, the tops must be cut back severely, to balance the root lost in transplanting from the nursery and to start the head at the proper height from the ground.

Growers' opinions differ as to the length of trunk an apple tree should have, and also as to whether the main trunk should be allowed to extend above the principal lower limbs. Formerly six feet (1.8 meters) was the usual length of trunk desired, but half that length now is preferred, and in the West Central states even less than that. Most growers agree that a few well-placed main limbs are better than a large number. These should start far enough from one another to avoid the danger of splitting under the load of fruit.

Principal limbs should be made to rebranch near the main trunk. Some of these branches should be trained upward and the others more horizontally, in order to develop a well-rounded, symmetrical top. Also trees with short bodies and low heads are less likely to be injured by wind and sunscald than those with high heads and long bodies. Four or five years are needed to establish the desired characteristics.

Soils and Fertilizers. Apples thrive in nearly all kinds of soils, certain varieties being better adapted to light soils and others to heavy. The great majority of varieties succeed best in medium or clayey loams, especially if the terrain is somewhat elevated, inclined or rolling, and the climate is clear and dry. Since air and water drainage are usually good in such places, the fruit produced is generally of fine color, flavor, and size. In lowlands and in damp climates the fruit is usually of inferior quality and the trees more susceptible to fungous attacks.

The preparation of the land does not differ materially from that for other crops such as corn or potatoes, either of which is often grown the previous season in order to fit the land for planting the orchard. The trees may be set out in spring or autumn, and the cost of cultivation may be met by cropping the land for the first few years with potatoes, melons, or some other low-growing, intertilled crop.

Nitrogen occupies a more important place in

orchard fertilizers than any of the other nutrient elements. Many apple orchards have grown to maturity and produced heavy crops when nitrogen was the only fertilizer applied. However, the value of potash, phosphate, magnesium, and other essential elements has more recently been shown in certain restricted areas.

Orchards in permanent sod or nonlegume cover crops require heavier fertilization than those in cultivation or in legume cover crops. If cover crops such as clover, vetches, or cowpeas are grown, they will supply all the nitrogen needed. Indeed, if such crops are long continued or if several very heavy crops are turned under, too much nitrogen may accumulate and recourse to a cereal crop may be necessary to remove the excess. Lack of nitrogen is indicated by pale green or yellowish foliage.

Harvesting. As the fruit ripens, the starch it contains becomes changed into sugar, the leaf green is replaced by tints characteristic of the variety, and the flow of sap into the fruit diminishes until the apple has attained full size and weight. Since the changes that subsequently take place are mainly chemical and continue independently of the tree, the fruit may be picked. Fruitgrowers agree upon this time, which they determine for each variety from experience. The fruits are still hard but have brown seeds, and having reached the proper development, may be picked by slightly twisting the stem without danger of breaking the twig upon which it is borne, thus preventing a loss of fruit-bearing wood. Fruits gathered at this time and ripened properly are superior to those allowed to hang longer upon the tree.

Apples should be stored as soon as possible after picking. The temperature should be kept uniform, just above 32° F (0° C), so as to check the ripening process. Drafts should be avoided, since they hasten decay and increase shriveling; hence closed packages are better than shelves. Odors should be excluded.

Apple Pests. Several hundred insects feed upon the apple, but most of them are so well controlled by their enemies or by natural checks that their injuries seldom are noticed. There are however, many insects that can be destructive. The following are the most common.

(1) Codlin moth (*Carpocapsa pomonella*) is perhaps the best known and most widely distributed apple pest. Its eggs are laid upon the fruit, and the larvae almost invariably enter the calyx, burrow through the flesh, and cause premature ripening. Since two or even three broods are produced in a season, the destruction of the first by spraying is of prime importance. This spraying must be done before the calyx closes, because the caterpillar's first meal must be poisoned.

(2) Apple maggot (*Rhagoletis pomonella*), the footless grub (⅕ inch [1.3 mm] long) of a two-winged fly, tunnels in the fruit and is especially troublesome in New York and New England. It attacks thin-skinned summer and autumn varieties.

(3) San José scale (*Aspidiotus perniciosus*) is a minute scale insect of enormous prolificacy which is found upon many species of woody plants. When full-grown it so closely resembles some of its relatives that a microscopic examination is necessary to determine its identity. When abundantly infested, the twigs have a somewhat scurvy appearance resembling a coating of ashes. The young appear from beneath the female scale,

crawl to a new feeding ground, fix themselves, and reproduce with great rapidity. It has been estimated from careful records of close observations that more than 3,000,000,000 scales may be produced in a single season from one female.

(4) Cankerworm is the larva of any one of certain moth species (*Anisopteryx* and *Paleacrita*), most common in the northeastern United States and adjoining Canada. The caterpillars attack the leaves of apple, pear, and some other trees, causing complete defoliation when infestation is especially abundant. The wingless females crawl up the trunks and lay their eggs upon twigs or bark. The larvae (measuring-worms) appear shortly after the foliage appears. When disturbed, they drop at the ends of silk threads; if they reach the ground they climb the trunk to resume feeding. Pupation occurs in the ground.

(5) Tent caterpillars, the larvae of a moth (*Clisiocampa americana*), attack various trees in a large part of the United States and Canada. The eggs are deposited in gluey-looking masses upon the twigs in summer and hatch in early spring. The larvae are gregarious, and spin a protective web from which they emerge to feed. When numerous they can strip the tree of foliage.

(6) Webworm (*Hyphantria cunea*) is a caterpillar similar in habits to the preceding, except that it encloses the foliage upon which it feeds inside a web. When nearly full-grown, the larvae disperse. The eggs are laid by the moth in late spring upon the undersides of leaves near the tips of branches of many trees. Bushes and even clover are also hosts.

(7) The round-headed and the flat-headed borers are serious pests. They bore into the young wood, the latter mainly near the ground in the trunk, the former more frequently in the larger limbs. They are the larvae of two beetles (respectively, *Saperda candida* and *Chrysobothris femorata*). Their presence is indicated by the presence of chiplike castings at the mouth of their burrows.

(8) Woolly aphis (*Schizoneura lanigera*), in England and Australia often called American blight, is a serious pest, especially upon young trees. Two forms of this insect appear: one above ground and the other upon the roots. The former, readily recognized by its woolly appearance, is controlled easily; the latter is hard to fight without injuring the trees. Tobacco dust worked into the ground seems to be the most effective and least harmful remedy. Nursery stock should always be carefully examined for this pest and treated, if necessary, before being planted.

(9) Bud moth (*Tmetocera ocellana*) is another apple pest. The larvae of this tiny insect appear in midsummer, pass the winter in the larval state, and in early spring, attack the opening buds and young leaves, over which they weave a little web.

(10) *Aphis fomi*, the green-apple leaf aphis, injures the leaves of young trees and stunts the growth of the fruit. It can be controlled by spraying with lime-sulfur solution in February or March, and by various insecticides, especially nicotine solutions, later on.

(11) Various caterpillars, especially the tent caterpillar, that of the gypsy moth (q.v.), and that of the brown-tail moth also are serious apple pests. The caterpillars of *Tmetocera ocelana* and *Eccopsis malana* attack the flower buds.

CHARACTERISTICS OF LEADING AMERICAN APPLES

Variety	Color	Main Food Uses	Some Common Apple Shapes		
BALDWIN	Medium Red	Culinary, Processing	**OBLATE** McINTOSH RHODE ISLAND GREENING		**SPHERICAL** BALDWIN JONATHAN ROME BEAUTY
BEN DAVIS	Striped, Medium Red	Culinary, Processing			
DELICIOUS	Medium Red	Dessert and Juice			
JONATHAN	Deep Red	Dessert and Freezing			
McINTOSH	Medium Red	Dessert			
NORTHERN SPY	Striped, Dull Red	Culinary, Dessert, and Processing			
RHODE ISLAND GREENING	Green Yellow	Culinary, Processing	**CONICAL** DELICIOUS WINESAP		**OVOID** BEN DAVIS NORTHERN SPY STAYMAN WINESAP
ROME BEAUTY	Medium Red	Culinary			
STAYMAN WINESAP	Dark Red	Culinary, Dessert			
WINESAP	Dark Red	Culinary, Dessert			

(12) The pear thrips also attack the blossoms.

(13) The plum curculio, *Conotrachelus menuphar,* attacks the fruit, and is controllable by the same methods as the codlin moth.

(14) The green-fruit worm (*Xyliner*) eats a cavity out of the side of the apple.

(15) Spider mites of the general family Tetranychidae recently have become extremely destructive orchard pests, and their control demands careful timing of miticide applications.

(16) The red-banded leaf roller, *Argyrotaenia velutinana,* has become important since the advent of certain organic insecticides that have reduced the number of natural parasites of this insect. See also INSECTICIDE.

Mice and rabbits are likely to damage young trees during the winter months, especially when the ground is covered with snow and food is difficult to find.

Apple Diseases. Apple scab (*Fusicladium dendriticum*) is probably the most serious apple disease, since it causes the loss of much fruit and injures the appearance of much more. It appears as black spots with grayish border on apples and pears that have not been sprayed. Often the abundance of the confluent spots prevents the normal development of the fruit, which becomes lopsided. The leaves are also attacked, but the markings are not so pronounced.

Rust (*Roestelia pirata*) appears upon the foliage in early summer as more or less confluent orange spots. The fruit is also destroyed. The spores of this fungus will not germinate upon the apple but find a congenial host in the juniper or cedar. These, when matured in the following spring, look something like orange-yellow sponge. The spores will not germinate upon the cedar, but will upon the apple. Sometimes the fungus perpetuates itself by its mycelium (branching filaments), which may live from year to year upon the young twigs and buds of the apple. Destruction of the cedars and spraying are effective.

Apple canker (*Nectria ditissima*) destroys the bark and younger wood, and eventually the tree, but small areas may be cut out and the wounds painted with Bordeaux mixture. In fact, since this disease gains entrance through wounds, these should all be similarly treated. Burning badly infested trees is the only means of checking the spread of this disease.

Powdery mildew (*podosphaera oxycanthae*), a grayish growth upon the foliage, is often troublesome in the South upon young trees and seedlings in the nursery. It may readily be controlled by a standard fungicide. Bitter rot (*Glomorella rufomasulans*) appears upon the fruit as brown spots extending until they often involve the whole apple. It may attack at any time and is especially destructive to the early varieties, more in the South than in the North.

Black rot (*Sphaeropsis malorum*) resembles bitter rot and is similarly controlled.

Two important bacterial pests are pear blight (*Bacillus amylavorus*), which causes cankers on the limbs and trunks, and crown gall (*Bacterium tumifaciens*), causing swellings on the trunk and roots just below the surface of the ground. Oregon canker is *Neofabraen malicorticis.*

COMMERCIAL ASPECTS

Commercial Varieties. In deciding which varieties of apples to raise for the commercial market, professional fruit growers take into consideration certain qualities in addition to the factor of anticipated yield. Obviously, all of the qualities described cannot be found highly developed in one variety.

Important qualities that the fruit itself should have are richness, which is dependent on the proportion of sugar to acid, and flavor, which is dependent on small quantities of a volatile oil. Firmness or sponginess, crispness or hardness, tenderness or softness, meltingness or juiciness are qualities related to the apple's cell structure.

Maturity (the variety should be ready to harvest at the same time) and firm adherence to the tree are qualities the grower must consider. Important in grading and handling the fruit are form, size and uniformity, smoothness and toughness of the skin, and good keeping qualities. Color and the culinary qualities of the fruit are important in the general market.

Grafting and long domestication have resulted in several hundred varieties. Even in Pliny's time, nearly 2,000 years ago, there were 22 varieties known to the Romans, many of them taking the name of the cultivator, a custom which prevails to the present day.

Varieties held in the highest esteem in the United States are: Delicious, Golden Delicious, McIntosh, Stayman Winesap, Jonathan, Grimes Golden, Wealthy, Gravenstein, Rome Beauty, Yellow Newtown, Winesap, Summer Rambo, Lodi, Yellow Transparent, Esopus Spitzenberg, York Imperial, Courtland, and Baldwin.

A matter of importance in the selection of varieties of apples is the determination of the fertility of the blossoms. Sterility is indicated by annual dropping of the fruit. It may result from one or a combination of the following causes: impotence of the pollen or the pistils (female organ) or the premature ripening of one or the other, and injuries to the blossoms by fungous attacks, rain, frost, or continued cool weather, or other causes more or less beyond the grower's control. On the other hand, sterility often results from impotence of the pollen to fertilize the pistil of the same variety. This type of sterility is noticed when trees stand singly or in blocks of one variety remote from other varieties. This may be prevented by having varieties that blossom at the same time planted in proximity, usually in alternate rows through the orchard, or by grafting such varieties in orchards already set.

A practice resulting from the problem of sterility and of the varying maturity of varieties with respect to fruit-bearing is the planting of "filler" trees in permanent orchards. The fillers are quick-maturing varieties of usually upright growth and small size. They are set alternately with the slower-growing, more-spreading permanent trees and cut out when crowding seems to threaten. For such practice four varieties usually are selected—two fillers and two permanents, each pair blossoming at the same time. Each pair is placed alternately with the other and each member of the pair alternately with its partner. Trees in such orchards often are planted 28 feet (8.5 meters) apart on the diagonal, so that when the fillers are removed the permanents will be left in rectangles of about 40 feet (12.2 meters), the usual distance recommended for large-growing varieties. Some growers plant as close as 30 feet (9.2 meters), but this is too close except for trees of small growth. No other tree fruit should be planted in an apple orchard, because no two fruits demand the same treatment, and where two are planted, one or the other, perhaps both, suffer. See also ORCHARD.

Production. World apple production varies greatly from year to year. In some years it falls to half the average annual output; in others it doubles. France, Germany, Italy, and the United States are the leading apple-growing countries, but their relative rank may change annually because of growing conditions or other factors.

APPLE PRODUCTION IN SPECIFIED COUNTRIES

	Annual average 1940–1949 (bushels)	Annual average 1950–1959 (bushels)	1960 (bushels)
Argentina	6,934,000	15,436,000	19,047,000
Australia	11,454,000	11,106,000	13,562,000
Austria	11,959,000	14,847,000	20,500,000
Belgium-Luxembourg	7,853,000	11,100,000	9,075,000
Canada	14,139,000	14,806,000	14,914,000
Denmark	5,948,000	9,471,000	12,070,000
France	104,122,000	157,170,000	239,699,000
Germany, West	...	59,476,000	114,316,000
Italy	17,430,000	50,678,000	84,151,000
Japan	9,628,000	26,494,000	40,239,000
Netherlands	6,750,000	14,005,000	17,683,000
Spain	5,851,000	10,528,000	12,038,000
Sweden	4,987,000	8,308,000	13,274,000
Switzerland	22,827,000	19,474,000	22,046,000
Turkey	3,840,000	6,600,000	9,186,000
United Kingdom	20,435,000	27,216,000	35,746,000
United States	109,793,000	111,848,000	108,515,000
Yugoslavia	8,339,000	7,947,000	7,527,000

Source: U.S. Department of Agriculture, *Agricultural Statistics*.

In the United States, apples are grown commercially in about 35 states, from the eastern seaboard to the Pacific coast. The five leading states—Washington, New York, Michigan, Virginia, and California—together produce about 65 percent of the national crop.

Over 10-year intervals, apple production tends to average about 110 million bushels annually, but crops of 135 million bushels are not unusual in individual years. Almost 70 percent of the crop is sold fresh; the rest is canned, dried, frozen, or converted into apple juice, cider, or vinegar.

UNITED STATES APPLE PRODUCTION

	Annual average 1940–1949 (bushels)	Annual average 1950–1959 (bushels)	1960 (bushels)
TOTALS	109,793,000	111,848,000	108,515,000
California	7,960,000	8,481,000	8,890,000
Colorado	1,511,000	1,154,000	800,000
Connecticut	1,206,000	1,323,000	1,050,000
Idaho	1,782,000	1,412,000	500,000
Illinois	3,117,000	2,403,000	2,100,000
Indiana	1,292,000	1,461,000	1,900,000
Maryland	1,441,000	1,268,000	1,300,000
Massachusetts	2,537,000	2,557,000	2,250,000
Michigan	6,850,000	10,260,000	11,300,000
Missouri	1,213,000	922,000	1,250,000
New Jersey	2,455,000	2,866,000	2,500,000
New York	14,007,000	17,525,000	17,500,000
North Carolina	893,000	1,490,000	2,500,000
Ohio	3,598,000	3,188,000	3,700,000
Oregon	2,788,000	2,260,000	1,800,000
Pennsylvania	7,168,000	6,955,000	7,000,000
Virginia	9,331,000	9,743,000	10,200,000
Washington	28,469,000	24,100,000	19,500,000
West Virginia	3,779,000	4,744,000	4,700,000

Source: U.S. Department of Agriculture, *Agricultural Statistics*.

The value of the commercial apple crop in the United States averaged about $235 million yearly in the 1960's. It generally exceeds that of any fruit crop except oranges.

Uses. When eaten raw, the apple is used as common food or as dessert at meals. It can be baked, roasted, stewed or boiled, or made into marmalades, jellies, tarts, pies, puddings, cakes, preserves, sauces, apple butter, Chinese chop suey, or French *raisiné*. The expressed juice of selected apples forms a sparkling sweet cider, much esteemed and commonly drunk wherever the apple grows. Very strong cider is made by separating the water from the fermented juice. This is sometimes done by freezing, and skimming off the ice. Verjuice is a product of the crab apple, *P. baccata*. Apples, when pared, cut, and dried in the sun, afford an excellent substance for pies and sauces.

Applewood is of fine grain and hard enough, when stained black, to pass for ebony. It is used in the manufacture of furniture, shoe lasts, small cogwheels, and buttons, and for Oriental imitations of olive wood. It is also excellent for use in the smoking of meats.

Dwarf apple trees sometimes are cultivated simply for ornament, forming very beautiful hedges when judiciously selected with regard to color of blossoms and fruit. They are also planted when a variety of fruit is required to be produced in a narrow space. Many varieties grafted on the wild crab seedling grow successfully and become dwarfed. The French paradise apple, a small variety, dwarfs other varieties grafted upon it. It is less dwarf than the crab and more dwarf than the Daucain or English paradise stock, another stock in common use for this purpose. The dwarfing of trees is carried to an astonishing extreme in China and Japan, where trees not more than a single foot high are produced and kept in flowerpots holding scarcely more than a quart. In England, France, and the Low Countries, apples are trained not only as dwarfs but more commonly as espaliers (trees trained to grow flat against a wall or trellis) and balloon-shaped trees.

Byproducts. Low-grade or inferior apples (culls) may be used in more ways than the culls of any other fruit crop, and each product finds a ready market, mainly at home. The better specimens are usually evaporated, and their cores and peelings are either utilized for cider making or, more frequently, dried and shipped to Europe for the manufacture of certain kinds of champagne and other wines. The canning of fresh apples has become an important industry, especially in the eastern United States. The others usually are made into cider, which in turn may be used to make jelly, applejack (apple brandy, a distilled liquor), or vinegar. When cider and apples are mixed and boiled with or without sugar the product is called marmalade, and if spices are added, apple butter. The pomace (as crushed fruit is called, especially after expression of the juice) is washed to obtain the seeds, which are dried and used for planting. See also FRUIT; FRUIT GROWING; FRUIT INDUSTRY.

Origin and Antiquity. The apple tree appears in the mythology, traditions, history, and archaeology of the most ancient nations. It is mentioned in the Bible, the Hindu *Code of Manu,* the Egyptian *Book of the Dead,* and Hesiod's *Theogony* (vs. 215). Its charred remains have been found in mud of the prehistoric lake dwellings of Europe, and it is represented in some of the most ancient stone carvings. It is mentioned in the earliest annals of China, Babylon, Phrygia, and Egypt.

Relying upon its hybrid origin, some horticulturists have assigned its origin to the Caucasus, where *P. malus* and *P. baccata* are most likely to have become associated. This theory, however, is contested by others, who advance many reasons for its origin in Asia Minor. However, all agree that the habitat of *P. baccata* is the Caucasus. There also are *baccata* that, unless they came from the Caucasus, are indigenous to America. Such are *P. ioensis,* or Prairie crab, and *P. coronaria,* or Eastern crab. The latter is a sweet-scented fruit about three fourths of an inch (1.9 cm) in diameter, which once grew wild in all the Northern and Middle states. The tree is about 15 to 20 feet (4.6 to 6.1 meters) high, with light-green leaves and rose-colored blossoms, which appear in May. This plant is now cultivated in many states. There is also the *P. rivularis,* with yellow-red fruit about the size of a cherry, native to the northern Pacific region, and the *P. angustifolia* of the Allegheny range. Both of them are native to North America.

C.P. HARLEY
United States Plant Industry Station

Further Reading: Gardner, Victor R., and others, *Fundamentals of Fruit Production,* 3d ed. (New York 1952); Shoemaker, James S., and Teskey, Benjamin, *Tree Fruit Production* (New York 1959); Tukey, H.B., *Dwarfed Fruit Trees* (New York 1964); U.S. Department of Agriculture, *Agricultural Statistics* (Washington, annually).

APPLE BRANDY. See APPLEJACK.

APPLE CIDER. See CIDER.

APPLEGATE, ap'əl-gāt, **Jesse** (1811–1888), American surveyor and rancher, who pioneered in the settlement of Oregon. He was born on July 5, 1811, in Kentucky. In 1821 he moved with his family to Missouri, where, having studied mathematics and surveying, he became a surveyor.

In 1843 he joined the "great emigration" of more than 900 persons to Oregon. As owner of one of the largest herds he was made commander of the slow-moving "cow column" (comprising 1,800 cattle), which he guided safely to its destination. He recorded this trek in a Western classic, *A Day with the Cow Column in 1843* (published with *Recollections of My Boyhood,* ed. by Joseph Schafer, 1934). A gifted writer, he influenced public opinion in later years with newspaper articles and correspondence.

Applegate settled in the Willamette Valley and, having proved his capacity for leadership on the westward migration, was elected in 1845 to the legislative committee of Oregon's provisional government, which ruled Oregon until it became a U.S. territory in 1849. He obtained the British Hudson's Bay Company's support of the provisional government, which brought political unity to the area for the first time. In 1845 he also led a group that opened up a southern route into Oregon.

In 1849, Applegate settled on a large cattle ranch in the Umpqua Valley of southern Oregon. After surveying and exploring much of the region, he promoted the construction of the Oregon and California railroad.

Applegate, a Republican, helped secure Abraham Lincoln's election to the presidency in 1860 and strongly supported the Union cause during the Civil War. He died in Oregon on April 22, 1888.

APPLEJACK, ap'əl-jak, is the name given in the United States to apple brandy. In France, the only other country where brandy distilled from apples is a popular drink, it is called *calvados.* It receives its name from the department of Calvados in Normandy, a center of French apple production.

The juice of special cider apples is extracted by grinding and pressing. It is fermented into hard cider and distilled. In the United States, the distillation takes place in large stills where the process is continuous. French distillers use the small pot still. The distilled liquor is stored in wooden casks for aging.

Applejack is sold after it has aged from 2 to 5 years. Calvados usually is aged for 10 years. The bottled drink in the United States is about 100 proof. In France the beverage is about 90 proof.

APPLESEED, Johnny. See CHAPMAN, JOHN.

APPLETON, ap'əl-tən, **Daniel** (1785–1849), American publisher, who, with his son William Henry Appleton, founded the firm of D. Appleton and Company, which was later renamed Appleton-Century-Crofts, Inc.

He was born at Haverhill, Mass., on Dec. 10, 1785. He operated a general store in Haverhill and then moved the business to Boston and began to import merchandise, including books, from England. In 1826 he moved again, this time to New York City, where he encouraged his son William to build up the store's book department.

In 1831 the Appletons began publishing books and in 1838 entered into a partnership under the name D. Appleton and Company. The first books of the new enterprise were primarily devotional or inspirational in character, but the firm later published general works of literature, textbooks, and reference books, including the popular *Appleton's Cyclopedia of Biography*. Daniel retired from business in 1848 and died at New York City on March 27, 1849. *Portrait of a Publisher*, Grant M. Overton's life of Daniel Appleton, was published in 1925.

WILLIAM HENRY APPLETON (1814–1899), Daniel's son, was born at Haverhill, Mass., on Jan. 27, 1814. After his father's retirement from the family business in 1848, William formed a partnership with his brothers to continue the house of D. Appleton and Company. William was especially interested in international copyright law and was president of the American Publishers Copyright League in 1887. He died at New York City on Oct. 19, 1899.

APPLETON, ap'əl-tən, **Sir Edward Victor** (1892–1965), British physicist and discoverer of the ionosphere, who received the 1947 Nobel Prize "for his work on atmospherical physics."

Appleton was born at Bradford, Yorkshire, on Sept. 6, 1892. He attended St. John's College, Cambridge, where he was a pupil of J.J. Thomson and Ernest Rutherford. After serving in World War I he returned to Cambridge, where he devoted himself to research on radio waves. In 1924 he was appointed professor of physics at the University of London. In 1936 he returned to Cambridge as professor of natural philosophy, but with the outbreak of World War II in 1939 he gave up this appointment to enter government service as secretary of the Department of Scientific and Industrial Research. In this capacity he administered Britain's development of the atomic bomb.

A series of experiments that he had begun in 1924 proved the existence of the ionosphere, the reflecting layer of the atmosphere about 60 miles (97 km) above ground. This discovery led to a great development of radio research. In 1926 he discovered another layer 150 miles (240 km) above ground, named at first the Appleton Layer, but later called the F_1 and F_2 layers of the ionosphere. (The original layer is called the E layer.) Further research to determine the height of reflecting layers of the ionosphere provided the basis for radar, which was developed a few years later by British scientists.

In 1927 Appleton was elected a fellow of the Royal Society, and in 1941 he was created a knight commander of the Order of the Bath. He was president of the Radio Industry Council from 1955 to 1957, and was principal of Edinburgh University from 1949 until his death at Edinburgh on April 21, 1965.

APPLETON, ap'əl-tən, **Nathan** (1779–1861), American businessman, banker, and politician, who contributed significantly to developing the American textile industry after the embargo on British imports during the War of 1812. Success in textile manufacture, he felt, depended on the use of power machinery, cheap female labor, and a separate selling organization. He served in Congress from Boston (1831–1833 and 1842) and drafted the protective tariff bill for President John Quincy Adams in 1832. As a banker, he favored a national bank—but with limited capital —in opposition to President Andrew Jackson. Another critical issue of his time—slavery—he dismissed as a local problem, but he argued against Southern secession.

Appleton was born in New Ipswich, N.H., on Oct. 6, 1779. Although he prepared for Dartmouth College, he entered the textile business instead. He was in partnership first with his brother Samuel and then in 1809 with his brother Eben. Their mills helped build the cities of Lowell and Lawrence, Mass., and Manchester, N.H. Appleton died in Boston on July 14, 1861, five days after his daughter, wife of the poet Henry Wadsworth Longfellow, was accidentally burned to death.

APPLETON, ap'əl-tən, is a city in eastern Wisconsin, on the Fox River, 105 miles (169 km) northwest of Milwaukee by road. The city is situated in a rich dairying and farming section. The rapid Fox River, including a 33-foot fall within the city limits, generates power for local needs and for an extensive public utilities service in the surrounding area.

Appleton is an industrial city and an educational center. It manufactures paper and paper products, wood products, farm machinery, knit and canned goods, and building materials. It is the seat of Lawrence University and two affiliated schools: the Lawrence Conservatory of Music and the Institute of Paper Chemistry. The latter's Dard Hunter Paper Museum has a collection devoted to the history of paper making.

Appleton was settled about 1833, incorporated in 1853, and became a city in 1857. A hydroelectric plant, believed to have been the first in the world, began operation there on Sept. 30, 1882, and a replica of it may still be seen. The city has a mayor-council form of government. Population: 57,143.

APPLIED PSYCHOLOGY. See PSYCHOLOGY, APPLIED.

APPLING, ap'ling, **Lucius (Luke) Benjamin** (1907–   ), American baseball player, who played a record 2,218 games at shortstop in a 20-year major league career with the Chicago White Sox. His durability, together with two batting championships and a .310 lifetime average, led to his election to the National Baseball Hall of Fame in 1964.

Appling was born in High Point, N.C., on April 2, 1907. After two years at Oglethorpe University, he signed with his hometown team, Atlanta of the Southern Association, in 1930. Chicago called him up in September of that year. By 1932 he was the regular shortstop for the White Sox, a position he filled for the next 18 years, with time off for military service.

In 1936 Appling won the American League batting title with a .388 average and in 1943 with a .328 average. During his playing career he became known for two unusual traits. He had an uncanny ability to hit foul balls, upsetting many pitchers by making them work harder and longer to dispose of him. He also complained frequently of imaginary ailments earning him the nickname "Old Aches and Pains."

Retiring as a player in 1950, Appling managed at Memphis and Richmond in the minor leagues and later coached for several major league teams.

BILL BRADDOCK, *New York "Times"*

APPOGGIATURA, ə-pôj-ə-tōōr′ə, in music, a grace note or embellishment affecting both harmony and melody. It is an ornamental note removed from the principal note usually by one scale degree above or below it.

The word comes from the Italian *appoggiare* (to lean upon). In older music the appoggiatura was almost always written as a smaller note, but in modern usage it sometimes appears as an ordinary notation. The appoggiatura has one half or more of the rhythmical value of the principal note, and the time required to play the appoggiatura is subtracted from the value of the principal note.

There are three main types of appoggiatura: long, short, and double. In the first, the accent falls on the appoggiatura itself. In the second, the accent is on the principal note. The double appoggiatura consists of two notes, written as sixteenths. One is usually below the principal note and may be any scale degree removed from it; the other is above the principal note and always one scale degree removed.

APPOMATTOX COURT HOUSE, ap-ə-mat′əks, the former seat of Appomattox County, is in south central Virginia, 68 miles (109 km) west of Richmond. It was the scene of the surrender, on April 9, 1865, of Gen. Robert E. Lee of the Confederate Army of Northern Virginia to Union Gen. Ulysses S. Grant in the American Civil War. The site now is included in the Appomattox Court House National Historical Park (972 acres, or 400 hectares).

Lee evacuated Petersburg, Va., where his army had been besieged for 10 months, on the night of April 2. He headed west, hoping to turn south and join the army of Gen. Joseph E. Johnston in North Carolina. Union forces followed, and the cavalry, led by Gen. Philip H. Sheridan, blocked his path at Jetersville. The Confederates lost heavily in engagements at Sailor's Creek (April 6) and Farmville (April 7). Lee concentrated his dwindling troops at Appomattox Court House on April 8, and the next morning there was a brief fight at Appomattox Station. Surrounded by overwhelming numbers, Lee agreed to surrender.

Lee and Grant signed the terms of surrender in the farmhouse of Wilmer McLean. Three days later Lee said farewell to his troops, and the 28,631 soldiers of his army laid down their arms and were paroled to their homes. The capitulation virtually ended the war, although scattered Confederate units held out for some time.

The area was established as a national historical monument in 1940 and as a national historical park in 1954. The park includes a restoration of the McLean house. The original was demolished in 1893.

Further Reading: Catton, Bruce, *A Stillness at Appomattox* (Garden City, N.Y., 1953; Davis, Burke, *To Appomattox: 9 April Days, 1865* (New York 1959).

APPONYI, op′pō-nyē, **Count Albert György** (1846–1933), Hungarian statesman. As minister of education in 1906–1910 he was responsible for legislation designed to Magyarize the children of non-Magyar nationalities, and his name became synonymous with oppression of minorities.

Apponyi was born in Vienna, Austria, on May 29, 1846. He served in the Hungarian parliament from 1872 to 1932 and, as a member of the Independence party, was chosen speaker of the

BRUCE ROBERTS FROM RAPHO-GUILLUMETTE

APPOMATTOX COURT HOUSE: The McLean house, scene of Lee's Civil War surrender, has been reconstructed.

lower house in 1901. His scholarship, commanding presence, and extraordinary facility for language made him an outstanding figure in Hungarian political life.

After Hungary's defeat in World War I, Apponyi headed the delegation that accepted the Treaty of Trianon (1920), which stripped Hungary of 71 percent of its land. He spent the rest of his life trying to have the treaty revised and promoting world peace. He represented Hungary at the League of Nations and at the Geneva conference (1932–1933) on armament limitation. He died in Geneva, Switzerland, Feb. 7, 1933.

ARTHUR J. MAY, *The University of Rochester*

APPONYI, op′ō-nyē, **Count György** (1808–1899), Hungarian political leader. He was born at Eberhard, Hungary, on Dec. 29, 1808. He belonged to one of the most prominent patrician families of Hungary, although he was the first of his branch of the family to attain public importance. As a young man he devoted himself to local administration, and in 1839 he was elected to the National Assembly. He championed the interests of the Croatian minority in Hungary and also of the Habsburg crown.

In 1844 he was appointed Hungarian court chancellor and took up residence in Vienna. Though he favored gradual constitutional reform for Hungary, he opposed the more radical currents which exploded in the revolution of 1848–1849. At that point he withdrew from public life, returning a decade later as an advocate of home rule for Hungary. He played a minor role in the negotiations that culminated in the *Ausgleich* (Compromise) of 1867, whereby Hungary gained autonomy in domestic affairs. Apponyi died at Eberhard on March 1, 1899.

ARTHUR J. MAY, *The University of Rochester*

APPORTIONMENT is the manner in which representation is assigned to the electoral districts, regions, states, or other subdivisions of a country or territory. A distinction should be made between apportionment, the electoral system, and the districting process. *Apportionment* is the manner in which representation is distributed; the *electoral system* is the way in which the representative is elected; and the *districting process* establishes the precise electoral boundaries of his district. Confusion sometimes arises because the three processes are frequently accomplished by the same statute, and the term "apportionment" is used loosely to cover all of them.

Two major principles govern modern apportionment practices. One is the assembly tradition of assigning equal value to the vote of each free citizen, which prevailed among such diverse peoples as the Iroquois of North America and the Greeks of the Athenian city-state. The other is the heritage derived from the royal courts and king's councils of medieval Europe, which were based on classes or estates. In the legislatures of nations that possess a long tradition of continuous representative government, such as Britain, vestiges of both principles may be discerned. Likewise, such bodies as the United States Senate are outgrowths of the king's council tradition, just as the House of Representatives is primarily of the assembly tradition. Newer nations, or those that have undergone successive revolutions, have adopted various apportionment formulas, which often are unrelated to national traditions but are used to meet prevailing conditions.

In general, four main criteria are employed in the distribution of membership in a legislative body: (1) representation on the basis of population, either on an exactly equal basis or in a specifically weighted manner; (2) representation by ethnic, national, occupational, educational, or social groups; (3) representation on the basis of governmental or geographical units; and (4) representation on the basis of wealth, generally determined by property assessments or tax payments.

Disparity in district sizes has been a political issue in Australia, Canada, the United States, and many European nations. The issue has arisen, however, only when egalitarian principles have gained sufficient popular support to challenge the oftentimes older tradition of representation by subordinate units of government. A frequent compromise assigns representation to the governmental units but varies the number apportioned to the population of each unit.

APPORTIONMENT IN THE UNITED STATES

There has been no universal pattern of apportionment in the United States. However, since 1964, all state legislatures have been required to be based substantially on population. In 1968 the Supreme Court extended this requirement to local governments—city, town, and county legislatures—as well.

Congress. The Congress of the United States consists of the Senate and the House of Representatives. The Senate represents units of government (the states), each of which is assigned two senators. Originally each state's senators were elected by its legislature, but direct election was instituted after the adoption of the 17th Amendment in 1913.

Membership in the House of Representatives is also assigned to the states but is apportioned according to population, except that each state is guaranteed at least one congressman. The Constitution established the number of congressmen to which each state was originally entitled and requires an enumeration to be made every 10 years for the purpose of determining future apportionments. Since 1941 the Bureau of the Census has used the system of equal proportions to determine the number of representatives to which each state is entitled. This method, which was developed in 1920 by Professor Edward V. Huntington of Harvard University, establishes the smallest possible difference between the representation of any two states, both with respect to the relative difference in the average population per district and with respect to the relative difference in the individual share in a representative. Each state legislature is responsible for establishing the district boundaries of the congressional seats apportioned to the state by the federal government. From 1842 to 1911, Congress required that all congressional districts be of compact and contiguous territory. That stipulation was not continued, and by the 1960's there were great disparities in the size of the districts within some states, due to the way their legislatures had drawn the boundaries.

State Legislatures. Traditionally there was no uniform pattern of apportionment for the state legislatures. Representation was unequal in most states: some sparsely populated districts had as many representatives as heavily populated ones, so that, in effect, a citizen's vote in a small district counted much more than a vote in a large one. For years, the U.S. Supreme Court refused to rule on this problem. Then, in 1962, it decided that malapportionment violated the 14th Amendment and that a citizen could sue in the federal courts on this ground. In 1964 the court held that state legislative districts must be "substantially equal" in population and that both houses of a state legislature must be apportioned on the basis of population. These decisions affected apportionment in every state.

At the time of these decisions, districting for the 99 state legislative chambers (Nebraska has a one-chamber legislature) was based on a variety of formulas. Many used only population; several used population, but with weighted ratios; about half considered both population and units of government; some gave equal representation to local political units, regardless of population; in a few, the state constitution fixed the apportionment, regardless of population changes; and one based its districts on state tax payment.

Both single-member districts and multimember districts were used in the distribution of representatives. Single-member districts were more common, although multimember districts had been more general in the colonial period and in the early years of the nation. Several states used multimember districts for the election of some senators, most states used multimember districts for the election of part of the lower house, and a few states used them for all elections.

Several states followed the so-called federal plan, by which the lower chamber was apportioned among the counties according to population, while the upper house was based on exactly equal representation for each county. Vermont reversed the process: it assigned one assemblyman to each town irrespective of population, while it apportioned senators according to population, except that each county was guaranteed at least one senator.

Many states granted each county at least one representative, irrespective of population. In several of these states such representation was effected in the lower house, which was the chamber with the larger membership. A combination of area and population criteria does less violence to the principle of popular representation when it is applied to the larger of the two houses than when it is applied to the upper house with its smaller membership.

Ohio had an apportionment formula that allowed total membership in the lower house to change from one legislative session to the next. Each county was assured at least one representative, and the remaining seats were distributed on the basis of a population ratio. Smaller counties were assigned an additional representative in accordance with the fraction of the ratio that they held over the basic requirement. A county with a population of one and three-fifths ratios, for example, would have one permanent member plus an additional representative in three of five sessions. After assignment of the first two representatives, a full ratio was required for each additional representative. The legislature was thus weighted in favor of the smaller counties. New Hampshire used a similar system based on towns instead of counties.

Discrimination in favor of rural as against urban areas was not unusual. All except a small minority of the state legislative houses showed rather pronounced favoritism to the rural element. As already noted, some states gave equal representation to each county in the senate. Others allowed two or more counties to be combined in a single senate district but limited each county to no more than one senator.

While slightly more representative, most lower houses were apportioned in favor of the less heavily populated areas. Such discrimination was the result of several factors: using population ratios that required a full ratio for large counties, while giving representation for partial ratios to smaller areas; assigning one representative to each county and apportioning the remaining seats according to population; drawing legislative boundaries so that there were many rural districts (with small populations) and only a few urban districts (with large populations); and the failure of legislatures to reapportion after each census.

In the 1960's several states adopted laws to make their apportionment systems fairer and more rational by removing the power of apportionment from their legislatures and vesting it in reapportionment commissions. Such bodies were usually responsible to the governor or were composed of public officials including the governor. The state supreme court had the power to issue orders to the commission if it failed to reapportion or if its reapportionment violated constitutional provisions.

Supreme Court Decisions on Apportionment. In March 1962 the U.S. Supreme Court ruled in favor of a group of urban voters in Tennessee who had brought suit (*Baker* v. *Carr*) against the state electoral commission on the ground that the apportionment of the legislature was unfair. The court's decision established the rule that a citizen may bring suit against legislative malapportionment when it deprives him of the equal protection of the laws guaranteed by the 14th Amendment. Previously the court had refused, in the case of *Colegrove* v. *Green* (1946), to accept jurisdiction in apportionment cases.

In *Baker* v. *Carr* (q.v.) the Supreme Court's decision was limited, although it did rule that if a system other than one based on population is used for apportionment, the resulting districts must not be "arbitrary" or "irrational" in composition.

In 1964 the Supreme Court extended the decision of *Baker* v. *Carr*. In the case of *Wesberry* v. *Sanders* (February 1964) it ruled that legislative districts for the national House of Representatives must be drawn so as to provide "equal representation for equal numbers of people." In suits that directly involved 15 states, the court ruled in *Reynolds* v. *Sims* (June 1964) that districts for state legislatures must also be substantially equal in population. Further extending the principle, the court ruled in *Avery* v. *Midland County* (April 1968) that if county, city, and town governments elect their representatives from individual districts, the districts must be substantially equal in population. And in February 1970 the court ruled that the principle applied in elections for school board members or other local officials.

APPORTIONMENT IN OTHER COUNTRIES

The apportionment systems in use throughout the world are extremely varied. Moreover, it is not uncommon for different methods to be applied in the allocation of representatives to the separate chambers of national and regional legislatures within a single country.

Traditions of representation on an assembly basis (equal value for the vote of each citizen) or by corporate bodies (subordinate units of government) still prevail throughout the world, often in combination within a single legislative chamber. However, just as suffrage rights have generally evolved toward greater equality, so apportionment formulas have gradually emphasized the distribution of representation by geographical districts of theoretically equal population.

The British House of Commons originally represented corporate bodies (towns, boroughs, or shires) without regard to differences in population. The Reform Act of 1832 introduced population as a partial consideration through an accounting of the number of houses and assessed taxation. Many of the rotten boroughs, as the districts of exceedingly small population controlled by the crown or by a single wealthy individual were called, were then eliminated. Later reforms were accomplished by the Reform Act of 1867, the Representation of the People Act of 1884, and the Redistribution of Seats Act of 1885. The double vote was not eliminated, however, until the election of a Labour party government in 1945 and the passage of the Representation of the People Act of 1948. Before that time, graduates of British universities had voted for candidates in the constituency in which they lived as well as for special university seats with a national constituency. Similarly, businessmen who had offices in the City of London had voted at their places of residence and also for City representatives. Meanwhile, beginning with the passage of the House of Commons (Redistribution of Seats) Act of 1944, the need for periodic redistricting and reapportionment was recognized. Boundary commissions for Northern Ireland, England, Scotland, and Wales were set up to work for equality in district sizes, and were required to report at intervals of from three to seven years.

Part of the agreement that led to the independence of Cyprus in 1960 was the establishment of a House of Representatives divided on communal lines, the Greek community electing 70 percent of the members and the Turkish community 30 percent. There are also Greek and Turkish communal chambers, which deal with the separate affairs of the two groups.

New Zealand has a unicameral Parliament (House of Representatives) apportioned on the basis of two sets of districts. The adult population of European descent chooses representatives from 76 districts, and the native inhabitants of the islands, the Maori, from 4 districts. Within each set, the districts are as nearly equal in population as possible, except that recent legislation has guaranteed the less populous South Island a specific number of representatives.

The Spanish Cortes and the Portuguese Corporative Chamber include representatives of labor, cultural, and professional organizations. Another type of corporative system prevailed in Fascist Italy, where representation in the Chamber of Fasces and Corporations was drawn in part from economic associations.

Among the many nations that use a system of bicameral federalism modeled after that of the United States are Australia, Brazil, Canada, and West Germany. Under this system one house is apportioned according to population, while the other represents subordinate governmental units. India also uses a federal system. The upper house, the Rajya Sabha, represents states that generally reflect linguistic-cultural groupings.

The Soviet Union's Constitution of 1936 established a two-chamber legislature. The Soviet of the Union is elected on the basis of 1 deputy for every 300,000 of the population, while the Soviet of Nationalities includes 25 deputies from each Union Republic, 11 from each autonomous republic, 5 from each autonomous oblast, and 1 from each national okrug.

Several different apportionment methods have been used in France. Under the Fifth Republic the National Assembly is based on population and is elected by direct vote. The Senate is representative of the departments, each of which, according to population, is entitled to from one to five members. The senators are chosen indirectly by deputies, departmental and municipal councilors, and other "grand electors."

An upper house based on rank, title, birth, or special accomplishment was prevalent in Europe before World War I. The most famous such body still existing is the British House of Lords.

See also ELECTIONS; MINORITY AND PROPORTIONAL REPRESENTATION; STATE GOVERNMENT, AMERICAN—State Legislatures.

                                WILLIAM J. D. BOYD
                        National Municipal League
Author of "Changing Patterns of Apportionment"

Bibliography

Baker, Gordon E., State Constitutions: Reapportionment (New York 1961).
Baker, Gordon E., The Reapportionment Revolution (New York 1966).
Boyd, William J.D., Changing Patterns of Apportionment (New York 1965).
Hacker, Andrew, Congressional Districting (Washington 1964).
Jewell, Malcolm E., ed., The Politics of Reapportionment (New York 1962).
McKay, Robert B., Reapportionment (New York 1965).

APPRENTICESHIP, ə-prent′əs-ship, is the procedure by which young persons acquire the skills necessary to become proficient in a trade, craft, art, or profession under the tutelage of a master practitioner. The apprenticeship system benefits three groups:

(1) Young persons who acquire skills that provide them financial and psychological security as trained craftsmen.

(2) The employer or master who receives productive work from apprentices during their training.

(3) Society at large, which receives continuing supplies of skilled labor and quality goods.

The apprenticeship system was highly formalized by the guilds of the early Middle Ages. The names of typical apprenticeable trades of the Middle Ages are preserved in surnames that are still common: Goldsmith, Blacksmith, Carpenter, Shoemaker, Taylor, Boatwright, and Weaver. Although apprenticeship declined with the rise of the factory system during the 19th century, there recently has been a marked revival of apprenticeship programs in many advanced industrial nations and developing nations such as Ghana and the United Arab Republic (Egypt). Such programs are sponsored by governments, trade unions, and industrial employers.

History. Apprenticeship systems probably have been operated since shortly after man began to engage in cooperative production effort. Apprenticeship was promoted, protected, and regulated by law in ancient states, as it is today. The Babylonian Code of Hammurabi provided that artisans teach their handicrafts to youths whom they adopted as "sons" to assist them in their work. Records from Greece in the 5th century B.C. contain contracts that paid high premiums to those providing apprentice sculptors and painters. There is evidence that ancient Egypt and Rome also had apprenticeship systems.

In England the guilds controlled apprenticeship through most of the 12th and 13th centuries. Parliamentary statutes of 1388, 1405, and 1437 sought to break down the excessive barriers to entrance to the trades established by the guilds for their own monopoly profits. The Elizabethan Statute of Artificers of 1563 established a system of statutory apprenticeship in England. Parliament repealed the Elizabethan act in 1814, inaugurating the modern period of voluntary apprenticeship contracts.

Indenture Terms and Wages. Apprenticeship thrived in colonial America, and the terms of the contract, or indenture, were similar to those that had prevailed in Europe for many years. Typically, the apprentice agreed to serve his master obediently and faithfully according to a carefully specified ethical code during the period of apprenticeship, usually seven years or until the apprentice reached age 21. The master agreed to teach the apprentice a trade and to provide food, lodging, washing, and adequate clothing. There usually were strictures on the behavior of the apprentice. Apprentices generally did not receive money, but there was an occasional exception: a cordwainer in 1705 was to receive three pounds at the end of every 12 months. The agreements often provided that the master teach the apprentice to read, write, and cipher and that, upon completion of the apprenticeship, the master was to supply clothing, money, and tools.

In ancient times the apprentice was no more than an indentured slave. In the Middle Ages his parent or guardian paid a premium to the master to take over his training, but the apprentice received no money wages. The conditions prevailing through the 19th century were not far superior. The workweek was six days and the workday was 12 to 14 hours. Pay scales of 5 cents an hour were not unusual.

Modern Apprenticeship in the United States. The present-day apprentice in American industry can expect $2 an hour or more for an 8-hour day and a 5-day week. General Electric Company's apprentice program, initiated in 1901, exemplifies private corporation programs. In the late 1960's, at GE's works in Schenectady, N.Y., from 200 to 300 apprentices were preparing for the trades of machinist, cabinetmaker, and patternmaker. A training period of 3½ years or 6,800 shop hours was supplemented by 720 hours of classroom instruction in a high school. The starting pay exceeded $80 per week. Today's apprentice is considerably more of an independent citizen than was his medieval counterpart. After three to five years of training he can expect to obtain a journeyman's rating in a craft or an appropriate job classification in a factory. In contrast to colonial days, when the apprentice typically began his indentured service by the age of 14, today the apprentice usually has completed high school before entering his occupational training.

Although the apprentice of early times was often required to complete a "masterpiece" to demonstrate his proficiency, today's apprentice is seldom required to do so. He becomes an economically productive worker as soon as he starts his apprenticeship, and specialization of tasks usually prevents the completion of any single item. But there are exceptions: patternmaker apprentices in Chicago complete a job order, which is judged by a committee; cash prizes are awarded to outstanding apprentices in the bricklaying, electrical, and foundry trades.

Throughout the 19th century many manufacturers hired only apprentices, used them until they qualified as journeymen, and then discharged them and hired more apprentices, thus keeping costs and prices down but leaving many journeymen unemployed for long periods. Craft unions understandably were driven to restrict the number of apprentices they admitted. However, until recently, in the United States a shortage of job opportunities presented more of a barrier to employment for apprentices than these restrictive practices did. Given the mobility of the modern worker, many employers have been reluctant to incur the expense of training apprentices whom they may not succeed in retaining once they have achieved craftsman status. Some employers consider it wiser to hire apprentices away from other employers. Such a policy, when made general, becomes self-defeating.

In the United States, interest in a national system of apprenticeship training began to revive markedly in the 1920's. In 1934 the Federal Committee on Apprenticeship was created, with members to be appointed by the secretary of labor. The National Apprenticeship Act (Fitzgerald Act) was adopted in 1937 and led to the creation of the Department of Labor's Bureau of Apprenticeship and Training. This bureau works with employers, labor groups, vocational schools, and others to promote and initiate apprenticeship programs in the trades and industry. In the mid-1960's thirty-one states had statutes designed to promote apprenticeship programs.

Nevertheless, apprenticeship programs declined in the United States. The 1950 census showed only one apprentice for every 68 "craftsmen, foremen, and kindred workers." By 1960 this ratio had dropped to one apprentice for every 105 skilled workers. The decline has prompted the federal government to take more positive steps to promote industrial training and vocational education. Trade unions have been stimulated into expanding old and initiating new training programs.

The Federal Committee on Apprenticeship has recommended that apprenticeship agreements contain provisions for the following: (1) a starting age of not less than 16; (2) a schedule of the work processes to be taught; (3) organized instruction to provide knowledge in technical subjects related to the trade; (4) a schedule of progressively increasing wages; (5) proper supervision of on-the-job training, with adequate facilities; (6) periodic evaluation and maintenance of records of the apprentice's progress; (7) employee-employer cooperation; (8) recognition for successful completion of apprenticeship; and (9) equality of opportunity for all qualified applicants.

Apprenticeship in Other Countries. Many nations are taking steps to revitalize existing apprenticeship programs and to stimulate new ones. Under the Vocational Training Coordination Act the federal government of Canada has entered into cost-sharing agreements with all provinces except Quebec and Prince Edward Island. Ghana, assisted by the International Labor Office, adopted in 1961 legislation and regulations for a national system of apprenticeship.

The United Arab Republic has been active since 1959 in promoting apprenticeship programs. India is giving government support to apprenticeship. Germany and Austria have led in the development of new apprenticeship programs for women, and Britain's Industrial Training Council is actively promoting apprenticeship programs in trade unions, government, and industry. The USSR has a multisided system of industrial training involving on-the-job training, apprenticeship programs, and allied vocational education programs similar to those in other advanced industrial nations.

Outlook. Automation, the computer, and the technological revolution of the 1960's have not made obsolete the traditional trades and crafts. Technological advances have given rise to the need for new types of skills that often demand more formal education, but they still require the kind of on-the-job training that for centuries has been the requisite for proficiency.

NORMAN A. MERCER, *Union College*

Bibliography
Clark, H.F., and Sloan, H.S., *Classrooms in the Factories* (Rutherford, N.J., 1958).
Liepman, Kate K., *Apprenticeship: An Inquiry into Its Adequacy Under Modern Conditions* (New York 1960).
National Manpower Council, *A Policy for Skilled Manpower* (New York 1954).
Serbein, O.G., *Educational Activities of Business* (Washington 1961).
U.S. Department of Labor, Bureau of Apprenticeship and Training, *Apprenticeship and Economic Change* (Washington 1964).
U.S. Department of Labor, Bureau of Apprenticeship and Training, *Apprenticeship Past and Present* (Washington 1964).
U.S. Department of Labor, Manpower Administration, *Training of Workers in American Industry* (Washington 1964).
Williams, Gertrude, *Apprenticeship in Europe: Lesson for Britain* (London 1963).

APPROPRIATION, ə-prō-prē-ā′shən, a sum set apart by a legislative body for a designated purpose. Historically, appropriation is the means by which the legislature controls the purse strings. By giving or withholding money, the legislature can secure the redress of grievances and influence the actions of the executive.

United States. Under the federal Constitution appropriations are made as prescribed by law. In the main, Congress is in the ascendant in the appropriation process, although the president's position was strengthened by the Budget and Accounting Act of 1921, under which he submits a budget containing a budget message, financial statements, and estimates.

Once it has reached Congress, the executive budget is broken up into a series of appropriation bills that custom requires originate in the House of Representatives. The bills follow no specific pattern. A separate bill is introduced for some departments, other departments are grouped together, and at least one bill is devoted to the independent establishments.

Hearings on the bills are conducted by the appropriations committees of each house. These committees are organized into subcommittees for each executive department and independent agency. The subcommittees call in and question department heads and their subordinates. Subcommittee chairmen have charge of the individual appropriation bills on the floor of each house. Whether in committee or in floor action, Congress never hesitates to assert its independence in the appropriation process. Like most state legislatures, it can increase, decrease, or eliminate items.

Appropriations may also be occasioned by authorizing legislation. First, legislation is passed, after review by program committees such as the agriculture or foreign affairs committees, that authorizes an expenditure. An authorization limits an expenditure to a specified amount. Since money can be made available only by appropriation, an authorization depends for its effectiveness upon an appropriation. Inasmuch as program committees tend to be sympathetic toward the programs they deal with, while the appropriation committees tend to be critical, the appropriation will often be less than the authorization.

For foreign aid programs, both the authorization and appropriation stages may involve drastic cuts in the president's requests. President Kennedy's first foreign aid program, for example, called for $3,575 million in direct appropriations. The Senate Foreign Relations Committee reported a reduction of $436 million, with the House Foreign Affairs Committee in near agreement. Subsequently, the House Appropriations Committee cut the authorized amount by a further $896 million; and Congress, in the ultimate appropriation, made a slight restoration by limiting the cut to $861 million.

After appropriation bills are enacted and differences between the houses are composed, the bills go to the president for signature. Since he has only a general veto power, he must approve or reject a bill as a whole. Congress' appropriation bills exist in considerable variety. The segregated-item type is very detailed and restrictive and allows little administrative discretion, while the lump-sum type includes only the principal totals and subtotals and permits the executive leeway for adjustment and economy.

Most appropriation acts authorize the agencies to incur obligations up to specified ceilings. The authority is usually limited to one year, but may be continuous, remaining available until all obligational authority has been used. Since the budget estimates are made up well in advance of the fiscal period for which appropriations are designed, unusual and unforeseen needs for funds sometimes arise. These are handled through deficiency appropriation estimates and bills.

Accounting controls, to compel the departments to stay within their appropriations, are imposed by several sources. Accounts must be kept as prescribed in a joint accounting program developed jointly by the Treasury, the Bureau of the Budget, and the General Accounting Office. The Treasury Department keeps accounts of funds. The Bureau of the Budget apportions appropriations by periods of the fiscal year. The comptroller general and his agency, the General Accounting Office, which is an arm of Congress, audits the departmental accounts.

State and local appropriation procedures are generally similar to the national. State and local governments are often limited by constitutional or legislative requirements that money derived from certain taxes be used for specified purposes. Legal restrictions on debts, taxes, and expenditures may greatly limit the legislature in determining the amount of expenditures. Some state governors and local executives have an item veto (as opposed to the president's general veto) for appropriations.

Canada. The British North America Act requires that all money bills originate in the House of Commons. A budget, developed from estimates prepared by the departments, is presented by the minister of finance. In considering the budget, the House resolves itself into a Committee of Supply. Estimates are considered department by department. No private member can move to increase any estimate, although he can move to decrease or strike out an item. After each of the departmental "votes" for spending money has been approved in committee, the minister of finance introduces an omnibus supply bill, which encompasses the estimates of all the departments and emerges as the appropriation act.

In the main, the cabinet controls finance. Support by the House of Commons of the cabinet's finance program is a matter of confidence. The Senate sometimes amends finance bills but does not reject them. Thus far its amendments have been supported by public opinion and accepted by the lower house.

Accounting controls are administered by the finance department. The auditor general, a legislative official, makes a postaudit and annually reports any irregularity to Parliament.

LOUIS W. KOENIG, *New York University*

Bibliography

UNITED STATES

Burkhead, Jesse, *Government Budgeting* (New York 1956).
Kimmel, Lewis H., *Federal Budget and Fiscal Policy, 1798–1958* (Washington 1959).
Wildavsky, Aaron B., *The Politics of the Budgetary Process* (Boston 1964).
Williams, Alan H., *Public Finance and Budgetary Policy* (New York 1963).

CANADA

Clokie, Hugh M., *Canadian Government and Politics* (New York 1945).
Dawson, Robert M., *Democratic Government in Canada* (Minneapolis 1949).

APPROXIMATION, ə-prok-sə-mā′shən, in mathematics, is any procedure, governed by rules, for calculating a value that differs from an exact value by an amount that can be made as small as is desired or required for accuracy in the computation. There are various methods of approximation. Some of the simpler ones are approximating a curve by a series of straight-line segments, approximating the area under a curve by a series of rectangles, and interpolation. In physical problems, it is often necessary to make approximate calculations rather than exact ones.

APPURTENANCE, ə-pûrt′ə-nəns, in law, literally means something which belongs to something else: an incidental property right or privilege which belongs to the principal property right. It is an adjunct that is necessary to the use and enjoyment of the main property, such as a right of way to land or buildings. It passes along with the principal property to a new owner.

APRA HARBOR, äp′rə, is a harbor in Guam, on the west coast of the island, 5 miles (8 km) southwest of the capital, Agaña. Also called *Port Apra*, it is the only good anchorage on the island. On its northeast shore, at Piti, is a well-equipped commercial port. In World War II, Apra Harbor was the scene of an Allied landing in the invasion of Guam on July 20, 1944.

APRAKSIN, ə-prá′ksyin, **Count Fyodor Matveyevich** (1671–1728), Russian admiral. He was born in 1671 and at the age of 10 became a page to Fyodor III. Two years later he entered the service of Peter the Great, with whom he grew up and whose protégé he became. In 1692 he was appointed governor of Archangel, and four years later he distinguished himself at the siege of Azov. As head of the admiralty from 1700 to 1706, he created the Russian Navy, constructing numerous ships and docking facilities. For his successful defense of St. Petersburg in 1708, he was made a count in the following year. In 1710 he captured Viborg. His defeat of the Swedish Navy in 1713 helped produce the Treaty of Nystad (1721), whereby Russia acquired the Baltic provinces. He died in Moscow on Nov. 10, 1728.

APRICOT, ap′rə-kot, a fruit-bearing tree native to China. It was brought to Europe in the time of Alexander the Great and now is cultivated also in the United States and Canada.

Characteristics. The apricot fruit resembles the peach in form but is less fuzzy or hairy; it has a characteristic orange skin color. Cultivated forms ripen earlier than cultivated peaches and plums. Most of them are orange-fleshed, but a few are white-fleshed. Most varieties also are less juicy but more highly flavored than the peach. The apricot stone or pit is generally smooth but prominently furrowed, like that of the plum. The kernels of most apricots are bitter.

As an ornamental tree, the apricot is notable for its dark-green, luxuriant foliage and its attractive white blossoms. The apricot blossoms earlier in the spring than the peach and most plum species, and later than the almond.

Growth Conditions. A good crop is obtained in areas where late frosts are unusual and in higher sites where air drainage (flow of cold air to lower areas) is excellent. Best results are obtained in loam soils suited for the apple. The land should

APRICOT tree bears peach-like fruit, an important southern California crop.

SUNSWEET GROWERS

APRICOT has white or pinkish blossoms in early spring.

C.G. MAXWELL

be situated on the downwind side of a large body of water or at higher sloping elevations that face north. The trees are set about 20 feet (6 meters) apart and cultivated like the peach. However, since the fruit-bearing habit is similar to that of the plum, the trees are pruned as plum trees are.

When properly managed and grown under favorable conditions, an apricot tree produces about as much fruit as a peach tree does. Systematic thinning is necessary to obtain large fruit size and to prevent alternate-year bearing.

Commercial Growth. The annual apricot production in the United States is valued at more than $25 million and averages close to 200,000 tons. Over 90 percent of the output comes from California. Washington and Utah produce nearly all the remaining tonnage. About 65 percent of the total production is canned, 20 percent dried, 10 percent marketed fresh, and 5 percent frozen.

Cultivated Forms. The apricot belongs to the rose family, Rosaceae. Its genus is *Prunus. P. armeniaca,* consisting of the botanical varieties *mandshurica* and *sibirica,* is the common apricot and contains all commercial cultivated forms. Other apricot species are the Japanese apricot (*P. mume*), which has striking double flowers; *P. brigantina;* and *P. dasycarpa* (probably an apricot-plum hybrid) and other plumcots.

Although 300 named cultivated forms (many still bearing their European names) are grown in United States and Canadian experiment stations, 10 varieties yield the commercial production. These are Royal, Blenheim, Tilton, Chinese, Riland, Perfection, Hemskirke, Newcastle, Moorpark, and Castleton.

Processing. Canned apricots require heavy syrup to balance high acidity and astringency. Much of the fruit is canned whole, without peeling. In some fancy packs, the fruits are lye-peeled and thoroughly washed before canning. Nearly all dried apricots are marketed as halves.

HAROLD W. FOGLE
U.S. Department of Agriculture

APRIL is symbolized in a della Robbia terra-cotta by a man training vines for the summer growing season.

APRIL, ā′prəl, is the fourth month of the year in the Gregorian calender. Called *Aprilis* in the Roman calendar (in which it was the second month), it probably derived its name from the Latin verb *aperire* (to open), indicating the season of the year when the buds begin to open. Another possible derivation of *Aprilis* is from *aper*, the Latin word for "wild boar," an important animal in early Italian religion and folklore.

There are two other theories of the word's origin: one is that there was a connection between the Greek *aphros* (foam), the root word of Aphrodite, the Greek goddess of love, to whom the month was sacred; the other, less tenable, theory is that it comes from the Vedic *áparas* (following), because as the second month, April follows the first.

In 45 B.C., Julius Caesar added the 30th day to the month. During Nero's reign, April was called *Neroneus*. The Anglo-Saxons called the month *Ooster* (Easter month), and Charlemagne, in his new calendar, called it "grass month." In the French Revolutionary calendar adopted by a decree of the National Convention in 1793, April lost its identity, becoming the last part of Germinal (bud month) and the first part of Floréal (flower month).

April 21 is observed as the traditional date of the founding of Rome in 753 B.C. Shakespeare was born near the end of April 1564 and died on April 23, 1616. The American Revolution began on April 19, 1775. Abraham Lincoln was shot on April 14 and died on April 15, 1865, and Franklin D. Roosevelt died on April 12, 1945.

The first day of April is observed by pranksters as April Fool's Day.

April is usually a rainy month, and there are countless literary allusions to April showers, including Chaucer's "Aprille with his shoures soote" and Sara Teasdale's "April shakes out her rain-drenched hair." T.S. Eliot called April the "cruellest month." Because April's weather is uncertain, the month is a traditional literary symbol for inconstancy.

The diamond is the birthstone for April.

See also CALENDAR.

APRIL FOOL'S DAY is the first of April, also known as *All Fools' Day.* On this day practical jokes are played, such as sending a friend on a fool's errand or duping him into doing or believing something absurd.

Although the practices of the day are of obscure origin, they are thought to have arisen with the celebrations of the vernal (spring) equinox. Many folklorists believe that the custom of playing someone for a fool on this day was begun in France in 1564 with the adoption of the reformed calendar. A person who resisted changing New Year's Day from April 1 to January 1 was victimized by pranksters on April 1 and became known as *poisson d'avril* (April fish).

Widespread observance of the day began in England in the 18th century. In Scotland, the custom of making April fools is known as *hunting the gowk* (cuckoo). In Mexico, *All Fools' Day* is celebrated on December 28.

APSE, aps, in architecture, the projecting semicircular or polygonal part of a building, roofed in by itself, and usually terminating the eastern end or transept of a church. The apse is of Roman origin. It was derived from the curved recess of the basilica or hall of justice in which sat the presiding magistrate and his assessors. In front of the apse stood an altar for public sacrifices. When the Christians received the protection of the state in the time of Emperor Constantine, basilicas were frequently used for their assemblies, the bishops occupying the seats of the assessors, and the altar still keeping its place.

In the earliest Christian churches the apse was situated at the western end of the church, and the priest officiated on the apse side of the altar facing eastward toward the congregation and the rising sun. In the 6th and 7th centuries, the ritual was changed so that the officiating priest stood on the side of the altar near the congregation; in order that he could continue to face the altar and the east the apse was placed at the eastern end of the church.

In Romanesque-style architecture smaller apses were frequently added at the ends of the side

APSE of Westminster Abbey, London, with the high altar in front. This area, the focal point of the abbey, is used for coronations and other ceremonies.

aisles, each apse having an altar dedicated to a particular saint. In addition, the apse end of the church itself was gradually expanded, with small chapels in apse form projecting out from an ambulatory. The apse wall was customarily richly decorated, usually with mosaics. English cathedrals generally have a square termination, though the apsidal form sometimes occurs.

APSHERON PENINSULA, äp-shə-rôn', in the Azerbaidzhan republic of the USSR, extending about 37 miles into the Caspian Sea, at the eastern end of the Caucasus Mountains. The peninsula is one of the richest oil-bearing areas in the world. The Samur-Divichi Canal brings water from the eastern Caucasus to the peninsula's arid terrain.

Baku, capital of the Azerbaidzhan republic and the largest port on the Caspian Sea, is on the peninsula. The main urban area of Baku is on the southwestern shore, but the entire peninsula is included in the city limits. Port Apsheron, on the east shore, is an oil-loading port.

APSIDES, ap'sə-dēz, are two opposing points in the orbit of an object. One apsis (the singular of apsides) is the point at which the object is closest to the body it orbits. The opposite apsis is the point at which the object is farthest away from the body. Orbits with apsides are elliptical; a circular orbit would not have apsides. The *line of apsides* is a straight line connecting the apsides; it corresponds to the major, or longer, axis of the orbit.

The apsides in the orbit of an object revolving around the earth are called *perigee* (the point nearest the earth) and *apogee* (the point that is farthest away). The corresponding apsides in the path of an object orbiting the sun are called *perihelion* and *aphelion*. The apsides in the moon's orbit around the earth shift slowly, moving in the same direction as the moon does, because of the gravitational influence of other heavenly bodies. This is called the *progression* of the moon's apsides. The apsides in the orbits of the planets around the sun shift in a similar manner, progressing slowly in the direction of motion of the planets. See also ANOMALY; APHELION; APOGEE; ELLIPSE.

THE APSIDES IN THE ORBITS OF THE MOON AND OF THE EARTH

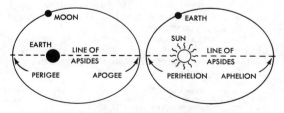

THE PROGRESSION OF THE MOON'S APSIDES

The line of apsides of the moon's orbit shifts slowly in the direction of the moon's motion. In the course of one lunar orbit, as from A to B, the progression is about 3°.

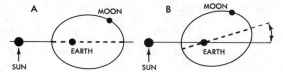

THE APTERYX, or kiwi bird, of New Zealand lays an egg that weighs about a pound and takes 80 days to hatch.

APTERYX, ap'tər-iks, is the generic name of the kiwis, flightless birds restricted to New Zealand and believed to be related to the extinct moas (see MOA).

Kiwis are about the size of a chicken. They have very stout legs and feet and a long snipelike bill, nearly one third of the bird's total length. The bill is flexible and equipped with very sensitive nostrils at the tip.

The plumage of the Kiwi is very thick, consisting of long, dark brownish and gray feathers that are incomplete in structure and resemble and feel like coarse hair. The wings are vestigial, reduced to stumps about two inches long; they have a degenerate bone structure and lack flight feathers.

Kiwis are active at night. They inhabit forest regions, and sleep or hide during the greater part of the day in thickets or burrows. Although they cannot fly, they are capable of running at great speeds when threatened.

The birds feed mainly on insects, worms, and snails. Kiwis search for their food by probing the ground with their long bills. Their sense of smell is said to be so acute that they can detect the presence of a worm underground before probing for it.

Kiwis lay one or two eggs at the end of a burrow dug by the female and furnished with a little dry fern or a few dry leaves. The eggs are very large—about one quarter the size of the bird and a pound (½ kg) or more in weight. The eggs are incubated by the male for a period of about 80 days.

The number of kiwis has decreased seriously because they are preyed upon by domestic and wild animals introduced to New Zealand by European settlers. Rigid protection has helped to check this decline to some extent, but many of the birds are still destroyed by dogs or by the ermines and ferrets brought into New Zealand to control rabbits. The kiwi is the emblem animal of New Zealand.

The kiwi belongs to the order Apterygiformes, suborder Apteryges, family Apterygidae. There is one living genus, *Apteryx australis,* and one fossil genus.

CHARLES VAURIE
Department of Ornithology
The American Museum of Natural History

APTITUDE TEST, ap'tə-tōōd, a test consisting of tasks chosen and standardized in such a way that the scores individuals make can be used to predict how successful they will be in future study or work. The difference between an achievement test and an aptitude test is that achievement test scores are used to evaluate present competence and aptitude test scores are used to predict future competence. In many instances the same test can serve both purposes, as when a test of achievement in mathematics is used to predict how successful applicants are likely to be in engineering school.

The items used in an aptitude test may or may not show an obvious resemblance to the work activities with which the test is concerned. For example, one type of mechanical aptitude test requires subjects to assemble small objects as rapidly as possible, but another that predicts just as well is a paper-and-pencil test requiring the subject to match geometric forms.

The crucial step in the production of an aptitude test is to obtain some sort of quantitative evaluation of how successful different individuals are in the work activities themselves. Such an evaluation is called a *criterion*. A test can then be validated by correlating test scores recorded for a group of subjects with their criterion scores obtained at a later date. Unless such a correlation is at least moderately high, an aptitude test cannot be considered valid.

Some aptitude tests, such as measurements of mechanical and clerical aptitude, are relatively short and are simple enough to be administered to any literate person. Others, such as assessments of suitability for medical or legal studies, are made up of several kinds of complex, difficult materials, and thus are appropriate only for college students who are almost ready to enter a professional school.

Scholastic aptitude tests attempt to predict how successful individuals are likely to be in school work. They are available for all school levels. Many intelligence tests are essentially scholastic aptitude tests, validated by correlating the scores persons make with their subsequent course grades or class ranks.

Aptitude tests have been used for two main purposes, *selection* and *guidance*. They have turned out to be better tools for the first of these purposes than for the second. For example, in selecting the best 10 candidates out of 20 who apply for a job, the use of even a moderately valid aptitude test may increase the proportion of those who ultimately succeed at the work and decrease the number of failures. But when the objective is to enable an individual to decide whether or not he is likely to succeed in a certain line of work, it is necessary to be very cautious about a conclusion based on a test score. Even if the validity of the test is high enough so that it correctly predicts success and failure in three quarters of the cases, an individual's score does not show whether he belongs to the three quarters for whom the test "works" or the one quarter for whom it does not.

Too much has been expected of aptitude tests on many occasions in the past. However, they can be useful instruments when employed with proper caution. For guidance purposes, the information that aptitude test scores furnish about individuals should be supplemented by information from other sources.

LEONA E. TYLER, *University of Oregon*

APUKHTIN, ə-pōōκ'tyin, **Aleksei Nikolayevich** (1840?–1893), Russian poet and novelist. He was born at Bolkhov, Orel Region, Russia, on Nov. 27, 1840 (or 1841). Following graduation from law school in 1859, he entered the Russian civil service. His poems of 1859–1862, appearing in various periodicals, met with great success and brought him the praise of Ivan Turgenev, Nikolai Nekrasov, and Afanasi Fet. His best poetry appeared after 1868, and some of his lyrics were set to music by Tchaikovsky.

Apukhtin's poetry, lyrical in quality, is characterized by sincerity and purity of feeling and a basic sadness. It is generally occupied with love themes. Although the poet does not concern himself with the important social and political questions of his day, his poetry frequently reflects his acquaintance with high society.

Apukhtin died in St. Petersburg (now Leningrad), on Aug. 29, 1893. Following his death his three novels were published—*From the Archives of a Countess, Diary of Pavlik Dolsky,* and *Between Life and Death.*

APULEIUS (born c. 123 A.D.), ap-ū-le'əs, was a Latin satirist and philosopher of the 2d century A.D., whose most celebrated work is the novel *The Golden Ass.* He was born at Madauros, Numidia, in North Africa. Neither the date nor the place of his death is known.

Apuleius studied first at Carthage and then at Athens, where he became an adherent of Platonic philosophy. From Athens he traveled widely, and while at Oea (modern Tripoli), he fell ill and stayed at the home of a former fellow student named Pontianus. About a year later he married Pudentilla, the rich widowed mother of Pontianus, first ensuring that Pontianus and his brother would not be disinherited. Pontianus died shortly afterward, and the relatives of Pudentilla accused Apuleius of using magic to gain her love. Apuleius' defense was his *Apologia sive oratio de magia,* a speech that is still extant.

Apuleius' most famous work is his *Metamorphoses* (published in English as *The Golden Ass*), the only Latin novel surviving in its entirety. A witty, trenchant satire, with some political overtones, *The Golden Ass* attacked the hypocrisy and debauchery of some orders of priests and assailed the vices that prevailed at the time. It also set forth the author's belief in the cults of Isis and Osiris. Later writers, including Cervantes and Boccaccio, drew upon various episodes in the novel for their own works. See also GOLDEN ASS.

Apuleius also wrote a number of works on philosophy and rhetoric. Among these were *Florida, De dogmate Platonis, De mundo,* and *De deo Socratis.*

Further Reading: Haight, Elizabeth H., *Apuleius and His Influence* (New York 1927); id., *More Essays on Greek Romances* (New York 1945).

APULIA, ə-pyōōl'yə, a region in Italy, extends along the Adriatic Sea from Mount Gargano in the north to Cape Santa Maria di Leuca in the south. It occupies the southeastern part of the Italian peninsula including the "spur" and "heel" of the Italian "boot." The region is made up of the provinces of Bari, Brindisi, Foggia, Ionio, and Lecce. Apulia's area totals 7,469 square miles. The land is mostly hilly, although there is a narrow coastal plain that widens to the north and south. The region is predominantly agricultural, and the chief products are wheat, barley, corn, peas, beans, cotton, flax, olive oil, wine, and tobacco. Sheep and cattle are raised, and salt and niter are obtained from coastal lakes. Apulia is very dry, but water for irrigation is supplied by an aqueduct from the Sele River in the western section of the Apennine Mountains. The most important river in Apulia is the Ofanto.

Originally settled by Italian peoples and colonized by the Greeks, Apulia came under Roman rule before the end of the 4th century B.C. It later formed, with Calabria, an administrative region of the Roman Empire. The Lombards conquered the region in 668 A.D., and it subsequently came under rule of the Byzantine empire. After the Norman invasion, Apulia became a county (1042) and then a duchy (1059). Later it was joined to the Kingdom of the Two Sicilies and the Kingdom of Naples. It joined the new nation of Italy in 1860. The Italian name for the region is *Puglia* or *Le Puglie.* Population: (1961) 3,421,217.

APURE RIVER, ä-pōō'rā, in Venezuela, formed by the union of the Uribante and Sarare rivers near Guadualito in western Venezuela. It flows about 300 miles eastward to the Orinoco River, draining a part of the Orinoco basin. Cattle are raised, and cotton, corn, and sugarcane are grown along the course of the river.

APURÍMAC RIVER, ä-pōō-rē'mäk, in Peru, arising as an outlet of Lake Villafro in the province of Arequipa not far from Cailloma. The Apurímac, which is probably the tributary of the Amazon rising nearest the Pacific Ocean, flows in a northerly direction through a mountainous country to join the Urubamba River and form the Ucayali, one of the chief tributaries of the Amazon. The Apurímac is between 500 and 600 miles in length.

AQABA, u'ko-bə, the only seaport of Jordan, is about 150 miles south of Amman. It is situated at the head of the Gulf of Aqaba, the northeastern arm of the Red Sea, and at the southern end of the Wadi Araba. Aqaba began to develop as a port in the early 1950's. By 1959 the main construction was completed, although expansion continued in the 1960's with the help of a loan from West Germany. The port handles more than 500 ships a year, with a total tonnage of about 850,000 tons. The chief exports are phosphates, and imports include petroleum products and food.

In ancient times the town was known as *Elath.* The modern Elath, in Israel, is nearby. Population: (1961) 8,908.

AQSU, äk'sōō', an ancient walled town in China, is located in western Sinkiang, on the southern slope of the Tien Shan mountains, about 250 miles (402 km) northeast of Kashgar.

Aqsu is an important caravan center. In the great bazaars, locally manufactured textiles, jewelry, carpets, and leather goods are sold. Sericulture and livestock raising are carried on in the surrounding area, and copper, iron, and lead are mined nearby. Aqsu was at one time the capital of the Khans of Kashgar and Yarkand. The town came permanently under Chinese rule in 1878.

AQUA REGIA, ak'wə rē'jə, is a mixture of one part nitric acid (HNO_3) and three or four parts of hydrochloric acid (HC). The mixture, which is by volume, was called aqua regia (royal water) by alchemists because it dissolves gold. It is also called nitrohydrochloric acid. It is a volatile, corrosive, yellow liquid used to dissolve not only gold, but platinum and other metals. It is also used to test amounts of precious metal in an alloy and to etch metals.

AQUAMARINE. See BERYL.

AQUAPLANING, ak'wə-plān-ing, is the sport of riding on the water on a wide board towed behind a speeding motorboat. The nearly flat board, called an *aquaplane,* is about 5½ feet long and 2½ feet wide, and ranges in weight from 20 to 70 pounds. It is constructed of laminated or solid wood. On the upper side of the board at the rear is a rough-surfaced foot pad, and fastened to the bow at each side are two hand ropes, knotted at the free ends; these help the rider obtain a firm stance.

A 50- to 75-foot towrope, threaded from the upper side of the board to the underside near the bow, links the board to the stern of the towboat. Though an aquaplane can float, it cannot support a rider in the water unless it is moving at least 10 to 14 miles per hour. It may be ridden as fast as 60 mph, but the most popular speed is about 20 mph.

In aquaplaning, the rider starts from a prone position on the board, legs trailing off the back. As the boat begins to pull the aquaplane, the rider grasps the sides of the board and the hand ropes. As the aquaplane accelerates, the rider moves to his knees on the pad and then to his feet, shifting his hand hold from the board to the hand ropes. By shifting his weight to one foot the rider can make the board steer to that side, even to the extent of going outside the boat's wake. If the water is rough, a slight pull on the hand ropes helps him to maintain balance and to keep the bow of the aquaplane from digging in. Skilled aquaplaners can ride without holding the ropes, and some can do acrobatics, such as handstands.

JACK ANDRESEN, *Author of "Skiing on Water"*

AQUAPLANING at full speed, this rider shows how a shift of weight will change the direction of the board.

FLORIDA CYPRESS GARDENS

OCEANARIUMS like this one at Marineland, Florida, are large aquariums. A diver is shown feeding the fish.

AQUARIUM, ə-kwâr′ē-əm, a tank or group of tanks for the display or study of fish or other aquatic animals. The basic requirement for keeping fish (except in small home aquariums) is to ensure the movement and treatment of large quantities of water, because the great majority of aquatic animals cannot endure the conditions that develop in small standing bodies of water. Particular requirements include filterage, clarification, temperature and chemical control, aeration, and storage. Most of these functions are performed in the operation of large aquariums, although the degree to which each is carried out may vary with local conditions. The limitations imposed by these requirements almost invariably cause any large aquarium to become a collection of relatively small tanks, each served by a circulation system isolated from that of the other tanks.

It was once thought possible to bypass some of these requirements in certain areas. Thus, in 1938, an entirely different kind of aquarium, called an *oceanarium*, was built at St. Augustine, Fla. This consisted of two very large tanks, open to the sky—one circular, 75 feet (23 meters) in diameter, the other roughly rectangular, 100 by 40 feet (30 by 12 meters), and each about 15 feet (5 meters) deep. Each tank had a number of glazed ports cut at various levels for viewing the fish. Water from the ocean was pumped directly into the tanks, and large populations of marine fish, mammals, turtles, and a few birds were placed in each tank. A number of modifications in the operation of the tanks became necessary, however, so that these tanks are now aquariums in the conventional sense of the word.

The operation of a domestic aquarium follows different principles from those governing the operation of large, institutional aquariums. The small aquariums are, by their nature, limited in the kind and number of fish that they can carry. Such aquariums work on the principle that fresh water, unless it is abused, overloaded, or poisoned, will improve as it ages and continue to support any of the kinds of fish that can live in it in the first place.

Stocking the Aquarium. In stocking a public aquarium or oceanarium, the animals first must be caught unharmed and then transported safely to their destination. This move also involves the transportation of water, which is as subject to deleterious change as is water in the aquarium.

A major fallacy once governed the stocking of small fish tanks. This was the principle of the so-called "balanced aquarium." The theory was that aquatic plants could take up the carbon dioxide released by the fish and use this carbon dioxide to release the oxygen needed by the fish. This simple principle gained widespread acceptance until it was shown that only under very strong light would the plants release oxygen. At other times, the plants actually competed with the fish for the available oxygen, which was entering the water through its surface. In actual practice, a small planted tank, in comparison to a similar unplanted tank, under normal conditions will carry more fish per unit of water only if kept in bright light continuously, day and night.

Aquatic Physiology and Aquariums. By their nature, fish and aquatic invertebrates are more intimately bound to their environment than are terrestrial animals. Proportionately, aquatic animals have less blood than terrestrial animals, for instance, because they are in osmotic balance with the water surrounding them (the concentration of salts in their blood is the same as the concentration in the surrounding water solution). Consequently, the aquatic environment must be more closely controlled both in temperature and in chemical conditions than either of these need be for terrestrial creatures. Also, noxious animal wastes slowly change the water chemistry; if allowed to accumulate, the wastes will kill the aquarium's inhabitants.

In aquariums or oceanariums where ocean water is pumped into tanks and returned to the sea, and where the inhabitants are from local

THERMOMETER

FILTER

AERATOR

HEATER

PUMP

THE AQUARIUM must provide a proper environment for aquatic life. Water is cleaned by the filter and supplied with oxygen by the aerator; the heater maintains the proper water temperature. Public aquariums operate on similar principles.

waters, much less control is needed than in inland aquariums. In these aquariums, water originally transported from the sea must be stored and continually recirculated.

Even in controlled aquariums, control of algae is a prime necessity because the metabolites developed by the higher organisms and by sunlight stimulate a prolific growth of algae that not only would limit visibility but also would destroy the exhibit animals. One way to control algae is to use copper, an excellent algicide. Unfortunately, many fish and invertebrates can tolerate a far smaller proportion of copper than is needed to destroy the algae.

A considerable financial saving in maintaining fresh aquarium water is possible with the use of fairly suitable synthetic seawaters. These are somewhat more limited than natural seawaters in the kind of fish that they will support. Synthetic seawater is prepared by adding to fresh water the proper proportions of most of the chemicals normally present in seawater. Some inland aquariums use a mixture of natural and synthetic seawaters to save money.

There are many other methods for the control of tank water and for the moving of aquatic animals. Most are the result of the experience of the workers in some specific aquarium, but the variations are numerous.

Assembling a Home Aquarium. Supplies and equipment for a domestic aquarium are available in most pet stores. The essentials are a tank, some fine gravel, plants, a thermostatically controlled heater, a thermometer, a net, and fish.

The tank, of any convenient size, should be installed in a suitable permanent place near, but not very close to, a window, and out of drafts. The gravel should be washed well and placed in the tank, sloping up from front to back. (Ore rocks or limestones should not be used in aquariums.) Some water should then be put into the tank to fill it about half way.

Plants should be planted and arranged in the back corners and along the back of the tank. Then the rest of the water should be put in without disturbing either the plants or gravel. The heater should be put into the water set to maintain a temperature of about 75° F. (24° C), and plugged in. The aquarium then should be left for a day or two to establish the proper temperature and release gases in the water. Then the fish, also available at pet stores, may be placed in the aquarium, making sure that they do not undergo a change of temperature.

A close-fitting cover glass should be placed over the tank. An electric lamp should be included either as a part of the cover itself or over the glass cover.

Since 1865, about 1,000 species of fish have been imported for domestic aquariums in the United States, but only about 150 species are regularly available. About 40 species of plants also are available for domestic tanks. The remainder of the complement of candidates for the home aquarium is made up of about 20 species of snails and other shellfish, a few species of newts and salamanders, the young of several species of freshwater turtles, and a few small frogs.

History. Keeping fish for amusement or for food is of ancient origin, going back to at least 2500 B.C., when pond culture of fish was practiced by the Sumerians. Later, the Chinese raised carp and goldfish, and the Romans of early Christian times maintained pet marine fish, spending considerable effort and money to arrange for constant changes of water by means of channels cut from the sea to their ponds. The use of glass-sided tanks as we know them today, containing both fish and plants, started in Britain about the middle of the 19th century.

In 1853, soon after the development of home fish keeping, the Zoological Gardens of Regent's Park, London, England, put a collection of standing water tanks into a small building called the Fish House, which became the first established public aquarium. Several other cities in England and on the Continent established aquariums within the next few years, but the difficulties inherent in the keeping of any fish other than the hardiest and most tolerant soon caused them all to close. However, several principles were becoming understood, and they were used in a new aquarium in Blackpool, England, in 1871, and in Brighton, England, and Frankfurt, Germany, in 1872. These were the first large public aquariums like those of today.

P.T. Barnum opened the first public aquarium in the United States in New York City in 1856. Like its English contemporaries, it did not last long, for it had all the faults of the English aquariums. There were very few aquariums in the United States until New York City opened its aquarium in 1896 at the remodeled fort Castle Garden (formerly Castle Clinton). This aquarium was the largest in the world for many years and, until it closed in 1941, was a leader in the development of aquarium management practices. The first stage of a new New York Aquarium was dedicated on June 5, 1957, on the ocean front at Coney Island, Brooklyn. The exhibitions consist mainly of marine mammals in an oceanarium type of tank and of tropical reef fishes, marine reptiles, and birds. Other oceanarium type aquariums are the Marinelands of Florida, in St. Augustine, and the Pacific, on the Palos Verdes Peninsula near Los Angeles.

CHRISTOPHER W. COATES, *New York Aquarium*

Bibliography

Axelrod, Herbert R., and Vorderwinkler, William, *Encyclopedia of Tropical Fishes* (New York 1957).

Barker, Philip, *Life in the Aquarium* (Newton Centre, Mass., 1960).

Coates, Christopher W., *Tropical Fishes for a Private Aquarium*, rev. ed. (New York 1950).

Emmens, Clifford W., *Keeping and Breeding Aquarium Fishes* (New York 1953).

Gray, William B., *Creatures of the Sea* (New York 1960).

Innes, William T., *Exotic Aquarium Fishes*, rev. ed. (New York 1964).

Janze, A.O., *Aquarium Techniques*, 2 vols. (New York 1964).

McInerny, Derek, and Gerard, G., *All About Tropical Fish*, rev. ed. (New York 1960).

Phillips, Craig, *Captive Sea: Life Behind the Scenes of the Great Modern Oceanariums* (Philadelphia 1964).

AQUARIUS, ə-kwâr′ē-əs, is a large but inconspicuous autumn constellation of the Northern Hemisphere. It is the 11th sign of the zodiac. The name means "water carrier," and Aquarius is usually represented as a man carrying a jug from which a stream of water pours toward the neighboring constellation Pisces. A number of ancient civilizations associated Aquarius with their rainy seasons; thus, the Egyptians connected its setting with the annual flooding of the Nile. There are no bright stars in the constellation. Two well-known meteor showers occurring in May and July have their radiant—the point in the sky from which they seem to come—in Aquarius.

AQUATIC ANIMALS are adapted to their environment by means of such anatomical features as shown in these four examples.

Bullfrog tadpole—gills

ALVIN STAFFAN, FROM NATIONAL AUDUBON SOCIETY

Mallard duck—webbed feet

LEONARD LEE RUE III, FROM NATIONAL AUDUBON SOCIETY

Atlantic walrus— blubber

NEW YORK ZOOLOGICAL SOCIETY

P. BERGEN, FROM NATIONAL AUDUBON SOCIETY

Sea turtle—flipper

AQUATIC ANIMALS, ə-kwät′ik, are animals that live constantly under water as well as those that swim on its surface or plunge beneath it for their food.

Aquatic Members of the Animal Kingdom. Aquatic animals are found at almost every level of the animal kingdom. Most crustaceans are aquatic, but a few, such as the wood louse and the sand crab, are modified for life ashore. There are both aquatic and terrestrial forms among the mollusks, and many other mollusks illustrate a structural transition from life in the water to life on land. The ascidians, or tunicates, are exclusively marine. Although the fishes are almost completely aquatic, a few, especially the air-breathing lung fishes, have a limited capability for life out of the water.

The transition from an aquatic habitat to a land habitat is seen in the individual life histories of the amphibians. In the frog, for example, the tadpole, or larval, form is fishlike with gills, but the adult frog has lungs and no gills. The black salamander of the Alps, whose life is entirely terrestrial, has no tadpole stage, but there is a gilled stage in the adult.

Among reptiles, there are numerous aquatic forms—turtles, lizards, snakes, and crocodiles. The absence of gill respiration in these forms, however, marks a progressive general adaptation to terrestrial life. Whereas terrestrial amphibians, such as the tree frog, seek water to rear their young, which are gill-breathing tadpoles, reptiles such as the sea turtle, which are aquatic, return to the land to lay their eggs. In both cases, the place in which the young are reared indicates the ancestral habitat of the adult.

Although birds occupy an aerial habitat, the structure of some, such as the penguin, has become adapted to a type of life that is almost exclusively aquatic.

Some of the land mammals have returned to the water. Familiar examples are the whale, the sea cow, and the seal.

Structural Adaptation to Aquatic Life. Animals in the water are subjected to environmental influences that are different from those on shore. Consequently, aquatic animals differ from terrestrial animals in modes of motion, form, respiration, and body temperature. There is also variation in the aquatic habitat itself—in composition, currents, pressure, food, and oxygen. Because of these differences, aquatic animals have a great diversity in structure.

Modes of motion vary among aquatic animals from the swimming bell of the jellyfish, which contracts and expands in the tide, to the paddling of the frog and duck. These modes of motion are both adaptations to and necessary results of aquatic life. Similarly, the smooth and frequently fishlike form, especially of locomotive water animals, is a very noticeable adaptive result of the condition of aquatic life.

Respiration is by gills in aquatic animals that have never left the aquatic environment. The blood is usually oxygenated by traveling through vessels spread out in feathery gills that trap the oxygen dissolved in the water. In terrestrial animal forms that have reverted to an aquatic habitat, respiration is by lungs and is accomplished at the surface of the water. (In some isolated cases of insects and spiders, the air is entangled in their hairs and conveyed into their submerged homes.) Transitional methods of respiration can be observed in larval insects, crustaceans, and fishes on land with a minimum of water about their gills, and also in the air- and water-breathing fishes.

The body temperature of aquatic animals is not much higher than that of the surrounding medium, and these animals often survive even the freezing of the water. Warm-blooded vertebrates that have returned to an aquatic habitat, however, have various modifications, such as thick fur or plumage, waterproof varnish, or blubber, that serve as protection against the cold.

AQUATIC PLANTS: Water lilies (*Nymphaea*), above left, have floating leaves that reach 18 inches (45.7 cm) in diameter and flowers that range in color from white to red and blue; lesser duckweed (*Lemna minor*), above right, is found floating on the surfaces of ponds; water hyacinths (*Eichhornia crassipes*), below left, have violet flowers and are found in the lakes and rivers of many warm countries; bladderwort (*Utricularia*), below right, a microscopic plant, has small, bladderlike floats.

AQUATIC PLANTS, ə-kwat'ik, are plants that grow in water. Such plants occur in almost every major group of the plant kingdom. They range from microscopic algae to the gigantic royal water lily, whose round leaves may grow as broad as 7 feet (2 meters) in diameter.

Aquatic plants are widely distributed throughout the world, inhabiting oceans and brackish lakes as well as freshwater lakes, rivers, and streams. Although most aquatic plants live only in water, some species may also live on land. In these species, however, the land-dwelling form often differs in appearance from the aquatic form. The aquatic arrowhead, for example, has limp, ribbonlike leaves, while the terrestrial form bears the stiff, arrowhead-shaped leaves from which the plant's name is derived.

Major Groups. Aquatic plants are generally divided into four major groups. Plants of the first group float freely on or below the surface of the water and have no connection with the soil. Among the best known of these plants is the salvinia, a small ornamental plant with whorls of oval leaves that are covered with stiff, bristly hairs on their upper surface. The salvinia is grown in home aquariums as well as in outdoor ponds.

The second group of aquatic plants is made up of plants whose leaves float on the water's surface but whose roots are anchored in the soil at the bottom. Among these leaf-floating plants are many popular ornamental species, including the white lotus and the royal water lily.

The third major group is composed of plants that live submerged in water, with their roots in the soil, but with their flower stalks rising above the water's surface. Included in this group is the riverweed.

In the fourth major group of water plants are those whose leaves, stems, and flowers grow above the water with their roots anchored in the soil. This group is the largest and contains the arrowhead, cattail, pickerel weed, and many other familiar plants.

Cultivation. When raising aquatic plants in outdoor ponds, it is important to consider the amount of light available, the depth of the pond, the kind of soil, and various other factors. Since most aquatic plants obtain nourishment from the soil, it is necessary to have a soil rich in organic matter. In most natural ponds the accumulation of humus at the bottom is excellent for plant growth. In some ponds, however, the bottom consists largely of sand or gravel that must be covered with a thick layer of rich soil. If the pond is very large, it is often easier to root the plants in earth-filled boxes or pots than to place a thick layer of soil over the entire bottom of the pond.

Most aquatic plants require large amounts of light and should not be grown in shaded areas. In some regions, it is also important to protect the plants from strong winds by growing shrubbery or other windbreaks near the edge of the pond. The depth of the water should be determined by the size of the plants. In many cases, a depth of 2 feet (61 cm) is adequate for most water lilies and other ornamentals.

The choice of plants to be grown depends largely on the size of the pond and the purpose for growing the plants. If fish are to be raised in the pond, it is necessary to grow plants that give off large amounts of oxygen into the water. Among the best known of these so-called oxygenators are arrowheads, eelgrass, and elodea. When aquatic plants are raised for ornament, it is sometimes useful to include some underwater plants that will conceal any boxes, pots, or other unsightly fixtures. Mare's tail and eelgrass are sometimes grown for this purpose.

Another consideration in selecting plants is their rate of growth. Some aquatic plants grow rapidly and form dense masses that hinder the flow of water and clog waterways. One of the most common of these plants is the water hyacinth, a serious pest in parts of the southern United States. It is generally controlled by dragging the water to remove the plants or by destroying them with chemical weed killers.

WALTER SINGER, *The New York Botanical Garden*

AQUATINT. See ENGRAVING; ETCHING.

AQUEDUCT, ak′wə-dukt, a structure that transports large quantities of water from a source to a point of use or distribution. The word "aqueduct" comes from the Latin *aqua* (water) and *ducere* (to lead).

Water is one of the necessities of life. Its availability partly dictated where the pioneers of any era settled and built their towns and cities. Thus, areas near rivers, lakes, and springs became the centers of population. When the source of supply became inadequate or unsatisfactory, water was brought from outlying areas by some form of aqueduct.

DESIGN AND CONSTRUCTION

Types of Aqueducts. There are two types of aqueducts. One carries the flow in a conduit that is not full and therefore not under pressure; in the other, the conduit is full and the water is under pressure. In a nonpressure aqueduct, water moves downhill under the force of gravity. Ancient aqueducts were usually of the nonpressure type.

Nonpressure or Grade Aqueducts. The main types of nonpressure aqueducts are *open-channel, cut-and-cover,* and *grade-tunnel* aqueducts.

The open-channel aqueduct, when excavated in soil, has a trapezoidal cross section. The channel usually is lined with an impervious material to prevent leakage, contamination, and erosion. A smooth surface is used to reduce the resistance to flow. When excavated in rock, the channel usually has a rectangular cross section. The top is uncovered.

In building a cut-and-cover aqueduct, a trench is dug along the route of the aqueduct and the conduit is built in place. Then the trench is filled, and the conduit is covered. Conduits are built of many materials, including quarried stone, brick, and poured concrete. A horseshoe-shaped cross section commonly is used because it provides strength and favorable flow characteristics. Vertical shafts provide ventilation and access for inspection and maintenance.

A grade-tunnel aqueduct is used in traversing a hill or mountain. A hole, either horseshoe-shaped or circular, is driven through the hill. The tunnel surface is then lined to prevent leakage and contamination. A smooth surface lining reduces the resistance to flow.

Pressure Aqueducts. The chief types of pressure aqueducts are *high-pressure pipe aqueducts* and *pressure-tunnel aqueducts.*

Steel and reinforced concrete pipes are used in most pressure aqueducts because they can withstand great internal pressures without bursting. The cross section of the pipe is circular.

Normally, the pressure in a pipe diminishes in the direction of flow. However, when a pressure aqueduct traverses a valley, the pressure in the pipe increases to a maximum at the valley floor and lessens thereafter. Such portions of the aqueduct are called inverted siphons or, simply, siphons. (These terms are misnomers because the internal pressure always exceeds atmospheric pressure in an inverted siphon, which is not the case in a true siphon.)

Pressure tunnels are used when an aqueduct must be built far below the earth's surface. A hole is drilled through the underlying rock, and the interior is lined with concrete. The concrete lining prevents leakage and contamination and provides a hydraulically smooth surface. The strength to resist the internal pressure is provided by the rock surrounding the tunnel.

Local circumstances control the type of aqueduct that is used. It is not uncommon for a single aqueduct to consist of several lengths of different types.

Design Considerations. For water to flow in any conduit, an expenditure of energy is required. The three types of energy involved are pressure

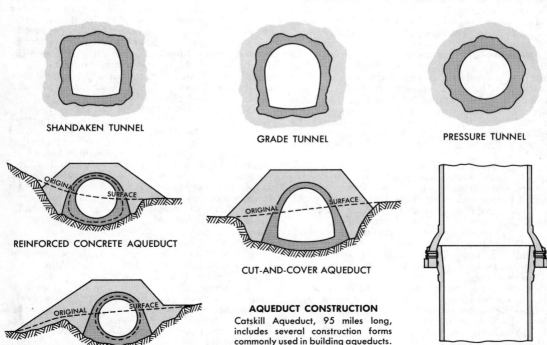

SHANDAKEN TUNNEL

GRADE TUNNEL

PRESSURE TUNNEL

REINFORCED CONCRETE AQUEDUCT

CUT-AND-COVER AQUEDUCT

STEEL PIPE SIPHON

AQUEDUCT CONSTRUCTION
Catskill Aqueduct, 95 miles long, includes several construction forms commonly used in building aqueducts. This aqueduct brings water from Catskill Mountains to New York City.

FLEXIBLE-JOINTED PIPE
NARROWS SIPHON

SECTION of Roman aqueduct, built 2,000 years ago, is now in the Smithsonian Institution, Washington, D.C.

energy, velocity energy, and elevation energy. At any cross section the velocity energy generally is small compared to the other types and therefore this quantity is neglected. The sum of the pressure energy and the elevation energy at any point is called the piezometric head. If a profile of the conduit is drawn and the magnitude of the piezometric head is measured and plotted vertically at several points, then a line drawn between these points is the hydraulic grade line (hydraulic gradient). The vertical distance between the pipe center line and the hydraulic grade line is a measure of the internal pressure in the pipe. If the internal pressure is no greater than atmospheric pressure, then the flow has a free water surface (the conduit is not full), and the aqueduct is a nonpressure aqueduct.

In a nonpressure aqueduct, water is moved by elevation energy. This type of aqueduct requires a channel of sufficient slope so that the work done by the force of gravity just balances the work necessary to overcome the frictional resistance of the channel. The smoother the channel surface, the smaller is the slope of a conduit that can maintain uniform flow at constant depth. Typical slopes vary from a few inches to a few feet per mile. Because it is unusual to find terrain that slopes uniformly along a straight line, aqueducts often twisted and turned as the builders sought to maintain the appropriate slope. As a result, an aqueduct often had a length considerably greater than the straight-line length between its termini.

An alternative design might allow the channel to follow the natural slope of the ground along a straight line across the valley. In general, this alternative is unsatisfactory because a channel slope that is greater than optimum produces destructive water velocities, and a channel slope that is less than optimum produces stagnation velocities.

The accompanying illustrations show several ways by which an aqueduct can cross a valley. In order to maintain a constant slope in the channel, supporting structures (bridges) were built. The height and length of the bridge depended on the characteristics of the valley. Often the bridge served the dual purpose of supporting the conduit and handling pedestrian traffic.

Another alternative is to encase the flow in a high-pressure pipe and allow the pipe to fol-low the natural slope of the terrain, such as down one side of a valley and up the other side. In this case the hydraulic grade line lies above the center line of the pipe. The vertical distance between these two lines determines the internal pressure that the pipe must resist.

Hills or mountains commonly intervene between the water source and the point of delivery. Often the early aqueduct bypassed such obstacles simply by going around them. A second alternative was to tunnel through the hill. There is considerable evidence that the ancients used grade tunnels for this purpose. The grade tunnel served as a passageway for an open channel or for pipes that were not full of water.

In modern hydraulic engineering practice, tunnels are used because they have several desirable and useful features. Tunnels lined with concrete have become integral parts of water supply systems because surface or near-surface aqueducts require extensive maintenance, utilize valuable surface area, and are susceptible to contamination and destruction.

HISTORY

Early Aqueducts. The first aqueducts probably were built in the Middle East. The earliest dated physical evidence is a tablet found in Moab, an ancient country east of the Dead Sea (now part of Jordan). Dated in the 10th century B.C., it states that "Mesho built two conduits, and since no cisterns were in the city of Karcho, Moab, he ordered the inhabitants to place a cistern in each house. He then had a conduit constructed by the Israelitish prisoners to supply water to the cisterns."

ROMAN AQUEDUCT still standing in Segovia, Spain, was built by the Emperor Trajan (reigned 98–117 A.D.).

DELAWARE AQUEDUCT pressure tunnel, shown while under construction, has a heavy steel interlining.

BOARD OF WATER SUPPLY, CITY OF NEW YORK

One of the earliest builders of aqueducts was King Sennacherib of Assyria, an engineering genius. The concept of an irrigation system was a secret brought back by his father after an invasion of Armenia in 714 B.C. In the 690's B.C., Sennacherib built several canals, one of which was remarkable for its time. It began about 30 miles (48 km) north of Nineveh and carried water from the Gomel River to the Tebitu River, which he had previously dammed as a source of supply. The channel, which was 65 feet (19.8 meters) wide, crossed a stream near Jerwan on an aqueduct bridge made of corbeled arches. The channel atop the bridge was lined with mortar to prevent leakage. The bridge, which was 30 feet (9.1 meters) high and 900 feet (274.3 meters) long, and the entire channel were completed in the remarkable time of 15 months.

About 600 B.C., Eupalinus of Megara built a notable aqueduct on the island of Samos. Its outstanding feature was a tunnel 8 feet (2.4 meters) in diameter and nearly a mile (1.6 km) long. A 3-foot-wide (0.9-meter) channel within the tunnel carried clay or wooden pipes.

Roman Aqueducts. Probably the greatest ancient builders of aqueducts were the Roman engineers. Italy, France, Spain, North Africa, Greece, and Asia Minor benefited from their engineering

COLORADO RIVER AQUEDUCT carries the river water to California. Inverted siphon section is shown.

METROPOLITAN WATER DISTRICT OF SOUTHERN CALIFORNIA

knowledge. Much is known about the works of these early builders, largely through the detailed writings of Sextus Frontinus, a water commissioner in about 97 A.D., and Vitruvius, a Roman builder who wrote *Ten Books of Architecture* about 15 B.C.

The accompanying table gives details on some of the early aqueducts. The dimensions listed are approximate. It was not possible to work to high degrees of tolerance with the materials available, and therefore the size of the conduit and its slope varied considerably along its entire length. The flows were computed by Claudio Di Fenizio (1916).

ROMAN AQUEDUCTS

Aqueduct	Date of construction	Total length (miles)	Length above ground (miles)	Flow (million gallons daily)
Aqua Appia	312 B.C.	10.3	0.1	20.0
Anio Vetus	272–269 B.C.	39.5	0.2	48.2
Aqua Marcia	144–140 B.C.	56.7	6.9	51.4
Aqua Tepula	125 B.C.	12.0	?	4.8
Aqua Julia	33 B.C.	14.2	6.4	13.2
Aqua Virgo	19 B.C.	13.0	1.1	27.5
Aqua Alsietina	2 B.C.	20.3	0.3	4.2
Aqua Claudia	38–52 A.D.	42.7	9.3	50.5
Anio Novus	38–52 A.D.	54.0	8.6	51.9
Aqua Trajana	109 A.D.	35.4	?	?
Aqua Alexandrina	226 A.D.	13.7	1.5	?

1 mile = 1.6093 km. 1 foot = 0.3048 meter. 1 gallon = 3.7853 liters.

Man's works reflect his knowledge, his technical abilities, and the materials available to him. This is clearly illustrated by the construction of the Roman aqueducts. The major portion of most of the early aqueducts was below ground. The technique of building great bridges had not yet been developed, the art of leveling had not been perfected, and there was a constant fear of destruction by enemies. Thus, ditches were dug in the ground, and large stone blocks, keyed with cement-filled slots, were put in the ditches. The bottom of the conduit consisted of flat blocks. The sides were two massive blocks cut to meet above the center line of the channel. The channel was lined with mortar.

The first three Roman aqueducts—Aqua Appia, Aqua Anio Vetus, Aqua Marcia—were built entirely of stone, which was abundant. About the 3d century B.C. it was discovered that a volcanic ash, when mixed with lime, water, sand, and gravel, made a concrete. Years later this new material was recognized as a valuable construction material. Aqua Tepula was the first aqueduct (125 B.C.) to be built of poured concrete, and most later Roman aqueducts also were built of this material. Being artisans, the builders faced the exposed portions with cut stone or brick.

The most striking feature of the ancient Roman aqueducts is the bridges that carry the channels over valleys near Rome. Aqua Marcia, built in the 140's B.C., was the first of several high-level aqueducts. The ability to build large, strong structures evidently had been fully developed by this time. The Roman builders were also practical men, so they commonly built several channels atop a single arcade. Some valleys were too wide and too deep to be bridged by arcade-type structures. However, the practice of using inverted siphons was known and understood by the Romans, as noted by Vitruvius.

Lead pipes and clay pipes were produced by the Romans. For a clay pipe to withstand any

PUMPING PLANT at Parker Dam reservoir has 1 billion gallons per day capacity. Plant is part of water system for Los Angeles.

BUREAU OF RECLAMATION

substantial pressure, it had to be encased in masonry blocks, and the joints had to be caulked. However, leakage still was a serious problem. Although lead was a sufficiently strong pipe material to resist the pressures developed in early aqueducts, the production of lead pipes mainly was limited to sizes much smaller than those needed to deliver the desired volume of flow. Consequently, Roman aqueducts were nonpressure aqueducts which followed tortuous routes that had a reasonably constant slope.

Aqua Alexandrina, built in 226 A.D., was the last of the ancient aqueducts. Throughout the period from 312 B.C. to 226 A.D., many of the aqueducts fell into disrepair or disuse. During the next centuries the aqueducts passed through many successive stages of restoration and deterioration. In 1585, Pope Sixtus V built an aqueduct, Acqua Felice, on the ruins of an old one. In 1870, Pope Paul V built Acqua Marcia-Pia, the first entirely new aqueduct in Italy in 1,644 years.

Other Ancient Aqueducts in Europe. The Roman emperor Hadrian spent six years building a 15-mile (24-km) aqueduct in Athens about 115 A.D. It ran 30 to 130 feet (9 to 40 meters) underground between 700 vertical shafts. Although the Greek government built an entirely new system between 1920 and 1931, the old aqueduct still supplies part of the city.

The Romans constructed numerous aqueducts in Gaul (France). In 19 B.C., Marcus Agrippa built an aqueduct at Nîmes. The outstanding feature of this structure, which is still standing, is the Pont du Gard. This bridge, which was built without cement or mortar, has three tiers of arches 160 feet (49 meters) high and is 900 feet (274 meters) long. In 50 A.D., Claudius I built an aqueduct at Lyon that contained three inverted siphons made of 8.625-inch-diameter (22-centimeter) lead pipe.

MODERN AQUEDUCTS

United States Aqueducts. In the United States, community water supplies were provided in some locations by about 1775. The Boston Aqueduct Corporation and the Manhattan Company in New York City were two of the earliest private enterprises for supplying water. In the early 1800's, several proposals were made for bringing water into New York City when the adjacent ponds and wells became unsafe and inadequate.

Croton Aqueducts. Between 1837 and 1843 the city's first great aqueduct, the Old Croton Aqueduct, was built. It is a 41-mile-long (66-km) masonry conduit of cut-and-cover construction, except at the crossings of the Harlem River and the Manhattan valley. The river crossing consists of two 36-inch-diameter (91-centimeter) cast-iron pipes carried on high masonry arches built in the style of the old Roman aqueducts. The Old Croton Aqueduct supplied 95 million gallons (359.6 million liters) per day (mgd).

Because of New York's phenomenal growth, the city required an additional supply. Consequently another aqueduct, the New Croton, was constructed in 1884–1893. It is a brick-lined, gravity-flow (grade) tunnel, with a horseshoe-shaped cross section, extending 25 miles (40 km) followed by a pressure tunnel extending 8 miles. The New Croton Aqueduct supplied about 300 mgd (1,135 million liters) for the city.

Catskill System. Despite the existence of the Croton aqueducts, the city's reserve supplies of water became alarmingly small after the turn of the century. Because the safe water yield of the neighboring area had already been realized, engineers were forced to develop the Catskill area.

Most projects for water resources development are carried out in stages. The first stage in the development of the Catskill system (1907–1917) provided 250 mgd (946 million liters). When the second, and final, stage was completed in 1927, the total supply from this system was 555 mgd (2,100 million liters). The Catskill system, which is 150 miles (240 km) long, uses gravity flow to deliver water with a head of 250 feet (75 meters) above mean sea level in lower Manhattan and Brooklyn. Because of the diversified terrain traversed by the aqueduct, a combination of cut-and-cover, grade-tunnel, pressure-tunnel, and steel-pipe-siphon constructions was used.

Delaware System. The Delaware system, which supplies some of the water for New York City, is another example of stage development, planned and built so that the available supply keeps pace with ever-increasing requirements. The Stage I aqueduct is a concrete-lined, 85-mile-long (137-km) pressure tunnel. It lies at depths of 300 to 2,500 feet (91 to 762 meters) below the ground. The diameter of the aqueduct varies from 13.5 to 19.5 feet (3.2 to 5.9 meters) as it approaches the city because provisions were made to carry

GATEWAY CANAL, part of Weber Basin project in Utah, is used to transport water for irrigating farms.

Catskill or Groton flow. Stage I completed in 1954, provides 235 mgd (889.5 million liters).

In 1955, Stage II was completed, including the East Delaware tunnel (25.5 miles long, 11.25 feet in diameter, 375 mgd capacity). In 1966, Stage III was completed, including the West Delaware tunnel (39 miles long, 11.33 to 13.33 feet in diameter, 310 mgd capacity). It is anticipated that the 1,820 mgd (6,857 million liters) of available supply from all components of the New York City water supply system will be adequate until the year 2000.

Aqueducts in the West. The Los Angeles River and ground water were the original sources of supply for Los Angeles. By 1908 these sources had been fully exploited, and a project was begun to bring water from the Owens River high in the Sierra Nevada Mountains. The Los Angeles aqueduct, completed in 1913, is about 215 miles (346 km) long. It includes about 60 miles (96 km) of lined and unlined canal, about 100 miles (161 km) of cut-and-cover construction and reinforced concrete conduit, about 43 miles (69 km) of lined tunnels, and about 12 miles (19 km) of concrete or steel pipe siphon. A jawbone siphon is the most notable part in this system. Though only 1.5 miles (2.4 km) long, it works under a maximum head of 850 feet (259 meters).

In this gravity-flow system, the first section of 60 miles (96 km) has a design flow of 580 mgd (2,195 million liters) and terminates in a reservoir with a capacity of 80 days' needs at full flow. The remainder of the aqueduct passes 270 mgd (1,019 million liters). Water is available to Los Angeles at a head of 575 feet (175 meters) above sea level.

Ten years after the Los Angeles aqueduct was completed, it was found that additional water supplies were necessary for the future development of the area. About 300 miles (483 km) east of Los Angeles flows the mighty, silt-laden Colorado River. However, downstream from Hoover Dam, the river water is clear and sparkling. Water rights were therefore obtained, and Parker Dam was built to provide the necessary storage for this water. Five pumping stations with a total lift of 1,617 feet (493 meters) are required along the 242 miles (389 km) of the main aqueduct, called the Colorado River Aqueduct. They deliver 1,030 mgd (3,999 million liters) to Lake Mathews, which is about 1,000 feet (305 meters) higher than the reservoir at Parker Dam. From Lake Mathews further distribution is effected entirely by gravity flow.

Lined-canal and cut-and-cover construction, which are almost equally cheap, account for 117 miles (188 km) of this aqueduct. Grade tunnels through the mountain ranges are 92 miles (148 km) in length, and 144 siphons, used only where necessary, have a combined length of approximately 30 miles (48 km). The first stage of the system was completed in 1941. Two branch aqueducts carry the flow to the San Diego area.

California's Department of Water Resources plans to construct multipurpose dams and other facilities on northern California rivers, where surplus runoff is available. An aqueduct will be built to transport this flow to water-deficient regions in southern California. The $2 billion water resources project has been under construction since 1957. Water was scheduled for delivery to parts of southern California in 1971.

The completed California Aqueduct will extend about 450 miles (724 km) from the Sacramento and San Joaquin delta to the Perris reservoir between Los Angeles and San Diego. It will include 400 miles (644 km) of trapezoidal canal lined with 4-inch-thick (9 cm) concrete. In design, the crossing of the Tehachapi Mountains includes 20- to 23.5-foot-diameter (6 to 7 meters) tunnels that have a total length of 8 miles (12.9 km).

The 19 pumping plants along this aqueduct provide a total lift of more than 3,000 feet (914 meters). The magnitude of the pumping requirements for the Tehachapi pumping plant surpasses all precedent in terms of combined volume of water and height of lift—2,660 mgd (10,069 million liters) through a single lift of 1,926 feet (579 meters). Hydroelectric power generation will be developed at nine locations. The completion date for the entire project is 1991.

Technology and Water Resources. The concept of an aqueduct has changed since the time of the Romans, even though the laws of hydraulics remain unaltered. Man's technological successes have enabled him to drill through miles of the hardest stone, to excavate thousands of cubic yards of earth in digging canals, and to make impervious embankments containing millions of cubic yards of material to dam rivers. Besides transporting water for domestic use and irrigation, modern practice includes the use of water for municipal disposal systems, industrial enterprises, and hydroelectric power generation.

Aqueducts and reservoirs do not produce water, of course. Rather, a reservoir allows discretionary use of available water, and an aqueduct makes it possible to determine its point of use. Only by far-reaching and imaginative design, using all existing and future tools of engineering, can water crises be averted.

See also HYDRAULICS; WATER SUPPLY.

ALBERT H. GRISWOLD, *New York University*

Bibliography

Ashby, Thomas, *Aqueducts of Ancient Rome* (Oxford 1935).
Board of Water Supply of the City of New York, *59th Annual Report* (New York 1964).
DeCamp, L. Sprague, *The Ancient Engineers* (New York 1963).
Herschel, C., *Frontinus: The Two Books of the Water Supply of the City of Rome* (London 1913).
Metropolitan Water District of Southern California, *25th Annual Report* (1963).
Sandström, Gosta E., *Tunnels* (New York 1963).
Southern California Metropolitan Water District, *Colorado River Aqueduct* (1950).
Times-Mirror Printing and Binding House, *Historical Sketch of Los Angeles Aqueduct* (1913).
Van Deman, E., *Building of the Roman Aqueducts* (Washington 1934).

AQUEOUS HUMOR, ā′kwē-əs hū′mər, the clear, watery, lymphatic fluid that fills the anterior and posterior chambers of the eye. (These chambers are located in front of the crystalline lens of the eye.) The aqueous humor is a slightly alkaline solution containing traces of sodium chloride, glucose, urea, and protein. It is secreted by the ciliary process and is drained from the eye through the canal of Schlemm. The pressure exerted by the secretion and drainage of the aqueous humor helps maintain the spherical form of the eyeball.

AQUIFER, ak′wə-fər, an underground bed of rock or other material that is porous enough to be a good carrier of groundwater. Beds of sandstone and gravel, the best aquifers, can extend for thousands of square miles, and may conduct groundwater to levels deep below the surface. Artesian wells tap such deep-lying water. Porous limestone is also a good source of water for wells and springs. Rock formations that contain channels of underground streams are also considered to be aquifers.

AQUILA, ak′wi-lə, a 1st century Christian associated with St. Paul. Aquila was of Jewish origin and a native of Pontus in Asia Minor. He first became acquainted with Paul at Corinth (Acts 18:1–3). Paul shared his lodgings and his trade as a leather worker (translated "tent-maker" in the Authorized Version). He later journeyed with Paul to Ephesus and remained there (II Timothy 4:19). None of the other Christians who aided Paul received such warm praise from his pen (Romans 16:3).

Another Aquila of Pontus, known as *Aquila Ponticus,* was a 2d century convert to Christianity and later to Judaism. He made a literal translation of the Old Testament into Greek, which was preferred to the Septuagint by Origen, Jerome, Augustine, and the Hellenistic Jews, but not by Christians generally. No complete copy of his work exists.

AQUILA, L′, äk′wē-lä, a city in Italy, is the capital of L′Aquila Province and of the Abruzzi region. It is situated 54 miles northeast of Rome, in the valley of the Aterno River. It is at the foot of the Gran Sasso d′Italia, the highest part of the Apennine Mountains.

The city is surrounded by medieval walls with seven gates. It is an archbishopric, and there are numerous interesting churches, including the romanesque Santa Maria di Collemaggio (1270–1280), which has a façade in white and red stone, and San Bernardino (1454–1472), rich in the works of local artists. A castle at L′Aquila is a typical, imposing example of 16th century fortifications.

L′Aquila was founded in 1240 by the Emperor Frederick II as a stronghold against the Papal States. Population: (1961) 29,462.

AQUILA, ak′wə-lə, is an autumn constellation of the Northern Hemisphere. It was known to several ancient civilizations by names meaning "eagle," but the mythology behind the name is not certain. Aquila lies in the Milky Way in the region known as the Rift. Altair, a yellowish first-magnitude star, is the brightest object in the constellation. A number of novae (see NOVA) have appeared in the region of Aquila, the most famous being the one of 1918.

AQUILEIA, ä′kwē-lā-yä, a town in northeastern Italy, in the province of Udine, is 21 miles south of the city of Udine. It is near the Adriatic Sea, in the Friuli-Venezia Giulia region. The town's Romanesque basilica, built in the 11th century on the foundations of a 4th century church, has brightly colored floor mosaics preserved from the original church. Nearby is a tall bell tower, begun in the 1300's and completed in the 1500's. The archaeological museum contains outstanding Roman antiquities including sculptures, mosaics, frescoes, glass, and ceramics.

Founded as a Roman colony in 181 B.C., Aquileia prospered as a military depot and a trade and art center. It was a favorite residence of the Roman Emperor Augustus (reigned 27 B.C.–14 A.D.) and was the site of an important church council in 381. It declined after 452, when it was destroyed by Attila, but revived in the 11th century, when it became the seat of the powerful patriarchate that held sway over Friuli, Istria, and Carniola. It began to decline again in the 1400's and 1500's, when it was seized by Venice (1420) and Austria (1509), and it never recovered its early preeminence. Population: (1961) 1,501.

AQUINAS, ə-kwī′nəs, **Saint Thomas** (1225–1274), Roman Catholic theologian and philosopher, often called the *Angelic Doctor.* He was born in Roccasecca, between Rome and Naples, Italy, in 1225 (some authorities give his birth year as 1224, others as 1226 or 1227). His father was Landolfo, count of Aquino, Belcastro, and Roccasecca, and his mother was Theodora, a Neapolitan noblewoman of Norman descent. Through them he was related to the imperial family of the Holy Roman Empire and to the royal houses of France, Aragon, and Sicily.

Career. About May 1230, Thomas became a Benedictine oblate at the nearby monastery of Monte Cassino, where a relative, Landolfo Sinibaldo, was abbot. Because of unsettled conditions, Thomas returned home, perhaps in April 1239. In the fall he entered the University of Naples, where he completed his liberal arts studies under Peter of Ireland and Peter Martin.

After his father's death in 1243 he decided to join the Order of Preachers, which had been

CULVER PICTURES, INC.

St. Thomas Aquinas

(Painting by Botticelli, c. 1480)

founded by St. Dominic in 1215, and against family opposition took the Dominican habit. On his way to Bologna he was seized by his brothers and held in the family castle for over a year. In 1245 he regained his liberty, again assumed the Dominican habit, and went to Paris, where he studied under St. Albertus Magnus. In 1248 he accompanied Albertus to Cologne, where he spent the following four years and was ordained a priest. In 1252 he began to lecture on Sacred Scripture at the University of Paris; in 1256 he started lecturing on theology and philosophy, and received his master's degree. He returned to Italy in 1259 to teach theology at the court of Pope Alexander IV at Anagni, and from 1261 to 1265 at the court of Pope Urban IV at Orvieto. From 1265 to 1267 he was at the Dominican house of studies at Santa Sabina in Rome, and the next year at Pope Clement IV's court at Viterbo. Late in 1268 he returned to Paris, and in the spring of 1272 was again in Italy, teaching at the University of Naples. At the request of Pope Gregory X, he started for Lyon in January 1274 to attend a Church council, but fell ill. He died in the Cistercian Abbey at Fossanova on March 7, which is the day of his feast.

Recognition of His Qualities. During his life, St. Thomas' great abilities as thinker and writer were recognized, as were his sanctity and other qualities. He was offered the abbacy of Monte Cassino, and Pope Clement IV wished to make him a cardinal and archbishop of Naples, but he declined in each case. His unceasing industry is evident in the vast extent and high quality of his works. His holiness of life, strength of character, and charm of personality, testified to by contemporaries, show through his writings. He was declared a saint by Pope John XXII on July 18, 1323, a Doctor of the Universal Church by Pope St. Pius V in 1567, and patron of all Catholic schools by Pope Leo XIII in 1880. In 1918 the *Codex Juris Canonici* (Code of Canon Law) directed that his philosophy be taught in ecclesiastical schools.

PHILOSOPHY AND THEOLOGY

St. Thomas Aquinas is both theologian and philosopher, but in his thought the two disciplines are kept distinct even in their closest alliance. Philosophy works to its conclusions by the unaided use of human reason; theology depends upon divine revelation and the teaching authority of the church. The theologian can use the methods and findings of philosophy, and philosophy is thus ancillary to theology but still distinct from it. The two sciences also differ in certain ways as to their subject matter. Some truths can be known only from revelation and belong to theology, for example, the mysteries of the Trinity and the Incarnation. Some truths are proper to philosophy, for example, the physical constitution of bodies. Other truths belong to both sciences. Thus the existence of God can be known both by revelation and through reason.

In his theory of knowledge Aquinas is a realist. There are no innate ideas; all our knowledge takes its origin from sense experience. The higher powers of the mind are then able to act upon the sense data and to form abstract and universal ideas. Aquinas' epistemology is in keeping with his psychology. Man is one single complete substance, made up of material body and spiritual soul united otgether. The soul is the substantial form, the animating and energizing principle; it is the principle of life and therefore of growth, sensation, thought, volition, and all other vital activities. Its highest powers are those of intellect, which has the place of primacy, and of will.

Methaphysics. In his metaphysics, Aquinas is again a realist: he is concerned with the existent being of finite things, but most of all with the supreme being in whom essence and existence are one and the same. He develops and applies Aristotle's basic distinction between the actual, or perfect, and the potential, or what is capable of perfection. In finite beings there is always found a mixture of the potential with the actual. An actual child is complete and perfect as a child, but it has many potentialities as yet unfulfilled: it is capable of being perfected in size, strength, knowledge, and the like. The only being that is devoid of all mere potentialities and is completely actual, or absolutely perfect, is God, the infinite being, pure actuality. Connected with this doctrine of actuality and potentiality are the doctrines of the four causes—material, formal, efficient, and final—and of matter and form in physical objects, both of which likewise derive from Aristotle.

Existence of God. This is not self-evident but can be proved by human reason in five ways, viz. (1) from movement or change, the passage from the potential to the actual; (2) from cause and effect; (3) from the contingent and the necessary; (4) from grades of perfection found in things; and (5) from order in the universe. Aquinas states the arguments succinctly and concludes from them that there must be a first unmoved mover in whom there is no mere potentiality (or lack), a first cause, a self-existent being, a supremely perfect being, and an adequate cause for the order found in the universe.

Each conclusion is a description of the one supreme and infinite being, God, creator and conserver, first cause and last end of all things. Man's mind cannot fully comprehend God's nature, but it can show that He possesses in a supreme degree whatever true perfections are found in creatures. Moreover, by "the way of negation" the mind must exclude from the concept of God every attribute that implies defect. Hence it is known that God is omnipotent, omniscient, all-good, immutable, and eternal. Although reason cannot demonstrate that the world is not eternal, that fact is known from revelation. As to whether this is the best of universes, Aquinas makes careful distinctions. Relatively, that is, as a means to God's purpose in creation, it is the best universe. In the absolute sense, God could have had a different end in view and therefore could have made a different and better universe. Aquinas gives a solution to the problem of physical and moral evil and shows that it is not incompatible with God's goodness and power.

Moral System. In the *Summa theologica* and elsewhere, Aquinas develops a complete moral system. He analyzes the nature of the specifically human act, the act done under the control of reason and will, and takes up the subject of virtues and vices. The three theological virtues of faith, hope, and charity and opposing vices and sins are discussed, as are the cardinal virtues, prudence, justice, fortitude, and temperance, and the contrary vices. All the basic ethical principles and problems are discussed and concrete solutions are given to problems, such as mendacity, homicide, and theft.

Aquinas lays great stress on the concept of law, "a dictate of practical reason, proceeding from the ruler who governs a perfect community," including the natural law, which is a participation in God's eternal law. He advances principles essential to just government and helpful to the growth of democracy. He emphasizes popular participation in government, the necessity of a well-ordered society, the advantages of a unified rule, and the evils of tyranny.

The physical sciences are not ignored. He suggests that the astronomical theory of Ptolemy may be supplanted, and that the earth's roundness is provable by physics and mathematics.

Philosophical Method. In the *Summa theologica* and certain other works, Aquinas brings to perfection the tripartite method of the medieval schoolmen. It consists of five steps. The first states a problem, as "Whether custom can obtain the force of law." The second gives arguments opposed to the author's own position, followed by a contrary opinion or doctrine. In the fourth step, which constitutes the body of each article in the work, Aquinas' own doctrine is stated, and finally the opposing arguments are answered.

Aquinas uses both deductive and inductive reasoning, appeals to experience and fact, and cites Sacred Scripture and other thinkers. He points out that in theology the argument from authority, that is, Scripture and the pronouncements of the church, is the strongest argument; but in philosophy an appeal to the opinion of other thinkers is the weakest. His knowledge of philosophical and theological literature is extraordinary. He makes greatest use of the writings of Aristotle and St. Augustine, but countless other men are quoted: great Greeks and Romans such as Socrates, Plato, Plotinus, Cicero, and Seneca; Fathers of the Church; Averroës, Avicenna, and other Arabs; and Jewish thinkers, such as Maimonides and Ibn Gabirol. Yet he never quotes without need. He is never harsh or captious in criticism and follows the rule that truth is to be respected rather than persons.

Aquinas' great analytical powers are surpassed by his powers of synthesis and construction. Making use of the best that had been accomplished by the patristic and earlier medieval thinkers, and of Aristotle's concepts, principles, and methods— and adding his own great contributions—he produced new syntheses in both philosophy and theology. He showed that there need not and could not be genuine conflicts between faith and reason, but that true theology and sound science aid one another. His work illustrates faith seeking understanding and faith as a way to understanding. Its spirit likewise illustrates the "*Amo ut intelligam*" of the mystics. He is always the intellectualist and the realist. Completeness, clearness, and exactness are his marks as thinker and writer.

Influence. St. Thomas' influence was great in his own time, and from the 13th century on he has never lacked followers. Although his influence waned between the 16th and the 19th centuries, the revival of Thomistic studies has been one of the most remarkable intellectual movements since the mid-19th century.

The extent of St. Thomas' influence is also suggested by the number of editions of his works, and the number of studies of his life and thought, that have been published. His books include *Scriptum super IV libros sententiarum magistri Patri Lombardi* (1254–56), a commentary on Peter Lombard's great textbook of the medieval universities and *Summa contra Gentiles* (1258–64), a defense of Christianity against Arab adversaries. His greatest work, *Summa theologica* (1266–73), was unfinished at his death.

JOHN K. RYAN
The Catholic University of America

Bibliography
Editions of St. Thomas' works include: the Leonine edition of *Opera Omnia* (Rome 1882–   ); the Parma edition of *Opera Omnia* (Parma 1852–73; New York 1948–   ); and *Summa theologica, Summa contra Gentiles,* and other works, tr. by the English Dominican Fathers (London and New York 1911–48). A.C. Pegis edited *Basic Writings of St. Thomas Aquinas* (New York 1945), and V.J. Bourke prepared *Thomistic Bibliography, 1920–1940* (St. Louis 1945).
Chenu, M.-D., *Toward Understanding St. Thomas,* tr. by A.M. Landry and D. Hughes (Chicago 1964).
Gilby, Thomas, *Political Thought of Thomas Aquinas* (Chicago 1958).
Gilson, Étienne, *The Christian Philosophy of St. Thomas Aquinas,* tr. by L.K. Shook (New York 1956).
Maritain, Jacques, *The Angelic Doctor,* tr. by J.F. Scanlan (New York 1931).
Meyer, Hans, *The Philosophy of St. Thomas Aquinas,* tr. by Frederick Eckhoff (St. Louis 1944).
Ryan, John K., ed., *Studies in Philosophy and the History of Philosophy,* 3 vols. (Washington 1961–65).
Walz, A.M., *St. Thomas Aquinas* (Westminster, Md., 1951).

AQUITAINE, ak'wə-tān, is an area comprising a large part of southwestern France. It was called *Aquitania* at the time of Julius Caesar, when it included the land between the Pyrenees and the Garonne River. The boundaries of the region have varied throughout its history. In the Middle Ages it was known as the duchy of Aquitaine, which in the 11th century extended from the Pyrenees north to the Loire Valley and east to the Rhône River. In the 10th century, Aquitaine also came to be known as *Guienne*, a name that supplanted "Aquitaine" in the late Middle Ages.

Little is known about Aquitaine prior to its occupation late in the 1st century B.C. by the Romans, but the inhabitants seem to have been Basques. Aquitaine became an integral part of the Roman empire and was one of the most thoroughly Romanized of the conquered provinces. When the empire broke up in the 5th century, most of Aquitaine was occupied by the Visigoths. Early in the 6th century Aquitaine was conquered by the Franks under Clovis and for 150 years was ruled by his Merovingian successors. In the middle of the 7th century Aquitaine became independent under a local noble styling himself duke. When the Muslims swept north of the Pyrenees early in the 8th century, the duke of Aquitaine had to ask for the military aid of Charles Martel, the de facto ruler of the Merovingian state. When the Muslims were repulsed, Aquitaine became a part of the Carolingian empire. In the last decade of the 9th century Charles the Simple bestowed Aquitaine on William the Pious, count of Auvergne.

Although tied to the French kings by feudal relations, Aquitaine remained virtually independent until 1137, when it went to King Louis VII by his marriage to Eleanor of Aquitaine, the daughter of Duke William X. In 1152, after her divorce from Louis VII, she married Henry Plantagenet, count of Anjou and duke of Normandy, who in 1154 came to the throne of England as Henry II. In the early 1200's, King John lost part of Aquitaine to the French king. The southern part (Gascony) remained English until the end of the Hundred Years' War in 1453.

BRYCE LYON, *Brown University*

ARAB, ar'əb, a name given to about 100 million persons who live in a group of independent nation-states in North Africa and the Middle East and have a common linguistic and cultural heritage. The religion of Islam has shaped this heritage, although about one tenth of the Arabs are not Muslims.

The Arabs occupy about 4,500,000 square miles (11,600,000 sq km) of land (an area approximately 50 percent larger than the continental United States) in the following independent countries: Morocco, Algeria, Tunisia, Libya, United Arab Republic (Egypt), Sudan, Jordan, Lebanon, Syria, Iraq, Saudi Arabia, Kuwait, and Yemen. About a million more live in territories along the southern and eastern coasts of the Arabian peninsula. Another 750,000 persons of Arab birth and descent, mainly from Lebanon and Syria, live in North and South America. Some 300,000 Arabs live in Israel.

On the basis of physical characteristics, the Arabs are regarded as Mediterranean: moderate to short in stature, slight in build, and dark in complexion. There are, however, wide physical differences among them, and this characterization is far from tenable along the land borders of the Arab world.

Linguistic Unity. Language is the basis of Arab cultural unity and of Arab efforts to achieve political unity. The Arabic language, which is one of the Semitic languages, is the principal cultural characteristic shared by all Arabs. As the language of the Koran, it is the Arab's link with the Islamic tradition. It is a vehicle of cultural and political expression among a people who readily respond to the evocative power it affords.

Classical Arabic has always been understood by the highly educated. In the case of modern Arabic, despite the existence of regional dialects, the media of mass communications have helped to develop a standard form of Arabic that is increasingly understood by all Arabs.

In adapting to a severe physical environment over thousands of years, the Arabs have constructed three kinds of community or social organization: nomadic, agricultural, and urban.

Nomadic Arabs. The nomads and seminomads (or bedouins), though declining proportionately to other Arabs, still number a few million. They occupy the vast deserts and steppes, over which they wander in regular patterns. Nomadic society is based on the family. The families are organized into larger groups of clans and tribes, which perform those functions that in other kinds of communities are carried out by more specialized agencies. Traditionally, the bedouins provided the manpower that carried Islamic and Arab rule far from its origin in central Arabia. Their values, such as courage, pride, generosity, and cunning, have become the values of all of Arab society.

Until the 20th century, bedouins were able to escape the controls of central governments, although bedouins have always maintained important if intermittent (and often predatory) relations with the villages and cities along their routes of travel and near their resting places. More recently, however, the governments have exercised greater control over bedouins, and most of them have "sedenterization" programs to facilitate the conversion of bedouins into peasants or urban workers. Even before the development of technology, which made this change inevitable, this process was set in motion by economic and political changes that reduced the importance of the bedouins as suppliers of animals and as paid protectors of travel routes.

Agricultural Arabs. Over two thirds of the Arabs live in agricultural villages built close to one another along the great rivers or more widely separated in the mountainous and steppelike areas. There land itself is the most important aspect of life. The family and religion influence attitudes, behavior, and expectations to a larger extent than in the other two types of communities.

There is greater division of labor and specialization than in desert society, but the structure of social classes remains simpler than in the cities. Among the agricultural Arabs the main difference has been between the families who own land and those who do not. During the 19th century a class of large-estate owners developed in several Arab regions under the influence of foreign and native rulers. Following World War II, however, independence, ideological change, and land reform combined to reduce or eliminate this class.

Despite a variety of plans for raising the standard of living in the villages, material conditions have not much improved, and most of the Arabs tied to the land are economically not much better off than the bedouins. Loyalties are changing in the village, yet they still cluster around the individual, the family, and religion. Effective loyalties to the nation, the state, and to wide economic or political associations are slow to develop.

Urban Arabs. Urban centers in the Arab world often grew out of religious or protective considerations. Cities have always dominated the hinterland and have exercised cultural, economic, and political influences far out of proportion to the number of their inhabitants. Economically, Arab cities have been centers of finance, commerce, and crafts. Only in the 20th century has there been an appreciable development of manufacturing—at first under foreign control, then through native private enterprise, and more recently under the direction and control of the governments.

Today there is a large migration to the cities from the poorer sections of the countryside. As a consequence, there is serious unemployment or underemployment in the cities. There are housing shortages in the center of the cities, and shantytowns have grown up on the outskirts. Arab cities are mixtures of old and new patterns, showing the effect of successive foreign influences on native foundations. Some cities have recently introduced urban planning, yet too often this has led to sheer display or has been neglected as the governments have concentrated on planning for economic growth.

The city has provided the impetus for the vast social changes that Arab governments, several of which are controlled by military regimes, have been trying to induce. Advancing technology, public education, and political ideologies all contribute to this urgent drive for "modernization."

Thus far, however, even those most anxious for change have had to admit that older values and institutions do not easily yield to exhortation. Few levers of spontaneous, widely based, profound, and self-perpetuating change have yet been found in the Arab world.

MORROE BERGER, *Princeton University*

ARAB CIVILIZATION.

ARAB CIVILIZATION. The Arabs were originally the people of the Arabian desert. Converted to Islam in the 7th century A.D., they conquered the Middle East from the Sassanian and Byzantine empires and established a succession of Arab-Islamic Middle Eastern empires, from Spain to central Asia and from the Caucasus to India. More profoundly, Islam, its laws and doctrines, and the culture associated with it became the almost universally accepted religion and culture of Persians, Turks, and many other peoples as well as Arabs. Islam gave Middle Eastern civilization a unity never before achieved. Religious learning, a brilliant literature, beautiful works of art (see ISLAMIC ART AND ARCHITECTURE), and the scholarly preservation of classical thought were among the achievements of the civilization. Although the Arab empires proved ephemeral, Islam continues to flourish as a religion and as the civilization of the Middle East.

CONTENTS

1. History

Arabia was the cradle of Islam and of Arabic civilization. In the 6th century A.D., it was a region with some sedentary agricultural and commercial life centered in Yemen and on the borders of Syria and Iraq, but the interior was the domain of camel-raising bedouin nomads. The bedouins were animists and polytheists in religious belief. They lived in small clans that migrated and fought in common and recognized no authority outside the patriarchal leadership of the clan sheikh. Disputes over water pasturage led to anarchic violence in Arabia. Yet at the same time, the politically and culturally backward peninsula was being influenced by the highly developed Byzantine and Sassanian empires that surrounded it. Military techniques, weapons, material goods, and above all, the ideas of the Jewish and Christian religions were spreading by settlements, itinerant preachers, and contacts with already converted border peoples.

The most advanced Arab communities were at the oases of Mecca and Medina. Mecca was a sanctuary settled in the 5th century A.D. by tribesmen called the Quraysh. Its shrine, the Kaaba, became a center for Arabian pilgrimage and trade, and thus the traditional sanctity of family ties and tribal values were undermined by commercial and political ambitions. Medina was an agricultural oasis, divided by bitter feuds among the Arab pagans and between the pagan and Jewish clans of the oasis.

ARAB EMPIRES AND ISLAMIC CIVILIZATION

The Prophet. Mohammed (Muhammad) the prophet was born in Mecca and earned his living in the caravan trading business of his wife Khadija. About 610 he received revelations (later put down in the book of the Koran) and founded a new religion, Islam. Mohammed taught monotheism to the polytheists, warned that God would judge men's deeds, and preached that they must live in pious fear of the wrath of Allah and strive for goodness. In many respects his preaching resembled Jewish and Christian beliefs, but it was nonetheless an original religious inspiration. Mohammed's early preaching won a number of converts but soon roused the opposition of most Meccans, because he challenged the traditional way of life and the authority of the elders. Opposition only confirmed the prophet in his conviction that God had chosen him, the last of His prophets, to warn Arabians of the coming last judgment. Opposition also showed him that to win converts he needed the support of a strong following and a community to practice his teachings. Thus, he accepted an invitation to arbitrate in strife-torn Medina. His emigration from Mecca to Medina in 622, called the Hegira (Hijra), marks the founding of the Muslim community and the first year of the Muslim era.

At Medina, Mohammed's work changed from preaching the principles of his faith to building the community that would embody it. Laws for religious life, family affairs, and other social concerns were revealed. Gradually, Mohammed welded the various clans of Medina, and the immigrants who accompanied him from Mecca, into one community. The Jews who would not accept his mission were destroyed, and the rest of Medina came to believe in him as their divinely inspired political and religious leader.

From Medina he waged war against Mecca and the tribes of Arabia until, in 630, Mecca capitulated and accepted Islam. The Kaaba was transformed into a shrine of the new faith. Whatever their kinship or tribal ties, all Muslims, who were those who accepted his revelations, became united by common religious beliefs.

Patriarchal Caliphate. Mohammed's death in June 632 called the survival of the Muslim community into question. But the clans in Medina decided to choose a successor, a caliph, to preserve Mohammed's religious legacy and political federation. Abu Bakr (reigned 632–634), an early convert and disciple of the prophet, was unanimously elected, but many of the bedouin tribes refused to recognize his authority. Abu Bakr attacked his tribal enemies (Wars of the Ridda), loosing chaos in Arabia. Tribes in flight, or seeking compensations for their losses, soon breached both the Iraqi-Sassanian and Syrian-Byzantine frontiers. Abu Bakr encouraged the raids into Palestine, where success emboldened the Arab tribesmen to merge forces and defeat a Byzantine army near Gaza in 634 (Battle of Ajnadayn). From then on, sporadic Arabian incursions became an invasion. The immediate causes of the Arab conquests were pressures and opportunities generated by wars among the Arabs themselves. Religious motives were very much in the background, although the improverishment and violence of Arabian life was tinder for the spark of the Ridda wars.

From Ajnadayn the Arabs seized the rest of Syria. Damascus was occupied in 636 after the Battle of the Yarmuk, and the rest of Syria by 641. Egypt was taken in 641–642, but the conquest of North Africa, begun in 634, required the remainder of the century. In Iraq the armies of the Sassanian empire were destroyed in 637 at the Battle of Qadisiya. Upper Mesopotamia was taken by 641, most of western Iran by 644, Fars by 649, and Khurasan by 654. Imperial armies were not adequate to check the Arab invaders, and many peoples readily accepted the victors.

Establishing an orderly government was the work of the second caliph, Umar (reigned 634–644). His basic principle was that the Arabs were to be a military ruling caste. They were not to settle or mix with the conquered people but were to be garrisoned in all-Arab cities—some created, some adapted for the purpose—where they could be organized for war and the distribution of pay. Masses of Arabs settled permanently throughout the Middle East. The conquered peoples were left entirely undisturbed in their religion, community life, and property on condition that they pay a tribute. Local notables and tributaries even cooperated in administration. The old imperial bureaucracies were set to work, and the old taxes were collected on behalf of the Arabs. Islam, in these circumstances, was the unifying tie between the various tribes of conquering Arabs and the basis of the authority of the caliphate. Conversion of the subject peoples was not encouraged. The Middle East was not conquered to spread Islam, but to be ruled by Muslims.

When the caliph Umar was killed in 644, a council of Meccans selected Uthman, of the Meccan Umayyad family, to be the new caliph. Uthman, however, became the focus of Arab resentments. The pious resented the increasing secularization of the caliphate and its absorption into military and administrative affairs. Medinians resented nepotism in the assignment of government posts and the distribution of lands. The tribesmen of the garrison towns were impatient of any superior authority as such and resented the administration's corruption and the withdrawal of surplus revenues to the caliph's treasury.

Uthman's ineptitude led to his assassination, and Ali, Mohammed's nephew and one of his most devoted followers, was elected in Medina. He was opposed by the old Meccan families, whom he defeated at the Battle of the Camel in 656. Muawiya, the Umayyad governor of Iraq, also refused to recognize Ali's authority, and as kinsman of the murdered Uthman, claimed vengeance. Ali was obliged by moderate allies to agree to Muawiya's proposal for an arbitration. In 659 the negotiators decided that Uthman's murder was not legitimate and that a council should be called to elect a new caliph. Ali was discredited, and Muawiya, biding his time until Ali's murder, benefited by the drift of Arab opinion in his favor and became caliph in 661. The civil war ended the moral and political supremacy of Mecca and Medina in the Arab empire, and the capital was transferred to Damascus. Its greatest consequence was a split in the Muslim world between the supporters of Ali, known as the Shiites, and the adherents of Muawiya, known as the Sunnites. The split eventually hardened into permanent religious, as well as political, differences.

Umayyad Dynasty. Muawiya (reigned 661–680) was the first caliph of the Umayyad dynasty (661–750). He strengthened the caliphate and kept the peace but could not suppress the antagonisms that caused the first civil war. At his death the second Arab civil war (680–692) broke out. Muawiya's son Yazid (reigned 680–683) succeeded him, but Husayn, the son of Ali, claimed the caliphate and was killed at Karbala in 681. Arabians and Iraqis then recognized Ibn al-Zubayr as caliph, but Yazid's successor, Abd al-Malik (reigned 685–705), defeated the rebels and suppressed bedouin tribal warfare by 692.

The civil war episode was a turning point in the history of the caliphate. Caliphs from Abd al-Malik to Hisham (reigned 724–743) generally relied less on the Arabs and built up the powers of the state and the forces of Syria. Administra-

tive centralization began in earnest. The Arab conquests were resumed. Spain, Transoxiana, and the Byzantine empire were all invaded. The translation of administrative records into Arabic, the minting of a new Arabic coinage, and monumental constructions dramatized the prestige of the caliphate and its services to Islam and the Arabs.

Despite this centralization of power, tribal disputes remained a latent threat to the stability of the caliphate. In addition, the gradual assimilation of the Arabs and their subjects to each other undercut the basic principles on which Umayyad government had been founded. Arabs became landowners, merchants, and peasants. Non-Arabs began to convert to Islam, and those who migrated to the garrison towns became clients or mawali of the Arabs. Mawali and other converts demanded equality in pay or in fiscal privileges, and their claims, though opposed by the Arabs, could not be ignored. The Mawali played a vital part in administration and an increasing role in the Arab armies and in religious and cultural life. The caliphate was trapped between conflicting demands from different segments of its supporters.

Umar II (reigned 717–720) sought to resolve these difficulties by embodying the principle of the equality of all Muslims in reforms that stressed equal pay for military service and in tax reforms that made land and property, rather than caste, the basis of fiscal obligations. Later caliphs, especially Hisham, made similar reforms, but caliphal efforts were only halfhearted and were obstructed by local Arab and bureaucratic interests.

The grievances of both Arabs and non-Arabs with the caliphate were exploited by the Abbasid family, which claimed legitimate title to the caliphate as descendants of Mohammed's uncle Abbas. For decades they carried on a secret movement. Exhausted by decades of military efforts and by the defeat of Syrian armies in Anatolia, Central Asia, and North Africa, sucked into renewed tribal disputes, harassed by bedouin rebellions and Shiite outbursts, Umayyad power collapsed by 749, and the Abbasids, led by Abu Muslim, swept out the Umayyads. Abu'l-Abbas was then declared the first caliph of a dynasty that was to rule for the next 500 years.

Abbasid Caliphate at Its Height. The new Abbasid dynasty effected a revolution in the Arab empire. The Abbasids accepted the equality of all Muslims, and privilege was no longer based on Arab blood but on service to Islam and the empire. The caliphate patronized religious activity and made itself responsible for the defense of Islam against heresy. Widespread conversions were made, although very substantial Zoroastrian, Christian, and Jewish communities persisted for centuries and had a strong influence on the development of Islam. Arabic, the official language of the empire, became a Middle Eastern lingua franca. Thus, the literature and religion of the Arabs was adopted by other Middle Eastern people.

In Abbasid government the Arabs had to share power and privilege with non-Arabs. The caliphate no longer relied on the Arab nation in arms for military support but on a professional army that, though basically Arab in composition, was recruited on the basis of service and loyalty. Arabs remained important as governors, generals, courtiers, and in religious life, but Persian scribes

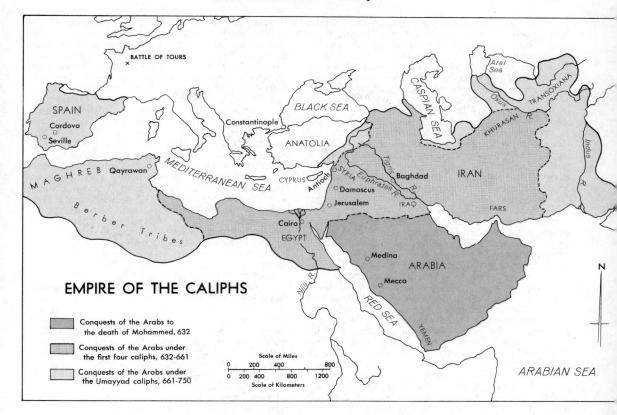

EMPIRE OF THE CALIPHS

Conquests of the Arabs to
the death of Mohammed, 632

Conquests of the Arabs under
the first four caliphs, 632-661

Conquests of the Arabs under
the Umayyad caliphs, 661-750

Scale of Miles
0   200   400   800
0 200 400   800   1200
Scale of Kilometers

were the backbone of an enormously strengthened bureaucracy. The Barmecid (Barmakid) family of viziers headed the government from about 750 to 803 and represented Iranian interests. In some of the provinces the caliphs appointed their own governors, but in others, local princes and notables continued to rule as vassals or tributaries. The empire was not rigidly organized; it adjusted flexibly to the realities of power in all provinces. The ultimate objective of government organization was taxation, and on the local level, government staffs, with some degree of collaboration from local notables, taxed the peasants. Abbasid government was thus based on the support of Arab populations and elites, the administrative classes, landowning and local ruling notabilities of every race and religion, the commercial classes favored by territorial unification, and, finally, on the *ulama* (*ulema*)—the religious elites, protected and organized by the empire.

The early Abbasid caliphs reshaped the empire into this form. Al-Mansur (reigned 754–775) founded the capital city of Baghdad and suppressed a variety of rebellious peoples. Al-Mahdi (reigned 775–785) began the persecution of heretics. The empire reached its apogee under Harun ar-Rashid (reigned 786–809), but Harun sowed the seeds of destruction when he deposed the Barmecids and made a complicated succession arrangement calling for the division of the empire between his two sons, al-Amin and al-Mamun. This led, in the reign (809–813) of al-Amin, to a civil war whose repercussions were ultimately to undermine the viability of the caliphate. Al-Mamun's victory resulted in the alienation of the Arab populations, who resisted what they regarded as the domination of his

Iranian supporters. Thus the alliance of Iranian notables and Arab elites, which had been the political foundation of the empire, was compromised.

The Caliphate in Decline. Al-Mamun (reigned 813–833) sought to regain popular support by manipulating religious beliefs, but his and other caliphal efforts only alienated the religious classes. Al-Mamun's efforts to rebuild the political bases of the caliphate were also ill-starred. Having come to power with the support of newly constituted Iranian armies, the caliph was in the power of the generals. He had to appoint Tahir Ibn Husayn governor of Khurasan as a tributary ally rather than a subordinate official, and the post became hereditary in the Tahirid family (820–873)—an important step in the decentralization of caliphal power.

Further difficulties stemmed from the efforts of al-Mamun and his successor al-Mutasim (reigned 833–842) to counterbalance Tahirid power. The caliphs recruited Central Asian regiments and Turkish slaves for a new army, but the new regiments became the masters rather than the servants of the caliphate. Between 833 and 870 they virtually destroyed the empire. Pursuing their own interests, the praetorian guards seized control of the caliphs and usurped control of the central administration. Worse still, chaotic fighting for spoils reduced the central government to impotence. Efforts of al-Mutawakkil (reigned 847–861) to find new military supporters and to revive popular support failed. By 870 the caliphate was at a nadir of power and influence.

Chaos at the center resulted in the separation of various provinces from central control. Some, such as Egypt under the Tulunids from 868 to

905, fell into the hands of Turkish officers who established their own dynasties. Others were seized by popular rebellions, such as the one led by the Saffarids, who controlled most of eastern Iran from 861 until 900. The caliphate did contrive to restore order by 905, but a total collapse of the imperial system was only postponed. Corruption of the central administration, the division of the bureaus into factions exploiting the government in their own interests, loss of control over taxable rural lands, and loss of revenue meant that military victories could no longer be followed up by routine government. Independent principalities and warlords burgeoned again. In the early 10th century the Samanids controlled Khurasan and Transoxiana; the Buwayhids, western Iran; the Hamdanids, Upper Mesopotamia; and the Ikhshidids, Egypt. Ultimately the Buwayhids seized Baghdad in 945, and full governmental powers, both military and civil, were vested in them. The caliphate, deprived of all effective power, remained for centuries the legitimate fount of all authority and the symbol of the religious unity of the Muslim community, but the empire as a Middle Eastern political unity was lost. The year 945 marks the effective end of the Abbasid empire.

Fragmentation. The demise of the unified empire meant the succession of a number of independent provincial dynasties. The Samanid house controlled Transoxiana and Khurasan until 999, when they were defeated by the Karakhanids, who took over Transoxiana, and the Ghaznavids of Afghanistan, who took control of Khurasan. Western Iran and Iraq were in Buwayhid hands until 1055. The Fatimids ruled Egypt (969–1171) and parts of Syria. Other petty princes ruled in Syria and Mesopotamia. These dynasties were relatively unstable and short-lived, disturbed by family quarrels and civil wars, by a general decline of bureaucratic organization in all regions except Egypt, and by the decentralization of control over the land and its taxable resources in favor of the leading army officers. Instead of revenues and salaries, centrally controlled, land was granted to the soldiers in return for military service. This arrangement supported armies composed largely of slaves, usually Turkish in origin, who became the ruling elite.

Political decentralization was accompanied in many places by economic regression. Exploitation of the peasantry and neglect of irrigation in Iraq and Iran led to severe losses in agricultural capacity. Long before the Mongol invasions the Middle East was losing productive resources.

Intense religious and social changes also began in the 10th century. The 10th and 11th centuries were a period of Shiite preeminence under the officially Shiite Fatimid, Buwayhid, and Hamdanid dynasties. Sufism (a form of Islamic mysticism) flourished. Islamic literature was translated and re-created in a new Persian language, making the culture accessible to non-Arabic speaking peoples, an important step in the spread of Islam as a world religion. In Iran and Central Asia, Zoroastrian and pagan peoples were converted to Islam. Finally, this period witnessed the consolidation of Muslim orthodoxy in the form of the Muslim schools of law and the emergence of the ulama-religious elites as the social and political chiefs of Muslim communities.

The Seljuks. These important internal changes were all furthered by the Seljuk (Saljuq) invasions. Turkoman pastoralists from Central Asia overran the Middle East in the middle of the 11th century, swept away the Ghaznavids, the Buwayhids, and the lesser Syrian principalities, and established the largest empire in the region since Abbasid times (1040–1193). The invasion introduced substantial Turkish populations into parts of the Middle East, furthered the decline of agriculture, and contributed to political instability. The invasions, however, did little to disturb Islam as a religion or the local communities built around it. The Seljuk conquest superimposed a new Turkish military elite over the Persian and Arab bureaucratic and religious functionaries, who continued to administer taxation and carry on local government. The Seljuk regime, based on an alliance of Turkish soldiers with native scribes and ulama, was passionately orthodox, repressed Shiism, and founded numerous madrasas, colleges of law and religion, which served for the training of scholars and scribes and for the standardization of orthodox Islam. Sunni Islam, after centuries of evolution, was consolidated into its lasting form and was made the prevailing religion of the Middle East.

Despite these important cultural contributions, there were family disputes, usurpations by governors, and a decentralization of fiscal power that resulted in the fragmentation of the Seljuk empire. Nomadic invasions of the Middle East culminated in the invasion by the Mongols under Hulagu, who in 1258 destroyed Baghdad and extinguished the Abbasid dynasty. For a time, in one place or another, the Mongols threatened to extinguish Islamic civilization.

Egypt and Syria. In other parts of the Middle East, the same tendencies toward political fragmentation, economic regression, and religious ferment, followed by the consolidation of Islamic orthodoxy, were manifest. Egypt was a partial exception to these trends. Shiite missionaries of the Ismaili sect founded the Fatimid empire in North Africa in 909 and in 969 conquered Egypt and some parts of Syria. The Fatimids appropriated the title of the caliph and sponsored an Ismaili missionary movement throughout the Islamic world to further their own ambitions for a universal Muslim empire. These missions had little success, and the Fatimid regime remained an Egyptian state, with African and Syrian possessions, supported by Berber and other foreign armies and a powerful centralized administration. After about a century the Fatimids lost their African and Syrian possessions and were undermined in Egypt by battles between their various army regiments. Deprived of effective power by their generals, deprived of authority by schisms within the Ismaili movement, the Fatimids succumbed finally to invasions from Syria in 1169, led by Saladin, a Kurdish emir from Syria.

Syria, from the fall of the Abbasids until the rise of Saladin, had been divided into small and contending principalities. The Fatimids controlled southern Syria and Damascus until 1076. The Byzantine empire, three centuries after the Arab conquests, reconquered Antioch and northern Syria, and the stand-off between the major contenders allowed small tribal states, independent cities, and sectarian communities to flourish. The Seljuks, invading in the latter half of the 11th century, brought Syria under their suzerainty, but they were unable to establish any lasting unity. The province remained divided and exposed to further invasions, this time from European Crusaders.

A product of papal and Byzantine politics, Norman ambitions, and French and European social unrest, the crusading armies seized Antioch, Edessa, Tripoli, Jerusalem, and most of Palestine between 1098 and 1109. The Muslims were at first too divided to repulse the invaders, but throughout the 12th century both Muslim power and Muslim determination to resist built up. Despite the frustrations of constantly shifting alliances, the Seljuk atabeg, Zangi of Mosul, managed to seize Aleppo in 1128 and Edessa in 1144. His son, Nur ad-Din, defended Damascus against the Second Crusade in 1147. In 1169 he sent his generals Shirkuh and Saladin to Egypt to seize the disintegrating Fatimid state and keep it out of the hands of the Crusaders.

Saladin's seizure of Egypt began a new epoch. Saladin accomplished, by 1183, what his predecessors could not—the unification of Egypt, Syria, and Mesopotamia into one state. In 1187 at Hattin he defeated the massed Crusaders' armies and recaptured Jerusalem and most of Palestine. Saladin's victories were built on widespread Muslim support rallied by vigorous espousal and patronage of Muslim orthodoxy.

When he died in 1193, Saladin was succeeded by his family, the Ayyubid dynasty (1193–1249). Family coalition replaced his unified government, and the Ayyubids reversed many of his policies, temporizing with the Crusaders, unwilling to risk new invasions or to compromise a flourishing and lucrative trade between East and West.

The Ayyubid house was extinguished in Egypt in 1249 by the revolt of slave soldiers called Mamluks, who appointed their own generals to be heads of state or sultans. To legitimize their government, the Mamluks refounded the Abbasid caliphate in Cairo and reinforced state collaboration with the religious elites. They defended Syria against the Mongols, defeated them at Ayn Jalut in 1260, and incorporated the province into their empire. By 1291 they also expelled the Crusaders from their last possession, Acre, in Palestine. There followed a long period—the Bahri Mamluk regime (1250–1382)—of relative stability and security for the populations of Egypt and Syria, but the succeeding Circassian period (1382–1517) witnessed the degradation of the state, economic decline, and social turmoil. In 1517 the Ottoman empire seized both Egypt and Syria and continued to control them until the end of World War I.

From the 7th to the 15th century, the Arabs founded a series of empires that served to create a new Islamic Middle Eastern civilization. From the 10th century, this civilization took definitive form, even though, almost paradoxically, centuries of political hardship followed. Eventually, the history of the Arab provinces became part of the history of the Ottoman empire.

The Arabs under Ottoman Rule. In many respects the Ottoman conquests did not involve substantial changes in Syria, Egypt, and the parts of Iraq that came under Ottoman rule. Ottoman domination substituted one elite for another, though in Egypt, the Mamluks continued to serve under Ottoman overlordship. However, Ottoman rule brought the Arab world into the historical rhythm of the larger empire. In the 16th and part of the 17th centuries, the Ottomans fostered irrigation and agricultural development, repressed bedouin violence, and managed a relatively tolerable and equitable system of taxation.

By the 18th century, however, the decline of the Ottoman empire undermined the security of the Arab provinces. Local governors established their effective independence of Istanbul. Factional and communal interests degenerated into fratricidal struggles. Bedouin violence grew unchecked. Agriculture declined. Taxation became rapacious and heedless of the security of the peasantry. In these conditions, Muslim religious and cultural life stagnated. Yet by the end of the 18th century, fresh energies mustered within the society and fresh stimuli from the European West opened new potentialities for the Arab peoples. The 19th century opened a new epoch in the history of the Middle East.

North Africa and Spain. The history of Muslim North Africa and Spain forms a separate chapter in the history of the Arab world. The Arab conquests proceeded slowly in this region, and only after the establishment of Qayrawan (Kairouan) in Tunisia in 670 was the whole of North Africa as far as the Atlantic brought under Muslim rule. Spain was invaded in 711 by Arab and Berber raiders, but their advances in Europe were checked at the Battle of Tours in 732.

The power of the caliphate in western North Africa (the Maghreb) and Spain was never fully established. In the 8th century, Arab rule was resisted by the Berbers of the Maghreb, who embraced the Kharijite form of Islam. The Idrisids established an independent Moroccan Berber kingdom lasting from the 8th to the 10th century. In Tunisia and Algeria the Aghlabid governors were effectively independent in the 9th century, though technically vassals of the Abbasids. In Spain an Umayyad family also established independent rule in 756.

At the beginning of the 10th century the Fatimids, appealing to Berber support for their Shiite claims to the caliphate, destroyed the Aghlabids and conquered most of North Africa and Egypt. In Spain the Umayyad ruler Abd ar-Rahman III (reigned 912–961) also claimed the title of caliph and contested Fatimid influence in Morocco.

In little more than a century both the Fatimid and the Umayyad states declined. The Zirid dynasty in Tunisia declared its independence of the Fatimids, while numerous Berber tribal states controlled Morocco and Algeria. Umayyad Spain collapsed into a multitude of tiny principalities, and the Christians began to conquer territory in Spain from the Muslims. Beginning in the 11th century, North Africa and Spain were overwhelmed by waves of bedouin invasions. The banu-Hilal (Beni Hilal) from the east destroyed most of Tunisia and Algeria. From the Sahara, Sanhaja Berber tribes united by the Almoravid religious movement led by Yusuf Ibn Tashfin conquered both Morocco and Muslim Spain, starting in 1053. The political unification of Morocco and Spain checked the Christian advances and permitted Hispano-Muslim culture to seep into North Africa. The Almoravids, however, were succeeded by another bedouin confederation and empire, the Almohad. Inspired by the religious reforms of Muhammad Ibn Tumart, the Almohads united most of North Africa and Spain between 1130 and 1269, when this empire also rapidly dissolved on all fronts. The Hafsids became independent in Tunisia from 1229 to 1574, while the Merinids inherited Morocco, which they ruled from the 13th to the 15th century.

The decline of the Almohads in Spain cost the Muslims control of the country. By 1248 the

Christians had recaptured both Cordova and Seville and reduced Muslim possessions to the kingdom of Granada, which survived until 1492. Although the Christians pressed their attacks against North Africa, Tunisia and Algeria came under Ottoman suzerainty, and Morocco was ruled by the Saadians until the 19th century.

IRA M. LAPIDUS
University of California at Berkeley

Bibliography

Bartold, Vasilii V., *Turkestan Down to the Mongol Invasion* (London 1959).
Bosworth, Clifford E., *The Ghaznavids* (Edinburgh 1963).
Bowen, Harold, *Life and Times of Ali ibn Isa* (New York and London 1928).
Lewis, Bernard, *The Arabs in History* (New York 1960).
Saunders, John Joseph, *A History of Medieval Islam* (London 1965).
Setton, Kenneth M., ed., *A History of the Crusades*, 2 vols. (Philadelphia 1955–62).
Watt, William Montgomery, *Muhammad at Mecca* (New York and London 1953).
Watt, William Montgomery, *Muhammad at Medina* (New York and London 1956).
Wellhausen, Julius, *The Arab Kingdom and Its Fall* (Beirut 1964).

ARAB REAWAKENING

Most scholars today place the beginnings of modern Arab history in the early 19th century. One of the most remarkable figures of that century, and perhaps the most important for modern Arab history, was the Albanian soldier of fortune, Mehmet (also Mehemet or Muhammad) Ali (1769–1849), who seized power in Egypt in 1805 and was then appointed viceroy of Egypt by Egypt's suzerain, the Ottoman sultan. Uninterested in Egypt or the Arabs for themselves, he determined to use them for his personal and dynastic ends. Impressed by the power of Europe and fearful of his suzerain, who was a reforming sultan, Mehmet Ali intended to build a powerful state by making modern soldiers out of the Egyptian peasants, by improving agricultural methods, by nationalizing commerce, by industrializing the country, and by educating a new class of technicians and bureaucrats in Europe or in Egyptian schools newly created along European lines.

Westernization of Egypt. Mehmet Ali failed in his grand design, but he laid the groundwork for later developments in the Arab world. In Egypt his new industry was largely abandoned even before his death; the European powers forced him to give up centralized control over the economy and commerce and to disband his military machine. But cultural impulses generated by his activities could not be stilled. Outside Egypt, in areas conquered by Egyptian armies, similar profound changes were in progress. Courting European favor, Mehmet Ali, acting, as he said, as "the armed missionary of civilization," welcomed Western merchants, clergymen, and diplomats and allowed Christians new freedom. The existence of his army created a new market, trade barriers were broken down, and economic investment was encouraged. American missionaries founded schools and clinics and eventually universities.

Old ways were judged outmoded, styles changed, new trade routes were established, new cities grew, and new social groups profited while some of the old were ruined. By mid-century, European merchants monopolized much of the commerce, industry, transport, and finance. The building of the Suez Canal, the cost of creating the new Egypt, and indulgence in European luxuries gradually brought the whole economy under European control and virtual foreclosure.

In turn, the pressures of Western merchants and creditors, the ambitions and fears of European powers, and the weakness of the Ottoman empire brought about de facto control by European advisors and consuls over many sensitive areas of Middle Eastern life.

Beginnings of National Consciousness. Only vaguely perceiving this pattern of events at first, educated Arabs eagerly embraced European mores and set themselves the task of translating Europe to their countrymen. As printing became common and cheap and the literate audience grew, not only European books but also the Arab classics became readily available. The rediscovery of the Arabic heritage during a confrontation with Europe gave birth to the first sense of national consciousness. By the 1870's a reaction against the West had begun.

This reaction took several different forms. The Wahhabis of Arabia, as well as other groups, tried to isolate Islam from Western Christian or secular "infection." Other Muslims tried to revitalize Islam. Outside the sphere of religion a succession of statesmen sought to defend themselves against European domination by becoming modern in the European sense, following essentially the pattern of Mehmet Ali. Still others tried military solutions. British invasions ended the career of the first modern Egyptian military leader, Ahmad Urabi (Arabi) in 1882. In 1898 the British also checked a Sudanese military uprising.

The failure of the soldier, the religious leader, and the modernizer to provide an effective defense against the West forced Arabs to consider more critically the basis of their corporate existence. A basis of nationality was sought in language, mainly by Christian Arabs who sought to minimize the importance of Islam. Gradually, the idea of nationalism spread in the Balkans, where the Ottomans were losing their foothold. And the Turks themselves set about creating their own ethnic and linguistic nationalism. But it was not until the eve of World War I, when European contempt for the weak and backward Arabs became manifest, that nationalism can be said to have become widespread. The first Egyptian political parties were founded in 1907 with the purpose of expelling the British. This movement was to come to a head in the "revolution" of 1919, when the Egyptians, determined to gain recognition of their national existence, demanded the right to send a delegation (*wafd*) to the Peace Conference.

World War I and the Demise of the Ottoman Empire. World War I and the alignment of the Ottoman Turks with Germany and Austria-Hungary provided an opportunity for Syrian and Arabian Arabs, supported by British arms and subsidy, to break loose from the Ottoman empire in the "Revolt in the Desert." (Westerners associate this revolt with Lawrence of Arabia.) At the war's end and with the collapse of the Ottoman empire, the leader of the revolt, Faisal, the son of the sharif of Mecca, had taken control of Damascus and much of Syria. At the Peace Conference he sought vainly to secure Syrian Arab national independence. When he failed at Paris, he returned to Damascus where he was proclaimed king. But when Syria was invaded by France, to whom the Peace Conference had awarded the mandate, Faisal was forced into exile.

Meanwhile, Britain had invaded Iraq and wrested the country from the Ottomans without

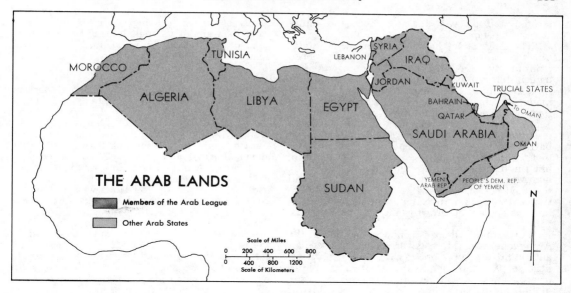

THE ARAB LANDS

■ Members of the Arab League

▨ Other Arab States

Scale of Miles
0   200   400   600   800
0   400   800   1200
Scale of Kilometers

N

any assistance from the Arabs. British policy was similar to that of the French in Syria. When a massive tribal revolt broke out against British rule in 1920, Faisal was retrieved from exile by the British and imposed on Iraq as its first king. Ironically, although Iraq was more backward than Egypt, Syria, or Palestine, it emerged from mandate status and achieved independence in 1932.

In Syria the French invasion left deep scars. The French were never able to create a government at once stable, friendly, and economical. Consequently, Syria lived under martial law virtually as an occupied state, suffering rebellions and repressions until the French were forced to evacuate in 1945 under British and U.S. pressure.

Palestine. In Palestine, which became a British mandate, a tragic and violent clash of nationalisms arose under British stimulus. As a means of encouraging Russian and American Jewish support for the Allies in World War I, the British government promised in the 1917 Balfour Declaration to allow "the establishment in Palestine of a National Home for the Jewish People." But the Arabs believed that the Husayn-McMahon correspondence of 1915–1916 had already promised Palestine to them as a part of the terms on which they revolted against the Ottoman empire. In the 1916 Sykes-Picot agreement the British also promised Palestine to the French.

After a period of bitter recrimination, the French bowed to the facts of British power. As in Syria, in Palestine the 1920's and 1930's were punctuated with violence, which after the enforced hiatus of World War II culminated in the 1948–1949 Arab-Israeli war and the flight and expulsion of the majority of the Arab population. The League of Arab States (see ARAB LEAGUE), formed in 1945, had signally failed in one of its purposes: to support the cause of the Arabs in Palestine. This failure of the Arab states led many Arabs to question the meaning of their nationalism, the health of their societies, and the politics of national security. Widespread disillusionment was a major cause of the series of coups that, over the next decade, toppled the governments of Syria, Lebanon, Egypt, and Iraq and resulted in the assassination of the king of Jordan. The "Palestine problem" became the major pre-

occupation of Arab thinkers and politicians. It was given further emphasis by the Israeli-French-British invasion of Egypt in 1956 and continued to be exacerbated by frontier hostility, arms races, and threats, which were so characteristic of the 1960's.

Although less pervasive in its impact on Arab thought, the Algerian war of independence dwarfed the Palestine war in length, cost, and savagery. Lasting seven years, occupying an average of nearly half a million French troops, involving the displacement of nearly three million people, and costing perhaps half a million lives and billions of dollars, it ended with the exodus of virtually the entire European population. Ironically, the war left behind in 1963 an exhausted and untrained population in possession of perhaps the most modern economic plant in the Arab world.

Arab World Today. Today, despite great diversity, differences, and hostility on political, economic, religious, and social issues, Arab governments agree on the need to gain strength and respect by modernizing their societies. All have programs that attempt to cope with rapid population growth by developing severely limited resources. Only in the oil-rich states of Saudi Arabia, Kuwait, Iraq, the Persian Gulf sheikhdoms, and Libya is capital sufficient for development needs. But in all the states a major transformation is in process, aimed at creating a modern industrial society in which, at least on the surface, little will survive from the past.

Perhaps the most fundamental changes are those resulting from education. In Egypt, the largest of the Arab states, the number of students enrolled in schools has increased nearly 25 times in the half century from 1920 to the mid-1960's. Even more important has been the growth of technical education since the mid-1950's. Not only the schools but also the army, the cinema, television, radio, and large works projects are significant means of instruction and stimulation. So great is the transformation resulting from these stimuli that it is possible to distinguish a new group in society different in motivation, discipline, education, and expectation. It is this group for which the development projects are created and on whose performance the future largely depends.

The Arab states have also attempted a state-directed industrial revolution. Progress has been painfully slow in Iraq, Syria, Morocco, and Jordan, faster in Egypt, and still faster in the states richest in oil. The greatest progress has been made in Lebanon and Algeria, which have profited from special relationships with Europe. A central problem has been the uneven spread of resources, capital, and people. Some attempts have been made, through lending by the oil states to their poorer neighbors, to spread the wealth, but this has been far less than the aid given by non-Arab states, notably the United States and the Soviet Union. Most of the Arab lands are showing some improvement, but all have high rates of population growth that tend to offset the gains.

Furthermore, there is a new radicalism in the Arab countries. Most governments are secular, authoritative, and *étatist:* with few exceptions, little scope is left for private initiative in politics or economics. Espousing what they call socialism, mobilizing mass opinion, and using the cold war to gain international assistance, such leaders as Gamal Abdel Nasser of the United Arab Republic (Egypt); Ahmed Ben Bella, who ruled Algeria until ousted by a coup in 1965; and Abdul Karim al-Kassem, who led the coup against the Iraqi monarchy and himself fell victim to another in 1964, appear to have taken Arab politics into a new sphere. It is, of course, too early to know whether their leadership has created its own counterbalance—with Ben Bella and Kassem replaced by more conservative governments and Nasser opposed by Saudi Arabian King Faisal and an Islamic movement. It is clear that vast and pressing problems remain and that the movements of transformation and cultural and political identification have not run their full course.

WILLIAM POLK, *University of Chicago*

Bibliography

Cremeans, Charles D., *The Arabs and the World* (New York 1963).
Gallagher, Charles F., *The United States and North Africa* (Cambridge, Mass., 1963).
Gibb, Hamilton A.R., *Modern Trends in Islam* (Chicago 1947).
Hourani, Albert H., *Arabic Thought in the Liberal Age* (London 1962).
Polk, William R., *The United States and the Arab World* (Cambridge, Mass., 1965).

2. Language

Arabic, Himyaritic (South Arabic), and Ethiopic belong to the southern group of the Semitic languages, of which Phoenician and Hebrew form the western, Aramaic the northern, and Accadian (Assyro-Babylonian) the eastern groups. Arabic shares with its sisters the characteristic features of Semitic speech, which include triconsonantal roots, inflectional endings, meagerness in mood and tense but richness in aspect, and capacity for expressing variation in meaning by a system for vocalic changes and by prefixes, suffixes, and other affixes. But it surpasses them all in its conservatism, copiousness of vocabulary, possibilities of syntactic distinction, and elaborateness of verbal forms—all of which combine to make Arabic the best surviving representative of the original Semitic speech, despite the fact that its recorded literature is one of the youngest of Semitic literatures. Arabic has succeeded in bringing out the potentialities of the Semitic family of speech to a higher degree of development than any of its cognates, most of which are dead or quasi-dead. It is the most widely used Semitic tongue.

South and North Arabic. South Arabic, also called Himyaritic or Sabaean, was the ancient tongue of Yemen and its environs and has survived in a few thousand inscriptions thus far discovered, the earliest of which dates from the 7th century B.C. South Arabic characters represent probably an early forking from the Sinaitic, which constitutes the connecting link between the Phoenician alphabet and its Egyptian ancestor.

Islam substituted North Arabic for South Arabic in the southern part of the peninsula, as it did in other conquered lands where other languages are spoken. North Arabic thus became Arabic par excellence, the language of Islam and the Koran.

Grammar. Arabic grammarians classify all the words of the language under three main categories: noun, verb, and particle. The noun includes adjectives and adverbs. All derived words, whether nouns or verbs, stem from a triconsonantal root. That root is the verb in its perfect form, third person masculine singular. By manipulating the root according to a recognized pattern, a modification of the basic meaning associated with that root is effected. Thus $q^at^al^a$ (he killed) may become $q^att^al^a$ (he massacred), $q^at^al^a$ (he sought to kill, fought), $aq\text{-}t^al^a$ (he caused to kill), $in\text{-}q^at^al^a$ (he suffered killing). By another system of affixes and case endings the nominal forms are produced: $q^at^il^un$ (he who kills), $q^at^il^un$ (he who is killed), and so on.

Alphabet. The Arabic alphabet, consisting of 28 characters, is an adaptation from the Aramaic alphabet, which in turn comes from the Phoenician. Arabic characters, as in the case of those of the other Semitic languages, are all consonantal, the vowels being signs inserted above or below the letters. The Arabic alphabet is used not only for this language but also for many other languages of Muslims. Arabic characters, next to Latin characters, are the most widely diffused in the world.

Script. Arabic script has two principal varieties: Naskhi (copy script) and Kufic. Naskhi is the ordinary cursive form used in correspondence and in writing books. Kufic, originally developed in al-Kufa on the lower Euphrates, is angular and was early employed in preparing costly copies of the Koran. It lends itself admirably to decorative purposes and has often been used in architectural ornamentation throughout the world of Islam.

Classical Arabic. In Arabic, distinction should be made between the written, or classical form, and the spoken, or colloquial. The classical is the form that, since the commencement of Arabic literature about a century and a half before the rise of Islam, has been used by Arabic-writing peoples in all their literature. Originally the classical form was used for poetical composition among the tribes of Arabia in pre-Islamic days —including the Quraysh, to which Mohammed belonged. It was later standardized by the Koran. The Koran was the first, and has remained the model, prose work in Arabic. As the word of Allah, its composition acquired sanctity in Muslim eyes. This miraculous character of the Koran was the only miracle claimed by the prophet Mohammed. Its rhymed prose has set the standard that practically every conservative Arabic writer even today strives to imitate. It is this book that has established the norm for the Arabic language and preserved its unity. Because of it alone, the various modern dialects of the Arabic-speaking peoples have not fallen apart into distinct languages, as has been the case with the Romance languages. Today an Iraqi may find it difficult to understand fully the spoken dialect of a Moroccan, but he would have no difficulty in understanding his written language, since in both countries—as well as in all other Arabic-speaking lands—classical Arabic, as modeled by the Koran, is closely followed.

The classical form is not only the literary form used by all Arabic-writing peoples but also the religious language of all Muslims, no matter what their native tongue may be. To Muslims, Arabic is the only appropriate language of approach to Allah.

Colloquial Arabic. Originally the humble dialect of tribes in the northern part of the Arabian Peninsula, Arabic is today the prevailing speech of the whole peninsula, of Jordan, Lebanon, Syria, Iraq, Egypt, Libya, Tunisia, Algeria, Morocco, of certain districts of the Sudan, districts on the curve of the Niger, and in Senegal, and Mauritania. In all, some 100 million people use it for daily communication.

The spoken forms in these varied countries take on dialectal differences. The dialect of North Africa, also called Maghribi, is somewhat distinct from that of Egypt, and both are distinct from the Syrian dialect. Iraq has its own colloquial, and so does Arabia proper. These differences are due to admixture of Arab tribes in medieval times, intercourse with foreign peoples, and the varied influence of the classical language.

This phenomenal spread of a language that was originally a tribal tongue was the direct result of the spectacular conquests of Islam. Once Arabic was written and spoken in Persia, Afghanistan, a part of the Iberian peninsula, (up to about 1500), the Balearic Islands and Sicily, the island of Pantelleria (up to the 18th century), Zanzibar, Madagascar, and the coast of Africa facing Madagascar. The language of Islam was then coterminous with its empire. As the political boundaries shrank, so did the linguistic boundaries.

Philip K. Hitti, *Princeton University*

3. Literature

Arabic literature is the expression not merely of a people or a family of related nations, but of a whole civilization embracing at different times (in addition to Arabs) Persians and Turks, southern and eastern "Europeans," Jews, Indians, Africans, and several peoples of central and southeast Asia. Writers from Spain to China, from Mongolia to central Africa have in the past contributed to this literature. In greater or lesser measure it has been shaped by the religion of that civilization, although not all writers have been necessarily wholehearted Muslims or even Muslims at all.

MEDIEVAL LITERATURE

Most standard critical studies include under medieval Arabic literature virtually all serious writing in Arabic from the late 6th century A.D. until the early 1500's. These studies deal not only with poetry and belles lettres but also with history, geography, classified biographies and encyclopedias, science and medicine, philosophy and theology, grammar and textual exegesis, law, mystical speculation, and many other disciplines. (It may be noted that in this period there is little recorded narrative fiction, virtually no epic material, and no drama whatsoever.) Such comprehensive coverage is no eccentricity or mere convenience but derives from the very nature of the material: for many of the "technical" writings are cast, wholly or in part, in literary form, while literary works themselves abound in "technical" allusions, often of an abstruse nature. Since several of these categories of writings are dealt with in other parts of this article, this section will be limited more nearly than is usual in this field to "literature" as commonly understood.

Coming into full flower only after the passing of the early, classically idealized period of "simple" Islamdom, medieval Arabic literature was at best the work and the delight of an educated, often professional elite, at worst the instrument of the talented to gain reward from the powerful or well endowed. Its content was rich and often highly refined, it followed an elaborate canon of rules and conventions, and it was couched in a script, a style, and even a vocabulary that became more and more inaccessible to the average man. Whatever this may mean for the role of Arabic literature within its own society, it has made it impossible to translate a great part of this literature into other languages in an effective or even meaningful way. This is especially so at the present time, when the spirit of the age runs so markedly counter to the whole notion of stylized classical forms, which can be understood and appreciated only after long study and with the aid of extensive annotations.

Poetry. The earliest and most abiding literary expression in Arabic is poetical. Moreover, through the nine centuries being considered here, although the poetry constantly changed its milieu and its purpose, it preserved an astonishing unity of matter (at least superficially) as well as of form. A classic Arabic definition of poetry is "Metrical, rhyming, meaningful utterance, of more than one line in extent." The typical genre is the *qasida*, a sort of ode that may run from 15 to some 100 couplets, though usually fluctuating between 30 and 50. While there are about 20 principal meters (all measured by syllable-length rather than stress, and all capable of many complex variations), the rhyme pattern is normally unvaried: aa, ba, ca, da, and so forth, for each pair of couplets. The standardized word-shapes of Arabic make this feasible.

In its pristine form the *qasida* vaunted the poet's tribe, his courage, the animal he rode, or his beloved (the lovers are usually figured as tragically separated). It sang the life of the desert, nature's beauties and terrors, feats of endurance and daring, and the ultimate tragedy of existence. It was pagan, heroic verse. Over the later centuries of sophisticated urban life, however, one or another element tended to be more heavily stressed within a given poem—the erotic, the bacchanalian, the moralistic, the panegyric, the satirical, and so on. The poem itself thus usually became fragmented, judged by earlier standards, although many later poems were very long indeed.

Some of the finest "nature" poetry and poetry of love was written in Spain between about 1000 and 1450 A.D. And one of the most remarkable developments of all was the adaptation of these verse forms as vehicles of sublime mystical expression. Poetry was never officially accepted by

THE KORAN

A page from a 16th-century Koran manuscript.

Islam (although Koranic commentators and grammarians cited ancient verses to support their interpretations). But the love of Arabic poetic utterance, with its contrasting long and short vowels and its rolling doubled consonants, lay too deep in most hearts to allow the art to die.

Of the anthologies, the best known, the *Muallaqat* (*Hung Poems* or *Golden Odes*), allegedly antedates Islam. It was, however, finally put together only in the 8th century A.D. Abu Tamman and Buhturi each compiled a *Hamasa* (*Book of Valor*) in the 9th century. And the multivolumed *Kitab al-Aghani* (*Book of Songs*) of Abu'l-Faraj al-Isfahani, a mine of incidental information on the cultural and social life of medieval Islam, belongs to the 10th century. Some of the greatest names are Abu Nuwas (died about 800), for anacreontic verse; the Egyptian Ibn al-Farid (died 1235), for mystical poetry; al-Maarri (died 1057), a pessimistic and original Syrian thinker in a class quite by himself; Ibn Zaydun (died 1071), the prince of Spanish-Arabic poets; and al-Mutanabbi (murdered 965 A.D.), often adjudged the master of all in language and technical skill and the most representative of the court panegyrists. Only the *Muallaqat* and the cream of Ibn al-Farid's verse have been fully and fairly successfully translated into English, both by A.J. Arberry and by others. Fragments of translation are found in many places.

The Koran. To treat the Koran as literature offends Muslims, for whom it is (more or less literally) the word of God, revealed to His ultimate Prophet, Mohammed, between about 610 and 632. However, its literary influence is incontestably enormous, and it is itself the object of a vast body of "technical" literature. The accepted version of 646 A.D. groups the basic verse-units (singular, *aya*) into chapters (singular, *sura*), the longest being placed first without regard to chronology or place of revelation. Content and style vary greatly throughout, from exhortation and prophecy through narrative to detailed legal prescription. The best modern English version is by A.J. Arberry (1955).

Histories and Travel Accounts. Two of the largest areas of Arabic literature that are fairly accessible to those with nontechnical, humanistic interests are historical chronicles and travel narratives. Save for the "Tunisian Toynbee," Ibn Khaldun (died 1406), Arabic historians tend to write annals and to amass unorganized detail. But the works of Tabari (died 923), Masudi (died 956), and Ibn al-Athir (died 1234), to name the three greatest, are essential tools for later researchers. To Western eyes, travel narratives have defects

somewhat similar to those of the histories, although once again their research value is high. Sir Hamilton Gibb has published several studies on the most famous of these "globe-trotters," Ibn Battuta (died 1377). Ibn Khaldun's *Muqaddima* has been translated into English by Franz Rosenthal (1958).

Belles Lettres. Belles lettres (*adab*) forms, with poetry, the other major pillar of the Arabic literary edifice. The most typical vehicle is the *risala* (epistle, essay), running from a page or two to a small book. In fact, many larger books or even multivolume sets may be seen as collections of *risalas* or as a *risala* greatly extended. The conventional framework of a "letter" to a friend or an enquirer allows an exhibition of linguistic brilliance, wit, polish, and learning, while the ostensible themes may range from mere witticisms through mystical or philosophical dissertations to essays on science or politics. The earliest practitioners were men of Persian origin, such as Ibn al-Muqaffa (died 757), and it is virtually certain that the form was brought into Arabic literature by the many Persians who staffed the state secretariat under the early Abbasid caliphs, for the writing of *risalas* was both a part of their training and a demonstration of their professional skill. But they were all outshone by al-Jahiz (died about 869), an errant, ill-favored genius of slave stock from southern Iraq. He had as little sense of intellectual discipline as of the path to worldly success, but his erudition was far-ranging and his skill as a prose writer was virtually unmatched in Arabic. His vast output includes smaller tracts on such unlikely subjects as "Thoroughbreds and Half-breeds," "Idols," "Men versus Women," and "Speech Better than Silence," the books *Misers* and *Eloquence*, and the multivolumed *Book of Beasts*. The latter is a perfect blending of the literary with the "technical," although it makes a most unorthodox manual of zoology. From the time of Jahiz the *risala*, in the hands of such writers as Ibn Qutayba (died 889), greatly extended its social range and its intellectual coverage.

Another type of belles lettres was the *maqama* (session), a sort of dramatic anecdote in elaborate rhymed prose, the two masters here being Badi az-Zaman (died 1008) and al-Hariri (died 1122). Little Arabic belles lettres has been translated, and much of it by its nature would not survive translation.

G. M. WICKENS, *University of Toronto*

Further Reading: Gibb, Hamilton, *Arabic Literature* (New York and London 1963); Nicholson, Reynold, *A Literary History of the Arabs* (New York and London 1953).

MODERN LITERATURE

The literary tradition that the 19th century Arab inherited from his predecessors called principally for verbal elaborations on conventional themes. But once Europe had demonstrated its power and had thrust on the Arab the claims of its cultural values, the need arose for more informative, direct, and purposeful literature.

In the early part of the 19th century, translators, such as Rifaah Rafi at-Tahtawi, and travelers, such as Ahmad Faris ash-Shidyaq, opened up European culture to their fellow Arabs. But by the end of the century there were men prepared to offer a creative revaluation of their heritage and a formulation of their present needs.

A galaxy of secularist writers, now known as Modernists, appeared in the early 20th century. They claimed that in seeking the best there was to be learned, even if it derived from foreign sources, they were not repudiating but renovating their heritage. Of these the one who was to have the longest and most distinguished career was Taha Husayn. The Diwan, one of the schools formed by those writing in the new vein, was inspired primarily by 19th-century English poets and critics. Its most prolific and scholarly member was Abbas Mahmud al-Aqqad. Most of the writers, however, were individual thinkers influenced to various degrees by contemporary French literature, and until World War II the intellectuals might fairly if none too precisely be characterized as romantic and liberalist. After the war, deepened insight and closer contacts with a variety of sources produced a literature in which existentialism and neoclassicism, Marxism and romanticism jostled each other as vigorously as in other major literatures.

Genres of Writing. The commonest outlet for prose writing was in literary journalism. Eventually, though poorly grounded in literary tradition, narrative fiction became popular. Mahmud Tymur remained preeminent in short-story writing from the 1920's to the 1960's. The earliest attempts at novel writing were episodic, digressive, or thin, or too closely modeled on Western patterns to be true to Arab life. However, forceful and talented novelists began to appear in the late 1930's. The most celebrated in the 1960's was Najib Mahfuz.

The theater had even fewer roots in the Arab past than the novel. In addition, the fact that literary Arabic differs from the spoken idiom created difficulties for it that have not yet been entirely overcome. Although there were successful stage presentations in Arabic from the middle of the 19th century, the first plays to be acclaimed as works of art were those of Ahmad Shawqi. These were historical dramas in verse, written shortly before his death in 1932. In the contemporary period, a versatile and stimulating playwright has been Tawfiq al-Hakim.

Poetry, the Arab literary form par excellence, did not immediately accommodate itself to adopted values. Ahmad Shawqi and Hafiz Ibrahim, whose poems reflected earlier models, dominated the field until the 1930's. Yet there have been other poets—for example, members of the Apollo group and Lebanese émigrés to the Americas, known as the Syro-American school—who have experimented with free verse forms, with the expression of tenderer and more intimate sentiment, and with a subtler use of images and symbols. They presaged the appearance in the late 1940's of a new school of poetry whose foremost members in the 1960's were Badr Shakir as-Sayyab and Nazik al-Malaikah.

PIERRE CACHIA, *University of Edinburgh*

Further Reading: Cachia, Pierre, *Tāhā Husayn* (London 1956); Landau, Jacob, *Studies in the Arab Theatre and Cinema* (Philadelphia 1958); Mazyad, A.M.H., *Ahmad Amīn* (Leiden 1963); Monteil, V., *Anthologie Bilingue de la littérature arabe contemporaine* (Beirut 1961).

4. Philosophy

Philosophy has been written in Arabic by Muslims of many nations and by Arabic-speaking Christians and Jews. The period of greatest vitality was from the 9th to about the 14th century. Islam provided the spiritual environment,

and the leading thinkers were Muslims. Yet philosophers maintained an independent, secular discipline. Proud to continue the tradition of ancient Greece, they based their search for true knowledge on reason and natural experience.

The Koran, though full of deep thought, was not a systematic treatise. The first systematic thought in the new Arabic-Islamic civilization was legal and theological, devoted to practical and theoretical questions raised directly by the scriptures of Islam. The earlier theologians built up terminology and a habit of close reasoning, which were taken over by the first Arabic philosophers. Meanwhile, the science and philosophy of the later Greeks were being kept alive in the Middle East by Christian scholars.

Arabic philosophy began two centuries after Islam, in the educated milieu of Baghdad, after the caliph Mamum (reigned 813–833) set Christians to translating the surviving body of Greek learning into Arabic. Besides much science, they translated most of Aristotle's philosophical works, later commentaries on them, summaries of Plato's dialogues, and later Greek mystical developments of Platonic thought (Nepolatonism).

Graeco-Muslim Tradition. The first Arabic philosopher, al-Kindi (died 867), shows some independence from the Greeks. For instance, he holds that the world was created from nothing and is not eternal. A similar independence is found in other early philosophers, such as Ibn Zakariyya ar-Razi (about 865–925), who disagreed with Aristotle on many points. The central Graeco-Muslim tradition was established by al-Farabi (about 870–950) and further systematized by Avicenna (Arabic, Ibn Sina; 980–1037). Al-Farabi was more rationalist and Aristotelian, Avicenna more mystical and Neoplatonist, and their successors show other variations. But it is possible to give a unified account of this tradition.

Philosophy was conceived in broader terms than it is in the modern analytic tradition and included large questions of science. In fact, it was distinguished from the regular sciences only in its concern for the general outlines of knowledge rather than the details. The method of reasoning adopted was Aristotle's syllogistic logic. The study of philosophy was thought to have a serious practical purpose: the attainment of happiness for the individual and society through the application of wisdom to life. Man must understand the universe and his place in it in order to choose the best way in life.

The highest branch of philosophy was metaphysics. The Arabic philosophers saw more clearly than Aristotle the distinction between essence and existence and realized that there is nothing in any ordinary concept that implies either the existence or nonexistence of instances of it. Avicenna found here a proof of God's existence: there must be one essence not thus logically contingent but necessary in itself, in order to bestow existence on all other essences.

Natural philosophy included cosmology, general physics, and psychology. The universe consists of eternal forms and eternal matter. Their combinations are unchangeable in the higher realm of stars and angels, but changeable in the sublunary sphere, which contains the earth. Man is composed of a mortal body and a soul, whose higher part, the intellect, is immortal in some sense (understood variously by different philosophers). The Aristotelian psychology of the intellect, as elaborated by the later Greek commentators, was taken over and elaborated further. A man's passive, potential, or material intellect receives "information" by illumination from the Active Intellect, which is outside the individual and connected with the sphere of the moon.

Political philosophy and ethics described the good life for society and the individual respectively, as known by reason. Supreme happiness is attained by a life of moral virtue and intellectual effort, culminating in the union of a man's intellect with the Active Intellect, in which state he sees truth by direct intuition. Few people achieve this perfect actualization of their mental powers.

Religious Critics and New Syntheses. This "perennial philosophy" was criticized as un-Islamic by theologians, especially by al-Ghazzali (1058–1111). He attacked three doctrines most sharply: the eternity of the world, God's knowledge of universals only (and not particulars), and the denial of bodily resurrection. The main burden of defense fell on Averroës (Arabic, Ibn Rushd; 1126–1198), who argued that when both Aristotle and the Koran were rightly understood, there was no disagreement between them.

Later Muslim philosophers diverged from the central Graeco-Muslim tradition by following out different tendencies in it. Averroës sought a return to the original Aristotle. Ibn Arabi (1165–1240) blended intellectual mysticism with Islam, viewing man as the highest reflection of God's nature and Mohammed as the most perfect man. Muslim theologians adopted philosophic techniques of reasoning and analysis without abandoning their more traditional approach and doctrines. Ibn Khaldun (1332–1406) developed a new science of society, which is related to the spirit of Aristotle. Of all these later developments, the world view of Ibn Arabi had the most profound influence on Arabic and Persian thought in the last premodern centuries.

Jews were writing vital philosophy in Arabic in the same period as the Muslims and were much influenced by them. The problems of harmonizing Greek philosophy with Judaism were similar, and there are noteworthy parallels between the solutions of Maimonides (1135–1204) and Averroës.

World Legacy. When philosophical studies revived in Christian Europe in the 12th century, the West recovered the major texts of Greek philosophy through their Arabic versions. These were eagerly translated into Latin, together with the summaries, commentaries, and independent works of Arabic philosophy. Avicenna, Averroës, and Maimonides had a great influence on Latin thought.

Much of medieval Arabic philosophy is of permanent interest: intelligent summaries of Greek thought, vast syntheses of philosophy and mysticism, the great debate of al-Ghazzali and the philosophers, and the attempts to harmonize philosophy with a revealed religion.

Modern Arab philosophers are restudying their heritage but are not yet able to match it in originality and power, being once again in the process of absorbing Western philosophy as their predecessors were in the 9th century.

GEORGE F. HOURANI, *University of Michigan*

Further Reading: Boer, Tjitze J. de, *History of Philosophy in Islam*, tr. by Edward R. Jones (London 1933); Watt, William Montgomery, *Islamic Philosophy and Theology* (Edinburgh 1962).

5. Science

The term "Arabic science" refers to the scientific achievements of men of various ethnic groups who in the medieval Islamic world wrote scientific treatises in the Arabic language. This important phase in the history of science began seriously in the middle of the 8th century with the translations into Arabic of Persian, Hindu, and especially Greek scientific, medical, and philosophical works. Most translations were made by Syrian-Christian and Sabaean scholars employed by the Abbasid caliphs. Arabic science reached its highest point in the 10th and 11th centuries and, after some sporadic and short-lived but important revivals in the 13th and 14th centuries, finally came to a virtual stop after the end of the 15th century. During the period of greatest productivity, Arabic science flourished in places as far apart as Baghdad, Cairo, and Cordova, to mention only three of its most important centers.

Position in the History of Science. A great deal of what the Arabic-writing scholars had acquired of Greek science and philosophy, and a great deal of what they built on this heritage, was transmitted in the 12th century to Europe through Latin translations from the Arabic. Thus Arabic science is continuous with Western science at both ends of its medieval life, and the names of Jabir Ibn Hayyan (alchemy and chemistry), al-Khwarizmi (algebra), al-Razi (medicine), al-Battani (astronomy), Avicenna (physics and medicine), al-Zarqali (astronomy and geography), and Alhazen (optics and mathematics) are as much part of the Western intellectual tradition as they are of Islamic culture. Their works enjoyed great prestige in Europe down to the 17th century.

Greek Influence. In essentials, Arabic science always remained predominately Greek in character. But Hellenistic science, the direct parent of Arabic science, had incorporated Eastern elements. Many of these elements found their way directly into Arabic science, such as the zero and the place-value system of reckoning, the so-called Arabic numerals, and certain trigonometric and astronomical techniques—all of which came from India. This cross-fertilization of Hindu and Greek ideas accounts for certain important advances in the fields of arithmetic, algebra, and astronomy and for certain features of the Arabic achievement not to be found in ancient Greek science.

Nevertheless, for the medieval Arabic-writing scientists the Greeks were the unsurpassed authorities: Euclid, Archimedes, and Apollonius of Perga in mathematics, Ptolemy in astronomy, and Galen and Hippocrates in medicine. This does not mean that the scientists of medieval Islam were slavish followers of their predecessors. Islamic civilization produced a fair number of original men of science with independent and critical minds: al-Razi, al-Masuudi, al-Biruni, and Alhazen (al-Hasan Ibn al-Haytham). But such innovations as those in observational astronomy, in clinical medical experience, and even in optics (a science that was given a new turn by Alhazen) were introduced within the general framework of earlier Greek disciplines or after Greek models, and the criticisms were formulated in terms fashioned by the Greek founders.

Arabic science did not produce a scientific revolution comparable to the one that matured in

Europe in the 17th century. But the view that the Islamic contribution merely consisted in preserving and later transmitting the scientific heritage of antiquity to Europe is only partly correct. Together with passing on this heritage, which they had kept alive by their enthusiasm and active participation, the Arabic scientists were in fact able to offer substantial results of their own.

Position in Islamic World. The role of Arabic science in Islamic civilization is not easy to define. The view that the "rational sciences of the ancients" (in contradistinction to the "Islamic sciences" of Koranic exegesis, traditions, jurisprudence, etc.) never became an integral part of Islamic civilization cannot be maintained: the rational sciences had a continuous and vigorous life in Islam for almost four centuries. And although the rational sciences never formed part of the curricula of state-organized education in medieval Islam, we know that they were positively encouraged, and not merely tolerated, by Muslim rulers of both the orthodox and Shiite sects of Islam.

The question of how far ideas derived from Greek science and philosophy penetrated various groups and layers of Islamic society cannot be answered in the same way for all periods of Islamic history. Educated people in 10th century Baghdad, for example, had a fair knowledge of Greek philosophy and used Greek methods of argumentation. Some of those who pursued the Arabic humanities, such as grammar and rhetoric, were characterized by their dependence on Aristotelian logic in their researches. Islamic theology adopted Greek dialectic and terminology almost from the first. Even the 11th-century orthodox theologian al-Ghazali, who suspected that the sciences of astronomy and mathematics had a pernicious influence, spared Greek logic from his attack, considering it a useful preparatory study in mastering Islamic jurisprudence. And both before and after Ghazali's time, astronomy itself was often claimed—sometimes by officials in charge of the Muslim calendar in the large mosques—to be of service to Islam as providing proof of the oneness of God (the fundamental tenet of Islamic religion) as well as of His perfection and wisdom.

Attempts were made to reconcile rational philosophy, of which mathematics and astronomy were conceived as parts, with Islamic religion. One of the most notable of these attempts, especially influential in Shiite circles, is represented by the Epistles of the Brethren of Purity (or Sincerity), composed in the 10th century. Although, on the whole, such attempts eventually failed, it would be wrong to construe their rejection as always implying a condemnation of Hellenic modes of thought. Some of those who, like the 10th-century philosopher Abu Sulayman al-Sijistani, had no use for reconciliation were sincere friends of Hellenic learning as well as practicing Muslims. In the final period of stagnation, only elementary sections of arithmetic and astronomy were cultivated for limited practical religious purposes, such as straightening out inheritance problems, keeping the Muslim calendar, and determining the direction of Mecca.

A.I. SABRA, *University of London*

Further Reading: Arnold, Thomas W., and Guillaume, A., eds., *The Legacy of Islam* (London 1931); Sarton, George, *Introduction to the History of Science*, 3 vols. (Baltimore 1927–48); Taton, René, ed., *History of Science*, vol. 1, Part 3 (London 1963).

ARAB LEAGUE, a regional organization founded on March 22, 1945. Its full name is the *League of Arab States*. The founding members were Egypt (later United Arab Republic), Syria, Lebanon, Saudi Arabia, Iraq, Transjordan (later Jordan), and Yemen. Membership was later extended to Libya (1953), Sudan (1956), Morocco (1958), Tunisia (1958), Kuwait (1961), and Algeria (1962). The permanent headquarters and secretariat are in Cairo. The post of secretary general has been filled by Abdur-Rahman Assam and Abdul-Khaliq Hassuna, both Egyptians.

The League charter invests authority in a council representing all members equally. On most major matters only unanimous decisions are binding. The council meets semiannually. Its functions are to promote political cooperation among its sovereign members; to deal with disputes or breaches of the peace; and to supervise collaboration in economics, communications, culture, social affairs, and other matters through the work of specialized committees. A League office administers a general boycott of trade and of communications with Israel and with foreign firms that have Israeli subsidiaries.

The League's chief success has been in nonpolitical fields, such as culture and communications. Economic cooperation, apart from the boycott of Israel, has progressed chiefly on a bilateral basis. In political matters the League has been chronically beset by disputes among members, first in the 1948 Palestine war and repeatedly since 1955, mainly between the Egyptian government and its rivals. A series of summit meetings in 1964 and 1965, devoted mainly to matters concerning Palestine, restored a measure of political harmony within the League.

MALCOLM H. KERR
University of California at Los Angeles

ARABI PASHA, ə-rä′bē pä′shä, **Ahmed** (1839?–1911), Egyptian nationalist, who fought against foreign influence in his country's government. He was born in 1839 or 1841 near Zagazig in Lower Egypt. Conscripted into the army, he was a lieutenant colonel in his early twenties.

Arabi became a leader of the Egyptian nationalist movement, seeking to end Franco-British control of the government. When in 1881, Khedive Tewfik Pasha, on French and British insistence, dismissed an Egyptian army officer, Arabi led a protest by a group of officers who forced the appointment of an Egyptian minister of war. Tewfik soon dismissed his new minister, and Arabi led a military march on the palace demanding total reorganization of the cabinet. Yielding, the khedive appointed an all-Egyptian cabinet, with Arabi as undersecretary for war.

In February 1882, Arabi was named minister for war. The following May the French and British sent warships to Alexandria, demanding the dismissal of the government. Arabi prepared for an anticipated British military intervention by strengthening the fortifications of Alexandria. The British bombarded the city on July 11 and two days later landed a force headed by Sir Garnett Wolseley. The khedive, placing himself under British protection, dismissed Arabi, who withdrew from Alexandria. Pursued by the British he was defeated at Tel el-Kebir. He was tried as a rebel and exiled to Ceylon. Pardoned by Khedive Abbas II in 1901, Arabi returned to Egypt, where he died in Cairo on Sept. 21, 1911.

L. GRAY COWAN, *Columbia University*

ARABIA'S GREAT DESERTS, though without agricultural value, yield great wealth in the form of oil and natural gas lying beneath their surface. Photos show seismographic tests under way in the desert (*above*) and an oil drilling rig (*left*).

run hundreds of miles in courses parallel to each other. Along the western and southern sides and part of the eastern side of the peninsula, rocky mountains provide scant space for farming or grazing.

Only parts of the far south close to the Indian Ocean enjoy fairly adequate rainfall. The aridity of most of Arabia has tended to restrict the growth of the population and to encourage emigration. Accurate figures are not available, but the population of the whole peninsula is probably well under 10 million, making it one of the most sparsely inhabited regions of the globe.

Although people were moving out of Arabia for thousands of years before the dawn of Islam in the 7th century A.D., the Islamic religion proved the chief motive power in the expansion of the Arabs. During the first Islamic century they reached France in the west and China in the east. Centers of Arab power and culture developed in Damascus, Baghdad, Cairo, and across Africa all the way to the Atlantic. In time the great majority of people calling themselves Arabs were to live outside Arabia.

Supreme political authority in the Islamic world also came to be concentrated in lands beyond Arabia. Muslims everywhere, however, continued to regard the Hejaz, the western part of Arabia, as their holy land. The holy cities of Mecca and Medina are in the Hejaz. Mecca is the home of the Kaaba, a cubical structure called by Muslims the House of God. Paying reverence to the Kaaba is the chief goal of the annual pilgrimage to Mecca, which draws the devout from every quarter of the Islamic world. In one corner of the Kaaba is set the Black Stone, the most sacred object in Islam, believed to be a sign sent by Allah to mankind. Mecca was the birthplace of the prophet Mohammed, but Medina was the capital of the Islamic state he founded, and in Medina he died and was buried. Pilgrims com-

ARABIA, ə-rā′bē-ə, is a peninsula with an area of slightly over 1,000,000 square miles (2,590,-000 sq km) in southwestern Asia. The peninsula is separated from Africa and from the rest of Asia by two narrow stretches of water: the Red Sea in the west and the Persian Gulf in the east. In the south, Arabia faces the Arabian Sea, the northwestern arm of the Indian Ocean, in which the large Arabian island of Socotra is located. In the north the stone-strewn wastelands of the Syrian Desert are divided between the kingdom of Saudi Arabia and its neighbors in the Fertile Crescent (Jordan, Syria, and Iraq). Surrounded on all sides by sea or desert, the peninsula deserves its Arabic name, *Jazirat al-Arab* ("the island of the Arabs").

Besides many barren, stony plains, Arabia has two vast sand deserts, the Nafud in the north and the Rub al-Khali (the Empty Quarter) in the south, which are joined by a narrow strip called the Dahna along which sand slowly migrates southward. The Rub al-Khali, with an area of about 200,000 square miles (518,000 sq km), is the largest continuous body of sand in the world. Some of its dunes are high enough to be considered sand mountains, and some of its sand ridges

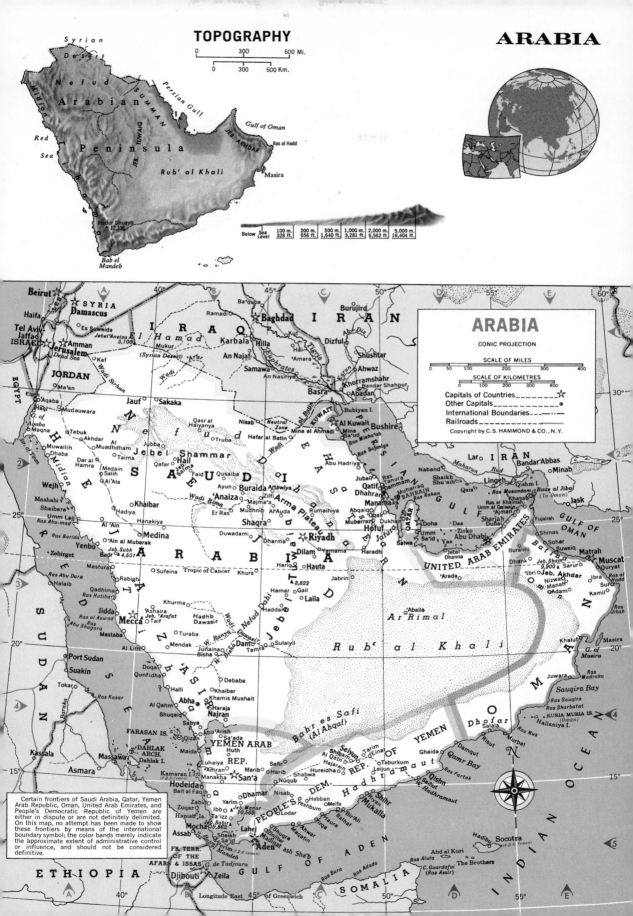

TOPOGRAPHY

0   300   600 Mi.

0   300   600 Km.

ARABIA

Syrian
Desert

Nefud

Arabian

SUMMAN

Persian Gulf

JEB. TUWAIQ

Gulf of Oman

JEB. AKHDAR

Ras al Hadd

Red
Sea

Peninsula

Rub' al Khali

Masira

Hadur Shuayb
12,336

Bab el
Mandeb

Below Sea Level | 100 m. 328 ft. | 200 m. 656 ft. | 500 m. 1,640 ft. | 1,000 m. 3,281 ft. | 2,000 m. 6,562 ft. | 5,000 m. 16,404 ft.

ARABIA

CONIC PROJECTION

SCALE OF MILES

0   50   100   200   300   400

SCALE OF KILOMETRES

0   100   200   300   400

Capitals of Countries _____ ☆
Other Capitals _____ ◉
International Boundaries _____ — · —
Railroads _____

Copyright by C.S. HAMMOND & CO., N.Y.

Certain frontiers of Saudi Arabia, Qatar, Yemen Arab Republic, Oman, United Arab Emirates, and People's Democratic Republic of Yemen are either in dispute or are not definitely delimited. On this map, no attempt has been made to show these frontiers by means of the international boundary symbol; the color bands merely indicate the approximate extent of administrative control or influence, and should not be considered definitive.

Beirut
Haifa
Tel Aviv
Jaffa
ISRAEL
Jerusalem
Dead Sea
Amman
JORDAN
EGYPT
Elath
G. of Aqaba
Maqna
Aqaba
Ma'an
Mudauwara

SYRIA
Damascus
Es Suweida
Jebel 'Aneiza 3,100
El Hamad
(Syrian Desert)
Mukur
Arar
Wadi Sirhan
Kaf
Jauf
Sakaka
Qasr al Haiyanya
Nisab

IRAQ
Ramadi
Ba'quba
Karbala
Hilla
An Najaf
Samawa
An Nasiriya

Baghdad
Kut
Amara
Basra

IRAN
Burujird
Dizful
Shushtar
Ahwaz
Khorramshahr
Bandar Shahpur
Abadan
Bushire

Neutral Zone
Hafar al Batin
Truba
Mina al Ahmadi
Mina Su'ud
KUWAIT
Al Kuwait
Ras Misha'ab

Laro
IRAN
Bandar Abbas
Minab

Haql
Tebuk
Dhaba
Dar al Hamra
Medain Salih
Al'Ala
Taima
Muadhdham
Jubba
Jebel Shammar
Hail
Jebel salma
Qusaiba
Ayun
Buraida
Anaiza
Majma'a
Mudhnib
Al'Auda
Rumaihiya
Abu Hadriya
Jubail
Qatif
Dhahran
Dammam
Muharraq
BAHRAIN
Manama
Dukhan

Ras Tanura
Ras Rakan

Qatar
Doha
Umm Sa'id

Naband
Shaikh Shu'aib
Qais
Lingeh
Ras Musandam 9,900 (To Oman)
Qishm I.
Khasab
Rus al Jibal
Jask

Muwailih
Wejh
Mashabi
Shaibara
Umm Lajj
Ras Abu-mad

Khaibar
Hadiya
Al 'Ain
Hanakiya
Medina
Shaqra
Riyadh
Duwadami
Dharma
Yamama
Haradh

Abqaiq
Ogair
Mubarraz
Hofuf

Das
Zirko
Umm Said'o
Abu Dhabi
Jalfar
Salwa
Jebel Dhanna

Sharja
Ajman
Ras al Khaima
Umm al Qaiwain
Dubai
Fujairah
Shinas
Sohar
Suwaiq

GULF OF OMAN
Matrah
Muscat
Quryat

HEJAZ
MIDIAN
Zebirget
Ras Abu Dara
Halaib
Ras Barida
Yenbo
Badr
Al 'Ain al Mubarak
Jeb. Subh 4,501
Mastura
Rabigh
Qadhima
Ras Hatiba
Jidda
Ras al Aswad
Abu Shagara
Mecca
Jeb. 'Arafat
Taif
Shaira

Tropic of Cancer
Sufeina
Khurma
Turaba
Mendak

ARABIA
UNITED ARAB EMIRATES
Buraimi
Dhank
Jeb. Shams 9,900
Nizwa
Manah
Adam
Jabrin
'Arada
Ibri
Jeb. Akhdar
Ibra
Sur
Kamil
Ras al Hadd

MASCAT
OMAN

Jiddah
Khamis Mushait

'ASIR
Doqa
Debaba
Khaibar
Halli
Abha
Al Qahm
Shuqaiq
Najran
Sabya
Haraja
Abu 'Arish

SUDAN
Port Sudan
Suakin
Tokar
Ras Kasar
Kassala
Massawa
DAHLAK ARCH.
Dahlak I.
Asmara

FARASAN IS.
Qizan
Sa'da
Maida

YEMEN ARAB REP.
Huth
Luhaiya
Amran
Manakha
San'a
Marib
Safir
Harib
Shabwa
Hureidha
Leijun
Nuqub

Ar Rimal
Rub' al Khali

'Aballa

Khalut
Juwara
Ras Madraka
Sauqira Bay
Ras Sauqira
Ras Sharbatat
KURIA MURIA IS. (Oman)
Hallaniya I.
Masira
G. of Masira
Ras Madraka

Bahr es Safi
(Al Ahqaf)

Seihun
Shibam
Tarim
Al Qatn
Tabur
Einat
Hadhramaut

Dhofar
Salala
Risut
Ras Nus

YEMEN
Ghaida
Qamr Bay
Damqut
Murbat
Ras Fartak

DEM. REP. OF YEMEN
Hodeida
Bait al Faqih
Zabid
Zuqar
Hanish Is.
Mocha
Jeb. Sabir 9,862
Assab
Perim
Bab el Mandeb
Dhamar
Yarim
Ibb
Ta'izz
Sheikh Sa'id
Lahej
Aden
Shuqra
Madinat ash Sha'b

Nisab
Lodar
Habban
Meifa
Ahwar
Baihan
Shihr
Ras Ali
Mukalla
Qishn
Saihut
W. Hadhramaut

Socotra (P.D.R. Yemen)
Hadibu
Abd al Kuri
Ras Alula
Ras Adado
The Brothers
C. Guardafui (Ras Assir)

FR. TERR. OF THE AFARS & ISSAS
Djibouti
G. de Tadjoura
Zeila

GULF OF ADEN
Ras Sura

ETHIOPIA

SOMALIA

INDIAN OCEAN

Longitude East 45° of Greenwich

ARABIA

AGRICULTURE, INDUSTRY and RESOURCES

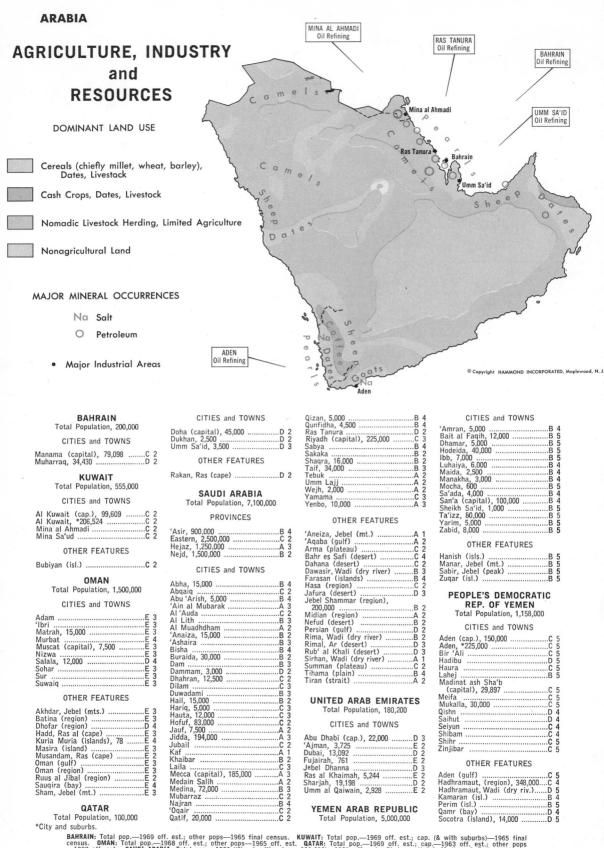

DOMINANT LAND USE

- Cereals (chiefly millet, wheat, barley), Dates, Livestock
- Cash Crops, Dates, Livestock
- Nomadic Livestock Herding, Limited Agriculture
- Nonagricultural Land

MAJOR MINERAL OCCURRENCES

- Na Salt
- ◯ Petroleum
- ● Major Industrial Areas

MINA AL AHMADI
Oil Refining

RAS TANURA
Oil Refining

BAHRAIN
Oil Refining

UMM SA'ID
Oil Refining

ADEN
Oil Refining

© Copyright HAMMOND INCORPORATED, Maplewood, N. J.

BAHRAIN
Total Population, 200,000

CITIES and TOWNS

Manama (capital), 79,098 ....C 2
Muharraq, 34,430 ....D 2

KUWAIT
Total Population, 555,000

CITIES and TOWNS

Al Kuwait (cap.), 99,609 ....C 2
Al Kuwait, *206,524 ....C 2
Mina al Ahmadi ....C 2
Mina Sa'ud ....C 2

OTHER FEATURES

Bubiyan (isl.) ....C 2

OMAN
Total Population, 1,500,000

CITIES and TOWNS

Adam ....E 3
'Ibri ....E 3
Matrah, 15,000 ....E 3
Murbat ....E 4
Muscat (capital), 7,500 ....E 3
Nizwa ....E 3
Salala, 12,000 ....D 4
Sohar ....E 3
Sur ....E 3
Suwaiq ....E 3

OTHER FEATURES

Akhdar, Jebel (mts.) ....E 3
Batina (region) ....E 3
Dhofar (region) ....D 4
Hadd, Ras al (cape) ....E 3
Kuria Muria (islands), 78 ....E 4
Masira (island) ....E 3
Musandam, Ras (cape) ....E 2
Oman (gulf) ....E 3
Oman (region) ....E 3
Ruus al Jibal (region) ....E 2
Sauqira (bay) ....E 4
Sham, Jebel (mt.) ....E 3

QATAR
Total Population, 100,000

*City and suburbs.

CITIES and TOWNS

Doha (capital), 45,000 ....D 2
Dukhan, 2,500 ....D 2
Umm Sa'id, 3,500 ....D 3

OTHER FEATURES

Rakan, Ras (cape) ....D 2

SAUDI ARABIA
Total Population, 7,100,000

PROVINCES

'Asir, 900,000 ....B 4
Eastern, 2,500,000 ....C 2
Hejaz, 1,250,000 ....A 3
Nejd, 1,500,000 ....B 2

CITIES and TOWNS

Abha, 15,000 ....B 4
Abqaiq ....C 2
Abu 'Arish, 5,000 ....B 4
'Ain al Mubarak ....A 3
Al 'Auda ....B 3
Al Lith ....B 3
Al Muadhdham ....B 2
'Anaiza, 15,000 ....B 2
'Ashaira ....B 3
Bisha ....B 4
Buraida, 30,000 ....B 2
Dam ....B 3
Dammam, 3,000 ....D 2
Dhahran, 12,500 ....C 2
Dilam ....C 3
Duwadami ....B 3
Hail, 15,000 ....B 2
Hariq, 5,000 ....C 3
Hauta, 12,000 ....C 3
Hofuf, 83,000 ....C 2
Jauf, 7,500 ....A 2
Jidda, 194,000 ....A 3
Jubail ....C 2
Kaf ....A 1
Khaibar ....B 2
Laila ....C 3
Mecca (capital), 185,000 ....A 3
Medain Salih ....A 2
Medina, 72,000 ....B 3
Mubarraz ....C 2
Najran ....B 4
'Oqair ....C 2
Qatif, 20,000 ....C 2

Qizan, 5,000 ....B 4
Qunfidha, 4,500 ....B 4
Ras Tanura ....D 2
Riyadh (capital), 225,000 ....C 3
Sabya ....B 4
Sakaka ....B 2
Shaqra, 16,000 ....B 2
Taif, 34,000 ....B 3
Tebuk ....A 2
Umm Lajj ....A 2
Wejh, 2,000 ....A 2
Yamama ....C 3
Yenbo, 10,000 ....A 3

OTHER FEATURES

'Aneiza, Jebel (mt.) ....A 1
'Aqaba (gulf) ....A 2
Arma (plateau) ....C 2
Bahr es Safi (desert) ....C 4
Dahana (desert) ....C 2
Dawasir, Wadi (dry river) ....B 3
Farasan (islands) ....B 4
Hasa (region) ....C 2
Jafura (desert) ....D 3
Jebel Shammar (region),
 200,000 ....B 2
Midian (region) ....A 2
Nefud (desert) ....B 2
Persian (gulf) ....D 2
Rima, Wadi (dry river) ....B 2
Rimal, Ar (desert) ....D 3
Rub' al Khali (desert) ....D 3
Sirhan, Wadi (dry river) ....A 1
Summan (plateau) ....C 2
Tihama (plain) ....B 4
Tiran (strait) ....A 2

UNITED ARAB EMIRATES
Total Population, 180,200

CITIES and TOWNS

Abu Dhabi (cap.), 22,000 ....D 3
'Ajman, 3,725 ....E 2
Dubai, 13,092 ....D 2
Fujairah, 761 ....E 2
Jebel Dhanna ....D 3
Ras al Khaimah, 5,244 ....E 2
Sharjah, 19,198 ....D 2
Umm al Qaiwain, 2,928 ....E 2

YEMEN ARAB REPUBLIC
Total Population, 5,000,000

CITIES and TOWNS

'Amran, 5,000 ....B 4
Bait al Faqih, 12,000 ....B 5
Dhamar, 5,000 ....B 5
Hodeida, 40,000 ....B 5
Ibb, 7,000 ....B 5
Luhaiya, 6,000 ....B 4
Maida, 2,500 ....B 4
Manakha, 3,000 ....B 4
Mocha, 600 ....B 5
Sa'ada, 4,000 ....B 4
San'a (capital), 100,000 ....B 4
Sheikh Sa'id, 1,000 ....B 5
Ta'izz, 80,000 ....B 5
Yarim, 5,000 ....B 5
Zabid, 8,000 ....B 5

OTHER FEATURES

Hanish (isls.) ....B 5
Manar, Jebel (mt.) ....B 5
Sabir, Jebel (peak) ....B 5
Zuqar (isl.) ....B 5

PEOPLE'S DEMOCRATIC REP. OF YEMEN
Total Population, 1,158,000

CITIES and TOWNS

Aden (cap.), 150,000 ....C 5
Aden, *225,000 ....C 5
Bir 'Ali ....D 5
Hadibu ....D 5
Haura ....C 5
Lahej ....B 5
Madinat ash Sha'b
 (capital), 29,897 ....C 5
Meifa ....C 5
Mukalla, 30,000 ....C 5
Qishn ....D 4
Saihut ....C 4
Seiyun ....C 4
Shibam ....C 4
Shihr ....C 5
Zinjibar ....C 5

OTHER FEATURES

Aden (gulf) ....C 5
Hadhramaut, (region), 348,000 ...C 4
Hadhramaut, Wadi (dry riv.) ....D 4
Kamaran (isl.) ....B 4
Perim (isl.) ....B 5
Qamr (bay) ....D 4
Socotra (island), 14,000 ....D 5

BAHRAIN: Total pop.—1969 off. est.; other pops.—1965 final census. KUWAIT: Total pop.—1969 off. est.; cap. (& with suburbs)—1965 final census. OMAN: Total pop.—1968 off. est.; other pops.—1965 off. est. QATAR: Total pop.—1969 off. est.; cap.—1963 off. est.; other pops —1962 off. est. SAUDI ARABIA: Total pop.—1968 UN est. cities (over 100,000)—1965 off. est.; Dhahran, Hofuf, Medina, & Taif—1962 off. est.; other pops.—1959 off. est. U.A.E.: 1968 prelim. census. YEMEN ARAB REP.: Total pop.—1966 UN est.; capital—1964 off. est.; other pops.—1959 off. est. P.D.R. YEMEN: Total and cap.—1966 off. est.; Socotra—1961 off. st.; other pops.—1965 off. est.

ing to Mecca often visit the prophet's tomb in Medina, although this is not an essential part of the pilgrimage rites. The rulers of various Islamic countries have often exerted themselves to ease the way for pilgrimages of their subjects, and on occasion these rulers have vied with each other for the honor of being the protector of the holy cities.

Political Divisions. The kingdom of Saudi Arabia occupies roughly four fifths of the total area of the peninsula. The kingdom's western province is the Hejaz; its central province is Najd, in which the kingdom's capital city of Riyadh is situated; and the eastern province is Hasa, which stretches along the Persian Gulf. The southern boundaries of the kingdom have not been fixed by international agreement, except for a part of the boundary with Yemen.

The size of the kingdom of Saudi Arabia and its special connection with Islam make it by far the most influential state in Arabia, even though its population may not greatly exceed 3 million.

Most of the southwestern corner of the peninsula is occupied by the Yemen Arab Republic, established as a republic in 1962. Its territory is much smaller than that of Saudi Arabia, but its population may be as large or even larger.

Along the western half of the southern coast lies the People's Republic of Yemen, formerly South Yemen. Britain granted it independence in 1967. The republic, comprising the territory of the former British colony of Aden and the former British Protectorate of South Arabia, took the place of the British-sponsored Federation of South Arabia, which had included Aden and 16 of the 20-odd sultanates, amirates, and sheikhdoms of the protectorate. Three large sultanates in the eastern part of the protectorate that had held aloof from the federation were incorporated in the republic, all the sultans being dethroned.

East of the People's Democratic Republic of Yemen is the Oman sultanate, which includes the rest of the south coast of Arabia and almost all of the Arabian coast of the Gulf of Oman. Though ranking as an independent state, the sultanate has relied heavily on British diplomatic and military support in its dispute with the imamate of Oman (which claims much of the interior of this part of Arabia) and in another dispute with Saudi Arabia over boundaries. The imamate now exists as a government in exile based in Saudi Arabia.

In the 19th century, Britain acquired predominant influence in the Persian Gulf, where it enjoyed special treaty relations with all the small Arab states. In 1968, Britain announced that it would withdraw its garrisons from the gulf by the end of 1971. Immediately thereafter the sheikhdoms of Bahrain and Qatar discussed the possibility of union with the Trucial States, consisting of seven sheikhdoms on the Persian Gulf and the Gulf of Oman. Rivalries · among the nine, however, prevented immediate union.

The remainder of the Arabian coast of the Persian Gulf belongs to Saudi Arabia and to the amirate of Kuwait in the far north. The full independence of Kuwait was established by an agreement with Britain in 1961. For administrative purposes Kuwait and Saudi Arabia have divided the Neutral Zone lying between them.

PEOPLE

Knowledge of the traditional system of Arab genealogy is necessary for an understanding of Arabian society, which is still largely tribal in structure. This system is elaborate and generally well organized, although it does contain some contradictions and inconsistencies.

Northern and Southern Tribes. The Arabs of Arabia look upon themselves as descendants of Noah's son Shem, which accords with the fact that their language is Semitic. Noteworthy in the early generations after Shem were Qahtan and Abraham. According to one version, Qahtan and Abraham belonged to separate lines, while another version made Qahtan a descendant of Abraham. In any event, Qahtan was regarded as the ancestor of the "true Arabs," the term applied to the tribes associated with the southern part of the peninsula, particularly Yemen. Among these southerners were Saba and Himyar, who gave their names to the Sabaean and Himyaritic civilizations.

According to the Arab genealogists, Abraham was the progenitor of the Hebrews by his wife Sarah and her son Isaac and the progenitor of the Ishmaelites by his concubine Hagar and her son Ishmael. One of the descendants of Ishmael was Adnan, the ancestor of the "Arabized Arabs," the term applied to the tribes associated with the northern part of the peninsula.

Both the southerners and the northerners were divided into many tribes. The members of each tribe usually recognized as a common ancestor one of the descendants of Qahtan or Adnan, whose name was given to the tribe. The tribes were distinguished from one another by differences in the dialects they spoke, with the distinction between the southern speech and the northern speech being particularly marked.

The lingua franca of the northerners, once it was accepted as the language of Allah and the angels in the Koran, became classical Arabic, taking precedence over the language of the "true Arabs" of the south. Classical Arabic, however, has remained largely a literary language, and dialectal variations still exist in Arabia.

The geographical separation of southerners from northerners was far from comprehensive. A number of southern tribes had moved into northern Arabia long before the beginning of Islam, and some northerners had gone south, and others east. Despite this mingling, tribal loyalties remained strong. Although feuds within a tribe were not uncommon, the members of a tribe tended to stick together. The southern tribes sided with one another against the northern tribes. When the Arabs spilled out of Arabia with the expansion of Islam, they took this rivalry with them, as far as Spain in the west and the borders of China in the east. The rivalry has endured to the present in some parts of the Arab world, notably in eastern Arabia.

The place of honor enjoyed by the "true Arabs" of the south in contradistinction to the "Arabized Arabs" of the north was lost when the prophet Mohammed appeared from the ranks of Quraysh, a northern tribe. Accorded the honorifics of "sharif" or "sayyid" ("noble" or "master"), his descendants are venerated throughout the Islamic world, and in Arabia they have had great influence, especially in the west and south.

While many tribes have moved about inside Arabia or left the peninsula to roam through the Islamic world, other tribes have shown a remarkable tenacity in staying in their original homes. The twin tribes of Hashid and Bakil, for example, held the mountains north of Sanaa in Yemen in pre-Islamic times and still hold the same mountains. In southwestern Saudi Arabia the tribe of Yam has inhabited the valley of Najran for countless centuries. Hudhail and other tribes living in the vicinity of Mecca in the time of the prophet Mohammed are still living there.

Dilution of Tribalism. With the passage of time, various tribes have disintegrated while new tribes have been formed, some of which are confederations embracing diverse elements. The absorption of strangers into the tribes through the institution of clientship has diluted the purity of descent. A few tribes are denied status because they are unconnected with any reputable ancestor.

Another distinction of great importance in Arabia sets the nomad apart from the townsman or oasis dweller, with the two often in conflict with each other. Nomadic society is completely tribal, and tribal ties also dominate the scene in many towns and oases. Some tribes once famous for their prowess in the desert are now settled, while other tribes with old urban connections have turned at least in part to nomadism.

A process of loosening the grip of tribalism on Arabia is under way. Abd al-Aziz Ibn Saud, founder of the kingdom of Saudi Arabia, relied heavily on the tribes during the first part of his career in the 20th century, but during the second part he brought them to heel and made them completely subordinate to the central government. Larger cities, such as Mecca and Jidda, have cosmopolitan populations made up of Muslims from all parts of the Islamic world for whom the tribal affiliations of Arabia have little meaning. Arabs educated abroad, whose number is steadily increasing, are likely to feel that tribalism is an unwanted relic of the past. The prophet Mohammed offered devotion to Islam as a substitute for tribal loyalties. The new leaders of Arabia offer national pride as well as religion. Many Somalis have come from Africa to work in Aden, and some have gone as far as the Persian Gulf. Other Africans have mixed with the population of Arabia through the institution of slavery, which until recently was legal there. Merchants and craftsmen from India and Pakistan are numerous along the eastern and southern coasts. Among the largest communities of foreign origin in Mecca are those from Indonesia (the so-called Javanese) and from what is now Soviet Central Asia (the so-called Bukharans). The oil business in particular has attracted Americans, Englishmen, and other Westerners, as well as Arabs from Jordan, Lebanon, and Syria, some of whom are Christians. The Jews, once well represented in Aden, Yemen, and southwestern Saudi Arabia, have all left.

THE LAND AND NATURAL RESOURCES

Geologically, Arabia is divided into two regions which differ strikingly from each other: the Arabian Shield and the sedimentary region. In the west is the Arabian Shield, a huge mass of igneous and metamorphic rock of ancient origin, closely related to the Nubian Shield on the other side of the Red Sea. The more recent volcanic activity in this region, which appears to have ceased only about 700 years ago, has covered large areas with desolate black lava flows. The Arabian Shield consists of a great bulge toward the east, beginning in the north at the head of the Gulf of Aqaba, reaching inland almost to Riyadh, the capital of Saudi Arabia, and finally receding westward down to the border between Saudi Arabia and Yemen. The

mountains of Yemen and the southern coast are physiographically very different from those of the shield, even though the constituent rocks may in some cases be similar. The highest peak in Arabia is Hadur Shuaib, with an elevation of 12,333 feet (3,760 meters). It towers west of Sanaa, the capital of Yemen. The mountains of Oman are more akin to the Iranian mountains on the far side of the Gulf of Oman than they are to the rest of the Arabian mountains.

North, east, and south of the shield lies the sedimentary region of Arabia or, in the broader sense, the Persian Gulf-Mesopotamia basin, a region that was submerged by seas in geologic times subsequent to the formation of the shield. The seas left sedimentary deposits, which reach a depth of about 4 miles (6.5 km) in some places. These deposits are mainly limestone, along with much sandstone and shale; within their interstices are tremendously rich stores of petroleum and natural gas. Saudi Arabia's proved reserves of petroleum are about twice those of the United States; Kuwait is not far behind Saudi Arabia; and other countries in Arabia have substantial deposits.

In antiquity many gold and silver mines were exploited in the region of the Arabian Shield. Modern attempts to revive this industry have had only moderate success. Large quantities of other minerals, such as iron and copper, have been found, but it remains to be determined whether tapping these supplies is economically feasible. Other resources, some of which are already being drawn upon commercially, are granite, marble, clays, barite, and chromite.

Most of Arabia lies within the temperate zone. Even the southwestern tip, which is not far north of 12° north latitude, has in places enough elevation to avoid the extremes of tropical climate. The southern coast, the coasts of the Red Sea and the Persian Gulf, and the Rub al-Khali, on the other hand, are subjected to the extremes, particularly in summer, when the combination of heat and humidity becomes very trying. The winter weather in these parts, occasionally refreshed by rain, is often balmy.

The general scarcity of rain has left Arabia with no lakes of any size and only one perennial river; a short one in the south. The peninsula depends for its water supply above all on springs, which are common in the oases, and on wells, some of which are in the oases and others of which are scattered throughout the deserts. The water problem has inhibited the growth of large cities in Arabia. No city there has a population as high as 200,000.

Arable land is easier to find than water. Many deserts tracts turn green with vegetation once they are irrigated. New sources of underground water are constantly being sought, and better control of existing surface water is being established. Paradoxically, excessive watering in some spots has given the soil an undesirably high salt content. Arabia's best hope for the future lies in large-scale desalting of seawater. Kuwait already has one of the world's largest desalting plants, and Saudi Arabia is working energetically on a desalting program.

Until a few decades ago, hunting was a profession and a pastime in which the bedouins were particularly proficient. More recently, large herds of gazelle have been virtually wiped out by hunting from motor vehicles. The oryx of the southern sands has become extinct or nearly so. The last ostrich was shot in 1938. Hares and game birds remain to be caught by highly trained falcons. Among the nocturnal creatures of the desert, snakes and lizards abound.

The natural pearls of the Persian Gulf are perhaps the finest in the world, but they are hard to get without mechanical equipment, the use of which is forbidden by tradition. In the 20th century there has been a serious decline in pearling. Both the Persian Gulf and the Red Sea have ample resources of fish and other forms of marine life.

ECONOMY

Contrary to popular belief, the bedouins, or nomads, of Arabia appear to be substantially fewer in number than the settled people. The bedouins rely chiefly on the camel. Its meat, hides, and hair are valuable products. During cool weather, when the bedouins range over great distances, they usually drink camel's milk rather than water. Good grazing can be found in many parts of the desert when wild plants spring up after even light rains. In summer the nomads ordinarily stay in encampments close to water wells. Before the introduction of motor vehicles the camel was the principal means of transportation in Arabia.

Most bedouins also keep sheep and goats, although the flocks are smaller than those found farther north. Horses were once among the main exports from Arabia, but very few are raised there now. Donkeys are widely used as work animals in the oases.

Attracted by opportunities in the developing industries, some bedouins have voluntarily taken to the settled life of the towns. The Saudi Arabian government has also elaborated a plan for bedouin settlement, a very expensive process if carried out on a large scale.

Agriculture has benefited from better farm machinery, fertilizers, and irrigation, but Arabia remains far from self-sufficient in food production. Almost everywhere the date palm is the mainstay of the oases, but it does not grow at the higher altitudes, and in a few spots along the southern coast it is replaced by the coconut. Arabs are fond of rice, but they grow very little of it themselves, doing better with wheat, barley, and millet. Yemen was once famous for coffee bearing the name of the port of Mocha, but many farmers there have turned their mountain terraces over to the cultivation of the more profitable plant called *qat*, the leaves of which are commonly chewed in the south as a mild narcotic. Frankincense, a noted product of ancient Arabia, still grows in the domains of Oman, but it is no longer a prime item of trade.

Industry. Until the end of World War II, Arabia had almost nothing in the way of industry, apart from native handicrafts. Oil was discovered in Bahrain in 1932, but not in large quantities. In 1938 oil was discovered in Saudi Arabia and Kuwait, but the war held up development. Since 1946 the oil business in both countries has been growing apace, and since the abortive nationalization of the Iranian oil industry in 1951, Saudi Arabia and Kuwait have been in stiff competition for the positions of fourth- and fifth-largest producers in the world. Other producers on the Arabian side of the Persian Gulf are Qatar and the Neutral Zone between Saudi Arabia and Kuwait. Especially rich deposits have been found offshore and on the mainland of Abu

Dhabi, which by 1965 became the third-largest producer in the peninsula. In 1966 oil was discovered in the Trucial state of Dubai. In 1967, Oman began exporting oil in considerable quantities from fields deep in the interior of the country. All the discoveries have been in the sedimentary basin of eastern Arabia, but hope has not been abandoned of finding oil along the Red Sea coasts of Saudi Arabia and the two Yemen republics.

The extraction of oil brings with it a number of supplementary industries, which are not always situated beside the producing fields. Of the larger refineries in Arabia, two are in the big-producing countries of Saudi Arabia and Kuwait, one is in the small-producing country of Bahrain, one is the People's Republic of Yemen, which has no production. Kuwait and Saudi Arabia have taken the lead in developing petrochemical and fertilizer factories. Other plants turn out such goods as cement, matches, detergents, and gypsum panels for buildings.

In the early days of technological growth in Arabia, during the first part of the 20th century, few inhabitants had the skills needed for the new enterprises. Governments and private companies have implemented training programs, and the people of Arabia are playing an increasingly important part in industrial development. Efforts have also been made to reduce the dependence of the Arabian countries on outside entrepreneurs and capital by making more extensive use of local resources.

The People's Republic of Yemen is the one part of Arabia where organized labor has become a strong political force. Bahrain and Kuwait have the next most sophisticated work force. Saudi Arabia does not allow trade unions, on the ground that unions might become centers of subversion and that the government is best qualified to safeguard the interests of labor.

Travel and Trade. Life in Arabia is being radically changed by remarkable improvements in communications, both internal and external. A network of paved roads is spreading across the peninsula, and sturdy vehicles have been introduced that can leave the roads and penetrate even the most formidable wildernesses of sand or rock. Regular airplane flights go to virtually every corner of Arabia, and international airports bring the outside world closer.

Until the 20th century, world trade tended to pass Arabia by. The three coasts of the peninsula had very few harbors capable of handling vessels larger than the native sailing craft. During the 20th century, modern docks and other equipment have been installed at Jidda, the port of Mecca, and at Yanbu, the port of Medina. The Soviet Union has built a new port for Yemen near the old port of Hodeida. Aden was, until the closing of the Suez Canal by the UAR, one of the world's foremost bunkering ports. In the Persian Gulf the modern ports of Kuwait and Bahrain are active, and Saudi Arabia uses Dammam for general cargo and Ras Tanura for the export of oil. As industry expands, the list of improved ports grows steadily longer.

Over the centuries the Mecca pilgrimage has kept Arabia in touch with distant lands, and many pilgrims have combined commercial dealing with their devotions. The rapid growth of the oil industry has helped make business in Arabia even more cosmopolitan than it was before. Japan, for example, holds oil concessions in the Neutral Zone between Kuwait and Saudi Arabia. A considerable amount of Arabian oil goes to Japan, and a wide variety of Japanese goods may be found in many Arabian bazaars.

HISTORY

Arabia may have been the original home of the Semites, but even if it was not, numbers of them have lived there since prehistoric times. From at least the 3000's B.C., people speaking Semitic languages have been moving from Arabia into the Fertile Crescent to the north and Egypt to the west.

Pre-Muslim Arabia. The evidence now available indicates that the camel was domesticated in Arabia during the 1000's B.C. When the Arabs are first mentioned, in an Assyrian inscription of the 800's B.C., they are associated with camels. These Arabs were in the northern part of the Arabian peninsula, where one of their groups or tribes was Saba, which may be identical with the Biblical Sheba. The Assyrian inscriptions speak of queens among the northern Aribi, who were probably tribal chieftainesses.

The name Saba recurs in southwestern Arabia, where the Sabaean civilization developed. The wealth that contributed to the growth of this civilization came from a monopoly of the export of incense and spices from the East to the West and from an elaborate irrigation system, the masterpiece of which was the great dam of Marib, whose ruins still stand in the interior of Yemen. The Sabaean states had commercial ties with northern Arabia and the Mediterranean world, where Sabaean remains have been found. Greek influence may be seen in sculpture, coins, and other aspects of Sabaean life. The Sabaeans also had close connections with Abyssinia on the other side of the Red Sea.

In the 6th century B.C. the capital of the Neo-Babylonian or Chaldean empire was established for a short time in Taima in northern Arabia. The Persian conquerors of Babylon created the satrapy of Arabaya. Scripts called Lihyanitic (Lihyanite) and Thamudic (Thamudene) came into extensive use in northern Arabia.

Alexander the Great of Macedon, who sent his navy to explore the Persian Gulf, was planning to conquer Arabia when death cut short his career in 323 B.C. During the 3d century B.C. the Ptolemies of Egypt began advancing southward in the Red Sea region. The Nabataeans, an Aramaean people with their capital at Petra in what is now Jordan, spread their influence into northern Arabia. In 24 B.C. the Nabataeans joined the Roman general Aelius Gallus in an expedition that ended in disaster after traversing almost the entire length of Arabia. Under Trajan (reigned 98–117 A.D.) the Romans converted Nabataea into what they called the province of Arabia. (See ARABIA, ROMAN PROVINCE OF.) The later period of the old civilization in southwestern Arabia is called Himyaritic, after the tribe of Himyar.

The Arabian commercial monopoly was gradually undermined by the Greeks and Romans in Egypt, who learned how to sail across the Indian Ocean with the monsoons. In the 3d century A.D. the Abyssinians won a foothold in Yemen but soon lost it. They came back in the 6th century, only to be evicted before long by the Persians, who also penetrated into eastern Arabia.

The oldest inscription in the proto-Arabic language of northern Arabia dates from the early 4th century A.D. The development of this language into what became classical Arabic was furthered by the eloquent poets of the period just before Islam. These poets were the founders of Arabic literature, although their poems were not written down until much later. Most of the poets, like the other inhabitants of Arabia, were pagans, although Christianity and Judaism had made some headway in the peninsula. The town of Mecca on the old trade route between Yemen and the north had a pagan sanctuary to which annual pilgrimages were made.

Cradle of Islam and Its Sects. Early in the 7th century the monotheistic religion of Islam was revealed to the prophet Mohammed, a native of Mecca. Mohammed made his hegira (flight) from Mecca to Medina in 622, which was taken as the year 1 of the Islamic era. In Medina the prophet built a state governed by the principles of the new religion.

Under the first caliphs—Mohammed's successors at the head of the Islamic state—the unification of Arabia, begun by the prophet, was completed. Muslim armies advanced beyond Arabia to win victories over the forces of the Byzantine and Persian empires. The lands of the Fertile Crescent and Egypt were annexed. Dissensions, however, set the Muslim leaders against one another. Ali, who was the prophet's son-in-law and fourth caliph, moved the capital from Arabia to Mesopotamia to strengthen his position; the Umayyad caliphs, who became supreme after Ali's death, moved it again to Damascus. A rival of the Umayyads held out in Mecca, but after his death in 692, Arabia became just a provincial part of the Islamic realm, important chiefly for the shrines in the holy cities.

The three great sectarian divisions within Islam had their origins in Ali's caliphate. The first to break away were the Kharijites (Outgoers), who were dissatisfied with Ali's conduct of affairs. When the Umayyads prevailed over Ali's line, Ali's followers formed the sect of the Shiites (partisans of Ali). The remaining Muslims, who have continued to constitute the majority, are known as the Sunnites.

Set off from the main centers of Islamic authority, Arabia became hospitable territory for Kharijism and Shiism, both of which preferred the title of "imam" to that of "caliph" for the head of the community. During the Umayyad caliphate, Kharijism flourished in Arabia, where it was usually called Ibadism. The first Ibadite imamate was established in the south in the 8th century, and another soon afterward in Oman, where it has lasted, with some interruptions, down to the present. The upsurge of the Ibadites in Arabia contributed to the downfall of the Umayyads in 750. The succeeding Abbasid dynasty built a new capital, Baghdad, in Iraq.

During the early Abbasid period the Shiites in Arabia gave the caliphs much trouble. In southern Mesopotamia, Shiites led a rising of Negro slaves, the prologue to the extremist Shiite movement of the Carmathians in Yemen and on the Arabian side of the Persian Gulf. In the early 10th century the Carmathians overran most of Arabia and carried off the Black Stone from the Kaaba in Mecca to their base in eastern Arabia. The stone was returned in the mid-10th century, but the Carmathians kept control of their eastern stronghold until late in the next century.

The extremist Shiites were not alone in rejecting Abbasid rule in Arabia. In the 9th century a more moderate Shiite faction, the Zaidites, founded an imamate in Yemen that has lasted, with some interruptions, down to the present. Independent secular dynasties also began to appear in Yemen, the first of these likewise dating from the 9th century. About the mid-10th century the government of the Hashemite sharifs was inaugurated in Mecca, where it endured until 1924.

Struggle for Supremacy. In the early 16th century the Portuguese established themselves in the Persian Gulf, although they were not strong enough to take either Aden or Mecca. To counter this new Christian danger, the Ottoman Turks moved into Arabia. On conquering Egypt in 1517, Sultan Selim was recognized as protector of the holy cities. The west coast of the peninsula, including Yemen, and part of the east coast were incorporated into the Ottoman empire.

In the 17th century the Ottomans lost their hold on eastern Arabia, where the Persians were advancing and the native Arab tribes were growing stronger, and on southwestern Arabia, where the Zaidite imamate was expanding. The British and the Dutch broke the commercial monopoly of the Portuguese, particularly in the Persian Gulf.

During the first half of the 18th century the Wahhabite reform movement, calling for a return to the original principles of Islam, was launched in central Arabia, where it received strong support from the house of Saud. In 1803 the reformers, who had won over most of the peninsula, entered Mecca. The Ottoman sultan called on his viceroy in Egypt, Mehmet Ali, to suppress the Wahhabites. The Wahhabite capital fell in 1818, but the movement did not die out.

From the end of the 18th century the British by stages secured political supremacy in the Persian Gulf and in southern Arabia through a system of protectorates and special treaties with local chiefs. Arabia was brought into much closer touch with the outside world by the opening of the Suez Canal in 1869, the Turkish reconquest of Yemen, and the completion of the Hejaz railway from Damascus to Medina in 1908.

Starting in 1902, Abd al-Aziz Ibn Saud rebuilt the Wahhabite state, which was renamed the kingdom of Saudi Arabia in 1932. Sharif Hussein Ibn Ali of the Hashemite dynasty in Mecca proclaimed the Arab revolt against the Turks in 1916 and took the title of king. The Turks also lost Yemen to the Zaidite imamate.

In 1924, Abd al-Aziz Ibn Saud defeated King Hussein and occupied Mecca, and in the following year he took Medina. In 1934, Saudi Arabia vanquished the Zaidite imamate in a brief war but allowed it to remain independent. A revolution established the Yemen Arab republic in 1962, and republican forces seized control of the main cities, but Imam Muhammad al-Badr, aided by Saudi Arabia, held out in the mountains. When Britain left Aden in 1967, South Yemen (later People's Republic of Yemen) was established.

GEORGE RENTZ
Hoover Institution, Stanford University

Bibliography

Doughty, Charles M., *Travels in Arabia Deserta,* abridged by Edward Garnett (New York 1955).
Ingrams, William Harold, *Arabia and the Isles,* rev. ed. (New York 1964).
Lebkicher, Roy, Rentz, George, and Steineke, Max, *The Arabia of Ibn Saud* (New York 1952).
Sanger, Richard H., *The Arabian Peninsula* (Ithaca, N.Y., 1954).
Twitchell, K. S., *Saudi Arabia,* 3d ed. (Princeton 1958)

ARABIA, ə-rā′bē-ə, **Roman Province of,** comprised the Sinai peninsula and the bordering country to the northeast. The Arabic-speaking Nabataeans, Aramaic in culture, dominated the area, with Petra as their capital. Through it passed the rich desert caravan trade from the Near and Far East, which Rome was eager to control and tax. About 65 B.C., the Nabataean state became a client kingdom of Rome, providing troops and accepting Roman dictation in internal affairs. When the Nabataean king Dabel died in 106 A.D., Trajan made it a Roman province with its capital at Bostra. The province declined when new routes diverted trade to Alexandria and Palmyra.

ELEANOR HUZAR, *Michigan State University*

ARABIAN DESERT, ə-rā′bē-ən, in Egypt between the Nile River and the Red Sea, with a southward extension into the Sudan. It derived its name either from its closeness to Arabia or from its having been the home of the first Arab nomads in Egypt. It is also called the *Eastern Desert.* Unlike the Libyan, or Western, Desert west of the Nile, the Arabian Desert is very mountainous and deeply dissected by wadis. Jebel Shayib, rising to 7,163 feet (1,183 meters), is the highest peak in Egypt. Some of the lower slopes of the mountains near the Red Sea are overgrown with grass after the winter rains.

THE ARABIAN DESERT in Egypt, barren and inhospitable to the living, was an ancient Muslim burial ground.

The Arabian Desert was a source of building stones for the ancient Egyptians. Its porphyry quarries were well known. When Egypt developed trade with southern lands, the main caravan route ran from the Nile bend near Thebes through Wadi al-Hammamat (the Valley of the Baths) to the coast near modern Quseir. In the 3d century St. Anthony, the first Christian monk, isolated himself in the desert, where his monastery still stands. In recent times transdesert traffic has declined, although rough motor tracks reach many parts of the area, and a few Mecca pilgrims travel through it. The desert is today a source of petroleum, extracted north of Hurghada, and of phosphate, mined near Quseir.

Three nomadic tribes inhabit the desert. The Maaza, originally from Arabia, reached the area in the 18th century. The Ababda and the Bisharin belong to the Hamitic-speaking Beja, although the Ababda are chiefly Arabic-speaking. The Bisharin raise handsome white camels of a superior breed.

The name "Arabian Desert" is also used for the deserts of the Arabian Peninsula.

GEORGE RENTZ
The Hoover Institution, Stanford University

ARABIAN NIGHTS, ə-rā′bē-ən, a collection of tales, of undefined extent and identity, that in the West ranks among the classics of literature. Outside the English-speaking world they are usually known as *One Thousand and One Nights*. They have frequently been adapted or plagiarized in literature, the theater, cinema, and opera, and watered-down versions were once fashionable as children's entertainment.

In the Arabic-speaking world, from which the West eventually received them, they hold no preeminent or even clearly defined status. Moreover, despite their long popularity in the West and an increasingly serious interest in them in their lands of origin, there is still no truly standard edition or translation. Individual tales and passages are included, omitted, or varied in haphazard fashion. Intensive research has sought answers to such questions as: where were these stories first told and by whom? how did they reach those who finally wrote them down in a form of Arabic? who were these scribes and when and where did they work? what changes did *The Arabian Nights* undergo, first in the East, later in the West? and how did the present working text gain acceptance? Research has served more to reveal the complexities of these problems than to solve them satisfactorily.

One cause of the difficulty is that fiction held a very lowly and insecure place in the formal civilization of classical Islam. Tales were told for the most part orally and, ostensibly, only by and for the common man. Their low-class, colloquial nature militated against their being recorded in a script and language normally reserved for the intellectual elite. Hence there is a lack of early documents from which to trace the tales' history.

Origins. Many of the stories are thought to be of Indian origin and to have undergone Persian transmission and remolding, both before and after the advent of the Islamic period in the 7th century A.D. For other stories, however, quite different times and places of origin are plausibly adduced—ancient Egypt, Babylonia, Israel, Greece, Arabia itself, and North Africa, to name only a few. They are supposed to have been first written down comprehensively in Mamluk Egypt by about the 15th century. Where their original linguistic form can be recognized through progressive "correction," they exhibit mainly Egyptian-Arabic elements; and much of their social background belongs to Egypt rather than to Baghdad of the 8th and 9th centuries, where they are so often circumstantially located.

Content and Style. *The Arabian Nights* is a classic example of the "frame story," similar to the frame stories found in Chaucer and Boccaccio. The individual tales are set within the framework of a ruse used by the newly married Scheherazade to preserve her life by her skill as a storyteller. But the boundaries are soon forgotten as the rich stream of anecdote moves from myths and legends of Alexander and Solomon, of shahs and caliphs, through fairy stories of the supernatural, to accounts of "boys making good" (like Aladdin, Ali Baba, and Sindbad). There are small novels of social and moral significance, romances, and farces.

The Arabic style is generally racy and unforced, although the tone varies and at times classical and learned modes are imitated as parodies or as embellishments. Unfortunately, most Western translations have been made in eras when the literary conventions, classical or Gothic, of the translator's day largely precluded a true display of the original style.

Western Translations. The earliest extended Western version was in French, published by the scholar, traveler, and civil servant J.A. Galland between 1704 and 1717. This translation-paraphrase served for a century as the basis of many others in a wide range of languages. Later, scholars of various nations returned to the original Arabic, discovering better texts and additional material, which resulted in a new series of original and secondary translations and reworkings. The English version by E.W. Lane (1839–41 and later) is accurate, if dull, and has excellent annotation. However, it is incomplete. The version of John Payne (1882–84 and later) is complete but less reliable and falsely florid and mock-Gothic. The famous version by Sir Richard Burton (1885–88 and later) has vitality and sweep but is often a mere plagiarism of Lane or Payne.

G.M. WICKENS, *University of Toronto*

Further Reading: Arberry, Arthur J., *Scheherezade* (London 1953), the first installment of a "modern" version; Littmann, E., "Alf Layla wa-Layla," *Encyclopedia of Islam*, new ed., vol. 1, pp. 358–364 (London and Leiden 1960).

ARABIAN SEA, ə-rā′bē-ən, the northwestern part of the Indian Ocean. It is bounded by Somalia and the Arabian Peninsula on the west, West Pakistan and India on the north, and the Malabar coast of India on the east. Two arms of the sea branch off westwards: the Gulf of Aden, which runs into the Red Sea, and the Gulf of Oman, which runs into the Persian Gulf.

The sea is generally very deep, and its few islands lie not far from the coasts. Socotra, in the west, is about 150 miles from the Somali coast, and the coral atolls of the Laccadives, in the east, are less than 150 miles off the coast of India. The chief ports are Bombay in India, Karachi in Pakistan, and Aden in Arabia.

Since early times the northeast monsoon in winter and the southwest monsoon in summer have facilitated direct crossings by sailing vessels.

The winter or fairweather monsoon is milder than the summer or wet monsoon. Storms are uncommon in winter, but the summer monsoon sometimes reaches gale force. Tropical cyclones occur in spring and fall, although with far less frequency than in the Bay of Bengal.

GEORGE RENTZ
The Hoover Institution, Stanford University

ARABIC. See ARAB CIVILIZATION.

ARABIS, ar′ə-bis, is a group of annual or perennial herbs widespread throughout the Northern Hemisphere. It is commonly called *rock cress.* The species are either hairless or hairy (with forked hairs) and bear simple, mostly toothed, leaves. The flowers are small, although often very numerous; they are white or purple with four petals and six stamens. The flowers are present over a long period, and a few species are sometimes used in rock gardens. The plants are hardy but should have full sunlight. The genus *Arabis* belongs to the mustard family Cruciferae.

RICHARD M. STRAW, *Los Angeles State College of Applied Arts and Sciences*

ARACAJU, a-rə-kə-zhoo′, is the capital of the state of Sergipe in northeastern Brazil. The city is situated on the Sergipe River near the river's mouth and has an excellent harbor. The commercial center of the state, it ships sugar, cotton, rice, and hides from its port. An airport provides commercial air service to other parts of Brazil. Population: (1960) 112,516.

ARACEAE, ə-rā′sē-ē, is the botanical name of a large family of plants, also known as the arum family. It includes more than 100 genera and over 1,000 species. The Araceae are characterized by a flower spike or inflorescence (spadix) that is usually enclosed by a sheath or blade that sometimes resembles a leaf. The members of the family (aroids) are mainly herbaceous plants but occasionally may be vines or climbing plants appearing to be shrubby and woody. Some aroids are epiphytes that grow on other plants; others have large tubers and subterranean stems.

In the tropics, aroids may reach gigantic sizes. The krubi (*Amorphophallus titanum*) from Sumatra, for example, has a spadix of 6 to 7 feet (1.8 to 2.1 meters) or more. In northern regions, aroids are comparatively small, like the jack-in-the-pulpit and the skunk cabbage.

Many aroids are popular ornamental plants. The anthuriums, native to the American tropics, are often grown for their colorful flowers, called "flamingo flowers," or for their luxuriant, satiny, colorful foliage. Vine-type aroids used for decorative purposes include the ceriman (*Monstera deliciosa*) and the philodendron. The ceriman and some other aroids, such as the taro and yautia, are also used as food plants in the tropics.

WALTER SINGER, *The New York Botanical Garden*

ARACHNE, ə-rak′nē, in Greek legend, was a young girl of Colophon, in Lydia, who was so skillful at weaving that even Athena (Minerva) could not compete with her. When she wove, into cloth, pictures depicting the loves of the gods and goddesses, Athena in a jealous rage tore the cloth to pieces. In despair, Arachne hanged herself, but was saved by Athena, who changed her into a spider and the rope into a cobweb.

ARACHNIDA, ə-rak′nə-də, is a large and important class of animals that includes scorpions, mites, ticks, daddy longlegs, spiders, and fossil spiderlike creatures. The class Arachnida belongs to the phylum Arthropoda and contains about 60,000 species, in 15 orders. Extremely diversified in appearance and size, arachnids range from the seven-inch-long giant black African scorpions to the tiny mites that live in the air tubes (tracheae) of insects. The absence of antennae, wings, and compound eyes and the possession of four pairs of legs differentiate arachnids from insects and crustaceans. Most arachnids are predators that feed on invertebrates, especially insects.

Common Arachnids. The omnivorous mites and ticks are atypical arachnids that are highly specialized. Half of them are parasitic—some only in one life stage but others in all—on a great variety of animals. Some are carriers of serious diseases of man and animals. The itch mites, chiggers, and various ticks are pests, and the red spider mites ruin crop plants.

With about 40,000 species, the true spiders are the most numerous in species of the arachnids. They have always attracted attention by their amazing web traps, extraordinary courtship behavior, and great structural variety. The species of *Latrodectus* (q.v.), which includes the black widow spider, and various scorpions from Durango and Guerrero in Mexico and from Arizona in the United States, have venoms that affect the nerves of their victims and are capable of causing death, particularly in young children.

Anatomy of the Arachnids. The bodies of arachnids are divided into two major sections, the cephalothorax (united head and thorax) and the abdomen. Each has distinctive appendages.

The cephalothorax, which is composed of eight segments, is fused to form a dorsal shield, the carapace. The first pair of appendages (the chelicerae) in many arachnids are pincerlike claws adapted for grasping and are used to hold and brush the prey during feeding. In spiders the venom sacs are located on these appendages—the second segment, which lacks pincers, is the instrument (fang) for injecting the venom.

The second pair of appendages are the pedipalpi. They may be simple, leglike sensory organs as in spiders or large pincerlike organs for grasping or seizing as in scorpions and whip scorpions. The first (coxal) segment of the pedipalpi is also modified into cutting or crushing organs for use during feeding, and in spiders, the last segment bears the male sexual organ. The remaining appendages of the cephalothorax are four pairs of usually similar walking legs. (The number may be three or even two pairs in larval mites.) Some of these appendages can have a sensory function or be the location of special copulatory organs.

The abdomen is either narrowly separated from the cephalothorax by a narrow basal portion or is broadly joined to it. It is normally composed of 12 or 13 segments and may be either elongate with free dorsal plates and tail segment, or short with less distinct segmentation and with a tail segment. The abdominal appendages are mostly lost, modified into lungs, or present as exposed combs and spinnerets (silk-producing appendages). The sexual ducts open through a single hole on the second segment beneath the base of the abdomen.

The respiratory organs are either book lungs, which are composed of thin folds of membrane at-

ARACHNIDA
DISTINGUISHING CHARACTERISTICS:

CEPHALOTHORAX UNSEGMENTED

SIMPLE EYE

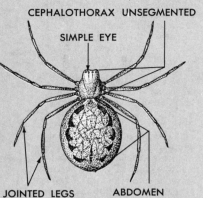

JOINTED LEGS   ABDOMEN
(UNSEGMENTED HERE)

ARACHNIDS HAVE a fused head and thorax, and an abdomen. There are four pairs of thoracic appendages. They have no antennae and no wings. Development is by molting. There are about 60,000 species grouped into 15 orders.

JOHN H. GERARD FROM NATIONAL AUDUBON SOCIETY   HUGH SPENCER FROM NATIONAL AUDUBON SOCIETY

TOM GREEN FROM NATIONAL AUDUBON SOCIETY   DADE THORNTON FROM NATIONAL AUDUBON SOCIETY

THE MAIN ORDERS OF ARACHNIDS ARE: 1. Mites and ticks, with cephalothorax and abdomen broadly joined. 2. Harvestmen, with long, slender legs and oval body. 3. Spiders, with abdomen and thorax joined by slender segment. 4. Scorpions, with abdomen ending in sting, and young born alive.

tached like the leaves of a book, or air tubes, depending on the order of Arachnida. The book lungs are derived from structures similar to the external gill-books of the king crab, and in various groups, they are modified into tracheal tubes analogous to those of insects.

The chief excretory organs are coxal glands that void wastes through small openings behind the first and third coxae. These glands, the silk- and venom-producing glands in the chelicerae of some arachnids, and the silk glands in the abdomen of spiders, are all thought to be modified nephridia (tubular excretory organs).

Lacking true jaws to aid in chewing, the arachnids must predigest their prey and suck the liquids through the simple mouth opening into the intestine by means of a powerful sucking organ. The sense of touch is remarkably developed among the arachnids and compensates for the imperfection of other senses. The eyes are always simple and never compound as in insects and crustaceans. Only in a few day-hunting spiders are the eyes notable for acuity.

Except scorpions, which bear their young alive, the arachnids lay eggs that hatch into small replicas of the adults. Development is gradual and direct, and change in size is accomplished by shedding the outer shell-layer.

Origin of the Arachnids. Arachnids are an extremely ancient type. They emerged from the seas as the first land animals 420 million to 510 million years ago (Cambrian period), long before insects or vertebrates. The arachnids and their nearest relatives, the Xiphosura (of which the king crabs are the only living types) and the extinct Eurypterida, probably arose from progressive relatives of the trilobites that lived in the Cambrian seas.

True scorpions lived 300 million to 360 million years ago (Silurian period) and spiders and mites 290 million to 330 million years ago (De-

vonian period). Most orders of the arachnids were well differentiated by 250 million years ago (Carboniferous period). Except for a few mites that have returned to aquatic life, the arachnids have remained terrestrial animals.

See also MITES AND TICKS; SCORPIONS; SPIDERS.

WILLIS J. GERTSCH
The American Museum of Natural History

ARAD, ä-räd', is a city in Rumania, in the western part of the country. It is situated on the Mureş River, about 15 miles from the Hungarian border and 265 miles northwest of Bucharest. Arad is the largest industrial center of western Rumania. It has distilleries, textile plants, sawmills, and plants producing electrical goods. It is also a trade center for the agricultural goods produced in the surrounding area. It is linked by air with Bucharest.

The existence of a settlement at present-day Arad is recorded as early as the 1200's. It was taken by the Turks in 1542 and heavily fortified, but was seized by the Austrians in 1685. Arad was held by Hungary during the revolution of 1849 against Austria, but it subsequently reverted to Austria. It was granted to Rumania after World War I, but there is still a large Magyar minority (about 30 percent of the population). Population: (1963) 114,494.

ARAFURA SEA, ar-ə-foor'ə, a part of the Pacific Ocean between the northern coast of Australia and the southern coast of New Guinea. It merges on the west with the Timor Sea, and is connected on the east with the Coral Sea by the Torres Strait. It is 800 miles (1,277.5 km) long by 350 miles (563.2 km) wide.

The Arafura Sea is on the main shipping route between eastern Australia and southern Asia. Its waters are shallow, and their numerous shoals are hazards to navigation.

ARAGO, à-rà-gō', **Dominique François Jean** (1786–1853), French physicist and astronomer who made pioneering experiments in light and electromagnetism. He was born in Estagel, France, on Feb. 26, 1786, and attended the Polytechnic School in Paris. After becoming a professor there in 1809, he investigated light and electromagnetism and studied planets and stars.

As a result of his studies and experiments, Arago promulgated the wave theory of light. With Jean Baptiste Biot, he measured the index of refraction of air and other gases and made the first precise measurements of the density of gases. His studies of light included experiments to compare the velocity of light in air, water, and glass. In 1811 he discovered the polarization of light in quartz crystals. Later he joined Augustin Jean Fresnel in research that established fundamental laws of the polarization of light.

In 1820, Arago showed that a copper wire attracted iron filings when it carried an electric current but that the filings fell off when the current ceased. In 1824 he showed that a rotating copper disk produced a rotation in a nearby magnetic needle. These experiments preceded Michael Faraday's explanation of induction.

Arago was made the director of the Paris Observatory in 1830. His work in astronomy included precise measurements of the diameters of the planets, an explanation of the scintillation of the stars based on the principle of interference, and studies of the sun's chromosphere and corona. He died in Paris on Oct. 2, 1853.

ARAGON, à-rà-gôn', **Louis** (1897–   ), French writer who was one of the founders of surrealism in literature and later became a leading propagandist for communism in the West. He was born at Paris on Oct. 3, 1897. With André Breton and Philippe Soupault, he founded the surrealist movement in the 1920's. His early poems—the volumes *Feu de joie* (1920) and *Mouvement perpétuel* (1925)—were surrealist works, as were his first novels—*Anicet ou le panorama* (1921) and *Le paysan de Paris* (1926). After a trip to the Soviet Union in 1931, he became a Marxist. His novels *Les cloches de Bâle* (1934; Eng. tr., *The Bells of Basel*, 1935) and *Les beaux quartiers* (1936; Eng. tr., *Residential Quarter*, 1938) paint life in France after World War I as corrupted by middle-class ideals and by capitalism.

During World War II, Aragon was a leader of the French underground. His revulsion with both the occupying Germans and the Pétain government at Vichy inspired him to attempt to recapture the traditional patriotic fervor of the French in two volumes of poetry published surreptitiously—*Le crève-coeur* (1940) and *La Diane française* (1945). In both books he employed a rhymed verse reminiscent of the *chansons* of the Middle Ages. His novels of this period, including *Aurélien* (1944), praised the selflessness of the proletariat. In 1949 he began *Les communistes,* a multivolume cycle of novels about communism. In 1959 he published *La Semaine Sainte* (Eng. tr., *Holy Week*, 1961), a large, sprawling, nonpolitical novel about the Napoleonic era.

In *Les yeux d'Elsa* (1942), *Les yeux et la mémoire* (1954), *Elsa* (1959), and *Le fou d'Elsa* (1963), Aragon wrote tender love poems to his wife, the novelist Elsa Triolet, whom he married in 1939. He also wrote literary criticism and essays on politics.

ARAGON, ar'ə-gon, is a region in northeastern Spain that was formerly a medieval kingdom. In 1833 it was divided into the provinces of Huesca, Saragossa, and Teruel. Its area of 18,382 square miles is bounded on the north by the Pyrenees Mountains and on the south by the Iberian Mountains. The region is drained by the Ebro River and its tributaries. The climate is characterized by little rainfall, extremes in temperature and high winds.

Although sheep and some cattle are raised, the main occupation is farming. The chief agricultural products are wheat, sugar beets, olives, fruit, and wine grapes. Manufactures include textiles, machinery, chemicals, and cement. Olive oil is processed and sugar is refined. There are important iron, sulfur, and lignite mines. Quarries produce marble and limestone.

Although hindered by lack of rain and poor communications, Aragon has slowly developed its industry and agriculture. Projects to conserve water, irrigate the land, and increase hydroelectric power have helped the economy. The manufacturing and commercial center of Aragon is Saragossa.

History. Aragon formed part of the ancient Roman province of *Hispania Tarraconensis.* It came under the control of the Visigoths during the 5th century A.D. When the Moors conquered Aragon shortly after 711, many Christians fled to the northern part of the area, where they maintained a small state with some independence. This state later came under the rule of Gothic counts. In 1035, under Ramiro I, Aragon established itself as an independent Christian kingdom. In 1076 it was linked with Navarre, but Navarre seceded from the union in 1134.

In constant conflict with the Moors, Aragon gradually expanded its territory, capturing Saragossa in 1118. In 1137 it was joined to Catalonia. During the next two centuries, Aragon extended its rule to the Balearic Islands, and at various times governed Sardinia, Sicily, and Naples. In 1479, ten years after the marriage of Isabella of Castile to Ferdinand of Aragon, the two crowns were united. When Charles I ascended the throne in 1516, the kingdom of Aragon became part of a unified Spain, but it preserved its *fueros,* regional systems of justice, taxation, military service, and currency, until the early 18th century. Population: (1960) 1,105,498.

ARAGONITE, ə-rag'ə-nīt, is a mineral form of calcium carbonate. It has the same composition as calcite and may change spontaneously into that substance. It belongs to a different crystal system than calcite does, however, and is somewhat heavier and much less common. Occasionally aragonite contains a little strontium, lead, or zinc. Its long, brittle crystals occur around hot springs, in stalactites, in clays and ore deposits, and in secretions by living organisms (such as the pearly layers found in many shells). The crystals are transparent to translucent, have a glassy luster, and are usually white or colorless. Good crystals have been found in Spain, England, and Sicily. In the United States, small deposits are found in New Mexico and Arizona. Aragonite, bromlite, witherite, strontianite, and cerussite, all carbonates in the same crystal system, are classified together as the aragonite group.

Composition: $CaCO_3$; hardness, 3.5 to 4.0; specific gravity, 2.9 to 3.0; crystal system, orthorhombic.

ARAL SEA, ar'əl, a large inland sea in Asia. It is in the Kazakh and Uzbek republics of the USSR, 175 miles east of the Caspian Sea. It is 266 miles long and 176 miles wide and has an area of 25,569 square miles.

ARALIA, ə-rā′lē-ə, is a widely distributed genus of shrubs, trees, and perennial herbs. The species have large, alternate, compound, deciduous leaves; small clusters of whitish flowers; and two- to five-seeded, variously colored, globular, berrylike fruits. All parts of the plants have a warm, aromatic taste.

The genus *Aralia* belongs to the family Araliaceae; there are about 20 species. *Aralia spinosa*—commonly called devil's-walking stick, angelica tree, Hercules'-club, or toothache tree, is an ornamental shrub or small tree that grows between 12 and 40 feet (3.6 to 12 meters) high. It is most often found in moist woods and along river banks from Pennsylvania to Indiana and southward to the Gulf of Mexico. Its very stout, prickly stems, large featherlike leaves, and clusters of flowers, which appear in midsummer, give a decided subtropical effect upon lawns in the South. It is not hardy in the North. *A. racemosa*, spikenard, is a widely branched herbaceous species, with large, spicy, aromatic roots and greenish-white flowers that appear in midsummer. It is common in thick woods from New Brunswick to Minnesota and southward as far as Georgia and Missouri. *A. nudicaulis*, wild sarsaparilla or small spikenard, is a nearly stemless herbaceous species with a single featherlike leaf a foot (30 centimeters) high. It is common in rocky and sandy places from Newfoundland to British Columbia and southward to an area extending from Georgia to Colorado. It bears from two to seven clusters of greenish flowers in late spring. The long, horizontal, aromatic roots are believed to be equal to those of sarsaparilla as a tonic. *A. hispida*, wild elder or bristly sarsaparilla, is a bristly stemmed perennial found from Newfoundland southwesterly as far as Minnesota. It bears several clusters of white flowers in early summer.

Among foreign Aralias, the Asiatic species are perhaps of most importance. Some, notably *A. cordata*, known as udo, are of value as human food; others, as stock food when grasses are scarce. *A. chinensis*, the Chinese angelica tree, is much like its American relative, *A. spinosa*, but is hardier and blossoms somewhat later.

Aralia (*A. hispida*, known as bristly sarsaparilla).

ARAM, ar'əm, **Eugene** (1704–1759), English philologist, who was one of the first scholars to assert that the Celtic languages belong to the Indo-European family. He was born at Ramsgill, Yorkshire, probably in September 1704. Self-educated, he learned Chaldee, Arabic, Welsh, Irish, and other languages. He began to compile a comparative dictionary of European languages, and he found that, contrary to scholarly opinion, Latin was not derived directly from Greek.

In 1745, Aram's intimate friend, Daniel Clark, and some stolen goods disappeared. Aram was tried for complicity in the theft but was acquitted. When Clark's skeleton was discovered 13 years later, Aram was arrested for murder. At his trial on Aug. 3, 1759, he conducted his own defense, vigorously attacking the doctrine of circumstantial evidence. He was convicted and hanged at York on Aug. 6, 1759. Thomas Hood's ballad *The Dream of Eugene Aram* (1829) and Bulwer-Lytton's novel *Eugene Aram* (1832) deal with the case.

ARAMAEANS, ar-e-mē′anz, were a Semitic people who lived in ancient Syria and Mesopotamia. Their language spread to the neighboring peoples, and this fact makes it difficult to determine the precise areas inhabited by the true Aramaean stock. It is now generally held that the Aramaeans moved before the 12th century B.C. from northeast Arabia into Syria, Mesopotamia, Assyria, and Babylonia. They established several important city-kingdoms, spread the knowledge of the alphabet, and generally exercised a great influence on the advance of civilization.

ARAMAIC LANGUAGE, ar-ə-mā′ik, a member of the Semitic language family. It was used in many different dialectal forms, chiefly in the northern parts of the Arabian peninsula, from the beginning of the 10th century B.C. to the end of the 5th century A.D. A modern form of Aramaic is still spoken in Syria and among the "Assyrians" living in Azerbaijan.

The Aramaic language in its eastern form is closely related to Syriac and in its western form to Hebrew. It is generally believed to have appeared at the end of the 11th century B.C. as the tongue of the Aramaeans who had settled in Damascus, although some philologists affirm that it was already in use in the 2000's B.C. In all probability, Aramaic was the language of the Laban-Rachel tribal groups which Biblical traditions connect with some of the ancestors of Israel. Hence, Aramaic was already exercising a profound influence upon the Hebrew language in the earliest period of Israel's history. Aramaeans remained in relatively close contact with Israelites during the monarchical period, especially during the reigns of Saul, David, and Ahab, and commercial and cultural exchanges entailed linguistic interaction.

Extent. By the time of the fall of Damascus and Syria (732 B.C.), Aramaic had become the lingua franca of the Fertile Crescent. Some of the Assyrian kings employed Aramaean scribes, and during the siege of Jerusalem by Sennacherib (701 B.C.), Aramaic was used as a diplomatic language by non-Aramaeans. It survived the falls of Nineveh (612 B.C.) and Babylon (539 B.C.) and remained the official language of the Persian empire (538–331 B.C.) Inscriptions in the Aramaic tongue or at least in Aramaic characters have been discovered in a vast area of the ancient world—from Asia Minor, Kurdistan, the Caucasus region, the territory south of the Ural Mountains, and Afghanistan to Egypt, the southwesternmost areas of Asia, the subcontinent of India, and the western border of China.

The Judeans, who were expelled from Jerusalem and Judah by Nebuchadnezzar in 597 B.C., settled chiefly in Egypt and in Mesopotamia, where they and their descendants, the Jews, adopted Aramaic as their native tongue and even came to use a form of the Aramaic script for writing Hebrew, which had by then become a sacred language. Thus, the so-called "square Hebrew alphabet" is actually Aramaic. The Hebrew Bible contains sections that were written originally in Aramaic, and several monuments of popular Jewish literature from the Hellenistic, Maccabean, and Roman periods were also composed in that language. See BIBLE—2. *Language of the Old Testament.*

Many Aramaic documents have been found in Egypt, especially at Elephantine, where a Jewish colony flourished in the 5th and 4th centuries B.C. Beginning with the 4th century B.C., Aramaic was adopted by some Arabs and evolved into Nabataean, which was spoken especially at Petra. There is ample evidence to show that Aramaic was widely used in Palestine in Roman times. Hence, Jesus and his direct followers spoke Aramaic, and words in that language have been preserved in the New Testament in transliteration as well as translation. Although the Gospels and the Acts of the Apostles appear to have been written originally in Greek, the Christian oral tradition concerning Jesus and the early church was begun in Aramaic.

As the Hebrew Bible was no longer understood by the common people of Palestine, translations in Aramaic were made in the synagogues, and their oral preservation led in due course to the written Targumin (Targumic Aramaic). Other dialectal forms of the language are Talmudic (Babylonian) Aramaic, Syriac, and Mandaean, in the East; and Palmyrene, Samaritan, and Talmudic (Palestinian) Aramaic, in the West.

Characteristics. The Aramaic language appears to have been more academic and prosaic than the other Semitic tongues in general and Hebrew in particular, but this characteristic may be due in large part to the type of literature in which it has been preserved. Phonetically, Aramaic is differentiated from the other members of the Semitic family by a predilection for the vocalic sound *a*, a reluctance to use pretonic vowels (which are, however, unchangeable if they appear at all), and various consonantal preferences, such as *d* for *z*, *t* for *sh*, and *n* for *l*. Lexicographically, many Aramaic words have been borrowed from foreign tongues, especially Akkadian and Persian. Morphologically, nominal, pronominal, and verbal inflections or conjugations are similar to those of the Hebrew language. However, there are several morphological differences from Hebrew: verbs in the third person plural active often assume a passive meaning; participles with pronouns tend to form a separate tense; participles and imperatives are commonly employed in the passive; and an emphatic ending replaces the use of the definite article. Syntactically, sentences are often long and repetitious; pleonastic expressions abound; direct objects are connected with verbs by the use of the prefix preposition *l*; the particle *di* is used to introduce relative clauses as well as to bind nouns together in the possessive relation, and also to supply, with the help of pronominal suffixes, the lack of possessive pronouns. These and other peculiarities of syntax betray the style of administrative, legal, and "bureaucratic" literary genres.

See also HEBREW LANGUAGE AND LITERATURE; SEMITIC LANGUAGES; SYRIAC LANGUAGE AND LITERATURE.

SAMUEL TERRIEN
Union Theological Seminary, New York

Bibliography
Bowman, R.A., "Arameans, Aramaic, and the Bible," *Journal of Near Eastern Studies,* 7:65–90 (1948)
Marshall, J.T., *Manual of the Aramaic Language of the Palestinian Talmud,* ed. by J.B. Turner (London 1929)
Rowley, H.H., *The Aramaic of the Old Testament* (New York 1929)
Stevenson, William B., *A Grammar of Palestinian Jewish Aramaic,* 2d ed. (New York 1962)
Torrey, C.C., "The Aramaic of the Gospels, "*Journal of Biblical Literature,* 61:71–85 (1942)

ARAN ISLANDS, ar'ən, in Ireland, three small islands in the Atlantic Ocean about 28 miles southwest of Galway, lying across the entrance to Galway Bay. Their Irish name, *Ara na Naomh,* means "Aran of the Saints." From northwest to southeast they are: Inishmore, or Great Island; Inishman, or Middle Island; and Inisheer, or Eastern Island. The rugged islands have attracted many artists and writers, as well as archaeologists and historians interested in the traces of early Celtic culture found there.

The islands are formed of carboniferous limestone and are lacking in topsoil. The inhabitants grow rye and potatoes in soil that they make from sand, seaweed, and manure. There is enough grazing land for cattle raising, which is the principal source of income. Other occupations are fishing and the burning of kelp for iodine manufacture. Kilronan, on Inishmore, is the largest town, with a population of 231.

There are many architectural relics on the islands, including churches, monasteries, fortresses, and rude huts. Some predate the 5th century, when Christianity was introduced in the islands. On Inishmore are ruins of the church of the islands' patron, St. Enda, and a huge fortress called Dun Aengus, rising above a 300-foot cliff.

John Millington Synge, the Irish dramatist, paid many visits to the islands. He wrote *The Aran Islands* (1907) and a well-known one-act tragedy, *Riders to the Sea,* about Aran fisherfolk. Life on the islands was dramatically portrayed by Robert Flaherty in 1934 in his documentary film *Man of Aran.* Population: (1961) 1,651.

ARANHA, ə-ran'yə, **Oswaldo** (1894–1960), Brazilian statesman. He was born in Alegrete, Rio Grande do Sul, Brazil, on Feb. 15, 1894, and was educated for the law in Rio de Janeiro. He held various public offices in Rio Grande do Sul and played a leading part in the revolution that brought Getúlio Vargas to power in 1930. Aranha became minister of justice in Vargas' first government and minister of finance in 1931.

Later he served as ambassador to the United States (1934–1938) and minister of foreign affairs (1938–1944), and he helped to bring Brazil into World War II on the side of the Allies. He served as Brazil's chief representative to the United Nations (1947–1948), and was finance minister under Vargas again (1953–1954). In the fall of 1947 he became president of the second session of the UN General Assembly. He died in Rio de Janeiro on Jan. 27, 1960.

ARANSAS BAY, ə-ran′səs, is an inlet on the coast of Texas between St. Joseph Island and the mainland. It is connected with the Gulf of Mexico by a channel known as Aransas Pass. The bay, which is about 25 miles (40.2 km) long and 5 miles (8 km) wide, is traversed by the Gulf Intracoastal Waterway. On the bay are the ports of Aransas Pass and Rockport.

Also on Aransas Bay is the Aransas National Wildlife Refuge, a sanctuary for many species of animals and birds, notably the almost extinct whooping crane.

ARANSAS PASS, ə-ran′səs, is a city in Texas, on Aransas Bay, an inlet of the Gulf of Mexico. It lies in San Patricio and Aransas counties, 20 miles (32 km) northeast of Corpus Christi. Commercial shrimpboats operate from Aransas Pass. The city is also a resort. The community adopted a city-manager form of government in 1952. Population: 5,813.

ARANY, o′ron-yə, **János** (1817–1882), Hungarian poet, whose epics, ballads, and lyric poems are among the finest productions of Hungarian nationalist literature of the 19th century. With Sándor Petőfi, Arany is regarded as a founder of modern Hungarian poetry. Writing in a simple, meditative style, with characteristic overtones of sadness, he utilized folklore materials in an original way.

Arany was born in Nagyszalonta (now Salonta), Rumania, on March 1, 1817. He left college at Debrecen to join a company of strolling players. Later he worked as a schoolmaster, village notary, and editor. From 1851 to 1860 he taught at the Nagykörös Gymnasium. He became a director of the Kisfaludy Society, a literary organization, in 1860, and from 1865 to 1879 he served as secretary of the Hungarian Academy. He died in Budapest on Oct. 22, 1882.

Arany came to public attention with his satirical epic *The Lost Constitution* (1845), which won the prize of the Kisfaludy Society. Two years later he published *Toldi,* the first part of a three-part epic based on Magyar traditions. The second and third parts of the trilogy are *Toldi's Evening* (1854) and *The Love of Toldi* (1879). This trilogy and the long narrative *King Buda's Death* (1864) are his best-known poems.

ARAPAHO INDIANS, ə-rap′ə-hō, a group of North American Plains Indians of Algonkian linguistic stock, closely associated with the Cheyenne Indians. According to their tribal tradition, the Arapaho were originally inhabitants of northern Minnesota and at some time migrated southwest to regions in the vicinity of the headwaters of the North Platte and Arkansas rivers in Colorado Territory. Some tribes are known to have ranged to the Yellowstone River and as far south as the Rio Grande.

The traditional sun dance of the Plains Indians was developed in its most elaborate form by the Arapaho and the Cheyenne, and it was their principal ceremony.

The tribes were divided into two main groups: the Northern Arapaho, who were assigned to the Wind River Reservation in Wyoming in 1876; and the Southern Arapaho, who were placed on an Oklahoma reservation by the Treaty of Medicine Lodge in 1867. The Atsine, or Gros Ventre, are considered a branch of the Arapaho.

ARARAT, ar′ə-rat, is the tallest mountain of the elevated eastern plateau of Turkish Anatolia. According to the Bible, it is the site where the ark of Noah came to rest after the Flood (Genesis 8:4). Ararat is the Hebrew form of the Assyrian *Urartu,* the name of a kingdom founded here in the 9th century B.C. The region continued to be so designated by its Semitic neighbors to the south long after it had become Armenia in the late 7th century B.C. In Turkish the mountain is called Ağrı Dağı, which is commonly distorted in speech to Eğri Dağ.

The mountain and its satellite, Little Ararat, to the southeast are extinct volcanoes jutting spectacularly out of the flat plain of the Aras (Araxes) River. About 17,000 feet (5,182 meters) in height, Ararat is taller than any mountain in Europe. Above 14,000 feet (4,265 meters) it is covered by perpetual ice and snow. It is an irregular, domed cone with prominent shoulders and buttresses, and on its northeastern side a deep, precipitous chasm extends from top to bottom. The last settled places on the mountain were destroyed by earthquake and landslide in 1840. The porous, ashy nature of the soil prevents the melting snows from forming rivers, leaving the lower slopes virtually barren of trees. It is connected by an eight-mile-long ridge to Little Ararat, a pointed cone of even greater aridity and barrenness, which attains a height of about 13,000 feet (4,000 meters).

Boundary treaties with Russia (1921) and Iran (1932) have left Ararat wholly within Turkish territory, straddling the eastern provinces of Ağrı and Kars. It was first climbed by Friedrich Parrot in 1829.

JOHN R. WALSH, *University of Edinburgh*
Further Reading: Bryce, James, *Transcaucasia and Ararat* (London 1877); Lynch, H.F.B., *Armenia: Travels and Studies* (London 1904); Navarra, Fernand, *The Forbidden Mountain* (London 1958).

ARAS RIVER, ä-räs′, in Turkey, the USSR, and Iran, rising in Turkish Armenia south of Erzurum. Flowing generally eastward for about 568 miles through dry and desolate country, the Aras forms part of the border between the Armenian and Azerbaidzhan republics of the USSR on the north, and Turkish Armenia and the Iranian province of Azerbaijan on the south. One branch of the river joins the Kura River, and another empties into the Caspian Sea. The Aras is not navigable. The Russian name for the river is *Araks.* Its ancient name is *Araxes.*

ARAUCANIAN INDIANS, ə-rou-kä′nē-ən, peoples of Chile and Argentina who speak dialects of the Araucanian linguistic group. Before the Spanish conquest in the 16th century, they occupied most of central Chile, including Chiloé Island and the Chonos archipelago, and extended into Argentina. The main divisions were the Picunche in the north, the Mapuche in the central zone, and the Huilliche in the south. Estimates of the total number of Araucanian-speaking Indians at the time of the Spanish conquest range from 500,000 to 1,500,000. In the mid-1960's there were about 200,000. The majority of these were Mapuche, living in south central Chile. In Argentina few Araucanians remained of the many who emigrated there after the Spanish came.

At the height of their power, the Araucanians were a loose confederation of farming tribes. The Picunche, smallest of the three groups, were soon conquered by the Spaniards. The other two groups, especially the Mapuche, warred almost constantly with the Spanish for over 300 years. The Mapuche retained their independence until the 1880's, when they were defeated and forced onto many small reservations in central Chile. Since then, much of the distinctive Araucanian culture has been lost through intermarriage, although the language is still widely spoken on the reservations. The Mapuche live by raising field crops, especially grain and potatoes. Many younger Indians have moved to towns.

Social structure on the reservations centers around patrilineal lineage groups. Members of the groups trace their descent, through their fathers, to a common ancestor. The traditional shamanistic religion now shows some influences of Christianity.

ARAUCARIA, ar-ô-kâr′ē-ə, is a genus of evergreen coniferous (cone-bearing) trees belonging to the pine family, Pinaceae. First discovered in the Arauco province of Chile, these trees are native to the temperate parts of South America and to Australia, New Guinea, New Caledonia, Norfolk Island, New Hebrides, and other Pacific areas. They are found in damp forests, coastal areas, and mountains.

Araucarias are tall trees; some may reach 200 feet (60 meters). They are characterized by regular, symmetrically whorled branches and stiff, pointed, flat leaves. Cones—both pollen-bearing and seed-bearing—are borne on short, axillary branches. The pollen-bearing cones produce large quantities of pollen, and the seed-bearing cones are large in size.

Some Species of Araucaria. The bunya-bunya tree (*Araucaria bidwillii*), a species native to Australia, grows to 150 feet (45 meters). It is cultivated in the southern parts of the United States for ornamental landscaping and in South Africa to reforest woodland areas. The seeds can be roasted and eaten. The white, soft, straight-grained, easily worked wood is used in building.

The Chilean pine, or monkey puzzle, tree (*A.*

Norfolk pine (*Araucaria excelsa*)

ANNAN PHOTO FEATURES

araucana), native to Southern Chile, now is found also in the United States and Great Britain. Its pollen-bearing cones produce up to 10 million grains of pollen each.

The Norfolk pine (*A. excelsa*) is an outstanding tree on Norfolk Island. This tree reaches 150 to 200 feet (45 to 60 meters) in height and up to 8 feet (2.5 meters) in diameter. It has symmetric tiers of lateral branches, which are horizontal or drooping. It is cultivated as a pot plant and as an ornamental tree in the U.S.

The hoop pine, or Moreton Bay pine (*A. cunninghamii*), is an important timber tree in Australia. Native to Queensland and the mountains of Dutch New Guinea, it grows to about 200 feet (60 meters) and provides excellent lumber for carpentry and construction.

The Paraná pine, or candelabra tree (*A. angustifolia*) of Brazil is a source of plywood.
WALTER SINGER, *The New York Botanical Garden*

ARAVALLI RANGE, ə-räv′ə-lē, a mountain range in India, situated in central and southern Rajputana, about 350 miles (563 km) in length and varying in width from 10 to 100 miles (16 to 161 km). It is also called the *Aravalli Hills*. The average elevation is 1,000 to 3,000 feet (305 to 915 meters); the highest point is Mount Abu (5,650 feet; 1,722 meters). The range, extending from the Gujarat plain to just north of Khetri, separates the Thar Desert on the west from the more fertile upland regions to the east. The southern portion of the hills is inhabited by the Bhil tribe.

ARAWAK INDIANS, a′rə-wäk, a group of American Indians in northeastern South America. Believed by some to have originated on the eastern slopes of the Andes, these Indians spread up and down the Amazon River and its tributaries; north into the Orinoco Valley; along the coasts of Venezuela, eastern Colombia, and the Guianas; and out into the Antilles. A few even settled on the Florida Keys during Spanish times. With such a broad distribution, there could be little uniformity of culture or racial type, and the Arawak are now distinguished chiefly by the fact that their languages, despite regional differences, belong to a single Arawakan stock.

The first Indians encountered by Columbus when he discovered the New World were Arawakan speakers, of a tribe known as the Lucayo which lived in the Bahamas. The Spaniards subsequently settled among the related Taino Indians of the Greater Antilles. A third group of Arawakan speakers, the Igneri, had previously lived in the Lesser Antilles, but had been conquered by the Carib Indians only shortly before the arrival of the Spaniards. However, it was not until the British explored Trinidad and the Guianas in the latter part of the 16th century that Indians named Arawak were heard of. These true Arawak are considered the best representatives of the Arawakan linguistic stock.

Indians of the Arawak group are still numerous in the Guianas, on the border between Colombia and Venezuela, and in various parts of the Orinoco and Amazon basins. As a distinct group, they have become extinct in the West Indies as the result of harsh treatment by the first Spanish settlers, epidemics of European diseases, and intermarriage with the Spaniards. Some 400 Indians still lived in eastern Cuba in 1900, but the local population later assimilated them.

PHOTO BY CHARLES UHT; COURTESY OF THE MUSEUM OF PRIMITIVE ART

WEST INDIAN ARAWAKS produced this idol (*zemi*) of carved wood with inlaid shell teeth. A rare specimen of Taino art, it dates from between 1000 and 1500 A.D.

When Columbus established the first Spanish settlements in Santo Domingo, he commissioned a friar named Ramón Pané to make a study of the Taino religion. Father Pané's account reveals an unusually high development of belief and ritual, the source of which is not known, although some authorities have attributed it to the Maya civilization in Middle America. The Taino worshiped idols called *zemis*, which they carved in wood, stone, and other materials. Zemis in the form of human and animal figures, collars, and three-pointed stones are still to be found in the Dominican Republic, Puerto Rico, and adjacent areas, as are traces of the ball courts and dance grounds on which the Indians conducted their ceremonies.

The Taino also had a relatively .elaborate system of rank and government. They were divided into four classes: slaves (*naborias*), commoners, nobles (*nitaynos*), and chiefs (*caciques*). The chiefs lived in special houses, were entitled to special food and clothing, and received special treatment from the other classes. Some ruled only their own villages, but the more important chiefs had control over districts or provinces. Each chieftainship was inherited in the female line, along with a set of titles and zemis which gave supernatural recognition and were a principal source of the chief's power.

The taino men wore a breech cloth (*nagua*) of cotton or palm fibers and the women an apron of the same materials, the length of which was a sign of rank. They cut their hair short and painted themselves with figures of their zemis on ceremonial occasions. Columbus reported the use of gold ornaments, particularly a pendant (*guanin*) worn by the chiefs as a sign of rank. None of these survived, however, and it is probable that Columbus exaggerated their use in order to impress the king and queen of Spain. The Taino were peaceful, and had difficulty defending themselves against the Carib and the Spaniards.

A number of Taino words, such as *canoa* (canoe), *hamaca* (hammock), and *tabaco* (tobacco), have become part of the English language. Their crops and form of house are still used in parts of the Antilles, although the irrigation system they established in Haiti has been abandoned. Each family had its own thatched hut, that of the chief being larger, differently shaped, and often accompanied by a special building for his zemis.

Further Reading: Lovén, Sven, *Origins of the Tainan Culture, West Indies* (Göteborg, Sweden, 1935); Steward, Julian H., ed., *Handbook of South American Indians*, Bulletin of the Bureau of American Ethnology No. 143, vols. 3, 4 (Washington, 1948); Steward, Julian H. and Faron, Louis C., *Native Peoples of South America* (New York 1959).

IRVING ROUSE, *Yale University*

ARBENZ GUZMÁN, är'bäns gōōs-män' **Jacobo** (1913–1971), Guatemalan leftist political leader, who was president of the country from 1951 until overthrown in 1954. He was born at Quezaltenango, Guatemala, on Sept. 14, 1913, and graduated first in his class from the national military academy. In 1944 he played a major role in the revolution that established Guatemala's first democratic government. The next year he became minister of defense under President Juan José Arévalo, whom he succeeded as chief executive in 1951.

As president, Arbenz attempted a program of agrarian reforms that provoked a revolt of the propertied classes on June 18, 1954. Assisted by exiles in Honduras and Nicaragua and sustained by other governments in Central America and by the United States, the revolutionists overthrew Arbenz on June 27. He and some 700 of his followers took refuge in Latin American embassies in Guatemala City, and he soon went into exile. A military regime was set up to replace his government, which had included a number of Communists.

The defeat of Arbenz evoked anti-American feeling among many Latin Americans. They believed that the United States government, in assisting the rebels, had meddled improperly in Central American affairs. Arbenz died in Mexico City on Jan. 27, 1971.

ARBITRAGE, är'bə-träzh, a commercial or financial transaction in which a purchaser buys commodities, securities, or bills of exchange in one market for simultaneous or nearly simultaneous resale in another market where the price quotations are higher. Arbitrage tends to equalize prices between two markets.

The arbitrager operates in stock and commodity markets, in precious metal markets, and in the foreign exchange departments of banks. In a stock market, for example, a company planning to split its stock two shares for one may have the old and new stock both listed briefly. If an arbitrager sees the old stock quoted at $103 and the new at $50, he sells the old for $103 a share and buys two new shares for $100.

ARBITRATION, är-bə-trā′shən, is the process of settling a dispute between two parties by submitting it to an impartial third party who renders a decision or makes an award. Any kind of dispute between two parties involving rights, interests, or claims may be submitted by mutual agreement to an arbitrator. A dispute may be submitted regardless of whether a previous agreement or contract exists, or whether a contract provides for arbitration. Most arbitration cases, however, arise from differences in interpretation of agreements or contracts between employer and labor union, buyer and seller, contractor and contractee, or professional practitioner and client, in instances in which the original agreements provide for the arbitration of disputes.

Arbitration clauses may provide for either compulsory or voluntary arbitration of disputes, and for either compulsory or voluntary acceptance of decisions and awards. Where submission to arbitration is voluntary, a refusal of either party to arbitrate usually results in carrying the dispute into court litigation. Obviously the usefulness of arbitration can be destroyed if either party has the right to reject the decision. Therefore most arbitration clauses provide for compulsory acceptance of the arbitrator's decision.

Arbitration is to be distinguished from *mediation* and *conciliation,* which involve the intervention of a third party to attempt a settlement of differences between the disputants through persuasion and compromise. Conciliation originally meant only the intervention of a third party to bring the parties together and keep them negotiating, but not to offer suggestions for solving the dispute. Mediation originally meant the intervention of a third party who actively proposed terms of compromise and means of solution. In recent years the terms "mediation" and "conciliation" have been used interchangeably. Neither a mediator nor a conciliator makes a decision for the disputants; the arbitrator does.

Because of the existence of the Federal Mediation and Conciliation Service and more than 20 state agencies that provide mediators and recommend arbitrators in the United States, arbitration may appear to be sponsored largely by government. However, it is primarily a private and voluntary institution with ancient roots.

The practice of arbitration goes back to the city-states of ancient Greece, and it was widely prevalent in medieval Europe for settling disputes between civil units. Its application to disputes between private parties evolved naturally from its use in governmental relationships. It is promoted and supported, as are many other private arrangements, by the principles evolved in common law and by statutory law. Statutory provisions for industrial arbitration began in the United States with New York and Massachusetts laws of 1886. The Federal Mediation and Conciliation Service evolved from legislative action beginning in 1913, which followed earlier acts applicable only to the transportation industries. In both world wars, boards were created for the compulsory arbitration of labor-management disputes in the United States and other warring nations. The Taft-Hartley (Labor-Management Relations) Act of 1947 established an advisory National Labor-Management panel and provided for the appointment of fact-finding boards for disputes involving the general welfare.

Under state as well as federal labor legisla-tion, fact-finding boards investigate causes of disputes involving broad public interests, clarify and report on the issues, and make recommendations for settling the disputes. But these boards lack power to make decisions or awards that are binding on the parties. The frequent acceptance of their implied or explicit recommendations for settlement is attributable primarily to the fact that neither party wishes to be saddled with the onus of refusing and thus losing public support.

Industrial Relations. More than 90 percent of labor-management contracts in the United States provide for the arbitration of disputes over the interpretation of contract terms. About 70 percent of these contracts provide for an outside agency to select an arbitrator if the parties cannot agree on a selection. The majority of the rest of the contracts provide for a permanent arbitrator.

If an outside agency is used, it is likely to be the American Arbitration Association, a private group; the Federal Mediation and Conciliation Service; or a state agency, such as the New York State Board of Mediation. Where arbitration clauses exist in contracts, the jurisdiction of the arbitrator is often restricted. For example, he may be prohibited from adding to or subtracting from the agreement or from ruling on certain subjects. Company managements typically have felt that matters not specifically dealt with in the contract are reserved to management and not subject to arbitration. In 1960, however, the U.S. Supreme Court ruled that, unless there is a specific exclusion in a written agreement or "the most forceful evidence" indicating that the party intended the arbitration clause not to be applicable, issues arising between parties to a contract are arbitrable. As a result of the court's decision, management, where it has had sufficient bargaining power, has restricted the arbitrator's discretion by inserting specific exclusions in contracts.

Disputes between unions and management arise both in the *determination* of the terms of the contract ("interests") and in the *interpretation* of the terms ("rights") once the contract is in effect.

Disputes over Interests. Disputes involving determination are concerned with interests that include the rights of union and management, the level and structure of wage rates, hours of work, fringe benefits, and general conditions of employment. Stalemates in negotiation of new contracts seldom result in arbitration. However, some employers and unions—for example, in printing and textile industries—have agreed to arbitration.

The parties to contractual agreements are likely to be jealous of their rights to include certain subject matters. Intervention by presidential fact-finding boards under the Labor-Management Relations Act, for example, is generally restricted to disputes arising in major industries affecting the public interest and where industry-wide bargaining is in effect. But even in such situations a board's findings and recommendations do not constitute an arbitration award.

Disputes over Rights. Most genuine cases of arbitration evolve from the failure to settle a dispute over rights of the parties as they interpret those rights in existing contracts. Problems not resolved by earlier steps of the grievance procedure may be submitted to arbitration by the terms of the contract or by mutual agreement. The problems typically include work assignments, job classifications, appropriate wage rates, and disciplining of employees for alleged violations of company rules. Hundreds of thousands of workers' grievances and management complaints of contract violations occur every year in United States commercial and industrial establishments, but most of them are settled at the first or second level of negotiations between the parties. Only a very small portion of the problems, perhaps less than 1 percent, ever reach arbitration.

Permanent arbitrators or boards are now firmly established in many key mass-production industries such as automobiles, steel, farm equipment, rubber, meat packing, and aluminum, as well as in many local industrial associations. The single arbitrator is increasingly receiving preference over the use of the tripartite board (representing labor, management, and public), largely, perhaps, because the neutral public member most often casts the deciding vote. Excessive resort to arbitration may indicate an immature approach to settlement of disputes by direct negotiation; a reduction in its use may indicate a lack of faith in the arbitration process.

Commercial Arbitration. Arbitration is being used increasingly as a means to settle disputes arising in commercial transactions. The most numerous cases concern construction contracts, insurance claims, sales contracts, leases, personal employment agreements, and patent licenses.

The advantages of arbitration over court litigation are lower cost, privacy, less rigid rules of evidence, quick disposition of the case, and access to the specialized experts who serve as arbitrators.

As an alternative to the courts in settling disputes, arbitration saves time and resources for the parties involved. Moreover, the result of the arbitration decision is simply a settlement, leaving the parties at least potentially amicable, whereas the result of a court decision is a victory and defeat likely to leave the parties hostile.

The American Arbitration Association in a typical year arranges hearings for about 6,000 disputes of the commercial type, and reports a steady annual growth in requests. The 16,000 members of arbitration panels of the association serve without fees, but the association itself collects fees on a sliding scale based upon the amount in dispute.

Arbitration Outside the United States—Britain. Britain's practices in arbitration have their roots in 19th century experience. The English Arbitration Act of 1889, substantially unchanged up to the 1960's and comparable to U.S. statutes, came well after the long-established use of commercial arbitration in exchanges and trade associations.

Canada. Arbitration statutes of the Canadian provinces are modeled after the English Arbitration Act. Arbitration of controversies arising in commerce between Canadian and American business concerns is promoted by the existence of a private international agency, the Canadian-American Commercial Arbitration Commission. This organization was established jointly by the American Arbitration Association and the Canadian Chamber of Commerce.

Australia. The nation's system of compulsory industrial arbitration was initiated by establishment of wage boards in the state of Victoria in 1896. The system is complicated by division of powers between federal and state authorities, as in the United States, and by the existence of two types of tribunals. One group of tribunals consists of one or more persons appointed by the government, independently of the disputing parties, to conciliate and arbitrate disputes over rights under contracts. The other tribunals are wage boards consisting of an equal number of representatives of workers and employers, with an independent chairman to settle matters of wages, hours, and working conditions. The wage boards concern themselves with interests as opposed to rights. Apparently from 85 to 90 percent of all private employees in Australia are now working under awards from industrial tribunals.

New Zealand. New Zealand's compulsory arbitration system is similar to Australia's. It dates from 1894. Even salaries of professional workers are now being determined by some form of arbitration.

International. Geneva conventions on arbitration provide ways to handle disputes over contracts made by parties of diverse nationalities.

The Arbitrators. The American Arbitration Association, a voluntary organization supported by membership fees and by fees charged for services rendered, is a principal source of arbitrators and of information on arbitration. The Federal Mediation and Conciliation Service and a number of state agencies also provide the names of arbitrators who may be selected by those having disputes.

Any person competent in a special field may serve as an arbitrator, and may apply to the federal or state services or the private association to be listed as a potential appointee. Even without such formal affiliation a person may be called upon by any party in a dispute.

Although lawyers dominate the panels in commercial fields of arbitration, they do not do so in the field of labor relations. College professors make up the second-largest group of arbitrators. Physicians, dentists, accountants, managers, and other professionals serve as arbitrators in cases where their specialized knowledge is essential.

The best sources of continuous information on arbitration matters are the publications of the American Arbitration Association: the monthly *Arbitration News*, the quarterly *Arbitration Journal*, the quarterly *Digest of Court Decisions*, the quarterly *Lawyers Arbitration Letter*, and frequent monographs and books. In the labor relations field, important sources of information and analysis are the *Monthly Labor Review* and the *Industrial Labor Relations Review*.

NORMAN A. MERCER, *Union College*

Bibliography

American Arbitration Association, *Labor Arbitration: Procedures and Techniques* (New York 1961).

Creswell, W.T., and Grieg, N.P., *Handbook of Procedure and Evidence in Arbitrations,* 2d ed. (London 1946).

Elkouri, Frank, and Elkouri, Edna A., *How Arbitration Works,* rev. ed. (Washington 1960).

Handsaker, Morrison and Marjorie L., *The Submission Agreement in Contract Arbitration* (Philadelphia 1952).

Kellor, Frances, *American Arbitration* (New York 1948).

McKelvey, Jean T., ed. *Challenges to Arbitration* (Washington 1960).

Perlman, Mark, *Judges in Industry* (Melbourne 1954).

Updegraff, Clarence M., and McCoy, Whitley P., *Arbitration of Labor Disputes,* 2d rev. ed. (Washington 1961).

Walker, Kenneth F., *Industrial Relations in Australia* (Cambridge, Mass., 1956).

Witte, E.E., *Historical Survey of Labor Arbitration* (Philadelphia 1952).

ARBITRATION, International, är-bə-trā'-shən. In the Hague Convention for the Pacific Settlement of International Disputes (1899; amended in 1907), international arbitration is defined as "the settlement of disputes between States by judges of their own choice and on the basis of respect for law. Recourse to arbitration implies an engagement to submit in good faith to the award." This definition differentiates international arbitration, on the one hand, from conciliation, inquiry, mediation, and other international procedures of a merely recommendatory character; and, on the other hand, from judicial settlement, which implies decision by a tribunal established independently of the parties to the particular dispute on the basis of law.

Some writers, such as John Bassett Moore (q.v.), have insisted that international arbitration is an essentially judicial process, but the predominant opinion accepts the view, implied by the term as used in private law, set forth by Secretary of State Elihu Root in instructions to the United States delegation to the Second Hague Conference in 1907:

> It has been a very general practice for arbitrators to act, not as judges deciding questions of fact and law, upon the record before them, under a sense of judicial responsibility but as negotiators effecting settlements of the questions brought before them in accordance with the traditions and usages and subject to all the considerations and influences which affect diplomatic agents. The two methods [arbitration and judicial settlement] are radically different, proceed upon different standards of honorable obligation, and frequently lead to widely differing results.

The Hague Conference of 1907 did not unequivocally accept this distinction. It did, however, draw up a convention for a judicial arbitration court composed of permanent judges to function parallel with the Permanent Court of Arbitration (Hague Tribunal), established by the First Hague Conference in 1899. The latter was not a real court but merely a panel of names from which arbitrators could be selected for a particular case by the parties. The judicial arbitration court never came into existence, nor did the international prize court also proposed at the Hague Conference of 1907.

The distinction between international arbitration and judicial settlement was recognized more definitely in the Covenant of the League of Nations. The Permanent Court of International Justice (World Court), established under authority of the League in 1920, functioned side by side with the International Bureau of the Permanent Court of Arbitration in the Peace Palace at The Hague.

The Geneva General Act for the Pacific Settlement of International Disputes, negotiated under the auspices of the League in 1928, also recognized this distinction. In successive chapters, procedures of conciliation, judicial settlement, and arbitration were set forth. All disputes between parties to the convention, which diplomacy failed to settle, were to be submitted to the procedure of conciliation. If the dispute concerned "the respective rights" of the parties, however, it was to be submitted to the World Court unless the parties agreed to submit it to a special arbitral tribunal. The latter procedure was obligatory for other disputes if the conciliatory procedure failed to result in an agreement. Under this treaty, therefore, arbitration was the ultimate resort if diplomacy and conciliation failed and if judicial settlement was not acceptable to the parties. Since arbitral awards are in

principle binding, definitive settlement of all disputes was in principle provided for. The General Assembly of the United Nations in 1949 revised the General Act of Geneva to conform to the new conditions created by the succession of the United Nations to the League of Nations, and of the International Court of Justice to the Permanent Court of International Justice.

This history makes it clear that international arbitration has come to be regarded as a procedure distinct from international judicial settlement. Because arbitrators are appointed by the parties with reference to the particular dispute and are less bound by law than are judges, arbitration is a more flexible procedure than judicial settlement, permitting more attention to be given to political exigencies.

History. International arbitration was utilized among the city-states of ancient Greece and among the feudal principalities of the Middle Ages. In the latter period and in early modern times, the pope was often accepted as arbitrator, notably in the controversy between Spain and Portugal concerning the division of their domains in the Americas and Asia. The Bull of Demarcation (1493) was generally favorable to Spain. As modified by the Treaty of Tordesillas (1494) and other treaties, the Americas, with the exception of Brazil, went to Spain, and southeast Asia, with the exception of the Philippines, went to Portugal.

During the following centuries, arbitration was seldom resorted to, but it was revived by Jay's Treaty, concluded between the United States and Britain in 1794. Under this treaty three arbitral commissions were established. The first consisted of three members, one each appointed by Britain and the United States and the third selected by these two. It met at Halifax and decided finally which river was designated as the St. Croix in a provision of the Peace of Paris (1783) defining the boundary between Maine and New Brunswick. The second commission consisted of five members, two each appointed by Britain and the United States and a fifth by these four. It sat at Philadelphia to determine the amount of confiscated debts due to British merchants, but difficulties arose and the claims were finally settled for $2,664,000 under a treaty negotiated by Rufus King in 1802. The third commission, which also had five members, sat at London from 1796 to 1799, when its proceedings were suspended. It renewed its sittings in 1802, and in 1804 gave final awards of $11,656,000 against Britain for illegal prize seizures, and of $143,428 against the United States for British losses from French vessels fitted out in violation of American neutrality. The latter award, though small in amount, established the principle of the responsibility of a neutral for belligerent losses resulting from violations of its neutrality and thus formed a precedent for the *Alabama* claims.

A list prepared by W. Evans Darby in 1904 indicates that 6 international controversies were settled by arbitration in the 18th century, 471 in the 19th, and 63 during the first three years of the 20th century. After this list was compiled, several dozen international controversies were settled by arbitration, but the accelerating development of arbitration up to World War I did not continue, due to the expanding use of judicial settlement by the World Court and of political settlement by the League of Nations and the

United Nations. By the middle of the 20th century the Central American Court of Justice (1907–1917; reestablished in 1923), the Permanent Court of International Justice, and the International Court of Justice had dealt with over 80 cases by judgment or advisory opinion, while the League of Nations and the United Nations had dealt with an even larger number of political controversies.

Employment by the United States. The United States has been active in the use of arbitration. Prior to World War I it submitted 83 controversies with 25 nations to this process, a number exceeded only by those submitted by Britain. Of these controversies, 17 were with Britain and 44 with Latin American countries. The remainder included controversies with France, Germany, Russia, Spain, Portugal, and the Kingdom of the Two Sicilies in Europe, and with China and Siam (Thailand) in Asia. These controversies covered a wide range of subjects. Some were of national importance, such as territory, boundaries, fisheries, and neutral rights and obligations; others consisted of the pecuniary claims of citizens arising from war, insurrection, mob violence, breach of contract, confiscation, maritime seizure, and other acts.

Among the most important were the four arbitrations with Britain provided for by the Treaty of Washington of 1871. The question of the maritime boundary in Juan de Fuca Strait (called Fuca Straits in the treaty) was submitted to Emperor William I of Germany and settled by him according to the United States contention in 1872. Pecuniary claims of citizens of each country against the other during the Civil War period were submitted to a tribunal of three, which awarded $1,929,819 against the United States in 1873, mostly for prize seizures. The British claim for compensation on account of the fishery concessions given by the treaty was placed before a commission of three, which awarded $5,500,000 in 1877. Most important, however, was the American claim for losses resulting from depredations by the *Alabama* and other Confederate war vessels fitted out in British territory during the Civil War. The British government had several times stated that the "national honor" was involved and that consequently the issue was not susceptible of arbitration; nevertheless, in the Treaty of Washington it expressed regret for the escape of the *Alabama* and agreed to submit the issues to a tribunal of five. The tribunal sat at Geneva and in 1872 made an award in favor of the United States of $15,500,000. (See also ALABAMA CLAIMS.)

Another important arbitration with Britain was the Bering Sea Controversy (q.v.), concerning the right of the United States to protect seals from indiscriminate dynamiting on the high seas by Canadian fishermen. In the arbitration of 1893 the United States rested its case mainly on the moral and economic iniquity of the practice, but the tribunal decided that international law recognized three miles as the limit of maritime jurisdiction. Consequently it recommended a treaty between the parties, a recommendation eventually carried out in the agreement of 1911 among the United States, Britain, Japan, and Russia.

The United States and Britain arbitrated the Alaska boundary dispute in 1903, the North Atlantic (Newfoundland) fisheries dispute in 1909–1910, and other disagreements. The United States has also arbitrated controversies with Mexico, including boundary controversies resulting from the changing course of the Rio Grande, and many private claims. Two commissions were established under an agreement made in 1923 to settle general and special claims arising from the Mexican revolution that began in 1910.

United States claims against Germany before World War I were submitted to arbitration under the treaty of peace of 1921, in which Germany recognized its responsibility for American losses resulting from submarine activity. Because of this treaty provision the responsibility of Germany under general principles of international law was not before the tribunal. The awards, which included losses resulting from the destruction of the *Lusitania,* approximated $250,000,000—more than all previous United States arbitration awards put together.

Finality of Awards. Arbitrations have dealt with very large sums of money, with principles of international law, and with territory and jurisdiction of great national importance. Yet the awards have almost always been carried out. It is an accepted principle of international law that arbitral awards are final and binding unless the arbitrators have gone beyond their powers or have committed a manifest error, unless there is discovery of fraud, or unless the agreement of submission expressly provides for revision. According to Article 83 of the Hague Convention of 1907, such a reservation should permit revision only after the discovery of new facts of decisive importance.

In three cases—the northeastern boundary dispute submitted to King William I of the Netherlands in 1827 (the award was made in 1831), the Paraguay pecuniary claims submission of 1859–1860, and the Chamizal Tract arbitration with Mexico of 1911—the United States, on losing, rejected the award on the ground that the arbitrator had gone beyond his powers. The northeastern boundary dispute, involving a large area claimed by both Maine and New Brunswick, was settled by compromise in the Webster-Ashburton Treaty of 1842. The Chamizal case, involving territory in El Paso, Texas, claimed by Mexico, was settled by treaty in 1963. In the Orinoco Steamship Company claim against Venezuela, the United States succeeded in getting the award of 1904 nullified by a new arbitration before the Hague Tribunal in 1910 on grounds of "excessive exercise of jurisdiction and essential error in judgment."

The award of the Hague Tribunal in 1922 of $12,239,852 to Norway for shipbuilding contracts requisitioned by the United States during World War I was severely criticized by the agent of the United States government and by Secretary of State Charles Evans Hughes on the ground that the method of arriving at this figure was not sufficiently explained by the opinion, but the award was paid nevertheless. A controversy also arose over the preliminary decision in 1926 of the United States-Mexican Special Claims Commission on the Santa Isabel case, holding Mexico not responsible for acts of insurgents whom she could not control. The United States commissioner strongly objected to the award. In 1934 a lump sum settlement covering all claims arising from the Mexican Revolution was arranged, and in 1937 the Special Mexican Claims Commission, established to distribute this sum, reversed the opinion in the Santa Isabel judgment. In the

United States-German Mixed Claims Commission after World War I, the umpire reopened the Black Tom sabotage case in 1936 on discovery of fraud in the original submission.

In three cases—involving Venezuela in 1868, Mexico in 1876, and Haiti in 1884—the United States voluntarily set aside awards in its favor on grounds of manifest error or fraud. In the Mexican case, however, the money already paid into the United States Treasury for the Benjamin Weil and La Abra Silver Mining Company claims was not returned to Mexico for more than 30 years. In several other cases the arbitral submission did not settle the dispute, either because the tribunal failed to make an award or because the award, while accepted as settling the legal rights of the parties, failed to satisfy their economic or political interests, so that further negotiations were necessary.

Types of Tribunals. Arbitral tribunals have been of two types: the sovereign of a disinterested state, usually named in the *compromis*, or special agreement; or a commission composed of persons with juristic qualifications. Tribunals of the latter type are more likely to justify their decisions in terms of international law. As there has generally been an odd number of arbitrators and as a majority is ordinarily competent to act, a decision has usually been reached. In some commissions, however, there has been an even number of arbitrators—half appointed by each side. The Alaska boundary question was submitted to such a commission, and President Theodore Roosevelt stated that since he would appoint Americans who would sustain the American contention, the United States could not lose and might win. He appointed Senator Henry Cabot Lodge, Secretary of War Elihu Root, and former Senator George Turner. Britain appointed two Canadians—Sir Louis A. Jetté and Allen B. Aylesworth—and Baron Alverstone, lord chief justice of England. As Lord Alverstone voted with the Americans, an award was made.

Since it is not certain in an even-numbered commission that an award will be made, these should be called mixed commissions rather than arbitral tribunals. Somewhat different from either are technical commissions, which have a limited authority to apply treaty provisions or arbitral awards. The most common function of such bodies is to mark a boundary on the spot. The United States has often utilized such commissions.

Arbitration tribunals have sometimes been asked to recommend on certain subjects in addition to giving awards on others. This was true of the Bering Sea and North Atlantic fisheries arbitrations. In performing this function, the tribunal acts as a conciliation commission.

Compulsory Arbitration. While frequently making use of arbitration, the United States has not always agreed to arbitrate disputes when requested to do so by the other party. In 1898 it rejected the Spanish proposal to submit to arbitration the issue of responsibility for the blowing up of the battleship *Maine,* and in 1912 it rejected the British proposal to submit the issues concerning discriminatory tolls to be levied in the Panama Canal. The first of these issues contributed to war; the second was settled in 1914, when Congress, at the suggestion of President Woodrow Wilson, abolished the special exemption of United States coastwise vessels from tolls.

The increasing use of arbitration during the 19th century led to a movement for compulsory or obligatory arbitration, established by conventions under which the parties agree to submit future disputes to arbitration. A number of such treaty commitments were concluded among the Latin American countries in the 19th century, and a provision urging, but not requiring, arbitration of future disputes was included in the Treaty of Guadalupe Hidalgo ending the war between the United States and Mexico in 1848. Compromissary clauses were sometimes inserted in a treaty requiring arbitration of disputes concerning the interpretation of that particular treaty. This was true of the treaty of 1796 between the United States and Tripoli, of the Anglo-Portuguese Treaty on African claims of 1891, and of several general treaties such as those establishing the Universal Postal Union (1874) and the Radiotelegraphic Union (1912).

The success of the arbitration of the *Alabama* claims stimulated interest in a permanent arbitration arrangement between the United States and Britain, and resolutions were passed in Congress and the House of Commons. Negotiations begun in 1895 resulted in the draft Olney–Pauncefote Treaty of 1897. It provided for the submission of all pecuniary claims to a tribunal of three with the requirement of unanimity or review by a tribunal of five if more than £ 100,-000 was involved. Territorial and national claims were to be submitted to a tribunal of six (three from the United States Supreme Court or circuit courts and three from the British Supreme Court of Judicature or the Judicial Committee of the Privy Council) which could not give an award if more than one judge dissented and either side protested. The treaty was endorsed by Presidents Grover Cleveland and William McKinley. Nevertheless, the Senate, after amending the draft to exclude all questions of importance and to require Senate concurrence for each submission, rejected the treaty by three votes.

The Hague Convention of 1899, while establishing the Permanent Court of Arbitration and procedures for arbitration, did not impose an obligation to submit disputes. The parties reserved the right to conclude special treaties to extend obligatory arbitration, however, and in 1903 France and Britain made such a treaty, providing:

> Article 1. Differences which may arise of a legal nature, or relating to the interpretation of treaties existing between the two contracting Parties, and which it may not have been possible to settle by diplomacy, shall be referred to the Permanent Court of Arbitration established at The Hague by the Convention of the 29th July 1899, provided, nevertheless, that they do not affect the vital interests, the independence, or the honor of the two contracting states and do not concern the interests of third parties.
>
> Article 2. In each individual case the High Contracting Parties, before appealing to the Permanent Court of Arbitration, shall conclude a special agreement defining clearly the matter in dispute, the scope of the powers of the arbitrators, and the periods to be fixed for the formation of the Arbitral Tribunal and the several stages of the procedure.

With this as a model, Secretary of State John Hay negotiated a series of treaties, but the Senate insisted on a reservation that each individual submission should be in the form of a treaty requiring Senate approval. President Roosevelt thought treaties with this amendment worthless and did not submit them to the other powers. After Hay's death in 1905, however, his successor, Elihu Root, renegotiated the treaties with the Senate amendment, and they became for many years the standard form of United States arbitration treaties. Because of the broad scope of the exceptions, however, they did not include a genuine obligation to arbitrate. John Bassett Moore stated that they made arbitration even more difficult for the United States, because it had been customary for the president to submit United States claims against other countries to arbitration by executive agreement and these treaties might require Senate concurrence for even such arbitrations.

In 1911, President William Howard Taft and Secretary of State Philander C. Knox, encouraged by a congressional resolution of June 25, 1910, set out to make arbitration treaties "which mean something." Draft treaties with Britain and France were negotiated to provide for submission of all justiciable disputes to the Hague Tribunal. They further provided for a joint high commission of six—three appointed by each party—to which all disputes which the parties could not agree to arbitrate should be submitted for investigation. If this body decided, with no more than one dissent, that the dispute was justiciable, arbitration was required. The Senate, however, so amended these treaties that they were never ratified. "The real reason for defeating them," wrote President Taft, "was an unwillingness to assent to the principle of arbitration without knowing something in advance, of whether we were going to win or lose. That spirit is not one that will promote the cause of arbitration."

Neither the League of Nations Convenant nor the United Nations Charter requires submission of disputes to arbitration, although the former (Art. 13) recognized as generally suitable for arbitration or judicial settlement disputes as to the interpretation of a treaty, as to any question of international law, as to the existence of any fact which, if established, would constitute a breach of any international obligation, or as to the extent and nature of the reparation to be made for any such breach. The optional clause (Art. 36, par. 2) of the Statute of the International Court of Justice requires accepting states to submit these classes of disputes to the court. The United States accepted this clause in 1946, but with important reservations, including one which gives the United States power to refuse submission of a dispute concerning a matter which it regards as within its domestic jurisdiction.

The Root treaties of 1908 were subject to renewal at five-year intervals, and in 1928, after conclusion of the Briand-Kellogg Pact (Pact of Paris), when these treaties came up for renewal, the United States introduced a new formula. The treaty with France, for example, provided:

Article 2. All differences relating to international matters in which the High Contracting Parties are concerned by virtue of a claim of right made by one against the other under treaty or otherwise, which it has not been possible to adjust by diplomacy, and which have not been adjusted as a result of reference to the above-mentioned Permanent Internationl Commission, and which are justiciable in their nature by reason of being susceptible of decision by the application of the principles of law or equity, shall be submitted to the Permanent Court of Arbitration . . . or to some other competent tribunal. . . .

Article 3. The provisions of this treaty shall not be invoked in respect of any dispute the subject matter of which (a) is within the domestic jurisdiction of either of the High Contracting Parties, (b) involves the interests of third Parties, (c) depends upon or involves the maintenance of the traditional attitude of the United States concerning American questions, commonly described as the Monroe Doctrine, (d) depends upon or involves the observance of the obligations of France in accordance with the Covenant of the League of Nations.

The treaty also provided that each particular dispute should be submitted by a treaty approved with advice and consent of the Senate. It is clear that the broad character of the exceptions makes it difficult to describe this treaty as one of obligatory arbitration.

The United States has concluded a few obligatory arbitration treaties for limited classes of claims. Among them are the Brussels General Act for the Repression of the African Slave Trade of 1890, which requires arbitration of seizure of slave-trading vessels in certain circumstances; and the treaty of 1909 with Britain in behalf of Canada, setting up the International Joint Commission with compulsory jurisdiction over questions of the use, obstruction, or diversion of boundary waters as defined by the treaty. Probably the most far-reaching arbitration obligation undertaken by the United States is in the Pan American Treaty of Arbitration of Pecuniary Claims of 1902, renewed in 1906 and modified in 1910, which provides:

The High Contracting Parties agree to submit to arbitration all claims for pecuniary loss or damage which may be presented by their respective citizens and which cannot be amicably adjusted through diplomatic channels, when said claims are of sufficient importance to warrant the expense of arbitration. The decision shall be rendered in accordance with the principles of international law.

The General Treaty of Inter-American Arbitration of 1929, to which the United States is also a party, may add something to this in requiring submission to arbitration of "all differences of an international character which have arisen or may arise between them by virtue of a claim of right." There are, however, important exceptions, which resemble those in the French treaty of 1928, although they are confined to matters within the domestic jurisdiction of one of the parties and to those which affect the interests or refer to the action of a state not a party to the treaty. It was thought that the latter phrase would in the case of a treaty among American states cover matters under the Monroe Doctrine. These exceptions give a broad opportunity for the United States to refuse to arbitrate a particular dispute.

While other countries have gone further than the United States in committing themselves to compulsory arbitration, no other country has been more vigorous in its formal support of arbitration. Thus, in his first inaugural address in 1897, President William McKinley recommended ratification of the pending general arbitration treaty with Britain with the words: "The adjustment of difficulties by judicial methods rather than force of arms has been recognized as the leading feature of our foreign policy throughout our entire national history." In 1916, Congress authorized United States participation in a conference on arbitration and disarmament with the declaration that it is "the policy of the United States to adjust and settle its international disputes through mediation and arbitration, to the end that war may be honorably avoided." In spite of its concurrence in this resolution, the Senate has been more reluctant to accept arbitral commitments than the president has been. This reluctance has undoubtedly hampered progress toward a general system of compulsory arbitration. Extensive acceptance of the optional clause of the International Court of Justice statute, however, has developed widespread obligations for compulsory judicial settlement.

It has often been contended in the United States that arbitration and judicial settlement between nations need no sanction other than good faith. The record of arbitrations is not conclusive, since submissions have generally been voluntary and there have been cases of nonfulfillment, usually on adequate legal grounds. If arbitration or judicial settlement is to be compulsory, good faith cannot be relied upon.

Article 94 of the United Nations Charter provides:

> If any party to a case fails to perform the obligations incumbent upon it under a judgment rendered by the Court, the other party may have recourse to the Security Council, which may, if it deems necessary, make recommendations or decide upon measures to be taken to give effect to the judgment.

No similar provision applies to arbitral awards. The Security Council could undoubtedly take measures to enforce an award if it felt that the situation threatened international peace and security, but the difficulties in its procedure ·make this sanction problematical.

The expectation, which was common in the period between the American Civil War and World War I, that international arbitration could eliminate war has not been justified by events. International arbitration is now recognized as only one among many procedures for pacific adjustment of international controversies. Article 33 of the United Nations Charter provides:

> The parties to any dispute, the continuance of which is likely to endanger the maintenance of international peace and security, shall, first of all, seek a solution by negotiation, enquiry, mediation, conciliation, arbitration, judicial settlement, resort to regional agencies or arrangements, or other peaceful means of their own choice.

If voluntary methods fail, the system of the United Nations depends primarily on recommendations by the Security Council or the General Assembly, utilizing judicial settlement through the International Court of Justice only if the parties have agreed to submit by special or general treaty. Article 36 (3) of the United Nations charter provides that in making recommendations the Security Council "take into consideration that legal disputes should as a general rule be referred by the parties to the International Court of Justice in accordance with the provisions of the Statute of the Court." The court, however, held in the Corfu Channel case (1949) that this provision did not authorize the Security Council to require states to submit to the court.

There has tended to be a differentiation between judicial and political processes. Arbitration, which has elements of both, has been less often employed than it was before World War I. Nevertheless, in some controversies, because of its very flexibility, arbitration may still prove useful. The reactivation in 1949 of the General Act of Geneva of 1928, which makes arbitration the ultimate resort, may contribute to a recognition of the importance of this process.

The International Law Commission began consideration of arbitral procedure in 1949. A code was finally completed by the commission and submitted in 1958 to the member states. Its procedures assure that the obligations undertaken in a general arbitration treaty cannot be frustrated because of inability of disputing states to agree on the composition of the tribunal or the precise issues to be submitted.

Several times the International Court of Justice has required states bound by an arbitral award to carry it out (*Honduras* v. *Nicaragua,* 1958), or, if bound by an obligatory arbitration treaty, to carry out their obligations (Ambatielos case, *Greece* v. *United Kingdom,* 1953).

While international arbitration between states differs from international commercial arbitration, the two procedures often have similar aims. After Iran had nationalized the Anglo-Iranian Oil Company in 1951, Britain claimed that it could invoke the arbitral provision in the concession agreement between Iran and the company. The International Court of Justice, however, held that this agreement was not a treaty and did not impose an obligation on Iran to arbitrate. Such controversies induced the United Nations to convoke a conference in 1958 on international commercial arbitration. Resolutions were passed urging the wider use of such arbitration and suggesting measures for assuring their effectiveness. A convention was signed by 25 states providing for enforcement of such awards.

QUINCY WRIGHT, *University of Virginia*

Bibliography

Darby, William E., *International Arbitration; International Tribunals,* 4th ed. (London 1904).
Fenwick, Charles G., *International Law,* 3d ed., rev. and enl. (New York 1948).
Habicht, Max, *Post-War Treaties for the Pacific Settlement of International Disputes* (Cambridge, Mass., 1931).
Higgins, Alexander P., *The Hague Peace Conferences* (Cambridge, England, 1909).
Hudson, Manley O., *By Pacific Means* (New Haven, Conn., 1935).
Moore, John B., *History and Digest of the International Arbitrations to Which the United States Has Been a Party,* 6 vols. (Washington 1898).
Schachter, Oscar, "The Enforcement of International Judicial and Arbitral Decisions," *American Journal of International Law,* vol. 54, no. 1, pp. 1–24 (Washington 1960).
Simpson, John L., and Fox, Hazel, *International Arbitration* (New York 1959).
Stone, Julius, *Legal Controls of International Conflict* (New York 1954).
World Peace Foundation, *Arbitration and the United States* (Boston 1926).

ARBOR DAY, är'bər, is an annual tree planting day observed in all states of the United States and in the District of Columbia, Guam, and Puerto Rico. Its purpose is to assist in foresting or reforesting scantily wooded areas or to beautify towns. It is generally held in cooperation with schools to impress children with the importance of conservation. In most Northern states, Arbor Day is proclaimed in April or May, or sometimes in March. Because of climatic differences, the day is observed in some Southern states in the winter months, and in November in Puerto Rico.

The Arbor Day movement began in the United States in the 1800's. A number of public-spirited persons, alarmed by the rapid deforestation of many sections of the United States, urged that trees be planted systematically. The publication in 1864 of George P. Marsh's *Man and Nature, or Physical Geography as Modified by Human Action* aroused widespread interest in the seriousness of the problem. Birdsey G. Northrop, secretary of the Connecticut Board of Education, suggested that states might profitably plant trees every year at the proper time, or supervise their planting. The first to propose a regular Arbor Day for the purpose was Julius

"ARBOR DAY," by Grant Wood (1932), depicts the planting of a tree at a rural school in northern Iowa.

S. Morton of Nebraska, who in 1872 succeeded in inducing his state to set apart a day, April 10 (in 1885, when the legislature made Arbor Day a legal holiday, it chose Morton's birthday, April 22). The first states to copy Nebraska's example were Kansas and Tennessee in 1875, Michigan and Minnesota in 1876, Ohio in 1882, and West Virginia in 1883. Within the next five years, 26 more states and territories adopted the observance.

ARBORETUM, är-bə-rēt′əm, a place set aside for the cultivation of trees and shrubs for scientific and educational purposes. An arboretum is a living collection of woody plants and usually contains many species not native to its own area. In line with its educational purposes, an arboretum usually has its collections arranged according to some predetermined order, as, for instance, their systematic relationships, their commercial uses, or their ecological associations.

Important United States arboretums include the Arnold Arboretum of Harvard University, Boston, Mass.; the National Arboretum, Washington, D.C.; the Missouri Botanical Garden, St. Louis, Mo.; and the Los Angeles State and County Arboretum, Arcadia, Calif. Especially noted

among European arboretums are the Royal Botanic Gardens, Kew, England; the Royal Botanic Garden, Edinburgh, Scotland; and the Jardin des Plantes, Paris. See also BOTANIC GARDENS.

RICHARD M. STRAW, *Los Angeles State College of Applied Arts and Sciences*

ARBORICULTURE, är′bə-rə-kul-chər, is the scientific cultivation and management of trees. It includes *silviculture,* the growing of forest timber trees; *pomology,* the culture of fruit trees; the cultivation of ornamental woody plants; and the study and control of tree pests and diseases. The methods of an arboriculturist vary with the use to which he intends his trees to be put. For ornamental purposes trees usually are well spaced and pruned in order to obtain symmetrical forms; in timber culture they are closely spaced to conserve space and to obtain a tall, erect, nearly branchless growth. Fruit trees are kept well spaced and are frequently pruned to a small stature to make harvesting easier; branching is encouraged to increase the yield.

ARBORVITAE, är-bər-vī′tē, is the common name of several aromatic, resinous, evergreen trees found in North America and eastern Asia. The trees are identified by their scaly bark and their pyramidal shape.

The arborvitae are members of the pine family, Pinaceae, and belong to the genus *Thuja.* There are six species, five of which are cultivated. *Thuja occidentalis* is the species native to northeastern North America. A slow grower, it is a conical tree that reaches a height of over 60 feet (18 meters). It has scalelike, overlapping leaves that lie flat against the twigs, and thin scaly bark that falls off in ragged strips on the older trunks. The cones are narrow, egg-shaped, and four to six inches (10 to 15 cm) long, with thin leathery scales. A second American species, *T. plicata,* is native to the Pacific Northwest. It is a large tree that reaches a height of 200 feet (10 meters). It has a stout trunk and short, horizontally spreading branches. Its soft, coarse-grained, but durable wood is used in construction and cabinetmaking and, formerly, by the Indians for canoes and totem poles.

The Chinese species, *T. orientalis,* includes many garden varieties. It is widely cultivated as an ornamental tree in the United States. This species has a pyramid or bushy shape. Extracts of the young twigs have been used for medicinal

ARBORVITAE, which may range from 60 to 200 feet tall, is found in North America and eastern Asia. Commonly grown as an ornamental, it has thin, scaly bark and scalelike leaves.

purposes. Two other cultivated species are *T. standishii,* a tree that grows to a height of 50 feet (15 meters) and is found in Japan, and *T. kordiensis,* which grows to a height of 26 feet (7.8 meters) and is found in Korea.

RICHARD M. STRAW, *Los Angeles State College of Applied Arts and Sciences*

ARBUTHNOT, är-buth′nət, **John** (1667–1735), Scottish physician and satirical pamphleteer, who published works on mathematics, numismatics, and medicine. He established John Bull as the popular symbol of Britain, although he did not invent the character.

Arbuthnot was born at Arbuthnot, Kincardine County, Scotland, on April 29, 1667. He taught mathematics for a time in London before entering University College, Oxford, in 1692. In 1696 he received his M.D. degree from the University of St. Andrews in Scotland. He was elected a fellow of the Royal Society in 1704 and a fellow of the Royal College of Physicians in 1710. He was physician to Queen Anne from 1705 until her death in 1714. He held no public appointment under George I, but after the accession of George II in 1727 he was appointed physician to Queen Caroline. He died in London on Feb. 27, 1735.

Arbuthnot published works on a great many subjects and even wrote a poem, *Know Thyself* (1734), but he is probably most famous for a series of five pamphlets issued in 1712 and collected under the title *The History of John Bull.* The pamphlets were in support of the efforts of the recently installed Tory ministry to bring to an end the long and costly War of the Spanish Succession. Originally titled *Law Is a Bottomless Pit,* the pamphlets satirized the war under the guise of a suit brought by John Bull (England) and Nicholas Frog (Holland) against Lewis Baboon (Louis XIV of France) for the estate of the late Lord Strutt (Spain). John Bull was depicted as bluff and hearty, but gullible, cheated by his associates, and worn out by the stubborn trickiness of his adversary. John Bull as the typical Englishman immediately took a place in popular speech which he has never lost.

About 1713, Arbuthnot formed, with Jonathan Swift, Alexander Pope, John Gay, and Thomas Parnell, the nonpolitical Scriblerus Club. The object of the club, said Pope, was "to have ridiculed all the false tastes in learning, under the character of a man of capacity enough, that had dipped into every art and science, but injudiciously in each." The resulting satiric essays were published by Pope in 1741 as *Memoirs of the Extraordinary Life, Works, and Discoveries of Martinus Scriblerus;* almost the whole work, except for Pope's own famous essay on *The Art of Sinking in Poetry,* was of Arbuthnot's writing.

Genial, erudite, and witty, Arbuthnot, as Lord Chesterfield said, placed his fund of wit at the disposal of his friends, without any thought of his own reputation. He had, indeed, a genius for friendship which endeared him alike to the arrogant Swift and the waspish Pope. The latter addressed to Arbuthnot the wittiest of all his poetic epistles; Swift, in his satiric lines on his own death, named Arbuthnot, after Pope and Gay, as the third and last of the friends who would sincerely grieve.

DeLANCEY FERGUSON, *Brooklyn College*

Bibliography
Biographies of Arbuthnot and texts of his works are in *The Life and Works of John Arbuthnot,* ed. by George A. Aitken (Oxford 1892), and Lester M. Beattie's *John Arbuthnot, Mathematician and Satirist* (Cambridge, Mass., 1935).
Allen, Robert J., *The Clubs of Augustan London* (Cambridge, Mass., 1933).
Teerink, Herman, *The History of John Bull* (Amsterdam 1925).

ARBUTUS, är-bū′təs, is a genus of trees and shrubs in the heath family (Ericaceae), comprising about 20 species native to southern Asia, the Mediterranean region, and western North and South America as far south as Chile. The species are characterized by smooth red branches, thin, scaly bark that continually peels off, and lustrous, evergreen, long-petioled leaves. The clustered flowers are small, ovate, and white to red in color; the fruits are globular, many-seeded, red berries. Especially common in cultivation in warm-temperate regions is the strawberry tree, *A. unedo,* a small southern European species with conspicuous fruits. Native in western North America is the madroña or madrone, *A. menziesii,* a handsome forest tree reaching over 100 feet (30 meters) in height, whose exfoliating bark leaves a highly polished trunk bright with shades of red, brown, and green. The Arizona madroña, *A. arizonica,* is a smaller tree with pale green leaves, red branches, and a pale gray or white trunk. Trailing arbutus belongs to the genus *Epigaea* (see TRAILING ARBUTUS).

RICHARD M. STRAW, *Los Angeles State College of Applied Arts and Sciences*

ARC, Joan of. See JOAN OF ARC.

ARBUTUS, native to western North America, exceeds 100 feet in height. A common type is the madroña. Its leaves are dark, oval, and leathery Orange berries appear in the fall.

ARC, ärk, in mathematics, a segment of a curve. The word most often is used in reference to the arc of a circle, where it is the segment of the circumference cut off by two radii or by a secant line. In angular measurement, the magnitude of an arc is expressed in degrees, minutes, and seconds of arc. In these units, the magnitude of the arc is identical to the magnitude of the central angle subtended by the arc.

When the sides of the central angle cut off a length of arc equal to the length of the radius, the central angle has a magnitude of one radian, which is another unit of measurement of an angle. When the central angle is known in radians, the arc length can be computed by multiplying the radian value by the length of the radius. Such computations are simplified if radians are used rather than degrees. Degrees can be converted to radians by multiplying the number of degrees by $\pi/180°$. Radius and arc length are expressed in linear measure—for example, inches.

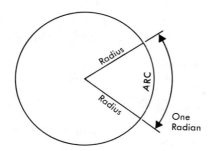

AN ARC is part of a curve, usually a circle. If the arc is equal in length to the radius of the circle, it is said to be 1 radian.

ARC WELDING. See WELDING.

ARCACHON, ár-ká-shôn′, is a town in France, in the department of the Gironde, on the Bassin d'Arcachon, 32 miles (51 km) southwest of Bordeaux. It is a major deep-sea fishing port and a center for the cultivation of oysters. It is also a popular resort, attracting summer visitors along the shore and winter residents to a colony of villas situated inland among pine groves. Population: (1962) 14,738.

ARCADE, är-kād′, in architecture, a series of arches supported by piers or columns, either standing free or attached to a wall. Arcades may be purely decorative, or they may form an intrinsic part of the structure of a building. They were first commonly used by the Romans, notably in the Colosseum. An outstanding example of the use of ornamental arcades in Romanesque structures is the baptistery and bell tower of Pisa Cathedral in Italy. Gothic churches, such as Westminster Abbey in London, make use of nave arcades. Handsome arcades are also found in such Renaissance buildings as the Farnese Palace in Rome.

ARCADIA, är-kā′dē-ə, is a residential city in southern California, in Los Angeles County, 13 miles (21 km) by road northeast of downtown Los Angeles. The community developed during the 1880's around Santa Anita Ranch, the estate of E.J. ("Lucky") Baldwin, at the foot of the

San Gabriel Mountains. On the grounds of the former estate are Santa Anita Racetrack, which opened in 1934, and the Los Angeles State and County Arboretum. The arboretum is a horticultural research center and park, with trees, plants, and flowers from all over the world. It includes a botanical library and several restored buildings of historic interest: the adobe house (1839) of Hugo Reid, Arcadia's first settler, and Baldwin's cottage and carriage house (1881). Arcadia was incorporated in 1903 and is administered by the city manager plan of government. Population: 42,868.

ARCADIA, är-kā′dē-ə, a city in Florida, is the seat of De Soto County. It is 80 miles (129 km) by road southeast of Tampa. Arcadia markets the cattle and citrus fruit of the surrounding Peace River valley. The city has citrus packing plants and makes naval stores and power transformers. There is an annual rodeo. The community adopted city manager government in 1961. Population: 5,658.

ARCADIA, är-kā′dē-ə, is a department in Greece, in the central part of Peloponnesus, bordering on the Gulf of Argolis. It has an area of 1,681 square miles (4,354 sq km). The terrain is generally mountainous, but there are fertile valleys in which grain, potatoes, wine grapes, and tobacco are cultivated and sheep and goats are raised. Industry is confined to the capital, Tripolis.

The modern department is almost coextensive with the ancient region of Arcadia, but the latter was landlocked. Cut off by mountains from the rest of Greece, it developed a pastoral civilization that came to be a symbol of rustic simplicity. Ancient Arcadia was mostly subject to Sparta until 370 B.C., when the Arcadian League was established with Megalopolis as its capital. In the following century part of Arcadia came under Macedonian influence. The region declined in Roman times. Population: (1961) 135,042.

ARCADIA, är-kā′dē-ə, is a pastoral romance by Jacopo Sannazzaro (q.v.), written between 1481 and 1504. It was only after his manuscript had been stolen and printed full of errors at Venice in 1502 that the poet decided to publish his work. Before doing so he corrected and revised the text, added a new chapter to complete the plot, and purified the language of all dialectal expressions. The first authorized version appeared in Naples in 1504. The Aldine edition, which appeared in Venice in 1514, still serves as the text of new editions of the work.

Consisting of 12 chapters of prose and 12 poems in a variety of meters, *Arcadia* blends autobiography and allegory in a rather dull narrative. An unhappy tale of love supplies dramatic unity to the work. Rebuffed by the lady of his heart, Sincero, a Neapolitan shepherd identified as the poet himself, has come to Arcadia seeking solace and diversion. He describes the conditions of his life in exile and depicts the dream world of pastoral simplicity. Through his characters, who are shepherds, Sannazzaro narrates the story of his own amorous misadventure and describes Carmosina, his Neapolitan mistress, among the nymphs of Mount Parthenion. In the end, oppressed by an evil omen, Sincero decides to return to his native land, only to find his ladylove dead. The work closes in a mournful but beautiful elegy of farewell to his shepherd's bagpipe.

The real interest in *Arcadia* lies in its gentle, graceful, and vivid idyllic descriptions of nature, drawn from Theocritus, Bion, Virgil, Ovid, Catullus, and other classical idyllists, and in its childlike, ingenuous pictures of human nature. Sannazzaro partakes of the life of his pastoral folk and describes their contests of song and dance, their herding and their hunting, and their rites and ceremonies. Throughout the work he assumes a serious and solemn tone.

Arcadia suffers from excessive Latinization in sentence structure and from the rhetorical exaggerations. Although the work lacks the clarity of truly great art, it has lasting interest because it reflects the pastoral emotions that were deeply and enduringly idealized during the Renaissance. It enjoyed great popularity in its own age, and its influence was immediate in France, Spain, Portugal, and England. Sir Philip Sidney derived from it some of the material for his own *Arcadia*.

HOWARD R. MARRARO, *Columbia University*

ARCADIA, är-kā′dē-ə, is a pastoral romance by Sir Philip Sidney (q.v.). Its full title is *The Countesse of Pembroke's Arcadia*. It is the longest and most famous work of prose fiction composed in English in the 16th century. It was completed in its earlier form about 1581, but a greatly revised and expanded version was left unfinished at the author's death in 1586. This incomplete recension was published in 1590. In 1593, Sidney's sister, Mary, countess of Pembroke, produced an enlarged edition in which the concluding sections of the original version were added to the unfinished second draft. In this composite form the work was circulated until 1926, when the complete text of the earlier version was at last printed from surviving manuscript copies.

As originally conceived, *Arcadia* was a pastoral love story modeled in part on its Italian namesake (1504) by Jacopo Sannazzaro. In this form the tale was in five books, or acts, separated by "eclogues" in prose and verse. It related the adventures of two princes, Musidorus and Pyrocles, and their loves for the princesses Pamela and Philoclea. It had, Sidney reminded his sister, been written hastily "in loose sheets of paper, most of it in your presence [at Wilton House, her country home], the rest by sheets sent unto you as fast as they were done."

In his unfinished revision, Sidney undertook to give the narrative more of an epic than a pastoral cast. The time sequence was altered to permit a conventional epic opening *in medias res;* warfare, captivities and rescues, and chivalrous deeds demoted the earlier love stories to relatively minor status. The first version was akin to Sannazzaro and to the Greek romances of Heliodorus and Achilles Tatius; the second was closer to *Amadis of Gaul* and *Morte Darthur*.

Arcadia continued to be widely popular throughout the 17th century: 14 editions appeared between 1590 and 1674; from it Beaumont and Fletcher borrowed the plot of *Cupid's Revenge*, and Shakespeare the story of Kent in *King Lear*. The most famous plagiarism, first detected by John Milton, was in the *Eikon Basilike*, where a prayer uttered by Pamela in book 3 of *Arcadia* was alleged to have been composed by King Charles I on the eve of his execution. Today the book is definitely a period piece, seldom read in its entirety except by special students of Elizabethan literature, who rightly regard it as a notable monument of English

prose style. But it may be doubted if many, even of these specialists, could from memory give a coherent outline of the plot. The most enduring element of *Arcadia* is in the verses interspersed among the prose. These include many of Sidney's finest sonnets and lyrics.

DELANCEY FERGUSON, *Brooklyn College*

Bibliography
The text of *Arcadia*, in the best modern version, is in Albert Feuillerat's edition of *The Complete Works of Sir Philip Sidney*, 4 vols. (Cambridge, Eng., 1912–26).
Bill, Alfred H., *Astrophel* (New York 1937).
Goldman, Marcus S., *Sir Philip Sidney and the Arcadia* (Urbana, Ill., 1934).
Myrick, Kenneth, *Sir Philip Sidney as a Literary Craftsman* (Lincoln, Nebr., 1965).
Zandvoort, Reinard W., *Sidney's Arcadia: A Comparison Between the Two Versions* (Amsterdam, Netherlands, 1929).

ARCADIUS (377?–408), är-kā′dē-əs, was the first emperor of the Eastern Roman (Byzantine) empire. Born in Spain, he was the son of Theodosius I, on whose death in 395 the empire was divided, Arcadius obtaining the East and his brother Honorius the West. Arcadius proved unable to govern for himself and was a tool in the hands of Rufinus, the praetorian prefect; then, until 399, of the eunuch Eutropius; then of his queen, Eudoxia (died 404); and finally of another praetorian prefect, Anthemius.

The reign was marked by Visigothic incursions into Greece, the revolt of the mercenary general Gainas (399–400), and the banishment of St. John Chrysostom (404). Arcadius died on May 1, 408.

ARCARO, är-kär′ō, **Eddie** (1916–   ), American jockey, who rode 4,779 winners in 24,092 races during a 30-year career. His 549 stakes victories included nearly every major American race. At the time of his retirement in 1961, he was the only jockey who had ridden as many as five Kentucky Derby winners and the only one to have ridden two "Triple Crown" winners. His lifetime riding purses totaled $30,039,543.

George Edward Arcaro was born in Cincinnati, Ohio, on Feb. 19, 1916. He became a stable boy at 13 and rode his first race in 1931. He booted home his first winner at Tijuana, Mexico, in 1932. He rode his first Kentucky Derby winner (Lawrin) in 1938. His other victories at Churchill Downs came aboard Whirlaway (1941), Hoop Jr. (1945), Citation (1948), and Hill Gail (1952). He completed racing's "Triple Crown" by winning the Preakness and the Belmont Stakes with both Whirlaway and Citation. Among his other well-known mounts were Gallorette, Devil Diver, Native Dancer, Shut Out, Nashua, Bold Ruler, Challedon, Busher, and Kelso.

A rough rider early in his career, Arcaro was suspended for a year in 1942–1943 before becoming one of racing's respected sportsmen. He was elected to the jockeys' Hall of Fame in 1955. After retiring as a jockey, he worked in insurance and served as a track official.

BILL BRADDOCK, *New York "Times"*

ARCATA, är-kā′tə, a city in northern California, is situated in Humboldt County, on Humboldt Bay, 8 miles (13 km) by road northeast of Eureka. The city has large lumber mills and is the seat of Humboldt State College. Founded in 1850, the community was incorporated in 1903. Arcata is governed under a city manager plan adopted in 1957. Population: 8,985.

ARCE, är'sā, **Manuel José** (1783?–1847), Central American political leader. He was born in San Salvador, El Salvador. He was twice imprisoned (1811; 1814–1819) for his role in the rebellion against Spanish rule. Subsequently he distinguished himself in the struggle to obtain Central American independence from Mexico.

After the formation of the Federation of Central America, he was elected its president, serving from 1825 to 1839. He led abortive revolts in 1831 and 1833, and in 1840 was an unsuccessful candidate for the presidency of El Salvador. Banished from the country after another revolt (1844), he returned shortly before his death, in San Salvador, on Sept. 14, 1847.

ARCESILAUS, (316–241 B.C.), är-ses-i-lā'əs, was a Greek philosopher who is considered the founder of the Middle or New Academy. His name appears also as *Arcesilas*. He was born in Pitane, Aeolis, and studied philosophy at Athens under Theophrastus and Crantor. On the death of Crates he became head of the Academy. Opposing the Stoics, Arcesilaus denied the certainty of intellectual and sensuous knowledge and recommended abstinence from all dogmatic judgments. He held that one must act on grounds of probability. Although he left no writings, he exerted a wide influence on philosophy.

ARCH, a structure composed of wedge-shaped stones, called voussoirs, and designed to span a void. The center stone at the apex or top of an arch is the keystone. The keystone is often emphasized architecturally, but from a structural point of view it is no more essential than any other voussoir. Indeed, in many Gothic arches there is no keystone; two voussoirs simply meet in a joint at the apex of the arch. The two voussoirs that begin the curve at each end of the arch are the springers. They rest on the imposts, the points of apparent support. The impost is generally emphasized by a block of stone that is given special treatment. The undersurface of an arch is called the soffit or intrados; the outer curve is the extrados. The haunch, where the thrust of the arch is usually greatest, is at a point located about one third the distance between the springer and keystone.

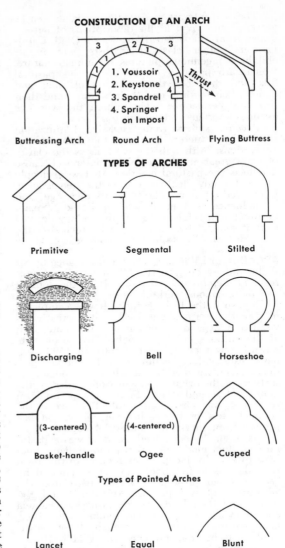

CONSTRUCTION OF AN ARCH

1. Voussoir
2. Keystone
3. Spandrel
4. Springer on Impost

Buttressing Arch   Round Arch   Flying Buttress

Thrust

TYPES OF ARCHES

Primitive   Segmental   Stilted

Discharging   Bell   Horseshoe

Basket-handle (3-centered)   Ogee (4-centered)   Cusped

Types of Pointed Arches

Lancet   Equal   Blunt

HORSESHOE ARCHES designed by the Moors fill the Grand Mosque (now the cathedral) of Córdoba, Spain.

FRITZ HENLE, FROM PHOTO RESEARCHERS

Structural Principle of the Arch. While an arch is being built, formwork or centering is required to support the voussoirs. When the arch is completed, the centering may be removed, because the wedge-shaped voussoirs cannot fall without pushing aside their neighbors. In other words, the voussoirs transform the vertical pull of gravity into a diagonal force known as thrust, or lateral thrust. The thrust must be overcome or the arch will collapse. It can be resisted by setting another similar arch against the first so that each presses against the other, as in an arcade. However, an arcade must eventually end, and at that point a buttress or buttressing is needed. A buttress is a mass of material heavy enough to absorb, through inertia, the diagonal thrust brought to bear upon it; in effect, it bends the diagonal thrust into a nearly vertical force. The arch is presumed to be safe if the resultant of the diagonal thrust of the arch and the vertical force of gravity of the buttress itself falls within the inner third of the buttress's thickness at ground level.

Basic Forms. Arches can be built in many shapes. The most common is the semicircular or

ARCHES played a prominent role in ancient Roman and in Gothic architecture. The Arch of Constantine (*left*) is one of Rome's triumphal arches. Wells Cathedral, England (*right*) is noted for its inverted Gothic pointed arches.

round arch. In Islamic architecture, horseshoe arches, consisting of more than a semicircle, are common. An arch of less than a semicircle is a segmental arch. It is even possible, using voussoirs, to construct a flat arch whose soffit is horizontal. If an arch rises vertically above the impost before the curve begins, the arch is said to be stilted. Gothic architecture uses many stilted arches. A full colonnette sometimes separates the impost from the springer that begins the curve of the arch. The pointed arch is a common feature of Gothic and some Islamic architecture. The centers of the two curves of a pointed arch are most commonly at the springer, creating an equilateral arch. If the centers are set outside the arch, the point becomes more acute—a lancet arch. If the centers are within the arch, an obtuse point and a blunt arch are the result. Elliptical or three-centered arches have sharp curves at the sides joined by a flatter curve in the center. In the late Gothic period, the four-centered arch came into favor; it has sharp curves at either side and flattish curves between, leaving a very blunt point at the apex. The late Gothic also made use of the ogee arch, with reversed curves at either side. A structural tour de force, the ogee arch must be relatively small. Finally, there are parabolic arches, which appeared first in Persia during the Sassanian period. In modern architecture the parabolic shape is frequently used for curved concrete slabs which, however, are not true arches because they are monolithic and involve no thrust.

History of Arch Construction. The principle of the arch was known to most early civilizations. The Egyptians used arches only in utilitarian buildings such as the granaries behind the Ramesseum at Thebes. Their obsession with the idea of permanence probably made the Egyptians distrust the arch, which can, of course, collapse if the buttress supporting the thrust is ever weakened. "The arch never sleeps," says a Greek proverb, referring to the eternal force of the thrust.

Lack of stone and timber forced the Mesopotamians to use brick and, consequently, a form of arched construction, because brick cannot span a void unless it is used as an arch. However, sun-baked brick is not strong and Mesopotamian arches were generally small, even in palaces of vast dimensions.

Roman builders were the first to exploit fully the possibilities of arch construction, which they inherited from the Etruscans. They also developed the vault—an extension of the principle of the arch to cover an area rather than a line. The impressive remains of Roman stone aqueducts may still be seen marching arch upon arch across the Roman countryside, in the Pont du Gard near Nîmes, France, and at Segovia, Spain. The Romans also built great triumphal arches such as those in Rome honoring the emperors Titus, Septimius Severus, and Constantine.

The construction of the later Middle Ages was dominated by the arch and vault. The early Christian basilicas, with their light arcades carrying thin walls and timber roofs, were superseded in the 11th and 12th centuries by great vaulted churches with transverse arches or ribs at intervals below the vault, and massive arcades to hold the thick walls. These arcades were often several stories high, each story having wider arches than the story below.

The most dramatic use of the principle of the arch is found in Gothic architecture. Buildings became skeletons of stone, with slender piers holding the pointed arches of the arcade, and above the arcade light vaults with a network of ribs. All openings—windows, doors, or the vast open spaces of the interior—were topped by pointed arches and the vaults they carry. An elaborate buttressing system was necessary to support these soaring arches and vaults. Spur walls were built at right angles to the church outside the aisles, with flying buttresses rising from them above the aisle roofs to support the nave vaults. The arch and vault construction of Gothic buildings made it possible to pierce the walls with large windows of stained glass. Architects of the Renaissance and later periods rejected the pointed Gothic arch, which they associated with barbarism, and brought the round Roman arch back into favor.

See also ARCHITECTURE; BRIDGES.

EVERARD M. UPJOHN, *Columbia University*

Bibliography
Branner, Robert, *Gothic Architecture* (New York 1961).
Conant, Kenneth J., *Carolingian and Romanesque Architecture, 800–1200* (Baltimore 1959).
Hamlin, Talbot, *Architecture, an Art for All Men* (New York 1947).
Rivoira, Giovanni T., *Roman Architecture* (London 1925).
Upjohn, Everard M., Wingert, P.S., and Mahler, J.G., *A History of World Art* (rev. ed., New York 1958).
Ward, Clarence, *Medieval Church Vaulting* (Princeton, N.J., 1915).

ARCHAEOLOGICAL INSTITUTE OF AMERICA. See THE AMERICANA ANNUAL—*Societies and Organizations.*

ALLYN BAUM, FROM RAPHO GUILLUMETTE

PETER THROCKMORTON, FROM NANCY PALMER

An archaeologist may excavate Inca ruins in Peru or dive for the cargo of an ancient wreck off Turkey. Wherever he works, his purpose is to find evidence of how peoples of earlier times lived by studying things they made and used.

ARCHAEOLOGY

CONTENTS

ARCHAEOLOGY, är-kē-ol'ə-jē. Both history and archaeology study the human past. However, history is dependent upon the written word and therefore concerns itself with the particular part of the human past that is recorded in documents. Archaeology, on the other hand, studies the past in terms of things that people made. In doing so it uses the methods both of history and of science. About 1 percent of the human past can be studied through written documents. The remaining 99 percent has left no written records and thus is outside the bounds of documentary history. This 99 percent of the human past is the main subject matter of archaeology. However, a portion of history's 1 percent of the human past also belongs to archaeology. This realm, in which archaeology and history particularly overlap, is called historic archaeology.

1. Scope of Archaeology

Insofar as the archaeologist deals with the histories of past cultures, he is doing something similar to what historians do. The essential difference is in the nature of the data. But when the archaeologist is studying culture in the anthropological sense of the term, he has moved from the area of the humanities, with their historical or fine-arts frames of reference, into the context of the social sciences or the natural sciences.

The Study of Culture. The term *culture*, in the anthropological sense, means an organized body or system of beliefs and understandings, manifest in acts and artifacts. Persisting through tradition, these beliefs and understandings characterize a human group. Culture consists of tools, weapons, utensils, ornaments, and the like, as well as customs, institutions, beliefs, myths, ideas, and acts. It is the means by which humans obtain their food, protection from the elements, and defense against their enemies. Culture is learned. It is transmitted from one person to another and one generation to another largely by language, which is also a part of culture. Culture is the agency through which humans interact with each other, with their own culture and other cultures, and with their physical environment. Without culture human existence is impossible.

Although both the historian and the archaeologist are interested in the study and knowledge of past cultures, the archaeologist focuses his attention on the material aspects of culture while the historian concentrates his efforts on the nonmaterial aspects of culture. Moreover, the historian, who needs written documents, must deal with the elaborated cultures that are called *civilizations*. The archaeologist may also study civilizations, but he often investigates the cultures of noncivilized or precivilized societies that are outside the boundaries of history. Whatever he studies, the archaeologist's work is intimately bound to the material aspects of culture, and the historian's is not.

Material culture consists of artifacts and other physical manifestations of human activity. An *artifact* is a product of human workmanship. Tools, weapons, utensils, amulets, charms, art objects, clothing, houses, buildings, monuments, walls, and the like are artifacts. Even a cemetery or a human burial in a grave is an artifact. The grave pit is an artifact, and the skeleton arranged in a particular way, especially a skeleton that has been fastened together, is an artifact. There is, however, a point at which the concept of artifact becomes somewhat obscure. Clearly a paved road is an artifact, but a path between two rivers may be only a byproduct of many people walking over the shortest route between two points. A carefully chipped knife of flint is clearly an artifact from which, with other examples of its class, an archaeologist can recover extinct notions of form, material, and to some degree methods of manufacture. Yet the flint chips or wastage that are a byproduct of the manufacture of the stone knife will usually convey more information about the method of making stone knives than the finished product itself. Thus the stone chips are man-made and are artifacts, even though they are not finished products intended for use. A small flint chip with an edge showing that it has been used as a cutting tool is an artifact just as much as a marble sculpture of a goddess is. Each in its own way is an equally important datum in the study of past cultures.

A kitchen midden, or refuse dump, although not an artifact, is certainly a physical manifestation of human activity and culture. The midden, or refuse pile, may contain fragments of broken tools, weapons, and utensils, various byproducts of manufacturing processes, and animal bones broken to obtain marrow or showing knife cuts from butchering. Such bones are not artifacts but they do manifest cultural behavior of groups of humans. Still other physical manifestations of past cultures and human behavior can be found: for example, discolored areas in soil where wooden posts of dwellings or other kinds of structures once stood; pollen and seeds of wild and cultivated plants; or concentrations of certain chemicals in the soil.

Because the kinds of material remains that constitute the record of past cultures are so variable and diverse, many sorts of skills and systems of interpretation are needed to recover the historical and scientific realities that the archaeologist seeks. In fact, much of archaeology is like detective work. To carry the comparison even further, a great part of the laboratory analysis done by or for archaeologists is similar to that done in the best crime laboratories.

Divisions of Archaeology. Because the materials of archaeology include a wide range of material cultural remains, archaeologists work with a great variety of skills, systems, and aims. Consequently archaeology has many divisions.

One kind of archaeologist, for example, may produce culture history from his studies, a history somewhat similar to documentary history but derived from data of a different kind. Another archaeologist may be interested only in the history of certain forms of art from one area and period. Such a person is operating in the branch of archaeology that is similar to art history. An archaeologist may also be interested in the evolution of cultures, or a comparative history of cultures, or the interaction of culture and physical environment, or comparative cultures and social processes, or some other kind of objective that places his kind of archaeology in the field of the natural or social sciences instead of in the humanities or the arts. Archaeology of this sort is a part of anthropology, which is a social science with a background in the natural sciences. Anthropology is the study and knowledge of man, culture, and society from the earliest times to the present. It is a combination of natural sciences and social sciences. In North America, anthropology is frequently divided into five separate fields or disciplines: (1) physical anthropology, (2) archaeology, (3) ethnology, (4) social anthropology, and (5) linguistics.

In North America most archaeologists receive their training in a university department of anthropology. Other archaeologists, however, may receive their training in a university department of fine arts, classics, or Oriental studies or in the humanities in general. Because of this diversity in training as well as the great range of materials to study, the field of archaeology includes many divisions and specializations. Some of these divisions concentrate on great civilizations and their antecedents, for example, the Greek, Roman, Egyptian, Chinese, Aztec, or Andean. Other divisions may be entirely regional, studying the various civilizations of Europe, Africa, North America, South America, or Oceania. There are divisions based on broad categories of subject matter—for instance, medieval archaeology, prehistoric archaeology, and colonial and historic archaeology. Underwater archaeology is really an extension of whatever division the remains under investigation belong to—for example, Roman archaeology. Yet underwater archaeology tends to become a speciality because of special skills and special equipment required. Thus far it has been easier to teach archaeologists to dive than to teach archaeology to those people who dive for sport and adventure.

Probably the best way to divide archaeology into reasonable segments is to think of it in relation to the totality of human culture. In the earliest stages of human existence or in later but marginal stages, most of man's attention was devoted to adapting to his environment. Cultures representative of such stages are in critical interaction with their physical environments and have relatively large technological systems in relation to their social and ideological systems. For example, they have to spend a great deal of time hunting for food and have little time for producing literature and art or for developing philosophies of religion. The archaeologists who specialize in the study of such cultures should have a good background in the natural sciences and in anthropology. In the latest stages of human existence the sociological and ideological aspects of culture are relatively larger than the technological aspect. Moreover, the physical environment is of relatively less importance. The archaeologist who concentrates on such cultures, which are representative of civilizations or near-civilizations, should have a background in the humanities and anthropology. The students of cultures that are intermediate between the prim-

ARTIFACTS help archaeologists to reconstruct past cultures. The term artifact includes anything made by human workmanship, whether small or large, simple or elaborate—whether made for ordinary use in the family or for rituals of religion. All the objects shown on this page are artifacts, from the thimble and pins to the columns at a temple gate.

18th century artifacts found when archaeologists dug on the site of Fort Michilimackinac on Mackinac Island in Michigan. Above are a scissors, a thimble, and pins.

(Right) A specimen of Inca pottery from the region of Cuzco in the Peruvian Andes.

Collection, Musee de l'Homme

(Right) Side plates from two 18th century muskets, made in the shape of dragons' tails.

(Left) Mexican incense burners dating from about 600 to 900 A.D.

Bernard G. Silberstein, from Rapho Guillumette

The arrowheads above and the medallion at left were recovered on Mackinac Island.

Above illustrations are from Mackinac Island Park Commission and Michigan State University

itive and the civilized should have as background a suitable combination of the humanities, anthropology, and natural sciences. The diversity of archaeology and its academic compartmentalization make archaeology somewhat difficult to classify but also give it a great strength. Only archaeology can provide a scientific over-all view of human existence from its earliest beginnings to the present time.

The ruins of a Roman temple at Baalbek (formerly called Heliopolis) in Lebanon are further examples of artifacts.

J. ALLAN CASH, FROM RAPHO GUILLUMETTE

2. Methods of Archaeology

Archaeologists work with a variety of purposes and techniques. One of the best ways to present the methods of archaeology is to describe a complete archaeological operation.

Organizing the Study. In the 1940's, Paul S. Martin, an archaeologist at the Field Museum in Chicago, became interested in an archaeologically unexplored area of the southwestern United States. He had good reasons for believing that the remains of a little known and at that time undefined prehistoric culture would be most abundant in west central New Mexico. Accordingly, under the sponsorship of the Field Museum, he organized and led an expedition to the area. A preliminary survey had located one large site that seemed to be well worth excavating, and there were believed to be other sites in the vicinity. Thus Martin decided that the expedition would combine excavation and a more detailed archaeological survey.

The expedition consisted of Martin and a trained field assistant, a photographer, several student assistants, and a cook. Local men were to be hired to do the heavy digging. The first job was to build a field headquarters consisting of a bunkhouse, latrines, kitchen, living quarters, storeroom, laboratory, and photographic dark room. Next a tank for water storage was installed so that there would be water for washing, drinking, developing and printing photographs, and cleaning specimens. In this case, water to fill the storage tank had to be hauled from a well about half a mile away.

The Archaeological Survey. The plan of the archaeological survey was to make an intensive search of an area of about two square miles in order to obtain a representative sample of the kinds of archaeological remains that existed in the region as a whole. The area to be covered by the survey was part of a large valley with two somewhat different topographical provinces. One was characterized by hills timbered with pine, cedar, juniper, and live-oak trees and by flat, broad valleys that were largely grassland.

The other province consisted of similarly wooded ridges and foothills with a network of shallow streams, springs, and dry washes. In either instance much of the area was covered by enough timber to make visibility difficult; thus the survey party found it necessary to use compass courses at selected intervals. These courses and measured intervals were then transferred to existing U.S. Geological Survey topographic maps.

The search was conducted on foot: the archaeologist, walking along his compass line, looked for evidences of past human occupancy of the area. In this instance three kinds of clues could be seen by a trained observer. First, there were clusters of flint chips or potsherds (small fragments of pottery). The stone chips, by-products of the manufacture of stone tools, and the fragments of broken earthenware are among the signs that the archaeologist is trained to recognize as evidence of past human occupancy. Another clue consisted of shallow depressions, about 12 to 24 feet in diameter, which were best seen in early morning light when the length of the shadow thrown by an otherwise nearly imperceptible rim could be noticed. Such depressions were the remains of partly underground houses. The roof timbers had long since rotted away, and the pit foundations had been filled by natural flowing and shifting of surface soils. Still another clue existed in the form of low mounds of rock overgrown with pines and junipers. These rock piles were the remains of the dry-laid masonry walls of small pueblos that had originally contained from two to twelve rooms. In some instances several clues might be found together; that is, the remains of a dwelling structure might be associated with surface finds of potsherds and flint chips or, on rare occasions, with finished artifacts such as a grinding stone or a flint knife. But, more often than not in this particular archaeological survey, the clues were distinctive and separate. When the survey was completed, the locations of the sites were placed on maps, the sites were classified as to types, and the pottery fragments, flint chips, and other artifacts were classified and analyzed. Finally, all the data were recorded and the records were filed for future use.

Excavation and Mapping. Meanwhile, the site that had been chosen for detailed examination was being excavated under the direction of Paul S. Martin, the leader of the expedition, and his assistant, Robert J. Braidwood. The site was a 2,000-year-old village of 20 or more pit houses (partly underground houses of round or oval outline with earth-covered roofs of poles and branches supported by posts). The village was situated on a gently sloping, well drained ridge extending outward from one of the foothills at the base of the San Francisco Mountains.

The field crew consisted of seven local men, four students, a surveyor-photographer, and Braidwood, who was in charge of the excavation. Work started at seven o'clock in the morning and stopped at half past four in the afternoon, with an hour and a half for lunch and rest at noon. All tools were brought by pickup truck from the expedition headquarters some three and a half miles away and were returned at night. Heavy digging equipment consisted of several large picks, axes, a crosscut saw, mattocks with the adze blade kept sharpened for dressing a vertical earth profile, a dozen light picks, and an equal number of light long-handled spades.

THE RIVER BASIN SURVEYS, SMITHSONIAN INSTITUTION

METHODICALNESS characterizes the work of archaeologists. When this artifact (a broken pottery vessel) was uncovered, it was marked with a number, an arrow to show direction, and a scale to show size. It was then photographed before it was moved from its original site.

A wheelbarrow and a scoop and team of horses, rented from one of the local workmen, were used for moving earth away from the excavations. Light digging and cleaning equipment included small army-style entrenching mattocks, geologists' hammers, a small army spade, kitchen spoons, whisk brooms and paint brushes, surveyors' lining pins used as probes, grapefruit knives, and pointing trowels. Several tarpaulins were kept handy for use in cases where it was not desirable to have the soil dry quickly and harden, as, for example, in clearing out burials. Dirt from particularly productive areas was sieved. An ordinary spray, with plunger for compression and a carrying strap, was used, with water, to dampen the soil in order to increase the color contrast between undisturbed earth (called "sterile" because it contains no artifacts) and the dirt containing cultural materials. The student members of the expedition were given the responsibility of distributing the light and heavy tools and water containers in the morning and checking them in again at the end of the day's work. The students also loaded the truck.

Each digging unit was equipped with one or more tight wooden fruit boxes for holding potsherds. At night the sherds were put in small cloth bags and tagged with their findspots, or exact proveniences, ready for washing, cataloging, and classification back at the expedition headquarters. As artifacts and related cultural remains were found, they were put in marked paper sacks; fragile or fragmentary pieces were wrapped in a cheap grade of tissue paper. Heavier stone artifacts were put in a special pile and returned to the camp laboratory as conditions warranted. At all times during the excavation of the site, every effort was made to maintain a high standard of neat and precise digging in order to ensure accuracy of records and counts of artifacts.

The actual methods of excavating the pit houses, according to Braidwood, were as follows: As the first step, lines for a straight trench about

EXCAVATION TOOLS enable the archaeologist to work with extreme care. These Maya figures were uncovered with such tools as a trowel, knife, and paintbrush.

1.5 meters (5 feet) wide were laid across a depression or an area suspected of being a pit house. Every attempt was made to lay the center of the trench through the middle of the depression. Then two workmen, picking back to back as closely as safety allowed, proceeded to dig downward in the trench for about half a meter (20 inches). If, at this depth, the dirt still had the blackened appearance of topsoil and was yielding occasional potsherds and flecks of charcoal, then the probabilities were excellent that it was now "fill," an accumulation of the debris of the earth roof of the original pit houses together with subsequently accumulated debris and humus. If, on the other hand, the depressed area was sterile, then this first operation in the center of the trench would encounter the orange-brown gumbo of the normal soil profile at much less than the half meter's depth. In such an instance, 4 or 5 meters (about 10 to 16 feet) of the length of the trench might be dug down to the compact surface of this sterile gumbo, to determine by the profile whether the trench had crossed the center of the depression or whether any smaller architectural feature such as a surface house had caused the apparent depression. In the first case, however, with the trench still yielding fill at a half meter's depth, the workmen were allowed to dig downward with care until the floor of the original substructure pit was reached. In every instance it was found that the ancient Indians had sunk their pits down into the oxidized and leached soil zone. Thus the surface of their original floor was differentiated from the accumulated fill by a change in color and density of the soils.

Once the presence and depth of the original floor had been ascertained, the center trench was continued out in both directions toward the rim of the depression, and the proper soil dump was started outside the anticipated area of excavation. In prolonging the trench both ways from the depth test in the center, the workmen were made to stay about 10 centimeters (4 inches, above the level of the floor. The final stage of the first operation ended when both ends of the central trench had made contact with the vertical wall of the pit. The vertical face of the pit-house wall, like the pit-house floor, showed an abrupt change in both color and density from the dark humuslike fill.

When the central or cross trench was finished, the encircling trench was begun. This was simply a tracing of the circuit of the vertical face or wall of the original pit, done with the light picks by flicking the fill away from the lighter-colored vertical face. The vertical wall showed the normal soil profile of gumbo and then oxidized and leached material below the topsoil. This trench needed to be no wider than convenience in picking, cleaning, and shoveling demanded, and was not dug deeper than 10 centimeters above the floor. When finished, this trench completely encircled the inner periphery of the pit house and also showed in profile the short entrance passage that usually was located at the east side. The earth fill from the entrance passage was easily recognized by the usual differences in soil color and texture and was removed by picking and shovelling.

At this stage of the excavation, the dumps were well established around the rim of the pit and were kept at least a pick handle's length back from the edge so that the loose earth would not fall back into the excavation. At this point the archaeologist could clearly see the outline of the particular pit house being worked on. The outer wall of the pit was encircled by a trench, and another trench bisected the circle or roughly oval form. But still to be dug were two areas of fill shaped like half circles and the 10 centimeters of fill that had been left above the floor.

The next step in this excavating procedure was the removal of the remaining segments of fill within the pit down to the 10-centimeter level above the floor. This was done by removing layers 25 centimeters thick and saving all cultural materials layer by layer. When this operation was completed, the remaining 10 centimeters of fill over the floor was carefully excavated, using only light tools such as trowels. All potsherds, chips, artifacts, and objects of cultural significance were collected and labeled as coming from this particular provenience. Groups of stones and large stone artifacts were left in place. The various subfloor features, such as pits and postholes, were outlined by digging them down several centimeters below the floor level. Then the floor was dampened by water from the portable sprayer to bring out the contents in soil colors, and the floor was carefully photographed.

The next operation was the removal of all the floor stones and artifacts and the removal of fill from all the subfloor features. This final digging was done with trowels, brushes, and other light tools. Along with the above activities, the final dressing of the pit house for mapping and photography was done. All vertical faces were checked for overhanging topsoil, roots were cut

FIELD WORK is illustrated in these views of excavations of Indian dwellings in South Dakota. These projects—undertaken in areas that were about to be flooded by new reservoirs—were part of a program called the River Basin Surveys, sponsored by the Smithsonian Institution.

Aerial photo shows the site of an Indian village in South Dakota. Earth lodges were on a small butte, and a palisade enclosed the entire village.

Close-range view of an earth lodge excavated at another site in South Dakota. The circle of small holes shows location of wall posts. Entrance was at left rear.

Diggers used spades, brooms, and even their fingers to clear earth from the floor of this Indian house. Post holes and other features were then carefully dug out.

off flush with walls or floor, and large root butts and large natural stones of light color were painted with muddy water to reduce their contrast in the photographs. The earth dumps were dragged back with the team and scraper, and the surface of the ground about the pit-house rim was then cleaned by trowel. A directional arrow of fixed length was placed pointing north on the floor of the pit house, and a meterstick for scale was placed against the pit-house wall. Then a plan photograph was made of the house from a tower 20 feet (about 6 meters) high. The photograph was taken with a large-view camera at a time when light-and-shadow conditions were at their best. The pit house was then mapped in detail, using surveyors' instruments, and the final notations were made.

All of the pit houses were excavated and mapped individually. Then a map of the entire site was made, showing the positions and pit shapes of all the houses in the village. At the end of the season all excavations were refilled with the team and scraper, and oats were planted on the loose soil to prevent erosion.

While the excavation crew was at work, other personnel at the expedition headquarters were carrying on important tasks. At the end of each day, for instance, the materials found at the dig were brought back to the expedition camp. At the dig these materials had been placed in sacks, each carefully marked with the provenience, or exact location, of the finds. The specially trained workers at the expedition headquarters washed, sorted, classified, counted, and recorded all the types and varieties of artifacts, potsherds, cultural remains, or other data of possible significance. Soil samples were studied. Maps, profile drawings, and field notes were checked against the actual digging operations and against one another to make certain there were no mistakes and that all the varying operations were as nearly perfect as possible.

Importance of Precise Techniques. The account of the investigation of an Indian village has stressed the care taken at every step. Such elaborate care is essential because, once an archaeological site has been excavated, it is completely destroyed as a scientific document. The layers of artifacts have been removed, the relationships of features, structures, and artifacts no longer exist in the earth. Even if walls are left standing or are restored, the site is not the untouched document that it was prior to excavation. If a historian found a valuable document, read it, and then destroyed it, no other historian would be able to read the same document. Historians do not, of course, destroy documents; they preserve them in special libraries and archives. But since the archaeologist destroys his site as a document when he digs it, he must make every effort to measure and describe it in such a way that what was once in the earth is transferred to words, maps, drawings, and pictures on paper. In fact, if the archaeologist has done his work properly, it should be possible to put the site back together, with every object, soil type, and the like just as he found it. There is, of course, no reason for doing such a thing. This theoretical ideal is presented here only as an indication of the high standards of excavation technique required of a responsible archaeologist who realizes that he cannot avoid destroying his document as he investigates it.

Laboratory Work. When the excavation and all the other field operations have been finished, the expedition returns to its sponsoring institution, usually a museum or university. Here, in the laboratory, the analyses, comparative studies, and interpretations take place. For each three months of field work, about nine months of laboratory work is required to prepare a finished archaeological report. In the laboratory all of the excavated materials are further cleaned, mended, restored when necessary, and otherwise prepared for analysis. All of these materials were cataloged in the field, but if more elaborate cataloging is required, it is done in the laboratory. Then the artifacts and other cultural materials are analyzed and described and measured in terms of shape, size, composition; biological, physical, and chemical properties; and construction, function, and anything else that the archaeologist thinks might be a clue to past human history and culture. As we have said, the archaeologist works somewhat like a detective or a technician in a crime laboratory. Often specialists from other fields of science are called in—a botanist, for example, to identify remains of plants. Finally, artifacts and other cultural materials are classified into types according to various systems that place like materials with like in the same class or grouping. For example, all stone tools made by one method may be grouped, and all pottery fragments with a characteristic design can be classified as a type.

Typology. As a methodological approach, typology varies greatly among archaeologists. The method may range from rather simple systems of grouping artifacts by material and design to sophisticated concepts supported by statistics and theories of probability. In its most simple form, a type is symbolic of its class and exhibits all of the attributes or characteristics that differentiate the type from all other types. When these types are sufficiently real and not imposed by the archaeologist, then the types represent formerly existing cultural realities, and the distinctions based on them can be interpreted in anthropological terms. That is, what the archaeologist concludes from studying a typical tool can be used as evidence of how an ancient group of people lived and worked. Most archaeologists

nowadays describe their concepts of types and give the context or frame of reference within which they have used the particular concept. When dealing with types that represent formerly existing cultural realities, the archaeologist must of necessity pay more attention to the data of ethnology and to the establishment of function for his types of artifacts. He notes clusters of types and aims his research at definition of different operational subsystems of the total cultural system he is studying. He distinguishes the types and type clusters that have their primary functional context in the interaction of culture and physical environment from those that have their primary functional context in the social subsystems or the ideological subsystem.

Types of Pottery. The concept of type is and has been applied to artifacts of any kind, from crude stone tools, harpoon heads, fishhooks, and milled grains to pyramids. The most common category of types, however, relates to pottery. Pottery is one of the most useful items among the unintentional records left by past peoples. Although a pottery vessel may break into a hundred or more pieces, or sherds (also shards) as they are called by archaeologists, each sherd is exceedingly durable and will remain intact in the earth for thousands of years. Moreover, pottery was easily made, easily broken, and used in abundance. Therefore, if an ancient culture used pottery, it usually left great quantities of sherds. From these sherds the whole vessels can be reconstructed. Except for museum exhibitions or illustrations in reports, however, this is not done. The archaeologist has had so much experience with pottery that he can tell vessel shapes, sizes, and ornamentation from the sherds. The sherds are classified into types. If this is done well enough, the types represent classes of vessels made by one group of people at one given place at one given time and for one purpose.

A knowledge of the purpose or function of pottery types can be obtained from distribution and cultural context within an archaeological site or sites. For instance, sherds of ceramic types found in hearths and cooking areas came from pots used in the storage, preparation, and serving of food. These pottery types, then, represent the technological and social subsystems of the extinct culture. Similarly, types of storage jars found at the site of a sunken ship are indicative of former trade in wines or oils and are a component of the technological and social subsystem of the extinct culture. Those pottery types found only in shrines, temples, and burial places are artifacts of religion and are a part of the ideological subsystem of an extinct culture.

Knowing how pottery was made can provide evidence on how the people of a given culture lived. In some cultures the pottery was made by hand without the use of a wheel or molds. This manufacturing process represents the technological level of the culture. At the same time the manufacturing process gives insight into the social structure. For instance, among uncivilized peoples whose culture was based on the sowing and harvesting of grain, descent may have been reckoned in the female line. Hence a number of related women and their husbands lived in one large house or cluster of houses owned by their lineage or clan. Pottery making usually was a part of the labor of such a group of women, and each woman learned to make pottery. A girl learning to make pottery by hand was taught by or under the observation of a number of women, her mother, sisters, aunts, and grandmother. There was a well established cultural pattern or ideal which the young beginning potter followed if she wanted the approval of her peers. The pottery representative of such a culture is exceedingly uniform in shape, size, and decoration. It generally is restricted to a very few types that were made in relatively large quantities. The archaeologist, after classifying the pottery types from such an extinct culture, knows or suspects the kind of social subsystem manifested by his artifacts. Then he looks for additional data among his archaeological records.

When studying a more elaborate level of culture, the archaeologist may find pottery that was made on a wheel and was stamped with the name or seal of the manufacturer. Such pottery is evidence that a people had reached an early form of civilization, with a social structure that included crafts and guilds. In studying the same kind of culture the archaeologist may find certain pottery types only in temples or other sacred places. With luck he might discover that such pottery was made only at the residences of the priests of the temples. He would then be justified in making the inference that the manufacture of this pottery as well as its use was regulated by religious beliefs and practices. Thus he would learn something about the ideological subsystem of this particular culture.

Publishing Reports. After all the laboratory studies have been completed, the archaeologist writes his report, usually intended for publication. The purpose of this report is to tell what the archaeologist did, present the facts he found and the concepts he used in classifying and analyzing his data, and tell what conclusions he reached. The archaeologist describes his site and how he excavated it. In this section of the report he uses pictures, drawings, site plans, maps, and profile drawings showing stratigraphy, construction, or soil differences. All photographs, maps, and drawings have to be clear and of a high professional quality. The archaeologist also describes and illustrates by drawings and photographs the classes and types of artifacts and other cultural materials found in his excavations. He explains his systems of classification and typology. In other sections of his report the archaeologist makes comparisons and contrasts with related archaeological phenomena. Finally, he presents his interpretations and conclusions. The finished report also includes a bibliography and usually an index.

The finished report is published by a museum or a university or some other nonprofit institution. Although published archaeological reports and monographs might be called the backbone of archaeology, they are expensive to publish and have to be subsidized by non-profit-making institutions. Commercial publishers are reluctant to publish such reports because they would not sell enough to make a profit. The kinds of archaeological books produced by commercial publishers, except for textbooks used in teaching, are for popular consumption and are of little or no use to archaeologists. The works upon which the discipline depends are usually published in editions of a few thousand copies or less and are distributed to scholarly libraries, museums, universities, scientific and other scholarly institutions, and archaeologists all over the world.

ESTABLISHING DATES is a problem in archaeology. In the southwestern United States, sites can often be dated by reference to a master key based on tree growth.

3. Chronology

One aspect of archaeological work that is important in both the field and the laboratory is time. By one means or another the archaeologist attempts to discover the time relationships among the cultures or segments of cultures that he analyzes and describes. The archaeologist wants to know if one culture is older than another or if it existed at the same or a later time. That is, he is concerned to establish a *relative chronology*. He may also want to date a culture in years B.C. or A.D. In this case he is concerned with *absolute chronology*.

Relative Dating. The most common and basic method archaeologists use for determining relative time or age is *stratigraphy*. This is a method of translating space, or position, into time. In its simplest form, stratigraphy is a system of dating by layers. For example, archaeologists have excavated caves that were used as shelters by prehistoric men and have found layers of debris and earth. In the ordinary course of events, the bottom layer is the oldest and the top layer is the youngest. In one famous instance, excavators found the remains of nine cities in one mound. The seventh from the top is believed to be the city of Troy, scene of the Trojan War. The higher layers represent later cities built on the same site.

Stratigraphy, however, is not always a matter of layers building up in a vertical column. There are a number of somewhat more complicated forms, one of which is *lateral stratigraphy*. To visualize lateral stratigraphy, think of a rather shallow garbage dump. Each load of garbage is dumped at the edge of the previous load so that the dump, or midden, grows laterally or

THE TIMES, LONDON, FROM PICTORIAL PARADE

CHRONOLOGY can be established if an object of a known date is found with objects of unknown age. The remains of an ancient ship were found in London—the ribs can be seen at the left. The small bronze coin (*above*) enabled archaeologists to identify the ship as a Roman vessel built in the first century A.D.

sideways instead of up. The layers of this dump are nearly vertical instead of horizontal. The oldest layers are at the end of the midden where the dumping began, and the youngest layers are at the opposite end of the dump. In excavating a midden such as this it would be a great mistake to assume that the lowest-lying materials were the oldest part of the dump. An experienced archaeologist would be on the watch for such a situation and most likely would be able to recognize the lateral stratification in the cleaned profile of the wall of a test trench.

Stratigraphy can be the result of either natural forces or cultural forces or a combination of both. For instance, layers of cultural remains separated by layers of culturally sterile silty soils may represent a series of floods that drove people from their river-valley settlements at various intervals. When the flood was over the people returned and established a new settlement on top of the water-deposited soils. Then another flood drove them away, and so on. A similar example would be a case in which layers of cultural remains were separated by culturally sterile windblown sands. This situation would suggest settlements that were abandoned during periods of drought when the rainfall was not sufficient to maintain the vegetation growth that held the soil in place. Blowing dust and sand covered the cultural remains. Then a shift to wetter climatic conditions produced vegetation, and humans again settled in the area. Another example would consist of alternate layers of cultural remains and volcanic ash.

A somewhat different example of natural stratigraphy is present in situations along seacoasts or large lakes where there have been changes in water level or land level. If the water has fallen in level or the land has been elevated by natural forces, there may be cultural remains associated with the fossil beaches. In such a case the oldest cultural remains are associated with the highest of the old beaches or former strand lines, and the youngest cultural remains are to be found in the youngest beaches. People kept moving down toward the water's edge.

Relative chronologies can be derived from *seriation*. This is a somewhat complicated method in which a stylistic variable of a class of artifacts or a type of some sort is ordered in terms of its relative frequency in relation to its level or position within a site or in a group of sites. For example, the number of specimens of one class of pottery found in each of several sites can be a clue to which site was used first. The system has been particularly useful with surface collections obtained in regional archaeological surveys.

In certain localized but important situations the chemical analysis of bone has been used to obtain a relative chronology. The best known of such analytic procedures is the *fluorine method*. In instances where bones are beneath the earth and the groundwaters contain small amounts of fluorine, the fluorine ions combine with the hydroxyapatite crystals of the bone to form fluorapatite. The longer a bone is buried, the more fluorapatite it contains. Thus the relative chronology of bones in a localized area can be based on the amounts of fluorapatite they contain. So far, the greatest usefulness of this system has been in determining whether bone artifacts and human bones found with those of extinct animals are of the same age as the extinct forms or whether they represent a later intrusion into the deposit containing the remains of the extinct animals.

All the dating techniques thus far described have one thing in common: they provide only a relative chronology. Stratigraphy or seriation can show that one thing or one culture is older than another, younger, or of the same age. But these methods cannot tell how old a thing or a culture is. Some system of determining absolute time is necessary for this.

Absolute Dating. One of the methods used for determining time according to an absolute chronology is dating by tree rings, or *dendrochronology*. This technique was developed by A.E. Douglass, an astronomer. Dendrochronology is not just the simple counting of growth rings in a tree stump on top of an archaeological site. It is a much more sophisticated system of dating based on the fact that trees respond to seasonal changes, to rainfall, and to drought, and that this responsiveness is manifested in the growth rings.

In wet years the growth rings are wide and in dry years the growth rings are narrow. Thus certain kinds of trees in situations where they truly and characteristically reflect patterns of climate will possess patterns of growth rings that belong only to specific periods of climatic history.

A master tree-ring chronology is constructed by first learning the patterns of living trees of known age, say a hundred years old. Then wooden beams from old buildings such as houses built seventy-five years ago are studied in terms of their ring patterns. The growth patterns of the old beams will overlap with the beginning growth patterns of the living trees of known age. If such beams are from trees that were two hundred years old when cut, the master chronology can be extended backward in time another two hundred years. By continuing to cross-date the patterns of tree growth from more ancient samples of wood with the growth patterns of the already established sequence it is possible to establish a master chronology or calendar covering centuries. For the southwestern United States there exists such a tree-ring calendar for the years since the time of Christ. There a sample of wood from an archaeological site of unknown age may be used to date the site. The growth rings of wood from charred roof timbers found in pit houses, small logs from dry cave sites, and roof beams from old pueblos may be compared with the ring patterns of the master tree-ring calendar and dated in terms of the correspondence of patterns. By knowing the date the wood was cut for use in the archaeological site, the site itself or parts of it can be dated. Then this absolute date can be used in conjunction with relative chronologies such as have been described previously.

At the present time the most widely used and satisfactory system for obtaining absolute chronology is the *radiocarbon method* of dating. Developed in the late 1940's by Willard F. Libby at the Institute for Nuclear Studies of the University of Chicago, the radiocarbon method revolutionized archaeological dating. In 1950 there was only one radiocarbon laboratory dating a few archaeological samples on an experimental basis. By the mid-1960's hundreds of such samples from a multitude of archaeological sites were being routinely dated each year in many different radiocarbon laboratories spread all over the world. The radiocarbon method of dating determines the age of things that lived during the past 40,000 years by measuring the amount of carbon-14 they contain and converting this amount into years. Carbon-14 is a radioactive, unstable form of carbon with an atomic weight of 14. It is being formed constantly in the earth's upper atmosphere as the result of the bombardment of nitrogen-14 atoms by cosmic rays or neutrons. In the upper atmosphere the carbon-14 combines with oxygen to form carbon dioxide, which then becomes mixed in the earth's atmosphere with the ordinary carbon dioxide containing carbon-12 atoms. After reaching the earth's atmosphere the carbon-14 enters all living things, which exchange materials with the atmosphere through their life processes. All living matter contains a constant proportion of carbon-14 because of the equilibrium between the rate of formation of carbon-14 and the rate of disintegration of the carbon-14 contained in the atmosphere, the ocean, and all living things.

When any living thing dies, it ceases to be

CHARLES W. HERBERT, FROM WESTERN WAYS PHOTOS

DENDROCHRONOLOGY was developed by A.E. Douglass, shown here with a core bored from a tree as a means to study the growth rate of the living tree.

in exchange with the atmosphere and thus ceases to take in carbon-14. However, the carbon-14 contained at death continues to disintegrate at a constant rate. The half-life of carbon-14 is 5,568 years. This means that the amount of carbon-14 at the time of death is reduced to half that amount in the first 5,568 years. The remaining amount of carbon-14 is reduced by half in the second 5,568 years, and so on, so that the amount of carbon-14 remaining at a given time is proportional to the time elapsed since death. Thus by knowing the carbon-14 content of living matter and the rate at which carbon-14 disintegrates, it is possible to ascertain the elapsed time since the death of a specimen of formerly living matter.

The archaeological materials that can be dated by the radiocarbon method are wood, charcoal, all kinds of plant materials, antler, burned bone, fur, skin, hair, shell, peat, dung, and many other organic substances. Bone that has not been burned is unreliable because it is easily contaminated by chemical alteration. Bone in general seems to register dates that are too young, whereas shells of various kinds give dates that are too old. Charcoal, however, is virtually perfect for dating purposes. Bits of charcoal from old hearths or from structural timbers or poles are frequently found in archaeological sites and at different stratigraphic levels.

Samples of the charcoal—or any other organic substance that is to be dated—are carefully collected and sent to radiocarbon laboratories. There the sample is prepared chemically for the measurement of the carbon-14 content. Unfortunately this chemical preparation destroys the sample for archaeological purposes other than dating; hence rare artifacts of wood and other organic materials usually are not dated. Fortunately, however, there are usually other sources of organic materials from a given archaeological site. Thus the problem of choosing whether to get a date or to preserve a rare or artistic artifact does not often arise. When the sample to be dated has been properly prepared in the radio-carbon laboratory it is placed in a specially constructed, exceedingly sensitive radiation counter that is something like a Geiger counter. Such a counter measures the amount of carbon-14 in the sample by registering the number of carbon-14 disintegrations over a period of time. The longer the run of the counter the greater the accuracy of the measurement.

The final result is a radiocarbon date, which is expressed, for example, as A.D. 850 plus or minus 30 years (often abbreviated 850±30). These plus-or-minus years attached to the date are a way of stating the probable error of the dating method. In the example given above there are 66 chances in 100 that the true date of the sample is within 30 years one side or the other of A.D. 850—that ·is, between 820 and 880. By doubling this particular error, the probability would be increased to 96 chances out of 100 that the true date of the sample was within sixty years (plus or minus) of A.D. 850.

Although radiocarbon dating dominates the archaeological scene today, other systems of determining absolute chronology are useful in particular situations. Among these methods is *glacial varve chronology*. Glacial varves are thin layers of clays deposited annually in basins of meltwater by the retreating ice of continental glaciers. Cultural remains associated with late-glacial and postglacial features, which are in a fixed position in relation to the varve count, can be dated by this method. However, this system has not worked well except in the Baltic region of northern Europe.

The *potassium-argon method* is most useful in dealing with dating problems of times so remote that they are beyond the range of radio-carbon measurements. The method is based on the radioactive decay of potassium 40 into calcium 40 and argon 40 and utilizes known proportions in terms of known rates of change. A notable application of this method was the dating of the geological context in Africa's Olduvai Gorge, where L.S.B. Leakey found fossil remains of *Zinjanthropus* and *Homo habilis*. The layer containing these remains was found to be 1,750,000 years old by scientists at the University of California, Berkeley.

Although it had been under development for some years, the *thermoluminescence technique* for dating pottery achieved the required standard of accuracy only as recently as 1965. The technique depends on the fact that radioactive elements (primarily thorium and uranium) in clay bombard other substances in the clay and raise electrons to unstable levels. When the clay is fired in the kiln, each electron falls back to its stable position and emits a photon of light. If a fragment of ancient pottery is reheated in the laboratory, small amounts of light are given off. The amount of thermoluminescence indicates how much radiation damage each electron has received. Hence the amount of thermoluminescence is a measure of the time that has elapsed since the pottery was first fired. New accuracy in use of this technique is the result of refinements developed at the University Museum, University of Pennsylvania. The improved method consists of bombarding pottery to be analyzed with X-rays, and of using a series of samples from one small piece of pottery for each assessment of age.

In colonial and historic archaeology the dating of undocumented sites or parts of sites is complicated by lack of depth of time. Often, not enough time has elapsed for observable stratification to occur. For such sites it is possible to establish chronology based on dated historic materials of known style and manufacture. Pipes, glass beads, silver ornaments, buttons, and iron knives are among the objects that have been used to construct chronologies of this sort. When objects that have been dated in historic time overlap in one site with older artifacts, it is possible to link history with prehistory.

One highly specialized method of dating in terms of absolute chronology is ideally suited to colonial and historical archaeology as well as to classical or other fields in which artifacts of glass are present. Glass that has been under water or buried in the ground for a long time becomes encrusted with variegated scales built up in iridescent layers. Although the destructive process causing these weathering crusts is not known exactly, scientists at the Corning Museum of Glass discovered that the number of decomposition layers on a given piece of glass is equal to the number of years that piece of glass has been submerged in water or buried in the earth. By counting the crust layers, which can be seen with a microscope, it is possible to tell how long an artifact of glass has been buried or submerged and thus to determine the date of the burial or submergence. For historic sites on land or underwater sites of shipwrecks that are only a few hundreds of years old, the method of dating by glass can scarcely be surpassed.

An unusual method of determining absolute time has been used with success on islands off the coast of Peru where artifacts were found in position in deep deposits of guano, or dung. Research indicated that the guano was deposited in annual layers that could be counted. Thus an artifact found at a depth of 1,000 layers beneath the fresh surface of a deposit of guano would be 1,000 years old.

There are a number of almost equally exotic ways in which chronology can be determined. Moreover, new concepts and methods of archaeological dating are being developed. The foregoing review, however, suffices to show that archaeologists use a great variety of dating methods and that they get help from chemists, botanists, geologists, and many other scientists.

4. Contributions of Other Disciplines to Archaeology

The discussion of dating illustrates one of the characteristics of modern archaeology. So many kinds of science are involved that this has become an interdisciplinary or multidisciplinary field. An archaeologist cannot expect to become expert in all of the disciplines that contribute to his field. Yet he must have sufficient background in a number of subjects so that he has some idea of what kinds of natural and physical scientists might be able to help him in the solution of archaeological problems. He must also have some idea of what kinds of problems would be of interest to these physical and natural scientists, who already have enough to do and will become professionally interested only in those problems of archaeology that have some relevancy to their own fields. How archaeologists work with scholars from other fields can be illustrated by describing a major study under the leadership of Richard S. MacNeish in Mexico.

Formulating the Problem. MacNeish set up his problem by asking the following questions. (1) How, where, and when did agriculture based on corn begin in the New World? (2) What cultural changes from savagery to civilization accompanied this development in the basic subsistence pattern? (3) What bearing would the answers to the first two questions have on the problems of how and why civilization arose anywhere in the world? In common with archaeologists everywhere MacNeish knew that the development of agriculture was basic to the rise of a civilization. He assumed that if he could find the origin of the systematic growing of corn (or maize) as a food crop, he would be able to contribute to the knowledge of where, when, and how civilization began in the Western Hemisphere. Thus his first problem was to find the area in the New World where maize was first domesticated.

MacNeish knew that botanists who had studied both modern and fossil corn had determined that corn had been developed in the New World. They knew the characteristics of primitive corn and believed that it probably was derived from a highland grass. Archaeological studies in Peru had already indicated the probability that corn had originated north of there. Archaeological finds of corn in northern Mexico and the southwestern United States had already shown that corn had been domesticated for at least five thousand years and that its origins were somewhere to the south of that general region. Other studies of fossil corn and of fossil pollen suggested an original homeland for corn in Mexico somewhere north of Chiapas and south of the valley of Mexico. In 1959, MacNeish conferred with Paul C. Mangelsdorf, director of the Botanical Museum of Harvard University and an authority on corn and its ancestry. Mangelsdorf and MacNeish decided that to seek information on the origin and development of corn, one must look in the region between southern and central Mexico for a highland area that possessed caves suitable for occupancy by humans and a dry climate suitable for the preservation of corncobs in the archaeological sites. They made a careful study of maps, charts, and data dealing with rainfall, climate, topography, and geography and reached the conclusion that there were likely areas in southern Oaxaca, the Tehuacán Valley, and the vicinity of the Río Balsas. In the winter of 1960 MacNeish made a brief archaeological survey in parts of Oaxaca and Puebla. Near the end of his survey he found a likely cave in the Tehuacán area of Puebla. His test trench showed that the cultural deposits in the cave were stratified. In a layer that could be dated at about 3600 B.C. he found very primitive corn cobs. This was the beginning of the interdisciplinary expeditions and researches that became the Tehuacán Archaeological-Botanical Project.

Arranging Sponsorship and Finances. With the archaeological and botanical problems defined and the geographical area for investigation found, the next problem for MacNeish was to decide what kind of organization could most successfully sponsor a program of the sort he had in mind. Should he choose a huge institution with many facilities and a large staff or should he choose a small, flexible institution with experience in handling interdisciplinary programs on a co-operative basis? He chose the latter type of institution and in the spring of 1960 approached

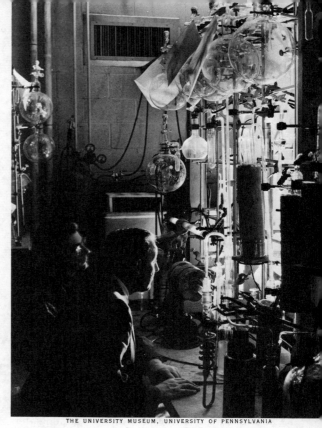

THE UNIVERSITY MUSEUM, UNIVERSITY OF PENNSYLVANIA

RADIOCARBON DATING illustrates how archaeologists call on experts from other fields. Physical chemists here watch the preparation of a specimen.

the Robert S. Peabody Foundation for Archaeology at Andover, Mass. This foundation, under the direction of two anthropologically oriented archaeologists, Douglas S. Byers and Frederick Johnson, has a history of successful interdisciplinary programs in archaeology and a proven ability to administer a project of the kind Mac-Neish planned. The Peabody Foundation was interested in his proposals and appointed him research associate of the foundation.

The next problem was that of financing the research and field work such a project would require. The Peabody Foundation was fortunate in obtaining the necessary funds from the National Science Foundation and the Rockefeller Foundation. Support and assistance were also received from the Instituto de Antropología e Historia of the government of Mexico and from other Mexican institutions. Thus the project acquired a sponsor and adequate funds, obtained permission to do archaeological research in Mexico, and enlisted an international coterie of cooperating scientists.

Organizing the Tehuacán Project. The basic organization of the Tehuacán project consisted of three divisions. Under the direction of Douglas S. Byers, the Peabody Foundation at Andover did the basic administration and planning, received and disbursed funds, and handled the accounting and receipts for all aspects of the venture. Business management is an important part of any expedition or large research project. The success of such undertakings is in great part due to the skill and experience of those operating the home office. It is important that they allow simplicity and flexibility in handling expenses in the field to suit varied customs and changing situations.

The field division of the Tehuacán project was under the direction of MacNeish, who took a leave of absence from his regular position as chief archaeologist in the National Museum of Canada. In the field MacNeish functioned as instigator of specific projects and general supervisor. He was also responsible for training personnel and for maintaining liaison with the technical consultants and local scientists. During the first year of the project he worked with Frederick A. Peterson, the assistant field director. The two men surveyed the Tehuacán Valley for sites and partly excavated some before turning them over to other archaeologists. Later in the season the important Coxcatlan cave site was completely excavated by Melvin L. Fowler, who was on leave from Southern Illinois University. Other sites, including the El Riego, San Marcos, Tecorral, and Abejas caves and the Ajalpan, Coatepec, and Quacheco sites, were subsequently excavated to establish the basic stratigraphy.

MacNeish also organized the field laboratory. After it was set up, the laboratory was taken over by Antoinette Nelken, a student of the Sorbonne who was on a fellowship at Escuela de Antropología in Mexico. About 30 workmen, some of whom became excellent field technicians, were hired locally and assigned to the various excavations under the direction of the archaeologists in charge of specific sites. Along with his other duties, Peterson kept the field headquarters running smoothly, handled local accounts, and did the local purchasing.

The field headquarters in Tehuacán consisted of a large rented house with rooms for sleeping and eating, baths, laboratories, storerooms, and an office. Mrs. Peterson ran the household at the headquarters, hired the necessary domestic help, and saw to it that the scientific staff was fed. An expedition depends upon these important and often difficult functions. Field equipment

consisted of shovels, trowels, screens, paint brushes, camping chairs, tables, tents, dark-room equipment, cameras, office supplies, and much more. The expedition purchased one Jeep station wagon, and cooperating Mexican institutions furnished a Jeep pickup truck and an army-type truck. Additional equipment for the Tehuacán project was supplied on loan from the Departamento de Prehistoria of the Instituto de Antropología e Historia of Mexico. Later, such items as a Landrover station wagon, a wide-carriage typewriter, and replacements for worn-out digging tools were purchased from expedition funds. The expedition was assisted in many ways by the people of the Tehuacán region. An unusual aspect of this cooperation was the guarding of the archaeological excavations by soldiers of the local Mexican army garrison.

The third division of the Tehuacán project included the work of botanists in the field and in their home-based laboratories, as well as the work of other specialized scientists called in as consultants. C. Earle Smith made a botanical survey of the region and identified plant remains found in the excavation of the cave sites. The fossil corn from the sites was analyzed by Paul C. Mangelsdorf and W.C. Galinat of the Botanical Museum of Harvard University and by Edwin J. Wellhausen and William C. Hathaway of the Rockefeller Foundation. The remains of squashes and pumpkins were studied by Thomas W. Whitaker of the United States Horticultural Field Section at La Jolla, Calif., and by Hugh C. Cutler of the Missouri Botanical Gardens. Irmgard W. Johnson of the Instituto Nacional de Antropología e Historia studied the remains of textiles. The planners of the project hoped that fossil pollen might be secured from the excavations to serve as a guide to climatic characteristics of the times represented by the archaeological deposits. However, conditions were such that no pollen was present from any but the most recent levels of sites, and this line of approach had to be abandoned.

Expanding the Project's Scope. As the Tehuacán project expanded, the operations of each division continued as before, but with significant additions. The increased staff of the laboratory processed greater amounts and kinds of archaeological material. The survey found an average of two new archaeological sites per day. At first MacNeish's main activity was testing new sites in order to choose which ones were to be excavated intensively. This testing consisted of digging trenches 1 meter (about 39 inches) wide and from 3 to 5 meters (about 118 to 197 inches) long across the cultural deposits of the sites, most of which were in caves. The test trench went as deep as the cultural refuse and was dug to establish stratigraphy. Additional archaeologists were placed in charge of the new sites selected for excavation while those archaeologists already in charge of excavation units continued with their sites. For a period the archaeologists from the home office in Andover, Mass., joined the field operations. Douglas S. Byers joined MacNeish in the excavation of the Ajalpan site designated TS204. Frederick Johnson collected carbon samples for radiocarbon dating and instructed the archaeologists on methods of collecting and treating samples suitable for radiocarbon measurement. He also organized the expedition's system for recording the radiocarbon dating of archaeological remains.

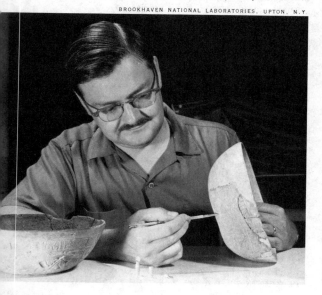

CHEMIST prepares to test a Mayan bowl to help archaeologists determine the region in which pottery was made.

BROOKHAVEN NATIONAL LABORATORIES, UPTON, N.Y.

BOTANISTS and other specialists cooperated in the Tehuacán Archaeological-Botanical Project. Archaeologists excavated open and cave sites in Mexico to find traces of ancient foods for botanical study. The trenches revealed earth layers in which artifacts and refuse could be found.

The botanists and other specialists were also busy. They studied the geology, geography, and fauna of the Tehuacán region. The scientists who were authorities on corn and squashes continued their work in the field and in the laboratory, and Lawrence Kaplan, a specialist on beans, was added to this division of the project.

The most unusual speciality added to the already brilliant spectrum of Tehuacán project specialities lay in the talents of Eric O. Callen of McDonald College of McGill University. Callen began the analysis of human fossil feces, or coprolites, found in the caves where they had been preserved by the dry climate. By chemical and physical methods, minute scraps of plant and animal material were recovered and analyzed microscopically. Not only was it possible to determine the diets of humans who died more than 7,000 years ago but also the presence of fats and starches, the probable time of year when the food was eaten, and methods of processing and cooking the food. Animal materials that had survived in the coprolites and could be identified microscopically included bones, cartilage, meat, and hair. Meat as such is recognized only by its decomposition products, but hair serves to identify sources of meat such as rabbit and deer. Small bones identify rodents, snakes, and lizards. Fragments of eggshell and turkey feathers were also identified. Vegetable material that could be identified in the sequence of coprolites covering a span of 7,500 years in the Tehuacán Valley included squash or pumpkins, corn, beans, grass seeds, peppers, prickly-pear cactus, organ cactus, agave, and starchy roots of a small silk-cotton tree.

Not all these plants were present at all periods in the span of time covered, but they serve to demonstrate the range of what could be identified by means of microcharacteristics of exceedingly minute and fragmentary materials.

Plant seeds ground into meal on a stone slab could be recognized as different from those pounded into meal in a mortar. It could also be determined that cooking of plant and animal food was done by a roasting method, although plant food also was eaten raw. In addition to the data on prehistoric food, the analysis of coprolites produced some information on human and animal parasites and on certain kinds of insects. The analysis also suggested differences between foods consumed by village dwellers of the later periods and their contemporaries living in areas away from the villages or perhaps on seasonal hunting trips.

Summary of the Tehuacán Project. The Tehuacán Archaeological-Botanical Project was in the field for more than three years. About 400 sites were selected for testing, and 13 major excavations produced 140 stratified floors and occupational zones. In the dry-cave sites the unusual conditions of preservation allowed recovery of cultural materials that gave a remarkably full picture of the mode of life of the ancient inhabitants, including how they made a living, what they ate, and the seasonal activities they pursued. More than 750,000 archaeological specimens were recovered, cataloged, and analyzed. Finally, more than 20 authors began to collaborate on a 6-volume report of the work and conclusions of the Tehuacán Archaeological-Botanical Project.

The project found evidence of a major step in man's climb toward civilization during the last 10,000 years. This evidence records the transformation of a wild highland grass into corn, the most productive of cereals, and a basic food plant not only of pre-Columbian America but also of modern America and much of the rest of the world. The work of all the scientists in this project stands as a prime example of the problem-oriented and interdisciplinary approach that characterizes modern archaeology.

5. Underwater Archaeology

By the second half of the 20th century, equipment and techniques had developed to such a point that scientific archaeology could be practiced underwater as well as on land. Underwater archaeology has the same aims and basic methods as archaeology on land; the difference is the environment in which the archaeologist works. As the necessity arose, archaeologists adapted themselves to work in high altitudes, low altitudes, deserts, dense forests, hard soils, soft soils, frozen soils, tropical climates, arctic climates, and any other kinds of environment the lands of this world had to offer. When technological advances made it possible to undertake proper archaeological researches beneath the surface of the water, archaeologists went into this new environment.

With the possible exception of certain kinds of caves, no environment is as different from normal experience as that faced by the archaeologist working underwater. He must have his own supply of air, must be protected against the cold, and must be able to see, move about, and communicate. Underwater currents, even mild ones, cause more problems than the winds on land. Because of this different environment, the archaeologist working underwater has had to employ special methods to achieve the same ends as he would expect to achieve on the land.

Much of what popularly passes for underwater archaeology is actually pot-hunting and looting of sites or at best is a kind of salvage. In general, people who dive for adventure or treasure are not archaeologists and become bored by the detailed and methodical procedures they have to follow when working under the direction of an archaeologist. Moreover, it is virtually impossible to expect an adventurer-diver to attend a university for the eight or more years it would take him to reach the doctoral level of archaeological proficiency. It is much more practical for the archaeologist to learn to dive. He can then supervise underwater excavation and direct and instruct more experienced divers in their archaeological tasks. Theoretically, a nondiving archaeologist could go underwater in a diving bell or similar apparatus and personally supervise the work of divers with whom he would be in direct communication by telephone. But by and large the archaeologists whose interests lead them to underwater sites should learn to use underwater breathing apparatus.

Recovery of a Bronze Age Cargo. High standards of underwater archaeological work have been achieved by George F. Bass, assistant curator of the Mediterranean Section of the University of Pennsylvania Museum. Bass directed the museum's underwater excavations at Cape Gelidonya and Yassi Ada in the Mediterranean Sea off the coast of Turkey. The Cape Gelidonya site was among those found in 1958–1959 by Peter Throckmorton, who was experienced in both diving and archaeology. Throckmorton's method of surveying underwater sites—shipwrecks in this instance—was somewhat parallel to the survey methods of land-based archaeologists. Instead of using farmers, herdsmen, road builders, and the like as informants about possible sites, he used sponge divers. Walking the bottom of the sea in search of sponges, these men obviously had information about what was beneath the water in the areas where they made their living.

Throckmorton spent part of a year living on a boat with a group of sponge divers. He dove with them, and questioned them about everything they had seen. He took notes and recorded the locations of ancient shipwrecks.

Although he learned of the Cape Gelidonya site at this time, it was not until the next year and by other means that he was able to reach the site. Then samples of the sunken ship's cargo were brought to the surface and were studied by experts. They reported that the wreck dated to about 1200 B.C. and belonged to the Late Bronze Age. At this point Throckmorton, on advice of the Council of Underwater Archaeology (an organization with headquarters in San Francisco), asked the University of Pennsylvania Museum for help. The result was an expedition led by archaeologist George F. Bass, who learned to dive at the YMCA. In addition to Bass, the expedition consisted of Peter Throckmorton as technical adviser, nine divers, and an archaeologist in charge of conserving and recording finds.

The expedition camp was situated on a narrow beach a few miles from the site. Each day the personnel were taken to the wreck in local sponge boats. Once there, each of the eight divers was able to work little more than one hour per day on the site, which lay 90 to 95 feet (27 to 29 meters) below the surface of the water. The site consisted of the remains of a wooden ship and its cargo, encased in a rocklike concretion with occasional protrusions of metal objects. The first step was a mapping of the concreted mass. This was done by a number of photographic montages. Positions of visible artifacts were plotted on sheets of frosted plastic. Then massive sections of the concretion-covered cargo were cut by divers, using hammers and chisels. These sections were hoisted by winch and cable to the sponge boat that was used as expedition tender. Then they were taken ashore and reassembled to reproduce the original mass. The positions of the sections could be determined from the photographic montages and from the location of visible artifacts plotted under water.

After the concreted sections had been reassembled on the beach at the expedition camp and had again been photographed, the actual excavation had begun. In effect, the site had been transferred from beneath the water to the land. The concretion was removed from the cargo portion of the site by means of assorted hammers and chisels and an electric vibrating point. The exposed artifacts and other cultural objects were mapped and photographed in place and in exactly the same relationship to one another as when the ship rested on the bottom of the sea. Concreted parts of the ship in which wood was still preserved had been gently raised by means of air-filled plastic balloons. Although very little of the ship remained, the wooden parts thus recovered provided information on the method of ship construction—the first such information for a ship of the Bronze Age.

The results of the Cape Gelidonya expedition were of great importance not only for the new information on ship construction but also for the chance to examine the cargo of copper ingots and bronze scrap that had been packed in wicker baskets. This cargo provided new data on Bronze Age sea trade and the nations participating in it. From the standpoint of underwater archaeology this was the "first methodical excavation carried to completion."

UNDERWATER ARCHAEOLOGY now uses the same precise techniques as archaeology on the land, even though work in the water has to be done in diving gear. Photos on this page were taken during the recovery of a ship that had been on the bottom of the Mediterranean since the 7th century. The wreck, with its cargo of 900 wine jars, was 120 feet below the surface. The ship was cleared of sand and weeds, photographed and mapped, and then raised to the surface, as described in the text on page 202.

(*Right*) Divers mapped the wreck using gridded plastic sheets. The wire grid laid over the cargo served as a guide.

(*Below*) Fragile timbers from the ship's hull were carried in wire baskets up the sloping sea bottom to the beach.

UNIVERSITY OF PENNSLYVANIA MUSEUM—NATIONAL GEOGRAPHIC SOCIETY EXPEDITION

UNIVERSITY OF PENNSLYVANIA MUSEUM—
NATIONAL GEOGRAPHIC SOCIETY EXPEDITION

UNIVERSITY OF PENNSLYVANIA MUSEUM—
NATIONAL GEOGRAPHIC SOCIETY EXPEDITION

(*Above*) One of the first jobs for the archaeologists-divers was to clear sand from the wreck. The large object is an iron anchor, with a wine jar from the cargo resting on it.

PETER THROCKMORTON, FROM NANCY PALMER

After the wreck had been mapped, wine jars and other objects were taken up to the surface to be examined, photographed, and stored.

Recovery of a Byzantine Ship. In 1961 and 1962 the University of Pennsylvania Museum, assisted by the National Geographic Society, undertook excavation of another wreck site charted by Peter Throckmorton on his underwater survey. At Yassi Ada, under the direction of George Bass, archaeology beneath the water achieved standards equal to those of the best archaeological work above water. The site was the wreck of a Byzantine ship which sank with its cargo in the 7th century A.D. It lay 120 feet (36.6 meters) beneath the surface of the Mediterranean off the coast of Turkey. Expedition headquarters were maintained on shore at Bodrum, 16 miles (25.7 kilometers) from the site, and on a flat barge securely anchored just above the wreck. The expedition staff of 15 experts included a classicist, an art historian, architects, draftsmen, photographers, a geologist, a medical doctor, and a mechanic. Though many of the staff members had no diving experience before they began this operation, the personnel of the expedition completed nearly 6,000 working dives in depths ranging between 100 and 150 feet (30.5 and 45.7 meters). This expedition is significant in the history of archaeology because, for the first time, a ship was excavated completely *in situ* on the bottom of the sea. Moreover, the whole project was done according to standards as exacting as those used on land.

First, the diving archaeologists cleaned the seaweed from the wreck with wire scrubbing brushes so that the site could be mapped and photographed. Then every visible object and significant point was labeled with a numbered plastic tag facing upward and held in position by a stiff wire pin so that tags could be identified in photographs. Next the mapping began. At first, specially constructed plane tables were used, and directions and elevations were recorded on sheets of frosted plastic pinned to the table tops. This method, however, required three divers and at times was hampered by poor visibility due to muddied water. Next a mapping frame was substituted for the plane tables. It consisted of a square of pipes, 5 meters (191.8 inches) on each side, which could be leveled to an absolute horizontal by means of adjustable legs. Right angles from two sides of the square were obtained by a sliding horizontal beam to which was attached an adjustable vertical pole. Both beam and pole were calibrated in centimeters. When the bottom of the vertical pole was placed on any object, the elevation of that object and its coordinates in the square were obtained. But finally an even faster and easier system of measuring was devised, a variation of one that is frequently used on land. A system of grids two and three meters (78.7 and 118.1 inches) square was constructed of metal frames and crisscrossing wires. These grids were laid over sections of the wreck, and the sections were drawn to scale by divers using gridded sheets of plastic and special pencils. Horizontal measurements were taken from the small wired squares within the grid, and then elevations were taken at the four corners of the grid frame either by plane table or by means of the large mapping frame, whichever was easier to use at the time.

After the objects had been photographed, mapped, and listed in place, they were removed by the divers, who began with the upper layer of cargo. The ship held 900 amphoras (large earthenware jars). About 100 were taken to the surface, while the others were stored underwater until needed for study or exhibition. A number of the amphoras were raised to the surface by being filled with air so that they rose slowly like balloons and were retrieved by expedition members on the barge.

The divers either used aqualungs or obtained their air supply from "hookah" hoses—so called because they resembled the tubes of Turkish water pipes. Hoses were hitched to air compressors on the barge. Each pair of divers had to decompress for 21 minutes at the end of their dives so that they would not get the bends, a paralyzing or killing condition that would result if they came to the surface too quickly. In order that this necessary decompression time not be wasted, short air hoses were run to the underwater decompression levels or stations beneath the barge. There the ascending divers transferred from their long hookahs to the shorter hoses, and the long hookahs were taken up to be used by descending divers. The divers waiting out their decompression time wrote reports of what they had accomplished on the dig. These reports were written with the aid of suitable clipboards and pencils hung by cords from the barge floating above. When the diver wished to send a written message to the barge, he pulled a string attached to a camel bell on the barge. The clipboard was then pulled up to the barge.

When the excavators had removed one level of cargo, there often remained a bare layer of sand above the next layer of cultural materials. To remove this sand and search for artifacts in it, a device called an airlift was used. The airlift is a kind of large vacuum cleaner with a suction hose made of metal, reinforced rubber, or plastic. Air from a compressor on the surface is pumped into the suction hose near its bottom. As the air rises to the surface it creates suction at the bottom of the tube, and this powerful suction pulls sand, mud, and cultural objects small enough to enter the tube to the surface.

The airlift used in the Bass operation had a tube about 6 inches (15.2 centimeters) in diameter that was securely anchored in place at the site and was held upright by a float. At its top end there was a large wire basket that funneled down into a large cloth bag. When the sand, mud, and cultural materials reached the wire basket, the currents carried away the sand and mud, but the cultural materials and fragments of shell and small stones passed into the cloth bag. When the bag was full, it was hauled to the barge by a rope; then the contents of the bag were handled as if on a land dig. Considerable skill is required in excavating properly with an airlift. Bass found that the best method was to keep the suction end of the tube a few inches away from the sea bottom and gently to sweep the sand and mud toward the tube with the hand. This much care is not necessary when using the airlift to excavate and remove sterile deposits or to cut a trench around a site.

As each layer of cargo and other cultural material was excavated from each section of the Byzantine wreck, these layers were not only mapped and drawn in place but also photographed as well. Underwater cameras were used to take photographs from fixed positions just above the part of the site that was to be recorded photographically. The fixed camera positions were at the tops of metal towers 4 meters (157.5 inches) high, which fitted on top of a rectangular scaffolding of angle iron constructed in 6-meter (236.2-inch) steps over the whole site. The steps were necessary because the wreck lay on a sloping sea bottom. The pipe legs supporting these steps were adjustable, allowing the archaeologists to keep them at fixed distances above the excavations and to keep them level with the aid of a spirit level. The underwater cameras fitted into a slot at the top of each photographic tower, thus assuring precise control of the underwater pictures.

Eventually the excavations reached the remains of the ship's timbers. By this time every scrap of material, cultural or noncultural, had been mapped and photographed in place, removed to the surface, cleaned, cataloged, described, and conserved. The architect incorporated the grid maps into a master plan containing every exposed portion of the site, both horizontally and vertically, with each individual find accurately plotted in its original position.

In excavating the remains of the ship's hull, the divers faced an unexpected situation. When uncovered, the wooden fragments drifted away with the current or were displaced by the slightest motion of the divers. To correct this situation Bass obtained about two thousand bicycle spokes and ground one end of each to a sharp point. The steel pins thus produced were pushed through pieces of wood, thereby holding the entire wreck together and to the bottom of the sea until it could be completely uncovered, examined, measured, photographed, and mapped. There was an accurate record of every surviving scrap of wood and every nail hole, bolt hole, score-line, mortise, and angle, as well as of the relationship of parts. The wood from the ship was raised gently by free divers who placed it in a special wire basket 18 feet (5.5 meters) long and walked it upslope to the shore of a nearby island. The raised wood was kept in tubs of water so that it would not shrink or disintegrate, as it would if allowed to dry without chemical treatment. One widely used treatment employs polyethylene glycol, which can be dissolved in water, soaks into wood cells, and replaces missing cell matter with a hard plasticlike substance as the water dries out.

The 7th century Byzantine ship excavated at Yassi Ada was a merchant vessel 70 feet (18.3 meters) long. The lower part of the hull was constructed in the routine Graeco-Roman manner with planks joined at their edges with tenons and ribs added later, but the upper part of the hull was built in the modern fashion with strakes or planks placed on a skeleton work of frames. The cabin was located toward the stern of the vessel. Inside the cabin on the left side was a hearth of flat tiles resting on a bed of clay supported by iron bars. The cabin itself seems to have had a roof covered by tiles. Inside the cabin were found the personal possessions of the captain and the crew. Just behind the cabin was the ship's large water jar. Among the furnishings of the ship were pottery, cooking utensils, and oil lamps. There were also steelyards for weighing the cargo and metal tools for cutting firewood and repairing the vessel. The ship carried 11 large iron anchors. The cargo carried by the vessel consisted of 900 amphoras, or large ceramic vessels, which originally contained wine and weighed about 100 pounds each when full. At some time in the 7th century this ship, while engaged in trade on the Mediterranean Sea, was wrecked off the coast of Turkey. There it lay unknown until the mid-20th century.

A brief summary cannot describe all the techniques of underwater archaeology. However, this study should show that undersea investigations can follow the exacting scientific standards that characterize the work of modern archaeologists in any environment.

6. The Profession of Archaeology

History. It is perhaps not a coincidence that the development of archaeology under the water has been similar to the development of archaeology on land. Their ancestral stages were neither scientific nor particularly scholarly. Early archaeology was characterized by the methods of adventurers, treasure hunters, and looters. On land, of course, this ancestral stage occurred several hundred years earlier than it did under the water. Archaeology can be said to have had its beginnings in the Renaissance when there was a rediscovery of the classic art of ancient Greece and Rome. When the word "archaeology" came into use in the 17th century, it meant merely the study of the classic art of antiquity. The objects studied were regarded as treasures and were gathered from the surface of the ground or dug from ancient sites by unskilled people. The objects thus obtained were sold to kings, noblemen, and rich churchmen, and col-

PROFESSIONALS in archaeology must be willing to do hard work and should not expect to find it in exotic places. Field projects may involve such tasks as clearing sand from a cave.

ON-THE-JOB TRAINING, in this case digging a test trench, helps students prepare for careers in archaeology.

lections of such objects became part of the treasures gained in war between nations and principalities. Scholars who studied the art treasures were interested only in the objects themselves. There was no real scholarly or scientific interest in the archaeological site as a document or record of the past. The approach to and methods of excavation of ancient sites were those of the treasure hunter and the looter.

Even men like Johann Joachim Winckelmann and Heinrich Schliemann, who appear in popular works as the "fathers of archaeology," did little more than systematize treasure hunting and the looting of sites. If "fathers of archaeology" must be named, more suitable candidates would be persons like the Danish scholar C.J. Thomsen, who as early as 1832 strictly employed the concept of stratigraphy in his excavations.

In any case, archaeology as it is known today had its significant beginnings between about 1880 and 1920 and underwent rapid development from 1920 to 1960. It would be difficult to give credit to the individuals who played significant roles in the history of scientific archaeology. There were many, and their backgrounds lay in such diverse fields as fine arts, epigraphy, classical studies, art history, ancient history, the natural sciences, the humanities, Oriental languages, anthropology, the social sciences, and the physical sciences. They had in common a sense of scholarship, the concept of the archaeological site as a document that was destroyed as it was excavated, and the idea that archaeology was a scholarly and scientific discipline.

Amateur Archaeologists. Unfortunately, the term "archaeologist" is still in popular use for anyone who digs up artifacts or recovers artifacts from beneath the water. Though such persons are frequently without training and knowledge, they claim to be amateur archaeologists. The term is a misnomer when applied to a treasure hunter. If "amateur" is used in its proper sense, the only difference between an amateur archaeologist and a professional archaeologist is that the latter is paid for his work. The true amateur, like the professional, meets exacting standards in excavation, recovery, preservation, and recording. Usually a professional is more broadly

trained, has a Ph.D. or equivalent, and covers a much wider area of interest and knowledge than the amateur.

The real strength of the amateur archaeologist lies in his or her knowledge of a particular local region. Frequently an amateur archaeologist knows more than anyone else about a small geographic area or a local expression of a particular period of the past. Some amateurs have collections of local artifacts that are as well cataloged as museum collections. When the professional archaeologist wants information on such subjects, he turns to the amateur for help. Moreover, when working in a region where there are amateur archaeologists, the professional will obtain information from them and enlist their aid in his excavations. In the United States the greatest contributions of the amateur archaeologists have come from those who wisely have refrained from excavation and have concentrated their efforts on the systematic recording of sites and surface collections.

In some parts of the world there are state and national archaeological societies to which both amateur and professional archaeologists belong. In such instances, there may be opportunities for amateurs to work alongside professional archaeologists and to obtain good field training. Many professional archaeologists, however, are doubtful about the value of men and women who claim to be amateur archaeologists and wish to be trained in excavation techniques. In some cases the person will turn out to be not an amateur at all but merely a collector of relics who wants to increase his proficiency in pothunting and looting. Such persons are not easily trained out of their habit of digging up or purchasing relics just for the pleasure of owning them, and an archaeologist often wastes his time if he attempts to train them.

A real amateur archaeologist may have trained himself by selective reading and association with professional archaeologists, but what really defines his position is his attitude towards excavation and artifacts. The amateur archaeologist keeps good records and has enough knowledge of surveying and stratigraphy to make good site maps and profiles if he excavates. Often he merely tests a site and then brings it to the attention of a professional archaeologist or an institution. Moreover, the amateur archaeologist writes reports, and these reports have to meet the standards of state or national archaeological societies that publish scholarly journals. In the long run, a real amateur archaeologist has to be good at his unpaid work and must get other satisfactions than money for what he is doing. No one who fails to meet these standards should be called an amateur archaeologist.

Careers in Archaeology. Just as archaeology as a hobby is personally satisfying to the amateur, so archaeology as a career is satisfying to the professional. This satisfaction is important because salaries of professionals are relatively low and opportunities for employment are relatively few. Moreover, archaeology is a field that requires a long period of training and a doctoral degree. The archaeologist spends as much time and money on his training as do those in professions such as law and medicine where the financial rewards can be much greater. Obviously it cannot be money that lures the archaeologist into his discipline. It is more likely to be the vision of intellectual adventure that is the drive of those engaged in pure science and other scholarly pursuits of which the practical application is left to others.

There are not a great many positions available for professional archaeologists. For most, the choice is between a museum, a college or university, and some division of federal or local government. The largest number of positions for archaeologists are in universities and colleges, where the research activities are combined with teaching duties. Depending upon his training and interests, a college or university archaeologist might be in a department of anthropology, fine arts, ancient history, Oriental languages, Far Eastern studies, classical studies, or some other area.

The next largest number of archaeological positions is found in museums, where archaeologists serve as curators. Again there is a division of work according to kinds of talents and interests. In anthropological museums or natural science museums with anthropology departments, there are usually curators with regional interests. For example, a large museum of this kind might have a curator of Far Eastern archaeology, one for Middle Eastern archaeology, a curator of Oceanian archaeology, a curator of Old World prehistory, and curators of North and South American archaeology. A big art museum might have a curator of Chinese archaeology, one for Egyptian archaeology, curators of Greek and Roman archaeology, and so on. A state museum might have a curator for the archaeology of that particular state. In addition to doing research, the museum-based archaeologist is responsible for the acquisition, maintenance, and preservation of collections and the planning of exhibits.

There are also archaeological positions in state and national governments. In the United States, for example, archaeologists are employed by the National Park Service and the agencies concerned with the construction of dams and reservoirs. In some states there are state archaeologists.

Salvage archaeology has also provided opportunities for trained archaeologists. Varying combinations of state, federal, and private funds have been used for emergency exploration and

CENTRAL PRESS, FROM PICTORIAL PARADE

ACCIDENTAL DISCOVERY by a ploughman led museum experts to this Bronze Age grave in Perth, Scotland.

excavation along the routes of new highways and pipelines. The River Basin Surveys program of the Smithsonian Institution has done emergency archaeological work in the areas flooded by the construction of new dams in various parts of the United States. A notable example of salvage archaeology was the removal of monuments that were about to be covered as a result of the construction of the Aswan High Dam on the Nile.

Preparation for a Career in Archaeology. Assuming that a young man wishes to become a professional archaeologist, how does he go about it? First of all, he should get rid of romantic notions of adventure in faraway places. Not all archaeologists work in exotic lands, and those who do soon find that the novelty is lost.

Next, the candidate must get a suitable education. The education of an archaeologist consists of the usual four-year college program leading to the bachelor's degree and three or more years of university graduate training leading to the doctoral degree, usually a Ph.D. In the four-year college program—and even in high school—the broadest possible education is the best foundation for graduate studies in archaeology. High

AMATEURS may work with professional archaeologists on such tasks as sorting and marking finds from a "dig."

THE TIMES, LONDON, FROM PICTORIAL PARADE

school and undergraduate courses should include human history, natural sciences, foreign languages, and English. An archaeologist must be able to write clearly and to read some of the major languages in which research is published, such as French, German, English, and Russian. In the United States two languages, such as French and German, are usually required for the doctorate. However, if an archaeologist plans to work in Mexico, he should also learn Spanish; to work in the Middle East, he should also learn Arabic, Turkish, or Persian.

With his broad, general education behind him, the prospective archaeologist must decide whether he chooses the fine arts-classical-humanities tradition of archaeology or the natural science-social science tradition. If he chooses the latter tradition, he will probably study in a department of anthropology where he will be concerned with the biological and cultural history of mankind in all parts of the world both past and present. In effect he will become a paleo-ethnologist. His interests may run from the most primitive systems of culture to fully developed civilizations. He will acquire enough knowledge of the natural and physical sciences to know what aspects of these will be of benefit to his archaeological studies. When he has completed his doctorate (or its equivalent), this type of archaeologist will be an anthropologist who specializes in archaeology. A *Guide to Graduate Departments of Anthropology in the United States, Canada, and Mexico* is published by the American Anthropological Association.

If the prospective archaeologist chooses the fine arts-classical-humanities tradition of archaeology, he will pick a graduate school where he may study in detail the extensive body of antiquities and monuments characteristic of the cultures of ancient Greece, Rome, Egypt, Mesopotamia, Hittite Anatolia, Persia, and the eastern Mediterranean Bible lands. He will learn the ancient languages so that he may read the written records of these old civilizations. He will study the history of the area of his interest and will learn the systems of artistic and historical criticism that best apply. He will also learn all the varieties of artifacts, art forms, buildings, monuments, and so on that relate to his field. In general, his interests and activities will be more concentrated and specialized and will be limited to civilized or near civilized cultures. Whatever field the prospective archaeologist studies, he must undergo a long period of university training and he must end up a scholar.

GEORGE I. QUIMBY
Burke Museum, University of Washington

For articles on major fields related to archaeology, see ANTHROPOLOGY; ARCHITECTURE; and ART. For special topics in or closely related to archaeology, see CIVILIZATION; MAN, PRE-HISTORIC TYPES OF; STONE AGE; CHRONOLOGY; RADIOCARBON DATING; ALPHABET; CUNEIFORM WRITING; HIEROGLYPHICS, EGYPTIAN; HIEROGLYPHICS, HITTITE AND CRETAN; HIEROGLYPHICS, PRE-COLUMBIAN AMERICAN; MEGALITHIC MONUMENTS; MOUND BUILDERS; PALEOLITHIC ART.

Asian and African Archaeology. See AEGEAN CIVILIZATION; AFRICA—11. *History;* ASSYRIOLOGY; BIBLE—6. *Old Testament History Including Archaeology and Chronology,* 14. *New Testament History Including Chronology and Archaeology;* INDIA—2. *The People,* 16. *Prehistory;* JAPAN—3. *The People,* 13. *Religion,* 17. *Architecture,* 20. *History;* ORIENTAL ARCHAEOLOGY.

European Archaeology. See FRANCE—25. *Prehistory;* GERMANY—16. *Art and Architecture;* GREAT BRITAIN AND NORTHERN IRELAND—20. *Archaeology,* 21. *History;* GREECE—2. *Ancient History;* ITALY—3. *Archaeology and Prehistory.*

The Americas. See INCA; INCA CIVILIZATION; INDIANS, AMERICAN; LATIN AMERICA—11. *Archaeology,* 12. *Pre-Columbian Art and Architecture;* MEXICO—16. *Pre-Hispanic Art,* 18. *Architecture,* 24. *Prehistory and Pre-Hispanic History;* PERUVIAN ARCHAEOLOGY; PUEBLO INDIANS.

Archaeological Sites. See ABU SIMBEL; CARNAC; CHICHEN ITZA; EASTER ISLAND; EPHESUS; LACHISH; MACHU PICCHU; NINEVEH; SUTTON HOO SHIP BURIAL; TELL EL AMARNA; TIRYNS; UR; WILLIAMSBURG; ZIMBABWE.

7. Archaeology Bibliography

Atkinson, Richard J.C., *Field Archaeology,* 2d ed. (London 1953).
Bass, George F., *Archaeology Under Water* (New York 1966).
Braidwood, Robert J., *Archaeologists and What They Do* (New York 1960).
Childe, V. Gordon, *A Short Introduction to Archaeology* (London 1956).
Clark, Grahame, *Archaeology and Society* (London 1947).
Heizer, Robert F., *A Guide to Archaeological Field Methods,* 3d rev. ed. (Palo Alto, Calif., 1966).
Kenyon, Kathleen M., *Beginning in Archaeology* (London 1952).
Meighan, Clement W., *Archaeology, an Introduction* (San Francisco 1966).
Meighan, Clement W., *The Archaeologist's Note Book* (San Francisco 1961).
Petrie, William M. Flinders, *Methods and Aims in Archaeology* (London 1904).
Piggott, Stuart, *Approach to Archaeology* (Cambridge, Mass., 1959).
Wheeler, R.E. Mortimer, *Archaeology from the Earth* (New York 1954).

For Specialized Study

Binford, Lewis R., "Archaeology as Anthropology," *American Antiquity,* vol. 28, no. 2. pp. 217–225 (Salt Lake City 1962).
Byers, Douglas S., "An Introduction to the Tehuacán Archaeological-Botanical Project," *XXXV Congreso Internacional de Americanistas, Actas y Memorias,* pp. 147–152 (Mexico City 1964).
Callen, Eric O., "Food Habits of Some Pre-Columbian Mexican Indians," *Economic Botany,* vol. 19, no. 4, pp. 335–343 (New York 1965).
Ford, J.A., and Steward, J.H., "On the Concept of Types," *American Anthropologist,* vol. 56, no. 1, pp. 42–57 (Menasha, Wis., 1954).
Gjessing, Gutorm, "Socio-Archaeology," *Folk,* vol. 5, pp. 103–111 (Copenhagen, Denmark, 1963).
MacNeish, Richard Stockton, "Ancient Mesoamerican Civilization," *Science,* vol. 143, no. 3606, pp. 531–537 (Washington 1964).
MacNeish, Richard Stockton, *First Annual Report of the Tehuacán Archaeological-Botanical Project* and *Second Annual Report of the Tehuacán Archaeological-Botanical Project,* Robert S. Peabody Foundation for Archaeology (Andover, Mass., 1961–62).
Mangelsdorf, Paul C., MacNeish, Richard S., and Galinat, Walton C., "Domestication of Corn," *Science,* vol. 143, no. 3606, pp. 538–545 (Washington 1964).
Martin, Paul S., *The S U Site. Excavations at a Mogollon Village, Western New Mexico,* 1941, Field Museum of Natural History, Anthropological Series, vol. 32, no. 2 (Chicago 1943).
Martin, Paul S., Rinaldo, John B., and Antevs, Ernst, "Cochise and Mogollon Sites, Pine Lawn Valley, Western New Mexico," *Fieldiana: Anthropology,* vol. 38, no. 1 (Chicago 1949).
Rainey, Froelich, "New Techniques in Archaeology," *Archaeology: Horizons New and Old,* Proceedings of the American Philosophical Society, vol. 110, no. 2, pp. 146–152 (Philadelphia 1966).
Rowe, John Howland, *Archaeology as a Career* (New York 1954).
Professional Journals: Antiquity Publications Limited, *Antiquity* (Cambridge, Eng., quarterly); Archaeological Institute of America, *American Journal of Archaeology* (Princeton, N.J., quarterly); Archaeological Institute of America, *Archaeology* (New York, quarterly); Society for American Archaeology, *American Antiquity* (Salt Lake City, quarterly).

GLOSSARY OF ARCHAEOLOGICAL TERMS

Abbevillian.—An early Paleolithic culture characterized by bifacial hand axes of stone. The culture is named for Abbeville, a town in northern France, where such stone tools were first found.

Acheulian.—An early Paleolithic culture characterized by hand axes and other bifacial stone tools with multiple cutting edges; named for St.-Acheul, a town in northern France, where such artifacts were first found.

Artifact.—Any tool, article, device, or ornament made by human beings. The term embraces anything from a needle to a pyramid made by man.

Assemblage.—A collection of artifacts from a single location or period, especially one that characterizes a certain culture or era.

Aurignacian.—A series of late Paleolithic cultures in central France, characterized by refinement of stone tools and the development of sculpture and cave painting; named for Aurignac, where such artifacts were discovered.

Azilian.—A Mesolithic culture characterized by flint microliths and antler harpoons. The Azilians were food gatherers and had domesticated the dog. The culture is named for Mas d'Azil, a region in southern France, where such artifacts were first discovered.

Barrow.—An artificial mound of earth or stones over a burial mound. In the United States, a burial mound.

Biblical Archaeology.—The branch of archaeology devoted to the discovery of places and artifacts of interest in the study of Biblical times and documents.

Blade Tool.—A narrow stone tool made by striking a prepared core and often shaped into a two-edged knife or into a burin or spokeshave. The Châtelperronian was the earliest of the known blade cultures.

Broch.—A prehistoric circular stone dwelling peculiar to northern Scotland, built of dry masonry with inner and outer walls.

Bronze Age.—An age that followed the Neolithic period, characterized by the production of bronze tools, weapons, and other artifacts. During this time civilization based on agriculture and urban life developed (see *Urban Revolution*). The Bronze Age began about 3500–3000 B.C. in the Middle East and about 2000–1500 B.C. in Europe. It was followed by the Iron Age, which began about 1500 B.C. in the Middle East and 900 B.C. in Europe.

Capsian.—A culture of the Stone Age in northern Africa, characterized by small stone tools and bone implements. The name derives from Capsa, the Latin form of Gafsa, a town in south central Tunisia where such artifacts were first discovered.

Carbon-14 Dating.—See *Radiocarbon Dating*.

Cenozoic.—The most recent geological era in the earth's history, in which mammals came to dominate animal life. It includes the Tertiary and Quaternary periods and began about 70 million years ago.

Chalcolithic.—A brief age largely preceding the Bronze Age, in which both stone and copper tools were used.

Châtelperronian.—An upper Paleolithic culture in central France, characterized by the two-edged knife, with one edge very sharp and the other curved and blunted. It is the earliest known blade culture.

Chellean.—The former name of the *Abbevillian*.

Choukoutienian.—An upper Paleolithic culture in northern China, characterized by core and flake tools of quartz and sandstone; named for Choukoutien, a town near Peking, where such artifacts and remains of *Sinanthropus* man were first discovered in caves.

Cire Perdue.—A process of casting figurines or statues developed during the Bronze Age. Molten bronze was poured into a wax mold coated with clay; the wax was melted by the heat and ran out, and the clay was then chipped away, leaving a seamless sculpture. The term in French means "lost wax."

Clactonian.—A lower Paleolithic culture coextensive with the Abbevillian and early Acheulian, characterized by coarse flake tools shaped by striking on an anvil; named for Clacton-on-Sea, a town on the east coast of England, where such artifacts were first discovered.

Clovis.—A Paleo-Indian culture in North America characterized by fluted stone projectile points, believed to be the oldest of their type; named for Clovis, N. Mex., where such artifacts were first found.

Cochise.—A Paleo-Indian culture of the southwest United States and northern Mexico, characterized by tools made by percussion flaking and by the use of milling stones, indicative of a food-gathering economy; named for Cochise, Ariz.

Colonial Archaeology.—The branch of archaeology dealing with the colonial period in American history, from the discovery of America to the establishment of the United States.

Complex.—A group of artifacts that serve to characterize a particular culture.

Core Tool.—A stone tool, such as a hand ax or cleaver, formed by chipping away pieces from a large nodule of flint or other stone material. Such tools were characteristic of Paleolithic culture.

Cromlech.—A circle of upright stones of prehistoric times. See also *Dolmen*.

Culture.—The learned behavior, social customs, ideas, and technology characteristic of a certain people or civilization at a particular time or over a period of time. In a more restricted sense (as in the term *blade culture*) culture signifies the artifacts or tool- and implement-making tradition of a people or a stage of development.

Culture Area.—A geographical region in which a cultural pattern distinct from the patterns of neighboring regions is predominant.

Culture Center.—The center of a culture area, so designated because it best represents the essential qualities of the culture.

Culture Change.—Any significant modification in the essential structure and elements of a culture over a period of time.

Culture Complex.—An integrated group of cultural traits functioning as a distinct system within a culture area.

Culture Sequence.—The order in which cultures or assemblages from different cultures follow one another. In successive levels of a stratified site, the oldest is usually at the lowest level.

Cuneiform.—An ancient system of writing using wedge-shaped characters inscribed on clay tablets, developed by the Sumerians, Babylonians, and Assyrians.

Dendrochronology.—A system of dating based on the study of annual rings formed on the trunks of trees, used especially in the southwestern United States.

Dig.—An archaeological excavation.

Dolmen.—A monument consisting of a flat stone laid across several upright stones, believed to be a type of tomb in Neolithic times.

Eocene.—A geological epoch in the earth's history, the second in the Tertiary period, in which the earliest forms of many modern mammals appeared and developed. The Eocene occurred after the Paleocene and before the Oligocene.

Eolithic.—A term used by some archaeologists for the earliest stage of human culture before the Paleolithic, characterized by very primitive stone tools, especially of flint. Such a stone tool is called an *eolith*, which means "dawn stone."

Epipaleolithic.—A term synonymous with *Mesolithic*.

Findspot.—A spot in an excavation where an artifact or other object of interest is found.

Flake Tool.—A stone tool, such as a burin or scraper, made by shaping a chip of flint or other stone. Chips detached from a nodule in preparing a core tool were often used for flake tools.

Flaking.—The removal of flakes from nodules of flint or other stone for making flake tools, done by pressure from another tool or by percussion.

Folsom.—A Stone Age culture of the western United States, characterized by refinement of fluted projectile points, marking a significant advance over the projectile joints of the earlier Clovis culture, named for Folsom, New Mexico, where such artifacts were first found.

Food-Producing Revolution.—A term applied by archaeologists and anthropologists to the development of farming and animal husbandry and the beginning of settled village life. The revolution occurred during the Neolithic. Associated with this change were great improvements in making stone implements.

Fossil.—The remains, impression, mineral replacement, or any trace of an animal or plant preserved in sedimentary rock or in the earth.

Gravettian.—An upper Paleolithic culture characterized by well-developed blade tools of flint and female figurines of ivory; named for La Gravette, a site in southwest France, where such artifacts were first discovered.

Hieroglyphics.—A system of writing using highly stylized pictures, symbols, and characters, essentially an advanced form of pictography. The best-known form is that developed by the Egyptians.

Historic Archaeology.—The branch of archaeology that deals with objects and events since the beginnings of recorded history.

Holocene.—See *Recent*.

Ice Age.—See *Pleistocene*.

Ideogram.—A picture used to represent an idea without signifying a spoken sound. Ideograms were the next stage in the development of writing after pictographs.

Industry.—A term denoting all the tools and artifacts made of a certain material or by a certain technique and found together; also, the technique itself. Examples: *flint industry, flake industry*.

Iron Age.—The period following the Bronze Age, when tools, implements, and weapons were first made of iron. It began at different times after 1500 B.C. in different parts of the world, according to the availability of iron ore and the state of knowledge. The age began about 1500 B.C. in the Middle East, about 900 B.C. in southern Europe, and about 400 B.C. and later in northern Europe.

Kitchen Midden.—See *Midden*.

Levalloisian.—A middle Paleolithic culture or industry characterized by the introduction and refinement of flake tools; named for Levallois-Perret, a town near Paris, where such artifacts were first discovered.

Lost Wax.—See *Cire Perdue*.

Magdalenian.—A late Paleolithic culture of western Europe. The people who produced this culture were chiefly fishermen and reindeer hunters. Its implements typically were stone burins and antler harpoons and lance heads, and its art centered chiefly about cave painting. It is named for La Madeleine, a site in southwestern France, where such artifacts were first discovered.

Maglemosian.—A Mesolithic culture of northern European people who inhabited bogs and fens and other low-lying places. The chief artifacts include flint microliths made by the core and flake techniques, bone fishhooks, and implements of antler. It is named for Maglemose, a site on Zealand island in Denmark, where such artifacts were first discovered.

Megalith.—Any of various prehistoric monuments built of very large blocks of stone, such as Stonehenge in England and Carnac in Brittany. Megalithic monuments are characteristic of the late Neolithic culture of western Europe.

Mesolithic.—The technical name for the Middle Stone Age, between the Paleolithic and Neolithic, characterized by the beginning of food production and the making of microliths. This age represents a transition and is not readily dated. It ended as early as 9000 B.C. in the Middle East and much later elsewhere.

Mesozoic.—A geological era in the earth's history before the Cenozoic, marked by the development of mammals, birds, reptiles, and flowering plants and the extinction of the dinosaur. It began about 200 million years ago.

Microlith.—Any of various very small flint tools made by flaking and carefully shaped, characteristic of Azilian culture of the Mesolithic.

Midden.—A mound of discarded bones, shells, and other refuse at a prehistoric habitation, a valuable source of archaeological data; also called *kitchen midden*.

Middle Stone Age.—See *Mesolithic*.

Miocene.—A geological epoch of the Tertiary period in the earth's history, in which many of the great mountain chains were formed and mammals came to dominate animal life. The Miocene occurred after the Oligocene and before the Pliocene.

Monolith.—A single block of stone in the form of a monument or sculpture, such as an obelisk or menhir. It usually is large and dates from prehistoric times.

Mousterian.—The flake technique of making flint stone tools and weapons; the technique is associated with Neanderthal man of the Middle Paleolithic; the name derives from Le Moustier, a cave near Les Eyzies, a village in northwest France, where such artifacts were first discovered.

Neolithic.—The technical name for the New Stone Age in the Old World following the Mesolithic. The Neolithic was characterized by the making of polished stone tools and weapons, the introduction of farming and livestock raising, and the establishment of villages. The Neolithic began about 8000–7000 B.C. in the Middle East and about 4000–3000 B.C. in Europe. It was followed by the Bronze Age, which began about 3500–3000 B.C. in the Middle East and about 2000–1500 B.C. in Europe.

New Stone Age.—See *Neolithic*.

Old Stone Age.—See *Paleolithic*.

Oligocene.—A geological epoch of the Tertiary period in the earth's history, after the Eocene and before the Miocene, in which many large mountain systems and herbivorous mammals began to develop.

Paleocene.—The earliest geological epoch of the Tertiary period in the earth's history.

Paleolithic.—The technical name for the Old Stone Age, which began in the Pliocene epoch. The age was characterized by the making of chipped or flaked stone tools and weapons and by a hunting and food-gathering way of life. It is usually divided into Lower, Middle, and Upper (or Late) Paleolithic. The Paleolithic began with the appearance of the earliest toolmakers and extended to about 10,000–8000 B.C. in some parts of the Old World.

Paleozoic.—A geological era in the earth's history before the Mesozoic, marked by the development of fishes, land plants, insects, and fernlike trees. It began about 500 million years ago.

Petroglyph.—A picture or writing carved into a rock, especially in prehistoric times.

Pictograph.—A picture used to represent a thing, action, or event. Pictographs were the earliest form of writing. Picture writing is called *pictography*.

Pleistocene.—A geologic epoch of the Quaternary period, during which large areas of the northern hemisphere were covered with ice. It ended about 10,000 years ago. Most present-day mammals appeared during the Pleistocene. It is also called the *ice age*.

Pliocene.—The latest geological epoch of the Tertiary period in the earth's history, in which mammals such as the elephant, horse, ox, and deer appeared, in addition to ancestors of man such as *Zinjanthropus* in Africa.

Potassium-Argon Dating.—A method of dating the age of a rock or mineral by measuring the rate at which potassium-40, a radioactive form of this element, decays into argon.

Potsherd.—A piece of a broken pot or other article of earthenware; also called *sherd* or *shard*.

Prehistoric Archaeology.—The branch of archaeology that deals with the times before the beginnings of recorded history.

Prehistory.—The history of the times before the appearance of written records; *prehistoric archaeology*.

Protohistoric Archaeology.—The study of the period just before the beginning of recorded history.

Quaternary.—A geologic period including the Pleistocene and the Recent (Holocene) epochs, marked by the appearance of near-humans and *Homo sapiens*.

Radiocarbon Dating.—A method of dating the age of a fossil or other organic specimen by measuring the rate of disintegration of radioactive carbon (or carbon–14).

Recent.—The present geological epoch in the earth's history, which began about 20,000 years ago; also called *Holocene*.

Salvage Archaeology.—The branch of archaeology devoted to the removal of artifacts from sites in localities scheduled to be affected by construction of dams, buildings, or highways or by other activities that will destroy or cover the sites.

Seriation.—The arrangement of the artifacts of a culture in an orderly sequence, according to one of several principles, to show how they have changed in time. It is also a way to establish chronology.

Site.—A single place in which excavation or other exploration has revealed objects or data or archaeological interest.

Solutrean.—A late Paleolithic culture or industry characterized by bifacial blade tools and weapons of flint; named for Solutré, a town in central France, where a cave containing such artifacts was discovered.

Stage.—A level of cultural development characterized by a technology and its associated social and ideological features.

Stela or Stele.—An upright tablet or pillar of stone used to mark a grave or as a monument, usually inscribed or carved in a traditional design.

Stone Age.—The prehistoric age embracing the Paleolithic, Mesolithic, and Neolithic. It was succeeded by the Bronze Age.

Stratigraphy.—The study or description of the strata of rocks, soil, or cultural debris, based on the principle that the lowest layer is the oldest and the uppermost is the latest. It is one of the chief ways of dating archaeological finds in terms of relative age.

Tardenoisian.—A Mesolithic culture characterized by the use of small stone tools with geometric shapes; named for Fère-en-Tardenois, a village in northern France, where such artifacts were first discovered.

Tell.—A mound produced by the successive building of mud or mud-brick structures on the ruins of the previous ones. It is an Arabic word occurring frequently in the place names of archaeological sites.

Tertiary.—The geologic period preceding the Quaternary in the Cenozoic era.

Tradition.—The persistence of artifact types in a given area over a period of time.

Typology.—The systematic classification of tools, weapons, ornaments, and other artifacts or remains according to type.

Urban Revolution.—A term applied by archaeologists and anthropolgists to the stage of human culture in the Neolithic and Bronze ages during which cities and urban life developed. This change was accompanied by great advances in metallurgy and other aspects of technology and a more specialized division of labor.

Varve.—One of a series of layers of sediment deposited annually by the melting of glaciers, used in determining the age of geological formations and in archaeological dating, especially in northern Europe.

Ziggurat.—A temple tower in which each story is smaller than the one below, leaving a terrace around each floor; characteristic of Sumerian, Assyrian, and Babylonian architecture.

ARCHAEOPTERYX, the earliest known bird form, was the size of a pigeon. It is shown here in a reconstruction.

ARCHAEOPTERYX, är-kē-op′tə-riks, is an extinct bird with reptilian characteristics. Generally considered a transitional form between reptiles and birds, it was common 125 million to 165 million years ago (Jurassic period) and is the earliest known bird form. Its birdlike characteristics were its feathers and the shape of its shoulder bones, feet, and parts of the hip bones. Its reptilian characteristics were the presence of teeth, a long bony tail, and lack of a horny bill structure. None of the bones of Archaeopteryx had air spaces. Its skeleton resembled that of the smaller, two-legged dinosaurs.

Archaeopteryx was about the size of a domestic pigeon, with a tail longer than its body. The tail contained about 20 separate vertebrae; each vertebra had a feather attached to either side of it. The wing skeleton had, at its end, three free fingers tipped with claws. Its wing feathers were arranged like those of modern birds. Because of the small size of the wing skeleton, the flying powers of *Archaeopteryx* were slight. *Archaeopteryx* probably glided from tree to tree or from the trees to the ground.

The genus *Archaeopteryx* belongs to the order Archaeopterygiformes, subclass Archaeornithes. Its uniqueness is emphasized by the fact that all other birds are placed in the subclass Neornithes.

Archaeopteryx is known from only two skeletons and a single feather, all found preserved in the lithographic limestone quarries of Solenhofen, Bavaria. The skeletons (one in the British Museum and the other in the Berlin Museum) are well preserved, and the impressions of the feathers are extremely clear.

ARCHANGEL, ärk′ān-jəl, a member of the second lowest rank of the angelic choirs (see ANGEL). The term also is used loosely to denote all orders above that of angel. The three angelic beings specifically named in Scripture generally are termed archangels: Michael (Daniel 10:13, 21; 12:1; Jude 1:9; Revelation 12:7); Gabriel (Daniel 8:16, 9:21; Luke 1:19, 26); Raphael (Tobit). Archangels served as special messengers and guardians to people close to God.

ARCHANGEL, ärk′ān-jəl, a city in the Russian republic of the USSR, is on the Northern Dvina River, 20 miles (32 km) from its mouth in the Dvina Gulf of the White Sea. The name in Russian is *Arkhangelsk.* The city is the administrative center of Archangel oblast. Archangel is the USSR's largest Arctic port. Its harbor is frozen six months of the year but can be kept open with icebreakers. It is the largest sawmilling center and lumber exporting port in the USSR. The port is the base for the Arctic Sea route to the Pacific Ocean, and supplies most of the Soviet Arctic expeditions.

Fishing is a major industry, and the city is the chief port for White Sea fishing boats. Most city industries are based on timber, fishing, or shipping. Besides sawmills, there are cellulose factories, shipyards, and fish canneries.

The city was founded in the 1580's and was called *Novo-Kholmogory* until 1613, when the name was changed to Arkhangelsk. In the 1600's it was Russia's only seaport. After the establishment of St. Petersburg (now Leningrad) in the 1700's, Archangel's importance as a port declined. It did not revive until the early 1900's, when lumber exports increased.

Archangel oblast is bounded on the north by the Barents Sea and includes the island groups of Novaya Zemlya and Franz Josef Land. Its most important geographic features are a large tundra area, dense northern forests, and the great rivers, the Dvina, Onega, Mezen, and Pechora. The inhabitants are mostly Russians, with small numbers of Nentses, Lapps, Karelians, and Chudes. Lumbering is the chief industry, and hunting and fishing are important occupations. In the southernmost districts, hemp and flax are grown. The region exports timber products, fur, and fish to the rest of Soviet Russia. Population: (1961) of the city, 271,000.

ARCHBALD, ärch′bôld, is a borough in northeastern Pennsylvania. It is situated in Lackawanna County, on the Lackawanna River, 10 miles (16 km) northeast of Scranton. An industrial community, it produces automobile parts, electrical instruments, and clothing. Nearby is Archbald Pothole, a geological curiosity of glacial origin. Archbald was settled in 1845 by Welsh and Irish immigrants and was incorporated in 1847. Until the 1930's, its economic mainstay was coal mining. The borough is governed by a mayor and council. Population: 6,118.

ARCHBISHOP, ärch-bish′əp, is the title accorded to a high ecclesiastical official by the Roman Catholic, Anglican, Orthodox, and Finnish and Swedish Lutheran churches. An archbishop is a bishop who, besides exercising jurisdictional authority over his own diocese (called an *archdiocese*), has certain prescribed supervisory responsibilities for other dioceses that fall within a specified geographical area. The territory made up of an archdiocese and subordinate dioceses is known as a *province.* The bishops within the province are *suffragans,* or subordinates, and the archbishop is their *metropolitan,* or superior (see BISHOP; METROPOLITAN). The archbishop's prerogatives include convoking and presiding over councils in his province and hearing appeals from the courts of his suffragan bishops.

In the early Christian church the congregations were concentrated in the principal city or metropolis of each Roman province. Each of these cities—for example, Corinth and Ephesus, which gave their names to the titles of New Testament epistles—had a religious leader called a bishop (*episkopos*). The date of the first appointment of an archbishop (*archiepiskopos*) is impossible to isolate. If the office of archbishop is interpreted as being the same as that of metropolitan, the office existed before 325. The Council of Nicaea, convened that year, was attended by many metropolitans. At the Council of Antioch, nine years later, a canon gave this instruction: "The bishops of every province must be aware that the bishop presiding in the metropolis has charge over the whole province." It was not until the 6th century, however, that the term "archbishop" itself came into use as a title for the metropolitan.

Many Protestant churches have no bishops, and most have no archbishops. The Church of England, however, maintains provincial sees, administered by archbishops, at Canterbury and York. A special position of honor is accorded the Archbishop of Canterbury as primate of all England. He crowns the sovereign and is also spiritual head of the Anglican Communion.

Some of the member churches of the communion have archbishops, including Ireland (Armagh and Dublin) and Scotland (called "Primus"). The Lutheran Church in Sweden has an archbishop at Uppsala; the Lutheran Church in Finland has an archbishop at Turku.

In the modern Roman Catholic church the authority of an archbishop, who may or may not be a cardinal, is strictly defined by canon law, which severely limits his right to interfere in the dioceses of his suffragans. A prelate who has the rank of archbishop because of diplomatic or other special duties, but who has no diocese to administer, is called a titular archbishop. The second Vatican Council decreed that dioceses be joined to archdioceses wherever possible. Thus the honorific use of "archbishop" for a bishop with only diocesan jurisdiction will eventually be eliminated.

In both the Eastern Catholic and Orthodox churches, archbishop is an honorary title. Unless the archbishop is also a patriarch, he has no more authority than a bishop. (See ORTHODOX EASTERN CHURCH.)

ARCHBOLD, ärch'bōld, **John Dustin** (1848–1916), American oil magnate who was one of the original nine directors of the Standard Oil Company and a dominant influence in its affairs after 1882. Archbold was born at Leesburg, Ohio, on July 26, 1848. He had a few years of schooling before becoming a clerk in a country store in Salem, Ohio. At 18 he joined the rush to the nearby Pennsylvania oilfields, where oil had been discovered in 1859. When John D. Rockefeller tried to destroy Pennsylvania oil producers by securing preferential freight rates for his company, Archbold—while still in his 20's—organized the Pennsylvanians to meet this threat. He formed the Acme Oil Company in Oil City, Pa., and became its president.

Recognizing Archbold's brilliance, Rockefeller made him a director of Standard Oil in 1875. Thereafter, Archbold acted as spokesman in many state and federal investigations of the firm. When the original company was dissolved as a monopoly in 1911, Archbold became president of Standard Oil of New Jersey. He died at Tarrytown, N.Y., on Dec. 5, 1916, leaving a huge estate.

ARCHDALE, ärch'dāl, **John** (c. 1642–c. 1717), English colonial administrator in America. The Gorges family sent him to Maine in 1664 to protect their interests, and in the 1680's he collected rents for the proprietors of the Albemarle settlements (North Carolina). In 1694 Archdale was appointed governor of Carolina, where his administration was considered particularly successful. He was elected in 1698 to the English Parliament, but, as a Quaker, he refused to take the oath and was not seated. He then retired from public life.

ARCHDEACON, ärch'dē'kən, a church dignitary, below a bishop in rank, who exercised disciplinary, supervisory, or pastoral authority over lower clergy in various Christian bodies during their history. The archdeacon's office originated in the 4th century. Originally he was the chief of the deacons and assistant to the bishop. From the 4th to the 8th century he served as confidant and representative of the bishop, exercised supervisory and disciplinary authority over subordinate clergy, and visited rural congregations. In the Eastern Orthodox church there was no further development of the office. In the West, however, from the 8th to the 12th century, archdeacons, several of whom might be found in large dioceses, developed independent jurisdictions. They were usually priests and often succeeded to the episcopal throne.

At the height of archidiaconal power, incumbents of the office might be appointed, independently of the bishop, by cathedral chapters or by the crown. Such a situation greatly restricted episcopal authority, and during the 13th century ecclesiastical synods began to restrict the power of archdeacons. In the 16th century the Council of Trent finally removed from them the authority to excommunicate and arbitrate in cases involving criminal acts of the clergy. After this time the office gradually diminished in importance.

In the Roman Catholic church today the office is honorary. In the Anglican communion, archdeacons may exercise administrative and pastoral authority on behalf of a bishop. A form of the office also exists among German Lutherans.

ARCHDUKE, ärch'dook', is a title that gives its holders authority and power superior to that of dukes. In modern times, the title was assumed only by members of the house of Habsburg. About a century after the duchy of Austria had been created by Emperor Frederick I Barbarossa in 1156, to counteract the power of his rivals, the Habsburgs acquired the duchy. In 1359, Duke Rudolf IV became the first Habsburg to call himself archduke. He hoped that the title would make the dukes of Austria equal to the electors of the Holy Roman Empire. In 1453, Emperor Frederick III confirmed Rudolf's claim and gave the title to Maximilian of Austria and his heirs.

ARCHEGONIUM, är-ki-gō'nē-əm, the female sex organ of mosses, ferns, liverworts, and conifers. It is usually flask-shaped, with a narrow neck and a bulb-shaped bottom portion containing an egg cell. As the archegonium matures, the cells in the center of the neck disintegrate and form a hollow canal. The remains of these cells are then released to the outside where they attract sperm produced by the same species. A sperm entering through the neck fertilizes the egg.

ARCHELAUS, är-kə-lā'əs, was a Greek philosopher of the Ionian school. He was born probably at Athens in the early 5th century B.C. Surnamed *Physicus* (the physicist) because of his devotion to physical science, he was a pupil of Anaxagoras, and according to Ion of Chios he became the teacher of Socrates and Euripides.

The outlines of his system were those of his teacher, but for the details of his cosmology he went back to the ideas of the earlier Ionic physicists. He postulated a primitive matter, acted upon by a ruling mind, which produced fire and water, and from them animal life. He held man to be superior to other beings by reason of his artistic and moral powers.

ARCHEOZOIC ERA, är-kē-ə-zō'ik, the earliest geologic era in the history of the earth. Together with the Proterozoic era it constitutes what is known as Precambrian time, extending from the formation of the earth's crust—more than 4 billion years ago—to about 600 million years ago. (The division into Archeozoic and Proterozoic eras is only an approximate one that some geologists use.) Archeozoic means "ancient life": it was during this era that primitive life first appeared.

Few fossil remains exist from Precambrian times, but radioactive dating techniques indicate that there may have been life as long ago as 3 billion years. Exposed Archeozoic rocks—mainly metamorphosed igneous rock—are found on all the continents. They have been studied most thoroughly in Finland and southern Canada. The best exposure of these ancient rocks in the United States is in the Grand Canyon. See also GEOLOGY.

ERA	PERIOD	
CENOZOIC	QUATERNARY	
	TERTIARY	
MESOZOIC	CRETACEOUS	
	JURASSIC	
	TRIASSIC	
PALEOZOIC	PERMIAN	
	CARBON-IFEROUS	PENNSYLVANIAN
		MISSISSIPPIAN
	DEVONIAN	
	SILURIAN	
	ORDOVICIAN	
	CAMBRIAN	
	PRE-CAMBRIAN TIME	
PROTEROZOIC ERA	LATE PRE-CAMBRIAN TIME	
ARCHEOZOIC ERA	EARLY PRE-CAMBRIAN TIME	

ARCHER, är'chər, **Branch Tanner** (1790–1856), American political leader in Texas. Born in Virginia, he studied medicine in Philadelphia and practiced in Virginia, where he also served in the legislature. He moved to Texas in 1831.

In Texas he became a leader of American settlers dissatisfied with Mexican rule. In November 1835, after the outbreak of war with Mexico, he presided over the "consultation" of settlers that formulated war aims. In 1836 he joined in a successful fundraising tour of New Orleans and other Mississippi River towns, but he failed to obtain aid from Washington. He was speaker of the lower house at one session of the 1st Texas Congress and was secretary of war during the administration (1838–1841) of Texas President Mirabeau B. Lamar. Archer died in Texas on Sept. 22, 1856.

ARCHER, är'chər, **William** (1856–1924), British drama critic, playwright, and translator, whose trenchant criticism was influential in raising the standards of the English theater. He was born in Perth, Scotland, on Sept. 23, 1856, studied law at Edinburgh University, but never entered practice. In 1878 he settled in London, where he became drama critic of *Figaro* and later of the *World*, the *Nation*, the *Tribune*, the *Manchester Guardian*, and other newspapers. His theatrical reviews for the *World* were collected and published annually as *The Theatrical World* (1893–97).

Archer became known particularly as a translator and popularizer of the works of the Norwegian dramatist Henrik Ibsen. Archer's version of *The Pillars of Society* was the first Ibsen play produced in London (1880).

Archer's writings on the theater include *Masks or Faces?* (1888), *Play-making* (1912), and *The Old Drama and the New* (1923). His plays include *The Green Goddess* (1921) and two plays written in blank verse, *Beatriz Juana* and *Lidia*, published posthumously in 1927. Archer died in London on Dec. 27, 1924.

ARCHERFISH, är'chər-fish, the *Toxotes jaculatrix*, one of eight species of fishes composing the family Toxotidae, found in coastal, fresh, and brackish waters of southeastern Asia, from India to the Philippines. It may grow to a length of 8 to 10 inches (20 to 25 cm) but is usually smaller.

The archerfish gets its name from its ability to shoot drops of water as far as 12 feet (3.5 meters), with 100 percent accuracy to 4 or 5 feet (1.2 to 1.5 meters). It directs these watery bullets at small insects and similar suitable prey, either at rest or in flight near the surface. The wetted insects usually drop within reach of the fish, which seizes and eats them. There is no external mechanism of projection, but the roof of the mouth contains a narrow groove which becomes a straight slender tube when the mobile tongue is placed against it. By closing the gill covers quickly, the fish propels water along the groove and out of the end of its mouth, which it has raised above the surface. The tip of the tongue probably controls the amount of water released.

THE ARCHERFISH captures its insect prey by "shooting" it with drops of water aimed from its pointed mouth.

LILO HESS—THREE LIONS

TARGET ARCHER takes a low anchor at full draw. This marksman, displaying perfect form, is using a bowsight.

ARCHERY, ärch'ər-ē, is the sport of shooting with bow and arrow. It is practiced in two forms: *target archery* and *field archery,* including *bow-hunting.* In target archery, target distances are fixed, and shooting is done with the aid of mechanical sights. In field archery, target distances are varied, and archers shoot either by the bare bow or special sight method.

Archery had its inception in primitive cultures as a method of self-preservation. For many centuries the bow and arrow was used as a weapon of warfare and as a means of providing food and clothing. During the 16th century, archery flourished as a sport, especially in England, where both kings and the rank and file of the citizens participated in contests.

In the United States the sport became organized with the founding in 1828 of the first archery society, the United Bowmen of Philadelphia, although the game did not become popular until after the Civil War. Modern archery in the United States really began in 1879 with the founding of the National Archery Association at Crawfordsville, Ind., and the holding of the first target archery tournament at Chicago. Field archery, a later development, was launched officially in 1939 with the establishment of the National Field Archery Association. The first national field archery tournament was held at Allegan, Mich., in 1946. Both the governing organizations provide separate classes of competition yearly for men, women, and juniors throughout the United States.

TARGET ARCHERY

In target archery, archers shoot a specified number of arrows at established distances from a target with prescribed scoring values. In tournaments, contestants shoot a definite number of *ends* (six arrows shot consecutively) at given distances, the total number of shots being called a *round.* A double round consists of shooting two rounds in succession.

The standard target face, mounted on a vertical butt, has a diameter of 48 inches and a marked series of five concentric rings (10 rings for international competition). A hit in the center (gold) ring scores the most points. Men's national championships include double York and American rounds; women's, double National,

American, and Columbia rounds. Other popular rounds include the Metropolitan and the Hereford. Younger competitors shoot shorter rounds. The winner of the championship is the archer who compiles the highest aggregate score.

STANDARD TARGET ARCHERY ROUNDS

Round	Total arrows	Distance (in yards)							
		100	80	60	50	40	30	20	
York (men)	144	72	48	24					N u m b e r o f a r r o w s
Hereford (men)	144		72	48	24				
American (men and women)	90			30	30	30			
National (women)	72			48	24				
Columbia (women)	72				24	24	24		
Metropolitan (men)	150	30	30	30	30	30			
Metropolitan (women)	120			30	30	30	30		
Junior American (boys)	90				30	30	30		
Junior Columbia (girls)	72					24	24	24	
Junior Metropolitan	90					30	30	30	

Other target archery activities are *clout, wand,* and *flight* shoots. A clout shoot is a long-distance event. The target, marked out on the ground, has a white flag in its exact center. Though marked and scored like the standard archery target, the clout is 12 times as large, having a diameter of 48 feet instead of 48 inches. The center (gold) area is 9.6 feet wide; the other rings each are 4.8 feet wide. Men's clout consists of a total of 6 ends at 180 yards; women's, 6 ends at either 140 or 120 yards.

A wand shoot is a novelty event, the object being to hit a 2-inch-wide strip of soft wood (wand) extending 6 feet above the ground. Men shoot 6 ends at 100 yards; women and juniors, 6 ends at 60 yards.

The several classes of flight shooting (distance) events are determined by the drawing weight of specially designed bows. In competition the archer shoots three arrows in each class and counts as official the one going the farthest.

FIELD ARCHERY

Field archers generally shoot at different-sized targets that are set at varying distances around a course. The Field Round and Animal Round are outdoor events; the Flint Round is an indoor event. Other activities for field archers include *archery golf, roving,* and *bowhunting.*

Rounds. A Field Round unit consists of 14 targets at distances of from 20 to 80 yards; two units, or 28 targets, comprise a round. The series of targets, placed in woods or countryside to simulate game-hunting situations, are arranged in cloverleaf fashion, so that the last target is stationed near the first. Four sizes of target faces are used, each containing a white inner ring with a small black center spot and a black outer ring. A hit in the white ring counts 5 points; in the outer circle, 3 points. The maximum possible score at each target is 20 points. A total of 112 arrows is shot.

In the Animal Round, archers shoot field arrows at animal-like faces on 28 targets at unknown distances. A maximum of 3 arrows is allowed, but shooting stops with the first hit. Scoring is designed to indicate the hunting archer's shooting skill. The Flint Round uses 7 targets

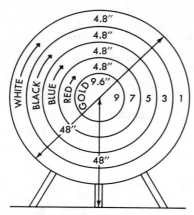

STANDARD TARGET FACE displays a gold bull's-eye and red, blue, black, and white concentric rings. Measurements and point values of the colors are shown here.

at distances from 20 feet to 30 yards and with 6- and 12-inch faces. Fifty-six arrows are shot.

Archery Golf and Roving. Archery golf combines certain characteristics of golf with those of flight and field archery. To start, the archer shoots a flight arrow from behind the first tee marker on the golf course. He continues from where the arrow lands. For an approach shot to the target he uses a roving or field arrow, and he completes each "hole" by hitting the bull's-eye at the green. This bull's-eye is a soft, white ball raised 18 inches above the ground. The archer who uses the fewest shots to hit all the balls on the course wins the game.

In roving, archers shoot at random marks, such as a stump, bush, or leaf. The one who hits the chosen target, or comes closest to it, wins points and selects the next target. This activity offers excellent practice for bowhunting.

Bowhunting. Bowhunting makes use of the bow and arrow for shooting big and small game as well as fish. Deer is the most widely hunted big game. Other big game shot regularly are elk, moose, bear, and wild pigs. The most popular small game are rabbits and squirrels. Common fish taken by bowfishermen are carp and garfish. Shooting is done either while wading or from small boats.

In the United States, bowhunting is legal in season in any place where hunting with a gun is permitted. A knowledge of legal restrictions, in addition to an archer's personal requirements, is essential in choosing the proper hunting equipment. For example, some communities specify a

BOWHUNTER takes a high anchor, from jawbone to cheekbone, for shooting at targets from short distance.

BEN PEARSON FILM LIBRARY

minimum weight or distance of cast for hunting bows; others regulate the size of broadheads (arrowheads) that can be used for deer.

Bowhunters must study the habits of game and execute the hunt with care. Hunting tactics can be influenced by many conditions, such as the terrain, direction of the wind, dampness or dryness of ground cover, and time of day.

EQUIPMENT

Essential equipment, or tackle, includes a bow of the right weight for the archer's strength, with a properly fitted bowstring, and arrows of the right spine for the bow weight. An archer also will need an armguard, a glove or fingertab, and a quiver.

Bow. The best modern bows are made of fiber glass over a hardwood core. The rigid center section (handle) contains the hand grip and the arrow rest—the shelf above the hand grip that holds the arrow at the exact spot each time the archer shoots. Both upper and lower limbs have a nock (notch) at their outer ends for attaching the bowstring. Bows vary in length from 5 to 6 feet. The surface area of each limb on the string side of the bow is called the belly; the side away from the string, the back.

Bow weight is determined by the number of pounds of effort necessary to pull the bowstring back to a distance equal to the length of the arrow an archer effectively draws. Most bows are marked with the pounds of pull indicated for 28 inches of draw.

Bowstrings vary in length, strength, and stretch. They are generally made of fine-thread Dacron. The serving on the string, usually of a snug-fitting nylon or cotton, has a marked nocking point for accepting the nock of the arrow.

Arrows. Arrows must be matched; that is, they must be of the same spine (stiffness and resil-

Component parts of the bow

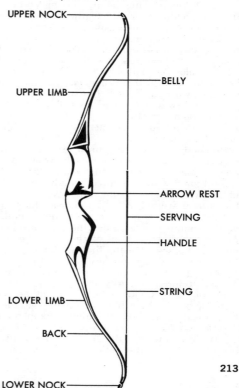

UPPER NOCK

BELLY

UPPER LIMB

ARROW REST

SERVING

HANDLE

STRING

LOWER LIMB

BACK

LOWER NOCK

iency of the shaft), weight, length, feather size, and pile. Hunting arrows average about 500 grains and are 26 to 30 inches long. Target arrows weigh approximately 300 grains and are 24 to 28 inches in length. Turkey feathers are used for fletching and are carefully selected and placed with regard to ballistic exactness. Increasing numbers of target arrows use plastic instead of feathers for fletching.

For both target archery and bowhunting, arrows of aluminum and fiber-glass tubing are used, although for bowhunting the most commonly used arrows still are made of wood. Target arrows have a tapered metal pile. Arrows with blunt heads are used for small game and for roving. Big game hunting arrows are equipped with sharp-edged broadheads.

SHOOTING

Learning to shoot a bow involves learning the proper techniques for taking the stance, nocking the arrow, drawing the bow, anchoring, aiming, releasing the arrow, and following through.

Stance. The archer's usual stance is with the body at right angles to the target and the shoulder of the bow arm pointing toward the target. The head looks over this shoulder, and the feet are placed about 12 inches apart. The bow is held with the heel of the bow hand resting on the grip, wrist behind the grip, and forefinger loosely encircling the handle and touching the thumb. Keeping the bow vertical, the archer raises the bow arm until it is parallel to the ground. His wrist must be straight, with the elbow slightly bent away from the string, and his shoulders must be level and in line with the direction of the flight.

Nocking the Arrow. In nocking the arrow, or putting the arrow on the string, the archer first grasps the arrow behind the fletching with the string hand. He then places the shaft on the arrow rest and fits the notched end onto the string at the nocking point, making certain that the cock feather (or odd feather) is up and that the arrow is perpendicular to the string.

Drawing. In preparation for drawing the bow, the archer places the forefinger of the string hand above the arrow nock and the second and third fingers below it. The string should rest along the first joint of all three fingers. As the bow is raised toward the target, the string-drawing arm pulls the arrow backward to full draw (to the anchor point on the face). At full draw the string-drawing arm becomes in effect a continuation of the arrow.

Anchoring. Anchoring must be performed in a precisely similar manner for each arrow. A target archer anchors under the chin, keeping the second joint of the forefinger snugly under the tip of the chin as the string touches the center of the chin and nose. A field archer anchors higher. He draws the arrow back until the second joint of the thumb lodges under the jawbone beneath the ear; the second joint of the forefinger commonly nestles into the hollow beneath the cheekbone, and the tip of the forefinger touches the mouth.

Aiming. Archers use three methods of aiming. Target archers ordinarily use a sight; few use a point of aim. Field archers aim either with a sight or by the bare bow, or instinctive, method. Regardless of method, the aiming point must be determined by trial and error.

With a bowsight the bead of the sight must be aligned with the center of the target. The

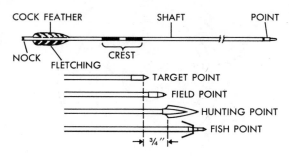

COCK FEATHER — SHAFT — POINT
NOCK — FLETCHING — CREST
TARGET POINT
FIELD POINT
HUNTING POINT
FISH POINT
¾"

ARROWS have specified lengths and weights and can be fitted with different kinds of points, depending on the archer's activity. Length is measured from the bottom of the nock to the position shown by the broken line.

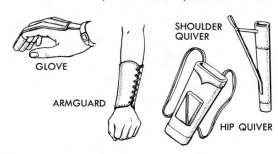

GLOVE — ARMGUARD — SHOULDER QUIVER — HIP QUIVER

SPECIAL EQUIPMENT shown here for the archer includes shooting glove, armguard, and two types of quiver.

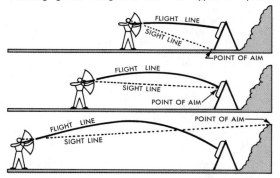

FLIGHT LINE — SIGHT LINE — POINT OF AIM
FLIGHT LINE — SIGHT LINE — POINT OF AIM
FLIGHT LINE — SIGHT LINE — POINT OF AIM

POINT OF AIM method of aiming uses three fixed marks: the eye, arrow point, and archer's anchor point. For short ranges, the point of aim is in front of the target (*top*). Farther back, it is closer to the target until, at one point, it coincides with the gold. This is called point blank range (*middle*). Still farther back, the point of aim is above the target (*bottom*).

sight, attached to the bow about 2 to 5 inches above the arrow rest, may have to be adjusted vertically or horizontally before the archer can aim properly.

In the point-of-aim method, archers sight the tip of their arrows in front of or beyond the target, depending on the distance from the target. Only at point-blank range can they aim directly for the gold.

In bare-bow shooting, archers usually tilt the bow to one side about 20 degrees, instead of holding it vertically. The arrow is anchored close to the corner of the mouth. Bare-bow archers focus on a spot on the target and aim the arrow at the mark, in a manner similar to that in aiming and throwing a stone.

Release and Follow-Through. Releasing the arrow is accomplished by relaxing the fingertips and permitting the elbow and forearm to move slightly backward. With a smooth action the fingers slip off the string, and the arrow flies to the mark. In a proper follow-through the archer retains the stance and form he held at the release until the arrow lands.

ARNOLD O. HAUGEN
Coauthor of "Field Archery and Bowhunting"

GLOSSARY

Anchor point.—The position on the face where the drawing hand rests while holding and aiming.

Armguard.—A device worn on the inner side of the bow arm to protect the arm from the slap of the bowstring.

Bare Bow Shooting.—Shooting with bows lacking any mark or sighting device.

Bow Hand or Arm.—The hand or arm that holds the bow in shooting.

Bow Weight.—The number of pounds of pull required to draw the string a specified distance.

Bowstring.—A cord fastened between the nocks at the ends of a bow to force it into a bent and stressed condition. It draws the bow and drives the arrow forward on the release.

Bracing the Bow.—Readying the bow for shooting by bending its limbs to attach the bowstring.

Butt.—The backstop that holds the target face. It consists of straw, excelsior, or earth.

Cock Feather.—The odd-colored vane that makes up part of the fletching.

Draw.—To pull the bowstring to the anchor point on the face.

Field Arrow.—An arrow with a spike-tipped point used in field archery. It usually is more rugged than a target-type arrow.

Finger Tab.—A device to protect the three string-pulling fingers, slotted for the arrow nock.

Fletching.—The vanes on an arrow, consisting of a cock feather and two hen feathers.

Flight Arrow.—A thin, light arrow for distance shooting, with small plastic vanes and a small point.

Full Draw.—The complete and consistent length a bowstring is pulled.

Hen Feathers.—The two vanes of the fletching of the same color, to distinguish them from the cock feather.

Hunting Arrow.—A blunt-tipped arrow for small game; also, an arrow with a broadhead for ducks, predators, and big game.

Instinctive Shooting.—Shooting without use of point-of-aim, bowsight, or other mechanical means. It also is called bare bow shooting.

Longbow.—A bow of 5 feet or more in length; also, the medieval English bow.

Nock.—The groove in the end of an arrow into which the bowstring fits. Also, the notch at either end of the bow that holds the end loops of the bowstring.

Nocking Point.—The place on the serving of the bowstring where the arrow is fitted.

Overbowed.—The condition of using a bow too heavy, or strong, for the archer; the opposite of *underbowed*.

Pile.—An arrowhead without cutting edges. It is usually cylindrical or conoidal and may be either pointed or blunt.

Quiver.—A receptacle to hold arrows for shooting. Quivers are hung on the back, worn in the hip pocket, or fastened at the belt or on the bow. Ground or floor quivers rest on the ground.

Serving.—The additional string around the center of a bowstring that protects it from wear by the fingers or the arrow nock.

String Hand.—The hand that draws the bowstring.

Vane.—One of the feathers on an arrow.

Bibliography
American Association for Health, Physical Education, and Recreation, *Official Archery—Riding Guide* (Washington, biennially).

Gillelan, G. Howard, *The Young Sportsman's Guide to Archery* (New York 1962).

Haugen, Arnold O., and Metcalf, Harlan G., *Field Archery and Bowhunting* (New York 1963).

Herter, George L., and Hofmeister, Russell, *Professional and Amateur Archery Tournament and Hunting Instructions and Encyclopedia* (Waseca, Minn., 1963).

Hodgkin, A.E., *The Archer's Craft* (New York 1954).

National Archery Association, *Official Tournament Rules* (Chicago, current ed.).

National Field Archery Association, *Official Handbook of Field Archery* (Redlands, Calif., current ed.).

Wambold, H.R., *Bowhunting for Deer* (Harrisburg, Pa., 1964).

ARCHETYPE, är′kə-tīp, is a term in psychology and literary criticism, meaning a pattern from which copies are made. In psychology, according to C.G. Jung's theory of the unconscious, an archetype ("primordial image") is essentially a mythological figure (for example, the dragon slayer) that "repeats itself in the course of history whenever creative fantasy is freely manifested." In criticism, archetypes are images, heroes, or story patterns that persist, with variations, from writer to writer. In Northrop Frye's theory of literature they are the most radical and powerful elements of which imaginative works are constructed.

Archetypes, like rituals, imitate prior models in a cycle of repetition similar to seasonal cycles. Religious myth is based on such cyclic materials, and literature draws much of its traditional coherence and enduring appeal from them.

ANGUS FLETCHER
Author of "Allegory: Theory of a Symbolic Mode"

ARCHILOCHUS, är-kil′ə-kəs, was a Greek lyric poet and lampoonist of the early 7th century B.C. He was born at Paros in the Aegean Islands. Of his life little is known save that he traveled widely, was a soldier of fortune, and died in battle. While he wrote choral hymns, elegies, and epigrams, experimented in various meters, and may have invented the epode, his fame is founded on his invention of iambic meter and on his vitriolic invectives. He calumniated his personal enemies so acidly that several victims of his satiric comments committed suicide. Later Greek and Roman poets esteemed Archilochus highly for his versatility and technique.

ARCHIMEDES (287?–212 B.C.), ärk-ə-mē′dēz, was a Greek mathematician, physicist, and inventor, who made original contributions in geometry and mathematics, founded the fields of statics, hydrostatics, and mathematical physics, and invented mechanical devices useful in war and peace. His range of subjects was almost encyclopedic—arithmetic, plane and solid geometry, mechanics, hydrostatics, optics, and astronomy—and many of his writings describe discoveries that he made. The achievements of Archimedes probably make him the foremost scientist until Newton.

Life and Major Discoveries. Archimedes was born about 287 B.C. in Syracuse, Sicily, a Greek colony. His father, Pheidias, was an astronomer. Archimedes studied at Alexandria, then the center of the scientific world, as a student of fol-

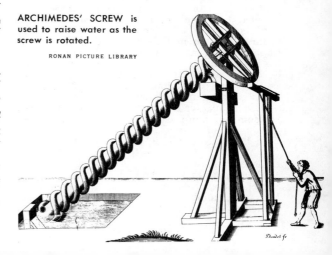

ARCHIMEDES' SCREW is used to raise water as the screw is rotated.

RONAN PICTURE LIBRARY

lowers of Euclid. During his stay in Alexandria he invented a "screw" for raising water from the Nile to irrigate fields. The design of the Archimedes screw is based on two geometrical forms, the helix and the cylinder. After his return to Syracuse, he devoted himself mainly to science.

In his treatise *Floating Bodies*, Archimedes stated that a body immersed in a fluid is buoyed up by a force equal to the weight of the displaced fluid. By means of this principle, known as Archimedes' principle, he determined that a crown was not pure gold. Hieron II, king of Syracuse, a friend and perhaps kinsman of Archimedes, ordered a crown of pure gold but suspected that the artist had fraudulently added alloys to the crown. Archimedes discovered the solution to this problem while lying in a bath, and it caused him so much joy that he hastened home from the bath undressed, crying "Eureka! Eureka!" (I have found it! I have found it!) The ratio of the weight of the crown to the weight of the water it displaced when completely immersed gave him what is now called the specific gravity of the material. Archimedes only had to take a quantity of pure gold and find its specific gravity by the same process. If the two specific gravities did not agree, the crown was not pure gold.

In his treatise *The Sand Reckoner*, Archimedes described a system for expressing immense numbers and gave an answer to his own question—how many grains of sand does the universe hold? Using Aristarchus' estimate of the size of the universe, Archimedes calculated that it would contain approximately 10^{63} grains of sand. Archimedes could express numbers as large as $(10^{8 \times 10^8})^{10^8}$, which is 1 followed by 80,000 million million zeros.

In a treatise on mechanics, he presented the solution to the problem of how to move a given weight with a given force. Legend has it that he told King Hieron: "Give me a point of support (fulcrum) and I shall move the world." When Hieron asked for a demonstration of some great weight moved by a small force, Archimedes moved a fully laden ship by using pulleys. He stated the principle of the lever in Proposition 6 in *Equilibrium of Planes*, "Commensurable magnitudes balance at distances reciprocally proportional to their weights."

In his *Measurement of the Circle*, Archimedes gave an approximation for the value of π, namely $3\frac{10}{70} > \pi > 3\frac{10}{71}$. He arrived at the upper and lower bounds on the value of π by starting with one hexagon that circumscribed a circle and another hexagon inscribed in the circle. He doubled the number of sides of each hexagon until both were 96-sided figures. By this procedure, the circumference of the circle was trapped between an upper bound (circumscribing figure) and a lower bound (inscribed figure).

In *Spirals*, Archimedes defined what is known as the spiral of Archimedes ($r = a\,\theta$, where r and θ are polar coordinates). In *Conoids and Spheroids* he gave the sum for the first n integers. He summed finite series and also infinite series $\sum_{0}^{\infty} 4^{-n}$, where n is 1, 2, 3 . . .), and he solved cubic equations.

In about 214 B.C., Archimedes' native city of Syracuse was besieged by the Roman general Marcus Claudius Marcellus. The defense of Syracuse was aided by military machines that Archimedes designed. These machines included catapults, missile throwers, and grappling hooks. One legend is that Archimedes also devised concave mirrors that burned Roman ships by concentrating the sun's rays on them. Tradition says that when the Romans finally gained possession of the city by assault in 212 B.C., Archimedes was sitting in the marketplace absorbed in contemplating some geometrical figures he had drawn in the sand. To a Roman soldier who addressed him, he is said to have cried out, "Disturb not my circle." But the soldier killed him.

Writings. Archimedes' treatises are characterized by rigor, imagination, and power. He gives strict proofs, for example, in finding the areas, volumes, and centers of gravity for figures such as circles, spheres, conics, and spirals. Works that have come down to us, besides those already mentioned, are *Sphere and Cylinder, Quadrature of the Parabola, Stomachion* (a geometrical puzzle), *Method, Book of Lemmas,* and *Cattle Problem.* Lost works include an investigation of polyhedra, a book dealing with the naming of numbers, books on balances or levers and on centers of gravity, *Sphere Making,* and *Catoptrica.* A text for *Method,* which had been lost, was found in 1906 by a Danish scholar, Johan Ludvig Heiberg. In this work, Archimedes attempts to explain his scientific method.

Bibliography

Archimedes, *Method,* ed by T.L. Heath (Cambridge, Eng., 1912).
Archimedes, *Works,* ed. by T.L. Heath (Cambridge, Eng., 1897).
Heath, T.L., *Archimedes* (London 1920).
Plutarch, *Lives* (any edition).
Sarton, George, *A History of Science* (Cambridge, Mass., 1959).
Whitehead, Alfred N., *Introduction to Mathematics,* American ed. (New York 1948).

ARCHIPENKO, är-kə-peng′kō, **Alexander** (1887–1964), Russian-American sculptor, whose major contribution to his art was the development of concave and negative space as an integral part of sculptural form. He was one of the first to adapt cubist tenets to sculpture. His influential innovations included the creation of a changeable, motor-driven painting (*Archipentura,* 1924); the use of color in sculpture; the combination of various materials in a single work; and the lighting of carved plastic sculpture from within.

Archipenko was born in Kiev, in the Ukraine, on May 30, 1887. He began studies in the Kiev art school but was expelled for his criticism of the "old-fashioned and academic" methods of the school. In 1907 he went to Paris, where he was briefly enrolled at the École des Beaux-Arts before setting up his own studio. Fascinated by cubism, he adapted its intersecting planes to sculpture and also began to develop his "sculpto-paintings," which are colored reliefs in combined media. His first one-man show was at the Hagan Museum in Berlin in 1912. During World War I he lived and worked in a suburb of Nice. Representative works of this period include *The Struggle* (1913), a painted plaster of intersecting forms, and *The Bathers* (1915), a sculpto-painting of colored wood, metal, and paper. From 1921 to 1923 he taught at his own art school in Berlin. He married the sculptor Angelica Bruno-Schmitz in 1921.

Archipenko moved to the United States in 1923 and established the École d'Art in New York City. His autobiography was published in 1960. He died in New York City on Feb. 25, 1964.

ARCHITECTURE

Architecture is concerned with the enclosure of space for human use. These enclosures range from houses for simple, everyday living to great structures for worship, such as the vaulted Pantheon in Rome (*right*).

ARCHITECTURE, är′kə-tek-chər, is the art of building. Virtually all architecture is concerned with the enclosure of space for human use. The precise activities to be housed in any specific building—ranging from an assembly line in a factory to a living room in a home—should dictate the size and shape of the several areas within. These spaces also must be arranged in some logical relation to each other. Furthermore, the movement of human beings within the building—"circulation" in architectural parlance—requires halls, stairs, or elevators whose size is governed by the expected load of traffic. The plan of a structure, always the first consideration of an architect, is the resolution of these different purposes into an organization of spaces that will fulfill the intent of the building. Good planning guides the visitor to his destination in the structure and impresses him, perhaps subconsciously, by visibly relating the several units of the edifice. Conversely, a bad plan results in inconvenience, waste, and visual confusion.

Furthermore, a structure must be well built; it should have such permanence as the purpose for which it is intended demands and as the materials chosen may allow. The raw materials of architecture—stone, brick, wood, steel, or glass —in part govern the forms of the building and are expressed by them. Stone can resist compression, the force that squeezes together, almost indefinitely. While it is possible to crush stone in a laboratory, for practical purposes its compressive strength is unlimited. On the other hand, stone is weak in withstanding tension, the force that pulls apart. Any beam spanning a void tends to bend downward between the supports, putting the lower half of the beam under tension. It follows from the tensile weakness of stone that

beams of this material must be comparatively short and supported at frequent intervals. Moreover, stone columns must be sturdy, rarely more than 10 times as high as they are wide. In stone buildings, windows, doors, and the spaces between columns are almost compelled to be taller than they are wide—the vertical rectangle of the stone aesthetic. Stone has been so dominant in the architecture of the Western world that forms appropriate to it have been preserved even in buildings constructed of wood, as in the American Georgian period. Stone, then, lends itself to the kind of construction in which walls support the floors and roof, to post and lintel construction with rather closely spaced columns, and to arch construction where the stresses are predominantly compressive.

Wood, a fibrous material, withstands tension as readily as it does compression. Wooden beams may be relatively longer than stone beams, and wooden posts slender and widely spaced. A horizontal rectangle, wider than it is high, results from the natural properties of wood, as may be seen in Japanese architecture. Steel also has tensile strength that is equal to or greater than its compressive strength. Anyone who has observed a steel building under construction must have noticed the gridiron of horizontal rectangles produced by the slender, widely spaced columns and the long beams of each floor. The nature of wood and of steel suggests frame construction— a skeleton to support floors and roof—with whatever surfacing material may be necessary. Wood and steel also permit cantilever construction in which beams project beyond the last point of support.

Finally, architecture must do more than meet the physical requirements of strength and space;

AMON-RA, the great temple at Karnak, Egypt, is a forest of columns that do not permit a sense of the vast interior.

it must also content the spirit of man. The building should form an aesthetic unity to which the several parts contribute. Thus, the sides and rear of a structure should bear sufficient correspondence to the front to make them all related parts of a single whole. The major internal divisions, too, require some expression in the external design. The nave, aisles, transepts, apse, and radiating chapels of Gothic cathedrals, for example, are all visible on the exterior, so that the visitor is subconsciously prepared for what he will find inside.

Architecture calls for good proportions—a pleasing relationship of voids to solids, of height to width, of length to breadth. Many attempts have been made to explain good proportions by mathematical formulas, such as the golden section (q.v.). These efforts have not found general acceptance, however, although good results have been achieved through the repetition of some dimension (for example, a module that is half the diameter of a column) throughout a design. Such repetitions help to produce the visible order that the human mind seems to crave.

A building also should have what architects call *scale;* that is, it should visually convey its true size. Such elements as benches, steps, or balustrades, though slightly variable in size, are, by their very purpose, related to the normal dimensions of human beings. They therefore become, almost imperceptibly, units of measurement for gauging the size of the whole edifice. Because these units are so small in comparison to the whole building, other elements of intermediate size are needed. Stairs and a balustrade may give a clue to the size of a doorway; that, in turn, to the height of a colonnade; and finally, the colonnade to the whole structure. The Petit Trianon at Versailles is perfect in scale. The absence of small elements in St. Peter's in Rome makes it difficult to perceive its vastness.

Although all decoration is rejected in some modern architecture, it was employed in the past either for its inherent beauty or to emphasize some point of importance in the building. Decoration or ornament may be used to contribute to character, the visible expression of the purpose of the building. Thus a bank should look like a bank, and a church should be immediately identifiable as such. Ideally, too, any building should seem to belong on its site, with some relationship to its architectural neighbors and to the local geography.

Through the related architectural forms shaped by their purpose, governed by the materials, proportioned and given scale and character by the designer, buildings become expressions of the ideals and aspirations of the generations that built them. The successive styles of historic architecture, reviewed in this article, are incarnations of the spirit of their times.

Egyptian. Herodotus characterized Egypt as the gift of the Nile. For over 1,000 miles its banks were irrigated and their fertility annually was restored by the inundations of the river, which also served for transportation and communication. The cliffs that bound the valley provided building stone, but in prehistoric times the Egyptians had used marsh reeds and mud for building. During the Old Kingdom (2664–2155 B.C.), shortly after recorded history began, architectural provision for the life after death absorbed the energies of the Egyptians. A peculiarity of their religion was the belief that part of the spirit of man required the preservation of the body for its permanent home. This they accomplished by mummification and ensured the preservation of the mummy by its concealment within the tomb. The pyramids at Giza (Gizeh), sepulchers of the pharaohs, faced the cardinal points of the compass. Most of the narrow passages in them were just wide enough to admit the sarcophagus, but after burial these passages were sealed with stone to protect the mummy. That desire for permanence, appropriate in a tomb, was expressed by the extremely stable shape, by the static mass, and perhaps by the size, which also testified to the pharaoh's power. The same desire to build for eternity was evident in the tombs of the nobles, called mastabas, solid blocklike masses of rough masonry sheathed in cut stone. Embedded within the mass were a small chapel decorated with paintings and relief sculpture depicting the owner of the tomb at work or play, an undecorated room (the serdab) for the effigy of the deceased and other statues, and a burial chamber, in the rock below the mastaba, entered through a shaft from the roof. The descendants of the owner might enter the chapel to make offerings, but the serdab and the burial chamber were cut off from the outer world, the latter by having its shaft blocked with stone after interment. The outer walls of the mastaba sloped inward on all four sides; that is, they were battered, a form that looked and was more stable than an ordinary wall.

AUDIENCE HALL of Xerxes at Persepolis was intended to impress visitors with the power of ancient Persian kings.

More interesting architecturally were the shallow, rock-cut tombs of the Middle Kingdom (2052–1786 B.C.). Here a colonnaded entrance hewn from the sloping face of a cliff led into the chapel. The shaft to the burial chamber was excavated in the floor of the chapel or perhaps from in front of the entrance. The 16-sided piers were speciously like the Doric columns of Greece, but it seems probable that the concept of the portico was derived from the poles that supported the tent flaps familiar to the nomadic ancestors of the Egyptians.

More elaborate than the tombs were the temples. In the best-preserved examples from the New Kingdom, or Empire, period (1570–1075 B.C.) and later, the plan contained four major parts. The pylon, two dignified masses of masonry, flanked the entrance; behind lay the peristyle, a courtyard surrounded by a colonnade; behind that was a colonnaded hypostyle hall; and finally, at the rear was the sanctuary with its subsidiary chambers. Even in the smaller examples the sense of enclosure and the progression from the sunlit court to the darker hall and to the still dimmer sanctuary impressed the visitor with the mystery of the god and the power of his servants, the priests, who alone were admitted to the sanctuary. Details and decoration enhanced this effect. Sphinxes lined the axial approach to the temple; the battered walls of the pylon, with colossal statues of the pharaoh in front, were covered with sculpture in low relief depicting the ruler triumphant over his foes. Within the hypostyle, stars studded the ceiling; birds were painted on the upper walls; and plants, animals, and human beings were pictured around the lower walls and on the bases of columns. In the sanctuary might occur scenes of ritual.

The early Egyptian methods of building left their traces in the columns. The clustered shaft looked like a bundle of reeds of the papyrus or the lotus, bulging outward very slightly above the base and bound together by thongs just below the capital. In some examples, such as the lateral columns in the Great Temple of Amon-Ra at Karnak, the reeds were smoothed out into a cylinder, although the bands below the capital and the bulge at the base, such as occur at the bottom of the stem of some plants, still re-

mained. The capitals of the columns likewise derived from plants: either the closed bud as in the side columns at Karnak or the open flower of the lotus used in the central colonnade, a form like an inverted bell. Petals and sepals were painted on the capitals. Though less obviously, the Egyptian cornice came from the same type of construction. The half-round molding at its base tied in vertical reeds that edged a mud wall; in time these reeds bent outward at the top in a quarter circle. Geography, too, had its influence. In this rainless climate a pitched roof was unnecessary; therefore, slabs of stone rested on beams, which were carried by the columns. To light so vast an interior as the hall at Karnak, the Egyptians raised the central part of the roof above the sides, thereby forming a clerestory (clearstory). This solution, starting in the Temple of the Sphinx at Giza of the Old Kingdom, ultimately reached its most dramatic expression in the medieval cathedral.

The forms of Egyptian columns and capitals were not remarkably expressive of their purposes from either a structural or an aesthetic point of view; the capitals provided neither the larger bearing surface to hold the beams nor a transition for the eye from the vertical lines of the column below to the horizontals of the beams above. Nor did their imitation of plant forms make them sensitive to the qualities of stone. Open interior space did not concern the Egyptians; huge as the hall was at Karnak, the forest of columns of the post-and-lintel system so cluttered the floor that no sense of space could be achieved. Furthermore, although their smaller temples exhibited a logical unity in their sequence of pylon, peristyle, hypostyle, and sanctuary, this unity was destroyed in the larger temples by adding extra halls, courts, and especially pylons to designs already complete. On the other hand, the Egyptian temple bespoke the character of Egypt's religion and society; the Egyptian love of permanence has made the pyramids recognized symbols of eternity; and finally the sheer size of the larger buildings created an imposing majesty of effect unrivaled by later peoples.

Mesopotamian and Persian. Civilization arose at least as early in the Tigris-Euphrates valley as in Egypt. But the remains in architecture are less extensive, chiefly because the region afforded neither timber nor stone for building. Hence the architects used the clay pits along the river valley to make sunbaked bricks. The small size of bricks did not encourage a post-and-lintel system of construction; although some brick piers were built, as for example at Telloh, and there is some evidence for the existence of cedar columns, the prevalent material forced the Mesopotamian builders to adopt the arch and vault as a means of covering their interiors. The true arch was known to these people at least as far back as 2400 B.C. However, sunbaked brick is not strong; hence the size of the vaults was limited, and their support necessitated heavy walls.

The principal feature of Mesopotamian religious architecture was the ziggurat, a pyramid of six or seven stories connected by ramps to allow access to the shrine on top. Like the pyramids in Egypt, these solid masses of brick were set in relation to the points of the compass; that is, they were oriented. However, in Mesopotamia the corners of the ziggurat pointed north, south, east, and west. The vertical walls of each story of the ziggurat were colored; in the Temple of Bel in Babylon, built by Nebuchadnezzar (6th century B.C.), the stories were colored white, black, blue, yellow, silver, and gold from bottom to top. The effect may have been garish, but at least it was striking.

The Palace of Sargon II at Khorsabad (8th century B.C.) stood on a bastion in the city wall, 60 feet (18.28 meters) high and measuring 1,050 feet (320.04 meters) by 1,140 feet (347.47 meters). To care for seepage within this mass of sunbaked brick, arched drains were provided. The palace itself contained a multitude of chambers, many of them narrow corridorlike rooms probably covered with brick vaults. The rooms were grouped around courts with more or less separated sections for men, women, service, and for the ziggurat connected with the palace. Although a few of the rooms seem to have been related to one another in plan, the arrangement strikes the modern observer as haphazard. It is only fair, however, to remember that our knowledge of the specific purposes of these rooms is meager and that their disposition may have been more logical than we can imagine. Most of the rooms were probably lighted from the courts, although some of the larger ones no doubt had skylights. The lower part of the walls was decorated with friezes in stone, carved in low relief and showing the triumphs of the rulers in warfare and the hunt which seem to have been the chief occupations of the military caste of the Assyrians, and confirm the ancient reputation of these people for ferocity. Rugs covered the floors, but these have vanished; on the other hand, since textiles would wear rapidly in such a location, the thresholds were paved with stone carved in the patterns of rugs. Guardian monsters—winged bulls or lions with human heads—flanked the entrance.

The influence of Mesopotamia spread to many areas, the most important being Persia under the Achaemenid rulers, whose immediate predecessors, the Medes, overthrew Nineveh in 612 B.C. For three centuries the Persians were to rule the western Asian world from India to the Nile. Unlike Mesopotamia, Persia offered its builders both stone and wood, and the consequence was a colonnaded architecture of slender shafts terminating in the peculiar Persian

capital of the forequarters of two bulls set back to back to support the wooden beams of the ceiling. In the large palaces, such as that at Persepolis (5th century B.C.), monumental gateways with winged monsters, similar to those in Assyrian palaces, and broad stairways whose sides were lined with friezes in low relief sculpture provided an imposing entrance to the halls and audience chambers of the King of Kings. In view of their scale and their costly materials, these square, colonnaded halls impressed visitors to Persepolis with the power of Persia. Architecturally, however, the large chambers do not seem to be related to each other in plan. At Susa, glazed brick, a common material in Mesopotamia, replaced the stone friezes at Persepolis.

Aegean. Until the discoveries of Heinrich Schliemann (q.v.) around 1870, the very existence of a great preclassical culture in Crete and the Aegean area was unknown. The ruins of the palace of Knossos (about 1800–1600 B.C.) testify to the high level of Aegean civilization. Clearly the Cretans were seafaring, and since Knossos was unfortified until late in its history, they feared no attack by land. Complicated though the plan of Knossos was, its principal chambers were organized in suites, one room or vestibule leading to another with a logic in plan absent in the later Mesopotamian and Persian palaces. Moreover, the need for three stories compelled the provision of light-wells around the stairways within the palace to supplement the light from the central court. The stone walls of the rooms and the wood columns in the stair halls supported the upper floors. The columns tapered downward from a cushion-shaped capital. The walls were enriched with frescoes of figures, birds, and plants and of men and women vaulting over the heads of bulls. Baths and extensive piping indicated a more developed knowledge of sanitation than western Europe was to know for 3,000 years.

The dominion of Crete extended through the islands of the Aegean Sea and the neighboring mainland of Greece and Asia Minor. However, toward the end of the 1000's B.C. the ancestors of the historic Greeks began to settle in the Peloponnesus. They absorbed something of Cretan culture but in time rejected the yoke of the sea kings. Their palaces, such as that at Tiryns, were smaller than that at Knossos, but with an arrangement of rooms in suites and with columns tapering downward like the Cretan examples. Their later chieftains, of whom Homer wrote in the *Iliad*, defended their strongholds with massive walls of stone, solid enough for protection by their sheer weight and thickness. Within these walls narrow passages covered with corbel vaults probably served for storage. Similar vaults covered their beehive-shaped underground tombs, like the Treasury of Atreus at Mycenae.

Greek. By the end of the 1000's B.C. the Mycenaean ancestors of the Greeks were overcome by new infiltrations of barbarian Greek tribes from the north. During the succeeding centuries the newcomers slowly became civilized and by the 7th century were so well settled that the city-states began to colonize the Black Sea and southern Italy and Sicily. They reached the purest expression of their culture between the end of the Persian Wars (479 B.C.) and the beginning of the Peloponnesian War (431 B.C.), a culture characterized by clarity of form in everything that they did. Each part of their buildings was a unit, shaped for its purpose and complete in itself and yet subordinate to the larger unity of the building, just as the choruses in Greek tragedy were complete poems forming part of the larger whole of the play, and that in turn of the trilogy. It was therefore inevitable that certain orders of architecture should develop; that is, certain types of column combined in established ways with other parts above and below. Through centuries of experiment, the parts of the Doric and Ionic orders and their relation to each other were perfected. The former can be identified by the low cushionlike shape of part of its capital, and the latter by the scrolls to either side of the capital. Each of these orders stemmed from early construction in wood, but both, by the 5th century, were adapted to stone. It is possible that some details of the Doric order may have been derived from the Cretan column, and it is almost certain that some features of the Ionic order trace their ancestry to Asia Minor; but these derivative elements, by the 5th century, were reshaped by the Greek passion for form so as to have a merely historic interest. During the late 5th century the third Greek order, Corinthian, developed, with a capital taller than those of the Doric and Ionic and adorned with rows of acanthus leaves, whose tips curl outward from the mass. The Corinthian order may have been first used in the Temple of Apollo Epicurius at Bassae (about 430 B.C.); it certainly appeared in the Tholos at Epidaurus (about 350 B.C.) and on the monument of Lysicrates in Athens, but its full popularity came only in Roman times.

Most Greek citizens lived more for the state than for themselves. Hence their architectural energies centered on temples erected by the city. The larger temples provided a single chamber as a home for the cult statue, perhaps with storage areas at the rear. Built on the pier-and-lintel system in stone, large free spaces on the interior were impossible, and there was no need for them. While the temple was open to visitors, nothing like the congregational worship of Christianity existed, and hence it was unnecessary to accommodate groups within the temple. Sacri-

ALISON FRANTZ—ART REFERENCE BUREAU

PARTHENON in Athens is an example of the architecture that expresses the classic Greek sense of form.

fices were offered to the gods at an altar outside the building. This clear form was then surrounded in the larger temples by a colonnade, and even in the smaller ones by porticoes on the front or at both ends. In the Heraeum (Temple of Hera) at Olympia (about 600 B.C.) the rectangle was about three times as long as it was wide. In the Parthenon in Athens (477–432 B.C.), the length was curtailed until it was little more than twice the width of the temple. The Parthenon, designed by Ictinus and Callicrates, illustrated the Greek sense of form. The unbroken lines of steps that create the platform on which the temple rests at once bespeak its shape and size. Shallow grooves or flutes then dramatize the columns as the principal supporting members. The Doric capital provides a larger bearing surface for the beams of the architrave and affords a progressive transition from the verticals of the columns to the horizontal members above them, thus serving both a practical and an aesthetic purpose. The entablature—consisting of the architrave, a frieze with alternating triglyphs and metopes, and an overhanging cornice—repeats the lines of the steps and clearly stresses the shape of the Parthenon. The mass of the temple was so defined that it seemed in-

STOA in Athens, reconstructed on its original site, was used by ancient Greeks as a promenade near the market.

AGORA EXCAVATIONS: AMERICAN SCHOOL OF CLASSICAL STUDIES

ROMAN BASILICA of Constantine combined groin vaults and barrel vaults (shown here) to increase enclosed space.

NATHAN PLETCHER

dependent of surrounding space; no projections from its sides or roof interrupted that clarity of form. The open colonnades did not exclude the visitor, as did the blank walls of Egyptian temples; in the democratic Greek city-state, the citizen was welcome to the temple. It was his monument.

The Erechtheum (435–about 408 B.C.) on the Acropolis in Athens brought the Ionic order to its culmination. The exquisite details attested to the Greek desire for perfection, regardless of cost. The temple was so important to the Greeks that few other types of building received much attention. The theaters, usually built on a hillside, centered their semicircular seats around the circular orchestra, the space reserved at first for the chorus in Greek drama. Behind the orchestra a low platform served as the stage, entered through doors in an architectural screen behind it. Finally, the stoa, a colonnaded hall or portico, provided a promenade for business purposes near the marketplace.

Roman. In the sixth book of the *Aeneid*, Virgil described the Romans as lawgivers, soldiers, and administrators but denied to them the greatest achievements in sculpture. From this it followed that the Romans in the decorative aspects of architecture were somewhat derivative; sumptuous as the detail was, it lacked refinement. The orders were borrowed from Greece and somewhat modified; the Romans added the Tuscan, a simplified version of the Doric, and the Composite, more elaborate than the Corinthian, to the traditional three orders. So, too, the Romans accepted from the Etruscans certain features of their temple plans and perhaps the principle of the arch. But Roman architecture was a great style, not because of these foreign elements but in spite of them. To be sure, such a temple as the Maison Carrée at Nîmes (16 B.C.) looked something like a Greek temple but differed in that the sanctuary was expanded to the full width of the temple, and therefore the surrounding open colonnade was supplanted by engaged columns— that is, columns partly embedded in the wall. Such columns were less structural and therefore less functional than the free-standing Greek columns. Since access to the temple was impossible on the back or sides, the steps whereon the Greek temple rested were confined in the Roman to the front only, with the temple raised above the ground on a pedestal or podium.

Unlike the Athenian, the imperial Roman civilization required vast, unencumbered interior spaces for crowds of people. Therefore the Romans turned to the arch and the vault, sometimes of stone, more often of concrete. The

masses of concrete were faced with brick, and the floors and walls of public buildings were sheathed in slabs of marble, often colored and set in patterns. The barrel vault, a half cylinder in shape, required continuous support along its sides, and since any arch or vault also pressed outward in the direction of its curve, the barrel vault had to have continuous abutment on both sides. The hemispherical dome on a ring of masonry must be buttressed on all sides. These simple forms did not combine well with other shapes in plan and were difficult to light. However, if two barrel vaults crossed at right angles, the resulting groin vault brought its weight and its outward thrust to bear only at the four corners of the square covered by it and thus needed support and buttressing only at those points; though more complex in shape and more difficult to construct, it could be combined with other groin vaults or with barrel vaults, and the interior that it covered could be lighted from any one or all four sides of the vault.

The Pantheon in Rome (about 120–124 A.D.) showed the possibilities of a single vault. The vast concrete dome created an interior with a maximum of spatial unity; it could be comprehended in its entirety from any point of view in contrast to the interiors of Greek or Egyptian temples, where files of columns broke up the space. So large a vault demanded a 20-foot-thick wall, somewhat lightened by seven niches and a doorway cut within its mass. Externally this cylindrical wall supported and partly contained the dome; that is, the lower part of the dome was embedded in the cylinder. Only the upper segment of the hemisphere was visible and even that had several rings of masonry, like steps, to add their weight to buttress the dome. A portico dignified the entrance.

Only rarely can an architectural problem be solved, as it was in the Pantheon, by a single chamber, however spacious. The architect ordinarily must combine a number of areas so that the building becomes a planned organization of volumes, each molded to its practical and expressive needs. Their plans were the Romans' greatest contribution to architecture. For example, the Basilica of Constantine or Maxentius in Rome (begun 306–312) had a central aisle covered by three groin vaults. In addition, barrel vaults were built on either side of each section of the groin vaults to extend the interior space. To light so large an interior from the end walls of the barrel vaults would be inadequate; therefore, the barrel vaults were built lower than the groin vaults, and windows in the sides of the groin vaults gave full light to the center of the building. Likewise, the solid supports between the barrel vaults resisted the outward pressure of the groin vaults and thereby held them in place. Although the Basilica of Constantine is the largest of the ruins in the Roman Forum, only one third of it is preserved.

Still more complex were such Roman bathing establishments as the Baths of Caracalla (211–217; see illustration accompanying the article on BATHS AND BATHING). In addition to dressing rooms and hot, tepid, and cold baths, they needed not only areas for exercising before ablutions, but also libraries and gardens for subsequent relaxation. Here the main building, planned around a pattern of intersecting axes, was set within lawns or gardens, bounded by smaller shops and other appurtenances. A stadium occupied one side of the gardens. The three principal units were ranged along the main axis; the cold plunge open to the sky, three groin vaults with a vestibule at either end in the main hall, and separate vaulted chambers on the principal axis for the tepidarium, or warm bath, and the caldarium, or hot bath. Each major unit along this main axis was crossed by secondary axes, and each of these minor axes in turn was terminated by some architectural feature, such as a niche, that gave visual expression to the fact of termination. This logical plan through its arrangement of many spaces so related them that the visitor was guided by the architecture to his destination and subconsciously was impressed by its complex organization. It is precisely because of this clarity of plan that Roman architecture has had so large an influence on later building. Although the system of crossed axes adopted by the Romans may not always produce the best arrangement, it proved adaptable to many building problems in the 19th and early 20th centuries.

The major Roman buildings were monumental in scale, but private homes were more modest. In the House of Pansa, Pompeii (1st century A.D.), a vestibule led into an atrium whose central pool was filled by drainage from the inward sloping roofs that covered its four walls. Rooms lined the sides, while alcoves at the farther end afforded an area for conversation where the owner might consult his *clientes* and give them their orders for the day. The atrium here became the business center of the house and provided accommodation for domestic slaves. The *tablinum*, opposite the vestibule, was the sanctuary where the household gods, the *lares* and *penates*, were venerated. Beyond this was the peristyle, a colonnaded courtyard surrounding a garden and lined with the family bedrooms and dining rooms. In the mild climate of Pompeii such a peristyle, its walls perhaps frescoed with copies of famous Greek paintings, must have been pleasant indeed. Being on a smaller scale, the columns of the peristyle could be more widely spaced in proportion to their height and perhaps more slender than the larger ones of public buildings.

India. To generalize about the architecture of the subcontinent of India, the home of many different races and religions, over a period of 2,000 years is extremely difficult. One may note, however, that most Indian styles, even though executed in stone, were translated from an architecture conceived in wood. Second, to Western eyes their temples, whether early or late, Buddhist, Hindu, or Jain, were overloaded with decoration. The first of these generalizations may be illustrated by Stupa No. 1 at Sanchi

ROMAN HOMES, such as the House of the Vettii, Pompeii, had rooms grouped about a peristyle and garden.

(70–25 B.C.), a memorial mound or reliquary, surrounded at its base and crowned above by stone railings exhibiting the characteristic horizontal rectangle of wood construction as does a rail fence. So, too, the gateways with their figural and decorative sculpture were based on a wood aesthetic. Even before this the Chaitya Hall at Karli (185–80 B.C.), though carved from solid rock, preserved the shapes of wooden ribs in its ceiling, where they had no function and could only indicate persistence of tradition.

Quite different from these Buddhist examples were such Hindu temples as the Durga Temple at Aihole (320–600 A.D.). Conceived as the home of the god, the flat or nearly flat roofed sanctuary was approached by a colonnaded porch on one or more sides, its supports and parapet enriched with sculpture. To this nucleus was attached a tower built in multiple layers with thin bands of shadow between them, its four sides curved inward toward the top to hold a finial with the emblem of the god on it. In some later examples, like the Parasuramesvara Temple at Bhuvaneshwar (8th century A.D.), the tower dwarfed the sanctuary; its surfaces were covered with carving.

The influence of India and of its religions spread throughout southwest Asia. Thus in Java the Barabudur or Borobudur (8th century) was a descendant of the earlier Buddhist stupas. Like them, the mass was solid and the round shape of the stupa was recalled by three circular terraces on top surrounding the symbolic parasol of Buddhism. Unlike the stupa, the six lower terraces were square in plan. All nine terraces were covered with hundreds of statues of the Buddha and with bands of sculpture in relief of Buddhist character. On the other hand, the Angkor Wat or Vat (12th century) in Cambodia was Hindu. The axial plan was composed of concentric rectangles of colonnades, their corners marked by towers that increased in size as the central tower was approached. The silhouettes of the larger towers curved somewhat like those of Hindu temples in India proper. Once more, miles of carvings lined the corridors and enriched the towers as they detailed the complicated scenes of Hindu mythology.

Chinese and Japanese. The Chinese trace their history at least to the 1000's B.C., but little extant work can be dated earlier than the 16th century A.D. For this the comparative impermanence of

EARLY CHRISTIAN CHURCHES copied the basilican architecture of Rome, as in the old St. Peter's. This church, shown here in a 16th century fresco, was pulled down to make way for the present St. Peter's.

their favorite building material—wood—was partly responsible, but only partly; successive dynasties obliterated the architectural monuments of their predecessors, whether those were executed in stone or in wood. However, it is known that under the Shang dynasty (1400 B.C.), wooden columns were erected on platforms of hard-packed earth, probably with the building units disposed around one or more courts and roofed with thatch. Walls enclosed and protected their towns; indeed, this was so ingrained in the Chinese mind that during the 3d century B.C. they built the Great Wall, which wandered over hills and mountains and was punctuated at intervals with towers to prevent invasion of China by the nomadic Huns from the north and northwest. Perhaps the Han period (202 B.C.–220 A.D.) reached the high point in Chinese architecture; certainly the building of the T'ang dynasty (618–906 A.D.) was fully developed. The main halls of palaces and temples alike faced a courtyard whose transverse axes terminated in minor halls. These units might be surrounded by a free-standing curtain wall. As in earlier times, the main colonnaded unit in wood or stone stood on a platform of earth paved and lined with stone. Hipped or gabled roofs covered with colored tile cast rich shadows over colonnades or walls; in later examples, the lower slopes of the roof curved in the manner popularly associated with all Chinese building, although this had not been true at first. More complex projects, such as the Forbidden City in Peking, were multiples of simple units in spacious plans designed around major and minor axes.

A fairly good idea of how the earlier Chinese temples probably looked can be had from the Japanese buildings that they inspired. Thus the form of the Shinto shrine at Izumo (now reconstructed) appears to date from the 6th century, while the temple halls of Horyuji (7th century)

and Toshodaiji (8th century) at Nara amplified that form. Widely spaced wooden posts were linked by horizontal members to produce the characteristic horizontal rectangle of wood construction, a shape present not merely in the larger structural units but also in the decorative features. The flaring eaves of the tiled roofs were cantilevered on brackets that in later times became overelaborate. Thus, the Yomeimon at Nikko (17th century) was so overlaid with decoration as to lose the structural quality of the earlier designs, although the marks of wood construction never disappeared.

Early Christian. This brief review of Oriental architecture has taken us far afield both geographically and chronologically. On returning to the West, we find that a half century (235–284) of revolution and economic chaos undermined the Roman empire. Although by no means the only Oriental cult in Rome, Christianity grew in importance until it became advisable for Constantine and Licinius finally to recognize the sect in 313. The Early Christian basilica was designed to meet the needs of the church. It grew in part from the Roman house, where the earliest Christians met for worship, and in part from pagan basilicas. At first, as in the original St. Peter's, Rome (4th century), the entrance was placed in the east end, but from the 5th century, churches regularly faced west and placed the altar near the east end of the building. A court or atrium with the font in the center stood before the church. On entering the building, one found a central aisle or nave, flanked by side aisles, to accommodate the congregation. Opposite the entrance was the apse, a semicircular area for the higher clergy with the altar directly in front of it and with a cross member at right angles to the nave separating it from the apse. Sometimes this cross member projected beyond the sides of the church to form transepts. A wooden roof rested on a clerestory that rose above the roofs over the aisles to light the church. The only vault in the building was the half dome over the apse; the costly and monumental vaults of the earlier Roman empire were abandoned because of the poverty of the times, and all available funds were lavished on decoration. Floors of patterned marble and a miscellany of columns from abandoned pagan temples, together with mosaics of colored glass or marble, created an interior that contrasted in splendor with the drab exteriors. In the classic temple the emphasis lay on the exterior; in the Christian church, on the inside.

So satisfactory did the basilica prove that it remained virtually unchanged in Rome itself for 1,000 years, and its parts both in plan and in elevation were basic through the later Middle Ages. A second form of building known as the central type was designed around a central vertical axis instead of a longitudinal one. The long, internal lines of the basilica carried the eye of the visitor from the door to the altar as the ritualistic climax of the structure. On the other hand, circular or octagonal buildings focused on the center. If the altar was not placed there, it appeared to be pushed into a corner; however, to place the altar in this position was undesirable, since the congregation should be in front of it. Hence, buildings of the central type were better adapted to votive churches or to baptisteries.

Byzantine. After the death of Theodosius the Great (395), the Roman empire was divided permanently into two parts: the Western with its center nominally in Rome, and the Eastern, with its capital at Constantinople. The Western empire collapsed in 476 under the impact of barbarian invasions. The Eastern empire, commonly called the Byzantine empire—although Constantine the Great in 330 had renamed Byzantium, its capital, after himself—survived for almost 1,000 years. Financed by the Eastern emperors, the vaulted churches of Constantinople had a magnificence beyond the reach of the early churches of western Europe. The plain, wood roof gave a sense of impermanence to the Early Christian basilica. The Eastern emperors therefore perfected the dome on pendentives. The pendentive, a device to enable the circular plan of a dome to be supported over a square area, probably was derived from late Roman architecture; a similar device, the squinch, may have come from Rome, or possibly from Sassanian Persia, where a vaulted style contemporary with the later Roman empire had been developed in brick. The possibilities of such a domed building can be seen best in Hagia Sophia in Constantinople (now Istanbul), begun in 532 by Anthemius of Tralles and Isidorus of Miletus, the architects of Justinian. The dome and half domes over the nave gave an extraordinary lightness to the building without loss of monumentality. The rich color in the mosaics on the upper walls and vaults, the marble revetment of the lower walls, and the polished marble columns spoke of the imperial wealth of Justinian. The columns no longer adhered to the classic orders. During the later Roman empire itself, the rules of the orders were modified, and under the Byzantines complete freedom reigned. The wealth lavished on the interior of Hagia Sophia was not evident on the exterior. If the outside was more interesting than the Early Christian basilica, it was because of the more complex mass, not from decoration.

After the Iconoclastic Controversy of the 8th and 9th centuries a second period of Byzantine architecture developed. The typical plan became a Greek cross (with four arms of equal length) inscribed within a square. A principal dome placed over the center was buttressed by the barrel-vaulted arms of the cross and by four smaller domes in the corners of the square. These churches were smaller than Hagia Sophia and less open in plan; decoration enriched their exteriors and expressed the structure. The Byzantine style of this period spread to Armenia, where the central dome was often encased in a tower. The sack of Constantinople by the Fourth Crusade (1204) undermined the strength of the Byzantine empire; although that empire revived somewhat in the later 13th and 14th centuries, the more important buildings of these centuries, probably influenced by western Europe, were created in the provinces, not in Constantinople itself. In Greece and in the Balkans, churches of the Greek cross form were altered by increasing the height of the ground story and by further emphasizing the vertical quality in towerlike domes. Beyond the Balkans the style spread to Russia, where it assumed an exotic character with its onion-shaped domes.

Islamic. In 622, Mohammed fled from Mecca to Medina; with this date the Muslims begin their chronology. The new religion spread rapidly from its center in Arabia north and east into Persia, west across North Africa to the Atlantic, and north into Spain and Sicily. The architecture of Islam was derived largely from Byzantium

HIRMER VERLAG: MÜNCHEN

HAGIA SOPHIA in Istanbul, begun in the 6th century, exemplifies the Byzantine use of domed interiors.

and Sassanian Persia. The former contributed to the type of columns and their combination with arches; the latter gave the domes of pointed outline supported on squinches, as well as the common use of the pointed instead of the round arch. If few structural innovations can be credited to them, the Muslims had the richest of colorful decoration. The mosques in Egypt and Syria were simply files of columns bearing arcades arranged around an open court, the colonnades multiplied on the side of the mihrab, a niche in the direction of Mecca. These features, together with the minarets, those slender towers whence the faithful are called to prayer, may be seen in the Mosque of Ahmed Ibn Tulun (about 879) at Cairo. Gradually the aisle leading to the mihrab was broadened and a domed sanctuary was built over the mihrab. In the mosque at Córdoba (begun about 785) were horseshoe arches, while those near the mihrab were fringed in scalloped-shaped forms.

Although the early Muslims lived in austerity, their descendants in Spain turned to luxury and to a degree of civilization far in advance of that in western Europe at the same time. Their great palace, the Alhambra at Granada (13th–14th century), was the most elegant in Europe (see ALHAMBRA). Its delicate decoration in stucco, gilded and painted, its slender columns, and its succession of courts and halls must have overwhelmed the visitor.

To the east, the mosques of Persia with their domed sanctuaries and vaulted chambers grew from the earlier Sassanian architecture of that country. These features in turn spread with Islam to India where in the Pearl Mosque at Agra (1646–1653) three marble domes rose beside a large courtyard. The most celebrated Islamic monument in India was the Taj Mahal at

NATHAN PLETCHER

ROMANESQUE CATHEDRAL of Pisa (*above*) added space and decoration to a basic Roman basilica design.

ST. ÉTIENNE (*left*), at Caen, France, Romanesque in style, anticipated the early phase of Gothic design.

JEAN ROUBIER

Agra (1632–1645), the tomb built by Shah Jahan for his wife Mumtaz Mahal. The beauty of the building lay in its clear plan, its exquisite proportions, its inlays of semiprecious stones, and in its setting of formal gardens and reflecting pools.

Romanesque. The collapse of the Roman empire in the West inaugurated five centuries commonly known as the Dark Ages. In the ensuing economic and political chaos, little of architectural significance could be produced, and it was not until the economic revival of the 11th century that extensive building became feasible. By then was born not one style but a family of diversified styles with some elements in common. The power of the higher feudal nobility made such areas as Auvergne, Normandy, and Aquitaine in France virtually independent, and since communications were poor, local styles arose. In this great age of the church some styles were affected by vague memories of classic forms, some by Byzantine, and still others by Islamic motives. Although generally characterized by the round arch, even this elementary form was not universal, and the churches ranged from wood-roofed basilicas to complex and prophetic vaulted buildings.

Thus Tuscany in Italy, as represented in the cathedral of Pisa (begun 1063), took the plan of an Early Christian basilica but enlarged the transepts and separated the apse from them by a full choir. The wood roof over the nave required only a light colonnade for its support, but its columns were so Corinthian that it is apparent the builders were familiar with Roman designs. The Pisans covered the entire exterior of the cathedral with tier upon tier of delicate arches on slender columns, with walls of lustrous white marble relieved by small patterns in mosaic. In contrast, Sicilian Romanesque was a mélange of elements borrowed from Rome, Constantinople, Islam, Normandy, and Lombardy, each of which left its mark on the island. For example, the cathedral of Monreale (1174–1189) was wood-roofed and basilican in plan. The nave columns and their capitals, and still more the mosaics that cover the walls, were Byzantine and gave the interior the colorful brilliance of its Eastern predecessor. Around the wall of the apse were two stories of interlacing arches, a favorite Norman motive, but composed of Islamic pointed arches at Monreale. In other Sicilian churches, such as

the cathedral of Cefalù (1145), the twin towers of Normandy flanked the façade.

These churches were unvaulted. Because a wood roof was flammable and since the greater churches housed valuable relics in their many altars, a stone vault was required. The great churches along the routes to Santiago de Compostela (begun about 1075) in northern Spain offered one solution. A nave and aisles of exceptional length were crossed by transepts in front of the choir. From the eastern side of the transepts and around the apse protruded chapels to provide altars for the additional relics preserved for the edification of pilgrims. To give access to these chapels, it was necessary to bend the aisle around the apse, thereby creating an ambulatory. A barrel vault, laced by ribs or arches, covered the nave and was buttressed by half-barrel vaults over the aisles. To pierce windows through the sides of such vaults was impossible; therefore the church was lighted only from the aisles and from the ends of the nave. These gloomy interiors were impressive in scale. Typical of the Romanesque was the clear separation of the several volumes that composed the church. Although the aisles opened on one side into the nave, the piers dividing the two were so massive that the aisles seemed distinct spatial units, not extensions of the space within the nave. The same was true of the exterior; nave, aisles, choir, apse, ambulatory, and chapels were each articulated, and the unity of the whole church was the sum of its parts.

Still other regions, like Lombardy, experimented with the ribbed vault. While an arch composed of wedge-shaped stones is being built, it must be supported until the arch is complete; this temporary support, known as centering, may then be removed. Timber for centering was expensive in Lombardy. By building ribs along the sides and across the diagonals of each vaulting compartment, the Lombards could rest the vault on them, at least partly. Since the ribs in Sant' Ambrogio in Milan (11th–12th century) seemed to concentrate the structural forces within the vault, each rib needed a separate colonnette in the pier to give it apparent support. The aisles, being half the width of the nave, required twice as many vaulting compartments and hence twice as many piers. However, the piers that supported only the aisle vaults could be smaller and simpler in design than those needed to hold the vaults of both nave and aisles. This resulted in a rythmic alteration of piers. Furthermore, the outward pressure of the ribs required a thickening of the wall into a buttress corresponding to each of the piers of the church. Logical as this system was, to light the church under such vaults was difficult. Moreover, the vaults appeared heavy and, being somewhat domical, overemphasized the independence of each unit. As buildings, they were less imposing, perhaps less expressive of the power of the church than other examples of Romanesque architecture; as structural experiments, they prepared the way for the Gothic style.

Thanks to Lombardy's intellectual prestige in the 11th century, its influence spread in all directions. German Romanesque cathedrals, like those at Mainz (12th century) and Worms (12th century), adopted but modified the Lombard system. More important, the Normans in St. Étienne (Abbaye-aux-Hommes) at Caen (begun about 1064) borrowed the ribbed vaults and membered piers but relied on thick walls for buttressing. Hence they reintroduced the clerestory to light the nave. Over each intermediate pier they constructed an additional rib across the nave, thereby converting the quadripartite vaulting of Lombardy, with its four triangles in each bay, into a sexpartite system that lived on into the early phases of the Gothic style. In La Trinité (Abbaye-aux-Dames), Caen (remodeled about 1140), the half arches under the aisle roofs buttressing each pier of the nave anticipated the flying buttress of Gothic architecture, as the twin towers on the façade foretold the front of Gothic cathedrals. With the conquest of England (1066) the Normans transported their architecture to the island. Although less concerned with structural problems than were the Normans on the continent, their expression of sheer power was greater. Durham cathedral (begun about 1093) was imposing through the immense mass of its supports, the ponderous rhythm that was created in the nave, and the clear definition of space. Geometric patterns applied to the moldings called attention to the more important structural members.

Gothic. About the middle of the 12th century the Gothic style developed in northern France. As time passed, communications improved. Moreover, with the growth of towns fostered by the king, the local variations of style typical of the Romanesque gave way to more unified styles. Thus we may speak of French, Spanish, or Italian Gothic, instead of Tuscan, Sicilian, or Lombard Romanesque. The Gothic style, generally characterized by the pointed arch, was the product partly of religious needs and partly of community pride. Thus, the ritual of medieval worship, with its elaborate processions and the veneration of relics calling for many altars, both inherited from the Romanesque, established the plan of the structure. The towns rivaled each other in the size or height of their cathedrals; the guilds supported chapels; and, in the case of Chartres (about 1194–1260), the townsfolk contributed their personal service in drawing carts loaded with stone for their cathedral.

The French Gothic style combined structural, spatial, and religious factors. The structural elements grew from the Norman Romanesque but were lightened and refined. Thus, ribbed vaults and membered piers reoccurred, but the vaults

CHARTRES CATHEDRAL exemplifies Gothic style that began in the northern area of France in the 1100's.

were higher, the ribs pointed, the clerestory larger, and the members in the pier both more consistent and more dramatic in their verticality. The pointed ribs were often stilted; that is, certain ribs began to curve at a higher level than others in the same group. This offered great flexibility in design, permitting the vaulting of rectangular, trapezoidal, or semicircular compartments, as well as the standard square bays of the Romanesque style. During the 12th century the Norman sexpartite system was often preserved, but in the 13th century there was a return to quadripartite vaulting. The wall as a supporting element was suppressed; at the clerestory level, windows extended from pier to pier. Because the vaults were so high, it became necessary to develop the flying buttress, a half arch of stone to transmit the lateral pressure of the nave vaults over the roofs of the aisles to the pier buttresses outside the church. The large windows required a network of stone tracery to hold the glass. The small size of the piers in proportion to the voids between them altered the spatial character. In the Gothic the aisles seemed to be extensions of the nave space instead of separate volumes; space flowed from aisle to nave or transepts. Also, since the wall was replaced by glass, there was no sharp distinction of internal and external space. On the exterior, the limits of the building, broken by the projections of buttresses and spires, fused, as it were, with surrounding space. In contrast to the Greek temple, which was devised as a complete shape resting on the ground, the Gothic had a quality of the infinite, a lack of definition, a parallel to the Christian concept of the divinity as infinite, whereas the Olympic deities were conceived in human form. The insistent verticality of the interior, with its arches pointing to heaven like arrows, contributed to this spirituality, as did the towers sometimes topped with spires on the exterior of the church.

From northern France, Gothic art spread through western Europe, but each country developed its own peculiarities of style. Thus in Italy and Spain, roofs tended to become flatter, windows smaller (since less light was necessary), and walls more extensive to exclude the southern heat. The Italians, particularly, ignored the structural elements of French Gothic, as in the gaunt interior of the immense cathedral of Florence (1296–1367). They tended to sheathe their churches with slabs of marble arranged in polychromatic patterns. In Germany, Cologne cathedral (begun 1248) was modeled on Amiens; more original were the hall churches, such as St. Elizabeth at Marburg (1235–1283), where the aisles were as high as the nave and where the slender piers hardly broke the unified interior space.

Unlike the French, many English cathedrals were monastic in origin, and most of the others were governed by secular canons who followed some of the practices of monasteries. In either case the cloister, rarely found in French cathedrals, appears quite regularly in England. Typically, the English minsters (monasteries) were surrounded by lawns and trees instead of the buildings of the town. They could be seen from all sides. Hence the building centered around a large central tower with a spire above it, as at Salisbury (begun 1220), although twin western towers were often retained. A square east end replaced the apse so that all the altars and chapels faced east. Transepts were often doubled, with one under the main tower and a second smaller one to the east, thereby producing an archiepiscopal cross plan. The eastern side of each bay in both transepts gave room for additional altars.

The Early English, or Lancet style (about 1150–1250) at Salisbury or Canterbury (begun 1175) preserved a large part of the Romanesque spirit. The structural system was not so logical as in French Gothic, the height was less extreme, and the heavy wall and massive piers of

SALISBURY CATHEDRAL, in the Early English Gothic style, preserves much of the Romanesque spirit.

MARBURG—ART REFERENCE BUREAU

the Romanesque were modified but not discarded. The great length of English churches stressed the horizontal line instead of the French vertical line. Early English vaults were simple, although the particular method of building the vault prompted the English to add ridge ribs along the apex of the vault down the length of the church and across each bay. Windows were simple, pointed shapes (lancet) without tracery. The reminiscences of the Romanesque were outgrown in the Decorated style (about 1250–1350); wider arches and smaller piers between nave and aisles created more flexible space, as in the Angel Choir (1255–1280) of Lincoln cathedral. Vaults became complex with a greater number of ribs, a logical outgrowth of the English method of vaulting. As the windows grew larger, many patterns of tracery were designed to support the glass. In the late 13th century these patterns within the arches at the top of the window were composed of circles and segments of circles, a geometric style that was replaced in the early 14th century with curvilinear designs involving complex reversed, or ogee, curves. The Perpendicular style (about 1350–1500) was so called because the vertical bars of tracery striped the window from top to bottom, braced at intervals by horizontal bars. Thus the pattern became a series of perpendicular rectangles. Vaulting was extremely complex; the fan vault in the cloisters of Gloucester cathedral (begun 1351) converted the ribs into a pattern on the undersurface of the vault without their earlier structural function. The virtuosity in vaulting reached its climax in Henry VII's Chapel (about 1500–1512) in Westminster Abbey.

Meanwhile in France the impulse that had produced the great cathedrals waned by 1300. Perhaps because the Hundred Years' War was fought on French soil, little architecture was then forthcoming. In the 15th century, building revived as Flamboyant Gothic was influenced by the English Decorated and Perpendicular styles. Similar vaulting patterns, elaborate tracery in flamelike lines, openwork gables and spires, and virtuosity in handling stone resulted in churches of great richness of design without the emotional impact of the earlier style.

Its churches did not exhaust the contributions of the Gothic period to architecture. As a matter of fact, civic and domestic building grew steadily in importance. The Cloth Hall at Ypres (13th century) testified to the power of the Flemish guilds, as did the Palazzo Vecchio (13th century) to the independence of Florence. In the earlier Middle Ages the castle with its keep or tower served the dual purpose of living and defense. Thick walls and small windows made Hedingham Castle in Essex, England (about 1130), safe from attack but hardly comfortable, since the warmth of open fireplaces was lost through unglazed windows, too small for adequate light. The germ of the later houses lay partly in such Norman castles, partly in manor houses like Oakham Castle (about 1180). From the latter came the hall as the focus of the patriarchal life of feudalism. Here, at first, the lord of the manor ate with his retainers, and there some of them slept. To one end of the hall were the kitchen, buttery, and pantry; to the other, the lord's solar and the lady's bower, their private quarters. As time passed and more rooms became available, the hall was less needed for communal eating, and not at all for sleeping, and therefore dwindled in size. Larger fireplaces added to comfort, and in the 15th century, window glass began to appear in the homes of the upper classes. Compton Wynyates, England (about 1520), was typical of these later manor houses. The frank acceptance of timber construction for the roofs, the indifference to symmetry, the unstudied directness of solution, the design for living made Compton Wynyates a perfect expression of its day in architecture.

Renaissance. Although anticipated earlier, the 15th century in Italy witnessed the first flowering of the Renaissance. The aspect of this period that most affected architecture was its deliberate revival of the classical past, that is, of Roman architecture, and its contemptuous rejection of the Gothic. Indeed the term "Gothic," meaning "barbarous," was coined in the 16th century to refer to the style of the later Middle Ages. Brunelleschi devoted years of enthusiastic study to Roman ruins. Therefore, when he designed San Lorenzo in Florence (1425), he avoided the pointed arches, vaults, tracery, towers, and spires of Gothic design and turned instead to the plan of the unvaulted Early Christian basilica. But he did not copy the basilica. No colorful mosaics on walls or floors remained in his monochromatic building. He tried to use the Roman orders and arches and to a certain extent succeeded, but he did not attain the spatial quality of Roman design. The Pazzi Chapel, Florence (about 1429), had a linear instead of a plastic design, as though the pattern of its columns, arches, and moldings had been designed in lines on a drawing board instead of in three-dimensional masses. Brunelleschi's attempt to revive Roman forms may be compared with the first lessons of a student in a foreign language; the words were recognizable but the grammar and accent from the Roman point of view were distorted. In fact, Brunelleschi created a new style, although his greatest work, the dome of the cathedral of Florence (begun 1418), had the boldness of the Renaissance but little of Roman inspiration. Its structure was derived in part from the dome of the Romanesque baptistery in front of the cathedral.

His successor Michelozzo, in the design of the Riccardi (Medici) Palace in Florence (begun 1444), translated the Gothic palace type of the Palazzo Vecchio into a Renaissance vocabulary. However, Leon Battista Alberti in the Palazzo

ALINARI—ART REFERENCE BUREAU

BRAMANTE'S TEMPIETTO in Rome anticipates on a small scale the later design for St. Peter's Basilica.

Rucellai in Florence (1451–1455) gave prominence to the orders of Roman architecture. The façade, though linear, has three orders of pilasters superposed, each with its own entablature. A scholar, Alberti grasped the principles of Roman planning and space, and made use of them in his design for Sant' Andrea at Mantua (begun 1470). In this design, not merely the orders but also the motive of the Roman triumphal arch fused with the temple front. Though not fully Roman in character, the building approximated the classical Roman style more than did the structures of Brunelleschi. This style reached a climax in the early 16th century at the hands of Bramante in Rome, whose Tempietto of San Pietro in Montorio (1501–1502), however small, had a monumentality and plastic form similar to true Roman designs. Bramante also began the reconstruction

CHAMBORD, vast château in the Loire Valley, France, combines elements of both Gothic and Renaissance styles.

BULLOZ—ART REFERENCE BUREAU

POST-RENAISSANCE ARCHITECTURE is exemplified by the Petit Trianon at Versailles (*above*), designed by Jacques Ange Gabriel as a retreat for King Louis XV, and by Francesco Borromini's ornate baroque church in Rome, San Carlo alle Quattro Fontane (*right*).

of St. Peter's in Rome (1506) on a vast scale, a design to be continued and modified through a century of building. The scholarly enthusiasm of Florence for the classical was not duplicated farther north in Italy. There it was the decorative Roman arabesques, rich surface patterns and color, that beguiled the designers. The façade of the Certosa (Carthusian monastery) at Pavia (begun 1491) by Giovanni Antonio Amadeo and others was so covered with carving and colored marbles as to bear no resemblance at all to antiquity. It was, however, this Lombard detail that affected French and German designers, perhaps because they saw that building when they first entered Italy.

Thus, at the beginning of the 16th century the French monarchy and aristocracy, familiar with Italian sophistication through the wars of Charles VIII, Louis XII, and Francis I, imported architects and craftsmen to design their châteaux. The style of Francis I as represented at Blois (south front, 1515–1519) was the child of a marriage of north Italian detail and French Gothic tradition. The verticality of the Gothic, its steep roofs and dormer windows, and its tracery and freedom underlay the pilasters, round arches, and arabesques brought from the south. The vast Château of Chambord (1526–1550) retains the courtyard of the Gothic castle and its round towers at intervals, alternating with somewhat lower links of building between them. On the other hand, substantial windows pierce the outer walls, showing that defense was no longer a primary consideration, and the detail has become Italianate in character, with horizontal moldings like strings tying together towers and links. By the middle of the 16th century under Henry II, the French designers better understood Renaissance ideas and produced a style that was restrained in comparison with the Rabelaisian exuberance of the style of Francis I. It may be seen in the part of the Louvre (1541–1548) designed by Pierre Lescot. The accented pavilions and subordinate links of the French tradition are still present, but the superposed orders of engaged columns and pilasters follow fairly closely the proportions and rules prescribed for them by Italian theorists.

A similar development occurred in Spain, beginning with the decorative extravagance of the Plateresque and merging in the mid-16th century into the sobriety of the more archaeological Griego-Romano. In England, too, the Renaissance began with the importation of Italian artists by Henry VIII. However, Henry's marital troubles led to the English withdrawal from the Roman Church and hence to a cessation of direct influence from the south. Under Elizabeth the English, affected by Protestantism, turned to Flanders and Germany. Unfortunately, the Germans themselves had little grasp of the principles of the Renaissance and their peculiarly heavy-handed style affected Burleigh House, Northamptonshire (1577–1587). The Elizabethan misunderstanding of the Renaissance may be seen in their use of Doric columns and blocks of entablature as chimney pots, as weird a distortion of the classical motive as can be imagined. Although no more classical, the Jacobean style of the early 17th century, a development from the Elizabethan, was better organized.

Post-Renaissance. The successors of Bramante in Italy modified his academic style. When Michelangelo was appointed architect of St. Peter's (1547), he announced his intention of returning to Bramante's plans, but his instinct as a sculptor led him to mold his building as a design in light and shade, with little consideration of the structural side of architecture. His love of the colossal found scope in the vast size of St. Peter's and caused him to suppress the smaller columns provided by Bramante, which might have conveyed to the observer the real scale of the building. Nevertheless, his design of the dome of St. Peter's, modified and completed after his death by Giacomo della Porta (1588), expressed the power and authority of the Roman Church in the Counter Reformation. Michelangelo's contradiction of the rules of classical architecture later served as the foundation of the baroque style. His contemporaries were less adventurous. Andrea Palladio (1518–1580) designed palaces in Vicenza and Venice with pilasters rising through two or more stories, well-proportioned and composed, and in admirable taste. His name is remembered in the motive

Palladio, an arch supported on columns and flanked by narrow rectangular openings, although he did not invent the motive. Palladio wrote books on architecture that recommended specific proportions for the units of the classical orders, books that had a profound influence in England and ultimately in America. Similar books by Giacomo Barozzi da Vignola influenced French architecture. His style was bolder than that of Palladio, and his Il Gesù in Rome (1568–1584) was typical of early Jesuit churches. Chapels, not aisles, lined the nave, the transepts were shallow; and the nave was broad, with a resulting compactness of space. This plan became standard for Roman baroque churches.

With Giovanni Lorenzo Bernini and Francesco Borromini the exuberant license of the baroque style was complete. Michelangelo's freedom in the handling of classical architecture prompted Borromini to disregard the accepted proportions and even the traditional membering of the orders, while the baroque love of movement led him to plan San Carlo alle Quattro Fontane, Rome (1638–1667), in the shape of an oval extended and broken by deep niches at either end, with shallower ones to the sides. Its façade alternates concave and convex bays. Borromini's star-shaped plan for Sant' Ivo alla Sapienza, Rome, is even more complex and dynamic. Bernini chose a similar elliptical plan for Sant' Andrea al Quirinale, Rome, as he did also for the colonnades of St. Peter's (1656–1663). This movement linked the baroque buildings with space, while the Renaissance designs had been defined within and separated from space. The most extreme examples of the baroque in space, in movement, and in profuse decoration were built in Spain, such as the Cartuja at Granada (late 17th century), and in Germany.

After the late 16th century wars of religion in France, Henry IV reestablished order. With returning prosperity, baroque influence impressed itself on the detail of Salomon de Brosse's design for the Luxembourg Palace in Paris (1615–1624), modeled on the newer parts of the Pitti Palace in Florence. However, the Luxembourg retained such elements of French tradition as the arrangement around a rectangular court, a faint reminiscence of the medieval castle, and a basic composition in vertical pavilions at the center and ends connected by horizontal blocks of building. François Mansart in the Château de Maisons-Laffitte (1642–1651) abandoned the enclosed court and also rejected the baroque license in handling the classical orders. Restraint

and beauty of proportions characterized his style. He prepared the way for the French classical style of Louis XIV, the supreme expression of the pomp and power of absolutism. Thus, the east front of the Louvre (1667–1674), designed by Claude Perrault, retained from the baroque chiefly the deep pattern of light and shade cast by the colonnade, whose proportions and membering were Roman. In Versailles the state apartments facing the gardens were so ordered as to impress the visitor with the majesty of the king of France. Order and organization of space did not prevent enrichment of the exterior by carved trophies on the skyline or of the interior by colored marbles, paint, sculpture, and gilding. The peculiarly French rhythm of accented pavilions with unaccented links between persists on the garden front of Versailles, but the roof finally disappears as a visible feature.

The formality of this age provoked its own reaction under Louis XV in the style of interior decoration known as the rococo. The salons of the 18th century were more intimate than the Hall of Mirrors at Versailles, designed for conversation and intrigue, not for assemblies of the court. Delicate patterns of curving lines adorned ceilings and walls and gave a feminine atmosphere. At the same time, men became aware of the inadequacy of the individual house as a unit in the larger design of the town. Hence the city of Nancy built whole streets and squares where the separate houses submerged their individuality in the larger units. In France, though not in Germany, the license of the rococo by 1760 gave way to the more sober and classical style of Louis XVI, some years before his accession to the throne. Thus, the Petit Trianon, Versailles (1762–1768), designed by Jacques Ange Gabriel as a retreat for Louis XV and his mistresses from the oppressive formality of court ritual, has the elegance and refinement of the rococo without its license. In terms of composition, proportion, and scale the Petit Trianon is one of the great masterpieces of architecture. The Panthéon (Ste. Geneviève) in Paris (1755–1780, or possibly 1764–1790) by Jacques Germain Soufflot, for example, used the colonnaded front of a Roman temple as an entrance and topped the building with a dome like that of St. Paul's, London. This style anticipated the eclectic revivals of the early 19th century, although it did not carry archaeology in architecture to an extreme.

England through the Jacobean period had been slow to grasp the principles of the

PALLADIO'S DESIGNS, such as Villa Rotunda (right), near Vicenza, Italy, had an influence on architecture that extended through 18th century Georgian in England.

PARSON CAPEN HOUSE at Topsfield, Mass., is an example of Gothic influence in American colonial homes.

Renaissance, but Inigo Jones almost brought his country into step with continental architecture. Nearly every detail in the Queen's House at Greenwich (1617–1635) and the Banqueting House, Whitehall, London (1619–1622) found a precedent in Palladio, and yet the buildings retain a peculiarly English flavor. But Jones' academic style yielded under the Restoration in the work of Sir Christopher Wren to a restrained baroque, influenced at times by Bernini and Borromini and at other times by French and Dutch architecture. While the plan of St. Paul's Cathedral (1668–1710) drew some elements from English medieval tradition, its western towers were somewhat Italian, and its façade was indebted to Perrault's colonnade of the Louvre. The dome, resting on a drum ringed with columns, was more structural than the dome of St. Peter's and hardly less effective visually. Wren's wealth of imagination found scope in the varied plans of his parish churches, designed to replace those destroyed in the great fire of London (1666). Each was adapted to its irregular site; and for each a steeple or tower of distinguished silhouette was provided.

The Georgian period preferred the Palladian style of Jones to the baroque vigor of Wren in its churches and in its mansions such as Prior Park at Bath (about 1736–1743) by John Wood. These dignified houses, with their pedimented porticoes, their balustrades above the main cornice, and their symmetrically placed pedimented windows, formed the immediate background of American architecture in the years just before and after the War of Independence. Toward the end of the century, partly under the influence of the newly excavated Roman houses at Pompeii, the Adam brothers introduced a semiclassical semidecorative style characterized by delicate surface ornament of urns, festoons, garlands, lyres, sunbursts, and other motives found in paint on the walls of Pompeian houses. The rooms in their houses were varied in volume, including circular, oval, and other shapes.

Early American. A thousand years before Columbus, the Mayan culture in Central America set its principal structures on mounds or pyramids of rubble masonry, approached by a steep staircase on one side. Corbel vaults roofed the narrow inner chambers, with a decorative section of pierced stone wall along the roof. Pro-

fuse carving in stone, painted in brilliant color, sheathed the outer walls, and where columns were needed they took the form of conventionalized serpents, whose heads jutted forward from the base of the wall, their bodies providing the height of the column and their tails protruding at the top to form a capital. Mayan culture influenced the later Aztec, but neither of these civilizations was destined to affect subsequent architecture. After the discovery of America the zeal of the Spaniards in spreading Christianity by force of arms led them to replace the earlier buildings by those of types then current in Spain, insofar as native labor could execute the designs of Spanish-trained architects. Thus, the cathedral in Mexico City (chiefly 17th century) belonged to the luxuriant Spanish baroque style, with domes resplendent in colored tile. From Mexico the style spread northward to Texas, New Mexico, and Arizona. In the missions of San Jose near San Antonio, Texas, and San Xavier near Tucson, Ariz., extravagant baroque façades loaded with decoration contrasted with the severe, thick walls of the body of the church. Thence the style spread through the chain of missions established by Padre Junípero Serra (1713–1784) along the California coast. These, however, generally lack the decorative façades of the older missions, although the front of Santa Barbara (1820) was based on the Spanish edition of the Roman architect and writer Vitruvius.

Along the Atlantic seaboard the dominant strain was English, although the early work in New York was Dutch. When the colonies were settled early in the 17th century, the homes of the middle class in England were not the aristocratic Jacobean style but rather the traditional Gothic. The type persisted almost unchanged throughout the 17th century in Virginia, but the best-preserved examples are in New England. The plan of the Parson Capen House in Topsfield, Mass. (1683), provided for two rooms of unequal size on either side of a central chimney with great fireplaces back to back for both warmth and cooking. The rooms were joined by a narrow hall (only as wide as the chimney), which contained the narrow stairs to the second floor. The structure, like many late Gothic houses in England and on the Continent, was half timber, the interstices between the timbers filled with brick or with wattle and daub (green twigs mixed with clay). This framework was left visible on the interior, like the ribs of Gothic vaults, and is visibly expressed on the exterior by pendants carved from the ends of posts that protrude below the overhanging second floor. English half-timber construction is often visible on the exterior; in the colonies it was covered with clapboards or shingles for additional warmth, sometimes perhaps, a few years after the house was built. The windows were small casements in the late Gothic style, either fixed in place or hinged at one side. They were filled with small panes of glass, or at the beginning, simply with paper soaked in linseed oil. None of the classical or Renaissance moldings or decorative accents appear. Very few churches of the time have been preserved. The Anglican St. Luke's, Smithfield, Va. (1632), preserved the buttresses, the pointed arches, and simple tracery of the Gothic, while the curved roof timbers of the Old Ship Meeting House, Hingham, Mass. (1681), bespeak the ship carpenters who built it for a Puritan congregation.

As wealth grew from plantations or trade, so modest a home was inadequate. In North and South alike the wealthier individuals turned to the English Georgian, assisted by carpenter's handbooks that offered models of design. Although the walls in Southern houses might be made of brick, and occasionally those around Philadelphia of stone, it was the woodworker whose supreme craftsmanship, evident in panels, doors, windows, fireplaces, or staircases, gave the style its character. The typical plan consisted of a central hall that contained the stairs and ran through the house from front to back flanked by two rooms on each side. Since each room required its own fireplace, a chimney was needed between each pair of rooms, or two chimneys might be built in both ends of the house. Roofs were less steep in pitch than in the 17th century and sometimes had a balustrade at the summit. Symmetry was the rule, with four windows and a central door on the ground floor and five windows on the second. The double-hung sash windows were larger than they had been, with fewer but bigger panes as glass became more available. The classical orders taken from the handbooks, usually as pilasters but rarely as engaged columns, accent the corners of the Royall House, Medford, Mass. (about 1747). They sometimes rise on either side of the door to the main cornice, which may then support a pediment in the center. Particularly in the doorway itself are the orders standard. The rooms are elegantly paneled or sometimes wall-papered, with plain plaster ceilings that give no hint of construction. The focus is on the fireplaces, which, though smaller in proportion to the room than they had been before, now have quite elaborate enframements and mantels drawn from the handbooks. Stairs become wider and less steep and are provided with exquisitely turned balusters. The few public buildings, such as Independence Hall, Philadelphia, are larger than private homes and often distinguished by a tower and belfry but adhere in design to the same essential features as the homes. Churches, whether Anglican, Congregational, or Baptist, are equally Georgian in character and often influenced by the English designs of James Gibbs. St. Paul's Chapel, New York, designed by Thomas McBean, with a graceful steeple at one end and a free-standing portico at the other, is a fine example of the type.

After the American Revolution, independence brought with it more complicated problems which called for architects as distinct from craftsmen. Charles Bulfinch in Boston and Samuel McIntire in Salem showed the influence of the Adam brothers sometimes in the plans of their buildings and regularly in decoration. The houses of this period often cease to be simple rectangles in plan. Instead, a free-standing porch or a pedimented portico the full height of the building may project in the center of the façade, while semicircular bays sometimes protrude from the ends of the house or from the rear, as in the White House, Washington, D.C., by James Hoban. Roofs become still lower in pitch so that the balustrade appears immediately above the cornice instead of at the top. Windows grow in size, and inside the house ceilings are higher than hitherto. Public buildings become more prominent. Charles Bulfinch designed the old State Capitol (now the City Hall) in Hartford, Conn., the State House in Boston (1795–1798), and the State House in Augusta, Me. The Boston State

POWEL ROOM, Philadelphia Museum of Art, shows colonial adaptation of the elegance of English Georgian.

House, distinguished in plan, in proportions, and in its handling of materials, started the tradition of a dome as a feature of state capitols—a tradition that lasted into the 20th century. Thomas Jefferson in Virginia preferred Roman architecture to the English sources of Bulfinch. His State Capitol in Richmond (1785–1798) was frankly modeled on the Roman temple called the Maison Carrée at Nîmes. The different purposes of the Capitol and its model forced Jefferson to introduce windows in his building, and the inadequacy of local craftsmanship compelled him to substitute the Ionic for the more complex Corinthian order. Jefferson modeled the pavilions, originally professors' houses and classrooms, of the University of Virginia at Charlottesville, (1817), on specific Roman buildings, so that they would present acceptable examples of architecture to the students. The library of the university is a small scale replica of the Pantheon, Rome, though here as in Richmond, it was necessary to add windows. Thus Jefferson was the first architect to adopt not merely a past style, but specific building forms of that style, and to force them to house new purposes.

Eclecticism. Eclecticism in architecture implies freedom on the part of the architect or client or both to choose among the styles of the past that which seems most appropriate. In a sense, the Renaissance was eclectic in its attempted revival of Roman forms. The eclecticism of the early 19th century was backed by archaeology. It revealed a sentimental nostalgia for past styles whose romantic forms seemed to offer an escape from the ungoverned industrialization of laissez faire economics and the sordidness of growing urbanization. Thus in the Madeleine in Paris (1807–1842) by Barthélemy Vignon, a Christian church has been forced into the form of a Roman temple. As western Europe learned more of Greek architecture, it, too, was laid under tribute. The Walhalla at Regensburg, or Ratisbon (1830–1842) by Leo von Klenze revived the Parthenon. Even in the United States the Lee Mansion in Arlington, Va. (1826), borrowed at least the front of a Greek temple both in proportions and in archaeological detail, although it was executed in wood, not stone. Contemporary with, but lasting somewhat later than, the Greek Revival was the Gothic Revival. At first, the picturesque and romantic aspects of the Gothic gave birth to such frivolous designs as James Wyatt's Fonthill Abbey (1796–1814). Early in the 19th century a serious study of medieval architecture was coupled with the revival in the Anglican Church known as the Oxford movement to produce a more correct version of the Gothic, whose best-known examples were the Houses of Parliament (1840–1860) by Sir Charles Barry and Trinity Church, New York City (1839–1846), by Richard Upjohn.

By the middle of the 19th century both the Greek and Gothic revivals were spent, to be replaced by a bewildering variety of styles. Italian villas and Swiss chalets jostled Victorian Gothic churches and Victorian classical post offices. These styles were superficial and interchangeable. They had in common, in this age of materialism and ostentation, plans whose outlines were broken by protruding bay windows, towers, or porches; restless silhouettes; senseless variety of crude and undigested details, as though the architects tried to prove their weath of imagination by multiplying motives; and ill-advised experiments in colored materials. Not all the Victorian buildings were bad; at least the best of them were bold, but the crass vulgarity of the style as a whole typified its age. In the United States the low point was reached in the Philadelphia Centennial Exposition (1876). The vigorous Romanesque Revival designs of Henry Hobson Richardson, based on the Romanesque styles of southern France and Spain, though ponderous, were well composed and expressive of stone in their rugged masonry. For 20 years after his design for Trinity Church, Boston (1872), his style held sway.

Beginning about 1890, eclecticism changed its flavor. Increasing wealth, greater speed of travel that made it easier to visit Europe, and the spread of photography familiarized architects and public alike with historic architecture as never before. Modern eclecticism was not only purer in style; it also understood something of the flavor of the past as well as its forms. A modernized classic style based on Greece, Rome, or the Italian Renaissance was popularized by McKim, Mead, and White in the Public Library, Boston (1888–1895). This style received such impetus through its adoption for the World's Columbian

Exposition in Chicago (1893) that for the next generation hardly a public building in America failed to adhere to it. At about the same time, Henry Vaughan, the firm of Cram, Goodhue, and Ferguson, and others suppressed the vagaries of Victorian Gothic to create a modernized Gothic for church, college, and occasionally domestic architecture. At best, modern eclecticism was marked by·scholarship, taste, and sympathy for the forms of the past and remarkable ingenuity in adapting central heating, plumbing, and electric lighting to those forms. The better eclectic buildings are less imitations than thoughtful adaptations of the past modified to suit new conditions. Thus in St. Thomas' Church, New York City (1905), by Cram, Goodhue, and Ferguson, the aisles of Gothic architecture have dwindled to mere passageways, since the elaborate processionals of medieval liturgy that brought aisles into being no longer obtained. In terms of composition, proportion, and scale, many eclectic buildings equal if they do not surpass the best buildings of the historic styles that inspired them. The almost complete acceptance of the eclectic approach through the first third of the 20th century may even mean that it was an answer to the spirit of the time. It is at least suggestive that the imperial character of modernized classical buildings coincides with the imperialist Spanish-American War and with the economic imperialism of big business.

Ancestry of the International Style. Every major style in the history of architecture was born because there appeared new problems for architecture to solve, new building materials, or new methods of principles of construction. Before the 20th century began, all three of these prerequisites had been fulfilled. The growth of industrialism, new means of transportation and communication, and new concepts of medicine or of education gave rise to problems unfaced by previous generations. Structural metals, concrete, glass, and fabricated materials offered fresh possibilities in design. Metal and concrete made it possible to exploit the cantilever as never before. The application of machines in the controlled conditions of factories to the production of materials and sometimes to whole sections of buildings, made obsolete the older styles based on handicraft methods.

Under its veneer of eclecticism the 19th century unwittingly laid the foundations of a new style. Improvements in metallurgy so lowered the price of iron (and later of steel) that it could be used for structure as well as decoration. The first iron bridge at Coalbrookdale, England (1779), had its members cast in the form of Gothic arches. Utilitarian buildings, such as the Halle aux Blés, Paris (1811), or the Marché de la Madeleine, Paris (1824), with metal columns and trusses, accepted the new material because of its practicality. An occasional public building, such as the Bibliothèque Ste. Geneviève, Paris (1843–1850), by Henri Labrouste, admitted iron for its inner supports. The Crystal Palace, London (1851), by Sir Joseph Paxton, was built for the exposition of that year as a frame of iron sheathed in glass.

Concrete, a mixture of sand, broken stone or aggregate, water, and cement, came into favor more slowly than metal. The Romans had used pozzolana, a natural cement, but modern concrete depends on the artificial portland cement invented in 1824 by an English bricklayer, Joseph

KAUFMANN HOUSE, Bear Run, Pa., illustrates Frank Lloyd Wright's contribution to the International style.

Aspdin. It found a modest use in foundations and canal locks where only compression was encountered, but it was relatively weak in withstanding tension. To give it the necessary tensile strength, it could be reinforced by embedded iron bars, a system patented in England in 1854 by William B. Wilkinson and in France the following year by François Coignet. In 1879, François Hennebique constructed the first reinforced concrete floor slabs, but the new material won acceptance very slowly. Perhaps the first important public building in concrete was St. Jean de Montmartre, Paris (1897–1904), by Anatol de Baudot, designed in simplified Gothic forms.

These early experiments rarely attempted to express the character of the new material in design. Thinking in terms of the material was the exception during the 19th century. One of Richardson's greatest contributions lay in his sympathy with the material—in his direct expression of stone construction in the Marshall Field Warehouse, Chicago (1885–1887) or of shingles and wood construction in the Stoughton House, Cambridge, Mass. (1882). Slightly later, Louis Sullivan in Chicago, influenced by Richardson's later work, developed the functional theory of architecture. According to this theory, any problem in architecture contained the germ of its own solution. The duty of the architect was to understand the problem so fully that the solution of both its utilitarian and its expressive aspects would become apparent without dependence on historic style.

The multistoried building was called into being by the desire of American businessmen engaged in the same type of enterprise to be close to their fellows. It could not exist without a metal frame to hold both floors and walls. It would not have been created without the elevator to provide vertical transportation; from the 1850's, elevators were installed. Probably in 1882, although the date has been questioned, Leroy S. Buffington in Minneapolis devised a method of supporting the walls and floors of multistoried buildings on an iron frame. The Home Insurance Building, Chicago (1883–1885), by William Le Baron Jenney, first applied this idea. Here two or three stories are grouped together with pilasters at the corners, the units stacked like a sectional bookcase. In Burnham and Root's Masonic Temple, Chicago (1892), the top half-dozen floors look like a German Renaissance townhouse that has unaccountably grown 22 stories under its roof. Only Sullivan saw that the new problem had to be solved on its own terms, that the skyscraper must be "a proud and soaring thing." In his Wainwright Building, St. Louis (1890–1891), the vertical continuity of the steel columns is frankly expressed. Likewise the discrete functions of the two lowest floors, the identical plan of the floors above, and the different nature of the top floor are all visualized. Thus Sullivan allowed the problem to suggest its own solution in terms of structure and purpose. His example, however, was not to be followed—for the time being at least. On the contrary, early skyscrapers until about 1913 were dressed in classical columns and entablatures or in the case of Cass Gilbert's Woolworth Building, New York City (1913), in Gothic detail.

The chaotic influence of the skyscraper on land values forced the adoption in 1916 of the New York Zoning Ordinance, which established

ROCKEFELLER CENTER, INC.

ROCKEFELLER CENTER COMPLEX, New York City, uses space between buildings to mitigate urban density.

certain limiting conditions on height and implied, although it did not prescribe, a type of design that found ready acceptance in such skyscrapers of the 1920's as the Barclay Vesey Telephone Building, New York City, by McKenzie, Voorhees, and Gmelin. Still more functional was the Philadelphia Savings Fund Society Building (1931–1932) by Howe and Lescaze, where one entire wall plane was cantilevered. Although a single skyscraper offered many advantages of light and air, to build them side by side sacrificed these benefits. Hence, Rockefeller Center, New York City, during the 1930's planned several skyscrapers as a group with space between them.

Virtually all the early skyscrapers were office buildings. With the rapid growth of city population in the 20th century the form was appropriated for living purposes also. The individual house in urban centers became an anachronism. As they became obsolete, they turned into slums which have been, and are being, torn down and replaced by tall apartment blocks, separated from one another like the buildings of Rockefeller Center to preserve light and air and to afford space for lawns and playgrounds.

Meanwhile, Frank Lloyd Wright, a disciple of Sullivan, brought his genius to bear on many problems and materials. Like Sullivan, he utterly rejected eclecticism. Like him, too, he showed extraordinary grasp of each separate problem. His Unity Church, Oak Park, Ill. (1930), was perfectly adapted as a skylit auditorium to the needs of this particular congregation. The church is designed from the inside out, so that each major part of the interior volume is given clear expression on the exterior. Here, too, for the first time in a public building, Wright demonstrated forms appropriate to concrete. The rectilinear shapes and the repetitive decorative motives on the posts between the windows are pecu-

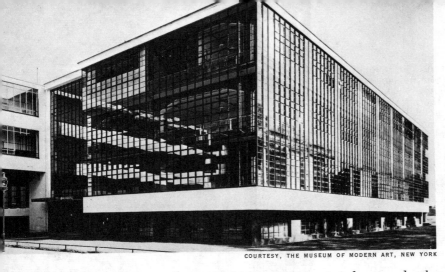

BAUHAUS, Dessau, Germany, designed by Walter Gropius, has a steel-frame and concrete interior that permits building a glass-wall exterior for light and openness.

liarly sympathetic to the material. His "prairie houses," like the Coonley House, Riverside, Ill. (1908), introduced the concept of flowing space that would be taken up and expanded later in the International style. Interior partitions are eliminated, except for the bedrooms and bathrooms, so that one can no longer speak of a living room or a dining room as distinct spatial entities. Instead there are areas whose volumes merge with one another. In addition, the windows are so extensive that space seems to flow from inside to out. The irregular plans of these houses also tend to fuse them with surrounding space. It is hard to say of them just where the house ends and out-of-doors begins. Indeed, in the Coonley House one must walk under more than half the depth of the house before reaching the door. Finally, the insistent horizontal lines of these houses adapt their design to the flat plains on which many of them are built. Wright's work became well known and much admired in Europe early in the 20th century. Although in the Kaufmann House at Bear Run, Pa. (1937–1939), he approximated the forms of the International style, he was too much an individualist and a romantic to accept any formalized doctrine of architectural theory and aesthetics.

In Europe, too, the more advanced architects dropped their inherited load of eclecticism. Antonio Gaudí turned from Gothic to purely fanciful forms for the Sagrada Familia in Barcelona, begun in 1882 and still little more than a shell in 1960. However visually exciting its lofty pinnacles and profuse seaweedlike decoration, this church is conceived not in terms of the human activity to be pursued within but, like abstract sculpture, as an object of perhaps symbolic value in its own right. Similarly free forms may be found in the short-lived Art Nouveau movement that particularly affected interior design in the 1890's and early 1900's. In the Tassel House, Brussels (1892), Baron Victor Horta applied the undulating lines of seaweed to floors, walls, ceiling, and stair rail. Comparable organic shapes dominate some of the entrances to the Paris Metro (1898–1900), designed by Hector Guimard. Charming though its results sometimes were, Art Nouveau languished because it was rooted in personal taste rather than in basic architectural problems.

More conservative architects, such as Sir Edwin Lutyens, did not reject the past quite so violently. His design of Deanery Gardens, Sonning (1900), retained the steep roof, casement windows, and other features of late medieval houses in England but not their tracery, buttresses, parapet, and other easily identifiable elements. And in Scandinavia the City Hall, Stockholm (1911–1923), by Ragnar Östberg, had so few eclectic features as to appear radical.

Other architects did not merely reject eclecticism but also anticipated elements that would later become part of the International style. Otto Wagner in the Postal Savings Bank, Vienna (1905), recognized that since the wall was supported by the frame within, it had lost its supporting function and had become a mere skin to exclude the weather. He therefore set the glass of the windows on the wall plane, thereby suggesting its thinness. Moreover, he applied to the surface of the walls repetitive patterns that, like wallpaper, have no structural implications. The building is really conceived in terms of its interior volume, not of its mass, although it has yet to be opened by extended window area. Steel, concrete, and glass were chosen by Peter Behrens for his A.E.G. Turbine Factory in Berlin (1908). The sides and large areas at the end of this building are window, thereby producing an openness to amplify the expression of volume.

The horizontal rectangle of steel or reinforced concrete construction and the precise surfaces of modern architecture were anticipated by other architects. Sullivan, in the Carson, Pirie, Scott department store, Chicago (1899), used the horizontal rectangle inherent in its steel skeleton. He accented intersections of verticals and horizontals with profuse decoration. Charles Rennie MacIntosh, in the façade of the Willow Tea Room in Glasgow (1904), accepted the horizontal window in which the glass was flush with the wall plane. In addition, he almost completely eliminated decoration in a design 20 years before such a style was generally accepted. In 1908, Adolf Loos in Vienna issued his ultimatum that "ornament is crime." Rightly or wrongly, he associated ornament with the tattooing of primitive peoples and of criminals and degenerates in civilized countries. The consequence of his doctrine, as one may see in the Steiner House, Vienna (1910), is that all decorations, even moldings, are stripped away from the severely precise surfaces, which become planes punctured by windows and doors.

International Style. It remained to bring these various innovations together and through them to create a coherent style. The resulting "International style," which crystallized in the 1920's, may be the first wholly original style in

TWO TYPES OF MODERN ARCHITECTURE in the International style: Ludwig Mies van der Rohe's Crown Hall at the Illinois Institute of Technology (*above*) emphasizes geometric precision; Le Corbusier's Notre Dame du Haut, Ronchamp, France (*right*) uses curves.

architecture since the Gothic. Traditional styles, based primarily on stone, had stressed mass and weight; the thickness of the wall was a direct expression of its strength and emphasized enclosure. The modern style substitutes volume for mass and openness for enclosure. Whole walls may be converted to glass, light in appearance and in fact. Wright's creation of flowing space eliminated interior partitions wherever possible. These concepts found expression in clean shapes whose obvious precision has a machinelike accuracy fostered by such modern materials as steel and concrete. Subtle modulations of surface, reminiscent of handicraft, could find no place here. Nor could ornament be tolerated; even moldings were suppressed to allow the planes of walls, ceilings, and floors to intersect abruptly. The resulting austerity of form seemed a direct response to function. And indeed, in the 1920's when the new style was struggling for acceptance, its proponents claimed for it a functionalism that they maintained was wanting in eclecticism. In the 1960's it is generally recognized that while some modern buildings are functional, the real motivation behind the modern style was more aesthetic than practical.

Perhaps the first man to accept the modern creed in its entirety and to illustrate it in his work was Walter Gropius. His Fagus Shoe Last Factory at Alfeld-an-der-Leine (1911) is already a fully mature work. It may be the first glass-walled building with the frame inside. Since both steel and concrete permit of cantilever construction, no support is needed at the corner, and glass may be taken around it. The very transparency of the wall planes reveals the concern with volume as distinct from mass. The Bauhaus, Dessau (1925–1926), carries this conception to its ultimate conclusion. The whole volume is cantilevered five or six feet (1.5-2 meters) beyond the limits of the ground floor, and the concrete floors and columns within are visible through the glass walls but do not interrupt their expanse. These walls manifestly hang from the cantilevered roof. As head of the Bauhaus, a school that stressed the impact of the machine on architecture and the allied arts, Gropius was singularly influential in Europe and later in the United States as senior critic in the School of Design at Harvard University.

Charles Édouard Jeanneret, commonly called Le Corbusier, was almost as important. His book *Vers une architecture* (1923) was a vitriolic con-

demnation of the traditional and an enthusiastic promotion of the new point of view. The Stein House, Garches (1927), has horizontal strip windows, running from corner to corner, forming dark bands that contrast with the white bands of wall between them, like the bars of a Neoplasticist painting by Mondrian. The living areas of the Savoye House, Poissy-sur-Seine (1929–1931), are raised a story above the ground on slender concrete columns. These living areas are half enclosed with glass; the other half is open terrace. The machinelike precision of the forms contrasts with nature, but the openness of the design provides direct contact with the out-of-doors, free from any enclosure of opaque walls.

Ludwig Mies van der Rohe was the third outstanding exponent of the International style. His German Pavilion for the Barcelona Exposition of 1929 consisted of a slab roof supported on slender steel columns, the space below punctuated, but not really divided, by thin slabs of fine marble or of colored glass. The effectiveness of the design rested on its manipulation of space and on rich materials used with clean-cut precision. His Tugendhat House, Brno, Czechoslovakia (1930), was largely enclosed for privacy on the street front but completely open in the living areas at the back. These areas, like those in the German Pavilion, suggest different functions through onyx or ebony screens but in effect continue Wright's concept of flowing space. Like Gropius, Mies van der Rohe came to the United States before the outbreak of World War II. His work there, notably his design of the Illinois Institute of Technology, Chicago (begun 1939), shows a calculated repetition of certain dimensions based on normal story heights and economical spacing of steel columns. Its effectiveness seems to rest on this mathematical precision of shapes and on a fastidious perfection of detail.

TWA TERMINAL at Kennedy Airport, New York City, was designed by Eero Saarinen to symbolize a bird in flight.

Somewhat different in character is the architecture of Eric Mendelsohn. Immediately after World War I, he designed the Einstein Tower, Potsdam (1919–1924), perhaps under the influence of German expressionist painting. Although its curvilinear planes convey the plastic nature of concrete, the tower was built of brick covered with plaster, perhaps because cement was difficult to obtain at that time or perhaps because wooden formwork for these shapes proved prohibitively expensive. Mendelsohn then turned to the International style in the Schocken Store, Stuttgart (1926–1927), with its horizontal rectangular bays and its staircase cantilevered within a half-cylinder of glass. The rise of nazism forced Mendelsohn to leave Germany for England, Israel, and ultimately the United States. After World War II he designed a number of synagogues remarkable for their flexible handling of interior space and for the freedom of their forms. In these buildings the mathematical austerity of the International style yields to a humanitarian approach. The Mount Zion Temple, St. Paul, Minn. (1950–1954), achieves a devotional spirit rare in the 20th century religious buildings. Its interior also shows a return to restrained decoration, not based on historical styles but adapted to the modernism of the building as a whole.

Through the 1920's and the 1930's the International style as handled by these and other architects showed an extreme, perhaps a doctrinaire, adherence to its program. Its undecorated forms were predominantly rectilinear, striped with horizontal bars of windows or formed of glass walls. Its opponents ridiculed it as the "shoebox style." Nevertheless, because it was the result of modern conditions, the new style prevailed. Perhaps it had to adhere strictly to its tenets at first, but after World War II, having completely replaced eclecticism, it no longer needed to be quite so rigid. While Gropius and Mies van der Rohe continued the program of Internationalism with comparatively little change, Mendelsohn modified it somewhat. Much more of a change appears in the later work of Le Corbusier. The forms of his church Notre Dame du Haut, Ronchamp (1950–1955), are curvilinear, not rectilinear; the roof appears to sag over the walls, and the windows are not horizontal bands as in his earlier Stein House, but small openings forming an apparently random pattern in the wall. The effect is more nearly like abstract sculpture than like the International style buildings of the 1920's. In his earlier Savoye House, Le Corbusier had gone out of his way to achieve smooth wall planes, but these had not weathered well. Whether for that reason or because his aesthetic taste had changed, the concrete of his High Court, Chandigarh, India (1951–1956),

shows clearly the imprint of the form work, giving a rough, almost brutal, character to the surfaces. Also utilizing free-flowing, curvilinear shapes, sometimes even before Le Corbusier, is his Brazilian admirer, Oscar Niemeyer, as in his fanciful terrace roof of the Baile Restaurant, Pampulha (1942). Another striking instance of the new freedom of form is the TWA Building at John F. Kennedy International Airport, New York City (1956–1962), designed by the American architect Eero Saarinen.

Since World War II, then, the International style has undergone change in its forms to a less austere and perhaps more human approach. It has done so with a complete acceptance of the architectural conditions of the 20th century and as such has become a logical expression of its own day, fulfilling Sir Henry Wotton's prescription of "commoditie, firmness, and delight."

EVERARD M. UPJOHN, *Columbia University*

Bibliography

Alex, William, ed., *Masters of World Architecture*, 11 vols. (New York 1960).
Andrews, Wayne, *Architecture, Ambition, and Americans* (New York 1955).
Blunt, Anthony, *Art and Architecture in France, 1500–1700* (Baltimore 1953).
Branner, Robert, *Gothic Architecture* (New York 1961).
Braziller, George, Inc., *The Great Ages of World Architecture*, 12 vols. (New York 1961–63).
Conant, Kenneth J., *Carolingian and Romanesque Architecture, 800–1200* (Baltimore 1959).
Condit, Carl W., *American Building Art*, 2 vols. (New York 1960–61).
Dinsmoor, William B., *The Architecture of Ancient Greece* (New York 1950).
Fletcher, Bannister, *A History of Architecture*, 17th ed. (New York 1961).
Frankfort, Henri, *The Art and Architecture of the Ancient Orient* (Baltimore 1959).
Giedion, Siegfried, *Space, Time, and Architecture*, 4th ed., rev. (Cambridge, Mass., 1962).
Hamlin, Talbot F., *Architecture, an Art for All Men* (New York 1947).
Hamlin, Talbot F., *Architecture Through the Ages*, rev. ed. (New York 1953).
Hamlin, Talbot F., ed., *Forms and Functions of 20th Century Architecture*, 4 vols. (New York 1952).
Hitchcock, Henry Russell, *Architecture, 19th and 20th Centuries* (Baltimore 1958).
Krautheimer, Richard, *Early Christian and Byzantine Architecture* (Baltimore 1965).
Morrison, Hugh, *Early American Architecture* (New York 1952).
Rivoira, Giovanni T., *Roman Architecture* (New York and London 1925).
Smith, Earl B., *Egyptian Architecture as Cultural Expression* (New York 1938).
Summerson, John, *Architecture in Britain, 1530–1830* (Baltimore 1954).
Tunnard, Christopher, and Reed, Henry H., *American Skyline* (Boston 1955).
Upjohn, Everard M., and others, *A History of World Art*, rev. ed. (New York 1958).
Webb, Geoffrey, *Architecture in Britain: the Middle Ages* (Baltimore 1956).
Wittkower, Rudolf, *Art and Architecture in Italy, 1600–1750*, rev. ed. (Baltimore 1965).
Zevi, Bruno, *Towards an Organic Architecture* (London 1950).

Abacus.—The uppermost member of a capital.

Ambulatory.—An aisle curved around an apse. In medieval architecture it afforded space for processions and gave access to the radiating chapels.

Anta.—A support made by thickening a wall and providing it with a simple base and capital to receive the end of a beam.

Apse.—A semicircular or semipolygonal area, commonly used as the sanctuary containing the principal altar in churches.

Arabesque.—A decorative motive in paint or low relief with foliate scrolls, intersecting bars, or other designs.

Arch.—A construction of wedge-shaped stones (voussoirs) spanning a void. The semicircular or round arch is common in Roman and Renaissance architecture and their derivatives. The pointed arch is characteristic of Islamic and especially Gothic architecture. Segmental arches are less than semicircles. A flat arch also may be built with voussoirs.

Architrave.—A beam spanning the void between columns; the lowest member of the classical entablature.

Ashlar.—Cut stone masonry. In *regular ashlar* the blocks are uniform rectangles; rectangles of varying sizes create *random ashlar.*

Atrium.—A courtyard lined with walks and open to the sky in the center. The atrium formed the center of smaller Pompeian houses. In early Christian times an atrium containing the baptismal font was set in front of churches.

Basilica.—A longitudinal, hall-like building, designed in Roman times for business and legal purposes. A similar form, perhaps influenced by pagan buildings, became the standard church in early Christian times.

Batter.—An inward slope given to a wall, increasing both its real and its apparent stability.

Bay.—The area, either two-dimensional or three-dimensional, between the centers of adjacent columns or piers. Also a semicircular or semipolygonal element projecting from a wall, as in a bay window.

Bond.—The overlapping of stones or brick so that the vertical joints between are staggered in alternate courses, or rows. *American bond* in brickwork has four or five courses of stretchers (the long side of a brick) with a sixth course of headers (the short end of a brick). *English bond* alternates courses of headers and stretchers. In *Flemish bond,* headers and stretchers alternate within each course.

Buttress.—A mass of masonry designed to withstand the lateral thrust of an arch or vault. Forms of buttresses range from a thickening of the wall in the Romanesque style to a section of wall set at right angles to the building in the Gothic style.

Cantilever.—A projection of a beam, floor, or roof slab beyond its last point of support. The inner end of the cantilever is held down by superposed or suspended weight.

Capital.—The group of moldings, carved or plain, at the top of a column or pier.

Centering.—A temporary support used to hold the wedge-shaped voussoirs of an arch or vault in place until it is completed; the centering may then be removed.

Chancel.—The sanctuary of a church reserved for the clergy. It includes the apse and the whole east end of the nave beyond the crossing.

Choir.—In medieval architecture, the part of the chancel in front of the apse where choristers were seated.

Circulation.—Those portions of a building, such as stairs and hallways, that provide for the movement of human beings.

Clerestory or **Clearstory.**—A part of a building that rises clear above adjacent parts on a wall that is pierced with windows.

Cloister.—A courtyard lined with walks, a common feature of religious, particularly monastic, buildings.

Colossal Order.—An order of columns or pilasters rising through two or more stories of a building.

Column.—An isolated support, usually circular in plan and provided with a base and capital.

Corbel.—A projection of a block of material from a wall surface, the block being held in place by the weight of the wall on its inner end. The corbel is essentially a cantilever on a small scale.

Cornice.—The group of moldings forming the topmost member of the classical entablature, projecting in front of the parts below and corresponding to the eaves of a wooden roof. The cornice may be used without the other members of the entablature.

Crossing.—The area of a church where the transept crosses the nave.

Elevation.—The vertical plane of the front, rear, or side of a building; also a drawing of any one of these views, providing measurements of height and width, but without perspective.

Engaged Column.—A column attached to and partly embedded in a wall.

Entablature.—That portion of a classical order above the columns, consisting of the beam, or architrave, the frieze, and the cornice.

Façade.—The front or less commonly the side or rear of a building.

Flute.—A vertical groove in a column.

Flying Buttress.—A half arch resting on a buttress and rising above a roof, its upper end pressing inward against a wall; its function is to transmit the thrust of high nave vaults over the aisle roof to the buttress outside the walls of the building.

Frieze.—A horizontal band sometimes sculptured or painted; particularly the middle member of an entablature.

Hypostyle.—A colonnaded hall, particularly in an Egyptian temple.

Lintel.—A beam spanning a void, particularly one over a door or window.

Metope.—A thin, square slab, sculptured or plain, alternating with triglyphs in the frieze of the Doric order.

Nave.—The central aisle of a church; liturgically, that part of the church intended for the laity.

Order.—A regularized combination of base, column, and entablature.

Pediment.—An isosceles triangle terminating a pitched roof, particularly in a classical temple. A similar form is often used over doors and windows. A *segmental pediment* substitutes a single curve for the diagonal lines of the common pediment; in a *broken pediment* the diagonal lines stop before the apex of the triangle is reached.

Pendentive.—A vaulted spherical triangle whose lower point rests on a pier and whose upper curve, combined with other pendentives, makes it possible to support a circular dome on a square plan.

Peristyle.—A colonnaded courtyard immediately behind the pylon of an Egyptian temple; also such an area behind the atrium in Pompeian houses.

Pier.—An isolated support in masonry, rectangular in plan or composed of groups of pilasters or colonnettes.

Pilaster.—A flat columnar form against a wall.

Portico.—A colonnaded porch.

Pylon.—The monumental gateway to an Egyptian temple, consisting of two tall masses of stone on either side of a lower entrance.

Reveal.—The distance between the plane of a wall and the plane of any windows or doors pierced through it.

Rib.—An arch below the surface of a vault.

Rustication.—A treatment of the exposed face of blocks of stone. There are many varieties of rustication, ranging from *drafted masonry,* in which grooves surround the perimeters of the blocks, to *rock-faced ashlar,* with irregular rounded surfaces as though the blocks had been roughly split from the quarry.

Sash.—The framework that holds the glass of a window. A *casement sash* is either immovable or hinged at one side. A *double-hung sash* slides up or down.

Shaft.—The principal part of a column between its base and its capital.

Spire.—A tall, pyramidal shape, usually octagonal in plan, rising above a tower in Gothic architecture.

Steeple.—A tapering design above a tower, consisting of one or more stories, each smaller than the one below and perhaps varying in design, and usually terminating in a small, slender pyramid. In post-Renaissance architecture it corresponds to the Gothic spire.

Stilt.—A vertical distance between the capital or impost on which an arch or rib rests and the point at which its curve begins.

Thrust.—The lateral or diagonal outward pressure of an arch or vault. It is a transformation of the vertical force of gravity into a diagonal force, caused by the wedge-shaped blocks of stone that compose the arch.

Tracery.—A pattern of stone bars in Gothic windows to hold the glass in place against wind pressure. Such windows are commonly divided by vertical bars, or *mullions,* perhaps by horizontal bars, or *transoms,* and within the curve of the arch they have many elaborate patterns.

Transept.—An area cutting across the length of a building and projecting beyond its side walls. This produces a cruciform plan in many medieval churches.

Triforium.—An interior story in medieval churches below the clerestory of the nave and above the arches that divide the nave from the aisles. It corresponds in height to the pitch of the roof over the side aisles.

Triglyph.—A group of three vertical cleatlike members separated by grooves. They alternate with the metopes in the Doric frieze.

Truss.—An arrangement of straight pieces of wood or steel in one or more triangles. Trusses have no lateral thrust and can be made to span a wider void than can be covered by beams or girders.

Vault.—An extension of the principle of the arch to cover an area instead of a plane. The basic vault forms are the hemisphere or *dome;* the half-cylinder, or *barrel vault;* and the *groin vault,* formed by the intersection of two barrel vaults at right angles. The groin vault supported by ribs ultimately produced the complex Gothic vaults.

Volute.—A scroll, usually at the sides of an Ionic capital or below the corners of Corinthian capitals.

CAREERS IN ARCHITECTURE

Architects and engineers are professional designers who, by means of drawings and words on paper, transmit their ideas to builders. Although at one time there was only one professional in the field of construction—the master builder—the increase in technical knowledge and the use of a wider variety of materials required greater specialization. As a result, individual architects began to concentrate their efforts on one or more of several general types of work, such as residential, commercial, industrial, religious, educational, recreational, and governmental. In addition, as more and more projects involved whole towns or large sections of rapidly growing cities, architecture was further subdivided into newly recognized professions involving city and regional planning and urban design. In engineering, too, separate professions were introduced, including civil, military, structural, mechanical, electrical, and acoustical engineering.

The Work of the Architect. An architect must have certain special talents. Foremost is the ability to analyze and evaluate, for once a client has commissioned him to plan a specific project, the architect must establish the initial spatial requirements (called the program). Using preliminary drawings, the architect tries various schemes in search of the one that best fits the program. Through his creative imagination he visualizes the form of the structure, then determines the most practicable plan and decides on the most suitable materials—all in harmonious combination. The documents he is required to submit to the builder must be precise and careful, for from the architect's plans and blueprints, the contract cost will be fixed and the structure built.

To accomplish this, there must be constant communication—by words, plans, and pictures—between the architect and his client. There must also be mutual understanding between the architect and those who assist him in drawing the plans, and between the architect and the builder to ensure that the plans are properly carried out. In the final analysis, the architect's success in meeting these responsibilities is the measure of his organizational and leadership ability.

The architect plans each project to achieve maximum safety, economy, utility, and comfort. He chooses materials for their durability and ease of maintenance. As a creative designer, he gives special attention to form, proportion, color, and surface, to achieve, through a combination of art and science, a building of utility and beauty.

These activities require many skills and talents and the cooperation of people in many fields, but it is the individual talent and skill of a particular architect that a client generally seeks. For this reason the greater proportion of architectural offices are small, individual enterprises in which the professional qualities of the architect may be exercised directly. Many offices consist of 30 or 40 persons, a few have about 100, some have even more, but as long as the services of consulting engineers are available, a small office can undertake work of a much wider scope than the number of its personnel would indicate.

The Training of the Architect. The prospective architect needs both formal training and practical experience to develop his latent talents. Because of the technical requirements involved in registering as an architect in the United States, it is becoming increasingly difficult to qualify for the profession merely by training in an architect's office while attending night school. Most candidates, consequently, go to a school of architecture at a college or university, where they frequently find that financial aid is available to qualified students.

Because he is concerned with creating the physical environment of human beings, the architect must know and understand as much as possible of the nature of his fellow man. Thus the education of an architect is not only tecnical but social and humanistic as well.

Schools of architecture in the United States are accredited by the American Institute of Architects (AIA), which seeks an educational program that is as balanced between liberal arts and technical courses as the requirements of the profession will permit. Most of the nearly 60 accredited schools of architecture in the United States give a five-year course leading to the bachelor of architecture degree. Graduate schools of architecture, which have a liberal arts or bachelor of architecture degree as a prerequisite for entrance, grant a master of architecture degree after an additional one to four years of study.

Because each school of architecture stresses a different aspect or branch of the profession—fine arts, architectural engineering, city planning, and the like—the prospective student of architecture should study carefully the curricula of several schools. He can then choose the school he thinks can best develop his particular talents or best serve his interests.

In general, after an architect receives his degree from an accredited school of architecture in the United States, he must have three years of practical experience in an architect's office before he is allowed to take the registration examinations. These examinations may be taken through the National Council of Architectural Registration Boards, which also may be of great assistance when an architect wishes to register in more than one state.

Opportunities in Architecture. Most young architects, after they have passed the registration examinations, will continue to get experience by working in other architects' offices until they have the initiative to establish their own firms or the opportunity to become partners in existing firms. About half of all architects in the United States have a private practice, either alone or in partnership. Most of the remainder are salaried employes of other architectural firms. Some architects work for building, engineering, or other businesses with extensive construction programs. Some work for government agencies, and a few teach.

The rewards of the profession include the stimulation derived from creativity and, because architectural services are in demand, good wages. Even the inexperienced beginner can expect a comparatively high salary. The most money, of course, is made by those who take the risks and face the responsibilities of private practice.

WALTER H. KILHAM, JR.
Fellow, American Institute of Architects

Further Reading: Hunt, William D., ed., *Comprehensive Architectural Services: General Principles and Practice* (New York 1965).

ARCHIVES, är′kīvz, are organized bodies of records, including papers, books, maps, sound recordings, and other documentary materials, made or received in pursuance of law or in connection with the transaction of business and preserved because of their enduring value. The term, derived from the Greek *archeion* (office building), applies to records of government agencies (public archives), institutions (institutional archives), business firms (business archives), and families and individuals (family and personal archives). Papers of families and individuals that lack the organic character of true archives are called historical manuscripts. A small part of the public archives becomes available in printed form as "government publications."

Archives have a twofold nature and use. They perpetuate the memory of the rights and activities of their creator and assist him in maintaining his rights and in planning his actions. They also furnish information on the political, economic, and cultural developments of the past, which cannot be fully understood by the scholar unless he has access to the rich store of human experience embodied in the archives.

European Countries. The technique of keeping archives was inherited from classical antiquity by the Roman Catholic Church and perfected in the evolving national states of western and central Europe. Statesmen of the period of absolutism recognized the advantage of concentrating in the custody of one agency the archives hitherto kept by the various offices of the government. Examples of such agencies were the General Archives of Simancas, Spain, established in 1543, and the Archives of the Dynasty, State, and Court, set up in Vienna, Austria, in 1749.

The idea of concentrating the care of government archives in the hands of a service agency (archival agency) was consistently applied in France. During the French Revolution, the National Archives in Paris became the depository for the records of the central government. Subordinate archival agencies in the provinces were made responsible for the records of the intermediate levels of government and charged, at the same time, with supervision over the archives of municipal and other local authorities.

Most nations of western and central Europe and of Latin America followed the French example and established networks of archival agencies geared to the administrative structure of the country. After World War I, Russia and other countries of eastern Europe made remarkable progress in establishing nationwide archives systems.

United States and Canada. In the United States, a movement for the establishment of a national archives was crowned with success when the American Historical Association and other scholarly groups joined agencies of the federal government in urging Congress to authorize a dignified depository for the nation's archives. Funds were appropriated in 1926 for the splendid archives building on Constitution Avenue in Washington, D.C., and the National Archives Act was enacted in 1934. As a result, the United States achieved an archival establishment that, in size and excellence of equipment, surpassed all comparable establishments in Europe. In 1949 the National Archives was transferred to the General Services Administration and renamed the National Archives and Records Service.

Inspired by the example of the National Archives, some states have made much progress in the administration of their archives. Churches, educational institutions, and business firms are also giving increased attention to the preservation of permanently valuable records.

The experience of the United States has had an influence in Canada, where older records of the Dominion government have been concentrated in the Public Archives in Ottawa. Of the provinces, Nova Scotia, Quebec, Ontario, and Saskatchewan are noteworthy for the care devoted to their archives.

Organizations. The Society of American Archivists, the professional organization of archivists in the United States and Canada, publishes the *American Archivist,* since 1938 the leading journal of the profession in America. The International Council on Archives was founded in 1948, and the first International Congress of Archivists was held in Paris in 1950.

ERNST POSNER
Author of "American State Archives"

Bibliography
Galbraith, Vivian H., *Introduction to the Use of the Public Records* (New York 1934).
Hamer, Philip M., *Guide to Archives and Manuscripts in the United States* (New Haven 1961).
Schellenberg, Theodore R., *Modern Archives: Principles and Techniques* (Chicago 1957).
Schellenberg, Theodore R., *Management of Archives* (New York 1965).

ARCHON, är′kon, was the title of the chief magistrate in many Greek states, especially in Athens. Though more is known of the Athenian archons, even here the origin and early evolution of the office remain obscure. Presumably the archon was created by the aristocracy in the latter half of the 8th century B.C. to act as a check on the power of the hereditary monarch. Two additional archons were subsequently created, and these three officials emerged as the most powerful figures in Athenian government. Before the time of Solon in 594 B.C., six additional archons were created, making a total of nine.

It is not known how the archons were originally chosen nor for how long. According to Greek tradition the office was at first hereditary, later held for a 10-year period, and finally in 683/682 reduced to a term of one year. Some modern scholars, however, believe that it was an annual office from its inception. Until 487 B.C., archons were elected annually by the assembly of the people, though only men from the upper two classes were eligible for the office. After 487 they were selected annually by lot. After a year in office, they were enrolled in the Areopagus (see AREOPAGUS) for life.

The nine archons did not serve as a body. The *archon eponymous* was the chief executive in matters of civic importance, responsible for protecting the property of all citizens, caring for widows and orphans, resolving family disputes, and trying inheritance cases. The *archon basileus* presided over the Areopagus and supervised the state cults. The *archon polemarch* commanded the military forces until 487 B.C., but thereafter was limited to minor religious duties and to trying cases involving foreigners resident in the city. The six other archons, called the *thesmothetai,* sat as a body and served as judges.

THOMAS KELLY, *University of Alberta*

Further Reading: Hignett, Charles, *A History of the Athenian Constitution to the End of the Fifth Century B.C.* (London 1952).

ARCTIC

ICEBERGS dwarf a 213-foot vessel, dramatizing the perils of navigation in Arctic and subarctic seas. Ships send warnings of these drifting masses.

ARCTIC, ärk'tik. The Arctic is commonly defined as the region around the North Pole lying north of the Arctic Circle (66° 30′ N). A more scientific definition describes the Arctic as the region north of the 50° F (10° C) isotherm. An isotherm (meaning "equal temperature") is a line on a climatic map between points with the same mean temperature. The 50° isotherm marks the southern limits of the region where the average monthly temperature never goes above 50° F, and the average for the coldest month is below 32° F (0° C). The 50° isotherm follows roughly the line of the Arctic Circle except in Canada, where it dips down to the northeastern coast of Newfoundland and across the southern part of Hudson Bay. It also makes a loop around the Bering Sea as far south as the western tip of the Aleutian Islands. Within these limits Arctic conditions prevail over the land areas.

Both definitions bear witness to the coldness of the Arctic climate—the isothermic measurement directly, the Arctic Circle indirectly. The Arctic Circle is determined by the angle at which the earth's axis is tipped in relation to the plane of its motion around the sun. As a result of this inclination, the sun's rays never shine straight down on the earth's surface north of the Arctic Circle and cannot effectively warm it. The earth's surface loses more heat into space here than it receives from the sun. This is the principal reason why the Arctic and the Antarctic —the similar area around the South Pole—are much colder than other regions of the earth.

But the distinctive fact about the Arctic is that most of it consists of an ice-covered ocean— unlike the Antarctic, which is an ice-covered landmass. The ocean lies between the continents of North America and Eurasia. It is commonly called the Arctic Ocean, although only the central body of water, around the North Pole, uniquely bears that name. Bordering the two continents are a number of seas, each with its own name but all forming part of the same ocean. Considering this ocean as a whole, it has

been determined that 90 percent of its surface is covered by ice in winter and 70 percent the year round. Yielding to stresses of wind and current, the ice is broken into floes, or pieces of ice, as it drifts slowly about the Arctic Ocean in two large gyres, or circles.

There are other scientific definitions that contribute to a description of the Arctic. To an oceanographer, the Arctic is the region where the temperature of the ocean water remains near the freezing point of salt water—about 29° F (−1.7° C)—and its salt content is about 32 parts per thousand. The Arctic can also be defined as the region beyond the tree line—where trees do not grow.

Not much land is included within the area defined as the Arctic. The northern coast of Siberia, most of Iceland, all of Greenland, northeastern Canada, and the north coast of Alaska are the landmasses above the 50° isotherm. But peripheral to the Arctic is the subarctic, which is almost entirely land. The subarctic is the region where the average temperature is not higher than 50° F for more than four months of the year (unlike the Arctic where the monthly average is never above 50°) and the coldest month is not more than 32° F (like the Arctic). The subarctic includes most of Siberia, western Russia north of Leningrad, most of Scandinavia and Canada, and all of Alaska except the Arctic coast and the Aleutian Islands.

Life in the Arctic. To most people the Arctic is simply a cold, bleak region—monotonous, inaccessible, and unproductive. But this stereotype is contradicted when we consider the region carefully. Actually, the coldest temperature in the Northern Hemisphere, −96° F (−70° C), according to Soviet sources, was recorded in the Oimyakon Basin in northeastern Siberia, not far north of the Arctic Circle. Fairbanks, Alaska, which is south of the Arctic Circle, records lower temperatures than Barrow, Alaska, which is north of it. It seldom gets colder in Barrow than it does in Minneapolis, Minn.

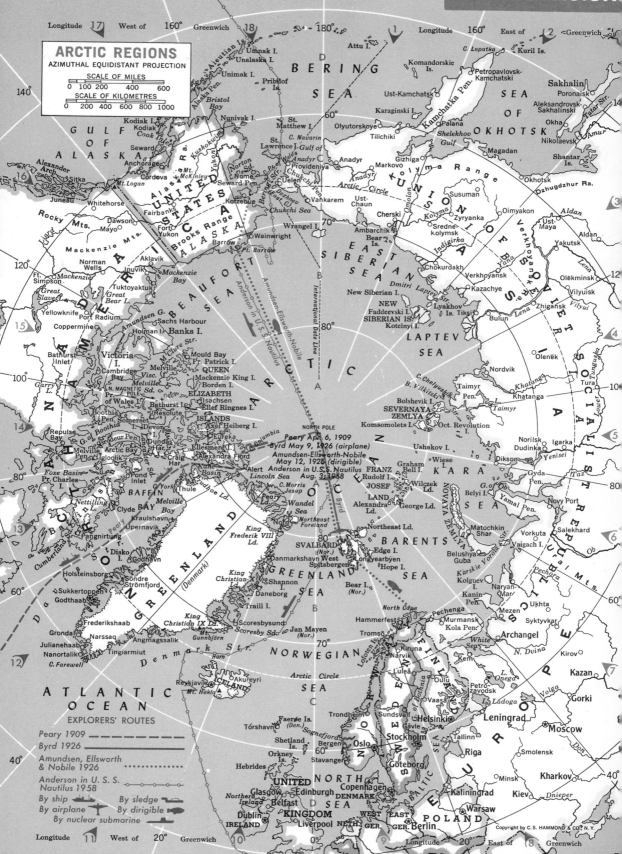

ARCTIC REGIONS
AZIMUTHAL EQUIDISTANT PROJECTION
SCALE OF MILES
0 100 200   400   600
SCALE OF KILOMETRES
0   200 400 600 800 1000

Longitude 17 West of 160° Greenwich 18 180° 1 Longitude 160° East of 2 Greenwich

EXPLORERS' ROUTES

Peary 1909
Byrd 1926
Amundsen, Ellsworth
& Nobile 1926
Anderson in U.S.S.
Nautilus 1958
By ship   By sledge
By airplane   By dirigible
By nuclear submarine

Longitude 11 West of 20° Greenwich 10 9 Longitude East of 20° 8 Greenwich

Peary Apr. 6, 1909
Byrd May 9, 1926 (airplane)
Amundsen-Ellsworth-Nobile
May 12, 1926 (dirigible)
Alert Anderson in U.S.S. Nautilus
Lincoln Sea   Aug. 3, 1958

NORTH POLE

Copyright by C.S. HAMMOND & CO., N.Y.

BERING SEA
SEA OF OKHOTSK
GULF OF ALASKA
UNITED STATES AMERICA ALASKA
CANADA
BEAUFORT SEA
EAST SIBERIAN SEA
LAPTEV SEA
KARA SEA
BARENTS SEA
GREENLAND SEA
NORWEGIAN SEA
GREENLAND (Denmark)
BAFFIN BAY
ATLANTIC OCEAN
NORTH SEA
BALTIC SEA
UNION OF SOVIET SOCIALIST REPUBLICS
EUROPE
ICELAND
ARCTIC OCEAN

ARCTIC REGIONS

To an inhabitant of San Francisco or Bern, Switzerland, the Arctic may seem bleak and monotonous, but what it lacks in majestic mountains and forests it more than makes up for in delicate beauty, in vastness, and in serenity. For men who sailed small wooden boats from temperate regions, the Arctic was indeed inaccessible, but modern technology now permits travel to any part of it any time of the year. It is unproductive in relation to temperate regions, but it has supported millions of caribou and reindeer, and there are bears, foxes, wolves, flocks of birds that darken the sky, insects, and a teeming ocean that may become a major food-producing area.

Extensive settlement in the Arctic seems still many years off. In North America only a small fraction of the land area lies in the Arctic. Actually it is the subarctic that is facing imminent settlement. It is to this region, sometimes called the Middle North, that we must first look for development. The temperatures are not continually so cold in this region, and man can live there if he wishes to. One adjustment the newcomer to the Arctic must make is to adapt to the changing cycle of light and darkness. In midsummer, north of the Arctic Circle, the sun never sets. In midwinter it never rises. Only in the spring and fall does the regular sequence of night and day take place. This causes a marked disruption in the normal patterns of men's lives. It is a factor that must be taken into serious consideration when choosing personnel for remote Arctic stations.

Another disrupting factor in the North American Arctic is the proximity of the north geomagnetic pole, which often plays havoc with radio communication. The northern pole of the earth's geomagnetic axis is located at 78° north latitude, near Thule, Greenland. It must not be confused with the north magnetic (or dip) pole— the one that affects the compass—which is about 500 miles (804 km) to the west. The ionosphere, the layer of upper atmosphere that reflects radio waves, is more often disrupted over the Arctic than over temperate regions, and radio communication is seriously affected. Such influences are not obvious, of course, except in the beautiful aurora borealis in the polar sky.

The exact behavior of radio waves and their propagation in the Arctic are undergoing careful study. The only fully dependable transmission modes there now are VLF (Very Low Frequency) and line-of-sight UHF (Ultra High Frequency). All others are subject to disruption by solar events and by fluctuations in the earth's magnetic field. On the other hand, it is probable that future voyagers into space will leave the vicinity of the earth through radiation-free "chimneys" over the North and South poles, which are not covered in space by the vast Van Allen radiation belts.

The newcomer to the Arctic must also adjust to the isolation. Man is a gregarious animal by nature, and this is especially true of civilized man. He craves the company of his fellows, and in the Arctic this is a difficult condition to fulfill. But that it can be done is evidenced by the 4 million residents of such beachheads of the Arctic as Resolute Bay, Canada, Norilsk, USSR, and others.

The Arctic and World Affairs. As the world's civilizations developed, northern expansion was at first slowed by the breadth of the lands in the Northern Hemisphere. But today national

WIDE WORLD PHOTOS

NORWEGIAN GLACIER above the Arctic Circle is seen from passenger plane on the north polar route.

boundaries reach the southern limit of the frozen Arctic Ocean, and the five nations bordering it are using their resources and manpower to research and develop the region. Canada, Denmark, Norway, the Soviet Union, and the United States each hopes to share in its bounty.

While nations have always tried to protect their borders from direct invasion, only today— with the current political environment—have nations separated by an ocean felt obliged to protect their lands from one another. The intercontinental missile and the nuclear submarine have made the Western and Communist nations realize that the shortest distance between them lies over the north polar region. Moscow is only about 2,300 miles (3,700 km) from the North Pole, while New York and Yalta are 3,400 and 3,100 miles (5,500 and 5,000 km), respectively, and San Francisco only 3,600 miles (5,800 km). The shortest distance (Great Circle) from New York to Moscow is 4,600 miles (7,403 km), and the route lies over Iceland. From San Francisco to Moscow is 5,800 miles (9,300 km), over northern Greenland. The shortest route from London to Toyko is 5,900 miles (9,500 km) and passes over much of Siberia. Most Americans think of the Soviet Union as being a great distance away. All Alaskans know it is only 48 miles (77 km) west of Cape Prince of Wales. Alaskan and Siberian Eskimos cross the boundary between the two countries with an abandon that flouts the cold war.

A significant step in the development of western Canada, Alaska, and Siberia resulted from the need to ferry aircraft from the United States to the USSR during World War II. A series of airfields was planned that would permit the planes to land and refuel. This necessitated building highways and developing waterways in order to construct and maintain the fields. The threatening world situation has required further improvement of these facilities.

New technologic developments after the war led to the installation of a series of radar stations

BMEWS STATIONS, like this one at Clear, Alaska, provide a warning system against a missile attack across the arctic regions.

across the North American Arctic. Huge quantities of equipment and supplies were ferried to the Arctic by ship and plane. Gradually, at 50-mile (80-km) intervals across the North American continent and Greenland, there sprang into being a complex electronic system, the Distant Early Warning Line, whose task it was to warn the more densely populated areas of possible attack. A similar system was erected at the same time in the USSR. Within ten years of their construction, new developments outdated them, and the United States began work on the three massive stations of the Ballistic Missile Early Warning System. These still more complex stations are located at Clear, Alaska; Thule, Greenland; and Flyingdales Moor, Great Britain. The sophisticated electronic systems in these three stations give earlier and better protection than their more numerous predecessors. While a constant watch goes on to warn of possible attack, the commercial jet aircraft of several Western

ESKIMO FAMILY wears leggings of reversed animal skins. The cups and cooking pot are new conveniences.

nations fly the "polar routes." Actually, these routes are not really "polar" but lie over Greenland and the Canadian Archipelago, so that emergency airfields may be used if needed.

Arctic Ocean. Scientists are still uncertain whether the Arctic Ocean can technically be called an ocean basin, because structurally it is smaller than some seas. It is more than 12,000 feet (3,600 meters) deep in some places, but so little is known of it that it has not been determined whether the rocks that underlie it are similar to those under the larger oceans. In contrast to these deep spots, great areas of the Arctic Ocean are only a few hundred feet deep and have been inundated only within the last few thousand years.

The perennial cover of sea ice that has made exploration of the Arctic difficult has also kept scientists from making the detailed studies they would like. It is known that areas of the ocean bordering more southerly waters are rich in marine life, but detailed information is still lacking. It is known, too, that there is a tremendous inflow of relatively warm saline water from the Atlantic Ocean northwest of Norway that sinks to a layer between 500 and 800 feet (150 and 240 meters) below the surface of the Arctic Ocean. The surface water of the Arctic is influenced mainly by the ice cover and the runoff from lands and islands, so it is generally colder and less saline. Some water does enter the Arctic from the Pacific Ocean by way of the Bering Strait, but it is not enough to influence the overall character of the ocean. It is doubtful whether the Soviet proposal to dam Bering Strait and pump water out of the Arctic Ocean, replacing it with warmer Atlantic Ocean water, would actually achieve its goal of melting the ice cover.

The ice that covers the Arctic Ocean comes from the freezing of seawater. During the course of a single winter the ice may grow to a thickness of six feet (1.8 meters). The growth is rapid at first because of the cold, but ice is a reasonably good insulator and the rate slows as the winter progresses. Winds and waves are constantly acting on the ice so that it is never a large unbroken sheet. Seldom will a single floe be larger than 10 square miles (26 sq km). While two floes may ride one upon the other, usually when they are forced together they crumble along their edges and form ridges of broken pieces. Such pressure ridges may rise 30 feet (9 meters) or more above the surface and make traveling on foot hazardous. Occasionally, floes that do not melt during the short summer season may grow to eight feet (2.4 meters) in thickness. After about a year the salt will have drained out of this thick ice, and when it is melted the water will be fresh.

One strange fact about the Arctic, which probably confused the early explorers, is the presence of ice islands. These are pieces of glacial ice that have broken off the ice shelf along northern Ellesmere Island and drifted out into the Arctic Ocean. Since they originate on land in association with mountains and rocks, they occasionally have remnants of moraines on their surfaces. These piles of rock and dirt probably led to the earlier belief that places such as

CARIBOU are among the largest Arctic mammals. A herd of Barren Ground Caribou, shown here, moves in July to a new feeding area in Alaska.

"Crocker Land" existed far north of where we now know land ends. Ice islands were first recognized in the late 1940's and since that time have become important as platforms on which to operate scientific research stations. Fletcher's Ice Island, T-3, was first occupied in 1952 and has been manned periodically with as many as 24 men supported by the U.S. Navy Office of Naval Research or the U.S. Air Force. ARLIS II (Arctic Research Laboratory Ice Station II) was operated by the Office of Naval Research from May 1961, when it was 93 miles (150 km) north of Barrow, until May 1965, when it entered Denmark Strait east of Iceland.

Geography and Geology. The landmasses of the Arctic and subarctic do not differ from their more southerly neighbors so much in their make-up as in the processes that act on them. There are three principal geological areas within the region that may be considered as extensions of the terrain in more temperate regions: shields, lowlands or plains, and cordilleras.

The shields are vast areas of very old crystalline rocks overlain with younger sediments that have been extensively glaciated during the major glacial epochs. They are now rocky lands with simple vegetation and many lakes. Along their seaward margins they often have substantial relief and numerous fjords.

The Canadian Shield, which lies between 60° and 100° W and surrounds Hudson Bay, is much larger than either the Baltic (Scandinavian) or Angara (Siberian) shields. It is the type of terrain that comes to the minds of many people when they try to picture the Arctic. Low-lying, with only scrub vegetation and grasses and filled with many lakes and meandering rivers, the Canadian Shield has been called the "Barren Land." However, on its eastern rim the Torngat Mountains rise as much as 7,000 feet (2,100 meters) above sea level and support many glaciers and some ice caps. In winter the low temperatures and lack of obstacles lead to periods of blowing snow in which visibility is less than one half a mile (0.8 km) for 24 to 36 hours. West of the Canadian Shield lie the Mackenzie Lowland (an extension of the prairie far to the south) and the Alaskan coastal plain. Both areas are lower than the shield and have only recently (in geologic time) emerged from the sea. West of the lowland lies the North American Cordillera, an extension of the great arc of mountains along the western edge of the North and South American continents. In Alaska these mountains form the Brooks Range and, in the Yukon and Northwest territories, Canada, the Richardson Mountains.

The Baltic Shield barely enters the Arctic, but topographically it is composed of the same peneplaned mountains that occupy the lower parts of Scandinavia. The Angara or Siberian Shield of central Siberia is made up of rolling hills and valleys. To the east of it lies a mountainous region that has not yet been fully mapped. Some peaks rise to 10,000 feet (3,000 meters). The north coast of Siberia is much like that of North America except for its greater size and the number of north-flowing rivers.

Two facets of the Arctic that make the land markedly different are permafrost and a lack of precipitation. Permafrost is the perennially frozen ground found in virtually all land areas within the Arctic Circle. Only the top layer, which may be three feet (0.9 meters) deep, thaws during the summer. Permafrost has been found to extend as deep as 1,200 feet (365 meters) and presumably is a condition left from the glacial periods. Because of it, ground water cannot percolate downward but must stay near the surface or run off into rivers. This is the reason that most of the tundra, or treeless plain, in the Arctic is studded with lakes. Although weather records are not as complete as in southern latitudes, enough is known to establish the Arctic as a desert that receives less precipitation than any other area on earth except the Antarctic. Total precipitation is less than 10 inches (25.4 cm) over much of the region, and only in the subarctic, where open oceans are close by, does this figure rise as high as 200 inches (508 cm).

As a result of permafrost and lack of precipitation, the processes of soil formation and erosion are different in the Arctic than elsewhere. Little chemical or organic weathering can take place, and since soils are poorly developed, the land cannot support a vigorous plant community. The mountains are not worn down by slow steady erosion but by mass wasting and solifluction. Solifluction is the process by which gravel, sand, and silt, weathering out of the rock, slump down slope in a relentless process of leveling the land.

Permafrost is an incompletely understood phenomenon. The behavior of the surface materials in the permafrost zone is unique. As a result of repeated freezing and thawing, the materials are sorted by size and are segregated into irregular areas known technically as polygons. When viewed from the air these polygons make striking patterns because the surface materials of different sizes support different forms of vegetation. In association with this strangely patterned ground there occur "ice lenses"—large wedge-shaped bodies of ice that can grow to over 10 feet (3 meters) wide, 50 feet (15 meters) long, and 50 feet deep. These lenses have posed many problems for inexperienced engineers and builders. If a structure, such as a road or a building, is constructed over a lens, it disrupts nature's balance. The lens melts, and the structure collapses into the void left by the melted ice. Only when proper insulation is added will such action be inhibited.

Natural Resources. Because a large portion of the Soviet Union lies above the Arctic Circle, that country has been foremost in developing its northern areas. Lenin was the first statesman in modern times to realize the potential wealth of this region. Since the 1920's, timber, coal, and minerals have been moving from their sources in Siberia to the factories of the USSR. Geography favors transportation of these materials in the USSR, where they are moved north down the great rivers of Siberia to the Arctic Ocean during the summer and convoyed by icebreaker to Murmansk, Archangel, and Vladivostok. Where there is mineral wealth, towns spring up. The Soviet Arctic is gradually being settled. However, some reports indicate that the Soviet Union's plan to settle the region by offering financial bonuses to settlers is not working any better than its counterpart in North America. Most settlers simply save enough from their earnings to move back to warmer climates nearer the heart of civilization. It requires determination at best—almost a special pioneer attitude—to move north. But many have done it, and more are sure to.

The exact extent of the mineral wealth of the Soviet Arctic is not well known, but it is certain to be vast. Nickel, copper, and coal are mined near Norilsk, and gold, uranium, diamonds, and other minerals have been found in quantity. The abundance of rivers and mountains means that power can be generated with relative ease and that further development is assured. In Sweden, high-grade iron ore is mined at Kiruna. Copper, cobalt, and associated minerals are mined by the USSR in the Pechenga fields near the Finnish border. In North America only natural gas and oil have been located and exploited above the Arctic Circle. As yet, the expense of bringing them to users in the south is too great to warrant full-scale development. In subarctic Alaska and Canada there is a wealth of both renewable and nonrenewable resources that are gradually being exploited. Iron at Knob Lake, Labrador, oil at Cook Inlet, Alaska, and in northern Alberta, uranium from the Northwest Territories, timber from the Pacific coast of Canada and Alaska—the list is long.

Flora and Fauna. The animal life of the Arctic is varied and colorful. Although there are not so many species as in equatorial regions, there are large populations of animals. Most common and best known are the caribou and its domesticated cousin, the reindeer. The people of Lapland have built their whole life and culture around herds of as many as 100,000 reindeer. The Lapps move with the reindeer almost continuously from their summer to their winter grazing grounds. Today the attractions of Western society have begun to draw the younger generation of Lapps into towns and cities, but the herds still remain.

An early attempt to introduce reindeer herding to Alaska has failed, but perhaps as many as one million caribou still range across Arctic Alaska and Canada, offering a potential food source that will doubtless be tapped someday. The other native animal that offers an interesting potential for man is the musk-ox. Hunted to the verge of extinction at one time, it is slowly increasing its number under government protection. Related to the goat, the musk-ox has a tasty meat, and experiments are under way to see if it can be domesticated. Not only would the animal prove an excellent food source, but it would also be able to provide for itself in a region where most domestic animals need to be sheltered and fed. The musk-ox also provides a fine wool, as light as cashmere but stronger. It seems certain to be one of the principal contributions of the Arctic to the people who settle there.

The most fabled and perhaps most misunderstood Arctic animal is the lemming. This small mouselike animal lives on grasses and roots and provides a large part of the diet of most carnivorous birds and animals in the tundra regions. Given a short gestation period and high fertility, a lemming population can expand immensely in a relatively short time. Probably depending on the availability of food, there is a marked and regular cycle of increase in the lemming population. Starting from a few animals in one area, the number grows to many thousands every fourth year. This large number draws in many predators—wolves, foxes, weasels, jaegers, even caribou—that prey on the lemming while the little animal itself is eating most of the available plants. Consequently, the following year the area can support only a few lemmings. But the lemming population has meanwhile grown so rapidly that it must spread out of the area in which it originated.

Almost nothing in nature will stem the course of a lemming migration, and herein lies the fable. Lemmings can swim, and if the body of water is not too wide they can cross it successfully. Their natural tendency is to move away from a center of high lemming population. Therefore, if the country is mountainous, like northern Norway, sometimes the migration will lead the animals to cliffs along the sea. Here the lemmings will swarm over the cliffs, intending to swim to the other side of the water. Thus was born the legend that lemmings try to "commit suicide" by jumping off cliffs into the sea. Actually, they cannot stand the overcrowding that results from their recurring "population explosions."

Most majestic of the Arctic animals is the polar bear. This graceful white creature is the undisputed king of the Arctic Basin. Born in snow banks on the Arctic coasts, it spends most of its life patrolling the ice pack for its dietary staple, the seal. Fearing nothing, it is thought to roam throughout the Arctic even in the dark and cold of the winter night. From the fringe of the ice pack to the limit of Arctic water, one finds a wealth of marine life. Seal, walrus, whale, and millions of fish thrive on the microscopic life that abounds in the chill waters. Birds, too, congregate in uncounted flocks during the Arctic summer—but virtually all will leave with the coming of fall, some traveling as far south as the rim of the Antarctic—a distance of some 20,000 miles (32,000 km).

KARL W. KENYON, FROM NATIONAL AUDUBON SOCIETY

T. GRANT, FROM NATIONAL FILM BOARD

STELLER SEA LIONS (*above*) gather at the water's edge on an Aleutian Islands beach. Polar bears (*right*), perhaps the most majestic animals of the Arctic, cast magnified shadows in the low sun as they cross an ice pan.

Practically none of the Arctic is forested, for one of the lines of demarcation is the treeline. North of this line is a world of grasses, shrubs, dwarf trees, and lichens. The lack of water is the principal reason for this limited vegetation. While much of the Arctic appears to be dotted with lakes, there is not enough free water during the short growing season to permit development of the plant communities familiar in temperate regions. Hybrid varieties of some crops have been developed for subarctic areas like those around Fairbanks or Whitehorse, in the Yukon Territory, but it may be many years before species will be developed for Arctic cultivation outside of greenhouses. Large areas of the subarctic will someday be used to produce crops and food, but the process will be slow since, in many places such as Alaska, the land must first be cleared of trees.

Future Development. Transportation to and within the Arctic has developed entirely within the political framework of the nations bordering the region. Most of the present routes lie in a north-south direction, connecting a specific, small outpost of the region to more developed centers in the south. Rivers are the most available and least expensive means of transport and have been used for the greatest length of time. The Lena, Yenisei, and Ob in the Soviet Union are among the world's ten largest rivers. The Mackenzie River is beginning to play an important role in the development of northwestern Canada, and Hudson Bay serves as an outlet for wheat grown in the northern prairies of Canada. Land routes, by rail and road, are few and difficult to maintain because of the permafrost. They are gradually inching into the Arctic, however, and as time passes, highways and railroads will become more common.

Much of the travel within the region is by small aircraft. They are the prairie schooners of the Arctic. Roads generally are constructed only within the towns. Tracked vehicles are of more use, and in winter tractor-crawlers pull long sled-trains of supplies across the frozen land and rivers, but this method is not satisfactory for large-scale development. Hopefully, air-cushion vehicles ("hovercraft") can be developed to fill a real need for year-round, all-surface mobility. The commercial air routes lie parallel to the roads and run north and south, the exceptions being the few so-called "polar" flights over the Arctic and a few east-west routes in the Soviet Union.

ARCTIC WILD LIFE

PTARMIGAN lives mostly in open country. The male whitetailed ptarmigan, shown here in its summer plumage, has a length of about 16 inches.

CHARLES J. OTT, FROM NATIONAL AUDUBON SOCIETY

The Arctic and subarctic hold enormous economic potential, but our knowledge of atmospheric processes is so slight that at present we cannot hope to change the environment there. All we can do is mitigate its harshness. Man will soon respond to the region and develop it—perhaps in a manner similar to a Soviet planner's scheme for building a city beneath a huge plastic dome. Someday there may be air-conditioned cities for people living in the northland and working to develop its vast natural resources.

For the history of exploration of the Arctic, see POLAR EXPLORATION, NORTH.

JOHN E. SATER, *Arctic Institute of North America*

Bibliography

Arctic Institute of North America, *The Arctic Basin* (Montreal 1963).
Arctic Institute of North America, *Arctic Institute Bibliography*, 12 vols. (Washington 1953–65).
Armstrong, Terence, *Russians in the Arctic, 1937–57* (London 1958)
Berg, Lev S., *Natural Regions of the U.S.S.R.*, tr. from the Russian by Olga A. Titelbaum (New York 1950).
Dodge, Ernest, *Northwest by Sea* (New York 1961).
Freuchen, Peter, *Adventures in the Arctic* (New York 1960).
Hayes, James G., *Conquest of the North Pole* (New York 1935).
Kimble, George H.T., and Good, Dorothy, eds., *Geography of the Northlands* (New York 1955).
Kirwan, Laurence P., *A History of Polar Exploration* (New York 1960).
Macdonald, Ronald, St.J., ed., *The Arctic Frontier* (Toronto 1966).
Stefansson, Vilhjalmur, *The Friendly Arctic* (New York 1921).

ARCTURUS, ärk-tōōr'əs, is a brilliant, golden-yellow star in the constellation Boötes. With a magnitude of about −0.05, Arcturus is the fourth-brightest star in the sky. Its brightness is due in part to its relative nearness, since the star is only 30 to 40 light years away from the earth. Arcturus is one of the few stars near enough and large enough for its diameter to have been measured. Its diameter is about 23 times that of the sun. The surface temperature of the star, however, is somewhat cooler than that of the sun. The name Arcturus is derived from Greek words that mean "guardian of the bear." This refers to the familiar constellation Ursa Major, or Great Bear, which is nearby.

ARDABIL, är-də-bēl', a city in Iran, is situated in the Third ostan, or province, (formerly the eastern part of Azerbaijan province), at the center of a fertile plain in the northwestern part of the country. The climate of the city, which is some 5,500 feet (1,675 meters) above sea level, is very cold in winter but temperate in summer.

A city was built on this site in the 400's A.D. There are remains of a mosque built in the 1100's, but the most important monument is the shrine of Shaikh Safi al-Din (1252–1334). One of his descendants, Ismail I (reigned 1501–1524), founded the Safavid dynasty, named for Safi al-Din. Treasures given to the shrine included the immense "Ardabil" carpet, woven in 1540 and now in the Victoria and Albert Museum, London; a collection of Chinese porcelain, now in the Teheran Archaeological Museum; and a great collection of Persian manuscripts, seized by the Russians in 1828. Population: (1956) 65,742.

DONALD N. WILBER
Author of "Iran: Past and Present"

ARDEN, Enoch. See ENOCH ARDEN.

ARDENNES, är-den', is the name of a district in Belgium, France, and Luxembourg. The area, known also as the *Forest of Ardennes*, covers parts of the Belgian province of Luxembourg, the Grand Duchy of Luxembourg, and the French department of Ardennes. The forest is best preserved in Belgium. A wooded plateau with much wild game, it rises in the northeast to a height of 2,283 feet (696 meters). In the cleared sections there is farming and livestock raising.

The present-day Ardennes covers part of the ancient forest of *Arduenna Silva*, described by Julius Caesar in his *Commentaries on the Gallic War*. During World Wars I and II it was the scene of heavy fighting, particularly in the winter of 1944–1945, when the Battle of the Bulge was fought around Bastogne and St.-Vith.

ARDMORE, ärd'mōr, is a city in southern Oklahoma, 100 miles (161 km) by road south of Oklahoma City. It is the seat of Carter County and the commercial center of a petroleum and farming region. Its industries include oil refining, food processing, and the manufacture of leather goods, fiber glass, electronics equipment, concrete, sportswear, and roofing material. A federal school for Indians is situated in the city. Within a few miles' drive are several recreational areas: Lake Murray State Park and Lake Texoma to the southeast, and Platt National Park and Turner Falls Park to the north. Ardmore adopted city manager government in 1921. Population: 20,881.

AREA, âr'ē-ə, the measure of a bounded plane surface, or region. A region consists of the union of two sets of points. One set comprises a limited surface; the other comprises a simple closed curve that is the boundary of the limited surface. Regions are characterized by the names of their boundaries; for example, a rectangular region is one that is bounded by a rectangle.

The area, or measure, of a region is expressed as a number. This number tells how many standard unit regions can be laid, without overlapping each other, on the region to be measured. For convenience in measuring, the standard units are square regions with sides one linear unit in length and sufficiently small to permit reasonably complete coverage of the region to be measured. Examples of standard units are the square inch and the square centimeter.

Fig. 1   Fig. 2

In the measuring process a grid of unit squares of selected size is matched with the region to be measured (Fig. 1). The area of the rectangular region *ABCD* is found by counting the number of unit squares required to cover *ABCD* completely. It is seen that neither the length nor the width of *ABCD* has an integral number of lengths of the unit squares. Thus the number of unit square regions required to cover *ABCD* completely must be estimated. This difficulty can be reduced by choosing a grid of smaller unit squares. A unit square with a side that is half the previous one would fit *ABCD* more nearly and would permit a more precise determination of its measure (Fig. 2).

LEE E. BOYER
Harrisburg (Pa.) Area Community College

AREA RULE, âr'ē-ə, is a concept used in the design of aircraft that fly at speeds near to or greater than the speed of sound. The area concerned—the overall cross-sectional area of the craft—is designed to overcome the excess aerodynamic drag that would otherwise result from the high speeds involved. An aircraft so designed has a cross section that increases from a minimum at the nose to a maximum near the middle of the craft, then tapers off again toward the rear. The concept was developed by Richard T. Whitcomb, a United States engineer, in the early 1950's.

ARECA. See BETEL NUT.

ARECIBO, ä-rä-sē'vō, is a seaport in Puerto Rico, on the north coast, at the mouth of the Arecibo River, 40 miles (64 km) west of San Juan. It is connected with San Juan by railroad and highway.

Arecibo, situated in a rich agricultural district, produces raw sugar, rum, and paper. A fleet of fishing boats operates from the harbor. There is an airport, and the town is popular with tourists. The Dos Bocas and Caonillas hydroelectric plants are situated a few miles to the south. Settled in 1556, Arecibo is one of the oldest towns in Puerto Rico. The British sacked the town in 1702. Population: 28,828.

ARENA THEATER, ə-rē'nə thē'ə-tər, is a form of theatrical staging in which an illuminated central acting area is surrounded, in whole or in part, by a darkened audience area. Its qualities of intimacy and simplicity enable it to develop greater emotional power and reveal more of the psychological subtleties of the play.

It is sometimes called *theater-in-the-round,* a general term used for almost any kind of arena theater and for other forms of flexible staging. Staging need not be in full round to be considered theater-in-the-round. Three-quarter round, for example, has only about 270° of viewing angle, but it is still called "in-the-round."

Development. The true, or full, arena theater, with its completely encircled acting space, is the only really new theatrical stage form since the Renaissance picture-frame stage replaced the Elizabethan platform. The concept seems to have originated with Adolphe Appia (1862–1928), a Swiss producer and scene designer, who was the spokesman for a scenic reform movement in the 1920's that demanded better use of stage light and space. Appia, Jacques Copeau, Kenneth MacGowan, and Robert Edmond Jones all explored the use of the encircled stage and other forms to free drama from its confinement within the picture frame. (Flexible staging was a term later applied to such innovations.) Gilmor Brown experimented with arena staging at the Playbox, a private experimental theater built in Pasadena, Calif., in 1929. In 1932, Glenn Hughes began the regular presentation of comedies in full arena at the Penthouse Theatre at the University of Washington. After World War II, arena theaters supported professional companies in all types of plays throughout the United States.

Notable Arena Theaters. The arena theater is popular chiefly in the United States, although it has been used in many other parts of the world. In addition to the Penthouse Theatre, the best examples of the true arena form are the Arena Theater at Tufts University in Medford, Mass., and Le Théâtre en Rond in Paris. Larger arena theaters, some convertible to three-quarter staging by the removal of one bank of seats, include the Arena Stage in Washington, D.C., the Alley Theatre in Houston, and the Pavilion at Pennsylvania State University.

KELLY YEATON, *Pennsylvania State University*

ARENARIA, ar-ə-nâr'ē-ə, is a group of low-growing annual or perennial herbs native to the temperate regions of the world. They are found especially in central and southern Europe and the United States. Commonly known as *sandwort,* the plant has clusters of white flowers and usually is cultivated as a garden border. The genus *Arenaria* belongs to the pink family Caryophyllaceae. There are about 250 species.

ARENBERG, ä'rən-berκн, was formerly a German duchy of the Holy Roman Empire. Later incorporated in Prussia, it is now part of the Rhineland-Palatinate, state in West Germany. The name also is spelled *Aremberg.*

The ancestral seat of the lords of Arenberg is near the village of Arenberg in the district of Adenau. Its rulers played a part of some importance in German history in the 1100's, but by 1280 the male line had become extinct. One of the female descendants married the count de La Marck (died 1328), the younger of whose

ARENA THEATER, TUFTS UNIVERSITY, MEDFORD, MASS.

ARENA THEATER, such as that at Tufts University (above), brings the audience close to the players.

two sons became the lord of Arenberg. In 1547 the male line again died out, but the heiress married into the Ligne family and her husband was made (1549) a count of the empire by Charles V. Because of the services rendered by his grandson to the emperor, the title was raised to that of duke (1645).

ARENDS, âr'əndz, **Leslie Cornelius** (1895–), American political leader. He was born in Melvin, Ill., on Sept. 27, 1895, and studied at Oberlin College. After serving in the U.S. Navy in World War I, he followed his father in a career in farming and banking.

In 1934, Arends was elected as a Republican to the U.S. House of Representatives from the 17th Illinois District, and he was regularly reelected thereafter. In 1943 he was designated Republican whip in the House, becoming responsible for maintaining party discipline.

A long-time member of the House Armed Services Committee, Arends at various times opposed measures for conscription and universal military training. He also served on the Patents Committee and the special committee on postwar military policy. He generally opposed legislation that he believed would strengthen federal control and diminish the powers of the states.

ARENDT, ä'rent, **Hannah** (1906–), German-American author and political scientist. She was born in Hannover, Germany, on Oct. 14, 1906, and raised at Königsberg (now Kaliningrad, USSR). She was educated there and at Heidelberg, where she received her doctorate in 1928. As a refugee from Nazi Germany, she worked for Jewish relief organizations in Paris during the 1930's and in New York from 1941 to 1952. Following publication of her first well-known book, *The Origins of Totalitarianism* (1951), she received teaching appointments at leading American universities.

Hannah Arendt's pessimistic view of the contest of good and evil in human affairs is reflected in *The Human Condition* (1958), *Between Past and Future* (1961), and *On Revolution* (1963). Her best-known book, *Eichmann in Jerusalem* (1963), is a controversial analysis of Nazi crimes based on her reports of the Adolf Eichmann trial in 1961.

ARÈNE, ȧ-rân, **Paul Auguste** (1843–1896), French poet, novelist, and dramatist, who was one of the leaders in the revival of the Provençal dialect, *langue d'oc*. He is noted for his colorful descriptions of his native Provence.

Arène was born at Sisteron on June 26, 1843. In 1865 he attracted wide attention with a one-act verse comedy, *Pierrot héritier*, presented at the Odéon in Paris. Among his other plays are *Jean des figues* (1870), *Les comédiens errants* (1873), and *Le duel aux lanternes* (1875). Arène collaborated with Alphonse Daudet in a collection of sketches, *Contes de Paris et de Provence* (1887). His novels include *Au bon soleil* (1879), *La chèvre d'or* (1889), and *Le canot des six capitaines* (1889). Arène died at Antibes on Dec. 18, 1896.

Further Reading: Duché, Robert, *La langue et le style de Paul Arène* (Paris 1949); Petry, Lorenz, *Paul Arène* (Halle 1911); Provence, Marcel, *Le roman d'amour de Paul Arène* (Avignon 1945).

ARENSKY, ə-ryān′skē, **Anton Stepanovich** (1861–1906), Russian composer whose musical style bears a strong resemblance to that of Tchaikovsky. Arensky was born in Novgorod on Aug. 11, 1861. In 1882 he graduated from the conservatory in St. Petersburg (now Leningrad), where he had been a pupil of Rimski-Korsakov. In the same year he was appointed professor at the Imperial Conservatory in Moscow, where he taught harmony and composition. Arensky's compositions began to attract national attention, and in 1894 he was made musical director of the Imperial Chapel in St. Petersburg. He held this position until 1901. He died of tuberculosis at a santatorium in Terijoki, Finland, on Feb. 25, 1906.

Arensky's most often performed works include the Piano Trio in D Minor, the Serenade for Violin and Piano in G Major, the Suite for Two Pianos, and *Variations on a Theme of Tchaikovsky*, for string orchestra. Arensky wrote three operas, *A Dream on the Volga* (1891), *Raphael* (1894) and *Nal and Damayanti* (1904). His other works include a collection of songs, many solo pieces for piano, a piano concerto, a violin concerto, and church music. He also wrote two textbooks, on harmony and on musical forms.

AREOPAGITICA, ar-ē-op-ə-jit′i-kə, is a tract by John Milton defending freedom of the press. Published in 1644, during the English Civil War, this work, along with his divorce tracts, marks Milton's break with the Presbyterian faction of the Puritan Revolution.

The title of the tract alludes to the *Areopagitic Discourse*, written by the Greek rhetorician Isocrates about 355 B.C., which it resembles chiefly in form (a "speech" to be read, not spoken) and in situation (a private citizen urging a change of policy upon the governing body of the state).

Milton's initial participation in the Puritan cause had been as the author of several tracts, published between 1641 and 1642, urging the abolition of episcopacy and a presbyterian reorganization of the Church of England. But the Presbyterian clergy's subsequent denunciation of Milton's arguments in favor of divorce (1643–1645) and their efforts to impose on England a religious system at least as rigorous and compulsive as the one they were trying to pull down brought Milton to the conclusion that "New Presbyter was but Old Priest writ large."

In June 1643 the Presbyterian-dominated Parliament had passed the Press Licensing Order restoring the requirement (which had lapsed with the abolition of the Star Chamber in 1641) that a manuscript must be approved by a licenser before it could be published. *Areopagitica* argues that neither true morality nor true religion can be protected by restrictions in publishing. It contends that morality demands not prelapsarian innocence, but a knowing and deliberate choice between good and evil. Religion, which requires free and understanding faith, is necessarily undermined by authorities who prevent the publication of searching questions or serious challenges to accepted doctrine. *Areopagitica* concludes that licensing of the press is basically only a means of fastening both an ecclesiastical and a political tyranny upon the country.

After a slow start, *Areopagitica* has exerted a widespread influence. It undermined the authority of the Press Act, which lapsed in 1695, and helped prevent its revival. Honoré-Gabriel Mirabeau's adaptation of the arguments of *Areopagitica* in the 18th century helped pave the way for the French Revolution.

ERNEST SIRLUCK, *University of Toronto*

AREOPAGUS, ar-ē-op′ə-gəs, one of several councils in ancient Athens. It received its name from the hill (*pagos*) of Ares, just northwest of the Acropolis, where it met when sitting as a court. When sitting as a council, it met in the agora.

The origin of the Areopagus is not clear, but it was probably the oldest Athenian council, having grown out of the council that advised the hereditary monarch. The *archon basileus* presided over it when it tried homicide cases, but at other times the *archon eponymous* may have been in charge.

The duties and functions of the Areopagus can be discerned more clearly after the reforms of Solon (594 B.C.), who defined but apparently did not greatly alter them. For more than a century afterward, the Areopagus possessed considerable power, primarily judicial and religious in nature. It tried cases of homicide, intentional wounding, arson, and impiety, and cases involving conspirators against the constitution. The Areopagus also had the power to hear complaints against, and to impose fines on, magistrates. This power generally deterred the magistrates from breaking the oaths they had taken to obey the laws. In this regard the Areopagus acted as protector of the constitution, but it does not seem to have been empowered specifically to veto any law that it regarded as unconstitutional.

From the time of Solon the Areopagus was composed of ex-archons, who became members for life. Since only the upper two classes were eligible to run for this office, the Areopagus was made up of members of the Athenian aristocracy, whose views it reflected. After 487/486 B.C., when archons were selected by lot rather than elected, its influence gradually declined. In 462/461 B.C. a democratic faction led by Ephialtes succeeded in transferring most of its duties to the *boule* or to the popular court. Thereafter the Areopagus retained only the right to try cases of homicide and minor religious offenses. It continued to exist even after Athens became part of the Roman empire. Although it remained a respected body, it never played an important role in Athens after 462/461 B.C.

THOMAS KELLY, *University of Alberta*

AREQUIPA, ä-rä-kē′pä, is the third-largest city in Peru and the capital of Arequipa department. It is situated just within the western edge of the Andes, at the foot of El Misti, a snowcapped volcano 19,088 feet (5,818 meters) high. The volcanoes of Chachani and Pichupichu, about the same height, are also visible from the city. The surrounding highlands are arid, but Arequipa lies in a fertile, well-watered oasis that produces cotton, food crops, and animal feed. The climate is dry and mild, with springlike average temperatures the year round.

Most of the buildings in Arequipa are made of a volcanic stone that gives the city a soft pearl-white gleam. The central square, the Plaza de Armas, is surrounded on three sides by arcaded buildings and on the fourth by the Cathedral, built in the 1600's. The smaller but more ornate Church of La Compañia dates from the same period, and there are numerous other churches and mansions of the Spanish colonial period. Indian markets and narrow cobbled streets add color and atmosphere to the city.

Arequipa is the transportation hub and commercial center of southern Peru. The city is on the Pan American Highway, 688 miles (1,107 km) southeast of Lima, on the route from Lima to La Paz, Bolivia. Railroads link it with Cuzco and the Pacific Ocean ports of Mollendo and Matarani. Arequipa is the chief market for alpaca, llama, and sheep wool produced on the southern Peruvian Altiplano, or high plain. The city has a large woolen mill and food-processing plants. Its handicraftsmen produce leatherwork and alpaca rugs.

The city is the seat of a Roman Catholic archdiocese. It also contains the University of San Agustín and an archaeological museum. There are two public stadiums, a racetrack, and good facilities for swimming, golf, and tennis. Three hot-spring resorts—Jesús, Yura, and Socosani—are within easy reach of the city.

Arequipa was an old Inca settlement when the Spanish conquered Peru. An aide of the conquistador Francisco Pizarro founded the Spanish town in 1540. Earthquakes have devastated Arequipa several times. Population: (1961) 156,657.

ARES, âr′ēz, in Greek mythology, was the god of war; he was called *Mars* by the Romans. The son of Zeus (Jupiter) and Hera (Juno), he was usually regarded as the lover of Aphrodite (Venus). The worship of Ares was important in Thebes, perhaps in Athens, and in other Greek communities, but it never achieved the prominence in Greece that the worship of his counterpart Mars attained later in Rome.

Ares' characteristic activities were making war and making love. In the Trojan War he sided with the Trojans, whose leader, Hector, he favored with his personal protection. Among his offspring by various goddesses and mortal women were Fear and Rout, and Cycnus, the plunderer, who was slain by Heracles (Hercules).

In art, Ares is often represented as a stalwart figure armed with a helmet, shield, and spear.

ARETAS, ar′ə-təs, is the Greek name of four kings of the Nabataeans in Arabia, whose capital was Petra.

ARETAS I is mentioned in II Maccabees 5:8 as the Nabataean king who refused to offer refuge to the high priest Jason in his flight from Jerusalem in 169 B.C.

AREQUIPA'S twin-spired cathedral rises on the central square, backed by the snow-covered peaks of the Andes.

ARETAS II is mentioned by the historian Josephus Flavius in his account of the siege of Gaza by the Jewish king Jannaeus Alexander in 96 B.C. Aretas encouraged the city's resistance to Jannaeus and promised his support.

ARETAS III (reigned c. 85 B.C.–c. 60 B.C.) took part in the war between the Seleucid king Antiochus XII Dionysus and his brother Demetrius III Eukairos. He vanquished and killed Antiochus near Cana and extended the Nabataean dominions to Coclesyria (Lebanon). He then defeated Jannaeus at Adida in Judea but soon after withdrew from Judea. In the civil war between the brothers Hyrcanus II and Aristobulus II of Judea, Aretas attempted to restore Hyrcanus to the throne. While besieging Aristobulus at Jerusalem, he was persuaded by the Romans under Pompey to withdraw his troops. He was pursued by Aristobulus, who defeated him in Transjordan. After Pompey took Judea in 63 B.C., Aretas was required to pay tribute to the Romans.

ARETAS IV (reigned 9 B.C.–40 A.D.). His name was originally *Eneas*, but when he took over the government of the Nabataeans, he changed it to Aretas. The most celebrated of the kings bearing this name, he was known in ancient inscriptions as "rāhem ammēh" (lover of his people). He came to the aid of Augustus in the Jewish wars that broke out in 4 B.C. after the death of Herod the Great. His daughter was the first wife of Herod Antipas, the Roman tetrarch who was a son of Herod the Great. When Antipas put her aside in favor of Herodias, Aretas attacked and defeated him. The imperial Roman army that was then mobilized against Aretas was demobilized at the death of Emperor Tiberius in 37 A.D., and the Nabataean kingdom remained independent throughout Aretas' reign.

In II Corinthians 11:32, Aretas is also described as the ruler of Damascus at the time of the conversion of the Apostle Paul.

ARETHUSA, ar-ə-thōō′zə, in Greek legend, was a wood nymph of Elis and one of the attendants of Artemis (Diana). Alpheus, a river god, saw her bathing and declared his love. She fled from him and begged for help from Artemis, who changed her into a fountain. In this form, she was transported to Ortygia, Sicily, where Alpheus in the form of a river united with her.

© THE FRICK COLLECTION, NEW YORK

PIETRO ARETINO, Italian Renaissance writer, from a portrait by Titian, which is now in the Frick Collection.

ARETINO, ä-rä-tē′nō, **Pietro** (1492–1556), Italian Renaissance author, whose works are a mixture of vitality, honesty, and venality, representing the best and the worst qualities of the Italian High Renaissance. Although Aretino had a great influence on 16th century literature, his writing is now mainly of historical interest.

Aretino was born in Arezzo on April 20, 1492, the son of a shoemaker. He studied painting and literature in Perugia. About 1516 he went to Rome, where he secured the protection of the banker Agostino Chigi. He soon attracted attention with his mordantly witty verse, winning the favor of Pope Leo X and Cardinal Giulio de′ Medici, whose candidacy for the papacy he later supported by writing libelous pasquinades about the other candidates. The ferocity of his satire earned him many enemies in Rome, and he went to Venice in 1527. He died there on Oct. 21, 1556.

Aretino was a Renaissance adventurer who succeeded in gaining fame and fortune through the power of his pen. Feared by many of the prominent men both in and outside of Italy, he was called the "Scourge of Princes." Widely known as the arbiter of men's reputations, he lived like a prince on the rich gifts and pensions given by those who feared his satire or by those who wished to buy the fame that resulted from his adulation. Among his most distinguished patrons were King Francis I of France and Emperor Charles V.

Aretino wrote a tragedy, *Orazio* (1546), and five comedies. The best of his comedies, *La cortigiana* (1526) and *La talanta* (1542), have a spontaneity and verve not found in other Italian writing of the era. Arentino's satirical dialogues, including *I ragionamenti* and *I dialoghi*, are vivid indictments of contemporary morals in Italy. His letters, which have been collected in six volumes, have a lively descriptive power that makes them important documents of 16th century history.

Further Reading: Cleugh, James, *The Divine Aretino* (New York 1966); Hutton, Edward, *Pietro Aretino, the Scourge of Princes* (Boston 1922).

AREZZO, Guido d'. See GUIDO D'AREZZO.

AREZZO, ä-rāt′tsō, a city in Italy, stands on a hill in the Tuscan Appennines, overlooking the Arno River, 39 miles southeast of Florence. It is the capital of Arezzo province. A trading center, Arezzo produces silk, wool textiles, furniture, machinery, silverware, wine, and olive oil.

Although the city has a modern appearance, it has fine medieval and Renaissance buildings. It is also rich in art treasures. On the highest point are the remains of the old citadel, from which many streets fan out toward the plain. The Church of San Francesco (1322) contains a famous group of frescoes by Piero della Francesca, illustrating the story of the Cross. The town's most notable buildings are the Romanesque-Gothic cathedral; the Romanesque Church of Santa Maria della Pieve, begun about 1287 and continued in the 1300's and 1500's; and the 14th century Palazzo dei Priori. There is an art gallery and museum in the Palazzo della Fraternità dei Laici, a charitable institution founded in the 1200's.

In ancient times the settlement, then called *Arretium,* was an important Etruscan town and later a Roman military station, famous for its red clay vases. In 1098 it became a free commune and extended its power over several neighboring towns. At the Battle of Campaldino (1289) the Ghibelline cities, led by Arezzo, were defeated by the Guelph forces, led by Florence. Arezzo reached the zenith of its achievement in the early 1300's, but declined after it was sold to Florence in 1384.

Arezzo province is mostly hilly, and its area of 1,248 square miles (3,232 square kilometers) is devoted chiefly to agriculture. Cereals, olives, and grapes are grown, and sheep and cattle are raised. Silkworms are also bred. Population: (1961) of the city, 43,868.

ARFE, är′fā, a family of Spanish goldsmiths and silversmiths of Flemish or German origin.

ENRIQUE DE ARFE (c.1470–c.1543) probably came from Harff, near Cologne, Germany. He settled in León, Spain, and executed tabernacles in the cathedrals of León, Córdoba, and Toledo.

ANTONIO DE ARFE (1510–c. 1578), his son, is noted for his ornamentation of the cathedrals of Santiago de Compostela and Medina de Ríoseco.

JUAN DE ARFE Y VILLAFANE (1535–c. 1603), the son of Antonio de Arfe, did the tabernacles in the cathedrals of Ávila and Seville.

ARFONS, är′fonz, **Art** (1926–   ), American automobile racer. While setting land speed records at the Bonneville (Utah) Salt Flat, he was one of the first to exceed 500 miles per hour in an axle-driven motor vehicle. *Arthur Eugene Arfons* was born in Akron, Ohio, on Feb. 3, 1926. A skilled mechanic, he used spare parts to build his own cars, most of which he called "Green Monsters." He adapted the parachute for use as a brake in 1959 and was the first drag racer to hit 200 mph. His first land speed record (the average speed for two runs made within one hour over a measured mile) of 434 mph, set on Oct. 5, 1964, was broken by Craig Breedlove. On Nov. 7, 1965, Arfons drove his 21-foot, 17,500-hp jet racer at 576.533 mph, but Breedlove raised the mark to 600.601 mph eight days later.

BILL BRADDOCK, *New York "Times"*

ARGALI, är'gə-lē, a wild sheep found in the mountains of central and eastern USSR, in China, and in Nepal. It is also known as the *Marco Polo sheep*. An herbivorous animal, the argali is from four to six feet long and weighs from 165 to 440 pounds. It has a narrow nose and pointed ears. The male has large spiral horns, whereas the female has small, slightly curved horns. The coat varies in color from creamy white to gray and brown; however, it is not woolly like that of the domesticated sheep. In some of the males, there is a fringe of long hair down the front of the neck.

The argali belongs to the order Artiodactyla, family Bovidae. Its classification is *Ovis ammon*.

ARGALL, är'gôl, **Sir Samuel** (died ?1626), English navigator and colonial official in America. He first achieved prominence as a navigator in 1609 by pioneering the northern route to Virginia, greatly reducing the sailing time between England and the colony. The next year he went to Jamestown with the new governor general, Thomas West, Baron De La Warr (Lord Delaware), arriving just in time to prevent the starving colonists from abandoning the settlement. Sent to the Bermudas for hogs, Argall made for Cape Cod instead, bringing back a cargo of fish for the settlers. Later he bought corn from the Indians to provide the needy colony with food.

In 1611, Argall went back to England with Lord Delaware, but he returned to Virginia the following year. Among his notable exploits was the capture (1613) of the Indian princess Pocahontas, whom he sent to Jamestown. Her father, Powhatan, was compelled to accept a peace treaty with the English settlers, and the peaceable development of the colony was thus assured.

In 1613 he had set out on his most far-reaching adventure, the destruction of the new French settlements of Mount Desert, St. Croix, and Port Royal, on the Maine and Nova Scotia coasts, which cleared the area for future English colonization. On the same expedition he forced the governor of the new Dutch colony on the Hudson to accept English suzerainty.

Appointed deputy governor of Virginia in 1617, Argall seems to have governed efficiently, though autocratically, at first. But he was soon accused of corruption, oppressing the poor, and diverting community property to personal use. These charges, never established or disproved, have long been a subject of controversy. Privateering was added to the list of his offenses, and he returned to England in 1619 to justify his conduct. He commanded a vessel against Algerian pirates in 1620, was knighted in 1622, and in 1625 served as admiral in a campaign against Spain, capturing prizes estimated at £100,000.

ARGELANDER, är-gə-län'dər, **Friedrich Wilhelm August** (1799–1875), German astronomer. He was born in Memel, Lithuania, on March 22, 1799. He studied at the Königsberg Observatory under Friedrich Wilhelm Bessel, whose assistant he later became (1820). In 1823 he was named astronomer and in 1828 professor at the observatory in Åbo, Finland. He became director of the observatory at Helsinki in 1832. In 1837 he was appointed professor of astronomy at Bonn.

Argelander carried out scientific observations of variable stars and added much to the knowl-

ARTHUR W. AMBLER FROM NATIONAL AUDUBON SOCIETY

THE ARGALI, largest of the wild sheep (*Ovis ammon*), is native to the Siberian highlands of central Asia.

edge of the progressive motion of the solar system through space. His great work, prepared with the assistance of Eduard Schönfeld, was the charting of the position and brightness of stars of the Northern Hemisphere to the 9th and 10th magnitudes. The results were published in volumes 3–5 (1859–62) of the *Astronomische Beobachtungen* (known popularly as the *Bonner Durchmusterung*), a catalog of over 324,000 stars, to which he added a celestial atlas in 1863. He died in Bonn, on Feb. 17, 1875.

ARGENSOLA, är-hän-sō'lä, Spanish poets and historians, known as the Spanish Horaces.

LUPERCIO LEONARDO DE ARGENSOLA (1559–1613) was born at Barbastro, Aragón, on Dec. 14, 1559. He was secretary to the duke of Villahermosa and to Maria of Austria, widow of Emperor Maximilian II of the Holy Roman Empire. In 1599 he was appointed royal chronicler of Aragón. In 1610 he went to Naples, where he served as state secretary until his death. In his early years Lupercio wrote three tragedies in the classical manner, which are no longer extant. He is remembered chiefly for a few sonnets, satires, epistles, and imitations of Latin poetry. He died at Naples in March 1613.

BARTOLOMÉ JUAN LEONARDO DE ARGENSOLA (1562–1631), Lupercio's brother, was born at Barbastro on Aug. 26, 1562. He was rector of Villahermosa and chaplain to Maria of Austria. Appointed royal historiographer at Aragón in 1613, he wrote the continuation of Jeronimo Zurita y Castro's *Anales de la corona de Aragón.* Bartolomé is noted for his elegant, witty satires and epistles as well as his excellent sonnets, translations of Horace, and a prose history, *Conquista de las islas Molucas* (1609). He died at Saragossa, Spain on Feb. 4, 1631.

Bartolomé's poetry is more polished than that of Lupercio but has less force and profundity. Both brothers wrote with simplicity and refinement in their attempt to counterbalance the effects of Gongorism, the cult of artificial, obscure versification that was strangling lyric expression in 17th century Spanish poetry. Their collected poems were published in 1634 under the title *Rimas* (modern ed., 2 vols., 1950–51).

Further Reading: Aznar Molina, Joaquín, *Los Argensola* (Saragossa 1939); Green, Otis H., *The Life and Works of Lupercio Leonardo de Argensola* (Philadelphia 1927).

ARGENSON, är-zhän-sôn′, was the title of a noble French family whose members were frequently prominent in French political and intellectual life. Surnamed *de Voyer*, the family originated in the old province of Touraine.

RENÉ DE VOYER, COUNT D'ARGENSON (1596–1651), the first notable figure of the family, was born on Nov. 21, 1596. He undertook diplomatic missions for Cardinal Richelieu and was later ambassador to Venice. He died on July 14, 1651.

MARC RENÉ DE VOYER, MARQUIS D'ARGENSON (1652–1721), the grandson of René, was born in Venice, Italy, on Nov. 4, 1652. One of Louis XIV's intimate advisers, he was lieutenant general of police (1697–1718). In 1709 he ordered the destruction of the Jansenist convent of Port-Royal des Champs. Appointed keeper of the seals and president of the Council of Finance in 1718, he was forced to resign two years later because of his opposition to John Law's schemes for enriching the government treasury. Marc René, a patron of letters, was admitted to the Académie Française in 1718. He died in Paris on May 8, 1721.

RENÉ LOUIS DE VOYER, MARQUIS D'ARGENSON (1694–1757), was born in Paris on Oct. 18, 1694, the elder son of Marc René. He was called *d'Argenson la Bête* because of his lack of sophistication. As foreign minister of France from 1744 to 1747, he tried to arrange a compromise peace during the War of the Austrian Succession (1740–1748), but the effort failed, in part because of his shortsighted policy of ignoring the growing might of Prussia and his fear of Austria, the traditional enemy of France.

After his dismissal, he was made president of the Académie des Inscriptions. D'Argenson was a friend of Voltaire and the Encyclopedists, and an advocate of political and social reform. His *Mémoires* are an excellent source for the literary and political history of the reign of Louis XV. Part of them were published as *Journal et mémoires du marquis d'Argenson* (9 vols., 1859–67). He also wrote *Considérations sur le gouvernement ancien et présent de la France* (1764). He died in Paris on Jan. 26, 1757.

MARC PIERRE DE VOYER, COUNT D'ARGENSON (1696–1764), was the younger brother of René Louis. He was born in Paris on Aug. 16, 1696. A civil servant, he was lieutenant general of police (1720–1724), councillor of state (1724), and intendant of Paris (1740). He became secretary of war in 1743, and for a time he and his brother, the foreign minister, virtually controlled the French government. He assisted in reforming the army and established the École Militaire (1751).

Although he was on good terms with Louis XV, he disliked and often opposed Mme. de Pompadour, the royal favorite, who obtained his dismissal as secretary of war in 1757. He was an intimate of Voltaire, to whom he gave material for the *Siècle de Louis XIV*, and was a patron of Denis Diderot and Jean le Rond d'Alembert, who dedicated the *Encyclopédie* to him. He died in Paris on Aug. 22, 1764.

MARC ANTOINE RENÉ DE VOYER, MARQUIS DE PAULMY D'ARGENSON (1722–1787), was the son of René Louis. He was born in Valenciennes on Nov. 22, 1722. Known as the marquis de Paulmy, he was secretary of war (1757–1758) after the dismissal of his uncle, Marc Pierre. He then served as ambassador to Switzerland, Poland, and Venice.

A member of the Académie Française, he edited and published his father's writings and compiled *Mélanges tirés d'une grande bibliothèque* (1779–88). His private library of over 100,000 volumes later formed the nucleus of the Bibliothèque de l'Arsenal. He died in Paris on Aug. 13, 1787.

MARC RENÉ DE VOYER, MARQUIS D'ARGENSON (1771–1842), was the grandson of Marc Pierre. He was born in Paris on Sept. 19, 1771. He was an aide-de-camp to the marquis de Lafayette, but having strong republican convictions, refused to leave France with the marquis in 1792. Under Napoleon I he held various official positions but did not hesitate to oppose the government when he felt it was unjust. After the Restoration of 1815, he entered the Chamber of Deputies and courageously protested against the White Terror and abrogation of the rights that had been won during the revolution. He died in Paris on Aug. 1, 1842.

ARGENTAN, är-zhän-tän′, is a town in France, in Orne department, on the Orne River, 23 miles (37 km) northwest of Alençon. The town produces lace, linens, leather goods, and stained glass, and is a trade center for horses and poultry.

There is an ancient château, now used as a courthouse and prison. There are also two interesting churches, St. Germain (15th–17th centuries) and St. Martin (early 16th century). Population: (1962) 11,724.

ARGENTEUIL, är-zhän-tû′yə, is a city in France, in Seine-et-Oise department, five miles (eight km) northwest of Paris, on the right bank of the Seine River. It is an important metallurgical center, producing tractors, rolling stock, automobile parts, and electrical equipment. It also has chemical and pharmaceutical plants, and rayon, rubber, and plaster are manufactured. The surrounding country has vineyards.

The town developed around a 7th century convent, famous as the retreat of Peter Abelard's beloved, Héloïse, who was its abbess until 1229, when it was turned into a monastery. The building was destroyed during the French Revolution. A sacred relic, said to be the Seamless Tunic worn by Christ and donated by Charlemagne, is enshrined in a church in the city. Population: (1962) 82,007.

ARGENTINA, La (1890?–1936), är-jən-tē′nə, Spanish dancer. She was born Antonia Mercé, in Buenos Aires, Argentina. After extensive training in operatic ballet, she devoted herself to Spanish dancing, achieving international reputation as a performing artist and choreographer. In 1925 she won acclaim for her original interpretation of Manuel de Falla's *El amor brujo*, and thereafter she popularized the music of other contemporary composers, including Isaac Albéniz and Julián Bautista. She is credited with having revived interest in the Spanish dance as a classical art form. She died near Bayonne, France, on July 18, 1936.

ARGENTINA

Coat of arms of Argentina

Sheep grazing on the Patagonia steppes symbolize Argentina's dependence on the land and its products.

TABLE OF CONTENTS

ARGENTINA, är-jən-tē′nə, is the second-largest country of South America in size and population, after Brazil. It occupies most of the southern part of the continent between the Andes Mountains and the Atlantic Ocean. Stretching from 22° to 55° parallel of south latitude, a distance of some 2,300 miles (3,700 km), it is shaped roughly like an inverted triangle, tapering southward from a base about 1,000 miles (1,600 km) broad. Argentina borders on five South American countries: Chile to the west, Bolivia and Paraguay to the north, and Brazil and Uruguay to the northeast.

Except for its northernmost fringe, which lies in the tropics, all of Argentina is in the Southern Hemisphere's temperate zone, which includes the world's most economically advanced regions south of the equator. Argentina shares with Australia the major land portion of this zone and like Australia is far removed from the world's centers of population and economic activity. Seven thousand miles (more than 11,000 km) of ocean separate its seaports from New York or the English Channel, and even the air age has not completely removed this handicap of distance.

In climate, size, and topography Argentina can be compared with the portion of the United States between the Mississippi River and the Rocky Mountains, although the North American region has colder winters. The humid lowlands of eastern Argentina, especially along the rivers of the Río de la Plata system, resemble the Mississippi valley. The savannas and swamps of the Chaco, in northern Argentina, find a parallel in coastal Louisiana. Westward, the humid Pampa (plain) of Argentina gives way to range land and finally to desert broken only by irrigated oases, just as the Great Plains of the United States become drier toward the west. The Andes present a far more imposing barrier than the Rockies, but both mountain systems mark the western end of the plains.

Both Argentina and its major river estuary, the Río de la Plata, were named for silver (Latin, *argentum;* Spanish, *plata*). The area rapidly deceived the dreams of the 16th century Spanish conquistadores, but today Argentina's more than 20 million inhabitants make up the most urbanized, well-fed, literate, and homogeneous nation

---

INFORMATION HIGHLIGHTS

Official Name: República Argentina (Argentine Republic).

Head of State: President.

Head of Government: President.

Legislature: Congreso Nacional (National Congress)—*Upper Chamber:* Senado (Senate); *Lower Chamber:* Cámara de Diputados (Chamber of Deputies).

Area: 1,072,067 square miles (2,776,656 sq km), excluding Falkland Islands and part of Antarctica, which are claimed by Argentina.

Highest Elevation: Aconcagua, 22,835 feet (6,960 meters).

Population: (1960) 20,005,691.

Capital: Buenos Aires.

Major Language: Spanish (official language).

Major Religion: Roman Catholic (official religion).

Monetary Unit: Peso, divided into 100 centavos.

Weights and Measures: Metric system.

Flag: Three horizontal bands, the middle one white with a golden sun at its center, the top and bottom bands light blue. See also *Flag.*

National Anthem: *Oid mortales, el grito sagrado* (O Hear, Ye Mortals, the Sacred Call).

in Latin America. Yet the 20th century has witnessed repeated periods of political chaos and economic stagnation in Argentina.

Two thirds of the people live in towns and cities; nearly half of the urban dwellers cluster in Greater Buenos Aires, one of the world's largest metropolitan areas, whose population of about 7 million is comparable in size to metropolitan Chicago's. The products of the land constitute most of Argentina's exports, and the majority of Argentines live and eat as becomes citizens of a leading producer of beef, mutton, hides, wool, wheat, and corn. The impulse provided by Domingo F. Sarmiento, the country's 19th century president-educator, has been transmitted to present generations in a national literacy rate of 91 percent and close intellectual ties to Europe. The heritage of an Indian or mestizo past survives near the frontiers with Bolivia, Chile, and Paraguay, but the overwhelming influx of European (largely Italian and Spanish) immigration since 1860 has produced a homogeneous people, both racially and culturally.

Despite these advantages, which often cause Argentines to reject labels of "underdeveloped" or even "Latin American," Argentina still finds itself painfully readjusting to the contemporary world, in which its prosperity and even its stability have been seriously compromised. The collapse in the 1930's of a commercial system that exchanged agricultural raw materials for European manufactures on favorable terms forced rapid and often unbalanced expansion of the industrial sector and gave rise to continuing conflict with agricultural interests. The political emergence of the urban middle classes at the beginning of the 20th century provided a façade of democracy behind which the enormous divisions between city and countryside, coast and interior, white-collar and laboring groups, were merely forgotten and not resolved. The personalistic appeal of President Juan D. Perón in the 1940's and 1950's shattered this façade, but left in its stead only vague appeals to the workingman and serious tensions between labor unions and military factions. The human resources of Argentina, however, combined with the agricultural wealth of the Pampa, the iron ore on the Patagonian coast, and the petroleum and natural gas along the Andes, hold forth the promise that eventually the potential of the "land of silver" will be realized.

JAMES R. SCOBIE, *Indiana University*

1. The People

The words that best describe the Argentines are "cosmopolitan" and "expressive." The people are a blend of many European nationalities, although the Spanish and Italian strains predominate. In temperament and way of life they are more "Latin" than the North Americans or British but more "Anglo-Saxon" than the Latins.

Most of the Argentine population is of relatively recent European origin, stemming from an immigration that was concentrated in the years 1880 to 1930, with a spurt after World War II. There are no Orientals, Negroes, or Indians to speak of, as there are in most South American countries.

The land offers much room for an increase in population, because most of it is habitable. In the mid-1960's, Argentina had 8 persons per square kilometer of territory, compared with 21 in the United States.

PROVINCES AND POPULATIONS

Provinces, Federal District, and Territory	Population (1960)	Capital
Buenos Aires	6,734,548	La Plata
Catamarca	172,407	Catamarca
Chaco	535,443	Resistencia
Chubut	142,195	Rawson
Córdoba	1,759,997	Córdoba
Corrientes	543,226	Corrientes
Entre Ríos	803,505	Paraná
Federal District	2,966,816	Buenos Aires
Formosa	178,458	Formosa
Jujuy	239,783	Jujuy
La Pampa	158,489	Santa Rosa
La Rioja	128,270	Rioja
Mendoza	825,535	Mendoza
Misiones	391,094	Posadas
Neuquén	111,008	Neuquén
Río Negro	192,595	Viedma
Salta	412,652	Salta
San Juan	352,461	San Juan
San Luis	174,251	San Luis
Santa Cruz	52,853	Río Gallegos
Santa Fe	1,865,537	Santa Fe
Santiago del Estero	477,156	Santiago del E.
Tucumán	780,348	Tucumán
Tierra del Fuego (territory)	7,064	Ushuaia
Total	20,005,691	

Argentina also claims the Falkland Islands (Islas Malvinas) and other islands in the South Atlantic that are administered by Britain, several islands south of Tierra del Fuego disputed with Chile, and a sector of Antarctica: population 3,254.

Spanish is universally spoken. Although many people of Italian descent speak Italian in their homes, they have little trouble with the closely related Spanish language. Nearly all the people are at least nominally Roman Catholic, although the larger cities have Jewish and Protestant minorities.

In the early 1800's the Argentines were noted for their fierce sense of nationalism, but this can hardly be called a strong characteristic today. Though proud of their national independence and sometimes suspicious of what they readily call "Yankee imperialism," they have been peaceable neighbors in the Latin-American world and a force for economic cooperation among nations.

Population Growth. Although Pedro de Mendoza and his Spanish adventurers founded a settlement at Buenos Aires in 1536, it was gradually abandoned, and new arrivals from Europe passed it by as they went up the Paraná River in search of silver and gold. The city was not refounded until 1580.

The men who settled on the Pampa, the flat plain of rich alluvial soil that radiates from Buenos Aires, were mostly sons of Indian mothers and Spanish fathers. For more than 200 years they and their descendants slowly populated the Pampa, fighting hostile Indians and eventually killing them off, as the North Americans were doing at the same time.

The gaucho, or cowboy, was the typical country dweller. He herded cattle, was an expert in breaking horses, and was said to be quick with his knife. Gauchos were the rank and file of the revolutionary army that won independence from Spain in the early 19th century. However, the ideas that inspired the rebellion came from the rising middle classes, who lived in the towns. An estimated 500,000 people lived at that time

POPULATION GROWTH

Census year	Population	Urban	Foreign-born
1869	1,737,076	27%	12%
1895	3,954,911	37%	25%
1914	7,885,237	53%	30%
1947	15,897,127	62%	15%
1960	20,005,691	68%	13%

ARGENTINA

AGRICULTURE, INDUSTRY and RESOURCES

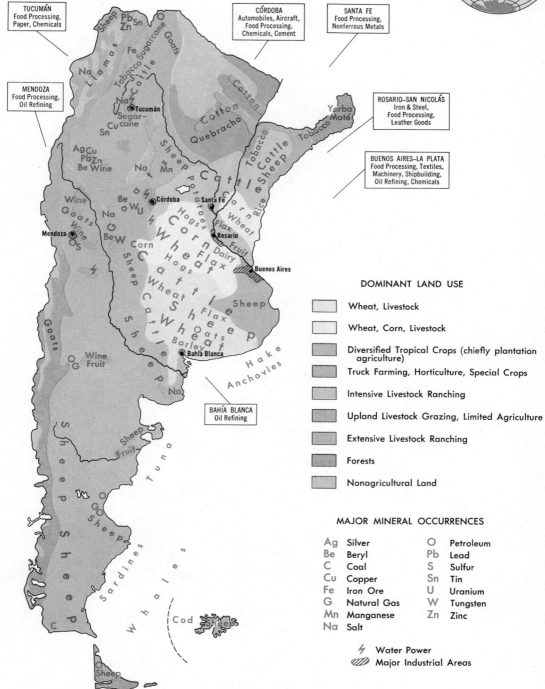

TUCUMÁN
Food Processing, Paper, Chemicals

MENDOZA
Food Processing, Oil Refining

CÓRDOBA
Automobiles, Aircraft, Food Processing, Chemicals, Cement

SANTA FE
Food Processing, Nonferrous Metals

ROSARIO–SAN NICOLÁS
Iron & Steel, Food Processing, Leather Goods

BUENOS AIRES–LA PLATA
Food Processing, Textiles, Machinery, Shipbuilding, Oil Refining, Chemicals

BAHÍA BLANCA
Oil Refining

DOMINANT LAND USE

- Wheat, Livestock
- Wheat, Corn, Livestock
- Diversified Tropical Crops (chiefly plantation agriculture)
- Truck Farming, Horticulture, Special Crops
- Intensive Livestock Ranching
- Upland Livestock Grazing, Limited Agriculture
- Extensive Livestock Ranching
- Forests
- Nonagricultural Land

MAJOR MINERAL OCCURRENCES

Ag	Silver	O	Petroleum
Be	Beryl	Pb	Lead
C	Coal	S	Sulfur
Cu	Copper	Sn	Tin
Fe	Iron Ore	U	Uranium
G	Natural Gas	W	Tungsten
Mn	Manganese	Zn	Zinc
Na	Salt		

⚡ Water Power
▨ Major Industrial Areas

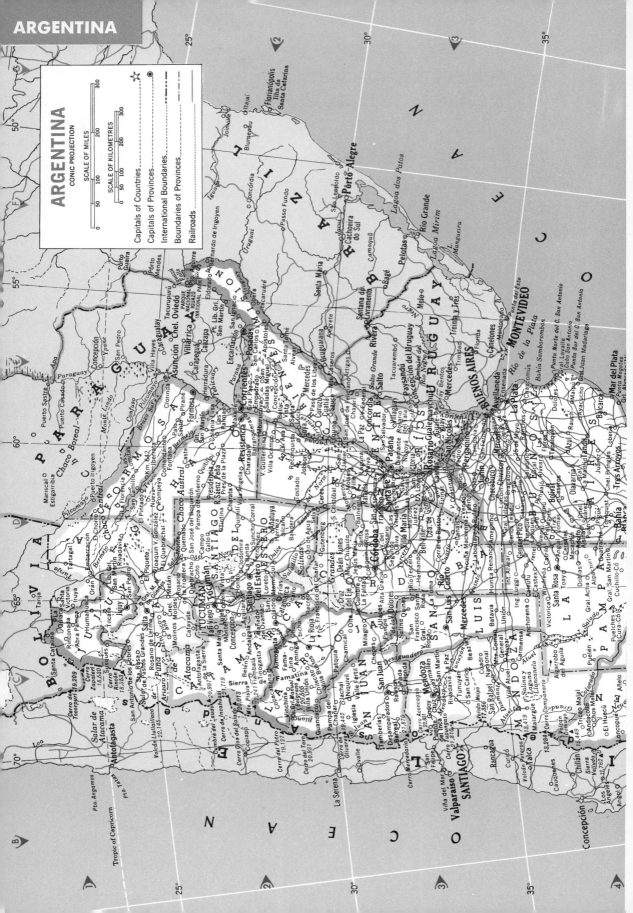

ARGENTINA

ARGENTINA
CONIC PROJECTION

SCALE OF MILES

SCALE OF KILOMETRES

Capitals of Countries
Capitals of Provinces
International Boundaries
Boundaries of Provinces
Railroads

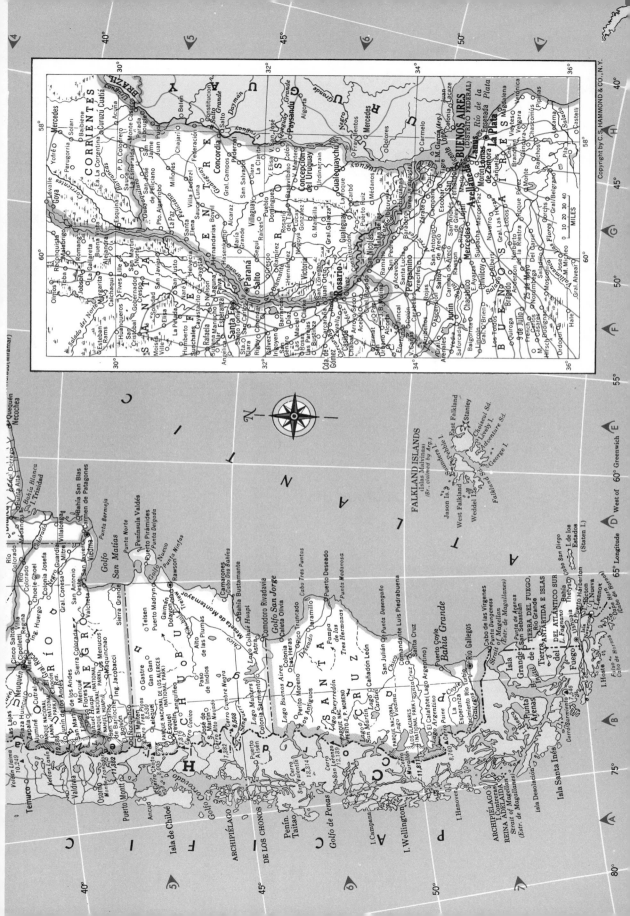

ARGENTINA

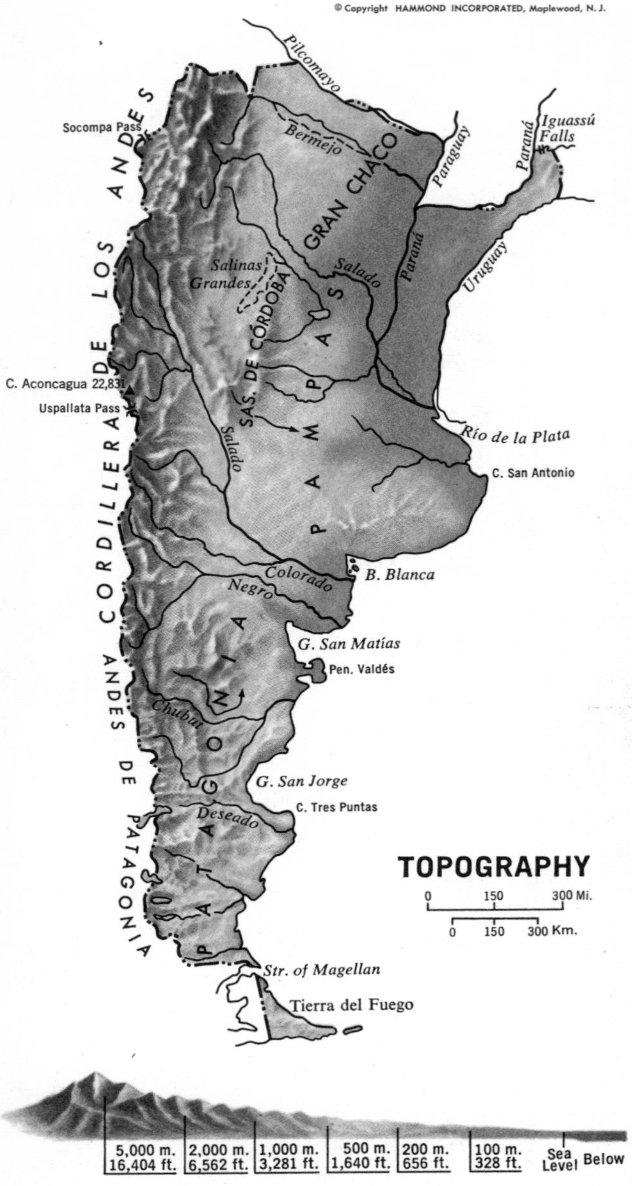

© Copyright HAMMOND INCORPORATED, Maplewood, N. J.
Pilcomayo
Socompa Pass
Bermejo
GRAN CHACO
Paraguay
Paraná
Iguassú Falls
Salinas Grandes
SAS. DE CÓRDOBA
Salado
Paraná
Uruguay
CORDILLERA DE LOS ANDES
C. Aconcagua 22,831
Uspallata Pass
Salado
P A M P A S
Río de la Plata
C. San Antonio
Colorado
B. Blanca
Negro
G. San Matías
Pen. Valdés
Chubut
G. San Jorge
C. Tres Puntas
Deseado
ANDES DE PATAGONIA
P A T A G O N I A
TOPOGRAPHY
0 150 300 Mi.
0 150 300 Km.
Str. of Magellan
Tierra del Fuego
5,000 m. 16,404 ft.
2,000 m. 6,562 ft.
1,000 m. 3,281 ft.
500 m. 1,640 ft.
200 m. 656 ft.
100 m. 328 ft.
Sea Level
Below

Total Population, 23,031,000

PROVINCES

Buenos Aires, 6,734,548 ....D 4
Catamarca, 172,407 ....C 2
Chaco, 535,443 ....D 2
Chubut, 142,195 ....C 5
Córdoba, 1,759,997 ....D 3
Corrientes, 543,226 ....E 2
Distrito Federal (fed. dist.), 2,966,816 ....H 7
Entre Ríos, 803,505 ....E 3
Formosa, 178,458 ....D 1
Jujuy, 239,783 ....C 1
La Pampa, 158,489 ....C 4
La Rioja, 128,270 ....C 2
Mendoza, 825,535 ....C 4
Misiones, 391,094 ....F 2
Neuquén, 111,008 ....C 4
Río Negro, 192,595 ....C 5
Salta, 412,652 ....D 1
San Juan, 352,461 ....C 3
San Luis, 174,251 ....C 3
Santa Cruz, 52,853 ....C 6
Santa Fe, 1,865,537 ....D 3
Santiago del Estero, 477,156.....D 2
Tierra del Fuego, Antártida e Islas del Atlántico Sur (terr.), 10,318 ....C 7
Tucumán, 780,348 ....C 2

CITIES and TOWNS

Abra Pampa, 1,391 ....C 1
Acebal, 2,026 ....F 6
Acevedo, 1,057 ....F 6
Acuña, 805 ....G 5
Adolfo Alsina, 5,836 ....D 4
Aguilares, 9,816 ....C 2
Aimogasta, 2,721 ....C 2
Alberti, 4,447 ....G 7
Alcaraz, 376 ....G 5
Alcorta, 3,781 ....F 6
Alejandra, 881 ....F 5
Allen, 11,389 ....C 4
Alpachiri, 733 ....D 4
Alta Gracia, 11,570 ....D 3
Alto de las Plumas, 182 ....C 5
Aluminé, 744 ....B 4
Alvear, 4,252 ....E 2
Ameghino, 2,770 ....D 3
Aminga, 480 ....C 2
Añatuya, 11,753 ....D 2
Anchorena, 862 ....C 4
Andacollo, 587 ....B 4
Andalgalá, 3,260 ....C 2
Angélica, 434 ....E 5
Anguil, 734 ....D 4
Antofagasta de la Sierra, 462....C 2
Apóstoles, 6,507 ....E 2
Arrecifes, 7,635 ....F 6
Arribeños, 1,739 ....F 7
Arroyo Seco, 5,193 ....F 6
Ascensión, 1,775 ....F 7
Astra, 1,019 ....C 6
Atamisqui, 1,122 ....D 2
Avellaneda, †329,626 ....G 7
Ayacucho, 9,220 ....E 4
Azul, 28,609 ....E 4
Bahía Blanca, †150,354 ....D 4
Bahía Thetys, †438 ....C 7
Baibiene, 380 ....G 4
Baigorrita, 1,206 ....F 7
Balcarce, 15,210 ....E 4
Balnearia, 4,306 ....D 3
Bandera, 2,035 ....D 2
Baradero, 10,194 ....G 6
Barrancas, 1,953 ....F 6
Barranqueras, 19,779 ....E 2
Barreal, 1,790 ....C 3
Basavilbaso, 6,614 ....G 6
Batavia, 457 ....C 3
Beazley, 1,070 ....C 3
Belén, 5,469 ....C 2
Bella Vista, Corrientes, 8,334 ....E 2
Bella Vista, Tucumán, 6,816 ......D 2
Bell Ville, 15,796 ....D 3
Bernardo de Irigoyen, 1,400 ......F 2
Bolívar, 14,010 ....D 4
Bovril, 1,955 ....G 5
Bragado, 16,104 ....F 7
Buenos Aires (cap.), 2,966,816....H 7
Buenos Aires, *6,762,629 ....H 7
Bustinza, 918 ....F 6
Cachi, 491 ....C 2
Cafayate, 2,407 ....C 2
Calchaquí, 2,782 ....F 5
Caleta Olivia, 3,639 ....C 6
Caleufú 1,197 ....D 4
Camarones, 501 ....D 5
Campana, 14,452 ....G 6
Campo Gallo, 2,336 ....D 2
Cañada de Gómez, 12,354 ....F 6
Cañadón León, 772 ....C 6
Canals, 5,359 ....D 3
Cañuelas, 5,614 ....G 7
Carabelas, 3,476 ....F 6
Carbó, 956 ....G 6
Carcarañá, 4,516 ....F 6
Carlos Casares, 7,558 ....F 7
Carlos Tejedor, 2,897 ....D 4
Carmen de Areco, 4,411 ....F 7
Carmen de Patagones, 5,423 ......D 5
Caseros, 4,975 ....D 4
Casilda, 11,023 ....F 6
Castelli, Buenos Aires, 3,263 ......H 7
Castelli, Chaco, 4,131 ....D 2
Catamarca, 45,929 ....C 2
Catriló, 1,794 ....D 4
Cayasta, 592 ....F 5
Cayastacito, 483 ....F 5
Ceres, 6,525 ....D 2
Chabas, 2,937 ....F 6
Chacabuco, 12,530 ....F 7
Chajarí, 9,075 ....G 5
Chamical, 3,756 ....C 3
Charadai, 1,872 ....D 2
Charata, 8,953 ....D 2
Chascomús, 9,105 ....H 7
Chepes, 2,941 ....C 3
Chicoana, 1,093 ....C 2
Chilecito, 9,809 ....C 2
Chivilcoy, 23,386 ....F 7
Choele-Choel, 3,079 ....C 4
Chos-Malal, 2,874 ....C 4
Chumbicha, 2,188 ....C 2
Cinco Saltos, 10,196 ....C 4
Cipolletti, 19,862 ....C 4
Clara, 1,557 ....G 5
Clarke, 506 ....F 6
Clodomira, 4,685 ....D 2
Clorinda, 10,043 ....E 2
Colón, Buenos Aires, 5,628 ....F 6
Colón, Entre Ríos, 6,813 ....G 6
Colonia Elisa, 1,338 ....E 2
Colonia Las Heras, 1,880 ....C 6
Colonia Sarmiento, 4,922 ....B 6
Comandante Fontana, 1,686 ....D 2
Comandante Luis Piedrabuena, 1,441 ....C 6
Comodoro Rivadavia, 35,966 ....C 6
Concepción, Corrientes, 2,593 ....E 2
Concepción, Tucumán, 15,832 ......C 2
Concepción del Uruguay, 36,486 ..G 6
Concordia, 56,654 ....G 5
Copacabana, 957 ....C 2
Córdoba, †589,153 ....D 3
Coronda, 4,656 ....F 6
Coronel Bogado, 1,264 ....F 6
Coronel Brandsen, 3,803 ....H 7
Coronel Dorrego, 7,245 ....D 4
Coronel Moldes, 1,695 ....C 2
Coronel Pringles, 12,844 ....D 4
Coronel Suárez, 11,133 ....D 4
Corral de Bustos, 3,900 ....D 3
Corrientes, 97,507 ....E 2
Cosquín, 7,746 ....D 3
Crespo, 5,706 ....F 6
Cruz del Eje, 15,563 ....C 3
Cuadro Nacional, 1,879 ....C 3
Curuzú Cuatiá, 16,567 ....G 5
Cutral-Có, 11,292 ....C 4
Deán Funes, 13,840 ....D 3
Del Carril, 475 ....G 7
Diamante, 10,948 ....F 6
Díaz, 1,288 ....F 6
Doblas, 902 ....D 4
Dolavón, 1,277 ....C 5
Dolores, 14,438 ....E 4
Dudignac, 1,503 ....F 7
Eduardo Castex, 4,020 ....D 4
El Bolsón, 2,607 ....B 5
El Calafate, 567 ....B 7
Eldorado, 2,778 ....F 2
Elisa, 579 ....F 5
El Maitén, 2,382 ....B 5
Elortondo, 3,514 ....F 6
El Pintado, 388 ....D 1
El Quebrachal, 1,212 ....D 2
Embarcación, 6,371 ....D 1
Emilio Ayarza, 1,357 ....F 7
Empedrado, 3,735 ....E 2
Ensenada, †35,030 ....H 7
Escobar, 3,693 ....G 7
Esperanza, 10,035 ....F 5
Esquel, 9,900 ....B 5
Esquina, 7,619 ....G 5
Famatina, 1,330 ....C 2
Federación, 4,247 ....G 5
Fernández, 3,115 ....D 2
Fiambalá, 1,450 ....C 2
Firmat, 4,051 ....F 6
Fives Lille, 667 ....F 5
Formosa, 36,499 ....E 2
French, 4,007 ....F 7
Frías, 11,862 ....D 2
Gaimán, 1,286 ....C 5
Gálvez, 2,475 ....F 6
Gálvez, 7,891 ....F 6
General Acha, 4,709 ....C 4
General Alvarado, 3,537 ....E 4
General Alvear, B. Aires, 2,548 ..F 7
General Alvear, Mendoza, 12,325..C 3
General Arenales, 2,182 ....F 7
General Belgrano, 3,789 ....G 7
General Campos, 1,400 ....G 5
General Conesa, 716 ....C 5
General Galarza, 2,435 ....G 6
General Juan Madariaga, 7,073......E 4
General La Madrid, 3,572 ....D 4
General Las Heras, 3,820 ....G 7
General Lavalle, 1,663 ....E 4
General Martín Miguel Güemes, 8,748 ....D 1
General O'Brien, 2,988 ....F 7
General Paz, 1,689 ....E 2
General Pico, 11,121 ....D 4
General Roca, 21,969 ....C 4
General San Martín, Chaco, 5,390 ....E 2
General San Martín, La Pampa, 2,501 ....D 4
General Villegas, 4,738..............D 4
Gobernador Crespo, 6,000 ....F 5
Gobernador Mansilla, 947 ....G 6
Godoy Cruz, 80,024 ....C 3
Goya, 30,011 ....G 4
Gualeguay, 16,542 ....G 6
Gualeguaychú, 29,863 ....G 6
Guandacol, 1,255 ....C 2
Guardia Mitre, 746 ....D 5
Guatraché, 1,259 ....D 4
Guaymallén, 85,718 ....C 3
Hasenkamp, 1,789 ....F 5
Helvecia, 3,390 ....F 5
Hernandarias, 2,788 ....F 5
Hernando, 4,869 ....D 3
Herradura, 1,679 ....E 2
Herrera, 1,685 ....D 2
Huinca Renancó, 4,391 ....D 3
Humahuaca, 2,530 ....C 1
Humberto, 3,434 ....F 5
Ibarreta, 4,366 ....D 2
Ibicuy, 3,356 ....G 6
Icaño, Catamarca, 1,114 ....C 2
Icaño, Santiago del Estero, 1,926 D 2
Iglesia, 575 ....C 3
Ingeniero Huergo, 3,083 ....C 4
Ingeniero Jacobacci, 2,656 ....C 5
Ingeniero Luiggi, 1,665 ....D 4
Intendente Alvear, 2,760 ....D 4
Irigoyen, 3,500 ....F 6
Itacaruaré, 422 ....F 2
Jáchal, 6,886 ....C 3
Jaramillo, 437 ....C 6
Jesús María, 6,284 ....D 3
Joaquín V. González, 3,274 ....D 2
Jobson, 7,667 ....F 5
José de San Martín, 1,143 ....B 5
José M. Micheo, 1,165 ....G 7
Juan B. Molino, 1,483 ....F 6
Juan Ortíz, 6,240 ....F 6
Juan Pujol, 625 ....G 5

ARGENTINA (Continued)

Juárez 7,602 .....D 4
Jujuy, 44,188 .....C 1
Juncal, 943 .....F 6
Junín, 36,149 .....F 7
Junín de los Andes, 1,183 .....B 4
La Banda, 23,772 .....D 2
Laboulaye, 9,032 .....D 3
La Clarita, 389 .....G 5
La Cumbre, 3,961 .....C 3
La Falda, 2,847 .....D 3
La Gallareta, 3,736 .....F 5
Lago Argentino (El Calafate), 567 .....B 7
Laguna Paiva, 7,196 .....F 5
Lanús, 381,561 .....H 7
La Paz, Entre Ríos, 11,028 .....G 5
La Paz, Mendoza, 2,502 .....C 3
La Plata, †330,310 .....H 7
La Quiaca, 6,290 .....C 1
La Rioja, 35,431 .....C 2
Larroque, 1,993 .....G 6
Las Flores, 9,287 .....E 4
Las Lajas, 1,805 .....B 4
Las Lomitas, 1,650 .....D 1
Las Palmas, 3,590 .....E 2
Las Parejas, 1,973 .....F 6
Las Rosas, 6,153 .....F 6
Las Varillas, 5,950 .....D 3
La Toma, 2,352 .....C 3
Lavalle, 1,571 .....G 4
Lezama, 1,962 .....H 7
Libertador General San Martín, Jujuy, 5,051 .....D 1
Libertador General San Martín, Misiones, 2,267 .....E 2
Lincoln, 12,695 .....F 7
Lobería, 7,916 .....E 4
Lobos, 8,372 .....G 7
Lomas de Zamora, †275,219 .....H 7
Loreto, 3,354 .....D 2
Los Antiguos, 709 .....B 6
Los Menucos, 1,749 .....C 5
Los Toldos, 5,342 .....F 7
Lucas González, 1,145 .....G 6
Luján, 19,176 .....G 7
Lules, 4,828 .....C 2
Macachín, 1,793 .....D 4
Maciel, 1,832 .....F 6
Magdalena, 4,114 .....H 7
Maipú, 5,469 .....E 4
Makallé, 1,462 .....E 2
Malabrigo, 1,532 .....F 4
Malargüe, 4,523 .....C 4
Manucho, 2,800 .....F 5
Maquinchao, 1,851 .....C 5
Marcos Juárez, 9,556 .....D 3
Marcos Paz, 4,115 .....G 7
Mar del Plata, 141,886 .....E 4
Margarita, 1,461 .....F 5
María Grande, 2,819 .....F 5
Mburucuyá, 2,555 .....E 2
Médanos, Buenos Aires, 2,229 .....D 4
Médanos, Entre Ríos, 647 .....G 6
Mendoza, 109,122 .....C 3
Mercedes, Buenos Aires, 16,932 .....G 7
Mercedes, Corrientes, 13,368 .....C 4
Mercedes, San Luis, 35,449 .....C 3
Merlo, 8,385 .....G 7
Metán, 12,849 .....D 2
Milagro, 1,967 .....C 3
Miramar (General Alvarado), 3,537 .....E 4
Moisés Ville, 3,166 .....E 5
Monte, 2,491 .....G 7
Monte Caseros, 12,930 .....G 5
Monte Común, 4,278 .....C 2
Monte Quemado, 4,083 .....D 2
Monteros, 11,938 .....C 2
Morteros, 5,993 .....D 3
Navarro, 2,547 .....G 7
Necochea, 17,808 .....E 4
Nelson, 866 .....F 5
Neuquén, 16,738 .....C 4
Niquivil, 1,301 .....C 3
Nogoyá, 10,911 .....F 5
Norberto de la Riestra, 2,809 .....G 7
Ñorquincó, 602 .....B 5
Nueve de Julio, 13,678 .....F 7
Oberá, 12,322 .....E 2
Ojo de Agua, 1,505 .....D 2
Olavarría, 24,204 .....F 7
Oliva, 8,701 .....D 3
Olta, 1,226 .....C 3
Orán, 14,286 .....D 1
Palo Santo, 1,123 .....E 2
Pampa del Chañar, 1,521 .....C 3
Pampa del Infierno, 1,261 .....D 2
Paraná, 107,551 .....F 5
Paso de Indios, 1,067 .....C 5
Paso de los Libres, 15,054 .....G 5
Patquía, 839 .....C 3
Paz, 2,495 .....F 6
Pehuajó, 13,537 .....D 4
Pellegrini, 2,310 .....C 4
Pérez, 3,433 .....F 6
Pergamino, 32,382 .....F 6

Perito Moreno, 1,587 .....B 6
Perugorría, 1,110 .....G 4
Pico Truncado, 1,527 .....C 6
Pigüé, 5,869 .....D 4
Pila, 1,009 .....H 7
Pilar, 2,508 .....F 5
Pipinas, 658 .....H 7
Pirané, 5,285 .....E 2
Plaza Huincul, 4,906 .....B 4
Pomán, 1,100 .....C 2
Posadas, 70,691 .....E 2
Pozo Hondo, 872 .....D 2
Presidencia de la Plaza, 4,568 .....D 2
Presidencia Roque Sáenz Peña, 14,381 .....D 2
Puán, 3,191 .....D 4
Pueblo Domínguez, 984 .....G 6
Puerto Deseado, 3,120 .....D 6
Puerto Madryn, 5,586 .....C 5
Puerto Pirámides, 425 .....D 5
Punta Alta, 19,852 .....D 4
Quemú-Quemú, 2,735 .....D 4
Quequén, 4,760 .....E 4
Quimilí, 2,902 .....D 2
Quines, 3,319 .....C 3
Quiroga, 1,827 .....F 7
Quitilipi, 5,217 .....D 2
Rafaela, 23,665 .....F 5
Ramallo, 4,824 .....F 6
Ramírez, 3,203 .....F 5
Ranchos, 2,475 .....H 7
Rauch, 5,274 .....E 4
Rawson, Buenos Aires, 2,425 .....F 7
Rawson, Chubut, 4,109 .....D 5
Reconquista, 12,729 .....D 2
Recreo, 2,834 .....C 2
Resistencia, 84,036 .....E 2
Rigby, 737 .....F 6
Rinconada, 782 .....C 1
Río Colorado, 5,892 .....D 4
Río Cuarto, 48,706 .....D 3
Río Gallegos, 14,439 .....C 7
Río Grande, 3,666 .....C 7
Río Segundo, 5,873 .....D 3
Río Tercero, 10,683 .....D 3
Rivadavia, 14,358 .....C 3
Rojas, 6,608 .....F 7
Roldán, 3,402 .....F 6
Romang, 1,906 .....F 4
Roque Pérez, 2,841 .....G 7
Rosario, †671,852 .....F 6
Rosario de la Frontera, 7,134 .....D 2
Rosario de Lerma, 4,241 .....C 1
Rosario del Tala, 7,350 .....G 6
Rufino, 10,987 .....D 3
Saladas, 3,883 .....E 2
Saladillo, 7,586 .....G 7
Salta, 117,400 .....C 1
Salto, 7,771 .....F 7
San Andrés de Giles, 5,392 .....G 7
San Antonio de Areco, 7,436 .....G 7
San Antonio de los Cobres, 1,439 .....C 1
San Antonio Oeste, 5,278 .....C 5
San Carlos, Corrientes, 1,858 .....E 2
San Carlos, Mendoza, 809 .....C 3
San Carlos, Santa Fe, 3,126 .....F 5
San Carlos de Bariloche, 15,995 .....B 5
San Cristóbal, 9,071 .....F 5
San Fernando, †91,644 .....G 7
San Francisco, Córdoba, 24,354 .....D 3
San Francisco, San Luis, 1,864 .....C 3
San Francisco del Chañar, 817 .....C 2
San Genaro, 1,522 .....F 6
San Ignacio, 2,106 .....E 2
San Isidro, 2,271 .....C 2
San Jaime, 1,997 .....G 5
San Javier, 2,961 .....F 5
San José de Feliciano, 3,721 .....G 5
San Juan, 106,564 .....C 3
San Julián, 3,649 .....C 6
San Justo, 6,571 .....F 5
San Lorenzo, 11,109 .....F 6
San Luis, 40,420 .....C 3
San Martín, 20,466 .....C 3
San Martín de los Andes, 4,567 .....C 5
San Miguel, 1,300 .....E 2
San Nicolás, 25,980 .....F 6
San Pedro, Buenos Aires, 12,778 .....F 6
San Pedro, Jujuy, 15,354 .....D 1
San Rafael, 46,599 .....C 3
San Salvador, 2,108 .....G 5
San Sebastián, 13,154 .....C 7
Santa Clara, 3,700 .....G 5
Santa Cruz, 1,178 .....C 7
Santa Elena, 8,174 .....F 5
Santa Fe, †259,560 .....F 5
Santa Lucía, Buenos Aires, 1,831 .....E 2
Santa Lucía, Corrientes, 2,930 .....E 2
Santa María, 2,826 .....C 2
Santa Rosa, Córdoba, 2,999 .....D 3
Santa Rosa, La Pampa, 14,623 .....C 4
Santa Rosa, San Luis, 2,880 .....C 3
Santiago del Estero, 80,395 .....D 2
Santo Tomé, Corrientes, 10,121 .....E 2
Santo Tomé, Santa Fe, 4,446 .....F 5
San Urbano, 1,721 .....F 6

Sauce, 3,448 .....G 5
Seguí, 2,161 .....G 6
Selva, 1,070 .....D 2
Sierra Colorada, 541 .....C 5
Sierra Grande, 512 .....C 5
Solari, 1,636 .....G 4
Soledad, 794 .....F 5
Suipacha, 3,006 .....G 7
Sunchales, 5,048 .....F 5
Suncho Corral, 2,693 .....D 2
Susques, 459 .....C 1
Tafí Viejo, 21,197 .....C 2
Tamberías, 1,129 .....C 3
Tandil, 32,309 .....E 4
Tapalqué, 3,018 .....E 4
Tartagal, 16,740 .....D 1
Tigre, †91,824 .....G 7
Tilcara, 1,675 .....C 2
Tinogasta, 3,557 .....C 2
Tintina, 1,500 .....D 2
Toay, 2,457 .....D 4
Tornquist, 2,782 .....D 4
Tostado, 5,234 .....D 2
Trelew, 11,852 .....C 5
Trenel, 1,206 .....D 4
Trenque Lauquen, 10,887 .....D 4
Tres Arroyos, 29,996 .....D 4
Tres Lomas, 3,425 .....D 4
Trevelín, 1,642 .....B 5
Tucumán, 271,546 .....D 2
Tunuyán, 9,781 .....C 3
Ulapes, 438 .....C 3
Unión, 630 .....D 3
Urdinarrain, 3,484 .....G 6
Ushuaia, 3,398 .....C 7
Valcheta, 1,697 .....C 5
Valle Fértil, 1,293 .....C 3
Vedia, 3,676 .....F 7
Veinticinco de Mayo, 9,063 .....F 7
Venado Tuerto, 15,947 .....D 3
Vergara, 1,077 .....H 7
Verónica, 2,405 .....H 7
Victoria, 15,108 .....F 6
Victorica, 2,475 .....D 4
Vicuña Mackenna, 3,032 .....D 3
Viedma, 7,253 .....D 5
Villa Ana, 5,413 .....D 2
Villa Ángela, 18,518 .....D 2
Villa Atuel, 6,027 .....C 3
Villa Bustos, 1,314 .....C 3
Villa Cañas, 7,099 .....F 6
Villa Constitución, 9,183 .....F 6
Villa del Rosario, 4,461 .....D 3
Villa Dolores, 13,835 .....C 3
Villa Elisa, 2,715 .....G 6
Villa Federal, 5,256 .....G 5
Villaguay, 12,463 .....G 5
Villa Guillermina, 7,471 .....D 2
Villa Mantero, 989 .....G 6
Villa María, 30,362 .....D 3
Villa Ocampo, 4,897 .....D 2
Villa Regina, 11,360 .....C 4
Villa San José, 2,188 .....G 6
Villa Unión, 1,696 .....C 2
Vinchina, 395 .....C 2
Winifreda, 1,063 .....D 4
Yacimiento Río Turbio, 3,506 .....B 7
Yofré, 826 .....B 4
Zapala, 7,497 .....B 4
Zárate, 35,197 .....G 7
Zavalla, 1,799 .....F 6

OTHER FEATURES

Aconcagua (mt.) .....C 3
Alerces, Los (park) .....C 5
Andes (mts.) .....C 7
Arenas (point) .....C 7
Argentino (lake) .....B 7
Arizaro (salt dep.) .....C 2
Arrecifes (river) .....G 6
Atacama, Puna de (reg.) .....C 2
Atuel (river) .....C 4
Barrancas (river) .....G 5
Bermeja (point) .....B 4
Bermejo (river) .....E 2
Blanca (bay) .....E 4
Blanco (river) .....C 2
Brazo Sur (river) .....E 1
Buenos Aires (lake) .....B 6
Campanario (mt.) .....C 3
Carcarañá (river) .....D 3
Cardiel (lake) .....B 6
Chaco Austral (reg.) .....D 2
Chaco Central (reg.) .....D 1
Chato (mt.) .....B 5
Chico (river) .....C 5
Chico (river) .....C 5
Chubut (river) .....C 5
Colhué Huapí (lake) .....C 6
Colorado (river) .....D 4
Cónico (mt.) .....B 5
Corrientes (river) .....E 2
Coyle (river) .....B 7
Cuarto (river) .....D 3
Cumbre Negra (mt.) .....B 5

Delgada (point) .....D 5
Desaguadero (river) .....C 3
Deseado (river) .....C 6
Desengaño (point) .....C 6
Diamante (river) .....C 3
Domuyo (vol.) .....B 4
Dos Bahías (cape) .....D 5
Dulce (river) .....D 2
Dungeness (point) .....C 7
El Chocón (res.) .....C 4
Estados (isl.) .....D 7
Fagnano (lake) .....C 7
Famatina (mts.) .....C 2
Feliciano (river) .....G 5
Flores, Las (river) .....G 7
Gallegos (river) .....B 7
General Manuel Belgrano (mt.) .....C 2
Glaciares, Los (park) .....B 6
Gran Chaco (reg.) .....D 1
Grande (bay) .....C 7
Grande (falls) .....C 3
Grande (river) .....C 4
Gualeguay (river) .....G 5
Guayaquilaró (river) .....G 5
Iguazú (falls) .....F 2
Iguazú (park) .....E 2
Incahuasi (mt.) .....B 4
Lanín (park) .....B 4
Lanín (vol.) .....B 4
Laudo (mt.) .....C 2
Lechiguanas (isls.) .....G 6
Lennox (isl.) .....C 8
Limay (river) .....C 4
Llancanelo (salt dep.) .....C 4
Llullaillaco (vol.) .....C 2
Magallanes (Magellan) (str.) .....C 7
Maipo (vol.) .....B 3
Mar Chiquita (lake) .....D 3
Martín García (isl.), 1,575 .....H 7
Mendoza (river) .....C 3
Mercedario (mt.) .....B 3
Mogotes (point) .....E 4
Montemayor (plateau) .....C 6
Murallón (mt.) .....B 6
Musters (lake) .....C 6
Nahuel Huapí (park) .....B 5
Negro (river) .....D 4
Neuquén (river) .....C 4
Norte (point) .....D 5
Norte del Cabo San Antonio (point) .....E 4
Nuevo (gulf) .....D 5
Ojos del Salado (mt.) .....C 2
Olivares (mt.) .....B 3
Pampa de la Salina (salt dep.) .....C 3
Pampa de las Tres Hermanas (plain) .....C 6
Pampas (plain) .....D 3
Paraná (river) .....E 2
Patagonia (reg.) .....B 5
Peteroa (vol.) .....B 4
Pilcomayo (river) .....E 1
Pissis (mt.) .....C 2
Plata, Río de la (est.) .....E 4
Potro (river) .....C 2
Pueyrredón (lake) .....B 6
Puna de Atacama (reg.) .....C 2
Quinto (river) .....D 3
Rincón (mt.) .....C 1
Saladillo (river) .....D 2
Salado (river) .....H 7
Salado (river) .....C 4
Salado del Norte (river) .....D 2
Salí (river) .....C 2
Salinas Grande (salt dep.) .....D 2
Salto (river) .....F 7
Samborombón (bay) .....E 4
San Antonio (cape) .....E 4
San Diego (cape) .....D 7
San Jorge (gulf) .....C 6
San Juan (river) .....C 3
San Lorenzo (mt.) .....B 6
San Martín (lake) .....B 6
San Matías (gulf) .....D 5
Santa Cruz (river) .....B 7
Senguerr (river) .....B 6
Staten (Estados) (isl.) .....D 7
Sur del Cabo San Antonio (point) .....E 4
Tarija (river) .....D 1
Tercero (river) .....D 3
Teuco (river) .....D 1
Tierra del Fuego, Isla Grande de (isl.), 7,064 .....C 7
Toro (river) .....B 2
Tres Picos (mt.) .....B 5
Tres Puntas (cape) .....D 6
Trinidad (isl.) .....D 4
Tronador (mt.) .....B 5
Tunuyán (river) .....C 3
Tupungato (mt.) .....B 3
Uruguay (river) .....D 5
Valdés (pen.) .....D 5
Vallimanca (river) .....F 7
Viedma (lake) .....B 6
Zapaleri (mt.) .....C 1

*City and suburbs. †Population of department.

Total pop.—1967 off. est.; provinces, capital (& with suburbs), departments, cities (over 100,000)—1960 prelim. census; cities (in all provs except Buenos Aires, Córdoba, Sta. Fe & La Pampa)—1960 final census; other pops—1947 final census.

LAKE NAHUEL HUAPI, churned by winds from the surrounding Andes, is the heart of a popular vacation area. Nearby is Argentina's best-known mountain resort, Bariloche.

BUENOS AIRES is Argentina's major seaport and industrial center, as well as the national capital. The port is on the broad Río de la Plata.

within the present borders of Argentina. No more than 2 percent were full-blooded whites, perhaps 63 percent were mestizos (part Indian and part white), 21 percent full-blooded Indians, 12 percent Negroes, and 2 percent mulattoes.

During the 19th century the population grew rapidly, and the first official census, in 1869, recorded about 1,750,000 people. From then on, growth was rapid, and the Spanish element lost its numerical dominance, although Spanish remained the official language. At the same time, the Negroes practically disappeared as a visible group, the Indians were reduced to a few thousand living on reservations in the western part of the country, and the visible mestizos decreased to 9 percent of the population by 1960. The Argentine population had become essentially white.

Immigration. European immigration was a large factor in the rapid population increase after 1860. The 1869 census counted 12 percent of the population as foreign-born. About half the population of Buenos Aires was foreign-born. After 1880, the stream of European immigration swelled to a torrent, as it did in the United States in the same period. The immigrants were largely Italian and Spanish. The greatest immigrant decade was 1901–1910, but this was almost matched by the postwar decades 1921–1930 and 1947–1957. The proportion of foreign-born reached a peak of 30 percent in 1944 and was still about 13 percent in 1960.

During the Nazi period in Germany, in the 1930's, there was a significant immigration of Jews from central Europe, and after World War II a substantial flow of refugees from eastern Europe.

Of the total out-migration from Europe between 1856 and 1937, Argentina received 11 percent, compared to 60 percent for the United States, 7 percent for Brazil, 9 percent for Canada, and 13 percent for other parts of the world.

Birth and Death Rates. Birth rates were much higher than death rates during the period of rapid population increase, thus adding a considerable natural increase to the growth by immigration. The birth rate dropped from over 40 per 1,000 population before 1900 to 38 in 1910 and 24 in 1940. It was 22 in 1960, with a death rate of 8. These figures are very similar to those of the United States and northern Europe and indicate that the growth of population will not be very rapid in the next years unless there is a new wave of immigration.

Social Structure. Since 1910 the Argentine nation has been more urban than rural. More than half of its people have resided in places of more than 2,000 population. In the 1960's about 70 percent of the population lived in urban places, which was similar to the situation in the United States. But, unlike the United States, much of urban Argentina is concentrated in one area, Greater Buenos Aires, where somewhat more than 25 percent of the Argentine population lives.

In spite of its high proportion of town dwellers, Argentina is by tradition a rural, agricultural country. Argentine meat and Argentine wheat have been the principal articles of export. And the transition since 1910 from a rural society and rural economy to an urban society and an industrial economy has created strains in the social structure.

Before 1905 the only city larger than 100,000

J. ALLAN CASH, FROM RAPHO GUILLUMETTE

MAR DEL PLATA, on the Atlantic Ocean in Buenos Aires province, is Argentina's most popular beach resort.

besides Buenos Aires was Rosario. Argentine society outside of Buenos Aires was rural, and that of the city was largely foreign-born. The present social structure has come about through the interaction of the two Argentinas of 1900—the native rural and the foreign-born urban.

The rural society was one of large landowners and their employees. There were very few small, independent landowners. The *estancieros*, or ranchers, were wealthy aristocratic families, often with a house in Buenos Aires and generally with some business or family connections there. The small independent farmers often rented land from large landowners, and when times were not prosperous they became foremen or managers for the large owners. Thus there came into existence a group of quasi-independent rural workers. There was also a large group of landless agricultural workers, or peons, who worked on the big estates for a bare living.

After 1900 the rural society became relatively less important in the national social structure, and the urban population came to dominate the situation. Industry developed and business flourished. Urban society was much like that of European countries, with a growing middle class of business and professional men.

By the end of World War II there was a major migration of rural workers to the cities in search of a better living. The pace of this migration has since increased. At the same time industry and commerce have grown substantially, requiring more workers.

This situation has brought about the growth of middle-sized cities, which are becoming important in the economic and political life of the country. The 1960 census reported 13 cities with populations over 100,000 without counting Buenos Aires and its suburbs. Also 40 percent of the 1960 population lived in cities of over 100,000 inhabitants.

Way of Life. Most Argentines are city dwellers. In the cities the majority of them live in multiple-family dwellings. Family life is close and affectionate among middle-class and stable working-class people. Women frequently work outside of the home, if they do not have young children.

CARL FRANK, FROM PHOTO RESEARCHERS

RENE BURRI, FROM MAGNUM

VIGOR AND ZEST distinguish the Argentine people. Soccer, full of swift action (*left*), is a favorite sport. A gaucho, the cowboy of the Pampa (*above*), stops his work for a drink of wine, obtained by squeezing the wineskin.

Not only do the Argentine people eat well, but their per capita consumption of meat is one of the highest in the world, partly because of the abundance of domestically produced meat. They also are well clothed, thanks partly to the abundance of good leather and woolen cloth that are produced in the country. The women of Buenos Aires have the reputation of being the best dressed in the Western Hemisphere.

Among sports, the Argentines favor football (soccer) and horse racing. They read widely, and have a tradition of public libraries going back to 1870, when President Sarmiento established 100 free libraries.

Buenos Aires, as the capital and center of culture and industry, represents the urbane, cosmopolitan, and modern aspect of Argentine society. It also has the worst slums and the most degrading vices of the country.

A typical day for a middle-class adult in Buenos Aires would be as follows. He rises at seven or seven-thirty in the morning, and has a breakfast of coffee and milk, rolls and butter. He walks or goes by subway to his place of work, where he begins the day at eight-thirty or nine. At noon he goes home for a warm luncheon, often taking a nap or reading the paper before he returns to work at two. Many shops and offices are closed during this period. About four or four-thirty, he steps out to a nearby café with friends and has a cup of tea or coffee, with a light sandwich or a piece of cake. If the weather is nice, as it is for most of the year, he may sit at a table of a sidewalk café. After 15 or 30 minutes he goes back to work and stays until seven or eight, when he is through for the day. Dinner is waiting for him at home at about nine

o'clock, though once or twice a week he will go with his wife and friends to a restaurant for dinner at nine-thirty or ten.

On a Saturday or Sunday he may go to the races or to a football game in the afternoon and to a theater or movie in the evening. The latest North American and European motion pictures are available, as well as some produced with Argentine film stars. Once or twice a month, he and his wife may attend an opera or a concert at the Teatro Colón.

At the butcher's or fish market, his wife (or the cook) will have a choice of excellent beef, lamb, and a wide variety of seafoods. He has his favorite wine merchant, from whom he can buy good Argentine white or red wine at the equivalent of 25 or 30 cents a bottle, plus a deposit for the bottle.

When he goes out to eat he has a choice among Italian and French menus, with a wide variety of seafood as well as Argentine beef. Cheese is good and cheap (Argentine Gorgonzola is a favorite). Argentine wine is good. As an alternative he may go to a steak house, generally run by an Argentine, where he has a choice of cuts of beef, with corn bread or other forms of corn, and a salad of fresh vegetables.

The Contemporary Crisis. Life is good, in the material sense, for the middle-class Argentine citizen and for the manual worker with a steady job. But the years since 1940 have been uneasy ones if he has an interest or concern for the political and economic welfare of his country. Argentina is caught in the grip of social change and cannot maintain prosperity simply as a producer of meat, wool, and grain. Industry must be developed, and a large bureaucracy of public officials and employees of railways and other services must be trimmed down or put to more productive work.

Under the Perón regime some first essential steps were taken, but there were also many missteps, and the established democratic ways of life were placed in jeopardy. Since 1955 there has been some further progress, along with much confusion. The average citizen feels frustrated and confused.

ROBERT J. HAVIGHURST, *University of Chicago*

2. The Land and Natural Resources

While Argentina is one of the less favored countries in terms of sources of mechanical energy, which are the controlling factor in economic development, its endowment in land is so

CITIES WITH OVER 100,000 POPULATION
(Excluding suburbs of Buenos Aires)

City	Province	Population (1960)
Greater Buenos Aires	Federal District and Buenos Aires	6,762,629
Buenos Aires	Federal District	2,966,816
Rosario	Santa Fe	671,852
Córdoba	Córdoba	589,153
La Plata	Buenos Aires	330,310
Tucumán	Tucumán	287,004
Santa Fe	Santa Fe	259,560
Paraná	Entre Ríos	174,272
Bahía Blanca	Buenos Aires	150,354
Mar del Plata	Buenos Aires (1958)	141,866
Salta	Salta	121,491
Corrientes	Corrientes	112,725
Mendoza	Mendoza	109,149
San Juan	San Juan	106,746
Santiago del Estero	Santiago del Estero	103,115

favorable that (1) it has enabled Argentina to develop a per capita output of goods and services that is second in Latin America only to oil-rich Venezuela; and (2) it has made its people not only the best fed in Latin America, but among the best fed in the world. Moreover, the remaining output has provided enough exports to finance the industrialization that characterizes modern Argentina.

Argentina has 11 percent of its total land in arable use, compared with less than 5 percent for Latin America as a whole. The potential for further expansion was estimated in 1965 to be more than 150 percent of the land then in arable use. Only 3.7 percent of the land under cultivation was irrigated.

Physical Characteristics. Argentina's area of 1,072,067 square miles (2,776,656 sq km) is about one third that of the United States. Although Argentina is much narrower than the United States—hardly 1,000 miles (1,600 km) from east to west at its widest point—it extends much farther from north to south. If placed in the corresponding latitudes of North America (22 to 55 degrees), Argentina would stretch from Cuba to Hudson Bay, a distance of 2,300 miles (3,700 km). Thus Argentina has a range of climates that support a broad diversity of vegetation, tropical as well as temperate. But the extreme temperatures that characterize comparable latitudes in North America are mitigated in Argentina by the oceanic influences affecting much of the country because of its situation on the relatively narrow landmass of southern South America. Almost all of Argentina is in the temperate zone, with climate ranging from subtropical in the extreme north to subantarctic in southern Patagonia.

Vegetation. The variety of vegetation types in Argentina is striking. In the south there is the Patagonian-Fuegian Steppe, characterized by a temperate or cold climate, windy and very dry. There are few trees, and the vegetation is dominated by very low plants bearing a cluster of leaves that grow in a dense cushionlike tuft. North and northeast are the desert and scrub regions of the interior parts of central and northern

Argentina. This desert-scrub area, known as the Monte, has a climate as dry as that of the Patagonian-Fuegian Steppe, but somewhat warmer and essentially without a winter season. Its vegetation is highly drought-resistant and consists partly of low trees. The scrub resembles that of northern Mexico and adjoining states of the United States. In the Chaco region of northern Argentina the vegetation is a mixture of forests and savannas. The trees often grow in salt-impregnated soils, marshes, or swampy areas. In the southern Andes region there are high intermountain valleys with dry grasslands and often subdesert shrubs and trees, many of which are deciduous.

In sharp contrast with such areas of limited economic efficiency is the vast Pampa region, the most extensive level grassland in South America, covering roughly one quarter of the nation. From its economic potential has been fashioned a great nation. The U.S. Department of Agriculture has commented without exaggeration that "the soil of the Argentine pampas can take as much punishment as can perhaps any other in the world." The extent of this region is particularly significant because, in South America, land with a slope of less than 8 percent that lends itself readily to cultivation is extremely scarce. Mobilization of the productive capacity of this area was accelerated by the extremely favorable conditions for railway construction. Railway lines running hundreds of miles with hardly a curve or gradient testify to this fact.

Classification of Regions. The Joint Argentine-United Nations Soil Utilization and Conservation Commission, seeking a classification for purposes of economic development analysis, identifies three "natural" regions of Argentina: humid, semi-humid, and arid.

The humid region consists of three zones. (1) The area in the east covers the Argentine Mesopotamia (the provinces between the Uruguay and Paraná rivers), the eastern sections of Chaco and Formosa, the greater part of Santa Fe, some of the eastern districts of Córdoba, and most of Buenos Aires. This region has an average annual precipitation of at least 28 inches (71

THREE LIONS

RUGGED COUNTRY shows the severe climate in parts of Argentina. Far south, in Tierra del Fuego (below), a tree is shaped by the winds. In the northwest, a road near Salta (right), crosses open Andes ridges.

JOHN G. ROSS, FROM PHOTO RESEARCHERS

IGUASSÚ FALLS, a famous attraction for visitors, are on the Iguassú River, on the border of Argentina and Brazil. More than 200 cataracts form the falls.

cm). The highest precipitation is in the extreme north of Misiones province, where it amounts to about 80 inches (203 cm) yearly. (2) The Tucumán-Salta zone extends about 435 miles (700 km) southward into Argentina from Tarija, in Bolivia. It varies greatly in width from a few miles to more than 60 (over 100 km), and it includes the ravines and eastern foothills of the mountains of Salta, Jujuy, Tucumán, and northeastern Catamarca. Precipitation varies from 32 inches to 60 inches annually (81–152 cm), with summer and autumn rainy seasons and dry winters. (3) The Andean-Patagonian humid zone, with an average annual precipitation of at least 20 inches (51 cm), includes the rim of the Andes from northern Neuquén to Tierra del Fuego. Precipitation reaches 120 inches (305 cm) in the areas of heaviest rainfall.

The semihumid region extends in the form of an arc from the Paraguayan border through eight provinces—Formosa, Chaco, Santiago del Estero, Santa Fe, La Pampa, San Luis, Córdoba, and Buenos Aires—to the Atlantic at Bahía Blanca. The average annual precipitation varies between 24 and 32 inches (61 and 81 cm).

The remainder of the country consists largely of arid or semiarid regions with an average annual rainfall of 4 to 24 inches (10 to 61 cm).

A more common classification by Argentine geographers follows distinctions long reflected in the economic activity of the respective areas:

The Pampa produces about two thirds of the nation's agricultural and pastoral output on its rich soil, providing 85 percent of agricultural and pastoral exports and in a typical year accounting for nine tenths of the cereal output and three fourths of the pastoral output. Here, in an area reaching from 30 to 40 degrees south latitude, average annual rainfall ranges from 20 inches (51 cm) in the west to 40 inches (102 cm) in the east; the winters are milder than in New York, and the growing seasons are longer.

The Andean region extends from the dry north to the heavily glaciated and ice-covered mountains of Patagonia and includes the very dry mountain and desert west of Córdoba and south of Tucumán. It embraces the provinces of Catamarca, San Juan, Mendoza, La Rioja, and a portion of Salta. From its irrigated valleys on the eastern slopes and foothills of the Andes, north of 40 degrees latitude, come important quantities of fruit for export. The Andean region includes the nation's chief wine-producing area, in Mendoza province.

Patagonia is a region of arid windswept plateaus, covering some 300,000 square miles (777,000 sq km), encompassing the provinces of Neuquén, Chubut, Río Negro, and Santa Cruz, and the territory of Tierra del Fuego. Except for some irrigated valleys, this is poor, scattered pasture land. In its far south, the weather is continuously cool and stormy, and there is no summer, although the winters are not severe.

The North consists of three areas. (1) The alluvial plain of the Chaco is rich in forest products, but its potential is limited in some sections by swamps and in others by periodic droughts. It has a tropical scrub vegetation and a subtropical climate with dry winters and very humid summers. Rainfall decreases from 60 inches (152 cm) in the northeast to 20 inches (51 cm) in the west, and temperatures reach 120° F (40° C). (2) Argentine Mesopotamia consists of floodplains in southern Entre Ríos province and gently rolling plains and numerous streams in Corrientes. (3) Misiones province produces tree crops like yerba maté, tung, and tea.

Forests. About 22 percent of Argentina's land area consists of accessible forests; another 3 percent, of inaccessible forests. In contrast, 16 percent of South America's land area is accessible forest; 38 percent inaccessible forest. Half of Argentina's accessible forests are government-owned. About 17 percent, or 10.25 million hectares (25.32 million acres), of the accessible forest is in productive use.

Since hardwoods and semihardwoods dominate the timber stands, the country has turned to the potential of reforestation to supply the softwood required for paper and other industries, for which it previously depended on imports.

The quebracho, from which tanning extract is obtained, has been the chief hardwood forest product and the only significant contribution of the forests to Argentine exports.

Minerals. Argentina is poorly endowed with minerals, but this judgment is subject always to the chance of new discoveries. For example, in 1965, mapping and geological studies along the eastern slope of the Andes disclosed five commercially exploitable mineral deposits, including an estimated 100 million tons (90.9 million metric tons) of copper.

Lead and zinc, tungsten, manganese, iron, and beryllium are among the minerals found in some abundance. Iron ore from Jujuy, with an average metal content of 50 percent, is exploited in some

CATTLE, like this herd on the grassy plains of Entre Ríos province, are a vital factor in the economy. Argentina is a leading nation in exporting meat.

quantity, and the Sierra iron-ore deposits, of high phosphorus content, in Río Negro province, offer some hope of substantial expansion.

But in terms meaningful to the world economy, the mineral-resource base offers no hope for the development of a great industrial concentration like the German Ruhr. In terms of locally significant industrialization, the mineral-deficient base means higher costs where domestic supplies are concerned and continuing drains on foreign exchange for imports.

Energy. In the all-important sources of mechanical energy, the resource base is again deficient, but again is subject to the possibility of new discoveries. For example, intensified drilling produced an immense expansion of petroleum output after 1958, from 36 million barrels to 97 million by 1965.

Long dependent on imported coal, Argentina has worked anxiously to develop some 250 million tons (227 million metric tons) of coal reserves in the Río Turbio area of Patagonia, despite the high cost and poor quality. But progress toward a target of a million tons per year has been slow. Petroleum resources consist of a major concentration near Comodoro Rivadavia (in Patagonia), and other fields along the Andes in Mendoza, Neuquén, Salta, and Jujuy provinces. Natural gas pipeline construction has paced a rapidly growing consumption of natural gas.

Fish. Argentina's fishing grounds have high potential, but although the annual catch has increased substantially, activity is minor. Warm waters from the north and colder waters from the south divide the fishing grounds into two zones: in the first, from the mouth of the Río de la Plata to the mouth of the Río Chubut, most of the commercial fishing is done in relatively warm water with fairly low salt content. Hake, croaker, and mackerel figure largely in the catch. The second, from the Río Chubut south, is less extensively fished. It offers haddock, codfish, and center fish and is rich in plankton nourished by the Falkland Current. Fish traditionally have not figured significantly in the Argentine diet, but consumption is growing, and the fish flour industry is expanding rapidly.

SIMON G. HANSON
"Inter American Economic Affairs"

3. The Economy

The per capita output of goods and services in Argentina is about one fifth to one quarter that of the United States. From the end of the post-World War II boom in 1949 through 1965 the annual per capita growth averaged just over 1 percent per year. Between 1961 and 1965 there were sharp fluctuations from year to year, but in 1965 per capita national income in meaningful terms was barely 1 percent over that of 1961.

These figures explain the concern with economic stagnation that characterizes any discussion of public policy in Argentina. Equally important is the fact that such increases as have occurred have been very unequally distributed: the share of wages in national income fell from 52 percent in 1950 to 45.5 percent in 1961 and was estimated at 46 percent in 1965, while the share of profits rose from 38 percent in 1950 to 46 percent in 1961. Real wages were stagnant in the period from 1950 to 1965.

From 1950 to 1963 the pace of growth in manufacturing was more than double that of agriculture, which barely matched the pace of growth in population. By 1965, manufacturing's share in the total output of goods and services was double that of livestock and agricultural activity. From 1960 to 1965 the relationship between components in gross domestic product did not alter substantially: agriculture and livestock contributed an average of 17 percent, manufacturing 33 percent, construction industry 4 percent, commerce 18 percent, and transport 7 percent, with the balance distributed among various elements.

Since agricultural and pastoral activity traditionally provided the exports that made possible the diversification of Argentina's economy and the import of its capital equipment, there has been a tendency to blame any relative stagnation on trends in this segment of the economy. Consistent with this concern, the Argentine National Development Plan for 1965–1969 contemplated roughly the same volume of investment for the agricultural and pastoral sector as for the industrial sector, in an effort to revive a suitable growth rate to pace the economy.

Agriculture and Livestock. In the mid-1960's Argentina was the world's third-largest producer of meat, the fourth-largest producer of wool, and fourth in numbers of cattle and sheep. Although

GROWTH OF GROSS NATIONAL PRODUCT

Cycle midpoint to cycle midpoint		Years in period	Rate of growth per year
1935–1938	to 1949–1952	14.0	3.40%
1949–1952	to 1952–1956	3.5	2.48%
1949–1952	to 1959–1963	10.5	2.81%
1952–1956	to 1956–1959	3.5	4.20%
1956–1959	to 1959–1963	3.5	1.76%

PATRICE HARTLEY, FROM RAPHO GUILLUMETTE

the pressure of enormous per capita consumption of meat at home strained its capacity to export, and in fact left only 20 percent of the beef for export, Argentina remained one of the world's great exporters of meat, wool, hides, and skins.

Geared to production for world markets, Argentina's pastoral activity arrived early at an advanced stage technologically, in selective breeding of its herds and flocks and in animal husbandry in general. But much remains to be done. For instance, it is estimated that foot-and-mouth disease causes annual losses of 16 billion pesos (U.S. $85 million), and it closes certain markets, like the United States, to Argentine beef.

In the Pampa, individual farm units are considerably larger than those in the United States corn belt. Much of the corn is exported, and cattle are grass-fattened on improved pastures. Hogs are relatively unimportant. In the mid-1960's Argentina had 49 million sheep, 47 million cattle, and 3.7 million hogs.

Argentina is one of the four most important exporters of wheat in the world and a major supplier of other cereals. In the mid-1960's it accounted for over half of the total world trade in flaxseed and linseed oil. It has been making significant strides in soybean production. It moves substantial quantities of fruit to world markets to complement seasonally local production. It has a substantial output of cotton. It has even been expanding its production of tea appreciably. In fact, the great variety of farm output makes Argentina self-sufficient, without sacrifice of diversity, except for such tropical imports as coffee, bananas, cacao, and certain specialty foods.

The wheat area is crescent-shaped, extending from Mar del Plata to an area north of Bahía Blanca and from there northward to Villa María and the region west of Santa Fe. The wheat region has very large farm units, permitting highly mechanized farming. Argentine wheat is of

AGRICULTURAL AND PASTORAL PRODUCTION
(tons)

	1948	1955	1965
Beef	1,958,000	2,147,000	2,100,000
Pork	148,000	156,000	190,000
Mutton	239,000	199,000	150,000
Milk	3,824,000	4,941,000	4,634,000
Wool	190,000	170,000	180,000
Wheat	5,198,000	5,250,000	5,640,000
Corn	5,200,000	2,546,000	6,500,000
Oats	733,000	723,000	460,000
Barley	613,000	951,000	426,000
Rye	304,000	654,000	266,000
Rice	116,000	172,000	268,000
Cotton fiber	86,000	114,000	136,000
Sugarcane	7,088,000	9,324,000	11,600,000
Flaxseed	1,513,000	238,000	760,000

good quality, although its protein content is lower than that of hard winter wheats of the United States. The failure of Argentina to share in the doubling of world wheat trade between the periods 1944–1948 and 1960–1964 has been a matter of great concern to the government.

The area suitable for growing corn in optimal conditions is limited, because most of the country is too dry or too cold. The provinces of Buenos Aires and Santa Fe contain over 75 percent of the corn acreage, with widely fluctuating yields from year to year. Oats grow on the fringe of the grain belt; rye grows well in the cooler areas of the grain belt and on the poorer soils west and south of the wheat area. Flaxseed grows mainly in Buenos Aires, Santa Fe, Córdoba, and Entre Ríos provinces, where the climate and soil are exceptionally favorable. Argentine flaxseed contains about one pound (0.45 kg) more oil per bushel than flaxseed grown in the northern United States.

Contrasting with its competitive capacity in cereals is Argentina's sugarcane production. The northwest has always been a sugar-producing area, but for generations the industry has been entangled in government regulations and subsidy arrangements as a result of overproduction early in the 20th century.

Agricultural Technology. Argentine agriculture is relatively well advanced in the improvement of its technological bases. In 1964 a United Nations Food and Agriculture Organization survey of wheat, cotton, and rice production rated Argentina "excellent" among producing nations in seed certification, production of improved seed, seed testing, seed distribution, and seed laws. Increased education for the rural population has helped in the advancement of agriculture.

Average capital assets per farm are relatively high. The number of tractors has expanded significantly: there were 25,000 units in use in 1949, 40,000 in 1954, and over 120,000 in 1965. The use of fertilizers more than doubled in the decade ending in the mid-1960's. The use of DDT increased more than fourfold from the mid-1950's to the mid-1960's.

Of the total increase in agricultural output from the late 1940's to the mid-1960's, roughly one tenth came from expanded area, two tenths came from changes in the crop pattern, and seven tenths derived from improved crop yields. But the estimated output from 1956 to 1960 per adult male employed in agriculture was only one third that of the adult male in United States agriculture.

Land Holdings. Agricultural holdings of substantial size are characteristic. It is estimated that one half of one percent of the farm units occupy one third of the agricultural land. In 1960, 5.9 percent of the rural properties occupied 75 percent of the land. Conversely, one sixth of the holdings occupied only 0.1 percent of the land, and 40 percent of the holdings occupied only 1 percent of the land.

Land Tenure. In 1960 half of the farm units were worked by owners, 14 percent by leaseholders, and 36 percent under other forms of tenure. This represented an increase in owner-operated farms of some 50 percent since 1947. The National Agrarian Council was set up to distribute titles to land not rationally cultivated, which it has expropriated or acquired by direct purchase or auction.

Agricultural Planning. Between 1950 and 1963 employment in agricultural and pastoral activity diminished by more than 30 percent while employment in manufacturing was rising 15 percent, and in transportation, 10 percent. In the decade ending in 1960 the number of agricultural holdings decreased by 14 percent and the average holding increased slightly in size. Consistent with the public policy of renewing the growth pace of agriculture, the plan for 1965–69 set forth production goals for 1969 which required increases over 1960–1964 of 56 percent for grains, 20 percent for oilseeds, and 19 percent for livestock. Changes in crop areas called for a reduction of 9 percent in natural pastures, increases of 48 percent in seeded pastures and 32 percent in grains; no changes were planned for oilseeds. Dairy and fruit production were to be promoted heavily, but output of cotton, sugar, potatoes, and grapes only enough to meet local needs. Investment was to come mostly from private sources.

Manufacturing. By 1966 the growing maturity of manufacturing was being demonstrated in a variety of ways: in the character of industries being set up; in the magnitude of investment in plant; and in the shift of management personnel from self-made men to professional managers.

Industries. The statistics are impressive. In 1965, Argentina produced about 195,000 motor vehicles, of which 120,000 were passenger cars. Nine tenths of the components were produced domestically. A decade earlier it had assembled some 6,000 vehicles, with the larger proportion of components coming from abroad.

In the mid-1960's Argentina was meeting about half of its iron and steel requirements. In 1965, for example, it produced 662,000 tons (602,000 metric tons) of pig iron a year, 1,347,-000 tons (1,225,000 MT) of crude steel, and 1,237,000 tons (1,125,000 MT) of finished steel. A single integrated producer was increasing its annual production from 850,000 tons to 1,100,000 tons (773,000 to 1 million MT). A decade earlier a quarter million tons (227,000 MT) had seemed a significant national achievement.

Great chemical complexes were coming into being. Typical was a fertilizer group known as Petrosur, designed to produce 135,000 tons (123,-000 MT) of fertilizer per year, to tie in closely with the revitalizing of farm growth. The complex would include five integrated plants, two to produce ammonia and sulfuric acid and the other three to make finished fertilizer products such as urea, ammonium sulfate, and mixtures of nitrogen, phosphate, and potash.

The country was manufacturing over 13,000 tractors per year. And Argentine factories were tooled up to meet local needs for office appliances and for the wide range of consumer appliances to which the middle classes were becoming accustomed.

Both old and new industries were expanding. In 1965, for instance, the older lines (such as food products, beverages, and textiles) expanded output by 8.2 percent while the newer lines (such as automobiles, chemicals, paper, and metals) rose 11.8 percent. There had been some interest in simple machine-tool fabrication for a half century, but now the automobile industry was creating an internal market for machine tools.

Investment. The magnitude of investment was also impressive. In 1961–1966, U.S. companies alone put $600 million into plant and equipment expenditures for manufacturing enterprises in Argentina, involving a modernization process for existing industries, as well as the introduction of new lines. European and local capital also was being mobilized for this purpose.

Much remained to be done to modernize the industrial plant. Industry had been successively stimulated by the two world wars, which had cut off foreign sources of supply, and by the great depression of the 1930's, which had made foreign exchange scarce for the purchase of foreign goods. Industry had enjoyed heavy protection from the government in the form of tariffs and through the encouragement of machinery imports by freeing them from certain taxes. The task now was to gain efficiency. Argentina's membership in the Latin American Free Trade Association (LAFTA) promised to provide a standard of comparison and a stimulus to create competitive capacity.

Management. The role of the professional manager was growing. Many industries had been started by small merchants or craftsmen, self-made men without serious training in management. Their enterprises were often family-financed. Their relations with labor often involved a paternalistic attitude, an unwillingness to share the prerogatives of management, and a tendency to evade labor laws and commitments involved in collective agreements. In the 1960's management was beginning to adjust to a new industrial society where the very scope of the operations, its importance in the economy, and the emerging ability of labor to challenge it promoted a search for professional managers. Meanwhile, industry's requirements for capital and the growth of an investing class able to participate in corporate financing had created a growing reliance on outside sources of capital, as distinguished from family financing.

For the average Argentine in the mid-1960's, "Made in Argentina" fairly well covered the range of his requirements of manufactured goods. The factories still imported many raw materials, and to become and remain competitive, they would long require machinery from abroad. But in reaching a point where it constituted one third of the gross product of Argentina, manufacturing was coming of age.

Transportation. The railroad network, about 25,000 miles (40,000 km) of route length, was built with foreign capital, mostly British and French. After World War II, the Argentine government purchased the properties, using foreign exchange accumulated during the war. The physical condition of the railways has deteriorated steadily. Surveys made in the 1960's illustrate this: two thirds of the locomotives were over 45 years old, and more than half the trackage was past the maximum life span for efficient operation. The financial condition of the railways had also deteriorated, making them the major source of Argentina's budgetary deficits. Costs were multiplied by an immense amount of featherbedding in the labor force, under political pressure.

During the 1960's Argentina worked to improve its 36,000 miles (58,000 km) of highways. The goal was to increase the proportion of paved highway mileage from one third of the total to two thirds. Inadequate attention to coordination of road and rail transport has been costly.

TRAVELERS in Argentina use many forms of transportation. The trans-Andean train (*below*) crosses the Aconcagua Range, and the amphibious plane (*right*) flies between Buenos Aires and Montevideo.

In the case of air transport, Argentina's experience has differed from that of countries that leaped from the oxcart to the airplane without going through transitional stages. Argentina's rail network was in place early. The Pampa offered few obstacles of water or terrain to easy transport, and there was a great concentration of population and economic activity in the capital. Thus the urgency of developing air transport was reduced. Currently, the country is served by a state-owned airline, as well as by private airlines.

Argentine ships carry about one sixth of the country's total ocean-borne cargo. The merchant fleet was acquired mainly because of the shortage of shipping in World War II. In the mid-1960's it totaled about 1.1 million tons (1 mil-lion MT). The government owns the principal company operating in international trade, as well as two river-fleet enterprises.

Communications. In 1965 Argentina reaffirmed its adherence to the agreements to establish a world commercial telecommunications system by space satellite, and stipulated that the ground station to be erected in Argentina should be operated by the national Telecommunications Secretariat.

Argentina has 40 to 50 percent of the telephones installed in South America, and the state-owned telephone system has been unable to keep up with demand. The telephone company also operates the television stations. Internal telegraph facilities and some circuits to nearby countries are wholly operated by the government. International cable service is provided by private enterprise.

Energy. Installed capacity to produce electric power has lagged behind demand, necessitating a rationing of power from time to time. Installed capacity has remained at a low percentage of economic potential. From 1950 to 1965, growth in power production failed to keep pace with that of Latin America as a whole.

In the case of petroleum there has been a similar lag behind demand and a similar failure to mobilize potential effectively. After 1958 the program permitting vigorous participation of foreign capital under production and drilling contracts with the state petroleum entity—Yacimientos Petrolíferos Fiscales—brought the country close to self-sufficiency in oil. But a slowdown followed the decision in 1963 to terminate the new contracts. Imports had been brought down from over $300 million per year to $57 million, after which they began to climb.

While Argentina has maintained a high level of domestic savings and investment, the immense requirements of capital for petroleum and electric power development have meant that the political pressure "to go it alone," largely to the exclusion of private foreign capital, has slowed the pace of expansion. The reluctance to permit private capital has militated against investment. Electricity is provided by state ventures, private companies, and mixed enterprises. In 1965 the government undertook a feasibility study on possible installation of an atomic power plant.

Foreign Investment. Argentina has traditionally provided a hospitable climate for foreign investment. The railways, packing plants, public utility enterprises, industrial factories—virtually every line of activity—have attracted foreign capital. Since 1945 the government has nationalized the railways, certain light and power companies, and the telephone services; but its respect for the doctrine of just, prompt, and effective compensation in the event of nationalization has been relatively impressive. Over $2 billion in private foreign capital is invested in Argentina. The United States share has been increasing. In the mid-1960's, direct investments from the United States were about $900 million, of which about $500 million were in manufacturing.

Role of Government in Business. Historically, nationalistic pressure for local ownership has been particularly strong in the case of the public utilities and the petroleum industry. All solid, liquid, and gaseous hydrocarbon deposits are the exclusive property of the national government, and private exploitation of these minerals is precluded. Coal development is virtually a government monopoly, partly because private capital has been uninterested in it. Government agencies for petroleum, solid fuels, and gas may call for bids and enter into agreements with private companies for exploration, drilling, pipeline and plant construction, and other services. Nuclear minerals are considered government property. Prospecting for and exploitation of other minerals are controlled by provincial authorities.

Besides owning or controlling fuel and nuclear mineral deposits, the railroads, part of the merchant fleet, an airline, the telephone and telegraph services, the television stations, and some light and power companies, the federal government owns packing houses that supply most of the meat for Buenos Aires, a meat-exporting plant, the only significant aircraft factory, and armaments factories.

Foreign Aid. Under the Alliance for Progress, Argentina has been a lesser beneficiary of aid from the United States than some other Latin American countries. In the first five years of the alliance it was given 5.7 percent of all aid rendered to Latin America. A larger portion of aid to Argentina consisted of loans at commercial terms rather than in the form of grants and "soft" loans (more generous terms).

This limited participation in aid reflects Argentina's more advanced stage of development. It has a relatively well-developed educational system from elementary school through university. The average life expectancy of its people is the highest in South America. Half the population has access to potable water systems. Sewerage service is available to one third of the urban population. The housing shortage is less severe than in many other Latin American countries. The greater part of housing construction is carried out by private enterprises.

Labor Organization. About 39 percent of Argentina's population is economically active. Almost half of all wage and salary earners are organized into labor unions. There are both craft and industrial federations, with the latter predominating. The largest number of unorganized workers are in the fields of agriculture and livestock. While the age and poor condition of much of the machinery in industrial plants have contributed materially to unsatisfactory productivity, manpower also has been a critical factor. Workers insist on strict adherence to job classifications, and highly skilled workers have been scarce. Many workers hold more than one job, thus lowering their efficiency. There is a high rate of absenteeism.

Argentina has a considerable body of advanced labor legislation and an extensive social insurance system. Industrywide collective bargaining has usually determined conditions of employment. The labor movement has also been deeply involved over the years in the politics of the country.

Public Finances. There are about one million public employees. A rather unsatisfactory system of budget formulation and implementation has been in process of improvement since the establishment of the National Budget Bureau in 1963. Substantial deficits are characteristic, arising in large part from deficits of such state-owned enterprises as the railways.

About one quarter of the revenues are collected from taxes on income and profits, slightly over one third from sales, turnover, and excise taxes, and one sixth from customs duties; the balance comes from other sources. On the expenditure side, national defense takes about 15 percent of the total—one of the highest proportions in Latin America. Defense outlay is estimated at 2.3 percent of the gross national product.

National Planning. The plan for 1965–1969 called for an average annual increase of 6 percent for gross domestic product—that is, 4.3 percent per capita—and for an investment rate equivalent to 21.2 percent of gross domestic product. The objectives of the plan were: (1) a rise in the growth rate per capita; (2) full employment; (3) more equitable distribution of income; (4) improved welfare standards; and

YACIMIENTOS PETROLIFEROS FISCALES

OIL REFINERY in Mendoza province is part of the state petroleum entity that is moving to develop the oil resources of the country.

EXPORTS AND IMPORTS
(1965)

Exports	Value	Imports	Value
Meat	$329,000,000	Foods	$ 69,000,000
Hides	50,000,000	Textiles	52,000,000
Wool	112,000,000	Chemicals and	
Dairy products .	29,000,000	pharmaceu-	
Other pastoral .	43,000,000	ticals	135,000,000
Fish	4,000,000	Paper	50,000,000
Cereals and		Lumber	87,000,000
linseed	576,000,000	Iron and steel .	190,000,000
Wheat flour ...	26,000,000	Machinery and	
Other farm		vehicles	277,000,000
items	219,000,000	Nonferrous	
Forest		metals	109,000,000
products	16,000,000	Stone and glass	20,000,000
Minerals	13,000,000	Fuel and lubri-	
Manufactured		cating oil ...	115,000,000
goods	75,000,000	Rubber, etc. ..	41,000,000
		Others	53,000,000

TRADING PARTNERS IN 1965

	Exports	Imports
Latin American		
Free Trade Area	$ 231,000,000	$ 256,000,000
Brazil	107,000,000	163,000,000
Others	124,000,000	93,000,000
European Common Market ..	603,000,000	271,000,000
Germany	99,000,000	110,000,000
Italy	238,000,000	80,000,000
Netherlands	161,000,000	19,000,000
Others	105,000,000	62,000,000
European		
Free Trade Association....	191,000,000	136,000,000
Britain	153,000,000	73,000,000
Others	38,000,000	63,000,000
United States	93,000,000	273,000,000
Communist Bloc	214,000,000	34,000,000
USSR	87,000,000	19,000,000
China	84,000,000	1,000,000
Others	43,000,000	14,000,000
Japan	32,000,000	44,000,000
Others	128,000,000	184,000,000
Total	$1,492,000,000	$1,198,000,000

(5) gradual elimination of inflationary pressures.

About 30 percent of the total investment was assigned to infrastructure, mainly electric power, roads, and railroads; 26 percent for social improvements, especially housing; 17 percent for agriculture and livestock; and 18 percent for the industrial sector. The plan contemplated financing chiefly by private internal savings, which would provide 91.4 percent of the $16.2 billion of gross fixed investment. External sources would provide the rest.

Foreign Trade. The Argentine economy has traditionally been oriented toward foreign trade. And the orientation of foreign trade has been toward Europe rather than the United States, because many of Argentina's leading exports are also produced in abundance in the United States. Foreign trade has been running about one tenth the magnitude of gross national product, but, in the case of agriculture and livestock, external trade represents 40 to 50 percent of total availabilities.

On the import side, consumers' goods declined as the industrial plant matured. Oil figured heavily until output was expanded from 1958 to 1963, and although expansion was balked by negotiations terminating drilling and production contracts with foreign companies in 1963, there is still hope for an approach to self-sufficiency. The great bulk of imports consist of raw materials for industry, iron and steel and nonferrous metals, machinery, and vehicles. Of the exports, livestock and agricultural products consistently provide 90 percent or more.

SIMON G. HANSON
"Inter-American Economic Affairs"

4. Education

A nearly universal system of education was initiated in the 1870's by President Domingo Faustino Sarmiento, who was a friend of Horace Mann, United States pioneer in the development of public schools. It was developed along European lines in the following decades, and today is most like the French system before World War II. All levels of education are offered by state-supported schools without tuition charges, although there are also at all levels private schools that charge fees. A child must attend school for at least seven years between the ages of 6 and 14. Some 91 percent of Argentines aged 14 and over are literate.

The costs of education are paid mainly by the national government, although some primary and secondary schools are supported by provincial governments. No schools are supported by local city or town governments.

The educational system is secular and public-supported to a greater degree than in most Latin American countries. While there are church-supported and church-operated schools at all levels, and also some independent private schools, they serve a relatively low proportion of students. About 10 percent of primary school pupils attend nonpublic schools, as do 40 percent of middle or secondary school pupils and 3 percent of university students.

Primary Schools. There are about 18,000 primary schools serving 3 million pupils. About 90 percent of primary school teachers are women. They are trained in secondary schools, called normal schools, with a five-year course beyond the primary grades. The school year commences in March and continues through November.

Middle or Secondary Schools. Though most of them are free of tuition charge, the middle or secondary schools require an examination for admission. They have about 850,000 pupils, or about 35 percent of the age-group 13–17, inclusive. About 50 percent of Argentine youth enter middle schools, and 25 percent graduate.

There is a variety of middle schools. Generally, the academic middle school is called a *liceo* if it is for girls and a *colegio* if it is for boys, although a number of colegios have become coeducational. Other types of middle schools include the normal school, which prepares students for teaching in primary school; the commercial school, which prepares young men and women for jobs in business; and the industrial school, which prepares students for trades and for technical jobs.

The middle schools have two cycles. The first, or basic cycle, consists of general studies. The second cycle is more specialized and leads either to a specific kind of job or to the university. The second cycle generally is a two-year course, although it is sometimes extended to three years. At graduation, the student receives a diploma as "Bachiller Universitario" or as an expert or technician in a specific vocational field.

The distribution of students among the various types of middle schools early in the 1960's was as follows: academic, 48 percent; normal, 16 percent; commercial, 20 percent; and indus-

CATHEDRAL AT JUJUY, capital of Jujuy province in northern Argentina, is a classic example of Spanish colonial architecture.

PAAR, FROM PIX

trial, 16 percent. The percentage for industrial schools is relatively high and reflects both the high level of industrial development and the high status of industrial work, as compared with other Latin American countries.

One problem of secondary education in Argentina is a shortage of space and a lack of modern equipment. Many schools operate on two or even three shifts a day, serving as a normal school in the morning, an academic school in the afternoon, and perhaps an academic school in the evening for older students, many of whom are employed during the day.

Higher Education. Education at the university level in Argentina has a substantial tradition. The oldest university is that of Córdoba, founded in 1622. The largest is the University of Buenos Aires, founded in 1821, which has some 75,000 students. There are, in all, about 150,000 university students, which is about 6 percent of the age-group 18–22, inclusive. This is a substantial number as compared with most other countries except the United States. One reason the number is so large is that many students study part-time only, particularly in Buenos Aires. Well over half of all university students are employed, most of them in full-time jobs. Especially in Buenos Aires, university classes tend to be scheduled after 5 P.M. to accommodate employed students.

A student in the university begins to specialize early, without much "general education" in the North American sense of that term. The university degree is the doctor's degree in philosophy, medicine, law, or another faculty, and may be achieved in six years. However, a student may earn a professional diploma after four or five years and not go on to the doctorate.

There are nine public universities: Buenos Aires, Córdoba, Cuyo (at Mendoza), La Plata, del Litoral (at Santa Fe), del Nordeste (at Corrientes), La Pampa (at Santa Rosa), del Sur (at Bahía Blanca), and Tucumán. All are supported by the national government. They were governed by councils made up of professors, alumni, and students until 1966, when the federal government abolished their autonomy and placed them under its department of education.

Several public teachers colleges for training secondary-school teachers operate at the university level.

There are four Roman Catholic universities. The law authorizing the creation of private universities was passed in 1958, over strong opposition from the state universities.

ROBERT J. HAVIGHURST, *University of Chicago*

5. Cultural Life

The cultural life of Argentina extends well back into the colonial period, during which the first university was founded and the first printing presses were brought to the country. But its most important manifestations date from the time of the revolutionary movement of 1810, which marks the birth of the country as a nation. In fact, the revolutionary movement owes much to the group of intellectuals who, like Mariano Moreno (1779–1811), secretary of the first revolutionary junta, were imbued with the ideas of the French Revolution.

19th Century Thinkers. Manuel Belgrano (1770–1839), a general of the revolutionary forces, also founded a school of mathematics. With Moreno and others of their group, he was anxious to break away from the overly scholastic training that Spanish rule had imposed on the colony and to modernize Argentine thinking through the study of science and the application of more liberal doctrines in the field of economics. Bernardo de Monteagudo (1785–1825) was one of the outstanding pamphleteers for the cause of independence—a Patrick Henry of the Latin American revolution. He was murdered at the height of his influence, after having served under both San Martín and Bolívar. After the war of independence, Bernardino Rivadavia, president in 1826–1827, attempted a new start in the cultural sphere by reorganizing free public instruction and university studies. But before the effects of his endeavors could be felt, the country was plunged into internal strife. Even so, exceptional individuals managed to develop their talent, and during the long dictatorship of Juan Manuel de Rosas, who ruled from 1832 to 1852, a new generation of intellectuals was in the making.

Practically all of this group had to emigrate at some point during the Rosas dictatorship. Outstanding among them was Esteban Echeverría (1805–1851). At the age of 20 he went to Paris to attend classes at the Sorbonne. After his return to Buenos Aires, he founded (1837) the May Society, whose ideals he formulated in *Dogma socialista,* an enlightened synthesis of political and social insight. He wrote a long romantic poem, *La cautiva,* and his story *El Matadero,* one of the most powerfully realistic documents of the time in its narration of the torture and murder of a young gentleman at the hands of the Mazorqueros, Rosas' storm troopers.

Another member of the May Society was the legal theorist Juan Bautista Alberdi (1810–1884). He spent most of his life in neighboring South American countries. After the downfall of Rosas, Alberdi wrote *Bases y puntos de partida para la constitución de la nación Argentina,* which sums up the principles of United States constitutional law, adapting them to the idiosyncrasies of the Argentine people. His document was basic in the drafting of the Constitution of 1853—with minor variations, the law of the land to this day. Alberdi may also be considered one of the founders of Pan American legal thought. His *El crimen de la guerra* (*The Crime of War*) is a classic on the subject.

Domingo Faustino Sarmiento (1811–1888) was a key figure in the cultural life of Argentina. Another enemy of Rosas, he worked his way up from humble beginnings to become one of the most learned men of his time. After the downfall of Rosas, Sarmiento was appointed Argentine minister in Washington and developed an almost fanatical admiration for the United States and what it stood for. By then (1845) he had written the classic *Facundo* (*Life in the Argentine Republic in the Days of the Tyrants*), in which he depicted the personality of Juan Facundo Quiroga, one of the most savage caudillos (local chieftains) of his time. The subtitle of this work, *Civilization or Barbarism,* made it clear that in the struggle between the anarchical forces of *caudillismo* and those of Western order, he stood decisively with the latter. Sarmiento was summoned from the United States to become president of Argentina in 1868, and he used this opportunity to carry out his ideas. With incredible energy he built schools at such a rate that by the turn of the century illiteracy had practically been eliminated. He also founded military and naval academies and many scientific and cultural organizations.

The other great figure of Argentine culture, José Hernández (1834–1886) wrote the epic poem of the Pampa, *Martín Fierro.* To understand the cultural personality of the Argentine people, it is as important to dwell on this poem as it would be to study Homer in order to know the Greeks. Hernández lived among the gauchos, and it was their destiny that concerned him.

In narrating the misfortunes of Martín Fierro, an honest gaucho who becomes an outlaw, Hernández expressed the plight of the contemporary rural worker, who was being legally dispossessed of the lands on which he worked by carpetbaggers from the city. But the poet went beyond the sociological dimension and reached universality in his vivid and passionate description of man's eternal struggle for wisdom and justice. *Martín Fierro* has become a national Bible, where Argentines find consolation, wise instruction, and strength.

Modern Writers. Leopoldo Lugones (1874–1938) marked a new era in Argentine intellectual history. He was one of the leaders of the literary movement known as *modernismo,* launched by the Nicaraguan poet Rubén Darío. Lugones, who was also a Greek scholar, had a decisive influence on Argentine letters. He had strong opponents and ardent followers.

Among those who parted with *modernismo* are some key figures of contemporary Argentine letters. They include Ricardo Güiraldes (1886–1927), author of the novel *Don Segundo Sombra,* the life of a boy who becomes a man through the experiences of gaucho life. Jorge Luis Borges, who has produced a huge quantity of poetry and prose, became the most widely known Argentine writer of the 20th century. His better-known works include such classics as *Ficciones.* Leopoldo Marechal, better known as a poet, also wrote *Adán Buenosayres,* a Joycean urban novel of epic dimensions. He had wide influence among the new generation of writers such as Julio Cortázar, whose metaphysical *Hopscotch* placed him among the most important writers of the 1960's.

Theater. The first important Argentine dramatists were Gregorio de Laferrère (1867–1913) and Roberto Payró (1867–1928), but the author who made the greatest impact was Florencio Sánchez (1873–1909), an Uruguayan who wrote in Buenos Aires. His dramas about the life of the Argentine proletariat and petty bourgeoisie belong among the world classics of plays devoted to depicting national life. Although theater production continues to add names like Carlos Gorostiza, Agustín Cuzzani, Osvaldo Dragún, and Omar del Carlo, these playwrights have not yet reached Sánchez' degree of dramatic perception.

Cinema. The Argentine cinema started in 1933, appropriately with a picture called *Tango.* Since then it has shown increasing vitality. After 1938, the directors Mario Soffici, Alberto de Zavalía, Luis Amadori, Daniel Tinayre, Luis Saslavsky, and Manuel Romero made films with scripts inspired by the writings of Argentine artists.

CARL FRANK, FROM PHOTO RESEARCHERS

GAUCHO DANCE, in its rhythms and colorful costumes, displays the vitality of a way of life that is traditional in the countryside.

TEATRO COLÓN, a center of Buenos Aires' cultural life, is famous among the opera houses of the world. The splendor of its foyer is typical of its design.

Actors such as Libertad Lamarque, Luis Sandrini, and Pepe Arias became popular.

In the 1940's fantastic success was achieved by *La Guerra Gaucha*, which starred Enrique Muiño. This film, with Mugica's *Así es la vida* and *Los martes orquídeas*, gave the Argentine cinema a fresh start. New talent after World War II included the director Leopoldo Torre Nilsson, whose work is based on the widely read novels of Beatriz Guido, and Fernando Ayala, Hugo del Carril, Lautaro Murúa, and David Kohn.

Music. Music can be traced at the level of classical composition to the first quarter of the 20th century, through such composers as Julián Aguirre and Alberto Williams, followed by Carlos López Buchardo, Felipe Boero, Gilardo Gilardi, and Luis Gianneo. In the 1960's Juan José Castro, Alberto Ginastera, and Juan Carlos Paz were considered the most original composers. Leading the path into the field of electronic music were Mario Davidovsky, Mauricio Kagel, and Hilda Dianda.

Visual Arts. The tradition of the visual arts has perhaps the best antecedents in the spectrum of Argentine culture.

Carlos Morel (1813–1894) was the first native Argentine painter of significance. But it was only with Prilidiano Pueyrredón (1823–1870) that Argentina can be said to have produced a first-rate artist. Pueyrredón painted the bucolic scenes of the Argentine Pampa with a purity of style reminiscent of Poussin's. Impressionism was introduced to Argentina by Walter de Navazio (1887–1921), Cesáreo Bernardo de Quirós, and Faustino Brughetti (1877–1956). Although Argentine painting had many strong personalities, it remained derivative in style, even though some of its creators participated actively in contemporary European movements, among them Emilio Pettoruti, who introduced futurism and cubism to Argentina in the 1920's. Opening the road to abstract art were painters like Juan del Prete. Important antecedents to the varieties of expression of the many contemporary trends were Raquel Forner, Antonio Berni (one of the major figurative artists in Latin America), Héctor Basaldúa, Horacio Butler, Ramón Gómez Cornet, Enrique Policastro, and Raúl Soldi.

In the 1940's a stylistic liberation took place, and although always linked to the international styles, artists accentuated their individual personalities. The "geometric-Op" style found important cultivators in Tomás Maldonado, J.A. Fernández-Muro, Alfred Hlito, Eduardo A. MacEntyre, Miguel Angel Vidal, and R. Polesello. The group of the "figurative lyrics" is represented by Leopoldo Presas, Raúl Russo, and Luis Centurion. Figuration became expressionistic under the influence of action painting with Romulo Maccio and Antonio Segni. The informalist movement gained momentum with Alberti Greco, Mario Pucciarelli, Kenneth Kemble, and Luis Alberto Wells. The "monsters" of Julio Renart were an outgrowth of this spirit.

Pop art produced a vision of its own through Martha Minujín, Delia Puzzovio, and Carlos Squirru, who also became active in staging "happenings." The Mexican muralist tradition was continued through the works of Roque Carpani, Mario Mollari, Juan M. Sánchez, Pascual Di Bianco and others. Its strong linear influence can also be detected in such abstract painters as Luis Barragán. Among the engravers, excellence has been achieved in the various technical fields: in metal, the refined abstractions of Mabel Rubli; and in wood, works by the painter Luis Seaone and by Albino Fernández.

Sculpture has important antecedents in the classical forms cultivated by Rogelio Yrurtia (1879–1950), sculptor of the outstanding monuments *The Death of Colonel Dorrego* and *Song to Toil*. Pedro Zonza Briano (1886–1941) shows the influence of Rodin. Among contemporary sculptors, the work of Sesostris Vitullo (1889–1953) marks a return to pre-Columbian forms. His pieces in wood and granite were given a one-man show in the Paris Museum of Modern Art the year of his death, and his work has influenced contemporary European sculpture. Alicia Penalba won the International Biennial of São Paulo (Brazil) in 1963 with her strong bronzes, also of pre-Columbian reminiscence. Libero Badii exercised powerful influence among the younger generation with his simple geometric forms. Hydraulic sculpture was practiced by Gyula Kosice and by Martha Boto. Luis Tomasello worked with reliefs in color.

Also working in three dimensions, using color effects in different materials, was the painter Julio Le Parc, whose kinetic constructions achieved substantial fame after he received the

1966 Venice Biennale's first prize for painting. Enio Iommi was a leading purist in spatial geometrical abstractions, together with Marino DiTeana. Of strong telluric flavor are the murals and totemic forms of Hugo Rodríguez.

Press. The press can be said to have started during the Revolution of 1810 with the *Gazeta de Buenos Aires,* founded by Mariano Moreno. Ever since, it has played an important role in developing the course of freedom. In 1869, José C. Paz founded *La Prensa,* and a year later Bartolomé Mitre started *La Naçión.* The two papers, published in Buenos Aires, have played leading roles in the life of the country ever since. Their Sunday literary supplements have counted among their collaborators, especially in the first quarter of the 20th century, outstanding intellectuals from all over the world, among them Miguel de Unamuno, Rubén Darío, and Arnold Toynbee. Other Buenos Aires dailies are *Critica, El Mundo, Clarín,* and *La Razón.* The last two have the largest circulation of any Argentine newspapers.

In the provinces there are important newspapers such as *La Capital* of Rosario, *La Gazeta* of Tucumán, *Los Andes* of Mendoza, and *Los Principios* of Córdoba.

Science. As a serious pursuit of any magnitude, Argentine science started during the last years of the colonial regime with the foundation of the first institutions of higher learning, the Nautical School and the Medical School, which led to the creation of the University of Buenos Aires in 1821. Argentine universities have played a major role in the development of science, along with other institutions such as the Sociedad Científica de Argentina para el Progreso de las Ciencias, founded in 1933 on the initiative of a team led by Bernardo A. Houssay. (Houssay was awarded the Nobel prize in physiology and medicine for 1947.) The society has a systematic program of fellowships and research and, since 1945, has published the excellent periodical *Ciencia e Investigación.*

The creation in 1933 of the National Commission for Culture, with its special council for scientific research, also proved a valuable source of aid in scientific development. Mathematics owes an important advance to the Spanish professor Rey Pastor, who arrived in Argentina in 1917 and devoted himself to teaching and promoting research, mathematical societies, and magazines. One outcome was the Institute of Rosario, founded in 1940. Physics had two associations, the Nuclear Physics Society founded in 1942, concerned with both scientific and technical research, and another under the auspices of the National Atomic Energy Commission founded in 1950. Important scientific work is also done at the Physics Institute of Bariloche. There is a special nuclear research institute with a computer center at the University of Buenos Aires. Chemistry found support in the Institute of Santa Fe, founded by Horacio Damianovich in 1929, and the Institute of Microchemical Research of Rosario, founded in 1936. Especially important is the Campomar Foundation, dating from 1947, which, under the direction of Luis T. Leloir, has achieved high international prestige. With a long tradition of scientific responsibility, the observatory of Córdoba has played a leading role in astronomical observation and research. The fields of botany and zoology have centers for development in the two great museums of Buenos Aires and La Plata.

Among those institutions that have promoted cultural activities in various fields, special attention should be devoted to the Instituto Torcuato Di Tella, founded in 1960. This important foundation has centers for visual arts, economic research, and neurological research, and it houses the Latin American Center for Advanced Musical Studies. These centers are all provided with the latest equipment in their respective fields and their hand-picked researchers have given the institute worldwide fame.

RAFAEL SQUIRRU
*Department of Cultural Affairs,
Pan American Union*

6. Government

The framers of the 1853 Constitution, which is still in force in Argentina, adopted in the first article "a representative, republican, federal form of government." The United States Constitution, especially as interpreted in the writings of the Argentine jurist Juan B. Alberdi, served as their model, and the Argentine Supreme Court has maintained this constitutional contact by repeated references to United States precedents. Despite this heritage, the Argentine president possesses more authority than his United States counterpart, particularly in his power to intervene in the affairs of the provinces and to declare a state of siege.

Argentine citizenship is acquired at birth or by petition after a stated period of residence. All citizens register at 18 years of age and are required to vote in national elections under penalty of being fined. Compulsory male suffrage was adopted in 1912 and female suffrage in 1947.

Division of Powers. The national government is composed of three branches: executive, legislative, and judicial.

The president and vice president are elected for six-year terms by an electoral college chosen by popular vote. Candidates must be Roman Catholics and native-born citizens; immediate reelection is not permitted. The president appoints all civil, military, and judicial officers and acts as commander in chief of the armed forces. In his capacity as chief executive he is assisted by a cabinet of appointed ministers. The vice president presides over the Senate and becomes chief of state in event of the death, resignation, or removal of the president.

Legislative powers are vested in the National Congress, composed of a Senate and a Chamber of Deputies. Each province, through its local legislature, elects two federal senators for nine-year terms, and two senators are chosen from the federal district (Buenos Aires) by a special body of electors. One third of the Senate is renewed every three years. The Chamber of Deputies is elected by direct popular vote in a system of proportional representation for four-year terms, half of the Chamber being renewed every two years. Senators must have been citizens for at least six years; deputies for at least four years. In addition to normal legislative functions, Congress writes federal codes in civil, commercial, penal, and mining law and must initiate any constitutional reforms. A two-thirds vote by each house is required to override a presidential veto and to approve international treaties negotiated by the executive. Congress also possesses impeachment powers over executive and judicial officers, including the president; the Chamber impeaches and the Senate tries such cases.

NATIONAL CONGRESS, the legislative body of
Argentina, meets in this Buenos Aires palace.

CARL FRANK, FROM PHOTO RESEARCHERS

NATIONAL CONGRESS, the legislative body of
Argentina, meets in this Buenos Aires palace.

The judiciary is composed of a Supreme
Court, five appellate courts, and at least one
district court in each province. Judges, appointed
by the president with the approval of the Senate,
hold life tenure and hear all matters within
federal jurisdiction, including any case involving
foreigners.

Finances. The national government derives its
revenues largely from tariffs and assorted excise
and income taxes; major expenditures, beyond
normal administration, occur in the operations
of the state-owned railroads, airlines, and telephone systems and in subsidization of industrial
development. In most years since 1945, expenditures have outstripped revenues, with the result
that domestic and short-term foreign debts have
risen steadily. Despite efforts by the Banco Central (established in 1934) to control currency
exchange, the depletion of gold reserves and
excessive public spending in the 1950's and 1960's
accentuated inflation, caused a sharp decline in
the peso's exchange value, and further complicated the problems of public finance.

Political Parties. Political party structure has
been dominated since the beginning of the 20th
century by the rise and subsequent divisions of
the Radical party, largely urban and middle
class in its origins, and more recently by the
personalistic and mass-oriented appeals of *pe-
ronismo.* The 19th century liberal landowning
elite has occasionally rallied under various conservative banners, but only in the 1930's did
it regain national power, while Communists,
Socialists, Christian Democrats, and other splinter
groups have been entirely unsuccessful in achieving a national appeal. Today, voting power is
divided roughly between the partly enfranchised
peronista groups and the two major Radical
groups, Radical Intransigente and Radical del
Pueblo, separated not so much by substance as
by personalities and tradition.

Armed Forces. Military service has been required of all male citizens since 1900; in the
1960's, one year's active service was compulsory
for men between 20 and 45, contributing to a
total strength of 500,000 in reserve and active
duty components. The three services—army, navy,
and air force—are autonomous (the last since
1945), and individual service schools for noncommissioned and commissioned officers stimulate
fierce service loyalty. The armed forces' representatives in the president's cabinet have played
an increasingly important political role since the
1930's, and the minister of war frequently has
held decisive control over a civilian government.

Public Services. Argentina boasts one of the
most extensive social-security systems in Latin
America, including maternity benefits, workmen's
compensation, severance pay, and family allowances. In the area of public health and sanitation, the national government, beginning with a
modest start in the federal district and several
of the provinces in the 1880's, has provided extensive direction and financial assistance. In the
realm of public order, the federal police possess
extensive law enforcement authority beyond the
federal district and supplement provincial law
agencies; for a time in the Perón period, the
federal police also acquired significant political
importance.

Local Government. Those powers not specifically assigned to the federal government belong
to the provinces; each of the 22 provinces has
its own constitution, governor, legislature, and
judiciary. Despite the centralized structure of
national government, there is therefore considerable provincial and municipal autonomy. Unfortunately, there is also a total lack of financial
resources at these levels.

JAMES R. SCOBIE, *Indiana University*

7. History

The Colony. At the beginning of the 16th century the area of present-day Argentina was sparsely settled by some 20 major Indian groups with
a total population estimated at 300,000. Most of
these tribes were nomadic hunters and food gatherers, although the political and cultural influence of the Inca empire reached into northwest Argentina. In the northeast the Guaraní
had developed an advanced slash-and-burn agricultural economy, felling and burning trees to
make land arable for cultivation.

First Spanish Settlements. The Spanish conquerors first intruded on Argentina by way of the
Atlantic coast. Following Amerigo Vespucci's
lead, one of Spain's chief navigators, Juan Díaz
de Solís, entered the estuary of the Río de la
Plata in 1516 in search of a passage around the
southern end of South America, but was killed
by warlike Indians on the coast. Four years later
Ferdinão de Magalhães (Magellan) wintered on
the southern Patagonian coast before pushing on
through the strait that bears his name, and in
1526–1528 Sebastian Cabot planted a temporary
settlement on the Paraná River not far from
present-day Rosario. Spain's appetite for new
lands, new subjects, and new wealth had been
whetted meanwhile by successes in Mexico and
Peru, and in 1536 the largest royal expedition
ever used in the conquest of the New World
arrived in the Río de la Plata under the command of a Spanish nobleman, Pedro de Mendoza.
But the absence of docile Indians and the lack
of mineral or agricultural wealth soon discouraged these first settlers of Buenos Aires, and the
expedition gradually withdrew upstream to Asunción (Paraguay).

Other Spaniards, however, soon reached into
northwestern Argentina from Peru and in 1553
planted the first permanent Spanish town on

CHRONOLOGY

1516 Río de la Plata estuary is discovered by Juan Díaz de Solís.
1536 Pedro de Mendoza founds temporary settlement of Buenos Aires.
1553 First permanent Spanish settlement on Argentine soil is established at Santiago del Estero.
1580 Spanish settlement at Buenos Aires is reestablished by Juan de Garay.
1776 Viceroyalty of the Río de la Plata is established, with seat at Buenos Aires.
1810 Inhabitants of Buenos Aires declare their political autonomy.
1816 Independence from Spain is declared at Tucumán.
1835 Juan Manuel de Rosas assumes supreme powers over the province of Buenos Aires and de facto control over the other Argentine provinces.
1852 Rosas is overthrown.
1853 The provinces accept a federal constitution.
1862 Bartolomé Mitre is inaugurated as president of all the Argentine provinces.
1880 City of Buenos Aires is federalized as a national capital.
1890 Middle-class Radical party elements force resignation of President Juárez Celmán.
1916 Radical party candidate, Hipólito Yrigoyen, is elected president.
1930 President Yrigoyen is overthrown by military revolt.
1943 Military revolt overthrows President Ramón S. Castillo.
1946 Juan Domingo Perón is elected president.
1955 Military revolt overthrows Perón.
1958 Arturo Frondizi is elected president.
1962 Military intervention removes Frondizi.
1966 Military junta deposes elected president, Arturo Illia, and installs Juan Carlos Onganía.
1971 Junta leader, Lieut. Gen. Alejandro A. Lanusse, assumes presidency.

Argentine soil at Santiago del Estero. Establishment of other towns in the interior followed rapidly. These Spanish towns thrived as centers of local industries, commerce, and administration. They were dependent on the agricultural production of the surrounding region and on the labor of "tamed" or Christianized Indians and, as the colonial period advanced, of Negro slaves. As the silver exploitation in Upper Peru (Bolivia) developed during the 17th century, the towns acquired substantial importance as suppliers of animals, food, and textiles for the mining area. Córdoba, where in 1622 the Jesuits founded the first university in the Argentine area, soon emerged as the interior's cultural and spiritual center.

The coastal region lagged significantly behind the interior in development. The colony at Asunción finally turned its energies outward toward the Atlantic, establishing Santa Fe in 1573, resettling Buenos Aires in 1580, and building a village at Corrientes in 1588. But the delay was sufficient to introduce a permanent dichotomy in Argentine development between the coast and the interior. For most of the colonial period the coastal towns remained rude settlements, dependent on the hunting of wild horses and wild cattle and tied to an increasing flow of contraband trade in hides, slaves, and silver.

Growth of the Coastal Area. By the 18th century the structure of the Spanish empire began to change. The mining economy of Upper Peru stopped expanding and then declined, and stagnation slowly spread to the supply centers of the Argentine northwest. The coast, on the other hand, showed signs of overcoming its earlier handicaps. The establishment in 1680 of a Portuguese emporium at Colonia do Sacramento (Uruguay), directly across the Río de la Plata from Buenos Aires, stimulated contraband trade as did the licenses given a limited number of English ships after 1713 to bring slaves to

Buenos Aires. The spread of wild horses and cattle across the fertile Pampa encouraged more rational exploitation of these animal resources than mere hunting. Gradually the animals were gathered in half-tamed herds by gaucho laborers; the still unsubjugated Indian tribes were pushed away from lands immediately surrounding coastal towns; finally the crown began to sell or grant the lands on which these herds roamed and the vast landed estate, or *estancia*, took root in Argentina.

In 1776, Spain established the viceroyalty of the Río de la Plata. Buenos Aires prospered as a port and capital. Silver bullion, formerly channeled through Lima, now passed through Buenos Aires to Spain. The town's population, which numbered 12,000 in 1750, rose to 50,000 by the end of the century. The export of hides, averaging 150,000 a year in the 1750's, increased to 700,000 a year by the 1790's. At the end of the century the development of the *saladero*, or meat-salting plant, enormously increased the value of herds by exploiting not only the hides but also the entire carcass.

The expansion of the coast's economy encouraged *porteño* domination of the Argentine area (domination by the port of Buenos Aires) and also stimulated latent desires for autonomy and independence from Spanish control. The economic interests of the *porteños* lay in the completely free exchange of agricultural products for imported manufactures—the direct antithesis of the interior's production of food, textiles, and local manufactures which needed protection in order to survive.

The Independence Movement. Efforts by Britain to capture the port in 1806 and 1807 probably hastened the area's separation from the Spanish empire. Although the Spanish viceroy fled, local militia twice defeated the redcoats and forced their evacuation from the Río de la Plata. Not only did the local inhabitants thus gain enormous confidence in their own abilities, but also the free entry, during several months, of British goods at Montevideo and Buenos Aires gave clear proof of the commercial advantages to be gained by free trade. In addition, the numbers of officials sent from Spain and the efforts at closer supervision over the viceroyalty through the establishment of a customhouse (1779), several intendancies (governorships) with military and fiscal responsibilities (1782), and an *audiencia*, or administrative court (1785), had led to increasing friction with the local, or creole, inhabitants.

In May 1810 the creole leaders, seconded by local militia units, exerted pressure on the town council, or *cabildo*, to replace the viceroy with a junta that would govern in the name of Ferdinand VII, who had been deposed from the Spanish throne by Napoleon. The junta, named on May 25, secured autonomy, not independence; but the restoration of Ferdinand VII, his refusal to recognize creole desires for self-government, and the development of a civil-war situation between Buenos Aires and royalist centers in Peru and Upper Peru led to an outright declaration of independence by representatives from several Argentine provinces at Tucumán on July 9, 1816.

Struggles for National Organization. A bewildering succession of juntas, triumvirates, and directors played out the drama, from 1810 to 1820, of *porteño* efforts to seize control of the viceroyalty versus provincial desires for local autonomy. *Porteño* military efforts to subjugate Asun-

MONUMENT honoring General José de San Martín, who is regarded as the liberator of Argentina early in the 19th century, is in a plaza in Buenos Aires.

ción and Montevideo failed immediately, and those two areas went their own ways—Paraguay emerging as an independent nation in 1813 and Uruguay in 1828. In the interior of Argentina the conflict was more confused because of royalist efforts from Upper Peru to reconquer the northwestern provinces, a move that was finally outflanked by the strategy of José de San Martín and his liberation of Chile (1817–1818) and Peru (1819–1822). Behind those external events, the congress of Tucumán had produced the highly centralized constitution of 1819 but was dissolved when faced with unanimous repudiation by the provinces. In this chaotic situation the individual provinces became autonomous units under their local chieftains, or caudillos, although Buenos Aires acquired a certain preeminence.

Bernardino Rivadavia. The province of Buenos Aires further developed its leadership under Bernardino Rivadavia, minister of government from 1821 to 1824. Among the progressive measures adopted were projects for immigration and port works to be supported by British loans, a major commercial treaty with Britain (1825), separation of church and state, and establishment of the University of Buenos Aires (1821).

Renewed efforts to implant a centralized constitution in 1826 resulted in Rivadavia's brief presidency over the United Provinces of the Río de la Plata, but the forces of provincial autonomy compelled him to resign the next year.

Juan Manuel de Rosas. The clash between the provincial, or local autonomy, position and the *porteño*, or centralist, tendency acquired new bitterness when troops shot a leading figure of the autonomist faction, Manuel Dorrego, a former governor of the province of Buenos Aires. A wealthy cattleman and local caudillo from southern Buenos Aires, Juan Manuel de Rosas, capitalizing on the reaction to Dorrego's execution, restored order under the autonomist banner and in turn was elected governor of Buenos Aires (1829).

Intermittent civil war over the issue of centralism versus autonomy afflicted Argentina for the next two decades, but Rosas, as the leader of the autonomist group, imposed a de facto control over the provinces, which had been unattainable within the framework of a centralist regime. In 1835, following a successful campaign to push the Indian frontier southward, Rosas was reelected governor of Buenos Aires with "supreme and absolute powers"—a position he was to retain along with authority to represent the other provinces in financial and external matters until his overthrow in 1852.

Rosas represented several significant trends in the early development of an independent Argentina. His own wealth and the position of his regime depended on the sale of products from a rudimentary cattle economy in the world market. Thus, despite his apparent political affiliation with the forces of local autonomy, his economic policies steadily undercut the interior and favored the coast. The *saladero* remained the keystone of this system, at least until mid-19th century, linking the vast reaches of the Pampa, the huge herds, the hard-riding gauchos, the town merchants, and the port in a viable economic unit. Rosas' political strength meanwhile rested in large measure on the leading landholding and commercial groups of the coast and on his charismatic appeal to the lower classes.

His major accomplishment was to hold the provinces together through the crises of civil war and several foreign interventions. His regime, however, encountered rising resistance not so much from the interior as from the other coastal provinces, which suffered from the trade monopoly maintained by Buenos Aires. In 1851 the governor of Entre Ríos, Justo José de Urquiza, raised the banner of revolution and joined in an alliance with Brazil and Uruguay to overthrow the "tyrant." Within a year Rosas had been defeated at the Battle of Caseros (Feb. 3, 1852) and had fled to exile in England.

Constitution of 1853. At Urquiza's instigation, representatives of the provinces gathered to draft the Constitution of 1853, modeled closely on that of the United States. Unity was not so easily decreed; the province of Buenos Aires, fearing that it would lose its dominant role in such a federal union, seceded. In 1854, Urquiza was elected as the first president of a strangely decapitated Argentine Confederation of thirteen provinces, lacking the customhouse, port, and traditional capital of Argentina. Six years later the wayward province temporarily rejoined the others under the presidency of Santiago Derqui, but it was an uneasy truce. Civil war once more broke out between the armies of Entre Ríos (leading the confederation) and Buenos Aires. Finally, in 1862, following the resignation of Derqui and the dissolution of the Confederation, Bartolomé Mitre, the governor of Buenos Aires, was elected president of the 14 united provinces of the Argentine Republic.

Formation of a Nation. The second half of the 19th century marked the emergence of a nation and saw the establishment of trends and patterns that still dominate Argentina. The election of Mitre in 1862 initiated the institutionalized and usually peaceful transfer of power. Men from the provinces occupied ensuing presidencies—Domingo F. Sarmiento from San Juan in 1868, Nicolás Avellaneda from Tucumán in 1874, Julio Roca from Córdoba in 1880—but they ruled in

PRESIDENTS OF ARGENTINA SINCE 1853

1854–1860	Justo José de Urquiza
1860–1861	Santiago Derqui, resigned
1862–1868	Bartolomé Mitre
1868–1874	Domingo F. Sarmiento
1874–1880	Nicolás Avellaneda
1880–1886	Julio Roca
1886–1890	Miguel Juárez Celmán, resigned
1890–1892	Carlos Pellegrini
1892–1895	Luis Sáenz Peña, resigned
1895–1898	José E. Uriburu
1898–1904	Julio Roca
1904–1906	Manuel Quintana, died in office
1906–1910	José Figueroa Alcorta
1910–1914	Roque Sáenz Peña, died in office
1914–1916	Victorino de la Plaza
1916–1922	Hipólito Yrigoyen
1922–1928	Marcelo Torcuato de Alvear
1928–1930	Hipólito Yrigoyen, overthrown
1930–1932	José F. Uriburu (provisional)
1932–1938	Augustín P. Justo
1938–1942	Roberto M. Ortiz, died in office
1942–1943	Ramón S. Castillo, overthrown
1943–1944	Pedro P. Ramírez (provisional)
1944–1945	Edelmiro Farrell (provisional)
1946–1955	Juan Domingo Perón, overthrown
1955	Eduardo Lonardi (provisional)
1955–1958	Pedro E. Aramburu (provisional)
1958–1962	Arturo Frondizi, overthrown
1962–1963	José M. Guido (provisional)
1963–1966	Arturo Illia, overthrown
1966–1970	Juan Carlos Onganía (provisional)
1970–1971	Roberto M. Levingston (provisional)
1971–	Alejandro A. Lanusse (provisional)

the interest of a national authority and not as pawns in provincial-*porteño* struggles. The climax of this process occurred in 1880 when, after a brief civil war, the city of Buenos Aires was federalized as the national capital. At the same time the power of local caudillos and their ability to revolt against the national government were gradually undercut, as railroads and telegraphs linked the country districts and Remington rifles replaced the lances of gaucho cavalry. Argentina's last foreign war in South America (1865–1870) had concluded with the defeat of Paraguay by Argentina, Brazil, and Uruguay.

Economic Changes. The growth of the economy transformed Argentina even more radically than political developments. After 1850, sheep displaced cattle on the grasslands nearest Buenos Aires. The first agricultural colonies established in Santa Fe and Entre Ríos provinces in the 1850's had encouraged use of the Pampa for crop farming. The 1870's brought the necessary internal and external tranquillity and a rising tide of European immigrants and capital to change the rudimentary *saladero* economy into a major world producer of wool, cereals, and fresh meats. The "conquest of the desert" (1879–1880) consolidated Argentina's claim to Patagonia and effectively eliminated the Indian menace. The completion of the first major railroad in 1870 from Rosario to Córdoba heralded rapid expansion, which by the end of the century covered the Pampa with 10,000 miles (16,000 km) of track. In those same 30 years, population climbed from less than 2 million to nearly 5 million; the last two decades of the century left a net balance of 1½ million European immigrants in Argentina, many attracted by the agricultural prospects. Cereal production, barely sufficient for local needs before 1870, contributed nearly half of the export trade by 1900. Experiments with refrigeration in the 1870's meanwhile enabled Argentina to ship frozen mutton and beef to Europe in the 1880's. Stimulated by related improvements such as barbed wire, blooded stock, and alfalfa pastures, these exports shifted increasingly to chilled meats after 1900.

Growth of Buenos Aires. The city of Buenos Aires, representing the administrative, commercial, and industrial core of the nation, grew even more rapidly than the rest of the country, to a metropolis of over a million inhabitants by 1900. Argentine concern with public education, evinced by Sarmiento, removed the church from a controlling position in education through anticlerical laws in 1884. A conscious cultural heritage, stimulated by two outstanding newspapers, *La Prensa* (1869) and *La Nación* (1870), found increasing reflection in the literate, cosmopolitan population of the cities, especially Buenos Aires. There was now no chance that the interior or the provinces could struggle against the predominance of the coast, and for many, especially for the outside world, Argentina became synonymous with Buenos Aires. This was the Argentina typified by the so-called oligarchy that ruled the nation from 1880 to 1916—enlightened, progressive trustees who owned the land, appointed presidents, encouraged investments and immigration, extended education, and modernized the cities, yet failed to unify the classes or regions within Argentina.

The Radical Movement. The first stirrings against this political structure occurred in the city of Buenos Aires itself, where a middle-class movement coalesced as the Unión Cívica Radical, or Radical party, in protest against the inflation and corruption of Miguel Juárez Celmán, Julio Roca's brother-in-law and successor. A brief revolution in July 1890, although defeated, resulted in the resignation of the president and led to fiscal and administrative reform by Vice President Carlos Pellegrini. The Radical movement continued its opposition, however, launching revolts in 1893, 1895, and 1905. Gradually it developed cohesion around a platform of abstention from politics until guaranteed free elections, and around the personality of Hipólito Yrigoyen. Similar sentiments underlay the formation of the Socialist party in 1894 by Juan B. Justo, although this party aspired to speak primarily for the urban workingman.

Roca became president for a second term in 1898–1904, years significant for the stabilization of the peso and the settlement of the boundary dispute with Chile, but also punctuated by widespread labor unrest and agitation. The economic boom of 1904–1912 once more stimulated railroad construction, immigration, public works, and urban development, but middle- and lower-class agitation continued in the cities. With the election of Roque Sáenz Peña in 1910, the reform wing of the oligarchy achieved power, and two years later the new president forced through Congress legislation establishing secret and compulsory voting for all men. In 1916 the Radical party won a closely contested election, and Hipólito Yrigoyen embarked on the presidency with a Jacksonian mandate of lower- and middle-class support.

Hipólito Yrigoyen. The Radical regime lasted until 1930 but introduced few changes. Yrigoyen maintained strict neutrality during World War I, and when the League of Nations in 1921 defeated an Argentine proposal to admit all states to membership, including Germany, he withdrew from that organization. Although friendly to university reform (especially as carried out by students at the University of Córdoba in 1918) and to social legislation, he vigorously suppressed labor agitation, notably the dockworkers' strike at

Buenos Aires in 1919. The creation of a national oil agency in 1922 symbolized support for Argentine exploitation of mineral resources but had little immediate impact on economic development. Yrigoyen's successor, Marcelo T. de Alvear, represented the more conservative wing of the Radical party and soon broke with Yrigoyen. The mid-1920's saw a return to economic prosperity based on cereal and meat production, renewed immigration, and a lessening of political strife. In 1928, Yrigoyen was overwhelmingly reelected, but he soon proved unable to stem the impact of the world depression on Argentina or to provide any effective political direction. On Sept. 6, 1930, Gen. José F. Uriburu, backed by the army and with the general support of most Argentines, removed Hipólito Yrigoyen from the presidency.

Depression and Postwar Years. For Argentina the world depression of the 1930's signaled the collapse of a trade system predicated on the exchange of agricultural products for manufactures. This and the military takeover in 1930 established the trends and problems of the nation's contemporary development. The haunting imbalance of trade, the conflicting demands of agrarian versus industrial growth, and the threat of military influence and intervention constantly intruded on post-1930 governments.

The 1930's and World War II. The initial corporate-state, pro-Fascist drift evident under Uriburu shifted toward renewal of oligarchical control with the election in 1932 of Agustín P. Justo, an anti-Yrigoyen Radical and former minister of war under Alvear. Supported by the military, by conservative groups, and by the right wing of the Radical party, Justo moved aggressively to institute a national economic recovery program with commercial controls, monetary reforms, social welfare measures, and public works.

The election in 1938 of Roberto M. Ortiz, another anti-Yrigoyen Radical, momentarily promised a return to political normalcy by curbing the controlled elections common to the Uriburu and Justo regimes. By 1940, failing health forced Ortiz to turn over authority to Vice President Ramón S. Castillo (Ortiz resigned and died in 1942), and under pressure of certain military groups the government evinced increasing support for the Axis powers during World War II. Industrialization and agricultural profits benefited the nation's economic growth, despite shortages created by the war. Yet in 1943 the military once again intervened and, with general public approval, removed Castillo from power.

Behind this move were several conflicting forces: unhappiness with Argentina's declining military and economic power alongside its traditional rival, Brazil; fear of the next presidential aspirant, a Conservative with clear pro-British ties; and an initial hope of overturning a pro-Axis regime. Under the leadership of Gen. Pedro P. Ramírez, however, the coup soon revealed itself as pro-Axis, instituted stringent political and economic controls, and invited church participation in public education. Under United States pressure, Argentina broke relations with the Axis in 1944, but internal reaction forced Ramírez to turn over authority to Gen. Edelmiro Farrell. Meanwhile the fortunes of Juan Domingo Perón, a leading participant in the 1943 coup, rose rapidly. In addition to his appeal and control over the labor movement, he emerged as minister of war and vice president under Farrell.

JUAN D. PERÓN, president of Argentina, 1946–1955, with his wife Eva. A military revolt ended his rule.

Argentina hastily declared war on the Axis in March 1945, signed the Act of Chapultepec, thus returning to good standing within the Pan American Union, and joined the United Nations. The end of the war brought with it increased discontent with military rule in Argentina and demands for a return to civilian government. For a moment in October 1945, Perón appeared as a scapegoat. He was arrested, but on October 17 a mass rally of workers in Buenos Aires forced his release from prison. A hastily assembled Labor party nominated him for the presidency, which he won easily in February 1946.

The Perón Era. The years of the Perón regime reflected many of the serious and unresolved problems of Argentine development: the gap between a burgeoning and cosmopolitan metropolis, which embraced one third of the national population, and a remote backward interior; the differences between urban and rural existence; the rivalry between middle and lower classes; the struggle between agricultural and industrial interests; and the increasing distrust between labor and military groups. Perón's first Five-Year Plan (1947–51) geared the nation to industrialization. A government institute purchased agricultural products from the farmers, sold them on the world market, and plowed the profits into industrial development. Under this stimulus, industry expanded and population flooded into the already crowded cities; but at the same time agricultural production and exports declined sharply and were further reduced by severe droughts in 1949 and 1952. In 1949 Perón revised the constitution to permit his immediate reelection and to introduce social welfare measures. The same year saw the establishment of the highly personalistic Peronista party. As repressive measures spread, the leading newspaper, *La Prensa*, was expropriated in early 1951, and a military revolt was put down harshly in September.

After the death of his wife, Eva, in 1952, and the burning of the Jockey Club and opposition political party headquarters in 1953, Perón's demagoguery declined, but so did his close relations with labor. A second five-year-plan, begun in 1953, attempted to reestablish an agricultural-industrial balance and to exploit oil reserves and energy resources. Negotiations with foreign oil companies and sharpened conflict with the church led, however, to rising public resentment. A military outbreak in June 1955 failed, but was accompanied by extreme violence and the burn-

JUBILANT CROWD hails the burning of Peronista papers in a street in Buenos Aires after the violent overthrow of the Perón government by a revolt in September 1955.

CORNELL CAPA, FROM MAGNUM

ing of churches in Buenos Aires. In September the military, after a sharp struggle, deposed Perón and permitted him to flee to exile.

After Perón. The governments after 1955 had little success in dealing with basic economic and political problems. A provisional government under Gen. Eduardo Lonardi restored the Constitution of 1853 and adopted a moderate policy toward *peronistas*. Certain military groups, which sought to eliminate *peronistas* and labor influence from the political scene, replaced Lonardi in 1955 with Gen. Pedro E. Aramburu. A *peronista* revolt was crushed in June 1956, but no positive development programs were undertaken. The constituent assembly convoked to reform the constitution dissolved in 1957 without acting.

In 1958, Arturo Frondizi, the candidate of the Yrigoyen wing of the Radical party, supported by *peronista* votes, won the presidency. He pursued an austerity program aimed at stabilizing the peso, promoting agriculture, and reducing imports, and he successfully negotiated the exploitation of oil deposits by foreign companies. Demonstrating amazing political versatility, he survived 33 coups against his regime, only to be removed from the presidency by the military in March 1962 when he permitted *peronista* candidates to run for office and to win in several key congressional and gubernatorial contests. The president of the Senate, José M. Guido, served as provisional president until the election in 1963 of Arturo Illia, the candidate of the conservative wing of the Radical party.

A strong nationalist posture led to Illia's cancellation of the Frondizi petroleum contracts with foreign companies, but in other respects his government was characterized by vacillation and uncertainty. After marked resistance against United States domination of the Organization of American States in the early 1960's on issues related to Cuba, Argentina increasingly sided with the United States, both in the OAS and in the United Nations. In 1964 the *peronista*-controlled labor movement took strong steps, including occupation of factories, to press their demands. Perón himself made a bid to return from his exile

in Spain in late 1964 but was turned back by Brazilian authorities in Rio de Janeiro. The 1965 legislative elections increased *peronista* representation, while the Illia government continued to struggle unsuccessfully with growing unemployment, inflation, and trade deficits.

In June 1966, the military again intervened, installing Gen. Juan Carlos, Onganía, a staunch conservative, as provisional president. Onganía suspended Congress and ruled for four years by decree. Economic conditions were partially stabilized, but unrest continued, building up to mass demonstrations and strikes in 1969. In June 1970 the military junta replaced Onganía with Gen. Roberto Levingston. Nine months later the junta's leader, Gen. Alejandro A. Lanusse, himself assumed the presidency of Argentina.

JAMES R. SCOBIE, *Indiana University*

Bibliography

Alexander, Robert J., *The Perón Era* (New York 1951).
Blanksten, George I., *Perón's Argentina* (Chicago 1953).
Bunkley, Allison W., *The Life of Sarmiento* (Princeton, N.J., 1952).
Burgin, Miron, *The Economic Aspects of Argentine Federalism, 1820–1852* (Cambridge, Mass., 1946).
Cochran, Thomas C. and Reina, Rubén E., *Entrepreneurship in Argentine Culture: Torcuato Di Tella and S.I.A.M.* (Philadelphia 1963).
Denis, Pierre, *The Argentine Republic,* tr. by Joseph McCabe (New York 1922).
Ferns, Henry S., *Britain and Argentina in the Nineteenth Century* (New York and London 1960).
Fillol, Tomás R., *Social Factors in Economic Development: The Argentine Case* (Cambridge, Mass., 1961).
Güiraldes, Ricardo, *Don Segundo Sombra,* tr. by Harriet de Onis (New York 1935).
Hanson, Simon G., *Argentine Meat and the British Market* (Stanford, Calif., 1938).
Hernández, José, *The Gaucho Martín Fierro,* tr. by W. Owen (New York 1936).
Jefferson, Mark, *Peopling the Argentine Pampa* (New York 1926).
Kennedy, John J., *Catholicism, Nationalism, and Democracy in Argentina* (Notre Dame, Ind., 1958).
Kirkpatrick, Frederick A., *A History of the Argentine Republic* (Cambridge, Eng., 1931).
Levene, Ricardo, *A History of Argentina,* tr. by W.S. Robertson (Chapel Hill, N.C., 1937; New York 1963).
Macdonald, Austin F., *Government of the Argentine Republic* (New York 1942).
McGann, Thomas F., *Argentina, the United States, and the Inter-American System, 1880–1914* (Cambridge, Mass., 1957).
McGann, Thomas F., *Argentina: The Divided Land* (Princeton, N.J., 1966).
Nichols, Madaline W., *The Gaucho* (Durham, N.C., 1942).
Pendle, George, *Argentina,* 3d ed. (London 1963).
Peterson, Harold F., *Argentina and the United States, 1810–1960* (New York 1964).
Rennie, Ysabel F., *The Argentine Republic* (New York 1945).
Rojas, Ricardo, *San Martín, Knight of the Andes,* tr. by Herschel Brickell and Carlos Videla (New York 1945).
Romero, José Luis, *A History of Argentine Political Thought,* tr. by Thomas F. McGann (Stanford, Calif., 1963).
Sarmiento, Domingo F., *Life in the Argentine Republic in the Days of the Tyrants* (New York 1961).
Scobie, James R., *Argentina: A City and a Nation* (New York 1964).
Scobie, James R., *Revolution on the Pampas: A Social History of Argentine Wheat, 1860–1910* (Austin, Texas, 1964).
Taylor, Carl C., *Rural Life in Argentina* (Baton Rouge, La., 1948).
Whitaker, Arthur P., *The United States and Argentina* (Cambridge, Mass., 1954).
Whitaker, Arthur P., *Argentina* (Englewood Cliffs, N.J., 1964).
White, John W., *Argentina: The Life Story of a Nation* (New York 1942).

ARGENTITE, är'jən-tīt, is a mineral, silver sulfide. When it occurs in large quantities it is an important silver ore, often called *silver glance* by miners. Usually it is found in association with veins of silver and with galena, or lead sulfide. The opaque, dark gray crystals of argentite have cubic shapes, which are often distorted. The freshly cut face has a metallic luster but soon tarnishes to a dull black. Argentite has been found in silver mines in Germany, Norway, Mexico, Bolivia, Chile, Peru, and other countries. In the United States it occurs in Colorado and Montana, and argentite was once an important ore at such famous deposits as the Comstock Lode in Nevada.

Composition: Ag_2S; hardness, 2.0 to 2.5; specific gravity, 7.2 to 7.4; crystal system, isometric.

ARGENTRÉ, är-zhäN-trä' **Bertrand d'** (1519–1590), French legal scholar and historian. He was born at Vitré, Brittany, and became seneschal of Rennes and president of the provincial court. In reaction to a 16th century revival of civil law on the Roman model, Argentré sought to legitimize the feudal law of the land. He was the first to state the doctrine that immemorial custom acquires the force of law. In *Commentaire sur les quatres premiers titres de l'ancienne coutume de Bretagne* (1568), he attempted to state the *coutume*, or common law, of Brittany. He also wrote a history of Brittany, *Histoire de la Bretagne* (1582).

ARGO, är'gō, or *Argo Navis*, is a large constellation of the Southern Hemisphere. In Greek mythology *Argo* was the ship used by Jason and his band of heroes. For convenience Argo is now divided into four constellations: Puppis (the Poop), Vela (the Sails), Pyxix (the Compass), and Carina (the Keel). Canopus, in Carina, is the second brightest star in the heavens. A dim star in the same constellation, Eta Carinae, has undergone great and erratic changes in brightness; in the 19th century it was nearly as bright as Canopus.

ARGOL, är'gəl, is a term applied to the crude acid tartrate (or bitartrate) of potassium, as deposited on the sides of the vats in which wine is fermenting. It exists in the grapes from which the wine is made, but is precipitated from solution in the vats by the alcohol formed during the fermentation. Like many other precipitates, argol brings down more or less of the coloring matter in the solution from which it is deposited, and it is white or red, according to the color of the wine from which it is formed.

When purified by recrystallization from its solution in hot water, argol is known in commerce as *cream of tartar*. The purified salt is used in baking powders and to a lesser extent in medicine. It is used in its crude state in metallurgy as a reducing agent in fire assaying.

ARGOLIS, är'gō-lis, a *nomos* (department) of Greece, occupies the northeastern peninsula of the Peloponnesus and extends inland to the plains around the city of Argos. It is bounded by the Saronic Gulf on the northeast. To the south is the Gulf of Argolis. Navplion (Nauplia), a port on the Gulf of Argolis, is the chief city and capital of the *nomos*.

In ancient times Argolis was famous as the home of the Argives–the Greeks who lived in Argos and the other small kingdoms of Mycenae, Tiryns, Troezen, Hermione, and Epidaurus. References in Greek mythology to the wealth and culture of many of these places as early as 2000 B.C. have largely been confirmed by archaeological discoveries, especially in Argos and Mycenae. The excavated palaces, tombs, temples, theaters, and other structures testify to their ancient splendor.

According to legend, King Pelops, for whom the Peloponnesus is named, came from Asia Minor and settled in Argos, where he founded a new and powerful dynasty. Among his illustrious decendants were Atreus and Agamemnon. Other notable Argives in Greek mythology include Adrastus, Eurystheus, and Diomedes. Population: (1961) 90,145.

ARGON, är'gon, is a chemical element, atomic number 18, that is a colorless, tasteless, and odorless gas in its ordinary state. The symbol for argon is Ar (changed from A by international agreement in 1957). Argon is a member of the helium group of elements, which are also called noble or inert gases. The elements in the helium group, besides helium and argon, are neon, krypton, xenon, and radon. The helium group of elements are in Group VIIIa of the periodic table.

Discovery. Argon was the first inert gas to be discovered. Its discovery took place in England over a period of 110 years, starting with the observation by Henry Cavendish in 1784 that atmospheric nitrogen could not be made to react completely with oxygen. In 1894, Sir William Ramsay and his assistant, Percy Williams, isolated a small sample of the nonreactive portion of atmospheric nitrogen and gave it to Sir William Crookes for spectrographic examination. The spectrum of the nonreactive gas was different from that of any of the elements then known. After this identification of a new element, the gas was named "argon."

Origin. Dry air contains 0.934 percent by volume (1.288 percent by weight) of argon. Argon is continually produced in the earth's lithosphere by the radioactive decay of potassium-40 in minerals that contain potassium. This argon works its way up through the earth's crust into the atmosphere. Although this process increases the quantity of argon in the atmosphere, the increase is so gradual that no change in the argon concentration can be detected in a lifetime.

Properties. Although argon is ordinarily a gas, it can readily be liquefied and also frozen to a solid. Its boiling point is $-302.6°$ F ($-185.9°$ C), and its melting point is $-308.9°$ F ($-189.4°$ C). The liquid and the solid are colorless.

Isotopes. Atmospheric argon is a mixture of three isotopes: argon-40 (99.6 percent), argon-38 (0.063 percent), and argon-36 (0.337 percent). Each of these isotopes has 18 protons in the nucleus, together with enough neutrons to bring the mass number up to 40, 38, or 36. The atomic weight of argon is the average of the weights of all atoms in a sample of atmospheric argon. Its atomic weight is 39.948 on the scale (adopted by international agreement in 1961) on which the atomic weight of the carbon-12 isotope is exactly 12.

Besides the three stable isotopes of argon, there are five radioactive isotopes. These have the mass numbers 35, 37, 39, 41, and 42, and their half-lives are 1.83 seconds, 35 days, 265 years, 110 months, and 3.5 years, respectively.

Chemical Activity. The chemical properties of any element are determined by the number and the configuration of the electrons outside the nucleus of the atom. In all atoms of argon there are 18 electrons outside the nucleus. They are arranged in shells (energy levels) of 2, 8, and 8 electrons, passing from the nucleus outward. The electrons in each of these shells are in a stable structure that is representative of the so-called "inert-gas configuration."

In a chemical reaction between two atoms, an outer electron of one atom is either donated to another atom or shared by the two combining atoms. In atoms of argon, and in the atoms of most of the other helium-group gases, the electrons are in such a stable configuration that they are neither shared nor donated. Thus the helium-group gases are quite unreactive. The molecule of argon contains only one atom, and no compounds (in the ordinary sense of the word) of argon have ever been prepared. However, argon does take part in formations called "clathrates," in which some argon, called the "guest," is held by weak adsorptive forces in a crystalline cage formed by a second substance, which is called the "host." Argon hydrate, for example, is actually a clathrate in which water molecules make up the host and argon is the guest.

Before 1962 it was thought that none of the helium-group gases could form any stable chemical compounds. In that year Neil Bartlett, then of the University of British Columbia, announced that he had succeeded in carrying out a true chemical reaction between xenon and platinum hexafluoride to form a stable compound of xenon. Since then a few other compounds of xenon, mostly fluorides, have been prepared by various investigators. Radon and krypton can also form a few compounds, but argon and the lighter helium-group gases apparently do not react, even with flourine. The names "inert gases" and "noble gases" for the elements of the helium group are still applicable because even xenon is monatomic and inert to most elements. The use of the word "noble" probably originated from the supposed aloofness of the nobility. The term "rare gases" applies strictly only to neon, krypton, xenon, and radon.

Production. Commercial argon is produced concurrently with oxygen and nitrogen by separation of the components of air. The air is liquefied and then distilled in a double distillation column of special design. Commercially pure nitrogen comes off the top, and oxygen is collected at the bottom. Crude argon is taken from a point in between. It is then redistilled in a separate column to produce a product that usually has a purity of at least 99.996 percent. A modern air-separation plant that produces 500 tons of oxygen per day can produce about 25 tons of argon per day. Argon is commonly shipped as a liquid in insulated railroad tank cars or in insulated tanks mounted on truck trailers.

Uses. The largest single use for argon is in inert-gas-shielded electric arc welding. In the electric welding torch the argon serves two functions: it is ionized to carry the electric arc, and it protects the torch and the parts being welded from attack by oxygen of the air. This protection at the high temperature of the welding process results from the fact that argon is a chemically inert gas.

An important use for argon is to provide a protective atmosphere around hot or molten met-als, such as titanium, that react readily with oxygen or nitrogen while they are being cast or shaped. In an increasingly important application, dissolved gases are swept out of molten steel by bubbling argon through it; this method provides a higher quality steel product.

Most ordinary electric light bulbs and fluorescent lamps are filled with argon or gas mixtures containing argon. In the ordinary tungsten-filament bulb the main function of the argon is to suppress evaporation of the hot tungsten and thus lengthen the life of the lamp. In the fluorescent lamp the argon is ionized and thus helps to maintain the electric discharge that excites the phosphor on the inside of the tube.

GERHARD A. COOK
Union Carbide Corporation

ARGONAUT, är′gə-nôt, or *paper nautilus,* an 8-armed cephalopod closely related to the octopus and having the same power of swimming backward by forcing water through its funnel. There are six known species of argonauts, and they make up the genus *Argonauta* of the family Argonautidae.

Argonauts are distributed throughout the warmer oceans. The females, which range in length from about 2 to 12 inches (5–30 cm), are about ten times larger than the males. The females, unlike the males, secrete a paper-thin spiral shell each year before mating. This delicate, semitransparent shell serves mainly as an egg case, sheltering the fertilized eggs. It may also serve as a hydrostatic organ, helping the female to float about. Unlike other animal shells, the shell of the argonaut is not connected to the body, and the animal may move out of it any time.

Mating occurs after the female's shell is built. One of the male's very short arms is a modified reproductive organ, the hectocotyle, which releases sperm to fertilize the female's eggs. During mating, the hectocotyle detaches from the male and remains in the female's body. Another hectocotyle is regenerated before the next spawning season. The hectocotyle, having independent powers of locomotion, is believed to be able to seek out a female after it detaches from the male.

GAGE CHASE ALLING

Model of female argonaut (*Argonauta argo*)

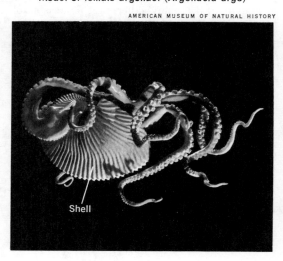

Shell

ARGONAUTS, är′gə-nôts, in Greek legend, the 50 Greek demigods and heroes who sailed the ship *Argo* to Colchis, a kingdom at the eastern end of the Black Sea, in quest of the Golden Fleece. The voyage was supposed to have taken place a generation before the Trojan War (traditionally 1194–1184 B.C.).

The legend appears abundantly in Greek and Latin literature with many variants of personnel and route, since various Greek city-states craved mention of their heroes and their sites in the voyage. It may represent a real exploit in the earlier period of Greek colonization (750–500 B.C.), when the adventures of explorers, navigators, and colonizers were commonly attributed to mythical heroes of a preceding age.

Pelias, who had usurped the Thessalian kingdom of Iolcus, agreed to surrender its sovereignty to Jason, his nephew and the rightful ruler, only if the latter would fetch the Golden Fleece from Colchis, where a dragon guarded it in a sacred grove. Jason accepted the proposal and collected companions from all parts of Greece. The *Argo*, built by Argus, conveyed the Argonauts from Iolcus first to Lemnos, an Aegean isle, where they stayed for a year as welcome guests of the Lemnian women, who recently had murdered all their men.

After additional adventures in the northern Aegean Sea, the Argonauts entered the Sea of Marmara by way of the Dardanelles Strait. Next, they successfully sailed through the Symplegades, clashing rocks that smashed ships attempting to enter the Black Sea. After engaging in other exploits along the Black Sea coasts, the Argonauts came to Colchis, where King Aeëtes promised the Golden Fleece to Jason, provided that in one day he would yoke two fire-breathing bulls to a plow, plow a hitherto unplowed field with them, sow it with the remaining teeth of the dragon of Cadmus, and slay the soldiers who would spring from these seeds. Aided by the magic of Aeëtes' daughter Medea, who had fallen in love with Jason, he accomplished these tasks.

When Aeëtes hesitated to keep his promise, Jason stole the fleece, took Medea and her brother Absyrtus with him, regained the *Argo* with his followers, and sailed for Iolcus. Aeëtes started in pursuit and was overhauling the Argonauts when Medea killed Absyrtus, cut his corpse to pieces, and threw them overboard, so that Aeëtes might be delayed by salvaging his son's scattered remains. The artifice succeeded, and the Argonauts escaped. But Zeus (Jupiter), angered at Medea's murder of Absyrtus, raised a storm that sent the *Argo* on a course that is described variously in different versions of the legend: (1) the same way as it had sailed to Colchis; (2) up the Phasis River (modern Rion) to earth-encircling Ocean, which the Argonauts followed until they entered the Mediterranean; or (3) up the Danube River and thence either into the Po River and the Adriatic Sea or into the Rhine River and the North Sea, whence it traversed the ocean and so came into the Mediterranean. The second and third routes allowed the Argonauts to have adventures on the Mediterranean coasts and islands, where Medea's magical arts assisted them. By any course, however, they returned to Iolcus, and Jason eventually came into his kingdom.

The chief account of the adventures of the Argonauts is in the *Argonautica* of Apollonius of Rhodes. In this work are combined earlier scattered materials into a connected and scholarly epic.

P.R. COLEMAN-NORTON, *Princeton University*

Further Reading: Graves, Robert, *The Greek Myths* (Baltimore, Md., 1955); Graves, Robert, *Hercules, My Shipmate* (New York 1957).

ARGONNE, àr-gôn′, a plateau in France in Meuse, Marne, and southern Ardennes departments. Also known as the *Argonne Forest*, it is a rocky, heavily wooded ridge about 10 miles wide, extending northwest-southeast for about 45 miles between the Lorraine and Champagne regions. It has an average altitude of about 1,150 feet and is drained by the Aisne and Aire rivers.

In 1792, Gen. Charles François Dumouriez checked the Prussians at Valmy in the Argonne. During World War I it was the scene of a major United States offensive in 1918. See WORLD WAR I—7. *Western Front: 1918—The Year of Decision.*

ARGOS, är′gəs, is a city in Greece in the northeastern Peloponnesus. It is located in the *nomos* (department) of Argolis and Corinthia, about 23 miles (37 km) southwest of Corinth, near the head of the Gulf of Argolis. Situated in the Argive plain at the foot of two hills—the Kastro and the Ayios Ilias—Argos is a railroad junction and market center for the surrounding agricultural area. Vegetables, tobacco, wheat, and corn are the leading crops. The modern city is built over the major part of the ancient city. The most important ruins are the remains of an amphitheater cut into the slopes of the Kastro, whose summit served as the acropolis of ancient Argos. The smaller Ayios Ilias was the site of a Mycenaean necropolis and a temple to Apollo and Athena. There is a museum of antiquities in the city.

Argos is reputedly the oldest city in Greece, its site having been occupied since the early Bronze Age (about 3500 B.C.). In the *Iliad* of Homer, its name was applied to all of the settlements on the Argive plain, the country of Diomedes and Agamemnon. After the Dorian invasion (about 1200 B.C.), Argos was probably the base from which the Dorians retained their overlordship of the Peloponnesus. Under King Pheidon (probably 7th century B.C.), who is said to have minted the first Greek coins, Argos became the most important city in Greece. But as the power of Sparta rose, beginning in the late 7th century B.C. and thereafter, Argos declined. It repeatedly aligned itself with Athens (in 461, 420, and 395 B.C.) against Sparta. Argos became a member of the Achaean League in 229 B.C., and, like the other members of that league, was subjugated by Rome in 146 B.C. It was successively part of the Byzantine and Ottoman empires. The city was sacked and burned in 1825 by Ibrahim Pasha in the Greek war of independence. During the war, Argos was the seat of Greek national assemblies in 1821 and 1829. Population: (1961) 16,712.

ARGÜELLO, är-gwä′yō, **Luis Antonio** (1784–1830), Mexican official in Alta California. He was born in San Francisco, Calif. His father, José Darío Argüello, was commandant of the presidio of San Francisco and later governor of Baja California (1815–1822). In 1821, while leading an exploratory expedition to the Columbia River, Luis Argüello discovered Lassen Peak. When Mexico gained independence from Spain, he was elected governor of Alta California (1822–1825), the first native Californian to hold the office. He died in San Francisco in 1830.

ARGUS, är′gəs, was the name of a number of figures in Greek mythology and legend.

One Argus was a giant who, in traditional accounts, had 100 eyes spaced throughout his body, half of which slept while the other half remained watchful. Hera (Juno) was jealous of Io, a favorite of Zeus (Jupiter), and appointed Argus to guard her. To prevent Hera from harming Io, Zeus had transformed Io into a cow. Hermes (Mercury), assigned by Zeus to rescue Io, lulled all of the giant's eyes to sleep with music and then cut off his head. Argus became a peacock or, in another version, his eyes were transplanted by Hera onto the peacock's tail.

Another Argus, the son of Zeus and Niobe, was the mythical ancestor of the Argives, and king of Argos in Greece.

In Greek legend, Argus was the name of the shipbuilder who built the 50-oared ship *Argo* for Jason, and became one of the crew (see ARGONAUTS).

ARGYLL, är-gīl′, is a county of Scotland, situated midway along the west coast. The county, also called *Argyllshire,* is bounded on the west by the Atlantic Ocean and on the southwest by the North Channel. Narrow arms of the sea extend deep into the coastline, cutting it into a fringe of peninsulas bordered by the many islands of the Inner Hebrides, such as Mull, Islay, Jura, Coll, and Tiree. These and other islands comprise about one fourth of the county's total area of 3,110 square miles (8,055 sq km). Argyll is a favorite resort area, noted for the wild beauty of its mountainous mainland as well as for its seacoast.

Agriculture, including sheep and cattle raising, is the basic economic activity. Croplands, where oats and hay are grown, are situated near the coast. There is some mining of coal and quarrying of slate. Other occupations are fishing, forestry, the resort trade, and employment in small plants that manufacture forest products (pulp and mine props), clothing, and pottery. The county town is Inveraray. Other towns are Dunoon, Campbeltown, Oban, Lochgilphead, and Tobermory.

Places of interest include the remains of a monastery on the island of Iona (see IONA) and the basaltic caves, notably Fingal's Cave, on the island of Staffa. The Campbells of Argyll are prominent among noble families of Scottish and British history. Population: (1961) 59,390.

ARGYRODITE, är-jir′ə-dīt, is a rare sulfide mineral in which the metallic element germanium was first detected (1886). The mineral is not, however, a commercially important source of germanium.

Argyrodite occurs in veins of sulfide ores. It has been found in Freiberg, Germany, and in Bolivia. The mineral's black or grayish crystals are tinged with red or violet and have a metallic luster.

Composition: Ag_8GeS_6; hardness, 2 to 3; specific gravity, 6.1 to 6.3; crystal system, isometric.

ARIA, är′ē-ə, a musical term applied to some vocal solos in operas, oratorios, and cantatas. It denotes a song, as distinguished from passages of declamatory recitative. With the emergence of opera in the 17th century, the aria rapidly attained prominence. *Lasciatemi morire* (*Let me die*) from Claudio Monteverdi's *Arianna* (1608) was the first popular operatic aria.

The term "aria" also designates compositions dominated by a single strand of melody, as opposed to contrapuntal works like motets and madrigals. In this sense, however, the term does not apply exclusively to vocal works; for example, Johann Sebastian Bach used it to refer to instrumental works where a single melody is stressed. See also AIR.

Early Forms. The term has no precise formal significance; it has been applied to various forms at different periods. Many early arias were written in simple two-part (binary) form; others were strophic, and when singers embellished the successive verses, the result was an air with variations. Alessandro Scarlatti (1660–1725) did the most to develop the expressive possibilities of the aria in binary form.

When the opening section of an aria is repeated at the end, the result is an *aria da capo,* a form that enjoyed great popularity in the early 18th century. Handel, who wrote hundreds of *da capo* arias, achieved a wide variety of effects within this form. In Handel's *da capo* arias the contrasting middle sections often bear some musical relationship to the repeated sections. Singers once were expected to add their own embellishments to the repetitions.

In Handel's day, arias had such special names as *aria di cantabile* (a sustained melody), *di portamento* (long-held notes linked by the singer), *di bravura* (runs, trills, and other ornaments), and *d'imitazione* (the phrases of the vocal line "answer" the same or similar phrases in the accompaniment). These terms, now outmoded, usually described different styles of *da capo* arias. The only one still somewhat current is *aria di bravura;* its equivalent in English is *coloratura aria.*

Later Forms. During the early 19th century other terms were introduced, such as *cavatina, canzone, romanza,* and *rondò.* These terms were used loosely. *Rondò* refers to airs with variations sung by prima donnas at the end of an opera; a famous example concludes Rossini's *Cenerentola.* It does not denote the *rondo* form used by Haydn and Mozart. *Cavatina* often describes a broad, expansive melody, yet Rossini calls *Largo al factotum,* Figaro's patter song in *The Barber of Seville,* a *cavatina.* French and German composers adopted these terms, but the French added *couplets*—a strophic song with refrain, such as the *Toreador Song* from Bizet's *Carmen.*

Wagner developed operas in which each act is a continuous musical fabric. His practice deemphasizes arias, because each episode of the opera flows directly into the succeeding one. Although Puccini imbedded arias in a continuous musical context, he usually ended them in such a way that applause would not greatly disrupt the continuity.

WILLIAM ASHBROOK, *Author of "Donizetti"*

ARIADNE, ar-ē-ad′nē, in Greek legend, was the daughter of Minos, king of Crete. Her lover, Theseus, killed the dreaded Minotaur—half man, half bull—which was confined in a labyrinth under the palace at Knossos, Crete. To find his way out, he followed a thread, given to him by Ariadne, which he had trailed behind on his way into the maze. Theseus took Ariadne to the island of Naxos, where he deserted her. Bacchus (Dionysus) found her and married her. Ariadne was a favorite subject of painting.

ARIANISM, âr'ē-ə-niz-əm, is the common designation for the teachings of Arius (about 265–356) and his followers, which deny the divinity of Christ. It had its roots in Greek theological speculation beginning with Gnosticism and may be regarded as an elaborate attempt to define the relation of Christ to God according to natural reason (see CHRISTOLOGY). Centered in Alexandria and Antioch, it was one of the most formidable challenges to orthodoxy in the history of the Christian church. During the greater part of the 4th century, its most flourishing period, it enjoyed the strong support of the Roman emperors and had a special appeal for the intelligentsia.

Doctrine. The basic doctrine of Arius may be summarized as follows: (1) God is unique and unbegotten (*agennetos*), and everything outside of God was created *from nothing* by the will of God. (2) The Logos (Word)–Christ–is an intermediary between God and the world. He was before time, but not eternal. *There was a time when the Word did not exist.* (3) The Word therefore was *created.* He was made (*genetos*). If it is said that He was born, begotten (*gennetos*), this is to be understood in terms of an adoptive sonship. (4) The incarnate Word (Christ), consequently, is inferior to God but is to be worshiped, since He is exalted above all other creatures and is both Ruler and Redeemer.

History. Arianism from the first was a fully developed doctrine. Hence, its history is the story of attenuations in the direction of orthodoxy and return to the original tenets of the church.

The Council of Nicaea (325) condemned the teaching of Arius and declared that the Son was of the same substance (*homoousios*, consubstantial) with the Father. However, Eusebius of Nicomedia, although he signed the formula of Nicaea, soon repudiated it. Through influence at the imperial court, he secured the recall of Arius from exile and the deposition of Athanasius of Alexandria, the leading champion of the Nicene definition. Eusebius represented a rigid form of Arianism. By the middle of the 4th century there were three main groups of Arians, all seeking and in part obtaining imperial support under Constantius II. The first group consisted of uncompromising Arians who maintained that the Son was unlike the Father (*anomoios*) and are called Anomoeans. The second group proclaimed in a Synod of Ancyra (358) that the Son is like in substance with the Father (*homoiousios*) and are called Homoeousians or Semi-Arians. The third group rejected the terms *homoousios, homoiousios,* and *ousia,* and maintained simply that the Son was like the Father. The position of the third group was not very different from that of the second.

The Homoeousians or Semi-Arians tended toward orthodoxy and were well received by Athanasius at the Council of Alexandria in 362. The Cappadocian Fathers, furthermore, showed that the doctrinal problem involved could be solved by recognizing *one nature* and three persons (*hypostases*). Despite the fanatical opposition of the Arian emperor Valens, Nicaean orthodoxy triumphed in the West and moved toward final victory in the East. The whole East subscribed to doctrines pronounced at Rome in 378 and 379, and the emperor Theodosius was an ardent champion of the Nicaean Faith.

The Synod of Constantinople (381), later recognized as the Second Ecumenical Council, reaffirmed the Nicene Creed with slight changes, thus completing the victory of Nicaea in favor of the full divinity of the Son. Arianism was soon suppressed within the empire, but it prevailed for a long time among the barbarians. The conversion of Clovis, king of the Franks, to the orthodox faith in 496 was followed by a decline of Arianism among the Teutonic peoples.

EDWIN KNOX MITCHELL
Revised by MARTIN R.P. McGUIRE
The Catholic University of America

ARIAS, ä'ryäs, **Arnulfo** (1897–   ), president of Panama. He was born into one of Central America's most powerful families. He studied at the University of Chicago and graduated from Harvard Medical School but immediately retired from medicine to enter the diplomatic service.

In 1931 he aided his brother, Harmodio Arias, in the revolt that placed Harmodio in the presidency. Arnulfo was made ambassador to Italy and, thereafter, to France and Britain. He was elected president in 1939 but was deposed in a bloodless coup in October 1941. During his year in office he switched from the Liberal to the Conservative party and rewrote the constitution on authoritarian lines. Adjudged a fascist sympathizer by the succeeding regime, he was exiled from 1941 to 1945. In 1949 he seized the presidency in a coup but was overthrown by a revolution 18 months later and barred by the National Assembly from seeking further office. Elected president again in 1968, he was overthrown in a military coup after only 10 days in office.

ARIAS, ä'ryäs, **Harmodio** (1886–1962), Panamanian lawyer, publisher, and political leader, who was patriarch of his country's most powerful family and president of Panama (1932–1936).

Arias was born in Panama on July 3, 1886, and was educated in England. After taking a law degree at London University, he became a successful lawyer and legal expert in Panama. He served on several constitutional commissions and was a delegate to the League of Nations. In the 1920's he was minister to Argentina and the United States. At the onset of an economic depression in 1931, he led a Panama City uprising that deposed President Florencio Arosemena. Arias became provisional president that year and served a four-year term, from 1932 to 1936. Thereafter he continued to influence Panama's politics as publisher of the nation's two largest newspapers. He died of a heart attack while on a flight from Boston to Panama on Dec. 23, 1962.

ARICA, ä-rē'kä, is a seaport city in northern Chile, on the Pacific Ocean, just south of the border of Peru. It lies at the edge of the Atacama Desert and has virtually no rainfall. Water is piped 150 miles (240 km) from the Andes Mountains. Arica is on the Pan American Highway and is the terminus of railroads from La Paz, Bolivia, and Tacna, Peru. The port carries a major share of the trade of Bolivia.

Formerly a part of Peru, the city was occupied by Chile during the War of the Pacific (1879–1883). The Treaty of Ancón, ending the war, stipulated that the Tacna-Arica area should remain under Chilean control for 10 years, after which a plebiscite would determine its permanent possession by Chile or Peru. The plebiscite was never held, but in 1929 a settlement awarded Arica to Chile and Tacna to Peru. Population: (1960) 43,344.

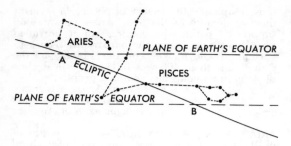

ARIES, one of the constellations of the zodiac, in ancient Grecian times marked the vernal equinox—the point (A) at which the sun's path through the heavens (ecliptic) crosses the plane of the earth's equator. Subsequent shifting (precession) of the equinoctial point now places the vernal equinox in constellation Pisces (B).

ARIES ar′ē-ēz, is a winter constellation of the Northern Hemisphere and the first sign of the zodiac. In Greek mythology, Aries was the ram that carried Phrixus across the Hellespont; its fleece became the Golden Fleece sought by the Argonauts.

The constellation is not conspicuous and contains no bright stars, but it has historical interest. When the ancient Greeks divided the ecliptic (the sun's apparent annual path among the stars) into the signs of the zodiac, the vernal equinox was in Aries. The vernal equinox, which occurs about March 21, is one of the two points where the ecliptic crosses the plane of the earth's equator. (The other point is the autumnal equinox.) Due to the slow "wobbling" of the earth's axis, known as precession, the position of the vernal equinox has shifted since Grecian times and is now in the constellation Pisces. Nevertheless, it is still called the *First Point of Aries,* although it will not return to the constellation Aries for another 22,000 years. See also EQUINOX.

ARION, ə-rī′ən, was a Greek lyric poet and musician of the 7th century B.C. He was born at Methymna, on the island of Lesbos, and lived most of his life at the court of Periander, tyrant of Corinth, where he demonstrated great skill with the lyre. According to Herodotus, Arion made a journey to Sicily, took part in a music competition there, won first prize, and was given many valuable gifts. On his return trip to Corinth, the sailors of his ship plotted to throw him overboard and seize his treasures. Arion's request to sing one last song was granted. His singing and playing of the lyre attracted a school of dolphins. When Arion jumped into the sea, he was rescued by a dolphin, which carried him home.

According to Herodotus and others, Arion was the inventor of the dithyramb, the ode in honor of Dionysus. However, his contribution probably lay in transforming an ancient ritual song into a formal literary work and in teaching choruses to perform it. Arion's name has been linked to the origins of tragedy, probably because of his significant contribution to the form of the dithyramb, which is regarded by many scholars as the first step in the creation of tragic drama. None of Arion's work survives.

LILLIAN FEDER
Queens College, The City University of New York

ARIOSTO, ä-rē-ôs′tō, **Ludovico** (1474–1533), Italian poet, who wrote *Orlando furioso,* the most celebrated narrative poem of the Italian high Renaissance.

Life. Ariosto was born in Reggio Emilia on Sept. 8, 1474. His father wanted him to study law, but Ariosto followed his own preference and studied literature instead. When his father died in 1500, Ludovico, the eldest of 10 children, had to support the family. In 1503 he was employed as a diplomatic attaché by Ippolito I, Cardinal d'Este. In Florence, in 1513, Ariosto met Alessandra Benucci who, after the death of her husband Tito Strozzi, became Ariosto's mistress and, in 1527, his wife.

Ariosto was unhappy in the service of Cardinal d'Este, chiefly because he had to spend so much time away from Ferrara, where he had settled. In 1517, after refusing to accompany the cardinal to Hungary, he entered the service of Alfonso I, duke of Ferrara, who was the cardinal's brother and Lucrezia Borgia's husband. In 1522 the duke sent him to govern the bandit-ridden Garfagnana region in the rugged Apuan Alps. After three years he returned to Ferrara, where he died on July 6, 1533.

Orlando Furioso. The romantic epic had long been popular at the court of Ferrara, which, in Ariosto's day, was still enthralled by the adventures and loves of Orlando (Roland in the medieval French epic) in Matteo Boiardo's uncompleted poem *Orlando innamorato.* In 1506, Ariosto began his continuation of Orlando's adventures in a new poem, *Orlando furioso,* first published in 1516 and revised in 1521 and 1532.

Boiardo had combined the epic, Carolingian tradition with the romantic, Arthurian tradition by changing the austere hero of the epic into a love-tormented knight. Ariosto went further. He had his Orlando go mad (*furioso*) because his love for the beautiful Angelica was not returned. The three main themes in *Orlando furioso* are (1) the wars between the Christians (led by Charlemagne) and the Saracens (led by Agramante); (2) the adventures of Orlando; and (3) the adventures, love, and marriage of the amazon Bradamante and the knight Ruggiero, the legendary ancestors of the Este family.

The poem is both comic and tragic, and achieves a successful blend of the real and the fantastic. Ariosto's narrative touch is sure, and his use of *ottava rima* skillful. *Orlando furioso* had a profound influence on such later poets as Tasso, Sidney, Spenser, and Lope de Vega.

Other Writings. Ariosto imitated the Latin plays of Plautus and Terence in his five comedies —*La Cassaria* (1508), *I suppositi* (1509), *Il negromante* (1520), *La Lena* (1528), and the unfinished *I studenti.* His plays had no great literary merit, but they inaugurated a vogue for classical comedy in the Renaissance. He also wrote seven *Satires,* beginning in 1514. These poems, in *terza rima,* are autobiographical.

CHARLES SPERONI, *Author of*
"Wit and Wisdom of the Italian Renaissance"

Bibliography
Texts of *Orlando furioso* in English include a poetic version by William S. Rose, 8 vols. (London 1823–31) and a prose version by Allan H. Gilbert (New York 1954). Selections from Sir John Harington's translation (1591) were edited by Rudolf Gottfried (Bloomington, Ind., 1963).
Croce, Benedetto, *Ariosto, Shakespeare and Corneille,* tr. from the Italian by Douglas Ainslie (London 1920).
Gardner, Edmund G., *The King of Court Poets* (New York 1906).

ARISTA, ä-rēs′tä, **Mariano** (1802–1855), Mexican soldier and political leader. He was born at San Luis Potosí on July 26, 1802. In 1820–1821, during Mexico's war for independence, he fought for the forces loyal to Spain. During the anarchy following the war he favored the moderate factions. He fought for Antonio López de Santa Anna in 1832 but went into exile after Santa Anna came to power in 1833. He returned in 1836, after Santa Anna was deposed.

Arista commanded the Mexican army defeated by Gen. Zachary Taylor at Palo Alto on May 8, 1846. From 1848 to 1851 he was minister of war in the administration of José Herrera. Arista was elected president on Jan. 15, 1851. Economic troubles and a conservative reaction to his moderate reforms led to his overthrow on Jan. 4, 1853. In exile again, he fell off a ship and drowned near Lisbon, Portugal, on Aug. 7, 1855.

ARISTAEUS, ar-ə-stē′əs, in Greek mythology, was the son of Apollo and the nymph Cyrene. As a god, he was worshiped as the protector of flocks and the originator of olive culture and beekeeping. He married Autonoë, daughter of Cadmus. When he declared his love for Eurydice, wife of Orpheus, she fled from him, was bitten by a snake, and died. His bees then died, but by propitiating the Dryads, Eurydice's companions, he was able to revive the bees.

ARISTAGORAS, ar-ə-stag′ō-rəs, was the regent of Miletus, an Ionian city in Asia Minor, about 500 B.C. He ruled in the absence of Histiaeus, tyrant of Miletus, who was forcibly detained at the court of Darius I of Persia. With Persian support, Aristagoras undertook to add the island of Naxos to his rule, but the attempt failed. Seeking to avoid punishment for his failure, he incited other Ionian cities in Asia Minor to revolt with him against Persia. He was unsuccessful in his bid for help from Sparta, but with the support of Athens and Eretria he attacked and burned Sardis in 499 B.C. He failed to take the citadel, however, and was driven off by the Persians. He afterward emigrated to Thrace, where he was killed by the Thracians.

ARISTARCHUS, ar-ə-stär′kəs (c. 217–c. 143 B.C.), Greek grammarian and critic who was a pioneer in literary scholarship. He was born in Samothrace and at an early age moved to Alexandria. He studied there under Aristophanes of Byzantium and later became librarian at Alexandria. His editions of the *Iliad* and the *Odyssey*, based on painstaking critical studies, have survived. Only fragments of his many other critical studies are extant. He died in Cyprus.

ARISTARCHUS OF SAMOS, ar-ə-stär′kəs, sā′mos, was a Greek astronomer of the 3d century B.C. He was the chief exponent of the heliocentric theory of the universe—that the sun stands still and the earth and the rest of the universe revolve around it. Because of this belief he was accused of impiety. He is supposed to have written extensively on astronomy, but all that survives is a short essay on the sizes of the sun and the moon and his estimates of their distances from each other and from the earth. He was the first to attempt to work out this problem by trigonometry. Though his theory was sound, his estimates were inaccurate because he did not have accurate instruments.

ARISTIDES, ar-ə-stīd′ēz (c. 530–c. 468 B.C.), was an Athenian aristocrat, statesman, and general. A selfless individual whose chief concern was the welfare of Athens, he achieved a reputation for justice and fairness and was commonly called Aristides the Just. He played a major role in the Greek defeat of the Persians in the Persian Wars and subsequently was instrumental in founding the Delian confederacy to keep the Persians in check.

Little is heard of Aristides before 490 B.C., the year in which he served as a general at Marathon. He probably distinguished himself in battle, for in the following year he was elected to the post of *archon eponymous* (see ARCHON). Except for a brief interval, he played a major role in Athenian politics for more than a decade thereafter. He was not a radical democrat, although he was one of several spokesmen for the anti-Persian faction. Aristides probably cooperated with Themistocles in 487/486 in supporting legislation that changed the method of choosing archons from election to selection by lot. The legislation also transferred military authority from the *archon polemarch* to an elected *strategos,* or general. Although both men represented the anti-Persian faction, Aristides bitterly opposed Themistocles a few years later when the latter advocated a strong navy. As a result of his opposition he was ostracized in 482, but was allowed to return to the city two years later under a general amnesty.

In 480, during the second phase of the Persian Wars, he was one of the ten generals elected to lead the fight against the Persians. In this capacity he cooperated fully with Themistocles. He was present at the Battle of Salamis and led an Athenian force to the island of Psyttaleia, where he defeated a Persian garrison. He was reelected general in the following year, and in 479 commanded the Athenian army in the final battle of the war at Plataea, in which the Persians were driven from Greek soil. In 478/477 he served as Athenian naval commander and convinced many Greek states in the Aegean islands and on the Asia Minor mainland that it was to their advantage to cast their lot with Athens rather than with Sparta. About 477 these states joined with Athens in founding the Delian League to present a united front against further Persian attack.

Aristides attended the first meeting of the Delian League as the Athenian representative. He was held in such high esteem by the representatives of the other states that he was entrusted with the task of determining how much each of the participating states ought to contribute to the common defense. It was his task also to decide which states ought to make their contribution in cash and which in ships. The total assessment of 460 talents was so fairly and justly distributed by Aristides that it remained in effect with little or no change at least until the middle of the 5th century.

Nothing is heard of Aristides after the year 477, but he appears to have remained influential in Athenian politics. He was a supporter of Cimon, who succeeded him as the leading figure in the Delian League, and he may have cooperated with him to secure the ostracism of Themistocles about 470.

THOMAS KELLY, *University of Alberta*

Further Reading: "Aristides," in Plutarch, *Lives* (any ed.).

ARISTIDES, ar-is-tī'dēz, **Marcianus,** Greek philosopher of the 2d century A.D., who was considered to be the first Christian apologist. His name is also spelled *Aristeides*. He was known as *Aristides of Athens*. Nothing is known about his life except that he taught philosophy at Athens and composed the earliest extant defense of Christianity, the *Apology of Aristides*. Written in Greek, the *Apology* may have been written to Emperor Antoninus Pius about 139.

The *Apology* was long considered lost, but in 1878 an edition of an Armenian fragment appeared at Venice. This was followed in 1889 by James Rendel Harris' discovery of a complete Syriac version in a monastery on Mount Sinai. Publication of this translation at Cambridge, England, in 1891 led to the discovery that a Greek text of the treatise had existed for centuries in the religious romance *Barlaam and Josaphat* (q.v.). Two portions of the Greek text were published in London in 1922 and 1924.

The *Apology* is brief, simple, and objective, but written in a lofty tone. It discusses the errors of Greeks, Chaldeans, Egyptians, and Jews concerning God, gives a summary of a seemingly primitive Christian belief, and emphasizes the righteousness of Christianity in contrast with the corrupt practices of paganism. Aristides seeks to demonstrate the reasonableness of Christianity by an appeal to facts.

P.R. COLEMAN-NORTON, *Princeton University*

Further Reading: The Syriac version of the *Apology of Aristides* is edited and translated into English by J. Rendel Harris (2d ed., Cambridge, Eng. 1893); the Greek fragments are in *The Oxyrhynchus Papyri*, ed. by Bernard P. Grenfell and Arthur S. Hunt (London 1922).

ARISTIDES OF MILETUS, ar-is-tī'dēz, mī-lē'təs, Greek writer who lived in the last half of the 2d century B.C. His name is also spelled *Aristeides*. Nothing is known of his life except that he was probably a native of the Ionian city of Miletus, where he wrote or compiled a collection, now lost, called *Milesian Tales* (q.v.). Considered the earliest examples of prose romance in Greek, they were translated into Latin by Lucius Cornelius Sisenna (120?–67 B.C.) and often were imitated by later Roman writers.

ARISTIDES QUINTILIANUS, ar-is-tī'dēz kwin-til-ē-ā'nəs, Greek musicologist of the 3d century A.D. His name is also spelled *Aristeides*. He lived in Smyrna (now İzmir, Turkey). His three-book treatise, which describes in detail six musical scales used by the Greeks, is the most valuable extant work on ancient Greek music. The best edition of the treatise is Heinrich Albert Jahn's *Aristidis Quintiliani de musica libri tres* (1882).

ARISTIPPUS (c. 435–c. 360 B.C.), ar-is-tip'əs, was a Greek philosopher who founded the Cyrenaic school. Born at Cyrene, Cyrenaica, he went to Syracuse where he taught rhetoric and was an attendant at the court of Dionysius the Elder, tyrant of Syracuse. He later went to Athens and became a student of Socrates.

Aristippus' school of Cyrenaics believed that all human sensations are reducible to two emotions, pleasure and pain. The highest good is pleasure, and virtue is the ability to enjoy pleasure and to avoid pain. Happiness is simply a continued pleasure, composed of separate—preferably immediate—gratifications. See also CYRENAICS; HEDONISM.

ARISTOBULUS, ə-ris-tə-bū'ləs, was the name of at least seven kings, princes, or high priests of the Jewish family of Hasmonaeans (less correctly called Maccabees, q.v.) in Palestine. The following were important:

ARISTOBULUS I (c. 140–103 B.C.) was a high priest and king of Judaea. He was also called *Judah*. Son of John Hyrcanus, he was the fifth successive Hasmonaean leader. After his father's death he imprisoned and murdered his mother, to whom his father had willed the government of Judaea. He did the same to most of his brothers and then took the title of king (reigned 104–103 B.C.), becoming the first king of the Jews since the Babylonian captivity. Aristobulus favored the Greeks in Judaea, supported the Sadducees, and conquered Galilee, where he Judaized the Ituraeans.

ARISTOBULUS II (died 48 B.C.) was a high priest and king of Judaea. He was the son of Alexander Jannaeus (Janneus), king of Judaea (reigned 103–76) and the nephew of Aristobulus I. Salome Alexandra, who was the widow of both his uncle and his father, became regent in 76. She appointed Aristobulus high priest and named as king his brother Hyrcanus II. But the brothers began a civil war in 67, when Aristobulus deposed Hyrcanus. Aided by Aretas III, king of Arabia Petraea, Hyrcanus besieged Aristobulus in Jerusalem until Pompey the Great intervened in 63, stormed Jerusalem, established Hyrcanus as ethnarch, and sent Aristobulus to Rome. In 57, Aristobulus escaped and returned to Judaea, where he renewed the war. Recaptured, he was again shipped to Rome. But Julius Caesar released him in 49 and selected him to superintend his anti-Pompeian interests in Judaea. There Aristobulus succumbed to poison administered by Pompey's adherents.

ARISTOBULUS (52–35 B.C.) was a high priest and prince of Judaea. He was the grandson of Aristobulus II and the brother-in-law of Herod the Great, king of Judaea. His mother, Alexandra, was indignant because Herod had bestowed the Jewish high priesthood on another. She endeavored to obtain office for Aristobulus through the influence of Cleopatra on Mark Antony, who was then the supreme Roman authority in the Middle East. Herod accepted Aristobulus as high priest in 36 B.C.; but he soon suspected Alexandra's and her son's ambition and arranged that the boy should be drowned. Aristobulus was the last Hasmonaean high priest.

ARISTOBULUS (died 6 B.C.) was a prince of Judaea. He was the son of Herod the Great and the father of Herod Agrippa I (Julius Agrippa I), who became king of Judaea, and of the infamous Herodias. From 23 to 17 B.C., Aristobulus was educated in Rome under the superintendence of Gaius Asinius Pollio, a patron of artists and authors. Soon after his return to Judaea, Aristobulus, whom Herod apparently had appointed his heir, became involved in his family's intrigues against Herod. He was accused three times of treason, but was absolved twice. On the third occasion he was tried by a royal council, which condemned him *in absentia*. Herod sentenced him to die by strangulation, and he was executed at Sebaste, in Samaria.

ARISTOBULUS was king of Chalcis and of Armenia Minor from 52 to about 75 A.D. He was the grandson of the preceding Aristobulus and the son of Herod of Chalcis. He received from the Romans his father's kingdom of Chalcis in

Coele-Syria in 52, after the Romans had removed its ruler, his cousin Herod Agrippa II (Marcus Julius Agrippa II), governor of Chalcis since 50. In 55, Nero, the Roman emperor, made Aristobulus king of Armenia Minor also, in order to secure that district as a buffer against Parthia. In 61, Nero enlarged Aristobulus' domain by adding part of Greater Armenia to it. The last certain notice of him is in 72, when he assisted the Romans in their war against Antiochus IV Epiphanes, king of Commagene. Aristobulus was married to Salome, who brought about the death of John the Baptist.

See also MACCABEES, THE.

P.R. COLEMAN-NORTON, *Princeton University*

Further Reading: Bickerman, Elias, *The Maccabees*, tr. by Moses Hadas (New York 1947); Finkelstein, Louis, *The Jews: Their History, Culture, and Religion*, 3d ed. (New York 1960); Mindlin, Valerie, and Cornfeld, Gaalyahu, *The Epic of the Maccabees* (New York 1962).

ARISTOCRACY, ar-ə-stok′rə-sē, in its original meaning in Western culture, meant the rule of the best citizens in the interest of all. The word comes from Greek (*aristos*, best) and was used in its original sense by Plato in the *Republic* and by Aristotle in the *Politics*. More generally, however, the term came to signify any system of government in which the right to govern is vested in a small privileged class. When the actions of this class are determined by selfish or corrupt motives, the form of government is termed an *oligarchy*, which Aristotle considered a natural corruption of the pure aristocratic form.

By extension, the term "aristocracy" is also used as the collective designation of the leading persons of a state (the patricians or nobles) or of those regarded as superior in rank, talent, intellect, or wealth. Both from its strict political meaning and from the fact that most aristocracies have been hereditary, the term has taken on the secondary significance of any hereditary caste that has claimed or has been accorded a superior rank.

The democratic principle of government stands in opposition to the aristocratic, and since the 18th century—the period of the Enlightenment and the French Revolution—the trend in the West has been toward the democratic and away from the aristocratic. Thus today the term "aristocracy" is used generally in a social, rather than political, sense.

In the Ancient World. In Greece the aristocracy originated in the Mycenaean period (about 1400–1200 B.C.) on a military basis. By Homeric times (about 1000–800 B.C.) it consisted of a hereditary landowning class, but gradually came to include those whose position was founded on other forms of wealth. Sparta, where only the Spartiates enjoyed full citizenship, was the most aristocratic of the Greek city-states. In Athens the aristocratic complexion of the government was altered progressively by democratic reforms in the course of the 6th century B.C.

Much of the history of the Roman republic recounts the struggle between the patricians and the plebeians. Citizenship, at first limited to the former, was extended to include plebeian property owners. Then, in 494 B.C., the office of tribune was established to curb the power of the patrician magistrates. Although public office was still a patrician privilege, the basis of citizenship was further extended in 471 B.C. Gradually, during the 4th century, the various offices were opened to plebeian candidates.

Meanwhile, however, new restrictions were imposed. These limited public offices to members of families, either patrician or plebeian, that had held office in the past. But as Rome expanded in the Mediterranean, a new wealthy class was created, and eventually it merged with the old aristocracy to form a new upper class, the *optimates*, which, under the leadership of Lucius Cornelius Sulla, fought the *populares* led by Gaius Marius in the 1st century B.C. The aristocratic party was finally defeated in 42 B.C., at the Battle of Philippi, where the forces of Mark Antony and Octavian (later Augustus) crushed the armies of Cassius and Brutus.

Transition to Modern Times. Although medieval feudalism in Europe involved the existence of privileged classes, the dominant characteristic of the system was a graduated hierarchy of absolute rulers. But with the breakup of feudalism, the formation of the Italian communes, and the subordination of the French and English petty lords to the king, the nobles again assumed power by virtue of their membership in a privileged class rather than by virtue of their territorial rule. Thus, in Italy, each commune was governed by a small group of minor nobles whose seats were in the surrounding countryside, and by a group of wealthy merchants whose establishments were in the town. Gradually, however, the power of the aristocracy in the communal governments was challenged by the growing middle class as well as by the lesser artisans. In the end, this struggle led to the establishment of hereditary rule by a single family, such as the Visconti in Milan and the Medici in Florence, and the loss of political power by the upper class. Only in Venice did a wealthy oligarchy retain actual power, until the dissolution of the republic in 1797.

Elsewhere in Europe, when a weak monarch or dynasty succeeded to the throne, as was the case with the house of Valois in France, it became easy for vigorous noble families to assume real control of the state. In France the power of the nobles was eventually crushed in the 17th century in the course of the nobles' rebellion known as the Fronde, during the minority of Louis XIV, after which the nobles were reduced to the role of mere courtiers.

In Britain, from the "glorious Revolution" of 1688 onward, and particularly after the accession of the Hanoverian dynasty to the throne in 1714, the government was generally controlled by the great Whig families. In the course of the 19th century, with the gradual extension of the franchise, government became democratized, and in 1911 the power of the House of Lords was sharply curtailed. The British aristocracy, however, still retains a measure of political power. Not only do members of noble families stand as candidates for seats in the House of Commons and become members of the cabinet, but they also fill many positions in the civil service.

Until 1918 the aristocratic system of rule survived to the greatest degree in central and eastern Europe, notably in Germany, Austria-Hungary, and Russia. In the German empire the great landowning families, the Junkers, formed a military caste on which Prussian, and imperial, power was based. See also GOVERNMENT—*Classifications of Governments.*

ARISTOGITON. See HARMODIUS AND ARISTOGITON.

ARISTOPHANES (c.450–c.385 B.C.) ar-is-tof'a-nēz, was the most important Greek comic dramatist and one of the greatest comic playwrights of all ages. Little is known about his life except that he was of Athenian parentage and either lived or owned land on Aegina, an island near Athens in the Saronic Gulf.

Aristophanes composed about 55 comedies, of which only 11 plays and about 985 fragments remain. Of his work for the Attic state festivals honoring Dionysus (Bacchus), the Greek god of wine, 4 plays achieved the first award, 3 took second place, and 1 received third place.

Aristophanes was the leading Athenian playwright of Old Comedy (c.485–c.400), treating fantastic subjects, burlesquing mythological concepts, and caricaturing everyday life, while aiming personal and often obscene abuse against contemporary politicians and other notable persons. However, Aristophanes also stood among the earlier masters of Middle Comedy (c.400–c.320), which diminished choral activity, paid less attention to obscenity, introduced a greater number of lyric passages, developed intrigue and love interest, emphasized the burlesque of mythological subjects, parodied tragic themes, and more realistically depicted commonplace existence.

Aristophanes' comedies are valuable aids to an appreciation of the Athenian culture of the late 5th century B.C., when Athens' participation in the Peloponnesian War affected Hellenic civilization as much as World War I influenced 20th century life and manners. But the reader must cautiously weigh the criticisms of a poet whose main purpose was to make people laugh. Aristophanes' writing is flavored with coarse invective, conservative prejudice, championship of rural life, animosity toward urban society, irresponsible lampoonery, and inconsistent buffoonery. Utilizing satire, he denounced new trends in education, literature, music, theology, philosophy, science, and politics, and he denounced or ridiculed personalities behind these innovations.

Plays. *The Acharnians* (425) is the first extant comedy and, like many of its successors, is named for its chorus. It deals with the fancy of a militant pacifist who constructs a private peace for himself while his state is at war. *The Knights* (424) assails Cleon, the radical demagogue, and confronts him with Agoracritus the sausage seller, a scurrilous ruffian. *The Clouds* (423) grossly caricatures Socrates as the representative of sophistry, atheism, and the new education, with the chorus of clouds symbolizing the mistiness of new thought. *The Wasps* (422) satirizes the huge popular courts buzzing with 500 to 2,000 jurors, who irresponsibly judge both law and fact according to their pleasure and the orators' persuasiveness. The play has many scenes of pure farce, as it depicts the conduct of cases in a court that has been instituted in a private house. *The Peace* (421) further develops pacifist protest against the Peloponnesian War by showing how farmers and other persons of good will extricate the personified Peace, who has been buried out of sight, and marry her to their leader, who has ascended to heaven on a beetle in order to find a way of ending the war. *The Birds* (414) sought to discourage the disastrous Athenian expedition to Sicily that took place at the time. The birds, who are the Athenians, are persuaded to construct the celestial city of Cloudcuckootown, which will sever the gods from connection with men and

F.E. WESTLAKE FROM NATIONAL AUDUBON SOCIETY
ARISTOLOCHIA, the genus of birthworts, commonly is represented by Dutchman's pipe, A. durior (above). It is a climber with yellow and brownish-purple flowers.

ARISTOLOCHIA, a-ris-tə-lō'kē-ə, is a group of perennial, erect, climbing or twining herbs or shrubs that are widely distributed in tropical and temperate regions. *Aristolochia* is noted for its peculiar flowers in which the inner circle of the floral envelope is missing and the outer circle is tubular and twisted, with spreading lips. The tropical members often have very large flowers. However, they are infrequently cultivated because of their lurid colors and bad odors.

Pollination of *Aristolochia* is carried out by flies that are attracted to the flowers and are entrapped until the pollen is shed. They then are released to fly to another blossom with the pollen on their bodies.

The genus *Aristolochia* belongs to the family Aristolochiaceae; most of its 300 species are tropical. The best-known species is *A. durior,* the Dutchman's pipe, which is native to eastern North America and is widely cultivated. It has large kidney-shaped or rounded leaves and small U-shaped flowers with purplish lips. Other species are *A. grandiflora,* the pelican flower, which is a climbing shrub native to Jamaica; *A. elegans,* calico flower, found in Brazil; *A. clematitis,* the birthwort, found in Europe.

Another species is *A. serpentaria,* the Virginia snakeroot, whose roots reputedly furnish a remedy for snakebite.

restore the birds as sovereigns over the earth.

Lysistrata (411) again assails the war, by demonstrating how the women plot to bring about peace by denying their husbands sexual relations during the war's duration. *The Thesmophoriazusae* (411) is a licentious portrayal of women celebrating Demeter's (Ceres') festival. It ends as a satire against Euripides, and condemns him for the misogyny in his tragedies. *The Frogs* (405) shows Dionysus searching in Hades for a tragic poet, since those on earth are worthless. Aeschylus contends with Euripides in a literary contest in which they exchange well-known verses and parodies. Aeschylus wins and returns with Dionysus, who seats Sophocles on the tragic throne of Hades during Aeschylus' temporary absence. Euripides is contemptuously dismissed. *The Ecclesiazusae* (393 or 391) portrays the Athenian women's seizure of the popular assembly (ecclesia) and the establishment of communism and of a community of wives, thus parodying the political theories found in Plato's *Republic*. *The Plutus* (388) tells how Plutus (Ploutus), the blind god of wealth, regains his sight by incubation in a temple of Asclepius (Aesculapius), the god of medicine, and shows the comic consequences when Plutus then visits only honest men. This is the last extant play of Aristophanes, and it has no chorus. An earlier edition (c. 408) is supposed to have had political allusions to the riches which Alcibiades' naval victories restored to Athens.

Criticism. Aristophanes' genius has many facets. His choral passages win him a high place among poets. As a dramatist, he is superb in caricature, parody, travesty, burlesque, wit, pun, farce, and invention of comic situations. Since he is an intellectual playwright, his comedies have little humor emanating from the emotions. Hampered by the theatrical tradition of his time,

BUST OF ARISTOPHANES, in National Museum, Naples.

his plots are weak in construction, and his characters, though brilliant as types, lack individuality.

No formal translation can recreate the atmosphere of an Aristophanic comedy—the cumulative hilarity of the exuberant rush of puns,

CHORUS OF "THE BIRDS" by Aristophanes, as produced by the Ypsilanti Greek Theatre in Ypsilanti, Mich.

surprises, and topical allusions. Only an impressionistic and viva-voce version, compact with up-to-date analogies and equivalents, can approximate Aristophanes' effects; but such a rendition, if printed, almost at once loses its flavor and becomes more obsolete than the original plays themselves. See also BIRDS, THE; CLOUDS, THE; FROGS, THE.

PAUL SHOREY
Author of "Platonism, Ancient and Modern"
Revised by P.R. COLEMAN-NORTON
Princeton University

Bibliography

Greek texts of the plays, with English translation by Benjamin B. Robers, were published in *Aristophanes*, 3 vols. (London 1924).
Croiset, Maurice, *Aristophanes and the Political Parties at Athens*, tr. by James Loeb (London 1909).
Ehrenberg, Victor, *The People of Aristophanes*, 2d ed. (Cambridge, Mass., 1951).
Lord, Louis E., *Aristophanes: His Plays and His Influence* (New York 1925).
Murray, Gilbert, *Aristophanes: A Study* (New York 1933).
Whitman, Cedric H., *Aristophanes and the Comic Hero* (Cambridge, Mass., 1964).

ARISTOPHANES' APOLOGY, ar-is-tof′ə-nēz ə-pôl-ə-gē, is a poem by Robert Browning (q.v.), written in 1874 and published in the following year. A sequel to *Balaustion's Adventure,* it describes a discussion, immediately following the receipt of the news of Euripides' death, between Balaustion herself and Aristophanes. While the latter defends his comic art, Balaustion, who serves as spokesman for Browning's own views, champions the tragic poet, supporting her case by reading his *Hercules Furens.*

ARISTOPHANES OF BYZANTIUM (c.257–c.180 B.C.), ar-is-tof′ə-nēz, bi-zan′shē-əm, was a Greek scholar and lexicographer. He was probably born in Byzantium or migrated there—hence his geographical epithet. He spent most of his life in Alexandria, where, after studying under directors of the Alexandrian library, he was head librarian from about 197 probably until his death.

Ancient and modern scholars have placed Aristophanes among the world's greatest philologists for his studies in general linguistics, accentuation and punctuation (each of which he either invented or improved), notation in prosody, grammatical science, textual criticism, and literary interpretation.

He edited many Greek political works, providing critical notes and scholarly introductions, and made a list of whom he considered to be the best Greek epic, lyric, and dramatic poets. In lexicography he not only compiled lists of rare and foreign words and of Greek phrases but also produced special studies arranged according to subject or to dialects. He collected proverbs into six books (two in verse and four in prose). In grammar, his essay on analogy answered his older contemporary Chrysippus, who had written on anomaly, and thus started the strife between these two schools. To Aristophanes are attributed studies on the antiquities of Thebes and Boeotia, a treatise on Athenian prostitutes, and a work on biology.

The best edition of his literary remains is still August Nauck's *Aristophantis Byzantini grammatici Alexandrini fragmenta* (Halle 1848).

Further Reading: Rose, Herbert J., *A Handbook of Greek Literature*, 4th ed. (New York 1951); Sandys, John E., *A History of Classical Scholarship*, 3d ed., vol. 1 (Cambridge, England, 1921).

ARISTOTLE (384–322 B.C.), ar′ə-stot-əl, was a major Greek philosopher and scientist. He was born of Greek parentage, at Stagira, a small town in Chalcidice, the peninsular section of Macedonia on the upper Aegean, or Thracian, Sea. Because of his birthplace he frequently was called the *Stagirite.* Aristotle's scientific and philosophical inclinations were largely determined by three prominent factors in his life. First, his father, Nicomachus, a member of the medical guild of the Asclepiadae, was the physician of Amyntas II at Pella, capital of Macedonia; through him Aristotle acquired an interest in biology and the scientific procedures of his age. Second, at the age of 17, Aristotle became a pupil of Plato at the Academy in Athens; this relationship was important in the development of Aristotle's concern for ethics, aesthetics, and early Greek philosophy. Third, Aristotle's interest in zoology and botany, as well as in the constitutions and forms of government in Greek states, was intensified by his association with Alexander the Great. There is reason to believe that, as tutor to Alexander, he composed at least two treatises on political science for the instruction of the 13-year-old prince. Subsequently, it is said, Alexander endowed Aristotle's library and museum at Athens and gave official encouragement to the collection of zoological and botanical specimens from the eastern Mediterranean area for the museum and for research activities.

While Aristotle, by his very nature, could not accept all the Platonic doctrines and interpretations, it was not until the death of Plato in 347 B.C. and the succession of Speusippus as director of the Academy that Aristotle discontinued his work there. As the reason for his break, Aristotle cites his dislike of the growing emphasis on mathematics at the Academy and the corresponding decline in philosophical investigation. From Athens he went to Mysia in Asia Minor, where he married Pythias, the niece and adopted daughter of Hermias, tyrant of Atarneus and former associate at the Academy. From Mysia he moved to the island of Lesbos; here he renewed his friendship with Theophrastus, another colleague of Academy days, who was destined to become a prominent associate of Aristotle and an exponent of his philosophy. Aristotle carried on much of his biological research in this eastern part of the Aegean.

In 335 B.C., Aristotle began his period of instruction in Athens, setting up a school in a grove sacred to Apollo Lyceus in the northeastern part of the city; his school came to be known as the Lyceum, from the name "Lyceum." Because of his practice of imparting instruction while walking about the grove with his pupils, the name *Peripatetics* was given to Aristotle's pupils. At the Lyceum, Aristotle is believed to have delivered lectures both popular and private or, in the terms that have been attributed to his pupils, exoteric and esoteric (that is, lectures easily comprehended by the public and lectures composed for his personally trained students).

Sentiment mounted in Athens against persons of Macedonian background after the death of Alexander in 323 B.C., and Aristotle was impelled to leave the city. He died at Chalcis in Euboea in the following year. Virtually nothing definite can be said about his appearance or character. There is reason to believe that he showed a quickness of mind toward all problems and mixed intensity of feeling with a good sense of humor.

Works. More than 400 separate treatises were attributed to Aristotle by ancient scholars. Of approximately 50 that have survived under his name, only about half will stand the tests of authenticity. It is customary to divide his creative scholarship into three main areas. (1) Works of a popular nature, written for publication beyond the needs and interests of his students. None of these has survived, although their popularity in antiquity is well attested, particularly one exhortation to the study of philosophy, entitled *Protrepticus*. (2) A collection of scholarly data, the result of his various interests in research, which he used in writing and lecturing and experimenting. The *Constitution of Athens* is Aristotle's only surviving work in this area. In this category also presumably belonged the didascalic notices for Greek drama, which are not extant. (3) The surviving works, the authenticity of which has been the subject of much debate. There is not sufficient evidence to establish whether these works, in the form in which they have survived, were Aristotle's notes for his lectures, a pupil's version of his lectures, or mere summaries of his principles compiled either by Aristotle or by a follower.

The extant writings may be divided conveniently into five groups, determined by the five aspects of his philosophical interest. In many instances the treatises are identified by the Latin titles that they have acquired. The first group, on logic, has been called the *Organon*. It embraces the six works devoted to reasoning and definition: *Categories, De interpretatione, Prior Analytics, Posterior Analytics, Topics,* and *Sophistici elenchi.* In the second group, which comprises principally the *Physics* and *Metaphysics,* Aristotle deals with the form and matter of reality, space, motion, and general existence. Three other treatises frequently are included in this group: *De caelo* (the earth in relation to the celestial bodies), *De generatione et corruptione* (conditions of existence), and *Meteorologica* (weather). Biological and psychological works are assigned to the third group: *Historia animalium* (classification and characteristics of animals), *De anima* (the soul), *De partibus animalium* (distinguishing parts of animals), and a collection of monographs on biopsychological aspects of animals known as *Parva naturalia.* In this group also are placed *De incessu animalium* and *De generatione animalium.* The *Nicomachean Ethics,* the *Eudemian Ethics,* and the *Politics* constitute the fourth group. The fifth and final group of extant works is composed of the *Rhetoric* and the *Poetics.*

The order of arrangement into these five groups is not precisely the order of composition. The chronological sequence is difficult to ascertain, but one criterion for determining it has been the degree of Aristotle's interest in and sympathy for Platonic principles. It generally is believed that Aristotle's earlier and popular works had the Platonic dialogue as their model. As Aristotle's own thought developed, he became more and more critical of Plato. Thus the more consistently his works reflect criticism of Plato and provide a distinctively Aristotelian solution to the problems raised, the later they are thought to have been composed. Excessive work by editors after Aristotle also must be taken into account, for some works, such as the *Politics* and the two treatises on ethics, show evidence of an editorial hand working to compile a larger work from separate monographs or essays.

ARISTOTELIAN PHILOSOPHY

To Aristotle the scientist and philosopher may be attributed several innovations in the examination and analysis of natural phenomena and human behavior. In the organization of his analysis, Aristotle divides the sciences into three classes: (1) theoretical or speculative philosophy (theological, physical and metaphysical, and biopsychological); (2) practical philosophy (ethics and political science); and (3) productive philosophy (rhetoric, aesthetics, and literary criticism). Plato sought to reconcile physical and moral phenomena with transcendental or idealized forms of nontemporal, nonspatial being; Aristotle, on the other hand, drew on the experience of the senses as interpreted by the emotions and the intellect and saw the universal residing or inherent in the particular object or state. Thus for him the particular object or state participated in the universal, and the universal provided a criterion of value for the particular. The universal and the particular are inalienably associated, and this affinity of participation underlies most of Aristotle's approach to the problem of causation. His teleology and epistemology are largely determined by this examination of reality and nature. Reality consists not of transcendental ideas but of individual, observable phenomena, with the application of the human intellect upon them. Motion and movement, deriving ultimately from what Aristotle calls the Prime Mover existing in the universe, cause the development from one form of existence to another and the transformation of matter. To motion may be assigned the transition from potentiality to actuality, for each object or state of being in nature has a potentiality of development that may be actualized or realized, in the course of time, in its growth.

In logic, Aristotle employs both the categories and the syllogism to define more precisely the essence of matter and form. An extension of the dialectic method displayed by Plato in his later dialogues, this analysis by deductive logic provides a basis for exploring the essentials of being. The syllogism attempts to separate one judgment from another by means of a middle term (for example, the original notion, the judgment on this notion, and the logical conclusion).

Since Aristotle maintains that all knowledge is gained from perception by the senses, he effects a close association between mind and soul on the one hand and body on the other. The soul may be identified with the principle of life, everywhere present in the human body. Through experience the mind develops in its capacity to govern action and choice. The chief good for man is said to be happiness, consisting of rational activity pursued in accordance with virtue. The virtues, as they are manifested by the individual man, may be divided into two groups, moral and intellectual. In discussing the several virtues Aristotle proposes the ethical mean, and each virtue is shown to occupy a middle position between the extremes of excess and defect (for example, courage is the main state between the extremes of rashness and cowardice). Character is determined by choice, and choice is governed by experience and the intellect or by the interrelationship of the two. In the field of government, Aristotle posits the constitutional democracy as the most effective type of state, since it aims at the greatest good for its citizens, the majority of whom, in turn, excel in virtue. Productive art is considered by Aristotle to be the result of reason, but it is conditioned by (1) the morality that it may convey to human beings and (2) the validity of the representation that it achieves. Thus, in imitating or representing facts and states of nature, art can be a strong determinant in the virtue and happiness of man.

Logic. Aristotle has written very fully in the area that has come to be identified as logic. His expressed purpose here is to define a method for the isolation and criticism of substance insofar as such isolation and criticism are pertinent to his scientific investigations. Logic is not properly a science in and by itself but an epistemological procedure whereby reality may be described accurately in language. It is an introduction to the pursuit of science. Perhaps the most basic isolation of being is provided in Aristotle's 10 categories. While Aristotle does not insist on analyzing matter in each of these categories, it will be observed that these 10 qualifications serve amply to identify the full nature of an object or being. Taking Socrates as the subject of his definition in the categories, Aristotle would make the complete analysis as follows: (1) substance (man), (2) quantity (five feet tall), (3) quality (white), (4) relation (married), (5) place (in the Athenian Agora), (6) date (400 B.C.), (7) position (sitting), (8) state (is sober), (9) action (drinking hemlock), (10) passivity (is convicted).

The relation of language as thought to material reality and being is conveyed further by the Aristotelian examination of the proposition. In the proposition, Aristotle analyzes the expression of judgment, notably the association between noun and verb. Thus he cites the distinction of meaning in the proposition: "man is" versus "man is not" versus "not-man is" versus "not-man is not." With the addition of a predicate adjective, such as "good," to the original proposition "man is," the variety of identification and analysis is increased.

In his treatment of inference Aristotle advances the syllogism. This he defines as an argument that produces a conclusion different from the assumptions employed in reaching that conclusion (for example, A is true of B; B is true of C; therefore, A is true of C). Aristotle was aware, however, of certain weaknesses in the combination of terms a syllogism employs, and subsequent logicians have supplemented his version. One difficulty that he recognized is the question of probability regarding the assumption used in developing the syllogism. There are certain basic principles that must be accepted as postulates, and from these is deduced the proof. Whereas the syllogism proceeds from the universal to the particular, Aristotle proposes induction as the method to reach the universal from the particular.

Finally, as it were to introduce his works on essence and being and to clarify his manner of approach, Aristotle effects the relationship of logic and science through a consideration of those premises that are not analyzed by means of demonstrative proof. It may be asked how man knows them and what validity they possess that makes them knowledgeable. Perception and ex-

THE BETTMANN ARCHIVE

ARISTOTLE, as portrayed in a Hellenistic sculpture.

perience are described as potentials that are actualized within the life of man; these enable him to move into the realm of universals, into the area where intuitive reason illuminates all universals. See also ORGANON.

Physics and Metaphysics. In the area of theoretical, or speculative, philosophy Aristotle explores the meaning and properties of being and of nature. He himself never employed the term "metaphysics," which arose from the analysis of what he called First Philosophy. The 10 books of his study of causation, which have come to be known as the *Metaphysics*, were placed by an early editor after (Greek *meta,* after) the works on physical phenomena. Physics may be described as the science that has for its subject the study of phenomena that are changeable, insofar as they possess a source of movement. These phenomena, such as are found in the study of the biological and natural sciences, may increase and decrease in growth, may come into being and pass away; yet they all are subject to certain established laws in the universe involving matter and motion. Motion that is to be found in natural objects effects the transition from potentiality to actuality. Motion, therefore, along with the actualization of potentiality in matter, defines the natural universe into a great scale of being, ranging from the most inorganic substance to the most highly developed being or form of reality. While this is not to be conceived of as a scale of evolution, it does provide an effective analysis of scientific phenomena in a universe that is forever changing. The responsibility of the scientist or the philosopher is the evaluation of matter within this scale with regard to the teleological questions: "What is the purpose of a physical phenomenon?" "What is its end?" "In what form will its development occur?"

Like most ancient philosophers, Aristotle was concerned with causation. He attempted to identify causation with the substance of matter itself. In First Philosophy, Aristotle seeks to isolate a principle of causation, and this he defines as a universal that is real and that is the formative principle of being. This principle may exist apart from motion, for motion presupposes a moving cause. The First Cause in the universe Aristotle calls the Prime Mover, which may be identified with God; in the isolation of other causes the Prime Mover serves as the norm. Motion is eternal because the Prime Mover is eternal; a degree of perfection may be observed in the material universe because this is communicated by the Prime Mover, who is perfect. In nature Aristotle enumerates four causes: material, formal, efficient, and final. Thus a work of art as well as a phenomenon in the natural universe can manifest cause in these areas: the substance is the material, the architectural plan is the formal, the execution or creation is the efficient, and the purpose is the final. The physical world, then, for Aristotle represents an intermediate being between the Prime Mover, who is perfect form, and the formless substance of matter. In the development of this explanation of causation and being, Aristotle places the greatest emphasis on the mind of man as an interpretative and creative principle, but the reasoning of this interpreation derives largely from the principles of his logic. His concept of the Prime Mover has been severely criticized, for without this First Cause the regress into the rationalized universe would be endless.

Biology and Psychology. Aristotle considered psychology a form of biological inquiry, and hence for him biology and psychology were inseparable. Within the field of biology his greatest contribution was the observation and classification of animals, their component parts, and their behavior. To classify animal life he effects an arrangement and classification by the form of reproduction (for example, viviparous like man, oviparous like birds, vermiparous like insects, and self-generative like mollusks), although another form of classification, distinguishing animals with blood from those that are bloodless, may be cited in broader terms. Each biological specimen may be considered according to its manner of reproduction, its feelings, and its actions and behavior. On the subject of reproduction Aristotle is concerned not merely with sex and heredity, but also with environmental factors and the fight for survival. He thereby analyzes the various functions and behavior in the light of the particular organs and parts as well as the classificatory nature of the animals themselves. In addition to analyzing generation, he examines the locomotion, growth, and nutrition of the human being. He always keeps before him the final cause or the purpose of life and reproductive creativity, which is the responsibility of the biologist to determine as he studies organic life.

Aristotle affirms the purpose of psychology to be the exploration of the nature, essence, and pertinent associations of the soul. Unlike Plato, he does not conceive of the soul as a spiritual entity. Rather it is inalienably associated with the organism of the body, and while it may be a source of motion and of knowing and is incorporeal in substantial form, it derives its growth from the function of the body's organs of sensation. Since the senses nourish the mind and the intellect of the body, the soul is the receptacle of experience in growth. Thus, of all the potentiality with which each body is endowed, it is the soul that becomes the first actuality of the body. The soul prominently actualizes other forms and aspects of potentiality. Through the function of the soul the moral and intellectual aspects of man are developed, and in this sense the soul provides the link between the bodily organism and the virtues, which the soul engenders in man through his conduct and behavior. The fourfold classification of functions of organic life—growth, sensation, motion, and thought—is maintained in Aristotle's dicussion of the soul.

As he discusses the soul, Aristotle always effects the distinction between man and the lower animals. All animals react to sensations, which affect the mind and fashion the intellect, with reflection and memory as results. Man, however, is able to exercise judgment based on experience, and this judgment represents the impact of the sensations on the soul, with the mind as the agent of interpretation for the activity of life. In associating the soul of man with the physical being of man, Aristotle contributes three outstanding attitudes toward psychology in the history of science: (1) he removes much of the mysticism previously associated in Greek science with the soul and its function; (2) he provides a method for dignified investigation of a scientific matter; and (3) he anticipates the psychosomatic interest of modern science.

Ethics and Political Science. Whereas knowledge is the end of such speculative sciences as physics and metaphysics, Aristotle construes the practical sciences, such as ethics and the art of government, according to their end, which is conduct, particularly good conduct. Ethics and politics are considered as two areas within the same science because both represent means of actualizing the potential that the speculative sciences have demonstrated to be inherent in man. Ethics has as its subject the study of virtue, with the purpose that the individual may identify and attain the supreme good both for his life and behavior and for his communal associations. In his own words Aristotle maintains that the study of ethics seeks not to impart information but to influence conduct. Political science, on the other hand, is concerned with man as a part of the living organism of the state, and this demands an analysis of the composition of government, including the citizenry, the relative merits of constitutions, the need for and the institution of laws, and the nature of living.

Aristotle defines the good for man as happiness, which may be interpreted variously as pleasure, honor, wealth, and contemplation. Within the individual he cites two kinds of virtues, moral and intellectual. Liberality, temperance, justice, courage, friendship, magnanimity, gentleness, and truthfulness are examined as moral virtues that are reckoned as mean states between the extremes of excess and defect. Similarly, the intellectual virtues in man—science, art, practical wisdom, intuitive reason, and theoretical wisdom— are also mean states and have a peculiar significance in that they illuminate the nature of the supreme good for man. Through these virtues and their pursuit, man arrives at the life of contemplation of truth, which is pronounced his highest activity.

Since man is by nature a political animal, conditioned by his associations with his fellow men under some form of government, man's actualization of his full potentialities occurs as he participates in a community or society. Just as in the speculative sciences and ethics Aristotle has observed growth toward a well-defined end or purpose, so he shows the state in its development toward the promotion of the noble life and the happiness of all its citizens. Thus he considers the family, the community, and the state as vehicles for morality and for the good life for man. In examining the various kinds of government, he finds virtue in monarchy, aristocracy, and what might be termed constitutional timocracy. For each of these forms of polity he cites a corruption: monarchy can develop easily into tyranny; aristocracy into oligarchy, where wealth becomes a qualification for office; and constitutional timocracy into disorganized democracy. Mob rule is one of the unfavorable features of democracy, although, with an enlightened citizenry and good educational opportunities, constitutional democracy may qualify precisely for the ideal form of government. Basically, however, the best state is the one that comes into being and achieves its end through the highest good as manifested by the citizens individually and collectively.

Aesthetics and Literary Criticism. Two treatises, the *Rhetoric* and the fragmentary *Poetics*, provide ample evidence of Aristotle's aesthetic theories or, more pertinently, of his examination of the productive imagination of man. Art seeks not merely to supplement nature, but also to imitate it by some form of representation. Artistic creativity, therefore, may be considered a natural function of man, because in the act of artistic creation man fulfills a natural desire and also participates in the universal. Through participation or activity in the productive sciences of the arts, man's life is enriched and ennobled morally and pleasurably, and his communal associations are enhanced.

At the base of Aristotle's discussion of rhetoric is a psychological implication, for he conceives rhetoric to be the ability to determine and to practice the possible ways of persuading men in any given subject. Rhetoric as an art of persuasion may function in three distinct categories: it may (1) indicate that some plan for the future is useful or harmful, (2) signify the legal implications of a previous action, and (3) illuminate the character or nature of an action in the present. The methods of persuasion, however, are divided into (1) the impact of the speaker's character upon his audience, (2) the arousing of the emotions, and (3) the advancement of pertinent arguments. Aristotle places great emphasis on style in this consideration of rhetoric, stressing the importance of the arrangement of words and arguments, lucidity, and choice of appropriate words and sentiments. Much of the *Rhetoric* has lost its significance with the increasing ease of communications, but this work is not without usefulness in formal debating or in any study where propaganda and the molding of public opinion are implicit.

The portion of the *Poetics* that discusses tragedy has survived. Aristotle observes several aspects of epic poetry, lyric poetry, and comedy insofar as these literary forms are related to tragedy, and from this discussion it is possible to discern his theory of imitation as well as several fundamental artistic principles. Poetry originates in man's desire to imitate and to represent the world about him. This is true of all forms of poetry, and it is only the varying degrees of emphasis in the act of representation and in the objects imitated

that account for the distinction of the several forms of poetic expression. In drawing a distinction between poetry and history, Aristotle maintains that poetry has greater philosophical value because it deals with universals, while history states particular facts. Plot, character (in this connection, Aristotle introduces the concept of the tragic hero and discusses the tragic flaw), philosophical content, spectacle, and choral music are examined as the component parts of tragedy. However, it is in his analysis of the purpose and function of tragedy that Aristotle's most significant and most discussed contribution to poetic criticism is to be found. Tragedy is said to be the imitation of an action with the end of arousing in the spectator the emotions of pity and fear, thereby effecting the catharsis of these emotions and a concomitant feeling of pleasure.

Thus it may be seen that in the productive sciences Aristotle maintains that interest in the biopsychological aspect of man that characterizes all of his philosophical system. In an even larger sphere his aesthetic theories figure characteristically in his concern with the phenomena of the world of which man is a part. See also POETICS OF ARISTOTLE.

JOHN ROWE WORKMAN, *Brown University*

Bibliography

Aristotle's Works were translated into English and edited by Sir David Ross and J.A. Smith, 12 vols. (New York and London 1910–52); *The Basic Works of Aristotle,* ed. by Richard McKeon (New York 1941), contains an extensive selection from the writings
Barker, Ernest, *The Political Thought of Plato and Aristotle,* rev. ed. (New York and London 1959).
Butcher, Samuel H., *Aristotle's Theory of Poetry and Fine Art* (New York 1951).
Cherniss, Harold F., *Aristotle's Criticism of Plato and the Academy* (Baltimore 1944).
Cooper, Lane, *The Poetics of Aristotle* (Boston 1923).
Jaeger, Werner W., *Aristotle: Fundamentals of the History of His Development,* tr. by Richard Robinson, 2d ed. (New York and London 1948).
Jones, John, *Aristotle and Greek Tragedy* (New York 1962).
Randall, John R., *Aristotle* (New York 1960).
Ross, William D., *Aristotle,* 5th ed., rev. (London 1949).
Spicer, Eulalie E., *Aristotle's Conception of the Soul* (London 1934).

ARISTOXENUS, ar-is-tok′sē-nəs, was a Greek philosopher and musical theorist who lived during the 4th century B.C. He was probably the greatest musical theoretician of antiquity. He was born in Tarentum, Italy, between 375 and 360 B.C. Trained in music first by his father, Spintharus, and then by Lamprus of Erythrae in Asia Minor, he went to Athens, where he became a pupil of Aristotle.

Although more than 450 works are attributed to Aristoxenus, only fragments of his *Principles and Elements of Harmonics* and *Elements of Rhythm* survive. Among the lost treatises by Aristoxenus are works on musical theory and instruments, as well as biographical, historical, and legal subjects.

Aristoxenus maintained that physical sense rather than mathematical reason must provide the principles of musical science and the criterion of the truth of its propositions. He systematized Greek music by clear definitions of terms and by orderly arrangement of scales.

P.R. COLEMAN-NORTON, *Princeton University*

Further Reading: Laloy, Louis, *Aristoxène de Tarente et la musique de l'antiquité* (Paris 1904); Macran, Henry, *Harmonics of Aristoxenus* (Oxford 1902); Westphal, Rudolf, and Saran, Franz, *Aristoxenus von Tarent: Melik und Rhythmik des classischen Hellenenthums,* vol. 2 (Leipzig 1893). Williams, Charles F., *The Aristoxenian Theory of Musical Rhythm* (Cambridge 1911).

ARITHMETIC, ə-rith'mə-tik, is sometimes defined as the science of numbers. The pupil studying the subject might be inclined to say: "It is the science of operating with numbers." But what are the "operations," and to what does the term "number" refer? Such questions merely stimulate one to search more widely and more deeply for the answer to the big question: What is arithmetic?

What arithmetic is can be discovered best by following the story of man's struggle to understand and control his environment. The origin and development of arithmetic can be seen in the way in which man's earliest ancestors recorded their efforts to describe quantities and shapes. On sticks they made notches to record counting. On rocks, in the sand, or in soft, muddy earth they made marks such as these to record counting and shapes:

● ● ●　∥　○　□

As people became more civilized, they tended to systematize and generalize their ways of describing quantities and shapes, and eventually they invented an abstract arithmetical vocabulary. They then named the ideas represented crudely by scratches or drawings "three," "two," a "circle," a "square," and so on. As these abstractions were organized and extended in one form or another, a body of pure arithmetic originated. People now learned and taught that 2 plus 3 equals 5. Multiplication tables came into being, and in due time such procedures as long division became standardized.

The earliest written evidence of arithmetic is found in Babylonian tables and in Egyptian handbooks of the 12th dynasty (1991–1786 B.C.). The Greeks were more interested in what has come to be called the theory of numbers (see NUMBERS, THEORY OF) than they were in practical or applied arithmetic. Among the celebrated Greeks who treated arithmetical problems were Pythagoras (late 6th century B.C.), the geometer Euclid (about 300 B.C.), Eratosthenes (c. 275–194 B.C.), and Diophantus (about 250 A.D.), of whose 13-book *Arithmetica* 6 books survive. The only important Roman writer on arithmetic was the philosopher Anicius Manlius Severinus Boethius (480?–?524 A.D.).

It was not from the Greeks and the Romans, however, that the modern numerical system was derived, but from the Hindus and the Arabs. The Hindus are credited with inventing the numerals and the way in which we use them, and the Arabs with spreading the system to the peoples of northern Africa and Europe. The first Arab work to use the Hindu numerals survives only in translation; it was written by Al-Khwarizmi (Arabic Muhammad ibn-Mūsa al-Khwārizmi, 780?–?850) and translated into Latin by Adelard of Bath (early 12th century). The *Liber abaci* (1202) of Leonardo da Pisa (Leonardo Fibonacci) was the most influential of the medieval Latin works on the Hindu-Arabic system.

The first printed arithmetic book was published in Italy in 1478. The first one to be printed in England was *De arte supputandi* (1522), a theoretical work by Bishop Cuthbert Tunstall. *The Ground of Artes* (1540), a popular textbook by Robert Recorde that went through many editions, was the first work in English. A major development was the introduction of decimal fractions by the Dutch mathematician Simon Stevin (1548–1620). Modern work on the theory of numbers began with the *Disquisitiones arithmeticae* (1801) of Karl Friedrich Gauss.

Although in the 20th century the frontiers of pure arithmetic still are being extended, the average person is interested mainly in applied arithmetic. He wants to know, for example, whether he should purchase an automobile on the installment plan or whether it would be more advantageous to postpone the purchase until he has saved enough money to pay for it in cash. In trying to understand the question "What is arithmetic?" One must recognize the existence of these two basic areas: pure (theoretical) arithmetic and applied (practical) arithmetic.

Numeral System. The core of pure arithmetic is a numeral system. Modern arithmetic uses the Hindu-Arabic system of integers, fractions, and decimal fractions. Of course there have been many other numeral systems, among them those of the Egyptians, Greeks, and Romans. Roman numerals sometimes are used today to number the chapters of books, to express dedication dates on buildings, and to indicate parts of an outline.

But what is systematic about the Hindu-Arabic numeral system? By comparing it with other systems, such as the heating system of a house or a railroad system, we find that there are the following similarities:

(1) The numeral system has a *name*.

(2) It has *elements* or *parts*: the numerals 1, 2, 3, 4, 5, 6, 7, 8, 9, 0; a base of 10; a decimal point.

(3) The elements or parts can be *used* or *operated with*. There are six fundamental operations: addition, subtraction, multiplication, division, involution (raising numbers to powers; for example, $8^2 = 64$, and $2^3 = 8$), and evolution (extracting the roots of numbers; for example, $\sqrt{25} = 5$, and $\sqrt[3]{27} = 3$).

(4) The system is *extendible*. No number is too large to be written, and no number is too small.

(5) The main elements of the system—the numerals—have a distinct *appearance* or *pattern*. All numerals can be made easily with circles or parts thereof and straight line segments. This is a tremendous advantage in teaching young children to write numerals, for any child can make a "ball" (circle) and a "straight line."

(6) There is a *relationship* among the parts of a numeral. This relationship sometimes is called the principle of position. In the numeral 333, for example, the 3 to the extreme left represents 3 hundreds, the middle 3 represents 3 tens, and the 3 to the right represents 3 ones. In the Roman numeral XXX, however, each X represents 10—no more, no less.

The Hindu-Arabic numeral system is so powerful, so readily applicable, and so easily written that it is used by scientists throughout the world even though they speak many different languages. In mathematical journals written in other languages such basic concepts as "food" and "shelter" may be written in what are to the reader strange foreign words, but the number concepts "four" or "eight" will be written with the familiar Hindu-Arabic 4 or 8.

One of the most fundamental services arithmetic renders is to enable people to describe the size of sets of things by the process called counting. Little reasoning need be done in order to specify the size of a set by using a number, as in the sentences: "Five persons are coming for dinner," and "The number of admission tickets sold for tomorrow evening's dance is 103."

Most of the elements of the numeral system came into existence to satisfy a need for either counting or measuring. Such was not the case, however, with the very special element zero (0), for the simple reason that if there were no animals to be counted or no distance to be measured, men did not engage in numerical activity. The invention of the zero symbol therefore was long delayed. Indeed, it was not until the abacus (q.v.) had been outmoded and the writing of numerals had become a pressing need that zero was invented as a placeholder. This fact is understood more easily when we realize that the number 103 can be represented quite adequately on the abacus by moving 3 beads on the ones wire, no beads on the tens wire, and 1 bead on the hundreds wire, but when we write 103 without the zero it appears to be 13 instead of 103.

The idea of using zero to represent an empty column on the abacus is regarded as one of the most significant events in the history of mathematics. It is not known when the symbol was invented, but the first recorded use of zero as a placeholder is in a Hindu inscription of 876 A.D. From the standpoint of arithmetical calculations it is interesting to observe that, with the invention of the zero symbol to represent the absence of quantity, it became possible to subtract one identical number from another, as 5 − 5 or 3⅔ − 3⅔, and record the remainder.

Describing the size of small finite groups or quantities is relatively easy in any of the ancient numeral systems, but when a large population figure, such as that of the city of London, is to be written, difficulty is encountered. Another limitation of the older systems becomes apparent if we think of using Roman numerals to describe the size of a common bolt 2 inches (5 cm) long and ½ inch (1¼ cm) in diameter, or of writing the value of π when using the formula $C = \pi d$ to find the circumference of a circle. See also NUMERALS.

One-to-One Correspondence. Basic to the fundamental process of describing the size of sets or groups of things in mathematics is the idea of one-to-one correspondence. The early tribesman made use of this idea when he cut notches in a stick to record the number of pelts he traded. The nomad shepherd used it when he placed pebbles on a pile when the sheep left the fold in the morning and picked them up when the sheep returned in the evening; if all the pebbles on the pile were picked up when the last sheep had entered the fold, he knew that none had met with a mishap during the day. When a child endeavors to "see" the sum of 5 plus 3 by looking at the 5 fingers on one hand and then at 3 fingers on the other hand, he lets each finger correspond to one of the things represented by the numbers 5 and 3. The alert kindergarten teacher emphasizes the basic mathematical idea of one-to-one correspondence when she urges the child to touch each object in succession as he counts 1, 2, 3.

Decimal System. The Hindu-Arabic numeral system is called a decimal (from Latin *decimus*, tenth) system because its base is 10. The base of any numeral system is determined by the number of unique symbols or digits that are used. Thus, in the Hindu-Arabic numeral system we use

the symbols 1, 2, 3, 4, 5, 6, 7, 8, 9, 0. After we have counted to 10, we continue with 11, 12, 13, and on up to 20; then 21, 22, 23, and on up to 30; and, later on, 101, 102, 103, 104, and so on. The extension of the system to represent very large, medium-sized, and very small numbers is achieved by giving each digit in a numeral two values: an absolute value and a positional value. In the numeral 333, for example, all the digits have the same absolute value, 3, but each has a different positional value. The positional values of the decimal system can be shown as follows, using the numeral 7123.64 as an example:

	THOUSANDS	HUNDREDS	TENS	ONES	DECIMAL POINT	TENTHS	HUNDREDTHS
POSITIONS					•		
VALUES	10^3	10^2	10^1	10^0		10^{-1}	10^{-2}
	7	1	2	3	.	6	4

Thus, 7,123.64 has a value of

$$7 \times 10^3 = 7 \times 1{,}000 = 7{,}000$$
$$1 \times 10^2 = 1 \times 100 = 100$$
$$2 \times 10^1 = 2 \times 10 = 20$$
$$3 \times 10^0 = 3 \times 1 = 3$$
$$6 \times 10^{-1} = 6 \times .1 = .6$$
$$4 \times 10^{-2} = 4 \times .01 = .04$$
$$\text{or} \qquad 7{,}123.64.$$

The concept of positional value may become clearer if we examine the binary numeral (base two) system, which is the system used by modern high-speed electronic calculating machines. The binary numeral system has only two symbols or digits: 1 and 0. Its positional values can be illustrated as follows, using the binary numeral 1101 as an example.

	THIRTY-TWOS	SIXTEENS	EIGHTS	FOURS	TWOS	ONES	
POSITIONS							•
VALUES	2^5	2^4	2^3	2^2	2^1	2^0	•
			1	1	0	1	.

Thus, 1101. has a value of

$$1 \times 2^3 = 1 \times 8 = 8$$
$$1 \times 2^2 = 1 \times 4 = 4$$
$$0 \times 2^1 = 0 \times 2 = 0$$
$$1 \times 2^0 = 1 \times 1 = 1$$
$$\text{or 13, in the decimal system.}$$

That is, the binary numeral 1101 represents the same size group as the decimal numeral 13 does. By making a similar table of values, we can check the binary counting shown above in which 111 is equivalent to the decimal numeral 7, and 1010 to the decimal numeral 10.

From the standpoint of teaching arithmetic, it should be noted that if the binary numeral system were used in the schools, the writing of numbers would be confined to 0's and 1's. There would be only four basic addition facts ($1 + 0 = 1$, $0 + 1 = 1$, $0 + 0 = 0$, and $1 + 1 = 10$), and four multiplication facts ($0 \times 0 = 0$, $1 \times 0 = 0$, $0 \times 1 = 0$, and $1 \times 1 = 1$).

Fractions. The numbers of arithmetic are not confined to the integers but include fractions as well. Early man felt the need for fractions when he wanted to describe a quantity that was only a portion, a broken (fractured) part, of a whole, as, for example, one half ($\frac{1}{2}$) of an apple or two thirds ($\frac{2}{3}$) of a certain length.

In fractions, the numerals beneath the lines are called denominators; they tell us into how many equal parts the wholes are divided. The numerals above the lines are called numerators; they tell us how many of the equal parts are being considered. If the numerator is less than the denominator, the fraction is called a proper fraction; if it is equal to or greater than the denominator, the fraction is called an improper fraction. It should be noted that with the use of fractions the quotient of any two numbers can be shown exactly, if zero is not a denominator.

Ever since the idea of a fraction became part of arithmetic there has been a tendency to expand the concept until it has come to have a variety of rather subtle meanings. The four principal meanings of a fraction are as follows:

(1) A fraction represents one or more equal parts of a unit; for example, a piece of pie may be $\frac{1}{8}$ of a whole pie.

(2) A fraction represents one of the equal parts of a group of units. In the following diagram, for example, it is seen that 3 eggs constitute $\frac{1}{4}$ of a dozen.

(3) A fraction represents an indicated division: for example, $\frac{7}{8}$ is $7 \div 8$.

(4) A fraction represents a ratio. If we compare two weights, such as 50 units and 100 units, the ratio of 50 to 100 is 1 to 2 or $\frac{1}{2}$.

There are two special kinds of fractions: those with denominators that are powers of 10, called decimal fractions; and those decimal fractions with denominators of 100, called percents.

In working with fractions it is often convenient and sometimes necessary to find equivalents. Thus, $\frac{1}{2}$ is equivalent to $\frac{2}{4}$ or to $\frac{10}{20}$, and $\frac{12}{16}$ is equivalent to $\frac{3}{4}$. Equivalent fractions are found or determined by using the fundamental law of fractions, which states: The numerator and denominator of any fraction may be multiplied or divided by the same number (other than zero) without changing the value of the fraction. If, for example, we wish to add (or subtract) the fractions $\frac{2}{3}$ and $\frac{1}{4}$, we meet with difficulty, for we cannot add (or subtract) thirds and fourths any more reasonably than we can add pencils and balls and get a meaningful answer. We therefore transform the thirds and fourths into like denominations by multiplying the numerator and denominator of $\frac{2}{3}$ by 4, ob-

taining $\frac{8}{12}$, and the numerator and denominator of $\frac{1}{4}$ by 3, obtaining $\frac{3}{12}$. The sum of $\frac{8}{12}$ and $\frac{3}{12}$ is $\frac{11}{12}$; and the difference, $\frac{5}{12}$. See also FRACTION.

FUNDAMENTAL OPERATIONS

The six fundamental operations of arithmetic have inverse, or opposite, relationships, as follows: (1) Subtraction is the inverse of addition. (2) Division is the inverse of multiplication. (3) Involution is the inverse of evolution. These relationships stem from the fundamental concepts of the operations. Thus, addition means a "coming together," the forming of one set by merging two or more smaller sets. Subtraction, on the other hand, means a "separation," the breaking up of one large set into two or more smaller sets.

Addition. The theory of sets underlies the concept of addition, which is probably the most basic of the six fundamental operations. The addition of two integers can be thought of as the union of two disjoint sets. (Disjoint sets are sets that have no elements in common.) Suppose set A contains five elements, and set B contains three elements not contained in set A. Then the set that represents the union of set A and set B contains eight elements. In using arithmetic symbols, this process can be represented as: $5 + 3 = 8$.

Subtraction. Largely because of vocabulary difficulties, the need for using the process of subtraction is less readily discovered than that of addition. Basically, subtraction refers to separation procedures: Ten ducks were in the pond, but six climbed to the bank to rest. How many remained in the pond? Although the operation of subtraction is suggested when we seek "the remainder," we also subtract to find "how many are left?", "what is the difference?", "how many more?", and "the amount to be added." Furthermore, the process of subtraction is used to find the "profit," "loss," "excess," "rest," "residue," "surplus," and a host of other things. In teaching subtraction, therefore, a special effort should be made consciously to connect the use of the process with these varied directive phrases. Like addition, subtraction is taught in terms of set theory.

Multiplication. Multiplication is a shortcut for the process of addition when the addends (numbers to be added) are identical. Thus, the total cost of several items each costing the same amount is found by multiplying the constant amount by the number of items. Multiplication facts always have been a difficult part of arithmetic. Knowing the tables, as these facts in their older rigid form and order were called, was a mark of achievement in the schools of yesterday. In the schools of today their mastery is still a task that challenges school, teacher, and child.

Early Egyptians avoided this extensive memorization of multiplication facts by doing their multiplication by a method called *duplation*. This method required only the doubling of numbers; an operation that could be done easily by mental addition.

Duplation is explained best by giving an example. Suppose we wish to multiply 176 by 19. First, we set up two columns of doubles headed by (a) and (b). Column (a) is begun always (that is, for all multiplication problems) by 1, 2, 4, etc. Column (b) always is started with the number to be multiplied, and this number also is

SETS IN ARITHMETIC

SET A

SET B

ADDITION

3 + 3 = 6

SUBTRACTION

6 − 4 = 2

doubled successively. Thus, for this example, we have:

(a)	(b)	(c)	(d)
1	176	1	176
2	352	2	352
4	704		
8	1408		
16	2816	16	2816
		19	3344

Column (a) is continued until the last number is just equal to or less than the multiplier. In this example the number that would follow 16 in column (a) would be 32 but that is *greater than* the multiplier, 19, so we terminate column (a) with 16. Next, from column (a) numbers are chosen such that when they are added, the

sum will equal the multiplier, 19. In this case, 16 + 2 + 1 = 19. These numbers that total 19 may well be rewritten in column (c) and opposite them, in column (d), the partner numbers found in column (b). The sum of the numbers in column (d) is the *product* of *176* multiplied by 19.

Another method of multiplication is the so-called lattice method. Its advantage lies in the fact that during the multiplications of the separate digits no mental carrying needs to be done. This method can be illustrated by multiplying 176 by 214. First the factors are written as shown in the accompanying diagram. Next the horizontal, vertical, and diagonal lines are drawn. Then the several products are placed in the rectangles with the diagonals separating the two-digit products. The next step consists in summing the digits between the diagonals as shown at the top of the next page.

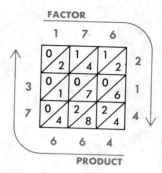

FACTOR

PRODUCT

Casting Out Nines. Because the process of multiplication is difficult, and errors need to be avoided, it is desirable to have methods of checking the work. One method that is used easily is called casting out nines.

In casting out nines we use *residues*. The residue of any numeral is the remainder after the sum of its digits is reduced by subtracting the highest possible multiple of 9. Thus the residues of the numerals 142, 678, and 675 are found by first adding the digits 1, 4, and 2; 6, 7, and 8; and 6, 7, and 5 to obtain the sums 7, 21, and 18. Then, upon subtracting multiples of 9 from 7, 21, and 18 we have the remainders 7, 3, and 0. These remainders are the residues of the numerals 142, 678, and 675 respectively.

Suppose we multiply 6,324 by 542:

$$542 \times 6,324 = 3,427,608$$

	11	15	30
Sum of digits	11	15	30
Casting out nines	9	9	27
Residues	2	6	3

If we multiply the residues 2 and 6 we obtain a product of 12 which has a residue of 3. This is identical with the residue of the product, 30, which is also 3. Thus, the multiplication is checked. In general, any arithmetical process can be checked by performing the same operation on the residues of the numbers involved and checking it against the residue of the result.

It should be noted that this process is not an absolute check, for if the digits totaling 30 were interchanged (if, for example, the product had been written erroneously as 7,324,806 instead of 3,427,608), the check still would have held. Such errors, however, are unlikely to occur.

Division. Division can be thought of as (1) finding the number of equal subtractions that can be made from a given quantity, or (2) partitioning a set into a given number of equal quantities. Thus, (1) if we have a 44-inch ribbon and want to know how many bows can be made from it if each bow requires 8 inches of ribbon, we wish to know how many 8-inch pieces can be subtracted from the ribbon. On the other hand, (2) if we want to know how long each piece will be if the ribbon is divided into 8 equal pieces, we are interested in partitioning the ribbon. Symbolically, our problem appears as:

$$8 \sqrt{\begin{array}{c} 5 \\ \overline{44} \\ \underline{40} \\ 4 \end{array}}$$

In the first case the 5 tells us how many bows can be made and the 4 tells the length in inches of the leftover piece. In the second case the length of each piece is 5⅛, or 5½, inches.

Evolution. Evolution is the process of finding the root of a number. In arithmetic the need for finding or extracting the square root is commonly encountered when we wish to find the length of the hypotenuse or the length of one of the other sides of a right-angled triangle using the Pythagorean theorem, which states that the square of the hypotenuse of a right triangle equals the sum of the squares of the other two sides.

The process of square root is useful in finding the length of a side of a square if its area is given. Cube root is needed to find the length of an edge of a cube if its volume is given.

Involution. Involution, the process of raising a number to a power, is used to find the area of a square if its side is given or the volume of a cube if its edge is given. Its use also is indicated in the evaluation of many of the common mensuration formulas of arithmetic.

LEE E. BOYER
Harrisburg (Pa.) Area Community College

Bibliography
Adler, Irving, *A New Look at Arithmetic* (New York. 1964).
Banks, J., *Elements of Mathematics*, 2d ed. (New York 1961).
Boyer, Lee E., *An Introduction to Mathematics*, rev. ed. (New York 1956).
Brueckner, Leo J., and Grossnickle, Foster E., *Making Arithmetic Meaningful* (Philadelphia 1953).
Buckingham, Burdette R., *Elementary Arithmetic: Its Meaning and Practice* (New York 1947).
Eves, Howard, *An Introduction to the History of Mathematics* (New York 1953).
Fujii, John N., *Numbers and Arithmetic* (New York 1965).
Willerding, Margaret F., *Elementary Mathematics, Its Structure and Concepts* (New York 1966).
Wren, F. Lynwood, *Basic Mathematical Concepts* (New York 1965).

ARITHMETIC SERIES. See SERIES.

ARIUS (c. 256–336 A.D.), ə-rī′əs, was a theologian who formulated the heretical doctrine known as Arianism, which denied the godhead of Christ (see ARIANISM). He is thought to have been born in Libya. Arius was a deacon when he was excommunicated in 311 by Peter, patriarch of Alexandria, for supporting the schismatic views of Meletius of Lycopolis. Reinstated by Peter's successor Achillas in 313, Arius was made presbyter of Baucalis, where he taught that Christ was created by God the Father and was less than God, although higher in the creation than man. To popularize his views, Arius wrote and distributed explanatory light verse among local workers. Although censured in 318, Arius persisted in his opinions. The ruling patriarch Alexander then convened a synod of bishops, who excommunicated Arius in 321.

Arianism was endorsed by Eusebius, bishop of Nicomedia, and gained further episcopal support, dividing the church in the East and dismaying Emperor Constantine. The emperor convoked the Council of Nicaea in 325, which anathematized and banished Arius. He then composed a rival pronouncement to the Nicene Creed. Impressed by Arius' creed, Constantine received him in 331 and ordered Athanasius, champion of orthodoxy at Nicaea, to receive Arius in communion. When Athanasius refused, he was deposed by the synod of Tyre (335) and exiled to Gaul. Constantine then commanded the bishop of Constantinople to restore Arius to communion, but Arius died on the day of the ceremony.

JOSEF MUENCH

THE GRAND CANYON is the finest of Arizona's natural wonders.

Great Seal of Arizona

CONTENTS

ARIZONA, ar-ə-zō′nə, a southwestern state of the United States, is young in statehood (the 48th state, admitted in 1912) but old in history. Spanish explorers strode its arid ground a quarter of a century before St. Augustine, in Florida, was founded and almost 70 years before the English came to Jamestown. Yet Arizona was so remote from the successful European settlements in North America and so inhospitable to the ways of civilization that it remained virtually a frontier until statehood. Since then, the wonders of 20th century transportation have brought it within hours of any part of the nation, and ingenious men have stored water for the dry land and cooled the hot air so that their environment almost can be made to order.

Ranking sixth in area among the states and varying in elevation from 100 feet (30.5 meters) to more than 12,000 feet (3,658 meters) above sea level, Arizona contains a rich variety of scenery and climate. The largest population centers are in the desert south, where great irrigation systems nourish the fertile land and the mild winters attract tourists and residents alike. But

---

INFORMATION HIGHLIGHTS

Location: In southwestern United States.

Area: 113,909 square miles (295,025 sq km); rank, 6th.

Population (1970 census): 1,772,482; rank, 33d.

Elevation: Highest—Humphreys Peak, 12,670 feet (3,862 meters); lowest—on the Colorado River in the southwest, 100 feet (30.5 meters).

Climate: Generally clear and dry, with wide variations between day and night temperatures; highest temperature of record, 127° F (52.8° C), lowest, −37° F (−38.3 C°).

Statehood: Feb. 14, 1912; order of admission, 48th.

Origin of Name: Probably from *arizonac,* Papago Indian for "small springs" or "few springs."

Capital and Largest City: Phoenix; population (1970 census), 581,562.

Number of Counties: 14.

Principal Products: Minerals—copper; farm products—cattle, cotton; manufactures—electrical and nonelectrical machinery, primary metals.

State Motto (adopted 1912): *Ditat Deus* (God enriches).

State Song (approved 1919): *Arizona.*

State Nickname: Grand Canyon State.

State Bird (adopted 1931): Cactus wren.

State Flower (adopted 1931): Blossom of saguaro cactus.

State Tree (adopted 1954): Paloverde.

State Flag (adopted 1917): A large copper star on a field half of blue and half of 13 rays, alternately red and yellow (see color plates under FLAG—*Flags of the States*).

Arizona is a state of mountains, forests, and high mesas as well. Evergreen woodlands—equal to any in beauty, with pure mountain lakes and streams and snow-covered peaks—are within two hours of Phoenix by automobile. Far in the northeast, remote tablelands—lonely except for the Indian hogan or trading post—stun the eye with canyons and majestic rock formations. Proudly Arizona claims the Grand Canyon of the Colorado River.

The mysteries of the ancient peoples of Arizona challenge the historian, archaeologist, and anthropologist as cliff dwellings stand deserted, dilapidated, and voiceless in all parts of the state, the hieroglyphics of their long-gone occupants discernible in the weathered rock face.

As its population and wealth grow, Arizona seems less and less a frontier state and more and more one of great cultural diversity. The rodeo and barbecue, western hats and cowboy boots still flourish, but these must share the affections of the people with cocktail lounge, backyard swimming pool, black tie, and symphony orchestra. Virtually every material thing available in New York or San Francisco can be bought in Arizona's cities, from fashionable women's wear to the art of Polynesia. Culturally and intellectually Arizona no longer is out of the mainstream. Excellent local orchestras, dramatic groups, and art collections are supplemented by frequent appearances of the country's great musical and theatrical companies.

Cultural diversity is matched by economic expansion. Founded upon agriculture and mining, Arizona's economy today has manufacturing as a mainstay. Copper production in Arizona still is the greatest among the states, and agriculture flourishes. Another important source of income is tourism, which has become big business.

Although as early as 1539 white men from New Spain (Mexico) began exploring the land that was to become Arizona, lasting settlements were not established until the time of Father Kino, the famous Jesuit missionary, in the late 1600's. Even then the Spaniards had a tenuous hold, subject as they were to the hazards of extreme isolation from their main settlements in Mexico and the capriciousness of their Indian neighbors. By the early 1820's when Mexico gained independence from Spain, Arizona's few white men had been virtually driven out by the marauding Apaches. The treaty ending the U. S.-Mexican War in 1848 brought most of present Arizona into the United States. Few were the prophets who would hold much hope for development of that arid wilderness, but forts were built, railroads planned, and mines developed. By Civil War times Arizona was a going concern. Congress made Arizona a territory of the United States in 1863, and slowly over the next half-century the march toward statehood went on. In 1911, President Theodore Roosevelt dedicated a dam named for him on the Salt River. This event signified that the way had been found to provide the water and electric power that would make central Arizona boom. Statehood came the next year.

Now, after more than 55 years of statehood, Arizona can document its achievements in many fields, and its people look forward to dynamic growth and broadening opportunity. But expansion creates problems, of which Arizona has its share. Long boastful of their clear air, people in the burgeoning metropolitan areas are confronted with increasing smog. Frequently the surrounding hills are blurred with the low-hanging brown pollution, and demands are heard to attack the menace before it is too late. A continuing problem is the financing of public institutions and services. But perhaps the fundamental need of an arid state is enough water for residential, agricultural, and industrial demands.

1. The People

When the Europeans first tentatively ventured into Arizona in the 16th century, they found the Indian peoples who would be known by such names as Papago, Pima, Mohave, Apache, Navajo, and Hopi. Some were peaceful folk. Others, proud and warlike, would resist the white man's aggressions until well into modern times. In present Mexico, the chief region of Spanish settlement, generations of intermingling of Europeans and native Indians produced a people who became the masses of that country. They came into Arizona under Spanish and Mexican rule and gave their culture, language, and religion to the region. The mid-1800's brought other newcomers—these (called Anglo-Americans, or Anglos) from the United States, carrying the language and culture of that country. They used such Mexican-American ways as suited them, but once the Anglos came, the Spanish cultural domination was doomed.

The Anglo-Americans came into Arizona from several directions. The years of the gold rush, in the late 1840's, saw men from Texas and the East crossing the territory headed for California. Some of these would come back, and through the years there has been a steady immigration to Arizona from California. From Utah, to the north, would come Mormon pioneers seeking new lands and converts. And always would come men seeking mild winters, health, mineral wealth, land for grazing and farming, and sometimes pure adventure or a chance to start life anew.

Components of the Population. About a third of Arizona's residents were born in the state. Foreign-born residents make up only a small percentage of the total population. Of the foreign-

MONUMENT VALLEY, in northeastern Arizona, is named for its picturesque rocky buttes and pinnacles.

HERBERT LANKS, FROM PIX

NAVAJO WOMAN weaving in Monument Valley on the Navajo reservation. A crafts museum is nearby.

zona's future as dependent on emulating the older and richer states.

Exceedingly rapid growth since 1950 explains much in Arizona. Expansion of population and the shift from rural to urban domination have meant that nothing could be static, and the old Arizona is vanishing as the cities take on the face of the southern California megalopolis.

Largest Centers of Population. Phoenix and Tucson dwarf other Arizona cities. The Phoenix metropolitan statistical area (coextensive with Maricopa county) is much more populous, however, since it includes such cities as Scottsdale, Mesa, Tempe, Glendale, and Chandler.

In the Tucson metropolitan area (coextensive with Pima county), Tucson is the only large center of population. Tucson, which is much older than Phoenix, is affectionately called the "Old Pueblo." The Spanish influence is more noticeable there than in other Arizona cities, but Tucson has not escaped the common pattern of uncontrolled growth, which makes one city look very much like another.

A characteristic of Arizona's large cities is decentralization. In 1950, Phoenix had a downtown business district appropriate to a city of 100,000; today virtually no retail businesses remain in that central district. Instead, the metropolitan area is dotted with large shopping centers, each with stores of every kind and acres of parking space. The people are almost entirely dependent upon the automobile for transportation. A few city buses run on infrequent schedules, but motor cars dominate the scene, clogging the streets and creating a demand for more and more freeways.

born, the largest numbers are natives of Mexico. Smaller numbers come from several other countries.

Of the 1,772,482 Arizonians enumerated in the 1970 federal census, the great majority were of the so-called Anglo-American group. Other large groups were those with Spanish surnames (chiefly Mexican-Americans), American Indians, and Negroes.

All the major religious groups of the United States are found in Arizona. The heavy proportion of Mexican-Americans helps make Roman Catholicism the largest single denomination, although Protestants are in the majority.

Until the mid-20th century more than half of the people in the state lived in rural areas. Today almost 80% of Arizona's residents live in urban centers.

Way of Life. Arizona is characterized by greater variety in way of life than most states. Since it contains more Indians than any other, large areas of the state, especially the northeastern section, are dominated by their ways, which reflect the ancient native culture invaded by the white man's influence. The large number of Mexican-Americans, most of whom are bilingual, means that their mode of living is prominent in Arizona.

Territorial Arizona was a land of miners and ranchers. Traditionally, the cowboy gained the spotlight with his broadbrim hat, high-heeled boots, and affection for horses. Economic forces, however, dictated that Arizona would not be simply a land of copper and cattle. Irrigation projects guaranteed large-scale farming, improved transportation and warm climate meant tourists, and the nation's industrial growth brought manufacturing. People from all over flooded into the state, and the culture grew increasingly eclectic. As Arizona residents, they cultivated informality, asserting that they had left stodgy ways behind. But a rising standard of living has brought increased sophistication, and the old informality is being eroded by newer residents who see Ari-

GROWTH OF POPULATION SINCE 1870

Year	Population	Year	Population
1870	9,658	1940	499,261
1880	40,440	1950	749,587
1890	88,243	1960	1,302,161
1900	122,931	1970	1,772,482
1920	334,162		

Gain between 1960 and 1970: 36.1% (U. S. gain, 13.3%). **Density (1970):** 15.6 persons per square mile (U. S. density, 56.2 persons per square mile).

URBAN-RURAL DISTRIBUTION

Year	Percent urban	Percent rural
1920	36.1 (U. S., 51.2)	63.9
1930	34.4 (U. S., 56.2)	65.6
1940	34.8 (U. S., 56.6)	65.2
1950	55.5 (U. S., 64.0)	44.5
1960	74.5 (U. S., 69.9)	25.5
1970	79.6 (U. S., 73.5)	20.4

LARGEST CENTERS OF POPULATION

City or Metropolitan area[1]	1970	1960	1950
Phoenix (city)	581,562	439,170	106,818
Metropolitan area	967,522	663,510	331,770
Tucson (city)	262,933	212,892	45,454
Metropolitan area	351,667	265,660	141,216
Scottsdale	67,823	10,026	...
Tempe	62,907	24,897	7,684
Mesa	62,853	33,772	16,790
Glendale	36,228	15,696	8,179
Yuma	29,007	23,974	9,145
Flagstaff	26,117	18,214	7,663
Chandler	13,763	9,531	3,799
Sun City (U)	13,670	...	...

[1] Standard metropolitan statistical areas. (U) Unincorporated, as of 1970 census.

2. The Land

Nature tried almost everything in Arizona—from pines to prickly pears, from Gila monsters to mountain lions, from snowy peaks to scorching deserts, from deep canyons to high mesas. Of Arizona's total area only about 16% is in private hands, and only 13% under state ownership. The Indians' holdings, included in some 20 Indian reservations, make up 27% of the total. The federal government holds the reservation lands in trust for the Indian tribes and individual Indian owners. The remainder of the state, all federally owned, consists of national forests, wildlife refuges, parks and monuments, and land-management areas.

Major Physical Divisions. Stretching diagonally across Arizona from southeast to northwest is a mountain region known as the Mexican Highland. Adjoining it on the southwest is a desert region called the Sonoran Desert. Both are sections of the great Basin and Range province of the western and southwestern United States. To the northeast of the mountain region are the Colorado Plateaus, which extend into Arizona from Utah, Colorado, and New Mexico.

The Mexican Highland and Sonoran Desert are characterized by numerous mountain ranges that rise abruptly from broad basins, or plainlike valleys. The highest of the ranges are in the highlands, or mountain region, which varies in width from 150 miles (241 km) in the southeastern part of the state to 60 miles (97 km) elsewhere. Most of the peaks do not exceed 8,000 feet (2,438 meters), although a few—such as Mt. Graham in the Pinaleno Mountains, Mt. Lemmon in the Santa Catalina Mountains, and Miller Peak in the Huachuca Mountains—are higher. In the desert region the ranges are lower and more sharply carved, and the valleys generally wider.

The Colorado Plateaus region, which covers the northeastern half of the state, is made up of individually named plateaus as well as valleys and mesas (isolated hills with steeply sloping sides and level tops). The plateaus vary in average elevation from 5,000 feet (1,524 meters) to more than 9,000 feet (2,743 meters). In several places the surface is surmounted by lofty volcanic mountains and deeply cut by canyons of the Colorado River system. Humphreys Peak (12,670 feet, or 3,862 meters), in the San Francisco Peaks north of Flagstaff, is the highest point in the state. Other high peaks are in the White Mountains, in east-central Arizona, near Springerville and McNary. Spectacular canyons, other than the Grand Canyon, include Oak Creek Canyon and Canyon de Chelly. The southern margin of the plateaus section is marked by rugged cliffs, known as the Mogollon Rim and the Mogollon Mesa.

Rivers and Lakes. Arizona's mighty river is the Colorado. Flowing into the state at the midpoint on the Arizona-Utah border, it turns abruptly westward into its 217-mile (349-km) canyon, then swings southward to form the boundry first between Nevada and Arizona and then between California and Arizona. This great river drains more than 90% of the state. Its tributaries include the Gila, which meets it at Yuma; the Little Colorado, which joins it at the beginning of the Grand Canyon; and the Bill Williams, which empties into it near Parker Dam.

Natural lakes are few in Arizona, but several man-made reservoirs are more than ample substitutes. The great man-made lakes partly or entirely in Arizona are those formed by the dams on the Colorado—Lake Powell, behind Glen Canyon Dam; Lake Mead, behind Hoover Dam; Lake Mohave, behind Davis Dam; and Havasu Lake, behind Parker Dam. On the Gila is San Carlos Lake, created by Coolidge Dam. The series of dams on the Salt River make a string of lakes called Theodore Roosevelt, Canyon, Saguaro, and Apache.

Climate. People move to Arizona because of its beneficial climate, particularly to the warm southern desert. A substantial part of the income of Arizonans is gained from serving winter tourists. Arizonans think of themselves as living outdoors more than people in the Midwest and East. The climate, then—except for the hot desert summer—is something to be praised and counted a natural blessing.

Temperatures vary drastically from one part of the state to another. A July day in desert Phoenix has an average high temperature of somewhat over 100° F (38° C). A January day in mountain Flagstaff has an average low of 14° F (−10° C). Phoenix's ideal time is March, when the average high is 75° F (24° C) and the low is 43° F (6° C). Flagstaff's best month is June, with an average maximum temperature of 77° F (25° C) and a minimum of 41° F (5° C). Precipitation is nowhere plentiful, the state's yearly average being about 13 inches (33 cm). The driest place is Yuma, with only 3 inches (7.6 cm) a year. Tucson averages 11 inches (28 cm), as compared to Phoenix's 7 inches (17.8 cm). McNary, in the White Mountains, records an average of 25 inches (63.5 cm), while Flagstaff has 18 inches (45.7 cm). Humidity generally is low.

Plants and Animals. The extreme ranges of elevation and temperature assure a great variety of flora. The trees of the high north country are aspen, fir, birch, ponderosa pine, spruce, oak, sycamore, cherry, and walnut. Those of the desert and oasis are citrus, Joshua, paloverde, cottonwood, palm, and olive. Cacti of all kinds abound. Symbolic of Arizona is the saguaro, towering over the desert. Others are the cholla, barrel cactus, and prickly pear.

GLEN CANYON DAM on the Colorado River is one of the largest power-producing dams in the United States.

ED FINLEY, FROM PHOTO RESEARCHERS

Most of the forest lands are included in national forests, which cover approximately one sixth of Arizona's total area. Management of the forests on a sustained-yield basis assures a continuing supply of timber.

The large animals of Arizona are elk, pronghorn antelope, desert bighorn sheep, brown bear, black bear, mule deer, white-tail deer, and mountain lion. Smaller animals include lynx, bobcat, jabalina (or javelina—wild swine), badger, beaver, fox, otter, raccoon, skunk, cottontail jackrabbit, porcupine, Kaibab squirrel and pocket gopher. More than 400 different kinds of birds are found in the state. Most of the freshwater fish of the United States can be found in Arizona's lakes and rivers.

Vicious crawling creatures are plentiful. In the desert regions, scorpions can show up almost anywhere. The tarantula and the black widow spider are familiar desert denizens, along with the centipede and the Gila monster (a large orange and black lizard). Rattlesnakes are found in all parts of the state.

Minerals. Arizona is well endowed with minerals. The chief metal deposits other than uranium and vanadium are found in the Basin and Range Province. These include copper, for which Arizona is famous, silver, zinc, gold, lead, molybdenum, manganese, tungsten, and mercury. Uranium and vanadium occur chiefly in the Colorado Plateaus, especially in the Four Corners area (the extreme northeast, where the corners of Arizona, Utah, Colorado, and New Mexico meet). The plateau region also contains nonmetallic minerals, including some mineral fuels—coal and comparatively recent discoveries of petroleum, natural gas, and helium. Other important nonmetallic minerals, found in various parts of the state, are sand and gravel, asbestos, lime, gypsum, cement materials, stone, feldspar, quartz, pumice, perlite, pyrites, and mica.

Conservation. Much of what Arizona is today can be attributed to conservation, particularly of water resources. The Federal Reclamation

LOUIS RENAULT, FROM PHOTO RESEARCHERS

GIANT SAGUARO CACTUS (*left*) grows in the dry country of southern Arizona. Fine specimens are abundant in the Saguaro National Monument area near Tucson. The blossom (below), near the tips of branches, is the state flower.

JOSEF MUENCH

Act of 1902 opened the way for the construction of (Theodore) Roosevelt Dam on the Salt River above Phoenix. This was the first of the four dams in the Salt River Project, which controls the irrigation water in the lakes behind the dams and the distribution of the electric power generated. This system also provides the flood control needed to protect Phoenix and its suburbs. With this great water conservation system, Maricopa county has more than one third of about 1 million acres (405,000 hectares) of irrigated land in the state. Other large irrigated area are around Yuma, in southwestern Arizona, and Casa Grande, in Pinal county, south of Phoenix.

The early 1950's saw the beginning of the Arizona's Watershed Program, a pioneer project among the states to bring together state, federal, and private agencies to seek means to save topsoil and recover rainfall. At about the same time the state government passed laws strictly controlling the drilling of new wells because of the rapidly diminishing water table. Since the water supply available from reservoirs is supplemented by wells, the restrictions meant that some cultivated lands have been abandoned.

Arizona's hopes for adequate water to guarantee its continued industrial and agricultural growth ride on the Central Arizona Project, a plan by which water from the Colorado River can be brought to the desert population centers around Phoenix and Tucson. In the 1920's the state began its efforts to obtain the right to a sufficient share of the water and to gain congressional approval of the project. A long dispute between California and Arizona over the division of the river's annual flow led Arizona to file suit in the U. S. Supreme Court in 1952. Eleven years later the court awarded Arizona 2.8 million acre-feet of that water annually. Even before this, in 1947, a plan now known as the Central Arizona Project, was introduced into the U. S. Senate. This bill and its successors finally won congressional approval in 1968.

The Central Arizona Project proposes to take water from the Colorado River at Havasu Lake behind Parker Dam and through an elaborate system of dams, aqueducts, tunnels, pumping stations, reservoirs, and long pipelines to bring it to the Phoenix valley. An aqueduct would serve Tucson.

3. The Economy

Arizona's economy is sometimes characterized by the five "C's"—copper, cotton, cattle, climate, and citrus. But this characterization omits a vital and growing element—manufacturing. When the Anglo-Americans became acquainted with the region in the mid-1800's, they could little envision how the economy would develop over the next 100 years. Mining and cattle raising were the principal means of livelihood in early territorial days, and these provided a living for relatively few people. But the early 1900's brought the practical application of irrigation and greater opportunities for farmers. Improved transportation made it possible to get manufactured products to markets throughout the country and for tourists and health-seekers to bring their spending power into the state.

After World War II, the economy expanded rapidly, and by 1960 the value added by manufacture in the state had leaped ahead of cash farm income and value of mineral production.

ARIZONA

TOPOGRAPHY

0   50   100 Mi.

0   50   100 Km.

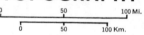

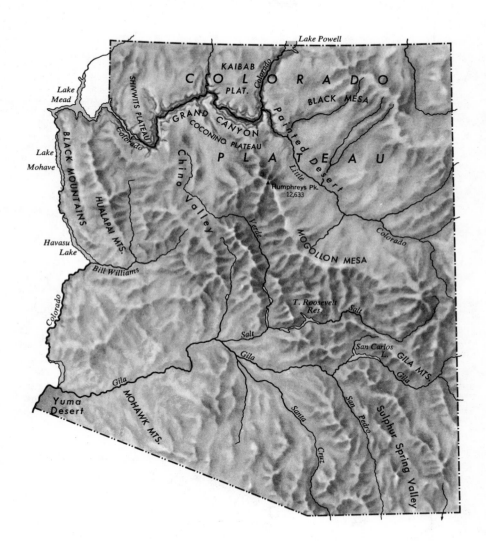

Lake Powell

KAIBAB PLAT.

C O L O R A D O

BLACK MESA

Lake Mead

SHIVWITS PLATEAU

GRAND CANYON

COCONINO PLATEAU

Colorado

Painted Desert

P L A T E A U

Colorado

BLACK MOUNTAINS

Lake Mohave

HUALAPAI MTS.

Chino Valley

Humphreys Pk. 12,633

Little

Havasu Lake

Bill Williams

Verde

MOGOLLON MESA

Colorado

T. Roosevelt Res.

Salt

Colorado

San Carlos L.

GILA MTS.

Salt

Gila

Gila

Gila

Yuma Desert

MOHAWK MTS.

Santa

San Pedro

Sulphur Spring Valley

Cruz

5,000 m. 16,404 ft. | 2,000 m. 6,562 ft. | 1,000 m. 3,281 ft. | 500 m. 1,640 ft. | 200 m. 656 ft. | 100 m. 328 ft. | Sea Level | Below

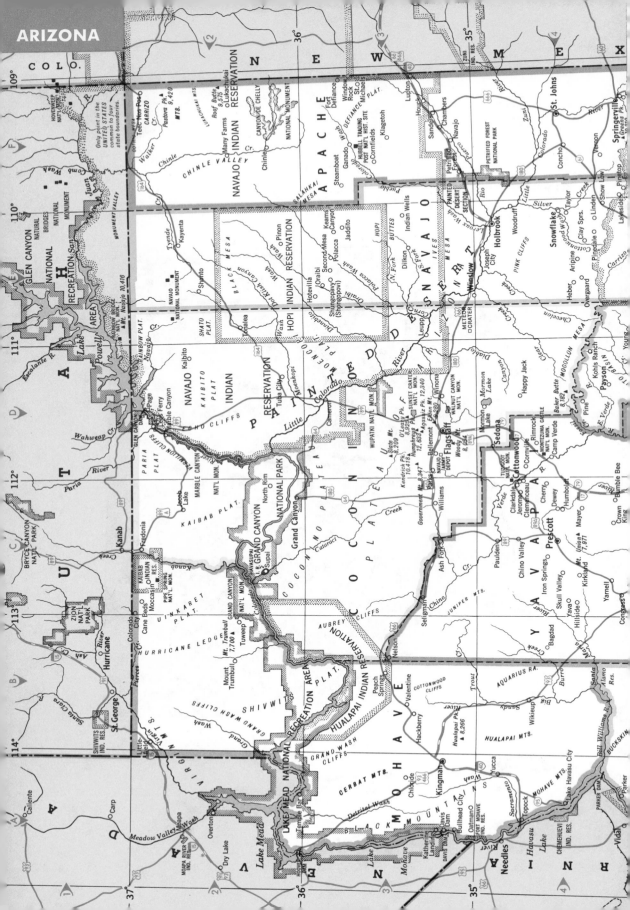

ARIZONA

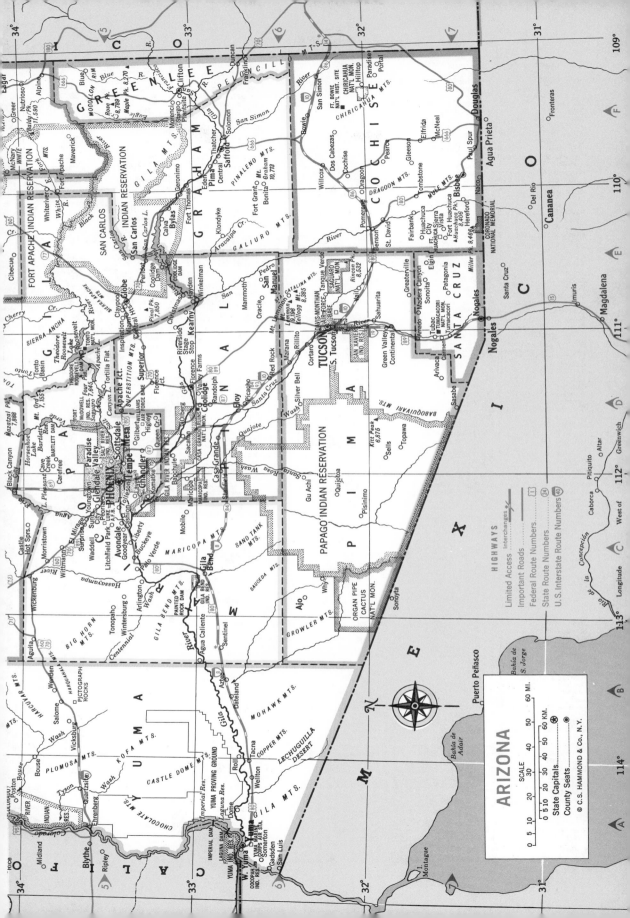

ARIZONA

ARIZONA

COUNTIES

Apache, 32,304 F 3
Cochise, 61,918 F 7
Coconino, 48,326 C 3
Gila, 29,255 E 5
Graham, 16,578 E 6
Greenlee, 10,330 F 5
Maricopa, 968,487 C 5
Mohave, 25,857 A 3
Navajo, 47,559 E 3
Pima, 351,667 D 6
Pinal, 68,579 D 6
Santa Cruz, 13,966 E 7
Yavapai, 37,005 C 4
Yuma, 60,827 A 5

CITIES and TOWNS

Aguila, 450 B 5
Ajo, 5,881 C 6
Alpine, 450 F 5
Apache Junction, 2,390 D 5
Arivaca, 165 D 7
Arlington, 950 C 5
Ash Fork, 800 C 3
Avondale, 6,626 C 5
Bagdad, 2,079 B 4
Bapchule, 300 D 5
Benson, 2,839 E 7
Bisbee⊙, 8,328 F 7
Black Canyon City, 600 C 4
Bouse, 200 A 5
Bowie, 600 F 6
Buckeye, 2,599 C 5
Bullhead City, 900 A 3
Bylas, 1,125 E 5
Cameron, 600 D 3
Camp Verde, 1,500 D 4
Carefree, 350 D 5
Carmen, 200 D 7
Casa Grande, 10,536 D 6
Cashion, 2,705 C 5
Cave Creek, 300 D 5
Central, 300 F 6
Central Heights, 2,289 E 5
Chambers, 500 F 3
Chandler, 13,763 D 5
Chinle, 500 F 2
Chino Valley, 970 C 4
Chloride, 225 A 3
Christmas, 201 E 5
Cibecue, 100 E 4
Clarkdale, 892 C 4
Claypool, 2,245 E 5
Clay Springs, 225 E 4
Clemenceau, 300 C 4
Clifton⊙, 5,087 F 5
Cochise, 150 F 6
Colorado City, 350 B 2
Concho, 100 F 4
Congress, 350 C 4
Continental, 250 D 7
Coolidge, 5,314 D 6
Cornfields, 200 F 3
Cornville, 425 D 4
Cottonwood, 2,815 D 4
Crown King, 100 C 4
Dateland, 100 B 6
Davis Dam, 125 A 3
Dewey, 100 C 4
Dilkon, 90 E 3
Douglas, 12,462 F 7
Dragoon, 150 F 6
Duncan, 773 F 6
Eagar, 1,279 F 4
Eden, 89 F 6
Ehrenburg, 93 A 5
Elfrida, 700 F 7
Elgin, 247 E 7
El Mirage, 3,258 C 5
Eloy, 5,381 D 6
Fairbank, 100 E 7
Flagstaff⊙, 26,117 D 3
Florence⊙, 2,173 D 5
Fort Apache, 500 F 5
Fort Defiance, 900 F 3
Fort Grant, 240 E 6
Fort Huachuca, 159 E 7
Fort Thomas, 450 F 5
Franklin, 300 F 6
Fredonia, 798 C 2
Gadsden, 250 A 6
Ganado, 300 F 3
Gila Bend, 1,795 C 6
Gilbert, 1,971 D 5
Glendale, 36,228 C 5
Globe⊙, 7,333 E 5
Goodyear, 2,140 C 5
Grand Canyon, 1,011 C 2
Green Valley, 3,800 D 7
Gu-Achi, 339 C 6
Hackberry, 250 B 3
Hayden, 1,283 E 5
Heber, 750 E 4
Higley, 500 D 5
Hillside, 100 B 4
Holbrook⊙, 4,759 E 4
Hotevilla, 600 E 3
Houck, 325 F 3
Huachuca City, 1,241 E 7
Humboldt, 424 C 4
Indian Wells, 150 E 3
Inspiration, 500 D 5
Iron Springs, 175 C 4
Jerome, 290 C 4
Joseph City, 650 E 4
Kaibito, 275 D 2
Katherine Landing, 102 A 3
Kayenta, 500 E 2
Keams Canyon, 400 E 3
Kearny, 2,829 E 5
Kingman⊙, 7,312 A 3
Kirkland, 100 C 4
Klagetoh, 200 F 3
Klondyke, 86 E 6
Kohls Ranch, 100 D 4
Komatke, 300 C 5
Lake Havasu City, 2,700 A 4
Lakeside, 700 E 4
Laveen, 800 C 5
Leupp, 150 E 3
Liberty, 150 C 5
Litchfield Park, 1,664 C 5
Lukachukai, 350 F 2
Lupton, 250 F 3
Mammoth, 1,953 E 6
Many Farms, 250 F 2
Marana, 2,900 D 6
Maricopa, 750 C 5
Mayer, 810 C 4
McNary, 950 F 4
McNeal, 100 F 7
Mesa, 62,853 D 5
Miami, 3,394 E 5
Mobile, 100 C 5
Morenci, 950 F 5
Morristown, 250 C 5
Naco, 750 E 7
Navajo, 100 F 3
Nogales⊙, 8,946 E 7
Oatman, 175 A 3
Oracle, 1,500 E 6
Oraibi, 600 E 3
Overgaard, 300 E 4
Page, 1,439 D 2
Palo Verde, 500 C 5
Paradise Valley, 7,155 D 5
Parker, 1,948 A 4
Parks, 175 C 3
Patagonia, 630 E 7
Payson, 1,490 D 4
Peach Springs, 525 B 3
Pearce, 300 F 7
Peoria, 4,792 C 5
Peridot, 950 E 5
Phoenix (cap.)⊙, 581,562 C 5
Phoenix, ‡967,522 C 5
Picacho, 1,200 D 6
Pima, 1,184 F 6
Pine, 800 D 4
Pinetop, 950 F 4
Pinon, 100 E 2
Pisinimo, 187 C 6
Plantsite, 1,077 F 5
Polacca, 500 E 3
Pomerene, 365 E 7
Poston, 500 A 4
Prescott⊙, 13,134 C 4
Quartzsite, 255 A 5
Queen Creek, 600 D 5
Quijotoa, 107 C 6
Randolph, 350 D 6
Red Rock, 100 D 6
Rillito, 400 D 6
Rimrock, 217 D 4
Riverside Stage Stop, 418 D 5
Roll, 700 A 6
Roosevelt, 125 D 5
Sacaton, 300 D 5
Safford⊙, 5,333 F 6
Sahuarita, 200 E 7
Saint David, 1,250 E 7
Saint Johns⊙, 1,320 F 4
Saint Michaels, 250 F 3
Salome, 684 B 5
San Carlos, 2,542 E 5
Sanders, 420 F 3
San Luis, 280 A 6
San Manuel, 4,332 E 6
San Simon, 400 F 6
Scottsdale, 67,823 D 5
Sedona, 2,022 D 4
Seligman, 950 B 3
Sells, 1,245 D 7
Shonto, 700 E 2
Show Low, 2,129 F 4
Shungopavy (Shongopovi), 570 E 3
Sierra Vista, 6,689 E 7
Silver Bell, 900 D 6
Skull Valley, 250 C 4
Snowflake, 1,977 E 4
Solomon, 700 F 6
Somerton, 2,225 A 6
South Tucson, 6,220 D 6
Springerville, 1,151 F 4
Stanfield, 150 C 6
Stargo, 1,194 F 5
Steamboat, 100 F 3
Sun City, 13,670 D 5
Supai, 190 C 2
Superior, 4,975 D 5
Surprise, 2,427 C 5
Tacna, 950 B 6
Tanque Verde, 850 E 6
Taylor, 888 E 4
Teec Nos Pos, 550 F 2
Tempe, 63,550 D 5
Thatcher, 2,320 F 6
Tolleson, 3,881 C 5
Tombstone, 1,241 F 7
Tonalea, 125 E 2
Topawa, 500 D 7
Topock, 325 A 4
Tubac, 140 E 7
Tuba City, 650 D 2
Tucson⊙, 262,933 D 6
Tucson, ‡351,667 D 6
Tumacacori, 100 D 7
Vail, 175 E 6
Valentine, 120 B 3
Valley Farms, 240 D 6
Waddell, 100 C 5
Wellton, 900 A 6
Wenden, 245 B 5
West Yuma, 5,552 A 6
Whiteriver, 900 E 5
Wickenburg, 2,698 C 5
Wikieup, 150 B 4
Willcox, 2,568 F 6
Williams, 2,386 C 3
Window Rock, 600 F 3
Winkelman, 974 E 6
Winslow, 8,066 E 3
Wintersburg, 400 B 5
Wittmann, 600 C 5
Woodruff, 120 E 4
Yarnell, 800 C 4
Young, 197 D 4
Youngtown, 1,886 C 5
Yucca, 250 A 4
Yuma⊙, 29,007 A 6

OTHER FEATURES

Agassiz (peak) D 3
Agua Fria (riv.) C 5
Alamo (res.) B 4
Apache (lake) D 5
Aquarius (range) B 4
Aravaipa (creek) E 6
Arizona (plat.) D 3
Aubrey (cliffs) B 3
Baboquivari (mts.) D 7
Baker Butte (mt.) D 4
Baldy (peak) F 5
Bartlett (dam) D 5
Bartlett (res.) D 5
Big Horn (mts.) B 5
Big Sandy (riv.) B 4
Bill Williams (riv.) B 4
Black (mesa) E 2
Black (mts.) E 5
Black (riv.) A 3
Blue (riv.) F 5
Bouse Wash (dry riv.) A 4
Buckskin (mts.) B 4
Burro (creek) B 4
Canyon (lake) D 5
Canyon de Chelly Nat'l Mon. F 2
Carrizo (creek) E 4
Carrizo (mts.) F 2
Casa Grande Ruins Nat'l Mon. D 6
Castle Dome (mts.) A 5
Cataract (creek) C 3
Centennial Wash (dry riv.) B 5
Cerbat (mts.) A 3
Cherry (creek) E 4
Chevelon (creek) E 4
Chinle (creek) F 2
Chinle (valley) F 2
Chino (creek) C 3
Chiricahua (mts.) F 6
Chiricahua Nat'l Mon. F 6
Chocolate (mts.) A 5
Coconino (plat.) C 3
Cocopah Ind. Res., 63 A 6
Colorado (riv.) A 5
Colorado River Ind. Res., 1,297 A 5
Coolidge (dam) E 5
Copper (mts.) B 6
Corn (creek) E 3
Coronado Nat'l Memorial E 7
Cottonwood (cliffs) B 3
Cottonwood Wash (dry riv.) E 4
Davis (dam) A 3
Davis-Monthan A.F.B., 5,100 E 6
Defiance (plat.) F 3
Detrital Wash (dry riv.) A 3
Diablo (canyon) D 4
Dinnebito Wash (dry riv.) E 3
Dot Klish (canyon) E 2
Dragoon (mts.) F 7
Eagle (creek) F 5
East Verde (riv.) D 4
Echo (cliffs) D 2
Elden (mt.) D 3
Fort Apache Ind. Res., 5,953 E 5
Fort Bowie Nat'l Hist. Site F 6
Fort Huachuca, 6,659 E 7
Fort McDowell Ind. Res., 280 D 5
Fort Mohave Ind. Res., 306 A 4
Fossil (creek) D 4
Four Peaks (mt.) D 5
Galiuro (mts.) E 6
Gila (mts.) A 6
Gila (mts.) F 5
Gila (riv.) B 6
Gila Bend (mts.) B 5
Gila Bend Ind. Res., 342 C 6
Gila River Ind. Res., 5,241 C 5
Glen Canyon (dam) D 2
Glen Canyon Nat'l Rec Area D 1
Gothic (mesa) F 2
Government (mt.) C 3
Graham (mt.) F 6
Grand Canyon Nat'l Mon. C 2
Grand Canyon Nat'l Park C 2
Grand Wash (butte) B 2
Grand Wash (riv.) B 2
Greens (peak) F 4
Growler (mts.) B 6
Harcuvar (mts.) B 5
Harquahala (mts.) B 5
Hassayampa (riv.) C 5
Havasu (lake) A 4
Havasupai Ind. Res., 270 C 2
Hoover (dam) A 2
Hopi (buttes) E 3
Hopi Indian Res., 4,966 E 2
Horseshoe (lake) D 5
Huachuca (peak) E 7
Hualapai (mts.) B 4
Hualapai (peak) B 3
Hualapai Ind. Res., 682 B 3
Hubbell Trading Post Nat'l Hist. Site F 3
Humphreys (peak) D 3
Hurricane Ledge B 2
Imperial (res.) A 6
Ives (mesa) E 3
Juniper (mts.) C 3
Kaibab (plat.) C 2
Kaibab Ind. Res., 60 C 2
Kaibito (plat.) D 2
Kanab (creek) C 2
Kellogg (mt.) E 6
Kendrick (peak) D 3
Kitt (peak) D 7
Kofa (mts.) B 5
Laguna (res.) A 6
Lake Mead Nat'l Rec. Area A 2
Lechuguilla (des.) B 6
Lemmon (mt.) E 6
Leroux Wash (dry riv.) E 3
Little Colorado (riv.) D 3
Lukachukai (mts.) F 2
Luke A.F.B., 5,047 C 5
Maple (peak) F 5
Marble Canyon Nat'l Mon. D 2
Maricopa (mts.) C 5
Maricopa Ind. Res., 240 C 6
Mazatzal (peak) D 4
Mead (lake) A 2
Meteor (crater) E 3
Miller (peak) E 7
Moencopi (plat.) D 3
Moenkopi Wash (dry riv.) D 2
Mogollon (mesa) D 4
Mogollon Rim (cliffs) F 5
Mohave (lake) A 3
Mohave (mts.) A 4
Mohawk (mts.) B 6
Montezuma Castle Nat'l Mon. D 4
Mormon (lake) D 4
Mule (mts.) E 7
Navajo (creek) D 2
Navajo Ind. Res., 71,396 F 2
Navajo Nat'l Mon. E 2
Navajo Ord. Depot D 3
O'Leary (peak) D 3
Oraibi Wash (dry riv.) E 3
Ord (mt.) D 5
Organ Pipe Cactus Nat'l Mon. C 6
Painted (des.) D 2
Painted Desert Section (Petrified Forest Nat'l Park) F 3
Painted Rock (dam) C 5
Papago Ind. Res., 5,506 C 6
Paria (plat.) D 2
Paria (riv.) D 1
Parker (dam) A 4
Pastora (peak) F 2
Peloncillo (mts.) F 6
Petrified Forest Nat'l Park F 4
Pictograph (rocks) B 5
Pierces (creek) B 2
Pinal (peak) E 5
Pinaleno (mts.) F 6
Pink (cliffs) E 4
Pipe Spring Nat'l Mon. C 2
Pleasant (lake) C 5
Plomosa (mts.) A 5
Polacca Wash (dry riv.) E 3
Powell (lake) E 1
Quajote Wash (dry riv.) D 6
Rainbow (plat.) D 2
Rincon (peak) E 6
Rio Puerco (riv.) F 3
Roof Butte (mt.) F 2
Rose (peak) F 5
Saguaro (lake) D 5
Saguaro Nat'l Mon. E 6
Salahkai (mesa) F 3
Salt (riv.) D 5
Salt River Ind. Res., 2,040 D 5
San Carlos (lake) E 5
San Carlos (riv.) E 5
San Carlos Ind. Res., 4,404 E 5
Sand Tank (mt.) C 6
San Francisco (riv.) F 5
San Pedro (riv.) E 6
San Simon (riv.) F 6
Santa Catalina (mts.) E 6
Santa Cruz (riv.) D 6
Santa Maria (riv.) B 4
San Xavier Ind. Res., 928 D 6
Sauceda (mts.) C 6
Shato (plat.) E 2
Shivwits (plat.) B 2
Sierra Ancha (mts.) D 5
Sierra Apache (mts.) E 5
Silver (creek) E 4
Slate (mt.) D 3
Sunset Crater Nat'l Mon. D 3
Superstition (mts.) D 5
Theodore Roosevelt (dam) D 5
Theodore Roosevelt (lake) D 5
Tonto (basin) D 4
Tonto (creek) D 4
Tonto Nat'l Mon. D 5
Trout (creek) B 3
Trumbull (mt.) B 2
Tumacacori Nat'l Mon. E 7
Tuzigoot Nat'l Mon. D 4
Tyende (creek) E 2
Tyson Wash (dry riv.) A 5
Uinkaret (plat.) C 2
Union (mt.) C 4
Verde (riv.) D 5
Vermilion (cliffs) D 2
Virgin (mts.) B 2
Virgin (riv.) B 2
Walker (creek) F 2
Walnut Canyon Nat'l Mon. D 3
White (riv.) E 5
Williams A.F.B., 3,443 D 5
Woody (mt.) D 3
Wupatki Nat'l Mon. D 3
Yuma Marine Corps Air Sta., 3,460 A 6
Yuma Proving Ground, 1,349 A 6
Zuni (riv.) F 4

⊙ County seat. ‡ Population of metropolitan area.

All figures available from 1970 final census are supplemented by local official estimates.

Agriculture. Income from crops usually makes up somewhat more than half the total farm income. Cotton is by far the largest cash crop, accounting for about one third of the crop value and occupying about the same proportion of the cultivated acreage. Other principal crops are feed crops—hay, sorghum grain, barley, and corn—vegetables, especially lettuce and cantaloupe, and citrus fruits.

In the livestock and livestock products category, cattle bring the largest proportion of the cash income. Dairy products rank second, followed by poultry and eggs and sheep and lambs. Although much of the income from cattle results from feedlot activities—by which cattle are shipped into Phoenix, Yuma, or Tucson, fattened in pens, and shipped out again—the rangelands of Arizona support a considerable quantity of breeding stock.

VALUE OF FACTORY, FARM, AND MINE PRODUCTION

	1965	1960	1950
	(Millions of dollars)		
Value added by manufacture	720	482	127
Cash farm income	513	442	278
Value of mineral production	580	416	207

Sources: U.S. Department of Commerce, *Census of Manufactures*; U.S. Department of Agriculture, *The Farm Income Situation*; U.S. Department of the Interior, *Minerals Yearbook*.

PERSONAL INCOME IN ARIZONA

Source	1965	1960	1950
	(Millions of dollars)		
Farms	192	163	150
Mining	144	112	53
Contract construction	195	239	63
Manufacturing	470	299	56
Wholesale and retail trade	516	394	156
Finance, insurance, and real estate	169	116	32
Transportation, communications, and public utilities	203	164	73
Services	453	296	110
Government	517	334	108
Other industries	11	10	3
	(Dollars)		
Per capita personal income	2,370	2,032	1,331
(Per capita income, U.S.)	(2,746)	(2,215)	(1,496)

Source: U.S. Department of Commerce, *Survey of Current Business*.

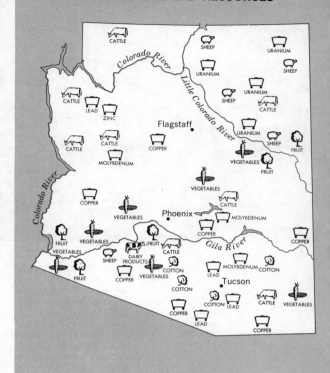

AGRICULTURE AND RESOURCES

The Apache, who occupy the San Carlos and Fort Apache reservations, are among the notable Indian cattlemen.

In the late 1960's, Arizona had some 6,500 farms with an average size of more than 6,000 acres (2,430 hectares) and an average value exceeding $300,000. Maricopa county, with the largest irrigated acreage, is by far the greatest crop-producing area in the state.

JOSEF MUENCH

TUCSON, second largest city in Arizona, spreads out in a valley under the Santa Catalina Mountains. Giant saguaros stand like sentinels outside the city.

IRRIGATION CANAL brings water from lakes created by dams on the Salt and Verde rivers to make an oasis of great desert areas near Phoenix.

Mining and Minerals Extraction. Since the early 1900's, Arizona has led the United States in production of copper. Its mines yield just over 50% of the U. S. total. Among the foremost "copper towns" are Bisbee-Douglas, Morenci, San Manuel, Ray, Globe-Miami, and Ajo. Copper usually accounts for at least 85% of the state's total mineral production, and other metals are produced in significant quantities. But a nonmetallic mineral—sand and gravel, for use in the construction industries—has ranked second in value to copper since the 1950's. Other than copper, the metals with greatest production value are molybdenum, silver, gold, zinc, lead, and uranium. The most valuable nonmetals, besides sand and gravel, include stone, lime, pumice, diatomite, mica, perlite asbestos, and gypsum.

Manufacturing. Manufacturing is a dynamic and expanding area of the economy, having been directly or indirectly responsible for the largest portion of economic growth since the 1950's. In value added by manufacture, the industries producing electrical machinery, chiefly electronic components, are the leaders, followed by the makers of nonelectrical machinery. Other important categories of manufacturing are primary metals; food and food products; stone, clay, and glass products; fabricated metals; and lumber and wood products.

The electronics industry boomed in Arizona in the era following World War II. The mild climate and excellent transportation facilities attracted an expanding industry. Phoenix and Tucson were especially attractive because they could draw skilled workers, the universities in their areas could give postgraduate work to engineers, and the nearby hydroelectric projects could furnish ample cheap electricity.

Power. Between 1950 and 1965, the installed generating capacity of Arizona's power plants increased from 843,000 kw-hrs to almost 4 million kw-hrs. More than half the total came from steam plants. The Colorado River is the principal source of hydroelectric power.

Tourism. Although the national parks and monuments attract many visitors, the bulk of Arizona's tourist business is centered in the winter desert playgrounds around Phoenix and Tucson. Tourist spending in Arizona in the late 1960's was estimated at $500 million annually.

Transportation. When the railroad came to Arizona in the 1880's, the isolation of the territory ended. Main rail lines cross both the northern and the southern parts of the state, playing a vital role in heavy shipping, especially for the mining industry, although their passenger business has diminished greatly.

Arizona is well served by commercial aviation. Several regularly scheduled airlines operate out of the big airports in Tucson and Phoenix, and there are more than a dozen other airports with scheduled services. Arizona also is well situated on main east-west highways, such as U. S. 66, 60, 70, and 80 and Interstate 40, 10, and 8. The automobile is the chief means of local transportation, since no subways or other rapid transit systems exist in the large cities.

Labor Force. In Arizona, as in many other states, government employment (federal, state, and local) is the single largest source of personal income. Next, ranking close together, are jobs in manufacturing, which have more than doubled since the mid-1950's, and in wholesale and retail trade. In terms of number of persons employed in each category, the ranking usually is somewhat different, with wholesale and retail trade and government each accounting for somewhat more than 20% of the total labor force, and manufacturing and the service industries for somewhat less than 20%.

For additional statistics on the economy of Arizona, see THE AMERICANA ANNUAL.

4. Government and Politics

Arizona entered the Union at the height of the Progressive era in 1912, and its constitution reflects the political science of those years: If the "selfish" interests could be controlled, democracy would flourish and evil would disappear from government. So the governor was given a short 2-year term. The legislature has 2-year terms in both houses, and its actions are subject to the initiative and the referendum. All elective officials are subject to recall.

Constitutional amendments may be proposed by a majority vote of the legislature or by initiative of 15% of the voters. Ratification requires a majority vote by the electorate. More than 100 amendments have been placed on the ballot since statehood, and the voters have adopted about half the number proposed. At the time of its adoption (in 1911, effective at statehood), the constitution was a liberal one, notable for providing woman suffrage and workmen's compensation and for barring trusts and monopolies.

Political Divisions. Counties are governed by 3-man boards of supervisors elected bi-annually, along with a sheriff, county attorney, assessor, and other officers. Cities and towns may be incorporated or unincorporated. Unincorporated places are controlled by the county. Incorporated cities and towns, according to state law, may follow the mayor-council form of government, or they may try to obtain a home-rule charter from the legislature. The larger cities have city managers, responsible to the city councils.

Public Finance. With only about 16% of its lands privately owned and with a relatively small population in proportion to its area, Arizona has a narrower tax base than states in which nearly all the land is economically productive. As a result, Arizona constantly is faced with a revenue problem, and some state services suffer. The principal sources of revenue are the sales tax, motor fuel taxes, the property tax, and the income tax. Education and highways are the chief areas of expenditure.

Social Services. Arizona's financial problems are reflected in its efforts to provide adequate modern social services. The state department of public welfare supervises vocational rehabilitation programs and administers aid to the blind, dependent children, and the aged. The state hospital for the mentally ill, in Phoenix, is administered by the director of mental health and retardation of the department of health.

Federal antipoverty programs have been introduced among underprivileged groups, including Negroes, Mexican-Americans, and Indians. These program have been helpful, although far from adequate to the need. Health and welfare services for Indians who live on reservations are provided by their own tribal councils and the federal Bureau of Indian Affairs.

Politics. Although Arizona came into the Union when a Republican, William Howard Taft, was president, it was thoroughly Democratic in the early days. Through the years an idea persisted that since the Democrats always would win in a general election, a voter had to be a registered Democrat to have a voice in the nomination of officials. To this day the registration lists show a Democratic preponderance of two to one. But this has not meant that the state has followed the liberal policies of the

GOVERNORS OF ARIZONA

TERRITORIAL

John N. Goodwin	Republican	1863–1866
Richard C. McCormick	Republican	1866–1869
A. P. K. Safford	Republican	1869–1877
John P. Hoyt	Republican	1877–1878
John C. Frémont	Republican	1878–1881
Frederick A. Tritle	Republican	1881–1885
C. Meyer Zulick	Democrat	1885–1889
Lewis Wolfley	Republican	1889–1890
John N. Irwin	Republican	1890–1892
Nathan O. Murphy	Republican	1892–1893
Louis C. Hughes	Democrat	1893–1896
Benjamin J. Franklin	Republican	1896–1897
Myron H. McCord	Republican	1897–1898
Nathan O. Murphy	Republican	1898–1902
Alexander O. Brodie	Republican	1902–1905
Joseph H. Kibbey	Republican	1905–1909
Richard E. Sloan	Republican	1909–1911

STATE

George W. P. Hunt	Democrat	1911–1919
Thomas E. Campbell	Republican	1919–1923
George W. P. Hunt	Democrat	1923–1929
John C. Phillips	Republican	1929–1931
George W. P. Hunt	Democrat	1931–1933
Benjamin B. Moeur	Democrat	1933–1937
Rawghlie C. Stanford	Democrat	1937–1939
Robert T. Jones	Democrat	1939–1941
Sidney P. Osborn	Democrat	1941–1948
Dan E. Garvey	Democrat	1948–1951
Howard Pyle	Republican	1951–1955
Ernest W. McFarland	Democrat	1955–1959
Paul Fannin	Republican	1959–1965
Samuel P. Goddard, Jr.	Democrat	1965–1967
Jack Williams	Republican	1967–

national Democratic party in the past 35 years. "Pinto Democrats"—those who are registered Democratic but are conservative in principle—join with Republicans to place the state in the middle of the road or to the right.

The year 1950 marked a turning point in Arizona politics: During the preceding 38 years of statehood, Republicans held the governorship

McMATH SOLAR TELESCOPE at Kitt Peak National Observatory near Tucson is one of the world's largest.

WESTERN ELECTRIC CORP.

GOVERNMENT HIGHLIGHTS

Electoral Vote—5. **Representation in Congress**—U. S. senators, 2; U. S. representatives, 3. **State Legislature**—Senate, 30 members; House of Representatives, 60 members; all 2-year terms. **Governor**—2-year term; may succeed himself; salary, $22,500. **Voting Qualifications**—Age, 18; residence in state 1 year, in county 30 days, in district 30 days. **Elections**—General and state, Tuesday after first Monday in November; primary, eighth Tuesday prior to general and state elections.

GAMMAGE AUDITORIUM, at Arizona State University at Tempe, was designed by Frank Lloyd Wright. The lighting at dusk dramatizes the effect of the building's circular motif.

for only 6 years. They had never sent one of their number to the U. S. House of Representatives and had sent only one (Ralph Cameron, who served from 1921 to 1927) to the U. S. Senate. In 1950, Howard Pyle surprised the political pundits by winning the gubernatorial contest. In 1952, Pyle was reelected governor, John J. Rhodes broke the Democratic monopoly on the seats in the U. S. House, Barry Goldwater was elected to the U. S. Senate, and the political picture in Arizona changed.

On the state legislative scene the Democrats had always been in control, but in 1966, for the first time, the Republicans gained a majority in both houses. This change followed the reapportionment of the legislative districts in 1966, when the one-man, one-vote rule dictated that the metropolitan areas would have much greater representation than formerly. Maricopa county (Greater Phoenix) was awarded half the seats in both houses, and the city voters elected a majority of Republicans.

5. Education and Culture

Effective public education in Arizona dates from the territorial governorship (1869–1877) of Anson P. K. Safford, and from that time the public system has been almost completely dominant at all levels. Arizona has only a handful of privately supported schools.

Elementary and Secondary Education. Free public education has existed in Arizona since the first territorial constitution, but it was not until shortly after Governor Safford's time that the office of superintendent of public instruction was created. The state superintendent is elected by the people, but the state board of education is appointed by the governor.

Enrollment in the public schools of Arizona increased from about 100,000 in 1950 to more than 400,000 in the late 1960's. Both teachers' salaries and average per pupil expenditure are well above the national average.

The Bureau of Indian Affairs operates numerous boarding schools and day or trailer schools on the reservations for Indian children who are without access to public schools. The state receives some federal aid for those enrolled in the public system. Income from mineral resources on their lands has enabled the Navajo to set aside several million dollars for scholarships.

Higher Education. In 1885 the territorial legislature established two institutions of higher education—the University of Arizona at Tucson and the 2-year Arizona Territorial Normal School at Tempe. The university was the land-grant college in the territory, and it still enjoys the financial and other advantages of that status. The territorial normal school, which underwent several changes in organization and purpose after its founding, became Arizona State University in 1958. A third college was founded in Flagstaff as a normal school in 1899. It became a state college in 1945 and was reorganized in 1966 as Northern Arizona University.

One of the most significant recent developments is the growing number of junior colleges. Eastern Arizona College, a public junior institution at Thatcher, traces its origins to an academy founded by the Mormons in 1891. Phoenix College was founded as part of the Phoenix Union High School District in 1920. In the 1960's a increasing demand for more 2-year schools resulted in the formation of a state system of junior colleges· and the rapid establishment of several new junior colleges, including those at Mesa, Glendale, Yuma, and Douglas.

Private 4-year colleges in Arizona are Grand Canyon College in Phoenix and Prescott College in Prescott. Both have limited enrollments, with no intention of growing very large. The American Institute for Foreign Trade, in Phoenix, is a private professional graduate school.

Research Centers. Important research is done in Arizona. Significant work in astronomy has been going on since 1899 at Lowell Observatory near Flagstaff. Scientists at that site discovered the planet Pluto and the "red shift" in the stellar spectrum. The Kitt Peak National Observatory, southwest of Tucson, houses the world's most powerful solar telescope.

The University of Arizona is widely known for its work in dendrochronology (a method of dating based on tree rings), radioactive (carbon-14) dating, anthropology, geology, archaeology, agriculture, atmospheric physics, ethnology, and water utilization. Arizona State University is strong in educational research electronics, solar energy research, rare earth chemistry, geology, experimental psychology, business research, and mathematics.

Other research agencies include the Museum of Northern Arizona, near Flagstaff, specializing in anthropology and archaeology; the Arizona Pioneers' Historical Society, in Tucson, specializing in history; and the Arizona Historical

ARIZONA

(Right) Peach trees blossom beneath majestic rock formations in Oak Creek Canyon, near the central Arizona town of Sedona.

DICK KENT, FROM SHOSTAL

(Above) A meal is prepared in Canyon de Chelly, on the Navajo reservation in northeastern Arizona.

RAY ATKESON

(Below) Roosevelt Dam, completed in 1911 on the Salt River northeast of Phoenix, provides water for irrigation.

ESTHER HENDERSON, FROM DE WYS

(Left) The "Ear of the Wind" in Monument Valley. *(Right)* Copper is mined by the open-pit method in Morenci.

Navajo Indians in Monument Valley herd a flock of sheep and goats.

Sunrise at Grand Canyon, as seen from Mather Point. The Colorado River flows in the deep canyon at center.

Foundation, a private foundation affiliated with Arizona State University, in Tempe.

Libraries. A young state with a very small population until recently, Arizona does not have large public libraries. The Arizona Territorial Library, established in 1864, evolved into the present state department of library and archives, in the capitol at Phoenix.

The largest libraries in the state are at the universities in Tucson and Tempe. The former has the larger collection, although both are growing rapidly. About 20 cities have public libraries, which usually are controlled by local boards appointed by the city councils. The department of library and archives maintains a statewide extension service, with more than 150 libraries and depositories and a bookmobile service that reaches remote communities.

Museums. Arizona has several excellent museums. At the university in Tucson are the Arizona State Museum, which is notable in the fields of anthropology and archaeology and has exceptional displays of dendrochronology, and the University of Arizona Art Gallery, with a first-rate collection of Italian art and contemporary American and European painting. The Arizona Pioneers Historical Society, in Tucson, has a fine collection of Arizona memorabilia.

In Phoenix are the Phoenix Art Museum, which has developed notably since the early 1960's, and the widely known Heard Museum of Anthropology and Primitive Art. The Arizona State University Collection of American Art, at Tempe, near Phoenix, covers most periods and schools of American painting.

The Museum of Northern Arizona, near Flagstaff, specializes in Indian exhibits emphasizing the cultural life of the ancient peoples of the northern part of the state. Displays of desert plants and animals may be seen at the Arizona-Sonora Desert Museum near Tucson, the Boyce Thompson Southwestern Arboretum near Superior, and the Desert Botanical Garden of Arizona in Phoenix. Museums or museum displays are maintained at most of the national parks and monuments and the state historical parks.

Other Cultural Organizations. The best-known musical organizations in Arizona are vocal groups, notably the Orpheus Men's Chorus of Phoenix and the Tucson Boys' Choir. They have appeared in other states, on national television, and in Europe. Symphony orchestras are maintained by private associations in Phoenix, Tucson, and Flagstaff, with the Phoenix Symphony being the premier orchestra in the state. Little theater groups flourish in large cities, and the music and drama departments of the universities and colleges present productions of all kinds.

Indian and Mexican arts and crafts are popular in Arizona, not only among tourists but among residents as well. Some of Arizona's most highly regarded resident artists draw their themes from the Indians and Mexican-Americans. There are active year-round art colonies in Tucson and Scottsdale and a very lively summer colony in Sedona and Oak Creek Canyon, near Flagstaff.

Communications. A newspaper appeared in Arizona before it was organized as a territory. The *Weekly Arizonian* came out in Tubac, an old settlement south of Tucson, in 1859. Today, Arizona has more than a dozen daily newspapers and some 60 weeklies. The papers with the largest circulation are those published in Phoenix and Tucson. *Arizona Highways*, the monthly publication of the Arizona Highway Department, is internationally known.

Arizona's pioneer radio stations were established in Phoenix in 1922, and its first television station began operating there in 1949. By the late 1960's there were more than 70 radio stations and about 10 television stations, including the educational stations at the universities in Tucson and Tempe.

6. Recreation

Within the borders of Arizona may be found virtually every kind of recreation except those that require ocean beaches. For persons who enjoy active sports there are skiing, mountain hiking and climbing, boating, swimming, hunting, fishing, and athletics of almost every kind. In the winter months the snow and ice sports are available in the north, while at the same time the sun sports are being enjoyed in the desert south. Recreation not confined to sports is amply found in the many scenic drives and in spectator events such as athletic contests, horse and dog racing, and camping and picnicking.

National Areas. Arizona contains a remarkable number and variety of national areas. Grand Canyon National Park, the most famous of them all, is so spectacular as to be counted one of the natural wonders of the world. Although most impressive at dawn or sunset, it offers an overwhelming panorama at any hour of the day, in any season of the year. And for the bold and hearty, a journey to the bottom of the canyon on muleback is an experience to be remembered. Petrified Forest National Park is less spectacular but still awesome. The pastel hues of the barren landscape and the huge logs lying like broken stone columns inspire a different kind of wonder.

More national monuments are found in Arizona than in any other state, and millions of people visit them each year, along with the national parks and other areas. The monuments present a variety of man-made and natural phenomena. About half of them, including Canyon de Chelly, Casa Grande Ruins, Montezuma Castle, Navajo, and Tuzigoot national monuments, are ruins of the dwellings of ancient Indians. Two—Organ Pipe Cactus and Saguaro national monuments—contain spectacular displays of desert plants. Sunset Crater National Monument preserves a volcanic cinder cone, and Chiricahua National Monument, a wonderland of rock formations. Others preserve historic

---

NATIONAL AREAS

AREAS ADMINISTERED BY NATIONAL PARK SERVICE:[1]

National Parks—Grand Canyon; Petrified Forest
National Recreation Areas—Glen Canyon; Lake Mead
National Monuments—Canyon de Chelly; Casa Grande Ruins; Chiricahua; Grand Canyon; Montezuma Castle; Navajo; Organ Pipe Cactus; Pipe Spring; Saguaro; Sunset Crater; Tonto; Tumacacori; Tuzigoot; Walnut Canyon; Wupatki
National Historic Sites—Fort Bowie; Hubbell Trading Post
National Memorial—Coronado

NATIONAL FORESTS (administered by Forest Service, U.S. Department of Agriculture):[1]

Apache; Coconino; Coronado; Kaibab; Prescott; Sitgreaves; Tonto

[1] For a brief description of each area, see articles *National Parks and Monuments*; *National Forests,* and separate articles as listed in Index.

places—a Mormon fort at Pipe Spring National Monument and a Spanish mission at Tumacacori National Monument. Historic places also are commemorated by Coronado National Memorial and Fort Bowie and Hubbell Trading Post national historic sites.

Arizona has two national recreation areas—Lake Mead, shared with Nevada, and Glen Canyon, shared with Utah. Recreational facilities of almost every kind are maintained in the seven national forests.

State Areas. The state parks board was created in 1957 to develop a system of state areas, including historic parks and monuments and recreational and scenic parks. Sites for the historic parks and monuments have been carefully chosen to present different aspects of Arizona's colorful past. Painted Rocks State Historic Park, near Gila Bend, encompasses an area with rocks bearing a notable collection of Indian inscriptions. Tubac Presidio State Historic Park preserves the site of the first European settlement in Arizona. Yuma Territorial Prison State Historic Park contains the ruins of the prison that was established in the 1870's and used until 1910 and was called the "hell-hole." Tombstone Courthouse State Historical Monument recalls the "Wild West" past when the courthouse at Tombstone stood as a symbol of frontier justice, and Jerome State Historic Park tells the story of mining, as represented in the once-flourishing "copper town" of Jerome.

Picacho Peak State Park, a scenic park, includes Picacho Peak (a well-known landmark) as well as Picacho Pass, the scene of a Civil War skirmish. Recreational parks include Buckskin Mountain and Havasu Lake state parks on the Colorado River and Lyman Lake State Park on the Little Colorado.

Other Points of Interest. Countless other attractions beckon the sightseer. Mission San Xavier del Bac, an 18th century mission on the Papago Indian Reservation near Tucson, still serves as a church and summons a feeling of the days of the Spanish pioneers who brought their religion to the Indians. Ghost towns dot the state.

Many people feel that Oak Creek Canyon, south of Flagstaff, offers the most beautiful scenery in the state. Although not so large or spectacular as the Grand Canyon, it is notable for its red and white rock cliffs, pine forests, and clear, rushing stream. A highway makes a pre-cipitous descent to the floor of the canyon, and the state maintains extensive campgrounds along the creek. A popular scenic drive close to Phoenix is the Apache Trail, which leads by the brooding pile of Superstition Mountain and on up toward Theodore Roosevelt dam and lake.

Other well-known attractions include the Painted Desert, a wide area of colorful plateaus and low mesas along the eastern side of the Little Colorado River valley, and Monument Valley, an area in Arizona and Utah where the forces of erosion have carved imposing monuments. Both are on the Navajo Indian Reservation, and the latter has been established as a Navajo tribal park. Since their lands include areas of exceptional beauty and interest, the Indians of Arizona are bidding for a share of the growing recreation industry. A few tribes, notably those of the Fort Apache, Navajo, Hopi, and Colorado River reservations, already have been notably successful. The Apache, for example, have developed a system of lakes and trout streams in the White Mountains, with motels, general stores, and camp and picnic sites.

Annual Events. Festivals and other events occur throughout the year. In the spring the Fiesta de los Vaqueros rodeo in Tucson and the Jaycees' Rodeo of Rodeos in Phoenix attract performers of national reputation. Gold Rush Days in Wickenburg and the Easter Sunrise Service at the Shrine of the Angels on the rim of the Grand Canyon attract thousands. The Fiesta de las Posadas in Tucson and the Parada del Sol in Scottsdale are widely attended. Early in July, people come from all over to see the Southwest All-Indian Powwow in Flagstaff and, later in the summer, the Navajo Tribal Fair at Window Rock.

7. History

Archaeologists can trace Indian cultures in the region of Arizona back 25,000 years, and evidence of ancient peoples is found all over the state in ruined cliff dwellings, mounds, and crumbling adobe walls. The period from about 500 B. C. to the 15th century A. D. saw the Hohokam culture flourish. The Hohokam (a modern Pima Indian name meaning "that which has vanished") had a well-organized and productive society. They practiced irrigated agriculture, and the remains of their canals still can be traced in the vicinity of Phoenix. But for reasons not entirely clear they disappeared around 1450.

FAMOUS RESIDENTS OF ARIZONA

Douglas, Lewis Williams (1894–   ), public official; businessman; ambassador to Britain, 1947–1950.
Ernst, Max (1891–   ), German-born surrealist painter and writer; resident of Sedona, 1946–1952.
Geronimo (1829–1909), Apache chief; dictated autobiography *Geronimo's Story of His Life*, 1906.
Goldwater, Barry Morris (1909–   ), U. S. senator, 1952–1964; Republican presidential candidate, 1964.
Greenway, John C. (1872–1926), industrialist; developer of Arizona's mining and hydroelectric resources.
Grey, Zane (1875–1939), novelist and writer of Western frontier romances, some with Arizona settings.
Hayden, Carl Trumbull (1877–   ), U. S. representative and senator for more than 50 years.
Hunt, George Wylie Paul (1859–1934), first state governor of Arizona; U. S. minister to Siam (Thailand), 1920–1921.
Jacobs, Helen Hull (1908–   ), tennis champion; writer; Women's Naval Reserve officer, World War II.
Kay, Ulysses Simpson (1917–   ), composer, winner of Rome Prize in Composition, 1949–1950 and 1951–1952.
Kino, Eusebio Francisco (1645?–1711), Jesuit missionary and explorer; founder of Arizona livestock industry.

Lowell, Percival (1855–1916), astronomer; founder of Lowell Observatory near Flagstaff.
Luke, Frank, Jr. (1897–1918), fighter pilot, World War I; first flier to receive Congressional Medal of Honor.
O'Neill, William O. (1860–1898), known as "Bucky," frontier sheriff; Rough Riders captain, Spanish-American War.
Patch, Alexander McCarrell (1889–1945), U. S. Army general, World War II.
Pickering, William Henry (1858–1938), astronomer; erected first telescope and dome for Lowell Observatory, 1894.
Poston, Charles Debrill (1825–1902), explorer; Arizona's first territorial delegate to Congress.
Tombaugh, Clyde William (1906–   ), astronomer; discovered planet Pluto (1930) while at Lowell Observatory.
Udall, Stewart Lee (1920–   ), U. S. representative, 1955–1961; U. S. secretary of the interior from 1961.
Weaver, Pauline (1800–1867), mountain man, prospector, scout, guide; named Paulino but known as Paulino.
Wright, Frank Lloyd (1869?–1959), architect; his Arizona home, Taliesin West, became a school for his disciples.

Spanish Exploration and Settlement. Less than 100 years later, the Spanish began to march up from New Spain (Mexico). In 1539, Marcos de Niza, a Franciscan, followed the legend of the fabulous golden Seven Cities of Cibola and returned to Mexico, imagining he had indeed seen the cities of gold (Zuñi villages in northeastern New Mexico). A military expedition then was fitted out with Francisco Vásquez Coronado as captain, and in 1540 the members of the expedition marched to the Zuñi villages, where they conquered the Indians. But these were not cities of gold, and about two years of frustrating search ended with the realization that Cibola did not exist. The door to Arizona was opened, however, and the Spanish continued their interest.

In the 1580's and the early 1600's, Antonio de Espejo and Juan de Oñate wandered to the remote regions of central and northern Arizona and found evidence of the minerals that one day would make Arizona rich. The middle 1600's brought increased Spanish interest, particularly in missions to the Indians, and by the 1670's the Franciscans had established several missions the Hopi. Then, in 1680, the revolt of the Pueblo Indians flamed through the settlements, and the infant Spanish outposts in Arizona and New Mexico were blotted out. But the missionaries were not deterred.

Eusebio Francisco Kino, a Jesuit, began his remarkable career about 1690. A dedicated missionary, Father Kino was also an entrepreneur, agriculturist, and explorer. He founded more than 20 missions, taught the Indians how to farm, stocked the ranges with cattle and sheep, and explored thousands of miles in Arizona and California. After his death in 1711, the Spanish hold on southern Arizona increased.

As miners and farmers slowly moved into the Santa Cruz Valley, the Indians resisted so relentlessly that in 1752, Tubac, near Tucson, was made a presidio as a reminder to the Indians of the Spanish military presence. Tucson later became a fortified place as well. The year 1781 brought a serious Yuman uprising, which all but obliterated the white colony at the confluence of the Gila and Colorado rivers. By that time the days of the Spaniards were numbered.

Mexican Period. During the first two decades of the 19th century, Mexico was engaged in a struggle for independence from Spain, and when independence came in 1821, Arizona became Mexican territory. Those years of turmoil left the white settlements at the mercy of the Apache, and the mission at Tumacacori and Mission San Xavier del Bac, near Tucson, had to be abandoned. This was the era of the mountain men from the United States—such romantic figures as Pauline (Paulino) Weaver and Kit Carson—who went among the Indians, trapping and trading. As a result of their activities Arizona began to move into the orbit of the United States. War between Mexico and the United States started in 1846, and when it was over in 1848, a vast territory stretching from Texas to California—called New Mexico, with its capital at Santa Fe—was stripped from Mexico and added to the victor's domain. Most of Arizona was a part of that territory.

Early U. S. Period. After the Mexican War, the United States extended its territory to the Pacific, and one of the dreams of the era was to connect East and West with railroads. Government survey showed that an excellent route from the

DE WYS INC.

PREHISTORIC CLIFF DWELLING, five stories high, is seen in Montezuma Castle National Monument.

lower Mississippi River to California would run through a region south of the Gila River, in Mexico. Accordingly, in 1853, the U. S. diplomat James Gadsden negotiated the purchase of the region between the Gila and the present Arizona-New Mexico boundary with Mexico.

In the few years between the Gadsden Purchase and the outbreak of the Civil War, settlers moved into Arizona, attracted mostly by the prospects of mineral wealth in an era dominated by the California gold rush. The people wanted to see Arizona organized as a territory separate from New Mexico, but no one in distant Washington, D. C., paid much attention. Forts were established to try to discourage Indian depredations, and stage lines, as well as steamboats on the lower Colorado River, found business to do. Then, thousands of miles away, Confederate guns fired upon the U. S. flag, and even remote Arizona felt the shock of civil strife.

Many of the U. S. settlers in the Gadsden Purchase area had come from the southern states, and early in 1862 the Confederate Congress, in an empty gesture, proclaimed Arizona a Confederate territory. But the Confederate ties were of short duration. In April 1862, a small force of Texas Confederates was defeated by Union troops from California in a skirmish at Picacho Pass, northwest of Tucson.

Territorial Period. The U. S. Congress was persuaded to create a territory of Arizona by a bill passed in 1863 and signed into law by President Abraham Lincoln. An important actor in the passage of that bill was Charles D. Poston, who is known as the "Father of Arizona Territory." Early in 1864 the first territorial governor, John N. Goodwin, established the temporary capital at Fort Whipple, near Prescott. A few months later the capital was moved to what is now Prescott and then, in 1867, to Tucson, where it remained for 10 years before it was moved back to Prescott. In 1889 it was established permanently at Phoenix. Although the Apache were far from subdued during the Civil War years, they were held in check, and a campaign led by Kit Carson crushed the Navajo in 1864.

The 25 years following the Civil War brought years of Indian war but also great progress. The

Apache fought the white man with cruelty and cunning. Steeped in the tradition of great chiefs like Mangas Colorados and led by resourceful men like Cochise and Geronimo, they defied the soldiers for years. Thousands of soldiers were tied down trying to control a few hundred fighting Indians. The most successful general in Arizona was George Crook. When Geronimo surrendered the last band in 1886, the general in command was Nelson A. Miles. The foundations of Arizona's economy were laid in those years. Gold and silver mining stimulated settlement, but the mineral future was in copper. The railroads entered Arizona in the early 1880's, at about the time that extensive copper deposits were discovered. Pioneers founded Pheonix in the late 1860's and began to utilize the ancient Indian canals to bring the water of the Salt River onto the land.

Statehood and Later Times. With the Indian menace at last removed and with substantial economic progress and considerable political experience in territorial government, the people of Arizona in the 1890's agitated for statehood. Congress, however, could not be persuaded until 1910 to pass an enabling act. The constitutional convention, dominated by Progressive thinking and presided over by George W. P. Hunt, drafted what was hailed by liberals as a model document, and in the summer of 1911, Congress approved statehood. President Taft, however, vetoed the bill because he opposed the clause permitting the recall of judges. Arizonans then removed the offending clause, and on Feb. 14, 1912, statehood was proclaimed. One of the first independent actions of the people was to restore the recall of judicial officers.

Hunt became the first state governor and served seven terms, although not in succession. The state had just taken its place in the Union when World War I, with its traumatic effects, began. Arizona suffered labor troubles in the mining district during the war years. In the "Bisbee deportation" of 1917, about 1,200 persons, most of them strikers, were arrested by the sheriff's deputies and armed citizens, loaded onto cattle cars, taken into New Mexico, and unloaded in the desert. The trouble was over radical agitation—or alleged radical agitation—of the IWW (Industrial Workers of the World).

The 1920's and 1930's were periods of tremendous development in water conservation and electrical power potential. Dams on the major rivers made it possible to irrigate thousands of acres and generate quantities of power. The Colorado River Compact of 1922, of which Arizona was a signatory, worked out the sharing of the precious water among seven states. The depression years shriveled the economy of Arizona, as it did the other states, but the World War II period brought a revival. The government needed copper for munitions and war machines, beef and hides, and cotton, and Arizona could supply them. Air bases sprang up in the clear, warm desert areas for the training of thousands of pilots, and lucrative government contracts were let. The boom was on.

The years since the end of World War II have been a time of phenomenal growth in virtually all aspects of human affairs. The population tripled between 1940 and 1955. Most notable were the rate of urbanization and the increase in manufacturing. The water problem was not solved, but a positive gain was recorded in 1963, when the U. S. Supreme Court upheld Arizona's claim to a major share of Colorado River water. In the same year the Glen Canyon Dam was completed. Plans for the Central Arizona Project, to bring Colorado River water to central Arizona, progressed slowly. Many Arizona leaders sincerely believe that the state's future will be secure only when that gigantic engineering feat is accomplished.

PAUL HUBBARD
Arizona State University

HISTORICAL HIGHLIGHTS

1539 Marcos de Niza entered present-day Arizona from New Spain (Mexico).
1540 Coronado began exploration of parts of Arizona.
1690 Eusebio Francisco Kino, Jesuit priest and mission builder, began work among Indians of Arizona.
1700 Mission San Xavier del Bac founded.
1752 Tubac established as a presidio.
1776 Presidio established at present site of Tucson.
1821 Mexico gained independence from Spain; Arizona became a domain of Mexico.
1848 At end of Mexican War, Mexico ceded a large area, including present Arizona north of Gila River, to United States.
1850 Arizona north of Gila River became part of New Mexico Territory.
1854 Ratification of Gadsden Purchase added land south of Gila to New Mexico Territory; copper mine opened at Ajo.
1858 Rich gold placers discovered in Arizona by this time.
1859 First Arizona newspaper published, at Tubac.
1862 Civil War skirmish fought at Picacho Pass.
1863 Arizona became a separate territory; important mining strikes made.
1886 Geronimo, Apache chief, surrendered to federal troops.
1889 Phoenix became permanent capital of Arizona.
1911 Completion of Roosevelt Dam marked beginning of large-scale irrigation projects.
1912 Arizona entered Union, February 14, as 48th state.
1919 Grand Canyon National Park established.
1936 Hoover Dam (then called Boulder Dam) completed.
1940 World War II brought industrial boom to Arizona.
1963 U.S. Supreme Court upheld Arizona's claim to major share of Colorado River water.
1966 State legislature reapportioned according to one-man, one-vote principle.
1968 Plan for Central Arizona (water) Project approved by U.S. Congress.

Bibliography

American Guide Series, *Arizona: The Grand Canyon State,* rev. ed. (New York 1956).
Arizona Highway Department, *Arizona Highways* (Phoenix, monthly).
Cross, Jack L., and others, eds., *Arizona: Its People and Resources* (Tucson 1960).
Krutch, Joseph Wood, *The Grand Canyon: Today and All Its Yesterdays* (New York 1958).
Lockwood, Francis (Frank) C., *Arizona Characters* (Los Angeles 1928).
Lockwood, Francis (Frank) C., *More Arizona Characters* (Tucson 1943).
Lockwood, Francis (Frank) C., *Pioneer Days in Arizona* (New York 1932).
McClintock, James H., *Arizona: Prehistoric, Aboriginal, Pioneer, Modern* (Chicago 1916).
McClintock, James H., *Mormon Settlement in Arizona* (Phoenix 1921).
Martin, Douglas D., *Yuma Crossing* (Albuquerque 1954).
Miller, Joseph, ed., *Arizona: The Last Frontier* (New York 1956).
Miller, Joseph, *Arizona Story* (New York 1952).
Paré, Madeline F., and Fireman, Bert M., *Arizona Pageant: A Short History of the 48th State* (Tempe 1965).
Peplow, Edward H., Jr., *History of Arizona* (New York 1958).
Wellman, Paul I., *Death in the Desert: The Fifty Years' War for the Great Southwest* (New York 1935).
Wyllys, Rufus Kay, *Arizona: The History of a Frontier State* (Phoenix 1950).

ARIZONA, ar-ə-zō′nə, **University of,** a state, co-educational, land-grant institution in Tucson, Ariz. It was established by act of the Arizona territorial legislature in 1885 and opened in 1891. There are colleges of agriculture, business and public administration, education, engineering, fine arts, graduate studies, law, liberal arts, mining, and pharmacy. Specialized areas of research include geochronology, lunar and planetary studies, numerical analysis, and tree-ring investigation. The university has an institute of atmospheric physics, an arid-lands program, a bureau of ethnic research, an observatory, and an archaeological field school.

The 135-acre campus is located in an area previously occupied by Indian tribes for over 10,000 years. Artifacts from their cultures are housed in the Arizona State Museum on the campus. The university library, with more than 400,000 volumes, has special collections on Arizona, Mexico, and the Southwest. A separate law library has 40,000 volumes. There is also a campus-based television station (KUAT).

Enrollment has shown a steady increase from 3,000 in 1940 to 6,000 in 1950 and to over 18,000 in the mid-1960's.

ARIZONA STATE UNIVERSITY, ar-ə-zō′nə, is a coeducational institution in Tempe, Ariz. Established in 1885 by act of the Arizona territorial legislature as Arizona Territorial Normal School, it was made a teachers college in 1925 and a state university in 1958.

There are colleges of liberal arts, business administration, education, engineering, and graduate studies; a school of nursing; and a graduate school of social service administration. An honors program is offered for outstanding upperclassmen, and there is a work-study program in engineering. Facilities for specialized research cover such fields as venomology, parasitology, meteorites, statistical processes, and numerical analysis.

The 310-acre campus, supplemented by a 320-acre model farm, houses an auditorium designed by Frank Lloyd Wright and a library of almost 500,000 volumes. Enrollment (4,000 in 1950) rose to over 17,000 by the mid-1960's.

ARK is the English translation of either *tēbhah* or *arōn*, two Hebrew terms used in the Old Testament. In Genesis, *tēbhah* designates Noah's vessel, built at God's command to save Noah from the flood (see NOAH). Noah's ark was 300 cubits (about 450 feet, or 137 meters) long, 50 cubits (75 feet, or 23 meters) wide, and 30 cubits (45 feet, or 14 meters) high. Constructed of "gopher" wood variously identified as cedar, cypress, or pine, the ark had three decks divided into "rooms," a skylight, and a door in the side. It was made watertight inside and out with pitch (Genesis 6:14 to 8:16). The same term, *tēbhah*, is found in Exodus to denote the receptacle of bulrushes in which the infant Moses was hidden (Exodus 2:3, 5).

In Exodus and subsequent books of the Old Testament the term *arōn* is used to mean the box containing the two stone tablets inscribed with the Ten Commandments. This ark was the most sacred vessel of ancient Israel. With its precious burden it symbolized the covenant between God and the Israelites and was called variously "Ark of the Covenant," "Ark of the Lord," "Ark of God," and "Ark of the Testimony." It was made of *shittim* (acacia) wood, 2½ cubits (3 feet 9

inches, or 114.3 cm) long, 1½ cubits (2 feet 3 inches, or 68.6 cm) wide, and 1½ cubits high. Its interior and exterior were overlaid with gold (Exodus 25: 10–11).

In the desert wanderings of the Israelites the Levites, the priestly assistants, carried the Ark by two gold-covered wooden staves, each of which passed through two golden rings fixed to either side of the Ark (Exodus 25: 12–15). An integral part of the Ark were the two golden cherubim, whose outstretched wings covered a golden seat placed on top of the Ark (Exodus 25: 17–22). This was believed to form God's throne on earth (1 Samuel 4:4–7). Talmudic scholars later elaborated on this theme, holding that here the *Shekhina,* God's Presence, visibly manifested itself and that the Ark derived miraculous qualities from this.

Although the ancient Israelites regarded the Ark as a palladium and carried it into battle in the belief that this would ensure their victory, the Ark was captured by the Philistines (I Samuel 4:11). Its sacredness, however, rendered the Ark inviolate, and its very presence caused havoc in the Philistine temple of Dagon (I Samuel 5: 1–5). Instant death resulted from an inadvertent touch (II Samuel 6:6–7).

The Ark was recovered during the reign of King David, who erected a tabernacle to house it. It was later installed in the innermost sanctuary of the Temple built in Jerusalem by King Solomon (I Kings 6:19). Only once a year, on Yom Kippur, the Day of Atonement, could the Ark be seen, and then only by the High Priest, who was protected from the radiance of the Ark by a cloud of incense (Leviticus 16:1–16).

There is no record of what happened to the Ark when the Solomonic Temple was destroyed by Nebuchadnezzar, king of Babylon, in 586 B.C. Talmudic tradition holds that the Ark had been hidden decades earlier by King Josiah of Judah, under the very place where it had stood.

The term *arōn,* or more fully, *arōn Hakōdesh,* "Holy Ark," is applied to the doored receptacle that, ever since Hellenistic times, has been placed in every synagogue against the wall that faces Jerusalem (in European and American synagogues, the eastern wall). This Holy Ark contains one or more handwritten scrolls of the Pentateuch, the Five Books of Moses known as the Torah. Readings from the Torah are basic to the religious services in a Jewish synagogue. The Holy Ark commands its historic place as the most sacred and revered part of the synagogue and is usually the most lavishly decorated feature in synagogue architecture. Suspended before the Holy Ark in Jewish houses of worship is the *Ner Tamid,* the Eternal Light, which is never allowed to go out and which symbolizes the constancy of Israel's faith and its covenant with God. See also TABERNACLE.

RAPHAEL PATAI, *Theodor Herzl Institute*

ARKADELPHIA, är-kə-del′fē-ə, a city in southern Arkansas, is the seat of Clark County. It lies on the Ouachita River, 75 miles by road southwest of Little Rock, in a region of diversified farming and lumbering. Manufactures include aluminum, clothing, and wood products. Arkadelphia is the home of Ouachita Baptist University and Henderson State Teachers College. Settled in 1810, it was incorporated in 1857 and is governed by a mayor and council. Population: 9,841.

RECREATION AND FLOOD CONTROL are provided by Bull Shoals Lake, typical of the numerous artificial lakes in the state.

diamond deposits ever to be discovered and mined in North America.

Conservatism, or wariness of change, long has been characteristic of Arkansas' people. An example is the legislative act passed in 1881 to preserve the traditional pronunciation of the state name. This conservatism has continued to affect much public thinking, particularly on civil rights issues, for it is fear of breaking with tradition, not racial animosity, that seems to motivate most Arkansas segregationists.

That the people as a whole are flexible is shown by their accomplishments toward both economic development and social justice. They appear determined to transform the promise of their state motto, "Land of Opportunity," into a reality. However, fulfillment of economic goals will require the continued inflow of federal aid and private investment capital. Further attainments toward social justice would seem to require moderate leaders within the state to reconcile the white majority's desire for gradual change with national guidelines for quick progress.

Although the conservatism of its people doubtless has contributed to the state's relatively slow development, Arkansas has also met numerous adversities over the years. Frontier Arkan-

Great Seal of Arkansas

CONTENTS

ARKANSAS, är'kən-sô, one of the South Central states of the United States, is situated on the west bank of the Mississippi River. Many different kinds of landscape can be seen within the borders of the state. There are hardwood-cloaked mountains, valleys cut by swift streams, rolling hills, thick pine forests, broad river plains studded with oxbow lakes, and even a few murky bayous lined with hanging moss. Man's labors are evidenced by orderly cotton fields and flooded rice lands, cattle browsing on fenced pastures, small farmhouses bordered by sprawling poultry sheds, reservoirs impounded by huge river dams, widely scattered cities and factories, a few oil derricks, and the only true

INFORMATION HIGHLIGHTS

Location: In west south-cental United States, bordered north by Missouri, east by Tennessee and Mississippi, south by Louisiana, southwest by Texas, west by Oklahoma.

Elevation: Highest—Magazine Mountain, 2,753 feet (930 meters); lowest—along Ouachita River near southern border, 55 feet (17 meters); approximate mean elevation—650 feet (198 meters).

Area: 53,104 square miles (137,540 sq km); rank, 27th.

Population: (1970 census): 1,923,295; rank, 32d.

Climate: Long, hot summers; mild winters; generally abundant rainfall.

Statehood: June 15, 1836; 25th state admitted.

Origin of Name: From a Siouan people, Ugakhpa or Quapaw (meaning "downstream people"), pronounced and written variously (Acansa, Arkansa) by French explorers.

Capital and Largest City: Little Rock.

Number of Counties: 75.

Principal Products: Farm products—cotton, poultry, soybeans; rice; manufactures—foods, lumber, wood and paper products; minerals—petroleum, stone, bauxite, natural gas.

State Motto: *Regnat populus* (The people rule).

State Song (adopted 1963): *Arkansas.*

State Nickname (adopted 1953): Land of Opportunity.

State Bird (adopted 1929): Mockingbird.

State Flower (adopted 1901): Apple blossom.

State Tree (adopted 1939): Shortleaf pine.

State Flag (adopted 1913): A large white diamond, bordered in blue, on a field of red (see color plates under FLAG—*Flags of the States*).

sas was bounded on the east by an undrained swamp, which made access to the interior difficult. Less than 25 years after achieving statehood, Arkansas joined what proved to be the losing side in a grim sectional struggle. After the Civil War the state was subjected to a political reconstruction of such nature that it still is resented by the people. Economic growth was slow in the late 1800's and early 1900's, and dependence on cotton as a cash crop became greater than ever before. Sharecropping—no respecter of races—entrapped landless white persons about as frequently as Negroes.

After 1940, however, there was an increase in the rate of industrialization, agricultural diversification, and urbanization. Since 1959 the state has had a small industrial boom.

Among Arkansas' assets are its many natural resources—including an abundance of rich soil, timber, minerals, cheap fuel, and pure water—and the desire of its people for progress. For this progress to continue, the state must attract more investment capital, further improve its roads, develop more technical skill, and provide the jobs required to halt the tendency of its most promising young people to leave the state after completing their education.

1. The People

Few Arkansans of today can trace descent from either the Indians or the early French and Spanish inhabitants of the area. By 1835 the last of the Indian tribes had been removed from Arkansas. These included not only the Caddo, Quapaw, and Osage, whose residence preceded exploration, but also the later arriving Choctaw and Cherokee. French and Spanish rule over the area from 1686 to 1803 did not attract many white settlers, nor did the early years of United States ownership. The census of 1810 enumerated a mere 1,062 non-Indian residents in the entire District of Arkansas.

The chief stock of permanent settlement were those Anglo-Saxon families that came after 1815 as a part of the westward movement. Originating along the Atlantic seaboard, but often taking up intermediate residence in Tennessee, Missouri, or Mississippi, they came to Arkansas in growing numbers during most decades of the 1800's, bringing whatever slaves they owned.

Characteristics of the Population. Arkansas' people are descended predominantly from English, Scotch-Irish, and Negro families who came from the older Southern states prior to 1900. More than three fourths of the inhabitants of Arkansas were born in the state. About 99% of the total population was born in the United States, and about 98 in 100 Arkansans are of parents who also were both native-born.

According to the census of 1970, the state contained more than four times as many white residents as Negroes. Most of the Negroes live in the lowlands, where they are in a majority in several southeastern counties. Numerous hill counties of the state have virtually no Negro residents.

Baptists are the largest church group, Methodists are second, and the two combined make up perhaps two thirds of the state's church membership. Other large church groups include Presby-

GROWTH OF POPULATION SINCE 1820

Year	Population	Year	Population
1820	14,273	1920	1,752,204
1840	97,574	1940	1,949,387
1860	435,450	1950	1,909,511
1880	802,525	1960	1,786,272
1900	1,311,564	1970	1,923,295

Gain, 1960–1970: 7.7% (U. S. gain, 13.3%). **Density, 1970:** 36.2 persons per square mile (U. S. density, 56.2).

URBAN-RURAL DISTRIBUTION

Year	Percent urban	Percent rural
1920	16.6 (U. S., 51.2)	83.4
1930	20.6 (U. S., 56.2)	79.4
1940	22.2 (U. S., 56.6)	77.8
1950	33.0 (U. S., 64.0)	67.0
1960	42.8 (U. S., 69.9)	57.2
1970	50.0 (U. S., 73.5)	50.0

LARGEST CENTERS OF POPULATION

City or Metropolitan area[1]	1970	1960	1950
Little Rock (city)	132,483	107,813	102,213
Metropolitan area	323,296		
Fort Smith (city)	62,802	52,991	47,942
Metropolitan area[2]	104,914		
North Little Rock	60,040	58,032	44,097
Pine Bluff (city)	57,389	44,037	37,162
Metropolitan area	85,329	81,373	76,075
Hot Springs	35,631	28,337	29,307
Fayetteville	30,729	20,274	17,071
Jonesboro	27,050	21,418	16,310
West Memphis (city)	25,892	19,374	9,112
Metropolitan area[2]	48,106		
El Dorado	25,283	25,292	23,076
Blytheville	24,752	20,797	16,234
Texarkana (city)	21,682	19,788	15,875
Metropolitan area[2]	33,385		

[1] Standard metropolitan statistical area. [2] Arkansas portion only.

terians, Roman Catholics, Episcopalians, and members of the Churches of Christ and the Assemblies of God.

Way of Life. As late as 1900, after the population of the state had exceeded one million, more than 90 in 100 Arkansans lived in rural areas. Parents of the early 1900's took their children by buggy to see the railroad engines, which did not reach most parts of Arkansas until the 1870's or 1880's. This rural isolation began to give way to a nonisolated farm life during World War I, when the state government began to coordinate the county road systems and telephones came into wide use. But, as late as 1940, Arkansas had only nine cities with as many as 10,000 residents,

BLANCHARD SPRINGS Recreation Area, in the Ozark National Forest, provides a natural pool.

and nearly 78 in 100 Arkansans were still classed as rural.

During and after World War II the state's urban areas grew markedly, as rural dwellers left the farms to seek employment in the larger towns and cities. For a time many also migrated to other states. As a result, Arkansas suffered actual population losses of 2 percent from 1940 to 1950 and 6.5 percent from 1950 to 1960.

In the 1960's the state gained more than 7% in population. In 1970 there were 1,923,295 people in Arkansas, an increase of 137,023 from the 1,786,272 inhabitants of the state in 1960. Arkansans continued to leave rural areas for the cities. By 1970, 50 in 100 residents of the state lived in urban centers.

Largest Centers of Population. Little Rock is the capital and largest city in the state. It is situated on the Arkansas River near the center of Arkansas. Directly opposite, on the north bank of the river, is North Little Rock. These two cities make up the largest metropolitan area wholly within the state.

Farther up the river, near the Arkansas-Oklahoma boundary, is Fort Smith, which has a population slightly larger than that of North Little Rock. A portion of the Fort Smith metropolitan area is in Oklahoma. Pine Bluff, Arkansas' fourth-largest city, is situated downriver from Little Rock.

All these cities are expected to become ports as a result of the opening of the Arkansas River to commercial navigation in June 1971.

2. The Land

Arkansas has a varied topography, a mild climate with ample rainfall, an abundance of plants and wildlife, and rich mineral resources.

Major Physical Divisions. The state consists of two major physical divisions, nearly equal in size. These are the eastern and southern lowlands and the northwestern highlands. The lowlands are subdivided into the Mississippi Alluvial Plain, covering the eastern third of the state, and the West Gulf Coastal Plain in the south. The highlands include the Ouachita Province in west-central Arkansas and the Ozark Plateaus adjoining it to the north.

Most of the Mississippi Alluvial Plain, which averages only 150 feet (45.7 meters) in elevation, is flat as far as the eye can see. It contains much of the state's best farmland, although some of the area is still in forests, hardwood flats, or swamps. Rising out of the northeastern part of this floodplain and delta region is Crowley's Ridge, a loess deposit up to 500 feet (150 meters) high at the north and from 1 to 12 miles (1.5 to 20 km) wide.

Entering the West Gulf Coastal Plain from the alluvial plain (along a line extending southeastward from Little Rock), one notices not so much the slight rise in elevation as the marked increase in trees. Timber growing predominates in the clays and sands of this gently rolling hill area of south Arkansas, where the elevation averages 300 feet (90 meters). But there is also considerable livestock grazing, as well as some general farming.

A traveler entering the Ouachita region from the coastal plain is less aware of changes in plant life than of the rising foothills of the Ouachita mountain system. The Ouachitas are sharply faulted, east-west ridges, with heights up to about 2,800 feet (850 meters) in the west. They are heavily wooded and sparsely populated. Northward, the ridges fall away to the wide Arkansas River valley, which is studded with mesa-like formations. One of them, Magazine Mountain, juts out of the valley floor to an elevation of 2,823 feet (860.5 meters), the highest point in the state.

The Ozark Plateaus, often called mountains, are eroded tablelands. The most rugged section, just north of the Arkansas Valley, is known as the Boston Mountains. Winding streams dissect the 2,000-foot (600-meter) surface to form steep, wooded gorges, from 500 to 1,400 feet (150 to 427 meters) deep. This section ends to the north in a sharp escarpment, from the base of which extend the Springfield and the Salem plateaus. These two lower plateaus have a gently rolling to rough surface, much of which is in hardwood forest, but they also contain stretches of good farmland in the northwest and northeast.

Rivers and Lakes. Arkansas' entire surface drains into the Mississippi River, which forms most of the eastern boundary of the state. The chief drainage basins are formed by the Red River in the southwest, the Ouachita in the south, the Arkansas across the central section of the state, the White in the north, and the St. Francis in the northeast. Arkansas has scores of lakes, well distributed. Most of the natural lakes were formed in the lowlands by changes in the river courses. A majority of the largest artificial lakes have been built in the highlands since 1940 as flood-control reservoirs. They also have provided

OZARK MOUNTAINS offer a sweeping view from White Rock Mountain, near Mountainburg. This area is in the Ozark National Forest.

BULL SHOALS DAM, in northern Arkansas, was erected for flood control and hydroelectric power. It made Bull Shoals Lake, a favorite with fishermen.

Arkansas with an ever-growing recreation and tourist industry.

Climate. The climate of Arkansas is usually mild and favorable to diversified agriculture and outdoor activities. Winter temperatures average 36°F (2°C) in the north and considerably higher in the south. Summer temperatures average 80°F (26.7°C) statewide. Most of the precipitation falls as rain.

The weather patterns are set by the interaction of southwesterly and southerly winds with cold fronts from the north and west. South winds prevent severe winters. Cold spells, with temperatures below 0°F (−17.8°C), are of short duration. The springs are long and pleasant. Very hot weather, with maximums above 100°F (37.8°C), occurs at times during July and August. The delightful autumns begin in September and, in the south, often continue into December.

Besides having a long growing season (from 180 to 230 days), Arkansas receives abundant precipitation, most areas having an average of from 40 to 50 inches (101.6 to 127 cm). The wettest months are December through May. Summer thundershowers make general droughts rare, and the relatively dry autumn season is favorable to harvest.

Plant Life. Vegetation grows luxuriantly in Arkansas' benign climate, and species are made numerous by the varying elevations and soil types. Over one half of the state is in forest, some of it virgin. Pine predominates in the south but becomes scarce to the north. Among the more than 200 other types of trees are oak, hickory, gum, ash, elm, and cypress. In early spring, dogwoods and redbuds flaunt blossoms on leafless branches; and in autumn scarlet sumac bushes accentuate the yellows and browns of the hardwoods. Among the colorful, smaller wild plants are the palmettos and water lilies of the lowlands and the irises, orchids, and azaleas of the hills.

Animal Life. The abundant wildlife includes several dozen species of mammals, more than 300 varieties of birds, and nearly 200 of fish. Rabbits and squirrels are everywhere present, deer have become plentiful again, and there is some trapping of skunks, opossums, raccoons, and mink for fur. The chief predators are foxes, bobcats, and a very few wolves. Among the more plentiful birds are mockingbirds, blue jays, robins, and cardinals. The principal game fowl are quail, migratory duck and geese, and a few turkey. The area around Stuttgart is widely known for its autumn hunting season, when large flocks of duck come to feed on the rice lands. Game fish include bass, trout, bream, crappie, and catfish. There is some commercial fishing in lowland waters. The shells of mussels, dredged from the White River and its tributaries, are used for making buttons and pearls.

Minerals. Arkansas possesses a great number and variety of minerals. Geologists are said to have identified some 75 different types at Magnet Cove, near Hot Springs. The fuels are petroleum, natural gas, coal, and lignite. The metallic group includes bauxite, iron ore, zinc and lead, manganese, cinnabar, and titanium. In the nonmetallic category are dolomite, sandstone, limestone, barite, marl, silica, gypsum, phosphate, asphalt, and bentonite. Diamonds, first uncovered near Murfreesboro in 1906, were mined there commercially for about a decade.

Conservation. Practices to conserve water are particularly varied. They involve the efforts of private interests as well as federal and state agencies, and they range from the damming of major rivers and the building of industrial and municipal reservoirs to the digging of farm ponds. The Arkansas Oil Association, in cooperation with the State Water Pollution Control Commission, has also taken steps to curb saltwater pollution in the oil fields. Timber conservation is practiced as avidly by most private landowners, assisted by the State Forestry Commission, as by the national Forest Service. Prudent land use is promoted by the 76 soil conservation districts, organized under state authority. The State Game and Fish Commission enforces hunting and fishing regulations and operates several fish hatcheries.

3. The Economy

Arkansas' early economy was largely one of self-sufficient agriculture, with cotton as the main cash crop. Sawmilling was the earliest industry, as would be expected in an area where the pioneers found more than 90 percent of the land covered with trees. Cotton and lumber are still important to Arkansas, but they no longer dominate the economy.

By the mid-1960's the state's poultry products almost equaled its cotton in value. Each brought about one fourth of the total cash farm receipts of nearly $1 billion. Even as a row crop, cotton no longer exceeds the combined value of soybeans and rice. Moreover, the rural simplicity of Arkansas' farms has ended, for the total net income per farm (about $5,000 in the mid-1960's) exceeds the national average, and even the traditional cotton crop is now increasingly flame-cultivated. (A flame cultivator, or flame thrower, uses flaming gas to destroy weeds.)

RICE CROP is reaped by a combine. The state's rice farms are rich producers. Their yield per acre ranks among the world's highest, due to use of machinery.

Although Arkansas' manufacturing income now exceeds its agricultural income, the state's basic wealth is still in its farms, forests, and mines. The processing of food, timber, minerals, and other local raw materials accounts for more than half of the total value added by manufacture.

Agriculture. Arkansas' poultry industry has expanded steadily since 1940 and has given a new source of income to areas where subsistence farming once prevailed. Cooperative enterprises are supplanting individual operations, with the major feed companies supplying the local growers with chicks and feed on credit and buying the broilers en masse for central processing and marketing. Egg production and turkey raising are following a similar trend. In cattle production the trend is toward the upgrading of herds and the enclosure of medium-sized ranches, often under absentee ownership.

Arkansas continues to be a major cotton-producing state, despite the near disappearance of cotton from many hill counties where it was an important crop before 1940. Much land once planted to cotton is now in soybeans, a crop important in the state before 1940. Soybeans also are rotated with rice in the Grand Prairie district of east-central Arkansas, which was mostly a brush-covered swampland until after 1900. Arkansas' rice farms are highly mechanized and prosperous, and their per-acre yields are among the world's highest. More than half the rice crop and significant amounts of soybeans, cotton, and poultry are exported.

Manufacturing. Although the larger cities had some industry before 1940, the typical Arkansas town often had no more than a sawmill and a cotton gin or two. Conditions improved markedly during and after World War II, and the state's later industrial boom was aided by a constitutional amendment of 1958 and a legislative act of 1959. Both of these enactments enable cities or counties to sell tax-free bonds for the construction of industrial plants. By the mid-1960's more than 175 bond issues totaling $333 million had been sold to build plants for new industry or to help existing industry expand. Almost every county or town of any size had attracted one or

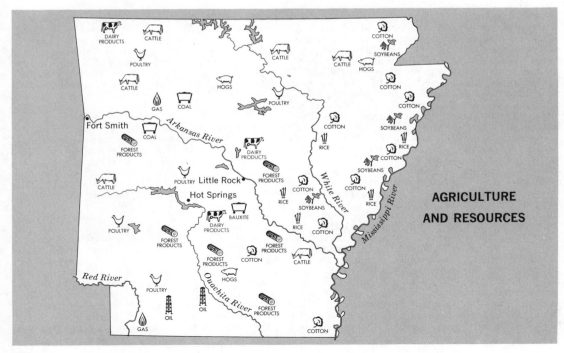

AGRICULTURE AND RESOURCES

ARKANSAS

TOPOGRAPHY

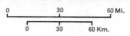

0   30   60 Mi.

0   30   60 Km.

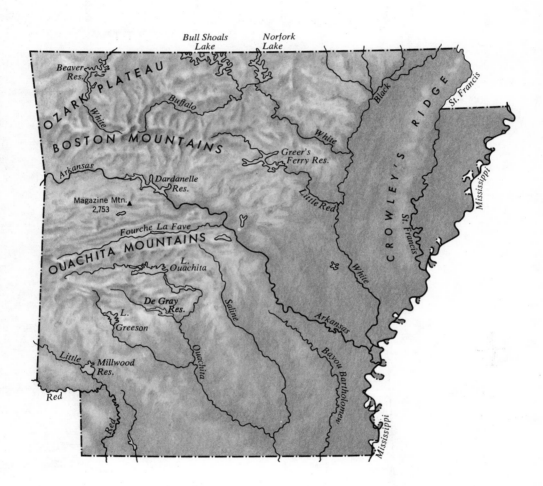

Bull Shoals Lake

Norfork Lake

Beaver Res.

OZARK PLATEAU

Buffalo

White

BOSTON MOUNTAINS

Arkansas

Dardanelle Res.

Greer's Ferry Res.

White

Little Red

Black

St. Francis

CROWLEY'S RIDGE

St. Francis

Mississippi

Magazine Mtn. 2,753

Fourche La Fave

OUACHITA MOUNTAINS

L. Ouachita

De Gray Res.

L. Greeson

Saline

White

Arkansas

St. Francis

Little

Millwood Res.

Ouachita

Bayou Bartholomew

Red

Red

Mississippi

Mississippi

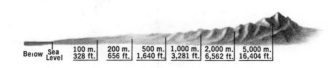

Below Sea Level	100 m. 328 ft.	200 m. 656 ft.	500 m. 1,640 ft.	1,000 m. 3,281 ft.	2,000 m. 6,562 ft.	5,000 m. 16,404 ft.

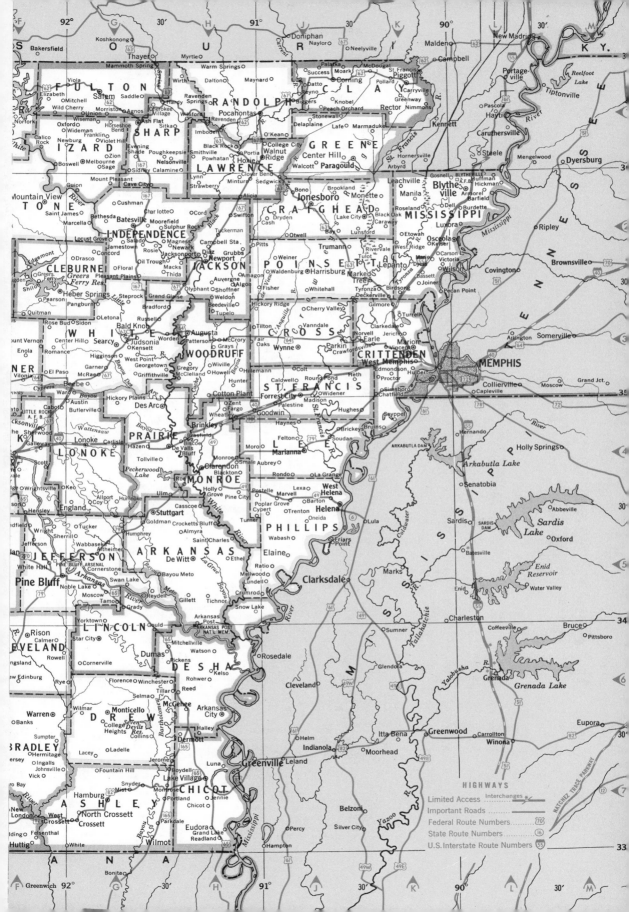

ARKANSAS

COUNTIES

Arkansas, 23,347 H 5
Ashley, 24,976 G 7
Baxter, 15,319 F 1
Benton, 50,476 B 1
Boone, 19,073 D 1
Bradley, 12,778 F 7
Calhoun, 5,573 E 6
Carroll, 12,301 C 1
Chicot, 18,164 H 7
Clark, 21,537 D 5
Clay, 18,771 K 1
Cleburne, 10,349 F 2
Cleveland, 6,605 F 6
Columbia, 25,952 D 7
Conway, 16,805 E 3
Craighead, 52,068 J 2
Crawford, 25,677 B 2
Crittenden, 48,106 K 3
Cross, 19,783 J 3
Dallas, 10,022 E 6
Desha, 18,761 H 6
Drew, 15,157 G 6
Faulkner, 31,572 F 3
Franklin, 11,301 C 2
Fulton, 7,699 G 1
Garland, 54,131 D 4
Grant, 9,711 F 5
Greene, 24,765 J 1
Hempstead, 19,308 C 6
Hot Spring, 21,963 E 5
Howard, 11,412 C 5
Independence, 22,723 G 2
Izard, 7,381 G 1
Jackson, 20,452 H 2
Jefferson, 85,329 G 5
Johnson, 13,630 C 2
Lafayette, 10,018 C 7
Lawrence, 16,320 H 1
Lee, 18,884 J 4
Lincoln, 12,913 G 6
Little River, 11,194 B 6
Logan, 16,789 C 3
Lonoke, 26,249 G 4
Madison, 9,453 C 1
Marion, 7,000 E 1
Miller, 33,385 C 7
Mississippi, 62,060 K 2
Monroe, 15,657 H 4
Montgomery, 5,821 C 4
Nevada, 10,111 D 6
Newton, 5,844 D 2
Ouachita, 30,896 E 6
Perry, 5,634 E 4
Phillips, 40,046 J 5
Pike, 8,711 C 5
Poinsett, 26,822 J 2
Polk, 13,297 B 5
Pope, 28,607 D 3
Prairie, 10,249 G 4
Pulaski, 287,189 F 4
Randolph, 12,645 H 1
Saint Francis, 30,799 J 3
Saline, 36,107 E 4
Scott, 8,207 B 4
Searcy, 7,731 E 2
Sebastian, 79,237 B 3
Sevier, 11,272 B 6
Sharp, 8,233 G 1
Stone, 6,838 F 2
Union, 45,428 E 7
Van Buren, 8,275 E 2
Washington, 77,370 B 2
White, 39,253 G 3
Woodruff, 11,566 H 3
Yell, 14,208 D 3

CITIES and TOWNS

Abbott, 210 B 3
Adona, 204 E 3
Agnos, 130 G 1
Alco, 90 F 2
Alexander, 297 F 4
Algoa, 50 H 3
Alicia, 246 H 2
Alix, 250 C 3
Alleene, 115 B 6
Allport, 307 G 4
Alma, 1,613 B 3
Almyra, 220 H 5
Alpena, 309 D 1
Alpine, 100 D 5
Altheimer, 1,037 G 5
Altus, 418 C 3
Aly, 50 D 4
Amagon, 136 H 2
Amity, 614 D 5
Antoine, 182 D 5
Aplin, 50 E 4
Appleton, 150 E 3
Arden, 80 B 6
Arkadelphia⊙, 9,841 D 5
Arkansas City⊙, 615 H 6
Arkansas Post, 15 H 5
Arkinda, 60 B 6
Armorel, 300 L 2
Ashdown⊙, 3,522 B 6
Ash Flat⊙, 211 G 1
Athens, 84 C 5
Atkins, 2,015 E 3
Atlanta, 50 D 7
Aubrey, 351 J 4
Augusta⊙, 2,777 H 3
Aurora, 30 C 2
Austin, 236 G 4
Auvergne, 150 H 2
Avoca, 173 B 1
Bald Knob, 2,094 G 3
Banks, 189 F 6
Barber, 28 B 3
Barfield, 40 L 2
Barling, 1,739 B 3
Barton, 400 J 4
Bassett, 265 K 2
Bates, 109 B 4
Batesville⊙, 7,209 G 2
Bay, 751 J 2
Bearden, 1,272 E 6
Beaver, 32 C 1
Beebe, 2,805 G 3
Beedeville, 144 H 3
Bee Branch, 50 F 3
Beirne, 140 D 6
Bella Vista, 500 B 1
Bellefonte, 300 D 1
Belleville, 379 D 3
Ben Lomond, 155 B 6
Benton⊙, 16,499 E 4
Bentonville⊙, 5,508 B 1
Bergman, 249 E 1
Berryville⊙, 2,271 C 1
Bestwater, 50 B 1
Bethel Heights, 284 B 1
Bethesda, 285 G 2
Bigelow, 258 E 3
Bigflat, 189 F 1
Big Fork, 45 B 5
Biggers, 372 J 1
Birdsong, 150 K 3
Birta, 36 D 3
Biscoe, 340 H 4
Bismarck, 200 D 5
Black Oak, 272 K 2
Black Rock, 498 H 1
Black Springs, 102 C 5
Blackton, 175 H 4
Blackwell, 75 E 3
Blevins, 265 C 6
Bloomer, 150 B 3
Blue Ball, 34 C 4
Blue Eye, 53 D 1
Blue Mountain, 108 C 3
Bluff City, 244 D 6
Bluffton, 198 C 4
Blytheville⊙, 24,752 L 2
Board Camp, 30 B 4
Bodcaw, 158 D 6
Bolding, 25 F 7
Boles, 163 B 4
Bonanza, 342 B 3
Bono, 428 J 2
Booneville⊙, 3,239 C 3
Boswell, 55 F 1
Boxley, 50 D 2
Boydell, 65 H 7
Bradford, 826 G 3
Bradley, 706 C 7
Branch, 325 C 3
Brasfield, 200 H 4
Brentwood, 30 B 2
Brickeys, 49 J 4
Briggsville, 200 C 4
Brightstar, 50 C 7
Brinkley, 5,275 H 4
Brookland, 465 J 2
Bruins, 90 K 4
Bruno, 130 E 1
Bryant, 1,199 F 4
Buckner, 392 D 7
Buckville, 65 D 4
Buena Vista, 40 D 7
Buffalo City, 25 E 1
Bull Shoals, 430 E 1
Burdette, 173 L 2
Butlerville, 50 G 4
Butterfield, 105 E 5
Cabot, 2,903 F 4
Caddo Gap, 125 C 5
Caldwell, 292 J 3
Cale, 75 D 6
Calico Rock, 723 F 1
Calion, 535 E 7
Calmer, 55 F 6
Camden⊙, 15,147 E 6
Cammack Village, 1,165 E 4
Campbell Station, 218 H 2
Canehill, 95 B 2
Canfield, 365 C 7
Caraway, 952 K 2
Carlisle, 2,048 G 4
Carryville, 50 K 1
Carson Lake, 100 K 2
Carthage, 566 E 5
Casa, 208 D 3
Cash, 265 J 2
Casscoe, 200 H 4
Cato, 75 F 4
Caulksville, 208 C 3
Cauthron, 50 B 4
Cave City, 807 G 2
Cave Springs, 469 B 1
Cecil, 234 C 3
Cedar Creek, 123 C 4
Cedarville, 50 B 2
Center Hill, 25 G 3
Center Hill, 1,201 J 1
Center Point, 144 C 5
Center Ridge, 220 E 3
Centerton, 312 B 1
Centerville, 100 D 3
Central City, 150 B 3
Chapel Hill, 154 B 5
Charleston⊙, 1,497 B 3
Charlotte, 158 H 2
Chatfield, 150 K 3
Cherokee City, 25 A 1
Cherokee Village, 1,300 G 1
Cherry Hill, 250 B 4
Cherry Valley, 556 J 3
Chester, 82 B 2
Chicot, 25 H 7
Chidester, 232 D 6
Chismville, 80 C 3
Choctaw, 97 F 2
Chula, 35 C 4
Cincinnati, 80 B 1
Clarendon⊙, 2,563 H 4
Clarkedale, 250 K 3
Clarksville⊙, 4,616 D 3
Cleveland, 74 E 3
Clifty, 50 C 1
Clinton⊙, 1,029 F 2
Clover Bend, 90 H 2
Coal Hill, 733 C 3
College City, 645 J 1
College Heights, 2,050 G 6
Collins, 26 G 6
Colt, 301 J 3
Columbus, 258 C 6
Combs, 100 C 2
Concord, 163 G 2
Conway⊙, 15,510 F 3
Cord, 60 H 2
Cornerstone, 107 G 5
Cornerville, 50 G 6
Corning⊙, 2,705 J 1
Cotter, 858 E 1
Cotton Plant, 1,657 H 3
Cove, 334 B 5
Coy, 240 G 4
Crawfordsville, 831 K 3
Crocketts Bluff, 70 H 5
Crossett, 6,191 G 7
Crumrod, 100 H 5
Crystal Springs, 75 D 5
Curtis, 500 D 6
Cushman, 427 G 2
Cypert, 29 J 5
Daisy, 100 C 5
Dalark, 132 E 5
Dalton, 52 H 1
Damascus, 255 F 3
Danville⊙, 1,362 D 3
Dardanelle⊙, 3,297 D 3
Datto, 142 J 1
Decatur, 847 A 1
Deckerville, 25 K 3
Deer, 100 D 2
Delaney, 150 C 2
Delaplaine, 145 J 1
Delaware, 200 D 3
Delight, 439 C 5
Dell, 358 K 2
Dennard, 89 E 2
Denning, 203 C 3
Denver, 45 D 1
De Queen⊙, 3,863 B 5
Dermott, 4,250 H 7
Des Arc⊙, 1,714 G 4
De Valls Bluff⊙, 622 H 4
De Witt⊙, 3,728 H 5
Diamond City, 282 E 1
Diaz, 283 H 2
Dierks, 1,101 B 5
Doddridge, 125 C 7
Dogpatch, 25 D 1
Donaldson, 500 E 5
Dover, 662 D 3
Drasco, 300 G 2
Driggs, 125 C 3
Dumas, 4,600 H 6
Dutch Mills, 75 B 2
Dutton, 28 C 2
Dyer, 486 B 3
Dyess■, 433 K 2
Eagle Mills, 149 E 6
Earle, 3,146 K 3
East Camden, 589 E 6
Edgemont, 125 F 2
Edmondson, 412 K 3
Elaine, 1,210 J 5
El Dorado⊙, 25,283 E 7
Elizabeth, 25 F 1
Elkins, 418 C 1
Elliott, 50 E 7
Elm Springs, 260 B 1
El Paso, 131 F 3
Emerson, 393 D 7
Emmet, 433 D 6
England, 3,075 G 4
Enola, 150 F 3
Ethel, 350 H 5
Etowah, 150 K 2
Eudora, 3,687 H 7
Eureka Springs⊙, 1,670 C 1
Evansville, 427 B 2
Evening Shade, 309 G 1
Everton, 124 E 1
Excelsior, 160 B 3
Fair Oaks, 270 J 3
Fargo, 206 H 4
Farmington, 908 B 1
Fayetteville⊙, 30,729 B 1
Felsenthal, 150 F 7
Felton, 50 J 4
Fisher, 361 J 2
Flippin, 626 E 1
Floral, 165 G 2
Florence, 75 G 6
Fordyce⊙, 4,837 F 6
Foreman, 1,173 B 6
Formosa, 224 E 3
Forrest City⊙, 12,521 J 3
Fort Smith⊙, 62,802 B 3
Fort Smith, ‡160,421 B 3
Forum, 75 C 1
Fouke, 506 C 7
Fountain Hill, 266 G 7
Fourche, 46 E 4
Fox, 200 F 2
Franklin, 117 G 1
Fredonia (Biscoe), 340 H 4
Friendship, 150 E 5
Fulton, 323 C 6
Galloway, 40 F 4
Garfield, 163 C 1
Garland, 321 C 7
Garner, 150 G 3
Gassville, 434 F 1
Gateway, 83 B 1
Genoa, 125 C 7
Gentry, 1,022 A 1
Georgetown, 137 G 3
Gilbert, 45 E 2
Gillett, 860 H 5
Gillham, 200 B 5
Gilmore, 461 K 3
Glenwood, 1,212 C 5
Goldman, 35 G 5
Goodwin, 125 J 4
Goshen, 95 C 1
Gosnell, 1,386 K 2
Gould, 1,683 G 6
Grady, 688 G 5
Grand Glaise, 50 G 3
Grand Lake, 30 H 7
Grandview, 50 C 1
Grannis, 177 B 5
Grapevine, 72 F 5
Gravelly, 300 C 4
Gravette, 1,154 B 1
Greenbrier, 582 F 3
Green Forest, 1,354 D 1
Greenland, 650 B 1
Greenway, 240 K 1
Greenwood⊙, 2,032 B 3
Greers Ferry, 389 F 2
Gregory, 311 H 3
Griffithville, 227 G 3
Grubbs, 442 H 2
Guion, 213 G 2
Gum Springs, 269 D 5
Gurdon, 2,075 D 6
Guy, 179 F 3
Hackett, 462 B 3
Hagarville, 123 D 2
Halley, 204 H 6
Hamburg⊙, 3,102 G 7
Hampton⊙, 1,252 F 6
Hardy, 692 H 1
Harmony, 50 D 2
Harrell, 269 F 7
Harriet, 50 E 2
Harrisburg⊙, 1,931 J 2
Harrison⊙, 7,239 D 1
Hartford, 616 B 3
Hartman, 400 C 3
Haskell, 239 E 4
Hasty, 25 D 1
Hatfield, 377 B 5
Hattieville, 163 E 3
Havana, 308 D 3
Haynes, 375 J 4
Hazen, 1,605 G 4
Heber Springs⊙, 2,497 G 2
Hector, 387 E 3
Helena⊙, 10,415 J 4
Hensley, 350 F 4
Hermitage, 399 F 7
Heth, 52 K 3
Hickman, 100 L 2
Hickory Plains, 200 G 3
Hickory Ridge, 410 J 3
Higden, 46 F 2
Higginson, 225 G 3
Highfill, 80 B 1
Hillemann, 25 H 3
Hindsville, 92 C 1
Hiwasse, 175 B 1
Hollis, 275 D 4
Holly Grove, 840 H 4
Holly Springs, 100 E 6
Hollywood, 175 D 5
Hon, 250 B 4
Hope⊙, 8,810 C 6
Hopper, 75 C 5
Horatio, 748 B 6
Horseshoe Bend, 321 G 1
Hot Springs National
Park⊙, 35,631 D 4
Houston, 200 E 3
Howell, 50 H 3
Hoxie, 2,265 H 1
Huffman, 150 L 2
Hughes, 1,872 J 4
Hulbert, 500 K 3
Humnoke, 398 G 4
Humphrey, 818 G 5
Hunter, 131 H 3
Huntington, 627 B 3
Huntsville⊙, 1,287 C 1
Huttig, 822 F 7
Imboden, 496 H 1
Ingalls, 75 F 7
Ione, 50 B 3
Ivan, 120 F 6
Jacksonport, 306 H 2
Jacksonville, 19,832 F 4
Jamestown, 116 G 2
Jasper⊙, 394 D 1
Jefferson, 250 F 5
Jennie, 172 H 7
Jenny Lind, 250 B 3
Jericho, 150 K 3
Jerome, 76 G 7
Jersey, 115 F 7
Jerusalem, 250 E 3
Jessieville, 248 D 4
Johnson, 274 B 1
Johnsville, 60 F 7
Joiner, 839 K 3
Jonesboro⊙, 27,050 J 2
Jones Mill, 850 E 5
Judsonia, 1,667 G 3
Junction City, 763 E 7
Keiser, 688 K 2
Kensett, 1,444 G 3
Keo, 226 G 4
Kerlin, 100 D 7
Kibler, 611 B 3
Kingsland, 304 F 6
Kingston, 200 C 1
Kirby, 300 C 5
Knobel, 375 J 1
Knoxville, 202 D 3
Lacey, 95 G 7
Ladelle, 35 G 7
Lafe, 160 J 1

⊙ County seat. ‡ Population of metropolitan area. ■ Name not shown on map.

All figures available from 1970 final census are supplemented by local official estimates.

CYPRESSES rise from a swamp in the Arkansas lowland. The trees have aerial roots, called "knees," that protrude above the water.

SKYSCRAPERS like the Tower Building (center) have altered skyline of the state capital, Little Rock.

ALUMINUM, after it has been smelted, is poured into pig-block molds at a plant in Arkadelphia.

more manufacturing firms, and many localities had issued the full amount of bonds allowable under state law.

More timber now is being grown in Arkansas than is being cut, and the State Forestry Commission's tree farm at Bluff City is breeding a superior type of southern pine for seeding. Indicative of the future direction of the state's forest industries is the dismantling at Crossett of what was once one of the nation's largest sawmills, now supplanted by other wood-products plants, including a container factory and a plant that makes flakeboards (boards composed of wood chips, or flakes, glued together under very high pressure).

Because of its abundance of water, natural gas and oil, power, and minerals, Arkansas is developing a promising chemical-processing industry—the type of large-investment, high-wage industry that the state needs in its next stage of economic growth. More than 60 corporations were engaged in the chemical business in the mid-1960's, including many of the nation's best-known firms, and several new plants were under construction.

Mining. Bauxite first was mined in Arkansas in 1896, natural gas first produced in 1901, and petroleum in 1921. Most of the nation's domestic bauxite has come from Arkansas. All the bauxite was shipped out of state in raw form until refineries were opened near Bauxite and Hot Springs during World War II. Today, finished aluminum products are manufactured within Arkansas for sale in other states.

The petroleum industry, which centers around Union, Columbia, and Lafayette counties, reached a peak in the 1950's, but there are still several thousand producing wells. The principal refineries are at El Dorado. Production of dry natural gas, from wells that yield no petroleum, centers around Fort Smith. Gas reserves are known to be tremendous.

For some time Arkansas has ranked about midway among the states in total annual value of mineral production (about $200 million in the mid-1960's). Crude petroleum accounts for the major share, followed by stone, bauxite, and natural gas.

Power. Most of the electricity used in Arkansas is produced within the state. There are numerous steam-generating plants, fueled by natural gas, oil, or coal; and several of the major river dams have hydroelectric plants.

Transportation. Although railroad mileage has decreased since 1910, most cities have railroad freight service, and almost every locality has motor freight service.

Arkansas did not seriously undertake the building of a state highway system until 1927. In the mid-1960's most of the state highways were paved, although many of the county roads were not. The chief problem is that, despite a high state gasoline tax, sparsely populated Arkansas does not have the money to build the local road system that it needs. Little Rock is the hub of the new federal interstate highways, as well as of most of the older federal highways, which cross all sections of the state. Several major airlines serve Arkansas, and lesser lines act as feeders.

River traffic, which was important in the early years, became insignificant after the 1880's because of the silting of the rivers and the coming of the railroads. Improvements on rivers such as the Ouachita in recent decades have helped to renew interest in water transportation, and the completion of the Arkansas River Project in the 1970's will make barge service available to several of Arkansas' principal cities. For additional statistics on the economy of Arkansas, see THE AMERICANA ANNUAL.

Economic Research. An experimental atomic power plant, internationally financed, was started near Fayetteville in 1964. The $25 million plant is one of several fast breeder reactors established in various parts of the nation and the world (see NUCLEAR ENERGY—*Nuclear Fission Reactors*).

The University of Arkansas provides assistance in solving the problems of agriculture and industry through its College of Agriculture, Bureau of Business and Economic Research, and Graduate Institute of Technology.

4. Government and Politics

The Arkansas state government is organized under the constitution of 1874, which replaced the Reconstruction constitution of 1868. The present constitution reflects a public reaction against the centralized, strong executive form of government that existed previously. It limits executive and legislative powers and requires the biennial election of most state and local officials.

Amendments may be proposed either by the General Assembly or by initiative petition, but they must then be approved by a majority vote in the next general election. More than a dozen proposed amendments reached the ballot during the years 1960–1964, but the voters adopted only three. These permitted the use of voting machines, abolished the poll tax as a voting requirement, and provided for the formation of tax districts to assist community colleges.

The 52 amendments to the constitution as of the mid-1960's had not greatly altered its basic

---

GOVERNMENT HIGHLIGHTS

Electoral Vote—6. **Representation in Congress**—U.S. senators, 2; U.S. representatives, 4. **General Assembly**—Senate, 35 members, 4-year terms; House of Representatives, 100 members, 2-year terms. **Governor**—2-year term; may succeed himself; annual salary, $10,000. **Voting Qualifications**—Age 18; residence in state 12 months, in county 6 months, in district 1 month. **Elections**—General and state, Tuesday after first Monday in November of even-numbered years.

GOVERNORS
TERRITORIAL

James Miller	1819–1825
George Izard	1825–1829
John Pope	1829–1835
William S. Fulton	1835–1836

STATE

James S. Conway	Democrat	1836–1840
Archibald Yell	"	1840–1844
Samuel Adams (acting)	"	1844
Thomas S. Drew	"	1844–1849
John S. Roane	"	1849–1852
Elias N. Conway	"	1852–1860
Henry M. Rector	"	1860–1862
Harris Flanagin		1862–1864
Isaac Murphy	Union	1864–1868
Powell Clayton	Republican	1868–1871
Ozra A. Hadley (acting)		1871–1873
Elisha Baxter		1873–1874
Augustus H. Garland	Democrat	1874–1877
William R. Miller	"	1877–1881
Thomas J. Churchill	"	1881–1883
James H. Berry	"	1883–1885
Simon P. Hughes	"	1885–1889
James P. Eagle	"	1889–1893
William M. Fishback	"	1893–1895
James P. Clarke	"	1895–1897
Daniel W. Jones	"	1897–1901
Jeff Davis	"	1901–1907
John S. Little	"	1907
John I. Moore (acting)	"	1907
X.O. Pindall (acting)	"	1907–1909
George W. Donaghey	"	1909–1913
Joseph T. Robinson	"	1913
J.M. Futrell (acting)	"	1913
George W. Hays	"	1913–1917
Charles H. Brough	"	1917–1921
Thomas C. McRae	"	1921–1925
Tom J. Terral	"	1925–1927
John E. Martineau	"	1927–1928
Harvey Parnell	"	1928–1933
J.M. Futrell	"	1933–1937
Carl E. Bailey	"	1937–1941
Homer M. Adkins	"	1941–1945
Ben T. Laney	"	1945–1949
Sidney S. McMath	"	1949–1953
Francis Cherry	"	1953–1955
Orval E. Faubus	"	1955–1967
Winthrop Rockefeller	Republican	1967–1971
Dale Bumpers	Democrat	1971–

restrictive nature. A proposal to replace the constitution, made by a special convention in 1918, was rejected by the voters; but constitutional revision or replacement is a recurring issue.

ARKANSAS STATE CAPITOL at Little Rock.

Structure of Government. The executive branch of the state government includes seven elected officials, chief of whom is the governor. Because of the governor's veto power and popular support, he also plays an important legislative role. The other executive officers are lieutenant governor, secretary of state, attorney general, auditor, treasurer, and land commissioner.

The bicameral General Assembly must conduct its business during a 60-day biennial session or during a special session convened by the governor for specific purposes. As a consequence, sessions of the legislature are called frequently. Its work is facilitated, however, by two joint interim committees—the Legislative Council, which gathers data about problems of legislative interest and reviews departmental budget requests, and the Legislative Auditing Committee, which postaudits state spending. The reapportionment of the General Assembly in 1965 may have placed the future balance of legislative power in the hands of the rapidly growing urban districts.

The judiciary consists of a supreme court, a circuit court system with criminal and civil jurisdiction, and a chancery court system with equity jurisdiction. The county judges, municipal judges, and justices of the peace make up a minor court system. All judges are elected.

Political Divisions. Arkansas' 75 counties are the basic governing units for the state. They tend to be small in area and population. In 1960 only a few more than half had as many as 20,000 people, although some have two county seats—holdovers from the days when travel was a major problem even within a small area.

The leading executive is the county judge, who is also the county business manager. Other elected officials include the sheriff, tax collector, assessor, treasurer, county clerk, coroner, and surveyor. The county judge and the justices of the peace make up the county legislative body, or quorum court.

Public Finance. Leading sources of state tax revenue are sales taxes and the state income tax withholding program, which became effective Jan. 1, 1966. Federal grants-in-aid provide a significant amount of the total state revenues. Among expenditures, those for education rank first, followed by those for highways and public welfare. Although the state of Arkansas spends less per capita on education and highways than most other states and its welfare payments are only average, its public expenditures for all three purposes per $1,000 of the personal income of its citizens are above the national average.

Arkansas' fiscal difficulties include the low per capita income of its citizens, the high number of its welfare clients, and the need for heavy state aid to equalize school services in the poorer districts. All these problems were aggravated by the population exodus of 1940–1960, which carried a large number of young adults out of the state, leaving behind a disproportionate number of the very young and the aged. But because the population decline has stopped and per capita income is rising, these problems may lessen in the future.

The chief sources of income for local governments include property taxes, state aid, and earnings of locally owned public utilities. Cities are pressed for funds because of recent growth; yet the state constitution restricts their sources of revenues and imposes a maximum 5-mill property tax for general operating purposes. Two separate

MAIN CAMPUS of the University of Arkansas at Fayetteville contains many schools of the university. Other schools are situated on a campus at Little Rock.

proposals by the legislature in recent years to remove this millage restriction by amendment were rejected by the state's voters.

Social Services. Arkansas offers the usual social services promoted through the federal health and welfare programs. The Children's Colony at Conway for retarded children and the state hospital unit at Little Rock for the treatment of mental illness are both outstanding. Tuberculosis sanatoriums are at Booneville and Alexander, and the Arkansas Rehabilitation Center is at Hot Springs.

Politics. In the mid-1960's, Arkansas was still a one-party (Democratic) state, with the Republican party having won no gubernatorial, presidential, or congressional contest since the Reconstruction period. Most county and local officials, almost all members of the legislature, and all state executives also were elected under the banner of the Democratic party. During the mid-1960's, however, Winthrop Rockefeller provided leadership toward creating an effective Republican party and thus a two-party system. In 1965 the legislature provided for the registration of voters on a free, permanent, and nondiscriminatory basis.

Nomination contests for most state offices in the Democratic primary are usually colorful, spirited, and highly personal. If a candidate fails to get a simple majority in the first primary, a runoff is held between the two top contenders. The Republican party usually nominates its candidates by convention.

5. Educational and Cultural Institutions

Arkansas' best-known early school, Dwight Mission, was opened for Cherokee Indians in 1820 near Russellville, Pope County, by Cephas Washburn, a missionary from Yale College. Classes for white youths were held in the same county in the summer of 1833 by Albert Pike, a former Harvard student. Pike was paid half his salary in money ($3.00) and half in pigs.

Elementary and Secondary Schools. Until 1868 "public" schools were at local option. The only state help was permission for the lease or sale of federally granted school lands. This system produced only 25 schools by 1860. They depended in part on tuition and were free only to those pupils whose parents could not pay. Many parents kept their children unschooled rather than admit to a "pauper" status, and paying parents tended to utilize the private academies.

The first schools for Negroes were opened by the Freedmen's Bureau after 1864. These schools were taken over by the state in 1868, when the carpetbag (Northern Republican) regime founded Arkansas' first tax-supported school system on a segregated basis. There is evidence that the freedmen (who were withdrawing from the white-controlled churches that, as slaves, they were required to attend) wanted the separate schools.

The constitution of 1874 required the retention of public schools, but the economy-minded Bourbons (conservative Democrats) gave them only meager support. The agrarian revolt of the early 1900's brought a demand for better schools, and since that time public education has been improved markedly by such means as a compulsory attendance law (1909), a school equalization fund (1929), and free textbooks (1937).

Controversy over desegregation of Arkansas' public schools drew wide attention in September 1957, when federal troops were used to force the admission of nine Negro students to Central High School in Little Rock. Most of those students remained in attendance throughout the school year, with federalized national guardsmen patrolling the school. In August 1958 a state law was passed permitting the closing of any school threatened with forced integration, and all the Little Rock high schools were closed for the 1958–1959 school year. Segregationist members of the school board were removed in a recall election, and the high schools were reopened in September 1959 on an integrated basis. A federal court invalidated the state law of 1958, and subsequently the legislature proposed a constitutional amendment that would repeal the requirement for public schools. But the people of the state rejected this local-option "school-closing" amendment by a vote of 3 to 1 in November 1960.

Higher Education. Arkansas' system of tax-supported higher education was launched on a segregated basis by the same political regime that launched tax-supported lower schools. The University of Arkansas was founded at Fayetteville in 1871, and a branch for Negroes (now a separate college) was opened at Pine Bluff in 1873. By 1966 the university and all state col-

HOT SPRINGS NATIONAL PARK is a famous spa owned by the U.S. government. It has 47 springs and many bathing facilities.

leges were desegregated, as were most of the private universities and colleges.

The University of Arkansas (see ARKANSAS, UNIVERSITY OF) and each of the state colleges has a separate board of trustees, but the budgets of all are approved by the Commission on Higher Educational Finance. The state colleges are at Arkadelphia, College Heights (near Monticello), Conway, Magnolia, Pine Bluff, Russellville, and State College (Jonesboro). The largest privately controlled institutions of higher education are Little Rock University in Little Rock, Harding College in Searcy, and Ouachita Baptist University in Arkadelphia.

The first in a system of state-aided community colleges, authorized in 1965, were Phillips County Junior College at Helena and Westark Junior College at Fort Smith. By the mid-1960's vocational technical training was authorized at several colleges and at numerous special trade schools.

Libraries. The State Library Commission maintains a central library at Little Rock and assists local libraries wherever there is help from local taxpayers. Almost every county has some kind of local public library, and two thirds of the counties participate in regional libraries with bookmobile service. The largest special library collections are at the University of Arkansas. The archives of the Arkansas History Commission in Little Rock are strong in materials on state history.

Museums. The Museum of Science and Natural History in MacArthur Park, Little Rock, is housed in the Old Federal Arsenal Building where Gen. Douglas MacArthur was born. Also in MacArthur Park is the Arkansas Arts Center, a municipal art center opened in 1963. The Old State House in Little Rock, which served as the state capitol from 1836 until the present capitol was occupied in 1909, houses the state history museum, with its portraits of famous Arkansans and collections of guns and battle flags. The Arkansas Territorial Capitol Restoration in Little Rock preserves historic buildings—government offices and the homes of prominent citizens—from the period 1821 to 1836.

The University of Arkansas Museum at Fayetteville is noted for its archaeological and mineral displays. Fort Smith National Historic Site at Fort Smith includes museum exhibits in the old commissary building.

Other Cultural Organizations. The Arkansas Arts Center operates an artmobile from Little Rock and sponsors statewide art, music, and drama activities. There are several local symphony orchestras, a summer opera workshop at Hot Springs, and many choral groups. The Schola Cantorum of the University of Arkansas placed first in international competition in Italy in 1962. Eureka Springs holds an annual Ozarks folk festival; Pine Bluff, a festival of art; and Magnolia, a sidewalk art show. The Arkansas Historical Association has published the *Arkansas Historical Quarterly* since 1942.

Communications. The *Arkansas Gazette*, first newspaper west of the Mississippi River, began publication at Arkansas Post in 1819. It was printed on a primitive hand press that the editor, William E. Woodruff, brought to the new territory from Tennessee. When the territorial capital was moved to Little Rock in 1821, the newspaper

PEA RIDGE, scene of a Civil War battle on March 7–8, 1862, is a National Military Park. Conditions similar to those shown existed during the struggle.

was moved there also. At present the *Arkansas Gazette* and the *Democrat*, both independently owned and both published in Little Rock, are the largest of the state's approximately 30 daily and 130 weekly newspapers. Arkansas Educational Television began operation in 1966, joining the numerous commercial television and radio stations in the state.

6. Recreation

One of Arkansas' early nicknames, "The Wonder State," accurately describes the number and variety of its recreational areas. These range from wooded mountains, laced by swift, clear streams stocked with rainbow trout, to swampy, cypress-studded lakes still populated by a few alligators. Such natural wonders help to make tourism Arkansas' fifth-ranked industry, with 20 million visitors from out of state each year.

National Areas. Arkansas has three national forests. The Ozark and the Ouachita national forests cover large areas of the highlands. The small St. Francis National Forest is in the lowlands, between Marianna and West Helena. The forests abound in streams and lakes with facilities for boating, fishing, swimming, and water skiing. Hunting is legal in season. The Forest Service maintains numerous campsites, which are supplemented by privately owned accommodations. Bird watching, nature study, and rock collecting are rewarding in the forests, and a drive along one of the highways or winding back roads is a memorable experience.

Hot Springs National Park is a widely known spa. The 47 thermal springs came under federal control in 1832, although the area did not become a national park until 1921. Besides thermal bathing facilities, the park offers mountain drives, foot and bridle paths, and a lookout tower. Surrounding the park is the resort city of Hot Springs.

Pea Ridge National Military Park memorializes the Civil War battle fought at Pea Ridge on March 7–8, 1862, called by some historians "the Gettysburg of the West." Now used as a park museum is Elk Horn Tavern, which served as a military hospital during the battle.

Fort Smith National Historic Site commemorates the founding (1817) of one of the earliest forts in the American West. Restorations there include the courtroom of Judge Isaac Parker, known as the "hanging judge" because of the large number of convictions for murder against train robbers and other fugitives who infested areas of his territory when he was federal judge of the western district of Arkansas (including Indian Territory) at Fort Smith during the years 1875–1896. Arkansas Post National Memorial preserves the site of the first permanent European settlement west of the Mississippi River.

State Areas. The state park system includes about a dozen completed recreational parks, nearly as many memorial sites, and one museum. A number of other areas, recently added, are being developed.

Petit Jean, Mount Nebo, and Queen Wilhelmina state parks, all noted for their panoramic views, are atop flat-crested mountains in the west-central highlands; Crowley's Ridge State

Park lies along a unique geological formation rising out of the northeast lowlands. Buffalo River and Devil's Den state parks both feature crystal-clear Ozark mountain streams; Bull Shoals, Lake Ouachita, Lake Catherine, and Daisy state parks all are situated beside large man-made reservoirs; and Lake Chicot State Park is on the shore of the largest natural lake in the state. Some of the parks operate the year round. Among the memorial sites are several Civil War battlefields. Hampson Museum in Wilson, the only museum in the state park system, houses an Indian artifact collection of the Mound Builder period.

Other Points of Interest. A few of Arkansas' many other interesting places include antebellum houses at Camden, Helena, and Arkadelphia; the Confederate state capitol at Washington; Diamond Cave at Jasper; Mystic Caverns at Harrison; and the Crater of Diamonds, site of former diamond mines at Murfreesboro, where visitors may search for diamonds. The White and the Buffalo river areas are well known for float fishing. Winrock Farm, near Morrilton, features Santa Gertrudis cattle and exhibits of antique automobiles. Eureka Springs is a picturesque resort town situated on a mountainside. Stuttgart offers exceptional duck hunting and fishing.

Annual Events. Most Arkansas counties hold fairs or livestock shows in the autumn. Little Rock is the site of the Arkansas State Livestock Show each October. Hot Springs holds a 43-day horse racing season, starting in February. West Memphis has dog racing from June through October. The Arkansas-Oklahoma Rodeo at Fort Smith is a major event in May. Numerous other annual events feature local products or specialties. These include the Apple Blossom Pilgrimage at Rogers; strawberry festivals at Marshall, Beebe, and Judsonia; a pink tomato festival at Warren; peach festivals at Clarksville and Nashville; a grape festival at Tontitown; a rice-cotton festival at Newport; a cotton-picking contest at Blytheville; and a duck-calling contest at Stuttgart.

7. History

A party of Spaniards under Hernando de Soto sought gold in Arkansas during the years 1541–1542, but because no gold was found, Spain lost interest in the area. The earliest French visitors were led by Louis Jolliet (or Joliet), who, in exploring the Mississippi River, descended it to the mouth of the Arkansas River in 1673. In 1682 René-Robert Cavalier, Sieur de La Salle, claimed the Mississippi Valley for France, naming it Louisiana. His aide, Henri de Tonty (or Tonti),

founded Arkansas Post in 1686. The French carried on missionary activities and Indian trade in the area until 1762, when France ceded its territory west of the Mississippi to Spain. In 1800 Spain secretly ceded the territory back to France, but Spanish occupancy continued until 1803, when the United States acquired the whole vast area through the Louisiana Purchase.

Territorial Period. Arkansas was made a separate district under the Missouri Territory in 1812, and Fort Smith was built in 1817 to protect the settlers from the Indians. In 1819 Arkansas became a separate territory. Its government first met at Arkansas Post but moved to Little Rock in 1821. As a territory, Arkansas obtained much federal aid, including the opening of

HISTORICAL HIGHLIGHTS

1541	Hernando de Soto explored the area for Spain.
1673	Louis Jolliet and party of Frenchmen descended Mississippi River to mouth of Arkansas River.
1682	La Salle claimed Mississippi Valley for France.
1686	Henri de Tonty (Tonti) founded Arkansas Post.
1762	France ceded western Mississippi Valley to Spain by secret Treaty of Fontainebleau.
1800	Spain retroceded territory to France by secret Treaty of San Ildefonso.
1803	United States bought territory from France.
1819	Territory of Arkansas created, with capital at Arkansas Post; *Arkansas Gazette* began publication.
1821	Territorial capital moved to Little Rock.
1836	Arkansas joined Union as 25th state (June 15).
1861	Arkansas seceded to join Confederacy.
1863	Confederate state capital moved to Washington, Hempstead County; Union forces captured Little Rock.
1864	Union state government formed at Little Rock.
1865	Confederate state government surrendered.
1868	Arkansas readmitted to Union.
1871	University of Arkansas founded.
1874	Present state constitution adopted.
1896	Bauxite first mined, near Little Rock.
1901	Natural gas produced near Fort Smith.
1906	Diamonds discovered near Murfreesboro.
1921	First petroleum produced, near El Dorado.
1935	State legislature enacted first sales tax.
1945	Revenue Stabilization Act passed to improve financing of state services.
1957	Federal troops helped enforce court order to desegregate Central High School, Little Rock.
1958	State constitutional amendment enabled cities or counties to sell tax-free bonds for construction of industrial plants.
1960	State voters defeated proposed "school-closing" amendment, ending major controversy over public school desegregation.
1963	Arkansas Arts Center opened in Little Rock.
1964	Contract signed for experimental atomic power plant near Fayetteville.
1965	Arkansas established its first permanent, free, nondiscriminatory voter-registration system.
1966	Work on $1.2 billion federal Arkansas River development program reached halfway point.

CRATER OF DIAMONDS at Murfreesboro in southwestern Arkansas, the site of old diamond mines. Visitors hunt for gem samples.

military roads, the clearing of snags from several rivers, and land grants for various purposes.

Early Statehood. When Arkansas was admitted as the 25th state in June 1836, it had barely the required minimum of 50,000 residents. One reason for the small population was that almost the entire eastern part of Arkansas was a vast swamp, which was virtually impassable in wet weather. This condition probably retarded immigration more than any other factor and was not fully remedied by levees and drainage until the late 1800's. The national panic of 1837 also hindered the new state by contributing to the downfall of its only two banks, chartered in 1836 to provide development capital. Despite such handicaps, Arkansas had nearly a half million residents by 1860 and was developing a promis-

FAMOUS RESIDENTS OF ARKANSAS

Anthony, Katharine Susan (1877–1965), biographer of famous women.

Barton, Thomas Harry (1881–1960), petroleum executive, civic leader, philanthropist.

Burns, Bob (1890–1956), comedian, known for homespun tales and performances on the "bazooka."

Caraway, Mrs. Hattie Wyatt (1878–1951), first woman elected to the U.S. Senate (1932) for a full term.

Couch, Harvey Crowley (1877–1941), utility and railroad executive, civic leader.

Davis, Jeff (1862–1913), leader of agrarian revolt in Arkansas, three times state governor; U.S. senator.

Dean, "Dizzy" (1911–   ), baseball pitcher, member of National Baseball Hall of Fame.

Faubus, Orval Eugene (1910–   ), only Arkansas governor to serve six terms.

Faulkner, Sandford C. (1803–1874), cotton planter, thought to have written the fiddle tune *The Arkansas Traveler*.

Fletcher, John Gould (1886–1950), Pulitzer Prize winner, 1939, for *Selected Poems*; prose writer and critic.

Fulbright, James William (1905–   ), U.S. senator; sponsor of Fulbright Act of 1946.

Garland, Augustus Hill (1832–1899), governor of Arkansas; U.S. senator; U.S. attorney general, 1885–1889.

MacArthur, Douglas (1880–1964), commander of Allied forces in Southwest Pacific during World War II.

McClellan, John Little (1896–   ), U.S. representative and senator.

McConnell, John Paul (1908–   ), U.S. Air Force officer; chief of staff from 1965.

Pace, Frank, Jr. (1912–   ), public official; U.S. secretary of the army, 1950–1952.

Parker, Isaac Charles (1838–1896), federal judge at Fort Smith, known as the "hanging judge."

Pike, Albert (1809–1891), pioneer teacher, lawyer, officer in Mexican and Civil wars, Masonic leader, poet.

Read, Opie Percival (1852–1939), writer; editor of *Arkansas Gazette* and *Arkansas Traveler.*

Rice-Meyrowitz, Jenny Delony (1866–1949), portrait painter.

Robinson, Joseph Taylor (1872–1937), U.S. senator; Democratic vice-presidential candidate, 1928.

Rockefeller, Winthrop (1912–   ), cattleman and civic leader; elected governor, 1966.

Snyder, John Wesley (1895–   ), banker and government official; U.S. secretary of the treasury, 1946–1953.

Somervell, Brehon Burke (1892–1955), U.S. Army officer, World Wars I and II.

Stephens, Wilton Robert (1907–   ), utility executive, securities and investment specialist.

Stone, Edward Durell (1902–   ), architect, known for art museums and other major buildings.

Warfield, William Caesar (1920–   ), concert singer, actor.

Washburn, Cephas (1793–1860), missionary, founder of Dwight Mission; his son, **Edward Payson Washburn** (1831–1860), painter, known for *The Arkansas Traveler.*

Wilson, Charles Morrow (1905–   ), writer on various subjects, including his native Ozarks.

Winslow, Thyra Samter (1893–1961), writer of popular novels and short stories, some about Arkansas.

Woodward, C(omer) Vann (1908–   ), historian, Sterling professor of history at Yale University from 1961.

Yell, Archibald (1797–1847), first U.S. representative from Arkansas, state governor, officer in Mexican War.

Mechanical pickers have almost entirely replaced hand labor in harvesting cotton, Arkansas' most important crop.

ARKANSAS

Natural gas, used as fuel in drilling for other gas deposits, is burned off at a drilling site in western Arkansas.

The colors of autumn begin to touch hardwood trees in the Ozark National Forest north of Russellville.

The Memphis and Arkansas Bridge, backed by two railroad bridges, crosses the Mississippi at Memphis *(foreground)*.

A sandy beach and cliffs for diving border a popular swimming area on the Buffalo River in the Boston Mountains.

Aluminum, processed in Arkansas from minerals mined in Arkansas, is now a major state industry. *(Left)* Strip mining for bauxite ore near the town of Bauxite. *(Below)* Continuous casting of aluminum ingots at a processing plant in Arkadelphia.

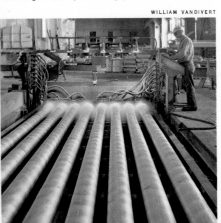

CAPITOL of the Territory of Arkansas from 1821 to 1836, when the state was admitted to the Union, is in a complex of restored buildings in Little Rock.

HAROLD PHELPS, FROM ARKANSAS PUBLICITY AND PARKS COMMISSION

ing farm economy, based in part on cotton and slave labor.

The Civil War. Arkansas seceded from the Union to join the Confederacy in May 1861, but only after war began and President Lincoln forced a choice of sides by calling on the state for troops. Loyalty to the federal government was strong in northern Arkansas, however, and more than 10,000 men fought for the Union. Many of the battles in frontier Arkansas were part of campaigns having objectives outside the state. One example was the Battle of Pea Ridge, where the defeat of a Confederate army moving north in March 1862 helped to secure Missouri for the Union. Because so many of Arkansas' Confederate troops served outside the state, Little Rock was an easy prey for Union forces when they could be sent against it after the fall of Vicksburg, Miss. As Little Rock fell in September 1863, the Confederate state government fled to Washington, in southwest Arkansas, where it functioned until the war's end. A government loyal to the Union was formed at Little Rock during 1864, under Isaac Murphy, an Arkansas Unionist. Thus for a time Arkansas had two state governments.

Reconstruction. In June 1865 the Confederate state officials yielded to the Unionist government, which extended its control over the entire state. Although the Murphy regime governed with popular support for several years, it was unable to gain recognition from the U.S. Congress and was replaced in 1868 by a Northern Republican, or carpetbag, regime under a new state constitution that enfranchised the Negroes. At this time Arkansas was readmitted to the Union.

Carpetbag control continued until 1873, when the state began to revert to home rule under Gov. Elisha Baxter, a local Republican who broke with the outsiders. Unquestionably, carpetbag rule was excessive, but it produced Arkansas' first system of free public education and brought renewed attention to the need for railroads and other improvements. It left Arkansas with a $10 million debt, but the voters repudiated this debt in 1884, and it is a moot question who was victimized— the people of Arkansas or the Northern speculators in Reconstruction state bonds.

Bourbon Rule and the Agrarian Revolt. Republican Governor Baxter worked so closely with the Democrats that they offered him their party's support for the governorship under the new constitution of 1874. When he declined, the position

went to Augustus H. Garland, under whom Arkansas returned to full conservative Democratic, or Bourbon, control. The Bourbons succeeded in having many railroads built and in attracting some industry; but because they allowed businesses to pay low taxes and to escape most state regulation, they aroused the displeasure of the small farmers, or agrarians.

In 1900 Jeff Davis (a native of Little River County, not to be confused with Jefferson Davis, president of the Confederacy) capitalized on agrarian unrest and sought the Democratic gubernatorial nomination on the promise to restore to the people those resources and rights that had been given away to business by the Bourbons. Stumping all 75 counties and using demagogic methods, Davis—who was elected governor three times—aroused the average voter as never before and heralded an age of popular politics that persists in Arkansas to this day.

Since 1900. Because Arkansans still associate the Republican party with Reconstruction and because Jeff Davis kept the agrarian revolt under the Democratic banner, Arkansas continued in the 1900's to be a strong one-party state.

The economy of Arkansas lagged behind even that of the South as a whole during the late 1800's and early 1900's. World War II brought some industry to Arkansas, and since the late 1950's the use of local bond issues to attract industry to the state has had promising results. Arkansas' agriculture and forest industries have been diversified, and recreation and tourism have become major factors in the economy.

ROBERT B. WALZ
Southern State College, Magnolia

Bibliography

Alexander, Henry M., *Government in Arkansas*, rev. ed., (Little Rock 1963).
American Guide Series, *Arkansas: A Guide to the State* (New York 1941).
Arkansas Almanac, Inc., *Arkansas Almanac* (Little Rock).
Arkansas Historical Association, *Arkansas Historical Quarterly* (Van Buren, Ark., 1942 to date).
Brown, Walter L., *Our Arkansas*, rev. ed. (Austin, Texas, 1964).
Ferguson, John L., and Atkinson, J.H., *Historic Arkansas*, Arkansas History Commission (Conway, Ark., 1966).
Fletcher, John Gould, *Arkansas* (Chapel Hill, N.C., 1947).
Harper, C. Armitage, and Kinkead, Ewing W., *Conservation in Arkansas*, 3d ed. (Little Rock 1956).
McKnight, Olin E., and Johnson, Boyd W., *The Arkansas Story*, rev. ed. (Oklahoma City 1960).
Thomas, David Y., ed., *Arkansas and Its People*, 4 vols. (New York 1931).

ARKANSAS, University of, är′kən-sô, a coeducational state university and land-grant college in Fayetteville, Ark. Founded in 1871, it was named Arkansas Industrial University; the present name was adopted in 1899. A second campus, at Little Rock, opened in 1879.

On the main campus at Fayetteville are the colleges of arts and sciences, agriculture and home economics, business administration, education, and engineering, as well as the graduate and law schools. Facilities are provided nearby on more than 7,000 acres for agricultural and forestry research. The school of medicine, the university hospital, and the schools of technology are at Little Rock.

Original research is encouraged by honors programs in the college of arts and sciences and in the medical school. University libraries house almost 500,000 volumes. Of special interest are a collection of Arkansas history and Ozark literature and folklore, and the John Gould Fletcher collection of English and American literature.

Enrollment at the university rose steadily, from almost 3,000 in 1940 to over 5,000 in 1950 and to more than 11,000 by 1970.

ARKANSAS CITY, är-kan′zəz, is in southern Kansas, at the confluence of the Arkansas and Walnut rivers, in Cowley County. Situated 60 miles (97 km) by road southeast of Wichita, the city is the trading and shipping center of a farming and oilfield region. Its industries include oil refining, flour milling, meat packing, tile manufacture, and railroad servicing. Arkansas City Junior College is situated here.

Founded in 1870, Arkansas City was the starting point for thousands of settlers at the opening of the Oklahoma lands in 1889 and 1893. It has a commission-manager form of government, adopted in 1931. Population: 13,216.

ARKANSAS POST, är′kən-sô, is a village in Arkansas, in Arkansas County, about 75 miles (121 km) southeast of Little Rock, on a high bluff overlooking the Arkansas River. The site of the first white settlement in the present state of Arkansas, it was founded in 1686 by Henri de Tonty (Tonti) and maintained by a few French soldiers during the next three decades. In 1719–1720, John Law, organizer of the Compagnie d'Occident, which was to become involved in the Mississippi Bubble (q.v.) scandal, sent some 500 Negroes and about 800 white settlers, mostly Alsatians, to start a community at Arkansas Post. Discouraged by hunger and privation and by news of the company's financial collapse, the settlers abandoned the site in 1721. During the later 18th century, Arkansas Post was a supply base for the French traders who penetrated the Southwest. Ceded to the United States by the Louisiana Purchase of 1803, it became the first capital (1819–1821) of the Arkansas Territory.

During the Civil War, powerful Confederate defenses that had been established here were reduced on Jan. 11, 1863, by the combined assault of a Federal army under Gen. John A. McClernand and a naval command under Adm. David D. Porter. After the war, river travel was superseded by railroads, and Arkansas Post, which had no rail connection, declined.

The Arkansas Post National Memorial, authorized in 1960 and administratively established in 1965, preserves the site of this historic settlement.

ARKANSAS RIVER, är′kən-sô or är-kan′zes, in the west central and south central United States, rising in Lake County, Colo., and emptying into the Mississippi River in Desha County, Ark. It is 1,450 miles (2,333 km) long. From its source in the Rocky Mountains of central Colorado, the Arkansas flows south, then east, through deep, narrow canyons, including the Royal Gorge, from which it emerges onto the plains of eastern Colorado near Pueblo. It flows generally east across Colorado and Kansas to the vicinity of Wichita, then southeast across northeastern Oklahoma and central Arkansas, passing Tulsa, Okla., and Fort Smith and Little Rock, Ark. It receives its largest tributaries—the Canadian, the Cimarron, and the Neosho rivers—in Oklahoma.

The Arkansas, one of the major western tributaries of the Mississippi, drains an area of approximately 160,000 square miles (414,400 sq km). Numerous water-storage, flood-control, and hydroelectric units have been developed in its basin. Major reservoirs on the river itself are the John Martin in Colorado, the Keystone in Oklahoma, and the Dardanelle in Arkansas. The lower third of the river is classified as navigable.

ARKHANGELSK. See ARCHANGEL.

ARKWRIGHT, ärk′rīt, **Sir Richard,** English inventor, who made important improvements in cotton-spinning machinery. He was born in Preston, England, on Dec. 23, 1732, the youngest of a family of seven children. His education was so limited that at the age of 50 he gave an hour each day to the study of grammar. Arkwright was apprenticed to a wigmaker at Kirkham, near Preston, and in 1750 entered the wigmaking shop of Edward Pollit at Bolton. When he was 20, he married Patience Holt; his son Richard was born on Dec. 19, 1755. Patience died the following year, and Arkwright in 1761 married Margaret Biggins of Leigh, by whom he had one daughter. He invested an inheritance from his father in a shop near the White Bear Tavern in Bolton. The discovery of a process of dyeing hair gave a new dimension to the wigmaking business, and Arkwright spent much of his time collecting hair at the fairs.

Arkwright soon became interested in cotton spinning. About 1767 he was far advanced on a model spinning frame using rollers and the flyer after the general pattern of the patents of Lewis Paul (1738 and 1758). With help on mechanical details from John Kay and financial support from John Smalley, Arkwright completed a model and exhibited it at Preston in the spring of 1768. Probably in June 1768, he set up a small mill, driven by horse power, in Woolpack Lane, Nottingham. Further financial support was secured through a partnership with Samuel Need and Jedediah Strutt. A patent on the throstle or water frame was granted on July 3, 1769.

To secure the full advantage of the productivity of the spinning frame, it was necessary to mechanize the preparatory processes of carding, drawing, and roving. In 1771, Arkwright purchased some property, at Cromford, that had a supply of water power, and as early as March 1772 some yarn was being produced at the mill that he built there. The yarn was superior in quality to the hand-spun or even the jenny yarn, which were too soft for use as warp.

In 1775, Arkwright secured a patent on the carding, drawing, and roving machines developed for the Cromford mill. The patent on the carding engine was opposed by the cotton spinners of Lancashire and Derbyshire, since the engine could be used to advantage in the jenny mills that were developing rapidly. Many of the spinners built carding engines without licenses from Arkwright, and in 1781 he brought suit against several infringers of the patent. The patent was declared invalid on the ground that the specifications were incomplete. Arkwright brought another suit, heard in March 1785, when he showed that the specifications were adequate. The cotton manufacturers secured a rehearing of the case in July, contending that the invention was not new when patented, that it was not original with Arkwright, and that it was not adequately specified. The court held against Arkwright on all counts. The patent was certainly vulnerable. Arkwright had added essential mechanisms to the carding engines previously developed, and he had made great improvements in the spinning and roving frames, but he could not defend the broad claims of comprehensive novelty made in the patents.

Arkwright's career as an entrepreneur was as distinctive as his work as an inventor. The Cromford mill of 1771 became the model for the power-driven spinning mill. By 1789 he was operating five mills in Derbyshire and three in other counties. There were 11 mills under other ownership in Derbyshire using his machinery. The business of selling machinery to licensees and prospective millowners was important, even after the patent of 1775 was declared invalid. At some of his mills, weaving shops were also set up.

Arkwright was knighted in 1786 by George III when he made the congratulatory address for his district after the king had escaped assassination. The following year he became the high sheriff of Derbyshire. He purchased the manor of Cromford in 1789; Willersley castle, which he began shortly after, was unfinished when he died in Cromford on Aug. 3, 1792.

ABBOTT PAYSON USHER, *Harvard University*

Further Reading: Baines, Sir Edward, *History of the Cotton Manufacture in Great Britain* (London 1835); Fitton, Robert S., and Wadsworth, Alfred P., *The Strutts and the Arkwrights, 1758–1830* (Manchester, Eng., 1958); Wadsworth, Alfred P., and Mann, Julia Delacy, *The Cotton Trade and Industrial Lancashire, 1600–1780* (Manchester, Eng., 1931).

ARLEN, är′lən, **Harold** (1905–   ), American composer. He was born *Hyman Arluck* in Buffalo, N.Y., on Feb. 15, 1905. His father, a cantor, gave him his earliest musical training. After graduating from high school, Arlen sang and played piano with jazz bands in the Buffalo area until 1927, when he moved to New York City.

He was working as a rehearsal pianist when he composed his first hit song, *Get Happy*, sung as the finale of the *9:15 Revue* (1928). From 1930 to 1933 he wrote some of his most successful songs for the Cotton Club revues in Harlem, including *Stormy Weather, I've Got the World on a String*, and *Devil and the Deep Blue Sea*. In 1939 he won a motion picture Academy Award for the song *Over the Rainbow*, which was sung by Judy Garland in *The Wizard of Oz*.

Other successful films with scores by Arlen include *Cabin in the Sky* (1940), *Blues in the Night* (1941), and *A Star is Born* (1954). He also wrote the music for Broadway productions, including *Bloomer Girl* (1944), *St. Louis Woman* (1946), and *House of Flowers* (1954).

ARLES, àrl, is a town in southern France, in Bouches-du-Rhône department, on the Rhône River, 45 miles (72 km) northwest of Marseille. The town's main trade is in olives, livestock, and wine. Industries include metalworking, boat building, chemicals, and sulfur refining.

Arles was an important town in both the Roman and the medieval periods. Among the Roman remains are the 2d century A.D. amphitheater (now used for bullfights), a cemetery (the Aliscamps), and a theater of the 1st or 2d century A.D. where the celebrated Venus of Arles was found in 1651. From the medieval period is the imposing Romanesque Church of St. Trophime (St. Trophimus Christianized the area), begun in the 11th century. Just outside the town is Montmajour Abbey, built in the 12th–14th centuries. Arles also has a museum of Provençal arts and crafts, founded by the poet Frédéric Mistral in 1899.

History. Called *Arelate* by the Romans, it became a flourishing commercial center after Gaius Marius connected it with the Mediterranean Sea by canal in 103 B.C. In 395 A.D. it was made the seat of the prefecture of Gaul. Emperor Constantine convened a synod in Arles in 314 that condemned the Donatists, a schismatic group that denied the right of a priest to administer the sacraments while in a state of sin. The town remained a Roman Catholic archiepiscopal see from about this time until the French Revolution.

Arles declined after its capture by the Visigoths in the 5th century, but it revived as a center of Provençal culture during the Middle Ages. In 933 it became the capital of the independent kingdom of Arles (also called the kingdom of Burgundy) that originally embraced most of southeast France and parts of Switzerland. Although the royal title passed to the rulers of the Holy Roman Empire in 1033, they exercised little direct control over the area. The counts of Savoy gradually assumed control over the northeastern and eastern parts of the kingdom, and the future King Charles VI of France acquired title to the rest in 1378. Population: (1962) 29,251.

ARLINGTON, är′ling-tən, **Earl of** (1618–1685), English statesman. He was born *Henry Bennet* and baptized at Little Saxham, Suffolk. He fought in the first Civil War on the king's side, joined the royal family in France, and in 1654 was appointed secretary to the future James II. After the Restoration he became a secretary of state in 1662 and was raised to the peerage as a baron (he was created an earl in 1672).

Instrumental in securing the dismissal (1667) of Edward Hyde, 1st earl of Clarendon, as Charles II's chief minister, Arlington was a leader of the so-called Cabal ministry, which succeeded Clarendon's. Assuming the duties of foreign secretary, he contracted the Triple Alliance with Holland and Sweden (1668). At Charles' direction, he betrayed this alliance, in the secret Treaty of Dover (1670), in favor of an alliance with France. This action led to the Third Dutch War (1672–1674).

Arlington's affected mannerisms were the object of much ridicule. In 1674, impeachment proceedings were brought against him on charges of embezzlement and Roman Catholic sympathies. The case was dropped, but he resigned from the ministry, retaining the office of lord chamberlain until his death, at Euston, on July 28, 1685.

ARLINGTON, är'ling-tən, a town in northeastern Massachusetts, is in Middlesex County, 6 miles (10 km) northwest of Boston, of which it is a residential suburb. Leather goods and wood products are manufactured. Arlington has many landmarks of the Revolutionary War, including the Jason Russell House, where a number of patriots sought refuge from British troops on April 19, 1775, the day of the battles of Lexington and Concord. The first settlement was made in 1630 in a part of Cambridge bearing the Indian name *Menotomy.* The town, incorporated as *West Cambridge* in 1807, obtained its present name in 1867. Government is by a limited form of town meeting, with a town manager named by the selectmen. Population: 53,524.

JUDITH E. STROMDAHL, *Robbins Library*

ARLINGTON, är'ling-tən, is a city in Texas, in Tarrant County, midway between Fort Worth and Dallas. It manufactures cans, rubber and paper products, trailers, machinery, and chemicals, and assembles automobiles. The city is served by the nearby Greater Southwest International Airport and is the home of Arlington State College of the University of Texas. Arlington was established soon after the Civil War and was laid out in 1876. It was incorporated in 1883 and adopted a council-manager plan of government in 1949. Population: 90,643.

JOHN A. HUDSON
Librarian, Arlington State College Library

ARLINGTON, är'ling-tən, a county in Virginia, is an urban community directly across the Potomac River from Washington, D.C. It is the fourth-smallest county in the United States (25.5 sq mi, or 66 sq km), and contains no incorporated cities or towns. It has some light industry and industrial research firms, but is principally a residential suburb of Washington. Federal installations in the county include Arlington National Cemetery (q.v.), Fort Myer, and the Pentagon, headquarters of the Department of Defense. Also situated here are Washington National Airport and Marymount Junior College.

Originally named *Alexandria County,* the area was ceded by Virginia to the federal government in 1789 to form part of the District of Columbia, but was returned to Virginia by the U.S. Congress in 1846. During the Civil War it was occupied by Union forces, who built here some 20 forts as part of the defenses of Washington. The name was changed in 1920 to Arlington, after the home of Gen. Robert E. Lee, which is situated within the Arlington National Cemetery reservation.

Arlington is governed by a five-member county board. Population: 174,284.

JEANNE ROSE
Arlington County Department of Libraries

ARLINGTON HEIGHTS, är'ling-tən hīts, a village in Illinois, is a residential suburb of Chicago. It is situated in Cook County, 30 miles (48 km) by road northwest of Chicago's Loop. Commercial activities include small manufacturing, publishing, and nursery farming. On the western edge of the village is Arlington Park Race Track. The community was settled in 1836 and was incorporated in 1887. It adopted managerial government in 1954. Population: 64,884.

ARLINGTON NATIONAL CEMETERY, är'ling-tən, is in Arlington County, Va., across the Potomac River from the city of Washington, D.C. It is the largest national cemetery in the United States, covering 420 acres (170 hectares). Arlington contains the graves of tens of thousands of Americans killed in war, other members or veterans of the armed services, and distinguished citizens who served the country. In some cases, members of their families also are buried there.

Among those buried in Arlington are Generals John J. Pershing and George C. Marshall, Admirals William F. Halsey, Robert E. Peary, and Richard E. Byrd, the political leaders William Jennings Bryan and John Foster Dulles, and Presidents William Howard Taft and John F. Kennedy.

In the Tomb of the Unknown Soldier lie three unknown dead, one each from World War I, World War II, and the Korean War. This tomb is guarded at all times by a sentry. Other military memorials in the cemetery include the Memorial Amphitheater, behind the Tomb of the Unknown Soldier; the Tomb of the Unknown Dead of the Civil War; the Confederate Monument; and the mast of the battleship *Maine,* sunk in Havana harbor in 1898. White marble stones mark thousands of individual graves.

The land was owned once by George Washington Parke Custis, adopted grandson of George Washington, and later by Gen. Robert E. Lee. The Custis-Lee family mansion overlooking the cemetery is now a national memorial. The U.S. Government acquired the land in 1864, and the first burial was made in that year.

FRED WARD, FROM BLACK STAR

ARLINGTON NATIONAL CEMETERY

The Tomb of the Unknown Soldier is situated in front of the Memorial Amphitheater.

ARLISS, är'lis, **George** (1868–1946), English actor, who was known for his character roles. He was born *Augustus George Andrews* in London on April 10, 1868. He made his theatrical debut in 1886 and scored his first London success in *Mr. and Mrs. Daventry* in 1900. He appeared chiefly on the New York stage from 1901 to 1928, notably in *Disraeli* (1911), *The Green Goddess* (1921), and *Old English* (1924).

Beginning in 1929, Arliss acted exclusively in motion pictures, recreating many of his stage roles. His film portrayal of Disraeli won him an Academy Award in 1929. Among his other films were *Voltaire* (1933), *The House of Rothschild* (1934), *The Iron Duke* (1935), and *Cardinal Richelieu* (1935). His last film, *Dr. Syn,* was made in England in 1937. He wrote two autobiographical works—*Up the Years from Bloomsbury* (1927) and *My Ten Years in the Studio* (1940). He died in London on Feb. 5, 1946.

ARM is the term used technically to denote the upper part of the limb of the body extending from the shoulder joint to the elbow. The term "arm" is used popularly, however, to denote both the arm and the forearm.

The arm proper has one large, strong bone, the humerus, which is covered by strong muscles that protect the blood vessels and nerves of the arm. The upper end of the humerus fits into one end of the shoulder blade (scapula), and with the collarbone (clavicle) forms the shoulder joint. The end of the humerus is held in the shoulder joint partly by ligaments, but mainly by the muscles attached to it.

The musculature of the arm permits it to move in several directions. Muscles known as abductors move the arm inward toward the chest. Adductors move the arm away from the body. Most of the muscles of the upper arm, however, go to the forearm and move that part. In all, there are 48 muscles that participate in the movements of the arm, forearm, and hand.

Blood is supplied to the arm by branches of the brachiocephalic artery on the right side of the body and from the arch of the aorta on the left side. These branches are the brachial arteries and they are the main arterial trunk in each arm. The brachial artery divides into two smaller arteries—the radial, supplying the outer side of the forearm, and the ulnar, supplying the inner side—at the bend of the elbow. The radial artery is the one felt most frequently in determining the pulse. The major veins of the arm are the cephalic and basilic; those of the forearm are the ulnar, the median, and the radial.

The nerve supply of the arm is derived from the brachial plexus, a group of nerves that includes the fifth, sixth, seventh, and eighth cervical nerves and the first, second, and third thoracic nerves of the spinal cord. Main branches of the plexus that go to the different muscles and skin areas of the arm are the median, ulnar, musculospiral, musculocutaneous, and circumflex.

ARMADA, är-mä'də, is the name applied to the great Spanish fleet that was defeated by the English in the summer of 1588. Few naval battles have had such far-reaching effects. The victory saved England from invasion. But it also marked a turning point in naval tactics, and it opened the way for the colonial expansion of England, Holland, and France by breaking the Spanish-Portuguese monopoly of overseas empire.

Ever since Queen Elizabeth had come to the throne in 1558, Protestant England had managed to steer a neutral course during the bitter religious wars on the Continent. The Catholics, with the powerful support of Philip II of Spain, were trying to stamp out Protestantism, especially in France and the Netherlands. Hoping to pave the way for maritime expansion, a group of bold and colorful English "Sea Dogs," led by John Hawkins and Francis Drake, engaged in successful but unneutral raiding of Spanish ships and ports in the Caribbean and more distant waters. Philip II put up with this for a quarter century but finally decided to invade England with his crack Spanish infantry, carried by an "armada."

Until this time most actions had been fought at close range, with ships lying alongside each other. In 1571 the Spaniards, with other Christian forces, had smashed Turkish naval power in the Mediterranean at Lepanto, using galleys, propelled by oars, of the general type used since Greek and Roman times. But for Atlantic action the English Sea Dogs were planning a very different sort of tactics, developing fast, low-lying maneuverable vessels that could get to windward and pound the enemy at long range with guns, safe from hand-to-hand contact with the redoubtable Spanish infantry on the ships.

In July 1588 the great Spanish-Portuguese force sailed for England, with 124 vessels of various sizes, carrying 1,100 guns and 27,000 men. The English had 197 ships with 2,000 guns and 16,000 men. The Englishmen were all seamen, while half the Spanish were soldiers. The English guns had the longer range.

The Spaniards met the new tactics along the south coast of England when the Sea Dogs pounded their huge, clumsy vessels from beyond the range of the Spanish guns. The Armada sought refuge in the French port of Calais, but Drake dislodged them with fireships—vessels filled with combustibles and set afire to drift into the enemy fleet. The English mauled the Spaniards badly until the English ran out of ammunition (having fired some 100,000 rounds), but by that time the heavy gales began to push the Armada northward around the tip of Scotland and then southward around Ireland. Many Spanish ships foundered while others were

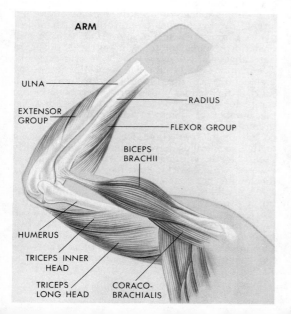

ARM

ULNA

RADIUS

EXTENSOR GROUP

FLEXOR GROUP

BICEPS BRACHII

HUMERUS

TRICEPS INNER HEAD

TRICEPS LONG HEAD

CORACO-BRACHIALIS

ARMADA'S huge ships (right) are attacked by light English craft. A Spanish galleon is captured (lower left).

wrecked on the coasts of Scotland and Ireland. Barely half the force that had set out in July limped home in September.

The new long-range tactics developed by the English were taken up by other naval powers. They continued in general use until the advent of steam and armor after 1850.

The defeat of the Armada marked a turning point in Spanish power. The Spaniards still were strong enough to keep their established colonies in Latin America and elsewhere, but they no longer tried to monopolize America north of Florida or to defend the Asian empire of Portugal then under Spanish control. The English, Dutch, and French moved into those two areas at once. The English East India Company was chartered in 1600, and the Dutch in 1602. The English settled Jamestown in 1607; the French settled Quebec in 1608; and the Hudson River was discovered for the Dutch in 1609. From those beginnings, new overseas empires grew rapidly.

ROBERT G. ALBION, *Harvard University*

Further Reading: Mattingly, Garrett, *The Armada* (Boston 1962); Woodroofe, Thomas, *Vantage at Sea* (New York 1958).

Nine-banded armadillo (*Dasypus novemcinctus***).**

ARMADILLO, är-mə-dil'ō, is any one of a group of mammals with few or no teeth. They are found in the south-central and southeastern United States and South and Central America. Armadillos are notable for their defensive armor. The armor consists of small roundish bony plates, hardened within the skin. In most members of the group, the plates are united to form solid shields, one over the shoulders, and one over the haunches. Between these shields are crosswise bands of movable plates that protect the body but leave freedom of motion to it. These plates are overlaid by a thin horny covering, and between them grow hairs varying in length and amount with the species, from almost none in some to a distinct coat hiding the shell in others. The unarmored undersurface is also hairy. The head has a shield entirely separate from that of the shoulders. In some species even the tail is protected by concentrically overlapping rings of armor. In others (the soft-tailed armadillos) the tail contains only scattered plates that are not firmly united to each other.

The armadillo belongs to the family Dasypodidae; there are 9 genera and about 20 species. The various species of armadillos are distinguished largely by the number of movable thin bands of plates lying between the large fixed anterior and posterior shields, up to as many as a dozen in the cabassous (*Xenurus*). Those of the genus *Tolypeutes* increase the value of the armor by their ability to roll themselves up into a ball so that the tender underparts of the body are completely protected. This ability depends upon the number of bands in the central portion of the armor case.

Although true edentates (mammals lacking teeth), armadillos have numerous small, nearly useless teeth, without true roots. The tongue is covered with a sticky fluid like that secreted by the tongue of an anteater.

Armadillos are timid, nocturnal animals, living on insects, carrion, and vegetable matter. Their legs and claws are adapted to burrowing, and when pursued they usually bury themselves more quickly than the pursuer can follow them. One of the most interesting of them all is the pichiciago (*Chlamyphorus truncatus*), found in Argentina, which lives entirely underground like a mole, and exhibits many peculiar structures. The body has a truncated appearance, as if the rear part had been cut squarely off, instead of ending in curved lines. It is very small, only five to six inches (.12½ to 15 cm) long. The giant armadillo (*Priodontes giganteus*) measures three feet, exclusive of the tail. Some of the armadillos range north and south as far as Texas and Argentina; among these is the nine-banded armadillo (*Tatusia novemcincta*). They are eaten by the South Americans and are considered to have a delicate taste.

Reproduction in *Dasypus novemcinctus*, a nine-banded form, is peculiar. The young, unless some mishap has taken place, are invariably quadruplets of the same sex. It is believed that the fertilized egg divides and redivides into four parts before each part becomes organized into a young armadillo.

Fossil armadillos have been found in both North and South America. One fossil species was six feet (1.8 meters) long. Another genus was *Eutatus*, which had a shield formed of 36 distinct bands, of which the last 12 were fused together. See also EDENTATA—*Fossil Edentates*.

G.H.H. TATE
The American Museum of Natural History

ARMAGEDDON, är-mə-gəd'ən, is the name given in the New Testament to the battlefield where the forces of good and evil will meet on Judgment Day in the final struggle for supremacy (Revelation 16:16). From this usage, the word has come to signify any climactic confrontation between irreconcilable forces.

Also written *Har-Magedon*, the name is thought to be derived from Megiddo, a hill or town on the plain of Esdraelon in Galilee, where many great battles were fought in the early history of the Israelites.

ARMAGH, är-mä', is the smallest county in Northern Ireland. Its area is 512 square miles (1,326 sq km). On the north it touches Lough Neagh, the largest lake in the British Isles, and on the south it borders the republic of Ireland. The county of Tyrone is on the west, and Down on the east. Armagh is hilly in the south, but around Lough Neagh the soil is black and fertile. Fruit and flax are the principal crops; linen milling is the chief industry. Population: (1961) 117,594.

The county town is Armagh, 33 miles (53 km) southwest of Belfast. It has been an ecclesiastical center for more than 15 centuries, although whether St. Patrick, the patron saint of Ireland, was the actual founder in 432 A.D. is a matter of scholarly dispute. Armagh is now a Roman Catholic and Protestant archiepiscopal see. Population: (1961) 10,062.

ARMAGNAC, är-mȧ-nyȧk', is a region in southwestern France, including parts of Gers, Landes, and Lot-et-Garonne departments. Once an important countship, it reached its greatest power and extent during the 14th and 15th centuries. The area is watered by several small rivers that descend from the Lannemezan plateau; the Gers River is the largest of these. The region, predominantly agricultural, is noted for its Armagnac brandy.

Under Roman rule, Armagnac was included in the Civitas Ausciorum, or district of Auch. Near the end of the 9th century the part now known as Fezensac became a hereditary countship. In 960, Armagnac separated from Fezensac. The counts of Armagnac increased their territory through marriage and purchase, and in time absorbed the countship of Fezensac.

During the Hundred Years' War the southern part of France, including Armagnac, was ceded to England by the Treaty of Brétigny (1360). Edward, the Black Prince, administered the area for his father, King Edward III of England. He soon alienated the nobles by giving privileges to the towns and levying heavy taxes. Until this time Armagnac had remained practically independent by shifting alliances, but the rule of the Black Prince was so harsh that the count of Armagnac appealed to the French king for help in 1369. By submitting themselves to King Charles V of France, noble families like the Armagnacs were able to retain much of their former power and assure themselves of protection.

In 1410 the daughter of Count Bernard VII of Armagnac was married to Duke Charles I of Orléans. Charles' father had been killed by supporters of the duke of Burgundy, who resented Orléans' influence on the king. After the marriage, the Armagnac family became associated with the party of King Charles VI against Burgundy, and the royal faction came to be called *Armagnacs*. Until his death in 1418, Count Bernard remained a bitter enemy of Burgundy. When Burgundy allied itself with England during the later stages of the Hundred Years' War, the friction between the two parties greatly increased. The two factions engaged in a bloody civil war that ended in 1435.

After peace was established, many veterans originally recruited by Count Bernard VII formed mercenary bands that also became known as the Armagnacs. Although they were in the service of King Charles VII, the Armagnacs became notorious far their rapacious plundering in the north of France. In 1444 they were sent to Switzerland on an expedition known as the *Armagnac War*, which culminated in a battle between the Swiss and the Armagnac mercenaries on Aug. 26, 1444. Although the Swiss were badly defeated, their determined resistance persuaded the Armagnacs to withdraw from Switzerland. Soon after, the Armagnacs were incorporated into Charles VII's regular army.

After the death of Bernard VII in 1418, the counts of Armagnac gradually lost their powerful position in southern France. In the late 15th century Count Jean V opposed King Louis XI. He was driven from the Armagnac lands and was killed by the king's soldiers in 1473. After the last count died in 1497, Armagnac was united temporarily with the crown. However, King Francis I gave the district to a nephew of the last count, and it subsequently passed by marriage to the family of Henry of Navarre. Henry became king of France as Henry IV in 1589 and joined Armagnac to the royal domain in 1607.

ARMAMENT, är'mə-mənt, broadly designates the military and naval equipment and forces of a nation. In its more limited meaning it designates the weapons with which these forces are supplied, such as ammunition, guns, and torpedoes. See AIRCRAFT CARRIER; AMMUNITION; ARTILLERY; GUNS; MACHINE GUN; MILITARY SCIENCE; MINE; MINE SWEEPING AND MINE CLEARING; NUCLEAR WEAPONS; PROJECTILES; SMALL ARMS; SUBMARINE; TANK; TORPEDOES; WARSHIPS.

ARMAND, är-mäN', **Charles,** MARQUIS DE LA ROUERIE or ROUARIE (1756–1793), French soldier. His real name was *Armand Tufin* or *Teffin.* He was dismissed from the French Army for fighting a duel about an actress.

He went to America in 1777 and was given a colonel's commission in the American Army. During the Revolutionary War, when Casimir Pulaski was mortally wounded at the siege of Savannah in October 1789, Armand succeeded him in command of the Pulaski Legion, which was soon renamed Armand's Partisan Corps. He was made a brigadier general in 1783. Returning to France, he was active on the Royalist side in the French Revolution.

ARMATURE. See ELECTRICAL TERMS.

ARMAVIR, är-mə-vēr', a city in the USSR, is situated in Krasnodar territory of the Russian republic, 100 miles east of Krasnodar, on the Kuban River. Founded in 1848, it is a trading and processing center for the surrounding rich agricultural area. Its factories produce agricultural machinery, nails, and wire. Population: (1961) 120,000.

ARMED FORCES DAY is a day designated in the United States to honor the nation's military services. In 1949 the Department of Defense, as part of its unification of the services, eliminated Navy Day, Army Day, and Air Force Day and created a single period to honor all the armed forces. This is the week ending the third Saturday in May each year. Open house is held at most military and naval installations for public visiting, and the week culminates on Saturday, which is Armed Forces Day, with parades and appropriate ceremonies. To make it possible to give emphasis in turn to each major service, the Army, Navy, and Air Force rotate annually as host force in each of the main military areas of the United States. Governors of many states and mayors of principal cities have joined in honoring the services by proclaiming observance of Armed Forces Day in their areas.

The Navy League of the United States continues to celebrate Navy Day on October 27 of each year, and the Marines observe the Marine Corps Birthday on November 10.

ROBERT H. BARNUM
Rear Admiral, USNR-R

ARMED FORCES STAFF COLLEGE, a joint staff college, located at Norfolk, Va., and serving the armed forces of the United States. This college, founded in 1946, conducts "a course of study in joint and combined [inter-Allied] organization, planning, and operations, and in related aspects of national and international security, in order to prepare selected military officers for duty in all echelons of joint and combined commands."

About 500 selected Marine, Army, Navy, and Air Force Officers (together with 50 civilian students from the executive departments that play a role in national security) attend the college each year for a 5-month course. The college relies largely on lectures, frequently by distinguished guests. In addition, the all-military faculty conducts seminars, map exercises, and field trips, all designed to contribute toward the student's mastery of military staff and management functions.

AMOS A. JORDAN, JR., COLONEL, USA
United States Military Academy

ARMED NEUTRALITY, nōō-tral'ə-tē, in international law, is the collective action of neutral states in employing armed strength for the purpose of compelling belligerents to respect their rights. The armed neutralities of 1780 and 1800 were formed by the northern European states (Denmark, Sweden, Prussia, and Russia), though other states later adhered, mainly for the purpose of bringing pressure to bear to compel Britain to respect specified neutral rights during the wars in which it was engaged with France.

The Armed Neutrality of 1780 provided specifically that free ships make free goods, that a blockade must be effective to be binding, and that contraband lists must be confined to articles of definitely military use. The British accepted these principles in the treaty of peace with France of 1783 but departed from them in the French Revolutionary wars. The British refused to recognize the claims of the armed neutrals, and in the case of the *Maria* a British prize court held (1799) that neutral vessels convoyed by warships were subject to capture because of constructive resistance. As a result, in December 1800, Russia concluded treaties with Sweden, Denmark, and Prussia, and the second Armed Neutrality became a fact. Most of the armed neutrals subsequently entered the war against France. The principles claimed by the armed neutralities were accepted in considerable measure by the naval powers in the Declaration of Paris of 1856, following the Crimean War.

The Declaration of London of 1909 accepted the right of neutral convoy, but it was not ratified, and during World War I, Britain refused to acknowledge this right. The arming of merchant vessels against German submarines in 1917 by the United States while it was still neutral was a form of armed neutrality and soon led to war between the United States and Germany.

The concept of armed neutrality during World War I contributed to the idea of a league to enforce peace, which led to the formation of the League of Nations and eventually of the United Nations. But the concept was extended from enforcement of neutral rights to enforcement of peace through common action.

QUINCY WRIGHT, *University of Virginia*

ARMED SHIP, a naval vessel or armed merchant vessel. The former must, according to the Hague Convention of 1907 on the conversion of merchant ships to warships, be commanded by a commissioned naval officer; the crew must be subject to military discipline; and the vessel must bear the external marks of a warship and observe the laws of war.

The question of the right to convert merchant vessels to naval vessels in time of war, especially in foreign ports and on the high seas, has caused much controversy, but agreement has not been reached. Armed merchant vessels were formerly authorized by governments, through instruments known as letters of marque and reprisal, to engage in hostilities against enemy commerce. This practice, known as privateering, was abolished by the Declaration of Paris of 1856. During World War I, Great Britain as a belligerent, and later the United States as a neutral, armed merchant vessels for defense against German submarines. Germany claimed that this was illegal, but most jurists recognized a distinction between privateering and armament for defense against attack.

QUINCY WRIGHT, *University of Virginia*

ARMENIA, är-mē′nē-ə, the historical land of the Armenians, at its zenith stretched from the Black Sea to the Caspian Sea and from the Mediterranean to Lake Urmia in what is now Iran. In classical times the land was bounded on the north by Iberia (modern Georgia) and Albania (modern Azerbaidzhan) and on the south by the Mesopotamian desert. The Anatolian provinces of Pontus, Cappadocia, and Cilicia bordered it on the west, and Lake Urmia and ancient Persia bordered it on the east. Translated into contemporary terms and based on a combination of historical and ethnic factors, the land of the Armenians would include the regions around Akhaltsikhe and south of Tbilisi (Tiflis) in the Georgian republic of the USSR, the Karabakh and Nakhichevan areas of Azerbaidzhan, Soviet Armenia in its entirety, the corner of Iran northwest of Lake Urmia, and the territories of Turkey around the cities of Van (including Lake Van), Trabzon, Erzurum, Sivas, Bitlis, and Diyarbakır.

The political boundaries of the country have been extremely elastic, frequently and convulsively altered by war, conquest, dismemberment, and internal political fragmentation. For over 3,000 years Armenia has been battered by war and occupation. The people of Armenia have been despoiled, transplanted, and decimated, and the country has been subjected to a succession of intruding tribes and peoples, who have intermingled with the indigenous inhabitants, superimposing upon the population their languages, religions, and cultures, all of which have left their imprint in varying degrees. Consequently, historical and ethnic claims to the area have often conflicted, and various nations have been equally fervent in claiming many of the regions of historical Armenia.

Land and Natural Resources. The Armenian plateau is rugged and varied, with an average elevation exceeding 6,000 feet (1,800 meters). It is marked by clusters of jagged volcanic mountains and cleft by ravines and gorges whose soft lava has been deeply carved by swiftly flowing streams. Four great rivers, the Tigris, Euphrates, Kura, and Araks (Aras, Araxes), have their sources in the mountains of Armenia. Three large lakes, Van, Urmia, and Sevan, are framed in triangular symmetry in the eastern part.

Much of Turkish Armenia is covered by recent volcanic outpourings, and the soil cover is frequently very thin or nonexistent. Most of the barren lava uplands are uninhabited. The rivers often lie several thousand feet below the level of the plateau, and although their upper reaches are too narrow for settlement, rich alluvial deposits lower down have invited cultivation.

Armenia's most famous and hallowed landmark, Mount Ararat, lies in modern Turkey. It rises majestically to over 17,000 feet, (5,100 meters), and its perpetually snow-clad summit is visible from virtually every corner of Soviet Armenia. The fertile Ararat plain lies in Soviet Armenia. Always the most densely populated section of Armenia, the Ararat plain today supports more than half the population of Soviet Armenia. Copiously supplied with water by the Araks River, the Ararat plain rivals the Lake Van basin as the Armenian heartland.

Overlooking the Ararat plain and the Araks valley from the north in Soviet Armenia are Mount Aragats (Alagez), more than 13,000 feet (4,000 meters) high and the Ara Mountains, whose alpine slopes have supplied livestock with rich pasturage for centuries. To the south of Ararat are two arching mountain chains, the Aladagh and the Taurus. To the east of the Ararat plain in present-day Azerbaidzhan are the Karabakh Mountains.

The climate of Armenia is extremely varied. The summers are short, hot, and arid in the lowlands but mild and pleasant in the highlands. The winters are long, extremely cold, and severe, and precipitation is abundant.

Armenia is not generously endowed by nature, but in the artifically irrigated lowlands, semitropical crops like tobacco, cotton, and apricots are cultivated as well as fine grapes, peaches, pears, apples, grains, rice, and nuts. Cattle and horse breeding is important in the north. The mountains are relatively rich in minerals and are mined for their copper, tin, iron, gold, and silver and quarried for their granite, tufa, basalt, and marble. The region is also endowed with abundant mineral springs.

HISTORY

Armenia first appears in recorded history in Assyrian inscriptions of the 9th century B.C. as *Urartu,* a powerful kingdom forged out of a union or confederation of indigenous tribes, which the Assyrians repeatedly assaulted and defeated but failed to subdue. Sometimes called the *Vannic* kingdom, the Urartean state was founded in the middle of the 9th century B.C. by Arame, whose memory has been preserved in Armenian tradition as the legendary national hero, Aram. Between 810 and 733 B.C., Urartu reached the zenith of its power and influence, extending from Lake Sevan and the Kura River in the north to the Euphrates River in the west and Lake Urmia in the east. Thereafter the kingdom declined. The Assyrians moved up from the south and plundered the country. The Scythians and Cimmerians swarmed down from the north, the Medes and Persians from the east, and the Phrygians and Armenians from the west.

The Armenians were a branch of the Thraco-Phrygian tribes that had crossed into Anatolia

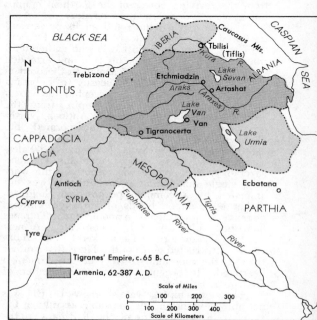

Tigranes' Empire, c. 65 B.C.

Armenia, 62-387 A.D.

Scale of Miles

Scale of Kilometers

from the Balkans. The name "Armenian" dates from the 6th century B.C. and seems to be the Persian designation for the Armeno-Phrygian conquerors of the area, who may have been called *Armens*. The Armenians established themselves as the new ruling aristocracy, imposed their Indo-European language upon the native population, and later intermingled with them to form the basic Armenian nation. This nation has tenaciously preserved its national and cultural identity for over 2,600 years, although repeatedly invaded, conquered, and ruled by others.

Armenia Under the Achaemenids and Seleucids. The Armeno-Phrygians acknowledged the suzerainty of the Medes and in this way were later incorporated into the Persian empire of the Achaemenids. The country emerged as Armenia for the first time in the famous Behistun inscription of Darius the Great, dating from 521 B.C., as a rebellious province (satrapy) of the Persian empire. When the Persian empire was conquered by Alexander the Great in 331 B.C., the Persian satrap of Armenia declared his loyalty to Alexander. However, much of Armenia in the north successfully resisted inclusion in Alexander's empire, retaining its independence under local kings and chieftains.

With the death of Alexander in 323 B.C., the former satraps of the Achaemenids in the Armenian territories acknowledged the nominal suzerainty of the Seleucids, Alexander's successors in the east, and Armenia was increasingly subjected to the beneficent influences of Hellenistic culture and civilization. In 189 B.C., after the Seleucid Antiochus the Great was defeated by the Romans at Magnesia, two Armenian princes, Artashes (Artaxias) and Zareh (Zariades), severed their loose bonds to the Seleucid empire and established two independent Armenian kingdoms: Armenia Major with Artashes as king and Armenia Minor (Sophene) under Zareh.

Artashes Dynasty. Artashes built a new capital, Artashat (Artaxata), and established a dynasty that not only preserved Armenia's independence from the Hellenistic kingdoms in Asia Minor and from the reviving power of the Parthian empire but also expanded Armenia's territory.

Armenia reached the zenith of its power and territorial expansion under Tigranes (Dikran) the Great (reigned 95–55 B.C.), who gathered all the Armenian lands under his rule and extended Greater Armenia from the Caspian to the borders of Egypt and from the Caucasus to Ecbatana (Hamadan). In 83 B.C. he accepted the crown of the diminished Seleucid empire from the strife-ridden ruling aristocracy of Antioch. Northern Syria and Cilicia were incorporated into Tigranes' domains as a satrapy, with Antioch as capital, and southern Syria, Lebanon, and Palestine remained vassal states recognizing Tigranes' suzerainty. His empire was essentially the work of a single dominating personality. It was not animated by a common purpose nor held together by common bonds of language, culture, or religion. Nevertheless, Armenia under Tigranes flourished culturally and economically. A new capital, Tigranocerta (Tigranakert), was audaciously constructed north of the Tigris River rather than in the mountain fortress of the Armenian heartland. It became an important center of Hellenistic culture.

Tigranes' empire was short-lived. He was not able to withstand the repeated assaults of the Romans in the west or of the Parthians in the east, and the empire finally became a client state of Rome. As a buffer battleground between Rome and the Parthian empire (and its successor, Sassanid Persia), Armenia was subjected to a prolonged period of invasion and was finally partitioned between the two empires.

The illustrious Artashes dynasty came to an ignominious end with Tigranes IV, who was deposed by Augustus around 1 A.D. For the next three centuries the Armenian throne was occupied by a succession of dynasties, most of them of Parthian origin. The most important of these dynasties, the Arshakuni (Arsacid), was quickly Armenianized and survived in Armenia. In Parthia it was deposed by the Sassanids.

Byzantine and Sassanid Rule. Roman influence prevailed in Armenia after the treaty of Nisibis with Persia (298 A.D.), and Tiridates (Trdat) III, an Arshakuni, was restored to the Armenian throne under Roman protection. Three years later, Tiridates was converted to Christianity by St. Gregory the Illuminator, and Armenia entered a new stage in its history as the world's first Christian state. This conversion inevitably plunged Armenia into renewed conflict with the fanatically Zoroastrian Sassanids of Persia. Armenia was partitioned between Byzantium (which had succeeded Rome in the east) and Persia, about four fifths of Armenia passing under Persian control in 387 A.D.

Both Byzantium and Persia governed their respective areas through native Armenian princes, called *nakharars*, who retained control over the population regardless of who exercised nominal suzerainty. Although the Persians frequently took punitive action against individual Armenian princes, they did not attempt to destroy the feudal system, whereas the Byzantines attempted to curb the power of the *nakharars* by abolishing hereditary claims to local office and instituting a system of appointment by the emperor.

In spite of the division and weakness of the country, Christianity provided a common bond that gave rise to a powerful sense of national distinctiveness, consciousness, and cohesion, which was almost immediately reinforced by the invention of the Armenian alphabet by St. Mesrop early in the 5th century. The refusal of the Armenian Church to accept the decisions of the Council of Chalcedon in 451 irrevocably transformed the Armenian Church into an ethnocentric rather than an ecumenical force. In the same year Vartan II Mamikonian rallied the Armenian nobility and peasantry around the twin standards of nationalism and Christianity in a revolt against the Sassanids. After a series of minor victories, the small Armenian force was decisively crushed and Vartan Mamikonian and the flower of the Armenian aristocracy perished on the battlefield.

The adoption of Christianity alienated and isolated Armenian from Zoroastrian Persia; the choice of a heretical path simultaneously alienated and isolated Armenia from Rome and Byzantium; the invention of a national alphabet severed Armenia's fragile cultural bonds with the West; and the martyrdom of Vartan Mamikonian provided Armenia with a national hero, further reinforcing the Armenian sense of isolation, self-reliance, and ethnocentrism. All of these factors contributed to the development of a strong sense of national consciousness, centuries before its advent on the western European scene.

Bagratid Dynasty. With the collapse of the Sassanid empire under the blows of the Arabs in the 7th century, the Armenian provinces of Persia passed under the nominal control of the Arab caliphate. By the terms of a treaty of 653, the Armenian *nakharars* accepted Arab suzerainty in return for the preservation of their local power and privileges. Armenia was plunged into constant turmoil not only by the attempts of the Byzantines to expand their power in Armenia at the expense of the caliphate but also by fierce internal rivalries among powerful princely families. Early in the 8th century the Bagratuni princes gained the ascendancy. In 885 the kingdom of Armenia was reestablished under Ashot V, a Bagratuni.

The Bagratid dynasty, however, was unable to consolidate and maintain its control over all the Armenian provinces. It was constantly challenged by other princes, who by the middle of the 10th century had succeeded in establishing five other autonomous Armenian kingdoms as well as several smaller principalities. The Bagratuni kings established themselves at Ani. Under King Gagik Bagratuni I (reigned 989–1020), the Bagratid kingdom ushered in a golden age in Armenia, in which culture, learning, trade, and commerce prospered; but Armenia's independence once again came to an end as Byzantium gradually annexed the Armenian kingdoms and principalities. In 1071, Byzantium itself was defeated at Manzikert by the Seljuk Turks, and the victors swarmed over eastern Anatolia and incorporated Armenia into their dominions.

Lesser Armenia. Seljuk domination of Armenia encouraged Armenian emigration into the Byzantine empire, particularly to Cilicia. Armenia itself was virtually denuded of its aristocracy, and its peasant population was abandoned to the mercies of its new overlords. Some of the Armenian nobility carved out small baronies and principalities on Byzantine territory. The most important of these, the principality of Cilicia (called Lesser Armenia), declared its independence under the Armenian Prince Rupen in 1080. Under Prince Levon II (reigned 1187–1219), this principality was transformed into a kingdom, which managed to survive for nearly 200 years.

Meanwhile, the Mongols had displaced the Seljuks in Armenia proper, and the country was subjected to unparalleled devastation and slaughter. Lesser Armenia hung on tenaciously until 1375, when it was incorporated into the Mamluk empire. It was the last independent Armenian state until the 20th century.

Ottoman Rule. After the death of the Mongol leader Tamerlane in 1405, Armenia was divided between the Ottoman empire and Persia. Persian Armenia, which was the smaller portion, developed close economic ties with neighboring Christian Georgia and in 1828 was incorporated into the Russian empire, which also absorbed Kars and Ardahan from Turkey in 1878.

After the fall of Constantinople to the Turks in 1453, the sultan established a new Armenian patriarchate of Constantinople in 1461 and invested it with supreme ecclesiastical and civil jurisdiction not only over all Armenians within the Ottoman empire but also over all other Eastern Christians except the Greek Orthodox. The various non-Muslim religious communities under Ottoman rule were allowed considerable internal religious and cultural autonomy as long as they refrained from political agitation. This was formally institutionalized in the millet system. As the head of the Armenian millet, the patriarch of Constantinople was in effect transformed into a combined ecclesiastical-political leader of the Armenian nation. Constantinpole inevitably became the real center of visible Armenian ecclesiastical and national life. By 1800 the Armenian community of Constantinople numbered about 150,000.

During the early centuries of Ottoman rule, the Armenian community was shown preferential treatment by the sultans. Out of the shattered ruins of the Armenian nation arose a new merchant bourgeoisie, whose loyalty to the Armenian Church and fidelity to Armenian traditions were unimpeachable, but whose dependence upon the good will of the Ottoman authorities for their economic prosperity and social status rendered them politically pliable, often servile and devious in demeanor, and willing instruments of the existing status quo. Inhabiting the main urban centers of the Ottoman empire, the wealthy, complacent Armenian bourgeoisie were geographically isolated and dispersed and politically and socially alienated from their peasant compatriots, who continued to languish in misery and oppression in the Armenian districts of eastern Anatolia and Cilicia. The Armenian merchants and bankers eschewed nationalistic politics. They eventually established oligarchical control of the partriarchate, and reduced it to an instrument of their vested interests rather than of the interests of the Armenian community as a whole.

The situation was mitigated by the growth of an Armenian petty bourgeoisie and intelligentsia, who were in turn encouraged and supported by the Ottoman government itself. The power of the oligarchs was finally broken with the promulgation of the Armenian National Constitution in 1863 as an imperial edict, providing for a more representative form of self-government. The leadership of the Armenian nation was seized by the Armenian revolutionary intelligentsia allied with the church. Inspired by the success of the Balkan peoples in their bid for independence, church and intelligentsia joined to produce a heady elixir of nationalism. The intelligentsia mobilized the support of the petty bourgeoisie and peasantry in their demands for an independent or autonomous Armenia.

Massacre and Dispersion of the Armenians. The growth of Armenian nationalism aroused the suspicion and wrath of Sultan Abdul-Hamid II (reigned 1876–1909). In 1876–1877 the Armenian quarter of Constantinople was burned and looted by Turkish soldiers and police. Then, in a frightful series of barbaric massacres beginning in 1894, nearly 200,000 Armenians were slain within two years. These wanton butcheries were both a cause of and a response to the series of sporadic acts of terrorism visited upon Turkish officials by Armenian terrorist groups, led largely by dedicated but inexperienced intellectuals, who thought that in this way they could simultaneously terrorize the sultan into granting reforms and arouse the European powers to intervene on behalf of Armenian independence.

The Young Turk revolution of 1908 raised false hopes of a Turkish-Armenian reconciliation, but the national interests of the two nations were by now incompatible and irreconcilable. The massacre of Armenians was resumed with renewed fury in 1909, this time in Cilicia, and was arrested only after the intervention of the great powers, including the United States. The outbreak of World War I sealed the fate of the

ARMENIAN CHURCHES of the 9th century, with typical conical domes, stand by the shore of Lake Sevan.

Turkish Armenians, whose unabashed sympathy for the Allied cause and enthusiastic embrace of the invading Russian armies impelled the Young Turk regime to attempt to settle the troublesome Armenian problem by physically annihilating the Armenians in Turkey. More than one million Armenians perished by deportation to the Syrian desert; thousands converted to Islam; another million survived the deportations or were evacuated by the retreating Russian armies on the Caucasian front.

The Allied promise to reestablish an independent Armenian state in its historic provinces was never carried out. Definitive frontiers for an independent Armenia, with access to the Black Sea at Trebizond, were drawn by President Woodrow Wilson in November 1920; but the area had already been overwhelmed in October by the resurgent Turks, who succeeded in detaching Kars and Ardahan from Russian Armenia as well. On Dec. 20, 1920, an Armenian Soviet republic was proclaimed in Yerevan by the Armenian Communist party, under the protection and control of Bolshevik Russia. See ARMENIAN SOVIET SOCIALIST REPUBLIC.

PEOPLE AND CULTURE

The People. Each invasion or conquest of Armenia and each migration into the land has left not only a genetic and biological imprint but also a linguistic, cultural, and religious stamp on the people of the region. But the Urartean origins of the Armenian people are still reflected in legend, myth, national traditions, place names, race, and language. Many legendary heroes (such as Haik, Aram, and Ara) and national myths of Armenia are pre-Indo-European in origin and are probably misty survivals of the Urartean or even pre-Urartean period.

Physically the Armenians reflect the genetic infusion and fusion of the various strains of the white, or Caucasian, race that have swept back and forth across the country. The Armenoid physical type, which is the most prevalent, represents a stabilized racial blend between Mediterranean and Alpine types, probably dating from Neolithic times. The Armenians appear to be the most authentic representatives of this physical type.

The Armenoid physical type is characterized by a round, high-vaulted skull and a prominent, high-bridged, convex nose. The hair is usually brown or black; the eyes are large, and hazel, brown, or black in color, often framed by bushy eyebrows; the skin color ranges from pinkish white to swarthy, with intermediate hues more in evidence; the height is moderate; and the body is stocky and sometimes generously endowed with hair. About 50 percent of the Armenians belong to the Armenoid type, while the Alpine and Mediterranean physical types account for about 20 percent each, and Nordic features are dominant in the remaining 10 percent.

Armenian colonies are found in virtually every corner of the globe. Each migration, invasion, or conquest has invariably resulted in the exodus of some Armenians. At the present time, of the approximately 3,700,000 Armenians in the world, about 3,000,000 live in the USSR. Of the approximately 700,000 Armenians living elsewhere, many in Europe and North America can no longer be described as a part of the Armenian nation-in-exile. However, the Armenian communities in the Middle East, with a total population of around 400,000, still largely regard themselves as part of the Armenian nation. Since World War II, over 100,000 Armenians have been repatriated to Soviet Armenia, mainly from the Middle East.

Language. The Armenian language is the only surviving member of the Thracian branch of the Indo-European group of languages. Thought to be an offshoot of Phrygian, Armenian has been a spoken idiom since before the 6th century B.C. but has been a written language only since the 5th century A.D. According to some philologists, the Armenian language represents the superimposition of an Indo-European language upon an ancient indigenous Caucasian language, probably that spoken by the Urarteans.

Words of Iranian origin, both Parthian and Persian, are numerous in the Armenian vocabulary and date from the earliest times. The vocabulary contains so many loanwords from Iranian dialects that at one time the language was mistakenly classified as an Iranian language. Words of Greek and Syriac origin are largely scientific and ecclesiastical. Turkish terms appear mainly in the vernacular language.

Written Armenian can be divided into classical Armenian (*Grabar*), which dates from the 5th century and is still employed as the scholarly and liturgical language, and modern Armenian (*Ashkharabar*), which dates from the middle of the 15th century and is the language of modern Armenian literature and newspapers. There are two main spoken dialects, Western Armenian and Eastern Armenian, the latter being closer to the classical language.

Both classical and modern Armenian are written in the same alphabet, which originally had 36 letters but now has 38. According to tradition, the alphabet was the creation of St. Mesrop, assisted by St. Sahak and a Greek named Rufanos, around 400 A.D. The Armenian alphabet appears to have been heavily influenced by the Greek alphabet, especially the vowels, the direction of the writing, and the upright and regular position of the characters. The Armenian alphabet is remarkably well suited to the phonetic values of the language, and it has undergone virtually no alteration in form or structure since its creation.

Religion. Before the adoption of Christianity as Armenia's state religion around 300 A.D., the religions of Armenia reflected the dominant polytheistic forms of pagan religious life prevalent in the Mediterranean and the Near East. Many of the local gods worshiped by the Urarteans later survived under new names, to be identified with or joined by a motley procession of Armenian, Greek, Persian, and Mesopotamian pagan deities.

About 150 years after it was Christianized, Armenia rejected the decisions of the Council of Chalcedon in 451 A.D. In doing so the Armenian Church irrevocably embarked upon the hazardous and lonely path of an independent, idiosyncratic national church to which only Armenians belong. To this day the small Armenian Church preserves its pristine national exclusiveness, recognizes the supremacy of no other spiritual jurisdiction, and considers itself the equal of Rome and Constantinople. See also ARMENIAN CHURCH.

Although the great majority of religious Armenians belong to the Armenian Apostolic Church, many Armenians are also affiliated with Rome or belong to various Protestant congregations. The Armenian Catholic Church, which acknowledges the supremacy of the pope in Rome, dates from 1740, but parts of the Armenian community have been affiliated with the papacy since the Crusades. The Armenian Catholic Mekhitarist orders, located in Venice and Vienna, have played an important role in preserving Armenian culture and learning.

Architecture. In the arts, the Armenians have exhibited their greatest originality in architecture, most notably in the fields of military and religious architecture. The Urarteans' architectural genius is clearly evidenced in the ruins of their fortresses, the excavated foundations of their palaces and temples, and their meticulously executed architectural models fashioned from metal. Just as the architecture of Urartu left its impact on Assyria, the architecture of Armenia and Armenian architects in Italy, in the Byzantine empire, and in the Balkans have had an impressive influence on Western church architecture.

Armenian church structures are usually modest in dimension, simple and compact, almost primitive in appearance, but strikingly original in design, if somewhat exotic in their external ornamental reliefs, decorative sculpture, and repeated blind arches. Even Armenian cathedrals are comparatively small in size. The churches are invariably constructed of native stone carefully cut and skillfully fitted together by local artisans. Isolated from the mainstream of Byzantine and Western cultural and art forms, Armenian architects were left largely to their own devices in designing and constructing their churches. According to some architectural historians, Armenian architects were responsible for the invention of the vaulted stone dome, which is usually mounted on a central floor plan, a triapsidal plan, a cruciform, or a quatrefoil.

The oldest surviving church in Armenia is the cathedral of Etchmiadzin, allegedly constructed by King Tiridates and St. Gregory the Illuminator in the early 300's. Its original wooden dome was later done over in stone, and the entire church has since been restored and enlarged in size. The most original period in Armenian church architecture and the most productive was the 7th century, when the definitive contours of Armenian church art were established and the Armenian dome assumed its characteristic inverted conical shape. The more notable churches of this period include St. Hripsimé (618) and St. Gayané (630), both located in Vagarshapat in

SOVFOTO

MEGRI, a town in Soviet Armenia near Iran, grows fruit on irrigated soil in a valley of the Zangezur range.

Soviet Armenia; the old church of Ani (622); the cathedral of Bagaran (631); the cathedral of Mran (635–640); the Church of Our Lady of Masters (650); the Church of St. Stepanos at Maghart; the Lady of Talin Church (690); and the cathedral of Zwartnots (641–666), an extraordinary triple-tiered structure, whose sculptured capitals with their motifs of eagles, grapes, leaves, and pomegranates lie in ruins in the middle of an arid wasteland.

Church construction was sporadic during the 8th and 9th centuries, but beginning in the 10th century Armenia experienced a cultural renaissance that produced a sudden flowering of churches and cathedrals in the various petty principalities and kingdoms of the time. In the Bagratid and Ardzruni kingdoms, in particular, a number of striking churches and cathedrals were erected, including the metropolitan church of Ani and the famous church on the island of Aghtamar, still visible from the shores of Lake Van. Simply but elegantly decorated with external sculptered reliefs and intricately carved scrollwork framing its arches, Aghtamar represents the crowning achievement of the period. Churches continued to be erected in abundance until the first half of the 13th century. However, all culture and art were arrested in Armenia with the coming of the Mongols and Tatars in the 14th century.

Painting. Armenian painting, both monumental and miniature, dates from at least the 6th century A.D. While the earliest dated illuminated manuscript is the Lazareff Gospel (887), at least four miniatures dating from the 6th century are preserved in the manuscript depository (Matenadaran) at Yerevan. Armenian pictorial art finds its most vivid expression in the illuminated manuscripts and miniatures of the Middle Ages. Monumental painting, most of which has been destroyed, was restricted mainly to church interiors and was probably not very extensively employed. But a series of photographs of the wall paintings of Aghtamar reveals a previously hidden originality in Armenian church murals.

Armenian illuminations and miniatures, many examples of which have survived intact, are without peer in Byzantine art, and their quality equals that of the finest miniatures of Western medieval art at comparable periods of development. The

Gospel of Etchmiadzin (989) has a primitive but luminous simplicity. More elaborate are the gospels and lectionaries of the Cilician miniaturists, Thoros Roslin and Sarkis Pidzak.

Although Armenian miniature art clearly shows its aesthetic debt to Byzantine and Syriac art, it was influenced only peripherally by Persian and Islamic art forms. Sassanid influences, however, are clearly discernible in the complicated geometric ornamentation and floral motifs sometimes employed by the Armenian masters for marginal decoration or to frame their depiction of Biblical figures and scenes.

Music. Armenian music, both secular and religious, is mainly of local significance. The ecclesiastical music is influenced largely by Greek sacred hymns and chants, and the secular is stamped with the Arabic imprint. Modern Armenian music has been equally lacking in distinction and originality, with the spectacular exception of the work of the Soviet Armenian composer Aram Khachaturian. Other modern Armenian composers of note are Aleksandr A. Spendiarov and the Armeno-Georgian Vano Muradeli, in the USSR, and the Armenian-American Alan Hovhaness.

Literature. Literature in the Armenian language dates from the 5th century A.D., but an oral tradition existed before the invention of the alphabet. There is much evidence to suggest the existence of Armenian writers, historians, and poets at the Armenian court who wrote in Greek.

The earliest Armenian historian to write in Armenian was Moses of Khoren (Movses Khorenatsi), known as the "Armenian Herodotus," whose 5th century history of Armenia is the prime source of information concerning the epics, legends, and folklore of ancient Armenia and the indispensable source of data on early Armenian history. Other notable historians of ancient and medieval Armenia are Ghazar Parbetsi (about 500 A.D.); Thomas Ardzruni (10th century); Matthew of Edessa, the passionate and partisan chronicler of Armenia during the Crusades; and Stephanos Orbelian (1258–1305), who recorded the depredations of the Mongols and Tatars.

Alongside Armenian history, there is the epic tradition, in which Western and Eastern forms have been intricately fused. Rich, passionate, and nationalistic, but at the same time marked by restraint and lucidity, Armenian epic poetry is unencumbered with the sensuality and abstruseness that characterize much of Eastern epic art. It was strongly influenced by Muslim popular poetry, particularly in form, although the content is conspicuously individualistic, Christian, and national. Love songs, lullabies, satirical couplets, prayers, hymns, rhymed stories, heroic ballads glorifying Armenia's folk and national heroes, and lamentations depicting Armenia's grief and misery are some of the rich and varied forms of the Armenian oral tradition. The most famous Armenian epic is *David of Sassoun*, which tells of the great hero who domesticated lions and tigers, slew tyrants, and delivered his people from oppression.

Armenian popular poetry was of two types, both sung by wandering troubadours. The first consisted of poems composed spontaneously and sung by professional minstrels, who often improvised on their own artistic creations. The second type consisted of more formal compositions, conveying considerable feeling and passion.

Modern Armenian literature is essentially the literature of Armenians abroad, since the cultural centers of Armenia itself had largely vanished after the 14th century. In Russia and Tbilisi, Russian and German influences were dominant in the development of Armenian writing, while Armenian authors in Constantinople, Smyrna, Venice, and Vienna were influenced by French, Italian, and Greek forms and styles.

The first Armenian novelist was Khachatur Abovian (1805–1848), whose novel *The Wounds of Armenia* clearly shows his Russo-German training at the University of Dorpat. Perhaps the most popular and outstanding writer was the nationalistic author Hagop Melik-Agopian (1835–1888), known as "Raffi," whose patriotically charged novels include *David Beg, Samuel,* and *Sparks*. These works enjoyed wide acclaim and served to infuse the revolutionary mood of the late 19th century with the romanticized heroism of Armenia's vanquished feudal aristocracy. While Abovian has always been persona grata with the Soviet regime, "Raffi," because of his blatant "bourgeois" nationalistic symbolism, was frowned upon until after the death of Stalin.

VERNON V. ASPATURIAN
Pennsylvania State University

Bibliography

Atamian, Sarkis, *The Armenian Community* (New York 1955).
Boyajian, Zabelle C., ed., *Armenian Legends and Poems* (New York 1959).
Der Nersessian, Sirarpie, *Aght'amar: Church of the Holy Cross* (Cambridge, Mass., 1965).
Der Nersessian, Sirarpie, *Armenia and the Byzantine Empire* (Cambridge, Mass., 1945).
Durnovo, Lydia A., *Armenian Miniatures* (New York 1961).
Kurkjian, Vahan M., *History of Armenia* (New York 1958).
Lloyd, Seton, *Early Anatolia* (Harmondsworth, Eng., 1956).
Lyashchenko, Peter I., *History of the National Economy of Russia to the 1917 Revolution* (New York 1949).
Morgan, Jacques de, *Histoire du peuple arménien* (Paris 1919); Eng. tr., *The History of the Armenian People* (Boston, no date).
Nalbandian, Louise Z., *Armenian Revolutionary Federation: The Development of Armenian Political Parties Through the Nineteenth Century* (Berkeley, Calif., 1963).
Oldenbourg, Zoé, *The Crusades* (New York 1966).
Rice, David T., ed., *The Dawn of European Civilization* (New York 1965).
Sanjian, Avedis K., *The Armenian Communities in Syria Under Ottoman Dominion* (Cambridge, Mass., 1965).
Vasiliev, Alexander A., *A History of the Byzantine Empire*, rev. ed. (Madison, Wis., 1964).

ARMENIAN CHURCH, är-mē′nē-ən, one of the larger Monophysite churches in the East and the first national Christian church. Its history during the first three centuries A.D. is somewhat obscure, but certain historic facts and traditional beliefs support its claim to be one of the oldest churches in Christendom. According to national tradition, the Gospel was preached in Armenia by the Apostles Thaddeus and Bartholomew during the 1st century. In the Armenian martyrologies we find the names of numerous Christian bishops of the 2d and 3d centuries, and the names of some of these martyrs are also included in the *Ecclesiastical History* of Eusebius of Caesarea. By such evidence, Armenians justify the apostolic origin of their national church.

The establishment of Christianity as the state religion in Armenia was consummated some time between 286 and 314 through the labors of St. Gregory, a missionary from Caesarea Mazaca (now Kayseri, Turkey) in Cappadocia. King Tiridates III became a convert to Christianity and, about 300, proclaimed it the religion of the country. St. Gregory, with the title of the Illuminator, became the first head of the church. From the beginning the church, as a national institution, aspired to autocephalic (independent) status, even though for more than a century its head as well as its bishops were consecrated by the bishop of Caesarea. In the 5th century complete autocephalic status was attained, when the Armenian Church openly rejected the orthodox decrees of the Council of Chalcedon (451) and adhered to the Monophysite doctrine, which holds that the divine and the human in Jesus Christ are one nature. (See CHALCEDON, COUNCIL OF) Thus was created the cleavage between the Greek Orthodox Church and the Armenian Apostolic (or Gregorian) Church.

In the ritual of the Armenian Church the liturgy occupies a most prominent place, and the beginnings of liturgical music with notations characteristically Armenian date back to the 11th century. The entire church service, except the sermon, is conducted in classical Armenian. The sermon, usually brief and considered less important, is in the modern vernacular.

The four distinct ranks in the higher hierarchy of the church are the supreme head of the church (catholicos), patriarchs, archbishops, and bishops. In addition, there are three ranks in the lower hierarchy: vardapets (doctors), priests, and deacons. Priests are allowed to marry, and deacons who do not intend to go beyond the priesthood also may marry, but all others must take a vow of celibacy.

As a national institution, the church has always played a most important role in Armenian history, and at times has assumed the task of political as well as spiritual leadership. In this dual role its authority has been supreme for centuries, and even in the mid-20th century it is of prime importance. In 428/429, when by the fall of the ruling dynasty the Armenian kingdom ceased to exist, the head of the church became and remained thereafter the symbol of national unity and the rallying point of patriotism. Through the centuries Armenians at home and abroad have regarded the catholicos of Etchmiadzin not only as the head of their church, but also as their spokesman and elected representative.

The catholicos is elected by the votes of electors representing all the faithful of the church. His seat is in the monastery of Etchmiadzin, near Yerevan (Erivan) in the Armenian SSR of the Soviet Union, which was built in 301. His see includes all Armenian communities everywhere except the small see reserved for the catholicos of Sis, named for the city of Sis (now Kozan, Turkey), in Cilicia. The present seat of the see of Sis is Antilyas, Lebanon. It includes Lebanon, Syria, and Cyprus. The supreme catholicos of Etchmiadzin exercises authority and leadership through the two patriarchs (in Istanbul and Jerusalem) and through numerous prelates in the several Armenian dioceses, who are elected locally and confirmed by him in their respective offices. Vazken I was elected supreme catholicos in 1955. Archbishop Khoren Paroyan was elected catholicos of the see of Sis in 1963 and enthroned as Khoren I.

There are one or more Armenian dioceses in nearly every country having Armenian communities. Before World War I there were some 30 dioceses in Turkey alone, but with the extermination and expulsion of the Armenian population

DIOCESE OF THE ARMENIAN CHURCH OF NORTH AMERICA

HOLY OIL for Armenian sacramental use is blessed by the catholicos (patriarch) of the church at Yerevan.

only one diocese remains, under the authority of the patriarchate in Istanbul.

In the United States the first Armenian Church was established at Worcester, Mass., in 1891, and the first diocese was created in 1902. Later, a second diocese was created in California. Of the estimated 250,000 Armenians in the United States, the majority are considered adherents of the Armenian Apostolic Church.

A.O. SARKISSIAN, *Library of Congress*

Bibliography
Arpee, Leon, *A History of Armenian Christianity from the Beginning to Our Own Time* (New York 1946).
Der Nersessian, Sirarpie, *Armenia and the Byzantine Empire* (Cambridge, Mass., 1945).
Nersoyan, Hagop, *A History of the Armenian Church* (New York 1963).
Ormanian, Malachia, *The Church of Armenia*, tr. from the French by G. Marcar Gregory, 2d rev. ed. (London 1955).
Sarkissian, Karekin, *The Council of Chalcedon and the Armenian Church* (London 1965).

ARMENIAN SOVIET SOCIALIST REPUBLIC, är-mē'nē-ən, the smallest of the 15 constituent republics of the USSR, with an area of 11,640 square miles (30,150 sq km). Located in the southern Caucasus, this completely landlocked republic is bordered by the Georgian SSR on the northwest, the Azerbaidzhan SSR on the east, Turkey on the west, and Iran and the Nakhichevan region of Azerbaidzhan on the south. The capital of the republic is Yerevan.

Land. Situated some 6,000–8,000 feet (1,830–2,440 meters) above sea level, Soviet Armenia is a rugged plateau located south of the Caucasus Mountains. The plateau is chopped up by short ridges, deep gorges and ravines, and narrow, pleasant valleys. Many small but turbulent rivers and streams carve its surface. The republic, a land of extinct volcanoes, reaches its highest point at Mount Aragats (Mount Alagez; 13,435 feet, or 4,095 meters), which is perpetually snow-capped. The terrain is rough, barren, and dry, with little forest land but excellent pasturage.

The principal lake of the republic is Sevan (541 sq mi, or 1,400 sq km), situated at an altitude of 6,300 feet (1,920 meters) and surrounded by extinct volcanoes. This lake is the main reservoir of the republic's irrigation water and the principal source of its electrical energy. The main rivers of Armenia are the Araks (Aras), which empties into the Caspian Sea, and its erratic and treacherous tributary, the Razdan (Zanga), which plunges precipitously from Lake Sevan in a series of steep, magnificent cascades some 3,200 feet (975 meters) to its confluence with the Araks on the Ararat plain. The taming of the wild Razdan and other rivers has provided the republic with more than half of its cultivated acreage and virtually all of its electrical power. The Ararat plain has been industrialized, and most rural regions have been electrified.

The climate is unusually varied and runs to extremes: chilly in the mountains, mild and cool in the highlands, and oppressively hot in the semiarid lowlands. The air is thin and dry, the winters severe, the springs brief, the summers hot, and the autumns cool and refreshing.

Centuries of war, conquest, and devastation have denuded Armenia of its rich natural forests, and virtually all the trees in the republic are the products of an extensive afforestation program. Trees now adorn all the cities, and the mountain slopes have been planted with oak, white beech, maple, chestnut, and ash, which provide the raw material for a burgeoning furniture industry. Natural vegetation continues to be sparse. However, the gray volcanic soil of the Ararat plain will yield two harvests if supplied with copious quantities of water.

Economy. Grain and cotton are grown on the Ararat plain, while fruit trees prosper in the higher brown earth regions, and the meadows provide the pasture for most of the republic's cattle and horses. The republic is irrigated by an elaborate system of canals, with new areas constantly being brought under cultivation. Other principal crops are tobacco, sugar beets, potatoes, geraniums, peaches, apricots, various vegetables, pomegranates, melons, and grapes, from which Armenia's famous cognacs are distilled.

The republic has little coal or iron ore. Its chief metal deposits are copper, mined from the rich lodes near Alaverdi, and smaller quantities

of zinc, lead, aluminum, molybdenum, and chromite. A rich variety of stone and marble supports a flourishing industry. Limestone, granite, gypsum, pumice, flagstone, slate, tuff, luxury marbles, and semiprecious stones are quarried and shipped to all parts of the USSR.

The republic manufactures cotton fabric, wool, and silks. The city of Yerevan produces electrical machines and instruments, watches, turbine generators, copper cables, lathes, synthetic rubber, tires, automobile and tractor parts, canned foods, cognac, and a wide variety of chemical products. Yerevan is also an important center of the Soviet plastics industry. Leninakan is a major rail junction and textile and food-canning center. Kirovakan is an important center for chemical production and leather goods.

The republic has less than 310 miles (500 km) of railroad; its main line connects Yerevan and Leninakan with Tbilisi and points north. The other main mode of access and exit is air travel.

There are nearly 200 important mineral springs in Soviet Armenia; the most significant are Arzni and Dzhermuk. Health resorts, spas, and sanatoria have been built near many of the springs. The waters of Arzni and Dzhermuk are bottled and shipped to all parts of Russia.

People. The Armenian SSR is one of the most densely populated and ethnically homogeneous republics in the Soviet Union. The population was officially estimated in 1965 at 2,164,000, up from 1,763,000 reported in the 1959 census. The population is 88 percent Armenian, 6.1 percent Azerbaidzhanian, 3.2 percent Russian, and 1.5 percent Kurdish. Of the approximately 3,400,000 Armenians estimated to inhabit the USSR in 1964 (up from 2,787,000 in 1959), nearly one half are found outside the republic, with about 1 million in the adjacent republics of Georgia and Azerbaidzhan (500,000 each) and about 300,000 in the Russian republic. Although the Armenians and the Armenian republic registered one of the highest population gains in the Soviet Union, the Armenians also exhibited one of the highest rates of denationalization, with 8.3 percent of all Armenians reporting Russian as their mother language in the 1959 census. Most of this group probably lived outside the republic.

When the republic was first established in 1920, only 10 percent of its population was urbanized; by 1940, urbanization had nearly tripled, and in 1965, 55 percent of the republic's population lived in urban areas, making Soviet Armenia one of the most urbanized republics in the USSR. The largest city is the capital, Yerevan, with a population that increased from 509,000 in 1959 to 623,000 in 1965. Little more than a mud village in 1920, Yerevan today is a modern city with wide, tree-lined boulevards featuring imaginatively designed buildings constructed and faced with native stone and marble in a neoclassical style reminiscent of Armenia's medieval church architecture. Located on the Ararat plain, near the site of the ancient, recently excavated Urartean fortress Erebuni (from which the name Yerevan may be derived), the city is the political, industrial, and cultural hub of the republic. The next largest cities are Leninakan and Kirovakan.

See also ARMENIA.

VERNON V. ASPATURIAN
Pennsylvania State University

Further Reading: Shaginyan, Marietta, *Journey Through Soviet Armenia* (Moscow 1954).

ARMENTIÈRES, är-mäN-tyâr', a town in France, is located in the department of Nord, on the Lys River, 9 miles (14 km) northwest of Lille. A trading and industrial center, it produces table linen, cotton goods, velvet, hosiery, lace, hemp, and beer.

During most of World War I, Armentières was only two miles behind the British lines. The Germans captured the town in 1918 during the Battle of the Lys. The town's name became famous during the war through the marching song about the legendary "Mademoiselle from Armentières." Rebuilt as a modern town after World War I, Armentières was occupied by German forces for over four years during World War II. Population: (1962) 23,168.

ARMIDALE, är'mə-dāl, is a town in Australia, in New South Wales, 240 miles (386 km) north of Sydney. It is on the New England Plateau, at an elevation of 3,313 feet (1,009 m). Cattle and sheep are raised nearby and there are some alluvial gold diggings. The town became a municipality in 1863. It has Anglican and Roman Catholic cathedrals, and New England University College and St. Patrick's College are located there. Population: (1961) 12,884.

ARMINIANISM, är-min'ē-ə-niz-em, is the religious teaching of Jacobus Arminius, a Dutch reformed theologian who challenged Calvinist orthodoxy on the crucial point of free will. After his death his followers, led by Episcopius, presented an expanded formulation of Arminius' beliefs to the Netherlands States-General in 1610. The document, called *The Remonstrances,* asserted: (1) all who believe in Christ can be saved; (2) atonement is universal, making it possible for all to be saved; (3) man cannot be saved without the grace of God; (4) God's grace is not irresistible; (5) whether grace, once granted, can be lost was a question demanding further study.

The "Remonstrants," as those who adhered to this document were called, thereby questioned the very foundations of Calvinism, and the Synod of Dort (1618–1619) was summoned to deal with them. Although it aspired to be an international council of the Reformed churches, the Synod of Dort was predominantly Dutch. Under the ultra-Calvinist leadership the synod wasted no time in condemning Arminianism. In refutation of *The Remonstrances* it issued the Canons of Dort (the "Five Points of Calvinism").

Although Arminianism is properly a Dutch controversy, the term twice came into conspicuous use in England. Under James I and Charles I the Calvinistic Puritans considered the Canons of Dort the touchstone of orthodoxy and described their Anglican opponents as "Arminian." The Grand Remonstrance adopted by the House of Commons in 1641 attacked the "Arminian party."

During the 18th century the term "Arminianism" was used frequently as a description of the common Anglican position of the period. John Wesley accepted it in his controversy with the Calvinistic wing of the Evangelicals, and called the theological journal that he founded in 1778 *The Arminian Magazine.*

The word "Arminian" is still applied occasionally to theologians, especially Protestant, who defend, against any kind of determinism, the free response of man to the gift of divine grace. See also ARMINIUS, JACOBUS; EPISCOPIUS, SIMON.

ARMINIUS (c. 18 B.C.–19 A.D.), är-min'ē-əs, was a brilliant leader of German revolts against Rome. A chief of the Cherusci, Arminius was an officer in the Roman auxiliary army and a Roman citizen of the equestrian order.

In 9 A.D., Publius Quintilius Varus was sent to Germany to increase Roman taxation and jurisdiction. Arminius united many of the recently conquered German tribes in rebellion. Luring Varus with three legions along an unfamiliar route, he annihilated 20,000 Romans in the Teutoburger forest. Varus committed suicide, and all the Roman captives were massacred.

Varus' defeat terrified Rome. The grief-stricken emperor, Augustus, promptly raised troops and halted the advancing Germans at the Rhine. Thus the Rhine became Rome's frontier, altering Rome's policy of unlimited expansion into Germany.

In 15 A.D., Tiberius' nephew Julius Caesar Germanicus again campaigned against the Germans. Allied with Segestes (Arminius' father-in-law), Germanicus captured Arminius' wife, Thusnelda. In the next year Germanicus, commanding eight legions, reached the Teutoburger forest and buried Varus' dead. He scored limited successes at high cost, and was recalled to Rome after part of his army narrowly escaped ambush by Arminius. To win raiding victories without permanent occupation appeared useless for Rome. Tiberius, like Augustus, judged Germany lost. Thereafter Tiberius intrigued to keep the German tribes divided by civil war.

In 17 A.D., Arminius and his allies crushed the powerful Maroboduus of Bohemia. But Arminius' ambition was too great. Aiming at absolute power, he was slain by his own kinsmen. He has survived in German legend as a bold warrior and a champion of German nationalism and liberty.

ELEANOR HUZAR, *Michigan State University*

ARMINIUS, är-min'ē-əs, **Jacobus** (1560–1609), Dutch theologian who founded Arminianism. The Dutch form of his name is *Jacob Harmensen* (or Hermansz). Born at Oudewater on Oct. 10, 1560, he entered the University of Leiden at 15. The Merchants' Guild of Amsterdam acknowledged his brilliance by financing his ministerial education, thus permitting him to study at Geneva with the eminent Calvinist Théodore de Bèze, as well as at Basel and Padua. After a prolonged stay in Rome he returned to Holland in 1588, where he was ordained and appointed pastor of the Reformed Church at Amsterdam.

When the teachings of Calvin were severely questioned, Arminius, as de Bèze's disciple, was asked to defend supralapsarianism—the Calvinist theory of predestination, which holds that even before the Creation and Fall, God elected some men to be saved without consideration of their worthiness. After careful consideration Arminius, recoiling against a teaching that he could not reconcile with the love and justice of God, reversed his theological views. Despite strong opposition to his new views, Arminius was awarded a professorship at the University of Leiden in 1603, where he and Franciscus Gomarus, a fellow professor and zealous Calvinist, clashed on the questions of predestination and free will and twice debated before the States-General of Holland. After Arminius' death at Leiden on Oct. 19, 1609, his followers codified his beliefs in *The Remonstrances* (see ARMINIANISM).

ARMISTICE, är′mə-stəs, in international law, an agreement between hostile armies or nations to suspend active fighting. A general armistice or *cease-fire* often is arranged so that peace negotiations may take place without being complicated by continued fighting. However, peace has been negotiated at times without an armistice, as in the case of the treaties of Westphalia (1648) ending the Thirty Years' War, the treaty of Ghent (1814) ending the War of 1812, and the treaty of Portsmouth (1905) ending the Russo-Japanese War.

A limited armistice or suspension of arms, sometimes called a *truce,* may be arranged for a shorter period of time to permit the opposing armies to rest, collect their wounded, or bury their dead.

An armistice normally assumes equality of the parties and eventual renewal of hostilities and, unless expressly forbidden, permits movement of troops and equipment and other acts short of actual fighting. It therefore differs from a capitulation or surrender, which implies that one party, either locally or generally, is incapable of continuing hostilities, even though the armistice may impose some obligations on the victor and is not, therefore, "unconditional."

Armistices usually are concluded by military commanders in the field, but if political conditions are included, they are not valid unless confirmed by the governments. The armistice concluded by British Gen. William Sidney Smith and French Gen. Jean Baptiste Kléber at El Arish, Egypt, in 1800 during the Napoleonic Wars, was repudiated by the British government, and the armistice arranged by Union Gen. William T. Sherman and Confederate Gen. Joseph E. Johnston in 1865 during the American Civil War was repudiated by the United States government, both on this ground.

Armistices and Peace Negotiations. Armistices must be differentiated from preliminaries of peace, although the two may be included in the same instrument as in that of Aug. 12, 1898, ending hostilities in the Spanish-American War. The armistice of Nov. 11, 1918, ending hostilities between the Allies and Germany in World War I, followed the preliminaries of peace of Nov. 5, 1918, in which these states accepted U.S. President Woodrow Wilson's Fourteen Points as the basis for peace negotiations. On the other hand, general armistices ending fighting in the Crimean War (1856), Franco-Prussian War (1871), and Russo-Turkish War (1878) preceded preliminaries of peace.

A general armistice differs from a treaty of peace in that the war continues in a legal sense during the cease-fire. However, the terms of an armistice may be such that one party cannot in fact continue the war. This was true of the armistice of Nov. 11, 1918, which, from a practical point of view, ended World War I as effectively as the "unconditional surrender" of Germany on May 7, 1945, ended World War II.

The treaty of Versailles, which came into force on Jan. 10, 1920, and the separate peace treaty between the United States and Germany, signed on Aug. 25, 1921, ended World War I in the legal sense. In the case of World War II, no treaty of peace with Germany was negotiated, but the Allies did, in fact, recognize peace with West Germany by unilateral declarations and by the establishment of diplomatic relations. The Soviet Union and other Communist states similarly recognized peace with East Germany. West Berlin, separate from both Germanies, remained occupied territory under the terms of the German surrender of 1945.

Success and Failure of Armistices. The United Nations has followed the practice of the League of Nations in attempting to end hostilities by inducing the hostile parties to accept an armistice. Efforts by the League or by the UN were successful in both ending hostilities and in achieving a settlement in the Graeco-Bulgarian (1926), Mosul (1926), and Indonesian (1946) incidents, and in crises involving the Suez (1956), Lebanon (1958), the Congo (1960), and the Dominican Republic (1965). Similar efforts failed, however, in Manchuria (1931), Ethiopia (1935), World War II (1939), and Hungary (1956). Armistices negotiated under UN auspices stopped the fighting in Palestine (1949), Kashmir (1949), Korea, after three years of fighting (1953), Yemen (1959), and Cyprus (1963), but the underlying disputes remained unsettled. Occasional lapses have occurred in these areas since, and small UN peacekeeping forces continue to police the armistices.

Armistices negotiated under the auspices of a special conference in Geneva in 1954 between France and the states of Vietnam, Laos, and Cambodia ended hostilities in the first Indochinese War. But the United States and the government of the southern zone of Vietnam were not parties to the armistices and did not accept the conference resolutions providing for a political settlement. Fighting was renewed after 1958, and, although a new agreement on Laos was concluded in 1962, the Vietnamese hostilities escalated to major war across the armistice line, with U.S. participation in the mid-1960's.

QUINCY WRIGHT, *University of Virginia*
Author of "A Study of War"

Further Reading: Hague Convention, *Rules of Land Warfare* (The Hague 1899, 1907); Phillipson, Coleman, *Termination of War and Treaties of Peace,* pp. 55–75 (London 1916); Spaight, James M., *War Rights on Land,* chap. 8 (London 1911); Wright, Quincy, *A Study of War,* 2d ed., pp. 891, 942, 1430, 1527, 1554 (Chicago 1965).

ARMISTICE DAY. See VETERANS DAY.

ARMITAGE, är′mi-tij, **Kenneth** (1916–   ), English sculptor who created a new, abstract idiom for the sculptural figure group. Working most often in bronze, he flattened and joined the figures in his groups to achieve the timeless quality of a wall or rock slab.

Born in Leeds, England, on July 18, 1916, Armitage studied at the Leeds College of Art (1934–1937) and at the Slade School, London (1937–1939). After serving in the British army during World War II, he began a 10-year period as the head of the sculpture department at the Bath Academy of Art. In 1952 he gained major recognition with his first one-man exhibition and by being represented in the Venice Biennale. He received the prize for the best sculptor under age 45 in the 1958 Venice Biennale.

Typical of Armitage's portrayal of human figure groups emerging from slablike formations is his *Family Going For a Walk* (1951), in the Museum of Modern Art, New York City. In much of his later work he abandoned flat formations and adopted a "rounded" quality, as in *Two Seated Figures* (1957) and *Figure Lying on its Side* (1958–59).

ARMOR, är′mər, is a covering to protect the body from injury by weapons. It may include a shield borne by the wearer. Primitive armor probably was made of hides and wood. This article is concerned with metal armor, particularly the type worn by European warriors.

The steps in the perfection of armor may be traced from its beginning in the Bronze Age, through the thousand years when mail made of iron rings was most in use, to the era of knights clad in plate armor. For connoisseurs, the finest period of the armorer's art occurred during the 15th and 16th centuries. But armor faded in importance as firearms became increasingly powerful and battle tactics changed, in the 17th century, from assaults by heavily armored troops to fast cavalry skirmishes. During the 18th century, armor became obsolete except for ceremonial occasions.

Bronze Age Armor. The earliest metal used for armor was bronze. Sumerian warriors of about 2500 B.C., wearing small conical helmets and cloaks apparently of leather or cloth with discs of metal attached, are represented in an inlaid panel in the British Museum. A limestone stele of about the same date in the Louvre shows other Bronze Age soldiers wearing conical helmets with nose bars surprisingly similar in shape to helmets worn in 1066 A.D. by the troops of William the Conqueror. An Egyptian wall painting of about 1500 B.C. shows in detail an armored garment of a type later known as a *jazeran,* which consisted of a cloth tunic entirely covered with overlapping bronze scales arranged in horizontal rows. Armor of this type was flexible yet gave good protection. It continued in use, especially in eastern countries, until nearly modern times, with iron scales replacing the bronze. Its disadvantages were, first, that its entire weight hung from the shoulders and, second, that a dagger or arrow point could penetrate between the scales.

As metallurgical skill developed and bigger pieces of bronze could be worked, it became possible to make larger helmets, shield coverings, breastplates, and other pieces of body armor. Soon after 1000 B.C. bronze armor of high technical and artistic quality was available. A Greek helmet of the 6th century B.C. (see illustration above right) now in the City Art Museum of St. Louis, Mo., afforded not only good protection for head and face, but it was also a magnificent work of art. Its silver crest was presumably a commander's insignia. The soldier in the ranks wore breast- and backplates, *greaves,* which covered his shins, and a helmet with nose and cheek pieces and a crest of horsehair directly above the skull piece. His arms and thighs were bare. He carried a large shield of round, elliptical, or hourglass form, of wood and leather with a bronze rim.

The Etruscans developed armor much like that of their colonial Greek neighbors in southern Italy. Both, in turn, influenced the emerging Roman civilization technically and artistically. More than 500 years after the Greek helmet shown above, a Roman bronze helmet (also shown) with face mask was ornamented with projecting busts in the round. This is now in Nijmegen, Holland. The mask itself is the surprisingly beautiful face of an idealized warrior.

Introduction of Iron. Iron first appeared about 400 B.C. and was well known by the beginning of the Christian era. It was difficult to produce and consequently expensive, so it was used at

RIJKSMUSEUM, NIJMEGEN, NETHERLANDS

GREEK AND ROMAN bronze helmets of unusual design. The Greek helmet (*left*) dating from 550–500 B.C., has a plume-like silver crest; the Roman one, a sculptured bronze face mask.

CITY ART MUSEUM OF ST. LOUIS

first only for small, important pieces such as lance points and sword and dagger blades. By the time of the Roman emperors, however, iron and steel (iron containing a small percentage of carbon which permitted it to be hardened and tempered) was readily available. The armor of legionary soldiers in the 2d century B.C. consisted of rings or pieces of chain sewn on a leather undergarment. By the end of the 1st century B.C., iron scales were similarly applied to leather, and by the 2d century A.D., overlapping horizontal iron strips were riveted or sewn to leather or cloth.

During the centuries after the fall of Rome (476 A.D.), both mail of interlocked rings and defenses of iron or steel plates, including scale armor and metal-studded cloth and leather, continued to be used. Garments were made of the jazeran type already mentioned. Others were made of scales held together by lacing only. Still others were of scales or of scales combined with larger plates riveted inside a cloth or leather garment. Defenses of this type were used in Scandinavia in the 14th century and in Italy and elsewhere in the 15th and 16th centuries. They were known as *brigandines.*

The Age of Mail. In central and western Europe, from the 11th century onward, mail of linked rings was predominant. When actually going into battle the mailed knight put on an iron helmet over his mail hood. At first this was a relatively small domed cap. It consisted of a circular rim around the head at the forehead, four vertical strips rising to meet at the top of the head, metal plates filling the spaces between them, and a bar descending from the forehead over the nose. Later these were replaced by larger—usually flat-topped and more or less cylindrical—helmets covering the face as well as the rest of the head. Only a horizontal slit was left for vision, with various smaller openings below it for ventilation.

After the latter part of the 12th century the suit of mail was reinforced here and there by additional defenses of quilted fabric, leather (both raw and hardened by cooking in oil), and metal plates. Usually the knees were the first parts to receive these additions, followed by the shins, elbows, and breast.

The trunk portion of the body was most fre-

341

GOTHIC ARMOR of the 15th century, the finest period, probably made by the noted Missaglia family of Milan.

quently protected by a "coat of plates" of the brigandine type. Additional small defenses of plate were applied to cover the joints of the shoulders, elbows, and knees. All were worn over the mail tunic (*hauberk*) and leg coverings (*chausses*). Additional defenses for arms and legs appeared. At first these were simple strips of metal attached by straps or lacings, but later they became complete tubular defenses opening on hinges (the inside of the thighs, however, was left unarmored for convenience in riding). Gauntlets, with overlapping finger scales, came into common use along with defenses of plate for the upper part of the foot. Collars of plate were added to protect the neck. On his head the knight wore a *basinet* style of helmet over his hood of mail, or the basinet alone with a neck-guard (*camail*) of mail attached to its lower edge and hanging down past the neck opening of the hauberk. For a major battle, a great *heaume* was worn over the basinet. This was solid plate armor, and covered head, face, and neck down to the shoulders. There was, of course, no official shape for heaumes. Some were flat-topped, some rounded, and some almost pointed. Knights sometimes wore, instead of any of these forms, a simple, rather broad-brimmed iron hat.

During the second half of the 14th century the various pieces of plate armor which had been added to the knight's defenses began to coalesce. The separate pieces protecting the forearms, elbows, and upper arms joined to form a single arm defense; the thigh, knee, and shin guards formed a complete covering for each leg. Breast-plates and backplates added horizontal lames (narrow plates) to protect the lower abdomen, and pendant plates, in addition to leg armor, to protect the upper thigh. As plate armor became more complete, the necessity for a full suit of mail beneath it vanished. In the 15th century, mail was usually confined to relatively small areas at exposed joints—armpit, elbow, crotch, and knee—although shirts or short shoulder-capes of mail might be worn instead of plate armor when immediate battle was not expected.

Types of Plate Armor. The so-called "Gothic" armor produced in the 15th century and in the first years of the 16th is the finest of all to the connoisseur. From the military standpoint it afforded the best combination of security and practicability; from the metallurgical standpoint it showed the greatest skill in manipulating a most intractable material; and esthetically it combined beauty of form without sacrifice of utility.

The best Gothic armor was made of a metal that, on the inner surfaces of the plates, was a soft, tough iron, almost of the quality of wrought-iron. Yet the exterior surface had been changed—by exposure to free carbon under great heat and subsequent quenching—to a steel of glasslike hardness. It was not a rolled sheet metal of uniform thickness, such as is used today for containers and automobile bodies. Rather, each part of a suit of armor was formed from a lump of metal hammered from the center toward the edges until the proper shape was attained. Thus the metal would be thickest at the most exposed part and thinnest at the edges.

There was no standard type of 15th century armor. Although the best specimens that have survived are of plain polished steel, there is ample evidence that armor was sometimes painted or chemically colored. Furthermore, it frequently had cloth or leather riveted to its plates, either inside or out. Variations in style ranged from the utilitarian to the most wildly fanciful.

The piece of armor which varied most in design was the helmet. This could be the steel hat, or *chapel-de-fer;* a *salade,* or bowl-type covering coming down to the mouth, with a slit at eye-level for vision; a *barbute,* deeper and more cylindrical, resembling a classical Greek helmet; a basinet, large and heavy, resting on the shoulders and having a movable visor in front of the face; or an *armet,* a small helmet completely enclosing the head, with a visor that could be raised to reveal the upper part of the face, and two hinged sidepieces enclosing the lower face and chin. If a helmet of the salade type was worn there was usually also a separate chin guard or *mentonnière,* attached to the top of the breastplate. With the armet there might or might not be a neck protection of mail.

Inside the helmet there might be a padded cap, or the helmet itself might have a lining of cloth attached by rivets around the lower edge of the metal. The same function—protection against chafing and temperature (for armor could get very cold in winter or hot in summer)— was served by padded cloth undergarments. These garments also had laces attached, to which the arm and leg units of the armor were tied. The laces passed through eyelets in leather tabs riveted to the top edge of the defenses.

In addition to the helmet, a suit of armor consisted of six main units: one for the trunk, another for the shoulders and neck, two for the arms, and two for the legs. Each of these in turn consisted of several smaller parts, connected either by being riveted to leather strips or by a series of interlocking studs, keyhole slots, and rotatable turning pegs. The trunk armor had a breastplate and a backplate, united by straps at the shoulders and sides. To the lower edge of each were attached horizontal lames which, sliding over each other, gave flexibility at the waist. This was accomplished by a rivet in the upper lame passing loosely through a slot in the lower one, allowing them to slide and permitting a certain amount of bending. To the lowest lame were attached *tuilles* (flat plates) or *tassets* (short groups of lames), which hung down over the tops of the leg armor.

The shoulders were protected by separate *pauldrons*, usually attached to a neck guard or *colletin* which might fit under or over the breast- and backplates. The arm guards consisted of a tubular defense, or *rerebrace*, for the upper arm; an elbow guard, pivoted to it front and back; and a forearm guard, or *vambrace*, also pivoted to the elbow guard. Each of these pieces might have one or more sliding lames at top or bottom for flexibility, but the three were usually attached to each other, and put on as a unit. The vambrace was generally made in two pieces, held together by a hinge with a spring catch so that it could be opened as the hand was passed through it and then clasped snugly around the forearm and wrist. The hands were protected by separate gauntlets, of hinged and sliding lames, and finger plates riveted to leather straps.

The leg armor was similar to that of the arm, except that the armor for the upper leg was open on the inside of the thigh. As with the arm, flexibility was provided by sliding lames at the top of the thigh, above and below the knee, and at the ankle. The feet were guarded by *sabbatons* or *sollerets* of hinged and sliding lames which covered the top of the foot only, but had a leather strap or sole to hold the plates in position. In addition to all these pieces many armors had also a pair of circular *rondels* hung from the shoulder straps of the breast- and backplates, or from the pauldrons, which gave extra protection to the shoulder joint. Further protection at the shoulder and elbow joint, the crotch, and the inside of the knee joint was usually given by mail. This might take the form of small pieces sewn to the undergarment, of sleeves or legs, or of an entire garment of mail worn under the plate armor.

The Art of the Armorer. Such a suit of armor would weigh from 55 to 65 pounds (25–30 kg), yet it was not particularly uncomfortable. Of course, it had to fit perfectly. The joints had to come at exactly the right places, and few adjustments were possible. This accounts for one of the common misconceptions about armor. The curator of an armor collection often hears the inquiry: "Weren't the people who wore armor as a rule quite a lot smaller then men today?" It is true that men today are generally larger than their European forebears, but not very much. The misconception arises because much of the armor now on exhibition in museums is the outgrown armor of young men. Their arms and legs grew so long that the joints no longer worked properly; their bodies grew too stout for their old breastplates. Therefore, they hung their old armor on the wall of the ancestral castle and ordered a new suit to fit their adult

stature. And, in all probability, they were buried in it. It was the outgrown armor which was preserved, unscarred by battle.

Another popular misconception is that armor was tremendously hampering; that a man, once fallen, could not rise without the aid of a derrick. Nothing could be further from the truth. Armor was practical—it had to be; men trusted their lives to it. Except in the case of mail, armor did not bear all its weight on the shoulders. The weight, which in total was no more than a modern soldier's field kit, was well distributed over the body. An armored man could lie down, rise again, climb stairs or a ladder, run (not very fast), descend a rope hand over hand (but hardly climb it, unless he were exceptionally strong). Any competent knight was expected to be able to run alongside his horse and vault into the saddle without using the stirrup.

The principal sources of armor were northern Italy and southern Germany. In a general way, the Italians preferred smooth, polished armor; its beauty was derived from excellence of form alone. The German armorers excelled in flutings, scallopings, and the addition of brass borders and ornaments. Among the great Italian armorers were the Missaglia family of Milan, Paulo and Filippo Negroli, Pompeo della Chiesa, and Bartolommeo Campi. Among the Germans were Wolf of Landshut, Jörg and Lorenz Helmschmied of Augsburg, Conrad Seusenhofer of Innsbruck, Coloman Colman, Matthäus Frauenpreiss, and Kunz Lochner. Excellent armor was also made in France, Spain, and England.

Influence of the Renaissance. As the 16th century wore on, styles in armor changed markedly. The chaste simplicity of the early Italian armor gave way to a decoration of parallel flutings favored by Emperor Maximilian I (1459–1519) of Austria and such armor was named after him. The pointed toes of Gothic foot defenses were replaced by exaggeratedly broad toe coverings. The salade helmets became less popular, and were replaced by closed armet or *burgonet* helmets, whose lower edges interlocked with the outturned top edge of the colletin. This type of helmet became a virtual turret which could be turned in any direction without exposing an opening at the neck. Arm defenses developed a similar rotating joint below the shoulder, and the

MAXIMILIAN ARMOR of German design, about 1505. More ornate than the Gothic, it was heavily fluted.

METROPOLITAN MUSEUM OF ART,
ROGERS FUND, 1904

KUNSTHISTORISCHES MUSEUM, VIENNA

TOURNAMENT ARMOR (left) was specially designed for man and horse. The armor above was inspired by a civilian's puffed and slashed doublet.

increasing use of sliding lames made armor ever more flexible and comfortable. In the most expensive armor, lames were also added at elbow and knee joints, eliminating the need for mail.

As armor improved mechanically it also acquired increasingly elaborate decoration, though at the sacrifice of the simple beauty of the Gothic period. With the flowering of the Renaissance, armor sometimes developed curious and fanciful tendencies. Helmets were made with grotesque face masks. Whole suits of steel were made to copy civilian cloth costume, with its puffed and slashed doublets and tight hose. Renaissance decoration was applied to armor in many ways. The surfaces might be etched with acid to form a roughened background to areas which had been protected from etching by acid-proof varnish. Gold was applied to the steel surface by evaporating gold amalgam, by burnishing gold leaf or wire onto a heavily roughened surface, or by inlaying gold into the steel. And, by the use of hammer and chasing tool, the surface of the armor might be embossed with designs in relief. But magnificent as this embossed decoration was, it deprived the armor of one of its principal advantages: the smoothness of surface that easily deflected a spear point or arrow. However, since such embossed armor was far too costly to be used for other than ceremonial purposes, this loss of practicality was not too serious.

With the 17th century there appeared two factors which radically affected the development of armor. One was a great improvement in the power and effectiveness of hand firearms (which had been in existence through the whole period of plate armor). The other was a change in cavalry tactics, favoring lightly-armed, swift-moving bands of skirmishers. More powerful bullets required thicker armor to resist them; fast cavalry skirmishing called for lighter riders on lighter, faster horses. So armor developed in the direction of thick, strong, bullet-proof breast-plates and helmets, increased flexibility from the use of sliding lames in place of solid plates, and the gradual elimination of arm and leg defenses.

Tournament Armor. Armor was fundamentally equipment for military activity. But there was one kind of armor intended only for sport—for the knightly tournament, one of the most exacting and exciting sports man has ever engaged in. And just as today's Olympic pistol champion uses a weapon which a soldier might deem fantastically impractical, so tournament contestants of the 15th and 16th centuries wore armor especially designed for that one purpose. Often, it would be grotesque and awkward for any other use.

There were many different kinds of tournaments, and there was tournament armor to fit each different set of rules. For some tournaments the knight could be suitably outfitted by merely exchanging his regular helmet for a special model and by adding two or three reinforcing pieces over his regular war armor. Other types of tournaments were so violent and dangerous that a special suit of armor had to be worn, with a huge helmet solidly bolted to breast- and backplates. Such a suit might weigh 90 to 100 pounds (41–45 kg), but it needed to be worn for only a short time. See also CHAIN MAIL.

THOMAS T. HOOPES, *City Art Museum, St. Louis*

Bibliography

Barraclough, Geoffrey, ed., *Social Life in Early England* (London 1962).
Blair, Claude, *European Armour* (New York 1959).
Grancsay, S.V., *Arms and Armor* (New York 1964).
Hoopes, Thomas T., *Armor and Arms* (St. Louis 1954).
Laking, Sir G.F., *A Record of European Armour and Arms Through Seven Centuries*, 5 vols. (London 1920–22).
Mann, Sir James, *European Arms and Armour*, 2 vols. (London 1962).
Metropolitan Museum of Art, *Arms and Armor* (New York 1964).
Metropolitan Museum of Art, *Handbook of Arms and Armor, European and Oriental* (New York 1930).
O'Neil, Bryan H., *Castles and Cannon* (London 1960).
Singer, C., Holmyard, E.J., Hall, A.R., and Williams, T.I., *A History of Technology*, 5 vols. (London and New York 1954–58).
Snodgrass, A., *Early Greek Armour and Weapons* (Edinburgh 1964).
Stone, George C., *A Glossary of the Construction, Decoration and Use of Arms and Armor* (New York 1961).
Thordeman, Bengt, *Armour from the Battle of Wisby*, 2 vols. (Stockholm 1959).
Yadin, Yigael, *The Art of Warfare in Biblical Lands*, 2 vols. (New York 1963).

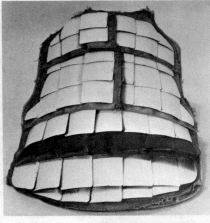

MODERN BODY ARMOR for infantry consists of helmet and liner, armored vest, and nylon groin armor. At right is the back of a different vest with nylon surface removed to show overlapping plates of titanium, each attached with two staples for protection without rigidity.

HEAD AND FOOT protection. Aviator's helmet with built-in sun visor and arrangements for earphones and microphone offers less protection than tank crewman's helmet. Shoe attachment deflects force of antipersonnel mines away from body.

U.S. NAVAL RESEARCH LABORATORY PHOTOS

MODERN ARMOR

Body armor is provided for the head, torso, and feet of military personnel to reduce the number of killed and wounded. The high percentage of casualties from grenade, mine, and shell fragments in the Korean War indicated the need for armor, but it had to be light enough for a foot soldier to wear in battle.

Effectiveness. Within the weight limitation, the most efficient armor materials available provide protection against relatively small fragments with velocities ranging from several hundred to a few thousand feet per second, depending upon their mass and shape. First used extensively in this century during the Korean War, armor was credited with reducing combat casualties by as much as 20 percent.

Protection against small-arms fire (caliber .30-inch or 7.62-mm and .50-inch or 12.7-mm bullets and armor-piercing projectiles) cannot be provided unless weights of from 10 to 20 pounds per square foot (48.8–97.6 kg/sq meter) can be borne, as is sometimes possible with air crew personnel or others engaged in sedentary work.

The armor material used for a particular application is selected for its relative effectiveness in protecting against anticipated missiles. The construction and contour of the garment are influenced by the nature of the material, the climates in which it may be used, and the shape of the part of the body to be protected. Armor materials protect against flying fragments by absorbing their kinetic energy.

Types of Armor. Armor for ground forces consists of a sleeveless torso jacket with detachable groin armor, a helmet, and special boots. Any

or all may be issued, depending upon the mission.

Torso Armor. The United States armed services have five types of torso armor, four of which are designed to protect against fragments. Three of these were designed for the foot soldier or marine. Torso armor for aviators is similar in construction and material to the infantry jacket but weighs considerably more, since a pilot can bear more weight and needs the additional protection.

Materials used in jackets for fragmentation protection include nylon fabrics, titanium, specially treated fiber staples, and Doron, a laminate of glass fabric bonded with a polyester resin. These are used singly or in combination.

Protection against small-caliber armor-piercing projectiles requires about seven times as much weight per unit of area as is used in fragmentation torso armor. In practice, the area of coverage is reduced. The resultant protective armor, used by air crews involved in low-altitude missions and close ground support, weighs about 25 pounds (11.5 kg) and consists of a hard outer surface to break the steel core of the projectile and a ductile backing to absorb the kinetic energy of the resulting fragments. Steel with a hardened surface is used to protect against these projectiles. For applications involving a low concentration of hits, a more efficient armor has been developed, consisting of a hard ceramic backed by a plastic reinforced with glass fiber.

Helmet. The U.S. infantryman's helmet consists of a nonmagnetic steel outer shell supported by a resin-bonded nylon fabric liner. The fabric, the same as that used in jackets and groin armor, is made of high-strength nylon yarn. The combination of the steel shell and bonded nylon liner provides almost the same protection as that of the foot soldier's torso armor.

Special helmets have been designed for aviators, crewmen of tanks, and communications personnel. Their functions require equipment that could not be accommodated in the infantryman's helmet, such as earphones, microphones, and tinted transparent sun visors.

Shoes. Armored boots or shoe attachments protect against spikes and antipersonnel mines. A sheet material, usually metal, is so shaped as to deflect much of the shock wave generated by an antipersonnel mine, thus reducing the damage.

History of Modern Armor. The development of firearms and the necessity for mobility on the battlefield led to the abandonment of body armor in the 1600's and 1700's, but the development of fragmentation ammunition for use against men and aircraft in the 20th century signaled body armor's return. The first item reintroduced was the helmet, worn in most major armies by the end of World War I. It remains the most universally used item. Most designs are similar except for the suspension system and the liner, which is omitted in some types.

During World War II the United States pressed for the development of materials and designs for fragment-protection garments. Most materials now in use were evaluated in battlefield trials near the end of that war. Armored vests, used extensively by the U.S. Army and Marine Corps during the Korean War, have been standard-issue items since then.

The recognition, development, and use of superior fragment-armor materials would not have been possible without the theoretical studies and concurrent development of laboratory evaluation techniques by government scientists. Nylon armor fabrics and Doron were developed through cooperative efforts of various laboratories of the U.S. Department of Defense and industry. Several titanium alloys of almost identical quality resulted from independent efforts of industry and government during the 1950's. Armored footwear research and development, garment design, and the introduction of the nylon laminate helmet liner were entirely government efforts, although industry produced prototypes and materials. Ceramic composite armor was introduced by American industry.

WILFRED J. FERGUSON
U.S. Naval Research Laboratory

ARMORED CARS have two general uses—commercial and military. Commercially they are designed for the transport of money and various types of valuable merchandise. They are built on a standard truck-type chassis. Armored cars are used mostly in cities for transferring cargo between depositories and business places.

The military armored car is different from the commercial vehicle. It is built to meet the battlefield requirements of mobility and protection—needs as old as war itself. The armored car had its genesis in the war chariot of early history, but the introduction of steel, gunpowder, and the internal combustion engine brought refinements to this war machine. During the 20th century, the skills of many kinds of experts in various countries contributed to the development of the modern armored car.

The modern armored car is designed to provide *high-speed mobility, protected firepower, and personnel protection.* Current tactics call for its use by ground combat elements engaged in reconnaissance, screening, pursuit, exploitation, and security missions.

In the strictest sense, the armored car is a wheeled vehicle. However, as with all military equipment, it undergoes constant tests, resulting in redesign and remodeling. As a result, the contemporary armored car classification is somewhat broad and flexible, embracing both wheeled and tracked vehicles.

Experimentation with various designs for increasing mobility has produced types of armored cars with conventional wheel systems, multiple wheel chassis, and combination wheel and track construction. Because the wheeled vehicle is essentially roadbound, the track has been incorporated to permit crosscountry operation in which vehicles must travel over rough terrain and surmount obstacles imposed by bad weather conditions. A familiar vehicle constructed with wheels in front and a half-track arrangement in the rear is the scout car.

The element of protection in armored cars is provided by metal armor of varying thickness, with primary attention given to the highly vulnerable front of the vehicle and lesser consideration given to the sides and rear. Some armored cars have overhead protection; others are constructed with an open top. The armor is protective against small arms and shell fragmentation but is not of sufficient strength and thickness to withstand antitank gun and direct artillery hits. The vehicle is dependent, therefore, upon its speed and maneuverability for protection.

The armored car has limited firepower, in keeping with its role. Normally its armament consists of a .30 caliber and a .50 caliber machine gun and a light artillery weapon of the 37mm type. Antiaircraft defense is usually within its capabilities, so far as low-flying aircraft are concerned, and ground mounts are carried to permit detachment and employment of the machine guns in foot operations. Individual arms are carried by crew members, and the ammunition load of the car includes a supply of hand grenades, smoke pots, and antitank mines.

The crew of the armored car may number from four, in the wheeled type of vehicle, up to a dozen in the half-track modification. The weight of the cars may range between six and ten tons (5.4 and 9 metric tons), the wheeled type being the lighter.

The U.S. Army acquired its first armored car in 1915, at a time when considerable experimentation with this type of vehicle had already been done by Russia, France, and Britain. A year later, three armored cars were made available to the New York National Guard through private financing. In 1928 the first armored car unit of the U.S. Army was organized at Fort Myer in Virginia.

Wide experience with all types of armor in World War II confirmed the superiority of the full-tracked vehicle over the wheeled type. This superiority indicates that the value of the armored car as a combat vehicle is decreasing, its role being taken by the light tank. However, the armored car continues in use as a training vehicle and is well adapted to occupation duty and internal security uses.

WILLIAM GARDNER BELL, *U.S. Cavalry Former Editor of "The Armored Cavalry Journal"*

ARMORED FORCES, along with infantry and artillery, are one of the combat arms, or branches, of an army. Armor is called the "arm of speed and violence." Armored forces are made up of mechanized infantry, armored cavalry, self-propelled artillery, engineers, and service elements, organized with tank units into a balanced striking combat force. Armor is thus a combined-arms force organized to conduct mounted combat, employing tanks and other armor-protected vehicles as the principal means of accomplishing its ground-combat mission.

A large armored unit, supported by military tactical aircraft, represents the most powerful striking force in an army. Organized for conventional as well as nuclear warfare, armored forces represent the combat arm most capable of fighting on an atomic battlefield. This is largely because of their armor protection, but also because of their mobility and firepower. Armored units can cover wide fronts and deep zones of action in dispersed formation and can concentrate rapidly. Using their great firepower, mobility, and shock action, armored forces conduct decisive, highly mobile warfare, primarily on the offensive.

Organization. One of the distinctive features of armored forces is the flexibility of their organization. Units of battalion, brigade, division, and even larger size generally organize and balance their task forces according to the particular combat mission to be accomplished. Thus, a task force might be organized with more tank than mechanized infantry units, or vice versa, or the balance might be equal. Armored units are well equipped with radio communications. This gives them great flexibility of action and rapid response. In addition to major armored units, such as armored divisions, brigades, and regiments, there are smaller units of tanks that are organic to or attached to infantry.

Combat Functions. There is general acceptance of the axiom that "the best antitank weapon is another tank." Tanks engage all enemy ground targets, and they are armed and protected for tank-versus-tank battle. Tank units fight almost entirely by direct fire. They seek to close rapidly with enemy forces, using fire, maneuver, and shock action. See also TANK.

Mechanized infantry units ride into battle on armored personnel carriers (APC's), but they normally fight on foot. By their own means of fire and maneuver they close with the enemy to destroy or capture him. A typical APC is a tracked vehicle that carries a squad of infantrymen. The vehicle's armor generally protects the men against small-arms fire and artillery fragments. Some APC's are amphibious. Mechanized infantry units and armored cavalry units perform reconnaissance and provide security for other units. They also engage in offensive, defensive, and delaying action.

Armored artillery units supporting tanks and infantry are a powerful means of influencing the course of combat. Such artillery consists of self-propelled guns and rocket launchers that move on tracks like tanks. (See ARTILLERY.) Armored engineer units serve to increase the combat effectiveness of the parent organization by removing mines, providing bridging, and so forth. Tactical air reconnaissance and close-air-support aircraft greatly assist armor in battle.

Tactics. Armored forces fight by a combination of fire and maneuver. These are called the

U.S. ARMY

ARMORED FORCES TANKS, such as this M-60, attack with speed and violence, spearheading army assaults.

base of fire and the *maneuver* element. The base of fire is designed to neutralize enemy capabilities; it usually comprises artillery and mortar units and tactical aircraft. The maneuver force has the mission of closing with and destroying the enemy; it is composed of tank and mechanized infantry units. It moves rapidly and continuously in mass, firing as it moves. The entire force advances as fast as possible on the enemy without halting, while the base of fire seeks to inhibit the enemy's ability to maneuver or advance. Tanks attack in mass formation.

Amphibious Armor. For land warfare the trend has been to produce vehicles that can cross rivers without bridging. The more modern APC's have this capability; tanks do not, except for one type of Soviet light tank. Some tanks can be equipped for fording rivers. For amphibious operations a variety of vehicles have been developed for ship-to-shore assault. The U.S. Marine Corps has pioneered in their development.

Limitations. The heavy weight of the vehicles and their high fuel consumption impose limitations. Bridges, for example, must be strong enough to bear them. High fuel requirements necessitate tanker supply vehicles and a large system of supply. Modern armored forces have shifted from gasoline to diesel fuel in order to reduce this burden of supply. In a tactical sense, armor is limited in its ability to fight in forests, mountains, and certain other terrain. In the strategic sense of being transported great geographical distances, armor must travel either overland or by sea, since only certain light vehicles can be transported by air.

Capabilities. Armor's operations in all types of conflict range from a threatening posture in cold war to action in general war. Particularly suited to nuclear conflict, its armor protection reduces significantly the effects on men of blast, heat, and radiation from nuclear bursts. Operationally, armor can conduct the following missions: deep penetration and wide envelopment, exploitation, mobile defense, destruction of enemy armor, reconnaissance/security, withdrawal operations, close support of infantry, and counterinsurgency operations.

History. Armored forces originated with the creation of the tank by Britain during World

ARMORED PERSONNEL CARRIER, U.S. Army M-113, is highly mobile, amphibious, and transportable by air.

War I. Designed to overcome machine guns, barbed wire, and the stalemate of trench warfare, tanks were first used in combat by the British in 1916 at the Battle of the Somme. The American Tank Corps, created on Jan. 26, 1918, first fought on Sept. 12, 1918, at St. Mihiel.

By the war's end, tank units had been used by the British, French, Americans, and Germans in 91 engagements. However, the potentialities of armored forces were not fully appreciated; most tacticians believed that the tank's role was to support infantry. In the 20 years after the war this belief was refuted. The leaders in the new concept of armored combat were Capt. Basil Liddell Hart in Britain, Generals Jean Baptiste Estienne and Charles de Gaulle in France, and General von Eimannsberger of Austria.

In their 1935–1939 organization of panzer divisions the Germans under Gen. Heinz Guderian were the first to create a single versatile armored force with greater mobility and firepower than the rest of the army. Each panzer division contained motorized infantry, artillery, engineers, and tanks. Panzer divisions, corps, and armies spearheaded the German army in its

ARMORED ARTILLERY, such as this self-propelled 155-mm gun, supports the infantry with long-range shelling.

blitzkrieg campaigns against Poland, France, and Russia. In 1941 some 3,500 frontline tanks struck the Soviet army's larger forces and destroyed or captured about 17,000 Russian tanks. German success caused expansion of other countries' armored forces.

In July 1940 the U.S. Army's Armored Force was created, while British and German-Italian armored forces clashed in the North African desert. In 1944, breaking out from the Normandy beachhead, Allied armor made spectacular advances across France and Belgium and did so again after the crossing of the Rhine. By 1945 the United States had 16 armored divisions in Europe. In the Pacific campaigns, U.S. infantry was supported by small tank units. In the latter half of the war, armored amphibious battalions were used successfully by the U.S. Army and Marine Corps.

By 1943 the USSR had reorganized its armor into a variety of mechanized formations, including tank armies. The greatest tank battle in history was the 1943 Battle of Kursk, where close to 3,000 tanks moved at one time. As the war progressed, Soviet armor gained a decisive role in Europe and Manchuria.

The Japanese used tanks with infantry against the Chinese in the 1930's and during World War II in the Malayan campaign and on Bataan in the Philippines.

In the Korean War, both sides used tank units with infantry. The classic use of armor was that of the Israeli forces in the Sinai campaign of 1956. France used armor in the Indochina War and in Algeria. American forces were making limited use of it in South Vietnam in the late 1960's.

Armored Forces of Various Countries. The U.S. Army usually maintains four armored divisions, two or three armored cavalry regiments, and a number of mechanized and tank battalions.

The USSR has the world's largest armored force. Its armor is made up of both motorized rifle divisions and tank divisions. The latter constitute about one third of the army. Both types of divisions have tanks, with the heaviest proportion in the tank division. Armies of the Warsaw Pact nations are similar. Communist China has very few armored divisions.

Britain maintains a small army of one armored division and several infantry divisions. West Germany's army is made up largely of armored infantry divisions; it also has several armored divisions. France possesses one armored division and some mechanized units.

ROBERT B. RIGG, *Colonel, Armor, U.S. Army*
Author of "How To Stay Alive in Vietnam"

Further Reading: Ogorkiewicz, Richard M., *Armor—A History of Mechanized Forces* (New York 1960); Rigg, Robert B., "Pictorial History of Armor," *Armor*, vol. 68, no. 5 (Washington 1959); U.S. Department of Army Field Manual 17-1, *Armor Operations* (Washington 1963); Whitehouse, Arch, *Tank* (New York 1960).

ARMORICA, är-môr′ə-kə, is the Latin form of the name used in Celtic, Roman, and Frankish times for the coastal region in northern France between the Seine and Loire rivers. The name was derived from the Celtic words *ar*, meaning "on," and *mor*, meaning "sea." With Caesar's subjugation of the Veneti tribe in 56 B.C. the area came under Roman rule. In the 5th century A.D., Britons emigrated to the northwestern section, which therefore became known as Brittany. The eastern part was incorporated into Normandy.

ARMORY SHOW, är′mə-rē shō, the popular name given to the International Exposition of Modern Art held in the 69th Regiment Armory in New York City from Feb. 15 to March 15, 1913. A portion of the exhibit later traveled to Chicago and Boston. The 50th anniversary of the show was celebrated in 1963 with a partial recreation of the exhibit at the Armory.

The show, which gave the American public its first glimpse of such European art movements as cubism and Fauvism, was one of the major moments in America's artistic coming-of-age. Despite an almost unanimous cry of outrage that greeted it, the show did succeed in bringing an end to America's artistic isolationism.

The exhibit was organized by the Association of American Painters and Sculptors, founded late in 1911 by a group of American modern artists. Arthur Davies, president, and Walt Kuhn, secretary, took the lead in organizing the show. They hoped to provide an outlet for the American artists who had no chance of being seen in the rigidly academic museum shows that dominated art in the United States at the time.

The show included about 1,500 paintings and sculptures, about 1,000 by American artists and 500 by Europeans. Americans represented included John Sloan, Guy Pène du Bois, John Marin, and Maurice Prendergast. In the European section the works of cubists, such as Picasso, Braque, and Léger were shown. Matisse, Rouault, and Vlaminck were represented among the Fauves. Independent painters such as Munch, Cézanne, and Kandinsky also were included.

The critics, the public, and the press reacted with a flood of hostility and ridicule, especially reviling the European "madmen." Marcel Duchamp's *Nude Descending a Staircase* was the special scapegoat. Nevertheless, the Armory Show opened the door to modern art in America, and, surprisingly, many of the European works exhibited were bought by American collectors. The show, in addition to dealing a heavy blow to academic art in the United States, revealed that allegedly progressive American artists were really somewhat derivative and timid.

ARMOUR, är′mər, **John Douglas** (1830–1903), Canadian judge. He was born near Peterborough, Ontario, on May 4, 1830. Educated at Upper Canada College and Toronto University, he was called to the bar in 1853. He served as chief justice of Ontario and president of the Court of Appeal (1900–1902), and as judge of the Supreme Court of Canada (1902–1903). He was one of the Canadian representatives on the Alaskan Boundary Commission in 1902–1903. He died at London, England, on July 11, 1903.

ARMOUR, är′mər, **Norman** (1887–   ), American diplomat. He was born in Brighton, England, on Oct. 14, 1887. After graduating from Princeton in 1909, he took a law degree at Harvard.

Armour's early diplomatic service was largely in Europe. For 10 years beginning in 1922, he held posts in Washington, Rome, Tokyo, and Paris. He was named U.S. minister to Haiti in 1932, and to Canada in 1935. From 1938 to 1945 he was ambassador successively to Chile, Argentina, and Spain. He became assistant secretary of state in 1947, retiring the following year. He later headed embassies in Venezuela and Guatemala (to 1955).

ARMORY SHOW (1913) challenged current tastes with works like Duchamp's *Nude Descending a Staircase.*

ARMOUR, är′mər, **Philip Danforth** (1832–1901), American businessman who was a leading organizer and innovator in the meat-packing industry in the post-Civil War era. Following a business partnership with John Plankinton started in 1863, he formed Armour & Co. in 1870, and by 1890 it had become one of the five firms that dominated meat packing in the United States.

Armour's innovations included the combining of slaughtering and packing operations, which led to mass-production efficiencies. His introduction of the refrigerated railroad car led to further efficiencies and extended the range of the market for fresh meat. In addition, Armour began canning meat. He achieved diversification by using almost every part of the hog or cow, and thus moved into new enterprises such as making soap. By 1890 he had a corporate fortune of more than $10 million.

Armour was born of Scottish-Irish and Puritan stock in Stockbridge, N.Y. on May 16, 1832. In early business ventures he produced sluices for miners in California, speculated in hog prices, and engaged in the wholesale grocery business in Milwaukee.

As a philanthropist he contributed to the Armour Mission, Armour Flats for workingmen's families, and the Armour Institute of Technology in Chicago. He died in Chicago on Jan. 6, 1901.
PAUL WEINER, *University of Connecticut*

ARMOUR, är′mər, **Richard Willard** (1906–   ), American teacher and author, who is known for his light verse and humorous prose. He was born in San Pedro, Calif., on July 15, 1906. Educated at Pomona College and Harvard, Armour taught at several universities before becoming professor of English at Scripps College in 1945.

His books include *Yours for the Asking* (1942), *Light Armour* (1954), *It All Started with Europa* (1954), *Twisted Tales from Shakespeare* (1957), *The Classics Reclassified* (1960), *Drugstore Days* (1960), *Going Around in Academic Circles* (1965), and *American Lit Relit* (1965).

ARMOUR, är'mər, **Tommy** (1896–1968), Scottish-American golfer, who won all three of the major professional golf titles of his era and who was the only golfer to represent two countries in international competition.

Thomas Dickson Armour was born in Edinburgh, Scotland, on Sept. 24, 1896. While serving in the British tank corps in World War I, he lost the sight of his left eye. In 1920 he won his first major championship, the French amateur title, and played with British teams in international amateur matches.

Armour went to the United States in 1922, turned professional in 1925, and two years later played for the U.S. team against the British in the first pro matches. (He became a U.S. citizen in 1930.) In 1927 he won the U.S. Open in a playoff with Harry Cooper. He took the Professional Golfers' Association (PGA) crown in 1930 by sinking a 12-foot putt at the 36th hole to defeat Gene Sarazen, 1-up. His most satisfying triumph, however, came in winning the 1931 British Open by one stroke. Armour was elected to the PGA Hall of Fame in 1940. He died in Larchmont, N. Y., on Sept. 11, 1968.

BILL BRADDOCK
New York "Times"

ARMS, ärmz, **John Taylor** (1887–1953), American etcher, who was noted for his delicate studies of medieval architecture. He was born in Washington, D.C., on April 19, 1887. He graduated from the Massachusetts Institute of Technology in 1911 as an architect but soon devoted himself to etching. Arms wrote the *Handbook of Print Making and Print Makers* (1934) and illustrated *Churches of France* (1929) and *Hill Towns and Cities of Northern Italy* (1932), both written by his wife, Dorothy Noyes Arms. Arms died in New York City on Oct. 13, 1953.

ARMS AND THE MAN is a comedy written in 1894 by George Bernard Shaw (q.v.), satirizing romantic notions about military glory. During a war between Bulgaria and Serbia, Raina Petkoff, the daughter of a Bulgarian major, saves Captain Bluntschli from Bulgarian troops by hiding him in her boudoir. Bluntschli, a reluctant soldier, returns after the war and wins Raina from her "heroic" fiancé Sergius. Sergius' reputation for heroism is based on his having led a foolhardy charge against the Serbs, in which he was saved only because the enemy guns had the wrong ammunition. Oscar Straus based his operetta *The Chocolate Soldier* on Shaw's play.

ARMSTRONG, ärm'strông, **Edwin Howard** (1890–1954), American pioneer in radio technology who invented the frequency modulation (FM) technique for radio communications. Armstrong was born in New York City on Dec. 18, 1890. As a youngster, he became interested in the new field of radio, and he successfully constructed his own radio station when he was 17. He entered Columbia University in 1909 and after receiving his degree in electrical engineering in 1913, he became an assistant to Professor Michael I. Pupin. In 1934, Armstrong became a professor of electrical engineering at Columbia. He died in New York City on Feb. 1, 1954.

After developing the regenerative (feedback) circuit in 1912, he investigated U.S. Army signaling methods during World War I. In 1919 he became enmeshed in a 12-year-long litigation with Lee De Forest (q.v.) in a suit involving the invention of the feedback circuit. After Armstrong lost the case, he made a grant of $50,000 to Columbia for a study of how courts decide complex technical cases.

Armstrong invented the superheterodyne circuit in 1918; this circuit is a basic component of nearly all modern radio receivers. After 1925, he worked on FM for many years, receiving a patent in 1933 and perfecting FM in 1939. In radio broadcasting, FM provides high-fidelity reception, reduced noise, and reduced interference. In 1953, Armstrong invented a system by which more than one FM program can be broadcast simultaneously on the same frequency.

Armstrong was awarded the Medal of Merit in 1947 for his contributions to military communications in World War II.

Further Reading: Lessing, Lawrence, *Man of High Fidelity: Edwin Howard Armstrong* (Philadelphia 1956).

ARMSTRONG, ärm'strông **George Buchanan** (1822–1871), American post office official who reorganized the railway mail service. He was appointed to the Post Office Department in Washington, D.C., about 1852 because of his mother's distant kinship to James Buchanan, then an important political figure and later (1857–1861) president of the United States. In 1858, Armstrong was named assistant postmaster at Chicago, and in 1864 he presented his plan for the reorganization of the railway mail service. His principal suggestion was that mail be sorted on trains instead of at distributing offices. While the idea was not entirely new, Armstrong was the first to demonstrate its feasibility. In 1869 he was appointed general superintendent of the newly established Bureau of Railway Mail Service.

Armstrong was born on Oct. 27, 1822, in County Armagh, Ireland, and emigrated to the United States with his family in 1830. They lived in Newark, N.J., and later in Virginia and Maryland. He died in Chicago on May 5, 1871.

ARMSTRONG, ärm'strông, **Henry** (1912–   ), American boxer, who in 1938 became the only fighter to hold three world championships simultaneously. Born *Henry Jackson* in Columbus, Miss., on Dec. 12, 1912, he fought first in amateur bouts under the name of *Melody Jackson*. He took the name Armstrong from his friend and adviser, Harry Armstrong. He turned pro in 1931.

In his first title fight, Armstrong stopped Petey Sarron in the sixth round for the featherweight (126 pounds) title on Oct. 29, 1937. He added the welterweight (147 pounds) championship by outpointing Barney Ross on May 31, 1938. Ten weeks later, on August 17, he defeated Lou Ambers, lightweight (135 pounds) titleholder, in 15 rounds for his third championship.

Armstrong relinquished the featherweight title in December 1938 and lost the lightweight crown back to Ambers on Aug. 22, 1939. He defended the welterweight title a record 20 times before losing to Fritzie Zivic on Oct. 4, 1940. Nicknamed "Perpetual Motion" for his swarming, aggressive style, he won 144 of 175 fights and had a 46-bout winning streak, including 27 in succession by knockouts. After retiring from the ring in 1945, he was ordained a Baptist minister in Los Angeles in 1951. In 1954 he was elected one of the first members of boxing's Hall of Fame.

BILL BRADDOCK
New York "Times"

ARMSTRONG, John (1758–1843), American army officer, diplomat, and public official. He was born in Carlisle, Pa., on Nov. 25, 1758. A student at the College of New Jersey (Princeton) when the American Revolution began, he served throughout the war, attaining the rank of major as aide to Gen. Horatio Gates. In camp at Newburgh, N. Y. (1783), he wrote the anonymous "Newburgh Addresses" or "Newburgh Letters" calling on Congress to pay arrears to soldiers before the army disbanded. George Washington was critical of these somewhat threatening letters until he learned the identity of the author.

Armstrong was elected to the Continental Congress in 1787 and married into the influential Livingston family of New York. He engaged in farming in Dutchess county, N. Y., until he was elected to the U. S. Senate in 1800. He served as American minister to France from 1804 to 1810, but his mission was not notably successful.

With the outbreak of the War of 1812, Armstrong was commissioned brigadier general and entrusted with the defense of New York City. The following year he became secretary of war. He was widely blamed for the failure of the Canada expeditions and for the British capture of the city of Washington. He retired in 1814 and died at Red Hook, N. Y., on April 1, 1843.

ARMSTRONG, ärm′strông, Louis Daniel (1900–1971), American jazz trumpeter, singer, and ensemble leader who became a major force in shaping jazz during the 1920's. An improviser who set new standards of melodic development and rhythmic flexibility, "Satchmo," as he was popularly known, was an exceptionally important jazz solo virtuoso on the trumpet. Before him, the collective identity of the ensemble had always been primary in jazz music, but Armstrong, more than anybody else, helped the soloist become preeminent.

Born into a poor family in New Orleans, La., on July 4, 1900, Armstrong was a street singer as a child. During his early teens he received his first instruction in music on the bugle and the cornet while in the Waif's Home in New Orleans. After an apprenticeship as a trumpeter in New Orleans cabarets and on Mississippi riverboats, Armstrong was called to Chicago in 1922 to play second cornet in the orchestra of Joe "King" Oliver, a well-known New Orleans-trained musician. He later was a featured soloist in the orchestras of Fletcher Henderson and Erskine Tate and by the end of the 1920's had become leader of his own group—the Louis Armstrong Hot Five, later the Louis Armstrong Hot Seven. During these years he recorded a series of performances that influenced jazz musicians throughout the world.

In the following decades, Armstrong led large bands and small ensembles and recorded regularly. Beginning in 1932 with a triumphant appearance in England, he traveled frequently throughout the world as the foremost "goodwill ambassador" of American jazz music abroad. He died in New York City on July 6, 1971.

Although Armstrong led groups of uneven quality, his own playing and singing were marked by an unusual consistency of achievement. The basic elements in his playing were a persistent use of blues coloration; disciplined power and technical mastery; a burnished clarity of tone; and a rhythmic resiliency rooted in a strongly pulsating sense of swing. His vocal work exemplifies the instrumentalized phrasing and textural resourcefulness that is essential to excellent jazz singing.

Armstrong did not adopt the more complex rhythmic and harmonic elements of the "modern jazz" that began in the early 1940's. Instead, he continued to perfect the classic, easily assimilated melodic improvising that he had developed during his early years. An expert in the more introspective nuances of the blues, he was essentially a lyrical player. His performances fused warmth, humor, and sheer joy in the act of creation—an artistry filled with exultant and sweepingly personal eloquence. See also JAZZ.

NAT HENTOFF, *Coeditor of "The Jazz Makers"*

Further Reading: Hentoff, Nat, and Shapiro, Nat, eds., *Hear Me Talkin' to Ya* (New York 1955); id., *The Jazz Makers* (New York 1957).

ARMSTRONG, Neil Alden (1930–   ), American astronaut, who was the first man to set foot on the moon. Born in Wapakoneta, Ohio, on Aug. 5, 1930, he became interested in aviation as a child and obtained a pilot's license at the age of 16. After entering Purdue University he left to become a Navy pilot and flew combat missions in the Korean War. Returning to Purdue, he took a degree in aeronautics in 1955 and then worked for the National Aeronautics and Space Administration as a research pilot until he was selected to become an astronaut in 1962.

Armstrong's first venture into space, in 1966, nearly ended in disaster when his two-man Gemini 7 spacecraft went out of control, but he brought the craft down safely in an emergency landing. In 1969 he was named commander of the first lunar landing mission, Apollo 11; the other astronauts on the flight were Edwin E. Aldrin, Jr., and Michael Collins. Armstrong and Aldrin set down on the moon in the lunar module of their craft on July 20, 1969. Armstrong's first words as he stepped out on the surface were, "That's one small step for a man, one giant leap for mankind." The astronauts brought back samples of rocks obtained from the moon. See also ASTRONAUTS; SPACE EXPLORATION.

ARMSTRONG, ärm′strông, Samuel Chapman (1839–1893), American educator who founded the Hampton Normal and Agricultural Institute (now Hampton Institute). He was born on Jan. 30, 1839, at Wailuku, on Maui Island, Hawaii. Both his parents were missionaries, and Armstrong derived much of his inspiration from them. He studied first at Oahu College, Honolulu. After his father's death in 1860, he moved to the United States and attended Williams College in Massachusetts.

The Civil War broke out while Armstrong was still a student. He entered the Union Army and became colonel of a Negro regiment. In 1866 he accepted a position with the Freedmen's Bureau that gave him full charge of a camp of emancipated Negroes near Hampton, Va. This experience, added to his observations during the war, led him to seek the establishment of a teacher training school for Negroes. Enthusiasm for his plans brought aid from the American Missionary Association and from friends in the North. In 1868, Hampton Normal and Agricultural Institute was founded with Armstrong as its first director. Armstrong died at Hampton, Va., on May 11, 1893. See also HAMPTON INSTITUTE.

ARMY, är'mē, in the usual military sense, is a term with two meanings: (1) the military organization of a nation for land warfare, and (2) the largest administrative and tactical unit of a land force, made up in modern times of a number of corps and divisions (sometimes called a *field army*). The first meaning may be applied to periods as early as 2500 B.C., when the Egyptians formally banded together the militia of their various provinces to repel incursions by barbarian tribes. The second meaning began to come into general use during the 19th century because of the marked increase in the size of national armies. Even in earlier times, when a nation conducted warfare on more than one front some subdivision of the national army usually was made. During the Second Punic War (218–201 B.C.), for example, the Roman Army was subdivided into three consular armies, each composed normally of 18,000 men—two Roman legions plus equal contingents from the Italian allies.

Early Middle Eastern and Indian Armies. Enough evidence exists to indicate that the Egyptians, Assyrians, Israelites, Aryans of India, and Persians developed formal armies with complex organization, specialized equipment, and a surprising appreciation of such matters as outposts, reconnaissance, staff work, and logistical support. Both the Egyptians and the Assyrians employed charioteers, heavy infantry in close formation, and lightly armed archers, slingers, and skirmishers. Cavalry, armed variously with the bow and the javelin, was the principal arm of the Persians. Both the Egyptians and the Aryans obtained their warriors through a caste system, while in Assyria (about 1500 B.C.) the army took on a more democratic complexion. The Persians, under whom the army system of the Middle East attained its highest point of development in the 6th century B.C., resorted to local levies or conscription in the event of a major war. Both the Assyrians and the Persians controlled their conquests with standing armies assigned to each province and organized according to arms, with separate contingents of spearmen, archers, and horsemen.

Greece. Unlike the Persians, the Greek city-states based their military system on universal service and on infantry instead of cavalry. Military service carried with it the responsibility to provide one's own equipment. Thus the nobility, who could afford mounts, made up the cavalry; the middle class formed the heavy infantry, ex-

emplified by the *hoplite,* or armored pikeman; and the poorer citizens composed the light infantry. In Sparta, though, the citizens had no choice of assignment. The age for military service was 20 to 40 in Athens, and 20 to 60 in Sparta. In later years, after long periods of external and internal fighting had sapped the enthusiasm of the citizen soldiers, mercenaries came to make up much of the strength of all the city-state armies.

Command in the Athenian Army was exercised by a board of ten elected generals, each of whom theoretically was supposed to take his turn at one-day overall command. Usually, however, either nine of the generals were left at home or the duties of commander in chief were assumed by a chief magistrate called the polemarch. The Spartans had less of a command problem although they had two kings: either each headed his separate army, or one of the two commanded by mutual consent.

The size of the Greek armies was held down by the inability of the city-states to confederate and by the reluctance of the citizen soldier to be away from home for extended periods. At Marathon (490 B.C.), for example, the Athenians numbered, according to Herodotus, only 10,000, while the invading Persians used 40,000 to 60,000 men. Much of the Greek power lay in the phalanx, a closely knit formation of armored pikemen that varied in depth and width in accord with the need to produce a shock effect or to outflank or avoid being outflanked.

Macedon. Alexander the Great's armies of conquest (4th century B.C.) were based on groundwork laid by his father, Philip II of Macedon. Since Philip's kingdom was not wealthy, the small class of nobles made up the bulk of the army, thus virtually compelling dependence on cavalry. Fleshing out this force with Greek mercenaries, Philip maintained the strong Greek phalanx in the center while correcting the weaknesses of the Greek flanks with his cavalry. Alexander, in turn, introduced a new class of infantry somewhere between the heavy and the light to connect the phalanx and the cavalry, as well as a distinctly new form of cavalry—the lancers—used primarily for reconnaissance and pursuit. For siege warfare he developed many varieties of engineering works and heavy siege artillery.

Under Alexander the true subdivision of the army became the grand phalanx of about 4,000 men, supplemented by cavalry, lancers, medium-

GREEK PHALANX was a tightly massed formation of *hoplites*—heavily armed infantry—who in attack protected themselves with overlapping shields. Bristling with spears, the phalanx was formidable but not very maneuverable.

light infantry, and auxiliary troops. Each phalanx was known by the name of its commander and was subdivided into four *chiliarchiae*, which in turn were subdivided into four 256-men *syntagmae*, the basic maneuvering force within the phalanx. The army was small, usually consisting of only 30,000 to 40,000 men. To a degree hard to comprehend today, Alexander was his own staff, his own strategic and tactical planner, his own logistician, and, finally, his own battle leader at the actual head of his column.

Rome. The phalanx met its peer in a new formation when Rome emerged as a military power and developed the legion. But the legion first had to stand the hard test of Carthage's attempt to dominate the western Mediterranean.

Carthaginian power reached its peak under Hannibal in the late 3d century B.C., but even the genius of a Hannibal could not fully overcome the obstacles posed by unenthusiastic support from the merchant class at home and by problems of discipline in an army of mercenaries hired only for short periods. The army, modeled on the Greek, relied on shock tactics exerted by the center, which was supported by strong cavalry on the flanks. At Cannae (216 B.C.), where Hannibal employed his cavalry to take the Romans in both flanks after enticing them with a weakened center, the army numbered about 40,000 infantry and 10,000 cavalry.

Backed by the solid institutions of Roman republicanism, the Roman legion was capable of withstanding the vicissitudes of both the Pyrrhic and the Punic wars, while its full effectiveness gradually evolved under a succession of capable leaders like Publius Cornelius Scipio Africanus. In the early Roman Army, citizens alone were permitted to bear arms. As in Athens, the citizen furnished his own equipment; also like the Athenian, the Roman was no natural horseman. Not until the Carthaginians had all too clearly demonstrated the cavalry lesson did horsemen emerge as a genuinely effective part of the legion.

Originally created as an administrative unit, the legion grew into the basic battle organization. It was tested directly against the phalanx at Pydna in 168 B.C., and was found superior, primarily because of maneuverability. The true genius of the legion organization lay in the ability of the tactical formations, maniples of 120 men each, to maneuver. Within the basic three-line formation of the legion each line contained 10 maniples, from front to rear made up of *hastati*, young men of some battle experience; *principes*, or seasoned veterans; and *triarii*, older men supplemented by light infantry of *velites*, or youthful novices. The cavalry similarly was formed into *turmae* of 30 horsemen. A turma of cavalry plus 3 maniples of heavy infantry and 1 maniple of 120 velites formed a cohort; 10 cohorts made a legion of approximately 5,100 men and 300 horses.

Like the Greeks, the Romans distrusted one-man command and instead rotated command among elected consuls. Not until about the 2d century B.C. did the system of personal command become established. Within the legions the field officers were the elected or appointed tribunes, six in number. The company officers, two to each maniple, were centurions of long service who rose from the ranks. No grade corresponded to the noncommissioned officer of modern armies.

By the end of the 2d century B.C., the army

CULVER PICTURES

MEDIEVAL CASTLES were built to foil attack, but an army could take a castle by storm or after a siege.

had become fully professional. It consisted, primarily, of the poorer citizens, both Roman and Italian, plus barbarians from the far reaches of the empire. In keeping with the change in personnel, a new organization gradually evolved, much of it the product of Gaius Marius, who constantly searched for greater maneuverability. Three maniples—one each of hastati, principes, and triarii—constituted a more or less self-contained cohort; then gradually the distinctions between hastati, principes, and triarii disappeared. Yet the basic legion organization continued into the years when the empire survived under the name of Byzantium and until the final dissolution in the 15th century A.D. Though intense patriotism no longer motivated the troops, leaders like Gaius Julius Caesar, Pompey the Great, and Augustus could command deep personal allegiance. For all the hodgepodge filling its ranks, the Roman Army probably reached the peak of its effectiveness under Caesar.

The Middle Ages. The barbarian tribes on the outer reaches of the Roman Empire created new circumstances in the history of armies that in many respects reached back 2,000 years, when armed hordes or migrating nations rather than formal armies held the stage of war. Among the tribes, the Germanic Franks adopted the Roman system as a legacy in defending the West against the fierce Muslims, even as the survivors of the true Roman system were holding out against the same enemy in Constantinople. For 200 years, during the 7th and 8th centuries A.D., the Muslims were the scourge of the Mediterranean until, in 732, a band of Saracens was defeated at Tours by a loosely knit Frankish force under Charles Martel.

There followed the piratelike raids of the Vikings and the banditlike incursions of the Magyars. Out of the problems of dealing with these invaders emerged a system of military service which was an integral part of feudalism. Basically local in character, the system involved hundreds of individual "armies," made up of vassals owing allegiance to a particular lord or landholder. On occasion, as in the 9th century under Charlemagne, contingents from the feudal estates might be combined into a genuine army but the accepted term of service of 40 days and the loyalty of the vassal to his immediate lord instead of to the king restricted the army's effectiveness. On other occasions considerable numbers of volunteers might be banded together with the promise of conquest and the spoils of war, as in the 11th century when William the Conqueror with 50,000 men invaded England.

Out of the feudal system emerged the individual knight, a kind of professional soldier, heavily armored and usually mounted. In the service of particular lords rather than of nations, the knight was a leader among the loosely organized volunteers who from the 11th through the 13th century conducted the seven campaigns or crusades to bring the Holy Land into the Christian world.

It was a military system based in the main on the knight and the feudal fortification—the castle—which had to withstand another barbarian invasion in the 13th century, when the Mongols pushed into Europe. The Mongols had a well-disciplined, highly organized army, capable of extended operations. They clearly were superior to the haphazard units of the West, which had forgotten so much of what Rome had known. It was difficulty at home which eventually turned back the Mongols, not military defeat.

The remainder of the Middle Ages, from about 1300 to the mid–16th century, a period when national coherence began more and more to emerge among the heterogeneous heirs of the Roman legacy, was marked by three major developments influencing the character of armies: (1) new weapons, (2) the decline of cavalry, and (3) a new kind of mercenary.

The first of the new weapons was the longbow, dramatically unleashed by Edward III at Crécy (1346). Far more effective than the first firearms, the cannon that Edward also introduced at Crécy, the longbow did not of itself bring about decline of cavalry, but its success against the French horsemen at Crécy made a definite contribution. It can be said that cavalry already was on the decline. As early as 1302, at Courtrai, infantry militia from the cities of Flanders had soundly defeated a superior force of French cavalry, the finest in Christendom. In the 1,000 years of cavalry preeminence, the cavalryman gradually had become obsessed with his superiority to the point of folly. At the same time, he had so burdened himself and his mount with armor that maneuver was almost impossible.

It took the ancient weapon of the pike in the hands of the Swiss to punctuate what Courtrai and Crécy had foreshadowed. Unable to afford horses and armor, the Swiss fell back on discipline and the solid mass formation of a new phalanx. While other nations copied the Swiss, the Spanish introduced a new version of the phalanx in the square, 2,500 men in 50 ranks and 50 files. They supplemented the Swiss pike with sword and musket (the harquebus), the latter being employed at the corners of the square so that the harquebusier might retire to the rear to perform the laborious task of reloading.

As the medieval period neared an end, armies became more professional than ever before. The Swiss, in particular, were in demand as mercenaries, but aside from the employment of individual mercenaries a new type of soldier for hire emerged. These were men who banded together as free companies—known variously as *condottieri* or lansquenets—and hired themselves out

as self-contained fighting units. Though these units introduced a measure of experience and discipline to warfare, the professionals in time displayed an aversion to bloodshed and a preference more for theatrics than for conclusive fighting.

Armies for the most part were relatively small. The Flemish at Courtrai had only 20,000 men; Edward III at Crécy, only about 25,000; Edward the Black Prince at Poitiers (1356), less than half that many; and Henry V at Agincourt (1415), only 15,000.

The Genesis of Modern Armies. The Thirty Years' War (1618–1648) marked the beginning of armies in the modern sense. As the war approached, a number of developments which were to be adapted and refined during the fighting already had appeared. The company, for example, 400 to 500 men strong and basically an administrative unit, had come to be grouped into tactical bodies of variable size, called Haufen, battles, battalions, and, in Germany, regiments, though the latter was a general term for any large command. These groupings were strictly tactical and varied from one fight to another. Men armed with a particular weapon—the cumbersome hand firearms, the pike, or the halberd, a kind of short pike with some aspects of the sword—were grouped administratively in separate units but on the battlefield had to be intermingled so that one weapon might complement the others. The Spanish, on the other hand, had adopted the tercio, in strength anywhere from 1,000 to 3,000 men, the first of the permanent tactical bodies large enough for independent use.

Though overall command of an army usually was retained by the king, actual command in the field might be entrusted to a deputy, variously called a constable, captain general, or marshal. Companies were led by captains, assisted by lieutenants, ensigns, and sergeants. A group of companies was commanded by a colonel, who also was one of the company commanders. Each arm had a chief responsible for training and equipment. Armies again were relatively small. In 1567, for example, Fernando Álvarez de Toledo, 3d duke of Alba, took 11,000 men into the Netherlands, and at Nieuwpoort (1600), Maurice of Nassau had 12,000 infantry and 1,600 cavalry.

In the Thirty Years' War the most far-reaching reforms were exhibited by Gustavus Adolphus, who has been called the father of modern war. Gustavus adopted universal military service while at the same time employing highly trained mercenaries. He studied weapons assiduously, lightening the musket and standardizing and increasing the numbers and mobility of artillery. He also fitted weapons to organization. In his small company of fewer than 150 men, he employed more muskets than pikes. A regiment consisted of 6 to 12 companies. Of the battle formation of both infantry and cavalry he made a permanent organization called a brigade, consisting of one to four regiments.

Gustavus integrated the action of artillery, cavalry, and infantry for maximum effect. The artillery was posted in front. Cavalry was trained not in the usual practice of firing by rank and then dropping back to reload, but in a novel procedure of charging the enemy and firing at the last moment before contact. Infantry fire was by rank, the front rank usually dropping back to reload, although on occasion two or three

NAPOLEON decisively defeated the Russians at Friedland in 1807 by his brilliant use of artillery. French cannon smashed the Russian infantry and cavalry at close range and cannonaded the bridges over the Alle River to cut off the Russians' escape.

ranks might fire together with the front rank kneeling. Gustavus developed the procedure of deploying his troops into two lines with a third in reserve in what was practiced widely in the 18th century as linear tactics.

The French added to the Swedish system a new type of troops known as dragoons, who rode to battle like cavalry but were trained to fight on foot. The French staff system took on distinctly modern aspects to include a second in command, a chief of staff, a *maréchal de bataille* who planned battle formations, and a *maréchal général des logis* who handled movements, supply, and transport. As tactical units became permanent, positions in the order of battle were assigned, according to the seniority of regiments. Cardinal Richelieu established a separate ministry of war. During the reign of Louis XIV, artillery was established as a distinct arm, and an engineer corps was created. Each arm had an inspector general.

In the War of the Spanish Succession (1701–1714) firepower superseded shock action as the decisive battle element, thus elevating linear tactics to the fore. The line became all important and had to be maintained at all costs. Battalions of 500 to 800 men became integral parts of the regiment. Artillery took position on the wings to the front of the infantry line. Armies still were small—John Churchill, 1st duke of Marlborough, and Eugene, prince of Savoy, together at Blenheim (1704) had 50,000 men—but the total number of men mobilized was beginning to foreshadow the conscript armies of the late 18th and 19th centuries.

Out of the Seven Years' War (1756–1763) emerged a new military genius, Frederick the Great, who accomplished impressive results not so much through revolutionary changes as through ingenuity in applying the linear tactics of the day and through discipline. His only basic innovation was the principle of fire and movement. Instead of halting to fire, his infantry fired while continuing to advance. Through incessant drill he taught his recruits to attain a much higher rate of fire than was common in other armies. Infantry began to deploy from march formation about 1,000 yards from the enemy and delivered the first volleys when within 100 yards. Deeming power less important than mobility, Frederick introduced horse artillery in which the cannoneers were individually mounted. He also attached light guns to the infantry battalions. Though Frederick's army numbered 150,000,

some of his more renowned engagements were fought with only a portion of this force. At Rossbach and Leuthen (both in 1757), he used 20,000 and 30,000 men, respectively.

In the meantime, British, French, and Spanish armies had been gaining experience of a new kind in colonial expeditions. While some military leaders were copying Frederick, others were advocating on the basis of experience in America more flexibility in the formal lines. Not for a long time would linear tactics disappear entirely, but light companies capable of a skirmish line approach soon became a part of every major army, including Frederick's.

The French Revolution and Napoleon. The American Revolution, when patriotism again became the motivating factor in armies, was a small-scale indication of what was to come. But it was in the French Revolution and the wars it fostered that the true national army with hundreds of thousands under arms came into being. As in the American war, units deployed in open formations, as much because firm discipline could not be instilled overnight in the masses as for any other reason. In 1793, when the French decreed universal conscription, armies had come full cycle from the days of the Persian hordes.

By the time Napoleon first came into prominence (1795), many changes in the army already had been instituted or begun. Divisional and corps organization, for example, involving permanent combinations of arms, had been advocated by the theorist Comte Jacques Antoine Hippolyte de Guibert, and to some extent had been practiced by George Washington in America. A permanent staff system complete with staff schools had been established in both France and Prussia. Though most weapons were about the same as those of Frederick's day, the Frenchman Jean Baptiste Vaquette de Gribeauval had made major changes in caliber, standardization, and mobility of artillery. Napoleon's predecessor, Lazare Carnot, developed the procedure of shifting battalion columns rapidly to reinforce success or to strike the enemy in unexpected places. Under Carnot the practice of firing from cover or concealment until the enemy was weakened, then charging forward en masse, already had become a feature of French tactics.

It remained for a Napoleon to assimilate and perfect all the developments and to fashion them to the peculiar nature of his manpower material. In his divisions he brought together all three major arms into a coordinated force and then

WIDE WORLD PHOTOS

ENTRENCHMENT caused long World War I stalemates. Germans await Russian attack by Vistula River in 1916.

combined them into corps of varying size and organization. Artillery closely supported the infantry in shock attacks, bringing the weight of fire and manpower together at a predetermined weak point. Flank attacks, envelopments, and counterattacks by mobile reserves were common. It was no iron-disciplined army, as indicated by some of the exhibitions of looting in various campaigns, but on the battlefield the troops usually found the incentive they needed in the very person of Napoleon.

Napoleon at his height of power normally took the field with about 150,000 men under his personal command, as at Jena (1806), yet on occasion his army compared to those of the early and mid-18th century, as at Austerlitz in 1805, when the French numbered 68,000.

An indirect outgrowth of the Napoleonic Wars was the concept of an army reserve. Limited after Jena to an army of 42,000 men, the Prussians continuously rotated recruits and soldiers so that a large army of trained civilians who might be called back into service was created. The practice of a trained civilian reserve soon became common and continues today.

American Civil War. The fighting in the United States in the 1860's provided the first demonstration of the impact of the Industrial Revolution on armies. The railroad, steam engine, telegraph—these and other technological developments created a need for sizable increases in the number of technical troops within the army. In the Department of War there were separate ordnance, medical, quartermaster, and other bureaus. In addition, the range and accuracy of infantry firearms were markedly increased, and rifling became accepted for both small arms and artillery.

The American war also showed more definitely than had the wars of Napoleon the tremendous impact of conscription on the character of armies. The Confederates had a peak strength of 900,000 men; the Federals, beginning with a professional force of only 17,000, eventually had 1,000,000. The theater of war embraced a stage

larger than all Europe, so that in effect there were several theaters of operations. Bodies of men the size of a normal European army sometimes had to be moved swiftly for literally hundreds of miles from one theater to another. In keeping with the vast stage and the unprecedented numbers of troops, each side kept in the field not one but several "armies." Thus Robert E. Lee had his Army of Northern Virginia, while others like the Army of Tennessee operated in the west; the Federals had their armies of the Potomac, the Cumberland, the Ohio, and the Tennessee. All the "armies" varied greatly in size and organization but usually consisted of two or more corps. On occasion several armies might be grouped under one commander in order to achieve unity of command.

The basic tactical organization was the regiment of 1,000 men. Two or more infantry regiments made a brigade; two to five brigades, a division, to which several regiments of artillery, a wagon train, and some engineers were attached. Cavalry was organized usually into separate divisions and sometimes into separate corps.

The Civil War demonstrated what changes were bound to follow wholesale adoption of arms of precision: looser fighting formations, advance by rushes, dismounted fighting by cavalry armed with firearms, increased use of the spade for both hasty and deliberate entrenchment, and diminished use of the sword and bayonet. The war also showed how complex armies soon would be. Yet many of the lessons were lost on European observers, with the possible exception of that of entrenchments, until the Franco-Prussian War of 1870–1871 had pointed them up.

World War I. By 1914 technological developments in fields both directly and indirectly connected with warfare were tremendous—the machine gun, airplane, motorcar, recoil mechanism for artillery, trench mortar, wireless. In planning their armies, the Continental powers made the mistake of assuming the new weapons would favor the offensive. A combination of the new weapons and massed manpower, they deduced, should prove overpowering.

A system of universal military service, which had gradually replaced conscription in Europe, provided adequate manpower for the equation. A new class of recruits became available annually for a year or more of training. At the same time, all the major powers with the exception of Britain and the United States maintained large standing armies of 500,000 to 1,000,000 men. In a matter of months the reserves could be mobilized around the professional army. The French could put 4,000,000 trained men in the field; the Germans, 5,000,000; the Russians, 6,000,000.

Organization took the form of divisions, corps, and "armies," the latter now a formal tactical and administrative subdivision of the national army in which two or more corps were grouped along with sufficient technical units to handle communications, supply, and other services. The Germans, for example, had eight armies, each known by a numerical name, such as the First Army and the Sixth Army. Like the divisions and corps, the armies possessed a general staff of four or five sections: administration, intelligence, operations, supply, and training, the last-named sometimes grouped with operations. At the start of World War I only the Americans had no organization larger than the regiment, the

British no organization larger than the division. In the field, armies of each nationality were controlled by an overall national commander. In later stages of the war the Allies attempted to achieve unity of command by subordinating the national armies first to a Supreme War Council of political leaders and later to a single military leader, the Frenchman Marshal Ferdinand Foch.

The three basic arms—infantry, cavalry, and artillery—still did most of the fighting, but so complex were the technological developments that a new corps of service troops, rivaling and even exceeding the numerical strength of the front-line units, made its appearance. Only in nations of lesser industrial resources, like Austria and Russia, was this tendency not present to a similar degree. These nations also depended more than did the others on cavalry, though of the major combatants only the Americans failed to put cavalry in the field.

The basic unit of infantry organization was the battalion of about 1,000 men divided into four to eight companies. A company included three or four platoons, each under the command of a lieutenant or an officer of similar rank. Some companies, such as machine-gun companies, were specialized. Three or four battalions, depending on whether the army employed a square or a triangular organization, made a regiment; three or four regiments, a division. Among European powers the division numbered 12,000 to 18,000 men, but United States divisions numbered 28,000. Cavalry was organized into squadrons of about 150 men, with three to six squadrons to a regiment. Artillery was grouped into batteries of four to eight guns; three to four batteries made a group (in some cases, a battalion), and two or three groups made a regiment. Some artillery was organic to a division, while other regiments were controlled by corps and army headquarters. Technical developments made it possible for artillery to fire indirectly, with high trajectory from a great distance, so that the pieces were seldom employed on the actual front line. Aircraft pilots were organized into squadrons, though their numbers were few, and the basic role of aircraft was that of reconnaissance.

Brought up on the theories of Karl von Clausewitz, the Continental armies placed their faith in mass. Massed artillery was to puncture the enemy line, whereupon masses of men moving in irregular but dense waves were to push through and pave the way for cavalry to exploit. But it soon became evident that the new weapons favored the defensive. Trench warfare came to the western front to stay, despite incessant attempts to break the stalemate by new tactics, like those of Oskar von Hutier; by new weapons, like the tank and poison gas; and by the increased use of automatic weapons. Artillery sometimes fired for hours and even days to weaken the enemy before an assault. In the face of the explosive weight of the new weapons the battlefield became a dreadful place of deadly and deafening noise and confusion. Casualty figures were appalling. Mental breakdowns were common. Though warfare along the eastern borders of Germany never settled down to the same kind of stalemate, the dependence on mass and the deadliness of the new weapons produced the same kind of losses. No genuine solution had been found when the war ended, so that the armies maintained their basic character of mass until the end. The big question of how to penetrate the solid defensive lines and move into the mobile warfare that everybody sought would remain for another generation to answer.

World War II. When the Germans invaded Poland in September 1939, they revealed the answer to the big question in effective coordination of two of the old arms—infantry and artillery—plus the substitution of massed tanks for the old cavalry and the addition of a new air arm. At the same time, they started a war that was to become as nearly total as the world has ever known and so technical as to challenge the imagination.

The basic army organizations of World War I remained: the battalions, regiments, divisions, corps, and armies, based in the main on the triangular as opposed to the square concept. The division numbered from 8,000 to 16,000 men. On the other hand, the technological developments wrought staggering changes in the character of armies and the nature of warfare. Perhaps the most obvious were increased firepower, despite a general reduction in numerical strength of individual units, and mechanization, which was based primarily on the internal combustion engine and the tank. The Germans were the first to use the panzer or armored division, both to deal a terrific shock blow and to exploit after infantry and artillery had achieved a penetration. The armored division usually contained about 200 tanks supported by infantry mounted in armored personnel carriers and by highly mobile artillery, sometimes self-propelled. Usually an armored division was incorporated into the existing corps framework with two infantry divisions, but some nations empoyed them in separate armored corps, and the USSR in separate mechanized armies. Separate tank battalions or brigades sometimes were attached to infantry divisions to give them some of the character of the armored division. Only the USSR retained any increments of horse cavalry.

The new air arm—both tactical and strategic in concept—usually formed a separate part of a nation's armed forces, with the notable exception of the United States. Yet in every case it was closely coordinated with the ground army. Indeed, no army could claim independence from

FORTIFIED BORDERS proved useless in World War II. U.S. armored forces cross Siegfried Line into Germany.

a nation's other armed services. In the Pacific, particularly, land warfare was closely interwoven with naval operations. The army itself became a thoroughly complex organization including in addition to the combat arms a variety of other units: engineer, quartermaster, ordnance, communications, chemical, transportation, military government. Each of these embraced a bewildering variety of specialized units like port battalions, railroad construction and operating units, heavy pontoon battalions, engineer amphibious brigades, truck companies, laundry companies, smoke generator companies, ordnance maintenance battalions, station and field hospitals, and graves registration units. In the United States Army, for example, only about 30 percent of the army's air and ground strength was in combatant units.

The infantry division contained a host of specialists in ordnance, medicine, transportation, and the like. Even the regimental combat teams (called *Kampfgruppen* by the Germans), which integrated the action of infantry, artillery, and tanks, and the battalion landing teams, used extensively in the Pacific, required specialists in communications, weapons, vehicular maintenance, and other fields. The multiplication of specialists increased the need for big and multicellular headquarters staffs. An Alexander or a Hannibal trying to act as his own staff might have foundered in the complexities.

Specialists were not confined to the supporting roles. Some units were specially trained for amphibious operations, others for parachute and airborne operations. British and Americans in Europe combined their airborne units into an Allied airborne army which had a potential strength of some eight divisions. Within the German Army existed an elite corps especially loyal to Nazi ideology, the *Waffen–SS*.

Armies numbered in the millions of men, a product both of the professional and reserve training before the war and of conscription. That of the USSR was biggest, some 12,000,000 men. The United States Army at peak strength exceeded 8,000,000. Engineer troops alone in most armies far exceeded the total strength Napoleon ever put in the field at one time. Though much of this strength was directed into technical channels, the armies in the field still were so large that a new type of tactical headquarters was created to control them. In the Allied and German armies it was called an army group. The Soviets called it an army front and gave it a definite geographical as opposed to a tactical connotation. An army group or front might control two to five armies and include considerably more than 2,000,000 men. The interrelation of army with air and naval forces gave rise to joint headquarters which included representatives from all three services. In each of the several theaters of operations the Allies created supreme headquarters which were both joint and allied. Women were incorporated into almost all armies, mainly as nurses or in administrative assignments.

Not all warfare was mobile in the new, grand sense of the word. Much of it still was plodding infantry fighting, yet the fighting formations were consistently open. In a small sector of Lorraine during the fall of 1944, for example, Americans and Germans together deployed about 10,000 men on the same terrain where French and Prussians in 1870 had disposed more than 330,000. Battles in the old sense were seldom decided in a matter of hours or even days but in weeks and even months, but once a penetration was achieved, the mobile columns might register gains of hundreds of miles in a few days. In some cases only the ability of the logistical echelons to provide the forward units with supplies restricted the extent of the advance.

Post World War II Armies. Research and development, so much a part of World War II within both the armies and the industries of the combatants, reached a zenith in the explosion of the atomic bomb and, later, of the hydrogen bomb. Despite the example of conventional warfare in Korea in 1950–1953, most major armies experimented through the 1950's with organizations geared to anticipated aspects of nuclear warfare. The tendency was toward smaller and more mobile units to counteract the effect of nuclear weapons against targets of mass. Considerable attention was given to movement by air of both men and matériel by means of helicopters and swift transport aircraft, including planes capable of short or vertical take-off and landing.

The U.S. Army during this period tested a pentagonal concept for its combat forces. Called the *pentomic division* and intended to provide battlefield flexibility, it consisted of a fixed base in the form of a division headquarters and supporting services, including artillery and armor, and five "battle groups." The number of battalions in each battle group was intended to vary according to the assigned tactical mission.

Other armies, particularly those of Britain and West Germany, were conducting similar experiments. Keeping the division as the fixed base in the same manner as did the Americans, the British organized brigade groups composed of the various arms and services that could be attached to the division base in numbers appropriate to varying missions. The Germans adopted a "building block" concept of separate infantry and armored brigades which could be attached to the division base to create various types of divisions—infantry, mechanized, or armored.

It was this latter system that the U.S. Army

AMPHIBIOUS ASSAULT on northern France typified massive Allied coastal invasions during World War II.

U.S. ARMY

had emulated in effect by the mid-1960's by a change from the pentomic division to the *reorganization objective army division* (ROAD). This new concept was based on the possibility that nuclear stalemate might preclude nuclear warfare, giving way to a pattern of guerrilla and conventional wars in various parts of the world. Under this concept, there would be four types of divisions (infantry, airborne, mechanized, and armored), each with a common division base. By combining a mixture of 10 or 11 infantry, armored, or airborne battalions in three brigades, the complexion of any division might be tailored to fit the locale and nature of the battle while at the same time retaining the flexibility deemed essential in the event of nuclear warfare. The infantry division under this concept has 8 infantry battalions, 2 armored battalions, and an aviation battalion, while the armored division, by way of contrast, has 5 infantry battalions, 6 armored battalions, and an aviation battalion. Divisional strengths vary from 13,500 men in the airborne division to 15,900 in the armored division. One division of a fifth type, an airmobile division, heavy in aerial transportation and weaponry, has also been created.

Whether Communist armies follow a similar organizational pattern for combat was not definitely known, but it was recognized that the army of the Soviet Union was strong in mechanized and armored units. The Soviets were believed to maintain about 150 divisions, 40 or 50 of them at about 80 percent of wartime strength, the others at about half strength. Upon mobilization, these would be rapidly filled out with reservists while other reservists were being organized into additional divisions. Almost all armies in the mid–1960's continued to maintain some form of reserve and militia system to augment the regular army in time of crisis.

A new feature of some armies, notably those of the U.S., Britain, and France, is the presence of an air-mobile force, specially organized with increments of air and ground forces ready for quick deployment to any trouble spot around the world. The British call this simply the *strategic reserve;* the French call it a *force of maneuver;* the Americans call it *strike command* (STRICOM).

Despite the tendency toward smaller combat units within divisions, the overall strengths of armies remained higher than in the pre–World War II period. The army of Communist China was probably the world's largest standing force with about 2½ million men. The army of the Soviet Union probably was next with about 2 million men, followed by that of the United States with 1.4 million. Other major armies as of the late 1960's had strengths as follows: Britain, 195,000; France, 350,000; Nationalist China (Taiwan), 400,000; South Vietnam, 320,000; North Vietnam, 250,000; West Germany, 350,000; Italy, 370,000; and Japan, 180,000.

The example of Korea, in which an international army fought under the aegis of the United Nations, had not been duplicated by the late 1960's, though several small international police forces had been organized and employed under UN auspices. A trend toward standardization of weapons among allies had nevertheless been sustained by the nations of the European Communist bloc under the Warsaw Pact, on the one hand, and by the Western allies under the North Atlantic Treaty Organization on the other.

WIDE WORLD

AIRBORNE INFANTRY strike and withdrawal became a major U.S. antiguerrilla tactic in South Vietnam.

Within the framework of NATO and the Western European Union (WEU), the Western victors of World War II had authorized an armed force of 400,000 men for West Germany.

See also AMPHIBIOUS WARFARE; ARMORED FORCES; ARMOR; ARMY RESERVE COMPONENTS; ARTILLERY; CONSCRIPTION; GUNS; INSIGNIA OF RANK, ARMED FORCES; LOGISTICS, MILITARY; MILITARY AERONAUTICS; MILITARY SCIENCE; NUCLEAR WEAPONS; SMALL ARMS; STRATEGY, MILITARY; TACTICS.

CHARLES B. MACDONALD
Office of the Chief of Military History
Department of the Army

Bibliography

Clausewitz, Karl von, *On War*, ed. by F.N. Maude, tr. from 3d German ed. by James J. Graham (New York 1961).
Dodge, Theodore A., *Great Captains* (Boston 1889).
Dupuy, R. Ernest, *Compact History of the U.S. Army* (New York 1956).
Earle, Edward Mead, ed., *Makers of Modern Strategy* (Princeton 1943).
Falls, Cyril, *A Hundred Years of War* (London 1954).
Falls, Cyril, *The Great War: 1914–1918* (New York 1959).
Fuller, John F.C., *A Military History of the Western World*, 3 vols. (New York 1955–56).
Fuller, John F.C., *Decisive Battles: Their Influence on History and Civilization* (New York 1940).
Greenfield, Kent R., ed., *The U.S. Army in World War II*, a multivolume series (Washington 1947–   ).
Leckie, Robert, *Conflict: The History of the Korean War 1950–53* (New York 1962).
Liddell Hart, Basil H., *A History of the World War: 1914–1918* (Boston 1934).
Lloyd, Ernest M., *A Review of the History of Infantry* (New York 1908).
Montross, Lynn, *War Through the Ages*, rev. ed. (New York 1960).
Nickerson, Hoffman, *The Armed Horde 1793–1939* (New York 1950).
Spaulding, Oliver L., *The United States Army in War and Peace* (New York 1937).
Spaulding, Oliver L., Nickerson, Hoffman, and Wright, John W., *Warfare* (New York 1925).
Weigley, Russell F., *Towards an American Army: Military Thought from Washington to Marshall* (New York 1962).

ARMY, Canadian. See CANADA—*Military System.*

Seal of the Department of the Army

ARMY, Department of the, a military agency of the United States government. It was created by the National Security Act of 1947, which, together with subsequent amendments, established the Department of Defense with authority over the coequal departments of the Army, Navy, and Air Force. The Department of the Army is the successor to the War Department, which was established by act of Congress on Aug. 7, 1789. In 1947 the secretary of defense replaced the secretaries of war and navy in the president's cabinet.

Functions. The Department of the Army includes the executive element of the U.S. Army and all field headquarters, forces, Reserve components, installations, activities, and functions under the control or supervision of the secretary. The Headquarters, Department of the Army, is the executive part and exercises directive and supervisory functions over the department. It does not consist exclusively of agencies and personnel located in the District of Columbia but includes dispersed agencies and personnel performing "national headquarters" functions as distinguished from "field" or "local" functions. The Army field commands are the part of the department not included in the Headquarters, Department of the Army.

Acts of Congress, executive orders of the president, and directives from the secretary of defense have broadened the scope of the department's responsibilities to include many activities not purely military in character.

The organization of the department changes periodically in pursuance of new tasks and more efficient operations. In 1962, in a reorganization more thoroughgoing than any since the establishment of the General Staff in 1903, the department began to abolish the traditional technical services in favor of a more functional organization.

Organization. The Office of the Secretary of the Army is composed of the secretary, an undersecretary, three assistant secretaries, the director of civil defense, a general counsel, and the chiefs of legislative liaison and of public information, together with their staffs.

The secretary of the army is a civilian appointed by the president and confirmed by the U.S. Senate. He has supreme authority in the department and is answerable to the president through the secretary of defense. He is responsible for developing improved weapons and equipment, maintaining high standards of train-

ing, and ensuring the institution of proper doctrine and methods. He is also responsible for improving waterways; developing facilities for flood control, power, and irrigation; surveying and charting the Great Lakes and international boundary waters; supervising, maintaining, and operating the Panama Canal and governing the Canal Zone; and operating the U.S. Military Academy at West Point. Since 1964, he has been in charge of the United States civil defense program.

The undersecretary of the army is the secretary's deputy and principal civilian assistant. He is responsible for manpower and personnel, including their health, morale, safety, welfare, and discipline, and for troop information and education programs. He administers civil governments in the Ryukyu Islands and the Canal Zone and is responsible for Panama Canal Company affairs. He also supervises military support of the civil defense program, special warfare, intelligence, and communications security.

The principal assistants to the secretary are authorized to act for him within their fields of responsibility, both in the department and with Congress and other governmental and nongovernmental organizations and individuals. Each assistant supervises the formulation, execution, and review of policies, plans, and programs in his area.

Army Staff. The Army Staff is that part of the secretary's military staff located at Headquarters. It furnishes professional advice and assistance to the secretary and his civilian assistants. It is presided over by a chief of staff, an Army general. Serving under the chief of staff and his principal assistant, the vice chief of staff, are a General Staff and a Special Staff made up of commissioned officers.

The General staff consists of deputy chiefs of staff for military operations, personnel, and logistics; the comptroller of the Army; chiefs for research and development, and for Reserve components; and assistant chiefs for force development and intelligence.

The Special Staff provides advice and assistance on specialized matters. It consists of the adjutant general, surgeon general, inspector general, judge advocate general, and provost marshal general; and chiefs of engineers, finance, chaplains, communications, the National Guard Bureau, information, military history, the Army Reserve, personnel operations, support services, and auditing.

MARTIN BLUMENSON
Office of the Chief of Military History
Department of the Army
Author of "Breakout and Pursuit"

ARMY, United States. See ARMY; ARMY RESERVE COMPONENTS; ARMORED FORCES; UNITED STATES —32. *Army.*

ARMY, NAVY, AND AIR FORCE VETERANS IN CANADA, the oldest veterans' organization in Canada. Founded under a royal charter in 1837 as the Army and Navy Veterans in Canada, it adopted its present name in 1946. It seeks to encourage service recruitments and promote welfare benefits for veterans and their dependents. The organization publishes a monthly magazine, *Veterans' Advocate.* Its national headquarters are at Ottawa, and there are regional headquarters in the six western provinces.

ARMY RESERVE COMPONENTS, är′mē ri-zûrv′ kəm-pō′nənts, a part of the United States armed forces. They consist of the Army National Guard and the U.S. Army Reserve (USAR).

The willingness of citizens to bear arms is the basis of United States defense philosophy. Although the international situation has required an increasingly large Active Army and continuation of the draft, the Army Reserve Components have continued to provide much of the national security forces. The highly trained Regular Army has been augmented substantially by reservists on extended active duty, many retained since World War II or the Korean War. In the late 1960's reservists made up over 60 percent of the Army's total of commissioned and warrant officers on active duty, a proportion unchanged since World War II.

Mission and Structure. The mission of the Reserve Components is to provide trained units and qualified individuals for active duty in time of war or national emergency and when required for national security. In addition, Army National Guard units may be called into federal service to preserve law and order and to uphold decisions of the federal courts. National Guard missile units have served since 1954 in key defense and industrial areas.

The National Guard has both state and federal responsibilities. In times of peace it assists in maintaining peace, order, and public safety under state authority. When ordered into federal service, National Guard units are commanded by the president and join the active forces.

In the late 1960's the Army National Guard consisted of some 4,000 federally recognized units, including 17 infantry and 6 armored divisions, of which 8 were high-priority units with increased manning and equipment. The Army Reserve comprised 3,610 units of all types, including 13 training divisions, 2 maneuver area commands, and 3 logistical commands.

The Reserve Components of the Army are divided further into the Ready Reserve, Standby Reserve, and Retired Reserve. Their combined total in the late 1960's was over 1,300,000.

Ready Reserve. Almost two thirds of the Army's over-all reserve force, including the entire Army National Guard and a large part of the Army Reserve, are in the Ready Reserve. The Ready Reserve includes all members of troop units who receive pay for attending training assemblies, as well as those individuals, not members of reserve units, in the Mobilization Reinforcement Pool. These units and individuals are available for immediate mobilization pursuant to the declaration of a national emergency or war by Congress. The president has authority to call up to one million Ready reservists of all the armed forces for a maximum of two years' active service. In the late 1960's almost 1,200,000 Army Ready reservists were organized into troop units, USAR schools, or control groups, or were mobilization designees. Control groups provide the administrative management for individuals in the Ready Reserve Mobilization Reinforcement Pool. The principal sources of manpower in this pool are personnel with a remaining period of military obligation who have been separated from the Active Army, transferred from Army Reserve units, or discharged from the Army National Guard. In the late 1960's the pool numbered nearly 500,000 men and women.

Troop-unit reservists participate in at least 48 scheduled training assemblies each year and in two weeks of field training during the summer. Some non-unit reservists may be ordered to an involuntary two-week active-duty training period annually for refresher training with troop units. Non-unit Ready reservists also may participate voluntarily in reserve training for education, for promotion credits, and for retirement points that will qualify them for a pension at age 60.

Troop units of the Ready Reserve are organized like Active Army units and are divided into the Immediate Reserve and the Reinforcing Reserve. The Immediate Reserve consists of units needed for early augmentation of the air defense of the United States, reinforcing the Active Army, providing division forces for early deployment, supporting specific contingency and partial mobilization plans, providing support for other services, and supporting initial expansion of the Army mobilization base. Over 80 percent of Army reserve forces are in the Immediate category. The Reinforcing Reserve consists of lower-priority Army National Guard units.

As a result of the expansion of U.S. operations in Vietnam and the president's decision not to call up the Reserve Components in 1965, certain reserve units were made a Selected Reserve Force. This group included 150,400 men in Army National Guard and Army Reserve units; major combat elements were three divisions and six separate brigades. All were authorized 100 percent strength, given high priority for equipment, and directed to accelerate training.

Standby Reserve. The Standby Reserve was established to provide greater equity in ordering reservists to active duty during emergencies and to prevent mobilization of individuals deemed essential to the country's economy. In the late 1960's it had 23,000 officers and 220,000 enlisted members. Army Reserve members are assigned to Standby status after completing four or more years of active duty or an equivalent combination of active duty and reserve training, or when in a critical civilian occupation. They can volunteer for unpaid reserve training. Standby reservists are subject to mobilization only during national emergencies that are declared by Congress.

Retired Reserve. Reservists who have completed 20 years of satisfactory military service, or are 37 years of age with 8 years' military service, may be assigned to the Retired Reserve. There were approximately 185,000 individuals in this category in the late 1960's. Members of the Retired Reserve do not participate in training. They are subject to mobilization in a national emergency declared by Congress, when there are not enough qualified Ready or Standby reservists to meet requirements. Reservists who have completed 20 years of satisfactory military service and have reached 60 years of age are eligible for retirement pay.

Training. The commanding general of the U.S. Continental Army Command supervises Reserve Component training. Army educational and training facilities, as well as maneuvers and field training exercises, are used to develop and train Reserve Component units and personnel. To ensure combat effectiveness, training programs are based on those of similar Active Army units and are supervised by Active Army officers assigned as advisers. This training includes regular participation in unit training assemblies, held in armories or at local field training areas, and active-duty field training. Beginning in 1966, unit training assemblies were four hours in duration; prior to that time they were two hours. This change encouraged the combining of several periods into a weekend training period and the use of local field training areas.

Educational opportunities for Reserve Component leaders begin with officer candidate school (OCS) and extend through the Army War College level. Reserve Component personnel are authorized to attend Active Army service schools, such as the Infantry School and the Artillery School. The Army extension-course program continues military education by correspondence. There are also 109 USAR schools with 189 satellites, paralleling Army service schools and the Command and General Staff colleges. Enrollment in the late 1960's totaled over 18,000 officer and enlisted students from both Army Reserve and Army National Guard.

Mobilization designees are Army reservists selected for specific jobs in the event of mobilization. They receive no weekly drill pay, although they sometimes meet and train as members of mobilization-designee detachments to keep abreast of military developments. Selected individuals also receive training through special active-duty tours; they may be attached to units for annual unit training, perform special projects, take part in special field exercises, attend short indoctrination courses, or serve with the staff or faculty of Army schools.

Qualified guardsmen and reservists can become officers by attending officer candidate school at Fort Benning, Ga., or Fort Sill, Okla., or by attending one of the similar schools conducted by the Army National Guard in each state, where a Reserve Component soldier can obtain a commission under the same standards as Active Army OCS without interrupting his civilian pursuits.

History. The U.S. Army Reserve in its present form began with the establishment of the Medical Reserve Corps in 1908, followed by the Army Reserve Corps in 1912. Some units of the National Guard trace their history to colonial militia of the early 1600's. The name "National Guard" first was applied to a state militia in 1824 when New York units took the title as a compliment to the visiting marquis de Lafayette, who had commanded the Garde Nationale in Paris in 1789. The National Guard remained a state organization, but in 1903 the federal government was made responsible for its training, equipment, and pay. The National Defense Act of 1916, amended in 1933, made it a reserve component of the U.S. Army.

The United States always has relied on reserves to expand its standing forces in great conflicts such as World War II and the Korean war. The partial mobilization in 1961 ("Berlin buildup") differed from previous mobilizations in that reserves were called up for a cold-war situation to help prevent a shooting war.

JOHN L. THROCKMORTON, *Lieutenant General*
USA Chief, Office of Reserve Components
Department of the Army

Further Reading: Derthick, Martha, *The National Guard in Politics* (Cambridge, Mass., 1965); Eliot, George Fielding, *Reserve Forces and the Kennedy Strategy* (Harrisburg, Pa., 1962); Elliott, James C., *Modern Army and Air National Guard* (Princeton 1965); Galloway, Eilene, *History of U.S. Military Policy on the Reserve Forces* (Washington 1957).

ARMY SERVICE SCHOOLS. The United States Army Service Schools make up the most comprehensive and varied military school system in the world. Altogether, the system comprises 37 separate schools conducting more than 500 courses for about 175,000 resident and over 200,000 nonresident students each year. No other army has devoted as much time or as many resources to schooling its personnel as today's U.S. Army. The courses of instruction at these schools (excluding the U.S. Military Academy) last from a few days (for students of the preservation and packaging of military supplies) to about a year (for missile technicians or students of Chinese). About 80 percent of the service school students are enlisted men, most of whom learn skills that cannot be mastered individually or through on-the-job training. The other 20 percent are officers engaged in professional education as well as technical or specialist training.

Army service schools are of several distinct types. There are 22 *branch schools*, 2 *Army colleges*, and 12 *specialist schools*. The Army is also responsible for the United States Military Academy at West Point, which gives prospective officers a four-year college education and preprofessional military schooling. (See UNITED STATES MILITARY ACADEMY.) The Army further provides education and training activities at most of its installations and enrolls its members in scores of civilian college and industrial and commercial courses to supplement its own school system.

Branch Schools. Branch schools offer career and specialist education and training for officers and enlisted men in the various specialized branches or "arms" of the Army. The schools include the Infantry School, Armor School, Artillery and Missile School, Air Defense School, Engineer School, Chemical School, Ordnance School, Quartermaster School, Transportation School, Adjutant General School, Army Security Agency, Civil Affairs School, Finance School, Intelligence School, Military Police School, Women's Army Corps School, Chaplain School, Judge Advocate General School, Medical Field Service School, Medical Service Veterinary School, and Signal School. In addition to the main Signal School, which is located at Fort Monmouth, N.J., there is a branch called the Southeastern Signal School, at Fort Gordon, Ga.

Collectively, the branch schools constitute the major part of the service school system. Resident students total about 130,000 annually, extension students about 185,000. The faculties number more than 22,000. Each of these schools teaches a number of courses of different lengths in the various subspecialties of the particular "arm." For example, the Infantry School at Fort Benning, Ga., teaches 12 courses of 2 to 35 weeks' duration, including ranger, airborne, pathfinder, heavy mortar, and nuclear weapons courses.

Among the most important of the branch school courses are the "basic" and "career" courses, comprising the first two tiers, or levels, of professional military education for officers. The basic course, the first level, is usually about 9 weeks long and furnishes the newly commissioned officer with the fundamentals of the profession and of his particular arm. Nearly half the basic course of study, taught in all branch schools, consists of "common" subjects such as military discipline and justice, map and aerial-photograph reading, personnel management, and control of civil disturbances. The remaining half consists of the tactical, logistical, and administrative subjects peculiar to the particular arm of the service.

The career course, attended by all officers, usually in about their sixth year of service, forms the second tier, or level, in the system. Career courses vary in length from 22 to 37 weeks in the various branches and, like the basic courses, are divided into common and particular topics. The career courses, however, are conducted on a higher and more intensive level than the basic courses. Career courses aim at preparing officers to command, or serve on the staffs of units at the battalion or brigade level, while basic courses prepare students essentially for duty as company officers.

In addition to teaching basic and career level courses, branch schools generally conduct research, participate with other Army agencies in developing doctrine and matériel pertinent to the branch, and publish training manuals and films.

Army Colleges. There are two Army colleges—the Command and General Staff College (C&GSC) at Fort Leavenworth, Kans., and the Army War College at Carlisle Barracks, Pa. The courses at these schools—the third and fourth levels, respectively, of Army professional education—are each about 10 months long. Only the top half of the officers, as graded by performance of service, attend the C&GSC, and only about one fifth go to the War College.

The C&GSC, founded in 1902, originated in the School of Application for Infantry and Cavalry, which was begun at Fort Leavenworth in 1882 when the fort was still a frontier post. The C&GSC student, who is generally a major with 12 years of service, studies the art of command, the fundamentals of military strategy, and staff planning and decision-making processes at the division, corps, and field army levels. Competition for one of the 1,600 annual places at the college is keen because of the high quality of instruction at Leavenworth. Almost 15,000 nonresident students are also enrolled in C&GSC courses. A small number of foreign officers from about 50 countries also attend the college. These foreign students have often honored the institution later by establishing counterpart schools in their own countries.

The Army War College is the pinnacle of the Army school system. It was founded in 1901 by Elihu Root, then secretary of war, and its home until World War II was at Fort McNair, on the outskirts of Washington, D.C. The National War College (operated by the Joint Chiefs of Staff) took over these facilities in 1946. The Army War College was temporarily located at Fort Leavenworth. In 1951 the college shifted to Carlisle Barracks, Pa., to the site once occupied by the famous Carlisle Indian School.

The Army War College is set up to prepare students, who are typically lieutenant colonels or colonels with about 20 years of service, for command and high-level staff duties, "with emphasis upon Army doctrine and operations." In contrast to the Command and General Staff College, the War College has no foreign students. Among its 200 students there are a few representatives from the Air Force, Navy, and Marines and from the civilian executive departments that deal with matters of national security (for example, the Department of State). There are no extension or nonresident students.

The War College curriculum is focused on the development of a national strategy for the United States and of appropriate supporting military programs. Students attend lectures and participate in seminars directed at aspects of this theme. Each student chooses a topic on which he writes one or more analytical papers. The wide-ranging, high-level courses include such subjects as "World Environment and Sources of Conflict," "Strategic Appraisal of the United States and the North Atlantic Community," "The Strategic Threat of the Communist Powers," "Strategic Implications of the Developing Areas," "Army and Joint Capabilities Planning," and "United States National Strategy and a Supporting Military Program."

Specialist Schools. Although each of the branch schools except the Women's Army Corps School teaches specialized, technical courses, the Army has created a number of specialist schools to deal with subjects that do not fit neatly into the responsibilities of any one of the arms or branches. Specialist schools are not marked by any common mission nor are they directed by any single authority. Of the 12 schools, 7 are especially for Army personnel: U.S. Army Aviation School; U.S. Army Chemical, Biological and Radiological Weapons Orientation Course; U.S. Army Combat Surveillance School; U.S. Army Management School; U.S. Army Ordnance Guided Missile School; U.S. Army Primary Helicopter School; and U.S. Army Special Warfare School. Over 27,000 resident students annually attend one or more of the 41 courses offered by these schools, and about 5,000 other students are enrolled in extension courses.

The Special Warfare School, which began in 1956 as an outgrowth of the Psychological Warfare School at Fort Bragg, N.C., affords an interesting example of the specialist school. "Special warfare" includes counterinsurgency operations, psychological operations, and unconventional warfare. Counterinsurgency instruction focuses on counterguerrilla operations, actions to improve environmental conditions so that insurgency cannot flourish, and measures to control resources and population to prevent their exploitation by insurgents. The psychological warfare course teaches the principles of propaganda and the use of various communications media. Instruction in unconventional warfare deals with guerrilla warfare, escape and evasion tactics, and politicomilitary techniques for operating in enemy-controlled territory. Altogether, the Special Warfare School offers nine courses annually in these subjects to American military and civilian officials and to selected foreign personnel. Included among the groups training at this school are the "Green Beret" units, prominent in the war in Vietnam.

Like other specialist schools, the Special Warfare School is also charged with research, development of doctrine, and production of training materials on the subjects it teaches. Since the early 1960's, the school has had the further mission of conducting a military assistance training adviser (MATA) course for selected personnel ordered to duty in South Vietnam. Besides the regular Special Warfare School subjects, MATA students learn about the Vietnamese countryside and society and acquire the rudiments of the Vietnamese language.

Within the specialist grouping there are also logistics and managements schools that are Army-operated but serve students from the entire defense establishment, especially its civilian members. These include the U.S. Army Logistics Management Center, the Army Management Engineering Training Agency, and the Joint Military Packaging training Center. In the mid-1960's about 11,500 resident students attend one or more of the 21 courses offered at these schools annually. Another 2,200 nonresident students were also enrolled.

The final category of specialist schools consists of two that were originally Army schools exclusively but have been broadened into Department of Defense schools operated by the Army. The first of these, the Defense Information School at Fort Benjamin Harrison, Ind., is set up to prepare military and civilian defense personnel for public affairs and information duties. It is a small school with about 120 students annually, offering about three courses focused on the use of mass communications media.

The second school in this category is the Defense Language Institute (DLI), with East and West coast branches at Washington, D.C., and Monterey, Calif. The institute "exercises technical control of all language training within the Defense establishment, except at the Service Academies."

Earlier, as the Army Language School, the West Coast branch of the DLI pioneered in the development of methods of language instruction that have been adopted throughout the world. Together, the West and East coast branches teach a total of 49 courses, ranging from 8 to 49 weeks in length. In the mid-1960's an annual average of about 2,000 full-time students spent 50 or more hours a week learning one of the 23 languages taught at the institute. Another 2,000 studied at civilian institutions in DLI-monitored programs.

In addition to all the Army service schools, Army personnel attend a number of other Department of Defense schools operated by other agencies—for example, the Armed Forces Staff College at Norfolk, Va., and the Industrial College of the Armed Forces and the National War College, both at Fort McNair near Washington, D.C.

Service Schools in Other Countries. Although not so comprehensive as the United States Army's service school system, the schooling arrangements of other principal military powers are also extensive. They bear a family resemblance to the American system. Britain, France, and Japan, for example, all have combinations of basic and advanced branch schools, specialist schools, and staff and war colleges. West Germany has schools on all except the war college level. The USSR maintains service schools for the Soviet army and, to an extent, for the armies of other Communist nations.

The similarity of scope and organization of the army service schools in most countries shows that a nearly universal pattern of training and education is demanded by modern military professionalism.

Amos A. Jordan, Jr., *Colonel, USA*
United States Military Academy

Further Reading: Department of the Army, *Military Education and Service Schools,* AR 350-5 (Washington 1966); Department of the Army, *Report of the Department of Army Board to Review Army Officer Schools,* 4 vols. (Washington 1966); Masland, John, and Radway, Laurence, *Soldiers and Scholars; Military Education and National Policy* (Princeton, N.J., 1957); Shelburne, James C., *Education in the Armed Forces* (New York 1965).

ARMY WORM, är′mē wûrm, a caterpillar, or larval stage, of a moth, *Cirphis unipuncta.* The adult moth measures about 1½ inches (3.8 cm) across the expanded brownish wings, each of which has a white spot near the middle. The eggs are laid at night in the folded blades or under the leaf sheaths of grains and grasses, usually in wet or sheltered places. They are whitish and considerably smaller than the head of a common pin.

The young caterpillars feed close to the ground and usually escape notice. Increasing quantities of food are consumed as the larvae grow. When all the food is consumed the caterpillars begin moving out in search of more. They move forward in a solid front, consuming everything in their path. When full grown, they are greenish with a broad blackish stripe on each side and another down the middle of the back.

Pupation takes place in the soil, where the larva wriggles around to form a smooth cell in which it transforms to a pupa, from which the adult emerges in about two weeks. The entire life cycle takes from seven to eight weeks, depending upon the temperature. There are two or more generations a year. The moths are strongly attracted to light and their presence in large numbers may indicate a serious outbreak.

The army worm belongs to the family Phalaeridae, order Lepidoptera. The fall army worm, *Laphygma frugiperda,* is also called grassworm. It originates in the extreme south of the United States and moves north as the summer advances. The army cutworm, *Chorizagrotis auxiliaris,* may be mistaken for the common army worm but it occurs in destructive numbers only west of the Mississippi River. The variegated cutworm, *Peridroma margaritosa,* often occurs in large numbers along with the army worm, especially where alfalfa and other legumes are grown, and is chiefly responsible for damage to these plants. All of these species march in the same way as the common army worm.

Among natural enemies of the army worms are many kinds of predaceous and parasitic insects. More than 40 kinds of birds feed upon them, and domestic fowl aid in reducing their numbers. Skunks also play an important part. Early control measures consisted chiefly of the use of poisoned bait for the destruction of the caterpillars. Present control measures consist of spraying or dusting DDT or one of the related insecticides over infested areas, airplanes being commonly used.

See also Cutworm.

Charles Howard Curran
American Museum of Natural History

Yellow-striped army worm

ROSS E. HUTCHINS

ARNAULD, ár-nō', was the name of a family that profoundly affected the religious, political, and intellectual life of 17th century France. Through the influence of members of the family the unorthodox religious beliefs called Jansenism gained popular acceptance in France. The doctrine took its name from a Flemish bishop, Cornelis Jansen. He was concerned with essentially religious problems of free will, grace, and salvation. However, people who endorsed Jansenism found themselves in conflict with the established Roman Catholic Church and the king (see JANSENISM).

Early History of the Family. The Arnaulds, who belonged to the lesser Provence nobility, were distinguished as early as the 12th century. They settled in Paris in 1557 when *Antoine Arnauld I, Lord of La Mothe* (about 1491–1591) was appointed attorney general to Queen Catherine de Médicis. He actively sympathized with the reform efforts of the Huguenots but returned to Catholicism in 1585. Like his father, *Antoine Arnauld II* (1560–1619) served as the queen's attorney general, enjoyed popularity at court, and entertained strict religious views. Because the Jesuits attempted to relax and reform some traditional religious practices, Antoine II became their resolute foe. In 1590 he delivered a celebrated speech, *Plaidoyer en faveur de l'Université*, in which he pleaded the cause of the University of Paris in its dispute with the Jesuits, whom he assailed as tyrants. He violently attacked them again in 1594 when he demanded their expulsion from France. The Jesuits remained, but Antoine's animosity continued undiminished. Ten of the 20 children who survived him were equally involved in religious struggles.

Port Royal. After Antoine II's death in 1619 his widow, Catherine Marion Arnauld, retired with their youngest son, *Antoine Arnauld III* (called *the Great*, 1612–1694) to the convent of Port Royal des Champs. Catherine's father had restored this Cistercian convent near Versailles for her daughter, *Jacqueline Arnauld* (1591–1661). As abbess of Port Royal, Jacqueline became famous under her religious name, *Mère Angélique*. Her reform movement restored the convent to its primitive austerity. Four of her sisters joined her and assisted her in the reform of Maubisson, a neighboring abbey.

As Port Royal's fame spread, more and more girls were sent there to be educated. Because of this expansion, Mère Angélique built a second convent, Port Royal de Paris, near the Louvre in Paris. Her nuns moved there in 1625, and the old convent at Champs was occupied by hermits. Most of these were men of the Arnauld family who wished to live monastically but took no vows.

In 1623, Mère Angélique had met the abbé de St.-Cyran, a supporter of Cornelis Jansen. St.-Cyran sincerely believed that Jansenism, a kind of Catholic Quakerism, could heal the scars of the Reformation. In 1633 he became the convent's spiritual adviser. He wielded tremendous influence over the Port Royalists and particularly over Angélique's sister, *Mère Agnès* (*Jeanne Arnauld*, 1593–1671). Agnes composed a little work, the *Secret Chaplet*, in which she contended that man is too soiled a receptacle to take the Eucharist frequently. This concept caused a theological furor. The Sorbonne condemned the work, but St.-Cyran published an anonymous defense. Finally convinced of the ethics of Jansenism, Angélique made Port Royal its bastion.

The Solitaires. In 1648 some of the nuns returned to Champs, where the hermits had opened "little schools" (*petites écoles*) for boys. The *solitaires*, as the hermits were called, included the four sons of *Catherine Arnauld le Maître* (1590–1651). Their advanced methods of education, reflected in the modern lycée, were surpassed only by their personal piety and scholarship. The poet Racine and Antoine Arnauld III were among the many brilliant students whom they imbued with Jansenism.

Antoine the Great. Antoine III had been tutored by St.-Cyran in Jansenism from his earliest days and was educated by the *solitaires*. In 1642, a year after Antoine's ordination, St.-Cyran died, and Antoine succeeded him as France's foremost exponent of Jansenism. In defending Jansenism, Antoine found it expedient to ridicule the longtime family foe, the Jesuits. In *On the Frequency of Communion* he accused the Jesuits of administering absolution for sins automatically and teaching heretical doctrines on grace and free will. As a theology professor at the Sorbonne, Antoine was in a position to proselytize. In 1653, however, Pope Innocent X condemned Jansen's book *Augustinus*, and since Antoine refused to heed the papal injunction and continued to teach Jansenism, he was dismissed from his professorship in 1656.

Blaise Pascal, the famed mathematician and longtime associate of Port Royal, was so enraged by Antoine's dismissal that he wrote his *Provincial Letters* in protest. This work derided the Jesuits with such ironic wit that it captured popular support for the Jansenist cause. Louis XIV and the French bishops were alarmed by this sudden surge of popularity and instigated steps to crush Port Royal. The French hierarchy issued a "formulary," or oath, that was administered to all the clergy in order to force them to disavow Jansenism. All at Port Royal refused to sign the formulary.

The Port Royal convent was put under interdict but still remained firm. It was only through the intercession of *Robert Arnauld d'Andilly* (1589–1674), elder brother of Angélique and Antoine III, that the convent was spared Louis XIV's wrath. Robert had been attorney to Louis' mother, Anne of Austria, and enjoyed her favor and friendship. He had retired to Port Royal in 1642 to spend his later years in contemplation and writing. Antoine had also retired there and occupied himself with literary projects. He and the *solitaires* translated the Bible and compiled the influential *Port Royal Logic*.

In 1662, a year after Angélique's death, the interdict against Port Royal was removed, and some years later Pope Clement IX received the Jansenists back into the church. In the 10 years that followed, Mme. de Longueville, the king's cousin and a Jansenist sympathizer, managed to protect the Arnaulds from further harassment. After her death in 1679, however, Louis XIV took immediate steps against the nuns. He ordered them to dismiss their novices and boarders, and Antoine was forced to flee to Brussels, where he remained for the rest of his life. In 1705, Louis achieved his long-sought victory—Clement XI unequivocally condemned the Jansenists. The nuns at Port Royal were dispersed, some were imprisoned, and in 1709 the buildings were razed. Although Jansenism was not destroyed by these measures, the Arnauld influence was permanently suppressed.

ARNDT, ärnt, **Ernst Moritz** (1769–1860), German poet and patriot, whose polemical writings aroused German feelings against Napoleon I. He was born in Schoritz, on the Island of Rügen (then part of Sweden), on Dec. 26, 1769. Arndt studied at Greifswald and Jena, in Germany, and in 1806 became assistant professor of history at Greifswald. That year he wrote the first part of *Geist der Zeit* (*Spirit of the Times*, 4 vols., 1806–18), which attacked Napoleon so fiercely that Arndt was forced to flee to Sweden when Napoleon won the Battle of Jena (October 1806). Arndt returned to Prussia in 1809, but was forced to flee again three years later, this time to Russia.

Arndt went back to Prussia after Napoleon's defeat in Russia and became professor of history at the University of Bonn in 1818, the year in which the final volume of *Geist der Zeit* was published. His criticism of the reactionary Prussian leadership caused his suspension from the university in 1820, and he spent the next 20 years in retirement. Reinstated in 1840, he continued teaching at Bonn until his death there on Jan. 29, 1860. A complete edition of his lyric poems was published that year. He also wrote songs, including the popular *Was ist des Deutschen Vaterland?*

ARNE, ärn', **Thomas Augustine** (1710–1778), English composer, who wrote the patriotic song *Rule Britannia*. He was born in London on March 12, 1710, the son of an upholsterer. Sent to Eton to study law, he studied music secretly and began his career as a composer of incidental music for plays. His full-length work, a musical setting of Addison's *Rosamond*, was produced in 1733. His musical adaptation (1738) of Milton's masque *Comus* established his reputation. *Rule Britannia* appears in his masque *Alfred*, produced in 1740.

Arne's other works include the operas *Eliza* (1754), *Britannia* (1755), and *Artaxerxes* (1762), and the oratorios *Abel* (1744) and *Judith* (1761). In a revival of *Judith* in 1773, he introduced a musical innovation—the use of female voices in oratorio chorus. Arne also composed music for harpsichord and organ and incidental music for Shakespeare's plays. He died in London on March 5, 1778.

Michael Arne (1741–1786), his son, was a composer and harpsichordist who wrote numerous works for the stage, including *The Artifice* (1780) and *The Choice of Harlequin* (1781).

ARNETH, är'net, **Count Alfred von** (1819–1897), Austrian historian and archivist. He was born in Vienna on July 10, 1819. After studying law and history there, he was appointed by Prince Metternich, Austria's foreign minister, to a position in the Austrian state archives. Arneth uncovered and published important sources of Austrian history, and was made director of the archives in 1868. He became president of the Academy of Sciences in 1879.

Arneth was also active as a politician and writer. He was elected to the Frankfurt Parliament in 1848 and became a member of the Diet of Lower Austria in 1861. Among his important historical works are *Prinz Eugen von Savoyen* (3 vols., 1858) and *Geschichte Maria Theresias* (10 vols., 1863–79). He also published *Aus meinem Leben* (1893), a 2-volume autobiography of his early life. Arneth died in Vienna on July 30, 1897.

ARNHEM, ärn'hem, an industrial city in the east Netherlands, is located on the north bank of the Lower Rhine, 36 miles (57 km) east of Utrecht. It is the capital of Gelderland province. Arnhem is surrounded by garden suburbs and has beautiful parks. It is a favorite residence of government officials. Its factories produce textiles, drugs, and electrical components. The city is also an important railroad junction. Possession of its railway bridge over the Rhine became the object of an Allied offensive in World War II.

Arnhem is believed to be the site of the town that the Roman historian Tacitus called *Arenacum*. By medieval times it had grown into a busy trading center, thanks to a favorable river location, and a member of the Hanseatic League for about two centuries. Arnhem was taken by the Dutch in 1585, by the French in 1672 and 1795, and by the Prussians in 1813. It was occupied by the Germans during World War II, and in 1944 it was the scene of a costly battle. The center of the city was reduced to ashes, but after the war it was rebuilt. Population: (1960) 120,091.

ARNICA, är'ni-kə, is a large genus of herbs of the thistle family. These herbs have yellow flowers and grow in the Northern Hemisphere. The roots of *Arnica montana*, the mountain herb, yield a small quantity of oil and resinous substance. From this a tincture was once prepared for treating sprains and bruises.

ARNIM, är'nim, **Bettina von** (1785–1859), German author, who is best known for a romanticized version of her correspondence with the poet Goethe. She was born *Elisabeth Brentano*, at Frankfurt am Main on April 4, 1785. Her correspondence with Goethe began after she met and became infatuated with him in Weimar in 1807. It continued over a four-year period, until Bettina's rudeness to Goethe's wife caused him to end the friendship. At Goethe's death in 1832, Bettina had her letters returned, and in 1835 she published from that material *Goethes Briefwechsel mit einem Kinde*.

For many years the authenticity of the correspondence was questioned, and it was not until the publication in 1879 of Goethe's actual letters to Bettina that her book was proved to be based on fact, although grossly distorted. Bettina herself translated the work into English as *Goethe's Correspondence with a Child*.

Her other works include two additional correspondences that mix fact and fiction: an exchange of letters with the poet Karoline von Günderode was published as *Die Günderode* (1840), and one with her brother as *Klemens Brentanos Frühlingskranz* (1844). Her *Dies Buch gehört dem König* (1843) was a plea to King Frederick William IV of Prussia for various reforms. Her works were collected in 11 volumes in 1853. She died in Berlin on Jan. 20, 1859.

Ludwig Joachim von Arnim (1781–1831), her husband, whom she married in 1811, was a romantic poet and novelist. In collaboration with Bettina's brother, Clemens Brentano, he published a collection of German folk songs and legends (*Des Knaben Wunderhorn*, 1805–08). His other works include *Ariels Offenbarungen* (1804), *Der Wintergarten* (1809), *Die Gräfin Dolores* (1810), and *Halle und Jerusalem* (1811), and an unfinished historical romance, *Die Kronenwächter* (1817).

ARNO RIVER, spanned in Florence by the Ponte Vecchio, flows across Tuscany on its way to the Ligurian Sea.

ARNIM är′nim, **Hans Georg von** (1581–1641), German soldier and diplomat, whose political role in the Thirty Years' War contrasted with that of his more famous contemporary, Wallenstein. Born in Brandenburg in 1581 of an old noble family, he served as an officer in the armies of Sweden, Poland, the Holy Roman Empire, and Saxony.

Known as a man of culture and of deep Protestant piety who lived an exemplary life, he became an articulate spokesman for a policy that gradually alienated him from Wallenstein. Arnim argued that both Protestants and Catholics had everything to gain from the preservation of the Holy Roman Empire, that the empire could not survive if the war were to continue, and that the weakening of the empire would strengthen its enemies, France and Sweden. He urged Wallenstein to find and enforce a *modus vivendi* between Protestants and Catholics and between the emperor and the princes.

When Wallenstein in 1630 turned toward his own idea of pacification through the defeat of the Habsburgs with the aid of Sweden, Arnim broke with him and in 1631 entered the service of Saxony. In 1635 he resigned his Saxon commission in protest against the Peace of Prague. He agreed to take a new command in 1641 but died in Dresden on April 18, 1641, before seeing action again.

GERALD STRAUSS, *Indiana University*

ARNIM, är′nim, **Count Harry Karl Kurt Eduard von** (1824–1881), German diplomat, noted for his opposition to Chancellor Bismarck. Born in Moitzelfitz, Pomerania, on Oct. 3, 1824, he trained as a lawyer and entered the diplomatic service in 1850. In 1864 he was appointed Prussian envoy to the Vatican. At the Vatican Council in 1869, Arnim supported the German bishops in their protest against the dogma of papal infallibility.

After leaving Rome in 1870, he participated in the negotiations to end the Franco-Prussian War. His effectiveness led to his appointment as ambassador to France in 1872. He came into conflict with Bismarck because he believed that Bismarck's support of the French republic would encourage antimonarchists in Germany. Arnim's closeness to the emperor prevented his immediate recall. He was accused of releasing diplomatic papers from the Paris embassy for publication in 1874, and was dismissed from his post.

Sentenced to three months' imprisonment for the theft of documents, Arnim left Germany. He published pamphlets blaming Bismarck's personal jealousy for his conviction. He died in Nice, France, on May 19, 1881, just after his demands for a new trial had been granted.

ARNO, är′nō, **Peter** (1904–1968), American cartoonist, whose rapier pen satirized the foibles of society matrons, debutantes, and members of exclusive men's clubs. Born *Curtis Arnoux Peters, Jr.,* in New York City, on Jan. 8, 1904, he attended Yale University, where he organized and played in a nine-man band, the Yale Collegians. Although Arno never studied art, he began to submit cartoons to magazines soon after leaving Yale in 1924. Before the *New Yorker* magazine published his first cartoon in 1925, he painted murals for New York restaurants and established himself as a member of the café society that he satirized in his drawings. Although associated primarily with the *New Yorker,* he also did cartoons for the *Saturday Evening Post, Cosmopolitan,* and the *Tatler* (in England).

Exhibits of Arno's work were held in New York, London, and Paris, and his cartoons were used in advertising by such corporations as General Motors and Pepsi-Cola. He also wrote humorous articles and stories and coauthored the Broadway musical *Here Comes the Bride.* Arno died in Port Chester, N.Y., on Feb. 23, 1968.

Collections of his cartoons include *Peter Arno's Parade* (1929), *Peter Arno's Circus* (1931), *For Members Only* (1935), *Man in the Shower* (1941), *Sizzling Platter* (1949), *The New Peter Arno Pocket Book* (1955), and *Hell of a Way to Run a Railroad* (1957).

ARNO RIVER, är′nō, one of the largest rivers of Italy. It rises in the Apennine Mountains to the east of Florence, and then turns southward toward Arezzo, after which it runs westward through Florence, more or less dividing the region of Tuscany. The river enters the Ligurian Sea seven miles below Pisa. In ancient times, when the river was known as the *Arnus,* Pisa was situated at its mouth, but the river's course eventually shifted to the south. Near Arezzo the Arno is connected with the Tiber River through the canalized portion of its tributary, the Chiana.

The Arno is fully navigable for only about 19 miles of its 150-mile course. Though its banks are protected by dikes, these were not sufficient to prevent serious flooding of Florence in 1966. The resultant damage to the city's art treasures was incalculable.

ARNOLD, är′nəld, **Benedict** (1615–1678), colonial governor of Rhode Island and greatgrandfather of the American Revolutionary War traitor of the same name. He was born at Ilchester, Somerset, England, on Dec. 21, 1615. He went to America in 1635, settled at Providence, and was a leader of the opposition to Samuel Gorton's settlement at Pawtuxet in 1641. His knowledge of Indian languages helped him effect important negotiations with the Indians in 1645.

In 1657, Arnold succeeded Roger Williams as president of the colony, and on the grant of a royal charter to the colony in 1663 he was made the first governor. He was reelected four times, the last in 1678. He took an active part in the reconciliation and union of the two colonies of Rhode Island and the Providence Plantation. He died at Newport, R.I., on June 19, 1678.

ARNOLD, är-nəld, **Benedict** (1741–1801), American Revolutionary War general and traitor. His treasonous acts in selling important information to the British overshadow his earlier feats as a successful and courageous military leader in the American cause.

Descended from a distinguished Rhode Island family, Arnold was born in Norwich, Conn., on Jan. 14, 1741, the son of Capt. Benedict and Hannah King (Waterman) Arnold. He was an active, mischievous boy and grew into a strong and daring youth.

Apprenticed at 14 to a firm of druggists, he ran away twice to fight in the French and Indian War but finally completed his apprenticeship. In 1762, after both his parents had died, he moved with his sister to New Haven, where he established himself as a druggist and bookseller, later expanding his business into general trade with Canada and the West Indies. On Feb. 22, 1767, he married Margaret Mansfield, by whom he had three sons.

At the start of the American Revolution, Arnold was captain of a Connecticut militia company. When news of the fighting at Lexington, Mass. (April 19, 1775), reached him, he assembled his company and marched to nearby Cambridge. Immediately he offered to seize Fort Ticonderoga, N.Y., and on May 3 was made a Massachusetts colonel empowered to raise a regiment for that purpose. With authority, but few recruits, he encountered Ethan Allen in Vermont with a force of Green Mountain Boys bent on the same mission. Arnold joined Allen, and together they led the assault on Fort Ticonderoga (May 10). Arnold then took 100 men of his own and sailed to the northern end of Lake Champlain, where he captured Fort St. John on May 18.

Mrs. Arnold died in June 1775, and Arnold's sister Hannah took over the care of his children. After a visit home, Arnold returned to the new army, now reorganized as a Continental force under the command of George Washington. Arnold proposed to Washington an expedition through the Maine wilderness to Quebec, to be carried out in conjunction with an already planned invasion of Canada via Lake Champlain and Montreal.

Washington agreed to his proposal, and Arnold set out in September 1775. His journey to Quebec with 1,100 men under incredible hardships is a classic march in military history. Reaching the St. Lawrence River on November 11, his force was too near exhaustion to attack Quebec. The other prong of the invasion, led by Brig. Gen. Richard Montgomery, took Montreal on November 12 and then moved up to join forces with Arnold. In a desperate, unsuccessful assault on Quebec (December 31), in a blinding snowstorm, Montgomery was killed and Arnold wounded in the right knee. Despite his wound he extricated his troops and maintained a tight blockade of the city during the winter. Congress promoted him brigadier general on Jan. 10, 1776.

Lake Champlain. The siege of Quebec was broken by British reinforcements in May 1776, and Arnold had no choice but to retreat via Montreal and Lake Champlain. The British, under Maj. Gen. Guy Carleton, pursued him with the intent of invading New York as far as Albany. The Howe brothers, Gen. Sir William Howe and Vice Adm. Richard Howe, were to capture New York City and control the Hudson, and thus New England would be cut off from the rest of the colonies. Exhibiting great energy, tenacity, and ingenuity, Arnold delayed the northern invasion by stubborn resistance down to Lake Champlain, forcing Carleton to make time-consuming preparations.

At length Carleton embarked at the northern end of the lake with a large army. Arnold was waiting for him behind Valcour Island with a hastily built fleet of crude ships manned by soldiers. He fought the superior British fleet to a draw on October 11 and escaped in the night. In the two days following he had to sacrifice his fleet, but it had served its purpose in discouraging Carleton. Beaten by a superior general who had turned trees into warships, Carleton returned to Canada, and the north was saved.

Again a hero, Arnold started south to join Washington's army in New Jersey but was ordered to Rhode Island to oppose the British, who had seized Newport. For several weeks Arnold tried to gather regiments for an attack. In February 1777, Congress promoted five brigadiers, junior in rank to Arnold, to be major generals. He was justly incensed, and even Washington complained of this injustice but persuaded Arnold not to resign. Visiting his home in April, Arnold heard of a British raid on Danbury, Conn. He dashed to the scene, rallied some militia, and harassed the retreating enemy. Congress promptly made Arnold a major general, but did not restore his seniority. Indeed, it began questioning Arnold's accounts from Canada, and in disgust he tendered his resignation in July. Washington asked him to withdraw it in order to take the field in the north, under Maj. Gen. Philip John Schuyler, as commander of the militia against advancing enemy troops. Arnold agreed.

Saratoga Campaign. To resume the strategy of the year before, the British planned a double descent from Canada in 1777. Gen. John Burgoyne was to follow the Lake Champlain route to Albany, while a smaller expedition under Col. Barry St. Leger was to disembark at Oswego, N.Y., and sweep across the Mohawk Valley to Albany. Sir William Howe was supposed to move up the Hudson again. St. Leger was besieging Fort Schuyler (formerly Fort Stanwix, near Rome, N.Y.) by the time Arnold reached northern headquarters on August 12, and Schuyler sent him with an inferior force to relieve the fort. Arnold adopted a ruse, sending ahead news that he was approaching with a vast army. First St. Leger's Indian allies and then the Loyalists melted away toward their homes. In helpless fury St. Leger had to flee back to Oswego and embark.

Arnold returned to headquarters, where he found that Maj. Gen. Horatio Gates had succeeded Schuyler in command. The Americans fortified Bemis Heights (near Stillwater, N.Y.) as the best defensive position to check Burgoyne's advance. Battle was joined at Freeman's Farm on September 19. Arnold commanded the left wing, and with his usual impetuosity ordered his men to attack, forcing Gates into a more general action than the latter wanted. Both sides claimed victory, but the British and their Hessian mercenaries lost twice as many men as did the Americans. In his report to Congress, General Gates omitted all mention of Arnold, and, when the latter objected, removed him from command of the left wing.

Indispensable but ignored, Arnold was still in the fortified camp on October 7 when the British attacked again. The Americans met the assault vigorously and turned the enemy's flanks, but the center stood firm. Arnold then appeared on the scene, rallied the men, and without any authority beyond the enthusiasm his appearance aroused, he broke the British center. Arnold's horse was killed, and he was shot again in the same leg that had been wounded at Quebec. Finally, one of Gates' aides caught up with him and ordered him to the rear. Burgoyne began a cumbersome retreat, which ended in his surrender at Saratoga on October 17. Congress belatedly restored Arnold's precedence in rank as a major general. The wounded Arnold was carried a hero to a hospital in Albany.

Prelude to Treason. In May 1778, Arnold joined Washington at Valley Forge, Pa. When the British evacuated Philadelphia, he was assigned as military commander of the city.

His extravagant style of living and his friendliness toward the city Loyalists, however, disgusted the patriots and aroused suspicions. Arnold had a passion for money, which he needed to give him the social standing his psychological insecurity demanded. He secretly entered a partnership to profit from the temporary closing of shops in Philadelphia. He even sought a forfeited Loyalist estate in New York.

Arnold's reputation was not improved by his marriage in April 1779 to Margaret (Peggy) Shippen, 18-year-old daughter of a Loyalist. Meanwhile he had resigned his command at Philadelphia in the face of accusations that he had misused public property and authority. Washington's delay in setting the date for his court-martial made him violent and unreasonable. Early in May he sent an emissary to New York to offer his services to the British. His motives were personal rather than political and appear to have been a lust for money, a piqued vanity, an urge to avenge himself on Congress and Pennsylvania for slights and grievances, and a desire for glory. After his treason, Arnold published his motives for changing sides: fear of the French alliance, dislike of independence, and objection to the tyranny of Congress. But these, the usual Loyalist arguments, were rationalizations after the fact.

In British Service. Arnold's offer of services were accepted with enthusiasm and promises of reward by Maj. John André, aide to Sir Henry Clinton, the British commander in chief. For five months Arnold supplied British headquarters with military intelligence, usually written in code. It is clear that Peggy Arnold knew of the correspondence and abetted her husband. Arnold was soon asking for £10,000 advance indemnification for the expected loss of his property and other assets when he openly joined the British. André boldly suggested "a little exertion," and Clinton refused to fix a sum for indemnification, preferring to pay on the basis of the importance of the services rendered.

Meanwhile Arnold had his long-delayed court-martial in December. The verdict was given in January 1780 and approved by Congress. Arnold was found guilty of using army wagons to haul private goods and of illegally granting a pass to a trading ship. He was sentenced to receive a reprimand from Washington. His public accounts were so entangled that Congress reported no decision on them; they were, in fact, never to be settled.

To have something of value to offer the British, Arnold now sought a naval command and, when refused, asked Schuyler and other friends to suggest him for the command of West Point, N.Y. At the same time (May 1780) he began converting his assets into cash that could be shifted to London.

On July 15, Arnold wrote to André that he had the command of West Point and its garrison and asked £20,000 for its surrender. Clinton agreed. After courier delays, an interview with André was arranged under a flag of truce and took place below King's Ferry, N.Y., on the night of September 21–22. Returning overland at Arnold's direction, André was captured in disguise, and incriminating papers were found in his boot. The intelligence was forwarded to Arnold on the 25th. Knowing the plot would be exposed, he immediately escaped down the Hudson, while Mrs. Arnold feigned hysterics to convince Washington, who had arrived on an inspection tour, of her innocence. She was allowed to join her husband in New York. André was executed on October 2 as a spy.

Arnold issued a proclamation attempting to justify his treason and urging other soldiers to follow his example. He was made a British brigadier but was able to muster only 28 deserters by December when Clinton ordered him into Virginia on a raiding expedition. After a successful campaign of destruction that further blackened his name, Arnold returned to New York in June 1781. In September he was sent to New London, Conn., where he destroyed Forts Griswold and Trumbull.

Later Life. After the surrender of British Gen. Charles Cornwallis at Yorktown, Va., in October 1781, Arnold and his family sailed to England with Cornwallis in December. In England, Arnold was offered no appointment and was ostracized socially. Gradually he realized he was not to be entrusted with another command anywhere. He attempted some unsuccessful commercial ventures in New Brunswick, Canada, and the West Indies, living in New Brunswick from 1787 to 1791. Repeatedly he tried to get more money from the British government and did obtain a grant of land in Canada, although it is difficult to believe he was in dire need. He had received £6,525 for his treason and was getting the half pay of a British colonel, £225 per year. Mrs. Arnold was receiving a pension of £500 a year minus commissions.

Arnold remained restless, grasping, and improvident until his death in London on June 14, 1801. His wife died in 1804. Both are buried in St. Mary's Church, Battersea (London). Besides the three sons by his first marriage, Arnold had four sons and a daughter by Peggy; all the sons held commissions in the British army.

HOWARD H. PECKHAM
William L. Clements Library
University of Michigan

Bibliography

Arnold, Isaac N., *Life of Benedict Arnold* (Chicago 1880)
Flexner, James T., *The Traitor and the Spy* (New York 1953)
Roberts, Kenneth L., ed., *March to Quebec,* rev. ed (New York 1940)
Sellers, Charles C., *Benedict Arnold* (New York 1930)
Van Doren, Carl, *Secret History of the American Revolution* (New York 1941)
Wallace, Willard M., *Traitorous Hero* (New York 1954).

ARNOLD, är′nəld, **Sir Edwin** (1832–1904), English poet and journalist, whose work was strongly influenced by the Orient. He was born at Gravesend on June 10, 1832. After graduating from Oxford in 1854, he taught for a while in Birmingham and then became principal of the Deccan College at Poona, India, where he rendered important service to the government during the mutiny of 1857–1858. Returning to London in 1861, he joined the editorial staff of the *Daily Telegraph.* In 1888 he was made Knight Commander of the Indian Empire.

In 1889, after 28 years of successful newspaper work, he began a series of trips to the Far East, about which he has left vivid and picturesque accounts in his books of travel. He frequently visited Japan and was attracted by the social and artistic side of Japanese life. He twice visited the United States on lecture tours. He died in London on March 24, 1904.

Of his original poetry, inspired by Oriental themes and legends, the most famous work is *The Light of Asia* (1879). Among his other works are *Pearls of the Faith* (1883), *India Revisited* (1886), *With Sa'di in the Garden* (1888), *The Light of the World* (1891), *Japonica* (1891), *Potiphar's Wife* (1892), *The Tenth Muse, and Other Poems* (1895), and *The Voyage of Ithobal* (1901). See also LIGHT OF ASIA.

ARNOLD, är′nəld, **George** (1834–1865), American poet. He was born in New York City on June 24, 1834. As a child he showed a talent for drawing, and for some time studied with a portrait painter in New York. He soon abandoned this career and, adopting literature as a profession, contributed prose and verse to *Vanity Fair,* the *Leader,* and other periodicals. The "Mc-Arone" papers established his reputation as a humorist. The *Jolly Old Pedagogue* is his best-known poem. His published volumes are *Drift: A Sea Shore Idyl* (1866), *Poems Grave and Gay* (1867), and *Poems* (complete ed., 1880).

During the Civil War he served at a fort on Staten Island. He died in Monmouth County, New Jersey, on Nov. 9, 1865.

ARNOLD, är′nəld, **Henry Harley** (1886–1950), American air force officer. As commanding general of the U.S. Army Air Forces during World War II, he was one of the most important military men of that period, in charge of nearly 2,500,000 men and over 75,000 aircraft. On June 3, 1949, President Harry S Truman appointed him to the permanent five-star rank of general of the air force, the first such commission ever granted.

Arnold was born at Gladwyne, Pa., on June 25, 1886. He was a flier in military aviation from its infancy. In 1911, four years after his graduation from the U.S. Military Academy at West Point, he was ordered to Dayton, Ohio, for flying instructions under Wilbur and Orville Wright. A year later he won the first Clarence H. Mackay Trophy for a 30-mile reconnaissance flight in an early type of Wright biplane. He won the trophy again in 1935 for commanding a squadron of 10 bombers on an 18,000-mile flight from Washington, D.C., to Fairbanks, Alaska, and back.

A lieutenant assigned to the aviation section of the Signal Corps, young Arnold was stationed in Panama when the United States entered World War I. He organized and commanded an aviation defense unit there, which was known as the 7th Aero Squadron (1917–1918). After a few months overseas in 1918, he was assigned to San Francisco, Calif., as department air service officer (1919–1922). His World War I experience convinced him that air power would be the decisive factor in future wars.

Soon after the start of World War II, General Arnold became deputy chief of staff for air (1940). In March 1942, when the Joint Chiefs of Staff was organized, he was appointed commanding general of the Army Air Forces. His promotion in March 1943 made him the first full aviation general. In December 1944 he was raised to the five-star rank of general of the army, with Gen. George C. Marshall, Gen. Dwight D. Eisenhower, and Gen. Douglas MacArthur. In that year he saw the establishment of the 20th Air Force, composed of B-29's. This force, which General Arnold kept under his direct command until the end of the war, dropped as much as 5,480 tons of bombs a day on the industrial cities of Japan in the summer of 1945. General Arnold retired as head of the Army Air Forces on Jan. 24, 1946, and was succeeded by Gen. Carl A. Spaatz. He died at Sonoma, Calif., on Jan. 15, 1950.

ARNOLD, är′nəld, **Isaac Newton** (1815–1884), American lawyer, antislavery legislator, and author. He was born at Hartwick, Otsego County, N.Y., on Nov. 30, 1815. Admitted to the bar in 1835, he moved in 1836 to Chicago, where he engaged in legal practice and politics. From 1861 to 1865 he was a member of Congress. In 1862 he introduced a bill to outlaw slavery in all territory subject to United States authority. The bill became law on June 19, 1862. On his retirement from Congress, President Andrew Johnson appointed him an auditor of the treasury of the Post Office Department.

Arnold retired from politics in 1866 and devoted himself to historical writing. A friend of Lincoln, he wrote *The History of Abraham Lincoln, and the Overthrow of Slavery* (1866) and *The Life of Abraham Lincoln* (1885). His *Life of Benedict Arnold* (1880) is an apologia. Arnold died in Chicago on April 24, 1884.

ARNOLD, är′nəld, **Matthew** (1822–1888), English writer, who ranks with Tennyson and Browning as one of the major Victorian poets and who was one of the four or five greatest English critics. In his own time he was best known as a literary critic, but he also wrote extensively on social, political, and religious matters.

Life. He was born in Laleham, Middlesex, on Dec. 24, 1822. His father was Thomas Arnold, a famous educational reformer and champion of liberal Christianity. The poet Wordsworth was a close personal friend of the Arnold family, and Matthew retained a lifelong admiration for him, writing *Memorial Verses* to Wordsworth in 1850 and the essay *Wordsworth* in 1879.

Arnold never supported himself by his literary activities. After graduating from Oxford in 1844, having distinguished himself there as a poet but not as a scholar, he became private secretary to Lord Lansdowne, a Whig elder statesman, in 1847. In 1851, in order to marry and rear a family, he took a job as a government school inspector, a post he held until his retirement in 1886. He died in Liverpool on April 15, 1888.

Poetry. Arnold's literary career began about 1847 and can be roughly divided into decades.

Most of his relatively small poetic output was produced in the first decade. As a young man, Arnold had seemed frivolous, supercilious, and elegant—the antithesis of his earnest, energetic father—and an urbane irony remained one of the distinctive marks of his prose style; but the seriousness and melancholy of his first volume of poetry, *The Strayed Reveller, and Other Poems* (1849), surprised even his family.

He employed a variety of narrative, lyric, and dramatic forms, but the characteristic mood of his poetry remained elegiac. Many of his poems express loneliness, isolation, and unresolved inner conflict. Frequently they show concern with the contemporary climate of cultural disorder and religious skepticism, and the emotional impact of this climate on the individual. He often used poets and philosophers, both ancient and modern, as symbols for different attitudes toward life.

In 1852 he published *Empedocles on Etna, and Other Poems;* in 1853, *Poems,* which was largely a selection of poems from his earlier volumes; and in 1855, *Poems* (second series), a further selection. Many of the poems in his final volume, *New Poems* (1867), had been written much earlier.

As early as 1853, Arnold had signaled his dissatisfaction with his own poetry by omitting *Empedocles on Etna,* his longest and perhaps best poem, from the volume *Poems.* Furthermore, he wrote a long preface condemning *Empedocles* for its lack of action and form. (He later argued that the classical sort of poetry he most admired could not be written in his time.)

Criticism. From 1857 to 1867, Arnold was professor of poetry at Oxford. This was an elective, largely honorary post, which he used as a platform to develop in theory and practice a broad conception of criticism. Of the volumes of literary criticism that derived largely from his Oxford lectures, the most important is *Essays in Criticism* (first series, 1865). In the book's key essay, *The Function of Criticism at the Present Time,* he defined criticism as "a disinterested endeavour to learn and propagate the best that is known and thought in the world." He asserted that it was the critic's responsibility to establish an "order of ideas" as a means of preparing the way for fruitful creative effort.

In the decade 1867–1877, Arnold turned from literary subjects to social, political, and religious matters. In 1869 he published his most brilliant sustained prose work, *Culture and Anarchy.* In it he argued that without the breadth of view provided by culture, England was mistaking narrow political and religious means for ends, and misdirecting its great practical energy and moral force. He held out culture ("a study of perfection") as an antidote to the anarchy threatened by the rise of individualism and democracy. Of the four volumes he devoted to religious questions during the 1870's, *Literature and Dogma* (1873) is the most important.

In his last decade he returned to literary criticism and produced some of his best and most influential essays—notably on the English romantic poets and *The Study of Poetry* in *Essays on Criticism* (second series, 1888). In *The Study of Poetry* he argued that since poetry should be a "criticism of life" and was destined to take the place of religion as man's principal moral guide, it was essential to establish standards of "high truth and seriousness" for judging it.

Matthew Arnold

(1822–1888)

Influences. Arnold once named four writers—Goethe, Wordsworth, Sainte-Beuve, and Newman—as the most decisive influences in shaping his mind. But the decisive influence in shaping his character was clearly his father's strong personality. By temperament Arnold was, like his father, a teacher, a reformer, a moralist, and a liberal. But his father was a representative Victorian in his strengths and limitations, and Matthew Arnold always sought to reconcile an earnest moral commitment like his father's with the contrary virtues of a free play of the mind and the integrity of the individual. This conflict underlies many of his poems and appears in the famous antithesis between "Hebraism" and "Hellenism" in *Culture and Anarchy.*

Contribution. A number of Arnold's poems—*The Scholar-Gypsy* (1853), *Dover Beach* (1867), *Thyrsis* (1867)—are assured a permanent audience. With less variety than Tennyson and less dramatic power than Browning, Arnold expressed better than either a mood of uncertainty and alienation that is both Victorian and modern.

Much of Arnold's social criticism remains timely because of his exploration of the problem of the individual and authority in modern society. Although he lamented the breakdown of traditional standards in literature, politics, religion, and morals, he believed that through culture and liberal education modern man could avoid anarchy without abandoning individual liberty to some coercive external authority.

In literary criticism Arnold's evaluation of past English poetry was standard for some 50 years, but after World War I, T.S. Eliot and others successfully challenged it—especially Arnold's emphasis on "high seriousness" in poetry. Arnold's way of looking at poetry in relation to its historical and social context has been widely accepted, however, and he gave to the words "criticism" and "culture" new meanings that have become part of the English language.

JOHN F. MCCARTHY, *Boston College*

Bibliography

Culler, A.D., *Imaginative Reason* (New Haven 1966).
James, David G., *Matthew Arnold and the Decline of English Romanticism* (New York 1961).
Johnson, Edward D.H., *The Alien Vision of Victorian Poetry* (Princeton, N.J., 1952).
Miller, Joseph Hillis, *The Disappearance of God* (Cambridge, Mass., 1963).
Trilling, Lionel, *Matthew Arnold,* 2d ed. (New York 1949).

ARNOLD, är'nəld, **Samuel** (1740–1802), English composer, who was an editor of the music of Handel. He was born in London on Aug. 10, 1740. In 1760 he was appointed composer at the Covent Garden Theatre, where he produced his pasticcio *The Maid of the Mill* in 1765. Arnold wrote nearly 100 operas and theater pieces between 1765 and 1802, including *Don Quixote* (1774) and *The Surrender of Calais* (1791). He also wrote a successful oratorio, *The Prodigal Son*, which was produced in 1767. He was appointed organist and composer of the Chapel Royal in 1783 and organist of Westminster Abbey in 1793. He died in London on Oct. 22, 1802.

Between 1787 and 1797, Arnold published a 40-volume collection of many of Handel's works. This collection, at first considered authoritative, was later found to contain many errors. He also published a 4-volume supplement to William Boyce's *Cathedral Music* (1790).

ARNOLD, är'nəld, **Samuel Greene** (1821–1880), American historian. Born in Providence, R.I., on April 12, 1821, he graduated from Brown University in 1841 and received an LL.B degree from Harvard in 1845. In 1852 he began the first of three terms as lieutenant governor of Rhode Island.

Arnold's best-known work is his *History of Rhode Island and Providence Plantation* (1859). He died in Middletown, R.I., on Feb. 13, 1880.

ARNOLD, är'nəld, **Thomas** (1795–1842), English educator and historian. He became famous as headmaster of Rugby School and was the father of Matthew and Thomas Arnold.

Arnold was born at East Cowes, Isle of Wight, on June 13, 1795. He graduated from Corpus Christi College, Oxford, in 1814. In 1818 he was ordained in the Church of England.

Arnold was elected headmaster of Rugby School in 1828 and served with vigor and distinction until 1842. He brought the school to prominence and put new life into English public school education. While his major aim was the development of "The Christian Gentleman," his stress on character education was paralleled by a striving for intellectual excellence. He believed that the main role of the schoolmaster was not to impart knowledge but to build an appetite for it and the means for gaining it. He advocated a Socratic type of teaching, leading pupils to understand principles, not just to acquire facts. He favored Greek and Latin as the central studies in the curriculum, but he also sought to use these languages as a means of extending the course of study beyond traditional emphases. Thus history, poetry, philosophy, and ethics found their way into the Rugby program, and he also incorporated modern languages and mathematics. He developed the prefect system, and his name became associated with public school fervor over games and athletics. His influence spread to other English schools. Thomas Hughes' *Tom Brown's School Days* reflects Arnold's influence.

In 1835 he became a member of the Senate of London University but resigned when an examination in the Scriptures was not included as a requirement for a degree. In 1841 he was appointed professor of modern history at Oxford. Here he concluded his well-known Roman history. He died at Oxford on June 12, 1842.

RICHARD E. GROSS, *Stanford University*

ARNOLD, är'nəld, **Thomas** (1823–1900), English writer and educator. He was born at Laleham, England, on Nov. 30, 1823, the younger brother of Matthew Arnold and son of Thomas Arnold, the famous Rugby headmaster. Educated at Rugby and Oxford, he was appointed clerk at the Colonial Office in 1847. From 1850 to 1856 he was colonial school inspector in Van Diemen's Land (Tasmania).

In 1856, Arnold was converted to Roman Catholicism, and in 1857 he was appointed professor of English literature at the new Catholic University of Ireland in Dublin. He became a close associate of Cardinal Newman, who was president of the institution. In 1876 Arnold became a lecturer at Oxford, and in 1882 he was appointed fellow of the Royal University of Ireland. He died in Dublin on Nov. 12, 1900.

ARNOLD, är'nəld, **Thurman Wesley** (1891–1969), American lawyer and legal scholar. Born in Laramie, Wyo., on June 2, 1891, he graduated from Princeton (1911) and Harvard Law School (1914). He practiced and taught law in Laramie in the 1920's. Arnold became dean of West Virginia University Law School in 1927 and transferred to Yale as law professor in 1930. During eight years at Yale he became known as an authoritative, often critical, student of American capitalism.

In March 1938, Arnold joined the Roosevelt administration as assistant attorney general in charge of the antitrust division of the Justice Department. He instituted 230 antitrust suits against business and labor monopolies before 1943, when he resigned to become associate justice of the U.S. Court of Appeals for the District of Columbia. He left the bench in 1945 to resume private law practice, and died in Alexandria, Va., on Nov. 7, 1969.

Arnold was the author of several books. The best known is *The Folklore of Capitalism* (1937).

ARNOLD, är'nəld, is a city in Pennsylvania, in Westmoreland County, on the Allegheny River, 15 miles northeast of Pittsburgh. Primarily a residential community, it has an aluminum plant and a plant that produces sheet window glass. The borough was named for Andrew Arnold, who owned the land in 1852. The site was originally incorporated in 1892 as part of New Kensington borough. Arnold was incorporated as a separate borough in 1896 and chartered as a city in 1939. Government is by a mayor and four councilmen. Population: 9,437.

ARNOLD OF BRESCIA (died 1155), är'nəld, brä'shä, Italian religious and political reformer. The Italian form of his name is *Arnaldo da Brescia*. He may have studied with Peter Abelard in Paris, but the first recorded event in his life is his expulsion from Italy by the Lateran Council in 1139. The following year he and Abelard were condemned by the Council of Sens. The basis for the censure of Arnold was his agitation for the clergy's return to the principle of apostolic poverty. Adoption of this principle would have required the church to surrender all lands and consequently to lose temporal power.

At Paris in 1141, Arnold preached against the reforms of Bernard of Clairvaux. Bernard enlisted King Louis VII's aid in expelling the "sower of schisms" from France. Arnold received protection in Zurich from Cardinal Guido, who arranged a reconciliation with Pope Eugene III at Viterbo (1145). Eugene had just escaped from the rebellious populace of the newly created Republic of Rome, but he ordered Arnold, as his penance, to make a pilgrimage there. Arnold remained in Rome, preaching religious reform. When he advocated that the church be ignored because of its decadence, the pope proclaimed him schismatic (1148). Arnold then entered secular politics, serving as the leader of the self-governing free commune of Rome. In 1155 the republic was shaken by Pope Adrian IV's interdict on the city. Days later it succumbed completely to Emperor Frederick Barbarossa. Arnold was tried and hanged, and his ashes were cast into the Tiber.

ARNOLDSON, är'noōld-sôn, **Klas Pontus** (1844–1916), Swedish author and winner of the Nobel Peace Prize. He was born at Göteborg on Oct. 27, 1844. A self-educated man, he was employed by the state railways from 1871 to 1881, during which time he became prominent as a writer of rationalistic philosophy. From 1882 to 1887 he served in the Riksdag (Parliament), where he advocated permanent neutrality for the Scandinavian countries. In 1908 the Nobel Peace Prize was divided between him and Fredrik Bajer of Denmark. Arnoldson's share of the money was devoted to peace purposes. He founded the Swedish Society of Peace and Arbitration and became a leader in the movement for world peace. His most important publication was *Hope of the Centuries: A Book on World Peace* (1900). He died at Stockholm on Feb. 20, 1916.

ARNOLFO DI CAMBIO (c. 1245–1310), är-nôl'fo dē käm'byō, Italian architect and sculptor who was the outstanding architect and one of the great sculptors of the Gothic period of Italy.

The essential qualities of medieval style are evident in all of Arnolfo's work, but within the medieval framework he evolved a strong personal approach. His sculpture, especially, is imbued with a new realism in form, movement, and emotion that heralds the Renaissance. His major architectural works, the Cathedral of Florence and the Church of Santa Croce in Florence, were greatly altered by later additions. Earlier theories that there were two Arnolfos, one an architect, and the other a sculptor, are now rejected.

Arnolfo was born in Colle di Valdelsa, then under the rule of the city of Florence. He was an apprentice of Nicola Pisano, with whom he worked from 1266 to 1268 on the pulpit of the Cathedral of Siena. After leaving Pisano's workshop, Arnolfo returned to Florence. It was probably at this time that he designed the Church of Santa Croce, which established his reputation.

In 1272, Arnolfo entered the service of Charles of Anjou (Charles I, king of Naples and Sicily). In Charles' service, Arnolfo probably spent much of his time in Rome, where his work includes the widely imitated tomb of Cardinal Annibaldi della Molara (died 1272) in the Church of St. John Lateran; the ciborium, or canopy (1285), for the high altar of St. Paul Outside the Walls; and the ciborium (1293) of Santa Cecilia in Trastevere. He also did portraits of King Charles (in the Capitoline Museum, Rome) and Pope Boniface VIII (in the Vatican) and the tombs of Cardinal Guillaume de Braye

(in the Church of San Domenico, Orvieto) and Pope Adrian V (in the Church of San Francesco, Viterbo).

By 1296, Arnolfo was again in Florence, this time to supervise the building of his masterwork, the Cathedral of Florence (then called Santa Reparata; now, Santa Maria del Fiore). The façade he designed, which was later replaced by a different façade, is depicted in a fresco in the Convent of San Marco, Florence. Vasari, in his *Lives of the Artists*, credits Arnolfo with helping to design other buildings in and around Florence, most notably the Palazzo Vecchio.

Further Reading. Mariani, V., *Arnolfo di Cambio* (Rome 1943); Pope-Hennessy, John, *Italian Gothic Sculpture* (New York 1955).

ARNPRIOR, ärn'prī-ər, is a town in Ontario, Canada, in Renfrew County, 37 miles west of Ottawa. Its picturesque location at the confluence of the Ottawa and Madawaska rivers has made it a popular resort. Lumber, paper, pulp, office furniture, electronic equipment, blankets, and processed foods are its chief products. Founded by Scottish settlers in 1831, Arnprior was built at the site of an old mill. It became a village in 1862 and a town in 1892. Population: 6,016.

ARNULF (850?–899), är'noōlf, the last of the Carolingian emperors, was the illegitimate son of Carloman, king of Bavaria. He inherited Carinthia, now in Austria, from his father. Arnulf later became involved in intrigues against the incompetent Emperor Charles III the Fat. When the East Frankish nobles revolted against Charles and deposed him in 887, Arnulf was elected king of the East Franks. The tradition of electing the king was to greatly weaken the monarchy in the future, but the immediate effect was to give Germany a strong ruler at a time when he was badly needed.

In contrast to Charles the Fat, Arnulf was able to defend his kingdom against the Northmen and the Moravians. The Northmen were defeated at the Dyle River near Louvain, Belgium, in 891. On the east, Greater Moravia proved a tenacious opponent but was held in check.

In 894, Arnulf invaded Italy at the invitation of Pope Formosus. He withdrew from Italy later in the year but returned in 895. Arnulf entered Rome late in the same year and had himself crowned emperor early in 896. Soon after, he left Rome to subdue northern Italy but was stricken with paralysis and had to return to Germany. After his death at Regensburg, Bavaria, on Dec. 8, 899, he was succeeded as king of the East Franks by his legitimate son, Louis III the Child, the last of the Carolingian kings in Germany.

AROMATIC COMPOUNDS, ar-ə-mat'ik kom'-poundz, are organic chemical compounds that contain atoms of carbon joined to form a molecule shaped like a closed ring. In contrast aliphatic compounds have carbon atoms joined to form an open, chainlike molecule.

During the latter half of the 19th century a large number of carbon compounds, mostly of vegetable origin, were called aromatic compounds because they had a characteristic odor that distinguished them from other compounds. These chemicals, which included oil of wintergreen, gum benzoin, coumarin, benzoic acid, cymene, and aniline, are still called aromatic compounds. However, after the German organic chemist Friedrich Kekulé proposed a structure for benzene (1865), aromatic compounds were differentiated from other types of compounds primarily on the basis of their structure. In Kekulé's conception of benzene, also developed by others, six carbon atoms and six hydrogen atoms are joined in the form of a hexagon. Each carbon atom has an attached hydrogen atom, and each carbon atom is attached to two other carbon atoms. (In the current view of this structure, fluctuating electrons rather than fixed bonds unite the atoms; that is, the electrons fluctuate between neighboring carbon atoms.)

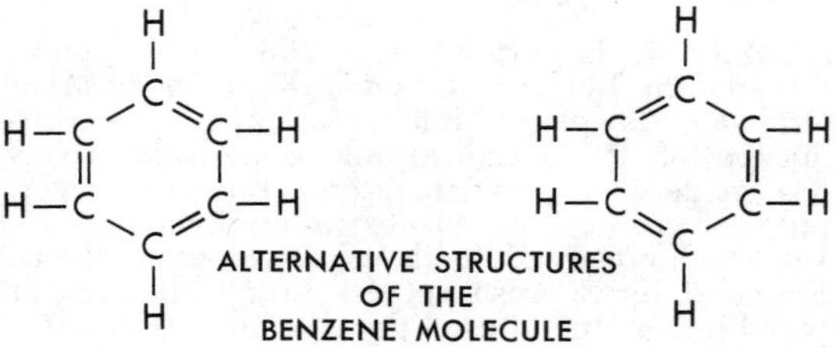

ALTERNATIVE STRUCTURES
OF THE
BENZENE MOLECULE

Aromatic compounds have a closed-ring benzene nucleus (C_6H_5). The benzene nucleus is pictured as having two bonds (four electrons) between some carbon atoms, a characteristic called unsaturation. Unsaturated compounds ordinarily react speedily, but the aromatics do not. An unsaturated aliphatic compound, such as acetylene (C_2H_2), reacts almost immediately with bromine, whereas benzene has a slow interaction with bromine at room temperature.

Another chemical distinction between aromatics and aliphatics is their different behavior with similar attached groups. The aliphatic halides are compounds of hydrogen and carbon with a chainlike molecule and an atom of fluorine, chlorine, bromine, or iodine substituting for a hydrogen atom. These halides react with boiling water solutions of alkali. In contrast, aromatic halides are relatively inert under the same treatment. The aromatic halides are compounds with the benzene nucleus and a fluorine, chlorine, bromine, or iodine atom substituting for a hydrogen atom. The benzene molecule alone, C_6H_6, is a very stable system compared with the molecules of the aliphatic compounds. For example, the aliphatic compound ethylene (C_2H_4) reacts with potassium permanganate in an alkaline solution even at a temperature of 32° F (0° C), but benzene is not changed by this chemical even at 212° F (100° C).

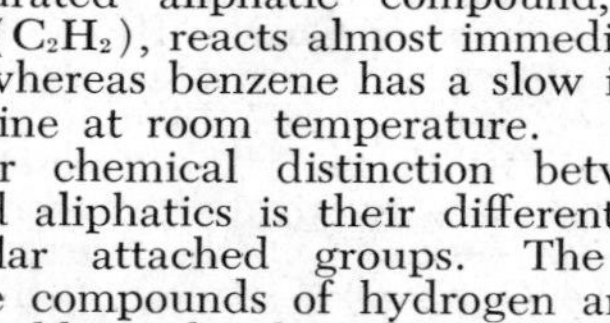

NAPHTHALENE

The aromatic compounds not only include compounds with the benzene nucleus as a part of the molecule but also include compounds with two and three joined benzene nuclei. For example, naphthalene has two benzene nuclei, and anthracene and phenanthrene have three fused benzene rings. Derivatives of these molecules also are called aromatic compounds. Molecules represented by a closed ring of eight carbon atoms have not yet been synthesized, but such molecules also would be aromatic compounds.

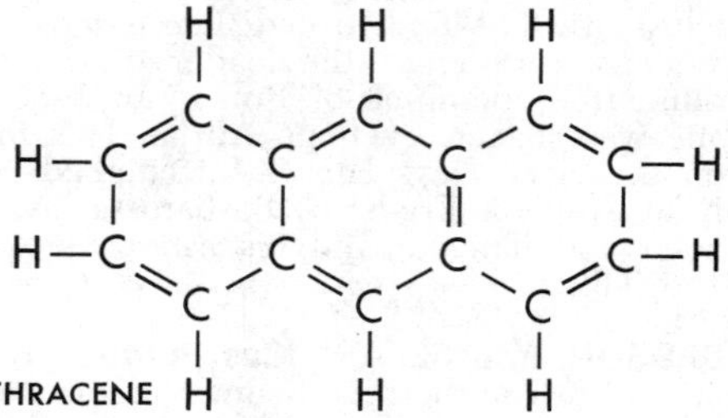

ANTHRACENE

Fluorine, chlorine, bromine, iodine, and many functional groups can be substituted for hydrogen in the benzene nucleus. Such substitutions form various types of aromatic compounds. Among the important types are carboxylic acids (characterized by the COOH group), ketones (characterized by the CO group), phenols (characterized by the OH group), amines (characterized by the NH_2 group), and nitro compounds (characterized by the NO_2 group).

MORRIS GORAN, *Roosevelt University*

AROOSTOOK RIVER, ə-rōōs′tŏŏk, in Maine, rising in Piscataquis County. It flows more than 140 miles in a circular course and enters the St. John River in New Brunswick, Canada. It falls 705 feet in its course within the state, affording valuable water power. Its valley is a rich potato-growing area. Possession of the region was in dispute between Maine and New Brunswick until the boundary between the two was fixed by the Webster-Ashburton Treaty in 1842.

AROOSTOOK WAR, ə-rōōs′tŏŏk, an undeclared, bloodless Anglo-American "war" that occurred in 1839. The peace treaty of 1783 concluding the American Revolution had not satisfactorily determined the boundary between New Brunswick and what is now Maine. The boundary dispute worsened after Maine gained statehood (1820) and, disregarding British claims, began granting land to settlers in the valley of the Aroostook River. The king of the Netherlands was asked to arbitrate the dispute, but the U.S. Senate rejected his award in 1832, although the British accepted it.

Canadian lumberjacks entered the Aroostook region to cut timber during the winter of 1838–1839, and in February they seized the American land agent who had been dispatched to expel them. The "war" was now under way. Maine and New Brunswick called out their militiamen, and Congress, at the instigation of Maine, authorized a force of 50,000 men and appropriated $10 million to meet the emergency. Maine actually sent 10,000 troops to the disputed area. President Van Buren dispatched Gen. Winfield Scott to the "war" zone, and Scott arranged an agreement (March 1839) between officials of Maine and New Brunswick that averted actual fighting. Britain agreed to refer the dispute to a boundary commission, and the matter was settled in 1842 by the Webster-Ashburton Treaty. See also WEBSTER-ASHBURTON TREATY.

AROSEMENA, ä-rō-sä-mä′nä, **Alcibíades** (1883–1958), Panamanian political leader, who was president of Panama in 1951–1952. He was born in Los Santos, Colombia (now in Panama) on Nov. 20, 1883. A political ally of the influential Arias family, he served as minister of finance in the government of Arnulfo Arias. Elected first vice president in 1948, he succeeded to the presidency on May 10, 1951. He remained titular head of state until Oct. 1, 1952, when Colonel José Antonio Remón, the power behind his government, became president. Arosemena died at Panama City on April 8, 1958.

AROUET, François Marie. See VOLTAIRE.

AROUND THE WORLD IN EIGHTY DAYS is a popular adventure novel by Jules Verne (q.v.), published in 1873. Its name in French is *Le tour du monde en quatre-vingts jours.* The novel tells of Phileas Fogg, an Englishman, who wagers with members of the Reformers' Club that he can travel around the world in 80 days. The bet is accepted, and Fogg agrees to appear at the club at a specified time. He sets out that very night, accompanied by Passepartout, his French valet, and by Detective Fix, who is assigned by the club to keep track of Fogg's travels. Fogg's voyage is filled with fabulous adventures in many lands, and his unfailing resourcefulness enables him to overcome seemingly insurmountable obstacles. Fogg wins the wager when he walks into the Reformers' Club at the specified time. Verne made a stage version of the novel in 1874. It also was adapted as a motion picture by Mike Todd in 1956.

ARP, Bill. See SMITH, CHARLES HENRY.

ARP, ärp, **Jean** (1887–1966), Alsatian sculptor and painter, who was a pioneer in abstract art. He is also known as *Hans Arp.* Arp was born in Strasbourg on Sept. 16, 1887. He studied art in Strasbourg, in Weimar (1905–1907), and at the Académie Julian in Paris (1908); but finding academic instruction stultifying, he sought refuge in poetry and in the work of various modernist painters, particularly the Blue Rider group. Not until 1915, around the time he met his future wife, the abstractionist Sophie Taeuber (1889–1943), did he produce his first "successful" picture, characteristically while playing with children's blocks.

He was a founder of the Dadaist movement in Zurich in 1916, the year he produced his first painted reliefs, and in the 1920's he joined the Surrealists.

Arp's first sculpture in the round dates from the early 1930's. He was awarded the grand prize for sculpture at the Venice Biennale in 1954. Simplicity, spontaneity, and an emphasis on biomorphic form are features of Arp's two- and three-dimensional constructions. Typical works are the oil and cut-cardboard *Mountain, Table, Anchors, Navel* (1925), and the cast stone *Human Concretion* (1935) at the Museum of Modern Art in New York City.

Arp also wrote essays and poems, published under the titles *On My Way* (1948) and *Dreams and Projects* (1951–1952). He died in Basel, Switzerland, on June 7, 1966.

Further Reading: Giedion-Welcker, Carola, *Jean Arp* (New York 1957); Soby, James T., ed., *Arp* (New York 1958).

ÁRPÁD (died 907), är′päd, is the national hero of Hungary. About 890 he was elected by the seven Magyar clans living in the steppes north of the Black Sea to succeed his father, Álmos, as their chief. Having united the Magyars, Árpád led them in 896 across the Carpathian Mountains, where they conquered what is now northeastern Hungary. They subsequently moved westward, settling among the tribes they had defeated in the region of present-day Budapest.

One of Árpád's descendants, Stephen I (St. Stephen), was the first crowned king of Hungary. In 1000 he founded the Árpád dynasty, which ended with the death of the childless Andrew III in 1301. The story of Árpád is told in the oldest Hungarian chronicles. It is one of the main components of the national legends and is the theme of many Hungarian folk songs.

ARPINO, Cavaliere d'. See CESARI, GIUSEPPE.

ARPINO, är-pē′nō, is a town in west-central Italy, 13 miles (21 km) east of Frosinone, in Frosinone province. It is situated near the Liri (Garigliano) River. In the town are the ancient churches of San Michele and Sant'Andrea, and nearby are ruins of megalithic walls and a gateway built in pre-Roman times. Woolens, paper, parchment, and leather goods are manufactured, and marble is quarried nearby.

Founded by the Volsci, *Arpinum,* as it was then called, became a municipal town under the Romans, who took it in 305 B.C. It was the birthplace of the Roman orator Cicero. Population: (1961) 2,207.

ARRAIGNMENT, ə-rān′mənt, in criminal law, usually describes the proceeding in open court when an accused person is first presented with the written charge that has been filed against him. He is then called upon to enter a plea to it of not guilty, guilty, or (with the judge's consent) nolo contendere. Depending on the defendant's plea, the circumstances of the case, and the nature of earlier proceedings, the judge may: (1) fix bail; (2) assign an attorney to represent the defendant; (3) set a trial date; (4) pronounce sentence, set a date for sentencing, or order preparation of a presentence report; or (5) set a date for other proceedings.

Some confusion surrounds the term "arraignment" because it is sometimes applied to the first appearance of an arrested suspect before a judicial officer for preliminary screening of the grounds for his detention. Many of the same things can be done then as at the formal arraignment, which occurs later.

RICHARD A. GREEN
Director, American Bar Association Project on Minimum Standards for Criminal Justice

ARRAN, Earls of. See HAMILTON (family); and for James Stewart (died 1596), STUART (family).

ARRAN, ar′ən, is an island in southwestern Scotland, in the Firth of Clyde. Its area is 165 square miles (427 sq km). Brodick and Lamlash are seaside villages on the island. Arran is rugged and picturesque, and its extensive deer forests attract numerous hunters in season. The island was occupied by Norse raiders for many years prior to 1263, when it was annexed to Scotland. Robert Bruce took refuge here in 1306. Population: (1961) 3,705.

ARRAS, à-räs', a city in France, 25 miles (40 km) southwest of Lille, is the capital of the department of Pas-de-Calais. It is a grain-trading center for the nearby area. Among its industries are metalworking, brewing, and tool manufacturing. The town's best-known buildings, which are the 16th century town hall, the 18th century cathedral, and the abbey of St. Vaast, were all badly damaged in World War I. Restored, they were damaged again in World War II.

Called *Nemetocenna* by the Romans, it was the chief town of the barbarian Atrebates in the time of Julius Caesar. It was ravaged by Attila in 451 A.D. In 863, Arras came under the rule of Baldwin I, count of Flanders. During the Middle Ages its weaving and banking operations brought it great wealth. The rich tapestries made in the city became so famous that the word *arras* in time was applied to tapestry wall hangings in general.

In 1180, Arras was part of the dowry of Isabella of Hainaut on her marriage to King Philip Augustus of France. About the same time it became the capital of the newly formed county of Artois and also received its city charter. The charter skillfully conciliated the powers of the nobles with the rights of the citizenry.

During the 14th century, Arras came under the control of Burgundy. After the death of Charles the Bold in 1477, Louis XI of France invaded Artois. When the people showed their resentment of the French garrison, Louis exiled the population, replaced them with other Frenchmen, and changed the name of the town to *Franchise.* The original name and the citizenry both were restored under Louis' successor, Charles VIII.

Arras gave its name to two important treaties. The first, in 1435, reconciled Burgundy and France during the Hundred Years' War, when Charles VII of France recognized Philip the Good as sovereign duke of Burgundy. By the second treaty, in 1482, Louis XI acquired most of the domain of Charles the Bold at the expense of Emperor Maximilian I. This treaty was superseded by the Treaty of Senlis (1493), which gave Charles' holdings to Maximilian. Arras remained in Habsburg hands until its capture by the French in 1640. By the Treaty of the Pyrenees in 1659, Arras again became part of the crown lands. Population: (1962) 40,969.

ARRAU, är-rä'ōō, **Claudio** (1903–   ), Chilean pianist who is noted for his romantic style of playing, especially of the works of Weber and Beethoven. His interest in romantic music is indicated by his statement that Beethoven's *Appassionata Sonata* is ". . . the most heroic spiritual battle waged . . ." in all music.

Arrau was born at Chillán, Chile, on Feb. 6, 1903. A child prodigy, he was sent by the Chilean government to Berlin for musical training when he was seven. He made his European debut in 1914 and during that season played in recitals in Germany and Scandinavia. In 1921 he went on an extensive concert tour of South America, and two years later he made his New York debut. Between World Wars I and II he lived chiefly in Germany, but in 1941 he went to the United States, where he divided his time between teaching and performing. As a performer, Arrau is noted for his cycle concerts, in which he plays all the works of one composer in the course of several evenings.

ARREST, in criminal law, occurs when a policeman or other law enforcement officer takes a person suspected of crime into custody, depriving him of his freedom of action. Usually it is the first in a series of steps in the criminal process leading possibly to the conviction of the suspect. Customarily, arrests are promptly followed by the suspect's being taken to a police station for fingerprinting, photographing, and "booking" (recording of the facts of the arrest and of the charge), and then being taken before a judge for the fixing of bail and for preliminary screening of the grounds for detention.

A person's previous arrest for a crime is often referred to as his criminal record. This has been criticized as unfair, since, despite his arrest, he may never have been convicted.

A person may be arrested by a policeman holding an arrest warrant. Most often, however, arrests are made without warrants in legal circumstances considered to be reasonable; that is, under provisions such as those contained in the 4th Amendment to the U.S. Constitution, which prohibit unreasonable seizures of persons (as well as of property). Generally speaking, either a policeman or a private citizen may legally arrest someone who is committing or attempting to commit a crime in his presence. A policeman or other law officer also may arrest a person who he has reasonable cause to believe has committed a felony outside of his presence.

In many states of the United States, until the 1960's, the questions of (1) precisely when an arrest took place and (2) whether it was made according to the requirements of the law had little impact on the determination of guilt or innocence of the suspect. This is because the primary purpose of an arrest is to ensure, so far as possible, that the suspect will be available for disposition of his case, whether he be kept in custody pending trial or under some such hold as bail. In most of the states, questions as to whether in fact the person was in custody and, if so, whether he was arrested legally arose mainly in connection with lawsuits instituted by the arrested person for false imprisonment. These suits, which can still be filed in all states, sought money damages from the arrester. In the 1960's, however, historic constitutional decisions by the U.S. Supreme Court added great significance to these questions. Under these decisions, the precise moment of the arrest and the amount of information then known by the police are factors that may determine whether evidence possessed by the police can be used at the trial to help prove a suspect's guilt of the crime with which he is charged.

One of the decisions (*Mapp* v. *Ohio*, 1961) applied to all of the states a rule—previously in effect in the federal court system but in only some of the states—that evidence taken as a result of a search of the suspect or of his immediate vicinity, without a search warrant, could not be used against him if the arrest was not made according to law. Known as the "exclusionary rule" because it calls for the exclusion of evidence from use at trial, it was developed by the courts because they considered it the best deterrent to improper police action.

Another Supreme Court decision (*Miranda* v. *Arizona*, 1966) was even more significant than its famous "parent case" (*Escobedo* v. *Illinois*, 1964). In *Miranda* v. *Arizona*, the court applied the exclusionary rule to a confession or other statement given by a suspect after his arrest, in answer to police questions, if the police did not follow certain requirements. These include advising the suspect of his constitutional privilege not to answer any questions, as well as of his right to have an attorney (provided by the state, under some circumstances) present to advise him during any questioning. (The Escobedo ruling had specified the right to an attorney.)

These developments have led to the reexamination of what contacts the police may have with a person before it can be considered that an arrest has taken place. One proposal is that police may stop a person on the street for general questioning and make a limited search of him for a weapon without its being considered an "arrest" or a "search" in the legal sense.

RICHARD A. GREEN
Director, American Bar Association Project on Minimum Standards for Criminal Justice

Further Reading: LaFave, Wayne R., *Arrest: The Decision to Take a Suspect into Custody* (Boston 1965).

ARREST OF JUDGMENT, in law, is the act of staying a judgment or refusing to enter it because of some defect in the record of the case. The procedure is employed in both civil and criminal cases. It amounts to a setting aside of the verdict for some reason apparent on the face of the record that would render a judgment on the verdict, if given, erroneous or reversible.

In a criminal case, a motion in arrest of judgment may be filed by a defendant after a verdict of guilty, as a means of challenging the legal sufficiency of the indictment or information on which the verdict was based. An arrest of judgment is granted if the court finds that the indictment did not state facts constituting a criminal offense or was deficient for some other reason. In a civil case, a motion in arrest of judgment similarly challenges the legal sufficiency of the pleadings or of some other part of the record.

ARRHENIUS, är-rā′ni-us, **Svante August** (1859–1927), Swedish chemist and physicist who received the Nobel Prize in chemistry in 1903 for his theory of electrolytic dissociation. He also developed an important equation for expressing the rate of a chemical reaction. His work laid foundations for the sciences of physical chemistry and electrochemistry.

Arrhenius was born near Uppsala, Sweden, on Feb. 19, 1859. In 1881, after five years at Uppsala University, he went to Stockholm, where he measured the conductivities of electrolytic solutions. In his Ph.D. thesis, submitted to Uppsala University in 1884, he described these measurements and presented a theory that explained the behavior of electrolytes in terms of molecular dissociation. This theory, which was a basis for his Nobel Prize award, was so revolutionary that it bewildered his examiners, who gave his thesis the lowest passing grade.

In 1887, Arrhenius wrote a refined version of his theory of electrolytic dissociation. He stated that some of the molecules of the electrolyte break up into positive and negative ions when in a water solution and that this dissociated state exists independent of the passage of electricity through the solution. He also stated that the degree of dissociation of the electrolyte increases as the electrolyte solution is made more and more dilute. Later experiments showed that this relationship was true in the case of weak electrolytes but not accurate in the case of strong electrolytes.

In 1889, Arrhenius discovered the remarkable speedup of chemical reactions with increasing temperature. Although the average molecule only increases its energy about one percent per degree of increase in temperature, the rate of reaction often doubles with a 10° rise in temperature. Molecules whose energy exceeds the average molecular energy by E are present in the proportion

$$n/N = e^{-E/RT}$$

where n is the number of activated molecules, N is the total number of molecules, E is an energy level above the average energy, R is the Boltzmann gas constant, and T is the temperature in degrees Kelvin. Arrhenius concluded that the rate of reaction was proportional to the concentration of activated molecules. Accordingly, for the specific reaction rate, k′, he wrote

$$k' = Ae^{-E/RT}$$

where A is a constant. This equation not only explained ordinary chemical reaction rates but many biological rates as well. The modern understanding of such processes is much broader and deeper, but Arrhenius' fundamental idea persists.

Arrhenius also proposed the remarkable hypothesis that life on earth may have come from other planets. He suggested that the first earthly organism may have been viable spores driven through space by the pressure of starlight.

Arrhenius was elected to the Swedish Academy of Science in 1901. He became director of the Nobel Institute of Physical Chemistry in 1905 and held this post for the rest of his life. He died in Stockholm on Oct. 2, 1927. His works include *Electrochemistry* (1901), *Worlds in the Making* (1908), *The Quantitative Laws in Biological Chemistry* (1915), *The Destinies of the Stars* (1918), and *Chemistry in Modern Life* (1923).

HENRY EYRING, *University of Utah*

ARRIAN, ar′ē-ən, Greek historian, philosopher, and administrator of the 2d century A.D., who wrote the most complete account of Alexander the Great. The Latin form of his name is *Flavius Arrianus.* Arrian was born in Nicomedia (modern Izmit), in Bithynia, Asia Minor, and was a student and disciple of the Stoic philosopher Epictetus. Like Xenophon, whom he admired and imitated, Arrian combined military and literary careers. Roman Emperor Hadrian (reigned 117–138) held him in high regard and made him a Roman citizen. He subsequently served as governor of Cappadocia (131–137), where he repulsed the invasion of the Alans in 134.

The most important of Arrian's extant historical writings is the 7-volume *Anabasis Alexandrou,* a narrative on the Asian expedition of Alexander the Great, which draws upon eyewitness accounts from Alexander's generals. Arrian's *Indica,* intended as a companion piece, deals with Alexander's retreat from India and includes a description of the voyage of Nearchus, one of Alexander's officers. Arrian is also credited with the authorship of *Tactica,* a treatise on tactics, and he was the editor of Epictetus' *Diatribai* and of the *Enchiridion,* a moral treatise containing an abstract of Epictetus' practical philosophy.

Further Reading: Robson, Edgar Iliff, ed., *Arrian,* Loeb Classical Library, 2 vols. (New York 1929–30).

ARRONDISSEMENT, à-rôn-dēs-mäN′, is a sub-division of the main French administrative district, the department. The arrondissement is headed by a *sous-préfet*. These subdivisions were established during the reign of Napoleon I. An arrondissement is also a city district in Paris and Lyon.

ARROW. See ARCHERY; BOW AND ARROW.

ARROW ARUM, ar′ō ar′əm, is the common name for the genus *Peltandra*, particularly *P. virginica*, a perennial herb of the arum family, Araceae. It is found in bogs from Maine to Florida and westward to Missouri. Its dark green leaves are shaped like arrowheads and it bears white flowers. *P. virginica* is sometimes grown in gardens.

ARROW WORMS. See NEMATHELMINTHES.

ARROWHEAD. See BOW AND ARROW.

ARROWHEAD, ar′ō-hed, is a common name for a group of plants distinguished by arrow-shaped leaves. The plants' unisexual flowers bear three green sepals, three white petals, and numerous stamens. The ovary has a great many one-seeded compartments, which are borne on a globular head. Arrowhead is found in tropical and temperate regions, mostly in the Western Hemisphere. Some species have been used medicinally, reportedly to cure such diseases as hydrophobia. The corms (bulblike parts of the stem) have been consumed as food, particularly in China and Japan, but they usually have an unpleasant acid taste.

Arrowhead belongs to the genus *Sagittaria*, family Alismataceae (Alismaceae). The most common species in the United States, *S. latifolia*, is often called the *duck potato* and is a valuable food for waterfowl. A few of the species are grown in water gardens for their attractive foliage and flowers.

Arrowhead (*Sagittaria latifolia*)

GOTTSCHO-SCHLEISNER

ARROWROCK DAM, ar′ō-rok, is a large irrigation dam on the Boise River in Idaho, east of Boise. It was built by the United States government in 1915. The dam is 354 feet (108 meters) high and about 1,100 feet (335 meters) long. It flanks Arrowrock Reservoir.

ANNAN PHOTO FEATURES

Arrowroot rhizomes

ARROWROOT, ar′ō-rōot, is an edible starch obtained from the rhizomes or underground stems of several tropical herbs. The starch is a tasteless whitish powder that crackles faintly when rubbed between the fingers. When mixed with boiling water, it swells up into a jellylike mass. It is an easily digested form of starch, and therefore is widely given to sick persons and children in the form of puddings and cookies. The refined arrowroot consists of about 85 percent carbohydrate and 15 percent moisture and contains only traces of other constituents. Because it lacks significant amounts of proteins and minerals, arrowroot starch has only slight nutritive value by itself.

The arrowroot herbs belong to the plant order Scitamineae. The principal source of arrowroot is a tropical American species called Bermuda or West Indian arrowroot (*Maranta arundinacea*, family Marantaceae). Bermuda arrowroot is cultivated in the West Indies for its jointed yellowish white underground stems, which measure 9 to 18 inches (22.5 to 45 cm) in length and ¾ inch (1.9 cm) in diameter. The underground stems are cut up at the end of a year of growth and soaked in water to make it easier to peel off the fibrous covering, which contains unpleasant tasting resins. The starchy core of the underground stem is next beaten to a pulp and washed repeatedly in water to separate the crude starch from the fibrous material. The starch settles out of the mixture or is extracted by centrifuging. The separated starch is finally dried in the sun and ground to powder. It is exported in sealed cases or barrels.

Arrowroot is commonly adulterated with potato, sago, manihot, curcuma, or other starches. The substitutions can be detected by microscopic examination of the starch grains. In true arrowroot, the grains are small and rounded, with a prominent scar marking the point of attachment of the seed.

Several botanical relatives of *Maranta arundinacea* also have underground stems that yield edible starch. *Curcuma angustifolia* and *C. leucorrhiza* of the ginger family (Zingiberaceae) are cultivated in India for their starchy underground stems, known as East Indian arrowroot. One species of the ornamental garden cannas,

Canna edulis (family Cannaceae), has starchy underground stems and is grown in the West Indies and elsewhere in the tropics for arrowroot starch. Extraction of the starch is accomplished by the same general methods as are used in the production of Bermuda arrowroot.

The so-called Brazilian arrowroot, which is more properly known as manihot, is a starch obtained from *Manihot esculenta* (spurge family, Euphorbiaceae), an important food plant of the Amazon region.

South Sea arrowroot is the starch prepared from the tubers of *Tacca leontopetaloides* (Taccaceae), which is cultivated in various parts of the tropics.

Portland arrowroot is produced in small quantities on the Isle of Portland off the south coast of England from the roots of *Arum maculatum* (Araceae). The starch is edible only after the removal of a poisonous irritant from the roots.

See also CASSAVA; CURCUMA; TACCA.

ARROWSMITH, ar′ō-smith, is a novel by Sinclair Lewis, published in 1925. In 1926 it was awarded the Pulitzer Prize, which the author declined.

Arrowsmith is concerned primarily with the state of American medicine in the early decades of the 20th century. It dramatizes the cleavage between the competent, idealistic, humanitarian physician and researcher, as represented by Martin Arrowsmith, and those examples of ignorance, quackery, political intrigue, and commercialism that are likely to be found in any profession. Arrowsmith's restless career carries him successively through the hardships of a small rural practice; the disillusionments of a politically controlled city health department; the intrigues in a fashionable metropolitan clinic; and the austerities, not quite free from rivalries and self-advertisement, of an endowed research foundation. In the end, Arrowsmith retires with a single associate to the complete independence of a Vermont farm, where they manufacture serum and pursue a number of research projects with objective rigor.

A novel of character as well as ideas, *Arrowsmith* is peopled by such important Lewis creations as Max Gottlieb, who vividly personifies the scientific spirit at its best; the notorious Almus Pickerbaugh, a blatant, gaseous, yet exuberantly vital ignoramus; the cyclonic Gustaf Sondelius; and Leora Tozer, Martin Arrowsmith's first wife, one of the most convincing and appealing portraits of a woman to be found in the entire range of Lewis' novels.

Arrowsmith is probably the most compassionate and "heroic" of Sinclair Lewis' major novels. At the same time, it ranks with *Main Street*, *Babbitt*, *Elmer Gantry*, and *Gideon Planish* in its vivid critique of some of the hypocritical aspects of modern American society.

ARROWWOOD, ar′ō-wŏŏd, is the common name of any of several unrelated shrubs that have slender, straight, lithe, and tough branches used for making arrows. The name is applied to such genera as *Cornus, Pluchea, Rhamnus, Viburnum, Oxydendrum, Holodiscus* (*Sericotheca*), and *Euonymus*. However, it is most commonly applied to certain species of the genus *Viburnum*, in the honeysuckle family (Caprifoliaceae), such as *V. dentatum*, the southern arrowwood. See also VIBURNUM.

ARROYO, är-rô′yō, is a town in Puerto Rico, on the south coast, at the head of Arroyo Harbor, about 40 miles (64 km) south of San Juan. It is the center of a sugar-producing area and exports molasses. Alcohol and rum are distilled there. Population: (1960) 3,741.

ARROYO DEL RÍO, är-rô′yō thel rē′ō, **Carlos Alberto** (1893–1969), president of Ecuador. He was born in Guayaquil, Ecuador, on Nov. 27, 1893. Admitted to the bar in 1914, he entered the national legislature two years later and became a senator in 1924. He held several municipal offices in Guayaquil and was dean and rector of its university. During his tenure as president of the Senate he became acting president of Ecuador in November 1939. Nominated by the Liberal party as its candidate, he was elected president in his own right on Jan. 12, 1940. Under his administration, Ecuador aligned itself with the Allies in World War II and broke off relations with the Axis countries. A coup d'état on May 29, 1944, forced his resignation. He died in Guayaquil on Oct. 31, 1969.

ARRUZA, är-rōō′sä, **Carlos** (1920–1966), Mexican matador, who was the most successful Mexican bullfighter ever to compete in Spain. In one season (1945) in Spain, he fought 108 bulls, winning a remarkable total of 219 ears, 74 tails, and 20 hoofs. A principal rival of Manuel Rodríguez (Manolete), he delighted the aficionados with his unorthodox and daring moves. The *arrucina*, a maneuver in which the matador holds the cape entirely behind his legs, exposing his whole body to the bull, was named for him.

Born in Mexico City on Feb. 17, 1920, Arruza became a millionaire at an early age, commanding sums as high as $20,000 for appearances. He retired as a matador in 1953, becoming a *rejoneador*, or mounted lance thruster, and bull breeder. He died in an automobile accident near Toluca, Mexico, on May 20, 1966.

ARS POETICA. See ART OF POETRY.

ARSACIDS, är-sas′idz, a dynasty of Parthian kings who ruled Iran from 247 B.C. until about 227 A.D. They took their dynastic name from that of their founder, Arsaces I.

The Parthians had come down from Transcaspia (east of the Caspian Sea) into what was later called Parthia (part of present Iran) after the main Iranian migration near the beginning of the Iron Age. They were then considered barbarians by the settled Iranian peoples, who resented their domination. After Arsaces I dislodged the Seleucids from Parthia in 247 B.C., the Arsacid kings gradually extended their rule over the region from the Euphrates to Afghanistan. They conquered Babylonia about 141 B.C. and reached the Mediterranean during the following century. In 53 B.C. the Roman general Crassus was routed by the Parthians at Harran. The Arsacid dynasty survived for more than four centuries until its last ruler, Artabanus V, was overthrown by the Sassanid king, Ardashir I, about 227 A.D.

During their domination in Iran the Parthians were converted to Zoroastrianism. They replaced Achaemenian art with that of the Seleucid Greeks and gave up the Old Persian script in favor of Aramaic. See also PARTHIA.

WILLIAM F. ALBRIGHT, *Johns Hopkins University*

ARSENIC, ärs′nik, is a chemical element that is classified as a metalloid because it has characteristics of both metals and nonmetals. Its symbol is As, its atomic number is 33, and its atomic weight is 74.91. Arsenic, which is between phosphorus and antimony in the Group V elements in the periodic table, exhibits properties intermediate between those two elements. The oxidation states of arsenic are +3, +5, and −3.

Elemental arsenic may have been first reported by the Greek historian Zosimus in the 5th century A.D., although some claim that Albertus Magnus, the 13th century German scholastic philosopher, was the first to isolate and identify arsenic as an element.

Occurrence. Arsenic is widely distributed in nature, even though it is one of the less plentiful elements in the earth's crust. The percentage of arsenic in the crust is comparable to that of tin and molybdenum. Virgin soils usually contain a few parts of arsenic per million, but the concentration often increases several hundredfold after several years of application of pesticides that contain arsenic. Arsenic is also found in seawater in concentrations of several tenths per million parts. Some deposits of elemental arsenic are known, but minerals in which arsenic exists as the arsenide, arsenite, or arsenate are much more common. Arsenopyrite, $FeS_2 \cdot FeAs_2$, is the most plentiful mineral.

Commercial arsenic is recovered as a byproduct of processing gold, silver, lead, copper, nickel, and cobalt ores. The United States, Sweden, and Mexico are the principal producers.

Allotropic Forms. Elemental arsenic exists in three allotropic forms. Black arsenic, which is amorphous, is obtained by the thermal decomposition of arsine (AsH_3). Yellow arsenic, which consists of As_4 molecules, is obtained when arsenic vapor is chilled rapidly. Yellow arsenic is quite volatile and is more reactive than metallic arsenic, to which it transforms easily. Gray, metallic arsenic has a layered crystal structure of high density. It is an excellent conductor of heat, but its electrical conductivity is only about 5 percent that of copper. It sublimes at 1130° F (610° C) under atmospheric pressure, melts at 1517° F (814° C) under a pressure of 36 atmospheres, and has a specific gravity of 5.7.

Reactions. Elemental arsenic burns at 752° F (400° C) to form the sesquioxide As_4O_6. It also reacts readily with chlorine and sulfur and with most metals to form arsenides. Arsenic does not dissolve in hydrochloric acid in the absence of oxygen and dissolves only slowly in its presence. It is insoluble in dilute sulfuric acid but reacts with the hot concentrated acid to form the sesquioxide but no sulfate. Warm, dilute nitric acid attacks it to form H_3AsO_3, and the concentrated acid forms H_3AsO_4.

Tests. The best-known compound of arsenic in its −3 oxidation state is arsine, AsH_3, a colorless gas. Arsine is formed by hydrolysis of an arsenide, reduction of arsenic compounds by zinc or tin in acid solution, or by electrolysis, using a mercury or lead cathode. In the Marsh test for arsenic, after formation of arsine, the gas is decomposed by heating in a small glass tube. The formation of a metallic mirror on the tube walls is proof of the presence of arsenic. A second test for arsenic, the Gutzeit test, depends on the reaction of arsine with a test paper impregnated with mercuric chloride or bromide. Arsine produces a brown coloration of the paper.

Because arsine is extremely poisonous, inhalation of the gas must be avoided in making tests.

Oxides. The oxides of arsenic are similar to those of phosphorus. Arsenious oxide, which is composed of tetrahedral As_4O_6 molecules, is known commercially as white arsenic or simply as arsenic. It is soluble in some organic solvents and is slightly soluble in water, in which it forms solutions of arsenious acid (H_3AsO_3). Arsenious oxide is amphoteric but has a slightly greater acidic character. It dissolves readily in alkalis to form arsenites. Arsenious oxide is extremely toxic (0.06 to 0.2 gram usually is fatal), although repeated consumption of small doses may lead to a higher tolerance. Suspensions of magnesium or ferric hydroxide are used as antidotes because they form insoluble arsenites.

Unlike phosphorus, arsenic does not react directly with oxygen to form arsenic pentoxide, As_2O_5. The pentoxide can be synthesized by oxidation of arsenic with nitric acid. On heating, the pentoxide readily loses oxygen to form arsenious oxide. The pentoxide is very soluble in water, forming solutions of arsenic acid ($H_3AsO_4 \cdot \frac{1}{2}H_2O$).

Halides. Arsenic trihalides are prepared by direct combination of the elements or by the reaction of the oxide or sulfide with a halogen. Arsenic does not form oxyhalides. The only pentahalide known is arsenic pentafluoride. The halides are reduced by hypophosphite, sulfurous acid, chromous chloride, or cuprous chloride. The volatility of arsenic trichloride has led to separation of arsenic from antimony and other heavy metals by volatilization of arsenic in a stream of chlorine.

Arsenates and Arsenites. Arsenates closely resemble the corresponding phosphates in solubility and crystal form, but they hydrolyze more than the phosphates. Sodium arsenate, $Na_3AsO_4 \cdot 12H_2O$, is used in printing inks, in dyeing textiles, and in preparing arsenates, such as lead and calcium arsenates, that are used in insecticides. Potassium dihydrogen arsenate, Macquer's salt, is used in the manufacture of flypaper and insecticides, in the dyeing of textiles, and in the preservation of hides. Sodium meta-arsenite, $NaAsO_2$, is used in the manufacture of soaps and insecticides, in dyeing, and in preserving hides. Arsenites of copper are used in Paris green as an insecticide and in Scheele's green as a pigment.

Sulfides. Arsenic forms the sulfides As_4S_3, As_4S_4 (red arsenic), As_2S_3 (yellow arsenic), and As_2S_5. The sulfides are acidic and dissolve in strong bases. Both red and yellow arsenic were used by the Greeks and Romans as color pigments. These compounds are still used for colors.

Organic Compounds. Organic compounds containing arsenic-carbon bonds can be prepared in numerous ways. The simplest way is to use Grighard reagents and arsenic halides. The trialkyl and triaryl arsines form many compounds with heavy transition metals. They also react with alkyl and aryl halides to form quaternary salts.

Effects on the Body. Arsenic causes acute inflammation of the stomach and also affects other parts of the body. Nevertheless, arsenic compounds have been used medicinally at least since the time of Hippocrates in the 5th century B.C. In 1909, Paul Ehrlich discovered that an organic compound containing arsenic could cure syphilis. However, antibiotics have now replaced arsenic compounds in most treatments.

GREGORY R. CHOPPIN, *Florida State University*

ARSENOPYRITE, är′sə-nō-pī-rīt, is a tin-white, opaque mineral with a metallic luster. It crystallizes in the orthorhombic system. Also called *mispickel*, it is a principal source of arsenic, and also contains iron and sulfur. Its formula is FeAsS (FeS₂·FeAs₂). The iron may be replaced by cobalt, in which case the mineral is known as *danaite*. The hardness of arsenopyrite varies from 5.5 to 6.0, and its specific gravity from 5.9 to 6.2.

Arsenopyrite occurs chiefly in crystalline rocks together with gold, silver, lead, and tin. It abounds in Austria, Germany, England, Switzerland, Scandinavia, and the United States (Connecticut, New Jersey, Maine, Montana, and Colorado).

Danaite, named for the American mineralogist James Dwight Dana, was first extracted at Franconia, N.H.

See also ARSENIC.

ARSINOË II (316–271 B.C.), är-sin′ō-ē, was a celebrated woman of antiquity, who was involved (as perpetrator or victim) in several instances of the violence characteristic of royalty in the Hellenistic world.

The daughter of Ptolemy I Soter of Egypt and Berenice I, she married Lysimachus, king of Thrace, about 300 B.C. Ambitious of securing the crown for her own children, Arsinoë persuaded Lysimachus to put to death Agathocles, the son of his former wife. This crime proved fatal to the Thracian king, because Lysandra, the wife of the murdered prince, fled with her children to the court of Seleucus I Nicator of Syria, who took up arms in her favor. In the course of the war, Lysimachus was slain, and his kingdom was taken by the conqueror (281 B.C.).

Arsinoë then fled to Macedonia, which was soon overrun by the Syrian army. In less than a year, however, Seleucus was assassinated by Arsinoë's half brother, Ptolemy Keraunos. Arsinoë, who held the city of Cassandreia (Potidaea) in Macedonia, was induced, under promise of marriage, to admit Ptolemy Keraunos within the walls; but no sooner had he entered than he had her two children butchered before her eyes.

Exiled to Samothrace, she succeeded in escaping to Egypt, where she became (276 B.C.) the second wife of Ptolemy II Philadelphus, her own brother, who banished his first wife, Arsinoë I, to Coptos. This marriage between sister and brother afforded a precedent for the unnatural unions that afterward became common among the Greek rulers of Egypt.

Ptolemy II, who was thoroughly enamored of Arsinoë II, gave her name after her death to a province of Egypt (Arsinoïtis) and to several cities in Egypt and elsewhere. He also intended to erect a temple to her but was prevented by his own death and that of the architect who had been commissioned for this work.

Further Reading: Macurdy, Grace Harriet, *Hellenistic Queens: A Study of Woman-Power in Macedonia, Seleucid Syria, and Ptolemaic Egypt* (Baltimore 1932).

ARSON, ar′sən, is most often defined as the willful and malicious burning of the real or personal property of oneself or another. It usually is committed covertly during the hours of darkness and out of sight of witnesses. There is usually no complaining witness as there is in other crimes, and since fire normally tends to destroy its own evidence, obtaining the legally required evidence or criminal origin is difficult. Arson has been called the easiest crime to commit and the hardest to detect, investigate, and successfuly prosecute.

Motives for setting fires are many and varied. They include revenge, spite, jealousy, intimidation, harassment, vandalism, excitement, and relief from tension. Arson also is committed in an attempt to defraud insurance companies or to conceal evidence of theft, embezzlement, and other crimes.

A term frequently associated with incendiarism is *pyromania*, or pathological fire setting. Pyromaniacs suffer from a mental disorder associated with morbid repetitive impulses to set fires. (See PYROMANIA.)

Statistics of the National Fire Protection Association show that in the mid-1960's, about 31,000 building fires of suspicious and incendiary origin occurred annually in the United States, causing damages estimated at nearly $70 million. While these represented only a small percentage of the total number of building fires, another area of possible incendiarism existed in 65,000 building fires of undetermined origin, with a monetary loss of nearly $500 million.

The Fraud and Arson Bureau of the American Insurance Association, which cooperates with authorities throughout the United States, conducted 4,393 investigations into fires of suspicious and incendiary origin in 1965. Of these, 836 fires were considered to have been set for recovery of insurance, which amounted to $46,221,000. A total of 671 persons were arrested during these investigations, including the so-called "pathologicals," unlawful intruders, revenge-motivated persons, vandals, and fraud firesetters. The Federal Bureau of Investigation's Uniform Crime Report shows that in the mid-1960's, arrests for arson averaged over 5,000 yearly, of which over 3,000 involved persons under 18 years of age.

Arson seminars, taught by experts, are now held annually at leading universities in the United States. Topics discussed include laws of search, seizure, and confession; tracing the origins of fires; electrical and other accidental origins of fires and explosions; collection and preservation of evidence; motivation of fire-setters; and forensic laboratory identification of evidence.

JOHN E. STUERWALD, *President*
International Association of Arson Investigators

Further Reading: Battle, Brendan P., and Weston, Paul B., *Arson: A Handbook of Detection and Investigation* (New York 1960).

ARSONVAL, är-sôn-val′, **Jacques Arsène d'** (1851–1940), French physicist and biophysicist. He invented the moving-coil galvanometer, an instrument for measuring small electric currents. He also pioneered in investigating the role of electricity in the functioning of the body. He developed a theory on the role of electric currents in muscular contraction and experimented with high-frequency currents in the treatment of disease.

D'Arsonval was born at La Borie, in the department of Haute-Vienne on June 8, 1851. After preparatory studies at a polytechnic school, he went to the College of France and studied under Claude Bernard. He became a doctor in medicine (1876), a director of the biophysics laboratory (1882), and a professor at the College of France (1894.) He died at La Borie in December 1940.

ART. The word "art" comes from Latin *ars*, meaning "skill," and it still retains this original meaning—for example, "the art of cooking". But it has come to have a wider significance. In the broadest sense, art embraces all the creative disciplines—literature, poetry, drama, music, dance, and the visual arts. However, as most commonly used today, art means the visual arts, those areas of artistic creativity that seek to communicate primarily through the eye.

The visual arts can be divided into three main categories: painting, sculpture, and architecture. (The graphic arts—woodcutting, etching, engraving, drypoint, wood engraving, and lithography—fall loosely within the category of painting.) Line, form or shape, color, space, and light and shade are the basic elements of the visual arts. In each specific art form some of these elements are relatively more important than others. Color, for example, is a more essential concern of the painter than of the architect.

Primitive Art.—From earliest known times man has created visual images. All primitive art, whether Paleolithic or 20th century African, seems to stem from the common needs of primitive peoples to protect themselves against forces of nature that they do not understand, to represent the sources of their food supply, and to honor and preserve the spirits of ancestors.

The oldest surviving examples of primitive art are paintings of animals on the walls of caves, such as those found at Lascaux, France, which date from 15,000 to 10,000 B.C. The Paleolithic artist who created these paintings, perhaps the inheritor of an older tradition about which we know nothing, portrayed the beasts that were essential to his survival, the bison and the bull. His paintings emphasized the aspects of the animals that were of most importance to him—the legs, which put the animal in motion, the mass of the body, which provided food, and the horns, which represented danger. Contemporary with these paintings are stone carvings of female goddesses, fertility symbols representing another aspect of man's survival. Masks for ritual spirit dances, an art form common to almost all primitive cultures, are one of the most important kinds of primitive visual expression. They range in form from the most highly realistic to the most bizarre and abstract.

Mesopotamia and Egypt. It was in Mesopotamia and Egypt, lands made fertile by great rivers, that an urban society and, concomitantly, a monumental architectural style first arose. In Mesopotamia, as early as 3500 B.C., the Sumerians raised enormous mountains of earth, called ziggurats, on top of which they built the temples of the gods who owned their cities. The ziggurat was an impressive sight as it rose from the flat plains of the Tigris-Euphrates river basin in western Asia.

The Egyptian culture, centered around the banks of the Nile River, reached its maturity between 2614–2181 B.C. During this period it produced in all three branches of the arts forms which were revolutionary in clarity of organization, both in individual forms and in the relationships between forms. Egyptian art was highly aristocratic, centering around the ruler, or pharaoh, and his court. It was also closely connected with Egyptian religious thought relating to death and the afterlife. On tombs, and much later also in temples, Egyptian artists lavished all of their considerable skills.

The Encyclopedia Americana offers a broad coverage of art. Articles on Africa, Asia, and major countries have sections on art and architecture. Techniques and forms are discussed under such headings as "Bas-Relief," "Fresco Painting," and "Pointillism." Periods and movements may be found in such articles as "Baroque Art" and "Impressionism." For a detailed guide for study, see the Index entries under *Art* and related subjects.

In painting the artist sought to represent the essential parts of the body in the most direct fashion. Shoulders and arms are seen straight on, while the legs and the face are seen in profile. Perspective and foreshortening were not used in Egyptian painting. Objects that extend in space are not shown as they appear to the eye, but as they actually are. For example, all four walls enclosing a garden would be represented in their absolute sizes as they relate to each other, rather than diminishing in size as they recede in distance. The Egyptians also strove for completeness in their representation of scenes from daily life. Wall decorations in the tomb of a king or noble, for example, represented the dead man accompanied by all of the things that he would want with him in the afterlife—his pleasures, his family, his slaves, and his animals.

Egyptian sculpture and architecture were massive, solid, and permanent. It was believed that the statue of the deceased became the permanent home of his soul in the afterlife. The statue was therefore carved of the hardest stone, and its blocklike, frontal character preserved visually the hardness of that stone. The statue was not intended to be an actual likeness, but a generalized representation incorporating those essential features of the body which the deceased would need in the afterlife.

The triumphs of Egyptian architecture were the pharaonic pyramid tombs, the greatest of which are those of Khufu (Cheops), Khafre, and Menkure, located at Giza. These pyramids, meant to be seen from the outside, have almost no interior space. The body of the pharaoh was placed in a small room inside the pyramid, which hopefully would never be violated, so that the deceased could enjoy his afterlife undisturbed. Few basic changes occurred during the 3,000-year history of Egyptian art, although it evolved through many beautiful and subtle variations.

Crete. After the year 2000 B.C. other major civilizations appeared in the regions surrounding the Aegean Sea, especially on the island of Crete, and later on the mainland of Greece. The early art of Crete is known as Minoan, after Minos, a legendary king of the island. It had two great periods of flowering, the first from about 2000 to 1700 B.C., and the second from around 1600 to shortly after 1500 B.C., when there occurred a mysterious catastrophe from which the Minoan civilization never recovered. During the first period great palaces became the centers of civilization, and pottery decorated with brightly colored, geometric patterns was produced. Large, elaborate palaces, such as the one at Knossos, are characteristic of the second phase of Minoan art. Painting, both on walls and on vases, turned from geometric to natural forms, such as the marvelously curvilinear aquatic creature that decorates the famous Minoan Octopus vase. The palaces, with characteristic columns tapering toward the base, were large, airy, well-planned, and without defensive structures. Military representations play almost no part in the art of the Minoans, who were a rather hedonistic race of traders. The only religious images are small statuettes of elegantly dressed goddesses, who are charming rather than awesome.

When the Minoan civilization fell, around 1500 B.C., certain cities on the Greek mainland reached a peak of artistic activity. One of them, Mycenae, has given its name to this period. The Mycenaeans built tombs that rivaled the pyramid tombs of Egypt in size. Mycenaean tombs, however, were built underground and shaped like beehives. The dead were buried wearing masks of gold and accompanied by intricately decorated gold artifacts.

Greece. From this background arose the art of ancient Greece, the foundation of all later Western art. From about 1100 to 700 B.C., Greek vase painters worked in what is called the geometric style, characterized in its earliest phase by rather strict geometric forms only, and later by the introduction of rudimentary human and animal forms, often arranged in very sophisticated patterns. About 700 B.C. a wave of influence from the East burst over Greece, introducing narrative figure composition from Sumeria and Assyria, as well as the Oriental costumes, hairstyles, and beards that appear in the vase painting of this period. Around 650 B.C. the Oriental style waned, and a new, specifically Greek style, the Archaic, came to the fore. In painting and in sculpture, the Archaic artist came to grips, for the first time in the history of art, with the problem of representing the human body, in all its complexity, as it actually appears to the eye. Ardent students of anatomy and admirers of the perfect beauty to which the body of a youth could attain, the Greeks sought to capture the momentary perfection (*acme*) of youth in the standing male figures known as *kouroi*. Throughout the Archaic period, these figures maintain the rigid frontal pose of Egyptian sculpture, with the left foot planted firmly in front of the right, and the hands held tightly to the sides, but a change, measurable almost year by year, is evident in the ease with which the sculptors rendered musculature and the moving parts of the body, such as the knees. The problem of representing the body in motion was taken up in vase painting and relief sculpture. These two approaches merged around 490 B.C., in the freestanding warrior figures of the east pediment of the temple of Aphaia at Aegina. For the first time we find a sculptor with such technical facility in the rendering of the human form that he could turn his attention to capturing the noble spirits of these warriors and the pathos at their moments of death.

The female form in Greek art before the 4th century B.C. is almost always clothed, whereas the male is generally shown "heroically" nude. By the end of the Archaic period, about 490–480 B.C., the representation of the female costume reached an extraordinary degree of elegance and refinement. The representations in relief of the goddess Athena (about 460), in very simple and severe dress, on the metopes of the Temple of Zeus at Olympia signals the emergence of the early or "severe" phase of the classical style that dominated 5th century Greek art. The classical style reached its culmination in both sculpture and architecture in the Parthenon in Athens, erected between 448 and 432 B.C. after the victory of the Athenians over the Persians. In the Parthenon sculpture there is an almost complete visual harmony of form, of motion, and of proportion—the same balance, harmony, and formal perfection, joined to the profound insight into the human condition that characterizes the tragedies of Sophocles and Euripides.

Greek architects sought perfection of form in a series of temples that were, in a sense, large pieces of public sculpture. Like the pyramids of the Egyptians, the Greek temple was meant to be seen from the outside. It consisted of a dark, rectangular interior, usually divided into a larger and a smaller space, surrounded on all four sides by an open colonnade. The interior spaces, reserved for cult images, were seldom seen by the public. In the Parthenon the architects employed the most subtle visual tricks to make the building appear more perfect than it actually was. The Greeks had observed that a straight horizontal line appears to sag in the middle and that a column with straight sides appears to narrow in the middle. They curved the lines of the buildings to compensate for these optical illusions. The base of the temple curves upward toward the center, and the edges of the columns are curved slightly outward. The effect of these visual tricks is to give the building a litheness, a sense of being almost a living form.

In the 4th century B.C. the center of political and artistic activity in the Greek world shifted from Athens to the Hellenized cities of the west coast of Asia Minor. Sculptors of the 4th century B.C. refined and developed concepts from the classic period in Athens, but by the late 3d century B.C. a new, far more active style reached its climax in the great frieze of the altar of Zeus at Pergamum, with its large, muscular gods and monstrous giants engaged in violent battle.

Rome. The Romans were the heirs of both the Greek and the Etruscan cultures. Etruscan civilization flourished in northern and central Italy from the 7th century B.C. until the end of the 3d century B.C., when it came completely under Roman domination. The Etruscans, combining Greek styles with a native interest in more angular lines and shapes, produced their own art forms, most notably terra cotta sarcophagi capped by reclining figures. The Etruscans also became masters in technical fields such as engineering, town planning, and metal casting, a legacy they passed on to their successors, the Romans.

Roman art was once considered to be only an unfortunate decline in Greek art, but this point of view is no longer held, especially for Roman architecture. Even in the republican period, to 60 B.C., when Greek forms were used, they were used with a new sense of pattern in light and shade and of relationships between solids and void. Imperial Roman architects, beginning in the reign of Nero, developed vaulted architecture on a grand scale for public, private, and religious buildings. Almost all previous architecture had used the post and lintel system of construction, but the Romans enclosed vast interior spaces with great brick and concrete vaults, such as that in the dome of the Pantheon (begun in 118 A.D.), which spans a circular area 145 feet (44.2 meters) in diameter. Not only did the Romans realize the visual possibilities of arches and vaults as forms, but they also realized, in a revolutionary fashion, the possibilities of interior space. The

WESTERN ART THROUGH THE AGES

Western art may be divided roughly into periods or cultures, beginning with prehistoric primitive art, such as the cave paintings found at Lascaux, France, and continuing to the abstract, non-representational art of the 20th century. The art of each period or culture has certain stylistic characteristics that differentiate it from that of the others.

CLASSICAL GREEK sculpture, from the east pediment of the Parthenon, idealizes the human form.

ARCHIVES PHOTOGRAPHIQUES—
ART REFERENCE BUREAU

PRIMITIVE PAINTINGS of animals (*above*), from the Paleolithic age, are on cave walls at Lascaux, France.

EGYPTIAN SCULPTURE, *Mycerinus and His Queen* (*right*), dated about 2525 B.C., shows massivity marking Egyptian art.

MUSEUM OF FINE ARTS, BOSTON

MARBURG—ART REFERENCE BUREAU

GOTHIC SCULPTURE called *Le beau Dieu* (13th century) is at the central portal of the west façade of the Amiens cathedral in France.

ALINARI—ART REFERENCE BUREAU

ANCIENT ROMAN painting (*above*), from the House of the Mysteries in Pompeii, shows rich style of mural decoration.

BYZANTINE mosaic (*right*) of Emperor Justinian and his courtiers is in the ancient church of San Vitale, Ravenna, Italy.

ALINARI—ART REFERENCE BUREAU

384

RENAISSANCE art reached a pinnacle in the work of Michelangelo, such as the *Creation of Adam*, on the Sistine ceiling.

BAROQUE paintings by Rembrandt, such as *Woman Bathing in a Stream* (above), marked the high point of the period of the great 17th century Dutch masters.

MODERN ART has evolved from works like Paul Cézanne's tranquil *Basket of Apples* (above) to the nonrepresentational art of the 20th century, like Constantin Brancuşi's sculpture *Bird in Flight* (left).

grandeur and vastness of their architectural space mirrored the grandeur and vastness of the empire.

In sculpture, Roman portraiture, based on Hellenistic prototypes, developed an incisive, rugged, and sometimes even brutal power of its own. We cannot be certain of the relationship of Roman to Greek wall painting, for no Greek examples have come down to us. But we know from the wall paintings at Pompeii that by the 1st century B.C. Roman painters had developed an elaborate style of mural decoration incorporating highly complicated architectural illusions and three-dimensional figures moving in a shallow but clearly defined space. In Rome, painters seem to have been as interested in rendering space as architects were in creating it, whereas Egyptian painting had had no three-dimensional space, and the only space in Greek vase painting is that displaced by the rather two-dimensional and linear figures.

Early Christian. The coming of Christianity gradually changed the whole course of Western art. After Emperor Constantine, who was converted to Christianity in 312, established it as the official religion of the empire, Roman architecture changed from the great vaulted space of the Basilica of Constantine (Maxentius) to large new churches, such as old St. Peter's, built under imperial patronage. These unvaulted churches were specifically designed to meet the requirements of the Christian liturgy, although they were loosely based on the basilica, an imperial architectural type of enormous variety. The simplicity of their spaces, contrasted with the complexity of space in previous imperial architecture, reflects the simplicity of faith which the early church emphasized.

Byzantine. After the 4th century A.D., Rome ceased to be a great center of artistic activity, and by the middle of the 6th century the artistic lead was taken by Constantinople, or Byzantium, the eastern seat of the emperors. With the reign of Justinian (527–565) a mature Byzantine style emerged, which, although based in part on earlier types, showed an entirely new attitude toward visual forms. Justinian and his courtiers as represented in the famous mosaic in San Vitale, Ravenna (about 546), are not portrayed as physical bodies, but as creatures of the mind and spirit, or soul. All weight has been removed from the figures; the bodies are hidden under an abstract pattern of drapery. They stand against a glittering gold ground, which cannot be interpreted as three-dimensional space. Justinian's great palace church, the Hagia Sophia in Constantinople (532–537), is as vast in scale as the Pantheon, but it also achieves a feeling of disembodiment. Individual spatial units are no longer clearly defined; light streams in through the walls and dome, destroying the sense of their mass, and the walls are covered with a profusion of mosaic and colored marble decorations that also deny their mass and strength. The Christian rejection of man's physical nature is mirrored in the art of the Christianized Eastern empire.

Carolingian and Ottonian. We know little of art in western Europe outside of Italy before about 700, when a vigorous school of manuscript illuminators appeared in Ireland and England. The style of these illuminations, incorporating intricately interwoven patterns of curving animal and plant forms, influenced painting at the court of Charlemagne, under whose reign northern Europe had its first artistic flowering. Charlemagne, crowned emperor in 800, attempted to revive the might of Rome, while his artists attempted, although in a crude and even barbaric way, to revive the visual world of the empire. Illuminations produced around Reims in this period combine figures in Roman togas with the nervous, linear excitement of the earlier Anglo-Irish school. Charlemagne's palace chapel at Aachen (Aix-la-Chapelle) reflects San Vitale in Ravenna, but with heavier and simpler forms. The elegance of the Byzantine style was replaced by an unsophisticated directness.

After the dissolution of the Carolingian empire, power in northern Europe gradually was funneled into the hands of the German rulers of Saxony known as the Ottonian emperors. The birth of German art can be traced to their court. It was an art deeply influenced by the elegance and linear complexities of the Byzantine style but infused with an emotionalism and power of expression that was entirely new. This style held sway in the north during most of the 10th century and into the first years of the 11th, when the new and powerful Romanesque style swept over all of western Europe.

Romanesque. The Romanesque architectural style was in part the result of reform movements within the Church seeking a return to a simple, direct Christianity. Thus this new architectural style, in the beginning, was almost totally undecorated. Using very simple architectural spaces and rhythms, the designers of these churches achieved powerful visual effects created by the great masses of the heavy stone walls themselves. The churches were dimly lit and had a fortresslike quality. This was the architecture of the church militant, and it was during the height of the Romanesque style, at the end of the 11th century, that the Crusades began. So great was the desire to build during the 11th century that, it is said, Europe was covered with a blanket of white churches.

In the third quarter of the 11th century, the Roman system of vaulting was revived and became common practice in western European architecture. The round arch was most commonly employed. Monumental sculpture also found new favor, especially in the early 12th century, when highly abstract figures, defined by a multitude of tightly curved lines, were produced. An example is the figure of Christ from the portal of the Church of the Magdalen at Vézelay, France. The figure, shown in glory and surrounded by a scene of the Last Judgment, was an awesome reminder of the judgment day to the faithful entering the church.

Gothic. During the 12th century, specifically in France, there slowly emerged out of the Romanesque a new style, which we now call Gothic. In architecture the style first appeared in the choir of the Church of St. Denis, near Paris, and in its purest form continued through the great cathedrals at Paris, Chartres, Reims, and Amiens. Romanesque architecture had emphasized the wall, but Gothic architecture sought to dematerialize the wall, replacing it with brilliantly colored stained glass windows which bathed the interiors in rich, flickering, red and blue light. The verticality of the Gothic church's enormous interior spaces, capped by pointed ribbed vaults, seemed to reflect a striving toward heaven.

Gothic sculptors moved away from the abstract, didactic Romanesque style toward a more realistic representation of the human body, without, however, losing the sense of an intensely religious motivation. The most important French Gothic sculpture adorned the portals of the great cathedrals. The late 12th century figures at Chartres are a unified part of the architecture. Gradually, in the course of the 13th century, the figures became more lively and detached from the wall, functioning more as individual pieces and less as architectural forms. By the early 14th century a very courtly and elegant style had arisen in France, and by the end of that century it had spread over Europe and become a true international style. Manuscript illumination, such as the Limbourg brothers' *Très riches heures du duc de Berry*, and the designing of stained glass windows generally occupied the attention of painters in northern Europe in these years.

Early Renaissance. In the late 13th and early 14th centuries in Italy, in the wealthy cities of Florence and Siena, monumental painting was, in a sense, reborn. Giotto, a Florentine, placed in his frescoes sober figures that once again were three dimensional, that existed in space, and that conveyed in their every gesture an unrivaled power of dramatic expression. In Siena, Duccio and his pupil Simone Martini combined a late Gothic linearity and dematerialization of the body with fresh observations of the material world and of man's environment.

Because of the ravages of the Black Death in Italy in the mid-14th century, it was not until the 15th century that the promise of Giotto and Duccio was fulfilled, and then primarily in Florence, since Siena never fully recovered from the plagues. The sculptors Ghiberti and Donatello, the architect Brunelleschi, and the younger painter Masaccio brought the Italian Renaissance into being. These artists sought a rational, homocentric art, based on the contemporary philosophy of humanism. They turned to the art of the Greeks and the Romans, which also centered on the human being, to find sources for the new style that they consciously sought to create. By the invention of one-point perspective, around 1420, Brunelleschi found a rational system for representing three-dimensional space on a two-dimensional surface. The Italian sculptors and painters studied anatomy, as well as proportion as used by the ancients in their figures. In architecture, after 1450, Leon Battista Alberti sought to revive not only the proportions and ornament of Roman building but also its principles of space, mass, and construction.

In painting, around 1480, Leonardo da Vinci fused the efforts of his predecessors into a more compact, dynamic style, to which he added fresh observations on the nature of light, on the way that light and shade define a three-dimensional form, and on proportions and physiognomy. Leonardo was as much a scientist as an artist. Indeed, art and science were practically interchangeable during this period, when both served man's efforts to discover and to understand himself and the natural world.

In the Low Countries, especially Flanders, a parallel development took place in the 15th century. Such painters as the Master of Flemalle and the brothers Hubert and Jan van Eyck began for the first time to exploit the possibilities of painting in oil, which allowed them to reproduce the colors, surfaces, and textures of the material world with a new fidelity and luminosity. Although little is known of Hubert van Eyck, Jan van Eyck's paintings, extremely meticulous in the rendering of visual details, glow like a collection of jewels. His realism and color established an unbroken tradition in northern European art. The style of the Flemish painters was still close in some ways to the sweeping elegance of the international late Gothic, yet their drapery folds are more angular, their colors far more true to life, and some painters, like Rogier van der Weyden, produced vivid new emotional effects.

High Renaissance. In Italy the impact of Leonardo paved the way for what is known as the High Renaissance, as personified by the painter Raphael. His rather sweet early style was transformed into something far more tightly organized, monumental, and "realistic" by his exposure to the paintings of Leonardo in Florence. In Rome, about 1510, Raphael produced paintings of extraordinary logic, balance, and harmony. He solved visual problems in the same logical spirit that his contemporaries, the Neoplatonist philosophers, applied to philosophical and theological problems. And in architecture, Donato Bramante, in his design for the new St. Peter's (1505), achieved a balance and harmony of parts that was altogether new. Bramante also had come under the influence of Leonardo, the universal man of the Renaissance.

Michelangelo Buonarotti neither attempted nor desired the balance achieved by Raphael. His sculpture, painting, and architecture—he took them up in that order—had a dramatic intensity, a preoccupation with the struggle of the soul for salvation, that gave his superbly muscular figures an unrivaled internal power. His paintings of the creation of the world, executed between 1508 and 1512 on the ceiling of the Sistine Chapel in the Vatican, made clear in visual terms the creation of man in God's image. Michelangelo's long career defies categorization. In his works almost all of the best possibilities of 16th century Italian art were stated. Even in architecture, his influence was enormous, as in his dome for St. Peter's in Rome, to which almost all subsequent domes pay tribute.

In Venice a separate tradition of painting grew up in the late 15th and 16th centuries. Venice was an enormously rich city, with close trade connections with the luxurious world of the Orient. Its painters reflected the love of luxury in which its citizens indulged themselves. The great phase of Venetian painting began with such men as Giovanni Bellini and Vittore Carpaccio, and entered a second phase with Giorgione, who drew directly on the canvas in oil paint, rather than transferring a pen or chalk design to the canvas. Venetians, as opposed to most Florentine and Roman painters, worked almost exclusively in oil, a technique imported from Flanders, which allowed them to depict the splendor of contemporary life in that city. Venetian painting reached its climax with Titian, whose sumptuous canvases, golden in his early years and silvery in his very last period, seem to glow from some inner richness of color and spirit. The leading painters of the latter part of the 16th century in Venice were Paolo Veronese, famous for his banquet scenes, and Tintoretto, whose diagonal spaces and freewheeling light effects foreshadow the movements of the 17th century.

Mannerism. The end of the High Renaissance coincides roughly with the death of Raphael in 1520. After about 1512, Raphael had begun to move away from the balance of his first Roman period, and from this late phase of his art came part of the inspiration for a new movement which is now known, rather uncomfortably, as Mannerism. Several later 16th century painters, among them Pontormo, Rosso Fiorentino, Giulio Romano, and Parmigianino, began to work in a style that seems consciously anticlassical and deliberately unbalanced. They were succeeded by a second generation of mannerists that included the Florentines Agnolo Bronzino and Giorgio Vasari. The latter also wrote the monumental *Lives of the Artists,* the first major piece of historical writing on art.

The mannerist style, a very complex one to define, and still not fully agreed upon by scholars, is characterized by a confusion of spatial effects, by bodies with hard outlines, silk-smooth surfaces, and elongated proportions. In almost all mannerist painters there is a latent eroticism and sometimes a psychological derangement. Often their color schemes employ harsh juxtapositions, and many of their paintings have a cruel elegance.

Baroque. The Reformation, or rather the Counter Reformation of the Catholic Church, had a profound effect on the art of the late 16th and 17th centuries. Mannerist religious painting was often too abstruse for popular devotional purposes, and so it was necessary to recapture or invent forms that would have a more general appeal. The baroque style, which developed out of a reaction against late mannerist excesses, was developed particularly in Rome by two painters from northern Italy, Annibale Carracci and Caravaggio. Annibale was deeply influenced by the early 16th century painter Correggio, a precocious artist whose soft, painterly style and brilliant illusionistic effects—a north Italian predilection—were largely ignored by his contemporaries. After he came to Rome from his native Bologna, Annibale tried to revive the "purer" and more classical style of Michelangelo and Raphael. Caravaggio, on the other hand, painted neither gods and goddesses nor elegant saints, but the man in the street, in peasant costume, with dirty hands. He also developed chiaroscuro, a technique that contrasts brilliant spotlight effects with areas of deepest shadow. His art, based on a type of lay Christianity popular at the time in Rome, was filled with dramatic intensity.

Studying in Italy at this time was Peter Paul Rubens, a Fleming who had a profound effect on the course of painting in the north of Europe. Rubens avidly copied all of the great masters of the Italian past, both recent and antique. When he returned to Antwerp in 1608, Rubens developed a free, brilliant, color-filled technique in oils, in which shadows ceased to be gray or black but reflected the surrounding colors. He is perhaps best known for his female figures, plump masses of vibrant pink and white flesh which move with great vigor and excitement in the infinite spaces he created for them.

In Rome the sculptor architect and painter Gian (or Giovanni) Lorenzo Bernini came to maturity around 1620. His work established the high baroque style in sculpture, just as Rubens more or less set the standard for high baroque painting. Indeed, Bernini sought to fuse all of the arts into a powerful dramatic whole which would totally capture the viewer. The marble of his *St. Theresa in Ecstasy,* in the Cornaro chapel in Rome, has an almost quivering life. A concealed light bathes the figures in a dramatic golden glow, emphasized by gilded bronze rays that come down behind the figures. The group is enclosed in a kind of architectural stage of curving polychrome marble. From boxes on the sides members of the Cornaro family, in marble, watch the event, and in the ceiling a frescoed, heavenly vision opens into infinite space.

The baroque, however, is a complex era. Standing beside the richness, freeness, and exuberance of Bernini and Rubens are the paintings of the Frenchman Nicolas Poussin, whose strict classical sense parallels that of his contemporary, the playwright Racine. The baroque in France had altogether a more classical flavor than its Italian counterpart. The great palace of the kings of France at Versailles, begun in 1669, is surely baroque in terms of scale, although it has a classical façade and its gardens are laid out with a rigorous sense of geometry.

In the Low Countries, Rubens represents only one trend, for painting in Protestant Holland took an entirely different direction, influenced by Caravaggio's dramatic use of light and scenes of common people. Dutch painting arrived at its greatest moment with the paintings of Rembrandt van Rijn. His early works have a strong baroque flavor, but in his middle and late periods, while maintaining his sensitive use of chiaroscuro, he became more concerned with representing the soul of man, delving deeply into human personalities and emotions. He used paint thickly and with great love to lay open man's innermost being, just as in his painting, *The Anatomy Lesson of Doctor Tulp,* the doctor lays open the arm of a cadaver for study. Late 17th century Dutch painting, however, could also reveal a consummate precision in the geometric ordering of compositional elements, as in the small, light-filled interior scenes of Jan Vermeer of Delft.

Rococo. By the 18th century the artistic center of Europe had shifted from Rome to Paris, the seat of the French court. There the rococo style, delicate, pastel in color, freely moving, curvilinear, and elegant, found its greatest expression in the paintings of Antoine Watteau, François Boucher, and Jean Honoré Fragonard. These painters chose for their subjects everyday events in the life of the courtiers and the bourgeoisie, depicted with gaiety, humor, charm, and an obvious delight in worldly pleasures.

In south Germany and Austria, on the other hand, there was a more direct continuation of the Roman baroque, often fused with the decorative devices of the French rococo. Architects, painters, and sculptors of these regions joined together to produce churches in which the three arts were fused together in an extraordinary and unequaled fashion. The spatial and rhythmic complexities and the elaborate sculptural and painted ornamentation of a church such as Johann Balthasar Neumann's Vierzehnheiligen (1743–1772), near Lichtenfels in northern Bavaria, are the visual counterpart of the elaborate counterpoint and ornamentation of a Bach fugue.

Toward the middle of the 18th century, a revival of interest in antique art produced the neoclassical movement, which reached its culmination in the works of Jacques Louis David, the great painter of the period of the French Revolution. In his geometrically ordered canvases, peopled with Greek heroes, art took on a profound political significance, reflecting the democratic aims of the French Revolution in scenes from classical antiquity. The severity of the style was a deliberate break with the aristocratic, rococo style of court art. And in Spain, David's contemporary, Francisco Goya, turned his virtuoso brushwork to biting social criticism and the exploration of the darkness in men's souls, which he mirrored in the vibrant blacks of his paintings.

19th Century France. Almost all of the great events of 19th century painting, except the development of English landscape painting by John Constable and J.M.W. Turner, took place in and around Paris. In that century a rapid succession of styles completely changed the general trend that art had taken since about 1400. The romantic painters, led by Eugène Delacroix, took up the color of Rubens and added an interest in current politics and the exotic worlds of North Africa and the Middle East. The realists, led by Gustave Courbet, rejected the romantic delight in the bizarre and painted the everyday world of the common man in a classical, monumental way deliberately reminiscent of Poussin but without his idealization.

Reacting perhaps to the contemporary development of photography, Édouard Manet, in paintings such as *Olympia* and *Déjeuner sur l'herbe* (both 1863), reaffirmed the essential artistic and visual functions of painting, as opposed to the literary and "realistic" trends that had dominated the art of the immediate past. The impressionists, including Auguste Renoir, Claude Monet, and Camille Pissarro, aware that light and color rendered form to the eye, described form only in those terms, using prismatic colors in what they thought was a scientific way. They never used black, which, according to science, does not exist in the spectrum. And because the eye can focus only on part of a scene in a given instant, they showed only part of a scene in focus, with the rest of the painting dissolving into a blur toward the periphery.

The styles of Manet and the impressionists were ill received by the French public and the styles that followed fared no better, and often worse. During the 19th century, ways of viewing the world, and the idea of the painter's role in that world, changed too rapidly for public taste to keep abreast of new developments. This was the beginning of that extensive gap that has since separated the artist from most of the public. Vincent van Gogh's turbulent, brilliantly colored, expressionistic view of the world found no more admirers than did Paul Cézanne's ordered, tranquil reduction of nature to its essential geometric elements. These two men are generally considered the fathers of 20th century painting. Cézanne attempted to represent space not from a static, single point of view, but as it is experienced in time. From his depiction of individual objects as seen from a few closely related points of view came cubism. Headed by Pablo Picasso, cubism fragmented objects by showing them from many different views simultaneously, exploring the relationship of visual space and time in a manner that has been related to Albert Einstein's contemporary theory of the relativity of physical time and space.

The beginning of modern sculpture may be dated from the work of the French artist, Auguste Rodin, in the last quarter of the 19th century. Rodin returned to the work of Michelangelo for inspiration, and infused sculpture with a sense of monumental grandeur that it had lacked for almost 200 years. The broken-up surfaces of his powerful bronzes helped to pave the way for cubist sculpture, and the freedom with which he used the human form liberated sculpture from the purely representational.

In Europe, the period before World War I produced many vigorous developments in painting. In France, the Fauves or "wild beasts," led by Henri Matisse, liberated color from its descriptive function and used it for emotional expression. Two groups in Germany, Die Brücke (The Bridge) and Der Blaue Reiter (The Blue Rider) used van Gogh's expressionistic style as a basis for further study of the inner man and for social criticism. Wassily Kandinsky transformed van Gogh's free brushwork and expressive use of color into the first "nonobjective" style, in which there is no subject matter except the act of painting itself, the quality of the paint, and the quality and relationships of the colors.

After World War I the deliberately antiart movement, Dada, flourished briefly, mainly in Switzerland. Surrealism, which was related to Dada, had more far-reaching consequences. Basing their work on the studies of the psychologists Freud and Jung, the surrealists explored the world of dreams and the subconscious, a world that is *sur* real, or of a "super-reality."

In sculpture such early 20th century masters as Constantin Brancuşi sought to reduce forms to their barest essentials. His *Bird in Flight,* with the machinelike perfection of its metal surface, shows the essence of the form of a bird moving swiftly through space. Purely nonrepresentational sculpture began in the period immediately following World War I with the abstract geometric forms of the Constructivists and, like nonrepresentational painting, reached full flower after World War II in the works of American sculptors such as David Smith.

United States. Some of the most important events of the post-World War II period have taken place in America, and by 1950 the art center of the world had shifted from Paris to New York. American abstract expressionists such as Jackson Pollock, Willem de Kooning, Franz Kline, and Robert Motherwell gave painting an enormous new freedom. Totally eschewing subject matter, these artists, often called "action

painters," attacked their enormous canvases with tremendous vigor. With large, bold brushstrokes or freely dripped paint, they showed that paint itself, using only color, form, and texture can produce powerful visual images.

American architecture had taken on international importance about a half-century before American painting. From the sophisticated and simplified use of Roman motifs by Thomas Jefferson, through all of the revival styles of the early 19th century, America produced no major innovations in architecture. In a sense, the work of H.H. Richardson in the 1880's represents a transitional phase. Although he used Romanesque motifs in the Marshall Field Wholesale Store in Chicago, he simplified and ordered the heavy, stone-arched elements of the exterior walls to give commercial architecture a fresh, clear dignity and personality of its own. Louis Sullivan, working primarily in Chicago around the turn of the century, was really the father of modern architecture. He insisted that form must follow function, meaning that the forms of buildings should be an honest reflection of their actual functions. His Wainwright Building in St. Louis, the first skyscraper, shows the unbroken vertical lines of its structural iron skeleton, rising on the exterior from the mezzanine to the great cornice that caps the whole. Sullivan's pupil and assistant, Frank Lloyd Wright, eventually discarded all traditional forms. For his prairie houses, such as the Robie House in Chicago, he used a long, low silhouette to match the landscape, and employed free-flowing, but highly organized interior spaces.

The International Style. Wright's work gave impetus to a new generation of architects in Europe. They, however, replaced the natural materials, such as wood and brick that had been favored by Wright, with products of the machine age—steel, glass, and reinforced concrete. Men such as Walter Gropius and Ludwig Mies van der Rohe, realizing that structural steel beams eliminated the function of the wall as a support, designed walls that are simple glass curtains between the exterior and the interior. This severe, rectilinear, "international style" of architecture is typified by the rectangular glass cages of Gropius' Bauhaus in Dessau, Germany. The most serious challenge to the international style came from the French architect, Le Corbusier. His most mature works of the 1950's and 1960's, such as the pilgrimage church at Ronchamp, France, show the sculptural and expressive power of freely moving concrete forms in space.

EUGENE JOHNSON
Williams College

Bibliography

Gombrich, Ernst, *Art and Illusion* (New York 1961).
Gombrich, Ernst, *The Story of Art* (New York 1966).
Hamlin, Talbot, *Architecture Through the Ages* (New York 1953).
Janson, Horst W., *History of Art* (New York 1962).
McGraw-Hill Book Company, Inc., *Encyclopedia of World Art* (London 1959–   ).
Panofsky, Erwin, *Meaning in the Visual Arts* (New York 1955).
Pevsner, Nikolaus, *An Outline of European Architecture*, Jubilee Ed. (Harmondsworth, Eng., 1960).
Read, Herbert, ed., *The Book of Art*, 10 vols. (New York 1965).
Read, Herbert, *The Meaning of Art* (Baltimore 1959).
Upjohn, Everard M., and others, *History of World Art* (London 1949).
Wölfflin, Heinrich, *Principles of Art History* (London 1932).

ART, Decorative. See DECORATIVE ART.

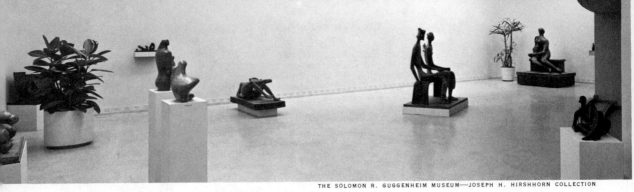

MODERN SCULPTURE COLLECTION of Joseph H. Hirshhorn, as shown at New York City's Guggenheim Museum.

ART COLLECTING, ärt kə-lek'ting, is the systematic accumulation of works of art by private individuals or by public institutions. A close connection exists between private and public collecting. Sir Kenneth Clark, British art historian, wrote: "When all is said, the world owes private collectors an enormous debt. Without them, many of the greatest works of art would have been lost or destroyed. Our public collections are, to a far larger extent than anyone realizes, private collections which have been accumulated and combined."

Earliest Collections. Art collecting began with the earliest civilizations—the Chinese, Indian, Sumerian, Egyptian, Cretan, Babylonian, and Persian. These early collections were prized less for their aesthetic value than for their religious significance and for the intrinsic worth of the precious metals and rare stones in the objects. The collections formed a kind of national treasury, a reserve of public wealth, and a symbol of the nation's credit. When the treasury outgrew the vault or strong room, it was taken into the sanctuary and the temple.

Classical Greece and Rome. The Greeks of the Hellenistic age were the first to collect art on a large scale. In Rome, the conquest of the ancient East brought plunder and new culture to the Eternal City. Senators of the republic and the caesars, as well as some private citizens, such as Virgil and Cicero, emerged as the foremost art collectors.

Renaissance. During the Middle Ages concern for art was insignificant. However, with the Renaissance, beginning in the 14th century, there was a reawakening of aesthetic consciousness, which largely had lain dormant in the Western world since Graeco-Roman times, and a renewed interest in art collecting. The collections of the Renaissance were true expressions of collecting in the grand manner, a far different thing from the haphazard accumulation of art that was characteristic of medieval princes.

Dominated by the ideals of humanism, Renaissance princes and popes became patrons of the great contemporary artists. Florence, the leading city of its day, was dominated by the Medici family, and for 150 years few European artists of major reputation, including Botticelli, Fra Filippo Lippi, Verrocchio, and Michelangelo, were left untouched by them.

Factual data regarding the prices paid for works of art during the Renaissance are scarce, but by the middle of the 15th century the artist had reached about the same economic level as the small shopkeeper. Raphael, Michelangelo, and Titian were the first artists to receive lucrative commissions. Michelangelo received the equivalent of $56,000 for painting the ceiling of the Sistine Chapel, but it took him four years to complete the work, and he had to pay his assistants out of that sum. Dürer became wealthy enough to leave an estate valued at $32,000. Van Dyck was paid $250 for his portrait of Charles I of England, now in the Louvre, and Rembrandt received about the same amount for his portraits. In France the court painters of Louis XIV received annual salaries of $3,000 in addition to free lodging and servants.

Between 1273 and 1806 the Habsburgs were, after the Medici and the popes, the most important patrons and collectors. The Habsburg Emperor Maximilian I was the patron of the Flemish painter, Bernard van Orley, and of many of the outstanding tapestry designers of Brussels. His encouragement of Dürer resulted in the incomparable print series, *The Triumph of Maximilian.* Margaret of Austria collected paintings by leading artists of the Netherlands, including Van Eyck, Memling, and Hieronymus Bosch.

During the Renaissance the collector was primarily a patron. His relation to the artist was that of master to servant, although there were exceptions, such as the painter Titian, who became a close and influential friend of his patron, Emperor Charles V.

Rise of the Open Art Market. The art market as it is known today dates from the mid-15th century, when a depression resulted in financial ruin for many Renaissance princes, particularly in Italy. Noble families were forced to sell many of the works of art they had accumulated over several generations. A more fluid art market arose as new millionaires offered to buy family treasures that had been acquired by the patronage system. Many of the great collections built after the 15th century were bought on the art market, rather than directly from the artist.

Post-Renaissance Collections. France, which during six centuries under the Valois and Bourbon kings gathered the masterpieces of Gallic culture, produced such leading 17th century collectors as Cardinal Richelieu, Cardinal Mazarin, and Jean Baptiste Colbert. In England, the most important collectors of the time were King Charles I, the duke of Buckingham, and the earl of Arundel. Charles I, who assembled works by Holbein, Dürer, Correggio, Rembrandt, Raphael, and Leonardo da Vinci, owned 28 Titians and was the patron of Rubens and Van Dyck. In Spain, King Philip IV, who was one of royalty's most passionate connoisseurs of art, was a patron of Velázquez. Elsewhere in Europe, Carl Eusebius, prince of Liechtenstein, began to assemble one of the greatest single family collections in the world. Queen Christina of

Sweden also bought art on a grand scale. During the 18th century Catherine the Great of Russia, Frederick the Great of Prussia, King Ludwig of Bavaria, and Pierre-Jean Mariette, a French scholar, were among the major collectors.

As trade and finance grew in Europe, art collecting by businessmen flourished. In Germany the Fugger banking family assembled a noted collection, and in France the banker Pierre Crozat brought together 19,000 drawings and 400 paintings.

Another type of collector was Herman Becker of the Netherlands, who established an immense collection by lending money to artists who repaid him in pictures. Rembrandt, for example, was in his debt and gave him at least two canvases. Becker was the precursor of Paul Durand-Ruel and Ambroise Vollard, the most important dealer-collectors of the French impressionists.

Modern Collections. Private collecting of art became "a legitimate end in itself" about the beginning of the 19th century, according to Francis Henry Taylor, former director of the Metropolitan Museum of Art in New York City. Since that time, "the work of art and its possession, its intimate relation to the tastes and curiosities of the man who owned it, has been a part of the texture of the life of the community. There is, in fact, one quality common to all of these collections, the quality of perspective enjoyed by every cultivated man. It is what Henry James called 'the sense of the past,' and what Edmund Burke meant when he spoke of 'the disposition to preserve and the capacity to improve.'"

Europe. After 1850, millionaires, rather than noblemen, assembled many of the great art collections. The Rothschild family brought together great collections in Frankfurt, Vienna, Paris, Naples, and London. Other modern European collections were formed by Emil Buhrle, Swiss gunmaker, and by Baron H. H. Thyssen-Bornemisza, German steel magnate.

In France, Victor Chocquet proved that it was possible to build a great collection without being wealthy. Chocquet, whom Renoir considered the greatest collector he knew, lived on the tiny income of a government official.

In the 1960's the most important European buyers of major works of art included Stavros Niarchos, Greek shipping tycoon; Gianni Agnelli, a member of the family that controls Fiat motors of Italy; Baron Heinrich von Thyssen, German steel magnate; Basil Goulandris and George Embiricos, Greek shipping operators; Charles Clore, British financier; and Heinrich Sprengel, West German chocolate manufacturer.

United States. In less than 150 years, the United States has become the greatest art-collecting country in the world, and one of the greatest depositories of works of art. Before the Civil War, art collecting was almost unknown in the United States. The only important exception was Thomas Jefferson, who assembled a collection of art objects, mainly paintings, at Monticello, his home in Virginia.

The vast wealth that developed in the United States after the Civil War made possible collecting on a large scale. In the mid-19th century August Belmont, John Jacob Astor, William Astor, William Vanderbilt, and other millionaires bought French academic painting. However, the taste of these early collectors is now generally considered to have been deplorable. There were only three discriminating collectors of note in the mid-19th century—Luman Reed, Thomas Jefferson Bryan, and James Jackson Jarves. Reed, a retired wholesale grocer, built the first American art gallery, in New York City in 1832. Bryan, who inherited a fortune, bought old masters, mainly Flemish, Dutch, and French. Jarves, heir to a glassmaking fortune, formed a collection of Italian primitives. Reed and Bryan were largely responsible for making art collecting fashionable in the United States.

During the 1880's and 1890's an expanding economy created an aristocracy of wealth in the United States. New American millionaires acquired a taste for the old masters of Europe and were soon transforming American collections into the world's best. Among these men was J. P. Morgan, the most prodigious collector of all time. He bought not only masterpieces of painting, but also precious Renaissance bronzes, vast collections of Byzantine enamels and ivories, Oriental porcelains, and illuminated manuscripts. Other American collectors were Benjamin Altman, the department store founder; Collis P.

PRIVATE ART COLLECTION and mansion of Henry Clay Frick is now open to the public in New York City. The collection's Fragonard Room is shown at right.

THE FRICK COLLECTION

Huntington, railway magnate; P.A.B. Widener, who made a fortune in meat and public transit; and Jules S. Bache, a Wall Street banker who gave his collection to the Metropolitan Museum of Art in New York City.

Many of these fabulous American collections of the 19th century provided the foundations of the nation's greatest museums. Henry Clay Frick, the steel industrialist, willed his art treasures and mansion in New York City to the public as the Frick Collection. Andrew S. Mellon gave 115 old masters and $15 million toward the establishment of the National Gallery in Washington, D.C. The Freer Gallery in that city holds the great collection of Oriental art assembled by Charles Lang Freer, a manufacturer of railroad cars. The Corcoran Gallery, also in Washington, was founded by William Corcoran, a banker and collector of American art. In Boston, the Isabella Stewart Gardner Museum, in the Venetian-style palace that was Mrs. Gardner's home, contains her collection of old masters. William Thompson Walters and his son, Henry Walters, assembled the collection that became the basis of the Walters Art Gallery in Baltimore.

Other 19th century collectors in the United States were Mrs. Potter Palmer of Chicago, who assembled the largest American collection of French impressionist paintings; the great corporation lawyer John G. Johnson, who bought Flemish primitives of the 15th and 16th centuries, as well as Italian Renaissance art; Henry O. Havemeyer, New York sugar refining magnate; Samuel H. Kress, department store millionaire; and William Randolph Hearst, owner of the Hearst newspaper chain.

After World War I, American collectors began to buy impressionist, post-impressionist and later European art, and finally contemporary American art. Among the early collectors of modern works were Albert C. Barnes, inventor of the patent medicine, Argyrol; Chester Dale, a Wall Street broker; and Duncan Phillips, heir to a steel fortune and founder of the Duncan Phillips Gallery in Washington, D.C. Heiress Peggy Guggenheim was one of the first collectors of abstract and surrealist art, which she assembled in her palace on the Grand Canal in Venice.

By the mid-20th century, more individuals and institutions were spending more money on art than at any other time in history. As a result, the supply of important works was dwindling, and in many countries governments began to put restrictions on the sale and export of art.

American collectors in the 1960's included the two children of Andrew Mellon, Paul Mellon and Mrs. Mellon Bruce; Norton Simon, West coast industrialist who paid $2.2 million for Rembrandt's *Titus;* and the Rockefeller brothers, especially David, Nelson, and John D., 3d. Others were John Hay Whitney, former American ambassador to London, and his sister, Mrs. Charles S. Payson, owner of the New York Mets baseball team; oilman Charles B. Wrightsman; Leigh Block, vice president of Inland Steel; Henry Ford, Jr., of the automobile family; and Jean Paul Getty, Texas oilman. Still others were Joseph H. Hirshhorn, who built a fortune in uranium in Canada; William S. Paley, chairman of the board of the Columbia Broadcasting System; Robert Lehman, New York investment banker; financier Henry Ittleson, Jr.; and Nathan Cummings, chairman of Consolidated Foods Corporation.

American art flourished in the period of national prosperity after World War II, and for the first time in history rose to a position of international importance. These factors combined to produce a growing awareness of art and a trend toward the formation of small private art collections by persons with moderate incomes. Graphic arts, drawings, small paintings and sculpture, and the work of young or unrecognized artists make up a large part of these collections. The trend stimulates the growth of small galleries, helps artists, and may shape a new concept of art collecting.

MILTON ESTEROW
New York "Times"; Author of "The Art Stealers."

Bibliography

Cabanne, Pierre, *The Great Collectors* (New York 1963).
Constable, William G., *Art Collecting in the U.S.A.* (Camden, N.J., 1964).
Cooper, Douglas, *Great Family Collections* (New York 1965).
Cooper, Douglas, *Great Private Collections* (New York 1963).
Gump, Richard, *Good Taste Costs No More* (Garden City, N.Y., 1951).
Horn, Jeanne, *Hidden Treasures* (New York 1963).
Reitlinger, G., *The Economics of Taste* (New York 1964).
Rigby, Douglas and Elizabeth, *Lock, Stock, and Barrel* (New York 1944).
Saarinen, Aline, *The Proud Possessors* (New York 1958).
Seligman, Germain, *Merchants of Art: Eighty Years of Professional Collecting, 1880–1960* (New York 1962).
Taylor Francis, *The Taste of Angels* (Boston 1948).

ART EDUCATION. See EDUCATION, ART.

ART FOR ART'S SAKE was the rallying cry of a group of 19th century artists, writers, and critics who formed a movement, also known as *aestheticism,* that defended the autonomy of art. Leaders of the movement in France were Théophile Gautier, Charles Baudelaire, and Gustave Flaubert; in England, James MacNeill Whistler, Walter Pater, and Oscar Wilde. Baudelaire cited the American poet Edgar Allan Poe as exemplifying the ideals of art for art's sake.

The movement was a reaction against the spreading blight of industrialism and the concurrent emergence of an affluent middle class with narrow utilitarian standards. Many contemporary artists and writers proclaimed that art should not serve any purpose, including representation, and opposed all theories that viewed art as didactic or as an instrument of reform. They received much of their inspiration from the romantic ideal of the artist as an especially sensitive, superior person alienated from society, and from the Kantian concept of art as having "purposiveness without purpose."

The "art for art's sake" movement defined what art ought to be—pure—and what ought to motivate the artist and how society should treat him. It held that the experience of art is in itself intrinsically valuable. The movement's ideal, the worship of beauty, was in direct opposition to the ideals of worship of contemporary society—goodness and power. Aesthetic appreciation of art called for subtle discriminations of beauty and the ability to appreciate unusual and alien things: the mysterious, the horrible, and even the criminal and satanic.

The best-known opponents of art for art's sake were John Ruskin and Leo Tolstoy. Generally, any didactic theorists who give art a function, such as the Marxists, oppose aestheticism.

GEORGE DICKIE
University of Illinois at Chicago Circle

ART GALLERIES are buildings or rooms used primarily for the exhibition of works of art. They include museums, showrooms of commercial dealers in art, and important public or semipublic collections of art objects.

Early History. Art galleries, in the modern sense of the term, date from the 1700's. The public exhibition of works of art, however, goes back to a much earlier period. In ancient Athens of the classical period the marble hall that formed the north wing of the Propylaea contained historical and mythological works of celebrated painters and was called the Pinacotheca, or gallery of pictures. But most of the Greek art that is in museums today was made originally for religious or votive purposes. The Greek temple treasuries, collections of votive offerings and military booty, probably were closer to the modern concept of a museum than the Propylaean Pinacotheca. These treasuries were considered to be essentially public property and were displayed in the agorae or pinacothecae and in the gymnasia.

The collecting of art of the past had its beginnings in republican and imperial Rome. The Romans, who worshiped the same gods as the Greeks, at first put their booty from military campaigns in Greece and Asia Minor at the disposal of their own deities and the state, displaying them first in temples and later in baths and in other public places. The beginning of private collections accompanied the growth of a wealthy upper class in Rome. This concentration of wealth soon led to lavish private collecting, and a whole quarter of the city was devoted to art dealers, booksellers, and antiquarians, very much in the style of East 57th Street in New York City or Bond Street in London today. Such collections were displayed in the private houses and villas of their owners for the delectation of guests rather than for the public.

Middle Ages. Throughout the Middle Ages there was no public exhibition as such of works of art. During the centuries of the medieval period, private wealth was at a minimum, and only the Christian monasteries made an effort to preserve the works of classical learning and art. The libraries they established, while not open to the public, contained the manuscripts and miniature paintings that were to be the source of nearly all religious art of the Middle Ages, as well as the backbone of the education of the nobility. During these centuries the churches constituted the nearest parallel to museums, in that they housed or incorporated paintings, sculpture, mosaics, and precious objects from the goldsmith's and lapidary's workshop made for ecclesiastical use. These works were public property in the sense that the church was public and universal and open to all believers.

Renaissance. With the renewal of private wealth during the Renaissance and a new emphasis on individuality, patrons and collectors began to form the nuclei of the great private collections that subsequently became public art galleries. In this way the collections of the Medici family in Florence evolved into the Uffizi and Pitti galleries, the collections of the popes formed the Vatican Museums, the Farnese collections became the Naples Museum, and the Louvre came into being as an agglomerate of the collections of the French kings and other royalty. Because of the revived interest in classical antiquity, the first public museums were composed almost entirely of works from ancient Greece and Rome. The systematic pillaging of Rome's art treasures by English, French, and German collectors led the popes to attempt to stop the flow of Roman treasures from the country. They began to buy in competition with other collectors, established the Vatican Museums in the early 18th century, and passed laws rigidly restricting the exportation of works of ancient art from Italy. Greece eventually established museums to house ancient works of art found and excavated in her territory, and similar steps have been taken more recently in the countries of the Near and Far East.

National Galleries. With the rise of representative governments, the idea of national, as opposed to royal, collections arose. The Louvre in Paris is perhaps the purest example of this change, since its new form was determined by the acts of the French Revolution. Until the revolution the Louvre Palace belonged to the king, and although a section of it, the Galerie d'Apollon, had been organized as a museum as early as 1681 under Louis XIV, it was for the use of the court only. Members of the Royal Academy of Fine Arts could obtain permission to see the king's pictures, but only through influence with the court. This was the general pattern of all royal and private collections with regard to artists. On Nov. 8, 1793, the Louvre was opened to the public for the first time by the First Republic, under the direction of a committee headed by the painter Jacques Louis David. Its use was at that time established chiefly for artists, and the general public had only limited access to it. In London the British Museum was created by act of Parliament in 1753 and was opened to the public in 1759. The Prado in Madrid and the National Gallery in London were established in the early 19th century, the former comprising the royal Spanish collections, the latter from English amateurs' private collections, which were threatened with exportation from England if not acquired by the state. In fact, the 18th and early 19th centuries saw the founding of most of the great public collections of Europe. This development was one of the results of the new political concept of the democratic right of a nation's citizens to the common use and enjoyment of the country's artistic heritage, as well as of their rights to education, liberty, and the pursuit of happiness.

United States. The United States, being formed when democratic concepts were new, saw the establishment of public museums almost side by side with the growth of private collections. The character of American museums today owes as much to democratic institutions as it does to the beneficence of private collectors. The American museum has no part of the tradition of royal collections as museums do in Europe. The special pattern of American museums was described by the late Francis Henry Taylor, former director of the Metropolitan Museum of Art in New York, who wrote: "The democracy of Jefferson and the enlightened cynicism of Dr. Franklin created a new and precious pattern . . . . It was to be the pattern of the great democratic museums of the United States, filled with objects donated by private capitalists and supported by taxation and popular subscription." Most large American museums are chartered as private corporations rather than as agencies of the nation. (The National Gallery and the galleries of the Smithsonian Institution, both in Washington, D.C., are exceptions to the rule.) In most cases, however, the

REPRESENTATIVE ART GALLERIES OF THE WORLD

UNITED STATES AND CANADA

Baltimore, Md.—Baltimore Museum of Art; Walters Art Gallery.
Boston, Mass.—Gardner Museum; Museum of Fine Arts.
Buffalo, N.Y.—Albright-Knox Art Gallery; Buffalo Fine Arts Academy.
Cambridge, Mass.—Fogg Art Museum.
Chicago, Ill.—Art Institute of Chicago; Oriental Institute.
Cincinnati, Ohio—Cincinnati Art Museum.
Cleveland, Ohio—Cleveland Museum of Art.
Dallas, Tex.—Dallas Museum of Fine Arts.
Denver, Colo.—Denver Art Museum.
Des Moines, Iowa—Des Moines Art Center.
Detroit, Mich.—Detroit Institute of Arts.
Edmonton, Canada—Edmonton Art Gallery.
Gainesville, Fla.—Florida State Museum.
Hartford, Conn.—Wadsworth Atheneum.
Honolulu, Hawaii—Honolulu Academy of Arts.
Houston, Tex.—Museum of Fine Arts.
Indianapolis, Ind.—Herron Museum of Art.
Kansas City, Mo.—Nelson Gallery and Atkins Museum.
Lawrence, Kans.—University of Kansas, Museum of Art.
Los Angeles, Calif.—Los Angeles County Museum of Art.
Milwaukee, Wis.—Milwaukee Art Center.
Minneapolis, Minn.—Minneapolis Institute of Arts; Walker Art Center.
Montreal, Canada—Montreal Museum of Fine Arts.
New Haven, Conn.—Yale University Art Gallery.
New Orleans, La.—Delgado Museum of Art.
New York, N.Y.—Asia House Gallery; Brooklyn Museum; Frick Collection; Gallery of Modern Art; Guggenheim Museum; Metropolitan Museum of Art and the Cloisters; Museum of Modern Art; Morgan Library; Whitney Museum.
Northampton, Mass.—Smith College Museum of Art.
Oberlin, Ohio—Oberlin College, Allen Memorial Museum of Art.
Ottawa, Canada—National Gallery of Canada.
Philadelphia, Pa.—Barnes Foundation Collection (in Merion, Pa.); Pennsylvania Academy of the Fine Arts; Philadelphia Museum of Art; Rodin Museum.
Pittsburgh, Pa.—Carnegie Institute Museum of Art.
Ponce, Puerto Rico—Museo de Arte de Ponce.
Portland, Oreg.—Portland Art Museum.
Princeton, N.J.—Princeton University Art Museum.
Quebec, Canada—Musée de la Province.
Rochester, N.Y.—Rochester Memorial Art Gallery.
St. Louis, Mo.—City Art Museum of St. Louis.
San Diego, Calif.—Fine Arts Gallery of San Diego.
San Francisco, Calif.—California Palace of the Legion of Honor; De Young Memorial Museum; San Francisco Museum of Art.
Sarasota, Fla.—Ringling Museum of Art.
Seattle, Wash.—Seattle Art Museum.
Toledo, Ohio—Toledo Museum of Art.
Toronto, Canada—Art Gallery of Toronto; Royal Ontario Museum of the University of Toronto.
Tulsa, Okla.—Philbrook Art Center.
Vancouver, Canada—Vancouver Art Gallery.
Washington, D.C.—Corcoran Gallery of Art; Dumbarton Oaks Collection; Freer Gallery of Art; National Gallery of Art; Phillips Collection; Smithsonian Institution, National Collection of Fine Arts; Washington Gallery of Modern Art.
Williamsburg, Va.—Abby Aldrich Rockefeller Folk Art Collection.
Williamstown, Mass.—Sterling and Francine Clark Art Institute.
Winnipeg, Canada—Winnipeg Art Gallery.

CENTRAL AND SOUTH AMERICA

Argentina—*Buenos Aires:* Museo de Arte Moderno de Buenos Aires; Museo Nacional de Bellas Artes. *Córdoba:* Museo de Bellas Artes.
Bolivia—*La Paz:* Tihuanacu National Museum.
Brazil—*Rio de Janeiro:* Museu de Arte Moderna do Rio de Janeiro; Museu Nacional de Bellas Artes. *São Paulo:* Museu de Arte.
Chile—*Santiago:* Museo Nacional de Bellas Artes.
Ecuador—*Quito:* Escuela de Bellas Artes; Museo Nacional de Bellas Artes.
Mexico—*Mexico City:* Museo Nacional de Antropología; Museo Nacional de Arte Moderno.
Peru—*Lima:* Museo de Arte.
Uruguay—*Montevideo:* Museo Nacional de Bellas Artes.
Venezuela—*Caracas:* Museo de Bellas Artes de Caracas.

EUROPE, AUSTRALIA, AFRICA, AND ASIA

Afghanistan—*Kabul:* Kabul Museum
Australia—*Melbourne:* Museum of Modern Art and Design of Australia; National Gallery of Victoria.
Austria—*Vienna:* Kunsthistorisches Museum; Museum des 20. Jahrhunderts; Österreichische Galerie.
Belgium—*Antwerp:* Musée des Beaux-Arts; Koninklijk Museum voor Schone Kunsten; Musée Mayer van den Bergh. *Bruges:* Musée Groeninge. *Brussels:* Musée d'Art Ancien; Musées Royaux des Beaux-Arts de Belgique. *Liège:* Musée des Beaux-Arts.
Britain—*London:* British Museum; National Gallery; National Portrait Gallery; Tate Gallery; Victoria and Albert Museum. *Birmingham:* Birmingham City Museum and Art Gallery. *Cambridge:* Fitzwilliam Museum. *Cardiff:* National Museum of Wales. *Edinburgh:* National Gallery of Scotland. *Glasgow:* Glasgow Museum. *Oxford:* Ashmolean Museum. *Royal Collections:* Hampton Court Palace; Windsor Castle.
Czechoslovakia—*Prague:* National Museum.
China—*Peking:* Palace Museum.
Denmark—*Copenhagen:* Ny Carlsberg Glyptothek; Statens Museum for Kunst.
Egypt—*Alexandria:* Graeco-Roman Museum. *Cairo:* Coptic Museum; Egyptian Museum; Museum of Islamic Art.
Finland—*Helsinki:* National Museum.
France—*Paris:* Musée Carnavalet; Musée Cernuschi; Musée de Cluny; Musée Guimet; Musée Jacquemart-André; Musée du Jeu-de-Paume; Musée du Louvre; Musée Marmottan; Musée National d'Art Moderne; Musée Rodin; Petit-Palais. *Versailles:* Musée National de Versailles et des Trianons. *Local Museums:* Amiens, Angers, Avignon, Bordeaux, Dijon, Le Havre, Lyon, Nantes, Orléans, Reims, Rouen, Saint-Omer, Strasbourg, Tours, Valenciennes.
Germany (East)—*East Berlin:* Bode Museum; Staatliche Museen zu Berlin. *Dresden:* Staatliche Kunstsammlungen. *Essen:* Folkwang Museum. *Leipzig:* Museum der bildenden Künste.
Germany (West)—*West Berlin:* Galerie des 20. Jahrhunderts; Museum Dahlem; Schloss Charlottenburg. *Brunswick:* Herzog Anton-Ulrich Museum. *Cologne:* Schnütgen Museum; Wallraf-Richartz Museum. *Freiburg im Breisgau:* Augustiner Kloster Museum. *Hamburg:* Hamburger Kunsthalle. *Munich:* Alte Pinakothek; Bayerisches Nationalmuseum; Glyptothek; Neue Pinakothek; Neue Staatsgalerie; Schleissheim Museum.
Greece—*Athens:* Acropolis Museum; Byzantine Museum; National Museum. *Delphi:* Delphi Museum. *Olympia:* Archaeological Museum.
Hungary—*Budapest:* Rath Museum; Szépmüvészeti Museum.
India—*Calcutta:* Indian Museum. *New Delhi:* National Museum. *Trivandrum:* Sri Chitra Art Gallery.
Ireland—*Dublin:* Municipal Gallery of Modern Art; National Gallery of Ireland.
Israel—*Jerusalem:* Israel Museum; *Tel Aviv: Tel Aviv* Museum of Art.
Italy—*Florence:* Accademia di Belle Arti; Galleria d'Arte Moderna; Galleria degli Uffizi; Museo Nazionale (Bargello); Palazzo Pitti. *Genoa:* Galleria di Palazzo Bianco. *Milan:* Castello Sforzesco; Museo d'Arte Antica; Pinacoteca di Brera. *Naples:* Museo Nazionale. Palazzo di Capodimonte. *Rome:* Galleria and Museo Borghese; Galleria Nazionale d'Arte Moderna; Museo Capitolino; Museo Nazionale Romano; Palazzo Farnese. *Siena:* Pinacoteca Nazionale. *Vatican City:* Vatican Museums and Galleries. *Venice:* Accademia di Belle Arti; Ca' d'Oro; Civico Museo Correr; Galleria d'Arte Moderna.
Japan—*Kyoto:* Kyoto National Museum. *Nara:* Nara National Museum. *Tokyo:* Japanese Folkcraft Museum; National Museum.
Netherlands—*Amsterdam:* Rijksmuseum; Jan Six Collection; Stedelijk Museum. *The Hague:* Bredius Museum; Maritshuis. *Haarlem:* Frans Hals Museum. *Rotterdam:* Museum Boymans-van Beuningen. *Utrecht:* Centraal Museum.
Norway—*Oslo:* Nasjonalgalleriet.
Pakistan—*Karachi:* National Museum of Pakistan. *Lahore:* Central Museum. *Peshawar:* Peshawar Museum.
Poland—*Warsaw:* National Museum.
Portugal—*Lisbon:* Museu Nacional de Arte Antiga; Museu Nacional de Arte Contemporanea.
Spain—*Barcelona:* Museo Arqueológico de Barcelona; Museo de Arte de Cataluña; Museo de Arte Moderno. *Madrid:* Museo del Escorial; Museo del Prado; Museo Lazaro Galdiano; Real Academia de Bellas Artes. *Toledo:* Museo del Greco.
Sweden—*Stockholm:* Nationalmuseum.
Switzerland—*Basel:* Kunstmuseum. *Zurich:* Swiss National Museum.
Turkey—*Ankara:* Archaeological Museum. *Istanbul:* Saint Sophia Museum; Topkapi Palace Museum.
USSR—*Leningrad:* State Hermitage Museum. *Moscow:* Folk Art Museum; State Museum of Oriental Folk Art; State Pushkin Museum of Fine Arts; State Tretyakov Gallery.

museum founders have seen fit to designate the museums as public institutions for the benefit and education of the general populace. For this reason, American museums have led the field in developing the currently accepted concept of museums as educational institutions. Museum practice in the United States now sets a pattern that is beginning to be emulated by administrators of museums in many other countries.

In the 19th century the European concept of the educational function of museums largely restricted their use to artists and industrial designers. The Victoria and Albert Museum in London was founded on this principle, in connection with an art school; its echo in the United States is the Museum of the Rhode Island School of Design in Providence.

But contemporary American practice has been guided by the principle of education for everyone. ' Every important museum in the United States devotes part of its effort to work with public educational systems, and nearly every one maintains a program of public lectures, special and educational exhibitions, popular publications, and facilities for the use of educational adult groups within its community. The 20th century saw enormous growth in these activities; hence museums have been able to demand more and more support from local and state governments, as agencies of public service. These activities are in addition to the important functions of the enlargement, care, and study of the collections.

Contemporary practice in the installation of collections has been affected by the educational concept. Whereas formerly paintings and sculpture were exhibited under conditions similar to those in early private collections—that is, crowded, badly lighted, often unclassified—the present tendency is to show each work to best advantage, often relating it to other works in the same gallery and lighting each gallery adequately. Thus the presentation of art objects is educational as well as visually enjoyable. Since about 1935, museums have been built with these considerations in mind, the most striking example being the Museum of Modern Art in New York.

The presentation of works of art from a historical and cultural point of view has led to special installations in the larger museums of "period rooms" and to the incorporation of architectural members from past art into the construction of the building, as at The Cloisters of the Metropolitan Museum in New York. This method of installation affords considerable historical and social knowledge to the casual visitor, in addition to its presentation of each single work as an aesthetic object.

Millions of people every year visit the collections of American art museums, and the attendance figures grow annually. Museums have become a recognized factor in the cultural life of the nation and its separate communities.

Museums and art galleries in the United States possess many collections that are the equal of similar ones in Europe. In the fields of Renaissance painting and sculpture and classical antiquities, however, European collections acquired many of the best works as they were produced or excavated, before American collections had been founded. For this reason many of the collections of highest quality in the fields of painting and sculpture in the United States are those of American and recent European art. It is also in these fields that the most stimulating activities among United States art dealers may be found.

The larger American museums have attempted to represent the entire history of art in their collections, rather than a single period or locality. Therefore they furnish some of the most valuable historical data in the country as well as a wide range of artistic products. Such museums are the Metropolitan Museum in New York, the Museum of Fine Arts in Boston, the Philadelphia Museum, and the Art Institute of Chicago.

See also ART COLLECTING; MUSEUMS.

BEATRICE FARWELL
The Metropolitan Museum of Art

Bibliography

American Association of Museums, *Museums Directory of the United States and Canada*, 2d ed. (Washington 1965).

Braider, Donald, *Putnam's Guide to the Art Centers of Europe* (New York 1965).

Cauman, Samuel, *Living Museum: Experiences of an Art Historian and Museum Director—Alexander Dorner* (New York 1958).

Junior Council of the Museum of Modern Art, *Guide to Modern Art in Europe* (New York 1963).

Low, Theodore L., *The Educational Philosophy and Practice of Art Museums in the United States* (New York 1948).

Spaeth, Eloise, *American Art Museums and Galleries* (New York 1960).

Taylor, Francis Henry, *The Taste of Angels: A History of Art Collecting from Rameses to Napoleon* (Boston 1948).

ART INSTITUTE OF CHICAGO, a museum in Chicago, Ill., with affiliated schools of art and drama. It was incorporated in 1879 as the Chicago Academy of Fine Arts, and given its present name in 1882. The institute occupies an Italian Renaissance-style building erected in Grant Park in 1893 in connection with the World's Columbian Exposition. The museum, one of the largest in the United States, contains collections of prints, furniture, decorative art, primitive art, and Oriental, European, and American painting and sculpture. There is also a special collection of American rooms in miniature. Modern additions to the building include the classrooms of the School of the Art Institute, one of the world's largest art schools. The institute's School of Drama uses the Goodman Theatre, adjoining the main building.

Collections. The Art Institute is best known for its collection of French impressionist and postimpressionist paintings. Outstanding works in the collection are Georges Seurat's *Sunday Afternoon on La Grande Jatte*, Auguste Renoir's *Two Little Circus Girls*, Edgar Degas' *Millinery Shop*, Claude Monet's *Gare St.-Lazare*, Vincent van Gogh's *Bedroom at Arles*, Paul Cézanne's *Auvers*, and Henri de Toulouse-Lautrec's *At the Moulin Rouge*.

Masterpieces of Flemish and Dutch art are represented by such paintings as Rogier van der Weyden's *Madonna and Child*, Gerard Terborch's *The Music Lesson*, Lucas van Leyden's *Adoration of the Magi*, and Rembrandt's *Young Girl at an Open Half-Door*. Spanish paintings include El Greco's *Assumption of the Virgin* and *St. Martin and the Beggar*.

Twentieth century paintings in the museum's collection include works by Pablo Picasso, Pierre Matisse, Amedeo Modigliani, Wassily Kandinsky, Fernand Léger, Joan Miró, Georges Braque, Edward Hopper, Jackson Pollock, and Willem de Kooning.

ART MUSEUMS. See ART COLLECTING; ART GALLERIES; MUSEUMS.

ART NOUVEAU influence on architecture is seen in facade of Gaudí's Sagrada Familia church in Barcelona.

ART NOUVEAU, är noo-vō′, was an aesthetic movement that flourished between 1875 and 1915, with a stylistic climax around 1900. The art nouveau style, which affected all the arts, is characterized by curvilinear patterns related to natural forms, and an emphasis on energy and restless movement. The term "art nouveau" was derived from Samuel Bing's shop in Paris, the Maison de l'Art Nouveau, which sold fine and decorative arts in the art nouveau style.

Perhaps the most important single influence on art nouveau was Japanese art, which was then being discovered in Europe. Japanese prints, especially, suggested a new aesthetic expression—two-dimensional, linear, asymmetrical, and unconcerned with creating the illusion of reality.

England provided sources for art nouveau in the work and theories of such men as J.A.M. Whistler, William Morris, Walter Crane, and, earlier, William Blake, and in the English arts and crafts movement, which called for a return to utilitarian, honest forms, and a unification of the arts (see ARTS AND CRAFTS MOVEMENT). Art nouveau also was indebted to the 19th century revival of the rococo, from which it drew a decorativeness and an emphasis on flowing curves; to the flat, moving-line patterns of Celtic art; and to the curving, linear designs of the Gothic revival in the 19th century.

The major center of the art nouveau movement was France, where the style flourished especially in Paris and Nancy. Nancy, which had been entirely transformed in the rococo style in the 18th century, provided a natural inspiration for the new movement. Émile Gallé, who dominated the movement in Nancy, designed fragile inlaid furniture and glass objects that used expressive plant forms, made in multicolored overlays.

In Paris the most influential figure was the architect Hector Guimard, who designed the gates of the subway stations in the late 1890's. He also created furniture with daring, rhythmic, free-flowing lines. Glass and jewelry designer René Lalique was another important artist working in the art nouveau style in Paris. The Exposition Universelle, held in Paris in 1900, represented the acme of the movement in France.

Belgium was also a major center of art nouveau. The most gifted artist within the movement in Belgium was Henry van de Velde, an architect, designer, and painter. His work shows a tendency away from natural forms toward the abstract. Another Belgian architect in the movement was Victor Horta, who designed the Tassel House (1892–93), the Van Eetvelde House (1895), and his own home (1898), all in Brussels, as well as a number of shops. The exuberant, writhing forms of the outside of his buildings are echoed within by cast-iron interior supports, stair-rails, and fixtures.

Scotland's Glasgow Group, headed by architect and designer Charles Rennie Mackintosh, helped to spread art nouveau to European countries. Mackintosh's best-known work is the Glasgow School of Art (1897–1909). The Glasgow Group's emphasis on simplified, rectilinear forms influenced the German and Austrian *Jugendstil*, as art nouveau was called in these countries. The style was introduced in Germany at the Decorative Arts Exhibition held in Dresden in 1897. The *stile floreale* of Italy and the architecture of Antonio Gaudí in Spain were southern European offshoots of the art nouveau movement. In the United States the glass designer Louis Comfort Tiffany made the most significant contribution to art nouveau. He favored exotic, irregular shapes, and often combined metal with glass of opalescent hues.

The sinuous lines and flat color patterns of art nouveau had a tremendous effect on poster art. The Austrian painter Gustav Klimt and the English illustrator Aubrey Beardsley were leading exponents of the style in their fields. Elements of art nouveau are also found in the work of such painters as Paul Gauguin, Toulouse-Lautrec, Edvard Munch, and Pierre Bonnard.

During the 1960's art nouveau enjoyed a revival in the United States and Europe. Its influence extended to advertising, illustration, interior decoration, and fabric design.

WILLIAM GERDTS, *University of Maryland*

Bibliography

Lenning, Henry F., *The Art Nouveau* (The Hague 1951).
Madsen, Stephen T., *Sources of Art Nouveau* (New York 1956).
Schmutzler, Robert, *Art Nouveau* (New York 1964).
Selz, Peter, and Constantine, Mildred, eds., *Art Nouveau: Art and Design at the Turn of the Century* (New York 1960).

TIFFANY GLASS, incorporating color and ornate design, as in the lampshade at left, best exemplify the American use of the art nouveau style.

ART OF FUGUE, ärt, fyoॕog, the last work of Johann Sebastian Bach, who wrote it in 1749 and was revising it for publication when he died in 1750. Its German title is *Die Kunst der Fuge*. Long regarded only as an instructional work, *The Art of Fugue* was eventually recognized as one of the greatest creations of musical art, testifying to the inseparability of Bach's practical educational purpose and his artistic ideal.

The score of *The Art of Fugue* was assembled carelessly by Bach's sons and published in 1752. They mistakenly included in it an earlier sketch of Bach's 10th fugue; two fugues for two claviers; an unfinished fugue with three themes, none of which is the subject of *The Art of Fugue;* and the chorale prelude for organ *Vor deinen Thron*. There is no evidence that Bach intended any of these works to form part of *The Art of Fugue*. The best of several corrected versions includes 13 fugues, which Bach called "counterpoints," and four canons.

The Art of Fugue centers on one tonality and is based on the following single theme:

The composition makes masterful and ingenious use of imitative counterpoint and demonstrates the vast possibilities of fugue writing. Bach did not specify any medium, either vocal or instrumental, for the performance of the piece, but transcriptions by later musicians include those for organ, string quartet, and two pianos.

CHARLES N. HENDERSON
*Organist and Choirmaster, St. George's Church
New York City*

ART OF LOVE, a poetical work by the Roman poet Ovid, written about 1 B.C. The title in Latin is *Ars amatoria*. Divided into three books, it is a pseudodidactic treatise on the conduct of amorous intrigues. The first book instructs a man in the ways of winning a woman's love; the second teaches him how to keep it; and the third provides similar advice for women. Designed for a sophisticated Roman audience, it is a masterpiece of erotic writing.

Emperor Augustus, attempting to reform public morals, was outraged by the work. Ovid believed this was the cause of his banishment from Rome in 8 A.D.

ART OF POETRY is a work of literary criticism written about 23–20 B.C. by the Roman poet Horace. The title in Latin is *Ars poetica*. Originally entitled *Epistula ad Pisones*, it is written in hexameters in the form of a three-part letter to a man named Piso and his two sons.

In the first part, Horace stresses the need for unity and harmony; style and vocabulary must be suited to the subject of the poem. In the second part, the problems of the drama are discussed insofar as these are applicable to other literary forms. In the third part, the poet treats originality and imitation, the avoidance of mediocrity, and the advisability of polishing a work before publishing it.

In general, Horace urges Latin poets to study the masters of classical Greece and, following their example, to create works of similar stature. *The Art of Poetry* was very influential in the 17th and 18th centuries.

ART STUDENTS LEAGUE OF NEW YORK, an art school organized in 1875 by a group of students who withdrew from the National Academy of Design in New York City. The school has been located in New York City at 215 West 57th Street since 1892.

The League is a nonprofit organization, operated by a membership society open to anyone who has been enrolled at the school for at least three months. At an annual meeting the membership elects six members to the Board of Control, and these six then elect six other board members. At least four members of the Board of Control must be currently enrolled students. The board directs the affairs of the League at no pay.

The school has no entrance requirements. The regular session lasts from mid-September through May, with morning, afternoon, and evening classes in life drawing and painting, composition, anatomy, portraiture, commercial art, lettering, sculpture, and print making. There are also regular evening lecture courses.

Former students include John Marin, Norman Rockwell, Alexander Calder, Jackson Pollock, Ben Shahn, Georgia O'Keeffe, Yasuo Kuniyoshi, Walt Kuhn, Reginald Marsh, and Charles Dana Gibson.

ARTA, är'tä, is a commercial and manufacturing city in northwestern Greece. It is situated on the Arakhthos River, 10 miles (16 km) from its mouth of the Ambracian Gulf. Arta is the shipping center for the cotton, grain, citrus fruit, almonds, olives, and tobacco grown in the surrounding area, which is irrigated from the Arakhthos River. The city has active fisheries, and its manufactures include leather goods, embroidery, and cotton and woolen textiles. It is the capital of Arta department, a region in southern Epirus.

Originally called *Ambracia*, the town was founded as a colony of Corinth in the mid-600's B.C. and was conquered by Philip II of Macedon in 338 B.C. In 294 it was taken by King Pyrrhus, who made it the capital of his kingdom of Epirus. The town was captured by Rome in 189 B.C. In Byzantine times a new town, called *Arta*, was established on the site. In the 1200's and 1300's it was the capital of the independent state of Epirus, but it was seized in 1430 by the Turks, who renamed it *Narda*. Held by the Venetians in the 1600's, Arta was taken by France in 1797 and by Ali Pasha in 1798. It reverted to Ottoman domination after Ali's death in 1822 and passed to Greece in 1881. Population: (1961) 16,899.

ARTAGNAN, är-tȧ-nyáṉ', **Seigneur d'** (1611–1673), French soldier. Born *Charles de Baatz* of a noble family in Gascony, he served brilliantly in the army during the several wars of territorial expansion that marked the reigns of Louis XIII and Louis XIV. He was killed at the siege of Maastricht in the Netherlands.

D'Artagnan's life furnished Alexandre Dumas with the inspiration for the immortal character d'Artagnan, hero of *The Three Musketeers* and its sequels. As his source Dumas used *Mémoires de M. d'Artagnan, contenant quantité de choses particulières et secrètes qui se sont passées sous le règne de Louis le Grand*, published in a three-volume edition in 1700. Though these memoirs were purportedly written by d'Artagnan, it is probable that they were actually the work of the novelist Gatein de Courtilz de Sandras (1644–1712). See also THREE MUSKETEERS.

ARTAUD, är-tō′, **Antonin** (1896–1948), French actor, director, and theorist of drama, whose "Theater of Cruelty" concepts have exerted a profound influence on avant-garde theater. Artaud was born at Marseille, the son of a shipowner. In his youth he suffered from mental illness, which was to recur throughout his life, resulting in several periods of institutional confinement. In 1920 he went to Paris, where he became associated with the theater. He acted on the stage and in films and engaged in two short-lived efforts to establish surrealist theater. However, his most important contribution to the theater was his essays, written mainly between 1932 and 1935, which developed his dramatic theories. He died in Paris on March 4, 1948.

"Theater of Cruelty" is the concept that forms the crux of Artaud's dramatic thinking. "The term Cruelty," he stated, "must be understood in its widest sense . . . as irreversible and absolute determinism . . . [and as] submission to necessity. Life is always the death of someone." His play *The Cenci* (1935) was a violent tragedy conceived as a demonstration of his theories.

Many movements of the contemporary theater have absorbed Artaud's ideas, incorporating his ritualistic use of music and dance, as well as his predilection for violence. The playwrights whom he influenced include Ionesco, Beckett, Genet, and Weiss.

ARTAXATA, är-taks′ə-tə, on the Araxes (Aras) River in western Asia, was the ancient capital of Greater Armenia. It was named for Artaxias, a general of Antiochus the Great, who founded the kingdom of Armenia about 190 B.C. According to tradition, the city was planned by Hannibal, destroyed by the Roman general Corbulo in 58 A.D., and restored by Tiridates I of Armenia. Its ruins are located near the modern town of Artashat in the Armenian Republic of the USSR.

ARTAXERXES, ärt-ə-zerk′sēz, was the name of three Persian kings of the Achaemenid dynasty.

ARTAXERXES I, surnamed LONGIMANUS, because his right hand was longer than his left, reigned 465–424 B.C. The second son of Xerxes I, he ascended the throne through the influence of Artabanus, the commander of the guard, who had arranged the murder of King Xerxes and his eldest son, Darius. Shortly afterwards, Artaxerxes turned on Artabanus and killed him. During his reign, Artaxerxes conquered the rebellious Egyptians, terminated the war with Athens by granting freedom to the Greek cities of Asia, and sanctioned the return of the Jews to Palestine. For the most part he governed his subjects in peace.

ARTAXERXES II, surnamed MNEMON, from his strong memory, reigned 404–358 B.C. He succeeded his father, Darius II, at the height of Achaemenid glory after Athens had been crushed in the Peloponnesian war. After vanquishing his brother Cyrus (died 401), who had allied himself with Sparta in an attempted rebellion, Artaxerxes made war on the Spartans and forced them to abandon the Greek cities and islands of Asia to the Persians. Favoring the Athenians, he endeavored to foment dissensions among the Greeks. Although Athens temporarily gained from Persian support, Artaxerxes in 388 concluded peace with Sparta and proceeded to crush Athenian expansionist ambitions. Toward the end of his reign, the Persian empire was weakened by dissension among the provincial governors.

ARTAXERXES III, originally called OCHUS, reigned 358–338 B.C. After causing the deaths of two of his brothers, he seized the crown on the death of his father, Artaxerxes II. To consolidate his control over the empire, he required the provincial governors to dismiss their Greek mercenaries. Between 345 and 343 he subjugated Phoenicia and Egypt, displaying great cruelty in both instances. He and his elder sons were killed by his favorite eunuch, the general Bagoas.

ARTEMIS, är′tə-mis, in Greek mythology, was a daughter of Zeus (Jupiter) and Leto (Latona), the twin sister of Apollo. She was identified by the Romans with Diana. Artemis was considered a virgin goddess, who assisted in childbirth and protected the young of humans and animals alike. As a goddess of the hunt, she was especially associated with bears. Like Apollo, she was a deity of light, but was particularly associated with the moon.

Artemis was probably of pre-Hellenic origin. She is thought to have been an Asian mother goddess, and she played a similar role in early Greek religion. In Arcadia she was related to Demeter and Persephone, and at times she was confused with Hecate and Selene. In Ephesus, an important center of her cult, she was represented as having many breasts—evidence of her role as fertility goddess. She was also worshiped in Attica, where there was a shrine of the moon goddess, thought to contain the image of Artemis brought from Taurus by Iphigenia.

LILLIAN FEDER
Queens College, The City University of New York

ARTEMISIA, är-tē-miz′ē-ə, is the name of two queens of Caria, in Asia Minor.

ARTEMISIA I lived in the early 5th century B.C. She ruled over Halicarnassus (now Bodrum, Turkey) and several of the Dodecanese Islands, as a vassal of Persia. It is reported that she fought with considerable bravery at the disastrous naval battle near Salamis (480 B.C.), while assisting Xerxes in his war against the Greeks.

ARTEMISIA II was the sister and wife of Mausolus, whom she succeeded as ruler upon his death in 352 B.C. At Halicarnassus, her capital, she erected a magnificent tomb to his memory. Known as the Mausoleum (q.v.), it was celebrated as one of the Seven Wonders of the World and gave its name to future sepulchral structures. Among the sculptors who labored in its decoration were Bryaxis, Scopas, Leochares, Timotheus, and possibly Praxiteles. Artemisia died about 350 B.C.

ARTEMISIA, art-ə-mizh′ə, is a group of odorous herbs and shrubs native to the Northern Hemisphere and southern South America. It is characterized by leaves that are opposite, usually divided into many slender segments, and often densely hairy. The yellowish, greenish, or purple flowers are small, inconspicuous. They may either be erect or hang in compound flower clusters.

The genus *Artemisia* belongs to the sunflower family, the Compositae. There are about 225 species, of which 60 occur in the United States. Several western American species, especially *Artemisia tridentata*, are properly called *sagebrush* (q.v.) and dominate vast areas of arid land.

ARTEMUS WARD. See BROWNE, CHARLES FARRAR.

ARTERIOSCLEROSIS, är-tir-ē-ō-sklə-rō′səs, is a disease that is commonly known as "hardening of the arteries." The term was applied because, as arteries age and undergo degeneration, calcium is often deposited in their walls, making them hard and brittle. Today, however, the term "arteriosclerosis" has been widely replaced by *atherosclerosis,* because hardening of the arteries is not always present and is not an important feature of the disease. Atherosclerosis indicates the presence of fatty deposits, called atheromas, on and within the inner layer of the artery wall. These deposits thicken and narrow the arterial channel, thus interfering with the flow of blood. Eventually a clot (thrombus) often forms at the site of the deposit and unless the clot is either dissolved or removed, it may completely obstruct the narrowed artery.

Mortality statistics for arteriosclerosis are not accurate because of the varied terminology, but in the United States in 1964 there were more than half a million deaths due to arteriosclerosis (atherosclerosis) of the coronary arteries, the small arteries supplying the heart. About 37,000 deaths were due to generalized arteriosclerosis of the arteries supplying the brain. See also ATHEROSCLEROSIS.

CHARLES K. FRIEDBERG, M.D.
Mount Sinai Hospital, New York

ARTERY, ar′tə-rē, one of the many blood vessels that carry blood away from the heart to the body cells. The largest artery is the aorta, which begins at the left ventricle of the heart and gives rise to several other arteries as it travels downward through the body. These other arteries soon branch and divide to form smaller arteries, which, in turn, branch and divide to form even smaller arteries. The smallest arteries, *arterioles,* connect with the capillaries, from which oxygen and food materials in the blood diffuse out to the body cells. At the same time that these materials are leaving the capillaries, carbon dioxide and other waste materials are entering the capillaries. These wastes are then carried back to the heart through a network of veins. These vessels, the arteries, capillaries, and veins, along with the heart, make up the circulatory system.

In addition to distributing blood to the body cells, the arteries help smooth out the flow of blood as it is pumped from the heart. With each contraction of the left ventricle, blood is forced into the aorta with a sudden spurt. To ensure that the body cells receive a rather steady flow of blood, not intermittent spurts, the arteries, especially the aorta and other large arteries, dampen the spurts to a degree by alternately expanding and contracting. As a spurt of blood enters the artery, the artery walls expand, and after the blood flow has ended, they contract to their normal size. By the time the original spurt of blood enters the smaller arteries, it has been evened out to a large degree.

Structure. All arteries consist of three basic layers. The innermost layer is called the *intima,* the middle layer is known as the *media,* and the outermost layer is the *adventitia.* Although these three layers are present in all arteries, they vary slightly in thickness and composition among arteries of varying size in the body. Like arteries, veins consist of three layers, but these layers are generally thinner than in arteries. In addition, veins differ from arteries in that the larger ones have flaps of tissue along their innermost surface at various intervals. These flaps, called valves, help keep the blood flowing in the direction toward the heart. Normally the flaps lie flat, but if the blood in a vein starts to back up and flow in the other direction, the flaps of tissue stand up and block the backward flow.

The intima, thinnest layer of the artery wall, consists of three separate sections. The innermost part is made up of endothelial cells, and the middle layer consists of connective tissue, mostly elastic and collagen fibers. In some of the medium-sized arteries this middle section may also have some smooth muscle fibers arranged longitudinally. The fibers are more abundant at the places where the arteries branch. The outermost section of the intima consists of a band of elastic fibers and is called the internal elastic membrane.

The media, usually the thickest layer of the artery wall, consists chiefly of smooth muscle fibers and connective tissue. As the arteries increase in diameter, the layer of muscle tissue

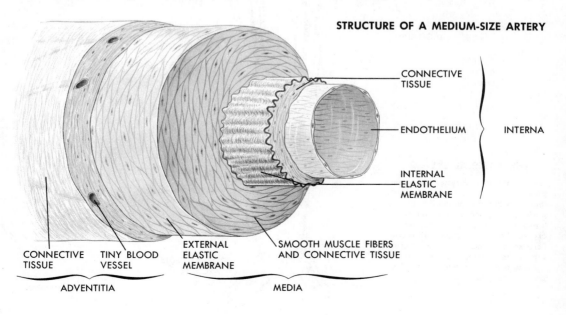

STRUCTURE OF A MEDIUM-SIZE ARTERY

CONNECTIVE TISSUE

ENDOTHELIUM — INTERNA

INTERNAL ELASTIC MEMBRANE

CONNECTIVE TISSUE   TINY BLOOD VESSEL   EXTERNAL ELASTIC MEMBRANE   SMOOTH MUSCLE FIBERS AND CONNECTIVE TISSUE

ADVENTITIA   MEDIA

becomes thicker. In small arteries the media may consist of only 3 or 4 muscle layers, but in medium-sized arteries there may be as many as 40 layers. The amount of elastic fibers in the connective tissue also varies with the size of the artery. In smaller arteries there are few elastic fibers, and they are scattered among the muscle cells. In medium-sized arteries they are much more numerous and form a circular network that extends throughout the entire media. In the largest arteries the amount of muscle tissue and elastic fibers decreases, and instead of encircling the artery they form bands that wind about in spirals.

The adventitia consists mainly of connective tissue. In small arteries it is a fairly thin layer. In medium-sized arteries it is thick, sometimes as thick as the media, and in the largest arteries it is thin again. The fibers of the adventitia are mostly arranged longitudinally, and the elastic fibers of the innermost section may make up a coarse network, sometimes forming a membrane known as the external elastic membrane. The outermost part of the adventitia consists of connective tissue that is continuous with the connective tissue surrounding the artery.

Diseases. The most common disease of the arteries is atherosclerosis, in which deposits of fatty materials line the inner walls. Other diseases of the arteries (described in separate articles) include chilblain, frostbite, and Raynaud's disease.

J. Willis Hurst, M.D.
Emory University School of Medicine

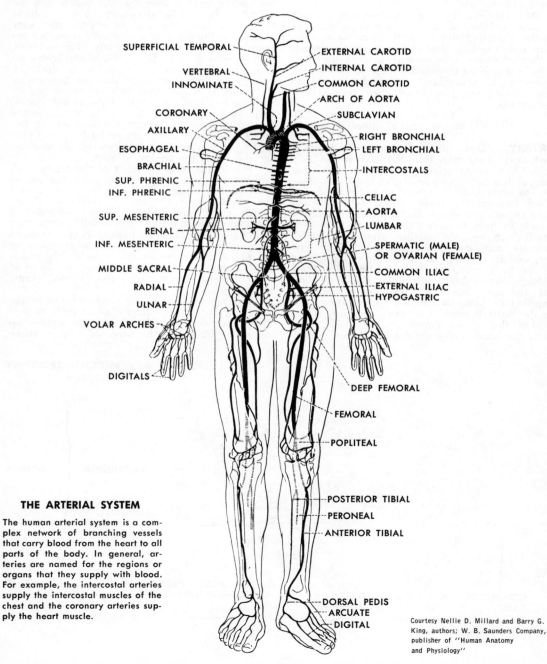

THE ARTERIAL SYSTEM

The human arterial system is a complex network of branching vessels that carry blood from the heart to all parts of the body. In general, arteries are named for the regions or organs that they supply with blood. For example, the intercostal arteries supply the intercostal muscles of the chest and the coronary arteries supply the heart muscle.

Labels (left side): SUPERFICIAL TEMPORAL, VERTEBRAL, INNOMINATE, CORONARY, AXILLARY, ESOPHAGEAL, BRACHIAL, SUP. PHRENIC, INF. PHRENIC, SUP. MESENTERIC, RENAL, INF. MESENTERIC, MIDDLE SACRAL, RADIAL, ULNAR, VOLAR ARCHES, DIGITALS

Labels (right side): EXTERNAL CAROTID, INTERNAL CAROTID, COMMON CAROTID, ARCH OF AORTA, SUBCLAVIAN, RIGHT BRONCHIAL, LEFT BRONCHIAL, INTERCOSTALS, CELIAC, AORTA, LUMBAR, SPERMATIC (MALE) OR OVARIAN (FEMALE), COMMON ILIAC, EXTERNAL ILIAC, HYPOGASTRIC, DEEP FEMORAL, FEMORAL, POPLITEAL, POSTERIOR TIBIAL, PERONEAL, ANTERIOR TIBIAL, DORSAL PEDIS, ARCUATE, DIGITAL

ARTESIA, är-tē′zhə, is a residential city in southern California. It is situated in Los Angeles County, 16 miles (26 km) southeast of downtown Los Angeles. Poultry, dairy products, fruits, and vegetables are raised in the surrounding region. Artesia produces feeds, feed mixers, and dairy equipment. It also has welding and machine shops, and hardware and sheet metal works. The Artesia Dairyland Fair and the Old Time Pit Barbecue are held here annually.

Founded in 1875 by the Artesia Land Company, the town derived its name from the many artesian wells that were drilled in the area. Artesia was incorporated in 1959. It has the city manager and council form of government. Population: 14,757.

ARTESIA, är-tē′zhə, is a city in southeastern New Mexico. It is situated in Eddy County, 45 miles (72 km) by road south of Roswell and 4 miles (6 km) west of the Pecos River. The city was named for the area's artesian wells, which tap vast resources of underground water used for irrigation. Besides farming and ranching, oil production and potash mining are important to the economy of the city. Artesia's main industries are oil refining, agricultural processing, and lumber finishing.

Centers of interest include the Abo Underground School and Fallout Shelter. The city holds an annual rodeo. Nearby Lake McMillan offers fishing and water sports, and the nearby Sacramento Mountains attract trout fishermen and deer hunters.

Artesia was settled in 1903 when the first artesian well was drilled there. The city was incorporated in 1905 and is governed by a mayor and council. Population: 10,315.

ARTESIAN WELL, är-tē′zhən, a well that pierces impermeable rock materials and obtains water from an underlying aquifer (a rock layer porous enough to carry ground water). The water in the aquifer is confined under sufficient pressure to rise above the top of the aquifer.

The term "artesian" derives from Artois, a former province at the northernmost top of France. Its flowing, bored wells of small diameter were famous during the Middle Ages, and the term "artesian" came to be applied to any deep well of small diameter that was constructed by means of boring.

These characteristics, however, are no longer considered definitive. It is true that many artesian wells are hundreds of feet deep; but others have depths of less than 20 feet (6 meters). Moreover, few artesian wells are bored today. Most are drilled or jetted by a variety of machines. The distinguishing feature of an artesian

ARTESIAN WELLS are primary sources of water in central Australia and other arid regions of the world.

well is that it taps water confined under a pressure that is sufficient to cause the water to rise above the aquifer. Thus, flowing wells are likely to be artesian, although not all artesian wells necessarily flow.

Background. The artesian wells of Artois were by no means the first to be constructed. The geologic conditions essential for artesian flow exist in many parts of the earth, awaiting only the capability for making a hole of sufficient depth. Egyptians long ago developed such techniques and kept the holes open by means of hollowed palm tree trunks. The ancient civilizations of China, Persia, and Syria also developed this ability.

The term "artesian" gained worldwide currency during the 19th century, chiefly because of the efforts of the city of Paris to obtain a satisfactory water supply by means of wells similar to those in Artois. A machine was constructed at suburban Grenelle for boring a hole 16 inches (40 cm) in diameter, and operations began in 1833. In 1841, after many tribulations, the hole tapped the aquifer at a depth of 1,965 feet (599 meters). Warm water rushed out, under sufficient pressure to rise 290 feet (87 meters) above the land surface. The flow, initially about 1,000,000 gallons (3,800,000 liters) a day, diminished to half that rate in the first three years and to a quarter of that rate during the 1850's. Another well was commenced at nearby suburban Passy in 1855. By 1861 it had reached the same aquifer, producing an initial yield of more than 5,500,000 gallons (20,800,000 liters) a day. Within a month after the Passy well was placed in service, the flow of the Grenelle well decreased sharply.

These wells in the Paris region are similar to those in many other areas of artesian flow.

ARTESIAN WELL

Artesian wells tap water-bearing layers of rock, called aquifers, lying beneath impermeable rock materials. Flowing water is obtained from a well situated below the level of the aquifer's recharge area, because of the pressure built up in the aquifer.

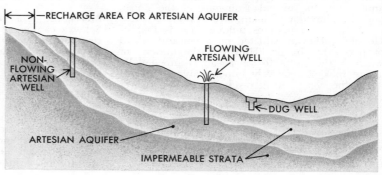

RECHARGE AREA FOR ARTESIAN AQUIFER

NON-FLOWING ARTESIAN WELL

FLOWING ARTESIAN WELL

DUG WELL

ARTESIAN AQUIFER

IMPERMEABLE STRATA

When the well is drilled, the pressure is great enough to cause the water level in the well to rise above the land surface. However, as the well continues to flow, the pressure and therefore the rate of flow diminish. Pressure and rate of flow are also reduced by flow from other wells tapping the same aquifer and causing interference.

Water Flow in Aquifers. Insofar as artesian wells obtain water confined under pressure, they are similar to the flowing wells, or gushers, that yield oil, gas, and water in petroleum fields. But whereas the fluids in oilfield reservoirs have been trapped and stationary for long periods of time, artesian waters characteristically are in continual, though perhaps very slow, motion as part of the hydrologic cycle. The direction of motion can be determined by measurements of the water levels or artesian pressures in wells when there is no pumping or other discharge occurring.

The water in an artesian aquifer may seep into or through the confining material. This is known as artesian seepage. In many places the water may flow naturally at the surface, forming an artesian spring. For any aquifer, artesian conditions exist in only a part of its flow system. Somewhere there must be an opportunity for water to enter the aquifer, either by seepage from streams, lakes, or canals, or by downward oozing of precipitated water. In these recharge areas the water in the aquifer is unconfined.

Wells pumping from an unconfined aquifer obtain water by dewatering the materials in the immediate vicinity of the well, whereas in artesian discharge the aquifer at the well remains saturated. The water is released from storage over a wider area but at a much lower rate per unit volume—hence the greater interference among artesian wells.

Occurrence of Artesian Aquifers. The Great Australian Artesian Basin is the largest in the world, extending over an area of about 600,000 square miles (1,500,000 sq km). Many wells there discharge water so hot that it must be stored in ponds before livestock can drink it. In the United States, the Dakota sandstone aquifer is one of the most extensive, including most of North and South Dakota and parts of adjacent states in the northern Great Plains.

In contrast to these extensive basins, most artesian aquifers are no more than a few tens of miles in extent. Many yield adequate quantities of water for irrigation or industrial or public supply, but pumping becomes necessary as artesian pressure decreases and demand increases. The aquifers occur in a variety of geologic environments. Among the most common in the United States are the gently sloping aquifers of sand and gravel in the alluvial fans of mountain valleys in the west, the coastal plains of the east and south, the glacial sediments of the north, and the alluvium of many river valleys.

A rare and perhaps unique case is that of Honolulu, Hawaii, situated on a volcanic island of permeable basalt. However, the outflow of water in the basalt to the ocean is impeded by a cap rock of relatively impermeable sediments along the coast. As a result, artesian pressures are developed.

See also WELLS AND WELL SINKING.

HAROLD E. THOMAS, *U.S. Geological Survey*

Further Reading: McGuinness, Charles L., *The Role of Ground Water in the National Water Supply Situation,* Water Supply Paper 1800, U.S. Geological Survey (Washington 1963); Thomas, Harold E., *Conservation of Ground Water* (New York 1951).

ARTEVELDE, är′tə-vel-də, a family of Ghent that was associated with the proud Flemish tradition of urban liberty and with the long struggle of the medieval county of Flanders to maintain independence from France.

JACOB VAN ARTEVELDE (c. 1290–1345) came from a well-known merchant and industrial family of Ghent, which made its money from the production of woolen cloth. The Artevelde family was active in urban affairs.

In 1337, when the Hundred Years' War broke out between England and France, Jacob argued that it would be catastrophic for Flanders to become involved in the war, since the Flemish woolen industry depended almost exclusively on England for its raw wool. Jacob soon dominated the urban council of Ghent and persuaded other towns, including Bruges and Ypres, to form a Flemish league devoted to neutrality. The efforts of the pro-French count of Flanders to involve the county on the side of his French overlord were thwarted, and in 1338 the count recognized the league and its policy of neutrality.

Between 1338 and 1345, Jacob was virtually a dictator in Ghent. He came to dominate the league, which expanded to include most of the Flemish towns. Under pressure from Edward III of England, who threatened to cut off exports of wool, Jacob embraced the English cause and proposed that the count of Flanders be removed in favor of Edward III's eldest son, Edward the Black Prince. This proposal plus the jealousy of other patrician families of Ghent led to Jacob's downfall. In the summer of 1345 the craft guilds of the woolen industry were incited to overthrow him, and an insurrection broke out. On July 24, 1345, he made a final appeal to the people but was shouted down and killed. Jacob became associated in romantic literature with the long struggle for Belgian liberty, especially after Belgium gained its independence in 1830.

PHILIP VAN ARTEVELDE (c. 1340–1382) was the youngest son of Jacob. When Ghent revolted against the count of Flanders in 1381, Philip was persuaded to become the leader of the revolt because of his name. He defeated the count and united all Flanders behind him. But with the military aid of the French king Charles VI, the count defeated the foot soldiers of the Flemish towns at the bloody Battle of Roosebeke on Nov. 27, 1382. Philip was among the Flemings who were slain.

BRYCE LYON, *Brown University*

ARTFUL DODGER, ärt′fəl doj′ər, the nickname of John Dawkins, a character in Charles Dickens' novel *Oliver Twist.* An expert pickpocket, the Artful Dodger introduces Oliver into the gang of young thieves led by Fagin.

ARTH, ärt, is a town in central Switzerland, in Schwyz canton, at the south end of Lake Zug. Its industries include lamp manufacturing. It was the scene of a disastrous landslide in 1806 when part of the Rossberg fell away, burying four villages. Population: (1960) 6,321.

ARTHABASKA, är′thə-bas-kə, is a town in Quebec, Canada, on the Nicolet River, 38 miles (61.1 km) southeast of Trois-Rivières. It is the seat of Arthabaska County. It has shirt and furniture factories, and is located in a lumbering and dairying region. The area is known for its fine hunting and fishing. Population: 4,479.

ARTHRITIS, är-thrīt′əs, is a general term used to denote an affliction, which may be inflammatory, of one or more joints. The symptoms of arthritis vary with the cause, but they usually include pain on motion, tenderness, swelling, warmth, and stiffness of the involved joints.

Types of Arthritis. *Osteoarthritis,* the most common form of arthritis, is frequently associated with aging (primary type) or trauma (secondary). See OSTEOARTHRITIS.

Rheumatoid arthritis, the second most common type, affects one percent of the U.S. population. It is twice as common in women as in men and may occur at any age. This chronic inflammatory disease may attack any moveable joint but most frequently affects small joints, especially the middle knuckles and the wrists. There may be stiffness about the joints lasting for more than half an hour after arising; muscle aching, particularly around the shoulders; fatigue; weight loss; and occasionally slight fever.

In this type of arthritis there is an overgrowth of inflammatory or scar tissue inside the joints (see JOINT). Irreparable destruction of the cartilage lining the joint space and the bone beneath the cartilage occurs and can be seen on X-ray. With prolonged disease there may be destruction of the joint capsule and the tendons that control the motion of the joint; partial dislocation of the joint; or fusion of the joint by scar tissue and new bone. Neighboring muscles tend to shrink from disuse.

Approximately 25 percent of all patients with rheumatoid arthritis develop painless nodules under the skin, especially on the elbows. Anemia, which often does not respond to iron therapy, also is found in about 25 percent of the patients. Occasionally, rheumatoid arthritis is associated with inflammation of the eyes, arteries, or nerves. Juvenile rheumatoid arthritis, which starts before puberty, may begin with a rash and fever and be associated with abnormal bone growth.

An abnormal protein called rheumatoid factor is present in the blood of 75 percent of adults with rheumatoid arthritis and 5 percent of adults without it. Those with the factor but without rheumatoid arthritis include healthy, often elderly, individuals and patients with liver disease, chronic infections, and other disorders. The erythrocyte sedimentation rate (ESR), a blood test that measures disease severity, is usually abnormally increased in rheumatoid arthritis, as it is in most other inflammatory diseases.

Rheumatoid arthritis often fluctuates in severity, and in 10 percent of the patients it may disappear permanently within one year. Many patients are no worse after 10 years of the disease than they were at its onset. Factors that predict severity are: onset of the disease early in adult life, persistent pain, nodules, and rheumatoid factor. Rheumatoid arthritis does not shorten life appreciably, except when it is complicated by vasculitis (inflammation of blood vessels), amyloidosis (a disease in which the protein amyloid is deposited in body tissues and organs), or misguided treatment.

Ankylosing spondylitis (Marie-Strümpell spondylitis) is a chronic inflammatory arthritis predominantly of the joints of the spine and pelvis, but in 15 percent of patients it also affects the joints of the hands and feet. It is five times more common in men than in women and usually begins in adolescence or young adulthood.

Early in the disease, patients may suffer

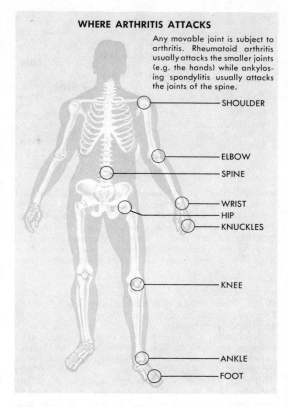

WHERE ARTHRITIS ATTACKS

Any movable joint is subject to arthritis. Rheumatoid arthritis usually attacks the smaller joints (e.g. the hands) while ankylosing spondylitis usually attacks the joints of the spine.

SHOULDER
ELBOW
SPINE
WRIST
HIP
KNUCKLES
KNEE
ANKLE
FOOT

stiffness on arising, malaise, and loss of weight. Later, the back and rib cage may become rigid because of calcification at edges of vertebrae, in intravertebral discs, and in adjacent supporting ligaments. In 25 percent of these patients there is inflammation of the eyes. Occasionally, disease of the aortic heart valve or amyloidosis, is present. The erythrocyte sedimentation rate is increased, and there may be anemia. Nodules under the skin and rheumatoid factor usually are absent. Life is not shortened by this type of arthritis, and most patients continue to lead a productive existence.

Arthritic symptoms are present in 80 percent of patients with *systemic lupus erythematosus,* a disease that may have many of the features of rheumatoid arthritis. This disease occurs mainly in women of child-bearing age. The disease may affect many organs and be associated with a falsely positive test for syphilis. Lupus erythematosus (LE) cells may be found in blood samples. (An LE cell is a white blood cell that has engulfed the nucleus of another white cell because of the presence of antinuclear antibodies in the patient's blood.) The disease, especially of the kidney and heart, may shorten life.

Two other types of arthritis, gout and rheumatic fever, are discussed in separate articles. Arthritis of any joint may result from bacterial infection in the joint (gonococcus, staphylococcus, or tuberculosis). Arthritis also is found in association with other diseases and conditions.

Treatment. The safest and most useful drug in the treatment of rheumatoid arthritis is aspirin (acetylsalicylic acid). Many patients take up to 15 five-grain aspirin tablets each day (see ASPIRIN). Indomethacin, introduced in 1962, seems to be an effective anti-inflammatory and

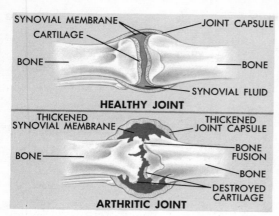

SYNOVIAL MEMBRANE
CARTILAGE
BONE
JOINT CAPSULE
BONE
SYNOVIAL FLUID
HEALTHY JOINT

THICKENED SYNOVIAL MEMBRANE
THICKENED JOINT CAPSULE
BONE
BONE FUSION
BONE
DESTROYED CARTILAGE
ARTHRITIC JOINT

AN ARTHRITIC JOINT compared with a healthy joint. In the healthy joint, synovial tissue produces a fluid which lubricates the articular cartilage covering the ends of the bones. In the arthritic joint the cartilage is destroyed, the joint capsule is thickened, and there may be an increase in the amount of synovial fluid. Very late in the disease the bones may become fused.

analgesic drug, the toxicity of which is still under study. Phenylbutazone may cause peptic ulceration or blood disease and therefore is seldom used for long periods of time. Gold compounds and chloroquine exert their effects only after months of use and are not always of lasting benefit. In severe rheumatoid arthritis, anti-inflammatory steroids may be needed. These drugs may produce temporary improvement but may be harmful and are not curative. Steroids may be given by mouth or injected directly into a joint. Narcotics are to be avoided.

Physical therapy is especially valuable in severe disease and should include range of motion exercises, warm moist heat, and rarely, night splints. Orthopedic surgery occasionally is useful to relieve pain or to improve joint function. Exhausting or unusually painful activity should be avoided. No special foods or vitamins, aside from an adequate diet, are of any benefit.

In ankylosing spondylitis, back exercises, a bed board, and elimination of a head pillow prevent fusion of the spine in a bent position while aspirin, phenylbutazone, or indomethacin provide relief of pain and suppress inflammation. Anti-inflammatory steroids, gold, and chloroquine rarely are useful in ankylosing spondylitis, and X-ray therapy is to be discouraged.

The treatment of systemic lupus erythematosus includes aspirin and often large doses of anti-inflammatory steroids when vital organs, such as the kidney or heart, have been attacked. Chloroquine and drugs thought to suppress immunological reactions in the body may be of value.

Causes of Arthritis. The cause of rheumatoid arthritis is not known. However, it is thought to be, at least in part, an aberration of the body's immune defense mechanism. The primary reason for this belief is the presence of rheumatoid factor (a gamma globulin). It has an antibody-like affinity for smaller denatured gamma globulin molecules, and it may be identified by its ability to agglutinate (collect into clumps) gamma globulin-coated latex particles or gamma globulin-coated red blood cells of sheep. Sometimes other such autoantibodies are present.

A popular theory supported by experiment holds that rheumatoid factor is an antibody to other antibodies that have become altered by interaction with their specific antigen so as to form an antigen-antibody complex. Animals, and probably humans, will make rheumatoid factor when subjected to any prolonged antigenic stimulus. Research suggests that white blood cells may cause damage in a joint by releasing enzymes from tiny intracellular packets (lysosomes) in response to the white blood cells' ingestion of rheumatoid factor. A vicious circle thus may be established, since the antigens produced by the action of the released enzymes theoretically could stimulate the formation of more rheumatoid factor. Transfusion of rheumatoid factor into individuals with no symptoms of arthritis does not produce arthritis. Conversely, replacing the blood of a patient with unaffected blood does not have a beneficial effect.

The finding of lymphocytes (a type of white blood cell) and plasma cells in the joints of patients with rheumatoid arthritis also points to an immune mechanism, since lymphocytes normally are known to play an active role in the body's immune defense system. Although no unique antigen has been found, the blood of patients with rheumatoid arthritis often contains large amounts of gamma globulin antibody.

An infectious cause of rheumatoid arthritis is suggested by the following observations. Viral diseases (such as German measles) occasionally cause an arthritis, and rheumatoid arthritis sometimes starts with a grippelike illness. An arthritis may be induced in swine by erysipelothrix (a bacterium) and in several other domestic animals by mycoplasma (microorganisms without a complete cell wall). Also, Bedsonia microorganisms have been isolated from some patients with Reiter's syndrome of arthritis, urethritis, and conjunctivitis. However, no causative organism has been found in rheumatoid arthritis, and the disease cannot be transmitted from person to person or to animals. It no longer is believed that foci of infection (such as bad teeth) contribute to rheumatoid arthritis.

It is not known whether rheumatoid arthritis can be inherited, and there is no evidence for a psychological, nutritional, endocrine, nervous, or occupational cause of this disease. Some research workers have suggested that rheumatoid arthritis is a metabolic disease, because the majority of patients excrete in their urine increased amounts of 3-hydroxyanthranilic acid, kynurenine, and histidine, with less histidine in the blood.

Except for the possible role of heredity, little is known about the cause of ankylosing spondylitis. The cause of systemic lupus erythematosus is not known but is thought to be similar to that of rheumatoid arthritis.

DONALD A. GERBER, M.D.
Downstate Medical Center
State University of New York

Further Reading: Hollander, Joseph Lee, ed., *Arthritis and Allied Conditions,* 7th ed. (Philadelphia 1966).

ARTHRODIRA, är-thrō-dī′rə, is an order of Devonian fishes in the class Placodermi. The Arthrodira were characterized by a bony dermal armor that typically consisted of a head shield and a thoracic shield which were movably articulated by a hinge joint. The group apparently included both freshwater and marine species; some of the latter, such as the *Titanichthys,* attained a length of 20 to 30 feet (6 to 9 meters).

ARTHROPODA
DISTINGUISHING CHARACTERISTICS:

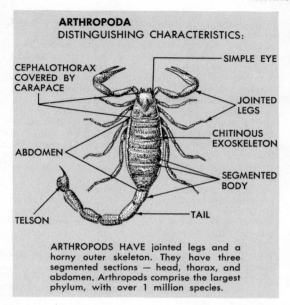

CEPHALOTHORAX COVERED BY CARAPACE

SIMPLE EYE

JOINTED LEGS

CHITINOUS EXOSKELETON

ABDOMEN

SEGMENTED BODY

TELSON

TAIL

ARTHROPODS HAVE jointed legs and a horny outer skeleton. They have three segmented sections — head, thorax, and abdomen. Arthropods comprise the largest phylum, with over 1 million species.

M.W.F. TWEEDIE, FROM NATIONAL AUDUBON SOCIETY

MAIN CLASSES OF ARTHROPODS: 1. Centipedes and other Myriapoda, with many pairs of legs. 2. Crustaceans (such as the crayfish), with specialized appendages. 3. Arachnids (garden spider), with four pairs of legs. 4. Insects (grasshopper), with three pairs of legs.

HUGH SPENCER

GEORGE PORTER, FROM NATIONAL AUDUBON SOCIETY

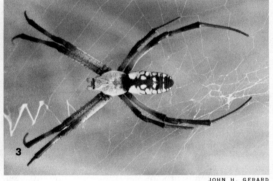

JOHN H. GERARD

ARTHROPODA, är-throp'ə-də, a phylum of the animal kingdom. It embraces a vast array of small animals including crabs, crayfish, insects, mites, spiders, centipedes, thousand-legged worms, and their relations. It far outnumbers all other known phyla in species and individuals, and only the phylum Chordata, which encompasses man and the other vertebrates, ranks higher on the zoological scale.

The name Arthropoda means "joint-footed," and this feature along with the segmented body structure and the chitinized outer skin are distinctive characteristics of the phylum. In the standard scheme of classification, the arthropods are divided into five classes: the Crustacea, Insecta, Arachnida, Chilopoda, and Diplopoda. Another class, the Onychophora, is sometimes included in this grouping, though it has certain wormlike features that set it apart from other arthropods.

Crustaceans are chiefly aquatic animals, living in both fresh and salt water. The members have a hard outer skeleton consisting of a cephalothorax (head and chest regions united) and abdomen. There are usually two pairs of antennae, and a single pair of legs for each segment. The most familiar examples are crabs, crayfish, lobsters, shrimps, and barnacles.

Insects are usually terrestrial, but some species inhabit fresh water, and many adult insects have a remarkable flying capacity. A defining feature of insects is the division of the body in its adult stage into head, thorax, and abdomen. There are three pairs of legs (hence the alternate name of Hexapoda to describe the class). Insects can be winged or wingless, and they can go through a simple or complex metamorphosis. Insects are by far the most numerous class of animals: An estimated 6,000,000 species exist, of which some 700,000 are known to science. The class includes cockroaches, crickets, earwigs, termites, lice, bugs, bees, beetles, wasps, butterflies, dragonflies, May flies, fleas, and grasshoppers. Grasshoppers are often cited as typical insects in their structure and habits.

The arachnids are mainly terrestrial, and have

segmented bodies consisting of head, thorax, and abdomen; they do not have antennae or wings. They usually have four pairs of legs, though in rare species two or three pairs may be found. The class includes mites, spiders, ticks, and scorpions. The horseshoe or king crab, often referred to as a "living fossil" because it belongs to an otherwise extinct order, is also commonly placed with the arachnids.

The class Chilopoda are terrestrial, wormlike animals whose anatomy consists of a head and many body segments, with one pair of legs attached to each segment. They are chiefly carnivorous, and undergo a simple metamorphosis. The common household centipede is the chief representative of the class. The nearest relatives of the Chilopoda are the diplopods. These are also terrestrial wormlike creatures, with elongated, many-segmented bodies. There may be one or two pairs of legs to each segment, as in the thousand-legged worm. Unlike the chilopods, they are chiefly vegetarian, and have a pair of short antennae.

In general, arthropods grow by a molting process: shedding their skins or shells as a new skin develops beneath the old. The cast-off skins, or exuviae, are often evident in colonies of leaf hoppers, aphids, and other arthropods.

All arthropods are comparatively small. The largest living crabs have a leg spread of 12 feet and the largest moths have a wing spread of 10½ inches, whereas the smallest species are scarcely visible to the naked eye.

Certain arthropods, especially the crustaceans, have long been a source of food for man. The catching, preserving, and distributing of crabs, lobsters, and shrimps constitute an important and highly developed food industry. Laws have been enacted to protect them from being exterminated, and means taken to increase their numbers.

Insects are not only the largest class of animals by number; they also present the most difficult problems for the human race. Some insects are beneficial to man, but the majority are not, and these cause incalculable damage through their biting, stinging, carrying of disease, and destruction of crops. Their small size, almost unlimited reproductive capacities, and adaptability to every type of climatic conditions create a constant challenge to man's ingenuity in his war against them.

The phenomenon called parthenogenesis, or reproduction without the fertilization of the female, sometimes occurs among the arthropods, especially in the insect class. A common example is to be found in the aphids or plant lice, which reproduce in tremendous numbers. In some species, males are unknown. In certain cases, only females are produced from the unfertilized eggs for long periods, until a generation evolves that resumes the sexual cycle. Among honeybees, the unfertilized eggs produce only male offspring.

Another phenomenon of the insect world is the condition of polymorphism, in which adults of two or more distinct forms of the same sex are designated as castes, each caste having a definite and specialized function within the insect colony. This phenomenon reaches its peak among such social insects as termites, ants, and bees.

E.O. ESSIG, *University of California*

ARTHUR, är'thər, **King,** a legendary figure who appears in literature as either a military leader or king of the Britons. If he actually existed, he was probably a 6th-century warrior and focal point of resistance to the Germanic invaders. Although he is credited by the Welsh writer Nennius (about 800) with the British victory at Mt. Badon (probably in what is now Dorset), the account of Gildas, the earliest native Welsh historian (about 540), does not mention him but has Ambrosius Aurelianus as the victor. Arthur is mentioned once in *Gododdin*, a Welsh song cycle, which in its earliest form is dated about 600, but because the text has interpolations, it is uncertain when his name entered it. In medieval literature Arthur evolved into a chivalric king, presiding over a Round Table of brave and courteous knights.

There is considerable agreement among scholars that Arthur while not a king, was an actual person of some national importance. Although it is now impossible to obtain certain proof, they contend that evidence points to the probability that he existed. Some scholars think Arthur may have been a Romano-Briton (a descendant of the Roman invaders).

See also ARTHURIAN ROMANCES.

CHARLES L. REGAN, *Boston College*

ARTHUR (1187–1203), är'thər, duke or count of Brittany. He was the grandson of King Henry II of England and the nephew of kings Richard I and John. In 1199, on the death of Richard I, who had declared him his heir, Arthur was proclaimed king of England by the nobles of Anjou, Touraine, and Maine, while the English lords decided in favor of John. King Philip of France supported Arthur, but after peace was concluded between John and Philip, Arthur came into John's power and soon mysteriously disappeared. According to general belief Arthur was murdered at John's command. The story of Arthur forms a portion of Shakespeare's *King John*.

ARTHUR III (1393–1458), är'thər, was a duke of Brittany. He was the third son of John IV, duke of Brittany, and Joan of Navarre, who later became the wife of Henry IV of England. Arthur received the earldom of Richmond in England through a brother, became a constable of France, and inherited the duchy of Brittany.

Arthur participated in the French civil war between the Burgundian and Armagnac factions during the reign of Charles VI, and in the last phases of the Hundred Years' War between France and England. He first fought for the Armagnacs and thereby obtained various titles and lands. In 1415 he fought against the English at the Battle of Agincourt, where he was wounded and captured. Held prisoner in England for five years, he gained the favor of Henry V and was freed. Through his English and French connections, Arthur helped arrange the Treaty of Troyes in 1420, which temporarily ended hostilities and gave most of northern France to England.

After his marriage in 1423 to Margaret of Burgundy, Arthur shifted his loyalty from the Armagnacs to the Burgundians. But when he received no high command from the Burgundians and their English allies, Arthur returned to the Armagnacs and loyally served King Charles VII to the end of the Hundred Years' War. As constable of France he helped plan the campaigns that gradually drove the English from France and ended the war in 1453. He died on Dec. 26, 1458.

BRYCE LYON, *Brown University*

21st President of the United States (1881–1885)

Birth—Oct. 5, 1830, in North Fairfield, Vt.
Higher Education—Union College (graduated 1848).
Religion—Episcopalian.
Occupation—Lawyer.
Marriage—Oct. 25, 1859, to Ellen Lewis Herndon (1837–1880).
Children—William Lewis Herndon Arthur (1860–1863); Chester Alan Arthur (1864–1937); Ellen Herndon Arthur (1871–1915).
Military Service—New York State Militia (1861–1863).
Nickname—"The Gentleman Boss."
Political Party—Republican.
Residence When He Became President—New York.
Position Prior to Taking Office—Vice-president.
Death—Nov. 18, 1886, in New York City, at age 56.
Burial Place—Albany, N.Y.

(Left) CHESTER A. ARTHUR, in his official portrait.

ARTHUR, Chester Alan (1830–1886), 21st president of the United States. He is remembered as the political spoilsman who, falling heir to the presidency, surprised his country with an honest administration. President Arthur supported and signed into law the reform Civil Service Act of 1883, which established a merit system of appointment to federal employment.

Early Life. Chester Alan Arthur was born in North Fairfield, Vt., on Oct. 5, 1830. His father, William Arthur, emigrated from Ireland and, after teaching school in Vermont and Canada, became a Baptist minister. His mother, Malvina Stone, was a descendant of English settlers in New Hampshire.

Young Arthur entered Union College at Schenectady, N.Y., at the age of 15. After his graduation in 1848 he studied law at home and earned his living as a teacher at North Pownal, Vt., and as principal of the academy at Cohoes, N.Y. He received his final training in New York City at the law office of Culver and Parker. Admitted to the bar in 1854, he formed his own law firm in 1856.

Rise in New York Politics. Soon after his arrival in New York City, Arthur became associated with the newborn Republican party, joining its ranks to make acquaintances and to find new clients. On Oct. 25, 1859, he married Ellen Lewis Herndon, who bore him three children, one of whom died in childhood.

Arthur worked assiduously for the reelection of Edwin D. Morgan as governor of New York, and when Morgan won in 1860, Arthur was given the post of state engineer-in-chief. In 1861, after the outbreak of the Civil War, he became the state's assistant quartermaster general, with responsibility for supplying barracks, food, and equipment for the New York militia. On July 27, 1862, three weeks after President Lincoln's call for 300,000 more men, he was advanced to the state quartermaster generalship.

When Governor Morgan was succeeded by the Democrat Horatio Seymour in 1863, Arthur returned to his law practice, but he retained close association with the city's Republican organization. The boss of the state's Republican political machine was Senator Roscoe Conkling. Arthur supported him, becoming one of his chief henchmen. Conkling obtained from President Grant an appointment for Arthur as collector of the port of New York; thus, in 1871, Arthur became the head of the customs house, a post that enabled him to give jobs to thousands of Republicans. Though personally honest, Arthur closed his eyes to unethical practices, incompetency, and graft in his office. During his first three years as collector his yearly earnings, mainly from percentages of fines, averaged $40,000.

In 1877, the year President Hayes took office, an investigation of the customs house was undertaken, and its lax management exposed. A prolonged and bitter fight between the New York party machine and Hayes ensued. Finally, Arthur was removed from office in 1878.

Vice President. At the Republican National Convention of 1880, Conkling's "stalwart" faction (which took the name by contrasting their own "stalwart" Republicanism with that of the reform elements in the party) supported former President Grant's nomination for a third term. Arthur was one of the 306 "stalwart" delegates who voted for Grant until the last ballot. However, the convention choice for president was James A. Garfield. To conciliate the defeated stalwarts, Arthur was suggested for the vice presidency. Conkling told him: "If you wish for my favor and my respect you will contemptuously decline it [the nomination]." But Arthur replied: "Senator Conkling, I shall accept the nomination and I shall carry with me the majority of the delegation." And he did.

After the election of the Garfield-Arthur ticket, the issue of the New York patronage flared up again. Conkling expected the new president to consult him on all federal patronage in New York State, and in this demand Arthur backed the senator, his old boss. When President Garfield stubbornly refused, both New York senators—Conkling and Thomas Platt—resigned their seats, mistakenly anticipating speedy reelection by the legislature. Meanwhile, a deranged office seeker, Charles J. Guiteau, shot President Garfield on July 2, 1881, exclaiming, "I am a Stalwart of the Stalwarts . . . Arthur is president now."

The Presidency. During the whole summer Garfield lay between life and death. Late on September 19 he died, and early the next day Arthur took the oath. "Chet Arthur, President of the

United States! Good God!" exclaimed a Republican, expressing a widely held feeling.

But those who feared that under Arthur the spoils system would become rampant and that political bossism would be the order of the day were to be much surprised. As chief executive, Arthur showed great responsibility. He filled federal offices with competent men, even though they were of the "stalwart" faction, and Conkling did not become the power behind the throne.

Arthur as president would not be the henchman of anyone. He gave the country an honest administration. His legislative program was moderate; he asked for tariff revision, for a reduction of excise taxes, for funds to rebuild the obsolete Navy, and for the creation of an up-to-date merchant marine. But Congress gave little heed to his recommendations. Despite the tremendous surplus pouring into the Treasury, taxes and tariff duties were not reduced.

President Arthur continued the prosecution of the Star Route swindlers in the Post Office Department, who had received large cutbacks from mail contractors. He vetoed a huge "pork barrel" appropriation of almost $19,000,000 for the improvement of rivers and harbors because he considered it to be wasteful and improper. He also vetoed a Chinese Exclusion Bill barring Chinese nationals from admission as immigrants to the United States, holding that the legislation was inconsistent with the existing treaty with China. Both presidential vetoes were overridden by Congress, however. Another law passed during his administration was the Anti-Polygamy Act, aimed at the Mormons in Utah.

In the midterm elections of 1882 the electorate gave the Democrats an overwhelming major-

ELLEN ARTHUR died before her husband became president.

THE LIBRARY OF CONGRESS COLLECTION

ity in the House, while in the Senate the Republicans had a scant majority. In the New York gubernatorial election the president threw his weight behind the candidacy of Charles J. Folger, and when Folger was defeated by the obscure mayor of Buffalo (Grover Cleveland), Arthur's political influence suffered so badly that his nomination for the presidency "in his own right" became improbable.

The lame duck session of Congress passed the Pendleton Civil Service Act, the first great step toward a merit system. It became law under Arthur's signature on Jan. 16, 1883 (See CIVIL SERVICE).

As Arthur's administration neared its end, public opinion about him changed. Many critics turned into supporters. Mark Twain said: "I am but one in 55,000,000; still, in the opinion of this one-fifty-five millionth of the country's population, it would be hard to better President Arthur's administration. But don't decide till you hear from the rest."

Arthur naturally hoped that the Republicans would nominate him in 1884. But as he had the support neither of the reform wing nor of the party bosses, his candidacy became an idle hope. On the first ballot he had 278 votes against frontrunner James G. Blaine's 334½, but on the fourth ballot the prize was Blaine's, with 541 votes against Arthur's 207. Blaine lost the election to Grover Cleveland.

His term completed, Arthur returned to his New York law practice. A year and a half later—on Nov. 18, 1886—he died in New York City of Bright's disease.

Aside from the quality of his administration, Chester A. Arthur will be remembered for being the most elegant and best-dressed president, in whose closet hung some 80 suits. Nicknamed "The Gentleman Boss," he read Scott and Thackeray, was an inveterate fisherman, enjoyed parties, and had an epicure's taste in food and drink. Handsome, dignified, and genial, he was a conscientious administrator, but never an inspiring leader of men.

STEFAN LORANT

Author, "The Presidency: A Pictorial History of Presidential Elections from Washington to Truman"

Further Reading: Clancy, Herbert J., *The Presidential Election of 1880* (Chicago 1958); Howe, George F., *Chester A. Arthur: A Quarter Century of Machine Politics* (New York 1934; reprint, 1957); Josephson, Matthew, *The Politicos, 1865–1896* (New York 1938).

PRESIDENT ARTHUR (in this 1885 engraving) reads to his young daughter, Nell, who was named for her mother.

CULVER PICTURES, INC.

ARTHUR, är'thər, **Timothy Shay** (1809–1885), American author. He was born at Newburgh, N.Y., on June 6, 1809. In 1852 he founded *Arthur's Home Magazine.* He wrote more than 100 moral and domestic tales, which had a large sale in both England and the United States. His most popular work was *Ten Nights in a Barroom and What I Saw There* (1854). He died at Philadelphia, Pa., on March 6, 1885.

ARTHURIAN ROMANCES, är-thōōr'ē-ən, a group of medieval tales, in prose and verse, concerning the legendary King Arthur (q.v.) and the chivalric knights of the Round Table. Arthur may have been an actual Briton or Romano-Briton who led the Celts against the Anglo-Saxons in the early 8th century, but he has become, through an overlay of mythological, legendary, and romantic elements, largely a fictitious figure. A corpus of written literature in which he is mentioned began to develop at least as early as the beginning of the 9th century. Nennius, probably a Welsh priest, in his Latin *Historia Brittonum* (about 800), has the earliest certain extant reference to Arthur, whom he calls *dux bellorum* (leader of battles) rather than king. Chosen 12 times to lead the Celts, Arthur bore the image of the Virgin and won 12 battles, the last being at Mt. Badon, in which he killed 960 of the enemy single-handed.

The next reference to Arthur is in the *Annales Cambriae* (about 950), an ancient history of Wales, where it is stated that Arthur and Medraut (Modred) fell in 537 in a Battle of Camlann. From the Welsh story "Kulhwch and Olwen," one of the *Mabinogion* (about 1100), it is evident that Arthurian narrative had grown up among the Welsh before it began to appear in French literature. In this story, moreover, several of the figures of Arthurian romance are already present. Although the society depicted is primitive, Arthur clearly presides over a court, which includes his wife Gwenhwyfar (Guinevere) and the figures, probably originally Welsh gods, Kei (Kay), Bedwyr (Bedevere), and Gwalchmei (Gawain). Probably, too, the Welsh stories were by this time being affected by Breton *conteurs* (storytellers). Descended from Britons who had fled to Armorica (Brittany) before the Germanic invaders, the *conteurs* now brought a continental tradition of the Arthurian story to the English-Welsh border. William of Malmesbury, in his *Gesta Regum Anglorum* (about 1125), speaks contemptuously of Breton mythologizing of Arthur but asserts his basic historicity. The legend of Arthur had by this time been enriched by motifs from Welsh folklore and by the transfer to Arthur and his companions of the deeds and traits of Irish heroes like Bran, an Odysseus-like figure, and Cuchulain, an Irish Achilles.

Geoffrey of Monmouth. The earliest extant formulation of the events of Arthur's career into a continuous narrative is in the Latin prose *Historia Regum Britanniae* (History of the Kings of Britain, 1137) of Geoffrey of Monmouth, a Welshman or Welsh-born Breton. Geoffrey devotes about a fifth of his work to Arthur and contributes several elements to the tradition, making Arthur the son of Uther Pendragon by an adulterous liaison with Igraine, and making Merlin, who was probably originally a Welsh deity, a magician. Geoffrey says that Arthur was taken to the Isle of Avalon while his wounds healed, and gives Arthur's capital as Caerleon

KING ARTHUR and the ladies of his court attend a joust. (From a French manuscript illumination, dated 1463.)

on the Usk. Geoffrey tells of Arthur's coronation, his defeat of the Saxons, his conquest of the Picts and Scots and of Ireland, Iceland, Gaul, and other nations, his routing the armies of Rome, the faithlessness of his wife Guanhamara and the treachery of his nephew, Regent Modred, and the final battle for Britain, in which Modred is killed and Arthur wounded. Geoffrey's veracity was suspect to some of his contemporaries, indisputable to others. Whatever his sources and however much he was indebted to them, Geoffrey set the pattern for subsequent treatments of Arthur. In Geoffrey's *Historia*, Arthur is a king, whose splendid court E.K. Chambers views as fashioned upon Charlemagne's. This remarkable work of pseudohistory has been called the wellspring of Arthurian romance.

Followers of Geoffrey. Several pseudohistorical poems followed closely upon Geoffrey's. Geoffrey Gaimar, a 12th century Anglo-Norman historiographer, made a French translation in rhyme of Geoffrey's work, and this was followed, in 1155, by the *Roman de Brut* of the chronicler Wace. Wace's poem is a reworking of Geoffrey's history, a paraphrase in octosyllabic couplets, in which the author adds and deletes at will. It makes the first extant reference to Arthur's Round Table and the first to Arthur's anticipated return from Avalon.

Although in the *Roman de Brut* Arthur is a French or Anglo-Norman chivalric king, he is thoroughly Anglicized in the *Brut* (about 1205) of Layamon (Laweman), a priest at what is now Areley Kings in Worcestershire. Layamon translated Wace's work into English, doubling its length. The main philological feature of Layamon's work is that it is almost completely English: only about a hundred words of French origin appear in it. Layamon's Arthur is a warrior, grim and fierce, an object of dread to friend and enemy; in short, an epic hero. To the tradition Layamon contributes a full account of the establishment of the Round Table and the magic origin of Arthur's lance (Ron) and sword (Caliburn). The *Brut* is both the first treatment of Arthur in English and the last for about a century.

French Romance. While in 12th century England Arthur was a figure of pseudohistory, in 12th century France he was one of romance. How he passed from Celtic legend to French romance has been variously described, but the most acceptable explanation is that the *conteurs,* who may have influenced Welsh treatments of Arthur, may equally well have communicated Arthurian stories to French-speaking people both in England and on the Continent. The language of the Bretons was close to Welsh; they became bilingual early and told their stories at the courts of France and Norman England.

The oldest extant Arthurian romances are those of Chrétien de Troyes, a Provençal poet who composed four poems, *Erec, Lancelot, Yvain,* and part of a *Perceval*—all concerned with knights of the court of Arthur. In another romance, *Cliges,* Chrétien tells a story that was originally Byzantine, but is here fused with the Arthurian milieu. The morality of *Erec* and *Yvain* is orthodox. *Lancelot,* however, treats of the adulterous love of Lancelot and Guinevere and is permeated with courtly love. In courtly love, the most important element was the lover's willingness to serve his lady, no matter what feats of bravery and endurance he might be required to perform. Physical consummation, even if adulterous, was permitted. Courtly love was alien to marriage, because love had to be freely given. Some of the events in Chrétien's plots have parallels in earlier Welsh and Irish literature, and the exact nature of his sources has long been disputed. In the 19th century, some scholars held that Chrétien fashioned a mass of Celtic folklore into a form it had not had before, but 20th century scholars are reluctant to credit Chrétien with the invention of Arthurian romance. At least one scholar believes that the immediate source of Chrétien's Arthurian poems were four long prose narratives, based on the accounts of the *conteurs* and accessible to Chrétien. Chrétien's works had a profound impact on the Germanic world. Some of them served as sources for Norse sagas and for poems by Hartmann von Aue. The *Parzival,* a *höfisches Epos* (courtly epic) of Wolfram von Eschenbach, a Middle High German work of the early 17th century, is at least partly indebted to Chrétien's *Perceval.*

The Two Traditions. There are differences between the Arthur of pseudohistory and the Arthur of romance. In the former he is always the strong, central figure; in the latter he is secondary and the stories are usually concerned with episodes in the lives of individual knights rather than with Arthur himself. Romantic treatments vary widely. In many works he is a background or peripheral figure whose presence is felt mainly as a social force or arbiter of chivalric excellence; sometimes he is a pathetic cuckold.

Arthur's court, however, remained devoted to the ideal, and heroes like Tristram and legends not originally Arthurian became part of it. Robert de Boron (1170?–?1212), a Frenchman, treated the Grail legend, originally a pagan theme, in a context of Christianity with Arthurian figures. Perceval, the Grail knight, was displaced in later romances by Galahad. In England, if the surviving romances are indicative, Gawain was the favorite Arthurian knight. Of the dozen works of which he is the hero, all of them dating from the late 14th century and the 15th century, *The Wedding of Sir Gawain and Dame Bagnell* (an analogue of Chaucer's "Wife of Bath's Tale," itself set in the Arthurian milieu) and the incomparable *Sir Gawain and the Green Knight* are outstanding. Lancelot, however, is the central figure of but two Middle English romances,

the stanzaic *Morte Arthur* (about 1400) and the late 15th century *Lancelot of the Laik.* The Grail quest, moreover, is treated in Middle English only by Sir Thomas Malory (1410?–1471), whose work was printed in 1485 by William Caxton as *Le Morte Darthur.* A manuscript found in 1934 led Eugene Vinaver to view Malory's work as a series of romances, not a unified whole. Malory's sources included several French romances and the Middle English alliterative *Morte Arthure* (about 1350). The early life of Arthur is treated in the English romance, *Arthur and Merlin* (about 1300). Only one romance, *Arthur,* an inferior English poem of the 14th century, is devoted to the entire career of the king.

Later Treatments. Interest in Arthur and his world did not die with the Middle Ages, but the materials were adapted to suit the interests and tastes of succeeding generations. Spenser, in the *Faerie Queene,* uses Arthur to represent magnificence and ideal manhood in an allegory in which virtues and vices are embodied in romantic knights, ladies, giants, and dragons. Milton contemplated an "Arthuriad" before he wrote *Paradise Lost.* The most distinguished treatment of Arthurian material in 19th century England is Tennyson's *Idylls of the King,* a series of 12 metrical romances, based in general on Malory, in which the full-bloodedness of Malory's knights gives way to refined Victorian sensitiveness. With the pre-Raphaelite enthusiasm for the culture of the Middle Ages, William Morris produced *The Defence of Guinevere* (1858), a dramatic monologue in which Arthur's queen answers Gawain's charge of adultery.

Although Arthur himself does not figure in them, Wagner's music dramas *Parsifal,* a treatment of the Grail legend, and *Tristan und Isolde* embody familiar Arthurian themes. In the United States, Mark Twain's *A Connecticut Yankee in King Arthur's Court* (1889) presents the collision of New England ingenuity and republicanism with medieval authoritarianism and superstition. Edwin Arlington Robinson wrote poetic versions of several of the Arthurian legends, including the Pulitzer Prize-winning *Tristram* (1927). In T.H. White's *The Once and Future King* (1958), Arthur, Guinevere, and Lancelot are humanized. Alan Jay Lerner and Frederick Loewe based their Broadway musical *Camelot* (1960) on this work.

See also ENGLISH CHRONICLES.

CHARLES L. REGAN, *Boston College*

Bibliography

Text of *Arthurian Chronicles* by Wace and Layamon, tr. by Eugene Mason with an introduction by Gwyn Jones (London 1912), was reprinted in New York in 1962. *Arthurian Romances* by Chrétien de Troyes, tr. with an introduction by William W. Comfort (London 1914) was reprinted in 1965. *The Works of Sir Thomas Malory* was edited in 3 vols. by Eugene Vinaver (New York 1947–48). Geoffrey of Monmouth's *The History of the Kings of Britain* was translated, with an introduction, by Lewis Thorpe (Baltimore 1966).

Brengle, Richard L., ed., *Arthur, King of Britain; History, Romance, Chronicle, and Criticism; With Texts in Modern English, From Gildas to Malory* (New York 1964).

Bruce, James D., *Evolution of Arthurian Romance From the Beginnings Down to the Year 1300,* 2d ed., 2 vols. (Gloucester, Mass., 1958).

Chambers, Edmund K., *Arthur of Britain* (London 1927).

Jackson, William T.H., *The Literature of the Middle Ages* (New York 1960).

Loomis, Roger Sherman, *Arthurian Tradition and Chrétien de Troyes* (New York 1949).

Loomis, Roger Sherman, ed., *Arthurian Literature in the Middle Ages* (New York 1959).

JOHN H. GERARD; (INSET) USDA

JERUSALEM ARTICHOKE (*Helianthus tuberosus*) is a sunflower and produces a cluster of edible tubers.

HERBERT C. LANKS, FROM FPG; (INSET) ROCHE

GLOBE ARTICHOKE (*Cynara scolymus*) is cultivated extensively in the southern United States and California.

ARTHUR'S SEAT, är'thərz sēt, a hill 2 miles east of Edinburgh, Scotland, that rises to a height of 822 feet (250 meters). Its steep sides are precipitous in places. A range of perpendicular basalt columns on the south side is called Samson's Ribs. The view from the summit includes the city of Edinburgh and Edinburgh Castle, the North Sea, the Firth of Forth, and the distant Grampian Mountains. On the north side are the ruins of a chapel and a hermitage dedicated to St. Anthony, and a spring called St. Margaret's Well. The origin of the name is obscure. There is a tradition that King Arthur surveyed the country from the summit and defeated the Saxons in the neighborhood.

ARTICHOKE, är'tə-chōk, is a tall perennial plant native to the Mediterranean region and the Canary Islands. It is a coarse, stout, thistlelike herb, usually 3 to 5 feet (1.0 to 1.5 meters) tall. It has spiny, feathery leaves, the lower ones often 3 feet (1 meter) or more long, and numerous small, scalelike leaves (bracts) associated with the flower clusters. The flowers are usually blue or white.

Artichokes are extensively cultivated in southern Europe. In the United States they are grown in the Southern states and California. They grow best in low ground near the seacoast. The plant is rather tender and must be protected from frost. If planted in rich soil and set 4 feet (1.2 meters) apart, the plants will yield two or three good crops before they are replaced with new plants grown from seedlings or suckers. If the plants are allowed to stand longer, the yield gradually diminishes.

Artichokes are cultivated for the edible thickened scales and bottoms, or hearts, of the immature flower heads, which sometimes exceed 4 inches (10 cm) in diameter before they become too old for eating. Anatomically, the scales are bracts and the heart is the receptacle of the flower head. Artichokes are eaten raw as a salad, pickled, or cooked like cauliflower.

Artichokes are members of the family Compositae. The common artichoke, sometimes called the globe artichoke or French artichoke, is *Cynara scolymus*. In Europe many types of artichokes are popular, but in the United States only the globe artichoke is raised commercially.

A perennial American sunflower (*Helianthus tuberosus*) is often called the "Jerusalem artichoke," although it is not an artichoke. The tuber of this plant is used as a vegetable. See SUNFLOWER.

ARTICLE, är'ti-kəl, a part of speech used before nouns to limit or define their application. In the English language, *a* and *an* are the indefinite articles, and *the* is the definite article. The German *ein* and the French *un* may be either the numeral "one" or the indefinite article, and the English indefinite article is a modified form of the Anglo-Saxon numeral adjective meaning "one." In Anglo-Saxon, the word had only one form, *ān*. But as English developed, because of the difficulty of pronouncing *an* before a consonant ("an book"), the *n* was gradually eliminated except before vowels. When a vowel takes on a consonantal pronunciation, such as *u* in union or *o* in one-sided, it also takes the article *a* rather than *an*.

There are traces in various languages showing that the definite article was originally a pronoun; thus, in English *the* is closely akin to *this* and *that*. Latin and most Slavic languages have no articles; Greek has only the definite. In some languages the definite article is prefixed to its noun; in others it is affixed to the noun. See also ADJECTIVE.

ARTICLES, Thirty-nine, är'ti-kəlz, a statement of doctrine issued by the Church of England during the Reformation period to present its position with reference to the theological controversies of the time. These articles continue to be accepted by the churches of the Anglican Communion as setting forth the doctrinal position of the communion. In practice, they are commonly interpreted in the context of the Book of Common Prayer.

Adoption. *The Thirty-nine Articles of Religion* (to give the formal title) were the last in a series of doctrinal formulations by the Church of England. During the reign of Henry VIII, as a result of conferences held in 1538 by Archbishop

411

Cranmer and other English clergymen with a group of Lutheran theologians, thirteen articles were agreed upon. These embodied some of the doctrine and phraseology of the Confession of Augsburg (see AUGSBURG CONFESSION). The substance of these thirteen articles, together with Calvinistic modifications in statements on the doctrine of the sacraments, was incorporated into the Forty-two Articles, compiled in 1551 on mandate from Edward VI.

Suppressed under Mary, the Forty-two Articles were revived and revised by Archbishop Parker and a Convocation of the English clergy early in the reign of Elizabeth. They were then reduced to thirty-nine and published in Latin and English in 1563. Article 29, however ("Of the wicked which do not eat the body of Christ in the Lord's Supper"), was suppressed until the final revision in 1571. At that time the clergy and candidates for ordination were required to state that they accepted the articles. In 1689 and again in 1772 attempts were made by the latitudinarian party to relax the requirement that the clergy subscribe to this formulation of doctrine, but these attempts were unsuccessful. The Articles are still binding on the clergy of the Church of England under a modified form of subscription adopted in 1865.

Interpretation. The articles were designed to embrace a considerable range of views on theology, while rejecting certain medieval teachings as well as Anabaptist radicalism. Because of their comprehensiveness, the Articles are in some places ambiguous and capable of diverse interpretation. Several undoubtedly reflect the Lutheran theology of the Augsburg and Württemberg Confessions. Some Anglicans have regarded the formulary as in no essential conflict with the dogmatic decrees of the Roman Catholic Council of Trent, yet others have seen in it an approximation to mild Calvinism. During the 17th century, the interpretation of the Articles was much in dispute between Anglicans and Puritans. Charles I issued "His Majesty's Declaration" (prefixed to the Articles of Religion in the English Prayer Book) in the hope of allaying controversy.

The American Episcopal Church adopted the Articles in 1801, but it has never required subscription by its clergy. The Twenty-five Articles of John Wesley (1784) for American Methodism represent a reduction of the Anglican articles, particularly at points that seemed to have Calvinistic implications.

Summary of Content. The following outline gives a brief analysis of the Thirty-nine Articles:

Articles 1–5. The Christian Faith: the Trinity; the Incarnation, atoning death, and resurrection of Christ; the Holy Ghost.

Articles 6–8. The Rule of Faith: Holy Scripture and the ancient creeds.

Articles 9–18. The grounds of man's salvation: Original sin, free will, justification by faith, good works and faith, predestination.

Articles 19–31. The corporate means of salvation: the Church, its authority and ministry; the Sacraments (Baptism and the Lord's Supper), rejection of transubstantiation, communion in one kind, the "sacrifices of masses"; the traditions of the Church.

Articles 32–39. Miscellaneous matters of practice and internal discipline.

PERCY V. NORWOOD
Author of "Tudor England and the German Princes"

ARTICLES OF CONFEDERATION, är'ti-kəlz, kən-fed-ə-ra'shən, the name of the first constitution of the United States. The Articles were the law of the land from 1781 until 1789, when the federal Constitution went into operation. Under the Articles, the 13 former colonies set up the first permanent central government in the new nation.

The Second Continental Congress moved to establish a committee to draw up a constitution on June 7, 1776—the same day a motion to declare independence was introduced. Heading the committee was John Dickinson of Pennsylvania, who became the chief author of the first draft of the Articles presented to Congress on July 12, 1776. Congress formally adopted the Articles on Nov. 15, 1777, but ratification by all the states was not completed until March 1, 1781.

Background. Many factors favored the formation of a central government in 1776. The military struggle for independence from Britain required a unified policy. There were also men in each of the 13 states who believed that when peace came, there would have to be a central government to regulate trade, control western lands, and limit paper money issues. Moreover, Americans shared many traditions that made possible some form of intercolonial union: a common language, common political ideas, and a common bond in their English heritage.

At the same time, strong forces were working against the creation of a central government. Americans had developed decidedly different customs, traditions, and economies in various sections of the country. New Englanders and Southerners had opposite views on many social, economic, and religious matters. Frontiersmen developed different ways of living from those of the coastal Americans. Moreover, the American people in general tended to be more loyal to the locality from which they came than to the nation as a whole. This powerful spirit of localism created rivalries that divided the states. Conflicts arose over boundaries, western lands, and the issue of slavery. Each state felt that it was contributing more to the war effort than its neighbor. Finally, the idea of a strong central government was repugnant to most Americans at this time; in many respects the Revolution itself represented a protest against the centralized political authority that had been imposed by the British.

Draft Negotiations. Dickinson's draft calling for a powerful central government did not meet with the approval of Congress. Most states insisted upon a central government that would be subordinate to the states and controlled by them. The final draft of the Articles adopted by Congress reflected this point of view; it provided for a weak central government with strictly delegated powers.

The controversy over the Articles in Congress, aside from states' rights, revolved around three main points—representation, money contributions, and western lands. Congress debated whether the states should be represented equally or in proportion to population. Representation, it was decided, should be equal, with each state having one vote. The second issue concerned the basis for determining the amount of money each state would contribute toward common expenses. Congress declared that contributions should be in proportion to the value of privately owned land within each state. The third and thorniest issue was over the control of western lands. Some states with fixed boundaries had no claims to lands in the west; they asked that control of all western lands be given to Congress. Those states with western land claims resisted such demands, and the dispute delayed ratification. Finally, to gain Maryland's consent, the landed states agreed to cede their claims to Congress, and the new constitution officially went into effect.

Characteristics. Under the Articles, the Confederation became a league of sovereign states. The central government consisted of a Congress of delegates chosen annually by the states. It was empowered to manage foreign affairs, declare war, make treaties, raise armies, build a navy, control Indian affairs, coin and borrow money, and establish post offices. All nonenumerated powers were retained by the states. Every important measure passed by Congress required the consent of 9 of the 13 states. No constitutional amendment could be added to the Articles unless approved by Congress and ratified by every state.

Under the Articles there was no chief executive or national judiciary. The central government had no right to collect taxes or control foreign commerce. Congress could pass laws but had no way of coercing the states to comply.

Practical Effects. Despite the weakness of the central government, the Congress during the Confederation period managed some notable achievements. The Revolutionary War was successfully concluded and a favorable peace treaty signed. A new territorial policy was worked out in the Northwest Ordinance. Executive departments were created to centralize some functions of the Congress, and four new officers were appointed: a superintendent of finance and secretaries of foreign affairs, war, and marine. In the view of some historians, the Articles might have secured the American union for many years. However, they had certain inherent defects.

The defects proved fatal to the Articles as a constitutional system. In spite of the numerous powers it possessed on paper, the central government was always dependent on the willingness of the states to accept its measures, and in many cases they refused to do so. Many states ignored or annulled the acts of Congress. Without the power to tax, the government was in constant financial difficulty. Lacking the power to regulate foreign commerce it could not establish a uniform commercial policy for the country. Britain, therefore, was able to raise barriers to American trade without fear of retaliation. None of these deficiencies could be corrected because it was practically impossible to make amendments to the Articles.

During the Confederation period, the country faced a postwar depression and serious threats to its security from Britain and Spain. The feeling grew that the central government would have to be strengthened if the nation was to survive. Political leaders like Washington, Hamilton, and Madison kept pointing to the flaws in the Articles and urging that something be done. In 1787 the Constitutional Convention in Philadelphia agreed to abandon the Articles, and it replaced them with the new federal Constitution that went into effect on March 4, 1789.

GEORGE A. BILLIAS, *Clark University*

Further Reading: Burnett, Edmund C., *The Continental Congress*, new ed. (New York 1964); Jensen, Merrill, *The Articles of Confederation*, 2d ed. (Madison 1959); id., *The New Nation* (New York 1950); Main, Jackson T., *The Antifederalists* (Chapel Hill 1961); Wright, Benjamin F., *Consensus and Continuity, 1776–1787* (Boston 1958).

ARTICLES OF WAR, är′ti-kəlz, wôr, the code of law by which members of the U.S. Army and U.S. Air Force were formerly governed. The body of statutes was comparable to the Articles for the Government of the Navy and the Disciplinary Laws of the Coast Guard, formerly used by the other military services. All of these codes were supplanted in 1951 by the Uniform Code of Military Justice.

Origins. The Articles of War, enacted in 1775 and later modified, were patterned on the earlier British Articles of War, a body of statutes enacted at various times. Probably the earliest code was that promulgated in England in the 14th century under the title "Statutes, Ordinances and Customs" of the armed forces. In 1642 the 3d earl of Essex, commander in chief of the Parliamentary army, replaced this brief code with one on the laws and ordinances of war. Both these instruments were designed to terminate the extreme and highly arbitrary action of military commanders in the enforcement of discipline. Cromwell himself on one occasion vented his rage on a group of officers by hastily putting them through the form of a court-martial in order to arrive at predetermined condemnation. He then promptly shot one of the condemned to expedite the job of disposal.

A serious mutiny in the reign of William and Mary was followed by Parliament's passage of the first Mutiny Act (1689). It extended the earlier laws governing military discipline and included a check on the crown's authority over such matters. The act reserved to Parliament sole power to establish and revise the military penal code. Annually reenacted and amended, the substance of this act remains in force today.

Enactment. When the American War of Independence confronted the Continental Congress with the need for a military penal code, the legislators, on July 30, 1775, adopted the English Mutiny Act, almost without change. Experience gained in fighting under the British flag had convinced them of the soundness of that code.

As modified by the Continental Congress on Sept. 20, 1776, these Articles of War consisted of three sections. The first announced "101 rules and articles by which the armies of the United States shall be governed." The second section dealt with the disposition of spies in wartime, subjecting them to the death penalty after trial by court-martial. The third section repealed the previous act of 1775. On April 10, 1806, the U.S. Congress enacted a further bill, slightly modifying the act of 1776. It remained on the statute books without substantial change until a revision of 1916 modernized the court-martial proceedings.

Most of the changes effected in 1916 moderated some of the penalties previously authorized, and in other ways eased the situation of the accused, thus bringing court-martial proceedings into closer harmony with those of civil courts. The immediate result was a reduction in the penalties suffered by the offenders. In addition, the reviewing authority was empowered to approve or disapprove the whole or any part of a sentence. The Articles were amended again in 1948 to liberalize them further, but shortly thereafter they were replaced by the Uniform Code. See also MILITARY COURTS-MARTIAL; MILITARY LAW–*Military Justice in the Armed Forces of the United States.*

ARTIFICIAL HEART. See ARTIFICIAL ORGANS.

ARTIFICIAL INSEMINATION

ARTIFICIAL INSEMINATION, ärt-ə-fish′əl in-sem-ə-nā′shən, is the injection of semen into the female genital tract by means other than normal mating. Cattle breeding, in particular, benefits from this practice, which makes it possible to improve herds by transmitting quickly and widely the characteristics of a superior sire. A bull selected for stud service can sire, through artificial insemination, 2,000 or more offspring in a year. The process used by breeders consists of collecting semen from a male, diluting it, storing it carefully under appropriate temperatures to ensure continued fertility, and then introducing it into the genital tract of a female. See also BREEDING.

In humans, too, a woman may be artificially inseminated with semen from a donor. The donor may be her fertile, but impotent, husband, or he may be an unknown donor selected by a physician. Accurate estimates of the number of artificially inseminated women are difficult to obtain. The rights of "test tube" babies produced in this manner and the question of whether the procedure would ever constitute adultery are legal problems as yet generally unsolved.

ARTIFICIAL LIMBS. See PROSTHESIS.

ARTIFICIAL ORGANS, ärt-ə-fish′əl ôr′gənz, are materials and mechanisms used to replace faulty organs in the body.

Artificial Kidney. The most significant developments in the design of artificial organs have taken place since the early 1940's. The earliest of these developments was the artificial kidney developed by W.J. Kolff in the Netherlands during World War II.

One of the functions of the kidney is to filter wastes (principally urea) from the blood. Kolff reasoned that an artificial membrane might be used to perform this task. For an artificial membrane, he used long tubes of cellophane designed for sausage casings. As the blood from the patient's body flowed through the cellophane tubes and back into his body, wastes passed from his blood through the porous cellophane by dialysis into the wash water (dialysate) that the tubes were bathed in. (Since the dialysate is free from wastes, the wastes pass from a region of greater concentration in the blood to the region of lesser concentration in the dialysate.)

Several types of artificial kidneys are in use. The membranes of all of them are made of cellophane, although much research is being done to develop better membranes. The two main types of artificial kidneys are the Kolff and the Skeggs-Leonard types. The Kolff System uses cellophane tubes. The Skeggs-Leonard type has cellophane membranes in many layers of flat sheets, and the blood and wash water pass through alternate layers.

The early artificial kidney was designed as an emergency device to take over for the kidneys temporarily until they could operate satisfactorily again or to help them rapidly remove great excesses of such material as sleeping pills or poisons from the blood. In 1960, however, Belding H. Scribner in the United States devised a method whereby the patient could be dialyzed repeatedly. Blood is shunted from an artery to a vein by means of a small permanent tube of Silastic silicone rubber and Teflon, which is surgically implanted in the patient's arm or leg. About twice a week the tube is opened and attached to the artificial kidney, and the patient's blood is dialyzed. Persons with no normal kidney function at all have been kept alive by this system for several years.

Much research is being done to reduce the cost of such treatment, which may be as much as $10,000 per year per patient.

Artificial Heart. Scientists also are studying the possibility of constructing artificial human hearts. The living heart serves only to pump blood through the body. However, it is a miracle of efficiency. It does an enormous amount of work with little input of energy, beating more than 100,000 times a day—40 million beats per year—for a lifetime, without tiring. The obstacles in duplicating such a mechanism are enormous. Research on the artificial heart is of two general types: devices for temporary assistance and complete heart replacement.

Heart-Assist Devices. The few hearts that have been placed in humans are of the temporary heart-assist type. Heart-assist devices are designed to keep the patient alive while heart damage heals so that the living heart can again function properly. When the heart is slightly damaged, it can continue to operate and keep the body alive until the damaged tissue heals. But if the damage is too extensive, the patient dies before healing can take place. The heart-assist device takes over some of the pumping work so that the damaged parts can heal. The American surgeons Adrian Kantrowitz and Michael DeBakey began placing heart-assist devices in human beings in 1966.

Heart Replacement. The two biggest problems in making actual artificial hearts are the materials to make them from and the means to operate them. Most investigators use Silastic silicone rubber for building the hearts, since it is the only rubbery material that can be implanted for long periods. Much research is being done both to improve this material's strength and its effect on clotting and to develop entirely new materials for implantation.

Artificial hearts now in use are double-walled bags powered by air pressure from an external source. When the air is forced between the two walls, the inner bag is collapsed, squeezing out the blood. When the air pressure is released, the inner bag again fills with blood. Valves keep the flow in the right direction, just as they do in the living heart.

Intensive research is being conducted on implantable power sources. Both atomic batteries

ARTIFICIAL KIDNEY machine in operation.

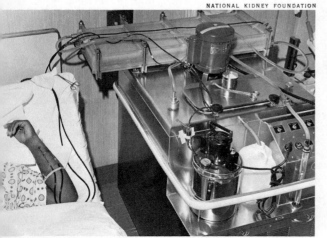

and fuel cells are being investigated as energy sources, but great problems are created by the large amount of power needed, the heat that must be dissipated, the fuel supply, tissue reactions, and many other obstacles. However, it is likely that these problems of materials and power sources will be surmounted and that artificial hearts will eventually be developed. Kolff has placed complete artificial hearts in calves, keeping the animals alive for up to two days.

Other Artificial Body Parts. Other body parts also have been replaced with man-made items. Stainless steel, chrome-cobalt, and silver have been used for years for pins, nails, plates, and screws, as well as for other devices for repair and replacement of bony tissue, such as faulty hip joints and defects in skulls and jaws.

Soft-tissue replacement, however, was almost impossible until the development of medical-grade silicones. All current heart valves utilize this material, and it is estimated that 20,000 persons are living useful lives because of modern heart-valve technology. Hydrocephalous shunts that serve to drain excess cranial fluid from the brain to the heart are made of Silastic silicone rubber and have been implanted in an estimated 100,000 persons. Dacron and Teflon arteries are

A COMPLETE artificial heart, developed by Willem Kolff, has been implanted in calves. It is made of Silastic-treated dacron mesh and has ball valves to direct blood flow.

NATIONAL INSTITUTES OF HEALTH PHOTO BY JERRY HECHT

carrying blood in many thousands of patients. Medical-grade silicone fluid and Silastic silicone rubber are used widely for reconstruction of tissue damaged by cancer, birth defects, and accidents.

Research is being done on artificial bile ducts, ureters, bladders, urethras, corneas, skin, joints, esophagi, tracheas, and many other body parts.

SILAS BRALEY
Dow Corning Center for Aid to Medical Research

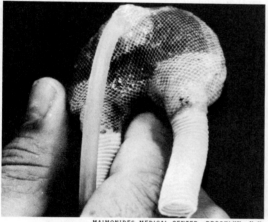

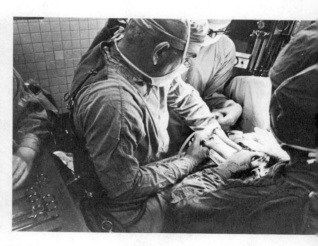

MAIMONIDES MEDICAL CENTER, BROOKLYN, N.Y.

A HEART-ASSIST DEVICE (*left*), developed by Adrian and Arthur Kantrowitz, has rigid outer and flexible inner tubes. The device is made of Silastic and has no valves. Implantation of the device is shown at right.

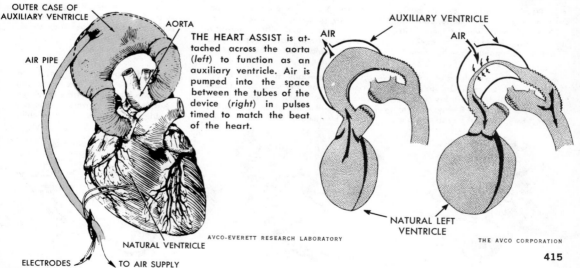

OUTER CASE OF AUXILIARY VENTRICLE

AORTA

AIR PIPE

THE HEART ASSIST is attached across the aorta (*left*) to function as an auxiliary ventricle. Air is pumped into the space between the tubes of the device (*right*) in pulses timed to match the beat of the heart.

AUXILIARY VENTRICLE

AIR

AIR

NATURAL LEFT VENTRICLE

NATURAL VENTRICLE

AVCO-EVERETT RESEARCH LABORATORY

THE AVCO CORPORATION

ELECTRODES

TO AIR SUPPLY

415

ARTIFICIAL RESPIRATION is the technique of forcing air into and out of the lungs when natural breathing ceases or seriously weakens. It is also used when breathing fails to begin in newborn infants. Its aim is not only to supply needed oxygen, but also to get the natural breathing mechanism working normally.

Natural breathing may be stopped or seriously impaired by drowning, strangulation, suffocation, or electrocution, or by inhaling poisonous gases or foreign bodies. Such emergencies require immediate action, since death or permanent brain damage will result if the brain's supply of oxygenated blood is cut off for 4 to 6 minutes.

When available, a mechanical device called a *resuscitator* is used to administer artificial respiration. For prolonged treatment, the *Drinker respirator,* popularly known as the "iron lung," is used. For emergency first aid, mouth-to-mouth, mouth-to-nose, or hand (manual) methods are applied. The Red Cross and other first-aid authorities prefer mouth-to-mouth or mouth-to-nose methods because they provide more ventilation and are more effective in keeping air passages open.

Mouth-to-Mouth and Mouth-to-Nose Methods. Artificial respiration by mouth-to-mouth and mouth-to-nose methods begins with measures to open the air passages so that air can move into and out of the lungs. Such measures are necessary because when a person loses consciousness and stops breathing, his jaw relaxes and his tongue drops backward, obstructing the throat. The best way to open the air passages is to place the victim on his back, lift the neck, and tilt the head back until the chin points straight upward. With the chin in this position, the jaw is drawn forward and the tongue is freed from the throat.

After clearing the victim's air passages in this way, the rescuer takes a deep breath, opens his own mouth wide, and places it over the mouth *or* nose of an adult victim (over the mouth *and* nose of a small child or an infant). He blows in the airway until he sees the chest rise and feels the resistance of the expanding lungs. Then he removes his mouth and allows the victim to exhale. This cycle is repeated about 12 times per minute for an adult, and at least 20 times per minute for a child. The rescuer should blow deep breaths for an adult, small breaths for a child, and only puffs of air for an infant.

Artificial respiration should be continued until the victim resumes spontaneous breathing. Evidence of a pulse on either side of the Adam's apple or a constriction of the pupils of the eyes generally precedes the return of normal breathing. When no pulse is present, it may also be necessary to administer artificial circulation. Only medical personnel or certified lifesavers should attempt artificial circulation.

Hand Methods. In both the *Silvester* and *Holger-Nielsen* hand methods, the rescuer kneels at the victim's head. In the former, the victim is placed on his back. His crossed arms are pressed against his lower chest and then pulled outward and upward over his head. In the Holger-Nielsen method, the victim is placed face down, with his head turned to one side and on his hands. The rescuer applies pressure on the victim's back and then draws the arms upward by the elbows.

ARCHER S. GORDON, M.D.
Lovelace Clinic, Albuquerque, N.Mex.

Further Reading: American National Red Cross, *First Aid Textbook,* rev. ed. (Washington 1957).

MOUTH-TO-MOUTH AND MOUTH-TO-NOSE RESPIRATION

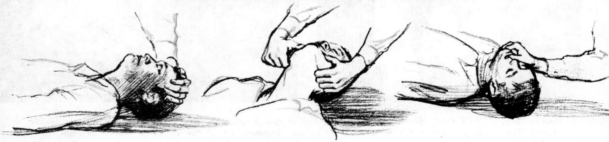

1. Place the patient on his back. Wipe any foreign matter out of his mouth with your fingers. Lift his neck. Tilt his head back so that his chin points straight upward.

2. You may also position the patient by grasping his lower jaw, as shown here, and lifting upward. But be careful not to press your fingers into soft throat tissue.

3. If his mouth is open, insert your thumb between his teeth to raise his jaw. These steps should open a pasage for air, by freeing the tongue from the throat.

4. Pinch his nostrils shut. Open your mouth as wide as possible, place it tightly over his mouth, and blow into him. Remove mouth; listen for rush of exhaled air.

5. Or, especially if his teeth are clenched, you may place your mouth over his nose and breathe into it. For a small child, place your mouth over his mouth *and* his nostrils.

6. If foreign matter blocks patient's throat, roll him onto side and slap him between the shoulders. Quickly resume blowing—12 times a minute for an adult, 20 for a child.

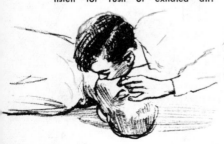

ARTIGAS, är-tē′gäs, **José Gervasio** (1764–1850), Uruguayan patriot. He is honored as the father of Uruguay's nationhood, although he himself did not finally lead the country to independence.

Born at Sauce, Uruguay, on June 19, 1764, Artigas was an officer in the colonial militia when Uruguay and Argentina were both part of the Spanish viceroyalty of the Río de la Plata. In 1811, after the struggle for independence from Spain began in Buenos Aires, Artigas raised an army of Uruguayans to support the revolution. Artigas' aim was to obtain autonomy for Uruguay within a confederation of Argentine states. By the end of 1812 he controlled most of Uruguay outside of Montevideo. However, the Portuguese invaded from Brazil, and Artigas led his followers on an historic exodus into Argentina.

In June 1814 the Argentines wrested Montevideo from the Spanish, but by that time Artigas had broken with the Buenos Aires government because it refused to recognize Uruguayan autonomy. He formed a federal league with several Argentine provinces in opposition to the central government, and in 1815 freed Uruguay from Argentine control. The next year the Portuguese again invaded Uruguay. After four years of fighting, they drove Artigas and his forces into Argentina. Artigas' former allies, the party favoring federal government, were now in power in Buenos Aires, but they refused to support him against the Portuguese. In the struggle that resulted, the Argentines defeated Artigas' army, and he went into exile in Paraguay in 1820. He took no further part in the Uruguayan independence movement and died in obscurity, at Asunción, Paraguay, on Sept. 23, 1850. See also URUGUAY—*History*.

ARTILLERY, är-til′ə-rē, is the collective term for cannon and guided-missile launchers of all sizes and calibers and the troops assigned to operate and care for these weapons. An artillery piece is a mounted gun or rocket launcher too large or too heavy to be classed as a small arm. The lower limit of size or caliber differs among the armed services, but the term generally is applied to any gun or launcher that uses ammunition of a caliber greater than one inch (25.4 mm) and that is not designed for hand or shoulder use.

In ancient times man increased the range of his weapons by using various types of catapults. These were great slings used to hurl stones and other large heavy objects over great distances. The history of artillery as we know it today dates roughly from the first use of gunpowder in Europe, about 1250 A.D., which brought into use the first smoothbore cannon.

Beginnings. The first firearms were large, heavy, and inefficient, and were difficult to move.

The development of cannon preceded that of small arms by about 50 years. The tube of a cannon was made like the barrel of those days—straight-sided and of wooden staves bound together with hoops of iron; it has been known ever since as a *barrel.*

The earliest artillery was used chiefly against the walls and gates of besieged towns, forts, and castles. The Hundred Years' War (1337–1453), in which English kings tried to add France to their kingdom, made the battlefields of France the proving ground for the new science of artillery. The first great land battle of that war, at Crécy in 1346, is most remembered because it proved English archers superior to heavily armored knights on horseback, yet it was also at Crécy that King Edward III of England introduced cannon—short-barreled *bombards.* Cannon proved their value in the ensuing siege of Calais, which Edward conquered after 11 months. Almost a century later (1428) in the same war, Joan of Arc is said to have aimed the French cannon herself, in a defensive use of artillery by a weak army. In 1436, King Charles VII of France organized the first permanent artillery department, for purposes of siege and defense, and headed it with a "master of artillery." See GUNPOWDER.

At the other end of Europe the Turks under Mohammed II used much artillery, some of great size, in their siege of Constantinople (Istanbul) in 1453. Their conquest brought about the final downfall of the Eastern Roman empire and the establishment of Constantinople as the new capital of the (Turkish) Ottoman empire.

The 16th Century. In the 1500's, brass guns and cast-iron projectiles came into general use throughout Europe. In Italy the mathematician Niccolò Tartaglia (1500?–1557) made great improvements in gunnery. In the late 1500's, shells were fired from mortars, lofting above walls to damage cities within, and case shot was invented. Case shot, consisting of a canister filled with pellets or fragments of metal, was highly effective against men and horses, whereas cannonballs were more useful against fortifications.

Artillery in the 1500's is important in both siege and field warfare. Hand firearms gradually became so effective that they supplanted the light artillery, which had been so successful in breaking up masses of foot soldiers armed with pikes. Heavy cannon with greater destructive power came into use. These were intended for frontline use ahead of the troops, but they were so cumbersome and so slow that they could not keep up with an advancing or retreating army and thus changed ownership repeatedly during a campaign. Increased weight brought increased effectiveness against targets, however,

ROMAN BALLISTA was powered by twisted cords pulling arms outward. Sixty-pound rock shot forth 500 yards.

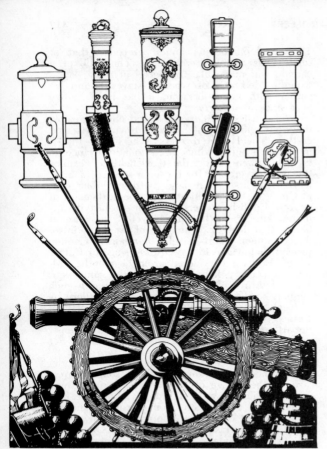

EARLY ARTILLERY includes 6-pounder bronze field gun (*bottom*) of Washington's army in the American Revolution (1775–83). In top row (*left to right*) are U.S. mortar (1861–65), Swedish siege gun (1620), French siege gun (1715–74), German breech-loading portable gun, and a mortar called the bombard of Rhodes (both 1400's). At center are early gunners' implements: cat to find holes in gun bore; wormer to remove cartridge-bag remnants; sponge to clean bore; ladle to insert powder; spontoon symbolizing artillery officer's rank; scraper to clean out bore. Linstock (*at lower left*) fired the cannon.

and in battles of fixed positions, such as the siege of a fortress, both attackers and defenders depended upon artillery.

The 17th Century. The period from 1600 to 1650 opened the modern era in the history of artillery. The Dutch leaders Maurice and Henry Frederick von Nassau advanced the use of artillery through discipline and training of artillerymen, but it was King Gustavus II of Sweden (Gustavus Adolphus, reigned 1611–1632) who first used artillery on the battlefield with true efficiency. Not only did he lighten equipment and begin to standardize matériel, but he also for the first time attached a pair of artillery pieces to each infantry regiment and brought artillery to a new height of mobility in the Thirty Years' War (1618–1648). Gustavus understood clearly the value of mobility, and moved his light field guns quickly and often, to obtain maximum efficiency. When he defeated the imperial Austrian army under Albrecht von Wallenstein at the Battle of Lützen (1632), Gustavus had 60 artillery pieces, including 4-pounder iron fieldpieces. The 4-pounder was a light cannon with attached

wheels, named for its 4-pound (1.5-kg) charge of case shot or grapeshot. The latter is a cluster of metal balls fired against troops. Gustavus greatly advanced the science of artillery, increasing its firepower and its rapidity of action.

Across the English Channel the arms laboratory at Woolwich Royal Arsenal, London, was established in 1672, and a reorganization of artillery took place in 1682 under Lord Dartmouth. But English artillery progress always lagged a bit behind its Continental contemporaries. The development of artillery was neglected in England mainly because of the great efficiency of English archers.

In France in 1671, King Louis XIV formed a regiment specifically for artillery duty, and in 1690 he founded the first artillery schools. During his reign (1661–1715), innovations in artillery included the elevating screw, by which a cannon's angle of fire could be precisely set; the prolonge, a rope and toggle for towing a gun carriage behind a wagon; and the priming tube filled with powder for improved control of firing.

The 18th Century. Prussian artillery, though backward before 1740, contributed several important improvements to the science under Frederick the Great (reigned 1740–1786). The inferiority of Prussian artillery in the face of the well-handled Austrian guns in the First Silesian War (1740–1742) impressed Frederick with the importance of giving more attention to this branch. He therefore increased the ratio of guns to infantry and cavalry and in 1759 established horse artillery in which the individual cannoneers were mounted.

After the Seven Years' War (1756–1763) the Austrians recognized the importance of artillery in warfare, and Prince Johann von Liechtenstein (1760–1836) was commissioned to reorganize the Austrian artillery. Jean Baptiste Vaquette de Gribeauval (1715–1789), a Frenchman who served as a field marshal in the Austrian army, was struck with the improvements effected in Austria and on his return to France strove to build a complete artillery system, with provision of separate personnel and matériel, for field, siege, garrison, and coast artillery. At first his reforms met with opposition, but in 1776 he became inspector general of artillery and was able to carry through his improvements. These consisted of lightening matériel and providing interchangeable parts. French horse artillery dates from 1791, and the last step in the complete reorganization of field artillery came in 1800, when the establishment of a drivers' corps ended the old system of hiring civilian teamsters to manage the horses used to haul artillery pieces. Napoleon used the Gribeauval artillery combination with great tactical success. In his wars, for the first time, massed guns produced a heavy concentration of fire with devastating effect. The Battle of Friedland (1807), in which Napoleon defeated the Russians, was perhaps the most brilliant use of artillery up to that time. The French killed some 25,000 Russians, against losses of about 7,500.

British artillery meanwhile had deteriorated greatly during the 1700's and was far below the standards reached by other countries. Late in the century, Britain introduced improvements, forming horse artillery in 1793 and a drivers' corps the following year.

The 19th Century. Most of the great powers continued to strive for superiority in artillery during the 1800's. Prussian artillery as of 1800

TYPES OF UNITED STATES GUNS

| Caliber | Mount or transport | Projectile | | | Classification |
		Kind	Weight (pounds)	Range (yards)	
40 mm	Towed or self-propelled	HE & AP	1.96	9,475	Antitank, antiaircraft
57 mm	Recoilless—hand or truck	HE & AP	2.75	4,930	Antitank, infantry
75 mm	Towed	HE	15.0	14,415	Antiaircraft
75 mm	Recoilless—tripod or truck	HE & AP	14.40	7,300	Antitank, infantry
76 mm	Self-propelled	HE & AP	15.44	17,000	Antitank
90 mm	Recoilless—tripod	HE & HEAT	7.95	820	Antitank
90 mm	Towed, self-propelled, tank	HE, AP, & Chem	23.4	21,400	Antiaircraft, antitank
105 mm	Self-propelled, tank	HEAT, AP, & HEP	42.0	3,250	Antitank
106 mm	Recoilless—tripod	HEP & HEAT	17.55	7,515	Antitank
120 mm	Recoilless—tripod	Nuclear	75.0	2,188	Infantry
155 mm	Recoilless—tripod	Nuclear	75.0	4,376	Infantry
155 mm	Towed or self-propelled	HE & Chem	95.59	25,715	Heavy field
175 mm	Self-propelled	HE & Chem	147.0	35,860	Heavy field
280 mm	Towed	Nuclear & HE	605.0	31,400	Heavy field

HE = high explosive.   AP = armor-piercing.   HEP = high explosive plastic.
HEAT = high explosive antitank.   Chem = gas, smoke, illuminating shell, and white phosphorus.

was powerful rather than mobile, but after several disastrous defeats by Napoleon in 1806–1807 its mobility was improved. In the Franco-Prussian War of 1870, Prussian artillery outgunned the formerly unsurpassed French artillery, after which the French developed remarkably superior guns.

Artillery was greatly improved between 1845 and 1885, and many features were adopted that are part of modern artillery. In artillery pieces themselves, faster and more efficient breech loading was substituted for muzzle loading; barrels were rifled (spirally grooved) to impart a steadying spin to projectiles; and the first crude recoil mechanisms appeared. Black powder was superseded by the much more efficient smokeless powder, and a new projectile gained broad use, the fragmentation type, containing explosives to blow it into many lethal pieces at the target.

Guns, howitzers, and mortars also began to have the distinct characteristics that they have now. In the artilleryman's vocabulary a *gun* fires its projectile with high muzzle velocity and a comparatively flat trajectory; a *howitzer* has a shorter barrel than a gun and fires with medium muzzle velocity and relatively high trajectory; a *mortar* has a wide-mouthed short barrel, usually with a smooth bore, from which it shoots with low muzzle velocity and at very high angles. The projectile can be fired over nearby hills or fortifications and fall vertically on the target. Guns and howitzers are breech loaded, but the mortar is muzzle loaded.

The Civil War in the United States brought the first extensive use of artillery in North America, although American technical skill already had made important contributions to the design and manufacture of artillery and the science of gunnery. Chief among the contributors were Thomas Jackson Rodman (1815–1871), John A.B. Dahlgren (1809–1870), and Robert Parker Parrott (1804–1877). The Civil War demonstrated the practicality of firing effectively at ranges longer than were possible before, in some instances as long as 2,500 yards (762 km). Moreover, the skillful and daring tactical use of artillery during the years 1861–1865 hinted at tactics that were used in the Franco-Prussian War of 1870.

In 1872, German artillery was reorganized, the field artillery of each army corps being augmented. There were also far-reaching technical improvements in matériel and transport that resulted in the powerful German artillery of World War I and brought to the battlefield such guns as the mammoth 42-centimeter (16.54-inch) howitzers that battered the Belgian forts of Liège

RIFLED FIELD PIECE of the Civil War with squad of Union Army soldiers. After cannon was fired, sponge at left was dipped in leather bucket of water and barrel was swabbed out. Man at right holds lanyard for firing.

8-INCH HOWITZER, the U.S. Army's M110, is self-propelled full-tracked heavy artillery. It fires a 200-pound projectile up to 18,500 yards.

and Namur until they surrendered. Austrian artillery was considered technically excellent before World War I, and Austria's artillerymen were well trained. The English and Prussian artillery reflected the general improvement but lacked the great number of artillery pieces required for modern war.

World War I. The four years of World War I brought changes in artillery tactics and matériel that were almost revolutionary, and it is safe to say that the artillery of all armies has been influenced to a remarkable degree by World War I trends.

The chief lesson of World War I was the extraordinarily large number of guns required for military operations. Then, too, there were increased ranges, new types of shell (gas and chemical, for example), and the improved methods of transport brought by the gasoline engine. Old tactics disappeared—for example, artillery was no longer positioned in front of infantry troops for direct fire. New tactics came into play: *barrage fire,* a curtain of artillery shell; *destructive fire,* to destroy concrete and barbed-wire-rimmed trench systems; and *neutralization fire,* to prevent enemy action.

New types of artillery never before used also came into being. Among these were the antiaircraft gun, the extremely high-angle-fire mortars, and the weapons to discharge gas and chemical projectiles exclusively.

World War II. Further changes in artillery tactics, technique, and matériel were introduced in World War II. The main new development was the effective use of rockets and jets in guided missiles. Probably the greatest change in technique was the rapid massing of field artillery fire through the use of fire-direction centers and improved communication facilities. Outstanding tactically was the use of field artillery in new close cooperation and coordination with the infantry, tanks, and other supported branches. Radar for surveillance, warning, and fire control was a major development in antiaircraft artillery and seacoast artillery. In general, developments in artillery matériel encompassed increased muzzle velocity of guns, greater ranges, increased penetrating power of projectiles, increased sensitivity and accuracy of fuzes, greater mobility, self-propelled weapons, recoilless infantry cannon, and the use of rockets and guided missiles, notably the German V-2 missile.

Post-World War II. World War II, with the proved effectiveness of bombing aircraft and naval mines, saw the obsolescence of seacoast, railway, and other types of heavy fixed and immobile artillery. Postwar artillery development concentrated on ammunition improvement, lighter weight, higher velocities, greater ranges, air-transportability, and recoilless and atomic artillery. Self-propelled artillery, lightweight towed artillery, free rockets, guided missiles, recoilless rifles, mortars, and tactical atomic weapons constitute the armament of modern artillery.

Types of Artillery. Modern artillery is the outgrowth of the artillery experience of World War

175-mm FIELD ARTILLERY GUN, very mobile, is used to support infantry and armored columns in battle.

60-mm MORTAR (*left*) fires a 3.7-pound shell up to 1,990 yards. 75-mm RECOILLESS RIFLE (*above*) is shown in action in Korea.

II and postwar development. This applies to matériel, tactics, personnel, methods of transport, gunnery, and fire control. Artillery may be classified according to its *mission, type,* or *size.*

Classified by mission, it consists of antiaircraft, antitank, and field artillery. *Antiaircraft artillery* includes cannon, small-caliber automatic weapons, rockets, and surface-to-air guided missiles, together with the equipment used or required in connection with antiaircraft operations. *Antitank artillery* consists of rockets, missiles, or artillery suitable for use against tanks or other armored vehicles. *Field artillery* includes rockets or guns, howitzers, and mortars that are mounted on carriages and mobile enough to accompany infantry or armored units in the field.

Classified by type, field artillery consists of *guns, howitzers, mortars, large recoilless rifles,* and *rockets.* The howitzer can be loaded with powder charges of various weights (called *zones*) for firing on a zone at a specified range and with the muzzle velocity and trajectory desired. Like the mortar, the howitzer can fire over hills or obstructions upon targets that are not available to the gun because of its practically flat trajectory. The recoilless rifle is a weapon consisting of a light artillery tube designed to let part of the propellant gases escape to the rear to eliminate recoil. According to its size, it may be shoulder fired or mounted on a tripod or lightweight vehicle. For discussion of artillery rockets see ROCKETS; GUIDED MISSILES.

According to size, or *caliber,* artillery is classified as light, medium, and heavy. *Light artillery*

includes all guns, howitzers, rockets, and recoilless rifles of 105-mm caliber (4.13 inches) or smaller. *Medium artillery* covers calibers greater than 105-mm and including 155-mm (6.1 inches). *Heavy artillery* consists of all artillery weapons greater than 155-mm caliber.

Organization. For tactical and administrative purposes, the basic artillery unit in the United States Army is the *battery,* operating two or more artillery weapons. Above the battery is the *battalion,* consisting of two or more gun batteries, a headquarters battery, and in some cases a service battery. The battalion normally is kept together as a unit. Battalions assigned to a division are called *division artillery* and operate under a division artillery headquarters, while other artillery is organized into *groups* of two or more battalions. In antiaircraft artillery two or more groups form a *brigade.*

Artillery Fire. The fires delivered by artillery are classified tactically in a number of ways:

(1) Fires are classified as to the effect sought. In order of decreasing severity, these are *destructive fire,* designed to render a target useless—such as fortifications or naval vessels; *neutralizing fire,* designed to render the enemy incapable of observing, moving, or using his weapons effectively; and *demoralizing fire,* designed to reduce the enemy's will to resist to such an extent that he does not recover immediately after fire is lifted and cannot, therefore, offer any effective resistance for a time.

(2) Fires are classified as to form. These are *concentration,* that is, fire delivered on a set area; *barrage,* a curtain of fire delivered on a line or a succession of lines; *standing barrage,*

TYPES OF UNITED STATES MORTARS

Caliber	Mount or transport	Projectile				Classification
		Kind	Weight (pounds)	Range (yards)	
60 mm	Hand	HE	3.7	1,990	Infantry
81 mm	Hand or truck	HE & Chem	9	3,200	Infantry
107 mm	Truck or self-propelled	HE & Chem	25	5,931	Infantry

HE = high explosive.   Chem = gas, smoke, illuminating shells and white phosphorus.

U.S. HOWITZERS

| Caliber | Mount or Transport | Projectile | | | Classification |
		Kind	Weight (pounds)	Range (yards)	
75 mm	Pack or self-propelled	HE	14.6	9,620	Light
105 mm	Towed or self-propelled	HE & Chem	33	12,330	Light
155 mm	Towed or self-propelled	HE & Chem	95	16,330	Medium
240 mm	Towed	HE & Chem	360	23,180	Very Heavy
8-inch	Towed or self-propelled	HE	200	18,510	Heavy

HE = high explosive; Chem = smoke, illuminating shell, and white phophorus.

a fire (normal or emergency) placed on a line 200 to 400 yards (183 to 366 meters) in front of the supported troops to bar the advance of the enemy; *box barrage,* a fire designed to isolate a portion of the enemy during a raid; and *rolling barrage,* a fire that advances in short bounds on successive lines ahead of attacking troops. The last-named is a supporting fire in an attack intended to sweep thoroughly a zone ahead of the attacking troops.

(3) Fires are classified as to prearrangement. *Scheduled fires* are planned fires, executed according to a time schedule or delivered on signal or call from the supported troops. *Fire on targets of opportunity* is delivered against unforeseen targets or on those that appear suddenly and are exposed for only a short period of time.

(4) Fires are classified as to preparation and conduct of fire. *Observed fire* is that in which an observer (who may be some distance from the firing battery, located either on the ground or in an airplane) gives the information on which adjustments are made. In *unobserved fire* the basic data are obtained from a chart.

(5) Fires are classified as to tactical purpose. *Supporting fire* is delivered when the troops supported are engaged. *Artillery preparation* is delivered immediately before an attack for the purpose of facilitating the subsequent advance of the infantry. *Counterpreparation fire* is utilized in a defensive action just prior to an enemy attack, to break up hostile troop formations, disorganize the enemy's command and communications systems, interfere with his artillery preparation, and impair his morale. *Counterbattery* is the fire delivered on the enemy artillery in position and is designed for either destruction or neutralization. *Interdiction fire* is that placed on points (such as crossroads or bridges) or areas that it is desired to prevent the enemy from using. *Harassing fire* is designed to interfere with the enemy's rest, curtail his movements, and lower his morale.

Both 105-mm and 155-mm calibers are suitable for the above types of fire except that the 105-mm is not a good weapon for counterbattery, although it may be so used. The 155-mm howitzer is an excellent counterbattery weapon.

The shells fired by artillery may be either armor-piercing, high-explosive, gas, or nuclear. *Armor-piercing projectiles* are designed for use against naval vessels and all types of armored vehicles and reinforced structures. The *gas shell* upon explosion releases toxic gases. Among the gases used in these projectiles are mustard, phosgene, blood, nerve, and tear gas. *Smoke shell* emits thick clouds of smoke and is designed to blind enemy observation. *Nuclear warheads and projectiles* have been developed for the larger-caliber artillery rockets and cannon.

JOHN D. BILLINGSLEY, *Colonel, U.S.A.*
United States Military Academy

Bibliography
Babcock, Leslie E., *Elements of Field Artillery* (Princeton, N.J., 1925).
Barnes, Gladeon M., *Weapons of World War II* (New York 1947).
Carman, William Y., *History of Firearms from Earliest Times to 1914* (New York 1956).
Comparato, Frank E., *Age of Great Guns* (Harrisburg, Pa., 1965).
Greener, W.W., *The Gun and Its Development* (London 1910).
Hayes, Thomas J., *Elements of Ordnance* (New York 1938).
Stevens, Philip H., *Artillery Through the Ages* (New York 1965).
Tunis, Edwin, *Weapons* (New York 1954).
U.S. Army, Office Chief of Ordnance, *Weapon Systems and Components,* ORDP 20–108, part 3 (Washington 1960).

ARTIODACTYLA, ärt-ē-ō-dak′tə-lə, is a suborder of hoofed mammals having an even, rather than odd, number of toes on each foot. Also, the central pair of toes on each foot is arranged symmetrically on each side of a vertical line running through the axes of the limbs. Included in this group are pigs, camels, llamas, alpacas, reindeer, cattle, yaks, buffalo, sheep, goats, hippopotamuses, giraffes, and pronghorns.

ARTOIS, àr-twä′, a former province of France, occupied approximately the same area as the modern department of Pas-de-Calais. Its most powerful neighbors were Flanders on the northeast and Picardy on the south and west.

Originally ruled by the dukes of Flanders, it was included in Isabella of Hainaut's dowry when she married King Philip Augustus of France in 1180. The acquisition of the rich weaving and banking province greatly increased Philip's income and extended his power toward the English Channel. Philip's son, Louis VIII, added Artois to the royal domain in 1223. Given by Louis IX to his brother Robert in 1237, it passed out of the control of the crown in the 14th century when Robert's granddaughter married a duke of Burgundy.

After the marriage of Mary of Burgundy to the Habsburg emperor Maximilian I in 1477, Artois remained under Habsburg rule until the 17th century. The French overran the area in 1640. By the Treaty of the Pyrenees in 1659, Artois was rejoined to the crown lands.

ARTS, ärts, in education, a name for certain branches of study. In the medieval universities they were called the "seven liberal arts" to differentiate them from mechanical arts. They comprised the *trivium* (grammar; dialectic, or logic; and rhetoric) and the *quadrivium* (arithmetic, music, geometry, and astronomy). Mastery of the trivium led to the bachelor of arts degree; mastery of the quadrivium led to the master of arts. These degrees are still widely used in 20th century universities, particularly for nontechnical students, and the faculty of arts is still a separate academic division.

ARTS AND CRAFTS MOVEMENT, a movement to reform the useful and decorative arts. It began in England in the second half of the 19th century and spread to continental Europe and the United States in the 1890's. Its adherents called for functional design, respect for the inherent properties of materials, and the abandonment of eclectic design and inappropriate ornamentation. The movement helped to break the hold of neo-Gothic and neoclassic eclecticism and laid the basis of modern design in industry and in the arts. Precursors of the movement included John Ruskin, who protested the sterility of machine-made products; Philip Webb, who led the revival of English domestic architecture; and William Morris, founder of the Kelmscott Press and designer of interior furnishings. The movement drew many of its allies from the craftsmen working in *art nouveau*, and further inspiration from Japanese design, which was seen in the international exhibitions of the time.

The movement reached its height in England in the 1880's with the founding of such organizations as the Century Guild for Craftsmen (1882), the Art Workers Guild (1884), and the Arts and Crafts Exhibition Society, which held its first show in 1888. The ideas of the movement were spread in *Hobby Horse* and *Studio* magazines.

The arts and crafts movement led to the founding of a number of craft schools, most notably London's Central School of Arts and Crafts, founded in 1896. Craft and design courses also were introduced at many art schools and colleges in the United States. In Germany the Weimar Academy of Art, reorganized in the craft school tradition in 1900, carried forward the ideals of the arts and crafts movement when it became the Bauhaus in 1919.

See also FURNITURE, MODERN; INDUSTRIAL DESIGN; POTTERY; PRINTING; WEAVING.

ARTUSI, är-tōō'sē, **Giovanni Maria** (c. 1540–1613), Italian composer and musical theoretician. He was born at Bologna, where he became canon-in-ordinary at the church of San Salvatore in 1562. A staunch musical conservative, he attacked the innovations of Monteverdi and other composers in his *L'Artusi ovvero delle imperfettioni della moderna musica* (1600). His compositions include a set of 4-part songs, *Canzonette* (1598); and an 8-part motet, *Cantate Domino* (1599). He died at Bologna on Aug. 18, 1613.

ARU ISLANDS, är'ōō, in Indonesia, a group of islands in the shallow Arafura Sea between New Guinea and Australia. *Aroe, Arru,* and *Arroe* are alternate spellings. There are five main islands, known collectively as Tanahbesar Island, and about 90 smaller islets. The total land area is 3,306 square miles (8,563 sq km). Dobo, on the island of Wamar, is the chief town. The people are of Papuan· and Malayan stock.

The islands produce sago, coconut, sugarcane, maize, tobacco, and palm products. Diving for pearls and fishing for sharks and trepang are important industries. Exports include pearls, mother-of-pearl, and tortoise shells. Another occupation is hunting birds of paradise for their plumes, notably the great bird of paradise (*Paradisaea apoda apoda*).

Other brilliantly hued birds in the islands' forests include the flightless, violet-necked cassowary (*Casuarius violicolis*), fruit pigeons, cockatoos, parrots, parakeets, kiwis, and kingfishers.

The archipelago lacks large mammals, but abounds in smaller pouched animals—kangaroos, wallabies, bandicoots, and phalangers. Butterflies also are abundant. There are forests of areca palms and pandanus plants (screw pines).

The islands were discovered by the Dutch in 1606 and were colonized after 1623. They were occupied and used as an air base by the Japanese from 1942 to 1946. Formerly a part of the Netherlands East Indies, they became Indonesian territory in 1947. Administratively, the Arus are in the Amboina division of Malaku province. Population: (1960) 20,000.

ARUBA, ä-rōō'bä, an island of the Netherlands Antilles (q.v.) in the Caribbean Sea, 18 miles (28 km) north of the Coast of Venezuela. Aruba is 19 miles (31 km) long and up to 5 miles (8 km) wide. The area is 69 square miles (179 sq km). The western part is mostly flat. The highest point is Arikok, 617 feet (188 meters). There are cliffs on the north coast and a coral reef along part of the south coast. The rock of Aruba is chiefly diorite, limestone, and phosphorite.

Aruba's dry climate restricts agriculture to some corn and beans grown in isolated spots, and a succulent desert plant, aloe, introduced in 1840, whose juice is used in medicines.

Gold was discovered in 1824, and calcium phosphate in 1879. Export of the latter supported all six islands of the Netherlands Antilles from 1882 to 1895. Mining of both minerals ceased in 1914. Since 1928 one of the world's largest oil refineries has been operated at Sint Nicolaas. The crude petroleum comes from Venezuela. Daily production averages almost 23 million gallons. About 58% of the exported oil products go to the east coast of the United States.

There were 8,300 refinery employees in 1949, but automation, started in 1950, caused an 80% reduction in 17 years. Fighting unemployment, the island government built a distillation plant to purify seawater—over 3.8 million gallons daily. The increased water supply fostered the building of chemical plants and of resort hotels along the 4-mile (7-km) white sand Palm Beach.

Oranjestad is the capital. Aruba has home rule and elects 8 of the 22 members of the Netherlands Antilles Staten (parliament), which meets in neighboring Curaçao. A lieutenant governor and 3 to 5 deputies form Aruba's executive, responsible to its 21-member Island Council. Population: (1968) 59,013.

JOHN HARTOG
Author of "Aruba Past and Present"

ARUM, ar'əm, is a small group of tuberous tropical and subtropical herbs found in Europe and Asia. Commonly called *callas*, they have simple leaves and diversely colored, twisted bracts (modified leaves) surrounding the flower clusters. Staminate (male) flowers are borne just above the pistillate (female) flowers on thick fleshy spikes. Arum is cultivated as an ornamental plant either under glass or, in the case of some hardy species, in the open air.

The genus *Arum* belongs to the family Araceae. *A. maculatum*—lords-and-ladies, cuckoo-pint, wake-robin—from Europe has many varieties and is perhaps the best-known hardy species grown in America. The leaves and corms (bulb-like parts of the stem) are acrid. Ripened corms contain starch, which may be extracted and used as a food.

ARUNDEL, ar'ən-dəl, **Thomas** (1353–1414), archbishop of Canterbury and chancellor of England, who took part in the overthrow of King Richard II. He was the son of Richard Fitzalan, earl of Arundel, whose prominence helped Thomas become bishop of Ely at the age of 25. The gifted son became involved in public affairs in 1386, when his brother Richard, who was then earl, and other feudal lords imposed a council of regency on King Richard, then 19 years old. The insurgents removed a number of Richard's friends from power and installed themselves in their place. Thomas Arundel was chancellor (1386–1389, 1391–1396), archbishop of York (1388–1396), and archbishop of Canterbury (1396–1397).

In 1397, Richard retaliated against the faction. He banished Thomas Arundel and beheaded Arundel's brother in a show of ruthlessness that foreshadowed his own downfall. Arundel joined Henry of Lancaster in European exile. He returned to England with Henry in 1399, attended Richard's abdication that October, and crowned Lancaster as Henry IV. Repossessing the see of Canterbury, Arundel devoted most of the next 14 years to church administration and the suppression of Lollards and other alleged heretics. He died at Canterbury on Feb. 9, 1414.

ARUNDELL, ar'ən-del, **Lady Blanche** (1583–1649), English royalist during the Civil War of 1642–1646. The daughter of the earl of Worcester, she was married to Thomas, Lord Arundell of Wardour, Wiltshire. In 1643, while her husband was fighting at Oxford, she defended Wardour Castle against the parliamentary soldiers, although she had only 25 men to their 1,300. The defenders held out for 9 days, continually besieged and unable to sleep. After two mines were set off under the castle, Lady Blanche was obliged to surrender. The defenders were spared, but the castle and grounds were ruined. When Lady Blanche left she was penniless. She died at Winchester, England, on Oct. 28, 1649.

HENRY ARUNDELL (1606?–1694), her son, regained the castle in 1644, but did not retain it or take up residence there.

ARUWIMI RIVER, är-ə-wē'mē, a tributary of the Congo River, in central Africa. Its entire course is in the Democratic Republic of Congo. The river rises near Lake Albert, where it is known as the *Ituri,* and flows for about 300 miles (483 km) south and west to Avakubi, where it becomes the Aruwimi. It continues westward for 320 miles (515 km), with many rapids, and enters the Congo River at Basoko. It is navigable for the last 75 miles (121 km). Sir Henry Morton Stanley explored the river in 1887–1889.

ARVADA, är-vad'ə, a city in Colorado, is a residential suburb of Denver, in the north central part of the state. Arvada is situated 9 miles (14.5 km) northwest of downtown Denver, directly east of the Front Range of the Rocky Mountains. It lies partly in Jefferson County and partly in Adams County.

Placer mining brought the first settlers to the area beginning about 1860, but truck farming proved more profitable than mining. When Arvada was incorporated as a town in 1904, it was an agricultural center with a population under 1,000. It became a city in 1951, with a population of 2,359. By 1960 the population had grown to nearly 10 times that much, and this figure was nearly doubled by 1965. In 1955 a home-rule charter was adopted, creating a council-manager form of government. Population: 46,814.

KENNETH E. DOWLIN
Arvada City Library

ARVAL BROTHERS, är'vəl, an order of 12 priests in ancient Rome. They are known also by their Latin name, *Fratres Arvales.* Their most important duty was to offer sacrifice for the fertility of the fields to Dea Dia, the Roman goddess of the harvest. This rite was performed each May in a three-day festival at the sacred grove of Dea Dia southwest of Rome. According to tradition, the cult began in the reign of Romulus, the legendary first king of Rome (said to have reigned 753–716 B.C.), but by republican times it was barely mentioned. It was revived during the reign of Augustus (27 B.C.–14 A.D.), and the cult still existed in 304 A.D.

The 12 priests of the brotherhood were chosen for life from the highest ranks in Rome and, under the empire, included even the emperor. Besides the celebration of the ancient cult rites, the priests maintained a series of *acta,* or minutes, of their annual proceedings. More than 150 of these records have been discovered, ranging from 21 B.C. to 241 A.D. The *acta* for 218 A.D. preserve the *Carmen Arvale,* the famous litany of the brotherhood, written in Saturnian meter during the 5th century B.C. It is one of the few extant fragments of early Latin literature.

Other duties of the Arval Brothers included prayers for special occasions in the imperial family or any imperial enterprise, all of which are dated in the *acta.* The *acta* thus provide an invaluable source for the chronology of the empire.

P. R. COLEMAN-NORTON
Formerly, Princeton University

ARVE RIVER, ärv, a tributary of the Rhône River, in Europe. It is 60 miles long (96 km). It rises in southeastern France, on the Mont Blanc massif, and flows southwest through the Chamonix Valley, then northwest, crossing the Swiss border and entering the Rhône in the suburbs of Geneva.

The Arve passes through picturesque gorges and forms cascades that supply hydroelectric power. On its bank north of Chamonix is a winter sports station that has a nine-acre skating rink—one of the largest in the world. The Arve also flows through the summer resort of Servoz (in France), below which are the ruins of the castle of Faucigny.

ARVERNI, är-ver'nē, an ancient people of France that contended with the Aedui for supremacy in southern Gaul. They gave their name to the Auvergne district of central France. Their power extended from the Atlantic to the Rhône, and from the Loire to the Pyrenees. In 121 B.C., the Romans restricted their rule to the region around Gergovia (near modern Clermont-Ferrand, which, as Augustonemetum, later became their capital). In 52 B.C. an Arvernian chieftain, Vercingetorix, unsuccessfully led the last Gallic revolt against Julius Caesar's Roman domination.

When Augustus reconstituted Gaul in 27 B.C., he deprived the Arverni of their suzerainty, but recognized them as a free community and probably relieved them from taxation. The Romanized Arverni vanished from history in 475 A.D., when the Romans ceded their territory to the Visigoths.

ARVIDA, är-vī′də, is a city in south central Quebec, Canada, situated on the Saguenay River, 110 miles (177 km) north of the city of Quebec. It is the site of large aluminum reduction plants for the refining of bauxite. Power is provided by hydroelectric developments on the river.

The city was founded in 1926 by the Aluminium Company of Canada (Alcan), which also manufactures abrasives and aluminum products there. The name Arvida was coined from that of the company president, Arthur Vining Davis. Arvida expanded during World War II. The company built both houses and urban facilities, creating a model community that is administered jointly by the company and the residents. Population: 18,448.

ARWIDSSON, är′vits-sôn, **Adolf Ivar** (1791–1858), Swedish poet. He was born at Padasjoki, Finland, on Aug. 7, 1791. In 1817 he was appointed docent of history at the University of Åbo, but was dismissed in 1822 after taking a strongly critical stand against the university authorities. Soon after, he was banished by the government and compelled to seek refuge in Sweden because of a controversial political essay that he had published. He found a position in the Royal Library in Stockholm, and in 1843 he became its director. He died at Viborg, Finland (now in the USSR), on June 21, 1858.

Arwidsson's chief work, *Svenska fornsånger* (1834–42), is a collection of Swedish folklore and songs. His original poems appear under the title *Ungdoms rimfrost af Sonen i Örnskog* (1832).

ARYA SAMAJ, är′yə sə-mäj′ is a Hindu reform movement, particularly strong in northern and western India. Its founder, Dayanand Saraswati (1824–1883), established the movement's first society in Bombay in 1875.

Rejecting post-Vedic Hinduism, the Arya Samaj (meaning "society of the Aryans") takes its theology from the Vedas, which are considered to contain ultimate revelations, including the basis for scientific discoveries. The movement criticizes Islam, Christianity, and Puranic Hinduism, and opposes temples, idol worship, polytheism, caste systems, and child marriage. It favors *yajnas* (fire rituals), equal rights for all, foreign travel, and proselytism. It accepts the doctrines of *karma* and rebirth, though they are not Vedic; it also accepts the fourfold division of society. Though not a political organization, the Samaj encouraged militant nationalism prior to India's independence.

In 1892 the Samaj split between the modernists and the purists; the former modernized the curriculum of the Dayanand colleges, while the latter set up academies for Sanskritic and Ayurvedic studies, including the famous Gurukul at Hardwar.

BRIJEN K. GUPTA, *Brooklyn College, New York*

ARYABHATA, är′yə-but-ə, was an Indian astronomer and mathematician of the 5th century. He was born at Pataliputra in 476. His only known work, the *Aryabhatiya,* is a mathematical treatise in verse.

In this work, by solving quadratic equations and applying algebra to geometry and astronomy, he anticipated some of the discoveries of modern algebra. He also announced the correct theory of the diurnal rotation of the earth and the correct explanation of solar and lunar eclipses.

ARYAN, ar′ē-ən, a name applied by the philologist Max Müller in the 1800's to the language family now known as Indo-European. The term survives in the name *Indo-Aryan,* a branch of the Indo-European language family that includes the languages of Pakistan and northern India, such as classical Sanskrit and modern Hindi and Urdu. Although properly a linguistic term, Indo-Aryan often is employed also to designate the early Indo-European-speaking peoples who entered the Indian subcontinent from central Asia about 1500 B.C. See also INDO-EUROPEAN LANGUAGES.

In a book published in 1854, the French writer Count Joseph Arthur de Gobineau gave a racial meaning to Aryan. De Gobineau held the white race to be superior to all others and the Aryan race to be supreme among whites. He identified Teutons as the purest modern representatives of the Aryans. This theory aroused interest in Germany and was espoused by the composer Richard Wagner among others. In the 20th century it was taken up by the German dictator Adolf Hitler, who equated Aryan with Nordic race and used the theory to justify his prosecution of Jews. Modern anthropologists reject the theory that there are "pure" or inherently superior human groups. See also RACES, NATURE AND ORIGINS OF.

ELIZABETH E. BACON, *Hofstra University*

ARZ VON STRAUSSENBURG, ärts fôn shtrou′sən-bōŏrкн, **Baron Artur** (1857–1935), Austro-Hungarian soldier. He was born at Hermannstadt, Transylvania (now Sibiu, Rumania), on June 16, 1857. At the start of World War I, he commanded the Austro-Hungarian 6th Army Corps on the Russian front, and succeeded Count Franz Conrad von Hötzendorf as chief of staff on March 2, 1917. The offensive he planned on the Isonzo River in northeastern Italy led to the Italian defeat at Caporetto in 1917. He died at Budapest, Hungary, on July 1, 1935.

AS I LAY DYING is a novel by William Faulkner (q.v.), published in 1930. The novel is divided into 59 short chapters in which 15 characters reflect on the events around them. It is one of Faulkner's important early efforts to use the stream-of-consciousness technique.

As I Lay Dying tells of the Bundrens, a poor white family who live in Faulkner's mythical Yoknapatawpha County in Mississippi. The central action springs from the death of Addie Bundren, the mother, and deals with the funeral journey conducted by her family in accordance with her wishes. In the course of the trip, the cortege meets with flood, fire, and physical injuries, and one of the sons, Darl, has an emotional collapse.

Faulkner once said of this novel: "*As I Lay Dying* took me just about six weeks [to write] . . . . I just thought of all the natural catastrophes that could happen to a family and let them all happen . . ." The effect is a mixture of dark comedy and deep anguish, both elements stemming from the stupidity and selfishness of the main characters. Yet Faulkner treats the Bundren family with compassion. Anse, the father, although physically lazy and mentally narrow, has comic qualities that make him memorable. Critic Frederick J. Hoffman pointed out that while death is central to the story, the truth with which the novel deals ". . . is not dying but the circumstances of being born and living."

AS YOU LIKE IT is a romantic comedy by William Shakespeare, probably written late in 1599 or early in 1600. It was entered in the Stationer's Register on Aug. 4, 1600, to establish copyright, but it was first printed in the Folio of 1623. Despite some misprints and inconsistencies, which suggest minor alterations, the Folio text is a good one and may have been based on the prompt-book.

In *As You Like It*, Shakespeare dramatized a charming but artificial pastoral romance by Thomas Lodge, *Rosalynde, or Euphues' Golden Legacie* (1590). He omitted much from his source; altered names, titles, and events; and cut the duration of time. But his most important departures from the original were his introduction of new characters, his development of those already in the story, and his relocation of the scene to England. Finally, he added the element of humor to a tale that had been simply a pastoral romance.

Though the plot of *As You Like It* is improbable and somewhat mechanical, it functions efficiently in providing situations for character development and witty dialogue. In the play, Rosalind becomes the leading figure; the pastoralism of Silvius and Phebe is ridiculed; Corin, Audrey, and William are made authentic rustics; and Jaques and Touchstone are invented to comment on the action. As William Hazlitt wrote, "It is not what is done but what is said that claims our attention."

The center of the comedy is Rosalind, the most joyous and clear-sighted of Shakespeare's heroines. The manipulator of her own love and the loves of others, Rosalind loses her heart to Orlando at first sight. Making sport of love, she delights in teasing Orlando, and in remaining in disguise as a boy while being wooed by him. On the other hand, she unconsiously reveals the sincerity of her affection through her spate of questions about Orlando to Celia, her friend and confidante. As a dramatic character, Orlando, while manly, is colorless in comparison with Rosalind, and his chief function in the play is as the object of her love. Celia, too, has a romance—this one conventional—with Oliver. But lest the play become sentimental or extravagant, Shakespeare inserts the more earthy affair between the country wench Audrey and the country bumpkin William, and parodies high-flown Arcadianism in the romance between Silvius and Phebe.

Healthy balance is further achieved by the deflation of sentiment through the cynicism of the sardonic Jaques and the witty mockery of Touchstone. Jaques has been a libertine; now he is a melancholy contemplative and a professed satirist of love and life. Yet Shakespeare can make fun with him and of him too, as Rosalind does. Touchstone, the court jester, is privileged to expose folly and pretension by word and by action. He reminds the other characters as well as the audience that love and marriage have other and earthier sources than romantic sentiment. Love is presented from many points of view in the play, but never tragically. Whether romantic or realistic, love is a comedy, permeated with songs and laughter and greenwood gaiety.

Despite its faults of plot and occasional prolixity, *As You Like It*, in its humor, characterization, and commentary, is a genuine delight and one of Shakespeare's major achievements in high comedy.

There is a tradition that *As You Like It* was played before King James I at Wilton on Dec. 3, 1603. Another more dubious tradition states that Shakespeare once acted the part of Adam, who, with Dennis, is one of the two servants of Oliver. The first verifiable record performance is that of 1740 at the Drury Lane Theatre in London, with James Quin as Jaques, Hannah Pritchard as Rosalind, and Kitty Clive as Celia. Since then revivals have been frequent. The Rosalinds in England have included Peg Woffington, Dorothea Jordan, Helen Faucit, Adelaide Neilson, and Lily Langtry.

Since 1786, when the play was first acted in the United States, Laura Keene, Ada Rehan, Mary Anderson, Julia Marlowe, and Katharine Hepburn have been among the outstanding Rosalinds in American productions.

ROBERT HAMILTON BALL
Queens College, New York

Bibliography
Texts of *As You Like It* were edited by Horace H. Furness, New Variorum edition, with commentary (Philadelphia 1890); Sir Arthur Quiller-Couch and John Dover Wilson, with a stage history by Harold Child (Cambridge, England, 1929); and George L. Kittredge (Boston 1939).

Brown, John R., *Shakespeare and His Comedies* (London 1957).
Palmer, John, *Comic Characters of Shakespeare* (New York 1947).
Parrott, M., *Shakespearian Comedy* (New York 1949).
Stoll, Elmer E., *Shakespeare's Young Lovers* (New York 1937).

ASA, ā'sə, in the Old Testament, was king of Judah about 915–875 B.C., succeeding his father, Abijah. He abolished the worship of idols and other heathen practices and brought the nation to its peak of prosperity.

In the 11th year of his reign, he was attacked by Zerah, the king or military commander of Ethiopia, whom he defeated decisively. In the 36th year of Asa's reign, Baasha, king of Israel, occupied Ramah, a city in the adjacent territory of Benjamin, and fortified it as an invasion point against Judah. With the aid of Benhadad I, king of Syria, Asa recovered Ramah but brought upon himself the rebuke of the prophet Hanani for seeking aid from one other than the Lord.

Asa died after a reign of 41 years and was succeeded by his son Jehoshaphat. Consult II Chronicles 14–16; I Kings 15.

ASAFETIDA, as-ə-fet'ə-də, is a gum resin obtained from the root of a group of herbs distributed throughout eastern Asia. It has an overpowering odor, which resembles that of garlic. Asafetida is highly prized in the East as a seasoning. In medicine it has been used as a stimulant to the sympathetic nervous system, as an antispasmodic, and as a stimulant for expelling gas from the alimentary canal.

Asafetida has a complex chemical structure consisting of resin, gum, ethereal oil, vanillin, and ferulaic acid.

Asafetida is obtained from three species of the genus *Ferula*—*F. narthex*, *F. fetidissima*, and *F. asafetida*. The main sources are *F. asafetida* and *F. narthex*. These are coarse herbs of the Umbelliferae family. To obtain the juice, the leaves of the plant first are cut off close to the ground as the plant is growing. The plant stump is then covered with leaves, and in five or six weeks a slice of the stump is cut off. A milky juice oozes out from the cut surface. The juice, after thickening, is the commercial asafetida.

ASAM, ä′zäm, is the name of two Bavarian artists who designed and decorated some of the most important German baroque churches. *Cosmas Damian Asam,* born in Benediktbeuern on Sept. 27, 1686, specialized in fresco painting. *Egid Quirin Asam,* his brother, born in Tegernsee on Sept. 1, 1692, did stuccowork and sculpture. Both were also architects.

The brothers studied under their father, Hans Georg Asam (1649–1711), a teacher of architecture at Prague and a fresco painter. From 1712 to 1714 they traveled in Italy, where they were strongly influenced by Italian baroque art. Cosmas died in Munich on May 10, 1739, and Egid died in Mannheim on April 29, 1750.

Most of their major works were done in collaboration. The Italian influence is apparent in such early structures as the monastic churches at Weltenburg and at Rohr, designed and decorated by them between 1717 and 1721. They were essentially baroque artists, but their later work was influenced by the growing fashion of French rococo, incorporating more ornate designs, diffuse light effects, and paler colors. Examples of this work include the interiors of monastic churches at Osterhofen, Fürstenfeld, and Straubing. In Munich they designed and decorated their residence and the Church of St. John Nepomuk, both outstanding examples of German baroque.

ASAMA, ä-sä-mä, is an active volcano in central Honshu, Japan, about 85 miles northwest of Tokyo. One of the country's largest active volcanoes, it rises 8,340 feet above sea level. Its most destructive eruption was in 1783.

ASARUM, as′ə-rəm, is a group of herbs widely distributed in shady woods throughout the Northern Hemisphere. They have odd chocolate or purplish bell-shaped three-lobed floral envelopes containing 12 horned stamens. The flowers, borne close to or upon the ground, are hidden by the kidney-shaped or heart-shaped leaves.

The genus *Asarum* belongs to the plant family Aristolochiaceae. *A. canadense,* wild ginger, or Canada snakeroot, is warmly aromatic. It is common in the eastern United States and is often cultivated in wild gardens, as are also the following species: *A. virginicum, A. arifolium,* both common from Virginia southward; *A. caudatum,* a Pacific coast species; *A. lemmonii* and *A. hartwegii,* both of the Sierra Nevada of California. *A. europaeum,* also cultivated, formerly served as an emetic and was also made into snuffs.

J. M. CONRADER FROM NATIONAL AUDUBON SOCIETY

Wild ginger

(*Asarum canadense*)

ASBESTOS, as-bes′təs, is a fibrous mineral substance that is used primarily as a fireproofing and insulation material in buildings, homes, and industrial installations.

In its natural state, asbestos is found encased in rocks. Its fibrous quality makes it a remarkable mineral. Asbestos is as dense as the rock in which it is encased, but it is a mass of tiny fibers that become as fluffy and light as thistledown when separated mechanically from rock.

The most important variety of asbestos is *chrysotile* ($H_4Mg_3Si_2O_9$). This variety provides most of the asbestos used in making asbestos products. About 90 percent of the fiber used in fabricating such products is chrysotile, and it is this variety that will be called asbestos here. Its fibers are valued for their ability to withstand heat and fire and for their fineness, flexibility, and toughness.

Occurrence. Asbestos is found in many parts of the world, but the province of Quebec, Canada, long has been the prime source. Important deposits also have been found in Rhodesia, the Republic of South Africa, the USSR, and Cyprus. Limited deposits are found in the United States, Italy, and a few other countries.

In the United States, asbestos is found chiefly in Arizona, Vermont, and California. Arizona produces excellent grades of fiber that are practically free of any iron content. These fibers are most desirable for electrical insulation. The deposits in Vermont are extensive. They contain large quantities of short-fiber mill grades but little of the long-fiber spinning grades. The United States is the major manufacturer of asbestos products, but imports most of the raw material from Canada. See also MINERAL WEALTH OF THE WORLD—*Nonmetallic Minerals*.

Quarrying. The recovery of asbestos from the earth is usually a quarrying operation. An asbestos mine generally is an open pit, occasionally of gigantic size. In a typical asbestos deposit the veins and veinlets of fiber run through the rock in every direction.

In developing a deposit, the first step is exploration. Core drills are used to take samples of rock. To start recovery operations, the topsoil may be removed before a working pit is cut into the rock. Once working faces have been cut, the quarrying operation consists of drilling holes in the rock, charging them with dynamite, and blasting a large mass of rock and asbestos into the pit. After a blast, men go down into the pit to recover the high-quality long-fiber asbestos, which is removed manually from the adhering rock by using a small hammer. However, most asbestos is recovered only after the rock has been broken into smaller pieces by a series of giant crushing machines. Between the various stages of crushing the broken rock is passed over vibrating screens. Large air hoods, which resemble huge vacuum cleaners, suck up the asbestos fiber from the screen.

Applications. In the manufacture of textiles, the long-fiber asbestos first is separated mechanically into a fine, fluffy mass, which goes to carding machines that are similar to those used in carding wool or cotton. Coming from the machines in the form of a roving, the material then is twisted or spun into yarn. From this stage the asbestos can be woven into cloth, packings, tape, brake linings, or other products in which the heat resistance or fireproof quality of the fiber is considered desirable.

The fireproof theater curtain is one major use for asbestos cloth. Fire fighters and rescue crews, especially those who must face the seething inferno of an oil well fire, are equipped with complete suits of asbestos cloth. Asbestos caps, gloves, aprons, overalls, leggings, and shoes are used by workers in hazardous occupations. High temperatures are created by friction when the brakes are applied in a speeding automobile, and no other material provides long-life, efficient brake linings better than asbestos. Heavy mechanized equipment such as giant power shovels, cranes, and tractors also depend on asbestos brake linings for sure, safe control.

Asbestos in the form of felt impregnated with asphalt or coal tar pitch is one of the most commonly used types of high-grade roofing for low-pitched roofs. This material also is used to wrap metal pipes before they are buried in the ground, to protect them against corrosion.

Asbestos fiber, when combined with cement under heavy pressure, can be formed into numerous strong, durable fireproof materials that are widely used in homes and by industry. One of these products, rigid asbestos shingles, provides enduring protection for the roof and outside walls of the home. Large panels of asbestos-cement composition, some with integral color and others with decorative surface treatments, are made for use on the inside walls and ceilings of the home. Because of the fireproof and corrosion-resistant character of asbestos-cement products, large corrugated sheets or flat sheets of this composition are used by industry for structural building walls, roofs, and partitions. This product is particularly in demand by industries in which corrosive fumes are developed in the manufacturing processes.

Asbestos also is used as an insulating material to prevent excessive loss of heat from furnaces, boilers, and pipes. Alternate sheets of plain and corrugated asbestos paper cemented together are used widely to insulate domestic heating systems. Laminated layers of asbestos felts in which tiny spongy particles are embedded provide a very efficient and durable commercial insulation. Asbestos fiber mixed with basic carbonate of magnesia forms one of the most widely used insulations for both home and industrial equipment. These forms of insulation using asbestos aid in the conservation of heat and the maintenance of accurate temperature control over a wide range of operating temperatures.

Asbestos paper, another widely useful product, is made in a way that is similar to the way in which paper is made from rags. Asbestos paper is used principally in the manufacture of corrugated insulations in various forms. It also is used to manufacture gaskets and protective pads; as a protection against heat or fire in walls, floors, and ceilings; and as a dielectric in domestic electrical appliances.

The foregoing examples are some of the many uses to which this versatile mineral is being put in the control of fire, heat, and motion, as well as to provide materials resistant to chemical and other destructive agents. See also FIRE-PROOF MATERIALS; INSULATION.

LEWIS H. BROWN, *Johns-Manville Corp.*

Further Reading: Berger, Hans, *Asbestos Fundamentals: Origin, Properties, Mining, Process, Utilization* (New York 1963); Bowles, O., *Asbestos, the Silk of the Mineral Kingdom* (New York 1946); Rosato, D.V., *Asbestos: Its Industrial Applications* (New York 1959).

ASBJØRNSEN, äs'byûrn-sən, **Peter Christen** (1812–1885), Norwegian folklorist and natural scientist who, with Jørgen Moe, collected and retold Norwegian folk tales and legends. He was born in Kristiania (now Oslo) on Jan. 15, 1812. Asbjørnsen met Moe when both were students. Their collaboration, begun in 1837, resulted in the publication of two volumes of *Norske folkeeventyr* (1841–44; *Norwegian Folk Tales*).

Asbjørnsen was also noted as a naturalist. He did research on marine fauna and later led explorations of Norway's peat resources. The author of many scientific essays, he acquainted his countrymen with the theories of Charles Darwin. But his interest in folklore never subsided, and on his own he published two volumes of *Norske huldreeventyr og folkesagn* (1845–48; *Norwegian Fairy Tales and Folk Legends*) and one more collection of *Norske folkeeventyr* (1871). He died in Kristiania on Jan. 5, 1885.

ASBURY, az'ber-ē, **Francis** (1745–1816), American Methodist bishop. He was born on Aug. 20/21, 1745, at Handsworth near Birmingham, England. His family was poor and could give him only a limited formal education. Their piety, however, inspired him to become a local Wesleyan preacher at 16. In 1767 he was admitted to the Methodist Conference as an itinerant preacher and four years later set out for America as a volunteer missionary.

At the outbreak of the Revolutionary War, which John Wesley opposed, the other Methodist lay preachers returned to England. Only Asbury remained active on the American scene. The decline of the Church of England during the war left the Methodists without adequate access to the sacraments. Many unordained preachers in the South threatened to split with the established church in order to administer the sacraments themselves, but Asbury persuaded them to wait for directives from Wesley.

Finally, in 1784, Wesley joined with other Anglican clergymen to ordain Methodist elders for America. He appointed Thomas Coke and Asbury superintendents of the Methodist societies. Asbury, however, insisted that both he and Coke be elected to their posts by the American preachers. As a result, the famous "Christmas Conference" was convened at Baltimore in 1784. There the American Methodist Episcopal Church was established, independent of the Church of England but based on Wesleyan principles. Coke and Asbury were elected superintendents; then Asbury was ordained deacon, elder, and superintendent on successive days. Soon, however, both were called bishops—a practice Wesley disliked.

Partially because of Coke's frequent absences but basically because of his own strong personality and iron will, Asbury emerged as the dominant influence in the young church. He was a driving organizer and strict disciplinarian, and some objected to his rule as autocratic. Throughout his long life he personified his belief in the itinerant ministry. He covered 300,000 miles under difficult conditions, preached an estimated 17,000 sermons, and presided over more than 200 conferences at which he appointed preachers to their circuits. He died at Spotsylvania, Va., on March 31, 1816, as he was hastening to a church conference at Baltimore.

ROBERT T. HANDY, *Union Theological Seminary*

Further Reading: Asbury, Francis, *Journal and Letters,* ed. by Elmer T. Clark, 3 vols. (New York 1958).

ASBURY PARK, az'ber-ē, a city in New Jersey, is in Monmouth County, on the Atlantic coast, 55 miles (89 km) by road south of New York City. While it is primarily an all-year resort and convention center, it is also developing light industry and manufacturing plants. It possesses a fine beachfront, for bathing, boating and swimming; a mile-long boardwalk, lined with modern hotels and places of entertainment; and a convention hall and auditorium.

The city was planned in 1869 by James A. Bradley, a New York businessman, as a haven for temperance advocates. He named it after Francis Asbury (1745–1816), the first Methodist bishop in America. Asbury Park became a borough in 1874 and was incorporated in 1897. In 1933 it adopted council-manager government. Population: 16,533.

VIRGINIA KIRK, *Asbury Park Free Public Library*

ASCALON, as'ka-lon, was an ancient city of Palestine that was destroyed during the Crusades. The Hebrew form of the name is *Ashkelon*. Ascalon was settled by 2000 B.C. and eventually became one of the five principal cities of the Philistines. Its location on the Mediterranean coast, 12 miles (19 km) north of Gaza, made it the key to the control of southwest Palestine.

The first recorded mention of Ascalon was in connection with the invasion of Palestine by the Khabiri (Hebrews?) in the 1300's B.C. The city passed successively under the domination of the Egyptians, Assyrians, Persians, and Greeks, with some intervals of independence. The Greeks hellenized the city. In 104 B.C. it came under Roman influence, and it remained under Roman domination until it was conquered by the Arabs in 636 A.D.

Ascalon prospered under Muslim rule, but the war between the Western Christians and the Muslims at the time of the Crusades led to its destruction. In 1153 it was captured by Baldwin III of Jerusalem, but in 1187 it was retaken by the Muslims under Saladin. In 1191, upon the approach of Richard I the Lionhearted, Saladin had the city partially destroyed. It was permanently destroyed by the Mamluk sultan Baybars I in 1270. The site is now desolate, but the imposing ruins testify to a brilliant past.

PETER CHARANIS, *Rutgers University*

ASCENSION, Right. See CELESTIAL SPHERE.

ASCENSION DAY. See ASCENSION OF CHRIST.

ASCENSION ISLAND, ə-sen'shən, is in the South Atlantic Ocean, 700 miles (1,130 km) northwest of St. Helena Island. Part of the British colony of St. Helena, Ascension measures 9 by 6 miles (14 by 10 km), with an area of 34 square miles (88 sq km). The island is of volcanic origin and reaches a height of 2,871 feet (875 meters). It has poor soil, but a small tract is cultivated for fruit and vegetables. Georgetown is the principal settlement.

Ascension was discovered by the Portuguese navigator João da Nova on Ascension Day, 1501. The British took possession in 1815. Ascension is the most distant island tracking station of the U.S. Air Force Eastern Test Range, which begins at Cape Kennedy, Fla., 5,160 miles (8,300 km) to the northwest. The station provides telemetry, radar, and optical coverage of missile and spacecraft flights. Population: (1963) 475.

ASCENSION OF CHRIST, ə-sen'shən, krīst, in the New Testament, the final appearance of Christ to His disciples after His resurrection. Jesus gathered with His followers on the Mount of Olives 40 days after His resurrection and assured them that they would receive power from the Holy Spirit enabling them to be His witnesses throughout the world. He then "was lifted up, and a cloud took Him out of their sight." While the disciples watched this event, two angels in white declared to them that the same Jesus whom they had seen ascend would return just as they had seen Him depart (Acts 1:1–11).

The Ascension is not mentioned by Matthew. Luke mentions the event (24:51), as does Mark (16:19). John refers to it (6:62, 20:17), but does not narrate it. Reference is also made in Ephesians 4:8–10, I Timothy 3:16, Hebrews 4:14, 6:20, 17:26, I Peter 3:22, and Revelation 3:21.

Since the 4th century, Ascension Day has been observed as a major feast on the Thursday 40 days after Easter. On Ascension Day in the Western church the Paschal, or Easter candle, is extinguished, after the reading of the Gospel, to symbolize Jesus' going into heaven. This candle is lit at the beginning of the Easter ceremonies to symbolize Jesus' resurrection and consequent defeat of death, and then burned at services during Eastertide.

ASCETICISM, ə-set'ə-siz-əm, is the practice of severe self-discipline, voluntarily undertaken, in order to achieve a higher or spiritual ideal. The term is derived from the Greek verb *askein*, which in Homer's time meant "to practice an art or a skill." It came to mean "to exercise"; thus "ascetics," in the earliest sense of the word, were the "skilled," particularly those skilled in athletics or the military arts. Various Greek philosophical schools, such as the Pythagoreans, Stoics, Sophists, and Cynics, used asceticism as a system of moral practices designed to free man from vices. Plato viewed asceticism as a means not merely of training the body but also of conditioning it to a point at which the soul—the sum total of ideals—could be free. The term seems to have come into Christian and Western use through the Hellenistic-Jewish philosopher Philo. In the New Testament the term appears only once (Acts 24:16), although it had previously been used in the books of Maccabees.

Varied Meanings of Asceticism. There is considerable ambiguity in the use of the term since it encompasses within itself two divergent elements. These are man's ability to recognize a higher good or ideal and, at the same time, his incapacity to attain the ideal because of his natural, physical limitations. In this broad sense, asceticism exists in all religions and philosophies of life, since they all accept in practice the discrepancy between ideals and ordinary human impulses. In primitive cultures, for example, trials of courage are required for full initiation into adult society. Even in a secularistic milieu, self-control and the discipline of regularity of life are considered a normal requisite for social acceptability. At the same time, in popular usage the term very often means more than discipline of the body (or "lower faculties") for some ultimate purpose. It suggests to many people a certain distrust of the body or "the natural," because in most religions and philosophies there exist elements of dualism—body-soul, material-spiritual, God-world.

In non-Western religions, such as Hinduism, austerity is often admired and prized as proper to "holy men." In chapter 18 of the *Bhagavad Gita,* however, the Lord Krishna says: "He who tortures his body and senses tortures Me who dwell within them." This suggests that the aim of asceticism is self-control. Between extreme austerity and extreme self-indulgence exists the "middle path," by which the Hindu can come to know the divine.

In the Old Testament true obedience to the Law of God is emphasized rather than extraordinary practices of austerity. Such obedience, of course, presupposes considerable asceticism, both exterior and interior ("Be holy, for I . . . am holy," Leviticus 19:2). The prophets, such as Isaiah (58:1–9), insist on interior mortification in controlling vices and unruly desires, and the later Wisdom literature insists on the struggle against pride, laziness, and other vices. Although extreme ascetic practices of a physical nature are not a major part of Jewish observance, certain groups did cultivate the type of austerity that is associated with monasticism. The Essenes, a sect of ascetic Jews who led eremitical lives in the desert, recorded their ideals in the *Manual of Discipline* found in the Qumran Scrolls. Later, too, Islam adopted observances (such as fasting) that are, in the broad sense, ascetic.

Christian Asceticism. In the New Testament, Jesus insists on a great deal of renunciation: "If any man would come after me, let him deny himself and take up his cross and follow me" (Mark 8:34). Thus self-denial and the positive following of Jesus became the Christian ideal of asceticism, although extraordinary fasting was not stressed (Matthew 9:14ff.). The Apostolic writings insist on the need for purity of life (II Peter 3), and Paul is insistent that the disciples engage in spiritual combat. Although he does not use the word "asceticism," Paul employs terms derived from *agon* and roughly synonymous with the primitive meaning of asceticism.

During the 2d and 3d centuries A.D., periods of frequent persecution, Christian asceticism stressed preparation for martyrdom. The Alexandrian theologians Clement and Origen lauded celibacy and self-renunciation; they were probably influenced in part by the tradition of Greek moral systems as well as by their desire to imitate Christ. After the period of persecution, monasticism became a characteristic expression of Christian asceticism as exemplified in the exhortations of Augustine, Basil, John Cassian, John Climacus, and other church fathers of East and West. Among monks, ascetic practices varied widely, from the extravagant austerity of Egyptian hermits to the work-oriented community life of St. Benedict and his disciples.

In the Middle Ages, notably during the 12th and 13th centuries, asceticism became identified more with conformity to the life and suffering of Christ. The friars, following St. Francis of Assisi and St. Dominic, stressed poverty and renunciation. Early in the 15th century Thomas à Kempis wrote the classic work *The Imitation of Christ,* which emphasized love of Christ and assimilation to Him and which heavily influenced the ascetics of the time.

The revival of interest in classical learning and science made the hyperasceticism of the Middle Ages repugnant to the humanists of the Renaissance. They preferred to attain knowledge of God through intellectual endeavors rather than through physical deprivations. During the Reformation the Protestants, too, reacted against severe asceticism. Luther and Calvin, as well as many other Protestant theologians, admired disciplinary asceticism as a means toward self-control. However, they did not regard asceticism as a means to salvation. The Protestant traditions of austerity in matters of drink and entertainment, notable among Baptists, Methodists, Quakers, and others, are considered to be manifestations of Christian conduct rather than expressions of asceticism. In the Roman Catholic Counter Reformation, the ascetic emphasis of St. Ignatius Loyola (founder of the Jesuits) and of most subsequent spiritual writers has been on interior renunciation and obedience rather than on exterior ascetic practices.

C.J. McNaspy, S.J., *"America" Magazine*

Further Reading: Chadwick, Owen, *Western Monasticism* (Westminster, Md., 1958); Gelpi, Donald, *Functional Asceticism* (New York 1966); Van der Weldt, James, and Odenwald, Robert, *Psychiatry and Catholicism* (New York 1957).

ASCH, ash, **Sholem** (1880–1957), Yiddish novelist and playwright. Born at Kutno, Poland, on Nov. 1, 1880, he was brought up in an orthodox Jewish atmosphere in a small Polish community. He went to Warsaw in 1899, and began his literary career with sketches of small-town Jewish life, written in Hebrew. He soon began writing in Yiddish and German, which remained his media of expression thereafter. Limited at first to Jewish themes and readers, Asch transcended linguistic and cultural bounds when his play *The God of Vengeance* was translated into German and produced in Berlin in 1910 by Max Reinhardt. In 1910, Asch visited the United States. He moved there in 1914 and became an American citizen in 1920. He later lived in many other parts of the world. He died in London, England, on July 10, 1957.

Asch's writings bring together characters of all conditions and backgrounds who are motivated by a common compulsion to find an ideal or faith they can share. His later books, especially his Biblical novels *The Nazarene* (1939), *The Apostle* (1943), *Mary* (1949), *Moses* (1951), and *The Prophet* (1955), have been interpreted as an attempt to provide a bridge between Judaism and Christianity. Other works include the novel *Mottke the Thief* (1917) and two volumes of short stories—*Tales of My People* (1948) and the posthumously published *From Many Countries* (1958).

ASCHAM, as'kəm, **Roger** (c. 1516–1568), English scholar, who played a central role in the intellectual and political life of England from the time of Henry VIII until the reign of Elizabeth I. He is noted in the history of education as author of *The Scholemaster,* one of the first educational treatises written in the vernacular in Europe.

Ascham was born at Kirby Wiske, Yorkshire, about 1516. At an early age he was practically adopted by Sir Humphrey Wingfield, who had him tutored with his own sons. In 1530, Roger's patron sent him to St. John's College, Cambridge. Young Ascham found the university an exciting center of educational change and also of unorthodox Reformation thought. He soon mastered much of the available Latin literature. He also developed an excellent Latin style that, coupled with his penmanship, led to many important opportunities. These eventually included appointment as university orator (with responsibility for official university correspondence) and as a writing tutor for the children of Henry VIII, notably Mary and Elizabeth.

Ascham gained his B.A. degree in 1534 and was then elected a fellow of St. John's. In 1537 he won his master's degree and began lecturing at the university. In 1545 he published *Toxophilus,* a popular essay on the English longbow, which was still viewed as an important element of national defense. The book was dedicated to Henry VIII. The king, an ardent archer, was pleased with the work and awarded Ascham an annual pension. In 1548, the year after Henry's death, Ascham was appointed tutor for Princess Elizabeth. His instruction of Elizabeth, especially in Latin and Greek, continued intermittently through the remaining 20 years of his life.

In 1550, Ascham was made secretary to Sir Richard Morison, newly appointed ambassador to Emperor Charles V. This gave Ascham an opportunity to visit Continental courts and schools and some of the scholars with whom he had corresponded, such as Melanchthon and Johannes Sturm in Germany. The death of Edward VI in 1553 brought about the recall of the diplomatic party. Ascham returned to Cambridge but soon succeeded in gaining appointment as secretary to Queen Mary. In spite of his Protestant leanings, he gained an increase in his pension and seems to have functioned well in the Catholic household. After Mary died in 1558, he continued as secretary to Queen Elizabeth and also as her private tutor almost until his death in London on Dec. 30, 1568.

Ascham wrote *The Scholemaster* in the last years of his life. It was published posthumously by his wife. The purposes of the book paralleled those of the great Renaissance educators—to contribute to the development of the good Christian gentleman. Ascham believed that the study of classical literature was the one sound base for a liberal education. The book contained little that was new, except for his method of double translation (for example, Latin to English and English to Latin) for the teaching of foreign languages. He drew extensively on the work of Quintilian and on ideas of his contemporaries, such as Erasmus and Sir Thomas Elyot.

RICHARD E. GROSS, *Stanford University*

Further Reading: Ryan, Lawrence V., *Roger Ascham* (Stanford, Calif., 1963).

ASCHE, ash, **Oscar** (1871–1936), English actor, producer, and writer. He was born *John Stanger Heiss* at Geelong, Victoria, Australia, on Jan. 24, 1871. His first stage appearance was in *Man and Woman* at the Opéra Comique in London in 1893. During the next few years he toured the United States, Australia, and South Africa, playing a variety of Shakespearean roles. Later, in London, he managed the Adelphi Theatre and His Majesty's Theatre, where he produced *As You Like It, The Taming of the Shrew,* and *Othello.*

In 1916, Asche wrote and produced the musical fantasy *Chu Chin Chow.* He and his wife, Lily Brayton, starred in this production, which ran uninterruptedly for five years, a record for its time. In 1921 he produced *Cairo,* another musical fantasy which was not as successful as its forerunner. His autobiography was published in 1929. Asche died at Marlow, Bucks, England, on March 23, 1936.

ASCITES, ə-sīt′ēz, is a pathological accumulation of a clear, watery, yellow fluid in the peritoneal cavity (abdominal region). Sometimes referred to as *dropsy,* the condition is brought about either by an increase in venous pressure or a decrease in blood plasma albumin. Ascites is not a disease itself but is a manifestation of one or several diseases, the most common being cirrhosis. Ascites may also accompany circulatory or heart disorders, kidney failure, and malignant disease of the abdominal organs.

The symptoms of ascites vary in proportion to the amount of accumulated fluid. If the amount is small, the symptoms may be absent, but as the amount increases, severe distension of the abdomen occurs, interfering with respiration, digestion, and elimination.

Treatment centers on eliminating the fluid by medication, decrease in fluid intake, and diet. If this fails, surgery may be used.

ASCLEPIAS, as-klē′pē-əs, is a group of weeds containing the milkweeds or silkweeds and found in North and South America and Africa. Mostly erect perennials with thick, deep roots, asclepias is common in pastures and waste places. Some of the plants furnish a fiber strong enough for ropes, and the silky down attached to the seeds is often used for stuffing pillows.

Asclepias is the principal genus of the family Asclepiadaceae; there are about 150 species. *A. tuberosa,* commonly known as butterfly-weed or pleurisy root, is a showy species found on dry banks from southern Canada to Florida. Other well-known American species are *A. rubra, A. purpurascens,* and *A. syriaca* (swamp milkweed). The few species cultivated for ornament in America are mostly foreign.

ASCLEPIUS. See AESCULAPIUS.

ASCOLI, äs′kō-lē, **Graziadio Isaia** (1829–1907), Italian philologist and dialectologist. He was born in Gorizia on July 16, 1829. At the age of 16 he showed remarkable originality in a paper he prepared on southern European dialects. Despite his lack of college training, he was appointed professor of linguistics at the Accademia Scientifico-Linguistica in Milan. His most important work is the multivolume *Studi orientali e linguistici,* on Oriental philology.

His *Studi ariosemitici* (1865) demonstrated the relationship between the Semitic and Indo-European languages. Ascoli edited the *Archivio glottologico italiano* (1873–1907), in which (vol. 8) he published *Italia: lingua e dialetti,* a definitive classification of Italian dialects. He died at Milan on Jan. 21, 1907.

ASCOLI PICENO, äs′kō-lē pē-châ′nō, is a city in Italy, in the Marches region, on the Tronto River, 87 miles northeast of Rome. It is the capital of Ascoli Piceno province, in a rich agricultural area. The city has numerous Roman and medieval remains and a fine Romanesque cathedral built in the 1100's and reconstructed in 1482. Plants in the city manufacture woolens, leather hats, glass, majolica ware, and chinaware.

Originally a Sabine town, it was captured by the Romans in 268 B.C. After the 700's A.D., it was ruled by bishops, and in 1185 it became a free republic. From 1504 until 1860 it was under the protection of the Holy See. Population: (1961) 33,825.

ASCOMYCETES, as-ko-mī-sē'tēz, are a large and important group of fungi (q.v.), so called because their spores are contained in asci (sacs). This group includes mildews, rusts, and smuts.

ASCORBIC ACID. See VITAMINS—*Vitamin C* (Ascorbic Acid).

ASCOT, as'kət, is a village in England, in Berkshire, 30 miles (48 km) southwest of London. Nearby is Ascot Heath, a famous racecourse inaugurated by Queen Anne on Aug. 11, 1711. Races are held in June, July, September, and October at distances ranging between 5 furlongs and 3 miles. The annual four-day Royal Meeting in June is notable for the royal procession that precedes the opening race each day, and for the Gold Cup stakes, a 2½-mile race established in 1807.

ASEN, à-sān', was the name of a Bulgarian dynasty founded by *Ivan Asen I* (died about 1196) and his brother *Peter Asen* (died 1197). They revolted against Byzantine rule in 1186 and established their own rule in Bulgaria, but their power was not secure until the final defeat of the Byzantines in 1196. Both Ivan and Peter were murdered by their boyars (nobles).

Peter was succeeded by a third brother, *Kaloyan* (reigned 1197–1207). Kaloyan conquered northern Bulgaria and defeated Emperor Baldwin I of Constantinople at Adrianople in 1205. Kaloyan was murdered in 1207 and was succeeded by his nephew *Boril* (reigned 1207–1218). In the second year of his reign Boril was severely defeated by the Franks. An unpopular ruler, he was overthrown and blinded by Ivan Asen's son, *Ivan Asen II* (reigned 1218–1241), who conquered Epirus, Macedonia, part of Albania, and Serbia.

The reigns of the two young sons of Ivan Asen II, *Kaliman I* (reigned 1241–1246) and *Michael I* (reigned 1246–1257), were characterized by declining power and extensive territorial losses. With the short reign of their cousin *Kaliman II* (reigned 1257–1258), the male Asen line died out, and the dynasty came to an end.

ASEPSIS. See ANTISEPTIC.

ASEXUAL REPRODUCTION. See PLANTS AND PLANT SCIENCE—*Sex in Plants*.

ASGARD, äs'gärd, in Scandinavian mythology, was the domain of the gods, corresponding to the Olympus of Greek mythology. It was also called *Asgarth* or *Asgardhr*. It was situated at the highest point between heaven and Midgard (Earth), and was accessible only by the bridge Bifrost (the rainbow). Chief among the gods who lived in Asgard was a pantheon of deities known as the Aesir, each of whom presided over a splendid mansion. Of these mansions, the most beautiful and lavish was Valhalla, the residence of Odin, the supreme god, where heroes slain in battle were brought.

The gods and goddesses led carefree lives in Asgard, with much feasting and merriment, until the giants from adjacent Jotunheim (enemies of the gods, like the Titans in classical myth) crossed over into Asgard and spread sin. See also AESIR; SCANDINAVIAN MYTHOLOGY.

ASH, ash, a genus (*Fraxinus*) of approximately 65 species of trees and some shrubs, native mostly to the north temperate zone of North America, Europe, and Asia, but extending south into Mexico and Java. It is classified in the olive family, Oleaceae. Ashes are important as a source of timber and as ornamentals.

The leaves of the ash are opposite, usually pinnately compound and composed of an odd number of leaflets (often 5 to 9), but in *F. anomala* of the southwestern United States, a leaf may consist of a single leaflet. The clustered flowers in many species are imperfect, the staminate (male) and pistillate (female) being on different trees; sometimes both occur on the same tree, however, and in some species, such as the blue ash, the flowers are perfect, with both stamens and pistils. A corolla is often lacking, but certain species, such as flowering ash, have 2 to 6 (commonly 4) narrow white petals. There are 2 stamens, and the single-seeded fruit is winged, suggestive of a minature canoe paddle.

The white ash, *F. americana*, is the most important timber ash of eastern North America, ranging from Nova Scotia and Ontario to Minnesota, and south to Oklahoma, Texas, and Florida. Its leaves are dark green above, and pale below. They are usually composed of 7 leaflets, with finely toothed or slightly wavy margins, and each leaflet is on its own short stalk. In autumn the leaves drop early, after turning pale yellow or, in some cases, a deep dull or reddish purple. The bark pattern is a finely ridged network, gray or tinged with brown, and the twigs are light gray. In rich, moist woodlands and along streams, where the white ash normally grows, it becomes a tall tree, occasionally over 100 feet (30 meters) high, with a thick trunk, and with the main branches stout and spreading. It is relatively free of insect and fungus pests.

LEFT, U.S. FOREST SERVICE; ABOVE, GOTTSCHO-SCHLEISNER

The white ash (*Fraxinus americana*), found in eastern North America.

The wood of the white ash, like that of hickory, combines elasticity with strength, but ash is not as tough, heavy, or expensive as hickory. Consequently it is used when resiliency, strength, and relative lightness are desirable, as in baseball bats, tennis rackets, hockey sticks, oars, the handles of agricultural tools, and the body frames of some station wagons. It is sometimes used for furniture, and pieces having a curly grain are especially valuable. The wood of several other eastern species is also sold as white ash, but it is generally inferior.

There are some 17 species of ash in North America, distinguished from each other mostly by detailed characteristics of the fruits. The black ash, *F. nigra,* is a fairly tall tree of wet habitats in eastern North America. Its leaves are composed of 7 to 11 finely toothed leaflets, which, unlike those of the white ash, are not stalked. The red ash, *F. pennsylvanica,* ranges from eastern Canada southward. It has leaves composed usually of 7 leaflets, with short stalks. The leaflets are silky haired underneath, and have nearly entire margins. The blue ash, *F. quandrangulata,* is found in the more-central areas of North America. It has 7 to 11 long-pointed, coarsely toothed leaflets, and its twigs are square in cross section. Unlike those of the other American species discussed here, its flowers have both stamens and pistils.

The only important commercial ash of the Pacific slope is the Oregon ash, *F. oregona,* which extends from British Columbia south through California. The leaves are usually composed of 7 pale green leaflets, oval and hairy beneath, with entire or slightly toothed margins. The uses of the Oregon ash are similar to those of the Eastern ashes, and its wood compares favorably in quality.

One of the most valuable timber trees in Europe is the European ash, *F. excelsior,* a native of Europe and Asia Minor. It may grow over 100 feet (30 meters) in height and has leaves composed of 7 to 11 sessile, toothed leaflets. It is used to make wagons, furniture, musical instruments, snowshoes, and wooden implements. Cultivated for many centuries, the European ash exists in numerous varieties, with leaflets marked or margined with yellow or white, with leaves simple or 3-parted, with leaf margins variously incised, and with pendulous branches.

The flowering ash, *F. ornus,* a smaller tree, is a native of southern Europe and western Asia. It is distinguished by its flowers, which are conspicuous, densely clustered, fragrant, white, and usually 4-petaled. Manna (q.v.), collected in Italy and Sicily and used medicinally as a gentle laxative, is a saccharine material obtained from the trunk of *F. ornus.* Manna exudes spontaneously in hot weather, but usually incisions are made in the bark with a knife to speed the flow. Several Oriental species of ash, especially *F. chinensis* and *F. Mariesii,* yield Chinese white wax.

The *mountain ash* (q.v.), in the genus *Sorbus,* is related to the pear and the apple and is not a true ash.

EDWIN B. MATZKE, *Columbia University*

ASH, ash, is the residue left after an organic material has burned completely. The main components of wood ash are silica, calcium oxide, magnesium oxide, and potassium carbonate. Wood ash is used to treat acid soils. Various types of ash from burned plants provide fertilizers.

All coal has ash. Such ash is made up of minerals from plants and varying amounts of sand, clay, and rock. Some coal ash is recovered and used as a building material, especially in cinder blocks.

The disposal of ash presents a problem because it is dusty and irritating to handle. Another problem is that ash is sometimes discharged from the stacks of coal-burning factories; this is one source of pollution of the atmosphere. Traps for stack ash have been developed. Other ash is placed in railroad cars, trucks, or barges for disposal.

ASH WEDNESDAY, ash wenz'dē, is the first day of Lent in the Roman Catholic, Anglican, and some other churches. It is so named from the ceremonial use of ashes as a symbol of penitence in the service for the day. The ceremony, which is of great antiquity, was confined at first to those engaged in public penance, which ended at Easter. Later the ceremony was applied to the whole congregation. In 1191, Pope Celestine III sanctioned its use throughout the church.

In the Roman Catholic Church, ashes from the previous year's Palm Sunday palms are applied by the priest to the foreheads of the devout. The priest marks with his thumb the sign of the Cross and says: "Remember, man, that you are dust, and to dust you shall return."

The Protestant reformers abandoned the old ceremony and (in England) substituted for it the *commination,* a series of curses pronounced upon sins (based on Deuteronomy 28). Churches of the Anglican Communion (including the Protestant Episcopal Church) and others have special services for Ash Wednesday, including the Litany. See also LENT.

FREDERICK C. GRANT
Union Theological Seminary

Further Reading: Shepherd, Massey H., *Oxford American Prayer Book Commentary* (New York 1950).

ASH WEDNESDAY, ash wenz'dē, is a poem by T.S. Eliot (q.v.), written in 1930, reflecting the poet's personal religious experience. The title derives from the first day of Lent, the traditional Christian season of penance and renunciation, and throughout the poem there are echoes of the Roman Catholic sacrament of penance. Employing allusions from Catholic liturgy and drawing material from both Christian and secular writing of the past, *Ash Wednesday* takes the form of a six-part prayer, spoken in the voice of a penitent who renounces the world and petitions for unity with God through the intercession of the Virgin Mary.

Parts 1 and 2 present the penitent refusing to return to the vain hopes and ambitions of his youth and attesting to his faith in God in a series of prayers to the Virgin. Part 3 evokes Dante's *Purgatorio,* wherein the penitent sees himself struggling with evil and proclaiming his unworthiness to God. Parts 4 and 5 invoke the aid of the Virgin and reaffirm the penitent's belief in God's existence. Part 6 presents the penitent still wavering between the world's attractions and his longing toward God, but finally beseeching: "And let my cry come unto Thee."

Further Reading: Eliot, Thomas Stearns, *The Complete Poems and Plays* (New York 1952; id., *Essays Ancient and Modern* (New York 1936); Smith, Grover, *T.S. Eliot's Poetry and Plays* (Chicago 1960).

ASHANTI, ə-shan′tē, an ethnic group that live mainly in the political division of central Ghana known as the *Ashanti region.* Numbering over 700,000, most of the Ashanti live in villages and small towns. Their one major city is Kumasi, the seat of the *Asantehene* (king of Ashanti), who is the guardian of the Golden Stool, the symbol of national unity.

The Ashanti are primarily a rural people, growing subsistence crops. Cocoa is the chief cash crop. Speaking a dialect of the Twi language, the Ashanti are related culturally to the Akan peoples of central and southern Ghana and the Ivory Coast. Their houses are mostly rectangular in shape and are built around a central courtyard in which the activities of everyday life are centered. Family membership and inheritance are determined by matrilineal descent.

The Ashanti nation was founded in the late 1600's by a confederation of several small Akan states. During the next two centuries the confederation greatly expanded its territory and the number of its constituent states, and exerted its political, military, and commercial influence over most of present-day central and southern Ghana. The British annexed Ashanti as a colony within the Gold Coast in 1901. The Ashanti maintained an identity of their own throughout the colonial period, and continue to be a distinctive ethnic group in Ghana, though politically integrated with the rest of the country.

ROBERT A. LYSTAD, *Author of "The Ashanti"*

ASHARI, Al- (c. 873–935), ash-a-rē′, Muslim theologian of Basra and Baghdad. His full name was *Abu'l-Hasan Ali Ibn Ismail al-Ashari.* Ashari initially taught the rationalistic theology of the Mutazilite school of Islam. When he was about 40, he embraced a more conservative doctrine, which he expounded in his later books. In them he argues that God has eternal attributes; that the Koran is His eternal Word and must be interpreted with as little rationalization as possible; that God wills all events, including man's evil acts; and that right action for man is obedience to God's commands, and wrong action is disobedience. The important Asharite school of theology was developed later from these teachings. Ashari also wrote an account of the sects of Islam.

GEORGE F. HOURANI, *University of Michigan*

ASHCAN PAINTERS of the early 20th century attempted to portray American city life realistically, as in John Sloan's *Sunday, Women Drying Their Hair* (1912).

ADDISON GALLERY, PHILLIPS ACADEMY, ANDOVER, MASS.

ASHBOURNE, ash′bōrn, **1st Baron** (1837–1913), Irish lawyer and politician. He was born *Edward Gibson* at Dublin, Ireland, on Sept. 4, 1837. Educated at Trinity College, Dublin, from which he was graduated in 1858, he was called to the Irish bar in 1860 and became a queen's counsel in 1872.

Entering politics as a Conservative, he represented Dublin University in the British Parliament from 1875 to 1885, and from 1877 to 1880 served as attorney general for Ireland. He was an excellent speaker and often expounded government policy on Ireland in the House of Commons. Raised to the peerage in 1885, he was appointed lord chancellor of Ireland, serving from 1885 to 1892 and from 1895 to 1905. He died in London on May 22, 1913.

ASHBURTON, 1st Baron. See BARING, ALEXANDER.

ASHCAN SCHOOL, a group of realistic painters in New York City in the late 19th and early 20th centuries. Also known as "The Eight," they were Robert Henri (1865–1929), John Sloan (1871–1951), George Luks (1867–1933), Everett Shinn (1876–1953), William Glackens (1870–1938), Ernest Lawson (1873–1939), Maurice Prendergast (1861–1923), and Arthur B. Davies (1862–1928). The epithet "ashcan school" was applied to them because of their use of such motifs as backyards and garbage cans. Shinn depicted an ash can as early as 1901, but the term was not actually coined until 1934, when Holger Cahill and Alfred Barr used it in their book *Art in America in Modern Times.*

The chief influences on the "ashcan" school were the realistic painting tradition of Thomas Eakins (q.v.) and the reportorial approach of newspaper illustrators. Henri, Sloan, Luks, Shinn, and Glackens all were newspaper illustrators in Philadephia in the 1890's. In time, they moved to New York City—first ·Luks, Glackens, and Shinn, then Henri and Sloan. In 1908, Lawson, Davies, and Prendergast joined the former Philadelphians in the historic exhibition of The Eight at the Macbeth Gallery. The group never repeated their joint showing.

Henri, the leader of the school, was primarily a portrait and figure painter. Sloan sought his subject matter among the people on the streets of New York and in backyards, bars, and skating rinks. Luks was a figure painter whose work shows overtones of social realism. Shinn remained essentially a reporter, his favorite subjects being the music halls of New York, London, and Paris. Glackens' discovery of Renoir's art led him to impressionism in his use of light and color, and his subjects were mainly urban parks and bathing beaches. Lawson, too, was essentially an impressionist—the landscape painter of the school. Prendergast was influenced chiefly by the French postimpressionists; he created brilliant, tapestry-like oils and watercolors of park scenes in New York and New England. Davies was an imaginative fantasist who created idyllic landscapes peopled by delicate nymphs.

Even those who disliked the "ashcan" school conceded that its art faithfully mirrored contemporary urban life. As critical opinion became increasingly favorable, the school's paintings became greatly sought after, collected, and exhibited.

WILLIAM GERDTS, *University of Maryland*

ASHEVILLE, business center of western North Carolina, lies in the shadow of the Blue Ridge mountain range.

ASHCROFT, ash'krôft, **Dame Peggy** (1907–   ), British actress, who is best known for her classical roles, but who also gave outstanding performances in modern plays. Born at Croydon, England, on Dec. 22, 1907, she began dramatic studies at the age of 16. She made her theatrical debut at the Birmingham Repertory Theatre in 1926 and first appeared in London in 1927.

She achieved recognition as a major actress in 1929 for her performance in the London production of *Jew Süss*. In 1932 she became a leading lady with the Old Vic Company, starring in a number of Shakespearean plays, as well as in Sheridan's *School for Scandal* and Goldsmith's *She Stoops to Conquer*. She made her New York debut in 1937 in Maxwell Anderson's *High Tor*.

Her other performances include leading roles in *Hamlet*, in John Gielgud's production in 1944; *Edward My Son* (1947); *The Heiress* (1950); *Hedda Gabler* (1955); and *The Good Woman of Setzuan* (1956). She was made Dame of the Order of the British Empire in 1956.

ASHEBORO, ash'bûr-ō, an industrial town on the Piedmont upland of North Carolina, lies 25 miles by road south of Greensboro, near the center of the state. It is the seat of Randolph County. The town has diversified industries, with factories producing hosiery, shoes, underwear, neckties, electric blankets, flashlight batteries, furniture, and concrete products.

The Asheboro area was once the home of several Indian tribes. The site of an Indian village was discovered near the town in 1936, and an Indian burial ground was excavated. The first white settlers arrived around 1740, and in 1779 the town was founded as the seat of the newly organized county. Incorporated in 1796, it was named in honor of Samuel Ashe, who was then governor of North Carolina. Asheboro adopted a city manager plan of government in 1942. Population: 10,797.

ASHER BEN YEHIEL (c. 1250–1327), ä'shər ben yə-Ḵēl', was an eminent rabbi and Talmudic scholar. Born in Germany, in a family of learned Jews, Asher studied under Rabbi Meir of Rothenburg and adopted Meir's orthodox teachings. To escape persecution, he fled in 1303 to Spain, where he became a rabbi at Toledo. Known as *Rosh* (head, or chief), he was soon recognized as the leading rabbinical authority in Spain. His strong emphasis on orthodoxy influenced the Spanish Jews to study the Talmud. Asher died in Toledo in 1327.

Asher possessed a vast knowledge of the Talmud and was distinguished for the terseness of his commentaries on it. His commentaries on Jewish law, especially his *Compendium* of the Talmud, are standard works. His *Responsa* is a source of Jewish history.

Jacob Ben Asher, his son, wrote the four *Turim,* a popular but profound codification of rabbinical law. Joseph Caro (Karo) directly based his code of Jewish law, the *Shulhan Arukh* (1564–65), on the *Turim.*

ASHEVILLE, ash'vil, a city in western North Carolina, is the seat of Buncombe County, and the economic and cultural center of a mountainous region. It is situated in the Blue Ridge Mountains at an altitude of 2,300 feet (701 meters) on a hilly plateau amid a complex of peaks and ridges. The Great Smoky Mountains National Park is about 50 miles (80 km) to the west. Mount Mitchell, 6,684 feet (2,037 meters) high, the highest point east of the Mississippi River, is 20 miles (32 km) northeast of Asheville.

Temperate climate and scenic beauty have established the city as a health resort and as a tourist, convention, and retirement center. The Asheville area also receives major economic support from diversified light industries. These include the manufacture of rayon, electronic components, instruments, rocket fuels, clothing and textiles, blankets, wood and paper products, and processed foods. Agriculture, though important in the economy, is restricted to a small amount of suitable terrain. Handwoven fabrics, handwrought jewelry, and native mountain crafts constitute a small industry of special interest to visitors.

Asheville-Biltmore College and Asheville-Buncombe Technical Institute are located in the city, and Warren Wilson College is at nearby Swannanoa. The surrounding area has many private schools, religious assemblies, and summer camps. Annual crafts fairs and folk music festivals continue to foster mountain traditions in the cosmopolitan atmosphere induced by residents from all parts of the United States.

Thomas Wolfe was a native of Asheville and drew heavily on the town and its people for his novels and short stories. His boyhood home, the "Dixieland" of his first novel, *Look Homeward, Angel,* is now a public memorial open during the tourist season. The house and the substantial collection of Wolfe material and memorabilia at the Pack Library are attractions for scholars and Wolfe enthusiasts.

Other points of interest in the Asheville vicinity are Biltmore House and Gardens, one of the most opulent estates in the United States, which was created by George W. Vanderbilt; the Blue Ridge Parkway, which offers spectacular mountain vistas north and south; Mount Pisgah and The Rat, a distinctive peak and ridge much loved by local people; the Zebulon Vance birthplace, restored pioneer home of a colorful North Carolina governor; and Riverside Cemetery, burial place of Thomas Wolfe, O. Henry (William Sydney Porter), and other contributors to Asheville's history.

History. Asheville was settled during the American Revolution on former Cherokee hunting grounds and was incorporated in 1797. It developed slowly until the coming of the railroad in 1880. Incorporated as a city in 1883, it began to profit from investments by George W. Vanderbilt and other capitalists. The collapse of a wild land boom in the late 1920's left Asheville prostrate during the depression. The city has recovered and now possesses a healthy, well-balanced economy. Asheville is governed by council-manager. Population: 57,681.

KENNETH BROWN, *Pack Memorial Public Library*

ASHI (352–427), ä-shē', was a Babylonian rabbi and scholar, who first compiled the Gemara in written form. Son of the wealthy and learned Simai, Ashi became head of the Talmudic academy of Sura, in Babylonia, while still young. He devoted his life to the collection and study of the explanations and discussions of the Mishna (Mishnah) that had been handed down in Babylonian Talmudic academies (see MISHNAH).

The result of these labors, in which Ashi was engaged for 52 years, was the first written compilation of the Gemara, the text accompanying the Mishna in the Babylonian Talmud. Ashi's work was concluded in 500 (or 499) A.D. by Rabina, another head of the Sura academy.

RAPHAEL PATAI, *Theodor Herzl Institute*

ASHIKAGA, ä-shē-kä-gä, a distinguished military family of medieval Japan, which established a shogunate that ruled from 1338 until 1573. Yoshiyasu, who founded the Ashikaga house in the 1100's, took the new family name from that of a village in central Honshu.

The Ashikaga were prominent in the affairs of the Kamakura shogunate (1192–1333), when the basic institutions of a feudal system were erected in Japan. Ashikaga Takauji vaulted the family to the political forefront when he supported Emperor Go Daigo, who sought to crush shogunal power. But after the downfall of the Kamakura shogunate in 1333, Takauji, dissatisfied with his position in the new government, turned against the emperor. Declaring Go Daigo deposed, Takauji placed Prince Yutahito (later Emperor Kōmyō) on the throne at Kyoto in 1336. Go Daigo, however, refused to surrender his imperial title and established a rival imperial court at Yoshino, thus inaugurating the era of the Northern and Southern Courts, which lasted until 1392. Takauji obtained the title of shogun from Emperor Kōmyō in 1338, becoming the first of 15 successive members of the Ashikaga family to hold the office.

The Ashikaga shoguns were never strong enough to control the many feudal lords. Maintaining their capital at Kyoto, the Ashikaga shoguns exerted their power mainly in the nearby provinces. Under the Ashikaga shoguns, the feudal system was extended throughout Japan. It was an era of chronic warfare.

In spite of the constant feudal strife, domestic commerce flourished, and a prosperous overseas trade was stimulated. With the encouragement of the Ashikaga shoguns, Chinese cultural practices, such as landscape painting, floral arrangement, the art of dwarf trees, and the tea ceremony, were adopted in Japan. The Nō play also became very popular.

The Ashikaga shogunate declined rapidly during the military upheavals of the 16th century. Yoshiaki, the last shogun of the Ashikaga house, was deprived of actual power by Oda Nobunaga in 1573 but retained the title of shogun until his death in 1597. A new shogunal line, the Tokugawa, was founded by Ieyasu in 1603.

HYMAN KUBLIN, *The City University of New York*

ASHKENAZIM, ash-kə-naz'əm, are the Jews whose ancestors lived in German lands. The name derives from *Ashk'naz,* the traditional Hebrew name for Germany. During and after the Middle Ages, Ashkenazi Jews spread all over Europe (except the Mediterranean countries). From there they migrated overseas, retaining their Yiddish language. They produced a rich religious and secular literature in Yiddish, a medieval German dialect with an admixture of Hebrew.

In the late 19th and early 20th century, however, the Ashkenazi Jews gradually adopted the languages of the non-Jewish majority in the countries where they lived. They began to assimilate with the majority population and to participate intensively in the national and cultural life of their host countries. At the same time, they remained tied to their local Jewish congregations and their Jewish consciousness. It was among Ashkenazi Jews that the idea of political Zionism emerged, leading ultimately to the establishment of the state of Israel.

Differences in tradition and ritual between Ashkenazi Jews and Sephardi Jews (see SEPHARDIM) led to the creation of separate congregations in lands, such as Holland, England, and Mexico, where both Ashkenazim and Sephardim live. In Israel, the supervision of religious life is divided between an Ashkenazi and a Sephardi chief rabbi.

In the late 1960's, Ashkenazi Jews numbered some 11 million, about 84 percent of the world Jewish population.

RAPHAEL PATAI, *Theodor Herzl Institute*

ASHKHABAD, ash'kə-bad, a city in the USSR, is the capital of the Turkmen republic in Soviet Central Asia. It is situated in the foothills of the Kopet Dagh, 25 miles (40 km) from the Iranian frontier, on the Trans-Caspian Railroad. The district, situated at the southern edge of the Kara Kum desert, is supplied with much of its water by the Kara Kum Canal, completed in the mid-1960's, from the Syr Darya river.

Ashkhabad's widely diversified industries produce window glass and glassware, cotton and silk textiles, farm implements, and furniture. As the cultural center of Turkestan, Ashkhabad is the seat of the republic's Academy of Sciences, a university, and medical and agricultural colleges. There is also a movie studio.

Russians make up 50 percent of the city's population, and the indigenous Turkmen people 30 percent. A variety of nationalities make up the remaining 20 percent.

Ashkhabad was founded in 1881 as a fortified outpost in the Russians' advance into Central Asia, and it flourished as a center of trade with Iran. The city has been largely rebuilt since its near destruction by an earthquake in 1948. Population: (1965) 226,000.

THEODORE SHABAD
Author of "Geography of the USSR"

ASHLAND, ash′lənd, an industrial city in northeastern Kentucky, is in Boyd County, on the Ohio River, 209 miles (336.2 km) east of Louisville. It is the chief city in this part of Kentucky and is included in the Huntington (W. Va.)-Ashland metropolitan area. The Kentucky-Ohio Interstate Bridge is located here. Commercial air service is provided at Huntington airport.

Natural resources of the region include coal, iron, gas, fire clay, limestone, shale, and hard timber. Ashland manufactures steel, petroleum products, fire brick, leather, and lumber products. The continuous sheet mill process of manufacture was developed in the steel roller mills of Ashland. The city is a retail, wholesale, and shipping center.

Ashland is built around Central Park (52 acres, or 21 hectares), which is notable for its Indian mounds and fine native forest trees.

The first white settlers arrived in 1815. The community was known as *Poage Settlement* until 1850, when it was laid out as a town and renamed in honor of the home of Henry Clay. Incorporated as a village in 1858 and as a city in 1870, it has a commission-manager form of government. Population: 29,245.

ASHLAND, ash′lənd, is an industrial city in northern Ohio, 85 miles (137 km) by highway southwest of Cleveland. It is the seat of Ashland County. Its rubber factories make a large percentage of the toy balloons produced in the United States, and a Balloon Festival is held in the city each year. Ashland also manufactures pipe fittings and water systems and has printing works. Despite its industries, Ashland preserves the mellowed appearance and quiet atmosphere often associated with communities in New England, from which many of its original settlers came.

Ashland was founded in 1815 and was named for the Kentucky estate of Henry Clay. The city was incorporated in 1844. Ashland College was established there in 1878 by the Brethren Church, an offshoot of the German Baptist Brethren. A monument commemorates John Chapman ("Johnny Appleseed"), the itinerant tree planter, who often passed through this region. Ashland has a mayor and council form of government. Population: 19,872.

ASHLAND, ash′lənd, a city in southwestern Oregon, is situated in Jackson County, at the southern end of the Rogue River valley, 15 miles (24.1 km) by highway southeast of Medford and 295 miles (474.5 km) south of Portland. Agriculture, including horticulture, is of first importance in the economy of the community; lumber ranks equally with tourism as a second source of income.

Ashland is the seat of Southern Oregon College, a state institution, and of the Oregon Shakespearean Festival, a summer event that began in 1935. Among other tourist attractions are nearby mountain streams and lakes for fishing, the Emigrant Lake Water Sports Carnival, and the Mt. Ashland ski resort.

The first settlers came in 1852 during a gold rush boom in nearby Jacksonville. The name Ashland Mills, given to the first sawmill and to the town as well, was later changed to Ashland. Incorporated in 1874, the city operates under a mayor-council form of government. Population: 12,342.

ASHLAND, ash′lənd, is a borough in eastern Pennsylvania, in Schuylkill and Columbia counties, 90 miles (144.8 km) northwest of Philadelphia. Anthracite coal is mined in the vicinity, and there are farms that raise grain, potatoes, and green vegetables. Ashland manufactures mine pumps, screens, store fixtures, and clothing.

The Ashland State Hospital is situated in the borough, as is the Mothers' Memorial, modeled in bronze after James Whistler's painting of his mother.

Ashland was settled in 1845 and incorporated as a borough in 1857. Since 1930 it has been governed by a manager and council. Population: 4,737.

ASHLAND, ash′lənd, a city in northern Wisconsin, is the seat of Ashland County. It is situated on Chequamegon Bay of Lake Superior, 67 miles (107.8 km) east of Superior. The Apostle Islands (q.v.) lie to the north and the Bad River Chippewa Indian Reservation to the southeast. The city is the seat of Northland College, a private institution established in 1892.

Possessing a fine natural harbor, Ashland is a shipping point for pulpwood and coke and a distributing center for coal received from ports on Lake Erie and Lake Ontario. Paper, logging machinery, foundry products, plywood, and clothing are manufactured.

Settlement began in 1854, but various disasters had virtually depopulated the community by 1870. Its later growth was due to lumbering operations and the mining of iron ore in the nearby Gogebic Range of Michigan. The iron mining has been discontinued. Ashland was chartered as a city in 1887. Government is by mayor and council. Population: 9,615.

ASHLEY, Anthony Cooper. See SHAFTESBURY.

ASHLEY, ash′lē, **James Mitchell** (1824–1896), American congressman, who proposed the constitutional amendment abolishing slavery. He was born on Nov. 14, 1824, in Allegheny County, Pa., and grew up in Portsmouth, Ohio. He had no formal schooling. Much of his childhood was spent traveling with his father, who was an itinerant preacher.

During this time, and as a cabin boy on an Ohio River steamboat, Ashley observed and learned to hate slavery. In his youth he was expelled from the state of Virginia for expressing militant abolitionist views. He settled in Ohio in 1841 and became a printer and subsequently editor for a Portsmouth newspaper. His intense abolitionist views drove him from the Democratic party to the Free-Soil party in 1848 and to the Republican party in 1854.

Elected to the U.S. House of Representatives in 1858, Ashley was a radical Republican congressman until 1869. In 1863 he introduced the first proposition to amend the Constitution to abolish slavery. The 13th Amendment became law in 1865. Ashley considered it the greatest achievement of his life.

Ashley's initiation of the unsuccessful impeachment proceedings against President Andrew Johnson and his increasingly harsh political criticisms brought an end to his congressional career in 1869. After a year's service as territorial governor of Montana, he became a successful railroad developer in Michigan. He died on Sept. 16, 1896.

ASHLEY, ash′lē, **William Henry** (c. 1778–1838), American fur trader, explorer, and public official. He was born in Chesterfield County, Va., and moved to Missouri in 1802. After farming, mining lead and saltpeter, and engaging in commerce, he entered the fur trade in 1822. He and a partner, Andrew Henry, advertised in the *Missouri Republican* of St. Louis on March 6, 1822, for "enterprizing young men" to ascend the Missouri River to its sources.

Famous trappers who got their start with Ashley were Jedediah Smith, James Bridger, Thomas Fitzpatrick, William and Milton Sublette, David Jackson (for whom Jackson Hole, Wyo., is named), and Etienne Provost (for whom Provo, Utah, is named). Smith and Fitzpatrick pioneered the Oregon Trail in 1823–1824 on one of Ashley's expeditions.

Prior to his fur-trading activities, Ashley had been active in Missouri's territorial militia, reaching the rank of brigadier general in 1812. He was elected lieutenant governor of the new state of Missouri in 1820. After his retirement from the fur trade he served in Congress as a Whig from 1831 to 1837, but was twice defeated in elections for the governorship of Missouri. He died near Boonville, Mo., on March 26, 1838. See also MOUNTAIN MEN.

KENNETH L. HOLMES, *Linfield College*

Further Reading: Morgan, Dale L., ed., *The West of William H. Ashley, 1822–1838* (Denver 1964).

ASHMOLEAN MUSEUM, ash-mōl′ē-ən, a museum at Oxford, England, that houses the art and archaeological collections of Oxford University. Opened in 1683, it was the first public museum in England. The collections were moved to the present building in the 19th century. The Ashmolean Museum now includes collections of paintings, drawings, sculpture, metalwork, ceramics, and other European works of art from the Middle Ages to the present; coins, medals, paper money of all periods; Japanese ceramics, lacquer ware, painting, prints, and metalwork; and Indian and Tibetan sculpture.

The museum derives its name from *Elias Ashmole* (1617–1692), English archaeologist and antiquarian, who in 1677 gave Oxford University the collections that formed the original nucleus of the museum. These consisted of his own collection of curiosities and antiquities and his library, together with the collections of his friend, the traveler and naturalist John Tradescant, which Ashmole had inherited. Tradescant's contribution included one of the earliest ethnological collections, with objects from North America, Africa, Polynesia, and other parts of the world.

ASHMUN, ash′mən, **Jehudi** (1794–1828), American colonial agent in Liberia. He was born in Champlain, N.Y., on April 21, 1794. After graduating from the University of Vermont in 1816, he entered the Congregational ministry, taught, and then went to Washington, where he edited a journal of the Episcopal church.

In 1822 the U.S. government sent him to Liberia with a party of 37 freed Negro slaves. On reaching the colony, which had been established earlier by groups sent out by the American Colonization Society, Ashmun discovered a disheartening situation: fever was rampant, supplies were short, the administrators had deserted, and native African leaders were on the verge of attacking. He led a successful defense of the col-

ony, and peace ensued. Ashmun helped the colonists to establish a permanent settlement and vigorously developed the colony until 1828, when, his health failing, he returned to America. He died in Boston on Aug. 25, 1828.

Ashmun was the author of *History of the American Colony in Liberia from December 1821 to 1823* (1826).

See also AMERICAN COLONIZATION SOCIETY.

ASHTABULA, ash-tə-bū′lə, is an industrial city in northeastern Ohio, in Ashtabula County. It is situated on Lake Erie at the mouth of the Ashtabula River, 56 miles (90.1 km) northeast of Cleveland. Ashtabula is a major port, receiving iron ore and shipping coal, and also is a trading center for the Lake Erie resort area. Its industries manufacture automobile forgings, bodies, and seat covers; truck and tractor brakes; electric motors; farm and garden tools; rubber and rubber foam products; corrugated boxes; dresses and sweaters; leather goods; and a variety of chemicals.

The city is the seat of the Ashtabula Center of Kent State University. Among its other cultural facilities are a playhouse supported by volunteers and a fine arts center.

Ashtabula's name, which means "river of many fish," is of Indian origin. The first white settlers, sent out by the Connecticut Land Company in 1803, brought with them New England traditions in architecture, religion, and government. The community was incorporated in 1831. In the 1850's it became a key terminus on the Underground Railroad, along which fugitive slaves were smuggled to freedom.

Ashtabula received its city charter in 1891. Since 1916 it has had a council-manager form of government, and since 1941 the city manager has been elected. Population: 24,313.

ASHTON, ash′tən, **Sir Frederick William Mallandaine** (1906–   ), English dancer and choreographer, whose romantic narrative ballets have become part of the repertories of most major ballet companies. Born in Guayaquil, Ecuador, on Sept. 17, 1906, he studied ballet in England with Léonide Massine and others. By 1926 he had staged his first ballet, *The Tragedy of Fashion*, with the Marie Rambert Dancers (later the Ballet Club). In 1935 he joined the Vic-Wells Ballet (later Sadler's Wells), for which he created such ballets as *Les Rendezvous* (1933, as guest choreographer), *Apparitions* (1936), *Les*

Sir Frederick Ashton
DUNGAN MELVIN
FROM BLACK STAR

Patineurs (1937), and *The Wedding Bouquet* (1937). He became a leading dancer and principal choreographer of this group. When Sadler's Wells received the title of Royal Ballet in 1957, Ashton became associate artistic director. He was selected to succeed Ninette de Valois as artistic director in 1964. He had been knighted in 1962.

Ashton's more than 70 ballets, while often romantic in locale or in their view of human relationships, range widely in subject matter. Comparatively few are abstract or plotless. What makes them unique is their elegance of phrasing, refinement of detail, and musical awareness. Among Ashton's evening-long ballets are *Cinderella* (1948), *Sylvia* (1952), *Romeo and Juliet* (1955), *Ondine* (1958), and *La Fille Mal Gardée* (1960).

DORIS HERING, *"Dance Magazine"*

ASHTORETH. See ASTARTE.

ASHUR, ä'shoor, was the chief god of the ancient Assyrians. The name is more correctly spelled *Asshur*, which is closer to the original form *Anshur*. In later times the name of the god Ashur was again written with the original *n* as *Anshar*, which by then had a cosmic significance, perhaps "totality of heaven."

Ashur's symbol was the winged solar disk, and in view of the history of this symbol among the Egyptians and Hittites it is reasonable to suppose that he was properly a sun god. His cult was identified with loyalty to Assyria. He is depicted as warlike and merciless, leading his nation—particularly its kings—in battle and exacting vengeance on its enemies. His worship continued in Assyria proper until the third century A.D., long after the empire's fall.

Although Ashur may have had an independent origin, he became identified with Bel-Marduk, the chief god of Babylonia, probably for political reasons, and took the latter's place as victor over the primordial dragon of chaos in the Assyrian myth of creation. To a similar origin may also be traced such cultic appellations for Ashur as "the great mountain," applied originally to Enlil, the head of the Sumerian pantheon.

WILLIAM F. ALBRIGHT, *Johns Hopkins University*

ASHUR, ä'shoor, was the first capital of ancient Assyria. It was probably named for the chief Assyrian god Ashur, whose temple was the most prominent building in the city. Assyriologists generally prefer the more correct *Asshur* for both the capital and the deity.

The city was situated on the west bank of the Tigris River at the site of modern Qalat Sharqat, Iraq, about two thirds of the way north from modern Baghdad to the southern foothills of the Armenian mountains. It was founded early in the 2000's B.C. and continued to be occupied with little interruption until its destruction by the Medes in 614 B.C. The original settlers appear to have been Sumerian, with a characteristically Sumerian art. Neither the name nor the site seems to have been known in Biblical and Graeco-Roman tradition, perhaps because Ashur ceased to be the political capital of Assyria after the early 800's B.C. though it retained its religious prestige until its destruction. There was a small town on the site in later times, and inscriptions prove that the old Assyrian divinities were still worshiped there in the 200's A.D.

The English traveler Claudius James Rich visited Qalat Sharqat in 1821 but without knowing its ancient name. Excavations were begun there by the British under Austen Henry Layard in 1847. Between 1903 and 1913 the Germans excavated there under Walter Andrae. Assyrian tablets found at the site give detailed descriptions of the city gates and temples, which have been identified in part by the excavators.

WILLIAM F. ALBRIGHT, *Johns Hopkins University*

ASHURBANIPAL, ä-shoor-bä'nē-päl, was king of Assyria in the 7th century B.C. His name is also spelled *Assurbanipal* or *Asurbanipal;* he was known to the Hebrews as *Asnapper,* to the Greeks as *Sardanapallos,* and to the Romans as *Sardanapalus.* He was the last great Assyrian ruler, a redoubtable warrior, and a notable patron of learning. In Ashurbanipal's reign, Assyria attained its highest level in art, architecture, literature, and science.

The son of Esarhaddon, Ashurbanipal ascended the throne in 668 B.C. The first war of his reign—for he lived in a time of troubles—concerned Egypt, which his father had conquered but which had revolted in 669. Ashurbanipal regained control of Egypt in 667, only to lose it to Taharqa of Ethiopia, whom Esarhaddon had removed from the Egyptian throne, replacing him with a system of native viceroys subject to Assyria. Ashurbanipal led a punitive expedition into Egypt, recaptured Memphis and Thebes, and in 664 installed Psamtik as regent. Psamtik subsequently made himself pharaoh. Ashurbanipal, engaged elsewhere, accepted this coup d'état, abandoning control of the Nile Valley in 654 because it was too costly in manpower. The two sovereigns later concluded an alliance.

After his return from Egypt in 664, Ashurbanipal reconquered several Phoenician cities that had defected in his absence. A number of states in Asia Minor then also acknowledged his suzerainty. Earlier, in 667, the Elamites had invaded Babylonia, where Ashurbanipal's brother Shamash-shum-ukin reigned (668–648). It required a series of wars to subdue the Elamites, but by 639 their kingdom had been absorbed by Assyria. Meanwhile, Shamash-shum-ukin concocted a grand conspiracy of Assyria's chief client kings and allies in the Middle East to overthrow Assyrian rule, but Ashurbanipal reasserted his power by a series of victories between 648 and 639.

Ashurbanipal's active career is difficult to follow after 639, when Assyrian records of his reign end, but it seems that he repulsed the Cimmerians about 637, and in 639 celebrated a magnificent triumph at Nineveh, his capital. Constant warfare had so weakened his empire, however, that his sons Ashur-etil-ilani and Sin-shar-ishkun, who successively succeeded him within four years, could not preserve their inheritance. Finally, in 612, a coalition of Babylonians, Medes, and Scythians conquered Nineveh, pillaged the empire and enslaved the people.

P.R. COLEMAN-NORTON, *Princeton University*

ASHURNASIRPAL, ä-shoor-nä'zir-päl, was the name of two Assyrian kings. The name is also spelled *Assurnasirpal* or *Asurnasirpal.* Ashurnasirpal II or III (reigned 883–859 B.C.) was the greater of the two. He extended the empire to the north, east, and west. With captives and tribute he rebuilt Calah (Kalakh) and erected luxurious palaces. He was succeeded by his son Shalmaneser III.

ASIA

CONTENTS

ASIA, ā′zhə, is the largest of the seven continents, covering (with outlying islands) a total land area estimated at 17,150,000 square miles (44,418,000 sq km) and containing a population estimated in 1966 at 1,890 million. Its vast expanse, roughly rectangular in shape, stretches from its mountain and sea boundaries with Europe and Africa eastward to the Pacific; and from the Arctic shores of Siberia and the Soviet Far East southward to tropical lands washed by the Indian Ocean.

Apparently none of the numerous peoples who have inhabited the huge land mass of Asia since the dawn of history ever devised a name for the entire area. The ancient Greeks, however, had a word for it; they used "Asia" in a general sense to refer to the various lands lying to the east of their homeland. Indefinite in scope and elastic in meaning, the name has been gradually extended to embrace the vast territory between the eastern Mediterranean and the western Pacific. The term "Asia" is thus rooted in a Western perspective of the continent.

Actually, the term is of limited usefulness. For centuries it adequately served the purposes of cartographers, geographers, and travelers. In the 20th century the idea of "Asia" has been manipulated by philosophers, geopoliticians, and littérateurs. But implying a unity that has rarely if ever existed, the term is of marginal worth to historians, social scientists, and scholarly students of lands, peoples, and cultures. Since the continent is preeminently characterized by numerous unique and complex civilizations and cultures, it is doubtless misleading to speak of an "Asian mind," "Asian values," "Asian psychology," and "Asian leaders." Differing in many fundamental ways among themselves, millions of Asians have more in common with the heirs of Western civilization than with their fellow inhabitants of the continent. Such terms as "Asia" and "Asian" should accordingly be employed discriminately. (The designation "Asiatic," with its nuances of barbarism and colonialism, is considered offensive by many Asians and is best avoided.)

Various other terms have been used as synonyms for Asia. Such nomenclature, coined by Europeans and Americans, has been designed to pose the cultural contrast between Asia, on the one hand, and the "West" or "Western civilization" on the other. The most commonly encountered phrases of this kind are "East and West" and "Orient and Occident." These expressions, being geographically imprecise and intellectually vague, are useful only for literary and popular purposes. The same may be said of the catchall phrase "the non-Western world," which includes areas other than Asia.

In addition to terms applied to all of Asia, there are names designating greater or lesser portions of the continent. The "Far East" is a rubric of indeterminate dimensions that has been widely employed to include many or all of the lands from China and Japan to India and Pakistan. Coming into vogue in the 16th and 17th centuries, when the fabled wealth of the Indies was for Portuguese merchant-explorers and their European successors literally far to the east, the term has remained intellectually fashionable until modern times. But to other Westerners who did not approach Asia by sailing around the Cape of Good Hope and across the Indian Ocean the term "Far East" was more convenient than accurate. For Spanish conquistadores and traders, who made their way across the Pacific from ports on the west coast of the Americas, as well as for many Americans of the 19th and early 20th centuries, "Far West" might well have been a more appropriate expression. With the unprecedented revolution in the technology of transportation and communications following World War II, the term "Far East" has lost much of its historical meaning and is less commonly resorted to by scholars and writers. And since the phrase embodies memories of the age of Western imperialism, many Asian peoples frown on its usage.

In a somewhat similar category to "Far East" are the expressions "Near East" and "Middle East." Their origins as well as the differences in their meanings are not entirely clear. The older term "Near East," which was applied to southwestern Asia and, at times, to the Balkan states, has been superseded in part by "Middle East" (q.v.), which became popular during World War II. Used loosely like other similar expressions, the term "Middle East" is ordinarily applied to the lands of Southwest Asia, extending

eastward from Turkey through Iran and southward into Arabia, as well as to Turkey in Europe, the United Arab Republic, and the Sudan, although other areas in the Balkans, North Africa, and South Asia have sometimes been included.

Other expressions, such as the "Levant" (the lands of the eastern Mediterranean), "Further India" (Southeast Asia), and "Central Asia" (Tibet, the Sinkiang-Uigur Autonomous Region of China, and portions of Mongolia and south central Siberia) also appear in scholarly and popular literature and speech. They have little geographical precision. Since World War II these terms, together with the synonyms for Asia in whole or in part, have gradually been replaced by more exact phraseology.

Cultural Regions. A useful standard for the classification of regions is offered by culture (in the anthropological sense), although it should be noted that in Asia, as elsewhere, cultural subdivisions are at times more meaningful than broad and general categories. Moreover, the configurations of culture do not always coincide with the distribution of races and languages. Despite these limitations, culture does furnish a convenient method for the definition of regions. In this series of articles data are generally organized according to the following scheme and terminology: (1) Southwest Asia, (2) South Asia, (3) Southeast Asia, (4) East Asia, (5) North Asia, and (6) Inner Asia.

Southwest Asia includes the lands to the south of the Union of Soviet Socialist Republics (European and Asian) extending as far as the Indian Ocean. Bounded on the west by the Mediterranean Sea, the region reaches to the frontiers of Afghanistan in the east. The inhabitants of the area are racially Caucasian, but many different languages are spoken. The commonest cultural denominator is Islam, although appreciably large communities of Jews and Christians exist.

South Asia denotes the region centering in the huge subcontinent of India. It includes not only the republics of India and Pakistan, but also Afghanistan to the northwest, the Himalayan states of Nepal, Sikkim, and Bhutan to the north, and the offshore island of Ceylon to the south. Although Buddhism and Islam have been and

still are vital cultural forces in the area, the civilization developed under Hinduism has enjoyed paramount influence.

Southeast Asia (q.v.), mainland and island, extends from the southern borders of China to the islands of the Southwest Pacific and from Burma in the west to the Philippines in the east. In this region, characterized above all by religious, racial, and linguistic pluralism, a special cultural classification must be employed. An overridingly important influence in the lives of

---

INFORMATION HIGHLIGHTS

Population (1965 estimate): 1,890,000,000 (57.5 percent of the world's population).

Land area (1965 estimate): 17,150,000 sq mi, or 44,418,000 sq km (33 percent of the world's land area).

Northernmost mainland point: Cape Chelyuskin, USSR.

Southernmost mainland point: Tanjong Piai, Malaysia.

Easternmost mainland point: Cape Dezhnev, USSR.

Westernmost mainland point: Cape Baba, Turkey.

Highest point: Everest, 29,028 feet (8,848 meters).

Lowest point: Dead Sea—surface: 1,292 feet (394 meters) below sea level; sea floor: about 2,590 feet (about 790 meters) below sea level.

Major mountain systems: Altai, Elburz, Himalaya, Hindu Kush, Karakorum, Kunlun, Pamirs, Taurus, Tien Shan, Urals.

Major rivers: Amu Darya, Brahmaputra, Chao Phraya, Euphrates, Ganges, Hwang Ho, Indus, Irrawaddy, Lena, Mekong, Ob, Salween, Syr Darya, Tigris, Yangtze, Yenisei.

Major lakes: Aral Sea, Baikal, Balkhash, Caspian Sea, Khanka, Koko Nor, Tonle Sap, Urmia, Van.

Major deserts: Dasht-i-Lut, Dasht-i-Kavir, Gobi, Karakum, Kyzylkum, Muyunkum, Nafud, Negev, Rub al-Khali, Syrian Desert, Takla Makan, Thar or Indian Desert.

most people has been the monsoon cycle, which has made possible the widespread practice of wet, or paddy-field, cultivation of rice.

East Asia embraces China, Japan, Korea, and the offshore islands of Taiwan (Formosa) and the Ryukyus. Although distinct ways of life have evolved in each of these areas and marked cultural subdivisions prevail, particularly in China, the entire region has been overshadowed by Chinese civilization based on Confucianism.

North Asia signifies the vast sweep of territory ranging from the Ural Mountains in the west to the North Pacific in the east, and from the Arctic Ocean in the north to the steppes and deserts of southern Siberia. Frequently referred to as Soviet Asia, it also includes the islands of Sakhalin and the Kurils, north of Japan. Culturally a backwater region, it has been drawn into civilized life only during the past few centuries.

POLITICAL DIVISIONS OF ASIA

Political division	Area (sq mi)[1]	Population: mid-1969 estimate	Capital
Afghanistan.........	253,861	16,516,000	Kabul
Bahrain.............	231	207,000	Manamah
Bhutan..............	18,000	770,000	Thimbu
Brunei..............	2,226	116,000	Bandar Seri Begawan
Burma..............	261,789	26,980,000	Rangoon
Cambodia (Khmer Rep.)	69,898	6,701,000	Phnom Penh
Ceylon.............	25,332	12,240,000	Colombo
China, People's Rep. of	3,691,500	740,000,000	Peking
China, Rep. of (Taiwan)[2]........	13,885	13,800,000	Taipei
Cyprus.............	3,572	630,000	Nicosia
Egypt (Asian portion: Sinai)[3]............	...	130,000	...
Gaza Strip[4].........	146	356,000	...
Hong Kong..........	398	3,990,000	Victoria
India[5]..............1,261,811		536,984,000	New Delhi
Indonesia...........	735,268	116,000,000	Djakarta
Iran................	636,363	27,892,000	Teheran
Iraq................	168,040	9,350,000	Baghdad
Israel[6].............	8,023	2,822,000	Jerusalem
Japan[7].............	143,659	103,294,000	Tokyo
Jordan[8].............	37,737	2,217,000	Amman
Korea, North[9].......	46,540	13,300,000	Pyongyang
Korea, Rep. of[9]......	38,022	31,139,000	Seoul
Kuwait..............	6,000	570,000	Kuwait
Laos...............	91,429	2,893,000	Vientiane, Luang Prabang
Lebanon............	4,015	2,817,000	Beirut
Macao..............	6	260,000	Macao
Malaysia............	128,570	10,581,000	Kuala Lumpur
Maldives............	115	108,000	Male
Mongolian People's Rep..............	600,000	1,240,000	Ulan Bator
Nepal..............	54,362	10,845,000	Kathmandu
Oman...............	82,000	565,000	Muscat
Pakistan[10]...........	365,037	111,830,000	Islamabad
Philippines..........	115,601	37,158,000	Quezon City
Portuguese Timor.....	5,830	590,000	Dili
Qatar..............	4,000	100,000	Doha
Saudi Arabia........	865,000	7,200,000	Riyadh, Jidda
Sikkim.............	2,745	191,000	Gangtok
Singapore...........	225	2,017,000	Singapore
Syria[8].............	71,665	5,866,000	Damascus
Thailand............	198,456	34,758,000	Bangkok
Trucial States........	30,000	185,000	...
Turkey (Asian portion).	287,117	31,408,000	Ankara
USSR (Asian portion)..6,499,000		58,963,000	...
Vietnam, North.......	61,293	21,340,000	Hanoi
Vietnam, South.......	66,263	17,867,000	Saigon
Yemen, People's Democratic Rep.....	100,000	1,220,000	Madinat al-Shaab
Yemen Arab Rep.....	75,000	5,000,000	Sana

[1] To convert square miles to square kilometers, multiply by 2.59.
[2] Population excludes Quemoy and Matsu islands and armed forces.
[3] Population in 1966. [4] Population in September 1967. [5] Including Jammu and Kashmir, the final status of which has not yet been determined. [6] Not including territory occupied during 1967 war. [7] Including Ryukyu Islands. [8] Including territory occupied by Israel in 1967 war. [9] Not including demilitarized zone of 487 square miles. [10] Not including Baltistan, Gilgit, and Jammu and Kashmir.

ASIA'S GEOGRAPHICAL BOUNDARIES AND ISLANDS

BOUNDARIES

Northern: Arctic Ocean, including Kara Sea, Laptev Sea, East Siberian Sea, Chukchi Sea.
Eastern: Bering Strait; Pacific Ocean, including Bering Sea, Sea of Okhotsk, Sea of Japan, Yellow Sea, East China Sea, South China Sea.
Southern: Indian Ocean, including Bay of Bengal, Arabian Sea.
Southwestern: Gulf of Aden; Red Sea; Suez Canal.
Western: Mediterranean Sea, including Aegean Sea; Dardanelles, Sea of Marmara, Bosporus; Black Sea; Caucasus Mountains; Caspian Sea; Ural River; Ural Mountains.

PRINCIPAL OUTLYING ISLANDS

Arctic Ocean: Severnaya Zemlya, New Siberian Islands, Wrangel Island.
Pacific Ocean: Komandorskiye Ostrova, Shantarskiye Ostrova, Sakhalin, Kuril Islands, the four main islands of Japan, Bonin Islands, Ryukyu Islands, Taiwan, Hainan, Philippine Islands, the islands of Indonesia (including West Irian).
Indian Ocean: Andaman Islands, Nicobar Islands, Ceylon, Maldive Islands, Laccadive Islands, Socotra.
Mediterranean Sea: Cyprus.

Inner Asia (sometimes called Central Asia) is a somewhat imprecise region comprising the western borderlands of China, especially the areas commonly known as Tibet, Chinese Turkestan (now the Sinkiang-Uigur Autonomous Region), Mongolia, and southeastern Siberia. Historically, this strategic region has been politically fluid and, despite its relatively sparse population, culturally complex. For hundreds of years, Lamaistic Buddhism and Islam have pervaded the local cultures.

Political Divisions. Even by reference to official sources it is not always possible to determine exactly the area and population of many Asian countries. Political frontiers have never been carefully drawn in some regions, with the result that from time to time, border controversies disturb relations between neighboring lands. Furthermore, some political areas have never been surveyed thoroughly and scientifically. It should therefore be understood that the statistics commonly cited for the areas of one or another of the countries of Asia, often varying by thousands of square miles, are no more than reasonable estimates.

What is true of area statistics is equally pertinent in the case of population figures. With several notable exceptions, few Asian governments have developed completely reliable systems for the compilation and analysis of statistics and for the conduct of accurate censuses.

HYMAN KUBLIN
The City University of New York

Bibliography

Berger, Morroe, *The Arab World Today* (New York 1962).
Cady, John F., *Southeast Asia: Its Historical Development* (New York 1964).
Cressey, George B., *Asia's Lands and Peoples*, 3d ed. (New York 1963).
Fisher, Charles A., *Southeast Asia* (New York 1964).
Fisher, Sydney N., *The Middle East: A History* (New York 1959).
Grousset, René, *The Civilizations of the East*, tr. from French by Catherine A. Phillips, 4 vols. (New York 1931–34).
Latourette, Kenneth S., *A Short History of the Far East*, 4th ed. (New York 1964).
Northrop, Filmer S.C., *The Meeting of East and West* (New York 1946).
Polo, Marco, *Travels of Marco Polo*, reprint (New York 1961).
Ward, Barbara, *The Interplay of East and West* (New York 1957).
See also special bibliographies following individual sections.

IN MONGOLIA, north of the Gobi, a herder grazes his sheep on the grassland near the city of Ulan Bator.

1. Geographical Features

Tradition separates Asia and Europe by an arbitrary line beginning in the Arctic Sea and following the Ural Mountains, the Ural River, and the Caspian Sea to the Greater Caucasus. From there it continues along a series of natural breaks in the Black Sea, the Bosporus, the Sea of Marmara, and the Dardanelles to the Aegean and Mediterranean seas. The separation of Asia and Africa is also partly arbitrary. While man has provided final cleavage by means of the Suez Canal, nature has provided the Red Sea passage to the Indian Ocean. Otherwise, Asia is rather naturally bounded by the Arctic Ocean on the north, the Pacific Ocean on the east, and the Indian Ocean on the south. On the southeast, however, the boundary between Indonesia and the islands of Melanesia is unclear, and scientists have therefore established lines demarcating flora and fauna (for example, Wallace's and Weber's lines). A similarly tenuous division exists farther north between Asia and Micronesia as well as Melanesia. In all, Asia is a giant rectangle, extending from 26° 4′ east longitude at Cape Baba, Turkey, to 169° 40′ west longitude at Bering Strait, and from 1° 16′ north latitude near Singapore to 77° 41′ north latitude at Cape Chelyuskin, Siberia.

It must not be assumed, however, that this vast and complex region is unified physically, ethnically, or culturally. In fact, diversity is among the few unassailable generalizations that can be stated about Asia. An attempt will therefore be made to divide Asia's 17,150,000 square miles (33 percent of the earth's land surface) and 1,890 million people (1966 estimate; 57.5 percent of the world's population) into physical and cultural segments that possess some aspects of similarity.

Certain key geographical features offer clues to man's history and presence in Asia. Basic are the implications of comparative size and position (latitude and longitude), both of which strongly influence the patterns of weather and climate and, in turn, those of soils and vegetation. Perhaps of equal importance is the general arrangement of landforms, especially the highlands that shield some areas from moisture-laden winds yet expose others, producing the drainage systems that have become vital to human development. Man has naturally tended to congregate where his livelihood has been simplest in relation to his technological development. The accompanying map of the population distribution of Asia demonstrates the combinations of physical influences relatively favorable for man, although the picture may change as he progressively masters his environment.

Topography. A relief diagram of Asia shows a complex east-west mountain core centered on the Pamir Plateau northwest of the Indian subcontinent. Stretching eastward across Eurasia (Europe and Asia) from the Atlantic to the Pacific in a series of parallel arcs, the mountains are punctuated by knots, especially in the west. Asia is said to be unique among the continents in having a mountainous heart. Flanking these heights on the north are the world's broadest flatlands, consisting either of virtually featureless plains, as in the west, or of higher land toward the east. Portions of this area, such as Mongolia and Tibet, are partly or entirely enclosed by giant mountain arms radiating from the Pamir. Outlying areas to the southwest, south, southeast, and east often defy these generalizations, being either archipelagic with unique qualities or simply ramifications of the features of the interior. In general, the landmass of Asia resembles a vast amphitheater, with highlands extending across the south central to northeastern portions, and with the northwestern to central portions sloping gently and almost uninterruptedly toward the Arctic. On the other hand, the climate of the sea-facing appendages, from the Arabian Peninsula in the southwest through South and Southeast Asia to the east coast and Siberia, exhibits few similarities.

Although Asia's highlands, being generally youthful, are both lofty and unstable, there are important exceptions, particularly in the Precambrian shields underlying parts of Arabia, India, Siberia, and China. It has been conjectured that these shields, now widely dispersed, were formerly contiguous and then drifted apart. The land between them has been subjected to pressures that have at times caused partial inundation by the surrounding seas or warping and buckling. The present configuration is typically ephemeral. The youngest formations are the high mountains and plateaus, capped by the Himalaya and Tibet. These highlands are thought to have been elevated in relatively recent times, during the Tertiary period, partially from the floors of an earlier sea called Tethys. Although Tertiary earth movement erased Tethys, residual bodies of water, such as the Caspian and Aral seas, Lake Balkhash, and the Black Sea, remain as evidence of the former sea. Meanwhile, parallel tectonic activity created smaller mountain complexes, as in the northeast, or caused gigantic lava flows, as may be seen in the volcanic overlays of the stable Deccan Plateau of India.

INDONESIAN RICE FIELDS, like these on Java, supply the staple food for most Southeast Asians.

Man has naturally preferred level land for settlement. Nevertheless, although much of Asia is level, drought and cold seriously limit vast areas, especially in the interior, as potential habitats. The inhospitableness of a large part of Asia is due mainly to the nature of the landforms and their arrangement and to the pattern of prevailing winds and pressures. Unlike the highlands of North America, those of Asia extend from east to west, blocking most of the interior from the beneficent influence of the warm offshore waters to the south and east, which do moderate the climates of the lands situated between the mountains and the sea. Permanent settlement is therefore found mostly in the flatter parts of this peripheral Asian crescent, from Iraq through the Indian subcontinent to the Sino-Japanese domain, but rarely far from the rivers and seas. The interior behind the mountain barrier has been left to sparse occupancy, usually by nomadic or semi-nomadic peoples. Notwithstanding some remarkable adaptation, especially by the Russians, the inhabitants of this area have failed to match the agricultural productivity and consequent population growth of the peripheral civilizations.

THE YANGTZE GORGES in China are famed for their scenic beauty, but are treacherous to navigate.

WAAGENAAR, FROM PIX

Rivers and Coastal Waters. Patterns of drainage in Asia have been fashioned by the highlands. In the north the drainage systems generally extend from the mountains of the south, center, and northeast toward the Arctic. In dry Inner (Central) Asia, from the Caspian to the Pamir and from the Tarim Basin eastward, however, there are about 5 million square miles of interior drainage where no river reaches the open sea. Throughout the Asian crescent the rivers originating in the high interior (especially in Tibet) radiate to the south, southeast, and east. Their courses are fashioned by the structure of the mountain chains, which droop to the southeast from the central mountain core but which in the northeast are unaligned. Between these highlands the runoff has shaped the floodplains and formed the deltas housing the major riparian societies of what has aptly been called monsoon Asia. China, India, Pakistan, and Japan boast the largest populations among these societies and are dominant in modern politics, but the smaller nations have contributed substantially to history and to contemporary affairs.

In the north, much of the Arctic Ocean is frozen almost all year, and a scarcity of coastal indentations has further limited the capacity of the region for trade and settlement. Nevertheless, the Soviet government has vigorously exploited these waters, establishing a seasonal northern sea route from Europe to the North Pacific. This seemingly barren land therefore contains a surprising number of settlements along the coast and, especially, along the navigable rivers. In general, Asia's coastal outline varies between the relative simplicity of Africa's and the complexity and usefulness of Europe's. With significant local exceptions, the northern and southwestern coasts are less useful than the southern, southeastern, and eastern. Moreover, inland waterways are poorly developed. The Yangtze River in China is the only route by which ocean-going vessels can penetrate the continent to an appreciable extent throughout the year. Nowhere else do the rivers and lakes of Asia rival those of Europe and North America in navigability.

The temperature and salinity of offshore waters are also vital to man in providing fishing grounds and, in the case of the Japanese, places where edible marine plants can be nurtured. Great banks for commercial fishing are usually found where warm and cold currents meet. In Asia, as in North America, these conditions are found ideally in the northeast. Off Japan, where the north-flowing Japan Current (Kuroshio) meets the cold countercurrent from Kamchatka, are some of the richest fishing banks in the world.

Climate. In general, Asia's climate is markedly continental, although the greatest population clusters have emerged where the continental influences are weakest. A continental climate implies wide seasonal and daily temperature ranges and limited precipitation. For most of Asia these conditions are general. Because of the enormous size of the landmass and the peculiar arrangement of its features, its climate is the most extreme in the world. Northeastern Siberia, for example, is the world's cold pole. January temperatures there average −59° F (−50.6° C), while the July temperature is about 60° F (15.6° C). The prevalence of a continental climate also means strong seasonal reversal of atmospheric pressures. The great mass of polar air of the Asian winter is accompanied by high pressure, which, being centered

ZAHLE, a small resort town in the Lebanon Mountains, provides a cool retreat from the heat of the coastal plain.

in the northeast, influences all but a few peripheral parts of the continent. Winter winds are generally offshore, dry, and cool. In summer these conditions are reversed. A low-pressure center in South Asia then replaces the winter high, and the landmass is heated, with the result that the prevailing winds become onshore, bringing moisture to the peripheral lands of the south and east between the mountains and the seas. This condition of seasonal wind reversal, known as the monsoon, joins the factor of continentality as a salient feature of Asian climate. In South Asia the monsoon cycle is almost ideally typical, probably because the mountainous periphery of the region confines and intensifies the effect. Southeast and East Asia, though less typical, also fall within the system.

The general pattern of yearly precipitation clearly demonstrates the effect of the monsoon. In winter the landmass as a whole receives less than one inch of rain. Exceptions are areas in the west, especially where the prevailing westerly winds bring moisture from the Atlantic and Mediterranean, and regions in the east where outgoing continental winds, warmed and humidified as they cross the open sea, are induced to release their moisture as they again encounter high land. The latter situation is characteristic of the area from Kamchatka through Japan and South Korea, proverbial in places for heavy snows, to south China, Vietnam, and Malaysia, including the oceanic Philippines and equatorial Indonesia. Southeastern India and Ceylon are also exceptions, since they interrupt the northeast continental winds that are warmed and humidified over the Bay of Bengal.

In summer, precipitation is ample except in the central plateaus and in the central and southwestern lowlands. The east and, especially, the south receive the heaviest accumulations. So much rain falls in some areas, notably along the range of the Western Ghats in peninsular India and the hills north of the Bay of Bengal, that despite dry winters they are in yearly averages among the world's wettest places. The famous rice agriculture of South, Southeast, and East Asia is critically dependent on these summer rains, all life being attuned to their rhythm.

Within this general pattern there are countless variations. Deserts abound from the southwest to the northeastern interior. There may be little or no seasonal change, as in parts of Indonesia, or extreme change, as in Siberia, while places like India have three seasons: a cool, dry winter, an intensely hot, dry spring, and a warm, humid summer. In much of East Asia the climate is similar to that of the eastern United States from Maine to Florida, although China is sharply divided by lateral mountains into a wet, temperate south and a dry, cool north.

Cyclonic storms, similar in character to but weaker than those of eastern North America and western Europe, are also influential in peripheral Asia, bringing winter moisture to parts of the extreme west as well as to south China, Korea, and Japan. In fall and winter, typhoons are common in an area extending from the Philippines in a broad arc from northwest to northeast. They exhibit even more regularity and violence than the hurricanes of eastern North America.

The climatic effect of mountains is especially noteworthy in Asia. In season the high mountains, while bathed in moisture on their windward slopes, serve as barriers to keep vast leeward areas drought-ridden. Moreover, because of the peculiar structure of the continent, where broad areas are elevated but flat, the climate may be of any variety locally and, depending on elevation, range from subtropical to subarctic.

See also CLIMATE—*Continental and Oceanic Climates;* MONSOONS; RAINFALL—*Distribution of the World's Rainfall* (Asia); TYPHOON.

Soils. In northern Soviet Asia soils are predominantly podzolic. Unless they are massively improved, they have limited agricultural potential. A zone of black earth (chernozem and similar soils) does, however, protrude deeply into Siberia from Europe, and it is mainly along this dwindling wedge that the Russians have settled and built lines of communication. The arid lands of the southwest and center, extending from the Arabian and Anatolian plateaus to Iran, Soviet Central Asia, and the Tarim and Dzungarian basins, and from the plateau of Mongolia eastward into China, have desert or semidesert soils. Their potential, though highly varied, is limited mainly by aridity. Apart from the modern exploitation of raw materials, in which man has chosen to disregard a hostile environment, occupancy of these dry lands has tended to be impermanent except in the areas that are near water sources.

ALFRED GREGORY, FROM PIX

THE HIMALAYA, highest mountains in the world, on whose southern slopes lie the trade routes to Tibet.

In several broad regions the soils have special qualities. The dry lands of northwestern China, for example, are noteworthy for their thick covering of windblown silt (loess); were it not for the aridity, its innate fertility might assure bountiful and continued production. There are also soils developed on basic volcanic ejecta, such as the thick, black, fertile soils (regur) of the Deccan Plateau and the volcanic soils of Java. Both help to support dense populations. Other important regions, among them Japan, have large areas of acidic volcanic soils, but these are generally low in potential despite their frequently remarkable supporting capacity, which has been developed by great effort.

The most productive soils of Asia consist of water-transported materials associated with the great river systems. Although they have often been overworked and depleted, intensive fertilization, crop rotation, and the natural refreshment of new alluvium have enabled them to support increasingly heavy populations. Rice, being a particularly nutritious grain, has been the chief product of alluvium. Wherever conditions have permitted, it has become a staple of the societies of the Asian crescent. Rice culture has been extended to higher latitudes, as in Japan, and to higher elevations, as in China, Japan, Java, and the Philippines. Where irrigated rice is the basic crop, populations have multiplied, and civilizations have tended to flower. Supplementing rice in alluvial lands during off-seasons and in places, such as north China or northwestern India, where aridity or cold have inhibited its growth, wheat and other grains as well as a rich variety of other food and commercial crops have been common. The exports of plantation agriculture have been derived from these soils, especially in the tropical south and southeast or wherever colonial economies were imposed.

Plants and Animals. The great flatlands of Soviet Asia present a classic example of the arrangement of vegetation in lateral zones. The most northerly of these zones, a mixture of Arctic meadow (tundra) and swamp, has generally paralleled the occurrence of the permanently frozen subsoil known as permafrost. Farther south, and usually associated with podzols, is an even broader zone of virgin coniferous forest called taiga. Although there are few species, they are so extensive as to constitute a major, though remote, natural resource. This zone gradually merges into more mixed forest and finally into cropland converted from the grasslands associated with the wedge of black earth. These northerly lands support a rich variety of fauna, including such large mammals as the bear, moose, and reindeer and such smaller varieties as the hare, lemming, and otter. Birds and insects are abundant, especially in summer.

Farther south, stretching across the vast arid interior from Arabia to China, the vegetation is xerophytic or drought-adapted, except in the many highlands of mixed forest, the limited barren sandy areas, and the oases. Although the fauna is not especially noteworthy, such domesticated animals as the horse, sheep, and camel have been invaluable to man in overcoming the hindrances of the environment.

The flora and fauna of monsoon Asia are extraordinary both in their variety and in their adaptation to human encroachment. Much of the vegetation is purely or partly tropical. Where moisture is minimal, as in northwestern India and Pakistan, there are savannas on which such large mammals as the tiger and the panther are present. But where rainfall is abundant, as in coastal India, East Pakistan, and Southeast Asia, tropical rain forest or its variants are found with appropriate fauna. The monkey, for example, is common from India to south China and Japan; large mammals, such as the Bengal tiger, are unusual. In the wetter parts of the monsoon forest there are exotic but widely dispersed varieties of tropical hardwood, including teak and ebony. Conditions favor the proliferation of small creatures, although it is here that the domesticated elephant is heavily used.

Elsewhere, in the highlands as well as at the higher latitudes of Japan, Korea, and Manchuria, the flora and fauna are similar to the mixed forest associations of North America and Europe. Local variations, such as the bamboo, are found farther north than in the Western Hemisphere. Regardless of environment, pests are omnipresent. Thus, throughout Asia man must cope with the rat, the crow, the flea, and the cockroach.

Natural Resources. Inaccessibility, caused by the limitations of environment and the vicissitudes of history, has delayed the discovery and exploitation of many of Asia's natural resources. For political reasons, too, their accurate whereabouts has often been obscured even after discovery. Generally, however, the resources of the continent are extremely rich.

Southwest Asia, especially the section near the Persian Gulf, is a leading supplier of petroleum, with much of the world's production and the major share of its known reserves. The remoteness of the area, however, has inhibited the exploitation of natural gas. Although some coal is mined in Iran and Turkey, and such materials as chromite in Turkey and potash in the Dead Sea area are exploited, the region as a whole is dominated by petroleum.

South Asia's major industrial resources are concentrated in India. Pakistan and Ceylon have specialized in agricultural products, particularly jute and tea (the production of natural graphite in Ceylon is an exception). With India's resources headed by rich supplies of iron and with good coal located nearby in the northeastern peninsula west of Calcutta, important heavy industries have developed in the vicinity. India also has export-

RICE FIELDS south of the Yangtze valley in Chekiang province, China, are well irrigated by the many rivers of the region.

able quantities of manganese, and there is some petroleum in Assam. In addition, varying amounts of other metallic and nonmetallic minerals exist. But although India has important resources, their exploitation, as is typical of monsoon Asia, has not been far advanced.

The production of such commodities as rubber, copra, fibers, hardwoods, and spices on the plantations of Southeast Asia is paralled by the exploitation of certain minerals, ranging from large-scale tin production in Malaya and coal and iron production in Indochina, Malaya and Indonesia, to a sizable output of bauxite, tungsten, copper, lead, zinc, and other materials throughout the region. Indonesia is especially noteworthy for its production of petroleum; there is also some petroleum production in Burma. In all, while Southeast Asia is potentially rich, its resources have been exploited largely for use outside the region. Its own industries are thus undeveloped, and its cities function for the most part as entrepôts.

Except for Manchuria, China's industrial base also suffers from late and inefficient exploitation. Widespread coal beds are the richest resource, especially in the middle Hwang Ho (Yellow River) region and in southern Manchuria, which has, additionally, iron ore and other basic substances. The latter area is well developed as a major industrial center. The Communist government has not only prospected vigorously for raw materials but has also developed and enlarged manufacturing elsewhere, notably in the middle Yangtze River and upper Hwang Ho valleys. The existence of large amounts of tungsten, tin, nickel, salt, bauxite, oil shales, and other substances has long been known, but these resources have been only partially exploited. In the early 1960's, claims were made of substantial petroleum reserves in the far west, and massive water power projects were under way, particularly in the Hwang and Yangtze river valleys.

For its size, Korea is rich in resources. Its deposits of coal, iron ore, and other materials, situated mostly in the north, have long been exploited. Under the Japanese, hydroelectric facilities were greatly improved. Taiwan (Formosa) has been similarly developed for the production of raw materials, especially coal and metals, while the Philippines are particularly rich in iron, chromite, and forest products.

Japan is a strong exception to the Asian rule of poor exploitation of resources, for its meager supplies have been worked to the point of depletion. Poor-quality coal is the chief item; there are also minimal amounts of copper, iron, and other metals as well as salt and sulfur. The conservation and use of hydroelectric and forest resources, however, have been highly developed. As one of the world's major industrial powers, Japan must import the bulk of its raw materials, the United States being a leading supplier. Industry has been accompanied by the growth and efficiency of transportation and communications. As a result, urbanization has developed on a scale unusual for Asia.

The Soviet Union possesses abundant supplies of such heavy industrial resources as coal, iron, and alloy materials in its Asian territories. Coal has been exploited chiefly in the Kuznetsk Basin, at the headwaters of the Ob and Yenisei river systems, and at Karaganda in Kazakhstan, northwest of Lake Balkhash. Iron ores are present in many areas, but the southern Urals are especially known for large-scale production. These resources have created important industries in both the Kuznetsk Basin and the Urals. While petroleum production has tended to shift from the Caucasus section of Asia to the middle Volga area of Europe, Caucasian oil and natural gas are still key exports. Perhaps the greatest Soviet Asian resource is the power potential of the major rivers falling from the mountain core to the northern lowlands. In the early 1960's, huge projects were in progress to harness this power and to create giant grid networks for its transmission throughout the Soviet Union.

See also sections on the land in articles on the various Asian countries; separate articles on major rivers, mountains, and other geographical features; COAL—4. *World Coal Resources;* CONTINENT; DESERT; FISHERIES—*World Harvest;* FORESTRY—*Forests of the World;* HYDROELECTRIC DEVELOPMENT—*World Hydroelectric Capacity and Potential;* IRON—9. *World Supplies* (Asia); MIDDLE EAST—1. *The Land;* WATERWAYS OF THE WORLD—*Asiatic Waterways.*

DAVID HENRY KORNHAUSER
University of Hawaii

Bibliography
Cole, John P., and German, Frank C., *A Geography of the U.S.S.R.* (London 1961).
Dobby, Ernest G.H., *Monsoon Asia* (Chicago 1961).
Freeman, Otis W., ed., *Geography of the Pacific* (New York 1951).
Ginsburg, Norton S., ed., *The Pattern of Asia* (Englewood Cliffs, N.J., 1958).
Ripley, Sidney Dillon, and the editors of *Life, The Land and Wildlife of Tropical Asia* (New York 1964).
Spencer, Joseph E., *Asia, East by South* (New York 1954).
Stamp, Lawrence D., *Asia* (part 4 of *Regional Geography*), 16th ed. (New York 1965).

ASIA'S POPULATION accounts for over half of the world's people. This scene is a marketplace in Bahri, India.

2. Population

As of 1966, Asia, with a total population estimated at 1,890 million, contained 57.5 percent of the population of the world. Between 1958 and 1963 its population had grown by an annual average of 1.8 percent. This high rate of growth was due to the intensive efforts of the major nations of the continent to modernize their economies and raise the levels of living of their peoples. Classified in what some population specialists call Demographic Group 3, most of the people of Asia were attempting through costly national economic plans to attain Group 2 status.

Group 3 nations have in common unusually high birth- and death rates, unusually low per capita national incomes, and unusually low per capita consumption of inanimate energy. In China and India, the two most populous nations of Asia, rapid economic progress, combined with successful campaigns to disseminate information about modern medical and sanitation techniques, has resulted in sharp declines in the death rates. These declines have in turn caused marked increases in the size of their populations, thus influencing strongly the population statistics for Asia as a whole. In these two nations, whose combined populations account for approximately two thirds of the people of the continent, birth- and death rates, national income, and levels of energy consumption are much closer to world averages than are those of most other Asian countries. Hence, China and India are much nearer to classification as Demographic Group 2 nations than most of their neighbors.

The few statistics available on the growth of the population of Asia since prehistoric times indicate that the degree of correlation between the stage of economic development of each nation, on the one hand, and the size, rate of growth, and age structure of its population, on the other, is very high. In nations in the primary stage of development, which corresponds roughly to Demographic Group 3, utilization of resources is generally limited to agriculture, fishing, lumbering, and mining. Since manual labor, supplemented by a meager use of draft animals, is the predominant form of energy, life is hard. Long hours and rigorous work, combined with poor facilities for health and sanitation, have resulted in high infant and general mortality rates. Life expectancies are short. At the same time, the economic need for children (particularly sons) to

work in the fields and the social need for sons to carry on the family name and traditions have kept birthrates high. Historically, the result has been low net annual rates of population growth, generally amounting to 1 percent or less. Such conditions have produced predominantly young populations.

Where Asian nations have undertaken modernization or industrialization programs, and where facilities for manufacturing, power, trade, transportation, communications, health, and sanitation have been developed to a high degree, national and personal incomes and levels of living have increased sharply. As a consequence, death rates have declined dramatically, and populations have "exploded." Japan, for example, entered this secondary stage of development, which corresponds roughly to Demographic Group 2, between 1870 and 1920. By the 1950's it had advanced to the tertiary stage of economic development, corresponding to Demographic Group 1.

In the tertiary stage of development (Group 1), occupations of the professional and service types are at least equal in importance to factory work as sources of income; ultimately they predominate. Urbanization, initiated in the secondary stage, has been completed, so that agriculture and similar occupations are of relatively minor economic and social importance. National and individual productivities have been increased either by lengthy, expensive, and distinctly superior education or by complex, expensive, and distinctly superior machinery or productive processes. Meanwhile, national and per capita incomes have risen, economic and social needs for children have been reduced, and the birthrate has declined nearly to the level of the death rate. The result is a low net rate of population increase. To an even greater extent than in the secondary stage, low infant and general mortality rates and longer life expectancies, attributable to improved health and sanitation facilities, produce an older population. It is toward such economic and demographic goals that most societies in Asia have been working.

Southwest Asia. Including nomadic tribes, for which few statistics are available, the population of Southwest Asia in the mid-1960's was estimated at between 85 million and 100 million. Of the total population, about one third was accounted for by the Asian portion of Turkey and one fourth by Iran, while the remainder comprised the 2,563,000 people of Israel and the

ASIA

TOPOGRAPHY

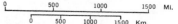

| 0 | 500 | 1000 | 1500 MI. |
| 0 | 500 | 1000 | 1500 Km. |

C. Dezhnev

NEW SIBERIAN IS.

SEVERNAYA ZEMLYA

Kara Sea

Laptev Sea

Taimyr Pen.

CENTRAL SIBERIAN PLATEAU

Lower Tunguska

Lena

Yenisei

Angara

L. Baikal

YABONOVY RA.

KOLYMA RA.

Kamchatka Pen.

Sea of Okhotsk

KURIL IS.

Sakhalin

Hokkaido

Amur

GREAT KHINGAN RA.

Sea of Japan

Honshu
Fuji 12,389

Shikoku

Kyushu

East China Sea

KYUKYU IS.

Taiwan

Hainan

Luzon

PHILIPPINE IS.

Mindanao

South China Sea

Celebes Sea

Borneo

Celebes

Timor

Java Sea

Sumatra

Java

SUNDA ISLANDS

Malay Pen.

Andaman Sea

G. of Siam

Indo-chinese Pen.

Mekong

Si

Red

Yangtze

Hwang

URAL MOUNTAINS

WEST SIBERIAN PLAIN

Ob

Irtish

ALTAI MTS.

Gobi

TIEN SHAN

Tarim

Taklamakan

KUNLUN

PLATEAU OF TIBET

HIMALAYA
Mt. Everest 29,028

Brahmaputra

Ganges

INDO-GANGETIC PLAIN

Indus

HINDU KUSH

Amu Darya

Syr Darya

L. Balkhash

Aral Sea

Caspian Sea

Ararat 16,945

PLATEAU OF ANATOLIA

Cyprus

Euphrates

Tigris

PLATEAU OF IRAN

Nefud

Arabian Peninsula

Rub' al Khali

Persian Gulf

G. of Oman

Arabian Sea

Socotra

LACCADIVE IS.

MALDIVE IS.

C. Comorin

Ceylon

Dondra Head

DECCAN PLATEAU

Godavari

WESTERN GHATS

EASTERN GHATS

Bay of Bengal

Yellow Sea

| Below Sea Level | 100 m. 328 ft. | 200 m. 656 ft. | 500 m. 1,640 ft. | 1,000 m. 3,281 ft. | 2,000 m. 6,562 ft. | 5,000 m. 16,404 ft. |

ASIA

POPULATION DISTRIBUTION

•......Cities with over 1,000,000
       inhabitants (including suburbs)

POPULATION DENSITY

under 1 PER SQ. KM.	under 2 PER SQ. MI.
1–10	2–25
10–25	25–65
25–50	65–130
50–100	130–260
100–200	260–520
over 200	over 520

ANNUAL RATE OF POPULATION INCREASE

1958-1964

PERCENT (%)

0-1	
1-2	
2-3	
3-4	
4-5	
Over 5	

U.S.=1.6%

Source: Statistical Office of the United Nations

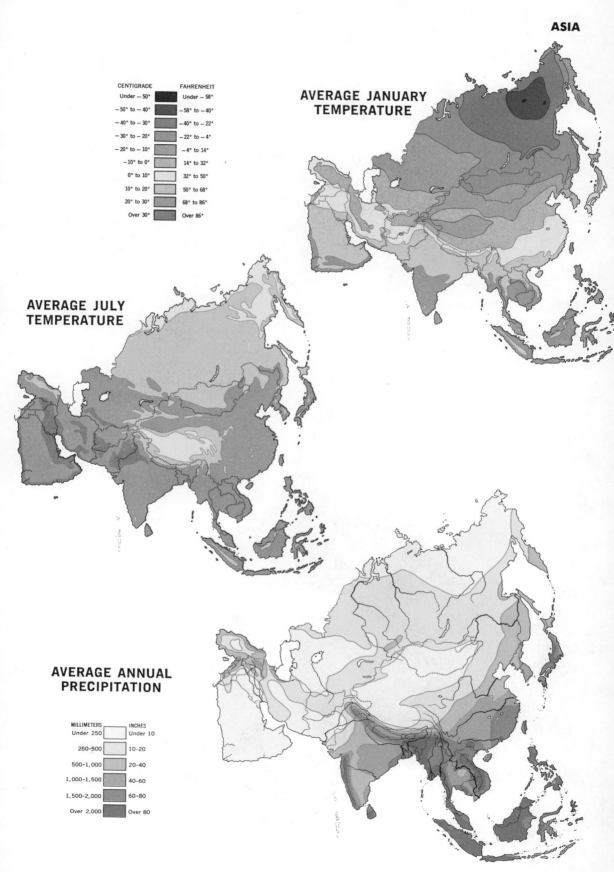

ASIA

AVERAGE JANUARY
TEMPERATURE

CENTIGRADE	FAHRENHEIT
Under − 50°	Under − 58°
− 50° to − 40°	− 58° to − 40°
− 40° to − 30°	− 40° to − 22°
− 30° to − 20°	− 22° to − 4°
− 20° to − 10°	− 4° to 14°
− 10° to 0°	14° to 32°
0° to 10°	32° to 50°
10° to 20°	50° to 68°
20° to 30°	68° to 86°
Over 30°	Over 86°

AVERAGE JULY
TEMPERATURE

AVERAGE ANNUAL
PRECIPITATION

MILLIMETERS	INCHES
Under 250	Under 10
250–500	10–20
500–1,000	20–40
1,000–1,500	40–60
1,500–2,000	60–80
Over 2,000	Over 80

ASIA

LAND TRANSPORTATION

Ankara • Sverdlovsk
Novosibirsk
Tselinograd • Irkutsk • Harbin • Vladivostok
Ulan Bator • Mukden • Tokyo
Baghdad • Teheran • Tashkent • Alma-Ata • Urumchi • Peking
Riyadh • Kabul • Lanchow • Chengchow • Shanghai
Rawalpindi • Chengtu • Wuhan • Taipei
Delhi • Chungking
Karachi • Lhasa • Hong Kong
Calcutta • Hanoi • Manila
Bombay • Rangoon
Hyderabad • Bangkok • Saigon
Madras
Singapore
Djakarta

Principal Railroads	———
Under Construction	- - - -
Connecting Roads	———
Under Construction	- - - -

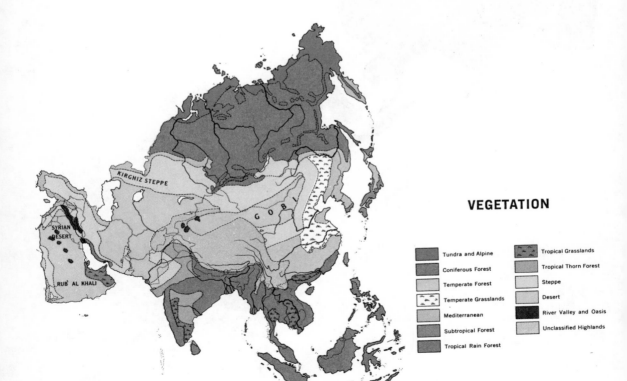

VEGETATION

KIRGHIZ STEPPE

SYRIAN DESERT

RUB AL KHALI

GOBI

▨ Tundra and Alpine		▨ Tropical Grasslands	
▨ Coniferous Forest		▨ Tropical Thorn Forest	
▨ Temperate Forest		▨ Steppe	
▨ Temperate Grasslands		▨ Desert	
▨ Mediterranean		■ River Valley and Oasis	
▨ Subtropical Forest		▨ Unclassified Highlands	
▨ Tropical Rain Forest			

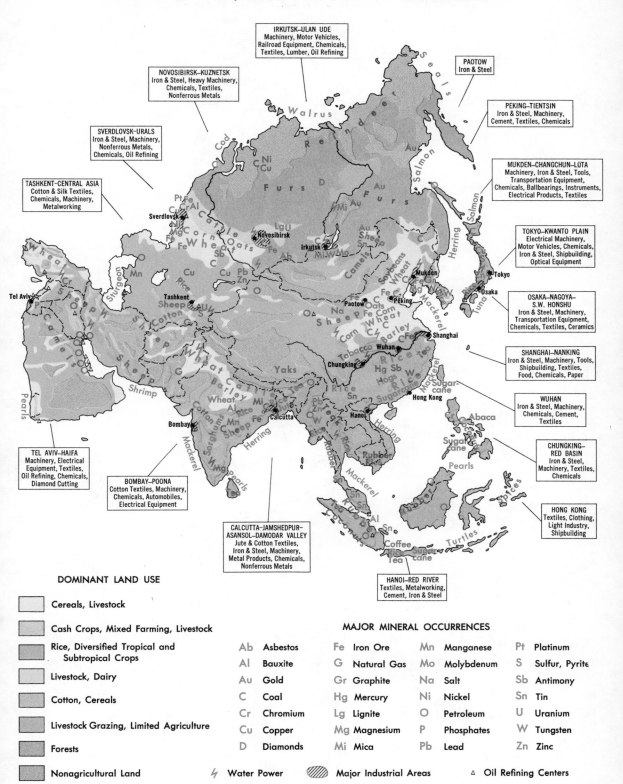

AGRICULTURE, INDUSTRY and RESOURCES

IRKUTSK–ULAN UDE
Machinery, Motor Vehicles,
Railroad Equipment, Chemicals,
Textiles, Lumber, Oil Refining

NOVOSIBIRSK–KUZNETSK
Iron & Steel, Heavy Machinery,
Chemicals, Textiles,
Nonferrous Metals

SVERDLOVSK–URALS
Iron & Steel, Machinery,
Nonferrous Metals,
Chemicals, Oil Refining

TASHKENT–CENTRAL ASIA
Cotton & Silk Textiles,
Chemicals, Machinery,
Metalworking

PAOTOW
Iron & Steel

PEKING–TIENTSIN
Iron & Steel, Machinery,
Cement, Textiles, Chemicals

MUKDEN–CHANGCHUN–LÜTA
Machinery, Iron & Steel, Tools,
Transportation Equipment,
Chemicals, Ballbearings, Instruments,
Electrical Products, Textiles

TOKYO–KWANTO PLAIN
Electrical Machinery,
Motor Vehicles, Chemicals,
Iron & Steel, Shipbuilding,
Optical Equipment

**OSAKA–NAGOYA–
S.W. HONSHU**
Iron & Steel, Machinery,
Transportation Equipment,
Chemicals, Textiles, Ceramics

SHANGHAI–NANKING
Iron & Steel, Machinery, Tools,
Shipbuilding, Textiles,
Food, Chemicals, Paper

WUHAN
Iron & Steel, Machinery,
Chemicals, Cement,
Textiles

**CHUNGKING–
RED BASIN**
Iron & Steel,
Machinery, Textiles,
Chemicals

HONG KONG
Textiles, Clothing,
Light Industry,
Shipbuilding

HANOI–RED RIVER
Textiles, Metalworking,
Cement, Iron & Steel

**CALCUTTA–JAMSHEDPUR–
ASANSOL–DAMODAR VALLEY**
Jute & Cotton Textiles,
Iron & Steel, Machinery,
Metal Products, Chemicals,
Nonferrous Metals

BOMBAY–POONA
Cotton Textiles, Machinery,
Chemicals, Automobiles,
Electrical Equipment

TEL AVIV–HAIFA
Machinery, Electrical
Equipment, Textiles,
Oil Refining, Chemicals,
Diamond Cutting

DOMINANT LAND USE

- Cereals, Livestock
- Cash Crops, Mixed Farming, Livestock
- Rice, Diversified Tropical and Subtropical Crops
- Livestock, Dairy
- Cotton, Cereals
- Livestock Grazing, Limited Agriculture
- Forests
- Nonagricultural Land

MAJOR MINERAL OCCURRENCES

Ab	Asbestos	Fe	Iron Ore	Mn	Manganese	Pt	Platinum
Al	Bauxite	G	Natural Gas	Mo	Molybdenum	S	Sulfur, Pyrite
Au	Gold	Gr	Graphite	Na	Salt	Sb	Antimony
C	Coal	Hg	Mercury	Ni	Nickel	Sn	Tin
Cr	Chromium	Lg	Lignite	O	Petroleum	U	Uranium
Cu	Copper	Mg	Magnesium	P	Phosphates	W	Tungsten
D	Diamonds	Mi	Mica	Pb	Lead	Zn	Zinc

⚡ Water Power   ▨ Major Industrial Areas   △ Oil Refining Centers

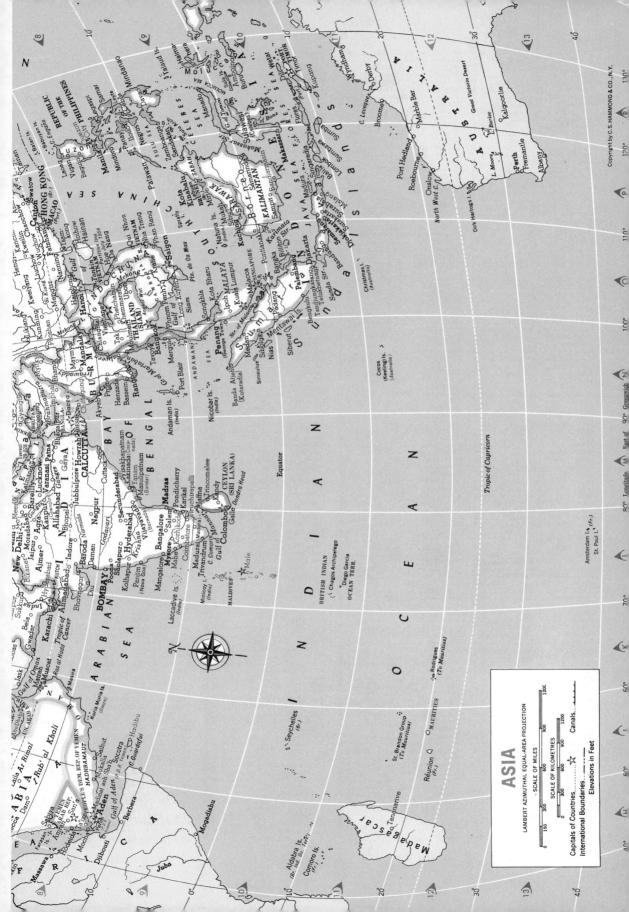

ASIA

LAMBERT AZIMUTHAL EQUAL-AREA PROJECTION

SCALE OF MILES

SCALE OF KILOMETRES

Capitals of Countries .... ☆
International Boundaries ....
Elevations in Feet

Copyright by C.S. HAMMOND & CO., N.Y.

ASIA

Abadan, Iran H 6
Abu Dhabi (cap.), United Arab Emirates J 7
Adana, Turkey G 6
Aden (cap.), P.D.R. Yemen H 8
Aden (gulf) H 8
Aegean (sea) F 6
Afghanistan K 6
Agra, India L 7
Ahmadabad, India K 7
Aigun, China R 5
Ajmer, India L 7
Akita, Japan S 6
Aktyubinsk, U.S.S.R. J 5
Akyab, Burma N 7
Alakol (lake), U.S.S.R. M 5
Aldan, U.S.S.R. R 4
Aldan (river), U.S.S.R. S 4
Aleksandrovsk-Sakhalinski, U.S.S.R. T 4
Aleppo, Syria G 6
Allahabad, India L 7
Alma-Ata, U.S.S.R. L 5
Altai (mts.) M 5
Altyn Tagh (mts.), China M 6
Amami (isls.), Japan S 7
Amboina, Indonesia R10
Amman (cap.), Jordan G 6
Amoy, China P 7
Amran, Yemen Arab Rep. H 8
Amritsar, India L 6
Amsterdam (isl.) L13
Amu-Darya (river), U.S.S.R. K 5
Amur (river) S 4
Anadyr, U.S.S.R. W 3
Anadyr (gulf), U.S.S.R. X 3
Anadyr (river), U.S.S.R. W 3
'Anaiza, Saudi Arabia H 7
Andaman (isls.), India M 8
Andaman (sea) N 9
Andizhan, U.S.S.R. L 5
Angara (river), U.S.S.R. N 4
Angkor Wat (ruins), Cambodia O 8
Ankara (cap.), Turkey G 5
Anking, China P 6
Antalya, Turkey F 6
Antung, China R 5
Anzhero-Sudzhensk, U.S.S.R. M 4
Aomori, Japan T 5
'Aqaba, Jordan G 7
Aqsu, China M 5
Arabia (peninsula) H 7
Arabian (sea) K 8
Aral (sea), U.S.S.R. J 5
Ararat (mt.), Turkey H 6
Arctic Ocean E 1
Argun (river) P 5
Ar Rimal (desert), Arabia H 7
Ashkhabad, U.S.S.R. J 6
Ayaguz, U.S.S.R. L 5
Ayan, U.S.S.R. S 4
Babol, Iran J 6
Babuyan (islands), Philippine Is. R 8
Baghdad (cap.), Iraq H 6
Baguio, Philippine Is. P 8
Bahrain J 7
Baikal (lake), U.S.S.R. P 4
Bali (island), Indonesia P10
Balkh, Afghanistan K 6
Balkhash (lake), U.S.S.R. L 5
Bam, Iran J 7
Banda Atjeh, Indonesia N 9
Bandar (Masulipatnam), India M 8
Bandar 'Abbas, Iran J 7
Bandjarmasin, Indonesia P10
Bandung, Indonesia O10
Bangalore, India L 8
Bangka (island), Indonesia O10
Bangkok (cap.), Thailand N 8
Bangladesh N 7
Barabinsk, U.S.S.R. L 4
Bareilly, India M 7
Barguzin, U.S.S.R. P 4
Barnaul, U.S.S.R. M 4
Baroda, India L 7
Basra, Iraq H 7
Bassein, Burma N 8
Batan (islands), Philippine Is. R 7
Batang, China N 6
Beirut (cap.), Lebanon G 6
Bela, Pakistan K 7
Belogorsk, U.S.S.R. S 4
Bengal (bay) M 8
Bengkulu, Indonesia O10
Berezovo, U.S.S.R. K 3
Bering (sea) X 4
Bering (strait) Y 3
Bezwada (Vijayavada), India L 8
Bhagalpur, India M 7
Bhamo, Burma N 7
Bhavnagar, India K 7
Bhopal, India L 7
Bhutan M 7
Bikaner, India L 7
Billiton (isl.), Indonesia O10
Bira, U.S.S.R. S 5
Birjand, Iran J 6
Black (sea) G 5
Blagoveshchensk, U.S.S.R. R 4
Bodaibo, U.S.S.R. P 4
Bolshevik (island), U.S.S.R. O 2
Bolshoi Lyakhov (isl.), U.S.S.R. T 2
Bombay, India L 8
Bone (gulf), Indonesia R10
Borneo (isl.) P 9
Brahmaputra (river) N 7
British Indian Ocean Terr. L10
Brunei P 9
Bukhara, U.S.S.R. K 6
Bulun, U.S.S.R. R 2
Buraida, Saudi Arabia H 7
Burma N 7
Bursa, Turkey F 6
Buru (island), Indonesia R10
Bushire, Iran J 7
Calcutta, India M 7
Ca Mau (point), S. Vietnam O 9
Cambodia O 8
Canton, China P 7
Caspian (sea) H 5
Cawnpore (Kanpur), India L 7
Cebu, Philippine Is. R 9
Celebes (Sulawesi) (island), Indonesia R10
Celebes (sea) R 9
Ceylon (Sri Lanka) M 9
Chagos (arch.), Br. Indian Ocean Terr. L10
Chamdo, China N 6
Chandigarh, India L 6
Changchun, China R 5
Changsha, China P 7
Changteh, China O 7
Changyeh, China N 6
Chaochow, China P 7
Chefoo, China P 6
Cheju (island), Rep. of Korea R 6
Chelkar, U.S.S.R. J 5
Chelyabinsk, U.S.S.R. K 4
Chelyuskin (cape), U.S.S.R. P 2
Chengtu, China O 6
Cherchen, China M 6
Cheremkhovo, U.S.S.R. N 4
Cherski T 3
Chiangmai, Thailand N 8
China O 6
Chinkiang, China R 6
Chita, U.S.S.R. P 4
Chittagong, Bangladesh N 7
Ch'ŏngjin, North Korea S 5
Christmas (island), Australia O11
Chukchi (pen.), U.S.S.R. X 3
Chumikan, U.S.S.R. S 4
Chungking, China O 7
Cocanada (Kakinada), India M 8
Cocos (isls.), Australia N11
Coimbatore, India L 8
Colombo (cap.), Ceylon L 9
Comorin (cape), India L 9
Cuttack, India M 8
Cyprus G 6
Dacca (cap.), Bangladesh N 7
Dairen (see Lüta), China R 6
Daito (islands), Ryukyu Is. S 7
Dam, Saudi Arabia H 7
Daman, India L 7
Damascus (cap.), Syria G 6
Da Nang, South Vietnam O 8
Darjeeling, India M 7
Davao, Philippine Is. R 9
Delhi, India L 7
Demavend (mt.), Iran J 6
Dezhnev (cape), U.S.S.R. X 3
Dhahran, Saudi Arabia H 7
Diego Garcia (isl.), Br. Indian Ocean Terr. L10
Dili (cap.), Portuguese Timor R10
Diu, India L 7
Diyarbakir, Turkey H 6
Dizful, Iran H 6
Djakarta (cap.), Indonesia O10
Djokjakarta, Indonesia O10
Dondra (head), Ceylon M 9
Dudinka, U.S.S.R. M 3
Dzhelinde, U.S.S.R. P 2
East China (sea) R 6
Elizavety (cape), U.S.S.R. T 4
Engaño (cape), Philippine Is. R 8
Erzurum, Turkey H 5
Euphrates (river) H 6
Everest (mt.) M 7
Faizabad, Afghanistan K 6
Fatshan, China P 7
Fengkieh, China O 6
Flores (island), Indonesia R10
Flores (sea), Indonesia R10
Foochow, China P 7
Formosa (Taiwan) (island), China R 7
Frunze, U.S.S.R. L 5
Fuji (mt.), Japan S 6
Fukuoka, Japan R 6
Galle, Ceylon L 9
Ganges (river), India M 7
Gartok, China L 6
Gaya, India M 7
George Town (Penang), Malaya, Malaysia N 9
Gilgit, India L 6
Gizhiga, U.S.S.R. V 3
Gobi (desert) O 5
Godavari (river), India L 8
Golchikha, U.S.S.R. M 2
Gorno-Altaisk, U.S.S.R. M 4
Grand (canal), China P 6
Great Khingan (range), China R 5
Great Wall (ruins), China O 6
Gurgan, Iran J 6
Guriev, U.S.S.R. J 5
Gwadar, Pakistan K 7
Gyangtse, China N 7
Hadd, Ras al (cape), Oman K 7
Hadhramaut (region), P.D.R. Yemen H 8
Hadibu, Socotra, P.D.R. Yemen J 8
Hail, Saudi Arabia H 7
Hainan (island), China P 8
Haiphong, North Vietnam O 7
Hakodate, Japan T 5
Halmahera (island), Indonesia R 9
Hamadan, Iran H 6
Hami, China N 5
Hanchung, China O 6
Hangchow, China R 7
Hankow (see Wuhan), China P 6
Hanoi (capital), North Vietnam O 7
Hanyang (see Wuhan), China P 6
Harbin, China R 5
Hauta, Saudi Arabia H 7
Helmand (river), Afghanistan K 6
Hengyang, China O 7
Henzada, Burma N 8
Herat, Afghanistan K 6
Himalaya (mts.) L 6
Hindu Kush (mts.) K 6
Hiroshima, Japan S 6
Hit, Iraq H 6
Hodeida, Yemen Arab Rep. H 8
Hofuf, Saudi Arabia H 7
Hoihow, China P 8
Hokkaido (island), Japan T 5
Hong Kong P 7
Honshu (island), Japan T 6
Howrah, India M 7
Hue, South Vietnam O 8
Huhehot, China P 5
Hwang Ho (river), China P 6
Hyderabad, India L 8
Hyderabad, Pakistan L 7
Ichang, China P 6
Igarka, U.S.S.R. M 3
Ili (river) L 5
Iloilo, Philippine Is. R 8
Imphal, India N 7
Inch'ŏn, Rep. of Korea R 6
India L 7
Indian Ocean L10
Indigirka (river), U.S.S.R. T 3
Indochina (region) O 8
Indonesia P10
Indore, India L 7
Indus (river) K 7
Inner Mongolia (region), China P 5
Ipin, China O 7
Ipoh, Malaya, Malaysia O 9
Iran J 6
Iraq H 6
Irkutsk, U.S.S.R. O 4
Irrawaddy (river), Burma N 7
Irtish (river), U.S.S.R. K 4
Isfahan, Iran J 6
Ishim (river), U.S.S.R. K 4
Islamabad (cap.), Pakistan L 6
Israel G 6
Issyk-Kul (lake), U.S.S.R. L 5
Iturup (island), U.S.S.R. T 5
Izmir, Turkey F 6
Jaffna, Ceylon M 9
Jaipur, India L 7
Japan S 6
Japan (sea) S 6
Jask, Iran J 7
Jauf, Saudi Arabia G 7
Java (island), Indonesia O10
Java (sea), Indonesia P10
Jerusalem (cap.), Israel G 6
Jerusalem, Jordan G 6
Jidda, Saudi Arabia G 7
Jordan G 6
Jubbulpore, India M 7
Kabul (capital), Afghanistan L 6
Kagoshima, Japan R 6
Kaifeng, China P 6
Kakinada, India M 8
Kalat, Pakistan K 7
Kalgan, China P 5
Kalimantan (region), Indonesia P10
Kamchatka (peninsula), U.S.S.R. U 4
Kanazawa, Japan S 6
Kanchow, China P 7
Kandahar, Afghanistan K 6
Kandy, Ceylon M 9
Kangting, China O 6
Kanpur, India L 7
Kara (sea), U.S.S.R. K 2
Karachi, Pakistan K 7
Karaganda, U.S.S.R. L 5
Karakorum (ruins), Mongolia O 5
Karbala, Iraq H 6
Karikal, India M 8
Karimata (strait), Indonesia O10
Kashan, Iran J 6
Kashgar, China L 6
Katmandu (cap.), Nepal M 7
Kayşeri, Turkey G 6
Kazakh S.S.R., U.S.S.R. J 5
Kazalinsk, U.S.S.R. K 5
Kazvin, Iran H 6
Keeling (Cocos) (isls.), Australia N11
Kemerovo, U.S.S.R. M 4
Keriya, China M 6
Kerman, Iran J 6
Kermanshah, Iran H 6
Kerulen (river) P 5
Khabarovsk, U.S.S.R. S 5
Khanaqin, Iraq H 6
Khanka (lake) S 5
Khatanga, U.S.S.R. N 2
Khatanga (river), U.S.S.R. O 3
Khemmarat, Thailand O 8
Khiva, U.S.S.R. J 5
Khotan, China L 6
Khyber (pass), Pakistan K 6
Kian, China P 7
Kiaohsien, China P 6
Kirensk, U.S.S.R. P 4
Kirghiz S.S.R., U.S.S.R. L 5
Kirin, China R 5
Kirkuk, Iraq H 6
Kitakyushu, Japan S 6
Kiuchüan, China N 5
Kobdo, Mongolia N 5
Kobe, Japan S 6
Kokand, U.S.S.R. K 5
Koko Nor (lake), China N 6
Kolhapur, India L 8
Kolyma (range), U.S.S.R. V 3
Kolyma (river), U.S.S.R. U 3
Komandorskie (islands), U.S.S.R. W 4
Komsomolets (isl.), U.S.S.R. L 1
Komsomolsk, U.S.S.R. S 4
Konya, Turkey G 6
Korea, North R 6
Korea, Republic of R 6
Korsakov, U.S.S.R. T 5
Kota Bharu, Malaya, Malaysia O 9
Kota Kinabalu, Sabah, Malaysia P 9
Kozhikode, India L 8
Krasnovodsk, U.S.S.R. J 5
Krasnoyarsk, U.S.S.R. N 4
Kratie, Cambodia O 8
Krishna (river), India L 8
Kuala Lumpur (cap.), Malaysia O 9
Kuching, Sarawak, Malaysia O 9
Kuldja, China M 5
Kumamoto, Japan S 6
Kunlun (mts.), China M 6
Kunming, China O 7
Kupang, Indonesia R11
Kure, Japan S 6
Kuria Muria (islands), Oman J 8
Kuril (islands), U.S.S.R. T 5
Kushiro, Japan T 5
Kustanai, U.S.S.R. K 4
Kutaradja (Banda Atjeh), Indonesia N 9
Kutch (region), India L 7
Kuwait H 7
Kweilin, China P 7
Kweiyang, China O 7
Kyakhta, U.S.S.R. O 4
Kyoto, Japan S 6
Kyushu (island), Japan S 6
Kyzyl, U.S.S.R. N 4
Kzyl-Orda, U.S.S.R. K 5
Labuan (isl.), Sabah, Malaysia P 9
Laccadive (islands), India K 8
Lahore, Pakistan L 6
Laila, Saudi Arabia H 7
Lanchow, China O 6
Laoag, Philippine Is. P 8
Laos O 8
La Pérouse (strait) T 5
Laptev (sea), U.S.S.R. R 2
Lebanon G 6
Legaspi, Philippine Is. R 8
Leh, India L 6
Lena (river), U.S.S.R. R 3
Leninsk-Kuznetski, U.S.S.R. M 4
Leyte (isl.), Philippine Is. R 8
Lhasa, China N 6
Likiang, China O 7
Liuchow, China O 7
Lombok (island), Indonesia P11
Long Xuyen, South Vietnam O 9

population of Cyprus and numerous small Arab nations.

Except for Israel, which by a wide variety of criteria may be classified in the tertiary stage of development, the nations of Southwest Asia are generally in the primary stage. In most of them, between 70 and 80 percent of the people live in rural areas and practice subsistence agriculture. Even these figures understate the situation, for many cities are little more than overgrown villages, and there are few professional and service people. The economic activity of the 7 to 10 million persons belonging to ethnic minority groups, organized in seminomadic and nomadic tribes, consists of little more than the pursuit and use of pasture for livestock.

While the ethnography, religions, and cultures of Southwest Asia are diverse, the demography is relatively uniform. In most parts of the region both birth- and death rates have been high, and the annual rate of population growth has tended to fluctuate around 1 percent. Since World War II the wider dissemination of Western medical and sanitation techniques in some areas has resulted in dramatically lowered infant and general mortality rates, longer life expectancies, and sharp increases in population. For most of the region, however, the demographic characteristics of economically underdeveloped nations (those in Group 3) have prevailed and will continue to do so for some time.

South Asia. The population of South Asia in the mid-1960's was estimated at approximately 620 million. India's 483 million people accounted for more than three fourths of the total, and Pakistan's 103 million for one sixth. Historically, the birthrate in the region has ranged from 40 to 45 per 1,000 of the total population, while with few exceptions the death rate has ranged from 30 to 40 per 1,000. The net annual rates of increase have thus been from 1 to 1.5 percent. By the early 1960's, when the death rate in India declined to less than 20 per 1,000, the net annual rate of increase for the area as a whole had risen to about 2 percent. Food shortages in the mid-1960's kept the rate of increase from rising.

One of the principal reasons for the sharp increase in the population of India has been industrialization, which has yielded significant improvements in agriculture and transportation as well as in manufacturing and has led to a general rise in levels of living. Another reason has been the wider dissemination of modern medical techniques, which have significantly reduced death rates and lengthened life expectancies. Efforts to disseminate birth control information and techniques in India have had only limited success in the more modern cities; they have failed in the rural areas, where deeply entrenched social mores and low educational levels have constituted almost insuperable obstacles. Little short of a combination of rapid technological progress, unusually large increases in literacy, and accelerated and radical changes in the country's sociological and economic structures would forestall further dramatic increases in population.

While India was in process of becoming a Group 2 nation (the secondary stage of development) in the 1960's, this was not generally true of its neighbors, which for the most part were modernizing their economies very slowly. For a wide variety of reasons based on geographic location, however, Ceylon had for some time been a Group 2 nation, with a population structure differing from the South Asian pattern. For the other nations of South Asia, classification in Demographic Group 3 (the primary stage of economic development) continued to be appropriate.

Southeast Asia. The nations of Southeast Asia have a total population estimated in the mid-1960's at almost 250 million. While their cultural, religious, and political structures vary widely, economically and demographically they have much in common. In general, high birthrates and moderately low death rates have combined to yield a net annual rate of growth for the region as a whole of about 2 percent. The high birthrates have reflected the traditional and still dominant socioeconomic outlook of the region; the low and rapidly declining death rates have signified its long history of contact with Western technology.

In both the colonial and post-World War II periods the extension of literacy, the improvement of health and sanitation facilities and knowledge, and the use of more rational and productive agricultural techniques have combined to raise incomes and ultimately to enlarge dramatically the size of the population and the economic problems of governments. The Southeast Asian nations export regionally diverse but nationally specialized agricultural and industrial raw materials and import manufactured consumer goods and capital equipment. Uncertainty concerning the demand and price for primary products has fostered a sense of insecurity in these nations, and numerous plans for economic development have been formulated. Unfortunately, relatively little progress has been made in diversifying economies and exports. As a consequence, economic structures have remained essentially dependent on external factors over which the Southeast Asian nations have no control.

By the 1960's the primarily agricultural nations of the region were much closer to classification as Demographic Group 2 countries than they were to the secondary stage of economic development. Given continued sharp increases in their populations without concurrent advances in industrialization, serious economic and demographic problems seemed likely to develop.

East Asia. In the mid-1960's, East Asia had the largest population of the major Asian regions. Estimated at about 860 million, this population was growing in absolute terms by at least 11 million and possibly by as much as 18 million each year. About 716 million of the total was represented by Communist China's population, while about 100 million people were in Japan, and about 40 million in Korea. The major role played by China in reaching these totals and the reportedly great variability of Chinese birth- and death rates (particularly the latter) made it difficult to evaluate the demographic structure of the region. In the 1950's, China's population, traditionally classified in Group 3, quickly began to assume Group 2 characteristics. The principal reasons for this change were rapid annual declines in the death rate, due to reported widespread improvement in health and sanitation facilities, sharp increases in agricultural and industrial output, and the expansion of facilities for producing inanimate energy. By the 1960's, however, a series of natural disasters and bad harvests had raised death rates again, and this, coupled with a reported breakdown of the industrialization program, signified retrogression to Group 3 status.

Korea's economic structure and demographic status are roughly comparable to those of China. Clearly Group 3 in character, Korea before World War II was a colonial supplier of raw materials as well as an outlet for Japanese capital and part of the overflow of the Japanese population. In 1945, primarily agricultural South Korea and partially industrial North Korea were separated from each other, and what had been a single viable economy became two nonviable ones. In both countries, despite economic assistance from the United States and Communist China, respectively, death rates have remained high, and life expectancies short. Net rates of natural population growth have thus been low. Large-scale movements of refugees from the north to the south have increased the economic pressures in South Korea. Both countries have remained in Demographic Group 3.

Japan's economic and demographic structures are far different from those of China and Korea, belonging clearly to the tertiary stage of development and Demographic Group 1. The country has a modern heavy industrial base, excellent transportation facilities, and high per capita levels of inanimate energy consumption and national income. Japan thus enjoys a very high level of living. Still, it is striking that, despite all these Group 1 characteristics, about one fourth of the population has remained on the land. Low birth- and death rates have yielded a net rate of increase of 0.9 percent, and by the 1960's Japan appeared to have achieved so low a net rate of population growth that the Malthusian specter of overpopulation, which threatened the country from 1870 on, had disappeared. While birth control programs, begun in 1948, have contributed to the achievement of this demographic stability, the chief reasons for success have been the urbanization process and changing social mores.

Soviet Asia. The population of Soviet Asia in the mid-1960's was estimated at about 55 million. In contrast to the other major Asian regions, the largest increases in population have been due to emigration from European Russia rather than to natural causes. The large scale of emigration is reflected in the ethnographic structure, for only one third of the population is of non-Slav origin. Although industrialization and urbanization of Soviet Asia have in general taken place concurrently with the development of other parts of the USSR, the region's character as an economic colony of European Russia has remained unchanged. Under Communist as under czarist rule, Soviet Asia has exported agricultural and industrial raw materials and imported the capital equipment and labor necessary to expedite these exports. As in much of the rest of Asia, most of the inhabitants are engaged in agriculture or mining. The few professional and service-type workers live mainly in the cities.

Few statistics are available concerning birth- and death rates, but the life-shortening work regimen of most of the people and a severe shortage of amenities suggest that death rates are higher and life expectancies lower than in European Russia. The size of the land area and resources of Soviet Asia in relation to its population have made it unlikely that measures to restrict the size of the population will be adopted for many years to come.

Summary. As a whole, Asia is underdeveloped. Such advances in economic development as have occurred in specific nations have resulted in sharp increases in the population, which in turn have retarded economic growth and restricted the rise in per capita levels of living. Historically, emigration within and without the continent has temporarily relieved population pressures in particular places, but with the passage of time the problem has recurred. Attempts to control birthrates have had only limited local success; on the national scale they have failed.

Where birthrates have declined, the decrease has been due to the impact of industrialization and urbanization on social mores and family economic aspirations. The resistance of these mores to change has been stronger than in Europe, where modern industrialization and urbanization processes originated. Perhaps the key to technological progress and orderly demographic change is education. With vastly enlarged educational facilities and much higher literacy rates, contrasts between the socioeconomic and demographic structures of Western and Asian nations can be made more apparent to people, who thus may be motivated toward change. It is in the remote, agriculturally oriented, and tradition-bound villages of Asia that the demographic trends of the future will be decided.

See also sections dealing with population in articles on various Asian countries; POPULATION.

SIDNEY KLEIN
Rutgers—The State University of New Jersey

Bibliography
Coale, Ansley J., and Hoover, Edgar M., *Population Growth and Economic Development in Low-Income Countries* (Princeton, N.J., 1958).
Davis, Kingsley, ed., *The Population of India and Pakistan* (Princeton, N.J., 1951).
Ho, Ping-ti, *Studies on the Population of China, 1368–1953* (Cambridge, Mass., 1959).
Taeuber, Irene B., *The Population of Japan* (Princeton, N.J., 1958).

3. Races

The size and location of Asia, combined with its varied topography, climate, flora, and fauna, have favored the development and retention within its limits of a high percentage of the races of mankind. Some of these races are represented by the descendants of recent migrants from Europe and Africa; others, such as the Negritos of the Andaman Islands, Malaya, and the Philippines and the pre-Dravidians of south India and Ceylon, are the remnants of ancient populations.

Efforts have long been made to classify the peoples of Asia, but they have never been very successful. The Egyptians pictured the Middle Eastern peoples with yellow skin, high heads, and curly beards, a pattern reflected also in Mesopotamian art, while Aristotle, with racial connotations, referred to Asian man. It remained, however, for Carl Linnaeus to attempt the first systematic classification (1758). He included all the peoples of Asia under the variety *Asiaticus luridus* (yellow). This scheme was modified in 1775 by Johann Friedrich Blumenbach, who designated five races of man and introduced the regional ethnic terms "Mongolian" and "Malayan," which still appear in anthropological literature.

Blumenbach's classification remained unchallenged until 1889, when Joseph Deniker introduced a sixfold division with many subdivisions. The new system employed hair form (woolly, wavy, or straight) as the primary classifier and placed secondary emphasis on skin color, stature, nose form, and head form (dolichocephalic, or longheaded; mesocephalic, or intermediate; and brachycephalic, or broadheaded). Of Deniker's 29 races, 11 are Asian: Assyroid, Arab or Semite, eastern European, Indo-Afghan, Turkish, Ugrian, Dravidian, Negrito, Indonesian, Mongoloid, and Ainu.

This classification was not seriously challenged until Alfred Cort Haddon's attempt in 1925. Using the same anatomical criteria, but in different sequence and orders of magnitude, Haddon added a few refinements and determined 26 races, of which 18 are located in Asia. In 1931, Earnest A. Hooton contributed the idea of 3 primary races (white, Negroid, and Mongoloid), with 13 subdivisions. Of the latter, he identified 8 with Asia and adjacent parts of eastern Europe: Mediterranean, Ainu, Alpine, east Baltic, Armenoid, Dinaric, classic Mongoloid, and Arctic Mongoloid (Eskimoid). He conceived also of composite or mixed races, of which several are preeminently Asian.

Two other schemes were devised in 1933, one by Egon von Eickstedt in Germany and the other by Georges Alexis Montandon in France. The former reverted to a trifold classification based on skin color, with subraces designed by location, language, or head form. Montandon conceived of 5 great races and 20 lesser ones. Jan Czekanowski and Stanislaw Klimek devised a similar scheme, with a comparable number of races and subraces, and in 1959 Renato Biasutti combined several older classifications and divided man into 4 subspecies and 16 races. The latter he fortified with Latin names and 52 secondary races—about half identifiable with Asia. Many other classifications might be cited.

The following 12 descriptions should be viewed not as a classification of Asian races, but rather as definitions of terms referred to as races. They represent idealized and highly subjective types, that though of questionable scientific significance, appear commonly in both scientific and popular literature.

Armenoid (Armenid, Assyroid, Anatolian).—Relatively stocky body; brachycephalic and high head; long and narrow face; high forehead; prominent and convex nose, with a high bridge and root; light to light brown skin; wavy, medium coarse, and brownish hair; found on the Anatolian plateau and eastward and southward into Iran and Arabia.

Eastern Mediterranean (Oriental, Arab, or Semitic).—Slender body; dolichocephalic head; long and elliptical face; aquiline nose, with a high root and thin tip; thin lips; wavy to curly, dark brown or black hair; dark and deep-set eyes, medium brown skin; found in the Middle East and eastward into Afghanistan.

Turanian (Turanid, Turkish, Turko-Iranian, Turko-Tatar).—Intermediate body; mesocephalic head; projecting cheekbones; slight inner (epicanthic) eyefold; light brown skin; light wavy to straight and dark brown hair; prominent and straight nose, with a high bridge; found in Central Asia.

Indo-Afghan (Irano-Afghan, Indo-Aryan).—Slender body; dolichocephalic to mesocephalic head; medium to dark brown skin; medium to dark brown eyes; light wavy and dark brown or black hair; straight nose, with a moderate root height; found in the Iranian plateau, West Pakistan, and northern India.

Dravidian (Dravido-Mediterranean, Deccanoid, Melano-Australoid, Melano-Hindu).—Slender body; dolichocephalic to mesocephalic head; deep-set and dark brown eyes; dark brown skin; wavy to curly and dark brown or black hair; concave or straight nose, with a depressed root; relatively thick lips, with little eversion; found in southern India and Ceylon.

Veddoid (Pre-Dravidian, Mixed Proto-Australoid).—Slender body; dolichocephalic head; dark brown skin; deep-set and dark brown to black eyes; curly, sparse, and black hair and beard; broad nose, with a depressed root; found in deep forests of southern India, Ceylon, and Malaya.

Negrito (Oceanic Negroid).—Extremely small body; brachycephalic head; bulbous forehead; dark skin; sparse, kinky, or woolly and black hair; concave nose, with a depressed root and flaring nostrils; concentrations found

among the Semang of Malaya and the Negritos of the Philippines (the Andaman Islanders are a variant, with an inner eyefold and light brown skin).

Indonesian-Malay (Paleo-Mongoloid, Southern Mongoloid, Proto-Mongoloid, Malayo-Mongoloid, Malayo-Indonesian).—Medium to stocky body; mesocephalic to brachycephalic head; straight black hair; slightly concave nose, with a depressed root; medium to dark brown skin; found in south China, Southeast Asia, and Indonesia.

Sino-Mongoloid (Mongoloid).—Rather stocky body; mesocephalic to brachycephalic head; pronounced inner eyefold; median incisors shovel shaped on the lingual surfaces; dark brown eyes; straight, coarse, and black head hair; sparse beard and body hair; yellowish to light brown skin; Mongoloid spot (pigment concentration on the skin at the base of the spine common during childhood); found in China, Korea, and Japan.

Tungus-Siberian (North Mongolian or Mongoloid, Paleo-Asian, Paleo-Siberian, Siberian Arctic).—Stocky and short-legged body; brachycephalic head; yellowish skin; coarse, sparse, and black hair; extreme inner eyefold; shovel-shaped median incisors; straight to concave nose, with a low root; eyes set far apart and very dark in color; prominent cheekbones; found along the Amur River and in northern Siberia.

Ainu.—Stocky body with short legs; dolichocephalic or mesocephalic head; heavy, wavy, and dark brown to black body and beard hair; light to medium brown eyes; no inner eyefold; light brown to tawny skin; pronounced browridges; broad nose, with a moderate root height and a fleshy tip; found in Hokkaido, Sakhalin, and the Kurils (Caucasoid or Proto-European connections have been presumed but not proved, and newer studies suggest possibly early Australoid and pre-Japanese Neolithic affinities).

Eskimo (Asian Eskimo).—Characteristics similar to the Tungus-Siberian but less extremely Mongoloid and generally mesocephalic; found along Anadyr Gulf in northeastern Siberia.

The difficulty with all morphological or typological classifications has been their general assumption that racial characteristics are fundamentally immutable, or breed true, and are not subject to change. Between 1930 and 1945 this notion was questioned, and increasing evidence was presented that races (or at least individuals identifiable by race) were subject to adaptive change. Especially significant were studies of Chinese, Japanese, and Korean immigrants to Hawaii and California and their children, in which marked increases in body size and modifications in head, ear, and nose form were noted. The discovery that similar modifications were occurring in the homelands as well as in other parts of Asia led to a revolt against the numerous methodological inconsistencies of previous classifications. As early as 1950, Carleton S. Coon, Stanley M. Garn, and Joseph B. Birdsell attempted a classification based on what they termed "adaptive function." They sought to interpret many so-called racial features, such as body build, skin color, hair form, nose form, and the prominence of cheekbones, as responses or adaptations to environment through natural selection over long periods of time. In this attempt mankind was reduced to 30 races, of which 13 are recognizable in Asia: Alpine, Ainu, Negrito, Dravidian, Hamite, Hindu, Mediterranean, classic Mongoloid, north Chinese, Southeast Asian, Tibeto-Indonesian, Mongoloid, and Turkic, terms conventionalized by common and recurrent usage.

Modifying this classification, Garn in 1961 applied Theodosius Dobzhansky's suggestion of large geographical races and referred to an Asian race whose composition corresponds more or less to the older, morphologically determined Mongoloid race. He added an Indian race and included the Middle Eastern peoples within a European geographical race. He also proposed the concept of local as well as micro (microgeographical) races, at least 13 of the former in Asia: Alpine, Mediterranean, Iranian, Turkic, Tibetan, north Chinese, extreme Mongoloid, Southeast Asian, Hindu, Dravidian, Pacific Negro, Ainu, and Eskimo.

PEOPLES OF ASIA

The peoples of Asia represent a high percentage of the racial groups of mankind. Represented here are the 12 basic types of Asians described in the accompanying text. Most of these types are actually made up of many divisions, and therefore none of the photos can be described as "typical." For example, the Sino-Mongoloid type, represented here by a Chinese farmer of North China, actually includes peoples of China, Japan, Korea, and other Asian countries.

GEORGE DANIELL,
FROM PHOTO RESEARCHERS

Armenoid
(Turkey)

UNITED NATIONS

Eastern Mediterranean
(Iraq)

VON MEISS-TEUFFEN,
FROM PHOTO RESEARCHERS

Turanian
(Pakistan)

JOHN BROWNLIE,
FROM PHOTO RESEARCHERS

Indo-Afghan
(India)

GEORGE DANIELL,
FROM PHOTO RESEARCHERS

Dravidian
(India)

DEANE DICKASON,
FROM EWING GALLOWAY

Veddoid
(India)

AMERICAN MUSEUM
OF NATURAL HISTORY

Negrito
(Philippines)

TIERS, FROM MONKMEYER

Indonesian-Malay
(Indonesia)

HENLE, FROM MONKMEYER

Sino-Mongoloid
(China)

ERGY LANDAU,
FROM RAPHO GUILLUMETTE

Tungus-Siberian
(Mongolia)

FUJIHIRA, FROM MONKMEYER

Ainu
(Japan)

AUTHENTICATED NEWS
INTERNATIONAL

Eskimo
(Siberia)

Another contemporary approach is that of using blood types and secretor genes as classifiers. In the conventional ABO blood group types, Chinese, Japanese, Koreans, and Siberians are relatively low (30 percent) in O but somewhat higher (35 to 40 percent) in B. The A_1 and A_2 genes, on the other hand, are quite rare. In the Rh (Rhesus) series, the distribution of the CDE gene is approximately 0.5 percent throughout the continent, whereas Cde is absent in East Asia and reaches 1.0 to 6.5 percent in western Asia. Gene cDE ranges from 7.9 percent in the Middle East to 30.8 percent among the Japanese, whereas cde shows the reverse distribution. Racial differences also appear in haptoglobins (hemoglobin-binding or stable proteins), but their racial significance has not been determined.

One of the problems of classification is that no relationship has been established between internal genetically determined factors and such externally discernible bodily traits of racial significance as hair form or nose shape. Meanwhile, anthropologists have been compelled to use a variety of techniques. Even paleontological evidence has been brought to bear on the problem of racial origins, and in 1962, Coon revived a proposal, originally advanced by Franz Weidenreich in 1946, that many of the morphological features of the Mongoloid race can be traced to Peking man of the second interglacial period. This proposal received only limited acceptance. Clearly, solution of the problem of racial classification of the peoples of Asia had only begun by the 1960's.

See also separate articles on various Asian peoples; sections on the people in articles on Asian countries; ANTHROPOLOGY—*Physical Anthropology;* MIDDLE EAST—*2. The People* (Physical Types); RACES, NATURE AND ORIGINS OF; SOUTHEAST ASIA—*The Land and the People.*

GORDON T. BOWLES, *Syracuse University*

Bibliography

Coon, Carleton S., *The Origin of Races* (New York 1962).
Dobzhansky, Theodosius G., *Mankind Evolving* (New Haven, Conn., 1962).
Hickey, Gerald C., *Village in Vietnam* (New Haven, Conn., 1964).
Le Bar, Frank M., and others, *Ethnic Groups of Mainland Southeast Asia* (New York 1963).
Mourant, Arthur E., *The Distribution of Human Blood Groups* (London 1954).
Patai, Raphael, *Golden River to Golden Road: Society, Culture and Change in the Middle East* (Philadelphia 1962).
Weidenreich, Franz, *Apes, Giants and Man* (Chicago 1946).

4. Languages

It is impossible to determine with any degree of precision the number and variety of languages spoken throughout Asia during the past several thousand years. For many centuries a considerable portion of the inhabitants of this huge area lived sedentary lives in one or another of the centers of civilization extending from the Mediterranean Sea to the Pacific Ocean. Their descendants today still speak languages that have evolved from the tongues used by their remote ancestors. But numerous other peoples, impelled by climatic changes, food shortages, war, and other factors, abandoned their traditional homelands and settled in new areas. Cultural absorption and physical extermination also worked constantly to alter the linguistic patterns of the continent. As a result, languages or dialects thereof disappeared from the knowledge and memory of man, while new, perhaps hybrid, languages were formed.

Since the late 18th century, tremendous strides have been taken in the development of philology, and considerable success has been achieved in the determination of basic language families and their component characteristics. Nevertheless, numerous languages have continued to defy philological classification, while many others have not been studied scientifically. In view of the impressive methods of analysis that have been devised and the brilliant triumphs of philology in the 20th century, however, it may be confidently predicted that most of the outstanding problems will be overcome.

Southwest Asia. The languages of Southwest Asia may be classified generally as Iranian, Turkic, or Semitic. The Iranian languages, which belong to the Indo-European linguistic family, are spoken mainly in Iran. Formerly called Persia, Iran derives its modern name from the Old Persian *ariya*, or "Aryan," the designation for the earliest ancestor of the Aryan or Indo-European languages. Persian itself is the chief representative of the Iranian subbranch of these languages in Iran.

There are also several closely related languages, including Luri and Bakhtiari in the south and Kurdish in the northwest. Of these secondary Iranian languages, Kurdish is the most important. The Kurds inhabit the mountainous areas where Turkey, Iraq, and Iran meet. Numbering approximately 5 million, they have long aspired to establish themselves as a separate nation. Another minority, the Turkic-speaking Azerbaijani, live near the Soviet republic of Azerbaidzhan. There is also an Arabic-speaking minority in the southwest.

Many of the Iranian languages, such as Kurdish, have at best only an oral literary tradition, but Persian has a written literature of high standing. The system of writing used by the Iranian languages was derived from Arabic. The Arabic script was also carried on waves of religious invasion into Turkey, where Turkish, the language of about 90 percent of the population, represents a western extension of the Turkic (Turko-Tatar) languages of Inner Asia and Siberia. In 1928 the Arabic writing system was replaced by a Latin script.

Apart from small minorities, such as the Greeks in Turkey, speakers of Semitic languages inhabit most of the rest of Southwest Asia. The most important of these languages is Arabic, spoken by the majority of the people except in Israel, where Hebrew, another major Semitic tongue, predominates. A third Semitic tongue, Aramaic or Syriac, is spoken by small groups in the region. The Semitic languages are represented by distinctive scripts (Arabic and Hebrew), which, written from right to left, consist of consonants only. Vowels are indicated chiefly by separate markings above or below the line of writing.

See also ARAB CIVILIZATION—2. *Language;* ARAMAIC LANGUAGE; HEBREW LANGUAGE AND LITERATURE; IRAN, LANGUAGES OF; MIDDLE EAST —2. *The People* (Languages); SEMITIC LANGUAGES; SYRIAC LANGUAGE AND LITERATURE; TURKIC LANGUAGES.

South Asia. In South Asia, out of a total population of about 620 million, less than 10 million persons speak Khasi, Munda, or Sino-Tibetan languages. Khasi is spoken in Assam, the Munda languages in the hilly areas of north central India, and languages of the Sino-Tibetan family on the northern Indian frontier and in Nepal, Bhutan, and Sikkim. The vast majority of the population in the two chief countries of South Asia, India and Pakistan, speak languages belonging to the Dravidian and Indo-European families.

Dravidian languages may in very early times have been spoken in most of the Indian subcontinent. They are now confined to the southern quarter or third of the peninsula, with enclaves in other areas. The four principal languages of this group are Tamil, Malayalam, Telugu, and Kannada (Kanarese). More than 90 million persons in India and Ceylon speak Dravidian tongues. The Dravidian languages have a well-developed literature dating back to the early centuries of the Christian era. Although pushed into the southernmost part of the country in ancient days by invading Indo-Aryans, Dravidians still retain a strong sense of their own identity.

The Indo-Aryan tongues of South Asia, which belong to the same linguistic family as the languages of Europe, are spoken by almost 475 million persons. Hindustani is spoken in northern India as well as in Pakistan, and it serves as a lingua franca in both countries. Baluchi (Balochi) is spoken in the Baluchistan area of West Pakistan, Pushtu (Pashto) on the northwestern frontier, and Sindhi at the southern end of the Indus Valley. Pahari prevails in the Himalayan areas, Kashmiri in the disputed region of Kashmir, and Assamese in the easternmost section of India. Panjabi (Punjabi) appears on both sides of the Indian-Pakistani border. Among other Indo-Aryan tongues in India are Marathi, Gujarati, Rajasthani, Bihari, Oriya, Bhili, and Bengali, the latter also being the chief language of East Pakistan.

In Afghanistan the two official languages, Pushtu and Persian, are Iranian. Lesser Iranian languages are spoken in the mountainous Pamir region of the northeast and in the south. In addition, speakers of Turkic languages are found in the north.

In Ceylon more than one fourth of the population speaks Tamil. The rest speak Sinhalese, an Indo-Aryan language with a strong intermixture of Dravidian.

Hindustani, the principal Indo-Aryan language in South Asia, may be divided into two segments on the basis of the ways in which it is written. Muslim speakers of this language in-

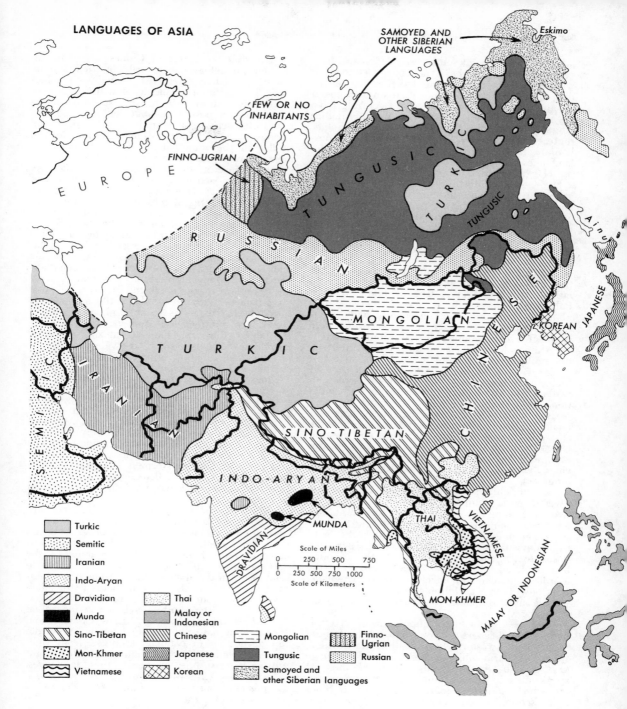

LANGUAGES OF ASIA

introduced many words of Persian origin and wrote in the Persian script, itself an adaptation of Arabic. The name Urdu has been adopted for both the spoken and the written forms of Hindustani in Pakistan. Hindu speakers of the language introduced many words from Sanskrit, the chief classical language of Hindu India, and used a distinctive script called Devanagari. The name Hindi has been adopted for both the spoken and the written forms of Hindustani in India.

When the Indian subcontinent was under British rule, English was extensively employed for purposes of education and official intercourse. It continues to have wide use despite attempts

to promote Hindi in India and Urdu and Bengali in Pakistan as national languages.

See also separate articles on the major South Asian languages; DRAVIDIAN; HIMALAYAN LANGUAGES; INDIA—9. Languages; PAKISTAN—8. Languages.

Southeast Asia. The peninsular area lying between India and China is inhabited by peoples speaking a wide variety of tongues. One group of languages, part of the Sino-Tibetan family and hence related to Chinese, includes as its main representatives Burmese, Thai (Siamese), Lao, and Vietnamese (Annamite). Dozens of lesser languages in this group are found especially in the northern mountain area, including the adjacent provinces of southwestern China. Many of these languages have not been reduced to writing. Burmese and Thai have scripts of Indian origin, while Lao and Vietnamese, spoken in areas formerly under French control, have been provided with Roman alphabets. Another language group, the Mon-Khmer, has as its chief representative modern Khmer, spoken in Cambodia. There are also many tribes speaking languages belonging to this group.

The Malay or Indonesian languages comprise a huge group of tongues extending from Madagascar to Malaysia, Indonesia, the Philippines, and Taiwan (Formosa). A relationship also exists between these tongues and such Pacific languages as those of Melanesia, Micronesia, and Polynesia. More than 200 languages and dialects of the Malayo-Polynesian group are found in Indonesia alone, and 90 in the Philippines. Numerically, the most important language of this group is Javanese, with approximately 40 million speakers. As is true of other Malayo-Polynesian languages, it has a very simple phonetic structure. The existence of wide variations within the language, based on differences in social level, is another distinguishing feature.

After Indonesia became independent in 1949, the problem of selecting a single national language was solved by the adoption of a form of Malay (the language of the Malay Peninsula and eastern Sumatra) that for centuries had functioned as a lingua franca in the islands. In comparison with most Malayan languages, this language, called Indonesian or Bahasa Indonesia, is simple in grammar, pronunciation, and vocabulary. It is also more democratic, lacking, for example, the socially oriented distinctions that characterize Javanese. It is written in a Latin alphabet.

In the Philippines the problem of linguistic diversity was compounded by the addition of two alien tongues, Spanish and English. Most educated Filipinos are conversant with one or the other of these languages, if not both. With the acquisition of independence in 1946, the desire for a common tongue led to the adoption of a modified form of the Tagalog speech of the Manila region as the official national language. It is now known as Pilipino.

See also BURMESE LANGUAGE AND LITERATURE; JAVA—*Language*.

East Asia. Of China's population of 716 million (1962 estimate), about two thirds, located in northern, western, and southwestern China, speak Mandarin Chinese, the principal language of the Sino-Tibetan family. Most of the rest speak other forms of Chinese, the exceptions being ethnic minorities in the southern and Inner Asian sections of the country. The various forms of Chinese are often referred to as dialects, but insofar as they ordinarily are mutually unintelligible, differing as widely as Dutch and English, they should properly be identified as separate languages. Among the non-Mandarin forms of Chinese are Cantonese, Wu (Shanghai), Kan-Hakka, Amoy-Swatow, and Foochow. All are located in the southeastern coastal area. Like the other forms of Chinese, Mandarin Chinese is subdivided into dialects, the most important being Pekingese (Pekinese), spoken in Peking. This dialect, known especially in its standard form as *kuo-yu* (national language), bears the same relation to other forms of Chinese as Parisian French does to other variations of French.

The different forms of Chinese vary mainly in their phonology, secondarily in their syntax. All are tonal languages with virtually no inflection. The position of elements within the sentence being all-important, Chinese is often referred to as a positional language. Chinese also has a distinctive ideographic script. Since the various forms of Chinese differ in sound but are similar in the grammatical order of their elements, newspapers and other publications in ideographic form can be read by any literate Chinese, who gives to each ideogram the pronunciation of his own dialect. The difficulty of the ideograms has led to attempts at reform. The People's Republic of China, besides promoting an approximation of the Peking dialect as the standard national language, has introduced many simplified ideograms. In addition, it has adopted an alphabetic script, called *p'in-yin* (spelling), as the official transcription. This script has been advocated by some reformers as a system of writing to replace ideograms in the future.

Japanese is spoken by about 100 million persons. The language has a simple phonetic system. Nouns are not inflected, and verbs are characterized by the piling up of suffixed elements. Particles called postpositions are widely used after phrases that function approximately as subject, object, and the like. A distinctive feature of Japanese word order is that almost all sentences end in a verbal element. The Japanese writing system is a mixture of borrowed Chinese ideograms (kanji) and indigenous syllabic scripts (kana), of which two are now used. Although some materials are published entirely in kana, it is common practice to use ideograms for the principal words and kana for inflectional endings and particles. Some reformers have advocated a romanization system called Romaji as a substitute for the complex writing system that is used in Japan.

Korean is spoken by about 40 million persons. The language is divided into two main dialects, northern and southern, the differences between them being mainly phonetic. The speech of educated citizens of Seoul has been adopted as the national standard. Attempts have been made to relate Korean to Japanese and to some of the languages of eastern Siberia, but there is still much uncertainty about the affinities of both languages. Korean is written with a syllabic script called *hangul* (formerly *onmun*). Like Chinese and Japanese, it has traditionally been written from top to bottom in columns arranged from right to left. Under Western influence, left-to-right writing has also been applied to these languages.

See also CHINA—*10. Language;* JAPAN—*18. Language;* KOREA—*10. Cultural Activities* (Creative Arts): Literature.

North Asia. Insofar as the number of speakers is concerned, by far the most important language in Siberia is Russian. The Russians are particularly numerous in the farmlands of western Siberia, along the line of the Trans-Siberian Railroad, and in the cities that have sprung up throughout the region. Russian is also the second language of many of the indigenous peoples. Among the latter are speakers of four distantly related representatives of the Ural-Altaic languages: Mongolian, Yakut, Tungusic, and Finno-Ugrian. The Mongols are centered in the Buryat Autonomous Soviet Socialist Republic. The Yakuts, a Turkic people, have their own administrative area, the Yakut Autonomous Soviet Socialist Republic, located on the upper reaches of the Lena River. The most widespread speech other than Russian is that included in the Tungusic family. Speakers of various Tungusic languages are thinly scattered over Siberia from 90° to 160° east longitude and from the Arctic Ocean to the area north of Lake Baikal and the Amur River. Among them the Manchus, who ruled China from 1644 to 1912, survive in small, scattered enclaves in Manchuria as well as in the Sinkiang-Uigur Autonomous Region. Speakers of Finno-Ugrian languages include the Ostyaks (Khanty), Voguls (Mansi), and Samoyeds (Nentsy) of western Siberia.

Most of the other Siberian peoples speak languages that are generally grouped together as Paleoasiatic (Paleosiberian). These peoples are believed to have inhabited most of the region before they were driven out and scattered by successive invasions, first by speakers of Ural-Altaic languages and then by Russians. There are now two chief groups of Paleoasiatic languages. One group, located in easternmost Siberia, includes Kamchadal, Chukchi, Koryak, and Yukaghir. Another, located along the Yenisei River and hence widely separated from the languages of the first group, is called Yenisei.

The indigenous languages of Siberia had little in the way of a literary heritage; most lacked even a writing system. Soviet authorities have devised alphabets where these did not exist, and all the languages of Siberia are now written in the Cyrillic script.

See also FINNO-UGRIAN LANGUAGES; MANCHUS; RUSSIAN LANGUAGE AND CULTURAL LIFE —1. *Russian Language*.

Inner Asia. The vast but sparsely populated lands of Inner Asia are inhabited by peoples of three main linguistic families, the Sino-Tibetan, Ural-Altaic, and Indo-European. In the Tibetan area of China and in the Chinese provinces adjacent to it are peoples who speak Tibetan and related languages of the Sino-Tibetan family. One of the distinctive features of Tibetan, which sets it apart from such relatives as Chinese, is the presence of initial consonantal clusters. Tibetan is written in a distinctive script borrowed from India in the 7th century A.D. The Chinese language is also represented in Inner Asia, particularly in areas adjacent to China Proper. It is important in the Sinkiang-Uigur Autonomous Region not only as the language of Chinese officialdom but also as the speech of merchants, Chinese settlers, and others.

The Ural-Altaic family of languages is represented in Inner Asia by two main branches, Mongolian and Turkic. Distinctive features of this family include vowel harmony and agglutination. Mongolian is spoken chiefly in the Mongolian People's Republic, in the adjacent area of China demarcated as the Inner Mongolian Autonomous Region, and in the Buryat ASSR around Lake Baikal. There are also outcroppings of Mongolian speakers in Manchuria and the Sinkiang-Uigur Autonomous Region. Most of these forms of Mongolian are mutually intelligible.

The Sinkiang-Uigur Autonomous Region is inhabited chiefly by Turkic-speaking peoples, the Uigurs alone accounting for almost three fourths of the population. Among other Turkic languages of the region are Kazakh, Kirghiz, Uzbek, and Tatar. Each of these languages is also spoken in adjacent areas of the USSR. Here linguistic criteria have had an important role in the establishment of the Kazakh, Kirghiz, and Uzbek Soviet Socialist republics as political-administrative regions. The Turkmen Soviet Socialist Republic, and the Kara-Kalpak Autonomous Soviet Socialist Republic within the Uzbek SSR, reflect in their names two additional Turkic languages, Turkmenian and Karakalpak.

The Tadzhik Soviet Socialist Republic was demarcated on the basis of the Tajik language spoken there. This language of the Indo-European family is most closely related to Persian; it is also spoken by a small group of settlers in the Sinkiang-Uigur Autonomous Region. The Russians are the largest group of speakers of an Indo-European language in Soviet Central Asia. Relative latecomers to the scene, they form a substantial proportion of the population of an area in which they first appeared as conquerors and remained as settlers and technicians and in other capacities.

See also ALTAIC LANGUAGES; MONGOLIA— *Language, Literature, and Theater Arts;* TIBET— *Ethnology and Language;* URAL-ALTAIC LANGUAGES.

Summary. Language changes during the evolution of the culture of which it is a part. Since the 16th and 17th centuries the ways of life of Asian peoples have been shaken by the intrusion of Western civilization. One of the more important effects of the impact of alien cultures has been the disturbance of the linguistic patterns of a substantial part of the continent, for with religion, trade, and imperialism the languages of the West were transferred to one section of Asia or another. Despite the emergence of numerous independent regimes in the wake of World War II, the languages of the former metropolitan countries have not only persisted as common means of communication, but also in some notable instances have been accorded official status. Thus English has been established as both a national and an international language in Asia, French is still widely used in the former Indochina and in parts of the Middle East, while Spanish and, to a lesser extent, Dutch are familiar to the educated classes in the Philippines and Indonesia, respectively. Russian is a first or second language for most of the inhabitants of Soviet Asia, while in Korea, Taiwan, and Okinawa the older generation at least is conversant with Japanese. In time the expansion of some of these languages and the decline of others in their extraterritorial locales may be anticipated.

The transfer of languages from Europe to Asia furnished more than additional means of communication. As a consequence of communication itself, both alien and local languages were enriched through the medium of loan words. An examination of the everyday vocabulary of English, French, and German or of Japanese, Hindi, and Arabic reveals numerous examples of linguistic interaction. With the constant increase in the mobility of people, the steady improvement of facilities for intranational and international communication, there is every reason to expect a continuation and intensification of this process. Such is the very nature of language.

See also LANGUAGE, SCIENCE OF; LANGUAGES OF THE WORLD.

JOHN DEFRANCIS, *Seton Hall University*

Further Reading: Matthews, W.K., *Languages of the U.S.S.R.* (London 1951); Meillet, Antoine, and Cohen, Marcel, eds., *Les langues du monde*, 2d ed. (Paris 1952); Pei, Mario A., *The World's Chief Languages*, 3d ed. (London 1949).

5. Social Organization

As applied especially to Asia, the term "social organization" implies a degree of unity or commonalty that can be quite misleading. In its collective sense the term should be understood to include the separate social organizations of all of the several hundred societies identifiable with the continent and not to represent a single unified system. Each of the societies has its own distinctive structural organization.

Asia occupies 32 percent of the earth's land surface and contains 57.5 percent of its population. It is not surprising, therefore, that there should be tremendous variability in social organizations just as there is in environment. Environment is especially important, for it has profoundly influenced and in many instances determined the economy or means of livelihood, which in turn has influenced the type of social organization. In regions where heavy demands are made on male labor, as among the hunters and herders of Siberia or the pastoral nomads of the Middle East or Inner (Central) Asia, or in regions depending on plow agriculture, social organizations tend to be structured along patrilineal lines of descent with patriarchal control. In economies requiring less arduous labor, such as the growing of root crops and leafy vegetables, or in fishing communities where the element of risk is great, circumstances may favor the equalization of the sexes or even the reckoning of descent through the maternal line and the adoption of matriarchal traits.

In spite of the many fundamental differences that exist among the various Asian social organizations, three features generally distinguish them from those of Europe. The first is the great range in size and in degree of complexity, from the relatively simple cultures of the Asian Eskimo of Siberia or the Negrito Semang of tropical Malaya to the great traditional civilizations of China and India. Many of the smaller and less complex cultures have persisted into the 20th century despite the fact that they may have been surrounded by the great traditional societies on which they have become dependent, and despite the penetrating influences of Western industrial civilization.

ASIAN FAMILIES, such as these Koreans, constitute a vital part of the continent's social structure.

UNATIONS

The second feature is the tremendous significance of kinship systems and such kin group extensions as clans, lineages, extended families, and castes. In all of the still tribally organized societies these are extremely important, but even in many of the great traditional societies they have preserved social cohesion and solidarity.

The third feature is the significant role played by religion in determining the philosophical and often the legal basis of social institutions and behavior. All the world's great religions had their origin in Asia, and all contributed to the development of the world's great civilizations. Except where Communist governments have assumed control or where complete secularization has occurred, religion still provides the basis for determining governmental and social structure. Even in secularized states, much of the political philosophy retains strong religious orientations.

Between 20 and 30 great civilizations are identifiable in Asia. Each at some time in the past had developed a system of writing, its own literature, philosophy, and fine arts, its own political system, and its own social organization. In general, however, the civilizations may be grouped both regionally and on the basis of their socioreligious philosophies into five major complexes: Judeo-Christian, Arab-Islamic, Indian-Hindu, Buddhist, and Sino-Confucian.

Judeo-Christian Societies. One of the clusters of complex civilizations originating in Asia, the Judeo-Christian, has come to be identified to a greater extent with Europe than with Asia. In Israel the population consists largely of recent migrants who are so mixed racially and culturally that the ancient social bonds of kinship, local community organization, and common language have all but disappeared. Reunion has been achieved on a sociopolitical level through the renewal of older institutions derived largely from the Torah and the Talmud, but so altered that the social organization bears little resemblance to that of the ancient past. Social as well as economic organization has been largely state-planned or state-encouraged. The use of Hebrew as a common language, participation in development projects and desert reclamation, and the kibbutz have been useful in achieving a degree of social cohesion and a sense of common community. These factors, however, are not so strong as the kinship ties of the former tribal society, which emphasized traceable genealogical descent from Abraham.

In the other nations of the Middle East the general catholicity of Islam has permitted the survival of Christian communities in every area except Arabia. Among these communities are the Armenians of Turkey and the USSR, the Maronites and other Christian sects in Lebanon, and the Nestorian remnants in Iran and Inner Asia. Scattered throughout the rest of the continent (apart from Siberia) are numerous small Christian communities. Among them are the Syrian Christians of the Malabar Coast and the Roman Catholic communities of coastal India and Southeast Asia, some of which might be designated as subcultures. The only Asian nations that can be identified generally with Christianity are the Philippines, Lebanon, and, to the extent that the Orthodox Church survives in the USSR, the Russian population of Siberia.

Arab-Islamic Societies of Southwest and South Asia. Arab social organization has been determined largely by shariah (sacred law), an essen-

FARMER'S HOME and buildings in Japan are squeezed together by the flooded rice paddies that surround them and nearly isolate them from the neighboring countryside.

tially social doctrine derived from the teachings of the Koran. Shariah has exerted a profound influence on all Arab and Islamic communities. It has tended to identify civic responsibility with religious duty and to condition social unity and solidarity primarily through the observance of social behavior and such religious rituals as ablutions, prayers, and pilgrimages.

In theory, Islam recognizes no social classes. All men are equal before God, and order is to be preserved through personal harmony with God's will. In practice, a distinction has been made between man's primary responsibility to God and his secondary responsibility to his fellowman. Differences in social rank among the various patrilineal families have led to heated claims and bitter rivalry, and kinship with Mohammed or descent through Biblical lines has become a symbol of status and prestige.

Among the pastoral nomadic Bedouin, the observance of many of the rituals of shariah has been lax. A number of pre-Islamic institutions have been retained, however, and the basic tribal hierarchy of traditional Arab social organization has been intensified. Each tribal group is composed of subtribes consisting of ranked patrilineages (ahls), within which the positions of the various family units are determined by seniority. Women are segregated within each tent encampment, and labor is fairly sharply divided between the sexes. Despite social restrictions, women share partially in inheritances, although animals are generally distributed among sons. In the selection of a bride, the preferred form is parallel cousin marriage, a young man being expected to marry a daughter of one of his father's brothers.

In the kingdoms and sheikhdoms of the Arabian Peninsula, political power and civic control are still vested in the matrix of the social structure. This is not generally true in the Islamic nations in other parts of the Middle East.

Turkish civilization is a fusion of older cultures from antiquity to the present, but the social organization has been so altered that it bears little resemblance to that of the Turkic tribes in the homeland of Inner Asia. Only among the pastoral nomadic Yuruks, descendants of the Seljuks, is a semblance of the older social structure preserved. With them, as with the Iranian-speaking Kurds, tribal patterns persist. Modern Turks, especially the descendants of the Ottomans, still preserve patrilineages, but the hierarchy of clans and tribes has almost disappeared. Turkey maintains unity primarily through common nationality

rather than through a kin-based social structure.

While economic and social reforms have been introduced in Iran, they have not fundamentally changed the traditional social organization, which is based on a stratified social hierarchy. Nor has the government succeeded in converting to a sedentary way of life such pastoral nomadic tribes as the Bakhtiari.

The ethnic and social complexities of Afghanistan are far greater than those of Iran. The majority of the population consists of Pushtun Afghans, Tajik Iranians, Turkomans, Uzbeks, and Hazara Mongols. There are also numerous nomadic tribes, each with its own social organization. A common characteristic of almost all these societies, however, is the retention of the general type of tribal hierarchy and genealogically interrelated patrilineages that also characterize the social organization of Arabia.

Although Pakistan was established originally on a religious rather than on a secular basis, the basic pattern of social organization, especially in the Bengali- and Panjabi-speaking areas, is in many respects closer to that of India than to that of the western Islamic countries.

See also MIDDLE EAST—2. *The People* (Way of Living).

Indian-Hindu Societies of South Asia. Traditional Indian society has often been characterized as the most conservative in Asia. The Vedic scriptures and the *Dharmasastra* recognized four varnas (colors) or classes: the priestly Brahmans (*Brahmana*), the warrior Kshatriyas (*Ksatriya*), the mercantile Vaisyas (Vaishyas; *Vaisya*), and the laboring Sudras (Shudras; *Sudra*). Below these were the outcastes. The first three classes were twice born (*dvija*) and hence full members of Hindu society; the Sudras enjoyed only limited privileges. The Brahman class formed a special priestly hierarchy, while the three lower classes were organized into hundreds of stratified jatis (castes).

Each caste had its own council and was organized on the basis of genealogical evidence into clanlike exogamous gotras, which also were ranked in accordance with tradition. Prohibitions existed against intercaste marriage, and there were dietary, commensal, and occupational distinctions and limitations as well. In a typical north Indian village there would usually be from 15 to 25 jatis. A village might be identified as Rajput (Kshatriya), with members of this class predominating numerically. A few Brahman families would be present to take care of the reli-

PRIMITIVE METHODS of trading characterize a cattle fair held in an arid area near the border of West Pakistan and India.

gious-ritual and educational needs of the community. Different artisan and service castes would also be represented, many of the latter being indentified traditionally with certain higher-caste families with whom they were hereditarily associated. In accordance with services rendered, the higher castes would be obliged to supply the serving castes with life's necessities. Each village community formed a cohesive social unit, and kin and marriage ties connected villages at various caste levels into superimposed networks.

In modern India caste is no longer recognized by law, and wages have largely replaced reciprocal socioeconomic relationships. Similarly, industrial jobs and contact with market and city have generally superseded dependence on intervillage exchanges. Nevertheless, behavior patterns characteristic of the various castes are still strong.

In their social organizations, Sikh, Jain, and minority Muslim communities have many features that identify them with Indian-Hindu society. There are also numerous tribal societies, some of which are being absorbed into Indian society, while others are resistant and retain their distinctive structure.

Buddhist, Islamic, and Hindu Societies of Southeast Asia. The Sinhalese, Burmese, Thai (Siamese), Laotian, and Cambodian civilizations of the primarily Buddhist nations of Ceylon and Southeast Asia share a number of social organizational traits. Usually there is a close association between individual families and their hereditary temples. While ritual observances vary considerably, every young man in a strict Theravada or Hinayana Buddhist community is expected to spend several months of his life in a monastery. In the larger society, distinctions still exist between the upper classes and the peasants, and extended family ties are remarkably loose. It is expected that social unity will be achieved primarily through cooperative economic and religious channels rather than through family lineages.

The only large Islamic nation on the Southeast Asian mainland is Malaysia, but there are numerous smaller Muslim communities, such as the Panthay and Arakanese of Burma and other communities in Thailand. In other parts of Southeast Asia and in western China there remain more than 100 culturally distinct societies, although many of them have been in contact with the great civilizations for centuries. Among

these are the Naga, Chin, Kachin (Chingpaw), Wa, Palaung, Miao, Yao, Lahu, Lashi, Lisu, Lolo, and Li. Such other societies as the Karen, Shan, Mon, and Khmer have developed their own complex cultures on an interrelated basis with the great civilizations.

Fully as complex is the situation in Indonesia. Apart from the nobility, Javanese society is stratified horizontally into an administrative and intellectual elite class and a commoner class. Possibly even more significant is the distinction between the *santri*, who follow the basic principles of Islam, and the more lax but preponderant *wongabangan*. The latter, for the most part commoners, are nominal Muslims who observe only the rituals called *slametau*, which are concerned with major events in the life cycle of the individual. Villagers tend to preserve a pre-Islamic reverence for ancestors and superstitious beliefs and practices, and they often fail to observe the daily Muslim prayers, the fasts, the pilgrimage to Mecca, and the prohibition against eating pork.

The social organizations of the Sundanese and the Madurese closely resemble those of the Javanese, but Balinese society retains the caste-class structure of Hindu society. Some of the social organizations of the smaller horticultural and agricultural Indonesian societies, such as the Atjehnese (Achinese), Bataks, and Menangkabau of Sumatra and the Dayaks (Dyaks) of Borneo, have been influenced by Islam.

See also SOUTHEAST ASIA—*The Land and the People.*

Sino-Confucian Societies of East Asia. Traditional Chinese society was based on the concept of the nation-family (*kuo-chia*) and on the Confucian doctrine that a perfect society was one in which each person lived in accordance with the duties imposed on him by his particular status and role. Below the imperial family and the nobility a social hierarchy of four classes was recognized: scholars, farmers, artisans, and merchants. Social mobility upward was possible through a nationwide examination system accessible to rich and poor alike. Persons from all walks of life might rise to positions of intellectual or administrative prominence and join the gentry elite. A kinship system based on exogamous clans also cut across class barriers and provided social solidarity at the community level. Villages or parts of villages were frequently composed of members of a single patrilineal clan with its own school, treasury, ancestral hall, cemetery, and clan lands for the benefit of the less fortunate members and, if possible, a clan temple. People of different villages tended to be bound together through a system of affinal ties, preference often being given to marriage between a son and his cross-cousin (his mother's brother's daughter). There was also a variety of clubs or associations at local, provincial, and national levels that catered to persons of common occupations or leanings.

The entire social organization depended on loyalty to the emperor as holder of the mandate of Heaven, but it was only right that a sovereign be overthrown if he failed to carry out the will of Heaven. Peasants have been known for their patience, but Chinese history is replete with instances of rebellion. Rulers were obliterated, dynasties were overthrown, and peasant leaders periodically seized power and redistributed lands, titles, and offices.

In Communist China the goal of the regime is to change the basic structure of the society and economy. Much of the ancient social organization has been altered since 1949, but there are numerous precedents in Chinese history for the methods employed and the patterns achieved. The social structure is changing, but it is changing within the framework of the patterns of the past.

Korean social organization was traditionally modeled on that of China, which it resembles in fundamentals. Where it differs, it tends to be like that of the old Manchu society.

Although traditional Japanese society borrowed many of its features from China, its organization was quite distinctive. Before the Meiji Restoration, clan surnames were generally restricted to the endogamous *bushi* (warriors) or aristocracy, who comprised no more than 8 to 10 percent of the total population. The peasants were named for the houses in which they lived; in most cases, houses were named for their locations. Since 1868 the social structure has undergone many changes. While the older extended household or family system of both the *bushi* and the peasants survives, corporate economic and social solidarity at the village level has largely been replaced by private interests of individual family units. Within the family itself individual interests have tended to supersede those of the group. The emperor retains his position as symbolic head of the Japanese family-nation, but the myths of his descent from the Sun Goddess and of the divine origin of the Japanese people are no longer credited within the framework of modern Japan, with its highly educated, industrialized, and largely urbanized society.

Societies of Inner and North Asia. Until the mid-20th century, Tibet and Mongolia generally maintained their northern Buddhist (Mahayana) civilizations, but under Communist pressures the religious and social institutions of both areas underwent drastic changes. Formerly, Mongol society, which had a pastoral nomadic economy, was divided into patrilineal descent groups known as *torel*. Grazing lands were divided into units known as aimaks, and these in turn into banner lands. The primary basis of everyday social solidarity was the aimak rather than the *torel*, which was important mainly for the selection of mates and for inheritance. In such a strongly patrilineal society, a woman lost her own kin status upon marrying and assumed that of her husband's household and larger lineage group.

CONSULATE GENERAL OF JAPAN, NEW YORK

WOMEN IN JAPAN handpick tea leaves, one of the major Asian agricultural commodities for export trade.

Overtly, Mongol Buddhism or Lamaism has generally disappeared, and efforts have been made to induce the Mongols to settle down to sedentary pastoralism and agriculture or industry. To some extent these efforts have been successful, but the aimaks and the *torel* have survived.

In Tibet, which has always been mainly agricultural, a marked distinction formerly prevailed between the landed aristocracy and the peasant commoners. Each family, however, was expected to send a son to its lamasery to be trained as a monk. Through excellence in scholarship and personal character, social mobility was therefore possible, and the child of even the humblest peasant might rise to a position of ecclesiastical eminence.

Apart from Russian migrants, by far the most numerous minority populations in the Asian USSR are the Turkic nations: the Kazakhs, Uzbeks, Karakalpaks, Turkomans, and Kirghiz. Some of the Uzbeks and most of the tribally organized nations were formerly nomadic pastoralists, but under Communist pressure, nomadism has generally been replaced by sedentary pastoralism, and a large part of the population has turned to agriculture and industry. These changes have drastically altered social structures, and tribal organization has virtually disappeared. The oasis dwellers and the nomadic pastoralists of Chinese Turkestan (Sinkiang-Uigur Autonomous Region) have been less influenced by political pressures, and the older tribal structures are still recognizable.

GORDON T. BOWLES, *Syracuse University*

Bibliography
Beardsley, Richard K., and others, *Village Japan* (Chicago 1959).
Berque, Jacques, *The Arabs: Their History and Future* (London 1964).
Binder, Leonard, *The Ideological Revolution in the Middle East* (New York 1964).
Cole, Fay Cooper, *The Peoples of Malaysia* (New York 1945).
Cressey, George B., *Crossroads: Land and Life in Southwest Asia* (Philadelphia 1960).
Dube, Shyama C., *Indian Village* (Ithaca, N.Y., 1955).
Fried, Morton H., *Fabric of Chinese Society* (New York 1953).
Jochelson, Vladimir I., *Peoples of Asiatic Russia* (New York 1928).
Murdock, George P., ed., *Social Structure in Southeast Asia* (Chicago 1960).
Myrdal, Jan, *Report from a Chinese Village*, tr. by M. Michael (New York 1965).
Nakamura, Hajime, *Ways of Thinking of Eastern Peoples: India, China, Tibet, Japan*, rev. ed., tr. by Philip P. Weiner (Honolulu 1964).
Rowan, Carl T., *The Pitiful and the Proud* (New York 1956).

6. Economic Systems

Asia is so huge a continent that its major regions, with vastly different economic histories, have evolved different economic systems and levels of development. Geographical, social, political, and military influences have been so diverse that one may justifiably speak of the five faces of economic Asia.

Southwest Asia. The economic history of Southwest Asia has been dominated by three factors: geography, agriculture, and petroleum. The region lies across all but one of the major land routes connecting Europe, Asia, and Africa. Moreover, enjoying access to the Mediterranean, Black, Caspian, Arabian, and Red seas, as well as to the Indian Ocean, Southwest Asia has for centuries been an integral part of the world's principal trade routes. For a wide variety of reasons, the region has been the source, channel, or destination of large numbers of migrants and invaders. In earlier ages, the Persians, Greeks, Romans, Arabs, and Turks, and, in later times, the British and French left the imprint of their economic institutions and practices on the region.

Between 70 and 80 percent of the population of Southwest Asia is engaged in some form of farming. Prevailing land-tenure systems and agricultural technology more closely resemble those of medieval Europe than the factory farms of the United States. Landownership is concentrated, and tenancy is widespread and insecure. Since land rentals are high and peasants assume most of the risks of cultivation, their incomes are generally low. Landlords, usually interested only in returns from rentals, rarely seek to improve their land or its productivity. In contrast to the situation in other parts of Asia, a fear of reprisals from landlords has generally retarded movements for land-tenure reform. Peasants have continued to accept subsistence levels of living as a way of life.

Farms in Southwest Asia are generally composed of small plots, frequently widely separated, and extensively rather than intensively cultivated. Since arable land is scarce, farm animals commonly graze on weeds. Soil fertility is replenished by allowing land to lie fallow. Manual labor is customary in plowing, sowing, reaping, binding, and agricultural construction work. Such implements as are used are primitive because of the availability and cheapness of labor and the high cost of modern machinery. The peasants have many economic, technical, and legal problems, but perhaps their greatest concern is the irregular and inadequate water supply. Lack of water is the chief limiting factor in crop production and grazing, and in few areas can farming be carried on without irrigation.

Petroleum has achieved a central economic importance in Southwest Asia only during the 20th century. Oil dominates the economies of Iran, Iraq, Saudi Arabia, Kuwait, and Bahrain, the primary producers, and of Jordan, Syria, and Lebanon, through which pipelines carry it to ports for distribution to western Europe and other parts of the world. In return for petroleum concessions, the supplying nations have received 50 percent of the profits, plus taxes on each barrel produced. The nations granting the right-of-way for pipelines have received sizable annual rentals; employment at relatively high wages in the oil ports has stimulated the development of the surrounding areas. Without petroleum, Southwest Asia would be even more dependent on agriculture and hence less developed than it is.

Modern factories exist in most Southwest Asian countries, but domestic or handicraft production predominates. As in medieval Europe, the means of production are man-powered. In the fashion of their ancestors, people everywhere in the region process food and make rugs, textiles, leather goods, ceramics, and metal and wooden objects. The tourist trade is an important outlet for some of these handicrafts. Extractive industries (except the petroleum industry) and such heavy industries as iron, steel, and chemicals are conspicuously absent. Because of the greater profitability of agricultural rentals, the wealthy do not invest in industry. As a result of some unpleasant experiences with foreign-owned companies, the various governments have generally discouraged foreign investment. Except in Israel, the consequence has been industrial stagnation.

The lack of industrial development is reflected in the domestic and foreign trade patterns and in the transportation networks of Southwest Asia. The cities and large villages serve mainly as supply and marketing areas. Except for products related to petroleum, the chief exports are agricultural, while imports consist largely of manufactured goods. Transportation facilities are satisfactory only in and between the large cities and ports. Air and sea transportation is generally excellent, but road systems vary considerably. Main roads, usually hard-surfaced, are serviceable the year round, but secondary roads are little more than dirt roads or desert tracks.

In general, the economic prospects of the Middle East have not been good. Internal political instability has discouraged prospective local investors, while rivalries and intrigues among the Arab states as well as expensive and unsuccessful military actions and boycotts against Israel have made foreign entrepreneurs wary. The poverty of the large majority of the population has not been relieved.

See also MIDDLE EAST—3. *Economic Life;* PETROLEUM—2. *Historical Survey* (20th Century): Middle East.

South Asia. In modern times the countries of South Asia were under British control and fulfilled the traditional economic roles of colonies. Providing cheap labor and low-priced raw materials, they in turn imported manufactured goods. Although the basic foreign trade pattern has remained the same since these countries became independent, some important changes have occurred. The South Asian nations, striving to modernize their economies, have been importing greater quantities of capital goods and technical assistance while lessening their former dependence on the West for consumer goods.

Although processes of industrialization are much in evidence in the cities, this is not true of the rural areas where most South Asians live. Earning their livelihood directly from the soil, they practice the technologically primitive agriculture of their ancestors. Crops are grown with much manual labor, while farm implements and tools are inefficient. Even in modern times, shortages of natural fertilizer, the high price of chemical fertilizer, and an inadequate water supply limit output to amounts barely sufficient to feed the large population of the region. Serious problems have also been caused by inadequate supplies of industrial raw materials.

The industrialization of South Asia has not proceeded rapidly enough for the needs of the growing population. In most nations of the region less than 15 percent of the labor force is engaged in manufacturing. Where modern factories exist, they are usually devoted to the processing of agricultural products and to the manufacture of textiles, ceramics, metalware, and other light consumer goods. Only in India and, to a lesser extent, in Pakistan are there modern iron and steel plants. In contrast, traditional handicraft industries continue to flourish. They, too, turn out a wide variety of textile, wood, metal, and glass products.

Contributing to the retardation of South Asia's industries are the quantitative insufficiency and qualitative inadequacy of the facilities for transportation and communications. Railroad facilities, quantitatively excellent in India, Pakistan, and Ceylon, are lacking in Afghanistan and the Himalayan states. Moreover, the variegated broad- (66-inch; 168-cm), meter- (about 40-inch; 100-cm), and narrow- (24- to 30-inch; 61- to 76-cm) gauge tracks, used in the construction of railroads in the past, have raised technical problems that hinder economic development. For most peoples and goods of the area, transportation still means the use of human feet and backs. In some areas people travel and transport their goods by bullock cart. Usually bicycles, buses, and streetcars are found only in the cities. Most roads in South Asia are little more than tracks. The excellent ports and airlines have barely touched the lives of the great majority of the population.

Still other factors retard the economic development of the region. Most important are the high rates of illiteracy. In the early 1960's more than 80 percent of the people in some countries could not read or write their own languages. Even in Ceylon, with the highest literacy rate in South Asia, approximately 40 percent of all persons of school age or older were illiterate. Although public education at all levels is expanding, many years will doubtless pass before this major barrier to economic progress can be overcome.

Cultural and religious obstacles to progress also exist. While the cultures and religious philosophies of South Asia are numerous and diverse, a common rigidity in socioeconomic matters results in an inefficient allocation of resources. The animosity between India and Pakistan, for example, stemming from religious friction between Hindus and Muslims, has obstructed the flow of trade between the two countries. There has thus been little application of the basic economic principles of specialization and exchange. The Indian caste system has prevented individuals of widely varying abilities from realizing their economic potential. The many ethnic groups of Afghanistan, adhering to their time-honored tribal traditions, have continued to cling to a subsistence and nomadic agriculture. Farm production of the capitalistic type, which would increase their incomes, has not been readily accepted.

The various plans for economic development adopted by India, Pakistan, and Ceylon since the early 1950's are encouraging. Although these programs have not been an unqualified success, they have nevertheless focused attention on the prevailing archaic economic systems.

Southeast Asia. The two outstanding features of the economic history of Southeast Asia are the location of the region and its unusually favorable man-land ratios. The area has long been a cross-roads for people, goods, and economic ideas and institutions emanating from South and East Asia and the Middle East. It has also been a major passageway for shipping from Europe, Africa, the United States, and other Asian areas. The excellent facilities for travel by water have historically dominated not only the transportation sectors of the economies of the region but much of the general economic activity as well. Through their ports most of the nations of Southeast Asia, as former colonies of European powers, have exported a wide variety of agricultural and industrial raw materials and imported manufactured goods.

About 70 percent of the labor force of the region is engaged in agriculture in all of its diverse forms. Unlike other Asian regions, however, Southeast Asia has a relatively small population in relation to the total land area. Less than 10 percent of the land is under cultivation. Although some sections are densely populated (and, indeed, are among the most heavily populated in the world), agriculture is basically extensive rather than intensive. In contrast to East and South Asia, Southeast Asia as a whole usually produces food surpluses, which are shipped to these less fortunate areas. Rice, dependent on the heavy but variable rainfall, is the commonest food crop.

While most small farmers in Southeast Asia raise food for subsistence, a small number of large estates have concentrated on the production of cash crops, principally in nonfood categories. These products, designed for export, include rubber, kapok, teak, hardwoods, sugar, tea, quinine, abacá, sisal, palm oil, tobacco, and copra. The generally favorable man-land ratio that has permitted cultivators to acquire arable land with relative ease is reflected in the absence of industrial development, except for that related to the extractive industries. Rich, easily accessible deposits of tin, iron ore, chromite, bauxite, lead, gold, copper, and zinc caused an influx of foreign capital for mining operations in the 19th and 20th centuries. In Indonesia, petroleum deposits have been exploited.

NATURAL RUBBER, here being tapped by an Indian laborer in Malaya, is an important resource in Asia.

BRIAN BRAKE, FROM MAGNUM

SHIPBUILDING, an industry in which Japan is a world leader, symbolizes Asia's growing mechanization.

Most of the nonextractive industries of the region are devoted to the processing of agricultural products and the manufacture of light consumer goods. Rice and sugar have been processed for local consumption, and silk and cotton textiles woven for home use. Village handicraft industries turn out glass, tile, pottery, baskets, and tobacco products. While foreign manufactured goods have offered some competition to handicrafts in the cities, they have not made any significant inroads in the rural areas.

The nonmaritime transportation facilities of Southeast Asia are poorly developed. Railroads are inadequate. Since World War II, airlines have established services between the major cities of the region, but most roads are poor. In Burma, Vietnam, and Malaysia the inland waterways have been especially important. Urban areas with access to waterborne transportation facilities have always been singularly important in the economic history of Southeast Asia. Such cities as Singapore, Rangoon, Manila, and Djakarta participate in both entrepôt and direct trade. It is to and through cities of this type that most of the commerce of the area passes.

In the mid-1960's United States participation in the war in Vietnam sharply stimulated production in and trade to, within, and from Southeast Asia. Employment, prices, and incomes rose in the area affected by United States war-goods purchases.

East Asia. The economy of the nations of East Asia is characterized by sharp contradictions. Perhaps the most striking is that, in a region overshadowed by the Chinese empire for several thousand years, it is Japan that has made the greatest economic progress in modern times. Until 1868 the Japanese economy was based on agriculture and domestic commerce. As a result of government policy after the Meiji Restoration, agriculture became capitalistic, modern banks and industries were organized, foreign and domestic trade was promoted, and modern transportation and communications facilities were constructed. By the end of World War I the country had become a world economic power. In the 1920's and 1930's, particularly after the seizure of Manchuria and the consequent enlargement of its resources base, Japan began to emphasize the development of heavy industry and the stockpiling of such scarce raw materials as petroleum in order to meet the demands of its armed forces. In 1945 it was forced to relinquish Korea, Manchuria, Taiwan (Formosa), southern Sakhalin, and the Kuril Islands, thus losing both its primary sources of raw materials and its largest markets. Soon, however, the United States and Southeast Asia replaced these areas as both buyer and supplier. A successful land-tenure reform program, the Korean War, and a constantly rising domestic demand for commodities of all types brought unprecedented prosperity in the postwar period.

The economic development of China has been radically different. In the early 19th century the country had the largest population and the most highly developed resources in Asia. Unsuccessful wars with Great Britain in the 1840's and 1850's, destructive rebellions in the 1850's and 1860's, and the decline of the Ch'ing (Manchu) dynasty led to general economic turmoil. In 1911–1912 the dynasty fell, and until 1949, when the Chinese Communist party gained control of the mainland, there were few years when a strong central government existed to direct, encourage, and finance economic development. Agriculture, the predominant form of economic activity, was stagnant. Farms were small, farm animals and implements were scarce, and fields were generally fragmented. At the village level there was a great concentration of landownership, and tenancy was widespread.

Because of the constant warfare among military leaders, who contended for power after the fall of the Ch'ing dynasty, economic life was insecure. Investment in industry, particularly of the heavy fixed type, was discouraged; few new transportation and communications facilities were built; the literacy rate remained low; and such natural disasters as floods, droughts, and typhoons, which seemed to strike annually, continued to take their toll. The difficulties of the Nationalist government increased after the Japanese attack in 1937.

In 1949, after defeating the Nationalists, the Chinese Communist government began to rehabilitate the damaged sectors of the economy. It implemented two economic plans, the First Five-Year Plan (1953–1957) and the Second Five-Year Plan (1958–1962). While the first was moderately successful, the second was not. The formation of communes in farming areas and some urban districts in 1958, together with long hours, hard work, separation from families, and low living levels, caused widespread dissatisfaction and heavy strains on the economy. As a result, Communist China's hopes for an economically bright future were greatly dampened.

Korea's economic history has been as unfortunate as that of China. Annexed by Japan in 1910, the country served as a colony until 1945. Rice, iron ore, coal, graphite, tungsten, copper, and other raw materials were exported, and a wide variety of manufactured goods was imported. Economic development, though rapid, was marred by a high degree of exploitation on the part of the Japanese. Few Koreans were permitted to acquire a higher education, occupy positions of importance in business and government, or enter the professions. About 80 percent of the population was engaged in manual labor in agriculture and industry.

In southern Korea, agriculture, particularly rice production, dominated the economy. As in China, the farms were small, and tools and animals were inadequate. In the villages, landownership was concentrated and in the hands of com-

Above left: Ankara, a forgotten city in western Asia, was selected capital of Turkey in 1923 and rebuilt along modern lines.

Above right: Although industrialization came late to Japan, today its production techniques are among the world's best.

ASIA

Right: Ujjain, one of the oldest inhabited sites in India, is a famous pilgrimage center where Hindus gather for their ritual baths.

Below: The Bank Umumnegara in downtown Djakarta once served the Dutch, and is now the hub of Indonesia's financial system.

Above: Islam is one of the major religions of Asia. This 17th century mosque in Lahore, Pakistan, is still used for worship.

Left: Home production plays an important role in the Asian economy. These women are weaving cloth in the Philippines.

Below: A food vendor sells his wares in an outdoor market in Kabul, the capital and largest city in Afghanistan.

(Top) Oppersdorf from Alpha; (left) José Sarmiento from Pix; (below) Peter Throckmorton from Nancy Palmer

Below: Rice, the food staple of Asia, is a leading crop on the Chengtu plain in China.

Brian Drake from Magnum

Above: Classical and modern Japan come face-to-face in a dress shop.

Above: Wearing traditional costumes, girls in Bali, Indonesia, perform a dance in pantomime.

Left: Land reform on Taiwan has created a new type of family farm.

Below left: Masked figures guard a royal tomb in the courtyard of the Grand Palace in Bangkok, Thailand.

Below right: A girl sells food staples from her sampan in Hong Kong Harbor, one of the busiest ports in Asia.

Above: The Tien Shan, among the highest mountains in Asia, separate the USSR from China.

ASIA

(Top) Ralph Gerstle from Photo Researchers; (left) Forbert from Alpha; (bottom) Annan

Left: Technician on duty in a modern Indian pharmaceutical plant in which antibiotics are manufactured.

Below: This technical high school for boys in Rangoon, Burma, is an excellent example of modern Asian architecture.

mercially oriented Japanese landlords, who took advantage of the large number of tenants dependent on them. Interest rates were high, water control was generally managed for the benefit of the landlords, and taxes were heavy. In northern Korea, mineral resources were exploited, power resources were developed, transportation and communications facilities and factories were constructed, and ports were improved. After Japan's surrender in 1945 and the division of the country along the 38th parallel, the nation's economy was split in two. Since then, South Korea has depended heavily on United States aid in the form of raw materials, machinery, and technical assistance; in North Korea, food shortages and political oppression resulted in the emigration of numerous refugees to the south. The Korean War (1950–1953) wrought great damage in both areas. South Korea's economic development since 1953 has been marked by much hesitancy, mismanagement, and profiteering. North Korea's raw materials, formerly shipped to Japan, have been exported to Communist China. While the North Korean government has issued favorable reports on industrial development, land reform, and other economic activities, they are at variance with the statements of refugees and other nonofficial accounts.

Soviet Asia. The economic history of what is now Soviet Asia dates back to the 16th century, to the early czarist interest in furs, gold, and silver. Not until the 19th century was Russian political control of the region extended and stabilized, however, and only in the 20th century has significant economic development occurred. Historically, the principal economic function of the region has been to supply precious furs and metals, industrial raw materials, and food to European Russia. Unlike other Asian areas, it has imported people rather than manufactured goods. The standard of living has for the most part been low.

The Russian rulers of Soviet Asia have largely used the resources of the area as they found them, and until the mid-20th century the development of nonextractive industries proceeded slowly. Most factories have been devoted to the processing of agricultural and forest products and industrial raw materials. Fish has been canned or converted into fertilizer; mills have turned out lumber, paper, and pulp; and mineral ores and petroleum have been processed.

The large-scale movement of raw materials and the development of widely scattered but mainly light industrial centers have been supported by barely adequate but growing transportation networks. The railroad system, begun in the late 19th century, consists of two major east-west lines and numerous important branches. The most significant and best-known line, the Trans-Siberian Railroad, extends from western Siberia to the key port of Vladivostok on the Pacific Ocean. Another important line, the Turkestan-Siberia (Turksib) Railroad, links the Trans-Siberian Railroad with Soviet Central Asia.

Because Soviet Asia's many rivers empty into the Arctic Ocean and are frozen for six months or more each year, they have contributed little to the economic progress of the region. By contrast, the numerous airlines have been of great use for long-distance hauls, although they are of only slight importance locally. The road system has been inadequate for both short- and long-distance transportation.

EASTFOTO

NEW STEEL MILL at Anshan, China, represents Asia's efforts to increase heavy industrial output.

While Soviet Asia is in absolute terms still an economically underdeveloped area with tremendous acreage and natural resources in relation to its population, in relative terms its rate of growth since World War II has been high. Aware of the potential of the region and its own economic needs, the USSR is not only investing heavily in its Asian territory but is also encouraging settlement.

Summary. The predominant economic factors in Asia have been the geography of the continent, the static nature of the agricultural sectors, and the direction and stimulus given to industrial development in specific nations by social, political, and military programs. In the 1960's and 1970's the basic patterns of economic life in most of Asia are not likely to be altered drastically. There, as in other parts of the world where large numbers of people and firmly embedded institutions and traditions are involved, change comes slowly.

See also sections on economic development in articles on various Asian countries; COAL—5. *Economics;* COLOMBO PLAN; MINERAL WEALTH OF THE WORLD; MINING—3. *Mining History;* RAILROADS—8. *Asia;* RICE; RUBBER; TEA; TIN.

SIDNEY KLEIN
Rutgers—The State University of New Jersey

Bibliography
Bonné, Alfred, *State and Economics in the Middle East,* 2d ed., rev. (London 1955).
Braibanti, Ralph J.D., and Spengler, J.J., eds., *Administration and Economic Development in India* (Durham, N.C., 1963).
Crane, Robert I., *Aspects of Economic Development in South Asia* (New York 1954).
Higgins, Benjamin H., and Higgins, Jean, *Indonesia: The Crisis of the Millstones* (Princeton, N.J., 1963).
Hughes, Trevor J., and Luard, David E.T., *The Economic Development of Communist China, 1949–1958* (New York 1959).
Leeman, Wayne A., *The Price of Middle East Oil* (Ithaca, N.Y., 1962).
Lockwood, William W., *The Economic Development of Japan* (Princeton, N.J., 1954).
Silcock, Thomas H., *Commonwealth Economy in Southeast Asia* (Durham, N.C., 1959).
Tawney, Richard H., *Land and Labour in China* (New York 1932).
United Nations, *Economic Survey of Asia and the Far East* (New York 1963).

7. Governmental Structures

Political Development. Asian governments are diverse in form, yet their political heritages have much in common. Political institutions in the continent originated with the early cultures of the Tigris-Euphrates, Indus, and Hwang Ho (Yellow River) valleys. Before 2000 B.C. governments of the city-state type existed in some of the communities along these rivers. Later, the city-states expanded into small empires ruled by autocratic kings.

The king in these areas was the spiritual as well as the temporal ruler. He was either the high priest of the state religion, as in Mesopotamia, or an emperor enjoying a mandate from Heaven, as in China. Ordinarily, he ruled through a hereditary group of priests and a privileged class of nobles who commanded military forces. Benevolent at first, such monarchs gradually became authoritarian and expansionist. They are exemplified by the rulers of the Assyrian empire, by Darius I of Persia (reigned 522–486 B.C.), by Asoka (Ashoka, reigned about 274–237 B.C.) of the Maurya dynasty in India, and by Shih Huang Ti, the first emperor of the Ch'in dynasty (reigned 221–210 B.C.), and Wu-ti (reigned 140–87 B.C.), of the Earlier Han dynasty, in China.

The trend toward military expansion, induced by the absolute power of authoritarian rulers, received further impetus from the Muslim conquests that began in the 7th century A.D. The Muslims did not distinguish between secular and religious power. They believed that the sole ruler of mankind was God and that His word, as revealed to Mohammed in the Koran, was both law and constitution. In their eyes the purpose of the state was to uphold the faith and to maintain and enforce the word of God. When Mohammed died, he was succeeded by a caliph who was the head of the Muslim religion as well as the chief of state.

Although the Muslims did not conquer East Asia, the Chinese and Japanese maintained similar attitudes toward their rulers. Chinese tradition dictated that the emperor be obeyed because he had ascended the throne with a mandate from Heaven. In Japan the emperor, believed to be of divine origin, was theoretically if not actually absolute. Hindu political theory also advanced the concept of obedience to the ruler.

Asian political systems, early cast in authoritarian molds, evolved steadily after the Muslim conquest. Absolutism reached its zenith with the Mongol (Yüan) dynasty in China (1260–1368) and with the Great Mughul (Mogul) rulers in India (1526–1707). Nor were the Ottoman sultans in Southwest Asia less powerful. Autocratic rule continued in China until the overthrow of the Manchu (Ch'ing) dynasty (1644–1912), while in Japan, military dictatorship prevailed under the shoguns (1192–1868).

With the arrival of Europeans in the 16th century, governments in many parts of Asia were slowly but deeply affected. The English East India Company, following a series of initial incursions into India, gradually consolidated its control and extended its rule over the subcontinent. After the Indian (Sepoy) Mutiny of 1857–1858, however, the British government took over administration from the company. The result was a series of legal and political reforms, which gradually modified governmental institutions and ideas

of long standing. Most important, political concepts that had evolved in England over a period of centuries became embedded in Indian thought. The influence of French and Dutch political ideas in Indochina and the East Indies, respectively, was to prove less durable.

While Britain was introducing political reforms in India, a revolution was taking place in Japan. After the country had been opened by Commodore Matthew C. Perry in 1853–1854, its leaders undertook to learn Western techniques. Utilizing newly acquired Western concepts, they initiated numerous reforms. A constitution modeled on European practices, especially those of Prussia, was proclaimed in 1889, and a Parliament of the British type was established in the following year. Limited national suffrage was also introduced; a universal manhood suffrage law was passed in 1925. The constitution was the earliest in Asia, and the Parliament (Diet) was the first Asian legislative body. These reforms of the Meiji period inspired similar movements elsewhere in Asia.

After the Opium War (1839–1842), nationalist movements were not long in rising in China. But the reforms proposed in the late 19th century were doomed to failure because of the reactionary policies of the Manchu court. In 1911–1912, when the Manchu dynasty was overthrown, it was replaced by a weak and ineffectual republican government. While the new government was striving to unify the country, the Bolshevik Revolution occurred in Russia (1917). With the formation of the Comintern in 1919, communism came not only to China but to other parts of Asia as well. Asia thus became a stage where traditionalism, modernism, and communism were all to play their parts.

When the Ottoman empire disintegrated after World War I, the countries of the Middle East that had been under Turkish rule became mandates of the League of Nations. In 1920, Syria and Lebanon were assigned to France for administration, while Britain received the mandates for Iraq and Palestine (including Transjordan). British and French colonial administrative systems were introduced in these areas.

While Britain and France were consolidating their position in the Middle East, Japan created the Manchurian incident in 1931. In 1937 the Japanese attacked China proper, and in 1941–1942 they swept over all of Southeast Asia. Although they preserved almost intact the traditional forms of government in Southeast Asia, they controlled state functions through their occupation commanders and advocated a policy of "Asia for the Asians." By the time Japan was brought to surrender in 1945 by the joint efforts of the Allied powers, all the Asian colonies and protectorates of Britain, France, and the Netherlands were bent on achieving freedom from Western domination and allowed the return of their former rulers only when provided with guarantees of independence. The defeat of Japan and the weakening of colonial power as an aftermath of the war created a power vacuum in Asia, and just as the former colonies began coping with the problems posed by independence, a difficult and menacing force arose in China in the form of that country's firmly entrenched (after civil war), expansionist, and militantly Communist new government.

The independence movements throughout Asia, themselves stimulated by nationalism, could not help but be deeply affected by the rising tide of communism, and in order to check it, some Asian political leaders advocated alliance with the United States and the espousal of democratic forms of government. However, in the ideological struggles of the 1950's and 1960's some Asians concluded that democracy had certain inadequacies. As a result, military leaders took over state power in a number of countries. Military government of this type, maintaining a constitutional or democratic façade, was a new phenomenon in Asian politics.

Characteristics of Asian Government. With military men as chiefs of state, many governments in Asia have partially returned in the post-World War II period to the ancient tradition of unitary autocracy. Autocracy of this type—in effect, dictatorship—is the first characteristic of Asian government. Chiefs of state of this type do not consult public opinion or representative bodies on important decisions. Since the entire life of the people is not regimented, however, this type of government differs from Western totalitarian regimes. Dictatorship, practiced in many Asian countries in the past, has prevailed in the years following World War II.

A second feature is the concept that government is the source of political authority, to which citizens must submit. Little changed in most Asian countries since ancient times, this tradition has allowed governments to become autocratic and to compel obedience. Consequently, Asian peoples seldom revolt against their governments unless life has become so wretched that it is the equivalent of the death that might result from rebellion.

A third characteristic is the personalizing of leadership. Personality, not systems or ideology, has dominated Asian politics.

A fourth feature is a desuetude of law. Although many Asian countries have excellent legal systems and codes of law, they have not always put them into practice. This tendency is due to a weak juridical sense, to a strong attachment to religious law, and to the force of a societal code of ethics.

Finally, there has been a general apathy toward politics on the part of the common people. Caring little about elections, ordinary citizens have had no ambition for public office. Politics in Asia has been the domain of small groups of upper-class persons.

In most Asian countries professional bureaucrats staff the various governmental posts. They are the political elite, who acquire their positions through family connections, examinations, or special appointment. They are transferred from one position to another with little regard for specialization or administrative responsibilities. Active and powerful pressure groups are almost nonexistent, except in a few countries with viable parliamentary systems, where labor, business, and other organizations may influence the formulation of policy. In the capitals or major cities of other Asian countries, professional organizations of businessmen, while not actual pressure groups, have close contacts with the government. Although they may not affect national policy, they attempt to influence officials in favor of their business or industry.

Political parties, uncommon in some Asian countries, may be found in Japan, India, Israel, Ceylon, Turkey, Cyprus, Burma, Malaysia, the Philippines, Lebanon, Iran, and Indonesia. These parties vary greatly in strength and efficacy. Certain countries, such as Afghanistan, Nepal, Thailand, Cambodia, Jordan, Saudi Arabia, Yemen, and Iraq, have, for all practical purposes, no political parties. In Pakistan, political parties were suspended from 1958 to 1962, and in the Republic of Korea (South Korea), political activity was banned from 1961 to 1963. Some Communist countries permit the existence of minor parties, but these function only as window dressing.

Aside from party politics, the landed gentry bring quite a force to bear on the administration of Asian rural districts. These groups are composed of village leaders, wealthy landowners, individuals prominent in caste or class, and persons who have political connections in local or central governments. Officially or unofficially, members of these groups conduct village affairs, serve as private judges to mediate disputes, settle family quarrels, advise individuals, and even arrange marriages. They also act as intermediaries between government officials and private citizens. Nevertheless, the landed gentry possess little power in shaping national policies.

An important political force everywhere in Asia consists of the military establishment and the police force. In most countries the police are commanded by centralized bureaus in the ministry of the interior of the national government. Provincial, county, and local police forces are usually headed by a national chief whose power is understandably great. Through pressures on voters he is able to influence elections, sometimes decisively. Military leaders in Asia differ from their counterparts in democratic nations. In a number of countries commanders consider soldiers to be their personal property, and because of their close relationship with their men, they cannot easily be removed from their commands. Soldiers may actually refuse to accept new commanders. Thus, military leaders may challenge the policy of the administration with threats of revolt. In the late 1950's and early 1960's, coups d'état occurred, and governments were taken over by military leaders, in Thailand, Burma, Pakistan, Turkey, South Korea, Iraq, Syria, Indonesia, and South Vietnam. The military is obviously a major social and political force in Asian government.

Students form a very important political and social force in all Asian countries. They are intellectuals and thus command followers and respect. Their sense of responsibility toward society and state is very strong, and this coupled with their youth evokes sympathy. It is often the student faction that organizes national demonstrations in support of political movements. It was the students' demonstration that brought down the Korean regime of Syngman Rhee in 1960, and students played a great part in causing drastic revisions in the government of Indonesia in 1966.

Constitutionalism. Except for Saudi Arabia and most of the sheikhdoms, every country in Asia has a constitution. The Indian Constitution is the longest document of its kind in the world. All the Asian constitutions contain provisions on the type of state, the structure of the government, the division of political power, civil rights, and political processes, but implementation falls short of the stipulations.

Insofar as distribution of power between central and local governments is concerned, most Asian countries are unitary states, with the exception of India, Malaysia, and Burma, which are federal unions rather than unitary states. The predilection for unitary government is due to the historical development of Asian political institutions. The central government has usually been organized first, provincial and county governments being created later. There are, however, two new trends: newly independent states tend either to give greater power to local provinces or to form federal unions.

Baron de Montesquieu's formula for the separation of power has been adhered to, at least in principle, by most of the countries. Government has usually been divided into legislative, judicial, and executive branches. The Republic of China (Nationalist China), with two supplementary branches, examination and control or investigation, has a five-branch system. Separation of power does not exist in Saudi Arabia or in most of the sheikhdoms and sultanates, while the Communist states are monolithic, the executive and judiciary being derived from the legislative assembly, usually called "the People's Congress." In such states the principle of checks and balances does not exist.

In most states except the sheikhdoms and sultanates, public administrative machinery has been established according to modern principles. There is, however, a lack of qualified and experienced administrative officers save in Japan, the Republic of China, Israel, and, to some extent, India. Japan, moreover, has maintained the most efficient civil service system, staffed by well-trained bureaucrats.

Since World War II there have been a number of conspicuous reforms in public policy. Some countries have carried out land reforms designed to raise the standard of living of the peasants and to provide an equal distribution of land. In order to cope with urbanization, city planning has begun in most countries. Taxation has been modernized, and new fiscal policies have been adopted. The welfare of the people has gradually been taken into consideration, although none of the Asian countries has a system of workmen's compensation or a social security plan on the United States model.

Governmental Trends. There is no doubt that democracy has made a deep impression on the minds of Asian peoples. Nevertheless, the conditions for democratic institutions are generally not ripe in the continent. Except in Japan, Israel, and, to some extent, Ceylon, no country, not even India, has maintained the necessary political stability. Political coups d'état, internal subversion by Communists, and external threats by neighboring states menace the stability of political institutions. The division of China, Korea, and Vietnam into warring sections poses festering problems that cannot be solved in a short time. And no adequate panacea for the Israeli-Arab conflict has been found. Revolution has been fomented in Southeast Asia as well as in the Middle East.

Another prerequisite for democracy is economic well-being. Citizens must be able to maintain minimum standards of living in order to take a real interest in political institutions. Excluding Japan, the Republic of China, Ceylon, and Israel, most peoples in Asia must struggle for their daily subsistence. There are also great differences in the economic life of city dwellers and of those who live in rural districts. The wealthy in the major cities often enjoy a standard of life approaching that of Western peoples, while the poor in the countryside barely earn the essentials of life.

A third essential condition for democratic institutions is an educated electorate. Unless citizens have the basic education to vote intelligently, to campaign, and to exercise other political rights, democratic institutions are unworkable. Only Japan, the Republic of China, Israel, Ceylon, and Cyprus have the necessary level of literacy.

A fourth requirement for democracy is the development of transportation and communications. These facilities make possible the transmission of governmental orders from the capital to every corner of the country and ensure the rapid movement of thought, news, and ideas. The great majority of Asian countries do not have the required communications and transportation systems, and some time may elapse before adequate systems are in operation.

Considering the lack of development of the preconditions for democracy in Asia, along with the growth of communism, supported by the People's Republic of China and the USSR, Asian nations faced serious challenges in the 1960's. In order to meet this problem, many of them had turned to military dictatorship. The future of political institutions in the continent would be determined by the struggle between the Communist system and anti-Communist military dictatorships, on the one hand, and between democratic-minded, progressive elements and conservative monarchical systems, on the other. Political revolutions and internal instability would very likely keep most of Asia in a state of turmoil for some time.

See also sections on government in articles on the various Asian countries.

JOHN B. TSU, *Seton Hall University*

Bibliography

Benz, Ernst, *Buddhism or Communism: Which Holds the Future of Asia?* tr. from the German by Richard and Clara Winston (Garden City, N.Y., 1965).

Brecher, Michael, *The New States of Asia: A Political Analysis* (New York 1963).

Bromke, Adam, ed., *The Communist States at the Crossroads between Moscow and Peking* (New York 1965).

Bronson, Albert, *Asia in Ferment,* rev. ed. (New York 1963).

Burks, Ardath W., *The Government of Japan* (New York 1961).

Kahin, George M., *Governments and Politics of Southeast Asia* (Ithaca, N.Y., 1959).

Kahin, George M., *Major Governments of Asia* (Ithaca, N.Y., 1958).

Kennedy, Donald Edward, *The Security of Southern Asia* (New York 1965).

Kublin, Hyman, *Asian Revolutionary* (Princeton, N.J., 1964).

Langer, Paul Fritz, *The Minor Asian Communist States: Outer Mongolia, North Korea, North Vietnam* (Santa Monica, Calif., 1964).

Lenczowski, George, *The Middle East in World Affairs,* 2d ed. (Ithaca, N.Y., 1956).

Linebarger, Paul M.A., and others, *Far Eastern Governments and Politics: China and Japan,* 2d ed. (New York 1956).

Palmer, Norman D., *The Indian Political System* (Boston 1962).

Saunders, J. Roscoe, *The Challenge of World Communism in Asia* (Grand Rapids, Mich., 1964).

Sayeed, Khalid Bin, *Pakistan, the Formative Phase* (Karachi 1960).

Sharabi, Hisham Bashir, *Government and Politics of the Middle East in the Twentieth Century* (New York 1962).

Ward, Robert E., and Macridis, Roy C., eds., *Modern Political Systems: Asia* (Englewood Cliffs, N.J., 1963).

Ward, Robert E., and Rustow, Dankwart A., eds., *Political Modernization in Japan and Turkey* (Princeton, N.J., 1964).

Wilcox, Wayne Ayers, *India, Pakistan, and the Rise of China* (New York 1964).

8. Religion

Asia is proverbially known as the birthplace of the great religions. It played this historical role partly because of the existence of several vast river-plain complexes, which, extending from the Hwang Ho (Yellow River) in north China to the Tigris-Euphrates Valley in Mesopotamia, facilitated the settlement and maintenance of large concentrations of population. Three of the principal centers of civilization—the ancient Middle East, India, and China—gestated the five important religions, Judaism, Christianity, Islam, Hinduism, and Buddhism, as well as an extremely influential social philosophy, Confucianism. All the great faiths of Asia, including Japanese Shinto, have survived for at least a millennium or two. In the 20th century, however, they have been challenged by a Communist movement dedicated to the destruction of all historical religions.

Southwest Asia. Southwest Asia is a region of more than ordinary interest to peoples throughout the world. There, in the western portion of the Fertile Crescent, are the places of origin of three religions—Judaism, Christianity, and Islam —that collectively have influenced the spiritual lives of a significant proportion of all the people who have ever lived. Unlike Hinduism, Buddhism, and Confucianism, whose influence has generally been localized in the eastern half of Asia, the religions that have evolved from the inspirations of Abraham, Jesus Christ, and Mohammed have become universal.

Exactly why the Middle East was so fertile in the production of brilliant systems of belief and values is difficult to say. In considering the many complex circumstances, however, it must not be forgotten that the earliest civilizations arose in this somewhat restricted area and that, by the time the Christian era itself dawned, man in this part of the world was heir to a heritage of more than 4,000 years of increasingly sophisticated and civilized life. In the earlier kingdoms and empires of Mesopotamia and Egypt, men had sooner or later reached the point of diminishing returns in deriving spiritual and emotional satisfaction from the prevailing animisms, pantheisms, shamanisms, and sundry religiopolitical cults.

Judaism, the germinal bed from which Christianity and Islam later sprouted, had its origins in several unique and marvelous insights by ancestors of the Hebrews almost 4,000 years ago. Hundreds of years elapsed, however, before their conception of monotheism flowered and before their culture, embodying novel ideals of truth, justice, and ethical behavior, was nurtured to maturity by the inner dynamic of their faith and by the processes of history. Their conviction that they were the chosen people of the Lord was a pillar of strength, supporting them through successive adversities at the hands of Egyptians, Babylonians, and Romans. Scattered into a Diaspora that ultimately included the entire globe, the descendants of the children of Israel have in the 20th century returned to the land of their forefathers, now a national home.

Christianity was, in the first instance, the offspring of Judaism. To the basic teachings of Jesus of Nazareth, stressing the existence of a compassionate God and the ideal of fraternal love, his followers contributed additional doctrines. As a result, not only did the community

FUJIHIRA, FROM MONKMEYER

ISLAM, major religion of Southwest Asia, calls the faithful to the Badshahi Mosque in Lahore, Pakistan.

of Hebrews suffer schism, but a new religion evolved before which the massive Roman empire, with its pagan gods, proved helpless. In many ways the initial triumphs of Christianity, occurring largely in the Mediterranean world and not in regions east of the Holy Land, foreshadowed the contours of its subsequent history. While it swept through the domains of the former Roman empire in Europe, the new faith itself was for long wracked by schisms in Southwest Asia. For more than 1,000 years, Asian peoples beyond the Fertile Crescent learned what little they did about Christianity from contacts with the sectarian Nestorians, Monophysites, and Jacobites. During the Mongol period, emissaries dispatched by the papacy in Rome fruitlessly sought to transmit Western Christianity to peoples in the East. Their successors, the Roman Catholic and, later, the Protestant missionaries of the 16th to 20th century, were not significantly more successful. The modern peoples of Asia are overwhelmingly non-Christian.

The last great religion to emerge in the Middle East was outstandingly successful in expanding into Asia. The message of Mohammed, calling for submission (Islam) to the will of Allah, was formulated in the 7th century A.D. His teachings united the perennially divided Arab tribes, whose armies advanced irresistibly in all directions during the next few centuries. In accounting for Islam's victories, particularly in Asia and Africa, it is misleading to overemphasize the persuasion of the sword and to overlook the intrinsic appeal of the Islamic gospel. Millions of converts unquestionably discovered in Islam more profound spiritual satisfactions than their own traditional faiths could furnish. Muslim soldiers, travelers, and traders were as often as not zealous missionaries. Not only were the majority of the inhabitants of Southwest Asia and their later conquerors, the Mongols and the Turks, led into the Islamic fold, but peoples far to the east, in Inner, South, and Southeast Asia, embraced the new religion. Since the 16th and 17th centuries the vast majority of Muslims have lived in Asia far beyond the Arab countries of the Middle East.

See also CHRISTIANITY; ISLAM; JEWISH HISTORY AND SOCIETY.

South Asia. In the popular mind, India denotes religion and concern for spiritual matters. This characterization may well be sound, but there is no doubt that, as a well-known scholar once commented, treatments of Indian civilization commonly suffer from a "surfeit of holiness." Be this as it may, it is clear that the range and variety of India's religious experience have not been excelled in any other society.

Little is known of the religious beliefs of the founders of the Indus River civilization of the 3d and 2d millennia B.C. Their conquerors, peoples of Indo-Aryan speech who came from the northwest, not only created a new civilization on the fertile Gangetic Plain, but also devised a remarkably durable religion and way of life. In continuity, Hinduism is surpassed only by Judaism. Like the faith of the Jews, it embodies both pristine beliefs and later embellishments derived from several thousand years of human experience. Although it has retained some essential features during the greater part of its history, Hinduism has undergone constant changes that have transformed it into an extraordinarily complex way of life. Since it embraces numerous sects and cults, accommodates a spectrum of thought ranging from simplistic to the sublime, and sanctions widely variegated rites and customs, no single definition of Hinduism would be satisfactory to its many followers at all times and places. Most Hindus, however, would probably agree that the Hindu must acknowledge himself as such, that the caste system be accepted, and that deference be accorded the traditional Vedic literature. They would also hold perhaps that, since life is an illusion, emancipation from its trammels and vanities may be achieved after a long succession of rebirths, in the course of which higher levels of understanding may be attained.

If Hinduism did not have a preeminent wise or holy man as its founder, this is not true of Buddhism, for centuries its foremost but usually friendly rival. Buddhism stems from the teachings of Siddhartha Gautama, the sage of the Sakya clan (Sakyamuni) who became the Buddha (the enlightened one); whether his message was a new point of spiritual departure or the fruition of older trends of thought is a matter of debate. Suffice it to say that, when Siddhartha enunciated his teachings in the 6th century B.C., he both adhered to and deviated from orthodox Hinduism. Stressing an ethical rather than a ritualistic approach to the realization of nirvana, and ignoring but not overtly attacking the caste system, his Four Noble Truths and Noble Eightfold Path furnished man with an explanation of life and its manifold problems. They also pointed the way to the discovery of truth, which alone could bring liberation.

About the 1st or 2d century A.D., Buddhism diverged into two main schools of belief. Theravada, often called Hinayana (Lesser Vehicle) but more appropriately Southern Buddhism, has generally adhered closely to the teachings of Siddhartha and has been upheld primarily in Ceylon and Southeast Asia. Mahayana (Greater Vehicle), or Northern Buddhism, on the other hand, has reflected accommodations to the beliefs and practices of Hinduism and other creeds. It is ironic that, while Buddhism sooner or later gained the allegiance of millions of persons, it steadily declined in India itself after the 7th century. Giving way before Hinduism and Islam, it is no longer a major Indian religion.

Another great test for Hinduism was posed by Islam. The gospel of Mohammed was borne to India by Arabs and by Islamic converts from Middle Eastern lands. For more than 500 years after 1000 A.D. the Islamic tide rolled over the Indian subcontinent and beyond, winning millions of converts, especially in the Indian northwest and northeast. Many Indians, particularly of the lower castes, were drawn to the monotheistic creed and social egalitarianism of their Muslim neighbors, while members of the higher castes were at times unable to resist the lure of Islamic philosophy and culture. Since Islam was the faith of the military conquerors of India, whose customs differed crucially from those of the Hindus, the groundwork was laid for the tensions and clashes that finally came to a head in the partition of the subcontinent into the two contentious nations of India and Pakistan in 1947.

In addition to Hinduism, Buddhism, and Islam, India has known other faiths. Jainism and Sikhism, both of native provenance, have in their own ways profoundly influenced Indian life. Judaism, Christianity, and the faith of the Parsis (Persian Zoroastrianism) came from abroad. Since World War II most Indian Jews have emigrated to Israel.

See also BRAHMANISM; BUDDHA AND BUDDHISM; HINDUISM; INDIA—13. *Religion and Philosophy;* JAINISM; SIKHS; ZOROASTRIANISM.

Southeast Asia. Southeast Asia is one of the major crossroads of the religions of the world. Few of the leading faiths have not penetrated the region and left a lasting impression on the local cultures. The uniquely rich religious heritage of Southeast Asians has been reflected not only in their spiritual values and patterns of behavior but also, until the upsurge of secular trends in the mid-20th century, in such cultural media as art, architecture, sculpture, music, dance, and drama.

As late as 2,000 or even 1,500 years ago Southeast Asia was inhabited largely by peoples who had not advanced beyond tribal stages of social organization and hunting and fishing economies supplemented by crude agriculture. The religious beliefs of the local peoples, animistic and centered in nature worship, did not differ significantly from those held by peoples at a comparable state of development elsewhere. Despite the later intrusion of sophisticated religions from other parts of Asia and from Europe, some of these animistic cults have survived, still being followed by descendants of the aboriginal inhabitants who now dwell in remote mountainous and jungle areas.

The initial filtration of Hinduism and Buddhism into Southeast Asia in about the 1st century A.D. was gradually followed by a swelling wave of Indian culture. The conversion of local ruling classes, in the early kingdoms of southern Indochina, in Java and Sumatra, and later in Burma and Siam (Thailand), to either or both of the Indian faiths had elevating effects on society and culture. Some rulers were thereafter occasionally successful in transforming their hitherto underdeveloped realms into mighty empires. The splendor of Hinduism, which in Southeast Asia has survived only in Bali, is still revealed in the magnificent cities and temples of the medieval Khmer empire in Cambodia. The shining example of Buddhist power and faith is perhaps best seen in the famous bas-reliefs of Borobudur in Java. Unlike Hinduism, Buddhism retained its appeal in Southeast Asia. Burma, Laos, Cambodia, South Vietnam, and Thailand are all preponderantly Buddhist countries, upholding mainly the Theravada position.

Islam was introduced into Southeast Asia at about the beginning of the 14th century by Arab

EAST ASIA'S MAJOR RELIGIONS are represented in these three pictures: (*left*) Buddhism, by the great bronze Buddha, or Daibutsu, at Kamakura, Japan; (*center*) Shinto, by the Itsuku-shima shrine near Hiroshima, Japan; (*right*) Hinduism, by a crowd of Hindu pilgrims bathing in the Gandak River of India, a tributary of the sacred Ganges.

merchants and later by converts from India. The teachings of Mohammed, disseminated by rulers and traders, won many new followers, especially in the port cities and islands. Ultimately most persons in the East Indies (Indonesia) and Malaya adopted Islam. Were it not for the advent of the religiously oriented Spanish in the late 16th century, all the Filipinos too might well have been brought into the Islamic fold. The northernmost advance of Islam in Southeast Asia is marked by the existence of Moros (Moors) in Mindanao and the Sulu Archipelago in the southern Philippines.

The Spanish friars were as successful proponents of Roman Catholicism in the Philippines as they were in the New World. In little more than three centuries they converted the great majority of the Filipinos to Christianity. Except for scattered minorities, Christianity's only other signal victory in Southeast Asia was scored in Vietnam. Intensive proselytizing by French missionaries after the middle of the 19th century resulted in the conversion of several million Vietnamese. During the Communist revolution after World War II, tens of thousands of Vietnamese Christians fled from North to South Vietnam.

See also SOUTHEAST ASIA.

East Asia—China. Chinese civilization, the oldest in the modern world, has had an almost incomparable experience of spiritual search and philosophical speculation for 4,000 years. Beliefs that may be traced to prehistoric times have endured beside some of the noblest ideas that have ever occurred to man. Rather than adhering exclusively to one faith, Chinese of more than a hundred generations have ordinarily been eclectic in religious matters.

The little that is known about the beliefs of the ancestors of the Chinese people suggests a primary concern with the forces and powers of nature. The so-called oracle bones, excavated at Anyang in north China beginning in 1928, reveal the practice of divination and scapulimancy by the priestly class of the Shang (Yin) dynasty (about 1523–1027 B.C.). An anthropomorphically conceived "heaven" may well have dominated the pantheistically viewed universe of some of the proto-Chinese. Propitiation and thanksgiving to heaven and other powers of the natural world were paramount among rites and sacrifices. Toward the end of the Shang and at the beginning of the Chou dynasty (1027–256 B.C.), a new religiopolitical concept, the mandate of Heaven, seems to have emerged. With later glosses it furnished the sanction for ruling houses in imperial China until the 20th century.

Since antiquity the Chinese have also acknowledged the beneficent and malevolent powers of feng shui (wind and water). The happiness and prosperity of men in this life and the next, it has been believed, necessitates the maintenance of a harmonious equilibrium of the forces of nature. Numerous decisions in daily life, such as the selection of a site for a home and the determination of proper burial places, have required the counsel of a feng shui expert or geomancer. Furthermore, most communities were from time immemorial devoted to tutelary deities, while ancestral worship in one form or another has probably been practiced since Neolithic times. Such beliefs and rites constituted the religious foundation on which later faiths and systems of thought were erected.

During the closing centuries of the Chou period, when the Chinese way of life underwent revolutionary changes, troubled men sought to discover social solutions for their problems. The result was an amazing outburst of philosophical and religious expression, which limned for centuries the principal contours of Chinese faith and thought. The preeminently this-worldly Confucianism and Legalism were rivaled by metaphysical Taoism and the more spiritual Mohism. If Confucianism finally triumphed, becoming the official state cult during the Han (202 B.C.–220 A.D.) and subsequent dynasties, it was not solely because of the strength of its ethical message. Its potential for the encouragement of social stability and harmony could not be overlooked by monarchs and scholar-bureaucrats. For 2,000 years, Confucianism, constantly enriched and carefully modified, was the philosophical and quasi-religious pillar of orthodoxy and tradition in imperial China.

471

The strongest challenge to Confucianism after its ascendancy during Han times was presented by Buddhism. Filtering into China in the 1st century A.D., and generously patronized by the Turkic rulers of north China in the 5th and 6th centuries, Buddhist teachings acquired widespread popular support during the brilliant T'ang dynasty (618–906). Although the expanding power and wealth of the Buddhist temples finally led to Confucian-inspired repression in the 9th century, the appeal of Buddhism could not easily be extinguished. But where oppression had failed, absorption succeeded. Savants of the Sung dynasty (960–1279) devised a syncretism integrating the social ethics of Confucianism, the metaphysics of Taoism, and the philosophy of Buddhism. Known as Neo-Confucianism, this religiophilosophical synthesis endured as orthodox doctrine until the 20th century.

Christian missionaries appeared in China from T'ang times on, becoming increasingly active once regular contact with the West began in the 16th century. Despite determined proselytizing as late as 1950, however, Christianity never succeeded in winning the loyalties of the great mass of the Chinese people. On the other hand, Islam, which penetrated China during the T'ang age, harvested million of converts among the inhabitants, Chinese and non-Chinese, of the western and northwestern regions.

Since the rise of the People's Republic of China in 1949, religion has come under attack. Critics claim that the antireligious Communists have been striving to replace the older faiths with a religion of their own—Marxist Leninism and, above all, Maoism.

See also CONFUCIUS; TAOISM.

Japan and Korea. The oldest and only indigenous faith of the Japanese is Shinto, which has existed in the archipelago since prehistoric times. Animistic beliefs and nature worship were not peculiar to the ancestors of the Japanese but were part of a congeries of cults dispersed throughout Korea and northeastern Asia. With the foundation of an imperial state in the 7th century A.D., an attempt was made to establish the primacy of the beliefs of the people of the Yamato kingdom. For more than 1,000 years thereafter the strength of Shinto depended largely on its efficacy in providing a rationale for the perpetuation of the reigning dynasty. Infused with nationalism in the late 19th century, the resultant Neo-Shinto remained the state religion of Japan until the end of World War II. After suffering a brief eclipse during the occupation years (1945–1952), Shinto, reflecting the resurgence of Japanese nationalism, staged an impressive revival.

Like all societies in East Asia, Japan was deeply influenced by the civilization of imperial China. Buddhism, transmitted via Korea in the 6th century A.D. and later directly from China itself, seized the imagination of the ruling class during the Heian period (794–1185). Its countrywide acceptance, however, accompanied the emergence of the so-called popular sects from the 11th through the 13th centuries. Not displacing but rather existing beside the nativistic Shinto, Buddhism endured as one of the two major faiths of the Japanese. Japan is now the leading exponent of Mahayana Buddhism. Confucianism, too, entered the archipelago during the first great influx of Chinese civilization, but for long it did not affect Japanese society as a whole. With the rise of a politically united country in the 17th century, however, Neo-Confucianism, selectively borrowed, was successfully introduced to foster social conformity and stability, and Neo-Confucian teachings, at times no longer recognizable as such, still pervade the behavioristic patterns of the Japanese people.

The last religion to enter Japan from abroad was Christianity. Experiencing remarkable successes in conversion between 1549 and 1638, the Western faith encountered the severe opposition of religious and political leaders. Almost uprooted by the Tokugawa shogunate, it was revived shortly after the opening of the country in 1853–1854. Although a following of as much as 3 percent of the population has been claimed, the strength of Christianity in Japan rests upon its influence on national leadership rather than upon numbers.

The Koreans have also had a long and varied experience with religion. The oldest faith, Sinkyo, is a blend of animism and shamanism; it has much in common with Japanese Shinto. Although Sinkyo has declined greatly, it persists in rural areas. Buddhism, introduced from China in the 4th century, gradually spread throughout the land during the next 1,000 years. With the advent of the Yi dynasty in 1392, however, its influence quickly waned. Today Buddhism in Korea, practiced largely by women, is neither well organized nor significantly influential. Confucianism, it is believed, came to Korea about the beginning of the 6th century. Patronized by the upper classes, it was long significant in Korean government, letters, and behavior, and traces of it may still be observed.

Although Korea's more than 1 million Christians constitute only a small percentage of the total population, their prestige and standing are scarcely rivaled by those of any other religious group in the country. Propounded clandestinely by Roman Catholic missionaries from the 17th century on, Christianity achieved no large-scale conversions until after the opening of the country in the late 19th century. With no strong opposition from local institutionalized churches, both Roman Catholicism and Protestantism made steady progress. Christian missions in Korea have been extremely active in social reform, especially in higher education and medicine. Many of the leaders in national life are graduates of missionary-founded and -operated schools.

See also JAPAN—13. *Religion;* KOREA—9. *Way of Living;* SHINTO.

Inner Asia. The religions of Inner Asia mirror the region's historical function as a political, cultural, and commercial meeting point of the Asian continent. While peoples of this area influenced the major civilizations of Eurasia, these societies in turn contributed directly and indirectly to the cultural formation of all the peoples inhabiting the area from Tibet to Mongolia. The intrusion of Buddhism from India into Tibet resulted in the modification of the indigenous shamanistic faith and in the formulation of Lamaistic Buddhism. In the 13th century this religion of the Tibetans was adopted by the Mongol conquerors of China. Soviet Central Asia and Chinese Turkestan (now known as the Sinkiang-Uigur Autonomous Region) were penetrated by Arab armies in the mid-18th century and thereafter converted to Islam. The Chinese Muslims have been designated a religious and ethnic minority by successive Chinese regimes.

Summary. For thousands of years the religions of Asia have furnished incalculable solace to multitudes of men. Until secular philosophies began to spread in modern times, the values of traditional religions pervaded the lives of all inhabitants of the continent, establishing and defining the purposes of life. Few if any basic social institutions failed to reveal the impress of religious values, while the gamut of the arts and of culture in general testified to a common concern with the spirit. Although the revolutionary storms of the 20th century have burst upon the time-honored faiths, with their deep roots in history the great religions are not likely to be swept aside; that they will undergo further change in the years to come, however, is very probable.

See also MISSIONARY MOVEMENTS.

HYMAN KUBLIN
The City University of New York

Bibliography

Anesaki, Masaharu, *History of Japanese Religions* (Rutland, Vt., 1963).

Ch'en, Kenneth Kuan Sheng, *Buddhism in China: A Historical Survey* (Princeton, N.J., 1964).

Conze, Edward, *Buddhism: Its Essence and Development* (New York 1951).

Finkelstein, Louis, ed., *The Jews: Their History, Culture, and Religion*, 2d ed., 2 vols. (New York 1955).

Geertz, Clifford, *The Religion of Java* (New York 1960).

Gibb, Sir Hamilton A.R., *Mohammedanism: An Historical Survey*, 2d ed. (New York 1953).

Harper, Edward B., ed., *Religion in South Asia* (Seattle 1964).

Holtom, Daniel C., *National Faith of Japan* (New York 1965).

Kitagawa, Joseph M., *Religions of the East* (Philadelphia 1960).

Landon, Kenneth P., *Southeast Asia: Crossroad of Religions* (Chicago 1949).

Morgan, Kenneth W., ed., *The Religion of the Hindus* (New York 1953).

Yang, C.K., *Religion in Chinese Society* (Berkeley, Calif., 1961).

9. Education

Three seminal cultures of Asia are the Islamic, Indian, and Sinitic (Chinese). These through diffusion strongly influenced many other, sometimes distant, societies. This influence may be observed particularly in the content of education and in traditional attitudes toward learning. In the Middle East and India, education and religion (in China, education and an official state philosophy) were inseparably intertwined, the values of learning being closely related to ethical and spiritual training.

With the spread of Islam through the Mediterranean Basin as well as eastward to Indonesia and parts of India and China, educational systems and practices were lastingly affected. The Confucian learning of China, transmitted to Korea, Japan, and Vietnam, molded society and education accordingly. And in Ceylon, Tibet, Burma, Thailand, Cambodia, and Laos, Buddhism, disseminated from India, became both the dominant religion and the principal vehicle of education.

In the 20th century, traditional Asian ways of life have been greatly affected by the impact of Western science and technology. Having won their freedom from imperialist control, the many lands of Asia have undertaken to construct new patterns of living. Education has commonly been accorded a high priority, and in the various plans to bring basic learning to the masses of the people are mirrored the numerous problems raised by the inevitable conflicts between the old and the new.

JEN YUNG-CHAO, FROM EASTFOTO

SCHOOL CHILDREN in Lhasa, Tibet, play before the Potala Palace, traditional seat of the Dalai Lama.

Southwest Asia. From the foundation of Islam in 622 A.D., learning was highly regarded. When Mohammed conquered Mecca two years later, he freed every moneyless captive who promised to teach 10 Muslims to read and write. The society he established was nonhierarchical, without distinction between sacred and secular, and unified in the belief that (1) "there is no god but Allah"; (2) Mohammed is the prophet of Allah; and (3) the Koran, written in Arabic, reveals Allah's divine guidance for living.

Traditional Islamic education used the tutorial-apprenticeship method. Through constant association with the teacher at the state-supported elementary mosque school, the pupil, aged six or seven, memorized the Koran, the first and basic textbook; learned the three R's; and was initiated through daily living into religious, moral, and social ways befitting a Muslim ("one who submits to the will of Allah"). For those not continuing in school and for the masses the mosques, with their prayers, sermons, lectures, and discussions of literary, poetic, and legal matters, served as educational centers. After mastering the elementary subject matter, students might enter the partially state-supported higher mosque school, where the curriculum of the Koran, hadith (tradition), "religious sciences," and the Arabic language was later supplemented by the Hellenic quadrivium and technical subjects.

At the highest level were the Bayt al-Hikmah (House of Wisdom), which opened at Baghdad in 830 with a royal endowment, and similar institutions established somewhat later. Strongly influenced by classical Hellenistic thought, these institutions became centers of learning and translation from Greek into Arabic. The Seljuk Turks, who were Sunnites, founded the heavily endowed Nizamiyah at Baghdad in 1065–1067 in opposition to the Shiite-oriented Bayt al-Hikmah. This new type of school, devoted to both the physical and the intellectual and spiritual development of its students, had one center for the study of Sunnite theology and law and another for the training of civil servants. A similar basic curriculum, originating at the great schools in Iraq, spread to Spanish and Indian Muslim schools. Higher education became the key to the professions and to the universities, centers of learning and research in philosophy, medicine, mathematics, and the physical sciences, which were later to enrich the West. Eventually, under the Ottoman Turks the curriculum, though further developed, became rigid.

In the 20th century, after successful struggles for independence, first from Ottoman Turkey during World War I and later from Western control, the new Islamic nations faced many problems: widespread poverty, illiteracy, deplorable health conditions, antiquated economies, and the opposition of orthodox religion. Having revolted against the status quo and the West, they groped toward a synthesis of the Islamic heritage and modern Western technology and education. By the 1960's, education, which had lagged behind political, social, and economic developments, was steadily closing the gap. Nevertheless, the various national educational systems generally were still in the planning stages; and in the attempt to meet internal and external pressures, curricula and methods of teaching formed a patchwork of the traditional, with its emphasis on religious instruction, and of undigested importations from the West.

Despite many obstacles, movements toward free, universal, and compulsory elementary education were under way by the 1960's. Adult and vocational education, education suited to rural needs, education for girls and coeducation (the special contribution of foreign missionaries), people's cultural centers, and the recruitment and training of teachers were other areas in which progress was being made. But until national budgets were increased, perhaps from petroleum royalties, there was little likelihood that education would be adequately financed.

Turkey, which is Islamic but not Arabic and, moreover, has always been an independent nation, consciously identified itself with Western culture early in the 20th century. In the 1920's, under Kemal Atatürk, the country began to strive for the realization of his ideal of a "republican, nationalist, populist, etatist, secular, and reformist" nation. In education, Turkey pioneered many reforms, including the use of a Roman alphabet (1928) to overcome the obstacles of the classical Islamic script. By the 1960's it had moved closer to the goals of free, compulsory, universal, secular five-year elementary education and an improved and expanded system of vocational and higher education. Through field trips and observations as well as individualized and socialized activities, education had been "life oriented."

See also sections on education in articles on various Southwest Asian countries; MIDDLE EAST —Cultural Life (Education and Law).

MELVIN E. LEVISON, *Brooklyn College*

East and South Asia. The major educational systems of East and South Asia are those of China, Japan, and India.

China. Confucian learning was the basis of traditional Chinese education. Confucius (551–479 B.C.) taught a practical philosophy that emphasized sincere motives and righteous conduct to foster good government and a harmonious society. Ancient wisdom was esteemed, while education was deemed necessary to cultivate the essentially good nature of man. When, beginning in the reign of the Han dynasty emperor Wu Ti (140–87 B.C.), the state decided to rely on Confucian scholars as administrators, schools were established to teach the Confucian classics, and examinations were devised to select the best scholars for office. Gradually an effective threefold institution emerged: Confucian schools leading to the civil service examination, which in turn led to the imperial bureaucracy. A principle, unique among nations, that government should be by the learned guided China for 2,000 years. In peaceful times this institution produced good government; in bad times, stagnation. Although Confucianism afforded China enduring cultural unity and high ethical and aesthetic standards, it also enthroned orthodoxy and caused the neglect of mass education.

The Confucian way of life was no match for Western ships and guns. Despite defeats by Great Britain in the Opium War of 1839–1842 and by Britain and France in 1856–1860, the Ch'ing (Manchu) dynasty's efforts at modernization were halfhearted and unsuccessful. Between 1862, when the first modern school was established, and the end of the 19th century, conservative Confucianists blocked real educational reform. The defeat by Japan in 1894–1895 made some Manchu leaders realize the need for modernization. The first modern school system, modeled on the Japanese, was founded in 1904. Strongly militaristic, it taught loyalty to the Manchu regime, Confucianism, and the three R's. From 1904 to 1912 the new education was under Japanese influence. Approximately 15,000 students went to Japan to learn the secrets of modernization, while Japanese instructors came to teach in Chinese agricultural colleges and military and police academies. Returned students from Japan helped overthrow the Manchus in 1911–1912.

In the early republican period (1912–1925), China's schools were based on American prototypes. American missionaries pioneered in establishing girls' schools, medical colleges, and hospitals. With Boxer indemnity money restored to China for educational purposes, hundreds of students were sent to the United States and then returned home to become leaders in education. When John Dewey visited China in 1919 at the beginning of the intellectual renaissance led by Dr. Hu Shih, his former student, his ideas of progressive education and democracy were widely accepted. In 1922 the educational system was reorganized, with American aims—individualism and education for living—and an American-style six-three-three school system. Confucian classics gave way to natural science and technology.

In 1928 a period of nationalist education, based on Sun Yat-sen's *Three People's Principles,* began. Education was centralized. Textbooks were rewritten, emphasizing China's humiliating experiences at the hands of foreigners. There was a reaction against American influence, and missionary schools were brought under government control. Liberal education gave way to indoctrination and an emphasis on uniform subject matter. Nevertheless, schools progressed rapidly: a national system with clear aims was achieved; a mass education movement under American-trained James Y.C. Yen began to reduce illiteracy; scientific and technical education was expanded; Mandarin was made the standard spoken language; and higher education was reorganized and developed. The Japanese attack in 1937 halted this advance. As the populous coastal areas were occupied, schools were closed. A total of 77 universities, colleges, and technical schools migrated to the interior, staff and students walking and carrying their books and equipment. World War II wrecked China's schools as well as its economy and morale.

When the Communists seized power in 1949, they turned their attention to schools, using them

AT THE TAJ MAHAL in Agra, India, a group of peddlers carry their merchandise across the Jumna River.

ON THE YANGTZE RIVER, in Chungking, China, sampans and junks are often used to supplement steamer crossing.

IN DOWNTOWN TOKYO, a monorail car has been put in operation in Ueno Park as an experiment in urban transit.

(1) to root out "feudal, compradore, and fascist ideology" among the people and replace it with Communist dogma; and (2) to train technicians for reconstruction. Confucianism, especially its conservatism, elitism, formalism, and contempt for labor, was attacked. Schools were now primarily for the workers and peasants. Education was combined with productive labor, and the educational system was placed under the leadership of the Communist party. The task was enormous, for more than 80 percent of the adult population was illiterate. Furthermore, the American-oriented intellectuals were resistant. A rigorous program of "thought reform" was launched to win their allegiance to the new regime, but it was not entirely successful. Nor did the attempt to rear a generation of new-type intellectuals of proletarian origin produce the leadership sought.

Communist schools followed the Nationalist six-three-three system, but with changes. Thousands of nursery schools were established to start indoctrination at an early age and to free mothers for productive labor. Elementary schools were expanded, and by the early 1960's it was claimed that 93.9 percent of all school-age children were enrolled. A system of part-time schools paralleling the academic track was established in factories, farms, shops, and ships to teach literacy and party dogma to workers and peasants without interfering with their jobs; as of the early 1960's it was claimed that 120 million persons were involved in the program. Through persuasion or conviction the Chinese, from 3 to 80, were going to school.

While the local Communist party organization controls education, mass education has been so expensive that the Ministry of Education has delegated responsibility for all costs, including those for much of higher education, to the provinces, cities, farms, factories, and communes. Since 1958 the government, in order to destroy the Confucian prejudice against work, has encouraged schools to found farms and factories with a half-work, half-study program of scheduled labor for each student. Factories, farms, and communes have established their own systems from nursery school to the university level. Although there is a severe shortage of teachers, and quality has been sacrificed to quantity, China has made the choice of inculcating both literacy and loyalty in the masses of its people.

See also CHINA—6. *Education, Religion, and Way of Living.*

Japan. For centuries, Japan was a part of the Sinitic (Chinese) cultural realm. Its written characters were Chinese, and its society and education were pervaded with Confucianism. Following the Meiji Restoration of 1868 the new leaders soon envisaged the modernization and unification of the country. They sought a universal and free public school system in order to provide technicians and to weld the people's loyalty to the emperor-state. Conditions were favorable for a cultural revolution; the people, of a single race and language, not only had the traditional Confucian respect for learning but also possessed a deep curiosity about the West. The government embarked on a two-way program of cultural borrowing, sending hundreds of students abroad to study specific technical subjects, to be introduced on their return, and importing foreign experts to teach their specialties.

The most important borrowing from the United States was made in the field of education.

Japanese leaders believed that the American public school system would be appropriate for their country, and in 1872 they sent a mission to the United States to inspect schools and collect advice and educational materials. An American adviser, Dr. David Murray, was employed to assist the returned Japanese officials in constructing a national public school system. For the first decade the Japanese used American textbooks and equipment, built their schools on American plans, and adopted the liberal philosophy and methods of the Swiss educator Johann Heinrich Pestalozzi, which they had learned at American normal schools. The American system did not entirely fit Japanese traditions and needs, however, and in the early 1880's there was a return to Shinto-Confucian ethical principles. In 1886 the education ordinances were rewritten, providing for a uniform, centralized school system. Instead of the earlier dedication to the interests of the individual, those of the state became paramount.

The next step, taken with the sanction of the emperor, was to codify a philosophy of education to guide the developing state system along traditional rather than alien lines. The Imperial Rescript on Education of 1890, destined to become one of the most influential documents in Japanese intellectual history, combined the Shinto ideology of emperor worship with Confucian concepts of loyalty, filial piety, and obedience to superiors. It crystallized these values into a catechism recited periodically by all students in formal religious ceremonies in the schools. Its principles, inculcated especially in a core course in morals required in all grades up to the university level, actually permeated all courses.

As a tool for nationalism, education was under the centralized control of the Ministry of Education from 1890 to 1945. In the 1930's it came increasingly under the influence of the militarists. Repressive thought control was enforced on students and intellectuals. Loyalty, patriotism, and a conviction of the divinity of Japan, the emperor, and the Japanese people, as well as a willingness to die for them, were taught in all schools. The system, though authoritarian, was effective in producing loyal subjects who were 98 percent literate. It also created a corps of technicians who made possible the first successful modernization and industrialization of an Asian country.

After World War II the Allied occupation moved into the vacuum caused by defeat. The program of democratic reforms, as prescribed by the Potsdam Declaration, required the Japanese to remove "all obstacles to the revival and strengthening of democratic tendencies among the Japanese people." Building on the liberal experiences of the Japanese during the 1870's and the 1920's, the occupation authorities introduced the latest democratic philosophy and techniques of education. Accustomed as they were to importing ideas, many Japanese educators accepted them enthusiastically. In March 1946 the United States Education Mission to Japan, working with a counterpart Japanese committee, drew up a blueprint for the reorganization of the educational system. The resulting system was strikingly similar to the American. The Fundamental Law of Education of 1947, based on a democratic philosophy, called for ". . . full development of personality, striving for the rearing of a people . . . who shall love truth and justice, esteem individual value, respect labor and have a deep sense of responsibility, and be imbued with an independent spirit." Other laws provided in detail for greater educational opportunity. The former complex multitrack system was streamlined into a nationwide single-track, six-three-three structure (six years of elementary school, three of junior high school, and three of senior high school). The number of free and compulsory years was increased by three to a total of nine, while scholarships were provided to enable needy children to obtain secondary and higher education. Coeducation at all levels and equal rights for women were perhaps the most revolutionary changes in the Confucian-oriented nation.

To make higher education more accessible, at least one national university was organized in each prefecture. Social studies were required in the lower schools, and general education in the universities. Teacher education was upgraded, given a professional character, and integrated into the program of the university. Teachers, urged to join unions, did so with alacrity, until soon 500,000 of them had become members. Control of the schools was decentralized through the institution of elected school boards.

Most of these reforms were permanent, but when sovereignty was returned to Japan in 1952, readjustments inevitably were made. In 1956, elected school boards were replaced by boards appointed by governors and mayors, which were more responsive to central control. By popular demand a course in moral education was restored in a modified form in 1958. The single track was divided in 1962, when an independent five-year technical college (combined senior high school and junior college) for the training of middle-grade technicians was introduced. Between 1958 and 1963 the American-style curriculum was revised, government courses of study and textbooks being prepared for all grades. Courses, formerly suggested, became universal and mandatory. The purposes of the revision were to toughen the curriculum, increase the number of hours devoted to mathematics, science, and the Japanese language, and ensure a prescribed coverage of Japanese history, geography, and morals for a better nationalist education.

The militant teachers' union (Nikkyoso), the radical students' federation (Zengakuren), and the Socialist and Communist parties have actively opposed most of these changes. Despite the frequent and violent controversies between the teachers' union and the Ministry of Education concerning educational issues, however, permanent gains have been made over prewar days. The doors of educational opportunity for women, the common people, and the handicapped are wider than ever before. Freedom has entered the classroom; activity programs are common at the elementary level; and children learn parliamentary procedure and participate in democratic self-government. Academic freedom is guaranteed by the constitution of 1947. Teachers even in remote areas are professionally trained in four-year universities. More than 99 percent of all children attend elementary and junior high schools, while 60 percent continue their education in senior high schools. The widespread use of educational television has brought high-quality programs to classrooms in all parts of the country. Japan has educational problems, but they are those of a sophisticated modern society, learning democratic ways.

See also JAPAN—14. Cultural Life.

India. From the time when the Indo-Aryans first entered the Indian subcontinent in the 2d millennium B.C., methods of transmitting religious traditions were developed. A common religious education contributed to the cultural unity that enabled the Indo-Aryans to conquer the earlier non-Aryan inhabitants. Boys of the higher castes, aged 8 to 20, were placed in the homes of teachers (gurus), subjected to rigid discipline, and required to learn the Vedic scriptures. The close teacher-pupil relationship provided character training.

Classical Sanskrit education met the needs of the higher Hindu castes. Other castes, based on occupation, devised apprenticeship systems to transmit skills from father to son. (Girls married early and did not receive a formal education.) Although it provided cultural continuity, the traditional system of education, with its rote learning of past wisdom, stifled the spirit of inquiry, fostered a rigid, static society, and prevented change.

After the British came to India in the early 17th century, they gradually eliminated the French and Dutch East India companies and defeated the native princes. Since England itself did not introduce public education until 1870, the English East India Company was, not surprisingly, unconcerned with educating India's millions. Faced, however, with the task of government, the company at first sought to communicate with Indian officials in the classical languages of Persian, Arabic, and Sanskrit. A few farsighted British civil servants mastered these languages and discovered a rich literature. Several governors general, such as Warren Hastings (served 1772–1785) and the 1st Marquess Cornwallis (served 1786–1793), founded religious colleges to train Indians in judicial administration. These cultural relativists, advocating education in the native languages, were known as the Orientalists. Opposed to them were the Anglicists in India and England, who held that the language of government, hence of education, should be English.

In 1835, Thomas Babington Macaulay, the new president of the Committee of Public Instruction in India, settled the controversy in favor of the Anglicists. Henceforth the medium of instruction was to be English, while education funds were to be used exclusively for the support of schools that taught in that language. Thereafter, aspirants to government jobs had to complete courses in English-language secondary and higher schools. Macaulay, an elitist who knew nothing about the indigenous culture of India, held that the "learned natives" could diffuse their enlightenment to the millions of Indians by a process of "downward filtration." This did not occur, and the educated clerks lost touch with their native culture.

The imposition of English education had advantages for India. With a common language, Indians of diverse groups developed a common modern culture of their own. English education opened a new world of thought in modern science, justice, democracy, and freedom, and this led in turn to political self-consciousness, a nationalist spirit, and a demand for independence.

During the 19th century, British colonial educational policy, favoring secondary and higher education in the cities, neglected mass education in the rural areas. The result was an educated elite and mass illiteracy. To salve its conscience, the government periodically called for the development of primary education, but instead of providing central support, it shifted responsibility to local public and private bodies, which could not handle the gigantic task. At the same time, government-supported higher education was strongly academic, after the pattern of Oxford, and failed to provide technical training for industrialization.

At the turn of the 20th century some Indian intellectuals began to demand national education. In the 1920's, Mohandas K. Gandhi found the British system inadequate and impracticable for Indians. The system stressed memorization, failed to prepare for life, created a bias against labor, encouraged competition rather than cooperation, and was dominated by an examination system. Gandhi's solution was presented to a conference held by the Indian National Congress at Wardha in 1937. His plan, termed "basic education," called for teaching a local craft as the center of instruction and relating all other subjects to it. Through the sale of the children's product or its use by themselves, the schools were to be self-supporting. Instruction, free and compulsory between the ages of 7 and 15, was to be in the mother tongue. Although the British government approved Gandhi's program for all of India in 1944, it also insisted on a minimum wage for teachers. Furthermore, since the element of self-sufficiency encouraged exploitation of the children, it was largely abandoned. (Having the craft as the sole center of teaching also proved unworkable.) When India became independent in 1947, basic education became the pattern for nationwide elementary education, and the central and state governments subsequently sought to convert all elementary institutions into basic schools.

Since basic schools have opponents among the general public as well as in the Ministry of Education, both basic and regular academic school systems are in operation. The basic system is craft-centered; the public schools, subject-centered, are characterized by a rigid curriculum, strict discipline, and competitive examinations. Basic schools, helping to break down the stigma accompanying manual labor, give the student a more meaningful experience and practice in community citizenship. Despite government encouragement, however, the development of basic education has been slow. Trained teachers have been lacking. By the 1960's only 35 percent of the schools, mostly rural, had adopted the pattern. Urban schools retained the British pattern, which still served to prepare youth for government service. Nevertheless, basic schools had moved into cities, and the gap between the two types of schools was being closed.

Although the constitution of 1950 guaranteed eight years of free, compulsory education by 1960, this goal was not achieved. Control and support of education have been decentralized in the various states, but within each state education has been highly centralized, with salaries, curriculum, textbooks, and fees being centrally determined and grants-in-aid allowed only if the local school has complied with the standards. The result has been a loss of local initiative and a lack of experimentation. At the national level, broad policies have been decided with the advice of all-India councils. India's overwhelming educational problems include (1) a shortage of classrooms and qualified teachers, resulting from national poverty, and at the same time, an increasing de-

CONSULATE GENERAL OF JAPAN, NEW YORK

JAPANESE ELEMENTARY SCHOOL children learn calligraphy in one of Asia's most modern school systems.

mand for education; (2) an academic bias in secondary and higher education, a heritage of the British period, and production of too many liberal arts graduates and too few technicians; (3) a complex language problem, compounded by an attempt to make Hindi universal in place of English; and (4) a British-derived system of external examinations, which results in cramming and orientation of the entire curriculum to the passing of examinations.

Although at the 1961 census only 23.7 percent of the population over 5 years of age was literate, educational progress had been made. Basic education had won a permanent place. It had brought practical education to rural villages, had influenced the building of comprehensive high schools, and had begun infiltrating university programs. The dispatch of rural extension workers under the Community Development Program, it was hoped, might provide more than 550,000 Indian villages with agricultural improvement, education, sanitation, and better group living. Indian education, moving forward slowly, was becoming Indian.

See also COEDUCATION—*Other Countries* (Asia); EDUCATION—2. *National Systems of Education;* INDIA—6. *Education.*

RONALD S. ANDERSON, *University of Hawaii*

Bibliography
Anderson, Ronald S., *Japan: Three Epochs of Modern Education,* U.S. Department of Health, Education, and Welfare, Office of Education, Bulletin 11 (Washington 1959).
Biggerstaff, Knight, *Earliest Modern Government Schools in China* (Ithaca, N.Y., 1961).
Blacker, Carmen, *The Japanese Enlightenment* (New York 1964).
Fraser, Stewart, ed., *Chinese Communist Education* (Nashville, Tenn., 1964).
Hu, C.T., ed., *Chinese Education Under Communism* (New York 1962).
Huq, Muhammad S., *Education and Development Strategy in South and Southeast Asia* (Honolulu 1965).
Kuo, Ping-wen, *The Chinese System of Public Education* (New York 1915).
Matthews, Roderic D., and Akrawi, Matta, *Education in Arab Countries of the Near East* (Washington 1949).
Shrimali, Kalulal, *Education in Changing India* (New York 1965).
Tritton, Arthur S., *Materials on Muslim Education in the Middle Ages* (London 1957).

10. Art

Asian societies are extremely diverse in their artistic genius. This diversity is founded on the radical differences in their experience of reality. The resulting art traditions vary both in the foci of their interests and in the modalities of their expression. This variety gives to the total art tradition of the continent a grandeur and a completion that could never be attained by any single tradition.

Yet the great centers of Asian art have not developed in complete isolation from each other. Since the Neolithic period, influences have traveled back and forth between these centers, particularly between Southwest Asia, India, and China. Thus, the entire complex of Asian societies constitutes a related artistic community. One can best appreciate the traditions within this community by studying each society in its distinctive characteristics and in its relations with the larger tradition of Asian art of which it is a part.

Southwest Asia. The transition from the primitive art of the Neolithic period to the art forms of the higher civilizations took place in Mesopotamia around 3000 B.C. During the era of Sumerian and Babylonian dominion, ending with the destruction of Babylon by the Hittites in about 1530 B.C., an exceedingly high level was attained in architecture, in stone and bronze sculpture, and in the lesser arts. This may be seen in the lovely white stone sculpture of a woman's head made at Erech, or Uruk (modern Warka), shortly after 3000 B.C.; in the stele of Naram Sin, dating from the second half of the 3d millennium B.C.; in the wall paintings at Mari (modern Tell al-Hariri), of the 18th century B.C.; and in the stone sculpture of the ancient lawgiver Hammurabi, who reigned from about 1728 B.C. to about 1686 B.C.

To understand the early art of Mesopotamia, it is necessary to appreciate the religious mystique that dominated the area throughout its early history. The wonder of man in the presence of the divine is depicted in the enlarged eyes of many statues of worshipers of the 3d millennium B.C.; those found at Tell Asmar are especially impressive. This wonder is also evident in the reverent stance and folded hands of worshipers, such as those of Gudea, governor of Lagash in about 2000 B.C. The religious attitude of the people may be seen even more clearly in the monumental architecture of the ziggurats, those vast elevated structures rising into the sky to serve as fitting places for the descent of a divine being to receive the worship of man. But if a sensitive artistic touch was needed to portray this early phase of man's religious experience, so awesome and even oppressive in its mood, a still more sensitive hand was required in the following, more intimate phase, when the human being was presented to the god by a heavenly mediator, generally in the form of a goddess. This challenge was met with unusual success in the seal engravings and the bas-reliefs of the Neo-Sumerian period.

The religious form of Sumerian art may be more fully appreciated by comparing it with the art of Assyria. Although this country was as theocratic as Sumer, its art is thoroughly secular in subject matter and in treatment. The principal dynamic is the exaltation of imperial might. At Dur Sharrukin (modern Khorsabad), at Calah

(Nimrud), and at Nineveh this art was intended to overwhelm the beholder with the terror of the king's majesty. The great narrative bas-reliefs, which constitute the finest artistic achievement of Assyria, give expression to violence and bloodshed, to armies and chariots charging the enemy, to the punishment of captives. When war is not the main theme, the Assyrian artists depict the slaying of fierce animals. Assyrian art is as exciting in its presentation as it is oppressive in its theme.

After the overwhelming grandeur of Assyria the Persian style of greatness offers the viewer considerable relief. Here, too, amid the remains of the great capital at Persepolis, may be found imperial majesty of awesome proportions. Architects raised columns of extraordinary height to sustain roofs over spacious areas fit for the residences of the men who had established the first organized empire of the ancient Middle East. Persian art was expressed principally in the construction and decoration of the great palaces at Persepolis, Susa, Ctesiphon, Firuzabad, and Shapur (Bishapur). There were no great religious temples of religious sculpture, for Zoroastrianism required no images. A simple fire altar in the open or in a small temple satisfied the demands of worship.

From the beginnings of Iranian prehistoric art at Susa in the 4th millennium B.C., a progressive understanding and delight in decorative beauty is evident. Appreciation of decorative art enabled Persia in later times to develop a world of rich and opulent splendor and deep aesthetic enjoyment. This art, of formal and highly stylized design, was directly opposed to the naturalism that basically characterizes Hellenistic and Western art. Of great significance in the art history of the world is the fact that Persia was responsible for halting the eastward expansion of a Hellenism that threatened to become the dominant force in the culture of the region. Except for the Graeco-Buddhist art of Gandhara in what is now West Pakistan, Hellenism was a subordinate rather than a dominant influence east of Persia.

Because of a capacity for spacious architecture and for decorative design, Persia was able to provide the basic inspiration for Islamic art, which is distinguished by the clarity and harmony of its structural form and by the decorative use of calligraphy, floral forms, and geometric motifs. The Persian contribution of an ornamental, nonreligious, and nonsymbolic art was invaluable to a religion that, in its earliest phase, cut itself off from the design of images, sacred or secular, in human or animal form. An impasse might have developed had there not existed, in Persia and in the Christian art of the Middle East, the foundations of a decorative art that offered Islam a suitable area for artistic initiative. If the resulting Islamic art is largely secular and devoid of warmth and human feeling, it nonetheless provides aesthetic satisfaction in the delicate and seemingly infinite interplay of motif and countermotif of a nonrepresentational order.

See also ISLAMIC ART AND ARCHITECTURE; MIDDLE EAST—4. *Cultural Life* (Islamic Art); ORIENTAL ARCHAEOLOGY (NEAR EAST); PERSIAN ART; SYRIA—8. *Art and Architecture.*

South Asia. Although India was strongly influenced by both traditions, its art is entirely different from that of Persia and Islam. A new intensity of spiritual and human feeling found expression in all the artistic media of the subcontinent. Despite the thoroughgoing naturalism characteristic of much of Indian art, there is a wider spiritual context within which works must be interpreted. The natural world with all its voluptuousness is considered an expression of the spiritual creative forces that permeate reality, providing a way to the divine as valid as the ascetic path of renunciation. This association of sensuous charm with high spirituality is one of the surest identifying characteristics of Indian art, and it is well exemplified in the artistic grandeur of the Buddhist stupas at Sanchi and Amaravati. Here the innocent beauty of Paradise seems to be reconstituted in works of a loveliness produced only in India and in countries influenced by Indian aesthetics.

Another characteristic of Indian art is its constant reference to symbolic values. This may be seen in the decorative details of the Rajput paintings of the 17th and 18th centuries, in which trees, vines, flowers, peacocks, colors, and cloud formations all reflect a highly symbolic language. Indeed, this language is part of an extensive mythology made up of innumerable accounts of the deeds of the gods. This must be thoroughly understood if either Hindu or Buddhist art is to be interpreted.

Indian art is further distinguished by the warmth of its portrayal of human life, although it does at times give expression to destructive natural and preternatural forces. Yet in depicting life itself as well as human conduct, it tends rather to portray a tender intimacy, distinguishable in the relations of persons with one another and with the natural world. This tenderness may be found in the great murals at Ajanta. There the beauty of the natural world is shown with particular affection on the ceiling of Cave No. 1. There are many touching domestic scenes, especially those of the king and queen in Vihara No. 17. These attractive human qualities may also be seen in the great rock sculpture at Mamallapuram, generally known as *The Descent of the Ganges*. The sympathetic portrayal of home and village life may be observed in even greater detail in the later Rajput paintings.

See also INDIA—7. *Architecture and Art;* PAKISTAN—7. *Architecture and Art.*

Southeast Asia. The main centers of higher artistic development in Southeast Asia are found in Indonesia, Cambodia, Vietnam, Thailand (Siam), and Burma. In each of these countries the art of India fused with the native artistic genius. This conjunction produced extraordinary results, especially in Indonesia and Cambodia. The Javanese people at Borobudur in the 8th century A.D. and the Khmer people at Angkor Wat in the 12th century built religious structures of more monumental dimensions, of greater doctrinal synthesis, and of a more consistent loveliness of expression than any in India itself. The Borobudur structure is Buddhist in inspiration; Angkor Wat is Hindu. These were exceptional achievements, however, and the high level of artistic accomplishment did not endure much longer than the dynasties responsible for their creation. Eventually these massive structures were swallowed up in the jungles originally cleared for their erection. Rediscovered and restored since the 19th century, they now stand forth among the greatest expressions of religious art known to man.

THE BUDDHA, a favorite subject of Asian artists, is seen here in a 5th century Indian stone carving.

The other major spiritual tradition in the region, especially in Indonesia, has been Islam. Yet the artistic influence of Islam has been of much slighter significance than that of Buddhism, Hinduism, or the native art traditions, and even in Indonesia there are no great Islamic religious monuments. There the outstanding work in the strictly native tradition is to be found in the textile arts and their decorative motifs. On the mainland, Buddhist art established itself as the dominant tradition. As Buddhist images and temple structures were adapted to native traditions, many impressive works were produced. These generally reflect the peaceful charm of the region.

See also INDONESIA—5. *Cultural Activities.*

East Asia—China. Although an impressive artistic tradition existed in Neolithic times, the history of Chinese art begins with the bronze vessels of the Shang dynasty (about 1523–1027 B.C.). Both in artistic conception and in technical execution they belong to a world of magical perfection. The fantastic being, the so-called *t'ao t'ieh,* that forms the principal motif of these vessels is highly stylized, but it seems to be glaring at us. The bulging eyes, horns, fangs, and claws reach out with startling realism. The entire work nevertheless embodies a certain serenity, harmony, and reassurance. Here are to be found the two major elements of Chinese art: the surge of a wild, almost violent inner dynamic; and a serene control that turns this force into a harmonious expression of the deepest rhythms of the universe.

After a period of decline in the middle Chou period (771–474 B.C.) this dynamic and harmony reappeared in late Chou (473–256) and Ch'in (221–207) times. Partially under the influence of the animal art of the North Asian steppes, a new intensity of motion was revealed. This may be seen quite clearly in a late Chou

JAPANESE INFORMATION SERVICE, CONSULATE GENERAL OF JAPAN

JAPANESE SECULAR ARCHITECTURE developed from 16th century castles such as this one at Himeji.

bronze vessel, now in the Stoclet Collection in Brussels, where a horned dragon peers over the rim. Here again the deeper forces of reality in the transhuman order are presented in one of the truly great art traditions of the world. For the moment this dragon is as still as an image of the Buddha; yet its wide eyes, its erect horns, and its claws gripping the vessel reveal a dynamic power about to unleash a swirl of motion. This captivating motif is also depicted in the bronze mirrors of the period and in the later dragon painting of Ch'en Jung (mid-13th century), now in the collections of the Boston Museum of Fine Arts.

In the art of Han times (202 B.C.–220 A.D.), order and classical harmony prevail over imaginative vigor. There is a superb perfection in Han work, as is evident in the mirrors of the period, but this very quality deprives it of the inventiveness that invariably distinguishes Chinese art in its more creative moments. Later, in the Buddhist art of the Wei period (386–556), the inner dynamic has been transferred from the cosmic to the spiritual plane, the meeting of Buddhist spirituality with Chinese humanism creating an art that achieves total reconciliation between the human and the divine. The lovely Maitreya statues of this period promise to heal all earthly sorrows. If the healing must wait, the vision granted of the transphenomenal world is immediate. This experience of the infinite attained through Buddhism went beyond anything that the Chinese had thus far known.

Thereafter the Chinese retained the memory of intense spiritual experience in their work. This new insight of Buddhism, combined with the intuitive vision of Taoism and the cosmic mystique of Confucianism, produced the su-

preme product of Chinese art, the landscape paintings of the 8th through the 14th centuries. During this period, paintings underwent many changes, from the muted tones of Wang Wei (699–759) to the grandeur of Li Ch'eng (died 967), Fan K'uan (early 11th century), and Kuo Hsi (about 1020–1090). It then progressed to the increasingly new, lighter, dramatic work of Hsia Kuei and Ma Yuan (early 13th century). Eventually it culminated in the amazing genius of Ni Tsan (1301–1374). These are but a few names in the long list of Chinese landscape painters of the period. Although their genius is infinitely varied, they were united in their efforts to present a hint of the final mystery of life. To some degree this goal had been achieved in the bronze work of the Shang period, in the animal motifs of late Chou art, and in Wei sculpture. But the final great effort of the Chinese to attain this objective was made in landscape painting, a tradition that has continued into modern times.

See also CHINA—*14. Art* and *15. Ceramics.*

Japan. In the Neolithic period and the early Bronze Age, in the centuries just before the Christian era, the Japanese had already manifested their peculiar artistic gifts in the form and in the decorative detail of their ceramic and bronze work. Later, in the grave mounds of the 4th and 5th centuries A.D., there emerged an even more advanced art, particularly in its presentation of the human form. The clay figurines known as *haniwa* are possibly unsurpassed in the simplicity of their realism.

Aesthetic delight in reality is so much the inner substance of life in Japan that even its experience with Buddhism has been equally aesthetic and religious. This accounts for the dominant attraction of the Japanese to the Shingon sect of Buddhism in the Heian period (794–1185) and to Zen Buddhism since the 13th century. Although both these schools favorably influenced the arts, in the beginning Buddhist art presented a challenge of massive proportions. Japan might have been absorbed artistically into this foreign orbit or have reverted to a simple folk art after the original impetus toward a higher art had passed away. But it achieved what Indonesia and Cambodia could not. In these countries, when the artistic impulse furnished by a foreign tradition had been exhausted, the development of native art could not continue on an equally high plane.

The native ability of the Japanese in architecture can be seen not only in the 7th century buildings of the Horyuji near Nara, erected under the first powerful influences of Chinese Buddhism, but also in the 11th century Hoodo (Phoenix Hall) in the Byodo-in at Uji and the late 14th century Kinkakuji (Golden Pavilion) at Kyoto. In sculpture, Japan produced impressive work in wood, bronze, and clay from the 7th through the 14th centuries. Of special importance are the works of the sculptor Unkei (1148–1223). Yet it is in the picture scrolls of the 12th through the 14th centuries that the artistic genius of the nation manifested itself most fully. This is not the narrative and illustrative art of the Persian and Mughul (Mogul) miniatures, or the contemplative art of the Rajput painters, or the intuitive art of the Chinese landscape scrolls. It is, rather, a great dramatic art of exceptional range in its presentation of Japanese life.

Later, Japan boasted the great Zen painters of the 14th and 15th centuries, the grand decorators of the 16th and 17th centuries, and the masters of the wood-block print from Hishikawa Moronobu (about 1618–about 1694) to Hiroshige Ando (1797–1858). In each of these periods individual artists produced works of genius, and together they form an artistic tradition that challenges comparison with the heritage of any society. Still, the essential character of Japanese art was revealed at its best by the creators of the great scroll paintings. There is above all a portrayal of Japanese life—from village simplicity to imperial pomp. All of society is depicted: the craftsmen, the peasants, the itinerant monks, and the warriors sweeping over the countryside to carry on their unending feudal struggles. The scrolls also show students at their books, lovers writing poems, and people dancing and watching cockfights. Here too, on the roads of medieval Japan, the oxen straining at their carts, the great processions of the nobility, and the monks on their tours of evangelization can be observed. The scrolls are the unique and superb art of the Japanese people.

See also JAPAN—16. *The Fine Arts* and 17. *Architecture;* JAPANESE CERAMICS; WOOD ENGRAVING AND WOODCUT—*Japanese Woodcuts.*

North and Inner Asia. In North Asia the master art in the Scythian-Siberian tradition is the portrayal of animal motifs in small bronze castings. Generally serving a functional purpose in the life of pastoral tribes, these works apparently contain no religious significance or symbolism. They constitute, rather, a humanistic art, revealing exceptional insight into the animal form in all its dynamic possibilities. It matters little whether the animal is shown placidly at rest or at the deadly moment of fierce conflict. While Scythian-Siberian art is highly stylized, it embodies a liveliness and a vigor of execution compelling attention in any survey of Asian art. Even though they represent in many ways extremely different traditions, the work of the Scythians was closely related to the Luristan art of Persia. The Scythian tradition developed in close relationship not only with Persian but also with Greek and Chinese art. The last great influence of the Scythians was exerted on the Chinese art of the late Chou period. Thereafter the animal art of the steppes declined, finally dying out at the beginning of the Christian era.

In Inner Asia the Tarim Basin (now part of the Sinkiang-Uigur Autonomous Region of China), as the meeting place of the great traditions of eastern and western Asia, has been a region of special importance in Asian art. It was at such centers as Khotan, Kucha, and Turfan, more than elsewhere on the vast continent, that the arts of Greece, Persia, India, and China mingled on a plane of equality. The Tarim Basin is no longer a crossroads of the Asian world and possesses no contemporary artistic significance. Nevertheless, it had its day of glory in the first millennium of the Christian era. Then and for centuries afterward it was a grand east-west highway through which men of many nations passed, bearing spiritual and material treasure. This treasure included artistic works, and the ideas embodied in them have had no small influence on the subsequent cultural history of mankind.

See also ARCHITECTURE; BRONZE AND BRASS IN ART; IVORY AND IVORY CARVING; LACQUER AND LACQUERWORK; PAINTING; PORCELAIN —*History;* POTTERY—*History.*

THOMAS W. BERRY
Fordham University

Bibliography
Binyon, Laurence, *The Spirit of Man in Asian Art,* reprint (New York 1965).
Chang, Chung-yuan, *Creativity and Taoism: A Study of Chinese Philosophy, Art and Poetry* (New York 1963).
Frankfort, Henri, *The Art and Architecture of the Ancient Orient* (Baltimore 1954).
Lee, Sherman, *A History of Far Eastern Art* (Englewood Cliffs, N.J., 1964).
Lloyd, Seton, *The Art of the Ancient Near East* (New York 1961).
Malraux, André, and Salles, Georges, eds., *The Arts of Mankind,* 8 vols. (New York 1961–66).
Paine, Robert T., and Soper, Alexander, *The Art and Architecture of Japan* (Baltimore 1955).
Pope, Arthur Upham, and Ackerman, Phyllis, eds., *A Survey of Persian Art,* 6 vols. (London and New York 1938–39); reissued, 13 vols. (Tokyo 1964–65).
Rowland, Benjamin, *The Art and Architecture of India* (Baltimore 1953).
Sickman, Laurence, *The Art and Architecture of China* (Baltimore 1956).
Skira, *Treasures of Asia,* 6 vols. (New York 1960–63).
Waley, Arthur, *An Introduction to the Study of Chinese Painting* (New York 1958).
Yashiro, Yukio, *2000 Years of Japanese Art* (New York 1958).
Zimmer, Heinrich, and Campbell, Joseph, *The Art of Indian Asia,* 2d ed., 2 vols. (New York 1955).

11. Music

There are as many musical traditions in Asia as there are language and culture groups. Moreover, thousands of years of high civilization and intercourse between nations have produced subtle admixtures of ideas on music as well as exchanges of forms, instruments, and compositions. The strong cultural traditions of many Asian nations have helped to preserve archaic

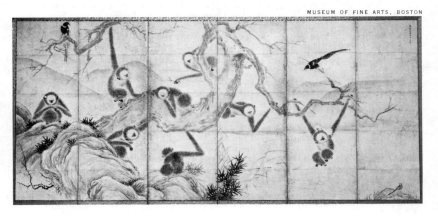

JAPANESE SCREEN PAINTING by Sesshu (late 1400's), a Zen priest, is in the spare, intuitively direct style derived from Zen Buddhist teachings.

CAST BRONZE vessel from Honan, China, dates from around 1100 B.C.

FREER GALLERY OF ART, WASHINGTON, D.C.

musical forms. In contrast to performances of ancient music in the West, these forms are the result not of historical reconstruction, but in many cases of an oral tradition continuing unbroken from teacher to pupil for more than 1,000 years.

Even before the great impact of Western culture that began in the mid-19th century, Asia had been slowly changing, discarding some musical styles and developing others. Certain nations with tenacious traditions of preservation, such as Japan, have maintained musical forms from almost every period of their history. Others with stronger creative energies, such as China and India, have created and discarded forms to such an extent that little in the tradition may confidently be said to be more than 100 years old.

With the overwhelming prestige of Western culture in the 20th century, many traditions are weakening or dying out completely. Both the popular music and the art music of the West are taking the place of the older traditions in the ideals of the younger generations, and from economic necessity ever-increasing numbers of musicians are seeking their fortunes along these paths. The governments of some Asian countries, however, have established schools for the training of young people in the native traditions.

Southwest Asia. The music of the Middle East shares many characteristics with that of India. There is a strong preference for a thin ensemble texture, consisting usually of a solo instrument or voice or of a small group of instruments playing essentially in unison. The preferred instruments are end-blown flutes, plucked lutes, bowed lutes, and vase-shaped drums.

The art music of Iran (Persia), based on the principle of improvisation and expansion of melodic and rhythmic formulas called *gushe,* is heard in its fullest form in the performance of the *dastgah,* a suite composed of several *gushe.* In such a performance most *gushe* are in free rhythm, performed on a solo instrument or voice, but certain sections, notably the opening and ending pieces, are in fixed rhythms and may be accompanied by the *tombak* (a single-headed drum). The principal melody-playing instruments are the long-necked, plucked lute (*tar*), the smaller long-necked lute (*sitar*), and the bowed lute (*kemanche* or *kamaniah*). The *santir,* a dulcimer struck with small, padded mallets, also figures prominently in the art music.

The art music of Turkey has a rich body of folk music from which to borrow. As in Persian music, a suite of compositions, here called *fasil,* is the mainstay of the performance. The several pieces are usually joined by a common mode and are contrasted by different styles and rhythms. The Arabic lute and the *darabukka* (a vase-shaped drum with a single head) are prominently employed. Other important instruments are the *kanun* (a trapezoid, plucked zither), the *kemanche,* and several varieties of the *saz* (a long-necked, plucked lute). Two other instruments widely employed outdoors are the *zurna* (a conical double-reed instrument) and the *dawul* (a double-headed drum).

Of all of the musical cultures of the Middle East, that of the Arabic-speaking peoples extends over the widest geographical area. Its influence has even permeated the styles of the non-Muslim minorities of the region. The human voice figures prominently in Arabic music, and the most frequently used instruments are the *ud* (lute), the *darabukka,* and the Western violin. The ancient classical theory is best manifested in the rather complex system of melodic music called *maqamat* and in the rhythmic patterns. As in Turkey and Iran, great emphasis is placed on elaboration by the solo voice or solo instrument.

See also MIDDLE EAST—4. *Cultural Life* (Performing Arts).

South Asia. The complex melodic and rhythmic theory of ancient Indian music undoubtedly influenced the music of the courts of Burma, Thailand, and Indonesia, and perhaps those of China and Japan as well. Unfortunately, little beyond literary and archaeological evidence remains of this music in India or Pakistan. The music of India in the 20th century is not designed for the large orchestras of former times but primarily for the soloist, who, within established theoretical limits, enjoys freedom for improvisation. He is supported by a drummer, who stabilizes the pulse while adding excitement to the performance. Lastly, an instrument venting only the main tones of the melodic system provides a continuous drone that envelops the ensemble in an atmosphere of sound.

Indian music may be divided into northern and southern idioms, that of the south being the more theoretically complex and systematized. The most commonly used solo instruments are the *vina* (a large lute with gourd resonators) and the transverse flute. The human voice is employed prominently. Whereas art music is widely performed and enjoyed by both amateur and professional musicians in the south, in north India there has been a tendency to relegate performance to professional musicians. The main instruments of the north are the *sitar* and the *sarod,* both of the lute type. The human voice is also widely employed, but in contrast to the practice in the south, the repertoires for vocal and instrumental music are distinct. Although the instruments are less frequently heard in the performance of art music, the transverse flute and the *shanai* (a double-reed pipe) are sometimes encountered. The accompanying drum of the south is the *mrdangam,* a large, double-headed, laced instrument played with the bare fingers. In north Indian music it is often replaced by a pair of small single drums called the *tabla.* The drone is usually supplied by a long-necked string instrument known as the *tambura.*

See also INDIA—8. *Dance, Music, and Drama.*

CHINESE SCROLL PAINTING, by Ku Hung-chung, depicts the amusements of a courtier in 10th century Nanking.

Southeast Asia. Bronze gongs in some type of frame and tuned to some tonal sequence have constituted the strongest element uniting the musical cultures of Southeast Asia. The bronze gong, it seems certain, originated in south China in prehistoric times. Not only have excavations revealed small ensembles of bronze gong drums in China, but bronze gongs also are still used similarly by the hill peoples of Burma, Laos, and Vietnam.

The traditional ensemble for Burmese music has been a circle of small, tuned bronze kettles called *saing-waing*. Sitting in the center of the circular frame, the player strikes the kettles with small mallets. A similar instrument is the *patt-waing*, consisting of a series of small, tuned drums hung in a circular frame. The ensemble also includes a small double-reed pipe called the *na*, a set of wooden clappers and bells, and a large hanging drum. It provides the musical accompaniment for the various types of *pwe* (Burmese theater). *Zat-pwe*, a combination of dances, mime, and comedy, is perhaps the most popular entertainment. Among other Burmese instruments, the *saung* (harp) is important as an accompaniment to the voice.

Despite individual differences, the musical cultures of Thailand, Cambodia, and Laos are joined by common practices and instrumentation. The gong circle in several sizes is known by the generic name *khawng wong*. The *ranat* (xylophone) in different forms serves as a supporting instrument together with various drums and single gongs and a small, strident double-reed instrument. Two types of ensemble may be distinguished: the *piphat*, composed of this basic instrumentation; and the *mahori*, characterized by string instruments of plucked and bowed lute types. There are two important dramatic styles. The *khon*, a masked play combining mime and dance, draws largely on the great Indian epic, the *Ramayana*, for its themes. *Lakhon* drama, which is not restricted to this epic, is most often performed by unmasked women.

The use of gong-chime ensembles is predominant in the Hindu-Islamic cultures of Indonesia and the southern Philippines. In Mindanao, Borneo, and parts of the Moluccas, small ensembles, composed of one set of gong chimes, permit melodies to be improvised according to a system of rhythmic modes and supported by gongs and drums for rhythmic punctuation. Compared with these light and flexible groupings, the large ensembles (gamelans) of the high cultures of Java seem ponderously complex. Assemblages of as many as 30 musicians are not uncommon.

There have been several different types of Javanese gamelan. Perhaps the most important

were the large ensembles found in the courts of Surakarta (Solo) and Djokjakarta. They have also been employed in the performance of all-night shadow plays based on modified texts of the *Ramayana* and the *Mahabharata*. These ensembles have been played in two styles: "loud," entailing the use of the main body of bronze metallophones; and "soft," requiring an addition to the basic ensemble of ornamenting instruments, such as the xylophone, flute, and two-stringed fiddles and the human voice. A special type of ensemble, known as *gamelan sekati*, has been used in connection with Muslim festivities.

Bali, with its small, isolated Hinduistic culture, has perhaps the highest degree of musical activity in Indonesia. Here the shadow play is accompanied by a quartet of high-pitched metallophones on which delicately ornamented music is played until dawn. *Gambuh*, a dramatic form with live actors, has an ensemble of great end-blown flutes, fiddles, and drums; its melodies have served as a basis for many other forms of Balinese music. A very large gamelan plays the music for the *legong*, a dance traditionally performed by three girls under the age of 13. A small group of instruments accompanying male and female singers and dancers, called the *djanger*, enjoys considerable popularity, but almost all other types of contemporary Balinese music have been influenced by the music for the dance known as *kebyar*, for which a very large gamelan is required.

East Asia. Musical instruments have been known in China since prehistoric times, and by the time of Confucius (551–479 B.C.) an elaborate theory and aesthetic of music had evolved. Military expansion and political influence left the imprint of the Chinese on the music of neighboring lands, among them Korea, Japan, the Ryukyu Islands, Mongolia, Tibet, and Vietnam. While the cultures of each of these countries have had easily distinguishable musical characteristics, they have also been linked by common musical practices. The most obvious are the use of large ensembles, associated with the royal courts and ceremonies of China, Japan, and Korea; a predilection for small, bowed lutes, plucked lutes, and plucked zithers; and a close bond between music and literature.

In China the large court ensembles have long been lost, and only the one employed in Confucian ceremonies has been maintained. Some of the oldest Chinese music is part of the vast repertoire of solo music for the seven-stringed zither, the *ch'in*. This ancient instrument has been especially honored and enjoyed by intellectuals. Its extremely detailed notation system furnishes directions for the proper finger with

JAPANESE MUSICAL INSTRUMENTS include the koto (foreground), samisen, and shakuhachi.

which to pluck each string and also dictates which finger is to be used to stop the string. A body of literature of a more dynamic character exists for the plucked lute, the *p'i-p'a*. A court instrument, the *p'i-p'a* was later taken up by wandering musicians as an accompaniment to the voice. The modern *p'i-p'a* repertoire, however, is almost entirely instrumental solo. A sparser body of literature exists for the small, plucked zither, which has movable bridges and as many as 16 strings. Known as the *cheng* or *tseng*, in its modern form it is a close relative of the Vietnamese *dan-tranh*. In its older form, employed in ancient court music, the *cheng* gave rise to the Japanese *koto*, the Ryukyuan *kutu*, and the Korean *kayagum*.

Of the many dramatic and literary forms of China, one of the most archaic was employed by the guilds of storytellers. As long epic or moral tales were recited, the storyteller, between the stanzas, beat a drum on a stand before him. The *san-hsien*, a three-stringed, long-necked lute with a snakeskin body, usually served as the accompanying instrument. The dramatic plays commonly called Chinese opera have included a great variety of styles. One of the oldest styles, the *k'un ch'u*, has waned in popularity, although it is still performed. The accompanying musicians sit on the stage to the side; their instruments include drums, gongs, the *san-hsien*, and the *ti-tzu* (a transverse flute). The later, more widespread *ching-hsi* (Peking opera) has employed essentially the same type of ensemble, but with the replacement of the softer flute by various types and sizes of the *hu-ch'in* (a bowed fiddle).

Although Korea has been overrun by China and Japan at various times in its history, it has maintained a remarkable degree of musical integrity and originality. The ancient Confucian ceremonial music, as well as special music for the death anniversaries of the Korean kings, has been preserved. This court music was performed by a large ensemble of instruments. In Cholla in southern Korea a number of important musical styles arose. The people of this area created several different vocal forms, as well as a form of instrumental music called *sanjo*. Usually improvised on the *kayagum* (a 12-stringed zither), with the accompaniment of a large drum, *sanjo* consists of several movements in increasingly faster tempos. The *changguk* is the only vocal dramatic form extant in the country. It is not true drama, but rather a long narration by a singer with drum accompaniment. It permits slight gestures as well as dancing. Another dramatic form, the mask play, exists in several slightly different types.

Japan has preserved the vocal and instrumental music of its courts from the 10th through the 12th centuries. Here, too, the music is entirely in large ensemble form. The repertoire consists both of songs, dances, and instrumental pieces of the court and of songs and dances used in conjunction with the rituals of Shinto. While this music was being transmitted by court nobles and a small group of hereditary musicians, the military class in the 14th century began to favor actors and musicians who were developing a new form, the distinctive *no* drama. Its singing style owes much to Buddhist cantillation. The accompanying instruments are a flute and three different types of drums, the function of which is to heighten the metric patterns.

The 13-stringed zither, the *koto*, is the central instrument of a genre of chamber music usually associated with the merchant class. It consists largely of vocal pieces, with short instrumental interludes, and of a few instrumental compositions performed either on the *koto* alone or in ensemble with the *shakuhachi* (an end-blown flute) and the *samisen* (*shamisen*), a three-stringed, long-necked lute. The *samisen*, related to the Chinese *san-hsien*, seems to have been introduced into Japan by way of the Ryukyus. This instrument achieved great popularity in each of these cultures because of its portability and suitability for vocal accompaniment. In combination with a strenuous vocal style, it became the mainstay of the *bunraku* (puppet play). Later, in an ensemble with the flute and drums of the *no* drama, it was used with live actors in the theater that became known as *kabuki*.

See also CHINA—13. *Music;* JAPAN—19. *Literature* (Drama); KOREA—10. *Cultural Activities* (Creative Arts): Music; MUSIC—*Oriental Music;* MUSICAL INSTRUMENTS.

ROBERT GARFIAS, *University of Washington*

Bibliography

Gosvami, O., *The Story of Indian Music* (Bombay 1957).
Lentz, Donald A., *Gamelan Music of Java and Bali* (Lincoln, Nebr., 1965).
Levis, John H., *Foundations of Chinese Musical Art,* 2d ed. (New York 1963).
Malm, William P., *Japanese Music and Musical Instruments* (Rutland, Vt., 1959).
Malm, William P., *Nagauta: The Heart of Kabuki Music* (Rutland, Vt., 1962).
Sachs, Curt, *The Rise of Music in the Ancient World, East and West* (New York 1943).
Van Aalst, J.A., *Chinese Music,* reprint (New York 1964).
Wellesz, Egon, ed., *Ancient and Oriental Music* (London 1957).

12. Literature

The designation "Oriental literature" is useful if a single term is needed to encompass the literatures of the Middle East, the Indian subcontinent, and East Asia, but the word "Oriental" is nevertheless a quaint survival of the Western heritage of parochial thinking about the non-Western world. The term "non-Western," with its implications of insider and outsider, is not wholly satisfactory. Moreover, by "non-Western literature" we do not normally mean such poetry as that of the Bakhtiari-speaking people of Iran or that of the Mon peoples of Southeast Asia, but only the literature of the major non-Western civilizations. The geographical classification of "Asian" or "Eastern" is even less satisfactory. One major corpus of the literature of the ancient Middle East, that of Egypt, was written in Africa. Arabic literature is written from Morocco to India and has been written even in Spain. On the other hand, Asian Russia is not Asian, Oriental, or non-Western in a literary sense. The term "Oriental" has always had some validity: in Europe it designated from Renaissance times some common religious and philosophical attitudes that had evolved chiefly through the spread of Hinduism and especially of Buddhism in large parts of Asia. In literature the term has been applied specifically to a large body of stories or tales. While these may once have been folktales, they have come to us through literary redactors and editors. There were collections of such tales in early times in India and China and later in the Islamic countries. Entering Europe first through Greek literature, they came in great numbers over the caravan routes in the Middle Ages and are represented in such collections as Giovanni Boccaccio's *Decameron* and the *Gesta Romanorum*. These tales can quite reasonably be referred to as Oriental tales, but it must be noted that their literary status has never been great and that it is greater in Europe than in the countries of their origin.

Cultural Divisions. Oriental literature can be separated into five cultural divisions, four of which represent major civilizations or groups of civilizations.

(1) The ancient Middle East was the birthplace of the great early civilizations of the Egyptians of the Nile Valley, the Hebrews of Palestine and Syria, the Sumerians, Babylonians, and Assyrians of Mesopotamia, and the Hittites of Anatolia. All these civilizations (the Hittite least) have left important literary remains with some common characteristics.

(2) After many centuries, Islamic civilization arose on the ruins of the ancient Middle Eastern world, and it produced two great literatures, Arabic and Persian. The origins of Persian literary culture go much farther back than Mohammed (570–632 A.D.), but the earlier heritage is most artistically exemplified in works of the Islamic period that glorify the Iranian past. Islamic literature burst out of the bounds of the ancient Middle East and extended itself along the North African coast to the Strait of Gibraltar and into Spain in the west and as far as Indonesia in the east. Arabic is a Semitic language, while Persian is an Indo-European one, and Arabic and Persian literatures are quite distinctive, although they share a common heritage.

(3) South Asia includes Pakistan, India, and Ceylon as well as Afghanistan and the Himalayan states. Although a considerable literature developed in Islamic India and later in Pakistan in Urdu (a Persianized form of Hindi), the great literary achievements of this area have been made in Sanskrit (an Indo-European language), and its recent descendants and have generally reflected the culture of Hindu India. Religious unity and the persistence of tradition have made the literature of this vast area more homogeneous than that of Europe.

(4) In literature, East Asia was dominated by China from ancient times. Powerful Chinese cultural influences moving down the Korean Peninsula made themselves felt in the earliest stages of Japanese civilization and literature and were periodically revived, although the spoken languages are dissimilar. But the Asian-Oceanic genius of the Japanese asserted itself so strongly both in modifying and nationalizing continental influences and in creating literary forms of its own that Japanese literature became great in its own right.

(5) From India to the west, from China to the north, and from the surrounding seas a multitude of literary influences—following waves of Hindu, Buddhist, and Muslim religious influences—poured into Southeast Asia. This is an area of considerable cultural achievements, though not most significantly in the domain of literature, which is eclectic (see below, separate section on *Southeast Asia*).

Whatever may be the case in religious or cultural history or anthropology, the first four of these literary groups have little in common with one another. The literature of East Asia has only some themes derived from Buddhism to connect it with the literature of the Indian subcontinent; in general, it does not resemble South Asian literature in its forms and techniques any more than it resembles Western literature. In certain aspects of literary theory the literatures of the Islamic world and South Asia are closer to the West than to Chinese and Japanese literature. Arabic and Sanskrit literary theory is Aristotelian, but the literary principles that govern the composition of the major genres of East Asian literature have no analogues in the West.

Literary Forms. The literary types of Oriental literature are extremely varied. The epic, or long narrative poem, celebrating the deeds of gods and heroes is a major genre in the literature of the ancient Middle East, Persia, and India. It does not exist for the Arabs, the Chinese, and the Japanese, although an equivalent prose form (but a minor genre) might be argued for Japan. A considerable number of dramatic texts are available from the ancient Middle East, but this form is virtually unknown in the Islamic world. From India, however, comes a great variety of major plays. Drama has always been a minor art in China, but two major, unique dramatic types, *no* and *kabuki*, emerged in Japan. Despite such collections as the Hebrew Song of Songs, lyric poetry either was not regarded as important or has not survived from the literature of the ancient Middle East. It is one of the great glories of Persian and Arabic literature but is less important in South Asia. The short poem is certainly the chief genre of Chinese literature, and in Japanese literature it competes for this honor only with drama.

The use of the terminology of Western genres in a discussion of Oriental literary forms is to a certain extent misleading: the Persian epic has little resemblance to Homeric or Indian epics; except for the presence of a stage and actors, Japanese drama is so far distant from Sanskrit drama as to seem a completely different art. We are left with the inescapable conclusion that there are five major literary complexes in the world's history, the four principal Oriental groups and the Western, and that both thematic and structural comparisons of these complexes are likely to be general and vague.

It is difficult to characterize briefly the literary spirit and the literary forms of even one of the four Oriental groups. Nonetheless, it is certainly not so hard a task as to try to characterize the dominant spirit or psychology of a people or group of peoples, although these two tasks are sometimes confused. What literary forms and styles did these peoples most delight in, value most highly, and take care to preserve? This is the question for the literary historian and critic. There is no "spirit" of Oriental literature in general, but some common characteristics may be found for the various literatures that comprise each of the four groups.

Ancient Middle East. The arid nature of the Middle East and the dramatic and life-giving onslaught of the rainy season brought forth in its ancient literature a number of religious poems and ritual dramas that have features in common. Thus, the Hebrew Genesis (see GENESIS, BOOK OF) and the Babylonian Gilgamesh epic (q.v.) share a myth of a great flood in the early history of the world. The religious rituals necessary to ensure the refertilization of the universe at the change of seasons are essentially dramatic in form, though closer in structure to Western medieval morality and miracle plays than to drama in the classical spirit. A number of these dramas have survived, and while they now seem the most static kind of pageantry, they do have dialogue and a rudimentary action, and they are complicated attempts to connect the necessary annual ceremony with the past and future history of the people through myth. A number of long religious poems, more philosophical than epic, also embody the myths of the various peoples and the legends of their early heroes.

From Sumerian literature much material survives, including fragments of at least 10 epics, many hymns, and numerous proverbs, but it is overshadowed by Accadian literature, which it fed and which succeeded it. From Babylonia came what is perhaps the greatest single work (the Old Testament is not a single work, but a library) of the ancient Middle East, the Gilgamesh epic. The hero of this epic is a man (if a superman) and not a god, and his adventures present a reading of human life analogous to that obtained from Odysseus' adventures in Homer's poem, although the epics are very different.

Beginning in 1929, a large body of texts was recovered from Ras Shamra in Syria, at the site of the ancient city of Ugarit. This literature, called Canaanite or Ugaritic, is written in a kind of proto-Hebrew, and Ugaritic culture influenced the later Hebrew literature and acted as an intermediary between the Egyptian and Assyro-Babylonian civilizations and Hebrew literature. At least three epics or parts of epics of great interest are among the Ugaritic texts, and the poetry is of importance for the study of Hebrew poetry.

Religious interest has made Hebrew literature the most important of all the ancient Middle Eastern literatures for the Western World. Much of the Old Testament is not literature, however, but historical narrative, and its beauties in Hebrew are different from its beauties in, for example, the English of the King James Version. Its most literary parts include the great poems of the Psalms, which contain some of the earliest material; the philosophical (and late) Book of Job; the compendium of wisdom in the Proverbs; such exciting historical narrative as the accounts of Rachel and Esther and of incidents in the lives of the patriarchs; the idyllic Book of Ruth; and the love lyrics of the Song of Songs. As a collection, the Old Testament represents the best and most varied literary offerings of the ancient Middle East. But Hebrew literature contains nothing remotely resembling the epic: the historical romances of Japan, the *monogatari,* are far more epical than Old Testament narrative. Hebrew literature also contains no drama, although the Book of Job may be viewed as a kind of static drama perhaps resulting from Greek influence. The Hebrew literary genius may well be lyrical: exquisitely artistic lyric poems survive, and we can gauge the importance of song from the Biblical account of David and his harp.

See also ASSYRIOLOGY; BIBLE; HEBREW LANGUAGE AND LITERATURE.

Islamic Literature. Hebrew civilization never attained the urban grandeur of the great cities of Egypt and Mesopotamia, and the Hebrews idealized in literature and life the hard existence of the nomad and the patriarchal leader of nomads. This is also true of the Arabs, a people without a past, who created a dynamic new civilization on the ruins of these many old ones in the 7th and 8th centuries A.D. Only some odes or epic lays, the *Muallaqat (Golden Odes),* survive from the days before the coming of Mohammed. But the verses of the sacred book of the Muslims, the Koran (q.v.), are excellent poetry and are, moreover, the actual words of the prophet. There are few Muslims who, regardless of their native languages, cannot quote some verses of the Koran. This fact, coupled with the historical position of the poet as historian of the tribe, chronicler of the deeds of its heroes, and inspirer to both love and battle, makes lyric poetry the dominant literary form, and a variety of lyric types has evolved. There are no epics (although the poems of the *Muallaqat* approach the epic lay) and no dramas. A second mode of expression for the Arab literary genius is found in prose fiction. The artistry of the *Thousand Nights and a Night (Alf Laylah wa-Laylah;* see ARABIAN NIGHTS) is well known; but its everyday equivalent is to be found in the tales told by a thousand and one Arab street-corner and coffee-shop storytellers.

Both Persian life and the Persian language were inundated by the Arab conquest, but independence and heterodoxy soon began to assert themselves. Persian is an Indo-European language, whereas Arabic is a Semitic one; the Persians had behind them a vast ancient history, but the Arabs leaped into history from nowhere. The basically different modes of Persian thought soon began to affect the literature. The Persians, like the Arabs, excelled in the short lyric but carried it perhaps to a higher level of genius in the poets Sadi (died about 1292) and Hafiz (about 1326–1389). Eventually the Persians revived in verse the pre-Islamic glories of Iran. The greatest of the Persian poets is Firdausi (Firdawsi, 940?–?1020), author of the *Shah Nameh* (q.v.), or *Shah-namah*, a powerful and lengthy epic. But where the Greek *Iliad* chronicles only the closing actions of the Trojan War —those events caused primarily by the anger of the hero Achilles—and begins *in medias res*, the *Shah Nameh* tries to cover the deeds of all the major Iranian heroes and is equivalent to an attempt to incorporate all of Greek mythology in a single poem. Nevertheless, the spirits of the Greek and Persian epics are similar, with emphasis on the heroes' prowess in battle and adherence to heroic codes of behavior. Objective in treatment, they include little that is romantic in the medieval Western or Indian sense. In his literary myths the Persian is heir to an ancient civilization that reared great cities, while the Arab is the nomad in the desert, with his stern virtues.

See also ARAB CIVILIZATION—*Literature;* ISLAMIC LITERATURE; MIDDLE EAST—*4.Cultural Life* (Journalism and Literature); PERSIAN LITERATURE.

South Asia. As we turn to India, religious elements become important in literature. Many religions have as part of their doctrine, or at least of their esoteric doctrine, the principle that there is no distinction between the sacred and the profane or secular, but Western modes of thinking usually make a sharp distinction here. Westerners do not regard the *Iliad* and the *Odyssey* as religious books, and it is not certain that the Greeks of classical times did. In general, this is true also of Arabic and Persian civilization, although symbolic and allegorical interpretations of lyric poems, similar to the Christian view of the Song of Songs, have been made. In the Hindu and Buddhist literature of the Indian subcontinent, however, the secular and the sacred, as Westerners see them, blend and integrate so throughly that the distinction, which is not made by Indians in any case, disappears. The most sacred book of the Hindus is perhaps the *Bhagavad Gita*, and this itself is part of the *Mahabharata* (qq.v.), a lengthy epic that is both a historical chronicle like the *Shah Nameh* and a compendium of religious legends. There are many gods, each of whom may manifest himself in countless ways. Among men there are kings and soldiers who operate in a "secular" sphere and priests and hermits who operate in a "sacred" sphere. But to the Hindu these things are two sides of a coin, as inseparable as the positive and negative qualities of an electric current.

The *Mahabharata* draws its subject matter mainly from the military history of early India; its sister epic, the *Ramayana* (q.v), tells the story of Prince Rama's quest for Sita, his love. But both epics incorporate much material from the sacred hymns of the earliest monument, the Vedas, and the commentaries on these scriptures, the Brahmanas and the Upanishads (*Upanisad*). To the Western reader these epics sometimes have the severity and objectivity of the *Iliad*, sometimes the fantasy and otherworldliness of medieval romance. The great later Indian drama of Kalidasa, *Sakuntala* (q.v.), though essentially a love story, is nevertheless permeated by the religious sentiment on which the plot turns. Indian literature is unique among the world's literatures in this amalgam of man's earthly and spiritual sides in an all-pervading unity.

See also articles on the literatures of the major South Asian languages; INDIA—*11. Literature;* PAKISTAN—*9. Literature;* SANSKRIT LITERATURE.

East Asia. If the spirit of Indian literature is religious, the spirit of Chinese literature is just as clearly philosophical. Although Buddhist miracles manifest themselves in Chinese religious thought, religion—especially Confucianism—is the creation of the sage and not of the divinely inspired prophet. The four books attributed traditionally to Confucius (551–479 B.C.) are not books of myth or tribal history or prophecy, but collections of *sententiae* illustrated with cunning examples. From the earliest times, poetry was the most valued literary mode, and the great early anthology of poetry, the *Shih Ching* (*Book of Odes*), is supposed to have been edited by Confucius. In every age of Chinese literature the lyric poem (a poem of about the average length of an English lyric, not the short Japanese forms) dominated the literature. There are many patterns for such poems, and intricate rules were laid down for their construction. All the normal aspects of upper-class life—love, journeys, pleasure, war, death, and royal and domestic events —form the subject matter.

The Western reader is likely to be impressed by the "literary" quality of Chinese philosophy and, in works like the 16th century *Hsi yu chi* (*Pilgrimage to the West;* translated into English as *Monkey*), by the "philosophical" quality of the literature. Chinese philosophical writings from the Confucian canon down are poetic in spirit. Truth does not come, it is believed, through logic, but through combinations of logic, wit, paradox, symbolism, fable, and aesthetic beauty. A great example of such writing is neither the Confucian books nor the important but more legalistic Mencius (Meng-tzu, 372?– 289 B.C.), but the almost legendary Lao-tzu (about 604–531 B.C.).

In general, Chinese literature yields to the Indian in imaginative qualities. It contains nothing like the rich tapestry of the Indian epic or the classical formality and poetic charm of the Indian drama. There is a considerable quantity of what is to Western readers highly interesting but somewhat formless fiction, as well as much drama, although the drama is a form on which little value was placed. Chinese literature reaches its heights in lyric poetry and in philosophical-poetic prose. It is certainly the most human and the most humane of the world's great literatures.

Much ancient and purely Japanese myth and legend were incorporated in early Japanese chronicles, but the development of literary culture cannot be traced until after a small but steady stream of Buddhist influence from China moved down the Korean Peninsula into Japan. With it came a cultural revolution that profoundly affected language and religion, as well as art, literature, and social customs and manners. At times, Chinese in Japan had the status of Latin in the European world: educated Japanese wrote in Chinese because they regarded it as a more civilized language than their own. But the Japanese are not racially or ethnically similar to the Chinese. They live in temperate islands, in a geographical milieu like that of Great Britain. The Japanese language is not related to Chinese, although the Japanese, with considerable difficulty, adapted the Chinese writing system to it. The highly individualistic Japanese early began to change Chinese Buddhist concepts of life and art into native Japanese concepts. After the early period there is scarcely a Japanese object of art that is easily confused with a Chinese one, and Japanese literature is quite distinct, save for some direct imitations of Chinese poetry written by Japanese in Chinese.

Poetry and drama vie with one another for the place of the most valued form in Japanese literature. There are many beautiful early lyrics of moderate length, somewhat comparable to Chinese odes, but more restricted in subject matter and more aesthetic in spirit. Many major later poets employ the very short 17-syllable *haiku* and 31-syllable *tanka,* which in their compression, their reliance on nuances, and their unexpressed implications are characteristic of the Japanese approach in literature. A unique combination of dance, mime, and poetic language makes the aristocratic *no* drama a subtle and evocative form. Finally, in prose fiction the Japanese reached a level not attained elsewhere in Asia and not in Europe until centuries later. The 11th century *Genji Monogatari* (see TALE OF GENJI) of Lady Murasaki Shikibu is a sophisticated psychological study of courtly society.

Some Western readers find Japanese literature less powerful and less varied than Chinese or Indian literature. It is true that the Japanese aesthetic involves the artistic arrangement of a small number of components, but this is done with infinite grace and with native genius. And despite the fact that, of all the Far Eastern countries, Westerners are drawn most easily to Japan, the Japanese spirit in art and literature is perhaps the most difficult for Westerners to penetrate.

See also CHINA—*11. Literature;* JAPAN—*19. Literature;* ORIENTAL THEATER.

G.L. ANDERSON, *New York University*

Southeast Asia. Southeast Asia is a region of considerable ethnic and linguistic heterogeneity; not surprisingly, this diversity is reflected in its literatures. For much of the region there exists, alongside indigenous folktales, sayings, proverbs, and riddles, a Hinduized literature that accompanied the spread of large-scale Indic influence. This literature of Indic origin is to be found, for instance, in the various reflexes of the famed epic, the *Ramayana,* known in Thailand and Laos as the *Ramakien,* in Cambodia as *Reamker,* in the Malay world as the *Hikayat Seri Rama,* and in Burma, after its acquisition from Thailand in the 18th century, as *Ramayagan.* The gigantic Indian epic *Mahabharata* has also left its mark in some parts of this region, especially in Indonesia.

The introduction of Theravada (Hinayana) Buddhism brought to Burma, Thailand, Cambodia, and Laos, and to a limited extent to Vietnam, a major contribution in the form of the *Jatakas,* stories of former births of the Buddha. Though virtually unknown to Indonesia, Malaysia, and the Philippines, these stories have exerted a profound influence on the literature of the rest of Southeast Asia and have been the source of, and inspiration for, an extensive court literature. Thai kings, for example, not only fostered but actively participated in literary endeavors.

While Theravada Buddhism was spreading over much of the mainland, Vietnam was undergoing a long history of Chinese cultural influence, which was to be reflected in such classics as the national Vietnamese poem, *Kim-van-Kieu* of Nguyen-Du (1765–1820), and the *Lament of a Warrior's Wife* of Dang-tran-Con (died ?1743). The latter poem, written originally in Chinese characters with a Chinese background and theme, was rendered into Vietnamese (Annamite) by Doan-thi-Diem and is still widely read.

In contrast with the Buddhist and Confucianist tenor of these literatures, the early writings of Malaysia and Indonesia possess an Islamic tone, about which Sir Richard Winstedt wrote: "The germ of every Malay romance is a folk-tale or cluster of folk-tales, nearly always Indian and manipulated by men wildly ignorant and intolerant of the unities of place and time and of historical truth." Incredibly involved, remarkably eclectic, and composite in nature, calling upon many legends, reminiscences, and mythology, upon Middle Eastern history, Sufism, and the *Mahabharata,* the Malay romances are anonymous hodgepodges that reflect the transition between Hinduism and Islam. Still read in Indonesia and Malaysia, they tend to appeal to the tastes of an older generation that enjoys accounts involving royalty, nobility, and all the trappings of that, to the younger reader, distant world.

Before the arrival of the Europeans, much of the literature existed in poetic form, usually quite rigid and stylized with little or no flexibility. Extant are some fragments of pre-European literature in the Philippines, but the coming of Christianity, which stemmed the tide of Islam, inevitably brought with it the beginnings of Western influence, a trend that has persisted unabated. From the literary point of view this contact with the West was reflected in the introduction into most of Southeast Asia of such Western literary genres as the novel, short story, drama, and essay and a flexibility of poetic forms. The sonnet made its appearance early in Indonesia, for instance. From this followed a period of imitation of Western models based on translations of Western writing; for example, *Robinson Crusoe* and *Der schweizerische Robinson* made their appearance in Burmese, Alexandre Dumas' *Les trois mousquetaires* in Indonesian, and *Hamlet* and *Macbeth* in Thai (Siamese).

Close on the heels of these translations and imitations appeared original work utilizing local themes to a large extent and often describing the conflicts between the old ways and the new, conflicts that were arising as a result of the introduction of Western ideas and mores and of the resistance of the traditional society to the new concepts. The earliest original novels in Indonesia and Vietnam, such as Marah Rusli's *Siti Nurbaja* (1922) and Hoang-ngoc-Phach's *To-Tam* (1925), were pioneers in depicting this conflict and had many imitators well into the 1930's.

During the decade or so before World War II, nationalist movements took shape in much of Southeast Asia. Hand in hand with the rise of nationalism went the development and stimulation of the modern vernaculars and a literary renaissance in all the modern genres, but with writers seeking and finding their themes to a large extent in the traditional cultures of their own lands. Perhaps a majority of these writers had received a Western education, and yet in some instances they tended to look to the East rather than to the West for their inspiration.

India was most often the magnet that attracted Southeast Asian writers, especially Indonesian, and the poetry and plays of Sanusi Pané exemplify this pull.

In the 19th century, Filipino writers of Spanish education drank deep of Spain's culture; this influence culminated in the famed inflammatory novel *Noli me tangere* (1886) of José Rizal, written in Spanish but published in Berlin for political reasons. From the beginning of the 20th century, however, with the advent of American rule and the spread of the English language, the Filipinos' best writing was and continued to be in an "alien tongue," and, with a few exceptions, vernacular literature tended to be generally second-rate.

Almost from the beginning of the colonial period in Southeast Asia some writing by indigenous writers in the pertinent Western language was to be found: in Dutch in Indonesia; in French in Indochina (now Cambodia, Laos, and Vietnam); and in English in Burma, Malaysia, and the Philippines. Thai literature has been written very largely in the Thai language, and only a few of the classics, notably *Khun Chan Khun Phan* and Sunthorn Bhu's *Phra Abhay Mani*, have been translated into English and other Western languages. The appearance in English in 1961 of Kukrit Pramoj's *Red Bamboo*, a novel of village life centered in the local *wat* (temple), is a notable exception. Only since the 1950's has Cambodia begun to encourage and to sponsor, through literary contests, writing in modern Khmer, while Laos is still endeavoring to edit and publish its older classics.

Of all the Western literary types represented in Southeast Asia (and nearly all are found), poetry and the short story have received by far the greatest emphasis. Poetry's history in the region is a long one, but the short story is a relatively modern innovation and as such is extremely popular. The reasons are probably obvious: stories can be written in a short time, and the writer can be assured of a quick return for his effort. They appear generally in weeklies, monthlies, or even newspapers and are readily accessible to the slowly growing reading public. The reading audience for creative writing in most of the Southeast Asian countries is remarkably small despite rapidly growing literacy. As a result of this slow response, the budding writer has sought in vain for adequate recognition and encouragement as well as for financial reward.

The novel and drama are somewhat less fully developed, but drama workshops, such as Severino Montano's Arena Theater in the Philippine provinces and the Indonesian Dramatic Academy in Djakarta, are quite active in stimulating an interest in plays. Southeast Asian writers are young men, and their novels tend to reflect this youth and immaturity. Writing novels takes time, and the questions "Where is the great Filipino novel? Who is working on the great Indonesian novel?" seem to pervade portions of Southeast Asia as much as similar questions have involved writers and their critics in the United States at various times. Few first-rate novels have appeared. Yet the Indonesian Achdiat K. Mihardja's *Atheis* (1949; *The Atheist*), a good novel by almost any criterion, has not been translated.

A serious lack in the evolving literatures and literary traditions of Southeast Asia is the existence of good or even mediocre literary criticism.

GOVERNMENT OF INDIA PRESS AND INFORMATION BUREAU

"SAKUNTALA," classical Sanskrit drama by Kalidasa, is the subject of this 18th century Indian painting.

There have been beginnings, but a stage of real sophistication has not been reached, and the need for critics is great. There is the further need for developing a discriminating reading audience. Creativity is present, and originality has emerged from time to time, but the literatures of Southeast Asia have tended by and large to be imitative, especially of the West. It is expected that this influence will be modified to the extent that younger writers succeed in their search for what they call a "national identity," a lack of which has been a matter of concern to some Southeast Asian intellectuals. A great deal of literary activity has taken place in this region of the world, but it has not found its way into the mainstream of world literature.

JOHN M. ECHOLS, *Cornell University*

Bibliography

Anderson, George L., ed., *Masterpieces of the Orient* (New York 1961).
Arberry, Arthur J., *Classical Persian Literature* (New York 1958).
Bownas, Geoffrey, and Thwaite, Anthony, eds. and trs., *The Penguin Book of Japanese Verse* (Baltimore 1964).
Casper, Leonard, *New Writing from the Philippines* (Syracuse, N.Y., 1966).
Clifford, William, and Milton, Daniel L., eds., *A Treasury of Modern Asian Stories* (New York 1961).
De Bary, W. Theodore, and Embree, Ainslie T., eds., *A Guide to Oriental Classics* (New York 1963).
Gibb, Hamilton A.R., *Arabic Literature: An Introduction*, 2d rev. ed. (New York 1963).
Keene, Donald, *Japanese Literature: An Introduction for Western Readers* (New York 1955).
Lee, Peter H., comp. and tr., *Anthology of Korean Poetry* (New York 1964).
Ming, Lai, *A History of Chinese Literature* (New York 1964).
Payne, Robert, ed., *The White Pony: An Anthology of Chinese Poetry* (New York 1947).
Raffel, Burton, ed., *Anthology of Modern Indonesian Poetry* (Berkeley, Calif., 1964).
Yohannan, John D., ed., *A Treasury of Asian Literature* (New York 1959).

EASTFOTO

CHINA'S FIRST ATOMIC EXPLOSION left a mushroom cloud over the Takla Makan Desert on Oct. 16, 1964.

13. Science and Technology

The immense structure and powerful momentum of modern science have shaped the character of the 20th century and affected every aspect of contemporary life. Yet the origins and development of science and technology are among the least-known areas of history. Paradoxically, these origins are to be found in Asia —which only now is being transformed by the full flowering of that science and technology whose earliest roots it nurtured.

Common Western usage of the term "science" equates it with natural science. Western educational tradition, with its assumption of a cleavage between natural science and other knowledge, makes it difficult to understand the interaction of science with other phases of human development. Thus, many of the early essentials in the development of science and technology do not, in the modern era, appear "scientific."

Prehistory. Science and technology have evolved from the earliest experiences of the human race, and their origins are to be found in the "records" of early man. The use of fire and the making of tools differentiate *Homo sapiens* from other primates. There is increasing support for the hypothesis that the use of such primitive implements as stones for throwing and sticks for digging was instrumental in the evolution of man from subhuman species. This hypothesis suggests that the use and production of tools—that is, technology—are not only fundamental characteristics of man but factors in his evolution as a species.

The Paleolithic period (Old Stone Age), which lasted for about a million years, represented a worldwide occurrence of similar levels of primitive technology. The men of this period developed a considerable variety of tools and weapons. The succeeding Mesolithic period (Middle Stone Age) and Neolithic period (New Stone Age) saw a marked advance. Neolithic culture included the arts of pottery making, domestication of animals, cultivation of grain, and spinning and weaving of fibers. These skills prepared the way for the transition to settled civilization and the growth of cities, which in turn made possible more advanced forms of science and technology.

Stone Age agriculture, as may be seen in the practices of surviving Neolithic cultures, quickly exhausted the fertility of land. This factor, which may have served to limit the size of many Neolithic communities, was present to a lesser degree in the great river valleys subject to seasonal flooding and natural fertilization. In such valleys as the Tigris-Euphrates, Indus, Ganges, Hwang Ho (Yellow), Yangtze, Chao Phraya (Menam), and Mekong, irrigation and drainage greatly extended the areas brought under permanent cultivation.

The establishment of grain agriculture and related techniques was followed by a rapid growth of population and advances in culture. In the Middle East most of the inventions basic to ancient civilization appear to have been made before 3500 B.C. One of the most important was the art of metallurgy, first the production of soft copper tools and then the discovery and systematic use of bronze, which ushered in the Bronze Age. The reduction of metal from ore had, in fact, begun much earlier, prior to 4000 B.C. and metal had been worked or wrought for many centuries before this.

See also COPPER—2. *History and Production* (Antiquity); METALLURGY—2. *History;* STONE AGE.

Early Civilizations. Although it is impossible to date accurately the beginnings of the various early cultures of Asia, mutual influences are known to have occurred among them. The extent to which similar techniques represent cultural borrowings or a converging of skills that were arrived at independently, however, is difficult to establish.

Mesopotamia. There were many similarities between Mesopotamian and Egyptian achievements, although the cultures of the two areas were generally not homogeneous. The greatest achievement conducive to the growth of scientific processes among the early peoples of both areas was the invention of writing, which took place before 3000 B.C. This invention permitted the accumulation of ideas and the improvement of techniques in mathematical calculation, astronomical observation, land measurement, and the systematic retention of data in general.

During the 3000's B.C. the Sumerians of southern Mesopotamia, by harnessing domestic animals to the newly devised plow, had entered the era of relatively large-scale field agriculture. They possessed boats and wheeled vehicles and used the potter's wheel. By about 3000 B.C. they had attained the highest achievements in Bronze Age metallurgy. Sumer itself was conquered by Semitic nomads from Akkad (Accad) to the north, and in time its civilization was absorbed into the mixed Babylonian culture. Invading Assyrians next added their influence to the Mesopotamian complex of cultures.

Generally speaking, Mesopotamian attainments in mathematics were higher than those of Egypt. Egyptian mathematics was essentially additive, tending to reduce multiplication to repeated additions. But Sumerian texts dating from about 2000 B.C., containing multiplication tables for squares and cubes, show a keen computational ability. They reveal a well-developed sexagesimal system of numeration superimposed on an earlier decimal system. Successive orders of magnitude were obtained by alternate use of the factors 10 and 6; there were also cuneiform symbols for 1, 10, 60, 600, 3,600, and so on. This double system was the basis of weights and measures, including the subdivisions of angular measurement of the circle, and other units, such as the fathom, foot, bushel, and the divisions of the day into hours, minutes, and seconds, which persist in modern usage. The mathematical-unit division of the Sumerians was not, however, the most significant feature of their achievement. Whereas the Egyptians had employed a new symbol for each higher unit, the Sumerians used the same symbol, but indicated value by position. Thus, 1 followed by another 1 designated 61. While not identical with the modern decimal system, positional notation furnished tremendous advantages for computation, comparable to the difference between computing with Arabic numbers and with Roman numerals.

Astronomical observation in Babylonia may be traced to at least about 1900 B.C., when accurate records for the rising and setting of Venus and other planets were kept. On the basis of some accurate knowledge, the Babylonians elaborated a fanciful body of astrology and magic. This linkage of scientific fact with magic, astrology, and religion is a feature of early cultures; it arose in part because learning and science were often the monopoly of the priestly classes. While astrological interests gave impetus to further accurate observation of the heavens, they constricted the bounds of understanding. The priestly scribes of both Mesopotamia and Egypt tended to record matters relevant to their duties and interests of keeping accounts, surveying, calendar making, astrological prediction, medicine, and the exorcism or propitiation of evil spirits. Not until relatively late times were the arts of craftsmen, such as chemists and metallurgists, recorded. The rift between clerical and craft traditions persisted to the detriment of the development of science and technology as elements capable of mutual reinforcement.

See also ASSYRIOLOGY; CALENDAR; WEIGHTS AND MEASURES, ANCIENT; WHEEL; WRITING.

India. Very little is known about the civilization that flourished in the Indus Valley in the 2000's and 1000's B.C. A Bronze Age agricultural society, it possessed a script, as yet undeciphered, and a decimal numerical system. That the rest of the world owes to India the unique numerical script commonly termed "Arabic" and the invention of the zero seems beyond doubt. It is not known precisely when the symbol of zero first came into use in India, but its earliest form, together with clearly recognizable signs for the numbers from one through nine can be found carved on Hindu monuments of the 6th century A.D.

Unfortunately, records of Indian science and technology before the Muslim invasions of the 8th century A.D. are extremely meager. Accounts of Hindu work in astronomy, dating from the 5th century, deal with the texts known as the Siddhantas, which had been written in an earlier period. Some of them were based on Greek and other astronomical sources to the west. Existing

TATA STEEL PLANT under construction at Jamshedpur, India, symbolizes Asia's drive for modernization.

evidence suggests that the Hindus were noteworthy for their mathematics rather than for their astronomy and that they were, in the main, in the algebraic tradition of Babylonian mathematics. Their most important contributions to world science were their numerical system and their development of generalized algebraic operations. Their concept of zero made it possible to use their other nine symbols to represent any number, regardless of magnitude.

See also INDIA—12. *Science.*

East Asia. The early historical period in China embraced the Shang (about 1523–1027 B.C.) and Chou (1027–256 B.C.) dynasties. Rich archaeological finds show that Shang Chinese developed a pictographic form of the present writing system, the potter's wheel, chariots, domesticated horses, rice and silk culture, and highly advanced bronze technology and art forms. Taken together, the Shang and Chou periods reveal perhaps a technological achievement as high as, or higher than, that of the early civilizations farther to the west.

Iron came to China at least as early as the 6th century B.C. (there is mention of it in texts of 513 B.C.). The state of Ch'in, which was associated with iron making, by 221 B.C. subdued and unified the warring states into which the Chou dynasty had deteriorated. The Han dynasty (202 B.C.–220 A.D.), which soon followed the Ch'in, brought China a period of almost four centuries of relative peace, during which important technical innovations were made. The orienting effect of the magnet was discovered in the 1st century B.C. Paper, invented during the Han period, gradually replaced bamboo slips and silk for writing purposes.

In the realm of ideas the Mohists, followers of the philosopher Mo Ti (Mo-tzu; late 5th and early 4th centuries B.C.), appear to have been substantially concerned with scientific matters. They taught a doctrine of universal love and the cultivation of strength, including the military arts. Their ideal was to assist weak states in resisting oppression. Investigation into the arts of defense led to the study of fortification, mechanics, physics, and optics. Observing reflections from various types of mirrors, they formulated empirical rules that related the size and position of the objects and images to the curvature of the mirrors. The Mohists also studied lever systems, though empirically and without formulating theories or employing geometrical constructions.

Although existing versions date from the Earlier Han dynasty (202 B.C.–9 A.D.), the first Chinese mathematical work is believed to have been written at the beginning of the Chou period. The problems of surveying and the determination of areas of triangles, circles, and other figures were dealt with. For some time the value of pi (π) was taken as 3, but by the first century A.D. it was assigned the value of the square root of 10 ($\sqrt{10}$). As in Egypt and Babylonia, mathematicians, astronomers, surveyors, and calendar makers were closely associated with the government.

Chinese astronomical calculations and compilations did not produce a scientific concept of the universe. In the mid-4th century B.C. the outstanding Chinese astronomer, Shih Ch'en, charted the relative positions of 800 stars and provided rules for the prediction of eclipses, and within a few hundred years other astronomers had discovered the precession of the equinoxes. But this activity in technical astronomy was generally separated from cosmological speculation, which remained largely untouched by scientific concepts. The T'ang period (618–906), like the Han, marked by relative peace and prosperity, saw further advances in technology. The manufacture of porcelain attained a very high level. During this period, too, the first block printing began in Buddhist monasteries. The wheelbarrow, invented in the 3d century, came into wide use. By the late T'ang period, gunpowder had been developed, and before the end of the Sung dynasty (960–1279), firearms had made their appearance.

Japanese and Korean science and technology of the premodern period must be regarded primarily as reflections of Chinese culture. In a few techniques, however, Chinese achievements were surpassed. A fine example is metalworking in Japan, where possibly the best swords in the world were and still are made. For centuries their fabrication was accompanied by magical or religious rituals, the theoretical principles involved in the metallurgical processes apparently not being understood. The steps in manufacture were kept secret. Eventually, they involved the blending of sections of hard and soft steel so that their different properties complemented each other. As a result of the modern study of two-phase materials, such as plastics reinforced with glass fiber, this ingenious craftsmanship has received full recognition. The Koreans have laid claim to various technological triumphs. Most important, perhaps, were printing with movable metal type in the 14th century and armored warships in the 16th century.

Influence of Greece. None of the early Asian civilizations developed a theoretical geometry. In none, moreover, did the concepts of the universe derive logically from observations made by astronomers. Nor do we find in ancient Oriental mathematics efforts toward what is now known as demonstration. Rules of procedure were prescribed but without logical argumentation. Some historians of science believe that mathematics and other sciences prior to Greek influence were never emancipated from the problems of technology and administration for the use of which innovations had been made. Others emphasize the limitations on scientific thought imposed by persistent habits of associating magic, astrology, and religion with the same phenomena with which science itself was concerned. The English historian and scientist Stephen F. Mason stresses the separation of theoretical and empirical inquiry that is characteristic of stratified society in most agricultural civilizations. His point is that the enhancement of science was closely related to the nature of such less static, commercialized civilizations as those of Greece and Renaissance Europe. Chinese society, typical of agricultural economic and political systems, was repressive of independent enterprise and related individualistic thought. The epitome of the independent man in traditional Chinese culture was the Taoist hermit, who rejected the expectations of his society but did so by retreating to the wilderness rather than by changing conditions around him.

In the 1st millennium B.C., Babylonia was occupied by a succession of invaders. Then, in 539 B.C., it was incorporated into the Persian empire, which was subsequently conquered by the Greeks under Alexander the Great (331 B.C.). For centuries before this time, however, great economic, social, and political changes had been occurring in the eastern Mediterranean Basin. Cities that had grown up along the coast of Asia Minor as well as on the Greek mainland were different in nature from the towns of the Bronze Age agricultural societies. These urban centers were the birthplace of a new milieu for human thought. There was a notable absence of well-established religion; while this may have led some inhabitants of these centers into mysticism, there is evidence that it also stimulated the growth of a rationalistic scientific outlook. This new Hellenistic outlook and civilization were a compound of Greek culture and Egyptian and Asian influences. The historian of science George Sarton has documented not only the great extent to which Greece Hellenized western Asia, most notably through the conquests of Alexander the Great, but also the extent to which Greece and eastern Europe were Orientalized by the westward flow of cultural influences.

The contribution made to science by the Greeks is no less than the formulation of the idea of science as we know it. So far as can be ascertained from earlier civilizations, data about the material world were studied for their possible practical use. The Greeks introduced what has continued to be the main theme of scientific inquiry: the desire to achieve a full understanding of the universe. The transformation effected by the Greeks has been put this way: they were concerned not with measuring triangular fields, but with all triangles. Although the Greeks apparently did not develop a consistent experimental method, they performed experiments in limited instances. Their genius for rigorous thinking was probably related to the existence of a considerable body of thinkers emancipated from the necessity of applied work because of the large number of slaves in their society. And this may well be the reason why the Greeks did not extend the application of science to new fields, although scientific thought itself was greatly enhanced through investigation and logic.

See also HELLENISM–*Hellenism of the Non-Greeks.*

Muslim World. Until modern European science and technology exerted an impact on Asia in the 19th century, the most important force for the spread of technology and scientific ideas in the continent was the extension of Arab power from the 7th century on. By the time Spain had been conquered in 711–713, the Arabs controlled a vast area within which cultural interchanges were greatly facilitated. As the Muslim empire spread, Arab learning was enriched by the cultures of the occupied peoples. This was true especially in the case of Persia. The new Muslim dynasty of the Abbasid caliphs (750–1258), with its capital at Baghdad, established a domain influenced essentially by Persian culture. Persian scholarship also transmitted contributions from Hindu Sanskritic sources (particularly arithmetic, trigonometry, and chemistry) and Greek sources (primarily logic, geometry, astronomy, and medicine). The Arabs obtained some of their arithmetical knowledge and forms from India, including the so-called Arabic numerals and the use of sines in trigonometry. The best-known Islamic mathematician, Muhammad Ibn Musa al-Khwarizmi (780––?850), wrote a book on algebraic calculation, of which the second word in the title, *Hisab al-Jabr w-al-Muqabalah*, gave rise to the term "algebra."

For 300 years vast numbers of translations were made into Arabic from Greek and various Asian languages, and Arabic became the leading language of learning in the Middle East, Central Asia, and much of the rest of the continent. Many treatises were written on theoretical mechanics, hydraulics, mineralogy, and chemistry. The Muslims transmitted the art of making crucible steel from India and made Damascus and Toledo famous as centers for the manufacture of damascene swords. Haran, site of a university, became a center for the production of scientific instruments for use in astronomy, calculation, and measurement. The Arabs developed the astrolabe for measuring angles and determining the position of stars; this was the forerunner of the navigational sextant. While the compass in an essentially modern form appears to have been developed later in Italy (possibly derived from the Chinese discovery of magnetic orientation), the Arabs used a compass of sorts in their extensive navigations in the Mediterranean Sea, Indian Ocean, and South China Sea.

The spread of Islam helped to transmit not only the collective cultural heritages of many civilizations, but also the new Arabic contributions to science. In contrast to Greek culture, that of the Arabs was notable less for individual genius than for progress in a wide range of fields. Their creative investigations and writings advanced knowledge in meteorology, optics, the measurement of densities, and medicine. They also enhanced trigonometry, which was derived from Greek and Hindu science.

It would not be an exaggeration to state that Arabic culture, enriched by many assimilated elements, was preeminent from the 8th through the 11th centuries. Arabic was the language of science and even of much European knowledge that had been submerged in the Dark Ages. The great centers of Islamic scientific learning were Baghdad and Cairo, while libraries and scientific academies were established in the 10th century in such cities as Toledo and Córdoba. Thus Spain, when recaptured by Christians, became the main route for the entrance of both ancient and Greek science into

MONKMEYER PHOTOS

JAPANESE SPACE CENTER at Kagoshima, a rocket testing ground, heralds Japan's entry into the space age.

western Europe. It was, in fact, the recovery of ancient science and philosophy in the 11th and 12th centuries that marked the beginning of the European scientific renaissance of the Middle Ages.

A strange interlude in the transmission of science and technology between Asia and Europe was provided by the Mongols in the 13th century. Although they were barbarians in their early days, the Mongols sometimes rose to the cultural levels of the civilized peoples they conquered. By the time their empire had reached its peak, travel and communication between East and West were far freer than they had previously been. The Mongols brought arms and gunpowder, the wheelbarrow, and the process of casting iron to the West, and from Europe they introduced into China such things as distilled alcohol and eyeglasses.

See also ARITHMETIC; CHEMISTRY—1. *History;* GEOMETRY—1. *History;* MATHEMATICS; MEDICINE, HISTORY OF; MIDDLE EAST—5. *History;* NUMERALS; TRIGONOMETRY—*History.*

Modern Period. The growth in Europe of truly modern science and technology began with the idea of experimental science, which first became influential in the early 17th century. The experimental method is characterized by either specially devised experiments, which allow events to take place under known or controlled conditions, or quantitative experiments, the results of which can be handled mathematically. With this major addition to the basic methods of science, the characteristics of the scientific approach in the modern period were rounded out.

The development of modern science and technology in Asia brought with it extraordinarily rapid change. What required centuries to evolve in Europe—the Renaissance and scientific revolution occurred between about 1500 and 1750, and the age of power and the Industrial Revolution took place from 1750 on—came to Asia abruptly and with immense impact, especially during the latter half of the 19th century. Western European mercantile expansion and colonial development, backed by military force, introduced the technical products of the West and some of its manufacturing processes to much of East Asia and the Middle East. In the main, Asian reactions were defensive and imitative. There were, for example, a few advocates of genuine modernization in China at

HIGH-TENSION LINES carry an increasing load of electric power across eastern China's countryside.

the end of the 19th century, but they were overshadowed by an officialdom that resisted scientific and technological innovation except insofar as Western gadgetry, as they regarded it, could be used in the defense of the nation against the West. In official Chinese records, early industrial establishments are described under the rubric of "sea defenses" against "barbarians," meaning Europeans and Americans. This disdain for the outsider and his ways led to a complete misunderstanding of the nature and forces of technology and science, although the threat to the traditional Chinese way of life was accurately sensed.

The Boxer Rebellion (Uprising) of 1900 was the last convulsive effort by traditionalist elements to keep China from being subjected to these forces. With its failure, which was ordained by the very sweep of science and technology, China was opened increasingly to the technological and intellectual influences of the West. The country did not, however, develop in a modern scientific sense for many years. Modern technology was in most instances introduced through imported machinery or through industrial plants, the patterns for which were transplanted from the West. Such basic innovations as the steam engine, mechanization of factories, interchangeability of mechanical components, central generation of electricity, internal combustion engines, heavier-than-air craft, and mass production were thrust on China without an indigenous technical or educational base. In the 1930's, before China had developed the processes for the manufacture of bicycles, it had airlines, automobiles, and radios.

To a large extent the pattern that prevailed in China was characteristic of much of Asia to the south and west. A notable exception was Japan. Like China, Japan felt the impact of the West, especially after the arrival of Commodore Matthew C. Perry's naval force in 1853. The Dutch and Portuguese had, to be sure, reached Japan by the 17th century and introduced ele-

ments of Western learning and technology, including the musket. But the country was closed in 1638–1640, and at the time of the Meiji Restoration in 1868 the levels of Japanese science and technology were comparable to those of pre-Renaissance Europe. In less than a century, however, the country had developed into one of the outstanding scientific and technological nations of the world. In the earlier decades of the 20th century, Japan's achievements were largely imitative, but they became increasingly original thereafter. In 1935, Hideki Yukawa postulated the meson, and after World War II the country made such contributions as the tunnel diode in electronics, new antibiotics, new fibers, and new lenses. Japanese patents were licensed to the United States and many European countries. The vigor of Japanese research by the 1960's is suggested by the publication of approximately 2,000 scientific periodicals. It could be said that Japanese had become the fifth language of world science.

Mainland China under the Communists and Taiwan under the Nationalists both entered the nuclear age and acquired operational research reactors. By the 1960's they were well along the way toward the development of nuclear power plants. Communist China launched a program not only to catch up with, but to surpass, the West scientifically and technologically. Substantial investment in education, research, and development was made governmental policy, and concerted industrialization become the order of the day.

In the mid-1960's, Asia was far from uniform in its levels of achievement in science and technology, but in nearly every country the promotion of scientific education and research and of technological development had been adopted as national policy. Foreign aid programs and international scientific and technical organizations were accelerating progress in this direction. Scientific methods were being applied to agriculture, health problems, and many forms of industrial production. In the perspective of history, what was occurring might be viewed as the completion of a great cycle. The fruits of Asia's ancient knowledge and techniques, transformed by the Greek spirit, preserved and enriched in the Islamic world, and applied and developed in the West, were being returned to the continent. Meanwhile, the West had moved into a new phase, characterized by the establishment and support of a large-scale industry of discovery. When Asia was in a position to enter this new mainstream of sustained and original scientific exploration, it would have truly joined the modern scientific and technological community.

See also JAPAN—15. *Scientific Research;* SCIENCE, HISTORY OF.

ROBERT BRUCE SHEEKS
National Academy of Sciences

Bibliography
Klochko, Mikhail A., *Soviet Scientist in Red China,* tr. by Andrew MacAndrew (New York 1964).
Needham, Joseph, *Science and Civilization in China,* 4 vols. (London and New York 1954–65).
O'Leary, DeLacey E., *How Greek Science Passed to the Arabs,* reprint (New York 1964).
Sarton, George A.L., *A History of Science: Ancient Science Through the Golden Age of Greece,* reprint (New York 1964).
Seal, Sir Brajendranath, *The Positive Sciences of the Ancient Hindus* (Delhi 1958).
Vucinich, Alexander S., *Science in Russian Culture,* vol. 1 (Stanford, Calif., 1963).

14. History: Earliest Times to 1350

Southwest Asia. Those ancient civilizations that might be called the ancestors of Western civilization flourished in the region extending from the Caspian and Black seas southward to the Persian Gulf and from the Aegean Sea eastward to Iran. By 5000 B.C., Paleolithic pursuits of hunting and food gathering had evolved into Neolithic agricultural and pastoral village life in Southwest Asia. The pioneers of post-Neolithic urban civilization in lower Mesopotamia were the Sumerians. Their numerous independent city-states were first brought under the control of the 1st dynasty of Ur in the 3d millennium B.C. After Lugalzaggisi of Uruk had conquered them, he in turn was defeated and killed by a Semitic chieftain, Sargon, in about 2360 B.C. Following a century of darkness the 3d dynasty of Ur (about 2060–1950 B.C.) regained control and greatly extended its empire. Power soon passed into the hands of a new Semitic dynasty, best known for its king Hammurabi (reigned 1728–1686 B.C.). This dynasty was subsequently overrun by the Kassites of northern Iran. The ancient Sumerians themselves disappeared from the pages of history, although some of their accomplishments survived as elements of later civilizations.

There were other important strands in the developing complex of cultures in Southwest Asia. The Hittites (q.v.), who established themselves in central Asia Minor and captured Babylon in about 1530 B.C., were finally divided into small Syro-Hittite kingdoms. Eventually, in the 8th century B.C., they were absorbed into the Assyrian empire. Then there were the Philistines, who often raided Syria and Palestine; the Hebrews, whose religion contributed much to the later development of Christianity and Islam; the Phoenicians, inventors of the alphabet, who built an extensive commercial empire in the Mediterranean Basin by 800 B.C.; and the Semitic Aramaeans, producers of great scribes, whose overland trade network covered most of the region.

Before the end of the 8th century the Assyrians made their military prowess felt beyond northern Mesopotamia. Syria was conquered in 732 B.C., and Babylon was sacked in 689. The Assyrians also reduced most of the Phoenician cities in Mesopotamia, extracted tribute from the king of Judah, occupied Egypt (670–654 B.C.), and built one of the most extensive empires Southwest Asia had yet known. After the death of Ashurbanipal (reigned 668–631 B.C.), the best known of their kings, the Assyrian empire was divided between the Neo-Babylonians (Chaldeans) and the Medes of Persia. The latter took the capital city of Nineveh in 612 B.C., as well as the northern possessions.

The domain of the Medes was overrun by the Persian Cyrus (reigned 559–529 B.C.). After his son Cambyses II conquered Egypt in 525 B.C., the Persian empire covered the larger part of the Middle East. The greatest accomplishments of the empire were made during the long and efficient administration of Darius I (reigned 522–486 B.C.). In 331 B.C. the empire was overthrown by Alexander the Great. Later, between about 250 and 100 B.C., the independent kingdom of Parthia constructed a second Persian empire. Engaged in continual conflict with Roman legions, the Parthian dynasty collapsed in about 226 A.D. The struggle against Rome was continued by the Sassanids, who ruled over a third Persian empire

GENGHIS KHAN, Mongol conqueror and military genius, gained control of an empire extending from the China Sea to the fringes of Europe.

CULVER PICTURES, NC.

until it too succumbed, to the invading Muslims in 641.

The birth of Islam in the Arabian Peninsula heralded a new era in the history of Southwest Asia. After Mohammed fled from his native Mecca to Medina in 622, he became not only the prophet of Allah but also the temporal ruler of Medina. Following numerous raids on the caravans of disbelieving Meccans, undertaken by Mohammed to finance his government, he returned triumphantly to Mecca in 630. The allegiance of sheikhs from all parts of Arabia was won in the process. After Mohammed's death in 632, one of his successors, or caliphs, Abu Bakr (reigned 632–634), suppressed the rebellious sheikhs and also attacked the Persians in Mesopotamia. The next caliph, Umar (reigned 634–644), conquering Persia by 641, completed the construction of a unified Muslim empire in Southwest Asia. Command of the eastern Mediterranean was wrested from the Byzantine navy in 655.

Under the Umayyad caliphate (661–750) the Muslim empire was extended across modern Afghanistan to the area of the Indus River (712). The Byzantines were driven back in Asia Minor, while in the west the Muslims conquered Carthage (698) and, beginning in 711, captured and controlled much of Spain. Crossing the Pyrenees, they engaged in unsuccessful raids on southern and central France. Meanwhile, power in Mesopotamia was seized by the Abbasid dynasty (750–1258), which in 762 established the caliphate in Baghdad. Although the Abbasids continued to rule until the middle of the 13th century, interdynastic rivalry had by 900 caused the disintegration of the Islamic empire.

In 1055, Tughril Beg, leader of the Seljuk Turks, seized Baghdad; he was named sultan in the following year. Seljuks invaded Armenia in 1071, capturing the Byzantine emperor Romanus IV Diogenes at Manzikert (now Malazgirt); others overran Asia Minor and founded independent kingdoms. By the time alarm at these conquests had brought the armies of the European Crusaders to Constantinople (Istanbul) in 1096, the Seljuks had dissipated their strength by quarrels among themselves. Various Christian leaders soon established kingdoms in Edessa (modern Urfa), Antioch, and Tripoli. Finally the Europeans, remembering the chief objective of the First Crusade, entered Jerusalem in 1099. By 1144, however, the Muslims had recaptured Edessa, and in 1187, under the leadership of Saladin, they recovered Jerusalem. During the next century other futile Crusades were launched.

In 1291 the last of the Crusaders' kingdoms in the Middle East vanished.

In 1220 the armies of the Mongol Genghis (Jenghiz) Khan invaded Persia and sacked many cities; by 1243 they had overrun most of Seljuk Asia Minor. In 1380–1381 a wave of marauding Turko-Mongols led by Tamerlane (Timur) devastated Persia; Baghdad was sacked in 1401. Shortly thereafter, when Tamerlane set out on his abortive campaign to conquer China, he left behind the smoldering ruins of much of Muslim civilization in Asia.

See also Assyria; Babylonia; Byzantine Empire; Caliphate; Crusades; Jewish History and Society; Middle East—5. *History;* Phoenicia—*History;* and sections on history in articles on the various Southwest Asian countries.

South Asia. The cradle of the ancient civilization that spread over South Asia was the Indus Valley in what is now West Pakistan. In prehistoric times, Paleolithic cultures had gradually evolved into the Kulli village cultures of Baluchistan and lower Sind, which apparently had some contact with Mesopotamia. Contemporary with or later than the Kulli cultures was the highly sophisticated civilization of Harappa in the Punjab and Mohenjo-daro in Sind, which flourished in the 2000's and 1000's B.C. From north to south this civilization extended 950 miles. Archaeological remains testify to an organized government, planned cities, and many other examples of high accomplishment.

Ancient India began to emerge from the prehistoric period with the invasions of seminomadic tribes from about 1500 to 1200 B.C. Their priests composed in their Indo-Aryan language a collection of religious and philosophical hymns known as the Rig Veda, a vital source for the history of the Vedic period. The three later Vedas, as well as the Brahmanas, the Upanishads, the Puranas, the *Ramayana,* the *Mahabharata,* and other religious literature, have also become part of Hindu tradition. The Bharatas, from whom modern India derives its name of Bharat, were one of the first Aryan tribes to settle in the Brahmavarta region between the Yamuna (Jumna) and Sutlej rivers in the eastern Punjab. Expansion eastward into India in the later Vedic period resulted in the establishment of the kingdoms of Kosala (modern Oudh), Kasi (modern Varanasi), Videha (northern Bihar), Avanti (Malwa), and Magadha (southern Bihar). Civilization gradually achieved greater sophistication, and after an interval of centuries, commercial and other relations with Mesopotamia were revived.

During the reign of Bimbisara (about 543–491 B.C.) of Magadha, and more particularly that of his son Ajatasatru (about 491–459), one of the truly large empires of ancient India was expanded to include most of these kingdoms. By the 4th century B.C., Magadha extended from what is now Varanasi (Benares) to Bengal and covered most of northern India. This century also saw the invasion of Alexander the Great. In 326 B.C. he crossed the Indus and the Jhelum. After a fierce battle he defeated the powerful Paurava (Porus), king of the Punjab. Fear of revolt in his army then forced him to turn back. In 323, Alexander died, and by about 317, Eudemus, the last of the generals he had left behind, lost control of the conquered territories.

Meanwhile, the rule of the unpopular upstart Nanda dynasty was overthrown by Chandragupta Maurya (reigned 321–297 B.C.). He was assisted by Chanakya Kautilya, author of the famous *Arthasastra* (Treatise on Polity). In about 304 B.C., Chandragupta, by defeating Seleucus I Nicator, one of Alexander's former generals, added parts of what is now Afghanistan to the Maurya empire. The greatest of ancient India's emperors, Asoka (Ashoka), grandson of Chandragupta, came to the throne in about 274 B.C. After his bloody campaign in Kalinga (modern Orissa) he abandoned aggressive war for conquest by righteousness (dharma). During his reign, Buddhism was launched on its career as a world religion. Although Asoka was a strong supporter of ahimsa (noninjury of living creatures) and the most humane of monarchs, he was also an eminent realist in the governance of his empire.

From the time of Asoka's death in 237 until about 184 B.C. the Maurya empire steadily declined, and a number of new kingdoms were established. Among the more important were those of Pushyamitra Sunga in Vidisa (eastern Malwa); the Satavahanas in Pratishthana (modern Paithan); and a Saka (Partho-Scythian) dynasty, known for its great ruler Rudradaman I (reigned about 130–150 A.D.), which controlled the states later known as Kathiawar, Malwa, Rajasthan, and Sind until 388. In the south, which was inhabited by Dravidian-speaking peoples, the seafaring kingdoms of the Cholas, Keralas, and Pandyas invaded Ceylon, colonized Southeast Asia, and were in touch with Egypt and the Roman empire.

In the 2d century B.C., Bactrian Greek invaders led by Demetrius and Eucratides occupied most of the Indus Valley, the Punjab, the Kabul Valley, and Taxila. The petty Greek kingdoms fell in turn to the invading Sakas (Scythians) in the 1st century B.C. Following a brief incursion by the Pahlavas of Iran, the Kushanas, a branch of the Yuechi (Yüeh-chih), made their appearance. Kanishka (flourished 1st or 2d century A.D.), the foremost Kushana ruler, controlled the western half of northern India as well as extensive territory in Inner Asia. Under his patronage, Buddhism began to spread to Inner and East Asia.

A new ruling dynasty, the Gupta, founded in 320 A.D., ushered in the age of Hindu imperialism. Under Chandragupta I (reigned 320–?330) and his son Samudragupta (reigned about 330–375/380) the empire stretched from Assam to the Punjab and held in vassalage the kings of Rajasthan and the eastern Deccan. Chandragupta II (reigned 375/380–about 413) defeated the Sakas in 388 and became the supreme ruler of northern India. He patronized Kalidasa, India's greatest poet and dramatist, and the arts in general. According to the Chinese pilgrim Fa-hsien, although Buddhism still flourished in his reign, Hinduism was ascendant. The succeeding emperors, Kumaragupta I (reigned about 413–455) and Skandagupta (reigned 455– about 467), were barely able to withstand the fierce attacks of the Huns, and by the early 6th century, western India had fallen into their hands. Following Skandagupta's death the Gupta empire disintegrated, and after 530 even the Huns lost their identity among the many small kingdoms vying for regional supremacy.

In 606 another northern Indian empire, centered in Thanesar and extending from Kathiawar to Bengal, arose under King Harsha (Harshavardhana, (reigned 606–?647). According to the Chinese pilgrim Hsüan-tsang, art, music, and literature flourished during his reign. Buddhism declined, and Hinduism was the dominant faith. When Harsha died without an heir, his many vassals became independent kings, and his empire vanished. In succeeding centuries, as aggressive Muslim forces gathered strength across the northwestern frontier, the Gurjara Pratiharas of Kanauj dominated northwestern India, though harassed by Rashtrakuta raids from the Deccan, while the Palas of Bengal and Bihar controlled the northeast.

In 986–988 a Turkish chieftain, Subuktigin (Sabuktigin) of Ghazni in Afghanistan, twice raided northwestern India, and his son Mahmud attacked the rich domains of the warring Hindu kings on possibly 17 occasions between 1001 and 1027. The celebrated shrine of Somnath in Kathiawar, the kingdom of the Chandellas in Bundelkhand, and the great cities of Mathura and Kanauj were sacked and plundered. Since Mahmud's chief interest was booty, his only territorial annexations were the North-West Frontier, the Punjab, and the petty Arab kingdoms established in Sind after 712. During the next century and a half no further Muslim invasions took place, but the conservative Hindu princes, who had learned nothing from the raids of Mahmud, continued warring among themselves. Beginning in 1175, Muhammad Ghuri, a new Turkish chieftain in Ghazni, conquered the Punjab and Sind and, after an initial failure at Tarain (Taraori) in 1191, defeated and killed the great Chahamana (Chauhan) king Prithviraja of Rajasthan on the same field in the following year. After his own assassination in 1206 one of his generals, Qutb ud-Din Aibak (reigned 1206–1210), became the first sultan of Delhi, with a domain that included Bengal, Bihar, and Bundelkhand. From then until the 18th century, Muslims dominated northern India.

While Hindu India was declining in the north, a vigorous synthesis of the Aryans and the Dravidians was taking place in the Deccan, which was generally controlled by Chalukya dynasties from the 7th until the late 12th century. Their rule, however, was interrupted by the Pallavas of Kanchi (modern Kanchipuram) and by the raids of the Rashtrakutas. The Chalukya empire was finally divided up by the Yadavas of Deogir (Devagiri, modern Daulatabad) in the northern Deccan, the Kakatiyas of Warangal in the east, and the Hoysalas in Mysore. The Pallava domains were absorbed by the Cholas in the 9th century. Under Rajaraja I (reigned 985–1014), the great Chola king of Tamil tradition, Ceylon was conquered. His successor, Rajendra Choladeva I (reigned 1014–1044), sent a naval expedition to Southeast Asia and occupied parts of Burma, Malaya, and Sumatra. In 1070 the Cholas were expelled from Ceylon, however, and by the 13th century their shrinking territories were shared by the Hoysalas and the Pandyas of Madurai.

While Ala ud-Din Khalii was sultan of Delhi (1296–1316), his general Malik Kafur crushed the kingdoms in the Deccan, and for a time various Muslim sultanates were established as far south as Madurai. In 1336, however, an independent Hindu kingdom called Vijayanagar was founded; its power eventually extended throughout the peninsula south of the Krishna River. A brilliant account of the splendor and prosperity of Vijayanagar was left by an Italian traveler, Niccolò de' Conti. The empire reached its zenith during the reign of Krishnadeva Raya (1508–1529/

1530), but in 1565 a coalition of Deccan sultans attacked it, utterly defeating the army of Rama Raya at Talikota. The city of Vijayanagar itself was sacked, and the last of the Hindu empires in the Deccan before the rise of the Marathas in the 17th century vanished completely.

See also AFGHANISTAN—11. History; CEYLON —7. History; INDIA—16. Prehistory and 17. History: 6th Century B.C.–1707.

Southeast Asia. The history of Southeast Asia is dominated by cultural influences emanating from India, China, the Middle East, and Europe, superimposed on a complex of Neolithic cultures that had evolved in the region since the end of the glacial periods. Largely because of the dominant use of perishable wood and bamboo for implements, archaeological evidence of these Neolithic cultures is scarce. Isolated pockets of peoples of Malayo-Polynesian languages and cultures still exist in a few islands of Indonesia and in the mountains of the Southeast Asian mainland, however, and similar cultural elements are found in the farthest Pacific islands and in Madagascar.

A major cause of the early introduction of Chinese culture into Southeast Asia was trade. Evidence suggests that tin was mined in the Malay Peninsula for use in the bronze-casting industry of China, which reached a point of perfection as early as the Shang dynasty. Subsequently the Chinese themselves came to Southeast Asia both as traders and as conquerors. Their influence ultimately became strongest in the border areas of modern Vietnam and Laos and, to a lesser extent, in Burma and Siam (Thailand). Elsewhere in the region the cultural exclusiveness of the Chinese communities reduced their influence to a minimum.

The initiative in bearing India's civilization to Southeast Asia was taken by colonizers and missionaries rather than by conquerors. Trade followed later. In about the 1st century A.D., colonizing expeditions were sent out from Kalinga and Bengal but much more extensively from the Tamil domains of the Pallavas. Hindu settlements were established in Java, Sumatra, Borneo, the Malay Peninsula, Cambodia, Burma, and Siam. The settlers spread the Hindu religion, the Sanskrit language, and Indian art and architecture. After a few centuries, however, Buddhism became the dominant religion, being overlaid on the composite of Southeast Asian Neolithic and Hindu cultures. The best known of the Hindu-Buddhist kingdoms in the region were the Srivijaya (Sriwidjaja) dynasty of Sumatra, the Sailendra dynasty of Java, the Khmers of Cambodia, and the Chams of Indochina.

At about the beginning of the 14th century, Islam came to Southeast Asia; by the end of the following century it had become a major religion of the region. Then, at the beginning of the 16th century, the Portuguese arrived, soon to be followed by the Spaniards, the Dutch, and the English.

See also sections on history in articles on the various Southeast Asian countries; SOUTHEAST ASIA—History.

PRABHAKAR S. AKOLEKAR
Clarion (Pa.) State College

East Asia—China. North China was the birthplace of East Asian civilization and remained its center throughout the ancient period of Chinese history. Its geographical setting, which was crucial to the very survival of primitive men, had much to do with the emergence of civilization in this area. North China benefited from accessible river valleys, vast inhabitable plains, fertile loess soil, and an invigorating climate. On the other hand, it suffered occasional natural disasters. From ancient days the Chinese contended laboriously, though sometimes futilely, with floods and droughts. The rise of civilization in early China was also influenced by the accumulating effect of time. During the 2000's B.C., Neolithic cultures, featuring pottery, agriculture, and domesticated animals, prevailed in north China. Then, in the 2d millennium, China entered the historic stage, characterized by the development of writing, the use of bronze, and the rise of cities.

Ancient China lacked the political foundation to support an effective centralized authority. Under the limited or nominal rule of the kings of the Shang (about 1523–1027 B.C.) and Chou (1027–256 B.C.) dynasties, the land long remained decentralized and feudal. How did a centralized empire eventually arise? From about the time of Confucius (551–479 B.C.), Chinese affairs gathered momentum. Through wars and annexations the numerous petty states were consolidated into several major entities. The period of contending states, as this era is traditionally labeled, continued for the next two centuries. As the warring rivals strove to increase their strength, their populations grew rapidly, trade and cities expanded, and copper money and iron tools came into use. The struggle for power was reflected also in the realm of thought. There was as yet neither an orthodox ideology nor a state religion; the marketplace for ideas was wide open. The challenging, competitive nature of the age was seldom matched in China until modern times. During this era of manifold growth an empire gradually came into being. By 221 B.C., one of the principal states, Ch'in, had destroyed all the others.

The first two major dynasties of the long imperial period of Chinese history were the Han (202 B.C.–220 A.D.) and the T'ang (618–906 A.D.). The rule of the Han coincided roughly with the hegemony of the Romans in the West. The two civilizations were comparable in power, wealth, and territory. Again to some degree paralleling Western history, the end of the Han dynasty was followed by "barbarian" invasions and critical divisions of the empire. The unity of the Chinese empire was eventually restored; however, the West remained divided. The new imperial dynasty, the T'ang, in many respects achieved even more than the Han. Under its rule, China was probably the most powerful and properous state in the world. The next major dynasty, the Sung (960–1279), is remembered for the refinement of its culture and the expansion of its trade. On the other hand, since it was militarily weak and territorially limited, the way was paved for conquest by another imperial dynasty, the Yuan, or Mongol (1260–1368).

Under the expansionist Han, T'ang, and Yuan dynasties, imperial China moved into Korea, Vietnam, Turkestan, Mongolia, and other borderlands. The object of the Han and T'ang emperors was mainly to subdue the nomads and not merely to acquire prestige. As testimony to China's sociopolitical stability, these two dynasties, together with the Sung, endured for a full millennium. The imperial system itself, which was established late in the 3d century B.C., survived until early in the 20th century. The Chinese monarchy, like the premodern monarchies of other countries, rested on absolute power, but in the absence of modern technology actual rule was far from absolute. The most significant feature of traditional Chinese government was its civil service examination system, whereby bureaucrats were recruited largely from among the most highly educated. The examinations played the role of modern elections. To the extent that they made possible the recruitment of talent, they narrowed the gap between government and the governed.

According to Joseph Needham, author of *Science and Civilization in China*, imperial China, possessing a long list of mechanical devices and inventions, was technologically ahead of Europe. Among other things, China contributed paper, printing, gunpowder, and the magnetic compass to the world. In economic affairs the Han dynasty was noted for its development of the Silk Road through Inner Asia, thereby establishing indirect trade with the Roman empire. This overland trade was expanded by the T'ang and the Mongols. The Sung, confined after 1127 to the area of south China, devoted its efforts to promoting maritime trade. Within China itself the south, from the end of the Han through the Yüan dynasties, was developing economically.

As early as the Han dynasty, north China supported a recorded total of approximately 60 million persons. The Chinese were then the largest ethnic group concentrated in a single region. By Sung times the population had risen to an estimated total of 100 million. Since this growth coincided with the increasing cultivation of the south, pressure on the land was not so serious as in later days. Meanwhile, in its philosophy and religion, arts and literature, ethics and customs, China had become a homogeneous community. The Chinese had developed a distinctive way of life, and although conquerors invaded the land, they were strongly influenced and sometimes even absorbed by the culture of the conquered.

China's accomplishments should not blind us to its basic problems. Because of its location and physiography, it was generally deprived of the benefits of contact with other major lands in early times. And even in its best days the Chinese government relied more on good men than on good laws. The trend in government during the Sung and Mongol periods was increasingly autocratic. Even when the economy flourished, the merchant class never enjoyed appreciable social prestige and political influence. While the Sung and the Mongols placed great emphasis on trade, other dynasties commonly favored the landed economy. With the passage of time, Confucian orthodoxy became more elaborate, refined, and thorough within its own sphere and thus more self-centered, self-reliant, and self-righteous. Science and technology, which scored such impressive triumphs in this period, soon lagged behind the achievements of the West. The basic cultural orientation and the socioeconomic system in China were not adapted to the consistent exploitation of nature. In short, conservatism in one form or another asserted itself ever more strongly the longer China lived in relative isolation. Later, Chinese society was to become even more mature and stable. In the end, this maturity and stability reached a point of stagnation.

See also CHINA—8. *History.*

Japan. The major strands of the ancient and early medieval history of Japan were the setting of the country, the cultural influence of China, and Japanese modifications of (and departures from) the Chinese pattern. An island country separated from the continent of Asia, Japan moved onto the historical scene much later than China. Moreover, barriers in the form of mountains and unnavigable rivers intensified social and political decentralization. In the early centuries of the Christian era the Japanese people were divided into numerous clans or tribes. Each major clan was largely self-sufficient and autonomous. The blood ties of clan members, the hereditary basis of leadership, and clan worship of a guardian deity contributed to the persistence of the system. In the course of clan rivalries the major group in the region of Yamato, originally one among many, gained or claimed increasing authority over the others. Its leader became recognized as the sovereign of the Yamato people and the head of an imperial line that has continued to reign to the present day, making it the oldest ruling house in the world.

Chinese cultural influence on Japan, which may be traced back to the prehistoric period, reached its height from the middle of the 7th to the middle of the 9th century. Sooner or later, almost all the major components of Chinese culture—the cultivation of rice, the use of bronze and iron, writing, literature, fine arts, Buddhism, Confucianism, legal codes, and the governmental system—were introduced into Japan. The overall result was the gradual transformation of Japanese culture. In political and economic matters, continental influence culminated in the adoption of the Taikwa (Great Reform) policy in the mid-7th century. Designed to introduce the imperial Chinese structure of centralization and to create a version of the T'ang dynasty, it sought to abolish the ancient clan system. These objectives were partially implemented in the 8th and 9th centuries, when for the first time a central authority appears to have flourished.

Gradually the alien institutions and ideas were adapted to native conditions. Partly because of the geographical factors, China was never able to impose its way of life on Japan by military or political pressure. Rather, Japan borrowed Chinese culture voluntarily and therefore had time to assimilate and modify it. While Chinese writing became the honored medium of expression, a native system of writing, a syllabary known as kana, was devised to meet the needs of Japanese pronunciation. Alongside Chinese literature and learning, Japanese prose and particularly poetry reached high standards by the 11th century. Moreover, Japanese painters, sculptors, and architects succeeded in mastering and changing Chinese styles. Although Buddhism, a highly developed religion, long dominated the rather primitive Shinto, the native cults were not swept aside. Rationalized as a local and familiar phase of the universal faith of Buddhism, Shinto survived. Buddhism in turn succumbed to Japanese social and aesthetic values, which were also expressed in Shinto. Instead of stressing theological subtleties, Japanese Buddhism was notable for its promotion of the arts and for the elaboration of its rituals.

In their political and economic systems the Japanese departed distinctively from Chinese ways. The Taikwa policy of centralized rule eventually broke down, for what had evolved on the continent during more than 1,000 years could not strike root in the islands. Chinese bureaucracy, based on competitive examinations, came in conflict with the Japanese tradition of a hereditary aristocracy. As the central authority declined, local strongholds reasserted themselves, and by the 10th century numerous tax-free, semi-autonomous, and armed private estates had emerged. Their rivalries and wars culminated in the leadership of the Minamoto clan, which late in the 12th century ushered in the shogunates (military dictatorships) and the Japanese brand of feudalism. Both endured until the middle of the 19th century. There were three successive shogunates; the first, named for its capital at Kamakura, lasted from 1192 to 1333. The shogunate was the government that counted, although it existed alongside the civil government, which was still headed by emperors who reigned but did not rule. Japanese feudalism was characterized by the rule of daimyo (lords) and samurai (warriors), who were in turn the vassals and subvassals of the shoguns, not of the emperors. The domination of the warrior class over a period of 700 years infused traditional Japanese culture with militaristic features that had not been really significant in earlier times.

See also JAPAN—20. *History: From the Earliest Times to 1853.*

Korea. Until the middle of the 7th century, Korea was politically divided. For about four centuries, from 108 B.C. to 313 A.D., China maintained colonial outposts in the northwestern section. Then, from the mid-4th to the mid-6th century, interlopers from Japan established strongholds along the south coast. During and after these foreign incursions three native kingdoms arose in rivalry with one another. Of the Three Kingdoms, Silla in the southeast succeeded with China's aid in unifying the country in 668. Thereafter, although ruling houses changed, Korea remained unified. In 935 the Silla dynasty was replaced by the Koryo, founded in 918. Both dynasties were vassals of China. Koryo rule endured until 1392, although during its last century the dynasty was dominated by the Mongols, who had also conquered China.

Linguistically and racially the Koreans and the Japanese were much more closely related to each other and to the non-Chinese Mongoloid peoples, especially the Tungusic tribes to the west and north, than to the Chinese. While their tribal kinsmen, who inhabited fundamentally different physical environments, remained nomads or seminomads, the Koreans (and the Japanese) shifted at an early time to an agricultural way of life. And Chinese culture, rising from an agrarian background, spread without great difficulty to comparable agrarian societies in both Korea and Japan but made little or no headway in the surrounding pastoral regions.

Like Japan, Korea adopted Confucianism and Buddhism as well as writing, literature, fine arts, a legal code, and a governmental system from China. While the Koreans were deeply influenced by the Chinese, they in turn contributed richly to Japanese culture. The Koreans, however, were not so skillful as the Japanese in transforming and adapting their cultural borrowings. Geographical propinquity, not to mention occasional invasions and migrations, doubtless accelerated and intensified the impact of Chinese civilization on Korea.

See also KOREA—12. *History.*

Inner Asia. Historically, various groupings of Mongolian and Turkic-speaking peoples have been scattered throughout Mongolia and Turkestan (Russian Turkestan and the Sinkiang-Uigur Autonomous Region of China). They have differed from their neighbors in China proper, India, Persia, and Russia in their physical environment (deserts, steppes, and mountains), ways of life (nomadism, diet, and customs), and cultural traditions (religions and languages). Occupying the central portion of Asia, they have played, in times both of peace and of war, the significant role of intermediaries. Through them, or at least through their region, the fully settled but widely separated lands of Asia established some contact in ancient and medieval times.

The nomads, widely dispersed and living under great physical difficulties, were never numerous, but they were often strong militarily. At such times they were usually well organized under capable leadership. Living on and moved by animals, they benefited from mobility, cavalry being their major and almost invincible striking force until firearms were invented. The pressure of frequent droughts and hunger, driving them to raid and plunder their neighbors, also fostered a martial spirit. Despite internecine rivalries, they had a common interest in expanding westward and southward.

In the early medieval period, Europe suffered from many major invasions launched by nomads originally emanating from Inner Asia. Both Persia and India were close enough to feel their pressure, while China was more often than not the major target. Upon the decline or collapse of every major Chinese dynasty the nomads threatened or partially occupied north China. The climax came in the 13th century, when the Mongols under Genghis (Jenghiz) Khan and his descendants created the largest empire the world has ever seen. At its peak its power extended from the Pacific Ocean to the Danube River. Dominating the historic scene for a century and more, the Mongols proved capable both in conquest and in administration. Their sensational achievements were made known to a disbelieving Europe by the incomparable traveler and employee of the Mongols, Marco Polo (q.v.). When they pulled back to the steppes, however, the Mongols left behind little of lasting cultural value.

In comparison with Mongolia and Turkestan, Tibet has been largely self-confined. Its massive physical barriers limited both domestic development and contact with the outside world. Instead of serving as a crossroads, this mountainous region prevented direct communication between China and India for thousands of years. The Tibetans never threatened China proper so often nor so seriously as did the Mongolian-Turkic peoples; China in turn did not direct its force specifically against Tibet until modern times. On the cold and desolate plateaus a small population eked out a bare living. The environment was not congenial to the creation of a sophisticated culture. Not until the 7th century did a small kingdom appear on the "Roof of the World." Buddhism, which then entered Tibet, was soon suppressed, but it was revived in the 8th century. In time it merged with the native shamanistic cults to produce Lamaism. Since the lamas, first of the Red Hat sect and later of the Yellow Hat sect, controlled both church and state, the government remained theocratic. In the 13th century, Lamaistic Buddhism spread from Tibet to Mongolia.

See also CHINA—*History*; MONGOLIA—*History*; TIBET—*History*; UNION OF SOVIET SOCIALIST REPUBLICS—*History*.

CHARLES K. CHU
State University College, Fredonia, N.Y.

Bibliography
Basham, Arthur L., *The Wonder That was India*, rev. ed. (New York 1963).
Charol, Michael (pseud. Michael Prawdin), *The Mongol Empire: Its Rise and Legacy*, tr. by Eden Paul and Cedar Paul, rev. 4th impression (New York 1964).
Hall, H.R., *The Ancient History of the Near East*, 11th ed. (New York 1960).
Lewis, Bernard, *The Arabs in History*, rev. ed. (New York 1960).
Morris, Ivan I., *The World of the Shining Prince: Court Life in Ancient Japan* (New York 1964).
Olschki, Leonardo, *Marco Polo's Asia*, tr. by John A. Scott (Berkeley, Calif., 1960).
Orlinsky, Harry M., *Ancient Israel*, 2d ed. (Ithaca, N.Y., 1960).
Sansom, George B., *A History of Japan to 1334* (Stanford, Calif., 1958).
Stein, Sir Aurel, *On Ancient Central Asian Tracks* (New York 1964).
Wilber, Donald N., *Iran: Past and Present*, 5th rev. ed. (Princeton, N.J., 1963).

15. History: 1350 to 1850

Asia experienced constant change after the disintegration of the Eurasian empire of the Mongols in the 14th century. Within the next few centuries some of the most powerful empires the world had yet known flourished in various parts of the continent. These regimes reflected the unprecedented resources in men and goods at the disposal of empire builders, as well as technologies that generally surpassed anything developed in Europe before the Industrial Revolution. The political consolidation of large areas facilitated trade and travel, with the result that Europeans ventured to the East. From a mere trickle in the days of Marco Polo the flow of merchants, missionaries, and adventurers steadily increased, especially after the Portuguese opened the Cape of Good Hope route to India in 1497–1499.

Until the 18th century, reports of European visitors commonly exuded admiration and envy. Tales of the marvels of the East, the wealth of its potentates, and the opportunities for profitable trade furnished an inexhaustible store of topics for table talk. Because of the impressive strength of the empires and kingdoms extending from the Red Sea to Japan, European merchants ordinarily did not presume to be arbitrary in their dealings; rather, they accepted the conditions imposed on them by local governments. To compound their difficulties, they were for a long time hard pressed to discover goods in their own part of the world for which there was a demand in Asia. As late as the early 19th century, Europeans were obliged to settle their accounts by shipments of bullion, supplied in large measure by Spanish America, and to resign themselves to a perennially unfavorable balance of trade.

After the Napoleonic Wars an epochal shift occurred in the relations of Europe and Asia. To the growing Western seapower, exercised successively by the Portuguese, Dutch, and British, new sources of strength were added. Discoveries in science, achievements in technology, and perceptions in philosophy and thought—all reflected in new sociopolitical systems—enabled western Europe to forge ahead of an Asia previously feared and respected. The triumph of the West was facilitated by the decline of the great Asian states. By the middle of the 19th century the tides of history had been reversed, and before long the West held much of the East in fee.

Southwest Asia. In the 13th and 14th centuries, Southwest Asia, historically a hunting ground for empire builders, was buffeted by invasions and wars. The older Byzantine, Arab, Seljuk Turk, and Persian empires, which controlled various parts of the region, not only engaged in internecine struggles, but also suffered the assaults of European Crusaders, Mongol cavalrymen, and the armies of Tamerlane (Timur). The ultimate victors were the Ottoman Turks, whose far-flung regime was for four centuries a leading political reality of the Eurasian-African world.

Contrary to popular belief, the Ottoman Turks did not charge out of Inner Asia, the traditional homeland of the Turkic peoples, to carve out an imperial domain. Rather, their empire evolved gradually from small border marches in central Anatolia, where their ancestors had settled before the 14th century, to its ultimate huge proportions. By steady advances the descendants of Osman (Othman; hence Ottoman) I (reigned 1288–1326) expanded their realm throughout the Middle Eastern world, one of their most decisive victories being the capture of Constantinople in 1453. In the next two centuries the Turkish dominions were extended northward into the steppes of southern Russia, eastward to the borders of the Persian empire, southward to Egypt, and westward along the coasts of Africa to the Atlantic Ocean. The entire Balkan area was overrun, and Turkish armies also penetrated central Europe. At its peak the Ottoman empire was rivaled only by the Mughul (Mogul) regime in India and the Ch'ing dynasty in China.

In their heyday the Ottoman Turks were superb soldiers and administrators, usually consolidating their conquests before undertaking new ventures. On the other hand, they were not particularly distinguished for cultural creativity; the great humanistic achievements made under their rule were ordinarily the product of other ethnic groups. By the 18th century their expansionist momentum had slackened, and thereafter they were harassed by new powers rising on their frontiers. Of especial significance was the pressure exerted by Russia and Austria-Hungary in the Balkans. Confronted also by chronic revolts and dissension in North Africa, the Ottoman empire was by the middle of the 19th century well on the way to becoming the Sick Man, not only of Europe, but of Asia as well.

See also BYZANTINE EMPIRE; CALIPHATE; EASTERN QUESTION; IRAN—6. *History;* MIDDLE EAST—5. *History;* TURKEY—3. *History.*

South Asia. For more than 1,000 years after the downfall of the Gupta empire in the 6th century, the Indian subcontinent remained fragmented. What common ties the peoples from the Himalaya to Cape Comorin possessed were provided primarily by their Hindu way of life, and even this was subjected to serious challenge after 1000 A.D. by expanding Islam. By the 16th century, Muslim power was firmly entrenched in large parts of the north, but it was only with the advent of the Mughul (Mogul) or Mongol invaders, descendants of the warriors of Genghis (Jenghiz) Khan and Tamerlane who had settled in Inner Asia, that the larger portion of the subcontinent was again united under an imperial system.

DEFEAT IN OPIUM WAR opened China to trade.

The Mughul monarchs of the 16th and 17th centuries, especially the celebrated Akbar (reigned 1556–1605), were able men who strove relentlessly to organize and expand their empire. Generous patrons of the arts, they fostered lasting contributions to the cultural heritage of India, particularly in painting, poetry, and architecture. The beautiful Taj Mahal, the mausoleum erected for his wife by Shah Jahan (reigned 1628–1658), ranks as one of the architectural wonders of the world. Under Shah Jahan's successor, Aurangzeb (reigned 1658–1707), the Mughul empire reached the height of its power. Weakened by Aurangzeb's ceaseless campaigns for the conquest of the western Deccan and south India, however, the empire disintegrated after his death. For more than a century and a half thereafter the sound of marching armies was rarely absent from the land as contenders for the mantle of the Mughuls struggled for advantage.

Among the principal rivals for power in the 18th and early 19th centuries were the tough Hindu Marathas of the western Deccan; the Sikhs, adherents of a martial, monotheistic Hinduist sect of the northwest; and the Muslim dynasties founded by former governors of the Mughul empire. In the east, from Calcutta to Madras, the British and French, who had come to India in the 17th century in search of trade, also became involved, their contest for empire being partly an extension of their competition in Europe and the New World. And in the north, on the broad Gangetic Plain, the shrunken realm of the Mughuls existed precariously in the shadow of numerous Hindu princely states. In the late 18th century the British East India Company began to forge ahead, and by the mid-19th century it was triumphant.

While the success of the British was aided by the sharp divisions among the Indians, the organization, wealth, technology, and devotion of the employees of the East India Company to the advancement of its interests should not be minimized. Beginning with the passage of the India Act in 1784, an imperial system was created that was greater than the company itself. The British Parliament continued thereafter to focus its sights on this state within the state, and once the bitter Indian (Sepoy) Mutiny had been quelled, the company was legislated out of existence in 1858. Great Britain itself then became the sovereign power in India.

The history of Afghanistan, always turbulent, was no less so in the post-Mongol period. Occupying a strategic position on the frontiers of the great empires of Southwest, South, and Inner Asia, the country had for centuries spawned conquerors and invited invaders. Overrun in 1219 by the Mongols under Genghis Khan, Afghanistan was also assaulted by Tamerlane. It was from Afghanistan that Tamerlane's descendant Babur (reigned 1526–1530) burst into northwestern India to lay the foundations of the Mughul empire. In the 18th and 19th centuries, after the decline of Mughul power, local dynasts and the Persians vied for control of the country. Perturbed by the continuing instability and fearful for the security of their respective empires, the British and the Russians maneuvered for hegemony in Afghanistan from the 1830's on.

Other outlying areas of South Asia sooner or later felt the impact of the shifting tides of political and military power in the post-Mongol period. In Ceylon, where government and people for hundreds of years had been deeply influenced by the civilization of the mainland, particularly Buddhism, the arrival of Western seapower was fateful. After parts of the island had been brought under the rule of the Portuguese (1505–1658) and the Dutch (1638–1796), all of Ceylon became a British crown colony during the Napoleonic Wars. As a consequence, too, of the rise of British power in India, protectorates were established over the Himalayan states of Nepal in 1816, Sikkim in 1817, and Bhutan in 1865 and 1910.

See also AFGHANISTAN—*11. History;* CEYLON —*7. History;* INDIA—*17* and *18. History.*

Southeast Asia. Southeast Asia remained a political no-man's-land until the 10th or 11th century. The region had been inhabited for thousands of years, and local cultures, though enriched by Hinduism, Buddhism, and Confucianism, continued to reveal the heritages of Neolithic times. With the exception of the Khmer empire, which developed in what is now Cambodia beginning in the 6th century, no really high civilization or majestic empire emerged during the 1st millennium of the Christian era. Thereafter, local cultures began to blossom, giving rise to kingdoms and empires of greater or lesser duration. In the East Indian archipelago the domain of the Majapahit empire (1293– about 1520) embraced much of the island world of Southeast Asia and, at times, portions of the nearby mainland as well. In Burma, Siam (Thailand), and Vietnam vigorous states arose and vied for primacy, breeding enmities that have lingered into the 20th century.

European power first reached the Southeast Asian world in the early 16th century. Strategically situated for the conduct of trade with Asia as a whole and wealthy in resources in perennial demand in both Asia and Europe, the region was gradually reduced to the control of several European powers. Understandably, the militarily weak and politically fluid states were the first to succumb. On Java the Dutch East India Company, chartered in 1602, established the bases from which the Dutch were to extend their sway throughout the East Indies over a period of three centuries. Few empires of the age of expansion consistently paid such lucrative dividends. In the Philippines the initial conquests were effected by the Spanish in 1565. In the next three centuries not only were the

islands reduced by Spanish power, but the Filipinos also were lastingly impregnated with Hispanic culture. Later, in 1819, Sir Thomas Stamford Raffles paved the way for Britain's imperial position in Southeast Asia by shrewdly purchasing the island of Singapore from a newly installed sultan of Johore. Within a century the various states of the Malay Peninsula had been transformed into British protectorates. Burma was acquired by the British in three wars after 1824, the annexation of Upper Burma (1885–1886) signaling the demise of the old kingdom. By 1860 only Siam and the five states of what later became French Indochina (Tonkin or Tongking, Annam, Cochinchina, Laos, and Cambodia) had completely eluded the grasp of the European imperialist powers.

See also COLONY; SOUTHEAST ASIA—*History;* and sections on history in articles on the various countries of the region.

East Asia—China. The expulsion of the Mongols and the founding of the Ming dynasty (1368– 1644) constituted a memorable event in Chinese history. For the first time since the fall of the T'ang dynasty in 906, imperial China was both united and free from "barbarian" rule. The Ming, however, were not sufficiently strong to reconstruct the traditional empire. Failing to vanquish the Mongol strongholds in the far northwest, they did succeed in establishing firm outposts in southern Manchuria and in bringing neighboring Korea under their mantle. Although the Japanese rejected a tributary relationship, they were willing to trade.

Ming frustrations in the western regions and difficulties in promoting trade along the historic routes probably induced the Chinese to turn elsewhere for commerce and glory. The period is notable for the extension of the maritime frontier. In the first half of the 15th century, at the very time when Prince Henry's mariners were exploring the coasts of northwestern Africa, China dispatched six major naval expeditions to Southeast and South Asia to foster commerce and to impress local rulers with Chinese might. Less than a century later, Portuguese traders arrived from India; in 1557 they were permitted to set up a trading post at Macao (q.v.).

Beginning in the late 16th century the Ming dynasty fell on troubled days. The invasion of Korea (1592–1598) by Hideyoshi Toyotomi, the Japanese Napoleon, weakened the Chinese empire, and subsequent pressure from the consolidated Manchu and Mongol tribes in the northeast brought about its downfall. The last "barbarian" conquerors of China founded the Ch'ing dynasty (1644–1912). This Manchu regime was the mightiest China had ever known, and until the late 18th century the Ch'ing empire was one of the world's most powerful and highly developed states. Through their tributary system the Manchus made their influence felt in much of East and Southeast Asia as well as in Tibet and Chinese Turkestan (now the Sinkiang-Uigur Autonomous Region). Confronted by this political colossus, European mercantile companies for years accepted restrictive conditions of trade with little protest.

The impressive success of Manchu rule may be attributed to the respect of the northern "barbarians" for Chinese civilization, their precautions to forestall cultural absorption by the numerically superior Chinese, and their willingness to share power and prestige, within limits, with China's vaunted scholar-bureaucrats. Until the twilight of the reign of Ch'ien Lung (1736–1796) the Manchu system worked astonishingly well. Thereafter, population pressure on the land, neglect of public works, and the growth of corruption stimulated a rash of peasant rebellions, which culminated in the titanic upheavals of the mid-19th century. Manchu troubles were further complicated by the increasing aggressiveness of Westerners, particularly the British. The result was the Opium War (q.v.) of 1839–1842.

See also CHINA—8. *History.*

Japan. The Ashikaga shogunate (1338–1573) was a dynamic era characterized by political confusion, military strife, economic growth, social change, and cultural creativity. The preceding shogunate, the Kamakura Bakufu, had fashioned the institutional framework of a feudal system, and the new order was now extended throughout the islands. The expansion of the cultivated domain, the spread of domestic commerce, the growth of foreign trade (including piracy on the high seas), and the stirrings of a money economy enabled the great feudal lords (daimyo) to construct formidable castles, maintain large standing armies, and vie for unprecedentedly high political stakes. With rich resources at their disposal, they also indulged themselves with new cultural importations from China. In the face of the mounting strength of the feudal lords, the emperors and the shoguns themselves became helpless nonentities. Finally, in the gigantic wars of the late 16th century, the triumvirate of Nobunaga Oda, Hideyoshi Toyotomi, and Ieyasu Tokugawa successively brought the feudal barons under control. The last shogunate, the Tokugawa (1603–1867), was founded by Ieyasu.

The early Tokugawa shoguns were capable political architects. Their system of centralized feudalism, resting on ingenious checks and balances, kept some 300 daimyo under control and preserved Tokugawa rule for more than two and one-half centuries. To arrest social change and to prevent collusion between ambitious lords and Europeans, the shogunate adopted a policy of national isolation. Except for a few Chinese and Dutch, foreigners were banned from Japan for two centuries, while the Japanese themselves were forbidden to leave the islands. Ultimately, Tokugawa policies led to stagnation. The pressures of power-hungry warriors, of a fettered commercial economy, and of the expanding West, symbolized by Commodore Matthew C. Perry's expedition, converged in 1853. Shortly thereafter the country was opened, the shogunate was overthrown, and the emperor was restored to power. The reign of the Meiji emperor (1868–1912) initiated the history of modern Japan.

See also JAPAN—20. *History.*

Korea. Under the Yi dynasty (1392–1910) old Korea, after attaining the zenith of its prosperity and culture, entered a long period of decline. In the 15th and 16th centuries a well-ordered state and trade with China, Japan, Okinawa, and Southeast Asia produced a golden age. These years also saw notable achievements in letters, art, and technology. The brutal invasions of Hideyoshi Toyotomi, the upsurge of Manchu power, and commercial competition from the Portuguese and Dutch had catastrophic effects, and in the early 17th century a policy of national seclusion was introduced. Although the Yi dynasty maintained its traditional tributary relationship with Manchu-dominated China, Korea became known as the Hermit Kingdom. The country, deprived of economic and cultural stimuli from the outside world, stagnated.

See also KOREA—12. *History.*

Inner Asia. The Mongol empire, pieced together by Genghis Khan and his successors, was unique. With a military force that was almost invincible during the 13th century, the Mongols succeeded in bringing much of Asia and eastern Europe under their sway. By the early 14th century, however, their domains, too large for effective administration, began to crumble. Before the century was out, they had disintegrated in many areas. With the collapse of the widespread order and security imposed by the great khans, trade and travel between Europe and Asia waned. Not until the 16th century, when Europeans blazed new sea routes around Africa and across the Pacific, was the flow of men and goods revived and expanded.

In the former Mongol empire several pockets of power remained. In the far west, on the steppes of southern Russia and southwestern Siberia, the Khanate of the Golden Horde lingered until the late 15th century, when it fell before the advance of rising Muscovite Russia from the north and the spreading power of the Ottoman Turks from the south. In the territories to the northwest of India the whirlwind campaigns (1380–1405) of Tamerlane caused a brief revival of Mongol power from the Tien Shan mountains eastward to the Mediterranean. Thereafter the region was divided into a multitude of bickering khanates. In the 15th and 16th centuries the rising power of the Dalai Lama of Tibet led to unprecedented unity in the mountainous borderlands of Inner Asia. In Mongolia and in large parts of Chinese Turkestan the numerous khans were able for several hundred years to resist the efforts of Ming dynasts to incorporate the region into the Chinese empire.

Beginning in the 17th century the precarious independence of the peoples of Inner Asia was gradually extinguished. The Ch'ing dynasty, in its westward drive, extended its hegemony into Mongolia, Chinese Turkestan, and Tibet. In no less persistent fashion, czarist Russia, advancing from the west, pushed its frontiers to the North Pacific, the Amur River, and the Tien Shan. And in the southern tier of Asia, British power, ascendant in the Indian subcontinent and later extended into Afghanistan and Persia (Iran) in the 19th century, came into dangerous confrontation with expansionist Russia.

See also MONGOLIA—*History;* TIBET—*History.*

HYMAN KUBLIN
The City University of New York

Bibliography

Goodrich, Luther Carrington, *A Short History of the Chinese People,* 3d ed. (New York 1959).

Harrison, Brian, *South-East Asia,* 3d ed. (New York 1966).

Hitti, Philip K., *History of the Arabs,* 8th ed. (New York 1966).

Ikram, S.M., *Muslim Civilization in India,* ed. by Ainslie T. Embree (New York 1964).

Lach, Donald F., *Asia in the Making of Europe,* vol. 1 (Chicago 1964).

Lane-Poole, Stanley, *Mediaeval India Under Mohammedan Rule* (Delhi 1963).

Lattimore, Owen, *Inner Asian Frontiers of China,* 2d ed. (Irvington-on-Hudson, N.Y., 1951).

Mason, Philip (pseud. Philip Woodruff), *The Men Who Ruled India* (New York 1964).

Reischauer, Edwin O., and Fairbank, John K., *East Asia: The Great Tradition* (Boston 1960).

Sansom, Sir George B., *A History of Japan,* vols. 2, 3 (Stanford, Calif., 1961–63).

16. History Since 1850

In the middle of the 19th century, Asia was in process of dynamic readjustment. In every part of the vast continent, political units were assuming their characteristic shapes, changing their structures, increasing or decreasing in size, and interacting in such a way as to augur imminent evolution or revolution. In the southwest the sprawling Ottoman empire, with the assistance of interested European powers, had in 1840 weathered a serious challenge by its African vassal, Egypt. Persia, engaged in accommodating foreign influences from both north and south, was being compelled to readjust its last claims to empire. Afghanistan also, on the Persian empire's eastern flank, was being pressed from the south.

In the south the vast Indian domains of the Mughul (Mogul) emperors had been rapidly fading away. Now almost nothing of importance was left. The larger part of Mughul territory had come under the direct rule of the British East India Company, while the rest had become company dependencies ruled by local princes. Areas along the Himalaya had similarly been drawn into the British orbit. In the southeast, once-expansionist Burma had been half paralyzed by British power penetrating its territory from India. Siam (Thailand) was still seeking glory at the expense of its neighbors, while Vietnam (Annam) was being subjected to French pressure. Farther south the British were beginning to penetrate Malaya. Beyond, the scattered sultanates of the East Indies, half subjugated in the port areas and half autonomous in the inland areas, were to undergo more thorough economic exploitation and further political integration by the Dutch.

In East Asia a largely surrounded Chinese empire, defeated in the Opium War (1839–1842) and seeking to regain its strength, faced incipient revolution. Its neighbor Japan was about to be torn from comfortable seclusion. Korea also was experiencing political and intellectual ferment, evidenced by the beginning of the nationalistic Tong-hak movement (later Chondogyo). And in the north, Russia was continuing its southward and eastward drive to bring new territories under its sway.

Southwest Asia. By 1850 the great Ottoman empire, which had long enjoyed suzerainty over most territorial units in Southwest Asia, was viewed as the Sick Man of the East by its covetous European neighbors, especially Great Britain and Russia. Their governments had already begun to talk privately about the eventual disposal of the empire. As the Crimean War of 1853–1856 testified, France was not far behind them. Russian, British, and French influences were to persist in the region thereafter.

Because of external exploitation as well as internal decay, the Ottoman ruling house suffered financial collapse in 1874. Soon rebellions broke out in its Balkan domains. When the Turks were defeated in a war with Russia in 1877–1878, control over Cyprus was ceded to Britain as a reward for the latter's part in the mediation of peace. The collapse of the empire's European flank was followed by the French occupation of Tunisia (1881) and the British occupation of Egypt (1882). Only the Asian domains remained to be disposed of.

Insurrection in the Armenian area in the 1890's marked the beginning of a new wave of disintegration. But a process of regeneration, signaled by the appearance of the Young Turk movement in 1896, also was inaugurated. It culminated in the revolution of 1908–1909. Two wars on the European flank were followed closely by World War I, which involved the Ottoman empire on the side of the eventually defeated Central Powers. Revolution, occurring again from 1919 to 1923, completed both the disintegrating and the regenerating processes. The old Ottoman empire was no more; a new Turkish nation, shorn of its outlying territories, came into existence as a republic. For after Turkey entered the war in November 1914, Britain not only annexed Cyprus outright, but also established a protectorate over Egypt. Then, between 1916 and 1918, the Ottoman empire's Arab subjects, desiring independence from Istanbul and prompted by the Allies, helped the British to occupy or penetrate Arab-populated areas. When an armistice was signed in October 1918, the Ottoman regime was obliged to surrender its garrisons in Iraq, Syria, Palestine, the Hejaz, the Nejd, and Yemen.

In Arabia, Yemen was immediately permitted to develop toward independence, especially after the British withdrawal in 1921. It remained an absolute monarchy until 1962, when a rebellion established a republic. Civil war between the new regime and royalist forces continued in 1966. Under Ibn Saud the Nejd expanded rapidly, at first with British support, in the hinterland of Arabia and ultimately took over the Hejaz and other areas. By 1926 the foundation had been laid for what became the Kingdom of Saudi Arabia in 1932.

In 1920 other Arab areas were allocated to Britain and France, roughly according to actual occupation, as League of Nations mandates. Iraq and Palestine came under British, and Syria (including Lebanon) under French, jurisdiction. The French immediately differentiated Lebanon from Syria, while the British separated Transjordan from Palestine in 1923. Lebanon and Syria finally achieved independence in 1944, during World War II. After the war, in 1948, part of Palestine became the independent republic of Israel. Transjordan became an independent kingdom in 1946 and, following the acquisition of part of Palestine, took the name Hashemite Kingdom of Jordan in 1949. Iraq, which had become an independent kingdom in 1932, overthrew the monarchy in 1958; in 1963, plans were made to draw it into the United Arab Republic with Egypt and Syria (the latter had been part of the UAR previously, from 1958 to 1961), but the projected federation failed to materialize.

To the east of the Ottoman realm lay what remained of the Persian empire. In the mid-19th century, pressed by expansionist Russia from the north and by the British from the east and south, the country was gradually subjected to political compression and penetration. The same foreign rivalry saved Persia from dismemberment. In a war with British India in 1856–1857 the country was forced to evacuate the Herat area of Afghanistan. This led to an over-all settlement of the Persian-Afghan frontiers in 1872. For decades thereafter, Persia's development was determined by Russo-British competition; joint military intervention occurred several times. The creation of Russian and British spheres of influence in 1907 notwithstanding, Persia remained a sovereign monarchy, becoming an original member of the League of Nations in 1920 and of the United Nations in 1945. During the interim, it sought to transform itself into a modern nation, assuming the ancient name of Iran in 1935. The discovery of oil in the early 20th century, however, continued to involve the country in various foreign rivalries.

The coastal and offshore areas of Southwest Asia, from the northeastern Mediterranean Sea via the Red and Arabian seas to the Persian Gulf, have shared a common experience since the 19th century. All first came under British domination and then sought independent status. Cyprus, for instance, completed this cycle in 82 years: occupied in 1878 and annexed in 1914, the island became independent of Great Britain in 1960. Kuwait required 62 years to pass through the same process, being made subject to protection in 1899 and becoming independent in 1961. The sheikhdoms of Bahrain and Qatar and the Trucial States came under British protection in the 19th century and retained relative autonomy thereafter. Qatar declared itself an independent sovereign state in 1970.

The port area of Aden was occupied by the British East India Company in 1839; long administered from India, it became a separate crown colony in 1937. Meanwhile, British expansion inland had resulted in the creation by 1914 of Aden Protectorate, consisting of a number of Arab principalities that came to be administered as Eastern Aden Protectorate (5 states) and Western Aden Protectorate (18 states). Such expansion, continued during and after World War I and also after World War II, caused border disputes with Yemen. In the 1950's an intensified process of integration took place under British auspices among the repeatedly divided and federated principalities of Western Aden Protectorate. The Federation of the Arab Amirates of the South, formed by six of these states in 1959, was expanded and, in 1962, renamed the Federation of South Arabia. Despite the opposition of Yemen and other Arab nations, Aden Colony (subsequently known as Aden State) became a member of the federation in 1963; with other additions, the federation then had 15 members. In the face of agitation, Britain promised in 1964 that independence would be granted to the federation by 1968. In 1967 the federal government collapsed, Britain withdrew, and Aden and South Arabia proceeded to form the independent People's Republic of Southern Yemen.

Muscat and Oman developed along similar lines. As a result of Franco-British rivalry in the general oceanic area beyond Arabia, both the port of Muscat and the hinterland had begun to accept British influence and authority by the mid-1850's. In 1862 the rivals agreed to respect the independence of Oman, which was then subject to the British-protected sultan of Muscat. By the 1890's, however, Muscat and Oman together became a virtual British protectorate, although treaties were usually concluded whenever agreements were called for. In 1920 the religious leader, the imam of Oman, obtained relative autonomy from the sultan. This status continued until 1954, when the new imam asserted outright independence, an act that led to the reconquest of Oman by Muscat with British assistance in the following year. Yet unrest continued, and the imam, who fled to Saudi Arabia after an unsuccessful revolt (1957–1959) in central Oman, received the support of most members of the Arab League. He subsequently raised his claims as legitimate ruler of Oman before the United Nations but failed to receive the necessary support.

See also EASTERN QUESTION; MIDDLE EAST—5. *History.*

South Asia. South Asia was fast being drawn into the British orbit in the mid-19th century. The 1st marquess of Dalhousie, governor general of India from 1848 to 1856, overshadowed the Mughul emperor, Bahadur Shah II, in every area of jurisdiction and authority. The latter, the last of the Mughul monarchs, was displaced by the Indian (Sepoy) Mutiny of 1857–1858, which also resulted in the replacement of the East India Company's rule by the authority of the crown. A viceroy now began to govern in fact and to expand the Indian realm in the name of the British empire, whose Queen Victoria was proclaimed empress of India in 1877. Neighboring Burma swelled the Indian domain after the British expeditions of 1852–1853 and 1885–1886, but in 1937 it was administratively separated from India. Under continued pressure, Afghanistan was forced to allow the integration of the Baluchistan area into British India (treaties of 1876–1891). A settlement in 1893–1895 added the Chitral territory in the extreme northwest, now separated from Russian territory by only a strip of Afghan land adjoining neighboring China. Except for the separation of Burma, British India remained generally unchanged from 1895 until 1947, although internal political reorganization often occurred.

Independence from Britain in 1947 divided the Indian subcontinent politically into two, and territorially into three, parts, with East and West Pakistan flanking India on both sides in the north. Kashmir remained in dispute. Between 1950 and 1954 the former French settlements of Chandernagor, Pondicherry, Karikal, Mahé, and Yanaon were transferred to sovereign India, as verified by treaties of 1951 and 1956, respectively. The Portuguese enclaves of Dadra and Nagar Haveli, as well as Goa, Daman, and Diu, were taken over by India in 1961. With a new constitution establishing it as a republic in 1950, India developed into an important power. Pakistan became an Islamic republic in 1956. As the result of a military coup in 1958, a government headed by Mohammad Ayub Khan took

MOHANDAS K. GANDHI, among the greatest of Asian leaders, inspired India to oppose British rule.

CHINESE DEFENSE OF SHANGHAI in 1932 failed to halt the Japanese drive for empire in Asia.

CULVER PICTURES, INC.

office. A new republican constitution was adopted in 1962.

Ceylon, off the southern tip of the Indian subcontinent, was merged into the Indian domain in 1796, became a separate British colony in 1798, and was granted independence in 1948. The Maldive Islands, a sultanate southwest of Ceylon under British protection since 1887, became independent in 1965.

Nepal was drawn into the British orbit in 1816, but it never came under direct British jurisdiction. Sikkim in 1817 and Bhutan in 1865 settled their boundaries with British India and acquiesced in Britain's power of arbitration, which overshadowed Nepal as well by the beginning of the 20th century. While the two smaller Himalayan states automatically came under Indian influence after 1947 (treaties were concluded in 1949–1950), Nepal developed in a more assertive manner. In 1951 the aristocratic rule exerted by the Rana family since 1846 was ended, and in 1959 a new constitution was adopted.

Following an initial conflict with British India in 1839–1842, a treaty of 1855 allowed Britain to protect Afghanistan from Persia. The British-Persian settlement of 1857 signified British ascendancy over Afghanistan. The country was now viewed as completely independent of Persia. In 1878–1880, however, a second conflict with British India resulted from the Russo-British struggle for power. Afghanistan, especially its foreign affairs and defense, came under British authority in India. Continued Russo-British expansion led to the establishment of the Durand Line between Afghanistan and India (now West Pakistan) in 1893 and to the partition of the Pamir between Afghanistan and Russian Turkestan in 1895. These developments transformed the country into a buffer between the Russian and British orbits. Following the rise of Soviet Russia a third conflict with British India enabled Afghanistan to become independent of British control according to agreements concluded in 1919 and supplemented in 1921. Thereafter, the USSR sought to gain the upper hand. Afghanistan's buffer status has, however, since been reflected in a neutralist outlook in world affairs.

Southeast Asia. The history of Southeast Asia, both mainland and island, from the mid-19th century on was one of progressive eclipse. Flanking the Empire of Annam (Vietnam), in competition with Britain, France achieved control of Cochinchina (southern Vietnam) in

1862, of Cambodia in 1863, of Annam itself and Tonkin (Tongking, northern Vietnam) in 1883–1885, and of Luang Prabang (Laos) in 1893. These acquisitions were made at the expense not only of the subjugated Annamese empire but also of Siam. A process of local integration began in 1887, when a customs union was formed by the French over Annam, Tonkin, Cochinchina, and Cambodia; Luang Prabang was added in 1899 after preliminary unification within its own area. The leased territory of Kwangchowwan, (Chankiang) in southeastern China was acquired in 1898. By 1911 general administrative unity of these areas had been established; as a whole, they became known as French Indochina.

In the meantime, Britain had absorbed all of Burma, thus approaching Siam from the west and north. In 1896, France and Britain agreed to make Siam a buffer state, with the Shan States in British Burma and Luang Prabang in French Indochina joined so as to insulate the country from China. Later the French and British projected their political influence into Siam and, in 1907, reached an agreement, never implemented, to divide the country into two spheres of influence.

The British had meanwhile been advancing in the Malayan area. With Singapore well established as a port by the East India Company, efforts were made to move northward in direct opposition to Siam's expansionist ambitions. Sufficient territory was acquired around the port area by 1867 to make the Straits Settlements a British crown colony. From 1874 to 1895 the British made further gains, resulting in the organization in 1895–1896 of four southern Federated Malay States with a capital at Kuala Lumpur. By 1909 four northern Malay states also had come under British control, and in 1914 a fifth state, Johore, accepted British authority and joined the group of five Unfederated Malay States. This completed British expansion in Malaya.

Allied during World War II to Japan, which occupied French Indochina as well as British Burma and Malaya, Siam made temporary territorial gains from all these areas with Japanese support. These gains were retroceded upon Japan's defeat and Siam's application to join the United Nations. The name of Siam had been changed at the beginning of the war in 1939 to Thailand, and at the end of the war in 1945 to Siam again. In 1949 the kingdom was again called Thailand.

In island Southeast Asia, among the 3,000 and more islands of the East Indies, a process of colonial replacement and integration took place after 1850. The year 1859 saw the final confinement of Portugal to the eastern half of Timor, this island at the southeastern extremity of the archipelago being divided thereafter between Portugal and its over-all successor, the Netherlands. The Dutch encountered temporary competition from the British in the 1870's over the control of Atjeh (Achin) in Sumatra and in the 1880's over the partition of Borneo and the detachment of southeastern New Guinea (Papua). German rivalry also appeared in the 1880's, over the detachment of northeastern New Guinea. The western half of Timor, West New Guinea, and southern Borneo, as well as all of Java, Sumatra, and other major and minor islands in the area, were retained and absorbed in the Dutch realm without further European opposition. The Philippines, after cession by Spain to the United States in 1898, was progressively integrated and Americanized, English being adopted as the official language in 1913. The constitution of 1935, which established its commonwealth status under the United States, signaled its early development toward independence.

The Japanese occupation of Southeast Asia in 1941–1942 was as much a shattering experience for the Western colonial powers as for the local political units. The return of these powers upon Japan's defeat was in most cases resisted by nationalists, Communists, or both, either by force or by political assertion. Thus, with differing speeds and success, through peaceful negotiation or war, the Philippines became officially independent in 1946, Burma in 1948, the East Indies (now called Indonesia) in 1949, French Indochina (now Cambodia, Laos, and Vietnam) in 1954, Malaya in 1957, and Singapore as an internally self-governing state in 1959 and an independent state in 1965.

Vietnam fought the French from the latter's initial attempt to reestablish themselves in 1945 until 1954, when the Geneva Conference divided the country approximately along the 17th parallel. As of 1966, guerrilla warfare by local rebels, supported from North Vietnam, continued in South Vietnam. To aid the badly harassed South Vietnamese regime, the United States mounted an ever more massive military buildup. The independent and neutral status of Laos required confirmation by another international conference, held at Geneva in 1962; the foreign-supported civil war in Laos continued, however, despite repeated international calls for a cease-fire.

Malaya, together with Singapore and two of Britain's Borneo territories (the colonies of North Borneo and Sarawak, which had come under British protection by 1888) formed the general Federation of Malaysia in 1963. At the same time, with United Nations and United States mediation, Indonesia's claims to West New Guinea (West Irian) resulted in an agreement with the Netherlands whereby the territory's administration was transferred to the United Nations in 1962 and to Indonesia in 1963. In a local plebiscite in 1969, West Irian chose to remain with Indonesia. In contrast to the Association of Southeast Asia (ASA) formed by Thailand, the Philippines, and Malaya in 1961, there developed a "confrontation" between Indonesia and Malaysia, which, however, eased off after domestic strife erupted in the former in 1965. Meanwhile, Singapore seceded from Malaysia to become an independent state in August 1965.

See also SOUTHEAST ASIA—*History.*

East Asia. Western expansionism achieved only limited success in East Asia. By 1850 the Chinese empire had been opened by Britain to international trade and intercourse. Hong Kong, already a colony of the British crown, was moving toward expansion, the Kowloon Peninsula being ceded by China in 1860 and the adjacent New Territories being leased in 1898. The empire also relinquished territories beyond the Amur and Ussuri rivers to Russia in 1858 and 1860; lost jurisdiction over the Ryukyu (Liuchiu) Islands to Japan in 1879; settled the Sinkiang frontier in the Kuldja (Ili) area with

PEKING'S CITY WALL withstood a prolonged siege by the Japanese before the city fell in 1937.

Russia in 1879–1881; and clarified suzerainty disputes over the Burma area with Britain, and over the Indochina area with France, in 1885–1886. In 1895 it ceded Taiwan (Formosa) and the Penghu Islands (Pescadores) to Japan; in 1896 acquiesced in the building by Russia in Manchuria of the Chinese Eastern Railroad as a shortcut for the Trans-Siberian Railroad (the line was completed by 1904); and in 1898 leased under duress the port areas of Kiaochow Bay, plus adjacent territory on the Shantung Peninsula, to Germany, nearby Weihaiwei (Weihai) to Britain, Port Arthur (Lüshun) and Dairen (Talien) on the Liaotung Peninsula to Russia, and Kwangchowwan to France. At this juncture, a short-lived court revolution, known as the Hundred Days' Reform, occurred. It led to the court-condoned Boxer Rebellion (Uprising) of 1899–1900. From the peace settlement of 1901 onward, however, no further territorial change was provided for or took place legally. The revolution of 1911–1912 therefore established the modern Republic of China over fairly well-defined territory.

Outer Mongolia and Tibet, however, both declared independence unilaterally. Negotiations with Britain and Tibet with respect to the latter's autonomous status and its frontier with British India in 1913–1914 proved fruitless, while the same process with Russia and Outer Mongolia in 1915 produced a treaty. Although Outer Mongolia returned to China's fold in 1919, it moved into the Russian orbit by 1921 as a result of fighting between Soviet and anti-Soviet forces. Local lama rule was replaced by a Soviet-type people's republic in 1924. A treaty of 1945 between the USSR and China confirmed Outer Mongolia's right to self-determination through a plebiscite. In 1946, China formally recognized the Mongolian People's Republic as an independent state. But China itself was divided in 1949 into a republic with headquarters on Taiwan and a people's republic on the mainland. In 1950 the latter regime confirmed, and in 1953 the Nationalist government rescinded,

COMMUNIST CHINESE hail a victory in the civil war that ended Nationalist rule of the Chinese mainland.

the 1945 treaty. In any case, Outer Mongolia was admitted to the United Nations in 1961 without positive opposition by the Republic of China. Tibet, on the other hand, was taken under Chinese control by the people's republic in 1950–1951, and after a revolt in 1958–1959 its government was abolished. The Dalai Lama fled the country, while the Panchen Lama remained to collaborate with Peking—only to be replaced by Ngapo Ngawang Jigme in 1965.

Korea, freed from Chinese suzerainty in 1895 and annexed by Japan in 1910, was released to Soviet-American supervision on its road to independence in 1945. This development led to the division of the country in 1948 into the Republic of Korea in the south and the Democratic People's Republic of Korea in the north, separated by the 38th parallel. The invasion of South Korea by North Korean forces in 1950 resulted in an international conflict involving the United Nations as well as Communist China. The armistice agreement of 1953 effected little territorial change.

Japan's fortunes exhibited the greatest fluctuations since the mid-19th century with respect both to its neighbors in East Asia and to non-Asian powers. Opened by the United States in 1853–1854, Japan occupied the Bonin Islands and secured the Kurils in 1875, incorporated the Ryukyus in 1879, and acquired Taiwan and the Penghu Islands in 1895. In 1905, southern Sakhalin was obtained, and in 1910 Korea was annexed. At the outbreak of World War I the Japanese moved into the German-held territory on the Shantung Peninsula as well as into the Caroline, Marshall, and Mariana Islands, over which they received a League of Nations mandate in 1920. After occupying all of Manchuria in 1931–1932, they invaded China proper from 1937 onward.

Then, following their lightning attack on Pearl Harbor in 1941, they seized Southeast Asia as well as large areas in the Pacific. Since all Western colonial powers in Asia east of India had been unseated in this process, Japan's defeat in 1945 left a vacuum that was filled by local forces. Japan's own territory, restricted to the home islands after World War II, was subjected to United States occupation until 1952. Between 1951 and 1953, portions of the Ryukyus were restored to Japanese control. Upon admission to the United Nations in 1956, Japan returned to the international community as a normal sovereign state. The Bonin and Volcano islands were returned to Japan in 1968.

North Asia. Russia's southern route of expansion in Siberia was directed toward two general areas: the Caucasus and Turkestan. In the former region the primarily military but also political effort exerted after the reign of Peter the Great (1682–1725) was finally crowned with success in 1859, when Shamyl, the last leader of Muslim resistance, surrendered. In 1864, Transcaucasia was organized as a province of imperial Russia. In the latter region a pincer drive, anchored in the 1850's at Orenburg on the Ural River and Semipalatinsk on the Irtysh River, facilitated the progressive annexation of the nomadic centers and principalities in Central Asia. The city of Turkestan, symbolic of the whole area immediately to the south of the well-established western Siberian territory, was taken in 1864. By 1867 an entire province named Turkestan had been organized. At the same time, the province of Semipalatinsk, adjoining China's Sinkiang area, was organized; this territory, soon expanded, was divided to create another province, Semirechensk, which also bordered on China. By 1873 the province of Samarkand, and by 1875 the province of Fergana, had come into being, rounding off the western Chinese frontiers. On the Caspian flank of the pincer drive, Krasnovodsk was founded in 1869, and a Transcaspian province was organized in 1883. When the Trans-Caspian Railroad, connecting Krasnovodsk in the west with Samarkand in the east, was completed in 1888, the entire Central Asian region was integrated into the Russian empire.

The eastward drive began where the southward drive ended. Having been appointed, in 1848, governor-general of eastern Siberia, which had yet to be defined, Count Nikolai Muravyov in 1850 advanced his headquarters from the Yenisei River, which divides Siberia into two regons, to the Irkutsk area directly north of Outer Mongolia. At the same time, he moved his naval base from Okhotsk, which divides eastern Siberia into its northern and southern parts, to Petropavlovsk on the Kamchatka Peninsula. From Irkutsk, the gateway to eastern Siberia, Russian expansion followed the Amur River to its lower valley. The territory along its north bank was secured from China in 1858. Interest in the island of Sakhalin began a new series of actions and reactions. Territory east of the Ussuri River, which joins the Amur not far from the Sea of Okhotsk, was obtained, again from China, in 1860. Vladivostok was founded that year. Later, in 1872, its new naval base replaced Petropavlovsk. Further expansion made it necessary for Russia and Japan to conclude in 1875 a treaty by which Russian sovereignty over all of Sakhalin island was confirmed.

In 1904 the Trans-Siberian Railroad was completed, uniting eastern and western Siberia, and in 1905 the Trans-Caspian Railroad was extended to Orenburg. With Transcaucasia a mere extension of the European territory, a Russia in Asia now assumed final shape. This gigantic process of absorption was not, however, complete in the political sense. Reorganization for administrative purposes continued in all these areas, especially after World War I and the Bolshevik Revolution. The Transcaucasian area, first organized into three republics, was merged into one in 1922. In 1936, when the new Soviet Constitution was adopted, the Ar-

VIETNAMESE REFUGEES fleeing from a battle zone portray the disruption of civilian life in the civil war in Vietnam.

KYOICHI SAWADA FOR UPI

menian, Azerbaidzhan, and Georgian Soviet Socialist republics were re-created. Meanwhile, between 1924 and 1936, five Union republics were formed in Central Asia: the Turkmen, Uzbek, Tadzhik, Kirghiz, and Kazakh Soviet Socialist republics. In eastern Siberia only one minor territorial change was made. In 1921, Tannu-Tuva, which had been detached from the Chinese empire and made into a Russian protectorate in 1911, was organized into a people's republic. In 1944, however, it was incorporated into the Russian Soviet Federated Socialist Republic as an autonomous oblast. Then, in 1961, the oblast became the Tuva ASSR. In the 1960's, sporadic border conflicts took place in these areas as a result of the Sino-Soviet ideological split.

See also COMMONWEALTH OF NATIONS—*History of British Empire and Commonwealth;* IMPERIALISM; SIBERIA—EASTERN SIBERIA; UNION OF SOVIET SOCIALIST REPUBLICS—*16. History of Russia and the USSR;* WORLD WAR I; WORLD WAR II; and sections on history in articles on the various Asian countries.

SHEN-YU DAI
Colorado State University

Bibliography

Beckmann, George M., *The Modernization of China and Japan* (New York 1962).
Borton, Hugh, *Japan's Modern Century* (New York 1955).
Cady, John F., *Southeast Asia: Its Historical Development* (New York 1964).
Clubb, Oliver Edmund, *Twentieth Century China* (New York 1963).
Fairbank, John K., and others, *East Asia: The Modern Transformation* (Boston 1965).
Fischer, Louis, *The Story of Indonesia* (New York 1959).
Griffiths, Sir Percival Joseph, *Modern India,* 4th ed. (New York 1965).
Hall, D.G.E., *A History of South-East Asia,* 2d ed. (New York 1964).
Jansen, Marius B., ed., *Changing Japanese Attitudes Toward Modernization* (Princeton, N.J., 1965).
Kublin, Hyman, *Asian Revolutionary: The Life of Sen Katayama* (Princeton, N.J., 1964).
Lee, Chong-sik, *The Politics of Korean Nationalism* (Berkeley, Calif., 1963).
Michael, Franz H., and Taylor, George E., *The Far East in the Modern World,* rev. ed. (New York 1964).
Payne, Robert, *Portrait of a Revolutionary: Mao Tse-Tung,* rev. ed. (New York 1962).
Peffer, Nathaniel, *The Far East: A Modern History* (Ann Arbor, Mich., 1958).
Peretz, Don, *The Middle East Today* (New York 1963).
Scalapino, Robert A., *North Korea Today* (New York 1963).
Trumbull, Robert, *The Scrutable East: Southeast Asia Today* (New York 1964).
White, J.A., *The Diplomacy of the Russo-Japanese War* (Princeton, N.J., 1964).

17. Asia in World Affairs

The individual regions of Asia, as well as the continent as a whole, have developed since the mid-19th century through interaction with extra-Asian forces, especially those of the traditional West, rather than through self-motivation. Russia, Britain, France, and, to some degree, the Central Powers of Europe changed the fortunes of Southwest Asia. In South Asia, Britain prevailed almost single-handed, while in Southeast and East Asia, Britain, France, the Netherlands, Russia, other European powers, and the United States achieved successes or encountered frustrations in their joint or separate expansionist activities. Russia, both czarist and Soviet, shaped the destiny of North Asia. It is small wonder that Asia's outlook in the modern world has generally been characterized by response and reaction and only in a very limited way by initiative and self-determination. The development of this generally passive outlook may be traced in three overlapping but fairly distinguishable periods: (1) the period of submission and retreat, 1850–1900; (2) the period of revolt and reaction, 1900–1945; and (3) the period of self-determination and limited initiative, since 1945.

Indicative of the helpless state of Asia in the face of European and North American power in the mid-19th century were the opening of Japan and the signing of unequal treaties between that country and the United States and European powers (1854–1858); the defeat of Persia by Britain (1856–1857); the crushing of the Indian (Sepoy) Mutiny by the British (1857–1858); the Taiping Rebellion in China and the signing of unequal treaties between the imperial government and Britain, France, and Russia (1858–1860); the progressively hopeless resistance of local forces to Russian expansion in North and Inner Asia; and the subjugation of Burma and the Indochinese and Malayan areas by France and Britain.

By 1904, Russia had completed the Trans-Siberian Railroad, which largely integrated the North Asian areas into its sprawling empire. Three years later, Russia and Britain established spheres of interest and influence across the continent from the Ottoman empire through Persia, Afghanistan, and Tibet to China proper. With Siam serving as a buffer, Britain and France did likewise in Southeast Asia (1896–1907), while the United States absorbed the Philippines (1899–1902). Meanwhile, in 1901, China had been defeated by a combination of seven European and American powers and an Asian neighbor.

At about the same time, however, nationalist movements arose in India, in China, and among both the Turks and the Arabs in the Ottoman empire. Japan, which had instituted a Western-type constitutional monarchy as early as 1889 and had adopted an industrialization program, formed an alliance with Britain in 1902. It was thus able, in the Russo-Japanese War of 1904–1905, to deal the first successful Asian blow against a European power. Profiting from the weakness of China and Korea, Japan had replaced defeated Germany in Asia and the Pacific area by the end of World War I; by the late 1930's it had closed the Open Door in East Asia to almost all other competing powers. In alliance with Germany and Italy, Japan then sought to deal with its last remaining competitor, the United States, but suffered instead total defeat in World War II.

Before 1945, Japan's reaction to the West was unique among the Asian states. Other states, however, were undergoing nationalist transformations. Among them were China, where the Manchu (Ch'ing) dynasty was overthrown in 1911–1912; Turkey, which became a republic in 1923; and Iran and Thailand. Before World War II the Philippines achieved commonwealth status, Burma was separated from British India, and several Arab states became independent. While such changes manifested the infusion of nationalism, parliamentary democracy, industrialization, and other Western ideas, they also represented the emergence of Asian revolt and renovation in general.

World War II ended Western domination of the continent. While Japan was going down in defeat, China was rising in its place as one of the world's Big Five powers. Together with India, yet to become independent, China began as early as 1942 to take part in the high councils of world affairs with the Western powers. In addition to China and India, seven Asian nations—Iran, Iraq, Lebanon, the Philippines, Saudi Arabia, Syria, and Turkey—became original members of the United Nations. By 1966, 19 others had been added: Afghanistan and Thailand in 1946; Pakistan and Yemen in 1947; Burma in 1948; Israel in 1949; Indonesia in 1950; Cambodia, Ceylon, Jordan, Laos, and Nepal in 1955; Japan in 1956; Cyprus in 1960; the Mongolian People's Republic in 1961; Malaysia and Kuwait in 1963; and the Maldive Islands and Singapore in 1965. In 1965, Indonesia became the first state ever to withdraw from the UN—but it resumed its membership again in 1966. The Arab League was organized in 1945 in the Southwest Asian area. And beginning with Vietnam and Indonesia, most Southeast Asian countries opposed the return of their former colonial masters. After 1947, India began to be recognized as a new leader in Asia. In 1951 it initiated a series of ambitious five-year plans. The French and Portuguese enclaves within its territory were absorbed, the former by treaty and the latter by force. Relations with China, friendly at first, deteriorated as a result of border clashes beginning in 1959 and a Chinese tactical offensive launched against India in late 1962. Following the withdrawal of this offensive, sporadic border clashes resumed.

In the most dramatic postwar development of all, mainland China, through a process of civil war and Communist revolution, became a people's republic in 1949. Although the Nationalist government, based on Taiwan (Formosa), remained in the United Nations, the new Communist regime enjoyed an unprecedentedly free hand in Asian and world affairs. It intervened in the Korean War on its northeastern periphery (1950–1953), supported North Vietnam in a resumption of traditional Chinese influence in the southeast (1950–1954), and assumed a menacing posture toward the Taiwan area (1954–1958). Beginning in 1960 it even revolted against the Soviet Union's strategy toward the Western World as a whole. Communist China also initiated close ties and aid programs with respect to its Communist and neutralist neighbors. At the same time, however, it instigated border troubles, concluded by treaties, with some of these neighbors: Burma (1956–1960), Nepal (1959–1961), and Pakistan and Outer Mongolia (1962–1963). By 1965 a theory or strategy of "people's wars," aimed at arousing "rural" Asia, Africa, and Latin America against "urban" western Europe and North America was publicized, with Peking the implied leader.

With the advent of the worldwide cold war, Asia's external relations took on a new character. In 1952, Turkey became firmly associated with the West through the North Atlantic Treaty Organization (NATO). New Arab states joined the Arab League, other Asian nations participated in the Central Treaty Organization, several adhered to the Southeast Asia Treaty Organization, and still other Asian states concluded bilateral defense treaties with the United States. A few Asian governments threw in their lot with the Soviet Union and the Communist world. These developments were evidence of Asia's increasing involvement in world affairs, the result of its postwar regeneration and its position in what geopolitical strategists have called the Heartland of the World Island. Asia's status in the 1960's was a far cry from the days when its fate was determined primarily by others.

See also Arab League; Central Treaty Organization (CENTO); Eastern Question; Far Eastern Affairs; Imperialism; Middle East—5. *History;* Southeast Asia Treaty Organization (SEATO); United Nations; World War I; World War II; and sections on history in articles on the various Asian countries.

Shen-Yu Dai, *Colorado State University*

Bibliography

Buss, Claude A., *Arc of Crisis* (New York 1961).
Fall, Bernard B., *Street Without Joy: Indochina at War 1946–1954,* rev. ed. (Harrisburg, Pa., 1964).
Fifield, Russell H., *Southeast Asia in United States Policy* (New York 1963).
Maki, John M., *Conflict and Tension in the Far East: Key Documents 1894–1960* (Seattle 1961).
Ogata, Sadako N., *Defiance in Manchuria* (Berkeley, Calif., 1964).
Smith, Roger M., *Cambodia's Foreign Policy* (Ithaca, N.Y., 1965).
Tinker, Hugh, *India and Pakistan: A Political Analysis* (New York 1962).
Tsou, Tang, *America's Failure in China: 1941 to 1950* (Chicago 1963).
Vinacke, Harold M., *A History of the Far East in Modern Times,* 6th ed. (New York 1959).
Zagoria, Donald S., *The Sino-Soviet Conflict, 1956–1961* (Princeton, N.J., 1962).

ASIA MINOR, ā′zhə mĭ′nər, is the westernmost peninsula of Asia, forming the greater part of modern Turkey. Also called *Anatolia,* it has an area of 292,260 square miles (756,954 sq km)—a little larger than Texas. The peninsula separates the Black Sea (on the north) from the Aegean Sea (on the west) and the Mediterranean Sea (on the south). The peninsula is itself separated from Europe by the narrow straits of the Bosporus and the Dardanelles. The straits are linked by the Sea of Marmara and thus connect the Black Sea with the Aegean. Asia Minor consists mainly of a central region of high plateaus and steppes enclosed by coastal mountains. These coastal barriers to rain-bearing winds give it a continental variety of climate and vegetation, which have diversified the human types and human activities of its distinctive regions.

In classical geography these divisions were, in the north, the Black Sea provinces of Pontus, Paphlagonia, and Bithynia, roughly marked off from one another by the Halys (modern Kizilirmak) and Sangarius (modern Sakarya) rivers. The lack of good natural harbors prevented an exclusively maritime orientation, and all three provinces extended southward beyond the Pontiac mountain system deep into the agricultural plain regions. Bithynia occupied also the eastern shores of the Propontis (modern Sea of Marmara). The three Aegean provinces of Mysia, Lydia, and Caria were the most favored in climate and fertility and enjoyed relatively easy access to the interior as well as commercial and cultural contacts with the active world of Mediterranean civilization. Their situation was in contrast with that of those provinces located on the Mediterranean itself, Lycia, Pamphylia, and Cilicia, which, lacking good harbors, were virtually isolated by the Taurus Mountains. The central provinces of Phrygia, Galatia, Lycaonia, and Pisidia, despite seasonal aridity and poor drainage, were the granary for the whole area, while Cappadocia in the mountainous east had always been more suitable for livestock raising.

The interior possesses only two large rivers, the Kizilirmak and the Sakarya, neither of which could serve as an avenue of communication because they are not navigable for any great distance. Most of the other rivers run short and often torrential courses. Encircled by mountains of forbidding height with easily defended passes, the area as a whole enjoyed security from foreign invasion, and although all the great cultures and religions of the Middle East did penetrate Asia Minor, each ultimately assumed distinctively regional characteristics.

History. Although Asia Minor is one of the world's oldest regions of settled habitation, artifacts of neither the Paleolithic nor the Neolithic period have been found in any significant quantity. There is evidence, however, of a widely distributed agricultural life, of uniform character, in the Aenolithic (Chalcolithic) period, about the 4th millennium B.C. In the succeeding millennium (Early Bronze Age), this life gave rise to a fused Anatolian culture.

At the beginning of the next millennium (about 1900 B.C.), archaeology is seconded by written records. At this time, eastern Asia Minor was held as a province by the Akkadians, who needed the metals of its mountains; the Aegean regions were the home of the people who founded level II of Troy; and the central plateau was inhabited by the obscure Hattites (Khatti). The Hattites had been largely absorbed by the Indo-European Hittites, the first phase of whose domination lasted until the end of the 19th century B.C. Excavations in the Hittite capital city of Khattusas (now Bŏgazköy) have revealed evidence of advanced social organization and familiarity with crafts.

Able to protect themselves against their aggressive neighbors in Syria and Mesopotamia, the Hittites were ultimately destroyed as a result of the development of navigation: about the middle of the 15th century B.C., the Achaeans had conquered Greece, and since then had been constantly attacking the coasts of Asia Minor, achieving their final success in bringing about the fall of Troy (1180 B.C.). This set in motion an eastward migration of the peoples they displaced, one of whom, the Phrygians, conquered the central Anatolian plain from the Hittites and broke their power. With the Dorian invasion of Greece in the early 12th century, further displacements of peoples took place, the repercussions of which were again felt in Asia Minor. Phrygia remained the one fairly stable political entity to the end of the 8th century B.C., when its neighbor to the west, Lydia, enriched by the

CONE-SHAPED FORMATIONS in Cappadocia's valleys once served as refuges for early Christian hermits.

MARC RIBOUD FROM MAGNUM PHOTOS

revenues of commerce and agriculture, attained supremacy. The invasion of the Persians under Cyrus in 546 B.C. restored unified political control to most of Asia Minor.

The Persians were driven out in 334 B.C. by Alexander the Great, and it was the wealth he acquired in its rich western provinces that financed his further Asian adventures. On the death of Alexander in 323, this section of his empire was parceled out among the generals who were his heirs, with Seleucus I Nicator receiving Phrygia and Cilicia, and Lysimachus the provinces of Mysia and Lydia, in addition to Thrace (in Europe). After Lysimachus was defeated by Seleucus in 281 B.C., the kingdom of Pergamum achieved its independence, and by virtue of its great wealth became a military power capable of encroaching on Seleucid territories. It supported the Romans in their invasion, which brought an end to Seleucid power at the Battle of Magnesia (190 B.C.), but in 129 B.C. Pergamum too was incorporated into the imperial province.

These Roman victories forced the native military manpower to flee northward toward the Black Sea provinces and eastward into Armenia. Thanks to these resources of manpower, Mithridates for a time held practically the whole peninsula and was even able to invade Greece, while Armenia expanded into the lands of its neighbors. As a result of the campaigns of Lucullus and Pompey between 73 and 68 B.C., however, Pontus was annexed by Rome, and Armenia was reduced to its former state of political insignificance. There was to be no further serious challenge to Roman authority until the rise to power in Persia of the Sassanid dynasty in 226 A.D. But, once arisen, the threat from this quarter proved so relentless that it could not be contained by a system administered by distant Rome. The pressure of the Sassanids in the east and of the barbarians in the north influenced Diocletian when he divided the Roman Empire into an eastern and a western branch in 286.

The new realities of the power politics of the world of that time were finally recognized when, in 330, Constantine transferred the capital of the temporarily reunited empire to Constantinople (modern Istanbul), the city he created on the site of Byzantium, on the European shore of the Bosporus. The transfer of the capital marked the beginning of the Eastern Roman or Byzantine Empire, which was finally separated from the Western empire in 395. Henceforth, Asia Minor was no longer a peripheral possession of the empire but its heartland, and it was held with such a concentration of power that not only could it maintain itself against Persian aggression, but it even withstood the Islamic Arab invasions of the 7th century. And this was to become the historic role of Constantinople: to hold the bastion of Christianity against the assaults of the Muslim east and the barbarian north. It was not until 1071 that the barrier it erected was broken by the Seljuk Turks at the Battle of Manzikert, and Asia Minor entered its modern historical phase as one of the political centers of Islamic power.

For later history, see TURKEY. See also MIDDLE EAST—*History*.

JOHN R. WALSH, *University of Edinburgh*

Further Reading: Bury, John B., *History of the Later Roman Empire*, new ed., 2 vols. (London 1923); Gurney, Oliver R., *The Hittites*, 2d ed. (Baltimore, Md., 1961); Lloyd, Seton, *Early Anatolia* (Baltimore, Md., 1956).

ASIR, a-sēr', is a province of Saudi Arabia, situated in the southwestern part of the kingdom. It borders on the Red Sea between Hejaz and Yemen, and extends for about 140 miles inland. Its area of approximately 42,000 square miles (108,780 sq km) consists basically of a coastal plain paralleled by a mountain range. The plain is hot, but the interior, with an average altitude of 6,500 feet (1,981 meters), is temperate and well watered, especially in the wadis, or gullies, which are filled with water during the rainy season.

The region's chief ports are al-Qunfidhah and Qizan, the lowland capital; the highland capital is Abha. Other important towns are Sabya and Abu Arish on the plain and Khamis Mushait in the mountains.

History. Before 1800, Asir consisted of petty principalities dominated sometimes by Hejaz, sometimes by Yemen. After the opening of the Suez Canal in 1869, the Ottoman Turks were able to assert their authority in both Asir and Yemen. But gradually the Asir plain came under the control of the Idrisi, the members of a religious movement formed by Ahmad Ibn Idris. Ahmad, a native of Fez, had died in Sabya in 1837.

In 1910 the Idrisi cooperated with the Yemenis in revolting against the rule of the Ottoman Turks, and in 1915 the British guaranteed the Idrisi independence in return for their neutrality in World War I.

Upland Asir passed under Saudi Arabian control in 1920, and in 1926 the Idrisi ruler, Hasan, concluded a treaty with Ibn Saud of Saudi Arabia that made lowland Asir a Saudi protectorate. In 1930, Hasan's authority became merely nominal, and in 1933 direct Saudi rule was substituted. Population: (1962) 900,000.

R. BAYLY WINDER, *New York University*

ASK, äsk, in Scandinavian mythology, was the first man, created by the gods together with Embla, the first woman. The name in Old Norse is *Askr*.

There are two slightly deviant stories about the creation, both naming Odin and two minor gods as creators. In the anonymous *Elder Edda* or *Poetic Edda* (about 9th century), Odin's companions are Hoenir and Lodurr (Lothur; unknown except in this passage). They find Ask and Embla "strengthless, fateless" on the land, without life, mind, or human shape. The three gods then proceed to bestow these traits on Ask and Embla, whose names suggest the names of the trees *ash* and *elm*.

In Snorri Sturluson's *Younger Edda* or *Prose Edda* (about 1221), Odin's companions are his otherwise unknown brothers, Vili and Vé. Here we are told specifically that Ask and Embla were made from trees that the gods found as they were walking on the seashore. The traits bestowed are almost the same as in the other version, but somewhat expanded. Odin gives "spirit and life"; Vili, "mind and feeling"; Vé "appearance, speech, hearing, and sight."

The origin of this myth is not known, but the possibility of influence from Hebraic-Christian tradition cannot be excluded. Yet the concept of man's creation from trees seems highly appropriate to Scandinavia, with its abundance of forests and its tradition of the sacred ash tree, Yggdrasill.

See also SCANDINAVIAN MYTHOLOGY.

EINAR I. HAUGEN, *University of Wisconsin*

ASKEW, as'kū, **Anne** (1521–1546), English Protestant martyr. Her name is also spelled *Askewe* or *Ascue*. She was born at Stallinborough, near Grimsby, England. A well-educated girl of good family, she was induced to become the wife of her deceased sister's fiancé, Thomas Kyme, and had two children by him. She was a staunch Protestant, and, upon being denounced by the family priest, was turned out of her home by her husband. She then went to London, where, in March 1545, she was arrested and charged with heresy. Although she was acquitted, her persistent devotion to her faith resulted in a second arrest, in June 1546. Despite torture on the rack, she refused to recant, and she was burned at the stake at Smithfield, London, on July 16, 1546.

ASMARA, az-mär'ə, is a city in Ethiopia, on the Hamasen plateau, at an elevation of 7,765 feet (2,367 meters). It lies 40 miles (64 km) southwest of the port of Massawa, with which it is connected by a railway. Asmara is the principal city of Eritrea, with fine public buildings and private villas. It serves as the trading and processing center for a fertile region whose crops include fruit, vegetables, coffee, and oilseeds.

Occupied by the Italians in 1889, Asmara became the capital of the colony of Eritrea, but it remained a small town until 1935, when it served as a base for the Italian attack on Ethiopia. In 1941, during World War II, it was captured by British forces. With the rest of Eritrea it became an integral part of Ethiopia in 1962. Population: (1961) 120,000.

ASMODEUS, az-mə-dē'əs, is the prince of demons in Hebrew mythology. In Hebrew the name is *Ashmedai*. Asmodeus is first mentioned in the apocryphal Book of Tobit as the slayer of seven husbands of Sarah, daughter of Raguel. Following the advice of the angel Raphael, Tobias exorcised him by burning a fish's liver. Asmodeus fled to Egypt, where he was bound by Raphael and rendered harmless (Tobit 3:8; 6:14; 8:2–4).

In the pseudepigraphic Testament of Solomon (1st century A.D.) and in later Talmudic literature, Asmodeus figures as the adversary of King Solomon. Solomon compelled him to help build the Temple in Jerusalem. Asmodeus later induced the king to lend him his magic ring, with which he flung Solomon into a faraway land, assumed his shape, and reigned in his stead, committing the sins attributed by Scripture to Solomon.

The derivation of the name and its meaning are uncertain, but "Asmodeus" is thought by some to correspond to *Aeshma-daeva*, the Persian demon of storm and wrath.

RAPHAEL PATAI, *Theodor Herzl Institute*

ASOKA (reigned c. 274–232 B.C.), ə-sō'kə, was the third emperor of the Mauryan dynasty and the greatest ruler of ancient India. The name is also spelled *Ashoka*. He is primarily known for his zealous propagation of Buddhism and for his great humanity. In his honor, modern India uses Asoka's lion-seal as its official seal.

In the eighth year of his reign Asoka conquered Kalinga, a vast unsettled area between the Mahanadi and Godavari rivers. Remorse over this war, in which 100,000 persons were killed, 150,000 taken captive, and many times that number made destitute, led Asoka to embrace Buddhism and the practice of *ahimsa* (noninjury of living creatures). He gave up hunts and the use of meat in his diet, opened animal sanctuaries, and established hospitals. Royal munificence was extended to all religions and sects. Armed forces and capital punishment were maintained.

With ardent zeal, Asoka began teaching *dhamma* (dharma), the Buddhist law of piety. On rocks, on pillars, on cave walls, he inscribed his message: obey parents, respect teachers and monks, tolerate all religious beliefs, show charity, truthfulness, and moderation. A bureaucracy was mobilized to instruct people in piety, and missionaries were sent to other Asian countries to propagate Buddhism. Asoka himself convened a council of Buddhists and suppressed schisms that were developing in the movement.

Asoka was a great builder. He is believed to have inspired the building of no fewer than 8,400 Buddhist temples. Huge sandstone pillars carrying his message of *dhamma* were erected throughout his vast realms. These pillars, some of which survive, have an exquisite polish that has never been duplicated in India. Bilingual inscriptions on many of them have helped modern etymologists decipher Kharoshthi and Brahmi scripts, and many of these pillars contain the so-called Arabic numerals, India's gift to mathematics.

Under Asoka the Maurya empire extended over an area larger than that of any later Indian empire. But within 50 years of Asoka's death, the empire had totally disintegrated.

BRIJEN K. GUPTA, *Brooklyn College, New York*

ASP, asp, is a general name applied to several venomous snakes. The snakes called asps include the Egyptian cobra (*Naja haje*), one of the horned vipers of the Sahara region (*Cerastes*), and a venomous snake (*Vipera aspis*) that has a wide range in central Europe and the Mediterranean region. These snakes rarely reach a length of over 2½ feet (75 centimeters). The sacred asp of the ancient Egyptians was the Egyptian cobra; it was the symbol of sovereignty and was represented on the crown of the ruler. Supposedly, it was this snake that caused Cleopatra's death.

PHOTO BY ISABELLE HUNT CONANT

Egyptian cobra (*Naja haje*), the sacred asp.

ASPARAGINE, ə-spar'ə-jēn, is a chemical compound found in the juice of most plants, especially asparagus and leguminous plants. It is believed to be a storage site for nitrogen. Asparagine, an amino acid, has the formula $C_4H_8N_2O_3$. It occurs in large amounts in germinating seeds and where plant growth is active.

Asparagine is obtained by filtering plant juice, evaporating the juice to a syrupy consistency, and separating it as white crystals. The crystals are soluble in water, acids, and alkalis, but are insoluble in alcohol or ether.

ASPARAGUS, ə-spar′ə-gəs, is any of a large group of erect or climbing plants widely distributed from Siberia to South Africa. Some species, such as the asparagus fern, are often grown for their decorative value, and one species is used in the florist trade, where it is erroneously known as smilax. The best-known and most widely cultivated species, however, is the common, or garden, asparagus, whose tender shoots, or spears, are widely eaten as a vegetable. The shoots are low in calories but contain relatively large amounts of calcium and phosphorus. They also contain vitamins A and C and the B vitamin niacin. Generally, the shoots are eaten either green or white. The green shoots are usually sold fresh, while the white ones are used mostly for canning or freezing.

A typical asparagus plant ranges in height from 6 inches to 2 feet (15.2 to 61 cm) and grows from either a tuberous root system or an underground stem called a rhizome. Unlike most other plants, the asparagus does not produce true leaves. Instead, it bears leaflike branchlets, called cladodes, that produce many small scalelike structures, called cladophylls, which perform the functions of true leaves. The flowers of the asparagus are greenish yellow in color and about ½ to ¼ inch (12.7 to 6.3 mm) in length. They are borne singly or in short spikes or flat-topped clusters, and in the fall each flower ripens into a small red berry.

Cultivation. Asparagus has been known and cultivated for more than 2,000 years, ever since early Roman times. Although the majority of species are found in tropical and subtropical climates, the common asparagus is most successfully grown in temperate regions, where the winter rest period is more favorable than a continuous growing season all year round. Asparagus plants grown in areas with a continuous growing season are spindly and become exhausted more rapidly than those grown in temperate regions.

Almost any kind of soil can be used for raising asparagus, as long as the soil is well drained and as long as the water level is about 4 feet (1.2 meters) below the planting level. Acid soils should be avoided, and the best soil is considered to be a mixture of sandy loams and loose clays. The soil should also be enriched with organic manure and chemical fertilizer. Generally, a field that is well cultivated should be productive for 10 to 15 years.

When an asparagus crop is started, the plants are raised from seeds that are grown in a nursery seedbed until they are at least one or two years old. At that time their crowns, or underground rootstocks, are transplanted to a field. The crowns are planted several inches below the ground, and those that are to be harvested as white shoots are planted in rows that are ridged or hilled up so that the growing shoots will be shielded from the sun and will not turn green. Generally, the rows for white asparagus are from 4 to 6 feet (1.2 to 1.8 meters) apart, while those for green asparagus are usually about 3 to 5 feet (91 to 152 cm) apart.

Diseases and Pests. While the plants are growing, they must be protected against various diseases and insect pests. Their most destructive enemy is asparagus rust (*Puccinia asparagi*), a fungus that is very difficult to control. The most effective method of combating this disease is to plant rust-resistant varieties, such as the Mary Washington. These varieties have been developed by asparagus growers as well as by the U.S. Department of Agriculture.

The most serious insect pests are the asparagus beetle (*Crioceris asparagi*), the garden centipede (*Scutigerella immaculata*), and various kinds of cutworms. The asparagus beetle and the garden centipede can often be controlled through the use of insecticides, and the best method of combating cutworms is to flood the field in late December or early January.

Harvesting. Harvesting should not begin before the third year, and the shoots are usually cut in early June. Harvesting is always done by hand. The white shoots are cut to a length of 4 to 7 inches (10.1 to 17.7 cm); the green shoots are cut from 5 to 8 inches (12.7 to 20.3 cm) long. The shoots are then graded, trimmed, and tied in bundles.

Immediately after harvesting, manure and fertilizer should be added to the soil to produce strong crowns for the next season. In warm regions where there is no winter resting period, the grower creates a resting period for the plants by stopping the supply of irrigation water.

Classification. Asparagus plants make up the genus *Asparagus* of the family Liliaceae (lily), and there are more than 150 species. The common asparagus is classified as *Asparagus officinalis*. The asparagus fern is *A. plumosus*, and the florist's species is *A. asparagoides*. Another popular ornamental is *A. sprengeri*.

WALTER SINGER, *The New York Botanical Garden*

ASPARUKH (died 701), äs-pä-rōōkh′, was a khan of the Utiguri tribe of the Bulgars. He is also called *Isperikh*. One of five sons of the khan Kubrat, who ruled all the Bulgars, Asparukh inherited one fifth of the kingdom. After obtaining the consent of Byzantine Emperor Constans II (reigned 641–668), Asparukh settled in Bessarabia about 668. He then moved south across the Danube River into the Dobruja and refused to recognize the authority of the next Byzantine emperor, Constantine IV (reigned 668–685), who sent out a punitive expedition to crush the Bulgars. The expedition was unsuccessful, and the Bulgars eventually settled in the region between the Danube and the Balkan Mountains about 679, thus founding the future kingdom of Bulgaria. Asparukh continued to rule until his death in 701. He was succeeded by Tervel (reigned 701–718), who consolidated the empire. See also BULGARIA—10. *History.*

ASPASIA (470? B.C.–410 B.C.), as-pā′zhə, was a celebrated woman of ancient Greece. She was born at Miletus, Ionia, and spent most of her life in Athens, where she was noted for her beauty, wit, and political influence. She won the enduring affection of the statesman Pericles, who repudiated his wife in order to live with Aspasia. Their home became the meeting place for the learned men of the time. When the Athenians were dissatisfied with Pericles, instead of attacking him they persecuted those whom he favored, and they accused Aspasia of contempt for the gods. Pericles defended her in the Areopagus, but it required all his influence to procure her acquittal. After his death (429 B.C.), Aspasia is said to have lived with a wealthy but obscure sheep owner by the name of Lysicles, who became an influential citizen in Athens. Her son by Pericles was legitimated by special decree.

ASPASIA THE YOUNGER, as-pā′zhə, was a Greek beauty who lived about 400 B.C. Originally named *Milto*, she was born at Phocaea, Asia Minor (now Foça, Turkey). She captivated Cyrus the Younger, a Persian prince, who renamed her Aspasia, after the accomplished mistress of Pericles of Athens. After Cyrus died in battle, his brother Artaxerxes II, king of Persia (reigned 404–358 B.C.), installed her in his harem. When he named his oldest son, Darius, as heir apparent, Darius claimed her for his concubine. Artaxerxes, not wishing to give her up, but finding that she favored Darius, appointed her priestess of Artemis, whose service required celibacy. The thwarted prince then plotted against Artaxerxes, but was detected and executed.

ASPEN, as′pən, is a resort city in west central Colorado, 100 miles (161 km) southwest of Denver (210 miles, or 337.8 km, by paved road). It is the seat of Pitkin County. On the western side of the Rocky Mountains, Aspen is situated at an altitude of more than 7,800 feet (2,397.4 meters) on the Roaring Fork River at the edge of White River National Forest and is surrounded by mountains rising to 14,000 feet (4,267 meters).

The city is noted for the activities of the Aspen Festival and Music School. There is a nine-week summer school, with orchestral concerts, recitals, and opera productions. Other summer events include the program sponsored by the Aspen Institute for Humanistic Studies, which offers films, lectures, and seminars; an annual design conference; and art schools and writers' workshops.

Aspen was founded in 1879 by silver prospectors, who named it for the aspen trees in the region. It became a richly productive silver camp. One of its notable mines was the Smuggler, where a nugget was found weighing 2,060 pounds (.91 metric ton), 93 percent pure silver. It was said to be the world's largest. By 1892, Aspen had churches, schools, banks, a hospital, an ornate opera house, and a luxurious hotel, but when silver was demonetized in 1893, Aspen became a ghost town, its population falling from 15,000 to 700. Several of its early buildings have been restored. Population: 2,404.

ASPEN, as′pən, is the name applied to several species of the genus *Populus*, especially to *P. tremuloides*, the trembling or quaking aspen, and *P. grandidentata*, the large-toothed aspen, both of North America; and to *P. tremula*, the European aspen. The trembling aspen is apparently the most widely distributed important forest tree in North America, extending, in several varieties, from northern Alaska across Canada into Labrador and Newfoundland, southward into Virginia and Kentucky, and in the west along the Rockies and into Mexico, California, and lower California.

The trembling aspen is a rather small tree, with yellowish green bark and oval, pointed, finely toothed leaves, 1 to 2½ inches (2.5 to 6.2 cm) across. The leafstalk is flattened at right angles to the blade, and therefore the leaves tremble in the slightest breeze. The leaves turn golden in the autumn. As in other poplars, the flowers are in wormlike catkins, the staminate (male) and pistillate (female) on different trees. The small seeds are numerous, hairy, and wind-blown. The tree seeds into denuded areas and initiates tree succession where the forests have

ART BILSTEN FROM NATIONAL AUDUBON SOCIETY

ASPENS in Colorado, photographed in fall foliage.

been cut or burned. The wood is light-colored, silky, soft, and not heavy. It is used for pulp, especially in making magazines and books; it is also used for boxes, tubs, matches, excelsior, and cores in plywood. The beaver feeds on the inner bark and builds dams with the stems.

The large-toothed aspen has much larger, coarsely toothed leaves, with blades 3 to 4 inches (7.5 to 10 cm) long, and hairy winter buds. It is found from southern Canada through the Great Lakes area down to Tennessee and North Carolina. The European aspen, native to Europe, northern Africa, and Asia, and widely distributed, has leaves like the trembling aspen, but with larger teeth. A weeping form, with graceful, pendulous branches, is often cultivated.

ASPENDUS, as-pen′dəs, was an ancient city in Pamphylia, Asia Minor, located about 25 miles (40 km) east of the modern city of Antalya, Turkey. It was situated on the Eurymedon River (now the Köprü River) about 10 miles (16 km) inland from the Mediterranean Sea. The Greek spelling of the name is *Aspendos*. According to tradition, the city was founded around 1000 B.C. by Greeks who may have come from Argos. The wide range of its coinage throughout the ancient world indicates that, in the 5th century B.C., Aspendus had become the most important city in Pamphylia. At that time the Eurymedon River was navigable as far as Aspendus, and the city derived great wealth from a trade in salt, oil, and wool.

In 333 B.C. Aspendus paid Alexander the Great a levy to avoid being garrisoned, but it ignored its agreements with him and later was occupied. In 190 B.C. the city surrendered to the Romans, who later pillaged it of its artistic treasures. Toward the end of the Roman period the city began a decline that continued throughout Byzantine times.

One of the best-preserved ancient structures in Asia Minor is Aspendus' splendid theater. Carved into a hill, it was built in the 2d century A.D. Nearly 40 tiers of seats were arranged in a semicircular enclosure with a circuit measure of about 310 feet (94 m). It had a seating capacity of about 7,500. Other ruins in or near Aspendus include an agora (market place), a nymphaeum (public rest building), and a series of aqueducts north of the city.

HOT ASPHALT MIXTURE for new highway is shown being laid down by paver (center) and packed by roller.

ASPHALT, as'fôlt, is a material used in building and paving since ancient times. Archaeologists have established that it is one of the oldest adhesives known to man. As early as 3800 B.C. it was being used as mortar for building stones and paving blocks. It made reservoirs, canals, and bathing pools watertight. Nabopolassar, the father of Nebuchadnezzar, is said to have paved the streets of Babylon with asphalt.

Natural Asphalt. The asphalt that mortared the ancient building blocks was natural asphalt found in scattered seeps or pools, where it had collected as a residue after the natural refining of petroleum deposits by geologic processes. Typical pools are the La Brea asphalt pits in Hancock Park, Los Angeles, Calif., where the remains of mastodons, woolly mammoths, saber-toothed cats, and other varieties of prehistoric fauna and flora have been found. Probably the best known of these natural asphalt pools is Pitch Lake on the island of Trinidad, where Columbus is said to have careened his ships for caulking on the way home to Spain. This lake and one in nearby Venezuela furnished most of the paving asphalt used in the United States before 1900. Thereafter, large-scale production of asphalt was achieved by controlled refining of crude petroleum. Most crude petroleums contain some asphalt. The amount varies from a few percent to 50 percent and more. A few crude petroleums contain no asphalt.

In addition to natural asphalt seeps and pools, deposits of asphalt-impregnated rock (called *rock asphalt*) are found at various places in the world. In the United States, there are deposits in several states, including Alabama, Texas, Missouri, Arkansas, California, Ohio, Kentucky, Wyoming, New Mexico, Oklahoma, and Kansas. Some of these deposits have limited local use for surfacing roads.

Another naturally occurring asphaltic material of commercial interest is *gilsonite*, which is found in the Uinta River basin in Utah. Gilsonite is used in paints, lacquers, and japans.

Exploitation of the lake in Trinidad and the Bermúdez deposit in Venezuela in the 1800's stimulated interest in street paving. The use of asphalt for this purpose in the United States began in 1870 with the laying of a stretch of pavement in front of the city hall in Newark, N.J. In 1876 the United States Congress directed that Pennsylvania Avenue in Washington, D.C., be surfaced with asphalt. Imported rock asphalt was used for part of the work; the remainder was done with Trinidad asphalt. By 1903 about 42 million square yards (35 million sq. meters) of streets in American cities from coast to coast had been paved with asphalt.

Petroleum Asphalt. The discovery and refining of asphaltic crude petroleum ended the feverish hunt for natural asphalt. With the advent of the motor age, American refineries began pouring out a torrent of petroleum products, including asphalt, a constituent of most petroleums. As a result, imports of natural asphalt became only a small fraction of the total market sales of asphalt in the United States. Virtually all asphalt used in the United States now comes from the refining of crude petroleum. (See simplified flow chart.)

U.S. Consumption. In 1920, total sales of petroleum asphalts and road oils in the United states amounted to only about 1,750,000 short tons (1,587,600 metric tons) of which about 810,000 tons (734,832 MT) were used in paving, 710,000 tons (644,112 MT) were used for roofing, and 230,000 tons (209,656 MT) were used for miscellaneous purposes. Twenty-five years later the United States Bureau of Mines reported that imports of natural asphalt were down to about 5,000 short tons (4,536 MT) while sales of petroleum asphalt and asphaltic road oils totaled 17 million short tons (15,422,-400 MT) with 12 million tons (10,886,400 MT) allotted to paving.

In 1965, sales of petroleum asphalt and road oil in the United States were about 26,373,000 short tons (23,975,000 MT). The United States produced 1,633,000 short tons (1,485,000 MT) of native asphalt and related bitumens in 1963. Sales of native rock asphalts and gilsonite in 1965 totaled 1,912,000 short tons (1,738,000 MT). Imports of petroleum asphalt and natural asphalt were 1,145,000 short tons (1,041,000 MT).

About 74 percent of the asphalt consumed in the United States is used for highway, airport, and other paving; 15 percent is used in roofing; and 11 percent is used for such miscellaneous applications as waterproofing, rubber compounds, insulating materials, pipe coating, and automobile undercoating.

Properties and Refining Methods. Asphalts are black or dark-brown solid or semisolid cementitious materials that gradually liquefy when heated. The predominating constituents are bitumens that occur in nature as such or are obtained by refining petroleum.

Chemically, asphalts are very complex mixtures of high-molecular-weight hydrocarbons. These hydrocarbons also contain nitrogen, oxygen, surfur, and other elements in trace amounts. By the use of solvents, the hydrocarbons can be separated into asphaltenes, resins, and oils.

Asphaltenes are brown to black, hard, brittle, semicrystalline solids. They contain aromatic and condensed-ring hydrocarbons that are insoluble in nonpolar paraffinic hydrocarbons. The average molecular weights of asphaltenes are higher than the average weights of any other asphalt constituents.

Resins are reddish to dark-brown amorphous solids that are soluble in most hydrocarbon solvents. Resins form highly adhesive films after the solvent evaporates. Hydrocarbons forming the resin fraction are structurally similar to the hydrocarbons in asphaltenes.

Oil fractions of asphalt resemble lubricating oils refined from petroleum. Generally, they are composed of saturated hydrocarbons that are lower in average molecular weight than hydrocarbons of other asphalt fractions.

It is believed that asphaltenes are dispersed by resins in the oily medium. This action forms colloidal micelles that tend to dissolve and disappear with increasing temperature.

Early refining methods consisted of a simple atmospheric distillation at high temperatures. Only the so-called asphaltic crude oils could be used for the production of asphalt. With the development of modern methods of fractional distillation and other refinery processes, the variety of crude oils that can be used for the refining of asphalt has increased greatly. However, even with modern refining methods, the selection of the crude oil for the economical commercial manufacture of asphalt is extremely important.

Crude oils can be classified by a number of methods. One method developed by the U.S. Bureau of Mines classifies petroleum on the basis of the gravity of two key distillation fractions obtained within specific temperature ranges. On this basis, crude oils are classified as naphthenic, intermediate, and paraffinic. Naphthenic and intermediate crude oils are most suitable for the refining of asphalt.

Several processes are used to refine asphalts. The most common process is atmospheric or vacuum distillation. In this process, steam often is used. Steam helps to separate light oils entrained in the asphalt and also prevents overheating of the asphalt. Another process is oxidizing or air-blowing of petroleum residues, primarily to produce roofing and industrial asphalts. Fractional precipitation with liquid propane is another method. This process, which can be used to produce extremely hard asphalts, must be performed under considerable pressure. Very often, two or more of the processes can be used to produce asphaltic material of particularly desired properties.

Use in Road Building. Historically, asphalt has been a road-paving material. It can be applied as a diluted emulsion spray on a graded roadbed or as a penetration treatment on a macadam rock base to fill the voids and bind the stones together in a waterproof mat. It can also be used as a hot or cold mix blended with stone, slag, sand, or gravel aggregates before it is spread on the prepared base. Asphalt has long been used to pave virtually all secondary roads in the United States and about 90 percent of U.S. city streets. Since World War II, it has been widely used also for surfacing primary highways and other heavy-duty roads because of its economy, speed of construction, durability, the ease with which it can be repaired, and the riding comfort it provides.

The most significant advance in the use of asphalt as a paving material has been the development of heavy-duty asphalt concrete. This,

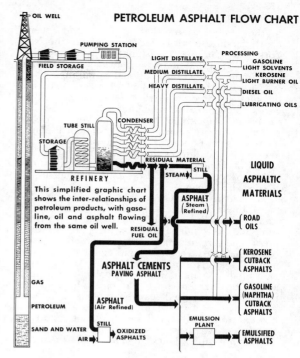

PETROLEUM ASPHALT FLOW CHART

This simplified graphic chart shows the inter-relationships of petroleum products, with gasoline, oil and asphalt flowing from the same oil well.

together with the development of the mechanical spreader, has established asphalt paving as a widely used surface for heavy-traffic highways. For example, the heavily traveled New Jersey Turnpike is a heavy-duty, deep-strength asphalt-concrete superhighway. Thousands of miles of the National System of Interstate and Defense Highways, scheduled for completion in the mid-1970's, are paved with asphalt.

The asphalt content of asphalt concrete pavement is approximately 5 to 6 percent. The asphalt cement is blended with crushed rock, slag, stone, or well-graded native aggregates. A quantity of mineral filler material often is added to this mixture to fill the voids between the larger aggregates. This mix, when laid and compacted to proper density, is a tough, flexible road surface that is capable of supporting the heavy wheel loads of modern vehicular traffic. In some cases where many heavy vehicles travel over the road, the asphalt pavement structure may be 10 or 12 inches (25 or 30 cm) thick. This cover may be supported by a prepared foundation of selected local materials of equal or greater thickness.

Other Uses of Asphalt. Asphalt lining for irrigation canals, ditches, and reservoirs has great promise for the semiarid regions of the western United States and the eastern regions where adequate water-retention facilities are needed. As much as one third of the irrigation water is lost in transit from the reservoir to the point of discharge when it is carried through unlined canals and ditches. This seepage also builds up an alkaline condition in the soil that reduces its productive capacity. Waterproof asphalt membranes and linings have been found effective in halting loss of water through seepage. They also furnish excellent protection as facing for dams. Sea walls and jetties constructed with asphalt are defending the world's shorelines against waves and wind.

Airport paving is another important use for asphalt. Five of the busiest commercial airports in the United States that dispatch and receive air traffic on asphalt-paved runways are the New York La Guardia, Washington National, Los Angeles International, San Francisco International, and Miami International airports.

In 1956 the development of a new extrusion machine resulted in increased use of asphalt for curbs along roads. Asphalt curbs can be laid easily and quickly in graceful curves. Asphalt-paved driveways have become standard equipment for thousands of new houses built after World War II during the greatest home-building boom in United States history. Suburban real estate developments also used asphalt-paved streets and driveways.

Department of Commerce figures show that more than 85 percent of the new roofing installed annually in the United States is asphalt shingling. Asphalt shingles, which are weatherproof and fire resistant, are composed of three basic materials: asphalt, impregnated felt, and mineral materials such as asbestos. Another type of asphalt roofing is built-up roofing—an asphalt and felt pavement on a flat or slightly sloping roof. Because asphalt can be processed to resist very low or very high temperatures, it is a popular roofing material in all climates and for all kinds of weather. See also PETROLEUM.

RICHARD C. DRESSER, *The Asphalt Institute*

ASPHODEL, as'fə-del, is the common name for various hardy, herbaceous, flowering plants, especially in the closely related groups *Asphodeline* and *Asphodelus*. Asphodels are found generally in the Mediterranean region and are common weeds in Greece.

The asphodels belong to the lily family, Liliaceae. The 14 species in the genus *Asphodeline* are recognized by their erect, leafy stems and yellow or white flowers. A common species is *A. lutea*, which grows in poor soil. It has fleshy roots; numerous, narrow, basal leaves; and a leafy flower stalk, 2 to 4 feet (0.6 to 1.2 meters) high, terminating in an elongated cluster of yellow, fragrant flowers. *A. lutea* is thought to be the asphodel used by the ancient Greeks to signify death and mourning.

The genus *Asphodelus* has about eight species. Its stemless plants are characterized by white, lilylike flowers on a leafless stalk, and clustered, elongated, narrow, basal leaves. The tuberous underground structures of *Asphodelus* were eaten in ancient times and still serve occasionally as food and in making adhesives.

Other plant groups referred to as asphodels are *Narthecium* and *Tofieldia*. The genus *Narthecium*, commonly called bog asphodel, has four species that are uniquely distributed—one in Europe, one in Japan, one in the pine barren swamps of New Jersey and Delaware, and one in northwestern North America. Found in bogs and moors, they have grasslike leaves and small, yellowish flower clusters. The genus *Tofieldia* is called the false asphodel. It has about 18 species in the northern hemisphere and the Andes.

ASPHYXIA, as-fik'sē-ə, is suffocation. In asphyxia, coma develops from the deprivation of oxygen, which causes low levels of oxygen and an accumulation of carbon dioxide in the body. This state is induced by decrease or suspension of respiration. Asphyxia is one of the most frequent of the immediate causes of death; it is responsible for some 10,000 deaths a year in the U.S.

Causes. Suffocation may result from several causes. Respiration may be decreased by foreign bodies, such as water in the lungs or inhaled irrespirable gases lodged in the air passages. Inflammation or swelling of the air passages, or external causes such as pressure and electrical shock may also be responsible for decreasing respiration. Respiration may be suspended by paralysis of or injury to the nerve respiratory center or to the respiratory muscles.

Types of Asphyxia. There are several types of asphyxia. Asphyxia of the newborn occurs in the first quarter hour of life, the mortality rate being some 2,000 times more than at any subsequent period. Asphyxia may occur inside or outside the mother's uterus and arises from a great variety of contributing causes. Prompt clearance of the air passages of the newborn and artificial respiration with administration of carbon dioxide and oxygen are lifesaving measures.

Drowning is a simple form of asphyxia due not so much to a large quantity of water in the lungs as to a lack of oxygen in the system. Treatment is by artificial respiration.

Electrical shock is also a simple form of asphyxia. Following the shock, the heart and circulation may be normal, but respiration ceases. Occasionally, recovery takes place after as much as three hours with early treatment by artificial respiration. If heart action has ceased, recovery is doubtful.

Carbon monoxide poisoning from gas heaters, automobile exhausts, and the like is more complicated than the foregoing types since carbon monoxide has an affinity for hemoglobin (the oxygen-carrying component of the blood) 300 times greater than that of oxygen. Recovery is therefore slow. Treatment should be administered by inhalation of a mixture of 93 percent oxygen and 7 percent carbon dioxide.

See also CARBON DIOXIDE; CARBON MONOXIDE; OXYGEN; RESPIRATION.

ASPIC, as'pik, is a clear jelly usually made from fish or meat stock and served cold as a garnish, a main dish, or a dessert. The derivation of the name "aspic" is not definitely known; according to one fanciful explanation it was coined from the word *asp* to suggest the icy coldness of a snake. It is generally thought, however, that "aspic" is derived from the Greek word *aspis*, meaning "buckle" or "shield," and refers to the shape of the molds that were first used for making aspics.

The stock used in making an aspic is made from animal parts that yield the most gelatin. These parts include calves' knuckles, calves' feet, fresh bacon rind, and bones. To make the stock, the parts are placed in a large pot, covered with water, and flavored with onions, carrots, and various herbs and spices. The mixture is boiled for 5 or 6 hours, and the liquid portion is then strained off and clarified. In clarifying, the liquid is mixed with egg white, simmered for 30 minutes, and strained through a moist cloth. A simpler method of preparing stock is to dissolve powdered gelatin in hot water. Canned bouillon may also be used as a substitute for homemade stock.

Once the stock is prepared, it is poured into a mold and chilled. Sometimes pieces of meat, chicken, fish, or vegetables are added, either before the aspic is chilled or after it has thickened slightly.

Aspidistra (*A. elatior*)

ASPIDISTRA, as-pə-dis'trə, is a genus of the lily family, Liliaceae. *A. elatior,* one of about six species, is widely known as a popular house plant. The leaves, 3 to 4 inches (7.5 to 10 cm) broad and from 12 to 18 inches (30 to 45 cm) high, spring from tough cordy roots that actually are underground stems. Stiff and glossy, the leaves are solid green or, in a variegated form, have white stripes. The brownish purple flowers bloom inconspicuously near the base of the leaves and should be pinched off to encourage hardy leaf growth.

ASPINWALL, as'pin-wôl, **William Henry** (1807–1875), American merchant and capitalist, who built a railroad across the isthmus of Panama in the early 1850's. He thus provided a short cut between New York and California, where gold had been discovered in 1849, and gained control of much of the gold-rush traffic.

Aspinwall was born in New York City on Dec. 16, 1807, and at the age of 30 became a partner in a shipping firm trading with England and the Mediterranean and Caribbean countries. After the Panama railroad was built, his company's ships served both the Atlantic and Pacific ends of the road, the eastern terminus of which originally was named Aspinwall (now Colón). At his death in New York on Jan. 18, 1875, he was one of the wealthiest men in the city.

ASPIRATOR, as'pə-rā-tər, a surgical instrument used for drawing off liquids from body cavities. It consists of a long metal probe connected by a hose to a container in which the liquids are collected. To draw liquids through the probe, a partial vacuum is created by a pump attached to the container. The aspirator is useful for draining air passages and body cavities during operations and for cleaning air passages during diagnostic examinations.

ASPIRIN, as'prən, is one of the drugs most widely used to reduce fevers (antipyretic) and to relieve pain (analgesic). It reduces fever by increasing the blood flow to the surface of the body, thereby promoting sweating and heat loss. The pain-relieving mechanism is far less understood. Once it was thought that aspirin acted directly on the brain, but now most authorities believe that it alters the blood flow or water balance, thereby reducing painful swelling and throbbing. However, aspirin is beneficial only for relieving low intensity pain, such as headache, or pain originating in muscles or joints, such as rheumatism; it is not effective in deep-seated pain originating in internal organs.

Chemically, aspirin is acetyl salicylic acid ($C_9H_8O_4$). It occurs as colorless crystals or as a white, crystalline powder. It is odorless and soluble in water.

Aspirin has been used since 1899 and is considered a safe drug. It is, however, toxic in overdoses. Several hundred children die annually in the United States from excessive ingestion of aspirin.

GEORGE GRIFFENHAGEN
American Pharmaceutical Association

ASQUITH, as'kwith, **Herbert Henry** (1852–1928), British statesman, who was prime minister for eight and a half years before and during World War I. He was born at Morley, Lancashire, England, on Sept. 12, 1852. The son of a wool spinner who died in 1860, Asquith received his early education at Huddersfield and at a Moravian boarding school near Leeds. In 1863 he entered the City of London School, where his brilliance attracted the notice of the headmaster, Edwin Abbott. Entering Balliol College, Oxford, in 1870, Asquith fulfilled his earlier promise and in his last term was president of the Oxford Union. Elected a fellow of Balliol in 1874, he entered Lincoln's Inn, which admitted him in 1876.

Asquith married Helen Kelsall Melland in 1877. For the next few years he added to his income by writing for the *Economist* and *Spectator* and began to devote his leisure to politics, as a Gladstonian Liberal. He entered Parliament in 1886 as member for East Fife, in Scotland, a seat he held for 32 years. He soon became an important voice in the House of Commons, where he opposed the policy of Arthur James Balfour, then chief secretary for Ireland. As junior counsel for Charles Stewart Parnell (q.v.) in 1888–1889, Asquith added to his reputation. In 1890 he became queen's counsel.

Herbert Henry
Asquith

(1852–1928)

Following the 1892 elections he became secretary of state for home affairs in the last Gladstone cabinet. The death of his wife in 1891 had left him a widower with five young children, and in 1894 he married Emma Alice Margaret (Margot) Tennant.

From 1895 to 1905, Asquith was out of office. When the Boer War (1899–1902) divided the Liberal party, he joined the imperialist wing in opposition to Sir Henry Campbell-Bannerman. In 1902, Asquith helped reconcile the party's opposing factions, and in 1905 he became chancellor of the exchequer under Campbell-Bannerman. Though he generally adhered to traditional economic policy, Asquith included some progressive elements in his budgets. His third budget made the first provision for an old age pension bill. On Campbell-Bannerman's retirement in April 1908, Asquith became prime minister.

Continual frustration of his social reform legislation by a Conservative majority in the House of Lords persuaded Asquith to mount a sustained effort to limit the power of the peers. His deftness in handling the constitutional struggle resulted in reduction of the upper house's power with passage of the Parliament Act of 1911. Asquith's home rule bill for Ireland was passed just after the outbreak of World War I but was not put into effect until after the war.

In 1915, Asquith formed a coalition cabinet that included one Labourite, but dissension within the cabinet caused Asquith's resignation in December 1916, and he was succeeded by David Lloyd George. The 1918 election practically destroyed the opposition Liberals, and Asquith himself was defeated in East Fife. A by-election at Paisley in 1920 returned him to Parliament, where he urged dominion home rule for Ireland and decried the methods of the Black and Tans. Home rule was granted finally in 1921.

Throughout his political life, Asquith felt that women should not be in politics. However, their role in the war and the overwhelming sentiment for their enfranchisement led him to support the act of 1918 giving them the vote, and to favor lifting restrictions that prevented their sitting in Parliament.

Defeated in Paisley in 1924, Asquith retired from politics. In 1925 he was created *Earl of Oxford and Asquith* and made a Knight of the Garter. He continued to lead the Liberal party until October 1926, when he resigned because of differences with Lloyd George.

In the year before his death he wrote *Memories and Reflections*, (1928), following his earlier *Genesis of the War* (1923) and *Fifty Years of Parliament* (1926). He died at Sutton Courtney, Berkshire, on Feb. 15, 1928.

Emma Alice Margaret (Margot) Tennant Asquith (1864–1945), his second wife, was a socially prominent wit and writer. The marriage offended many of Asquith's conventional Victorian friends, but the match was a very happy one. Margot Asquith was a brilliant hostess, and she aided her husband's career considerably. Her *Autobiography of Margot Asquith* (1922) is a lively account of her early life. Among her other writings are *Places and Persons* (1925), *More Memories* (1933), and *Off the Record* (1944), a collection of 11 sketches of British prime ministers. She died in London on July 28, 1945.

Further Reading: Jenkins, Roy, *Asquith: Portrait of a Man and an Era* (London and New York 1965); Spender, John Alfred, and Asquith, Cyril, *Life of Herbert Henry Asquith, Lord Oxford and Asquith* (London 1932).

STROHMEYER & CARPENTER

Jackass

ASS, a type of Old World horse characterized by a short mane, long ears, and short tail hairs. It generally is considered to be a form midway between the zebra and the true wild horse. The ass belongs to the horse family, Equidae, and the genus *Equus*. There are several species. Male asses are popularly known as *jackasses*.

The kiang, or Tibetan wild ass (*Equus kiang),* is the largest member of the group. Its height is sometimes four feet (1.2 meters) at the shoulders. It is pale underneath, but the color above is dark red with a narrow black stripe along the mane and backbone from head to tail. This animal is found on the high plateaus of Tibet.

Another of the Asiatic forms, the Mongolian wild ass (*Equus hemionus hemionus*), is slightly smaller and lighter in color than the kiang. Although now restricted to almost inaccessible regions of Mongolia, this animal and its close relatives once occurred from southern Siberia and western Manchuria west across Mongolia to Sinkiang. The variety found in Iran and Syria may be the one mentioned in Old Testament writings. The American naturalist Roy Chapman Andrews reported that the Mongolian wild ass was abundant in the Gobi Desert and moved about in herds of up to 1,000 individuals. Andrews noted the speed and endurance of this species, timing a male ass at 40 miles per hour. Another male ass was run to a standstill only after a chase of 29 miles, during which he averaged 30 miles per hour for some 16 miles. These two Asiatic species differ in ability to withstand cold as well as in size and markings.

The Abyssinian wild ass (*Equus asinus somalinensis*) and the Nubian wild ass (*Equus asinus africanus*) are the major African representatives of the group. The latter species has a bluish tint and the very large ears that characterize the donkey. The dark stripe on the back is crossed at the withers by another, stretching across the shoulders; the hair of the mane differs little from that of the body. It is the most widely distributed of the African species, being found in all the open regions of northeastern Africa and westward through the Sahara and the Sudan. Like the Asiatic ass it is extremely wild and fleet. The domesticated ass, or *donkey*, has probably been derived from this species.

EDWARD HODGSON, *Columbia University*

ASSAB, as'ab, in Ethiopia, is a port on the Red Sea. It is situated in southeastern Eritrea, on a dry plain about 60 miles (96.4 km) north of Bab el Mandeb Strait. Assab has long been important as a trade and caravan center. Today the port is linked by a modern road with the highway to Addis Ababa and handles one third of Ethiopia's foreign trade. Salt evaporation is the chief local industry.

The Assab region was the first African territory to pass to Italian control. An Italian steamship company bought the area in 1869, and it was taken over by the government of Italy in 1882. During World War II, when the Allies defeated the Italians in Ethiopia and Eritrea, the British entered Assab on June 12, 1941. Assab became an important part of Ethiopia with the federation of Ethiopia and Eritrea in 1952. Population: (1963) 8,400.

ASSAI, ä-sä̇e', is a food made from the fruit pulp of various species of Brazilian palms and largely used in the lower Amazon region. A thick, creamy, purplish beverage with a rather pleasant flavor is also made from the pulp; it is generally eaten with starchy foods.

The principal sources of assai are the species *Euterpe edulis* and *E. catinga. E. edulis* grows in tide-flooded swamps and reaches a height of 90 feet with a diameter of only four to five inches. It produces small pea-like purple fruit with a thin firm pulp and a hard seed. The fruits of *E. edulis* are kneaded in warm water to produce the beverage.

E. catinga grows on dry, sandy, upland soil. Although this species yields a smaller quantity of fruit thn *E. edulis,* it furnishes a sweeter assai.

ASSAL, Lake, ä-säl', in French Somaliland, a salt lake in the Danakil Desert about 9 miles (14.5 km) from the Gulf of Tadjoura. It is 500–600 feet (150–180 meters) below sea level. Salt flats comprise its western section.

The first information about the lake was published by the ·English geographer Charles Tilstone Beke in the early 1840's.

ASSALÉ, á-sá̇-lä̇', **Charles** (1911–   ), Cameroonian political leader and trade unionist, who was the first prime minister of the independent Cameroon Republic. He was born in November 1911 at Ebolowa, in Kamerun (later French Cameroons), and studied in a Protestant mission school. From 1935 to 1946 he was a leader in the trade union movement and played an active role in organizing unions in the Cameroons. Assalé was a member of the Economic Council in Paris from 1947 to 1951.

Elected to the territorial assembly in the Cameroons in 1952, Assalé allied himself with other deputies to form the Mouvement d'Action Nationale du Cameroun. He was reelected to the territorial assembly in 1956 and to the new legislative assembly in 1957.

He entered the new government of Prime Minister Ahmadou Ahidjo in 1958 as minister of finance, a post he held until 1960 when he became prime minister of the Cameroon Republic following independence. After unification of the republic with the former British Southern Cameroons in 1961, Assalé remained prime minister of East Cameroon.

L. GRAY COWAN, *Columbia University*

ASSAM, ə-sam', one of the 17 states of India, is located in the easternmost extremity of the country, north and east of East Pakistan. One of the most isolated of the Indian states, Assam has no seacoast and is connected with the rest of India by only a narrow corridor between Nepal and East Pakistan. The state comprises Assam proper and the North East Frontier Agency, a group of five hilly or mountainous tracts along the Chinese and Burmese frontiers administratively attached to Assam. The area of Assam proper is 47,091 square miles (121,966 sq km) and of the North East Frontier Agency, 31,438 square miles (12,138 sq km). Before December 1963, Assam also included what is now Nagaland state, made up of the former Naga Hills district and the Tuensang Area.

The capital of Assam is Shillong (1961 population: 72,438), and other cities of importance are Gauhati (1961 population: 100,707) and Tezpur (1961 population: 24,159), both on the Brahmaputra River.

Land. There are three major physical divisions: the Assam Valley, the Himalayan and Indo-Burmese mountains, and the Shillong Plateau. A smaller but heavily populated area is the Cachar plain in the southwest angle where the Shillong Plateau joins the Indo-Burmese mountains. The Assam Valley is an alluvial belt some 450 miles (724 km) long and about 50 miles (80 km) wide. It is enclosed on all sides by mountains and hills except in the west. Through the valley from east to west flows the great Brahmaputra in a broad channel. Settlements are typically located on high ground near rivers and swamps and are hidden in groves of mango and plantain trees and clumps of bamboo.

The Himalayan and Burmese mountains form a great hairpin bend around the head of the valley. The Himalaya rise from the northern flanks of the valley to snow-clad peaks over 20,000 feet (6,000 meters) high, but the range is cut through in the east by the Brahmaputra (called the Dihang at this point) rushing through an immense gorge some 18,000 feet (5,400 meters) deep. The Indo-Burmese system, comprising the Naga, Patkai, Lushai, and other ranges, is less spectacular, the highest peak being Saramati (12,553 feet, or 3,826 meters).

The Shillong Plateau projects westward from Burma and consists of the Garo, Khasi, and Jaintia hills. Summit elevations range from 4,500 to 6,000 feet (1,350 to 1,800 meters).

Assam's climate is characterized by high humidity and moderate temperatures, with the year divided into a cool, dry season from October to February and a warm, wet season from March through September. Annual rainfall varies from about 67 inches (170 cm) at Gauhati in the Assam Valley to an astonishing 452 inches (1,148 cm) at Cherrapunji on the south slope of the Shillong Plateau, the wettest place on earth. Heavy floods are frequent.

The region is subject to earthquakes. Those of 1897 and 1950 were particularly severe.

Much of Assam, especially the hills, is covered by forest. A common tree is Sal (*Shorea robusta*), which is of economic value. In the Himalaya and on the Shillong Plateau are pines, oaks, tropical evergreen and deciduous species, and bamboo jungles. Orchids, azaleas, and rhododendrons are common. These forests and wild lands shelter a rich fauna that includes elephant, rhinoceros, tiger, leopard, deer, bison, wild dog,

ASSAM STATE in India is traversed laterally by the Brahmaputra. Long, narrow boats are used for river crossings, as at this landing near Gauhati.

and bear. Birds and insects abound. A sanctuary at Kaziranga in the Assam Valley shelters the Indian one-horned rhinoceros, now rare.

People. In 1961, Assam proper had a population of 11,872,722, an increase of 34 percent over the 1951 figure. The majority of the people live in the Assam Valley and Cachar plain. The average density in the plains is 432 persons per square mile, and in the hills is 58. The population is overwhelmingly rural, only about 8 percent being classed as urban. Assamese and Bengali are the chief languages, although Tibeto-Burman languages prevail in the hills.

There is probably a greater ethnic mixture in Assam than in any other Indian state. The chief contrast is between the lowlanders, many of whom are of Indian origin, and the hill peoples —the Nagas, Khasis, and Lushais—who have Burmese and Indo-Chinese affinities. Most of the hill tribes long remained remote and hostile, the Nagas practicing headhunting into the 20th century. In addition, immigrants, brought in by the tens of thousands from the states of Bihar and Orissa to work the tea estates, have added another element to the population.

Economy. Agriculture accounts for over half of Assam's income. The chief crops are rice, jute, tea, oilseeds, and fruits. The Assam Valley produces over 80 percent of all these except oranges and pineapples, which are a specialty of the Khasi Hills. Yields are generally higher than for India as a whole, but production has not kept pace with the growth of population. Most of the hill peoples practice a type of shifting cultivation called *jhuming*.

Tea is the most important single crop, accounting for a fifth of the state's income and employing about half a million people. It is produced chiefly on large estates in the upper valley. Current annual production is about 360 million pounds (163 million kg), much of which enters foreign trade.

The state has very little industry. Forest-based industries, still underdeveloped, produce plywood, lumber, railroad ties, and fuel. More important are the oil fields at Digboi, Moran, and Naharkatiya in Lakhimpur district, which are the only producing fields in India at present. Annual production is about 2.7 million tons (2.5 million metric tons). There are refineries at Digboi and Gauhati. Coal is mined in Lakhimpur district, and there are large untouched reserves in the Khasi Hills. Current production is about 600,000 tons (545,000 metric tons) annually. Assam has an enormous potential for hydroelectric power generation.

History. The remote history of Assam is little known. In early times, however, migrant peoples entered from adjacent parts of China, Tibet, and Burma. These and later movements from the same places account for the Mongoloid racial elements distinctive of the Assamese people. In the 13th century the valley was invaded by Ahoms, a Shan tribe of Burma. After establishing themselves in the upper valley, they extended their domains westward and, except for temporary reverses, were masters of the Assam Valley until late in the 18th century.

In 1816 Assam suffered the first of several invasions by the Burmese, who soon threatened the British East India Company's territories in neighboring Bengal. This and other provocations led to the First Anglo-Burmese War. The Burmese were defeated, and in 1826 they ceded Assam to the East India Company. At first, actual rule was left to local chiefs, but as time went on, one area after another was annexed to British territory because of misrule or hostilities. Cachar, Jaintia, the Garo Hills, the Naga Hills, and other areas were annexed in this way. The semi-independent Khasi Hill States were incorporated into Assam in 1950.

During World War II, Assam was of strategic importance in the defense of India against the Japanese advance in Burma, and it was a staging and supply base for the Allied reconquest of Burma. Parts of the Indo-Burmese hills were occupied by the Japanese, and bitter fighting occurred at Imphal (in Manipur) and Kohima (in Nagaland). Numerous roads and airfields were built, including the famous Ledo (Stilwell) Road, connecting with the Burma Road.

More recently, the North East Frontier Agency was attacked from Tibet by Chinese forces. In October 1962, Chinese columns advanced toward the valley, overrunning several Indian positions, first in the Kameng Frontier division and later in the Siang and Lohit divisions. In November, after taking Bomdila in the Kameng division, the Chinese unilaterally announced a cease-fire and withdrew.

Since the creation of Nagaland state in 1963, agitation has persisted there and in Assam's Mizo Hills for complete independence.

JOEL M. ANDRESS
Central Washington State College

ASSAMESE, as-ə-mēz', is a language spoken by about 5,000,000 people living in the Brahmaputra valley in Assam state, India. It is classified in the Sanskritic group, Indic branch, Indo-Iranian sub-family, of the Indo-European family of languages. In grammar Assamese is closely related to Bengali (q.v.); in vocabulary it is of the same character as Sanskrit. Tibeto-Burman dialects have affected it in vocabulary, structure, and phonetics, but Bengali has been the chief influence in accentuation. Assamese literature goes back to the 13th century and covers a wide field; it is especially rich in *buranjis*, or historical works.

ASSAROTTI, äs-sä-rôt'tē, **Ottavio Giovanni Battista** (1753–1829), Italian educator who founded the first Italian school for deaf-mutes. His teaching methods were based on those of Abbé Charles Michel l'Épée, who had founded the first French school for the deaf in 1770 in Paris.

Born in Genoa on Oct. 25, 1753, Assarotti was a professor of theology before devoting himself to the education of deaf-mute children. He founded his school for them at Genoa in 1805. Later it was endowed with annual subsidies by Napoleon I and the king of Sardinia. Assarotti wrote a number of books on the teaching of deaf-mutes. He died in Genoa on Jan. 24, 1829.

ASSASSIN BUG, ə-sas'ən bug, a medium- to large-sized, black or brown, winged insect that frequently bites man. It has a long, narrow head with a necklike portion behind the eyes. The antennae are long and conspicuous. The abdomen is wide at the middle.

The assassin bug belongs to the order Hemiptera, family Reduviidae; there are several common species. Among these is *Triatoma sanguisuga*, a bloodsucking form that in South America carries the organism that causes Chagas' disease, a type of sleeping sickness.

ASSASSINATION, ə-sas-ə-nā'shən, is the killing of a prominent public figure—usually a ruler or political leader—by a treacherous act. The motive may be a desire to avenge a real or imagined personal wrong or to lead to the overthrow of an existing political or other order. The term is usually not applied to the execution of a public figure if it is carried out with at least an appearance of legality.

The assassination of a president of the United States became a federal crime in 1965, after the murder of President John F. Kennedy. Congress passed a law making it a federal crime to kill, kidnap, or assault a president, vice president, president-elect, or acting president.

HISTORIC ASSASSINATIONS

Name	Date of Death
Philip II, king of Macedon	336 B.C.
Tiberius Sempronius Gracchus, Roman tribune	133 B.C.
Gaius Julius Caesar, Roman dictator	March 15, 44 B.C.
St. Thomas à Becket, English archbishop	Dec. 29, 1170 A.D.
Albert I, Holy Roman emperor	May 1, 1308
Edward II, king of England	Sept. 21, 1327
James I, king of Scotland	Feb. 21, 1437
Henry VI, king of England	May 21, 1471
Edward V, king of England	1483
Alessandro de' Medici, duke of Florence	Jan. 5, 1537
David Beaton, chancellor of Scotland and cardinal	May 29, 1546
David Rizzio, secretary to Mary, Queen of Scots	March 9, 1566
Lord Darnley, husband of Mary, Queen of Scots	Feb. 10, 1567
William I, prince of Orange	July 10, 1584
Henry III, king of France	Aug. 2, 1589
Henry IV, king of France	May 14, 1610
Albrecht von Wallenstein, Austrian general	Feb. 25, 1634
Gustavus III, king of Sweden	March 29, 1792
Jean Marat, French revolutionist	July 13, 1793
Jean Baptiste Kléber, French general	June 14, 1800
Paul I, emperor of Russia	March 23, 1801
Abraham Lincoln, president of United States	April 15, 1865
Michael, prince of Serbia	June 10, 1868
Alexander II, emperor of Russia	March 13, 1881
James Garfield, president of United States	Sept. 19, 1881
Sadi Carnot, president of France	June 25, 1894
Antonio Cánovas del Castillo, premier of Spain	Aug. 8, 1897
Elizabeth, empress of Austria	Sept. 10, 1898
Humbert I, king of Italy	July 29, 1900
William McKinley, president of United States	Sept. 14, 1901
Alexander I Obrenovich, king of Serbia	June 11, 1903
Sergius, grand duke of Russia	Feb. 17, 1905
Carlos I, king of Portugal	Feb. 1, 1908
Luiz, son and heir of Carlos I	Feb. 1, 1908
Pyotr Stolypin, premier of Russia	Sept. 18, 1911
George I, king of Greece	March 18, 1913
Francis Ferdinand, archduke of Austria	June 28, 1914
Jean Jaurès, French Socialist	July 31, 1914
Rasputin (Grigori Novikh), Russian monk	Dec. 31, 1916

Name	Date of Death
Venustiano Carranza, president of Mexico	May 21, 1920
Walther Rathenau, foreign minister of Germany	June 24, 1922
Álvaro Obregón, president of Mexico	July 17, 1928
Paul Doumer, president of France	May 7, 1932
Anton Cermak, mayor of Chicago	March 6, 1933
Engelbert Dollfuss, chancellor of Austria	July 25, 1934
Alexander I, king of Yugoslavia	Oct. 9, 1934
Jean Louis Barthou, foreign minister of France	Oct. 9, 1934
Sergei Kirov, Russian political leader	Dec. 1, 1934
Huey Long, U.S. senator	Sept. 10, 1935
Armand Călinescu, premier of Rumania	Sept. 21, 1939
Leon Trotsky, Russian revolutionist	Aug. 21, 1940
Jean Darlan, French admiral and political leader in North Africa	Dec. 24, 1942
Mohandas K. Gandhi, leader of Indian independence movement	Jan. 30, 1948
Count Folke Bernadotte, Swedish diplomat	Sept. 17, 1948
Abdullah ibn-Husein, king of Jordan	July 20, 1951
Liaquat Ali Khan, prime minister of Pakistan	Oct. 16, 1951
José Antonio Remón, president of Panama	Jan. 2, 1955
Anastasio Somoza, president of Nicaragua	Sept. 29, 1956
Carlos Castillo Armas, president of Guatemala	July 26, 1957
Faisal II, king of Iraq	July 14, 1958
S.W.R.D. Bandaranaike, prime minister of Ceylon	Sept. 26, 1959
Hazza Majali, premier of Jordan	Aug. 29, 1960
Patrice Lumumba, Congolese leader	Feb. 12, 1961
Rafael Trujillo Molina, dictator of Dominican Republic	May 30, 1961
Sylvanus Olympio, president of Togo	Jan. 13, 1963
John F. Kennedy, president of United States	Nov. 22, 1963
Martin Luther King, Jr., American clergyman and civil rights leader	April 4, 1968
Robert F. Kennedy, U.S. senator	June 6, 1968
Sir Abubakar Tafawa Balewa, prime minister of Nigeria	Jan. 15, 1966
Hendrik F. Verwoerd, prime minister of South Africa	Sept. 6, 1966
Tom Mboya, economics minister of Kenya	July 5, 1969
Abdirashid Ali Shermarke, president of Somalia	Oct. 15, 1969
Wasfi al-Tal, premier of Jordan	Nov. 28, 1971

ASSASSINS, ə-sas'inz, is the popular name for a secret order of the Ismailite sect of Muslims. The order was founded in the late 11th century, in Persia, by Hasan ibn-al-Sabbah. In 1090, Hasan seized the fortress of Alamut, near Kazvin, Persia, to use as a base for his operations. His followers supposedly were aroused by use of the drug hashish to commit murder in the name of religion, and it is generally assumed that the name *Assassins* was derived from the name of the drug. Crusaders in the 1100's encountered the order in the Holy Land, and they took the term *assassin* back with them to Europe. The order was generally suppressed by the end of the 1200's, but peaceful survivors are still found in India, Iran, and Syria. The Aga Khan of Bombay is their titular head. See also MOSLEM SECTS—*Seveners.*

ASSATEAGUE ISLAND, as'ə-tēg, is a narrow barrier island about 32 miles (51 km) long, off the Atlantic coast of southeastern Maryland and eastern Virginia. The island is divided between these states. Highway bridges connect the northern part of Assateague with the mainland of Maryland and the southern part with Chincoteague Island and the Eastern Shore Peninsula of Virginia.

Both Assateague and Chincoteague, to the west, are inhabited by wild ponies. The last Thursday of July each year is Pony Penning Day, when the animals are rounded up for auction at Chincoteague, Va. The abundant wildlife of Assateague Island also attracts hunters and fishermen. The only regular inhabitants are a coast guard crew.

Assateague Island is one of the last areas of undeveloped Atlantic beach between Cape Hatteras, N.C., and Cape Cod, Mass. Conservationists fought for years to prevent commercial exploitation of the island's natural beauty. In 1965, Congress authorized the purchase of all privately owned land on the island for the Assateague National Seashore, to be operated as a park by the Department of the Interior.

ASSAULT, ə-sôlt', is an intentional act threatening bodily harm to another person, coupled with ability or apparent ability to do such harm, but falling short of physical contact. If one raises his fist or a cane to strike, or swings and misses, and the requisite intent and ability are present, assault is committed. An *aggravated assault* is an assault with intent to commit some additional crime, or a particularly outrageous one, such as assault with a deadly weapon. Where force is actually applied by the aggressor to the victim, a *battery* occurs; hence the common term *assault and battery* (see BATTERY).

Intent either to harm or to cause apprehension of danger may be a basis of assault. The court looks to the aggressor's conduct and attending circumstances and considers how they would appear to the victim. For example, when one points a gun in a threatening manner, it is assault, although the assaulter may know the gun is unloaded. The act is reasonably calculated to create in the victim apprehension of immediate harm, in spite of the assaulter's inability to do harm in the manner threatened. Mere abusive language without threatening action is not assault. Thus, threats over the telephone, even at short range, do not constitute assault, since there is no present and immediate danger.

CURRAN C. TIFFANY, *Member of the New York Bar*

ASSAYING, a-sā'ing, is the process of determining the amount and type of metals present in ores, alloys, scrap, furnace products, and other mixtures. Assays are made to evaluate mining property, to determine the quality of ores for buying and selling, to control the processing of ore, to control metallurgical processes, and to evaluate scrap. The degree of accuracy required in the assay depends on its purpose. For example, greater accuracy in assaying is needed in buying or selling ore than is needed for the control of processing, because assays for processing control are made periodically, and errors can easily be detected.

The two major types of assaying methods are *dry processing* and *wet processing.* In dry processing (also called *fire assaying*), a heat source is used to melt the materials and promote chemical reactions. In wet processing, a chemical solution is used to decompose the materials and obtain the desired chemical reactions.

In the dry process, the metal or metals of interest are separated from impurities by melting and collecting them. Then the weight of the metal is compared to the weight of the original sample. The precious metals, such as gold, silver, and metals of the platinum group (platinum, palladium, iridium, ruthenium, and osmium), are assayed by the dry process.

The wet process is used to determine the amount of iron, copper, or lead in ores or alloys. This method can be adapted to the quantitative analysis of many other metals. In the wet process, the metallic ingredients of the sample under test are acted on by chemicals in a solution. Different wet process methods are used, depending on what type of measurement is desired, such as a measurement of volume or a measurement of weight. Wet process methods also are varied to meet the conditions for assaying different metals and different mixtures of substances in which the metal for assaying is found.

In general usage, the term "assaying" applies only to determining the type and amount of precious metals that are assayed by the dry process. Only dry assaying will be discussed further.

Sampling. In assays, only a very small amount of the metal is obtained and, therefore, it is very important to obtain a representative sample of the ore. Samples can be taken in three different ways: a spot sample can be taken from a single place; the samples can be taken at random; or the samples can be taken at regular intervals throughout the ore body. It is difficult to get a representative sample, but the method of taking samples at regular intervals is considered to be the best way to do so.

In the simplest procedure, a small sample of rock is crushed and divided into two portions, one of which is crushed and divided again. This procedure is repeated until the assay portion is obtained. When large amounts of rock are to be sampled, the sampling can be done by hand or by machine. One way to do hand sampling is to take shovel samples of the material at regular intervals. The shoveled material is arranged in four conical piles. Two piles are retained, and the procedure is repeated until the assay portion is obtained. Another way to do hand sampling is to take pipe samples. A pipe is driven into the material, and the core of material that clings to the inside of the pipe is brought up for assay.

Both stationary and mobile machine are used as mechanical samplers. Stationary machines have a fixed cutter, which continuously takes a portion of the stream of ore. Mobile machines cut across a falling stream of ore at intervals, taking the entire stream of ore within the interval.

In reports on assays of precious metals, quantities are expressed as troy ounces (31.1035 grams) per avoirdupois ton (2,000 pounds). However, a special unit of weight, called the *assay ton,* is used for weighing the ore that is to be taken for the assay process. The assay ton, which weighs 29.166 grams, has the same relation to the milligram as the avoirdupois ton has to the troy ounce. Thus, one milligram of gold per assay ton is the same as one troy ounce per avoirdupois ton. The number of assay tons of material obtained for sampling depends on the expected amount of precious metals in the material. The accuracy and the cost of the assay increase with the number of assay tons.

Preliminary Assay. Two preliminary assay methods are used for the precious metals: the *crucible assay* and the *scorification* assay. Gold and silver assays, simpler than those of the platinum-group metals, will be used as examples. In the crucible assay method, a portion of the sample is melted with fluxes in a fireclay crucible. The bottom of the crucible is filled with lead monoxide (PbO), which is reduced to lead by controlling the chemical reactions. The lead collects gold and silver from the sample. This collection of materials is called a *lead button.* The lead button is treated further (see section on *Cupellation*) in another step toward determining the gold and silver content.

In the scorification assay method, a shallow fireclay dish called a scorifier is used. A small quantity of ore, a small amount of acid fluxes, and a large amount of granulated lead are placed in the scorifier. Oxidizing conditions are maintained by admitting air to the oven in which the scorifier is placed. The molten lead oxidizes, and the lead oxide fluxes the ore. The molten lead collects the gold and silver. The lead button is then treated in the same way as the lead button obtained from the crucible assay.

The crucible method for the precious metals can be adapted for assaying all types of ores and metallurgical products. However, before proceeding, the assayer must determine the general nature of the ore sample. He then must choose the proper fluxes for melting the ore and the right reagents for controlling the formation of the lead button. The type of flux depends on whether the ore is acidic or basic. Control of the reduction of the lead oxide depends on the oxidizing or reducing power of the ore minerals and the added reagents. Ores can be neutral, or they may have oxidizing or reducing power.

Crucible assaying can be performed either in a single-stage process or in a two-stage process. In the single-stage process, the amounts and types of the materials are adjusted so that fusion (the decomposition of the assay portion by melting with fluxes and reagents), the reduction of the lead oxide, and the collection of precious metal occur within the crucible. In the two-stage process, the first stage is a preliminary treatment to destroy the reducing effect of the ore or to remove impurities that are difficult to flux. The separate second stage is the reduction of lead oxide and collection of precious metal.

The scorification method is best adapted to assays of ores that are so rich in gold or silver that small samples can be used. The scorifica-

KENNECOTT COPPER CORPORATION

ASSAY FURNACES are used for assaying precious metals. The furnace temperature is controlled electronically. Fumes escape as exhaust through the hood.

tion method also is suitable for assays of products that contain oxidizable forms of zinc, tin, manganese, copper-free nickel, cobalt, or lead.

In the scorification method, a weighed amount of granulated lead, equal to half the total amount of lead that is required, is spread on the bottom of the scorifier dish. The weighed ore is then added and mixed. The remaining half of the lead is placed over the mix, and borax glass is sprinkled on top. The scorifier is placed in a muffle furnace, which keeps the assay sample separated from the heat source and its combustion products. The scorifier is heated at 500° to 600° C until the lead is melted. Air is admitted to the furnace, and the temperature is raised to 900° C. Heating is continued until the slag covers the lead. The temperature is raised to 1000° or 1050° C to enable a cleaner separation in pouring. Pouring out the contents of the scorifier separates the lead button and the slag.

Cupellation. The lead buttons produced by crucible or scorification assays contain the precious metals. The buttons are treated in an absorbent vessel known as a *cupel;* this process is called cupellation. Cupels are porous cylinders or inverted-cone frustrums of refractory material, such as bone ash, cement, or magnesia.

Cupellation is the fundamental part of all fire assay procedures. During this process, the lead is oxidized to lead oxide, which is absorbed by the cupel. The remainder in the bowl of the cupel is a bead of gold, silver, and any platinum metals that may be present.

The cupellation process includes the following steps: preheating the cupel, placing the lead button in the cupel, melting the lead button, and recovering the bead of precious metals. A muffle furnace usually is used for cupellation, and temperature control is very important.

Cupels are preheated to 850°–900° C to drive off any volatile constituents in them, such as water or carbon dioxide. After the cupel is preheated, the lead button is placed inside it, and the draft and door of the muffle furnace are closed. As the temperature rises, the lead melts and becomes covered with a crust of lead oxide. The lead oxide crust melts, and it is absorbed by the cupel. The draft is adjusted so that there is a definite flow of air through the muffle. This air flow, under the proper temperature conditions, causes the lead to oxidize.

Toward the end of cupellation, the proportion of lead in the button decreases rapidly, and the melting point of the alloy rises toward that of the finished bead. Cupellation is finished when the last trace of lead has been oxidized and removed from the bead by being absorbed by the cupel. After cupellation and when the cupel has been cooled, the bead is removed from the cupel. Any particles of the cupel that adhere to the bead are broken off by flattening the bead with a hammer. Impurities or platinum metals can be detected because each produces distinctive effects on the structure and appearance of the bead.

Parting and Weighing. In the process called parting (dissolving), there are two objectives. One is to separate the gold from the silver and any base metals that may be present in the bead. The second objective is to leave the gold in a form, preferably a single piece, so that it can be worked without losing any of the gold. In determining the gold and silver content, the beads from cupellation are weighed, and the results are recorded as the weight of the gold-silver alloy, which is commonly called *doré bead.* The silver is then dissolved in acid, and the gold remainder is washed, dried, annealed, and weighed. The weight of the silver, which is also recovered, is determined by subtracting the weight of the gold from the weight of the doré.

An alloy containing up to two times as much silver as gold will not part, even in strong acid, and additional silver must be added. If the lack of silver is known in advance, a known amount of silver can be added before or during cupellation. To aid in the parting process, the gold-silver bead either is flattened with a hammer or is rolled thin and then coiled into a spiral form.

Bullion Assays. The term "bullion," which is used in assaying and metallurgy, refers to alloys that contain a sufficient proportion of precious metals to make it worthwhile to estimate their quantities or to recover them from the alloy.

Lead bullion is a bullion in which lead is dominant. For ordinary lead-smelter bullions, simple cupellation is satisfactory for the assay.

Copper bullion contains more than 50 percent copper and not more than 10 percent base metals other than lead or copper. In a copper bullion assay, most of the copper must be removed by scorification assay, crucible assay, or acid treatment before cupellation.

Silver bullion contains more than 50 percent precious metals (including silver), at least 25 percent silver, and not more than 10 percent base metals other than lead or copper. The assay of silver bullion can be performed either by cupellation or by a volumetric analysis.

Gold bullion contains more than 50 percent precious metals (including gold), at least 25 percent gold, and less than 10 percent base metals other than lead and copper. The general method of assaying gold bullion at mints and assay offices is to use cupellation and parting. This procedure is accompanied by another assay as a check for errors introduced in cupellation.

The assay of gold bullion, silver bullion, and some other bullions is expressed in parts per thousand—the so-called scale of fineness. Gold bullion that contains 990 parts of gold per 1,000 parts of bullion is referred to as 990 fine.

Assay Offices. Although commercial mining and smelting organizations maintain their own assay offices, all buying and selling of gold in the United States is based on government assays conducted under the direction of the United States Mint. Government assay offices are maintained at the mints in San Francisco, Denver, and Philadephia. A separate assay office is located in New York City. The United States gold depository is located at Fort Knox, Ky., and the silver depository is located at West Point, N.Y.

Gold and Silver Prices. The price of gold in the United States was fixed at $35 per ounce by presidential proclamation on Jan. 31, 1934. Silver prices ranged in the early 1960's from about 90 cents to about $1.30 an ounce.

ALVIN S. COHAN, *Scientific Design Company*

Bibliography

Agricola, Georgius, *De re metallica* (1556), tr. by Herbert Clark Hoover and Lou Henry Hoover (New York 1912).

Bugbee, Edward E., *Textbook of Fire Assaying*, 2d rev. ed. (New York 1933).

Newton, Joseph, *Extractive Metallurgy* (New York 1959).

Shepard, Orson C., and Dietrich, Waldemar F., *Fire Assaying* (New York 1940).

Wise, Edmund M., *Gold: Chemistry, Metallurgy, and Applications* (Princeton, N.J., 1964).

ASSEMANI, äs-sä-mä′nē, **Giuseppe Simone** (1687–1768), Syrian Orientalist. He was born in Tripoli, Syria. His name in Arabic was *al-Samani.* Educated at the Maronite college in Rome, he made extensive journeys to the Near East in 1717 and 1735, collecting Oriental manuscripts and ancient coins for the Vatican Library. On his return from the second voyage he was named titular archbishop of Tyre and Vatican librarian. At the order of Pope Clement XI, he edited the important work, *Bibliotheca Orientalis Clementino-Vaticana* (4 vols., 1719–28), reproducing the Syriac codices in the Vatican Library. Other parts of the work, planned to include Vatican Library manuscripts in Arabic and other Eastern languages, were incomplete at his death, in January 1768, in Rome.

STEFANO EVODIO ASSEMANI (1709?–1782), a nephew, succeeded him as Vatican librarian, publishing (1742) a catalog of Oriental manuscripts in the Laurentian and Palatine collections.

SIMONE ASSEMANI (1752–1821), a grandnephew of Giuseppe Simone, was born in Tripoli, educated at Rome, and served as a missionary in Syria. He was appointed professor of Oriental languages at the University of Padua in 1785, and subsequently published an important treatise on ancient coins, *Museo cufico naniano illustrato* (2 vols., 1787–88), and a study of the pre-Islamic culture and literature of the Arabs.

ASSEMBLAGE, ə-sem′blij, in art, is a form of relief or free-standing construction made wholly or in part from natural or manufactured materials, fragments, or objects. Assemblage differs from relief and from sculpture in its use of nontraditional materials—shells, driftwood, machine parts, and any other kind of object, from stuffed animals to furniture. Collage (q.v.) is sometimes considered a form of assemblage, although a distinction is usually made between the two-dimensional collage and the three-dimensional assemblage.

The word "assemblage" was first used as a generic technical term in the title of an exhibition "The Art of Assemblage," held at the Museum of Modern Art, New York City, in 1961. The term applies to both the technique and the art works.

Although works made from such materials as shells, bones, and feathers have long been common in primitive and folk art, the modern art of assemblage began as an extension of the collage technique originated by Picasso and Braque in 1911–1912. Assemblage was not widely practiced until after 1916, when it was adopted by the Dadaists—partly as an anti-art gesture. The Dadaist artist Kurt Schwitters, who is regarded as the "old master" of the technique, developed assemblage to the scale now known as an "environment".

Surrealist artists such as André Breton, Max Ernst, Salvador Dali, and Joan Miró also created a form of assemblage in their "surrealist objects." These objects use the disquieting juxtapositions intrinsic to the surrealist aesthetic.

After 1955 assemblage became a widely practiced technique used by many artists, including Joseph Cornell, Robert Rauschenberg, Richard Stankiewicz, John Chamberlain, Jean Tinguely, Bruce Conner, Edward Kienholz, and Lucas Samaras. The untrained artist Simon Rodia created one of the masterpieces of assemblage, the fantastic sculptural towers of cement, bits of metal, glass, and other objects that he built in Los Angeles.

WILLIAM SEITZ, *Author, "The Art of Assemblage"*

ASSEMBLAGE construction, called *Poetic Object,* was done in 1936 by Joan Miró.

COLLECTION, THE MUSEUM OF MODERN ART, NEW YORK. GIFT OF MR. AND MRS. PIERRE MATISSE.

ASSEMBLIES OF GOD

ASSEMBLIES OF GOD, a religious body in the United States, organized in a constitutional convention at Hot Springs, Ark., April 2–12, 1914. It is one of the largest of the Protestant groups commonly designated "Pentecostal." In the mid-1960's there were nearly 8,500 churches (assemblies) with an enrolled membership of about 556,000 and nearly 9,000 Sunday schools with a total enrollment of over 1,000,000.

The organization is based on a combination of Congregational and Presbyterian principles. The local congregations are autonomous in the choice of pastors and in the management of local affairs. The sovereignty of the local congregation was guaranteed in the preamble to the constitution which was adopted at the first General Council in 1914. At that time, the Bible was recognized as the all-sufficient rule for faith and practice. Later (1916) a statement of truth was adopted as a standard of fundamental doctrine essential to a full-gospel ministry.

Doctrinally the denomination is Arminian, following basically the Methodist pattern. Emphasis is laid on the new birth, divine healing, the baptism in the Holy Spirit accompanied by the sign of speaking in tongues (Acts 2:4), and the premillennial return of Christ. It is held that the pattern set forth in the Acts of the Apostles is the norm for Christian experience and growth. The denomination is intensely evangelistic and missionary in spirit and practice. Mission stations are found on every continent and in over 70 different countries.

The form of organization is democratic. All ordained ministers and one lay delegate from each affiliated, cooperative congregation constitute a general council, which meets biennially. The officers of the General Council are the general superintendent, four assistant general superintendents, the general secretary, the general treasurer, and the foreign missions secretary. These, together with four others, constitute an executive presbytery. To them is committed the management of the various departments of the denomination, including home and foreign missions, youth, publications, education, and benevolences. The executive presbytery is supplemented by a general presbytery composed of three representatives from each of the district councils and two from each of eight foreign-language branches. These branches include churches using European languages, and others using Latin American languages. There are 45 church districts, whose boundaries mainly follow state lines. They are organized similarly to the general council and meet annually. The foreign-language branches function under the supervision of the Home Missions Department.

The Assemblies of God puts out a weekly newspaper, the *Pentecostal Evangel,* and maintains a publishing house for religious literature. The denomination administers Bethany Bible College, Santa Cruz, Calif.; Eastern Bible Institute, Green Lane, Pa.; Evangel College, Springfield, Mo.; Northwestern Bible College, Kirkland, Wash.; and South-Eastern Bible College, Lakeland, Fla. The denomination belongs to the National Association of Evangelicals and to the Pentecostal Fellowship of North America.

ASSEMBLY, Legislative. See LEGISLATIVE ASSEMBLY.

ASSEMBLY, Right of, ə-sem'blē, the right of citizens to assemble peaceably. It is deeply rooted in the constitutional law of all countries where the basic rights of man are recognized and respected. Thus, the 1st Amendment (1791) to the U.S. Constitution provides that Congress shall make no law abridging "the right of the people peaceably to assemble, and to petition the Government for a redress of grievances."

Anglo-American Law. The right of assembly was closely connected historically with the right of petition, which in England was mentioned as early as Magna Carta (1215) and was given classic formulation in the Bill of Rights (1689). Today the right of assembly is spelled out in the constitutions of most American states. It is regarded as such a fundamental right that the U.S. Supreme Court in *DeJonge* v. *Oregon* (299 U.S. 353 [1937]) read it into the liberty secured against state action by the due process clause of the 14th Amendment.

Like other rights, the right of assembly is not unlimited under U.S. law. It does not extend to an assembly having a criminal purpose, nor does it justify riot or the use of unlawful force. Above all, the concept of unlawful assembly limits the scope of the right. Unlawful assembly is generally defined by U.S. courts as a gathering of three or more persons that has the common intent to attain a purpose, whether lawful or unlawful, that will interfere with the rights of others by committing acts in such fashion as to give firm and courageous people in the neighborhood reasonable ground to apprehend a breach of the peace.

On the other hand, it is well established in U.S. law that a meeting cannot be prohibited merely because it advocates unpopular views or changes in the status quo. The right of assembly extends to the holding of meetings in such public places as parks and streets. Such meetings are subject to reasonable regulation, though regulation may not go so far as to vest undefined or arbitrary discretion in public officers.

Freedom of Association. The right of assembly, when read in conjunction with such related rights as that of free speech, is part of the broader concept of freedom of association. Although this phrase does not appear in the U.S. Constitution, it is regarded as falling within the scope of the 1st and 14th amendments.

Since the rise of a militant civil rights movement for greater equality of rights, freedom of association has been involved in a great deal of litigation testing the limits of that freedom. This is mainly the result of efforts by Southern states to weaken or drive out the National Association for the Advancement of Colored People (NAACP). Thus, the U.S. Supreme Court ruled in *NAACP* v. *Alabama* (357 U.S. 449 [1958]) that a state may not constitutionally compel the NAACP to disclose its membership lists, since this would expose its members to economic reprisals, threats of violence, and other manifestations of community hostility.

This decision was the first in which the Supreme Court used the phrase "freedom of association" in a forthright constitutional holding. Since then the court has repeatedly struck down attempts to interefere with the NAACP through required disclosure of membership lists (*Louisiana ex rel. Gremillion* v. *NAACP*, 366 U.S. 293, [1961]) or the names of its contributors (*Bates* v. *City of Little Rock*, 361 U.S. 516 [1960]).

Again, as in the case of other rights, the freedom of association is subject to reasonable restraints where public interests outweigh the individual's claim to associational privacy. Examples include the case of an association committed to violent and unlawful activities (*Bryant* v. *Zimmerman*, 278 U.S. 63 [1928]) or where subversive activities may be involved (*Uphaus* v. *Wyman*, 360 U.S. 72 [1959]). However, a mere assertion that such activities exist does not suffice to justify disclosure of names (*Gibson* v. *Florida Committee*, 372 U.S. 539 [1963]).

DAVID FELLMAN, *University of Wisconsin*

Further Reading: Fellman, David, *The Constitutional Right of Association* (Chicago 1963).

ASSEN, äs'ən, a town in the northern Netherlands, is the capital of Drenthe province. It is located 15 miles (24 km) south of Groningen on the Smildervaart, a canal that connects it with Meppel. Assen is an important transportation junction situated on the route of the main railway and highway from Amsterdam to northern Germany. The town is a farm-produce market and the butter-control station of Drenthe province. There is also some canning of foods.

Assen is built around an old nunnery whose 17th century church is now the town hall. An annex of the 13th century cloisters houses an archaeological museum. Nearby are tumuli, ancient grave mounds built of stone by prehistoric Celts. First mentioned by the Roman historian Tacitus (1st century A.D.), they were found to contain wooden and stone implements. Population: (1960) 25,216.

ASSENT, ə-sent', in law, is the act of agreeing, consenting, concurring, or approving. The implication generally carried by the term is that of an implied acceptance rather than an affirmative expression of agreement. Knowledge on the part of the person assenting is necessary, however, since the word connotes a meeting of the minds. An assent ordinarily applies only to concurrence before or at the time of doing an act. As a general rule, mere silence or inaction does not constitute assent to an offer, except where the relations between the parties or other circumstances are such as to justify the offer in expecting a reply.

ASSER (died 909/910), as'ər, was a Welsh monk, who wrote a chronicle of Alfred the Great and served as bishop of Sherborne. Born in Wales, he became a monk of St. David's monastery and, according to Giraldus Cambrensis, was bishop there. About 885, King Alfred took him into the royal household, where Asser spent six months of each year teaching Alfred and recording the events of his reign. As a reward he was made bishop of Sherborne and given extensive lands in Cornwall and the west. His death date is mentioned in the *Anglo-Saxon Chronicle* as 910, but William Stubbs, in his *Registrum Sacrum Anglicanum* (1858), a calendar of English bishops, gives the date as 909.

Asser's accounts of Alfred do not include the later aprocryphal stories of the burning of the cakes or the founding of Oxford University. In spite of interpolations and additions by later writers, Asser's life of Alfred (*De rebus gestis Aelfredi Magni*) remains a primary source for Anglo-Saxon scholarship. It includes a history of the period from 849 to 887.

ASSER, äs'ər, **Tobias Michael Carel** (1838–1913), Dutch expert on international law, who shared (with Alfred H. Fried) the Nobel Peace Prize in 1911. Born in Amsterdam, Netherlands, on April 28, 1838, he was professor of international law at the University of Amsterdam from 1862 to 1893, a member of the council of state in 1893, and minister of state in 1904. He was a Dutch representative at the Hague peace conferences of 1899 and 1907 and a member of the Permanent Court of Arbitration in 1900. The Institute of International Law, which he helped found in 1873, received the Nobel Peace Prize in 1904, seven years before his personal Nobel citation. He died at The Hague on July 29, 1913.

ASSESSMENT, ə-ses'mənt, broadly defined, is the exaction of a contributive share from each of a group of persons, to be applied toward a common object and computed according to the benefits received. It also includes the procedural steps necessary to compute and collect such a fund or to impose a tax. The term is used in a variety of contexts, including the laws of taxation, corporations, clubs, associations, eminent domain, shipping, and trade unions.

In municipal government, a "local" or "special" assessment is a charge in the nature of a tax, levied to pay all or a part of the cost of local improvements in a municipality. The charge is placed upon the various pieces of property presumed to have been especially benefited by the construction of the improvement in question. It is thus distinguishable from an ordinary tax, the purpose of which is to raise revenue for general governmental purposes. It also differs from a tax in that it can be levied only on land.

As a general rule, a local assessment is constitutional if there is a special benefit to the property charged and if this benefit bears a reasonable relationship to the amount exacted. Examples of the kinds of improvement for which local assessments are made are bridges, parks, sewage systems, and flood protection.

In the law of property taxation, the term "assessment" refers to the processes of listing the persons and property to be taxed and the valuation of the property, and includes the entire statutory means of imposing the tax. *In income tax law,* "assessment" usually means the formal determination of the amount of tax due prior to its collection, but the term is sometimes used in a broader sense to include collection.

In corporation law, the term "assessment" is used with reference to both paid and unpaid subscriptions. Where payment of subscriptions to the stock of a corporation is made in installments, as is often the case, an assessment is the same as a "call" or "installment," and denotes an official declaration by the directors that all or part of the sum subscribed is due. With reference to paid-up stock subscriptions, assessment is the pro rata amount levied on each stockholder above the par value of the stock, generally for the purpose of satisfying the demands of the creditors. Assessments cannot be made on fully paid stock unless authority is conferred by statute or contained in the corporate charter.

With respect to clubs, an assessment is an amount collected from members in addition to their membership fees and regular dues. The authority to levy assessments must be provided for by statute or in the club's charter.

ASSESSOR, ə-ses'ər, an officer chosen to assess property for taxation; a person chosen to determine or estimate benefits to be charged, or compensation or damages to be allowed, in a particular case; a quasi-judicial officer who participates in the determination of questions of law or fact in a particular court or other tribunal; a technical or legal adviser to a judge.

A municipal assessor is an appointed or elected officer, whose duties are generally to make lists of persons and property, and establish valuations on property for purposes of taxation.

Assessors, also called *associates,* are sometimes used in extraterritorial consular and treaty courts to advise consuls and consular judges.

ASSETS, as'ets, in law, means all property of any description and all property rights owned by a person. The term includes real and personal property, as well as intangibles, such as accounts receivable, the goodwill of a business, and a beneficiary interest in a trust fund. Assets are the opposite of *liabilities* (what one owes to others). The *net worth* of a person or business organization is the excess of assets over liabilities.

ASSHUR, ASSHURBANIPAL, ASSHURNASIR-PAL. See Ashur; Ashurbanipal; Ashurnasir-pal.

ASSIGNAT, as-ēn-yä', a form of paper money issued during the French Revolution. After the lands belonging to the church had been confiscated by the National Assembly in 1789, bonds were issued whose security was based on these lands. The bonds, called assignats, bore interest of 5 percent and entitled holders to repayment in property of the same value as the face value of the bonds.

The purpose of the assignats was not only to supply financial relief to the government but also to commit the middle class to the revolutionary cause by making them owners of the confiscated land. The first issue in 1790 of 400,000 francs brought some relief to the government, but purchases were generally slow because the clergy was still in possession of its property.

In August 1790 the government's need for greater income forced a change. The assignats no longer bore interest and thus became equivalent to currency. Their value dropped sharply as more and more assignats were issued. Price controls instituted in 1793 proved effective in halting inflation for a short time, but with their removal in December 1794 the assignats' value decreased rapidly. By 1795 they were worth less than 1 percent of their face value.

In March 1796 the assignats were withdrawn from circulation and redeemed at a thirtieth of their value by "territorial mandates" (*mandats territoriaux*), a new kind of paper currency that empowered the holder to take possession of public lands equal in value to the face value of the mandates. This measure also proved a failure because the public's lack of confidence resulted in very small sales.

In 1797 the government terminated the paper money experiment and returned to a metallic currency. The inflation caused by the large issues of paper money had ruined many of the bourgeoisie, who held the greater part of the state's debt, and turned them against the revolution. It also created a new bourgeoisie that had made its fortune speculating on the various issues.

ASSIGNMENT, ə-sīn'mənt, is the transfer of a property right or a legal interest from one person to another. Though sometimes applied to the conveyance of title to real estate, the term is usually confined to the transfer of intangible rights.

Among the interests that can be assigned are rights under a contract that has not yet been performed, interests in a decedent's estate, rents, choses in action (legal claims not yet reduced to judgment), and salaries and wages not yet earned. The assignability of the expectant interest of a prospective heir in the estate of a living person is not clearly established; most courts hold that the assignment of such an interest is enforceable in equity, if not at law.

Ordinarily, business contracts are assignable unless they involve personal skill or services, or a relationship of special confidence, such as a contract to paint a picture, write a book, sing, or render professional services. Similarly, a contract involving reliance on the character, credit, or solvency of another person is unassignable. A covenant not to engage in a competing business, executed by the seller of a business, is assignable to a person subsequently acquiring the business. Since such a contract is regarded as a part of the good will of the business, an express assignment is generally not necessary.

A right of action arising out of a breach of a contract (one type of chose in action) is now almost universally assignable, although the early common law rule recognized no assignment of any kind of choses in action. A chose in action resulting from the commission of a tort may be assignable, depending upon the nature of the wrong and the terms of the controlling statute. Generally, a chose in action is assignable where, due to statutory enactment, it survives the death of the person against whom the tort in question was committed.

To be valid, an assignment must in general meet the requirements of an enforceable contract. It must be executed by parties having the legal capacity to contract, must be supported by consideration, and must not be fraudulent or illegal. It may be made orally or in writing.

ASSISI is famous for the 13th century church of Saint Francis of Assisi, built over the saint's tomb.

FRITZ HENLE, FROM MONKMEYER

ASSIMILATION, ə-sim-ə-lā'shən, is a sociological term for the process by which two or more groups having different attitudes, values, and customs become alike in these respects. As a result of the process, the groups involved lose their sense of being clearly separated and come to regard themselves as members of one larger society and culture. Assimilation often involves a blending of cultures. But the culture of a subordinate group may be submerged—or it may even be destroyed—by the culture of a dominant group.

Assimilation can be illustrated by the experience of immigrant groups in the United States. These groups, with different ethnic origins, languages, religious faiths, and social patterns successfully adapted to American society. They tended to give up their original languages, costumes, and many customs and to take on the speech, attitudes, and other characteristics of American society. On the other hand, they often kept their religious beliefs and otherwise preserved at least some of the flavor of their homelands.

ASSINIBOIN INDIANS, ə-sin'ə-boin, a tribe of North American Indians of Siouan linguistic stock. Originally members of the Yanktonnai tribe of Dakota Indians, they separated from the parent nation before the mid-1600's and settled in the territory between the Saskatchewan and Missouri rivers.

Physically and culturally they were similar to other Sioux Indians, and depended for their livelihood on the buffalo. Their descendants are chiefly in reservations at Fort Belknap and Fort Peck, Montana, and in southern Alberta and Saskatchewan, Canada.

ASSINIE, à-sē-nē', is a historic port in Ivory Coast, west Africa, 50 miles (80 km) southeast of Abidjan. French traders settled there in 1702 and established the town as a trade center. In the 20th century Assinie's importance faded. Its port activity almost disappeared, and its population fell to a few hundred.

ASSISI, äs-sē'zē, is a town in Italy, in Perugia province, Umbria, 15 miles southeast of Perugia. Situated on a spur of Mount Subasio, the town has a fine view over the Tiber and Topino rivers. Its manufactures include hemp, wrought iron products, fertilizers, and pumps. There are olive groves and mineral springs in the surrounding region.

Assisi is famed as the birthplace of St. Francis, founder of the Franciscan Order, and of St. Clare, founder of the Poor Clares. The town's Franciscan monastery and its two churches (a lower and an upper church, making a single building) were begun in 1228 and completed in 1253. These fine examples of Gothic architecture contain many valuable old paintings, including frescoes by Giovanni Cimabue, Giotto, and Pietro Cavallini. The Church of Santa Chiara, containing the tomb of St. Clare, was begun in 1257. It has a simple Gothic interior that is enhanced by massive lateral buttresses and a fine rose window. Another interesting church is San Damiano, where St. Francis renounced the world and where St. Clare became a member of the Franciscan Order. Assisi has a medieval castle, which was built by Cardinal Albornoz in 1367. Population: (1961) 5,302.

ASSIZE, ə-sīz', is a term used in British law to denote a sitting or session of an assembly or court. In medieval England "assize" was the name given to a court or session of the king with his councilors. Later it came to mean the decrees or enactments made at such a council. These enactments were known either by the name of the place where the council was held or by the subject with which they dealt. Examples of the first kind were the assizes of Clarendon (1166) and Northampton (1176), famous for their introduction of a new procedure for arraigning criminals. Representative of the second kind were the Assize of Arms (1181), the Assize of the Forest (1184), and the periodic assizes of bread and beer.

From enactments such as these came new procedures and new forms of action at law that also took the name "assize." The *grand assize* (about 1179) was a procedure that allowed a defendant in an action concerning title to land to choose to be tried by the oath of a body of 12 knights in preference to trial by battle. The assizes of *novel disseizin, mort d'ancestor* and *darrein presentment*—all from the time of Henry II (reigned 1154–1189) and known collectively as *possessory assizes*—were forms of action begun by royal writ and designed to give a speedy, though perhaps temporary, settlement to disputes about the possession of land and church patronage. All made provision for trial by the oath of local neighbors, and these men, like the knights in the grand assize, were called an assize. The assize in this sense was an early form of jury, deciding the case on its own knowledge of the facts.

For the convenience of litigants, royal judges were sent through the country with a commission to determine cases involving the possessory assizes. They were said to "take the assizes" and were known as justices of assize. For this purpose the country was divided into circuits which the judges traveled alone or in groups, hearing assizes and also criminal cases. The courts they held were, and still are, called *assize courts,* or *assizes;* and so, by this curious route, the word has returned to its original meaning.

The commission of assize, initially confined to the determination of possessory assize cases, was extended by the Statute of Westminster II (1285) and later enactments to include the hearing of civil pleas of every sort. However, pleading, arguments of law, and judgment took place at Westminster until the Judicature Acts of 1873–1875. Since that time the court of a commissioner of assize has been a court of the High Court of Justice, and it has full power to determine the civil pleas brought before it.

A modern judge of assize in England and Wales tries criminal cases under commissions of "oyer and terminer" and "gaol delivery," and civil cases under a commission of assize. His title, court name, and civil commission are anachronisms; possessory assizes were ended in 1835.

G. D. G. HALL, *Oxford University*

ASSOCIATED PRESS. See PRESS AGENCIES AND SYNDICATES.

ASSOCIATION FOOTBALL. See SOCCER.

ASSOCIATION OF AMERICAN PUBLISHERS, an organization of publishers of general books and educational materials. The association was created by the consolidation of the American Book Publishers Council and the American Educational Publishers Institute on July 1, 1970. These predecessor associations had been providing services to the book industry for almost three decades—the American Educational Publishers Institute since 1942 and the American Book Publishers Council since 1946.

One objective of the association is the development of better public understanding of the essential role of general books and instructional materials. Another goal is to furnish a vehicle for cooperation with members of the public, government agencies, and trade associations interested in the uses of books and educational materials. The association provides members with information and statistical data pertinent to the book industry, pursues legislative matters relating to the interests of members, and cooperates in research on improvement in the design and preparation of books and educational materials.

The association is organized into college, general, map, reference book, professional, and religious book divisions. In addition, services are provided by general committees on copyright, freedom to read, international trade, marketing, postal matters, and reading development. The National Book Committee, a nonprofit citizen group affiliated with the association, sponsors National Library Week (with the American Library Association), the National Book Awards, and the National Medal for Literature.

Membership in the association is open to all Americans and U. S. partnerships and corporations that have been actively engaged for at least one year in the creation, production, and publication of books or copyrightable types of educational materials in the United States. Associate memberships may be granted to qualified foreign publishers doing business in the United States.

A Board of Directors elected by the membership oversees the general business of the association. The headquarters is in New York City, with branch offices in Washington, D. C., and Chicago.

SANFORD COBB
Association of American Publishers

ASSOCIATION OF IDEAS is the name of a theory of how ideas are connected in the mind. Of great importance in the history of psychology and modern philosophy, the term was first used by John Locke in a supplementary chapter included in the fourth edition of his *Essay Concerning Human Understanding.* Plato, however, had already described the ways in which ideas are related and recollected (*Phaedo,* 73), and in *De memoria et reminiscentia* (*Memory and Reminiscence*) Aristotle stated these principles—the laws of association—more concisely. Ideas, he said, are associated by contiguity, similarity, and contrast. Sir William Hamilton, who surveyed the extant literature thoroughly in the 19th century, observed that several other older writers (for example, Juan Luis Vives) also had expounded these principles. Thomas Hobbes incorporated the concept into his system of psychology, but it was David Hume who gave major emphasis to it. In *A Treatise of Human Nature* (1739–40) he wrote about a "gentle force" that joins ideas together; it is through association that simple ideas are built up into complex ideas.

Hartley and Mill. David Hartley in his *Observations on Man* (1749) not only developed the concept further, but also grounded it in physiological theories ("nerve-vibrations") which he adduced from Newtonian physics. Vibrations affect various parts of the brain, and, if they are set up by simultaneous or successive sensations, they may become connected. Contiguity and repetition are most likely to establish these associations. Furthermore, they tend to fuse or coalesce into complex ideas.

These views were more cogently expounded by James Mill, who rejected, however, Hartley's fanciful theories of brain physiology. In the *Analysis of the Phenomena of the Human Mind* (1829) he states that there are nothing but individual ideas associated in simultaneous or successive configurations. So-called abstract ideas are, likewise, nothing but configurations of individual ideas with names associated with them. Thus, he believed, psychology can be made into a science as precise as mechanics. Mental life consists of compounds analyzable into elements which have been associated by contiguity. To these views his son, John Stuart Mill, took exception. There is not a mosaic of ideas in the mind; rather, ideas become associated into unanalyzable patterns. As a result of an intricate process of compounding, in which some ideas may drop out, others coalesce, and still others undergo modifications, association effects an entirely new configuration of ideas.

Bain. A contemporary of the Mills, Alexander Bain, whose textbooks were widely used in English-speaking countries, also emphasized the concept of association of ideas. All higher mental phenomena are outgrowths, through the processes of association of ideas, of lower mental phenomena. Unlike the previous writers on this subject, Bain appreciated the significance of the genetic method of study in psychology. According to him, associations are established in the progressive experience of the individual, and the school is an institution designed to facilitate the formation of desirable associations. Concentration is of particular importance in the formation of associations which promote mental development.

James. Many of Bain's theories about the association of ideas were enriched by William James, who brought them to the attention of thousands of students in the United States and Canada through his book *The Principles of Psychology* (1890). "Cerebral laws" determine the orderly association of ideas in the mind, James wrote. There is a reason for each sequence, though it may be difficult for us to account for the connection. In *Psychology, Briefer Course* he wrote: "Habit, recency, vividness, and emotional congruity are, then, all reasons why one representation rather than another should be awakened by the interesting portion of a departing thought." The associations may be spontaneous—a stream of consciousness—or they may be voluntary or intentional. James forcibly rejected the notion that associations are determined by chance alone. The mind can select among those ideas "which the associative machinery introduces" to it.

Applications of the Concept. The concept of associated ideas has been abandoned as too atomistic by modern, more dynamically orientated psychology (see GESTALT PSYCHOLOGY). However, the idea of association appears in a modified form in behaviorism and in Ivan Petrovich Pavlov's theory of conditioned reflexes. Moreover, in psychological testing the association of ideas has come to play an important role in assessing a person's mental and emotional reactions. Thus, in free association experiments the subject responds to each stimulus word with the first word he can think of. Sir Francis Galton was the first to devise this type of experiment, which, he wrote, lays "bare the foundations of a man's thought with a curious distinctness, and exhibits his mental anatomy with more vividness and truth than he would probably care to publish to the world."

Experimental investigations of that kind have been developed through a variety of techniques. Not only have lists of words been employed, but also pictures and inkblots are now commonly used. The Rorschach test, for example, has gained great popularity in many countries since its development in 1921. By eliciting free associations it is said to be a "royal road to the unconscious." In the United States another widely used technique is the Murray-Morgan series of pictures called the "thematic apperception test," in which pictures are used to stimulate fantasies in the subject. Such psychological devices, which have considerable use in arousing the flow of associations, are referred to as projective tests, since the tested person is likely to project his own conflictual tensions into the responses he makes to the inkblots, pictures, or other materials. In other, more conventional experiments, Hermann Ebbinghaus demonstrated the manner in which ideas are associated, retained, and recalled.

Impetus to novel uses of this concept was given by Sigmund Freud, who employed free association as a major technique in psychoanalysis. While explorations of the "stream of consciousness" had previously attracted the interest of William James, Freud realized the possibilities of eliciting data about the unconscious determinants of behavior by encouraging free or unrestricted associations from his patients. Brought to the attention of the academic world at a Clark University symposium in 1909, Freud's method stimulated many ingenious experiments by psychologists in the United States and elsewhere. It also influenced writers, many of whom made use of the stream of consciousness. James Joyce in *Ulysses* used this method most effectively.

The concept of the association of ideas is one of the oldest attempts to account for the manner in which learning takes place. Opposing the doctrine of inherent faculties, it claims to offer an empirical explanation for the origin and formation of complex elements of consciousness. Many 20th century theories of learning may be regarded as restatements of this concept. Moreover, this concept was made the basis of a system of psychology known as associationism, or association psychology. According to associationism, the association of ideas is the basic principle of memory, thought, and learning. This school of psychology had its genesis in England and was also taught by leading scholars in America until the end of the 19th century, when interest shifted to experimental psychology.

PHILIP L. HARRIMAN
Editor of "Encyclopedia of Psychology"

Further Reading: Copleston, Frederick, *History of Philosophy*, vols. 5, 7 (Westminster, Md., 1959–63); Mandler, George and J.M., eds., *Thinking: From Association to Gestalt* (New York 1964); Warren, Howard C., *History of Association Psychology* (Boston 1921); Woodworth, Robert S., *Experimental Psychology*, rev. ed. (London 1955).

ASSOCIATIONISM. See ASSOCIATION OF IDEAS.

ASSOCIATIVE LAWS. See ALGEBRA.

ASSONANCE, as'ə-nəns, in poetry, is the repetition of vowel sounds, without regard to the consonants, as a substitute for rhyme. Examples include *dwell* and *tread, sleep* and *feel, gloaming* and *boating.* It is most common in languages in which vowel sounds predominate over consonants, most notably the Romance languages. Its repeated use in English is often unpleasing to the ear or unintentionally amusing, and it has generally been replaced by rhyme.

Assonance was used in both Greek and Latin writing, and it is a distinguishing characteristic of the lyrical and dramatic literature of Spain and Portugal. In France, assonance was used in the romances of the *trouvères,* but it was rejected early in the history of French poetry, and modern attempts to reintroduce it have met with little encouragement.

Assonance occurs in its most elaborate form in Celtic poetry, where perfect rhyme is almost unknown. In this poetry, the original terminal assonance was developed and a system invented wherein the last word of one line corresponds with the middle word of the next, and words in the same line also chime with one another. Assonance is also common in Scottish poetry. Among poets writing in English, Elizabeth Barrett Browning made frequent use of assonance. See also RHYME; VERSIFICATION.

ASSOS, as'əs, was an ancient Greek city and port in Asia Minor. It was located on the Gulf of Adramyttium (Edremit), opposite the north shore of the island of Lesbos and southwest of the site of the modern village of Ayvacık, Turkey. Its Latin name was *Assus.* Founded about 900 B.C. by Greeks from Methymna, a city on Lesbos, Assos was long an important port. Its public buildings were built on terraces that rose above an artificial harbor. In the 4th century B.C. it was the center of a school of Platonists at which Aristotle taught. In the 1880's, Assos was thoroughly explored by archaeologists, who unearthed the ruins of an agora, a senate house, bath, theater, gymnasium, and seven Christian churches.

ASSUMPTION OF THE BLESSED VIRGIN MARY, the doctrine that Jesus' Mother "at the conclusion of her life on earth was assumed body and soul into heavenly glory." Pope Pius XII used these words in 1950 when he defined this as a divinely revealed truth. His consultation with the bishops of the church had shown that Catholics throughout the world already believed in the Assumption. The corresponding liturgical feast is celebrated on August 15.

This doctrine may suggest the ancient picture of a three-level universe—hell, earth, and heaven —with God at the top. For the Catholic faith, however, that image is neither identical with the religious truths it has helped to express in the past nor guaranteed by divine revelation as scientifically accurate. Is heaven a place; and if so, where is it and how (other than by God's power) was Mary conveyed there? These may or may not be religiously significant questions. The doctrine of the Assumption makes no pretense of answering them. It rather proposes Mary as already sharing more perfectly than any other human being in the effects of Christ's redemption. Uniquely, in body as well as in soul, she is with God, even before the rest of material creation reaches its final consummation.

THE ASSUMPTION OF THE VIRGIN, painted by the Spanish artist El Greco in 1577.

The Second Vatican Council called Mary the first or preeminent among the redeemed. In such a perspective, her Assumption means that the new creation, sign and effect of Christ's victorious grace, has already reached in her a degree of material perfection which the other Saints yet await.

CARL J. PETER
The Catholic University of America

ASSURBANIPAL. See ASHURBANIPAL.

ASSURNASIRPAL. See ASHURNASIRPAL.

ASSY, ä-sē', is a region in the French Alps, in Haute-Savoie department, France, near the border of Italy. Its full name is *Plateau d'Assy.* The plateau, at an altitude of 3,450 feet (1,050 meters) in the foothills of Mont Blanc, is noted for its beautiful scenery and healthful climate. Primarily an agricultural district, the plateau is also a winter sports area. The village of Passy is located here.

The most notable feature of the area is the modern church of Notre Dame de Toute Grâce, begun in 1937 and consecrated in 1950. It was designed by the architect Maurice Novarina, and many outstanding modern artists contributed to its decoration, including Fernand Léger, Jean Lurçat, Germaine Richier, Marc Chagall, Jacques Lipchitz, and Georges Rouault. The church was built through the efforts of Father M.A. Couturier, a Dominican priest, who sought to revitalize church architecture through the contributions of the best contemporary artists regardless of their faith.

ASSYRIA, ə-sir'ē-ə, was the ancient name of the district on both sides of the Tigris River, varying in size but generally confined to the region in the northern part of modern Iraq between the present Syrian frontier and the Little Zab River. On the west it was bounded by the desert plateau of central Mesopotamia, and on the east by the mountains of Kurdistan; to the north lay Armenia, and to the south Babylonia. The heart of the land was fertile alluvial plain, but most of it consisted of desert plateau and rolling limestone ridges, with arable valleys between the ridges. The climate of this district is cooler and rainier than that of Babylonia, but it is still Mediterranean, with rain only in winter. Irrigation was thus essential for the production of sufficient food to maintain its people. In the course of time the Assyrian Empire grew in all directions, but particularly toward Syria. With this westward extension came a shift in the use of the name. It is now certain that the name "Syria" is derived from the older "Assyria."

The original capital of the country, to which it owes its name, was Ashur (Asshur), modern Qalat Sharqat, on the western bank of the Tigris above the mouth of the Little Zab. About 60 miles (97 km) to the north lay Nineveh (modern Kuyunjik), which was founded long before Ashur and became the capital of the later empire. Between them lay Calah (modern Nimrud), which was the capital of the empire during part of the 9th and 8th centuries B.C., and northeast of Nineveh was Dur Sharrukin (modern Khorsabad), the capital during the reign of Sargon II (721–705 B.C.). The most important secondary cities were Arbela (modern Erbil or Arbil), southwest of Nineveh, and Haran, the principal center of late Assyrian power in western Mesopotamia and the last capital of Assyria (after the fall of Nineveh in 612 B.C.).

Exposed to the incursions of wild mountain tribes from the north and east, and of equally wild nomads from the west and south, the Assyrians early learned the art of defense. Very mixed in blood and always subject to new intermixture, the Assyrian people developed striking national vitality, and the cold winters which contrasted with the warmer Babylonia helped to prevent them from becoming lethargic. The tenacity of their special form of Mesopotamian culture may be gauged from the fact that most of the essentials of their 7th century culture may be traced back over a thousand years. In almost all periods the Assyrians were more militarily minded and less interested in higher culture than the Babylonians; their religion and literature drew heavily from their more cultured southern neighbors. Assyrian laws were much harsher than Babylonian, and the royal inscriptions are chiefly devoted to accounts of brutal military campaigns. In Babylonia, on the other hand, we scarcely ever find any reference to warfare in the royal inscriptions after the 22d century B.C. In this respect Assyria has not unjustly been compared to Sparta or Prussia, while Babylonia resembled Athens or Austria in its comparative lack of interest in military matters.

Chronology. Our knowledge of Assyrian history greatly surpasses that of any other country of the ancient East, and there is every reason to believe that it will continue steadily to increase. From the wealth of detail preserved in the royal inscriptions and official documents, we know a great deal about the geography and history of all neighboring countries, of which we would otherwise be almost totally ignorant. We possess detailed historical inscriptions of nearly all the kings of Assyria from the late 10th to the late 7th century B.C., as well as of a number of kings from earlier centuries. Deeper excavations in the ancient capitals will eventually yield much more information for more ancient periods. Lists of kings, and especially lists prepared by the yearly officials (*limmu*), after whom most documents were dated, have made it possible to establish the exact dates of nearly all historical events from about 640 B.C. back to the late 10th century. A reference to a total eclipse of the sun under one of these annual officials makes it possible to date the entire series, as far back as it is preserved. The chronology thus established agrees throughout to the year with the overlapping part of the Canon of Ptolemy, a list of Babylonian (and Assyrian) kings that was translated into Greek and preserved for astronomical purposes. Because of these records, we have a more exact chronology for these centuries than we have for almost any other period of ancient history anywhere in the world. This is particularly important for Biblical chronology.

When we go back to the 2d millennium B.C., we find that Assyrian chronology is fixed to within a decade as far as the early 15th century B.C. Before this, the Khorsabad List, which contains the names of kings and most of their regnal years back to the beginning of the 2d millennium, may give us a reliable chronological basis. Unfortunately, however, its figures sometimes seem to disagree radically with scattered dates given by various Assyrian kings for rulers who lived in earlier times, and there are also serious discrepancies between the statements of these later kings about earlier chronology. The chronology here adopted is based on a combination of Babylonian and Assyrian data, as well as of various astronomical calculations. It was independently proposed by William F. Albright and Friedrich Cornelius in 1942; its dating is about 64 years later than that given by Sidney Smith and about 120 years later than the chronology of Albrecht Goetze, but is over 20 years higher than that of Ernst F. Weidner—to mention only the more generally recognized alternatives. However, careful archaeological investigation of an increasing number of contacts with Egypt, whose chronology is fixed astronomically back to the beginning of the 20th century B.C., has convinced many scholars that the lower alternatives are preferable to the higher chronologies. Radiocarbon datings have completely disproved the excessively high dates for still earlier Mesopotamian history which were current in the early years of the 20th century.

Beginnings of Assyrian History. From the excavations of Ephraim A. Speiser at Tepe Gawra (1926–1928), followed by the work of Campbell Thompson at Nineveh, of Max Edgar Lucien Mallowan at Tell Arpachiya (1937–1939), and of Fuad Safar at Hassuna (to mention only the most important undertakings in this field), we possess a detailed knowledge of the succession of sedentary cultures in this region from the beginning of village settlement to the introduction of writing about 300 B.C.

The discovery by Robert J. Braidwood in 1950 of prepottery Neolithic settlements at Qalat Jarmo, Iraq, just beyond the southeastern limits of Assyria, has been followed by similar finds all around the periphery of northern Mesopotamia, including sites in Assyria proper. In the river valleys and alluvial plains, sites of such remote periods (chiefly between 7500 and 5500 B.C.) are buried under the modern water table and are thus inaccessible to excavators.

Not later than the early 6th millennium B.C. pottery was invented somewhere in the ancient East, and its use spread with great rapidity. Remains of neolithic pottery from the first half of the 5th millennium B.C. are found at Nineveh and elsewhere in Assyria. This phase was followed by a series of cultures characterized by painted pottery: the Hassunan, Samarran, Halafian, and Obeidian cultures, each named after the site where it was first clearly distinguished. There is a rather steady advance in elaboration of techniques and in complexity of decorative motifs until the height of the Halafian, somewhere about the second quarter of the 4th millennium B.C.

During the Obeidian, in the middle centuries of the same millennium, pottery styles were simplified, presumably because earthenware was being displaced by stone and metal containers, but there was a remarkable development of architecture. Babylonia, which was not settled as early as the northern valleys of Mesopotamia, then gained a cultural ascendancy which was never lost in later history. It is certain that the pottery styles of the Obeidian period were largely borrowed from the south, and it is highly probable that the complex brick architecture of Tepe Gawra temples was also imitated from the similar constructions of contemporary Babylonia, best known from the Iraq excavations at Eridu and the chronologically later German finds at Erech (Warka).

We know from archaeological finds at Ashur, Tell Khuweira (just west of Assyria proper), and other sites that Assyria participated in the early dynastic culture of Sumerian Babylonia. From contemporary finds and later allusions we know that Assyria formed part of the empire of Sargon of Akkad and his successors (about 2300–2200 B.C.); it was also subject in part, at least, to the Babylonian kings of the 3d dynasty of Ur III (about 2050–1950 B.C.). Since the publication of the Khorsabad King-List in 1942 it has become evident that the Assyrian scholars of the 8th century B.C. knew little about the history of their country before the end of the 3d millennium. With characteristic honesty they admitted that no *limmu* dates were preserved before Erishum (about 1885–1845 B.C.). Of the 32 earlier kings whose names appear in the list, the last 17 are certainly, in the main, historical, since several have left inscriptions and others are mentioned in documents from the second millennium.

The Assyrian Empire, about 700 B.C.

ADAPTED FROM PLATE XI(A) IN THE ''WESTMINSTER HISTORICAL ATLAS TO THE BIBLE,''
COPYRIGHT 1945 BY THE WESTMINSTER PRESS, AND USED BY SPECIAL PERMISSION

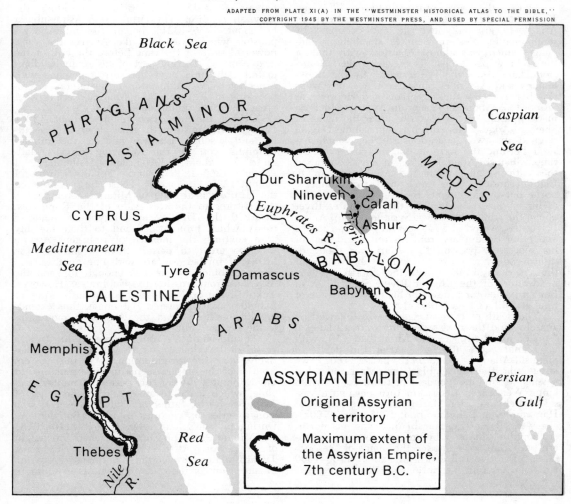

But the first 15 kings, who are said in the list to have "dwelt in tents," bear strange names, which may in part be of mythological origin. It is curious that the second of these should bear the name "Adam (u)," like the progenitor of mankind in Hebrew tradition.

Old Assyrian Empire. We reach solid ground with the reign of Puzur-Ashur I, who reigned about 1950 B.C. During the two centuries covered by his reign and those of his successors, the political power of Assyria expanded in all directions, and it became a wealthy commercial empire, with merchant colonies and trading posts hundreds of miles away. Ilushumma overran Babylonia about 1900 B.C., and his four successors organized a very lucrative trade with Asia Minor, documented from thousands of economic tablets discovered at Kanish (now Kultepe) and elsewhere in Cappadocia. The language of these tablets is Old Assyrian, and they are dated by the Assyrian eponyms of the year (*limmu*). Curiously enough, our knowledge of the Old Assyrian language is still derived almost exclusively from economic texts found in far-off Anatolia, at least 700 miles (1,130 km) away over the roads of that time. These trading stations lasted nearly a century (between 1875 and 1775 B.C.), and they provide a unique example of stable relations between foreign merchants and local rulers (Hittite) nearly four thousand years ago.

During the two centuries between 1950 and 1750 B.C., the settled regions of southwestern Asia were gradually overrun and occupied by seminomadic Western Semites speaking a language which was almost identical with that of the Hebrew patriarchs. They were called *Amurrium*, later *Amurru*, "Westerners," by the Babylonians and Assyrians; in later times this word was borrowed by the Egyptians and Hebrews as "Amorite." About 1748 B.C. an Amorite chieftain made himself king of Assyria under the name of Shamshi-Adad. He and his son, Ishme-Dagan, reigned for two generations, during which Assyria became the most important power of the time. Shamshi-Adad I claims to have conquered the entire region from the Mediterranean to Elam (southwestern Iran), and this claim is borne out by documents found in different parts of his empire. At Mari, on the Euphrates River above the frontier between Syria and Iraq, André Parrot discovered in 1935 several thousand letters and other documents from his reign and that of his successor, proving that Mari was then administered by a son of the king as a province of the Assyrian Empire. Further north, at the headwaters of the Khabur River, Shamshi-Adad built a palace for himself in his new residence of Shubat-Ellil (Chagar Bazar).

The death of Ishme-Dagan I was followed by anarchy, and the next seven rulers are all labeled "son of a nobody" in the Khorsabad List, with no regnal years attached. After the death of Shamshi-Adad I about 1716 B.C. (1780?) we know from the Mari tablets that Mari and other vassals became independent of the great Assyrian king. Weakened, Assyria in turn became a vassal of Babylon after Mari's fall before armies of Hammurabi of Babylon about 1696 B.C. (1760?). Ten years later Hammurabi died and his northern empire collapsed before attacks from northern barbarians who flooded the plains of Mesopotamia. For two full centuries (about 1700–1500 B.C.) no Assyrian inscriptions are known and the country must have been politically weak, if not a vassal state. We know that Horites (Hurrians) and Indo-Aryans from the east and north then migrated in force into Syria and Palestine, and it appears probable that Assyria was at least part of the time under their domination. About the middle of the 17th century B.C. one Bel-bani, son of Adasi, became king and founded a dynasty that still held the throne of Assyria, according to the claim of Esarhaddon, a full thousand years later.

Middle Assyrian Empire. With Ashurnirari I, about 1500 B.C., Assyrian inscriptions begin again. During the following century the fortunes of the state seem to have been unstable. We hear of treaties between Assyrian and Cossaean (Kassite) Babylonia, which at least prove that Assyria was an independent state during part of the time, but we also learn that Assyria was at war with the Indo-Aryan kingdom of Mitanni to the west and that Nineveh was in Mitannian hands. It would appear that Assyria became a vassal of Mitanni during part of this period. When Thutmose III of Egypt conquered Syria and drove the Mitanni forces beyond the Euphrates, about 1450 B.C., the king of Assyria is reported to have sent him rich gifts—doubtless as a token of union against the common Mitannian foe. It was, however, not the Egyptians but the Hittites who finally brought Mitanni to its knees about 1360 B.C. and made it possible for Eriba-Adad (about 1383–1357) to begin rebuilding the Assyrian Empire. The latter's son, Ashur-uballit I (about 1356–1321) began the military expansion which was to make Assyria the most powerful state of the time before the end of the next century. During part of his reign he dominated Babylonia, and his correspondence with Amenhotep IV (Akhenaton), the famous "heretic" king of Egypt, in the Amarna Letters is of great historical significance.

During the next two reigns (about 1320–1299) Assyrian strength grew slowly but steadily, and a solid basis was laid for the military triumphs won by the following kings: Adad-nirari I (about 1298–1266), Shalmaneser I (about 1265–1236), and Tukulti-Ninurta I (about 1235–1199 B.C.). These kings conquered the Hittite vassal state of Mitanni, forcing back the Hittites to the west side of the Euphrates. In 1270 the Hittites and Egyptians made a treaty which brought an end to their hostility of a century; the menace of resurgent Assyria was too great to permit them to indulge the luxury of further warfare with one another, and their combined power was enough to keep the Assyrians from crossing the Euphrates. However, Tukulti-Ninurta I defeated Kashtiliash, king of Babylon, and conquered Babylonia, thus extending his territory from the Armenian mountains to the Persian Gulf.

Tukulti-Ninurta's son became in his turn a vassal of Babylonia, and Assyria remained relatively weak for several reigns. Yet the western frontier of the empire seems to have remained at the Euphrates during this period of military decline, which came to an end with the reign of Asshur-resh-ishi, father of Tiglath-pileser I, who won a series of victories over the Babylonians. During his son's long reign (about 1116–1078) the Middle Assyrian Empire reached the height of its power. At the beginning of his reign Tiglath-pileser drove the Phrygians (Assyrian Mushke) out of their advanced posts in southern

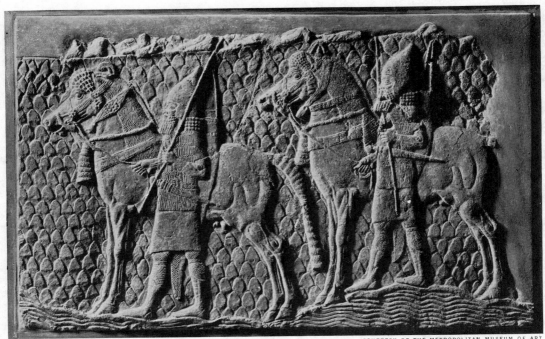

ASSYRIAN ALABASTER SLAB from the palace of Sennacherib (704–681 B.C.) at Nineveh shows war regalia.

Armenia, to which they had penetrated after the collapse of the Hittite Empire (about 1200 B.C.). Farther west he occupied Syria and Phoenicia, and carried out a long series of campaigns against the Aramaeans in Mesopotamia and Syria. The mountain peoples of Armenia and the Zagros Mountains were subdued. On the other hand, he did not succeed in crushing the kings of the 4th dynasty of Babylon, though he forced them back into their own borders and captured Babylon.

We have a wealth of written material from the Middle Assyrian period, illustrating the solid bureaucratic organization of the state and the efforts made to preserve order. The Middle Assyrian laws, discovered in the palace of Tiglath-pileser I, are particularly instructive, since they indicate a systematic attempt to preserve the ancient mores by imposing extremely severe penalties for crimes and even for acts which we should regard as mere misdemeanors. In this respect the Assyrian laws are much more drastic than any other laws preserved from the ancient East; they may be compared with the attempt of Draco to stamp out crime and raise moral standards in Athens by punitive legislation some five centuries later.

After the death of the great king, his successors steadily lost ground before the advancing Aramaeans. Under Ashur-rabi II (about 1012–972) the Aramaeans drove the Assyrians from their ancient Euphrates frontier, and under his grandson, Tiglath-pileser II (about 966–935), they advanced as far as the Tigris, confining Assyria to its narrowest recorded limits. Assyria was reduced to dire straits, and the poverty of its people is vividly described in the inscriptions of Asshur-dan II (934–912), under whom the Assyrian Empire began its long climb back to its former power.

Late Assyrian Empire—First Phase. Asshur-dan II and his son Adad-nirari II (911–891) were chiefly concerned with the restoration of Assyrian strength by procuring cavalry horses and increasing the area of cultivated land. Again and again they struck back at the ring of Aramaean tribes and states that had become established around the western and southern borders of Assyria proper. The father conquered the Aramaean states in the Tigris Valley itself, northwest of Nineveh, and his son captured Nisibis (modern Nusaybin). Raids as far as the Euphrates brought in booty and tested the strength of the Aramaeans. The next king, Tukulti-Ninurta II (890–884), continued the task of subjugating the Aramaeans in the Khabur basin (northeastern Syria) and southward as far as the Babylonian frontier. His son, Ashurnasirpal II (883–859), fought the Aramaeans in campaigns of unprecedented terrorism, laying waste their territory and butchering their population to the accompaniment of savage torture. In all the Assyrian records of war, replete as most of them are with harrowing details of savage cruelty, no other inscriptions approach the sadistic ferocity which throughout characterizes his military narratives. Yet he possessed an energy which carried his armies across the Euphrates to the Mediterranean, thus restoring the empire of Tiglath-pileser I, more than two centuries earlier.

The next Assyrian king, Shalmaneser III (858–824 B.C.), seems to have had his father's drive for power without his unequaled ferocity; so it is scarcely surprising that he was able to continue the consolidation of the empire without the constant revolts that were a feature of his father's reign. The first years of his reign were devoted mainly to strengthening his position in western Mesopotamia and the northernmost part of Syria, in preparation for an all-out attack on a coalition of Aramaean, Phoenician, Palestinian, and other states, headed by Hadad-ezer (Ben-hadad II) of Damascus. The Syrians also prepared elaborately to resist the Assyrian irruption: Hamath (which was directly in the path of the enemy) contributed 1,200 chariots, 700 cavalry, 10,000 infantry; Damascus sent 1,200 chariots, 1,200 cavalry, and 20,000 footmen; while Ahab of Israel provided 2,000 chariots and 10,000 footmen. The head of the Arab tribes of the Syrian Desert sent a thousand camel-riders, and even Egypt contributed a thousand archers. The battle was joined in 853 B.C. at Qarqar on the Orontes. The Assyrians seem to have won the day, but at such a cost that they retired to their own land in order to reorganize. In subsequent invasions of Syria the allies continued to stand their ground, but internecine conflicts broke out (such as that between the Syrian king and Ahab of Israel), and after the death of Hadad-ezer (Benhadad II) the latter's successor, Hazael, was forced to abandon his capital and fortify himself in the mountains (841 B.C.). Israel (under Jehu) and many other former members of the coalition submitted to Assyria, thus further weakening the Aramaeans. However, Shalmaneser was unable to conquer Damascus, and even later in his reign Aram still proved too hard a nut to crack. Elsewhere Shalmaneser gained numerous victories, and he finally succeeded in subjugating Babylonia.

Two years before Shalmaneser's death one of his sons rebelled against him and was supported by most of the empire. The rebellion was not suppressed until two years after the accession of the legitimate king, Shamshi-Adad V (823–811), and by this time Assyria had lost its recently conquered vassals all around the periphery of the empire. Incidentally, this respite from Assyrian attack enabled Hazael of Damascus to conquer Israel (about 815 B.C.). Shamshi-Adad died prematurely, and his young heir, Adadnirari III (810–783), was for four years under the control of the queen-regent Sammuramat, the legendary and mythical Queen of Assyria.

The tremendous impression made on the warlike Assyrians and Aramaeans by this interlude of female rule is vividly illustrated by the way in which later historical tradition is dominated by the towering figure of Semiramis, as the Greeks called her. After Adadnirari had been freed from his mother's control, he at once began a hitherto unparalleled career of conquest, which brought the subjugation of Damascus and acknowledgment of vassal status on the part of other Syro-Palestinian states (including Israel but not Judah), the conquest of Babylonia, and the reduction to vassalage of a large part of Media, as far as the Caspian Sea. Only in the north is no advance of Assyrian arms recorded; there, the kingdom of Urartu was growing rapidly and was already powerful enough to put the Assyrians on their guard.

It would seem that something happened to interrupt the advance of Assyrian arms in the middle of Adadnirari's reign as sole monarch, since all recorded victories of consequence appear to date from the first half of his reign of 28 years, and because—contrary to the practice of all other successful rulers of the Neo-Assyrian Empire—we have no detailed annals or other records of his campaigns. At all events, from about 797 on, we hear nothing of further invasions of Syria and virtually nothing about any military exploits. His three successors, whose reigns covered the period from 782 to 745, continued to lose the ground won by Adadnirari during the first years of his reign. Syria was left almost entirely to itself, after repeated thrusts had failed to win any decisive success. It thus became possible for several strong states to be established in Syria and Palestine, and they were to try the mettle of the next king. In Armenia the increase in the power of Urartu was so spectacular as to threaten Assyria proper; Argistis and Sarduris of Urartu controlled the whole of Armenia and the territories immediately to the west, north, and east. Revolts abroad were followed by revolts at home. Assyria was still the most powerful nation in southwestern Asia, but its prestige was ebbing fast.

Second Phase. In 746 a rebellion in the city of Calah brought Tiglath-pileser III to the throne. We know nothing about his background, and the evident hostility of later kings to his memory suggests that he was not of royal blood. In any case, he proved to be a ruler of extraordinary ability, who restored Assyrian prestige and founded the last and greatest phase of the Assyrian Empire. At his accession he found Assyrian fortunes at their lowest point since the early 9th century. His first campaign was aimed at the subjugation of the Chaldaean tribesmen of southern Babylonia and the restoration of that rich land to its normal state of Assyrian vassalage. He then pacified the eastern frontiers of Assyria in the Zagros Mountains and western Media.

In 743 he fought and won a decisive battle with Sarduris of Urartu on the upper Euphrates and began the reconquest of Syria. According to the Assyrian story, Uzziah of Judah was apparently the mastermind behind elaborate plans for resistance. But Uzziah died about 742 and the coalition fell apart. Arpad, the northernmost of the hostile states of Syria, was taken in 740, after a blockade of two years. In 734 the Assyrians swept down the Philistine plain and captured Gaza; the next year Israel was overrun and the territories of Galilee, Megiddo, Dor, and Gilead were detached and turned into Assyrian provinces. Two years later Damascus fell.

Shortly afterwards Tiglath-pileser broke with the time-honored practice of appointing Babylonians as vassal kings and took the title of king of Babylon himself. Had it not been for the stubborn resistance of the still only half-settled Chaldaean tribes, the Assyrian Empire might have become a dual monarchy. He broke with tradition in another, even more important way. Instead of enslaving or exterminating chronic rebels he executed some of the leaders and moved the bulk of the population to other regions which had been or were being pacified in a similar way. While this method was little more humane, and was scarcely intended to be, it broke nationalistic movements without reducing the Assyrian vassal states to unproductive wastes. Thereafter it became the standard Assyro-Babylonian method of crushing intransigent rebels. To be sure, it broke the spirit of the entire empire, whose various nationalities lost their own particularisms without becoming loyal Assyrians. With the disappearance of patriotism, Assyria was unable to resist aggressors, and it finally collapsed with unprecedented speed.

After the short reign of Tiglath-pileser's son, Shalmaneser V (726–722), Sargon II became king (721–705), reviving a famous name of much earlier centuries. Sargon's predecessor had laid siege to Samaria, but the Israelite capital did not fall until the first months of the new king's

PALACE OF ASHURNASIRPAL II (883–859 B.C.) at Calah (Nimrud) yielded this limestone wall slab.

reign; the Israelite population of the rump state left by the surgery of Tiglath-pileser was deported to the northern and eastern provinces of the Assyrian Empire. The same fate soon afterwards befell the major states left in Syria; Hamath fell in 720 and Carchemish in 717. Three years after completing the pacification of Syria, Sargon II was ready for the chief campaign of his reign—the invasion of Urartu (Armenia), in 714. Thanks to a vivid description of this campaign in the longest preserved Assyrian historical text (the Eighth Campaign of Sargon), we are able to follow details and even to admire the rugged scenery of the mountain regions through which the Assyrian army passed. It resulted in the complete devastation of the richest provinces of Urartu, whose power was effectively broken. In Babylonia, Sargon was less successful, and throughout his reign he had trouble with a redoubtable Chaldaean chieftain, known in the Bible as Merodach-baladan, who sent an embassy to Hezekiah in order to solicit the latter's aid in his rebellion against Assyria. Perhaps because he wished to break with the immediate past, Sargon removed his capital from Calah to the new site called Dur Sharrukin (modern Khorsabad) after his own name. Since virtually all buildings and objects found here can be dated to his reign, excavations have been of great value to historians.

Sargon's son, Sennacherib (704–681), lacked either his father's ability or his good fortune—possibly both. Scarcely had he become king when rebellions began to break out, first in Babylonia and then in Phoenicia and Palestine. The Chaldaeans continued to make trouble for him in Babylonia throughout his reign, and his rule was so oppressive that the native Babylonians welcomed them as liberators. In 701 he invaded the west and swept through it with fire and sword to the Egyptian frontier. Hezekiah, king of Judah, was reduced to abject submission, and a heavy payment of tribute was imposed on him, recorded in nearly the same figures (30 talents of gold and 300 or 800 talents of silver) in Biblical and cuneiform records. Ten years later the Babylonians and Elamites levied a strong army and succeeded in defeating Sennacherib at Khalule, east of the Tigris. This sensational disaster brought new rebellions in the west, led apparently again by Hezekiah, with the encouragement of Tirhakah, the young Nubian king of Egypt (689–664). Before taking the road against the western rebels, Sennacherib stormed and destroyed Babylon itself (689). However, the Assyrian invasion of the west, which followed before Hezekiah's death in 686 B.C., was terminated abruptly by pestilence (according to the brief but vivid Biblical account). We learn nothing more about the reign of Sennacherib until he was assassinated by his two sons.

The triumph of the parricides was brief; they were defeated by their brother Esarhaddon (680–669) and forced to flee to Armenia. In spite of his short reign, Esarhaddon ranks among the greatest kings of Assyria. He rebuilt Babylon and made it one of his chief capitals, consolidating Assyrian control of Babylonia. He regained control of parts of Media and Arabia that seem to have been lost by his father. He invaded Egypt, and after an initial setback he captured Memphis. In the northwest he blunted the force of the onslaught of the Cimmerians and Scythians, who had crossed the barrier of the Caucasus Mountains and had broken through the ring of small states which formed the outer defenses of the Assyrian Empire. Though Assyria lost much ground there, it was at least spared a disastrous barbarian invasion at that period in its history.

Esarhaddon's son, Ashurbanipal (Assurbanipal), who reigned for about 36 years (668–633), was the last great king of Assyria. He was known to the Romans as Sardanapalus, who figured in sensational legends in which he was confused with other Mesopotamian rulers of the same general period. After finishing the conquest of Egypt, begun by his father, he had to return to the Nile Valley to suppress another rebellion, headed by the Nubians. Thebes was sacked in 663, and there is no definite record of further rebellion, though Psammetichus (Psamtik I), founder of the 26th dynasty of Egypt, was able to assert his independence and later appears as Assyria's ally instead of as its vassal. Esarhaddon had divided the Assyrian Empire between two of his sons who were full brothers, Ashurbanipal and Shamash-shum-ukin. The latter became king of Babylon. However, he resented his inferior status, and a bloody war broke out, ending in 648 with a ghastly massacre of the inhabitants of Babylon.

The four years' war had greatly weakened the empire, especially since most of the outlying satellites of Assyria had joined the rebels. Ashurbanipal proceeded to crush the Elamites and the Arabs. The destruction of the powerful Elamite kingdom opened the way for the rise of a new Aryan state, already called "Persia," whose first known king, Cyrus I, accepted Assyrian suzerainty after the collapse of Elam. The struggle with the Arabs took longer, owing to the difficulty of carrying on successful warfare in the desert, but they too submitted in the end. However, the Arabs seem to have continued to occupy most of the agricultural areas which they had taken over at the beginning of the rebellion. The apparent triumph of Assyrian arms everywhere was crowned by the nominal submission of the king of Urartu (Armenia) and of Gyges, king of Lydia.

Under Ashurbanipal the higher culture of Assyria reached its climax. Never before had the fine arts been so cultivated, nor had they reached such technical perfection as in his reign. The king claimed to have become an expert in the complex system of cuneiform writing, and he certainly devoted part of his time to the encouragement of learning. His scholars were sent to the old towns of Babylonia to collect and copy rare tablets in Sumerian and Akkadian (Assyro-Babylonian). His great library at Nineveh contained tens of thousands of tablets (many of which are now in London's British Museum), all copied in the beautiful and remarkably legible script which was cultivated for calligraphic purposes. To the king's scholarly interest we owe much of our knowledge of Assyrian and Babylonian literature as well as of higher culture in general.

The death of the great king (probably in 633) was followed by a period of rapid decline, in which it speedily appeared that the seeming might of the empire was only a sham façade, covering the total bankruptcy of the ancient social organization of the state. We have no more historical inscriptions from the last Assyrian kings (about 633–606), and if it were not for the valuable tablet (published in 1923) of the Babylonian Chronicle, which contains the annals of the years 616–609, we should know next to nothing about the last decades of the Assyrian Empire.

Apparently a struggle for power broke out between the two successors of Ashurbanipal, in the course of which the Chaldaean governor of Babylonia, Nabopolassar, declared his independence and entered into an alliance with Cyaxares, king of Media. This struggle began before 616, and the Medes and the Babylonians rapidly beat down the Assyrian defenses. In 614 the ancient capital, Ashur, was stormed and destroyed by the Medes, and two years later Nineveh itself met with the same fate, King Sin-shar-ishkun perishing in the siege. Ashur-uballit II then became king and set up his capital at Harran in western Mesopotamia, in close proximity to his Egyptian allies, who had taken advantage of the situation to annex Palestine and Syria to their own empire although they were ostensibly aiding Assyria. Harran fell to the Medes between 608 and 606, and the Assyrian Empire collapsed completely, to the great delight of its former subjects, who had suffered from the cruelty and rapacity of their overlords for so long. So far as we know, no attempt was ever made to restore the Assyrian state, though the ancient gods were still worshiped in Parthian Ashur as late as the 3d century A.D.

Assyrian Literature. As already indicated, the Assyrians were more interested in military achievements than in the arts of peace, and they seem always to have looked up to the primacy of Babylonia in religion, science, and literature. Nearly all Assyrian literary texts that have been preserved to us in the libraries of Ashur, Nineveh, Harran, and other cities, are copied or adapted from Babylonian originals. Even the royal inscriptions of the Assyrian kings were mostly written in standard contemporary Babylonian, and later Assyrian literature is nearly all composed in the same Middle Babylonian literary language as was used in the south. The Assyrian dialect of Akkadian was used in the earliest historical inscriptions from the Old Empire, as well as in the economic texts from Cappadocia. It appears in a later form in Middle Assyrian letters, business documents, and ritual tablets, and was revived in a still later form in Late Assyrian times. From the 7th century B.C. we have a highly interesting collection of official letters and oracles in the native dialect; the latter throw much light on life and religion in this period, which is of such great interest to students of contemporary Biblical literature.

See also ASSYRIOLOGY, BABYLONIA; and articles on the principal kings and cities mentioned in this article.

WILLIAM F. ALBRIGHT
Johns Hopkins University

Bibliography

Gadd, Cyril John, *The Stones of Assyria* (Toronto 1936).
Hall, Harry R.H., *The Ancient History of the Near East*, 8th ed. rev. by Cyril J. Gadd (London 1932).
Luckenbill, Daniel D., ed., *Ancient Records of Assyria and Babylonia: Historical Records of Assyria* (Chicago 1926–1927).
Olmstead, Albert T.E., *History of Assyria*, reprint (Chicago 1960).
Poebel, Arno, "The Assyrian King List from Khorsabad" in *Journal of Near Eastern Studies*, vols. 1, 2 (Chicago 1942–1943).
Pritchard, James B., ed., *Ancient Near Eastern Texts Relating to the Old Testament*, rev. ed. (Princeton, N.J., 1955).
Rogers, Robert W., *A History of Babylonia and Assyria*, 5th ed. (New York 1915).
Smith, Sidney, *Early History of Assyria* (London 1928).

A ROYAL BANQUET for King Ashurbanipal (668–633 B.C.) is depicted in this slab from his palace at Nineveh.

ASSYRIOLOGY

ASSYRIOLOGY, ə-sir-ē-ol′ə-jē, is the study that deals with the language, literature, society, and history of the ancient peoples of Assyria and Babylonia, which together are called by the Greek name "Mesopotamia." Since the Assyrian and Babylonian empires extended far beyond the valleys of the Tigris and Euphrates rivers and because their cuneiform system of writing was borrowed by the Horites and Hittites, Amorites and Canaanites, Elamites and Old Persians, as well as by the ancient Armenians and other peoples north of Mesopotamia, the term "Assyriology" is often used to cover these related fields as well.

As a rule, the Assyriologist specializes in the inscriptions and their interpretation, but since it is exceedingly hard to differentiate clearly between inscriptions and their content, and between higher and lower culture, he also becomes historian and sociologist, geographer, and anthropologist, as well as philologian. In no field of study, except perhaps Egyptology, is it quite so necessary to understand an entire civilization in order to interpret both written documents and other archaeological objects.

Owing to the relative indestructibility of clay tablets, enormous masses of them have survived under the ruins of buried settlements. They carry us back to a higher antiquity than any other written documents of mankind, and they furnish more firsthand evidence for man's institutional life and higher culture before the second half of the last thousand years B.C. than Egyptian, early Biblical, Vedic, and early Chinese literary remains taken together. Of the greatest value for the historian and the student of cultural anthropology is the fact that cuneiform inscriptions may all be dated within narrow limits. Also, their contents are indisputably older than parallel phenomena in other cultures.

History of Assyriology. Curiously enough, not a single description of cuneiform writing has come down to us from antiquity, and this script itself seems to have become extinct not long after the 1st century A.D., to which belong the latest dated tablets yet found. In contrast to the wealth of true and false information about Egypt preserved by Graeco-Roman authors, relatively few data about ancient Mesopotamian history and civilization were handed down, and what has been transmitted has mostly proved to be misleading. In early modern times no scholar or traveler had the least idea about the wealth of art and literature hidden under the soil of Assyria and Babylonia.

It was not until the early 17th century that the Italian explorer Pietro della Valle showed sufficient curiosity to copy a few signs in Old Persian cuneiform at Persepolis and to take a few stamped bricks from the ruins of Babylon. In 1711, Jean Chardin, a French traveler, published the first copy of a cuneiform inscription (a trilingual text in Old Persian, Babylonian, and Elamite), and other copies were published in the following decades. Toward the end of the century the Danish explorer Carsten Niebuhr published a considerable group of these inscriptions from Persepolis, and work on their decipherment began in 1798. Georg Friedrich Grotefend, a German, succeeded in laying a sound basis for interpretation in 1802, but so great was the prejudice against such innovations that he was unable to publish his revolutionary discoveries until 13 years later. Progress then became more rapid, and the publication (1846–1851) of the great rock inscription of Darius I at Behistun (Bisitun) in Media (western Iran) by the Englishman Sir Henry Rawlinson gave a solid basis for reading both Old Persian and Babylonian. By 1850 it had become possible to translate simple Assyrian inscriptions with general accuracy.

The period of excavation was begun by the French in December 1842, with Paul Émile Botta's first work at Nineveh, followed by his long and very successful campaign at Khorsabad (northern Iraq), the ancient city of Sargon II. In 1847 a selection of the monuments uncovered by Botta was exhibited at the Louvre and created a sensation. In 1845 the Englishman Austen Henry Layard began excavation at the old Assyrian capital of Calah (Nimrud), followed by other brilliantly successful excavations, whose chief finds were placed in the British Museum. French and British scholars vied with one another in interpreting the new documents, and by 1860 the period of decipherment may be said to have been completed. Meanwhile the outbreak of the Crimean War in 1854 put an abrupt end to the first period of excavations, which were not resumed for 18 years. This period of enforced inactivity in the field was fortunately characterized by activity in British and French research, as well as by the beginnings of German interest in Assyriology.

In 1872 excavations were resumed in Assyria by the British with great success, particularly in recovering Assyrian tablets. Five years later the French began the extraordinary series of campaigns at Telloh (ancient Lagash) in southern Babylonia that disclosed the civilization of the Sumerians, who had preceded the Semites in Mesopotamia. The Americans entered the scene in 1889, digging at the great site of Nippur in central Babylonia until 1900, with sensational results, as described by Hermann Volrath Hilprecht. Unfortunately, all excavations undertaken in Mesopotamia up to that time, with scarcely an exception, were badly recorded or not recorded at all, the entire emphasis being placed on the discovery of museum objects and inscriptions.

A new phase began in 1899 when the Germans began to excavate at Babylon (until 1917), under Robert Koldewey. Four years later, work began at Ashur (Asshur), the oldest capital of Assyria, under Koldewey's assistant, Walter Andrae. Both men were trained historical architects, and the work was fully and exactly recorded in a series of splendid volumes. The introduction of rigidly scientific method into Mesopotamian archaeology through their example was to revolutionize our knowledge of the subject, replacing vagueness by precision and chaos by order. Unhappily, the first German excavators neglected to have the inscriptions studied by specialists and rejected the use of pottery for dating purposes, so that all their engineering and architectural skill was still not fully adequate to present-day requirements. Yet they were far superior to all other excavators who worked in Mesopotamia during the same period. Scarcely any subsequent expedition has had such large funds at its disposal, and no one has dared to resume the formidable task of excavating the great city of Babylon.

After 1919 work continued actively; between the two World Wars the number of excavations increased until there were as many as a dozen expeditions in the field at one time. Most important among these undertakings were campaigns by the Englishman Sir Charles Leonard Woolley at Ur (1922–1934), and by Julius Jordan, Arnold Nöldeke, and others at Erech (modern Warka) in southern Babylonia (1927–1939). These excavations were particularly important in their attention to all aspects of excavation, architecture, inscriptions, and pottery; they vastly enlarged our knowledge of the earliest periods of Babylonian history, before the middle of the 3d millennium B.C. Next to these major excavations must be placed the well-organized and well-conducted work of the Oriental Institute of the University of Chicago in several mounds in the valley of the Diyala River in northeastern Babylonia (between 1930 and 1938), under the direction of Henri Frankfort and Pinhas Delougaz. The same organization also undertook important excavations elsewhere, notably in Sargon's capital of Dur Sharrukin (modern Khorsabad).

Starting about the time of World War II the Iraqi government entered the field of excavation with numerous small and large digs, among which the excavation of Eridu in the extreme south of Babylonia, beginning in 1946, is particularly important. Among other undertakings were the resumption of German excavations at Erech (Warka) and of British digs at Calah (Nimrud), as well as of American work at Nippur. Important excavations in more peripheral regions include the epoch-making work of the Frenchman André Parrot at Mari on the middle Euphrates (1933–1939, and after 1950).

Without adequate progress in systematizing and interpreting the results of excavation, they would remain of little value. In 1872, German scholars, headed by Eberhard Schrader and Friedrich Delitzsch, began to publish systematic treatises and special investigations, employing the rigidly scientific philological method developed by German classical and Oriental scholarship in the early 19th century. This method was characterized by the utmost attainable accuracy in publishing the new material, and by application of strict principles of inductive and deductive logic, constantly testing inferences by applying them to new material. Delitzsch published the first systematic Akkadian (Assyro-Babylonian) and Sumerian grammars and dictionaries, based on comprehensive collection and methodical classification of all words and grammatical forms. His pupils carried his method further, and their pupils are now continuing the work of organizing the mass of cuneiform data into manageable form. Bruno Meissner, Delitzsch's student, classified the material found in the inscriptions with special reference to legal and economic institutions, arts and crafts, and the like. Heinrich Zimmern did the same for religion, and his pupil Benno Landsberger has contributed brilliantly to almost every branch of Assyriology. There are now scores of active Assyriologists in the United States, Britain, France, Germany, Iraq, and elsewhere, who are continuing the best traditions of the great German school.

Sumerian Script and Language. The cuneiform script of later Mesopotamia was probably invented by the Sumerians during the last centuries of the 3000's B.C. When we first find it used on clay tablets for business records, about 3100 B.C., the original picture writing had been simplified and phonetic elements already appear. In the following five centuries or so, the cuneiform ("wedge-shaped") appearance of the strokes, which were impressed on clay to form characters, grows steadily, as we know from successive groups of tablets from the intervening centuries. The form of characters carved on stone monuments remained much more archaic, and at certain periods the difference is most pronounced.

The Sumerian language has not been connected successfully with any other known tongue of ancient or modern times, though there are still a number of inadequately explored possibilities. It had already split up into a number of dialects with striking phonetic differences before the middle of the 3d millennium; for example, *dug* ("good") in the standard dialect is *zeb* in the next most important dialect. In view of such facts, it can hardly have been brought into Mesopotamia after the beginning of sedentary occupation there in the early 3000's. An even earlier date for its first appearance in the Tigris and Euphrates valleys is suggested by the fact that the names of the rivers in the region can nearly all be easily derived from Sumerian. The structure of Sumerian is semi-incorporating; that is, it incorporates clauses and even whole

INTRICATE MOTIFS appear in this relief from the palace of Sargon II (721–705 B.C.) at Dur Sharrukin.

sentences into the verb complex. It is less bound in this respect than some of the American Indian languages, and the verbal structure is less agglutinative than Turkish or Horite. Sumerian had broken down phonetically to such an extent in the earliest fully intelligible inscriptions that a great many words had become monosyllabic and could scarcely have been distinguished without the use of pitch tones, as in Chinese and Indo-Chinese languages.

Sumerian Written Texts. Texts in Sumerian occur on stone monuments of every size from a large stele to a little cylinder seal, but chiefly on clay tablets, cylinders, and prisms. Nearly 300,-000 are known to have been excavated by official expeditions and by Arabs searching for antiquities. Unilingual texts, written only in Sumerian, date between about 3100 and 1600 B.C.; very few are later. Bilingual texts, in Sumerian and Akkadian, virtually all date from between 1400 B.C. and the beginning of the Christian era. Down to about 1700 B.C., most Sumerian texts are of economic character, such as business contracts, bills of sale, receipts, promissory notes, lists of rations, and inventories. These documents are found in nearly every century, but they are most abundant (partly on account of accidents in locating sites, and partly because of real shifts in the amount of business recorded by scribes) in the late pre-Sargonic age (the 24th century B.C.) and the 3d dynasty of Ur (about 2050–1950 B.C.). There are also legal documents, among them wills, adoptions, records of court cases and decisions, and administrative letters.

Historical texts are relatively rare, less than a thousand being known among a quarter of a million economic and legal texts. Most of them are short dedications and records of building operations, amounting to little but prayers on behalf of the king. However, there are longer texts, some of them of specifically political and military character, like the Stele of Vultures, erected by Eannatum (Eanatoum) of Lagash in the 25th century B.C., and some of them legal and administrative, like the famous decrees of Urukagina of Lagash (about the late 24th century B.C.). Some again are chiefly religious in nature, like the two big cylinders of Gudea, governor of Lagash about 2100 B.C., which form our longest prose texts in pure Sumerian.

Religious and literary texts were handed down by word of mouth until comparatively late periods, just as in many other ancient lands. Discoveries at the sites of Tell Salabikh (near Nippur) and Tell Fara (Shuruppak) have yielded Sumerian literary texts from Early Dynastic II, about the 26th century B.C. They are, accordingly, much the earliest copies of literary texts found anywhere in the world. Our extant unilingual material goes back in substance to the 3d millennium—probably to all parts of it. It is not likely, however, that any appreciable amount of it was put in writing before the time of Ur III, about 2000 B.C. Nearly all preserved copies of this literature come from Nippur and date from the 18th and early 17th centuries B.C., when Sumerian was still the literary language of the land and could be understood by the scribe who copied the texts.

The several thousand literary tablets in Sumerian that have been recovered are written in a minute hand which requires long specialization and a good eye to transcribe correctly. Competent Sumerologists are rare. Most active in the study and publication of these Sumerian texts has been, since 1938, Samuel Noah Kramer of the University of Pennsylvania. From the work of Kramer, materially aided by the investigations of Thorkild Jacobsen and Adam Falkenstein, we now possess a good knowledge of the scope of

Sumerian religious and didactic literature. It comprises mainly epics and myths, hymns and lamentations, proverbs and other didactic writings. A dozen epic tales deal with the exploits of legendary heroes of the past , such as Gilgamesh, Lugalbanda, and Enmerkar; others deal with cosmogonic themes, such as the destruction of the primordial monster of chaos by some god (the hero varies in different forms of the myth). Of particular interest are the proverbs and didactic texts, which prove that "wisdom" literature was as early as any other form of composition in Babylonia.

After 1800 B.C., Akkadian scholars tried their hands at composing Sumerian historical and religious texts, often translating from their own Semitic tongue back into the ancient sacred language. Since they always made mistakes and the errors became greater as time went on, there is seldom any difficulty in detecting the late date of the Sumerian compositions in question. It is an extraordinary fact that Babylonian scholars tried to compose in the old sacred language at least a thousand years after it had become extinct. Sumerian was still read as late as the Christian era, and perhaps even later, or nearly two thousands years after it had ceased to be spoken.

Akkadian Script and Language. The Sumerian script was used to write Akkadian (Assyro-Babylonian) at a very early date—probably well before the oldest Sumerian inscriptions from Lagash, which date from about 2500 B.C. Our oldest inscriptions in Akkadian come from Mari and belong to the 25th century B.C. When Sargon I of Akkad conquered Babylonia about a century later and established the oldest known empire in southwestern Asia, Akkadian (called after his capital, where it first attained court status) became the official tongue of his empire, though Sumerian was still used in southern Babylonia. This stage of Akkadian is now well known from many hundreds of historical and economic texts from the 24th–22d centuries B.C. Sumerian signs were taken over with their ideographic and their phonetic values, but a selection of both meanings and sounds was made for the purpose of simplifying the otherwise impossibly complex system. Since the sounds of Sumerian were often quite different from those of Semitic Akkadian, many adaptations of signs for sounds unknown in Sumerian had to be made. In the course of the subsequent history of Akkadian writing we find a gradual shift in the phonetic values in common use, and many new signs were formed out of old ones, with new phonetic values. In standard Assyro-Babylonian of the last two thousand years B.C. we find an elaborate system of ideograms (that is, word signs adopted from Sumerian and sometimes used with a number of different Akkadian renderings, usually differentiated by adding phonetic complements); determinatives (ideograms prefixed to phonetically or ideographically written words to indicate the class of objects to which they belong: men, women, trees, plants, lands, etc.); and phonetic signs. The last represented either syllables beginning and ending with a consonant (for example, *bar*, *kal*), syllables containing consonant and vowel (e.g., *ra*, *mu*, *ti*), vowel and consonant (e.g., *ar*, *um*, *it*), or simple vowel (*a*, *e*, *i*, *u*).

After Old Akkadian, which was spoken in most of the empire in the late 3d millennium, Akkadian split into dialects and stages of speech.

The most important dialects were Babylonian and Assyrian, which may be divided respectively into Old, Middle, and Late, dating roughly from 2000 to 1500, 1500 to 1000, and 1000 to 500 B.C. After about 500 B.C. Babylonian continued to be written, but Aramaic had become the tongue of the people, and the Akkadian of the latest tablets became more and more artificial, just as Sumerian had a thousand years earlier. In the last centuries of Babylonian higher culture there were actually two extinct languages of learning, both of which are found transcribed into Greek for teaching purposes.

Akkadian Written Texts. Just as in the case of the earlier Sumerian tablets, the overwhelming majority of all known Akkadian texts are economic, administrative, and legal in character. While we have examples from nearly every period in some parts of Mesopotamia, by far the largest number consist of tablets from the dynasty of Larsa and the 1st dynasty of Babylon (18th–16th centuries B.C.), and from neo-Babylonian times (7th–5th centuries B.C.). Very interesting collections come from the Old Assyrian colonies in Cappadocia (19th–18th centuries B.C.), from the Horite (Hurrian) population of the east Tigris country around Kirkuk (15th–14th centuries B.C.), from Middle Assyrian times (14th–11th centuries B.C.), from Kassite (Cossaean) Babylonia (14th–12th centuries B.C.), and from late Assyrian centers (9th–7th centuries B.C.).

Historical inscriptions in Akkadian are abundant, and date from the same general periods as the texts just described. The Old Akkadian historical records contain details about the military operations and conquests of the kings, and this tradition was continued in Assyria, as we know from scattered historical texts of the rulers of the Old Empire (19th–18th centuries), as well as from the royal inscriptions of later times. In Babylonia, curiously enough, we have no official royal inscriptions which mention military activities of any kind, except in passing, though much information about external affairs may be extracted from other inscriptions. Late Assyrian historical records are extraordinarily full and are sources of primary importance for the history of all southwestern Asia and Egypt during the period which they cover (9th–7th centuries B.C.). Some of the longer ones attain a high degree of literary excellence.

Religious and didactic literature first appears in the 1st dynasty of Babylon, about 1700 B.C. and later. Most of it seems to have been transmitted orally from the last centuries of the 3d millennium, though it is still possible that we will find written texts of this type from the dynasty of Akkad. The most archaic class, the so-called hymnal-epic literature, consists of hymns and poetic narratives in literary Old Akkadian, somewhat modified to adapt it to Old Babylonian taste. Nearly all of these texts disappeared and were replaced by Old Babylonian compositions which we know mostly from later copies. In general, all standard Babylonian literary, religious, and other categories of material were carefully edited in the Cossaean (Kassite) period and given a canonical form, which they preserved for over a thousand years.

Akkadian religious literature is exceedingly diversified in character. Most interesting are the epics of mythological or quasi-mythological type, like the Creation Epic (in seven tablets) and

CUNEIFORM WRITING, probably in the Sumerian language, is carved on this marble fragment dated 2600 B.C.

the Gilgamesh Epic (in twelve tablets originally containing about 5,000 lines). There are also a great many hymns and prayers to the gods, ritual and liturgical series, and numerous series of tablets dealing with magic and divination. Divination covered many different types of telling the future by observed omens, which were classified in great detail; there are, for example, astrological omens dealing with astronomical events, hepatoscopic omens describing the appearance of the liver of a sacrificial sheep, omens dealing with monstrous births, and others concerned with the movement of a drop of oil in water. Magic is difficult to separate from medicine, and in late Assyrian times the physician was chiefly a sorcerer.

Science was also cultivated in ancient Mesopotamia. In Old Babylonian times there was great interest in pure and applied mathematics, and astonishing progress was made in the field of algebra. The Babylonians attained distinction in architecture and engineering, but their most remarkable achievements were in astronomy. They were able to predict lunar eclipses by the 8th century B.C. The fact that they were bilingual in two languages of completely different grammatical structure and were accustomed to treating abstract cuneiform signs as bearers of many more or less related meanings, gave them a taste for abstract thought and a facility for dissociating concepts from words that have no counterpart in the ancient world before the 5th century B.C.— and in some respects not even then. They drew up elaborate grammatical tables and dictionaries of signs and words; they also prepared classified lists of gods, animals, plants, and stars, to mention some of the subjects which attracted them.

Besides legal texts dealing with actual cases in social and family life, we have several Akkadian law codes, in particular the Eshnunna Code of the early 18th century B.C. and the Code of Hammurabi (now in the Louvre) of the early 17th century. The latter was copied on clay tablets for more than a thousand years, illustrating its normative character in Babylonian judicial thinking. The Assyrian code from about 1100 B.C. is particularly interesting because of the drastic penalties that it imposes for what we should consider minor offenses. There are also proverbs, fables, and colloquies between exponents of different theories of life, such as the so-called Babylonian Job. Some of these texts are strikingly skeptical in outlook.

Epistolary literature is exceedingly varied and informative. We have official and private letters from every period that is represented by economic texts. Among the richest collections are the administrative letters from 18th century Mari, thousands of which were found by André Parrot in 1935; the administrative letters of King Hammurabi from about the same time; the Amarna Letters, written in Akkadian cuneiform to the Egyptian pharaohs of the early 14th century and discovered in Egypt in 1887; and the royal Assyrian letters from 7th-century Nineveh.

Other National Cuneiform Texts. Owing to the fact that cuneiform was so widely used in antiquity, the Assyriologist finds it necessary to deal with tablets in Akkadian and non-Akkadian cuneiform from many countries around the periphery of Mesopotamia. Particularly important are the Horite (Hurrian) and Hittite cuneiform inscriptions, nearly all on clay tablets like the Assyro-Babylonian. Horite documents are still comparatively few in number, but they are found in many places in Mesopotamia, Syria, and Asia Minor and date between the 24th and 13th centuries B.C. It is now certain that the Horites, with their strange agglutinative tongue, played a considerable part in spreading Babylonian culture. Cuneiform Hittite tablets come mostly from the ancient Hittite capital of Hattusas near modern Ankara in Turkey. They are very numerous and cover almost as diversified a field as contemporary Akkadian tablets from Mesopotamia. The Elamites in later Susiana (southwestern Iran) and the Urartians in Armenia both borrowed the Akkadian cuneiform script for their own languages. On the other hand, the Canaanites of the Mediterranean coast and the Old Persians of Iran invented new quasi-alphabetical scripts, put together from different combinations of simple wedges. Though cuneiform in appearance, they have nothing directly to do with Akkadian but are quite original inventions. The Canaanite (Ugaritic) cuneiform "alphabet" was invented not later than the 15th century B.C., and the Old Persian "alphabet" was introduced not later than the 6th century B.C.

Mesopotamian Civilization. Owing to the extraordinary wealth of material contained in more than half a million cuneiform texts already unearthed, and owing to the way in which the information extracted from them dovetails into other data obtained by excavation, numerous special studies have developed in the field of Assyriology. For example, cuneiform law and legal institutions have become a treasure house for students of comparative law, especially in Europe, where Roman law is still taught in many faculties of law. For the history of marriage, of slavery, of business, and other institutions, the cuneiform sources are of unequaled value because of their great age and their varied character. The study of Mesopotamian flora and fauna, and especially of agriculture and plant and animal breeding, form engrossing subjects. There is a very large body of material bearing on arts and crafts that is important for ethnographic research and for the history of technology. Comparative religion has, however, become the leading study to be influenced by cuneiform research, profiting from the great extent of space and span of time that these records cover.

WILLIAM F. ALBRIGHT
Johns Hopkins University

Bibliography

Chiera, Edward, *They Wrote on Clay*, ed. by George G. Cameron (Chicago 1938).
Frankfort, Henri, *Cylinder Seals* (New York 1939).
Gelb, Ignace J., *Old Akkadian Writing and Grammar* (Chicago 1952).
Heidel, Alexander, *The Gilgamesh Epic and Old Testament Parallels*, 2d ed. (Chicago 1949).
Heidel, Alexander, *The Babylonian Genesis*, 2d ed. (Chicago 1963).
Hilprecht, Hermann V., *Explorations in Bible Lands* (Philadelphia 1903).
Kramer, Samuel N., *Sumerian Mythology* (Philadelphia 1944).
Kramer, Samuel N., *The Sumerians* (Chicago 1963).
Lloyd, Seton, *Foundations in the Dust* (London 1947).
Oppenheim, Adolf Leo, *Ancient Mesopotamia* (Chicago 1964).
Pallis, Svend A.F.D., *The Antiquity of Iraq: A Handbook of Assyriology* (Copenhagen 1956).
Perkins, Ann L., *The Comparative Archaeology of Early Mesopotamia* (Chicago 1949).
Pritchard, James B., ed., *Ancient Near Eastern Texts Relating to the Old Testament*, rev. ed. (Princeton, N.J., 1955).

ASTAIRE, ə-stâr′, **Fred** (1899-   ), American dancer, actor, and singer, whose light sophisticated style dominated American motion picture musicals from the 1930's through the 1950's. He was born *Fred Austerlitz* on May 10, 1899, in Omaha, Nebr. He appeared in vaudeville performances in New York as early as 1906, with his older sister Adele as a dancing partner. They changed their name to Astaire and made their Broadway debut in 1917 in Sigmund Romberg's *Over the Top*. Together they starred in a series of hit musicals including *For Goodness Sake* (1922), *Lady Be Good* (1925), *Smiles* (1930), and *The Band Wagon* (1931).

Adele retired from show business in 1932, and Fred began a new career in motion picture musicals, dancing with Ginger Rogers. The Astaire-Rogers team appeared in a series of motion picture hits, including *Flying Down to Rio* (1933), *Roberta* (1935), *Top Hat* (1935), *Shall We Dance?* (1937), *Carefree* (1938), and *The Story of Vernon and Irene Castle* (1939). Astaire's other dancing partners included Eleanor Powell (*Broadway Melody of 1940*), Rita Hayworth (*You Were Never Lovelier*, 1942), Leslie Caron (*Daddy Long Legs*, 1955), and Cyd Charisse (*Silk Stockings*, 1957). In 1958 he made his television debut in *An Evening with Fred Astaire*, for which he won nine Emmy awards. He was married in 1933 to Phyllis (Livingston) Potter, who died in 1954. Astaire's autobiography, *Steps in Time*, was published in 1959.

ASTARABAD. See GURGAN.

ASTARTE, as-tär′tē, was a Semitic goddess of sexual activity, fertility, maternity, love, and war. She was the female counterpart of Baal (q.v.). The chief goddess of the Phoenician Sidonians, she was worshiped as far away as Cyprus, Sicily, Sardinia, and Carthage. Her worship by the Israelites was denounced as idolatry in the Old Testament, where she is referred to derogatorily as *Ashtoreth*, a form of the name derived from the Hebrew word *bosheth*, or "shame."

Astarte appears in records as early as 1478 B.C. in the annals of Thutmose III. She is depicted as goddess of sexual activity in the Babylonian Gilgamesh epic and is cited as such by Lucian, Herodotus, and Strabo. The fact that the Greeks later identified her with Aphrodite is further evidence of her role in this respect. As goddess of fertility and maternity, she appears in Babylonian and Assyrian art with a child in her arms, and she has affinities with ancient Semitic matriarchs, bearers of the children of the tribe. A reference to her as a war goddess is made in I Samuel 31:10, when the armor of Saul is placed in a Philistine temple to her as a trophy. There was also a statue of her in armor at the Phoenician colony of Cythera. The opposition of her warlike aspect is reconciled in the tradition of Semitic matriarchy in which the mother of the tribe often leads it in battle.

Attempts have been made to identify Astarte as one of many manifestations throughout eastern Asia of the Babylonian goddess Ishtar (Istar), but the relationship seems unlikely. Astarte was more widespread among Semitic peoples than any other Babylonian god, and there are linguistic and phonetic reasons ruling against any Ishtar-Astarte identity. Furthermore, the cult of Ishtar had a close tie-up with the planet Venus, a connection not evident in the worship of Astarte.

ASTATINE, as′tə-tēn, a radioactive element, is the heaviest member of the halogen series of elements, which includes fluorine, chlorine, bromine, and iodine. The atomic number of astatine is 85, and the atomic weight of the longest-lived isotope is 210. Its symbol is At. The name "astatine" was taken from the Greek word *astatos,* meaning "unstable." All isotopes of astatine are highly radioactive; that is, astatine has no stable isotopes. No astatine has been isolated from natural sources. It is a synthetically produced element.

Astatine was first produced by Dale R. Corson, Kenneth R. MacKenzie, and Emilio Segrè in 1940. They identified the isotope At-211 in targets of bismuth that were bombarded with energetic helium ions in the 60-inch cyclotron at the University of California, Berkeley. The nuclear reaction can be represented as:

$$Bi^{209} + He^4 \rightarrow At^{211} + 2 \text{ neutrons.}$$

This isotope has a half-life of 7.5 hours. In 60 percent of its disintegrations, it transmutes itself by the nuclear capture of an orbital electron. In these cases, it transforms to Po-211, which decays to Pb-207. In 40 percent of its disintegrations, it decays by the nuclear emission of an alpha particle. In these cases, it transforms to Bi-207.

Other isotopes of astatine have been synthesized by nuclear transmutation reactions, and some information is available on more than 20 isotopes. Of these isotopes, At-210 has the longest half-life, 8.3 hours. It is unlikely that any isotope of astatine with a longer half-life will ever be discovered.

Chemical studies of astatine must be made by tracer methods because it is highly radioactive and is obtained only in small quantities. Most studies have been designed to develop procedures for isolating radiochemically pure solutions from the complex mixtures of radioactive contaminants produced in nuclear reactions. Other experiments have been designed in order to explore the tracer properties of an element in Group VIIa of the periodic table.

Astatine exhibits several oxidation states that more or less closely resemble the known states of iodine. However, experiments with astatine are performed in extremely dilute solutions. The interpretation of the experiments is complicated by the fact that iodine in extremely dilute solutions shows behavior markedly different from that normally observed.

Astatine has oxidation states with coprecipitation characteristics that are similar to those of iodide ion, iodate ion, and free iodine. Under oxidizing conditions, several positive oxidation states, including an astatate ion, can be formed. In the free state, astatine is quite volatile. It is readily taken up by organic liquids such as ethyl ether aliphatic ketones or tributyl phosphate. It resembles polonium in the ease with which it plates metals such as copper and silver. It can be removed from an aqueous solution by using a freshly formed precipitate of tellurium metal.

Astatine has some physiological importance because it is readily taken up by the thyroid gland, as is iodine. Absorption of At-211 has possible clinical usefulness because the heavily ionizing alpha radiations can cause localized destruction of thyroid tissue. See also RADIO-ACTIVITY.

EARL K. HYDE
University of California, Berkeley

ASTEN, as′tən, **Friedrich Emil von** (1842–1878), German astronomer, who is remembered for his observations of Encke's comet (see ENCKE, JOHANN FRANZ).Asten was born in Cologne, Prussia. In 1870 he began work in the national observatory at Pulkovo, Russia, and in 1887 he published his work on Encke's comet which discussed the comet's appearances between 1819 and 1875. Asten also undertook studies of the asteroids. He died in St. Petersburg (now Leningrad), Russia.

ASTER, as′tər, is a group of mostly perennial herbs found in North America, Europe, Asia, and South America. Commonly cultivated for their flowers, the asters are freely branching plants bearing their flowers generally in clusters. The outer part of the composite flower may be white, pink, purple, blue, or violet; the tubular flowers in the center are usually yellow, turning red, brown, or purple with age. The asters bloom in late summer.

The approximately 600 species of asters are classified in the genus *Aster* and in several closely related genera of the Compositae. Since there is frequent natural and artificial hybridization, the species are hard to classify. Among the more common American species are the New England aster, *A. novae-angliae;* the common blue wood aster, *A. cordifolius;* and the purple-stemmed aster, *A. puniceus.* Eurasian species include *A. alpinus, A. himalaicus, A. sibericus,* and *A. tartaricus.* The China aster, *Callistephus chinensis* (Reine Marguérite), is the common annual grown in flower gardens.

JOHN H. GERARD

Wild aster (*Aster oblongifolius*).

ASTERISM, as′tə-riz-əm, in crystallography, is a six-rayed star that is seen in certain crystals when light is shone on or through the polished crystal. It is produced by the reflection of light from bits of foreign matter within the crystal or by peculiarities of the crystal structure itself. Asterism is well exhibited in star sapphires and some types of quartz.

ASTEROID, as'tə-roid, one of many small planetary bodies orbiting the sun. Asteroids are sometimes called *planetoids* or *minor planets*. The orbits of more than 1,600 asteroids have been calculated, and thousands of other asteroids have been observed. These small planets travel around the sun in elliptical paths that with a few exceptions lie in the zone between the orbits of Mars and Jupiter. Probably no undiscovered asteroid of any size exists within the orbit of Mars. In the zone beyond Jupiter, on the other hand, only an asteroid of unusual size would stand much chance of being observed.

Discovery. From the time when the relative distances of the planets from the sun were made known by Johannes Kepler (1571–1630), the tremendous gap between Mars and Jupiter was noticed. In 1781, when Uranus was discovered, it was found that the new planet's distance agreed excellently with the distance predicted by Bode's law. This empirical law, published in 1772, expressed an apparent numerical relation between the average distances of the planets from the sun. Bode's law predicted a planet in the zone between the orbits of Mars and Jupiter, and the discovery of Uranus strengthened the hypothesis.

Near the end of the 18th century an association of 24 astronomers, mostly in Germany, was formed to search for the missing planet. An unexpected object was sighted on Jan. 1, 1801, by Giuseppe Piazzi, an Italian. The object, a seventh magnitude "star," changed in its position among the other stars on succeeding nights. Piazzi carefully followed the object for six weeks, apparently thinking he had found a peculiar sort of comet. He fell ill, and on his recovery the object was no longer in a position favorable for observation. The news of his observations reached Germany, however, and it was believed that the new body was the missing planet. Piazzi gave it the name Ceres.

It now became necessary to rediscover Ceres. The problem of its location was solved by Karl F. Gauss, a young German mathematician at the University of Göttingen, who devised a new method of computing an orbit from only three observations. Baron Franz Xaver von Zach subsequently rediscovered the planet on Dec. 31, 1801. No one expected other planets to be found, and so there was great surprise when Heinrich W.M. Olbers announced that on March 28, 1802, while searching for Ceres, he had found another object instead. Olbers named the asteroid Pallas.

Astronomers were now fired with a desire to add to the asteroid group. The first to be re-warded was Karl L. Harding, who on Sept. 1, 1804, discovered an object that he named Juno. After these discoveries, Olbers, who had observed that the orbits of the three asteroids crossed each other in the constellation Virgo, advanced the hypothesis that they might be the remains of a shattered planet. He searched for other fragments and on March 29, 1807, found a fourth, which he named Vesta.

For several years afterward laborious searches for other asteroids were carried out by many men. They were not rewarded because they did not look for sufficiently faint objects. Not until 1845 was a fifth asteroid, Astrea, with a magnitude of 10, discovered by Karl Hencke, an amateur astronomer in Berlin. Three more asteroids were found in 1847, and from then on every year has witnessed fresh discoveries.

Methods of Observation. It must be remembered that in the mid-19th century there were no photographic atlases of the sky that showed faint stars. Only for isolated regions did any chart exist for objects fainter than a magnitude of 7 or 8. Therefore the asteroid hunter often had to plot laboriously a region of the sky and then later plot it again, afterwards comparing the charts to see if there were any changes.

By 1891, celestial photography was sufficiently advanced to furnish a new method of observation. A telescope with camera attached was turned to a chosen area of sky, usually in the zodiac, and a driving clock was started. The exposure could be continued for up to two or three hours. The observer in the meantime kept a guiding star centered on the cross wires of the guiding telescope. This, incidentally, has to be done in all celestial photography with instruments of any size or focal length. Differential refraction, vibrations, and the like would cause imperfect images if one trusted wholly to the driving clock, which cannot allow for these abnormalities.

When a plate exposed in this way is developed, the stars appear as round dots, their sizes varying according to their brightness. Any asteroid in the region would have moved slightly among the stars during the exposure. It appears as a short trail among the dots and can at once be picked out, and its position measured with respect to the stars. Three observations, at intervals of a week or two, are generally enough to permit the calculation of a preliminary orbit.

One serious disadvantage is that the asteroids appear as lines instead of fixed dots. A faint asteroid would thus escape discovery because its light would not be concentrated by the time exposure. A modification of the method

ASTEROIDS vary greatly in size, but even the four largest asteroids are small in comparison to the moon.

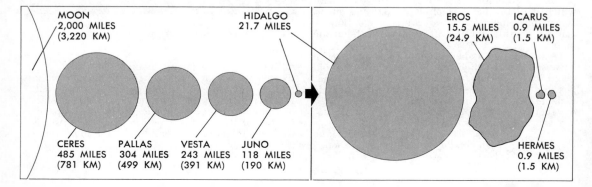

MOON 2,000 MILES (3,220 KM)

HIDALGO 21.7 MILES

CERES 485 MILES (781 KM)

PALLAS 304 MILES (499 KM)

VESTA 243 MILES (391 KM)

JUNO 118 MILES (190 KM)

EROS 15.5 MILES (24.9 KM)

ICARUS 0.9 MILES (1.5 KM)

HERMES 0.9 MILES (1.5 KM)

avoids this difficulty to a large extent. The probable average hourly motion of the asteroid is calculated and the driving clock slowed up accordingly, so that the asteroid appears as a dot while the stars are drawn out into lines. This method permits much fainter asteroids to be detected.

Although three observations of an asteroid can provide a preliminary orbit, at least five or six, spaced over as many weeks, are required for a more exact calculation. Asteroids are first designated by the year in which they are discovered, followed by two capital letters—for example, 1932 HA. After a good orbit has been computed, the asteroid is given a permanent number. When asteroids were first being discovered the names of female deities were assigned to the bodies. As more and more were found, however, all mythologies began to give out. Names of cities, countries, and even modified proper names were used instead. Most asteroids discovered today go without names.

Physical Properties. The diameters of only a few of the largest asteroids can be measured. Using the 36-inch Lick refractor, Edward E. Barnard in 1894–1895 obtained the following values: Ceres, 485 miles (781 km) in diameter; Pallas, 304 miles (499 km); Vesta, 243 miles (391 km); and Juno, 118 miles (190 km). (Values obtained by other observers may vary from these somewhat.) Barnard considered the diameter of Juno about the very limit of measurability. All but a very few of the other asteroids are too small, even when closest to the earth, to show disks of appreciable diameter.

The only way that the diameters of most asteroids can be computed, therefore, is by observing their brightness when they are at known distances from the earth and the sun. By assuming their reflecting power per unit area—their albedo—the astronomer can calculate how large an asteroid must be to appear so bright at the given distance. An albedo equivalent to that of Mars is perhaps about correct on the average, but it is known that not all the asteroids have the same albedo. Diameters calculated by this method have indicated asteroids down to about half a mile (less than 1 km) wide. There seems no reason to set this as a lower limit of size, however, and very small asteroids may be literally innumerable.

Mass. Practical considerations limit the ability of astronomers to determine the mass of an asteroid. The only way in which the mass of such a body can be calculated is by observing its gravitational effect upon some other body, but no such effect has been observed for an asteroid. However, if Ceres (the largest asteroid) is assumed to have the same density as the moon, its mass would be 1/7,200 that of the earth. It can be assumed that the mass of the average asteroid is very insignificant. It has been calculated that the combined masses of all the known asteroids, together with the probable combined masses of those unknown, must amount to less than 1/500 the mass of the earth.

Shape. There are many reasons for believing that most asteroids are irregular rather than spherical in shape. This is indicated by the periodic changes of brightness observed in a significant percentage of the asteroids that have been studied thoroughly with the photometer. (On the other hand, there are asteroids that have shown no periodic variations.) The changes

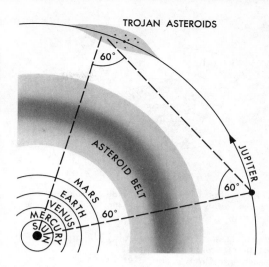

TROJAN ASTEROIDS

THE TROJAN ASTEROIDS lie beyond the asteroid belt. One group of Trojans orbits the sun 60° ahead of Jupiter; another (not shown) travels 60° behind the planet.

can be accounted for by supposing that asteroids are rotating bodies of irregular shape. In some cases the changes may also be the result of different sides of an asteroid having different reflecting powers. In general it might be said that if an average-sized mountain could be taken and thrown out into space, it would make an asteroid of respectable size and shape.

Surface Conditions. Because of the small masses of the asteroids, the gravitational pull at their surfaces is far less than the gravitational pull on any of the planets. A man weighing 100 pounds (45 kg) on earth would weigh about 4 pounds (1.8 kg) on Ceres. On an asteroid 10 miles (16 km) in diameter he would weigh just over one ounce (28.3 grams). It is obvious that the asteroids cannot hold an atmosphere, which in turn means that any known form of life could not possibly exist there.

Orbits. The orbit of every asteroid is an ellipse, with the sun at one focus of the ellipse. Every known asteroid travels around the sun in a counterclockwise direction, as the planets do. A very wide diversity is found, however, among particular asteroid orbits.

Asteroid Zones. Most of the asteroids remain within the zone between the orbits of Mars and Jupiter, but that zone is by no means uniformly occupied by asteroid orbits. Jupiter's period of rotation about the sun is 11.86 years, and there is a conspicuous absence of asteroids having periods one half, two fifths, and one third of this period. It is generally believed that this is a resonance effect. Should an asteroid be placed in one of these gaps, it would undergo perturbations by Jupiter with each revolution. In the long run its orbit would be shifted either nearer to or farther from Jupiter's orbit.

Less prominent gaps are also found at distances having values one fourth, one fifth, three fifths, and three sevenths of Jupiter's period. Why similar gaps are not found at some other larger fractions, such as two thirds and three fourths, is not clearly understood. In fact, there are somewhat more asteroid orbits with periods near to these latter values than would be expected mathematically. In any case, the relative proximity of all asteroid orbits to that of Jupiter, the most massive of the planets, is surely

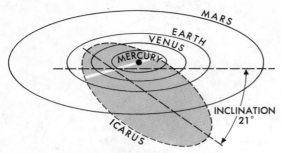

ICARUS and a number of other small asteroids have very eccentric orbits that resemble the orbits of comets.

(if as yet somewhat obscurely) the main reason for their present distribution.

Eccentric Orbits. The asteroids in the zone between Mars and Jupiter generally have planetary orbits. That is, their paths around the sun are not very exaggerated ellipses but are more or less circular. The orbits of some asteroids, however, are highly eccentric. Such asteroids travel around the sun in flattened ellipses that may take them far within the orbit of Mars or beyond the orbit of Jupiter. Orbital eccentricity is indicated by values ranging from 0 to 1. An orbit with 0 eccentricity would be perfectly circular; the more eccentric an orbit is, the more nearly it approaches a value of 1.

Another kind of orbital variation is the inclination of an orbit to the ecliptic (the plane of the earth's orbit around the sun). Many asteroids travel in the same orbital plane as the earth does, and therefore have an inclination of 0° Some asteroids, however, have orbits that are tilted in comparison to the earth's orbit.

About 7 percent of the asteroids have eccentricities greater than 0.25, and 6 percent have inclinations exceeding 20°. In most cases, an asteroid with a very eccentric orbit also has a high degree of inclination (although this is not an invariable rule). Hidalgo, for example, has an eccentricity of 0.65 and an inclination of 43°. At aphelion, its point of greatest distance from the sun, it approaches the orbit of Saturn. Icarus, an asteroid with an estimated diameter of 0.9 mile (1.5 km), has an eccentricity of 0.79 and an inclination of 21°. At perihelion, its point of closest approach to the sun, Icarus passes within the orbit of Mercury. The orbits of asteroids such as Icarus and Hidalgo and a number of others are called cometary orbits, because they resemble the orbits that comets follow. In fact, comets and such asteroids may be related. Thus, Hidalgo may be the nucleus of a comet whose coma has disappeared.

Close-Approaching Asteroids. Icarus has passed within a few million miles of the earth, and so has the larger asteroid Eros. There are several small asteroids that come even closer. Hermes, at the time of its discovery, sped past the earth at a distance of perhaps 600,000 miles (966,000 km). Such asteroids move by quickly, and even with the use of powerful telescopes it is only a brief time before they fade out of sight. They are also perturbed by the earth's gravitation. Discovered by merest chance, with orbits calculated from a very few observations, some of these close-approaching asteroids are now "lost," and their rediscovery will be largely a matter of luck. None of these faint, small asteroids has so far

come near enough to make a collision with the earth possible; but, given time, such a collision might someday occur.

Trojan Asteroids. A few asteroids travel at the same distance from the sun as Jupiter does. They represent one solution to the so-called three-body problem, a classic problem in celestial mechanics: the determination of the effects that three bodies will have on each other's motions. The problem has been solved for two simple cases, one being when the bodies lie at the vertices of an equilateral (equal-sided) triangle. The bodies will then form a stable system.

In 1904 the German astronomer Max Wolf discovered the asteroid Achilles, whose position fitted this description. That is, Achilles lies at the same distance from the sun as Jupiter but approximately 60° ahead of the planet, forming an equilateral triangle with the sun and Jupiter. Since Wolf's discovery, several more asteroids have been observed near the position of Achilles. Another group has been found traveling about 60° behind Jupiter, forming another equilateral triangle with the planet and the sun.

These asteroids are all named after heroes of the Trojan War and are therefore known as the Trojan asteroids. None is brighter than the 12th magnitude, but the larger ones must be about 80 miles (129 km) in diameter to appear so bright at that great distance. Largely because of Saturn's disturbing influence, the Trojans do not remain at fixed distances from Jupiter, but vibrate back and forth somewhat. Their orbits have high inclinations but small eccentricities. Perhaps some of the present Trojans may succeed in escaping from their positions, but other asteroids wandering too near the danger limit may in turn join the group.

Theories of Formation. Kiyotsugo Rigakushi Hirayama, after a long study of asteroid orbits, found certain groups whose orbits suggested a common origin. These groups are usually designated as "families." Hirayama identified five families, and other less numerous or well-defined ones can be added. Hirayama conjectured that each family was the product of the disruption of a larger primitive body. He did not agree with Olbers' hypothesis that all asteroids were the product of the disruption of a single planet. Should such a disruption have taken place, it can be proved that no matter what the shape of the orbit of any fragment, the fragment would have to pass through the point of disruption on its next revolution around the sun. It would continue to do so indefinitely unless its orbit were changed by perturbations. No such common point can now be found.

It then becomes the task of the mathematical astronomer to show whether perturbations through the ages could result in the asteroid orbits as they now exist, if they all originally passed through a common point. It seems difficult to believe that all the asteroids ever did this, especially with the discovery of small asteroids like Hidalgo that have unusual orbits.

The problem of how asteroids were formed is far from being settled. But, for that matter, there is no absolute certainty as to the formation of the solar system itself. If the latter were definitely known, probably the former would be obvious. The original theory that a planet broke up to form the asteroids is, in the opinion of some astronomers such as Gerard P. Kuiper, still the best.

Collision Theory. A breakup of a planet might be possible in four ways: explosion, rapid rotation, tidal disruption, and collision. Kuiper dismisses the first three as improbable or impossible. The last—the collision theory—may be considered as an oblique collision of two small bodies, a small relative velocity being sufficient to produce the breakup. In Kuiper's theory of the formation of the solar system, it is predicted that five to ten "condensations" or embryonic planets might have existed in the present asteroid zone. A collision between two of these would certainly be possible.

Once the first collision had taken place, further collisions between fragments would be far more frequent, and families of asteroids would come into being. It has been calculated that if fragments of a larger body had relative velocities of only 0.06 to 0.12 mile (0.1 to 0.2 km) per second, the present distribution of the families of asteroids could be accounted for. Kuiper's hypothesis, like Carl von Weizsäcker's before it, veers away from the catastrophic theories of the formation of the solar system and resembles, rather, the older nebular hypothesis of Pierre Simon de Laplace.

A collision origin of asteroids also fits certain facts about these objects. Thus, many of them must be quite irregular in shape, and their orbits differ greatly in size, shape, and inclination. Also, many meteorites have orbits similar to the asteroids' and may perhaps be considered as smaller debris. The structure of meteorites indicates that they were once fragments of much larger bodies.

Short-period comets have orbits resembling those of some of the more eccentric asteroids. There is speculation that these two types of bodies therefore may have some relation to each other, and some of the asteroids may possibly be the remains of comets. Finally, considerable work has been done on the possibility that certain asteroids, like the Trojans, are lost satellites of Jupiter, or that the small outer satellites of Jupiter may be captured asteroids.

Conclusion. The subject of asteroids is receiving increasing attention everywhere. Asteroids are very useful to astronomers as reference points and for making distance determinations. They have been employed in careful measurements of the solar parallax (the angle subtended by the earth's radius at the center of the sun) and the astronomical unit (the mean distance of the earth from the sun). Several of the larger United States observatories have been carrying out extensive programs for the observation of asteroids. Much theoretical work is also being done at the Cincinnati, Berkeley (University of California), and Yale observatories.

In Europe, the Astronomisches Recheninstitut of Heidelberg, Germany, and the Academy of Sciences in the USSR publish an immense number of asteroid orbits, as well as the perturbations of these orbits. Notable work is also being done on asteroids at some other European observatories, as well as in Japan and in the Republic of South Africa.

See ASTRONOMY; CELESTIAL MECHANICS—*The Asteroid Group*; COSMOGONY; SOLAR SYSTEM.

CHARLES OLIVIER, *University of Pennsylvania*

Further Reading: Cole, Dendridge M., and Cox, D.W., *Islands in Space* (New York 1964); Rother, Gunter D., *The System of Minor Planets* (Princeton 1963); Watson, Fletcher G., *Between the Planets*, rev. ed. (Cambridge, Mass., 1956).

ASTHMA, az′mə, is a disorder of the lung resulting in difficult breathing, characterized by attacks of coughing and shortness of breath, and accompanied by an audible wheeze or whistling sound during breathing. In severe attacks there may be varied degrees of anoxia (oxygen deficiency). Attacks may occur suddenly or have their onset insidiously, and may last from a few minutes to hours or days. During an attack there is difficulty in both inspiration and expiration so that the expiratory effort is continuous, interfering with talking and swallowing.

Symptoms and Causes. The symptoms of asthma are a result of the simultaneous spasmodic contraction of the muscles of the bronchioles (small bronchial tubes), a swelling of the tissues of the bronchial tubes, and the retention of the secretions of the bronchial glands. Numerous theories have been advanced as to the mechanism of the attack. The best evidence would indicate that there is a release of certain chemical substances (histamine, acetylcholine) within the lung tissue which in turn causes the bronchial muscle spasm, increased bronchial secretions, and swelling of the bronchial tubes. In the vast majority of cases, there seems to be a hereditary predisposition to the disease. In the presence of such a hereditary factor, the actual attack may be initiated by allergy to foods, drugs, miscellaneous inhalants (pollen, molds, pillow and mattress dust, animal danders, and a wide variety of air contaminants); or the attack may be precipitated by various emotional and psychic stimuli, nonspecific irritants such as smoke and gaseous fumes, or by upper respiratory infections (common cold).

Hay fever of the seasonal or year-round variety and atopic eczema may also be present in patients with asthma. This combination of conditions is slightly more frequent in men than in women. It is seen in all races and nationalities and is encountered throughout the world. It may be present in the mountains or at the seashore, although a change of locality is often an important factor for relief of the affliction.

Asthma may be present at any time of the year, but is more common in the summer and autumn, possibly due to the presence of pollen, mold spores, and dust in the air at these seasons. Exposure to cold air, upper respiratory infections, sinusitis, nasal polyps, and certain types of glandular disturbance may be contributory factors in some patients.

Several conditions produce symptoms similar to those of true asthma. Disorders of the kidneys or heart may cause labored breathing, and these are called respectively renal and cardiac asthma. Foreign bodies, such as peanuts, teeth, or coins, when aspirated into the air passages, may cause symptoms of asthma. Tumors within the lung or bronchial structure or pressing against the bronchial tubes from the outside may also produce a form of asthma. Pulmonary emphysema (dilated air sacs), bronchiectasis (dilatation and destruction of bronchial walls), tracheobronchial tuberculosis, and other lung infections also may cause people to wheeze and must be differentiated from true asthma.

An asthmatic attack may start at any time but it most frequently occurs during the night after a few hours of sleep. The patient will notice a choking sensation, tightness in the chest, shortness of breath, and audible wheezing which may produce thick, mucoid sputum. The appearance of the patient during an asthmatic attack is impressive. He will be sitting upright in order to use all the auxiliary muscles of respiration. The face is pale and anxious, the voice is gasping and speech is difficult, the eyes become prominent, the lips may take on a bluish hue, and beads of cold, clammy perspiration are seen on the forehead and face; breathing is seen to be labored and extremely difficult. The attack may reach its apex in a few minutes and persist for a brief period of time, or it may persist for hours or days. Once it is over, the person feels perfectly well, except for fatigue, until the onset of the next attack.

Prevention and Treatment. To prevent asthma it is necessary to know its cause. This may be determined by a careful and detailed history, a thorough physical examination with the aid of X-rays, certain laboratory studies, and skin tests in selected instances. Prolonged observation of the patient, with historical association between trigger agents and the attacks, frequently must be made. The ultimate prognosis for relief is good provided that the allergic cause, such as foods and inhalants, is properly identified and eliminated or protected against by means of allergic injections. Correction of chronic infections, an adequate liquid intake, and correction of psychic disturbances are all important adjunct therapeutic procedures.

There are a number of ways and procedures by which an acute attack of asthma may be relieved. These procedures are not curative but are simply for the purpose of arresting the attack, although all of them may be repeated over and over again with therapeutic effectiveness. Probably one of the oldest asthmatic remedies is the inhalation of fumes from burning cigarettes or powders containing stramonium leaves (atropine) and saltpeter (potassium nitrate). The odor is pungent and offensive, so that at present it is not used extensively. Inhalation of a vapor of adrenalin atomized from a nebulizer has proved to be effective and is used extensively. Potassium iodide and other iodide salts have been used for centuries for the treatment of chronic asthma. Injections of adrenalin or administration of aminophylline or ephedrine have also proved to be exceedingly effective in stopping the paroxysms, often within a few minutes' time. Corticotropin (a hormone manufactured by the pituitary gland) and adrenal corticosteroid hormones have demonstrated their value in the symptomatic relief of asthma, especially in the chronic types.

Children withstand attacks better than adults, and in their cases asthma is apt to disappear at puberty. Persons beyond middle age are less likely to have a complete remission, although asthma, as such, rarely shortens life. Much, however, can be done to prevent future symptoms if the cause of the attacks can be determined and proper treatment instituted.

JOHN M. SHELDON, *University of Michigan*

Bibliography

Arnoldsson, Hans, *Long-Term ACTH and Corticosteroid Therapy in Bronchial Asthma* (Copenhagen 1959).
Banzsky, Laszlo, *Modern Treatment of Asthma*, 2d ed. (Baltimore 1960).
Hirt, Michael L., ed., *Psychological and Allergic Aspects of Asthma* (Springfield, Ill., 1965).
Kemp, Robert. *Understanding Bronchitis and Asthma* (London 1963).
Oliver, Harold G., *The Bronchitis-Emphysema Eczema-Asthma Complex* (London 1965).
Rowe, Albert H., and Rowe, Albert Porter, *Bronchial Asthma* (Springfield, Ill., 1963).

ASTI, äs'tē, is a city in northwestern Italy, in the Piedmont region, 28 miles (45 km) southeast of Turin. It is the capital of Asti province. The province, 583 square miles (1,511 sq km) in area, is a hilly country known for its production of wines, especially the sparkling Asti spumante. Wheat, corn, and vegetables are the chief products, and silkworms and raised. The largest river is the Tanaro.

The city of Asti, located on the Tanaro River, became the capital of Asti province when it was formed in 1935 from Alessandria province. The city is the trade center for the products of the area. Asti has many churches, towers, and palaces that were built in the Middle Ages.

An ancient Ligurian town and later a Roman colony, Asti became a free commune in the 11th century. It then became involved in the struggles of the Lombard cities against the Holy Roman Empire and in wars with neighboring principalities. It passed into the possession of the house of Savoy in the 16th century. Population: (1961) 44,455.

ASTIGMATISM, ə-stig'mə-tiz-əm, is a condition of the eye in which part of an object being viewed appears blurred while part is clear. In astigmatism a ray of light passing through the eye is bent so that the light does not focus to a single point on the retina. Mild astigmatism is unnoticed by the viewer; however, refractive errors of appreciable size will prevent the eye from forming a clear image and thus decrease visual acuity.

Symptoms of astigmatism vary from a mild frontal headache or drowsiness related to the use of the eyes, to more severe pain, irritability or fatigue, and occasionally nausea. If a marked astigmatic error is not corrected, congestion of the membrane covering the eyeball and inner eyelid or infection of the lid margins may result.

Astigmatism is grouped into two types: irregular and regular.

Irregular Astigmatism. The multiple radiating lines of light that appear around a faint source of light, such as a star, are a common example of the small amount of irregular astigmatism that is present in all eyes. However, if a marked amount of irregular astigmatism is present visual acuity will be poor.

This type of astigmatism results from the interruption of light rays caused by a disorder of the cornea, lens, or the jellylike material in the eye. The interruption usually is a result of injury to or disease of one of these eye parts, causing an irregularity of the surface and a consequent distortion of the light rays as they pass through.

In irregular astigmatism, a perfect retinal image cannot be formed by lens correction. Instead the condition that causes the irregular refraction must be removed or corrected. For example, a cone-shaped corneal surface can be made spherical by the use of special therapeutic contact lenses, or an irregular crystalline lens of the eye can be removed.

Regular Astigmatism. In regular astigmatism, different regions of the eye, instead of focusing on the center of the retina (normal), focus on different posterior planes of the eye—that is, either in front of the retina (nearsighted), or behind the retina (farsighted). The effects of regular astigmatism can be demonstrated by viewing two lines that are at right angles to each other. In every case of regular astigmatism, there is one direction in which lines are most distinct and one at right angles to this in which they appear most blurred or confused.

In *simple astigmatism,* which is one type of regular astigmatism, one region of the eye is normal while the other is either nearsighted or farsighted. Thus, when viewing two perpendicular lines, the line that represents the farsighted or nearsighted error is out of focus and appears fuzzy, while the other line is in clear focus.

There are two other types of regular astigmatism. In *compound astigmatism,* both regions of the eye are either farsighted or nearsighted; in *mixed astigmatism,* one region is farsighted while the other is nearsighted.

The simple form of astigmatism is corrected by cylindrical lenses that redirect the rays of light only in the regions of the eye that are out of focus. In the combined and mixed forms, the cylinder is added to spherical lenses in order to produce a clear image on the retina.

ROY O. SCHOLZ
Wilmer Institute, Johns Hopkins Hospital

ASTON, as'tən, **Francis William** (1877–1945), British physicist who won a Nobel Prize in chemistry in 1922 for his discovery of the isotopes of a large number of nonradioactive elements. He made his discoveries by using the mass spectrograph, an instrument he developed.

Aston was born in Harborne, England, on Sept. 1, 1877. He was educated at Malvern College and the Universities of Birmingham and Cambridge. In 1910 he joined the British physicist J.J. Thomson in research work that led to the development of the mass spectrograph. During World War I, Aston was an aircraft engineer. In 1919 he took up his previous work and constructed a mass spectrograph that provided an accuracy of measurement of 1 part in 1,000.

Aston returned to Cambridge in 1920 and worked under British physicist Lord Rutherford in the famous Cavendish Laboratory. He continued doing research there until his death, making important contributions to the study of the chemical elements. By means of the mass spectrograph, he proved that most elements occur as a mixture of similar atoms of different weight; these atoms are called isotopes. Some of the isotopes he found were for the elements neon and chlorine. This work clarified why some elements have an atomic weight that is not an integer.

Aston received the Royal Medal of the Royal Society in 1938. He died in London on Nov. 20, 1945. He wrote *Isotopes* (1922) and *Mass-Spectra and Isotopes* (2d ed., 1942).

ASTON, as'tən, **Hugh** (c. 1490–c. 1550), English composer. Few details of his life are known, but he received the bachelor of music degree at Oxford in 1510 and was master of choristers at St. Mary's College, Leicester, from about 1525 to 1548.

Aston was one of the first composers to write music especially for keyboard instruments, rather than only adapting choral music to instrumental use. He may have been the first to write music for the virginal, and his *Hornpype* is the oldest known extant set of variations for that instrument. Other keyboard pieces ascribed to Aston include *Lady Carey's Dompe* and *The Short Measure of My Lady Winkfyld's Rownde.*

THE GRANGER COLLECTION

John Jacob Astor

ASTOR, as'tər, **John Jacob** (1763–1848), American fur merchant and capitalist who cornered the nation's fur trade. He created the first American trust and built what was said to be the largest American fortune of his day.

He was born in the village of Waldorf, near Heidelberg, Germany, on July 17, 1763. His father was a butcher. Astor left Germany at 16 to work in his brother's piano and flute factory in London. In 1783 he emigrated to the United States to be the agent of his brother's firm, Astor and Broadwood, in New York City.

Two years later, Astor traveled up the Hudson River to trade for furs. By the mid-1790's he was one of the leading fur merchants in the United States. Through friendship with a London official of the East India Company, Astor obtained a charter in 1796 authorizing him to trade freely in any port monopolized by that company. The charter opened the way for Astor's commercial transactions with China, then the world's richest fur market. He founded his own shipping line to carry his furs to Canton, and to St. Petersburg, London, and New York.

Appointed executive agent in the Northwest by President Jefferson, Astor organized the American Fur Company in 1808 to challenge the North West and Hudson's Bay companies, which controlled the North American fur trade. He also added subsidiaries to operate in different parts of the country. In 1811, while organizing the Pacific Fur Company to obtain control over the flourishing fur trade with the Orient, he founded Astoria (q.v.), at the mouth of the Columbia River, the first permanent American settlement in the Pacific North West. In 1822 pressure from private traders led by Astor and his American Fur Company induced Congress to abandon the government's 26-year-old program of maintaining fur trading posts. By 1827 he had won a virtual monopoly by buying out rivals.

Astor was adept at using political pressure and friendships with presidents. His friendship with Jefferson enabled him to be appointed executive agent in the Northwest. Also, Jefferson permitted an Astor ship to sail for Canton while the embargo of 1807 was in force. This venture provided a profit of over $200,000. Astor, along with Stephen Girard and David Parish, helped finance the War of 1812 by taking over the unsubscribed part of a government loan and selling it to the public at a profit. Astor, Girard, and Parish were instrumental in obtaining passage of the congressional act establishing the Second Bank of the United States, which strengthened the nation's financial condition. They enriched themselves as large holders of government securities, the price of which increased greatly.

In 1834, Astor withdrew from the fur trade to deal in New York City real estate and other investments. He built Astor House, the forerunner of a series of family hotels. At his death in New York on March 29, 1848, he left a fortune of over $20 million. His will, among other bequests, benefited New York libraries. His contemporaries were almost unanimous in viewing him as selfish, grasping, and ruthless, a "self-invented money-making machine."

IRVING GERSHENBERG, *University of Connecticut*

Further Reading: Porter, Kenneth W., *John Jacob Astor* (New York 1965); Terrell, John Upton, *Furs by Astor* (New York 1963).

ASTOR, as'tər, **John Jacob** (1822–1890), American businessman. He was born in New York City on June 10, 1822, the first son of William Backhouse Astor. He graduated from Columbia College in 1839 and from Harvard Law School in 1842. He managed the family estate and with his wife gave large sums to public institutions in New York City, including Trinity Church, the Astor Library, and the Metropolitan Museum of Art. He died in New York City on Feb. 22, 1890, leaving a fortune estimated at $75 million to $100 million.

ASTOR, as'tər, **John Jacob** (1864–1912), American capitalist and inventor, who built the Astoria Hotel in New York City. It was combined later with the hotel next door to become the Waldorf-Astoria. Astor was born at Rhinebeck, N.Y., on July 13, 1864, the great-grandson of John Jacob Astor (1763–1848), the fur merchant. He majored in technical studies at Harvard and received his B.S. degree in 1888. He patented a triple bicycle brake for solid-tire bicycles, an improved marine turbine, a vibrating disintegrator for getting power gas from peat, and a pneumatic road improver that won first prize in the Chicago exposition of 1893. In 1894 he wrote *A Journey in Other Worlds*, a semiscientific novel exploring the world of the year 2000.

In the Spanish-American War, Astor made his yacht available to the U.S. Navy, outfitted an artillery battery at a cost of over $100,000, and served in Cuba as a lieutenant colonel. Besides the Astoria, he built the Knickerbocker and St. Regis hotels, New York City landmarks. He actively directed the family fortune and was a director of such companies as Western Union, Equitable Life Assurance, the Illinois Central Railroad, and the Mercantile Trust Co. He died on April 15, 1912, when the steamship *Titanic* struck an iceberg and sank in mid-Atlantic. Soon after the catastrophe, his wife, who had been saved from the *Titanic*, gave birth to an heir, John Jacob Astor 5th.

IRVING GERSHENBERG, *University of Connecticut*

ASTOR, as'tər, **John Jacob,** 1ST BARON ASTOR OF HEVER (1886–1971), British publisher. He was born in New York City on May 20, 1886, the younger son of William Waldorf Astor, 1st Viscount Astor of Hever Castle. He was educated at Eton and Oxford, and during World War I he fought in France and was seriously wounded. In 1922, after the death of Viscount Northcliffe, Astor bought the London *Times* and published it thereafter. From 1922 to 1945 he served in Parliament as a Conservative member for Dover, and in 1956 he was created a baron. He moved to France in 1962 to avoid heavy British death duties. He died in Cannes on July 19, 1971.

ASTOR, as'tər, **Nancy,** VISCOUNTESS ASTOR (1879–1964), American-born British political leader. She was born *Nancy Witcher Langhorne,* in Greenwood, Va., on May 19, 1879. Her marriage to Robert Gould Shaw ended in divorce in 1903. In 1906 she married Waldorf Astor (q.v.). When her husband entered the House of Lords, Lady Astor was elected to his seat in Commons as a Conservative member for Plymouth. She was the first woman to sit in Parliament, retaining the seat until 1945. She died at Bourne, Lincolnshire, England, on May 2, 1964.

During her long parliamentary career, she distinguished herself as a crusading advocate of temperance, a champion of women's and children's welfare, and a spirited opponent of socialism. In the late 1930's her political reputation suffered when she was generally identified as a leader of the "Clivenden set," which was accused of fostering appeasement of Germany. Despite a propensity to irreverent polemics, she won popularity as one of the wittiest and most colorful figures in British public life. Her book, *My Two Countries,* was published in 1923.

ASTOR, as'tər, **Vincent** (1891–1959), American businessman and publisher. *William Vincent Astor* was born in New York City on Nov. 15, 1891, the son of John Jacob Astor (1864–1912). He left Harvard when his father died and began to manage his vast inherited real estate holdings in New York City. Breaking with the family's conservative traditions, Astor espoused social reforms, sold many of his slum properties to the city on easy terms for housing projects, and supported the New Deal in its early years. He continued to engage actively in real estate operations and from 1937 headed the corporation that published *Newsweek* magazine. He died in New York City on Feb. 3, 1959.

ASTOR, as'tər, **Waldorf,** 2D VISCOUNT ASTOR OF HEVER CASTLE (1879–1952), British publisher and public official. He was born in New York City on May 19, 1879, the first son of William Waldorf Astor, 1st Viscount Astor. He was educated at Eton and Oxford, and in 1906 married Nancy Langhorne Shaw (see ASTOR, NANCY). He represented Plymouth in Parliament from 1910 to 1919, when he succeeded to his father's title, and from 1915 was the publisher of the London *Observer.* He was chairman of the Royal Institute of International Affairs (1935–1949) and lord mayor of Plymouth (1939–1944). He and Lady Astor were among the leaders of the "Cliveden set" (named after his estate in Buckinghamshire), which was accused of favoring the appeasement of Hitler before World War II. Astor died at Cliveden on Sept. 30, 1952.

THE ASTOR PLACE RIOT, May 10, 1849, from a contemporary wood engraving that appeared in the *Illustrated London News.*

ASTOR, as′tər, **William Backhouse** (1792–1875), American businessman, who was known as the "Landlord of New York" because of his extensive real estate holdings in that city. Born in New York City on Sept. 19, 1792, the son of John Jacob Astor (1763–1848), he was educated in public schools and at the universities of Heidelberg and Göttingen in his father's native Germany. In 1815 he became a partner in John Jacob Astor & Son, a fur-trading company that had invested heavily in New York City real estate. Upon his father's death in 1848, he inherited the major portion of a $20 million estate.

Astor continued his father's policy of buying real estate in the heart of rapidly growing New York City. His disregard of living conditions in his tenements brought him much condemnation, and in 1861 he began replacing many of the older structures. He built the Astor Library in 1853, for which his father had left $400,000, and added another building to it in 1859 at a cost of about $550,000. The library later became a component of the New York Public Library. Astor more than doubled his inheritance, and at his death in New York City, on Nov. 24, 1875, he left an estate of nearly $50 million. This he bequeathed equally to his sons John Jacob Astor and William Astor.

ASTOR, as′tər, **William Waldorf,** 1st Viscount Astor of Hever Castle (1848–1919), American–British businessman and publisher. He was born in New York City on March 31, 1848, the son of John Jacob Astor (1822–1890). He graduated from Columbia Law School (1875), entered the New York State legislature (1878), and from 1882 to 1885 was U.S. minister to Italy.

Developing a strong aversion to American life, Astor established himself in London in 1890 after inheriting a large fortune from his father, part of which he used to construct the Waldorf section of the old Waldorf–Astoria Hotel in New York. In 1899 he became a British subject, using his great wealth lavishly to win a place for his family in English society. In 1893 he purchased the *Pall Mall Gazette* and the *Budget* and founded the *Pall Mall Magazine;* in 1911 he also acquired the *Observer,* but three years later suddenly disposed of all his publications.

In 1916 he was created Baron Astor of Hever Castle (once owned by the family of Anne Boleyn and restored by Astor at great expense), and in 1917 he was made a viscount. His elevation to the peerage, regarded as a reward for financial contributions to conservative political causes, was criticized by the press. He died in Brighton, England, on Oct. 18, 1919.

ASTOR PLACE RIOT, as′tər, a riot on the evening of May 10, 1849, in Astor Place, New York City. It was the climax of a long-standing feud between the American actor, Edwin Forrest, and the English tragedian, William Charles Macready (qq.v.), but its deeper causes lay in anti-British passions and class bitterness.

On an acting tour of England four years earlier, Forrest was affronted by one of his audiences and blamed Macready's influence. The feud gained momentum when Forrest retaliated by hissing at a performance by his rival. In America, the controversy developed along social lines: the upper classes backed Macready, while the rank and file ardently supported the American.

The affair finally erupted into tragedy during Macready's 1848–1849 tour of America, on the occasion of his farewell performance in *Macbeth* at the Astor Place Opera House. A mob of Forrest partisans stoned the theater, smashed windows, and were trying to seize Macready when the militia was summoned. When the rioters began fighting the troops (7th Regiment), the order was given to fire into their ranks. The mob dispersed but not before about 30 were killed and 36 wounded. Macready fled the scene in disguise and sailed for England soon after. Although many blamed Forrest for the fateful clash, there is no evidence of his participation.

Further Reading: Moody, Richard, *The Astor Place Riot* (Bloomington, Ind., 1958).

ASTORIA, as-tôr′e-ə, a city in Oregon, is the seat of Clatsop County. It is situated on the Columbia River near its mouth, 70 miles (113 kilometers) northwest of Portland. Astoria is the trading center of a diversified farming region in the lower Columbia River area. Its principal industries are fishing, shipping, and lumbering. The city has also become the focus of a thriving tourist industry, chiefly because of its long and colorful history. Astoria has a council-manager form of government.

The new Astoria Bridge, completed in August 1966, replaced an old ferry. The bridge, which spans the mouth of the Columbia for 4.1 miles (6.6 kilometers), filled the last gap in U.S. Pacific Highway 101. The city is the site of a maritime park and museum in addition to the Clatsop County Historical Museum. Clatsop College, a two-year community college, was established at Astoria in 1958.

High on a hill back of the city stands the colorful Astor Monument, a column 124 feet (38 meters) high. Depicted on it, in a spiral ascending its sides, is a representation of the history of the lower Columbia region of Oregon and Washington.

History. Lewis and Clark spent the winter of 1805–1806 near the site of Astoria, within view and hearing of the Pacific. They explored the region and left in the spring for their long trek back to Missouri. A replica of their winter headquarters, Fort Clatsop, and a historical museum associated with it have been built and are operated by the National Parks Service as a national memorial. Astoria is to be the western terminus of a projected major federal and state program marking the Lewis and Clark Trail.

Fort Astoria was established by John Jacob Astor's Pacific Fur Company in 1811. During the War of 1812 the post was sold to the Northwest Company of Montreal, but in 1818 it was returned to the United States. It languished for a number of years while Fort·Vancouver at the juncture of the Willamette and Columbia rivers became the center of the fur trade in the Oregon country. When American settlers arrived in the early 1840's, they found only the ruins of the old fort.

After the Oregon boundary was settled between the United States and Britain in 1846, Astoria became a center of American activity. The first United States post office on the Pacific coast was opened there in 1847, and the first customs district and port of entry were established in 1849. A salmon cannery was built in 1864, and the city became a major center of the fishing industry. Population: 10,244.

KENNETH L. HOLMES, *Linfield College*

ASTRAEA, as'trē'ə, in Greek mythology, was the goddess of justice. In art she is usually represented carrying scales and wearing a crown of stars on her head. The daughter of Zeus and Themis, she was a regular inhabitant of the earth during the Age of Gold. In the Age of Brass, however, when men began forging weapons of war, she fled to the skies, where she formed the constellation Virgo in the zodiac.

ASTRAGALUS, ə-strag'ə-ləs, is a group of leguminous herbs and undershrubs found on dry soils throughout the world, except in Australia. Also known as *milk vetch*, they sometimes are grown in rock gardens. The group is characterized by compound leaves with the leaflets on either side of the leaf stem, and white, yellow, or purple flowers arranged in elongated clusters.

The genus *Astragalus* belongs to the pea family, Leguminosae; there are about 1,600 species. *A. gummifer* yields tragacanth gum, which is used in the arts and pharmacy. Other species in the western United States, called *locoweeds*, are poisonous to grazing animals.

ASTRAKHAN, às'trə-ᴋнən, is an oblast in the southeastern part of the Russian republic of the USSR. It consists of two semidesert steppes adjoining the Caspian Sea and separated by the lower Volga River.

Livestock raising is the main occupation in the interior. Sheep, horses, and camels are the chief herds, and the most important products are meat and wool. Some cotton, rice, and fiber crops are grown on irrigated land along the Volga River. Although the oblast is sparsely populated, it cannot produce enough food to supply its needs and must import grain from upriver regions. Population: (1963) 762,000.

ASTRAKHAN, às'trə-ᴋнən, a city in the USSR, is the capital of Astrakhan oblast in the Russian republic. It is about 800 miles (1,290 km) southeast of Moscow, in the delta of the Volga River near the Caspian Sea.

Astrakhan is the largest fisheries center in the Soviet Union, specializing in sturgeon and caviar. Fish canning, the manufacture of fish nets, and shipbuilding are the chief manufactures. There is also a woodworking industry that obtains its raw timber from log rafts floated down the Volga from the northern regions of European Russia. Astrakhan is situated on an important railway linking the Caucasus Mountains with the Volga Valley and the Ural Mountains. Airlines connect the city with Moscow, the Caucasus, and the Black Sea coast.

In volume of traffic, Astrakhan is one of the greatest seaports of the USSR. Huge quantities of oil arrive across the Caspian Sea from Baku and are shipped up the Volga River. In return, timber coming down the Volga to Astrakhan is sent by sea to Central Asia and the Caucasus. The sea and river are connected by a ship roadstead 12 feet deep, and cargoes have to be transferred to special canal craft at the port.

Because of its location, Astrakhan was in ancient times a great trading center on the Volga-Caspian route between Russia and Persia. During the Middle Ages it became a Tatar capital. It was conquered by Russia in 1554 during the reign of Ivan IV. The city was held briefly by groups of peasant revolutionaries whose leaders were Stepan Razin (in 1670–1671) and Yemelyan Pugachev (in 1773–1774). Population: (1961) 313,000.

ASTRAKHAN, as'trə-kən, is a fabric treated to resemble the fur of Karakul (q.v.) sheep. It formerly was used as an alternate name for the fur itself. The curled, looped pile of the fur can be closely matched by a textile process that steams wool, or cotton, thread before spinning, and the name is commonly applied to this fabric. Men's hats, made of the fabric or fur, are called simply Astrakhans.

ASTRINGENTS, ə-strin'jənts, are substances that have the property of precipitating albumin and other proteins. When astringents are used on mucous membranes, they contract the tissues, diminish the blood supply, decrease the mucus, and modify the sense perceptions. They cause puckering in the mouth. Their action is purely local. Vegetable astringents all contain tannic acid, which is their active agent. Most mineral salts are astringent when used well diluted with water. (In concentrated solution their coagulant action is so strong that they cause death of the tissue.) The most serviceable of the vegetable astringents are tannic acid and its compounds. Solutions of copper sulfate, zinc sulfate, iron sulfate, silver nitrate, and alum are among the most useful of the mineral salts.

ASTROLABE, as'trə-lāb, an instrument developed in ancient Greece for measuring the altitude of a heavenly body. The user sighted the body along a pointer that pivoted across the face of a vertical disk marked off in degrees of a circle. In the late 15th century the German geographer Martin Behaim adopted·the astrolabe for navigational use in determining latitude. The sextant replaced it in the 18th century.

ASTROLOGY, a-strol'ə-jē, is the belief in the occult influence of heavenly bodies on human affairs and the practice or technique of divining events from astronomical observations. Astrology is based on the assumption that the position of the sun in relation to the stars and planets affects the auspiciousness of certain days in general and the fortunes of individuals in particular.

In its origins, astrology everywhere was linked to astronomy and religion. In the Western world, however, astronomy and religion have developed their separate identities. Astrology, in spite of attempts to establish itself as a science, must be considered a pseudoscience and a divinatory art.

Contemporary astrology is a widespread and lucrative practice. Newspapers all over the world publish daily astrological forecasts; books and periodicals devoted exclusively to astrology have a large readership; and many astrologers prepare elaborate predictions for thousands of believers. In the Orient, auspicious days for important activities are selected by astrologers; in Korea, China, and Japan, for example, they give advice on the appropriate days for weddings.

In addition to its concern with auspicious days for individuals, astrology has found collective applications. Comets, eclipses of the sun or the moon, and other unusual astronomical events have been seen as portents of wars and calamities. Among the most famous of the old astrological treatises are the so-called prophecies of Nostradamus (published in 1555), who at one time in his life was the court physician to Charles IX of France. In times of crisis, astrological works such as those of Nostradamus have had astonishingly large sales. During World War I and World War II many people consulted Nostradamus and claimed that he foretold events.

History. Western astrology can be traced directly to the theories and practices of the Chaldeans and Babylonians of the 2000's B.C. In its beginnings, astrology was an attempt to make practical application to human affairs of astronomical observations and calculations. In fact, astrology remained linked to astronomy from the time of the Chaldeans to Ptolemy, through the Middle Ages, and down to the period of Tycho Brahe and Johannes Kepler.

Astrological as well as astronomical concepts are based on observations of the regularity or periodicity of the movements of the sun, the moon, the stars, and the planets. For agricultural peoples, such as the ancient Chaldeans, Babylonians, Egyptians, Indians, and Chinese, these regularities and their associations with the seasons, the rains, and the growth cycles of plants were of the greatest importance. The Chaldeans and Babylonians, aided by mathematical conceptions more complex than those available to the Egyptians, developed refined astronomical observations and calendars. Their work was the basis of all subsequent astronomical studies as well as astrological conceptions and traditions. The movements of the heavenly bodies were linked to a complex mythology and cosmology, which, in somewhat modified form, became the basis of astrological interpretations in the West. Their astrological and astronomical studies were preserved and developed further by the Greeks and the Arabs and became increasingly popular in Europe from the 13th century on, when European courts included royal astrologers.

Underlying Chaldean and later astrological concepts is the image of the zodiac, with its

SYMBOLS OF ASTROLOGY
SIGNS OF THE ZODIAC

♈ ARIES	MAR. 21–APR. 19	♎ LIBRA	SEP. 23–OCT. 23
♉ TAURUS	APR. 20–MAY 20	♏ SCORPIUS	OCT. 24–NOV. 21
♊ GEMINI	MAY 21–JUN. 21	♐ SAGITTARIUS	NOV. 22–DEC. 21
♋ CANCER	JUN. 22–JUL. 22	♑ CAPRICORNUS	DEC. 22–JAN. 19
♌ LEO	JUL. 23–AUG. 22	♒ AQUARIUS	JAN. 20–FEB. 18
♍ VIRGO	AUG. 23–SEP. 22	♓ PISCES	FEB. 19–MAR. 20

SIGNS OF THE SUN, MOON, AND PLANETS

♄ SATURN		♀ VENUS
♃ JUPITER	☉ SUN	☿ MERCURY
♂ MARS		☽ MOON

Diagram of astrological houses and the life conditions they are said to influence. Each house stands under one sign of the Zodiac. Used in casting a horoscope.

series of mythological animals. A different set of zodiacal animals is used as a basis of Chinese astrology, which is the kind that is best known in Japan, Korea, and Southeast Asia.

Astrological systems, linked to astronomical observations and a highly accurate calendrical system, were developed by the Mayas of southern Mexico and Guatemala. Among the books that the Spanish found at the time of the conquest of Mexico were numerous astrological treatises.

Horoscope. A horoscope is a diagram of the heavenly bodies showing the relative positions of the sun, moon, stars, and planets at a given time. To make up an individual's horoscope, the astrologer must know the exact time and place of his birth. Each of the 12 signs of the zodiac is believed to be associated with definite aspects of character, temperament, physiology, aptitudes, and the like. By establishing the relative positions of the heavenly bodies at the exact time of a person's birth, astrologers claim to be able to predict his future or advise him on courses of action or decisions. See also ZODIAC.

ERIKA BOURGUIGNON, *The Ohio State University*

Further Reading: Lyndoe, Edward, *Astrology for Everyone* (New York 1960); MacNeice, Louis, *Astrology* (New York 1964); Neugebauer, Otto, *The Exact Sciences in Antiquity* (Providence, R.I., 1957).

ASTRONAUTICS, as-trə-nô'tiks, is the science and technology of space flight. With the rapid expansion of technology, this relatively new term was required to cover the broad range of scientific and engineering activities related to the exploration of space.

There are two major landmarks in the history of this group of disciplines. The first was Isaac Newton's formulation of the laws of celestial mechanics. In fact, Newton noted the possibility of creating an artificial satellite. The second was the development of large rockets for space travel. The Russian mathematician Konstantin Tsiolkovsky pointed out the possibilities of rocket flight in the 1890's. Robert Goddard, the American physicist, pioneered the development of the rocket for exploration of the upper atmosphere of the earth in the 1920's and 1930's, and a German group under Hermann Oberth undertook studies on interplanetary travel during the 1920's.

PRINCIPLES OF ASTRONAUTICS

Astrodynamics, with which this article is primarily concerned, is the foundation of astronautics. It is the mathematics and physics of the motions of bodies—in this case, spacecraft—in space flight. Astrodynamics concerns itself with the motion of the center of mass of a spacecraft, as well as with the motions of the craft about that center of mass.

Mass should not be confused with weight. In the Newtonian sense, mass is a property possessed by all matter and is defined for any particle in the universe by its ability to attract another particle. Weight is a force resulting from the attraction of the earth (or other body) on the particle and is best defined as being proportional to the mass of the particle times the acceleration produced by the earth. A satellite in orbit has mass but no weight, whereas if the spacecraft were on the earth, it would have weight as well as mass.

Figure 1. LAUNCHING OF A SPACECRAFT

The launch vehicle lifts off from the launching pad (0) and the engines of the first stage accelerate the vehicle upwards (1). The first stage then separates from the rest of the vehicle and falls back to earth (2). The engines of the second stage are fired (3) and the vehicle coasts upwards to the desired orbital height (4). After the second stage separates and falls back to earth (5), the third-stage rocket is fired (6). The spacecraft is given sufficient thrust to inject it into orbit (7).

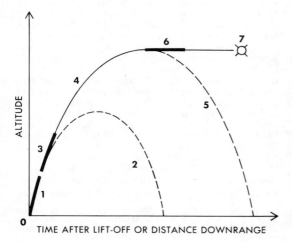

TIME AFTER LIFT-OFF OR DISTANCE DOWNRANGE

The physicist, in calculating the motions of bodies in space, thinks of each body as a point in which all the body's mass has been concentrated. This point is called the *center of mass,* or center of gravity, of the body. It is a particularly useful concept when the bodies under discussion are separated by distances that are large in comparison to their sizes.

Laws of Gravity and Motion. Underlying these astrodynamical studies are the physical laws governing the motions of particles through space. These laws apply to the motions of all bodies, and an understanding of them is essential to an understanding of the problems of space flight. The laws were formulated by Isaac Newton in the 1680's and form the basis of modern physics, although in some aspects the laws are only good approximations.

Newton's law of gravitation states that any particle of matter in the universe is attracted to any other particle with a force equal to the product of the two masses divided by the square of the distance between them. Thus, suppose that the gravitational force between two particles a certain distance apart is calculated. If these particles were twice as far apart, the force between them would be only one fourth as great as that force first calculated.

The laws of motion state that: (1) a particle moving through space tends to move in a straight line unless acted upon by some force; (2) the strength of such a force can be calculated as the acceleration it produces times the mass of the particle; and (3) for every force there is an equal and opposite reacting force. The concept of equal and opposite reaction is necessary to the understanding of the operation of a rocket. A rocket is propelled forward in reaction to its ejection rearward of small but rapidly moving particles of hot gas.

These laws of gravity and motion apply to all particles or bodies in space: the stars, the planets, the moon, and artificial satellites and spacecraft. However, generalized mathematical solutions to the equations of motion are possible only when no more than two bodies are involved—the so-called "two-body" problem. If three or more bodies are involved—the earth, the moon, and a spacecraft, for example—only approximate, computer-produced solutions can be obtained.

Kepler's Laws. Other laws governing the motions of bodies in space can be derived from the basic law of gravitation. Thus, Newton generalized Johann Kepler's laws concerning orbits about 70 years after Kepler had deduced them from observations made by Tycho Brahe.

Kepler's laws state that: (1) the orbit of any planet (body) about the sun (another body) is an ellipse, with the sun as one focus of the ellipse; (2) an imaginary line joining a planet and the sun would sweep over equal areas of space in equal intervals of time; and (3) the squares of the periods of any two planets, each multiplied by the sum of that planet's mass and the sun's mass, are in the same proportion as the cubes of their average distances from the sun.

The first two laws are of particular importance to space flight. The third law is of more interest in theoretical astronomy.

APPLICATIONS OF ASTRONAUTIC PRINCIPLES

Space flight can be categorized and discussed usefully as being either earth orbital or planetary flight. The laws of motion and gravitation apply to each category, but the conditions and results involved are different.

Earth Orbital Flight. In earth orbital flight the gravitational field of the earth dominates the motion of the spacecraft. For this discussion the effect of the earth's atmosphere (which creates drag on the spacecraft, causing it to slow down and eventually fall back to earth) can be neglected. So can the effects of such phenomena as the shape of the earth, the lunar and solar gravitational attractions, and other small but nonetheless real perturbations of the motion of the spacecraft.

A spacecraft flight begins with the ignition of the engine or engines of the booster rocket. As thrust builds up to an amount where it is greater than the weight of the space vehicle (booster rocket plus spacecraft), the vehicle rises. It climbs faster and faster as its weight is decreased by the burning propellants. The trajectory (Fig. 1) is determined by the guidance equipment in the space vehicle, usually augmented by a radio guidance system. Each stage of the booster rocket adds to the velocity required to orbit the spacecraft. Injection of the spacecraft into orbit occurs when it is at the desired altitude and is given the proper amount of thrust parallel to the surface of the earth.

The Newtonian laws explain why the spacecraft stays in orbit and account for the other properties of its motion around the earth. Thus, the spacecraft would tend to travel in a straight line unless acted upon by some force. The force causing it to follow a curved path around the earth is the earth's gravitational attraction. If the velocity of the craft is too low, it falls back to earth; if too high, the craft may escape the earth's attraction.

At intermediate velocities there is a balance of forces acting on the craft, which moves around the earth in an elliptical path (Fig. 2). The ellipse has the center of gravity of the earth as one of its foci. The speed of the spacecraft is greatest at perigee (the point of closest approach to the earth) and lowest at apogee (the point of maximum distance from the earth). An imaginary line connecting the spacecraft and the earth's center of gravity would sweep out equal areas of space in equal intervals of time.

Planetary Flight. In planetary flight the objective is to have the spacecraft approach—either to land on or to fly by—the moon or one of the planets. The launch trajectory may be the same as for earth orbital flight except that the injection velocity is higher. (See Table.) The trajectory is influenced by the gravitational attraction of the earth for the first few days of flight. Then it is influenced for a long period by the attraction of the sun. For the last few days of approach to the moon or planet the spacecraft's trajectory is influenced by the gravitational attraction of that planet.

The solar system lies in a flat disk with the planets orbiting the sun in nearly circular paths of different periods. The motions of the planets limit the times of day and the years during which spacecraft can be sent to the planets. The trajectory and duration of such a flight are determined by the velocity with which the spacecraft starts out. A spacecraft moves under the gravitational influence of the sun for most of its flight, so that it follows Newtonian laws and travels along an ellipse with the sun at one

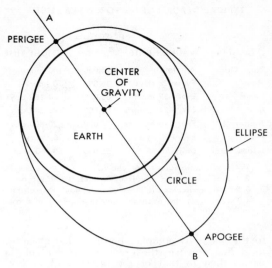

Figure 2. EARTH ORBITS

The elliptical orbit, unlike the circular one, has an apogee (point farthest from the earth) and perigee (point closest to the earth). The line AB is the major axis of the ellipse and the earth's center of gravity is one of the ellipse's foci.

focus. If the spacecraft misses the target planet, it ultimately falls back toward the sun along the other half of the ellipse and becomes a tiny "planet" orbiting the sun.

An important aspect of flight trajectories (whether planetary or earth-orbiting) is that they are essentially ballistic. That is, the spacecraft is given a push much as a rifle ejects a bullet, although more gently and slowly. The craft then coasts along the largest part of its trajectory, responding to the gravitational pull of the nearby astronomical bodies. Successful space flight therefore requires precise aiming, because the target is small and far away. It requires precise timing of the launch as well, because the target is moving and because the launch site is itself a moving platform—a certain latitude on the earth—with a velocity determined by the rate of the earth's rotation and the latitude.

Aiming and timing cannot be absolutely accurate, however, and the concept of midcourse correction becomes very important. For example, on a flight to Mars a small rocket engine is carried on the spacecraft to provide midcourse velocity correction. For a few days after launch the craft is tracked by radio, and its speed and direction are precisely determined. The change in velocity required to make the spacecraft hit the target area (which may be simply a "hole" in space if the mission objective is to fly by the planet) is computed, and the spacecraft rocket is fired at the right time and for the right duration to provide the required velocity correction.

Since there are a great many variables to consider in planning a flight to a planet, graphs are the best way of showing the required data. In Fig. 3 is shown the trajectory of a flight to Mars. In the Table, various targets and the times required to reach them under minimum energy conditions are listed.

Flight to the Moon. The flight to the moon is of special interest because it is the first target for manned space exploration beyond the immediate environs of the earth. The trajectory

TYPICAL OPPORTUNITIES FOR SPACE FLIGHT[1]

TARGET	LAUNCH DATE	VELOCITY AT INJECTION (FEET PER SECOND)[2]	FLIGHT TIME
Earth Orbit	Anytime	26,000	100 minutes[3]
Moon	Every 28 days	36,000	60 hours
Venus	Every 19 months	38,000	150-180 days
Mars	Every 24 months	38,000	180-240 days
Jupiter	Every 13 months	48,000	650-800 days
Pluto	Every 12 months	52,000	50 years
Nearest Star	Daily	55,000	80,000 years[4]

1 Approximate values are shown
2 1 foot per second equals 0.305 meters per second
3 Period of circular orbit of 400 miles (640 km) altitude
4 Traveling at the average velocity required to escape the solar system

to the moon is complex because the spaceship must first move in the gravitational field of the earth, then in that of the moon, and in both cases the sun is also acting on the ship.

There are a number of different flight plans possible for the flight to the moon and back. Thus, a space vehicle can be launched from the surface of the earth at the right time and in the right direction to fly directly to the moon, using rockets in the spacecraft to slow it to a gentle landing on the surface. (This is the way the U.S. Surveyor unmanned landings were made.) An alternative is to orbit the earth first, then fire a rocket engine and transfer to the moon, using the engine again to slow down and land directly on the lunar surface. Another alternative is to orbit the earth, then transfer to the moon and enter a lunar orbit, finally descending and landing by retrorocket (Fig. 4).

Figure 3. TRAJECTORY FOR A FLIGHT TO MARS

The trajectory below is one that requires a minimum expenditure of energy. When the spacecraft is launched (0 days), Mars is well in advance of the earth. Subsequent positions of the planets and the spacecraft during the flight are indicated. When the spacecraft encounters Mars 240 days later, it is 85,000,000 miles (136,-000,000 km) away from the earth.

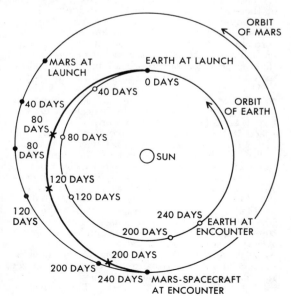

Each alternative has its advantages. The first requires the least number of maneuvers. In the second a larger rocket can be assembled during the earth-orbital phase by using several launches and having the parts rendezvous in space. The third method requires the least amount of propellants, however, and it is the one chosen for the U.S. Apollo mission.

Jupiter and Beyond. Space flight to Mars and Venus and beyond, particularly out into the solar system beyond Mars, is now possible and of great interest for scientific and technological reasons. The first major planet beyond Mars (and the largest planet in the solar system) is Jupiter. As it turns out, Jupiter is the key to the exploration of the entire solar system, because it is possible to play a kind of "celestial billiards" with the giant planet.

A mission to Jupiter would have the same characteristics as those to other planets. The initial velocity would have to be about 50,000 feet (15,000 meters) per second in order to reach Jupiter within 600 days. The spacecraft would move under the gravitational attraction of the sun for most of the journey.

By passing close to Jupiter, however, it becomes possible to go beyond Jupiter to the limits of the solar system, to fly out of the orbital plane of the planets, or to turn back and pass very close to the sun. The reason for this is that the powerful gravitational field of Jupiter can be used to change both the speed and the direction of the spacecraft—in a sense, to toss it farther out into space or back toward the sun. The advantages of this use of the gravity of Jupiter are particularly apparent in the fact that the time of flight to Saturn is shortened from five years to three years by this method.

Manned Flight. The principles of space flight that have been discussed apply equally well to a manned spacecraft or an unmanned spacecraft. Whether a space flight is manned or unmanned is determined by the mission objectives. The reasons for manned flight are many. Space is a new frontier that man as a pioneer wants to explore, for the same reasons that he has explored the limits of the earth on which he lives. Space exploration is a means of increasing his knowledge and understanding of the universe. It is a means of applying new tools, such as those developed in the fields of meteorology and communications, for the benefit of all mankind. Although most of the objectives of space exploration could be accomplished by unmanned automatic spacecraft, man will go into space because it is in his nature to do so.

Man in space, whether as a pilot, explorer, or scientist, brings new dimensions and new difficulties to space flight. He is small, adaptable, and an extraordinarily efficient computer. But he must be carefully protected from the hostile environment of space, where there is no atmosphere to breathe, to keep him warm, to protect him from the radiations of the sun, and to shield him from the cosmic rays or the micrometeorites and other bits of matter moving through space at high velocities.

Thus, a vehicle carrying man into space must be designed to get him there safely, protect him while there, and bring him back without injury. It is a shelter that must provide man with the oxygen, water, and food he requires and that must remove the toxic wastes that would in time bring about death. For all these reasons the structures, the machinery, and the supplies required to maintain man in space add up to a considerable amount of weight. The Apollo command module needed to house and support three men on a 14-day lunar mission weighs 11,000 pounds (4,950 kg).

PRESENT AND FUTURE DEVELOPMENTS

The astrodynamic aspect of astronautics is highly developed today, largely because of the availability to the mathematician-physicist of large, fast digital computers. In determining the motions of bodies in space, exact analytical solutions to problems are possible only when no more than two bodies are involved. Thus the multibody problems that arise in space exploration, where trajectories involve the gravitational effects of many bodies, cannot be solved analytically but only through the use of computers. With computers a series of approximate numerical solutions are made to a problem, the approximations becoming quite exact after many repetitions and many hours of computation.

Although there have already been many remarkable achievements in space exploration through the use of such methods, more difficult problems remain. Thus, there is still no adequate mathematical procedure, either numerical or analytical, to handle the problem of a spacecraft moving through interplanetary space under continuous thrust or propulsion. This problem, quite important for long-distance space flight using nuclear propulsion, remains unsolved as yet.

As a discipline, astronautics has developed rapidly by drawing on a wide range of scientific and technological fields: mathematics, physics, engineering, biology and biosciences, management, and so forth. In large part the initial pioneering is over and the early objectives of astronautics have been realized. The basic techniques and skills required for extensive manned and unmanned space flight have been developed and demonstrated. The facilities—research and development laboratories, launch complexes, and manufacturing plants—have been built. Man is about ready to undertake the systematic and definitive exploration of space.

Future Objectives. The immediate objectives of astronautics can be identified. One is the development of an earth-orbiting research laboratory occupied continuously by 6 to 24 men. From this station in space, spacecraft can be launched to more distant objectives; meteorological and communications research and operations can be conducted; and surveys of the oceanographic, agricultural, hydrological, geographic, and human resources of the world can be carried out. The laboratory will afford the opportunity for solar and stellar research in all regions of the electromagnetic spectrum and will permit the development of the basic skills required for man to live and work in space for long periods of time.

The construction of a permanently manned lunar base is another possible objective. This would be desirable if there is a need to exploit any mineral wealth found on the moon. Also, the moon may prove to be a superior site for the establishment of an astronomical observatory. In any event it is likely that lunar bases manned for periods of up to 90 days will be necessary for the extensive and definitive physical study and exploration of the moon.

Another objective of the not-too-distant future—perhaps in the next 20 years—could be a

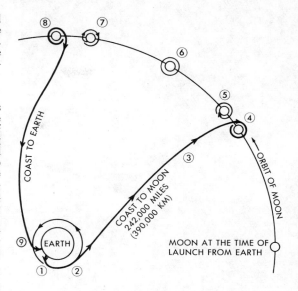

Figure 4. THE U.S. APOLLO MISSION PROFILE

A number of maneuvers are involved in the lunar-orbital type of flight plan chosen for the U.S. Apollo mission to the moon. The spacecraft is launched into earth orbit (1), then enters a lunar trajectory (2). Midcourse corrections of velocity are made during the coasting flight (3). After going into orbit around the moon (4) the lunar excursion module of the spacecraft descends to the lunar surface (5) and the men aboard disembark for a brief period of exploration (6). The craft then returns to lunar orbit (7), after which it enters a coasting trajectory back to the earth (8) for final reentry into the earth's atmosphere (9).

manned flight to Mars, including a landing on the surface. The primary goal of manned exploration of the Martian surface would be the search for extraterrestrial life, either past or present, since Mars is considered to be the planet that is most amenable to life as man understands it.

Of great scientific interest for future space flight is the exploration of the atmosphere of the sun as it moves outward through the solar system. Unmanned missions to and beyond Jupiter will be required. Difficult technological problems will have to be solved to accomplish this objective. The communications distances are enormous, and the spacecraft will be far from the sun, so that solar heating and solar power will be quite limited. The future development of astronautics could introduce one of the most challenging and creative periods of man's history.

See also ASTRONAUTS; ASTRONOMY; CELESTIAL MECHANICS; SPACE RESEARCH; SPACE VEHICLES.

WILLIAM G. STROUD
National Aeronautics and Space Administration

Bibliography

Abell, George, *Exploration of the Universe* (New York 1964).
Alexander, Thomas, *Project Apollo* (New York 1964).
Clarke, Arthur C., *Interplanetary Flight: An Introduction to Astronautics,* 2d ed. (New York 1960).
Gatland, Kenneth W., *Spaceflight Today* (Los Angeles 1964).
Hilton, W.F., *Manned Satellites: Their Achievements and Potentialities* (New York 1966).
Seifert, Howard S., and Brown, Kenneth, *Orbital Space Flight* (New York 1964).

For Specialized Study

Berman, Arthur I., *The Physical Principles of Astronautics* (New York 1963).
Ehricke, Krafft A., *Space Flight: vol. 1, Environment and Celestial Mechanics* (Princeton 1960).
Park, Robert A., and Magness, Thomas, *Interplanetary Navigation* (New York 1964).
Szebehely, Victor G., *Celestial Mechanics and Astrodynamics* (New York 1964).

ASTRONAUT Edwin Aldrin of Apollo 11, first moon landing by man, poses for camera of Neil Armstrong.

NASA

ASTRONAUTS, as'trə-nôts, is a term that means "sailors of the stars." Until the beginning of the space age in the mid-20th century the word belonged to the realm of science fiction. However, with the launching of the first artificial satellite in 1957 and the initiation of serious government projects to send men beyond the earth's atmosphere, a whole new space-age terminology was required. The word "astronaut" was adopted by the United States about 1959, when the National Aeronautics and Space Administration (NASA) began to select and train pilots for its space projects. In the USSR the comparable term is *cosmonaut*, or "sailor of the universe."

Astronaut's wings are awarded to the NASA space pilots who have flown suborbital and orbital missions. In addition, the U. S. Department of Defense awards the rating of pilot-astronaut to military pilots who fly higher than 50 miles (80 km). Thus Air Force pilots Robert M. White and Robert A. Rushworth, who flew the X-15 experimental rocket-powered plane higher than 50 miles, are pilot-astronauts. Joseph A. Walker (killed in 1966 in an air accident) did not receive this rating, although he reached a height of 67 miles (107.9 km) in the X-15, because he was not a military pilot.

Astronaut Selection. The first seven astronauts selected in 1959 for Project Mercury had to have an academic degree or equivalent experience in engineering or in a physical or biological science. They had to be graduates of a military test-pilot school and to have a minimum of 1,500 hours flying time. Because of the small size of the Mercury capsule, they could be no more than 5 feet 11 inches (180 cm) tall. The age limit was 40 years. One member of this group, Donald K. Slaton, was later barred from space flights when a slight irregularity was detected in his heartbeat, but he remained in the U. S. program.

Five more groups of trainees were selected thereafter for the Gemini and Apollo programs. Some of the criteria were revised. Thus the nine men chosen in 1962 could be 6 feet (183 cm) tall but not more than 35 years old, and civilian test-pilot experience was acceptable. In the third group of 14 men, selected in 1963, six were not test pilots, and several had advanced academic degrees. Four men of these early groups of astronauts were later killed in airplane accidents, and three died while testing a spacecraft at its launch facility. The six men selected in 1965 were called scientist-astronauts, because they were primarily scientists and only secondarily pilots. Nineteen more men were named in 1966 and 11 in 1967. Of these, one man was later killed in an automobile accident, while a number of the scientist-astronauts quit because they were not named to make Apollo flights.

The first Russian cosmonauts were experienced jet pilots, but some of the later Soviet missions were carried out by men without a military or piloting background. The Russians also differed from the Americans in selecting a woman to make a space flight. Six women had applied for the U. S. program but were rejected.

Astronaut Training. An astronaut has to be prepared for the emergencies that may arise during his mission and must be psychologically stable in order to cope with them under the unfamiliar and dangerous conditions of space. His training must prepare him to endure the stress of extended periods of extreme confinement and the disorientation and physical discomfort resulting from weightlessness.

Astronauts are trained intensively to familiarize them with the power, control, communications, and life-support systems they use in their missions. Their studies include aerodynamics, physiology, astronomy, basic mechanics, space navigation and communications, and computer theory. Each astronaut, on a rotating basis, is given specific assignments in areas such as trajectory aerodynamics, instrumentation, cabin layout, environmental control systems, aeromedical monitoring, and countdown procedures. The astronauts are also consulted by space contractors at the design stage in many projects, and become acquainted with the construction of the rockets and craft they are to use.

A good deal of actual training involves the simulation of space-flight conditions and activities. Full-scale models are located at the Lyndon B. Johnson Space Center in Houston, Texas, and several other installations. There the astronauts familiarize themselves with spacecraft layout, and they carry out simulated docking and lunar-landing maneuvers. They are also placed in simulated emergency situations to prepare them for such occurrences in actual flight.

High-gravity conditions experienced at liftoff and reentry are simulated by large centrifuges, while weightlessness is simulated to some degree by suspension devices, underwater work, and certain aircraft maneuvers. In addition, each astronaut takes part on the ground in some way in each actual space flight.

Training procedures for the Soviet cosmonauts are probably similar to those of the astronauts. Soviet programs also include intense physical exercises, sports, and parachute jumping.

See also SPACE EXPLORATION—*Manned Space Flights; Space Achievements* (table); SATELLITE, ARTIFICIAL.

ASTRONAUT David R. Scott stands in open hatch of Apollo 9 command module during an earth orbital mission in 1969. The picture, taken from the lunar module (*foreground*), also shows the Mississippi River valley (*center*).

NASA

ASTRONAUTS AND COSMONAUTS

WIDE WORLD

NASA

NASA

EDWIN EUGENE ALDRIN, JR., an Air Force colonel and scientist, was born in Montclair, N. J., on Jan. 20, 1930. Graduating from the U. S. Military Academy in 1951, he flew 66 combat missions in the Korean war and won the Distinguished Flying Cross and the Air Medal. He earned a doctorate of science at Massachusetts Institute of Technology and became an astronaut in 1963.

Gemini 12, earth orbital mission; Apollo 11, lunar landing mission.

WILLIAM ALAN ANDERS, an Air Force lieutenant colonel and nuclear engineer, was born in Hong Kong on Oct. 17, 1933. He graduated from the U. S. Naval Academy in 1955, earned a master's degree from the Air Force Institute of Technology, and was an engineer and instructor pilot at the Weapons Laboratory in New Mexico before becoming an astronaut trainee in 1963.

Apollo 8, lunar orbital mission.

NEIL ALDEN ARMSTRONG, a former Navy aviator, was born in Wapakoneta, Ohio, on Aug. 5, 1930. After flying 78 combat missions in Korea, he entered Purdue University and earned a degree in aeronautical engineering (1955). In 1962 he won the Octave Chanute award for his work as test pilot with the X-15 rocket plane, and in the same year was selected to become an astronaut.

Gemini 8, earth orbital mission; Apollo 11, lunar landing mission.

ALAN LAVERN BEAN, a Navy captain, was born in the town of Wheeler, Texas, on March 15, 1932. After graduating from the University of Texas he entered the Navy, received pilot training, and served as project officer on aircraft for preliminary evaluation trials and final board of inspection and survey trials. Bean was selected for training as an astronaut in 1963.

Apollo 12, lunar landing mission; Skylab 2 crew; Skylab space station.

PAVEL IVANOVICH BELYAYEV, a Soviet Air Force colonel, was born in Chelishchevo, USSR, on June 26, 1925. He had ten years of schooling and worked in a war plant. After training to be a pilot in 1943, he flew with an air squadron in the Far East in 1945–1946. Belyayev went to the Soviet Air Academy in Moscow and graduated in 1959 before selection as a cosmonaut.

Voskhod 2, earth orbital mission.

GEORGI TIMOFEYOVICH BEREGOVOY, a Soviet Air Force major general, was born in the Soviet Union in 1921. He joined the air force in 1938 and was a fighter pilot in World War II. After the war he became a test pilot, attended a school for higher officers, and he graduated from the Soviet Air Academy in Moscow in 1956. He joined the cosmonaut program in 1964.

Soyuz 3, earth orbital mission.

FRANK BORMAN, an Air Force colonel, was born in Gary, Ind., on March 14, 1928. Graduating from the U. S. Military Academy in 1950, he took pilot training and served with fighter squadrons for five years. He earned a master's degree and became an instructor at West Point. He was an instructor at a flight school before being selected for astronaut training in 1962.

Gemini 7, earth orbital mission; Apollo 8, lunar orbital mission.

VALERI FYODOROVICH BYKOVSKY, a Soviet Air Force lieutenant colonel, was born in Pavlovski-Posad, USSR, on Aug. 2, 1934. He completed secondary school, joined the Young Communist League, began flying lessons, and entered the army in 1952. Later he graduated from pilot school and became a jet fighter pilot and an expert parachutist and served as an air force instructor.

Vostok 5, earth orbital mission.

SOVFOTO

WIDE WORLD

PICTORIAL PARADE

SOVFOTO

NASA

NASA

MALCOLM SCOTT CARPENTER, a Navy commander, was born in Boulder, Colo., on May 1, 1925. He entered flight training in 1943, graduated from the University of Colorado in 1949, and received further flight training in 1949–1951. He flew combat patrols in the Korean War. Carpenter retired from the astronaut program to direct the Sealab II underwater-living project.

Aurora 7, earth orbital mission.

LEROY GORDON COOPER, JR., an Air Force colonel, was born in Shawnee, Okla., on March 6, 1927. After serving in the Marine Corps (1945–1946), he attended the University of Hawaii, entered the Air Force, and flew for four years. He earned an engineering degree in 1956, went to flight test school, and served as a test pilot before being selected as an astronaut in 1959.

Faith 7, earth orbital mission; Gemini 5, earth orbital mission.

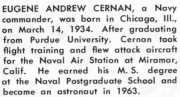

NASA

NASA

EUGENE ANDREW CERNAN, a Navy commander, was born in Chicago, Ill., on March 14, 1934. After graduating from Purdue University, Cernan took flight training and flew attack aircraft for the Naval Air Station at Miramar, Calif. He earned his M. S. degree at the Naval Postgraduate School and became an astronaut in 1963.

Gemini 9, earth orbital mission; Apollo 10, lunar orbital mission; Apollo 17, lunar landing mission.

WALTER CUNNINGHAM, a scientist and Marine reserve officer, was born in Creston, Iowa, on March 16, 1932. After graduating from UCLA with an M. S. degree in physics, he joined the Navy in 1951 and took flight training. He worked as a research scientist for the Rand Corporation, studying problems of missile defense, before he joined the space program in 1963.

Apollo 7, earth orbital mission.

SOVFOTO

MICHAEL COLLINS, an Air Force colonel, was born in Rome, Italy, on Oct. 31, 1930. After he graduated from the U. S. Military Academy in 1952, he transferred to the Air Force and was a test pilot at Edwards Air Force Base, Calif., where he tested the control characteristics of experimental craft (primarily jet fighters). He was selected for astronaut training in 1963.

Gemini 10, earth orbital mission; Apollo 11, lunar landing mission.

GEORGI T. DOBROVOLSKY, a Soviet Air Force lieutenant colonel, was born in Odessa on June 1, 1928. He won acceptance to an Odessa secondary school that trains boys for service in the air force, and he became a fighter pilot after attending flying school at Chugayev. On his first space flight, in June 1971, Dobrovolsky and his two fellow cosmonauts were killed.

Soyuz 11, Salyut space station.

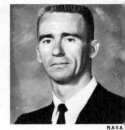

NASA

CHARLES CONRAD, JR., a Navy captain, was born in Philadelphia, Pa., on June 2, 1930. After graduating from Princeton University in 1953, he entered the Navy, became a pilot, and worked as a flight instructor, safety officer, test pilot, and pilot instructor. He was selected as an astronaut in 1962.

Gemini 5, earth orbital mission; Gemini 11, earth orbital mission; Apollo 12, lunar landing mission; Skylab 1 crew; Skylab space station mission.

CHARLES MOSS DUKE, JR., an Air Force lieutenant colonel, was born in Charlotte, N. C., on Oct. 3, 1935. A graduate of the U. S. Naval Academy in 1957, he earned a master's degree in aeronautics and astronautics from Massachusetts Institute of Technology in 1964. He taught at the Air Force Aerospace Research Pilot School before becoming an astronaut in 1966.

Apollo 16, lunar landing mission.

UPI

APOLLO 11 CREW—Neil Armstrong, Edwin Aldrin, and Michael Collins—are launched into space on July 16, 1969, beginning the mission in which man first walked on the moon.

NASA

DONN FULTON EISELE, an Air Force captain, was born in Columbus, Ohio, on June 23, 1930. He graduated from the U. S. Naval Academy (1952), earned an M. S. degree in astronautics at the Air Force Institute of Technology, and graduated from pilot school. He became a project engineer and experimental test pilot in New Mexico and joined the space program in 1963.

Apollo 7, earth orbital mission.

SOVFOTO

YURI ALEKSEYEVICH GAGARIN, a Soviet Air Force colonel, was born near Gzhatsk, USSR, on March 9, 1934. After graduating from vocational school in 1951, he studied foundry technology and aviation in Saratov. He entered an air force school, was commissioned in 1957, and is believed to have been a test pilot. He died in a plane crash near Moscow on March 27, 1968.

Vostok 1, earth orbital mission.

NASA

RONALD ELLWIN EVANS, a Navy commander, was born in St. Francis, Kans., on Nov. 10, 1933. He graduated from the University of Kansas in 1956 and received a master's degree in aeronautical engineering from the U. S. Naval Postgraduate School in 1964. He flew F8 aircraft in Vietnam operations before becoming an astronaut in 1966.

Apollo 17, lunar landing mission.

NASA

OWEN KAY GARRIOTT, a civilian scientist, was born in Enid, Okla., on Nov. 22, 1930. He graduated from the University of Oklahoma in 1953. In 1957 he received a master's degree in electrical engineering and in 1960 a doctorate from Stanford University. He then served there as an associate professor of physics. He spent 53 weeks in jet-pilot training before becoming an astronaut in 1965.

Skylab 2 crew, Skylab space station.

SOVFOTO

KONSTANTIN PETROVICH FEOKTISTOV, a Soviet engineer, was born in Voronezh, USSR, on Feb. 7, 1926. He volunteered for service in World War II at the age of 16 and was wounded. He later earned an M. S. degree in engineering at Bauman Higher Technical College in Moscow, and helped launch the first Sputnik. He was selected as a cosmonaut in 1963.

Voskhod 1, earth orbital mission.

NASA

JOHN HERSCHEL GLENN, JR., a former Marine colonel, was born in Cambridge, Ohio, on July 13, 1921. He attended Muskingum College, took Navy flight training, flew missions in World War II and Korea, and became a test pilot. He was selected as an astronaut in 1959. In 1964 he resigned to run in Ohio for the U. S. Senate but gave up the campaign after an injury.

Friendship 7, earth orbital mission.

PICTORIAL PARADE

ANATOLI V. FILIPCHENKO, a Soviet Air Force colonel, was born in Davydovka, USSR, in 1928. The son of a Communist party official, he graduated from the Zhukovsky Air Force Engineering Military Academy and was a pilot before he joined the space program as a cosmonaut. Filipchenko served as the backup pilot for Shatalov's solo Soyuz 4 flight in January 1969.

Soyuz 7, earth orbital mission.

PICTORIAL PARADE

VICTOR V. GORBATKO, a Soviet Air Force colonel, was born in the Kuban region of the North Caucasus Mountains, USSR, in 1934, to a peasant family. A research engineer, Gorbatko graduated from the Zhukovsky Air Force Engineering Academy. Gorbatko was the backup pilot for Yevgeny V. Khrunov's flight in Soyuz 5 in January 1969.

Soyuz 7, earth orbital mission.

NASA

LUNAR MODULE carries astronauts Neil Armstrong and Edwin Aldrin to a rendezvous with the Apollo 11 command and service module in July 1969 after they had completed the first manned lunar landing mission. The earth is seen above the lunar horizon.

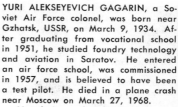

NASA

RICHARD FRANCIS GORDON, JR., a Navy commander, was born in Seattle, Wash., on Oct. 5, 1929. After earning a degree in chemistry from the University of Washington, he won his Navy wings in 1953. In 1957 he became a test pilot for the F4H Phantom and other planes and later studied at the Naval Postgraduate School. He was selected as an astronaut in 1963.

Gemini 11, earth orbital mission; Apollo 12, lunar landing mission.

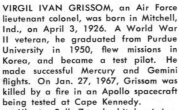

NASA

VIRGIL IVAN GRISSOM, an Air Force lieutenant colonel, was born in Mitchell, Ind., on April 3, 1926. A World War II veteran, he graduated from Purdue University in 1950, flew missions in Korea, and became a test pilot. He made successful Mercury and Gemini flights. On Jan. 27, 1967, Grissom was killed by a fire in an Apollo spacecraft being tested at Cape Kennedy.

Liberty Bell 7, suborbital mission; Gemini 3, earth orbital mission.

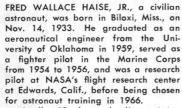

NASA

FRED WALLACE HAISE, JR., a civilian astronaut, was born in Biloxi, Miss., on Nov. 14, 1933. He graduated as an aeronautical engineer from the University of Oklahoma in 1959, served as a fighter pilot in the Marine Corps from 1954 to 1956, and was a research pilot at NASA's flight research center at Edwards, Calif., before being chosen for astronaut training in 1966.

Apollo 13, lunar landing mission (aborted).

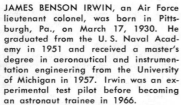

NASA

JAMES BENSON IRWIN, an Air Force lieutenant colonel, was born in Pittsburgh, Pa., on March 17, 1930. He graduated from the U. S. Naval Academy in 1951 and received a master's degree in aeronautical and instrumentation engineering from the University of Michigan in 1957. Irwin was an experimental test pilot before becoming an astronaut trainee in 1966.

Apollo 15, lunar landing mission.

JOSEPH PETER KERWIN, a Navy commander, was born in Oak Park, Ill., on Feb. 19, 1932. He received a B. A. degree from the College of the Holy Cross in 1953 and a doctor of medicine degree from the Northwestern University Medical School. He entered the Navy in 1958, completed flight training in 1962, and served as a flight surgeon before being selected as an astronaut in 1965.

Skylab 1 crew; Skylab space station.

NASA

YEVGENY V. KHRUNOV, a Soviet Air Force lieutenant colonel, was born in Prudy, USSR, on Sept. 10, 1933. After finishing an agricultural secondary school, he became interested in aviation and attended air force training schools. He then served as a fighter pilot and became a cosmonaut in 1960. He graduated from the Zhukovsky Air Force Military Engineering Academy.

Soyuz 5, earth orbital mission.

UPI

VLADIMIR MIKHAILOVICH KOMAROV, a Soviet Air Force colonel, was born in Moscow on March 16, 1927. He attended a special air force school in Moscow and was a jet fighter pilot after World War II. He graduated from the Zhukovsky Air Force Engineering Military Academy in 1959. Komarov was killed on April 23, 1967, while returning from his second space flight.

Voshkod 1, earth orbital mission; Soyuz 1, earth orbital mission.

SOVFOTO

VALERI N. KUBASOV, a Soviet engineer, was born in Vyazniki, northeast of Moscow, in 1935. He attended the Moscow Aviation Institute and obtained a master's degree in technical sciences. Kubasov served as backup pilot for Aleksei S. Yeliseyev in the flight of Soyuz 5 in January 1969 before making his own flight in Soyuz 6 in October of that year.

Soyuz 6, earth orbital mission.

PICTORIAL PARADE

VASILY G. LAZAREV, a Soviet Air Force lieutenant colonel, was born in Siberia in 1928. He graduated not only from an air force flying school but also from a medical school. He served in the air force for 12 years as a flight instructor, jet pilot, and physician before becoming a cosmonaut in 1966.

Soyuz 12, earth orbital mission.

NOVOSTI, FROM SOVFOTO

ALEKSEI ARCHIPOVICH LEONOV, a Soviet Air Force lieutenant colonel, was born in Listvyanka, Siberia, on May 30, 1934. After completing secondary school in 1953, he went to aviation school. He graduated in 1957, joined the Communist party, and then served two years as a fighter pilot. He became an expert parachutist before being selected for training as a cosmonaut in 1959.

Voskhod 2, earth orbital mission.

SOVFOTO

JACK ROBERT LOUSMA, a Marine major, was born in Grand Rapids, Mich., on Feb. 29, 1936. He received a B. S. degree in aeronautical engineering from the University of Michigan in 1959, entered the Marine Corps that year, and completed flight training in 1960. He received the degree of aeronautical engineer from the U. S. Naval Postgraduate School before becoming an astronaut in 1966.

Skylab 2 crew, Skylab space station.

NASA

JAMES ARTHUR LOVELL, JR., a Navy captain, was born in Cleveland, Ohio, on March 25, 1928. After graduating from the U. S. Naval Academy in 1952, he took flight training and was a test pilot. He was a flight instructor at Oceana, Va., and was selected for astronaut training in 1962.

Gemini 7, earth orbital mission; Gemini 12, earth orbital mission; Apollo 8, lunar orbital mission; Apollo 13, lunar landing mission (aborted).

UPI

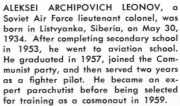

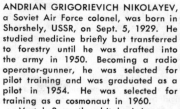

JAMES ALTON MCDIVITT, an Air Force colonel, was born in Chicago, Ill., on June 10, 1929. Entering the Air Force in 1951, he flew fighter missions in Korea. Returning to school, he graduated first in his class at the University of Michigan. As a test pilot, he logged about 3,000 hours of flying time before being selected by NASA as an astronaut trainee in 1962.

Gemini 4, earth orbital mission; Apollo 9, earth orbital mission.

WIDE WORLD

ANDRIAN GRIGORIEVICH NIKOLAYEV, a Soviet Air Force colonel, was born in Shorshely, USSR, on Sept. 5, 1929. He studied medicine briefly but transferred to forestry until he was drafted into the army in 1950. Becoming a radio operator-gunner, he was selected for pilot training and was graduated as a pilot in 1954. He was selected for training as a cosmonaut in 1960.

Vostok 3, earth orbital mission.

SOVFOTO

OLEG G. MAKAROV, a Soviet spacecraft design engineer, was born near Kalinin in 1933. He graduated from the Bauman Higher Technical School in Moscow in 1957. He worked on the design and construction of spacecraft before being selected as a cosmonaut in 1966.

Soyuz 12, earth orbital mission.

NOVOSTI, FROM SOVFOTO

VIKTOR I. PATSAYEV, a Soviet civilian flight engineer, was born in the Soviet Union on June 19, 1933. He graduated from an industrial institute in Penza, a city of central Russia, and was a design engineer of precision instruments before becoming a cosmonaut in 1968. On his first space flight, in June 1971, Patsayev and two fellow cosmonauts were killed in Soyuz 11.

Soyuz 11, Salyut space station mission.

SOVFOTO

THOMAS KENNETH MATTINGLY II, a Navy lieutenant commander, was born in Chicago, Ill., on March 17, 1936. He obtained an aeronautical engineering degree from Auburn University in 1958, entered the U. S. Navy, and was on aircraft carrier duty before becoming a student at the Air Force Aerospace Research Pilot School. He was selected as an astronaut in 1966.

Apollo 16, lunar landing mission.

NASA

PAVEL ROMANOVICH POPOVICH, a Soviet air force lieutenant colonel, was born in Uzin, near Kiev, Ukraine, on Oct. 5, 1930. A son of a sugar-refinery worker, he completed vocational school, graduated in 1951 from an industrial-technical school at Magnitogorsk, and entered the army. Transferring to an aviation school, he became a fighter pilot before selection as a cosmonaut.

Vostok 4, earth orbital mission.

SOVFOTO

EDGAR DEAN MITCHELL, a Navy captain, was born in Hereford, Texas, on Sept. 17, 1930. He graduated from the Carnegie Institute of Technology in 1952 and the U. S. Naval Postgraduate School in 1961, and obtained a doctor's degree in aeronautics and astronautics from the Massachusetts Institute of Technology in 1964. He entered the astronaut training program in 1966.

Apollo 14, lunar landing mission.

NASA

STUART ALLEN ROOSA, an Air Force lieutenant colonel, was born in Durango, Colo., on Aug. 16, 1933. He graduated from the University of Colorado in 1960 with a degree in aeronautical engineering, and he served as an Air Force maintenance test pilot and experimental test pilot at Edwards Air Force Base before being selected as an astronaut in 1966.

Apollo 14, lunar landing mission.

NASA

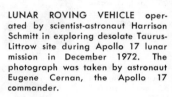

NASA

LUNAR ROVING VEHICLE operated by scientist-astronaut Harrison Schmitt in exploring desolate Taurus-Littrow site during Apollo 17 lunar mission in December 1972. The photograph was taken by astronaut Eugene Cernan, the Apollo 17 commander.

SOVFOTO

NIKOLAI N. RUKAVISHNIKOV, a Soviet civilian test engineer, was born in Tomsk, Siberia, in 1932, to a railroad family, his mother and stepfather having helped to build railroads across the Soviet Union. He graduated from the Moscow Physics and Engineering Institute in 1957 and was a design engineer in the automation and computer field before becoming a cosmonaut.

Soyuz 10, Salyut space station rendezvous mission.

VLADIMIR ALEXEYEVICH SHATALOV, a Soviet Air Force lieutenant colonel, was born in Petropavlovsk, Kazakhstan, in December 1927. He attended special military flying schools and worked as a flying instructor before graduating from an air force college in 1956. He began his training as a cosmonaut in 1963.

Soyuz, earth orbital mission; Soyuz 8, earth orbital mission; Soyuz 10, Salyut space station rendezvous mission.

CAMERA PRESS—PIX

WALTER MARTY SCHIRRA, JR., a Navy captain, was born in Hackensack, N. J., on March 12, 1923. After attending the Newark College of Engineering and graduating from the U. S. Naval Academy in 1945, he took flight training and flew 90 combat missions in Korea. He was selected for training as one of the original astronauts in 1959.

Sigma 7, earth orbital mission; Gemini 6, earth orbital mission; Apollo 7, earth orbital mission.

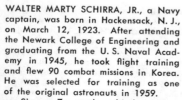

NASA

ALAN BARTLETT SHEPARD, JR., a Navy rear admiral, was born in East Derry, N. H., Nov. 18, 1923. After graduating from the U. S. Naval Academy in 1944, he saw combat duty in World War II. He won his wings in 1947, served as a fighter pilot, and later became a test pilot. When selected as an astronaut in 1959 he was aircraft readiness officer for the entire Atlantic fleet.

Freedom 7, suborbital mission; Apollo 14, lunar landing mission.

NASA

HARRISON HAGAN SCHMITT, a civilian geologist, was born in Santa Rita, N. Mex., on July 3, 1935. He received a B.S. degree in geology from the California Institute of Technology in 1957 and a doctorate in geology from Harvard University in 1964. He worked for the U. S. Geological Survey in New Mexico and Montana before becoming an astronaut in 1965.

Apollo 17, lunar landing mission.

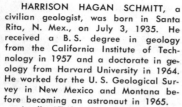

NASA

GEORGI S. SHONIN, a Soviet Air Force colonel, was born in Balta, near Odessa, USSR, in 1935. He enrolled in a flight school when he was 15 years old, became a cadet at a naval air force school, and was an honors graduate of the Zhukovsky Air Force Engineering Military Academy. He served as a pilot before entering the space program as a cosmonaut.

Soyuz 6, earth orbital mission.

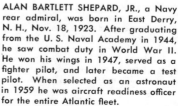

PICTORIAL PARADE

RUSSELL LOUIS SCHWEICKART, a former Air Force aviator, was born in Neptune, N. J., on Oct. 25, 1935. He earned an M. S. degree in aeronautics and astronautics at the Massachusetts Institute of Technology in 1963 after his military service, and worked there as a research scientist in atmospheric physics and applied astronomy before his selection as an astronaut.

Apollo 9, earth orbital mission.

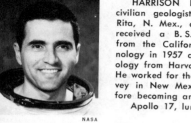

NASA

THOMAS PATTEN STAFFORD, an Air Force colonel, was born in Weatherford, Okla., on Sept. 17, 1930. After he graduated from the U. S. Naval Academy in 1952, he transferred to the Air Force and became a pilot. Before being selected for training as an astronaut in 1962, he was a test pilot, an author of Air Force manuals, and an aviation school administrator.

Gemini 6, earth orbital mission; Gemini 9, earth orbital mission.

NASA

DAVID RANDOLPH SCOTT, an Air Force colonel, was born in San Antonio, Texas, on June 6, 1932. After graduating from the U. S. Military Academy in 1954 he transferred to the Air Force and became a test pilot. At Massachusetts Institute of Technology he earned an M. S. and engineering degree in aeronautics and astronautics. He was selected as an astronaut trainee in 1963.

Gemini 8, earth orbital mission; Apollo 9, earth orbital mission.

NASA

JOHN LEONARD SWIGERT, JR., a civilian astronaut, was born in Denver, Colo., on Aug. 30, 1931. Graduating from the University of Colorado in 1953 as a mechanical engineer, he obtained a master of science degree in aerospace science from Rensselaer Polytechnic Institute in 1965. Swigert was a research engineering test pilot before becoming an astronaut in 1966.

Apollo 13, lunar landing mission (aborted).

NASA

VITALI I. SEVASTIANOV, a civilian Soviet cosmonaut, was born in Krasnouralsk, USSR, on July 8, 1935. He grew up in Sochi, attended the Moscow Aviation Institute, and earned a master's degree in engineering in 1965. The author of more than 20 scientific works, he was one of the first teachers at the cosmonaut training center and joined the program in 1967.

Soyuz 9, earth orbital mission.

SOVFOTO

VALENTINA VLADIMIROVNA TERESHKOVA, a Soviet Air Force captain, was born in Maslennikovo, near Yaroslavl, USSR, on March 6, 1937. After seven years of school she worked seven years in a cotton mill and took a correspondence course in cotton-spinning technology. She became an expert parachutist, was accepted for cosmonaut training, and entered the air force.

Vostok 6, earth orbital mission.

SOVFOTO

SOVFOTO

GHERMAN STEPANOVICH TITOV, a Soviet Air Force lieutenant colonel, was born in Verkhneye Zhilino, USSR, on Sept. 11, 1935. After early schooling he entered the Elementary Military Flying School in 1953, was assigned to advanced training at the Stalingrad Flying Academy in 1955, and graduated in 1957. He served in the Leningrad area prior to cosmonaut training.

Vostok 2, earth orbital mission.

BORIS BORISOVICH YEGOROV, a Soviet physician and army medical corps captain, was born in Moscow on Nov. 26, 1937. He specialized in aviation and space medicine at Moscow's First Medical Institute, and upon graduation in 1961 became a researcher in medicine and mechanics. Selected as a cosmonaut, he also kept the cosmonauts' health records and wrote about balance.

Voskhod 1, earth orbital mission.

SOVFOTO

PICTORIAL PARADE

VLADISLOV N. VOLKOV, a Soviet engineer, was born in Moscow in 1935 to a family long associated with aviation. His father was an aviation design engineer and his mother had worked in aircraft factories for many years. Volkov was educated at the Moscow Aviation Institute. He and two fellow cosmonauts were killed in June 1971 on the Soyuz 11 flight.

Soyuz 7, earth orbital mission; Soyuz 11, Salyut space station mission.

ALEKSEI S. YELISEYEV, a civilian flight engineer, was born in Zhizdra, USSR, in 1934. He grew up near Moscow, where he graduated from a technical school. He showed an interest in mathematics and physics and became concerned with problems relating to the development of space technology. He began cosmonaut training in 1966.

Soyuz 5, earth orbital mission; Soyuz 8, earth orbital mission; Soyuz 10, Salyut space station rendezvous mission.

PICTORIAL PARADE

UPI

BORIS V. VOLYNOV, a Soviet Air Force lieutenant colonel, was born in Irkutsk, USSR, in 1934. He attended secondary school and then went to flying schools, graduating from an aviation college in 1956. He became a fighter pilot and logged 613 flying hours. During his training as a cosmonaut, he graduated from the Zhukovsky Air Force Engineering Military Academy.

Soyuz 5, earth orbital mission.

JOHN WATTS YOUNG, a Navy commander, was born in San Francisco, Calif., on Sept. 24, 1930. A graduate of the Georgia Institute of Technology (1952), he entered the Navy and by 1959 was program manager and test pilot for the F4H fighter. He was selected for astronaut training in 1962.

Gemini 3, earth orbital mission; Gemini 10, earth orbital mission; Apollo 10, lunar orbital mission; Apollo 16, lunar landing mission.

UPI

NASA

PAUL JOSEPH WEITZ, a Navy commander, was born in Erie, Pa., on July 25, 1932. He graduated from Pennsylvania State University in 1954, became a naval aviator in 1956, and received an M. S. degree from the U. S. Naval Postgraduate School in 1964. He flew in the Vietnam War before being selected as an astronaut in 1966.

Skylab 1 crew, Skylab space station mission.

ASTRONAUT Paul Weitz gets medical checkup on recovery ship after spending 28 days on Skylab in 1973.

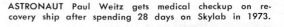

NASA

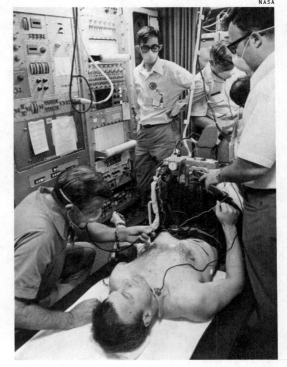

UPI

EDWARD HIGGINS WHITE II, an Air Force lieutenant colonel, was born in San Antonio, Texas, on Nov. 14, 1930. A graduate of the U. S. Military Academy (1952), he transferred to the Air Force and later graduated from the University of Michigan. The first American to walk in space, White and two other astronauts were killed on Jan. 27, 1967, by a fire in an Apollo craft.

Gemini 4, earth orbital mission.

NASA

ALFRED MERRILL WORDEN, an Air Force major, was born in Jackson, Mich., on Feb. 7, 1932. He graduated from the U. S. Military Academy in 1955 and received a master's degree in engineering from the University of Michigan in 1963. Thereafter he served as a pilot and attended test and research pilot schools before being selected as an astronaut in 1966.

Apollo 15, lunar landing mission.

ASTRONOMY

Astronomers have learned in this century that beyond our own Milky Way lie billions of other galaxies. A dark band of dust and gas is visible around the nucleus of galaxy M104 in the constellation Virgo.

ASTRONOMY, əs-tron'ə-mē, is the branch of science that includes the study of the universe beyond the earth, and all that it contains. The astronomer seeks to understand the nature of the objects he observes in the universe and to explain the events taking place there. These great problems have intrigued man since he first began to study the heavens in prehistoric times, and they continue to puzzle him today.

THE GROWTH OF ASTRONOMY

The earliest recorded astronomical studies dealt with the sun, eclipses of the sun and the moon, and the track of the sun across the sky. Thus, the records of the early astronomers of China and of the Mesopotamian Valley show that they had learned to distinguish between the *ecliptic* (the annual path of the sun across the celestial sphere) and the *celestial equator* (the plane of the earth's equator extended to the celestial sphere). In fact, the early Greek astronomers noted that the intersection points of these two circles—that is, the *equinoxes*—were slowly moving, or precessing, from year to year.

Pythagoras and his followers undoubtedly made use of this knowledge in propounding the cosmological view that the earth and the planets revolve around the sun—the *heliocentric* theory that was most fully developed by Aristarchus about 300 B.C. Prior to that time the *geocentric*, or earth-centered, view of the Chaldean astronomers had prevailed. According to the geocentric view, the sun and planets move around the earth, and the stars hang from a great dome encompassing the whole of the universe.

It was unfortunate that the great astronomer Hipparchus, in the mid-2d century B.C., rejected the heliocentric theory and reverted to the geocentric theory of the universe. His theory was refined about 150 A.D. by the Alexandrian astronomer Ptolemy, and the Ptolemaic model of the universe held sway until after 1600 A.D., when astronomy finally broke free of astrology. Astrological studies had been valuable despite their in-

CONTENTS

sistence that human events are influenced directly by celestial events. However, astrology became more concerned with directing men's lives than with the pursuit of knowledge.

The Copernican Revolution. The Ptolemaic view was first seriously challenged by Copernicus in 1543. Copernicus argued for the heliocentric view because the geocentric view was becoming very cumbersome in explaining the detailed motions of the planets. However, the Copernican view was not accepted immediately, not only because it heretically placed the sun instead of man at the center of the universe but also because it seemed to require that the stars show parallax (a relative change in position due to the earth's orbital motion). The instruments of that time revealed no such parallax, and the immensity of the distances to the stars was not yet realized. Besides, what would keep a man from flying off of a turning earth?

Several events, along with the intellectual ferment of the times, conspired to do away with the Potolemaic view. Thus, when the newly invented telescope was applied to the heavens by Galileo in 1608, it revealed many things never before observed, such as features on the moon. The conclusion that could be drawn from the latter observation—that the moon is a body like the earth—ran counter to the accepted view of celestial objects. Then, in 1618, Johannes Kepler propounded his three laws of planetary motion, with which the positions of Mars were successfully predicted. Isaac Newton's formulation and proof of the law of gravity, later in the century, removed any really serious objection to the heliocentric viewpoint.

The death knell of the geocentric view was not actually sounded until 1727, when James Bradley demonstrated the aberration of starlight (the apparent change in direction of light from the stars that results from the earth's motion across the line of sight). This unequivocally showed that the earth moves around the sun. A little more than 100 years later the so-called classic proof of the heliocentric view, stellar parallax, was demonstrated. Only then did it dawn upon man how far away the stars really are, and how vast the universe really is.

Changing Views of the Universe. For a while the belief developed that the sun holds the central place in the universe, a truly heliocentric outlook. This outlook was based on the fact that star counts seemed to reveal that in every direction the stars thin out. Careful studies of photographs confirmed this observation. In less than 100 years, however, the whole cosmological picture changed. Thus, in 1918, Harlow Shapley demonstrated that the center of stellar concentration was not the sun and that in fact that the sun is more than 35,000 light years away from the center of the stellar universe as it was known at that time.

The heliocentric view was dead; it was replaced by the *galactocentric* view. The center of the universe was now taken to be the vast group, or *galaxy*, of stars to which the sun belongs and which is known as the Milky Way.

The galactocentric view was in turn quickly abandoned. In 1924, Edwin Hubble demonstrated that the so-called Andromeda Nebula actually is not a nebula (a cloud of gas and dust) but another galaxy more than a million light years distant from the Milky Way. Subsequently many more star systems were identified that rival or exceed the glory of our own galaxy.

Spectroscopic studies of the light from other galaxies, begun by Vesto Slipher, revealed that the more distant galaxies are all moving away from our galaxy. Thus it appeared for a while that the Milky Way might be the center of the universe. But astronomers had learned that such assumptions should be mistrusted. With the development of relativistic mechanics a simple cosmology evolved which held that the universe appears essentially the same from any galaxy in the universe. This might be called the *universal* view as opposed to the heliocentric or galactocentric view. With this view, astronomers could now ask critical questions about the composition, size, and age of the universe with reasonable hope of finding meaningful answers.

Modern Astronomy. The development of astronomy has thus kept pace with the accelerating development of modern technology. Curiosity about the heavens was one aspect of the expanding intellectual interests that led to the Industrial Revolution, and astronomy in turn benefited from the resulting changes. The discoveries of modern astronomers could not have been made without great advances in instrumentation; for example, detailed models of stellar interiors would be impossible without high-speed computers. Giant new telescopes, increasingly precise instrumentation, and the orbiting of astronomical spacecraft promise even more rapid advances in astronomy in the future.

Modern astronomy can be loosely divided into several general subject areas: the sun, the solar system, stars, the interstellar medium, galactic structure, and extragalactic systems. These subjects, which will be discussed separately later, may be studied in a number of ways, depending on the region of the electromagnetic spectrum that is being used in the observations. Thus, an astronomer may speak of gamma-ray, X-ray, optical, infrared, and radio astronomy, each dealing with a portion of the electromagnetic spectrum. However, the boundaries between the divisions are not very rigorously defined.

TECHNIQUES OF MODERN ASTRONOMY

The fundamental techniques of the astronomer—astrometry, photometry, and spectroscopy—may be applied in all the different areas of study. To the information gathered by these

An observer sits in the prime-focus cage above the 200-inch mirror of Mount Palomar's Hale telescope, the largest optical reflector in the world. Telescopes are the basic tools used by astronomers to collect light.

ANCIENT ASTRONOMY

PREHISTORIC

The study of the heavens became important in Neolithic times with the rise of agriculture. Primitive peoples came to recognize the seasonal changes in the position of the rising and setting sun, the regularly recurring phases of the moon, and the motions of the planets. Crude methods were devised to help measure the passage of time, constellations were established, and cosmologies began to be developed by primitive man.

EGYPTIAN
  (c. 3000 B.C. to
  Greco-Roman times)

Egyptian astronomers developed fairly accurate calendars for practical or ritual needs. They divided their year into 12 months of 30 days each, with five extra feast days. Their calendar fell behind one day every year, and 1,456 years were required for it to coincide again with the astronomical year—a period called the "Sothic Cycle." They developed simple instruments for sighting stars, but their mathematics remained crude. Special constellations called *decans* helped them divide their year into 36 parts.

MESOPOTAMIAN
  (c. 2000 B.C. to
  Greco-Roman times)

The later Mesopotamian cultures may be said to have founded astronomy as a science. Following earlier Sumerian achievements, their astronomy reached its height in the last three centuries B.C. and was known by the Greeks. The Babylonians were less interested in explaining celestial events than in dealing with them mathematically. They were able to predict eclipses, although their calendar was inferior to that of the Egyptians.

CLASSICAL ASTRONOMY

THALES
  (c. 634–c. 546 B.C.) Greek

Thales was indicative of the trend of Greek science in his search for rational explanations of observed phenomena, his concern with underlying principles, and his interest in a geometric approach. He is reputed to have successfully predicted a solar eclipse.

PYTHAGORAS
  (c. 585–c. 495 B.C.) Greek

The school founded by Pythagoras in southern Italy (c. 530) became a center of astronomical speculation. Pythagoras further developed geometry, noted the inclination of the moon's orbital plane, and taught that the earth is a sphere. His school originated the concept of heavenly spheres (later used by Plato) to account for planetary motions. Philolaus, a member of the school, speculated (c. 450) that the earth moves through space.

ANAXAGORAS
  (c. 500–c. 420 B.C.) Greek

Accounting for eclipses and lunar phases as the result of the motion of these bodies through space, Anaxagoras speculated that the earth and the heavenly bodies are similar in nature. He saw the earth as a flat disk that rested on nothing (or on air).

EUDOXUS
  (c. 368 B.C.) Greek

A pupil of Plato, Eudoxus further developed Plato's system of concentric spheres to account for planetary motions, a system Aristotle expanded to include 55 concentric spheres.

HERACLIDES
  (c. 390–c. 310 B.C.) Greek

Although a pupil of Plato and maintaining his geocentric outlook, Heraclides suggested that the earth rotates and that the planets revolve around the sun (which in turn circles about the earth)—a step toward a heliocentric theory of the universe.

PYTHEAS
  (c. 305 B.C.) Greek

Pytheas, a navigator, was the first to note a relationship between the moon and the tides, a concept that was not fully accepted for centuries, until the time of Newton.

ARISTARCHUS
  (c. 320–c. 250 B.C.)
  Alexandrian

Aristarchus was a careful astronomer who is remarkable for developing a heliocentric picture of the universe and suggesting that the stars are at a very great distance. He was unable to convince others of his time, however, of the validity of his theory.

ERATOSTHENES
  (c. 275–c. 194 B.C.)
  Alexandrian

Eratosthenes is best remembered for his close determination of the size of the earth by measuring angles of the sun's declination. The value he obtained was considered too large by his contemporaries.

HIPPARCHUS
  (c. 190–c. 120 B.C.) Greek

Hipparchus stressed observation. He discovered the precession of the equinoxes and determined the moon's parallax. He devised a system of mapping stars and classifying them according to magnitudes. He held to a geocentric view and is usually considered to have developed the system of deferents and epicycles (to account for planetary motions) that was perfected by Ptolemy, who also used his observations.

POSIDONIUS
  (c. 135–c. 51 B.C.) Greek

The philosopher Posidonius obtained the best of the ancient measurements of the sun's distance and diameter, and was the first to take account of atmospheric refraction in making his measurements.

PTOLEMY
  (c. 100–c. 170 A.D.)
  Alexandrian

Ptolemy synthesized and further contributed to the work of previous astronomers, especially Hipparchus. His geocentric model of the universe—the Ptolemaic system—dominated astronomy until the Renaissance. His work, which was translated into Arabic about 800 and into Latin in the 12th century, is still known under its Arabic title, the *Almagest*.

THE MIDDLE AGES

ARABIAN
  (c. 800–c. 1300)

With the fall of the western Roman Empire, the Arabian cultures fell heir to Greek science and, through their conquest of Persia, to the science and mathematics of India and China as well. They preserved and added to the observations of the Greeks, and developed an experimental approach. While they contributed to spherical astronomy, chronometry, and spherical trigonometry, they did not really improve on the Ptolemaic system (although dissatisfied with it), and they ignored subjects in the area of astrophysics.

ARYABHATA
  (c. 500) Indian

Aryabhata applied algebra to geometry and astronomy. He maintained that the earth rotates and explained the mechanics of solar and lunar eclipses. In the next century Brahmagupta further extended algebraic techniques.

AL-KHWARIZMI
  (c. 780–c. 850) Arabian

Al-Khwarizmi prepared a book on algebra, drawing from Greek and Indian science. He drew up the first astronomical tables in Arabic, using the Hindu system of numerals.

AL-BATTANI
  (c. 850–c. 929) Arabian

Al-Battani (better known as Albategnius) corrected some of Ptolemy's observations, such as the constant of precession and the length of the year. He introduced trigonometric methods of computation, such as the use of sines.

AL-TUSI
  (1201–1274) Arabian

Working at Il-Khanid Observatory in Persia, al-Tusi obtained a very accurate value for solar precession. He also sought an alternative to the Ptolemaic system of epicycles.

ALFONSO X
  (1221–1284) Spanish

Under the direction of King Alfonso X of Castile, new planetary tables were drawn up in 1252 to supplant Ptolemy's. The Alfonsine Tables were not different from others drawn up earlier by previous Arabian astronomers, but they remained the best for 300 years.

REGIOMONTANUS
  (1436–1476) German

Regiomontanus (baptized Johann Mueller) accepted the Ptolemaic theory but made many important observations that improved the Alfonsine Tables. He further developed mathematical methods of computation, and also carried out studies of a comet.

FROM COPERNICUS TO THE PRESENT

COPERNICUS, NICOLAUS
(1473–1543) Polish

Copernicus worked out in mathematical detail, for the first time, a heliocentric model of the universe. However, he still maintained the Ptolemaic system of circular orbits and epicycles to account for planetary motions.

BRAHE, TYCHO
(1546–1601) Danish

Last and greatest of the naked-eye observers, Brahe did not accept the Copernican theory, but his accurate tables of planetary motions helped Kepler to develop the Copernican system further, and led to the Gregorian reform of the Julian calendar.

GALILEI, GALILEO
(1564–1642) Italian

Galileo championed the Copernican system; his experiments disproved Aristotelian physics and anticipated Newton. In 1609 he initiated telescopic astronomy, using a telescope that he made himself. His discovery of the phases of Venus provided evidence for a heliocentric universe; he also observed sunspots and features on the moon.

KEPLER, JOHANN
(1571–1630) German

Using Brahe's data, Kepler established that the orbits of the planets were elliptical instead of circular, thus eliminating the need for Ptolemy's epicycles. He communicated his views to Galileo, and Newton made use of his laws of planetary motion.

HUYGENS, CHRISTIAN
(1629–1695) Dutch

Huygens ground his own lenses and made many new observations. He introduced accurate time measurement by devising a pendulum clock, and he and French astronomer Jean Picard also introduced the techniques of making accurate angular measurements of the stars.

NEWTON, ISAAC
(1642–1727) English

By developing and codifying his laws of gravitation and motion (published in 1687), Newton answered remaining objections to the Copernican system and accounted for the overall structure of the universe. Newton also devised the first reflecting telescope.

HALLEY, EDMUND
(1656–1742) English

Halley was the first to note (in 1718) that the stars have proper motion and are not fixed. He also determined that the comets actually are members of the solar system.

BRADLEY, JAMES
(1693–1762) English

Bradley discovered the aberration of light in 1728 and, on the basis of this discovery, measured the speed of light more accurately than had the Dane Ole Rømer in 1676.

HERSCHEL, WILLIAM
(1738–1822)
German-English

Herschel recognized Uranus as a planet in 1781. He carried out the first systematic study of double and variable stars, discovered star clusters, and worked out a reasonable picture of our Milky Way galaxy (although placing the sun at its center).

PIAZZI, GIUSEPPE
(1746–1826) Italian

Piazzi was the first to discover an asteroid (Ceres, in 1801). He also found that proper motions are the rule rather than the exception among stars.

LAPLACE, PIERRE SIMON
(1749–1827) French

In cooperation with Joseph Lagrange (who had found solutions to the three-body problem), Laplace worked out complex gravitational problems of the solar system and established the field of celestial mechanics. His speculative "nebular hypothesis" of the origin of the solar system, modified and developed, is largely accepted today.

BESSEL, FRIEDRICH
WILHELM
(1785–1846) German

Bessel was the first to determine the parallax of a star (61 Cygni) and calculate its distance; he announced his results in 1838. He and a pupil, Friedrich Argelander, also published excellent star catalogs, the last to be drawn up without aid of photography.

LEVERRIER, URBAIN J.J.
(1811–1877) French

Leverrier shares credit with the English astronomer John Couch Adams for the discovery of Neptune in 1846. He also worked out the motions of the solar system, although not accounting for certain (later important) discrepancies in Mercury's orbit.

HUGGINS, WILLIAM
(1824–1910) English

Along with Pietro Secchi, Huggins was the first to apply the recently developed techniques of spectroscopy to astronomy, establishing the field of astrophysics. In 1864 he observed a red shift in the spectrum of Sirius and measured the star's radial velocity. He and Secchi were also among the first to use photographic techniques.

KAPTEYN, JACOBUS
CORNELIS
(1851–1922) Dutch

Through a statistical study of the stars, Kapteyn determined the lens-shaped structure of our galaxy. He also observed that the stars in the galaxy share a common motion, but did not interpret this result as a rotation of the entire galaxy.

EINSTEIN, ALBERT
(1879–1955)
German-American

Einstein's special theory of relativity (published in 1905) and his general theory (1915) accounted for the results of the Michelson-Morley experiment and for the discrepancies in Mercury's orbit. Einstein showed that the hypothesis of FitzGerald and Lorentz (that the velocity of light was a universal constant) could be deduced, and he established the relationship between mass and energy.

RUSSELL, HENRY NORRIS
(1877–1957) American

In 1914, Russell published his independent discovery of the relationship between a star's color and luminosity and its spectral class, a relationship observed earlier by Danish astronomer Ejnar Hertzsprung (hence, the *Hertzsprung-Russell* diagram).

SHAPLEY, HARLOW
(1885–   ) American

Together with Henrietta Leavitt, Shapley developed the period-luminosity curve for Cepheid variables in 1914. He worked out a relatively accurate estimate of our galaxy's size, and determined that its center is several thousand light years away.

EDDINGTON, ARTHUR
STANLEY
(1882–1944) English

Eddington determined the relationship between high pressures and high temperatures within stars, and from this he worked out the mass-luminosity law in 1924.

HUBBLE, EDWIN POWELL
(1889–1953) American

In 1924 Hubble determined that there are galaxies beyond our own, and worked out a classification of the galaxies. Through studying the red shifts in their spectra, he announced in 1929 that the galaxies are receding at a speed proportional to their distance—an expanding-universe concept that was earlier suggested by Willem de Sitter.

LEMAÎTRE, GEORGES
ÉDOUARD
(1894–   ) French

Lemaître worked out what has become known as the "big-bang" theory of the creation of the universe (1927), a concept further developed by physicist George Gamow.

JANSKY, KARL
(1905–1950) American

An engineer, Jansky detected radio noises from space in 1931. Grote Reber, an American amateur astronomer, built the first actual radio telescope in 1937, but radio astronomy came into its own after World War II with Bernard Lovell and Jan Oort.

BETHE, HANS ALBRECHT
(1906–   )
German-American

In 1938 Bethe developed the details of the nuclear reactions from which stars derive their energy. Carl F. Weizsäcker independently worked out the same details, as well as a more sophisticated version of Laplace's "nebular hypothesis."

BAADE, WALTER
(1893–1960)
German-American

In 1942 Baade classified stars as being either Population I or Population II stars. In 1956 Baade corrected the period-luminosity curve and reestimated the distance to other galaxies, more than doubling the figures for these distances.

GOLD, THOMAS
(1920–   )
Austrian-American

Gold introduced the "steady-state" theory of the universe, postulating the continuous creation of matter, in 1948. This theory was further developed by Fred Hoyle.

Radio waves are brought to a focus by the 140-foot dish of this radio telescope situated at Green Bank, W. Va.

techniques, discussed below, an astronomer can then apply his special knowledge of mechanics, physics, chemistry, or other fields, in order to deduce further the nature of what he is studying. If his concern is with the elementary composition of celestial objects, their sources of energy, and the distribution of energy in their spectra, he is working in the branch of astronomy called *astrophysics*. If, on the other hand, his concern is primarily with the motions of the objects he is studying, his field of interest is *celestial mechanics*. A worker in *cosmology* is concerned with the general distribution of galaxies in the universe, and with the explanations for that distribution.

Astrometry. Astrometry concerns itself with the accurate measurement of the positions of celestial objects. As such, it is concerned with the precise determination of time, with the motions of stars and planets (and a reference system for determining these motions), with the distance to the stars, and with any information that can be derived from these studies. For example, knowledge of stellar masses is obtained primarily from astrometric studies of binaries—stellar systems composed of two stars gravitationally linked.

Photometry. Photometry, which might be called gross spectroscopy, is concerned with measuring the intensity of radiation coming from a celestial source. A photometer is used for this purpose. Measurements of radiation intensity of a source, taken at two or three different wavelengths and corrected to the values they would have if measured outside the atmosphere, lead to knowledge of the temperature, color, and spectral index of the source. A knowledge of what the absolute intensity of the radiation should be leads to a determination of the distance of the source from the earth.

Spectroscopy. The purpose of spectroscopy is to look at the radiative output of a celestial source in more detail. The basic instrument is the spectroscope, which separates the light from

a source into its component colors. The features of such spectra—the continuum, absorption lines, emission lines—tell the astronomer a great deal about the sources (and also about the intervening space). For example, the realtive intensity of certain spectral lines can reveal the temperature of the star or other celestial source under study.

TOOLS OF THE ASTRONOMER

The Telescope. Since the time of its invention, the telescope has been the basic tool of the astronomer. So far as is known, the first telescope was happened upon by accident by the Dutch spectacle maker Hans Lippershey in 1608. He combined a long-focus lens with a short-focus eye lens and found that distant objects could be magnified by this combination. Accidental or not, the discovery ranks with the invention of the wheel in the vistas it has opened to man's inquiring mind.

From the crude scaffolding and crane-suspended optics of early telescopes, the instrument has developed into a rugged yet delicate research tool. In most cases, the moving parts of modern telescopes weighing more than 150 tons are driven with a precision so fine as to be almost unbelievable; the degree of error is commonly held to less than 0.5 second of arc. This is equivalent to a wobble in the drive no larger than the width of a hair as seen from about 35 feet (10.7 meters). Although the basic design of the conventional all-purpose optical telescope has not changed much over the years, some special-purpose optical telescopes have been built, such as the coronagraph, the Schmidt telescope, the Maksutov-Bowers telescope, the astrometric reflector, and the metal-mirror light collector.

The purpose of the telescope is twofold. It collects light, and it increases resolving power. Both attributes increase as telescopes become larger. Thus a 100-inch (254 cm) telescope collects 10,000 times more light than a 1-inch telescope. Also, a 100-inch telescope can resolve angles 100 times smaller than the angles a 1-inch telescope can resolve.

Although astronomers make many efforts to obtain the most efficient use of their telescopes, the full resolving power of a large telescope is never realized, at least at the surface of the earth. The atmosphere is a turbulent mixture of gases, and it causes a point source of light (such as a star) to have an apparent angular size of 1 second of arc. An angle this size can be resolved by a 10-inch telescope; generally speaking, telescopes larger than this are simply collecting more light. On the other hand, the image size decreases as the atmosphere gets drier and thinner, which is why large telescopes are placed on high mountains.

There are two basic types of optical telescopes, differing in the objectives they use in focusing radiation on the image plane. A refracting telescope, or *refractor*, uses a lense. Isaac Newton was the first to use a curved mirror as an objective instead; such a telescope is called a reflector. The larger telescopes built today are usually reflectors, which are compact and require smaller domes than do refractors of the same aperture. Furthermore, reflectors reflect all the light to the same focus, and since the light does not pass through the mirror, the glass used to make the mirror need not be perfect.

PLATE 1

ASTRONOMY

The Great Nebula in Andromeda, a celestial neighbor of our own Milky Way galaxy, shines with the light of its billions of stars. This spiral galaxy is the most distant object that can be seen with the naked eye.

The Great Nebula in Orion, one of the largest in our galaxy, was the first nebula ever photographed (1880). Its full splendor is evident in this photo by the 200-inch telescope at Mount Wilson and Palomar Observatories.

Horsehead Nebula in Orion, a dark cloud of interstellar material, obscures part of the bright region beyond.

Stellar groups may range from very loose galactic clusters, containing a few stars, to the vast star islands known as galaxies. *(Above)* The globular cluster M3, in the constellation Canes Venatici. *(Right)* The Whirlpool galaxy and a smaller, irregular galaxy. *(Below)* The familiar Pleiades cluster, a group of young, hot stars within our own galaxy.

(Right) The complex Lagoon Nebula in Sagittarius gets its name from the dark band of obscuring material that crosses bright gases of the nebula.

The Rosette Nebula in Monoceros is fluorescent. Its gases are made to glow by radiation from stars.

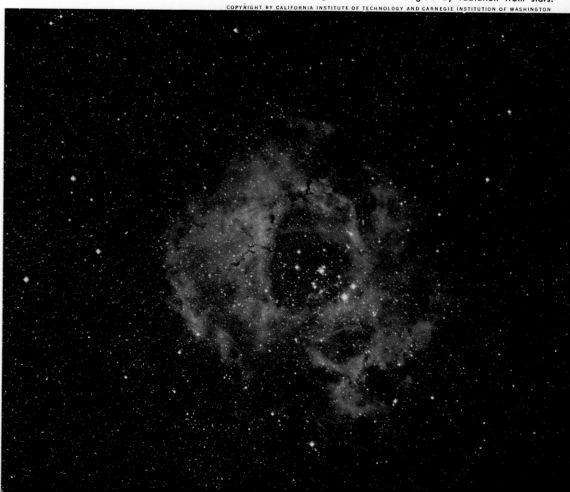

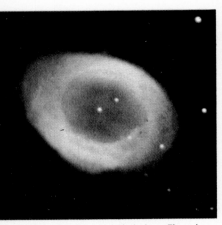

(*Above*) The Ring Nebula in Lyra. The sphere of glowing gases was emitted by a star at the center of this so-called planetary nebula.

(*Above*) The Crab Nebula, a strong source of radio noise, is the remnant of a great stellar explosion.

PLATE 4

(*Left*) The Veil Nebula in Cygnus, like the Crab Nebula, represents remnants of a supernova.

HREE OF EARTH'S PLANETARY NEIGHBORS AS THEY APPEAR IN COLOR PHOTOGRAPHS

MARS

SATURN

JUPITER

Reflecting telescopes are distinguished by the focus being used. For example, if the image from the objective (often referred to as the "primary" or main mirror) is used directly, the telescope is being used as the *prime focus*. If a mirror intercepts the converging beam and reflects it to one side before it reaches the prime focus, the telescope is being used at the *Newtonian focus*. Other focal arrangements are possible, some having the purpose of extending the focal length of the telescope.

The Photographic Plate. Telescopes are seldom "looked" through for serious research purposes, notable exceptions being the measurement of visibly double stars and the making of observations with various meridian instruments. Even in these cases, experiments are well under way for replacing the human eye at the telescope. The primary auxiliary instrumentation for telescopes has been the photographic plate. Most telescopes act as large cameras, collecting light and focusing it on such plates, which can store the image of thousands of stars in a single exposure. The plates are permanent records, the information they hold being available to the astronomer as he requires it. This is especially important to astrometry.

The virtue of the photographic plate as a permanent record leads to its frequent use in storing information furnished by other instrumentation attached to a telescope. A prime example would be the storing of information obtained by a spectroscope, which in such a combination is referred to as a spectrograph. A considerable portion of the observing time of the largest telescopes is spent in collecting light to be fed into spectrographs.

The Photomultiplier Tube. Despite the usefulness of the photographic plate, it has been superseded by the photomultiplier tube in the accurate measurement of the intensity of starlight from a given source. There are several reasons for this. Cathodes (a basic part of such tubes) are generally more sensitive to light than are photographic emulsions, and cathodes respond linearly to light whereas plates do not. (That is, five photons always yield one electron for the cathode, independent of the time element, but the response of the plate depends in a logarithmic way upon the number of photons as a function of time.) Furthermore, the photocurrent from the cathode can be multiplied and amplified. Special high-gain, low-noise amplifiers are available, thanks to advances in solid state electronics.

The auxiliary instrument using a photomultiplier tube is referred to as a photoelectric photometer. In some cases such a photometer is used to scan the spectrum yielded by a spectroscope, taking advantage of the efficiency of the photoelectric process and making direct reading and analysis of the spectrum possible.

The Image-Intensifier Tube. The so-called image-intensifier tube utilizes the sensitivity of the photocathode and the storage capacity of the photographic plate. In this tube, an image from the telescope, spectroscope, or other instrument is formed on a photocathode. The resulting electrons are accelerated and made to strike a phosphor screen. The resulting bright image is then photographed and stored on a plate.

Such tubes yield the additional advantage that the astronomer can select a phosphor that yields light at the peak sensitivity of the photographic plate. Also, since cathodes can be made sensitive to a broad range of wavelengths, regions outside of the visible spectrum can be converted by the phosphor to visible light. Thus the infrared region, which is poorly handled by a photographic plate, can be converted to efficiently handled blue light. An image-intensifier tube accomplishing this is therefore often referred to as an image converter tube.

The Radio Telescope. The instruments known as radio telescopes are among the more recently developed tools of the astronomer, the first ones having been built in the 1940's. These telescopes are used to study the radiation being emitted by celestial objects in the radio region of the electromagnetic spectrum. The objective of a radio telescope must be much larger than that of an optical telescope because of the longer length of radio waves.

Radio telescopes commonly take the form of large, steerable parabolic antennas. Special radio telescopes, however, may consist of large fields of antenna arrays—for example, the Mills Cross in Australia. Others may be giant parabolic dishes fixed on the ground, such as the Arecibo telescope in Puerto Rico. Numerous other smaller and special-purpose radio telescopes are under construction or being planned. Of special note is the so-called Very Large Array proposed by the National Radio Astronomy Observatory, consisting of 85 radio telescopes of 85-foot (26-meter) aperture in a circular area covering many square miles.

Astrometric Advances. Major advances in astrometric techniques are being made mainly in instrumentation and data handling. Automatic plate-taking devices are being developed, and automatic measuring machines are being introduced. The data from such devices can then be reduced by digital computing machines, leading to a continual improvement in accuracy.

In the determination of time the tables have, in a sense, been turned, in that they no longer depend basically on astrometric determinations. That is, the development of atomic clocks has led to an accuracy that has supplanted the rotation of the earth and the revolution of the moon as the basic timekeeper of the astronomer. This applies, of course, to shorter intervals of time only; epochs must still be determined by astronomical methods.

The Interferometer. Because of the wave nature of light, the astronomer is making more and more use of the principles of interferometry in instrumentation.

In an interferometer, light interference is produced in order to obtain very precise measurements of wave lengths. The adaptation of interferometric techniques to spectral recording and analysis is perhaps the most important development in modern spectrometry. It is conceivable that the interferometer, along with photoelectric equipment, will comprise the basic instrumentation for almost all of the principal areas of astronomy in the future.

AREAS OF ASTRONOMICAL STUDY

The instruments and techniques of modern astronomy are being used to tackle and solve a whole host of problems in all of the different areas of astronomical study, taken up separately below. Each of these areas illustrates further some of the special problems faced by the astronomer today and the techniques he has developed for dealing with them.

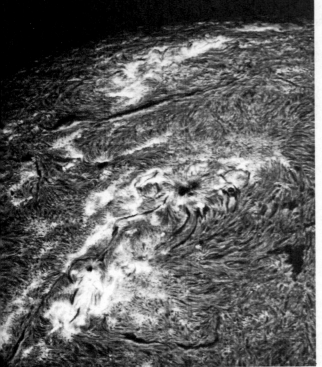

MOUNT WILSON AND PALOMAR OBSERVATORIES

Spectroscopic methods are used to study sunspot details. This spectroheliogram was taken in hydrogen light.

The Sun. The first of the areas of astronomical study is the sun, the nearest star. The importance of the sun has been recognized since ancient times. Various civilizations have feared and worshipped the sun because of its obvious relation to activities on earth, and the sun's passage through the sky was the basis of many early calendar systems. Beyond their records of daily and yearly solar motions, however, ancient astrologers and astronomers could learn very little about the sun.

Chinese astronomers, many thousands of years before the invention of the telescope, are reported to have noticed spots on the solar surface; but the first fully documented discovery of sunspots was not made until the 16th century,

The solar corona, an area of intense brightness surrounding the sun, is clearly visible in this total eclipse.

NASA-AMES PHOTO FROM UPI

when Galileo noted the markings with his small telescope. Through this discovery Galileo determined that the sun rotates, and he established the tilt of the sun's axis. He conjectured that the stars are bodies like the sun, and that—since they appear as mere points of light—the universe must be much vaster than had been thought.

Today the sun is of great astronomical interest for a number of reasons. While the sun was long felt to play a direct role in human affairs, it is now realized that this astrological view was valid in ways that the ancients never suspected. Thus there are many direct relationships between solar activities and activities on earth and in surrounding space. A large portion of current astronomical research is devoted to studying the interaction of the sun's radiation and magnetic field with the earth's magnetic field and atmosphere. The sun is also important in providing detailed information on the workings of a star, information that it is impossible to obtain from other, much more distant stars.

By studying the solar spectrum astronomers have been able to determine the elements making up the sun, their abundance, and the temperatures at which they exist there. This information is obtained from the absorption lines in the spectrum. The tenuous solar atmosphere absorbs some of the light coming from the hotter *photosphere*, or visible surface of the sun, below it.

The Sun's Interior. Underneath the photosphere lies a broad zone where energy from deeper in the sun is transmitted outwards by convection. Below this zone is another broad zone where energy is transported outwards by radiation. The energy coming from the sun's core is generated by nuclear fusion reactions in which hydrogen nuclei fuse to produce helium nuclei. Other nuclear reactions are possible in other stars; which one is operating depends on the type of star, its age, and its mass. Such nuclear reactions, along with radiative and convective transfer of energy and problems related to these systems, are under active consideration by theoretical and observational solar astronomers today.

The Photosphere. Activities at the surface of the sun are also of great importance. Thus, the sunspots appearing in the photosphere are one of the major areas of study. Sunspots are regions of great activity, somewhat cooler than the surrounding photosphere. They are associated with the general solar magnetic field, which increases greatly in strength in the sunspots. The sunspot cycle, during which the number of sunspots increases to a maximum and then decreases again, takes about 11 years.

At maximum activity there is a great outpouring of radiation that often interacts with the earth's atmosphere, causing geomagnetic storms. The radiation is of great concern to manned space flight, and sunspot activity is being intensely studied by instruments on the earth, carried by balloons and rockets, and orbited in satellites. Intense sunspot activity also gives rise to solar prominences and flares, which can be studied from the X-ray to the radio region of the spectrum.

The Chromosphere and Corona. Above the photosphere and the main portion of the solar atmosphere lies the chromosphere. This is a very tenuous and transparent region that eventually merges with the still higher corona. The pearly white corona is best seen during an eclipse of the sun, but since such eclipses are infrequent

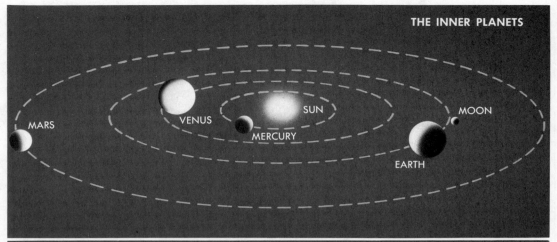

THE INNER PLANETS

MARS
VENUS
MERCURY
SUN
MOON
EARTH

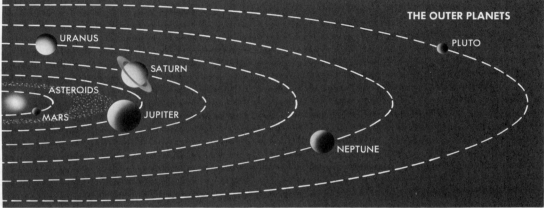

THE OUTER PLANETS

URANUS
PLUTO
SATURN
ASTEROIDS
MARS
JUPITER
NEPTUNE

SCHEMATIC DIAGRAMS NOT DRAWN TO SCALE

and inconvenient to observe, astronomers use a coronagraph to produce an artificial eclipse of the sun when photographing the corona.

The corona has a very high temperature, hence all or most of the material it contains is ionized. In fact, the energy source of coronal temperatures is one of the problems currently under intensive study by solar physicists. According to the laws of thermodynamics, temperatures should continue to decline as distance from the sun increases (as they do in the photosphere and lower chromosphere), but in the corona the temperatures actually increase. Another aspect of coronal study is that oscillations in the corona give rise to interesting radio spectrum phenomena. These are under intense investigation.

The Solar Wind. The outer boundary of the corona is anybody's guess and depends a great deal on how the corona is defined. Beyond the corona there remains a continuous outward stream of radiation and electrically charged particles. Occasionally, during outbursts in the chromosphere, great clouds of particles move away from the sun. The continuous stream of radiation and particles, together with these occasional clouds, constitute the solar wind that follows the convolutions of the sun's magnetic field out into the depths of the solar system.

The Solar System. The planets, satellites, asteroids, comets, and meteors that make up the rest of the solar system have long attracted the attention of astronomers. The early Greek astronomers invented the name *planet*, which means "wanderer." Mars, with its very noticeable changes of brightness over an 18-year period and

its ruddy color, was of special interest to the ancients. Fittingly, Mars was also the object that Kepler used to develop his laws of planetary motion, and it is again an object of intense study today.

The true nature of the solar system was first satisfactorily solved by Copernicus. As the proofs of his theory became positive, astronomers shifted their interest more and more to the physical characteristics of the objects in the solar systems, the evolution of the solar system, and the possibility of life on these other worlds. The coming of the space age has reemphasized these questions and problems, and a discussion of a few recent developments in this area will also indicate some modern methods of astronomical study and the kind of information they can provide.

The Moon and the Terrestrial Planets. The question of the moon's origin is of primary interest to astronomers. The moon and the earth may have been a two-planet system from the time of their formation, or the moon may have broken off from the earth in the geological past, or it may have been an independent planet that was captured by the earth's gravity. Studies of the features and composition of the moon have progressed rapidly in the space age; unmanned probes have photographed and tested its surface, and men have landed there and brought rock samples back to earth for analysis. Further study of the lunar interior is needed, however, before the history and nature of the moon is fully understood.

The terrestrial planets—Mercury, Venus, Earth, Mars, and the asteroids—are so called because they have rather large, "earthlike" den-

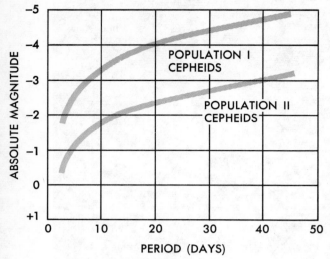

POPULATION I CEPHEIDS

POPULATION II CEPHEIDS

ABSOLUTE MAGNITUDE

PERIOD (DAYS)

sities as compared with the outer, gaseous planets. Studies of the terrestrial planets have yielded many interesting results in recent years.

Thus radar techniques were used to determine that Mercury rotates once on its axis every 59 days, contrary to the previous assumption that the planet always keeps the same side facing toward the sun. Similar techniques determined that Venus, unlike other planets, rotates in a retrograde fashion—that is, opposite to the rotation of the earth—and completes one rotation every 246 days. Radar echoes also showed that two highlands are on the hidden surface of Venus. Recent evidence indicates that the temperature of the planet is high, perhaps because of a greenhouse effect caused by the large amounts of carbon dioxide in the atmosphere of Venus. Russian and United States space probes failed to detect a magnetic field around the planet.

Space probes that were sent past Mars have returned the interesting information that the surface of Mars is marked with craters much as the surface of the moon is—a thesis already proposed in the late 1950's. The same probes indicated that if Mars has a magnetic field, it must be very weak and hence of little use in protecting the Martian surface from bombardment by charged particles from the sun. Atmospheric pressure at the planet's surface, about $1/100$ of that at the surface of the earth, further indicates that life on Mars seems unlikely in anything but very elementary states. Space missions of the future can tell astronomers more about the planet and how it fits into the puzzle of the solar system's origin and evolution.

The Outer Planets. Concentrated studies of Jupiter are being made. This massive, gaseous planet has been shown to have a strong magnetic field and a source of internal heat. Speculation as to Jupiter's origin and nature—is it almost a dwarf star?—have therefore increased. The radio spectrum of the planet is also of great interest, being characterized by strong bursts of radio energy. The other gaseous planets—Saturn, Uranus, and Neptune—are not being studied as intensively as Jupiter.

Pluto, the farthest known planet in the solar system, is another puzzle for modern astronomy.

It lies beyond the gaseous giants. Yet, if its mass is as large as the perturbations it produces in the orbits of other planets indicate, and its size is as small as it appears to be, Pluto is a very dense planet. Further studies of the diameter and mass of Pluto are urgently needed.

Comets. Comets are also of great interest to modern astronomers. They are thought to be composed of frozen water, methane, ammonia, and other gases, with some amount of solid debris—a picture that is consistent with the observed effects of solar radiation upon comets. A large store of such debris is thought to exist far beyond the confines of the visible solar system, held only loosely by the sun's gravitational attraction. Perturbations by the planets would occasionally cause deflections of some of this material toward the sun in the form of comets.

If these ideas are correct, some of the original material that formed the solar system is contained in comets. Also, such objects from the outskirts of the solar system have sampled very large regions of space for very long periods of time. The detailed study of cometary material would therefore be of great interest to astronomers. The ultimate wish of such studies would be to explain the origin and evolution of the solar system.

Origin of the Solar System. The current theory of the solar system's origin is that a large nebula, or gas cloud, began to condense into individual small clouds, the protostars, a few billion years ago. One of these protostars was our solar system. This cloud had smaller condensations, the protoplanets, and these in turn had condensations that gave rise to the major satellites. The central mass of the cloud, the *protosun,* eventually became large enough to contract, grow hot, and start to glow. When nuclear reactions set in within the sun, the resulting radiation swept the remaining uncondensed material out of the solar system. This simple picture does not explain all of the details, such as whether the asteroids are debris from the original cloud or fragments from a planetary collision or explosion, but it is probably close to the general truth.

The Stars. The next extension of astronomical study beyond the solar system is the observation of the stars, which constitute the major population of our Milky Way galaxy and the other galaxies. Ancient civilizations sometimes thought of the stars as small lights hanging from a celestial dome or as holes in the dome through which the fires of hell could be seen. The Greek astronomers alluded to the stars as suns, and the Arabic astronomers were aware of this possibility as well, but it was not until the time of Copernicus, that stars were definitely established as bright, distant objects. In following years it was determined that stars are balls of hot, glowing gases. However, men did not learn the source of stellar energy until recent decades.

Distance and Brightness Measurement. The ability to measure immense distances is essential to the study of stars. Astronomers have had to develop new techniques and adopt new units of measurement. Thus stellar distances are usually expressed in light years or parsecs. A *light year* is the distance that light travels in one year, moving at approximately 186,000 miles, or 300,000 kilometers, per second. One *parsec* is equivalent to 3.26 light years.

Measurement of distances to nearby stars is relatively straightforward, the method employed being similar to that of the surveyor. The radius of the earth's orbit is used as a baseline and also as a distance unit called the *astronomical unit*. The position of a nearby star is observed in relation to the background of more distant stars. The star is again observed from the opposite point of the earth's orbit, and its relative position is seen to have changed. This is called *parallax,* and the angle subtended by the astronomical unit at the distance of the star is called the *parallactic angle.*

If the star's apparent brightness is measured, the astronomer can then compute the actual brightness of the star. For convenience, 10 parsecs is used as the standard distance for expressing actual brightness. That is, the brightness of the star as it would appear at a distance of 10 parsecs from the earth is considered to be its actual brightness, or *absolute magnitude.*

Magnitude. In expressing stellar brightness, astronomers reduce their measurements to a convenient power relation that has its origins in the response of the eye to light. This response is measured in *magnitudes* and is related to the intensity of the stimulus on a logarithmic scale. The term magnitude has been used to express stellar brightness since the days of the ancient Greek astronomers, who thought that a star's brightness depends simply on its size, or magnitude. (It is now known that other factors are involved as well.)

The Hertzsprung-Russell Diagram. If the absolute magnitudes of a large number of stars are determined and plotted against the temperatures of these stars, a diagram known as the Hertzsprung-Russell (H-R) diagram results. This type of diagram is fundamental to astronomy because it reveals that there is a systematic organization to the physical properties of the stars.

The H-R diagram is of immediate interest here, however, because it is also of importance in the measurement of stellar distances. The astrometric technique used for measuring distances to nearby stars cannot be used for greater distances because the parallactic angle simply becomes too small to measure. However, if an astronomer can identify where a distant star would lie on an H-R diagram, he then knows its absolute brightness and can determine its distance. Since an astronomer can measure very feeble light sources, this photometric method is a powerful method indeed.

The Period-Luminosity Relation and Hubble's Law. Nature has provided two other methods of establishing stellar distances. One method involves true variable stars—pulsating stars with a periodic change in brightness that is related to their changes in size. The period of pulsation of any gaseous sphere is related in a simple way to the density of the sphere. Basically, the more dense a star is, the shorter is its period of pulsation. Also, the more dense a star is, the smaller it is, and hence the smaller is its surface area. Other things being equal, therefore, the denser a star is, the fainter is its absolute magnitude.

Astronomers have established a period-brightness, or period-luminosity (P-L relation), for pulsating stars. All that they need to do to use the P-L relation is to measure the period of pulsation of a star. They then know the star's absolute magnitude and can compute its distance. Pulsating stars are very easily recognized even in other nearby galaxies, and the distances to these

galaxies can therefore be measured.

The other method of measuring distances pertains to the galaxies themselves. When galaxies are far enough away, they all appear to be moving away from us. The speed of their recession seems to follow a simple law called Hubble's law (after Edwin Hubble), which states that the speed is proportional to the distances of the galaxies. Using this law, astronomers can measure the great distances of the universe.

Stellar Masses and Composition. Distances do not tell astronomers how stars are born, evolve, and die, however. To obtain such information they must also be able to measure the mass and determine the composition of stars.

Mass is a difficult property to measure, because it is necessary to weigh a star against something. That "something" can only be another star, and for this reason astronomers study binaries (double-star systems in which two stars revolve around one another). From such studies it has been deduced that there is a fundamental relation between a star's mass and its luminosity —the so-called *mass-luminosity relation.* This relation holds true for most stars but there are exceptions, notably those stars known as white dwarfs. To increase knowledge about stellar masses a considerable amount of work must be done over the coming years.

The problem of composition is even more perplexing. A spectrogram of a star reveals only those elements contained in the star's atmosphere,

This nebulosity in Moncoceros is an example of the dust and gas clouds that occur in interstellar space. (The star "halos" are telescope-produced optical effects.)

mainly the lower chromosphere. From such information an astronomer has to infer the composition of the main body of the star. All of the available evidence leads to the conclusion that, in general, stars are composed of 70 percent hydrogen, 28 percent helium, and 2 percent heavier elements by weight. Different stellar models can be set up and studied on a computer by varying these percentages. In this way an astronomer can look at stellar evolution in theory and then test the theory by observation.

Classification of Stars. Spectrographs are also used in the classification of stars. That is, the spectral classification of a star is determined by the presence or absence of certain lines in its spectrum and by the strength and shape of those lines. Since the appearance of the lines depends primarily upon the brightness and temperature of the star, it is possible to simplify the identification of stars to the point where an astronomer need only look at the spectrum of a star to do this.

The basic classification system in general use today is the Morgan-Keenan system, referred to as the MK Classification. It is essentially an excellent extension and refinement of an earlier Harvard Classification. In the MK system, stars are assigned the letters O, B, A, F, G, K, or M, in order of decreasing temperature. Each letter type is further subdivided into 10 classes, 0 through 9, again in order of decreasing temperature. There are also certain types of stars that do not fit into the general system and are instead assigned special letters. Thus carbon, or C, stars are similar to the cool M stars in temperature but have quite different spectra.

Stars of the same spectral type and lying at about the same distance from the earth are often quite different in brightness. Since the stars must have the same surface temperature, this can only mean that they have different surface areas—that is, they are different in size. This in turn leads to the concept of luminosity classes and the fact that there are dwarf stars, giant stars, and even supergiant stars. In the MK Classification these types are indicated by additional numerals, ranging from 0 for the most luminous supergiants to VI for subdwarfs. For example, the sun is a type G2V star; a G2III star would be a giant with the same temperature as the sun.

Giant stars are objects of great interest in modern astronomy. These huge stars are very tenuous. In fact, their density is so low that it is possible for matter to escape from them, and this has been observed to occur. Intensive studies of this mechanism of loss of mass, with subsequent enrichment of the interstellar medium, are currently under way.

Stellar Evolution. Another area of interest to modern astronomers is the study of stellar evolution. It is thought that there is an evolutionary order to the types of stars, and that the life history of a star like the sun can be described in the following way.

The star begins as a cloud of dust and gas in the interstellar medium. Somehow, perhaps because of magnetic fields, the cloud exceeds a certain density and begins to collapse inwards. Pressure in the protostar's center causes it to glow. In order to reach a stable configuration, convective currents carry heat to the surface of the protostar, which rapidly contracts until it is one of the main sequence of stars on the H-R diagram and is generating its energy by nuclear fusion. This process takes about a million years. The star then remains stable for billions of years until a large portion of its core is converted to helium by nuclear reactions. At this point the star expands because of increased internal temperatures and becomes a giant, until continuing reactions cause the core to collapse slowly again. The star continues to contract until it becomes a white dwarf. The dying star takes billions of years to cool off and become a black dwarf, a burned-out sun.

For stars a little less massive than the sun the evolutionary process may take much longer, whereas stars much less massive may proceed directly towards becoming black dwarfs in only a few million years. On the other hand, events in stars much more massive than the sun are more drastic and proceed at a much faster rate. In such stars it is thought that the collapse of the core after the giant stage occurs in a catastrophic way, producing what is known as a *nova*—an exploding star. If the star is very massive, it may become a *supernova*. After the explosion a white dwarf remains, with a great amount of ejected material being returned to the interstellar medium. In this process the content of the interstellar medium is altered, and the next stars formed from it will be quite different.

Studies of such evolutionary concepts have only begun. Testing the results of these studies requires a combination of observational efforts covering the entire electromagnetic spectrum. One area of study that may be very useful is that of binary systems in which the stars are quite close to one another. Spectroscopic evidence indicates that such stars are constantly exchanging mass—that is, one star is gaining mass at the expense of the other. In some close binaries the stars are both losing mass, which is streaming away from the system in a great pinwheel pattern. In all such systems the stars are evolving faster than they ordinarily would and provide interesting subjects for evolutionary studies.

The Interstellar Medium and the Galaxy. Of fundamental importance to these evolutionary studies and to the study of galactic structure in general is knowledge of the interstellar medium. The gas, dust, and other materials between the stars have revealed their presence and properties in a variety of subtle ways. The very sharp lines of calcium and sodium found in the spectra of these materials have been studied extensively, as has the small amount of polarization of starlight caused by the interstellar medium and its magnetic field. It was the discovery of this polarization that revealed the magnetic field of our Milky Way galaxy.

Because of the comparatively heavy concentration of dust and other material in the plane of the galaxy, the use of optical astronomy techniques in the study of the Milky Way is limited to a few thousand parsecs. Radio waves, however, penetrate the interstellar dust, and radio astronomy has therefore greatly extended man's knowledge of the galaxy. Similar studies of nearby galaxies, using the 21-centimeter line of hydrogen, are also yielding insights into the interpretation of the results obtained from the studies of the Milky Way.

Galactic Structure. A detailed picture of the galaxy is emerging from all of these studies. The galaxy appears to have several very high energy sources in its central region, along with billions of stars. About 3,000 parsecs from the

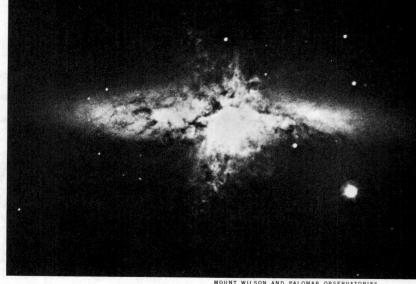

Galaxy M82, about 10 million light years away fom the earth, is peculiar in that a cataclysmic event of enormous magnitude appears to have taken place in its nucleus at some time in the past. Filaments of ejected material extend 10,000 light years to either side.

center there is an expanding ring of hydrogen. This is about where the arms of the galaxy begin. The arms spiral outward in a plane, and the galaxy rotates in the sense that the arms are trailing. The arms themselves may be due to a shockwave phenomenon.

Interstellar gas and dust are concentrated in the arms of the galaxy, and it is here that stars are being born. Thus, new stars are associated with gas and dust. Such stars lie on the main sequence of the H-R diagram and are known as *Population I stars.* Surrounding the galaxy is a halo of quite different stars, a continuation of the great concentration of stars at the center of the galaxy. Occasionally there is a smaller spherical concentration, called a *globular cluster,* in this distribution of stars. The stars in the galactic center and the expanding halo are called *Population II stars,* and their H-R diagram is quite different from that of the Population I stars. Evidence points to Population II stars as being "old" stars. Of course, distinctions are seldom sharp, and there appears to be every shade of stellar type between the two populations.

Galactic Evolution. This fact may give astronomers a clue toward understanding the evolution of the galaxy. Two possibilities are readily apparent. One is that an enormous gas and dust cloud, the *protogalaxy,* began to condense and form the Population II stars. The remaining material then collapsed into a relatively thin surrounding disk, where the Population I stars were formed. The other possibility is that the collapse was in successive stages, leaving a number of ellipsoidal distributions of intermediate-population stars centered about the core of the galaxy.

These two possibilities must be tested. Such tests would involve the distribution of the various constituents of the interstellar medium and might also involve the open or galactic clusters. Thus clusters born in a pure hydrogen cloud should be quite different from those born in a metal-enriched medium. A number of peculiar types of stars may aid in such studies as well. For example, some A-type stars have measureable magnetic fields that vary in strength and even in polarity. Were the magnetic fields generated after the stars formed, or did they result from conditions in the interstellar medium? And how do the peculiar stars called planetary nebulae and

shell stars (stars that are surrounded by an expanding shell of hot, tenuous gases) fit into the evolutionary scheme of the galaxy? Astronomers do not know how to answer these questions as yet.

Extragalactic Systems. Our Milky Way is one of a cluster of perhaps 19 galaxies referred to as the Local Group by astronomers. Billions of other galaxies lie scattered through the depths of space beyond the Local Group. For the most part they also occur in clusters, one such cluster containing approximately 10,000 galaxies. In the great voids between the clusters lie individual galaxies and, probably, a few stars that have escaped from galactic systems altogether.

Galaxies range from 10,000 to 40,000 parsecs in diameter and contain from 100 million to 100 billion stars or more. In some cases, the amount of gas and dust they contain is equal to the total mass of their stars.

A study of the relatively nearby galaxies has led to a system of galaxy classification based upon appearance. (Such a classification may or may not have anything to do with the evolution of galaxies.) Thus, in Hubble's early classification, some galaxies are spherical or elliptical with little gas or dust present. Disk-shaped galaxies such as the Milky Way seem to branch into two groups. One group has normal spiral arms and is classified according to the size of the galactic centers. The other group has a bar from which the arms trail. According to the classification system, both groups seem to terminate in amorphous galaxies referred to as irregular galaxies.

There are also so-called peculiar galaxies in which cataclysmic events of enormous magnitude appear to have occurred. An example is the galaxy M82, in which a completely disrupting event took place in the center of the galaxy at some time in the past. An analysis of the distribution of stars and particularly of the hydrogen in one region of our galaxy indicates that possibly a similar but smaller cataclysmic event took place long also in its spiral region.

The Universe. The size of the universe that the astronomer looks out upon today can only be estimated. The nearest galaxies are about a million light years away, and other galaxies are much more distant. Not only are these distant galaxies moving away from the Milky Way, but the more distant they are the faster they are receding. The most distant galaxies that could be viewed would be those with velocities approaching that of light. That velocity would occur at a distance of 10 billion light years, approximately, which is therefore the radius of the known universe. It is meaningless to inquire further, because anything beyond that distance could not be observed by the astronomer.

The lower limit of the age of the universe is also determined by the limit of size. Thus, a galaxy traveling at the velocity of light ever since the event that started it in motion would reach the limit of the observable universe in about 10 billion years. If that initial event is assumed to be the beginning of the universe as well, the universe must be at least 10 billion years old.

The Cosmological Principle. Studies of the size, shape, and distribution of galaxies, along with their brightness and color, have led astronomers to certain other conclusions about the universe. It has been observed that beyond a certain distance, all galaxies are speeding away from our own galaxy. The old geocentric and heliocentric view of the universe having been discarded long ago, there seemed no reason to think that a "galactocentric" view would be any more valid, but the fact that other galaxies are speeding away from us in all directions seemed to imply this. However, the development of relativistic mechanics provided a solution to the problem. According to relativistic mechanics, an observer located in any galaxy in the universe would also see his galaxy as the center of an expanding universe.

This outlook is known as the *cosmological principle.* Without its acceptance, assumptions about the universe as a whole could not be made from observations of local conditions in the Milky Way. If the cosmological principle is accepted, however, there are still several ways in which the universe may be described. Thus the universe may be expanding at an increasing pace, expanding uniformly, or expanding but slowing down. The first two cases would suggest a single origin to the universe some eons ago. The third case would admit to a pulsating universe infinite in time, but only traceable through one of its pulsations.

The Steady-State Theory. Since light has a finite velocity, the astronomer not only looks far out into space, but also far back in time. Thus the outer reaches of the universe ought to look quite different from the nearer parts if the universe is expanding and changing. For a long time, however, this appeared not to be the case, which led to an extension of the cosmological principle. This extension required that the universe appear the same in general nature at any place and point in time, which implies a constant density. This is the famous steady-state theory, and it requires the continuous creation of matter in order to comply with the cosmological principle.

However, high-resolution radio surveys of the universe have turned up the fact that some galaxies have a very large radio energy output. Such galaxies are called *radio galaxies.* From statistical counts of radio galaxies it became apparent that the farther away one went from the Milky Way, the more of these galaxies there are. Hence the universe is not everywhere the same in time, and it would seem that astronomers must abandon the steady-state theory.

Optical studies of very distant galaxies now seem to indicate that the expansion rate of the universe is slowing down. That is, the universe is apparently pulsating. But much more work must be done to satisfy all astronomers that this is so.

Quasars. Radio surveys have also turned up other very unusual objects that have greatly excited astronomers. These are the *quasistellar* (starlike) *radio sources,* which for brevity are called *quasi sources,* or *quasars.* That is, certain radio sources, thought at first to be galaxies, proved—unlike galaxies—to be smaller than the telescopes could resolve. These point sources of radio energy also had very unusual radio spectra. Radio astronomers called attention to the need for other observations of these objects.

Spectrograms of the objects revealed a number of rather broad emission lines on a generally blue, starlike continuum. The emission lines could not be identified, and it was thought that they might be due either to unknown elements or to elements in a condition never before observed. Neither possibility was very attractive. The problem was resolved when the emission lines of two quasi sources were identified with lines of well-known elements, but with large redshifts. The objects were, according to the redshifts, receding at velocities comparable with the most distant objects known. In fact, some quasi sources later studied proved to have redshifts as large as 0.8 times the velocity of light— the largest ever observed. Hence the quasi sources appeared to be at the limits of the known universe.

The objects presented several contradictions, however. Thus, the light of some quasi sources appears to vary in a periodic manner ranging from days to months. The periodic oscillation of an object cannot be shorter than the time needed to communicate between the two farthest points of the object; therefore quasi sources could be, at most, only a few light-months in diameter. However, at the great distances at which the objects were presumed to be, their energy output must be on the order of 10^{47} ergs per second, far greater than the energy output of the largest galaxies.

Another contradiction was that, according to certain absorption lines in their spectra, the quasi sources could not be very dense, since such lines arise only in low-density, high-temperature regions. Thus quasi sources presented a real dilemma to astronomers. The only objects at all resembling them are the planetary nebulae, shell stars, and novae at maximum brightness. But none of these objects have velocities at all approaching those of the quasi sources.

Current efforts to resolve the problem of quasi sources take two directions. One is to consider the sources as being at great distances and to accept the energy problem as unsolved. The other is to consider the sources as being relatively nearby and accept the problem of explaining the large redshifts in their spectra. If the latter direction is taken, one possibility is that the quasars are material ejected from violent events inside a galaxy.

There are arguments in favor of taking the former direction, however. That is, certain galaxies called *Seyfert galaxies* have highly condensed nuclei that are extremely bright and almost point sources of light. Spectra of these nuclei reveal some broad emission lines similar to those found in the spectra of quasi sources. There may therefore be a smooth transition from radio galaxies to Seyfert galaxies to quasi sources.

NEW OBSERVATORY at Cerro Tololo in Chile is operated by the Association of Universities for Research in Astronomy, Inc., and houses several large telescopes. The site, 7,200 feet (2,200 meters) above sea level, affords excellent atmospheric conditions for viewing Southern Hemisphere skies.

CERRO TOLOLO INTER-AMERICAN OBSERVATORY

It may be noted in passing that the Seyfert galaxies can serve as ideal reference points in astrometric work; the positions of stars in the Milky Way can be referred to these essentially fixed positions. Such work is already well under way.

ASTRONOMY IN THE FUTURE

The cosmological problem presented by quasi sources may rank with the greatest problems that astronomy has ever faced. Other challenges for astronomers multiply continuously as well. The details of star formation and the death of stars are yet to be worked out; there are many unsolved problems relating to the solar system; and astronomers have only begun to understand the interstellar medium. Thus the list grows and grows.

The Search for Life on Other Planets. There is also the fascinating question of whether life exists elsewhere in the universe. It is hard to conceive that life might not have arisen on some celestial body besides the earth. There are something like 10^{22} stars in the observable universe, and some percentage of these stars must almost certainly have planets, some of which must in turn resemble the earth.

At least one object of a planetary nature beyond the solar system has been discovered, a companion of the nearby star called Bernard's Star. In this instance the planet is far too massive for life as we know it, and its eccentric orbit precludes the possibility of other earthlike planets around the star. Most stars are too distant for possible planets to be detected at all. However, serious efforts have been made to discover intelligent life elsewhere in the universe. Perhaps with more sophisticated techniques the search may be rewarded.

The Development of Observational Techniques. Many more astronomers and many more telescopes are needed to obtain the answers to the problems that astronomy faces in the future. Much greater use will be made of space platforms for the mounting of instrumentation. The earth's atmosphere absorbs much of the ultraviolet radiation falling on it; in the radio region of the spectrum, wavelengths of over 40 meters

NASA

PROJECT SKYLAB of U. S. space program offers scientist-astronauts the chance to make astronomical observations from space. Skylab consists of a modified third stage of a Saturn 5 rocket (right) and a telescope mount (above) joined to a docking adapter. An Apollo command service module, used by the astronauts as an earth shuttle, is shown docked to Skylab (left).

(131 feet) are reflected back into space by the ionosphere. Only from above the atmosphere can these regions of the spectrum be observed.

Astronomers will also develop more sophisticated instruments to be placed on telescopes. There will be a far greater reliance upon computer systems for data handling, and a much more detailed approach to astronomical problems will be made by theoreticians. With the building of special purpose earth-based telescopes, and diffraction-limited telescopes for use in space, astronomers will uncover new information from which new problems will unfold.

See also ASTROPHOTOGRAPHY; ASTROPHYSICS; CELESTIAL MECHANICS; COSMOGONY; QUASI-STELLAR SOURCES; SPECTROSCOPY.

LAURENCE W. FREDRICK
Leander McCormick Observatory
University of Virginia

Bibliography

Abetti, Giorgio, *The History of Astronomy* (New York 1952).
Baker, Robert H., and Fredrick, Laurence W., *An Introduction to Astronomy* (Princeton, N.J., 1967).
Bok, Bart J., and Bok, Priscilla F., *The Milky Way*, 3d ed. (Cambridge, Mass., 1957).
De Vaucouleurs, Gérard, *Discovery of the Universe* (New York 1957).
Glasstone, Samuel, *Sourcebook on the Space Sciences* (Princeton, N.J., 1965).
Hoyle, Fred, *Astronomy* (Garden City, N.Y., 1962).
Lyttleton, Raymond A., *The Modern Universe* (New York 1957).
Menzel, Donald H., *Our Sun*, rev. ed. (Cambridge, Mass., 1959).
Miczaika, Gerhard R., and Sinton, William M., *Tools of the Astronomer* (Cambridge, Mass., 1961).
Page, Thornton, and Page, Lou W., *The Origin of the Solar System* (New York 1966).
Page, Thornton, and Page, Lou W., *Wanderers in the Sky* (New York 1965).
Shapley, Harlow, *Galaxies,* rev. ed. (Cambridge, Mass., 1961).
Struve, Otto, *The Universe* (Cambridge, Mass., 1962).

GLOSSARY OF ASTRONOMICAL TERMS

Aberration.—The small apparent variation in the position of a star as a result of the motion of the earth across the line of sight.

Absorption Lines.—The dark lines in the continuous spectrum of light from the sun or other star, produced by and identifying the layer of cooler gases in the atmosphere of the star.

Altitude.—The angular distance of a celestial object vertically above the plane of the celestial equator.

Aphelion.—The point in the elliptical orbit of a member of the solar system when it is most distant from the sun.

Apogee.—The point in the orbit of the moon, or of an artificial satellite, when it is most distant from the earth.

Asteroid.—One of many minor planets, or planetoids, orbiting the sun, principally between the orbital paths of Mars and Jupiter. A few asteroids have eccentric orbits that take them close to the sun.

Astronomical Unit.—The average or mean distance of the earth from the sun, used as a unit of measurement.

Astrometry.—The technique of astronomy that is concerned with the accurate measurement of the positions of celestial objects.

Astrophysics.—The branch of astronomy that deals with the physical nature of celestial objects.

Azimuth.—The horizontal angle between a celestial object and the south point of the horizon, measured clockwise in a plane parallel to the horizon.

Big-Bang Theory.—See *Expanding Universe.*

Binary Star.—A system composed of two stars orbiting one another. A *visual binary* can be detected on photographic plates; a *spectroscopic binary* can be detected only by spectroscopic means. The orbital plane of an *eclipsing binary* is so oriented with respect to the earth that the stars periodically eclipse one another.

Celestial Mechanics.—The branch of astronomy concerned with the motions and gravitational interactions of celestial objects.

Celestial Sphere.—The apparent sphere of the heavens as seen from the earth. The *celestial equator* is the projection of the earth's equator upon this sphere.

Cluster, Star.—A group of stars having a common origin and common motion through space. A *galactic cluster* is a loose collection of up to several hundred stars; a *globular cluster* consists of many thousands of stars in a compact globular formation.

Coelostat.—A clock-driven mirror system used with telescopes or other instruments, which follows the path of a celestial object under observation across the sky and allows the main instrument to remain still.

Comet.—A diffuse aggregation of gas and dust particles clustered in a "coma" and moving about the sun in an eccentric orbit. In the region of the sun a comet may exhibit a tail.

Constellation.—A pattern formed on the celestial sphere by stars. Modern astronomy still employs the constellations for describing the approximate positions of celestial objects.

Coronagraph.—A telescopic device that produces an artificial eclipse of the sun by means of an occulting disk, permitting photography of the solar corona.

Cosmogony.—The study of the possible origin and evolution of the universe. See *Expanding Universe; Steady-State Universe.*

Cosmological Principle.—The assumption that the universe would appear the same in over-all structure from any galaxy in the universe.

Cosmology.—The study of the structure of the universe as a whole.

Declination.—The angular distance of a celestial object north or south of the celestial equator, in a plane perpendicular to the equator.

Double Star.—See *Binary Star.*

Eccentricity.—In an elliptical orbit, the degree of flattening of the ellipse. A circular orbit has 0 eccentricity; the more eccentric the orbit, the more nearly it approaches a value of 1.

Eclipse.—The obscuration of the light from one celestial object by the interposition of another object between it and an observer. See *Occultation.*

Ecliptic.—A great circle representing the apparent annual path of the sun upon the celestial sphere. Because of the tilt of the earth's axis, this path is inclined to the celestial equator.

Electromagnetic Spectrum.—The entire range of wavelengths of electromagnetic radiation. It includes gamma rays, X-rays, ultraviolet rays, visible light, infrared rays, microwaves, and radio waves.

Emission Lines.—The bright lines in the spectrum of light emitted by a glowing gas.

Equinoxes.—The two points where the great circle of the ecliptic intersects the great circle of the celestial equator on the celestial sphere. The *vernal equinox* occurs about March 21 and the *autumnal equinox* about September 23. See *Precession.*

Expanding Universe.—A 20th-century theory that the universe is expanding as the result of an explosion, billions of years ago, of a nucleus containing all of the matter in the universe; also known as the "big-bang" theory.

Galaxy.—A vast system, light-years in extent, containing hundreds of millions of stars and, usually, large clouds of interstellar dust and gas. The galaxy of which our sun is a member is known as the *Milky Way.*

Harmonic Law.—The third of Kepler's three laws of planetary motion, which states that the squares of the periods of any two planets are in the same proportion as the cubes of their average distances from the sun.

Hertzsprung-Russell (H-R) Diagram.—A diagram in which the temperatures of a group of stars are plotted against their absolute magnitudes. The stars fall into a number of spectral classifications in the diagram.

Hubble Sequence.—A sequence devised by Edwin Hubble of the different types of galaxies (elliptical, spiral, and irregular).

Image-Intensifier Tube.—An instrument that increases the brightness of an image from a telescope by means of a combination of photocathode and phosphor screen.

Interferometer.—An instrument that produces interference patterns of light for the precise measurement of wavelengths and other minute distances.

Interstellar Medium.—The dust and gas lying between the stars, from which the stars are formed.

Kepler's Laws.—The laws of planetary motion published by Johannes Kepler in 1609 and 1618. The first states that the orbit of each planet is an ellipse with the sun at one of its foci. The second states that each planet revolves so that the imaginary line between it and the sun sweeps over equal areas of space in equal intervals of time. For the third, see *Harmonic Law.*

Light Year.—A unit of astronomical measurement; the distance that light travels in one year, or approximately 6,000,000,000,000 miles (9,500,000,000,000 km). One light year equals 63,240 astronomical units.

Luminosity.—The intrinsic brightness of a star compared with the brightness of the sun.

Magnitude.—A logarithmic scale of stellar brightness. The *apparent magnitude* of a star is its brightness as seen from earth; its *absolute magnitude* is its brightness as it would appear at a distance of 10 parsecs (see *Parsec*).

Main Sequence.—The band, or sequence, into which the majority of stars fall in a Hertzsprung-Russell diagram. Our sun is a main-sequence star. Other types of stars include white dwarfs, red giants, and supergiants.

Meridian.—A great circle on the celestial sphere, passing through the zenith, nadir, and the north and south points on the horizon.

Meteor.—A particle of rock or metal, usually very small, that orbits the sun (often in a stream or swarm of other meteors); also called *meteoroid*. A meteor entering the earth's atmosphere glows, melts, and disintegrates because of friction with the air, and may be seen as a "shooting star."

Meteorite.—When a meteor entering the atmosphere is large enough for a portion to reach the ground, the portion is known as a meteorite. Sometimes the term is used to indicate a fragment of meteoric origin, whether encountered on the earth or in space.

Milky Way.—See *Galaxy.*

Monochromator.—A device used for obtaining a desired narrow band of wavelengths from a light source by means of a prism or diffraction grating and a system of slits.

Nebula.—A diffuse cloud of interstellar matter. *Bright nebulae* are found near stars and reflect their light, also emitting radiation of their own. *Dark nebulae* do not glow but obscure the celestial objects that lie beyond them. *Planetary nebulae* are bright shells of expanding gas that surround some stars.

Newton's Law of Gravitation.—The gravitational force between two bodies is directly proportional to the product of their masses and inversely proportional to the square of the distance between their centers.

Newton's Laws of Motion.—(1) A body at rest remains at rest and a body in motion remains in uniform motion unless acted upon by an outside force. (2) The acceleration produced by that force is directly proportional to the force and inversely proportional to the mass of the body, and takes place in the direction in which the force acts. (3) For every action there is an equal and opposite reaction.

Nova.—A star that in a matter of hours may be seen to increase in brilliance by several magnitudes, probably as the result of an explosive ejection of surface material. A *supernova* is a far more violent explosion and occurs much more rarely than novae.

Occultation.—A term applied especially to eclipses of the stars and planets by the moon. The satellite of a large planet such as Jupiter may also be said to undergo occultation when, as viewed telescopically, it passes behind the body of the planet.

Optical Double.—A pair of stars that, as seen from the earth, appear to form a binary system but are actually widely separated in space.

Orbit.—The path of revolution of a secondary celestial body around a more massive primary, or of both bodies around a common center of gravity.

Parallax.—The apparent change in position of a celestial object (compared with a background of more distant objects) when it is viewed from opposite sides of the earth or from opposite sides of the earth's orbit.

Parsec.—A unit of astronomical measurement. One parsec is equivalent to about 3.26 light years, or 206,265 astronomical units. See *Light Year.*

Perigee.—The point in the orbit of the moon, or of an artificial satellite, when it is closest to the earth.

Perihelion.—The point in the orbit of a member of the solar system when it is closest to the sun.

Period.—The time taken to complete a cycle of events; as, a revolution of a planet about the sun. In the term *period-luminosity relation* it refers to a completed cycle of luminosity changes of a variable star.

Period-Luminosity Relation.—A relation that has been established between the periods of certain variable stars, called Cepheids, and the intrinsic brightness of these stars. By observing the period of a Cepheid, its luminosity and distance can be calculated.

Perturbation.—A disturbance in the regular motion of a celestial body around its primary, produced by the presence of a gravitationally acting third body or by a nonuniform distribution of mass in the body around which the revolution occurs.

Photometry.—The technique of astronomy that is concerned with measuring the intensity of radiation coming from a celestial source.

Photomultiplier Tube.—A tube using a photocathode for the accurate measurement of the intensity of light from a celestial source. The auxiliary instrument employing a photomultiplier tube is referred to as a *photoelectric photometer.*

Planet.—In the solar system, one of the nine massive bodies revolving around the sun and shining by its reflected light. The asteroids are minor planets, or *planetoids.* Many other stars may also have planetary bodies revolving around them.

Precession.—The slow shifting of the celestial equator as a result of a motion of the earth's axis about a line perpendicular to the plane of the earth's orbit. This motion is produced by the gravitational pull of the sun and the moon on the earth's equatorial bulge.

Proper Motion.—The apparent angular motion of a star across the observer's line of sight. It does not take into account the star's radial velocity. Nearby stars with a motion that is transverse to the line or sight show the largest proper motions.

Pulsating Universe.—A variation of the concept of an expanding universe. The universe is considered as expanding from and then contracting again to a primeval nucleus, possibly repeating this cycle forever.

Quasi-Stellar Radio Source.—One of several powerful sources of light and radio energy, apparently at the very limits of the known universe. The nature of these point sources of energy is unknown. Also called *quasi sources,* or *quasars.*

Radial Velocity.—The linear velocity of a star along the observer's line of sight, either approaching or receding. Radial velocity is measured by a spectrograph.

Radio Astronomy.—The study of radio energy sources in space by means of large reflecting instruments called *radio telescopes.*

Red Shift.—A phenomenon observed in the spectrum of an object receding from the earth. The spectral lines are shifted toward the red end of the spectrum. If the object is approaching the earth, the lines are shifted toward the violet end. The amount of the shift, in either case, is proportional to the speed of the object.

Reflector.—See *Telescope.*

Refractor.—See *Telescope.*

Satellite.—A moon of one of the planets. There are 31 satellites in the solar system, not considering the particles making up the rings of Saturn. Men have orbited many *artificial satellites* of the earth.

Schmidt Telescope.—See *Telescope.*

Solar Wind.—A continuous stream of radiation and electrically charged particles moving outward from the sun and following the convolutions of the sun's magnetic field.

Solstices.—The two dates on which the sun reaches positions farthest north and south of the celestial equator; also, the two positions involved. The northern solstice occurs about June 21 and the southern solstice about December 21.

Spectrograph.—An instrument combining a spectroscope and photographic equipment, used for studying the spectra of celestial objects. The plates on which the spectra are recorded are known as *spectrograms.*

Spectroheliograph.—A spectrograph that is specially modified for study of the lines of the sun's spectrum.

Spectroscopy.—The detailed study of the radiative output of a celestial source.

Spectrum, Visible.—The portion of the electromagnetic spectrum that can be detected by the human eye.

Star.—A massive, hot, glowing ball of highly ionized gases, having an internal temperature of many millions of degrees and deriving its energy from nuclear reactions. The sun is the closest star to the earth. Stars may vary widely in size, density, temperature, and other physical properties. See *Main Sequence.*

Steady-State Universe.—A theory of the universe opposed to that of an expanding or pulsating universe and requiring the continuous creation of matter. The theory states that the universe maintains a uniform density and that it appears the same in general nature at any place and point in time.

Supernova.—See *Nova.*

Telescope.—An instrument for collecting light from celestial objects and resolving the images of the objects. A reflecting telescope, or *reflector,* has a mirror as an objective for forming the image; a *refractor* has a system of lenses as an objective. A *Schmidt telescope* is a reflector with a spherical mirror as an objective and is used for wide-angle photography.

Transit.—The passage of a smaller body in front of a larger one (as seen from earth), such as the transit of Mercury or Venus across the disk of the sun, or of a satellite of Jupiter across the disk of that planet. Transit may also mean the passage of a celestial object across the meridian of a place.

Variable Star.—A star that varies in intrinsic brightness. There are several classes of variable stars, some with short-term and others with long-term periods of variation. There are also irregular variables. An eclipsing binary is not a true variable star.

Zodiac.—An imaginary band on the celestial sphere, having the ecliptic as its middle line and divided into 12 zones.

ASTROPHOTOGRAPHY, as-trō-fə-tog′rə-fē, is the application of photographic techniques to the field of astronomy. The invention of photography and its use in the study of the heavens has changed the entire course of astronomical research. Except for special problems—such as the study of the surface features of planets from the surface of the earth, or the measurement of the separation of close binary (double) stars—photographic methods have entirely replaced the method of visual telescopic observation.

History. Photography was first applied to astronomy soon after the invention of photography in the 19th century. In a historic experiment performed in New York in 1839, John William Draper obtained an image of the moon on a daguerreotype plate after a 20-minute exposure. Following this achievement, daguerreotypes of the moon and stars were obtained by William Cranch Bond and his son George Phillips Bond at the Harvard College Observatory in 1848 and 1850. In the next two decades many other people made additional experimental photographs of the brighter stars and of the sun.

The daguerreotype process was slow and cumbersome, however. Serious, extensive use of photography did not come about until the invention of the dry-plate process in the 1870's. In this process, silver bromide crystals were imbedded in a transparent gelatin and deposited on a glass surface. The glass plate could be handled easily at the telescope and could also be stored with little difficulty after processing.

Steady increases in the sensitivity of photographic materials have been made since the development of the dry-plate process. Today the speed of emulsions is fully 10,000 times faster than the original daguerreotype plates. Photographs of the moon can be obtained now in considerably less than 1 second, compared to the 20 minutes required by Draper's equipment. Exposures of less than 1 hour with a modern photographic telescope—such as the Palomar 200-inch (508 cm) reflector—can record stars that are 10 million times fainter than the eye can see.

Applications. Photography is used in astronomy for a number of purposes. Thus, daily photographs of the sun are made at several observatories to provide a stable, permanent record of the size and position of sunspots, the presence

A photographic plate is placed in the prime-focus observing position of the 200-inch (508 cm) Hale telescope.

of solar flares, and the appearance of other active regions. Direct photography of star fields provides information on the positions, brightness, color, and motions of the stars and reveals that some of the stars are actually binaries or multistar systems.

The permanency of the photographic plate permits comparison of pictures taken long ago with pictures taken recently. By means of this method of comparison, astronomers can detect changes in brightness of variable stars and observe motions of stars across the line of sight. Astronomers could not hope to record and catalog such phenomena by visual observation only.

Similarly, photographs of nebulae and of galaxies reveal details of form far richer than can be seen by visual observation. In fact, much information on the nature of galaxies and the structure of the universe has been obtained through photography with the 100-inch (254-cm) photographic telescope. Also, the precise determination of time is accomplished with special photographic telescopes pointed toward the zenith to record the passage of certain catalog stars across the meridian.

Equipment. Photographic emulsions are made today with a wide range of spectral sensibilities. That is, they can record wavelengths of light ranging from the short ultraviolet rays to the longer near-infrared. This ability permits studies of the colors of stars to be made by using several emulsions of different color sensitivity, together with special filters that isolate precisely the portion of a spectrum to be studied.

Telescopes. Special telescopes have been designed to exploit the potentialities of the photographic method. For example, wide-angle Schmidt cameras that accept photographic plates 14 inches square (35.6 cm square) are used for mapping the sky in different colors. Long focal length reflectors are used for detailed photographs of smaller areas of the sky in different colors.

The comparison of photographs of nearby stars, taken at six-month intervals with special parallax telescopes, provides data on the distances to the stars. The data are obtained through measurement of the displacements of the stellar images relative to more distant background objects, the displacement resulting from the motion of the earth about the sun. Knowledge of the distances to other astronomical objects is based on such measurements.

The wide camera attached to this 26-inch (66 cm) refractor is used for taking pictures of double stars.

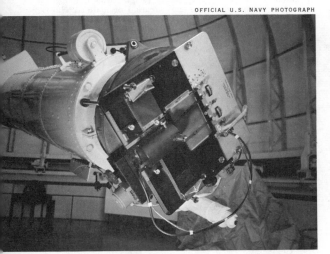

This galaxy in Centaurus (*left*), a source of radio noise, was photographed with the giant Hale reflector. The 100-inch (254 cm) Mount Wilson telescope was used to photograph the central region of the Andromeda galaxy (*right*).

Spectrographs. The use of spectrographs attached to large telescopes permits photographic recording of the spectra of stars and of other astronomical objects. The spectra provide information on temperatures, pressures, chemical compositions, and radial velocities.

The measurement of red shifts in the spectra of distant galaxies—that is, the shift of the spectral lines toward the red end of the spectra, indicating that the galaxies are moving away from us—is accomplished entirely by astrophotography. (Such measurements led to the concept of an expanding universe.) Spectrographs of great speed are used in these measurements, the spectrographs being designed specifically around the properties of the photographic plate.

Emulsions. New photographic emulsions of higher speed, greater resolution, and higher efficiency are continually being developed for astronomical purposes. The sensitivity of photographic plates has increased by a factor of 10, at least, since the 1930's, and even greater increases in sensitivity are expected in the future.

A variety of emulsions is available, offering different resolutions, different sensitivities, and different color properties. Selection of the correct emulsion for a given photographing problem requires skill and knowledge on the part of the astronomer.

Continuing Importance of Astrophotography. The astronomer must be familiar with photographic processing methods and with the variations of these methods that are needed to produce the desired contrast and limiting magnitude for a particular problem. The science of astronomical photography is therefore part of the training of every astronomer. Although photoelectric devices, in some applications, supplement astrophotography in the analysis of light from astronomical objects, astronomers will continue to use photographic methods for many years.

See also ASTRONOMY; ASTROPHYSICS; OBSERVATORY; PHOTOGRAPHY; SPECTROSCOPY; TELESCOPE.

ALLAN R. SANDAGE
Mount Wilson and Palomar Observatories

Dr. Walter Baade (1893–1960), who established a new scale of interstellar distances through his studies of the Andromeda galaxy, is shown examining a photographic negative of a star field. Such negatives reveal details with great clarity.

ASTROPHYSICS, as-trō-fiz′iks, is the branch of astronomy that deals with the physical and chemical nature of celestial objects and events. This covers a vast scope, since everything that lies beyond the dominant influence of the earth falls naturally into its domain. In contrast to the wide variety of objects that are studied in astrophysics, the means of studying them are very limited, because for obvious reasons the objects cannot be subjected to controlled experimentation. Although the advent of space research has somewhat modified this situation, the basic characteristic of astrophysics (as of astronomy in general) is its observational nature.

Astrophysics has sometimes been defined as the application of physical laws to astronomical objects. This definition would include *celestial mechanics*, which studies the motions of planets and other bodies in the solar system. Actually, celestial mechanics is never considered a part of the field of astrophysics.

While astrophysics had its origins in the development of special means of observation that will be discussed in this article, the scope of astrophysics has changed with the passage of time. In order to obtain a clear understanding of this branch of astronomy, its historical development must first be studied.

BACKGROUND OF ASTROPHYSICS

Positional Astronomy. Historically it was the positions of shining objects in the sky that first caught the attention of men. This developed into what is called positional astronomy. Observations of the night sky convinced men of early civilizations that there were two kinds of celestial objects. There were the fixed stars that moved across the sky without changing their positions relative to one another. There were, in contrast, the planets (from a Greek word meaning "wandering") that moved across the background of the fixed stars. The study of the motions of planets provided the clue for the formulation of Newton's laws of gravitation in the 17th century. It led also to the measurement of the positions of the stars, or *astrometry*, and eventually to the determination of the distance and brightness of stars. Although astrophysics depends on these results, positional observations in themselves are not considered a part of the field of astrophysics.

Photometry. Another directly observable quantity of celestial bodies is their apparent brightness—their brightness as seen from the earth. The study of stellar brightness is astronomical *photometry* and may be traced back to the ancient Greeks, who graded the stars according to their apparent brightness. The Greeks, who thought that the brightness of a star depended only on its size, spoke of brightness as *magnitude*. This terminology is still in use.

Magnitude. When the brightness of a star is measured, the region (in the spectrum of electromagnetic radiation) of the wavelengths of light being measured must be specified. In the early days, when the human eye was used directly for such measurements of brightness, the measurements involved visible light only. This is known as the *visual magnitude* of stars. With the development of photographic methods, the measured brightness refers to the spectrum of wavelengths to which the photographic plate is sensitive. This is known as the *photographic magnitude* of stars.

By proper choice of light filters and of detecting instruments, astronomers today can measure the brightness of a star at any particular wavelength—that is, at any particular color—they desire. The color of a star is related to its temperature. The different brightness readings obtained when the same star is measured at different colors gives the astronomer a good estimate of the temperature of the star.

The most important brightness measurement should perhaps be one that takes into account all the different wavelengths of electromagnetic radiation, from the long radio waves to the very short gamma rays. A measurement of this type is known as the *bolometric magnitude*. The earth's atmosphere absorbs wide ranges of wavelengths in the electromagnetic spectrum, however, and the bolometric magnitude of a star is not a directly measurable quantity for earthbound astronomers. (This is especially true of hot blue stars, whose radiation lies mostly in the ultraviolet region of the spectrum.) The situation is being changed by the development of earth satellites that make astronomical observations above the atmosphere.

Photometric Studies. It was mentioned that photometric measurements are useful in determining the temperature of a star. Furthermore, if the distance to a star is known, the apparent brightness of the star can be converted directly into its *intrinsic brightness*, or *luminosity*—the star's actual rate of energy output.

In addition to temperature and luminosity determinations, photometric observations also are used to study the ways in which the brightness of some celestial objects varies with time. These studies are very rewarding, because they reveal some of the physical events that can take place in celestial objects. Thus, the study of novae, supernovae, and similar objects indicates that stars can explode catastrophically, increasing suddenly in brightness by several million times. Other less drastic variations indicate that some stars pulsate or in other cases that one star is traveling around another star and eclipsing it periodically.

A relationship was discovered in 1912 between the period of pulsation and the luminosity of a group of pulsating stars being studied. This discovery had a far-reaching impact on the determination of distances of cosmic objects. It also stimulated the further study of the nature of such pulsating stars, or *variables*. It has been found that there are several different kinds of variables, each having a distinct period-luminosity relationship of its own. Pulsating variables are an outstanding problem in astrophysics.

Astrophysicists also owe to photometric studies much knowledge concerning the properties of the material between the stars. Interstellar space is not entirely empty but is permeated with gases and dust at very low densities. This material affects the electromagnetic radiation passing through it. First, starlight is dimmed through scattering and absorption by the material, and stars therefore appear fainter than they would if space were entirely empty. Second, the dust particles in interstellar space scatter blue light more effectively than they scatter red light, which is of longer wavelengths. The removal of blue light leaves starlight redder as it spreads through interstellar space. This is known as "interstellar reddening" and can best be studied through photometry of hot, distant stars.

Polarization. A special means of photometric study that is of great importance to the understanding of interstellar media is polarization. It was discovered in 1949 that light from distant stars becomes polarized when the light passes through clouds of interstellar matter. That is, the lightwaves now vibrate in planes parallel to each other. The polarization is believed to be caused by the alignment of elongated dust grains in interstellar space. There is no difficulty in supposing this, because laboratory experiments show that crystal growth tends to produce particles of just such a shape. However, the question of why they are aligned—possibly because a weak magnetic field prevails in interstellar space—has created for the astrophysicist many new problems concerning the proposed magnetic field and the particles themselves.

Surface Photometry. A final area of photometric study concerns the larger or nearby objects that appear as more than point sources of light. Thus, the surfaces of the moon, the sun, and the planets provide interesting subjects for study, either visually or by photograph. Other such objects are the distant star groups, or galaxies, which can be classified on the basis of their structural appearance—spiral, elliptical, or irregular. These studies may be regarded as photometric because, basically, they involve light distribution—that is, the surface photometry of an extended object. They provide a quick, revealing, over-all description for extended celestial objects.

SPECTROSCOPIC OBSERVATION

With photometric methods alone, scientists could not have succeeded in comprehending the physical nature of celestial objects. The founding of astrophysics had to await the development of another means of observation, stellar spectroscopy. Before it became possible to analyze the light from celestial objects spectroscopically, it was meaningless to ask about the chemical composition and the physical state of the objects.

Development. As early as 1666, Isaac Newton demonstrated the basic procedure of spectroscopy when he broke sunlight into the colors of the visible spectrum by means of a prism. If the light is first passed through a slit, dark lines are seen crossing the solar spectrum. These lines were first noticed in 1802 by the English chemist and physicist William Hyde Wollaston, who made no effort to investigate the lines.

The spectroscopic study of celestial objects may be said to have started with Joseph von Fraunhofer, a Bavarian optician. Fraunhofer investigated the dark lines of the solar spectrum and published his results in 1817. He showed by experiments that the dark lines and bands—now known as Fraunhofer lines—were intrinsic to the nature of the sun's spectrum and did not result from light diffraction or optical illusion. Fraunhofer measured hundreds of these lines and to the heaviest ones assigned letters—A, B, C, and so forth—some of which remain in use today. He did not have any idea of the meaning of the lines, however.

Kirchhoff's Laws. Perhaps Gustav Kirchhoff, a German physicist, should be credited with the founding of astrophysics, because from his interpretation of the Fraunhofer lines emerged the possibility of learning the physical nature of celestial objects. In collaboration with Robert Bunsen, a German chemist, Kirchhoff studied the spectra of flames and of metallic vapors in an electric arc. Such spectra appear as bright lines against a dark background. The men discovered that a bright double line in the spectrum produced by a sodium flame coincided in wavelength with the dark D lines in the solar spectrum. After determining a number of similar coincidences between the bright lines in the spectra of other vapors and the dark lines of the solar spectrum, Kirchhoff enunciated the famous laws that now bear his name.

SPECTROSCOPY has made it possible to determine the chemical composition of stars. The first element to be identified in a star was sodium, whose characteristic D-line was found in the absorption spectrum of the sun.

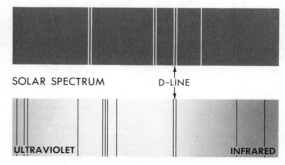

LINE SPECTRUM OF SODIUM VAPOR

SOLAR SPECTRUM   D-LINE

ULTRAVIOLET   INFRARED

The first law states that each chemical species has its own characteristic spectrum. The second law states that each chemical species absorbs radiation at the same wavelengths at which it can emit radiation.

Thus, the surface, or photosphere, of the sun (and other stars) emits continuous radiation. If this light were directly received by instruments on earth, it would produce a *continuous spectrum*, just as an incandescent light does. However, vapors in the so-called *reversing layer* immediately above the solar surface selectively absorb some of this radiation, according to the chemical nature of those vapors. The absorption takes place because the reversing layer is at a lower temperature than is the photosphere, and it results in the Fraunhofer lines of the solar *absorption spectrum* observed on earth. By identifying the absorption lines in the sun's spectrum, Kirchhoff was able to announce in 1861 the presence of various chemical elements in the solar atmosphere, such as sodium and calcium.

The importance of this discovery is obvious. The chemical composition of stellar atmospheres could now be determined. The discovery also demonstrated that even at the surface of the sun, temperatures are high enough to vaporize metals. The realization that stellar matter is in a gaseous state had far-reaching consequences, because the study of matter in a gaseous state is simpler than the study of liquids or solids. Thus, the density of a gas is related in a direct way to the temperature of the gas and the pressure to which it is subjected. As a result, the internal structure of stars could be studied theoretically, and a mathematical theory of stellar structure could be established from such studies.

The term "astrophysics" was first introduced to denote vaguely the physical problems resulting directly or indirectly from the spectroscopic observation of celestial objects and events. It acquired a more definite meaning and became a term of common usage when the American astronomers George Ellery Hale and James Edward Keeler, in 1895, founded the *Astrophysical Journal*, subtitled "An International Review of Spectroscopy and Astronomical Physics."

Fields of Spectroscopic Research. Stellar spectroscopy opened up many areas of astrophysical research. A discussion of these areas of research follows.

Line Identification. Line identification is a continuation of Kirchhoff's original work. Lines found in the spectra of celestial objects are compared with the spectra that are produced by vapors in the laboratory. Straightforward as the identification process may seem to be, this work is not yet completed. There are many lines arising from celestial sources that are still unidentified. Most of these lines must be produced by molecules.

Chemical Abundance Determination. From the identification of lines in a spectrum to the determination of the abundance of the chemicals identified is a logical step. Abundance is determined by the strength of the observed lines. The actual procedure is tedious, however, and it depends on the nature of the object producing the spectrum—that is, whether the object is a star, a nebula, or interstellar material. Results have shown an approximate uniformity of chemical abundance in the universe, with some noted exceptions. Hydrogen is by far the most abundant element. It is followed by helium, with much smaller amounts of carbon, nitrogen, and oxygen, and traces only of all the other elements.

Spectral Classification. As a result of the chemical uniformity of stars, differences in the spectra of the majority of the stars can be attributed to differences in temperature and pressure in the stellar atmospheres. These differences in temperature and pressure affect the appearance of stellar spectra because they affect processes taking place in the stars on the atomic and molecular level.

Furthermore, pressure is related to the surface gravity of a star, which in turn depends on the size and consequently the luminosity of the star. Thus, the pressure in the stellar atmosphere can be expressed in terms of the star's luminosity. In this way an astrophysicist can tell the temperature of a star as well as its luminosity by looking at its spectrum.

When a group of stars is studied, it is useful to prepare a diagram in which the luminosity of the stars is plotted against their temperature. This is known as a *Hertzsprung-Russell*, or *H-R* diagram. The diagram describes the physical nature of the constituents in the group at a glance. That is, stars in general do not appear randomly scattered on the H-R diagram. Instead they form different sequences, and from these sequences astrophysicists have determined a great deal about the various types of stars and the processes of stellar "evolution"—the birth, growth, and death of stars. The sequence formed by a particular group of stars therefore indicates the physical nature of the group. The H-R diagram is a powerful tool for studying stellar evolution in star clusters.

Emission Line Studies. Emission lines appear in the spectra of some celestial objects. The presence of the lines raises many interesting possibilities of investigation, because there are several circumstances under which the lines can be formed in celestial sources. The appearance of some kinds of emission lines often presents the

HERTZSPRUNG-RUSSELL DIAGRAM showing the major types of stars. Much information about a group of stars can be obtained by studying the sequences that are formed when the stars are plotted on an H-R diagram.

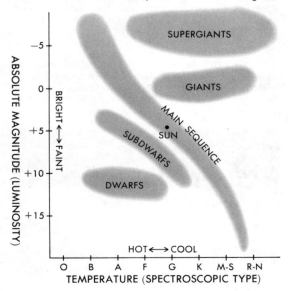

astrophysicist with clues to the nature of their origin. For example, the emission lines in the spectra of gaseous nebulae led to the proposal in 1927 that they could be emitted only by gases of very low density. Another example was the identification in the early 1940's of emission lines from the solar corona as being produced by highly ionized atoms. This helped to establish that extremely high temperatures prevail in the solar corona.

Radial Velocity Studies. The positions of the lines in the spectra of celestial objects are shifted slightly from the positions of corresponding lines in laboratory-produced spectra. That is, the lines in the spectra of celestial objects appear at slightly different wavelengths than the lines produced in a laboratory.

This shifting of line position is caused primarily by the Doppler effect resulting from the motions of the celestial objects relative to the earth. Thus, the wavelengths of light from an object approaching the earth are slightly shortened, so that the lines in its spectrum are shifted toward the region of shorter wavelengths—the ultraviolet end of the spectrum. Conversely, the lines in the spectrum of an object traveling away from the earth are shifted toward the infrared end of the spectrum, because the wavelengths of light are increased. This shift toward the infrared is known as the "red shift."

By studying line-shifting in the spectrum of a celestial object, an astrophysicist can thus determine the line-of-sight component of the object's motion with respect to the earth—that is, its *radial velocity*. Since the earth is itself in motion around the sun, it is actually the usual practice to subtract this motion from measured values and to refer to the motion of a celestial object with respect to the sun as the object's radial velocity.

Much of the present understanding of the universe comes from the measurement of radial velocities. Of foremost significance was the establishment by Edwin Hubble in 1920 of a simple relationship between the shifting of the spectral lines of galaxies and the distances of the galaxies from the earth. Interpreted as being produced by the Doppler effect, the red shifts of the galactic spectral lines indicated that the universe is expanding. That is, the galaxies are flying away from each other, and their rates of motion increase as the distances between the galaxies grow larger. This concept of an expanding universe (combined with the general theory of relativity) provided the first scientific theory of the nature of the universe, although today other theories are also under consideration.

The radial velocities of stars supply important data concerning the motions of groups of stars, such as the slow rotation of our own galaxy, the Milky Way. Traditionally the study of galactic structure has not been regarded as part of astrophysics, because it is not concerned with the physical and chemical nature of the galactic system. But it has become increasingly difficult to separate the astrophysical problems of the relation between stellar and galactic evolution from the purely structural problems.

Binary Stars. Radial velocity measurements are used in the study of two-star systems, or binary stars, which are quite common. Although the two components of such a system may not be visually separated on a photographic plate, their orbital motions cause their spectral lines to

RED SHIFT

LIGHT FROM A STAR MOVING TOWARD THE OBSERVER APPEARS BLUER

LIGHT FROM A STAR MOVING AWAY FROM THE OBSERVER APPEARS REDDER

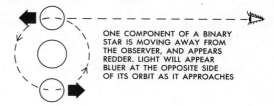

RED SHIFT IN A BINARY STAR SYSTEM

ONE COMPONENT OF A BINARY STAR IS MOVING AWAY FROM THE OBSERVER, AND APPEARS REDDER. LIGHT WILL APPEAR BLUER AT THE OPPOSITE SIDE OF ITS ORBIT AS IT APPROACHES

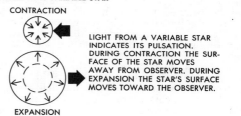

RED SHIFT IN A VARIABLE STAR

CONTRACTION

EXPANSION

LIGHT FROM A VARIABLE STAR INDICATES ITS PULSATION. DURING CONTRACTION THE SURFACE OF THE STAR MOVES AWAY FROM OBSERVER. DURING EXPANSION THE STAR'S SURFACE MOVES TOWARD THE OBSERVER.

oscillate back and forth with time. A binary detected by such means is called a *spectroscopic binary.* Sometimes two sets of lines are observed, corresponding to the two stars, but in most cases one of the components is too faint for its spectrum to be seen. Although the study of spectroscopic binaries concerns dynamics, it has traditionally been regarded as part of astrophysics because it relies on stellar spectra. And truly astrophysical problems do exist in connection with binary systems if the separation between the two stars is so slight that the outer portions of the stars physically interact.

The variations in radial velocity resulting from the orbital motion of binaries, moreover, provide important means for measuring stellar masses. Thus, the velocity of orbital motion reflects the amount of gravitational attraction between the two stars of a binary system. This attraction is determined by the masses of the stars as well as by the distance between them. This is true not only for binary systems but also for all systems in a state of dynamic equilibrium. Thus, the mass of an entire galaxy may be estimated from the velocity of its rotation.

Variable Stars. Radial velocity measurement is also of great importance in the search for an understanding of such variable stars as pulsating and exploding stars. In fact, it was radial velocity measurements that conclusively showed that the light variations of some stars are produced by the actual pulsation of the stars and not by their being eclipsed periodically. It was radial velocity measurements, as well, that indicated that novae and supernovae are actually catastrophic stellar explosions. That is, the measurements indicated that matter is ejected at high velocities from such stars when they suddenly increase in brightness.

Line Broadening Studies. The lines in the spectrum of a star are ordinarily narrow. However, in stellar atmospheres there are many effects, such as thermal motion and turbulence, that can broaden the lines. But by far the most conspicuous cause of line broadening in stellar spectra is the axial rotation of the stars. When a star rotates, various parts of the stellar disk move at different velocities. Thus, the spectral line produced by an element at the stellar surface is shifted by varying amounts, according to the location of the element at the surface. Taken as a whole, the various shiftings of the line show up as a broadened single line. Therefore, the speed of the star's rotation can be estimated by the extent of the line's broadening.

Zeeman Effect Studies. If a star has a sufficiently strong magnetic field, the field will affect the spectral lines of the star by splitting them into two or more components. This effect, known as the Zeeman effect, is caused by energy changes in the atoms within the stellar magnetic field. The separation between the split lines is small and is obscured by the line broadening already discussed. However, the different components of a spilt line are polarized in different ways, so that the presence of the splitting can be detected by means of polarization studies.

Through observations of the Zeeman effect the strengths of stellar magnetic fields can be determined. In the case of the sun, field strengths at different points of the solar disk can be obtained by what is called a *solar magnetograph*, which makes use of polarization differences. Much has been learned about stellar magnetic fields, although the cause and effect of magnetism in stars has yet to be determined fully.

Spectroheliograph Studies. A final area of spectroscopic study is the observation of the sun's surface by means of a spectroheliograph. This is an instrument designed to study the solar surface in the light of a single spectral line at a time, through the blocking out of the rest of the spectrum. Spectroheliograph observations aid in the understanding of solar activities.

Many avenues of astrophysical research are opened up by spectroscopic observations. Such observations are the foundation of astrophysics. At the same time it should be recognized that mathematical theoreticians have contributed greatly to the growth of this branch of science. Some of them—the Indian-born American astrophysicist Subrahmanyan Chandrasekhar, for example—have never made an actual observation, but the influence of their work is felt in every area of astrophysics.

FURTHER DEVELOPMENTS IN ASTROPHYSICS

In order to gather sufficient light for spectral analysis or photometric measurement, or to penetrate deeply into space, a large telescope is required. The development of astrophysics has gone hand in hand with the construction of larger and larger telescopes.

With the construction of several very powerful telescopes before World War II, therefore, one might have thought that astrophysics was about to enter a golden age. With the advantage of hindsight, however, it can be seen that this was not true. The period was one of hesitation on the part of astrophysicists. They further developed what they already knew, but they failed to grasp a concept that would eventually turn out to be revolutionary in its scope.

It should be recalled that astrophysics is supposed to study the physical and chemical nature of all objects lying beyond the earth's atmosphere, by whatever means available. For centuries the only means available for making contact with celestial objects was light—that is, electromagnetic radiation in the optical region of the spectrum. Thus, astronomy and consequently astrophysics invariably were associated with the optical telescope. The association resulted purely from expediency but gradually became a tradition after centuries of practice. As a result, astronomy and astrophysics became synonymous with optical observations through telescopes and the interpretation of such observations. This concept remained valid until the early 20th century, but after the 1930's it was no longer true.

Two Important Discoveries. One aspect of the change was the discovery of *cosmic rays*—the high-energy particles from outer space. Here scientists encountered something coming from extraterrestrial sources that could not be studied with conventional telescopes. Cosmic rays provided a new contact with cosmic events and might be expected to yield new information about celestial objects. For the time being, however, and for good reasons, astrophysicists kept busy with their telescopes and let physicists work with cosmic rays. But in retrospect this was the first sign that a centuries-old tradition in astronomy was going to be broken.

The other tide of revolution came at about the same time when, in 1932, Karl Jansky, an American scientist, discovered radio noise coming from outer space while he was investigating interference in radio reception. In later years this was to lead to the development of radio astronomy. At the time, astrophysicists were slow to realize the investigatory value of radio emissions from cosmic sources. Astrophysics was still imprisoned in the optical observatory.

However, as scientists in other fields came to be interested in the solution of certain astrophysical problems, they helped to liberate this branch of science. Physicists, for example, with their knowledge of atomic nuclei, turned their attention to the problem of determining the source of stellar energy. When it was established that this energy comes from thermonuclear reactions, the processes of stellar evolution also became more understandable.

Development of Radio Astronomy. The development of radar techniques during World War II helped to set the stage for the rapid progress of radio astronomy after the war. This progress depended on the designing of instruments to deal with the special problems of radio astronomy. Radio waves have the advantage of not being weakened easily as they pass through interstellar space. However, because of the much longer wavelengths involved, compared with those of light, the resolving power of a radio telescope having the same aperture as an optical telescope would be very poor. Therefore the central aim in the design of radio telescopes has been to increase the effective aperture and to obtain a higher resolving power. Radio telescopes today range from fixed or movable parabolic antennas, used singly or in pairs, to enormous cross-shaped installations with arms that extend a mile (1.6 km) or more.

Unlike the optical region of the electromagnetic spectrum, where spectral lines abound, the radio region of the spectrum has only a few lines. By far the most important is the 21-centimeter line generated by hydrogen. With this line, astrophysicists can study the distribution of neutral hydrogen clouds in our galaxy and other galaxies and the motions of these clouds. The arms of our galaxy were traced by this means.

The observation of the skies by radio telescope has opened many important lines of study. Thus, there is a general background of radio noise both inside and outside our galaxy. The question of what produces this noise has provided material for theoretical investigation and may have an important bearing on cosmological theories. Indeed, the existence of this continuous background noise may have advanced the theory of an expanding universe, as opposed to the competing theory of a steady-state universe.

More immediately rewarding lines of study are provided by the investigation of individual sources of radio waves. These sources fall into three groups: sources in the solar system (such as the sun and Jupiter), sources in our galaxy (such as the Crab Nebula, the remains of an exploding star), and sources beyond our galaxy. The radio emissions of these objects have helped astrophysicists to understand the physical nature of the objects.

For example, radio emissions from the sun have been found to be related to activities on the solar surface. The study of these emissions thus becomes an important part of solar physics. Similarly, radio observations of Jupiter and other planets can reveal a great deal about these planets, such as the existence of magnetic fields and of radiation belts that may surround them. The study of more distant radio objects may help to identify the sources of cosmic rays.

Quasars. The most significant astronomical discovery of the early 1960's came as a result of studying extragalactic sources of radio emission. Through the combined efforts of radio and optical observation, a number of individual radio sources were identified on photographic plates with the optical objects to which they must correspond. The objects thus identified, it was found, had very large red shifts in their spectra. According to the general theory of relativity, the shifting of the lines could be caused by very strong gravitational fields. However, it is now generally assumed that the shifting is caused by the great velocities at which these radio objects are receding from the earth.

If this is so, these objects—which are called quasi-stellar radio sources, or quasars (abbreviated QSRS or QSS)—must be very far away, at the frontiers of the observable universe. It follows that the quasars must be extremely bright. Both their great distances and their enormous luminosities make quasars some of the most interesting objects in the universe. There is no doubt that the nature of quasars will be one of the central problems in astrophysics for years to come.

Future Developments. Astrophysics made great advances through the development of radio astronomy. Perhaps even more spectacular results may be obtained through observations made above the atmosphere of the earth. The atmosphere absorbs electromagnetic radiations in all wavelengths except for two narrow bands, in the optical and the radio ranges of the spectrum.

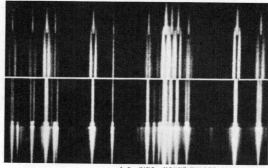

A.S. KING, MOUNT WILSON OBSERVATORY

ZEEMAN EFFECT, the splitting of spectral lines, results from a strong magnetic field surrounding a star.

By conducting observations above the atmosphere, astrophysicists are able to study the whole range of the electromagnetic spectrum. Even in the first years of the space age the discovery of X-ray sources in the galaxy has been of the utmost importance to astrophysics. Their discovery led to many speculations about the nature of these sources. They will provide much work for astrophysicists in the future.

The effect of space research on astrophysics is felt most strongly in the study of objects within the solar system, because men are now developing the ability to send space vehicles to these objects and have already begun investigations of the moon, Venus, and Mars. It is a matter of time before manned planetary landings will be accomplished and the probing of comets will have begun. The exploration of the solar system needs the cooperation not only of physicists and chemists but also of geophysicists, geologists, and biochemists.

There are very many objects in the solar system. If it is remembered how great the task has been (and continues to be) of studying the earth alone, the extent of work lying before men in making similar studies of the moon, planets, satellites, asteroids, comets, and the interplanetary medium can be grasped only faintly. If peace reigns on the earth, it seems safe to predict that men will spend vast amounts of energy in this exploration of the solar system during the coming centuries. In the meantime, the astrophysicist finds himself entering a new age.

See also ASTRONOMY; ASTROPHOTOGRAPHY; COSMIC RADIATION; DOPPLER'S PRINCIPLE; OBSERVATORY; QUASI-STELLAR SOURCES; SPECTROSCOPY; STARS; SUN; TELESCOPE; UNIVERSE.

SU-SHU HUANG, *Dearborn Observatory*
Northwestern University

Bibliography

Gamow, George, *A Star Called the Sun* (New York 1964).
Gamow, George, *The Creation of the Universe* (New York 1952).
Goldberg, Leo, and Aller, Lawrence H., *Atoms, Stars and Nebulae* (New York 1946).
Struve, Otto, and Zebergs, Velta, *Astronomy of the Twentieth Century* (New York 1962).
Sullivan, Walter, *We Are Not Alone* (New York 1964).

For Specialized Study

Baade, Walter, *Evolution of Stars and Galaxies*, ed. by C. Payne-Gaposchkin (Cambridge, Mass., 1963).
Brown, Robert H., and Lovell, A.C. Bernard, *The Exploration of Space by Radio* (New York 1958).
Chandrasekhar, Subrahmanyan, "The Present Revolution in Astronomy," *The University of Chicago Magazine* (Chicago, Dec. 1966).
Hoyle, Fred, *Galaxies, Nuclei and Quasars* (New York 1965).
Morrison, Philip, "Neutrino Astronomy," *Scientific American*, vol. 207, pp. 90–98 (New York 1962).

ASTURIAS, äs-tōō′ryäs, **Miguel Ángel** (1899–), Guatemalan writer and diplomat, who won the 1966 Lenin Peace Prize and the 1967 Nobel Prize in literature. Born in Guatemala City on Oct. 19, 1899, he took a doctorate in law at the National University there in 1923, worked for a time as a journalist, and was elected to Congress in 1942. In 1946 he entered the diplomatic service but was forced into exile in 1954 for his political activities supporting President Arbenz' regime. He returned to Guatemala in 1966 after a change of administration and was appointed ambassador to France in 1967.

Asturias began his literary career as a poet but became better known as a novelist. Many of his novels strike at conditions in his own country, and several speak out against the United States. *El señor presidente* (1946; Eng. tr., *Mr. President*, 1964) attacks dictatorship, and *Mulata de Tal* (1963; Eng. tr., *Mulata*, 1966) is a satirical retelling of a Mayan legend. Other major works include his anti-United States trilogy— *Viento fuerte* (1950), *Papa verde* (1954), and *Los ojos de los enterrados* (1960)—and *Weekend en Guatemala* (1956), a collection of stories about the 1954 uprising against Arbenz.

ASTURIAS, äs-tōō′ryäs, is a region and former kingdom in northwestern Spain. It now forms the province of Oviedo. The rugged Cordillera Cantábrica, which rises to more than 8,000 feet (2,438 meters) in Asturias, extends across the region from east to west, forming deep fertile valleys where corn, vegetables, apples, and other fruit are grown. The chief rivers are the Nalón, Lena, Navia, and Sella. The abundant rainfall in Asturias promotes extensive forest growth and a rich pasturage, on which excellent breeds of horses and cattle are raised. There are fisheries along the high rocky coast.

The richest coal mines in Spain are located in Asturias. Other important minerals produced are iron, zinc, lead, manganese, and copper. The city of Oviedo is one of Spain's major industrial centers, producing iron and steel, armaments, glass, chemicals, and processed foods. Gijón, Avilés, and Mieres are other leading cities.

History. Asturias claims to be the cradle of Spanish nationalism. Conquered by the Romans in the 3d and 2d centuries B.C. and by the Visigoths in the 5th century A.D., Asturias became the refuge of Christian nobles during the Moorish invasion of Spain in the 8th century. Under Pelayo, who in about 718 founded the kingdom of Asturias, the reconquest of Spain was begun. Gradually expanding southward, Asturias merged with León in the 10th century, forming the kingdom of Asturias and León. In 1230 it united with Castile. The heir to the Spanish throne bore the title of prince of Asturias after 1388, when John I of Castile created Asturias a principality for his eldest son. By the marriage of Isabella to Ferdinand in 1469, Castile was joined to Aragon. Thereafter the history of Asturias is merged with that of Spain. Population: (1960) 989,344.

ASUNCIÓN, ä-sōōn–syôn′, is the capital and largest city of Paraguay. With one sixth of the country's population, it is the center of Paraguay's political, economic, religious, and intellectual life. It is Paraguay's chief river port and its major trade outlet, because the country has no seacoast. Three fifths of Paraguay's exports and three fourths of its imports pass through Asunción. The city is the seat of a Roman Catholic archbishop. It also contains Paraguay's two universities and its major libraries and institutes.

Asunción stands on a low hill rising from a bay of the Paraguay River. Argentina is on the other side of the river. The city has air connections with Buenos Aires, 625 miles (1,000 km) to the south, and with several other South American capitals. Formerly, it could be reached conveniently only by train or river steamer from Buenos Aires.

The city was founded in 1537 and was named Nuestra Señora de la Asunción (Our Lady of the Assumption) because it was dedicated on August 15, the feast day of the Assumption. Although the city is old, most of the public buildings date from the mid-1800's. Between 1840 and 1870, the dictators Carlos and Francisco López tried to make Asunción look like a European capital. The colonial cathedral was torn down and replaced by a structure with an imposing front and an elaborate interior. A government palace was built in the style of the Louvre in Paris, and a Pantheon of Heroes (finished in 1937) was modeled after the Invalides, Napoleon's burial place. Asunción's poor sections still have houses showing the Spanish-Moorish style of architecture. Population: (1962) 305,160.

ASVINS, as′vinz, in the Vedic mythology of ancient India, the twin gods of light, Dasra and Nasatya. Husbands of Surya, daughter of the sun god, they accompanied her, bringing the light of the sun to the world each morning. People prayed for health to the Asvins, who were supposed to cure all infirmities. Their parallels in Greek mythology were Castor and Pollux.

ASWAN, a-swän′, is a city in Upper Egypt, in the United Arab Republic. The capital of Aswan province, it is situated on the east bank of the Nile River, near the first cataract, about 500 miles (800 km) south of Cairo. In the river opposite the city is historic Elephantine Island; Philae Island is 6 miles (10 km) upstream.

Known as *Suwanu* to the ancient Egyptians and as *Syene* to the Greeks, Aswan acquired its present name from a Coptic word meaning "market," referring to its former prominence in commerce; the Arabic name is *al-Swanou*. The city was the capital of a principality of pharaonic Egypt and a major customs port. Strategically located at the gateway to Nubia, it held command of the first cataract and communications routes to the south and therefore of river commerce and desert caravans. Its quarries furnished red granite for colossi, obelisks, sarcophagi, and other monuments. In modern times a sleepy agricultural town and a winter resort, Aswan is destined to play an increasing role in Egypt's industrial economy because of the hydroelectric facilities afforded by the Aswan High Dam, 7½ miles (12 km) south.

The Aswan region, with its striking rocky landscape, resembles adjacent Nubia more than the Nile lands of northern Egypt. Among the archaeological remains are Egyptian and Graeco-Roman temples. Other interesting points are the mausoleum of Aga Khan III and St. Simeon's Monastery. The administrative headquarters of the Aswan High Dam authority, new industrial plants, and tourist hotels lend a modern touch. Population: (1960) 48,393.

ALFRED G. GERTEINY, *University of Bridgeport*

ASWAN DAMS, a-swän', two large dams regulating the flow of the Nile River near its first cataract, just south of the city of Aswan in the United Arab Republic (Egypt). They provide irrigation water and hydroelectric power for a vast area of the Nile Valley and adjacent desert.

The older, known as the *Aswan Dam,* situated 3½ miles (5.6 km) upstream from Aswan, was completed in 1902 and expanded in 1912, 1934, and 1960. A gravity-type masonry dam, it is 175 feet (53 meters) high and 7,062 feet (2,152 meters) long, with 180 sluices, and has a hydroelectric capacity of 345,000 kilowatts. Its reservoir, storing 6,900,000,000 cubic yards (5,300,000,000 cu meters) of water, irrigates 1,400,000 acres (570,000 hectares).

The newer dam, known as the *Aswan High Dam,* situated 4 miles (6.4 km) farther upstream, was constructed in the 1960's. The world's 10th-largest rock-fill dam, it is 375 feet (114 meters) high and 11,811 feet (3,600 meters) long and has a hydroelectric capacity of 2,100 megawatts. Its reservoir, Lake Nasser, is the world's second-largest artificial lake, extending 310 miles (499 km) in length and about 2,000 square miles (5,000 sq km) in area. It has a storage capacity of 204,000,000,000 cubic yards (157,000,000,000 cu meters), sufficient to irrigate 2,000,000 acres (800,000 hectares) in Egypt and 5,000,000 acres (2,000,000 hectares) in Sudan.

Actually a complex of three dams, the High Dam has two subsidiary structures: an upstream cofferdam channeling the flow of the river to a diversionary canal, and a downstream cofferdam preventing the waters from backing into the main dam site. The diversionary canal has a bed 262 feet (80 meters) deep, 6,400 feet (1,950 meters) long, and a minimum of 131 feet (40 meters) wide. It is capable of passing 388,500 cubic feet (11,000 cu meters) of water each second; in this respect it is the world's largest artificial canal. The main dam is protected against water infiltration by a vertical grout curtain descending some 690 feet (210 meters).

At the downstream end of the spillway tunnels, a 12-turbine hydroelectric plant produces low-cost energy in excess of 10,000,000,000 kilowatt-hours annually. Lake Nasser guarantees an annual draft of 96,800,000,000 cubic yards (74,000,000,000 cu meters) of irrigation water.

President Gamal Abdel Nasser announced plans for the High Dam in 1953 as part of his economic development program. The project was delayed because in 1956, Western nations withdrew their offers of aid for political reasons. Ultimately the dam was financed by loans from the Soviet Union. On Jan. 9, 1960, Nasser set off the first charge of dynamite for the dam's construction. In the succeeding decade 40,000 workers participated in the billion-dollar project.

Although the dam inundated several Nubian villages and obliterated some archaeological treasures, it augments by at least one third the nation's cultivable area and provides power potential to revolutionize the economy. Other benefits are year-round river navigation, increased fish production, and additional employment opportunities stemming from subsidiary industrial development. Some 60,000 Nubians were resettled in villages north of Aswan, and the most precious antiquities, the temples at Abu Simbel (q.v.), were salvaged through an international operation sponsored by UNESCO.

Alfred G. Gerteiny, *University of Bridgeport*

ASYLUM, ə-sī'ləm, a place of shelter, safety, or protection. The term is also used to denote the protection afforded by such a refuge and the right to grant such a refuge. In international law, asylum, often called *political asylum,* is the right or privilege of a state to offer protection to a foreign national who seeks it. Although in ancient times a fugitive could claim asylum in a place of sanctuary, modern political asylum is not the right of the fugitive to demand protection but the right of the state to provide it. Individuals may seek asylum, but they have no legal claim to it.

A state may grant asylum in its own territory (*territorial asylum*) or in its legations, consulates, warships, or other public agencies abroad (*diplomatic* or *extraterritorial asylum*). Neutral states have the right to grant asylum to belligerent forces fleeing to their territory. In a special sense, the term "asylum" also is used to refer to the duty of ports to give shelter to ships in distress from weather or mutiny.

Ancient Right of Sanctuary. Under the Mosaic dispensation, cities of refuge or asylum were recognized, to which a slayer might flee and gain protection from revenge. In the Graeco-Roman world, temples, statues of the gods, and altars, consecrated for that purpose, constituted refuges for persons generally, and it was deemed an act of impiety to violate such asylum. Emperor Tiberius (reigned 14–37 A.D.) abolished all places of asylum except the Temple of Juno and Aesculapius. Under Constantine the Great (reigned 306–337 A.D.), however, all Christian churches were made asylums from arrest by officers of justice and from private violence. Theodosius II, emperor in the East, extended these privileges in 431 A.D. to all courts, gardens, walks, and houses belonging to the church.

In 631 A.D. a synod of Toledo extended the limits of asylums to 30 paces from every church, and this privilege was generally accepted in western Europe. Under the influence of the Cluniac movement of the 10th century, the Peace of God exempted all church buildings and their environs from feudal war and violence, thus providing places of general asylum, as did the Truce of God, which forbade private war on certain days of each week and at the time of religious festivals. These institutions were maintained by the threat of papal excommunication and interdict during the 12th and 13th centuries. They broke down, however, with the decline of the authority of the church and the rise of national monarchies in the 15th and 16th centuries. In modern times asylum, in the sense of a place of sanctuary, usually refers to an institution for the protection and care of the poor, blind, deaf, insane, or others incapable of caring for themselves.

Political Asylum—Territorial. Because of the respect which every state owes to the territorial rights of others, each state may permit fugitives from another to take asylum in its territory. In the period of absolute monarchy, the duty of states to prevent acts hostile to another in its territory was thought to permit asylum to ordinary criminals but not to political refugees who, from a safe refuge, might plot against the government from which they had fled. Even in the 19th century a number of treaties between conservative monarchies provided for refusal of asylum to political refugees. After World War I, the Netherlands government gave asylum to Emperor William II, who had been indicted by the Allies for high crimes, but in doing so the Dutch government put him under guard and took measures to prevent his engaging in political activities.

With the rise of political freedom, however, the practices with respect to political and criminal fugitives generally have been reversed. States mutually recognize each other's administration of ordinary criminal justice and conclude extradition treaties for turning over fugitives from ordinary criminal justice, but in deference to the right of political dissent or even of revolution, they give asylum usually to political fugitives. Extradition treaties usually expressly except "political offenses." Liberal countries have frequently given asylum to political refugees from oppressive regimes and refused to return them to the country of origin, even when the latter has sought their return. The right of United Nations powers to give asylum to prisoners of war from the Communist side who did not wish to be repatriated caused prolonged debate during the armistice negotiations which ended the Korean hostilities in 1953.

Diplomatic Asylum. The practice of giving asylum to political fugitives in embassies, legations, consulates, and warships has been highly controversial. In the 16th and 17th centuries when the state system was taking form, states claimed exterritoriality for their embassies and legations, thus permitting them to accord asylum in their premises as they would in their own territories. This practice was subject to abuse. Diplomatic officers sometimes rented buildings which they sublet to malefactors who were willing to pay exorbitant rents for the opportunity which the exterritoriality of these buildings gave them to escape the local police. The diplomatic quarters enjoying the *franchise des quartiers* or freedom of the area, became notorious for this reason in Madrid, Venice, Rome, and other cities.

As a result, international lawyers like Hugo Grotius, Cornelis van Bynkershoek, and Emmerich von Vattel criticized the practice. They denied the exterritoriality of diplomatic premises, and asserted that the immunity from local police, which international law extended to diplomatic premises and personnel, was limited to the functions for which those immunities were essential and was accompanied by a duty of the sending state not to permit asylum to fugitives from local justice.

This principle has been accepted in many treaties, as for example that between the United States and Persia in 1856 (Art 7) and, with exceptions, in the Havana Convention of 1928 between the United States and several Latin American states (Art. 1), and it seems to be established in customary international law. The Harvard Research draft convention on diplomatic privileges and immunities says, "A sending state shall not permit the premises occupied or used by its mission or by a member of its mission to be used as a place of asylum for fugitives from justice."

In spite of this position, diplomatic asylum continues to be given to political refugees, especially in Latin America. One notable example concerned the ousted dictator of Argentina, Juan Domingo Perón. After an army revolt ended his regime, Perón was granted diplomatic asylum in the Paraguayan embassy in Buenos Aires on Sept. 20, 1955. From there he fled successively to Paraguay, Nicaragua, Venezuela, and the Dominican Republic, finally settling in Spain. Perón made a much publicized attempt to return to Argentina in December 1964, but his plane was turned back in Rio de Janeiro, Brazil.

Diplomatic asylum was recognized in several agreements among the American republics, including the Havana Convention of 1928, the Montevideo Convention of 1933, and the Caracas Convention of 1954. The Havana Convention, while forbidding diplomatic asylum to persons "accused of, or condemned for common crimes," did permit asylum to "political offenders," but only "in urgent cases, and for the period of time strictly indispensable for the person who has sought asylum to insure in some other way his safety." It was also specified that "while enjoying asylum, refugees shall not be allowed to perform acts contrary to the public peace."

The United States in ratifying this convention reserved on the exception, though its diplomatic instructions of 1927 state that while it did not look with favor on asylum, it permitted its missions to give "temporary shelter" to persons in "actual danger," such as that arising from mob violence, violence at the hands of revolutionists, or the threat of illegal acts by authorities. This very strict interpretation of diplomatic asylum was relaxed somewhat when the United States granted asylum to Joseph Cardinal Mindszenty in its legation in Budapest during the Hungarian revolt against the Communist regime in November 1956.

The legal status of diplomatic asylum and the interpretation of the Havana Convention was considered by the International Court of Justice in the Haya de la Torre case. Victor Raúl Haya de la Torre, head of a leftist political party in Peru, sought asylum in the Colombian embassy in 1949. Peru, claiming he was a common criminal, demanded that he be turned over. Colombia refused, claiming he was a political refugee, and the matter was submitted to the court. In its judgment of Nov. 20, 1950, the court held that Peru had not proved that Haya de la Torre was not a political refugee, but that Colombia's characterization of the fugitive as a political offender was not binding upon Peru; therefore Peru was not obliged to issue a safe-conduct. Furthermore, Colombia had not proved that the political urgency requisite for asylum existed. In two subsequent opinions on this case, the court declined to clarify the award or to tell the parties what actions they should take, but suggested that diplomatic negotiations were available. Such negotiations eventually resulted in Peru's permitting Haya de la Torre to leave its territory. The juridical result seems to have been a restrictive interpretation of the privilege of diplomatic asylum for political refugees.

Warships are subject to similar restrictions in giving asylum to political refugees, and persons fleeing from mob violence. The Havana Convention, in fact, places warships, military camps, and military aircraft in the same category as legations in this respect. United States Naval Regulations generally deny the right of asylum and instruct naval officers not to invite refugees to accept asylum and to refuse applications for asylum "except where required in the interests of humanity in extreme or exceptional cases, such as the pursuit of a refugee by a mob."

Merchant vessels are generally subject to the

local jurisdiction and so cannot, in principle, offer asylum. However, in practice they have sometimes done so, and governments have sometimes protested when fugitives were removed by local authorities from merchant vessels without clear warrant of law.

Treaties have often expressly forbidden the use of consulates for purposes of asylum, but the practice of giving asylum in consulates to political refugees is permitted in certain countries; some, such as Brazil, recognize the practice in national regulations, but only for humanitarian purposes and not to thwart local justice. The Harvard Research draft on the legal position and function of counsuls (Art. 32) says, "A sending state shall not permit its consul to allow the consular office to be used as a place of asylum by fugitives from justice."

Asylum for Belligerent Forces. A neutral state is permitted to give asylum to belligerent forces by the Hague Conventions of 1899 (II, Arts. 57–60) and 1907 (V, Arts. 11–15) on condition that it intern them for the duration of the war unless they have come in as prisoners of war. Neutral states may also give asylum to belligerent warships, but must intern them unless they leave within 24 hours (Hague Convention 1907, XIII, Art. 24). A prize of war brought to a neutral port must be released unless it enters under necessity, but it must leave when the necessity is ended or unless it accepts sequestration during the war (Hague Convention 1907, XIII, Arts. 21–23). In World War I the United States refused to apply the provision concerning sequestration in the case of the *Appam*, a British vessel captured by the Germans, brought to an American port, and returned to its original owners by orders of the U.S. Supreme Court.

Asylum for Distressed Vessels. International law has distinguished between the normal entry of foreign merchant vessels into a port of sojourn, subjecting them to the law of the port, and the abnormal entry of such vessels for shelter or asylum because of weather or other unavoidable necessity. In recognition of this right, an arbitral tribunal in 1853 required Britain to pay damages to the United States because of the liberation of slaves on the American brig *Creole* while it was seeking asylum in Nassau in the Bahama Islands in 1841 because of mutiny. Although slavery had been abolished in the Bahamas, it was held that American law continued to apply in an American vessel seeking asylum. See also CITIES OF REFUGE; EXILE; EXTRADITION; EXTRATERRITORIALITY; REFUGEES; SANCTUARY, PRIVILEGE OF.

QUINCY WRIGHT, *University of Virginia*

Bibliography

Garcia Mora, Manuel Ramón, *International Law and Asylum as a Human Right* (Washington 1956).
Harvard Research in International Law, *American Journal of International Law*, supplement, vol. 26, part 1, "Diplomatic Privileges and Immunities"; part 2, "The Legal Position and Functions of Consuls" (Washington 1932).
Hyde, Charles Cheney, *International Law*, 2d ed., vol. 1, p. 743 ff., and vol. 2, pp. 828 ff., 1284 ff., 1540 (Boston 1945).
International Court of Justice, *Reports of Judgments, Advisory Opinions and Orders, Colombian-Peruvian Asylum Case, 1950*, pp. 266, 399 (New York 1951); *Haya de la Torre Case (Colombia vs. Peru)*, 1951, p. 71 (New York 1952).
Moore, John Bassett, *Digest of International Law*, vol. 2, pp. 358, 755, 845 (Washington 1906).
Organization of American States, *Convention on Diplomatic Asylum, Caracas, 1954* (Washington 1954).
Satow, Sir Ernest, *A Guide to Diplomatic Practice*, 4th ed. by Nevile Bland (New York 1957).

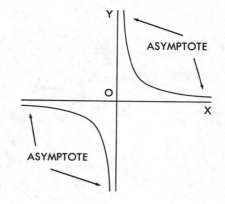

ASYMPTOTE, as′əm-tōt, is a line that becomes a tangent to a curve at a point infinitely distant from the origin. More precisely, an asymptote is a line that is a limit of a series of lines tangent to the curve as the point of tangency approaches infinity along the curve. Asymptotes are classified as vertical, horizontal, and oblique. If the abscissa x of the point of tangency approaches a value a as the point moves along the curve, and its ordinate y becomes infinite, then the line $x=a$ is a vertical asymptote. Similarly, if x becomes infinite as y approaches a value b, then $y=b$ is a horizontal asymptote. Some curves have asymptotes, and others do not. For example, the hyperbola has two asymptotes, and the parabola has none.

ASYUT, as-yōōt′, is a city in Egypt about 250 miles (400 km) south of Cairo, on the Nile River, at the head of the Ibrahimiya Canal to El Faiyum. It is the largest city and chief commercial center of Upper Egypt, and is the capital of the governorate (province) of Asyut.

As ancient *Siut*, in the time of the Middle Kingdom (2052–1786 B.C.), the city was the seat of an important nome (petty state) whose nomarchs (lords) rose to considerable power, as evidenced in records found in their rock-cut tombs behind the city. South of Asyut, near El Badari, are the remains of a Neolithic culture, the Badarian, which flourished around 4500 B.C. and was noted for the use of imported copper and for pottery model boats—indicating a preoccupation with trade.

Present-day Asyut is still known for its pottery and for fine wood and ivory carving. Cotton yarn, fabrics, shoes, and refrigerants are also manufactured. A mile (1½ km) north of the city is the Asyut Barrage, important for irrigation. Population: (1960) 127,485.

ATA, ä′tä, a primitive people numbering about 7,500, living on the northwestern and western slopes of Mount Apo in Davao province, on Mindanao Island, in the Philippines. Their name—*atas* in the local dialect—means "people living on the upper slopes of the mountain." A tall people with long curly hair, the Ata are believed to be a mixed Indonesian-Papuan type. They may be descendants of an early invading people who intermarried first with the Negritos and later with others whom they contacted in the Davao vicinity. Their bodies are elaborately tattooed with designs similar to those embroidered on clothing worn by the Bagobo, a neighboring tribe. The Ata hunt with the bow and arrow and practice shifting agriculture.

DONN V. HART, *Syracuse University*

ATACAMA DESERT in Chile is one of the world's driest regions. In some parts rainfall is unknown.

ATACAMA DESERT, at-ə-käm′ə, a virtually rainless plateau in northern Chile. It is one of the driest regions in the world. It extends 600 miles (965 km) south from the border of Peru to the area near Copiapó, Chile. Its average width is 90 miles (145 km). The Pacific coastal mountains lie to the west, and the Cordillera Domeyko, foothills of the Andes, to the east. The desert's average elevation is about 2,000 feet (609 meters).

The desert consists of a series of salt basins interspersed with broad tracts of sand and lava. Rain is unnknown in many parts of the plateau, but a few summer showers fall in the foothills. There is no vegetation except at a few small oases or where irrigation systems have been established. The region has the world's largest natural supply of sodium nitrate, which formerly was mined on a large scale. There are rich deposits of copper and other minerals.

ATACAMITE, at-ə-ka′mīt, is a comparatively rare copper ore. It is found in association with deposits of other copper minerals in arid regions such as southern Australia and the Atacama Desert of Chile. No important deposits of atacamite occur within the United States. The crystals are small, thin, and have a glassy luster. They range from transparent to translucent in various shades of green. Before blotters came into use, atacamite often was used as a sand to dry ink.

Composition: $Cu_2Cl(OH)_3$; hardness, 3.0 to 3.5;· specific gravity, 3.75 to 3.77; crystal system, orthorhombic.

ATAHUALPA, at-ə-wäl′pə (c. 1500–1533), Inca emperor of Peru.

He was born probably at Quito, now in Ecuador. The accounts of his life handed down in Spanish chronicles and Indian traditions are contradictory on many points. Atahualpa (also called *Atabalipa*) appears to have been the son of the Inca emperor Huayna Capac by a daughter of the chief of Quito. Huayna Capac had rounded out his father's conquests in that region, and died suddenly at Quito (1527?) without designating his successor. One of his sons, Huáscar, was installed as emperor at Cuzco, the Inca capital. Atahualpa, however, fell heir to the superb Inca army that had followed his father north.

At first Atahualpa controlled only the small part of the empire north of the Gulf of Guaya-quil, and he seems to have accepted Huáscar's suzerainty. Soon after, when war broke out between them over Cañari (just east of the gulf), Atahualpa appears to have claimed that Huayna Capac had willed him half the empire. Finally, as his prospects improved, he set out to make himself sole ruler. His army advanced steadily southward under his father's generals, defeated and captured Huáscar near the Apurímac River, entered Cuzco, and massacred the leaders of Huáscar's party.

At almost the same time Francisco Pizarro, at the head of a small Spanish expedition, landed on the coast (1532). Atahualpa, who was following his army south, halted and awaited Pizarro outside Cajamarca. The Spaniards entered the town unopposed. When the unsuspecting Atahualpa visited them (Nov. 16, 1532), and made a gesture which they interpreted as a refusal to accept Christianity and become a vassal of Charles V, they boldly seized him and dispersed his escort with great slaughter. Atahualpa is said to have had his subjects fill an entire room with gold to purchase his freedom, but he then was accused of plotting against the Spaniards and of having secretly caused the death of Huáscar. He was put to death at Cajamarca on Aug. 29, 1533. The Inca state, shaken by the recent civil war, speedily succumbed to the superior weapons and military organization of the Spaniards.

ATALANTA, at-ə-lan′tə, in Greek legend, was a beautiful girl celebrated for her skill in archery, her hunting prowess, and her fleetness of foot. She was cast out at birth by her father, who had wanted a son, and was nursed by a she-bear and raised by hunters. She later sailed with the Argonauts to Colchis and took part in the Calydonian boar hunt. As the first to wound the boar, she was awarded the boar's head and hide as a prize by Meleager, the hero who had killed the animal.

On her return, Atalanta became reconciled with her father, who wished her to marry. She agreed, on this condition: that her suitor would have to compete with her in a foot race; if he won, she would marry him; if he lost, she would kill him with a dart. After several men failed and were killed, Meilanion bested her in a race by dropping before her three golden apples, which she stopped to pick up. After they were married, they were transformed into lions by Zeus for lying together in a grove that was sacred to the god.

In some versions, Atalanta is the daughter of Iasos, king of Arcadia; in others, she is the daughter of Schoenus, a king of Boeotia, and her husband is Hippomenes.

ATALANTA IN CALYDON, at-ə-lan′tə, kal′ə-don, is a poetic tragedy in the Greek style by Algernon Charles Swinburne (q.v.), published in 1865. This work and the *Poems and Ballads* of 1866 established Swinburne as the most sensational English poet since Lord Byron.

The play is based on the legend of the great wild boar of Calydon, as related by Homer and Ovid. At the birth of Meleager, son of Oeneus and Althaea, it was foretold that he would live only until a brand on the hearth was consumed. Althaea quenched the brand and hid it. When the boar laid waste to Calydon, the Greek champions gathered to help Meleager. With them came Atalanta, the Arcadian huntress, and her arrow gave the beast its first wound. Meleager finally slew it, and gave the spoils to Atalanta because she had dealt the first blow. His uncles, Toxeus and Plexippus, contested the award, and in the ensuing brawl Meleager killed them both. On hearing the news, Althaea in her grief and anger flung the fateful brand into the fire, and Meleager perished.

In form, *Atalanta in Calydon* is probably the most successful adaptation of Greek drama ever made in English. It is closer in method to Euripides, whose choruses are lyric interludes, than to Aeschylus or Sophocles. In tone, however, the play is hardly Greek at all. Swinburne writes as a 19th century rebel and freethinker; instead of Greek acceptance of fate, he hurls curses at "the supreme evil, God."

His blank verse, in the narrative portions, is rich and flexible, but his finest poetry is concentrated in the choruses. The opening one, "When the hounds of Spring," with its amazing stanza contrived from ottava rima by shifting the position of the couplet, is merely the first sampling of a metrical virtuosity unrivaled in English verse.

DeLancey Ferguson, *Brooklyn College*

ATARGATIS, ə-tär′gə-təs, was the Syrian goddess of fertility, similar to the Babylonian Ishtar and the Phoenician Astarte. Her chief temple was at Hierapolis; another great shrine was at Ashkelon (Ascalon) in Palestine, where she was worshiped under the name of Derceto and represented as half woman and half fish. Her cult spread to Egypt and to some extent to Greece, Italy, the Danubian provinces, and even England. As a fertility goddess, the Greeks sometimes identified her as a form of Aphrodite.

ATASCADERO, ə-tas-kə-der′ō, is an unincorporated town in western California, in San Luis Obispo County, 210 miles (338 km) northwest of Los Angeles. It is a shopping center for a large agricultural area that produces mainly grain and poultry and some cattle and horses. The Atascadero school district serves pupils residing within a 1,200-square-mile area. The Atascadero State Hospital, a mental institution, is here.

Atascadero was founded as a model community in 1913 by Edward Gardner Lewis, a newspaper and women's magazine publisher, of St. Louis, Mo. Its architectural design was patterned after that of University City, in St. Louis, which Lewis also had founded. Population: 10,290.

Lois King Crumb
San Luis Obispo County Free Library

ATASI, ə-tas′ē, **Hashim al-** (?1875–1960), president of Syria. He was born in Homs, Syria, possibly in 1865, though official records give 1875. He was educated at Istanbul University. In 1920 he was King Faisal's prime minister. Elected president of the Syrian republic in 1936, he secured a treaty of independence from France, but resigned in 1939 over the French refusal to ratify it. Again elected president in 1950, he resigned in 1951 after a military coup by Adib al-Shishakli. When Shishakli was ousted in 1954, Atasi resumed the presidency until his term expired in 1955. He died in Homs on Dec. 5, 1960.

Malcolm H. Kerr
University of California at Los Angeles

KEMAL ATATÜRK, founder of the Turkish Republic.

ATATÜRK, ä-tä′türk, **Mustafa Kemal** (1881–1938), Turkish soldier and statesman, the founder and first president of the Turkish republic. He was born in Salonika (now in Greece), which was then the port city of Turkish Macedonia. He entered the military secondary school in Salonika in 1893. Mustafa was strong-willed and proud even as a child. The stern patriotism that was to motivate him throughout his life was kindled by the slights to which he saw his people exposed by the Greeks, Bulgarians, and Serbs, who were openly preparing to expel the Turks from Europe. In 1895, Mustafa Kemal (*kemal,* meaning "perfection," was a nickname given him by a teacher) entered the military academy at Monastir, graduating in 1899.

Early Military Career. He attended the war college in Istanbul and then the staff college. After graduating with the rank of captain in 1905, he spent a few months in prison because of his political activities. On his release he was assigned to the Damascus garrison, where he organized a secret revolutionary group among his brother officers. This group was almost immediately swallowed up in a more powerful movement, the Committee of Union and Progress, which launched the Young Turk revolution in 1908. After suppressing a counterrevolution in April 1909, the Committee deposed the sultan and took the reins of government into its own hands. Mustafa Kemal, distrusted because of his ambition and his outspoken criticisms of the Committee, was excluded from the center of power. In the Balkan Wars of 1912–1913 he was allowed to play only a minor part, and when World War I broke out in 1914, with Turkey as an ally of the Central Powers, he was serving as military attaché to the embassy in Sofia.

Although opposed to his country's entering the war, the disastrous outcome of which he clearly foresaw, he gained the only significant Turkish victory when the units under his command repulsed the massive Allied invasion of Gallipoli in 1915. He held the rank of general when the Ottoman government signed an armistice with the English at Mudros on Oct. 30, 1918.

Founder of the Republic. The Committee leaders fled the country, and the sultan and his ministers bowed to the demands of the Allies. But Mustafa Kemal still voiced open defiance. It was probably to rid the capital of his embarrassing presence that he was sent to Anatolia in May 1919 as inspector general, charged with disbanding still-mobilized army units. This coincided with the occupation of Smyrna by the Greeks, a move on the part of the Allies that was to revive Turkish national pride and turn resignation and despair into fierce resistance. Kemal began to organize the local resistance groups into a unified force, and in July 1919 he convened at Erzerum a congress of nationalist delegates representing the eastern provinces. From this emerged the National Pact, a manifesto proclaiming the right of self-determination for the Turkish people, defining the irreducible boundaries of its territories, and resolving to protect these at all costs.

Proclaimed a rebel by the sultan, Kemal defiantly convened a more widely representative congress at Sivas in September, at which a provisional government claiming to speak for the nation was formed under his leadership. The sultan felt obliged to respond by allowing elections for a new parliament, but when most of the delegates returned were found to be nationalists, the British occupying forces caused it to be dissolved. This gave Kemal the pretext for convening his own parliament, the Grand National Assembly, in Ankara, under his presidency. The sultan's government betrayed its complete separation from the popular will when it assented to the crippling terms imposed by the Allies in the Treaty of Sèvres in 1920.

Encouraged by the British, the Greeks now launched a drive into Anatolia, hoping to win additional territory, but in June 1921 the Turkish armies under Kemal halted their advances, and in August 1922 he was again victorious. An armistice was concluded with the Allies in October.

By the new peace treaty negotiated in 1923 with the Allies at Lausanne, Switzerland, nearly all the objectives outlined in the National Pact were obtained, and Kemal directed himself to the re-creation of Turkey as a modern state in the Western pattern. Convinced that the Islamic faith and the attitudes it induced were keeping his people backward, he focused his assault on all its manifestations in civil and political life, brooking no opposition. The sultanate had been abolished in 1922, and on Oct. 29, 1923, Turkey was proclaimed a republic, with Kemal the only choice for its president.

Reformer. Earlier in 1923, he had founded the country's only political party, under his own leadership. Thus he controlled the chief sources from which organized protest might arise. Kemal began his reform campaign in March 1924 by abolishing the caliphate—the religious counterpart of the sultanate—and expelling from Turkey all members of the Ottoman dynasty. At the same time, the theological schools and the religious courts were closed. One year later the dervish orders were outlawed, and superstitious expressions of popular Islam were discouraged. To be Western one had to look Western, so the wearing of the traditional fez was prohibited.

In February 1926 the *çeriat* (shariat)—the Holy Law of Islam—was replaced by the Swiss Civil Code. An additional link with the past was severed in November 1928, when it was made obligatory to use Latin instead of Arabic characters for writing Turkish. Opposition to these measures did occur, notably a Kurdish revolt in 1925 and an assassination attempt against Kemal in 1926, but the opposition was ruthlessly suppressed. His last reform that changed Turkish society was the extension of the franchise to women in 1934. In the same year the Turks were compelled to adopt surnames, Kemal choosing Atatürk (meaning "Father of the Turks").

In the international field, Atatürk had given Turkey a new prestige, achieving her entry into the League of Nations in 1932 and bringing former enemies into friendly relations by mutual defense arrangements in 1934. On Nov. 10, 1938, Atatürk died, mourned by a grateful nation that acknowledged its very survival as a debt to him. However lacking in compassion, however vindictive and cynical he may at times have appeared, scandalizing the deepest religious and moral sentiments of his people by his public and private behavior, the true measure of this complex and contradictory man is to be found in the achievements of the new generation of Turks, which he originated and directed and to which he remains both an inspiration and an ideal.

JOHN R. WALSH
The University of Edinburgh, Scotland

Further Reading: Kinross, Lord, *Atatürk: The Rebirth of a Nation* (New York 1964); Lewis, Bernard, *The Emergence of Modern Turkey* (New York 1961).

ATAXIA, ə-tak'sē-ə, is lack of coordination of muscular movement. It is a symptom and not a disease and may be due to a number of causes, among them alcoholism and *tabes dorsalis* (locomotor ataxia, q.v.). Among specifically named ataxias, *Friedreich's ataxia* (named after Nikolaus Friedreich, 1825–1882) is a hereditary disease, accompanied by degeneration of the nerve tracts in the brain and spinal cord. A victim staggers with his feet wide apart. Although the mind is not effected, there is often a speech disturbance. *Marie's hereditary ataxia* (named after Pierre Marie, 1853–1940) is also caused by cerebellar disease and resembles Friedreich's ataxia.

The name *static ataxia* is given to those cases in which there is lack of muscular coordination in standing still or in fixed positions of the limbs. It is found in some varieties of insanity (catatonic phase of schizophrenia). The term *vasomotor ataxia* refers to instability of the circulatory mechanism due to lack of coordination between the sympathetic and parasympathetic nervous systems. The commonest form of ataxia is seen in *tabes dorsalis*, which exhibits characteristic signs, notably inability to stand still in the dark (Romberg's sign, named after Moritz Heinrich Romberg (1795–1873).

HAROLD WELLINGTON JONES, M.D., *Former Editor, "Blakiston's New Gould Medical Dictionary"*

ATBARA RIVER, ät'bä-rä, in Africa, a tributary of the Nile, about 500 miles long. Its ancient name was *Astaboras*. It rises in Ethiopia to the northwest of Lake Tana, flows north, receiving such tributaries as the Mareb and Takkaze, and enters the Nile at Atbara, in the Sudan. At Atbara, Gen. Horatio Kitchener defeated the Mahdists on April 8, 1898.

ATCHAFALAYA RIVER, a-chaf-ə-li′ə, in Louisiana, flowing out of the Red River at the northern tip of Pointe Coupee Parish, near the confluence of the Red and Mississippi rivers. It flows southward about 170 miles (273.4 km), entering the Gulf of Mexico through Atchafalaya Bay after passing through Grand Lake. Normally fed by the Red River, in flood stages it forms an outlet for the Mississippi as well. The West Atchafalaya and Morganza floodways afford protection to the surrounding area during high-water stages of the two parent rivers.

ATCHISON, ach′ə-sən, **David Rice** (1807–1886), American political leader. He was born in Frogtown, Ky., on Aug. 11, 1807. He was educated for the bar in Lexington, Ky., and began practicing law in Missouri in 1830. After two years as judge of the Platte County Circuit Court, he was appointed United States senator (1843) to fill a vacancy. Reelected in 1849, he was president pro tempore of the Senate 16 times. (The theory that he was technically president of the United States for one day, March 4, 1849, because Zachary Taylor was not inaugurated until March 5, is not legally sound.)

A leading proslavery Democrat, Atchison helped to secure passage of the Kansas-Nebraska Bill (1854). After losing his Senate seat in 1855, he led border raids from Missouri against the free-soil settlers in Kansas. He died in Gower, Clinton County, Mo., on Jan. 26, 1886.

ATCHISON, ach′ə-sən, is an industrial city in northeastern Kansas, on the west bank of the Missouri River, 60 miles (96.5 km) northeast of Topeka. Its manufactured products include oilfield equipment, tools, industrial alcohol, textiles, flour, and feed. It is the distributing point for an agricultural region that raises corn, wheat, oats, alfalfa, fruit, hogs, cattle, and poultry.

Atchison is the seat of two Roman Catholic colleges—St. Benedict's College for men and Mount St. Scholastica Academy and College for women. The Kansas Children's Receiving Home also is situated there.

Atchison was settled in 1854, chiefly by immigrants from Missouri, and was named for David Rice Atchison, a United States senator from that state. During the struggle between free-soil and slavery parties for political control of Kansas in the 1850's, Atchison was headquarters of the proslavery faction. The *Squatter Sovereign,* a vigorous antiabolitionist journal, was published there. The city, incorporated in 1855, has a council-manager government. Population: 12,565.

ATCHISON, TOPEKA AND SANTA FE RAILWAY SYSTEM, ach′ə-sən, tə-pē′kə, săn′tə fā, one of the world's largest privately owned rail systems and the only U.S. railroad that offers single-line service between Chicago and California. The lines of the Santa Fe, as it is known to the traveling public, cover more than 13,000 route miles (20,921 km) in 12 states and operate almost 15,000 diesel locomotives that haul over 85,000 freight cars and about 1,500 passenger cars. They extend westward from Chicago to Los Angeles and San Francisco, as far north as Denver, and as far south as Galveston and El Paso. System headquarters are in Chicago.

The Santa Fe owes its reputation in large part to such premier passenger trains as the Super Chief, which covers the 2,222 miles (3,576 km) between Chicago and Los Angeles in 39 hours and 30 minutes. But the Atchison, as it is known in the stock market, owes its blue-chip rating to its freight service. In the 10-year period ending in 1965, the Santa Fe's annual freight revenues rose from $491.5 million to $551.8 million; freight ton-miles (one ton of freight hauled one mile) climbed from 33.9 billion to 41.4 billion; and the average freight haul increased from 523 miles (841.6 km) to 573 miles (921.08 km) (in contrast to a national average of 470 miles, or 756.37 km). In the same period, passenger-train revenues dropped from $44.6 million a year to $38.9 million and the number of passengers carried fell from 3,192,000 to 2,317,000.

Mergers. The merger fever that swept the railroads in the 1960's did not bypass the Santa Fe. Its overtures to the Western Pacific Railroad, the Missouri Pacific Railroad, and the St. Louis-San Francisco Railway came to nothing. But the Santa Fe became a principal in a case involving rival applications of the Union Pacific Railroad and the Chicago & North Western Railway for control of the Chicago, Rock Island & Pacific Railroad. The Southern Pacific Railroad supported the Union Pacific, on condition that the Southern Pacific be permitted to buy 3,500 miles (5,631.1 km) of Rock Island lines that would give it access to Kansas City, Mo. With its two principal competitors thus aligned together, the Santa Fe entered the fight on the side of the Chicago & North Western—on condition that the Santa Fe be allowed to buy 2,500 miles (4,023.25 km) of Rock Island lines providing access to St. Louis, Mo. The continuing litigation became the most hotly contested railway merger in U.S. history.

History. The founder of what is now the Atchison, Topeka and Santa Fe was Cyrus K. Holliday, a farmer and lawyer who was also the first mayor of Topeka, Kans. He dreamed of a railway to supplant the prairie schooners then plying the Santa Fe Trail between Independence, Mo., and Santa Fe, N. Mex. In 1868, Holliday obtained a charter and raised capital, and by the following year his trains were running between Topeka and Carbondale, Kans.

By 1890 Holliday's successors had battled rugged mountains, Indians, and rival railroaders to build or buy 9,000 miles (14,483.7 km) of track, and the dream had become a reality. But the panic of 1893 caught the Santa Fe overextended and the railroad went into bankruptcy. It was picked up by Edward Payson Ripley, who added 2,000 miles (3,218.6 km) of track by 1920, quadrupled gross earnings, and put the company in a strong financial position. In the following decades, conservative financial practices, coupled with progressive operating techniques, helped to put the Santa Fe in the forefront of U.S. railroads.

LUTHER S. MILLER, *"Railway Age"*

ATE, ā′tē, in Greek mythology, was the goddess of discord and mischief, causing men to perform actions ruinous to themselves. Homer identified her as a daughter of Zeus, while according to Hesiod she was the daughter of Eris (Strife). For her evil influence, Zeus banished her from Olympus. In her travels through the world, she was followed by her sisters, the Litai, kindly goddesses who restored to goodness those who had been ruined by Ate.

ATELECTASIS, at-ə-lek′tə-səs, is an imperfect or incomplete expansion of the lungs at birth (congenital atelectasis), or a collapsed or airless state of the lungs caused by the plugging or blocking of a bronchus with subsequent absorption of the retained air. This condition may occur through some external pressure such as fluid in the pleural cavity or by a tumor pressing on a bronchus. It may arise during the course of pneumonia, following an operation, or as an aftermath of spinal anesthesia when respiration has been greatly depressed. The symptoms may be few or may be those of partial asphyxia with dyspnea (difficult respiration). Unless large areas of the lung are involved, the collapse may not be at all serious. The diagnosis can be established by an X-ray picture of the chest. As a rule uncomplicated cases require no specific treatment.

ATELIER, at-əl-yā′, an artist's studio where informal classes are held for students of art. The word is French for "studio" or "workshop." Ateliers attained special importance in the 19th century, when most serious art students, including those who later became the leaders of the impressionist movement, studied at one or another of the many ateliers in Paris.

There were two kinds of ateliers in Paris. One kind, called *atelier libre* (free studio), provided studio facilities for a fee, with a model posing at set times, but with no instruction by a teacher. The most famous *atelier libre* was the Atelier Suisse, which was opened in Paris between 1825 and 1830 by a model named Suisse.

In the other kind of atelier, students worked under the guidance of a teacher as his private pupils. Many of these ateliers were run by teachers from the École des Beaux-Arts and were intended to prepare students for admittance to that school. The most famous of these was the Académie Julian, founded by Rudolphe Julian in 1860. The artists who studied there included Pierre Bonnard, Édouard Vuillard, Henri Matisse, André Derain, Fernand Léger, and Marcel Duchamp.

Although most of the teaching ateliers offered strict academic training, the approach of individual teachers varied. The Atelier Couture encouraged slavish copying of nature and outline drawing in the tradition of Ingres. The Atelier Gleyre, on the other hand, permitted more freedom. This studio attracted such painters as Claude Monet, Alfred Sisley, Auguste Renoir, and Paul Cézanne.

WILLIAM GERDTS
University of Maryland

ATGET, at-zhā′, **Jean Eugène Auguste** (1856–1927), French photographer, who documented Paris and its environs in the early 1900's. He was born at Libourne, near Bordeaux, on Feb. 12, 1856. He was raised by an uncle, and was a sailor and an actor before taking up photography. He died in Paris on Aug. 4, 1927.

From the beginning, Atget's ambition was to create a collection of photographs of Paris. He photographed its historic buildings, its fountains, statues, shops and streets, and its people. His technique was not advanced, and his figures were obviously posed, but the directness and sensitivity of his work show that he recognized photography as an independent art form. He sold some photographs to Paris museums, and some to painters for reference. A few of his pictures were printed in the magazine *La révolution surréaliste* in 1926.

Atget's importance was not recognized until the American photographer Berenice Abbott arranged for a posthumous exhibition of his work. His photographs were first seen in the United States in 1930, and had a strong influence on the style of young American photographers. Some 60 of his photographs form part of the permanent collection of the Museum of Modern Art in New York City.

Further Reading: Abbott, Berenice, *The World of Atget* (New York 1965).

ATHABASCA RIVER, ath-ə-bask′ə, in Alberta province, Canada, rising in the Rocky Mountains, near Mount Columbia, in southwest Alberta. It traverses the province and empties into Lake Athabasca in Alberta's northeast corner.

In the mid-1960's, a refinery near Fort McMurray on the lower Athabasca began producing synthetic crude oil from heavy oil extracted from sands along the river. The potential yield of these sands has been estimated at 370 billion barrels of oil, roughly equal to the free world's present conventional oil reserves.

Lake Athabasca extends across the Alberta border into northwest Saskatchewan. It is about 200 miles (321.8 km) long and discharges into the Slave River. Uranium City is on the northern shore of the lake.

ATHALIE, à-tà-lē′, is a drama by Jean Baptiste Racine (q.v.). Completed in 1691, it was called "the masterpiece of the human intellect" by Voltaire and Racine's "most beautiful work," by Boileau, and most modern critics would accord it at least the second place among his dramas. The play was slow in winning general recognition, however. After Racine's *Esther* had been produced with much éclat in 1689 by the aristocratic young ladies of Mme. de Maintenon's foundation at St. Cyr, Louis XIV ordered the poet to compose for the same amateur stage a new tragedy drawn also from the Scriptures. Two years later *Athalie* was ready, but Mme. de Maintenon had developed scruples as to the disturbing effect of dramatic representations on her educational wards. As a result, *Athalie* was accorded only a chamber performance without costumes in 1691. It was first presented to the theater-going public on March 3, 1716.

The subject of the play is the revolt of the loyalist priesthood under Jehoiada against the usurping Queen Athaliah, the anointing of the child king Jehoash, the destruction of the temple of Baal, and the slaying of his priest Mattan and, finally, of Athaliah, as told in II Kings 11, supplemented by the account of II Chronicles, 22 and 23. In the poet's hands this rather crude account of dynastic rivalries and sacerdotal ambition has become a splendid picture of religious enthusiasm and a superb plea for the divinity that was supposed to hedge true royal blood, at the court of Versailles as well as in Jerusalem.

Racine's *Athalie* is a grandly tragic portrayal of a commanding woman who knows no law but the feverish pursuit of the objects of her inconsequent passion. Prone to superstition, she struggles wildly with the portents of her fears, dashing herself against righteous fate to ruin.

ATHANASIAN CREED. See CREEDS AND CONFESSIONS.

ATHANASIUS, ath-ə-nā′zhəs, **Saint** (c. 295–373), early Christian bishop, theologian, and doctor of the church. He was born, probably at Alexandria, of Christian parents. He received his classical and theological training in Alexandria and was ordained deacon in 319 by Alexander, bishop of that city, whom he served as secretary and accompanied to the Council of Nicaea in 325.

Bishop of Alexandria. Upon the death of Alexander, Athanasius was chosen bishop of Alexandria on June 8, 328, over the opposition of the Arians and the followers of Meletius. Although Arius had been condemned at Nicaea, his supporters continued to oppose Athanasius because of his adherence to Nicaean teaching (see ARIANISM). Athanasius' refusal to admit Arius to communion, as ordered by Emperor Constantine, hardened the opposition. Under the leadership of Eusebius of Nicomedia, Athanasius' enemies deposed him at the Synod of Tyre in 335. In the same year, Constantine banished him to Trier.

After the emperor's death on May 22, 337, Athanasius returned to his see. Soon, however, the Eusebian faction succeeded in placing Gregory of Cappadocia in the see of Alexandria, whereupon Athanasius fled to Rome in 339. Pope Julius I received him and in a synod in 341 declared Athanasius innocent of the charges made against him. The Council of Sardica in 343 confirmed the findings of the synod and made it clear that Athanasius was the lawful bishop of Alexandria. After Gregory's death in 345, Athanasius returned to his diocese.

Three more banishments, however, awaited Athanasius within the next decade. Expelled during the reign of Constantius, he found asylum among the monks of the Egyptian desert. Banished by Julian the Apostate, he fled to the Thebaid. Under Emperor Valens he was forced to leave Alexandria again, and if the reports in early church histories are accurate, Athanasius spent four months hiding in the ancestral tomb near Alexandria. Of the 45 years of his episcopate he spent 17½ years in exile. Athanasius died on May 2, 373. His feast is observed May 2.

As the intrepid defender of the Nicene faith, Athanasius was called "the pillar of the Church" by Gregory of Nazianzus. Neither imperial threats nor Arian intrigues could sway him. Athanasius was not a speculative theologian but held fast to "the tradition, teaching, and faith proclaimed by the apostles and guarded by the fathers" (*First Letters to Serapion*). Against the rationalistic tendencies of his opponents he maintained the primacy of faith over reason. His Trinitarian theology taught that the Son is of the same substance (*homoöusios*) with the Father, as is also the Holy Spirit. His teaching on the Logos furnished the basic ideas for the development of later Christological doctrine. As a friend of the monks of Egypt he fostered the ascetic life in the East and brought a knowledge of monasticism to the West.

Writings. Authentic Athanasian writings can be grouped in five categories:

Apologetical and Dogmatic Works. Two titles —*Against the Pagans* and *On the Incarnation of the Word*—constitute a single work in two parts. The first refutes pagan practices and beliefs; the other presents patristic teaching on the redemption. *Discourses Against the Arians* is Athanasius' chief dogmatic treatise.

Historicopolemical Works. This group includes four titles: *Apology Against the Arians,*

Apology to the Emperor Constantius, Apology for His Flight, and *History of the Arians.*

Exegetical Works. These commentaries, chiefly on books of the Old Testament, are known through excerpts: *Genesis, Song of Songs, Psalms.*

Ascetical Works. These include *The Life of St. Anthony, Discourse on Virginity,* fragments of a treatise *On Sickness and Health,* and a brief tract on *Love and Self-Control.*

Letters. The surviving letters are valuable for the light they shed on the history of the Arian controversy and the development of Christian doctrine. Most widely known are the *Festal Letters,* written annually to the suffragan bishops of Alexandria concerning the time for Lent and the celebration of Easter and discussing important ecclesiastical matters. Especially noteworthy is the letter of the year 367, which lists the 27 books of the New Testament canon. *Letter Concerning the Decrees of the Council of Nicaea* is an account of the proceedings of the council.

Of the pseudo-Athanasian works, the best known is probably the so-called Athanasian Creed (called *Quicumque,* from its opening word). From the 7th to the 17th century this work was ascribed to Athanasius. This profession of faith is probably of Gallican origin, dating from the second half of the 5th century.

HERMIGILD DRESSLER
The Catholic University of America

Further Reading: Cross, Frank L., *The Study of St. Athanasius* (New York 1945); Daniélou, Jean, and Marrou, H., *The Christian Centuries,* vol. 1 (New York 1964); Musurillo, Herbert, *The Fathers of the Primitive Church* (New York 1966); Quasten, Johannes, *Patrology,* vol. 3 (Westminster, Md., 1960).

ATHAPASKAN LANGUAGES, ath-ə-pas′kən, a closely related group of North American Indian languages. The name is also spelled *Athapascan.* The group is made up of a number of smaller stocks: Kutchin, Tsetsaut, Tanana, Koyukon, Tanaina-Ingalik, Carrier-Chilcotin, Tahltan-Kaska, Sekani-Beaver-Sarsi, Chipewyan-Slave-Yellowknife, Dogrib-Great Bear Lake-Hare (all in western Canada and Alaska); the Pacific Coast stock (Hupa, Kato, Mattole, Wailaki, Tolowa, Chastacusta), scattered from Washington to northern California; and Apachean (Navaho, San Carlos, Chiricahua, Mescalero, Jicarilla, Lipan, Kiowa-Apache) in Arizona, New Mexico, and Oklahoma. The Apachean and Pacific Coast tribes undoubtedly came from the north, the original home of the Athapaskan languages.

Today most Athapaskan languages have only a few speakers (100 to 400), and some (for example, Mattole, Wailaki, Lipan) are nearly extinct. However, the language of the Navaho, one of the largest Indian tribes north of Mexico, has over 85,000 speakers. No Athapaskan tribe had a writing, but scholars have recorded many of the languages, and the United States Indian Service has devised an alphabet for Navaho, for the printing of school texts and a newspaper.

Athapaskan is sometimes included in the larger Na Dene stock, together with Tlingit and Haida (two groups of languages spoken on the Pacific Coast of British Columbia and Alaska). However, this grouping is still provisional.

HARRY HOIJER, *University of California*

Further Reading: Driver, H.L., *Indian Tribes of North America* (Bloomington, Ind., 1953); *Linguistic Structures of Native America,* Viking Fund Publications in Anthropology, No. 6 (New York 1946); McQuown, Norman, "Indigenous Languages of North America," *American Anthropologist,* vol. 57 (Washington 1955).

ATHEISM, ā′thē-iz′əm, commonly speaking, is the denial of God. Theism (from Greek *theos*, "God") is belief in or conceptualization of God; atheism is the rejection of such belief or conceptualization.

The meaning of atheism, then, depends upon the theism that is being denied. Hence the word has been used traditionally in at least three ways. (1) Most precisely, atheism is the denial that there is any being or power deserving the name of God or the reverence accorded God. (2) Frequently, atheism is the name applied to any conviction that rejects the prevailing beliefs in the God or gods of a given culture. (3) Sometimes atheism refers simply to the practical rejection or ignoring of God.

Because the word is often used in argument or accusation, the three meanings are frequently confused. The ambiguity of the term can be illustrated by the fact that the 17th century philosopher Spinoza was called both "the God-intoxicated man" and an atheist. The essential factor in atheism is some element of denial or rejection, not simply the skepticism or doubt known as agnosticism.

Atheism in the Ancient World. In the ancient world atheism was rarely a clearly formulated position, because it could not be defined against any clearly formulated theism. But there were many atheistic or semiatheistic expressions in the ancient religions. Confucianism and Taoism are sometimes interpreted as atheistic religions, even though popular religion in China assumed the reality of many gods and spirits. Most scholarly opinion regards the original Buddhism of Gautama as an atheistic discipline of self-mastery and self-reliance, though later (Mahayana) Buddhism affirms divine beings.

In ancient Greece, Socrates was accused of atheism (consult Plato, *Apology*). However, he angered the judges at his trial by telling them, "I shall obey God rather than you." The atomists, Democritus and the Epicureans, allowed for the existence of gods, in interstellar space, but they gave a materialistic explanation of the world in which divine beings had no influence.

The Bible contains no evidence of any absolute atheism. The saying of the fool, "There is no God" (Psalms 14:1 and 53:1) might better be translated as a scoffing declaration, "God is not here." Far more familiar is the painful cry over the absence of God; for example, "My God, my God, why hast thou forsaken me?" (Psalm 22:1; Mark 15:34). In later centuries Christians were commonly known in the Roman empire as atheists, because they denied the gods of the imperial cult. Arnold Toynbee, in *A Study of History*, cites a letter of Emperor Julian in which the "atheists" turn out to be the "Galileans."

It is often held that the prophetic tradition of the Bible, continued in Christianity, makes thoroughgoing atheism possible for the first time. Prophecy, in its protest against idols, de-divinizes nature and the state, the two most common objects of worship. The remaining alternatives are radical monotheism, centered on a transcendent deity, or atheism.

Modern Forms of Atheism. In any case, thoroughgoing, systematic atheism appeared in force as a protest against Christian orthodoxy in the modern West. It is helpful to differentiate between two forms of atheism which, even though they frequently interact and occasionally are indistinguishable, contrast in motive and dynamism.

These are the rationalistic and romantic forms.

Rationalistic atheism arose out of the modern confidence that scientific reason could offer an explanation of the world that made religious superstition obsolete. The origins of the movement in Renaissance and post-Renaissance thought are obscure, but it reaches full tide during the Enlightenment of the 18th century.

The French *philosophes* included several outspoken atheists. It is reported that the Scottish skeptic, David Hume, told his host in Paris, Baron d' Holbach, that he had never met a real atheist. Holbach's reply was, "It may interest you to know, Monsieur, that you are dining tonight with seventeen of them."

Romantic atheism, emerging in the 19th century, was a radical protest against God as an enemy of human power and morality. Dostoyevsky's Ivan Karamazov defied God on moral grounds, then asked the nihilistic question, "If there is no God, is everything permitted?" The romantic complaint against God swept through the poetry and prose of western Europe.

Meanwhile, Ludwig Feuerbach had already united the rationalistic and romantic strains. His romanticism appeared in his effort to turn theology into anthropology for the sake of a passionate affirmation of man. His rationalism came out in his naturalistic materialism, which explained God as a projection of the human mind—a theme that Sigmund Freud was later to develop in psychological terms.

The chief heir of Feuerbach was Karl Marx, whose atheism had several roots. On the one hand he was a romantic humanist who was anti-God in order to be pro-man. On the other, he was a rationalist, claiming to refute God with a scientific materialism. Reinforcing both themes was his protest against religion as the ideological prejudice of the bourgeoisie, who sanctified the status quo and offered the proletariat consolation in heaven instead of justice now. The Marxist complaint against religion is in many ways a repetition of the attack of the Hebrew prophets upon cult as a substitute for justice.

The romantic impulse to atheism, untouched by rationalism, erupted again in Friedrich Nietzsche. In cryptic writings he let his "madman" declare: "God is dead. God remains dead. And we have killed him." For Nietzsche this murder of God was a tremendous deed for which men could atone only by becoming gods.

The Nietzschean strain persists, in a rationally disciplined form, in some of the 20th century existentialists, most notably Jean-Paul Sartre. Sartre affirms that, since there is no God, man is the creator of his own values, and he must determine what is good by his act of decision. (Existentialism, as a system of thought, is neither theistic nor atheistic; prominent existentialists belong in both camps.)

Faith and Atheism. It is no longer possible, if it ever was, to regard faith and atheism as opposite limits. As in the writings of Dostoyevsky, the two intermingle. Many a theologian of the 20th century has written with profound appreciation of serious atheism; examples are the Jewish Martin Buber, Eastern Orthodox Nikolai Berdyaev, Roman Catholic Jacques Maritain, and Protestant Paul Tillich.

Maritain, while dismissing the glib atheist, ranks the serious atheist near to the saint. Such an atheist, says Maritain, has a "greatness and generosity" in his protest against the evils of the world; and he shows courage in his dismissal of the idols of conventional religion.

Thus believer and atheist frequently find common cause in criticizing the complacency of popular religion. They reject the dogmas that foment holy wars between "Christian democracy" and "atheistic communism." When Vatican Council II set up a new secretariat to encourage conversations with nonbelievers, several of the bishops urged that the church take seriously the aims and ideals of atheism at its best.

One variation on the believers' appreciation of atheism appeared in the "death-of-God theologies" of the 1960's. Despite their dramatic language, most of these theologies, upon inspection, proved to be only pseudoatheistic. The effort to combine rejection of God with an absolute affirmation of Christ proved inherently unstable, and such theologies usually reverted to some concept of God. The new concept was often radically revised from the traditional idea of God.

In at least one respect, however, these theologies marked the recovery of an orthodoxy that originates in the Bible. It is the affirmation that any belief in God must take account of the experience of God's absence, and any conceptualizing of God must purge itself of its own tendency to idolatry.

Militant atheism is now less common than agnosticism, which assumes a smaller burden of proof. Even in Marxist eastern Europe there is some tendency to qualify dogmatic atheism in the direction of an inquiring agnosticism. And agnosticism, since it must make practical commitments in life, is bound to wonder about the relation between its commitments and religious faith.

So long as men confront the mystery and meaning of their origins, their decisions, and their destinies, it is probable that atheism, agnosticism, and belief in God will all remain live options. It may be that the various perspectives and commitments will all be chastened and made wiser by virtue of their mutual conversation. See also AGNOSTICISM.

ROGER L. SHINN, *Union Theological Seminary*

Bibliography

Altizer, Thomas, and Hamilton, William, *Radical Theology and the Death of God* (Toronto 1966).
Feuerbach, Ludwig, *The Essence of Christianity* (New York 1957).
Lubac, Henri de, *The Drama of Atheist Humanism* (Cleveland 1963).
Maritain, Jacques, "The Meaning of Contemporary Atheism," in *The Range of Reason* (New York 1952).
Russell, Bertrand, "A Free Man's Worship," in *Mysticism and Logic* (New York 1929).
Sartre, Jean-Paul, *Existentialism* (New York 1947).

ATHELSTAN (895–939), ath'əl-stan, was a king of England. His name is also spelled *Æthelstan* and *Ethelstan*. His father, Edward the Elder, king of Wessex, arranged to have Athelstan raised at the Mercian court. After Edward's death in 924, Athelstan succeeded to both thrones, uniting the kingdoms of the south for the first time. In 927 he expelled the Norse rulers of Northumbria and obtained recognition of his supremacy from the kings of Cumberland and Scotland.

Within the next four years he extended his authority throughout most of England. By force or persuasion he extracted homage and an annual tribute from the Britons of Wales and established the Wye River as the national frontier. Shortly thereafter he broke Cornish power east of the Tamar River. In 937 he repulsed an assault of his enemies at Brunanburh. His influence on the European continent, based on security at home and royal marriages of five of his sisters, was greater than that of any earlier English king. He died on Oct. 27, 939.

ATHENA, ə-thē'nə, in Greek mythology, was the goddess of war and the patroness of the arts and industry. The Greek form of her name is *Athēnē*. She was also known as *Pallas Athena*. The city-state *Athens* was named in her honor. The Romans identified her with *Minerva*.

According to most accounts, Athena was born fully grown and armed from the head of Zeus. Zeus had swallowed his wife Metis to prevent the birth of a child for fear that the child might displace him. When Zeus complained of headaches, Hephaestus (Vulcan) or Prometheus laid open his head, permitting Athena to emerge.

As a war goddess, Athena emphasized justice and skill, as opposed to the wild fury of Ares (Mars). In the Trojan War, she sided with the Greeks and especially favored Odysseus (Ulysses). As patroness of the arts and industry, she inspired many great works, such as the building of the wooden horse by Epeius and of the ship *Argo* by Argus, for Jason and the Argonauts.

The olive tree, the serpent, the lance, and the owl were sacred to Athena. In art she is represented as wearing armor and carrying a shield (see AEGIS) and a golden staff.

ATHENAEUM, ath-ə-nē'əm, was the general name applied to all temples in ancient Greece dedicated to Athena, especially the celebrated temple in Athens where poets and men of learning assembled to read their compositions. The Roman emperor Hadrian used the name for the institute of learning he founded in Rome about 135 A.D. It flourished under his successors until the 400's. There scholars gathered to exchange ideas, and, in time, many were given salaries so that they could teach and pursue their studies.

More recently the name was applied to secondary schools in some countries. It also became a popular title for many literary journals, and was sometimes used as a name for literary and scientific clubs such as the Athenaeum in London and the Athenaeum in Boston.

ATHENAEUS, ath-ə-nē'əs, was a Greek scholar who lived about 200 A.D. A native of Naucratis in Egypt, he resided later in Alexandria and finally in Rome. He was the author of *Deipnosophistai* (*Sophists at Dinner* or *Connoisseurs in Dining*), written in 15 books probably after 192 A.D. It is in the form of a conversation among learned men assembled at a banquet. They discuss food in all of its aspects and a variety of other subjects, including philosophy, law, literature, and music. The work is valuable in that it preserves many quotations from Greek comedy and other literature that otherwise might have been lost.

ATHENAGORAS, ath-ə-nag'ə-rəs, was a Greek philosopher of the 2d century A.D. His chief surviving work is an *Apology for the Christians*, written in Greek and addressed in 177 to Emperor Marcus Aurelius Antoninus. The work is primarily a defense of the Christians against charges of atheism, incest, and cannibalism. Athenagoras frequently combined the beliefs of the Greek poets and philosophers, particularly Plato, with the doctrines of Christianity.

ATHENAGORAS I, ä-thē-nä-gôr'ás (1886–1972), ecumenical patriarch and archbishop of Constantinople (Istanbul), was the spiritual leader of some 150,000,000 members of the Orthodox Eastern Church. Born in northern Greece in 1886, he became head of the 15 independent national Orthodox churches in 1948. As patriarch, Athenagoras sought to minimize long-standing differences between the church and the Turkish authorities and to promote a dialogue between Christians of East and West. He died in Istanbul on July 7, 1972.

The historic conference of Athenagoras with Pope Paul VI in Jerusalem in January 1964 was the first meeting between leaders of the Orthodox and Roman Catholic churches since 1439. In 1965 the Patriarch and the Pope revoked the mutual excommunication decrees of 1054.

ATHENS, ath'ənz, a city in Alabama, is the seat of Limestone County. It is 10 miles (16 km) north of the Tennessee River and 98 miles (157.7 km) northwest of Birmingham. Athens is the center of an agricultural area where cotton, livestock, corn, hay, poultry, and truck crops are produced. In the city are cotton gins, stockyards, grist and lumber mills, and a garment factory. Athens College, now coeducational, was established as a college for women in 1842.

Athens was incorporated in 1818, a year before Alabama became a state. The area had been part of Mississippi Territory. Athens became the county seat in 1819. It was occupied early in the Civil War by Union troops and was the scene of much fighting. Public buildings were burned, and municipal records were destroyed. Confederate forces under Gen. Nathan Bedford Forrest recaptured it in 1864 when Col. Wallace Campbell surrendered his Federal troops.

In 1934, Athens, by vote of its citizens, became the first city in Alabama to use electric power supplied by the Tennessee Valley Authority. It has a mayor and council form of government. Population: 14,360.

ATHENS, ath'ənz, a city in Georgia, is an industrial and educational center of the northeastern part of the state and the seat of Clarke County. It is situated on a hillside in a bend of the Oconee River, about 75 miles (120 km) northeast of Atlanta. Athens is the site of the University of Georgia. It manufactures textiles, cotton garments, cord, tire fabric, cottonseed products, fertilizer, dairy products, wood products, electrical transformers, clocks, and cartons for dairy products. It also processes poultry from the surrounding agricultural area, which it serves as a trading center. Athens is served by a municipal airport.

The city is noted for its stately pre-Civil War homes, built in Greek Revival style. A unique double-barreled cannon, produced in Athens during the Civil War, stands at the city hall.

Athens was created as the result of the decision of a committee in 1801 to establish a state university on the site. The land was donated to the university by the legislator John Milledge. Part of the land was sold to individuals, who thus became the first settlers of the community. Athens' growth was accelerated by an influx of refugees during the Civil War. Athens was incorporated in 1806 and became the county seat in 1872. Government is by mayor and council. Population: 44,342.

ATHENS, ath'ənz, the capital and largest city of Greece, is one of the world's most historic and beautiful cities. At the summit of its golden age during the 400's B.C., Athens was the capital of Attica and the cultural center of the Mediterranean world. Because of the great contributions made by Athenians to art, literature, philosophy, and law, historians have called ancient Athens the fountainhead of Western culture. The modern city of Greater Athens, including the busy port of Piraeus and several residential suburbs, remains the hub of Greek political, economic, and cultural life. Population: (1961) Athens, 627,564; Greater Athens, 1,852,709.

Athens is in the southeastern part of Greece, on a plain cut by limestone ridges. Several of the higher ridges stretch along three sides of the city. On the west is Aigaleos (1,535 feet); on the north, the Parnes (4,635 feet); on the northeast, Lycabettus (909 feet) and Pentelikon (3,637 feet); and on the east, the Hymettus range (3,367 feet). Metropolitan Athens lies across a series of lower ridges. The ancient city was built originally on the Acropolis, a hill that rises 412 feet above sea level. As the city developed, it spread across other hills—the Areopagus, to the northwest of the Acropolis, and the Pnyx and Museum Hill to the southwest.

The Saronic Gulf, an inlet of the Aegean Sea, lies a few miles southwest of Athens. Athens' two historic rivers, the Cephisus to the west of the city and the Ilissus on the east, flow into the gulf. They are now insignificant streams.

The climate is temperate and dry. Temperatures range from an average of about 45° F (7° C) in winter to 80° F (27° C) in summer. Rainfall averages about 20 inches a year.

Modern Athens. Greater Athens is the economic center of Greece, and its port of Piraeus is one of the busiest in the Mediterranean Sea. With its extensive shipping facilities and rail and road connections to all sections of the country, it handles almost all of Greece's foreign trade. Together, Athens and Piraeus account for almost 45 percent of the nation's industrial output. In addition to shipbuilding and repair yards, there are flour and paper mills, machinery works, textile mills, tanneries, breweries, and distilleries. Other important manufactures include glass, tiles and bricks, soap, paper, and chemicals.

Athens is linked by highway and rail lines to all the major cities of Greece. Hellenikon airport is served by Olympic Airways, the domestic airline, and by many international airlines.

The Marathon Reservoir, formed by a dam made of Pentelic marble, supplies the city's water. The dam, the only one in the world made of marble, was completed in 1931 by American engineers. Electric power is supplied by thermal power plants at Hagios Georgios Keratsiniou, and Neon Phaleron.

Modern Athens is distinguished by carefully planned, wide streets and plazas. Many of its public buildings follow classical styles of architecture. The most striking are the National Library, the Academy of Science, the National University, and Gennadeion Library. Next to the Old Palace, now the parliament building, are the royal gardens designed by Queen Amalie in the 1800's.

Athens is rich in museums and educational institutions. The National Museum and the Acropolis Museum contain collections of classical antiquities; the Museum of Epigraphy has

THE CITY OF ATHENS, as viewed from the Acropolis.

a vast quantity of ancient inscriptions. Other notable institutions are the Byzantine Museum, Historical and Ethnological Museum, National Gallery of Art, and Benaki Museum, the last containing a remarkable collection of Greek costumes through the ages. The National Library has a collection of more than 2,300 ancient manuscripts. The National Theater continues the traditions of the Greek stage.

The National and Capodistrian University of Athens, founded in 1837, has more than 11,000 students in its five faculties. Athens also has a technical university, colleges of agriculture, fine arts, music, and drama, two business colleges, a teacher-training college, and an ecclesiastical college. There are also numerous research societies and institutes, including the Academy of Science.

Outstanding contributions to classical learning have been made by the Greek Archaeological Society, founded in 1837, and by foreign archaeological schools in Athens: the French, founded in 1846; the German, in 1874; the American, in 1882; the British, in 1886; the Austrian, in 1898; and the Italian, in 1909. Most of the important archaeological work in the first half of the 20th century was done by Americans. Bert Hodge Hill directed excavations on the Acropolis, beginning in 1906. Theodore Leslie Shear and Homer A. Thompson, directing operations in the 1930's and 1940's, respectively, unearthed portions of the Agora, the Athenian place of assembly or market

place. Excavation of the site has continued.

Monuments of the Ancient City. Athens is rich in monuments of the preclassical, classical, Hellenistic, Roman, and Byzantine periods. On the Acropolis, Pnyx, and other hills, traces have been found of prehistoric dwellings cut in the rock. There are also vestiges of defense works and dwellings of the pre-Hellenic Pelasgian and Minyan settlers.

The Acropolis, center of the ancient city's religious life, affords the most abundant display of archaeological treasures. Few traces remain of the structures that existed before the Persians sacked Athens in 480 B.C. and burned the Hecatompedon, the principal temple on the Acropolis, but many sculptured pieces of that period have been unearthed. The most notable comprises a beautiful series of figures of maidens, suggesting Ionian and Oriental influences in early Athenian art.

The city's destruction by the Persians cleared the ground for the construction of new temples on the Acropolis. A period of rebirth was inaugurated by Pericles, who commissioned the architects Ictinus and Callicrates to build the Parthenon (temple of Athena Parthenos), a magnificent Doric structure 228 feet long and 101 feet wide. It has columns on all four sides: 8 outer columns on the east and west, and 17 on the north and south, if the corner columns are counted twice. Completed about 432 B.C., the Parthenon still stands as a model of classic purity. It was em-

THE ACROPOLIS, crowned by the majestic Parthenon, towers over the modern city. Both the Parthenon and the Erechtheum (*at left*) were built in the 5th century B.C. The building atop Mt. Lykabettos (*right*) is a monastery.

DE WYS, INC.

bellished with statues, reliefs, and decorative sculpture. The frieze, pediments, and metopes, ascribed to Phidias, are of unsurpassed beauty; they are in great part preserved in the British Museum in London (see ELGIN MARBLES). The frieze represents the procession of the greater Panathenaic festival (see PANATHENAEA). The pediments portray the birth of Athena and her contest with Poseidon for the allegiance of Athens. The metopes depict battles of gods and giants, centaurs and Lapithae, the siege of Troy, and other scenes. A large statue of Athena by Phidias, now lost, once stood inside the Parthenon. The unclothed portions of the statue were of ivory, and the drapery was of gold plate. In 1687, the Parthenon was bombarded by Venetian forces under Francesco Morosini. The attackers exploded a powder magazine, causing great damage to the structure. Much of the damage was repaired by the Greek Archaeological Society in 1931.

At the western approach to the Acropolis stands the Propylaea (Greek *Propylaia,* meaning "outer gates"), a fine Doric building of white Pentelic marble erected in 437–432 B.C. It overlooks the winding processional road and marble stairway leading up from the city. The north wing is in perfect condition; the inner wall with its five gateways still stands. Near the Propylaea is the tiny temple of Athena Nike, of almost ethereal lightness in its Ionic elegance. It was destroyed in 1687 but was reassembled from the original materials in 1835. When water seepage threatened the foundations in 1930, the temple was taken down and reassembled by the Greek Archaeological Society.

On the north side of the Acropolis is the Erechtheum (435–about 408 B.C.), a composite Ionic temple dedicated to Athena, Poseidon, and Erechtheus, possibly symbolizing in its somewhat confused architecture an awkward compromise among these tutelary deities in their legendary struggle for possession of Athens. The caryatid porch is famous for its imposing female figures.

On the south slope of the Acropolis are the Theater of Dionysus; the Asclepieum, or shrine of Aesculapius; the Odeum (*Odeion,* or concert auditorium) of Pericles; and the Roman Odeum of the orator and scholar Herodes Atticus. In the solid and spacious remains of the Roman Odeum, performances of Greek tragedies and symphony concerts are given.

Conspicuous in the lower city are the so-called Theseion or temple of Theseus (probably a temple of Hephaestus), in the Doric style, the best-preserved Greek temple in the world, on whose metopes are represented the labors of Hercules and Theseus; and the Olympieum or temple of the Olympian Zeus, largest in Athens, begun by Pisistratus in the 500's B.C. and continued at intervals until its completion by Hadrian in 129 A.D. The Olympieum was 354 feet long and about 135 feet wide, and was surrounded by 104 columns 56½ feet high and 5½ feet in diameter, 15 of which are still standing. Most graceful is the monument of Lysicrates (335 B.C.), the only remaining monument of many commemorating successful *choragoi* (wealthy citizens who provided at their own expense the dramatic chorus appearing in Greek plays). It is a small circular edifice of Pentelic marble only nine feet in diameter, with slender Corinthian columns embedded in the wall and a frieze.

The Agora was the center of civic and business activity in ancient Athens. In it stood the Stoa Poikile (painted colonnade or portico), adorned with frescoes by great artists, from which the Stoics took their name because Zeno taught there. The Agora also contained the Bouleuterion or council hall of the 500 elected representatives of the people. In the square in front of the hall were shrines and monuments of heroes and a statue of Hermes, god of merchants and sometimes protector of thieves, who presided over activities in the Agora.

THE PARTHENON, greatest monument created by ancient Athenians, is a model of classic architectural purity.

THE ERECHTHEUM, an Ionic temple named after a legendary king of Athens, is the best preserved specimen of Greek Ionic architecture. The six statues within the famous Porch of the Maidens are among the finest surviving sculptures of ancient Athens.

In the 400's B.C., Athens was connected with Piraeus and the adjoining harbors by two massive walls set 550 feet apart, called the Long Walls. During enemy incursions into Attica, the rural population and livestock took refuge between the walls. Sparse remains of their foundations still exist. To the south was a third wall, the Phaleric, which extended from Athens to the coastal town of Phaleron and protected the bay connecting it with Piraeus. On the south shore of Piraeus are traces of the defensive wall built by Themistocles beginning in 493 B.C.

An interesting structure is the Horologium (*Horologion,* or hour recorder), erected by the astronomer Andronicus of Cyrrhus. This is a well-preserved octagonal marble tower, popularly known as the Tower of the Winds because the eight winds are represented in relief on its upper sides. A vane operating a pointer showed the prevailing wind, and a series of sundials on the walls indicated the hour.

Under the Roman emperor Hadrian (reigned 117–138 A.D.), a whole new city, Novae Athenae, rose around the Olympieum. The Arch of Hadrian, still extant, was the gateway to this district. The Panathenaic Stadium, built by the orator Lycurgus about 330 B.C., was reconstructed about 143 A.D. by Herodes Atticus. In 1896 it was restored for the first modern Olympic games. It accommodates 44,000 spectators. Under Hadrian, the Romans began construction of a water supply system from the springs of Mount Pentelikon. It was completed under Antoninus Pius (reigned 138–161). The underground aqueducts, made of huge blocks of stone, were so solidly built that they have been incorporated in the modern system.

The Byzantine era bequeathed to Athens and its environs several small churches of great beauty. Most graceful among them is the 12th century Little Metropolitan Church (Small Cathedral), nestling in the shadow of the ungainly modern cathedral. The mosaics in the church at Daphne on the road to Eleusis are unique.

History. Athens was named for Athena, goddess of wisdom, the city's patron. When the city first appeared in history, its population was grouped in families and tribes. Athens was governed by kings claiming descent from Erechtheus, who according to legend was an early king of Athens and later was deified. In the late 700's and early 600's B.C. the monarchy was superseded by an oligarchy of archons (magistrates) elected by the Athenian aristocracy.

A social crisis led to constitutional and economic reforms promulgated by Solon in 594 B.C. Pisistratus seized power in 560 and, except for two brief intervals, ruled as a popular and benevolent dictator until his death in 527. He was succeeded by his sons Hipparchus and Hippias. After Hippias was overthrown in 510, a struggle broke out between those who favored oligarchy and those who favored democracy. The democrats won and in 508 Cleisthenes introduced reforms that made Athens the first democracy.

In 480 B.C., the Persians under Xerxes I captured and burned Athens. In the struggle that followed, Athens emerged in ruins but victorious, and its authority as leader of the Ionian Greeks was firmly established. Its geographical position ensured rapid commercial progress. Under the leadership of Cimon (about 468–461) and Pericles (about 461–429), Athens became a great imperial power. The 60 years following the Persian Wars were the great creative age in Athens.

Aeschylus, Sophocles, Euripides, Aristophanes, and Socrates all flourished at this time. But the Peloponnesian War (431–404) impoverished Athens. The city surrendered to Sparta and took second place in Greek affairs.

In the 300's B.C., Athens revived, but it struggled unsuccessfully against the rising power of Macedon. Athens retained a measure of autonomy under Alexander the Great (reigned 336–323) and kept its cultural preeminence. In 146 B.C., when the Greek cities were placed under the Roman governor of Macedonia, Athens kept its autonomy, but the city was sacked by Sulla, in the year 86, and in 27 it became part of the Roman province of Achaea. Although Athens ceased to be politically important, it was regarded as the great university city of the Roman world. In the 100's A.D., under Hadrian and the Antonines, it revived as a great commercial center.

After about 300 A.D., Athens began to decline as a cultural center. Under Byzantine rule from the late 300's to 1453, the city was unable to compete with Constantinople. After the Latin empire was established in 1204, the de la Roche family was awarded the lordship of Athens. Later the city came under Catalan and Florentine rule. Under the Turks (1458–1821), Athens dwindled to an impoverished village with a population of less than 5,000.

In the Greek War of Independence (1821–1829), Athens and its ancient monuments were badly damaged. The Acropolis became a military garrison and changed hands between Greeks and Turks several times. After Greece won her independence, Athens was chosen as the capital of the new nation in 1834. As the city grew in the next 100 years, it became again one of the great commercial and cultural centers of the Mediterranean area.

Athens was occupied by German troops during World War II from 1941 to 1944. The city's monuments survived the war intact, but the Germans wrecked the harbor of Piraeus and inflicted heavy damage on Athens' industrial establishments.

In the 1950's and 1960's, with substantial American aid and some help from foreign loans, Athens repaired most of its war damage and expanded its industrial and commercial capacity to well beyond its prewar level.

See also GREECE.

ANDRÉ MICHALOPOULOS
Fairleigh Dickinson University

Bibliography

Burn, Andrew R., *Pericles and Athens* (New York 1949).
Forster, Edward S., *A Short History of Modern Greece* (London 1941).
Gardner, Ernest A., *Ancient Athens* (New York 1902).
Hambidge, Jay, *Parthenon and Other Greek Temples* (New Haven 1924).
Hignett, Charles, *History of the Athenian Constitution to the End of the Fifth Century B.C.* (New York 1952).
Jones, Arnold H.M., *Athens of Demosthenes* (New York 1952).
Lancaster, Osbert, *Classical Landscape with Figures* (Boston 1949).
Miller, William, *History of the Greek People, 1821–1921* (New York 1923).
Penrose, Francis C., *An Investigation of the Principles of Athenian Architecture* (London 1888).
Procopiou, Angelo, *Athens: City of the Gods* (New York 1964).
Robinson, Charles A., Jr., *Athens in the Age of Pericles* (Norman, Okla., 1959).
Rodenwaldt, Gerhart, *Acropolis* (Norman, Okla., 1958).
Sicilianos, Dimitrios, *Old and New Athens* (Chester Springs, Pa., 1960).
Weller, Charles H., *Athens and Its Monuments* (New York 1913).

ATHENS, ath'ənz, a city in southeastern Ohio, is the seat of Athens County. It is situated on the Hocking River, 75 miles (120 km) southeast of Columbus. The surrounding region is principally agricultural. The city's industries include the manufacture of business machines and systems, tire molds, forged hand and bench tools, midget automobiles and trucks, scooters, and building materials.

Athens is the seat of Ohio University which was founded in 1804 and was the first college in the Northwest Territory. The community was founded in 1800 and incorporated as a city in 1912. Government is by mayor and council. Population: 23,310.

ATHENS, ath'ənz, a borough in northeastern Pennsylvania, is situated in Bradford County, between the Chemung and Susquehanna rivers, 80 miles (130 km) by road northwest of Scranton and 3 miles (5 km) south of the New York border. Its main industry is the manufacture of pneumatic tools. An important Indian village called *Tioga Point* occupied the site before 1778, when American troops burned it in revenge for the Wyoming Massacre (see WYOMING VALLEY). Athens was settled in 1786 and was incorporated in 1831. Population: 4,173.

ATHENS, ath'ənz, is a manufacturing city in southeastern Tennessee and the seat of McMinn County. It is situated midway between Knoxville and Chattanooga, which are about 50 miles (80 km) from the city. Athens manufactures textiles, furniture, paper, animal feeds, and chemicals. The surrounding farms produce chiefly tobacco, beef cattle, and milk. Tennessee Wesleyan College (founded 1857) is in Athens.

The city was laid out in the early 1820's and incorporated in 1868. Government is by a city manager. Population: 11,790.

ATHENS, ath'ənz, a manufacturing city in Texas, is the seat of Henderson County. It is situated 70 miles (112 km) by road southeast of Dallas. Athens' industrial establishments include cotton gins, a cotton-oil mill, oil- and gas-processing works, a food-processing factory, and plants manufacturing brick, tile, glass, pottery, television sets, clothing, furniture, and hardwood lumber. A regional power plant serves the area. The county's Memorial Library and Henderson County Junior College are in the city. Athens was settled in 1848 and was incorporated in 1856. It is governed under a city manager plan adopted in 1960. Population: 9,582.

ATHENS, ath'ənz, **National University of,** a co-educational state institution in Athens, Greece. Founded in 1837 by King Otto I, it was nationalized in 1862 and named the *National and Capodistrian University* in honor of Greek patriot John Capodistrias (1776–1831). Adjoining the university, and considered part of its facilities, are the National Library, housing 500,000 volumes, and the Academy, with a collection of rare coins. There are faculties of theology, law, medicine, philosophy, and science; a school of dentistry; and departments of English and French, supplemented by 70 institutes, clinics, and laboratories. Each unit has its own library, and there are numerous museums. Master's degrees are given in all disciplines; doctorates are also granted. Enrollment averages about 8,500.

ATHEROSCLEROSIS, ath-ə-rō-sklə-rō'səs, is a disease in which deposits of cholesterol and other fatty substances line the walls of the arteries. At first, these deposits involve only the innermost layer of the artery wall, but as the disease progresses, they affect the entire wall, causing it to become thick and inelastic and narrowing the channel through which the blood flows.

In the advanced stages of atherosclerosis, various complications may occur. One of the most serious of these complications occurs when a blood clot forms in the narrowed artery. Unless the clot is dissolved or is removed through surgery it may cut off the flow of blood to the tissue normally supplied by the artery, resulting in the death of the affected tissue. This kind of complication often occurs in the major arteries that carry blood to the brain and to the extremities. It also frequently occurs in the coronary arteries, the small blood vessels that supply the heart tissue, and is a major cause of heart attacks.

Incidence and Mortality. At the present time, atherosclerosis, particularly of the coronary arteries, is the most widespread illness affecting the populations of the United States and other economically developed countries. In 1965 nearly 40 percent of all deaths in the United States were due to heart attacks caused by atherosclerotic heart disease. Of these deaths, nearly one third occurred in people under the age of 65. Today there is about one chance in five that the average American male will develop coronary disease before the age of 60. The chance that he will die of the disease before 60 is about 1 in 15. For most middle-aged women the chances of developing atherosclerosis are much lower than for middle-aged men. After menopause, however, a woman's chance of developing the disease rises considerably.

Causes. There is no single cause of atherosclerosis. Instead, the disease has many causes, with

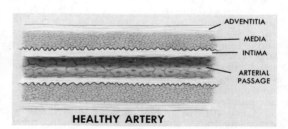

HEALTHY ARTERY

In the early stages of atherosclerosis, cholesterol and other fatty substances are deposited on the inner wall of an artery. As the disease progresses, these deposits interfere with the flow of blood through the artery and cause the artery wall to become thick and inelastic.

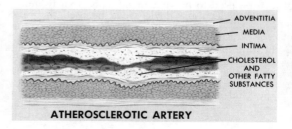

ATHEROSCLEROTIC ARTERY

the various factors having different relative roles in different people. Diet is generally a key factor. Diets rich in calories, saturated fats, cholesterol, sugar, and salt have been found to play an important role in producing several of the traits and abnormalities that intensify the disease process. Among these abnormalities are obesity, high blood pressure, diabetes mellitus, and high levels of cholesterol and other fatty substances in the blood. All four of these traits are important risk factors; their presence is associated with a significant increase in the probability of developing an atherosclerotic disease.

Cigarette smoking is another major risk factor, and a lack of exercise also increases a person's tendency to develop the disease. Other traits that have been implicated include high levels of uric acid in the blood plasma and certain personality traits and behavior patterns. In addition, it has been found that a susceptibility to atherosclerosis may be inherited. A person whose close relatives suffer the disease prematurely is more likely to develop atherosclerosis than a person with no family history of the disease.

Symptoms. The symptoms of atherosclerosis vary greatly, depending on the organ involved and the severity of involvement. Often the disease is present for years but produces no symptoms. When illness finally develops, it frequently takes the form of heart disease, usually a heart attack, heart failure, or angina pectoris (chest discomfort brought on particularly by exercise, meals, or excitement). Stroke is another major manifestation of atherosclerosis. In addition, the disease may produce high blood pressure, especially if it involves the arteries supplying the kidneys. If the disease involves the major arteries supplying the legs, it may produce pain in the calves of the legs after walking.

Prevention and Treatment. As a result of our knowledge of the causes of atherosclerosis, the disease can often be prevented. Rich diets, sedentary habits, and cigarette smoking can almost always be avoided or corrected. High blood levels of cholesterol and uric acid, as well as hypertension, obesity, and diabetes can be detected in early adulthood and can usually be controlled through special diets, drugs, or exercise. Mounting evidence indicates that this approach is indeed effective. It is also effective in the long-term care of patients who have recovered from one or more episodes of atherosclerotic disease, for purposes of preventing recurrent attacks.

Once atherosclerotic disease is present, there are many forms of treatment for bringing relief and aid to the patient. These measures include closed-chest heart resuscitation and intensive care for patients during the first days after a heart attack. For patients with angina pectoris there are various drugs (for example, nitroglycerin) to relieve pain and dilate the heart and coronary arteries. Digitalis and diuretic drugs are helpful for heart failure patients, and anticoagulants can be used to prevent blood clots from forming. Various electronic devices can be used to break episodes of abnormal heart rhythms or to pace the heart (establish a proper heart rate) when it is beating at an abnormally slow rate. In addition, there are surgical procedures that can be used to make the blood bypass severely atherosclerotic arteries, restoring the normal flow of blood to the vital organs.

JEREMIAH STAMLER, M.D.
Chicago Health Research Foundation

ATHERTON, ath'ər-tən, **Charles Gordon** (1804–1853), American political leader, who introduced in the U.S. House of Representatives one of the gag rules aimed at balking antislavery legislation.

Born at Amherst, N.H., on July 4, 1804, he was graduated from Harvard College in 1822. He served in the New Hampshire House of Representatives for four years (the last three as speaker). He was a Democratic congressman in 1837–1843, and a member of the Senate in 1843–1849. Elected to the Senate again in 1852, he was prevented from taking his seat because of a paralytic stroke. He died at Manchester, N.H., on Nov. 15, 1853.

The "Atherton gag" resolution, which he introduced in the House in 1838, provided that all bills or petitions on the subject of slavery be tabled. A more sweeping version was adopted two years later, but it was finally repealed in 1844 (see also GAG RULES). Atherton appears to have been motivated in this effort by his strict constructionist view of the Constitution, holding that states' rights prevented the federal government from acting against slavery.

ATHERTON, ath'ər-tən, **Gertrude** (1857–1948), American author. She was born *Gertrude Franklin Horn,* in San Francisco, on Oct. 30, 1857. She was educated at private schools in California and Kentucky. In 1876 she married George Henry Bowen Atherton, by whom she had two children. After her husband's death in 1887, she traveled extensively and pursued a literary career, writing novels with varied backgrounds, ranging from ancient Greece, France, and Germany to the West Indies and California. She died in San Francisco on June 14, 1948.

Her most popular books include *The Conqueror* (1902), a fictional biography of Alexander Hamilton, for which she went to his birthplace in the West Indies to gather information, and *Black Oxen* (1923), a novel inspired by her own experience with the Steinach method of rejuvenation. Among her other works are *The Doomswoman* (1892), a novel about California in 1840; *Before the Gringo Came* (1894), short stories; *Senator North* (1900), a novel; *The Bell in the Fog* (1905), short stories; *Rezanov* (1906), a novel; *California: An Intimate History* (1914); *The Immortal Marriage* (1927), a story of personages of ancient Greece; *Dido, Queen of Hearts* (1929), a novel; *Adventures of a Novelist* (1932), an autobiography in which she revealed her dislike for the conventional; *The Horn of Life* (1942), a novel of San Francisco; *Golden Gate Country* (1945), a history; and *My San Francisco* (1946), a book of reminiscences.

Mrs. Atherton received the Legion of Honor in 1925 for her relief work in France during World War I. In 1947 she received a gold medal from the city of San Francisco. She was awarded honorary degrees by the University of California and by Mills College.

ATHERTON, ath'ər-tən, a city in California, is in San Mateo County, 22 miles (35 km) southeast of San Francisco, near the base of the San Mateo Peninsula. Atherton is primarily residential in character. It was developed on land acquired in 1860 by Faxon D. Atherton, father-in-law of the author Gertrude Atherton, and was named for him. Incorporated in 1923, Atherton has a mayor and council form of government. Population: 8,085.

ATHETOSIS, ath-ə-tō'sis, is an abnormal movement, usually of the hands and fingers, occurring after some destructive process in the brain. The movement is slow and purposeless, the fingers flexing and extending separately in an irregular manner. The whole hand is affected and sometimes the arms, toes, and feet. The condition usually arises from a brain injury.

ATHLETE'S FOOT, ath'lets foot, is a fungus infection of the feet that is very common in adult males and less usual in adult females and children. It is caused by the fungus *Trichophyton mentagrophytes* and related fungi.

Description. Small, deep blisters appear on the foot and often lead to a wearing away and cracking of the skin. Chronic lesions are characterized by dry scaling of the skin. The skin between the fourth and fifth toes is most commonly involved. Sometimes, deep blisters appear on the soles of the feet, especially over the instep. Eventually, the infection spreads to the nails, causing gross distortion and discoloration. Occasionally the fungus may produce blisters (dermatophytids) on the palms of the hands.

The symptoms of athlete's foot are variable, and some chronic infections may show no symptoms. In the acute phase of the infection, intense itching may occur. Pain may be caused by deep fissures and inflammation in the surrounding areas. Bacteria may gain access to the fissures and cause local redness, pain, and swelling. The infection may spread to the leg, causing red streaks (lymphangitis), and to the groin, causing painful enlargement of the lymph glands. In severe diabetic cases, poor circulation may cause the infection to result in gangrene.

Prevention. Athlete's foot is not easy to prevent. It is usually contracted in public showers, dressing rooms, and swimming pool areas where bare feet may come in contact with the fungus. One should avoid walking barefoot as much as circumstances or comfort permit. Perspiration, which can aggravate athlete's foot, should be diminished by the use of dusting powders. Shoes should be light and airy.

Treatment. Fungicidal chemicals are used in the treatment of athlete's foot, but they frequently fail to contact the fungi located within the horny layers of the skin. Whitfield's ointment—a mixture of benzoic and salicylic acids—is valuable because it peels off the infected skin. Certain fatty acids—propionic, undecylenic, and caprylic—found in commercial powders and ointments may also be effective. Extensive infections may be treated with an oral agent—Griseofulvin—that inhibits the growth of fungi. In acutely inflamed lesions, soothing wet applications should be applied for several days before any other agent is used.

IRVING SOLOMON, M.D.
Mt. Sinai School of Medicine, New York City

ATHLETICS. See OLYMPIC GAMES; PHYSICAL EDUCATION; SPORTS, ATHLETIC.

ATHLONE, ath-lōn', **1st Earl of** (1874–1957), British soldier and Commonwealth official. He was born *Alexander Augustus Frederick William Alfred George Cambridge,* at Kensington Palace, London, on April 14, 1874. He was the son of Francis of Hohenstein, duke of Teck, and Princess Mary Adelaide, granddaughter of King George III. His sister, Mary, married George,

duke of York, later King George V.

Cambridge was educated at Eton and the Royal Military College, Sandhurst, and fought in the Boer War and World War I. In 1904 he married Princess Alice of Albany, granddaughter of Queen Victoria. George V created him 1st Earl of Athlone in 1917.

He was named governor general designate of Canada in 1914, but the outbreak of World War I prevented his appointment. He was governor general of the Union of South Africa from 1923 to 1931, when he was appointed governor of Windsor Castle and chancellor of London University. He served as governor general of Canada from 1940 to 1946. He died at Kensington Palace on Jan. 16, 1957.

ATHLONE, ath-lōn', is an urban district in Ireland, in Westmeath County, on both sides of the River Shannon, 70 miles (112 km) west of Dublin. It is an important rail junction of the Irish Transport System (Córas Iompair Éireann) and a military depot. The main transmitting station of Radio Eireann is here. Athlone has wool and cotton mills, a mineral-water works, and an eel fishery. It is a convenient center for visitors to the Irish midlands.

Lough Ree, where the Shannon widens to form a long, beautiful lake, is just north of Athlone. Just south of it is Clonmacnoise, where St. Ciaran founded a monastery in 548 A.D. Clonmacnoise became the most famous of the "monastic cities" of Ireland. During the next 1,100 years it was often plundered—and rebuilt—until its final despoliation by English troops under Oliver Cromwell in the mid-17th century. Ruins of eight churches and two round towers remain. Population: 9,624.

ATHOL, ath'ôl, is an industrial town in northern Massachusetts, on the Millers River, in Worcester County, 40 miles (64 km) by road northwest of Worcester. It is on the historic Mohawk Trail. Its manufactures include precision tools and instruments, shoes, artificial leather, wooden toys, plastics, paint, and furniture.

Athol, settled in 1735, was called Pequoiag until its incorporation in 1762. Then, John Murray, a prominent landowner in the area, renamed it for the ancestral seat of the Murrays, who were dukes of Atholl in Scotland. Athol has a selectmen-representative form of government. Population: 11,185.

ATHOLL, ath'əl, **Duchess of** (1875–1960), British political leader and author. She was born *Katharine Marjory Ramsay,* daughter of the Scottish historian Sir James Ramsay. In 1899 she married John George Stewart-Murray, 8th duke of Atholl. She was created a dame in 1918 in recognition of her war work as commandant of Blair Castle Hospital (her converted home).

From 1923 to 1938 the duchess was a Conservative member of Parliament. As parliamentary secretary to the board of education from 1924 to 1929 she was the first woman minister in a Conservative government. In 1938 she broke with the party over its policy of accommodation with Nazi Germany and retired from office, but she continued her efforts to rouse the British for the approaching war. She was the author of several books on international affairs, and she also composed songs. The duchess died at Edinburgh on Oct. 21, 1960.

MOUNT ATHOS is the site of 20 Greek Orthodox monasteries; many cling to the rocky coast.

JERRY FRANK

ATHOS, ath′os, **Mount,** in Greece, the easternmost extension of Chalcidice peninsula, jutting into the Aegean Sea. It is also known as *Akte* peninsula. The area, 30 miles (48 km) long and about 5 miles (8 km) wide, constitutes the administrative district of *Hagion Oros*, a semiautonomous monastic community. At the southeastern end of the prong is Mount Athos proper (6,670 feet; 2,033 meters). Karyai, the capital, is the only town.

Mount Athos first came into prominence during the Greek wars with the Persians. In 491 B.C. part of the Persian fleet was destroyed in the treacherous waters at the head of the cape. In 483–481, Xerxes prepared for his invasion of Greece by building a canal through the neck of the peninsula to avoid a similar disaster.

Hermits began settling in the region in the 9th century A.D., and by the 10th century they were organized into small monastic communities, or *lavra*. In 963, Athanasius the Anchorite founded the Grand Lavra, which today contains the finest religious art on Mount Athos. Under the Byzantine emperors, the monasteries greatly increased in number after the 10th century. In th 15th century some monasteries broke away from the strict cenobitic rule to form more liberal, idiorrhythmic communities, in which the monks could have personal property.

Despite outside pressures, the monks of Mount Athos maintained their independence until after World War I. The Greek constitution of 1927 confirmed their status as a theocratic republic under Greek sovereignty. Mount Athos is governed by a council composed of a representative from each of the 20 monasteries and by an executive committee of four monks. The monks still ban women from their retreat, but male tourists are allowed to visit.

The monasteries have the same general plan. Each is enclosed by a rectangular wall, which in one corner has a large tower that usually serves as a library. In the interior courtyard is the church, with a refectory on the shorter side of the rectangle. The church and refectory are decorated by frescoes. Population: (1961) 2,687.

ATITLÁN, Lake, ä-tēt-län′, is a resort lake in Guatemala, 40 miles (64 km) west of Guatemala City. Four volcanoes overlook the lake, which is 1,050 feet (320 meters) deep and is thought to be an ancient valley dammed by volcanic ash. Its area is 53 square miles (137 sq km). Good food fish can be caught in its waters. The chief town on the lake is Atitlán.

ATJEH, ä′che, is a province of Indonesia, in the extreme northern part of the island of Sumatra. It is often called by its former name, *Achin*. Once the most powerful sultanate in northern Sumatra, dominating trade in the area, Atjeh now is primarily an agricultural region.

The province extends over an area of 21,381 square miles (55,377 sq. km), most of it very mountainous, with long ranges running parallel to the coast and several peaks exceeding 9,000 feet (2,743 meters) in height. Except in the extreme north, there is a fairly wide coastal plain. The rivers are short and run down sharply to the coast. Kutaradja, the capital, is situated on the Atjeh River, at the northwest extremity, some three miles (4.8 km) from the sea. Its harbor and Atjeh's main port is at Uleelheue.

The Achinese (Atjehnese), a Malay people, are engaged mainly in cultivating rice, the principal subsistence crop, and rubber, copra, and spices, the chief export crops. Local industries include silk weaving and wood carving. Fishing is an important activity, and there is a considerable coastal trade.

History. European penetration was begun by the Portuguese in 1506, when Achin was visited by Alvaro Tellez, who had gone to the Indies with the fleet of Tristão da Cunha. The Dutch and English East India companies established settlements here in 1599 and 1602, respectively. The sultanate of Achin was at the peak of its power between 1607 and 1636, when Sultan Iskandar Muda controlled the entire western tip of Sumatra and parts of the Malay Peninsula.

In 1819 the British made a treaty with the sultan of Achin to exclude all other foreigners from permanent settlement, but in 1824 they exchanged their settlements in Sumatra for Dutch settlements elsewhere in Asia. The Dutch had great difficulty in establishing control over the Achinese, and after 1873 they were constantly involved in military operations against the population. Achin was never fully pacified by the Dutch or by the Japanese, who occupied the area during World War II. To satisfy the desire of the Achinese for more autonomy, the government of Indonesia made Atjeh a separate province in 1956. Population: (1961) 1,628,983.

ATKINSON, at′kin-sən, **Brooks** (1894–   ), American theater critic, who as reviewer for the New York *Times* was once called the "autocrat of the aisle seat" because of the influence he exerted on the success or failure of Broadway productions. He was born *Justin Brooks Atkinson* in Melrose, Mass., on Nov. 28, 1894. After receiving his B.A. degree from Harvard in 1917, he taught for a year at Dartmouth, then joined the Boston *Transcript*. In 1922 he became a book reviewer for the New York *Times*. He edited the newspaper's Sunday *Book Review* until 1925, when he became the *Times'* theater critic.

From 1942 to 1946, Atkinson served as a foreign correspondent for the *Times*, first in

Chungking, China, and then in Moscow. His series of articles on the Soviet Union won him a Pulitzer Prize in journalism in 1947. In 1946 he resumed his post as theater critic, from which he retired in 1960.

After his retirement, Atkinson wrote for the *Times* an occasional column, "Critic at Large," in which he expressed his opinions on a wide range of subjects. His books include *Henry Thoreau, the Cosmic Yankee* (1927), *Cingalese Prince* (1934), *Broadway Scrapbook* (1947), *Tuesdays and Fridays* (1963), and *Brief Chronicles* (1966).

A theater in New York City was named for Atkinson after his retirement as drama critic.

ATKINSON, at'kin-sən, **Henry** (1782–1842), American army officer. He was born in North Carolina; little else is known about his early life. He joined the army in 1808 and served as a colonel in the War of 1812.

In 1819 and again in 1825 he led expeditions to the Yellowstone River. The first of these was of little consequence, but the second, during which he concluded several treaties with the Indians, was an important factor in consolidating the frontier.

Atkinson oversaw the establishment of Jefferson Barracks (south of St. Louis), which was later his home, as well as of Fort Leavenworth, on the Kansas frontier. He was the successful commander of the troops in the short Black Hawk War (1832), and subsequently he directed the removal of the Winnebago Indians from Wisconsin to Iowa. He died at Jefferson Barracks on June 14, 1842.

ATKINSON, at'kin-sən, **Ted** (1916–   ), American jockey, who won 3,795 of 23,661 starts in a 21-year racing career. His mounts earned a total of $17,449,360. *Theodore Frederic Atkinson* was born in Toronto, Canada, on Sept. 18, 1916, and grew up in Corning, N.Y.

Atkinson began to ride when he was 20 years old, and got his first mount and first winner at Beulah Park, Ohio, in 1938. Six years later, "The Slasher" (so called by fans for the way he used the whip) led U.S. jockeys in winners with 287. He won riding honors again in 1946 with 233. He became a racing official after a chronic sacroiliac condition forced him to retire from riding in 1959.

BILL BRADDOCK, *New York "Times"*

ATKYNS, at'kinz, **Sir Robert** (1621–1709), English judge and public official. He was born in Gloucestershire into a family of distinguished lawyers. In 1659 he entered Parliament and, as a partisan of Stuart restoration, was knighted at the coronation of Charles II.

He became recorder of the City of Bristol in 1659 and judge of the Court of Common Pleas in 1672. Thereafter he increasingly became politically disaffected by what he regarded as corruption under Charles. He was forced into retirement in 1679.

Following the overthrow of Charles' successor, James II, in 1688 and the accession of William and Mary, Atkyns was named lord chief baron of the exchequer (1689–1694) and speaker of the House of Lords (1689–1693). His scholarly defenses of the common law were collected in *Parliamentary and Political Tracts* (1734). He died in Gloucestershire on Feb. 18, 1709.

ATLANTA, ət-lan'tə, the capital of Georgia, has become the distribution, financial, and communications capital of the southeastern United States. It has thus fulfilled a prophecy of its destiny by Union general William Tecumseh Sherman, after he had burned the city in 1864 during the Civil War.

The circumstances of its founding foreshadowed its development. On July 11, 1842, a final location for the southeastern terminus of the Western and Atlantic Railroad was selected. The surveyor's stake was placed in an area described as in the north central part of the state "in a perfect state of nature—a wild, unmolested forest." The inland town that began there, first called *The Terminus*, then *Marthasville*, became Atlanta in 1845.

"A child of the railroads," Atlanta has made the most of its central situation to become the regional hub of transportation and business. The city is on five federal highways and is a center of bus and truck transport. Seven railroads serve it. Seven airlines use its large modern terminal. Its airport is a U.S. customs port of origin for processing and shipping freight and merchandise direct to international airports.

Post-Civil War Change. Atlanta alone among cities of the pre-Civil War cotton states chose not to turn back to the past in spirit or culture when the war was over. Being burned on General Sherman's orders was part of its good luck. It could not, had it wished, become a quaint old city, caught flylike in the amber of its past and that of its region. Atlanta could start anew—and give Sherman a cordial welcome when he came on a visit a few years later.

Even in the postwar years, except for a few diehards, there was no hatred of "Yankees." Those who had come during the Reconstruction years and who had character and know-how in construction and commerce were encouraged to stay and help rebuild a city. The best of them did remain, and without them the postwar task of making a new city could not have been accomplished.

Factors in Growth. A major explanation of the dynamics of Atlanta has been its continued enrichment by the annual addition to the population of young men from the ranks of trained managers and the professions. They have come from all regions to staff the offices of the many national and local corporations doing business in the city. The presence in Atlanta of five formerly all-Negro colleges and universities and a large interdenominational theological center has been a positive force in the continued enrichment and stability of the city.

Atlanta's success in handling racial decisions, beginning with the U.S. Supreme Court decree in May 1954 that racial segregation in the public schools is unconstitutional, set it apart from other Southern cities. The mayor and city government of that period, the newspapers, most of the clergy, the businessmen, and the Negro leadership all worked to do what had to be done and what was long overdue. Negro voters, who have voted freely in Atlanta for many years, have aided enormously in attaining and maintaining good government in the city.

The long-term stability of the city's government, administered by a mayor and board of aldermen, is shown by the tenure by the mayor's office by William B. Hartsfield, a nationally known expert in municipal affairs, for almost 25

ATLANTA STADIUM and a network of expressways near clustered skyscrapers testify to the city's vitality.

years. He retired at the end of 1961 and was succeeded by Ivan H. Allen, Jr., who carried on in the same tradition and with equal efficiency.

These are some of the essential ingredients of a city whose modern story is more meaningful and important to the present than the romantic tales of war and slavery. Atlanta is unique in that long ago it put together a coalition of political, business, and press media leadership. This included Negro representatives in these three fields. Atlanta's surge in national prominence stems from this coalition of leadership dedicated to the city.

Population and Area. Atlanta's population, as of the 1970 census, was 496,973. Its area is 131 square miles (339 sq km), including 82 square miles (212 sq km) added in 1952 to expand the city's cramped limits.

The population growth has been consistent, as shown by the following U. S. census figures:

1900	89,872	1940	302,288
1910	154,839	1950	331,314
1920	200,616	1960	487,455
1930	270,366	1970	496,973

The Atlanta metropolitan area had a population of 1,390,164 in 1970, compared with 1,053,-000 in 1960 and 726,989 in 1950.

Construction and Urban Renewal. By the mid-1960's, Atlanta was changing rapidly. In new construction, the primary index of growth, the city had the nation's second-highest percentage gain in 1965. Building permits for 1962–1965 inclusive totaled more than $500 million, a gain of 22½ percent over the previous 4 years.

Atlanta has been participating in urban renewal since 1958. Seven urban renewal projects completed in 1965–1966 covered more than 1,474 acres (596.5 hectares). Of these, 765 acres (310 hectares) were acquired for redevelopment. More than $45 million had been invested in these acres, $25 million by private enterprise. The improvements due to private investment were expected nearly to triple the properties' annual yield of tax revenue.

The Economy. As a center of transportation and trade, Atlanta has expanded its facilities to meet enlarging demands. More than half of the city's planned 120-mile (193-km) expressway had been completed and was in use in the mid-1960's. Perimeter roads take through traffic around the city. But, as in other growing cities, motor traffic is a problem.

An Atlanta Rapid Transit Authority has been created. It includes representatives of five counties adjoining Fulton County, of which Atlanta is the seat. Success of its plans for rapid transit will be important to Atlanta's future.

The Atlanta airport is among the foremost in the nation in commercial use and in the number of passengers who board planes. Runways have been expanded to handle jet traffic, but future traffic projections present new demands. The airport's status as a customs port of origin means that a continuing and increasing volume of air freight will move from Atlanta to world points.

Industry and Trade. There are more than 1,000 manufacturing plants in the Atlanta area. Their products are widely varied, including steel, paper, chemicals, furniture, fertilizers, candy, and processed foods.

Employment opportunities are high in the city. In 1966 its unemployment rate averaged about 2½ percent, one of the lowest in the nation. A "Forward Atlanta Campaign" goal of 10,000 new jobs a year from 1961 through 1965 was surpassed by 125 percent each year.

During the 1960's the city's rate of growth in retail sales surpassed the rate of the nation's top 25 cities. In 1965 it showed the second-largest gain among the nation's 25 largest urban centers.

Education and Culture. Atlanta has 11 institutions of higher education—the Georgia Institute of Technology, Georgia State College, Oglethorpe College, Emory University, Atlanta University, Clark College, Morehouse College, Morris Brown College, Agnes Scott College, Spelman College for women, and the Interdenominational Theological Center. The Atlanta school system is rated among the best in the South. The system began integration without serious incident.

Construction of the $9 million Atlanta Memorial Cultural Center was begun in 1966. It was financed by a private donor who gave $6.5 million, and by public subscription, which raised $2.5 million. It was planned to provide a concert hall, a theater for the performing arts, a theater for productions by small groups and by children, an accredited art school, and an expansion of the High Museum of Art.

Communications. Three daily newspapers are published in the city. The Atlanta *Constitution*, first published on June 16, 1868, is the oldest. The Atlanta *Journal*, an afternoon paper, was founded in 1883. The Atlanta *Daily World*, a Negro-owned paper with many white subscribers and advertisers, is published daily and Sunday.

Several commercial television stations, educational television stations operated by the city and by the state, and more than 30 radio stations serve the area.

Recreation. The $18 million Atlanta Stadium, built on redevelopment land at no tax increase, brought major league baseball (Atlanta Braves) and football (Atlanta Falcons) to the city in 1966.

Atlanta maintains 47 major parks. Grant Park, one of the largest, has a modern zoo and a zoo for children. In a special building in Grant Park is the huge Cyclorama, a painting of the Civil War Battle of Atlanta.

History. Cherokee Indians, who occupied much of the state north of where Atlanta was founded, did some of the labor on the railroad which was to bring Atlanta into being. Creek Indians had ceded the territory in the central area southward from the Atlanta area in 1831.

When General Sherman came here in 1879, he was asked by a reporter for the Atlanta *Constitution* why he burned the city. Sherman asked the reporter to hold out a hand. The general said that when he reached Atlanta in late 1864, what was left of the Confederacy was something like a hand. Atlanta was the palm. If he destroyed the palm, he destroyed also the Confederacy's capacity to endure. Atlanta, the center of transport and supply, would be gone. With the palm destroyed, he would not need to fight his way along the several rail lines running into and from the city. And, with the palm gone, the fingers were useless.

"The military reasons causing me to burn the city will be those making you a great city in the future," he concluded.

See also ATLANTA CAMPAIGN.

RALPH McGILL
Publisher of the Atlanta "Constitution"

ATLANTA CAMPAIGN, ət-lan′tə kam-pān′, one of the decisive campaigns of the American Civil War. Waged by the Union army of Gen. William T. Sherman from May to September 1864, it culminated in the capture of Atlanta, Ga., a key railroad and supply center, and established a Union force in the heart of the Confederacy.

At the beginning of the campaign, Sherman had about 100,000 men, organized into the Army of the Cumberland led by Gen. George H. Thomas, the Army of the Tennessee under Gen. James B. McPherson, and the Army of the Ohio under Gen. John M. Schofield. Opposing him were about 60,000 Confederates commanded by Gen. Joseph E. Johnston.

Sherman started toward Atlanta from the northwest corner of Georgia on May 7. As part of the Union's grand strategy, his move was made simultaneously with Gen. U.S. Grant's advance against Gen. Robert E. Lee in Virginia. Johnston, a canny defensive fighter, retreated slowly. Several engagements were fought, notably at Resaca (May 13–16) and New Hope Church (May 25–28), but Sherman generally avoided direct attacks and moved around the Confederates' flanks, compelling them to withdraw to avoid encirclement. A frontal assault on the Confederate position at Kennesaw Mountain (June 27) failed with heavy loss, but by July 2, Johnston's army had been pushed back to the Chattahoochee River only 8 miles (13 km) from Atlanta. Gen. John B. Hood relieved Johnston in command on July 17 and withdrew into the city.

Hood sent his troops against Sherman's besieging forces in the battles of Peachtree Creek (July 20), Atlanta (July 22), and Ezra Church (July 28), but was repulsed with serious losses. Atlanta was virtually destroyed by Sherman's artillery and by burning, and Hood evacuated the city on Sept. 1. Sherman entered the next day.

His victory cleared the way for other climactic campaigns. On November 15 he began his famous "march to the sea" across Georgia that destroyed much of the Confederacy's agriculture. Sherman took Savannah on December 21, and in the spring of 1865 he drove north through the Carolinas.

ATLANTA UNIVERSITY, ət-lan′tə, is a private, coeducational institution in Atlanta, Ga. Together with Clark, Morehouse, Morris Brown and Spelman colleges and the Interdenominational Theological Center, it forms the Atlanta University Center.

The university was established in 1865 and college instruction began in 1872. First professional and master's degrees are conferred in schools of library service, social work, business administration, and education. A graduate school of arts and sciences gives doctorates in biology and in guidance and counseling. Enrollment in the mid-1960's totaled about 600.

ATLANTIC, ət-lan′tik, a city in southwestern Iowa, is the seat of Cass County. It lies 60 miles (96.5 km) northeast of Omaha, Nebr. The city is a trading and processing center for a farm area, and has feed mills and food-packing plants.

Because it was thought to be halfway between the Atlantic and Pacific oceans, the community was named *Pacific* on the toss of a coin, but the name was changed to Atlantic because several other Midwestern towns were called Pacific. Incorporated in 1869, Atlantic is governed by a mayor and council. Population: 7,306.

ATLANTIC, BATTLE OF THE, the name given to the World War II submarine campaign by which Germany attempted to deny the Allies the use of the seas. The leader of the campaign was Adm. Karl Doenitz, the World War I U-boat commander who reestablished Germany's undersea force in 1935. His strategic concept was not to cut the enemy's sea lines of communication but to destroy its merchant shipping.

At the start of the war Doenitz had a trained force of 57 submarines, 39 of which were operational. By early 1943 there were 219 operational boats. The primary unit was the Type VIIC U-boat, of 770 tons displacement, carrying a crew of 44. A total of 659 of these were built.

The submarine campaign ranged over all the oceans, but its major phases were fought in the North Atlantic. The first began in July 1940, after the fall of France enabled Doenitz to use bases on the Bay of Biscay. The merchant tonnage destroyed was less than in later phases of the war, but the losses were serious because Britain was then alone in the war and her merchant marine was smaller than in World War I. Surface escorts were inadequate, but the critical lack, both in numbers and range, was aircraft. Convoy air cover was not possible over one third of the North Atlantic route. This phase ended in late 1941 when Hitler sent U-boats to the Mediterranean to help avert collapse there.

The second phase was the ship slaughter along the Atlantic coast of the United States from January to August 1942, for which the U.S. Navy was unprepared. Losses were the highest in the war, inflicted by the few U-boats Doenitz could send from the Mediterranean. Coastal convoys were organized in May, and Doenitz shifted his U-boats to the Caribbean.

Germany's submarine defeat came in the convoy battles of early 1943. Doenitz' "wolf packs" met their match in the new Allied antisubmarine forces. By May the Battle of the Atlantic was over. Between that month and September the Germans lost 73 U-boats. In August, Allied ships were being built faster than the Germans could sink them.

Thereafter the Germans used submarines as a threat to force the Allies to devote large resources to antisubmarine warfare while advanced types of U-boats, equipped with schnorkels or hydrogen peroxide engines, were developed. Their production came too late.

See WORLD WAR II—12. *Developments in Naval Warfare* (Antisubmarine Operations).

JOHN D. HAYES, *Rear Admiral, USN (Retired)*

ATLANTIC & PACIFIC TEA CO., The Great, the largest retail grocery chain in the United States. The A&P markets its products mainly on a cash-and-carry, self-service basis. Subsidiaries produce many items, including baked goods, butter, and canned fruit and vegetables. The company operates coffee-roasting and fish-processing plants and has coffee-purchasing offices in Brazil. The A&P has more than 4,600 stores in the United States and Canada which had over $5 billion annual sales in the mid-1960's. Its headquarters are in New York City. The George Huntington Hartford Foundation, named for the company's founder, owns one third of the firm's stock, and gives aid to medical education and research.

COURTNEY ROBERT HALL
Author of "History of American Industrial Science"

ATLANTIC CHARTER, a statement of principles formulated in World War II by President Franklin D. Roosevelt and Prime Minister Winston Churchill. The charter, announced publicly on Aug. 14, 1941, resulted from a series of conferences (August 9–12) between the two leaders aboard the U.S.S. *Augusta* off Newfoundland.

The text of the document reads as follows:

The President of the United States of America and the Prime Minister, Mr. Churchill, representing His Majesty's Government in the United Kingdom, being met together, deem it right to make known certain common principles in the national policies of their respective countries on which they base their hopes for a better future for the world.

First, their countries seek no aggrandizement, territorial or other;

Second, they desire to see no territorial changes that do not accord with the freely expressed wishes of the peoples concerned;

Third, they respect the right of all peoples to choose the form of government under which they will live; and they wish to see sovereign rights and self-government restored to those who have been forcibly deprived of them;

Fourth, they will endeavor, with due respect for their existing obligations, to further the enjoyment by all states, great or small, victor or vanquished, of access, on equal terms, to the trade and to the raw materials of the world which are needed for their economic prosperity;

Fifth, they desire to bring about the fullest collaboration between all nations in the economic field with the object of securing, for all, improved labor standards, economic adjustment and social security;

Sixth, after the final destruction of the Nazi tyranny, they hope to see established a peace which will afford to all nations the means of dwelling in safety within their own boundaries, and which will afford assurance that all the men in all the lands may live out their lives in freedom from fear and want;

Seventh, such a peace should enable all men to traverse the high seas and oceans without hindrance;

Eighth, they believe that all of the nations of the world, for realistic as well as spiritual reasons, must come to the abandonment of the use of force. Since no future peace can be maintained if land, sea or air armaments continue to be employed by nations which threaten, or may threaten, aggression outside of their frontiers, they believe, pending the establishment of a wider and permanent system of general security, that the disarmament of such nations is essential. They will likewise aid and encourage all other practicable measures which will lighten for peace-loving peoples the crushing burden of armaments.

Although not an official document, the Atlantic Charter was employed effectively as a propaganda weapon against the Axis powers during World War II. The United Nations Declaration, signed in Washington, D.C., on Jan. 1, 1942, by the Allies, then numbering 26 states, endorsed the principles of the charter. Subsequently, in 1945, the Charter of the United Nations affirmed some of the points of the Roosevelt-Churchill statement. Prime Minister Churchill and President Eisenhower, in June 1954, reaffirmed the charter's principles.

ATLANTIC CITY, ət-lan′tik, is a New Jersey resort and convention center that attracts millions of visitors each year. The city is situated in Atlantic County, on Absecon Island off the Atlantic coast, 62 miles (99 km) southeast of Philadelphia.

The city's seashore location ensures it a relatively moderate temperature in summer and winter. Its gently sloping free beach is well protected and safe for bathers. Along the beach stretches the famous Boardwalk, over 4 miles (7 km) long and up to 60 feet (18 meters) wide, lined with shops, hotels, and motels. Five piers projecting into the ocean, including the famous Steel Pier, offer recreation, exhibits, and entertainment. The municipal Convention Hall on the Boardwalk seats 41,000 and covers 7 acres (2.8 hectares). It has the largest auditorium in the world, and its pipe organ is the largest musical instrument ever built. The Absecon lighthouse, a city landmark, was decommissioned in 1933 and is now a public park.

The main industry of Atlantic City is providing service and entertainment for visitors. There is also a considerable employment in boat building and the manufacture of clothing and salt water taffy.

Important annual events include the Easter Parade, the Boardwalk Art Show in May, and the Miss America Pageant in early September. The Atlantic City Race Track, the National Aviation Facilities Experimental Center, and the Brigantine National Wildlife Refuge are in the vicinity.

The first permanent settler on Absecon Island was Jeremiah Leeds in 1783. The island itself is a sand bar 10 miles (16 km) long, separated from the mainland by small bays and inlets. Dr. Jonathan Pitney, the "father of Atlantic City," was instrumental in bringing the railroad to it in 1852. Richard B. Osborn, chief engineer for the newly formed railroad, the Camden and Atlantic Railroad Company, gave the resort its name in 1853. The city was incorporated the following year. Atlantic City claims a number of firsts: the first ocean boardwalk was built there in 1870; salt water taffy originated in Atlantic City in 1883; and the first picture postcards were introduced there in 1893.

Atlantic City has a commission form of government. Population: 47,859.

RUTH SMITH WILSON
Free Public Library of Atlantic City

ATLANTIC COAST LINE RAILROAD COMPANY, a major freight and passenger carrier serving the southeastern United States, known especially for its luxurious streamliners plying between the populous East and the Florida resort areas. Coast Line represents the unification, completed in 1900, of more than 100 small railroads, of which the earliest to receive a charter was the Petersburg Railroad (Feb. 10, 1830). In the mid-1960's, Coast Line operated 5,500 miles of main track southward from Richmond, Va., to Jacksonville, Fla., with important secondary lines reaching Norfolk, Va., and Wilmington, N.C., in the east; and Columbia, S.C., Augusta and Atlanta, Ga., and Birmingham and Montgomery, Ala., in the west. Annual operating revenues in the mid-1960's amounted to about $200 million, of which about 75 percent came from freight service. In 1967, Coast Line merged with the Seaboard Air Line Railroad to form the Seaboard Coast Line Railroad.

ATLANTIC CITY'S hotels rise behind the ocean beach. The city is a year-round resort and convention center.

ATLANTIC HIGHLANDS, ət-lan′tik hī′ləndz, is a residential borough in eastern New Jersey, in Monmouth County, on Sandy Hook Bay. It is 20 miles (32 km) south of Manhattan, but 42 miles (68 km) by road. Is has a large yacht harbor. Mount Mitchell (266 feet, or 81 meters), one of the highest points on the United States Atlantic coast south of Maine, is located here. The site was visited by Henry Hudson in 1609. Atlantic Highlands was incorporated in 1887. Government is by mayor and council. Population: 5,102.

ATLANTIC INTRACOASTAL WATERWAY, ət-lan′tik in-trə-kōst′əl, a protected route for pleasure craft and small commercial vessels along the Atlantic coast of the United States from Norfolk, Va., to Key West, Fla. It follows natural and artificial waterways—sounds, bays, rivers, and canals—for 1,081 miles (1,740 km). Passage is toll-free. The waterway is under the jurisdiction of the U.S. Coast Guard. Principal cities along the route are Beaufort, N.C., Charleston, S.C., and Jacksonville and Miami, Fla. A route for coastwise traffic from Norfolk to Boston, partly in open ocean, sometimes is called a part of the Atlantic Intracoastal Waterway. A sheltered route along the Gulf of Mexico from Carrabelle, Fla., to Brownsville, Tex., is called the Gulf Intracoastal Waterway. Small craft may cross Florida from Stuart to Fort Myers and enter the Gulf route after running up the west coast.

ATLANTIC MONTHLY, ət-lan′tik, now the *Atlantic,* an American periodical that for more than 100 years has published scores of poems, essays, and short stories that have become a permanent part of American literature.

The *Atlantic Monthly* was founded in Boston, Mass., in November 1857 by the publishing firm of Phillips, Sampson & Company. Since 1908 it has been owned by the Atlantic Monthly Company, a stock corporation. In its earliest years the magazine published almost exclusively the works of leading New England writers, including James Russell Lowell (who was also the first editor of the magazine, 1857–1861), Oliver Wendell Holmes, Longfellow, Emerson, and Whittier. Under the editorship of William Dean Howells (1871–1881), it began to publish the work of other prominent American literary figures, including Mark Twain and Bret Harte. In the 20th century it broadened its scope to include economic, scientific, and political articles.

ATLANTIC OCEAN, ət-lan'tik, the second-largest of the three great oceans of the world. The Pacific Ocean is larger, and the Indian Ocean is smaller.

The waters of the Atlantic, Pacific, and Indian oceans compose 70.8 percent of the earth's surface, the Atlantic covering 20 percent, or over 41 million square miles (more than 106 million sq km). The division of the oceanic area into three oceans, in which we include the inland seas that have natural outlets, is to a certain extent arbitrary. According to this conception, the Atlantic extends from Antarctica to the North Polar Regions, including the Arctic Ocean. The Atlantic is bounded by the North and South American continents, and by Asia, Europe, and Africa. It is separated from the Pacific Ocean by a natural boundary at the Bering Strait, and an artificial line forming the shortest distance south from Cape Horn, South America, (70° W) to the South Shetland Islands. On the east it is separated from the Indian Ocean by the meridian (20° E) of the Cape of Good Hope.

The Atlantic Ocean is divided and subdivided into many different parts. The boundaries may vary according to the features of the ocean that are being delineated. For instance, the major division is into the North and South Atlantic, with the boundary at the equator. But when the general circulation of waters is under discussion the boundary between the North and South Atlantic does not lie on the equator but north of it. Also, the waters surrounding Antarctica are sometimes referred to as the Antarctic Ocean, but the boundaries of this ocean depend entirely on the distribution of such things as the temperature and salinity of the water, and the position of the northern boundary is constantly shifting.

Three subdivisions of the North Atlantic Ocean are the Arctic Mediterranean, the American Mediterranean, and the European Mediterranean. The Arctic Mediterranean includes all those waters north of the latitude of Iceland, and is again subdivided into the North Polar Sea (Arctic Ocean), Norwegian Sea, Baffin Bay, and the waters of the Canadian Archipelago. The American Mediterranean consists of the Caribbean Sea and the Gulf of Mexico. The European Mediterranean has many well-known divisions and includes the Black Sea. Further subdivisions of the North Atlantic include the Baltic Sea, Hudson Bay, the North Sea, the Irish Sea, and the Gulf of St. Lawrence.

Bottom Topography. Vast reaches of the oceans have not been sounded even today, yet it is felt that the major features are known.

The principal feature of the bottom topography of the Atlantic Ocean is the Mid-Atlantic Ridge, which extends from Iceland in the north to the latitude of Cape Horn in the south. The depth of water over this ridge is generally less than 1,500 fathoms (2,743 meters), but the bottom is very irregular, and what has been termed a Rift Valley extends over the greater part of its length. The Azores, and the islands of St. Paul, Ascension, Tristan da Cunha, Gough, and Bouvet rise from the ridge. There is one break in the ridge—the Romanche Trench near the equator—where the depth of water is as great as 4,300 fathoms (7,864 meters).

The Mid-Atlantic Ridge separates two vast troughs of the Atlantic Ocean, where the depths average between 2,000 and 3,000 fathoms (3,657 and 5,486 meters). Transverse ridges running from the Mid-Atlantic Ridge to the continents separate the two major troughs into numerous basins. The largest basins in the North Atlantic are the North American and Guiana basins in the west, and the Canaries and Cape Verde basins in the east. The four correspondingly large basins in the South Atlantic are the Brazil and Argentina basins in the west and the Angola and Cape basins in the east.

The Caribbean basins are separated from the open Atlantic by a particularly steep-sided and rugged ridge which rises in many places above sea level to form the numerous West Indian islands. Just north of Puerto Rico is the Puerto Rico Trench, the deepest depression in the Atlantic Ocean. A similar deep is located in the South Atlantic. This is known as the South Sandwich Trench and is 4,518 fathoms (8,262 meters) deep.

The North Polar Basin is separated from the main portion of the North Atlantic by two ridges and the relatively shallow Norwegian Basin. The ridge from Greenland to Scotland, from which rise Iceland and the Faeroe Islands, is the northern boundary of the North Atlantic proper.

Another important feature of the bottom topography in all the oceans is the continental shelves. These are the shallow areas less than 100 fathoms (183 meters) deep, bordering the continents. About 13 percent of the Atlantic is shelf area. The broadest shelves are in the North Polar Sea off the coasts of Siberia and North America. The narrowest shelves are generally found off mountainous coasts, while the widest appear off glaciated coasts. The discovery of oilfields on the continental shelves, such as those on the relatively broad shelf in the Gulf of Mexico, has stimulated the study of these large shallow water areas. These are also the regions where the great fisheries are located, notably the Grand Banks, the Scotian Shelf off Nova Scotia, Georges bank off Cape Cod, and the Bahama Banks, all in the western North Atlantic. Off Europe, the North Sea, the Irish Sea, and the waters along the ridge toward Iceland are all fishing areas. In the South Atlantic the continental shelves are generally narrow except off the coast of the southern tip of South America where the shelf extends to the Falkland Islands.

Water Masses and Currents. The Atlantic Ocean also can be subdivided on the basis of the distribution of its water masses. Over large regions the water has certain temperature and salinity characteristics which differ from those found in other areas. For instance, the northern boundary of the Antarctic Ocean, which is called the subtropical convergence, is a region where the surface water temperatures show a sharp increase from south to north. The Sargasso Sea is an example of a subdivision of the North Atlantic

---

INFORMATION HIGHLIGHTS

Area: With adjacent seas, 41,105,000 square miles (106,463,000 sq km); without adjacent seas, 31,830,000 square miles (82,441,000 sq km).

Volume: With adjacent seas, 85,087,000 cubic miles (354,679,000 cu km); without adjacent seas, 77,635,000 cubic miles (323,613,000 cu km).

Depth: Greatest, 27,498 ft (8,381 meters) in Puerto Rico Trench; mean, 12,877 ft (3,926 meters).

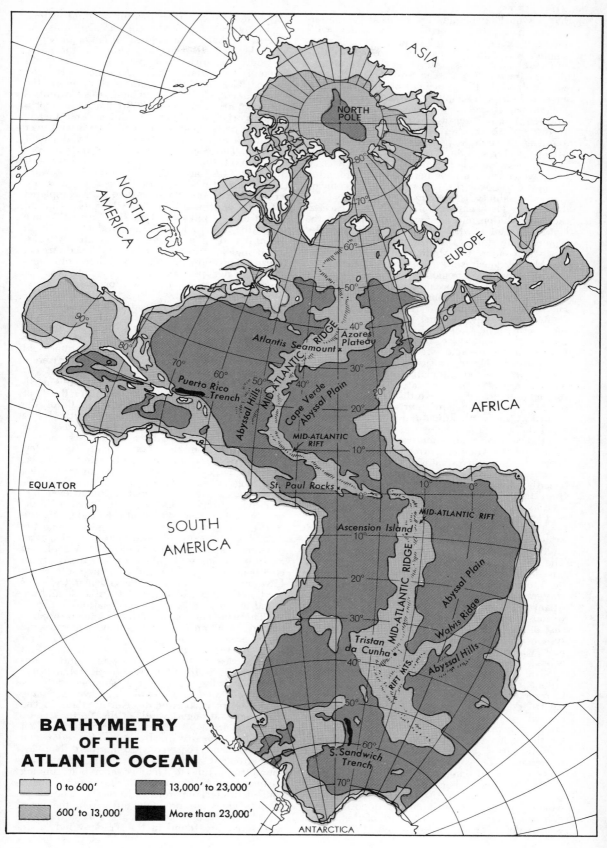

BATHYMETRY
OF THE
ATLANTIC OCEAN

☐ 0 to 600'		☐ 13,000' to 23,000'	
☐ 600' to 13,000'		■ More than 23,000'	

ASIA

NORTH POLE

NORTH AMERICA

EUROPE

AFRICA

Atlantis Seamount

Azores Plateau

MID-ATLANTIC RIDGE

Puerto Rico Trench

Abyssal Hills

Cape Verde Abyssal Plain

MID-ATLANTIC RIFT

EQUATOR

St. Paul Rocks

SOUTH AMERICA

Ascension Island

MID-ATLANTIC RIFT

MID-ATLANTIC RIDGE

Abyssal Plain

Walvis Ridge

Tristan da Cunha

RIFT MTS.

Abyssal Hills

S. Sandwich Trench

ANTARCTICA

that has no land boundaries, or fixed geographical boundaries, but is surrounded by waters with different temperature and salinity ratios.

The water masses have vertical as well as horizontal boundaries. All water masses assume their characteristics at the surface of the sea when subject to the influences of such factors as solar radiation, precipitation, and evaporation. The subsequent location of these masses depends on their relative density. Hence water formed at the surface of the Antarctic Ocean is later found at the bottom beneath the North Central Atlantic water.

The highest salinity in the Atlantic Ocean, when we consider all component seas, is found in the eastern end of the European Mediterranean. Here the salinity is greater than 39 parts in a thousand. The evaporation in this sea exceeds the precipitation and freshwater runoff from the land. In winter when this high salinity water is cooled, it sinks to the bottom. Atlantic surface water enters the Mediterranean at Gibraltar and Mediterranean subsurface water flows out.

The boundary regions between the large water masses in the ocean are where the major ocean currents are found. In the Northern Hemisphere the lighter, warmer water is on the right (facing downstream) of the currents. In the southern hemisphere it is on the left. Although the winds are the primary source of power for the oceanic circulation, it is this unequal distribution of density of the water masses that maintains the circulation, even when the wind is absent. The circulation is clockwise in the main body of the North Atlantic. In the southern part, shallow currents, collectively known as the North Equatorial Current, move toward the west propelled by the Northeast Trades. Off the coast of South America these currents are joined by the Guiana Current, which is an offshoot of the South Equatorial Current, generated by the Southeast Trades of the South Atlantic. Together these currents pass through the Caribbean to pour out again from this land-locked area as the mighty Florida Current in the straits of Florida.

This is the beginning of the Gulf Stream System, which includes the Florida Current, the Gulf Stream, and the North Atlantic Current. The Florida Current is the northern moving water as far as Cape Hatteras; the Gulf Stream is the more easterly moving water between Cape Hatteras and the Grand Banks; and the North Atlantic Current is the collective name for the various northerly and easterly moving currents east of the Grand Banks. One extension of this system of warm currents is the Norwegian Current, which flows north along the coast of Norway to enter the Polar Sea.

The cold water currents of the North Atlantic originate in the Polar Sea. The East Greenland Current flows south carrying large quantities of ice from the Polar Sea. At Cape Farewell this current recurves toward the north into Davis Strait, becoming the West Greenland Current. On the western side of Davis Strait the Labrador Current carries cold, relatively fresh water and numerous icebergs south as far as the southern tip of the Grand Banks.

At the equator, beneath the South Equatorial Current, there is an Equatorial Undercurrent which flows west to east—in the opposite direction to the surface flow. The core of this current is at a depth of about 40 fathoms (73 meters)

and is more saline than the surrounding waters.

In the South Atlantic the circulation is the reverse of that in the North Atlantic, or counterclockwise instead of clockwise. Off the bulge of South America, that portion of the South Equatorial Current which does not form the Guiana Current turns south and becomes the warm Brazil Current. Although this current is the counterpart of the Gulf Stream in the north it transports only about 10 million cubic meters of water per second as compared with well over 50 million cubic meters transported by the Gulf Stream. The South Atlantic Current is a continuation of the Brazil Current and flows east from near the latitude of Buenos Aires toward the southern tip of Africa. The counterclockwise circulation of the South Atlantic is completed with the northward flowing Benguela Current in the east. Unlike the Canaries Current, which forms the eastern link of the gyral in the North Atlantic and is a vague, slow, southerly drift, the Benguela Current is a better defined stream, transporting approximately 16 million cubic meters of water per second. Along the coast of Argentina there is a branch of the Antarctic Circumpolar Current. This is the Falkland Current which carries cold water north along that coast, to the counterpart of the Labrador Current in the Northern system.

Climate and Weather. Because of the greater heat capacity of the oceans, the maritime and oceanic climates are less subject to the extremes of temperature associated with continental climates. The warmest area of the Atlantic is north of the equator in a belt running from the Gulf of Guinea westward toward the mouth of the Amazon River and then more northerly to the Yucatan Peninsula. The coldest areas of the Atlantic can be shown by a brief description of ice conditions. In the South Atlantic in winter, sea ice, which is formed by freezing seawater, covers a large area off the coast of Antarctica extending at times farther north than the latitude of Cape Horn. Icebergs are found even farther away from Antarctica, their average northern limit being at 40° south latitude. In the North Atlantic in winter, sea ice covers the Polar Sea and extends south along the east coast of Greenland to Cape Farewell. Unnavigable sea ice also extends south along the North American continent to Newfoundland and the Gulf of St. Lawrence. Icebergs from the Greenland glaciers are limited to the western North Atlantic and are found as far south as 40° north latitude.

The winds are an important factor in oceanic climate, not only because they generate the major ocean currents, but also because of their effect on the roughness of the sea surface. An extreme case of high velocity winds and mountainous seas is found in the tropical hurricane. These cyclones occur in late summer and fall, during a period of generally light winds, in the southwestern portion of the North Atlantic. The consistently strongest winds of the North Atlantic are found from November to February in a belt running northeastward from the Labrador and Newfoundland coasts toward northern Norway. The strongest winds in the South Atlantic are found from July to October in a belt running eastward across the ocean in the vicinity of 40° south latitude (the "roaring forties"). The winds in both areas are predominantly from the west.

The most persistent winds, rarely reaching gale force, are found in the Trade Wind areas.

In the North Atlantic the Northeast Trades blow from the northwest coast of Africa toward the northern coast of South America. In the summer these winds are more easterly than in winter, and in late summer and fall they are less constant in direction than during the rest of the year. The Southeast Trades of the South Atlantic blow across the equator. They blow persistently, over 80 percent of the time, from the southwest African coast in a northwesterly direction.

The greatest percentage of calms in the Atlantic is found from December to February, in the doldrums, an area between 5° and 10° north latitude extending off the coast of Africa.

When warm air blows over colder water the water vapor in the air condenses and forms fog. Fog occurs to the greatest extent in the northwestern North Atlantic. These fogs occur during the spring and summer months, being reported on the Grand Banks over 30 percent of the time. The second most important areas of fog are the Polar Regions. See also GULF STREAM; OCEAN.

FREDERICK FUGLISTER
Woods Hole Oceanographic Institution

THE ATLANTIC IN WORLD HISTORY

The Atlantic Ocean has been an enormous factor in human history. Situated west of the landmass of Eurasia, which had been inhabited since earliest times, it was the natural avenue for the expansion of populations. When the New World was colonized from Europe, the ocean was at first a barrier beyond which the new cultures developed in their own ways. With advances in technology, it became a means of communication among nations.

During ancient and medieval times, the Mediterranean Sea was the center of maritime activity, while the Atlantic marked the outer edge of European civilization. Once Columbus discovered the way to America, the westward push of the European seeking adventure, wealth, or new homes led to steadily increasing settlement overseas. The stormy 3,000-odd miles (4,800 km) of the North Atlantic became the busiest and most vital of all sea lanes, the highway between the Old World and the New.

There had been, to be sure, some Atlantic sea-

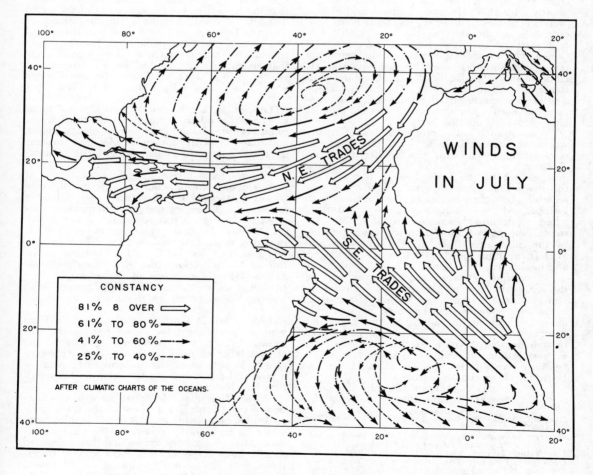

This chart shows the mean position, for July, of the Northeast and Southeast Trades in the Atlantic Ocean. The Northeast Trades are in their most northerly position during this month. The arrows do not give any indication of the average force of the winds but only the dominant direction and constancy.

faring even before Columbus. Traders became acquainted with the coastal waters of western Europe, while the Scandinavian Vikings or Northmen had ventured out to Iceland, Greenland, and briefly, around 1000, to North America. Systematic exploration dates from 1415, when Prince Henry the Navigator began to push Portuguese expeditions down the west coast of Africa in the South Atlantic. The Azores, Madeira, the Canaries, and the Cape Verde Islands were settled by Europeans.

The climax of the new discoveries came in the 30 years between 1492, when Columbus discovered America, and 1522 when one of Magellan's ships completed the first voyage around the world. During those years, various voyagers explored the Caribbean and South America, while John Cabot in 1497 crossed the North Atlantic and found the rich Grand Banks cod fisheries, off Newfoundland. The next year Vasco da Gama reached India by way of the Cape of Good Hope at the southern end of Africa, thus developing an important trade route through the South Atlantic.

Almost immediately, Spain and Portugal began to develop colonies in America, and their ships were soon plying the Atlantic with silver from Mexico and Peru and sugar from Brazil. Shortly after 1600, Holland, England, and France founded colonies in America, and trade flourished, especially on the ships of the transplanted English settlers in New England. Venice and Genoa, which had long dominated Mediterranean trade, were overshadowed by ports on the Atlantic—Lisbon, Seville, Bordeaux, Hamburg, Amsterdam, London, and others. The North Atlantic shuttle soon surpassed all other sea routes. Neither the Pacific nor the Indian Ocean, then or later, could match that activity.

With transatlantic crossings taking many weeks, it was difficult to keep the American colonists in touch with the mother countries. The result was that most of the colonies became independent by the early 1800's. But in 1818 the Black Ball square-riggers, sailing on regular schedule, brought America in closer contact with Europe, and the crossing was speeded up further when steamships began service in 1838. Instantaneous news transmission was made possible by the cable after 1866. By the time of World War II, aviation had begun to move passengers and mail across the Atlantic in a matter of hours.

In warfare, a nation enjoying command of the sea could use the Atlantic as a highway for attacking others. Formerly, it could also use the ocean as a protective moat against invasion from abroad. However, the advent of the long-range bomber and then of the intercontinental ballistic missile sharply reduced this protection. In communications as well as in warfare, new inventions brought the opposite sides of the Atlantic far closer than in earlier days.

ROBERT G. ALBION, *Harvard University*
Author of "Square-Riggers on Schedule"

Bibliography

Gaskell, Thomas F., *Under Deep Oceans* (New York 1960).
Huxley, Anthony, ed., *Standard Encyclopedia of the World's Oceans and Islands* (New York 1962).
Life Nature Library, *The Sea* (New York 1961).
Outhwaite, Leonard, *The Atlantic* (New York 1957).
Sverdrup, H.U., and others, *The Oceans; Their Physics, Chemistry, and General Biology* (New York 1942).
U.S. Department of Agriculture, Weather Bureau, *Atlas of Climatic Charts of the Oceans* (Washington 1938).
U.S. Hydrographic Office, *Ice Atlas of the Northern Hemisphere* (Washington 1946).

ATLANTIS, ət-lan′tis, is a legendary island in the Atlantic Ocean, near the Strait of Gibraltar. It was also called *Atlantica.* The chief sources of the legend of Atlantis are two Platonic dialogues. In *Timaeus,* Plato tells of the Athenians' conquest of Atlantis, and in *Critias* he discusses the island as an ideal commonwealth. Atlantis, a rival of ancient Athens, was a beautiful, productive, and wealthy island, governed according to the precepts of Poseidon (Neptune). The island was divided into 10 sections, each administered by one of Poseidon's sons, with Atlas, the eldest son, as its king.

According to the *Timaeus,* the legend of Atlantis was related to Solon by an Egyptian priest who admired the great achievements of the prehistoric Athenians. When the rulers of Atlantis, which was larger than Asia Minor and Africa, and extremely powerful, threatened to overwhelm all of Europe and Asia, the Athenians, on behalf of all the Greeks, defeated the people of Atlantis and removed the threat of enslavement. Later, as a result of earthquakes, Atlantis was swallowed up in the sea.

There is no certainty that Atlantis existed, but medieval scholars believed in it and later writers tried to identify it with an actual country. Some 20th-century archaeologists believe that the legend may have arisen out of an actual disaster. Volcanic eruptions on the island of Thera in 1450 B.C. may have destroyed that island and caused an earthquake and tsunamis that ruined civilization on Crete. The legend grew that an entire continent had been destroyed.

LILLIAN FEDER, *Queens College*
The City University of New York

ATLAS, at′ləs, a collection of geographical maps or charts bound in a volume. The term is applied also to a bound collection of charts, plates, and material in the form of tables that presents information on one subject, as an atlas of anatomy or ethnography.

Geographical atlases contain many types of maps—topographical, climatic, geological, economic, and political. They may also include a gazetteer, a listing of geographical names. Passages of descriptive text sometimes are included.

Ortelius' *Theatrum orbis terrarum* (1570) is regarded as the first modern atlas. The term "atlas" was used first by Gerardus Mercator in the title of his collection *Atlas sive cosmographicae* (1585–95). Frontispieces of earlier map collections had shown the mythological figure of Atlas holding the globe on his shoulders.

ATLAS, at′ləs, in Greek mythology, was a Titan who, as punishment for taking part in the war against Uranus, was condemned by Zeus to the eternal labor of holding up the sky. As represented in art, especially in sculpture, Atlas is a powerful figure bearing the earth on his shoulders and hands.

When Hercules (Heracles) went to the Garden of the Hesperides in quest of the three golden apples, he asked that Atlas pluck them for him, while he temporarily relieved Atlas of his burden. Atlas plucked the apples and then suggested that he himself should carry them back to Eurystheus, who had sent Hercules on his 12 labors. Hercules asked Atlas to let him find a pad to ease the load and thus tricked Atlas into taking the earth back on his shoulders. Hercules then took the apples and went on his way.

THE ATLAS MOUNTAINS form a backdrop for the outdoor market at Telouét, Morocco. In springtime, as shown in this photo, the peaks retain a covering of ice and snow.

ATLAS MOUNTAINS, at′ləs, a mountain system in northwest Africa, extending approximately 1,500 miles (2,414 km), southwest to northeast, from the Atlantic Ocean through Morocco, Algeria, and Tunisia to the Gulf of Gabès in the Mediterranean Sea. *Atlas* is the European name for the system, reflecting the ancient Greeks' belief that it was the home of their god Atlas. In Arabic it is called *Djezira el-Maghreb* (Island of the West) because it is an "island" of relative fertility in a desert region.

The Atlas system comprises several roughly parallel ridges, including three major ranges in Morocco (from north to south: the Middle Atlas, the High or Great Atlas, and the Anti-Atlas) and lesser ranges in Algeria and Tunisia, of which the Maritime or Tell Atlas along the Algerian coast and the Saharan Atlas to the south are most important. The High Atlas, stretching across central Morocco, is the most impressive range, with an average elevation of 10,000 feet (3,048 meters). Its highest peak, Djebel Toubkal in western Morocco, towers 13,661 feet (4,164 meters).

The northern flanks of the Atlas are covered with oak, walnut, pine, and cedar. Here fertile valleys and plateaus intersperse the mountains. Southward the slopes that face the desert are barren. Iron, copper, manganese, lead, marble, limestone, and basalt are the system's mineral deposits, and some oil and gas is exploited.

Geologically the Atlas Mountains are more European than African. They were born of the same global convulsions that reared the Alps and the Himalaya, the course of which may be traced eastward through Sicily to the Italian Apennines and westward far out to sea in the Canaries. The main foldings occurred in the Jurassic period and continued into the Miocene, but there are older Paleozoic and Archeozoic rock formations.

The Atlas region is rich in legend and history. Phoenician sailors venturing into the Atlantic told tales of snow-capped peaks far inland on the African continent, and the Greeks believed that their Titan, Atlas, who bore up the heavens, dwelt there. The Atlas ranges once sheltered Carthage from the hostile tribesmen of the Sahara. The native people, like most mountain dwellers, have always been brave and freedom loving. Numidian horsemen of the Atlas region provided Hannibal's army with an effective mobile striking force. Native Berbers swelled the armies that overran Spain to establish the kingdom of the Moors. Later, Muslim corsairs preyed upon Christian shipping. Riffian tribesmen long defied Spanish armies and yielded to France only after repeated campaigns. Mountaineers of the Atlas region participated actively in the rebellions that brought Morocco, Tunisia, and Algeria their independence from France in the 1950's and 1960's.

FERDINAND C. LANE
Author of "The Story of Mountains"

Further Reading: Hooker, John Dalton, Ball, John, and Maw, George, *Journal of a Tour in Morocco and the Great Atlas* (London 1878); Huxley, Anthony, ed., *Standard Encyclopedia of the World's Mountains* (New York 1962); Lane, Ferdinand C., *The Story of Mountains* (Garden City, N.Y., 1950); Slouschz, Nahum, *Travels in North Africa* (Philadelphia 1927).

ATLATL, at′lat-əl, was the Aztec name for the spear-thrower, an important weapon of primitive man. The atlatl consisted of a slender flat or rounded piece of wood, about 2 feet (61 centimeters) long, with a raised hook or spur at one end to engage the butt end of the spear. A hunter or warrior held the spear and atlatl in one hand and hurled the spear with an overhand motion, the thrower being retained in the hand. The atlatl lengthened the throwing arm and gave greater velocity to the spear than was possible with the unaided arm.

The spear-thrower is believed to have been invented before the bow. The thrower was used by European peoples in the Paleolithic era, and by Eskimos and other American Indians until more recent times. The Aztecs used atlatls in battles with the Spaniards. The Australian aborigines continued to employ spear-throwers in the mid-20th century.

ATMORE, at′mōr, is a city in southwestern Alabama, in Escambia County, near the Florida state line and 50 miles by road northwest of Mobile. It is the trading center of an area that raises cotton, soybeans, fruit, cattle, and hogs. Cotton ginning and textile and lumber milling are leading industries. Little River State Forest, 15 miles north of the city, is a recreational area.

The community was settled in 1880 and was known as *Williams Station* until 1897, when it adopted its present name. Incorporated in 1910, it has a mayor and council type of government. Population: 8,293.

ATMOSPHERE, at′mə-sfir, the nearly transparent envelope of gases and suspended particles that surrounds the earth. Although human senses respond to the atmosphere only in limited ways, so that a man is usually more aware of trees, hills, and other objects than of the atmosphere, the atmosphere plays a crucial role in most sensory perceptions, and life could not exist without it.

The atmosphere provides virtually limitless sources of oxygen, carbon dioxide, and nitrogen, which are essential to animal and plant life. It also provides the water that is essential to life, and it dissipates through its far reaches many of the waste products of life and of man's industries. The atmosphere transmits the radiation from the sun that is essential to photosynthesis. At the same time it shields the earth from lethal ultraviolet radiation as well as from powerful cosmic rays and from the meteors that constantly shower down on the earth from space. Furthermore, the atmosphere acts as a blanket, maintaining a generally higher temperature on the earth than would occur if it were absent. It also moderates the earth's climate, warming the polar regions and cooling the tropical regions.

The atmosphere is essential to communications. It readily transmits sound and electromagnetic (light and radio) waves; and an electrically conducting layer in the upper atmosphere reflects radio waves, thereby permitting communication beyond the limit of the horizon. Finally, properties of the atmosphere permit flight by aircraft except under special conditions.

The sun's energy, as it falls on the earth, keeps the atmosphere in a ceaseless state of turbulent motion. From weather satellites orbiting at heights of hundreds of miles above the earth, complex and constantly changing patterns of clouds may be observed that indicate this turbulence. Some of the clouds are thousands of miles across, while others are much smaller; some appear simple in shape, while others have a detailed structure.

PHYSICAL PROPERTIES

The atmosphere extends outward from the earth for a distance of several hundred miles, where it gradually merges with the very thin gases of interplanetary space. Because of the earth's gravitational pull, however, 99 percent of the matter making up the atmosphere is confined to within about 20 miles (30 km) of the earth's surface. A vertical column of air having a cross section of 1 square inch (about 6.5 sq km) and extending from sea level to outer space weighs about 15 pounds (6.8 kg). The atmosphere presses down with this force on each square inch of the earth's surface.

Composition of the Atmosphere. The atmosphere consists of a mixture of permanent gases (primarily nitrogen and oxygen), gases of variable concentration (such as water vapor), ions (electrically charged atoms and molecules), and various solid and liquid particles suspended in the air.

The concentrations of the permanent atmospheric gases are shown in Table 1. Throughout most of the atmosphere—from the surface of the earth to a height of 50 to 55 miles (80 to 90 km) —the permanent gases are uniformly mixed except for small changes during short periods and over limited areas. The concentrations of the variable atmospheric gases are shown in Table 2.

Water is introduced to the atmosphere through evaporation at the earth's surface and is re-

Table 1—PERMANENT ATMOSPHERIC GASES[1]

Gas	Percent by volume
Nitrogen (N_2)	78.110 ± 0.004
Oxygen (O_2)	20.953 ± 0.001
Argon (Ar)	0.934 ± 0.001
Neon (Ne)	$(18.18 \pm 0.04) \times 10^{-4}$
Helium (He)	$(5.24 \pm 0.004) \times 10^{-4}$
Krypton (Kr)	$(1.14 \pm 0.01) \times 10^{-4}$
Xenon (Xe)	$(0.087 \pm 0.001) \times 10^{-4}$
Hydrogen (H_2)	0.5×10^{-4}
Methane (CH_4)	2×10^{-4}
Nitrous oxide (N_2O)	$(0.5 \pm 0.1) \times 10^{-4}$

[1] After R.G. Fleagle and J.A. Businger, *An Introduction to Atmospheric Physics* (New York 1963).

moved through condensation and precipitation. Carbon dioxide is introduced through the exhalation of animals and through combustion and is removed by photosynthesis. Large quantities of carbon dioxide are absorbed and released by tiny plants (algae) within the ocean.

Ozone (triatomic oxygen) is created from oxygen atoms and molecules by absorption of ultra-

Table 2—VARIABLE ATMOSPHERIC GASES[1]

Gas	Percent by volume
Water (H_2O)	0 to 7
Carbon dioxide (CO_2)	0.01 to 0.1 (average 0.032)
Ozone (O_3)	0 to 0.1 (at 30 km)
Sulfur dioxide (SO_2)	0 to 0.0001
Nitrogen dioxide (NO_2)	0 to 0.00002

[1] After R.G. Fleagle and J.A. Businger, *An Introduction to Atmospheric Physics* (New York 1963).

violet solar radiation in the region 12 to 30 miles (20 to 50 km) above the earth. It is destroyed by absorption of radiation from other wavelengths and by oxidation.

Except for ozone nearly all the oxygen within 50 miles (80 km) of the earth's surface is in diatomic form (two atoms in each molecule). Above 65 miles (100 km), however, absorption of ultraviolet solar radiation maintains oxygen in the monatomic (single atom) form. In the region of 50 to 185 miles (80 to 300 km) above the earth there are sufficient ions to create important electrical and magnetic effects. Above 300 miles (500 km) helium is probably the major atmospheric gas. It gradually gives way to hydrogen at heights of 1,800 miles (3,000 km) or more, until at last the atmosphere merges with the gases of interplanetary space.

The solid and liquid particles that are suspended in the atmosphere come from many different sources. Solid particles are swept up from dry surfaces of the earth, or they may originate from evaporation of sea spray. Volcanoes and fires produce dust and smoke particles. Man also affects the composition of the air through his burning of fuels and introduction of industrial pollutants into the atmosphere. Meteors that vaporize before reaching the earth's surface add about 1 ton of matter to the atmosphere every day. Most of this material ultimately is deposited on the surface of the earth.

Matter from the sun enters the outer regions of the atmosphere. A continuous stream of elementary charged particles, known as the solar wind, flows outward from the sun in all directions. The particles (protons and electrons) interact with the magnetic fields of the sun and the earth. As a result the intensity of the solar wind fluctuates and in turn affects the shape of the earth's magnetic field. The particles do not reach the earth's surface. Instead, they are deflected by the earth's magnetic field or are trapped in the Van Allen radiation belt that surrounds the earth at a height of 2,000 to 20,000 miles (3,000 to 30,000 km). (See also VAN ALLEN RADIATION BELTS.)

Finally, the atmosphere receives a continuous shower of very high-energy particles (mostly protons) from outer space. The particles, called cosmic rays, are partly deflected by the earth's magnetic field but have enough energy to penetrate the atmosphere and strike the earth's surface. As they pass through the atmosphere, they collide with air molecules, producing great numbers of secondary cosmic rays, some of which may reach the earth's surface.

The total composition of the atmosphere, therefore, is determined by a complex balance of processes. These processes include the absorption of carbon dioxide and exhalation of oxygen by plants, the inhalation of oxygen and exhalation of carbon dioxide by animals, the discharge of gases from volcanoes, the evaporation and condensation of water, photochemical processes, and the addition of particles from the earth's surface and from outer space. Man, as well, introduces gases and pollutants into the atmosphere. There is also some loss of matter caused by the escape of atoms of light gases (principally hydrogen and helium) from the exosphere. It is not certain whether or not the total mass of the atmosphere experiences a net gain or net loss.

Structure of the Atmosphere. The atmosphere may be described as being subdivided into several layers, each characterized by a distinctive temperature distribution. The layers have been given names with the suffix "-sphere," and the boundaries between the layers have been given names ending with the suffix "-pause."

The *troposphere* is the lowest layer of the atmosphere, closest to the surface of the earth. The prefix "tropo-" means "turning or changing," because this is the layer in which the changing atmospheric conditions known as weather occur. The troposphere extends to a height of 10 to 11 miles (16 to 18 km) in tropical regions, and 5 to 6 miles (8 to 10 km) in regions nearer the poles. About four fifths of the atmosphere's mass is contained in the troposphere. Temperatures within this layer decrease as the height increases. The temperatures at the upper boundary of the troposphere, called the tropopause, range from −60° to −110° F (−51° to −79° C).

Above the tropopause lies the layer of air called the *stratosphere*. In the lower part of this layer, temperature is nearly constant with height, but higher up temperature increases with height. At a height of about 30 miles (50 km) maximum temperatures of about 45° F (7° C) are reached. This height marks the stratopause, or upper boundary of the stratosphere. Above the stratopause lies the *mesosphere*, in which temperatures may drop to about −100° F (−73° C) at a height of 50 miles (80 km).

Above the mesopause, or upper layer of the mesosphere, lies the *thermosphere*. Here the temperature again increases with height until it reaches about 2250° F (1232° C) at a height of 300 miles (480 km). Temperatures in the thermosphere probably vary by several hundred degrees between day and night.

Above 300 miles (500 km) lies the fringe region known as the *exosphere*, where the earth's atmosphere merges with the gases of interplanetary space. Individual molecules moving rapidly

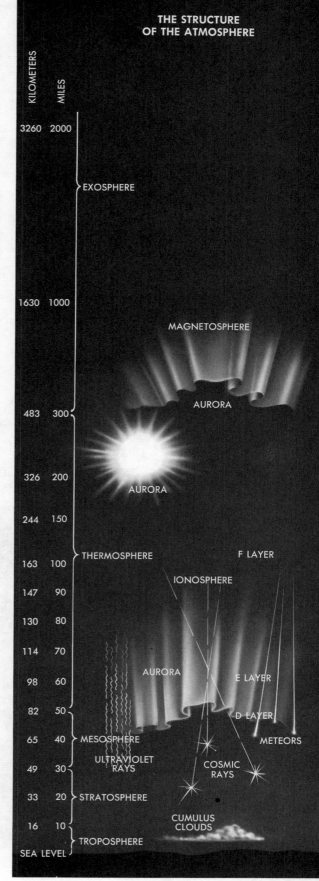

THE STRUCTURE
OF THE ATMOSPHERE

upward may escape from the earth's gravitational field before colliding with other molecules. Hydrogen atoms, formed by the dissociation of water vapor and of methane, may escape readily in this way.

The atmosphere also may be divided into regions on the basis of electrical properties. Below a height of 50 miles (80 km) the atmosphere consists mainly of neutral molecules of air whose motions are controlled by pressure forces and by the gravitational field of the earth. Here, a vertical potential or "voltage" difference amounting to about 400,000 volts is maintained between the earth (negative) and the ionosphere (positive). Thunderstorms occurring all over the earth generate and maintain this potential difference.

From a height of 50 to 300 miles (80 to 480 km) the atmosphere contains many electrically charged particles, or ions, as well as neutral molecules. This region, therefore, is referred to as the *ionosphere*. It is the region of auroral displays and is also the region that is used in radio communications for reflecting radio signals over long distances.

Above a height of 300 miles (480 km) lies a region of the atmosphere called the *magnetosphere*. It is so named because here the behavior of the ions and atomic particles is controlled almost entirely by the earth's magnetic field. Between 2,000 and 20,000 miles (3,000 to 30,000 km) lies a "radiation zone" containing many high-energy ionized particles. This zone, called the *Van Allen radiation belt,* was first detected by James A. Van Allen of the United States and Sergei N. Vernov of the Soviet Union through the analysis of data that had been obtained from artificial satellites.

Clouds. Nearly all clouds are found in the lower half of the troposphere. They are composed of small water droplets and ice crystals, and they assume a great variety of forms, differing widely in vertical extent and in horizontal scale. The fair weather cumulus, the cumulonimbus, and other clouds of small extent can be identified by an observer on the ground. Other more extended forms found in hurricanes or in still larger storms may be readily identified on weather satellite pictures taken from outside the atmosphere.

Clouds are formed as a result of the cooling of a mixture of water vapor and dry air to the *dewpoint*, or temperature at which that particular mixture becomes saturated. Typically, cooling occurs when warm air rises to regions of lower pressure and expands. The water vapor from which the clouds are formed comes from evaporation that has taken place over some moist land or water surface. The vapor-enriched air has risen to a height at which it becomes saturated, often very far from the original source.

The form of a cloud reveals something of the atmospheric currents that created it. Towering, billowy clouds are formed by *convection cells,* or tall chimneys of air rising at a rapid rate. Precipitation from such clouds is characteristically heavy as a result of the rapidity with which the air rises and cools. Smooth-layered clouds that spread over a wide area are formed in air that flows upward at a very gradual slope and at a low rate of speed. Clouds that are arranged in rows with clear spaces between them are formed by atmospheric waves on an *inversion surface*— a surface above which temperature increases with height. Clouds that are formed by atmospheric waves often are observed in the lee of hills or

The earth and its atmosphere as viewed from a height of 475 miles (760 km) by the Gemini 10 astronauts, who passed through part of the Van Allen radiation belt. A tropical storm is seen near the Strait of Gibraltar.

mountains, but they also may exist far from such obstacles.

Condensation Nuclei. Condensation of water vapor always occurs on minute solid or liquid particles that are called condensation nuclei. These particles vary greatly in size. If the particles were reduced to spherical shapes, their radii would vary from 0.005 to 20 microns (1 micron equals about 0.00004 inch, or 0.001 mm). Particles with a radius between 0.1 and 1 micron (called large nuclei) are the most effective nuclei for clouds. Near sea level the atmosphere contains hundreds or thousands of these large nuclei in each cubic inch, and even in the upper troposphere the concentration usually exceeds 10 nuclei per cubic inch. These nuclei probably originate as smoke particles from fires and as salt particles from the breaking of small bubbles at the surface of the ocean. Because condensation nuclei are present everywhere in the atmosphere, clouds form readily and promptly whenever air is cooled to the dewpoint.

Newly created cloud droplets grow rapidly to a size that is determined by the size of the condensation nucleus, the temperature, and the amount of water vapor in the air. After a radius of about 20 microns has been reached, the droplet begins to fall in relation to smaller droplets and consequently may grow by sweeping up smaller droplets that lie in its path. By the time the droplet has reached a radius of 100 microns, it falls at a rate of about 20 feet (6 meters) per second relative to the air and may be considered a rain droplet. In falling through the cloud it may grow to a diameter of 0.04 inch (1 mm) or larger. This process of rain-droplet growth is called *accretion*.

Some particles—probably crystalline—may act as nuclei for the formation of small ice crystals, but such ice nuclei are much less numerous than condensation nuclei. Ice nuclei originate as dust from the earth's surface and possibly as meteoric dust in the upper atmosphere. Man can influence the formation of ice crystals by adding artificial nuclei to the atmosphere. Silver iodide acts as an ice nucleus at about 23° F (−5° C); naturally occurring crystals require somewhat lower temperatures.

Because ice nuclei vary in concentration and effectiveness, many clouds exist at below-freezing temperatures. A few ice crystals forming in such a supercooled cloud may grow very rapidly at the expense of the water vapor within the cloud. This leads to evaporation of the liquid droplets. The ice crystals may grow to a size at which they precipitate, or the cloud may be transformed rapidly into an ice-crystal cloud. This process of precipitation is probably most important in supercooled *stratiform* (layered) clouds, whereas the accretion process of precipitation probably is most important in *cumiliform* (bulging) clouds.

Convective clouds (clouds formed by convection cells) in which small droplets are freezing act as huge electrostatic generators. Electrical charges are separated, the positive charges being carried to the upper part of the cloud and the negative charges to the lower part. When the voltage difference between the upper and lower parts of the cloud—or between the lower surface of the cloud and the ground—becomes great enough, a lightning flash occurs. The electrical storms of the earth as a whole maintain the charge of the ionosphere at about 400,000 volts positive with respect to the surface of the earth.

ANSEL ADAMS FROM MAGNUM

Towering billowy clouds such as these formations above Kings Canyon National Park, Calif., are formed by rapidly rising columns of air called convection cells.

ENERGY TRANSFER

The earth's total environment is one in which complex transformations of energy are constantly occurring. These transformations determine the behavior of the atmosphere, the weather, and climate. They also determine biological processes on which man depends for survival.

Solar Energy. The sun is the source of virtually all the energy that drives the great air currents of the atmosphere. The energy falling on a square centimeter of surface perpendicular to the sun's rays at the top of the atmosphere amounts to about 2 calories per minute. This is called the *solar constant*, although there is no reason to expect it to be strictly constant. The solar energy falling in one minute on a square surface 30 miles (50 km) on a side is equivalent to the energy released by the explosion of a small atomic bomb.

Atmospheric Absorption and Emission. The solar energy that falls on a square centimeter at the earth's surface is considerably less than the solar constant. It varies with elevation, with the angle of the sun (season, latitude, and time of day), with the amount of air traversed by the

Rows of clouds separated by clear spaces are the product of atmospheric waves on an inversion surface—a boundary of air above which temperatures increase abruptly with height.

AMERICAN MUSEUM OF NATURAL HISTORY

solar energy, and with the amount of cloud cover. On the average, about 18 percent of the solar energy striking the atmosphere is absorbed in the atmosphere and about 35 percent is reflected or scattered back into space by clouds, by the earth's surface, and by the atmosphere itself. The remaining 47 percent of the solar energy is absorbed by the earth's surface. The radiation absorbed by the earth and its atmosphere is the energy source that drives the winds and ocean currents and supports all biological processes on earth. Wide variations in the average percentages of absorption and reflection of solar energy occur with differences in latitude, season, time of day, type of ground surface, and cloud conditions.

The sea and the land differ in their manner of absorbing the sun's radiant energy. The sea surface absorbs almost all the radiation falling on it, and this energy is mixed efficiently by local currents so that little over-all change in temperature occurs. A dry land surface, on the other hand, is heated rapidly by the radiation falling on it, and this heating is confined to a thin surface layer. This variation explains the contrast between the mildness of a maritime climate and the harsh extremes of an inland continental climate.

The earth's surface emits radiation upward at a rate that increases with temperature. This radiation, called infrared radiation, is not detected by the eye, but the energy radiated is comparable to that received from the sun. Under clear skies, roughly 60 to 70 percent of the radiation given off by the earth's surface is absorbed by the water vapor and carbon dioxide in the atmosphere. The remainder escapes directly into space. The absorbing gases reemit the absorbed energy both to the earth and to space. Thus, water vapor and carbon dioxide act as a blanket, keeping the earth's surface warmer by about 65° F (36° C) than it would be if there were no atmosphere. Cloud layers absorb nearly all the infrared radiation falling on them and reradiate this energy, thus further insulating

the earth's surface. The phenomenon is commonly called the "greenhouse effect." The term is actually a misnomer, since a greenhouse maintains its temperature primarily by preventing convective, rather than radiative, transport of heat.

Since the net amount of cooling or warming by radiation always depends on the small difference between the rates at which radiation is absorbed and emitted, the effects of radiation are among the most difficult to account for or predict.

Effects of Energy Transfer. Only a few of the many complex interactions involving energy transfer are discussed here. The effects of energy transfer can be clearly recognized in some cases, as when fog forms in cold air over warm water or in moist air over a field on a clear night. But even in these relatively simple examples, the processes of energy transfer interact in such a way that predictions of fog formation are uncertain.

The surface layer of the sea or land may store energy for a season or longer. Ultimately, the energy absorbed is released in a variety of ways. Ocean currents may transport energy from the tropics to higher latitudes. Of the energy transferred from the earth's surface, some is in the form of infrared radiation, some is transmitted to the atmosphere by conduction, and some is transferred as latent heat associated with the water vapor evaporated from the earth's surface. Heat conduction and evaporation depend in a complex way on the nature of the earth's surface and on the vertical distribution of temperature and wind speed in the air close to that surface. All of these factors influence the turbulence of the air, and atmospheric turbulence is the primary mechanism by which heat and water vapor are carried upward from the earth's surface.

The energy involved in evaporation over the oceans greatly exceeds that involved in heat transfer. There is less evaporation over land areas, the greatest amount taking place in equatorial jungle regions, and precipitation over land

As a result of energy transfer, fog may form in cool air over warm water or in moist air above a field at night.

areas exceeds evaporation. This means that the atmosphere transports water from ocean to land. Furthermore, evaporation exceeds precipitation over the ocean in subtropical regions (about 30° latitude); but in the middle latitudes (about 50° latitude) and at the equator precipitation exceeds evaporation. This means that water is transported by wind from subtropical regions to middle latitudes and to equatorial regions.

Heat energy also is transported by ocean currents, particularly by the Gulf Stream of the Atlantic Ocean and the Kuroshio, or Japan Current, of the Pacific Ocean. The effects of these currents on the weather and climate of the Northern Hemisphere are considerable, although the total energy they carry is less than the energy carried by the atmosphere.

ATMOSPHERIC MOTIONS

One of the most important effects of energy transfer is to drive the wind systems and to generate storms. The winds also provide an additional means for energy transfer, which is one more evidence of the complex interactions occurring in the atmosphere.

Atmospheric motions take place in response to the following forces acting on the air: friction, gravitation, pressure, and (in the ionosphere and magnetosphere) electromagnetic forces. To these must be added the centrifugal and Coriolis forces, which arise from use of a coordinate system fixed on the surface of the rotating earth.

The friction force is commonly neglected, except near the ground and at heights above 60 miles (100 km). However, in discussions of turbulence and small-scale motions, friction plays an important role. (Electromagnetic forces have a negligible effect on atmospheric motions below

the ionosphere and will not be discussed here.) The force of gravitation is directed vertically downward toward the center of the earth, and its chief effect is to compress the atmosphere against the surface of the earth. The vector sum of the force of gravitation and the centrifugal force of the earth's rotation is called the force of gravity; this sum defines the vertical direction everywhere over the surface of the earth. There is also a very small gravitational force due to the moon and the sun. This force varies with the positions of the moon and sun relative to a point on earth.

The remaining forces—pressure and Coriolis forces—may act horizontally and therefore are important to an understanding of winds. Pressure at a point in the atmosphere is proportional to the weight of the air column extending from that point to the top of the atmosphere. Horizontal pressure forces, therefore, arise from differences in the weight of air columns; these differences represent horizontal differences in temperature. As air temperatures change, therefore, changes in horizontal pressure forces occur.

The Coriolis force may be experienced by a person in attempting to walk across a rotating platform. He finds himself impelled at right angles to the direction in which he tries to walk. Similarly, air moving over the surface of the rotating earth is deflected to the right of the direction of motion in the Northern Hemisphere, and to the left in the Southern Hemisphere. The deflecting force is called the Coriolis force.

The resultant of all the forces acting on a unit mass of air, as required by Newton's second law of motion, equals the acceleration of the air. In many cases the forces are nearly balanced, and the acceleration is correspondingly small. An

Collisions of ions with air molecules produce auroras.

important case occurs when the pressure and Coriolis forces are balanced. The pressure force is directed toward lower pressure; but if the air is moving at appropriate speed counterclockwise around a low in the Northern Hemisphere, the Coriolis force balances the pressure force. This condition may be identified on weather maps when the wind blows parallel to the lines of constant pressure.

Complex and variable patterns of airflow may be developed by the interaction of forces. Some of the major patterns are discussed here.

Large-Scale Atmospheric Motions. From the point of view of an observer looking at the earth from above the North Pole, the earth and its atmosphere rotate in a counterclockwise direction about the polar axis once every 24 hours. From above the South Pole the rotation would appear to be clockwise. The atmosphere has, on the whole, a somewhat faster rate of rotation than that of the earth itself. Air therefore flows in a great vortex about the poles.

Planetary Waves. Air velocities vary in all three space coordinates of latitude, longitude, and height. The distribution of these velocities is changing continuously. However, certain atmospheric motions known as planetary waves recur persistently on a global scale. They are linked closely to the extratropical storms that dominate the winter weather outside the tropics. The waves may cover thousands of square miles and take several days to develop. There are usually 2 or 3 planetary waves in polar regions, distributed around a latitude circle, and 8 or 10 waves at about 45° latitude. Disturbances at about 60° latitude develop the greatest intensity.

Another characteristic of planetary waves is that the air rises when flowing from warmer to colder areas—that is, from equator to pole—and sinks when flowing in the reverse direction. The vertical velocity is less than one percent of the north-south velocity, but this is often sufficient to produce clouds in the area of rising air (south winds) and clear skies in areas of sinking air (north winds).

Planetary waves are effective mechanisms in transporting water vapor and heat from the abundant supplies of low latitudes to higher latitudes. Planetary waves develop when the cold dense air masses of the polar regions sink in moving toward the equator while the warm air masses of the low latitudes rise in moving poleward. During this process some of the potential energy of the systems is converted into kinetic energy of wave motion. This transformation of energy occurs most efficiently for planetary wavelengths of about 3,000 miles (5,000 km). Waves of about this size, therefore, predominate in the atmosphere. The large-amplitude planetary waves also contribute to the kinetic energy of the zonal atmospheric currents known as the middle latitude *jet streams*.

In the tropical regions, where the Coriolis force is of minor importance, air rises in concentrated areas along the intertropical convergence zone and flows poleward in the upper troposphere. Some of the air sinks earthward at about 30° latitude in the subtropical anticyclones (to be discussed later), and the tropical circuit of air currents is completed by the surface trade winds.

Airflow in the stratosphere appears to be more or less independent of the troposphere. The time scale of major disturbances in the stratosphere is weeks or months rather than days. Data are scarce, and questions remain concerning the description of the general circulation of the stratosphere and its relation to the circulation of the troposphere.

Cyclones. There are numerous examples of atmospheric wind systems in which the air flows "cyclonically," or roughly circularly, about a center. These systems include small vortices ("dust devils") seen in desert areas, tornadoes, hurricanes, and the winter storms of middle and high latitudes.

Extratropical cyclones are large wind systems that occur in the middle or high latitudes. They often are called depressions, or, in the terminology of weather reports, "lows." In the Northern Hemisphere the wind in such cyclones flows in a counterclockwise sense, as seen from above, whereas in the Southern Hemisphere the wind flows in a clockwise direction.

Extratropical cyclones are associated with planetary waves and may be regarded as another aspect of the same phenomenon of atmospheric motion. A series of extratropical cyclones often is associated with a single planetary wave. The most intense of these cyclones develop into very large vortices that extend from the earth's surface into the stratosphere.

The following features are characteristic of the structure of fully developed extratropical cyclones. Winds blow counterclockwise around a central region of low air pressure. The warm moist air on the east side of the cyclone rises, cools by expansion, and then precipitates its water vapor in the form of rain or snow. The cold air on the west side of the cyclone sinks and is warmed by compression, so that clear dry weather prevails there. As the cyclone develops, the boundaries between the warm and the cool air become progressively sharper and are spoken of as "warm fronts" and "cold fronts." Subsequently, other cyclones may form along this meeting of warm and cool air. At a later stage of development the warm air is forced upward by the overlapping, or *occlusion*, of the cold and warm fronts. The source of warm moist air thus is cut off, or at least reduced, and the energy of the storm is dissipated gradually.

Tropical cyclones are smaller, more intense storms. As their name implies, they occur in the tropical latitudes where the widespread storm systems characteristic of middle and high latitudes rarely form. Tropical cyclones develop in the summer and early fall, generally on the western sides of the oceans. In the western Atlantic and the Indian oceans the storms are called hurricanes or cyclones. In the western Pacific they are known as typhoons, and in the region of the Philippines they are called baguios. In the Southern Hemisphere tropical cyclones occur in the western Pacific and the Indian oceans, but very rarely in the Atlantic Ocean. The storms develop from small disturbances in the easterly winds over the tropical oceans, which form along a belt of converging winds from the Northern and Southern hemispheres.

It is characteristic of tropical disturbances that the lowest several miles of the atmosphere are nearly saturated with water vapor, so that the lifting of this air may release large quantities of latent heat. Only rarely do tropical disturbances develop into tropical cyclones.

Tropical cyclones are probably the most destructive of all atmospheric phenomena. Their winds often exceed 100 miles (160 km) per hour near the earth's surface. They create enormous ocean waves, which may overrun low-lying islands hundreds of miles from the path of the storm. Rainfall of 20 inches (50 cm) is common, and as much as 100 inches (250 cm) has been reported. The daily transformation of energy occurring through condensation within these storms is many times greater than the energy released by a thermonuclear explosion.

The tropical cyclone feeds on a layer of moist air a mile or so thick, which lies next to the ocean surface. In the life of a tropical storm this layer, extending over a region equivalent to the land area of the United States east of the Mississippi River, may be pumped through the vortex of the storm and lifted 6 miles (10 km) or more. Near the surface of the ocean the air spirals inward and is warmed and further enriched with water by its violent passage over the sea. Long converging spirals of clouds mark the regions of ascending air. These spirals meet in an inner core—a circular band of thick clouds, violent turbulence, and heavy rainfall. Inside this region is found the "eye," a circular region of relative calm and sometimes clear skies, 6 to 36 miles (10 to 60 km) in diameter. The boundary of the eye slopes outward with height.

Extratropical cyclones and tropical disturbances may be considered the primary engines that drive the general circulation of the atmosphere by converting the latent heat and available potential energy to kinetic energy. They provide the first stages of the large-scale upward transport of water vapor and heat and probably most of the downward transport of ozone and radioactive fallout as well.

Anticyclones are regions of high pressure within which the air flows around the region of

BOB TAYLOR

A lightning flash produces radio waves that may travel along the earth's magnetic field for long distances.

highest pressure. The flow is clockwise in the Northern Hemisphere and counterclockwise in the Southern Hemisphere. Anticyclones tend to be larger than cyclones, but the wind velocities are usually smaller. Anticyclones are characterized by sinking air and by clear, calm weather. In the terminology of weather reports they are known as "highs."

Small-Scale Atmospheric Motions. Disturbances of a considerably smaller scale than extratropical and tropical cyclones also influence the weather significantly. Among these small-scale systems are thunderstorms, sea breezes, gravity waves, and tornadoes. In these systems the wind speeds are often as great as, and sometimes greater than, those encountered in the larger cyclones. But because of their limited horizontal extent of 6 miles (10 km) or less these smaller phenomena do not play an important direct role in the general atmospheric circulation.

The *convection cell*, the tall chimney of rising air of which the thunderstorm is the most dramatic product, is one such small-scale system. Development of a convection cell depends on the temperature of the air, which must drop at a sufficiently rapid rate, as height increases, to allow rising warm air to gain in buoyancy as it rises. If the temperature drops more than about 30° F per mile increase in altitude (about 10° C per km), the air is said to be statically unstable, and vertical convection is likely. The rising, cooling air often becomes saturated with water vapor at

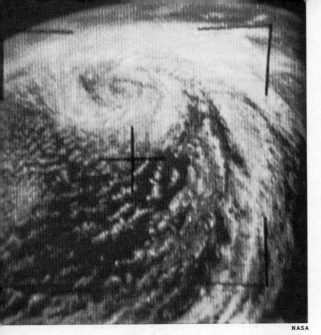

A Tiros satellite photographs the vortex of an extra-tropical cyclone over the eastern North Atlantic.

a height that may be clearly identified as the base of a cumulus cloud. If the temperature within the cloud decreases more than 15° F per mile rise in altitude (about 5° C per km), the cloud is statically unstable also. (The difference between the critical vertical temperature gradients inside and outside of clouds is due to the latent heat release that accompanies condensation of water vapor within the cloud.) As a result, clouds are often convection cells of very violent updrafts. If the convection cell extends high enough ice crystals are likely to form in the upper portion. This provides the necessary conditions for the separation of electrical charges within the cloud and for the production of lightning.

The *sea breeze* is an example of the effect of differential heating of the earth's surface on a very small scale. As the land is heated during the day, cool air from the sea displaces the warm air, which rises and moves out over the sea. In the complex thermal and topographic conditions that are common over much of the earth a similar mechanism produces a bewildering array of winds, many of which remain mysteries to the meterologist as well as to the farmer or sailor.

Gravity waves are analogous to waves on the surface of the ocean. They often form within layers of cold air lying below warmer air. They may be recognized, especially in the lee of mountains, by the crests of the waves, which are marked by evenly spaced, lens-shaped clouds. Large gravity waves may develop a very sharp leading edge, just as large sea waves sometimes do. Gravity waves passing over an observation point are detected by the occurrence of an abrupt rise in pressure as the wave passes.

The most violent of all atmospheric phenomena, the *tornado*, is associated with the static instability that sometimes develops as part of a convective storm in the warm moist air ahead of an advancing cold front. The tornado appears as a funnel-shaped cloud, roughly 300 feet (100 meters) in diameter. The cloud is in violent rotation about a small, intense, central low-pressure area. The tornado probably forms as a result of strong vertical convection currents together with large-scale rotation of the air mass in the vicinity of the storm. As air flows inward toward the convection cell, it rotates more and more rapidly. The centrifugal effect prevents filling of the funnel and permits the tornado to persist as a stable entity for many minutes.

Turbulent Motions. The motions discussed thus far are organized in fairly simple ways. There are also much smaller-scale motions that are chaotic and more or less random. These turbulent motions play a dual role. They provide the primary mechanism for the transfer of heat energy and matter from near the earth's surface into the free air. They are also the means by which the kinetic energy of atmospheric motions is dissipated. That is, the energy is passed from larger to smaller-scale motions and ultimately to the molecular motions that constitute thermal energy. Turbulence thus plays an important part in both the prologue and the epilogue of atmospheric motions.

Turbulence usually is generated by air flowing over rough surfaces, or wherever there is a rapid change of wind velocity with distance. Turbulence also is generated by the buoyancy that results from the heating of the earth's surface. Where air rises freely and winds are active, turbulence is an efficient agent in energy transfer. On the other hand, where winds are light and the temperature of the air increases with increase in height (temperature inversion), turbulence is suppressed. When temperature inversions occur over large cities, they trap smoke and fumes near the surface of the earth, producing the irritating and sometimes dangerous condition known as "smog."

Turbulence is particularly important in influencing the properties of clouds. Condensation and ice nuclei are carried aloft by turbulence and are distributed through large volumes of air. Turbulence also makes possible the great range in the size of water droplets, which is essential for efficient rain production, and it maintains the supply of moisture to the growing droplets of water.

OTHER ATMOSPHERIC PHENOMENA

The atmosphere abounds in optical and acoustic phenomena, which are sometimes beautiful and spectacular, sometimes subtle and hardly noticeable. The refraction, or bending, of light produces many remarkable effects. It occurs when there is rapid change of temperature in the direction perpendicular to the light beam. Perhaps the most familiar example of refraction is the *inferior mirage* seen on the surface of a highway on a hot sunny afternoon. Light rays from the sky are refracted upward to the motorists' eyes. In a *superior mirage* a distant object appears elevated in the sky as the light rays from the object are refracted downward from a higher layer of warm air. Refraction by turbulent air produces the twinkle of stars. Normal atmospheric refraction bends the light reaching the earth from the stars, the moon, and the sun. In this way it extends by several minutes the period during which these celestial objects are visible above the horizon.

The refraction of light rays by ice crystals produces *halos* around light sources. When one looks at the moon or sun through a thin cloud contain-

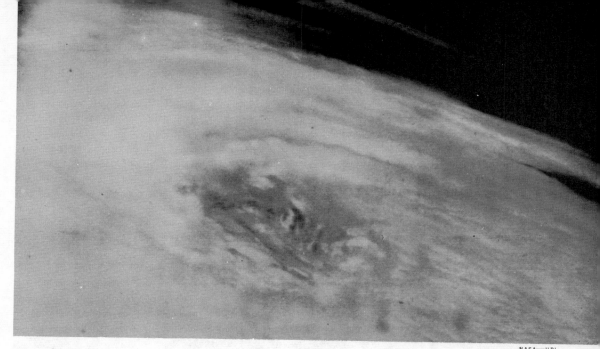

NASA—UPI

Tropical cyclones such as hurricane Debbie (1961) are smaller, more intense storms than extratropical cyclones.

ing hexagonal-shaped crystals, a bright ring with a radius of about 22° (as measured by the observer) appears around the moon or sun. A cloud containing rectangular ice crystals, however, produces a ring that is about twice as large in diameter. The various wavelengths of visible light are refracted differently, so that the halo may appear varicolored, with red on the inside and blue on the outside. *Sundogs,* or *mock suns,* bright spots that appear in the sky at the same altitude as the sun and about 22° to either side of it, are produced by hexagonal plate-like ice crystals that are horizontally slanted. Because of this orientation of the crystals a halo is not seen.

Refraction by water drops produces the familiar *rainbow* and in some instances produces a higher-order rainbow as well, with a larger radius. Clear and colorful rainbows result from large drops of water. Very small drops produce a white, primary bow.

Lightning produces electromagnetic waves, ranging from the ultraviolet to very long radio waves. The longer waves are detected in nearby radio receivers as static. Waves of audio frequency may penetrate the ionosphere, travel along the earth's magnetic field, and reach the earth again in the opposite hemisphere at a latitude corresponding to the latitude at which the lightning flash occurred. The higher frequencies arrive before the lower frequencies, so that a listener hears a whistle of descending pitch on a radio equipped to detect very low frequencies. Observations of these *whistlers* may be used to determine the density and activity of electrons along the path of the whistlers.

Geomagnetic Phenomena. Phenomena associated with the earth's magnetic field are more subtle than those already discussed, but they are important nevertheless to an understanding of the earth's environment. They are important also in the consideration of problems relating to radio communication, navigation, and space travel. The magnetic field has its source in the interior of the

earth and extends many thousands of miles into space. Its general structure is that of a sphere whose axis is at an angle of 11.5° to the earth's axis of rotation. This angle changes, however, over a period of decades or centuries. The magnetic field is vertical to the earth's surface at the geomagnetic poles and horizontal to the earth's surface at the geomagnetic equator. The field grows rapidly weaker as its distance from the earth increases. At the distance of about 80,000 miles (128,000 km) the field has about 0.1 percent of the strength it has at the surface of the earth.

The solar wind—the stream of protons and

The vortex and "eye" of hurricane Donna (1960) show up clearly on a radar screen. Hurricanes are probably the most destructive of all atmospheric phenomena.

U.S. WEATHER BUREAU

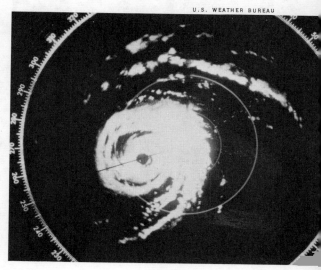

U.S. DEPARTMENT OF COMMERCE, WEATHER BUREAU

Cumulonimbus clouds are characterized by heavy precipitation. Here a violent thunderstorm is in progress.

A tornado, like a thunderstorm, is a small-scale atmospheric motion, but it can be violently destructive.

FPG

electrons coming from the sun—"compresses" the geomagnetic field on the side nearest the sun. Changes in intensity and direction of the solar wind create fluctuations in the strength and configuration of the geomagnetic field. Ions from the solar wind may be captured by the geomagnetic field and may be impelled to move along the magnetic lines of force with a spiraling motion. They are reflected near the geomagnetic poles, so that they oscillate—move back and forth rapidly—from pole to pole. At the points where they are reflected the ions may come within 60 to 600 miles (100 to 1,000 km) of the earth's surface and in doing so may excite neutral air molecules by colliding with them. The molecules then may emit visible light to produce the *aurora borealis,* or "northern lights," and the corresponding *aurora australis* of the Southern Hemisphere (see AURORA). The mechanisms involved in auroral displays are not fully understood. By studying the auroras with spectroscopes, however, scientists have gained much of their basic information concerning the composition and temperature of the atmosphere at those heights.

The much less energetic ions in the atmosphere that are produced by absorption of ultraviolet solar radiation are influenced also by the earth's magnetic field. There are sufficient ions in the region between 60 and 180 miles (100 to 300 km) above the earth to make it electrically conducting. The neutral molecules in this layer are much more numerous, however, and they take part in the tidal motions of the atmosphere. The ions are carried along in the atmospheric tide, but when they cross lines of magnetic force, they are impelled to move at right angles to the tidal motion. In this way an ionospheric current of some 60,000 amperes is made to flow constantly in the upper atmosphere. The presence of the

636

current can be detected by a regular daily fluctuation in the earth's magnetic field, amounting to about 0.1 percent of the permanent field over most of the earth. A particularly strong daily "electrojet" current flows along the magnetic equator. Electrojets often are associated with the appearance of auroras at high latitudes as well. Another effect of ultraviolet solar radiation on the earth's atmosphere is the production of the airglow, a faint glowing of the upper air, which results from photochemical reactions involving oxygen and nitrogen at heights between 50 and 70 miles (80 and 110 km).

Atmospheric Modification. Man's extensive activities—burning of fossil fuels, clearing of forest and grass areas, irrigation of fields, and so forth—have already modified the atmosphere in important ways. For example, the carbon dioxide content of the atmosphere has probably increased by 25 percent in this century and may continue to increase, and pollutants are being added to the atmosphere over large cities in increasing amounts. The effects of such inadvertent modification are only partially understood, but there is increasing reason to believe that they may be important and far-reaching.

Possibilities of deliberate modification of the atmosphere present both an opportunity and a nightmare. For example, it is technologically possible to melt the ice covering the Arctic Ocean. It is not known, however, what the effects would be—what increase or decrease in precipitation might take place, what shifts in distribution of precipitation or sunshine might occur, or whether or not the ice would form again. Similarly, there is increasing evidence that cloud seeding offers great possible benefits, especially in increasing water supplies in mountainous areas. But here again, as in all such cases, the consequences must be understood before extensive experiments are carried out.

An essential step in achieving the necessary understanding is to observe the atmosphere accurately and completely. A major effort of the International Council of Scientific Unions and the World Meteorological Organization is to develop a system of observation satellites and balloons circling the earth at prescribed heights. This system is intended to provide, for the first time, descriptions of the entire atmosphere and of the changes that are taking place in it.

See AIR; AIR POLLUTION; CLIMATE; IONOSPHERICS; METEOROLOGY; SPACE RESEARCH; VAN ALLEN RADIATION BELTS; WEATHER; WEATHER FORECASTING.

ROBERT G. FLEAGLE, *University of Washington*

Bibliography
Battan, Louis Joseph, *The Nature of Violent Storms* (New York 1961).
Loebsack, Theo, *Our Atmosphere* (New York 1961).
Orr, Clyde, Jr., *Between Earth and Space* (New York 1961).
Riehl, Herbert, *Introduction to the Atmosphere* (New York 1965).

For Specialized Study
Craig, Richard A., *The Upper Atmosphere: Meteorology and Physics* (New York 1965).
Fleagle, Robert G., and Businger, J.A., *An Introduction to Atmospheric Physics* (New York 1963).
Fletcher, Neville Horner, *The Physics of Rainclouds* (London 1962).
Pasquill, Frank, *Atmospheric Diffusion: The Dispersion of Windborne Material from Industrial and Other Sources* (London 1962).

ATMOSPHERIC PRESSURE. See ATMOSPHERE—*Motions*; BAROMETER; CLIMATE; METEOROLOGY; PRESSURE; SPACE MEDICINE; WEATHER FORECASTING; WINDS.

ATOLL, a′tôl, a roughly ring-shaped mass of reef-building coral and calcium-containing algae, found in the open sea. Atolls differ from fringing reefs and barrier reefs (see CORAL AND CORAL REEFS) in that an atoll encircles a shallow central lagoon. Water depths in atoll lagoons average 150 feet (45 meters). The largest known atoll—Kwajalein in the Marshall Islands—is 42 miles long and 32 miles wide (67 by 51 km). There are usually shallow channels through atoll reefs, allowing ships to pass into safe harbor within the lagoons. Surmounting an atoll reef in many places are islands of carbonate sand, rarely rising more than a few feet above the high-tide line. They tend to support a restricted flora of mangrove, coconut palm, and breadfruit trees.

Reefs are typically found in clear shallow waters of tropical and subtropical regions from about 30° north to 30° south latitude, chiefly in the Pacific Ocean. The mean annual water temperature in these regions is 70° F. (21°C). The coral and reef-building algae grow best on the seaward portion of the reef mass, where a constant supply of oxygen and nutrients is brought by waves and ocean currents. Vigorously growing reef-building organisms can be found in the range from slightly above low-tide line to depths of about 50 feet (15 meters). It is generally believed that the lower depth of reef development is controlled by the depth of penetration of sunlight, which is required for photosynthesis by the algae living in the tissues of the coral polyps.

Charles Darwin, from observations he had made, concluded that atolls grew around volcanic islands that had subsided beneath the ocean surface. Drilling into one Pacific atoll has revealed a foundation of volcanic rock at a depth of about 4,100 feet (1,200 meters) below present sea level, and this is consistent with Darwin's theory. Atolls and organic reefs may also form if upward growth of coral is stimulated by a general rise in sea-level.

W.E. YASSO, *Columbia University*
C.G. TILLMAN, *Virginia Polytechnic Institute*

FORMATION OF AN ATOLL

Charles Darwin concluded that as a volcanic island erodes and at the same time gradually subsides beneath the ocean surface, the fringing reef growing around the island becomes a barrier reef and, finally, an atoll. This theory is widely accepted.

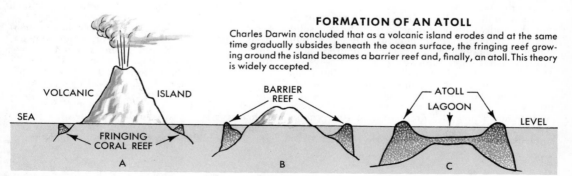

VOLCANIC ISLAND — BARRIER REEF — ATOLL — LAGOON

SEA — FRINGING CORAL REEF — LEVEL

A   B   C

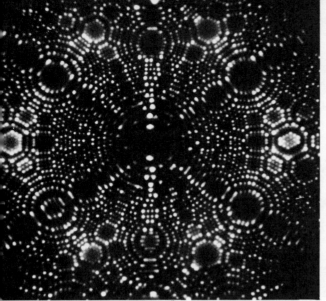

ATOMS in a tungsten crystal appear as small dots in this photograph of the point of a tungsten needle, taken with a field-ion microscope. The magnification is about a million diameters.

ATOM, at'əm, traditionally, the smallest and most fundamental building block of matter. The word comes from the Greek *atomos,* meaning "indivisible." In present-day usage "atom" is the name for a particular subunit of matter—not at all the smallest—consisting of an elaborate organization of particles into which it can be divided.

ATOMIC STRUCTURE AND PROPERTIES

In chemical terms the atom is the smallest unit of matter that has the characteristic properties of one of the 103 known elements, such as iron or hydrogen. This definition differentiates the atom from the *molecule,* which is a combination of atoms forming a chemical compound such as iron oxide or water. However, the definition is inadequate because some of the characteristics of materials depend on the group properties of atoms even when the atoms are of the same kind. For instance, atomic hydrogen composed of individual atoms has different chemical properties from the usual molecular hydrogen gas composed of double hydrogen atoms bound together.

A more meaningful definition of "atom" can be made in terms of the internal structure, which has been well understood at least since 1927. In these terms the atom is the unit of matter that contains a small, dense, positively charged *nucleus* surrounded by sufficient negative *electrons* to make the whole electrically neutral.

Structure. All atoms are about the same size, and this fact is a clue to the nature of their structure. The atomic diameter is about 2×10^{-8} cm (2 hundred-millionths of a centimeter). Since this is only $\frac{1}{1000}$ of the wavelength of visible light, atoms cannot be seen in the ordinary sense, even with microscopes.

Fifty million ($\frac{1}{2} \times 10^8$) atoms are ranged side by side in one linear centimeter of solid matter. A cubic centimeter of any solid will therefore contain about 10^{23} (one hundred thousand billion billion) atoms. ($\frac{1}{2} \times 10^8 \times \frac{1}{2} \times 10^8 \times \frac{1}{2} \times 10^8 = \frac{1}{8} \times 10^{24} \approx 10^{23}$.) Since a cubic centimeter of a solid element ranges in mass from about 0.1 gram for hydrogen to 20 grams for uranium, the individual atomic masses must range from 10^{-24} gram to 2×10^{-22} grams. All but $\frac{1}{20}$ of 1 percent of this mass is in the nucleus; the rest is carried by the electrons.

The nuclei of atoms of the various elements differ in size, in a way that would be expected if the nuclei were composed of closely packed unit spheres, each containing about the same mass and the same size. In such an arrangement the diameter is proportional to the cube root of the volume, which in turn is proportional to the number of subunits. The lightest atom, hydrogen, contains only one of these subunits in its nucleus and has a nuclear diameter of about 3×10^{-13} cm—about $\frac{1}{100,000}$ of the atomic diameter. One form of uranium, the heaviest of the naturally occurring elements, has 238 of these subunits in its atomic nucleus. The nuclear diameter is therefore about $\sqrt[3]{238} \times 3 \times 10^{-13}$ cm, or about 6 times that of hydrogen. Even in this case, however, the atomic diameter is about 10,000 times greater than the nuclear diameter.

The rest of the space within the atom is filled with electrons and the electromagnetic fields that bind them to the nucleus. To comprehend the scale of such a structure, consider that if an atom were enlarged until its diameter was $\frac{1}{2}$ mile, the nucleus would be a small sphere at the center ranging in size from a marble, for hydrogen, to a baseball, for uranium.

Atomic Number and Mass Number. The nuclear subunits are positively charged *protons* and electrically neutral *neutrons.* They have about equal mass, although the neutron is about $\frac{1}{1,000}$ heavier. The chemical properties that distinguish the various elements are determined by the number of electrons bound to each nucleus, and this number is equal to the number of protons in the nucleus. The usual hydrogen nucleus consists of a single proton, and the atom possesses only one electron. Uranium has 92 protons in the nucleus and 92 electrons bound in the atom. The number of protons (or the number of electrons) is called the *atomic number.*

The neutrons in atomic nuclei add to the mass but do not affect the number of bound electrons or the chemical behavior. There are roughly equal numbers of protons and neutrons in the nuclei of light atoms, but heavier atoms contain more neutrons than protons. For instance, the most common uranium atom has 146 neutrons and 92 protons. The sum of the number of protons and neutrons is called the *atomic mass number,* or *mass number.* Usually, the atomic number and the atomic mass number are written as subscript and superscript around the symbol for the particular element; for example, $_{92}U^{238}$.

Isotopes. It is possible to have different numbers of neutrons with a particular number of protons. These various combinations are known as *isotopes.* For example, hydrogen can exist in three such forms. Regular hydrogen has no neutrons ($_1H^1$); heavy hydrogen, or deuterium, has one neutron ($_1H^2$); and there is a yet heavier form called tritium with two neutrons ($_1H^3$). Tritium is unstable and has a radioactive half-life (see *Glossary*) of 12.4 years. Most elements have only a few stable isotopes, one of which usually makes up the bulk of the substance. Man-made radioactive isotopes have different neutron-proton ratios from naturally occurring ones; usually, the greater the difference, the shorter the half-life.

ANCIENT ATOMIC SPECULATIONS

Any attempt to reduce the stupendous variety of forms of matter leads to speculation that there may be only a few basic forms that combine to produce all the others. One school of Greek philosophy, exemplified by the teachings of Empedocles (5th century B.C.), thought that there were four primary substances—earth, air, fire, and water. These, acted upon by a few influences, mixed in various ways to form all the materials of our world, including spirit and mind. Opposed to these notions of continuous, jellylike substances were the ideas of the atomists. They pictured matter as being made up of small, hard particles, all consisting of the same material but differing in size and, therefore, "subtlety." The infinite number of combinations of these infinite numbers of particles gave rise to all substances, including intangibles.

Aristotle and other ancient philosophers credit the origin of atomic philosophy to Leucippus (5th century B.C.), but Democritus (460–370 B.C.) is usually credited with the first complete development of the theory. One feature of the theory was that the space between atoms was a vacuum in which the atoms could move and rearrange themselves. For this reason, Aristotle (384–322 B.C.), who held that nature abhorred a vacuum, believed that the atomic theory was untenable. Subsequently, in the teachings of Epicurus (342–270 B.C.), the atomic theory became associated with a materialistic philosophy with implications of godlessness.

The atomic theory was revived and given a remarkable exposition by a Roman, Lucretius (c. 99–55 B.C.). He wrote a long treatise in the form of a poem, *De rerum natura* (*On the Nature of Things*). Claiming Epicurus as his inspiration and intellectual master, Lucretius provided elaborate explanations of the nature of substances in terms of the interactions and motions of atoms. Although the poem was known to the contemporaries of Lucretius, it had no influence on scientific or philosophic thinking. The atomic theory itself, with its antireligious implications, went underground for 1,600 years.

The story of these early speculations is of historical interest largely because of the importance of the atomic idea in the development of philosophy. Historians of science differ about the degree to which the ancient theories influenced the thinking of chemists in the 1600's and 1700's. Certainly, the ancient notions were not a theory in our present meaning of the term. The Greek philosophers neither based their ideas on physical measurements nor tried to prove their ideas by any experimental tests.

THE THREE ISOTOPES OF HYDROGEN differ in atomic mass number (number of protons and neutrons together), although they have the same atomic number (number of protons in the nucleus), as shown here.

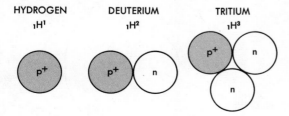

| HYDROGEN | DEUTERIUM | TRITIUM |
| $_1H^1$ | $_1H^2$ | $_1H^3$ |

BEGINNINGS OF MODERN ATOMIC THEORY

With the beginning of freer thought and modern science the stage was set for a revival of various ancient philosophies long suppressed or ignored. In the 1600's a French philosopher and mathematician, Pierre Gassendi, dared to attack the Aristotelian tradition and defend both the atomism and moral philosophy of Epicurus. Meanwhile, alchemy was turning into chemistry through the exact measurements made by many experimenters of the 1600's. Joachim Jung used the word "element" in our modern sense, influencing the thoughts of Robert Boyle. With the use of vacuum pumps, which Otto von Guericke invented in 1654, Boyle and Robert Hooke isolated and experimented with known volumes of air and other gases. Boyle explicitly used the idea of atomism in describing matter, and the basic notion was accepted by most educated people from then on. The existence of some form of basic particles is implicit in the work of Christian Huygens and of Isaac Newton.

Dalton's Theory. Although the connection between modern ideas of atomicity and the Greek speculations is tenuous and to some extent wishful, there is a clear historical line leading from the present back to the work of John Dalton at the beginning of the 1800's. Dalton made minor contributions in a number of scientific fields, particularly meteorology, but his main importance lies in his elaboration and defense of an atomic theory to explain chemical facts. In particular he cited data to demonstrate the law of multiple proportions. This law states that if two elements combine in different proportions to form different compounds, the ratios of weights of the same elements to each other will be small whole numbers. Whenever ratios of physical quantities appear in the form of small integers, the existence of definite, whole, fundamental units is implied. (There are numerous other examples in nature of integral multiples of a basic unit, such as the quantity of electric charge, the amount of angular momentum of a bound system, and the masses of the elements.) Thus, the law of multiple proportions is evidence for the atomic structure of matter.

Dalton expounded his atomic theory in *A New System of Chemical Philosophy*, first published in 1808. Although this was a major attempt to reconstruct a theory to fit experimental results and to use the theory to predict other results, it was largely wrong in its details. According to Dalton atoms of different elements were of different sizes and could expand or contract indefinitely, depending on the temperature. He accepted the caloric theory of heat. Caloric was supposed to be a fluidlike substance that could permeate solid matter. Conduction of heat was explained as the flow of caloric from one substance to another, and the rise in temperature when an object was rubbed or beaten was believed to result from driving out the caloric.

Dalton supposed that static atoms were surrounded with the heat fluid, which could expand. He therefore disagreed with the theory of his contemporary Amedeo Avogadro that correctly required equal volumes of gases at equal temperatures and pressures to contain equal numbers of the units of gas (which Avogadro proposed might contain two atoms of the gas). Dalton discarded the experimental results of Joseph L. Gay-Lussac on the combining volumes of gases, although these results also displayed ratios that were small whole numbers. Despite the arbitrary selection of data to be used or denied and the completely false picture of the atomic details, Dalton's treatise established the atomic theory for most subsequent experimenters.

Periodic Table. Because of the importance of the weights of combining elements, much of the work of chemists in the early 1800's was devoted to determining and cataloging precise atomic and molecular weights. The cataloging was important because data from different sources often were inconsistent. In 1869, Dmitri I. Mendeleyev assembled many of the facts about the elements and arranged the elements in a system known as the periodic table. This classification scheme, which others had tried to arrange with only partial success, grouped together elements with the same general chemical activity. The periodic table did not explain the nature of the atoms that could give rise to it, but it did serve as a major testing ground for all subsequent theories of atomic structure. See also PERIODIC LAW.

Equivalence of Heat and Energy. Other fields of scientific study during the 1800's led to the formation and acceptance of an atomic theory of matter. As recently as 1850 the caloric theory was the most widely accepted view of the nature of heat. The triumph of a kinetic atomic model over the caloric was due to the experimental work of Benjamin Thompson (Count Rumford) in 1798, the proposals of Julius von Mayer in the 1840's concerning the equivalence of heat and energy, and the synthesis of theory and experiment by James Joule. In a paper written in 1847, Joule used a model of atoms held together by mutual attraction and vibrating about their equilibrium positions. With this model he explained qualitatively many facts about the thermal behavior of matter and even made crude quantitative calculations concerning the required atomic properties.

Other scientists soon made more extensive calculations using this kinetic atomic model. Success in explaining many phenomena was startling, particularly in the deduction of the gross gas laws, starting with the statistical behavior of free particles in collision. Names associated with this endeavor are Hermann von Helmholtz, James Clerk Maxwell, Ludwig Boltzmann, and Josiah Willard Gibbs. In spite of the successes there were a number of problems that either were not solved or were first noticed because of the general success of the theory. These were associated with the division of energy among the atoms under various conditions, and in some cases were major clues leading to a later understanding of the interior structure of the atom.

Atomic Spectra. Yet another body of scientific knowledge requiring an atomic hypothesis was being investigated during the 1800's. This concerned the properties of light emitted by matter under various conditions. The emission of light must be explained in terms of the structure of matter from which the light comes. The nature of emitted light under different conditions of emission is extremely complex. Not only are the color and intensity of light from different sources obviously different, but when the light is spread out into a spectrum by a prism or grating it can be seen that the detailed structure of colors is far greater than is apparent. Bright lines characteristic of different elements appear in the spectra of light emitted by those elements.

All during the 1800's scientists were observing and eventually photographing the spectra produced by different elements at various temperatures and under various conditions of solid or gaseous states. Although many spectral lines were cataloged and it was learned that each element produced a unique spectrum, no theory related these light patterns to the atomic structure that clearly was responsible for their presence. Like the chemical regularities, the spectra served as a testing ground for the various atomic models proposed at the beginning of the 1900's. See also SPECTROSCOPY.

Other Evidence for the Atomic Theory. Other scientific discoveries between 1880 and 1900 implied atomicity of matter, although that interpretation was not always obvious at the time. The improvement of vacuum technology allowed investigators to deal with what we now recognize as individual particles under conditions such that the particles could travel appreciable distances without colliding with the relatively few gas molecules that always remain in any evacuated chamber. Thus, X-rays were discovered by Wilhelm Roentgen in 1895 while he was working with an evacuated discharge tube in which a current was passed between high-voltage terminals (see X-RAYS). In 1897, J.J. Thomson identified the negative current in such a tube as a stream of individual particles (electrons).

Heavier particles with positive charge also were observed. These were ions, atoms from which the electrons had been torn. Such a hypothesis fitted earlier experiments in which it was assumed that individual charge carriers migrate through a solution. In 1896 radioactivity was discovered by Henri Becquerel. Subsequent revelations of the process of radioactive decay and the nature of the decay products clearly demanded an explanation of atomic structure.

TWO EARLY MODELS OF THE ATOM are shown below. In the Thomson model (A), negative electrons were symmetrically embedded in a continuous distribution of positive charge, like raisins in a raisin pudding. In the early Rutherford-Bohr model (B), electrons moved in orbits about a small, dense, positively charged nucleus.

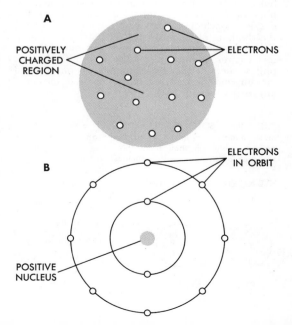

A

POSITIVELY CHARGED REGION

ELECTRONS

B

ELECTRONS IN ORBIT

POSITIVE NUCLEUS

THEORIES OF ATOMIC STRUCTURE SINCE 1900

Until the 1890's there were still respectable arguments against the atomic theory. Until that time the atom could not be isolated, and the regularities of chemical and optical behavior could be explained in a general way in terms of resonances of continuous matter (see RESONANCE).

A sizable body of scientists was opposed to atomic explanations, which they considered to be based on theoretical speculations without any experimental evidence. Ernst Mach, the Austrian physicist and philosopher, saw no need for such interpretations, and F. Wilhelm Ostwald, the great physical chemist, was not convinced until 1905, when Albert Einstein successfully explained the Brownian motions (see BROWNIAN MOVEMENT) on the basis of individual atomic bombardment. In the 1895 edition of the second volume of his *Introduction to the Kinetic Theory of Gases,* Boltzmann expressed the hope that even though he spoke against the prevailing opinion in assuming atomicity, the successes of such an idea should be recorded for future generations.

By 1900, however, most physical scientists were concerned not with whether matter was atomic but with the nature of the atom. The assumption was that the atom must have an internal structure with smaller parts, a conclusion forced by the experimental production of electrons that apparently came out of all kinds of matter and by the emission of helium gas from radioactive materials.

Early Atomic Models. The first atomic models were based on attempts to combine positive chunks of matter and large numbers of electrons so that they would be internally stable. Philipp Lenard in 1903 proposed a model of an atom composed of yet smaller neutral particles, which he called "dynamids." These charge doublets were supposed to occupy only a small fraction of the atomic volume. J.J. Thomson proposed a model with electrons embedded in a positive sphere in various equilibrium positions.

These models presented the atom as a complex assemblage that would vibrate in various modes if disturbed. The problem was to design the structure so that the electrons would vibrate at all the required frequencies for the emission and absorption of light, produce the chemical binding forces, and still remain attached to the central structure if undisturbed. Thomson's atom did seem to produce approximately the same resonant vibrations as those of light frequencies but with only a small amount of the required complex regularity. In 1904, Hantaro Nagaoka proposed a solar-system type of atom with the electrons existing in belts, much like the rings of Saturn. However, no quantitative results from such a model agreed with the atomic facts.

Discovery of the Nucleus. Lenard had pictured the atom as an almost empty region because he had experimented with the transmission of high-speed electrons through very thin foils of metal. Thomson's model could also explain the transparency of solid atoms. If most of the mass is distributed over the whole volume of the atom with the electrons embedded in it like raisins in a pudding, the density of the atomic material is approximately that of ordinary matter. High speed bullets can travel through water, slowing down and scattering slightly, just as electrons do when going through a thin foil. In 1910, Ernest Rutherford suggested a similar penetration and

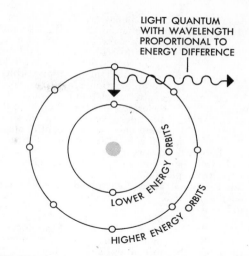

LIGHT QUANTUM WITH WAVELENGTH PROPORTIONAL TO ENERGY DIFFERENCE

LOWER ENERGY ORBITS

HIGHER ENERGY ORBITS

THE BOHR ATOM successfully explained the spectral lines of hydrogen in terms of light quanta emitted by electrons that were falling from allowed orbits of higher energies to vacancies in orbits of lower energies.

scattering experiment to a graduate student, Ernest Marsden. Alpha particles (now known to be helium nuclei) from natural radioactive materials were used as the projectiles. Marsden discovered that a few alpha particles were scattered from the foil at wide angles and even in a backward direction. In the words of Lord Rutherford, "It was almost as incredible as if you fired a 15-inch shell at a piece of tissue paper and it came back and hit you." Rutherford realized that the alpha particles must be bouncing off something in the foil more massive than themselves and that this must imply that the atomic mass was concentrated in a small region.

Subsequent experiments by Marsden and Hans Geiger provided the quantitative data that Rutherford used to demonstrate that the scattering was due to the electrostatic repulsion of the positive alpha particle from a positive core no larger than $1/10,000$ of the atomic diameter. Furthermore, the amount of the positive charge on the core, measured in electron charge units, proved to be approximately one half the atomic mass number. The number of negative electrons outside the core must therefore be about one half the atomic mass number.

Henry G.-J. Moseley gave an important confirmation of this picture in 1913 when he showed that each element bombarded by high-speed electrons in an X-ray tube gives off a unique spectrum of X-ray wavelengths. These spectra are basically simpler than the visible light spectra produced by each element, and certain characteristic wavelengths are related in a simpler way to the atomic number—that is, to the number of positive charges in the nucleus. These results agreed with those of the alpha-scattering experiments. The importance of the atomic number rather than the atomic mass was therefore clear. The characteristic X-rays must be generated from the interior of the atom in a region dominated by the positive nucleus and not shielded by the atomic electrons. The periodic table of the elements, which Mendeleyev had organized on the basis of chemical behavior, was really organized on the basis of atomic number, which in turn controlled the behavior. See ELEMENT.

Rutherford's nuclear atom theory had serious flaws. It did not explain how the electrons were associated with the positive core. They could not simply hover nearby, or they would be drawn into the nucleus. If they rotated in planetary orbits, they were subject to an electromagnetic problem. Orbiting particles are accelerated toward the center, and an accelerated electric charge emits electromagnetic radiation. An electron in such an orbit would radiate energy away continuously and so spiral into the central nucleus. Furthermore, there was no apparent relationship between the electron behavior and the known chemical and spectroscopic data.

The Bohr Atom. Niels Bohr solved many of these problems in 1913 with an atomic model that abandoned several fundamental laws of the physics of the 1800's. He suggested that the electrons do circulate in orbits around the nucleus but that they do not radiate away their energy continuously because they can change energy only in specific amounts, called quanta.

Having once established the stability of the system by this rather arbitrary assumption, Bohr then proposed that emission or absorption of electromagnetic radiation occurred if the electron abruptly changed orbits. Presumably, an electron would be stable in the orbit of lowest energy. If excited to a higher orbit by absorbing the appropriate energy from heat or electrical discharge, it would then jump down again, emitting a packet of light whose energy content is equal to the energy difference of the orbits. The energy of the light quantum determines its wavelength. Thus, spectral lines correspond to differences between electron orbits. This simple but radical model was particularly easy to deal with in the case of the hydrogen atom, which contains only one electron. Calculations of the possible wavelengths in the hydrogen spectrum were spectacularly accurate and complete. See also QUANTUM THEORY.

Bohr extended his theory to atoms of higher atomic number. Through a series of speculative arguments he concluded that the two electrons of helium could occupy the smallest orbit, but that the third electron of lithium would have to move in the next larger orbit. He adopted the

positions of atoms in the periodic table as guidelines in determining the orbital positions of the various electrons. Thus he assumed that in the case of an alkali metal, such as lithium, the outermost electron must occupy an orbit by itself, with the rest of its electrons distributed in the lower orbits. A very satisfactory qualitative picture was thus developed for the atomic basis of chemical activity. The quantitative predictions for the spectra of the larger atoms were not very satisfactory, however. Alkali metals, with their single valence electron, produce hydrogen-like spectra, and the general details of these could be satisfactorily explained. Such a simple atom as helium, however, produces a complex double spectrum that could not be explained with Bohr's simple model. During the ensuing 12 years many complicated additions were made to the model by various investigators. For instance, combinations of elliptical orbits were tried that successfully explained the "fine structure" or close neighboring wavelengths of many spectra.

Electron Spin and the Exclusion Principle. The next great step in understanding the atom came with the proposal by Samuel Goudsmit and George Uhlenbeck in 1925 that the electron must possess an intrinsic spin. When this theory was linked with the general exclusion principle of Wolfgang Pauli, which says that no two electrons occupy exactly the same state, the organization of multiple electron atoms and the main explanations of their spectra were complete.

The helium atom can contain two electrons in the lowest orbit, but only because the spins of the two electrons are opposite each other. Spin, being angular momentum, must be quantized; it can change only in integral multiples of h, Planck's constant, the basic unit of the quantum theory. If the electron has intrinsic spin ½ h, then it can change by one unit of h if it flips to the opposite direction where it would have a spin of -½ h relative to the first position. A third electron cannot exist in the first orbit, because its spin would be in line with one or the other of the two electrons already there and two of the electrons would then occupy the same state.

THE PRESENT VIEW OF THE ATOM

Very often, when a theory becomes too complex and can explain phenomena only with the addition of extra assumptions, it is time for a completely new theory or a recasting of the old. Such was the situation by the 1920's with the "old" quantum theory of Bohr. The new insights came rapidly and dramatically during the years from 1924 to 1928, with contributions made by many physicists. In 1924 Duc Louis de Broglie (later Prince de Broglie) proposed that particles should show wave behavior under certain circumstances, and Clinton Davisson and Lester Germer observed this effect with electrons. Erwin Schrödinger proposed in 1925 that particle motion could be described with an equation that under certain approximations has solutions implying that particles exhibit wavelike properties. This equation was applied with great success to a wide range of problems, from the behavior of the hydrogen atom to the emission of alpha particles from radioactive nuclei. The various ad hoc assumptions that had been necessary to patch up the Bohr atom were implied by this equation as necessary features of the theory.

A corresponding development in 1926 by Werner Heisenberg, using matrix mathematics,

DE BROGLIE WAVES of one, two, and three wavelengths are represented as standing waves associated with the allowed electron orbits in the Bohr atom.

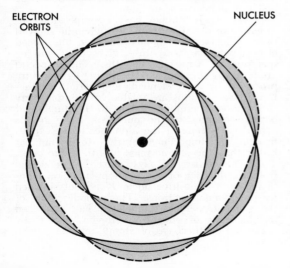

ELECTRON ORBITS

NUCLEUS

was shown to be mathematically equivalent to Schrödinger's equation. In 1928, Paul A.M. Dirac revised the theory slightly to make it compatible with the requirements of relativity. His mathematics yielded solutions that he interpreted as requiring the existence of antiparticles, one of which was soon found in cosmic rays.

Problems with a Mechanical Model of the Atom. The Bohr atom and the quantum conditions on which it was based are still useful first approximations in describing some atomic phenomena. The more accurate quantum mechanics developed in the 1920's yield results that are harder to picture in terms of a mechanical model. These new and successful equations make no pretense of describing the exact position and motion of the individual electrons in orbit around the nucleus. Such position and motions, as a matter of fact, can never be determined experimentally, at least with the precision implicit in the formulas of classical mechanics. All that can be determined experimentally are the differences between one energy level and another and the approximate radial position of the electrons. Quantum mechanics gives the probabilities for finding these various quantities, predicting only what actually can be observed.

The wave properties of all particles, including the electron, provide an example of the inappropriateness of taking the old solar-system model of the atom too seriously. The particles are not themselves waves, but the mathematics that predicts certain aspects of their behavior is similar to the mathematics describing waves. The wavelength associated with an electron in an atom is about the same length as the distance from the electron to the nucleus. But this wavelength is the only meaningful measure of the size of the particle itself. In trying to make a mechanical model of such a situation we should have to picture the electron as if it were as large as the entire region in which it can exist—approximately as large as the atom! Furthermore, although the probability of finding the electron a certain distance from the nucleus can be calculated, neither theory nor experiment can make any comment about the angular location of an electron. Under such circumstances it is meaningless to talk about an electron "orbit."

Picturing the Atom. The best we can do is to picture the atom as a tiny nuclear core surrounded by cloudy regions where electrons probably may be found. These probability zones correspond roughly to the main orbital regions of the Bohr model. To picture the location of the electrons in atoms, consider what happens if electrons are added to bare nuclei. In the case of hydrogen the electron could drop either from high energy levels to slightly lower ones or directly to the lowest level. As the electron is trapped in this process, it loses energy, which is radiated as light. The same amount of energy would have to be provided to lift the electron out of its final position. In the case of helium another electron can also fall to that same lowest energy level, but only if its spin is opposite to that of the first electron. For nuclei with greater positive charge the lowest energy level corresponds to a probability zone of smaller radius. As a result, the radius of the zone of the outer electrons is about the same for all atoms.

After the lowest energy level closest to the nucleus is filled, any other electrons must exist in higher energy zones further from the nucleus.

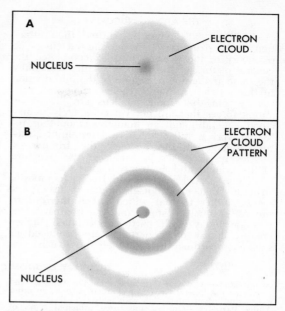

THE ELECTRON CLOUD PATTERNS for two atoms may be represented as shown. The hydrogen atom (A) has a single zone, while the sodium atom (B) is more complex.

The third electron of lithium and the third and fourth electrons of beryllium fit into a spherical zone around the nucleus, which is larger but concentric with the lowest energy level. The extra electrons of the next six atoms of increasing atomic number—boron, carbon, nitrogen, oxygen, fluorine, neon—find themselves in probability zones that are not spherically symmetric around the nucleus but whose energy is not too different from that of the second spherical zone. The probable energies of electrons in these regions and the rules that determine with what probability an electron will transfer from one zone to another are all given by quantum mechanics.

Quantum mechanics also predicts how the outer electrons will arrange themselves to provide chemical binding when two or more atoms are close together. These outer probability zones are usually not at all symmetric about each of the atoms but rather form complex regions encompassing the joined atoms. In the case of crystals these outer zones become more the property of the whole assembly of atoms.

Summary. Thus, in a special sense, the problem of the atom was solved by 1927. The basic particles were known; the electromagnetic forces among them were understood; and the quantum laws governing their interaction had been written down. Chemical behavior, the emission and absorption of electromagnetic radiation, and the gas kinetic laws were all solvable in principle. In practice the overlapping interactions of many particles created problems of such complexity that only qualitative trends could be deduced from the general mathematical statements. Solid-state physics—the study of the dynamics of large arrays of atoms—became a major field of study after World War II. Very little modern work, however, is being devoted to the correlation of spectral wavelengths with atomic structure. The opinion in the late 1960's was that no basic mysteries remained in the study of the atom.

THE ATOMIC NUCLEUS

In the 1930's physicists shifted their attention to the structure of the atomic nucleus. The discovery of the neutron in 1932 completed the general picture of the atom, a picture essentially the same as the one presented in the introduction to this article. Although the neutrons and protons within the atomic nucleus are bound by strong forces that are not yet completely understood, and although an immense amount of research work is still devoted to determining structural details of the nucleus, the frontier of physics research lies in exploring the structure of the protons and neutrons themselves.

These particles do indeed have a composite structure that makes itself apparent in experiments similar to that which led Rutherford to propose a nuclear atom; but the bombardment is done today with particles of much higher energy. Many other particles are produced in such bombardments, and their brief existence can be traced. It appears that each generation finds that the "atom" of the previous generation is really divisible and is composed of—or can be described in terms of—more fundamental particles. Where the process will end, or whether there is an end, is not now clear. See also NUCLEUS, ATOMIC.

CLIFFORD E. SWARTZ
State University of New York at Stony Brook

Bibliography

Adler, Irving, *Elementary Mathematics of the Atom* (New York 1964).
Andrade, E.N. da C., *Rutherford and the Nature of the Atom* (New York 1964).
Boorse, Henry A., and Motz, Lloyd, eds., *The World of the Atom* (New York 1966).
Cline, Barbara Lovett, *The Questioners* (New York 1965).
Conn, George K.T., and Turner, Henry D., *Evolution of the Nuclear Atom* (New York 1966).
Gamow, George, *The Atom and Its Nucleus* (Englewood Cliffs, N.J., 1961).
Korsunskii, M.I., *Atomic Nucleus* (New York 1965).
Livesey, Derek L., *Atomic and Nuclear Physics* (Waltham, Mass., 1966).

GLOSSARY OF ATOMIC AND NUCLEAR TERMS

Accelerator.—A device for increasing the velocity and hence the kinetic energy of charged particles in order to study their interaction with matter.

Alpha Particles.—One of the three principal types of nuclear radiation. Alpha particles are helium nuclei and are thus positively charged.

Angstrom.—A unit of length used to measure the wavelengths of light or of subatomic particles. One Angstrom unit (A) is equal to 10^{-8} centimeter.

Angular Momentum.—The property of a rotating body that determines the torque required to bring the body to rest in a given time; a measure of the quantity of a body's rotary motion.

Annihilation.—The conversion of the rest masses of a particle-antiparticle pair into energy.

Antiparticle.—A subatomic particle whose charge and magnetic moment are opposite to those of a more frequently encountered particle of the same mass and spin. Since a particle and its antiparticle, such as the electron and the positron, annihilate each other, only one member of the pair can normally exist.

Atom.—The smallest subdivision of an element that retains the chemical properties of the element.

Atomic Number.—The number of unit charges on the nucleus of an atom; that is, the number of free protons in the nucleus. The atomic number of an element determines its position in the periodic table.

Atomic Weight.—The weight of an atom based on a scale in which the most abundant isotope of carbon is assigned a weight of exactly 12.

Avogadro's Number.—The number of atoms in a gram of hydrogen or of particles in a mole. Value: 6.0247×10^{23}.

Barn.—A unit of area used in measuring nuclear cross sections. One barn equals 10^{-24} square centimeter.

Baryon.—Any of a class of particles with a mass equal to or greater than that of the proton. All nucleons and hyperons are baryons. Baryons are strongly interacting particles with half-integer spin and are thus classified as fermions.

Beta Rays or Beta Particles.—One of the principal types of radiation given off during radioactive decay. Beta rays consist of high-speed electrons or positrons.

Boltzmann's Constant.—A constant that relates the kinetic energy of a system of free particles to their equilibrium temperature. The value of Boltzmann's constant (k) in cgs units is 1.3805×10^{-16} erg per degree C.

Boson.—Any of a group of particles that are described by the Bose-Einstein statistics. Bosons have integer or zero spin and symmetric wave functions, and include the photon and various mesons.

Bubble Chamber.—A device for detecting charged particles by the formation of tiny bubbles along their tracks in a superheated liquid.

Chain Reaction.—A self-sustaining series of nuclear reactions whereby products of individual reactions initiate new reactions.

Cloud Chamber.—A device for making the paths of charged particles visible; it contains a supersaturated vapor that condenses into minute droplets along the path of such a particle.

Complementarity Principle.—A fundamental principle, closely connected with wave-particle duality, which states that nature has a number of complementary aspects impossible to study in a single experiment.

Compton Effect.—The lengthening of wavelength of electromagnetic radiation, usually X-rays or gamma rays, when it is scattered from a free electron.

Correspondence Principle.—The principle that requires that quantum mechanical descriptions must approach the descriptions of classical mechanics and electromagnetic theory as a limit in the case of macroscopic systems.

Cosmic Rays.—High-energy particles, mainly protons, that enter the earth's atmosphere from space; also, the secondary radiation produced by the interaction of such particles with the earth's atmosphere.

Critical Mass.—The minimum mass in which a chain reaction can be sustained in a fissionable substance.

Cross Section.—The apparent or effective area of nuclei and subatomic particles.

Curie.—A unit of radioactivity. One curie is equal to 3.7×10^{10} disintegrations per second.

Deuterium.—The isotope of hydrogen with mass number 2; also called heavy hydrogen.

Deuteron.—A nucleus of deuterium, containing one proton and one neutron.

Duality.—The characteristic of both particles and waves whereby particles exhibit wavelike properties and waves behave like particles. This dual nature of both particles and waves is the basis of the complementarity principle.

Einstein Mass-Energy Relation.—The relationship $E = mc^2$, where E is energy, m is mass, and c is the speed of light, developed by the special theory of relativity.

Electromagnetic Radiation.—Energy in the form of oscillating electric and magnetic fields propagating through space. It includes radio waves, visible light, X-rays, and gamma rays.

Electron.—A subatomic particle with a rest mass of about 0.5 Mev and one unit of negative charge. Electrons are leptons and have half-integer spins. The electrons in an atom determine the atom's chemical properties.

Electron Volt.—The unit of energy equal to the energy gained or lost by an electron in passing through a potential difference of 1 volt. One electron volt (ev) is equal to 1.60209×10^{-12} erg. Masses of particles are often given in millions of electron volts (Mev).

Element.—A substance consisting of atoms having the same atomic number.

Energy Level.—A permissible value for the energy of a system of particles. For example, the electrons in an atom can occupy only certain discrete energy states.

Fermion.—Any of a group of particles that are described by the Fermi-Dirac statistics. Fermions have half-integer spin and antisymmetric wave functions, and include leptons and baryons.

Field Emission.—The emission of electrons from matter caused by an electric field at the surface that is strong enough to overcome the attraction of the electrons to the surface of the matter.

Fine Structure.—The splitting of spectral lines caused by the spin of the electron. Additional slight splitting caused by the interaction of orbital electrons with the magnetic moments of nuclei or by isotopic mass differences is called *hyperfine structure*.

Fission.—The splitting of a heavy nucleus into two smaller nuclei of approximately equal mass with the release of other particles and energy.

Frequency.—The number of wavelengths of a wave-like disturbance that pass a fixed point in a given unit of time. Frequency is equal to the speed of the waves divided by their wavelength.

Fusion.—The union of two light nuclei to form a single heavier nucleus with the release of a large amount of energy. Fusion can take place only at very high temperatures; for this reason it is also called a thermonuclear reaction.

Gamma Rays.—High-energy electromagnetic radiation. Gamma rays are one of the three types of nuclear radiation.

Geiger Counter.—A device for detecting charged particles by the ionizing discharge that they cause in a gas.

Half-Life.—The time required for one half of a given mass of a radioactive substance to decay.

Heavy Water.—Water composed of deuterium and oxygen. Heavy water (D_2O) is used as a moderator in reactors.

Hypercharge.—A fundamental quantity of subatomic particles equal to twice the average charge of a multiplet.

Hyperon.—Any baryon heavier than a nucleon.

Ion.—An atom or molecule from which one or more of the electrons have been removed.

Ionization Potential.—The electric potential required to overcome the attraction of an electron to an atom, permitting its removal and producing an ion.

Isotope.—Any of two or more different forms of an element differing in atomic weight.

Lepton.—Any of a class of light subatomic particles that do not participate in the strong nuclear interaction. Leptons are fermions and thus have half-integer spin. They include the electron, the muon, and the neutrinos.

Light Quantum.—A "bundle" of electromagnetic radiation, also called a photon, whose energy is equal to Planck's constant h times the frequency of the light v.

Magic Numbers.—Numbers of either protons or neutrons in a nucleus that result in particularly stable nuclei. The magic numbers are 2, 8, 14, 20, 28, 50, 82, and ~126.

Magnetic (Dipole) Moment.—The intrinsic magnetism of a particle (nucleus, electron, molecule, and so on). Circulating electric currents or rotating-charge distributions produce magnetic fields. Many atomic-scale particles have intrinsic, unchanging currents that give rise to permanent magnetic fields associated with these particles. The strength of these fields is measured by the particles' magnetic moments.

Magnetic Resonance.—The condition in which a system can interact strongly with a magnetic field because the frequency of the field is such as to induce transitions between the energy levels of the system.

Mass Number.—The sum of the numbers of protons and neutrons in a nucleus.

Mass Spectrometer.—A device for measuring the masses of charged particles by determining their deflections in electric or magnetic fields.

Meson.—Any of a class of strongly interacting subatomic particles with integer or zero spin. Mesons are bosons and have masses intermediate between those of leptons and those of baryons. The pi meson, or pion, is thought to be responsible for the force holding nuclei together.

Moderator.—Any material, such as graphite or water, used to slow down fast neutrons.

Molecule.—Two or more atoms held together by electrical forces; generally the smallest subdivision of a chemical compound.

Multiplet.—A group of subatomic particles having approximately the same mass and equal spin but differing in charge. The proton and neutron form a multiplet.

Muon.—A subatomic particle with a rest mass of about 105 Mev. The muon was originally classed as a meson but has since been termed a lepton, having a spin of ½ and resembling the electron in many aspects.

Neutrino.—A neutral subatomic particle classed as a lepton, having zero rest mass and a spin of ½. Two types of neutrinos, each with its own antiparticle, have been discovered; one is associated with the production and absorption of electrons, and one with muons.

Neutron.—A neutral subatomic particle with a rest mass of about 940 Mev. It is a nucleon.

Nucleon.—Either of the two particles, the proton and the neutron, that make up atomic nuclei.

Nucleus.—The heavy, positively charged, central core of the atom, composed principally of protons and neutrons.

Orbital.—A wave function that describes the probability of finding an electron in a given orbit of an atom.

Pair Production.—The simultaneous production of a particle and its antiparticle. The term is commonly applied to the production of electron-positron pairs by high-energy electromagnetic radiation.

Parity.—An intrinsic property of subatomic particles related to the mirror-image symmetry of space. Parity is conserved in an interaction when the "handedness" of the coordinate system does not affect the interaction.

Particle.—Any of a large number of minute distinguishable subdivisions of which matter is composed. The term "elementary particle" is often used to refer to those particles, such as the electron, that do not appear to be composed of still smaller particles.

Pauli Exclusion Principle.—The principle that two fermions cannot occupy the same atomic or nuclear state simultaneously.

Periodic Table.—The arrangement of the elements in such a manner that elements with similar chemical properties fall naturally into recurring groups.

Photoelectric Effect.—The emission of electrons from atoms, caused by the action of light.

Photon.—A light quantum; a massless subatomic particle associated with electromagnetic radiation.

Pion.—A multiplet of subatomic particles classed as mesons. Charged pions have a rest mass of about 140 Mev. The pion is associated with the nuclear binding force.

Planck's Constant.—The fundamental constant of quantum theory. Planck's constant h is equal to 6.625×10^{-27} erg-sec.

Positron.—The antiparticle of the electron, that is, a positively charged lepton with a rest mass of about 0.5.

Probability Cloud.—A region about an atom, described by a wave function, in which an electron is likely to be found.

Proton.—A positively charged subatomic particle with a rest mass of about 940 Mev and a spin of ½. The proton is a nucleon and, with the neutron, is one of the chief components of nuclei.

Quantum.—A basic, indivisible amount of a physical quantity, such as mass and some forms of energy. Mass or energy can be gained or lost only in multiples (quanta) of this basic amount.

Quantum Electrodynamics.—The study of the interaction of matter and electromagnetic fields in which the ordinary field variables are replaced by quantized variables.

Quantum Mechanics.—A study of atomic and nuclear processes characterized by the principle that certain physical quantities can exist only in multiples of a basic amount, or quantum.

Radioactivity.—The spontaneous emission of radiation from certain nuclei.

Reactor.—A device in which a controlled nuclear chain reaction can be produced.

Relativity.—A principle that postulates the equivalence of different frames of reference for the description of events in terms of physical laws.

Rest Mass.—The mass of an object in a system in which it is at rest. The energy associated with an object at rest is given by the Einstein mass-energy relation.

Roentgen.—The amount of X- or gamma radiation that produces 1 electrostatic unit of charge in 1 cubic centimeter of dry air at 0° C and 1 atmosphere pressure.

Secondary Emission.—The emission of electrons from the surface of a material when it is bombarded by other electrons. One incident electron can cause the ejection of several secondary electrons.

Shells, Atomic.—Configurations into which electrons in an atom can be grouped according to their orbital angular moments.

Spin.—The intrinsic angular momentum of a particle, measured in units of Planck's constant h divided by 2π. Only integral or half-integral values are possible.

Strangeness.—A fundamental property of subatomic particles closely related to hypercharge. For baryons, strangeness is $Y - 1$, one less than hypercharge (Y); for antibaryons, strangeness is $Y + 1$.

Strong Interaction.—The short-range nuclear force that is responsible for binding strongly interacting particles together in atomic nuclei.

Symmetry Laws.—Physical laws resulting from observed symmetries in the physical world. Each symmetry is closely associated with a conservation law; for example, the conservation of momentum is due to a symmetry with respect to the translation of space.

Uncertainty Principle.—A theoretical principle of the quantum theory that places a limitation on the accuracy with which certain pairs of quantities can simultaneously be measured. For example, position and momentum cannot both be determined exactly at the same time because the measurement of one disturbs the original state of the other.

Wavelength.—The distance between corresponding points of two successive phases of a wave motion; for example, the distance between successive crests.

Weak Interaction.—The short-range nuclear force that governs the decay of several strongly interacting particles and certain radioactive nuclei.

ATOMIC BOMB. See MANHATTAN PROJECT; NUCLEAR WEAPONS.

ATOMIC CLOCK, ə-tom'ik klok, a device for measuring time intervals with extreme accuracy by using the oscillations of atoms or molecules. When the operating frequency of a maser is used for defining a time interval, the maser is called an atomic clock.

In any clock, it is necessary to count the number of oscillations to measure a time interval, just as the hands of an ordinary clock add up or count the total number of oscillations of the

COURTESY OF N. F. RAMSEY

ATOMIC CLOCK is constructed from a hydrogen-beam maser. Magnetic shields are removed to show the device.

balance wheel. Most atomic clocks use an extremely high frequency of oscillation—roughly 1,000 to 30,000 megacycles per second—and, therefore, the counting usually is done indirectly. This is accomplished by electronically synchronizing a lower-frequency, very stable quartz-crystal clock to the atomic clock. The quartz-crystal clock serves as a secondary time standard, and its accuracy is checked against the atomic clock. The atomic clock serves as a primary time standard because it is extremely accurate.

The basic unit for measuring time is the second. The second was defined in terms of the length of the solar day, but greater precision in determining and measuring time intervals was desired in order to obtain greater accuracy in scientific work. The fact that atoms and molecules absorb and emit energy at specific frequencies and that they can be stimulated to an energetic state became the basis for the development of the atomic clock.

Efforts relating to the development of a time standard based on the properties of atoms and molecules were under way in the late 1940's. In 1949 the National Bureau of Standards built a clock that depended on the properties of the

ammonia molecule (NH_3). In 1954 the first maser oscillator was built by Charles H. Townes and two colleagues. An atomic oscillator of very high precision that used a beam of cesium atoms was built in England in 1955. A hydrogen-beam maser was developed in the United States in 1960.

The cesium-beam atomic clock with a frequency of 9,192,631,750 cycles per second became the provisionally accepted primary time standard in 1963. The cesium-beam clock has an accuracy of at least one part in 10^{11}. The hydrogen-beam maser has an accuracy of one part in 10^{12}. With improvements in atomic clocks in progress, it can be expected that accuracies of one part in 10^{13} or perhaps one part in 10^{14} will be achieved. An accuracy of one part in 10^{14} corresponds to a gain or loss of only one second in three million years. See also MASER; TIME, MEASUREMENT AND DETERMINATION OF—*Atomic Time.*

HAROLD LYONS, *Lyons Research Associates, Inc.*

ATOMIC ENERGY. See NUCLEAR ENERGY.

ATOMIC ENERGY COMMISSION, ə-tom'ik en'-ər-jē, the federal agency created by the U.S. Congress to direct and control the production and use of atomic energy for national defense and for a wide variety of peaceful applications in such fields as biology, medicine, health, agriculture, and industry. The AEC is charged with encouraging the use of atomic energy for peaceful purposes, including the production of electricity from nuclear fuels, and is responsible for seeing that programs are developed and maintained for the protection of health and promotion of safety in the nation's nuclear energy program.

History. The AEC was established by the Atomic Energy Act of 1946, which was signed by President Truman on August 1 of that year. On Dec. 31, 1946, the agency succeeded the Manhattan Engineer District of the U.S. Army Corps of Engineers, created during World War II to develop the atomic bomb.

Major programs inherited from the Manhattan District and continued by the AEC included the production of fissionable materials; the declassification of atomic energy data (to the extent consistent with national security); the production and distribution of radioisotopes; studies concerning the possibilities of producing electric power from the atom; nuclear aircraft studies; accident prevention and health programs; health and biology research; training in the handling of radioisotopes; compilation of scientific data; and numerous research programs in reactor physics, metallurgy, and other fields.

While a start had been made on peaceful atomic applications, by far the major share of Manhattan District work was devoted to military requirements. Meeting these needs continued to be a major responsibility of the AEC but increasing emphasis was placed on nonmilitary uses of atomic energy.

The great aim of the 1946 act was to place the vast new power of the atom in the hands of a civilian agency that would continue to direct the use of nuclear energy in the United States. Under the act, however, all fissionable materials and most facilities to produce and use them had to be government-owned. A complete revision of the act, resulting in the Atomic Energy Act of 1954, removed this restriction by permitting private ownership, under AEC license, of facilities for using and producing fissionable materials. An amendment in 1964 went one step further in fostering development of the burgeoning nuclear power industry by providing for private ownership of nuclear fuels.

Operations. The agency is headed by five commissioners who are appointed to five-year terms by the president with the advice and consent of the Senate. One commissioner is named chairman and reports directly to the president. Operating functions of the AEC are directed by a general manager, and licensing and regulatory functions are directed by a director of regulation, each of whom reports directly to the commission. AEC headquarters are located at Germantown, Md., near Washington, D.C., where the agency also maintains an office. Thirteen AEC field offices throughout the country are supervised from the general manager's office.

Most of the AEC's work is done by contractors, who in the mid-1960's had some 130,000 people in their employ. The commission itself employed about 7,000 people. The agency's investment in manufacturing plants, laboratories, and various other facilities totaled more than $8 billion.

The Commission's extensive program of peaceful atomic uses represented approximately 50 percent of its annual operating budget of $2.5 billion in the mid-1960's. Light-water reactors for nuclear power had become competitive with conventional plants in many parts of the United States, and major utilities were turning to these reactors more and more as a source for power.

Radioisotopes were virtually indispensable in many applications. Nuclear desalting, ship and space propulsion by nuclear energy, and the use of peaceful nuclear explosions were among uses under study and development by the AEC. Broad programs of research in physics, chemistry, and the life sciences, as well as in other fields, were continuing.

Fermi Award. The commission's highest award is the annual Enrico Fermi Award, named for the leader of the scientific group that achieved the first sustained nuclear chain reaction at Stagg Field, Chicago, on Dec. 2, 1942. First awarded in 1954, it is given for outstanding scientific or technical achievements related to the development, use, or control of nuclear energy. The award consists of a citation, gold medal, and $25,000 cash prize.

GLENN T. SEABORG
Chairman, Atomic Energy Commission

ATOMIC FALLOUT. See FALLOUT, RADIOACTIVE.

ATOMIC NUMBER. See ATOM; PERIODIC LAW.

ATOMIC PHYSICS. See ATOM; NUCLEAR ENERGY; QUANTUM THEORY.

ATOMIC POWER. See NUCLEAR ENERGY—*Nuclear Fission Reactors.*

ATOMIC STRUCTURE. See ATOM; SPECTROSCOPY—*The Interpretation of Spectra;* X-RAYS—*Physics of X-Rays.*

ATOMIC SUBMARINES. See SUBMARINES.

ATOMIC WEAPONS. See NUCLEAR WEAPONS.

ATOMIC WEAPONS CONTROL. The explosion of American atomic bombs equivalent to 20,000 tons of TNT on Hiroshima and Nagasaki, Japan, on Aug. 6 and 9, 1945, heralded an era of military weaponry with graver potential consequences than any the world had known before. The unleashing of the energy locked in the atom represented a momentous scientific breakthrough of great future benefit to mankind. Unfortunately it was followed by the East-West ideological conflict and thus triggered an arms race of unprecedented dimensions.

Within two decades the Hiroshima weapon was dwarfed by thermonuclear weapons with two and three thousand times its power. The development of massive nuclear arsenals, plus the means of delivery, by the United States and the Soviet Union achieved a crude kind of stability by deterring major acts of aggression. But if this power were ever put to destructive use, the survival of civilization as it is known today would be placed in great doubt. Even vying nations saw the need for nuclear weapons control.

The Arms Race. The Soviet Union tested its first atomic weapon in 1949 and its first hydrogen bomb in 1953, a scant nine months after the first U.S. test of such a device. By the mid-1960's both nations possessed thousands of nuclear warheads; Britain, France, and Communist China had joined the "nuclear club"; and other nations were acquiring the basic resources to do so. Accelerating technologies had made it possible to orbit weapons of mass destruction and to offset offensive weapons, to some degree, with nuclear antimissile defenses. At this time neither of these programs was under way to any significant degree. The decision to proceed with either of them would put the arms race in a new upward spiral.

When the United States and the Soviet Union —the two "superpowers"—developed their nuclear arsenals, the peace was kept by a highly unstable "balance of terror" between them. Fear of surprise attack on the exposed bomber and missile forces of both nations kept trigger fingers nervous. In time both nations came to recognize a common interest in seeking more stable conditions that would reduce the incentive to make a "preemptive" attack for fear that the other was about to do so. By the mid-1950's it was already clear that this could not await prior agreement on sweeping disarmament schemes.

Deterrence Doctrine. Out of this insight American strategic thinkers in the late 1950's evolved a set of doctrines that came to be known as "arms control"—that is, measures other than arms reductions to lessen the risk of war. Focusing on the problem of surprise attack, they developed a doctrine of "stabilized deterrence" that both powers came to accept implicitly. This doctrine recognized that the best deterrent to a nuclear first strike, whether planned or unplanned, is the capacity to hit back in unacceptable strength after such an attack.

Stabilized deterrence calls for strategic retaliatory forces that are invulnerable to sudden assault, good information about the other party's actions and the means to communicate instantly in times of crisis, and conventional forces adequate to handle local conflicts and prevent them from escalating. Much of the history of the 1960's was a history of the two major powers' understanding and acting on this doctrine.

Dangers of Proliferation. The stability of

mutual deterrence is not a particularly reassuring prospect for the future. But a dimension of the arms race posing a still greater threat is the prospect of more and more countries acquiring nuclear weapons. Although some have argued that nuclear deterrence might work between parties to other conflicts—such as Communist China and India, or Egypt and Israel—the dangers of nuclear spread are obvious. The stability of the balance between the Soviet Union and the United States was preceded by years of dangerous instability, which can also be anticipated in the early stages of other nuclear arms races. Furthermore, the number of decision-makers able to choose between peace and nuclear war will increase, as will the danger of technical accidents. Finally, moves by either of the superpowers to erect ballistic missile defenses against third-power irrationality might well destabilize the existing balance of power.

A nation's decision to acquire a nuclear capability depends both on its technical capacity to develop the bomb and on political and military incentives to take such a fateful step. Technically, there are few secrets left in bomb manufacture. The requisite raw materials are widely available. Nuclear reactor programs for peaceful use have spread, and some nations have research reactors that are not supervised by any outside source, national or international. Sophisticated delivery systems represent perhaps the greatest bar to poorer nations, but, in a pinch, a commercial airliner would make an adequate bomb carrier. Although the acquisition of a weapons capability is likely to remain very expensive, China has shown what a poor country can do with skilled manpower.

Political incentives are more important than technical considerations. Countries that could have become nuclear powers—Canada, West Germany, Japan, Sweden, Switzerland, and Italy, for example—have not done so. But India appears to have a potent incentive to offset Communist Chinese nuclear blackmail power, and Israel may see nuclear weapons as an "equalizer" against the Arab states that threaten to annihilate it. In an age of rampant nationalism, nuclear weapons may come to seem an indispensable status symbol.

Steps Toward Control. Three months after the American attack on Nagasaki, the United States, Britain, and Canada issued an "Agreed Declaration," which called for placing atomic weapons under international control. In 1946 the United States put before the United Nations the Baruch Plan, under which an international authority would own or control all atomic materials, from the mining of the ore to the finished product. The Soviet Union denounced the plan on the grounds that it would encourage espionage and permit interference in internal affairs. In all the subsequent years of negotiation on armaments the Soviet objection to outside intrusion, except within a framework of total disarmament, has proved the major stumbling block to schemes calling for unimpeded inspection.

Nevertheless, there has been some progress toward nuclear weapons control. Based on U.S. President Eisenhower's "Atoms for Peace" proposal to the United Nations in 1953, the International Atomic Energy Agency (IAEA) was established in 1957 to further the peaceful uses of atomic energy. Since 1963 the Soviet Union and the United States, as donor countries of

nuclear assistance for research and industrial reactors, have supported safeguard agreements, through the IAEA, against the diversion of nuclear resources to military purposes. The two superpowers also have refused to transfer nuclear weapons to their allies, although Soviet technical help prior to 1959 enabled Communist China to proceed toward producing the bomb and the United States has made nuclear weapons potentially available to its NATO allies under a dual-control arrangement.

The most significant advances in controlling the arms race have been in the area of collateral measures, commonly called arms control. In June 1963, as a result of bilateral negotiation, the so-called "Hot Line" agreement was signed, instituting a direct teletype communications link between Moscow and Washington. Three months later the two powers signed a limited test-ban treaty banning nuclear tests in the atmosphere, under water, and in outer space—an agreement to which an overwhelming majority of countries subsequently adhered, with the notable exceptions of two nuclear powers, France and Communist China. In October the UN General Assembly made general an agreement between the U.S. and the USSR not to place weapons of mass destruction in space. Three years later the United Nations adopted a treaty barring the orbiting of nuclear weapons and the use of the moon or other celestial bodies for clearly military activities.

Other proposals for limited nuclear control under discussion in the mid-1960's included a ban on underground nuclear tests, a safeguarded cessation of the production of fissionable materials and a freeze on the production of strategic delivery vehicles, and the establishment of regional nuclear-free zones. The key problem undoubtedly remained the prevention of the further spread of nuclear weapons capabilities.

Far-reaching control agreements were bogged down in the knotty issue of general disarmament. The 18-nation disarmament committee, meeting in Geneva since 1962, had before it two draft treaties—United States and Soviet—on general and complete disarmament. Both drafts called for the elimination (USSR) or reduction (U.S.) of nuclear delivery vehicles to be supervised by an international disarmament organization; both would outlaw all weapons test explosions; and both would prohibit transferring control or transmitting information on manufacturing to nonnuclear states.

General disarmament and intermediate steps toward nuclear weapons control depend on the climate of East-West relations. The emergence of China on the nuclear stage complicates the issue. But given the dangers inherent in a world without arms control, there is no alternative to the search for a workable agreement.

LINCOLN P. BLOOMFIELD
Massachusetts Institute of Technology

Bibliography

Beaton, Leonard, *Must the Bomb Spread?* (Baltimore 1966).

Bloomfield, Lincoln P., Clemens, Walter C., Jr., and Griffiths, Franklyn, *Khrushchev and the Arms Race: Soviet Interests in Arms Control and Disarmament, 1954–1964* (Cambridge, Mass., 1966).

Bull, Hedley, *The Control of the Arms Race*, 2d ed. (New York 1965).

Dean, Arthur H., *Test Ban and Disarmament: The Path of Negotiation* (New York 1965).

Lefever, Ernest W., ed., *Arms and Arms Control* (New York 1962).

Schelling, Thomas C., and Halperin, Morton H., *Strategy and Arms Control* (New York 1961).

ATOMIC WEIGHT, the average weight of the atoms of an element as it occurs in nature, expressed in terms of a unit equal to $\frac{1}{12}$ of the weight of an atom of carbon-12. Since an element can consist of two or more isotopes having atoms that differ in mass, the atomic weight of such an element depends on the relative proportion of its isotopes—the atomic weight of natural carbon is 12.01115 because its composition is 98.89% carbon-12 and 1.11% carbon-13. These two are the only stable isotopes of carbon.

Carbon-12 has six protons and six neutrons in its nucleus; thus the unit of atomic weight is approximately equal to the weight of one proton or one neutron. The mass number of an element is equal to the total number of neutrons and protons in its nucleus; thus it is close to its atomic weight. See ELEMENT.

ATOMISM, at'ə-miz-əm, is a philosophic doctrine that views indivisible units or entities as the ultimate reality of the physical universe. Usually these entities are conceived as material particles, and the physical universe is seen as embracing all reality.

In ancient Greek philosophy, Leucippus and Democritus, in the 5th century B.C., held that all of reality consists of an infinite number of indivisible, impenetrable, material particles moving in all directions in the void. These atoms are invisible and indestructible, differing from one another only in size and shape. Their random collision produces vortices or whirls, in which, by a sifting action, atoms of like size and shape are brought together. Innumerable worlds, and all things therein, result from such aggregation and combination. Thus all qualitative differences in things are reducible to quantitative difference and mechanical action. Soul consists of the finest and subtlest atoms. Change and variety are explicable as rearrangement of indestructible material particles. In this concept of the universe there is no need for either an ordering intelligence or a divinity.

Following its eclipse in medieval Christian thought, atomism reappeared during the period of early modern science in the mechanistic account of nature given by Pierre Gassendi in the 17th century. It also played a role in the thought of Boyle, Newton, and such Enlightenment thinkers as Diderot and d'Holbach.
MURRAY GREENE, *New School for Social Research*

ATOMS FOR PEACE PROGRAM, a formula for international cooperation in the peaceful uses of atomic energy. It involves the distribution of nuclear materials and equipment, the training of qualified persons in nuclear science and technology, research, and exchange of technical information. The plan, proposed by President Eisenhower in an address to the UN General Assembly on Dec. 8, 1953, originated as an effort to curb the nuclear arms race.

When the U.S. Congress voted into law the Atomic Energy Act of 1954, the way was opened for the United States to pursue the Atoms for Peace program. By the mid-1960's, under agreements for cooperation negotiated between the United States and other nations, the program included impressive worldwide efforts in the peaceful uses of the atom in industry, agriculture, medicine, and research.

International Organizations. The principal international organizations promoting the peaceful uses of atomic energy are the International Atomic Energy Agency (IAEA), the European Atomic Energy Community (Euratom), the European Nuclear Energy Agency (ENEA), and the Inter-American Nuclear Energy Commission (IANEC).

The IAEA, established in 1957, had 96 member nations by the mid-1960's. More than 20 of these countries had received United States nuclear materials and equipment and had agreed to the agency's safeguards against possible diversion of such equipment to military purposes. The United States had voluntarily placed four reactors under IAEA safeguards, including the Yankee Atomic Power Reactor in Rowe, Mass.

Euratom, composed of France, West Germany, Italy, Belgium, Luxembourg, and the Netherlands, was established in 1958. The United States has provided the organization with special nuclear materials and has entered into a comprehensive program for technical cooperation in the nuclear field, including a joint program to construct U.S.-designed power reactors in France, West Germany, and Italy.

Since the inauguration in 1958 of ENEA, the atomic arm of the Organization for Economic Cooperation and Development, the United States has provided information and other assistance for its activities. For example, technical personnel and heavy water were furnished to the boiling-heavy water reactor project in Halden, Norway.

The Council of the Organization of American States established IANEC in 1959 to facilitate consultation and cooperation on nuclear energy among its members. The United States has provided IANEC with technical and financial aid.

International Programs. The United States has developed over 40 major technical information exchanges with other countries. For example, it exchanges information with Canada on the development of heavy-water power reactors, and it exchanges with Australia information and personnel concerned with high-temperature gas-cooled reactor technology. Numerous reciprocal visits of scientists have taken place with the Soviet Union.

Between 1955 and 1965 over 3,000 persons from 67 countries were trained in nuclear science and technology in United States facilities. Foreign nationals participated in unclassified research in Atomic Energy Commission (AEC) laboratories. Nuclear establishments in Turkey, Korea, Colombia, Greece, Thailand, and Taiwan were assisted through arrangements with the Brookhaven (N.Y.), Argonne (Ill.), and Oak Ridge (Tenn.) national laboratories and with the Puerto Rico Nuclear Center. The United States maintained abroad nearly 80 technical atomic energy libraries that are major sources of information on nuclear science and technology. AEC exhibits in Europe, Asia, Africa, and Latin America encouraged understanding of the atom and its peaceful uses.

By the mid-1960's the United States had committed more than 100,000 kilograms of uranium-235 for civilian uses abroad, and American industry had built about 15 power reactors in other countries, totaling about 4,000 megawatts of electric power capacity. Emphasis was placed on developing dual-purpose, nuclear-power water desalting plants to help ease water shortages in many parts of the world and on utilizing nuclear power for space exploration.
GLENN T. SEABORG, *Atomic Energy Commission*

ATONAL MUSIC, ā-tōn′əl, is music organized without reference to a central keynote. When it was introduced, the concept was so revolutionary and so little understood that the music that resulted was called *atonal* (literally, "not tonal"). The adjective "atonal" and the noun derived from it ("atonality") survive in discussions of modern music, particularly in connection with the compositions of Schönberg, Berg, and Webern.

Although there were a few earlier atonal compositions, atonal music was most prominent from about 1908 to about 1921. This period began with tentative departures from tradition and ended with the emergence of the 12-tone system of composition.

Tonality. Atonality can be understood only in relation to tonality, which uses the 12 pitches of the chromatic scale. In a tonal composition one pitch is designated as primary and is called the tonic (key) of the work. Two other pitches are in harmony with the tonic, and the resulting collection is called the tonic triad or tonic chord.

The development of tonality is one of the most remarkable artistic and intellectual achievements of Western culture, and virtually every musical work composed between 1650 and 1900 uses triadic tonality. The operation of this system gives tonal music its characteristic coherence and permits a comparison of the music of one tonal composer with the music of any other tonal composer.

Although atonality represents the most extreme departure from the tonal tradition, there were other startling trends in musical composition in the 20th century. In general, however, these trends remained substantially tonal, using, for example, a centric pitch or sonority or a pervasive pattern, such as an ostinato figure (see MUSICAL ELEMENTS AND TERMS). Such procedures, exemplified in the innovational works of Claude Debussy, Igor Stravinsky, Béla Bartók, Charles Ives, and Paul Hindemith, may be called "systems of nontriadic tonality."

Atonality. Atonality occupies a central position in the history of modern music. In the mid-19th century it became apparent to some theorists, notably the Belgian composer François J. Fétis, that tonality was but one of many possible ways of organizing music. Isolated instances of experimentation with other techniques of organization occurred later in the century. Perhaps the most noteworthy of these are Franz Liszt's late piano pieces, which he composed in the five years or so preceding his death in 1886. Among these works there is even a remarkably prophetic miniature, *Bagatelle ohne Tonart* (*Bagatelle without Tonality*), but these pieces were not published until long after Liszt's death, and it cannot be claimed that they influenced musical practice.

In the decade preceding World War I a complete detachment from the traditional system took place in the work of several composers. Between 1904 and 1911 the American Charles Ives composed *A Set of Pieces for Theater or Chamber Orchestra*, a work that exhibits none of the familiar organizational characteristics of tonality. In 1908, Béla Bartók wrote *Fourteen Bagatelles for Piano* (Opus 6), which, like the Ives composition, does not depend on tonality for its structural unity. At almost the same time, the Russian Alexander Scriabin was writing equally revolutionary compositions, the best known of which is *Prometheus* (Opus 60, 1908–1910). And in Vienna, Arnold Schönberg composed the song cycle *Book of the Hanging Gardens* (Opus 15, 1908–1909). At the same time his students Anton Webern and Alban Berg began composing similarly nontraditional music.

These compositions were not experimental in any trivial sense, for the atonal works that Schönberg and his students produced up to about 1921 are among the most significant musical statements of the modern period. They include Schönberg's *Pierrot Lunaire* (Opus 21, 1912), for chamber orchestra, and *Five Orchestral Pieces* (Opus 16, 1909); Webern's *Six Pieces for Large Orchestra* (Opus 6, 1910); and Berg's opera *Wozzeck* (Opus 7, 1919).

Schönberg preferred not to use the word "atonal," and the revised edition of his book on harmony, *Harmonielehre* (1922), stressed that the new music was logical and based on an integrity of structure equivalent to that of tonality. Two observations can be made with certainty. First, atonal music is not random but exhibits regularities of pattern that can be effectively studied by applying appropriate analytic techniques. Second, atonal music should not be studied as a kind of distorted tonal music, even though it may be regarded, in a limited sense, as the precursor of 12-tone music.

The 12-Tone System. Atonality was largely superseded by the 12-tone system, known in Britain as the 12-note system and on the Continent as dodecaphony. The 12-tone system developed from compositional experiments undertaken by Schönberg, possibly as early as 1914, in preliminary studies for his incomplete oratorio *Die Jakobsleiter*. The earliest instance of this new system in a complete work is found in the waltz movement of Schönberg's *Fünf Klavierstücke* (Opus 23, 1920–1923).

From quite primitive beginnings the 12-tone system gradually evolved into a complex structure that has influenced many contemporary composers. The system may be characterized, briefly, by taking as its elements the 12 pitches of the chromatic scale. For a given work a particular ordering of these pitches, called a 12-tone set, or row, is designated as prime, and by means of certain transformations the entire composition is derived from this pattern. The term "serial music" is generally applied to works in which ordered patterns of fewer than 12 pitches are used.

When the 12-tone system first emerged, it was regarded as merely an extension of atonality. Consequently, "atonal" and "atonality" were applied indiscriminately to the early 12-tone compositions of Schönberg, Berg, and Webern. There is, however, a distinct difference between the terms "atonal" and "12-tone."

ALLEN FORTE
*Yale University; Author of
"Contemporary Tone-Structures"*

Bibliography

Austin, William W., *Music in the 20th Century* (New York 1966).
Basart, Ann P., ed., *Serial Music; A Classified Bibliography of Writings on Twelve-Tone and Electronic Music* (Berkeley, Calif., 1961).
Forte, Allen, *Contemporary Tone-Structures* (New York 1955).
Lang, Paul Henry, ed., *Problems of Modern Music* (New York 1962).
Perle, George, *Serial Composition and Atonality* (Berkeley, Calif., 1962).
Redlich, Hans F., *Alban Berg: The Man and His Music* (New York 1957).
Schönberg, Arnold, *Style and Idea* (New York 1950).

ATONEMENT, ə-tōn′mənt, is the act of effecting reconciliation ("at-one-ment") with another person or persons who have been alienated by offense or injury. It also signifies the means used to effect such a reconciliation.

In theology, atonement means reconciliation with God (or the gods) by means of sacrifice or offering. Thus in the Bible the Jewish law required that "you shall offer a bull as a sin offering for atonement" (Revised Standard Version: Exodus 29:36). Even the altar, and also the smaller altar of incense, had to be "atoned" once a year (Exodus 30:10; Leviticus 16:18). Although the sacrifice might be eaten as food, it was effective (Exodus 29:33).

The elaborate ritual of the Day of Atonement (Yom Kippur) is described in Leviticus 16. In addition to the sacrifice of a bull and a ram, two goats were presented to the Lord. On the head of one of the goats the sins of Israel were laid symbolically (but, in ancient thought, really), and it was then led into the wilderness and left to die. This meant the removal of the people's sins, because the goat bore them "to a solitary land." The necessity of such a rite is clear from the early conception of sin as pollution, which defiled the land (Leviticus 18:24–30; Deuteronomy 21:1–4; 32:43; Isaiah 47:11) and caused plagues (Numbers 8:19). Sin was conceived as an infection or corruption that could be transmitted to a group or an individual (compare Numbers 12:11), much as in the early Greek religion, where a *pharmakos* (a human or animal scapegoat) could remove or overcome it. See also Yom Kippur.

This conception was far older than the idea of sin as personal guilt deserving punishment (compare Exodus 32:30), and lies behind such a realistic conception as that in Isaiah 53:4–6, where some individual (or the people of Israel) has "borne our griefs" and "carried our sorrows," and upon whom has been meted out "the chastisement that made us whole," since "the Lord has laid on him the iniquity of us all." This passage provided the foundation for the Christian doctrine of the atonement through the death of Christ, chiefly as set forth in the teaching of St. Paul and later elaborated by church fathers and theologians.

Definition of Terms. The term "atonement" is one of several words used in theology to describe the act or process of reconciliation. It involves something done or given to effect the renewal of good relations between men and God, and since man cannot give anything really adequate or satisfactory, God Himself must provide the gift (I Peter 1:18ff.; Hebrews 9:11–15). "Reconciliation" describes the resulting restoration of good relations. "Expiation" is a quite different term, and, originally, meant what must be done to restore a broken order in the invisible world, the peace of the gods (*pax deorum*), the supernatural system of relations between gods and men. "Propitiation" meant winning back by a gift or sacrifice, especially by self-sacrifice, the favor or goodwill of an offended deity; this conception is on a lower level than the one found generally in the Bible. "Redemption" implies purchase, especially buying back someone whose life or liberty has been forfeited by sin or disobedience. It involved paying a price (Leviticus 5:18; 25:47–52).

All these terms are deeply embedded in ancient religion—Hebrew, Greek, Roman, and other —and are retained in Christian theology as expressing various aspects of the central theme of restoration to divine favor, chiefly through the death of Christ. But they are not interchangeable, and to use them as equivalent or synonymous terms leads only to confusion of thought. For example, to describe the death of Christ as the "propitiation" of an angry God is a total perversion of Christian teaching. The real depth of man's need is clear in the Bible and in all religious teaching based on it; it is also clear from modern psychoanalysis, which has distinguished levels of consciousness. Guilt, pollution or alienation, and fear are different states of mind, requiring different kinds of treatment.

Pauline Interpretation. The origin of the Christian doctrine of atonement is reflected in the New Testament, especially in Paul's letters. His teaching was based upon three sources: first, his interpretation of the Old Testament; second, the tradition of Jesus' life and teaching, death, and resurrection; and, third, the Christian experience of reconciliation with God and of the new life in Christ (compare Romans 3:25).

The early Christians lived in a world where, for countless centuries, sacrifice had been the normal expression of religious worship and devotion, and the recognized mode of reconciliation or reunion with God (or the gods). Thus it was natural for them to relate their new experience of acceptance and fellowship with God to the death of the Messiah, whom God had sent to be their Savior (I Corinthians 15:3). His death had been voluntary—He made no effort to escape it (Philippians 2:5–11)—and it had resulted in His exaltation to Lordship over the universe, at God's right hand. To be a Christian was to be "in Christ," that is, united to Him. This mystical idea underlies the whole conception of atonement ("onement"), for it means that those who are "one with Christ" have "died with Him" and "risen again" in His death and resurrection (Romans 6:3–14). Therefore, whatever the mysterious transaction that was effected on the cross (Colossians 1:20), as God's victory over Satan or the demons or the evil astral spirits—the powers that hitherto ruled the universe—it made possible the reconciliation of men to God and the imparting of a new life "in Christ" (Colossians 2:13–15). But Paul was a legalist as well as a mystic, and the language he used was often one-sided when for the moment he stressed one aspect rather than others; a fair statement of his theology requires a balance of several elements in his thought.

Christ as Ransom. Among the earliest church fathers, Christ's suffering and death were often viewed as an example of humility, patience, and obedience "even unto death." But with Irenaeus, Origen, and Tertullian, in the 2d and 3d centuries, came a theory that dominated Christian theology (at least in the West) for several hundred years, warped its symmetry, and introduced a note that completely distorted the New Testament teaching. This was the theory that Christ's death was a "ransom" paid to the devil. This theory is based on Mark 10:45, "For the Son of Man . . . came . . . to give his life as a ransom for many"; but the new exegesis added details and a general setting that amplified but distorted the meaning of the text.

From the Gnostics whom he controverted, Irenaeus had taken the view that the whole world is subject to evil (compare I John 5:19), that is, to Satan; God could redeem mankind only by tricking Satan into accepting the sacrifice of Christ on the cross under the impression that he could thereby count Him among his subjects. But Christ proved invincible, and the Victor had thereupon vanquished man's enemy and released his captives (compare Mark 3:27). Irenaeus' theory is a good example of a metaphor—or a series of metaphors—growing into a dogma.

With St. Augustine (354–430) a full-fledged, thoroughgoing, logical theory of the Atonement entered Christian theology. His whole system of doctrine centered in the idea of redemption, chiefly by the death of Christ. Man is now by nature evil as a consequence of the Fall, since Adam's sin corrupted the very nature of his descendants. (Augustine never wholly abandoned the Manichaeanism of his youth, or the Neo-Platonist antimaterialism of his middle years.) The death of Christ was the means chosen by God to counteract this tragic state that had overcome the human race, but only for those predestined to salvation, the "elect"—not for all men. The means by which the merits or benefits of Christ's death are applied to the saved are the sacraments of baptism, the Eucharist, repentance, and fasting—all in the communion of the visible church. The influence of Augustine's theology on later Christian teaching and speculation is obvious, especially among the medieval Schoolmen and the Protestant reformers.

Scholastic Explanations. The leading theologians of the early Middle Ages wrestled with Augustine's theology, and some of them definitely rejected it. St. Anselm of Canterbury would have nothing to do with the theory of a ransom to Satan (which Augustine still retained); instead, thinking in terms of contemporary feudalism, he believed that the death of Christ was the necessary reparation or "satisfaction" to God's offended (or injured) "honor"—a reparation that only God (that is, God-in-Man, Christ) could offer in the name of helpless humanity. By dying, Christ (the God-Man) earned infinite merit, which was far in excess of the injury done by man's sin and therefore effective in removing it. But the theory is a lawyer's parable, designed to illustrate and describe (not explain) the blessed results of Christ's self-sacrifice. It presupposes ideas of God, and of the transferability of guilt from one person to another, that are incompatible with the highest religion and ethics.

Another Schoolman, Peter Abelard, taught a much simpler doctrine: the voluntary death of the innocent Son of God moves the sinner to penitence, faith, love, and gratitude; that is, to reconciliation with God. "I think," said Abelard, "the purpose and cause of the Incarnation was that He [God] might thus enlighten the world with His wisdom and enkindle it with love for Himself."

The final eclectic systematization of Scholastic theology by St. Thomas Aquinas includes elements from most of the earlier speculations and theories. It clings tenaciously to Scripture, as understood by earlier fathers and theologians, and applies the newly recovered full philosophy of Aristotle (brought to the West about 1225). Thomism has since become the standard theology of the Roman Catholic Church, and has had an immense influence upon the whole Christian church, including Protestantism and even the Eastern churches. But there is no universally accepted Christian dogma on this subject.

Protestant Views. Martin Luther and John Calvin, who viewed Christ's sacrifice as a "substitute" for the death, suffering, and punishment of sinners; the Puritans; the English Evangelicals—in brief, most orthodox Protestants to this day—usually adapted or reemphasized one or another phase of the ancient classical theology of the church fathers and Schoolmen. In modern times more attention has been paid to the actual fact of reconciliation and the new relation to God thus effected, that is, to the experience of the new life in Christ, and far less to any theory of the *modus operandi* of the divine act that made this both possible and actual. The prayers and hymns of all the modern churches are filled with this theme.

FREDERICK C. GRANT
Union Theological Seminary

Bibliography
Aulen, Gustaf, *Christus Victor*, tr. by A.G. Herbert (New York 1934).
Brunner, H. Emil, *The Mediator* (New York 1947).
Denney, James, *The Death of Christ: Its Place and Interpretation in the New Testament* (London 1902).
Forsyth, Peter T., *The Work of Christ* (Naperville, Ill., 1952).
Hodgson, Leonard, *The Doctrine of the Atonement* (New York 1951).
Hughes, Thomas H., *The Atonement: Modern Theories of the Doctrine* (New York 1949).
Moberley, R.C., *Atonement and Personality* (London 1901).
Mozley, John K., *The Doctrine of the Atonement*, 6th ed. (Naperville, Ill. 1951).
Rall, Harris F., *Religion as Salvation* (New York 1953).
Rashdall, Hastings, *The Idea of Atonement in Christian Theology* (London 1919).
Thornton, Lionel S., *The Doctrine of the Atonement* (London 1937).
Taylor, Vincent, *The Atonement in New Testament Teaching*, 2d ed. (Naperville, Ill. 1954).
Turner, Henry E.W., *The Patristic Doctrine of Redemption* (London 1952).

ATONEMENT, Day of. See YOM KIPPUR.

ATP, ātēpē, is the commonly used abbreviation for *adenosine triphosphate*, a key compound in the energy-handling machinery of all living tissue. Its structure is similar to that of adenylic acid, a structural unit in many nucleic acids. This similarity in structure suggests that, in the lifeless primeval ocean of the earth, the processes that led to the formation of nucleic acids must also have led to the formation of ATP. The presence of both of these compounds represented giant steps toward life itself.

Chemistry of ATP. Adenylic acid is the combination of one phosphate group with a compound called adenosine; therefore adenylic acid may be referred to as adenosine monophosphate, or AMP. Adenosine triphosphate, or ATP, is the union of three phosphate groups with adenosine:

A phosphate group attached to a compound like adenosine is an example of a low-energy phosphate group. When such a group is hydrolyzed (hydrolysis is a chemical reaction, involving water, in which a bond is split), only 2 to 4 kilocalories of energy are liberated per mole. When a phosphate group is attached to another phosphate group (as in ATP), this is an example of a high-energy phosphate group. When this group is hydrolyzed, 5 to 10 kilocalories of energy are liberated per mole—more than two times the amount liberated when a low-energy phosphate group is hydrolyzed.

It is common to symbolize the ordinary low-energy phosphate group as $- \text{P}$, the high-energy phosphate group as $\sim \text{P}$, and the adenosine portion of the molecule as A. In that case, adenylic acid can be symbolized as $A - \text{P}$ and ATP as $A - \text{P} \sim \text{P} \sim \text{P}$.

The Role of ATP. Hydrolysis of ATP supplies the energy required for the energy-consuming processes of living tissue. For example, muscle

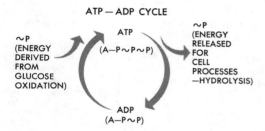

ATP — ADP CYCLE

tissue contains an enzyme called adenosine triphosphatase, which catalyzes the hydrolysis of the third phosphate group of ATP, leaving adenosine diphosphate. This is abbreviated as ADP and can be symbolized $A - \text{P} \sim \text{P}$. The energy liberated in this hydrolysis is utilized by the muscle cell when it contracts; indeed, it could not contract without the energy made available by the hydrolysis of ATP to ADP. ATP also supplies the energy that makes it possible for the nerve cell to initiate and transmit an impulse; for the kidney cell to filter the waste products out of blood; and for any cell to build complex energy-rich compounds out of simple energy-poor ones.

Renewal of ATP: The ATP-ADP Cycle. The ATP supply of the body is very small, and if there were no provision for its renewal, it would be able to support the activities of living tissue for a brief period only. But actually there is provision for its renewal.

The complex molecules of food (carbohydrates, fats, and proteins) are made up largely of carbon and hydrogen atoms. These molecules are broken down within the body, and the atoms combine with oxygen to form carbon dioxide (CO_2) and water (H_2O). In particular, the removal of hydrogen from such molecules (dehydrogenation) and their combination with oxygen liberates a great deal of energy—from 35 to 70 kilocalories per mole for every pair of hydrogen atoms removed. This is too large a quantity of energy for living tissue to use directly without enormous waste. The various energy-consuming processes of living tissue can make more efficient use of energy in smaller packets. Therefore the hydrogen atoms are removed from the food molecules through a long series of chemical reactions. In the course of these reactions, phosphate groups are added to molecules formed in the process.

These molecules then undergo changes that convert the phosphate groups into the high-energy variety. The high-energy phosphate groups formed during dehydrogenation then are capable of passing their phosphate to adenosine diphosphate (ADP) once more.

For each pair of hydrogen atoms removed from a complex food molecule, two to four molecules of ATP are formed. The large energy packets produced in the course of dehydrogenation are thus broken up into the more convenient "small change" of ATP, and it is this "small change" that all known forms of life utilize for the daily energy transactions of their tissues.

Rebuilding the Food Molecules. If ATP is expended and then rebuilt at the expense of the breakdown of food molecules, the question remains: What rebuilds those food molecules? To be sure, one of the tasks of ATP is to make it possible for organisms to build up complex molecules out of simple ones. These complex molecules would serve as food for any creature eating the organism. However, there is unavoidable waste at each stage, so that a given quantity of food brings about the formation of ATP containing less energy, which in turn brings about the formation of new food supplies containing still less energy, and so on. It takes perhaps 10 pounds of grass to make 1 pound of cattle and 10 pounds of cattle to make 1 pound of man. The food supply soon would vanish if this sort of waste were allowed to continue unchecked.

The basic renewal of food is found in green plants. These contain a substance called chlorophyll, which by absorbing the energy of visible sunlight becomes capable of breaking up water molecules (H_2O) into hydrogen and oxygen. When some of the resulting hydrogen atoms recombine with oxygen, ATP molecules may be formed. This process is called photosynthesis.

In photosynthesis, then, ATP is formed at the expense of the limitless energy of sunlight. When food molecules are formed by way of the ATP so produced, the energy of the food is indirectly derived from solar energy. Green plants thus grow at the expense of sunlight, and all animal life (including human beings) also is supported by sunlight, by way of the green plant.

See also BIOCHEMISTRY.

ISAAC ASIMOV, *Boston University Medical School*

ATRATO RIVER, ä-trä′tō, in Colombia, in the northwestern part of the country, in Chocó department. The river rises in the western Cordillera Occidental near the city of Quibdó and then flows in a northerly direction over a course of approximately 350 miles. Through its extensive delta it enters the Gulf of Urabá, a southern arm of the Gulf of Darien. The Atrato has often figured in plans for a canal linking the Atlantic and Pacific oceans.

ATREK RIVER, ä-trek′, in northeastern Iran. The name is also transliterated *Atrak*. The river rises in the Turkmen-Khurasan Mountains near Quchan and flows generally westward to its confluence with the Sumbar River. Thereafter it flows southwest to the Caspian Sea, forming part of the international boundary between Iran and the Turkmen republic of the USSR. Its mouth is on the Soviet side of the border. The river is about 300 miles (480 km) long. Its lower course is a spawning ground for sturgeon.

ATREUS, ā′trē-əs, in Greek legend, was a king of Mycenae and the son of Pelops, king of Pisa (in Elis), and Hippodamia. The curse on the houses of Atreus and his brother Thyestes is a major theme in Greek tragic literature.

After killing their half-brother Chrysippus, their father's favorite, Atreus and Thyestes fled to Mycenae. When King Eurystheus died, Atreus became king and married Aërope. The jealous Thyestes seduced Aërope and was banished by Atreus. Thyestes then persuaded Atreus' son Pleisthenes, whom he had raised, to kill his father. Atreus did not know his own son and killed him.

When Atreus learned that Thyestes had planned his death, he invited his brother to a banquet and served Thyestes the flesh of two of his sons. Thyestes cursed his brother and fled to Sicyon.

Thyestes did not know that he had a son, Aegisthus, by his daughter Pelopia. When Atreus came to Sicyon to seek Thyestes, he met and married Pelopia and ordered the infant Aegisthus exposed. Raised by shepherds, the boy later came to Mycenae and was accepted by Atreus. Thyestes was brought back to Mycenae by Atreus' sons (or grandsons) Agamemnon and Menelaus and was thrown into prison. Atreus then ordered Aegisthus to kill his father. But Thyestes recognized his son and persuaded him to kill Atreus.

ATREUS, Treasury of, ā′trē-əs, a stone construction of the Bronze Age set into a hillside in Mycenae, Greece. In reality the "treasury" is a royal tomb built about 1300 B.C. Shaped like a beehive, it is about 50 feet (15 meters) in diameter and nearly 50 feet high at the apex. The stones are laid in overlapping circular tiers crowned at the top by a single stone. Nail holes indicate that the walls were probably faced with bronze plates. The inner lintel in the long entrance consists of a single stone weighing about 120 tons. The structure was named "Treasury of Atreus" (for Mycenae's legendary king) by Pausanias, a Greek geographer of the 2d century A.D.

ATRI, ä′trē, a town in south central Italy, is in Teramo province, in the Abruzzi region. It is situated near the Adriatic Sea. The town produces flour, macaroni, terra-cotta, and licorice.

The town, known in ancient times as *Hatria Picena*, was taken by the Romans in 282 B.C. The modern town is the seat of a Roman Catholic diocese and has a cathedral, built in 1285, with 15th century frescoes and a handsome 16th century tabernacle. Population: (1961) 4,696.

ATRIPLEX, a′trə-pleks, is a genus of annual and perennial herbs and shrubs commonly found in salt deserts and along ocean shores. The genus is widely distributed. Most American forms are called *saltbushes*. Atriplex has small, green flowers. The female flowers are surrounded by two modified leaves that enlarge and fuse about the mature fruits. The leaves are located either alternately or oppositely on the plant stem. The plant often is covered with flakes or mealy scales or hairs, which are grayish in color.

The genus *Atriplex* belongs to the goosefoot family, Chenopodiaceae, of about 140 species. A common species, found in the southwestern United States, is the desert holly, *A. hymenelytra*. A few species are raised for greens, for forage crops in arid regions, or for ornamentals.

ATRIUM of the Romanesque basilica of Sant'Ambrogio in Milan is surrounded by an arcade built about 1150.

ATRIUM, ā′trē-əm, in Roman domestic architecture, the interior court surrounded on all sides by the rooms of the house. In early Christian churches, the atrium was an open rectangular court in front of the church, usually surrounded by an arcade or colonnade.

The Roman atrium evolved from the main room of the earliest Roman houses, which usually had at its center the family cooking hearth. Later houses had an opening in the roof above the cooking hearth. After the 2d century B.C., when the hearth had been moved to another room, the atrium was used to provide light to the interior of the house, and for catching rainwater, which fell into a shallow pool, called an *impluvium*, from the opening in the atrium roof, called a *compluvium*. The larger houses of Roman times had several atria, the largest serving as a reception hall, called a peristyle. The ruins at Pompeii show various forms of atria, including some that were richly paved and had ornamented ceilings.

The early Christian churches adopted the atrium concept for a kind of forecourt, or public reception area in front of the church. An arcade or colonnade surrounded the atrium, which usually had a fountain for ablutions in the center. Among the best remaining examples of these atria are those of the basilical churches of Sant'Ambrogio in Milan, and of San Clemente in Rome.

ATROPHY, a′trə-fē, is a reduction in size of an organ, tissue, or cell that previously has reached normal dimensions. It differs from hypoplasia, or aplasia, a condition in which the tissues do not reach full development. The names of many specific diseases include the term "atrophy," since their most prominent feature is a wasting of the part.

There are two types of atrophy—temporary or permanent. Temporary atrophy occurs, for example, when a limb is fractured and cannot be used for a time. Permanent atrophy occurs in such cases as infantile paralysis, injury to the nerves, and nerve degeneration caused by progressive muscular atrophy or syphilis.

Atrophy may be a result of any of several causes. The basic effect of any of these causes is usually an alteration in the metabolism of the affected region. Thus atrophy of body parts may be caused by senility, especially when there is a decrease in the blood circulation. It may also occur in the general aging process not associated with senility. Examples of this type are the decrease in size of the thymus (a gland in the throat region) and closure of the fetal structures in the heart at birth.

Atrophy may be caused by the loss of motor nerve supply to muscles, as in poliomyelitis. Atrophy also occurs when the nutrition of a particular region is reduced or cut off by prolonged pressure, as sometimes happens in tissue that is near a tumor.

Atrophied tissue is recognized readily. Atrophic skin is thinner than normal skin and often has a glazed appearance. It is more susceptible to injury, and wounds in it heal slowly. Atrophied joints show a thinning of the cartilage, and atrophic muscles waste away rapidly. X-rays of atrophic bone show a marked reduction of the internal structure.

ATROPINE, a'trō-pēn, is a poisonous white crystalline alkaloid used for many purposes in medicine. First isolated in the early 1830's, atropine is obtained from a variety of plants of the family Solanaceae, including deadly nightshade (*Atropa belladonna*), henbane (various species of *Hyoscyamus*), and jimson or Jamestown weed (*Datura stramonium*). It can also be synthesized and prepared in a variety of salts, including sulfate and hydrochloride.

Medical Uses. The medical uses of atropine are many and varied. Atropine has an inhibitory effect on the motility of the gastrointestinal tract and is used to relieve spasms, such as those associated with a peptic ulcer. It can also be used as a nasal decongestant, as an antidote for some insecticides and nerve gas, and for the dilation of the pupil of the eye (mydriasis).

Mode of Action. Atropine acts in competition with acetylcholine for receptor sites in smooth muscle, cardiac muscle, and various glandular cells. When atropine occupies the receptor sites, the normal action of acetylcholine in the transmission of nerve impulses is blocked. An inhibition or paralysis of secretory glands and smooth muscle fibers results.

Atropine Poisoning. Atropine is an extremely potent drug, and overdoses produce distinct signs of poisoning such as rapid heart rate, dilated pupils, dry mouth, and hot, dry, and flushed skin. Weakness and giddiness sometimes also occur. Respiration may become shallow, and death may follow. Treatment for an overdose includes measures to relieve the symptoms as well as the use of activated charcoal and gastric lavage.

GEORGE GRIFFENHAGEN
American Pharmaceutical Association

ATTACHMENT, ə-tach'mənt, in law, is the act of taking, apprehending, or seizing a person, his goods, or his estate by virtue of a writ, mandate, or other judicial order. It is distinguished from the process of *arrest* because an arrest lies only against the body of a person, whereas an attachment lies often against the property only or sometimes against the body and the property.

In the United States attachment may be defined as taking into the custody of the law the person or property of one already before the court, or of one whom it is sought to bring before the court; it is also a writ for this purpose. To some extent it is of the nature of a criminal process. In some states, at the beginning of an action to recover money, a plaintiff can attach the property of the defendant as a security for the payment of the judgment expected to be re-

covered; in case of recovery the property is applied in satisfaction of the judgment. But the more usual rule is that there can be no seizure of property, except in specified cases, until the rights of the parties have been settled by judgment of the court. The exceptions are chiefly in cases where the defendant is a nonresident or a fraudulent debtor, or is attempting to conceal or remove his property.

In some states, attachments are distinguished as foreign and domestic—the former issued against a nonresident having property within the jurisdiction of the state, the latter against a resident in the state; jurisdiction over the person or property is necessary for an attachment. An attachment issued under a state law not adopted by Congress, or by a rule of court, cannot be sustained in a United States court.

ATTAINDER, Bill of, ə-tān'dər, a legislative act that pronounces an individual or a specific group guilty of a crime, usually treason or a felony, without a court trial. The legislative body thus exercises the powers of a judge and jury, determining guilt and fixing punishment without the safeguards of trial procedure.

Bills of attainder usually are products of politically troubled times when "necessity" is said to render existing laws and judicial trial inadequate. In English common law, the punishment provided by a bill of attainder was the death of the person declared guilty, the forfeiture of his property, and the barring of any inheritance from him. By 1870, Parliament had abolished all such bills except that of forfeiture of property after outlawry. As used in the U.S. Constitution, the term also has been held to apply to bills involving lesser punishments.

Bills of attainder passed in the American states during and just after the Revolution led to a constitutional provision against them (Article III, section 3). This assurance of judicial process for accused persons was amplified in the Bill of Rights and later amendments.

Courts in the United States have held that some laws of the post-Civil War and post-World War II eras were unconstitutional as bills of attainder. Most such laws have required the taking of an expurgatory, or "purifying," oath. A loyalty oath provision of the Missouri constitution requiring a clergyman, before entering the ministry, to state that he never had aided the enemy during the Civil War was the first law declared invalid as a bill of attainder. This decision was made by the U.S. Supreme Court in 1886.

PETER D. WEINSTEIN
Member of the New York Bar

ATTALEA, ə-tä'lē-ə, is a group of palms of tropical America, with large, erect, featherlike leaves. It is related to the coconut. The genus *Attalea* contains about 20 species. Leaf stalks of *A. funifera* are a source of piassava fiber, used for coarse brushes and brooms, as in street-sweeping machines. Walking sticks and handles of umbrellas sometimes are made from the hard shell of the fruits (coquilla nuts); the kernal is a source of oil. *A. excelsa*, occasionally cultivated, is native to Brazil, where its fruits are used in smoking rubber. *A. cohune*, cohune palm, of Central America, sparingly grown in Florida, is now classified as *Orbignya*. It furnishes soap oil, leaves for thatching, and a beverage.

EDWIN B. MATZKE, *Columbia University*

ATTAR (1119?–?1230), àt-tär′, was a celebrated Persian poet. His full name was *Farid ud-Din Attar* (sometimes transliterated *Ferid Eddin Attar*). He was born in Nishapur and, after traveling widely in his youth, became a druggist (*attar* means druggist) there. Attar was a prolific author, his most famous work being *Language of Birds* (1184–87), an allegorical poem about the life and doctrines of the Sufis. The *Book of Counsels* is a moral treatise. His principal prose work is *Memoirs of the Saints*.

He is generally said to have been killed by the Mongols in Nishapur in 1230 but may have met his death when they captured the city in 1220.

ATTAR OF ROSES, at-ər, is a strong fragrant oil that is obtained from rose petals. It is used in making perfumes and cosmetics. The red *Rosa damascena* and the pink *Rosa centifolia* are the two chief sources for the rose oil. About 350 roses provide a pound (0.45 kg) of petals, and about 3,500 pounds (1,575 kg) of petals yield a pound (0.45 kg) of oil. To obtain the oil, the rose petals are mixed with water in a vat, and the mixture is heated until a vapor rises. The vapor is collected and cooled to form a liquid. The rose oil is then skimmed off the top of the liquid. The oil is shipped to perfume or cosmetics manufacturers in copper flasks. Bulgaria is the principal producer of attar of roses. France, Syria, and Turkey also produce it.

ATTAVANTI, àt-tä-vän′tē, **Attavante degli** (c. 1452–c. 1517), Italian miniaturist and illuminator. His full name was *Attavante di Gabriello di Vante di Francesco di Bartolo degli Attavanti*. He was born in Castelfiorentino, Tuscany.

His work is linked to that of Ghirlandajo and Leonardo, whose compositions he sometimes copied. He illuminated a number of books for such notables as King Matthias I Corvinus of Hungary and the Medici family. Attavanti's works include the *Satyricon* of Martianus Capella (now in the Biblioteca Marciana in Venice); the famous Bible he made for Lorenzo de' Medici, duke of Urbino, and the illuminated missal he executed for Matthias I Corvinus (both of which are in the Biblioteca Vaticana); and a Bible in seven volumes (in the monastery of the Jeronimos at Belém, near Lisbon, Portugal).

ATTEMPT, in criminal law, an act that is done with intent to commit a crime and that, if not prevented, would result in commission of the crime. Three elements are present in an "attempt" to commit a crime: (1) intent to commit it, (2) performance of some act toward its commission, and (3) failure to carry it out. For example, a person who reaches through an open window to steal a wallet lying on the table, but fails because the owner snatches it away from his grasp, commits an attempted theft. An assailant who fires a gun with intent to murder, but misses, commits attempted murder.

In an attempt, there must be some overt act, beyond mere preparation, that would ordinarily result in the commission of the intended crime were it not for the intervention of extraneous causes. Without criminal intent, however, no act is an "attempt," no matter how well it is adapted to an apparently criminal result.

PETER D. WEINSTEIN
Member of the New York Bar

ATTENTION, the attitude or "set" that is the major influence on perception. The importance of attention is shown by the fact that people perceive the world around them in a selective fashion. They do not "see" and "hear" everything that is within the range of their sight and hearing. A driver may say after an accident, "I never saw the other car," even though the car was in his field of vision.

Attention involves the whole body. Watching for something requires turning the head and focusing the eyes, and nerves and muscles in the rest of the body are involved as well. Psychologists have been able to detect small muscle movements and changes in blood pressure and nerve impulses in people who are apparently sitting still but are in a state of alertness. The central nervous system is, of course, involved in the process of directing attention. This fact has been demonstrated with hypnotized subjects, who can be instructed to respond to certain stimuli and ignore others.

Factors in Attention. A number of factors influence attention, but the most important is interest or motivation. This factor can be demonstrated experimentally with a device called a tachistoscope, which presents pictures for very brief intervals. When subjects are given brief views of pictures, they usually recall few details, though they may have an impression of size or color. If, however, they are told to look for certain details, they are much more successful in detecting and reporting them.

The influence of this kind of preparatory set is often illustrated in everyday life. A mother whose child is playing in the street will hear screeching brakes and tires, while a guest in the same room may not notice a thing. A student who is attentive in class usually hears and remembers more than a student whose interest is focused elsewhere. The alert student may be motivated by enthusiasm for the subject or by a desire to win the reward of a good grade. In any case, he is giving voluntary attention, and this helps him learn. In general, anything that arouses an expectant attitude makes a person attentive. See also ATTITUDE.

Although interest is basic to attention, a number of objective factors are also important in making objects and events stand out. Large size, unusual shape, bright color, and changing position are effective, and advertisers make use of these factors in signs and displays. Loud sounds can be used to attract involuntary attention.

Repetition can be used to make people attend to a message, as when advertisers repeat a television commercial or display hundreds of posters on the streets. However, there is a point of diminishing effect in repeating a stimulus. A message that is heard repeatedly over days and weeks may become monotonous; it may then move out of the focus of attention and become part of the background noise of the environment.

Novelty is useful in arousing attention. Hence teachers try to pose challenging questions, and advertisers search for fresh approaches in pictures and copy. Contrast will often compel attention. As a familiar example, a green lawn would be highly noticeable in an arid country but would not seem remarkable in England or New England. Yet interest may be the most influential factor. A salesman for lawnmowers is likely to notice every lawn he passes.

ATTERBOM, ät'tər-bŏŏm, **Per Daniel Amadeus** (1790–1855), Swedish poet and philosopher, who was a leader of the romantic movement in Sweden. Born in Åsbo, Östergötland, on Jan. 19, 1790, he studied at the University of Uppsala from 1805 to 1815 and was appointed professor of philosophy there in 1828. He died at Uppsala on July 21, 1855.

Atterbom was the founder of the Aurora League, which became the center of the romantic movement in Swedish literature. The league published a journal, *Phosphoros,* edited by Atterbom. Members of the league, known as the "fosforister," after the name of the journal, were greatly influenced by the German idealistic philosophers and by Goethe and Schiller.

Atterbom's outstanding works were two verse plays, the uncompleted *Fågel blå* (*1818; The Blue Bird*) and *Lycksalighetens ö* (1824–27; *The Isle of Bliss*), an allegory. His work was collected in 13 volumes (1854–70).

ATTERBURY, at'ər-bər-i, **Francis** (1662–1732), English Anglican bishop. He was born on March 6, 1662, at Middleton Keynes, Buckinghamshire, where his father was rector. Educated at Westminster and Christ Church, Oxford, he stayed at Christ Church as a tutor after graduation. Ordained in 1687, he gained fame as a pulpiteer and was appointed chaplain to William and Mary and preacher at Bridewell Hospital. He settled in London following his marriage to Katherine Osborn. In 1697 he published "A Letter to a Convocation Man," a strong defense of the clergy's right to parliamentary assembly. Because of the state's ascendancy in religious matters, this right had virtually been suppressed.

A brilliant orator, Atterbury led the High Church's bitter opposition to the Latitudinarians, who minimized the necessity for a system of dogma or an ecclesiastical organization. In 1713, after a succession of posts and honors, he was raised to bishop of Rochester and dean of Westminster. Swift, Newton, Addison, and especially Pope were among his friends and admirers in England's literary circles.

Initially, Atterbury had accepted the accession of George I, but his sympathies for the Stuarts' claim to the English throne led to his involvement with the Jacobites. When correspondence came to light linking him with the plot of 1722 to overthrow the Hanoverian monarchy, he was arrested. Found guilty, he was stripped of his offices and banished. He settled in France, spending his last years in study, correspondence, and service to the Pretender. He died in Paris on Feb. 22, 1732. (See also CONVOCATION; JACOBITES.)

ROBERT T. HANDY, *Union Theological Seminary*

ATTERBURY, at'ər-ber-ē, **William Wallace** (1866–1935), American railroad official, who directed transportation of American troops and matériel on French railroads in World War I. He was then vice president of the Pennsylvania Railroad. He received a brigadier general's rank and was later honored by the Allied countries for his wartime services. Previously he had helped with American logistics in the Mexican border war.

Atterbury was born on Jan. 31, 1866, in New Albany, Ind. Graduated from Yale in 1886, he became an apprentice with Pennsylvania Railroad. In 1925 he became president of the line. He died at Bryn Mawr, Pa., on Sept. 20, 1935.

ATTERSEE, ät'ər-zā, is a lake in Austria, in Upper Austria province in the Eastern Alps. It is situated in a beautiful mountain and lake region known as the Salzkammergut. The lake, also called the *Kammersee,* is about 12 miles (19 km) long and reaches a width of 2 miles (3 km) and a depth of 560 feet (170.5 meters). Its outlet is the Ager River, which drains through the Traun River into the Danube River.

Near the southern end of the lake are the summer resorts of Weissenbach (with a fish hatchery) and Unterach. At the northern end, the market town of Schörfling has an ancient ruined castle rising above it.

ATTESTATION, a-tes-tā'shən, is the verification of a legal instrument, as a will, by the signature of a person or persons to a memorandum stating that it was executed in his or their presence. The purpose of the attestation of a document is to furnish a record of the names of disinterested persons who were present at the execution of the document in order that they may later, if necessary, appear as competent witnesses to testify as to the attendant circumstances.

In many states two attesting witnesses only are required to wills devising land, but in some states three are necessary. Deeds do not require attestation in common law, but the provision has been modified largely by statute. See also WILL.

ATTICA, at'i-kə, is a *nomos* (department) of Greece. Its capital is Athens. The Greek spelling of the name is *Attiki* or *Attike*. Roughly triangular in shape, it occupies 1,303 square miles (3,375 sq km) of the easternmost promontory of central Greece. To the north is the neighboring nomos of Voiotia (Boeotia) and the large island of Evvoia (Euboea). The Aegean Sea washes the eastern coast, and the Saronic Gulf the southern coast. Attica extends as far west as the shores of the Gulf of Corinth and now includes part of Megaris, an area on the isthmus between central Greece and the Peloponnesus that in ancient times was a separate district. The island of Salamis in the Saronic Gulf is also included in the nomos.

The physical features of Attica are varied. Most of the nomos consists of small plains separated by hilly uplands and mountain ridges. The principal plains surround the cities of Athens, Eleusis, and Marathon. As in most of Greece, the soil is dry, light, thin, and calcareous, unsuitable for most agriculture other than the growing of olives and figs. Some success has been achieved, however, in the cultivation of grapes for wine. Wheat was grown in Attica in ancient times, but even then the scanty harvest compelled the importation of much grain.

Attica's natural riches lie in its mountains. In the hilly and barren southeast are the mines of Mount Lavrion, which produced vast quantities of silver in ancient times but are now worked for lead. Marble is quarried on Mount Pentelikon, northeast of Athens, and on Mount Imittos (Hymettus; famed also for its honey), a mountain ridge east of the city. Potter's clay is found in most of the hilly uplands.

Throughout Attica the mountain slopes provide excellent pasturage for sheep and goats. In antiquity the reckless cutting of timber denuded the hills. The grazing of the flocks ever since has prevented reforestation, but the country in the north is well wooded, mostly with pine.

Besides those already mentioned, the best-known mountain ridges are Kithairon and Parnis, both near the Attica-Boeotia border; Aigaleos, west of Athens; and Geraneia, on the Megaris isthmus.

The Kifisos and Ilissos rivers, both of which empty into the Saronic Gulf, form the main drainage system of Attica. They are, however, little more than mountain torrents, full only in winter or after heavy rains and almost dry in summer. About 15 inches (38 cm) of rain fall each year. The climate in Attica, tempered by the sea, is known for its mildness. Both the clarity of the Attic air and the brilliance of Athenian sunsets have been celebrated for centuries.

The leading port in Greece and the country's foremost industrial center is Piraievs (Piraeus), located on the Saronic Gulf about 5 miles (8 km) southwest of Athens, with which it forms a continuous urbanized area. Developed as the port of Athens, it has been Attica's chief seaport since the 5th century B.C. The indented southern shoreline with its fine sandy beaches provides excellent shelters for numerous small fishing craft.

History. Archaeological evidence indicates that Attica was a center of Mycenaean culture in the 1000's B.C. The story of its subsequent development is rooted in tradition and legend. According to tradition, the mythical king Cecrops divided Attica into 12 independent communities. These waged intermittent and internecine wars until Theseus, a later legendary monarch, united them into one state. By historic times (about 700 B.C.), Attica was unified under the central control of Athens, which extended its citizenship to all freemen in Attica.

From earliest times the people were divided into 4 phylae, or tribes, which were dominated by a landowning aristocracy. Cleisthenes, a member of a noble family important in Athenian politics, instituted reforms in 508 B.C., reorganizing the state on a more democratic basis. A new organization based on topography was substituted for the old based on family groups. Citizens were redistributed into 10 new phylae, each of which was composed of *demes* (local administrative communities) scattered throughout the area so that the three topographical sections of plain, hills, and coast were represented in each tribe. Since the topographical subdivision generally corresponded with the economic interests of the dwellers in each area, a broader-based democracy was achieved.

With the adoption of an aggressive foreign policy by Athens in the 5th century B.C., Attica became merely an extension of Athens and shared its subsequent political history. Population: (1961) 2,057,974.

See also ATHENS.

P.R. COLEMAN-NORTON, *Princeton University*

ATTICA, at'i-kə, a city in Indiana, is situated in Fountain County, on the Wabash River, 65 miles (104 km) northwest of Indianapolis. It lies in a farming area, the main products of which are grain, tomatoes, livestock, and poultry. Sandstone quarries are near the city. Its industrial establishments produce steel castings, bricks, cement vaults, canned foods, clothing, and electronic equipment.

White settlement began in 1827, on the site of a former Indian village. Attica was first incorporated in 1867 and was chartered as a city in 1905. Government is by mayor and council. Population: 4,262.

ATTICUS, at'i-kəs, **Titus Pomponius** (109–32 B.C.), Roman literary patron. He was born in Rome of a wealthy family, one of the most distinguished of the equites (knights). About 88 B.C., while still a young man, he moved to Athens to avoid the civil warfare between Sulla and Marius in Italy, and there lived the life of an Epicurean philosopher, devoting himself to study. His surname derives from this long residence in Attica. When peace was restored to Rome he returned there in 65 B.C., inheriting ten million sesterces from his miserly uncle, Quintus Caecilius. His house on the Quirinal became a literary gathering place.

Atticus, adhering to his policy of personal political neutrality, became and remained the friend of such diverse figures as Caesar, Pompey, Brutus, Cassius, Marcus Antonius, and Octavian, but his closest friend was Cicero, whose brother, Quintus Cicero, married Pomponia, the sister of Atticus.

Atticus wrote several works, including a history of Cicero's consulship, none of which have been preserved. In 32 B.C. he was seized with an illness he believed to be incurable, and starved himself to death. A panegyrical biography of Atticus by Cornelius Nepos survives, as well as Cicero's *Letters to Atticus.*

ATTILA (c. 406–453), at'i-lə, king of the Huns, was known to Roman Christendom as the "scourge of God" because of the devastation he wrought throughout the Roman empire. He is remembered for his savagery and his unattractive, even brutal, appearance.

The Huns, whose language belonged to the Ural-Altaic family, had swept out of Asia across central Europe in the 4th century, pushing the Ostrogoths westward toward Gaul and the Visigoths southward into the Roman empire. Subsequently, the Huns controlled a large area north of the Danube and, on several occasions, invaded Roman territory. Only by annual payments in gold was Rome able to stall further depredations.

In 433, Attila and his brother Bleda inherited the kingship of the Huns from their uncle. Attila arranged a treaty with the Romans under which the annual payment was set at 700 pounds of gold. Among other things, the Romans agreed to ransom their nationals held captive by the Huns and to return to Attila deserters from his own realm. Occupied with extending his empire north and east of the Danube, Attila did not molest the Romans until 441, when he took advantage of the absence of Roman troops engaged in Sicilian and Persian campaigns to invade the eastern part of the empire. He advanced toward Constantinople along the great Roman highway that ran through Viminacium, Margus, and Naissus (in the Balkans), but the return of the Roman troops induced him to sign a new treaty with Rome. It was more advantageous to the Huns in that it raised the tribute to more than 2,000 pounds of gold a year.

After Attila had his brother Bleda killed, he made another incursion in 447 all the way to Constantinople, which, however, he was unable to capture. Nevertheless, this time even better terms were secured from the Romans—so much better that Attila did not bear a permanent grudge when a Roman plot to assassinate him failed a year or so later.

About 450, Attila turned his attention to the West. With an army of Huns, Ostrogoths,

Gepids, Heruli, and Alans, along with some Burgundians and Franks, he invaded Gaul in 451. His most formidable opponent was the Roman general Aëtius, who also persuaded the Visigoth king Theodoric to take the field. After some maneuvering, the battle sometimes referred to as the Battle of Châlons took place, although the actual site has never been identified. Theodoric was killed, yet his side was victorious and might have inflicted further damage on Attila if Aëtius had not wished to spare the Huns for some long-range scheme of his own. Attila then invaded Italy in 452, announcing his intention to claim the emperor's sister Honoria as his bride.

Attila never reached Rome. According to tradition, he was visited in his camp by an embassy headed by Pope Leo I and was persuaded to withdraw. It was said that the apostles Peter and Paul also appeared to second the pope's recommendation. It is known that plague and famine raged in the camp of the Huns at the time. Moreover, when Roman reinforcements arrived from the East, Attila was compelled to retreat northward and leave Italy.

By 453, Attila, the "scourge of God," was dead. Perhaps he was the victim of assassination, but the most popular and romantic version of his passing was that he burst a blood vessel on the night of his marriage to Hilda, a beautiful Gothic maiden.

The great kingdom of the Huns did not survive its great king. The subject peoples revolted, and the Huns themselves weakened and dispersed. One group under the sons of Attila is reputed to have been known as the Bulgarians and to have become the founders of Bulgaria.

TOM B. JONES, *University of Minnesota*

ATTIS, at′is, in Greek legend, was a handsome shepherd of Phrygia. His name is also spelled *Atys*. He was loved by Cybele, goddess of the earth, fertility, and wild nature. Cybele discovered that Attis was in love with the daughter of the Phrygian king, and in a jealous rage she caused him to lose his senses. In this deranged state, Attis castrated himself and died. Cybele transformed Attis into a pine tree, which became her sacred tree, and she transformed his blood into violets.

The legend of Cybele and Attis is one of many versions of the death-and-rebirth motif: the pine tree represents winter or death, and the violets represent spring or rebirth. Parallel legends are those of Isis and Osiris in Egypt, Ishtar and Tammuz in Babylonia and Assyria, and Venus and Adonis in Rome.

Following the pattern of the death of Attis, men in the cult of Cybele voluntarily became eunuchs in their initiation to the priesthood. See also CYBELE.

ATTITUDE, at′ə-tōod, a predispositon to respond in a certain way to a person, object, situation, event, or idea. The response may come without conscious reflection. A person who shows a certain attitude toward something is reacting to his conception of that thing rather than to its actual state. An attitude is more enduring than a mood or whim; it produces a consistent response. For example, a man who has an unfriendly attitude toward foreigners will show dislike of most foreigners he meets or hears about.

Attitudes are closely related to opinions. A distinction can be made, however, in that a person can state his opinions in words but may not be able to express his attitudes in the same way. He will reveal his attitudes by his actions and only indirectly by the content of his statements. Attitudes are also related to prejudices. A prejudice is a rigidly fixed attitude, usually unfavorable, though a favorable prejudice is also possible. An attitude becomes a prejudice when the predisposition is so strong that no attention is paid to evidence that might call for a changed reaction. If a man says that all government employees accept graft, he is showing an attitude. If he refuses to accept proof that many government employees are honest, he has developed a prejudice.

Attitudes are formed as a result of some kind of learning experience. In some cases the experience is one single dramatic or damaging event. If, for example, a man is robbed by a member of a certain ethnic group, he may thereafter fear all members of that group. Attitudes may also be learned simply by following the example or opinion of a parent, teacher, or friend. A child may take on his parents' prejudices about politics, for example. Attitudes are often built up more slowly, however. Growing up in a happy home may contribute to a favorable attitude toward marriage. In addition to the home, important builders of attitudes are schools, churches, and media such as newspapers and television. The agencies that help form attitudes can also change attitudes, though reshaping a deep prejudice may take years of effort —or even be impossible.

The attitudes people hold can profoundly influence the way they act in personal and larger situations. For this reason psychologists and sociologists are concerned with how attitudes develop, how they affect behavior, and how they can be changed. To study attitudes, social scientists have prepared measuring scales. One form of scale requires a respondent to read a number of statements, ranging from strongly favorable to strongly unfavorable, about a topic. He then picks the statement he most fully agrees with. For example, a scale to assess attitudes about labor might include statements ranging from "All working men and women should be union members" to "All labor unions should be outlawed." Responses to a number of such items can be given a numerical score. Attitude scales in this and other forms have been designed to measure many kinds of attitudes—toward war, toward minorities, toward political figures, toward schools, and toward parents, to name a few. Scales can be applied to the same group at intervals in order to measure changes in attitude as a result of education or other influences.

ATTLEBORO, at′əl-bur-ō, is an industrial city in Massachusetts, in Bristol County, 10 miles by highway northeast of Providence, R.I. Its leading industry is the manufacture of jewelry. Other products made there are silverware, scientific instruments, machine tools, fabricated metal products, and paper goods.

Settled in 1634, the community was incorporated as a town in 1694 and was named for Attleborough in Norfolk, England. It began to manufacture jewelry in 1780. During the 19th and early 20th centuries it was also an important textile center. Attleboro received a city charter in 1914 and is governed under a mayor and council. Population: 32,907.

PICTORIAL PARADE

CLEMENT ATTLEE, photographed on his 80th birthday.

ATTLEE, at'lē, **Clement Richard** (1883–1967), British political leader, who was prime minister of Britain from 1945 to 1951. He was the leader of the British Labour party from 1935 until 1955, when he was created *1st Earl Attlee and Viscount Prestwood.*

Clement Attlee was born at Putney on Jan. 3, 1883, the seventh child of an eminent London lawyer. After graduating from Haileybury College and Oxford, he became a barrister. His politics were mildly conservative. In October 1905, Attlee visited the East End of London, then a place of stark poverty and grinding unemployment. Its impact on him was immediate and profound. He abandoned his pleasant career, and in a passion for social service that was akin to a religious conversion he went to live and work in the Limehouse slums. He remained there for nearly 20 years, interrupted only by World War I, during which he served with distinction in Gallipoli, Mesopotamia, and France, and was wounded.

After the war he returned to the East End. In 1922, on the fall of the Lloyd George coalition, the East Enders prevailed on him to run for the Limehouse seat in Parliament in the general election. He won by a big majority. In the same year he married Violet Helen Millar.

These early years provide an essential key to Attlee's character and his subsequent role. He was small in stature, modest, unassuming, and without much public glamour or oratorical skill; but he had a deep sense of public service and an unmistakable integrity that earned him the abiding loyalty of the East End. This loyalty, almost accidentally, brought him to the leadership of his party, for in the crisis election of 1931 which reduced the Parliamentary Labour party from 287 to a tiny group of only 46 members and robbed it of almost all its best-known figures, Attlee was one of the few to survive. He became deputy to the beloved veteran George Lansbury, and when Lansbury resigned in 1935, Attlee was elected leader in his place. Everyone, including himself, assumed the appointment was merely a stopgap; but when the general election of November 1935 brought back most of the better-known Labour leaders, Attlee was re-elected leader. He remained leader longer than any man in the party's history.

As leader of the Labour party, Attlee in 1942 became deputy prime minister under Winston Churchill in the wartime national government, after refusing to serve, in any circumstances, under Neville Chamberlain. Attlee was in the war cabinet longer than any man except Churchill.

When party politics resumed at the end of the war in Europe, the majority of the nation, including most of the armed services, unexpectedly turned to this quiet and essentially unassuming man in preference to Churchill. Attlee became prime minister after Labour's election victory in July 1945. Churchill fought as Conservative leader, but reaction against Conservative rule, particularly of the prewar period, was strong. On the other hand Attlee's calm, logical assessment of postwar problems proved to have a powerful appeal.

Although it was against Attlee's nature to play a buoyant role as a national leader, he proved a firm and decisive master of his cabinet. His qualities as prime minister were those of an administrator of ideas rather than a creative thinker. He lacked his predecessor's imagination and also his ability to communicate to a mass public a sense of participation in history. In the end his government, which was inevitably caught up in serious postwar economic shortages and had to deal with the transitions required by Britain's altered position in the world, suffered in popularity. But within its range, Attlee's vision was clear, precise, and orderly, informed by a deep moral purpose, but practical and realistic and salted with an agreeable wit. He never lacked the courage to do what he thought was right, however unpopular. He was quick to perceive the danger of a Russian advance in Europe after the war and, at considerable national sacrifice, put Britain's remaining power in its way. In his dealing with Indian independence and his conception of Britain's future role in relation to her old colonial empire, he displayed great qualities of imaginative statesmanship.

Possibly Attlee's greatest contribution to the political life of his own country was that, essentially moderate and pragmatic in his socialism, he enabled Britain to carry through a postwar economic and social revolution without a breakdown in basic national unity.

Attlee was the author of *The Social Worker* (1924), *The Will and the Way to Socialism* (1935), *The Labour Party in Perspective* (1937), *Purpose and Policy: Selected Speeches by C.R. Attlee* (1946), *The Labour Party in Perspective and Twelve Years Later* (1949), *As It Happened* (1954), and *A Prime Minister Remembers,* with Lord Francis-Williams (1962). Attlee died in London on Oct. 8, 1967.

LORD FRANCIS-WILLIAMS OF ABINGER
Author of "The Rise of the Labour Party"

Further Reading: Jenkins, Roy, *Mr. Attlee: An Interim Biography* (London and New York 1948).

ATTORNEY, Power of, ə-tûr'nē, a written authorization to another person to perform specified acts. The person thus designated as agent is called an "attorney in fact," as distinguished from an "attorney at law." In general, any person having legal capacity to appoint an agent can execute a power of attorney. In the absence of an express statutory requirement, the instrument need not be recorded or acknowledged. A power of attorney, except when coupled with an interest, may be revoked by the principal at any time, and is terminated by death of either party.

RICHARD L. HIRSHBERG, *Attorney at Law*

ATTORNEY GENERAL, ə-tûr′nē jen′rəl, the chief legal officer of a government. His principal duties are to advise the executive branch of the government on questions of law, to represent the government in legal controversies to which it is a party, to appear personally in the courts in important cases, to supervise the prosecution of criminal cases, and to institute legal proceedings in matters affecting the welfare of the people or of the state at large.

United States. The attorney general of the United States is a member of the cabinet, appointed by the president with the advice and consent of the Senate. As the chief legal officer of the federal government, he renders legal opinions to the president of the United States and to the heads of the executive departments of the government; supervises the administration of the Department of Justice; directs special matters relating to national defense; directs the federal penitentiaries and other penal institutions; supervises the work of the United States attorneys and their assistants and the United States marshals and deputy marshals; approves abstracts of title for lands acquired by the government for various civil and military uses; supervises all civil and criminal litigation to which the government is a party; represents the United States in legal matters generally; appears in the Supreme Court of the United States in matters of exceptional importance; and provides special counsel for the United States in cases where such action is required. The published opinions of the attorney general, although not having the force of law, are recognized as providing authoritative guidance on the subjects covered.

The post of attorney general was created by the Judiciary Act of 1789. In 1870, Congress passed a law establishing the Department of Justice, in recognition of the great expansion of the office of the attorney general during the years since its creation. This enactment made the attorney general the head of the newly established department, provided for a solicitor general and two assistant attorneys general, gave to the attorney general the direction and control of United States attorneys and all other counsel employed on behalf of the United States, and vested in him supervisory powers over the accounts of district attorneys, marshals, clerks, and other officers of the federal courts. In 1871 Congress began the long series of enactments providing for the control and supervision of federal prisons and prisoners by the attorney general. The Federal Bureau of Investigation, established in 1908, developed from a force of examiners at first hired by the attorney general from other departments.

The attorney general exercises most of his functions through the Department of Justice, which he heads. His chief aides are the deputy attorney general, the executive assistant to the attorney general, the solicitor general, nine assistant attorneys general, the directors of the Federal Bureau of Investigation and the Bureau of Prisons, the associate commissioner of federal prison industries, the pardon attorney, the commissioner of immigration and naturalization, the chairmen of the Board of Immigration Appeals and of the Board of Parole, and the director of public information. The attorney general also supervises all United States attorneys and marshals, as well as the field office personnel of the Federal Bureau of Prisons and of the Immigration and Naturalization Service.

The deputy attorney general, who is the second-ranking official of the Department of Justice, assists the attorney general in the overall supervision and direction of the department, maintains liaison between the department and Congress, and handles legislative proposals prepared in the department or referred to it for its views. He performs all the duties of the attorney general in his absence or in the event of a vacancy in the office. The solicitor general is directly in charge

ATTORNEYS GENERAL OF THE UNITED STATES

Name	Term of service	Presidents under whom served
Edmund Randolph	1789–1794	Washington
William Bradford	1794–1795	Washington
Charles Lee	1795–1801	Washington, J. Adams
Levi Lincoln	1801–1804	Jefferson
Robert Smith	1805	Jefferson
John Breckenridge	1805–1806	Jefferson
Caesar A. Rodney	1807–1811	Jefferson, Madison
William Pinkney	1811–1814	Madison
Richard Rush	1814–1817	Madison, Monroe
William Wirt	1817–1829	Monroe, J.Q. Adams
John McP. Berrien	1829–1831	Jackson
Roger B. Taney	1831–1833	Jackson
Benjamin F. Butler	1833–1838	Jackson, Van Buren
Felix Grundy	1838–1840	Van Buren
Henry D. Gilpin	1840–1841	Van Buren
John J. Crittenden	1841	W.H. Harrison, Tyler
Hugh S. Legaré	1841–1843	Tyler
John Nelson	1843–1845	Tyler
John Y. Mason	1845–1846	Polk
Nathan Clifford	1846–1848	Polk
Isaac Toucey	1848–1849	Polk
Reverdy Johnson	1849–1850	Taylor
John J. Crittenden	1850–1853	Filmore
Caleb Cushing	1853–1857	Pierce
Jeremiah S. Black	1857–1860	Buchanan
Edwin M. Stanton	1860–1861	Buchanan
Edward Bates	1861–1864	Lincoln
James Speed	1864–1866	Lincoln, A. Johnson
J. Hubley Ashton	1866	A. Johnson
Henry Stanbery	1866–1868	A. Johnson
Orville H. Browning	1868	A. Johnson
William M. Evarts	1868–1869	A. Johnson
Ebenezer R. Hoar	1869–1870	Grant
Amos T. Akerman	1870–1871	Grant
George H. Williams	1871–1875	Grant
Edwards Pierrepont	1875–1876	Grant
Alphonso Taft	1876–1877	Grant
Charles Devens	1877–1881	Hayes
Wayne MacVeagh	1881	Garfield
Samuel F. Phillips	1881–1882	Arthur
Benjamin H. Brewster	1882–1885	Arthur
Augustus H. Garland	1885–1889	Cleveland
William H.H. Miller	1889–1893	B. Harrison
Richard Olney	1893–1895	Cleveland
Judson Harmon	1895–1897	Cleveland
Joseph McKenna	1897–1898	McKinley
John K. Richards	1898	McKinley
John W. Griggs	1898–1901	McKinley
John K. Richards	1901	McKinley
Philander C. Knox	1901–1904	McKinley, T. Roosevelt
William H. Moody	1904–1906	T. Roosevelt
Charles J. Bonaparte	1906–1909	T. Roosevelt
George W. Wickersham	1909–1913	Taft
James C. McReynolds	1913–1914	Wilson
Thomas W. Gregory	1914–1919	Wilson
A. Mitchell Palmer	1919–1921	Wilson
Harry M. Daugherty	1921–1924	Harding, Coolidge
Harlan F. Stone	1924–1925	Coolidge
James M. Beck	1925	Coolidge
John G. Sargent	1925–1929	Coolidge
William D. Mitchell	1929–1933	Hoover
Homer S. Cummings	1933–1939	F.D. Roosevelt
Frank Murphy	1939–1940	F.D. Roosevelt
Robert H. Jackson	1940–1941	F.D. Roosevelt
Francis Biddle	1941–1945	F.D. Roosevelt
Thomas C. Clark	1945–1949	Truman
J. Howard McGrath	1949–1952	Truman
James P. McGranery	1952–1953	Truman
Herbert Brownell, Jr.	1953–1957	Eisenhower
William P. Rogers	1957–1961	Eisenhower
Robert F. Kennedy	1961–1964	Kennedy, L. Johnson
Nicholas deB. Katzenbach	1964–1967	L. Johnson
Ramsey Clark	1967–1969	L. Johnson
John N. Mitchell	1969–1972	Nixon
Richard Kleindienst	1972–1973	Nixon
Elliot L. Richardson	1973–	Nixon

of all government litigation in the Supreme Court of the United States. He supervises the preparation of briefs and the presentation of oral arguments, and appears in person or is represented by members of his staff in court. The chief divisions of the department, each headed by an assistant attorney general, are the Criminal Division, Antitrust Division, Tax Division, Lands Division, Civil Division, Civil Rights Division, Internal Security Division, and the Office of Legal Counsel. In addition to these eight assistants, an administrative assistant attorney general is responsible for management, fiscal, and personnel matters in the department.

The duties of the attorneys general of the individual states vary according to the statutory provisions establishing the office. Most of the statutes are more or less declaratory of the common law, and it is usually held that the attorney general, in addition to the powers expressly conferred by the legislature, has all the common law powers and duties pertaining to the office. He represents the state in all litigation of a public character, and can participate in private litigation that has a bearing on the interests of the general public or affects its welfare. He also gives legal advice to the chief executive and heads of departments on questions arising from their official duties. Among particular proceedings that can be instituted by a state attorney general are actions to abate public nuisances, to enforce charitable trusts, and to recover public offices from those who wrongfully assume to be their lawful occupants.

Canada. The attorney general of the Dominion of Canada is the chief legal adviser of the government and a cabinet minister. Bearing also the title of minister of justice, he is the head of the Department of Justice. His principal assistant is the solicitor general. The attorney general appears on behalf of the government in important cases in the courts, has general responsibility for the courts and their employees, and supervises the Royal Canadian Mounted Police. The enforcement of criminal law is usually left to provincial officials; consequently, the federal attorney general confines his work in this field to supervision, the exercise of the royal prerogative of mercy, and the administration of penitentiaries.

The attorney general of Canada has an additional special function, arising out of the negative legislative attorney that the federal cabinet possesses in the provincial field. Any act of any provincial legislature may be rendered void by an order-in-council passed by the cabinet within one year after the receipt of such act by the federal government. This power of veto, or "disallowance," generally invoked only where provincial legislation is illegal or unconstitutional, where it conflicts with federal legislation on the same subject, or where it adversely affects national interests, is exercised by the cabinet upon the recommendation of the attorney general.

Britain. The office of attorney general in England began to assume its modern shape only during the 16th century, and did not substantially attain it until the end of the 17th century. By that time, the attorney general and the solicitor general had become legal advisers of the crown and, either in person or by their deputies, appeared on behalf of the crown in the courts. They gave legal advice to all departments of the state and appeared for them in court cases. They were from time to time summoned to appear before the House of Lords to give advice. Either the attorney general or the solicitor general was always a member of the House of Commons. They came to be regarded as the leaders and representatives of the bar, and as their position became increasingly important they were made members of the ministry.

In modern times, the attorney general is the chief legal officer of the crown, and is a member of the ministry and sometimes of the cabinet. The office is conferred by patent and is held at the pleasure of the crown. The attorney general is assisted by the solicitor general, also a member of the ministry, but not of the cabinet, upon whom his duties devolve during his absence or incapacity. The crown is represented by separate law officers for Scotland, Northern Ireland, Lancaster, and Durham.

The attorney general is the head of the bar, represents the crown in the courts in all matters in which rights of a public character come into question, and is the legal adviser to all public departments. He is responsible for the conduct of all suits, civil or criminal, in which the crown is interested, and has general supervisory powers in connection with the administration of the criminal law. He advises the crown on peerage cases, and acts as prosecutor both for the House of Lords and for the House of Commons. Where the institution of an action is necessary to enforce the execution of a charitable trust, to remedy any abuse or misapplication of charitable funds, or to administer a charity, the attorney general is the proper plaintiff, acting either on the initiative of the crown or at the request of a private individual, called a "relator."

RICHARD L. HIRSHBERG, *Attorney at Law*

Further Reading: Clokie, Hugh M., *Canadian Government and Politics*, 2d ed. (New York 1945); Deener, David R., *United States Attorneys General and International Law* (New York 1957); Holdsworth, William S., *History of English Law*, vol. 6, chap. 8 (London 1927); Schwartz, David, and Jacoby, Sidney B., *Government Litigation, Cases and Notes* (Fairfax, Va., 1963).

ATTRACTIVE NUISANCE DOCTRINE, ə-trak′tiv noō′səns, in law, a principle defining the legal responsibility of anyone who maintains on his property something of potential danger to children that, by its nature, will attract them. This may be an object, a condition, or any agency that is dangerous because young children are not able to discern and recognize peril. An example would be an unprotected backyard swimming pool or a scaffold left unsafe and unprotected on a construction site. The owner of premises must take precautions against injury from any attraction that can induce children to play on the site.

ATTU, a′tōō, is the westernmost of the Aleutian Islands in Alaska. The island, rugged and almost barren, is 30 miles (48 km) long and 8 to 15 miles (13 to 24 km) wide.

During World War II, the Japanese seized Attu in June 1942, but the United States recaptured it a year later. The few Aleuts who lived on Attu before the war were fishermen and fur traders. In the late 1960's there was no permanent population. See also ALEUTIAN ISLANDS.

ATTUCKS, at′əks, **Crispus** (c.1723–1770), American patriot. Attucks, "6 feet 2 inches high, short curl'd hair, his knees nearer together than common," ran away from his master in Framingham, Mass., on Sept. 30, 1750. He was then "about 27 Years of Age," according to the advertisement that ran in the Boston *Gazette* offering £10 for his recapture. Twenty years later, toughened by a life at sea and now concerned for the freedom and dignity of his country as he had once been concerned for his personal freedom and dignity, Crispus Attucks became the first hero of the American Revolution.

On the morning of March 5, 1770, what was to be the Boston Massacre (q.v.) began with a small band of courageous Americans confronting a detachment of British redcoats in Boston's King Street. At issue were the excessive taxes required of the colonists and the humiliation of having to support the royal troops garrisoned among them to enforce collection. The redcoats fired on the men who stood in their way, and Attucks, the ex-slave who stood in the vanguard, was the first American to be killed. All told, five men died in the massacre. They were buried in a common grave.

The Crispus Attucks Monument dedicated to their memory stands on the Boston Common.

C. ERIC LINCOLN
Union Theological Seminary, New York

ATWATER, at'wô-tər, **Caleb** (1778–1867), American pioneer and author. He was born in North Adams, Mass., on Dec. 25, 1778. He graduated from Williams College in 1804 and moved to New York City to study for the ministry, but he soon gave up this calling in favor of law. After a business catastrophe he decided to go west. In 1815 he settled with his family in Circleville, Ohio, where he remained until his death on March 13, 1867.

In Ohio, Atwater devoted himself to the improvements within the state, including the development of a system of public education, and in his spare moments, to the history and antiquities of the region. In 1822 he ran for Congress, but was defeated. As one of three commissioners appointed by President Andrew Jackson to negotiate with the Indians near Prairie du Chien, Wis., in 1829, he successfully concluded the treaties and delivered them to Washington, where they were ratified by the United States Senate.

Atwater was deeply concerned with the social problems of the expanding Middle West. He founded the school system and wrote the first history of Ohio, and was among the first to call attention to the need for forest conservation. His writings include *The Writings of Caleb Atwater* (1833); *A History of the State of Ohio, Natural and Civil* (1838); and *An Essay on Education* (1841).

ATWATER, at'wô-tər, a city in California, is in Merced County, in the San Joaquin Valley, 60 miles (97 km) northwest of Fresno by road. It is a trading and shipping center for an irrigated farming area noted for its sweet potatoes, peaches, and melons. The city has food processing industries. Castle Air Force Base (formerly Merced Field) lies just northeast. Atwater was settled in 1872 and was incorporated in 1922. It has the mayor-council form of government. Population: 11,640.

ATWOOD, at'wŏŏd, **George** (1746–1807), English mathematician and physicist who invented *Atwood's machine*. He was born in London.

After graduating from Trinity College, Cambridge, he became a fellow and tutor there. He left Cambridge in 1784 and obtained a position in the customs service through the aid of William Pitt.

In *A Treatise on the Rectilinear Motion and Rotation of Bodies* (1784), Atwood describes a mechanical apparatus (Atwood's machine) that he invented to illustrate the principles governing the motion of falling bodies. His other works include *Analysis of a Course of Lectures on the Principles of Natural Philosophy* (1784), *Dissertation on the Construction and Properties of Arches* (1801), and several treatises on mathematics.

Atwood was elected to the Royal Society in 1776. He died in London on July 11, 1807.

AUBE, ōb, a department in France southeast of Paris, was formed in 1790 out of the southern part of Champagne and a small part of Burgundy. Because of the chalky soil the northern and northwestern districts are almost barren. The southern districts are much more fertile, and it is here that the chief agricultural products, grain and grapes, are raised. The capital, Troyes, is the center of hosiery manufacturing, the only important industry in the department. The area is 2,327 square miles (6,027 sq km). Population: (1962) 255,099.

AUBER, ō-bâr', **Daniel François Esprit** (1782–1871), French composer, who is regarded as the founder of French grand opera. The son of a violinist, he was born in Caen, Normandy, on Jan. 29, 1782. His first compositions, including a violin concerto, attracted the attention of Luigi Cherubini, who accepted him as a pupil. Auber's first publicly performed operas, *Le séjour militaire* (1813) and *Le testament et les billets doux* (1819), met with unfavorable receptions, but when his comic opera *La bergère châtelaine* was produced in 1820, he became a popular composer. Auber was named to the French Academy in 1829. In 1842 he succeeded Cherubini as director of the Paris Conservatory and was appointed court chapel master to Napoleon III in 1857. Auber died in Paris on May 13, 1871.

Auber wrote some 40 operas, many of them in collaboration with the librettist Augustin Eugène Scribe. His operas frequently had their premieres at the Opéra-Comique, where the composer was famous for never having attended a single performance of his work. It is claimed that he said, "If I had attended even one of my works, I would never have written another note of music." His operas include *La muette de Portici* (1828), his most serious opera; *Fra Diavolo* (1830); *Le philtre* (1831); *Le serment* (1832); *Gustave III* (1833); *Le cheval de bronze* (1835); *Le domino noir* (1837); *Le lac des fées* (1839); *Les diamants de la Couronne* (1841); *La part du diable* (1843); *Haydée* (1847); *L'enfant prodigue* (1850); *Marco Spada* (1852); *Jenny Bell* (1855); *Manon Lescaut* (1856); *La Circassienne* (1861); and *Rêves d'amour* (1869).

AUBERT DE GASPÉ, ō-bâr' də gàs'pā, **Philippe Joseph** (1786–1871), Canadian lawyer and author, whose only novel, *Les anciens canadiens*, became a classic of French-Canadian literature. He was born in Quebec on Oct. 30, 1786, to a family that had migrated from France in 1665. He attended the Quebec seminary, studied law, and was admitted to bar in 1813, and in 1816 became high sheriff of the Quebec district. Following bankruptcy and imprisonment for debt (1834–1841), he spent the rest of his life in seclusion at the family manor at St.-Jean-Port-Joli. He died there on Jan. 29, 1871.

Les anciens canadiens (1863; Eng. tr., *The Canadians of Old*, 1864, 1890) is a historical romance based on the burning by British troops of the St.-Jean-Port-Joli manor house during the Seven Years' War. Its digressions on society and folk traditions make the novel a prime source of social customs of late 18th century Quebec. In 1866, Aubert de Gaspé published *Mémoires*, a collection of legends and stories of historical interest that had been excluded from the novel.

GORDON ELLIOTT, *Simon Fraser University*

AUBIGNÉ, ō-bē-nyā', **Agrippa d'** (1552–1630), French poet and Huguenot soldier, who wrote some of the best examples of French baroque poetry. His full name was *Théodore Agrippa d'Aubigné*. Born near Pons in Saintonge, on Feb. 8, 1552, he received a good education and traveled widely during his youth. An ardent Protestant, he joined the Huguenot forces at the age of 16 and fought under Henry of Navarre, who later became King Henry IV. After Henry renounced Protestantism in 1593, Aubigné retired to his estate, but in 1620 he was condemned to death for his continuing hostility to the Roman Catholic Church. He fled to Geneva, where he died on April 29, 1630.

Aubigné's best-known work is *Les tragiques,* a long poem in seven cantos, published in 1616. Basically a poem of praise to God and a statement of faith in the ultimate triumph of the Huguenot cause, the work encompasses many subjects, including natural science and military tactics. The tone of the poem varies from sharp satire to religious ecstasy. Aubigné's youthful love poems, published as *Le printemps* in 1874, are also prized for their vital and original baroque style. Among his other works are *Histoire universelle* (1616), a history of the Huguenots, and several satirical and polemical works in defense of Protestantism.

Further Reading: Buffum, Imbrie, *Agrippa d'Aubigné's "Les tragiques": A Study of the Baroque Style in Poetry* (New Haven 1951); Sauerwein, Henry A., *Agrippa d'Aubigné's "Les tragiques"* (Baltimore 1953).

AUBREY, ô'brē, **John** (1626–1697), English author and antiquarian, whose *Brief Lives* of eminent 16th and 17th century Englishmen is a classic among biographical writings. Born at Easton Pierse (or Percy), Wiltshire, on March 12, 1626, Aubrey was a student for a short time at Oxford (1642); he later studied law in London but never became a lawyer. Inspired by Sir William Dugdale's topographical history, *Antiquities of Warwickshire* (1656), he began his own study of the antiquities of England. From 1655 to 1673, Aubrey collected materials for Dugdale's *Monasticon Anglicanum,* and in 1663 he was made a fellow of the Royal Society. Having dissipated his family fortune by 1670, he was mainly supported thereafter by his friends, though in 1671 a royal commission aided him in making antiquarian surveys. He died at Oxford in June 1697.

The only book by Aubrey published during his lifetime was *Miscellanies* (1696), a collection of ghost stories, dreams, and other occult subjects. His best-known work was published in 1813 under the title *Minutes of Lives,* though

modern editions are usually titled *Brief Lives.* The work is a collection of biographical sketches, and it is noted for its lively style, colorful anecdotes, and historical details. *Brief Lives* includes biographies of Francis Bacon, John Milton, Thomas Hobbes, and Sir Walter Raleigh. Aubrey's most important antiquarian study, *The Natural History of Wiltshire,* was published in 1847.

Further Reading: Aubrey, John, *Brief Lives. Chiefly of Contemporaries, Set Down Between the Years 1669–1696* (Ann Arbor, Mich., 1957); Powell, Anthony, *John Aubrey and His Friends* (New York 1964).

AUBURN, ô'bərn, the home of Auburn University, is a city in eastern Alabama, 50 miles by road northeast of Montgomery. Though primarily a university town, it is also a trading center for a lumbering and cotton-farming district in Lee County. Auburn was settled in 1836 and adopted city manager government in 1958. Population: 22,767.

AUBURN, ô'bərn, a city in northern California, is the seat of Placer County. It is on the American River, 30 miles (48 km) by road northeast of Sacramento. It was founded in 1848 by prospectors who discovered gold there while on their way to the original California gold strike at nearby Sutter's Mill. Their settlement, called *Wood's Dry Diggings,* was renamed the next year by prospectors from Auburn, N.Y. Many buildings of the early 1850's survive in the "Old Town" section. In the 1880's, after the gold rush was over, fruit trees were planted on the hillsides around the town, and fruit-growing is now the mainstay of Auburn's economy. Stockraising and lumbering also are carried on. Auburn adopted city manager government in 1957. Population: 6,570.

AUBURN, ô'bərn, a city in northeastern Indiana, is on Cedar Creek, 15 miles (24.1 km) by road north of Fort Wayne. It is the seat of De Kalb County. Located in an industrial and farming area, Auburn manufactures automotive parts, rubber products, foundry and metal products, stokers, oil burners, calendars, and greeting cards. It was settled in 1837, and was incorporated as a city in 1900. Auburn pioneered in the development of the automobile industry in the United States. It was the home of the Auburn Automobile Company, established in 1902 and disbanded in 1933. The city has a mayor-council form of government. Population: 7,337.

AUBURN, ô'bərn, in southwestern Maine, is an industrial city 30 miles (48 km) north of Portland. It is the seat of Androscoggin County. Auburn is situated on the west bank of the Androscoggin River opposite the city of Lewiston. Auburn and Lewiston are called the Twin Cities.

Auburn is a major shoe-manufacturing center. The shoe industry was begun there in 1835. Other manufactures include shoe dies, paper shoe linings, glass fabrics and rubberized rayon cloth, bakery products, livestock and poultry feeds, concrete, and brick. An airport at Lewiston provides commercial service.

The site of Auburn was occupied by the Anasagunticook Indians before it was settled by whites about 1786. Auburn was incorporated as a town in 1854 and as a city in 1869. It was the first city in Maine to adopt a city manager form of government (1917). Population: 24,151.

AUBURN, ô′bərn, a town in Massachusetts, is located in Worcester County, five miles (8 km) southwest of the city of Worcester, of which it is a residential suburb. The community has the town meeting form of government.

Settled in 1714, the town was incorporated under the name of *Ward* in 1778 and under its present name in 1837. Robert Hutchings Goddard, pioneer in modern rocketry, fired the first liquid-fuel rocket at Auburn in 1926. Population: 15,347.

AUBURN, ô′bərn, a city in New York, is the seat of Cayuga County. It is situated about 25 miles (40.2 km) southwest of Syracuse on the north outlet of Owasco Lake, one of the Finger Lakes. Auburn is the business and industrial center of a fertile agricultural region. Among its most important manufactures are diesel locomotives, electrical rectifiers, air-conditioners, rope, and plastics.

The city is famous in penal circles as the home of Auburn state prison, which was erected in 1817, and as the birthplace of Thomas Mott Osborne, well-known American prison reformer. Other noted residents of Auburn have included William H. Seward, Abraham Lincoln's secretary of state, who was instrumental in the purchase of Alaska from Russia in 1867; Harriet Tubman, a slave who escaped to the North in 1849 and helped other slaves to freedom; Logan, a famous Indian chief; and Enos Throop, governor of New York in 1830–1832. Among the city's places of interest are the 19th century houses of Seward and Harriet Tubman, the monument to Logan in historic Fort Hill Cemetery, Auburn Community College, Cayuga Museum, and the Seymour Library.

The city is the home of Auburn Theological Seminary, which since 1939 has been associated with the Union Theological Seminary of New York.

Auburn was founded in 1793 by John Hardenbergh, a surveyor and army captain in the American Revolution. It became the county seat in 1805 and was chartered in 1848. Government is by city manager, mayor, and council. Population: 34,599.

NORBERT BERNSTEIN, *Seymour Library*

AUBURN, ô′bərn, a city in northwestern Washington, is in King County, 15 miles by road northeast of Tacoma. It is a railroad division point and service center. It is governed by a mayor and council. Founded in 1887, Auburn was named *Slaughter* for a hero of the Indian wars. Its present name, adopted in 1893, is derived from Oliver Goldsmith's line: "Sweet Auburn! loveliest village of the plain." Population: 21,817.

AUBURN UNIVERSITY, ô′bərn, is a state-controlled, land-grant, coeducational institution in Auburn, Ala. It was founded in 1857 by the Methodist church as the East Alabama Male College, and was reorganized in 1872 as the Alabama Agricultural and Mechanical College. Twenty years later it became the first school of higher education in Alabama to admit women on an equal basis with men. In 1899 it was again reorganized, as the Alabama Polytechnic Institute, and in 1960 it was renamed Auburn University.

Auburn has schools of agriculture, chemistry, engineering, science and literature, pharmacy, veterinary medicine, architecture and the arts, education, and home economics. It also has schools of military, naval, and air science and tactics.

Studies leading to the master's degree are offered in most areas. Doctoral studies are offered in agriculture, biology, entomology, zoology, chemistry, mathematics, education, English, and electrical and mechanical engineering.

The university library of about 350,000 volumes includes special collections of early Americana and Alabama history. It also serves as a depository of Atomic Energy Commission papers. Enrollment, which reached 4,000 in 1940, rose steadily to about 10,000 by the mid-1960's.

AUBURNDALE, ô′bərn-dāl, is a city in central Florida, in Polk County. It lies 40 miles by road east of Tampa, and is situated on Ariana Lake. The processing and packing of citrus products is the main industry. Auburndale was incorporated in 1884 and adopted city manager government in 1949. Population: 5,386.

AUBUSSON, ō-bü-sôɴ′, **Pierre d'** (1423–1503), French Crusader and grand master of the Order of St. John of Jerusalem. He was born in 1423, and as a boy he fought under Duke Albert of Austria against the Turks in Hungary.

After campaigning for Austria during its war with Switzerland in 1444, Pierre d'Aubusson went to the island of Rhodes and became a knight of the Order of St. John of Jerusalem. At Rhodes he distinguished himself in fighting the Saracens, and in 1476 he was elected grand master of the order. Four years later he successfully defended Rhodes against a Turkish attack under the command of Mohammed II.

In 1489, Pope Innocent VIII made him a cardinal, not only as a reward for his military feats, but also in recognition of his efforts to organize a league of Christian nations against the Turks. He died in 1503.

AUBUSSON, ō-bü-sôɴ′, is a town in central France, 58 miles northwest of Clermont-Ferrand, in the department of Creuse, on the Creuse River. It is noted for the manufacture of fine tapestries and carpets. A school of decorative arts helps to maintain the artistic standards of the industry. Population: (1962) 5,595.

Aubusson Tapestries. According to a local tradition, the Saracens made tapestries here as early as the 700's A.D. It is more probable, however, that the craft began when nobles of the region brought in Flemish weavers during the Middle Ages to make hangings for the walls of their castles.

King Henry IV (reigned 1572–1610) permitted Aubusson carpets to enter Paris duty free, but it is only from the reign of Henry's son, Louis XIII, that an exact account of them can be traced. In 1655 they were given the right to be called "Royal Manufacture," but in 1685, with the revocation of the Edict of Nantes, the Protestant weavers left the city, and the industry suffered a blow from which it did not recover until the 18th century.

During the reign of Louis XV the painter Jean Dumont and a skilled dyer, Fimazeau, began making beautiful tapestries from designs by Jean Baptiste Oudry based on animals, the chase, and the fables of Jean de La Fontaine. Consequently, Aubusson regained its prestige. In the 17th and 18th centuries its fabrics were known as "Auvergne tapestry." See also TAPESTRY.

AUCASSIN AND NICOLETTE, ō-cà-saɴ', nē-kō-let', is a 13th century French romantic narrative by an unknown author. It tells the love story of Aucassin, son of a lord of Provence, and Nicolette, captive daughter of a Saracen king of Carthage. It is written in the form of a *chantefable* (song-story), composed alternately in prose, to be recited, and in verse, to be sung.

The only surviving manuscript of *Aucassin and Nicolette*, rediscovered in 1752, is in the Bibliothèque Nationale in Paris. Written in the Picard dialect, it is one of the earliest masterpieces of French literature. The verse, in seven-syllable assonanced lines, has a light grace that contrasts charmingly with the elegant, sophisticated prose sections. Fantasy and reality intermingle and alternate in the narrative. The characters are vividly portrayed, and realistic detail brings the scenes to life. Among the best-known English translations of *Aucassin and Nicolette* are those by Andrew Lang (1887) and Laurence Housman (1930).

The story is about Aucassin's love for the Saracen captive Nicolette. The romance is opposed by his father, the lord of Beaucaire, who has planned a noble match for his son. Nicolette is thrown into prison to prevent the couple from meeting, but she escapes and Aucassin goes in search of her. After he finds her, they make their way to the coast. There they board a ship that takes them to the fantastic castle of Torelore, where they spend three happy years. The Saracens then attack the castle and separate the lovers, taking Nicolette to Carthage, where the king recognizes her as his lost daughter. Aucassin is carried off on another ship and is eventually shipwrecked near his own home in Provence. His father having died, he becomes lord of Beaucaire. To escape marriage to a Saracen king, Nicolette disguises herself as a minstrel and goes in search of Aucassin. She finds him and sings to him the story of their romance. He recognizes her and the lovers are reunited.

AUCH, ôsh, a town in France, is capital of Gers department. It is on the Gers River, about 42 miles (68 km) west of Toulouse. Auch is a trading center for Armagnac brandy and the wine, cereals, and livestock produced in the region. Its manufactures include agricultural tools, leather, and vinegar.

The city consists of a lower and upper town united in several places by flights of steps. Its most imposing sight is the Gothic Ste.-Marie Cathedral, with its classic façade and stained glass windows, built in the 15th to 17th century.

While it was the chief town of the Ausci, a Celtiberian tribe, it was known as *Elimberrum*. After the Romans conquered the area, the town was renamed *Augusta Auscorum* and became one of the main centers of Gaul. It was the capital of Armagnac for many centuries and later was capital of Gascony. Population: (1962) 16,109.

AUCHINCLOSS, ô'chin-klōs, **Louis Stanton** (1917–   ), American novelist, whose characters and plots are drawn from the world of wealth and social position. His subject matter, his emphasis on character analysis, and his careful literary craftsmanship place him in the tradition of Edith Wharton and Henry James.

Auchincloss was born in Lawrence, N.Y., on Sept. 27, 1917. He attended Groton and Yale, and received a law degree from the University of Virginia in 1941. After working briefly in a New York law firm, he enlisted in the Navy when the United States entered World War II. He served in the Panama Canal Zone, saw active duty with amphibious forces in the Atlantic and Pacific theaters of war, and took part in the Normandy invasion of 1944. After the war he returned to the practice of law.

Auchincloss' first novel, *The Indifferent Children*, about New York society during the war years, was published in 1947. He then began to contribute short stories to the *New Yorker,* the *Atlantic Monthly,* and other magazines. Eight of his stories were published in 1950 under the title *The Injustice Collectors*. His second novel, *Sybil,* appeared in 1952. In the following years he established a reputation as a major American writer with *A Law for the Lion* (1953), *The Romantic Egoists* (1954), *Venus in Sparta* (1958), *Pursuit of the Prodigal* (1959), *The House of Five Talents* (1960), *Reflections of a Jacobite* (1961), *Portrait in Brownstone* (1963), and *Powers of Attorney* (1963). In *The Rector of Justin* (1964) and *The Embezzler* (1966) Auchincloss created powerful character studies by presenting his protagonists from the point of view of their friends and acquaintances.

AUCHINLECK, ô-kən-lek', **Sir Claude John Eyre** (1884–   ), British field marshal. He was born in Aldershot, Hampshire, England, on June 21, 1884, the son of an army colonel. He graduated from Wellington College and Sandhurst Royal Military College before entering the Indian Army in 1904. In World War I he served in Egypt (1914–1915), Aden (1915), and Mesopotamia (1916–1919). His subsequent career was closely associated with the development and command of the armed forces of India. After appointment to the Staff College at Quetta (1930–1933), he directed victorious operations in 1933 and 1935 against the Mohmands on India's northwest frontier. In 1938 he became commander of the Meerut district.

When the Germans invaded Norway in World War II, Auchinleck was sent there as commander of the Allied forces that briefly occupied Narvik in May-June 1940. He then became commander in chief of the Southern Command in England and organized the country's first defenses against a threatened Nazi invasion. He returned to India as commander in chief in December 1940.

Auchinleck replaced Gen. Archibald P. Wavell as commander in chief of the British armies in the Middle East in 1941. He achieved a sweeping success over the German forces by advancing across Libya, but later he had to fall back toward Egypt and abandon Tobruk (June 1942) to German Gen. Erwin Rommel. His strategy in North Africa caused some controversy, but in 1960 the official British war history vindicated his role in the campaign as "turning defeat into counterattack."

Succeeded by Gen. Sir Harold R.L.G. Alexander in the Middle East command, Auchinleck assumed his old post in India in 1943. In defending India against Japanese invaders from Burma he enhanced his reputation as a brilliant organizer and military leader. He was knighted in 1945 and in 1946 promoted to the rank of field marshal. His service in India ended with the country's independence in 1947.

AUCKLAND, 1st Baron. See EDEN, WILLIAM.

AUCKLAND, ôk′lənd, is the largest city and a leading port of New Zealand. Located on North Island at the base of North Auckland Peninsula, the city lies between two excellent harbors. The main port facilities are on Waitemata Harbour, which opens into Hauraki Gulf. Manukau Harbour lies about 5 miles (8 km) to the south and provides access to the Tasman Sea. The city has an international airport and is linked by rail and highways with all parts of the country.

Auckland is the leading industrial center of New Zealand. Manufactured products include woolens, clothing, tobacco, furniture, electrical goods, fertilizer, and food products. There are automobile assembly plants, breweries, and engineering works in the suburbs.

The city has numerous parks and public reserves, several of which are situated on volcanic hills that afford excellent views of the city and its harbors. The University of Auckland, located in the center of the city, was founded in 1882. The War Memorial Museum has an outstanding Maori collection. The city also has an art gallery and public library, a teachers' college, and a zoological garden.

Auckland was founded as the capital of New Zealand in 1840 by Capt. William Hobson, the first governor of New Zealand. It remained the capital until 1865 when the seat of government was moved to Wellington. Auckland was made a borough in 1851 and became a city in 1871. Population: (1961) 143,583.

HOWARD CRITCHFIELD
Western Washington State College

NEW ZEALAND CONSULATE GENERAL, N.Y.

AUCKLAND is the largest city of New Zealand. Aerial view of city shows its business district and waterfront.

AUCKLAND ISLANDS, ôk′lənd, an uninhabited island group in the South Pacific Ocean about 290 miles (461 km) south of South Island, New Zealand. The island group, at latitude 50° 32′ S and longitude 166° 13′ E, belongs to New Zealand. The total area is 234 square miles (377 km). Auckland Island, the largest of the group, is about 27 miles (44 km) long and 15 miles (24 km) wide and very mountainous, rising to 2,000 feet (610 meters) above sea level. The group has several good harbors: that of Port Ross is one of the best in the world.

The island group was discovered in 1806 by Abraham Bristow, a British sea captain. A whaling station was established in 1850, but it was abandoned two years later. The New Zealand government maintains a depot on Auckland Island with supplies for shipwrecked sailors.

AUCTION, ôk′shən, the public sale of property to the highest bidder. The auctioneer acts primarily as the agent of the seller, his authority being defined by their mutual arrangements and by the general usages of the business. An auctioneer generally has no power to warrant the goods on behalf of the seller, unless such authority has been expressly granted. Fraudulent conduct or misrepresentation by an auctioneer, on the other hand, gives rise to a right of legal action against the seller, if he benefits and the purchaser is injured, even though the fraud is unauthorized by and unknown to the seller.

The terms and conditions of sale may be advertised beforehand or announced at the time of the auction. The seller must expressly make provisions if he wishes to fix a minimum price below which the property shall not be sold, or if he wants to reserve the right to bid himself. Unless an auction is announced to be "without reserve,"

the property may be withdrawn at any time before the fall of the hammer and, conversely, a bid may also be withdrawn at any time before that event. The majority rule in the United States is that fictitious bidding by any agent of the seller for the purpose of inflating the value of the property (also called "by-bidding" or "puffing") is considered a fraud on legitimate buyers and entitles the successful bidder to avoid the contract of sale. The former English rule, adopted by a minority of American jurisdictions, is that a seller may employ a "puffer" as a defensive measure to prevent a sacrifice of his property, provided he acts in good faith. Agreements not to bid, made for the purpose of stifling competition, are generally held to be invalid, but agreements to buy jointly are permissible, if the primary purpose is not to suppress competition.

RICHARD L. HIRSHBERG, *Attorney at Law*

AUCUBA, ô′kū-bə, is a group of evergreen shrubs native to the Himalaya, China, and Japan. They are grown outdoors for ornamental foliage in the warmer parts of the United States and under glass in the cooler climates. The shrubs are unisexual (having either male or female flowers) and have either green leaves or leaves blotched with yellow or white.

The genus *Aucuba* belongs to the dogwood family, Cornaceae; there are three species. *A. japonica*, commonly known as the gold dust tree, is a rounded laurellike shrub that bears bright scarlet berries in the spring and is cultivated in city gardens. *A. chinensis* and *A. himalaica* also are cultivated.

AUDE, ōd, is a department in southern France, bordering on the Mediterranean Sea. The capital is Carcassonne. It is mainly covered by foothills of the Pyrenees and Cévennes mountains and is traversed by the Aude River and the Canal du Midi. Wine is the chief product; wheat, oats, and fruit also are important crops. Minerals in the region include iron, gold, silver, manganese, salt, and marble. The department has an area of 2,448 square miles (6,340 sq km). Population: (1962) 269,782.

AUDE RIVER, ōd, a river in France, rises in the eastern Pyrenees, in Pyrénées Orientales department. It flows north into Aude department to Carcassonne and then east through Aude, emptying into the Mediterranean Sea about 12 miles (19 km) east of Narbonne. Before reaching Carcassonne, the river flows through deep gorges that have been harnessed for hydroelectric power. From Carcassonne to the Mediterranean it is paralleled in places by the Canal du Midi. The Aude has a length of about 138 miles (222 km).

AUDEN, ô′dən, **Wystan Hugh** (1907–1973), British-American poet, who became one of the dominant voices in 20th century English verse. He exerted a formative influence not only on poetry and prose but also on people and opinions—in the 1930's as a romantic radical and after 1940 as a convinced Christian. Auden conveys his moral acuteness and concern in a graphic, varied, and rich vocabulary. His verse is marked by a fierce and sometimes macabre wit and by a facility that recalls Byron or Browning. His mental landscape, like his geographical, is "Northern," with fells, rocks, scarps, and worn hills, as well as industrial debris, suggesting the polar peril of a new ice age.

Life. W.H. Auden was born in York, England, on Feb. 21, 1907. His father was a distinguished physician; his mother had been a nurse. Both grandfathers were Anglican clergymen. His home atmosphere, as a result, was both scientific and devout. He intended to become a mining engineer, but in March 1922 a friend asked him, "Do you write poetry?" He never had, but from that instant he knew what he wanted to do, and his first poem was published in 1924. In 1925 he went to Christ Church, Oxford, where he studied English and coedited *Oxford Poetry, 1926* and *Oxford Poetry, 1927.* He dominated his companions in a father-confessorly way. In 1928 the poet Stephen Spender handprinted 26 of Auden's poems in an edition of 45 copies.

After leaving Oxford in 1928, Auden spent a year in Germany, where he "fell in love with the language" and was influenced by the playwright Bertolt Brecht and by German cabaret and theater songs. He also acquired a passion for politics and psychology. On his return from Germany he became the most exciting social poet in England, the leader of the literate left and the poet analyst of a sick society. Auden's *Paid on Both Sides,* a poem published in 1930 in T.S. Eliot's quarterly *Criterion,* was dedicated to the poet C. Day Lewis, whom Auden succeeded that year as an English master at Larchfield Academy, Helenburgh, Scotland.

In 1936, although he had not previously met her, Auden married Erika Mann, the daughter of the German novelist Thomas Mann, to provide her with a passport so she could leave Nazi Germany. They remained married until Erika died in 1969. In 1937, during the Spanish Civil War, he went to Spain as a stretcher-bearer. That same year he was awarded King George's Gold Medal for poetry. In 1938 he and Christopher Isherwood went to China, then together wrote the play *On the Frontier* (1938) and an essay in prose and verse, *Journey to a War* (1939).

In 1939, Auden settled in the United States. He became an American citizen in 1946. He received the 1948 Pulitzer Prize in poetry for *The Age of Anxiety* (1947). From 1956 to 1961 he was professor of poetry at Oxford. Then, in 1972,

Wystan Hugh Auden

CAMERA PRESS—PIX

he again made his home in England as poet in residence at Oxford University. He died in Vienna, Austria, on Sept. 28, 1973.

Writings. *Poems* (1930) made Auden's reputation. It included *Paid on Both Sides* and 30 other poems and was published by Faber and Faber, where T.S. Eliot was an editor. *Poems* castigates and satirizes the bourgeoisie as doomed from without by the inevitable march of Marxism and from within by the interior death-wish that motivates its noisy resistance. However, both writer and reader are part of that bourgeoisie, which Auden loved and later also prayed for. These ideas are expanded in *The Orators* (1932).

Auden and Isherwood collaborated on two more plays, *The Dog Beneath the Skin* (1935) and *The Ascent of F6* (1936). Auden and Louis MacNeice, a fellow poet, went to Iceland in 1936, then collaborated on *Letter From Iceland* (1937), a volume of prose and verse.

Among Auden's later volumes of poetry are *For the Time Being: A Christmas Oratorio* (1944), *The Shield of Achilles* (1955), and *Epistle to a Godson* (1972). He translated Dag Hammarskjöld's *Markings* (1964) and, with Chester Kallman, wrote librettos for the operas *The Rake's Progress* (1951), *Elegy for Young Lovers* (1961), and *The Bassarids* (1966).

ANNE FREMANTLE
Author of "This Little Band of Prophets"

Further Reading: Beach, Joseph W., *The Making of the Auden Canon* (Minneapolis, Minn., 1957); Blair, John G., *The Poetic Art of W. H. Auden* (Princeton, N.J., 1965).

AUDIENCIA, ou-dē-en′sē-ə, any of the territorial and regional law courts formerly appointed by the Spanish crown to exercise jurisdiction in provincial Spain and Spanish colonial America. The term also applied to the jurisdictional districts of those courts.

The first audiencias in America were introduced in the early 16th century to check the independent authority of the conquerors of Mexico and Peru. Audiencias were established in Santo Domingo in 1511, Mexico in 1527, Panama in 1535, Peru in 1542, Guatemala in 1543, New Galicia in 1548, and New Granada in 1549. They were made up of four or more judges or auditors, called *oidores,* who had supreme judicial authority in their districts. Persons aggrieved by acts of the civil administrators of the colonies and subsequent viceroyalties could appeal to the audiencia. Consequently the audiencias soon became consulting bodies of the administrators.

Initially the system of colonial audiencias was effective in protecting individual rights. In the 17th and 18th centuries, however, the courts fell victim to the increasing corruption in Spanish colonial administration.

AUDIOVISUAL EDUCATION, ô'dē-ō-vizh'ōō-əl ej-ə-kā'shən, is education by such means as slides, tape recordings, models, television, and motion pictures. The methods of educational communication by sight and by sound developed more or less separately, and the name of the field evolved accordingly. In the 1920's and early 1930's it was called "visual education" and included the use of blackboards, charts and graphs, maps and globes, bulletin boards, exhibits, models, museums, field trips, slides, opaque projectors, flat pictures, photographs, silent motion pictures, and other primarily visual media. When disc, wire, and tape recordings, radio, and sound motion pictures came into use in the schools in the 1940's, the field broadened and became known as "audiovisual education." The new media were used in varying degrees to supplement the traditional media of instruction—the teacher's voice and the printed page.

Today an increasing array of communications media combine photographic, mechanical, and electronic devices into teaching-learning systems for individual as well as for large-group instruction. The essential purpose is to employ modern communications technology to help solve the educational problems arising from the population boom, the explosion of human knowledge, the complexity of the information to be taught and learned, the need for individualized instruction, and the shortage of qualified teachers in certain critical areas. The result of this combination of forces has been a shift in emphasis; the field is becoming known as "educational communication" or "audiovisual communication."

DEVELOPMENT OF AUDIOVISUAL EDUCATION CONCEPT

Since ancient times, pictures and sculptures have preserved and transmitted an interpretive record of events and values. Formal education, however, was generally limited to verbal exercises until the educational reform movements of the 17th and 18th centuries, inspired by John Amos Comenius and Johann Heinrich Pestalozzi.

Comenius, a Moravian bishop, preached a doctrine that was the forerunner of the modern audiovisual education movement. His influence was greatest in the reforming of language teaching and textbook writing. He believed that systematic instruction using both words and pictures would alleviate some of the meaningless verbalism practiced by teachers of his time. His reader, *Orbis pictus (The World Pictured)*, included some 150 pictures, each providing a topic for a lesson. Pestalozzi, too, believed that children learned best by concrete experience, and his school was based primarily on direct observation and education of the senses.

The study of science, by its very nature, contained many elements of what later became known as visual education, including field trips, drawings, exhibits, models, and the like. The 19th-century scientists Louis Agassiz and Thomas H. Huxley advocated the teaching laboratory as a place for demonstrations, observations, and a problem-solving approach to the study of biological science, rather than sole reliance on textbooks and lectures. This philosophy is expressed today in the "discovery" approach to science teaching and in the preparation of audiovisual materials in this field.

Most formal educational systems in 19th century western Europe, however, continued to be based on bookish knowledge and on learning by rote. The emphasis of the Latin grammar schools of New England, which derived their methodology from the British schools, was on memorization, recitation, and lecture. There is little mention of even the simplest instructional devices, such as the blackboard, until 1800, and the use of slates by individual students was not common until mid-century. In the grammar schools and academies that spread across the United States in the early 19th century, simple spelling books—the "hornbook" and "blue-back speller"—were not replaced by the illustrated McGuffey readers until almost midcentury. Later, there were significant improvements in maps, projected images, and the printing of pictures in textbooks thanks to the development of photography and the half-tone process. But the concept of audiovisual education made very little progress in formal education from the colonial period to 1900. The real experiences and preparation for living for most young people in the United States during this period were limited to their lives on the farms and in the small towns of the growing nation.

SIGHT AND SOUND are used in new ways in the school. Left: filmstrip viewer for individual study. Center: headset for questions and answers in an electronic classroom. Right: overhead projector shows an experiment to the class.

HAYS FROM MONKMEYER   GEORGE ZIMBEL FROM MONKMEYER   LEW MERRIM FROM MONKMEYER

Progress in the 20th Century. The importance that these firsthand, concrete experiences have in the learning process was pointed up and implemented in the significant contributions that John Dewey made to American education in the late 1800's and early 1900's. Dewey saw education as life, rather than as simply a prelude to life. A philosophical climate was thus established in which audiovisual instruction should have flourished—and, in fact, it did so to a limited degree. But in the United States, members of the Progressive Education Association (PEA) laid an almost exclusive claim to possession of this philosophy, and they applied it with a rigidity that limited the logical growth of audiovisual education. Despite the criticisms of enlightened educational leadership, including Dewey himself, the influence of the PEA inhibited the development of audiovisual education until the World War II era.

In the decade 1940–1950 the use of audiovisual materials and methods of instruction was amplified by wartime needs through the U.S. Office of Education, the Armed Services, and industry training programs. Stimulated by the instructional and propaganda needs of a nation at war, much impressive evidence on the effectiveness of audiovisual education emerged. Certain doubts were raised, however, about the direct applicability of these methods to public school education. The traditional role of the teacher seemed to be at stake; the differences between "training" and "education" were sharpened; the financial resources of the public schools were compared unfavorably with those of the military; and doubts were expressed that schools could teach "the Army way."

Yet, during this period and shortly after, many of the wartime audiovisual instruction methods were effectively transferred to industry, advertising, and some educational settings. A number of professional associations were also founded, including the Educational Film Library Association (EFLA) and the Division of Audiovisual Instruction (DAVI) of the National Educational Association, and professional publications such as *Educational Screen* (now *Educational Screen and Audiovisual Guide*) began to appear.

The 1950's and 1960's. The decade 1950–1960 was marked by intense interest in educational television, much of which was researched by the Armed Forces. The Ford Foundation sponsored investigations of the effectiveness and acceptability of TV in teaching university courses. It also contributed to the development of airborne television transmission (Midwest Program for Airborne Television) in areas where conventional teaching programs, especially in science and language, were weak. Hagerstown, Md., became the center of the country's most extensive closed-circuit experimental television project. Teaching by TV was regularly scheduled in all schools in an entire county.

In 1958 the National Defense Education Act was passed by Congress. Title VII of the act provided for "Research and Experimentation in More Effective Utilization of Television, Radio, Motion Pictures, and Related Media for Educational Purposes." An initial amount of about $500,000 was appropriated for 1958, and $5 million was authorized for each of the next three years (1959–1961). This opened a whole new era of research, production, testing, and utilization of media in education. By 1960 expressions such as "the technological revolution in education," the "communications revolution," "information explosion," and "population explosion" were found in almost every major exposition of the problems and needs of modern education.

The shortage of qualified teachers, the dramatic increase in the quantity and complexity of modern knowledge, and the success of Soviet Russia's space-blazing Sputnik I (1957) accelerated the development and sophistication of audiovisual methods of communication. There were also significant changes in curriculum, especially in the teaching of the physical sciences, that contributed to this development. Leadership in audiovisual instruction broadened from a small dedicated group of pioneers, practitioners, and theorists to include subject-matter specialists and such national professional organizations as the Physical Science Study Committee, the School Mathematics Study Group, and the Biological Science Curriculum Study. New emphases were also given to the study of foreign languages by film, tape, and text, and the language-laboratory idea took firm hold.

At the same time, other related streams of educational thought began to merge. In many cases they complemented each other, but the combined effect was always to change significantly the traditional concepts of curriculum, the media of instruction, the role of teacher and learner, and even the nature of the school itself. These new educational practices included team-teaching; ungraded, continuous-progress schools; special programs for the gifted, the handicapped, and the culturally-deprived; and programmed instruction. There was a major shift from teacher-centered to learner-centered instruction, and audiovisual methodology was applied both to large-group instruction and to individualized, independent study programs.

To this situation was added the explosive (sometimes described as "implosive") impact of technological discoveries that made possible mechanical-photographic-electronic information systems. Their rapid development was in contrast to the earlier, slow-paced emergence of isolated media in the attack on educational problems. With these enormously significant improvements, audiovisual education came of age almost overnight.

The large-scale introduction of audiovisual methods in education met with criticism in the 1950's from literary figures, like Joseph Wood Krutch; educators, like Arthur Bestor; prominent public figures, like Admiral Hyman Rickover; and communications specialists, like Rudolph Flesch. They took the classic view of education in "intellectual discipline," rather than discovery, and attacked recent trends as "concessions" that resulted in inferior, undisciplined, and undistinguished end products. The critics charged that audiovisual instructional methods contributed to the unwillingness or inability of students to read or to profit from lectures. Other critics warned of the "dehumanization" of education and the "replacement of the teacher" by instructional technology.

By the mid-1960's, events seemed to prove otherwise, however. Audiovisual methods of teaching and learning seemed to be requiring the services of more and better-qualified teachers, and technology seemed to be relieving the instructor of many of his purely information-dispensing functions as well as some of his multiple clerical

LANGUAGE LABORATORY allows a roomful of students to practice speaking and hearing a foreign tongue. Right: students in booths. Lower picture: teacher in control room.

duties. More creative uses were being found for films, television, and even computers, and educators were acquiring a more balanced view of the importance of all communications media as they became experienced in the theory and technology of audiovisual education.

DEVELOPMENTS IN AUDIOVISUAL TECHNOLOGY

Beginnings. The sources of what is now known as audiovisual technology are many and varied. Some of them lie in the distant past, although most of the important developments occurred during the 19th century. As early as 1500, Leonardo da Vinci described the principle of image formation by means of light in his camera obscura. Joseph Nicéphore Niépce produced the first photograph in 1826. Several British and French inventors perfected the photographic process during the 19th century, and George Eastman, an American, popularized photography with the box camera he introduced in 1888.

Printing from movable type originated with Johann Gutenberg, whose Bible, printed about 1455, showed his mastery of the craft. High-speed printing and photoengraving were developments of the 19th century. The rotary press was invented in 1845, and the first photoengraved halftone was published in 1869.

The projection of pictures probably owes its origin to Athanasius Kircher, a German Jesuit priest, who described the magic lantern in a work published in 1644. The illusion of movement—from a series of still pictures—was first conveyed by a machine invented in 1832. In 1889, Thomas A. Edison, who had invented the phonograph in 1877, developed his Kinetoscope—the ancestor of present-day motion picture mechanisms.

The first little step toward electronic communication may have been taken in 1745 when Pieter van Musschenbroek discovered that the discharge from a Leyden jar could be conducted by a wire. Samuel F.B. Morse invented the telegraph in 1835, and Alexander Graham Bell, the telephone in 1876. Guglielmo Marconi first sent messages through the air in 1895.

The 20th Century. Electronic communication, as we know it today, began with Lee De Forest's invention of the "audion" in 1907. This three-element vacuum tube made possible the practical amplification of electrical signals and thus the development of radio and later the sound motion picture. The first scheduled commercial radio program in the United States (KDKA, Pittsburgh) went on the air in 1920. The Ohio School of the Air began broadcasting to schools in 1929—although 12 years later only 55 percent of the

Ohio schools had radios, and only 37 percent had equipment for playing records and recordings.

The silent motion picture, which flourished in the early 1900's, found very limited school use until the development of 16-mm "safety" film that was noninflammable and required less cumbersome and expensive projection equipment. After 1927, when Warner Brothers added sound to theatrical motion pictures, the 16-mm sound film became the world standard for educational motion pictures.

In 1936 the first public broadcast of television was presented from Alexandra Palace in London. By 1942 magnetic tape, developed in Germany, had completely replaced earlier methods of sound recording on magnetized wire and practically all original recordings on disc. Video tape recording—the next advance—had both visual and audio information on a single magnetic tape. Subsequently, the sound filmstrip, much used during World War II, was adapted to industrial and educational uses, and the 2x2-inch color slide largely supplanted the earlier 3¼x4-inch photographic slide. The microprojector, overhead pro-

TEACHING MACHINE, shown here in a high school library, allows individual study of programmed material.

jector, and the opaque projector became more sophisticated, both in design and use. Wide-screen and three-dimensional pictures were used both in military and industry training programs but found little application in education.

Interest in the 8-mm motion picture, which had first been developed in 1932 and to which magnetic sound had been added by 1947, was revived in the early 1960's along with the use of short "single-concept" or "single-idea" 8-mm films in preloaded cartridges for use in automatic rear-screen projectors. By the mid-1960's several types of 8-mm film production and projection systems had developed in the United States, and at least one in Japan. In Europe, trade interests and educators favored the continued use of standard 8-mm. The multiplicity of noncompatible equipment in this medium, along with differences of opinion about desirable disc playback speeds (78, 33⅓, and 45 revolutions per minute), pointed up the growing need for education-industry cooperation in setting standards.

Progress in the 1960's. Advances in electronics, the miniaturization of equipment, and the linking of photographic and electronic media produced rapid, almost explosive developments in communications technology in the 1960's. These developments were particularly evident in self-threading cameras and projectors, instant photographs (with Polaroid cameras), transistor radios, midget tape recorders, and small slow-scan video tape recorders, using one-inch or half-inch tapes, designed for home and school use. The emphasis on language instruction resulted in push-button carrels for the independent study of audio tape in what were called "language laboratories." Later, with the addition of programmed tapes on other subjects, they became known as "listening laboratories." The instructional laboratory expanded with the addition of film, television, and other visual components available to students in cen-

tral stations. Dial-access systems make it possible for students to get information in activities centers, libraries, and even in dormitories by dialing code numbers on a telephone that is linked to a central source of data.

After the first educational television station went on the air in 1950 (WOI-TV Ames, Iowa), this medium captured the imagination of educators. In 1952 the Federal Communications Commission, convinced by a small group of dedicated professors, school administrators, and audiovisual specialists of the potential of this medium, reserved 242 of the nation's limited number of broadcast channels for educational television (ETV). Millions of dollars were poured into experimentation by the Armed Forces, the Ford Foundation, and by federal and state governments. By the mid-1960's, in addition to 250 AM and 32 educationally-owned and operated FM radio stations, there were 109 educational television stations on the air. There was also significant growth in closed-circuit television (CCTV) systems for transmission to a limited number of receivers, by cable or by microwave. By this means, programs could be presented to a specialized audience, generally within the same building or complex of buildings in an educational plant.

The advent of programmed instruction also brought about a boom in what are called "teaching machines." These mechanisms present information in words, pictures, or both, on some sort of display surface. The information is presented one step at a time in a systematized but sometimes flexible manner, and the individual student is required to respond to each step. In 1961 about 90 percent of the programs involved the use of rather complicated machines, and 10 percent were found in programmed-book form. By 1963 these figures were almost exactly reversed as it became evident that many successful programs of study did not require expensive mechanical systems for the kind of information and response involved.

In many parts of the world where pressing educational needs of unsophisticated populations had to be met with low budgets, the simpler audiovisual media seemed to be most effective. The chalkboard, slide projector, maps, charts, the feltboard, the overhead projector, battery-operated radios, and simple demonstrations and field trips proved successful and, from the teacher's point of view, most practical.

In the United States, however, education at the public school and university level, stimulated by federal funds, spent an estimated $237 million on audiovisual equipment and materials in 1964, much of it allocated to the newer, more sophisticated equipment and materials of instruction. In that year an estimated 1,200 educational films were produced; there were 227,000 operable 16-mm motion picture projectors in use in education; and continuing growth of combinations of several conventional, audiovisual media in a single, sometimes computer-centered, teaching-learning system.

These developments in the technology of audiovisual instruction were accelerated as industry began to exhibit intense interest in the commercial possibilities of the once limited education market. The result was a rapid growth of new products, bringing with them the problems of standardization mentioned earlier. The mid-1960's was a period of consortiums in the audiovisual field—consolidations of industries producing the equipment ("hardware") and companies designing the programs or materials of instruction ("software"). Several mergers took place between electronics firms and publishing houses.

Educational leadership in the field, although by no means exclusively concentrated in professional audiovisual organizations, continued to be exerted by such organizations as the National Audio-Visual Association (NAVA), the Department of Audiovisual Instruction of the National Education Association (DAVI), the Educational Film Library Association (EFLA), the National Association of Educational Broadcasters (NAEB), and the National Society for Programmed Instruction (NSP). An interassociation organization, the Educational Media Council (EMC), was organized to coordinate and implement the efforts of groups in the field of audiovisual education and instructional communication. Its aim was to bring order and purpose to an expanding galaxy of developments that included lasers, computers, thermoplastics, fiber optics, information satellites, and other technological extensions of man's senses.

THE PSYCHOLOGY OF AUDIOVISUAL EDUCATION

There is an easy tendency to describe the field of audiovisual education in terms of equipment and materials, but the effectiveness of these methods obviously depends upon the support and direction provided by research in the process of teaching and learning.

The psychology of audiovisual instruction is based on the principle that learning results from new experiences gained through the senses and that audiovisual impressions may be effective substitutes for some forms of direct, sensory experience. With sense impressions the process of abstraction begins and develops (provided the environment is favorable to educational achievement). In addition, any adequate psychology of audiovisual education takes into account that education is a social process, even though learning is done by the individual. This social interpretation of education is very important, since it sets the stage for the use of audiovisual materials in group as well as in individual instruction.

Research in the audiovisual field began during World War I, picked up momentum in the period 1920–1940, and expanded in the military and civilian training programs of World War II. Studying the effectiveness of media, especially the motion picture, psychologists determined that these means could be used to impart information, teach skills, and change attitudes, although the exact nature of attitudal change could not always be predicted, since it would be conditioned by the learner's previous experiences. Early research that attempted comparisons of the effectiveness of one medium over another—print versus film, for example, or a "live" classroom lecture versus a taperecording—gave way to more meaningful studies of listener motivation, individual differences, and ways to improve the design of instructional materials.

A common finding was "no significant difference" between media-mediated instruction and good teacher-centered conventional classroom procedures. But one important fact was established: audiovisual materials could perform most of the information-imparting functions of the average teacher, and just as effectively. Audiovisual methods were readily recognized as especially useful in the simultaneous presentation of common experiences to learners under controlled conditions requiring rapid, mass instruction. Radio, the motion picture, and television were first used and studied almost exclusively.

With the work of the Harvard psychologist B.F. Skinner and a revival of the earlier work of the psychologist Sidney Pressey, the idea that information could be systematically programmed for individual learners by the application of technological methods began to influence the audiovisual field. The use of slides, filmstrips, audio tape, and even films and television for individual as well as group instruction, began to be recognized. It became evident that new analytical, problem-solving techniques could be developed using systems of presenting audiovisual stimuli (sometimes linked to computers) to feed and respond to the learner's needs—and even to shift the program when these needs changed—as in the "branching" techniques developed by Norman A. Crowder.

The importance of "feedback," or response, in the psychology of audiovisual instruction has changed the concept of media from "one-way" to "two-way" communication—from imparting in-

MODELS in a museum display help boys study communications technology. Through earphones they listen to explanations of the models as they look at them.

CLASSROOM TELEVISION:
The use of TV for demonstrations is made easy by this mobile unit which can record programs to be shown on many classroom screens.

formation to stimulating thinking. It has led to the use of media to evoke the right questions quite as often as to give the right answers.

The widespread concern with communicating large quantities of information to students will probably be matched by an increasing concern with the selection of essential and meaningful information, and the development of new intellectual skills applicable in a wide variety of circumstances. This trend permits an improvement in the student's understanding and judgment without requiring an appreciable extension of the time required to cope with the ever-increasing quantity of information accumulated by scholarly and scientific research.

The effect of this new psychology—provided it proves successful—could be enormous. The curriculum could be selectively simplified with a gain rather than a loss of educational effectiveness, and audiovisual methods of teaching and learning could finally play an integral, rather than a peripheral, role.

The study of the production, use, and theory of audiovisual education, including the recent emphasis on programmed instruction, has unquestionably strengthened the quality of education. It has served to remind everyone concerned with education of the importance of sequential presentation, logical planning, strategic use of a rich variety of audiovisual stimuli, follow-up, testing, repetition, relevancy, motivation, and individual differences—all factors whose importance in the learning process has long been recognized by educators everywhere. Attention to audiovisual methods of instruction has also helped refocus attention on the objectives of education and the nature of curriculum, and has contributed to enlarging the mainstream of thought about communication as a basic and all-encompassing study of human behavior.

Much work remains to be done in the development of the psychology of audiovisual education. A great deal is known about how and under what circumstances people learn. However, very little is known about many of the psychological mechanisms involved, and there is wide disagreement about the organization and structure of audio and visual perception. Even less is known about the subliminal processes involved in perceiving and communicating. These gaps in our knowledge are particularly critical with reference to the long-range effects of mediated experiences, and the way in which

children learn to understand and come to terms with both audio and visual symbols in an increasingly abstract, image-oriented world.

AUDIOVISUAL EDUCATION AND SOCIETY

Developments in audiovisual instruction reflect the values and problems, as well as the technological progress of the society which produces them. The informal, out-of-school influences of the mass media, especially the motion picture, radio, television, and, to a lesser extent, comic books and paperbacks, have been the subject of academic studies, legislative investigations, and public criticism.

The motion picture, in its early days, was practically the only contact many people had with distant places and different ways of living. Radio was the first means the average man had of bringing the world into his home in a vital, contemporary way. Today, television is typically the child's initial contact with the world outside his own home and neighborhood, a contact he experiences long before he spends his first day in school.

By 1950 children were spending, on the average, three to four hours daily in television viewing. An estimated 52.6 million American homes (excluding Alaska and Hawaii) were equipped with one or more TV sets. In the mid-1960's well over 90 percent of American homes had television. Elementary school pupils were spending an average of 29 hours a week watching it and about 7 hours a week listening to radio; and they were going to theatrical films on an average of once every two weeks. In a study made in Chicago by Paul Witty of the School of Education of Northwestern University, about half the pupils stated that help in their schoolwork was obtained from TV, and about one fourth cited movies as helpful, too. Definite relationships were established between reading and visual experiences; both films and television tended to stimulate the reading of books and to produce gains in vocabulary. Most studies, however, show little definite relationship between television-viewing and academic achievement.

Critics of the media continue to point out possible relationships between juvenile delinquency and the violence and other negative social values portrayed on films and television. The Payne Fund studies on motion pictures and youth, made in 1929, had shown that about one

LARGE-SCREEN projection allows 300 students to view TV or motion picture programs in the instructional resources center at an American university.

third of the motion picture audience was composed of young people under the age of 20. The research pointed to the following conclusions: (1) Children gained considerable information from films. (2) The lasting effect on the social attitudes of children was probably the result of a specific reaction of a given child to a given film; it was not easy to predict that all or most children would respond in the same way. (3) There was some kind of relationship between films and emotional stimulation and sleep patterns. (4) The film experience filled gaps in children's needs not satisfied by the school, home, or church. Most of these findings seem to hold true of television (and films) today.

While most studies of the influence of the mass media on the general public cannot show direct relationships, some of the questions raised in regard to mass media and young people apply to adults as well. Whole populations are being subjected to audiovisual impressions in massive quantities in the form of entertainment, education, advertising, political propaganda, and news and information. Along with the inexperienced young, few adults find themselves able to cope with the flood of audiovisual impressions, appeals, messages, exhortations, and directives that reach them in their homes, offices, and even in their cars while speeding along superhighways.

Undoubtedly the need is for a general public specifically educated to evaluate and cope with the media of communication and with the audiovisual symbolism that is becoming a part of their personal lives. Parents need to be taught how to help their children discriminate not only in the matter of books and literature but also in the growing array of audiovisual stimuli that abound in the home and community.

Teachers need formal studies on the kinds of audiovisual imagery their students are absorbing in the long hours spent out of school, and this implies a new and extended role for the teacher beyond the duties of the classroom. The pupils' understanding of out-of-school television, for example, may help them utilize in-school television, and other experiences, better. Because these out-of-school audiovisual influences affect the in-school program, teachers need to be trained in both the technology and programming of the media of communication.

Many educators and social scientists believe that one of the major fallacies of American education is the assumption that almost everything to be learned must be taught in a formal course. The major thrust of the audiovisual education movement has been to establish the fact that people learn best from an arrangement of vital, exciting experiences that help the learner learn and the teacher teach, wherever or however these experiences occur. Once this premise has been accepted, the pattern of teacher training, the roles of teacher and learner, curriculum planning, school building architecture, and the nature of the educational system itself may be radically changed, improved, and better designed to meet the realities of the world in which we live.

CHARLES F. HOBAN, *University of Pennsylvania*
ROBERT W. WAGNER, *The Ohio State University*

Bibliography

Brown, James W., and others, *A-V Instruction; Materials and Methods*, 2d ed. (New York 1959).
Brown, James W., and Norberg, Kenneth D., *Administering Educational Media* (New York 1965).
Cherry, Colin, *On Human Communication* (Cambridge, Mass., 1957).
Dale, Edgar, *Audio-Visual Methods in Teaching*, 3d ed. (New York 1965).
De Grazia, Alfred, and Sohn, David A., *Revolution in Teaching; New Theory, Technology, and Curricula* (New York 1964).
Glaser, Robert, ed., *Teaching Machines and Programmed Learning, II: Data and Directions* (Washington 1965).
Hoban, Charles F., Jr., and Van Ormer, E.B., *Instructional Film Research 1918–1950*, U.S. Dept. of Commerce, Technical Report No. SDA 269-7-19 (Washington 1950).
Kinder, James, *Using Audio-Visual Materials in Education* (New York 1965).
Miller, Neal E., *Graphic Communication and the Crisis in Education*, Department of Audiovisual Instruction, NEA (Washington 1957).
National Education Association, "The Changing Role of the Audiovisual Process in Education: A Definition and Glossary of Terms," *Audio-Visual Communication Review* (Washington 1963).
Schramm, Wilbur, ed., *Mass Communications* (Urbana, Ill., 1960).
Trow, William, *Teacher and Technology; New Designs for Learning* (New York 1963).

AUDIOMETER, ô-dē-om′ət-ər, an electrical device used for the measurement of the acuity of hearing. It is of value as an aid in medical diagnosis of the state and cause of a hearing deficiency, as well as in the adaptation of a hearing aid to the needs of an individual. Sounds of definite and adjustable frequency and intensity are presented to the subject, and determinations are made of the minimum sound intensity which he can hear at any given frequency. The results for any individual are plotted as a curve, which is known as an *audiogram*.

AUDITOR, ô′də-tər, in accounting, originally "one who hears," because he performed an audit by listening to the reading of the accounts. The increased complexities of business have made it necessary for the auditor to see as well as to hear, but his title has not been changed. An audit consists of an examination of original documents and accounting records as well as a review of methods and procedures so that the auditor can reasonably issue an opinion as to the fairness of the statements. There are two types of auditors—independent (or external) and internal.

Independent Auditor. A practitioner-client relationship exists between an independent auditor and a firm. The independent auditor's primary function is to issue an opinion determining the fairness of the firm's financial statements. Originally, the report issued by the auditor was referred to as a certificate. Currently, it is felt that to certify to the correctness of statements gives a false impression of accuracy. Now such a report is referred to as the auditor's opinion.

Because published statements are used by stockholders, creditors, and the public, they should be free of bias. Thus it is important that statements be reviewed by an independent auditor and that he issue an opinion. To assure objective accuracy, the audit should be performed by a professional accountant. The professional ability of an auditor may be relied on if he is a certified public accountant (CPA). In many instances the opinion must be signed by a CPA.

Internal Auditor. An employee-employer relationship exists between an internal auditor and a firm (or a government agency or other employer). He conducts functional audits and responsibility audits. In a functional audit a single activity is reviewed and evaluated. In a responsibility audit all activities under the jurisdiction of one person are reviewed and evaluated.

Differences. Some important differences between independent and internal auditors are: (1) The independent auditor usually reports to the board of directors; the internal auditor usually reports to the controller or a vice president. (2) The independent auditor's report is used by the general public; the internal auditor's report is used by management. (3) The independent auditor is interested primarily in determining the fairness of financial statements; the internal auditor is interested in determining how well policies and procedures are followed and how they can be improved.

W. ASQUITH HOWE, *Temple University*

AUDITORIUM BUILDING, ôd-ə-tōr′ē-əm, a structure in Chicago that is one of the early landmarks of modern architecture in the United States. It was designed by Louis Henri Sullivan (q.v.), who at the time was a member of the firm of Adler and Sullivan. His partner, Dankmar Adler, was responsible for the technical aspects of the building, including the nearly perfect acoustics of the theater. The building, between Michigan Avenue and Wabash Avenue, on Congress Street, now houses Roosevelt College.

Built in 1887–1889, the structure was intended primarily to provide a permanent auditorium for the city, with hotel rooms and offices added to bring in additional revenue. Sullivan handled this problem by designing the theater within a shell of hotel rooms, with the offices in a tower over the theater entrance on Congress Street. The exterior design of the building is in the Romanesque revival style popularized by Henry Hobson Richardson. It is remarkable chiefly for the sensitive massing of the arcaded façades, which rise from a three-story base of heavily rusticated granite. Sullivan's originality is most evident in the interior, especially in the careful proportions and rich ornamentation of the theater, the bar, and the staircase.

AUDITORY NERVE, ô′də-tōr-ē, the nerve of hearing and of the sense of position necessary to maintain equilibrium. The auditory nerve, or *eighth nerve,* has its origin in two distinct portions of the ear, in reality, being two distinct nerves, the *cochlear* and the *vestibular,* both of which are sensory in function. The cochlear nerve originates in the cells of the organ of Corti in the cochlea of the ear, the one that carries sound impressions to the brain. The vestibular nerve has its origin in the semicircular canals and is the nerve of the sense of localization of position. Both nerves join and run together, lying for some distance in the same sheath as the seventh or facial nerve.

In head injuries there is often a disturbance of the cochlear portion of the auditory nerve, especially where the temporal bone is fractured and extensive bleeding occurs at the base of the skull. There is usually diminution of hearing, with islands of deafness revealed by the audiometer. One or both ears may be affected and complete restoration of hearing seldom takes place. In many cases head noises and ringing in the ears (tinnitus) are so intense and persistent as to keep the affected person bedridden. If the vestibular portion is damaged, disturbance of equilibrium may be a prominent aftereffect. Sudden changes in the position of the head accentuate the dizziness and may be disabling. See also EAR; ORGAN.

AUDLEY, ôd′lē, **Sir James** (1316?–1386), English knight. Audley, or *Audeley,* served with valor under Edward III and the Black Prince in France, and in 1344 was honored as a founding knight of the Order of the Garter. In 1350 he distinguished himself in the naval engagement with the Spaniards off Sluys, the Netherlands. For his conspicuous bravery at the Battle of Poitiers in 1356, Audley was retained by the prince as his own knight and received a revenue of 500 marks. Informed that Audley had given the money to his squires, the delighted prince bestowed a further annuity of 600 marks on the knight. In 1362, Audley was appointed governor of Aquitaine; and in 1369, grand seneschal of Poitou. He died near Poitiers in 1386.

AUDLEY, ôd′lē, **Thomas** (1488–1544), English lord chancellor. In 1529 he became speaker of the Parliament that ultimately abolished papal jurisdiction in England. In 1532 he was knighted, and in the following year he became lord chancellor, after supporting Henry VIII in his attempt to divorce Catherine of Aragon.

As lord chancellor he presided at the trial of Sir Thomas More, whom he had succeeded, and at that of Bishop John Fisher. He was also the presiding judge at the trials of the supposed accomplices of Anne Boleyn, and of the paramour of Catherine Howard. Completely subservient to Henry VIII, and devoid of moral scruples, he was rewarded with a peerage (1538) as *Baron Audley of Walden.* Audley founded Magdalene College, Cambridge, in 1542. He died on April 30, 1544.

AUDUBON, ô′də-bən, **John James** (1785–1851),
American painter and naturalist, who is famous
for his drawings of birds in their natural habitats. Audubon was born on April 26, 1785, at Les
Cayes, Haiti, the illegitimate son of Jean Audubon, a French sea captain and planter, and
Jeanne Rabine, a Breton peasant woman who
died a few months after his birth. Brought to
Nantes, France, in early childhood, he was
legally adopted in 1794 by his father and Anne
Moynet Audubon. From 1796 to 1800 he served
as a first-class cabin boy at Rochefort-sur-Mer,
but he finally failed his officer training tests. In
1800 he was baptized *Jean Jacques Fougère
Audubon,* but in French lawsuits he remained
Jean Rabine.

In 1803, in order to avoid conscription during
the Napoleonic Wars, Audubon fled to the United
States, where he called himself *John James
Audubon* and was thus naturalized in 1812. In
America, while living at Mill Grove farm near
Norristown, Pa., he was supposed to study farm
and mine management and to learn English, but
when he was not in the woods and fields, he was
courting his English-born neighbor Lucy Bakewell. Audubon's illegitimacy and sporadic education made him boast to her that he had studied
with the Paris artist Jacques Louis David. However, Audubon's early artwork, and the voluminous
papers of David, belie this claim, which he often
repeated.

In 1805, Audubon returned to France to
inform his father of troubles on their farm and
to ask consent to wed. A local physician, Charles
Marie d'Orbigny, introduced him to some aspects
of French ornithology, and Audubon began his
first serious attempts at drawing birds. Accompanied by a business partner, Ferdinand Rozier,
he returned to America in 1806. Following a
year's apprenticeship in New York City under
Lucy's uncle, Benjamin Bakewell, a merchant, he
went with Rozier in 1807 to set up a store in
Louisville, Ky. In 1808, Audubon married Lucy.

In 1810, after the partners had moved to
Henderson, Ky., a visit from ornithologist Alexander Wilson (q.v.)—whose work on American
birds was just emerging—had its effect. Audubon's heart was so set on surpassing Wilson that
he spent more and more time at hunting and
drawing, while business suffered. When, in 1800,
Rozier elected to settle in Missouri, Audubon
continued alone in Henderson until 1812. Lucy's
brother Thomas then became his partner in a
store and gristmill, but these were doomed no
less by Audubon's preoccupation with birds than
by wartime. Deserted by Thomas in 1817 and
bankrupt by 1819, Audubon drew chalk portraits
and taught art in Louisville for six months. In
1820 he worked for several months as a taxider-
mist in Cincinnati for the Western Museum.

With the artist Joseph Robert Mason, who
was to paint botanical accessories for the bird
portraits to be made in the South, Audubon
sailed down the Ohio and Mississippi rivers in
October 1820. (In later years Mason was succeeded by George Lehman, Maria Martin, Audubon's son John, and various unidentified artisans.)
Not until December 1821 did Lucy and sons
Victor and John join Audubon in New Orleans.
Except for a futile trip east to seek a publisher
in 1824, Audubon remained in the South until
May 1826, when he sailed to England. Gambling
all on success abroad, he left Victor to clerk in
Louisville and young John with Lucy at Beech

NATIONAL AUDUBON SOCIETY

JOHN JAMES AUDUBON, a self portrait.

Woods plantation, near Bayou Sara, La., where
she was a neighborhood schoolteacher.

Valuable introductions and successful exhibitions in Liverpool and Manchester led Audubon
to Edinburgh. There, in 1827, William H. Lizars
engraved the first 10 of 435 hand-colored aqua-
tints of Audubon's 4-volume classic, *The Birds
of America,* which was finished in London by R.
Havell & Son from 1827 to 1838. Fewer than
200 sets were printed, and they sold by subscription for $1,000 each. It was largely this work
that established Audubon's reputation as a drafts-
man and watercolorist and naturalist-observer of
the first rank.

While this work was in progress, Audubon
revisited America repeatedly between 1829 and
1838 to draw and redraw needed species of birds.
His observations, *Ornithological Biography* (5
vols., 1831–39), he published with the editorial
aid of William Macgillivray. Before leaving England for good in 1838 he published his *Synopsis
of the Birds of America.*

Upon settling in New York City, Audubon
and his sons published an octavo-size edition of
his *The Birds of America* (5 vols., 1840–44).
Then, from 1845 to 1848, they published his
folio *The Viviparous Quadrupeds of North America,* two volumes of mammals, with nearly half
the drawings by John Woodhouse Audubon. J.T.
Bowen of Philadelphia lithographed and hand-
colored the plates for both of these later works.

For *The Viviparous Quadrupeds of North
America* Audubon made his final expedition, a
journey to the upper Missouri, in 1843. A year
or so later his eyesight failed, and by 1847 his
mental faculties declined. From then on his sons
Victor and John and his friend and collaborator
John Bachman of Charleston, S.C., carried Audubon's later editions through to completion in the
1850's. Bachman edited *The Viviparous Quadrupeds of North America* and wrote much of the
text. Audubon died on Jan. 27, 1851, at his
estate, Minnie's Land, in New York City.

ALICE FORD, *Author of "John James Audubon"*
Further Reading: American Heritage, *The Original
Water-color Paintings by John James Audubon for "The
Birds of America,"* 2 vols. (New York 1966); Herrick,
Francis, *Audubon the Naturalist* (New York 1938).

AUDUBON, ô′də-bən, a residential borough in southwestern New Jersey, is situated in Camden County about 4 miles (6.4 km) southeast of Camden. Incorporated in 1905, it was named for John James Audubon, who studied the birds of the area in 1829. It has a commission form of government. Population: 10,802.

AUDUBON SOCIETIES, ô′də-bən, are organizations dedicated to the conservation of wildlife and other renewable natural resources. The major purpose is to advance public understanding of the value and need of conserving soil, water, plants, and wildlife and to encourage appreciation of the importance of their intelligent use for human progress.

In the United States, the National Audubon Society has branches and affiliated clubs in more than 300 communities. With more than 300,000 junior and adult members it is one of the largest and most active organizations in the country engaged in conservation efforts. There are 12 state Audubon societies and about 200 local and county Audubon societies, all autonomous.

History. The name "Audubon Society" was originated in 1886 by the naturalist George Bird Grinnell in honor of John James Audubon, whose widow had been Grinnell's early teacher in New York City. In 1895, Audubon societies were organized in Massachusetts and Pennsylvania. Their example was soon followed in other states by groups of men and women seeking to save a wide range of bird and mammal species from threatened extermination at the hands of plume hunters for the millinery trade and by other commercial destroyers. Because of the interest generated by the society a model bird-protection law was adopted by 32 states in the decade from 1895 to 1905.

The National Association of Audubon Societies was incorporated in New York City in 1905, with William Dutcher as president. (The name was changed to National Audubon Society in 1935.) The association was instrumental in obtaining passage in New York of the Audubon Act (1911), prohibiting the sale of feathers of native wild birds in the state, and the federal Migratory Bird Treaty Act (1918), prohibiting the killing or capturing of most nongame species.

The association was successful in the early 1900's in saving from decimation and possible extinction such now abundant species as the American and snowy egrets and various terns, gulls, waterfowl, and some species of insectivorous birds. The society's campaign was also a basic factor in the establishment of hundreds of government wildlife refuges and sanctuaries.

Major Programs. The society cooperates closely with federal resource-use agencies, state conservation departments, and private organizations in furthering a wise use of natural resources. National Audubon sanctuaries include more than 40 areas, ranging from small islands to a 26,000-acre (10,500-hectare) coastal marshland in Louisiana. The Florida and Massachusetts Audubon societies have jurisdiction over a number of important sanctuaries. Many other state and local Audubon groups also maintain sanctuaries for nature preservation and educational purposes.

Staff research experts are engaged in efforts to save such rare species as the whooping crane, bald eagle, California condor, and Key deer from extermination. In addition the society carries on a continuing campaign in behalf of such persecuted species as hawks and predatory mammals. It stresses the interrelationships among various forms of life and warns of the biological consequences of interference with them.

The society's Nature Centers Division was formed in 1961 by a merger with Nature Centers for Young America, Inc. The division offers technical assistance and a variety of publications to communities that wish to establish nature centers as a means of creating among youth and adults a greater appreciation of nature and the need for conservation. The society itself owns and operates nature centers at Greenwich and Sharon, Conn.; Dayton, Ohio; and El Monte and Tiburon, Calif.

The society has enrolled as junior members more than 10 million children. Its has distributed to them and their teachers over 50 million copies of a great variety of leaflets presenting the fundamentals of bird recognition, natural resource conservation, and nature study. The society operates summer camps for teachers, youth leaders, and other adults. These camps offer instruction in outdoor methods of teaching natural history, ecology, and conservation. Audubon camps are located at Medomak, Me.; Greenwich, Conn.; Sarona, Wis.; and Dubois, Wyo.

Publications and Films. The society issues a variety of publications. *Audubon Magazine,* published six times a year, presents nontechnical articles and illustrations on nature and conservation topics. *Audubon Field Notes,* also issued six times yearly, publishes the results of bird watching, including seasonal reports and bird censuses. *Audubon Nature Bulletins,* for teachers and youth leaders, are issued from time to time. *Leaders Conservation Guide,* a semimonthly for Audubon leaders, is also available, by subscription, to the public.

Audubon Wildlife Films bring the finest available color motion picture photography, with expert naturalist speakers, to audiences totaling more than 500,000 each winter season in more than 200 North American cities and towns.

Administration. The National Audubon Society occupies its own building, Audubon House, at 1130 Fifth Avenue, New York City. It houses a library containing one of the most comprehensive collections in the United States of books and articles on ornithology, conservation, and general natural history. The photo-film department has photographs and films of hundreds of American wild mammals and birds. Regional offices operate in Miami and in El Monte, Calif. The society's income is derived from endowments, membership fees, special gifts, and funds from lectures, camp enrollments, and other sources.

Canadian Society. The Canadian Audubon Society, formed at Toronto in 1948, is a national nonprofit organization dedicated to the advancement of public understanding of the need to conserve wildlife, plants, soil, and water. Besides conducting many educational and research programs the society publishes *Canadian Audubon* (formerly *Canadian Nature*), a bimonthly magazine. The magazine's sponsorship of the Audubon Junior Clubs of Canada in 1942 led, six years later, to the incorporation of the Audubon Society of Canada (now the Canadian Audubon Society).

KENNETH D. MORRISON
Mountain Lake Sanctuary, Lake Wales, Fla.

AUE, Hartmann von. See HARTMANN VON AUE.

Mallard Duck

Flamingo

Brown Pelican

AUDUBON

Passenger Pigeon

Summer Tanager

Roseate Spoonbill

A SELECTION OF AUDUBON'S FAMOUS BIRD PAINTINGS

Right: Through demonstration lectures at Audubon Camp of Maine, adults learn from naturalists, so as to teach young people.

Below: At the Audubon Center in Greenwich, Conn., a botanist and students pause to identify a wildflower.

Above: At the Maine camp, on a forested island just off the coast, campers study birds at close range.

AUDUBON SOCIETIES

Left: Visitors navigate a swamp during an Audubon wildlife tour in Everglades National Park, Fla.

Below: A bird being banded by a staff expert—one of the society's many research activities.

(All photos) National Audubon Society: G. Sickles, Charles C. Daly, Thomas N. Lineaweaver

AUE, ou'ə, is an industrial city in East Germany, in Karl-Marx-Stadt district, 13 miles (20.9 km) southeast of Zwickau, on the Mulde River. Formerly in the old German province of Saxony, it became a center of uranium production after World War II. The nearby Erzgebirge (Ore Mountains) on the East German-Czechoslovakian border provide the uranium ore that is processed in Aue. Other manufactures include metal goods, machine tools, textiles, and chemicals. Aue received its town charter in 1629. Population: (1964) 31,720.

AUER, ou'ər, **Leopold** (1845–1930), Hungarian violinist. He was born in Veszprém, Hungary, on June 7, 1845. He attended the conservatories of Budapest and Vienna and was a pupil of Joseph Joachim in Hannover, Germany. He was concertmaster of orchestras in Düsseldorf (1863–1865) and Hamburg (1866–1867).

In 1868, Auer was appointed head of the violin department at the Imperial Conservatory in St. Petersburg (now Leningrad), Russia. At St. Petersburg, his pupils included Efrem Zimbalist, Mischa Elman, and Jascha Heifetz. From 1887 to 1892 he also held the directorship of the Imperial Music Association.

Auer left Russia in 1917 and a year later settled in the United States, where he became a citizen in 1926. He died in Loschwitz, near Dresden, Germany, on July 15, 1930.

Auer was the author of *Violin Playing As I Teach It* (1921) and *My Long Life in Music* (1923).

AUERBACH, ou'ər-bäкн, **Berthold** (1812–1882), German author, who is known for his tales of peasant life. Auerbach was born in Nordstetten, Württemberg, on Feb. 28, 1812. He intended to become a rabbi but turned to literature after studying at the universities of Tübingen, Munich, and Heidelberg. An admirer of Spinoza, he wrote the novel *Spinoza* (2 vols., 1837) and in 1841 published a complete translation of Spinoza's works, with a critical biography.

Auerbach's very popular series of novelettes on rural German life began with the first volume of *Schwarzwälder Dorfgeschichten* (*Black Forest Village Tales*), published in 1843. The series, which attempted to combine realism with romanticism, has been criticized for portraying the peasants as too refined and "literary." The novelettes, of which the most popular were *Die Frau Professorin* (1846), *Diethelm von Buchenberg* (1853), and *Barfüssele* (1856), inspired a flood of literature in Germany with similar themes. Auerbach's other works include *Auf der Höhe* (1865) and *Waldfried* (1874). He died in Cannes, France, on Feb. 8, 1882.

AUGEAN STABLES, ô-jē'ən stā'belz, in Greek legend, a series of stalls housing 3,000 oxen belonging to Augeas, king of Elis. The stables had not been cleaned for 30 years. As one of his 12 labors, Hercules (Heracles) had to clean out the filth in a single day, in return for which Augeas promised to give him one tenth of the cattle.

Hercules accomplished this task by diverting the waters of the Alpheus and Peneus rivers through the stables, washing away all the filth. When Augeas refused to honor the agreement, Hercules killed him. The expression *Augean stable* has become a synonym for any filthy or excessively untidy place.

AUGER EFFECT, ō-zhā' i-fekt', the photoemission of an electron from an outer shell of an atom, caused by the absorption of an X-ray quantum produced in a special manner. Electrons emitted under these conditions are called *Auger electrons*. The effect was discovered in 1925 by the French physicist Pierre Auger.

In order for the outer-shell electron emitted to be called an Auger electron, the X-ray quantum absorbed by it must have been produced by the filling of a vacancy in the K shell—the innermost shell—by an electron from a higher-energy shell or from outside the atom. The initial K-shell vacancy may have been produced in a number of ways, such as bombarding the atom with electrons from an outside source.

SAMUEL OLANOFF, *Bard College*

AUGEREAU, ōzh-rō', **Pierre François Charles** (1757–1816), French soldier, an important aide of Napoleon. He was born in Paris on Nov. 11, 1757. Joining the Revolutionary army, he was a division general in Napoleon's campaign in Italy in 1796. He had a leading role in the victory at Lodi on May 10 and in the capture of the village of Castiglione delle Stiviere on August 5. Napoleon entrusted him with a major role in the military coup in Paris on Sept. 4, 1797, that overthrew royalist and moderate elements in the French government. Later he commanded troops in many of Napoleon's battles.

Augereau was named a marshal of the empire in 1804 and duke of Castiglione in 1806. When Allied armies entered France in 1814 and Louis XVIII became king, Augereau submitted to him and was made a peer. He tried to rejoin Napoleon in 1815, but the emperor declared him a traitor. Augereau died at La Houssaye, near Melun, on June 12, 1816.

AUGIER, ō-zhyā', **Émile** (1820–1889), French dramatist, whose plays are noted for their realism and their strong emphasis on morality. He was born *Guillaume Victor Émile Augier* at Valence, Drôme, France, on Sept. 17, 1820. Trained in the legal profession, he became a playwright exclusively after the success of his first work, *La ciguë*, in 1844. He died at Croissy-sur-Seine on Oct. 25, 1889.

Working both alone and in collaboration, Augier wrote a number of successful plays that are among the first and best representatives of the "theater of ideas." They concentrate largely on social and political themes, and combine didacticism with a skillful handling of character. *Le gendre de Monsieur Poirier* (1854), written in collaboration with Jules Sandeau, deals in a witty manner with the conflict between the aristocracy and the bourgeoisie. Some critics consider this to be the best French drama of the 19th century.

Augier's other plays include *Le mariage d' Olympe* (1855), an unsympathetic picture of a "reformed" prostitute; *Les effrontés* (1861), an attack on the corrupting power of the press; *Maître Guérin* (1864), a fine study of a country lawyer; and *Les Fourchambault* (1878), a naturalistic portrait of an upper-middle-class family. *Madame Caverlet* (1876), a play dealing with divorce, helped to convert French public opinion to the need for reestablishing legalized divorce.

Further Reading: Gaillard, H., *Émile Augier et la comédie sociale* (Paris 1910); Marsan, Jules, *Théâtre d'hier et d'aujourd'hui* (Paris 1926).

AUGSBURG is the site of the Fuggerei, a group of about 50 small houses built for poor Roman Catholic workers by the wealthy Fugger banking family in 1519.

AUGSBURG, ouks'bŏōrкн, is a city in West Germany, in the state of Bavaria, 34 miles (54.7 km) northwest of Munich. The capital of the government district of Swabia, it is on a point of land formed by the junction of the Wertach and Lech rivers, at an altitude of about 1,500 feet.

Industries. Augsburg is one of the most important industrial centers in southern Germany. There is a large and long-established textile industry. Other manufactures include machinery, engines, chemicals, paper products, precision instruments, leather goods, and jewelry. Before and during World War II submarine engines and Messerschmitt airplanes were produced there.

Architecture. Until the severe bombings of World War II, there were many beautiful buildings of the medieval and Renaissance periods in the city. One of the buildings that survived is the cathedral, begun in 994. It is a Romanesque edifice with later Gothic additions. The city hall (Rathaus), built in 1615–1620 and containing the great Golden Hall, was badly gutted by fire in World War II. St. Ulrich's Church, begun in the 15th century, is in late Gothic style. There are also many 16th century fountains.

The wealthy Fugger banking family, which originated in Augsburg, contributed to the architectural history of the city. The town house of Jakob II Fugger, built between 1512 and 1515,

still stands. The Fuggerei, a group of about 50 small houses built in 1519 by the Fuggers for poor Roman Catholic families, was badly damaged by fire during World War II.

History. Known in ancient times as *Augusta Vindelicorum*, Augsburg was founded as a Roman outpost about 15 B.C. by the Roman general Drusus Senior during a campaign to subdue the barbarian tribes in the area. In the 5th century A.D. the city was devastated by the Huns, but it recovered sufficiently by the next century to be made an episcopal see. Charlemagne captured Augsburg early in the 8th century.

By the 10 century Augsburg had come under the control of Swabia, a duchy in south central Germany that was under the suzerainty of the emperor of the Holy Roman Empire. In 955, invading Magyars from Hungary overran southern Germany and beseiged Augsburg. Emperor Otto I united the quarreling German duchies and crushed the Magyars near Augsburg in the important battle of Lechfeld. The battle marked the end of the Magyar threat to Germany. Augsburg grew to be a prosperous city of the Holy Roman Empire, especially after it was made a free imperial city in 1276.

Because of its location at the northern Alpine exit of the trade routes leading north from Venice, Augsburg was one of the wealthiest cities of Europe by the Reformation. The great banking and commercial families of Fugger and Welser added to the city's fame. During the late 15th and early 16th centuries, Augsburg became well known as a cultural and artistic center. The two painters, Hans Holbein the Elder and his son, the Younger, were both born in Augsburg. Hans Burgkmair, a painter and wood engraver, was also a native of the city.

Several imperial diets were held in Ausgburg, and the Ausgburg Confession (1530) and the Peace of Augsburg (1555) were drawn up there. The city suffered severely during the Thirty Years' War of the 17th century and did not recover its prosperity for many years. On the dissolution of the Holy Roman Empire in 1806, it was joined to Bavaria. During World War II, Augsburg was captured by United States forces in April 1945. Population: (1961) 208,659.

AUGSBURG, League of, ouks'bŏōrкн, a league concluded at Augsburg, Bavaria, on July 9, 1686, for the maintenance of the treaties of Westphalia (1648) and Nijmegen (1678–1679) and the Truce of Ratisbon (1684), and to resist the encroachments of King Louis XIV of France. William III, stadtholder of Holland and later king of England, was instrumental in forming this league, whose contracting parties were Emperor Leopold I, the kings of Spain and Sweden, and the rulers of several German states, including the electors of Saxony, Bavaria, and the Palatinate. By the terms of the league, all members of the confederacy were to come to the aid of any member state that might be attacked. England, Holland, and Savoy later joined the league, thus forming the Grand Alliance of 1689. This alliance opposed France in the War of the League of Augsburg, which began when Louis XIV invaded the Rhenish Palatinate to enforce a questionable claim to that district. The conflict, also known as the War of the Palatinate, the Orleans War, or the War of the Grand Alliance, lasted from 1689 to 1697. The parallel conflict in the American colonies was called King William's

War. The war had great colonial and commercial implications.

In the War of the League of Augsburg the French forces were well led and prevented the allies from invading the country. On the sea they were less successful, and the French expedition to Ireland to aid James II (who had been replaced on the English throne by William III in the revolution of 1688) proved disastrous, as William III defeated the Jacobite forces in the Battle of the Boyne (1690). The English and Dutch decisively defeated a French fleet at Cap La Hogue in May 1692, but the English under William III were defeated by French troops led by the duc de Luxembourg at Steenkerke (1692) and at Neerwinden (1693).

Savoy signed a separate peace with France in 1696, and French conquests were restored to Savoy. By the Treaty of Ryswick (1697), the French restored to Spain various lands taken over since the Treaty of Nijmegen, gave a favorable commercial treaty to the Dutch, abandoned claims to the Palatinate, allowed the Dutch to fortify the Spanish Netherlands, and accepted William III as king of England. Louis XIV kept Alsace, but all conquests between France, England, and Holland were restored.

AUGSBURG, ouks′bŏŏrкн, **Religious Peace of,** a convention agreed to by the Catholic and Protestant estates of Germany and by Ferdinand, brother of Emperor Charles V, at a meeting of the Imperial Diet in Augsburg, Germany, on Sept. 25, 1555. It marked a culmination not only of the German religious controversy but also of the half-century-old movement for the political reconstitution of the Holy Roman Empire.

Distracted by his wars with France and by the Turkish menace, the emperor had been powerless to stop the gathering momentum of Protestantism until the early 1540's. The best hope for religious peace until then had seemed to lie in a general Christian council, but Charles' victory in 1547 over the Protestant powers of the Schmalkaldic League reversed this situation temporarily and indicated religious reunification by force. But when the war was renewed the emperor met with little success, and in the Treaty of Passau (1552) Lutheranism won legal recognition in the empire.

Unable to bring himself to accept religious compromise, Charles transferred his powers to his brother Ferdinand, who met the estates in Augsburg. As set out in the *Abschied,* or final decree, of the Diet, the agreement postponed reunification until a more opportune time and substituted what was thought to be a temporary pacification based on the current positions of Protestants and Catholics. Estates professing the Augsburg Confession, that is, the Lutherans (Calvinists and other Protestant groups were excluded) were to be left unmolested.

Freedom of religious choice was granted to estates (but not to individual subjects), with the reservation that spiritual rulers who converted would forfeit their ecclesiastical properties (Article 18). In Protestant lands, Catholic jurisdiction was suspended, and all ecclesiastical affairs were placed under territorial rulers (Article 20). Individuals who could not accept their ruler's religion were to be allowed to sell their property and emigrate (Article 24). Special provisions were made for imperial cities with religiously mixed populations (Article 27), but there was no mention of individual religious freedom nor was there provision for religious tolerance. Each territorial government had the right to enforce religious compliance.

Although intended only as a temporary measure during the religious schism, the Augsburg decree in fact perpetuated the split by establishing the principle of the territorial church. Though intended to preserve the peace, it prepared the way for future trouble by excluding Calvinists from the settlement. Its real importance lies in the realm of German constitutional history, representing one of the final stages in the demise of the medieval empire in favor of the territorial state.

GERALD STRAUSS, *Indiana University*

AUGSBURG CONFESSIONS, ouks′bŏŏrкн kən-fesh′ənz, documents of faith prepared in 1530 by the Lutheran theologian Philipp Melanchthon. They had their origin in a meeting of the Swiss religious reformers Zwingli and Oecolampadius with the German reformers Martin Luther and Melanchthon. These leaders met at Marburg, Germany, in 1529 to discuss a union of their two movements. The concordat that resulted, called the Marburg Articles, was an elaboration of their common beliefs. A final clause acknowledged their differences but enjoined their followers to practice tolerance. The Marburg Articles were, in turn, expanded into two other Protestant statements: the Articles of Schwabach, phrased with a view to reunion with the Roman Catholic Church, and the more polemical Articles of Torgau.

When Emperor Charles V convoked the German Diet at Augsburg on April 8, 1530, he was determined that one of the ruling body's major objectives should be a conciliation of the Lutheran and Roman Catholic factions. Since Luther had been banned from attending the Diet, the burden of representing Protestant religious views fell to Melanchthon. To help achieve a compromise, he prepared for the Diet's consideration a statement of Lutheran objections to, and agreements with, Catholic doctrines and practices. His work, called the Augsburg Confessions (*Confessio Augustana*), was primarily based on the articles of Schwabach and Torgau, but the language was softened to render the presentation more acceptable to the Catholics. Luther approved both the theology and the diplomatic phraseology of the Confessions. The first 21 of its 28 articles dealt with Lutheran views on such doctrines as the nature of God, traditional creeds of the Catholic Church, the sacraments, transubstantiation, good works, ecclesiastical rights, free will, and the saints. The last 7 articles are condemnations of what were considered Catholic abuses: distributing Communion under one form, forbidding the clergy to marry, accepting payment for offering masses of expiation, making confession compulsory, equating grace with participation in fasts and festivals, lack of monastic discipline, and the misuse of authority.

The Confessions were presented to the Diet on June 25, 1530, by seven Lutheran princes and two independent imperial cities. The doctrinal statements were then given to a committee of Catholic theologians for study. The theologians replied negatively in a report read to the Diet on Aug. 3, 1530. Thus reunion failed. The Confessions of Augsburg, however, have survived as the basic profession of Lutheran beliefs. See also LUTHERANISM; MELANCHTHON.

AUGUR, ô′gər, an official Roman diviner who sought to discover how the welfare of the state could be preserved by interpreting the will of the gods. "Augur" probably comes from the Latin *augere* (to increase), suggesting the augur's original function of increasing fertility through sympathetic magic. This original responsibility gradually declined, leaving only traces in festival rites: blessing spring crops, protecting grain from rust, and blessing the life of the state at peace. Such fertility functions shifted to interpreting certain natural signs—especially the flight, feeding, and cries of birds—as the conventional language of the gods for letting men know their will.

Apparently augury was Italian in origin. The Etruscans added elaborate Eastern rites and made the forms of augury so complex that the augurs became a board of experts in secret lore. Their earliest *collegia* had three, then five, members. All early augurs were patricians until the Ogulnian Law of 300 B.C. added five plebeian augurs. Sulla increased the college to 15; Caesar, to 16. The members originally filled their own ranks, but the Domitian Law of 104 B.C. decreed popular election.

Augury in Practice. The augural college met monthly. During the monarchical period the king, an augur, presided. Under the republic the augurs held equal rank and deliberated according to their ages. Once consecrated, a man remained an augur for life. The office gave great prestige and could be held concurrently with other offices. It was therefore much sought after in all periods.

Helping to take the auspices and "inaugurating" officials, cities, and sacred places were the augur's main responsibilities. The rituals were strictly defined. The augur marked out a rectangular area with his curved stick. From its center he marked out a similar rectangle in the sky in which the omen must appear. Then he posed a yes-or-no question to the gods. A magistrate watched the sky for birds, then consulted the augur for interpretation. The augur's word was final, and if the ritual suffered a flaw or oversight, the augur nullified the omens.

Auspices thus did not foretell the future but revealed whether the gods approved or disapproved a proposed action. Auspices were taken on all important occasions: laying out the sacred boundary of a new city or temple, waging war, or installing officials. Even marriage needed favorable auspices. Chance omens, especially thunder and lightning, also showed the will of the gods, but augurs were not obliged to note unsought omens. In essence, the augur and magistrate watching the omens could approve or veto all legislation and elections. Even after the passage of a bill, the augur could belatedly announce an omen or flaw and thus nullify the action. He could postpone an action by announcing that he was "watching the sky." Thus, Cicero could call augurs "the highest and most responsible authorities in the state."

As real faith in religion waned, the power of the augurs was easily abused by political involvement. Political leaders supported the state religion as a patriotic duty, without faith. Sulla, Pompey, Cicero, Antony, Caesar, and Pliny were all augurs, using augural power to block their opponents. In imperial times the augurate became subservient to the will and purpose of the emperors.

ELEANOR HUZAR, *Michigan State University*

August is symbolized in a della Robbia terra-cotta by a husbandman ploughing his fields with a yoke of oxen.

AUGUST, ô′gəst, is the eighth month of the year in the Gregorian calendar. In the ancient Roman calendar it was the sixth month; hence its original name, *Sextilis*. In 8 B.C. the name was changed to *Augustus* in honor of the first Roman emperor, Augustus Caesar. *Augustus*, in turn, is a Latin adjective derived from the verb *augere* (to make greater), and the word carries the connotations of majesty and grandeur.

In the original Roman calendar the month had 29 days; in the Julian calendar, 30 days; in the Augustan and Gregorian, 31 days. Although they do not coincide exactly, August in the Gregorian calendar corresponds to the month called *Metageitnion* in the ancient Greek calendar. An important Roman Catholic holy day of obligation, the Feast of the Assumption, is celebrated on August 15. The carnelian is the birthstone for August.

August was an important month in both world wars. August 1914 was the month in which the great powers declared war on each other in World War I: Germany against Russia on August 1, Germany against France on August 3, Britain against Germany on August 4, Austria against Russia on August 6, and Japan against Germany on August 23. August was also the month in which World War II ended, after the United States dropped the atomic bomb on Hiroshima, Japan, on Aug. 6, 1945, and on Nagasaki on August 9. V-J Day (victory over Japan) was Aug. 15, 1945.

Columbus set sail from Spain on his first voyage to the New World on Aug. 3, 1492. Virginia Dare, the first English child born in America, was born on Aug. 18, 1587. Among persons in the arts born in August were the poet Alfred, Lord Tennyson (Aug. 6, 1809) and the composer Claude Debussy (Aug. 22, 1862). Benjamin Harrison, the 23rd president of the United States, was born on Aug. 20, 1833, Herbert Hoover, the 31st president, was born on Aug. 10, 1874, and Lyndon B. Johnson, the 36th president, was born on Aug. 27, 1908. President Warren G. Harding died in office on Aug. 2, 1923.

AUGUSTA (1811–1890), ô-gus′tə, queen of Prussia and empress of Germany. She was born in Weimar, Germany, on Sept. 30, 1811, the daughter of Charles Frederick, grand duke of Saxe-Weimar. Her full name was *Marie Luise Katharina Augusta.* She was educated at the Weimar court where she became acquainted with Goethe.

In 1829 she married William, then crown prince of Prussia, who became king of Prussia in 1861 and emperor of Germany in 1871. Their two children were Frederick William, who became Emperor Frederick III, and Louise, who married Frederick I, grand duke of Baden. Augusta died in Berlin, Jan. 7, 1890.

AUGUSTA, ô-gus′tə, an honorific title originally bequeathed by Emperor Augustus of Rome to his wife, Livia. It was conferred afterward by Gaius I (Caligula) on his grandmother, Antonia Minor. Claudius I granted the title to his fourth wife, Agrippina Minor, and Nero bestowed it on his wife, Poppaea Sabina.

From Domitian's time (late 1st century A.D.) the title was normally conferred, on the initiative of the Senate, upon the mother, wife, sister, or daughter of the reigning emperor.

AUGUSTA, ou-gōōs′tä, is a town in Italy, located in Siracusa province, Sicily, about 12 miles (19 km) north of the city of Siracusa on the southeastern Sicilian coast. For many centuries before the mid-1800's it was known as *Agosta.*

The town is a seaport, situated on a small island that is connected by two bridges with the mainland of Sicily. There is a good harbor with a naval base. Olive oil, wine, fruit, cheese, fish, and salt are the chief products.

Founded by Emperor Augustus in 42 B.C., the town was sacked by barbarians and by the Muslims and rebuilt by Emperor Frederick II in 1232. It was burned by Turkish forces in 1551 and badly damaged by an earthquake in 1693. Off the port of Augusta in 1676, Adm. Michel Adriaanszoon de Ruyter, commanding a Dutch-Spanish squadron, was defeated and mortally wounded by French forces under Marquis Abraham Duquesne.

The town was badly damaged by bombing in World War II and was taken by British forces in July 1943. The ruins of the ancient Greek colony of Megara Hyblaea are close by. Population: (1961) 25,774.

AUGUSTA, ô-gus′tə, was the name of many ancient European towns. Some of the more famous were *Augusta Auscorum,* now Auch, France; *Augusta Emerita,* now Mérida, Spain; *Augusta Praetoria,* now Aosta, Italy; and *Augusta Suessionum,* now Soissons, France. Others were *Augusta Taurinorum,* now Turin, Italy; *Augusta Treverorum,* now Trier, Germany; and *Augusta Vindelicorum,* now Augsburg, Germany.

AUGUSTA, ô-gus′tə, a city in Georgia, is the seat of Richmond County. It is situated 161 miles (259 km) east of Atlanta at the head of navigation on the Savannah River. The city is rich in historical associations. Modern Augusta is the main trading center for the Central Savannah River Area (CSRA), comprising 13 Georgia and 5 South Carolina counties. One of the most important economic components in the CSRA is the U.S. Atomic Energy Commission's huge Savannah River plant near Aiken, S.C., which produces radioactive isotopes for military and peacetime use. Fort Gordon, a permanent army post in Richmond County, 12 miles (19 km) from the city, also contributes to its prosperity.

The CSRA has diversified industries and agriculture. Its large deposits of clay and kaolin are used in Augusta to manufacture brick and clay products. Other important manufactures in the city are pulp and paperboard, chemicals, and textiles. The area's forestry and agricultural products include timber, livestock, soybeans, cotton, peanuts, pecans, fruit, and tobacco.

Among educational institutions are the Medical College of Georgia, founded in 1828; Paine College, established for Negroes in 1882; and Augusta College, which became a four-year institution in 1965. Cultural attractions include the Augusta Symphony, the Augusta Players, the Gertrude Herbert Institute of Art, the Augusta Choral Society, and the Augusta Museum.

Clark Hill Reservoir, 22 miles (35 km) to the northwest, is a favorite recreation area. It has 1,200 miles (1,931 km) of shoreline and is bordered on the east by Sumter National Forest. Augusta's National Golf Club is world famous for the Masters Golf Tournament played there each year.

Other places of interest are St. Paul's Church; the Signers' Monument, honoring three Georgian signers of the Declaration of Independence; the Mackay House, built in the 1750's; and the boyhood home of Woodrow Wilson.

History. Gen James Edward Oglethorpe, first governor of Georgia, ordered the site for Augusta to be marked out in 1735, and the following year he built Fort Augusta as a trading post for the Indian fur trade. It was probably named for Princess Augusta, wife of the British prince of Wales, whose son became King George III. In 1763 representatives of five Indian nations and four colonial governors met here to settle boundaries and trade terms. During the American Revolution, the British captured the fort and renamed it Fort Cornwallis, but it was recaptured by the Americans. Augusta served intermittently as Georgia's seat of government during some of the chaotic years during and immediately after the Revolution. In 1798 it was chartered as a city. By 1811 cotton had replaced tobacco as the principal commodity traded there.

In the Civil War, Augusta was important to the Confederacy as a railroad junction and for the manufacture of gunpowder. The U.S. Arsenal was seized by the Confederates in 1861 without bloodshed.

In 1908, the Savannah River overflowed its banks and the city suffered serious damage. Bonds for a levee along the river were issued in 1912. Today Augusta is protected from floods by the Hartwell and Clark Hill dams.

The city has a mayor and council form of government. Population: 59,864.

AUGUSTA, ô-gus′tə, a city in southern Kansas, is in Butler County, 25 miles (40 km) east of Wichita by road. Augusta is situated in grain-farming, stockraising, and oil country. Oil refining and allied industries are important. The city has a historical museum. Butler County State Park recreational area is nearby.

Settled in 1861, the community was named for Augusta James, the wife of its founder. Augusta adopted the city manager plan of government in 1951. Population: 5,977.

AUGUSTA, capital of Maine, lies in the southwestern part of the state. The State House was designed by Bulfinch.

AUGUSTA, ô-gus'tə, a city in south central Maine, is the capital of the state and the seat of Kennebec County. It is situated on both sides of the Kennebec River, at the head of navigation about 35 miles (56 km) from the Atlantic Ocean and 60 miles (96 km) by road northeast of Portland. In Augusta the ground rises steeply on both sides of the river. Near the southern approach to the city, landscaped Capitol Park leads up from the river to the old state house, which was designed in 1829 by the American architect Charles Bulfinch. The river is spanned by three bridges, and Kennebec Dam is in the city.

Augusta is the business center of a tourist vacation area, a fertile agricultural region, and rich timberlands. Among its many nearby lakes are Belgrade, China, and Cobbosseecontee. There are summer camps, resorts, and golf courses. The chief agricultural products are apples, potatoes, poultry, and garden produce. The timber is used to manufacture pulp and paper in the city. Other principal manufactures are cotton textiles, shoes, food products, carbonated beverages, and poultry feed. Near the Augusta airport is Camp Keyes, home of the Maine national guard. Augusta's newspaper is the *Daily Kennebec Journal,* founded in 1825. A branch of the University of Maine was opened in 1965.

There are many interesting buildings in and around Augusta. The state house has retained the Bulfinch façade, although it was rebuilt in 1909–1910. The Kennebec County courthouse dates from 1830. Across the street from the old state house is the executive mansion, which was formerly the home of James G. Blaine, U.S. secretary of state from 1889 to 1892. Among the newer buildings in Augusta are the computer center of the Central Maine Power Company and the U.S. post office and federal building.

On the east side of the city is Augusta State Hospital, one of two large mental hospitals maintained by the state. It was begun in 1840. The U.S. Veterans Administration Facility at Togus, 4.5 miles (7 km) east of Augusta, was established in 1866 as a home for Civil War veterans. Its hospitals and other buildings now occupy a 1,752-acre (709-hectare) reservation.

Augusta occupies the site of the Indian village of Cushnoc, where the Plymouth Colony set up a trading post in 1628. Its first agent, John Howland, shared his quarters in 1634 with John Alden, the reticent hero of Longfellow's poem *The Courtship of Miles Standish.* John Winslow, of another famous colonial family, was in charge of the post from 1647 to 1653. Fort Western, now a museum, was built there in 1754. Its first and only commander was Capt. James Howard. He later bought the fort and is therefore reputed to be Augusta's first settler.

The settlement that grew up around Fort Western became a trading and shipping center called *Hallowell.* It developed as two communities, one named *Cushnoc,* near the fort, and the other called the *Hook,* after Bombahook Stream. In 1797 differences between the two sections became acute, and the town divided. The Hook kept the name Hallowell, and Cushnoc became *Harrington.* Later that year, Harrington was renamed Augusta, supposedly after Pamela Augusta Dearborn, daughter of Henry Dearborn, a Revolutionary general.

Augusta was incorporated as a town in 1797. It became the county seat in 1799 and the state capital in 1832. A dam was built across the Kennebec in 1837, and Augusta became a manufacturing town. In 1849 it was chartered as a city. Government is by council-manager. Population: 21,945.

MARGARET A. WHALEN, *Maine State Library*

AUGUSTAN AGE, ô-gus'tən, a cultural period marked by adherence in literature to the style and ideals of classical Rome. The literature of such an age is extremely formal, emphasizing learning and reason rather than the emotions. Historically the term refers to the reign (31 B.C.–14 A.D.) of Emperor Augustus of Rome. This was the time of the great poets Horace, Ovid, and Virgil, and was the golden age of Roman literature.

In England the literary era in the reign of Queen Anne (1702–1714) or, more broadly, the time of Addison, Swift, and Pope, is called the Augustan age. The term was given currency by the contemporary dramatist and editor Nicholas Rowe, who believed that the formalism and polish of Roman writing were appropriate to his own time. Writers of the era were consciously "Augustan." They followed such Latin forms as the satires and odes of Horace, incorporated Roman themes in their works, and frequently compared London to Rome. Pope even addressed George II satirically as "Augustus." In France the era of Corneille, Racine, and Molière also has been called an Augustan age.

AUGUSTAN HISTORY, ô-gus-tən, the name commonly given to a collection of 30 biographies of Roman emperors who reigned between 117 and 284 A.D. Its Latin name is *Historia Augusta.* The history begins with a biography of Hadrian and ends with one of Numerianus. It is modeled on Suetonius' *Lives of the Caesars* (about 121 A.D.). The authorship is attributed to six writers, but little or nothing is known of the authors; many of their names may be pseudonyms. Even the date of composition is uncertain. Dedications to Diocletian and Constantine suggest that the work was written in the period 284–337 A.D., but scholars generally agree that the collection in its present form probably was not written before 350 A.D.

The work is valuable chiefly because it often provides the only full account of certain emperors; for example, Antoninus Pius, for whose reign other major sources are lacking. Its historical value, however, is uneven. The earlier biographies are the most reliable, but the later ones are padded throughout with letters, documents, and speeches, all of which are fabrications.

TOM B. JONES, *University of Minnesota*

AUGUSTINE, ô'gə-stēn, **Saint** (died 604/609), first archbishop of Canterbury. He was prior of the Benedictine monastery of St. Andrew at Rome when chosen by Pope Gregory the Great to lead a band of missionaries to England. This marked the revival of the Roman church's interest in missionary work. England also became the first foreign area of Benedictine expansion, as Augustine took both the papal jurisdiction and the Benedictine rule to Britain.

Accompanied by a small number of monks, he reached the Kentish coast in 597. He was courteously received by Ethelbert, king of Kent, whose Frankish wife Bertha was a Christian. The king gave protection to the monks, permitting them to become established at Canterbury and to preach. Ethelbert himself was baptized, as were his people after him. Augustine went the same year to Arles, in France, and was consecrated bishop by Virgilius. In 601 Gregory gave him jurisdiction over Britain as archbishop.

In the interests of Christian unity, Augustine attempted to come to terms with the Celtic bishops. These bishops represented a Christianity already in existence for some centuries in England, but it had been driven into the west and north by German invasions 150 years before Augustine's time. The Celtic bishops refused to cooperate with the Roman mission or to give up their customs regarding baptism and the date of Easter. At Augustine's death (sometime between 604 and 609) the Roman mission hardly extended beyond Kent, but after his death a joint effort by the Roman and Celtic churches converted all England to Christianity in less than 100 years. His feast day is May 26.

ST. AUGUSTINE of Hippo, Christian theologian and philosopher of the 4th and 5th centuries, from a painting by El Greco and his school (Museo de Santa Cruz, Toledo).

BETTMANN ARCHIVE

AUGUSTINE, ô'gə-stēn, **Saint** (354–430), Christian bishop, Doctor of the Church, theologian, and philosopher. He was born at Tagaste, Numidia (now Souk-Ahras, Algeria), on Nov. 13, 354. He was the son of Patricius, a Roman official, who remained a pagan until shortly before his death in 370, and of Monica (or Monnica), a Christian. Although Augustine was traditionally known by the Latin name *Aurelius Augustinus,* there is no evidence that he received the name Aurelius at birth or baptism or that he used it. He had a brother named Navigius and a sister, traditionally called Perpetua, who became a nun. He was enrolled as a catechumen shortly after his birth, but he was not baptized and did not receive much Christian instruction.

Education and Early Career. Augustine's first training in grammar and arithmetic was in Tagaste, where he was badly taught. He hated Greek and never acquired a thorough knowledge of it. When he was about 11 years old, he was sent to school at Madauros, a center of paganism. There he gained a deep knowledge of Latin literature, but the pagan environment adversely affected his moral and religious development. He spent the year 369–370 at home in idleness, but a reading of Cicero's *Hortensius* made a lasting impression on him and turned his mind toward philosophy. In 370, through the generosity of Romanianus, a fellow citizen, he went for further study to Carthage, where he lived with a mistress who bore him a son, Adeodatus, in 371. There also he became a Manichaean and attempted to make converts to the sect. In 373–74 he taught grammar at Tagaste, and for the following nine years he conducted a rhetoric school at Carthage. He then went to Rome, where he established a school of rhetoric, abandoned Manichaeism, and turned to the skepticism of the New Academy. A year later he established a school at Milan.

Conversion to Christianity. Various influences, among them St. Ambrose's preaching, his friend Simplicianus' counsel, and the study of Neo-Platonic philosophy, contributed to his entry into the Christian church. The long prayers of Monica were answered when Augustine and Adeodatus were baptized on Easter, April 25, 387. Soon after, he and his family (he had previously dismissed Adeodatus' mother) started back to Africa. At Ostia, the port of Rome, St. Monica died after scenes and conversations beautifully recorded by her son in his *Confessions.*

Augustine was not physically strong and suffered frequently from ill health, but he was unceasing in both physical and intellectual labors. In him were united emotional intensity, immense intellectual power, tenacity of will, deep spirituality, and heroic sanctity. After his conversion he gave himself entirely to God and to the service of his fellow men.

After Augustine returned to Tagaste in 388 he sold his patrimony and gave the money to the poor, keeping only a house which he turned into a monastic community. Among its first members was Adeodatus, now a youth of brilliant intellect, who died in 389/390. Augustine did not intend to become a priest, but in 391 he was ordained in the nearby city of Hippo (modern Annaba, Algeria), almost by popular demand.

Bishop of Hippo. In 395–396, Augustine was consecrated auxiliary bishop of Hippo and shortly after succeeded to the diocese. Hippo was a city of about 30,000, but the Christian church was not strong there because the population was mixed in religion and race. As administrator, preacher, controversialist, correspondent, and writer, Augustine worked to defend and spread the Catholic religion.

The last years of Augustine's life were years of war and disaster for the Roman empire in the West. What remained of Roman rule was crumbling rapidly under the impact of constant barbarian infiltrations. In August 430 the Vandals, who had marched west after seizing Carthage, were besieging Hippo. In the midst of the assault on his city, on Aug. 28, 430, Augustine died in the sanctity and poverty in which he had lived for so many years. After the conquest of the city, the Vandals destroyed all of it except Augustine's cathedral and library, which were left untouched. According to tradition his body rests in Pavia, Italy. The date of his death is celebrated as his feast.

AUGUSTINIANISM

The body of philosophical and theological doctrines originated by St. Augustine, or developed and stressed by him, is called Augustinianism. One of the most independent thinkers in the history of Western thought, Augustine rightly belongs to its best tradition. It was by a reading of Cicero's *Hortensius*, an exhortation to the philosophical life based on Aristotle's *Protrepticus*, that Augustine was first drawn to philosophy. However, far greater than any Aristotelian influence on him was that of Plato and Plotinus. These Platonic and Neo-Platonic influences united with Augustine's religious beliefs, qualities of mind, and cast of character to place mystical elements in his work and inspire him to express them with eloquence and beauty.

Augustine sometimes wrote in haste, but he was one of the greatest of writers as well as one of the greatest of thinkers. Among his masterpieces are: *On the Trinity* (*De trinitate*, 400–16), *Confessions* (*Confessiones*, 397–401), and *The City of God* (*De civitate Dei*, 413–26). His vast body of writing also includes *On the Happy Life* (*De beata vita*, 386), *On Order* (*De ordine*, 386), *On the Immortality of the Soul* (*De immortalitate animae*, 387), *Soliloquies* (387), *Concerning the Teacher* (*De magistro*, 389), *On True Religion* (*De vera religione*, 389–91), *On Free Will* (*De libero arbitrio*, 388–95), *Against the Manichaean, Faustus* (*Contra Faustum Manichaeum*, 400), *On Nature and Grace* (*De natura et gratia*, 415), *Retractions* (*Retractiones*, 426).

On God. Augustine's thought may be said to center upon two poles, God and the self, but it is more correct to say that all his thought is centered upon God. Thus he writes: "I wish to know God and the soul. Nothing more? Nothing more whatever"; and "O God, Thou who art always the same, I would know myself and I would know Thee." Early in his *Confessions* he puts the words: "For Thyself hast Thou made us, O God, and our heart is restless until it rests in Thee." To show that the mind can arrive at truth is one of his first tasks. Against the skeptics of the new Academy, who held that only probability is possible, he argues that the very notion of probability involves that of truth. If a man asserts that a doctrine is probable, he holds that it is like the truth. Hence he must have some perception of the truth. Again, Augustine points out that if a man doubts, he lives, and even "if I am in error, I am." Here he anticipates Descartes' "I think; therefore I am," but he is on firmer philosophical ground and makes better use of the principle. By these and other arguments he shows that skepticism is untenable and that we can arrive at certain truths. He distinguishes carefully between sense knowledge and the higher knowledge that comes from intellect and reason.

The soul is a true substance and not a mere accidental reality, that is, an attribute or aspect of the body. It is simple, or devoid of parts, immaterial, and spiritual. For its immortality Augustine advances various proofs which derive from Plato. The soul is possessed of imperishable truths, and is therefore itself imperishable. It is rational, and in essence it is a living substance; therefore it cannot die. Because of his soul, man is in the image and likeness of God, and in the soul's powers of memory, understanding, and will Augustine finds a reflection of the Blessed Trinity—Father, Son, and Holy Spirit.

The existence of God can be known by reason, and Augustine accepts the traditional proof from order in the universe, and the proof from consciousness. Characteristically, his principal argument is Platonic in nature and is based upon the mind's possession of eternal and immutable truths. Because there are such truths, there must be an eternal Truth. This Truth is God, or if there is a being more excellent than Truth, then that being is God. For Augustine, however, Truth is a favored name for God. Like Plotinus, he teaches that God is above all categories. God's greatest attributes are eternity, wisdom, and blessedness. He is infinite, omnipotent, omniscient, all-good, and unchangeable. He is Beauty, ancient yet ever-new, as well as eternal Truth.

So unified is Augustine's thought that it would be wrong to isolate and overstress this proof for God's existence It represents an attitude and an approach as well as a formal argument. If the *Confessions* can be described as one long prayer, so can Augustine's entire philosophy be taken as a turning to God and a view of things in His light. Just as God is the source of all reality, so does all knowledge depend on Him. Hence his theory of knowledge is one of divine illumination. God floods His light into the human mind and enables it to perceive the eternal and immutable truths. Ultimately, in all acquisition of knowledge, in all learning, God is the teacher. In Augustine faith and reason are most closely allied. Hence it is wrong to departmentalize his mind and to think that he offers an exclusively rational and purely philosophical approach to God.

On the Works of God. Augustine rejects the Plotinian doctrine that the universe emanates from God. It was in God's eternal plan to create the universe, and with its production out of nothing time began. Material things belong to the lowest level of being. Within them God has implanted certain *rationes seminales*; because of these "seedlike causes" or potencies, new forms appear in the course of time. On the problem of time he is especially effective. Its difficulties are summed up in his epigram: "What is time? If you do not ask me, I know; if you ask me, I do not know." Although influenced by Aristotle, he goes beyond Aristotle in his stress upon the psychological aspect of time and regards time as "a distention of the soul."

On the Problems of Man. In various writings Augustine teaches that evil is not something real and positive but rather a privation of the good. Hence it has a *causa deficiens* rather than a *causa efficiens*. Moral evil, or sin, is due to man's free will. Every man has the will to be happy, but not every man wills those things which are necessary for true happiness in this world and eternal happiness in the world to come. Every sin is a turning away from eternal things and an acceptance of something temporal. Among the particular moral problems that he considers are those concerned with veracity, self-preservation, chastity, and peace and war. For a just war there must be lawful authority, a just cause, and a right intention, and the war must be a last resort. War is not contrary to the divine law and evil in itself. However, it can be justified only by its relation to peace, the tranquillity of order. Augustine points out that whereas the good soldier is rightly praised, a higher glory belongs to those who will slay war itself with the word, that is, by the use of reason. His teaching on war and peace has been the accepted doctrine in Western Christendom.

In *The City of God*, Augustine produced the first and the greatest philosophy of history. Its occasion was the capture and sack of Rome by the barbarians. As this could lead to anti-Christian charges, Augustine's first purpose was apologetic, but as he wrote he broadened his view and developed the doctrine of the two cities, the earthly city and the heavenly city. Jerusalem, the city of God, is the Catholic Church; Babylon, the earthly city, is the state, or more precisely the pagan state. Just as within the individual man there are two warring loves, the love of God and the love of the world, so also there are two opposing loves in human society. In developing this basic theme, he discusses many subjects and brings to bear on them his great knowledge of history and literature as well as that of theology and philosophy. *The City of God* provided the Middle Ages with a political theory and ideal. In the judgment of Augustine himself and of later readers, this is his greatest work.

On Doctrine. Following his conversion, Augustine's knowledge of Sacred Scripture and of Catholic doctrine became ever deeper and wider. Outstanding among his contributions to theology is that which gives him the title of "the Doctor of Grace." The Pelagian heresy had repudiated the supernatural order in man, in the sense that it held a completely naturalistic theory as to human freedom and responsibility. Man's will was said to be entirely independent of God, so that by his unaided powers a man could attain to perfection. Hence also, a man is completely responsible for even his slightest offenses. Against this extravagant and rigoristic doctrine Augustine's solution safeguarded both God's omnipotence and man's freedom. God controls the human will, as He does all things, and His grace is necessary for salvation. Yet even when God gives His efficacious grace to a man, he can accept or reject such grace. When God freely and out of His infinite love offers His grace to a man, He likewise knows that that man will freely accept it. Augustine's doctrine on grace, predestination, and free will has been a constant subject of study and discussion and an enduring influence among both Catholic and Protestant thinkers.

Among other Augustinian contributions are his profound study of the incarnation and the redemption, his emphasis upon the church as the mystical body of Christ and the way in which men are incorporated into it, his teaching on the sacraments, and his doctrine on Christian charity. Although he stressed the primacy of faith and showed the relation of reason to faith, he did not clearly define their two realms, as was done by later thinkers.

His Influence. So great was the genius of "the greatest of the doctors of the Church" that he decisively affected subsequent thought in the Western world. Throughout the Middle Ages the representative teachers appealed to his authority, although some, like St. Anselm, are more formally Augustinian than others. His influence is strong in the work of St. Thomas Aquinas, St. Albertus Magnus, Peter Lombard, the members of the Franciscan and Victorine schools, and many others. In later times he was used in many quarters, although not always with understanding and justice. Although he was not neglected in the earlier modern period, there has been a greatly increased interest in him in the contemporary world, and he has attracted to himself thinkers who have perceived clearly that he can still teach men about God, the soul, and countless other subjects. Because of what he was and did, he remains one of the greatest and most influential figures in the history of thought.

See also CONFESSIONS OF SAINT AUGUSTINE; CITY OF GOD.

JOHN K. RYAN
The Catholic University of America

Bibliography

Translations of Augustine's writings include *The Works of St. Augustine*, 15 vols., ed. by M. Dods (Edinburgh 1871–76); *The Basic Works of Saint Augustine*, ed. by W.J. Oates (New York 1948); volumes in the Fathers of the Church series (Washington 1948–) and the Ancient Christian Writers series, ed. by J. Quasten and J.C. Plumpe (Westminster, Md. 1946–); *The Confessions*, tr. by John K. Ryan (Garden City, N.Y. 1960); and *The City of God*, tr. by G.G. Walsh (New York 1958). His complete works in Latin are found in *Patrologia Latina*, ed. by J.P. Migne, and the Vienna Academy's *Corpus Scriptorum ecclesiasticorum Latinorum*.

Bertrand, Louis. *Saint Augustine* (New York 1914).

Bourke, V.J., *Augustine's Quest for Wisdom* (Milwaukee 1945).

Chabannes, Jacques, *St. Augustine*, tr. by J. Kernan, (Garden City, N.Y., 1962).

Guitton, Jean, *Modernity of Saint Augustine* (Toronto 1959).

O'Meara, John J., *The Young Augustine* (London 1954).

For Specialized Study

Boyer, C., *L'idée de la vérité dans la philosophie de saint Augustin* (Paris 1920).

Figgis, J.N., *The Political Aspects of St. Augustine's City of God* (London 1921).

Gilson, E., *The Christian Philosophy of Saint Augustine*, tr. by L.E.M. Lynch (Toronto 1960).

AUGUSTINIANS, ô-gəs-tin′e-ənz, are religious orders and congregations of Roman Catholic priests, brothers, and nuns who follow the rule of St. Augustine of Hippo (354–430). Although St. Augustine never delineated a detailed rule, such as that of St. Benedict, he advocated certain ascetic principles throughout his works and particularly in a letter addressed to a community of nuns in 423. From the time of his conversion, St. Augustine's personal adherence to monasticism set an example that others were to emulate. Many of his friends joined him on his father's estate at Tagaste (now Souk-Ahras, Algeria) to pursue a life of prayer and study. To this early monastic compound the Augustinian Fathers trace their origin.

Augustine's appointment as bishop in 395 forced him to abandon the Tagaste retreat but not his monastic way of life. He required that his clerics live with him in a form of common life fitting to their more worldly state; the Canons Regular of St. Augustine trace their origins to this innovation. The 70 or more other orders and congregations which follow the rule of St. Augustine were founded later or resulted from reform movements. Among the more important are the Recollects of St. Augustine, Discalced Augustinians, and Augustinians of the Assumption.

Augustinian Fathers. Formerly the Order of Hermits of St. Augustine, they originated at Tagaste in 388 and expanded to 19 communities by the time of the Vandal invasions of Africa in the 5th century. The evidence of the survival in Europe of these early communities is at best tenuous. Documents yield no information until the 11th and 12th centuries at which time many communities who followed the rule of St. Augustine and whose monks identified themselves as Hermit Brethren of St. Augustine were flourishing throughout France, England, Germany, Hungary, and Italy. This wide geographical distribution indicates an origin in antiquity; and in 1256, after Alexander IV granted the hermits canonical status and joined certain larger hermit groups

THE AUGUSTINIAN HABIT is black, belted by a leather cincture, and topped by a cape with attached hood.

to the existing Order(s) of St. Augustine, the title of Hermits was retained to indicate the order's early founding.

By the time of Martin Luther (1483–1546), who had been an Augustinian monk before his estrangement from the church, Augustinian membership had swelled to 20,000. During the Reformation, however, the order suffered losses. After the 16th century, it was suppressed in France, Germany, Austria, and Italy and suffered reverses in Spain, Mexico, Russia, and the Philippines.

The Augustinian Fathers have been established in the United States since 1796. Two provinces, one in the Middle West, another in the East, and a vice-province in the Far West have a total membership of 700 religious. The provinces conduct parishes, high schools, and three colleges —Merrimack, Biscayne, and Tolentine—and one university, Villanova. The order as a whole has a membership of 4,000 professed religious, and an Augustinian order of nuns numbers 1,700 religious.

Recollects of St. Augustine. Formed in 1574 by the Spanish friars of the Hermits of St. Augustine to emphasize the contemplative aspect of Augustinianism, the movement grew rapidly. It assumed a semiautonomous status, until in 1912, Pope Pius X established the Recollects as a distinct order with its own superior general and constitution. Its 1,600 members are active chiefly in South America. A Recollect province was founded in the United States in 1944, with a motherhouse in West Orange, N.J.

Discalced Augustinians. Formed in Spain in 1592–1599 by Friar Thomas of Andrada, like the Recollects they sought to be more rigid in rule than the Hermits. The Discalced (Barefooted) Augustinians gained autonomy in the 17th century and independence in 1910. The monks, who serve as missionaries in South America, numbered fewer than 200 in the mid-1960's.

Canons Regular of St. Augustine. Although St. Augustine attempted to organize his clerics into a semimonastic community (one of his disciples, Gelasius, emulated this ideal in Rome in 492), it was not until the reform of Gregory VII (reigned 1073–1085) that communities of clerics who sought to live the common life of poverty, chastity, and obedience in imitation of the Early Christians became legion. Approved by the Lateran synods in 1059 and 1063, they rapidly expanded throughout Europe. Due to the Reformation and subsequent political suppression, however, the "Black Canons," as they were called because of their distinctive black hoods, declined in numbers. The Canons were confederated in 1959. Their abbot primate is located in Switzerland.

Augustinians of the Assumption. Also called the Assumptionist Fathers, they were founded in 1843 at Nîmes, France, by the Rev. Emmanuel d'Alzon and approved by the Holy See in 1864. They have sought to rechristianize Europe and reunite the Eastern Orthodox and Roman Catholic churches. They maintain houses of 2,000 religious. The United States province in New York City was founded in 1946.

Further Reading: Dickinson, John C., *Origins of the Austin Canons and Their Introduction into England* (New York 1951); Orozco, Alonso de, *Rule of St. Augustine* (Westminster, Md., 1956); Roland, Thomas F., *Hermits of St. Augustine in the United States* (Villanova, Pa., 1947).

AUGUSTULUS, Romulus. See ROMULUS AUGUSTULUS.

AUGUSTUS (63 B.C.–14 A.D.), ô-gus′təs, first emperor of the Roman empire. His original name was *Gaius Octavius*. After his adoption by Caesar, he was known as *Gaius Julius Caesar Octavianus*, which has become anglicized to *Octavian*. He was the grandnephew of Julius Caesar, who, having no son of his own, took an interest in him. When Caesar was assassinated in 44 B.C., Octavian was a student in Illyricum, where he was awaiting Caesar, intending to go with him on an invasion of Parthia. The Roman world received a shock when it learned that Caesar had adopted the youth—then only 18 years old—as his son and heir.

Struggle for Supremacy. Octavian immediately set out for Rome to claim his inheritance. By the time he arrived in Italy, many of Caesar's veterans had flocked to his standard, and Octavian from the very beginning demonstrated the political acumen that was to characterize his whole career. He found that Mark Antony, one of Caesar's lieutenants, had taken possession of Caesar's papers and wealth and was determined to shunt Octavian aside.

Octavian threw in his lot with Cicero and the senatorial party. In 43 B.C. they defeated Antony at Mutina. After Octavian returned victorious to Rome and Antony seemed no longer to be a threat, the senators decided that they, too, could ignore the young man. Octavian turned to Antony, who in the meantime had joined his forces with those of Lepidus, another of Caesar's lieutenants, and the three of them marched on Rome late in 43 and secured the passage of a law that named them triumvirs for the purpose of reorganizing the state. In the following year Lepidus, the least important of the three, was left behind in control of Rome while Antony and Octavian went to Greece and there at Philippi defeated Brutus and Cassius, the assassins of Caesar. After the battle Antony stayed in the East and Octavian returned to Rome.

In 41 B.C., Antony's wife, Fulvia, led a revolt against Octavian. Relations between the two men became so strained that they decided to meet in 40 at Brundisium, in southern Italy, where they effected a reconciliation. The triumvirs divided the Roman empire among themselves. Antony took the East; Octavian, the West; and Lepidus, Africa. To cement their renewed friendship, Antony, whose wife had died, married Octavia, the sister of Octavian.

In the West, Octavian had one major problem. Sextus Pompey, the son of Pompey the Great, commanded a large fleet and, in defiance of the triumvirate, held the island of Sicily, from which he periodically attacked Italy. In 37 B.C., Octavian and Antony met again, this time at Tarentum. Antony agreed to give Octavian a fleet in return for several legions. Octavian received the fleet but did not send Antony his legions. In the following year he defeated Sextus Pompey. At the same time he eliminated Lepidus, who had decided to join forces with Pompey. There were now only two rulers in the Roman empire—Octavian, who now controlled all of the West, and Antony.

Octavian methodically began to prepare for a confrontation with Antony, whose invasion of Parthia in 36 B.C. had been unsuccessful. By this time Antony's relationship with Cleopatra, queen of Egypt, was a public scandal. Octavian, in a skillful propaganda campaign, convinced many Romans that Antony intended to move the capital

THE GRANGER COLLECTION (PIC NO. 114.02)

AUGUSTUS, first emperor of the Roman world, is portrayed in this statue in the Louvre in Paris.

of the empire to Alexandria and to make the unpopular Cleopatra the queen of the Romans. He had Antony's authority abrogated and secured a declaration of war against Egypt. In 31 B.C. the forces of Antony and Cleopatra met those of Octavian at Actium, and in a great sea battle Octavian emerged victorious. Antony and Cleopatra fled to Egypt, where they committed suicide in the following year. Octavian thus became the sole ruler of the Roman empire.

The Principate. Like his adoptive father Julius Caesar, Octavian had eliminated most of the opposition. But Caesar had been unwise. By his monarchical behavior he had provoked a conspiracy of assassination. Octavian was determined to avoid this precedent. He directed his attention to the creation of a stable government that he could rule without alienating the republican sentiments that the Romans had traditionally held so dear. Up to the time of his victory over Antony, Octavian had been the leader of a faction, but he now found it necessary to transform his faction into a national party by incorporating into it all elements of Roman society.

For a few years he temporized, but finally in January of 27 B.C. he announced his plans before a meeting of the Senate. He said he had decided to restore the republic. He offered to resign his offices and turn over all his provinces to the control of the Senate. Almost certainly this meeting of the Senate had been well organized in advance by Octavian and his supporters. After his speech, individual members of the Senate rose to protest that the Roman state could not survive without him. He allowed it to appear that he had been persuaded to take back some of the provinces and to continue as consul. For his apparent self-sacrifice many honors were bestowed upon him, including the name "Augustus," by which he was afterward known.

Despite the restoration of the republic, the settlement left Augustus firmly in control. He took as his provinces the old military commands of Spain, Gaul, and Syria. Most of the Roman armies were stationed in those provinces, and Augustus, as their commander, remained by far the most powerful man in Rome. He had succeeded in disguising his own monarchy in the cloak of republicanism.

In 23 B.C. he again altered his position in the state. He resigned the consulate, making it possible for more senators to hold that office. But he took in its place the tribunician power, which gave him the right to initiate legislation and to convene the Assembly. Most of the functions he had lost by giving up the consulate were restored to him when he was given a proconsular *imperium maius*, allowing him to continue governing his provinces from Rome, which he had previously done as consul. Since his *imperium* (command) called *maius* (greater), he had authority superior to that of the other proconsular governors. He was soon given the right to call meetings of the Senate, to submit the first item of business, and to sit between the consuls at meetings of the Senate. Later, in 12 B.C., he became *pontifex maximus* (see PONTIFEX), and in 2 B.C. the Senate gave him the title *Pater Patriae* (Father of His Country).

Augustus' position in the state resulted from several titles and grants, but he was careful to maintain the fiction that he was merely one of many elected officials in the Roman government. He turned down some offices that were offered to him on the grounds that they were unconstitutional. He never accepted the tribunician power or the *imperium maius* for life, preferring to have them periodically renewed at intervals throughout his reign. The title that he favored was *Princeps*, an old Roman designation that gave its bearer little power but proclaimed that he was first among equals. The government that Augustus created is therefore called the "principate."

Augustan Policies. Augustus considered himself a second Romulus. He hoped to restore the old Roman virtues, which had lapsed during the late republic. As one step in this direction he reformed the religious structure of Rome by filling the vacancies in the priesthoods and by repairing old temples and building new ones. He also encouraged the people to worship his own *genius*, fostering in the provinces the development of an imperial cult whereby he himself was worshiped as a god. By his social legislation he sought to reform society. In 19 and 18 B.C. he passed several laws to encourage marriage, restore family life, and discourage childlessness.

Roman literature flourished under his reign, and he himself tried to forward the efforts of the poets. Virgil wrote the *Aeneid* at Augustus' suggestion. The emperor was quick to recognize the value of an intellectual elite favorable to his reign, and he personally supported many literary men, while his friends supported others. In addition to Virgil, whose works sing the praises of the new regime, there was Horace, who was selected by Augustus to write a hymn for the secular games celebrated by the emperor in 17 B.C. Literary men who dared criticize the Augustan ideals did so at their own peril. In 8 A.D., Ovid, who had written erotic poetry and condoned adultery, was banished from Rome. Cassius Severus was similarly exiled because of his writings.

The hand of the emperor was felt in many other areas. He reorganized the Roman army and created a permanent navy. He suppressed abuses in provincial administration, both in his own provinces and in those of the Senate. During most of his reign he conducted an aggressive foreign policy and expanded the Roman empire to its "natural" frontiers, the Rhine and Danube. After the loss of three legions in Germany in 9 A.D. at the battle of the Teutoburger Forest, he gave up the idea of further expansion across the Rhine. In the East he was more cautious, preferring to rule with client kings where possible and abandoning Caesar's and Antony's dream of conquering Parthia.

He was most unsuccessful in his attempts to find a successor. Afraid that Rome would revert to the chaos of the late republic when he died, Augustus sought to groom a successor within the ranks of his own family, but he had no son of his own. First he selected his nephew Marcellus, then his friend Agrippa, then his grandsons Gaius and Lucius, but they all died before him. Finally, in 4 A.D., by that time a saddened and embittered old man, he chose his stepson Tiberius, whom he disliked. Because of these and other family frustrations (he had been forced to exile his daughter and granddaughter for adultery), he became in his last years more tyrannical, arbitrarily controlling elections and invoking censorship, establishing precedents that were followed by his successors.

The growth of absolutism was one of the chief characteristics of Augustus' reign. By the time he died in 14 A.D., there were few men alive who could remember the free institutions of the republic. Despite this, his achievements were remarkable. He introduced an era of peace, the *Pax Romana*, that was to continue almost unbroken for two centuries. Under his leadership Rome prospered, and when he died at the age of 76, he was deified.

ARTHUR FERRILL, *University of Washington*

Further Reading: Buchan, John, *Augustus* (Mystic, Conn., 1947); Holmes, T.R.E., *Architect of the Roman Empire*, 2 vols. (New York 1928–31); Rowell, Henry, *Rome in the Augustan Age* (Norman, Okla., 1962); Syme, Ronald, *Roman Revolution* (New York 1939).

AUGUSTUS (1526–1586), ô-gus′təs, elector of Saxony, was the younger son of Henry the Pious of the Albertine line of Saxon dukes. He was born on July 31, 1526, at Freiberg. Augustus was the brother of Maurice of Saxony, whose opportune change of sides in the German religious wars won electoral status for Albertine Saxony. Until his brother's death in 1553 raised him to the throne, Augustus played a minor role in Saxon affairs. Augustus devoted himself to the consolidation of his power in the duchy and pursued a pacifying and mediating policy toward the emperor and the Catholic states, as well as toward rival Protestant princes in order to retain his electorship.

An enormous man of great strength and vigor, quick to anger and capable of great cruelty, Augustus became a resourceful power politician and a practitioner of a ruthless mercantilism. His great achievement was the modernization of administration, finance, and commerce in his duchy. He improved roads and waterways and tried to reduce the maze of commercial restrictions that encumbered traffic on the Elbe River. He expanded mining in silver, gold, and iron, promoted technical innovations, and encouraged new manufactures. He reorganized judicial administration and the police.

In religious affairs, his reign saw the triumph of doctrinaire Lutheranism through the promulgation of the *Formula Concordiae*. Though originally an adherent of the more flexible Philippist strain in Lutheran thought, Augustus came to accept orthodox Lutheranism, perhaps through the influence of his wife Anna, daughter of King Christian III of Denmark and a zealous Lutheran. In his religious as in his political and economic ideas, he represented the authoritarian elements emerging in the German territories.

Following his wife's death in 1585, Augustus remarried. He died a few weeks later on Feb. 12, 1586, at Dresden.

GERALD STRAUSS, *Indiana University*

AUGUSTUS II (1670–1733), ô-gus′təs, king of Poland and, as Frederick Augustus I, elector of Saxony. He was born in Dresden on May 12, 1670. Called "the Strong" because of his prodigious strength, and notorious for his drinking bouts and sexual prowess, Augustus was a man of vast ambitions and unscrupulous egotism.

He became elector of Saxony at the death of his childless brother in 1694. His desire for glory soon drove him to press his candidacy for the elective throne of Poland. To improve his chances Augustus converted to Catholicism, a religion that suited his baroque tastes better than his native Lutheranism. Though he won the votes of only a minority of the Polish nobles, he was crowned king after agreeing to the *Pacta Conventa*, which placed many restrictions on his power.

Augustus' reign ushered in the most disastrous period in Polish history. He sought to turn his rule into an absolute monarchy. By ceding territory to would-be allies, he began the dismemberment of Poland that led to its disappearance as a state in the 18th century.

Augustus entered the Great Northern War by concluding an alliance with Peter the Great of Russia in 1699. Though the aim was to recover Livonia, a former Polish possession, Poland refused to be drawn into the conflict, and the military burden fell on Saxony. A series of stunning Swedish victories under the youthful Charles XII soon cut the ground from under Augustus. On Swedish insistence he was deposed from the Polish throne in 1704, but the Russian victory over the Swedes at Poltava in 1709 allowed him to regain his throne.

His absolutist ambitions were more successful in Saxony than in Poland. He replaced the privy council with a cabinet of ministers responsible to himself, and he made the Saxon army an up-to-date instrument of war. He had some modern ideas for economic improvement of his lands, but in this, as in all else except the pursuit of his pleasures, he lacked consistency of purpose.

Augustus lived apart from his sternly Lutheran wife, Christiana Eberhardine. Of his many illegitimate children, Marshal Maurice de Saxe was the most famous. His only legitimate heir was Frederick Augustus, who succeeded him in both his titles after Augustus II died in Warsaw, Poland, on Feb. 1, 1733.

GERALD STRAUSS, *Indiana University*

AUGUSTUS III (1696–1763), ô-gus′təs, king of Poland and, as Frederick Augustus II, elector of Saxony. The son of Augustus II, he was born in Dresden on Oct. 17, 1696. As Augustus II's only legitimate son he became the tool of his father's dynastic ambitions, which included marriage into the Catholic house of Habsburg. Forced to abandon the rigorous Lutheran faith in which his mother had raised him, Augustus married Maria Josepha, eldest daughter of Habsburg Emperor Joseph I, in 1719.

He succeeded his father as elector of Saxony in 1733, but a surging national reaction to his father's rule in Poland prevented Augustus from assuming the Polish crown immediately. The majority of the Polish nobles supported the French candidate, Stanislas Leszczyński, but Augustus was aided by nearby Russia. A Russian invasion of Poland forced Leszczyński to flee, and Augustus was confirmed as king in 1736, a symbol of Poland's impotence to decide her own fate.

Like his father, he was a thoroughly bad ruler. While his father had at least been energetic and ambitious, Augustus II was indolent and cared nothing for affairs of state. His passion was the opera at Dresden, and he also liked painting and the plastic arts. In both Saxony and Poland he was content to entrust government to favorite courtiers, chief among them the unscrupulous Count Brühl, who had risen to eminence under Augustus II and who soon contrived to make himself indispensable to the son.

Augustus III did nothing to save Saxony from devastation in both the War of the Austrian Succession and the Seven Years' War. His reign was an unmitigated disaster for both Saxony and Poland.

Augustus III died in Dresden on Oct. 5, 1763, succeeded by his son Frederick Christian in Saxony and, in Poland, by Catherine the Great's former lover Stanisław Poniatowski.

GERALD STRAUSS, *Indiana University*

AUGUSTUS, ô-gus′təs, **Mausoleum of,** the tomb of the Roman emperor Augustus (63 B.C.–14 A.D.), and of the principal members of his family. It is located in Rome on the Campus Martius between the Via Flaminia and the Tiber River.

Built in 28 B.C., it is a circular structure 292 feet (89 meters) in diameter. It was originally covered by a mound of earth planted with evergreens and probably crowned by a statue of Augustus. On each side of the portal stood an obelisk. One of the obelisks is preserved in the Piazza dell' Esquilino and the other in the Piazza del Quirinale.

The structure was used as a fortress by the Colonna family in the 12th century. In the 18th century it was an amphitheater. It was later converted into a concert hall and used as such until 1936. It has since been restored to its original appearance.

AUGUSTUS, ô-gus′təs, was originally a name conferred by the Roman Senate on Octavian, the first of the Roman emperors, on Jan. 17, 27 B.C. It was assumed by subsequent emperors and soon became a title rather than a name.

According to the Roman historian Dio Cassius, the title implied that its bearer was "something more than human." In Latin its meaning lies somewhere between *humanus* (human) and *divinus* (divine).

ARTHER FERRILL, *University of Washington*

Razorbill auk.

AUK, ôk', a marine bird found in the Arctic Ocean and the northern Atlantic and Pacific. Ranging from about 8 to 19 inches (20 to 48 cm) in length, auks have squat bodies, small narrow wings, and short necks and tails. Their dense plumage is black above and white below or, in some of the smaller auks, all brown. Auks are rather poor flyers because of their small wings. Their whole structure is adapted better for diving or pursuit under water, where the wings are used as in flight.

The auks belong to the family Alcidae, order Alcae. There are 11 living genera and 19 living species. The largest member of the family was the great auk (*Alca impennis*); however, it was exterminated by man and became extinct in 1844 (see GREAT AUK). This species was about the size of a goose, stood erect, and was flightless because its wings were reduced to paddlelike appendages. It closely resembled the penguin.

The only two auks which breed in the Atlantic are the razorbill (*A. torda*), which measures about 16 inches (41 cm) long (see RAZOR-BILLED AUK), and the dovekie or little auk (*Plautus alle*) which is about half that size and therefore not much larger than a robin. In the northern Pacific this last species is replaced by five other small auks, called auklets, some of which are still smaller than the dovekie. Their English names are Cassin's, the paroquet, the crested, the least, and the whiskered auklets.

During the breeding season the heads of the males in the auklets are adorned with whiskerlike plumes or quaint little crests which curl forward. The auks build no nest and usually lay one egg, sometimes two, more or less concealed among rocks or boulders in crevices or under stones; Cassin's auklet often digs a burrow in the earth. All species are social, breed in colonies, and gather in large flocks on the open waters after the breeding season. About half of the food consumed by the razorbill consists of fish, the rest of it and virtually all of that of the dovekie and auklets consisting of small crustaceans or plankton. The auks and their eggs are an important source of food to the Eskimo.

CHARLES VAURIE
The American Museum of Natural History

AULARD, ō-làr', **François Alphonse** (1849–1928), French historian specializing in the French Revolution. He was born at Montbron on July 19, 1849. After completing his education, he taught in provincial universities for several years and then went to the Sorbonne, where he held the first chair of the history of the French Revolution (1887–1922). His commanding position as a student of the French Revolution proved influential in shaping scholarly views of the period.

Taking an anticlerical, patriotic, and republican view of his subject, he defended the revolution and found its chief hero in Georges Jacques Danton. Aulard's ablest pupil, Albert Mathiez, broke with his teacher by identifying himself with the Jacobin point of view and upholding Maximilien Robespierre as the leading statesman of the revolution.

Aulard founded the Société de l'Histoire de la Révolution and its journal, *La Révolution française*, which he edited from 1887 to 1927. He wrote extensively on the period and published several collections of source materials. Among his most significant works was *Histoire politique de la Révolution française* (1901), translated into English as *The French Revolution, a Political History*. He died in Paris on Oct. 23, 1928.

AULD LANG SYNE, ō lang zīn, is a song with words in the Scottish dialect written by Robert Burns about 1788. It has become a traditional song of friendship, and is sung at parting and at midnight on New Year's Eve to mark the passing of the old year. The title words mean "old long since," or "long ago." The melody, based on an old Scottish folk tune, was first published together with the words in the *Scots Musical Museum* (1796). The text of the poem follows.

Should auld acquaintance be forgot
    And never brought to mind?
Should auld acquaintance be forgot,
    And auld lang syne!

Chorus: For auld lang syne, my jo,[1]
        For auld lang syne,
We'll tak a cup o' kindness yet
        For auld lang syne.

And surely ye'll be your pint stowp![2]
    And surely I'll be mine!
And we'll tak a cup o'kindness yet,
    For auld lang syne.

We twa[3] hae run about the braes,[4]
    And pou'd[5] the gowans[6] fine;
But we've wander'd mony[7] a weary fitt,[8]
    Sin auld lang syne.

We twa hae paidl'd[9] in the burn,[10]
    Frae morning sun till dine;[11]
But seas between us braid[12] hae roar'd,
    Sin aud lang syne.

And there's a hand, my trusty fiere![13]
    And gie's[14] a hand o' thine!
And we'll tak a right gude-willie-waught,[15]
    For auld lang syne.

---

[1] *jo*, dear (now usually substituted); [2] *ye'll . . . stowp*, you'll pay for your pint measure (of drink); [3] *twa*, two; [4] *braes*, hills; [5] *pou'd*, pulled or plucked; [6] *gowans*, daisies; [7] *mony*, many; [8] *fitt*, foot or step; [9] *paidl'd*, paddled; [10] *burn*, brook; [11] *dine*, dinner time; [12] *braid*, broad; [13] *fiere*, friend; [14] *gie's*, give us; [15] *gude-willie-waught*, good-will draught.

AULIC COUNCIL, ô'lik, one of the two highest courts of the Holy Roman Empire. Known in German as the *Reichshofrat*, it developed from an advisory group around the emperor. Emperor Maximilian I set it up in 1498 as a rival to the Imperial Chamber, or *Reichskammergericht*, which had been forced upon him by the Diet. The name "Aulic Council" stems from the Greek word *aulikos*, which means "hall" or "court."

Its powers were curtailed by the Peace of Westphalia in 1648, but six years later it was formally constituted as one of the two supreme courts of the empire, the equal of the Imperial Chamber, and the highest court of appeals in the empire. In this form it consisted of a president, a vice president, the vice chancellor of the empire, and 18 councillors, all selected and paid by the emperor. Its seat was at the imperial residence, Vienna. Its jurisdiction included the reserved rights of the emperor, appeals on the part of the states from decisions in minor courts, and whatever concerned the empire in Italy.

The council was dissolved on the death of the emperor and had to be reinstituted by his successor. Six of the councillors were Protestants, whose unanimous vote could not be set aside by the majority. Although the council retained its judicial powers, it gradually lost its executive strength. On the fall of the empire in 1806 the council ceased to exist, but the title was used by the council of state of the Austrian empire.

AULIS, ô'ləs, in ancient Greece, was a seaport in Boeotia noted for its temple of Artemis and as the gathering place of the Greek fleet before the Trojan War.

AULNOY, ō-nwä', **Countess d'** (c. 1650–1705), French author, who is best known for *Contes nouvelles ou les fées à la mode*, a collection of fairy tales published in 1698. Her other works include the romance *L'histoire d'Hippolyte, comte de Douglas* (1690), *Mémoires de la cour d'Espagne* (1679–81), *Relation du voyage d'Espagne* (c.-1690), and *Histoire de Jean de Bourbon* (1692).

She was born *Marie Catherine Le Jumel de Barneville*, at Barneville in Normandy. After she and her mother were discovered in a plot to bring charges of treason against her husband, the count d'Aulnoy (also spelled *Aunoy*), they were forced to flee from France. They went first to England and in 1679 to Spain. Eventually they were allowed to return to France as a reward for secret services rendered the government. The countess died at Paris on Jan. 14, 1705.

AURANGABAD, ou-rung'gə-bäd, a city in India, is situated on the Deccan Plateau, in the northern part of Maharashtra state. It stands on the banks of a small tributary of the Godavari River, about 175 miles (282 km) northeast of Bombay. The city was founded early in the 1600's and increased greatly in importance when Emperor Aurangzeb made it the headquarters of the Mughul government. It rose to be a commercial center, but its importance decreased with the growth of Hyderabad. In the mid-20th century it again became an agricultural trade center for the surrounding area, with silk, silver, and gold handicraft industries. The city contains the ruins of the palace of Aurangzeb and a mausoleum erected to the memory of his favorite wife, Rabi'a Daurani. Aurangabad is the home of Marathwada University. Population: (1961) 87,579.

AURANGZEB (1618–1707), ä'ōō-rəng-zāb, was the sixth and last effective Mughul (Mogul) emperor of India. His harsh reign was beset by revolts, and his death signaled the disintegration of the empire. He was also known as *Alamgir* (Conqueror of the World).

Aurangzeb came to the throne in 1658 after having imprisoned his father, Emperor Shah Jahan, and subdued and killed his brothers in a war of succession. The fratricidal war was waged by Aurangzeb in the name of Sunni Islamic orthodoxy, in opposition to the more liberal views of Dara Shikoh, his brother and rival.

During his 50-year reign, Aurangzeb expanded the empire to a point near its zenith; in 1690 it reached from Cape Comorin in the south to Kabul in the north. In doing so, however, he aroused the Marathas, who rose in defiance under Shivaji. His religious persecution resulted in the revolt of the Jats, Rajputs, and Sikhs. The empire, shaken by these uprisings, could not endure, and Aurangzeb's successors faced anarchy.

Under Aurangzeb, Mughul culture was set back. Music and art lost royal patronage, and the position of women declined. Heretics and apostates were killed as traitors, Shia kingdoms were reduced, Hindu temples were destroyed, and the *jizya*, or poll tax, was reinstated.
BRIJEN K. GUPTA, *Brooklyn College, New York*

AURELIAN (c. 215–275 A.D.), ô-rēl'yən, was emperor of Rome from 270 to 275 A.D. His name in Latin was *Lucius Domitius Aurelianus*. A high-ranking officer, Aurelian was the choice of the troops to succeed Emperor Claudius Gothicus. He wrested the throne from Quintillus, Claudius' brother, and then dealt with a series of barbarian invasions, some of which penetrated Italy itself. Victorious by a narrow margin, he returned to Rome, where he instituted the building of a great wall around the city. Portions of the wall still stand. About the same time, he began a much-needed monetary reform, which continued throughout his reign.

After a brief campaign along the Danube, Aurelian in 271 moved against Queen Zenobia of Palmyra, who, at the time, dominated the eastern provinces. Asia Minor, Syria, and Egypt were soon recovered, and Zenobia herself was taken prisoner. Despite subsequent uprisings, the eastern provinces were secure in Roman hands by 272, allowing Aurelian to move against Tetricus, who ruled an independent empire in Gaul. Tetricus was defeated and captured in 273. Having thus reunited the empire, Aurelian proudly took the title *Restitutor Orbis* (Restorer of the World).

A soldier-emperor, he emphasized the cult of *Sol Invictus* (Unconquerable Sun God). Rome was deprived of a potentially great emperor when Aurelian was murdered by officers who had been led to believe that he was plotting their downfall.
TOM B. JONES, *University of Minnesota*

AURELIAN WALL, ô-rēl'yən, the city wall of ancient Rome, built mostly during Emperor Aurelian's reign (270–275 A.D.). Constructed in great haste in anticipation of a sudden attack by the barbarians, it in many places embodied garden walls, houses, tenements, tombs, or other standing structures that lay in its path. Its purpose was more to repel a raid than to stand a siege. The wall was almost 12 miles (19 km) long. It was originally about 20 feet (6 meters) high, but its height was later doubled by the addition of a gallery. Placed at intervals of about 100 feet (30 meters) were towers, about 380 in number, which connected the higher fortifications with inner arcades. The main gates, 16 in all, were located at the intersections of the principal roads of the city. There were also at least 6 postern gates. The wall was refurbished during the reign of the emperor Justinian (527–565 A.D.) and a large ditch was dug in front of it. Much of the wall is still standing.

AURELIUS, Marcus. See MARCUS AURELIUS ANTONINUS.

AUREOMYCIN. See ANTIBIOTICS.

AURICHALCITE, ô-rə-kal′sīt, is a native basic carbonate of copper and zinc, usually occurring in beautiful bright blue or green, pearly incrustations, composed of ill-defined crystals or scales. It has been found in European countries and in fine specimens at Morenci in Arizona, Magdalena in New Mexico, and in Colorado, Montana, and Utah.

AURICULA, ô-rik′yə-lə, is a hardy perennial herb, *Primula auricula,* found in the mountainous parts of central Europe. The wild plant has a cluster of small yellow flowers on a short stalk, which rises from a rosette of basal leaves. By selection, a very large number of varieties have been produced. These have long stalks and very diversely colored, fragrant, large flowers, for which the plant is widely cultivated in Europe. Auricula belongs to the primrose family, Primulaceae.

AURICULAR CONFESSION. See CONFESSION, SACRAMENTAL.

AURIESVILLE, ô′rēz-vil, an unincorporated village in Montgomery County, N.Y., is the site of the shrine of Our Lady of Martyrs, honoring the first Roman Catholic martyr saints of North America. Situated in the Mohawk Valley of east central New York, the place was originally occupied by an Indian village called *Ossernenon.* The land was purchased as a shrine by the Society of Jesus in 1884.

The shrine, including a coliseum, chapel, and Indian longhouse, is dedicated to a group of French missionary martyrs: three Jesuits (Father Isaac Jogues, Father Anthony Daniel, and Brother René Goupil) and Jean de la Lande, a layman. These four voyaged to America in the mid–17th century to convert the Mohawks and subsequently were killed by them. The martyrs were canonized on June 29, 1930. Their feast day is celebrated on September 26.

An adjoining grotto honors Blessed Kateri Tekakwitha, an Indian girl known as the "Lily of the Mohawks." This young convert, who died in 1680 at the age of 24, was given the title Venerable by Pope Pius XII in 1943.

AURIGA, ô-rī′gə, in astronomy, is the Charioteer or Wagoner, a constellation of the Northern Hemisphere, containing as its chief luminary, Capella, a star of the first magnitude. In 1892 a new star was discovered in the foot of Auriga. At its brightest it showed as a star of the fourth magnitude. It remained visible to the naked eye for about a month and then rapidly became invisible. After several months it again reached the 10th magnitude, but its spectrum had undergone a great change, having become assimilated to the nebular type. It has since resumed its stellar character and is of the 13th magnitude.

AURIGNACIAN, ôr-ēn-yā′shən, in archaeology, an epoch in the Upper Paleolithic period, or late Stone Age. It corresponds to the Würm glaciation period in geology. Aurignacian stone implements were of the flake variety, similar to those of the preceding Mousterian epoch, although a number of tools and ornaments of bone, horn, and ivory were introduced.

The most characteristic achievements of this epoch were cave drawings and sculptures, first discovered at Aurignac, in southern France, from which the epoch takes its name.

AURILLAC, ō-rē-yȧk′, is a city in south central France, on the Jordanne River, 105 miles (169 km) northeast of Toulouse. It is the capital of Cantal department. Aurillac is noted for its ancient buildings, among which are the Church of Notre Dame aux Neiges, constructed in the 14th century, and its 11th century castle of St. Étienne. The town manufactures jewelry, copper articles, paper, and umbrellas. Since the Middle Ages, it has been an important market center for cattle and Cantal cheeses.

The town grew up around a Benedictine monastery founded in the late 9th century by St. Géraud. The first French pope, Sylvester II, was born in the town and trained for church at the monastery. During the 14th and 15th centuries, the English besieged Aurillac several times. The town also suffered during the French wars of religion in the 16th century. Population: (1962) 23,179.

AURIOL, ô-ryôl′, **Vincent** (1884–1966), president of France. He was born at Revel, Haute-Garonne, on Aug. 27, 1884, the son of a prosperous baker. After receiving a law degree from the University of Toulouse, he became an active member of the Socialist party and an associate of Jean Jaurès. Auriol became editor in chief of a Socialist journal, *Le Midi socialiste,* in 1909, but continued his law practice as well. In 1912 he married Michèle Aucouturier, daughter of a glassworker.

Soon after his election to the Chamber of Deputies in 1914, Auriol began to specialize in finance. He was exempt from army service in World War I, having lost an eye in childhood. In 1919 he was appointed general secretary of the Socialist delegation in Parliament. When the French Socialist party split in 1920, Auriol chose to follow the reformists under Léon Blum rather than the more extreme Marxist faction.

With Premier Édouard Herriot he went to London in 1924 to negotiate with the British government concerning the Dawes Plan, evacuation of the Ruhr, and the Geneva Protocol for arbitration, disarmament, and collective security. The following year he accompanied Finance Minister Joseph Caillaux to Washington to negotiate settlement of the French war debt.

After the Popular Front victory of 1936, he became finance minister in the Blum cabinet and in October agreed to devaluation of the franc. After the fall of France in 1940, he was one of the minority of legislators who voted against full powers to Marshal Pétain and dissolution of the Third Republic. Imprisoned, he was released under surveillance in 1941. He helped the French resistance until 1943, when he escaped to London and joined Gen. Charles de Gaulle's Free French government-in-exile.

After the war he was president of the Consultative Assembly that drafted a new constitution. As president he shaped the compromises that brought the Fourth Republic into being. In November 1946 he was chosen president of the National Assembly, and on Jan. 16, 1947, he was elected president of France. During his term, he helped prevent the shifting French political alliances from degenerating into anarchy.

Auriol remained in political retirement from 1954 until 1958, when the Algerian crisis threatened the Fourth Republic. The publication of an exchange of letters between him and de Gaulle, together with Auriol's arguments inside the Socialist party, was decisive in swinging Socialist support to de Gaulle. In 1960, however, he publicly broke with de Gaulle, criticizing the general's assumption of personal power. Auriol died in Paris on Jan. 1, 1966.

AURISPA, ou-rē'spä, **Giovanni** (1369–1459), Italian scholar who helped spread classical Greek learning in Italy. He was born in Noto, Sicily. In 1418 he went to Constantinople to study Greek. When he returned to Italy some years later, he brought with him over 200 valuable manuscripts, including some of the writings of Pindar, Aeschylus, Sophocles, Plato, Plutarch, and Empedocles. He then taught Greek literature at the universities of Bologna and Florence, and later moved to Ferrara. From 1433 to 1436 he traveled in Germany, where he obtained manuscripts of Pliny's *Panegyricus,* the *Panegirici veteres,* and other classical works that had been unknown during the Middle Ages. In 1438, at the Council of Basel, Aurispa attracted the attention of Pope Eugene IV, who made him his secretary in 1441. He was reappointed to the same post by Pope Nicholas V in 1447. Aurispa also translated many Greek works into Latin. He died in Ferrara in 1459.

AUROCHS, ou'roks, the European bison (*Bison bonasus,* or *Bison europaeus*) called by Germans *auerochs* and in the Slavonic languages *subr* or *suber.* This great bison stands six feet (1.8 meters) or more in height at the shoulder and closely resembles the American bison or buffalo. It is believed that the American animal descended from the ancestral race of aurochs. When the Romans spread northward into Europe they found these and other oxen in the forests of Europe, and in the time of Charlemagne, aurochs were hunted in Germany. They are now practically extinct. See also BISON.

"Aurochs" is sometimes applied to the urus, the ancient wild ox of Europe (*Bos primigenius*), the supposed ancestor of modern cattle.

AURORA, ô-rôr'ǝ, the fourth-largest city in Colorado, is an eastern suburb of Denver. Though primarily residential, it has aviation, electrical, and fishing tackle industries. Fitzsimons General Hospital (U.S. Army) is in Aurora, and Stapleton Field Municipal Airport and Lowry Air Field Base lie just west of the city line.

Aurora was settled in 1891 and was incorporated in 1907. It is governed under the city manager plan, adopted in 1953. Population: 74,974.

AURORA, ô-rôr'ǝ, is an industrial city in Illinois, situated on the Fox River, 38 miles (61 km) west of Chicago. It is the center of a four-county trading area. The city has more than 200 manufacturing plants, which produce steel lockers and shelves, office furniture and equipment, brushes, electric and pneumatic tools, women's dresses, pumps, plastic toys, typewriter supplies, and heavy grading, road building, and conveying machinery. Division shops of the Chicago, Burlington & Quincy Railroad are here.

Aurora College (Advent Christian, coeducational), founded in Mendota, Ill., in 1893, moved to Aurora in 1912. The Bellarmine School of Theology, of Loyola University, and Mooseheart, a vocational school for orphans sponsored by the Loyal Order of Moose, are north of the city. The Aurora Historical Museum, in a 20-room house built in 1856, contains a world-famous astronomical clock, mastodon bones, Indian artifacts, and items of early Aurora history.

Samuel McCarty, who is called the founder of Aurora, arrived in 1834 from Elmira, N.Y., a few months after his brother Joseph, searching for a sawmill site, had settled here. The site then was occupied by a Potawatomi Indian village led by Chief Waubonsie, who had befriended the whites after the Fort Dearborn massacre at the site of Chicago in 1812. Samuel McCarty acquired land and platted the original town. By 1836 about 30 families had established homes here. McCarty persuaded a stagecoach line to come through the village, and the line served until the founding of the Burlington railroad here in 1850.

The village was called *McCarty's Mills* until 1837, when it acquired a post office and was renamed Aurora after an early settler's home town in New York. The rival villages of Aurora and West Aurora united in 1857. The city claims that its electric streetlighting system, installed in 1881, was the world's first.

Aurora has a commission form of government. Population: 74,182.

ROBERT W. BARCLAY, *Aurora "Beacon-News"*

AURORA, ô-rôr'ǝ, a city in southwestern Missouri, is in the scenic Ozark mountain country, in Lawrence County, 35 miles by highway southwest of Springfield. Shoe manufacturing is the city's largest industry. Aurora also has food-processing industries and a photoengraving plant, and it manufactures photoengraving equipment, heating and air-conditioning equipment, and clothing. One of the state's largest game-fish hatcheries is situated nearby. Aurora was laid out in 1870 and was incorporated in 1886. Population: 5,359.

AURORA, ô-rôr'ǝ, in classical mythology, was the goddess of the dawn, known to the Greeks as *Eos.* She rose in the east from the ocean in a chariot drawn by white horses and with her rosy fingers dispersed the darkness and shed light upon the earth. She was the daughter of the Titans Hyperion and Theia and the sister of Helios (Sun) and Selene (Moon). By the Titan Astraeus, she was the mother of the winds Boreas (North), Zephyrus (West), Notus (South), and Eurus (East), as well as of the star Hesperus.

Notable among Aurora's mortal lovers was the Trojan Tithonus, by whom she was the mother of Memnon, the youth who was slain by Achilles in the Trojan War. Aurora's mourning for Memnon was a favorite subject in classical art.

THE AURORA BOREALIS, in draperylike form, illuminates the night sky with its many long, thin rays. The base of the auroral display is about 70 miles (110 km) above the earth.

VICTOR PETER HESSLER

AURORA, ə-rô′rə, a light, visible at night, that is produced in the upper atmosphere of the earth at irregular intervals. The aurora observed in the Arctic and subarctic regions is called the *aurora borealis*. The corresponding phenomenon in the Southern Hemisphere is called the *aurora australis*. In North America the most likely places for seeing an aurora are northern Alaska, the central part of Hudson Bay, and Labrador. In Europe the auroral zone passes through northern Norway and Sweden and on through the northern coast of Siberia. The auroral zone in the Southern Hemisphere lies mostly in Antarctica.

Appearance. When their light is bright enough for colors to be distinguished, aurorae usually appear yellowish green. Aurorae exceptionally high in the atmosphere are red, however, and exceptionally low aurorae may have an orange lower border. Occasionally, high aurorae seen at twilight may appear violet.

Aurorae occur in various shapes and with various degrees of activity. Thus, an aurora may take the form of a steady, homogeneous arc. This form usually extends some tens of miles vertically into the atmosphere, gradually fading out toward the higher altitudes. The arc is often less than 1 mile (1.6 km) thick in the north-south direction. However, it may stretch from east to west for several thousand miles around the earth. The lower boundary of an aurora is about 70 miles (110 km) above the surface of the earth.

Active aurorae appear as draperies, coronas, or other forms. They are made up of long, thin rays that may extend upward for several hundred miles. The rays are aligned parallel to the earth's magnetic field. Individual rays generally are short-lived, but often disappear and reappear in the same position every few seconds. Occasionally, bright red patches are seen that last for a few minutes. Perhaps the most spectacular type of display is the so-called flaming aurora, in which wavelike patches of light start low in the north—or south—and rise high into the sky, disappearing within a second or so.

Auroral displays usually are confined to a northern and southern circular zone around the geomagnetic poles; these zones lie from 20 to 25 degrees from the poles. In the Northern Hemisphere the geomagnetic pole is found near Thule in northwest Greenland. Strong aurorae occasionally extend to middle latitudes. They are accompanied by small but important changes in the earth's magnetism.

Cause of the Aurora. It has been found that auroral displays are more frequent during periods of intense sunspot activity. During the active periods of the 11-year solar cycle, for example, displays of the aurora borealis are frequently visible from the northern United States, where otherwise they are rarely seen.

The aurora is therefore associated with activity on the sun, as well as with the earth's magnetism. These associations suggested to scientists that the aurora results from bombardment of the earth's upper atmosphere by electrically charged particles from the sun. The concept was supported by the discovery by Norwegian scientist Lars Vegard in 1939 that a small portion of the auroral radiation is produced by hydrogen. Hydrogen is a rare element in the earth's atmosphere but is the major constituent of the sun. In 1950 more precise studies of auroral radiation (conducted in the United States by Aden B. Meinel and Carl W. Gartlein) showed that the hydrogen producing some of the radiation was impinging on the atmosphere at speeds of several thousand miles per second. This finding reinforced the view that the aurora is caused by charged particles—protons and electrons—coming from beyond the atmosphere.

Later studies by Anders Omholt in Norway and others demonstrated that the most important source of auroral energy is the bombardment of the atmosphere by electrons. Various theories have been proposed but not proved to account for the propagation of solar particles through interplanetary space, the capture of some of these particles by the earth's magnetic field, and their subsequent bombardment of the earth's atmosphere.

Early Studies of the Aurora. The aurora drew scientific attention as far back as the time of Aristotle in the 4th century B.C. Detailed, systematic investigation began in the early 18th century and was developed through the efforts of men of many nationalities. Thus, Mikhail Lomonosov in Russia, John Canton in England, and Benjamin Franklin in the American colonies all noted a similarity between the aurora and lightning. They therefore began to modify their theories about lightning to encompass the aurora. The general idea that the aurora was a gigantic electric discharge in the atmosphere—somewhat akin to a stroke of lightning—was prevalent almost until the beginning of the 20th century.

During this period a large body of statistical information was accumulated about the aurora. In 1733, Dortous de Mairan, in France, published a treatise on the aurora in which he showed the relationship between frequent auroral displays and periods of maximum sunspot activity. He also noted a tendency of aurorae to occur within a month or so of the equinoxes—that is, in the periods of March-April and September-October. That aurorae exist most commonly in the two so-called auroral zones was first realized through work published in Germany in the mid-19th century.

Modern auroral physics had its beginnings in Norway at the start of the 20th century. At that time an Oslo scientist, Kristian Birkeland, performed some experiments in which he fired ions—electrically charged atoms—at a magnetized sphere that served as a model of the earth. The sphere was coated with a phosphor, a substance that emits light when excited by radiation. The firing of the ions produced a zonal glow around the sphere, corresponding to the auroral zones.

A young Oslo mathematician, Carl Størmer, excited by Birkeland's experiments, developed a mathematical theory of the motion of charged particles in the neighborhood of a magnet. His theory postulated that the particles all had the same charge and moved at the same speed, and that they did not interfere with one another. (These assumptions are now known to be incorrect so far as the natural aurora is concerned.)

Auroral Height Determination. Størmer spent a long, fruitful life devoted to the perfection of his theory and to a variety of observations on the aurora, in order to clarify some of the more mysterious aspects of its nature. It had been known for some time that the aurora appeared high above the earth, but previous measurements had been so few and so poor that there was considerable uncertainty as to the precise region of height involved. Størmer and his many dedicated students and assistants carried out a long program of photographing the aurora simultaneously from two widely separated stations. Then they determined auroral heights by triangulation, in the same manner that a surveyor derives distances that he cannot measure directly.

Spectroscopic Studies. A great deal more was learned about the aurora through study of the auroral spectrum. While such studies had been conducted before his time, it was Lars Vegard of Norway who initiated an extensive program of photographing the spectra of aurorae and of analyzing them for the information they yielded.

By breaking down the light of the aurora into its component colors—that is, its spectrum—one

NATIONAL BUREAU OF STANDARDS

AURORAE result when charged particles from the sun strike the upper atmosphere near the magnetic poles.

can learn which kinds of atoms and molecules are responsible for the auroral radiation. It is as though each atom and molecule possesses its own identifying thumbprint of colors that it emits when excited. For example, the usual green color of the aurora is emitted by atomic oxygen. The reddish glow that is occasionally seen is produced by atomic oxygen emitting at extremely low pressures—that is, at extremely high altitudes in the atmosphere. Occasionally an aurora is observed that has a slightly different shade of red at the lower border of an otherwise green aurora. Molecular nitrogen produces this red. These strong emissions are easily observed, but by using the methods of spectrum analysis a scientist also can detect the thumbprints of many emissions that are weaker and harder to observe.

Later Investigations. During the first half of the 20th century, several theories were developed concerning the passage of clouds of particles from the sun to the earth. Some speculations were offered as to how these particles penetrate the earth's magnetic field and strike the upper atmosphere in the auroral zones. Størmer's theory, developed under the inspiration of Birkeland's experiments, was but one approach to this problem. Rather different pictures were drawn by Sydney Chapman and V.C.A. Ferraro in England and by Hannes Alfvén in Sweden. None of these theories, however, gave a very satisfactory explanation or description of the observed phenomena. The theories were highly involved.

Although it is not clear just how a proper theory should be constructed, a wide variety of information has in the meantime been obtained on the behavior of the aurora. The range of speeds of the protons and electrons striking the atmosphere and producing the visible glow has become known, thanks largely to rocket experiments in recent years. Today scientists even have some information about the nature of the orbits of these particles in space just above the atmosphere.

Beginning with the International Geophysical Year (IGY) in 1957, networks of observing stations were established in many countries. From observations of aurorae and of the magnetic and other changes that accompany them, it was established that there is a close relationship between aurorae occurring in the Northern Hemisphere and those occurring at corresponding positions in the Southern Hemisphere. The particles that produce the aurorae apparently are trapped in the earth's magnetic field before bombarding the atmosphere, possibly only for very short periods of time. The particles oscillate back and forth between the hemispheres along the lines of force of the magnetic field. As the magnetic field lines converge nearer to the surface of the earth, the lines tend to form a trap—somewhat like the converging exit of a funnel. This causes the particles to be reflected back from one hemisphere to the opposite hemisphere, where the same kind of reflection occurs again.

The emerging view, therefore, is that the following sequence of events takes place in the formation of an aurora: Particles of matter—electrons and protons—are ejected from the sun by violent disturbances taking place there. The particles travel through interplanetary space. Some of them reach the earth and are caught by the outer fringes of the earth's magnetic field. The particles are trapped in the field in much the same way as the higher-energy particles of the Van Allen radiation belt are trapped. Eventually they are dumped onto the upper atmosphere, where they strike the atoms and molecules of air, producing the visible aurora. The mechanism of the dumping process is not yet well understood. However, it is thought to arise from some type of instability in the proton-electron gas trapped above the atmosphere. This instability permits the particles to slip past the points where they would otherwise be reflected back and forth between the earth's magnetic poles.

Artificial Aurorae. For many years scientists have attempted to produce artificial aurorae in the laboratory in order to gain further understanding of the physical processes responsible for auroral displays. More recently, the explosion of nuclear bombs in the upper atmosphere has produced artificial aurorae at tropical latitudes.

For example, the explosion of a hydrogen bomb high above Johnston Island in the Pacific Ocean produced such an aurora. This aurora was seen from American Samoa, which, although located some 2,000 miles (3,200 km) away, is linked to the island by the geomagnetic field. Although the energies and composition of the particles from a nuclear explosion are different from those responsible for the natural aurora, there is every reason to believe that the basic physical processes are much the same.

See also SUN; TERRESTRIAL MAGNETISM; UPPER ATMOSPHERE.

JOSEPH W. CHAMBERLAIN
Kitt Peak National Observatory

Further Reading: Chamberlain, Joseph W., *Physics of the Aurora and Airglow* (New York 1961); Harang, Leiv, *The Aurorae* (New York 1951); Petrie, William, *Keoeeit: The Story of the Aurora Borealis* (New York 1963); Störmer, Carl, *The Polar Aurora* (New York 1955).

AURORA LEIGH, ô-rôr′ə lē, is a romantic narrative poem in blank verse by the English poet Elizabeth Barrett Browning (q.v.), first published in 1856. It is the poet's longest work and the one in which she expresses her "highest convictions upon Life and Art." An immediate success, the book became enormously popular.

The heroine of the poem, Aurora Leigh, is a half-English, half-Italian woman living in mid-Victorian England. The story of her life, told in the first person, parallels in some respects that of Elizabeth Barrett Browning herself. Aurora is a studious girl, dedicated to poetry, who is raised by an unsympathetic aunt. She has a wealthy cousin, Romney Leigh, who is active in philanthropic and reform movements. However, Leigh's arrogant and dogmatic manner repels Aurora, and she refuses his proposal of marriage. The struggle between their respective approaches to human problems gives the poem its theme:

" 'Tis impossible
To get at men excepting through their souls.
And poets get directlier at the soul
Than any of your economists."

Ultimately, after Romney discovers through experience that his approach to human problems is doomed to failure, he and Aurora Leigh fall in love.

Aurora Leigh has flashes of Elizabeth Barrett Browning's lyric brilliance. However, modern readers usually find the poem too didactic, rhetorical, and diffuse, with little action and rather stilted characters. It is usually read today for its accurate representation of Victorian England, with its complacent wealth and appalling poverty, and for the insight the poem offers into the mind of Elizabeth Barrett Browning, who had a great sympathy for the victims of the contemporary English social order.

AURUNGZEB. See AURANGZEB.

AUSABLE CHASM, ô-sā′bəl kaz′əm, in Essex County, New York, is a gorge on the Ausable River near its mouth on Lake Champlain. Below Horseshoe Falls the river narrows to widths of 10 to 50 feet (3 to 15 meters) and becomes much deeper. Smooth vertical walls of layered and blocked Potsdam sandstone, cut with deep lateral slots, rise to heights of 175 feet (53 meters) on both sides of the river. Ferns grow in crevices of the richly colored rock and evergreens overhang the chasm. In spring, flood waters rise more than 40 feet (12 meters), flush out accumulated debris, and wash the standstone walls in a grand housecleaning.

The gorge was created during a relatively brief postglacial period by the cutting force of the swift Ausable River. The river falls nearly a mile (1.6 km) in its 50-mile (80 km) course from Mount Marcy to Lake Champlain.

Although waste from an upstream pulp mill has turned the water of this Adirondack river opaque, the chasm has lost little of the attraction it had a century ago when it rivaled Niagara Falls as a spectacle. Each year, from May to October, thousands of tourists visit this sculpture gallery hewn by time and the river. Visitors may gain access to the 1.5-mile (2.4-km) length of the chasm by stairs, walks on ledges guarded by railings, and a guided boat tour of the terminal flume and rapids.

PAUL F. JAMIESON
Editor of "The Adirondack Reader"

AUSCULTATION, ô-skəl-tā′shən, is a method of examining the body by means of sound. The naked ear may be used, or instruments such as the stethoscope and the phoneidoscope may be used. The natural sounds alone may be investigated, such as breathing sounds or heart sounds; or an organ or the area near it may be tapped, or percussed, to determine variations in the resonance. All parts of the body may be investigated by these means.

Auscultation is probably, next to inspection, the oldest mode of investigation. Hippocrates used it extensively, but it was not until René Laënnec, in 1816, gave his demonstrations that the method came to be recognized as one of the most important in the diagnosis of diseased conditions. Early views held that the sounds produced were capable of revealing directly the nature of disease, but Joseph Skoda first demonstrated (about 1840) that they were only manifestations of peculiar physical states of the body. See also PERCUSSION.

AUSLANDER, ôs′lan-dər, **Joseph** (1897–1965), American poet. He was born in Philadelphia, Pa., on Oct. 11, 1897. After graduating from Harvard College in 1917, he was appointed an instructor of English there. He studied for a time at the Sorbonne, in Paris, and from 1929 to 1937 lectured in poetry at Columbia University. From 1937 to 1943 he was a consultant in English poetry at the Library of Congress.

The death of young men in war is a recurring theme in Auslander's later poetry. His best-known work is *The Unconquerables* (1943), a collection of poems addressed to the Nazi-occupied countries of Europe. His other poems were collected in *Sunrise Trumpets* (1924), *Cyclops' Eye* (1926), *Hell in Harness* (1930), *No Traveler Returns* (1933), *More than Bread* (1936), and *Riders at the Gate* (1939).

In 1933, Auslander married the poet Audrey Wurdemann, who received the Pulitzer Prize for poetry in 1935. They collaborated on two novels, *My Uncle Jan* (1948) and *The Islanders* (1951). Auslander died in Coral Gables, Fla., on June 22, 1965.

AUSONIUS, ô-sō′nē-əs, **Decimus Magnus** (c. 310–c. 395 A.D.), Roman poet of the 4th century A.D. He was born in Burdigala (Bordeaux), in Gaul. He studied under several distinguished masters and eventually became professor of rhetoric in his native city, from which his fame extended through the whole empire. Emperor Valentinian I entrusted to him the education of his son, Gratian, and later appointed him quaestor and praetorian prefect. After Gratian became emperor, he showed his gratitude to his preceptor by appointing him consul in Gaul in 379. After the murder of Gratian in 383, Ausonius retired to an estate at Burdigala, where he died.

Because Valentinian was a Christian, probably Ausonius was also. Many of his writings confirm this conjecture. Critics are not unanimous about his importance as a poet. He was undoubtedly learned and ingenious, but his style and versification have the blemishes of the age, and his Latin is impure. He wrote numerous idyls, epigrams, eclogues, and letters. Among his works the most famous are his summaries of the *Iliad* and the *Odyssey; Mosella*, a travel narrative; and the *Caesares*, verse tributes to the Roman rulers after Julius Caesar.

EWING GALLOWAY

JANE AUSTEN'S house in Chawton, Hampshire, is typical of the English country homes described in her novels.

AUSTEN, ôs′tən, **Jane** (1775–1817), English novelist, whose narrative world—"the little bit (two Inches wide) of Ivory on which I work with so fine a Brush"—has gained in literary reputation with the passage of the years. Her novels are poised in time between the neoclassicism of the 18th century and the lyricism of the romantic movement. Her spare, witty style and satiric insight are in the 18th-century tradition; her imaginative values share the sensitivity of the romantic poets.

Life. Jane Austen was born in Steventon, near Basingstoke, on Dec. 16, 1775. She was one of many children of a clergyman whose income was sufficient to support his family's gentility and whose literate tastes created an urbane atmosphere in the Austen home. She enjoyed an affectionate intimacy with her brothers and her sister, Cassandra. Jane never married but resided and worked in her family's home. The Austens lived largely in the English countryside, and Jane came to know all of county society, from the village apothecary to the landed aristocracy. She died in Winchester on July 18, 1817, and was buried in the cathedral.

Writings. The principles of English neoclassicism as expressed in the critical essays of Joseph Addison, the ethics of Samuel Johnson, and the fiction of Henry Fielding provided Jane Austen with a literary heritage. She was familiar with the preromantic poetry of Collins, Gray, and Cowper, and with the salacious wit of Laurence Sterne. Among the romantics her references are mainly to Scott and Byron. The major English novelists of the 18th century collectively influenced her work, but Richardson, Fanny Burney, and Maria Edgeworth were perhaps the most significant. She was always capable of satirizing the sentimentality of her sources, and she began early to parody the Gothic sensationalism of Horace Walpole and Mrs. Radcliffe.

Jane Austen's early pieces, written mainly in the 1790's, caricature the incongruities of contemporary fiction. In her "juvenilia" she satirizes the insipid sentimentality that had prevailed in English fiction since Richardson, as her comic heroines faint or issue dire warnings against fainting. Parody allowed the young writer to purge her fiction of inert conventions and facile affectations. As her skill increased, her pieces became more serious and more complex. Satire on Gothic horror tales was subtler, for example, in *Northanger Abbey*, perhaps her first extended novel, although it was published only after her death. Here, while the heroine's sensational fantasies are satirized, there is a simultaneous revelation of "Gothic" brutality beneath the conventionally courteous surfaces of her characters.

In *Sense and Sensibility* (1811) sentimentality is seriously attacked as a source of emotional insufficiency; here the values are more complex—reason and imagination are no longer set in opposition but are ironically interrelated. *Pride and Prejudice* (1813), the most popular and wittiest of her novels, resembles the 18th-century comedy of manners with which her work has been too generally associated, and she herself was later dissatisfied with the sustained "playfulness and epigrammatism of the general style." *Mansfield Park* (1814), though it includes sequences of brilliant comedy and bitter verisimilitude, has seemed too serious for some generations of readers; but a growing awareness of the figurative and ironic elements in her novels may alter this response. It is clear that irony is a pervasive and significant element in her fiction, and in *Emma* (1816), perhaps the most perfectly patterned of her narratives, she employs her ironic vision to explore the heroine's delusions. By contrast, *Persuasion* (published posthumously in 1818) reveals a delicately lyric insight characterized by an especially poetic use of natural imagery. *Persuasion* was her last completed novel; during the final months of her life she began to write *Sanditon*, a fragment reverting partly to the manner of her earlier parody.

Evaluation. Jane Austen's novels deal with a comparatively affluent society, but scenes set in the urban and sometimes sordid contexts of Bath and Portsmouth suggest not a restricted range but a purposeful limitation of subject that resulted in the perceptive precision of her art. During her life her work was not widely known, although from the first it elicited rare but revealing critical response. Sir Walter Scott, her contemporary, Macaulay in the mid-1800's, and Kipling in later years were ardent admirers, but her work tended to remain the province of cultists until its reappraisal in the 1900's, when Virginia Woolf and others initiated serious criticism of her fiction.

Her novels had little influence on later writers, except as a source of resentment or delight. Her work has been derided as prim and trivial by novelists and critics in search of social significance. On the other hand, E.M. Forster paid tribute to the subtleties of her technique.

Jane Austen's greatest admirers among writers are no more like her in manner than are her most hostile critics. "Of all great writers," Virginia Woolf remarked, "she is the most difficult to catch in the act of greatness." No successor has been able to assimilate her methods. As a result, her fiction has been, from the first, in fact, inimitable.

JOHN W. LOOFBOUROW
Author of "Thackeray and the Form of Fiction"

Bibliography

Chapman, Robert W., *Jane Austen: A Critical Bibliography* (New York 1953).
Lascelles, Mary, *Jane Austen and Her Art* (New York 1939).
Litz, A. Walton, *Jane Austen; a Study of Her Artistic Development* (New York 1965).
Mudrick, Marvin, *Jane Austen: Irony as Defense and Discovery* (Princeton, N.J., 1952).
Watt, Ian, ed., *Jane Austen: A Collection of Critical Essays* (Englewood Cliffs, N.J., 1963).

AUSTERLITZ, Battle of, ous'tər-lits, a great victory by the French emperor Napoleon over the Austrians and Russians. It was fought on Dec. 2, 1805, near the town of Austerlitz, 12 miles (19 km) southeast of Brünn, Austria (now Brno, Czechoslovakia). The French were led by Napoleon, the Austrians by Emperor Francis II, and the Russians by Emperor Alexander I; hence it is sometimes called the "Battle of the Three Emperors." The French numbered about 70,000, and the Allies more than 80,000. By a feint, Napoleon threw the Allies' center off balance and broke through to scatter their armies. The French suffered about 9,000 casualties; the Allies, about 25,000. As a result of the battle, the third coalition against Napoleon dissolved, and Austria concluded peace with France, making important territorial concessions. The battle was fought on the first anniversary of Napoleon's coronation as emperor.

AUSTIN, ôs'tən, **Alfred** (1835–1913), English poet and journalist, who was poet laureate from 1896 to 1913. His verse serves as an example of the Victorian penchant for pompous rhetoric and banal sentimentality.

Born at Headingly, near Leeds, on May 30, 1835, Austin graduated from London University in 1853, and was called to the bar in 1857. He soon abandoned law, however, and devoted himself to writing. His first successful volume of verse was *The Season* (1864).

In 1867, Austin joined the staff of the *Standard,* the most influential daily newspaper in London at the time. Through his editorials, reviews, and biographies, he so dominated the *Standard* that it was humorously called "The Daily Alfred Austin." From 1883 to 1893, he also served as editor of the magazine *National Review.*

Austin's appointment as poet laureate came in 1896, nearly four years after the death of his predecessor, Lord Tennyson. The appointment caused much indignation in literary circles because Austin's greatest contemporaries, Rudyard Kipling, Algernon Swinburne, and William Morris, whose verse was not acceptable to Queen Victoria, were not considered for the appointment. Admired primarily by those who shared the Tory views he upheld, Austin published more than 20 volumes of epic, dramatic, and lyric verse, including *Savonarola* (1881), *The Conversion of Winckelmann* (1897), and *Sacred and Profane Love* (1908). His most popular book was the prose work *The Garden That I Love* (1894). His *Autobiography* appeared in 1911. He died at Ashford, Kent, on June 2, 1913.

AUSTIN, ôs'tən, **Benjamin** (1752–1820), American political leader. He was born in Boston on Nov. 18, 1752. During the American Revolution he published patriotic articles in the Boston press. He made his name with *Observations on the Pernicious Practice of the Law* (1786), in which he urged such legal reforms as the abolition of lawyers. Inheriting Samuel Adams' mantle as leader of the radical Boston Republicans (Democrats), he served in the state senate in 1787, 1789–1794, and 1796. Extremely anti-Federalist, he wrote inflammatory articles and encouraged public riots. After 1796 he lost his influence with the public. In 1803, President Jefferson appointed him a federal loan commissioner. He died in Boston on May 4, 1820.

AUSTIN, ôs'tən, **Herbert** (1866–1941), British automobile manufacturer, who designed one of the first cars produced in Britain and later brought the automobile within reach of people with modest incomes. Like Henry Ford, he was a practical engineer who began his career as an apprentice and learned every phase of the manufacture and sale of automobiles. He was born at Little Missenden, Buckinghamshire, on Nov. 8, 1866. In 1895 he designed his first Wolseley car. With another car he had designed and driven, he won first place in its class in the Thousand Mile Trial of 1900. From 1901 to 1905 he was manager of the Wolseley Tool and Motor Company.

In 1905 he formed the Austin Motor Company, which became one of Britain's largest automobile manufacturers and now is part of the British Motor Corporation. His Austin Seven, first produced in 1922, won popular acclaim because it sold for only about $225. Built within the dimensions of a large motorcycle-and-sidecar combination, it had a 4-cylinder engine rated at slightly less than 8 horsepower. He was created Baron Austin of Longbridge in 1936. Lord Austin died at Lickey Grange, Worcestershire, on May 23, 1941.

RAMON KNAUERHASE, *University of Connecticut*

AUSTIN, os'tən, **John** (1790–1859), British legal theorist, who was the architect of modern jurisprudence. He was born at Creeting Mill, Suffolk, on March 3, 1790. He joined the army when he was 17 but left it five years later to study law. Chronic poor health and dissatisfaction with his work forced him to abandon practice in 1825.

In 1826, Austin was appointed professor of jurisprudence at University College, London. He prepared himself for the post by studying Continental authorities for a year (1827–1828) at Bonn. Although John Stuart Mill and a few other brilliant students were profoundly influenced by Austin's teaching, his lectures were not well attended, and in 1832 he reluctantly resigned his post. In 1833–1834 he served on a criminal law commission appointed by the government, but his intellectual scrupulousness forced him to view the project with disdain. He was happier and more effective as a member of a commission that in 1838 examined the grievances of the natives of Malta. For ten years thereafter he lived abroad and, after 1848, at Weybridge, Surrey, where he died in December 1859.

He published one major book on law—*The Province of Jurisprudence Determined* (1832). After his death his accomplished wife, Sarah Taylor Austin, whom he married in 1818, republished this work, adding to it the larger body of lecture material to which it was intended to be an introduction. It appeared in 1863 as *Lectures on Jurisprudence.* Austin's reputation rests entirely on this slender foundation.

There were two reasons for the success of the *Lectures.* The author stuck single-mindedly to his theme, and his theme was appropriate and acceptable to the age in which it appeared. Austin's thesis was that law is based on power. As he saw it, law is a command from a powerful superior, the sovereign, to a weak inferior, the subject. Its content expresses the sovereign's desire; its authority derives from his position and power. To disobey is to render oneself liable to sanctions. In this analysis, indeterminate criteria of law such as the common good or the will of the people are abandoned in favor of hard objective phenomena.

The analysis rejected moral principles as determinants in the operation of law. International and constitutional law were swept into a limbo inhabited by laws of fashion and etiquette, the limbo of positive morality. Custom became law only when adopted by the courts.

Austin's ideas were not entirely original. The philosophy of natural law had already been demolished by David Hume. The philosophy of positive law had been created by Austin's friend and inspiration, Jeremy Bentham. The systematic development of jurisprudential concepts had been accomplished by Friedrich Karl von Savigny. However, Austin is deservedly credited with having been the first to make a sharp distinction between legal and moral criteria in the analysis of law.

Discussions of Austin's theories appear in most standard textbooks on jurisprudence. His *Lectures* are available in several reprintings.

COLIN TAPPER, *Oxford University*

Further Reading: Eastwood, Reginald, and Keaton, G., *Austinian Theories of Law and Sovereignty* (London 1929).

AUSTIN, ôs'tən, **Jonathan Loring** (1748–1826), American diplomatic agent. Born in Boston on Jan. 2, 1748, he graduated from Harvard in 1766, and engaged in trade until 1775, when he entered the American army. For a time he was secretary of the Massachusetts Board of War, and in 1777 he was sent to Benjamin Franklin and the American commissioners in Paris with the news of Burgoyne's surrender at Saratoga. In early 1778 he was in England as Franklin's agent. Afterward he was secretary to the commissioners at Paris.

On his return with dispatches to America in 1779, Austin was reimbursed for his expenses by Congress, which thus recognized the value of his services to the nation as a whole. The following year he was sent to Spain and Holland to negotiate a loan for Massachusetts but was captured by a British privateer on the way. Although he was soon released, his mission proved unsuccessful. He later held the offices of state secretary and treasurer in Massachusetts. Austin died in Boston on May 10, 1826.

AUSTIN, ôs'tən, **Mary Hunter** (1868–1934), American author, whose best-known books are about the people and life of the western United States. Her work shows a strong strain of mysticism and a sympathetic understanding of Indian life. She was born in Carlinville, Ill., on Sept. 9, 1868. After her graduation from Blackburn College in 1888, she moved west, lived in Carmel, Calif., and finally settled in Santa Fe, N.Mex., where she died on Aug. 13, 1934.

Her first book, *The Land of Little Rain* (1903), containing 14 sketches of desert life, was an instant success. Her other works include *The Basket Woman* (1904), *The Flock* (1906), *Lost Borders* (1909), *Christ in Italy* (1911), *A Woman of Genius* (1912), *The Man Jesus* (1915), and two collections of poetry, *American Rhythm* (1923) and *The Children Sing in the Far West* (1928). She also wrote a play, *The Arrow Maker,* produced in 1911, and an autobiography, *Earth Horizon* (1932).

Further Reading: Pearce, Thomas, *Mary Hunter Austin* (New York 1965).

AUSTIN, ôs′tən, **Moses** (1761–1821), American merchant, mine owner, and colonizer. He was born in Durham, Conn., on Oct. 4, 1761. In 1783 he became a member of a Philadelphia merchant firm, which he and his brother, Stephen, expanded. Moses went to Richmond, Va., and, by 1789, he had bought lead mines in what is now Wythe County, Va. In 1796 he extended his interests to the lead fields in Missouri, where he received a grant from the Spanish governor near present Potosi, Mo., which he founded.

The panic of 1819, however, cost him his fortune, and he applied to the Spanish government for a permit to settle 300 families in Texas. This was granted on Jan. 17, 1821, but Austin's death in Missouri on June 10, 1821, prevented his completing the project. It was carried out by his son, Stephen Fuller Austin (q.v.).

AUSTIN, ôs′tən, **Stephen Fuller** (1793–1836), American colonizer. As founder and administrator of the principal Anglo-American colony in Texas, he displayed extraordinary qualities of leadership. His astute dealings with the Mexican authorities permitted the settlement to develop until it was strong enough to resist Mexican tyranny when it arose and to win independence. Devoted to Anglo-American principles of common law, he was legalistic in his approach to problems, yet pragmatic in their solutions.

Austin was born in Austinville, Va., on Nov. 3, 1793, the eldest son of Moses Austin (q.v.) and Maria (Brown) Austin. At the age of five he moved with his family to Missouri. He attended Colchester Academy in Connecticut and Transylvania University, Lexington, Ky. Returning to Missouri, he had varied experiences as a trader, land speculator, and a lead miner and manufacturer in association with his father. He also served in the territorial legislature in 1814–1820 and as an officer in the militia.

In 1821, Moses Austin received a grant to settle 300 Anglo-American families in Texas, then a Spanish province. He died in June 1821, bequeathing the grant to his son. In December of that year, with the consent of the Spanish governor of Texas, Stephen established the colony along the Gulf of Mexico on the lower reaches of the Colorado and Brazos rivers. (Under later contracts, he settled about 750 additional families.) As civil and military leader, he assumed the responsibilities of liaison with civil authorities and of organizing defenses against hostile Indians.

Because of unsettled political conditions in Mexico, Austin spent much of his time in clarifying the legal position of the Anglo-American colonists in Texas. To this end he made two trips to Mexico City, the first in March 1822. On the advice of the governor of Texas he sought validation of his grant by the Mexican government, which recently had been organized after winning independence from Spain in 1821. Uncertainties in Mexico forced Austin to remain until April 1823 to assure continuance of authority in Texas.

Austin made a second journey to Mexico City in 1833. By that time, tensions between the Mexican government and Texas had become severe, resulting from increasing efforts of the Mexican government to assert control over Texas and to limit the influence of the rapidly growing Anglo-American population. After a revolution in Mexico gave promise of improved conditions, Texans met in convention in 1832 and the following year to prepare petitions asking redress of certain

STEPHEN F. AUSTIN (1793–1836), American colonizer. (Painting in the Texas state capitol, Austin.)

grievances and requesting Mexican statehood independent of Coahuila, to which Texas had been joined in 1824. Austin agreed to deliver the petitions to the Mexican government. In 1834, President Antonio López de Santa Anna granted some requests of the Texans, including the repeal of an anti-immigration decree of 1830. He denied, however, the appeal for separate statehood.

While returning to Texas, Austin was arrested in Saltillo and sent to prison in Mexico City. The charge against him, though never pressed, was an allegedly seditious letter that he wrote while frustrated in talks with Santa Anna's predecessor concerning the petitions. When finally released in 1835, Austin had abandoned hope for the future of Texas as a part of Mexico. Thus upon returning in September he joined a movement in Texas calling for the assumption of a strong stand against the growing tyranny of Santa Anna. Austin accepted chairmanship of the Committee on Public Safety, which had been organized to watch over relations with Mexico; and when a general convention was called to define Texas' new status, he was elected its president.

Meanwhile, military action of the Texas Revolution had begun on Oct. 2, 1835. Austin left the convention and joined a Texas army congregating at Gonzales. Elected commander in chief, he led a campaign against San Antonio, Mexico's military headquarters in Texas. While he was directing a siege against the city, the convention in November appointed him as one of three commissioners to the United States to seek recognition of Texas if independence was declared, to raise material aid, and to enlist volunteers. This business kept him out of Texas during the main phase of the Texas Revolution.

Austin reluctantly agreed to be a candidate for the first presidency of the Republic of Texas after his return in June 1836. Defeated in the election by Sam Houston, he accepted an appointment as secretary of state and was serving in that capacity when he died at Columbia, Texas, on Dec. 27, 1836.

DAVID M. VIGNESS, *Texas Technological College*

Stephen Austin Bibliography

Barker, Eugene C., *The Life of Stephen F. Austin* (Nashville, Tenn., 1925).

Richardson, Rupert N., *Texas, the Lone Star State*, 2d ed. (Englewood Cliffs, N.J., 1958).

Vigness, David M., *The Revolutionary Decades* (Austin 1965).

Webb, Walter P., ed., *The Handbook of Texas*, 2 vols. (Austin 1952).

AUSTIN, ôs′tən, **Warren Robinson** (1877–1962), American legislator and diplomat. He was born in Highgate, Vt., on Nov. 12, 1877. Educated at the University of Vermont, he studied law in his father's offices at St. Albans (1899–1902), was admitted to the Vermont bar in 1902, and remained with his father's firm until 1916. That year he represented the American International Corporation in negotiating a $130 million loan for railway and canal construction in China. From 1917 to 1931 he practiced independently at Burlington and became an eminently successful trial and corporation lawyer.

Entering politics in 1904, Austin was elected state's attorney for Franklin County and mayor of St. Albans (1909). He seconded the nomination of Herbert Hoover at the Republican National Convention of 1928. In defiance of Vermont Republican state machine politicians, he won nomination to the U.S. Senate, was elected on March 31, 1931, and was subsequently returned to office in 1934 and 1940.

An independent conservative in domestic policies, he vigorously opposed New Deal legislation while strongly supporting President Franklin D. Roosevelt's foreign policy. Growing increasingly fearful of the effect on the world of the detached American role in international affairs, he became a leading Republican internationalist. In 1937 he called for an alliance of the United States with the League of Nations to impose sanctions against Japan, and during the same period he advocated American collaboration with Britain in halting German and Italian imperialism.

In the Senate, Austin supported lend-lease legislation and revision of the Neutrality Act, and in 1940 he was coauthor of the first Selective Service Training Act. In 1944 he was made a member of the Senate Foreign Relations Committee and took a prominent part in discussions preceding and subsequent to the Dumbarton Oaks agreement, which laid down the foundations of the United Nations.

Appointed by President Truman in June 1946 to succeed Edward R. Stettinius, Jr., as permanent United States delegate to the United Nations, Austin officially assumed office on Jan. 14, 1947. In this capacity, he insisted on firm unified action against aggression, particularly during the Korean crisis of 1950, called for military action against the North Koreans, and was outspoken in defense of United States foreign policy as being designed only to promote and ensure international peace. Austin retired in 1953; he died in Burlington, Vt., on Dec. 25, 1962.

AUSTIN, ôs′tən, **William** (1778–1841), American author. He was born in Lunenberg, Mass., on March 2, 1778, and was educated at Harvard University and at Lincoln's Inn, London. In 1803 he settled in Charlestown, Mass., where he successfully practiced law and took an active part in state and local politics. He died in Charlestown on June 27, 1841.

Of Austin's five short stories, the best-remembered is the striking and original tale *Peter Rugg, the Missing Man*, which first appeared in the *New England Galaxy* of Sept. 10, 1824. A New England variant of the Wandering Jew legend, the story tells of Peter Rugg's journey home toward Boston in the face of a threatening storm. Rugg, who swears an oath that he will reach home that night or never, is punished by being forced to drive for 50 years toward Boston in a phantom chaise that is drawn by a black, white-footed mare. Pursued throughout his journey by a thunderstorm, he is permitted to stop only long enough to ask the way. The story has an eerie atmosphere that influenced both Hawthorne and Poe, and, like Irving's *Rip van Winkle*, it has become a part of American folklore.

AUSTIN, ôs′tən, a city in southeastern Minnesota, is on the Cedar River, 95 miles (152.8 km) by road south of Minneapolis. The principal industry is a large meat-packing plant. Other industries in Austin are publishing and the manufacture of cans, containers, and paper boxes. The city is the home of Austin Junior College and of Hormel Institute, a unit of the graduate school of the University of Minnesota that conducts research on fats and oils and their connection with heart disease. The Mower County Pioneer and Historical Center, in Austin, includes a museum.

Settled in 1853, the community was voted the county seat in 1857 after two of its citizens had dramatized the issue by carrying off the county records from Frankfort. Austin was incorporated as a city in 1873 and is governed by a mayor and council. Population: 25,074.

AUSTIN, ôs′tən, a city in central Texas, is the state capital and the seat of Travis County. It is situated on the Colorado River, 75 miles (120 km) northeast of San Antonio. As the seat of state government and the site of the University of Texas, Austin has a special professional character. It is also a shipping and receiving center for a large agricultural area. Austin's industries produce boats, brick and tile, candy, chemicals, concrete pipe, feed, food products, furniture, structural steel, and research and electronic equipment. Bergstrom Air Force Base adjoins the city on the southeast. Austin is a major convention center and the headquarters of about 200 state, national, and regional associations.

Besides the University of Texas, institutions of higher learning in the city are St. Edward's University, Huston-Tillotson College, the Austin Presbyterian Theological Seminary, Episcopal Theological Seminary of the Southwest, and Lutheran Concordia College. The Austin Symphony Orchestra, Austin Civic Theater, and Austin Ballet Society contribute to the cultural life of the city.

Lake Austin, impounded by the Tom Miller Dam, and Town Lake within the city limits provide recreational facilities. Barton Springs, in Zilker Park, which produces 27.3 million gallons (103 million liters) of pure cold water daily, is a popular bathing resort. The Highland Lakes country stretches for nearly 100 miles (161 km) northwest of the city through wooded hills and picturesque cliffs along the Colorado River valley. O. Henry (William Sydney Porter), the short-story writer, called Austin the "City of the Violet Crown" because of the purplish mist that rings the surrounding hills in the evening.

The present Texas capitol, built of Texas granite, was completed in 1888. Other notable

AUSTIN is the home of the University of Texas, whose campus lies in the center of the city.

homes and buildings include the governor's mansion, built in 1855; the home of the German-born sculptor, Elisabet Ney, which is now a museum; the Texas Memorial Museum; the O. Henry Museum; the French Legation, which is a house built in the early 1840's for the French representative to the Republic of Texas; Laguna Gloria Art Museum; and the Texas State Archives and Library Building. Confederate General Albert Sidney Johnston, Stephen F. Austin, and other famous Texans are buried in the state cemetery in Austin.

A distinctive feature of the city is its "tower lights," 27 iron towers capped with mercury-vapor lamps 150 feet (45.7 meters) high, which were erected in the 1890's.

History and Government. In 1730 three Spanish missions were moved from east Texas to the vicinity of Barton Springs. In 1833 the present site of Austin lay within the territory of a Mexican land grant sought by Stephen F. Austin. In 1838, Edward Burleson named the village springing up at the site Waterloo. Another early settler was William Barton, for whom Barton Springs was named. In April 1839 a joint congressional commission of the Republic of Texas reported its selection of Waterloo as the capital of its republic. The government offices moved to the new capital in October, and the village was renamed Austin in honor of the principal colonizer and "Father of Texas."

Frequent Indian raids and a Mexican invasion of Texas in March 1842 caused the seat of government to be moved to Houston. Austin citizens retaliated by holding on to the government archives in what came to be known as the "Archives War." The capital was returned to Austin in 1845, the year Texas was annexed to the United States. In 1850 a state referendum made Austin the capital until 1870, and in 1872 it won the designation permanently.

During the Civil War, Austin supported the Confederacy, although Travis County voted against secession. The city manufactured ammunition, raised a company of light infantry, and contributed many volunteers to Terry's Texas Rangers.

After the Civil War, Austin grew rapidly. The Chisholm Trail, an important route for cattle, crossed the eastern part of the city, and the railroads reached Austin in the 1870's. Its selection as permanent capital in 1872 and the establishment of the University of Texas in 1883 determined the future development of the city. Completion of a city-built dam on the Colorado River in 1893 made Austin one of the first cities in Texas to operate its own electric plant. This dam, destroyed by a flood in 1900, was finally replaced by the Tom Miller Dam in 1940.

Since 1926, Austin has had a council-manager form of government. City council members serve without pay and select one of their number to serve as mayor. Population: 251,808.

Dorman H. Winfrey, *Texas State Library*

AUSTRAL ISLANDS. See Tubuai or Austral Islands.

AUSTRALASIA, ôs-trə-lā′zhə, is a geographical term meaning literally "south of Asia" (from Latin *australis*, "southern"). The term was used in the early days of exploration to refer to the lands thought to exist south of Asia. It is still used, with various meanings, but is generally not favored, because of lack of precision in its definition and the likely confusion with *Australia*.

In its broadest meaning, "Australasia" is used as a synonym for *Oceania* to denote all the islands of the Pacific Ocean. In this sense it includes a vast extent of the earth's surface with a total land area of about 3,300,000 square miles (8,500,000 sq km).

More recent usage limits the term to only a part of Oceania—namely, Australia, New Zealand, and surrounding islands. In this usage the other parts of Oceania are Polynesia (including French Oceania; the Niue, Cook, and Tokelau islands of New Zealand; and the islands of Tonga, Samoa, and Hawaii), Melanesia (including New Guinea and the Bismarck Archipelago), Micronesia (including the islands of the Marshall, Marianas, Caroline, and Gilbert groups; Guam; and Nauru), and the Malay Archipelago (including Indonesia and the Philippines).

AUSTRALIA

DAVID MOORE, FROM BLACK STAR

AUSTRALIA, the leading sheep producing country in the world, uses as grazing land its vast outback—a rugged region with sparse vegetation and little rainfall.

Australia's coat of arms

CONTENTS

AUSTRALIA, ô-strāl′yə, is a self-governing member of the Commonwealth of Nations that lies wholly in the Southern Hemisphere. It comprises the island continent of the same name and also includes the adjacent island of Tasmania to the south and lesser coastal islands. Australia is geographically isolated from the other continents by vast expanses of water: the Timor and Arafura seas on the north, the Coral Sea on the northeast, the Pacific Ocean and the Tasman Sea on the east, and the Indian Ocean on the south and west. The total area of continental Australia and the adjacent islands is 2,967,909 square miles (7,686,893 sq km), or about the size of continental United States exclusive of Alaska. Because of its over-all flatness and regular coastline, Australia has been described as a "sprawling pancake."

The Commonwealth of Australia, official name of the country, is a national federation of six states and two federal territories. Its parliamentary government is similar to Britain's, but its federal system, which divides power between national and regional governments, resembles that of the United States.

External territories under Australian administration include Papua, Norfolk Island, the Ashmore and Cartier islands, the Heard and McDonald islands, the Cocos (Keeling) Islands, Christmas Island, the Australian Antarctic Territory, and the UN trusteeships of New Guinea and Nauru.

Modern Australia is a "new" country whose people are mainly of British ancestry. Although it is basically an urban nation, with two out of three of its citizens living in large cities, its vast hinterland remains sparsely populated. Away from the cities and beyond the developed areas in the east and south there are still open, genuinely untouched areas. Combining modern city and frontier, Australia retains some of the mystique associated with it since 17th century mariners first related tales of its unusual landscapes, exotic animals, and primitive tribesmen.

Lying just beyond the chain of islands stretching out from southeastern Asia, northern Australia was subject to intermittent exploration by Malay fishermen and other Asian voyagers, but presumably because of the uninviting terrain there was no large-scale influx of immigrants until European settlement began in the late 1700's. Across the continent the aborigines' Stone Age culture remained unchanged. The tribespeople were nomads who did not till the soil or plant crops. Their only domesticated animal was the dingo, or hunting dog, and the people lived the simple lives of hunters, supplementing their diet with fish, seeds, and plant roots. At no time did they exceed 300,000 in number; yet they remained in undisputed possession of the land until the arrival of the white man.

Once European mariners entered the Indian and Pacific oceans, speculation grew about the nature of the still-unexplored regions. Sixteenth century cartographers filled the great void south of Asia by drawing an imaginary coastline on their maps, which they labeled *Terra Australis Incognita* (Unidentified South Land). From their trading posts in the East Indies, the Portuguese learned of an uninviting land to the south, while the Spaniards, reaching the Philippines from America's shores, speculated that King Solomon's gold mines might be somewhere in the mythical South Land; but it was the Dutch who made the first extensive explorations of Australia's northern and western shores after they ousted the Portuguese from the East Indies. However, when their efforts to trade with the aborigines of "New Holland" proved unsuccessful, the Dutch abandoned any thought of acquiring the land.

The British showed their first serious interest in Australia after Lt. James Cook discovered and charted the fertile east coast in 1770 and took possession of it as New South Wales. Favorable reports by Cook and fellow voyagers led to the founding in 1788 of the first settlement, at Sydney. After a few years settlements were established at other points along the temperate-zone coastline and in Tasmania.

From the 1820's English wool spinners drew increasing supplies from Australia's expanding flocks of sheep, which spread across the grasslands of New South Wales and Tasmania. However, after 50 years of settlement, little of the continent had been explored and the total population was barely 150,000. By 1851, when gold was discovered, the population was 400,000; thereafter the country experienced a period of extraordinarily rapid growth as rich gold finds lured a steady stream of settlers. Within a decade the population had trebled. Agriculture was stimulated, pastoral activities were expanded, and in gold-rich Victoria the rudiments of an industrial economy were established. Investment from abroad supported the construction of railways. By the 1890's the already self-governing Australian colonies were moving toward federation. The Commonwealth of Australia came into being with the adoption of a constitution on Jan. 1, 1901.

Unification of Australia under a single customs administration and adoption of a policy of tariff protection for domestic industry helped to stimulate manufacturing. During World War I shortages of goods led to industrial expansion, which continued in the 1920's as Australia became self-sufficient in steel production. Gradually the range of manufactures was extended, and during and after World War II major enterprises, including some heavy industry, were developed. By the 1960's home appliances, automobiles, farm implements, locomotives, ships, and precision-engineering products were manufactured, as were chemicals, textiles, and paper. Of the total work force, three out of every ten were employed in manufacturing. A significant part of the industrial expansion, which went hand-in-hand with a sustained government-sponsored immigration program, resulted from investment by overseas business enterprises, particularly British and American firms.

Rural enterprises also expanded, although because of mechanization fewer workers were required. Output of most products showed strong gains. In the late 1960's, Australia led the world in the export of wool, lead, and rutile, was second in zinc, sugar, and meat, and third in wheat. Vast deposits of bauxite and iron ore gave the nation the world's largest store of these minerals. The country's first oilfield went into production in 1965.

Until World War II, Australia followed Britain closely in foreign policy. Thereafter, its distinct role as a Pacific nation was more frequently stressed. Traditional concern over the pressures of overcrowded Asia grew more intense in the 1950's as Communist power was consolidated in China and Communist influence expanded in some of the newly independent countries of Southeast Asia. Australian spokesmen emphasized the need to overcome the prevailing poverty, disease, and hunger in underdeveloped lands with rising populations. In furtherance of this aim Australia supported the Colombo Plan (q.v.) and other measures aimed at economic advancement throughout the region. Steadily, however, Australia came to recognize military dangers arising from Communist-backed subversion in Southeast Asia, and from the early 1960's defense outlays were increased.

While continuing close and active partnership with Britain, Australia established a firm and direct relationship with the United States. It joined the ANZUS pact with New Zealand and the United States in 1951 and SEATO, the wider Southeast Asian collective defense treaty, in 1954. In 1963, Australia and the United States concluded an agreement for the establishment of a U.S. Navy communications base in Australia's far northwest on the Indian Ocean. By that time it was recognized that Australia was bound to remain an important partner in the furtherance of U.S. defense policies in the whole western Pacific and Indian Ocean region.

R.M. YOUNGER
Author of "The Changing World: Australia"

Bibliography

Australia, Bureau of Census and Statistics, *The Official Year Book of the Commonwealth of Australia* (Canberra, annually).
Chisholm, Alexander H., ed., *The Australian Encyclopedia*, 10 vols. (Sydney 1965).
Fitzpatrick, Brian C., *The Australian Commonwealth: A Picture of the Community, 1901–1955* (Melbourne 1956).
Grattan, Clinton Hartley, ed., *Australia* (Berkeley, Calif., 1947).
Grattan, Clinton Hartley, *The Southwest Pacific to 1900* (Ann Arbor, Mich., 1963).
Grattan, Clinton Hartley, *The Southwest Pacific Since 1900* (Ann Arbor, Mich., 1963).
Horne, Donald, *The Lucky Country: Australia Today* (Baltimore 1965).

INFORMATION HIGHLIGHTS

Official Name: Commonwealth of Australia.

Head of State: The monarch of the United Kingdom and Australia (represented by a governor general).

Head of Government: Prime minister.

Legislature: Commonwealth Parliament (House of Representatives and Senate).

Area: 2,967,909 square miles (7,686,893 sq km).

Boundaries: Timor and Arafura seas, north; Coral Sea, northeast; Pacific Ocean and Tasman Sea, east; Indian Ocean, south and west.

Elevation: Highest point, Mount Kosciusko (7,314 feet, or 2,229 meters); lowest point, Lake Eyre (39 feet, or 11.9 meters, below sea level).

Population: (1965 estimate) 11,478,703.

Capital: Canberra (population, 1965 est., 85,690).

National Language: English.

Literacy Rate: 99% of population, excluding aborigines.

Major Religions: Protestantism, Roman Catholicism, Judaism.

Monetary Unit: Australian dollar (100 cents) = U.S. $1.12; Australian pound (20 shillings) = U.S. $2.23.

Chief Products: Wheat, oats, barley, sugarcane, fruit; wool, meat; lead, zinc, iron, copper, gold.

Flag: Dark blue field with Union Jack at upper left, seven-pointed federal star directly below, and stars of the Southern Cross to the right (see Flag).

National Anthem: God Save the King (or Queen).

SYDNEY HARBOR, in the heart of the city, is spanned by the Sydney Harbour Bridge, one of the largest steel arch bridges in the world.

1. Population

Political Divisions and Population. The Commonwealth of Australia comprises the five mainland states of Queensland, New South Wales, Victoria, South Australia, and Western Australia; the island state of Tasmania; and two federally controlled territories, the Northern Territory and the Australian Capital Territory, the latter an enclave in New South Wales. The states and territories, with their areas, populations, and capitals, are shown in the accompanying table. The principal cities, with their estimated populations (including suburbs) as of June 30, 1965, are Sydney, 2,349,590; Melbourne, 2,121,900; Brisbane, 677,000; Adelaide, 615,500; Perth, 465,000; and Hobart, 123,967. Canberra, the federal capital, had 85,690 inhabitants.

AREA AND POPULATION OF AUSTRALIA
(official estimate Dec. 31, 1965)

State or territory	Area (square miles)[1]	Population[2]	Capital
New South Wales	309,433	4,237,514	Sydney
Victoria	87,884	3,233,938	Melbourne
Queensland	667,000	1,615,384	Brisbane
South Australia	380,070	1,064,629	Adelaide
Western Australia	975,920	820,063	Perth
Tasmania	26,383	379,107	Hobart
Northern Territory	520,280	34,253	Darwin[3]
Australian Capital Territory	939	93,815	Canberra[4]
Total	2,967,909	11,478,703	

[1] 1 square mile = 2.59 sq km. [2] Exclusive of full-blooded aborigines. [3] Administrative center. [4] Federal capital.

The population of Australia passed the 10,000,000 mark in 1959 and the 11,000,000 mark in 1963. Throughout the 1950's and into the 1960''s the increase averaged slightly more than 200,000 annually, representing an annual rate of about 2 percent. In most years from one-third to one-half of the population increase was provided by immigration. With a steadily declining natural increase (excess of births over deaths) after 1960 and rising immigration, the relative contributions varied. In the year ended June 30, 1957, for example, the natural increase was 129,144 and the net intake from overseas, 86,377; while for the year ended June 30, 1965, the corresponding figures were 123,446 and 100,555 respectively. The birth rate in the 1950's varied from 23.3 to 22.5 per 1,000 population; in 1965 it was down to 19.61 per 1,000. The death rate throughout the 1950's and 1960's remained fairly constant at about 8.75 per 1,000. In 1965 the death rate for infants under one year of age was 16.48 per 1,000 live births.

R.M. YOUNGER
Author of "The Changing World: Australia"

Immigration and Population Growth. The non-aboriginal population of Australia is almost wholly of European origin and is composed principally of descendants of earlier immigrants from Great Britain and Ireland. The census of 1961 showed that 83 percent of the population was Australian-born, a slight decline from the percentage in earlier years, probably reflecting the success of the aggressive immigration program. However, it was not until approximately 1870 that persons born in Australia outnumbered those born overseas. This fact emphasizes the relatively recent origin of European settlement in Australia.

The first settlers, who arrived in New South Wales beginning in 1788, were chiefly convicts, military personnel, or government officials. Until about 1830 the transportation of convicted persons remained the main source of population increase; thereafter the immigration of free settlers began to accelerate sharply. By 1850, when the total population reached 400,000, population growth was the result of free immigration and natural increase. Between 1851 and 1860, the decade of the gold rushes, over 600,000 immigrants arrived in Australia and swelled the population to 1,145,585 by 1860.

After 1860 natural increase was the most important element of growth. Nevertheless, for the three decades preceding 1891 the net gain from immigration exceeded 740,000 or 35 percent of total population growth. From 1891 until about 1907, during a period of economic collapse, there was little immigration. Yet, on the eve of federation it amounted to 593,000, but the influx was far from constant—194,000 persons arrived between 1906 and 1915, and 313,000 between 1921 and 1930. In both periods passage assistance—traditionally the price Australia paid to compete with the great immigrant countries closer to Europe, particularly the United States—played an important role. In the first four decades of the 20th century more than 421,000 immigrants were assisted financially to reach Australia.

A feature of non-British immigration of the 1920's and 1930's was the increasing number of southern Europeans, all of whom came without government assistance. The German-born element declined steadily, from 46,000 in 1891 to 22,400 in 1921, and the number of Scandinavians also declined, from 16,000 to 14,000. By contrast, there was a slow but steady increase in Greek-born immigrants, from a few hundred in the early 1900's to 3,700 in 1921 and to 8,300 in 1933. The greatest increase was in Italian-born immigrants, whose number rose from 5,700 in 1901 to 8,100 in 1921 and to 26,800 in 1933. The Australian people in 1933 were still essentially the descendants of British immigrants. Their political, religious, legal, and social insti-

MELBOURNE is an important commercial and industrial center. The business section of the city, looming beyond the Prince's Bridge, is on the northern bank of the Yarra River.

tutions bore the marks of their origin, but they had taken on certain features that were peculiarly Australian. The people had come overwhelmingly from the lower middle and working classes of the British Isles, and their society lacked the formal class divisions of the parent countries; yet they were unmistakably British, even if Australian British. Nevertheless, while non-British Australians were fewer than 160,000 in 1933, they played an important role in the nation's life. Pockets of non-British residents had long been identifiable throughout the country, as in the predominantly German areas of South Australia and southern Queensland in the 19th century; the enclaves of Italians in coastal fishing villages or more significantly in the canefields of northern Queensland in the 20th century; and the concentration of Greek settlers associated with the restaurant and fruit-vending trades in the cities.

Economic recession after 1929 brought about two sudden changes: the cessation of immigration and a sharp fall in the birth rate. The volume of births declined to 110,000 in 1933 and 1934, as compared with 136,000 in 1920 and 117,000 in 1910. The birth rate, which had been as high as 35 per 1,000 in 1890, dropped to 25 by 1920 and to less than 17 by 1933. To some extent, this sharp fall was due to the postponement of marriages and births, but substantially it marked the consolidation of the trend to the small family, typical of Western societies, with an average of about 2.5 children.

The economic recession of the 1930's was accompanied by a pessimistic attitude toward the future population of Australia. Estimates of Australia's capacity to sustain its population, which had been as high as 100 million in the optimistic 1920's, were brought as low as 15 million in the 1930's. Immigrants were feared as competitors for labor, rather than welcomed as incentives to capital investment. By 1939 these pessimistic attitudes had been moderated slightly, but it was felt that immigration would have to be highly selective and controlled in terms of job opportunities.

World War II temporarily curtailed any substantial increase in immigration, but the events of the war, particularly in the Pacific area, encouraged a new and more constructive approach to the question of population building. The cry was less the "populate or perish" slogan of the 1920's than a recognition that Australia had to

secure population rapidly to make efficient use of the continent's known resources. More manpower was needed, it was felt, not so much to settle the land as to increase the nation's industrial strength. The official reaction to this mood was the government's initiation in 1945 of a long-term immigration program which would bring a steady stream of immigrants at the annual rate of 1 percent of the population. A mission was sent abroad to study the prospects of European immigration, and plans were laid to assist non-British as well as British settlers. This assistance to non-British immigrants on a large scale was new in Australian history. Thoroughly traditional, on the other hand, was the planning of the new program within the strict framework of the policy which since federation had virtually prohibited the entry of any Asian person for permanent settlement.

Shipping problems delayed full operation of the program, but by 1948 positive results were evident, particularly in the flow of British immigrants. The recruitment of non-Britishers from Europe was also showing results in 1948, but the flow from this source became a flood when the Australian government cooperated with the International Refugee Organization by accepting thousands of displaced persons. By 1951 about 171,000 displaced persons had been received in Australia. Flows from other sources, predominantly the United Kingdom, also increased sharply, and the total intake of persons declaring their intention of settling for a year or more jumped from 65,700 in 1948 to 167,700 in 1949 and to 174,500 in 1950. This rate of increase had scarcely been exceeded for a century and was greater than the gain from natural increase.

The decrease in the number of displaced persons after 1950 brought a decline in permanent arrivals to 132,500 in 1951, and thereafter a minor economic recession checked the flow further, but after 1953 the inflow continued considerably above 100,000 a year. The net gain each year was somewhat smaller, for permanent departures (those leaving Australia to reside abroad for a year or more) averaged about 35,000 annually after 1951, but even so the years after World War II were remarkable in Australia's immigration history. In the period 1946–1965, Australia received 2,356,569 permanent new arrivals; the immigrant gain was approximately 2 million—the largest 20-year increase from immigration on record.

PERTH, capital of Western Australia, lies on the Swan River 12 miles from the port of Fremantle. A major rail terminal, Perth is the trading center for products of the vast hinterland.

This increase was not strictly in the Australian tradition, since almost 50 percent of all permanent arrivals were assisted immigrants and close to half of these were from non-British lands. In all, about 30 nationalities were represented. By far the largest non-British element was the Italian (about 290,000 arrivals), while the inflow from Greece (140,000) and the Netherlands (139,000) was also substantial. Other significant groups were Poles (82,000 arrivals) and Yugoslavs (54,000). A small but steadily rising element was the migrant inflow from the United States; by the mid-1960's more than 4,000 Americans a year were arriving to take up residence.

A further departure from traditional immigration policy, announced early in 1966, was the relaxation of laws governing the entry of non-Europeans. Regulations for non-Europeans seeking permits for limited residence were eased, and the period of residence for citizenship was shortened from 15 years to 5 years, the same as for Europeans. It was thought that the new laws would apply mostly to Asians with special skills and would not increase non-European immigration substantially above the 700 permitted to enter annually in the mid-1960's.

While large-scale immigration in the 20th century changed the composition of the non-British minorities, it did not greatly reduce the proportion of the population of British origin compared with that of the late 19th century. The census of 1961 enumerated 83 percent of the population as Australian-born and a further 7 percent as being born in British countries, leaving 10 percent of the entire population foreign-born.

For several years after 1947 the rapid growth through immigration was matched by a great increase in births; during the 1950's the birth rate averaged 23 per 1,000 (compared with a figure of slightly over 17 in the 1930's). In 1961 there were 239,986 births, but from that year there was a slow but steady decline as the number of births fell by a few thousand each year; in 1965 the rate was below 20 per 1,000 for the first time since 1943. The levels of infant and maternal mortality, which were among the lowest in the world, were still being reduced—infant mortality was below 19 per 1,000 live births in 1965—and this was associated with an increased life expectancy (over 70 years), which was one of the highest in the world.

The occupational pattern was broadly similar to that of the United States. Throughout, the long-term trend toward urban concentration continued. The 1961 census showed that 55.6 percent of Australia's population resided in the six state capitals, and 26.4 percent in other urban areas, leaving 17.8 percent living in rural areas and 0.2 percent migratory. Associated with an increasingly industrialized economy was the expansion of commercial activities and service industries, and a corresponding growth in the white-collar element of the work force, accompanied by a decline in the number engaged in pastoral and agricultural pursuits. As of 1961, only 13 percent of all employed men were engaged in rural industries as compared with 25 percent in manufacturing. Because of the country's size and dispersed population, transport continued to involve a relatively high proportion of the work force.

Australia had become one of the world's most highly industrialized nations as well as a great producer and exporter of food, fiber, and minerals; yet it remained the world's most sparsely populated continent. In the 1960's relatively few Australians knew or had cause to know the arid interior. It was still the fertile coastal fringe, the great capital cities, and a few developing industrial zones in coastal areas that absorbed the bulk of the population increase.

WILFRED D. BORRIE
The Australian National University

Australian Aborigines. Anthropologists usually classify the Australian aborigines as a separate race or subrace, the *Australoid,* because they exhibit certain anatomic characteristics distinct from the Caucasoid, Mongoloid, and Negroid traits. They are a dark-skinned people of medium height with narrow heads, black wavy or curly hair, deep-seated eyes, broad noses, and a plentiful growth of hair on face and body. Apparently coming from the Malaysian region, they reached the northern coasts of Australia in simple watercraft, bringing the dingo with them. The approximate period of their arrival has not been determined.

Adaptation to Environment. Before the coming of the white men the aborigines lived solely by hunting and food gathering, but their economy was not haphazard. Each group accumulated detailed knowledge of the habits, cycles, and food values of the plants, insects, reptiles, mar-

AUSTRALIAN NEWS AND INFORMATION BUREAU

ABORIGINES hunt game in Western Australia with a nonreturning boomerang (*at left*) and a spear and woomera, or spear-thrower.

supials, and fish found in its area, and developed methods and equipment for obtaining them and, when necessary, for making them edible. The environment was a system of associated elements. The year was divided into seasons according to the succession of temperatures, winds, and condition and availability of various food sources, and the behavior of one insect, plant, or animal was a sign of the condition or appearance of certain others, each in its own place and time.

Population density varied with the fertility of the country. When a group increased beyond the number that could live on the food obtainable within practical range, some of its members moved to the next satisfactory unoccupied area, although they maintained kinship and social, economic, and ritual ties with the parent group. By this hiving-off process all of Australia was occupied. Through varying degrees of separation in space and time, differences arose in language, in material equipment, in customs, and in ritual. Basically, however, the aborigines retained a common culture, language, system of values, and philosophy.

The fundamental principle of aboriginal life and thought was complete dependence on nature —on what it provided unaided by gardening and herding. Life depended on intelligent adaptation to nature through knowledge and skill, including provision for contingencies. Such provision was made by regarding natural species and phenomena as part of the same social order as man himself. Each clan or other social group consisted of human beings and also of specified plants, animals, and natural objects, whch were regarded as close relations. The former, who were called totemites, generally refrained from hurting or eating their associated natural species, called totems. The latter, by their behavior in the totemites' waking or dream life, helped, strengthened and warned them. Above all, the human members ensured through ritual the normal increase of essential species or phenomena—for example, rain—in due season. This ritual was so vital that knowledge of it and of its mythology was imparted only to men who had been tried, disciplined, and taught through a long process of initiation into the secret life.

Impact of the European. The equilibrium of man and nature in aboriginal Australia was upset catastrophically by European settlements from 1788 onward. The newcomers appropriated the better lands, and the food-gathering, social, and ritual activities of the aborigines were curtailed and eventually rendered impossible. Some unequal clashes occurred, but the inevitable result was the pauperization of the aborigines.

Groups in the vicinity of white settlements, no longer regularly on the move in quest of food, became unhealthily sedentary and relied more and more on an unbalanced diet obtained from settlers and officials. They used unaccustomed clothing and blankets unhygenically, fell prey to new diseases, and developed a defeatist attitude. In all such situations they were reduced to remnants within a few decades.

As settlement spread to less-favored areas and became slower and sparser, however, local tribes had time to adjust themselves to the new factor in their environment. The settler depended on the aborigines' labor, and the aborigines came to desire some of the settlers' goods. Through its elders each tribe or subtribe evolved a *modus vivendi* with the settler on its country. The aborigines, while continuing much of their tribal life, worked for the settler, but expended just enough effort to keep him going and to get from him all they could in return. On his side, the settler, and later the pastoralist, accepted the situation, recognizing that his native workers were generally inefficient and uninterested. This was not a progressive solution of the problem of intrusion and did not prevent aboriginal decrease, but in the central and northern parts of the continent it enabled sufficient full bloods to persist long enough to ensure the survival of the race.

Development of Aboriginal Policy. The aborigines were British subjects wherever the proclamation of British sovereignty became operative through actual settlement. As such they were, according to official instructions, to be treated with "amity and conciliation" and to receive the blessings of Christianity and civilization. This early attempt at assimilation failed because of the speed of settlement with its resultant clashes, many marked by atrocities, and because of the aborigines' rapid decrease. Consequently, the mid-19th century policies of protection were adopted to ease their "inevitable passing," for they seemed unable to cope with the sudden change from the Stone Age to modern civilization.

In the 1920's, stimulated by ideas inherent in the mandate principle of the League of Nations, the white settlers began to feel misgivings about their attitude toward the aborigines. From 1931, positive policies were advocated, based on the conviction that with appropriate health, education, and employment measures the aborigines would increase and contribute to Australian life. From the late 1930's the states, which remained responsible for aboriginal policy and administration within their borders, and the federal government, which was responsible for the Northern Territory, actively adopted such policies. Anthropologists threw new light on the aborigines as a people, and the welfare work of religious missions helped lay a foundation for their advancement. By the 1950's, with the federal government setting the pace, administrators were taking measures to hasten aboriginal development with the object of eventual assimilation into the life of the nation as a whole.

The efforts of various nongovernment bodies interested in aboriginal welfare were coordinated in 1958 with the formation of a federal Council

AN ABORIGINE FAMILY (*above*) in front of their wurley, or hut. Aborigine children (*right*), who are often fair-haired and comparatively light-skinned until adulthood, are digging for water in a dry creek.

for Aboriginal Advancement. Three aborigines were among the 25 people who formulated a "charter" embodying five basic principles: equal rights; a standard of living "adequate for health and well-being, including food, clothing, housing and medical care"; equal pay for equal work; free and compulsory education for detribalized aborigines; and retention of all remaining aboriginal reserves.

In 1959 all aborigines came under the provisions of federal social-welfare laws qualifying them for pensions and maternity allowances. Vocational and other training was also provided not only for children but also for adults who could benefit from it. Some of the states provided university scholarships for aborigines, and an aborigine was graduated from an Australian university in 1966. Increasingly aborigines and part-aborigines were employed as stockmen, mechanics, and handymen on the cattle properties and in the towns.

A conference of federal and state ministers in 1960 resolved that the practice of isolating aborigines in reservations should be abandoned as soon as possible and that measures should be taken to assist in their assimilation into the mainstream of contemporary Australian life. A survey disclosed that fewer than 2,000 bush primitives remained, and even these nomads of the northwest interior, mostly in the Northern Territory and Western Australia, were beginning to make contact with civilization.

A measure to enfranchise aborigines was enacted by the federal parliament in 1962; it left the matter of enrollment to individual choice. The way was opened for aborigines eventually to attain the same mode of living as other Australians, with the same rights, privileges, and responsibilities. However, assimilation proceeded very slowly. There was evidence that the aborigines preferred a separate communal existence, and some aboriginal spokesmen expressed concern over what they feared to be the threatened extinction of their people's separate cultural and social identity.

The aboriginal population, sometimes estimated to have been as great as 300,000 in 1788, had been greatly reduced over the years. According to the 1961 census, the full-blood aboriginal population totaled 40,081; the largest groups were in the Northern Territory (17,386), Western Australia (10,121), and Queensland (8,686).

Part-Aborigines. Part-aborigines in all states and the Northern Territory probably total about 30,000. In each generation many pass into the general community. Traditionally the mixed bloods were deprived of good home life, full education and economic opportunity, and they harbored resentment; but this situation has improved. Many are now employed in trades, and some have become teachers, nurses, and musicians. The remaining problem is a matter of attitude and personal and group relations rather than of administrative policy. Many unofficial groups of white citizens have extended both friendship and practical assistance, and in this way the remaining barriers to assimilation are expected to be removed.

A.P. ELKIN, *University of Sidney*

Bibliography

Appleyard, Reginald T., *British Emigration to Australia* (Toronto 1964).
Berndt, Ronald M., and Berndt, Catherine H., *The World of the First Australians* (Chicago 1964).
Bleakley, J.W., *The Aborigines of Australia* (Brisbane 1959).
Coleman, Peter, ed., *Australian Civilization: A Symposium* (Melbourne 1962).
Davies, Alan Fraser, ed., *Australian Society: A Sociological Introduction* (New York 1965).
Elkin, Adolphus P., *The Australian Aborigines*, 5th ed. (Sydney 1964).
Foxcraft, Edmund J.B., *Australian Native Policy* (Melbourne 1941).
Hasluck, Paul M.C., *Black Australians* (Melbourne 1942).
Holt, Harold E., and others, *Australia and the Migrant* (Sydney 1953).
Horne, Donald, *The Lucky Country: Australia Today* (Baltimore 1965).
McLeod, Alan L., ed., *The Pattern of Australian Culture* (New York 1963).
Price, Charles A., *Southern Europeans in Australia* (Melbourne 1963).
Simpson, Colin, *Adam in Ochre: Inside Aboriginal Australia*, 5th ed. (Sydney 1962).
Tindale, Norman B., and Lindsay, Harold A., *Aboriginal Australians* (Brisbane 1963).

GREEN ISLAND, one of the coral cays, or low islands (*left*), at the edge of the Great Barrier Reef, off the coast of Queensland. Thousands of visitors annually view the multicolored corals and tropical fish that are found in the clear waters (*above*).

R.M. YOUNGER

2. The Land and Natural Resources

Topography. Australia is for the most part a vast, undulating plateau. Its 12,210-mile (19,-650-km) coastline is characterized by long stretches of sandy surf beaches. Off the northeast coast the Great Barrier Reef, the longest coral reef in the world, stretching for 1,250 miles (2,012 km), fringes the continental shelf. Unlike every other continent, Australia lacks mountains of truly alpine structure and elevation.

The chief highlands, known as the Eastern Highlands, occur in a zone 50 to 200 miles (80–322 km) wide along the eastern seaboard. Mount Kosciusko (7,314 feet or 2,229 meters) is the highest peak, and there are only a few others that rise above 6,000 feet (1,829 meters). The Eastern Highlands consist mainly of dissected plateaus containing many residual high plains or tablelands cut by deep river gorges. Through this complex of ranges runs a main divide or water parting. The western slopes of the highlands lead down to interior plains which, with a few interruptions caused by prominences of bedrock or by residual tablelands, extend to the Flinders and Mount Lofty ranges in South Australia and to the low but rough range country around Mount Isa and Cloncurry in western Queensland, at the borders of the Barkly Tableland.

Beyond this great belt of plains, which extends from the shallow Gulf of Carpentaria in the north to the sea in South Australia, lies the Great Plateau, comprising more than half the continent and rising gradually to a level of 2,000 feet (610 meters) at Alice Springs. Above the general level of the plateau are many prominent peaks and ranges, some of which attain a height of 5,000 feet (1,524 meters). Mount Olga and Ayers Rock (see picture on page 714), two monolithic mountains of hard conglomerate, rise like islands from the sandy plains south of the Macdonnell Ranges.

Along the west coast the plateau breaks sharply down to narrow coastal plains along the Darling scarp in the hinterland of Perth. To the south, along the Great Australian Bight, the old rocks are covered by flat-lying Tertiary limestones which form the treeless Nullarbor Plain. In the far northwest the Kimberley Plateau, separated from the Great Plateau inland from Broome by the Great Sandy Desert and the Fitzroy River valley, is a rugged and inaccessible wilderness. The plateau of Arnhem Land, at the northern limit of the Northern Territory, is a similar

wasteland, but many fine gorges cut its edges and afford dam sites for the monsoon-fed rivers of the region.

The desert and semidesert areas of Australia are notable for their endless array of parallel sand ridges. Formed for the most part in a more arid period, the ridges are partly fixed by vegetation, and in places the rivers flood out between them during the wet season. They afford the largest area of sand-ridge deserts in the world.

The greatest river system in Australia is that of the Murray and its major tributary, the Darling. These streams rise in the well-watered Eastern Highlands and spread out in complex systems of anabranches and distributaries in the Riverina district of New South Wales, especially along the Lachlan and Murrumbidgee rivers. After receiving the Darling, the Murray gains no additional tributaries but flows through the semiarid Mallee in a much more restricted flood plain. Originally it was subject to great reduction in flow in summer, but its level is now maintained by dams, weirs, and locks.

In the well-watered eastern and southeastern coastal ranges many permanent streams flow directly to the sea, although only a few have extensive catchments. The largest is the Burdekin in Queensland, which rises west of the highland axis and passes through a gorge on its way to the sea. A great engineering project was undertaken in the 1950's in the Kosciusko area of the Snowy Mountains, where the headwaters of the Snowy River were turned westward to discharge into the Murray River system.

Thousands of square miles in the Great Plateau are riverless, and those water courses in which temporary streams flow only rarely after rain are marked by lines of shallow salt pans, which appear on maps as lakes. The largest are permanent streams, but all the major streams of monsoonal northern Australia are subject to marked variations in flow. A very extensive area of the Northern Territory, western Queensland, and northern South Australia drains toward Lake Eyre (39 feet or 11.9 meters below sea level). The streams flowing toward the lake are fed only during the wet season, and in their slow passage downstream the floodwaters spread out in numerous distributary channels that form a natural irrigation system and yield excellent cattle pastures in a large part of southwestern Queensland.

Geology. Compared with the other continents, the Australian land mass is geologically very old and stable. The western two thirds of the

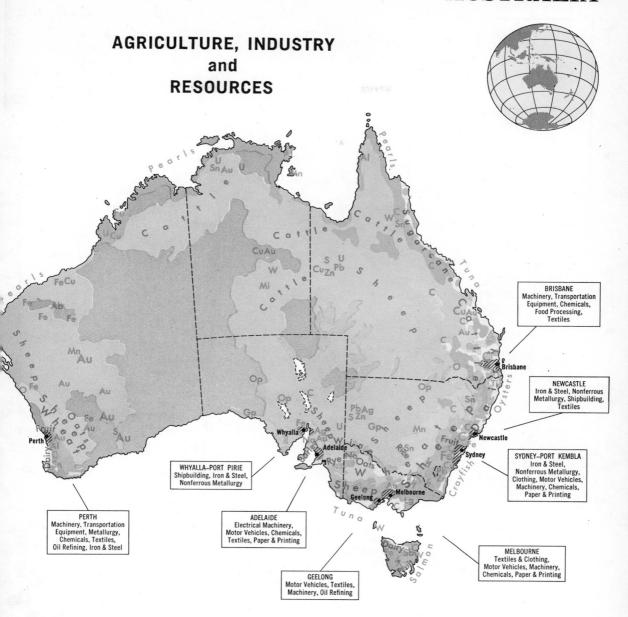

AUSTRALIA

AGRICULTURE, INDUSTRY and RESOURCES

BRISBANE
Machinery, Transportation
Equipment, Chemicals,
Food Processing,
Textiles

NEWCASTLE
Iron & Steel, Nonferrous
Metallurgy, Shipbuilding,
Textiles

SYDNEY–PORT KEMBLA
Iron & Steel,
Nonferrous Metallurgy,
Clothing, Motor Vehicles,
Machinery, Chemicals,
Paper & Printing

WHYALLA–PORT PIRIE
Shipbuilding, Iron & Steel,
Nonferrous Metallurgy

PERTH
Machinery, Transportation
Equipment, Metallurgy,
Chemicals, Textiles,
Oil Refining, Iron & Steel

ADELAIDE
Electrical Machinery,
Motor Vehicles, Chemicals,
Textiles, Paper & Printing

MELBOURNE
Textiles & Clothing,
Motor Vehicles, Machinery,
Chemicals, Paper & Printing

GEELONG
Motor Vehicles, Textiles,
Machinery, Oil Refining

DOMINANT LAND USE

- Cereals (chiefly wheat), Livestock
- Dairy, Truck Farming
- Cash Crops, Horticulture, Fruit
- Pasture Livestock
- Range Livestock
- Forests
- Nonagricultural Land

MAJOR MINERAL OCCURRENCES

Ab	Asbestos	Na	Salt
Ag	Silver	O	Petroleum
Al	Bauxite	Op	Opals
Au	Gold	Pb	Lead
C	Coal	S	Sulfur, Pyrites
Cu	Copper	Sb	Antimony
Fe	Iron Ore	Sn	Tin
Gp	Gypsum	Ti	Titanium
Lg	Lignite	U	Uranium
Mi	Mica	W	Tungsten
Mn	Manganese	Zn	Zinc

Water Power

Major Industrial Areas

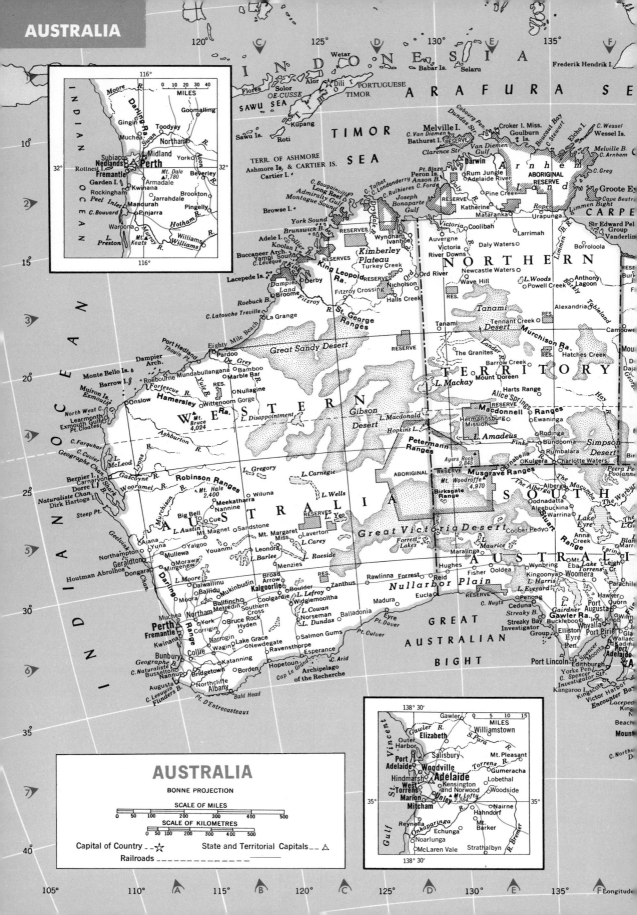

Copyright by C. S. Hammond & Co., N. Y.

AUSTRALIA

TOPOGRAPHY

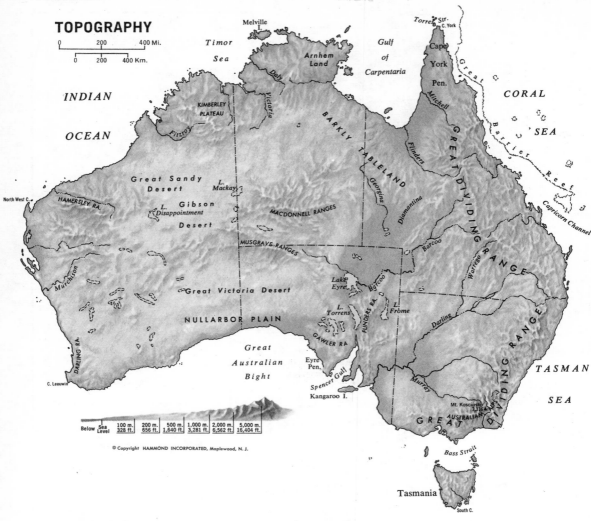

0   200   400 Mi.

0 200 400 Km.

Timor Sea

INDIAN

OCEAN

KIMBERLEY PLATEAU

Arnhem Land

Gulf of Carpentaria

CORAL

SEA

Great Sandy Desert

L. Mackay

MACDONNELL RANGES

BARKLY TABLELAND

GREAT DIVIDING RANGE

HAMERSLEY RA.

North West C.

L. Disappointment

Gibson Desert

MUSGRAVE RANGES

Lake Eyre

L. Torrens

FLINDERS RA.

L. Frome

GAWLER RA.

Great Victoria Desert

NULLARBOR PLAIN

MURCHISON

DARLING RA.

C. Leeuwin

Great Australian Bight

Eyre Pen.

Spencer Gulf

Kangaroo I.

Mt. Kosciusko

GREAT AUSTRALIAN ALPS

GREAT DIVIDING RANGE

TASMAN

SEA

Torres Str. C. York

Cape York Pen.

Mitchell

Flinders

Georgina

Diamantina

Barcoo

Bogoo

Murray

Darling

Murrumbidgee

Great Barrier Reef

Capricorn Channel

Below Sea Level | 100 m. 328 ft. | 200 m. 656 ft. | 500 m. 1,640 ft. | 1,000 m. 3,281 ft. | 2,000 m. 6,562 ft. | 5,000 m. 16,404 ft.

© Copyright HAMMOND INCORPORATED, Maplewood, N. J.

Bass Strait

Tasmania

South C.

AUSTRALIA
Total Population, 12,522,000

AUSTRALIAN CAPITAL TERRITORY
Total Population, 103,573

CITIES and TOWNS

Canberra (capital), 92,308 ....H 7
Canberra, *127,750 ....H 7

CORAL SEA ISLANDS TERRITORY
Total Population, 3

Bougainville (reef) ....H 3
Cato (isl.) ....K 4
Coral (sea) ....H 2
Coringa (islets) ....H 3
Great Barrier (reef) ....H 3
Holmes (reef) ....H 3
Lihou (reef and cays) ....J 3
Magdelaine (cays) ....J 3
Saumarez (reef) ....J 4
Willis (islets), 3 ....H 3

NEW SOUTH WALES
Total Population, 4,300,083

CITIES and TOWNS

Albury, 23,379 ....H 7
Armidale, 14,984 ....J 6
Auburn, 48,961 ....L 3
Ballina, 4,931 ....J 5
Bankstown, 159,981 ....L 3
Bathurst, 17,222 ....H 6
Bega, 3,925 ....J 7

Blacktown, 103,037 ....K 3
Blue Mountains, 30,731 ....J 6
Botany, 31,871 ....L 3
Bourke, 3,262 ....H 6
Broken Hill, 30,014 ....G 6
Camden, 3,427 ....K 4
Campbelltown, 22,801 ....L 3
Casino, 8,502 ....J 5
Cessnock, 15,331 ....J 6
Cessnock, *34,515 ....J 6
Cobar, 2,348 ....H 6
Coffs Harbour, 7,667 ....J 6
Condobolin, 3,571 ....H 6
Cooma, 9,103 ....H 7
Coonamble, 3,396 ....H 6
Cootamundra, 6,219 ....H 6
Cowra, 7,076 ....H 6
Deniliquin, 6,239 ....H 7
Dubbo, 15,561 ....H 6
Forbes, 7,369 ....H 6
Glen Innes, 5,737 ....J 7
Goulburn, 20,871 ....J 7
Grafton, 15,951 ....J 5
Griffith, 9,537 ....H 6
Gunnedah, 7,507 ....H 6
Hay, 2,952 ....H 6
Hurstville, 64,851 ....L 3
Inverell, 8,413 ....J 5
Junee, 3,904 ....J 6
Kempsey, 8,181 ....J 6
Kiama, 3,814 ....J 6
Kogarah, 47,654 ....L 3
Lake Cargelligo, 1,128 ....H 6
Lismore, 19,734 ....J 5
Lithgow, 13,165 ....J 6
Liverpool, 60,597 ....L 3
Maitland, 23,112 ....J 6
Manly, 38,141 ....L 3
Moree, 8,031 ....H 5
Mudgee, 5,372 ....J 6

Murwillumbah, 7,311 ....J 5
Muswellbrook, 6,312 ....J 6
Narrabri, 5,953 ....H 6
Narrandera, 4,905 ....H 6
Narromine, 2,465 ....H 6
Newcastle, 233,936 ....J 6
Nowra, 9,633 ....J 6
Nyngan, 2,584 ....H 6
Orange, 22,196 ....H 6
Parkes, 8,438 ....H 6
Parramatta, 106,996 ....K 3
Penrith, 35,979 ....K 3
Port Macquarie, 7,063 ....J 6
Quirindi, 2,730 ....J 6
Randwick, 113,634 ....L 3
Rockdale, 81,463 ....L 3
Ryde, 81,291 ....L 3
Scone, 2,915 ....J 6
Singleton, 6,188 ....J 6
Strathfield, 26,704 ....L 3
Sutherland, 131,739 ....L 3
Sydney (capital), †2,446,345 ....L 3
Tamworth, 21,680 ....J 6
Taree, 10,560 ....J 6
Temora, 4,536 ....H 6
Tenterfield, 3,270 ....J 5
Wagga Wagga, 25,819 ....H 7
Waverley, 63,607 ....L 3
Wellington, 5,825 ....H 6
Willoughby, 54,576 ....L 3
Wollongong, *162,153 ....K 4
Yass, 4,098 ....H 6
Young, 5,754 ....H 6

OTHER FEATURES

Australian Alps (mts.) ....H 7
Botany (bay) ....L 3
Byron (cape) ....J 5
Darling (river) ....G 6

Great Dividing (range)...........J 6
Kosciusko (mt.) ....H 7
Lord Howe (isl.), 267 ....K 6
Murray (river) ....G 6
Murrumbidgee (river) ....H 6
Nepean (river) ....K 3

NORFOLK ISLANDS
Total Population, 1,147

CITIES and TOWNS

Cascade ....L 5
Kingston ....L 5

OTHER FEATURES

Anson (bay) ....L 5
Ball (bay) ....M 5
Pitt (mt.) ....L 5

NORTHERN TERRITORY
Total Population, 39,556

CITIES and TOWNS

Adelaide River, ‡300 ....E 2
Alice Springs, 6,037 ....E 4
Anthony Lagoon, ‡162 ....F 3
Charlotte Waters ....F 5
Daly Waters, ‡265 ....E 3
Darwin (capital), 18,042 ....E 2
Hatches Creek, ‡74 ....F 4
Hermannsburg Mission ....E 4
Katherine, 1,302 ....E 2
Kulgera, ‡229 ....E 5
Mataranka, ‡114 ....E 2
Melville Island ....E 2
Newcastle Waters ....E 3

*City and suburbs. †Population of metropolitan area. ‡Population of district.

Total & cap. (with suburbs)—1970 off. est.; states—1967 off. est.; other pops—1966 final census.

Pine Creek, ‡577 ... E 2
Tennant Creek, 1,001 ... E 3
Wave Hill, ‡289 ... E 3

OTHER FEATURES

Amadeus (lake) ... E 4
Arafura (sea) ... E 1
Arnhem Land (region) ... E 2
Ayers Rock (mt.) ... E 5
Barkly Tableland ... F 3
Bathurst (isl.) ... D 2
Carpentaria (gulf) ... F 2
Cobourg (pen.) ... E 2
Dundas (strait) ... E 2
Goulburn (isls.) ... E 2
Groote Eylandt (isl.) ... F 2
Limmen Bight (river) ... F 3
Macdonnell (ranges) ... E 4
Melville (isl.) ... E 2
Murchison (range) ... E 4
Roper (river) ... E 2
Simpson (desert) ... F 5
Sir Edward Pellew Group (isls.) ... F 3
Tanami (desert) ... E 3
Van Diemen (cape) ... D 2
Victoria (river) ... E 3
Wessel (cape) ... F 2
Woods (lake) ... E 3

QUEENSLAND

Total Population, 1,688,529

CITIES and TOWNS

Ayr, 8,674 ... H 3
Barcaldine, 1,779 ... G 4
Beenleigh, 2,026 ... L 2
Biloela, 3,537 ... J 4
Bowen, 5,144 ... H 3
Brisbane (capital), †718,822 ... K 2
Brisbane, *732,686 ... K 2
Bundaberg, 25,402 ... J 4
Cairns, 29,326 ... H 3
Charleville, 4,871 ... H 5
Charters Towers, 7,602 ... H 4
Chinchilla, 3,336 ... J 5
Cloncurry, 2,149 ... G 4
Collinsville, 1,887 ... H 4
Corinda, 12,643 ... K 2
Cunnamulla, 1,980 ... H 5
Dalby, 8,860 ... J 5
Emerald, 2,193 ... H 4
Gladstone, 12,426 ... J 4
Gold Coast, 49,354 ... J 5
Goondiwindi, 3,529 ... H 5
Gympie, 11,279 ... J 5
Home Hill, 3,507 ... H 3
Hughenden, 2,033 ... G 4
Ingham, 5,354 ... H 3
Innisfail, 7,432 ... H 3
Ipswich, 53,394 ... K 2
Kingaroy, 5,080 ... J 5
Longreach, 3,871 ... G 4
Mackay, 24,578 ... H 4
Mareeba, 4,799 ... H 3
Maryborough, 20,393 ... J 5
Moorooka, 16,801 ... K 2
Mossman, 1,614 ... G 3
Mount Isa, 16,877 ... F 4
Mount Morgan, 4,055 ... H 4
Proserpine, 2,951 ... H 4
Redcliffe, 27,011 ... K 1
Rockhampton, 45,376 ... J 4
Roma, 5,996 ... H 5
Sandgate, 22,621 ... K 2
Sarina, 2,422 ... H 4
Stanthorpe, 3,641 ... J 5
Thursday Island, 2,551 ... G 2
Toowoomba, 52,139 ... J 5
Townsville, 56,768 ... H 3
Tully, 2,860 ... H 3
Warwick, 10,065 ... J 5
Winton, 1,667 ... G 4
Wynnum, 23,191 ... K 2

OTHER FEATURES

Albatross (bay) ... G 2
Bentinck (isl.) ... F 3
Bowling Green (cape) ... H 3
Broad (sound) ... H 4
Bulloo (river) ... G 5
Cape York (pen.) ... G 2
Capricorn Group (isls.) ... J 4
Carpentaria (gulf) ... F 2
Coral (sea) ... H 2
Cumberland (isls.) ... H 4
Diamantina (river) ... G 4
Endeavour (strait) ... G 2
Fitzroy (river) ... J 4
Flattery (cape) ... H 2
Flinders (river) ... G 3
Fraser or Great Sandy (isl.) ... J 5
Georgina (river) ... F 4
Gilbert (river) ... G 3
Great Barrier (reef) ... H 3
Great Dividing (range) ... G 3
Great Sandy (Fraser) (isl.) ... J 5
Gregory (range) ... G 3
Grenville (cape) ... G 2
Hervey (bay) ... J 4
Hinchinbrook (isl.) ... H 3
Keerweer (cape) ... G 2
Leichhardt (river) ... G 3
Manifold (cape) ... J 4
Melville (cape) ... G 2
Mitchell (river) ... G 3
Moreton (bay) ... K 2
Moreton (isl.) ... L 1
Mornington (isl.) ... F 3
Norman (river) ... G 3
Pera (head) ... G 2
Prince of Wales (isl.) ... G 2
Sandy (cape) ... J 4
Simpson (desert) ... F 5
Sturt (desert) ... G 5
Thomson (river) ... G 4
Torres (strait) ... G 2
Wellesley (isls.) ... F 3
Whitsunday (isl.) ... H 4
York (cape) ... G 2

SOUTH AUSTRALIA

Total Population, 1,107,178

CITIES and TOWNS

Adelaide (capital), †727,916 ... D 7
Bordertown, 1,758 ... G 7
Ceduna, 1,406 ... E 6
Coober Pedy ... E 7
Elizabeth, 32,949 ... D 7
Gawler, 6,645 ... D 7
Gladstone, 1,035 ... F 6
Hindmarsh, 11,352 ... D 7
Jamestown, 1,282 ... F 6
Kadina, 3,022 ... F 6
Kensington and Norwood, 11,928 ... D 7
Kingscote, 1,071 ... F 7
Leigh Creek, 1,014 ... F 6
Loxton, 2,418 ... G 6
Maralinga and Woomera, 4,745 ... E 6
Marion, 66,950 ... D 8
Mitcham, 49,470 ... D 8
Moonta, 1,122 ... F 6
Mount Barker, 1,934 ... E 8
Mount Gambier, 17,251 ... F 7
Mount Pleasant, ‡1,433 ... E 7
Murray Bridge, 5,957 ... F 7
Naracoorte, 4,378 ... F 7
Peterborough, 3,117 ... F 6
Pinnaroo, ‡1,717 ... G 7
Port Adelaide, 39,823 ... D 7
Port Augusta, 101,103 ... F 6
Port Lincoln, 8,888 ... F 6
Port Pirie, 15,566 ... F 6
Quorn, 588 ... F 6
Renmark, 6,275 ... G 6
Reynella-Noarlunga, 11,818 ... D 8
Salisbury, 35,762 ... D 7
Strathalbyn, 1,449 ... E 8
Streaky Bay, ‡2,134 ... E 6
Unley, 39,721 ... D 8
Victor Harbor, 3,128 ... F 7
Waikerie, ‡3,818 ... G 6
Wallaroo, 2,094 ... F 6
West Torrens, 46,222 ... D 7
Whyalla, 22,121 ... F 6
Woodville, 73,878 ... D 7
Woomera and Maralinga, 4,745 ... F 6

OTHER FEATURES

Barcoo, The (Coopers) (creek) ... F 5
Coopers (creek) ... F 5
Encounter (bay) ... F 7
Everard (lake) ... E 6
Eyre (lake) ... F 5
Eyre (peninsula) ... F 6
Flinders (range) ... F 6
Frome (lake) ... G 6
Gairdner (lake) ... F 6
Gawler (range) ... F 6
Great Australian (bight) ... D 6
Harris (lake) ... E 6
Investigator (strait) ... F 7
Investigator Group (isls.) ... E 6
Kangaroo (isl.), 3,375 ... F 7
Lacepede (bay) ... F 7
Murray (river) ... G 6
Musgrave (range) ... E 5
Northumberland (cape) ... F 7
Nullarbor (plain) ... D 6
Nuyts (cape) ... E 6
Peera Peera Poolanna (lake) ... F 5
Saint Vincent (gulf) ... D 7
Simpson (desert) ... F 5
Spencer (gulf) ... F 6
Stuart (range) ... E 5
Sturt (desert) ... G 5
Torrens (lake) ... F 6
Yorke (peninsula) ... F 7

TASMANIA

Total Population, 376,212

CITIES and TOWNS

Burnie, 18,611 ... H 8
Deloraine, 5,205 ... H 8
Devonport, 16,757 ... H 8
Hobart (capital), 53,257 ... H 8
Hobart, †119,469 ... H 8
Launceston, 37,217 ... H 8
New Norfolk, 5,770 ... H 8
Queenstown, 4,393 ... G 8
Ulverstone, 6,842 ... H 8
Wynyard, 3,355 ... H 8
Zeehan, 1,017 ... G 8

OTHER FEATURES

Banks (strait) ... H 8
Eddystone (point) ... H 8
Flinders (isl.) ... H 7
Furneaux Group (isls.), 1,234 ... H 8
Hunter (isls.) ... G 8
King (isl.), 2,462 ... G 7
Legge (peak) ... H 8
Macquarie (harb.) ... G 8
South West (cape) ... H 8
Tasman (pen.) ... H 8

VICTORIA

Total Population, 3,271,993

CITIES and TOWNS

Ararat, 8,233 ... G 7
Bacchus Marsh, 3,707 ... L 6
Bairnsdale, 7,785 ... H 7
Ballarat, 41,026 ... G 7
Ballarat, *56,290 ... G 7
Bendigo, 30,159 ... G 7
Bendigo, *42,208 ... G 7
Brighton, 40,617 ... M 7
Camberwell, 99,908 ... M 7
Caulfield, 76,119 ... M 7
Chelsea, 24,789 ... M 7
Coburg, 68,568 ... M 6
Dandenong, 31,054 ... M 7
Echuca, 7,043 ... G 7
Essendon, 58,258 ... L 6
Footscray, 58,823 ... L 7
Frankston, 38,718 ... M 7
Geelong, 18,129 ... L 7
Geelong, *105,059 ... L 7
Hamilton, 10,054 ... G 7
Heidelberg, 63,929 ... M 6
Horsham, 10,562 ... G 7
Maryborough, 7,707 ... G 7
Melbourne (capital), ‡2,110,168 ... H 7
Mildura, 12,931 ... G 6
Mordialloc, 28,076 ... M 7
Mornington, 7,349 ... M 7
Port Fairy, 2,579 ... G 7
Port Melbourne, 12,591 ... L 7
Portland, 6,690 ... G 7
Preston, 89,767 ... M 6
Richmond, 32,530 ... M 7
Ringwood, 29,141 ... M 6
St. Kilda, 58,129 ... M 7
Sale, 8,640 ... H 7
Sandringham, 36,671 ... M 7
Stawell, 5,909 ... G 7
Swan Hill, 7,381 ... G 7
Wangaratta, 15,175 ... H 7
Warrnambool, 17,499 ... G 7
Werribee, 8,228 ... L 7
Williamstown, 30,499 ... L 7
Wonthaggi, 4,026 ... G 7
Yallourn, 4,250 ... H 7

OTHER FEATURES

Australian Alps (mts.) ... H 7
Bass (strait) ... H 7
Discovery (bay) ... G 7
Murray (river) ... G 6
Otway (cape) ... G 7
Port Phillip (bay) ... M 7
Snowy (river) ... H 7
Wilsons (promontory) ... H 7

WESTERN AUSTRALIA

Total Population, 863,744

CITIES and TOWNS

Albany, 11,419 ... B 6
Armadale, 3,463 ... B 2
Beverley, ‡1,773 ... B 2
Boulder, 5,234 ... C 6
Bridgetown, 1,569 ... B 6
Brookton, ‡1,341 ... B 2
Broome, 1,570 ... C 3
Bruce Rock, ‡2,142 ... B 6
Bunbury, 15,459 ... A 6
Busselton, 4,278 ... A 6
Carnarvon, 2,956 ... A 4
Collie, 7,628 ... B 6
Coolgardie, ‡162 ... C 6
Corrigin, ‡2,099 ... B 6
Derby, 1,424 ... C 3
Esperance, 2,677 ... C 6
Exmouth Gulf, ‡2,248 ... A 4
Fremantle, 25,284 ... B 2
Geraldton, 12,125 ... A 5
Gingin, ‡1,021 ... B 1
Goomalling, ‡1,567 ... B 1
Halls Creek, ‡1,728 ... D 3
Jarrahdale, ‡1,728 ... B 2
Kalgoorlie, 9,174 ... C 6
Kalgoorlie, *19,908 ... C 6
Katanning, 3,506 ... B 6
Kwinana, 1,272 ... B 2
Lake Grace, ‡1,986 ... B 6
Leonora, ‡623 ... C 5
Mandurah, 2,730 ... B 2
Marble Bar, ‡567 ... C 4
Meekatharra, ‡1,011 ... B 5
Merredin, 3,599 ... B 6
Midland, 9,335 ... B 2
Mingenew, ‡978 ... B 5
Moora, 1,185 ... B 6
Mount Magnet, ‡1,016 ... B 5
Mukinbudin, ‡869 ... B 6
Mullewa, ‡1,825 ... B 5
Nannup, ‡1,272 ... B 6
Narrogin, 4,861 ... B 6
Nedlands, 23,320 ... B 2
Norseman, 1,863 ... C 6
Northam, 7,400 ... B 2
Northampton, ‡2,021 ... A 5
Onslow ... B 4
Perth (capital), †499,969 ... B 2
Pingelly, ‡1,453 ... B 2
Port Hedland, 1,778 ... B 3
Rockingham, 3,767 ... B 2
Roebourne, ‡702 ... B 4
Subiaco, 16,621 ... B 2
Toodyay, ‡1,388 ... B 2
Wagin, 1,750 ... B 6
Waroona, 1,013 ... B 2
Williams, ‡1,193 ... B 2
Wittenoom Gorge ... B 4
Wyndham, 1,156 ... D 3
Yampi Sound ... C 3
York, 1,421 ... B 6

OTHER FEATURES

Admiralty (gulf) ... C 2
Ashburton (river) ... B 4
Barlee (lake) ... C 5
Barrow (isl.) ... A 4
Bougainville (cape) ... D 2
Bruce (mt.) ... B 4
Buccaneer (arch.) ... C 3
Carey (lake) ... C 5
Carnegie (lake) ... C 5
Cowan (lake) ... C 6
Cuvier (cape) ... A 4
Dale (mt.) ... B 2
Dampier (arch.) ... B 4
Dampier Land (region) ... C 3
Darling (range) ... B 6
D'Entrecasteaux (point) ... B 7
Dirk Hartogs (isl.) ... A 5
Disappointment (lake) ... C 4
Drysdale (river) ... D 2
Exmouth (gulf) ... A 4
Farquhar (cape) ... A 4
Fitzroy (river) ... C 3
Flinders (bay) ... A 6
Fortescue (river) ... B 4
Garden (isl.) ... B 2
Gascoyne (river) ... B 5
Geelvink (channel) ... A 5
Geographe (bay) ... A 6
Geographe (channel) ... A 4
Gibson (desert) ... C 4
Great Australian (bight) ... D 6
Great Sandy (desert) ... C 4
Great Victoria (desert) ... D 5
Hale (mt.) ... B 5
Hamersley (range) ... B 4
Houtman Abrolhos (isls.) ... A 5
Joseph Bonaparte (gulf) ... D 2
Kimberley (plateau) ... D 3
King (sound) ... C 3
King Leopold (range) ... D 3
Koolan (isl.) ... C 3
Lacepede (isls.) ... C 3
Latouche Treville (cape) ... C 3
Leeuwin (cape) ... A 6
Lévêque (cape) ... C 3
Londonderry (cape) ... D 2
Lyons (river) ... B 4
Macdonald (lake) ... D 4
Mackay (lake) ... D 4
Montague (sound) ... C 2
Monte Bello (isls.) ... A 4
Murchison (river) ... B 5
Naturaliste (cape) ... A 6
Naturaliste (channel) ... A 5
North West (cape) ... A 4
Nullarbor (plain) ... D 6
Ord (river) ... D 3
Recherche (arch.) ... C 6
Rottnest (isl.) ... A 2
Saint George (ranges) ... D 3
Shark (bay) ... A 5
Talbot (cape) ... D 2
Timor (sea) ... D 2
York (sound) ... C 2

THE EASTERN SLOPE OF MOUNT KOSCIUSKO is the site of Guthega Dam, which was the first project of the Snowy Mountains hydroelectric complex.

continent is a shield area of Precambrian igneous and metamorphic bedrock perhaps three or four billion years old. East of the shield the land was built up within the last 500 million years—the eastern coastal region and Tasmania largely during Paleozoic times, and the great east-central depression largely during Mesozoic times.

To the west of a line joining Cloncurry and Mount Isa in western Queensland with Broken Hill in western New South Wales, widespread Precambrian rocks constitute the Australian Shield. Smaller Precambrian areas occur in the Cape York Peninsula and Tasmania. The oldest rocks recognized (about 3,000 million years old) are submarine pillow lavas and tuffs that constitute the older greenstones of Kalgoorlie and the Warrawoona series of the Pilbara Goldfield. Similar greenstones occur around Mount Isa. The Yilgarn series which overlies the greenstones in the southern and central goldfields of Western

Australia is also Archean. It comprises mainly metasediments, in places including cyanite, sillimanite (fibrolite), staurolite, and sericite schists. Also regarded as Archean are granitic gneisses and granites in many parts of South Australia, south Western Australia, and the Eastern Territory. The oldest rocks in the important Broken Hill lead-zinc mining field are those of the Willyama series, which consist of sillimanite and garnet gneisses, representing a transformed sedimentary succession of Archean age.

The Archean rocks are overlaid unconformably by the Mosquito Creek series in the Pilbara Goldfield, and possible equivalents of this series are recognized in other parts of the Australian Shield as Lower Proterozoic in age (about 1,250 million years). These rocks have been mapped in the Pine Creek geosyncline south of Darwin, where they include *Collenia* reefs; in the Mount Isa belt; in the Yampi Sound area of Western Australia, where they include bedded hematitic iron ore deposits; and in Eyre Peninsula of South Australia, where the bedded hematitic iron ore deposits of the Middleback Range occur. Lower Proterozoic rocks are invaded by the younger granites, which also are responsible for the many ore deposits in the Pine Creek area, Mount Isa, and the Pilbara Goldfield.

Upper Proterozoic rocks are separated from all older Precambrian rocks by a violent angular unconformity, but in several places they are seen to pass conformably up into fossiliferous Lower Cambrian. In the Pound quartzite of South Australia the remains of primitive jellyfish and arthropods occur 300 feet (91 meters) beneath the lowest Cambrian zones. The Upper Proterozoic rocks include a variety of sediments and, in Western Australia, volcanic rocks. The sediments are both transgressive over the Australian Shield and geosynclinal in facies, the Adelaidean geosyncline containing a development of Upper Proterozoic followed by Cambrian and possibly Ordovician rocks. Tillites (Sturtian tillites in South Australia; Torrowangee tillites at Broken Hill) indicate continental glaciation. Cambrian seas were widespread. In

AYERS ROCK (*left*), over 1½ miles long, rises 1,100 feet above the plains of the Great Plateau. Sandhills (*right*) mark a desert area of Western Australia.

"THE NUT" (left) is a volcanic rock rising above the town of Stanley on the northwest coast of Tasmania. Tasman Peninsula (below), on the rugged coast of Tasmania, is the southernmost point of the continent.

the Barkly Tableland of Northern Territory and nearby areas the rocks are chiefly transgressive and still remain virtually undisturbed, and in the Adelaidean geosyncline they are strongly folded. Lower Cambrian Archaeocyathus limestones are prominent in South Australia. In the far north of Western Australia, Lower Cambrian basalts are widespread in the Antrim Plateau, and in Victoria thick submarine basic lavas of the same age pass up into submarine tuffs and cherts, with local lenses of limestone. Well-preserved trilobite faunas are known from South Australia, Northern Territory, and Victoria.

Ordovician rocks occur in all major geosynclinal zones of Australia. In Western Australia graptolitic calcareous shales are known from Price's Dome in the Fitzroy Valley (Westralian geosyncline), and in central Australia the Larapintine series of the Amadeus trough contains rocks of the shelly facies which are also represented as transgressive formations in the Australian Shield. Victoria has some 16,000 to 18,-000 feet (4,877–5,486 meters) of entirely graptolitic facies with a complete succession of fossil zones from Tremadocian to Upper Ordovician in strongly folded graywackes and slates. In New South Wales both shelly and graptolitic rocks occur, and there are also interbedded volcanics, which are absent elsewhere. In Tasmania the Ordovician Gordon River limestone covers almost the whole area with rocks of the shelly facies. Possibly Ordovician schists occur also in the eastern coastal belt of Queensland and northern New South Wales. These Ordovician sediments in eastern Australia mark the first clear evidence of the Tasman geosynclinal zone, which was a feature of Australian geology until the epi-Permian foldings destroyed it.

Silurian rocks in Australia are entirely marine, being found in the Westralian geosyncline north of Perth and in the Tasman geosyncline in the east from Chillagoe in northern Queensland to Tasmania. The rocks include graptolitic and shelly facies, with acid volcanics in New South Wales, where reef limestones are also well displayed at Jenolan Caves. *Baragwanathia*, the oldest known vascular land plant, occurs in the Upper Silurian of Victoria, where it was washed into marine rocks.

The distribution of Devonian rocks is similar to that of Silurian, except that transgressive sandstones occur in the Fitzroy Valley and in western New South Wales and Victoria. Fossil fish, including the primitive dipnoan *Dipnorhynchus*, are numerous in the marine Middle Devonian, and freshwater fish are found in the Upper Devonian.

Carboniferous rocks likewise are found chiefly in the major geosynclinal belts, on the east and west of the continent, with the Silurian and Devonian. At the top of the Carboniferous in New South Wales occur the first important tillites of the Permocarboniferous glaciation, during which the whole continent suffered severe climatic conditions. The Permian period also saw fluctuating glaciation with interglacial periods. Well-preserved labyrinthodont amphibia occur in the black coal measures of New South Wales. The plant fossil assemblages are typical of the *Glossopteris* flora, with Gondwana affinities. Deposits of Permian black coal also occur at Collie in Western Australia. The marine Permian faunas of Western Australia show affinities with Timor, notably in the presence of the aberrant crinoid *Calceolispongia*, while those of eastern Australia have Pacific affinities.

At the close of the Permian and in the Triassic periods strong orogeny in eastern Queensland and New England in New South Wales was accompanied by the formation of important ore deposits. Elsewhere, beyond the line of serpentine intrusions marking the edge of the fold belt, Permian and Triassic rocks are conformable or nearly so. The orogeny destroyed the marine Tasman geosyncline, and the Triassic and Jurassic in eastern Australia are entirely lacustrine. Large lakes extended beneath the broad sag of the Great Artesian Basin, and these persisted into the Cretaceous period. The climates of the Mesozoic era were warm and moist, and small coal basins, as at Ipswich in Queensland, Wonthaggi in Victoria, and Leigh Creek in South Australia, were numerous. In the vicinity of Sydney and in the Blue Mountains thick Triassic sandstones form characteristic stony tablelands transected by steep-walled river gorges. During the Cretaceous period shallow seas transgressed great areas of western Queensland and the Eucla Basin at the head of the Great Australian Bight. Blue and gray clays rich in fossils form the impervious cover of the water-bearing beds of the Great Artesian Basin. In Tasmania great dol-

AUSTRALIAN NATIONAL TRAVEL ASSOCIATION

AUSTRALIAN NATIONAL TRAVEL ASSOCIATION

DE WYS, INC.

LAKE AMADEUS (*above, left*), one of the salt-encrusted lakes found in central Australia, is rarely filled with water. Sawtooth cliffs (*above, right*) extend into the waters of the Great Australian Bight. Pleasant, sandy beaches, such as this one in Victoria (*left*), are characteristic of much of the coastline of the country.

eritic sills as thick as 1,500 feet (457 meters) were intruded, probably in Jurassic times.

Marine Tertiary rocks are restricted to transgressions into the Murravian Basin, parts of southern Victoria and Tasmania, the Eucla Basin, and the Westralian geosyncline, especially around Exmouth Gulf. Nowhere is a thickness greater than a few thousand feet known. Uneconomic petroleum occurs at Lakes Entrance in Victoria, but of great economic importance are the immeasurable Victorian brown coal deposits of the Latrobe Valley, which are of Eocene and Oligocene age. The alluvial gold deposits and deep leads of Victoria and New South Wales formerly afforded rich yields, but most of the gold has been worked out. A volcanic belt with lavas ranging from basalt to rhyolite existed throughout much of the Tertiary in eastern Australia, but all the volcanoes are now extinct.

During the Pleistocene period, Australia experienced first a wetter and then a more arid climate than prevails today. Especially during the wetter period giant marsupials, including *Diprotodon,* kangaroos up to 10 feet (3 meters) high, and marsupial "lions" and "tigers" were numerous. During the arid period most of the parallel sand ridges of the semidesert area were built up, and many large marsupials became extinct as the freshwater lakes dried or became saline. Because of eustatic falls of sea level, Tasmania was at times joined with Australia during the Pleistocene period. A notable feature of many stretches of coast is afforded by dune complexes, including calcareous dunes and beach deposits carrying ilmenite, rutile, zircon, and other valuable minerals.

EDWIN S. HILLS, *University of Melbourne*

Climate. In general the climate of Australia is warm and dry with mild winters and warm to hot summers. Seasons are the reverse of those in the Northern Hemisphere. The major climatic zones are arranged fairly simply, chiefly because of the scarcity of large marine gulfs, the predominant east-west extent, and the lack of high mountains and plateaus.

Some 38.6 percent of the continent lies within the tropical zone, and the north has a tropical though somewhat uncertain monsoonal climate, with a wet season extending generally from January to April. The rains of the summer monsoon diminish in amount from north to south. Small areas of the far north—the Kimberley Plateau, Arnhem Land and the Darwin area, and Cape York Peninsula—receive from 40 to 60 inches (102–152 cm) of rain annually, but much of it falls on infertile soil in uninhabited country. In the interior the rain is more unreliable and much less abundant, and the temperature increases so that a large area on either side of the Tropic of Capricorn has a January mean temperature of over 85° F (29°C). The coastal belt north of the tropic has a high rainfall, which attains more than 100 inches (254 cm) in the vicinity of Cairns in northern Queensland, where the southeast trade winds and the summer monsoonal influences combine.

South of Capricorn the climate is influenced chiefly by the great pressure belts of the Southern Hemisphere—first, the high-pressure belt near the tropic; then the low-pressure belt of variables, which influences particularly the southern states; and finally, the roaring forties, which consistently affect Tasmania. The low-pressure variables extend as far north as the Darling Downs in southern Queensland, and because of the combined influences of tropical air masses, trade winds, and variables, New South Wales enjoys a rainfall that varies little throughout the year. As the pressure belts move north and south with the sun's annual march across the tropical zone, the zones affected by them change correspondingly. In winter the variables bring rain to the southwest corner of the continent, to southern South Australia, and to Victoria and New South Wales, whereas in summer the high-pressure belt swings south, and these parts experience summer drought. Swanland, at the southwest corner of Western Australia, has a typical

Mediterranean climate, but Victoria is influenced also by the southeast trades, by tropical lows and, especially in the east, by altitude. The west coast of Tasmania has more than 60 inches (152 cm) of rain, but the east is drier, and a small area receives less than 10 inches (25 cm).

A strongly marked weather cycle of about a week's duration is one of the notable features of southern Australia. A succession of high- and low-pressure areas moves across the continent from west to east, with consequent sharp changes in wind direction, temperature, and precipitation. Hot northerly winds may raise temperatures to over 100° F (38° C) in Melbourne and Adelaide, but the southerly air moving in as a cold front causes sudden squalls, rainstorms, and temperature drops of 30° or more.

Two factors materially affect the usefulness of rainfall in Australia. The first is variability, which is very great except in the coastal belt. The second is distribution, both throughout the year and daily or hourly during storms. Like the variability, the incidence of rainfall in many areas is unfavorable. In addition, evaporation is extremely high in the areas of lower precipitation, so that the number of months during which plants experience growth conditions drops to zero in the central third of the continent where annual rainfall is less than 10 inches (25 cm). Three fifths of the continent has a growing season of less than five months. Nevertheless, the actual area of Australia with favorable climatic conditions is still large, the dryness of the continent is conducive to healthy existence, and there are extensive regions in the southwest and southeast that enjoy perhaps the most favorable and pleasant climate of any part of the globe.

Plant Life. Australian flora not only is extremely rich but also exhibits a number of peculiarities associated with the high degree of endemism resulting from geographic isolation. It can be classified into three elements—the Australian, the Indo-Malayan, and the Antarctic.

Usually it is assumed that the angiosperms evolved in the Northern Hemisphere, and that speciation and migration were rapid. Groups of plants migrated into Australia to supplant the then dominant gymnospermic flora, which has persisted as a conspicuous element only in certain restricted areas. Having established themselves on the continent, the angiosperms underwent rapid speciation to produce a large number of endemic genera, of which *Eucalyptus*, with its 600 recorded species, is the most noteworthy. Later the Indo-Malayan element, whose component species are related to those of southeast Asia, entered Australia to occupy the more fertile soils of the northern and eastern sections. Speciation among this group of plants likewise occurred within the continent, so that most of the species are endemic. Mainly mesophytic plants, they constitute the rain forests of the warmer and wetter areas. The Antarctic element, typified by the beech (*Nothofagus*), has affinities with the South American flora. The means of entry of this element is purely conjectural. The species, which are endemic, are confined to the colder parts of Australia and Tasmania.

The common species which characterize the Australian element of the flora belong to four families—Myrtaceae, Proteaceae, Leguminosae, and Rutaceae—none of which is endemic. There are indeed only five endemic families, none of which is widely distributed. Other large families well represented in Australia are the Compositae, Gramineae, Orchidaceae, and Cyperaceae. Endemic genera, on the other hand, are abundant, aggregating some 500. Of these, *Eucalyptus* and *Darwinia* (Myrtaceae); *Banksia, Hakea,* and *Petrophila* (Proteaceae); *Pultenaea, Dillwynia,* and *Jacksonia* (Leguminosae); and *Boronia* (Rutaceae) are of particular interest.

Although the Australian continent is relatively dry, it is well vegetated, and many perennial species capable of surviving under desert conditions have evolved there. Even in the driest

NATIVE EUCALYPTI, in the forest country of the Australian Alps (*left*), provide an excellent supply of valuable hardwood timber.

THE RAIN FORESTS of Queensland are being preserved in the many large national parks (*right*) in the eastern part of the province.

THE MALE LYREBIRD (*left*) has a tail spread of over five feet. The kookaburra (*center*) is known also as the laughing jackass because of its loud cry. The emu (*right*), standing five feet tall, is a flightless bird. It appears with the kangaroo on the Australian coat of arms.

THE ECHIDNA is a monotreme, or egg-laying mammal. This anteater is protected by its sharp quills.

BIRDS

AND MAMMALS

OF

AUSTRALIA

THE PLATYPUS, an aquatic animal found only in Australia, is the world's only other known monotreme.

localities, where rainfall averages only five inches (13 cm) a year, perennial swards of saltbush (*Atriplex*) occur on the heavier soil types, while the sandy soils in such areas support scrubs of the mulga (*Acacia aneura*). A few dune areas are devoid of vegetation, while others are clothed with hummocks of the curious porcupine grass (*Triodia irritans*).

Areas which receive an average of 12 inches (30 cm) or more of rain each year are covered mostly with communities dominated by species of *Eucalyptus* or, in a few cases, by scrubs of *Acacia*. In the driest of these areas the eucalypts are dwarfed and assume a mallee form characterized by the presence of a large, woody, underground lignotuber producing many small stems usually less than 12 feet (4 meters) in height. With higher rainfall the height of the communities increases. Woodlands in which the trees are so spaced as to form a parkland occupy the areas of intermediate rainfall, while forests with trees exceeding 300 feet (91 meters) in height, develop in the wettest areas (the east coast and southwestern Western Australia), where the annual rainfall is in excess of 30 to 40 inches (76–102 cm). As a rule, communities of different structural form are dominated by different species of *Eucalpytus*. Undershrubs and herbaceous plants occur below the trees. A general feature of all the species in these forests, woodlands, and mallees is the xeromorphic nature of the leaves; some of the plants possess phyllodes or cladodes.

A KOALA MOTHER AND HER BABY (*left*) eat the leaves of eucalypti. These animals are marsupials.

THE KANGAROO (*right*) is also a marsupial. The young live in the mother's pouch for several months.

Interspersed among the tall *Eucalyptus* forests of eastern Australia are small areas of rain forest which are structurally similar to but floristically different from other tropical and subtropical rain forests. Occupying the soils of higher fertility, they are characterized by the broad, soft-leaved Indo-Malayan element of the flora. Small areas of beech-dominated rain forest (Antarctic element) are to be found at higher elevations on the mainland and in Tasmania.

Apart from desert and semiarid grasslands, only small areas of natural treeless grassland occur; these are found in central and southwestern Queensland and northern New South Wales. The dominant genera are *Astrebla* and *Stipa*. Most of the grassland used for grazing has been induced by the clearing of timber (chiefly *Eucalyptus*), followed by the introduction of fodder plants, notably clovers.

Australian plants as a whole are of little value as food, but timber is produced in abundance by certain species. Many of the Indo-Malayan species yield valuable softwoods. Two conifers are cut extensively: the bunya (*Araucaria bidwillii*), which occurs in the rain forest of Queensland, and the cypress pine (*Callitris glauca*), which is found in association with *Eucalyptus* on the western slopes of the Eastern Highlands and on the nearer western plains. Eucalypts produce a variety of valuable timbers, including hardwoods for construction work and furniture. A few yield tannin, and several species are sources of honey. In addition, a large number of tree species produce good fodder, particularly in the drier areas.

NOEL BEADLE
University of New England, Australia

Animal Life. The Australian fauna is one of the most interesting in the world. The continent has long been separated from other land masses, and at the time of its severance was populated with the representative life of the period. This isolated fauna, lacking competition with the superior types which developed subsequently in other parts of the world, has remained fundamentally unchanged. The place of origin of the original fauna is unknown, but it probably has been isolated since the early Tertiary period or even since the late Mesozoic era.

Although the ancient origin of the fauna is best exemplified by the furred animals, it is by no means confined to them. The primitive shrimplike crustaceans *Phreatocopsis* and *Phreatoicus* are living fossils, and the inch-long bulldog ants (*Myrmecia*) exhibit many primitive insect features. The bivalve mollusk *Neotrigonia* is known in other parts of the world as a fossil shell, and the lungfish (*Neoceratodus*) and Port Jackson shark (*Heterodontus*) are among the last living remnants of their ancient type of fish.

Australia's fauna, however, is best known for its peculiar furred animals. The unique egg layers (*monotremes*) and many of the varied forms of pouched mammals (*marsupials*) are restricted to the Australian continent. The monotremes are true, warm-blooded, fur-covered mammals that nourish their young with mother's milk; yet their reproductive organs are so primitive that they lay leathery-shelled eggs—like the eggs of their reptilian ancestors—from which the young subsequently hatch. The platypus (*Ornithorhynchus anatinus*) is an aquatic animal with a flattened, naked muzzle similar to the bill of a

duck. It lays two eggs each year in a nest made at the end of a long burrow in a riverbank; the eggs are nearly spherical and about half an inch (1.3 cm) in diameter. The echidnas, which are found in New Guinea as well as in Australia, are the only other egg-laying mammals known; they usually lay one egg each year.

The numerous species of Australian marsupials are very diverse and occupy many different habitats. They have a number of anatomical peculiarities, of which the most salient is the female's pouch, situated in the abdominal region, which contains the teats of the mammary glands. The young, born in an imperfect condition, enter the pouch and remain there until they are fully developed. Small insectivorous-carnivorous marsupials, such as the marsupial "mice" (*Sminthopsis*) and "rats" (*Antechinus*), live under stones and logs. Slightly larger carnivorous forms, misleadingly called native cats (*Dasyurus*), make their homes in hollow logs; the Tasmanian devil (*Sarcophilus*) and Tasmanian wolf (*Thylacinus*) are as large as a terrier and an Alsatian dog, respectively. Truly arboreal forms embrace some 23 species of Australian opossums ranging in size from the tiny dormouse opossum (*Cercartetus* or *Cercaërtus*), a nectar- and insect-eating animal, to the gray opossum (*Trichosurus*), which is as large as a domestic cat and is herbivorous. Some opossums have developed a parachutelike body membrane which allows them to glide from one tree to another. Allied to the opossums is the well-known koala (*Phascolarctos*), a large-eared arboreal marsupial that feeds on eucalyptus leaves. Of the kangaroolike animals (Macropodidae), characterized by their hopping gait on elongated hind legs, there are over 50 species. The rat kangaroo (Potoroinae) may be smaller than rabbits, while the larger species (Macropus) can measure six feet (1.8 meters) when erect. These animals inhabit forests and open plains and are herbivorous. (See also *Marsupialia*.)

Although the flight of birds has allowed much intercontinental migration, there is a typical Austral-Pacific avifauna. Flightless birds possessing primitive features, are represented by the cassowary (*Casuarius*) and the emu (*Dromaius*). The former is confined to the rain forest of the northeast, while the latter is distributed throughout the continent. Parrots (Psittaciformes) are well represented, with more than 50 species, and the nectar-feeding honey eaters (Meliphagidae), number about 70 species. Perhaps the most widely known Australian bird is the lyrebird (*Menura*), a mimic of tremendous voice found in the damp fern gullies of the eastern coastal mountains. Such cosmopolitan groups as quail, birds of prey, waterfowl, waders, and perching birds also are well represented.

The reptilian fauna is typically Indo-Australian. Geckos (Gekkonidae), monitor lizards (Varanidae), dragons (Agamidae), and skinks (Scincidae) are widely distributed. There are no true adders (Viperidae), but many species of elapid snakes (Elapidae) with toxic venom are present. The largest of these, the taipan (*Oxyuranus*), reaches a length of 11 feet (3 meters), and species such as the tiger snake (*Notechis*), the copperhead (*Denisonia*), the brown snake (*Demansia*), and the so-called death adder (*Acanthophis*) are all lethal, although few exceed 5 feet (1.5 meters) in length. The python family (Boidae) is represented by

AUSTRALIAN NEWS AND INFORMATION BUREAU

TUMUT POND DAM is part of the Snowy Mountains Hydroelectric Scheme, which has increased Australia's irrigated area and electric output.

the Queensland python (*Liasis*), which attains a length of 21 feet (6 meters), and some 10 species of smaller rock pythons (*Liasis*), carpet snakes (*Morelia*), and rock snakes (*Aspidites*).

C.W. Brazenor
National Museum of Victoria

Natural Resources. Australia provides an example of the great practical importance of climate as compared with soil. Wherever the climate is suitable for agriculture, soil deficiencies can be corrected artificially.

Soils. Physically, the mountains have not been stripped of their surface soils, as has happened in some countries with longer settlement, and the most widespread physical defects of Australian soils are the presence in large areas of deep sands and of ironstone, either as gravel or as massive rock. Chemically, Australian soils range from rich to very poor, but the relative area of poor or very poor soils is greater than in most other parts of the world.

Lack of phosphorus is the most obvious shortcoming. This element is in low supply everywhere in the country except in a few districts along the east coast. The average content of phosphorus in Australian surface soil is approximately 200 parts per million, or about half as much as is considered normal. Large areas of soil are also naturally deficient in one or more of the trace elements, such as copper, zinc, and molybdenum, which though present in plants only in quantities of a few parts per million, are as essential for growth as are phosphorus and nitrogen.

Deficiencies can be cured by adding these minerals to the soil. Superphosphate, a compound containing 10 percent phosphorus, is commonly added to the soil in proportions amounting to 100 pounds or more per acre (121 kg per hectare). This fertilizer has played a great role in Australian agriculture, first in restoring wheat yields in the early years of the 20th century and later in establishing good pastures. If the native grasses, which are adapted to soil poverty, are to be replaced by the introduced, more productive grasses and clovers, it is necessary first to add superphosphate. Trace elements, where needed, are added in smaller quantities—perhaps a pound or two of copper or a few ounces of molybdenum per acre.

Australians have become used to the idea of turning poor country into good by adding fertilizers and by growing clovers, which are all im-

ported species. These practices have been financially beneficial in the stock-raising land with an annual rainfall of 20 inches (51 cm) or more, neighboring the south and east coasts.

G.W. Leeper
University of Melbourne

Water Resources. Australia is the driest of all continents. Areas with sufficient rainfall for normal cultivation are limited largely to the coastal highlands and to semitropical coastal regions in the north. The mean annual runoff for the whole of Australia is little more than 1 inch (2.5 cm), as compared with 9.75 inches (24.77 cm) for the land areas of the world. Agricultural and pastoral development is dependent on irrigation and utilization of ground water.

Irrigation. Early in the history of land settlement in Australia, it was realized that only with irrigation could intensive production be maintained away from the areas of relatively high rainfall around the eastern, southeastern, and southwestern coasts. A start was made in Victoria in 1886, when an Irrigation Act nationalized surface water resources and so prevented the establishment of privately owned riparian rights. Thereafter, many irrigation projects were initiated by local trusts. Finally, in 1905, Victoria set up what was then a new form of instrumentality—a corporate body known as the State Rivers and Water Supply Commission—to take over all irrigation works from the trusts and to develop the water resources of the whole state. Most of the other states followed Victoria's lead, and by the 1960's the irrigated area of Australia aggregated 2,000,-000 acres (800,000 hectares). Of the total, about 85 percent was watered by the Murray and its tributaries, the Murrumbidgee and Goulburn rivers. One half of the total irrigated area was within Victoria.

Control and distribution of Murray River waters among the states is administered by an interstate body, the River Murray Commission, which is not a constructing authority, but which arranges for its works to be designed, built, and operated by state instrumentalities. Two large storage areas have been provided: 1,385 miles (2,229 km) from the mouth of the Murray and 950 miles (1,529 km) downstream. In addition, there are 14 regulating weirs along the river and barrages close to its mouth to exclude seawater.

The chief irrigated crop in Australia is pasture for dairy, meat, and wool production. Lucerne (alfalfa) is grown to some extent, but it is being replaced increasingly by mixed pastures of clovers and grasses. The clovers are of two types—perennial and annual. The perennial clovers are grown with mixtures of perennial grasses and are used mostly for the grazing of cattle, mainly dairy cattle. On highly developed farms these pastures carry up to one milking cow per acre throughout the year without supplementary feeding. Similar pastures are used for growing and fattening beef cattle. The annual pastures, which consist chiefly of subterranean clover and an indigenous annual rye grass called Wimmera rye, are used mostly for sustaining sheep; fine to medium crossbreeds, rather than Merinos, are grazed, with revenue coming mainly from the turnoff of fat lambs.

Other important irrigated crops in Australia are soft fruits for canning in the Goulburn and Murrumbidgee valleys; dried vine fruits and wine grapes along the lower Murray in New South Wales, Victoria, and South Australia; rice in New South Wales; sugarcane and tobacco in Queensland; and cotton and safflower in northern New South Wales and Western Australia.

L.R. EAST, *State Rivers and Waters Supply Commission, Victoria*

Underground Water. The utilization of subsurface water supplies has been of great importance to Australia's pastoral development, and large areas of the principal sheep and cattle raising country depend on artesian supplies to provide drinking water for livestock. Since artesian water was discovered in 1879, many thousands of bores have been put down, and the daily free discharge exceeds 350 million gallons (1,325 million liters). The artesian water is drawn from depths down to 4,000 feet (1,219 meters) or more. Subartesian bores, in which the water must be pumped to the surface, number more than 200,000.

Artesian basins underlie approximately one third of the total land area. The Great Artesian Basin, which occupies well over 600,000 square miles (1,554,000 sq km) extending from the Gulf of Carpentaria southward throughout Queensland into New South Wales and South Australia, is the world's largest artesian waterbearing area. Other major basins are the Murray River basin, to the south, and the Eucla basin, on the Great Australian Bight, both subartesian; the Coastal Plain Basin of Western Australia; the Northwest Basin; the Desert Basin of Western Australia; and the Barkly Basin, in Northern Territory and Queensland.

The artesian water is generally of the alkaline carbonate type, but its mineral content varies. In general, it is suitable for livestock, though not for irrigation. The temperature range is considerable, and in some bores the water reaches the surface at over 200° F (94° C). Subartesian water usually has a lower mineral content, and in some areas it is suitable for all purposes, including irrigation.

R.M. YOUNGER
Author of "The Changing World: Australia"

Minerals. Mineralization is widespread in the Precambrian and Paleozoic rocks, which outcrop or come close to the surface over much of the Australian continent but are masked in many places by desert sands or surface debris. These ancient rocks were subjected to prolonged and deep weathering in the Tertiary period. As a result, many deposits disintegrated and, except for gold and tin, which were reconcentrated in numerous placer deposits, the mineral content was dispersed. The prolonged weathering gave rise to deposits of bauxite and laterite. The areas of Precambrian mineralization occupy the western two thirds of the continent, the eastern margin of the Precambrian shield being hidden by Mesozoic sediments of the Great Artesian Basin. In Western Australia gold was long the chief economic mineral; the discovery of immense deposits of iron ore and bauxite changed that position in the 1960's. In addition there are significant deposits of manganese and chromite, and minor deposits of copper, tin, lead, tantalum, and various pegmatite minerals.

The eastern edge of the shield is marked by a zone of copper deposits in South Australia (Wallaroo-Moonta, Kapunda, Burra) and western Queensland (Mount Isa, Cloncurry district) and by the major lead-zinc-silver lodes of Broken Hill, New South Wales, and Mount Isa. Scattered deposits of uranium, gold, copper, tin, lead, and tungsten ores occur throughout Northern Territory and extend into western Queensland.

Paleozoic mineralization forms a belt about 200 miles (322 km) wide, extending down the entire eastern edge of Australia into Tasmania. Western Tasmania contains the lead-zinc deposits of Rosebery and Zeehan, the copper ores of Mount Lyell, and the tin ores of Mount Bischoff, Renison Bell, Heemskirk, and Moina. Iron ores (magnetite) occur near Zeehan and the Savage River, and nickel, osmiridium (iridosmine), and asbestos are associated with the ultrabasic rocks of the region. In northeastern Tasmania there are gold-quartz veins, alluvial tin deposits, and the tin-tungsten veins of Aberfoyle and Storey's Creek, while on King Island there is a major scheelite deposit.

Central Victoria contains an intense gold-quartz mineralization (the saddle reefs of Bendigo and the indicator veins of Ballarat), together with rich placer deposits, which led to the spectacular gold rushes of the 1850's. Gold-quartz veins are associated with a swarm of basic dikes in the Walhalla-Woods Point belt of eastern Victoria, and at a number of places there are gold-antimony veins and isolated tin and molybdenite deposits extending into New South Wales.

Southern New South Wales has numerous small deposits of gold, copper, tin, bismuth, and molybdenum, and there is a significant lead-zinc deposit at Captain's Flat. Strong gold mineralization occurs in the Mudgee and Cobar districts, and at Cobar is associated with copper and lead-zinc ores. In the New England section of northeastern New South Wales, rich alluvial tin deposits, now largely exhausted, extended into the Stanthorpe district of Queensland. The source granites also contained numerous pipes of tin, molybdenum, and bismuth ores, together with small manganese and antimony deposits.

Gold and copper ores predominated in southern Queensland, at Mount Morgan, Cracow, Charters Towers, and Gympie, with a little chromite at Marlborough and mercury at Kilkivan. In the north, tin predominates at Herberton, Mount Garnet, and Cooktown, with molybdenite and tungsten at Wolfram Camp and Mount Carbine. Gold ores predominate at Croydon and the Palmer River.

Coal. Australia coals range from anthracites to brown coal (lignite), and the reserves, though not comparable with those of North America, Europe, or Asia, are ample. Since the principal coalfields lie close to the major cities and to the seaboard, interstate shipments are facilitated.

The main coal measures of New South Wales, which are of Permian age, form an elongated basin truncated by the coastline. The basin occupies an area of 16,500 square miles (42,735 sq km) and extends 200 miles (322 km) along the coast. The deepest part is near Sydney, where the top coal seam was worked at a depth of 2,884 feet (879 meters). The seams rise to north, south, and west, to outcrop at Newcastle, Bulli, and Lithgow. Excellent gas and steam coals occur near Maitland, while good coking coals are available near the steel centers of Newcastle and Port Kembla. Excellent coking coals are also available in the Permian coalfields of Bowen, Queensland, where the coal measures extend for 400 square miles (1,036 sq km); and good gas and steam coals occur near Ipswich. Subbituminous Permian coals at Collie provide southwest Western Australia with electricity, but coal for gas is imported from New South Wales. South Australia mines subbituminous Triassic coal at Leigh Creek, 380 miles (612 km) north of Adelaide. In Victoria, Tertiary brown coals in seams 200 to 500 feet (61–152 meters) thick, with an overburden of 30 to 50 feet (9–15 meters), are open cut mechanically to provide electricity, briquettes, and town gas (Lurgi process). Surplus gas yields about 60 million gallons (227 million liters) of liquid fuels annually. The briquettes can be made into good metallurgical coke. Thinner seams of brown coal occur in South Australia at Moorlands and Inkerman.

Petroleum. Petroleum was first discovered in isolated wells in the 1950's, but it was 1962 before the first commercial oilfield was discovered, at Moonie, in southern Queensland. Production began two years later. Soon afterward oilfields of commercial proportions were discovered at Alton, south of Moonie, and at Barrow Island, Western Australia.

Large deposits of natural gas have been revealed since 1962 in the Roma and Gilmore areas, in Queensland; in the Gilpealpa area, South Australia; and in the Amadeus basin, Northern Territory. Gas has also been discovered in Western Australia, at Gin Gin (north of Perth) and on Barrow Island. In 1966 an important oil and gas deposit was revealed in Bass Strait, close to the Victoria coast; its proximity to the industrially developed areas gave it special significance.

From the mid-1960's the search for oil was being undertaken on a greater scale than previously. Studies of sedimentary petrology, palynology, paleontology, and photogeology were being pursued by government experts and representatives of commercial oil-search interests, and over 200 wells a year were being drilled.

Iron. Australia's iron-ore resources are commensurate with its coal resources. Production is from two major deposits—the Middleback Range deposits in South Australia; and the Yampi Sound deposits, 200 miles (322 km) northeast of Broome, in Western Australia. In the Middleback Range, hematite bodies, totaling about 150 million tons (136 million metric tons) with a 65 percent iron content, occur in structural traps associated with vast tonnages of sedimentary Precambrian taconites, which are amenable to concentration. At Yampi Sound, bedded hematite deposits, totaling 100 million tons (90.7 million metric tons) with a 65 percent iron content, are associated with large tonnage of generally similar taconite. Similar types of hematite (magnetite below the water table) occur at Wilgi Mia and Koolyanobbing in Western Australia, and additional deposits have been discovered north of Koolyanobbing. In the Pilbara district (Hamersley Range area) of Western Australia, immense deposits of high- and medium-grade iron ore of similar type have been discovered over an area of 30,000 square miles (77,200 sq km). By 1966 surveys had established reserves of more than 50 percent iron in 15,000 million tons (13,600 million metric tons), and export of ore had begun.

Many small contact metamorphic deposits of magnetite are known in the Paleozoic rocks of eastern Australia and Tasmania, and a significant deposit of magnetite has been found in the Savage River area of Tasmania. Extensive sedimentary oölitic hematite-siderite formations have been explored in northwest Queensland and the Northern Territory.

Ferroalloy Ores. Tungsten is in plentiful supply in Australia. The main deposits are in Tasmania. There, at the King Island open-cut scheelite mine, a contact metamorphic deposit with reserves of 2,875,000 tons (2,608,142 metric tons) at 0.48 percent tungsten trioxide is worked, and at Aberfoyle and Storey's Creek are large tungsten-cassiterite veins. Other deposits are found in Northern Territory and in eastern Australia. Molybdenum, once abundant, is in short supply; small, pipelike deposits occur in granites in eastern Queensland, New South Wales, and Victoria. Massive deposits of medium-grade manganese ore at Groote Eylandt, in the Gulf of Carpentaria, are the basis of greatly expanded production of ferroalloys in Tasmania. Manganese also occurs, as small rhodonitic deposits, in New South Wales, and, as surface ores, in Western Australia, at Horseshow and Peak Hill and near Pilbara.

Small chromite deposits occur in serpentines near Rockhampton, Queensland, and there is a major deposit at Coobina, 700 miles (1,126.5 km) northeast of Perth, in Western Australia. In Queensland, cobalt ore occurs in the Cloncurry and Chillagoe districts as a minor constituent of various copper and lead-zinc ores. Small bodies of good nickel ore occur near Zeehan, Tasmania, and a weak nickel mineralization in Sudburylike rocks exists in South Australia.

Gold. By the mid-1960's, Australia had produced more than 170 million fine ounces (5,287,-510 kg) of gold, of which approximately 40 percent came from Victoria, 15 percent from Queensland, 10 percent from New South Wales, and the remainder chiefly from Western Australia. Close to 900,000 fine ounces (27,993 kg) was being produced annually, largely from lode deposits in Western Australia (Kalgoorlie and Norseman), Northern Territory (Tennant Creek), Queensland (Mount Morgan), and Victoria (Chewton, Woods Point).

Base Metals. Supplies of copper are ample; major ore bodies occur at Mount Isa and Mount Morgan, in Queensland; Mount Lyell, Tasmania; Peko, Northern Territory; and Ravensthorpe, Western Australia. Copper mineralization is widespread in northern Queensland and central South Australia.

Australia has about one fourth of the world's reserves of lead, zinc, silver, and cadmium. The Broken Hill lode, which has yielded 70 million tons (63.5 million metric tons), contains another 60 million tons (54.4 million metric tons) of ore averaging 15 percent lead, 12 percent zinc, and 5 ounces (142 grams) of silver per ton. The Mount Isa lodes have proved reserves of 14 million tons (12.7 million metric tons) of 8 percent lead, 8 percent zinc, and 6 ounces (170 grams) of silver per ton, together with much larger, incompletely tested reserves of lower-grade ore (about 6 percent lead). Smaller deposits are mined at Rosebery and Zeehan, Tasmania, and at Captain's Flat, New South Wales; and large deposits have been discovered at Rum Jungle and Borroloola, Northern Territory.

Remaining tin reserves appear to be limited. The rich placers of New England, Stanthorpe,

MOUNT MORGAN, a huge open-pit copper, gold, and pyrites mine near Rockhampton, in the state of Queensland, is one of the world's largest man-made excavations.

and northeastern Tasmania are largely exhausted, as are the famous lode deposits of Mount Bischoff in northwestern Tasmania. Rich veins of tin-tungsten ore occur at Aberfoyle and Storey's Creek in northeastern Tasmania, and there are a number of small cassiterite ores rich in sulfides at Renison Bell and elsewhere in western Tasmania. Rich tin ores also occur at Maranboy, Northern Territory. Placer deposits are mined at Greenbushes, Western Australia, and in northern Queensland.

Titanium and Zirconium. Australia produces nine tenths of the world's rutile and most of its zircon from beach sand deposits on the south coast of Queensland and the north coast of New South Wales, as well as some ilmenite and monazite. Valuable ilmenite sand deposits occur in southwest Western Australia.

Uranium. Pitchblende occurs at Rum Jungle and other localities in the Northern Territory and at Mary Kathleen, near Cloncurry, Queensland, while davidite ore outcrops at Radium Hill, South Australia. Hundreds of uranium occurrences of minor significance have been discovered, generally in Precambrian areas.

Aluminum. Bauxite deposits totaling hundreds of millions of tons occur on the west coast of Cape York peninsula; and there are other large deposits at Gove peninsula and Wessel Islands, Northern Territory, and in the Darling Range, east of Perth, Western Australia. These, together with lesser deposits in southern Queensland, New South Wales, Victoria, and Tasmania, give Australia reserves estimated at approximately 3,000 million tons (2,722 million metric tons).

Nonmetals. Among other substances mined in significant amounts in Australia are antimony, barite, beryl, bismuth, clays, crocidolite (blue asbestos), diamonds, diatomite, dolomite, emery, feldspar, fluorspar, glauconite, graphite, gypsum, limestone, magnesite, mica, mineral pigments, monazite, opal, osmiridium, perlite, pyrite, salt, sillimanite (fibrolite), spodumene, tantalite, and vermiculite. Exports of salt and gypsum have increased in recent years.

Fertilizers. No deposits of elemental sulfur or phosphate rock are known. Pyrite is mined at Norseman, Western Australia, and at Nairne, South Australia, for its sulfur content, and, together with pyritic concentrates from Mount Morgan, Mount Lyell, and Captain's Flat, and zinc concentrates from Broken Hill and Rosebery, is used as a source of sulfur for sulfuric acid, consumed largely in the production of superphosphate. Phosphate rock is imported from Nauru, Ocean, and Christmas islands. Potash is available in alunite deposits in Western Australia and New South Wales.

A.B. EDWARDS, *Commonwealth Scientific and Industrial Research Organization*

Bibliography

Andrews, John, *Australia's Resources and Their Utilization* (Sydney 1957).
Audas, James W., *The Australian Bushland* (Melbourne 1950).
Audas, James W., *Native Trees of Australia* (Melbourne 1954).
Australia, Department of National Development, *Atlas of Australian Resources: Physical Features, Geology, Temperature, Rainfall, Drainage Systems* (Canberra 1953 to date).
Australia, Department of National Development, *Atlas of Australian Resources: Rainfall, Conservation of Surface Water, Underground Waters, Mineral Deposits* (Canberra 1953 to date).
Australia, Department of National Development, *Atlas of Australian Resources: Vegetation Regions, Soils, Forest Resources* (Canberra 1953 to date).
Campbell, Lindsay, *Moonie and Oil Search: The Story of the Discovery of Oil in Australia* (Sydney 1964).
Chisholm, Alexander H., *Bird Wonders of Australia*, 4th ed. (Sydney 1956).
Commonwealth Scientific and Industrial Research Organization, *The Australian Environment*, 3d ed., rev. (Melbourne 1960).
Dakin, William J., *Australian Seashores* (Sydney 1960).
Dakin, William J., *The Great Barrier Reef*, rev. by Isobel Bennett (Sydney 1963).
David, Sir T.W., Edgeworth, *The Geology of the Commonwealth of Australia*, 3 vols., ed. by William R. Browne (London 1950).
Davidson, B.R., *The Northern Myth* (Melbourne 1965).
Frauca, Harry, *The Book of Australian Wildlife* (London 1965).
Gillett, Keith, and McNeill, Frank, *The Great Barrier Reef and Adjacent Isles* (Sydney 1959).
Harris, Thistle Y., *Wild Flowers of Australia*, 5th ed. (Sydney 1962).
Keast, Allen, and others, eds., *Biogeography and Ecology in Australia* (The Hague 1959).
Laseron, Charles F., *The Face of Australia*, 2d ed. (Sydney 1961).
McKeown, Keith C., *Insect Wonders of Australia*, 2d ed. (Sydney 1944).
Stephens, Charles G., *A Manual of Australian Soils*, 3d ed. (Melbourne 1962).
Taylor, Griffith, *Australia*, 7th ed. (London 1960).
Troughton, Ellis, *Furred Animals of Australia*, 6th ed. (Sydney 1957).
Tweedie, Alan D., and Robinson, Kenneth W., *The Regions of Australia* (Croydon, Victoria, 1963).
Wadham, Sir Samuel, and others, *Land Utilization in Australia*, 4th ed. (New York 1964).
Wills, Neville R., ed., *Australia's Power Resources* (Melbourne 1955).

SHEEP await sale in pens on the plateau of Tasmania. The raising of sheep is an important industry in Australia, the world's leading producer of apparel wool.

3. The Economy

Australia has a modern industrial economy with a rapidly expanding gross national product and national income. Living standards and per capita income are among the highest in the world. Labor is highly organized, and arbitration well developed. Although the nation is the world's foremost wool producer and a leading producer of wheat, meats, minerals, and other primary products, manufacturing represents the largest single source of productive wealth—contributing about one third of the gross national product and employing one third of the working force. Despite a strong international demand for Australian exports, the nation frequently has an unfavorable trade balance because of the rising import needs of its affluent society. Transportation and communication services are extensive, and the government plays a primary role in all public utilities.

Agriculture. Australian farming has progressed technically, and research has solved many of its problems. Periodic droughts are still the main depressant to improved production. While high labor costs have made mechanization essential, most farms are large enough to carry the necessary capitalization. Naturally, profitability depends on the available markets. For most products except wool, the home market is the most attractive, especially as effective internal marketing organizations have been developed for the majority of products. As in the case of other exporting countries, difficulties often appear where the ratio of export to home consumption is high, as is true of dried fruits, dairy products, and wheat.

Wool. Australia's main claim to international distinction in farming lies in the production of apparel wool, which developed as the staple industry of the wide plains that occupy large areas between the coastal ranges and the semideserts of the interior. There the natural ground vegetation and the browsing shrubs offer feed of fair quality, parasites are relatively few and the dingo is the only predator. In the early days, wherever water was available, the country was occupied by pastoralists intent on running Merino sheep for their wool, although cattle were kept where the country was too rough or the water points were too far apart for sheep. By 1860 this grazing industry had spread over the continent to the desert margins. Except where droughts brought disaster, stock numbers increased until 1891, but the worldwide depression of the 1890's, coupled with a series of dry years and the rapid increase in rabbits, reduced the sheep population. Between 1891

and 1902 the number of sheep declined from 106.4 million to 53.7 million.

With improved economic conditions, a second period of expansion then set in. Old runs were reoccupied, and a more intelligent outlook toward the grazing industry gradually developed, especially in areas with better rainfall. Pasture management was studied, and scientific research helped control parasitic worms, blowflies, and disease. Sheep numbers reached 125 million in 1942, but two years of bad drought reduced them to 96 million. Since then, greater knowledge of pastures, and especially of the importance of traces of copper, zinc, and molybdenum on certain soil types, has improved management, and myxomatosis has held the rabbit in check. The high price of wool also gave farmers money to make capital investment. By 1960, the sheep population exceeded 155 million. Meanwhile, production of wool increased from 983.6 million pounds (446,-153 metric tons) in the year 1938–1939 to an annual average of approximately 1,700 million pounds (771,107 metric tons), or about 30 percent of the total world production, in the 1960's.

Meat. The development of refrigeration made the export of meat practicable and opened the way to markets for surplus sheep, especially fat lambs, and for beef. The fat lamb industry required sheep with a better body configuration than that of the Merino, and such British breeds as Lincolns, Border Leicesters, Romneys, and Southdowns were used to provide suitable stock, either crossed with the Merino or on their own. In keeping with the idea of holding wool quality with superior frames, two new crossbred types, the Corriedale and the Polwarth, emerged. The cattle population also increased, especially in Queensland, but the high hopes for large beef exports disappeared before the vast supplies to world markets from Argentina in the early 1920's. Prices were so low that the industry made little progress until after World War II, when Argentinian supplies were disturbed and Britain entered into a long-term meat agreement with Australia. Overall production of meat rose from 2,165 million pounds (982,028 metric tons) in 1938–1939 to an annual average of more than 3,300 million pounds (1,497,000 metric tons) in the early 1960's. By this time new markets for meat had been developed in Japan and other countries of the western Pacific as well as in the United States.

The chief cattle areas are in the northern half of the continent, where rainfall is uncertain and limited to a few months and distances from ports

ABERDEEN ANGUS herd is watered on a cattle station, or ranch, in New South Wales, in one of Australia's richest, most settled pastoral regions.

of shipment are long. Elsewhere, the cattle industry is usually associated with sheep raising or dairying. The beasts are grass fed with occasional supplements of hay. Pigs are raised mainly for lard and they are nothing but a sideline to dairy farming.

Dairy Products. Dairying is practiced where the soil type and the rainfall or irrigation encourage prolific pasture growth over a large part of the year, southern Victoria and some of the river valleys of coastal New South Wales being the most favorable districts. Dairy farmers seldom grow crops; instead, they rely on conserved pasture hay or silage to feed their cows in off seasons. Milking is done by machine. The average dairy herd contains 40 to 50 cows, and the chief product is factory butter. Whole milk supplies are organized in each state on a contract basis by a milk board. Yield of milk varies with the season, but production averages close to 15,000 million gallons (56,780 million liters) a year. Butter production is about 450 million pounds (204,117 metric tons), and cheese, over 130 million pounds (58,967 metric tons) a year.

Crops. Australia's chief crops are winter cereals. Wheat, barley, oats, and, to a limited extent, rye are grown down to the 10-inch (25-cm) annual isohyet in the south. Summer cereals are not widely grown; few areas have the high summer rains and the freedom from hot winds that are necessary for corn production.

PRODUCTION OF LEADING AUSTRALIAN CROPS, 1950–1964

Crop and unit of production	Average 1950–51 1954–55	1956–57	1963–64
Wheat ('000 bushels)	181,910	135,000	327,912
Barley ('000 bushels)	31,351	49,300	43,395
Oats ('000 bushels)	42,252	35,400	68,234
Corn ('000 bushels)	4,654	5,500	6,722
Cane sugar ('000 short tons)	1,132	1,353	1,900
Rice (million pounds)	170	156	313

Of all the cereals, wheat is by far the most important, because it is usually worth most on the world market. In the early days, when transportation was a problem, it was grown for local consumption, and the South Australian plains north of Adelaide, with their numerous small ports, constituted the first large area of true wheat land to be developed. In other states, railways built across the coastal ranges from 1860 onward opened the way to the present wheat belt. In the 1920's, expansion toward the drier interior was rapid, but yields were often low and following

was introduced. Super-phosphate fertilizer was found to be essential except in northern New South Wales and Queensland.

The depression of the 1930's brought about a reassessment of the industry; marginal lands were returned to grazing, and nearly all wheat growers began to keep sheep as well. The adoption of a longer period between crops and the introduction of clover not only arrested the fall in soil nitrogen on many farms but also increased yields and caused an improvement in the soils.

Sugarcane is grown in a series of fertile coastal areas stretching from northern New South Wales to Cairns in northern Queensland. The industry is technically efficient and operates under an all-Australian agreement whereby the local population is supplied at an agreed price irrespective of the world market. In order to keep the export of sugar within the bounds set by international agreements, the area on each farm is assigned so that the local mills can keep production within their quotas.

SAMUEL M. WADHAM
University of Melbourne

Forestry. The main forest areas of Australia aggregate 186,791 square miles (483,789 sq km), only 6.3 percent of the total land area. For the most part, they are confined to the humid coastal

WHEAT FIELDS cover much of the area of central New South Wales. An important export, wheat is often grown on land that has been treated with chemical fertilizers.

BAUXITE PLANT at Weipa on the northwest coast of Cape York Peninsula, Queensland. The world's largest known bauxite deposit was discovered at Weipa in 1955.

strips and highlands of the southwestern and eastern parts of the mainland and to Tasmania. Two main types are recognized—the sclerophyll and the rain forest. The sclerophyll type, forming about 95 percent of the commercial areas, is dominated by species of the genus *Eucalyptus*, which is indigenous to Australia and contains over 650 species and varieties. The trees vary from forest giants, 200 to 300 feet (61–91 meters) in height, to the dwarf types (mallees) of the drier inland areas. The tropical rain forests of northern coastal New South Wales and coastal Queensland are most complex, and more than 300 species of trees have been recorded in them.

The country is deficient in native softwoods, and since softwoods make up the bulk of the lumber imports, large plantations of conifers have been developed by government and private organizations. The main species planted is the Monterey pine (*Pinus radiata*) of California. In 1966 the federal government began an accelerated afforestation program, in which trees native to Asia and southern Europe, as well as to North America, would be planted, mostly to replace existing poor-quality forests.

There are over 3,000 sawmills throughout the continent (many of them, however, with very limited output). The species cut are the medium- and light-weight eucalypts, some of the rainforest timbers, and plantation thinnings. The products are employed for building, manufacturing, furniture, cabinetwork, and other purposes. Because of the incidence of collapse (abnormal shrinkage), care must be taken in seasoning some of the eucalypt timbers, but this condition can be corrected by a reconditioning (steaming) process. The denser eucalypts, many of which are highly durable, are valuable for heavy construction, poles, posts, piles, and railway ties. Hardwoods and softwoods from the rain forests are used in the manufacture of plywood, the annual production of which was about 250,000,000 square feet (23,226,000 sq meters) on a 3/16-inch (0.5-cm) basis in the mid-1960's. Second-quality eucalypt timbers form the raw material of the fiberboard industry; more than 40,000,000 square yards (33,445,200 sq meters) of manufactured boards were being produced annually.

An important development has been the establishment of a pulping industry, using lightweight eucalypt timbers as well as plantation conifers. All grades of paper are manufactured. Production of newsprint averages about 95,000 tons (86,182 metric tons) a year; fine writing and printing paper, over 130,000 tons (117,933 metric tons); kraft, about 150,000 tons (136,077 metric tons); and paperboard, over 250,000 tons (226,795 metric tons).

Minor products of the forest include essential oils from eucalypt leaves, which are used medicinally and for flotation processes; and tannin extracts from wattle bark, mallet (*Eucalyptus astringens*) bark, and the timber of wandoo (*Eucalytpus wandoo*). Crude rutin is extracted from the leaves of *Eucalyptus macrorrhynca*.

The value of forestry production exceeds $A100 million (Australian dollars) a year. In terms of importance to the economy, forest products rank higher in Tasmania than in any other Australian state. In 1964, the Australian Forestry Council was formed, bringing together Commonwealth and state governments for the purpose of research into matters related to forest protection and utilization of forest products.

H.E. DADSWELL, *Commonwealth Scientific and Industrial Research Organization*

Mining and Metallurgy. The record of the exploration and development of the mineral resources of Australia is in many ways an impressive one. Settlement of the country received its first great impetus from the gold discoveries of the 1850's, and, although the peak of production in that generation was attained only six years after the main discoveries in Ballarat, Bendigo, and other centers of Victoria, the penetration of the interior had been initiated, and the promise of rich rewards in gold and base metals led intrepid prospectors into the arid, trackless country of the mainland and the rain forests of Tasmania. In more fortunately endowed sections of the continent, the first mining settlements were subsequently consolidated by pastoral and agricultural activities, although mining itself was short-lived in many cases. In other instances, such permanent mining towns as Broken Hill, Kalgoorlie, and Mount Isa were established as the principal outposts of settlement in their respective states. Discoveries in the southeastern coastal areas included the coalfields of New South Wales, Queensland, and Victoria, and the iron-ore fields of the Middleback Range (South Australia).

In the mid-20th century, important mineral discoveries in sparsely settled tropical regions established populations at remote points, including the uranium fields of Mary Kathleen (Queensland) and Rum Jungle (Northern Territory), the important bauxite fields at Weipa (Queensland) and Gove (Northern Territory), the manganese deposit on Groote Eylandt, and massive iron-ore deposits at Yampi Sound and in the Pilbara district of Western Australia. At the same time, important discoveries were made in southern coastal regions, including iron-ore and bauxite fields near Perth, and the beach-sands deposits of New South Wales, Queensland, and Western Australia.

Economic Significance. The combined effects of the mineral discoveries and the establishment of mining and of metallurgical reduction plants have made possible a striking degree of industrialization. Australia is self-sufficient in steel, copper, lead, zinc, aluminum, nickel, solid fuels, and the great majority of the nonmetallic minerals of commerce; is partly supplied with tin and manganese, and produces sulfuric acid from pyrites and furnace recovery. The country is a substantial exporter of lead, zinc, copper, gold, uranium oxide, rutile, zircon, asbestos, bauxite, and iron ore. The only important deficiencies are in petroleum, sulfur, and phosphate rock. Mining is third among Australia's primary industries in value of output, following wool and wheat.

In the early 1960's new prospects were opened by a quick succession of rich mineral discoveries—manganese, iron ore, and bauxite in vast deposits, and added reserves of copper and silver-lead. Together with the discovery of oil, these were significant not only to the future of mining in Australia but also to the course of development of the economy as a whole. By 1966 export of iron ore and bauxite to Japan had begun, and new processing and refining facilities were coming into operation, involving large-scale investment, much of it from abroad. At the same time the prospect raised by oil discoveries was that petroleum imports might be progressively reduced over coming years.

Production. Coal has been the most important mineral in Australia's industrial development to date, and its continuing significance is indicated by the fact that it accounts for 30 percent of the value of mine output. Coal is produced mainly by the Newcastle, Port Kembla, and Lithgow fields, New South Wales; the Ipswich and Bowen fields, Queensland; Collie, Western Australia; and St. Mary's, Tasmania. Brown coal comes from the Latrobe Valley field, Victoria, and Leigh Creek, South Australia. Exports of coal have been rising.

Next in importance are lead and zinc, which together account for about 24 percent of mine output in terms of value. The Broken Hill field continues to be the principal producer; other important fields are at Mount Isa, Queensland, and Rosebery, Tasmania. Copper, representing about 11 percent of the value of mine production, is produced mainly at Mount Isa and Mount Morgan, Queensland; Mount Lyell, Tasmania; and Tennant Creek, Northern Territory. Rutile and zircon are produced by a number of small operators on the east coast of New South Wales and Queensland. Beginning in the early 1950's, the output of both minerals rose strongly in response to overseas demand.

PRODUCTION OF LEADING AUSTRALIAN MINERALS, 1953–64

Mineral and unit of Production	1953	1957	1964
Coal ('000 tons)	18,411	19,799	27,402
Brown coal ('000 tons)	8,257	10,741	19,033
Lead ('000 tons)	269	332	375
Copper (tons)	36,585	56,613	104,642
Gold ('000 fine ounces)	1,075	1,084	965
Zinc ('000 tons)	239	292	345
Iron ('000 tons)	2,132	2,465	5,668
Tin (tons)	1,553	1,938	3,638
Bauxite ('000 tons)	0	0	841
Petroleum, crude ('000 barrels)	0	0	1,491

New port facilities had to be built in the early 1960's at Weipa, on Cape York peninsula, Queensland, to exploit the great bauxite deposits of the area. At first the ore was exported, mainly to Japan, but in 1965 construction of the largest alumina plant in the world began at Gladstone, Queensland. Other major developments in mineral-processing facilities were the Townsville copper refinery, handling Mount Isa ore, and the

COAL mined by the open-cut method at Yallourn in the Latrobe Valley of eastern Victoria. The output is used chiefly to generate electricity for use in the state.

alumina plant built near Geelong, Victoria, to process Western Australian bauxite. A third bauxite reduction plant was planned to handle Gove (Northern Territory) ore. Manganese from Groote Eylandt was being shipped to Bell Bay, Tasmania, where the capacity of the ferro-manganese furnace was being extended.

Facilities for developing the iron-ore deposits of the Pilbara district of Western Australia were begun in 1966. Plans called for the construction of complete new townships as well as for the laying of rail lines and the installation of handling and portside equipment. Money for the projects was provided largely from abroad. Meanwhile, expansion of the domestic steel industry has continued. In 1965 the Broken Hill Proprietary Company opened a new steelworks at Whyalla, South Australia, with a planned ingot capacity of 900,-000 tons (816,462 metric tons) a year. The company has a continuing program to expand its existing plants and to decentralize its steelmaking facilities.

Fisheries. Fish is not an essential item in the Australian diet. Unlike many other countries, Australia is well supplied with a variety of foodstuffs, and there is no great urgency to exploit fisheries even as an export industry. Nevertheless, the nation holds an important place with regard to some fisheries: it is, for example, the principal world supplier of pearl shell and makes substantial contributions to crayfishery and whaling. Moreover, there are abundant but not yet fully exploited stocks of tuna and prawns. Since all these stocks are expected to be subjected to increasing exploitation with the growth of population, the various state governments have taken steps to see that they are not overexploited.

The main marine products are pearl shell, trochus (top shell), cultured pearls, prawns, mullet, a species known locally as salmon, tuna, oysters, barracouta, and crayfish (spiny lobster). The shell of the Australian species of pearl oyster (*Pinctada maxima*) has proved capable of producing the world's largest pearls, commanding top market prices. Since commercial production began in 1957, fifteen pearl culture farms have been established along the northern coastline. Mullet and salmon are caught on both the east and west coasts, whereas oysters are farmed mainly in New South Wales. Prawns are caught principally in

AUSTRALIAN NEWS AND INFORMATION BUREAU

LOBSTERS, like these taken at the port of Coff's Harbour, New South Wales, are a major marine product.

New South Wales and Queensland, and tuna in New South Wales. The barracouta fishery is centered mainly in Bass Strait. Crayfish caught in Western Australia and the southern states constitute an important export commodity.

Until 1963, when an international prohibition on the taking of humpback whales was imposed, four whaling stations were in operation. Whaling is now confined to the sperm whale, and one station remains open in Western Australia.

There are nine fisheries departments in Australia: seven regional and two that act for the whole country. The regional departments, though concerned partly with exploitation and scientific research, are occupied mainly with the administration of regulations in inland and territorial waters. The Fisheries Division of the Department of Primary Industry is responsible for development and administration outside territorial waters, and the Division of Fisheries and Oceanography of the Commonwealth Scientific and Industrial Research Organization, for scientific research in all waters.

G.F. HUMPHREY, *Commonwealth Scientific and Industrial Research Organization.*

Manufacturing. Australia is highly industrialized, and the range of its manufactured products is wide. Among them are refined lead, zinc, aluminum, and petroleum; steel, including special steels; automobiles; ships; jet aircraft; heavy earthmoving equipment; electric and electronic equipment; a great variety of chemicals, including such plastics as polyethylene as well as plastic articles; textiles of wool, cotton, and synthetic fibers; and food products.

Historical Development. The policy of imposing import duties to promote manufacturing goes back to the 1860's in Victoria. While federation (1901) brought freedom of trade within the continent, it was combined with protection of domestic manufacturers from outside producers. World War I not only reduced the supply of imported goods; by breaking links between Australian mines and overseas refineries, it led to a great extension of nonferrous metal refining. It was at this time also that the steel industry was firmly established.

Expansion during the 1920's was marked by the development of automobile assembly and body production. Several measures taken to deal with the depression of the early 1930's including the depreciation of the Australian pound against sterling and a general reduction of wages, strengthened the Australian manufacturer against overseas competition. Among the industries that expanded most rapidly in the 1930's was textile production. The total volume of manufactured production was perhaps two thirds higher in 1927–1930 than before World War I, and it expanded by approximately 40 percent between 1927–1930 and World War II.

Apart from the heavy task of replacing imports, World War II meant that United States as well as Australian troops had to be supplied for fighting in the Pacific and the Far East. During the war, aircraft, machine tools and other machinery, and chemicals were the chief fields of expansion. Factory employment increased by about one third.

In the postwar years expansion continued, and between 1946–1947 and 1956–1957 the number of factories rose from 35,000 to over 50,000. Wartime experience in engineering formed the basis for the large-scale production of capital equipment and consumer durable goods; chemical manufacture, so important to a modern manufacturing economy, continued to grow; and petroleum refining was rapidly developed to a point where almost the entire range of refined products was being produced from imported crude oil. Associated with the development of oil-refining capacity, were several petrochemical units, set up to produce various intermediate chemicals, plastics, detergent alkylates, and synthetic rubber.

By the mid-1960's the number of factories exceeded 60,000, and investment in plant extensions was rising without interruption. Industries showing the greatest expansion were those associated with the treatment of nonmetalliferous mine and quarry products, and basic industries—notably engineering, metals, chemicals, and paper. As a result of expansion and diversification, manufacturing industries produced almost the entire range of items required by a community with high living standards.

Character of Manufacturing. Apart from industries processing rural and mining products, Australian manufacturing traditionally has been a home market activity. With such important exceptions as steel, manufacturing costs tend to be high. The high cost level stems from a number of factors: for some industries, and in comparison with some countries, high wages are important; but for modern continuous-production industries, such as chemicals, a more significant factor is the smallness of the home market, in comparison, for example, with the United States.

Because of high costs, the export of manufactured goods has grown slowly. Nevertheless, in the 1960's Australia was able to sell abroad a wide range of manufactured goods. A major part of the export trade was directed to New Zealand, but various other countries and territories were buying goods of Australian manufacture. Although there continue to be heavy imports of producers' capital equipment and some other commodities, the strong growth of manufacturing has resulted in a per capita reduction in imports.

Since World War II, expansion of manufacturing has been a prime objective of federal policy. Manufacturers have been protected not only by

AUSTRALIA

Above: Wollongong, an industrial complex 40 miles south of Sydney, is a coal mining and manufacturing center.

Right: The wattle is extremely widespread, and has become a national emblem. Shown here is the Cootamundura wattle (*Acacia Baileyana*).

Bottom left: Devil's Coach House, one of the famous Jenolan Caves, formed by the Jenolan River, about 70 miles west of Sydney.

Bottom right: Sheep ranch in Tamworth, busy agricultural center in New South Wales.

(Top) Jerry Cooke from Photo Researchers; (center) John Nisbett from Shostal; (bottom left) George Leavens from Photo Researchers; (bottom right) David Forbert from APA

Left: Fall coloring comes in May to landscape in Victoria while hills stay green with pine.

Above: Perth is capital of Western Australia and hub of activity in developing the west.

Right: Copper mine near Queenstown on west coast of Tasmania. Copper is the third most valuable mineral product of the Commonwealth of Australia.

Left: More than half the people of South Australia live in Adelaide or its pleasant suburbs.

(Top left) De Lisle—FPG; (top right) Australian News and Information Bureau; (center) Rhonda Small from Photo Researchers; (bottom left) Alpha

Above: Surfers Paradise on "gold coast" south of Brisbane has smart shops and gay restaurants.

Right: Center of continent near Ayers Rock, Northern Territory, is arid red sand desert.

Left: Spinning machines in port of Melbourne, Victoria, produce large quantities of wool yarn.

Right: Victoria's reliable rainfall assures water and lush pasture for sheep. Australia is world's leading producer of apparel wool.

(Top left) H. B. Green from Alpha; (top right and bottom right) De Lisle—FPG; (center) Australian News and Information Bureau

AUSTRALIA

Above: Close-up of colorful underwater formations on the 1,250-mile-long Great Barrier Reef, the world's most famous coral deposit.

Left: Sailing has been popular in Australia almost since the time of the first settlement.

Right: Aboriginal boy with nose plug made of bone.

Bottom: Hobart, capital and chief port of the small island state of Tasmania.

(Top right) Frank Hurley from Rapho Guillumette; (top left) Jerry Cooke from Photo Researchers; (center) Annan; (bottom) Pan American Airways

tariffs but, at crucial times—as in the period from World War II to 1960—by a system of import restrictions. Since the late 1950's each of the state governments has been increasingly active in encouraging establishment of new industrial undertakings within its borders. Some concern has been expressed about the burden of dividend payments to many overseas firms operating in Australia. However, the federal government has continued to encourage investment from abroad, considering the benefits of accelerated industrialization on an efficient basis as being of paramount importance, while urging that, whenever possible, the overseas investment should be on a basis of partnership with Australian capital.

Principal Manufacturers. The largest of the Australian manufacturing firms is the Broken Hill Proprietary Company, Ltd., which dominates the steel industry and employs, directly or through subsidiaries, over 35,000 persons. It is mainly owned and controlled in Australia, although there are many overseas stockholders. The company owns virtually all the Australian blast furnaces and all the steelmaking capacity; and, to transport its ore and steel, it operates a shipping line and shipyards. Its annual output of steel increased from 1.4 million long tons (1.42 metric tons) in 1950–1951 to more than 5.5 million tons (5.6 million metric tons) in 1965–1966. Ingot capacity in 1966 exceeded 6 million tons (6.1 million metric tons). (The company name is a somewhat misleading relic of its history: it retains little connection with Broken Hill, the nonferrous mining center in western New South Wales, or with the nonferrous industry in general.)

The leading automobile firm is General Motors —Holden's Ltd., a subsidiary of General Motors, Inc. In the mid-1960's, domestic sales of its distinctive car, the Holden, exceeded 150,000 a year, and approximately 20,000 a year were being exported. Encouraged by tariff protection and under pressure from the federal government, a number of other overseas producers, mainly American, British, and German, also have increased the proportion of Australian components in their vehicles. As a result, the automotive industry has developed from a minor assembler of motor vehicles to a point where it has a productive capacity of some 400,000 units a year and is able to produce component parts.

The chemicals industry also benefits from foreign capital and technology. The chief chemicals firm is an offshoot of Imperial Chemical Industries of the United Kingdom; others are controlled by the Monsanto Chemical Company and Union Carbide Corporation of the United States; and still others have strong links with American or German capital. Oil refineries and petrochemical plants are owned mainly by British or American firms. Rayon yarn is produced by an Australian affiliate of the British firm, Courtaulds, Ltd., and nylon by a subsidiary of British Nylon Spinners. The rubber industry is shared by British, Australian, and American firms. Most of the appliance manufacturers are associated with overseas firms, but control generally remains in local hands.

Glass, like steel, is an example of near-monopoly and mainly Australian ownership in a large-scale industry, the producer being Australian Consolidated Industries. There are several big firms in the paper industry, but each specializes in a particular range of paper or cardboard.

FRANK GEOFFREY DAVIDSON
University of Melbourne

GUTHEGA DAM, a major installation of the Snowy Mountains hydroelectric project, in New South Wales.

Hydroelectric Power. Possible hydroelectric installations in Australia are generally limited to a narrow strip in the eastern Highlands, and the principal power potential is confined to the southeastern portion of the continent in the Australian Alps. It is expected that the limited extent of the hydroelectric power resources will result in their use for peak-load generation in a predominantly thermal system in multipurpose developments.

In the mid-1960's, the installed capacity of all hydroelectric plants in Australia was approximately 2.5 million kilowatts. The total hydroelectric power resources that are considered capable of ultimate economic development are estimated at approximately 9.9 million kilowatts, of which 7.5 million kilowatts are available from the continent and 2.4 million kilowatts from Tasmania. Of the mainland resources, approximately 4 million kilowatts are capable of economic development in the New South Wales and Victoria sections of the Australian Alps. There, the Kiewa project and the Snowy Mountains undertaking will develop some 4 million kilowatts by the mid-1970's.

New South Wales. Of a total hydroelectric potential of approximately 5.4 million kilowatts, 1.8 million had been installed by 1966. The installed capacity consisted of 1.04 million kilowatts in the operating sections of the Snowy Mountains project and 140,000 kilowatts in small plants in other parts of the state. Works under construction in the Snowy Mountains will add 2.7 million kilowatts of capacity by 1975. This includes the Tumut 3 project, which will have a generating capacity of 1.5 million kilowatts and will be the first pumped storage project in Australia. The remaining New South Wales potential of about 1.5 million kilowatts lies mainly in the coastal Clarence, Macleay, and Shoalhaven rivers.

Victoria. The principal Victorian hydroelectric developments are the Kiewa project in the southern section of the Australian Alps and the Eildon and Rubicon installations on the Goulburn River. Total hydroelectric resources of the state are estimated at 1.5 million kilowatts, of which 368,000 kilowatts had been installed by 1966: 224,000 kilowatts at Kiewa, 136,000 kilowatts at Eildon Reservoir, and 8,000 kilowatts at Rubicon.

Queensland. Of an estimated hydroelectric potential of about 600,000 kilowatts, 135,000 kilowatts had been developed by 1966. Most of the installed capacity was centered on the northeast coast where the Tully Falls and Barron River projects, with a combined capacity of 132,000 kilowatts, supply power to the Cairns, Innisfail, and Townsville areas.

Tasmania. Tasmania is unique among the states in that all of its power requirements are met from hydroelectric resources. Its potential hydroelectric capacity of 2,400,000 kilowatts is about one third that of the mainland. By 1966 the installed capacity in service reached 808,000 kilowatts, and additional undertakings were planned, including a 300,000-kilowatt project in the northern part of the state. Investigations of the undeveloped resources in the rugged west coast area were under way.

Other States. Hydroelectric power developments would appear to be unlikely in South Australia and Northern Territory. In Western Australia, hydroelectric power generation would appear to be economical only in conjunction with irrigation or with such town water supply projects as Wellington Dam, where a 2,200-kilowatt plant has been installed.

SIR WILLIAM HUDSON, *Snowy Mountains Hydro-Electric Authority*

Public Utilities. By tradition and circumstances, railroads, electric power, town gas supplies, irrigation and water supply, telephone service, some of the shipping and air transportation, and some housing are the responsibility of state governments or of statutory authorities set up by them. There are also minor state instrumentalities engaged in coal mining, engineering, shipbuilding, and brickmaking. This strong entrenchment of public ownership is due perhaps to an over-all shortage of risk capital and to a general political climate in which there is an underlying belief in the desirability of maintaining public control over basic services and of supplying such services at the lowest possible cost. Federal experiments with public ownership of air and shipping services since World War II have been concerned with the need to maintain effective competition. At the same time, however, the government has relinquished its holdings in some commercial enterprises established with public funds in earlier years.

The tendency for railroads to become the monopoly of state governments was apparent from the early days. At the local level this trend toward public ownership in the field of transportation was extended to streetcar and bus services, and at the national level it led to the creation of Trans-Australia Airlines (1945) and of the Australian Coastal Shipping Commission (1956), successor to the Australian Shipping Board. In addition, a major interest in an international airline, Qantas Empire Airways, was acquired by the federal government in 1947.

In every state, the generation, reticulation, and distribution of electricity are almost exclusively in the hands of public corporations, set up by acts of Parliament and able to control their own revenue and raise loans for capital funds. Of these utilities, the largest is the State Electricity Commission of Victoria, founded in 1918, which controls virtually all of the state's electricity for public supply. The commission also is responsible for the development of Victoria's immense brown coal deposits for both the generation of electricity and the manufacture of briquettes, and for the development of hydroelectric resources. In New South Wales, about 96 percent of the power is generated by the Electricity Commission, which sells it to distributing authorities and to some large industrial users.

The largest single public project in Australia is that undertaken by the Snowy Mountains Hydro-Electric Authority, a federal instrumentality. Developed after 1949, this combined power and irrigation project, involving the diversion and damming of rivers in the Australian Alps, is designed to provide 2,800,000 kilowatts of electric power and 2,000,000 acre-feet (2,467 million cubic meters) of water for irrigation.

For the whole of Australia, capital expenditure on public works rose from $A156 million in 1960's, with about three fourths of the expenditure undertaken by state governments and local authorities. Expenditures were principally for roads (about 22 percent of the total outlay), railways and other transportation and communications (12 percent), electricity (18 percent), water supply and sewage (10 percent), educational facilities (8 percent), and such developmental undertakings as irrigation, land settlement, and afforestation.

R.M. YOUNGER
Author of "The Changing World: Australia"

Labor—Labor Force. Since the 1890's, the proportion of the population of Australia in the labor force has been fairly constant, constituting about two fifths of the total. At the 1961 census, women workers comprised 25 percent of the labor force, compared with 15 percent in 1871, and almost one fourth of all Australian women were in paid employment. This expansion of the employment of women has been accompanied by a trend away from personal and domestic service in favor of other occupations. Junior workers under 21 years of age comprised about 15 percent of the labor force, and 75 percent of the males and 65 percent of the females between the ages of 16 and 20 years were at work. The proportion of junior females at work was among the highest in the world. Although, as in other industrialized countries, the proportion of men over the age of 65 in the labor force had declined markedly, about one in four men in this age group was still at work in the 1960's.

As a modern economic pattern has been established, the distribution of the labor force among the various industries has undergone considerable change. The proportion engaged in primary industries has fallen sharply over the past two or three generations, while that employed in manufacturing and service industries has greatly expanded. In 1871, 44 percent of the employed population worked in primary industries (agricultural, pastoral, mining, and forestry); by the early 1960's this proportion was down to about 12 percent. On the other hand, manufacturing (including employees in wholesale selling and distribution of factory products) and building/construction had expanded from 26.5 percent to about 38 percent and transportation/communications from 3.6 to 9 percent. Commerce occupied about 20 percent, compared with 8 percent in 1871, while personal and professional services and other occupations had moved up to 21 percent from 17.6 percent in 1871. Because of mechanization of agriculture and the growth of manufacturing, the proportion of the labor force engaged in urban occupations was exceeded in only a half dozen nations.

An important feature of the Australian labor force is the extent of government employment. Railroads, urban passenger transportation, and electricity, gas, and water supplies are almost entirely government operated. In addition, there are large government enterprises in the fields of civil aviation, radio broadcasting, and telecommunications. State education and health services also employ large numbers of workers, as do government construction agenices. In the 1960's, almost 30 percent of those in civilian employment were employed by federal, state, or local governments or by statutory authorities.

Labor Organizations. Australian labor is highly unionized. In 1911 over one fourth of all employees were union members, and ten years later the proportion was one in two. During the 1940's, union membership increased markedly, and since then the proportion has been a steady three-in-five of all employees.

With the progress of industrialization early in the 20th century, industrial unionism began to replace the craft unionism of the 19th century. In addition, a trend toward nationwide federation of state unions resulted in a decline in the number of unions from 573 in 1911 to 355 fifty years later. Nevertheless, some craft unions remain strong, and it is not unusual for more than one union to exist in an industry. Unions vary in size from less than 50 to nearly 200,000 members, with the larger unions accounting for a greater proportion of the total membership. The industrial distribution of union membership has changed in accordance with the changing distribution of the labor force, rising in engineering and manufacturing and falling in the pastoral and agricultural industries.

The basic unit of union organization is the local or state branch, which is usually much more significant than the organization at the plant or federal level. At the branch level, a district or state council of trade unions, known as a labor council or a trades hall council, coordinates interunion relations and policies, although some unions are not affiliated with these bodies. The Australian Council of Trade Unions (ACTU), founded in 1927, acts as a coordinating body at the national level. It represents both the state labor councils and the federal unions. The largest union, the Australian Workers' Union, which has nearly 200,000 members, mainly in rural occupations, remains unaffiliated, as does the state labor council in Western Australia. The most important functions of the ACTU and the state labor councils are representation of the union movement in negotiations with employers and governments, and control and direction of important industrial disputes affecting more than one union. Although the ACTU has grown in strength and influence, it exerts only limited power over the constituent unions.

The rules and conduct of the internal affairs of Australian trade unions are regulated by government tribunals, which give a considerable degree of protection to the rights of individual members, including control of elections if necessary. Funds are not large, staffing is modest, and there are few research or educational activities. A number of unions publish small newspapers. Most unions contribute to Australian Labour party funds.

Historically, the Australian labor movement is a stream diverted from the main flow of social reform in Britain, the accumulated pressure of which carried it forward over the unresisting terrain of a new society lacking a rigid class structure. It is a pragmatic and pluralist movement, concerned little with ideologies but much with practical results. Once described as "socialism without doctrines," Australian unionism's general objective has been to improve wages and conditions and, if necessary, to use political organization to this end. Although socialism has figured in the labor program over a long period, for the most part this aim has been tempered to the demands of practical politics. A certain tension exists between the unions and the Labour party, even though the unions supply many members and leaders of the parliamentary party.

Labor-Management Relations. Negotiations between unions and employers are commonly industrywide, and on certain key issues they are economywide. Negotiations at the plant level deal for the most part with matters internal to the plant rather than with wages and general working conditions. The growth of industrywide and economywide negotiations has been strengthened by government machinery for the settlement of industrial disputes. Strong employers' associations try to ensure that all negotiations are channeled through them in order to prevent unions from winning concessions from a few employers and using these gains as precedents when putting their claims before a tribunal. In this way, plant bargaining is discouraged and industry bargaining fostered. Under the arbitration system, nationwide negotiation has been encouraged by unions using gains in one industry as an argument in favor of adjustments in others in order to restore the original relation between the various industries. Moreover, early in their history the tribunals adopted the principle of the basic wage, a standard minimum wage for unskilled labor in all industry, which is essentially an economywide concept. Later, the establishment of margins for skill above the basic wage were dealt with in the same way, applications to vary the margins in certain industries being treated as test cases that would, in effect, set the pattern for changes throughout the economy. This procedure has also been applied to other key issues, including standard working hours and vacations.

Thus, relations between individual unions and individual employers always develop against a background of industrywide and economywide negotiation and arbitration. The actual form of the federal and state tribunals and the legislation under which they operate vary considerably, and there has been a good deal of experimentation since the early 1900's, when most of the tribunals were founded. Aimed at instituting "a new province for law and order," most of the systems envisaged the settlement of industrial disputes by arbitrators drawn from the judiciary and the legal profession. Although all systems provide for nonlegal, "practical" men to act as arbitrators, most of them retain a considerable degree of legalism, imposing fines and other penalties on unions and employers that engage in illegal stoppages or break arbitrators' awards. The tribunals have developed a complex system of industrial relations law. Employers' federations and large firms employ industrial advocates to conduct cases before tribunals, and such duties are an important part of a union official's work.

AUSTRALIAN NEWS AND INFORMATION BUREAU

COINS, minted for the new decimal system using dollars and cents, feature a picture of Queen Elizabeth II on one side and wildlife on the other. Animals shown: feather-tailed glider (1c), frilled lizard (2c), echidna (5c), lyrebird (10c), platypus (20c), and kangaroo and emu (50c).

The federal tribunal, the Commonwealth Court of Conciliation and Arbitration, has come to dominate the other tribunals. Since 1926, a federal award prevails over state legislation or awards that would apply in the absence of a federal award, and since the 1930's, the state tribunals have usually followed the federal lead on major issues, some being legally required to incorporate the federal basic wage in their awards. The federal tribunal has become the nation's forum for debating wage policy, and its decisions are a conscious attempt to adjust wages to the demands of the current economic situation.

The power of the federal tribunal as an agent of economic policy is, however, limited. In the first place, state parliaments and industrial tribunals at times take an independent line on industries within state jurisdiction. Secondly, the federal tribunal's actions on wages are not coordinated directly with such other key economic controls as central bank policy and budget policy. Thirdly, its intentions regarding the level of real wages may be frustrated by the operation of market forces that cancel out the effects of changed money wages on real income.

In the mid-1960's the trend within the federal wage tribunal appeared to be toward the creation of a "total wage" concept rather than perpetuation of the existing basic-wage-plus margin system. At the same time there was a tendency for the tribunal's jurisdiction to shrink as a result of a marked shift toward state awards and over-award wage payments, which lessened the effectiveness of award judgments.

Although available statistics are inadequate, they support this limited view of the impact of the industrial tribunals on economic policy. Real wages have kept pace with rises in productivity during the 20th century in the United Kingdom and the United States as well as in Australia, and there is no evidence that the arbitration system has had a substantial effect either on the general level of real wages or on the relative distribution of income. It has certainly strengthened organization among employees and employers and has made it easier for unions to bring lagging employers into line with leading employers, but beyond that its impact is doubtful.

Compulsory arbitration has not achieved the dream of complete industrial peace, and the evidence suggests that it has had mixed effects on industrial relations, improving the situation in some industries and worsening it in others. Many disputes never get to the tribunals: they are settled amicably by negotiation, and in isolated instances the industrial affairs of an industry are largely determined by the processes of collective bargaining. Agreements freely negotiated can be brought under the Conciliation and Arbitration Act without going through the formal process of arbitration. Nevertheless, arbitration has established itself as an enduring institution in Australia, and the community shows no disposition to abolish it.

KENNETH F. WALKER, *University of Western Australia*

Banking and Finance. *Weights and Measures.* The British system of weights and measures prevails in Australia. The unit of distance is the yard of 3 feet, or 36 inches (.9144 meters); the unit of weight is the long ton of 2,240 pounds (1.0160 metric tons); and the unit of liquid measure is the imperial gallon of 4 quarts or 8 pints (4.5459 liters), which is equivalent to 1.20094 United States gallons.

Monetary System. The unit of currency is the Australian dollar ($A), equivalent to 8 shillings sterling and US$1.12 at the 1966 exchange rate. Denominations are notes of 1, 2, 10, and 20 dollars and coins of 1, 2, 5, 10, 20, and 50 cents. The decimal currency system was adopted officially on Feb. 14, 1966, when the Australian pound was replaced by the dollar on the basis of £A1 = $A2.00, but the old currency remained in circulation, along with the new, for two subsequent years. Paper currency, issued by the Reserve Bank of Australia under the authority of the Commonwealth government, is legal tender within the territories of the Commonwealth of Australia.

Banking System. The banking system comprises the central bank, the 15 trading or commercial banks, and savings banks—some government sponsored and the others established by the major trading banks.

Under legislation passed in 1959 the central bank, hitherto part of the Commonwealth Bank of Australia, was made a separate unit and renamed the Reserve Bank of Australia. The Reserve Bank is controlled by a board comprising the governor and deputy governor of the bank, the federal secretary to the Treasury, and seven other members. The board has the statutory duty to direct the bank's monetary and banking policy to the greatest advantage of the people of Australia by contributing to "the stability of the currency, the maintenance of full employment, and the people's economic prosperity and welfare." In the event of a difference of opinion arising between the board and the government on whether any policy is so directed, the governor general of Australia, acting with the advice of the Executive Council, may determine the policy to be adopted by the bank.

In carrying out its policy, the Reserve Bank not only uses the powers of direction conferred upon it but also consults freely with members of the general banking system. The bank's duties, powers, and activities are similar to those of central banks elsewhere. They include management of the note issue, regulation of bank lending and of bank interest rates, operations in government securities, acting as banker and financial agent of the federal government, and administration of overseas exchange control. The bank also has a responsibility to protect the interests of bank depositors. Through a system of statutory deposits, the bank regulates the liquidity of the various trading banks. By agreement, the trading banks maintain a certain minimum level of liquidity in their own hands. A rural credits division of the Reserve Bank is designated as the authority to make short-term advances to statutory marketing boards and cooperative societies for the purpose of financing the marketing of primary produce.

Under the 1959 legislation, the Commonwealth Banking Corporation took over the other activities of the government-owned Commonwealth Bank. The corporation became the controlling body of the Commonwealth Trading Bank and the Commonwealth Savings Bank, and also of the newly formed Commonwealth Development Bank, whose function is to provide financial and other assistance for rural or industrial activities as an encouragement to smaller enterprises in these fields.

The Commonwealth Trading Bank competes actively with the 15 "private" banks providing general banking facilities. These banks are joint stock companies, most of whose capital has been subscribed in Australia or in Britain. The British system of branch banking is followed. Total deposits of the trading banks exceed $A4,000 million.

Savings banks play an important role in the general financial system. A large proportion of deposit funds is invested in government and semi-government securities; the remainder is invested mainly in fixed loans, particularly for housing, either directly or through cooperative building societies. Deposits with all savings banks exceed $A4,000 million.

Insurance. Companies, persons, or associations of persons carrying on insurance business in Australia are required to lodge a deposit with the Commonwealth treasurer. Money so deposited is invested in prescribed securities selected by the depositors, and all interest is paid to depositors. Deposits remain as security against liability to policyholders and are available to satisfy judgments obtained in respect of policies. Under the Life Assurance Act 1945–1965, an insurance commissioner exercises active supervision over life insurance companies with a view to securing the greatest possible protection for policyholders.

Economic Activity. With a gross national product of $A19,124 million and a population of about 11.5 million, Australia's per capita income in 1964–1965 was over $A1,650—one of the highest in the world. In the early 1960's

an average annual increase of about 5 percent was recorded in gross national product (GNP); the largest single source of productive wealth was manufacturing. Between 1961 and 1965, a period of strong economic expansion, the number of people in civilian employment increased by more than 600,000. During the same interval, total expenditure rose by $A6,200 million, or 43 percent.

CONTRIBUTIONS TO GROSS NATIONAL PRODUCTS
(Average 1960–1965)

Industry	Percentage of GNP
Manufacturing, power, and water supply	31.9
Commerce	15.4
Rural industries and mining	14.9
Transportation and communications	8.0
Building and construction	7.8
Other:	22.0
Community and business service	6.5
Public administration and defense	4.0
Ownership of buildings	4.0
Finance and property	5.5
Miscellaneous	2.0

Capital Formation, Prices, and Wages. After World War II, Australia sought to achieve a considerably higher rate of economic growth, in terms of population and productivity, than had been attained in the economically stagnant period between the two world wars. In order to carry a population increase of about 2.5 percent a year and to achieve a satisfactory increase of productivity, it allocated to capital formation almost 30 percent of its gross national product in the postwar years, compared with less than 20 percent in the interwar period. The relative contributions of public works and private fixed investment to this capital formation, however, remained approximately constant. Greater expenditures on defense and public services were balanced approximately by a decreased service on overseas debt, while the allocation of resources to consumption was reduced by nearly the full amount required to provide increased capital formation.

Since World War II personal savings have made a substantial contribution to capital formation. This resulted from the generally satisfactory—though fluctuating—level of export prices, which yielded relatively high incomes to farmers, who tend to save a substantial portion of any increase in their income. In the mid-1960's, total personal savings amounted to 7.5 percent of the gross national product. Other private savings (mainly undistributed profits, increases in insurance funds, and allowances for depreciation) maintained a stable relation to the gross national product. The government surplus on current account—the excess of tax revenues over expenditure on public services, defense, interest, and cash social benefits—rose substantially in response to the need for greater savings.

A main source of economic disturbance in Australia is the marked fluctuation of export prices and, to a smaller extent, of farm production as a result of changes in seasonal conditions. Because of climatic conditions and world prices, farm income varies considerably in relation to the gross national product. In the 1950's the combined effect of a high level of internal demand maintained by a high rate of economic growth, and of generally high prices for export commodities and for imports, brought sizable increases in prices and wages. As a result of fiscal and monetary measures introduced in 1960, the inflation was checked, and the trend in the 1960's was toward greater stability, with consumer demand remaining relatively stable and prices showing little rise. After 1963, capital expenditure on both public and private accounts showed a marked rise, and defense spending also began to move up sharply.

Aided by good seasons and by improving efficiency of production, farm output showed a generally upward trend, making possible a big increase in the volume of rural exports until 1965, when widespread drought sustained the rise. Most branches of industrial production had also been rising; building and construction went on apace, and there was all-around growth in transport and communications and in tertiary employments. With an easing of demand, output of various factory industries levelled off in 1965, but output of basic materials continued to rise, reflecting the efforts being made to divert manpower and materials to plant expansion, development projects, and defense.

Overseas Investment. In the eight years from 1947–1948 to 1955–1956, net capital inflow into Australia totaled approximately $A1,164 million, and in the following nine years (through 1964–1965), it exceeded $A3,221 million. Over the entire period, the smallest annual inflow was in 1952–1953 ($A51 million) and the greatest in 1964–1965 ($A528 million).

In all, overseas investment represented about 10 percent of private and public gross investment during the period. Of the total $A4,385 million, about 88 percent consisted of direct investment in subsidiaries or branches; about one third of this investment derived from the reinvestment of undistributed profits accruing to overseas investors, while two thirds consisted of new capital inflow.

About 52 percent of the inflow came from British sources, and 36 percent from United States and Canadian sources. During the period, however, the proportion of U.S. capital rose substantially, from under 20 percent in 1947–1948 to over 40 percent in the early 1960's, and in terms of the annual inflow of new capital the United States was the principal source from about the mid-1950's.

In spite of the buildup in industrial investment, the net interest burden on overseas debt was relatively lower than before World War II, amounting to only about 2 percent of national income. Nevertheless, some anxiety was being expressed about the prospective growth of the burden of overseas debt and about the dangers of overseas control of important segments of Australian industry. The government, while encouraging further investment from abroad, made clear its hope that companies setting up operations in Australia would take in a substantial proportion of Australian equity capital wherever possible.

External Trade. Australia's export income, depending mainly on wool and other rural products, is subject to wide variations because of changes in seasonal conditions and in overseas prices, both of which are beyond Australia's control. Substantial reserves of international currency are held in order to permit the maintenance of a reasonably stable level of imports, especially of the equipment and materials required for full employment and economic growth.

Direct control over imports (by volume) was abandoned in 1960, and thereafter the volume of imports moved up to record levels.

In international trade negotiations, Australia has been active in efforts to overcome impediments to trade in primary products and raw materials. Additionally, it has sought to cooperate with other exporting and importing countries in moderating excessive price fluctuations in commodities through international agreements.

Balance of Payments. Between 1949–1950 and 1964–1965, the value of Australian exports rose from $A1,210 million to $A2,586 million, and that of imports from $A1,076 million to $A2,754 million. The marked swings in Australia's fortunes in overseas trade were reflected in changes in the balance of payments.

BALANCE OF INTERNATIONAL PAYMENTS
($A million)

	1949–1950	1950–1951	1954–1955	1955–1956	1963–1964	1964–1965
Exports (f.o.b.)	1,210	1,976	1,556	1,576	2,740	2,586
Imports (f.o.b.)	1,076	1,484	1,694	1,640	2,251	2,754
Trade balance	134	492	−138	−64	489	−168
Other current items	224	282	378	406	539	586
Current balance	−90	+210	−516	−470	−50	−754
Net capital inflow	428	138	232	324	509	460
Movement in international reserves	+338	+348	−284	−146	+459	−294
Reserves at end of period	1,294	1,642	856	710	1,708	1,414

Commodities. Australia's major exports remain wool, wheat, minerals, and meat, and its principal imports, machinery, motor vehicles, and petroleum. However, the export base has been broadened, and a better balance has been achieved in commodity composition. As late as 1953–1954, wool and sheepskins accounted for 52 percent of all exports, with wheat 8 percent

LEADING EXPORTS, 1964–1965
($A million)

Wool	806
Wheat and flour	334
Other grains	57
Butter and cheese, milk and cream	101
Coal, iron and steel, copper, lead, gold, ores, and concentrates	283
Machines and machinery	42
Meat	260
Sugar	113
All other items	586
Total exports	**2,582**

LEADING IMPORTS, 1964–1965
($A million)

Motor vehicles and parts	253
Machines and machinery (agricultural, mining and metallurgical, textile working, and others)	507
Electrical machinery and appliances	139
Chemicals, drugs, and fertilizers	185
Aircraft	86
Plate and sheet, and other forms of iron and steel	103
Petroleum	206
Paper	53
Apparel, piece goods, and yarns	143
Plastic materials	62
Rubber	60
All other items	1,108
Total imports	**2,905**

and metals, metal manufacturers, and machines 8 percent. In 1964–1965 the picture was different: wool, although exported in greater quantity and earning slightly more, represented only 33 percent of total exports, with wheat and flour up to 13 percent, metals, metal manufactures, and machines at 12 percent, meat 11 percent, and miscellaneous items, 14 percent.

Markets. Traditionally, trade with the United Kingdom has been of major significance in the external commerce of Australia. Britain remains the single largest purchaser and supplier, but its predominance has declined from the period 1936–1939, when Britain supplied 40 percent of Australia's imports and received 56 percent of its exports, and the year 1948–1949 (51 percent of imports and 42 percent of exports) to the point where, in 1964–1965, only 20 percent of Australia's export trade was with Britain and 27 percent of imports came from that source.

An unremitting trade expansion and diversification drive has been under way for some years, aimed at spreading the pattern of Australia's export trade by opening new markets. Special emphasis has been placed on New Zealand, as a buyer of manufactured goods, and on Japan, as a market for wool, foodstuffs, and minerals. Elsewhere in the western Pacific and in the Indian Ocean area, significant markets have been developed, and whereas in 1938–1939 Asian lands took only 11 percent of Australia's exports, by the 1960's the proportion going there had trebled. In imports, the United States had moved up to second position, immediately behind Britain; at the same time, exports of meat to the United States had increased considerably.

TRADE WITH PRINCIPAL COUNTRIES, 1964–1965

	($A million, f.o.b.)	
	Exports	Imports
United Kingdom	516	761
Canada	40	117
Hong Kong	37	24
India	55	41
Malaysia	83	52
New Zealand	158	46
Other Commonwealth countries	166	111
Arabian states	14	104
China (mainland)	136	23
France	112	67
West Germany	84	161
Italy	85	51
Japan	441	259
United States	264	692
Other foreign countries	442	392
Total	**2,633**	**2,901**

RICHARD I. DOWNING
University of Melbourne

Transportation. Because of its vast expanse and the great distances from its principal commercial partners, Australia early in its history recognized the need for extensive transportation—local, transcontinental, and international. Its modern transport systems are centered on the industrial areas at the main seaports, which are linked by railroads, roads, coastal shipping services, and air. Australia leads the world in freight-ton miles and is second to the United States in passenger miles per capita.

Road construction was one of the main accomplishments of the early colonial governors of Australia, but by 1850 the available labor force had dwindled, and responsibility for road maintenance passed to local administrators. What had been by contemporary standards a good (though limited) road system then went into decline. As settlement spread inland, unpaved tracks carrying the bullock wagons of the settlers and the stagecoaches of Cobb & Co. became the principal channels of communication.

DAVID MOORE, FROM BLACK STAR

CAHILL EXPRESSWAY, connecting Sydney with its eastern suburbs, bypasses the central area of the city and eases traffic congestion on the Sydney Harbour Bridge.

Railway construction, which began in the 1850's, was accelerated after 1880 in order to reach rural resources beyond the confines of the closest settlement. In 1870 there had been only 1,000 miles (1,600 km) of railroad, but by 1890 there were 10,800 miles (17,400 km), the building of which had been financed largely by government loans raised in London. Expansion continued with sustained British investment until 1920. Thereafter, few routes were built, but services were intensified on existing routes.

After World War I, road construction reemerged as a major form of public works, and with the spectacular advance of the automotive industries road transport became an important factor, complementary to existing facilities in many respects and competitive in others. Later, air transport emerged as a new competitor, particularly in the passenger field, and as a valuable multipurpose facility in the remote interior and in the island territories.

From the earliest period of Australian history, shipping has been of special importance. The isolated nature of the Australian community made it particularly dependent on overseas shipping as a carrier of settlers and supplies and of agricultural and mineral exports. With the development of heavy industry and of the sugar industry, interstate shipping became important.

By the late 1960's, coastal shipping had lost most of its passenger trade and faced stiffer competition from road and rail transport in freight handling. However, more efficient methods for the handling of general cargo, including the packing of goods in standard containers to eliminate multiple handling and the use of roll-on/roll-off ships, coupled with a substantial increase in bulk cargoes moved by sea, pointed to a revival in interstate shipping. There are few internal waterways, and transportation on the Murray-Darling river system was significant only from 1880 to 1900.

In freight handling, sea transportation leads in ton-miles, but roads carry most of the tonnage.

FREIGHT TRANSPORTATION, 1962–1963

Means of trans-portation	Ton-miles ('000,000)	Percent of total ton-miles	Tons carried ('000)	Percent of tons carried
Sea	22,280	51.16	19,977	5.39
Road	11,611	26.67	273,034	73.62
Rail	9,624	22.10	77,783	20.97
Air	31	0.07	65	0.02
Total	43,546	100.00	370,859	100.00

In public passenger transportation, about two out of every three journeys are made by bus or streetcar. Nevertheless, this represents a sharp decline from records from the early 1950's. The number of passenger journeys by rail also fell sharply. The balancing factor has been the striking increase in the number of cars and motorcycles on the roads—up from 1,026,000 in 1952 to 2,810,000 in 1965.

PASSENGER MOVEMENT BY PUBLIC TRANSPORTATION, 1962–1963

Means of transportation	Number of journeys ('000)	Percent of total
Sea:		
Coastal ships	115	0.01
Ferries	17,028	1.26
Rail	465,329	34.51
Road (buses, trolleys, and streetcars)	863,043	64.01
Air	2,833	0.21

Railroads. The first steam-traction rail line in Australia was a 2-mile (3.2-km) route, extending from the heart of Melbourne to the suburb of Sandridge, which was opened to traffic on Sept. 12, 1854. Constructed by the Melbourne and Hobson's Bay Railway Company, it was 5 feet 3 inches (160 cm) in gauge. Carriages and wagons were delivered from England, but the locomotive was built locally; land and some money were granted by the governor of Victoria. While suburban lines were opened by various companies in Melbourne, these were amalgamated and, in 1878, bought out by the government. Outside the metropolis, private capital could not surmount the financial difficulties involved in rail construction, and the Victoria government had to take it in hand. Construction continued intermittently until the late 1920's. The total route mileage exceeded 4,400 (7,100 km) in the mid-1960's. The suburban system, progressively electrified since 1918 and converging on a single central terminal in Melbourne, covered some 445 route miles (716 km).

In New South Wales a 13-mile (21-km) line (4 feet 8.5 inches or 143.5 cm, in gauge) between Sydney and Parramatta was opened in 1855. Construction was begun by a private group, but the government, after advancing large sums, was forced to step in and complete the line. Another company began construction of a line in the Newcastle area, but by 1855 it, too, was in financial difficulties, and the government completed the line, which was opened in 1858. Construction was continued under government aegis, and by 1885 the mileage had increased to 1,732 (2,787 km). Connection was made with the Victorian and Queensland systems in the 1880's. In the mid-1960's, 6,055 route-miles (= 9,744 km) of line were in operation.

From the beginning, railroads in Queensland were built by the government, and for reasons of economy a gauge of 3 feet 6 inches (107 cm) was adopted. Construction of a line running 21 miles (34 km) inland from Ipswich began in 1863. A second line, extending from Rockhampton, was opened in 1867, and in 1875 a 4.5-mile (7-km) section was completed in Brisbane. By 1885, Queensland had 1,433 miles (2,306 km) of line. In the mid-1960's there were 5,954 miles (9,002 km) of government-owned railroads, as well as some private lines, most of very narrow gauge, for the haulage of sugarcane.

Construction of railroads in South Australia was first proposed in 1846. A company formed in London authorized a 7.5-mile (12-km) line to the harbor, but interest soon flagged. The government then voted funds for the work and in 1851 began a broad-gauge line that was the first government-owned railroad on British soil; it was opened in 1856. Other lines were constructed, the less important on a gauge of 3 feet 6 inches (107 cm), including a 478-mile (769-km) line north from Port Augusta to Oodnadatta, which was built sectionally between 1878 and 1891 and was intended to form part of a transcontinental line. It was extended to Stuart (now Alice Springs) in 1929 by the federal government. A 77-mile (124-km) line (3 feet 6 inches or 107 cm in gauge) south from Palmerston (now Darwin) was opened in 1888; in 1929 it was extended to Birdum. By 1885 the route mileage in South Australia was 1,203 (1,936 km), and connection with the Victorian system was made two years later. In the mid-1960's, route mileage of the state system was 2,514 (4,046 km), about 65 percent of which was at a gauge of 5 feet 3 inches (160 cm) and the remainder, at the smaller gauge of 3 feet 6 inches (107 cm).

The first railroad in Western Australia was a 12-mile (19-km) line opened in 1871 by a lumber company. Construction of other lines was initiated by the government, but work was slow, and by 1885 there were only 124 miles (200 km) of government-owned railroad, all of a gauge of 3 feet 6 inches (107 cm) for reasons of economy. Some private lines were acquired by the government, and by 1903 the total mileage in use was 1,424 (2,292 km). In the mid-1960's state-owned railways extended over 3,677 miles (5,917 km), but some privately owned lines still existed, of which a 277-mile (446-km) link of the Midland Railway Company was the most important.

In Tasmania, a broad-gauge line from Launceston to Deloraine was opened in 1871, but the operating company soon found itself in financial difficulties, and the line was taken over by the government. Subsequently, the line was converted to a gauge of 3 feet 6 inches (107 cm). A line between Hobart and Launceston, completed in 1876, was sold to the government in

1890. Extension of the Tasmanian system was slow. In the mid-1960's there were 500 miles (800 km) of government-owned line in operation. This represented a decline from the previous decade, due to the closing of several short lines.

The longest railroad constructed in Australia at one time is the federal government's 1,051-mile (1,691-km) Trans-Australian Railway of a gauge of 4 feet 8.5 inches (143.5 cm), which extends from Kalgoorlie in Western Australia to Port Augusta. Construction began in 1912, and the line was opened in 1917.

From 243 miles (391 km) in 1861, the route mileage of Australia's railroads increased to 13,551 miles (21,808 km) in 1901 and 26,202 (42,167 km) in 1921. Construction then tapered off, and the total was 27,956 miles (44,990 km) in 1941, after which some uneconomic lines were closed. Operating route mileage declined to 26,800 (43,129 km) in 1952, and over the next ten years an average of about 120 miles (193 km) of track a year was closed to traffic. In the mid-1960's there were less than 25,200 miles (40,550 km) of publicly owned lines in operation and about 650 miles (1,050 km) of private line in use.

Five rail gauges are in use in various parts of Australia, although three of these represent virtually the entire route mileage. The longest rail journey possible in the continent—from Meekatharra, Western Australia, to Dajarra, Queensland, a distance of 5,500 miles (8,850 km)—involves five breaks of gauge.

ROUTE MILEAGES OF GOVERNMENT-OWNED RAILROADS, 1964

System	GAUGE					
	5 feet 3 inches	4 feet 8.5 inches	3 feet 6 inches	2 feet 6 inches	2 feet	Total Mileage
State-owned systems:						
New South Wales	....	6,055	....	....	...	6,055
Victoria[1]	4,000	202	....	9	...	4,211
Queensland	....	69	5,855	....	30	5,954
South Australia	1,655	....	859	....	...	2,514
Western Australia	....	....	3,677	....	...	3,677
Tasmania	....	....	500	....	...	500
Commonwealth Railways[2]	....	1,330	922	....	...	2,252
Total	5,655	7,656	11,813	9	30	25,163

[1] Including 204 miles of 5-foot 3-inch gauge line extending into New South Wales. [2] Embracing mileages in South Australia (871), Western Australia (454), Northern Territory (490), and the Australian Capital Territory (5).

The confusion in gauges began in the earliest days of rail construction. In 1848, when New South Wales sent its proposals to London, a gauge of 4 feet 8.5 inches (143.5 cm) was approved, and the Sydney Railway Company intended using that gauge for its projected line. In 1850, however, the company's engineer advocated the adoption of a gauge of 5 feet 3 inches (160 cm). This was officially approved two years later, and the governors of Victoria and South Australia were so advised. Soon thereafter, however, a new engineer came out in favor of 4 feet 8.5 inches (143.5 cm), and in 1853 the company secured a new law sanctioning it. By this time the Melbourne and Hobson's Bay Railway Company and other companies had ordered rolling stock for a gauge of 5 feet 3 inches (160

cm), and Victoria and South Australia therefore decided to adhere to the broad gauge. In other colonies narrower gauges were introduced as an economy measure.

From 1897 on, many conferences were held on the question of unification of the various gauges. In 1921 an expert committee recommended adoption of a standard gauge of 4 feet 8.5 inches (143.5 cm), but the cost of conversion balked attempts to put its recommendation into practice. Finally, in 1957, preliminary work was begun on the construction of a 197-mile (317-km) standard-gauge line between Albury (New South Wales) and Melbourne, roughly paralleling the existing broad-gauge track; this section was opened to traffic in 1962. By the mid-1960's, construction was under way on a new standard-gauge section for the 380-mile (612-km) link between Kalgoorlie (Western Australia) and Perth and its ports of Fremantle and Kwinana, and the 255-mile (410-km) Port Pirie (South Australia)-Broken Hill section; a 130-mile (209-km) line from Port Pirie to Adelaide also was planned. On completion of this construction, every mainland capital would be accessible by the common 4-foot 8.5-inch (143-cm) track.

Tramways. In Australia, streetcars have been confined to the principal cities and larger provincial centers, and by the 1950's they were generally replaced by buses except in Melbourne. Almost all of the tramways are owned either by state governments or by independent governmental authorities.

A 1.7-mile (2.7-km) tramway, opened in 1862 between Sydney and Parramatta Junction, was soon abandoned, but another line was established in 1879 in the city proper. Horse, and later steam, traction was used, with double-decked cars. On some lines cable trams were used, the first electric tramway being opened in 1893. The Melbourne Omnibus Company, founded in 1869, proposed in 1878 to introduce streetcars in the city and its suburbs. Various municipalities subsequently set up a tramway trust, and by 1891 there were 43 miles (69 km) of cable lines and 4.5 miles (7 km) of horse tramways. Other municipalities then became active, and most of them introduced electric streetcars. The Melbourne and Metropolitan Tramways Board, established in 1915, extended and converted the network, and by the mid-1960's it was operating 156 miles (251 km) of double-track electric tramway services and over 100 route miles (161 km) of bus services. In other states private capital established tramway systems, but by the early 1900's they had become publicly owned.

Roads. The roads of Australia range in quality from primitive tracks to first-class highways. Of the 532,000 miles (856,000 km) of roads in the country used for general traffic, 208,000 miles (335,000 km) or 39 percent are surfaced (most with gravel or crushed stone, but some with bitumen or concrete) and the remainder are unsurfaced. The federal government levies taxes on fuel and tires as well as a sales tax on motor vehicles and parts, and it makes grants to the states for the construction and maintenance of roads.

In proportion to population, Australia is among the world's leading users of motor vehicles, with one for every 3.3 persons. In the mid-1960's, registered motor vehicles of all types numbered 3,216,000, including 2,720,000 cars, station wagons and "utilities," 399,000 trucks and smaller delivery vehicles, 14,000 buses, and 83,000 motorcycles. The size and carrying capacity of road vehicles have been limited to some extent by the quality of roads and the capacity of bridges, but larger vehicles have been introduced in recent years. They include refrigerated vans, bulk tankers, low loaders, and livestock transport. As a result of cooperation between railway authorities and road transport operators, piggy-back operations have extended, with complete trucks carried on railroad flattops.

In varying degree, state governments exercised control over both interstate and intrastate road transportation operations until 1954, when their regulations controlling interstate traffic were held unconstitutional. The result of this decision was a very rapid growth in the volume of goods moving by road between states. Intrastate transport is still subject to direct state control, but the levels of license fees and the conditions under which permits are granted to road haulers vary between the states.

Shipping. Interstate and intrastate shipping handles about 18,000,000 tons (16,329,000 metric tons) of cargo a year. In the mid-1960's, there were 125 vessels of over 200 gross tons (180 metric tons) engaged in the coastal trade, with an aggregate gross tonnage of about 475,000 (431,000 metric tons). Of this fleet, 105 ships were interstate vessels (either Australian or New Zealand owned) and the remaining 20 were smaller vessels operated on intrastate runs.

A noticeable trend in coastal shipping has been a decline in the tonnage of general cargo and an increase in ironstone, limestone, petroleum products, and other bulk cargoes, which by the mid-1960's represented more than three fourths of the total. Improved handling methods, including use of standard containers, were introduced to win back a larger share of the general cargo.

Between 1952 and 1964 the number of entrances and clearances (combined) at Australian ports by overseas vessels rose from 4,136 to 7,601. Over the same period, overseas cargo discharged rose from 14,400,000 tons (13,063,000 metric tons) to 27,700,000 tons (25,129,000 metric tons), and cargo shipped out increased from 5,700,000 tons (5,171,000 metric tons) to 22,-400,000 tons (20,321,000 metric tons). Ships of United Kingdom registry are the largest factor in overseas commerce, carrying 27 percent of the tonnage entering Australia; other Commonwealth countries, with New Zealand and Hong Kong predominating, account for 5 percent; foreign flag carriers discharge almost 60 percent of the total tonnage, with Norwegian, Greek, Liberian, and Japanese ships of particular significance.

Airlines. *Domestic Airways.* After World War I, Australia adopted measures for the development of civil air transportation similar to those of other countries. A civil aviation branch, formed in 1920 as part of the Department of Defense, promoted air services to remote inland areas. Although large initial subsidies were required to establish these services, their operation proved highly successful. Interurban services, which were not subsidized, had to await improvements in aircraft design to operate profitably, and it was not until 1939 that they accounted for the bulk of domestic air traffic. The principal operator, Australian National Airways (ANA), expanded its operations to such an extent during World War II that by 1945 it car-

ried about 80 percent of all domestic air traffic. In addition, it had secured financial control over a number of the remaining airlines.

In 1945 the Labour government attempted to secure a government monopoly over domestic air services. An act passed by Parliament in that year gave the Australian National Airlines Commission exclusive rights to operate interstate and territorial airline services, but these rights in respect of interstate services were subsequently disallowed by the High Court of Australia. The government then established Trans-Australia Airlines (TAA) as a domestic airline operator on a competitive basis. In 1951 the Liberal-Country party government announced a domestic airline policy that would favor neither government nor private monopoly, and measures to secure equitable competition between TAA and ANA were enacted. Despite the economies of rationalization, however, the two lines remained barely profitable. As a result, ANA approached the government in 1957 to suggest a merger with TAA; this proposal was rejected, but subsequently ANA was taken over by another private line, Ansett Airways, and the combined airline of Ansett-ANA was larger than its government-owned competitor. The Ansett group already had a number of intrastate airlines, and subsequently it took over others. By the mid-1960's its entire fleet totaled more than 100 aircraft, compared with about 70 owned by TAA. Both major operators introduced jet airliners on their main trunk routes in 1964. Small independent feeder-type airlines operate also in the Northern Territory, Western Australia, and Papua-New Guinea.

The domestic airlines function under complicated legal restraints. Under the constitution, the federal government has no general right of regulation, but in practice the Department of Civil Aviation enjoys complete authority in all matters relating to air safety. The volume of domestic passenger air traffic moved up from 722 million passenger-miles (1,829,000 passengers) in 1952 to more than 1,600 million passenger-miles (3,763,000 passengers) in 1965. Freight moved up more slowly, from 26 million ton-miles in 1952 to 34 million ton-miles in 1956, but Australia retained its world lead in freight-ton miles per capita.

International Services. Australia was the target for a series of long-distance flights after World War I. In 1919 the Australian government offered a prize of £10,000 for an England-Australia flight. Many attempts were made, but only one machine, a Vickers Vimy whose crew was led by Sir Ross Macpherson Smith and Sir Keith Macpherson Smith, fulfilled all conditions and finished within the stipulated 30-day limit. In 1926, Sir Alan Cobham flew from England to Australia in 40 days and returned in 34; two years later, Capt. Herbert J.L. Hinkler cut the time to 16 days in the first solo flight; and in 1930, Amy Johnson made a solo flight in 19 days. In the 12 months ending in June 1934, there were 10 successful flights, the most spectacular being the solo, 7¼-day flight of Sir Charles Edward Kingsford Smith. By this time the route had been well surveyed, and a London-Melbourne race was practicable. Prizes (£10,000 for the speed section and £2,000 for the handicap) were offered, and 20 machines left London in October 1934. A Comet piloted by C.W.A. Scott and T. Campbell-Black made the flight to Melbourne in 70 hours 54 minutes. Scott and Black took first place in both sections, but since the rules prevented the award of both prizes to one entrant, the prize for the handicap section was awarded to K.D. Parmentier and J.J. Moll, who, flying a DC-2 and representing KLM Royal Dutch Airlines, were in second place in that section.

Since 1931, experimental mail flights had been made by Imperial Airways from London to Darwin, with Queensland and Northern Territory Aerial Services, Ltd. (Qantas) taking over at Darwin. The interests of the two lines were linked in 1934, and Qantas became Qantas Empire Airways. It operated a weekly service to Singapore, which became triweekly in 1938. By 1959, Qantas operated four flights weekly in each direction between Sydney and London via Singapore and the Middle East. The 1,200-mile (1,931-km) crossing of the Tasman Sea to New Zealand, which presented many hazards, was first flown in 1928, but the regular service by Tasman Empire Airways (owned jointly by the Australian and New Zealand governments) did not begin until 1940. In 1928 Kingsford Smith made his historic transpacific flight in the *Southern Cross*, a trimotor Fokker, with Charles Ulm (Australian) as copilot and two Americans as navigator and radio operator, the 7,389-mile (11,891-km) flight from Oakland, Calif., to Brisbane occupying 83 hours 38 minutes flying time. The first regular transpacific service from Australia to San Francisco, Calif., was operated in 1946 by ANA under charter to British Commonwealth Pacific Airlines (owned jointly by the British, New Zealand, and Australian governments). In 1954, Australia took over the other interests in BCPA, and the route was operated thereafter by Qantas, which in 1958 extended it via New York to London. Jets were introduced on the transpacific service in 1959 and subsequently on other international routes. Meanwhile, in 1952, Qantas opened a route across the Indian Ocean to South Africa. In addition, Qantas operates regular services to Japan and Hong Kong via the Philippines, to New Zealand, to New Caledonia, and to Mexico via Tahiti. In the mid-1960's, the Qantas international network covered more than 72,000 route miles (116,000 km) and carried some 350,000 passengers a year.

Non-Australian airlines that connect Australia with other countries are Pan American World Airways, Air India, Air New Zealand, Alitalia, British Overseas Airways Corporation, Canadian Pacific Air Lines, KLM Royal Dutch Airlines, Lufthansa, Philippine Air Lines, South African Airways, and UTA French Airlines.

Communications—Postal, Telegraph, and Telephone Services. The official postal history of Australia began in 1803 with regulations issued by the governor of New South Wales fixing the charges for private letters carried by boatmen between Sydney and Parramatta. A step toward the establishment of an organized postal service was the appointment in 1809 of a postmaster in Sydney. Hobart opened a post office at about the same time. Brisbane followed in 1824, Perth in 1827, Adelaide in 1837, and Melbourne in 1837. After 1825 post offices were also established at the principal rural centers, and mail services were extended throughout the settled areas. The six colonial postal administrations each issued distinctive stamps, the first issues being made by New South Wales and Victoria in 1850, Tasmania in 1853, Western Australia in 1854, South Aus-

tralia in 1855, and Queensland in 1860. After federation the separate states continued to issue stamps until 1913, when designs for the Commonwealth were released. The Australian colonies together constituted a member of the Universal Postal Union from 1891, Australia being admitted as a separate member country in 1907.

The first telegraph line for public use was erected between Melbourne and the suburb of Williamstown in 1854. Sydney and Melbourne were linked in 1858, and Adelaide soon thereafter. In 1872 a line was built from Adelaide to connect with the overseas cable terminating at Darwin. Since the laying of the Pacific cable connecting Australia with New Zealand and Canada (1902) and the establishment of radio communication with other parts of the world (1927), the overland telegraph line has lost its original significance, but it is still used as part of the communications system.

The Post and Telegraph Act of 1901 established a central administration to control postal and telegraph services on a national scale. There were then more than 6,000 post offices of various types; by the 1960's the total exceeded 8,200. Airmail services reach all parts of the mainland and neighboring islands. No extra charge is made for airmail to isolated areas, and letters to and from Tasmania are flown across Bass Strait at ordinary postal rates. Approximately 90 percent of all overseas letters are carried by air.

Telephones were introduced into Australia in 1878. Privately owned exchanges were opened in Melbourne and Brisbane in 1880 and in Sydney in 1881, and a government exchange was established in Sydney in the following year. In 1907, Melbourne and Sydney were linked by telephone, and in 1912 the first automatic exchange was opened at Geelong, Victoria. Telephone communication was established between Sydney and Brisbane in 1923, and in 1930 a trunk line was completed between Perth and Adelaide. With the laying of a telephone cable between the mainland and Tasmania in 1936 the interstate communication system was complete.

In the mid-1960's there were more than 2,-800,000 telephones in the country, or approximately one for every four persons. A coaxial cable linked Canberra, Melbourne, and Sydney; other main trunk lines were equipped with carrier-wave multichannel systems, and some of them operated over radio links.

Besides collecting, dispatching, and delivering mail, transmitting and delivering telegrams, and providing telephone service, the Postmaster General's Department conducts a money order and postal note business, provides all teleprinter services, and plays a major part in the provision of radio and television broadcasting services. It also performs many tasks for other government agencies, including the payment of federal pensions and the transaction of savings bank business.

Radio and Television. Radio and television services in Australia are operated under the Broadcasting and Television Act, separate services in both fields being provided by the Australian Broadcasting Commission and by interests with commercially sponsored backing. The Australian Broadcasting Control Board supervises the licensing of all stations and transmission standards and watches the public interest in matters of program content. Most of the revenue for the national services is provided by radio listeners' licenses and television viewers' licenses. In the mid-1960's the former numbered almost 2 million and the latter over 1.6 million; there were also more than 430,000 combined licenses.

The Australian Broadcasting Commission provides the programs of the national services, while transmission facilities are the responsibility of the Postmaster General's Department. In each capital city the commission maintains an orchestra of high standard, which provides regular broadcast programs and also presents public symphony concerts. Leading conductors are brought to Australia by the commission, and concerts by celebrities are arranged on an extensive scale. The commission itself gathers the news, which it presents eight times a day. Commercial broadcasting stations are operated under licenses granted and renewed by the postmaster general after consultation with the Broadcasting Control Board. The 110 commercial radio stations are linked in a federation that acts for them in matters of common concern. Some of the stations form networks, and others join together from time to time to suit advertising commitments. News broadcasts by commercial stations are provided by arrangement with newspapers.

After the first television stations were opened in Melbourne and Sydney in 1956, the television industry grew rapidly. Within 10 years more than 70 stations were broadcasting; of these, 30 were operated by the Australian Broadcasting Commission (including one in each of the capital cities) and 42 by commercial interests.

Programming tends to follow the pattern prevailing on commercial stations in the United States, with all stations drawing heavily on imported screenplays, detective mysteries, and Western-type dramas. Commercial stations devote considerably less time to cultural aspects than do the state-owned stations.

The shortwave overseas radio service of the Australian Broadcasting Commission, known as Radio Australia, broadcasts more than 40 hours a day through several transmitters and has programs in English and seven foreign languages. The programs, directed to nearer neighbors in Asia and the Pacific area, provide news and information as well as entertainment.

Newspapers and Magazines. A free and vigorous press has been a feature of Australian life since quite early in the settlement of the country. Although official policy and requirements were reflected in the first newspaper—the four-page Sydney *Gazette* issued by the government printer, George Howe, in 1803—an independent newspaper, the *Australian*, was published by William Charles Wentworth in 1824. Wentworth clashed with Governor Sir Ralph Darling, who in 1827 sought to enact a law under which newspapers could be issued only if they were licensed. This act was not certified, and an alternative act imposing a prohibitive stamp duty was not enforced. Henceforth the press was free from government control, and editors could print whatever they chose within the bounds of the laws of libel. The *Australian* ceased publication in 1850, and the oldest surviving newspapers in the country are the Sydney *Morning Herald* (founded in 1831) and the Melbourne *Herald* (1840). Ten newspapers were in existence in New South Wales by 1840, and in that year the Sydney *Morning Herald* became the first paper to be published daily. Political writing was a feature of the newspapers of this period, and the radical press, which advocated Chartist principles, was strong from 1848

to 1858. Under David Syme the radical Melbourne *Age* achieved extraordinary political power from 1856 to 1900; by the 1950's the paper had veered to liberal conservatism. Its great rival, the *Argus* (founded in 1846), once a newspaper of world standing, closed in 1957.

Ownership of most city newspapers has been transferred from families to public companies. While political comment tends to favor conservative groups, no newspaper is directly the mouthpiece of a political party. Each paper jealously guards its right to an independent point of view, and between elections there is frequently strong criticism of the government. Circulation has increased steadily since World War II, but the number of newspapers has declined. Among provincial papers there has been a trend toward amalgamation; at the same time major technical advances have been made, and local or regional news is featured as a counter to the metropolitan dailies. Smaller communities are served by papers published once, twice, or three times a week.

Australia ranks fifth among the nations of the world in per capita circulation of daily newspapers. In the 1960's there were approximately 640 papers, of which 56 were dailies and 7 were Sunday newspapers, all with large circulations. The over-all breakdown shows a total of 16 metropolitan dailies, more than 450 provincial newspapers (mainly weeklies), and more than 160 suburban newspapers (almost all weeklies). Among the dailies the *Sun News-Pictorial*, a Melbourne tabloid founded in 1923, had the highest circulation —620,000 copies daily. *The Australian*, established in 1964 as a national daily, is published in Canberra and printed simultaneously in both Sydney and Melbourne.

The leading newspapers maintain bureaus in New York and London and representatives in other centers to supplement the basic news service provided by Australian Associated Press–Reuter, which gives world cable coverage. For Australian news, country papers as well as some metropolitan dailies subscribe to Australian United Press.

Periodicals cover a wide range. Those with the largest circulations are the *Australian Women's Weekly*, founded in 1933, which publishes 830,000 copies each edition, and the Australian edition of *The Reader's Digest*. News reviews include Australian editions of *Time* and *Newsweek* and the locally owned weekly, the *Bulletin*. Among the more than 1,300 publications directed toward special-interest groups those dealing with trade and commerce and associations and organizations are most numerous. Technical, scientific, educational, and professional interests; religion and sports; and rural, foreign-group, and community matters also are well represented.

Federal Economic Policy. The Commonwealth Parliament has power to make laws with respect only to subjects specified in the federal constitution, residual powers being reserved to the six state parliaments. The more important economic subjects specified for Commonwealth control are: trade and commerce with other countries and among the states; taxation; currency, coinage, and legal tender; banking; insurance; weights and measures; immigration and emigration; and conciliation and arbitration for the prevention and settlement of industrial disputes extending beyond the limits of any one state. In addition the Commonwealth can make grants, with or without conditions, to the states.

The large financial powers of the Commonwealth and a number of judgments by the High Court of Australia sympathetic to an extension of other Commonwealth powers have led to a substantial degree of centralization of economic power since the establishment of the federation in 1901. In particular the Financial Agreement of 1927 gives the Commonwealth virtually complete control of borrowing by states, by local governments, and by semigovernmental authorities, and the Commonwealth's uniform tax legislation of 1942 has won it a complete monopoly of the right to levy income tax in addition to its exclusive rights over most commodity taxes. As a result the states have become almost wholly dependent on the Commonwealth for all their revenues.

Nevertheless, and especially because of the provision that interstate commerce shall be absolutely free, there remain serious constitutional (not to mention political) obstacles to the implementation by the Commonwealth government of an effective economic policy. While the Commonwealth government can vary all taxes (including tariffs) as it wishes, can license imports, can usually set an upper limit to public borrowing, and can control credit, banking, and monetary policy, it cannot directly undertake expenditure in the many fields reserved to state governments, and it cannot impose direct controls over prices, wages, employment, production, and distribution.

R.M. YOUNGER
Author of "The Changing World: Australia"

Bibliography

Amstey, Cecil E., and Hoskins, W.M.G., *Australian Business Principles and Practice* (Sydney 1965).
Australia, Forestry and Timber Bureau, *Statement on Forestry in Australia, 1951–1955* (Canberra 1956).
Blainey, Geoffrey, *The Rush That Never Ended: A History of Australian Mining* (Melbourne 1964).
Bishop, Dwight R., *Recent Trends in Australia's Livestock Industry*, U.S. Department of Agriculture, Foreign Agricultural Service, M-134 (Washington 1962).
Condliffe, John Bell, *The Development of Australia* (Sydney 1964).
Davidson, F.G., *The Industrialization of Australia*, 3d ed. (Melbourne 1962).
Downing, Richard L., *National Income and Social Accounts*, 9th ed. (Melbourne 1965).
Ellis, Malcolm H., *The Beef Shorthorn in Australia* (Sydney 1932).
Foenander, Orwell de R., *Industrial Conciliation and Arbitration in Australia* (Sydney 1959).
Gifford, John L.K., and Wood, J. Vivian, *Australian Banking* (Brisbane 1955).
Holden, Willis S., *Australia Goes to Press* (Detroit 1961).
Hughes, Helen, *The Australian Iron and Steel Industry 1848–1962* (Melbourne 1964).
Hunter, Alex G., ed., *The Economics of Australian Industry* (Melbourne 1963).
Meade, James E., and others, *Development in Monetary Policy* (Sydney 1956).
Munz, Hirsch, *The Australian Wool Industry* (Melbourne 1964).
Newell, Hugh H., *Road Engineering and Its Development in Australia, 1788–1938* (Sydney 1938).
Nicholson, Donald F., *Australia's Trade Relations* (Melbourne 1955).
Roughley, Theodore C., *Fish and Fisheries of Australia* (Sydney 1951).
Shann, E.O.G., *An Economic History of Australia* (Melbourne 1963).
Shaw, Alan G.L., *The Economic Development of Australia*, 4th ed. (London 1964).
Wadham, Sir Samuel M., and others, *Land Utilization in Australia*, 4th ed. (New York 1964).
Walker, Kenneth F., *Industrial Relations in Australia* (Cambridge, Mass., 1956).
Wedlick, Lance, *Fishing in Australia* (Sydney 1962).
Wilkes, John, ed., *Australia's Transport Crisis* (Sydney 1956).
Woodward, O.H., *A Review of the Broken Hill Lead-Silver-Zinc Industry*, 2d ed. (Sydney 1965).

AUSTRALIAN NEWS AND INFORMATION BUREAU

TENNIS COACHING SCHOOLS, found throughout Australia, have contributed greatly to making the country one of the leading tennis-playing nations of the world.

4. Way of Living

To many residents of Australia, as well as to those who have never visited the country, the prototype of the Australian is a tall, rangy, sun-browned countryman with wide-brimmed hat and faithful horse and dog. Even if this picture were at one time accurate, it is so no longer. In reality the average Australian lives in a predominantly urban society, either in a crowded coastal city or in the narrow strip of land extending down the east coast and along the south coast of the continent. The hinterland is sparsely populated. Perhaps the only thing the idealized prototype and the statistical reality have in common is that both manifest an egalitarian attitude toward their fellow men and impose this attitude on the community in which they live.

Australians live in a relatively classless society. Although standards of living cover a considerable range, an extensive system of social services has lessened the pressures of poverty and personal hardship at one end of the scale, while a high income tax, considerable legislative control over commercial enterprise, and a well-developed and aggressive trade union movement have limited financial prizes at the other. Nevertheless, the egalitarianism of the community is more obvious in the Australian's attitude than in any objective assessment of the financial, social, or political circumstances of the country. Throughout Australia there is a settled dislike of social pretension and personal affectation and there is also a strong tendency to support the underdog, even if he deserves to be the underdog. This attitude fosters self-confidence, self-reliance, and individual initiative, while it tends at the same time to place a high value on comradeship and on unaffected, cordial, and equal collaboration between individuals. It makes for personally generous and hospitable relationships and generates a social mobility akin to that in the United States and Canada.

No well-defined high society has emerged in Australia nor are there many families of continuing social or political prominence. The squatters, as the great ranchmen are called, might well have formed such a social group, but they did not develop traditions of community responsibility or produce many political leaders. The same is true of the other financially privileged groups. Indeed, only among the professional groups, and to a lesser degree among the senior branches of the civil service, are traditions of community service to be found, but among these groups high ethical standards and levels of skills have come to be expected.

Considering its geographic magnitude and its climatic diversity, there is a surprising uniformity about life in Australia. In the north, of course, tropical conditions have led to an even more informal dress and a more leisurely, relaxed approach to life than is to be found in the more temperate south, but such regional differences are slight. Even the distinctive broad *a* and nasal consonants of Australian speech have a sameness throughout the continent, and the only noticeable distinction is a product of education rather than of geography, the more highly educated being less typically Australian in their speech.

One facet of this egalitarian society is an exaggerated suspicion of both the integrity and the competence of persons in positions of political, industrial, or social prominence. Likewise, there is a general disinclination to trust experts, as well as a preference to rely in matters of government and commerce on practical experience rather than on academic training or specialized qualifications. This suspicious attitude is not, however, extended to the prominent sportsman—footballer, cricketer, jockey, tennis player—who tends to receive generous adulation.

Sport, indeed, plays an important part in the Australian way of life. There is greater participation in sporting activities than in other countries, and skill in one or another sport tends to be expected of everyone. The climate is generally favorable to outdoor sports, and a communitywide stress on technical skill has led to the provision of excellent facilities and, in relation to population, to remarkable successes in international competition. Although hours of work are comparable with those in North America and Britain, greater stress is placed on leisure.

The egalitarian attitude in Australia has resulted in a stress on individual freedom and a resistance to authority and to any extensive political regulation of life. Thus in World War I the Australians twice voted strongly against conscription, although they enlisted for war service to such an extent as to yield a higher proportion of the community in the armed services than most other countries produced by conscription. In World War II they rejected conscription for overseas service and yet sent rather large units of volunteers overseas. Considerable government control is, however, exercised and accepted over primary production and industrial and commercial enterprise. The acceptance of this type of control of individual enterprise may reflect desire to improve working conditions, limit the amount of effort needed to achieve reasonable standards of living, and guarantee to all a minimum standard of life.

In Australia the trade union movement is of great significance politically as well as industrially. Politically it expresses itself through the Labour party, which is more subject to trade union influence and control than is its British counterpart. Although Australia was in the vanguard of political experimentation with secret and compulsory voting, invalid, old-age, and unemployment payments, and compulsory education, the general attitude of the Australian to political and community affairs is pragmatic. He tends to judge political suggestions and developments by the test of practicality rather than by concordance with any generalized political philosophy. This attitude has been described as "politics without doctrine," and all the major political parties share in it. The Labour party has nominally espoused a platform with many left-wing planks, but its actual political activities have tended toward day-to-day improvements in working conditions and the achievement of social security throughout the country. The same pragmatism is to be seen in the principal right-wing parties, which also have eschewed abstract political philosophy and have manifested social purposes similar to those of the Labour party, while giving greater support to the businessman and the back-country man.

In his attitude toward international affairs the Australian has been moving steadily away from the parochial outlook that was dominant until the 1950's. Reluctantly the average citizen has come to an awareness of the implications of Australia's geographic isolation from kindred Western communities and its occupancy of a sparsely populated continent immediately south of overcrowded and nationally self-conscious Asian lands. Concern over "pressures from the North" has led to reassessment of the national role. One result has been a closer identification with and understanding of American views and policies. However, as in national affairs, there has been a marked tendency to avoid a doctrinaire approach in international affairs.

Even in his religious life the Australian tends to avoid doctrinal disputations. Relatively little bigotry exists, there is a considerable degree of collaboration among the churches in charitable and social service activities, and a man's religious belief is considered to be his own affair. There is little public discussion of beliefs. This attitude gives religious life a generally noninstitutional, personally friendly, and tolerant quality in which tradition and reverence for church hierarchies play a minor part.

In general the fundamental liberties and freedoms are not constitutionally guaranteed or

SKIING among the eucalyptus trees at Thredbo, a leading resort in the Snowy Mountains. Sports-minded Australians participate in year-round outdoor activities.

SAILING is a popular sport in Australia's coastal waters. Here, a variety of boats in Sydney harbor are silhouetted against the famous Sydney Harbour Bridge.

protected in Australia, although they are protected by the traditions of the courts and the political and social attitudes of the people. One of the few constitutionally protected freedoms, however, is that of religious belief and exercise, and there is a constitutional prohibition of governmental discrimination based on religious belief. For the most part, the churches exercise neither a direct nor a great influence on political life.

Housing in Australia is influenced by the Australian's firm belief in his right to his own block of land and house. In the cities and in the country, among both the more and the less financially privileged groups, there is a remarkably high level of home ownership. Much time and attention is given to the care of gardens.

The position of women in the Australian community deserves special consideration. When Australia ceased to be a penal colony, it became a frontier grazing society with a dash of gold rush. In such a community individual enterprise and self-reliance were considered the most desirable personal qualities, and the friendly collaboration of "mates" was a community need. This was what was expected of men, however, not of women. While a man was expected to demonstrate these qualities in all his activities, and particularly in his equal relationships with other men, the task of the wife was that of making a home in what was for her a difficult and lonely environment. Whatever the causes, it is true that the social freedom and vigor of the Australian way of life are more noticeable among men than among women, and that women play a lesser role in political, professional, and community affairs than one might expect in an otherwise egalitarian society. Although women are playing a greater part in professional and community life and are employed increasingly in commercial activities, their role in the community has remained within the home more than has that of their North American counterparts. This position of women in community life can even be observed in social gatherings. The visitor from overseas attending a party in an Australian home is often surprised to find the sexes segregated, the men herding together to discuss sport, politics, and business affairs, while the women gather separately for domestic chatter.

In recent years male fashions have followed American trends. The once characteristic attire of gray trousers and sports coat has been largely replaced, and a greater formality is apparent. In Sydney, Brisbane, and Perth many younger men abandon the jacket in summer, but in the southern capitals more formal habits prevail. Women have developed a smart casualness in their dress that suits their outdoor life and the lack of rigid convention in social attitudes and behaviors.

Australians are among the world's greatest meat eaters. In the backcountry it is by no means uncommon for meat to be served at all three daily meals, seven days a week. Both in the home and in many restaurants grilled steak and eggs figure prominently in the menu. Australians also are credited with an unusually high per capita consumption of beer. However, the large-scale immigration has had a noticeable effect on eating habits. Newcomers from central and southern Europe have brought with them eating and drinking patterns entirely different from those that developed within Australia, and in the main cities foreign restaurants serving exotic dishes and beverages are well patronized. Steadily rising prices for meat have also helped to change diet habits in many families.

By the mid-1960's about every ninth person living in Australia had come from abroad. This massive immigration appeared to be enriching the Australian way of life and to be rendering it more diverse and culturally stimulating at a time of rising living standards based on advancing prosperity and greater spending power throughout the community.

NORVAL MORRIS, *University of Adelaide*

Bibliography

Boyd, Robin G.P., *The Australian Ugliness* (Melbourne 1963).

Caiger, George, ed., *The Australian Way of Life* (Melbourne 1953).

Clarke, Colin, *Australian Hopes and Fears* (London 1958).

Davis, A.F., ed., *Australian Society* (Melbourne 1965).

McLeod, Alan, *The Pattern of Australian Culture* (Ithaca, N.Y., 1963).

Palmer, Vance, *National Portraits*, 3d ed. (Melbourne 1954).

Phillips, Arthur A., *Australian Tradition: Studies in a Colonial Culture* (Melbourne 1958).

Ward, Russell B., *The Australian Legend* (Melbourne 1960).

5. Religion

The Australian Constitution guarantees religious freedom. It provides that there shall be no established church and no law imposing any religious observances or prohibiting the free exercise of any religion. In addition no religious test may be required as a qualification for federal employment.

Religious Affiliation. According to the 1961 census 88.2 percent of the population of Australia acknowledges affiliation with some Christian church, and about 0.6 percent is Jewish.

RELIGIOUS AFFILIATION, 1961 CENSUS

Religious group	Number	Percent of total
Church of England	3,668,931	34.8
Roman Catholics	2,620,000	24.6
Methodists	1,076,395	10.2
Presbyterians	976,528	9.3
Other Christians (including Lutheran, Greek Orthodox, Baptists, and other denominational groups)	932,272	8.9
Jews	59,343	0.6
Others[1]	1,174,717	11.6
	10,508,186	100.0

[1] Including 1,102,930 persons who did not state their religion.

Australians of English or Scottish descent are generally Protestants, while those of Irish descent, as well as many recent European settlers, are mainly Roman Catholics. The only substantial changes in the over-all pattern of affiliation since World War II—rises in the proportions of Catholic, Lutheran, and Greek Orthodox adherents—have been caused by migration. Protestants form the great majority of the population in all states and territories and in practically every local area, so that representatives of the leading religious groups often meet in a single group. In the more remote areas, Protestant churches are virtually nondenominational, although efforts aimed at developing a united Protestant church have not achieved success. Roman Catholic schools are widespread, and in the larger cities each Protestant denomination supports schools giving religious instruction that supplement the secular state schools. The various universities all have residential colleges of the principal denominations.

Historical Development. The first Anglican service in Australia was conducted by the chaplain of the First Fleet on Feb. 3, 1788, within a few days of its arrival, and the first church was opened in 1793. The Rev. Samuel Marsden, who arrived in Sydney in the following year, was a notable early figure who gained distinction for his work both as a practical farmer and as a clergyman. At first the Church of England in Australia was under the control of the bishop of London. Then, in 1814, it was transferred to the bishop of Calcutta, and 10 years later it became an archdeaconry. The colony was raised to a separate see in 1836, when William Grant Broughton became the first bishop. Tasmania became a separate diocese in 1842, and by 1847 four separate sees had been established on the mainland. Subsequently, these also were divided. Meanwhile, the possibility of the Church of England's becoming the state church had been ruled out by a law of 1836 that placed all religions on an equal footing. After 1905 the question of reconstructing the Anglican Church of Australia on an autonomous basis was discussed in successive synods, and in 1962 the title "Church of England in Australia" was adopted.

The first Roman Catholic Mass in Australia was celebrated in 1803. In 1817, Father Jeremiah O'Flynn arrived with the title of prefect apostolic, but since he had not obtained official permission, he was deported in the following year. Protests in England resulted in the sending of two officially recognized priests in 1820. The senior of these, Father John Joseph Therry, came to be regarded as the founder of Roman Catholicism in Australia, although it was Father William Bernard Ullathorne (who arrived in 1833 as vicar general) who put the church on a sound footing.

The first Presbyterian free settlers were established on the Hawkesbury River in 1802, and although a church was built, no minister was appointed until 1831. The dominant figure was John Dunmore Lang, who arrived in 1823 and played a conspicuous role both in the Presbyterian Church and in public life, making a deep and lasting impression by his forthright advocacy in politics, education, and journalism, as well as in religion. An outstanding figure of the 20th century was the Rev. Dr. John Flynn, who in his work with the Australian Inland Mission was inspirational in founding the Flying Doctor Service, which now operates over two thirds of the continent to bring medical comfort to settlers in remote areas.

Methodism dates from 1812, and the first Methodist chapel from 1817. A Baptist preacher arrived in 1831, and the first church was established in 1836.

The first Jewish place of worship was opened in Sydney in 1831. There are now synagogues in all the larger cities.

R.M. YOUNGER
Author of "The Changing World: Australia"

Further Reading: Border, Ross, *Church and State in Australia, 1788–1872* (London 1962); Robinson, James C., *The Free Presbyterian Church in Australia* (Melbourne 1947); Suttor, T.L., *Hierarchy and Democracy in Australia, 1788–1870: The Formation of Australian Catholicism* (Melbourne 1965).

R.G. MENZIES BUILDING of the Library of the Australian National University, Canberra, houses some 350,000 volumes. It was opened by Queen Elizabeth II in 1963.

6. Education

Although Australia is not densely populated, it has a wide range of educational institutions that provide instruction resembling, both in variety and in standard, that found in other English-speaking countries. Between 1872 and 1893 all six colonies introduced universal and compulsory education, and illiteracy is therefore almost nonexistent. Australia has pioneered methods of teaching children living in isolated areas. Chief among these methods is education by correspondence, to which has been added the use of radio not only for regular school broadcasts but also for contact with individual pupils over the network of communications associated with the Flying Doctor Service.

In secondary and higher education the situation is not so strong as it is in the primary field, and the proportion of the population continuing its formal education after the age of 14 or 15 years is lower than it is in the United States. Educational standards are high, however, at secondary and higher levels, and facilities for higher education in both general and technical fields have been expanded in response to the needs of industry.

Public Education. Along with other social services public education was left in the hands of the six states when the federal government was constituted in 1901. Each of the six state systems operates under a professional head, who is responsible to the state minister of education, and a highly specialized staff. All administrators and teachers in the system are public servants with permanent tenure of office. With minor exceptions the state departments of education train their own teachers.

In marked contrast to all other English-speaking countries, there is no local participation in the control of the public schools or in the appointment of teachers. Each Australian state system is centralized to a high degree. Two states, New South Wales and Queensland, have set up regional directorships, but this has resulted in improved services in the outlying areas rather than in any transfer of autonomy for the regions involved. Since all public school expenditure is derived from the consolidated revenues of the state, even the large cities play no part in controlling schools or in deciding what schools will be established in their areas. Voluntary associations of parents and citizens do raise considerable sums to assist the schools in obtaining supplementary equipment, however, and in all states officially recognized lay committees are associated with each school and are given minor powers of action and of expenditure.

Although the federal government has no constitutional responsibility for conducting schools, it has steadily increased its participation in matters related to education. The first formal body, the Universities Commission, was set up in 1943 to organize postwar education and training for ex-service men and women. The Education Act of 1945 gave permanent form to the commission and also established the Commonwealth Office of Education, which became the central coordinating body for Australia's contact with UNESCO and other international groups in the field of education.

An innovation of the early 1950's was the introduction of a unique system of instruction by two-way radio—the School of the Air—designed to supplement the comprehensive system of education by correspondence for children in remote sections of the country. By the late 1960's ten schools-of-the-air were operating throughout the hinterland in conjunction with the radio facilities of the Flying Doctor Service. In 1963 the federal government undertook to provide aid to the teaching of science in all secondary schools. In addition it provided thousands of scholarships for students and made supplemental grants to the states to assist them in meeting the higher costs incurred in education generally.

Government schools enroll more than 75 percent of all schoolgoers, and more than one fourth of all expenditure by state governments is devoted to education in some form. The ratio of students to teachers is about 29:1. Enrollments in the various states follow the same general pattern as the population breakdown, with New South Wales having one third of the total.

AUSTRALIAN NEWS AND INFORMATION BUREAU

GRADUATION CEREMONY at the University of Melbourne is held in modern Wilson Hall. The university, the second oldest in Australia, was established in 1853.

In the 1950's all school systems had to develop rapidly to meet the needs of an expanding population and the special pressures of an education-minded generation. Reflecting the high birthrate of the war and postwar years, the total number of students rose steadily by about 100,000 a year to reach 2 million before 1960. Outlays for education in all schools amounted to 3.4 percent of the gross national product in the 1960's.

Nongovernmental Education. Church schools, although affiliated with some religious denomination, usually are controlled by school councils, and even within a single denomination these councils may be appointed in a variety of ways. The schools sponsored by the Roman Catholic Church are organized more closely, however, and in each state the church authorities appoint a director of education. Since the 1950's their facilities have been strained as a result of immigration from Europe.

Higher Education. Since students go direct from secondary education to a university, there is no general educational institution corresponding to the college in the United States. Australian universities are selective in character, and admission is gained through a statewide examination over which the university has direct or indirect

THE SCHOOL OF THE AIR instructs children in remote areas over two-way radio. Here one of the boys questions his teacher by speaking into the microphone.

AUSTRALIAN NEWS AND INFORMATION BUREAU

control. No degree-granting institution can be set up without legislative authority, nor are there any private universities in the sense that they operate without state aid. All except the University of Western Australia charge fees. University revenues are derived partly from fees, partly from endowments, and, increasingly, from state and Commonwealth grants. Despite this aid, however, the universities exercise full autonomy over their own affairs.

The two oldest universities are those of Sydney (1850) and Melbourne (1853). Over the next six decades each of the other states set up a university in its capital city, the University of Adelaide in 1874, the University of Tasmania in 1890, the University of Queensland in 1909, and the University of Western Australia in 1911. Subsequently, the following institutions were established: Canberra University College (1930), the University of New South Wales (1949), Newcastle University College in New South Wales (1951), the University of New England in New South Wales (established as a college in 1938 and as an autonomous university in 1954), Monash University in Victoria (1961), La Trobe University in Victoria (1967), and Macquarie University in New South Wales (1966). The Australian National University, established in 1946 at Canberra, is a postgraduate institution catering to research studies in the social sciences, medicine, the physical sciences, and Pacific studies.

Increased demand for university education beginning in the 1950's produced a crisis in accommodation. Facilities at existing universities were extended, new institutions were established, and plans for further universities in provincial centers were under discussion. University enrollments rose from 30,000 in 1955 to more than 75,000 in 1965 (of whom about 30 percent were women). Meanwhile the proportion of higher-degree students had risen sharply. In 1957 a federal committee investigating the situation recommended emergency grants; two years later the Australian Universities Commission was invited to advise on the financial needs and balanced development of tertiary education. By the 1960's, the federal government was providing many thousands of scholarships for undergraduates.

Technical and Vocational Education. Senior technical colleges and agricultural colleges conducted by each state offer courses covering all the major occupations. Students intending to go into clerical positions often receive their training at private business colleges. Each state has an apprenticeship program, and the classroom training received during apprenticeship is provided at the technical schools of the education department concerned. Basically, however, technical education has remained tied to the apprenticeship system of on-the-job training, and in the 1960's new efforts were being made to improve standards of teaching, accommodation, and equipment in technical-training institutions. In certain occupations—for example, accountancy, law, and librarianship—the profession itself through its association plays an important part in regulating standards by establishing requirements for various grades of membership and sometimes by providing courses and conducting examinations.

Adult Education. Each state has a program for voluntary attendance by adults at classes of a nonvocational character. The system of control and the proportion of funds received from government grants vary from state to state. Originally the programs were based on the Workers' Educational Association movement, a form of university extension that had started in England. There are still close links with the universities, but functions have been broadened to cover such nonacademic activities as drama and music. Some states, too, have taken special steps to reach rural areas and populations by means of summer schools, traveling troupes, exhibitions, and the like.

Museums, Art Galleries, and Public Libraries. Each capital city established museums, galleries, and libraries at an early date. In most cases a single board of trustees controlled all three institutions on a single site. This early start and the absence of challenging contact with other countries caused Australia to lag behind developments elsewhere in the first quarter of the 20th century. In the 1930's, however, this complacency was challenged, particularly by the Munn-Pitt survey of public library services sponsored by the Carnegie Corporation of New York. Thereafter most states made considerable progress in extending public library services to the population as a whole, and progress was also made in modernizing museums and in improving art galleries. The principal Australian galleries and museums are the National Gallery of Victoria, which because of the Felton bequest (1904) possesses a number of paintings of world fame, and the National Museum of Victoria, Melbourne; the National Gallery and the Australian Museum, Sydney; the Queensland National Art Gallery and the Queensland Museum, Brisbane; the National Gallery of South Australia and the South Australian Museum, Adelaide; the Art Gallery of Western Australia and the Museum of Western Australia, Perth; the Tasmanian Museum and Art Gallery, Hobart; and the Queen Victoria Museum and Art Gallery, Launceston.

Historical and Geographical Influences. The educational and cultural aspects of Australian life find their primary source in the British tradition and outlook, although there has been considerable American influence. Textbooks used in higher education, for example, are about equally divided between British and American works, with, of course, a sprinkling of locally produced books. In some directions, however, Australia has departed markedly from both the British and the American pattern. In most cases these departures have been brought about by geographical, economic, and governmental conditions. The centralization of educational control, for instance, is due partly to a determination to provide a good primary education for all children, partly to the scattered nature of much of the population, and partly to reliance on state action for equalizing opportunities for all.

K.S. CUNNINGHAM
Australia National Research Council

Bibliography
Austin, Albert G., *Australian Education 1788–1900* (Melbourne 1959).
Australian Council for Educational Research, *Review of Education in Australia, 1955–1962* (Hawthorn, Victoria, 1964).
Australian Institute of Political Science, *Tertiary Education in Australia* (Sydney 1965).
Butts, Robert F., *Assumptions Underlying Australian Education* (New York 1955).
Fogarty, Ronald, *Catholic Education in Australia, 1806–1950* (Melbourne 1959).
Wheelwright, E.C., ed., *Higher Education in Australia* (Melbourne 1965).

7. Cultural Life

The development of the creative arts in Australia has been shaped by the interplay of local forces on the basic British heritage. Before an intellectual and artistic culture that was not merely imitative could evolve, these factors had to be blended on equal terms. The opening up of a new country precluded the slow evolution of literature from folklore, while the basic problem in the pictorial arts was the discovery of a satisfactory interpretation of a countryside markedly different from that of the homeland. In the first 100 years of settlement, therefore, only very tentative attempts were made to develop a distinctively Australian approach to the arts. Before the end of the 19th century, however, a sense of national unity, sustained by a way of life that in its essentials was the same over the whole continent, had emerged.

This feeling of unity proved to be a determining factor in the genesis of an indigenous culture. No longer was the land seen as something alien to which adjustment must be made; rather, it became a familiar setting that had positive qualities to be treated with understanding. At first there was a rather aggressive assertion of the new-found nationalism, with marked self-consciousness and exaggeration, and it was several decades before artists and writers were able to delineate the Australian scene without flaunting it.

With all its shortcomings the Australian effort in the creative arts since the 1880's has been one of remarkable achievement in which much talent and some brilliance are evident. The early nationalist writers and artists helped make Australians feel at home in their inscrutable continent, while later artists were able to look beyond their country without ceasing to belong to it.

Literature. The first descriptions of Australia were written with an eye to publication in Britain. Some of the early explorers were quite gifted writers, and during the gold rush period a host of visitors to the continent competently recorded their observations and impressions.

In Australian literary history poetry preceded the short story, and the short story preceded the novel. The first poet of any significance was Charles Harpur (1813–1868), who applied himself with some success to the interpretation of the country and its scenes, but the later work of Henry Kendall (1839–1882) had more authentic poetic quality. An interesting early work of fiction was *The Recollections of Geoffrey Hamlyn* (1859), an idealistic pioneering story by Henry Kingsley (1830–1876), who after five years in Australia began his career as a writer in England with its publication. *For the Term of His Natural Life* (1874), a reconstruction of early convict days by Marcus Clarke (1864–1881), and *The Mystery of a Hansom Cab*, a pioneer detective story by Fergus Hume (1859–1932), were among the few early writings of lasting interest. Although there were recognizable Australian characters in the exciting *Robbery Under Arms* (1888) by Rolf Boldrewood (pseudonym of Thomas Alexander Browne, 1826–1915), neither he nor contemporary authors established real contact with the country or the developing ideas of its people.

By the 1880's, however, a marked trend toward the creation of a distinctively Australian manner was apparent. No longer were stories written primarily for British audiences. Habits of life and thought brought from Britain had begun by that time to show cumulative change, the sense of a separate life had grown with the increasing proportion of Australian-born among the population, and the emergence of a national consciousness had set the stage for the development of a national literature. A definitive expression of this trend came with the growth of the *Bulletin,* a weekly founded in 1880 by John Haynes and John Feltham Archibald. Through this medium writers interpreted Australians for themselves, and a folk culture based on the pastoral hinterland began to emerge. The so-called bush idiom, in which Australian speech is particularly rich, was absorbed into writing and brought to print a multitude of expressions developed in the outback.

The first notable Australian literary form was the bush ballad, but the same characteristics later shaped the short story. The new writing was the product of a pioneering land, and the writers were themselves engaged in the practical work of its development. Their output was simple and sometimes crude, but it was individual and, above all, vital. Among the first balladists was Adam Lindsay Gordon (1833–1870), whose influence on those who followed was strong. Perhaps the greatest of the balladists—certainly the most popular—was Andrew Barton ("Banjo") Paterson (1864–1941), but Henry Lawson (1867–1922) was the outstanding figure of the movement. Lawson was also the author of short stories, in which he was perhaps supreme. His compassion and realism touched many persons of succeeding generations, who have considered him the voice of much that is finest in the Australian tradition. The printing of short stories in periodicals was sometimes followed by collections in book form, and *The Bulletin Story Book* (1901) contained the work of 60 writers. There was scant encouragement for authorship in longer forms, however, and few novelists appeared. Only one is notable: Joseph Furphy (1843–1912), who as Tom Collins wrote *Such Is Life* (1903), a work of exceptional complexity and breadth. Furphy was largely neglected in his own time, but he has since been recognized as one of the most significant Australian writers. Meanwhile, in 1901, the first novel of Miles Franklin (1879–1954), *My Brilliant Career,* appeared. It has been described

as the first truly Australian novel, and Miss Franklin's later work maintained the strong Australian note.

Among the poets Victor Daley (1858–1905) early established a reputation as a lyrist, but the work of John Shaw Neilson (1872–1942) and Hugh McCrae (1876–1958) proved more durable. McCrae stands as the most accomplished verbal artist of his generation, although his contemporaries William Baylebridge (pseudonym of William Blocksidge, 1887–1945) and Bernard O'Dowd (1886–1953) were poets of intellectual force. Another intellectual, and a poet almost entirely divorced from his environment, was Christopher Brennan (1870–1932). Furnley Maurice (pseudonym of Frank L.T. Willmot, 1881–1942) can be said to have been the first to develop a style that was at once poetically acceptable and genuinely Australian. The poems of Dame Mary Gilmore (1865–1962), whose work appeared over a period of 50 years or more, showed a strong social content as well as a marked lyrical gift.

Perhaps the best-known work of description is *We of the Never-Never* (1908), by Jeanne (Mrs. Aeneas) Gunn (1870–1961), a simple account of the author's experience in the Northern Territory in the early 1900's. *My Crowded Solitude,* by Jack McLaren (1887–1954), tells of the author's lonely life as a planter in northernmost Queensland. *The Confessions of a Beachcomber* (1908), by Edmund James Banfield (1852–1923), won recognition, as did a later work, *The Pea Pickers* (1942), by Eve Langley (1908–). Also of interest is *On the Wool Track* (1910), by Charles E.W. Bean (1879–), which presents an engagingly veracious description of the dry pastoral country of New South Wales.

Based as it was on the secluded distinctiveness of the outback, the early national movement lost its momentum as modern transportation and communications developed. The isolation of the spacious pastoral age was passing, and under the pressure of mass media local writing lost its direction. From 1905 to about 1925 little of note was produced in longer form. An exception was the outstanding trilogy *The Fortunes of Richard Mahony,* a classic treatment of the theme of immigration and assimilation, written in England by

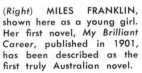

(*Left*) **ANDREW BARTON ("BANJO") PATERSON,** most popular of the bush balladists, pioneered in a new literary form based on folk culture of the Outback.

(*Right*) **MILES FRANKLIN,** shown here as a young girl. Her first novel, *My Brilliant Career,* published in 1901, has been described as the first truly Australian novel.

Henry Handel Richardson (pseudonym of Henrietta Richardson, 1870–1946).

Beginning in the late 1920's, however, a steady stream of novels of quality appeared. Among the earliest were *Working Bullocks* (1926), set in Western Australia, by Katharine Susannah Prichard (1884–   ) and *A House Is Built* (1929) by M. Barnard Eldershaw (pseudonym of Marjorie Barnard, 1897–   , and Flora Eldershaw, 1897–1956). Other notable books showing rare descriptive qualities were *The Passage* (1930) by Vance Palmer (1885–1959) and *The Man Who Loved Children* (1941) by Christina Stead (1902–   ). One of several writers who employed authentic backgrounds was Frank Dalby Davison (1893–   ), whose stories are set mainly in the cattle country of southern Queensland. The central and northern interior regions formed the scene of works by William Hatfield (1892–   ) and Arthur William Upfield (1888–1964), and the latter continued to use that setting for detective stories that brought him a large following abroad. *Capricornia* (1939), the only novel of Xavier Herbert (1901–   ), is a work of distinction.

Novels of Australia's developing urban life also made their appearance. Eleanor Dark (1901–   ), the first novelist to make use of latter-day urban scenes, published *Prelude to Christopher* (1934), *Return to Coolami* (1936), and other novels interpreting behavior psychologically, while sociological implications were strong in novels of the depression years by Kylie Tennant (1912–   ). *Flesh in Armour* (1932), a story of Australian troops in World War I by Leonard Mann (1895–   ), is still the most notable Australian war novel. The later *We Were the Rats* (1944), by Lawson Glassop (1913–   ), deals with the Tobruk campaign of 1941–1942. *The Winds Are Still* (1947), by John Hetherington (1907–   ), is concerned with the escape of Australian soldiers from Greece following the German invasion, as is *The Sea Eagle* (1944), by James Aldridge (1919–   ). The English writer Nevil Shute (pseudonym of Nevil Shute Norway, 1899–1960) introduced local settings for some of the popular novels he wrote after settling in Australia in 1950. The work of Patrick White (1912–   ) showed a modern intellectuality, and with *The Tree of Man* (1955) and *Voss* (1957), both set

in Australia but using universal themes, he won high praise abroad. White's reputation was sustained by *Riders in the Chariot* (1961). On his return to Australia, Morris West (1917–   ) ignored Australian subjects in *The Devil's Advocate* (1959) and in other best-sellers written for a universal readership in the early 1960's. John O'Grady, writing under the pseudonym Nino Culotta, won success in Australia with *They're a Weird Mob*, an impish story of a young Italian-born laborer-turned-journalist living in Sydney. Other writers of note included Jon Cleary (1917–   ) and Ruth Park, whose *Harp in the South* was followed by other well-constructed novels. Excellent short stories were being written—among them many outstanding examples by Hal Porter, whose extensive collection, *A Bachelor's Children* (1962), showed the fine polish of his writing, and D'Arcy Niland (1920–   ), whose work appeared in numerous anthologies.

In poetry a new phase developed in the 1930's with the work of Robert David FitzGerald (1902–   ) and Kenneth Slessor (1901–   ), whose poems revealed the rare gift each possessed for imparting color and creating imagery. They were joined by other mature craftsmen, who in the 1950's gave a new impetus to poetry; they included Alec Derwent Hope (1907–   ), whose first book of verse, *The Wandering Islands,* appeared in 1955; James McAuley (1917–   ), who won wide acclaim for the epic poem *Captain Quiros* (1964); and Vincent Buckley, whose *New Land for My Family* linked the quest for an earthly paradise with the dreams of Australian immigrants in general. Also notable for their significant contributions were Judith Wright (1915–   ), Max Harris (1917–   ), and Douglas Stewart (1913–   ).

Interest in nonfiction in the mid-20th century was reflected in an improved quality of writing and a greater diversity of books dealing with various aspects of the Australian scene. Serious but lively biographies, books of reminiscences and essays, and penetrating studies on numerous phases of the nation's history, politics, and development were being written.

Among the magazines that shared with the *Bulletin* the inspiration of the early literary movement were the *Bookfellow*, the *Lone Hand*, and the *Triad*, but all three had ceased publi-

(Left) KATHARINE PRICHARD, leading Australian novelist, has had her books published in Britain and the U.S., as well as in translation in the Soviet Union and France.

(Right) MORRIS WEST, award-winning novelist, whose books —such as *The Devil's Advocate*, *Shoes of the Fisherman*, and *The Ambassador*— are international best sellers.

cation by the mid-1920's. The quarterlies *Meanjin* (founded in 1940 as *Meanjin Papers*) and *Southerly* became important influences on taste, and their encouragement of original writing and penetrating criticism, like that of the *Bulletin*, was significant at a time when mass circulation media ignored such work. From the late 1950's the paucity of serious journals was alleviated by the appearance of two reviews devoted to subjects of cultural as well as political interest: the *Nation* and the *Observer* (the latter subsequently merged with the *Bulletin*). Beginning in 1938 writers received assistance through a literary fund established by the federal government.

Drama and Ballet. Despite sustained public support of the theater in Australia there has been no appreciable development of native drama. Some critics consider that this results from using available theaters almost exclusively for the staging of established successes, but it is probably truer to say that audiences have shown a marked preference for the more sophisticated stage presentations from London and New York. Repertory companies have provided almost the only outlet for the Australian playwright. Since its establishment in 1954 the Elizabethan Theatre Trust has stimulated interest in the performing arts. The launching by the trust of the Australian Institute of Dramatic Art led to an improvement in technical standards.

Efforts were made to provide dramatic entertainment from the earliest days of settlement, the first play being an improvised performance (1789) of George Farquhar's *Recruiting Officer*. In 1833 a properly constituted theater was opened in Sydney. A series of "Dramatic Amusements" was announced in the same year in Hobart, and in 1837 the Royal Victoria Theatre (later renamed the Theatre Royal) was built there by public subscription. Adelaide had a theater in 1838, and at about the same time plays were first presented in Perth. Melbourne's first theater was opened in 1841. By 1856, Sydney had three theaters in full production, and during Melbourne's boom many of the world's leading artists played to packed houses.

Actors from Britain and the United States, seeing opportunities for wealth and prestige, brought their talents for theatrical organization to Australia. George Selth Coppin (1819–1906), a British actor who arrived in 1843, appeared in Sydney, Hobart, and Adelaide before settling in Melbourne, where he won distinction as player and entrepreneur. Another influential figure was Bland Holt (1853–1942), Australian-born but British-trained, who presented some spectacular productions. The most far-reaching influence was that of the American actor-manager James Cassius Williamson (1845–1913), who reached Melbourne in 1874. In 1884 he joined two English managers, Arthur Garner and George Musgrove, to form the Comic Opera Company, a dominant force for four decades. The name of J.C. Williamson is still a vital one, for the firm he founded remains the principal Australian theatrical organization. Fresh companies were brought in, theaters were built, and such international celebrities as Sarah Bernhardt and Irene Vanbrugh appeared. Shakespearean plays and Gilbert and Sullivan operettas, as well as comedy melodramas and such dramatic successes as *Camille* and *A Doll's House*, were presented. Nor did the local theater depend solely on imported talent, for a number of Australian stars developed, among them Nellie Stewart (c. 1860–1931), who began her career in the 1870's, and Oscar Asche (1871–1936), who made several tours of his homeland between successful engagements in Britain and the United States.

Interest in the theater flagged under the impact of motion pictures, however, and many theaters were converted to film showings. After 1930 commercial stage presentations were confined mainly to such assured successes as musical comedies and light plays. Significant drama was found only in the smaller theaters. The little theater movement, made up largely of amateur groups but including semiprofessionals and some professionals, helped to keep interest alive, and the Independent and Metropolitan theaters in Sydney, and the Arrow and Union theaters and the National Theatre Movement in Melbourne, gave excellent productions of classical and modern plays. It was here that native playwrights found some support, although their work generally had literary rather than theatrical value. Greater success was achieved in radio drama, which received encouragement from the Australian Broadcasting Commission.

Interest in serious theater revived after World War II. Great English actors—Dame Sybil Thorndyke, Sir Lewis Casson, Sir Ralph Richardson, and Sir Laurence Olivier—visited Australia. The Elizabethan Theatre Trust, created in 1954, provided sponsorship for drama, ballet, and opera; but even so there was little stimulation for intellectual theater, and in the commercial theater support was seldom available for any production other than an established success from London or New York. Hopes that Australia was about to produce distinctive drama were awakened by the success of *Summer of the Seventeenth Doll* by Ray Lawler (1921–   ), which was presented in Melbourne and Sydney in 1956 and became the first local drama to achieve success in the theater on a fairly broad plane and to be well received in London. *The Shifting Heart* by Richard Benton did well in London, and *The One Day of the Year* by Alan Seymour scored a success in several European capitals; but thereafter the initiative faded.

In the main cities drama was kept alive in professional repertory or "little" theaters, which provided a stage for Australian plays as well as for experimental or controversial work from abroad. Adelaide's biennial Festival of Arts encouraged Australian playwriting. The Adelaide University Theatre Guild staged Patrick White's *The Ham Funeral* (1960), *Season at Sarsaparilla* (1962), and *Night on Bald Mountain* (1964). Generally, however, hopes for the creation of a nonimitative national theater seemed as far from attainment as ever.

A significant aspect of the theatrical scene is the growing popularity of ballet. The initial impetus was given by a tour that Col. Vasili de Basil's Ballet Russe de Monte Carlo made of Australia in 1936. Thereafter, Australian groups developed, among them the Borovansky Ballet, founded in Melbourne by Édouard Borovansky, a member of the Monte Carlo group who left the cast in 1939; the Bodenweiser Ballet, a modern expressive dance group that reached Australia in 1939; and the National Theatre Ballet of Melbourne. After Borovansky's death (1959) direction of the company was taken over by English dancer Peggy van Praagh, who in 1963 became the first artistic director of the Australian Ballet

Company, a national company and advanced ballet school established with government support. Van Praagh was joined in 1965 as codirector by dancer-choreographer Robert Helpmann, who had returned after 30 years in London. By this time Marilyn Jones, the leader of the company, was being hailed as Australia's first truly classic ballerina.

Motion Pictures. Although motion pictures have been made in Australia from the earliest days of the cinema, most commercial productions have been undertaken on small budgets, and few Australian films have gained serious attention in other countries. In order to capitalize on the distinctive Australian landscape efforts were made to set up a local center as an offshoot of British or American production; *The Overlanders* (1946), *On the Beach* (1959), and *The Sundowners* (1960) were made under these conditions, but the initiative was not sustained.

Even in documentary film production the story has been disappointing. In the 1940's and 1950's several official productions of the film division of the Australian News and Information Bureau won international awards, including *Kokoda Trail* (1942), *School in the Mailbox* (1948), and *Down in the Forest* (1953). The Shell Oil Company's production *Back of Beyond*, a documentary of the desolate inland, gained first prize at Cannes in 1953. After this period documentary film making declined, in large measure because greater rewards were to be earned in television. The National Film Board, which had been advising on the official film production program since 1945, found it necessary to limit the effort to narrow-purpose films, with the emphasis on utility. The distribution of educational films in each state is handled by a state-operated film center.

Music. Music is the most highly developed of the arts in Australia, and many of the country's singers and instrumentalists have become celebrated. Beginning in the 1870's, when rich talent first appeared, singers went abroad to be acclaimed; later, instrumentalists and composers also achieved world recognition. Teaching—instrumental, vocal, and theoretical—is of a high standard, and the effects of close cooperation with educational authorities are reflected in the fine music work that is a feature of both primary and secondary schools. Despite the amount and quality of musical composition, however, there has been little indigenous expression, and Australian composers have mostly followed Old World traditions.

Melbourne's Philharmonic Society, a choral group, was founded in 1853, and choral music of a high order has also been produced in Sydney and Adelaide. The development of orchestral music dates from 1888, when a full orchestra under Sir Frederick Cowen was brought to Melbourne, where it gave 241 concerts in six months. In 1890, Adelaide became the first Australian city to have a chair of music at its university. The University of Melbourne created one in the following year, and by 1894 it also had a conservatorium directed by the professor of music. This departure from general university practice was a result of the vision of the country's first great musical personality, George W.L. Marshall-Hall (1862–1915). Besides founding and conducting an orchestra he built up a school that continued to provide performers and teachers whose influence on Australian musical life has been great.

DAME NELLIE MELBA, as she appeared in *Manon*. One of Australia's many singers who achieved international fame, she starred in opera throughout the world after making her operatic debut at Brussels in 1887.

WIDE WORLD

In 1906, Alberto Zelman (1874–1927) founded the Melbourne Symphony Orchestra, which he conducted until his death. The University Symphony Orchestra, recruited from past and present students, and the University Conservatorium Orchestra were combined in 1932 under Sir Bernard Heinze (1894–   ) to form a new Melbourne Symphony Orchestra. Meanwhile, in Sydney the State Conservatorium of Music of New South Wales had been established in 1916 under Henri Verbrugghen (1873-1934). Verbrugghen added distinction to the school with the creation of a string quartet. The University of Sydney founded its chair of music in 1948.

Beginning in 1870 opera attracted sizable audiences. Companies from other countries presented French and Italian operas and, later, those of Richard Wagner. One of the greatest of of all operatic performers, Dame Nellie Melba (real name Helen Porter Mitchell Armstrong, 1861–1931), heads a long list of Australian singers who have won international fame. She made her operatic debut in Brussels in 1887 and later gained outstanding success in London, Paris, and New York. Madame Melba returned to Australia for many visits and did much to stimulate Australian musical life. Melba had many distinguished Australian contemporaries, including Ada Crossley (1874–1929) and Peter Dawson (1882–1961).

Between World War I and World War II Australian performers who won acclaim while spending most of their time in Britain, Europe, and the United States included the singers Malcolm McEachern (d. 1945), John Brownlee (1900–   ), Marjorie Lawrence (1908–   ), Stella Power, Florence Austral, and Dorothy Helmrich. Operatic soloists prominent in the 1950's and 1960's included Joan Sutherland, Sylvia Fisher, Max Worthley, Lorna Sydney, Stanley Clarkson, June Bronhill, Marie Collier, Una Hale, and John Lanigan. Miss Sutherland received a tumultuous welcome in Australia when she returned home in 1965, after 14 years abroad as the star of her own touring company.

Among internationally known instrumentalists were the pianists Una Bourne and Eileen Joyce (1912–   ), the violinists Florence Hood and Ernest Toy, and the organists Sir William Neil

JOAN SUTHERLAND, Australian soprano, in *Lucia di Lammermoor* at her Metropolitan Opera debut in 1961.

McKie (1901–   ). Percy Grainger (1882–1961), long a resident of the United States, and Arthur Benjamin (1893–   ) attained distinction as composers. John Henry Antill (1904–   ) scored his greatest success with the ballet suite *Corroboree* (1946), while Alfred Hill (1870–1960) wrote fine overtures and concertos.

The greatest single impetus to professional music came with the establishment in 1932 of the Australian Broadcasting Commission, which not only has fostered wider appreciation of music but has also helped to provide greater opportunities for performers. An enthusiastic and discerning following has been developed. The commission brings eminent soloists from Europe and the United States, and it has created symphony orchestras in each of the states that together provide nearly 800 concerts annually. In addition financial support from its subscribers and sponsors has made it possible to support tours by Australian artists. Resident and visiting conductors of world standing have helped to build up the symphony orchestras, which can now provide assured employment for trained musicians. Wider audiences have been dveloped through the commission's educational work as well as through the children's orchestral concerts founded in Melbourne in 1929 by Sir Bernard Heinze.

The Sydney Symphony Orchestra, established in 1946 as a full-time body of 82 players, has financial support from the government of New South Wales and the Sydney City Council as well as from the Australian Broadcasting Commission. Its conductors have included Sir Hamilton Harty (1934), Sir Malcolm Sargent (1936, 1938–1939, 1945), Georg Schneevoigt (1937–1940), Sir Thomas Beecham (1940), Eugene Ormandy (1944), Walter Susskind (1946), Rafael Kubelik (1947–1949), and Otto Klemperer (1940, 1950). From 1947 to 1956 Sir Eugene Goossens, permanent conductor of the Australian Broadcasting Commission and director of the State Conservatorium of Music of New South Wales, controlled the orchestra, and on his resignation Nicolai Malko was appointed conductor; in 1965, Dean Dixon was appointed musical director. The orchestra participated in the 1965 British Commonwealth Arts Festival, in London, and gave concerts in the Philippines, Japan, Hong Kong, and India.

In other cities state and municipal authorities have also helped to support symphony orchestras.

The Brisbane Symphony Orchestra of 50 players was established in 1947 with John Farnsworth Hall as conductor, and a Tasmanian orchestra of 25 players (Clive Martin Douglas, conductor) became a permanent unit in 1948. In 1949 the Victorian Symphony Orchestra (72 players) was established; Walter Susskind was its conductor from 1954 to 1956, followed by Kurt Woess; later it became the Melbourne Symphony Orchestra. A South Australian orchestra (55 players) was constituted in 1949; its resident conductor in the 1960's was Henry Krips. In 1964 the West Australian orchestra was enlarged to 50 players, and Thomas Mayer took up the position of resident conductor in 1966.

Architecture. There has been very little local creative development in architectural design in Australia. The promise of early colonial building was submerged fairly quickly, and building methods and traditions have been largely those of Britain, with a strong American influence in the 20th century.

The earliest buildings were mere shelters. It was some time before use of the local hardwoods was mastered and Sydney's fine sandstone was shaped for the first substantial structures. Francis Howard Greenway (1777–1837), an English architect who arrived in Sydney in 1814, achieved a strong and simple architectural expression. His style, now known as colonial, was a transition from the Georgian with original modifications in the form of verandas to suit the Australian climate. The economy of materials enforced simplicity, and in Hobart buildings of some charm were produced. Meanwhile, in the hinterland, the country home was developing, as the first rough shelters were replaced by more permanent and spacious buildings with extensive verandas. At first roofs were made of split shingles, but the danger of fire in a dry summer brought about the use of corrugated galvanized iron sheets, which came to dominate the Australian building scene.

The Gothic Revival style, everywhere considered a proper form for churches, appeared on the Australian scene in the middle of the 19th century. There, partly because of the simplification demanded by local conditions, an almost distinctive manner was achieved. When the growth of cities prompted the erection of cathedrals, Gothic was commonly adopted. Impressive public buildings were constructed in the capitals of all the colonies. The most remarkable were those of Melbourne, which were built in the grand period of the city's expansion, from the 1850's to 1890. Commercial buildings, some 11 or 12 stories high, included the world's tallest in their day.

Terrace houses appeared in great numbers in the late 19th century, but since then the trend has been to individual cottage-type dwellings rather than the town houses generally typical of older cities. The cottage has in fact become the characteristic type of domestic architecture. The rise of the individually built house resulted in the emergence of a typical Australian house plan, which only in the mid-20th century began to give way to more varied layouts.

One of the architects whose work had a continuing influence was Walter Burley Griffin (1876–1937) of Chicago, whose design for the national capital, Canberra, won a worldwide com-

petition in 1912. Griffin, whose work was planned basically for function, also designed many buildings in Melbourne and Sydney. After World War I the first organized architectural schools appeared. The University of Sydney established a complete course of study, and the University of Melbourne a less extensive one, but both relied on on-the-job training in practical building.

While Spanish and Italian influences have been strong in 20th century town and country architecture, sound contemporary design, introduced by young architects who had traveled in continental Europe, Britain, and the United States, has become more generally accepted. The Australian public has shown less interest in multiple-dwelling units than in small houses, and there are relatively few apartment blocks. An emphasis on simplicity is noticeable, and contemporary American influence is strong. In commercial building, functional styles, following international trends, are dominant in the glass-fronted steel and concrete office blocks in the principal cities.

Two great structures, each of exceptional character, took shape in the 1960's: one was the harborside Sydney Opera House, designed by Danish architect Joern Utzon as a center for the performing arts, with vaulting white-tiled roof shapes simulating billowing sails; the other was Melbourne's Cultural Center, a highly individual design comprising three structures—rectangle, triangle, and elongated cone—created by Australian architect Roy Grounds.

Painting and Drawing. Among the earliest representations by Europeans of the Australian scene are sketches made by the topographical draftsmen who accompanied Capt. James Cook. The scientific recording of fauna and flora followed, and explorers who pushed inland usually made sketches that were reproduced in the books about their journeys. After 1835, when an art school was established in Sydney, the field widened slightly, and with the expansion of the pastoral industry, landholders and merchants were able to lend limited patronage to the arts.

Conrad Martens (1801–1878), a landscape painter, produced some delicate watercolors in which he used space, light, and color well. Other painters attempted to capture the adventurous pioneering life of the pastoralists. Their works, reproduced or exhibited in England, helped to stimulate the interest of prospective migrants. Then, with the discovery of gold in 1851, a number of artists arrived to depict the life of the fields. Representative of this period was Samuel Thomas Gill (1818–1880), whose popular lithographs give a vivid picture of colonial life and manners. Among other artists of quality were John Skinner Prout (1806–1876), William Strutt (1825–1915), and Nicholas Chevalier (1828–1902).

Still, little progress had been made in interpreting the Australian landscape. The form of the eucalyptus—thin in outline, with a heavy trunk and light, scattered foliage—created problems no more easily solved than those of the quality of the pervading light and of the vast spaces of subtle coloring. John Glover (1767–1849), who arrived in Hobart from England in 1830, produced some sound work, but the first to paint the landscape with insight was (Abram) Louis Buvelot (1814–1888), who arrived in Melbourne in 1865.

Victoria, growing rapidly, set up a commission on the fine arts in 1863 and artisans' schools of art and design in 1867. In the 1870's national galleries were established in Melbourne and other colonial capitals. These moves, combined with an appreciable degree of local patronage, made possible the emergence of an Australian art form, a development that coincided with the growth of the national spirit in writing. What Henry Lawson did with his pen to stimulate a national sentiment based on the pastoral tradition, Frank Mahony (1862–1916) furthered in painting and drawing.

The final step in the evolution of a distinctive approach to landscape painting followed the return to Melbourne in 1885 of Tom Roberts (1856–1931), who during his stay in Europe had become interested in the work of the French impressionists. He was soon joined by a group of painters that included the landscapists Federick McCubbin (1855–1917), Sir Arthur Streeton (1867–1943), and Charles Conder (1868–1909) and the portraitist Sir John Langstaff (1862–1941). This group, which became known as the Heidelberg School from the locale of one of its painting camps outside Melbourne, succeeded in creating a new form of Australian painting in which plein air and impressionist principles were applied to the interpretation of the local landscape.

In the 1890's a subjective note appeared as artists tended to capture subtler and more reflective moods in landscapes and portraiture. However, deterioration in economic conditions made it difficult for artists to sell their work, and by 1900 many of those who had helped develop an Australian approach had gone abroad. Conder, George Washington Lambert (1873–1930), Rupert Bunny (1864–1947), and Emanuel Phillips Fox (1865–1915) won international recognition. In Australia itself lighter and more tonal watercolors became increasingly popular in the hands of such men as Blamire Young (1863–1935), Norman A.W. Lindsay (1879–   ), and Jesse Jewhurst Hilder (1881–1935).

A munificent bequest made by Alfred Felton in 1904 to the National Gallery of Victoria was of some assistance to Australian painters, although the bulk of the money was spent on foreign works. In 1916 the periodical *Art in*

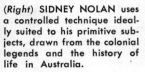

(Left) GEORGE RUSSELL DRYSDALE with a painting in progress which depicts the typical theme of his work— the lonely man living on the great Outback of Australia.

(Right) SIDNEY NOLAN uses a controlled technique ideally suited to his primitive subjects, drawn from the colonial legends and the history of life in Australia.

AUSTRALIAN NEWS AND INFORMATION BUREAU

DAVID MOORE, FROM BLACK STAR

Australia was established by Sydney Ure Smith, who was to play an important role in gaining a wider critical following for art.

By the 1920's the first fine flush of a national school had lost some of its inspiration, and, although some excellent work was being done by the leading landscapists, the Australian style was becoming stereotyped. One of the few innovators was Sir Hans Heysen (1877–   ), known for his gnarled eucalyptuses set against immense distances. Another was Kenneth Macqueen (1897–1960), one of the first painters to search for design and rhythm rather than form and tone in the Australian landscape.

In 1926 the Contemporary Art Group was formed in Sydney, and in 1931 George Bell (1878–   ) and Arnold Shore (1897–1965) founded an art school in Melbourne. Following successful exhibitions of contemporary British and French works, Australia's Contemporary Art Society was founded in 1938.

An enterprising approach to Australian painting began in the 1940's. By this time the painting of representational landscapes had come under challenge, and an earlier interest in stylized aboriginal art forms—fostered especially by Margaret Preston (1883–1963)—also was starting to fade. In a great surge of artistic energy many gifted individuals came to the fore, and the public responded with an enthusiasm and support for art quite new in Australia. Sir William Dobell (1899–   ) painted distinctive, though controversial, portraits, and George Russell Drysdale (1912–   ) drew upon the myth of the "Great Australian Loneliness," showing attenuated figures dramatically isolated against the astringent ochre-red inland landscape. Others who captured the spirit of the Australian environment included Sidney Nolan (1917–   ), whose extreme simplification of expression suited his subjects derived from colonial legends and Australian history; Arthur Boyd (1920–   ), a painter of mysterious allegories in dark and tangled landscapes; and Albert Tucker (1914–   ), whose work symbolizes the pioneer's struggle for survival in an arduous land. By the mid-1960's more than fifty "new" artists were turning out work of vitality and quality. The phase in which the main function of Australian painting had been to reveal to the ordinary citizen the natural beauties of his country had given way to an approach in which the painter showed awareness of his art in its relation to a universal medium.

An important contribution to the wide appreciation for art in Australia had been made by immigrant artists, some of whom imported the traditions of their native lands, particularly those of central Europe. These artists introduced a style of painting that is low-keyed, sonorous, and romantic, yet robust; and their influence, though less direct than that of the leading Australian figures, was nonetheless significant.

Cartooning and other black-and-white work have been features of Australian art since the 1890's, when the *Bulletin* began to support a group of first-rate men. Among the most notable exponents of this school, most of whom were connected with the *Bulletin*, were Phil May (1864–1903), Norman A.W. Lindsay, Sir Lionel Lindsay (1874–1961), William Henry Dyson (1883–1938), David Low (1891–1963), and Livingston Hopkins (1846–1927), an American who became known as Hop. Later artists, particularly some who came from Europe, have been responsible for new progress in a form of expression that in Australia has traditionally shown vitality as well as good draftsmanship and fine technique.

Sculpture. There has been no marked trend toward the development of a national school of sculpture, and Australian sculptors have followed the British tradition. The first exhibition of work of Australian origin, which was held in Sydney in 1854, consisted largely of the work of Charles Abrahams, who modeled and carved busts of wealthy Australians. Charles Summers (1827–1878), who had been trained in Britain at Royal Academy schools, secured a position as a modeler in Melbourne in 1853, and later was commissioned to erect a memorial to the ill-fated Burke and Wills expedition of 1860–1861. This work is the largest bronze modeled and cast in Australia. The first Australian-born sculptor to be acclaimed at home and abroad was Sir Bertram Mackennal (1863–1931), who studied at the National Gallery of Victoria and at Royal Academy schools and executed an amazing body of work in London. W. Leslie Bowles (1885–1954), who was awarded a traveling scholarship, also studied at the Royal Academy. After serving as an assistant to Mackennal, he returned to Melbourne, where he received commissions for a number of statues. Major commissions were few, however, and sculpture barely survived until the mid-20th century, when interest in it revived. The Victorian Sculptors' Society, which had been discontinued, was re-formed in Melbourne in 1947, while in Sydney, Lyndon Dadswell (1908–), who was head teacher of sculpture at East Sydney Technical College from 1938 to 1949, had great influence. The college became a training ground for established sculptors and promising newcomers.

Graphic Arts. Standards in the graphic arts improved noticeably in the 1950's. Artists and designers from abroad and Australians trained overseas helped raise design quality, while typography and printing techniques also progressed. In advertising, where expenditures are proportionally higher than in the United States, more attention has been paid to all aspects of presentation, and by the 1960's the best Australian advertising art could be ranked with the finest work done elsewhere.

Industrial Design. With the expansion of manufacturing activity and increased competition, product design received greater attention in the 1950's, and by the 1960's the Australian consumer no longer had to accept plainer styling than that available to his North American counterpart. The Council of Industrial Design is an important influence in this field.

Ceramics. The branch of Australian handicrafts of most interest is ceramics. The emergence of the artist-potter is a development of the 20th century, but by the 1950's most of the country's largest technical schools provided classes in pottery making, and in the principal cities a good deal of attention was paid to advanced pottery work. The first Australian potter with an authentic style was Merric Boyd. First-class work has also been done by William Cox (Joliffe), Allan Lowe, David and Hermia Boyd, Carl Cooper, and John Percival, and the influx of European nationals has had a marked influence in raising standards.

R.M. YOUNGER
Author of "The Changing World: Australia"

Science and Invention. Public recognition of the importance of scientific research and development to the life of Australia dates from the end of World War I. Until then interest in research in science and technology was confined largely to the universities. The few secondary industries were satisfied to obtain scientific knowledge from overseas, while the agricultural industries, though beset by many major problems, had but meager indigenous scientific resources to which they might turn for aid.

Nevertheless, Australian inventiveness had been expressed from the mid-19th century onward by the production of a number of devices that enabled the country's young agricultural and pastoral industries to overcome the shortage of labor and the distance from overseas markets. These devices included perhaps the first stripper harvester, which was invented by John Ridley (1806–1887) in 1843; one of the earliest header harvesters; the first sheepshearing machine; and a method of commercial refrigeration based on the evaporation of ammonia, which was patented in 1867 and which by 1880 made possible the shipment of frozen mutton and beef to Britain, 12,500 miles (20,100 km) away.

The turn of the century was marked by two major scientific advances. The first of these came from the pioneering work of William James Farrer (1845–1906) on the cross-breeding and selection of wheat varieties suited to the Australian environment, to which the great expansion of the wheat industry over the next two decades was largely due. The second was the development in 1900–1902 of the flotation process for the separation and recovery of metals from the rich silver-lead-zinc lodes at Broken Hill in western New South Wales, which had a decisive influence on metal mining throughout the world.

Research Organizations. The most important stimulus to scientific research in Australia was given by Prime Minister Stanley Melbourne (later Viscount) Bruce in 1926, when he established a national research organization, the Council for Scientific and Industrial Research, known since 1949 as the Commonwealth Scientific and Industrial Research Organization (CSIRO). Bruce saw to it that the new organization was not subject to political control, and that it was free to select its own programs of research into the problems of primary and secondary industry, to carry out or sponsor basic research, and to establish scholarships for the training of young Australian scientists at home or overseas. The first chairman of the organization was Sir George Alfred Julius (1873–1946), a distinguished consulting engineer and the inventor of the automatic totalizator. By the 1950's the CSIRO, with a staff of over 1,200 scientists, was the largest research body in Australia, and the work of its 30 major divisions and sections covered practically all branches of primary and secondary industry and many fields of basic science.

Since the 1940's, research resources of the older universities have been greatly enlarged and emphasis has been placed on the scientific faculties of the new universities. The Australian National University is an entirely postgraduate and research institution with four research schools: the John Curtin School of Medical Research, the Research School of Physical Sciences, the Research School of Social Sciences, and the Research School of Pacific Studies. Among other notable additions to the Australian scientific scene are three federal government agencies: the Bureau of Mineral Resources, Geology and Geophysics; the Atomic Energy Commission; and the Defense Scientific Services. The last-named is responsible for Australian participation in the joint programs of the Australian–United Kingdom Long Range Weapons Establishment in South Australia. Medical research is centered mainly in the university medical schools and great teaching hospitals, in state government medical research institutes in Adelaide and Brisbane, and in the Walter and Eliza Hall Institute of Medical Research in Melbourne. Federal grants for such research are disbursed by the National Health and Medical Research Council in Canberra.

In the 1950's various manufacturing companies established industrial research laboratories and made large contributions to the Nuclear Research Foundation of the University of Sydney, and the wool, wheat, and tobacco growers contributed to national research funds for the investigation of the problems of their respective industries. In 1953 the Australian Academy of Science was founded to represent Australian science in general; it received a royal charter from Queen Elizabeth II in 1954.

Scientific Achievements. The widespread appreciation of the place of science in national development that existed by the 1950's was due to the spectacular dividends yielded by research over the preceding 30 years, particularly in relation to the agricultural industries. Between 1926 and 1936, 60 million acres (24 million hectares) of arable and pasture land in Queensland were cleared of a dense forest of prickly pear as a result of the introduction of the *Cactoblastis cactorum* moth to parasitize the plant. The rabbit population, for decades the most serious cause of the denudation of pastures, soil erosion, and catastrophic drought losses, was reduced to insignificant numbers over an area of 750,000 square miles (1,940,000 sq km) between 1950 and 1954 by the introduction of the myxoma virus.

The work of veterinary pathologists, parasitologists, and entomologists has elucidated and brought under a large measure of control a wide range of bacterial and parasitic diseases that formerly exacted a heavy toll in the livestock industries. In particular, Australian research workers have made notable contributions to the understanding of the metabolic diseases of plants and animals caused by the deficiency, excess, or imbalance of trace-element nutrients in the soil or pasture plants. The essential role of cobalt in animal nutrition was first demonstrated by research workers in the CSIRO and the University of Western Australia.

Similarly, CSIRO workers discovered that the infertility of 2 million acres (800,000 hectares) of so-called desert soil in South Australia was due to the lack of minute quantities of zinc and copper essential for vegetative growth and for the reproduction of clovers and other legumes. Additional CSIRO research showed that molybdenum is essential for the metabolism of legumes and that, by its use in conjunction with superphosphate, sparse natural pastures could be replaced with sown grasses and clovers over more than 10 million acres (4 million hectares) of "infertile" soils in southern Australia. As a consequence of these discoveries, the agricultural potential of the nation was reevaluated.

Another achievement of Australian science has been the development of a flourishing pulp and paper industry in the face of an almost complete lack of indigenous softwoods. The complementary investigations of the pulp and paper companies and the CSIRO have led to the successful employment of Australian hardwoods (eucalyptuses) for the production of newsprint and fine writing papers.

In a country that is for the most part semiarid, and that in the better-watered coastal fringe suffers from marked irregularity of rainfall, it is understandable that scientists should study factors affecting rainfall and water conservation. The long-term study of the physics of clouds by the CSIRO Division of Radiophysics has thrown much light on the physical conditions needed for the occurrence of natural precipitation and has begun to define the limitations and possibilities of artificial rainmaking. A controlled cloud-seeding experiment over an area of 1,000 square miles (2,590 sq km) in the southern portion of the Australian Alps has led to an apparent increase in rainfall of 20 percent. Water conservation studies on farm dams and inland town water supplies, where evaporation losses may be as much as eight feet (2.4 meters) annually, have demonstrated that, by the use of a monomolecular film of cetyl alcohol, evaporation may be reduced by 35 percent at low cost.

In medical research outstanding achievements have been made in the field of virology at the Walter and Eliza Hall Institute of Medical Research in Melbourne. The institute's director, Sir Frank Macfarlane Burnet (1899–   ), who made notable contributions to knowledge of the influenza and poliomyelitis viruses and developed one of the foremost schools of virus genetics, shared a Nobel Prize in 1960 for work in immunology. In 1963 the noted neurophysiologist Sir John Carew Eccles (1903–   ), professor of physiology at the John Curtin School of Medical Research, Australian National University, Canberra, shared a Nobel Prize for his work on transmission between nerve cells. Earlier the association between rubella (German measles) contracted by mothers during the early months of pregnancy and congenital cataract, blindness, and other deformities of their offspring was first recognized by Sir Norman McAlister Gregg (1892–1966), a Sydney clinician. During World War II the work of Australian medical scientists led to an understanding of, and did much to reduce losses by, scrub typhus

(Left) SIR FRANK MACFARLANE BURNET, corecipient of the Nobel Prize in 1960 for his work in immunology, has made major contributions to our knowledge of viruses.

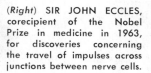

(Right) SIR JOHN ECCLES, corecipient of the Nobel Prize in medicine in 1963, for discoveries concerning the travel of impulses across junctions between nerve cells.

among the Allied troops in the Pacific islands. In England the Australian-born pathologist Sir Howard Walter Florey (1898–   ), did research on penicillin that made him a corecipient of the Nobel Prize in medicine in 1945.

Although a high proportion of scientific effort has been devoted to practical ends, a sign of increasing maturity is the rapid expansion of research in the basic sciences, not only in the universities but also in medical research institutes and the CSIRO. In particular, strong research groups are found in genetics, biochemistry, and protein chemistry; in chemical physics, metal physics, and nuclear physics; and in the physics of the upper atmosphere, solar physics, astronomy, and radio astronomy. The Department of Astronomy of the Australian National University, with its observatory at Mount Stromlo, has greater resources than are found elsewhere in the Southern Hemisphere. The radio astronomy group of the CSIRO, under Edward George Bowen (1911–   ), has been in the forefront of this scientific field, developing techniques and equipment that have been widely adopted in other countries. Bernard Yarnton Mills (1920–   ), formerly of the CSIRO team and subsequently professor of astrophysics at the University of Sydney, was responsible for the design of the Mills Cross type of radio telescope. The status of the Australian effort in radio astronomy was demonstrated in 1964, when Cornell University in the United States and the University of Sydney initiated a plan to create the world's largest radio astronomy and cosmic ray research agency by pooling instruments and related facilities and interchanging research and technical staffs.

IAN CLUNIES-ROSS
*Commonwealth Scientific and
Industrial Research Organization*

Bibliography

Berndt, Ronald M., ed., *Australian Aboriginal Art* (New York 1964).
Bonython, Kym, *Modern Australian Painting and Sculpture* (Adelaide 1960).
Ewers, John K., *Creative Writing in Australia*, 3d ed. (Melbourne 1959).
Green, Henry, *A History of Australian Literature*, 2 vols. (Sydney 1962).
Hope, Alec D., *Australian Literature, 1950–1962* (Melbourne 1963).
McGuire, Paul, *The Australian Theatre* (Melbourne 1948).
Roderick, Colin A., *An Introduction to Australian Fiction* (Sydney 1950).
Smith, Bernard, *Place, Taste and Tradition* (Sydney 1945).
Wright, Judith A., *Preoccupations in Australian Poetry* (Melbourne 1964).

8. Government

The six British colonies established in Australia after 1788 were to a large extent governed from London until the middle of the 19th century (in the case of Western Australia, until 1890). Local self-government was then established under legislation of the Parliament of the United Kingdom, and by the end of the century the colonies were self-governing in practice, although as a matter of law the British Parliament had full power to legislate for them. The colonies made their own laws, imposed their own taxes, and spent their own revenues.

The Commonwealth of Australia, which consists of six states, two federal territories, and various external territories, was established by a statute passed by the Parliament of the United Kingdom in 1901. In 1931, by the Statute of Westminster, the British Parliament formally stated that it would not legislate for the Commonwealth except upon Commonwealth request. Thus the Commonwealth of Australia is self-governing and independent. Nevertheless, although legal ties with Britain and control from London are no longer factors in Australian affairs, Australia remains closely associated in policy, interest, and sentiment with Britain and with the other members of the Commonwealth of Nations. Not only are there bonds of trade and commerce, but also those of a shared tradition, a like culture, and a common parliamentary system of government. Frequent consultations take place between the governments of Britain and Australia, and this voluntary, cooperative association constitutes a major feature of Australian policy.

Constitution of the Commonwealth. The Australian Constitution is similar in many respects to that of the United States, upon which it is largely based. In each case federal powers are defined and limited by the constitution, and all other powers belong to the states.

The constitution is the supreme law of the land, binding upon all the parliaments, federal and state, the courts, and the people. Thus a statute of the Commonwealth Parliament duly made in pursuance of a power given to it by the constitution is valid, but if it is not so made it is invalid, and the courts will so declare. This principle, established in the United States by the case of *Marbury* v. *Madison* (1803), is accepted without question in the courts of Australia. Similarly, a state statute that deals with a matter excluded by the constitution from state legislative authority is invalid. When the Commonwealth Parliament and a state parliament have concurrent legislative powers in relation to a subject, the Commonwealth act prevails over the state act in case of inconsistency.

The Commonwealth Parliament is empowered to make laws with respect to more than 40 enumerated subjects: among them, foreign and interstate trade; quarantine; taxation; borrowing on the credit of the Commonwealth; naval and military defense; immigration and emigration; external affairs; postal, telegraphic, telephonic, and like services (held by the High Court of Australia to include radio and television broadcasting); currency, coinage, and legal tender; census and statistics; banking other than state banking; insurance other than state insurance; weights and measures; bankruptcy and insolvency; copyrights and patents, designs, and trademarks; naturalization and aliens; marriage and divorce; and invalid and old age pensions, maternity allowances, and other social services.

The Commonwealth Constitution does not contain a set of guarantees like those of the American Bill of Rights. There is, however, a provision (Section 116) that prevents the enactment of any federal law for establishing any religion or for imposing any religious observance, or for prohibiting the free exercise of any religion, and it is also provided that there shall be no religious test as a qualification for any office or public trust under the Commonwealth.

Section 92 of the constitution provides that, on the imposition of uniform customs duties, all trade, commerce, and intercourse among the states, whether by means of internal carriage or ocean navigation, shall be absolutely free. This vague provision has been responsible for endless litigation and political confusion. It has been interpreted and applied many times by the High Court of Australia, and on several occasions by the Privy Council in London upon appeal from the High Court, and its implications are still being worked out. This section has prevented the establishment of a government monopoly in civil aviation and in banking, has limited the operation of price control and of taxation of road haulers, and has invalidated a number of federal and state statutes in their application to interstate commerce.

The constitution makes provision for the exercise of the three functions of government: legislative, executive, and judicial. Section 1 provides that the legislative power of the Commonwealth shall be vested in the federal Parliament, which shall consist of the British sovereign, the Senate, and a House of Representatives. Section 61 provides that the executive power of the Commonwealth is vested in the British sovereign and is exercisable by the governor general as his or her representative. Section 71 provides that the judicial power of the Commonwealth shall be vested in a federal supreme court, to be called the High Court of Australia, and in such other federal courts as Parliament creates and in such other courts as it invests with federal jurisdiction.

Although distinct grants of power are made to the federal legislative, executive, and judicial organs, the British system of separation of powers did not have so great an effect in Australia as in the United States. The power to make laws has been interpreted in Australia as power to make such laws as have been made for many years in Britain and Australia. Thus a law upon a federal subject may give power to the executive to make relevant regulations. Further, the ministers who execute the law, and who with the governor general constitute the Commonwealth executive, must (subject to an exception for only three months) be members of Parliament. Insofar as judicial power is concerned, however, a strict doctrine of separation of powers has been established by judicial decision. It is settled that courts established under the constitution have for their exclusive purpose the performance of judicial functions, and that it is impossible to impose or confer upon them duties or authorities of another order. Thus a power of industrial arbitration cannot be given to a court, and an industrial tribunal cannot impose penalties or commit persons for contempt.

Parliament and Political Parties. All parliaments in Australia, federal and state, are elected by adult suffrage. In the Commonwealth Parliament the lower house, the House of Representatives, has 122 full members and 2 members with limited voting rights who represent the Australian Capital Territory and the Northern Territory. Seats are allotted among the states on the basis of population, with provision for a minimum of 5 seats, which now applies only to Tasmania. All six states are equally represented by 10 senators each in the Senate. Originally, the Senate was intended to protect and promote state rather than federal interests, but, like the House of Representatives, it consists of members belonging to political parties and is divided along party lines.

The principal party alignment is between the Liberal and Labour parties, but there are also the Country party and the Democratic Labour party. All Commonwealth political parties support the United Nations and the maintenance of the Commonwealth of Nations, and all of them advocate a policy of defense, with some difference as to means and methods, and a policy of full employment. All support welfare services. The Liberal party, which emphasizes the importance of the individual and of individual initiative, is opposed to state ownership of any service or business enterprise "which can be financed or operated efficiently by private enterprise." It believes "that no Government can plan a nation into prosperity," and opposes socialism, which it identifies with "a rigid direction of all economic activities."

The Australian Labour party, on the other hand, has constantly pressed for greater government intervention in economic affairs. At different times the Labour party has placed emphasis on varying aspects and in doing so has advocated nationalization of (1) banking, credit, and insurance; (2) monopolies; (3) shipping; (4) health services; (5) radio and television; and (6) sugar refining.

In 1972, after the Liberal party in coalition with the Country party had been in office in the Commonwealth for 23 years, the Labour party assumed power.

Section 92 of the constitution, according to the now-established interpretation, prevents any of these proposals from being carried out, because the requirement that interstate trade and commerce shall be absolutely free bars a government monopoly of any trading or commercial business with substantial interstate activities. Accordingly, the Labour party further advocates amendment of the constitution to clothe the Commonwealth Parliament with unlimited powers and with the duty and authority to create states possessing delegated constitutional powers. The Liberal party, on the other hand, advocates the maintenance of the federal constitution with possibly some rearrangement of powers between states and the Commonwealth.

The Country party generally, but not always, collaborates with the Liberal party. It supports assistance for rural industries by subsidies and other methods and conducts a campaign for the creation of new states. The Democratic Labour party consists of former Labour party members who became dissatisfied with the attitude of the Labour party toward communism. The continued existence of the Democratic Labour party was at first considered unlikely, but proposals for settling differences within the Australian Labour party failed to get anywhere. By the mid-1960's it seemed assured that the Democratic Labour party would maintain its identity, even though its chances of winning significant representation in Parliament were slim. Its main aim appeared to be to thwart the ambitions of the Australian Labour party, and in this effort it was successful. The Democratic Labour party maintained a strong stand on international issues, advocating close identity with United States policy, and on the question of government aid to private schools, which it considered essential in the light of modern educational requirements.

Executive Government. According to Section 61 of the Australian Constitution, the executive power extends to "the execution and maintenance of the Constitution, and of the laws of the Commonwealth." The British sovereign is represented in the Commonwealth by the governor general

AUSTRALIAN NEWS AND INFORMATION BUREAU

FEDERAL PARLIAMENT HOUSE in Canberra (*left*) is the home of the House of Representatives and the Senate. Queen Elizabeth II (*below*) in 1954 became the first reigning monarch to open the Parliament.

WIDE WORLD

and in each of the states by a governor, who are appointed by him or her upon the advice of the relevant government. As a matter of course the governor general and the governors act upon the advice of their ministers, except that a government's request for the dissolution of Parliament may be refused when another government can be formed from the existing Parliament.

Australia follows the English system of cabinet government under which the ministers who constitute the executive government must be members of the Parliament, as distinct from the United States system under which the members of the executive branch are excluded from Congress. A government can remain in office only so long as it retains the support of the lower house of Parliament; if a government loses this support, it must resign in favor of a successor. If no workable government can be established, however, the lower house (in special cases, both houses) of Parliament may be dissolved, and an election then takes place. Thus a government in office always speaks with the authority of Parliament.

Judicial System. A federal system, where a constitution confers only limited powers on a legislature, which by itself is unable to amend the constitution, is necessarily legalistic. The interpretation of the constitution and the determination of the powers of Parliament or other federal agencies rests with the courts.

Judges of the federal courts are appointed by the governor general in council—that is, by the government. This is the rule also in the states, and no judges in Australia are elected. Federal judges must be appointed for life, but in the states there are age limits of 70 or 72 years. Judges can be removed from office only upon an address from both houses of Parliament.

At the head of the judicial system is the High Court of Australia, which has a limited original jurisdiction and an appellate jurisdiction from such other federal courts as the Court of Bankruptcy and from the supreme courts of the states. Legislation provides means whereby constitutional questions will be decided by the High Court. Appeals can go from the High Court by special leave, and from the supreme courts in certain cases, to the Judicial Committee of the Privy Council in London, but Section 74

of the constitution provides that there can be no such appeal "from a decision of the High Court upon any question, howsoever arising, as to the limits *inter se* of the Constitutional powers of the Commonwealth and those of any State or States . . . unless the High Court shall certify that the question is one which ought to be determined by His (Her) Majesty in Council." The Judicial Committee of the Privy Council consists of judges of the highest tribunal in England, who "advise" the queen in each particular case, and she always acts upon their advice. Since the establishment of the Commonwealth only one certificate for appeal to the Privy Council has been given by the High Court, but important decisions have been given by the council upon constitutional questions, such as the meaning of Section 92, which do not involve a question of limits *inter se* of federal and state powers.

The decisions of the High Court have built up an extensive system of constitutional law. Soon after the establishment of the High Court in 1903, the courts adopted the principle of immunity of instrumentalities (federal and state) which had been established in the United States by the cases of *McCulloch* v. *Maryland* (1819) and *Collector* v. *Day* (1871). This doctrine of mutual noninterference was associated with a doctrine of implied prohibitions, according to which certain powers not expressly conferred upon the Commonwealth were treated as reserved to the states and were therefore held to be exempt from any interference or impediment created by federal law. These principles were difficult to apply in practice and to justify in theory, and in 1920 they were reviewed in the *Engineers' case,* 28 C.L.R. 129, in which it was decided that the constitution should be construed according to its terms upon ordinary principles of interpretation without any implications derived from some supposed reservation of powers to the

759

states. While the Commonwealth Parliament could exercise only the powers granted by the constitution, it could exercise those powers fully. State parliaments possessed the residue of legislative power, but the terms of the positive grant to the Commonwealth were not to be limited in interpretation by assumptions as to the extent of the residue left to the states. The new doctrine was applied in the case of industrial awards made by the Commonwealth Court of Conciliation and Arbitration. It was held that these awards could properly control state employees in industry conducted by a state. Such awards prevail over state awards and state laws.

The Commonwealth Court of Conciliation and Arbitration was established in 1904 in pursuance of the power conferred upon the Commonwealth Parliament by Section 51, paragraph 35, of the constitution, which enables Parliament to make laws with respect to conciliation and arbitration for the prevention and settlement of industrial disputes extending beyond the limits of any one state. The interpretation of this provision by the High Court has established that the federal power is not a power to make laws with respect to industrial conditions, but only to establish authorities for the purpose of dealing, by the particular methods of conciliation and arbitration, with industrial disputes that extend beyond a single state. It is easy in practice to make an industrial dispute extend beyond a single state, and accordingly conditions in a large number of industries in Australia are controlled by awards of the Commonwealth Court of Conciliation and Arbitration. The result is that this tribunal is an economic authority of great significance in determining wages and conditions of labor.

All the states have industrial commissions, courts, or tribunals of various kinds that make awards or determinations relating to conditions in industry, and state parliaments have the power (which the Commonwealth Parliament does not possess) of making laws with respect to industrial conditions. Thus an industry may be subject to a federal award for some employees and to a state law or a state award for others. Numerous attempts to procure a constitutional amendment in order to eliminate the resulting confusion have failed.

Public Finance. The principal sources of public revenue in Australia are income tax and customs and excise duties. Only the Commonwealth Parliament has the power to impose customs and excise duties. While both the Commonwealth and the states imposed income taxes until World War II, a single income tax imposed by the Commonwealth was adopted in 1942. Thus the money available to the state governments for such necessary services as the administration of justice, police, transportation, water supply, irrigation and drainage, health and—most significantly—education, has come to depend principally upon the amount the Commonwealth has been prepared to provide. Increasingly the Commonwealth has come to assume responsibility for maintaining the states' programs. Details of the federal-state financial relationships are hammered out each year at the premiers' conference and associated loan council meeting.

Of the total revenue of the Commonwealth government, which was about $A 4,400 million annually in the mid-1960's, the largest portion, 52 percent, was furnished by income tax; excise duties accounted for about 15 percent; postage,

9 percent; sales tax, 8 percent; customs duties, 6 percent; payroll tax, 3.5 percent; and other sources, 6.5 percent. The principal categories of expenditure were payments to or on behalf of the states; social services; defense services; business undertakings, including the postmaster general's department; railways; broadcasting services; and the federal territories.

The revenues of the six states—omitting business enterprises, such as railways—amounted to almost $A 1.4 billion annually in the mid-1960's. Only 25 percent was derived from state taxation, while 60 percent came from federal grants. The latter included tax reimbursements, road grants, financial assistance and special grants, and interest on state debts and sinking fund payments on behalf of such debts, which are paid by the Commonwealth under the terms of the Financial Agreement of 1927.

By that agreement the Commonwealth took over the liability to the bondholders on the debts of the states and agreed to make contributions toward both interest and sinking fund thereon. The agreement provided for the establishment of the Australian Loan Council, consisting of the prime minister of the Commonwealth and the premiers of the states or their deputies, which determines the amount of money to be sought on the loan market each year. All borrowing on behalf of the states is done by the Commonwealth.

The public debt of the Commonwealth in the mid-1960's stood at about $A 3.8 billion, and that of the states at $A 7.1 billion. Of the total $A 10.9 billion, 86 percent was held in Australia. The interest payable annually on the debt is about $A 442 million.

Foreign Affairs. The constitution expressly gives the Commonwealth Parliament power to make laws with respect to external affairs. In the prefederation era the Australian colonies had no concern with foreign affairs, and their relations with countries outside the British Empire were negligible. The position was much the same when the Commonwealth first assumed control of foreign affairs. After World War I, however, the full autonomy of the British Dominions—Canada, Australia, South Africa, and New Zealand—was recognized by their admission as foundation members of the League of Nations, and the independence of the Dominions was formally acknowledged in the Balfour report adopted by the Imperial Conference of 1926.

Until 1940, Australia maintained high commissioners in Britain, Canada, and the United States but had no diplomatic representatives abroad, and there were no such representatives of other countries in Australia. In that year ministers were sent from Australia to Washington and Tokyo. By the late 1960's Australia was represented at the ambassadorial level in 22 countries and had high commissioners stationed in 11 Commonwealth countries; in addition it maintained consulates in 5 countries, a legation in another, and trade or migration missions in 8 others. Some 33 countries were represented in Canberra by ambassadors, high commissioners, or ministers, in addition to consular posts elsewhere in Australia.

The foreign policy of Australia supports the United Nations, in which Australia takes an active part, and is characterized by the fullest possible cooperation with Britain and the other Commonwealth nations. All have the same interest in the preservation of peace, but Australia is especially concerned with security in the Pacific. The Tripartite Security (ANZUS) Treaty between Australia, New Zealand, and the United States (1951) contains guarantees of mutual help in case of aggression; and the Southeast Asia Collective Defense Treaty (1954), establishing the Southeast Asia Treaty Organization (SEATO) with Australia, Britain, the United States, New Zealand, the Philippines, Thailand, France, and Pakistan as members, provides for mutual assistance in the case of aggression by armed attack against any of the parties. The positive part of Australian foreign policy is largely concerned with Southeast Asia. The countries constituting this region are visited frequently by the minister for external affairs, and Australia provides technical assistance and material grants to these and other Asian nations under the Colombo Plan (q.v.).

Defense. Defense policy is based on the concept of collective security, operating through the Commonwealth Strategic Reserve, established in 1955, and through SEATO and ANZUS. From the late 1940's a sizable long-range weapons testing establishment has been operated, in conjunction with the United Kingdom, at Woomera, in the desert northwest section of South Australia.

The military services send representatives to discussions by Commonwealth chiefs of staff, Australian vessels take part in combined exercises with the navies of other Commonwealth countries, and Australian officers maintain liaison with the services of the Commonwealth countries as well as with the United States. Joint air and naval exercises are held with the United States from time to time. Australia's close association with the United States in defense and in space tracking work has made possible a striking advance in defense science.

In the mid-1960's the Royal Australian navy had approximately 13,500 active personnel, with another 4,000 reserves; the army had approximately 27,000 officers and men; the Royal Australian air force had 17,700 regulars; and the Citizen Military Forces numbered about 30,000. A major defense plan then underway provided for expansion of the navy and air force, with emphasis on guided-missile antisubmarine patrol craft. United States-built missile destroyers and Australian-built Mirage fighter aircraft, equipped with air-to-air missiles, were purchased. A submarine base was to be developed at Sydney, forward bases for the air force were planned near Wewak and elsewhere in New Guinea and at Cocos-Keeling island, while airfields were to be established at Learmouth in Western Australia and on Manus Island.

Public Health and Social Services. Public responsibilities in relation to health, which formerly fell largely upon the state governments, have become increasingly a concern of the Commonwealth as well. While hospitals and medical education fall within the state sphere, the Commonwealth provides substantial financial assistance.

Social services are well developed in Australia. Most of them are provided by the Commonwealth from tax revenue, and are not on a contributory basis. The services include invalid and old age pensions, maternity allowances, child endowment, unemployment and sickness benefits, widows' pensions, funeral benefits, and a rehabilitation service for disabled persons. Except for the maternity allowances and child endowment, all of the benefits are subject to a means test.

State and Local Government. The theory of a federal system of government is that the central government should be independent in its sphere and that the states or provinces should be independent in their respective spheres. In practice, however, this theory is greatly modified by the fact that major economic policy respecting trade and credit, the issues of war and peace, and relations with other countries are controlled by the federal government. The Commonwealth Parliament has an unrestricted power of taxation, except that taxation must be uniform as between the several states, and the states can enter the field only after federal needs have been satisfied. But the people of the states are the same as the people of the Commonwealth, and so some practical compromise is reached that enables the states to carry on, though not always to their own satisfaction.

In Australia each state has a full apparatus of government—a governor, a cabinet, a Parliament (bicameral except in Queensland), and a Supreme Court and other courts. The states make and administer most of the laws that closely touch the lives of ordinary people, but these laws, the result of long tradition, do not present so many politically controversial features as those that are derived from federal authority. The states control property law, the law of contracts and torts, the law of trusts and the administration of the estates of deceased persons, company law, the law as to shops and factories, the general criminal law, forestry, mining, education, hospitals, and charities. Housing is a state activity, but the states receive much financial assistance for this purpose from the Commonwealth, and this is also true in relation to universities, hospitals, and homes for the aged.

The local government of cities, towns, and rural areas is controlled by state local government acts. Local councils or boards are elected, generally by those who pay municipal rates based on the valuation of landed property. The councilors or board members are unpaid. With financial assistance from the state, the municipalities make and maintain bridges and streets and roads other than main highways. They also make and administer bylaws relating to health, sanitation, sewage and drainage, disposal of rubbish, nuisances, markets, pounds, offensive trades, traffic, construction of buildings, and other local matters, and they may provide and maintain parks and gardens and libraries.

J.G. LATHAM
Former Chief Justice, High Court of Australia

Bibliography

Caldwell, Arthur A., *Labour's Role in Modern Society* (Melbourne 1965).
Cowen, Zelman, *Federal Jurisdiction in Australia* (New York 1959).
Crisp, Leslie F., *The Australian Federal Labour Party, 1901–1951* (London 1955).
Crisp, Leslie F., *The Parliamentary Government of the Commonwealth of Australia* (London 1962).
Eggleston, Sir Frederic W., *Reflections on Australian Foreign Policy* (Melbourne 1957).
Ellis, Ulrich, *A History of the Australian Country Party* (New York 1964).
Jupp, James, *Australian Party Politics* (Melbourne 1964).
Miller, John D.B., *Australian Government and Politics*, 3d ed. (London 1965).
Overacker, Louise, *The Australian Party System* (New Haven, Conn., 1952).
Santamaria, B.A., *The Price of Freedom* (Melbourne 1964).
West, Katherine, *Power in the Liberal Party: A Study in Australian Politics* (Melbourne 1965).
Wynes, William A., *Legislative, Executive and Judicial Powers in Australia*, 3d ed. (Sydney 1962).

9. History

The history of European occupation and development of the island continent that, with Tasmania, was to become an outpost of Western civilization in the South Pacific began with the British convict settlement at Port Jackson (Sydney), New South Wales, in 1788. After the Blue Mountains had been crossed in 1813, the progress of the pastoral industry successfully challenged the concept of a purely penal establishment near the coast. Then the subsequent rural squattocracy, as the group of wealthy pastoralists came to be called, was itself challenged by a combined immigrant and emancipist small settler opposition, which by 1840 had secured the end of regular convict transportation to the mainland. In 1851 the young colonial society of eastern Australia was rudely disturbed by the influx of diggers seeking fortunes on the goldfields of New South Wales and its southern daughter colony, Victoria, which had acquired separate colonial status in that year. The aftermath of these gold rushes not only sharpened controversies already present in the closing decade of the first half of the 19th century but also added new problems and opened new trends of political, social, and economic evolution. Many of the distinctive features of Australian life were thus determined before the establishment of the federated Commonwealth of Australia on Jan. 1, 1901.

Conditions had indeed varied considerably in the federating colonies of New South Wales, Victoria, and their four neighbors. South Australia had been founded in 1836 as an experimental free society on the principles of Edward Gibbon Wakefield. Tasmania, which had been a penal offshoot of New South Wales from 1804, became a separate colony in 1825 but continued to receive convicts until 1853. Another six years passed before the mother colony's northern neighbor, Queensland, also received separate status. The isolated and sparsely settled Western Australia, which covered one third of the continent, had barely held its own from its foundation in 1829 as a free settlement until convicts were admitted from 1850 to 1868 for service on public works and in private employment; in the late 1880's and the 1890's it, too, enjoyed its gold rush and belated prosperity. In none of the six colonies, however, was the pastoralist to regain the political and social primacy that he had enjoyed in the pre–gold rush era. The infant Australian Commonwealth continued to shape its own peculiar form of political and social democracy in a setting that became increasingly urban and industralized as the new century lengthened, and this despite the persistent importance of the pastoralist's wool as a staple export and the growing significance of wheat exports and all the economic changes that two world wars brought to the now more diversified Australian economy.

Discovery. The discovery by Europeans of the mainland of Australia, like that of the Americas, was largely accidental. The 17th and 18th century voyages that resulted in the charting of the greater part of the coastline were designed mostly for other purposes. The Portuguese and Spaniards, who in the 16th century had reached Java, the Moluccas (Spice Islands), the north coast of New Guinea, the Philippines, and the Solomons by extending Vasco da Gama's track northeastward from the Cape of Good Hope (1497–1498) or Ferdinand Magellan's route northwestward

from the strait that bears his name (1520), or, like the Spaniard Álvaro de Mendaña de Neyra, by venturing from Peru (1567), had been concerned chiefly with the location of speedier routes to the coveted Spice Islands.

When also moved, like Mendaña, by the traditional conviction that a considerable land mass lay awaiting discovery in the southern seas, these Spanish and Portuguese navigators had sought not an island continent but the mythical great south land, Terra Australis Incognita, which was supposed to balance Europe and Asia by stretching southward unbroken to the pole. Thus, Pedro Fernandes de Queirós, a Portuguese who had served under Mendaña in the latter's second and unsuccessful voyage of 1595, later sailing from Peru for King Philip III of Spain, reached the New Hebrides Islands in 1606 and was convinced that he had found the great southland. His more spirited lieutenant, Luis Vaez de Torres, who lost his leader in a storm, proved that the New Hebrides were not part of the continent and was on his way to the Philippines when circumstances diverted him from the normal course north of New Guinea and led him through the dangerous strait to the south of the island. If, as is possible but improbable, he then sighted Cape York, he was ready enough to include it among the "very large islands" that he had seen. No Spaniard or Portuguese got nearer to the mainland than had Torres in 1606. On the other hand, the north coast of New Guinea, which had been discovered accidentally by the Portuguese Jorge de Meneses as early as 1526, was further explored by several Spaniards, including Álvaro de Saavedra (1527) and Íñigo Ortiz de Retés (1545).

The Dutch navigators, who are credited with most of the discoveries on the Australian coast before the voyages of the Englishman Capt. James Cook, came upon the west and northwest shores of the continent by their seeming misfortune—an untimely delay in their passages to and from the rich Spice Islands, of which they had dispossessed the Portuguese. Blown off the course then thought most favorable, Dirk Hartog in 1616 nailed a pewter dish to a post on the island that bears his name outside the entrance to Shark Bay, halfway up the coast of what is now Western Australia. Three years later another Dutch captain, Frederik Houtman, sighted the coast farther south and followed it north to Dirk Hartog Island after narrowly escaping disaster on an Abrolhos reef. Upon these treacherous reefs, still known as Houtman Rocks, the *Batavia*, a Dutch man-of-war commanded by Frans Pelsaert, was wrecked in 1629. In similar fashion other pieces of the west coast were discovered by Dutch captains off their course—Cape Leeuwin at the southwest corner in 1622 and De Witt's Land near North West Cape in 1628.

Dutch discoveries were not entirely fortuitous. Some of these errant captains found curiosity too much for them and deliberately extended their wanderings. In 1627 the *Gulden Zeepaard* pressed eastward along the south coast of what was called Nuyts Land as far as the head of the Great Australian Bight. In the northern waters more than one attempt was made to solve the mystery of what lay east and south of New Guinea. A few weeks before Torres had proved the existence of a strait between New Guinea and the mainland, the *Duyfken* coasted down the west side of Cape York Peninsula. In 1623 the

LANDING OF CAPTAIN COOK on the east coast of Australia in 1770 is depicted in a painting (*right*) by Australian artist E.E. Phillips Fox. The cottage in which Capt. Cook was born (*below*) is now in a Melbourne park.

Dutch sailors of the *Pera* and *Arnhem* under Jan Carstensz made another attempt, and failed again, but charted farther down into the Gulf of Carpentaria, the coast of which they treated as continuous with New Guinea—so little known was the discovery of Torres until it was confirmed by Cook after 164 years.

The best-known name in the story of Dutch discovery in Australian waters is that of Abel Janszoon Tasman, to whom fell the task of piecing together the knowledge of the north and northwest coasts of New Holland (the Dutch name for Australia) in his voyage of 1644 from the Gulf of Carpentaria to North West Cape, and, on a famous voyage two years earlier, of carrying further the search for the great south land. It was then that he discovered the southern portion of Van Diemen's Land (now Tasmania) and sailed up part of the west coast of New Zealand, establishing its separation from New Holland but wrongly assuming it to be the northwestern extremity of the mythical Terra Australis Incognita. That further discoveries were not made by the Dutch in the century that followed Tasman's great voyage was due partly to the poor reports that Dutch navigators had given of the western mainland and its people. In this they were strongly supported by the first British navigator to touch Australia, the buccaneer William Dampier (1688–1689). As yet the pleasant coastal country of the southern and eastern sections of the continent had not been explored, and Dampier's account of "a dry and dusty soil" in-

habited by "the miserablest people in the world" remained the general impression of what had actually been seen of Australia and Australians until the second half of the 18th century.

Speculation concerning the unknown nevertheless continued. By the 1760's, French as well as British writers had whipped up sufficient interest to induce their respective governments to assist further voyages in the southern seas. Capt. Samuel Wallis, who sailed in 1766, discovered Tahiti for the British in the following year, and Louis Antoine de Bougainville, who set out three months later and came within sight of the track of Torres, southwest of New Guinea, was the first of a line of distinguished French navigators in Australian waters. Bougainville's departure rather than his actual discoveries stimulated fresh British voyages to forestall French discovery of rich lands that might compensate France for the loss of Canada. Alexander Dalrymple and other geographers assured the British government that the great south land would be found south and east of Tasman's New Zealand. This mythical land was still more enticing than the unknown spaces between Van Diemen's Land and the Gulf of Carpentaria.

The efforts of Dalrymple and his friends to continue the search were aided by the desire of British scientists to dispatch a ship to the South Pacific to observe the transit of Venus in 1769. This done, exploration might be renewed. The British government agreed, and before Bougainville returned to Europe the voyage of the *Endeavour* had begun under the command of Lt. (later Capt.) James Cook of the Royal Navy. The transit was duly witnessed at Tahiti in June 1769. Early in October of the following year the *Endeavour*'s commander reached Batavia after having effectively disproved the alleged connection of New Zealand with the continent and having confirmed the almost forgotten discovery of Torres that a dangerous strait separated New Guinea from the land around the Gulf of Carpentaria. In addition Cook had charted the east coast of the continent from Point Hicks to Cape York, opening the way for the first European settlement on the hitherto unattractive mainland and for the founding of the first British colony in the Pacific.

Foundation and Early Settlement, 1788–1820. Most Australians celebrate January 26 as Australia Day or Foundation Day in commemoration

"THE FOUNDING OF AUS-TRALIA" recreates the un-furling of the British flag at Sydney Cove on Jan. 26, 1788. January 26 is now celebrated as Australia Day.

of Jan. 26, 1788, when Capt. Arthur Phillip landed a company of over 1,000 (including 717 convicts, of whom 188 were women) and with his officers toasted success to the infant colony of New South Wales. In making this settlement the British government had no intention of claiming the whole continent, nor was New South Wales strictly speaking a colonial settlement. The very site of the convict prison was itself a second choice. Phillip had sailed direct for Botany Bay, which had been specified in his instructions as "the most eligible situation upon the coast for the first settlement." There he landed on January 18, but was not long in sat-isfying himself that there was little to substanti-ate what had been stated by Joseph Banks, the naturalist who had accompanied Cook on the *Endeavour*, concerning Botany Bay's suitability for a settlement. Phillip therefore ordered the 11 vessels of his fleet to move north along the coast to the more attractive site he had discovered inside Port Jackson, a harbor that Cook had seen only from a distance.

Fortunately, Phillip, who served as the first governor, was a man of vision as well as cour-age. He refused to regard the colony as merely a convict settlement, and he frequently urged upon the government the desirability of encour-aging free settlers. Though the future character of the colony as a free settlement had not been determined, Phillip's successful efforts to make it self-supporting prepared the way. Ill supported by many of his officers, who regarded themselves for the most part as jailers, handicapped from the first by the poor quality of the human ma-terial upon whose labor he could draw, and often faced with the threat of starvation, which was increased by the arrival of fresh batches of convicts, Phillip nevertheless persevered. He spared no effort in the attempt to demonstrate the soundness of his view that New South Wales would one day rank among the most valuable parts of the British Empire. When Phillip retired in 1792, his goal of a self-supporting colony had not been reached, but the first governor of a penal colony had succeeded in laying the founda-tions of free British settlement in Australia.

Some measure of Phillip's contribution is in-dicated by the chaos that developed after his

withdrawal, when direction of the young settle-ment passed into the hands of lesser men. The officers of the New South Wales corps, which had been sent out to aid the governor in main-taining order, obtained a corner in trade and en-dangered the future of the colony by traffic in rum. This became the recognized currency of the community with disastrous effects on its morals and its economic welfare. The officers openly challenged Phillip's naval successors, Capt. John Hunter (1795–1800) and Capt. Philip Gidley King (1800–1806), and played a prominent part in the so-called Rum Rebellion against another naval governor, Capt. William Bligh (1806–1808).

Lt. Col. Lachlan Macquarie, the soldier who replaced Bligh in 1809 and held the governor-ship until 1821, left a mark on the colony no less significant than that of Phillip. His claim to recognition as the greatest of the early governors lies in his determination to make New South Wales more than a convict prison but less than a colony of free settlers—a colony of reformed con-victs reshaping their lives in a new environment. He succeeded in the former aim but failed in the latter. Whatever may be the ultimate judg-ment of history on Governor Macquarie, the sur-prising thing is that he should have achieved so much in the teeth of opposition from a home government that could see no further than a con-vict prison and from the more prosperous free settlers, brave but grasping, whose imagination reached beyond the limits of a closely controlled community of peasant proprietors. Under Mac-quarie the population of the colony rose from 11,590 in 1810 to 38,778 in 1821, and farmland under cultivation from 7,615 to 32,267 acres (3,082 to 13,058 hectares). But Macquarie could not withstand the main stream of colonial development, for the economic potentialities of the colony had been revealed by the crossing of the Blue Mountains in 1813. The pathway was thus provided to the pasture lands on which would graze the flocks descended from the Merino sheep bred by the governor's greatest rival, John Macarthur. By the time of Macquarie's departure there were nearly 300,000 sheep in the colony, as compared with only about 26,000 at the time of his arrival.

Regular convict arrivals in New South Wales did not cease until 1840, and Macquarie's successors as governor ruled with legal authority but little restrained by the nominated legislative councils of 5 to 7 and 15 members established in 1823 and 1828, respectively, and by the two-thirds elected legislative council of 36 constituted in 1842. Nevertheless, the so-called age of the tyrants was giving way to the era of squatters.

The term "squatter," transplanted first from North America to Van Diemen's Land and thence to the parent colony of New South Wales, originally expressed contempt for those occupying land outside settled areas. A certain undesirable element among the first Australian squatters was, however, soon dwarfed in numbers and importance by the more enterprising free settlers who sought greater opportunities beyond the 19 counties near the coast, an area within a radius of about 150 miles (241 km) from Sydney within which government policy in New South Wales sought to restrict settlement. Authorities in Sydney were eventually forced to admit the economic value of the fleeces shipped to expanding English woolen factories by squatters from runs to which they had no legal title and for which at first they paid no rent. From mere "poaching beyond the pale" squatting by the 1840's had become a pursuit both respectable and—drought periods excepted—profitable. It was still far from providing the pseudoaristocratic life it came to offer in the 1860's and 1870's, after the first squatters had made the runs, and their descendants the fortunes. Many battles had yet to be fought before the squatters' constantly changing, unfenced runs gave place to fenced stations with comfortable homesteads and boundary riders who replaced nomadic shepherds. Squatters' claims for security of tenure and compensation for improvements were resisted, on the whole without success, by colonial governors like Sir George Gipps (1838–1846) and small-farmer interests who sought to deny titles in perpetuity that might restrict intensive agricultural development. But the squatting age had come to stay in New South Wales and also to exercise its influence on the extension of settlement far beyond the confines of the mother colony.

Extension of Settlement, 1820–1850 and After. Political and economic considerations were closely interwoven in the extension of British settlement in Australia. Economic opportunity stimulated the expansion from Port Jackson into the interior, but political factors were largely responsible for the first coastal settlements in the more distant regions to the south, west, and north. By 1829 the whole continent was claimed for the British.

Convict transportation, which was abolished gradually between 1840 in New South Wales and 1868 in Western Australia, certainly had an effect on Australia's development, but three schools of thought appraise its influence differently. One school regards the convicts as more sinned against than sinning and stresses the valuable contribution made to Australian political and social democracy by those who were sent out for political offenses as well as the services of those who provided much needed labor in government gangs or as assigned servants, or who, as emancipists, founded some highly respectable pastoral families of a later era. A second school points to the known depravity of some of the convicts and insists on recognition of the widespread degradation caused by the severity of the system in the early days of New South Wales, in Queensland, and, in particular, in Tasmania, to which many of the worst felons were retransported. Others go further still and find in the regimentation of convict days one of the predisposing causes of the allegedly excessive government interference with the Australian economy of the 20th century.

The New South Wales Hinterland and Queensland. The reversal in the early 1820's of Macquarie's rigid emancipist policy encouraged a steady stream of free settlers who were ready to make a moderate outlay on the purchase of land on which to raise sheep for wool with the aid of convict labor. Such an increase in the occupation of extensive pasture lands necessarily implied expansion into the interior. This took the form of a series of movements westward beyond the excellent pasture lands around Bathurst (founded in 1815 after Gregory Blaxland's conquest of the Blue Mountains); northwestward to the Liverpool Plains, New England, and the Darling Downs; southward across the Murrumbidgee River; and southwestward into the more distant but equally rich pastoral districts of Australia Felix, the existence of which was confirmed by the explorations of Charles Sturt and Sir Thomas Livingstone Mitchell in 1828–1830 and 1836, respectively. The attempts of Governor Sir Ralph Darling (1825–1831) to restrict settlement to the 19 counties were therefore doomed to failure. Squatters were, however, debarred from effecting the natural economic expansion beyond the Darling Downs to the Moreton Bay district by the decision in 1824 to establish a convict settlement at the mouth of the Brisbane River. It was not until shortly after transportation had ceased, in 1840, that this district was thrown open to free settlement. Therefore, Brisbane gradually became the port, and later the capital of a predominantly pastoral community.

Settlement gradually pressed farther north and northwest and, in 1859, compelled the recognition of Queensland as a self-governing colony separate from New South Wales and in some ways peculiarly distinct from all the other Australian colonies. Its special tropical conditions were emphasized by the extension of settlement northward along the coast of sugar plantations as well as northward and northwestward into the interior for pastoral purposes. This latter expansion led to the inclusion in the colony, in 1861, of the Albert region south of the Gulf of Carpentaria.

Victoria. Meanwhile the pastoral development and inland exploration southwest of Sydney, together with the colorful exploits of independent settlers from Tasmania—the Hentys at Portland Bay in 1834, and John Batman and John Pascoe Fawkner at Port Phillip Bay in 1835—prepared the way for a new southern colony. Officials in Sydney were, however, slow to recognize or to encourage it. The failure of officially authorized establishments at Port Phillip in 1803 and at Westernport in 1826, inspired by fear of the French, had exhausted the enthusiasm of Sydney officials for extending the range of an administration already proving difficult, but economic forces once more proved too strong for officialdom. Accordingly, a police magistrate from Sydney formally represented the New South Wales governor in Melbourne from 1836 to 1839, when the British government sent out Charles Joseph Latrobe as superintendent of this Port Phillip district of squatters. Port Phillip remained part of the colony of New South Wales until the Australian Colonies Government Act, 1850, gave separate representative institutions to a separate colony of Victoria (1851).

Tasmania. Economic pressure was thus mainly responsible for the extension of settlement to the northern and southern colonies of the eastern mainland. But the island of Tasmania—smallest of the six states of the 20th century Commonwealth, yet first of the daughter colonies to attain separate colonial status (1825)—owed its settlement, if not its development, to the endemic fear of the French that possessed successive governors in Sydney. The first British settlement in Van Diemen's Land, made by Lt. John Bowen at Risdon Cove on the Derwent River in 1803, was in the following year taken over and transferred to Hobart by Lt. Col. David Collins, who had been sent to forestall the French in Port Phillip, where he did little but compose pessimistic reports for Governor King. In 1804 another settlement under Lt. Col. William Paterson was made on the Tamar River, but was transferred to the present site of Launceston two years later.

The early development of Van Diemen's Land was aided by the transfer of free settlers and convicts from Norfolk Island. This island, which had been occupied in 1788 to forestall "any other European Power," was gradually abandoned between 1806 and 1813. It was reoccupied in 1825 and governed thenceforward by New South Wales, except for a period of Tasmanian control from 1844 to 1856, until the Commonwealth took over in 1914. Tasmanian development was also assisted by the growth of a profitable whaling industry centered at Hobart and, later, by the rapid progress of the wool industry after Macarthur's experiments in New South Wales. Further development of the colony was retarded by gross mishandling of the native question and by the steady influx of convicts. In 1821 the grim Macquarie Harbour was established in the western part of the island for the worst type of convict, and the first independent governor, Col. George Arthur (1824–1836), though he replaced Macquarie Harbour by a new prison at Port Arthur, regarded Van Diemen's Land as primarily a convict settlement. The number of convicts increased rapidly after transportation to the mainland stopped in 1840. Transportation to Van Diemen's Land did not cease until 1853, when the island's name was also changed to Tasmania.

Western Australia. The first British station in the largest of the states of the 20th century Australian Commonwealth was also due to fear of the French and not to economic factors favorable to settlement. Although Albany, in the southwest corner, can boast of a continuous history from the arrival of Maj. Edmund Lockyer in 1826, the extension of settlement in Western Australia came from the Swan River Settlement on the west coast. In 1827, Capt. James Stirling had explored the river with the approval of Governor Darling, who was much concerned that "so advantageous a position should not be taken possession of by the French." The problems of the colonists who came with Stirling to the Swan in 1829 and of those who followed him during the next few years were caused by poor land, marked shortage of labor, and difficulties with the aborigines. In 1832 the population was only 1,500, and the lack of further immigration accentuated the labor problem until it was met by

the British government's decision to grant the colonists' request for convict labor. The first group arrived in 1850. Transport was also provided for a small number of free settlers.

This costly British subsidy to the colony had substantial economic results. When transportation ended in 1868, expansion into the enormous hinterland had begun. Settlement extended eastward across the Darling Range around York, Northam, and what was later known as Toodyay. Fresh settlers established themselves on the southwest coast—at Australind near Bunbury, where an abortive settlement had been attempted in 1841; and from Augusta north to the Vasse River, where the Bussell family pioneered with more success from 1831. Geraldton was founded in 1851. In the 1860's, adventurous settlers pressed north with sheep and cattle as far as the De Grey district, and by the 1880's the pearling industry was established in the northwest, and gold prospectors as well as pastoralists were at work in the Kimberleys.

South Australia. The extension of settlement to what is now the state of South Australia was due less to strategic considerations and owed more to the influence of ideas than was the case with any other Australian colony. Six men are inseparably associated with this settlement. Charles Sturt, by his epic voyage down the Murray in 1830, drew attention to the rich lands near the river's mouth. The difficulties that attended the ill-planned settlement at the Swan River emphasized the need for closer coordination of land, labor, and capital in any new colony, and Edward Gibbon Wakefield provided a reasoned theory of coordination and was instrumental in founding the South Australian Association, which engineered the passage of the Foundation Act of 1834. George Fife Angas was one of the ablest and least doctrinaire of the commissioners appointed under the act to share with the colonial office the organization of the new settlement. As the promoter and main supporter of the privately owned South Australian Company, Angas also made possible the land sales necessary to bring the act into operation. William Light, who arrived as surveyor general in August 1836, determined the site of and laid out the future capital city of Adelaide. George Gawler, the second governor (1838–1841) of the colony but the first with unified authority, had to face the consequences of the speculation in land that had prevented the Wakefield theory from operating smoothly and that threatened the colony with starvation while settlers were still pouring in. By a vigorous policy of public works financed by bills drawn on the authorities in London he prevented the colony from collapsing. Recalled in 1841 and virtually disgraced by a home government that at first refused to honor his promissory notes, Gawler had nevertheless given the colony the equipment in roads, buildings, and country services necessary to its future development, which followed the vital reconstruction and rigorous economy ruthlessly effected by his capable successor, George Grey (1841–1845). Thereafter the extension of settlement in South Australia proceeded more steadily than in Western Australia. The land itself was more uniformly good, and what convicts did for the western colony was more than equaled by the natural stimulus afforded to South Australian agriculture by the markets opened up after the silver, lead, and copper discoveries in the colony

GOLD RUSH TOWN in New South Wales in the 1870's is typical of those that sprang up all over Australia to house the men who came to seek wealth.

itself in the early 1840's and by the gold of Victoria and New South Wales a decade later.

Northern Territory. Political and economic influences both played a part in the extension of settlement to what is now the Northern Territory of the Commonwealth. Anxiety to forestall French settlement in the north combined with the hope of developing East Indian trade led to abortive settlements at Melville Island in 1824 and at Raffles Bay in 1827, and to a settlement at Port Essington, which lasted from 1838 to 1849. Inland exploration in the 1860's, which resulted in the crossing of the continent from south to north, evoked new interest in the Northern Territory, and Queensland and South Australia cast ambitious eyes on the unsettled north. The temptation was too strong for the more venturesome politicians in Adelaide, and in 1863, with the consent of the British government, the boundaries of South Australia were extended to the north coast. Conditions less favorable than those obtaining in Queensland and the absence of a native population to serve as plantation laborers help to explain the slight progress made in settlement during the 48 years of South Australian administration, despite considerable expenditure by the government and the construction of an Adelaide-Darwin telegraph line and part of a south-north railway. Finally, in 1911, the Commonwealth assumed control over the territory.

The Gold Rushes and Their Aftermath, 1850–1890. Five of the six colonies had been independently established and Queensland was within sight of separate status before the gold rushes of the early 1850's. Self-government had also been foreshadowed by the Australian Colonies Government Act, 1850, at the same time that it separated Port Phillip from the mother colony. This act authorized all four colonies except Western Australia, whose convict period (1850–1868) delayed representative government until 1870 and responsible government until 1890, to draw up their own proposals for the modification of existing constitutions. To attribute Australian political institutions or ideas exclusively to the gold rushes would therefore be as misleading as it would be to ignore the economic and social potentialities of small settler resistance to squatter predominance in the second quarter of the century. Yet it must be recognized that the men of all classes and creeds who flocked to the east-

ern diggings in the 1850's and 1870's and to the western goldfields in the 1890's exercised a profound influence on the political, social, and economic evolution of all the Australian colonies. Australian history does not begin in 1851, but it was deeply affected by the aftermath of the discovery of gold at Bathurst by Edward H. Hargraves in February of that year.

Although gold had been found in New South Wales on at least four occasions between 1823 and 1842, further investigation had been officially discouraged. Transportation to the mother colony had, however, ceased by the time the riches of the California goldfields had whetted the appetites of colonial prospectors and colonial governments alike. The latter were now more attracted by the wealth than they were fearful of the social consequences of the discovery of gold in large quantities. Hargraves was therefore rewarded, and by the middle of 1851 the first Australian gold rush had begun. The most colorful features of life on the Australian diggings were to be seen after the much richer finds made in August and December 1851 at Ballarat and Bendigo, comparatively near the Victorian capital of Melbourne. But all colonies felt the direct effects of rushes to their own fields (as in Queensland and Western Australia during the 1870's and 1890's, respectively) or the indirect influence of the sudden migration of laborers to goldfields in neighboring colonies and the subsequent development of new markets there.

The political and economic effects of the gold rushes are more readily apparent than their social consequences. Although the immigrant diggers were not the only 19th century democrats in Australian colonial societies, the relatively high proportion of politically disaffected among the many thousands who came from Great Britain and Ireland, from continental Europe, and from North America to the goldfields in the 1850's was an important factor in the successful attack made upon the privileged classes in the responsible colonial legislatures of the 1860's. Vote by ballot became law in Victoria in March 1856 and in South Australia the following month. Modern historians tend to minimize the immediate political significance of the rebellion at the Eureka Stockade on the Ballarat fields toward the end of 1854, when four of the attacking military force, which had been rushed to the scene of the riot, and some 30 rebels lost their lives. This direct conflict with authority gave place to a more constitutional opposition to vested interests after the advent of capitalist mining in the 1860's.

Most diggers were then absorbed into the ranks of an urban proletariat or became more or less disgruntled small farmers seeking to take advantage of Victorian and New South Wales legislation for "free selection before survey" in a largely vain attempt to force squatters to "unlock the land." The former diggers certainly provided a new and welcome labor force, which made possible the manufacturing industries created in Victoria under the dominant influence of David Syme and his protectionist program. They gave new significance to the development of the Australian trade union movement, which had begun in the 1830's. Population in Australia increased from 405,356 in 1850 to 1,145,585 in 1860. Similar results were to follow the opening of the Western Australian fields some 25 years later; the western colony's population rose from 39,-584 to 179,708 between 1886 and 1900, when gold indeed put Western Australia on the map. The colony's exports multiplied ten times in value during the period, and responsible government, foreshadowed before the gold rushes and granted in 1890, became an effective instrument in agricultural expansion after the decline of gold mining early in the 20th century.

The social consequences of the gold rushes, like those of convict transportation, are not easily assessed. But it must be recognized that the mass migrations of the gold rushes had some leveling influence during the common search for fortunes on the fields and in the less spectacular search for a living when the alluvial gold had petered out. A certain ethnic infusion should also be recognized. Though the proportion of non-Britishers among the diggers was surprisingly small—the census of 1861 put it as low as 7.5 percent—the intermingling of English, Scottish, and Irish immigrants with colonial diggers helped to produce a distinctively Australian stock from which Asian strains were excluded. This was partly the result of the vigorous policy of immigration restriction—a policy owing much to the hard feelings between Europeans and Chinese on the goldfields. The policy eventually was embodied in the Immigration Restriction Act, passed immediately upon the establishment of the Commonwealth (1901).

One clearly understandable consequence of both convict transportation and gold discoveries was the increase in bushranging, or frontier violence. The final outburst of lawlessness in sections of an almost empty land was brought under control in 1880 with the destruction of the notorious Kelly gang led by Ned Kelly.

Economic Depression and Prelude to Federation, 1890–1901. The most serious sequel to the gold rushes, the land boom of the 1880's, had long-term results that were political and social as well as economic. The boom of the late 1880's and the acute depression that followed its bursting in the early 1890's, when 23 banks failed within two years, had many contributory causes. In the traditional interpretation of the boom of 1890 paramount importance is attached to the colonial self-confidence that had followed the gold rushes long after the gold yield had begun to decline. The significance of this single causative influence has, however, been challenged in view of the steady and healthy growth of many urban manu-

facturing and building industries between 1860 and 1885. Gold production throughout Australia nevertheless decreased more than 50 percent in value between 1860 and 1886, though falling world prices in manufactured goods helped to offset the reduction in gold exports as long as world prices for wool remained high. Eastern Australia also experienced an unusually long run of good seasons in the 1870's and 1880's, which helped to disguise a relative decline in efficiency of some expanded pastoral properties.

This expansion and some unhealthy urban building ventures were assisted by money from English and Scottish sources, which was freely invested in Australian banks and other private enterprises. Colonial governments also had no difficulty in raising loans on the London market, which were spent on developmental works whose economic soundness was too seldom subjected to careful scrutiny. Overseas interest commitments trebled between 1861 and 1890, and the situation was aggravated by unwise banking policy. Banks that had once given overdrafts on wool and stock in process of sale extended their credit until eventually the land itself was considered sufficient security. Speculation in land values made this security more than doubtful, especially when the advances were made on city blocks, in which an orgy of speculation developed in the 1880's. The reappearance of drought in New South Wales and South Australia between 1884 and 1886 checked the overconfidence of Sydney and Adelaide speculators, but Victoria continued to enjoy good seasons. People poured into the southern colony from other parts of Australia, and huge sums from overseas were invested between 1886 and 1890. Stock exchange activities in mining shares and the scrip of land companies nearly doubled between 1887 and 1888. Melbourne became a veritable boom city. When the banks endeavored to call a halt to the speculation, which their overgenerous advances had encouraged, land companies took advantage of Victorian legislation of 1888 to convert themselves into banks. They had little difficulty in obtaining financial support in the United Kingdom, and speculation in land values extended from the capital to country towns until the whole colony was affected.

There was no sudden bursting of the bubble, but the price of wool was an indicator. Steady from 1875 to 1884, it dropped each year thereafter until it was down to half of the 1884 price in 1894. British investors were also alarmed by failures in Argentina in the late 1880's and the sources of private and public loans began to dry up. The pinch was felt in Melbourne by the close of 1889, when a building association suspended payment. Building construction stopped suddenly in the early part of the following year, and most of the land companies collapsed in 1891 and 1892. The associated banks held on until January 1893, when the first of their number, the Federal Bank of Australia, went down.

Resolute action by the government of New South Wales checked panic in Sydney and made possible the use of the gold resources of the mother colony to assist reconstruction elsewhere, but rehabilitation was a slow and painful process. Millions of pounds of British deposits were locked up in the form of preference shares in reconstructed banks, and colonial investors had to settle down to a period of lean years from which many of them never recovered. Between 1898 and 1900, however, recovery was rapid despite the recurrence of drought conditions.

When financial, commercial, and rural interests had adjusted themselves to postboom conditions, they were faced with labor forces that themselves had undergone a difficult period of readjustment following a trial of strength with employers, while the boom was still at its height, from which the trade unions had come off second best. The Australian labor movement, which in its pre-goldfields phase had been influenced largely by British trade unionism, was strengthened and refashioned in the 1860's as a "unionism native to the country" by former diggers absorbed into older urban and rural industries, the new capitalized mining ventures, and the young manufacturing industries. The growing strength of the trade unions was displayed in a series of strikes in the 1870's and 1880's. Other landmarks in their rapid development were the formation of a coal miners' mutual protective association in the Hunter River district in 1874, the holding of the first intercolonial conference of trade unions in 1879, and the launching of the Amalgamated Shearers' Union (1886), which by 1894 was to become the powerful Australian Workers' Union (AWU), embracing shearers and shed hands in Victoria, New South Wales, South Australia, and New Zealand and joined a decade later by the Queensland Shearers' Union. The AWU thus organized by William Guthrie Spence, with a membership of 50,000, was to remain one of the most influential Australian trade unions, whose nationwide organization swept across political boundaries and absorbed minor rural unions. Elsewhere, craft unionism continued to retain a considerable hold on the labor movement, while geographical and political factors reinforced craft union arguments in favor of federation rather than amalgamation.

Meanwhile, the whole trade union movement, with its emphasis on industrial rather than on political activity, received a shattering blow from the failure of the great shipping strike of 1890, which both sides treated as a trial of strength. Although shearers and miners struck, the approach of the depression, already reflected in falling prices and increasing unemployment, and the strength of the political and press support for employers spelled disaster for the unions. After both leaders and rank-and-file members had retired to lick their wounds and to share in the general suffering caused by the bursting of the boom, Australian labor reemerged in a new political phase in which it rapidly rose to leadership in what became the federal and state parliaments of the new Commonwealth of Australia.

Although labor's advent as an organized political party dates from the 1890's, political pressure had been exercised by unions long before, as is shown by the general adoption of an eight-hour day by colonial legislatures between 1873 and 1896 and the passage of various factory and mines acts. A labor member had been elected to the legislative assembly of Victoria as early as 1859, and to that of New South Wales in 1880 and 1883. Such political intervention was merely incidental, however, and industrial activities were considered the real concern of trade unionists. The growing difficulties of the 1880's had suggested to some the need for a change of tactics, and the disastrous defeat in the shipping strike

of 1890 brought many more round to this point of view, which was strengthened by the payment of members of the New South Wales Legislative Assembly in 1891, following the lead of Victoria in 1871 and South Australia in 1887.

New South Wales and Queensland were most active in this new political phase of the labor movement. Some 36 Labour party members were elected in New South Wales in 1891, and 27 in 1894, only to be split on the fiscal issue by the superior tactics of Premier Sir George Dibbs. From 1895 on, the reunited party, though still in the minority, held the balance in the Legislative Assembly. Increasingly skillful tactics—the party now included two future Labour prime ministers of the Commonwealth, John Christian Watson and William Morris Hughes—made possible the making and unmaking of ministries. Labour thus secured the passage of important social legislation before it obtained a majority of the assembly in 1910 and formed the first Labour ministry in New South Wales, under James S.T. McGowen, though not the first in Australia. That distinction belongs to Queensland, where Anderson Dawson became premier in 1899. The Dawson ministry lasted only a week, but it included the second Labour prime minister of the Commonwealth, Andrew Fisher.

The fortunes of the Labour party in the various states in the early years of the 20th century were affected by local issues, reflecting to some degree the level of economic development reached in each. However, by this time the Australian labor movement was concentrating more and more of its political attention on the Commonwealth Parliament, to the creation of which organized labor had made an indirect contribution—though the influences leading to federation were concerned with external as well as internal affairs and in both respects considerably antedated the political phase of the labor movement.

It is difficult to estimate the relative importance of these external and internal influences. The need for coordination in defense policy and for joint action in external affairs undoubtedly played an important part in transforming vague aspirations for political federation into positive action. This was especially evident after the early 1880's, as the activities of foreign nations in the Pacific continued to alarm the several colonial communities in eastern Australia. But both the main stimulus and the most persistent opposition to federation came from the growing divergence of the domestic policies of the several colonial governments and from increasingly acute local rivalries and jealousies. There was a pressing need to find some way of coordinating the customs policies of neighboring colonies. Particularly glaring was the contrast between free trade New South Wales and protectionist Victoria after the late 1860's. Other common needs might be met from time to time by intercolonial conferences, which did indeed produce agreement concerning ocean mails, lighthouses, and the like. Some such ad hoc method might also have resolved the difficulties involved in the navigation and use of the waters of the Murray River, in which three colonies were closely interested, but without some more general and permanent machinery the search for a customs agreement was bound to be fruitless. On the other hand the very sharpness of the contrast between Victoria and New South Wales made a common tariff policy almost as elusive.

The first project for central government to achieve prominence dates from 1837, when Earl Grey suggested the establishment of a general assembly for the several colonies. The Australian Colonies Government Act of 1850 did contain such a provision in its first draft, but the centrifugal tendencies in Australian development made such attempts fruitless, although there were men in the colonies—Edward Deas-Thomson, William Charles Wentworth, and John Dunmore Lang—who early recognized the need of a machinery for common action. In the 1870's and 1880's the stiffening of Victoria's protectionist policy and the urgency of Murray River problems gave support to the convictions of three political leaders in Victoria, New South Wales, and Queensland, respectively—James Service, Henry Parkes, and Samuel Walker Griffith—to whom the cause of federation owed much. Events in the Pacific then played their part. In 1883 the British government refused to confirm Queensland Premier Sir Thomas McIlwraith's annexation of New Guinea, although it was supported by colonial opinion elsewhere. Service and Griffith then endorsed the earlier suggestion of Parkes for a federal council of Australasia, which was duly established in 1885 by an act of the British Parliament.

The first practical step in the movement toward federation was endangered by its founders' attempt to create a comprehensive unit including New Zealand and Fiji. The council's powers were also too limited, for they excluded defense and the question of tariffs. To make matters worse Parkes, who had been in England in 1883–1884 while his colleagues were somewhat hastily drafting the constitution of the new body, failed to persuade New South Wales to become a member. The federal council, indeed, fell far short of the federation of which Parkes dreamed, and for which he began an active campaign in the late 1880's.

The national convention that met in Sydney in March 1891 did not have sufficient popular drive behind it to overcome the partly factious opposition in all colonies. Nevertheless, it brought together a number of able men (including representatives of New Zealand) who, under the leadership of Parkes and Griffith, produced a draft embodying the details of a federal constitution to be submitted to the British Parliament after the endorsement of the colonial legislatures had been obtained. The colonial parliaments of 1891 failed, however, to give the necessary confirmation. Opposition, led by George Houstoun Reid, was strongest in Sydney, where there were real fears for the prosperity that had been built up by free trade. The opposition in the other colonies, though not so serious except in Western Australia, was sufficient to prevent the governments concerned from moving without the assurance of New South Wales cooperation, and there was no organized nonparty federal movement strong enough to force the issue.

The second national convention, held in 1897–1898, was the direct result of the rapid rise of such an organized popular movement. A conference of federal leagues and the older Australian Natives' Association, which assembled at Corowa in 1893, reflected the sentimental enthusiasm for union and the practical search for more efficient government inspired by the collapse of the land boom and the widespread depression of the early 1890's. Political changes

and retirements also provided parliamentary leaders for the federal movement. Edmund Barton in New South Wales and Alfred Deakin in Victoria gave steady support, while Reid, though still hesitant, was shrewd enough to recognize the political significance of the popular movement and give it the equivocal support that later earned him the nickname of "Yes-No" Reid. The popular side to the federal movement in the 1890's was reflected in the composition of the second national convention. Its members, following the procedure recommended by Dr. John Quick at Corowa, were elected by the people of the several colonies (except in Western Australia, where they were again appointed by the British Parliament, and in Queensland, which was not represented). Additional popular support was invited by the decision to submit the convention's revised version of the draft constitution of 1891 to the electors of the several Australian colonies.

The course was now set for federation, but opposition again sprang up in New South Wales and Western Australia. At Reid's instigation the legislature of New South Wales had made an 80,000 affirmative poll a condition for its further action, and the referendum of June 1898 produced an affirmative majorty vote totaling only 71,595. Despite clear majority votes in Victoria, South Australia, and Tasmania, followed by a similar result in Queensland, a position of stalemate was thus reached. Further negotiations led in January 1899 to a premiers' conference at Melbourne, where it was agreed to resubmit the bill with certain amendments concerning, among other subjects, financial clauses and the alteration of the constitution, and providing for the establishment of the federal capital within the boundaries of New South Wales, but more than 100 miles (161 km) from Sydney. A revival of opposition in Sydney threatened still further delay, but affirmative votes, with increased majorities, were obtained in all the colonies except Western Australia. There the government of John Forrest was at length persuaded, and a referendum held on July 31, 1900, produced the necessary affirmative vote. Meanwhile, the other five colonies had proceeded to London with their bill, and the Commonwealth of Australia Constitution Act came into operation on Jan. 1, 1901. Barton became the first prime minister of the new Commonwealth, with Deakin as his attorney general and leading colleague.

From Federation Through World War II, 1901–1945. The first Australian Commonwealth of 1901 would be scarcely recognizable to those who have known only the nation that emerged from the second of the two world wars that so deeply affected the first half century of its development. Its behavior in its first 14 years reflected its colonial parentage as well as its overseas ancestry. In many respects the young Commonwealth was but old colonial societies writ large. Leading figures at the seat of federal government—in Melbourne until 1927, thereafter at the new federal capital city of Canberra—were men of local political experience. The first prime minister had been both attorney general of New South Wales and a speaker of its Legislative Assembly; his attorney general had been premier of Victoria; five other members of his first ministry—John Forrest, Sir George Turner, Sir William John Lyne, Charles Cameron Kingston, and Sir Philip Oakley Fysh—has held the premiership in Western Australia, Victoria, New South Wales, South

Australia, and Tasmania, respectively. The official leader of the opposition, George Reid, had given up his colorful political career in Sydney for what was to be a somewhat indifferent success in federal politics, though he was to hold the office of prime minister in 1904–1905. John Christian Watson, Andrew Fisher, and William Morris Hughes, the first three Labour prime ministers of the Commonwealth, were also members of its first Parliament.

Apart from the problems peculiar to the new federal governmental system, it had to take on the many issues that had already been hammered out in the several colonies. In the formative period of the young Commonwealth preceding World War I most of these issues were clarified in general with very substantial common consent—a fact that helps to explain their high degree of subsequent acceptance.

In many cases the colonial antecedents are readily detectable in legislation passed in the early years. Protection, which became the accepted fiscal policy in 1908 after an initial compromise, was a victory for Victorian as against New South Wales practice—a victory made inevitable by the support of the Labour minority in the House of Representatives. The peculiarly Australian system of industrial arbitration developed in the Commonwealth Court of Conciliation and Arbitration set up by the Commonwealth Parliament in 1904 was modeled on New Zealand experience embodied in Kingston's Conciliation and Arbitration Act of 1894 in South Australia, Bernhard Ringrose Wise's New South Wales Arbitration and Conciliation Act of 1901, and the Western Australia Court of Arbitration created in 1900, although the system was also influenced by the minimum wage boards introduced in Victoria in 1896, in Queensland in 1908, and in Tasmania. As noted above, the Immigration Restriction Act of 1901 was the sequel to an agitation that dated back to goldfields rivalries and had already found expression on the prefederation statute books of more than one colony. The decision to repatriate and exclude South Sea Islanders was made by general consent through the Pacific Islands Labourers Act of 1901, and the concurrence of Queensland cane sugar interests was secured by a tariff designed to compensate for the additional cost of white workers in the cane fields.

Some of the measures passed in the first 14 years reflected the growing influence of the Labour party. Though lacking a clear majority until 1910, Labour, under Watson until 1907 and then under Fisher, had a strong ally in Alfred Deakin. This made possible many of the reforms that gave the prewar Australian Commonwealth a reputation for pioneering social legislation. The year 1908 witnessed the introduction of old-age and invalid pensions. A maternity allowance (1912) followed Labour's advent to power in 1910, and 1911 saw King O'Malley's act for the establishment of the Commonwealth Bank of Australia. However, the electors of the Commonwealth refused Labour the necessary votes at referendums held in 1911 and 1913 to extend federal powers under the constitution to speed up its gradualist policy of "socialism in our time."

Public as well as parliamentary interest centered mainly on domestic affairs in the prewar years, but substantial progress was made in the related fields of defense, imperial relations, and external affairs that had greatly influenced the establishment of the Commonwealth. The decision to create the Royal Australian Navy (1909) had the support of all political parties, and the new Australian military system established by Deakin's legislation of 1909, as amended by Labour's minister for defense, Senator George Foster Pearce, in the following year, provided for a citizen army based on the principle of compulsory training for home defense.

The early leaders of the Commonwealth had no difficulty in reconciling a sturdy Australian nationalism with retention of the imperial tie, but Deakin in particular was not afraid of frank speech in rejection of imperial federation, in denunciation of the "disdain and indifference" with which British enterprise in the Pacific was treated by the Colonial Office, and in advocacy of an imperial secretariat of officials appointed by the several Dominions to maintain direct contact between their governments and United Kingdom departments of state. Deakin's demand for a greater share by the Dominions in the shaping of imperial policy was reinforced by Fisher, but the United Kingdom's control over foreign relations affecting Australia remained virtually unfettered down to the outbreak of war in August 1914. The Australian government had also shown its readiness to qualify its economic nationalism by a mild form of imperial preference (1908). The existence of a portfolio of external affairs in prewar ministries was, indeed, justified chiefly by such legislation as the Navigation Act of 1913, designed to implement the domestic social policy of the Australian Commonwealth by denying interstate coastal trade to ships whose crews did not enjoy the conditions and wages prescribed for Australian seamen.

To the nation at large World War I thus came as a shock, and the reaction was instinctive and emotional rather than reflective of a considered responsibility in foreign affairs. Both as leader of the opposition and as prime minister from September 1914, Fisher pledged "our last man and our last shilling to see this war brought to a successful issue." The wartime record of the young Australian navy in its Indian Ocean sinking of the *Emden* (1914) and in service with the Royal Navy, the capture of German New Guinea (1914), and the contribution of some 329,000 volunteer servicemen (from a total population of less than 5,000,000) were rightly regarded as a national baptism of fire.

Service on the battlefields also won a place for Australian politicians in the councils of peace at the end of the war, as well as in imperial war cabinets. The nation was behind William Morris Hughes (who had succeeded Fisher as prime minister in 1914) when he insisted before and during the Paris Peace Conference that Australia should secure all of Germany's Pacific possessions south of the equator, with or without the nominal restrictions of a League of Nations mandate. Hughes had nevertheless failed to carry a majority of the Australian people with him when he sought by successive referendums (1916 and 1917) to replace voluntary enlistment by conscription for overseas service.

These conscription referendums had a profound and lasting effect on Australian politics, for they split the Labour party as well as the nation. Hughes and most of his lieutenants left the federal party, which went embittered to the wilderness and remained there until 1929. Hughes led his wartime non-Labour allies until

1923, when he was succeeded as prime minister by Stanley Melbourne (later 1st Viscount) Bruce.

During the postwar and predepression decade of the 1920's most Australians again were preoccupied with domestic affairs. Prime Minister Bruce, aided by substantial overseas loans and extensive projects of assisted immigration (both mainly from the United Kingdom), grappled with the three related problems of men, money, and markets that confronted an Australia now intensifying its wartime industrialization with more speed than efficiency or discrimination. Bruce was a conservative and restraining influence on Canadian, South African, and Irish Free State representatives at the imperial conferences of 1923 and 1926. Australia was more concerned with economic arrangements that would increase her preferences in United Kingdom markets and with improved machinery for imperial consultation and cooperation than with discussions of the legal rights of the Dominions or with elaboration of constitutional formulas for the British Commonwealth of Nations, which was replacing the British Empire. Successive Australian governments declined until 1942 to ratify the Statute of Westminster of 1931. However, despite preoccupation with domestic matters, little social legislation was passed during the interwar years.

Labour, returned to office under James Henry Scullin in 1929, found its hands tied by a hostile majority in the federal Senate, though Labour governments controlled several state parliaments, including that of New South Wales. When the worldwide depression hit Australia, under circumstances strikingly similar to those of the early 1890's, the Labour party once more split. The majority followed Scullin into opposition to a national government headed by his lieutenant, former Tasmanian Labour Premier Joseph Aloysius Lyons. The latter remained in office as prime minister, with the future High Court chief justice, J.G. (later Sir John) Latham, as his right-hand man, until the death of Lyons in 1939 brought Robert Gordon Menzies to the prime-ministership. In this office, notwithstanding his replacement by successive Labour leaders John Curtin and Joseph Benedict Chifley between 1941 and 1949, Menzies was to establish an all-time record for length and quality of service before his retirement in 1966.

In September 1939, however, Menzies led into World War II a divided coalition government and a nation almost as ill prepared as it had been in 1914, both psychologically and in defense equipment, despite the Lyons government's efforts in rearmament from 1933 onward. The replacement of the Menzies government by the Curtin Labour administration of 1941 made possible increasing manpower controls that might otherwise have been resisted by the trade unions. Wartime industry was thus enabled to provide munitions and machine tools and, with increasingly mechanized agriculture, made possible United States use of Australia as a base.

During World War II, Australian troops repeated their previous role in voluntarily recruited service overseas in the Middle East and also in Malaya, where an Australian division was trapped at the fall of Singapore. Troops then recalled from the former theater were joined by compulsorily recruited militia, whose home service was extended to the Pacific Islands; together they held the Japanese in the jungles of New Guinea, while the Royal Australian Navy and the Royal Australian Air Force fought alongside other British Commonwealth and United States forces in various parts of the world. Of Australia's total population (1943) of 7,229,864, nearly 1,000,000 were in uniform; there were 95,561 wartime casualties.

Post-World War II Period. World War II made Australia more sharply aware of the responsibilities of nationhood. The inability of the Royal Navy to defend Australia's shores unaided, the Japanese bombing of Darwin, Wyndham, Broome, and other northern outposts, and the submarine threats to Sydney's harbor shocked the nation into its first recognition of the proximity of Asia. With the help of an expanded Department of External Affairs the nation settled down to work out the realities of a belated but fairly distinctive three-pronged foreign policy. This policy aimed to preserve and make the most of the historic link with the United Kingdom and older Commonwealth members; to welcome increasing association with Australia's wartime ally and powerful trans-Pacific partner, the United States; and to work for increasingly close economic, diplomatic, and strategic links with Australia's northern neighbors, whether through Commonwealth of Nations or United Nations membership, or by direct regional relationships.

This threefold postwar foreign policy was largely bipartisan, though some significant differences of emphasis appeared from time to time. A former High Court judge, Dr. Herbert Vere Evatt, as minister for external affairs in the Labour governments of Curtin and Joseph Benedict Chifley (who had succeeded to the prime-ministership on Curtin's death in 1945), made vigorous use of Australia's membership in the United Nations General Assembly (of which he was president in 1948–1949) and Security Council. Evatt, an exponent of the new "open door" diplomacy, sought to maximize the role of lesser nations and tended to give the impression of emphasizing divergences between Australian and United Kingdom or United States policies. By contrast his successors as minister for external affairs, Sir Percy Spender (1949–1951) and Richard Gardiner (later Lord) Casey (1951–1960), endeavored to resolve these differences through diplomatic and personal channels. The Evatt initiative in support of Indonesian independence in 1947–1948 attracted much attention and provoked some anti-Labour domestic criticism, but Spender's initiative over the Colombo Plan (q.v.) in 1950 continued to reflect the new policy of strengthening Australian-Asian ties. A gradual relaxing of the administrative of immigration regulations, without any major modification of the principle of denying permanent residence to Asians, made possible substantial educational facilities within Australian schools, technical colleges, and universities for Asian students.

Successive electoral victories consolidated the Liberal party (which had been formed in 1944 at the initiative of Robert Gordon Menzies) and enhanced the prestige of its leader, opening the way for the Menzies government to move toward its objective of formal regional defense arrangements. The signing in 1951 of the ANZUS pact (bringing together Australia, New Zealand, and the United States) was a turning point in Australian diplomacy, assuring United States participation in the defense of the area. As concern mounted over the nationalist-Communist threat in Southeast Asia, Australia supported the formation of the Southeast Asia Treaty Organization (SEATO), which came into being in 1954. Ratification of these two pacts was secured without difficulty, although the Labour party was more critical of the latter pact than of the former.

As the postwar era lengthened there was increasing divergence between the Liberal-Country party government and the official Labour opposition, which was led by Evatt after Chifley's death in 1951. Evatt continued to stress the need of finding solutions to international differences and of lessening international tension through the closest possible suport of the United Nations; Menzies, on the other hand, considered that integration within the framework of British and American policies (and the resolving of any differences that might arise between Washington and London) represented the only sound policy for Australia to follow.

Australia followed the lead of the United States rather than Britain in relation to Communist China, refusing recognition of any type —a stand strengthened by events in Korea, where Australia was an active participant after hostilities broke out there in 1950. When Australian troops were sent to join other Commonwealth forces in Malaya (1955), Labour was critical. The division was even sharper when Menzies took a stand in support of Anglo-French intervention in the Suez Canal area (1956), and there were dissidents even among Menzies' own followers. Therefore, Australian policy became more closely attuned to Washington, and a hard line in relation to the "neutralist" countries of Asia and Africa was discernible in Canberra.

The substantial contribution made by successive Labour and non-Labour governments to the economic and social development of Australia, as well as to the clarification of its foreign policy in the postwar decade, was undoubtedly obscured by the rapid deterioration in domestic politics that followed Chifley's death. Increasing uneasiness on ideological grounds had been revealed inside as well as outside the Australian Labour party during the last year of the Chifley administration. The Labour prime minister's insistence on forcing the issue of bank nationalization not only contributed to his party's electoral defeat in December 1949 but also sharpened the resistance of its right wing to the growing influence of Communists within key trade unions. The right wing, having strengthened its position and recaptured certain of those unions through the formation of anti-Communist industrial groups within them, openly challenged Evatt's allegedly left-wing leadership in the early 1950's.

The split in the labor movement attracted great attention because of the personalities involved and the widely publicized allegations, on the one hand, of the Labour party leader's Communist sympathies and affiliation and, on the other, of Catholic Action's association with the industrial group movement. The latter allegation invited attention to the unavowed but widely recognized link between the once predominantly Irish priesthood of the Roman Catholic Church in Australia and the Irish-born workers in the 19th century Australian trade union movement. Changes by the mid-20th century in the economic and social status of many Australians of Irish descent or birth no doubt helped as much as the church's worldwide postwar ideological

hostility to communism and socialism to bring about increasingly uneasy relations between many Roman Catholics and the official Labour leadership after 1951.

The emotions released in the resultant internecine party strife were still further charged by the 1954 incident of the defection of Vladimir M. Petrov, a ministry of state security (MVD) official at the Soviet embassy at Canberra. Though a royal commission's report of 1955 failed to reveal evidence of a link between any person prominent in Australian politics and the Soviet espionage activities uncovered by the Petrov disclosures, much mud was flung by opposing factions.

The eventual emergence of a separate right-wing group, the Australian Democratic Labour party (so named after 1957) caused a major shift in political balance. Although the dissident group was itself almost annihilated when its members faced the polls, the split contributed to Liberal party successes in both federal and state elections.

The bitterness inevitably associated with the Labour split of the early 1950's and the deep-seated personal antagonism frequently displayed between prime minister and opposition leader did much to obscure the steady continuity in the postwar policies of the Commonwealth, domestic and foreign, to which the Suez crisis and banking legislation may perhaps be regarded as significant exceptions. However, both Labour and non-Labour governments revealed their determination to maintain and extend the material achievement that the war effort had called forth.

A significant illustration was the decision of the Chifley government, with Arthur Augustus Calwell as minister for immigration, to set aside Labour's traditional suspicions of organized immigration that might threaten living standards in a time of economic distress. Calwell sponsored a postwar migration policy which laid unprecedented stress on non-British immigration of displaced persons. As a result of this policy, which the Menzies government continued after 1949 and later expanded, some 2 million new settlers reached Australia over a 20-year period. The proportion of effective British immigration remained about 50 percent of the total. Some social effects of European immigration on the substantially homogeneous Anglo-Saxon society of Australia were clearly discernible. But government policy aimed at maximum assimilation proved extremely successful with younger age groups and with the children of European settlers.

In addition to the welcome given by all political parties to overseas workers, postwar Australia also eagerly sought—and received—assistance from overseas capital willing to participate in the development of an increasingly diversified economy. United States as well as British and European businessmen and investors appeared to appreciate the high degree of continuity in government policies and the economic prospects for continued expansion. A substantial inflow of capital and of technical know-how helped in the modernization and expansion of Australian industrial and transport undertakings. Productive capacity was built up in rural as well as manufacturing industries and in all phases of transportation, and as a result the total outpouring of goods and services increased more than 4 percent a year. With greater efficiency in evidence in various facets of the economy, general prosperity was enhanced, making it possible for Australians to undertake greater expenditures for consumer goods and services and to increase their savings.

Much more serious attention also was given by the Commonwealth government in the postwar years (notably under the ministerial direction of Paul M.C. Hasluck after 1951) to the development of the Northern Territory and to the Commonwealth's external territories—Norfolk Island, Papua, the trusteeship territories of New Guinea and Nauru, the Territory of Heard and McDonald Islands, the Australian Antarctic Territory, the Territory of Ashmore and Cartier Islands, Cocos (Keeling) Islands (transferred from the United Kingdom in 1955), and Christmas Island (transferred in 1957). In spite of special problems there, New Guinea was advancing economically and politically. Increasing numbers were being drawn into a modernized economic system, giving up the old subsistence horticulture. Successive degrees of representative government were granted: in 1960 the territory's legislative council was expanded to 37 members, eliminating the administration's former official majority, and in 1964 an elective house of assembly was instituted.

In these varied fields of activity, Australian governments and the Australian people worked their way into the second half of their first century of federation with increasing confidence in new technical, managerial, and promotional skills, but with a somewhat sobered recognition of their need for increased external cooperation, political and economic, from friends old and new, in Asia as well as in Europe and North America.

Meanwhile, distances were continually shrinking within Australia. A beginning was made belatedly in 1957 to overcome the differences in railway gauges on major interstate lines, air transportation was growing rapidly, and television was inaugurated in Sydney and Melbourne in 1956. The widespread expansion of transportation and communication, together with such peculiarly Australian experimental ventures as the Flying Doctor Service and correspondence schools, was breaking down the isolation of the remotest regions in the island continent and Tasmania and in its adjacent territories overseas.

Throughout the 1950's the national effort was directed toward the strengthening of the economy, and, with available resources fully committed, the defense effort was maintained at minimum levels. Changes in the international scene —particularly Indonesia's belligerency over the future of Dutch-held West New Guinea (incorporated into Indonesia in 1963)—caused concern, and by the early 1960's the government recognized the necessity for a greater defense effort. Concern was reinforced by Indonesia's violent reaction to the creation of the Federation of Malaysia (1963) and the increasing Communist infiltration in South Vietnam. Australia supported the United States stand on South Vietnam, believing the commitment of American forces and resources to be vital if the balance of power were to be maintained in Southeast Asia.

In 1962 new commitments were undertaken "in sharing the American determination to see that Asian communism made no further territorial gains." The growing complexity of Australia's strategic position was recognized by the creation of a standing cabinet committee, the Defense and Foreign Relations Committee, to coordinate policies. Australia became directly involved in the United States Asian defense policy when an agreement to erect a radio communication base at North West Cape (Western Australia) for use by the U.S. Navy was ratified in 1963.

In successive elections Prime Minister Menzies maintained office until his retirement in January 1966. Throughout, he skillfully exploited divisions within the Australian Labour party on foreign policy and defense and on domestic issues such as the provision of government aid to private schools (which the Labour party continued to oppose). Menzies steadily drew Australia into a closer working relationship with the United States on defense matters and in space programs. Harold Holt became prime minister in January 1966, and he was succeeded on his death in December 1967 by John Gorton. Gorton was replaced as Liberal party leader and prime minister by William McMahon in March 1971.

In December 1972 the Labour party was swept into office, and Labour party leader Gough Whitlam became prime minister. Whitlam immediately announced the end of the military draft and the beginning of talks to establish diplomatic relations with Mainland China.

FRED ALEXANDER
University of Western Australia

Bibliography

Cannon, Michael, *Who's Master, Who's Man: Australia in the Victorian Age* (Verry 1972).
Clark, Charles M. H., *A History of Australia*, vol. 1, *From the Earliest Times to the Age of Macquarrie* (Melbourne Univ. Press 1968).
Clark, Charles M. H., ed., *Select Documents in Australian History*, 2 vols. (reprint, Angus 1969).
Crawford, Raymond M., *Australia*, 3d ed. (Hutchinson 1970).
Ellis, Malcolm H., *Lachlan Macquarrie* (Angus 1947).
Encel, Solomon, *Cabinet Government in Australia* (Melbourne Univ. Press 1971).
Fitzpatrick, Brian, *The British Empire in Australia: An Economic History, 1834–1939* (Melbourne Univ. Press 1941).
Fitzpatrick, Brian, *British Imperialism and Australia, 1783–1833* (Allen, G. 1939).
Grattan, Clinton Hartley, *The Southwest Pacific to 1900* (Univ. of Mich. Press 1963).
Grattan, Clinton Hartley, *The Southwest Pacific Since 1900* (Univ. of Mich. Press 1963).
Greenway, John, *Australia: The Last Frontier* (Dodd 1972).
Greenwood, Gordon, ed., *Australia: A Social and Political History*, 3d ed. (Verry 1964).
Greenwood, Gordon, and Harper, Norman D., eds., *Australia in World Affairs* (Angus 1958).
Harper, Norman D., and Sissons, David, *Australia and the United Nations* (Manhattan Pub. 1959).
Legge, John D., *Australian Colonial Policy: A Survey of National Administration and European Development in Papua* (Angus 1956).
McKnight, Tom L., *Australia's Corner of the World* (Prentice-Hall 1970).
Millar, Thomas B., *Australia's Defence* (Melbourne Univ. Press 1965).
Miller, John D. B., and Jinks, Brian, *Australian Government and Politics*, 4th ed. (Dufour 1971).
Moorehead, Alan, *Cooper's Creek* (Harper 1963).
O'Brien, Eris M., *The Foundation of Australia 1786–1800*, 2d ed. (Angus 1950).
Reese, Trevor R., *Australia in the Twentieth Century: A Political History* (Burns & MacEachern 1964).
Scott, Sir Ernest, *Australian Discovery by Land* (Dutton 1929).
Scott, Sir Ernest, *Australian Discovery by Sea* (Dutton 1929).
Scott, Sir Ernest, *A Short History of Australia*, 7th ed. (Oxford 1947).
Serle, Percival, *Dictionary of Australian Biography*, 2 vols. (Angus 1949).
Starke, Joseph G., *The ANZUS Treaty Alliance* (Melbourne Univ. Press 1965).
Younger, Ronald M., *Australia and the Australians* (Humanities 1970).
Younger, Ronald M., *The Changing World of Australia* (Watts, F. 1963).

AUSTRALIAN ALPS, ô-strāl′yən alps, a mountain range in Australia, extending eastward from central Victoria and then north into New South Wales. It consists of a group of ranges forming the continent's principal upland area. The southern portion, called the *Victorian Alps,* is a broad plateau with peaks rising above 6,000 feet (1,830 meters). North of the border, in New South Wales, the plateau narrows, and the names *Snowy Mountains* and *Kosciusko Massif* are applied to portions of the range. Mount Kosciusko (7,316 feet; 2,229 meters), the highest point in Australia, is located here.

The Australian Alps are part of the Great Dividing Range (Eastern Highlands), which forms the watershed between the rivers flowing to the east and south coasts and the westward-flowing rivers of the Murray-Darling river system. There are resort areas and many large forest reserves in the range.

The mountains were first explored by white men in 1839–1840 and were surveyed between 1846 and 1850. Their streams constitute a valuable source of irrigation water, and also represent the most important hydroelectric power potential of the Australian continent. An estimated 4 million kilowatts of power could be developed economically in the Australian Alps. The Kiewa project in Victoria and the Snowy Mountains project in New South Wales have a potential generating capacity of about 3.1 million kilowatts.

AUSTRALIAN BALLOT. See BALLOT.

AUSTRALIAN CAPITAL TERRITORY, a territory in Australia, chosen in 1908 under the Australian Constitution as the seat of the federal government and containing the capital, Canberra. An enclave of 911 square miles (2,359.5 sq km) in the southeastern part of the state of New South Wales, it was transferred to the federal government in 1911, and until 1938 was known as the Federal Capital Territory. Most of the population of the territory lives in Canberra and is involved in government service. Sheep raising is the main occupation of the rural leaseholders.

In 1915 an additional area of 28 square miles (72.5 sq km) at Jervis Bay, on the coast about 80 miles (128.7 km) to the east, was acquired by the Commonwealth government to serve as a federal port and as the seat of the Royal Australian Naval College. After the college was moved to Victoria, the Jervis Bay area was developed as a tourist resort. Population: (1961, including Jervis Bay) 58,828.

R.M. YOUNGER
Author of "Changing World of Australia"

AUSTRALIAN NATIONAL UNIVERSITY is a coeducational institution in Canberra, Australia. It was founded in 1946 by an act of Parliament to provide for postgraduate research. The act was amended in 1960 to include Canberra University College (founded 1929) for undergraduate study. The Institute of Advanced Studies has schools of medicine, physical and social sciences, and Pacific studies. The undergraduate School of General Studies has faculties in law, science, economics, and the arts. The libraries of both units house a total of 240,000 volumes. Average enrollment in the mid-1960's was 150 graduate students and 320 full-time and 650 part-time undergraduates.

AUSTRALOID, ôs′trə-loid, in anthropology, a designation applied to a subgroup of the Caucasoids, one of the three historical divisions of the human species (the other two being the Mongoloids and the Negroids). Although some anthropologists, such as Melville J. Herskovits and A.L. Kroeber, have expressed uncertainty about how to classify the Australoids, many authorities are in general agreement as to their geographical distribution and physical characteristics. Australoids are described as dark-skinned, wavy-haired, and large-toothed, with moderate to abundant body hair.

In many tabulations of human races, the Australoids are listed as including chiefly the aboriginal inhabitants of Australia, the Vedda of Ceylon, the Dravidians of southern India, and the Ainu of Japan. Carleton Coon, however, extends the designation to include the Melanesians and Papuans and various Negritos of South Africa and Oceania.

Further Reading: Beals, Ralph L., and Hoijer, Harry, *An Introduction to Anthropology,* 2d ed. (New York 1959); Coon, Carleton, *The Origin of Races* (New York 1962); Herskovits, Melville J., *Cultural Anthropology* (New York 1958); Kroeber, A.L., *Anthropology* (New York 1948); Montagu, Ashley, *Man's Most Dangerous Myth: The Fallacy of Race,* 4th ed. (Cleveland 1964).

AUSTRALOPITHECINES, ôs-trə-lō-pith′ə-sēnz, in anthropology, a group of manlike primates, the fossil remains of which were discovered at various excavation sites in South Africa. They are classified by many authorities as a subfamily within the family Hominidae. Their teeth and dental arches and pelvic, leg, and foot bones were very similar to those of modern man. Australopithecines were between 4 and 5 feet tall, walked or ran upright, and had hands capable of forming and using simple stone tools. Their brains, however, were no larger than those of apes.

Notable among several genera of this group are *Australopithecus,* reckoned to be between 500,000 and 1,000,000 years old, and *Zinjanthropus,* estimated to be at least 1,750,000 years old. Another genus, *Paranthropus,* has been classified by some authorities as virtually identical with *Australopithecus,* although it appeared somewhat later.

See also MAN, PREHISTORIC TYPES OF—*Australopithecus;* AFRICA—*History.*

AUSTRASIA, ô-strā′zhə, derived from a Germanic word meaning *east,* was the eastern dominion of the Merovingian Franks. Also called *Ostrasia,* it included much of eastern France, a portion of modern Germany, and what is now Belgium. The capital was at Metz, France.

The Merovingians, especially under Clovis I, had greatly increased Frankish influence in northwestern Europe. After Clovis died in 511, his realm was divided among his four sons, with Austrasia passing to Thierry I. For over 150 years, Austrasia alternated between being a separate kingdom and being united with Neustria, the western part of the Merovingian holdings.

During the late 7th century a family later known as the Carolingians became the hereditary mayors of the palace, or chief ministers, of the Merovingians. The Carolingians gained control of Austrasia and then Neustria. In 751, Pepin III (the Short) deposed the last Merovingian and was elected king himself. By the time Pepin's son Charlemagne came to the throne, Austrasia no longer existed as a subdivision of the Frankish empire.

AUSTRIA

Austria's coat of arms

DAVIS PRATT, FROM RAPHO GUILLUMETTE

AUSTRIA'S MOUNTAIN HAMLETS are transformed by heavy snowfalls into attractive centers for winter sports.

CONTENTS

AUSTRIA, ôs'trē-ə, is a federal republic of central Europe. *Österreich* is the German form of the name. The Austrian republic was established in 1919, following the end of World War I and the breakup of Austria-Hungary.

Austria is the product of unique historical and geographic factors. Consolidated in the 10th century as an eastern march, or borderland, of the Holy Roman Empire, it was to become in time a leading German state. Austria was above all a dynastic state; its history was for centuries the history of the house of Habsburg, from among whose members, after the 15th century, the emperors of the Holy Roman Empire almost automatically came. Through dynastic marriages the Habsburgs extended their hegemony to Spain, the Netherlands, and Italy, and they became a pivotal power in European affairs.

Austria for many years was the defender of Germany against the French. On the other hand, looking east, it was the defender of Europe against the Turks, eventually driving back the Ottoman Turks from east central Europe. The expansion of the Austrian state added to the largely Germanic population many other ethnic elements, including various Slavic groups, Italians, and Magyars.

To a remarkable degree the Habsburg rulers were devoted to music, and many great musicians were attracted to Vienna. The dynasty sur-

rounded itself with splendor and magnificence. Architecture and all the decorative arts flourished under the Habsburgs. Vienna became the center of a rich culture, blending East and West. It was renowned for its music and lighthearted charm.

In the 19th century the empire began to decline, as Prussia gained hegemony over the rest of Germany. Following the revolutions of 1848, Austria and Prussia competed at length for leadership in Germany. Austria was defeated by Prussia in the Austro-Prussian War of 1866 (known also as the Seven Weeks' War). There followed a serious confrontation with the Hungarian part of the empire, which ended in 1867 with the creation of the dual monarchy of Austria-Hungary.

The continuing conflict between Slav, German, and Magyar brought increasing political problems, yet Vienna remained a great cultural center. Despite the strictness and frugality of the regime of Emperor Francis Joseph (reigned 1848–1916), Vienna was a colorful city with outstanding opera, theater, and concerts. The Viennese had become famous for their *Gemütlichkeit:* their easygoing approach to life, their warmth and gaiety, their love of music, and their cosmopolitan outlook.

INFORMATION HIGHLIGHTS

Official Name: The Republic of Austria (Republik Österreich).

Head of State: President.

Head of Government: Chancellor.

Legislature: Bundesversammlung (Federal Assembly): Upper chamber, Bundesrat (Federal Council); Lower chamber, Nationalrat (National Council).

Area: 32,369 sq mi (83,835 sq km).

Boundaries: North, Czechoslovakia; east, Hungary; south, Yugoslavia and Italy; west, Switzerland and Liechtenstein; northwest, Germany.

Elevation: Highest point, 12,461 feet (3,798 meters; Grossglockner Peak); lowest point, 377 feet (115 meters; Neusiedler See).

Population: 7,255,000 (mid-1965 est.).

Capital: Vienna (population, mid-1963, 1,634,253).

Major Languages: German (official language), Croatian, Slovenian, Magyar, Czech.

Major Religious Groups: Roman Catholics, Protestants.

Monetary Unit: Schilling (100 Groschen).

Weights and Measures: Metric system.

Flag: Red, white, and red horizontal bars.

National Anthem: *Land der Berge, Land am Strome* (music by W.A. Mozart; text by Paula von Preradovic).

Following Austria-Hungary's defeat in World War I, the Austrian republic was created. By the Treaty of St.-Germain of Sept. 10, 1919, Austria was stripped of all but 26.63 percent of the territory and 24.40 percent of the population of the Austrian half of the dual monarchy. Austria gained the province of Burgenland, formerly part of Hungary. Austria thus became very nearly a completely German state, instead of a complex of nationalities as before.

After World War I there was a strong movement for union with Germany (*Anschluss*), although this had been forbidden by the Treaty of St.-Germain. When Hitler's forces marched into Austria in 1938, *Anschluss* was established, but it did not survive the defeat of Germany. After Austria was liberated at the end of World War II, it was occupied by American, British, Soviet, and French forces. On May 15, 1955, two months after the four occupying powers and Austria signed the State Treaty, Austria regained its full sovereignty, and parliament subsequently enacted a statute pledging Austria to a policy of neutrality.

1. Land and Natural Resources

Approximately 71 percent of Austria is classified as mountainous, as compared with 62 percent of Switzerland. Within its boundaries there are also forested highlands and the plain of the Danube Basin. Visitors are particularly drawn to Austria by the spectacular scenery of its mountains and lakes. The mountains also attract winter sports enthusiasts.

General Topography. The corner of Austria north of the Danube River, where the country borders on Germany and Czechoslovakia, includes a part of the Bohemian Massif, characterized by its undulating hills, occasional rocky crags, and thick woods, especially in the so-called Waldviertel area in the province of Lower Austria. In some places the massif extends south of the Danube and accounts, for example, for the Gorge of Grein and the Gorge of Wachau in Lower Austria. In general, however, the massif gives way on the south to the long valley of the Danube, which extends for 217 miles (349 km) from west to east. Relatively narrow in the west, this valley broadens out as it nears Vienna and merges into the great Hungarian plain.

To the south of the Danube Valley rises the Eastern Alps, which dominate Austria. These can be divided roughly into three longitudinal ranges. The Northern Limestone Alps, made up of numerous minor groups such as the Tuxer Gebirge, the Kitzbühel Alps, and the Eizenerz Alps, are separated from the Central Alps by a series of valleys. These valleys stretch from the Arlberg Pass in the west, along the upper waters of the Inn, Salzach, Enns, Mur, and Mürz rivers, to the Semmering Pass in the east. As the first three rivers bend north to find their way to the Danube, and the last two find their way south to the Drave (German, Drau), they provide important north-south passes through the mountains. These and lesser passes make Austria one of the most accessible of mountainous countries.

The second great longitudinal range is formed by the Central Alps. These are, from west to east, the Rhätikon, Silvretta, Ötztal, and Stubai Alps, which run along the Austrian-Swiss-Italian border west of the Brenner Pass, and farther east, the Zillertal Alps, the Hohe Tauern, the Niedere Tauern, and the extensions of the Gurktal

CHALETS AND CASTLES, like these in Kufstein, are typical of Austria's provincial towns in the mountains.

and lesser chains leading into Yugoslavia. The Hohe Tauern contain Austria's highest peak, the Grossglockner (12,461 feet; 3,798 meters). The Grossglockner alpine highway, completed in 1935 and subsequently widened, is more than 35 miles (56 km) in length and rises to a height of more than 8,200 feet (4,300 meters) above sea level. This road has become one of the most popular scenic mountain highways in the world.

The Southern Alps are most clearly marked off from the Central Alps in the easterly reaches. The most important ranges are the Carnic Alps and the Karawanken, which run along the border between Austria's southernmost province of Carinthia and Italy and Yugoslavia. Within the Southern Alps lies the Klagenfurt Basin, with its beautiful lake, the Wörthersee. The mountains taper off to foothills in the east, and there is a continuous belt of land from west of the Mur River around the whole eastern end of Austria to north of the Danube, which is less than 1,650 feet (500 meters) above sea level.

Climate. The mountainous terrain that predominates in most of Austria accounts for a varied climate. There is ample precipitation in all sections, the average annual rainfall measuring between 40 and 50 inches (102–127 cm).

The seasons are for the most part clearly defined, the winter in the mountain sections often being very severe, with deep snow and high winds. The cold is at times moderated by a warm, dry south wind—the Föhn—that prevails when a low-pressure area passes north of the Alps. Its effects are felt particularly in the Inn River valley of Tyrol. The Föhn helps to melt the snow, but at times it produces an extremely uncomfortable cold fog.

A FARMER cultivates a mountain slope in the Tyrol.
The small farm is still important to Austria's economy.

The lowlands of eastern Austria are under
continental climatic influences. Vienna has a
moderate climate with an average temperature
just under 50° F (10° C). The days are short
in winter and largely overcast. Spring and fall
in Austria usually are mild, while the summers
are short and moderate.

Natural Resources. Considering Austria as a
whole, more than one third of its land area is
forest, of which approximately 84 percent is coniferous, mainly spruce. The remainder is predominantly beech, with considerable oak in the eastern
lowlands. Arable land constitutes some 20 percent of the total area, with an additional 1
percent devoted to gardens and vineyards. Meadow and pasture land comprise 29 percent of
the area, while 13 percent is uncultivable.

Austria has large deposits of salt, magnesite,
iron ore, and lignite or brown coal. There are
also noteworthy deposits of bituminous coal,
graphite, lead, zinc, and copper ore. Many other
minerals, including mica, quartz, gypsum, bauxite,
antimony, and talc, also are mined. These, together with important oil and natural gas fields
and the great power potential of its lakes and
rivers, constitute Austria's rich endowment of
natural resources.

Provinces. Nine provinces—Vorarlberg, Tyrol,
Salzburg, Carinthia, Styria, Burgenland, Upper
Austria, Lower Austria, and the city of Vienna—
make up the compact Austrian republic, and their
inhabitants are in the main alike in such important characteristics as ethnic background, language, and religion. Geography and history have
nonetheless tended to produce and perpetuate
distinct provincial traits, occupations, and traditions.

At the narrow western tip of Austria is Vorarlberg ("beyond the Arlberg"). Rugged and mountainous, this "Little Province" (*das Ländle*), as
it is affectionately called, has many textile mills
and hydroelectric stations. Its people speak an
Alemanic dialect, like the neighboring Swiss, and
there was a movement after World War I among
the populace to join the Swiss confederation. The
Swiss, however, opposed such a union, and Vorarlberg remained a part of Austria. Its capital,
Bregenz, is located on Lake Constance. Vorarlberg, also famous for its skiing, is separated
from Tyrol by mountains, which are traversed
only by the Arlberg Pass (5,900 feet; 1,798 meters) and by the famous Arlberg railroad tunnel
that runs beneath the pass.

Tyrol (German, Tirol), one of the most distinct historical entities of the republic, developed
as a state around the Alpine lands controlling the
Brenner Pass (4,494 feet; 1,522 meters). In
1363 the territory came into the possession of the
Habsburgs, and it has always maintained a certain separate status and independence. The Tyrolese, among the Habsburgs' most faithful and
loyal subjects, had the special privilege of ad-
dressing the emperor with the familiar form
"thou." When all Austria had bowed to Napoleon, the Tyrolese continued to oppose him under their great peasant leader Andreas Hofer.
Finally captured and executed by the French in
1810, Hofer has remained a symbol of the ardent
local patriotism of the Tyrolese.

Part of South Tyrol had an Italian-speaking
population, and at the end of World War I this
region (called the Upper, or Alto, Adige by the
Italians) was ceded to Italy. The boundary, however, was drawn so as to give Italy control of
the heights of the Brenner Pass. This arrangement meant that about 250,000 German-speaking
Tyrolese were incorporated into Italy, and East
Tyrol was cut off from the rest of the province
by a tongue of Italian territory. Because of the
rugged mountain terrain, the East Tyrolese must
communicate with their capital city (Innsbruck)
either via Italy or through the Austrian provinces
of Salzburg and Carinthia.

Salzburg, taking its name from the famous
old salt mines of the region, is the third of the
three mountainous provinces that are usually considered to constitute western Austria. Salzburg
is strategically located, with the chief lines of
Alpine communication intersecting on its territory. After 10 centuries of control by prince
bishops of the Roman Catholic Church, Salzburg
was secularized in 1802 and joined to Austria at
the close of the Napoleonic Wars. The province's
chief glory is its capital, the city of Salzburg.
One of the most beautiful cities in the world,
Salzburg is located on both sides of the turbulent, glacial Salzach River, overlooked by the
fortress of Hohensalzburg and several picturesque
peaks. The city benefited from the patronage of
the arts by many of its ruling prince bishops,
and it is the most perfect example of Austrian
high baroque. Salzburg is now perhaps best
known for its summer music festivals, presented
as a tribute to Wolfgang Amadeus Mozart, who
was born there in 1756.

East of Salzburg, Austria broadens out like
the face of a tennis racket. In this area about
87 percent of the Austrian population is concentrated. To the south lies the province of Carinthia. It has high mountains on the north,
west, and south; the eastern regions slope toward
the Hungarian plain. The valley of the Drave,
which enters Yugoslavia 20 miles (32 km) east
of Klagenfurt, has done much to shape the life
of Carinthia. Slovenes settled early in the valleys
near the present southern frontiers. In 1919,
Yugoslavia laid claim to these territories, and
the Allied powers arranged for a plebiscite in
the Klagenfurt district. It was divided into two
parts: Zone A, the largest and most southerly
section, was inhabited predominantly by Slovenes.
Zone B, containing the city of Klagenfurt, the
capital of Carinthia, was inhabited largely by
Germans. When Zone A voted 22,025 to 15,279
for remaining with Austria, no further balloting
was held. Carinthia has many beautiful lakes,
and because of its somewhat milder climate the

AUSTRIA

AGRICULTURE, INDUSTRY and RESOURCES

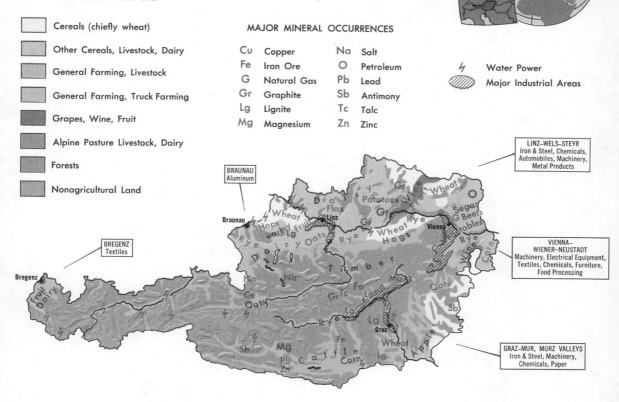

DOMINANT LAND USE

- Cereals (chiefly wheat)
- Other Cereals, Livestock, Dairy
- General Farming, Livestock
- General Farming, Truck Farming
- Grapes, Wine, Fruit
- Alpine Pasture Livestock, Dairy
- Forests
- Nonagricultural Land

MAJOR MINERAL OCCURRENCES

Cu	Copper	Na	Salt
Fe	Iron Ore	O	Petroleum
G	Natural Gas	Pb	Lead
Gr	Graphite	Sb	Antimony
Lg	Lignite	Tc	Talc
Mg	Magnesium	Zn	Zinc

⚡ Water Power

▨ Major Industrial Areas

LINZ–WELS–STEYR
Iron & Steel, Chemicals, Automobiles, Machinery, Metal Products

BRAUNAU
Aluminum

BREGENZ
Textiles

VIENNA–WIENER–NEUSTADT
Machinery, Electrical Equipment, Textiles, Chemicals, Furniture, Food Processing

GRAZ–MUR, MÜRZ VALLEYS
Iron & Steel, Machinery, Chemicals, Paper

TOPOGRAPHY

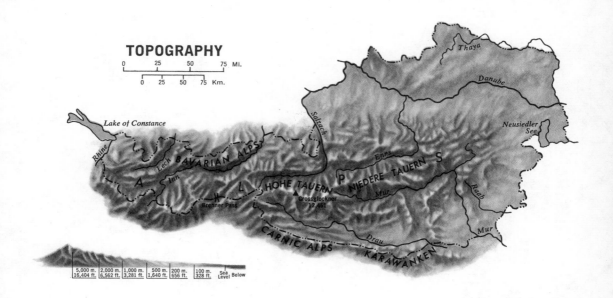

0   25   50   75 Mi.

0   25   50   75 Km.

| 5,000 m. 16,404 ft. | 2,000 m. 6,562 ft. | 1,000 m. 3,281 ft. | 500 m. 1,640 ft. | 200 m. 656 ft. | 100 m. 328 ft. | Sea Level | Below |

© Copyright HAMMOND INCORPORATED, Maplewood, N. J.

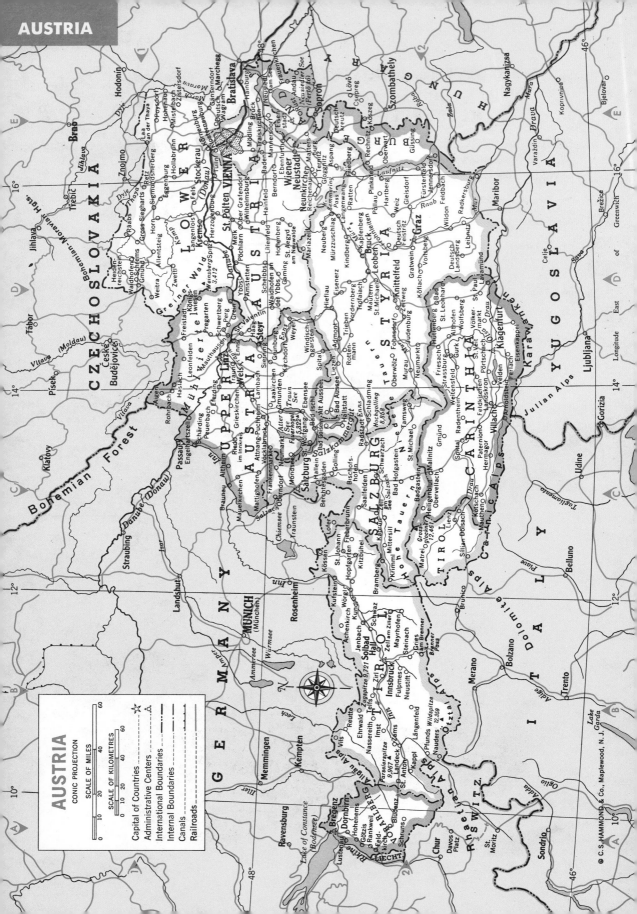

AUSTRIA

province is often referred to as the "Austrian Riviera." The most important natural product of Carinthia is wood, although there are rich deposits of iron ore, lead, zinc, and magnesite.

To the north of Carinthia lies Styria, known as the "Green Province" because nearly 50 percent of its surface is woodland. For centuries iron ore has been strip-mined on the Erzberg, a rust-colored mountain that rises in a series of gigantic terraces to a height of 2,500 feet (762 meters). This ore has an iron content of from 30 to 32 percent, and a manganese content of 1.5 to 2 percent, with traces of phosphorus and sulfur. Graz, situated on the Mur River, is the capital of Styria and the second-largest Austrian city. It is not only important industrially but is also, with its university and technical institutes,

an important educational center. Also within Styria is the town of Mariazell, Austria's most famous place of pilgrimage.

East of Styria is the province of Burgenland. Inhabited largely by Germans, this province was detached from Hungary and joined to Austria after World War I. Hungary retained a small portion of the prewar Burgenland—the city of Odenburg (Sopron) and eight adjoining villages—as a result of a plebiscite held Dec. 14–15, 1921. Burgenland lies to the east of the Leitha River, which for many years formed the boundary between Austria and Hungary. Primarily a flat agricultural land, Burgenland has long supplied neighboring Vienna with vegetables and milk. Burgenland, whose capital is Eisenstadt, has the largest lake in Austria, the Neusiedlersee.

THE MOUNTAINS OF AUSTRIA attract devotees of both summer and winter sports. (*Left*) Skiers descend a slope near Kitzbühel in the Eastern Alps. (*Above*) Mountain climbers scale the Serles mountain in Tyrol.

Constituting the northern rim of eastern Austria are the two provinces that bestride the Danube: Upper Austria, the province above the Enns River, and, to the east, Lower Austria, with its close association with Vienna. Vienna not only has the status of an Austrian province but also serves as the capital of both Lower Austria and the nation. Long the administrative center of a vast empire, Vienna has many palaces, monuments, and museums recalling glorious former days and still lending an air of grandeur and distinction to the city. While the past is ever present, the modern luxury shops and hotels, the throbbing industry, and the surging traffic are evidence that Vienna changes with the times. Nevertheless, now as formerly, the great Gothic Cathedral of St. Stephen with its magnificent spire is the focal point of Vienna. The cathedral is encircled by the Inner City, which in turn was surrounded until 1857–1858 by a great chain of fortresses. These were razed to make way for the famous Ringstrasse; sections of this boulevard have since been adorned by monumental public buildings and gardens.

The Danube enters Upper Austria at Passau, and Linz, the provincial capital, lies on its banks. Here is located Austria's most impressive industrial enterprise, the great United Austrian Iron and Steel works (VÖEST). A new method of steel production, the Linz-Donawitz (LD) Oxygen Blast System, which was developed by this concern after World War II, has been adopted by steel manufacturers throughout the world. Upper Austria, like Salzburg, has many salt mines, concentrated in a particularly beautiful mountainous section of the province, the so-called Salzkammergut. It has become an important winter sports area and also has many famous spas: Bad Ischl, once the summer residence of Emperor Francis Joseph as well as of the composer Franz Lehár; Bad Hall (iodine, bromine, and lime springs); Bad Schallerbach (sulfur), and Bad Goisern (iodine-sulfur). The province's picture-book lakes—Traunsee, Attersee, Mondsee, Wolfgangsee, Almsee, Zellersee, to name only a few—have for years attracted many visitors.

As the Danube enters Lower Austria it approaches the Wachau, the loveliest part of the entire Danube Valley. Here the river is symbolically guarded by two of Austria's most beautiful and historic Benedictine monasteries, Melk and Göttweig. To the north of the Danube the woods of the Waldviertel give way opposite Vienna to the extensively cultivated Weinviertel, noted for its many vineyards, and then, to the east of Vienna, to the rich plains of the Marchfeld. Lower Austria is the principal granary of the country, but in this province, north of the Danube, are also located great oilfields, their discovery dating back to 1914. South and west of the Danube lie the Vienna Woods (Wiener Wald), which rise from Vienna's suburbs to the Semmering Mountains and the Schneealpen (Snow Alps).

2. People

It is not surprising that the people of Austria have a mixed ethnic background, for the country is at the juncture of important trade routes. Conquering armies also have swept across Austria, which in turn conquered and governed neighboring peoples of different races. Austrians are, in general, of South Germanic stock with strong Slavic admixtures.

Population Changes. The population of the republic has remained comparatively stable since its establishment in 1919. By the census of 1961 the population totaled 7,073,807, an increase of approximately 500,000 over 1923. About one quarter of the total population lives in greater Vienna. Other leading cities in descending order of population are Graz, Linz, Salzburg, Innsbruck, and Klagenfurt. Over-all population density is 218 persons per square mile, but because of the mountainous nature of the country the population is unevenly distributed.

World War II greatly affected the population of Austria. Of the 800,000 Austrians drafted into the armed services, 280,000 were killed and 100,-000 were listed as missing in action. Disabled veterans numbered 305,000 as compared with 169,000 in World War I. There were 24,255 civilian dead, most of them killed in Allied air raids. The years of German rule brought the exodus, expulsion, or extermination of the Jewish population, which numbered 191,481 on a religious basis in the census of 1934. According to the racial definition used by Hitler, however, the number was much larger.

The end of the war found an estimated 1,650,-000 displaced persons, refugees, and expellees in Austria. By June 30, 1947, when the United Nations Relief and Rehabilitation Administration (UNRRA) was discontinued, some 900,000 of these displaced persons had been returned to their homes through the efforts of UNRRA. In 1950 it was announced officially that there were 300,000 *Volksdeutsche* (German-speaking) refugees in Austria, 80 percent of them having come from areas that had been part of the Austro-Hungarian monarchy until 1918. Most of these refugees have since been admitted to Austrian citizenship. The Hungarian revolution of 1956 brought a new wave of refugees, but most of these, with the aid of international agencies, were passed on to other countries. From 1956 to 1965 —not counting Hungarian refugees—54,000 East Europeans sought asylum in Austria.

Language and Minorities. Although World War II brought diverse peoples to the country, the Austrian republic remains as it was when established, an overwhelmingly (98.7 percent) German-speaking state. Many local dialects exist, but literary German is understood everywhere. The minority languages used in everyday speech by somewhat over 1 percent of the population are Croatian, Slovenian, Windisch (a dialect close to Slovenian), Magyar, and Czech.

The minorities in Austria have been given equitable treatment and have not caused the government any difficulties. On the other hand, sympathy for the German minority in South Tyrol, which was transferred to Italy after World War I, has led the Austrian government to engage in protracted and difficult negotiations with Italy.

Religion. The country has been overwhelmingly Roman Catholic since the days of the Counter Reformation. Today full religious liberty prevails. Civil marriage is compulsory, and divorces are permitted. Religious instruction is a regular but not compulsory offering in the elementary and secondary schools. According to the 1961 census, 89 percent of the total population was Roman Catholic and 6 percent Protestant (Lutheran and Reformed). The small remainder of those with other religious affiliations included Old Catholics, Uniates, and Jews.

The Roman Catholic Church in Austria is divided administratively into two archbishoprics and six bishoprics. One archbishop resides in Salzburg, while the archbishop of Vienna is primate of Austria; he usually is also a member of the College of Cardinals. His seat is the Cathedral of St. Stephen (Stephanskirche). The cathedral was badly damaged in the last days of World War II but was restored by popular subscription.

3. Education

Austria's educational system, like the systems in most of Europe, traces its origins to the monastic schools of the Middle Ages. The Benedictine Schottengymnasium, a world-famous secondary school, was founded in 1155 and still exists. Major educational reforms were made in the second half of the 18th century under Maria Theresa and Joseph II. The Educational Reform Act of 1774 provided for six years of compulsory education. Required school attendance was extended to eight years by significant school legislation passed between 1867 and 1869, which remains in large part the legal basis for the present-day educational system. These laws, which increased state influence over the schools, engen-

THE HOHENSALZBURG FORTRESS overlooks the Renaissance and Austrian high baroque churches of Salzburg.

dered a *Schulkampf* (school struggle) with the Roman Catholic Church. Although, technically, the state won, the church remained strong through its control of teacher-training institutes and its influence on government authorities.

The 1920 constitution of the republic, which still prevails in amended form, provided that "In the domain of schools, education, and adult education the respective powers of the federal government and the states are to be regulated by a separate federal constitutional law." So far, no such law has been passed. During the period of Nazi domination of Austria, its schools came under the control of the German ministry of education. However, with the reestablishment of independence the prewar school system was, for the most part, reinstated. Education remains a field shared by the federal, provincial, and municipal governments, and although the public system predominates, private schools, controlled mostly by the Roman Catholic Church, are free to function if they meet state standards.

Illiteracy is almost unknown in Austria. Education is compulsory and free for all children between the ages of 6 and 14. For the first 4 years all attend the *Volksschule*. The pupils then may continue for another 4 years in the *Volksschule* (the usual practice in rural areas) or transfer either to the *Hauptschule*, which offers a 4-year practical terminal course and prepares for trade schools, or to the *Mittelschule*, which prepares students for the universities and higher technical schools.

Secondary education is dominated by the *Mittelschulen*, which offer an 8-year course, divided into upper and lower divisions. Admission requirements for *Mittelschulen* are the completion of 4 years at a *Volksschule* and the passing of an entrance examination, although under special conditions exceptional students may transfer from a *Hauptschule*. There are four types of *Mittelschulen*: *Gymnasium* (Latin, Greek, one modern language); *Realgymnasium* (more attention to science, Latin, one modern language); *Realschule* (emphasis on science, two modern languages); and *Frauenoberschule* (for girls, includes courses in home economics and child care). The curricula of all schools include such subjects as German, foreign languages, history, geography, mathematics, science, music, art, and physical education. The number of hours of required study for each subject varies. Other types of secondary schools

LOUIS GOLDMAN, FROM RAPHO GUILLUMETTE

THE DANUBE CANAL in places is bordered by apartment houses as it winds through Vienna, the capital.

designed to accommodate the needs of students in special circumstances play a minor role.

The successful passing of a final examination at a secondary school qualifies a student for admission to an institution of higher learning. Three universities—Vienna (founded 1365), Graz (1585), and Innsbruck (1677)—have faculties of philosophy, law and political science, medicine, and Catholic theology. In addition, Vienna has a faculty of Protestant theology, which has been part of the university since 1922. The University of Salzburg, founded in 1928 but dating back to 1619 as a theological seminary, had only a faculty of Catholic theology until 1964–1965, when a faculty of philosophy was added.

In addition there are 10 *Hochschulen* or *Akademien*, which give instruction at the university level in technology (Vienna, Graz), mining (Leoben), agriculture and forestry (Vienna), veterinary medicine (Vienna), business (Vienna), fine arts (Vienna), applied arts (Vienna), and music and dramatic arts (Vienna and Salzburg). The Diplomatische Akademie for the training of diplomats was opened in 1964. There are also numerous theological seminaries, teacher-training institutions, and trade schools.

4. Economy

The Austrian population suffered severely during the last months of World War II. The policy of wholesale requisitioning adopted by the liberating Soviet forces and the quartering of excessively large numbers of troops in Austria caused great hardship.

On April 5, 1946, the United Nations Relief and Rehabilitation Administration (UNRRA) approved a grant of $59 million for supplies for Austria. During the next two years this agency provided over $136 million in aid. Other countries, but primarily the United States under the Marshall Plan, then poured relief funds and materials into Austria. The coverage was uneven, although there was supposedly four-power agreement on the distribution of food supplies. Lower Austria, the chief granary of the country, was in the Soviet zone, and many agricultural properties there were confiscated. The Russian and

French occupying forces, more than the British and American, lived off the land. A strict system of rationing was enforced in all Austria and was not relaxed until the summer of 1949.

The Potsdam agreement of Aug. 2, 1945, granted the Russians the right to German assets in their occupation zone, as a step toward meeting Soviet claims for reparations. Disputes soon arose as to what constituted German assets; did they include, for example, Jewish property seized by the Germans after 1938? The Soviet authorities defined German assets as they pleased, dismantling many factories and sending the machinery to the Soviet Union. About 400 industrial enterprises were seized and brought together in a Soviet-controlled corporation. The most important of the industrial prizes taken over by the Russians were the Danube Shipping Company and the oilfields concentrated at Zistersdorf.

Postwar Recovery. Both in the years before *Anschluss*, and particularly in the period 1938–1945 when Austria was a part of Hitler's Greater Germany, the Austrian economy was linked closely with Germany's. Overnight, this union was ended, and old trade associations were broken. Spare parts for agricultural and industrial machinery, much of it worn out by heavy use during the war, were no longer available. Partly as a move to liquidate German assets in Austrian industry, the Austrian parliament on July 26, 1946, and March 26, 1947, passed far-reaching nationalization laws. The Soviets refused to recognize these laws in their zone, and the other occupation powers followed suit as long as the laws were not universally applied throughout Austria.

In spite of ostensible disapproval by the occupying powers, the Austrian government did manage to take over some 70 of the great industrial enterprises. Since private capital was not available to get the industries going, the nationalization policy was strengthened. It was also furthered by the need for governmental authorities to supervise and invest the approximately $1.6 billion in aid that was extended to Austria in the years 1945–1955. The nationalization laws provided for compensation to the previous owners under terms to be fixed later by a federal law. Such nationalization compensation laws were finally adopted on July 7, 1954, and Dec. 18, 1959.

Production got under way rather slowly, but by 1947 marked improvements were to be noted monthly. The general industrial index (compared with average monthly industrial production in 1937) stood at 56 percent in June 1947, 61.3 percent in November, and 71.7 percent in March 1948, and had reached 98 percent in October 1948. Production continued to improve steadily; 1954 and 1955 were boom years, when the growth rate of the gross national product stood at 8.6 and 11.1 percent, respectively.

By that time Austria was strong enough economically to undertake the heavy financial payments that were part of the price for its obtaining independence under the State Treaty of 1955. Austria was obligated to deliver to the USSR $150 million in specified goods over a period of 6 years, to pay $2 million in cash for the Danube Shipping Company, and, in addition, to dispatch 1 million tons of oil annually to the Soviet Union for 10 years in payment for the return of the oilfields. In July 1958 the USSR agreed to a 50 percent reduction of the 7 million tons of oil still to be delivered. Austria was able to meet its payments, and in February 1964 the Soviet

Union formally confirmed the fact that Austria had fulfilled its obligations under the 1955 treaty.

Austria in turn received a number of benefits from the treaty. For many years the cost of the occupying armies had been a heavy drain on Austrian finances. The United States on July 1, 1947, returned most of the payments it had received and agreed that henceforth it would pay its own occupation costs. Russia did not waive its occupation costs until 1953; Britain and France, not until the following year. The State Treaty brought the departure of the occupying forces and the end of various controls that the Allied powers had exercised. Requisitioned property was restored to Austrian hands. Withdrawal of the troops placed approximately 375,000 additional acres of farm and forest lands at Austrian disposal. Russia handed over 398 confiscated industrial enterprises in addition to the Danube Shipping Company and the oilfields.

Character of the Economy. The return of the Russian-controlled industries, particularly the oilfields, raised anew the question of nationalization. The issue was complicated by an agreement that the Austrian government had signed—in connection with the State Treaty—with Britain, the United States, and France on May 10, 1955, providing compensation for Nazi-confiscated, foreign-owned oil properties. This agreement, although known to the Russians and sanctioned by the leaders of the two coalition parties, had been kept secret from the Austrian public. Debate over how the oil industry was to be run led to a governmental crisis and new elections in 1956. The new coalition government agreed on a federally controlled, limited liability company to manage all nationalized industries. The oil industry was placed under the Austrian Petroleum Administration, which was to be controlled by the federal government.

The economy of Austria as it has developed since World War II is actually based on the concept of private property and private ownership. Retail trade is largely in the hands of small shopowners, and there are important producers', consumers', and credit cooperatives. Agriculture and, to a great extent, forestry are in the hands of many small owners. There are over 102,000 handicraft enterprises (making such products as wood and leather goods, ceramics, glassware, costume jewelry, and specialized fabrics) that employ over 20 percent of Austria's nonindependent, gainfully employed persons. There are few large manufacturing companies. National, provincial, and municipal administrations exercise considerable direct and indirect influence on the conduct of business and industry. This practice accords both with a traditional paternalistic concept of government and the influence of the Socialist party, which has long been strong in Austria.

Industry. In 1956 a government holding company, the Österreichische Industrie- und Bergbauverwaltungs-Gesellschaft m.b.H., was created to administer all nationalized companies with the exception of the electrical industry. This holding company, however, was dissolved in 1959, and its powers and duties were divided between the full federal cabinet and a special Section IV (Nationalized Industries) of the chancellor's office. In 1966 jurisdiction over the nationalized industries was given to the ministry of transportation. Most nationalized firms are organized and operated like private firms, each managed by and responsible to its own directors.

UNITED AUSTRIAN IRON AND STEEL WORKS at Linz is Austria's largest industrial enterprise.

Public ownership is dominant in heavy industry. Nationalized industries produce 99.6 percent of the iron ore, 99.4 percent of the iron, 95.6 percent of the steel, 69.3 percent of the aluminum, 99 percent of the natural gas, over 90 percent of the oil, 85.5 percent of the bituminous coal, and 95.6 percent of the lignite. In net value of production the rank of these industries in descending scale is: iron and steel, oil, electricity, machine tools, metals (aluminum, lead, zinc, and others), chemicals, and coal. Nationalized industries contribute just over 25 percent of Austrian exports.

Power. In the era of Greater Germany all of Austria's power stations were incorporated into the German national network. Much new construction was undertaken, and a number of plants were completed. With nationalization, a single holding company, the Österreichische Elektrizitätswirtschaft A.G., was established, and it, unlike the other nationalized industries, is under the supervision of the minister of communications and power. In 1956, the peak year of the European Recovery Program (Marshall Plan), about 78 percent of the funds allocated to Austria went to electrification projects.

In the 1960's a plan was implemented for the construction of 13 hydroelectric plants and dams along the Danube, with the additional aims of furthering flood control and facilitating river traffic. All dams were to have two ship locks so as to permit free movement in both directions, day and night. There were also to be smaller hydroelectric plans on the Enns River. In addition, Austria cooperated with Bavaria in planning a chain of five power plants along the lower Inn River. In 1964 export of electricity (to Italy, Switzerland, and West Germany) accounted for 3 percent of Austria's total exports.

To even out the seasonal flow of energy from the hydroelectric stations and to meet the demand at peak periods, Austria greatly expanded its thermal power stations. Thermal electricity is generated mainly by bituminous coal, lignite, oil, and natural gas.

Transportation. At the close of World War II, 41 percent of the Austrian railways were out of action. Many bridges had been destroyed, and

THE REFRESHING WINES made from the grapes grown on the hills around Vienna are drunk while still young.

two thirds of the rolling stock was unserviceable. No construction of new major lines was undertaken, but there was considerable double tracking and rapid electrification. In 1952 a new tunnel through the Semmering Pass was completed. The state-owned and operated Austrian Federal Railways have a network of 3,370 miles (5,623 km) of standard gauge, and 315 miles (508 km) of narrow gauge, lines, of which about a third are electrified. The main line from Vienna to the Swiss frontier—the route of the Orient Express —is now electric-powered all the way, as is the route from Vienna to the Italian frontier at Tarvisio. There are 19 small private railroads that operate approximately 390 miles (628 km) of largely narrow gauge track. After the war there was extensive construction of cable railways, chair lifts, and ski tows, which contributed to the opening up of the mountain regions.

Even the remotest areas are covered by vastly expanded bus lines operated by both the Austrian railways and the Austrian Postal and Telegraph Service. Austria has an excellent highway system, with an autobahn from Vienna to Salzburg.

Of the rivers, only the Danube is navigable, and it provides a major artery for the transport of bulk cargo—mostly coal, coke, iron ore, steel, oil, and grains. Major ports are Linz, Vienna, and Krems, and the largest shipping company is the government-owned Danube Steamship Company, which provides both passenger and freight service. Ships of all the riparian states ply the Danube. As a member of the International Danube Commission, Austria shares in regulating this traffic.

During the period of four-power occupation Austria was not allowed to operate an airline of its own. In September 1957 the Austrian Airlines began operation. It engages in extended domestic and international service. There are numerous civilian airfields. Major fields are at Vienna (Schwechat), Salzburg, Linz, Graz, Klagenfurt, and Innsbruck.

Agriculture and Lumbering. It was not until 1953 that Austrian agriculture equaled prewar production. Thereafter, productivity increased steadily, thanks largely to the wider use of commercial fertilizers and better seed and in general to the employment of more scientific methods. Whereas, before the war Austria supplied 72 percent of its own needs, in the mid-1960's the percentage was in the neighborhood of 83 percent. In some sectors (chiefly dairy products) there is a surplus for export, while fruits, vege-

tables, eggs, poultry, and vegetable oils are among the chief food imports.

As mechanization increased, the number employed in agriculture decreased. Between 1934 and 1961 the number employed declined by 30 percent. The decline of small farm enterprises was less marked because of the many vineyards and truck gardens; Austria remains a land of small agricultural establishments.

Sixty percent of Austrian forest and woodlands are privately owned, some 40 percent by individuals who have small tracts of less than 123.55 acres (50 hectares). About 10 million cubic meters of wood are felled yearly, lumber and paper being among Austria's most important exports. A rigorous policy of selective cutting and of reforestation is followed.

Labor and Social Insurance. After World War II there was on the whole a more than adequate labor supply to undergird the economy. For a time there was a serious problem of unemployment, but this condition eased with economic recovery. When shortages in some fields developed in 1964 Austria began to recruit workers from nearby frontier countries. According to the census of 1961, 164 persons per 1,000 were engaged in agriculture and forestry, 428 in industry, handicrafts, and personal services, 133 in trade and commerce, 51 in the professions, 47 in public service, and 7 in domestic service.

Of the total labor force of 3.4 million (60 percent are men), over two thirds belong to the 16 unions that make up the Austrian Trade Union Federation. All workers and wage earners must belong to their respective chamber of labor (*Arbeitskammer*). These chambers are organized on a provincial basis and serve as a liaison with the government. Many union officials are elected officials of the chambers. Sometimes the chambers (but more frequently the unions) negotiate the collective agreements establishing wages and working conditions. The 8-hour day is fixed by law, and the 45-hour week is the standard set by the collective agreements. Thanks to the effectiveness of the collective bargaining system, strikes are relatively few and of short duration.

Workers benefit from an extensive and well-established social insurance system that goes back to the second half of the 19th century. On Jan. 1, 1956, a new social insurance law, which codified existing legislation, came into force. The following year social pension insurance was extended to include farmers and craftsmen carrying on their own business. Normally, old-age pensions begin at 60 years for women and 65 for men. Social insurance, compulsory for all dependent workers and for most independent workers as well, is financed by employer and employee contributions and by a government allocation from general tax funds. In addition to widely held health, accident, unemployment, old-age, disability, and survivors' insurance, there are social benefits in the form of housing and children's and mothers' allowances.

Banks. The economy is further supported by a sound banking system. The Austrian National Bank (formed in 1923, taken over by the German Reichsbank in 1938, reestablished in 1945) is a joint stock company in which the federal government owns 50 percent of the shares and controls the rest. It serves as the nation's central bank, with offices in Vienna and branches in each province. The National Bank issues Austria's bank notes, fixes the official discount rate, and in general supervises the currency and credit of the nation.

In 1946 the three largest joint-stock banks —the Creditanstalt-Bankverein, the Österreichische Länderbank A.G., and the Österreichische Creditinstitut A.G.—were nationalized. Marking a slight trend away from nationalization, 40 percent of the shares of the Creditanstalt and the Länderbank were sold to the public in 1956, three fourths of the shares being preferred and nonvoting. The number of private banks decreased after World War II, but they continued to play an important role. The federal government operates a postal savings system that also provides many of the usual banking services.

Foreign Trade. Austria's constantly strengthened and expanding economy brought a steady increase in foreign trade. Imports have usually exceeded exports, but the growth in the tourist industry has done much to right this imbalance. In 1949–1950 tourism brought in 376 million schillings in foreign currency, and by 1964 this amount had grown to over 13 billion schillings.

Austria was a charter member of the Organization for European Economic Cooperation (OEEC) and participated enthusiastically in its trade liberalization policies. In 1960 it joined in establishing the European Free Trade Association (EFTA, or Outer Seven). Tariffs on industrial products in internal trade among the association members were reduced gradually. In the mid-1960's EFTA nations supplied about 15 percent of Austrian imports and purchased about 17.5 percent of its exports. Austria has endeavored unsuccessfully to join the European Economic Community (EEC, or Common Market), which in the mid-1960's furnished about 60 percent of its imports and took 47 percent of its exports.

The Federal Republic of Germany is Austria's most important trading partner, accounting for approximately 42 percent of its imports and 28 percent of its exports. Italy, Switzerland, and Britain rank next. In the mid-1960's, eastern Europe accounted for about 11 percent of Austria's imports and 15 percent of its exports, while Austria's trade with the United States and Canada was practically balanced at about 5 percent for both imports and exports. Austria has four free-trade zones (Linz, Solbad Hall, Graz, and Vienna), where foreign goods may be displayed, stored, or repaired without permits or duty charges. These free zones have developed into permanent display areas for foreign merchandise.

5. Government, Political Parties, and the Press

Austria is governed under the constitution of Oct. 1, 1920, as amended in 1929, although many of its existing laws date back to earlier periods. The constitution establishes a democratic federal republic. Powers not specifically delegated to the federal government belong to the nine provinces.

The central government has the predominance of power, and its share has constantly increased, in part because of the amendments of 1929 and also because of growing federal control of the economy. In addition to such fields as foreign affairs, currency, and civil law, over which it has sole jurisdiction, it can prescribe fundamental principles on a variety of subjects. The provinces have the power to supplement this legislation, a power that is limited in practice because these laws are often very detailed and specific. More important than their legislative activity is the role played by the provinces in

administration, in respect to both federal and local laws.

The Presidency. Originally, the constitution provided that the president should be elected by the legislature for a term of four years. This procedure was changed in 1929 to direct election by the people for a term of six years, although the change was not implemented until after World War II. If a candidate fails to receive a majority of the votes cast, a runoff election, limited to the two candidates who received the highest vote, is held. A president can hold office for no more than two successive terms.

The constitutional amendments of 1929 gave the president slightly greater powers than he originally held, but his functions remain largely nominal and ceremonial. He represents the state in foreign affairs, signs treaties and laws, and appoints the ministry and other officials. He also calls the legislature into session, prorogues it, and can dissolve it (but not more than once for the same reason).

The Legislature. The Federal Assembly (Bundesversammlung) is composed of an upper chamber, the Federal Council (Bundesrat), and a lower chamber, the National Council (Nationalrat). The Federal Council is made up of 50 members chosen by the provincial legislatures, seats being distributed in proportion to the population of each province. The National Council, consisting of 165 representatives, is elected from 25 constituencies for a four-year term by direct ballot, according to the principles of proportional representation. Candidates must be at least 26 years of age. Suffrage is universal for citizens of 21 years of age and over, and balloting must take place on a Sunday or public holiday. Legislation needs the consent of both houses for enactment, but the National Council is the more important of the chambers.

The Cabinet and Coalitions. The ministry, headed by a chancellor and including a varying number of ministers, is responsible only to the National Council. Although ministers do not have to be members of parliament, with rare exception they are. From 1920 to 1934, when Chancellor Engelbert Dollfuss established his single-party corporative state, the Christian Socialists dominated the cabinets, but usually in coalitions with one of the small conservative parties.

Karl Renner, a Socialist, headed the first coalition government after World War II. The first national election in November 1945 gave a victory to the People's party, successor to the prewar Christian Socialists. The People's party's majority was small, and by an agreement that was favored by the occupying powers, a coalition was formed with the Socialists and Communists, with Leopold Figl as chancellor. The only Communist in the government resigned in November 1947 in protest over currency reform and the Marshall Plan. Henceforth, until the spring of 1966, the governments consisted of a two-party coalition: the chancellor was from the People's party and the vice chancellor was a Socialist.

The basis of each coalition was laid down in an agreement drawn up while the cabinet was being constituted. It defined the policy to be followed on all important questions and demarcated certain spheres of authority in advance. In line with this policy most legislation was drawn up by a coordinating committee in negotiations between the two parties before being submitted to parliament. The result was that while

THE PARLIAMENT HOUSE in Vienna was erected in Greek classical style in the second half of the 19th century. In the background rises the tower of the Neo-Gothic city hall.

there were debates in parliament, they had little significance. Individual members exercised little influence, and the party leaders determined policy. In 1963 the coalition agreement provided for the first time that certain legislative matters should be exempt from prearrangement between the parties.

In hammering out each coalition agreement, there was a good deal of jockeying between the parties for the control of certain ministries, often leading to the creation of an undersecretary post that went to a member of the party that did not get the top post. The election of March 6, 1966, gave the People's party a clear majority, and after long negotiations the Socialists decided to go into opposition rather than accept the demands of the victors.

Political Parties. The Declaration of Independence of April 27, 1945, was signed by representatives of three parties that had been reconstituted shortly before. These were the Socialist party, successor to the former Social Democratic party founded in the 1880's; the People's party, lineal descendant of the Christian Social party founded by Karl Lueger in the 1880's; and the Communist party, organized from a splinter group of the Social Democrats after World War I.

The Socialist party has given up much of its Marxism, as well as its ardent anticlericalism, and has concentrated on adherence to democratic methods and opposition to dictatorship either of left or right. Its stronghold is in Vienna, and it regularly controls the government of the city. The People's party has become less clerical but is still inherently conservative. It embraces important vocational organizations such as the Federation of Farmers, the Tradesmen's Federation, and the Federation of Salaried Employees and Workers. It is strong in rural areas and controls most of the provincial governments. The Communist party, although it has appealed to various splinter groups, has steadily lost ground.

A few small parties also appeared after 1945. The League of Independents, a rightist party drawing its chief support from former Nazi sympathizers and from the old Landbund (Country party), emerged in 1949. It joined with the Freedom party in 1956. A dissident left-wing Socialist group under the leadership of Franz Olah, a labor union leader and former minister of the interior, organized the Democratic Progressive party in 1965. It was unable to win a seat in the parliamentary elections of 1966, but polled 3.28 percent of the vote and thereby contributed to the People's party victory in that election. The small parties have played only a minor role,

and Austria's political scene continues to be dominated by the People's party and the Socialists.

The Courts. The constitution is protected by a special Constitutional Court, which is empowered to decide jurisdictional disputes between provinces and the federal government. Under certain conditions this court can also pass on the constitutionality of both provincial and federal legislation. Not only the administrative courts but also the ordinary civil and criminal courts are under federal jurisdiction. Judges are appointed, and their independence is assured by provisions carefully regulating appointment, tenure, removal, or transfer.

Local Government. Each of the nine provinces has a unicameral legislature (Landtag), varying in size from 26 to 100 members, elected on the same basis as are members of the National Council. All provincial legislative enactments must be submitted to the proper federal ministry before promulgation. If the ministry vetoes the legislation, the veto can be overridden by a second passage of the act by the Landtag, with at least half of its members present. However, the federal ministry of finance has an absolute veto in financial matters. The Landtag elects the provincial governor (*Landeshauptmann*), who has the dual responsibility of acting as chief executive of the province and of implementing decisions of the federal government.

The Press. The constitution and special press laws guarantee the freedom of the press in Austria. Each publication must appoint an editor who is legally responsible for it. In cases of penal action the editor and, in some situations, the publisher, printer, and distributor will be held accountable. In addition to daily and weekly papers, Austria has several "Monday papers" (*Montagblätter*). There are also numerous trade and learned journals.

The *Wiener Zeitung*, founded in 1703 and one of the oldest newspapers in the world, is owned by the state and published as well as printed by the Government Printing Office. It combines the function of a daily paper with that of a government gazette, publishing official news and notices. Statutes, ordinances, and texts of treaties appear in the official *Bundesgesetzblatt*. The independent dailies have grown stronger and account for more than 60 percent of the over-all circulation. Among the 10 Vienna dailies are *Arbeiter Zeitung* (Socialist), *Volksblatt* (People's party), *Volksstimme* (Communist), *Express* (nonaffiliated, liberal), and *Kurier* (nonaffiliated, conservative). In the provinces the nonaffiliated dailies tend to be the strongest.

6. History

Before its conquest by the Romans in about 14 B.C., much of the territory that is now Austria was inhabited by the Celts, who had organized the kingdom of Noricum. At the time of the conquest, the territory north of the Danube River was inhabited by German tribes, while in the areas bordering modern Switzerland the ancient Raetians lived. The Romans, who did not press beyond the Danube at this time, established the provinces of Raetia, Noricum, and Pannonia. Some of the more important Roman settlements and garrisons were at Vindobona (Vienna), Juvavum (Salzburg), Valdidena (Innsbruck), Ovilava (Wels), and Brigantium (Bregenz).

In a later period, Roman civilization also brought Christianity to the region, but it largely disappeared with the barbarian invasions that swept over the land as Roman power declined. The region was ravaged by the Huns (5th century) and then by the Avars, whose kingdom in the 6th and 7th centuries centered to the east in the Hungarian plain. Under the Avars, toward the end of the 6th century, the Slovenes, a Slavic people, began to settle the southeastern areas, where they have remained to this day.

Various German tribes at times occupied portions of the region, only to move on to other areas. When the Lombards moved south into Italy in 568, it was the Bavarians, already in occupation of lands between the Lech and the Enns rivers, who moved eastward and to the south to do battle with the Avars and the Slavs. They greatly expanded their territories, and about the middle of the 8th century, in return for aid against the Avars, the duke of Carinthia acknowledged the suzerainty of Bavaria. It was in this period of Bavarian expansion that missionaries reestablished the Christian church.

The dukes of Bavaria, who had long maintained a tenuous relationship with the Frankish kings, were finally subdued in 787–788 by Charlemagne, who incorporated Bavaria into the Frankish kingdom. Charlemagne was now confronted with the task of halting Avar raiding expeditions. He led three successful campaigns (791, 795, 796) against them and established a series of marches—border districts—to defend the eastern frontiers of his empire. The establishment of the marches brought more Germans, but now as feudal lords, retainers, peasants, traders, and missionaries, and not as tribal migrants.

With the disintegration of Charlemagne's empire in the 9th century, Frankish supremacy in these eastern areas vanished. The marches were overrun, first by raiders from Moravia and then by the Magyars, who by the end of the 9th century had firmly established themselves in the valley of the middle Danube and the Theiss.

A new era began in 955 when Otto I, who later became emperor of the Holy Roman Empire, decisively defeated the Magyars on the Lechfeld near Augsburg. To keep them in check, Otto founded a strong march along the Danube to the east of the Enns. Otto, more than Charlemagne, is the real founder of Austria.

The position of the territory in respect to Germany and particularly to Bavaria accounts for its name. The term *Ostarrichi* first appears in a charter of 996, and the German *Österreich*—eastern realm—is derived from it. The Latin form "Austria" appears for the first time in a document of Conrad III (1093–1152). The German term *Ostmark,* used often in modern historiography, was not employed in early medieval sources.

The House of Babenberg. In 976, Emperor Otto II granted the eastern march to Margrave Leopold of the house of Babenberg, and it remained in the hands of this family until 1246. Under their vigorous administration the march was expanded until it reached along the Danube to the Leitha River, which became the traditional frontier between Austria and Hungary. In about 1140, Vienna became the capital. To the west the Babenbergs obtained the lands between the Inn and the Enns in 1156, and in the same year Emperor Frederick I (Barbarossa) raised Austria to the rank of a duchy, conferring on it certain privileges. As a result of an inheritance pact, Styria passed into Babenberg hands in 1192. In 1229 a large part of Carniola was purchased from the bishop of Freising.

Other territorial bits were added, and when the last Babenberg fell fighting the Magyars in 1246, Babenberg lands stretched along the Danube from Passau almost to Bratislava (Pressburg). The major Austrian territories had been gathered in. Salzburg was developing as an important ecclesiastical state; in the Tyrol a number of counties had been formed, some lay and others under the control of ecclesiastical princes. Carinthia, which had been separated from Bavaria as an independent duchy in 976, continued on its separate path, although it had suffered significant territorial losses.

Austria prospered under the Babenbergs largely because of the developing trade along the Danube. Christianity was firmly established, and important monastic centers were founded, among them Göttweig (1072), Melk (1089), Klosterneuburg (1106), and Heiligenkreuz (about 1150).

Soon after the death of the last Babenberg the estates elected as their duke Ottokar, son of the king of Bohemia. Ottokar, who later also became king of Bohemia, duke of Styria, and duke of Carinthia, provided a beneficent rule.

Accession of the Habsburgs. In 1273, Rudolf of Habsburg was elected emperor, thus ending the period of strife and conflict in the Holy Roman Empire known as the Great Interregnum (1254–1273). With only small hereditary possessions in Switzerland, Alsace, and Swabia, he needed to increase the wealth and power of his family in order to hold his own among the nobility. As emperor, Rudolf questioned the title of Ottokar to the duchies of Austria, Styria, and Carinthia and was able to seize control of these lands.

In 1363 the Habsburgs obtained Tyrol and Vorarlberg (whose borders were not then the same as they are today). These acquisitions were important, for the Habsburgs now controlled the best route (Arlberg Pass) to their possessions in Switzerland and along the upper Rhine. Also, by acquiring the Brenner Pass, they commanded the easiest road from Germany to Italy.

The following year Carniola was made a separate hereditary duchy. Part of Istria was acquired in 1374, and in 1382, Trieste submitted voluntarily to Austria. The Habsburg lands, to which other fragments were added from time to time, now extended from the Danube to the Adriatic; the family ruled over Germans, Slavs, and Italians.

In this period the house of Habsburg, sometimes called the house of Austria, was not governed by the law of primogeniture, and the territories were divided among the sons. Despite constant territorial expansion, these divisions greatly diminished the role of the Habsburgs in the affairs of the Holy Roman Empire. In a century and a half only one Habsburg was elected to the imperial throne, and the Habsburg realm was not raised to the dignity of an electorate in the Golden Bull of 1356. Austria did not officially achieve the status of an archduchy until 1453. This status was unique, and the title of archduke (or archduchess), peculiar to Austria, was subsequently borne by all members of the imperial house.

Territorial Acquisitions in the 15th Century. In 1437–1439 the crowns of Bohemia and Hungary as well as the crown of the Holy Roman Empire were briefly united in the person of a Habsburg, Albert V of Habsburg (Albert II of the empire). His successor, Frederick III (reigned 1440–1493), was driven from Vienna by Matthias Corvinus of Hungary, who took over Austria, Styria, and Carinthia. Nevertheless, Frederick laid down the foundation for the future glory of the state. He arranged a marriage in 1477 between his son Maximilian and Mary of Burgundy, who had just inherited the Netherlands and the rich Burgundian lands from her father, Charles the Bold. Already the defenders of the empire against the Turks, the Habsburgs now also became its defenders in the west against France.

Since Emperor Rudolf had acquired the Austrian lands in the 13th century, the fortunes of the Habsburgs, with acquisitions and losses, had gradually shifted to the east. Though they had lost many of their Swiss possessions, they still had scattered positions along the Rhine. Now, with the great acquisitions that came with the Burgundian marriage, the Habsburgs again turned their attention to the west. At this time France was much involved in Italy, and hostility to France led the Habsburgs to look also to the south.

Long before his father's death Maximilian had become the driving force in the administration of the country. His position had been bolstered by his selection as German king in 1486. In 1490 the Tyrol, gateway to Italy, became Maximilian's. When in 1493 he came into full possession of all the Habsburg lands in his own right, he ruled over a realm that extended from the Netherlands to the Leitha. It was not a compact territory, but this was the rule rather than the exception for princely holdings in that period. That same year he was chosen emperor.

Maximilian attempted to breathe new life into the moribund Holy Roman Empire by making administrative changes. He also sought to centralize the government of his Austrian territories. He was able to bring a measure of administrative unity to Upper and Lower Austria, as well as to the Tyrol and the Austrian lands to the west. The estates in the various local diets tried with greater or less success to retain their privileges, yet he did start the long process, never fully achieved, of bringing uniform government to the Habsburg lands.

Maximilian also added to his territories. Long a widower, in 1494 he married the daughter of Ludovico Sforza of Milan, which involved him anew in Italian political ventures. In 1500 he acquired the county of Görz (Goritza). In general, he established the Austrian boundaries with Italy that were to last until after the War of the Spanish Succession at the beginning of the 18th century. By timely intervention in a disputed succession in Bavaria in 1505, he obtained the territories of Kufstein, Kitzbühel, and Rattenberg on the Tyrolean border.

Austrian and Spanish Habsburgs. These and various other acquisitions in Germany were minuscule compared to the vast territories that came to the Habsburgs as a result of the marriages Maximilian arranged for his descendants. The most famous of Maximilian's nuptial pacts was the marriage of his son Philip to Juana, the daughter of Ferdinand and Isabella of Spain. Their son, the future Emperor Charles V, was to hold dominion not only over the empire and all the Habsburg and Burgundian lands but also over Spain, with its rich possessions in the New World and in Italy. Maximilian also arranged Habsburg marriages with the children of the king of Bohemia and Hungary.

When Maximilian died on Jan. 12, 1519, he was succeeded as ruler of all the Habsburg lands and also as emperor by his grandson Charles V. Already the monarch of Spain and the Netherlands, Charles partitioned his territories with his brother Ferdinand. By an agreement reached at Worms in 1521, Ferdinand was to receive the so-called five Austrian duchies: Upper Austria, Lower Austria, Styria, Carinthia, and Carniola. A year later (Brussels Pact, 1522) Ferdinand received, in addition, Tyrol and its outlying territories to the west as well as certain northern Italian lands. This territorial partition brought a division of the Habsburg family into Spanish and Austrian branches. Henceforth, the Austrian line, though deeply involved in German affairs through its ties with the empire, was to direct its attention primarily to the east.

Expansion to the East. Ferdinand had hardly taken possession of his territories when he became involved in renewed conflict with the Turks. The Ottoman sultan, Suleiman the Magnificent, had captured Belgrade in 1521, and his forces were soon raiding across the Danube. In 1526, Louis, king of Bohemia and Hungary, met defeat and death at the Battle of Mohács. In the hope of receiving German aid against the Turks, the Bohemian estates elected Ferdinand as their king.

In Hungary the estates divided. One group elected Ferdinand, but the so-called National party chose John Zápolya, prince of Transylvania, as their king. The latter became a vassal of the sultan and received his support. Thereafter, the aim of Ferdinand and his successors was to assert their rights over all of Hungary. This meant almost continual conflict not only with Turkey but also with the Hungarian National party and it resulted in a diversion of attention from imperial affairs. The union of the Austrian, Bohemian, and Hungarian crowns in 1526 by Ferdinand formed the basis of the future Austrian empire. From this time until 1918 the histories of Austria, Bohemia, and Hungary were intertwined.

Soon after the Battle of Mohács, the Turkish armies withdrew from Hungary, and Ferdinand was able to force Zápolya to flee to Poland. Ferdinand was crowned king of Hungary on Nov. 3, 1527, but he never was able to win Turkish recognition. Turkish forces attacked Carniola in 1528, and Suleiman undertook a siege of Vienna in the fall of 1529. Although the Turks were forced to retreat, Ferdinand, unable to secure a peace treaty, had to content himself with truces that were no sooner made than broken.

In 1538, by the Treaty of Grosswardein, Ferdinand and Zápolya reached agreement. Hungary was to be divided, Zápolya receiving the

AUSTRIA-HUNGARY and its constituent areas at the time of the outbreak of World War I in 1914.

larger portion and the royal title. But he was to be succeeded by Ferdinand. When Zápolya died two years later, this agreement was abrogated, and the National party elected Zápolya's young son, John Sigismund, to be their king. The sultan recognized John Sigismund, and Ferdinand, unable to gain substantial support from Germany, was forced to conclude a new series of truces. In 1544 a five-year armistice was concluded on the condition that Ferdinand pay tribute for the small fringe of Hungary that remained in his possession.

For the next century and a half, until the Turks were driven from the country, Hungary remained divided into three sections: one part under the Habsburgs, the central portion under direct Turkish rule, and an eastern section, centering in Transylvania, under native rulers.

Reformation. Emperor Maximilian had been able to sidestep the problems raised by the Protestant Reformation, but this was impossible for his heirs, Charles V and Ferdinand I. As emperor, Charles had the immediate responsibility, but Ferdinand, too, was deeply involved. In 1521, Charles made him president of the council of regency (Reichsregiment), which was to govern Germany during the critical years while Charles was absent. In 1531, Ferdinand was elected German king. Because of their personal concerns—Charles with the Netherlands, Spain, Italy, and the wars with France, Ferdinand with Austria, Bohemia, Hungary, and the wars with Turkey—they were unable to give their full support to the Catholic cause. Their desire to have the aid of the Protestant princes in Germany for the struggle against their enemies, especially against the Turks, led both Charles and Ferdinand to agree to compromises that eventually gave legal recognition to Lutheranism in the empire by the Peace of Augsburg (1555).

Political, social, cultural, and religious conditions in Austria were not unlike those in Germany, and many people—governing officials, soldiers, scholars, and traders—traveled between the two regions. Protestant doctrines spread rapidly. In 1523, Ferdinand felt it necessary to prohibit all Protestant writings in his lands, a ban that had as little effect as his general manifesto against Lutheran doctrine issued in 1527. By that time the new teachings had penetrated even the Slovene and Croatian regions of Carinthia and Carniola.

It has been estimated that by the middle of the 16th century the majority of the inhabitants of all Austrian lands had accepted the new doctrines. The most overwhelmingly Protestant provinces were Upper and Lower Austria, where some 90 percent of the inhabitants were Protestant. The Slavic southeastern provinces were the least affected by the new doctrines. In Bohemia, where the Hussite movement had prepared the way, Protestantism swept the country. It also spread to Hungary, where Calvinism became dominant.

Both Charles and Ferdinand were loyal sons of the church and hoped that a religious compromise could be worked out. But when the Roman Catholic Council of Trent (1545–1563) refused to make concessions, and reconciliation failed, Ferdinand accepted the verdict and pursued a pro-Catholic religious and political policy.

In 1556, Charles V abdicated, and Ferdinand received the imperial crown to add to his many others. On Ferdinand's death in 1564 his lands were divided, as he had ordained, among his three sons. Maximilian, already king of Bohemia and Hungary and German king as well, was to receive Upper and Lower Austria and the imperial dignity; Ferdinand obtained Tyrol and Vorarlberg; and Charles, the Inner Austrian lands with the territories on the Adriatic.

Counter Reformation. Maximilian ruled as Emperor Maximilian II from 1564 to 1576. In general, he followed a liberal policy toward Protestantism. His son Emperor Rudolf II (reigned 1576–1612), a devout Catholic, was not an able administrator, and disorder was widespread. A peasant revolt in Upper Austria (1594–1597) was suppressed, Catholicism was restored there, and Protestant churches were closed. But successful revolts in Transylvania and Hungary obliged Rudolf to grant the Protestants of Hungary equal status with the Catholics. In 1609 he was also forced to grant to the nobility and royal cities of Bohemia the free exercise of religion and the right to form a committee of "Defensors" to protect their privileges. Later curtailment of these privileges was to play a part in bringing about the Thirty Years' War.

Rudolf's brother Matthias was crowned king of Bohemia in 1611, and on the death of Rudolf in the following year Matthias was elected emperor (reigned 1612–1619). He too was unable to curb the nobility, and disorder continued. Childless, Matthias sought to secure the succession for his cousin, Ferdinand of Styria. The latter was a narrow-minded, Jesuit-trained exponent of the Counter Reformation who had assumed the rule of Inner Austria in 1596. There he had ordered Protestants to accept Catholicism or leave the country. Although Ferdinand was hated by the Protestants, Matthias was nevertheless able to engineer Ferdinand's election as king of Bohemia and as king of Hungary.

In Bohemia a bitter dispute soon broke out over the interpretation of the royal charter of 1609. Antagonism increased when Ferdinand appointed 10 governors, 7 of them Roman Catholic, to administer Bohemia. Two of these governors, attempting to negotiate with the Protestant "Defensors," were thrown from a window of the palace (the Defenestration of Prague, May 23, 1618). The Bohemian nobility subsequently deposed Ferdinand. On the death of Matthias, Ferdinand was elected emperor (reigned 1619–1637).

The suppression of the Bohemian revolt initiated the Thirty Years' War (1618–1648), in which the Austrian Habsburgs as champions of the Catholic imperial cause played a leading role. (See THIRTY YEARS' WAR.) The Peace of Westphalia (1648) formally recognized Lutheranism, Calvinism, and Catholicism as legal religions in the empire. But the religious provisions of the peace were specifically excluded from the hereditary territories of the Habsburgs.

By this time the Habsburgs had successfully furthered the reconversion of all Austrian provinces and Bohemia to Catholicism. In 1623 all Protestant clergy were ordered to leave Bohemia; the following year all worship but that of the Catholic Church was forbidden, and in 1627 all Protestants were banished. Similar measures were introduced in Austria.

The old Habsburg territories in Alsace were given to France by the Treaty of Westphalia. This loss diminished the influence of Austria in the empire. The empire emerged from the long conflict weaker than ever before. And yet the Habsburgs clung to the imperial crown, for even if it represented little actual power, it at least lent a certain luster and prestige to the dynasty.

The Habsburgs and Hungary. Disturbances in Transylvania and renewed Turkish activity in Hungary led to a brief Austro-Turkish War (1663–1664). Emperor Leopold I (reigned 1657–1705) undertook a vigorous anti-Protestant policy in Hungary, curtailing many of the old privileges. A group of Hungarians under Imre Tököly asked Turkey for aid. The Turks in 1683 dispatched a large expedition that swept across Hungary and laid siege to Vienna (July 17–September 12). A German army under Charles of Lorraine and Polish forces under King John III Sobieski arrived barely in time to save Vienna. Leopold, his armies strengthened by German contingents, now undertook to drive the Turks from Hungary. Budapest was taken in 1686, and a resounding victory at Mohács, on Aug. 12, 1687, forced the Turks to abandon most of Croatia and Slavonia.

So impressed were the Hungarian magnates by these victories that in 1687 they agreed that the Hungarian crown should henceforth be hereditary in the house of Habsburg. In the Peace of Karlowitz (1699), Austria acquired all of Hungary, except the Banat of Temesvár. Transylvania had already been united to the Hungarian crown in 1697, and Croatia-Slavonia was now again a part of Hungary.

By freeing Hungary from Turkey, Leopold had completed the task Ferdinand I had undertaken in 1526. With his armies had come the Jesuits and the Counter Reformation. So severe were the measures taken against the Protestants that sharp protests were made by Sweden and a number of the Protestant German states. The Protestant strongholds were restricted to the northeastern corner of Hungary (Debrecen) and Transylvania, which had been bypassed by the Austrian forces as they pursued the Turks.

Gains in Italy. By the treaties of Utrecht, Rastatt, and Baden (1713–1714), which marked the close of the War of the Spanish Succession, Austria acquired the Spanish Netherlands, Milan, Mantua, Naples, and Sardinia. Sardinia was exchanged in 1720 with the duke of Savoy for Sicily. Later in the century, by the Peace of Vienna (1738), which concluded the War of the Polish Succession, Austria exchanged Naples and Sicily with Spain for Parma and Piacenza. At the same time, Emperor Charles VI's son-in-law, Francis of Lorraine, was compensated with Tuscany for his cession of Lorraine to France. By these exchanges the Habsburg territories in Italy became more compact.

On the east, Austria gained the Banat of Temesvár in 1718 after a two-year war with Turkey. Although Austria also gained Little Wallachia and northern Serbia by the same treaty, the Habsburgs were obliged to give these back to Turkey after the Austro-Turkish War of 1736–1739.

Maria Theresa. Charles VI was greatly concerned over the problem of succession. In 1713 he issued a new order of succession known as the Pragmatic Sanction. The Habsburg territories were to be indivisible and inseparable and were to descend to his son if he should have one, or if not, to his daughters in order of seniority, and to their issue. Heretofore succession had never devolved on a female of the Habsburg line. Charles VI won approval of this settlement from the estates of all his lands, as well as from the major European powers. The Pragmatic Sanction was an important constitutional document of the developing Austrian state. By it all the estates acknowledged the unity of the Habsburg territories and pledged themselves to accept a common sovereign. It was the one mutually recognized tie between Austria and Hungary.

In spite of all Charles' diplomatic preparations, on his death in 1740 a dispute arose over the succession. When his eldest daughter, Maria Theresa, assumed control of the Habsburg lands, the most serious challenge came from Frederick II the Great of Prussia, who laid claim to Silesia. Charles Albert of Bavaria claimed all the Habsburg lands and was also a candidate for the imperial throne, to which he was elected in 1742. On his death in 1745, Maria Theresa was successful in furthering the election of her husband, Francis of Lorraine, who as Francis I was emperor from 1745 to 1765. Henceforth it was the house of Habsburg-Lorraine that ruled both the empire and the various Habsburg lands.

The War of the Austrian Succession (1740–1748) in its various phases developed into an international conflict in which, at times, Prussia, Bavaria, Saxony, Sardinia, Spain, and France opposed Austria and Britain. In the Peace of Aix-la-Chapelle (1748), Frederick II's possession of Silesia was confirmed, and Austria was forced to cede some of its Italian lands to Sardinia and Spain. The powers, however, agreed to recognize the Pragmatic Sanction and also Francis I as emperor. The War of the Austrian Succession was continued in the Seven Years' War (1756–1763), when Maria Theresa made an unsuccessful attempt to repossess Silesia from Prussia. This time Austria was aided by France and Russia, while Britain allied itself with Prussia. Only the death of Czarina Elizabeth of Russia in 1762, which brought the withdrawal of Russia, saved Frederick the Great of Prussia from defeat. Silesia remained in his hands by the terms of the Treaty of Hubertusburg (1763).

The losses in territory that Maria Theresa sustained were offset by the acquisition of Galicia and Lodomeria in the first partition of Poland (1772). In recognition of Austria's neutrality in its war with Russia, Turkey in 1779 acquiesced in Austrian occupation of Bukovina. These additions brought substantial numbers of Poles, Ruthenians, and Jews to Austria's conglomeration of nationalities.

Maria Theresa's wars necessitated financial reforms and greater centralization of administration. She established a state council, which was to act in an advisory capacity, and the Austrian and Bohemian chanceries were united. She did not abolish the local diets but simply neglected them. Even the important Hungarian Diet was called only four times during her reign. She enlarged the bureaucracy, which was chiefly composed of German-speaking officials.

Joseph II, an "Enlightened Despot." When Joseph II became sole ruler in 1780 on his mother's death, he attempted to centralize the realm overnight, feeling that it must become one territory with similar institutions and obligations. He divided the country into 13 new administrative districts with directors appointed by the crown. He gave serfs the right to leave their lands and to marry without the consent of their lords.

He was also an innovator in religious policy. His Toleration Patent of 1781 brought political equality to Protestants. Lutherans, Calvinists, and Orthodox were guaranteed free private exercise of their religion, but their churches could not have a tower, a bell, or an entrance from a main street. Joseph dissolved 700 monasteries, some of them long in a state of decrepitude. State-controlled seminaries for the education of priests were erected; all higher clergy were to be appointed by the crown. In general, Joseph so increased the restrictions on the Catholic Church that the term "Josephinism" came to be applied to his system of state control of the church.

Joseph was an exponent of the ideas of the Enlightenment. One of the most worthy recipients of the accolade "Enlightened Despot," he alienated many by his vigorous policy of reform from the top. His ventures in foreign policy, notably his various attempts to acquire Bavaria, failed. He suffered disastrous reverses in a war with Turkey, in which he was an ally of Russia. In the Spanish Netherlands he was confronted by a revolution in 1789. Sick and discouraged, on Jan. 28, 1790, he rescinded all his innovations except the abolition of serfdom, the Toleration Patent, and the Religious-Educational Fund.

Turn of the Century. It was the task of Joseph's brother Leopold II (reigned as emperor 1790–1792) to make peace with Turkey and by judicious concessions to pacify the Belgians and other peoples of the realm. The policy of centralization was halted; the old diets and estates resumed their traditional powers. Although the religious laws were not repealed, the Catholic Church regained much of its old supremacy.

The events of the French Revolution and its repercussions in Belgium and Germany forced Leopold to take action. On Feb. 7, 1792, Austria and Prussia signed an offensive and defensive alliance. Leopold died before war broke out, and his son Francis II had to bear the burdens and defeats of the wars of the French Revolutionary era. Austria did not share in the Second Partition of Poland (1793) but did join with Russia and Prussia in the final dismemberment of that country in 1795.

After Napoleon had been proclaimed emperor of France in 1804, Francis, foreseeing the end of the Holy Roman Empire, proclaimed himself hereditary emperor of Austria on Aug. 11, 1804. His new ennoblement did not change the legal basis of his various lands, and he still carried his many subsidiary titles. For two years he wore the two imperial crowns, but after Napoleon had established the Confederation of the Rhine, Francis laid down the old imperial crown, and on Aug. 6, 1806, the Holy Roman Empire came to an end. As Francis II he was Holy Roman emperor (1792–1806); as Francis I he was emperor of Austria (1804–1835).

The disastrous campaigns of the first three coalitions against France led to many territorial losses. When Metternich replaced Johann von Stadion in 1809 as minister of foreign affairs, Austria drew closer to France for a time. Marie Louise, the daughter of Francis I, was married to Napoleon in 1810. Austria as France's ally was forced to supply a contingent for Napoleon's Grand Army when he invaded Russia in 1812. It was less than half-hearted cooperation, however, and Austria subsequently joined in the final coalition that brought Napoleon's downfall in 1814.

The Congress of Vienna. To straighten out the affairs of Europe, the powers assembled in Vienna (September 1814–June 1815). Here Francis I played host to the sovereigns of Europe. In spite of the continual round of receptions and parties, the Congress of Vienna under the presidency of Metternich accomplished a great deal. Austria regained many of its old territories, including Salzburg and most of Galicia, but not Cracow, which became a free city. The cession of Belgium to the Netherlands and the loss of Breisgau were more than offset by the acquisition of new Italian territories in Lombardy, Venetia, and the Illyrian provinces (Dalmatia). In addition, by dynastic agreements, Austria won dominance over many of the other Italian states, becoming the leading power in Italy. In Germany it managed to maintain a certain influence by assuming the presidency of the German Confederation, which succeeded the Holy Roman Empire.

The Age of Metternich. So completely did Metternich control the foreign policy of Austria and cast his influence over all Europe that the period 1815–1848 is often referred to as the Age of Metternich. In order to maintain the peace, he joined with the other great powers in holding periodic conferences. Austria played host to the Conference of Troppau (1820), where the powers agreed in a famous protocol to unite in suppressing revolution wherever it might occur, and to the conferences of Laibach (1821) and Verona (1822), which decided respectively on coercive measures to suppress revolutionary uprisings in Italy (undertaken by Austria) and in Spain (undertaken by France).

In the Diet of the German Confederation, Metternich sponsored the Carlsbad Decrees (1819), which provided for control of the universities, established a strict censorship of all publications, and vastly extended the police powers. He was able for a time to keep the powers from intervening to support the Greek Revolt (1821) against the sultan. After Russia did go to war with Turkey, the emperors of Austria and Russia and the crown prince of Prussia met at Münchengrätz in 1833, where new measures were agreed upon for the suppression of revolutionary agitation. In addition, Russia made a fateful promise that if partition of the Ottoman empire should become necessary, Russia would act only in agreement with Austria.

Internal Policies Under Francis I and Ferdinand I. Metternich's influence on Austrian internal policy did not match his leadership in foreign affairs. He is quoted as saying, "I have sometimes governed Europe, but Austria never." Francis I, rigid, slow-witted, and determined to maintain his personal authority, insisted that the heads of each department deal directly with him. In 1825, Count Kolowrat, a personal antagonist of Metternich, became finance minister and more than any other official controlled internal policy. Finances were perpetually in a sad state, and tariff reforms did not alter the tariff frontiers that separated Hungary from Austria.

Emperor Francis was succeeded by his son Ferdinand I (reigned 1835–1848), an epileptic whose mind was impaired. It was necessary to establish a state conference, consisting of Archduke Louis, Prince Metternich, and Count Kolowrat to carry on the government. The last two were great rivals, and partly out of fear of each other they ventured upon nothing.

In 1824 the Jesuits, who had been banned in 1783, were again permitted in all Austria. Under Ferdinand the church tightened its control over the schools. The schools were there to provide the emperor with God-fearing, obedient subjects.

Dissaffection Within the Empire. In spite of strict censorship and an ever-increasing reliance on the police, opposition to the government manifested itself. Liberal agitation was complicated by a rising spirit of nationalism among the various peoples of the empire. The Hungarian Diet, which had not been summoned since 1811, assembled again in 1825 and rapidly became a center of Magyar nationalism. A series of laws were enacted that made Magyar virtually the exclusive state language. A new Slavic consciousness also appeared, which inevitably led to a demand for more political rights. In Italy, meanwhile, the kingdom of Sardinia was fanning the spirit of discontent with Austrian rule. In 1846, when the Poles in Cracow and Galicia agitated, resulting in Cracow's annexation by Austria, the Austrian authorities called on the largely Ruthenian peasantry to turn on their Polish landlords. The promised abolition of feudal restrictions did not meet expectations, and discontent grew.

The business and professional classes, particularly in Vienna, wanted a more unified state with a central parliament. The conservative aristocracy, irritated by ceaseless bureaucratic control, favored local particularism and the reassertion of the rights of the estates in the local diets of the non-Hungarian areas. Everywhere there was dissatisfaction but no united program of action.

Constitutional Change. This was the situation when, in 1848, Louis Philippe was deposed in France. Soon Germany was aflame, and rioting and insurrection broke out also in Vienna, Budapest, Prague, and in the cities of northern Italy. Metternich, forced to resign on March 13, 1848, fled to England. The emperor on April 4 granted a constitution for his non-Hungarian lands, but a second uprising in Vienna won the concession that the parliament scheduled to be elected should be considered a constituent assembly. This Reichstag, minus representatives from Hungary, met in Vienna on July 22, 1848, and began to chart a new constitution. It was this body that abolished serfdom on Sept. 7, 1848—one of the lasting revolutionary reforms.

Renewed agitation in Vienna caused the emperor to flee the city on October 7, and on October 22 the Reichstag was adjourned to Kremsier, a small town in Moravia. General Windischgrätz, who had previously suppressed the insurrection in Prague (June 17), now occupied Vienna. On Dec. 2, 1848, Emperor Ferdinand abdicated and was succeeded by his nephew Francis Joseph (reigned 1848–1916), then a youth of 18 years. Prince Felix Schwarzenberg, as prime minister, directed the affairs of state.

At Kremsier the Reichstag drafted a constitution that would have established a decentralized, federal Austria. However, Schwarzenberg dissolved the Reichstag and on March 4, 1849, promulgated the Stadion Constitution providing for a strongly centralized state. It aroused great opposition in Hungary. In 1851 the Stadion Constitution was revoked, and thereafter the emperor alone ruled the Habsburg lands.

When Schwarzenberg died on April 5, 1852, the minister of interior, Alexander Bach, became the most influential man in the government. He developed a strong centralized government, administered by a German-speaking bureaucracy and controlled by a greatly expanded police force. Bach tempered his absolutism by introducing a number of reforms. He carried out the liberation of the serfs, he built roads and railroads, implemented a common tariff, and modernized the judicial and legal system.

Foreign and Domestic Reverses. Austria became involved in war with Italy in 1859. The war was the work of Count Cavour, who as premier of the kingdom of Sardinia had negotiated a secret alliance with Napoleon III of France. The victory of these allies forced Austria to cede Lombardy and to acquiesce in the unification of Italy. Austria retained Venetia, but it was no longer the dominant power in the peninsula. At home the military defeat and chronic financial troubles forced the Austrian authorities to introduce constitutional reforms.

In an effort to meet some of the demands of various national groups, particularly the Magyars, Francis Joseph on Oct. 20, 1860, issued the October Diploma, giving more power to the local diets, which were controlled by the propertied classes and nobility. This did not satisfy liberal demands, and the emperor almost im-

Prince Metternich (*left*), chancellor of Austria and leading statesman of Europe after fall of Napoleon.

Emperor Francis Joseph (*right*), Habsburg ruler of Austria and Hungary, 1848–1916.

mediately replaced the diploma with the February Patent of 1861, which provided for a centralized government. However, the Hungarians, Czechs, and Poles refused to send delegates to the legislature (Reichsrat) it established.

Meanwhile, events in Germany were leading to a conflict between Austria and Prussia for leadership of the German Confederation. Together these two powers had defeated in 1864 a Danish attempt to annex Schleswig-Holstein, but soon differences over German affairs led to the Seven Weeks' War of 1866. Bismarck, the Prussian leader, arranged an alliance with Italy; Austria had as its allies most of the German states, including Bavaria, Saxony, and Hannover.

Austrian arms were successful in Italy, but the Prussian victory at Königgrätz (Sadowa) on July 3, 1866, forced Austria to capitulate. As a result of the war, Austria lost Venetia and had to acquiesce in Prussian seizure of various German lands and the establishment of the North German Confederation. Although Austria ceded no territory to Prussia, it had been removed by Bismarck's policy of "Blood and Iron" from both Italian and German affairs.

The Dual Monarchy. It was now imperative for Francis Joseph to end the disaffection in Hungary. Friedrich Ferdinand Beust, appointed foreign minister in October 1866, and Ferencz Deák and Gyula Andrássy, as leaders of the dominant party in Hungary, worked out a new constitutional settlement. Known as the Austro-Hungarian Compromise (*Ausgleich*) of 1867, it established a dual monarchy—an empire of Austria and a kingdom of Hungary. Each state was to have its own parliament and ministry but, true to the Pragmatic Sanction, would have a common sovereign. In addition, there were to be three common ministries—those of finance, foreign affairs, and war—to manage joint affairs. A common representative body known as the Delegations, made up of 60 delegates from each parliament, was to serve as a link between the two state governments.

On Dec. 21, 1867, the Austrian Reichsrat adopted a series of five fundamental laws, which brought about a revision of the Patent of 1861. By these laws the competence of the central parliament was limited in favor of the provincial diets. These laws also provided for implementation of many liberal ideas, such as freedom of religion and education, equality of citizens before the law, ministerial responsibility, establishment of a supreme court to decide questions of competence, and interpretation of public law. The fundamental laws recognized the equal rights of all languages and nationalities in the empire, but the exact meaning of this was not clear.

The bicameral Reichsrat was to consist of a House of Lords, made up of certain hereditary nobles and high ecclesiastical personages in addition to 150 to 170 persons nominated by the emperor for life in recognition of special services rendered to the state; and a House of Deputies, elected by the provincial diets. (There were important franchise reforms in 1868; in 1873, when election of deputies was transferred from the diets to a direct vote by the people; and in 1896 and 1907.)

Internal and Foreign Affairs, 1868–1914. After 1867, Austria and Hungary went their separate ways in internal affairs. In Austria, Count Eduard von Taaffe, prime minister from 1879 to 1893, made important concessions to the various nationality groups and formed a coalition of Slavs and clericals in opposition to the German liberals. When Count Badeni, who formed a government in 1895, made further concessions to the Czechs, the Germans feared for the unity of the empire. Thereafter, short-term ministries succeeded each other to the end of the empire. The cabinets governed mostly by emergency legislation enacted by the emperor, and the Austrian Reichsrat was reduced to impotence by the bitter conflicts among the nationalities.

During this period the imperial house suffered two tragedies. On Jan. 30, 1889, Crown Prince Rudolf committed suicide at Mayerling, taking with him in death his mistress, Baroness Mary Vetsera. He was succeeded as crown prince by his cousin Archduke Francis Ferdinand of Habsburg-Este. On Sept. 10, 1898, Francis Joseph suffered a second personal loss when Empress Elizabeth, the idol of his Hungarian subjects, was assassinated by an anarchist in Geneva.

The defeat of France in the Franco-Prussian War and the establishment of the German empire in 1871 forced Francis Joseph to abandon all hope of regaining a leading position in German affairs. The emperors of Austria-Hungary, Germany, and Russia formed the League of Three Emperors (1872–1873), in which they promised to consult each other on any problems on which they might have divergent interests or that threatened the peace of Europe.

Prior to the Russo-Turkish War of 1877–1878, Austria and Russia had come to an understanding on Near Eastern affairs: Austria was to remain neutral in any future Turkish-Russian conflict and was free to occupy Bosnia-Herzegovina when it saw fit to do so. But in the Treaty of San Stefano of March 1878, drawn up by Russia and

Turkey at the end of the war, Austria was accorded no rights in these provinces. This and other provisions of the treaty displeased the Austrian statesmen. Together with the British leaders, the Austrians were primarily responsible for calling the Congress of Berlin (1878), which revised the Treaty of San Stefano. At the Congress, Austria-Hungary was given the right to occupy and administer Bosnia-Herzegovina, which, however, was to remain under Turkish suzerainty. In addition, Austria-Hungary was given permission to station troops in the sanjak of Novibazar (Novi Pazar), a step designed to prevent the territorial union of Montenegro and Serbia. The occupation of Bosnia-Herzegovina in 1878 required the use of over 145,000 troops, and the army suffered over 5,000 casualties.

Alliance Systems. Bismarck began to fear a possible Russian attack after the Congress of Berlin and in 1879 concluded a dual alliance with Austria-Hungary. To Bismarck's disappointment, Austria refused to undertake any obligation against a possible French attack on Germany. The result was a pact that limited their mutual aid to the event of an attack by Russia or Russian intervention in a war in which either ally was attacked by another power. The treaty was to be kept secret. It lasted until the end of World War I.

Russia, fearing an attack by Britain, concluded another Alliance of Three Emperors on June 18, 1881, in which it was agreed that if any of the three contracting powers were involved in a war with a fourth great power, the other two would preserve a benevolent neutrality.

Austria strengthened its position in Serbia in 1881 by negotiating a treaty of alliance with Serbia that was to last until 1895. In 1882 the dual alliance of Austria and Germany became a Triple Alliance when Italy joined the grouping. In this treaty Austria and Germany agreed to help Italy if it was attacked by France, while Italy agreed in turn to aid Germany if Germany was attacked by France. Austria still fought shy of promising direct aid in case France attacked Germany. The alliance system was extended in 1883 by a treaty between Rumania and Austria to which Germany and Italy adhered. This latter treaty was directed against an attack by Russia.

Meanwhile, Austria's relations with Russia had deteriorated as each country sought to strengthen control over areas in the Balkans. Russia, having negotiated an alliance with France (1891–1894), gradually drifted further away from both Austria and Germany. In 1897, Austria and Russia agreed to maintain the status quo in the Balkans. If this proved impossible, European Turkey was to be divided among the existing Balkan countries but with the addition of an independent Albanian state. This agreement did not hold up for long. Russia concluded an alliance with Bulgaria in 1902, and Serbian policy also became oriented toward Russia. Under Russian patronage, Bulgarian-Serbian treaties of friendship and of alliance were concluded in 1904 with a view to establishing close economic relations between the two states. In order to prevent this development, Austria imposed economic sanctions against Serbia. Tariffs and sanitary regulations were aimed at the Serbian export of pork. The Pig War (1905–1907) was successful for Austria, inasmuch as it prevented the establishment of a customs union between Serbia and Bulgaria, but it fanned Serbian nationalism and intensified Serbian hostility toward Austria-Hungary.

Bosnia and Herzegovina. In 1908, Russia attempted to win Austrian approval for the opening of the Turkish Straits to Russian warships, in return for Russian consent to the annexation of Bosnia-Herzegovina. The complicated negotiations were not completed when the Young Turks threatened to summon delegates to the parliament in Istanbul from Bulgaria and Bosnia-Herzegovina, both of which were still technically components of the Ottoman empire. In part to forestall this action, Bulgaria on Oct. 5, 1908, proclaimed its independence. On the following day Austria-Hungary announced the annexation of Bosnia-Herzegovina. The annexation aroused vociferous opposition in Serbia and Montenegro, and a grave international crisis developed. Although German diplomacy prevented it from exploding into war, Serbian as well as Russian hostility to Austria was intensified by this turn of events.

The Balkan Wars of 1912–1913 increased Serbian nationalism and stimulated dissatisfaction among the Slavs within the empire. When it became clear that it would be impossible to maintain the status quo in the Balkans, Austria, desirous of preventing Serbia from reaching the Adriatic, insisted on the establishment of an independent Albania. The powers agreed to this and in laborious negotiations determined the boundaries of this state. When Serbia at the close of the Second Balkan War refused to evacuate Albania, Austria-Hungary on Oct. 18, 1913, sent an ultimatum to Belgrade demanding the withdrawal of Serbian troops within eight days. Although Serbia yielded, it became even more determined to form a united South Slav state.

On June 28, 1914, Archduke Francis Ferdinand and his wife were assassinated at Sarajevo in Bosnia. The Austrians were convinced that the Serbian government was behind the plot. Austria dispatched an ultimatum to Belgrade, and the Serbian government took conciliatory steps toward meeting the Austrian demands. Certain key demands, however, were rejected, and Austria declared war against Serbia on July 28, 1914. The Austrian-Serbian conflict, which the Austrian leaders planned as a local one, quickly mushroomed into World War I.

World War I and the Collapse of the Dual Monarchy. The Austrian parliament had been prorogued on March 14, 1914, and was not summoned again until May 30, 1917. A military dictatorship and strict censorship were established. Civil tribunals and jury trial gave way to courts-martial. Large segments of the populace, especially in Bohemia and the South Slav provinces, opposed the war from the start, and as the conflict ground wearily on, dissatisfaction with the general internal situation mounted.

On Nov. 21, 1916, Emperor Francis Joseph died. The new emperor-king, Charles I (reigned 1916–1918), attempted to inaugurate a change in policy. New premiers were appointed in both Austria and Hungary, and a change was made in the military command. The Austrian parliament was called into session on May 30, 1917, and rapidly became a sounding board for the grievances of all the peoples of the empire.

On July 2, 1917, the emperor on his own initiative issued a general amnesty for all those who were imprisoned under the emergency decrees. This liberated some of the most able national leaders, who immediately took up their agitation again.

Hunger, internal nationality conflicts, and military defeat hastened the political collapse in the summer of 1918. On Oct. 7, 1918, the government applied for an armistice. In a final effort to save what he could, Emperor Charles on October 16 issued a manifesto announcing that the empire was to be transformed into a federal state. Representatives of each national group in the Reichsrat were to withdraw and form national councils. The emperor's manifesto had a profound effect, for it offered a peaceful basis for the disintegration of the empire.

On November 3 the three common ministers signed the Austrian armistice and then resigned. Finally, on November 11, Emperor Charles withdrew from Austrian affairs; two days later he laid down his Hungarian crown. In neither case did he abdicate, a technicality that meant that if either Austria or Hungary chose a monarchic form of government, the claims of the Habsburgs to the throne remained intact.

Establishment of the Austrian Republic. Each of the national councils staked out its claim to a portion of old Austria, which led to many disputes. In the Treaty of St.-Germain of Sept. 10, 1919, between the republic of Austria and the victorious Allies, the boundaries of the republic were defined, and certain former Austrian territories were awarded to other states. Other territorial allotments came later, with the following results: 26.63 percent of the area of imperial Austria went to the new Austrian republic; 26.48 percent to Poland; 26.21 percent to Czechoslovakia; 9.34 percent to Yugoslavia, 7.86 percent to Italy, and 3.48 percent to Rumania. All these states also received portions of the former kingdom of Hungary.

The Austrian National Council, in proclaiming its independence as a republic on Nov. 12, 1918, had carefully chosen the name *Deutsch-Österreich* (German-Austria) and inserted in its fundamental laws a provision that it was to form a part of the German republic. The terms of the *Anschluss*, or union, were to be worked out later, but all German Austrians were looking forward to being united with Germany. It was the Allies who forced them to change the name to Austria and to insert in their constitution a denial of any intention of joining Germany.

The Interwar Period. The Social Democrats, led by Karl Renner, formed the first government. The elections of 1920 ended their rule, although they retained control of the city of Vienna. From this point on, the Christian Socialists, ably led by a Catholic priest, Ignaz Seipel, dominated the coalition cabinets. The German National party under Johann Schober usually sided with the Christian Socialists. Extrapolitical organizations soon sprang up. The Heimwehr, led by Ernst Rüdiger von Starhemberg, recruited most of its followers from the rural districts, was conservative in outlook, and usually associated with the Christian Socialists. The Social Democrats formed the Schutzbund, which drew its members from Vienna and other industrial centers.

The Treaty of St.-Germain saddled Austria with heavy financial burdens, which the young republic was unable to meet. The League of Nations provided loans that revived the economy. In 1931, Austria and Germany projected the formation of a customs union, but the International Court of Justice held 8 to 7 that it was contrary to the Treaty of St.-Germain, and the plan was abandoned.

The bankruptcy of the Creditanstalt on May 11, 1931, and the resulting economic crisis led to political unrest, which was enhanced by the rise of Hitler in Germany. On March 3, 1933, Chancellor Engelbert Dollfuss suspended parliament and established his own brand of dictatorship. Ever since 1930, when Italy and Austria concluded a treaty of friendship, Mussolini had encouraged fascist elements in Austria. Mussolini rather than Hitler inspired Dollfuss.

In February 1934, Dollfuss dissolved all political parties except his own Fatherland Front, a coalition of Christian Socialists, Agrarians, and the Heimwehr. When the Social Democrats resisted and barricaded themselves in some of the great municipal housing projects, Dollfuss ordered the buildings bombarded. The Socialists never forgave him this bloodbath and turned a cold shoulder when it came to aiding him against the Nazis. He strengthened ties with Italy and Hungary by signing the Rome Protocols on March 18, 1934.

A putsch of July 25, 1934, carried out by Austrian Nazis but directed from Berlin, ended in the assassination of Dollfuss. Mussolini sent troops to the Brenner Pass, making it clear to Hitler that he could not take over Austria at that time. Kurt von Schuschnigg, a lawyer who had taken an active part in Catholic political activities, became the new chancellor-dictator, with Starhemberg as vice chancellor.

Schuschnigg went quietly ahead, concentrating power in his own hands. On April 1, 1936, he reintroduced military conscription in Austria. Starhemberg was forced out of the cabinet, and the Heimwehr was disbanded. Supposedly absorbed into the Fatherland Front militia, many Heimwehr members actually developed ties with the Nazis. By an agreement of July 11, 1936, Hitler promised to respect the independence of Austria, and Schuschnigg agreed to pursue a policy friendly to Germany. As Mussolini became involved in Ethiopia and Spain, he sacrificed Austria's independence for German friendship.

Anschluss. The Austrian dictator began to cultivate closer relations with the Little Entente (Czechoslovakia, Rumania, and Yugoslavia). Hitler objected and invited Schuschnigg to pay him a visit in February 1938 at Berchtesgaden. Hitler demanded that Arthur Seyss-Inquart, the leader of the Austrian Nazis, be made minister of the interior and that the Nazis be permitted to join the Fatherland Front. Schuschnigg decided to stage a plebiscite on the issue of Austrian independence. Hitler realized the maneuver was aimed against Germany and demanded that the plebiscite be canceled. When the Austrian Nazis fomented disturbances, Schuschnigg gave in. He canceled the plebiscite and resigned. Seyss-Inquart, the new chancellor, promptly appealed for German troops to restore order. They entered Austria on March 12, 1938. The next day the union of Austria and Germany was proclaimed.

Austria now became the *Ostmark* with Seyss-Inquart as governor, and the coordination of Austrian life and economy with those of Germany proceeded smoothly. In many ways it was but the exchange of one dictatorship for another, and incorporation into Germany brought more prosperity. The Jews suffered, but the Austrians were not inclined to take a stand on their behalf.

Reestablishment of the Republic. At the Moscow Conference of 1943 during World War II, the Soviet Union, the United States, and Britain formally declared their wish to see a free and independent state of Austria. It was the Soviet army that began the liberation of Austria, occupying Vienna in April 1945. With the approval of the Russians, Karl Renner established a provisional government for all Austria on April 27, 1945.

On May 1 this government reintroduced the constitution of 1920, as amended in 1929. At the cessation of hostilities, in accordance with agreements reached earlier, Austria was established as a separate administrative territory within its 1922–1937 boundaries, under joint occupation by the United States, Britain, the Soviet Union, and France. Each power administered a zone of occupation. Vienna, lying deep in the Russian zone, was likewise partitioned into four occupation sectors, with the Inner City administered by the four powers.

The four powers and Austria signed the State Treaty on May 15, 1955, and on July 27, 1955, Austria regained its full sovereignty. In line with pledges made before the signing of the treaty, Austria adopted a law, effective Nov. 5, 1955, that decreed the permanent neutrality of the nation. On November 5, Austria celebrated the opening of the rebuilt Vienna opera house with Beethoven's *Fidelio*—and with no foreign troops on its soil.

On Dec. 14, 1955, Austria was admitted to membership in the United Nations. In 1960 it brought the dispute with Italy over South Tyrol before the UN Assembly. In establishing the region of Trentino-Alto Adige, Italy united the predominantly German-speaking South Tyrol province of Bolzano with the Italian-speaking province of Trento. Austria charged that this action along with other policies deprived the German-speaking Tyrolese of the autonomy envisaged in an Austrian-Italian agreement of 1946. The Assembly recommended resumption of direct discussions between Austria and Italy. Some advances were made, but no settlement of the long-festering dispute was reached.

E.C. HELMREICH, *Bowdoin College*

7. Culture

Through the centuries, Austrians by birth or adoption have made impressive cultural contributions to the world. The beginnings of culture in Austria date from the founding of Christian monasteries and churches. Monastic establishments in the lonely countryside were shrines of culture as well as of religion.

Austrian ruling dynasties—the Babenbergs from the late 11th into the 13th century and then the Habsburgs until 1918—fostered the things of the mind and the spirit. The Renaissance court of Emperor Maximilian I compared favorably with that of the Medicis in Florence. Landed aristocrats, who erected châteaus and palatial mansions, were patrons of the arts. The universities, first at Vienna (founded 1365) and later at Graz, Salzburg (which lay outside of Habsburg sovereignty until 1816), and Innsbruck, were milestones in the cultural betterment of the country.

Recurrent warfare with Hungarians and Turks and the Protestant upheaval followed by the Counter Reformation greatly hampered cultural progress. But in the century following the last Turkish invasion (1683), Austria experienced a glorious epoch in music, art, and architecture. Vienna was firmly established as the supreme focus of Danubian culture. The house of Habs-burg enlarged its domains by acquiring lands to the east, the north, and the south. As the capital of this multinational monarchy, Vienna came to have larger importance for Austria than, for instance, Paris for France. Yet provincial cities jealously preserved their cultural identity and imitated Vienna in providing new facilities for cultivated living. Even so, Austrian masters in music, in art and architecture, and in literature tended to gravitate to the "Queen City" on the Danube. And more and more the aspiring middle classes replaced the church and the aristocracy as the principal patrons of culture.

A new golden age began soon after the middle of the 19th century. Immigrants to Austria enriched nearly every branch of civilized existence; of special significance were Jewish newcomers, who concentrated in Vienna. From about 1880 into the 1930's, Jews predominated in cultural and intellectual affairs.

When the Habsburg monarchy collapsed as a result of World War I, Austria, which had been the core of a realm as large as Texas, was suddenly reduced to an Alpine republic the size of Maine. For a time drastic political and social changes interrupted advances in culture, but Austrians soon demonstrated remarkable qualities of resilience. Then the approach of the catastrophic Hitlerian epoch drove scores of the culturally gifted, Jews especially, to seek asylum elsewhere. The Nazi absorption of Austria in 1938 was followed by World War II and then the occupation of Austria by the Allies until 1955. Despite the resultant dislocations, cultural activity revived rapidly. Municipalities and the national government subsidized the arts to an unparalleled extent. By reason of its location and the status of neutrality adopted in 1955, Austria was able to resume its age-old mission as a cultural bridge between Western society and the peoples of eastern Europe.

MUSIC

The greatest cultural glory of Austria derives from musical composition and performance, both instrumental and vocal. From the earliest period, the Christian church, especially in its Benedictine monasteries, fostered music. Some of the most outstanding Austrian compositions are church masses and sacred oratorios. A Christian hymn borrowed the tune of the Habsburg imperial anthem, written in 1797 by Joseph Haydn, and no Christmas carol is more widely sung than *Silent Night, Holy Night*, written by the Austrian Francis X. Gruber.

Folk music and military songs were freely appropriated by the most illustrious masters of instrumentation. Flutists, fiddlers, trumpeters, and zither players enlivened local gatherings. Babenberg dukes and Salzburg prelates encouraged minnesingers—kinsmen in spirit of the French troubadours. Maximilian I generously supported musicians; his favorite, Paul Hofhaimer, author of secular and sacred pieces and an accomplished organist, was known throughout Europe. The Vienna Boys' Choir, formally organized in 1498, is the oldest Austrian ensemble. Leading communities of the country set up schools to train choristers and promoted singing in other ways. As early as the 1500's foreigners commented on the universal popularity of music in Austria.

Dutch immigrants and, later, Italians, who brought opera with them, enhanced the stock of musical literature. To satisfy the demands of the

VIENNA OPERA HOUSE, badly damaged during World War II, was reconstructed after the war.

Habsburg court and of elegant society, Italian musicians prepared as many as a dozen operas a year. Daughters of the imperial and aristocratic households danced in ballet, and several emperors composed music—Leopold I is credited with over 150 pieces. An archbishop of Salzburg, Wolf D. von Raitenau (died 1612), and his successors underwrote operatic productions and founded an important center of musical instruction in Salzburg.

Classicism in the 18th Century. The outstanding Austrian musical personality of the early 18th century, Johann J. Fux, came of Styrian peasant stock. In addition to conducting, he wrote operas and religious music, as well as a book on the theory of music and counterpoint, *Steps to Parnassus*. The Artaria publishing house of Vienna, specializing in musical scores, began its long career in 1778, and at about the same time professional critics attained recognition, although their superficial appraisals often infuriated the leading composers of the day. By then the superb Austrian classical school dominated the musical scene. The cosmopolitan Christoph Gluck, called by a contemporary "the Sophocles of music," effected radical alterations in operatic writing. As is demonstrated in *Orpheus and Eurydice*, Gluck stressed simplicity and directness in orchestration, intense emotional expression, and engaging libretto. Like Gluck, Joseph Haydn was born into a humble home. He, too, liked to experiment with musical forms and ideas, and his works solidly established the ascendancy of Austria in the world of music. He displayed inexhaustible freshness, lyrical beauty, and flashes of humor in a large quantity of chamber and vocal pieces, symphonies, operas, and masses. Haydn's creativity reached a peak in two oratorios, *The Seasons* and *The Creation*.

The most gifted of the classical composers, Wolfgang Amadeus Mozart, was born and spent his early years in Salzburg. More than 600 compositions carry his name. Into his best-loved creations he infused rich orchestral emotion, bold harmonies, and rugged strength. The operas *Don Giovanni* and *The Magic Flute*, together with the Symphony in C Major (called the *Jupiter*), alone would have earned Mozart immortality.

Beethoven and the 19th Century. Moving to Austria from the Rhineland, Ludwig van Beethoven greatly enriched the musical literature of his adopted country. The diversified artistry of this towering genius represented a bridge between classical formalism and the age of romanticism. Vitality of expression, rare nobility of spirit, and technical perfection distinguish the works of Beethoven. His nine symphonies and two masses

and his overtures, concertos, sonatas, and string quartets exerted a lasting influence upon composition and never lost their appeal for music lovers. The remarkable orchestration and the songs in *Fidelio*, Beethoven's only opera, have made it a perennial favorite for state occasions in Austria.

Wealthy patrician families maintained orchestras of their own and attached musical artists to their household staffs. Fickle aristocratic audiences quickly tired of new compositions and insisted upon something newer. For the sophisticated middle classes performances by professionals and amateurs in public squares and parks attained unprecedented popularity. On November 22, the feast day of St. Cecilia, patroness of music, Austrian communities presented special concerts. Gradually, financial and industrial magnates supplanted the aristocracy and churchmen as the principal patrons of music and composers.

Lyric songs, rich in melodic beauty, by Franz Schubert, a precocious son of Vienna, became and remained prized possessions of the world of music. When Schubert died at the age of 32, it was fittingly lamented, "Death has here buried a rich treasure, but much richer hopes."

In the early part of the 19th century, Austrian waltz music acquired the status of an art form. Josef Lanner and Johann Strauss the elder produced waltzes for dancing and popular concerts. To foster musical culture the important Vienna Society of the Friends of Music was organized in 1812. In 1841 the Vienna Philharmonic Orchestra started on its celebrated career, and it soon had a rival in the Symphony Orchestra. New concert halls were built in Austrian cities, universities created chairs in musicology, and choral societies, military bands, and clubs for critical discussion of music were very active. Firms like Streicher and Bosendörfer set international standards in the making of instruments. Ambitious young Europeans regarded study at the Vienna Conservatory—subsequently the Academy of Music—as a necessity, and European composers coveted the praise of Austrian critics.

The most respected, and by some the most detested, professional critic, Eduard Hanslick, disparaged the thunderous operas of Richard Wagner and praised the music of Johannes Brahms. During his Austrian years, Brahms fashioned symphonies and sonatas, choral and chamber pieces, and the majestic *German Requiem*. The music of Anton Bruckner, especially his *Te Deum*, his *Mass in D Major*, and his Seventh Symphony, took its place in the library of great serious music. Hugo Wolf's boisterously orchestrated symphonic poem *Penthesilea* and his songs for voice and piano won him enduring international acceptance. Under the baton of Hans Richter the Vienna Philharmonic experienced a golden era. A sumptuous new opera house, completed in 1869, and a succession of outstanding conductors, artistic directors, and performers enhanced the international prestige of Austria in the realm of music.

Compositions by Johann Strauss the younger shaped the image of the "Queen City" on the Danube as a carefree fairy-tale community. Gay waltz tunes, crowned by *The Beautiful Blue Danube*, and a profusion of operettas, notably *Die Fledermaus* (The Bat) and *The Gypsy Baron*, made Strauss world-famous. Imitating him, Franz Lehár wrote 30 operettas, including *The Merry Widow*, which captivated audiences everywhere.

The 20th Century. Gustav Mahler, who like Wolf had been influenced by Bruckner, wrote music that was both intellectual and romantic. As the Eighth Symphony demonstrated, Mahler was a perfectionist, and, with him as director, Vienna opera reached a high level of excellence. He transplanted Austrian tastes in music to the United States, as did his protégé, Bruno Walter. In later years, Vienna-trained Erich Leinsdorf (a former assistant of Walter) and Eugene Ormandy followed the example of these masters. Great musical skill and singular artistic beauty distinguished such operas as *Elektra* and *Der Rosenkavalier* by Richard Strauss, born in Germany but for years a resident of Vienna. Outstanding soloists, including Selma Kurz, Maria Jeritza, and Leo Slezak, sustained the musical eminence of Austria. The violin virtuoso Fritz Kreisler afforded pleasure to listeners on two continents for six decades.

A fresh chapter in Austrian musical inventiveness opened with the bold innovations of Arnold Schönberg. Universally regarded as a major force in modern composition, he developed the 12-tone system, which led to heated controversy in professional circles. Yet his musical system, which gave birth to the Vienna Atonal School, deeply impressed many younger composers, especially Anton von Webern and Alban Berg. Authorities classified *Moses and Aaron* by Schönberg and Berg's *Wozzeck* (only marginally in the style of the "new music") among the operatic triumphs of the 20th century. Ernst Křenek, who had insinuated jazz rhythms into the opera *Johnny Strikes Up the Band*, eventually edged into the Schönberg circle.

Before and during World War II music lovers filled Vienna's opera house and concert halls. Able conductors—Franz Schalk, for one—directed singing stars like Elizabeth Schwarzkopf and Vera Schwarz, and the dramatic tenors Eric Zimmermann and Hermann Gallos. Bombing and fires during World War II severely damaged Vienna's music halls, yet within a matter of months after the fighting stopped, repairs had been effected and the Philharmonic and Symphony orchestras quickly reestablished their enviable reputation. It was a different story, however, with the opera house, which warfare had ruined. By 1955, however, it had been rebuilt; for the gala reopening Karl Böhm directed *Fidelio*. At the Volksoper, dating from 1898, lighter fare was offered to capacity audiences. Favorites were Strauss operettas and American musicals.

At ease with all kinds of musical culture, Herbert von Karajan, artistic director and conductor at the opera as well as of the Philhar-

monic, gained international recognition as one of the foremost personalities in his profession. The temperamental Karajan resigned his posts in 1964 and went abroad to conduct. Postwar singers approached the standards of Austria's best artists. Leonie Rysanek, Christl Goltz, Walter Berg, and Paul Schöffler were widely acclaimed.

The leading mid-20th century Austrian composer of opera, Gottfried von Einem, dramatized prevailing human anxieties in *The Trial* and strengthened his reputation with *The Death of Danton*, noted for its graceful ballet rhythms. While Joseph Marx wrote songs in the tradition of Wolf, Hans Jelinek and Hans E. Apostel wrote music more in the tradition of their master, Schönberg. Josef Lechthaler led the way in an authentic renaissance of church music.

Austrian summer musical festivals prospered to an unprecedented degree after 1945. Crowds of foreigners were lured annually to Salzburg, for instance, where a rich variety of offerings, including the works of Mozart, were performed. At Vienna native and foreign artists presented music appealing to all tastes, from the classic to the avant-garde.

ART AND ARCHITECTURE

Many historic Austrian monasteries and churches testify to changing tastes in architectural thinking and in painting, sculpture, and wood carving. Romanesque patterns are well exemplified in the severe lines of the Franciscan church in Salzburg and in the Cistercian chapterhouse at Zwettl, in northern Austria. Gurk Cathedral near Klagenfurt exhibits the transition to the Gothic style. Admirable examples of later Gothic are the Cathedral of St. Aegidius in Graz and the village church at St. Wolfgang, which contains a winged altar and paintings by Michael Pacher.

But the noblest Gothic edifice in Austria is Vienna's Cathedral of St. Stephen. The decorations of this masterpiece are mostly Gothic, but the "giant's door" on the western façade, its flanking sculptures and two towers, and part of the nave are Romanesque.

In the 16th century the simpler, dignified Italian Renaissance style was admirably expressed in arcades and balconies at Innsbruck and most impressively in the court church there. This church enshrines the most prized Austrian artistic triumph of the age: a massive, black marble sarcophagus, originally intended to be the tomb of Maximilian I. Marble reliefs recall key episodes in his colorful career and 28 tall bronze statues personify ancestors and contemporaries of Maximilian or heroes of antiquity. The elaborately arcaded courtyard of Graz' Landhaus and of Schallaburg castle near Melk are also superior examples of Italian Renaissance architecture. It was in this period, too, that Habsburg princes began to assemble paintings, sculptures, and other art treasures from all over western Europe.

Ascendancy of the Baroque. It was in Salzburg that the lush exuberance of baroque architecture and decoration was first manifested, notably in the cathedral, university church, and Mirabell palace. Old Benedictine monasteries were reconstructed on a distinctively Austrian baroque pattern. Noteworthy are the imposing, lavishly ornamented structures at Melk and Göttweig along the Danube and at Kremsmünster. While Jacob Prandauer served as the principal architect of the rural monasteries, Johann B. Fischer von Erlach, his son, and their contemporary, Lukas von Hildebrandt, designed baroque ecclesiastical and secular buildings in Austrian cities. The involved, grandiose Karlskirche in Vienna is the supreme creation of the von Erlachs, and the nearby Belvedere palace complex exhibits the talent of Hildebrandt at its peak.

Magnate families—the Liechtensteins, the Trautsons, the Schwarzenbergs, for example—had large, showy Vienna residences constructed, usually with princely gardehs attached. Testifying to Habsburg grandeur were the massive Schönbrunn summer palace and park. This establishment contrasted sharply with the Hofburg, the Vienna winter quarters of the Habsburgs; a vast array of structures interspersed with courtyards incorporates six centuries of changing fashions in architecture.

Intense building activity in the 1700's stimulated the decorative arts. Unusual creative qualities in ornamental paintings and frescoes were exhibited by Johann M. Rottmayr and Daniel Gran. Franz A. Maulbertsch also excelled in grand frescoes and altar paintings. To honor the master of the Belvedere, Balthasar Permoser carved a majestic "Apotheosis of Prince Eugene" of Savoy. This cultured prince and the Liechtensteins accumulated extraordinary collections of art objects. Raphael Donner created a famous fountain in lead for Vienna's Neuer Markt (New Market) and an exquisite copper grouping, *Crucifixion*, for Gurk Cathedral.

The 19th Century. A fresh wave of construction swept over Vienna in the second half of the 19th century. Along the Ringstrasse—laid out on ground formerly occupied by medieval walls—Austrian and north European architects erected monumental edifices, traditionalist in design. The Ringstrasse became one of the world's show places with its impressive buildings: an opera house in French Renaissance style, a parliament house imitative of Greek classicism, a Neo-Gothic city hall, a handsome Gothic Votivkirche, a new university structure and museums of art and natural history reflecting the style of the Italian Renaissance, and a new imperial theater (Burgtheater) laid out on a late Renaissance pattern.

A master of photographic realism, Ferdinand G. Waldmüller painted memorable landscapes and portraits. The monumental Ringstrasse building inspired vast painting projects, chiefly on historical themes, by Hans Makart, dean and arbiter of Austrian fine arts for many years.

Sculptors adorned the Habsburg metropolis with memorials to eminent worthies. For instance, Anton D. Fernkorn carved for the Square of Heroes a bronze equestrian statue of Archduke Charles, commander in an inconclusive battle with Napoleon, and a statue of Eugene of Savoy. Victor O. Tilgner produced a statue of Mozart.

Toward the end of the 19th century new currents swept over Austrian art and architecture. Imaginative artists founded the "secession" school in 1897 and executed daringly unconventional paintings. One of the leaders, Gustav Klimt, who painted society ladies and sensuous female nudes, attracted great critical acclaim in Europe. A second rebel, Oskar Kokoschka, in his Austrian period mirrored the mental states of the people he painted. At the outset of World War I he depicted grim military realities, and later in Germany and England he achieved front rank among the artists of his time.

New Currents in the 20th Century. Architect Otto Wagner inaugurated a new era. He em-

ST. STEPHEN'S CATHEDRAL in Vienna is a mixture of styles, with its Gothic spire and Romanesque towers.

phasized the function that a building was to serve and exploited new construction materials. A radical exponent of the "new objectivity," Adolf Loos, who had studied American architecture to good purpose, stressed functionalism and a minimum of ornamentation.

Between the world wars municipalities and other governmental bodies commissioned architects and artists to design and embellish residential blocks like the colossal Karl Marx Hof in Vienna. Herbert Boeckl won acclaim for his unusual decorative painting, suggestive of the baroque style, in Seckau Cathedral near Graz. Abstract expressionists such as Anton Kolig used boisterous color. In addition to sculptures for communal apartment houses, Anton Hanak carved busts of politicians and portrayed the concern of "Red" Vienna for child welfare in a splendid symbolic group, *The Great Mother*.

After World War II, Austrian cities witnessed the greatest spurt in construction they had ever known. Wrecked railway stations in Vienna, Graz, and Innsbruck were rebuilt on larger, brighter, and gayer lines. Gutted St. Stephen's Cathedral was restored nearly to its prewar condition, and the ruined opera house and Burgtheater were rebuilt with important improvements. Erich Boltenstern designed high-rise office structures. Municipal apartment blocks were built or repaired. An enormous residential complex was named the George C. Marshall in gratitude for postwar help from the United States.

A set of young artists, including Josef Mikl, imitated the abstractionist styles fashionable in France and Italy. Two technically proficient painters of the new movement, Ernest Fuchs and Anton Lehmden, best demonstrated "fantastic realism." Students of Hanak perpetuated the teachings of their master; Fritz Wotruba, for one, experimented with original techniques for representing the human form. Austrians generally disliked a gigantic war memorial raised by the Soviet occupiers in central Vienna, but they applauded the erection in 1964 of the much loftier Danube Tower in the heart of a new park in the capital city. Designed by Hannes Lintl, the

DAVIS PRATT, FROM RAPHO GUILLUMETTE

THE BURGTHEATER is on Vienna's famous Ringstrasse.

monument symbolized the post-1945 reinvigoration of Austrian cultural traditions.

LITERATURE AND DRAMA

The first literature of significance in the German language appeared in Austria. Verses and local chronicles written by monks preceded the poetry of court minnesingers. The most illustrious of the minnesingers, Walther von der Vogelweide, who died about 1230, and his followers composed lyrics on knightly ways of life and love. Intense patriotism was blended with witty satire. The old German literary epic, *Song of the Nibelungs,* was collected in the Danube Valley. It combined ancient myths of the German folk with realities of the age when chivalry flourished. Religious drama flourished especially in the Tyrol, and the actors were generally ordinary villagers. Secular plays, earthy in dialogue, were staged in marketplaces or wine-houses.

Creative literature prospered during the reign of Maximilian I. The greatest of German humanists, Conrad Celtis, moved to Austria and organized the Danube Literary Society, which fostered literature of all types in Latin. Lyric poems by Celtis had no equal in German Europe before Goethe. During the Counter Reformation, Jesuit priests wrote scores of religious dramas, in which the German language gradually superseded Latin. Plays became an integral feature of the curricula of Jesuit-operated educational institutions, and well-appointed theaters run by the Jesuits made the stage increasingly popular in Austria. Itinerant Dutch and English troupes also added to the theatrical fare of the country.

Prose writings by Abraham a Sancta Clara, a dynamic court preacher who died in 1709, left an enduring stamp on Austrian thinking. Although he was a staunch champion of the existing social order, he denounced the privileged classes for loose living and savagely condemned Austrians outside the Roman Catholic communion. Official

poets surrounded the Habsburg court of the 18th century; their most notable achievement, illustrated by the works of Metastasio, took the form of texts for operas.

Expansion of the Theater. New centers of entertainment in drama were erected in Vienna: the Carinthian Gate theater in 1709 and the Burgtheater, attached in 1752 to the Hofburg. The Burgtheater, which generally presented classical productions, came to be recognized as the foremost stage in German-speaking Europe. Several theaters were built in the suburbs of the capital. Of first importance was the Theater an der Wien, which was completed in 1801. It offered varied fare and was the scene of many famous premieres, including Beethoven's *Fidelio.* Ordinary townsmen preferred a variety of farce called *Hanswurst,* which dealt with manners and personalities of the age in dialogue that was comical or unconventional. The star actor in this form of theater was Anton Stranitzky.

If permitted by government censors, dramas by the 19th century playwright Franz Grillparzer were performed at the Burgtheater. In his historical plays he wrote in flattering accents of the Habsburg dynasty and realm. His finest production, *The Waves of the Sea and Love,* became a permanent favorite. Under the management of Josef Schreyvogel and Heinrich R. Laube the Burgtheater gained even greater eminence. Actors coveted starring roles there more than any other distinction.

The 19th century German-born Christian F. Hebbel, author of *Agnes Bernauer* and *The Song of the Nibelungs,* pioneered in psychological and social dramas, while Ferdinand Raimund created fairyland folk farces that are still popular. A contemporary, Johann Nestroy, established a new theatrical tradition with sardonic satires on the realities of everyday living.

Fiction and Poetry in the 19th Century. Best among the fiction writers of the first half of the 19th century was Adalbert Stifter, noted for short stories and regional and society novels. *The Priest of Kirchfeld* by Ludwig Anzengruber faithfully depicts Austrian rural concerns; Anzengruber also exposed the harsh elements in the daily life of Viennese commoners. Intense pessimism pervaded the poetry of Nicolaus Lenau, reflecting his Hungarian homeland and a harrowing American adventure. Political verse was written by the aristocratic Anastasius Grün, who boldly assailed the repressive literary censorship.

Later in the 19th century, Marie von Ebner-Eschenbach and Bertha von Suttner gained a wide readership. Fiction by the former vividly portrayed all social groups, and more particularly the interests and shortcomings of her own patrician class. *Lay Down Your Arms* by von Suttner was a sensational novel preaching pacifism. The author was the first woman awarded a Nobel Peace Prize. From Styria came two excellent tellers of stories of country living: Peter K. Rosegger and Rudolf K. Bartsch. And two Styrian poets, Robert Hamerling and Wilhelm Fischer, gained European recognition, as did Adolf Pichler with his entertaining tales of his native Tyrol.

The 20th Century. Another Tyrolean, Karl Schönherr, united imaginative fancy, stark realism, humor, and earnestness in his plays. Works like *Faith and Home* deal mostly with timeless human perplexities and Tyrolean history. Arthur Schnitzler presided over a psychological school of imaginative literature. In novels, dramas, and short stories he analyzed motives and mental aberrations in a manner that prompted Sigmund Freud to hail him as a colleague. A grand stylist, Schnitzler was fond of barbed dialogue and cynical wit. *Light-O'-Love,* a searing portrayal of the human triangle, and *Professor Bernhardi,* touching lightly on the Jewish question, typify the writings of Schnitzler. Close to him in spirit was Richard Beer-Hofmann, most appreciated perhaps for the play *The Count of Charolais.* Karl Kraus, best known for *The Last Days of Mankind,* became a potent moral force by reason of his slashing attacks, especially upon politicians and journalists.

Gifted as a lyricist and serving as a European conscience, Rainer Maria Rilke shone most brilliantly in philosophical verse—*Stories of God* and *Duino Elegies,* the latter finished in Switzerland. As a youth, Hugo von Hofmannsthal won applause for his dramatic poem *Yesterday.* His superb mastery of diction and his fascination with the past are both evidenced in his play *The Death of Titian.* He composed the libretto for *Der Rosenkavalier* and other operas by Richard Strauss and exerted a considerable influence on later Austrian poets.

Hofmannsthal also worked with Max Reinhardt, the most influential theatrical impresario of his age. Together they annually staged Hofmannsthal's version of the mystery play *Everyman* at the Salzburg Festival. Reinhardt delighted in impressionistic techniques and gigantic fantasies replete with color and pageantry.

Two novelists, Franz Werfel and Franz Kafka, earned worldwide fame. Abominating war and social injustice, Werfel dwelt on the theme of human salvation through brotherly love. His creative qualities are amply revealed in a collection of short stories, *Twilight of a World,* and in the novels *Forty Days of Musa Dagh* and *Song of Bernadette.* The pages of Kafka are filled with the grotesque. His unusual capacity for penetrating thought is exhibited in *The Castle,* which has had a substantial influence on other writers. In the unfinished, though stylistically attractive, *The Man Without Qualities,* Robert Musil mingled skepticism with mysticism as he brooded on the passing of the Habsburg monarchy. Widely known for semifictional biographies, Stefan Zweig also wrote a valuable self-portrait, *The World of Yesterday.*

European acclaim was won by the lyricists Josef Weinheber, Anton Wildgans, and Christina Lavant. During World War I the playwright Franz T. Csokor dramatized the noble and the tawdry in warfare, and subsequently in *November 3, 1918* he recaptured the mood of the Habsburg realm's demise. On the eve of the Nazi annexation of Austria many prominent authors fled abroad, but a few, like the dramatist-poet Max Mell, who expounded Christian values in morality plays, chose to stay in their homeland. No fresh literary talent of importance emerged during the Hitler era.

Following World War II, while the ruined Burgtheater underwent reconstruction, classical dramas were performed in a cramped downtown playhouse. Opera was presented until 1955 at the historic Theater an der Wien, which thereafter was completely modernized. Within a few years after the war a score of Vienna theaters and nearly as many more in provincial centers were staging performances. Cellar or "little act" playhouses furnished stages for the creations of younger authors. Among the newer dramatists of high distinction, Fritz Hochwälder chose to recall historical episodes: *The Holy Experiment* is an account of a Jesuit enterprise in Paraguay. Hans F. Kühnelt's *It Is Later Than You Think* portrays the dawning atomic age, while in *Ulysses Must Travel Again,* Kurt Klinger addressed himself to current social issues.

So enthusiastic were the admirers of Hermann Broch, author of *The Death of Virgil,* a sordid novel about human existence, that they proposed him for a Nobel Prize. Better known outside of Austria is Heimito von Doderer, whose long, ambitious, and thoughtful *The Demons* pictured Vienna youths of all sorts struggling to adjust themselves to conditions after World War I. *Nineteen Eighty-four* by Orwell had an Austrian counterpart in Friedrich Heer's *The Eighth Day.* Helmut Qualtinger, master of satirical monologue, sturdily upheld the sardonic traditions of Nestroy and Kraus.

ARTHUR J. MAY, *University of Rochester*

Bibliography

Crankshaw, Edward, *The Fall of the House of Hapsburg* (New York 1963).

Gulick, C.A., *Austria from Habsburg to Hitler,* 2 vols. (Berkeley, Calif., 1948).

Hantsch, Hugo, *Die Geschichte Österreichs,* new ed., 3 vols. (Vienna 1959, 1962).

Jászi, Oscar, *The Dissolution of the Habsburg Monarchy* (Chicago 1929; paperback, 1961).

Jenks, William A., *Austria Under the Iron Ring* (Charlottesville, Va., 1965).

Kann, Robert A., *The Multinational Empire: Nationalism and National Reform in the Habsburg Monarchy, 1848–1918,* 2 vols. (New York 1950).

Leeper, Alexander W.A., *A History of Medieval Austria* (New York and London 1941).

MacDonald, Mary, *The Republic of Austria, 1918–1934* (New York 1946).

May, Arthur J., *The Hapsburg Monarchy, 1867–1914,* reprint (Cambridge, Mass., 1965).

May, Arthur J., *The Passing of the Hapsburg Monarchy, 1914–1918,* 2 vols. (Philadelphia 1966).

Mecenseffy, Grete, *Geschichte des Protestantismus in Österreich* (Graz 1956).

Pribram, A.F., *The Secret Treaties of Austria-Hungary, 1879–1914,* 2 vols. (Cambridge, Mass., 1920–21).

Redlich, Joseph, *Austrian War Government* (New Haven 1929).

Redlich, Joseph, *Emperor Francis Joseph of Austria* (New York 1929).

Redlich, Joseph, *Das österreichische Staats- und Reichsproblem* (Leipzig 1920–26).

Rothenberg, Gunther E., *The Austrian Military Border in Croatia, 1522–1747* (Urbana, Ill., 1960).

Sugar, Peter F., *Industrialization of Bosnia-Hercegovina, 1878–1918* (Seattle 1963).

Taylor, Alan J.P., *The Habsburg Monarchy, 1809–1918; a History of the Austrian Empire and Austria-Hungary,* new ed. (London 1948).

Uhlirz, Karl, and Uhlirz, Mathilde, *Handbuch der Geschichte Österreichs und seiner Nachbarländer Böhmen und Mähren,* 4 vols. (Graz 1927–44).

Zeman, Z.A.B., *The Break-up of the Habsburg Empire, 1914–1918; a Study in National and Social Revolution* (New York 1961).

Zöllner, Erich, *Geschichte Österreichs von den Anfängen bis zur Gegenwart,* 2d ed. (Vienna 1961).

Culture

Bourke, John, *Baroque Churches of Central Europe* (London 1958).

Graf, Max, *The Legend of a Musical City* (New York 1945).

Kann, Robert A., *A Study in Austrian Intellectual History* (New York 1960).

May, Arthur J., *Vienna in the Age of Franz Josef* (Norman, Okla., 1966).

Mayer, Franz M., Kaindl, R.F., and Pirchegger, H., *Geschichte und Kulturleben Deutsch-Österreichs,* 3 vols. (Vienna 1929–37).

Preyer, David C., *The Art of the Vienna Galleries,* new ed. (Boston 1926).

AUSTRIA-HUNGARY. See AUSTRIA—*History;* HUNGARY—*History.*

AUSTRIAN SUCCESSION. See SUCCESSION WARS.

AUSTRO-PRUSSIAN WAR, a struggle between Austria and Prussia in 1866 for supremacy in Germany. The causes of the war, frequently called the *Seven Weeks' War,* lay in the 18th century conflicts between the Habsburg empire under Maria Theresa and Prussia under Frederick the Great. Austria maintained its dominant position in the German Confederation of 1815, and a compromise with Prussian was reached. When Bismarck became Prussian prime minister in 1862, he sought to unify Germany under Prussian supremacy, with the exclusion of Austria.

The last incident before open hostilities was a quarrel with Austria over the administration of Holstein. Supported by an alliance with Italy, Prussia started the war by invading Saxony in June 1866. The great majority of German states joined Austria, but most gave only token support. The war was decided by the Prussian victory at Königgrätz (Sadowa) on July 3, when three Prussian armies converged on the battlefield according to the plans of the brilliant chief of staff, Count von Moltke, and defeated the Austrians under the far inferior command of General von Benedek.

Even though Austria's defensive campaign against Italy was successful, it ceded Venetia to Italy in order to concentrate all its forces against Prussia. Nevertheless, by the end of July, Austria had to sue for peace, and on August 24 the definitive Peace of Prague was signed. Bismarck, who saw in defeated Austria a potential ally for the future, did not insist on territorial annexations, although Hannover, Hesse-Kassel, and Frankfurt am Main were incorporated into Prussia. Bismarck had achieved his main objective—Austria's withdrawal from German affairs. The further unification of Germany under Prussian auspices was determined in principle by the peace treaty.

ROBERT A. KANN, *Rutgers University*

AUTHORIZED VERSION OF THE BIBLE, ô'thə-rīzd vûr'zhən, the English translation of the Bible, often known as the *King James Version.* Its preparation was authorized by King James I in 1604, the year following his accession to the English throne (see BIBLE—*History of the English Bible*). The work was completed and published in London in 1611.

Whether or not the Bible was ever actually "authorized" to the exclusion of other versions cannot be ascertained. It may be that the original order of authorization has been lost: all records of acts by the Privy Council from 1600 to 1618 were destroyed in the fire at Whitehall in 1618. But whether this version was actually "authorized" or not is scarcely decisive now. The version was a revision of the Bishops' Bible and was intended to be authorized. It was afterward accepted as authorized, and for 350 years and more has been known as the "Authorized Version."

The Authorized Version has undergone two considerable revisions, known as the Revised Version (late 19th century) and the Revised Standard Version (mid-20th century). Even those churches that formerly emphasized its authorization now permit the use of alternate versions.

FREDERICK C. GRANT
Union Theological Seminary
Further Reading: *Facsimile Edition of the Authorized Version* (London and New York 1911); Grant, Frederick C., *Translating the Bible* (Edinburgh and Greenwich, Conn., 1961).

AUTHORS LEAGUE OF AMERICA, a national organization of authors and dramatists in the United States, organized in 1912 to protect the rights and properties of writers who produce copyrightable material. Included among the founders were Arthur Train, Will Irwin, Booth Tarkington, and Kate Douglas Wiggin. The novelist Winston Churchill was the first president; Theodore Roosevelt, the first vice president. In 1919 the league formed within it the Authors Guild and the Dramatists Guild. Subsequently the Radio Writers Guild and the Television Writers Group developed as component parts of the league, and the Screen Writers Guild as an affiliate. These three groups formed the separate Writers Guild of America in 1954.

In 1964 a reorganization resulted in three membership corporations: the Authors League of America, which handles matters such as copyright and freedom of expression; and the Authors Guild and the Dramatists Guild, which handle problems such as contract terms and subsidiary rights and publish the *Authors Guild Bulletin* and the *Dramatists Guild Quarterly.* A member of either guild automatically becomes a league member.

MILLS TEN EYCK, JR.
Authors League of America, Inc.

AUTO-DA-FÉ, ô'tō-dȧ-fā, was the name of the ceremony at which judgment was pronounced on those convicted of heresy by the Spanish Inquisition. It was essentially a religious ceremony, taking its name from a Portuguese phrase meaning "act of faith." Persons convicted by the ecclesiastical courts of the Inquisition were expected to recant their heresy at this time, thus performing the act of faith, and the public was encouraged to witness this act. Those who refused to recant or who protested their innocence were turned over to the civil authorities. The civil authorities executed the sentence, which often was death by burning at the stake. Ultimately, the term "auto-da-fé" also came to mean this death by fire.

The ceremony, known originally as the *sermo generalis* (general sermon) from the opening address of the inquisitor, was a long-established procedure of the Inquisition, which began as an institution in 1232. It was from the Spanish Inquisition, however, dating from 1479, that autos-da-fé received historical notoriety. The ceremony was preceded by a procession and a Mass. The condemned wore the *sanbenito,* a yellow penitential garment embroidered in front and back with a cross and symbols of the crimes of which he was convicted. After the opening statement, during which the invitation to recant was issued, civil authorities were sworn in to carry out the sentence. Decrees of mercy, ranging from a reduction of sentence to freedom, were announced for some of those already under sentence for heresy. Finally, new sentences were pronounced and those condemned to death were taken to the place of execution.

Autos-da-fé continued until 1808, when the Spanish Inquisition was halted by Joseph Bonaparte, king of Spain. They were reintroduced by Ferdinand VII of Spain in 1814 but were finally abolished about 1820. It has been estimated that about 2,000 autos-da-fé took place in Spain, Portugal, and their dependencies between 1480 and 1825, and about 30,000 persons were put to death. See also INQUISITION.

AUTOBIOGRAPHY, ô-tə-bī-og′rə-fē, is literally a man's recording of his own life. Autobiographical documents can be found in all cultures and all ages, but autobiography as a deliberate literary product is brought into existence only under certain conditions. While both ancient Greece and Rome produced outstanding examples of biography, even the finest examples of classical "autobiography" (if it can be called such) lack the introspection and self-dissection that characterize the best examples of the form. Xenophon's *Anabasis* contains a few elements of autobiography but is more truly an account of the expedition of a Greek mercenary army into Persia in 401 B.C. Caesar's *Commentaries* are less autobiographical than they are an explanation and justification of his campaigns in Gaul (58–55 B.C.). The romantic age, on the other hand, when introspection and extreme self-awareness were part of the prevailing intellectual climate, produced a number of genuinely autobiographical testaments; and the 19th century saw the emergence of autobiography in many countries: Goethe in Germany, Rousseau in France, Wordsworth in England, and Thoreau in America, to name only a few outstanding examples.

Related Forms. As a literary form, autobiography is to be distinguished from those types of self-revelation most closely related to it, the diary, the journal, and the memoir. The diary is a record of daily experience, the preservation of the day-by-day process of one's own life, without regard to patterned development, narrative continuity, or dramatic movement toward a climax. Samuel Pepys' *Diary* (1660–69), for instance, often achieves continuity but does so intermittently and without conscious design. Autobiography sees separate occurrences, even in early life, as moving toward and completing a pattern finally achieved in later life. *The Education of Henry Adams* (1907) illustrates how the author's maturity fulfilled the destiny implicit in the events of youth.

The memoir devotes more attention to occurrences around and outside the writer than to the writer himself, as in *The Personal Memoirs* of Ulysses S. Grant (1885–86), and the *Memoirs* of President Harry S Truman (1955–   ). From the memoir we learn a great deal about the society in which the subject of the memoirs moved, but little about the writer himself. On the other hand, *The Autobiography of Lincoln Steffens* (1931) not only recorded the events of a changing America in the late 19th and early 20th centuries, charting in great detail the movement of social reform, but also noted those events as they affected the autobiographer himself.

The journal concentrates largely on the interior life of the writer, often excluding events outside the reveries or meditations of the author's memory and imagination. Henry David Thoreau's *Walden* (1854) is more a lyric celebration of innocent solitude than a diary or autobiography, and André Gide's *Journals* (1949–50) is primarily concerned with his developing artistic craft and not with his exterior life.

In some instances, all the related forms of diary, memoir, journal, and autobiography may be welded together to achieve a particularly thorough review of one's life or portion of it. One of the best examples of such a combination is Fyodor Dostoyevsky's *The House of the Dead*, which is the intimate account of his four years spent in a Siberian penal colony and his last-minute rescue, in 1849, from death before a firing squad.

Types. Autobiography has been provoked by a variety of motives. It may be confessional, in which the motive is to unburden one's self of a feeling of guilt; apologetic, in which the writer attempts to declare and to justify the course of his life or a particular action thereof; exploratory, when he uses the act of writing as an instrument of research and a probing into his own hitherto unexamined behavioral patterns; or simply egocentric portraiture, when the writer assumes that his life is worth sharing with others.

While autobiography usually results from a compound of such motives, and only rarely from one motive alone, it is possible to define the central motive in the most famous examples of the form. Thus, the *Confessions* of St. Augustine (about 400), generally recognized as the first instance of true autobiography, was prompted mainly by the desire to recount and thus absolve a sense of guilt. John Bunyan's spiritual autobiography, *Grace Abounding to the Chief of Sinners* (1666), is in this respect Augustinian autobiography, as is Jean Jacques Rousseau's *Confessions* (1782) and, in many ways, Benjamin Franklin's *Autobiography* (1789).

The autobiography of justification is represented by Peter Abelard's *History of My Calamities* (written in the early 1100's), in which he explained his tragic and notorious romance with Héloïse; and by John Henry Cardinal Newman's *Apologia Pro Vita Sua* (1864), in which he retraced the events leading to his conversion to Roman Catholicism.

The exploratory autobiography is finely illustrated by John Stuart Mill's *Autobiography* (1873), which treats dispassionately of a spiritual crisis in Mill's life; and by Edmund Gosse's *Father and Son* (1907), an amazingly frank examination of his own relationship with his father. Autobiography of portraiture ranges from the startlingly boastful *Autobiography of Benvenuto Cellini* (1558–66) to the symbol-ridden *Autobiographies* (1926) of the poet William Butler Yeats and the analytic and judicious *Summing Up* (1938) of Somerset Maugham.

The autobiographical impulse has frequently been satisfied, not in autobiography proper, but in literary work of more than usual personal import. Charles Dickens' *David Copperfield* (1849–50) is an obvious re-creation of the author's own early life, as is James Joyce's *Portrait of the Artist as a Young Man* (1916) and Thomas Wolfe's *Look Homeward, Angel* (1935). Unlike these novels, however, true autobiography avoids conscious fictionalizing.

General Significance. Nevertheless, a certain amount of "unconscious fictionalizing" may take place in autobiography, for an author may be psychologically unable to reveal certain of his motivations, untrained in his analyses of his own behavior, or simply unconscious of his true motivations, in which case it remains to the reader to make the proper interpretation of the autobiographical details.

It is an interesting feature of autobiography that even when he is discreet or reticent, the writer does reveal himself: for what a writer obscures is often as significant as what he recounts. It may well be true that there can be no psychoanalytic autobiography as there can be psychoanalytic biography, inasmuch as the achievement of an analyst-patient relationship toward one's self is possible only at the cost of schizophrenia. But even the most cautious and self-protective of autobiographies can be read from a psychoanalytic viewpoint.

In addition to satisfying curiosity about the author himself, autobiography has been a valuable guide to the manners and customs of the ages and societies in which it was produced. Girolamo Cardano's *Book of My Life* (1576), *The Booke of Margery Kempe* (1436), Richard Baxter's *Reliquiae Baxterianae* (1696), and *An Apology for the Life of Colley Cibber* (1740), for all the differences in the lives of their authors—Cardano was a scientist, Margery Kempe a mystic, Baxter a Puritan evangelist, and Cibber an actor, playwright, and theater manager—have proved to be indispensable documents for the historian determined to recapture the times in which these so-different people lived.

Future historians will undoubtedly find the 20th century unmatched in the richness of autobiographical materials, for not only has the professional man of letters put his hand to autobiography (for instance, Evelyn Waugh's *Little Learning: The Early Years*, 1964), but so too have important religious leaders (Mahatma Gandhi), military and political figures (Dwight D. Eisenhower), and representatives of human dignity and courage (Helen Keller, Eleanor Roosevelt, and Albert Schweitzer). When the time has come for the 20th century to be recorded in full, there will be no shortage of materials demonstrating, from an autobiographical point of view, its achievements and vagaries.

RICHARD E. HUGHES, *Boston College*

Further Reading: Garraty, John A., *The Nature of Biography* (New York 1957); Pascal, Roy, *Design and Truth in Autobiography* (Cambridge, Mass., 1960); Shumaker, Wayne, *English Autobiography* (Berkeley, Calif., 1954); Wethered, Herbert N., *The Curious Art of Autobiography* (New York 1956).

AUTOBIOGRAPHY OF ALICE B. TOKLAS,

a book of memoirs by Gertrude Stein (q.v.), first published in 1933. It is written in the first person, supposedly by Alice B. Toklas, Gertrude Stein's friend of many years. It was the first of Miss Stein's books to receive the attention of major critics, who had largely ignored her earlier work, and it is still her most popular work. Less abstract than some of Miss Stein's other writing, the *Autobiography* retains her characteristic whimsicality, egocentricity, and simple, cadenced language.

The book outlines briefly Miss Stein's early years in the United States, but dwells particularly on the years after 1907 when she and Miss Toklas lived in Paris.

The book is full of anecdotes about the artists and writers of that revolutionary epoch, including Picasso and his mistress Fernande Olivier, Georges Braque, Marie Laurencin, Guillaume Apollinaire, Ernest Hemingway, Jean Cocteau, and Sherwood Anderson. It recounts the famous banquet given in 1908 by Picasso at his studio for the primitive painter Henri Rousseau. It also tells about, and contributed further to, the feud between Miss Stein and the novelist Ernest Hemingway, her former protégé.

The *Autobiography* provoked *Testimony Against Gertrude Stein* (1935), a critical rejoinder from various Parisian artists and writers. The contributors to the book challenged the accuracy of the *Autobiography* and its author's knowledge of art and literature.

AUTOCRACY, ô-tok′rə-sē, is a form of government in which unlimited power is formally vested in a single person, presumably uniting in himself the legislative and executive functions of the state. Many governments in the ancient and more recent East were of this character. Among European rulers the late czars of Russia alone bore the title of autocrat, thus signifying their constitutional absoluteness. (See DICTATORSHIP.) The philosopher Kant used the word to denote the mastery of reason over the rebellious propensities—the self-government of the soul.

AUTOCRAT OF THE BREAKFAST TABLE, ôt′ə-krat, a work by Oliver Wendell Holmes, consisting of imaginary conversations around a boarding-house table. The characters are introduced to the reader as the Autocrat, the Schoolmistress, the Old Gentleman Opposite, the Young Man called John, the Landlady, the Landlady's Daughter, the Poor Relation, and the Divinity Student. The book was the most popular of Holmes' works. His ease of style, wit, humor, kindly sympathy, and love of humanity are nowhere more clearly shown. *The Autocrat of the Breakfast Table* was first published serially in the *Atlantic Monthly* in 1857–1858 and appeared in book form in 1858.

AUTOGRAPH, ô′tə-graf, any handwritten document, page of manuscript, or letter, with or without a signature. It is sometimes called *holograph*. In popular usage, "autograph" is a synonym for "signature." The word is derived from the Greek word *autographos*, meaning "self written."

Collecting autographs had its start in ancient times. Before paper came into use, collections of cuneiform writings on baked clay tablets were carefully preserved. With the advent of paper, the collecting of autographs became widespread. *Alba amicorum* first became popular in medieval times. These were notebooks corresponding to modern autograph books in which friends or prominent personalities of the day inscribed cordial messages for the owner. Such collections were chiefly made for sentimental reasons and have little intrinsic historical value. Today it is fully accepted that autographs as written records of the past are a rich source of material for historians and biographers and a lively educa-

Letter from President Lincoln to General G.B. McClellan

tional approach to history and literature for students.

There are today many thousands of collectors of autograph signatures only. Serious collectors scorn this type of collecting and seek rather letters or manuscripts of famous characters in history, literature, science, and the arts, especially those that are meaty in substance. This group of collectors, which includes both institutions and private collectors, is smaller in number, and in the United States totals less than 2,000. Among them are those who generalize, acquiring items of interest, no matter by whom written or when.

Among the great institutions which generalize are the U.S. Library of Congress, the British Museum, and the National Archives of France. Specialist collections, public or private, may be devoted to a period, to a general subject, to a particular subject, to matters of special local interest, or to material pertaining to an individual. Among the specialist institutions in the United States, for example, are the Roosevelt Library at Hyde Park, N.Y., and the Rutherford B. Hayes Library at Fremont, Ohio. Again, institutions frequently contain specialist collections within their general collections. Yale University, which has a splendid general collection, is particularly noted not only for its great Western collection, but also for its Boswell-Johnson papers and its Benjamin Franklin papers. Historical societies are keenly interested in material of local interest. Private collectors are often the greatest patrons of institutions, bequeathing them their collections or making generous gifts of manuscript material during their lifetimes.

There is a definite market for autograph material, and dealers and auctions throughout the world handle such items constantly. Prices vary from a few cents to thousands of dollars, depending on supply and demand. The contents of a letter is one of the main factors to influence prices.

The most popular set of autographs in the United States, whether signatures or letters, is the set of presidents. Some collectors undertake to complete sets of the signers of the Declaration of Independence, but this is difficult because of the rarity of two of the signers, Button Gwinnett of Georgia and Thomas Lynch, Jr., of South Carolina, whose signatures alone on documents fetch thousands of dollars. More easily and less expensively made are sets of autographs of the signers of the Constitution.

MARY A. BENJAMIN
Director, Walter R. Benjamin Autographs
New York City

Further Reading: Hamilton, Charles, *Collecting Autographs and Manuscripts* (Norman, Okla., 1961); Lazare, Edward, ed., *American Book-Prices Current* (New York, annually); McNeil, Donald R., *American Collector* (Madison, Wis., 1955); Munby, A.N.L., *Cult of the Autograph Letter in England* (New York 1962).

AUTOLYCUS, ô-tŏl'i-kəs was a Greek astronomer and mathematician who lived about 310 B.C. at Pitane, Asia Minor. He wrote the earliest Greek mathematical treatise which is extant in its entirety.

Autolycus also compiled a work on the risings and settings of celestial bodies. The first describes a revolving sphere's concentric circles. The second explains how variations in the brightness of the sun, the stars, and the planets determine the distance of these bodies from the earth.

AUTOMATIC CONTROL, ô-tə-mat'ik kən-trōl', is process of maintaining a satisfactory relationship between the input and the output of a system without human intervention. Automatic control is used in preference to simple manual control to relieve man of tedious or difficult tasks, to permit control in an environment hostile to man, to obtain amplification of signals, to produce a desired effect at a remote location, and for many other reasons. Thus, automatic control systems now are widely used in the home (temperature control), in industry (automatic machine tools; petroleum refineries), in space vehicles (automatic control of attitude and trajectory), and in military applications (aiming and firing guns).

Development. One of the first applications of automatic control was James Watt's use of the flyball governor in 1787 to control the speed of a steam engine. An even earlier example was the use of a small pilot windmill (fantail) to keep a large windmill faced into the wind so that it would provide maximum power. Whenever the wind direction changed, the fantail would turn the large windmill back into the wind. This type of windmill was invented by Edmund Lee in England in 1745.

Following the invention of the vacuum tube early in the 20th century, the development of electronics laid the technological foundations for great advances in the design of automatic control systems. About the beginning of World War II, interest in such systems increased greatly because of the need to improve the speed and accuracy with which searchlights, guns, and radar antennas could be aimed at moving targets.

Operation. A simple form of automatic control system is represented in the illustration, which shows the use of *feedback* as a means of automatic control. The system output—the variable being controlled—is subject to undesirable variations because of disturbing influences. The system input—in this case the desired value of the variable being controlled—is the reference quantity. The system output is fed back and compared with the input in a *comparator*, or error detector. In this device, the controlled variable, c, is automatically subtracted from the reference input, r. The difference thus obtained is the error, e, in the variable being controlled ($r - c = e$). If the error is positive ($r > c$), the system output is too small, and the controller acts on the controlled process so that the value of the controlled variable is increased. If the error is negative ($c > r$), the system output is too large, and the controller acts on the controlled process so that the value of the controlled variable is decreased.

In many cases the characteristics of the particular process being controlled cause such a simple control system to exhibit a "hunting" behavior, which is very undesirable. When a control system persistently overcorrects for error, the error alternately becomes positive and negative. The system then appears to be "hunting" continually for the desired value of the controlled variable. In such cases, to improve the response, the controller is designed to respond to the error signal in a more intricate manner, usually by anticipating future error by measuring the rate at which the present error is changing.

Types of Systems. There is a large class of automatic control systems in which the input may change from one level to another occasion-

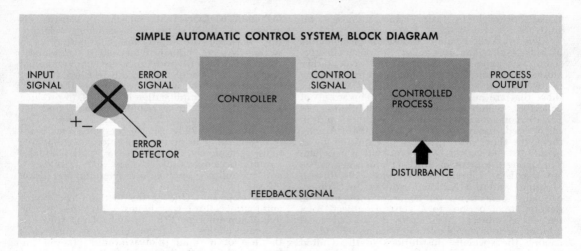

SIMPLE AUTOMATIC CONTROL SYSTEM, BLOCK DIAGRAM

INPUT SIGNAL — ERROR SIGNAL — **CONTROLLER** — CONTROL SIGNAL — **CONTROLLED PROCESS** — PROCESS OUTPUT

+ −

ERROR DETECTOR

DISTURBANCE

FEEDBACK SIGNAL

In this simple automatic control system, disturbances in a process are compensated for by measuring the output and comparing the resulting signal with the input signal. Errors are then corrected by the controller.

ally but is constant at all other times. The primary function of such systems, termed *regulators,* is to compensate for the effects of unwanted disturbances acting on the controlled process. Familiar regulators include thermostatic temperature-control devices for ovens, air conditioners, and heating systems. The thermostat serves as the comparator in a regulator that maintains a desired constant temperature in spite of disturbances caused by the opening of doors and the changes in outdoor temperature.

There is another large class of control systems, termed *servomechanisms,* in which the output is a mechanical displacement of some object. In these systems the input may vary rapidly over a wide range, unwanted disturbances may act on the controlled process, and the system output is often at a location that is remote from the location of the input.

For most automatic control systems, feedback is essential to compensate for outside disturbances and unpredictable variations in the process being controlled. If no unwanted disturbances act on the controlled process and if the characteristics of the controlled process are known and unchanging, feedback is not required for automatic control. The controller can then be designed so that the system output is approximately proportional to the input with no use of feedback and hence no error detection.

Research. Although the scope of automatic control is already broad, it is still increasing rapidly. Attempts are being made to apply automatic control theory to production and inventory control systems and to large-scale economic systems. Some of the more exciting areas of current research—including pattern recognition, self-organization, adaptive control, automatic control of automobiles on transcontinental expressways, and the use of digital computers for complete control of large manufacturing plants—will have a major impact on our way of life. See also SERVOMECHANISM.

GORDON J. MURPHY, *Northwestern University*

AUTOMATIC PILOT, ô-tə-mat′ik pī′lət, or *auto-pilot,* an electronic system on an aircraft that carries out automatically a sequence of flight functions at the command of the human pilot,

thus freeing him for other important flight duties. The autopilot detects and corrects deviations from the flight program that has been selected by the pilot, such as variations in heading (direction), roll, and pitch of the aircraft.

Operation. The deviations from the flight program are detected by a number of sensors. The electrical signals from the sensors are combined, mixed, and amplified in an electronic computer. In response to these signals, coordinated commands are produced by the computer and fed to servomotors that move the control surfaces (ailerons, elevator, and rudder) of the aircraft. The commands produce the desired flight conditions that will achieve the previously selected flight program. The autopilot controller permits the pilot to command maneuvers (such as turns, climbs, or dives) that require a coordinated movement of the control surfaces.

Sensors. A vertical gyroscope is used to detect changes in the pitch or roll of the aircraft, and a directional gyro detects changes in heading. The gyroscope's inherent tendency to maintain a fixed direction in space provides the necessary reference. Rate gyros or accelerometers on the axes of the aircraft are used to detect how fast these changes occur. The combination of displacement (how much) and rate (how fast) information indicates very precisely the control action needed. Altitude information is supplied to the autopilot by a barometric altitude sensor.

Navigation and Radio Aids. At the pilot's discretion, an assortment of navigation and radio aids can be coupled to the autopilot for automatic navigation. Navigational aids include inertial navigation systems, Doppler radar navigation system, and radio navigation beacons. In addition, instrument landing system (ILS) beams, installed at major airports throughout the world, can be used to assist in making landings at the destination airport under adverse weather conditions. When coupled to the autopilot, ILS will bring the aircraft to the desired glide path and align it with the selected runway.

See also AIR NAVIGATION; GYROSCOPE.

DONALD M. McLEAN
Sperry Gyroscope Company

AUTOMATIC WRITING. See AUTOMATISM.

AUTOMATION thinned the ranks of workers needed to compile and transmit stock market tables for the Associated Press at its New York headquarters. A battery of tabulators (*left*) was replaced by a computer system (*right*).

AUTOMATION, ô-tə-mā′shən. A simple example of automation is the thermostatically controlled heating system in a home. The furnace provides the heat, but the thermostat automatically turns the furnace on and off to keep the temperature of the home constant. One machine starts and stops another. A more elaborate example of automation is the computer complex that controls an automobile production line or prepares a company payroll.

Automation may be defined as any continuous, integrated operation of a production system that uses electronic computers or related equipment to regulate and coordinate the quantity and quality of what is produced. Automatic control of production is achieved in factories by transfer machines, which move a product from place to place for successive operations.

Computers, transfer machines, and related equipment use the principle of "feedback," a concept of control in which the input of machines is regulated by the machines' own output. Although the use of machines dates back to the steam engine of the 18th century and to the assembly line of the early 20th century, feedback is a new development truly unique to automation. (Under this definition, a farm cannot be called automated merely because of the hugeness of its tractor, since the principle of feedback is lacking.)

Automation covers the output of both physical products and of services. It may be used to administer work in any large organization, as in manufacturing, to produce automobiles, or in the insurance industry, to process data on vast numbers of policies. Automation may be used even by labor unions, churches, and other organizations that are large enough to need and afford the equipment. It has been reliably estimated that most of the recording activities of the New York Stock Exchange could be handled by one electronic computer and two operators.

Technology—of which automation is a component—is the application of science to practical uses. Man lived hundreds of thousands of years without it, until the Industrial Revolution in the 18th century, but only about 10 percent of the people were able to live above minimum subsistence, and they usually did this by enslaving the rest. Since the first Industrial Revolution, and during the present-day "automation revolution," the number of people living in poverty in industrialized countries has fallen to about 20 percent.

Nearly everybody knows that technology can solve a multitude of problems. Spectacular economic growth has been due in great part to advances in technology. Untold millions of people, especially in the underdeveloped parts of the world, fully expect science and technology to solve all of their most pressing problems.

Too few persons recognize that although technology solves countless old problems it also creates many new ones. Not all technological improvement is a net gain. In the first place, some new technology is necessary just to cure the ills of previous technology; for example, if afterburners are perfected for automobile exhaust, then the air will merely be as clean as it was before the automobile contaminated it. Secondly, some new technology is workable but not yet economical, as in the case of solar energy. Thirdly, nearly all forms of technology have enormous potential for human betterment but, if they are not clearly understood, technological advances can do more harm than good. This is especially true of automation.

Mass-production techniques, however, have produced a mental and physical dependency on machines. The complete effects of this dependence are not yet fully recognized. Although living standards in the industrialized world are the highest in history, much of industry has become dependent on automated machinery, and as a consequence people generally have become dependent on automation's products, such as washers, dryers, and automobiles. Reliance on these machines often tends to make society measure culture not in terms of intellectual or artistic accomplishment but in terms of such new concepts as automobile horse-power, cigarette mildness, and deodorant durability.

CONTRIBUTIONS

Automation as a Benefactor. Wernher von Braun, the rocket engineer, once said, "We can lick gravity but the paperwork is overwhelming," referring to the fact that the most powerful computers are needed to do the millions of calculations required to guide rockets as they take off into space. The staggering amount of arithmetic required for each space mission could never be done by human beings alone in time for the results to be useful.

The memory drum of a computer at a medical college holds millions of pieces of evidence regarding the results of certain types of treatment based on particular symptoms. Patients benefit because doctors no longer must rely on their own memories of a few similar cases. Other computers benefit science and education by holding Russian-English dictionaries in their memory drums and translating automatically (although not by any means perfectly, because single words have so many different meanings).

Some jobs cannot be done without automation. Because of their speed of operation, automatic transfer machines, electronic computers, and other automation equipment perform tasks that otherwise could not be accomplished, no matter how much power was used or how well the work was organized and managed. Manipulating an atomic pile or controlling a rapid chemical reaction could not be done without automation. Some new products, such as polyethylene, a soft but strong plastic used for making thousands of consumer products, could not have been produced without automation. Color television would not be possible without automatic control machinery because human beings by themselves cannot put the hundreds of thousands of colored dots in their right places in the tubes. In addition, automatic sensing devices operate under conditions that would be deadly to man—in intense heat, in bitter cold, in poisonous gases, and in areas of atomic radiation.

In the pottery industry, silica dust has long been a hazard, but closed silos and automatic conveyors now handle all dust-producing materials. In a major automotive stamping plant, scrap steel formerly was collected at individual scrap collection areas, then was baled and moved on open conveyors to the central collection area. Workmen were exposed to physical dangers, and there were frequent injuries. Automatic equipment now enables the scrap to be put into balers, and closed conveyors move it to the collection area where the scrap is loaded automatically.

Automation generally has resulted in greater efficiency and over-all cost savings for companies, and consumers have benefited from lower prices on a wide variety of products.

Automation as an Employer. Although many jobs have been eliminated by automation, others have been created. Before one of the Bell System telephone companies installed several electronic computers for office work, the processing of information to go into the company's operating plan required the accounting department to employ all available workers for nights, weekends, and holidays, and additional persons had to be borrowed from other departments. Everyone worked under great pressure until the plan was processed. After computers were installed, the company reported that the plan was handled in stride and with no strain. A deck of cards, automatically punched, replaced a mountain of laboriously typed reports. Nevertheless, more clerical workers had to be added. The explanation is

that prior to automation most of the employees had not had time to do what they were supposed to do. Important analysis and planning had been postponed because of the burden of routine. Thus, the efficiency and comprehensiveness of the clerical work was greatly increased by means of automation.

How many new jobs may be created permanently in the manufacturing, selling, and servicing of computers is not yet known, because the industry itself is undergoing rapid change. There is some indication that the manufacture of automation equipment itself may become automated. In the manufacture of automation equipment—the "instrument production" industry—employment declined sharply beginning in 1955. Employment in the production of nonconsumer machinery had risen by an average of about 12,000 jobs a year from 1900 to 1930 and by about 80,000 a year from 1939 to 1947, but then remained relatively constant until 1958 (while investment in machinery hit new records), and has fallen steadily ever since. Regardless of whether these trends continue, the jobs created by automation will be far different from the jobs destroyed and will require workers to obtain more education and training.

EFFECTS ON WORKERS AND JOBS

Advantages to Workers. Automation has many advantages for workers. It improves working conditions in several ways. Safety is improved by means of mechanized materials handling, elimination of the most hazardous jobs, and the reduction of the number of persons in direct production areas through the use of remote controls. For instance, dangerous operations are monitored with an electric eye or television equipment. As a result, hernia, eye troubles, and foot accidents have been greatly reduced in many automated plants.

In general, automation improves working conditions by permitting plants to be cleaner, neater, and more pleasant. Automated grain mills have eliminated all dust. Some foundry workers never touch molding sand except out of curiosity, and there are oil refinery workers who could wear dinner jackets and white gloves on the job and never get them soiled. Automation thus has certain esthetic advantages.

Job Losses. Mushrooming technological changes have had a much more serious effect on factory jobs than office jobs. Although automation has increased factory output enormously the total number of production workers has declined. The number of workers in factory production in the United States decreased from 40 percent to 30 percent of the labor force from 1950 to 1960, while over-all production increased about 45 percent and the population rose 20 percent.

Displacement of labor takes several forms. First, a worker may be laid off permanently with loss of seniority and other job rights. A second direct form of displacement involves transfer of the displaced worker to another department of the same firm. Several case studies have found departmental transfer to be a common occurrence. The decline in employment of production workers in the automobile industry has included both of these types.

Third, indirect displacement may arise when automation makes large plants so much more efficient but so much costlier that smaller firms are forced out of the market by competition.

THIS COMPUTER helps bake cakes. It weighs ingredients for each product and monitors baking processes.

President Walter Reuther of the United Automobile Workers aptly remarked that "automation in Detroit causes unemployment at South Bend," referring to the fact that the Studebaker Company, which quit making automobiles at a plant in South Bend, could not compete with the more highly automated companies in Detroit.

Fourth, there is also hidden unemployment caused by the downgrading of jobs. Automation renders many skills obsolete and dilutes other skills by further division of labor. Because the new skills in automation require extensive training and education, workers are not able to move easily into the new jobs. As a result, workers are often downgraded in the kinds of jobs they do even though their pay may not be reduced. Unfortunately this underemployment is not measurable.

Fifth, the skill and technical requirements of computer jobs should not be overestimated. Many studies show that most employees, even those over 45 years of age, can be retrained easily for the new jobs required by automation.

Sixth, both theory and recognized practical evidence indicate that the ability to adjust to new conditions, learn new skills, and benefit from formal education do not decline proportionately with increasing age but are a function of mental alertness. Some persons are apparently ready for retirement by the age of 30, while others do not reach true maturity in genuinely creative thinking until decades later.

Automation apparently has proceeded slowly enough so far to allow the normal job turnover to disguise some of its effects. For example, a study by the U.S. Bureau of Labor Statistics showed that a manufacturer of television sets had laid off no employees as a result of automation. In fact, new job classifications and new machine-tending jobs had been created. The manufacturer simply cut back on hiring new workers when employees left their jobs. Therefore, the problem became not the worker who was fired but the worker who was not hired. This is called "silent firing."

Quality of Automated Job. Automation has improved working conditions, but contrary to popular belief, it does not seem to have upgraded employees. According to testimony at congressional hearings on automation, 23 new activities were created by automation, but in only four of these were engineers required to have special training.

A U.S. Labor Department study showed that prior to automation a plant had 450 employees performing 140 tasks in its central accounting area. Automation eliminated about 50 percent of the tasks and substantially changed 30 percent of the remainder. Relatively few workers lost their employment, but nearly 90 percent had to develop new skills or move to new locations, or both.

But with all this dislocation there was no significant upgrading in skills required. Before automation the range of jobs had been classified from grades 3 to 13, with an average job grade of 8. After automation the average rose almost imperceptibly to between 8.1 and 8.2. Even some of the highest grade and supervisory tasks were programmed for the computer.

Bigger Investment Per Worker. According to a French study, automation has increased the ratio of capital investment per worker in France to three or four times more than that of conventional mechanization. In the United States, many highly automated plants have a capital investment per worker of over $100,000. The 10 firms in the United States with the highest ratio of assets per employee are all in the highly automated oil refining industry. The range of investment per worker, including clerical employees, is from $81,000 to $138,000. The average for the entire oil industry (of those firms included among the 500 largest American industrial firms) is an investment totaling over $61,000 per employee, as contrasted with $20,000 in all industries and $10,000 in the textile and electronic appliance industries.

Although automation offers many possible advantages to small enterprises in certain industries, the required investments reduce the chances of success for the smallest firms, and even for many medium-sized firms.

PATTERNS FOR SOCIETY

Attitudes. A sign on a backwoods road reads: "Choose your rut carefully. You'll be in it for a long time." Many persons get great satisfaction from burying themselves in routine activities. They resist strongly any threat of change because it strikes at their basic emotional security. Industrial workers are no exception. Often they believe they are dependent for their livelihood on a unique combination of machines, plant organization, and their own highly specialized skills. Sometimes they are right; but, right or wrong, where this belief exists, workers can be expected to resist automation in a thousand subtle ways. Despite official acceptance of automation by union leadership and even after installation of equipment, workers in some cases are still able to sabotage automation effectively. Serious obstacles to automation loom where management fails to foresee this attitude and forestall its consequences. Many employee attitudes may be made more positive through better planning, communication, consultation, and education.

Courses Open to Management. There are some who would try to hold back the tide of technological change. This idea is not new. Walter Hunt, of New York City, who invented the sewing machine in the 1830's, refused to patent it for fear it would lead to mass unemployment of seamstresses. But the answer does not lie here. A nation must advance technologically if for no other reason than to compete effectively with other nations that are advancing rapidly in their technology.

A DATA CENTER continuously checks all mechanical equipment in the University of Chicago Medical Center, a five-building complex. It watches 400 points for off-normal conditions, such as low oxygen pressure.

Private management must continue to do most of the retraining of workers if the United States is not to become a second-rate power. Management must recognize that although the federal government has approved hundreds of millions of dollars for general retraining, this amount is only a fraction of the need. It is less than the cost of two nuclear-powered aircraft carriers.

Second, and more important, private management should support private and governmental efforts to double, at least, the rate of economic growth of the United States. There is no single, easy solution to the complex problem of job losses due to automation. Tax cuts, shorter work-weeks, and private or government retraining are only partial solutions. The first solutions to complex problems are as complex as the problems themselves. Several things need to be done at once.

It must be remembered that people are still important to the economic process—perhaps more so than ever. The authoritative National Bureau of Economic Research has reported that two thirds of the enormous increase in output in recent years resulted not from any increase in capital equipment but from the ideas and skills of average workers. But thinking does not come automatically. The word "commencement" at graduation means what it says—the diploma is not the end but the beginning of learning. Everyone must plan to spend his entire life in continuous reeducation or retraining.

The traditional idea of property rights has been weakened by the enormous growth of American business enterprises. Corporations have become so big that the men who manage them rarely own them. This growth, in large part, has been due to automation. Separate studies at both Harvard University and the University of Pennsylvania show that corporate growth has also been a major cause in increasing the rate of separation of management from ownership.

Industry becomes more efficient as automation prods it into mobility, flexibility, and ration-

ality, but an excess of these traits makes pirates out of businessmen and gypsies out of workers. These traits, carried to excess, create irresponsible citizens who do not own property, vote, or assume civic responsibilities. On the other hand, a lack of mobility, flexibility, and rationality leads to provincialism, ignorance, waste, and a great loss of potential accomplishments.

Courses Open to Workers. If the worker displaced by automation is young and energetic, he can be trained for promotion to one of the new, highly skilled jobs created by advancing technology. If he is only moderately adaptable, he may be trained or developed to keep pace with changing job requirements as his trade evolves. If he no longer has the zest, ability, or youth to learn higher or newer responsibilities, he may be transferred laterally to another job with requirements similar to those of the job that has just been abolished.

The barriers to labor mobility have always been formidable, yet even in the face of increasing concentration of capital, it is likely that labor is more mobile and flexible today than it ever was. Cheap transportation, improved communications, and the disintegration of family and community ties, which specialization and industrialization have encouraged, tend to make for labor flexibility among firms in the same industry or firms offering similar jobs. However, movement from one occupation to another, particularly to more highly skilled jobs, entails great costs for training and in some cases, for moving the family which individual workers cannot normally bear. Yet this is exactly the kind of mobility that automation requires.

Economic Freedom and Stability. The human mind is the greatest underdeveloped area in the world. If computers ever control people, it will not be because minds are less intelligent than machines, but because they are lazier. But ideas must be kept in perspective.

Although automation has contributed greatly to the large size of today's enterprises and to an excessive dependence on large organizations, society no longer has to accept over-all economic recessions or high levels of unemployment, either in certain geographical areas or among certain groups of people. In the case of these modern economic diseases, just as in physical diseases such as the once-dreaded smallpox, the causes are well known and the remedies are effective when properly applied.

Prosperity itself is a potential threat to continued stability. The abundance of production that increases living standards also frees people from spending all their incomes unless they so desire. Whenever basic necessities can be secured by most people with only a part of their incomes, full employment and stability become precarious because prosperity is then sustained by that portion of total spending dependent on confidence rather than on physical needs. A prosperous economy tends to be unstable in the sense that small changes in expectations can have magnified effects. Yet this is not so bad as the starvation threatening nearly two thirds of the world—the "unautomated world"—and the cures are much easier.

Sheep may be marched without protest to slaughter, even though they can look ahead and see the results at the end of the line, but people have an instinctive sympathy for others and will fight to save them, not only for humane considerations but because they can see that they, themselves, may be the next victims.

Abraham Lincoln once said that freedom seldom means the same thing to a wolf that it means to a lamb. If a shelter is built to protect the lambs, the wolves howl that the lambs have lost their freedom. Of course, public programs and collective bargaining restrict some kinds of freedom, but they may safeguard or create other kinds of freedom of greater importance. Unemployment and insecurity can destroy freedom more effectively than laws and regulations can. Freedom to change jobs requires that there be other jobs to change to. In fact, the freedom to make a living, to pursue happiness, and to enjoy the blessings of democracy in a highly industrialized economy requires full employment and some degree of individual job security. Only stability and prosperity can ensure that everyone will have the economic freedom upon which political democracy must rest. Automation can make the prosperity possible, but at the same time it makes the stability indispensable.

See also ABUNDANCE; COMPUTERS; INFORMATION STORAGE AND RETRIEVAL; MACHINES; UNITED STATES—*Industry* (Impact of New Technology).

WALTER BUCKINGHAM
*Author of "Automation:
Its Impact on Business and People"*

Bibliography

Bagrit, Sir Leon, *The Age of Automation* (New York 1965).
Buckingham, Walter, *Automation: Its Impact on Business and People* (New York 1961).
Diebold, John, *Beyond Automation* (New York 1964).
Myrdal, Gunnar, *Challenge to Affluence* (New York 1962).
Philipson, Morris, ed., *Automation: Implications for the Future* (New York 1962).
Seldin, Joel, *Automation: The Challenge of Men and Machines* (New York 1965).
Shils, Edward B., *Automation and Industrial Relations* (New York 1963).
Simon, Herbert A., *The Shape of Automation* (New York 1965).
Weeks, Robert P., ed., *Machines and the Man: A Sourcebook on Automation* (New York 1961).

AUTOMATISM, ô-tom′ ə-tiz-əm, is behavior that is neither initiated nor directed by conscious thought processes. The term has been used in two different though related senses, one primarily philosophical and the other psychological. In philosophy, automatism is the metaphysical doctrine that the behavior of organisms can be accounted for without introducing conscious choice as a determinant of action. In the more strictly psychological sense, automatism denotes any form of behavior executed while the individual is unaware of what he is doing. Automatic writing and actions performed under the influence of hypnotic suggestion are examples of automatism in this sense.

Automatism as a metaphysical theory was advanced by the 17th century French philosopher René Descartes. He held that the behavior of animals consists entirely of automatisms, and that man alone possesses cognitive powers. His English contemporary Thomas Hobbes believed that consciousness had no directive part in human action but only had the appearance of being the guide of action.

In the 19th century, Thomas Henry Huxley advanced the automaton theory a step further by stating that men are "conscious automata." According to Huxley, there is no proof in men or animals that any conscious state causes actions; "our mental conditions are simply the symbols in consciousness of the changes which take place automatically in the organism."

This concept of automatism furnished the basis for nonrational systems of psychology such as that of the radical behaviorists. They tried to reduce behavior to a machinelike level. They believed that stimuli bring forth responses without any thought or intent on the part of the individual. They referred to those who held that reasoning was a primary factor in behavior as "armchair psychologists." This behaviorist position was criticized by the philosopher-psychologist William James in his 2-volume work, *Principles of Psychology*, first published in 1890. Deriding what he termed the "automaton-theory," James held that habitual actions are obviously automatic but that when a man has to make a decision, he brings consciousness and choice into play.

In the 20th century, automatism is used almost exclusively by psychologists. Philosophers prefer to speak of freedom or free will versus *determinism.* As psychologists use the term, automatism refers to any complex action of a nonreflex type performed without the conscious guidance of the performer. Such acts as breathing and digestion are not automatisms. But acts that normally require attention, such as speaking and writing, are automatisms when they are not under conscious control.

Gertrude Stein and Leon R. Solomons conducted many experiments designed to explore the limits of such automatic behavior in normal persons. James, who directed their research, had long been interested in the automatism of hypnotized individuals. He explained this behavior by referring to the then popular theory of dissociation of consciousness. According to this theory, certain parts of consciousness become "split off," either through the influence of a hypnotist or, as in the case of Stein and Solomons, as a result of prolonged training. The consequent behavior then assumes an automatic character.

Automatic Writing. A well-known example of automatism is automatic writing. This is the act of writing with attention concentrated on the content rather than on the writing act. Usually the writer does not see what he is putting on paper. It is produced with either semiconscious or unconscious control. The agent may, in some cases, feel a loss of sense of agency about the action. He may even be completely unaware of what is being written and even of the fact that he is writing. Automatic writing may be carried out under hypnosis or some other form of suggestion.

Although automatic writing and related phenomena can be symptoms of serious psychological disturbances, they can also be experimentally produced in normal, healthy individuals.

Automatic writing is sometimes done with a planchette, a device resembling a small three-legged stool, with a pencil in place of one leg. The writer rests his hand on the device and concentrates on a topic or question. He is not aware of the muscle movements that actually move the planchette and spell out words.

The ouija board, which was once a popular parlor game, is a similar device. In this case, a three-legged pointer is moved about on a board that has the alphabet displayed on its surface. By pointing to letters it spells out words in answer to specific questions.

AUTOMOBILE

CONTENTS

AUTOMOBILE, ô-tə-mō-bēl′, a self-propelled wheeled vehicle designed to transport passengers on highways and streets. Its power unit may utilize steam, electricity, gas, or some other energy source. Because early experiments proved the superiority of the internal combustion engine as a power unit and also proved the superiority of liquid fuel, generally gasoline, as an energy source, the term "automobile" is usually applied to vehicles employing these agents.

Automotive vehicles carrying a large number of passengers are called *buses*. Commercial vehicles are called *trucks*. Agriculture, various industries, and military organizations use specialized types of automotive units, which are called by distinct names, such as *tractor* or *tank*. All these are produced by the automotive industry, but common usage describes as an automobile a vehicle driven by a gasoline engine and designed to carry a few passengers (seldom more than seven). This usage will be followed in this article except where basic principles or the entire automotive industry are being discussed. In the United States familiar terms for the passenger automobile are *auto* or *car*. In other countries *motorcar* or *motor* is often used. In England a truck is called a *lorry*.

1. Impact of the Automobile on Civilization

Wherever the automobile has been manufactured and distributed in large volume, striking economic and social changes have followed. Since the United States has mass-produced automotive vehicles in greater numbers than all other countries combined, the impact of the automobile will be discussed here in terms of that country. Similar effects have occurred in other countries in proportion to the level of automobile production and use attained.

Economic Effects. Automobile manufacturing was an infant industry in the United States in 1900; by the 1920's it had grown into a giant, and it has continued to expand although hampered by depression and war.

Deprived of the civilian market during the World War II years of 1942–1945, the industry proved its vitality by converting its productive potential to trucks, tanks, machine guns, and aircraft engines for the war effort. After the war, with the enormous civilian market again available, it resumed its expansion to larger totals in automobile production. By the mid-1960's the industry had lifted its annual production to more than 11 million units—passenger cars, buses, and trucks.

The industry has become a major force in the American economy. By the 1960's approximately one in every seven persons employed in the United States was engaged in some form of enterprise related to highway motor transport, and approximately one business in six depended on the manufacture, distribution, servicing, or use of motor vehicles.

The complexity of the automobile, requiring hundreds of varied items, stimulated other industries whose products were needed for automobiles, such as steel and other metals, glass, natural and synthetic rubber, plastics, textiles, and chemicals. The phenomenal growth of the oil industry is traceable directly to the demands of the automobile and related vehicles. Hardly less impressive than the expansion of these ancillary industries has been the appearance of thousands of repair shops, garages, and service stations to maintain, store, and supply the huge automotive fleet.

Through various special taxes and toll charges, the manufacture, distribution, service, and use of motor vehicles are a major source of revenue to federal, state, county, and city government agencies in the United States. In 1932 these agencies collected $990 million in motor vehicle taxes. In the 1950's, special motor vehicle taxes averaged about $7.5 billion annually; in the 1960's, they averaged about $11.5 billion annually. Truck taxes rose from an average of $1.9 billion a year in the 1950's to $3.5 billion a year in the 1960's.

Not all of this has represented a net economic gain. Older types of enterprises, especially those concerned with horsedrawn vehicles, have all but disappeared. The bicycle business, a sizable industry, was adversely affected for a time. The railroads, which once held a virtual monopoly on fast transportation, have suffered severely in competition with automotive vehicles in both their passenger and freight lines. The vast expansion in road building, involving multilane expressways and throughways, bridges and vehicular tunnels, has strained the resources of federal and state governments and compelled a rise in gasoline taxes and the establishment of road tolls. Traffic problems have become staggering, particularly in and near large cities. The high cost of most automobiles has driven a large proportion of purchasers into installment buying, increasing individual indebtedness and adding materially to the car's cost.

See also INSTALLMENT BUYING AND SELLING; MOTOR TRANSPORTATION; ROADS AND HIGHWAYS; TRAFFIC AND TRAFFIC CONTROL; TRUCK TRANSPORTATION.

Social Changes. As the automobile has become a virtual necessity in the United States, it has brought revolutionary social changes. No longer need the industrial worker or the white-collar employee live near his job. His automobile can carry him over fast roads to a suburb or rural area where living may be more comfortable and rewarding. Motor transport conveys perishable foods and other commodities to distant communities. The average automobile owner can enjoy longer and more frequent pleasure trips than were possible before the days of motors and smooth highways. To serve these travelers, resorts, motels, cabins, and restaurants have risen throughout the country. The automobile trailer has opened to many a nomadic way of life.

Some social impacts of the automobile have been sinister. It has made the escape of the criminal easier. Sociologists have pointed out adverse effects of the motorcar on American family life. It has been described as a contributing factor in juvenile delinquency. The most grimly portentous problem, especially in the United States, is the high rate of accidents, frequently fatal. The increase of leisure time, the greater speed of new-model cars, and the licensing of young and incompetent drivers had brought the total of automobile fatalities to a million by 1951. The annual death toll during the 1950's averaged about 37,000; during the first half of the 1960's this average had risen to 42,000. See also AUTOMOBILE SAFETY.

The automobile has become a permanent fixture in modern civilization because it satisfies so many human needs and desires. Without the passenger car and related vehicles the modern world could hardly function effectively. The advantages that it has brought to millions are undeniable. The problems and evils resulting from its improper use must be combated by wise public officials and an informed public.

2. History of the Automobile

The automobile was not invented; that is, no individual can be named as its inventor, nor can its development be credited to the work of experimenters in any one nation. It evolved from some 200 years of tinkering by the French, Germans, British, Americans, and others. Some historians have tried to trace the evolution of the idea of a self-propelled vehicle. For clarity, it seems preferable to assume the existence of an ancient dream of such a vehicle and to describe simply the principal steps in its realization. Until men knew what could be done with certain energy sources and something of how to apply them to controlled motion, it was idle to talk about workable self-propelled vehicles. The automobile is really a product of the industrial and mechanical age, and its background history begins properly with the 18th and 19th century experiments in attempting to achieve locomotion with the power devices that were becoming known.

Experiments with Steam. The earliest progress in exploring the possibilities of steam as a power source was made in Britain. Thomas Newcomen (in 1705) and James Watt (in the 1760's) developed steam engines that were useful in British mines and factories (see STEAM ENGINE—History). Applications of steam to vehicles appeared with the steam-propelled gun tractor of Nicolas Joseph Cugnot, a French army officer, in 1769; the Englishman Richard Trevithick's steam coach in 1801; and the steam-propelled dredge of Oliver Evans, an American, in 1805. The first practical use of steam vehicles was made in Britain, where such designers as Sir Goldsworthy Gurney, Walter Hancock, and William Church developed steam coaches or "road locomotives," some of which could accommodate 12 or 16 passengers. These

MOTOR VEHICLE REGISTRATION OF MAJOR PRODUCING COUNTRIES

Country	Passenger cars 1934	1954	1964	Trucks and buses 1934	1954	1964	Total units 1934	1954	1964
Australia	452,685	1,200,555	2,599,329	142,666	605,735	852,641	595,351	1,806,290	3,451,970
Britain	1,408,801	3,131,700	8,436,193	462,821	1,085,600	1,798,801	1,871,622	4,217,300	10,234,994
Canada	952,427	2,682,420	5,121,750	166,840	937,580	1,203,000	1,119,276	3,520,000	6,324,750
France	1,410,240	2,087,900	7,960,000	504,321	1,230,100	1,826,000	1,914,561	3,318,000	9,786,000
Germany	755,000	1,512,029[1]	8,689,689[1]	213,000	626,665[1]	956,709[1]	968,000	2,138,694[1]	9,645,762[1]
Italy	266,737	744,299	4,631,829	111,170	436,928	619,829	377,907	1,181,227	5,251,658
Japan	53,012	141,894	1,672,359	76,800	660,379	3,266,091	129,812	802,273	4,938,450
USSR	33,500	225,000	926,000	146,500	2,375,000	3,465,000	180,000	2,600,000	4,391,000
United States	21,430,503	48,498,870	71,950,198	3,502,900	10,123,677	14,346,935	24,933,403	58,622,547	86,297,133
World total	28,880,608	66,643,334	130,097,437	6,169,515	21,828,829	35,988,422	35,050,123	88,472,163	166,085,859

[1] West Germany only. Source: Automobile Manufacturers Association, *Automobile Facts and Figures.*

and Trevithick's later models ran on regular schedules out of London and other British towns. The peak of this business was reached before 1840; competition by the railroads and, later, strict antispeed laws put an end to it in Britain by 1865, but in France and the United States experiments with steam continued well into the age of the gasoline automobile.

Early Internal Combustion Engines. Meanwhile inventors were trying to utilize the energy developed by explosive gases. Étienne Lenoir, a Frenchman, devised in 1860 an internal combustion engine that ran on illuminating gas. The German inventors Nikolaus August Otto and Wilhelm Otto and Eugen Langen made important improvements in Lenoir's engine in the next decade. A key figure in organizing the Otto and Langen engine factory in Cologne, Germany, was an experienced industrial engineer, Gottlieb Daimler. He became more interested in making some application of the Otto engine to locomotion than in helping manufacture it for stationary use. Before he was able to work out his plans, however, two other inventors had some success with vehicles powered by internal combustion engines. Lenoir apparently had placed his engine in some sort of vehicle and run it for six miles in 1863; Siegfried Marcus of Vienna is said to have operated such a vehicle in 1864. Neither device has survived, but a later model built by Marcus in 1875 is still preserved in a Vienna museum. It proved operable as late as 1950 and may be the oldest existing internal combustion vehicle.

It is interesting to note that while visitors to the International Centennial Exposition at Philadelphia in 1876 were gazing in wonder at the huge Corliss steam engine, few noticed seven smaller engines exhibited nearby. Six of these were late models of the Otto and Langen engine, still operated by illuminating gas; the other, designed by George Brayton, an inventor from Boston, Mass., ran on crude petroleum. Among the visitors attracted to this engine was George B. Selden, a lawyer with a mechanical turn of mind, who returned to his home in Rochester, N.Y., and began to design a self-propelled vehicle that would utilize the Brayton type of power plant. Three years later, in 1879, Selden applied for his famous patent, which was the cause of perhaps the most disturbing legal battle in American automobile history (see section 3. *Automobile Industry in the United States:* Selden Patent Litigation).

Daimler, Benz, and the Moving Vehicle. By 1882 Daimler had left his post at the Otto and Langen engine plant and set up his own shop in Bad Cannstatt, a suburb of Stuttgart, Germany, to experiment with adapting the Otto engine to a moving vehicle. He had read the important essay by the French engineer Alphonse Beau de Rochas, which demonstrated the practicability of the 4-stroke-cycle principle. He concluded that a liquid fuel must be found to free the Otto-type engine from dependence on city gas mains. Nikolaus Otto also had seen the Brayton engine at Philadelphia and had brought back two engines to Cologne to study. He designed a new engine, using the 4-stroke-cycle principle, which won great acclaim at the Paris Exposition of 1878 and was soon introduced commercially in several countries. But Daimler concluded that the engine, although improved, was too heavy and slow to suit his purposes, and that its ignition system was faulty. He therefore designed a lighter and faster engine, using the Otto 4-stroke cycle, fired by "hot tube"

ignition (instead of by an open flame that entered the cylinder via a slide valve, as in Otto's). The new engine, which utilized a mixture of gasoline vapor and air, was completed in 1883.

Meanwhile another German inventor, Karl Benz, had been studying the same problem in Mannheim. It is a curious fact that both men, working independently, developed similar engines, mounted them in vehicles, and operated them successfully at the same time, between 1885 and 1887. Daimler placed his on a bicycle frame; Benz used a tricycle. Soon both cycle frames were replaced by 4-wheeled vehicles. An important step in automotive propulsion had been achieved.

Benz, whose device seemed to function better than Daimler's and who apparently received more acclaim as the "inventor" of the gasoline automobile, rushed immediately into the manufacture of his product. Daimler proceeded more slowly, and with his associate Wilhelm Maybach experimented further. They improved the ignition system and carburetion, with the result that by 1890 their company was in the lead, with a production of 350 cars, and was soon issuing licenses to automobile manufacturers in foreign countries.

See also INTERNAL COMBUSTION ENGINE—*History.*

Panhard's Automobile. One of the licensees of the Daimler vehicle was the firm of Panhard and Levassor, French carriage builders. Through skillful designing by Émile Levassor, a version of the Daimler engine was mounted in front on a chassis, from which the power was transmitted to the rear wheels by a clutch, gearbox, differential gear, and transverse axle, using a chain-drive arrangement. In several particulars the new Panhard, as it was usually called, was an almost modern vehicle; some have called it "the first automobile." The term already had been used popularly. In 1895 the French Academy officially sanctioned it.

Influence of the Bicycle. Before the horseless carriages of Benz, Daimler, Panhard, and others were in production, the bicycle had created something of a furor. By the 1890's this small vehicle, weighing only a few pounds but able to support humans of more than 10 times its weight, was appearing in great numbers along the bypaths and streets of Europe and America. The automobile, as first conceived, owed much to the bicycle, for early cars often adopted its chain and sprocket drive, the same type of steel tubing for their frames, and bicycle-type wheels. Pneumatic tires, invented by the Scot John Boyd Dunlop, appeared in time to serve the needs of both kinds of vehicles, as did the development of cheaper steel by the Bessemer process.

Later Steam Developments. Despite these accomplishments, inventors still were unwilling to abandon experiments with other types of powered vehicles. In the United States and France, especially, work on steam vehicles continued. The oldest existing self-propelled American vehicle is probably the steam carriage evolved by Richard Dudgeon in 1867. This ran on four solid wooden wheels. The two rear ones were connected to steam cylinders mounted on each side of a horizontal boiler at the front of the vehicle. Passengers sat on benches arranged along each side, while the operator sat at the rear on a small depressed platform. The car is now in a private collection at East Greenwich, R.I.

Other types soon appeared: tricycles, bicycles, and steam buggies, some of them rather elegant

1600
Sailing chariot designed by
Simon Steven of Holland.

1769
First self-propelled road vehicle
built by Nicolas Cugnot of France.

1801
First steam carriage built by
Richard Trevithick in England.

1804
First American self-propelled
vehicle built by Oliver Evans.

1827
First differential invented by
Onésiphore Pecqueur of France

1832
First three-speed transmission patented
by W. H. James in England.

1886
One of first gasoline-engine-powered
automobiles, German Daimler.

1893
First American gasoline-powered automobile, built by Duryea brothers.

1902
First volume-production car—
the curved-dash Oldsmobile.

1912
First electric self-
starter installed.

1923
Lacquer finishes first
used in production.

1923
Four-wheel brakes become
standard on a production car.

1934
Turret top provides added safety and
knee-action gives smoother ride.

1940
Sealed-beam headlight system
adopted by automobile industry. Automatic transmission introduced.

1949
High-compression engine increases
economy. Redesigned bodies and more
glass give greater visibility.

1960's
Shape changes to sleek, wide, flat, and
almost square. Transmission, power
steering, and power braking improved.

IN THE EARLY DAYS OF AUTOMOBILES, gasoline cost the motorist only 10 cents a gallon (see the sign in the top photo) and a cross-country tour represented high adventure. *Above:* A Metz two-seater attracts admirers. *Right:* Henry Ford, 33 years old in 1896, poses in his new "quadricycle." *Below:* Even though equipped with tire chains, a Pierce Arrow finds the going difficult in an American Automobile Association tour of 1907.

models in the form of a hansom cab, with two passengers sitting in a comfortable canopied chair and the driver on an elevated seat in the rear. In France Amédée Bollée, the marquis de Dion, and Léon Serpollet designed successful steam models in the 1870's and later. Several American manufacturers, notably the White Company, Locomobile, and the twin brothers Francis E. and Freelan O. Stanley, were still making and selling steam carriages in the early 20th century. A Stanley, cut down into a racer, captured the world speed record of more than two miles a minute at Ormond Beach, Fla., in 1906.

Electric Vehicles. Electrically powered vehicles, although they had to await the development of stored electric power, which was available by 1892, enjoyed a measure of popularity. They appealed to feminine taste and the luxury trade in general, but their slow speed and short driving range limited their usefulness. By 1900, however, the electric was the quietest and smoothest operating car made. It was the first automotive vehicle to carry an enclosed body. Electric cabs were operated in New York and other cities. Light electric delivery cars achieved some success.

U.S. Gasoline Automobiles. At the turn of the century the automobile, still something of a curiosity and certainly a luxury, was available in

three types—powered by an electric battery, a steam boiler, or an internal combustion engine. But the dependability and flexibility of the gasoline automobile captured the fancy of the public. In the development of the gasoline automobile the United States took an early lead.

The brothers Charles E. and J. Frank Duryea of Springfield, Mass., built the first successful American gasoline automobile, a one-cylinder buggy type, which was ready for operation on Sept. 21, 1893. A second Duryea car, with two cylinders and pneumatic tires, won the first American automobile race, in the Chicago area, in 1895. A third Duryea won an English race from London to Brighton the next year. In 1895 the Duryea brothers established the first American automobile firm.

By the end of 1896, Elwood Haynes, Charles B. King, Ransom E. Olds, Henry Ford, and Alexander Winton had built or designed successful gasoline-powered vehicles. Many of the early automobile inventors publicized their products by designing special racer models in which they or trained bicycle racers such as Barney Oldfield competed against each other in speed trials. Ford's Model 999 and Winton's various Bullets took part in many of these. Automobile racing stirred great public enthusiasm, especially after the series of Vanderbilt Cup races was begun on Long Island in 1904 and the annual 500-mile race at Indianapolis, Ind., was inaugurated in 1911. See also AUTOMOBILE RACING.

Long-distance trials and special tours demonstrated the power of the new machine. In 1903 the first transcontinental trips were made by Winton and Packard cars. The first to complete this grinding journey over muddy roads was a two-cylinder Winton driven by Nelson Jackson, which arrived in New York City after a 63-day trip from San Francisco. The first of the Glidden Tours, in 1905, an 870-mile round trip between New York City and the White Mountains in New Hampshire, was won by a Pierce Arrow. Another advertisement of the merits of the new vehicles was the annual automobile show. The first, in 1900 at the old Madison Square Garden in New York City, attracted 40 exhibitors and about 300 types of vehicles. Many famous names in the history of the American automobile already had appeared: Packard, Pierce, Cadillac, White, Winton, Oldsmobile, and Locomobile.

The second show, in 1901, marked the change from the horseless buggy to the French body type, with a tonneau fitted behind the driver's seat, with seats for two passengers. In 1902 the Locomobile became the first American car to display a four-cylinder, water-cooled, front-mounted engine. Packard obtained in the same year a patent for an "H" gearshift slot, which became the standard for American automobiles. In the 1905 show, 177 of 212 exhibitors featured gasoline vehicles, and the trend toward large cars was evident. Only four steamers were shown; the remaining exhibits were electric passenger cars and trucks.

By this time the French tonneau had been replaced by longer car bodies, with side doors. Many other improvements appeared: folding tops, fans to cool the engine, Goodyear universal rims to take either clincher or straight-side tires, and tire chains as a safeguard against skidding. Makers sought to strengthen structural parts by using more chromium-nickel steel and phosphor bronze. By 1906 the trend toward multicylinder cars was emphasized by the appearance of many six-cylinder models, including National, Stevens-Duryea, Ford, Franklin, and Pierce Arrow.

General Motors and Henry Ford. In 1908 two events of maximum importance took place in the United States. The General Motors Corporation was organized and began to absorb several of the leading independent companies, and Henry Ford began to manufacture the Model T. The latter revolutionized the automobile industry by making available to the masses of Americans a small car that a substantial proportion of them could afford to buy. With these steps, the history of the automobile ceases to be an account of how a number of makers competed to interest the wealthy in acquiring a luxury or an exciting plaything. The manufacture of high- and medium-priced cars continued, but the smaller firms were integrated into a few larger ones. Ford and eventually others created vast markets by making inexpensive cars on an enormous scale. The story thereafter becomes one of the development of a massive industry.

3. Automobile Industry in the United States

The United States automotive industry is the largest of its kind in the world, and probably the largest of all industries if the collateral enterprises that it supports almost completely are included. There were several basic reasons for the country's ability to build such an industry. The nation had quantities of raw materials such as iron, coal, hydroelectric power, petroleum, lumber, and chemicals. American industry in general had developed swiftly since the Civil War and by the turn of the century was matching and in some cases exceeding the capacity of such nations as Britain, France, and Germany. The nation was growing rapidly; immigration and a relatively high standard of living had helped virtually to double the population from 1870 to 1900, supplying an abundance of skilled and unskilled labor. The inventive talents of the American worker were at least equal to those of his European contemporary.

Early Financial Problems. Although basic conditions were favorable, financial leaders were not convinced at first that the self-propelled vehicle was a sound investment venture. Poor highways did not encourage its use. Public interest in the new vehicle seemed sluggish. The confusion over what type of power vehicle, if any, could be produced extensively had not been clarified by the experience of European designers, none of whom had been able during the 19th century to attract more than a luxury market. For these reasons, no generous financial assistance was available to manufacturers for some years. Many who later became leaders of the industry possessed no substantial capital. Ransom E. Olds was a machinist. Henry Ford was a watchmaker and power-plant employee. John N. Willys and the brothers John and Horace Dodge were bicycle dealers. Walter P. Chrysler was a railroad worker. They and other early manufacturers had to use their savings or their limited credit to get a start and begin operations in a small way. Many went bankrupt.

Olds and Quantity Production. Ransom E. Olds was the first American manufacturer to achieve anything like quantity production of cars. As early as 1887 he built and drove a three-wheeled steam carriage; and by 1893 he built one on four wheels, which was sold to a firm in Bombay, India, to become probably the first American-made car sold abroad. But Olds was not to become a steam-automobile manufacturer, for in his early years he had helped his father make some of the first Otto-type engines to be produced in the United States, and he retained a conviction that the car of the future would be powered by an internal combustion engine.

Olds designed such a car in the mid-1890's and sought capital among his friends in Lansing, Mich., to establish a factory to make it. The Olds Motor Vehicle Company was organized in 1897 but was unsuccessful; a second firm was formed in 1899 with the help of a wealthy lumber and copper operator, Samuel L. Smith. This company operated modestly for a time by manufacturing stationary engines, while experiments went on with electric and gasoline vehicles. A little runabout with a curved dashboard, powered by a one-cylinder gasoline engine and mounted on bicycle wheels, was not regarded seriously at first. Yet this model was all that was saved from a fire at the Olds works in 1901 that destroyed electric and other gasoline-powered vehicles, stored engines and accessories, patterns, and machinery.

To salvage anything from the disaster, a different approach to production had to be improvised. The little runabout with the curved dashboard was hauled out, patterns were made directly from the machine, and orders for parts were rushed to

CONTRASTS IN ASSEMBLY: *left,* a modern plant producing Chevrolets; *right,* a pioneer Cadillac assembly line.

various Detroit machine shops. The Leland and Faulconer firm, which had first developed precision standards in engine manufacture, that were later put to effective use in Henry M. Leland's Cadillac Automobile Company, was engaged to supply engines for the new runabout. John and Horace Dodge agreed to make the transmission gears; Benjamin and Frank Briscoe, the radiators; C.R. Wilson and Fred J. and Charles T. Fisher, the car bodies. A bicycle dealer named William E. Metzger was induced to sell the finished product. An empty factory building, obtained by Olds' Lansing friends, became the assembly plant, and soon the little curved dashboard runabout was being produced in quantity: 425 in 1901; 2,500 in 1902; and 5,000 by 1904.

Olds and the people whom he had brought into his operation had created the mass-production system, so skillfully enlarged by Henry Ford a few years later. Olds had done more than this: he had evolved the idea of subcontracting for precision parts and devised the means of obtaining the capital needed to continue his production by enlisting agents who would pay cash for the cars as they ordered them. One of the runabouts made a daring trip over wretched roads from Detroit to New York City in time to be exhibited in the automobile show of 1901. This stunt dramatized the worth of the small inexpensive automobile and gained the company a single order for 1,000 cars. But while Olds can be credited with original advances in car manufacturing and selling, he was not the perfecter of large-scale manufacture. In 1905, having made a fortune, he sold the business. Later he returned to the industry as the maker of the more expensive Reo car.

Henry Ford's Start. The experience of Henry Ford, the great genius of the industry and the most successful financially of all individual automobile makers, illustrates many of the difficulties that beset the pioneers. He went to Detroit from a farm, intending to make and sell cheap watches. When this venture did not prosper, he set to work designing engines, and late in 1893 he began to assemble from junkyards and scrap piles his first car. He fitted four bicycle wheels together with gas-pipe hubs; a two-cylinder engine, water-cooled, was made of cast-off pipe. Between the wheels he attached an old buggy seat and a dashboard. A tank for gasoline was fastened under the seat. The first Ford, the "quadricycle," had

two forward speeds of 10 and 20 miles per hour. It could not move in reverse. After a few weeks Ford sold this contraption for $200 and began to build another. During these early experiments he supported himself and his wife by working days for the Edison Illuminating Company.

By 1899, Ford was able to interest a number of people in joining him to form a company to make his cars. In August of that year the Detroit Automobile Company was set up with the support of William C. Maybury, mayor of Detroit; a wealthy lumber dealer named William H. Murphy; Ellery I. Garfield of the Fort Wayne Electrical Company; and about 10 others. Ford became superintendent of the new firm with a small block of shares, assigning his patents to the firm, and operations began.

The company had its troubles, and only a few cars were produced. There were arguments among the directors over what type of cars should be built. Especially bitter were disputes between Ford and Henry M. Leland, which led to Ford's resignation. Leland merged his Leland and Faulconer firm with the Cadillac Motor Company, while Ford in 1903 organized the Ford Motor Company, bringing into it a coal dealer, Alex Y. Malcolmson, and the latter's bookkeeper, James Couzens. A little later the Dodge brothers came in as makers of automobile parts.

Model T and Mass Assembly. At first the Ford company produced three types of cars, with prices up to $2,800. The first year brought good profits from the sale of 1,700 units, but sales dropped off seriously in the next two years, which led Ford to believe that the wise course for the future would be to concentrate on a cheap one-model car. With this purpose in mind, he secured control of his company by 1907 and planned the production of his Model T, which appeared on the market in October 1908. The fabulous success of the "Tin Lizzie," of which 15 million were sold at prices from $850 down to $290 before it was discontinued in 1927, is the most astounding chapter in automotive history. Several innovations marked the Model T: the foot-controlled gear-band system; the left-side drive; the detachable motor head; the en bloc casting of the cylinders; and the use of a vanadium steel alloy.

Ford actually devised a completely new type of manufacturing. Until this time all automobile production had been largely an assembly process in which the many parts were made in other shops and put together slowly in the automobile factory. Necessary alterations were made by skilled workmen in what really was a large assembly shop. Although standardization of parts had long been the rule in other industries, such as watch and firearms manufacture, it had not been used in the early automobile industry except in the case of Leland's engines and to some extent in the work of Olds with Leland's help. The automobile of 1908 had become so large and intricate that the industry could not advance to extensive production until tools and machinery had been contrived to produce the hundreds of identical cylinders, pistons, crankshafts, axles, gears, and frames that would allow the erection of assembly lines and thus accelerate the entire process.

Ford's decision to concentrate on a single type of car enabled him to make the chassis of each the duplicate of every other and to manufacture motors exactly alike, whether for sedan, roadster, or delivery car. Standardized parts could therefore be made by the thousand without change of patterns, readjustment of lathes, or resetting of other machines. Even the testing and measuring of parts to make sure that they conformed to specifications became a machinelike process. Under these conditions the Ford concern could produce huge quantities of finished parts and arrange the plant on an assembly-line basis, with the unfinished cars moving steadily from station to station as the standard parts were affixed to them. After the final assembling and testing, the Fords rolled off as completed cars. Ford's accomplishment in mass production changed the entire course of automobile making. To a large extent all manufacturers were forced to adopt the same system or withdraw from the field.

On May 31, 1927, after nearly 20 years of manufacture, the Ford Motor Company terminated its production of the Model T. After a six-month changeover period, Ford introduced the Model A, a conventional gearshift car; on April 18, 1932, a Model B, last of the four-cylinder type, appeared. On March 31, 1932, just before the Model B emerged, the Ford V-8 began production. In the first six years of manufacture, five million V-8's were assembled. Thus the Ford Company accomplished a successful transition to mass production of conventional multicylinder cars.

Selden Patent Litigation. A legal action early in the 20th century was of significance to the entire industry. George B. Selden had designed a self-propelled gasoline vehicle and sent his drawings with a model of the proposed machine to the United States Patent Office in 1879. In 1895 he was granted a patent for his idea. Four years later Selden made a contract with the Electric Vehicle Company of Hartford, Conn., to enable it to manufacture gasoline vehicles under a Selden license. In 1903 the Association of Licensed Automobile Manufacturers was formed with 10 charter members, each of whom agreed to pay Selden a royalty of 1¼ percent (later reduced) on the retail price of all cars sold. At its peak, the association included a large majority of all makers of cars in the United States.

Ford had refused to deal with the association, and a suit was filed against him in October 1903 for infringement of the Selden patent. Ford lost the case but appealed the decision, and in 1911 the patent was upheld only as far as it involved the Brayton engine as a power unit. Since the

Brayton was no longer used, the attempt to prove infringement failed, and the association was soon dissolved. Selden did not produce a gasoline-powered car until 1904, when he and his son Henry constructed one as an exhibit in the legal proceedings. This car utilized the original Brayton engine, which Selden had built in 1877.

Expansion of the Industry. The industry made basic progress between 1900 and World War I. Factors that gave it permanence and stability were mass production, begun by Olds and expanded by Ford; release from the licensing system by the litigation of 1903–1911; almost total concentration on the gasoline car as the most feasible for large-scale production; growing public interest; and the appearance of many new corporations and a wider variety of models. Improvements in the reliability and safety of cars, such as battery ignition and the electric self-starter, were being made steadily. The trend toward six- and eight-cylinder cars in larger and heavier models continued.

A hint of the future character of the industry appeared in the enormous growth of the Ford Motor Company and the absorption by General Motors of the Buick, Oldsmobile, and Oakland companies in 1908, the Cadillac concern in 1909, and Chevrolet in 1918. Largely as a result of World War I demand, trucks became an important feature; Packard, Pierce, General Motors, Hudson, Nash, White, and other companies produced large numbers, many for the military.

After World War I the American automobile industry began the giant strides that carried it to the top position in the nation's economy. More than a million automotive units had been sold in the United States in 1916; more than five million were sold in 1929. Though seriously depressed during the 1930's and hampered by the loss of its civilian passenger-car business during World War II, the industry regained its momentum after the war. Sales of motor vehicles tripled between 1946 and 1955. After dips in sales in the late 1950's and the early 1960's, the industry reached a productive level of more than 11 million units annually by the mid-1960's.

Refinements in the Automobile. While production was booming, the passenger car changed drastically. Originally it was merely a device that would go and get you there—as had been said humorously but truthfully of the early Fords and other cars. Now it was an amazing complex of mechanical marvels, electrical gadgets, and decorative embellishments. Much of this complexity was a response to consumer taste and whim, but much was due also to the originality and skill of automotive designers working to enhance the safety, speed, reliability, and beauty of their product.

By the end of World War I the trend began toward universal use of the electric self-starter, devised by Charles F. Kettering and introduced by Cadillac in 1912. Although by 1916 five makers were producing 12-cylinder cars, eighteen had settled on the V-8 type, and gradually 6- and 8-cylinder engines became the rule. Automobile backup lights appeared by 1921; balloon tires and air cleaners in 1922; four-wheel brakes, power-operated windshield wipers, headlight dimmer switches, and lacquer body finishes in 1923. Shockproof or safety glass was first installed on Rickenbacker and Stutz models in 1926 and later, in greatly improved form, became a standard feature. After 1929, 90 percent of all cars were closed models, while 10 years earlier the same

Long Island Automotive Museum

1900 Columbia electric surrey.

Culver Pictures

1913 Mercer touring car.

Brown Brothers

1916 Packard limousine.

Chrysler Corporation

1948 Chrysler convertible.

General Motors Corporation

1958 Chevrolet Bel Air sports coupé.

percentage had been open models. By 1933 independent front-wheel suspension was introduced, and power brakes appeared on a number of models. Types of automatic and semiautomatic transmission existed on some models before World War II but became common only after the war.

By the mid-1950's most cars had radios, sealed-beam headlights, independent front-wheel suspension, and safety glass in all windows. The majority were equipped with automatic transmission systems, and there was a strong trend toward power steering and power brakes. The outside running board had disappeared years before, as sides became streamlined and car bodies were built lower to combat air resistance. Long models with picturesque tail fins created at least the illusion of great aerodynamic capability. Research evolved more durable tires, superior fuels, and more efficient lubricants.

In the 1960's, a marked increase in mechanical air conditioning took place; protruding bumpers gave way to recessed bumpers; tail fins were abolished; and most of the round appearance atop the hood and trunk assemblies was gone. The car of the 1960's developed into a sleek, wide, flat vehicle that appeared almost square.

The Safety Movement. Much of the change in automotive engineering in the 1960's was closely related to a revival of interest in safer motorized travel. Strong pressure was evident among the general public and in Congress, where Sen. Abraham A. Ribicoff of Connecticut headed a subcommittee that challenged the automobile industry on the safety of its models. As continuous coverage by press, radio, and television stimulated public discussion, Congress enacted a law in 1964 ordering the General Service Administration to devise safety requirements for all cars purchased for government use. The rules devised by the GSA for 1967 models included improved seat-belt anchorages, better door latches, dual braking systems, and standard gearshifts on cars having automatic transmission.

After much argument whether the main responsibility for accidents lay with the maker or the driver, it became evident by late 1965 that private industry was making an effort to meet the public demand for greater safety. Five or six of the government requirements were included in some 1966 cars. General Motors reported early in 1966 that it had developed a collapsible steering column for all its 1967 models, and American Motors said it would buy the column from GM for its 1967 models. At the same time, the four largest manufacturers planned dual braking systems and optional front-seat shoulder harnesses for their 1967 models. Meanwhile engineers worked on long-range features such as brakes that would prevent wheels from locking, greater visibility in tail lights, redesigned instrument panels, and stronger passenger compartments.

Concentration of the Industry. According to the Automobile Manufacturers Association, some 1,500 manufacturers have made more than 3,000 types of cars since the industry began in the United States. Most of the cars were financial failures, and only a few makes were still being produced in the 1960's. Only one firm, the Ford Motor Company, had lasted as such since its original organization in 1903. Although dominated by only a few companies, the industry increased its yearly sales steadily from $43 billion in the mid-1950's to $77 billion in the mid-1960's.

These figures include retail sales of cars plus sales of batteries, tires, accessories, and gasoline. The value of automotive exports from the United States climbed to a total of more than $2 billion by the mid-1960's.

Influx of European Cars. The popularity of European-made cars in the United States has troubled U.S. manufacturers. This trend, which began to be noticeable about 1955, illustrated the public interest in economical compact cars and in sports cars and racers. Import figures climbed from more than 100,000 units in 1956 to more than 700,000 in 1959, indicating the immense postwar growth of European automotive manufacturing as well as its inroads on the American domestic market.

Some American manufacturers had foreseen this possibility and established factories in other countries to make cars that would meet European or other preferences and price ranges. Ford built a plant in Denmark in 1924 and later built plants in Germany, France, Britain, and Canada. General Motors set up a Chevrolet plant at Hendon, near London, in 1924, purchased the Vauxhall Motor Company in Britain two years later, and in 1929 acquired the Opel firm in Germany. But these moves and others did not prevent small British, French, German, and Swedish cars from finding a ready market in the United States during the 1950's. To cope with this condition American manufacturers designed and added to their offerings several compact cars.

Nevertheless, by the mid-1960's, imports from two of the smaller producing countries, Canada and Sweden, approximately doubled. Imports from the larger ones, such as West Germany, Britain, France, Italy, and Japan, continued to maintain their earlier levels.

COUNTRIES LEADING IN AUTOMOBILE PRODUCTION

Country	1934	1954	1964
Australia		54,794	411,750
Britain	354,806	1,039,190	2,332,376
Canada	116,852	357,083	670,582
France	201,644	600,093	1,582,129
Germany	173,014	680,509[1]	2,909,657[1]
Italy	43,416	216,700	1,090,078
Japan	2,845	162,517	1,702,469
USSR	72,466	500,000	603,100
United States	2,753,111	6,601,071	9,307,860
World	3,735,841	10,348,996	21,727,002

EXPORTS OF PRINCIPAL PRODUCING COUNTRIES

Country	1934	1954	1964
Australia			22,394
Britain	57,649	492,816	847,989
Canada	43,368	28,740	51,909
France	24,987	141,216	519,007
Germany	13,236	298,154[1]	1,498,964[1]
Italy	9,434	44,136	331,122
Japan	349	1,106	131,848
USSR	307		
United States	236,311	357,692	360,863
World	338,653	1,395,516	

IMPORTS OF PRINCIPAL PRODUCING COUNTRIES

Country	1934	1954	1964
Australia		140,972	31,802
Britain	12,519	5,344	69,695
Canada	2,905	45,182	97,313
France	1,772	8,282	170,500
Germany	5,559	5,415[1]	187,379[1]
Italy	117	2,453	124,848
Japan	1,846	16,317	12,813
USSR	21,732		
United States	585	35 033	532,027
World	73,831	703,376	

[1] West Germany only. Source: Automobile Manufacturers Association, *Automobile Facts and Figures.*

Long Island Automotive Museum
1911 Stanley Steamer touring car.

Long Island Automotive Museum
1923 Pierce Arrow coupé sedan.

Culver Pictures
1940 Lincoln Continental coupé.

Ford Motor Company
1953 Ford sedan.

American Motors Corporation
1966 Ambassador Hardtop.

The Bettmann Archive

1893 Benz (Germany).

Long Island Automotive Museum

1928 Bugatti Royale (France).

Long Island Automotive Museum

1949 Sunbeam Alpine (Britain).

Simca

1962 Simca (France).

Long Island Automotive Museum

1963 Fiat 1200 Spyder (Italy).

4. Automobile Industry in Other Countries

Outside the United States most automotive industry is concentrated in a few European countries, although substantial progress is being made in Japan, Canada, and Australia. The leading European makers in the 1960's were West Germany, Britain, France, and Italy, in that order.

European automotive manufacture has been characterized by individualism rather than by standardization as in the United States. Until the appearance of the small automobile, which has been typical of European design since the 1950's, makers concentrated on producing small numbers of individually styled, carefully made models, often the product of hand workmanship, designed for the luxury trade. Even when the small compact automobile came into production, there was no such huge development of mass-production tooling as in the United States. The comparatively low per capita income of middle class Europeans made even the compact models expensive for them and usually prevented any but the wealthy from buying imported American cars. High tariffs on foreign models, the scarcity of gasoline, and high excise taxes seriously constricted the European market for both foreign and domestic cars. The destruction and displacement caused by two world wars interrupted and hampered the efforts of European manufacturers to develop large automotive production.

Germany. The Daimler-Benz firm is probably the oldest of all motorcar companies and is still one of the leaders in West Germany. It assumed its present form in 1926, when the original Daimler Motoren Gesellschaft of 1890 was combined with the Benz firm of an even earlier date. Heavy investment by the banker Emil Jellinek led to successful production; the famous Mercedes and Mercedes-Benz models were named for Jellinek's daughter. The Mercedes has earned renown as a racer, winning the Grand Prix and Indianapolis races and many others.

Another successful German car is the Opel, named for its original producer, Adam Opel of Rüsselsheim, who began his factory in 1898 after making sewing machines and bicycles. An early Opel was entered in the Gordon Bennett Cup race in 1904. The Opel firm was purchased in 1929 by General Motors, and after World War II it produced many small cars, which sold extensively in Germany and abroad.

The Volkswagen was designed by Ferdinand Porsche, a sports-car maker, who later manufactured cars under his own name. It was ordered by Adolf Hitler as a car for the German public, but very few were available for the subjects of the Third Reich. After World War II the Volkswagen developed into the largest of German automotive ventures. Daimler-Benz, Opel, Volkswagen, and Ford of Germany became the Big Four of the German automotive industry, with the major share of production.

Most of the German automotive firms have retained their original centers of operations in western Germany, but have decentralized parts production. Assembly lines and automation have been introduced. The industry's climb to an annual production of nearly 3 million units annually in the mid-1960's demonstrates the resilience of German industrial capacity, especially in such related fields as electric power, steel, and machine tools, which were damaged but not destroyed by war.

Britain. The British automotive industry began operations in 1896 after the repeal of restrictions on the speed of vehicles. At first it was situated in the West Midlands area, in towns near and north of Birmingham, where raw materials and ample skilled labor were found. More recently there has been considerable development in the area from Oxford east to London and in towns north of London.

During its first 25 years the British automotive industry was small, producing mainly luxury cars. The general public in Britain showed a preference for the high-powered American car, which by mass-production methods could easily undersell the Rolls-Royce in Britain despite high import duties. After World War I the British government, by increasing these duties to the prohibitive rate of 33⅓ percent on all imported vehicles, encouraged the rise of a larger domestic industry.

The Morris works at Coventry began the trend toward flow assembling in 1924 with large-scale production of small low-powered cars. Most British manufacturers followed this lead. Because the government taxed gasoline heavily and levied £1 per horsepower on all makes of cars, the small-car business grew steadily. It benefited also from the decline of the motorcycle business after insurance on motorcycles was made mandatory by law. American imports were nearly eliminated, and British automobile production climbed to nearly 500,000 units annually by the eve of World War II.

Several factors helped the British to secure a large export business after World War II. Germany, always a great industrial competitor, was slow to recover its world position; there was a dollar shortage in many countries; American industry was busy supplying the domestic demand for cars; personal incomes were higher in many countries. In the 1950's British automotive exports surpassed those of the United States. In Canada, Australia, South Africa, and even in the United States, British cars sold briskly. The Baby Austin, the Morris MG, the Hillman Minx, and the Jaguar, the last-named especially prized by sports-car owners, became familiar sights on American highways.

The industry in Britain went through a process of integration, not unlike that of the United States. In the 1950's Morris, Austin, MG, and others merged into the British Motor Corporation (BMC). By the mid-1960's BMC was still the largest maker of cars, followed in order by English Ford and Vauxhall (controlled by General Motors). The Standard-Triumph firm and Rootes Motors were smaller but were growing fast.

Much of the swift progress of the British motor industry in the 1960's was due to the continued popularity of English sports cars, especially those made by BMC, Jaguar, Standard-Triumph, and Rootes. Rootes made an agreement with Chrysler to market its sports cars in the United States. Rolls-Royce, famous producer of luxury automobiles as well as aircraft engines, began a determined effort in the mid-1960's to expand its American market.

France. One of the pioneer nations in the field, France has created a vigorous automotive industry. The French began well before 1900 with the Panhard-Levassor company, soon followed by the Peugeot, de Dion, and Delahaye firms. Panhard adopted a Knight sleeve-type engine and made excellent racing and sports cars. Another

Authenticated News

1898 Opel (Germany).

Long Island Automotive Museum

1948 Citroën (France).

Long Island Automotive Museum

1960 Lancia Appia convertible (Italy).

Long Island Automotive Museum

1963 Datsun sports car (Japan).

Volkswagen of America

1966 Volkswagen fastback (West Germany).

823

old firm is Renault, which began operations in 1898 and developed one of the largest automobile factories in Europe. It eventually broadened its production to include diesel engines, tractors, trucks, and marine engines. Renault was one of the first cars to have four-wheel brakes, and Renault taxicabs made an early appearance on New York City streets. World War II injured the firm's business, but it recovered to produce successful low-priced cars, of which the Dauphine, appearing in 1956, is the best known.

One of the newer French firms, whose long name is simplified to the initials Simca, has become with Renault, Citröen, and Peugeot one of the four largest in the nation's industry. Its specialty has been sports cars. One popular model was the Simca Aronde, introduced in 1951. Simca manufactured thousands of Jeep engines for the Allies late in World War II. Peugeot and Citröen have featured principally small cars and racers.

The French have concentrated the bulk of their motor industry in the Paris region, which has a large pool of skilled workers, many factories geared to the making of automotive parts, and the most advantageous automobile markets. The manufacturers of luxury cars also are located in the Paris neighborhood. A limited movement to decentralize the industry, especially assembly plants, began early in the 1960's, when the larger firms established plants in Le Mans, Rouen, Strasbourg, Rennes, and the Lyon area. Renault, with more than 50,000 employees, was the largest firm, producing about one third of all French automotive units. The Ford Motor Company has one of the most modern plants in Europe at Asnières, a few miles northwest of Paris.

Soviet Union. The automotive industry of the Soviet Union has developed entirely under communism and was initiated under the various five-year plans. The first plan, designed to produce 125,000 units per year by 1932, fell far short of this total; the second, with a goal of 200,000 units per year, attained its quota of vehicles but failed in such items as spare parts and accessories. The third plan, intended to double the previous total by 1942, was wrecked by the German invasion. World War II forced the Russians to disperse a part of the industry when it appeared that the Moscow-Gorki area, where it was mostly concentrated, would fall into German hands. New plants were built in Minsk (southwest of Moscow), in Ulyanovsk and Miass to the east, and even in Novosibirsk in Siberia, where a diesel truck factory was set up late in the war. Destruction by the German invasion was less than might have been expected, although a plant in Leningrad was badly bombed and the Rostov-on-Don assembly plant was ruined.

Since World War II, production has been slowly rebuilt, with heaviest concentration again in the Moscow-Gorki area. One large establishment at Gorki produces nearly half of all Russian automotive units; another, at Moscow, possibly one third of the remainder. Each of these, known respectively as GAZ and ZIL, has a cluster of conveniently situated subsidiary factories. Russian passenger-car production is small, mostly of 33- and 66-hp Moskvich cars, many of which are made in Moscow's small-car plant. There are few private owners because of the high cost of these cars. Russia's total production, which passed 500,000 annually by 1950, is mostly devoted to trucks, tractors, bulldozers, and similar badly needed types.

The mid-1960's brought a modest increase in domestic sales of pleasure cars, mostly the small Moskvich models. Though figures are lacking for most phases of the Soviet motor industry, it appeared that in the mid-1960's trucks and buses outnumbered pleasure cars in use by nearly 4 to 1.

A radical change in Soviet production policy took place in 1966 with the signing of an $800 million contract with the Fiat company of Italy to build automotive facilities in the USSR. This contract, the largest ever made by the USSR with any Western company, was in line with a proposed increase in private-car production to 800,000 yearly by 1970. That goal was announced in the Soviet's five-year plan adopted in 1966. The site selected for the Fiat plant was Togliatti, formerly Stavropol-on-the-Volga, 500 miles east of Moscow.

The USSR, later in 1966, designated Renault, the French company, to rebuild the Moskvich automobile plant in Moscow in order to increase output fourfold.

Italy. Italy has a sizable automotive industry, largely centered in Turin, where the principal plant of Fiat is situated. Fiat also manufactures diesel engines, buses, stationary engines, airplanes, machine tools, and refrigerators. The Lancia car also is made in Turin. Other automotive centers are Milan, which makes the Alfa Romeo; Modena, which produces world-famous Maserati and Ferrari sports cars and racers; and Brescia. Italian automotive production increased markedly in the 1960's, mostly because of the growth of Fiat, which became the fifth largest producer in the world.

Japan, Canada, Australia. Outside of Europe and the United States, the leading producers of motorcars are Japan, Canada, and Australia. Japanese automotive operations were well developed by 1935, after initial American engineering aid. A leading center of the Japanese industry is in the Nagoya area. Total annual production passed 1 million units early in the 1960's. Small passenger cars, such as the Datsun, have become popular, but the bulk of Japanese production is in trucks. The Nissan firm, maker of the Datsun, also manufactured the Austin after 1952 by agreement with the British company. Japanese makers—Nissan, Toyota, and others—converted to aviation engines during World War II and worked for the occupation forces afterward. Japan imports few foreign cars but has a small export business with Thailand, Okinawa, Taiwan, and several Latin American countries. The Nissan and Toyota firms were making more than half of Japan's motor vehicles by the mid-1960's.

Canada and Australia ranked eighth and ninth, respectively, among producing nations in the mid-1960's. Both developed their automotive industries by close cooperation with large industrial nations, especially Britain and the United States. For many years the leading U.S. firms have collaborated with Canadian companies in setting up factories and assembly plants in that country. In Australia, the Holden Company of Melbourne assembles Chevrolets and Pontiacs by agreement with General Motors and manufactures the Vauxhall car and Bedford commercial vehicles by agreement with their British and American manufacturers.

See also separate articles on individual countries mentioned.

COURTNEY ROBERT HALL
Author of "History of American Industrial Science"

5. Modern Automobiles

Modern automobiles give customers a wide choice of body style, size, and engine power. Among American cars a perennial body favorite is the 4-door sedan. Other popular styles are 2-door and 4-door hardtops—cars having no supporting side pillar between the windshield pillar and the rear quarter panel; 2-door sedans; 4-door station wagons; and convertibles—cars with soft retractable tops.

The smaller cars have engines in the order of 80 to 100 horsepower. Engines used in larger automobiles usually range from 140 to 340 hp. Present engine size and car weight combinations give a broad performance range. For example, acceleration from 0 to 60 miles per hour (0 to 97 km per hour) may require from 9 to more than 20 seconds. A high-performance extra-cost engine (some exceeding 400 hp) is available in almost every model if the buyer wishes better performance.

Major Components. An understanding of the modern automobile is best assured by considering its four major components: (1) engine, or power plant; (2) power-transmission system (power train); (3) chassis (including the frame, suspension, steering, and brakes); and (4) body.

The basic function of the engine is to transform the chemical energy of an air-fuel mixture into the mechanical energy required to propel the car. Quite simply, the burning of fuel inside the engine produces mechanical energy in the form of a rotating shaft. This working energy then is delivered to the driving wheels of the car by the power-transmission system.

Through suitable coupling devices and gears, operated either manually or automatically, the power-transmission system permits the driver of the car to control the delivery of power from engine to driving wheels. The system (Fig. 1) includes some form of clutch, a transmission, a propeller shaft, and a final-drive assembly. The clutch serves to engage or disengage the engine from the power-transmission system, depending on whether the driver wishes to start, stop, or change gears.

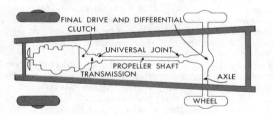

Fig. 1. Power-transmission system of an automobile.

Space considerations make it desirable that the automotive power plant be as small as practicable. The engine therefore must be run at fairly high speeds to develop the torque (rotating force) required for acceptable car performance. Because of the wide range of speed and power requirements, some means must be provided to ensure optimum matching of engine power and vehicle performance. The transmission satisfies this requirement by providing suitable gear combinations between the engine and the final-drive unit. Engine power flow is through the transmission and thence, at reduced revolutions per minute (rpm), to the final-drive unit via the revolving propeller shaft. The final-drive unit consists of a gear set and two axles that drive the rear wheels. The gear set provides further speed reduction and torque multiplication as well as the necessary right-angle drive for the rear-wheel axles.

The automobile frame is the basic structure to which every other major component of the vehicle is attached. Made of steel side rails and cross members, it serves as a rigid mounting platform for the engine, power train, suspension system, and body. The weight of the frame, body, engine, and transmission is transferred to the wheels through a spring suspension system that absorbs most of the road shock picked up by the wheels. The brakes are used to slow or stop the car; the steering system provides a means for changing the car's direction of travel by turning its front wheels.

The body consists of that portion of the car enclosure behind or ahead of the engine compartment that houses driver, passengers, and luggage. Made of welded steel, it may be either bolted to the frame or incorporated with the frame to form a single integral unit.

In the following paragraphs, a detailed description of the automobile and its production is given, under 14 headings: engine; lubrication system; cooling system; fuel system; fuel; electrical system; power transmission; chassis; body; optional equipment and accessories; new-model development; production; road testing; and warranty. For additional information on the engine and its auxiliary systems, see separate articles ENGINE; INTERNAL COMBUSTION ENGINE.

ENGINE

Despite challenges from steam, electricity, and more recently the gas turbine engine, the 4-stroke-cycle (Fig. 2) gasoline-burning piston engine still is considered the most suitable power plant for automobiles. During the 1960's more than half of all United States passenger cars were equipped at the factory with V-8 engines; that is, engines with 8 cylinders arranged in the shape of a V. The shorter crankshaft of the V-8 offers several advantages over the in-line engine: a rigid construction that permits the use of higher compression ratios; less engine vibration and noise from crankshaft "whipping"; and shorter over-all engine length. At the same time, car manufacturers continued to offer a wide choice of other engine configurations: straight 6, slant 6, V-6, and pancake 6; straight 4 and slant 4; front-mounted and rear-mounted; water-cooled and air-cooled. Four-cylinder engines ensure maximum economy in cars of modest size, while the larger and more powerful 6-cylinder engine provides reasonable economy and better performance in standard cars. Horsepower ranged from 80 to 425, and compression ratios hit a high of 13.5:1 with an average standard compression ratio of 9.16:1.

Four-Stroke Cycle. The basic unit of the internal combustion engine commonly used in automobiles is a cylinder, closed at one end, in which a piston is free to move up and down. When a mixture of air and gasoline is burned above the piston, the resulting expansion drives the piston down into the cylinder. This vertical thrust is transmitted by a connecting rod and suitable bearings to an offset crankshaft journal, where it is converted into rotary motion.

All United States automobile engines operate on the 4-stroke cycle (Fig. 2), in which each piston travels alternately from the top to the bottom of the cylinder four times as it completes the following cycle of events:

Intake Stroke.—Piston moves down, pulling a mixture of air and gasoline into the cylinder through the open intake valve.

Compression Stroke.—Intake valve closes; piston moves up and compresses the mixture.

Power (Expansion) Stroke.—Near the top of the compression stroke the highly compressed charge of air and gasoline is ignited by the spark plug and, expanding rapidly, forces the piston back down to the bottom of the cylinder.

Exhaust Stroke.—Exhaust valve opens; piston moves up and sweeps the cylinder clear of burned gases.

At the end of the exhaust stroke the piston is at the top of the cylinder, with the exhaust valve closing, ready to begin the cycle again.

Cylinder Block. Basically, the modern multicylinder automotive engine consists of cylinders that have been cast into an integral grouping or "block" and provided with a common crankshaft. Although most automotive engine blocks are made of cast iron, American car producers have been offering lightweight aluminum engines in some models since 1960. The relatively soft aluminum castings are fitted with cast-iron sleeves for moving parts, to provide acceptable wear resistance.

In water-cooled engines, the block is cast with passages in it to accommodate a flow of cooling water around the cylinders, valves, and combustion chambers. Air-cooled engines dissipate their heat via integral fins that permit maximum exposure of the engine's hot exterior surfaces to a stream of blower-driven air.

Piston and Connecting Rod. The piston, together with its connecting rod, transmits the force of combustion-chamber explosions to the engine crankshaft. To provide the tight piston-to-cylinder seal necessary to prevent the escape of high cylinder working pressures, split steel and cast-iron rings are installed in grooves cut into the outer wall of the piston. The upper, or compression, rings are plain; slots are cut into the bottom ring to facilitate the return of excess lubricating oil to the engine crankcase. All pistons in American-made cars are made of lightweight aluminum alloys.

An I-beam-section connecting rod, made of forged or cast steel, links the piston to the crankshaft. Its upper end is connected to the piston by a steel wristpin; its lower end—fitted with precision steel-backed bearing shells of copper-lead, babbitt, or aluminum alloys—is split to permit its installation on the crankshaft.

Cylinder Head. Bolted to the top of the cylinder block, the cast-iron or aluminum cylinder head provides a separate combustion chamber of specific volume and shape immediately above each piston. In these spaces and the cylinder bore occur the four events that make up the 4-stroke operating cycle of the automotive gasoline engine.

There are two types of cylinder heads: (1) L-head, which contains no valves (intake and exhaust valves are arranged in the cylinder block); and (2) overhead-valve, in which both intake and exhaust valves are installed in the cylinder head. Virtually all modern passenger car engines are of overhead-valve design. The cylinder head for an overhead-valve engine carries not only the spark plugs and cooling water jackets, but also the valves and most of the valve-actuating mechanism. A gasket of copper-clad asbestos or sheet steel provides a tight seal between cylinder head and cylinder block.

Crankshaft. The function of the engine crankshaft is to convert the straight-line, reciprocating (back-and-forth) movement of the pistons into a rotary motion. The crankshaft is supported by and free to turn in split precision journal bearings at the bottom of the cylinder block. Journal bearings are steel shells lined with copper-lead, babbitt metal, or aluminum alloys. Those portions of the shaft that run in the bearings are called journals; the U-shaped cranks between journals are known as crankpins.

Crankshafts may be forged from plain carbon steel or made of special cast iron. Some manufacturers cast crankshafts with hollow journals, a design that permits a double saving in weight and materials because of the reduced counterweighting requirements. Counterweights are positioned opposite the crankpins to minimize engine vibration and reduce centrifugal-force loads on bearings at high engine speeds. Crankshafts are balanced statically (at rest) and dynamically (in motion) at the factory by drilling precise amounts of metal from the counterweights.

Power impulses transmitted to the offset crankpins actually twist the crankshaft, and when these forces are relieved, the crankshaft has a tendency to unwind. Because of the inertia and elasticity of the shaft, these vibrations tend to become increasingly severe. In fact, if the torsional (twisting) vibrations should match the natural frequency of the shaft, the resulting vibration could be severe enough to break the crankshaft.

In American cars a torsional vibration damper is installed on the forward end of the crankshaft. It consists of a steel-disk inertia weight that is elastically connected to the crankshaft by a rubber mounting ring. Under the stress of crankshaft torsional vibrations, the rubber deforms and permits relative motion between the crankshaft and the inertia weight. By vibrating out of phase with the natural frequency of the crankshaft, this device prevents any destructive buildup of torsional vibrations.

Because each cylinder is producing power during only one stroke of the 4-stroke cycle, some means must be provided to keep the crankshaft rotating during the other three strokes. A flywheel bolted to the rear crankshaft flange provides the necessary inertia by storing enough energy during the power stroke to carry the crankshaft through the rest of the cycle. Since there is an overlapping of power strokes in a multicylinder engine, the weight of the flywheel is reduced as the number of cylinders is increased.

Valve Mechanism. One intake and one exhaust valve are provided for each cylinder. These valves have three distinct functions: (1) the intake valve admits an air-gasoline mixture from the carburetor and intake manifold; (2) both intake and exhaust valves seal off the combustion space during the compression and power strokes; and (3) the exhaust valve opens to permit the discharge of exhaust gases from the cylinder.

The poppet valve, consisting of a circular head and stem in one piece, is universally used in American automotive engines. The underside of the outer edge of each valve is machined to a 30° or 45° angle, and a corresponding seat is cut into the cylinder block or cylinder head.

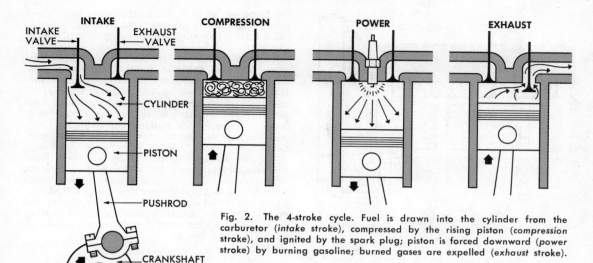

Fig. 2. The 4-stroke cycle. Fuel is drawn into the cylinder from the carburetor (*intake* stroke), compressed by the rising piston (*compression* stroke), and ignited by the spark plug; piston is forced downward (*power* stroke) by burning gasoline; burned gases are expelled (*exhaust* stroke).

The valves are opened in a correctly timed sequence by the revolving camshaft; they are returned to their seats, and held tightly against them, by helical steel springs. The gastight seal thus formed prevents any loss of compression or firing pressures from the engine cylinders.

Engines are identified by their valve arrangements as L-head or overhead-valve engines. In the L-head engine the valves are arranged along one side of the cylinder block and actuated by valve lifters that bear directly on the camshaft lobes. In the overhead-valve engine the valves are installed in the cylinder head and operated either by an overhead camshaft or, more commonly, by a rocker-arm, push-rod, and valve-lifter arrangement.

Combustion-chamber temperatures range from 150° to 5000° F (65.5°–2760° C). Although the intake valve is cooled effectively by the incoming charge of air and gasoline, the exhaust valve must transfer its heat to the engine-cooling water jackets through the valve seat and valve guide. To resist warping and subsequent leakage of cylinder pressures, exhaust valves generally are made of age-hardenable high-chromium austenitic steels; intake valves, of medium carbon steels.

Valve seats are machined directly into the cast-iron block or cylinder head, then induction-hardened by electromagnetic heating for long life. Hard-steel inserts are used in both the intake- and exhaust-valve seats of aluminum engines. Hydraulic valve lifters ensure quiet valve action by maintaining zero lash (no clearance) between valve-stem and rocker-arm faces.

LUBRICATION SYSTEM

The engine lubrication system serves two purposes: it reduces metal-to-metal friction and wear between rotating and sliding parts, and it carries excess heat away from the engine. Among the important surfaces requiring lubrication are the crankshaft journal bearings, connecting-rod bearings, wristpins, cylinder walls, piston skirts and rings, camshaft bearings, valve mechanism, and timing gears.

An oil supply of 4 to 5 quarts (or liters), depending on engine size and design, is maintained in the crankcase. A screened, floating oil intake is provided at the suction side of a camshaft-driven lubricating-oil pump. Located in the deepest part of the crankcase, the intake rises and falls with the oil level. Oil is picked up by the circulating pump and delivered at a pressure of approximately 40 pounds per square inch (3 kg/cm²) to a main gallery that runs the length of the cylinder block. Branch passages then conduct the oil to the valve mechanism, timing gears, camshaft bearings, and crankshaft main bearings. From the main-bearing journals it flows through the drilled crankshaft to the connecting-rod bearings, passing up through drilled holes in the I-beam connecting rods to the wrist-pins and piston bosses to which they are attached. Cylinder walls and piston skirts are lubricated by oil thrown from rotating parts; excess oil is scraped from the cylinder walls by the oil-control rings and drained back down into the crankcase.

A gauge or signal light on the instrument panel indicates the state of the oil pressure. The oil level in the crankcase is measured either by a graduated "stick" type of gauge or by a direct-reading gauge on the instrument panel.

Prior to 1962, American cars were equipped with breather tubes that discharged unburned crankcase gases directly into the atmosphere. Since 1962, however, they have been equipped at the factory with internal venting devices by means of which these unburned gases are led back to the engine combustion chambers and burned. This ventilation system was devised to reduce air pollution caused by crankcase vapors.

COOLING SYSTEM

The internal combustion engine generates a large amount of heat that is not transformed into useful energy. To keep engine temperatures within a range in which the fuel will not preignite spontaneously, and to prevent any destructive buildup of engine heat, some type of cooling system must be used to dissipate excess heat.

Water-Cooled System. The overwhelming majority of American automobile engines are water cooled. In this system (Fig. 3) relatively cool water is drawn from the bottom of the radiator and circulated by a small centrifugal pump through jacketed spaces in the cylinder head and block. Absorbing heat as it is pumped through the engine, the water is returned to the top of the radiator, where, as it passes down through

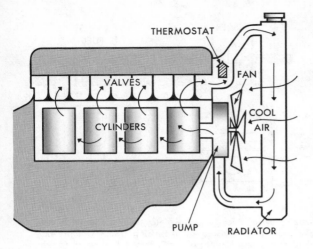

THERMOSTAT

FAN

VALVES

COOL
AIR

CYLINDERS

PUMP   RADIATOR

Fig. 3. Cooling system. Water in radiator is cooled by air sucked through the radiator by the fan. A pump drives cooled water from the bottom of the radiator through ducts in the engine block and cylinder head. As it becomes hot, the water transfers heat from engine to radiator where the heat is transferred to the air. A thermostat prevents water circulation in a cold engine.

the many small copper tubes of the radiator core, it transfers waste heat to the airstream passing through the radiator.

Mounted directly behind the radiator, the typical cooling fan has four to six blades (unevenly spaced to reduce noise) and is driven by a V-belt from the crankshaft. Its main function is to pull air through the radiator when the car is motionless or moving slowly. At road speeds above 45 miles per hour, the forward motion of the car forces enough air through the radiator to cool the engine adequately. Ideally, then, the cooling fan should absorb no engine horsepower at high road speeds. In one fan design a viscous fluid clutch inside the fan hub automatically regulates fan speed in response to temperature changes in the air passing through the radiator core.

Optimum engine operating temperatures ($160°$–$180°$ F or $71°$–$82°$ C) are maintained by a thermostat. This device responds to temperature changes in the engine water jackets, restricting the flow of water discharged into the radiator until the engine is up to normal operating temperature.

A pressure cap on the radiator increases cooling-system capacity by raising the temperature point at which the water boils. In this sealed system the expansion of water as it absorbs heat from the engine puts the entire cooling system under pressure. Because the boiling point of water is raised about $3°$ F for every pound per square inch ($1.7°$ C for every kg/cm^2) of pressure above atmospheric, pressurizing the system increases its heat capacity. Pressure caps are variously calibrated to maintain a pressure of 12 to 17 pounds per square inch (0.8–1.2 kg/cm^2).

Water expands as it freezes; therefore, an antifreeze solution must be added to the cooling system to prevent cracking the cylinder block, head, or other components at temperatures below $32°$ F ($0°$ C). Nonevaporative ethylene glycol, as well as less expensive but faster-evaporating

solutions of alcohol or methanol, afford good protection against damage from freezing. Chemical inhibitors usually are added to retard corrosion.

Air-Cooled System. In the air-cooled system, waste heat is rejected to the atmosphere by circulating a large volume of air over the engine. Built-in cooling fins on the exterior surfaces of the cylinder block and head increase the surface area exposed to the cooling air. Heat transfer is further improved by making the cylinder block and head of aluminum, an excellent conductor of heat.

A circulating fan, driven by a V-belt from the crankshaft, directs air to the engine through sheet-metal ducts. Engine temperature is controlled by a thermostat-operated damper that regulates the volume of cooling air blown over the engine fins. In addition, the engine-lubricating oil is cooled by circulating it through a small air-cooled heat exchanger.

FUEL SYSTEM

The fuel system consists of a fuel tank, fuel pump, carburetor, intake manifold, and exhaust manifold. The fuel tank, ranging in capacity from 14 to 26 gallons, generally is located beneath the body or in the fenders at the rear of the automobile. A filler pipe with removable cap extends to the outside of the body for convenient refueling, and the interior of the tank is fitted with baffles to restrict the surging of gasoline due to car movement. A float within the tank operates an electrical gauge on the instrument panel to indicate the fuel level.

The flexible diaphragm of a mechanical fuel pump (Fig. 4), actuated by a special cam on the camshaft, maintains a constant level of gasoline in the carburetor float chamber at all road speeds. A sediment bowl and filter keep foreign matter out of the carburetor.

Carburetor. The purpose of the carburetor is to meter and atomize the fuel, mix it with a suitable quantity of air, and deliver it to the engine cylinders via the intake manifold. The theoretical air-fuel ratio that provides the exact quantity of air required to burn the fuel is about 14.7:1. However, the carburetor has provisions for varying the mixture ratio automatically for different operating conditions. For example, a rich mixture is required for acceleration, hill climbing, and high speeds; for level driving, maximum economy is ensured by running the engine on a leaner mixture. Fig. 5 shows the automotive fuel system, and Fig. 6 the basic carburetor. Air enters the top of the air horn, flows down through the venturi, past the throttle valve, and into the intake manifold. With the throttle valve closed, only a very limited amount of air is drawn past it. This creates a vacuum on the engine side of the throttle valve as the pistons move down on the intake stroke. However, an idle discharge hole is located below the throttle valve, and enough fuel is drawn to run the engine at idling speeds. As the throttle valve opening is increased, the valve uncovers a second idle discharge hole, and additional fuel is supplied to the engine. When wider throttle openings further increase the flow of air through the carburetor throat, the vacuum created by the venturi also will draw gasoline from the main nozzle.

When the throttle is opened quickly, the flow of gasoline from the carburetor lags behind the rapid increase in air flow and causes a momentary lag in engine power. An accelerating pump connected to the throttle linkage provides the necessary temporary enrichment by injecting a stream of gasoline directly into the carburetor air horn.

Gasoline does not vaporize readily in cold weather, and the air-fuel ratio often must be reduced to as low as 1:1 to start the engine. To provide this ratio, a choke valve in the upper part of the air horn limits the amount of air entering the carburetor, and a richer mixture is drawn into the engine cylinders. In most automobiles, the choke valve functions automatically under the control of a thermostat.

A combination air cleaner and silencer, connected to the carburetor intake, keeps abrasive dirt particles out of the engine by trapping them in a filtering element. Filter elements may be made of pressed paper, polyurethane foam, or metal gauze. Pressed-paper elements are discarded at recommended mileage intervals, and new paper elements installed; elements of polyurethane foam or metal gauze may be cleaned, reoiled, and used indefinitely. Incorporated in the air-cleaner design is a resonance muffler, tuned to reduce the noise of air rushing into the carburetor intake.

Superchargers, available as optional equipment on some American passenger car engines, improve engine performance by packing more air into the cylinders than normally would be drawn in by the pistons. Basically an air compressor, the supercharger may be driven by a gear train, a

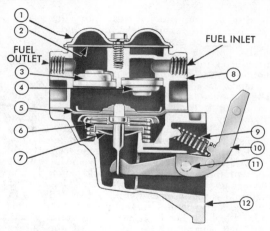

Fig. 4. Typical diaphragm fuel pump. (1) Pulsator cover. (2) Pulsator diaphragm. (3) Outlet valve. (4) Inlet valve. (5) Diaphragm assembly. (6) Diaphragm spring. (7) Oil seal. (8) Fuel cover. (9) Rocker-arm return spring. (10) Rocker-arm-and-lever assembly. (11) Pivot pin. (12) Pump body. Rocker arm, moved by a cam on the camshaft, springs back, causing down-up motion of diaphragm to suck in fuel and pump it to carburetor.

V-belt, or a turbine wheel spun by engine exhaust gases. See also SUPERCHARGER.

Fuel Injection. Fuel injection was first offered by an American automobile maker in 1957. In-

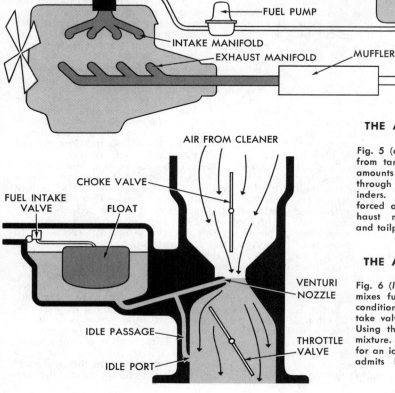

THE AUTOMOBILE FUEL SYSTEM

Fig. 5 (*above*). Fuel pump moves gasoline from tank to carburetor, where measured amounts are mixed with air and sprayed through the intake manifold to the cylinders. After ignition, burnt gases are forced out by the pistons through the exhaust manifold, exhaust pipe, muffler, and tailpipe, and then into the atmosphere.

THE AUTOMOBILE CARBURETOR

Fig. 6 (*left*). The carburetor measures and mixes fuel and air for various operating conditions. The float regulates the fuel intake valve to keep fuel in the carburetor. Using the choke cuts off air for a richer mixture. The idle port admits fuel enough for an idling engine, and using the throttle admits both more air and more fuel.

stead of the conventional carburetor, this system utilizes a high-pressure gear pump and a metering/distributing system to deliver gasoline to the intake port of each cylinder. Metered air is introduced into the cylinder through an intake manifold. See also FUEL INJECTION.

Intake Manifold, Exhaust Manifold, and Muffler. The gasoline and air mixture formed by the carburetor is conducted to each cylinder of the engine by a ducting system called the intake manifold. The intake manifold generally is made of cast iron or aluminum and has flanged connections for the carburetor and cylinder ports.

Exhaust gases are conducted from the exhaust ports of the engine by a manifold connected to the exhaust pipe and the muffler. The exhaust manifold is made of cast iron and provided with the necessary flanges for connection to the cylinder block or head. It usually contains a section that surrounds the portion of the intake manifold immediately below the carburetor mounting flange. This section, or "stove" as it sometimes is called, heats the incoming air-fuel mixture in the intake manifold during engine warm-up. A thermostatically controlled valve permits heat to be added to the air-fuel mixture when the engine is cold and also prevents heat from being added after the engine has warmed up to operating temperature. The engine exhaust, leading from the exhaust manifold to the muffler, usually is made of steel tubing.

Mufflers are cylindrical or oval chambers of sheet steel installed between the exhaust pipe and tailpipe. They contain perforated baffles that effectively reduce the noise of engine explosions without raising the exhaust-system back pressure sufficiently to cause engine overheating and loss of power. The environment of the automotive muffler is highly corrosive and coatings of zinc, aluminum, or ceramic often are used to extend muffler life. Increasingly, cars are being equipped with mufflers made wholly or in part of stainless steel. Exhaust gases are led from the muffler by a tailpipe and discharged into the atmosphere at the rear of the vehicle.

FUEL

Gasoline, which first became available in the 1860's, is a complex mixture of hydrocarbons that meets all the requirements of a satisfactory automotive engine fuel: it has a high heat content per unit of weight or volume, high volatility, and good antiknock characteristics. Although the volatility of gasoline must be sufficiently high to ensure its combining with air to form a good combustible mixture, it also must be kept low enough to minimize evaporation from the tank and carburetor float chamber, both of which are open to the atmosphere. Equally important are the antiknock characteristics of a gasoline. Any engine knocking caused by the spontaneous ignition of portions of the fuel charge will result in increased engine temperatures, loss of power, and objectionable noise. In general, gasolines of high octane number have less tendency to cause engine knock.

The term "compression ratio" expresses the relation of cylinder volumes when the piston is (1) at the bottom of its stroke and (2) at the top of its stroke. Fuel burns more efficiently at higher compression ratios; for example, with a compression ratio of 6:1 only 25 percent of the potential energy of the fuel is converted into mechanical power by the engine, but with a com-

pression ratio of 12:1 the efficiency is close to 32 percent. As engine compression ratios go higher, however, it becomes increasingly difficult to control the burning of the air-gasoline mixture within the combustion chamber. The addition of various chemicals to both gasoline and lubricating oil has made possible the design of passenger-car engines with compression ratios as high as 11.1:1, and they generally vary from 8:1 to slightly more than 11:1. Some manufacturers also build special-purpose automobile engines with compression ratios up to 13.5:1. See also GASOLINE; PETROLEUM.

ELECTRICAL SYSTEM

The automotive electrical system consists of a storage battery, a direct-current (d-c) or alternating-current (a-c) generator, a starting motor, the ignition system, lighting, and such accessories as a radio, indicating gauges, and the driving motors for power windows, power seats, and heater circulating fans.

Battery and Generator. The primary current source for the electrical system is a 12-volt, 6-cell storage battery of the lead-plate and acid type. Six-volt systems were discontinued by all American car makers in 1956. The battery is kept charged by a d-c generator or an alternator (a-c generator) driven by a V-belt from the engine. Voltage and current regulators automatically increase or decrease the charging rate, depending on the condition of the battery and the electrical load on the system. A signal light on the instrument panel (or, less often, an ammeter) indicates whether the battery is being charged or discharged.

By the late 1950's the growing use of electrical accessories made it advisable to increase the capacity of the automobile generator, particularly at engine-idling speeds. However, because of the destructive high-speed effects of centrifugal force on the segmented commutator of conventional d-c generators, it was considered impractical to increase electrical output simply by increasing generator revolutions per minute (rpm).

The alternator first appeared on an American passenger car in 1960. It offers these advantages over a d-c generator of comparable performance: (1) a basic design that permits safe operation at high rpm; (2) half the size and weight; and (3) fewer parts. The alternator's a-c output is changed to the d-c required by automotive electrical systems by six silicon rectifiers pressed into one end of the alternator housing.

Starting Motor. The starter is a series-wound, high-torque electric motor that drives the engine until it is running on its own power. The starting motor is geared to the flywheel ring gear at a ratio of approximately 15:1, a reduction that provides sufficient torque for engine-cranking speeds up to 200 rpm. Current practice is to energize the starter through the contacts of a relay, the relay itself being controlled either by the ignition switch, a button on the instrument panel, or the accelerator pedal. When the starting motor begins to turn, a pinion gear on the motor shaft slides axially into engagement with the flywheel ring gear and turns the engine over. Once the engine starts, the pinion gear is automatically disconnected from the flywheel.

Ignition System. The function of the ignition system is to ignite the combustible mixture in each engine cylinder at the instant that will yield approximately maximum power and efficiency from the explosion. Ignition is accomplished by a high-tension spark that jumps a gap between two electrodes in the combustion chamber. The electrodes are contained in a spark plug, which is composed of two parts: a center electrode and an outer steel shell held together by a removable bushing (metal lining) or, more commonly, sealed at the time of manufacture. The outer steel shell, threaded into the cylinder head, is grounded to the engine; the center electrode, consisting of a steel wire surrounded by insulating ceramic, is connected to the high-tension source. The spark gap varies in width from 0.025 to 0.040 inch (0.6–1 mm), measured from the face of the center-electrode wire to a wire extending horizontally from the steel shell. The spark plug must be able to withstand high pressures without leaking, and the insulation between shell and electrode must be of high insulating quality, able to withstand high temperatures and shock loads, and be a good conductor of heat. If heat is not conducted away from the electrodes, preignition may result.

The source of high-tension current is a coil that is sealed in a cylindrical metal case. The coil consists of primary and secondary windings wrapped around a central core of soft iron. When current is passed through the primary winding from the system's 12-volt battery, a strong magnetic field is formed around the windings. Every time the current flow in the primary winding is interrupted, the rapid collapse of the magnetic field induces an electrical potential of up to 20,000 volts in the secondary winding, sufficient to cause a spark to jump between the spark-plug electrodes.

The distributor has two functions: it periodically interrupts the flow of current through the primary winding of the coil, and it delivers high-tension current from the secondary winding to the spark plugs. In effect, the distributor is a rotary switch. Its insulated rotor, mounted atop a vertical shaft, conducts high-tension current from coil to spark plugs at the proper time and in the proper sequence. On the shaft just below the rotor is a cam equipped with as many lobes as the engine has cylinders. By successively opening and closing a set of tungsten breaker points, this cam interrupts the primary circuit at exactly the right instant to deliver a high-tension spark across the electrodes of each spark plug. Breaker points are positioned automatically for various conditions of speed and load (1) by centrifugal weights on the distributor shaft and (2) by an actuating diaphragm under the control of engine intake-manifold vacuum.

The fully transistorized ignition system was introduced as an optional equipment item in 1963. It utilizes a magnetic pulse distributor in which a rotating timer core and magnetic pickup assembly have eliminated the mechanical switching performed by the conventional cam and breaker-point arrangement. A modification of this system retains the cam and breaker points, but the points handle only the low current used for switching a transistor on and off. The transistor, in turn, controls the higher current flowing through the primary winding of the ignition coil. This reduced current flow through the points (which open and close from 10,000 to 12,000 times a mile) minimizes arcing and prolongs the useful life of the tungsten contacts. Other advantages are better cold-weather starting and improved engine performance at high speeds.

THROWOUT FORK
THROWOUT BEARING
DIAPHRAGM SPRING
CLUTCH COVER   CLUTCH DISK   FLYWHEEL

Fig. 7. Disk clutch. Transmission shaft, fixed to disk, revolves when disk is pressed against turning flywheel.

Lighting. The front of every American vehicle displays either two or four headlights. Each assembly—filament, reflector, and lens—is hermetically sealed for better lighting and long lamp life. A control switch, either manual or automatic, also is provided to switch headlamps from low-beam illumination (city driving) to high-beam illumination (country driving). Mounted near the headlight on each side of the vehicle is a combination lamp for parking and turn signaling. (Pre-1963 cars used white-light units; cars built later use amber-light units.) The rear of the vehicle carries a shielded white lamp for license-plate illumination, and red combination tail, stop, and turn-signal lamps. Many cars also are equipped with white backup lamps that operate only when the transmission lever is moved to the reverse position. See also ELECTRICAL LIGHTING—4. *Exterior Lighting Techniques* (Automobile Headlights).

POWER TRANSMISSION

Clutches. The clutch is a mechanism for connecting and disconnecting the engine and the attached manual transmission in cars equipped with a hand-operated gearshift. This operation is necessary when shifting gears from one ratio to another, when starting the car from rest, or when the car is to be stopped with the engine running. Pressure on a pedal disengages the clutch, allowing the engine to run free of the transmission. The single dry-plate friction clutch is used almost universally for passenger cars equipped with manual transmissions. This clutch consists of a disk, shown in Fig. 7, which is keyed to the transmission shaft. By means of a spring-loaded pressure plate, the disk—which is faced on both sides with a friction material—is sandwiched between the smooth flywheel face and the pressure plate. By applying pressure gradually, power is transmitted smoothly from the flywheel to the disk and thence to the transmission.

The development of the hydraulic coupling, or "fluid flywheel," led to fully automatic transmission. In the hydraulic coupling, power is transmitted through a fluid rather than a friction disk. It is essentially an efficient centrifugal pump consisting of two members: a driving member attached to the engine and a driven member attached to the transmission shaft. Its operation can be compared to two electric fans facing each other at close range. Air from the driving fan turns the driven fan, making the

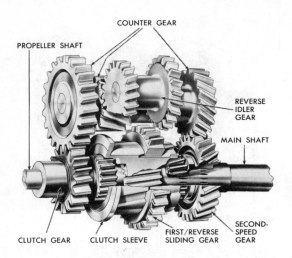

Fig. 8. Manual transmission. Three forward-speed gears and reverse are in constant mesh to prevent clashing.

combination, in effect, a coupling. In the fluid-flywheel mechanism, oil is the medium of power transfer instead of air, and a great deal less slippage takes place.

Manual Transmission. The manual transmission (Fig. 8), or gearbox, provides three or four forward speeds and one reverse. In the United States, 3-speed transmissions are standard on passenger cars, with 4-speed transmissions offered as an option. Low gear (first speed) gives an average gear ratio of approximately 2.6:1 between the engine and the propeller shaft; intermediate gear, or second, approximately 1.6:1; and high gear, or third, a direct 1:1 coupling. Reverse gear has a ratio of approximately 3.4:1. Actual engine-to-wheels ratio will vary with the rear-axle ratio selected.

The forward gears are used in sequence for starting the car from a standstill and are selected according to driving conditions. Highest forward torque is available in first gear; third or fourth gear offers highest road speed and best economy for level driving.

Synchronous meshing permits an unskilled driver to shift through the forward speeds of a manual transmission, either up or down, with no clashing of gears. The 3- and 4-speed manual transmissions used in American passenger cars are of the synchronized constant-mesh type. In most cases, these transmissions are constructed so that all forward gears are continuously in mesh. See Fig. 8.

An overdrive is offered in conjunction with standard transmissions, adding a higher gear ratio for better economy and quieter engine operation at high road speeds. The overdrive usually is set between the transmission and the drive shaft. It is controlled automatically by a governor-operated solenoid switch that causes the overdrive unit to engage at a predetermined speed. It also can be disconnected manually.

Automatic Transmissions. Introduced in 1939, fully automatic transmissions have become optional or standard equipment on every American passenger car. The driver merely has to depress the accelerator pedal, and the hydraulically controlled transmission automatically will shift through its entire low to high range as the auto-

mobile gathers speed. Conversely, it will automatically provide the proper gear ratio as the car loses speed. Automatic transmissions are of two general types: step-ratio shifter and torque converter.

Step-Ratio Shifter. In this type the changing of gear ratios is controlled by governors within the transmission. Responding to throttle-position and vehicle-speed changes, the governors cause hydraulically operated brake bands or clutches to lock the appropriate section of a planetary-gear set. Planetary gears are employed in step-ratio shifter transmissions, as this type of gear arrangement permits shifting under power without disengaging the transmission. A fluid coupling is used between transmission and engine to cushion the shock of changing gear ratios. The automatic step-ratio shifter transmission provides three forward gear ratios, reverse, and neutral. Another model of this same transmission offers a fourth forward gear ratio. When the transmission has shifted through its complete forward-speed range, the engine is connected directly to the drive shaft through the fluid coupling.

Hydraulic Torque Converter. Unlike the step-ratio shifter type of automatic transmission, the hydraulic torque-converter transmission provides what amounts to an infinite number of gear ratios by continuously and smoothly changing the torque at the drive shaft through the entire range. The torque converter resembles a fluid coupling, but with one important difference: the fluid coupling is the same as a friction clutch in that the transmission receives no more torque than is available at the engine crankshaft, but the torque converter multiplies engine torque in much the same fashion as a gear transmission does. The addition of a stationary element, or stator, makes the difference. Oil is thrown out from the driving member by centrifugal force and directed against the vanes of the driven member, or turbine, to which the drive shaft is attached. The turbine is so constructed that the oil not only imparts torque to the turbine but also leaves the turbine faster than it entered. The stator then catches the oil and redirects it with little loss of energy, and it reenters the pump at a speed greater than that at which the pump is being driven. This swiftly moving oil is given a further increase in velocity by the pump, thus multiplying the speed of the oil and hence the torque on the turbine. As the turbine begins to turn, the multiplication factor gradually becomes smaller because of the centrifugal reaction from the turbine and because the oil now enters the stator vanes at a more and more disadvantageous angle. Finally, at the cruising speed of the automobile, the unit is nothing more than a fluid coupling with the turbine rotating at the same speed as the engine, minus slippage.

Torque converters are equipped with planetary-gear sets to multiply torque further and to provide a reversing gear. See also HYDRAULIC DRIVE.

Propeller Shaft and Universal Joints. The propeller shaft, or drive shaft, carries the power from the transmission back to the final-drive gears and rear axles. The propeller shaft may be either exposed or enclosed in a stationary torque tube. Inasmuch as an automobile's rear axles are suspended from springs, the rear end of the propeller shaft will move up and down, and the distance from transmission to rear axles will change slightly. This angular motion of the drive shaft is accommodated by one or more universal joints. In addition, a splined (keyed) slip joint takes care of the changes that occur in drive-shaft length.

The most commonly used universal joint is the double yoke and cross joint, consisting of two U-shaped members placed at right angles to each other and connected by a cross, an arrangement that permits relative motion along both the horizontal and vertical axes. This type of joint will transmit power through an angle of 6° to 8° with little loss in efficiency. The slip joint, which must be used with the universal joint, normally consists of external splines (keys) on one shaft meshed with internal splines on the other. This allows axial movement both toward and away from each member, while at the same time the splines cause the shafts to rotate together.

With torque-tube drive, only one universal joint is required, and this is located at the transmission end of the propeller shaft. With the Hotchkiss drive, in which an exposed tubular drive shaft is used and the rear springs are designed to absorb both braking and driving torque, a universal joint must be used at each end of the drive shaft.

Final Drive and Differential. The final drive provides a right-angle transfer of power from the propeller shaft to the rear axles and wheels. It consists of a ring-gear-and-pinion set in which the center line of the pinion is offset from the center line of the ring gear (Fig. 9). The pinion meshes with the lower half of the ring gear so that the automobile chassis can be lowered without interfering with the movement of the drive shaft. The relatively large amount of sliding friction between the ring and pinion gear teeth requires a special high-pressure lubricant. A further reduction of the engine-to-rear-axle ratio is accomplished by keeping the pinion gear much smaller than the ring gear. The standard rear axle ratio of American passenger cars varies from approximately 2.8:1 to 3.6:1.

When an automobile turns a corner, the outside wheels travel farther than the inside wheels; consequently, it is necessary to turn the outside rear wheel faster if the torque transmitted from the engine is to be divided equally between the two wheels. In order to make this possible, two differential gears are splined to the inner ends of the axle shafts. Meshed between these are small bevel gears called differential pinions, which are carried in the differential case. The differential case is riveted to the ring gear and also serves to hold the differential gears in mesh with the pinions (Fig. 10).

Power is transmitted from the propeller shaft through the final-drive pinion and ring gear to the differential case, from which it is transmitted through the differential pinions to the differential gears splined to the rear axles. When power is applied and the two rear wheels are turning at equal speeds, the differential pinions will not revolve. However, if a corner is being turned, there is movement of the differential pinions about their own axes, causing one axle shaft to revolve faster than the other. As the speed of one axle shaft accelerates, the other one is slowed by an equal amount. (Offered as optional equipment, the limited-slip differential directs power to the rear wheel that offers the most resistance to torque. As long as one tire is resting on a surface that provides good traction, the car can be moved.)

Fig. 9. Drive-shaft pinion powers ring gear on axle.

The final-drive gears and the differential case are assembled in the differential carrier, which in turn is mounted in the rear-axle housing. The differential carrier also holds the bearings that support the differential case and the drive shaft. Two tubular extensions of the differential housing enclose the rear-axle shafts. Sufficient high-pressure lubricant is carried in the housing to lubricate the entire final-driving unit.

Rear Axle. Power from the differential is transmitted to the wheels through the rear axles. Each axle is splined to a differential gear at one end and secured to a wheel at the other. Most cars use what is known as the semifloating axle, in which the weight of the car is carried on two bearings between the axle housing and the axle itself. Bending stresses are distributed along the axle between the differential and the outer axle bearing.

Fig. 10. Rear-axle assembly. The rear wheels usually revolve at the same speed, but the differential gears permit one wheel to revolve faster than the other when car turns. (1) Pinion drive flange. (2) Oil seal. (3) Front pinion bearing. (4) Pinion bearing spacer. (5) Rear pinion bearing. (6) Ring gear. (7) Differential pinion. (8) Axle housing. (9) Differential side gear. (10) Differential case. (11) Differential pinion shaft. (12) Differential side bearing. (13) Adjusting sleeve lock. (14) Axle shaft. (15) Adjusting sleeve. (16) Pinion shim. (17) Carrier. (18) Drive pinion.

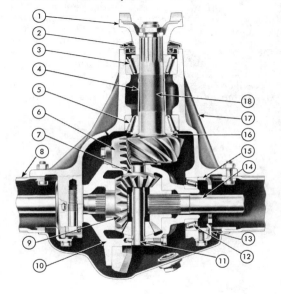

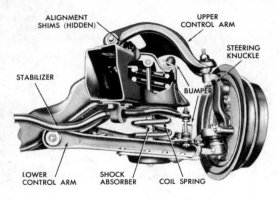

Fig. 11. Independent front-suspension system.

CHASSIS

The term "chassis" is used to designate the complete car minus the body. The chassis therefore consists of the engine, power-transmission system, and suspension system all suitably attached to, or suspended from, a structurally independent frame. Although this construction is widely used, an almost equal number of automobile makers employ a design in which the frame and body are welded together to form an integral unit.

Usually of all-welded steel construction, the frame may consist of either (1) box-girder side rails with reinforced center X; (2) full-length box-girder side rails with box-girder cross members (ladder type); or (3) center X construction with no side rails, braced front and rear with box-girder cross members.

The chief design requirements of the automobile frame, whether it be structurally independent or an integral part of the body, are that it provide great strength with minimum weight. It must be rigid enough to absorb the road impacts and shocks transmitted by wheels and axles, and it must be able to withstand the torsional stresses encountered under operating conditions.

To save weight, side members are made deepest at the location of greatest bending moment, tapering off as the bending moment decreases. The frame is made narrower at the front to allow the front wheels to turn when steering; it also features a "kickup" at the rear to lower the center of gravity of the car and still allow sufficient room for effective rear-spring action.

Front Suspension. The front wheels of most passenger cars are independently suspended from the frame (Fig. 11). Independent suspension re-

duces the front-end vibration associated with the rigid front axle that formerly was used, and it also improves vehicle riding and handling qualities. The movement of each front wheel is, within the limitations discussed below, completely unaffected by the movements of the other.

The most common independent suspension system mounts a steering-knuckle-and-wheel-spindle assembly between upper and lower pairs of nearly parallel control arms. The inner ends of the control arms pivot in rubber-mounted steel bushings secured to the frame; the outer ends terminate in ball joints that support the steering knuckle and wheel spindle. Because the lower arms are longer than the upper, the relation of their up-and-down movements is such that, in turning maneuvers, the outside and more heavily loaded wheel remains more nearly vertical with respect to the road surface.

Front suspensions may incorporate either torsion bars or coil springs. Torsion bars, one on each side, run parallel to the front-to-back center line of the vehicle. A torsion bar is a steel member, usually cylindrical, that absorbs front-wheel deflections by twisting about its own horizontal axis. One end of the torsion bar is fastened rigidly to the frame at some point toward the rear of the car; the other end is linked to the suspension system so that the shaft alternately twists and untwists in response to the vertical movements of the front wheel.

When coil springs are used, they are mounted under compression between the frame and the upper or lower control arms. In addition, a stabilizer bar often is linked to the lower control arms to balance tire loading and to prevent excessive sway when the car is cornering. Whenever one spring deflects more than the other, the stabilizer equalizes the deflection by transferring part of the load to the other tire.

Rear Suspension. Although a few American cars feature independent, or swing-axle, rear-wheel suspension (Fig. 12), the majority use a fixed rear axle suspended from either laminated (layered) leaf springs or a coil-springs-trailing control-arm arrangement. Whichever suspension system is used, it must be designed not only to absorb road shocks but also to provide a means for absorbing the torque reactions resulting from driving and braking.

When laminated leaf springs are used, one end of each spring is fastened to the frame of the car by a pivot joint. The other end is connected to the frame by a shackle, or swinging joint, that compensates for the changes in over-all length that occur when the spring flexes. Connection bushings are steel sleeves mounted in oil-resistant rubber. Leaf springs usually are clamped to the rear-axle housing with U-bolts at a point approximately midway between the ends of the spring.

In a coil-spring rear-suspension system the springs are mounted under compression between the frame and the axle housing. Because of the nature of coil springs, transverse (crosswise) radius rods are used to restrict sidewise movement of the axle housing relative to the frame. To absorb torque reactions, special torque bars are installed between the axle housing and some reinforced point on the frame just ahead of the axle housing.

Shock Absorbers. The shock absorber is a hydraulic damping device that controls the oscillations of the springs and prevents their being excessively compressed or expanded. Most commonly used is the direct-acting type, involving

Fig. 12. Independent rear-suspension system.

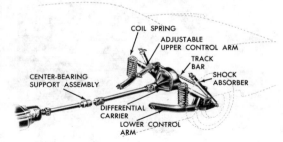

a double-acting piston-and-cylinder arrangement. Rear shock absorbers are installed between the axle housing and the frame; front shock absorbers usually are mounted inside the coil springs between the lower control arm and the frame.

Optional-equipment rear shock absorbers are available that provide adjustable load-carrying capacity, an especially useful feature for station-wagon owners. In one design the upper portion of a hydraulic shock absorber is surrounded by a metal-encased rubber boot that can be inflated with air from a connection inside the vehicle. By varying the air pressure within the boot from approximately 30 to 90 pounds per square inch (2.1–6.3 kg/cm²), the driver can have a soft, comfortable ride when the vehicle is empty or a ride that is firm and controlled when the vehicle is heavily loaded.

Brakes. All American automobiles are equipped with two independent brake systems: 4-wheel hydraulic service brakes operated by a pedal (Fig. 13) and mechanical parking brakes usually operated by a lever. In some older cars the parking brake consists of a brake-drum-and-band arrangement mounted on the propeller shaft directly behind the transmission. More commonly, however, the parking-brake system consists of steel cables and linkage that mechanically actuate only the rear-wheel service-brake shoes. By incorporating a positive mechanical lock, most automatic transmissions provide what is, in effect, another parking brake. Its engagement is controlled manually through the transmission-selector lever.

When the service-brake pedal is depressed, the master cylinder transmits equal pressure through high-strength tubing to hydraulic cylinders at all four wheels. Each wheel cylinder then forces a pair of brake shoes outward against the revolving drum with sufficient force to slow or stop the car. Maximum braking is attained when the pressure of the shoes against the drums is such that the wheels do not quite lock. Brake shoes are faced with a friction material that is either bonded or riveted to the shoes.

Depending on many variables—including the heating properties of lining and drum materials, car speed, deceleration rate, and (least significant) ambient temperature—the surface temperature at the drum while braking may exceed 1000° F (538° C). The forward motion of the car causes a flow of cooling air to sweep over the drum, effectively removing most of this heat.

Brake-drum material is usually cast iron; however, some manufacturers are taking advantage of aluminum's high heat conductivity and are using ribbed aluminum drums lined with cast iron at the wearing surfaces. Brake-drum ribbing has two functions: (1) it improves the radiation of heat away from the brakes by increasing the surface area of the drum, and (2) it provides an additional structural stiffness that enables the drum better to resist high-temperature distortion and accompanying brake fade.

Braking system improvements include the following: the provision of an extra margin of safety through the use of independent hydraulic systems for front and rear brakes; the introduction of self-adjusting brakes as standard equipment on a great many cars; the adoption of disk brakes long popular on European cars; and the use of linings of sintered (specially heat-treated) metal for heavy-duty braking service. Increasingly, American cars are being equipped with power brakes to reduce the pedal effort.

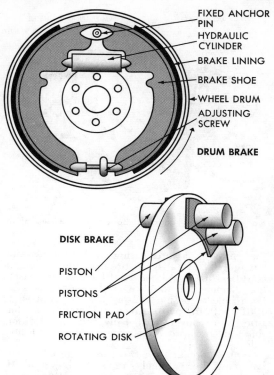

FIXED ANCHOR PIN
HYDRAULIC CYLINDER
BRAKE LINING
BRAKE SHOE
WHEEL DRUM
ADJUSTING SCREW

DRUM BRAKE

DISK BRAKE
PISTON
PISTONS
FRICTION PAD
ROTATING DISK

Fig. 13. Two kinds of brakes. In drum type, stopping occurs when brake shoes are pressed against wheel drum. In disk type, friction pads press rotating disk.

Wheels and Tires. The automobile wheel has progressed from the original wooden-rim-and-wire-spokes affair borrowed from the bicycle to the present all-steel safety wheel designed specifically for automotive applications. Made of two steel stampings welded together, the modern wheel combines great strength with relatively light weight. Most compact cars are equipped with 13-inch-diameter wheels (33 cm); all other American cars use either 14- or 15-inch wheels (36 or 38 cm).

Tires also have undergone some radical changes over the years. For example, pressure has dropped from the 65 pounds per square inch (4.6 kg/cm²) used in early tires to the 24 pounds per square inch (1.7 kg/cm²) now commonly recommended for low-profile tires. The tubeless tire, introduced in 1955 and now standard equipment, has added considerably to automotive safety.

Increasingly, automobile manufacturers are regarding the tire as an integral part of the car and not just as an accessory that is fitted arbitrarily into an already completed design concept. More attention is being paid to the skidding characteristics of tires, and the scientific designing of tire treads and casings is contributing importantly to both automobile handling and passenger safety. Tires claimed to be virtually punctureproof are available to the American motorist. Some feature a separate inner chamber that assumes the load if the regular tire casing loses its air; others utilize a gummy substance stored inside the tire to seal off leaks.

In tire construction, the term "ply" refers to one of the layers of rubber-impregnated cords

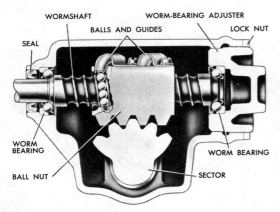

Fig. 14. Ball-nut gear at bottom of steering shaft.

that provide a tire casing with stiffness and strength. Thus a 4-ply tire has four layers of cord beneath its rubber tread face. By increasing the diameter of the tire cords, engineers have been able to design a 2-ply tire (introduced in 1961) with the performance and safety characteristics of a conventional 4-ply tire. In addition, the 2-ply tires provide a softer, more comfortable ride.

Once popular as a tire cord material, cotton has now been largely replaced by synthetic fabrics, such as nylon and rayon. Cotton deteriorates when moisture leaks through small cracks in the sidewall rubber and is therefore less desirable than the synthetic materials.

Steering Gear. Through a suitable mechanism and connecting linkage, the steering gear permits the driver to control the vehicle's direction of travel by simultaneously changing the angle of both front wheels. Rotary motion applied to the steering wheel rim is transferred via a steel shaft to a lubricant-filled steering mechanism bolted to the frame of the vehicle. Here it is translated into the lateral movement required to position the steering-wheel linkage.

The translating mechanism may be one of several types: cam and lever, worm and sector, worm and roller, or recirculating ball nut. Most American cars now employ the recirculating ball nut. In this design (Fig. 14), recirculating steel balls cause a grooved nut to move along the steering-shaft worm gear when the steering wheel is turned. The nut, in constant mesh with a toothed sector, imparts a rotational movement to the output shaft of the steering-gear mechanism.

A short steering arm—called the Pitman arm—is splined to the other end of the output shaft. It links the translational mechanism to the steering linkage via a ball-joint connection (Fig. 15).

Steering tie rods and drag links, of varying lengths of steel rod or thick-walled steel tubing, transmit Pitman-arm movements to a steering knuckle at each road wheel. Ball joints throughout keep friction low and ensure freedom of linkage movement in any direction. Both the steering mechanism and the geometry of the steering linkage offer a mechanical advantage that makes steering comparatively effortless for the driver. In American cars, the steering ratio—which is the ratio of the gear reduction provided by the steering-gear translational mechanism—ranges from 15.7:1 for power-assisted steering to 24.1:1 for manual steering.

BODY

The body is the part of the car that accommodates the passengers and their belongings. It does not include the front fenders, hood, or grille. Body styling is extremely important to the sales success of the product.

Automobile bodies are constructed by fabricating a number of subassemblies and then welding these sections into a single solid unit. The various component parts are formed on presses that range from relatively small units to enormous machines, used in stamping the body top. The subdivision of the body can be accomplished in several ways, depending on the basic body design and the manufacturing facilities available for its production. In one method, the breakdown consists of a cowl-and-dash-panel subassembly, doors, windshield, center and lock pillars, rear-quarter panels, trunk lid, underbody, and roof panel. Rear fenders are part of the rear-quarter-panel assembly.

Once the body is assembled, it is treated with a rustproofing process and painted. The roof and flat side areas usually are painted with a mechanical sprayer; the remainder of the body is hand sprayed. Drying is accelerated by routing the body through ovens. Upholstery, seat cushions, and interior trim are added as the painted body shell moves along the assembly line.

The completed body is bolted to the frame on the final car-assembly line. To prevent squeaks or other noises that would result from body-to-frame contacts, rubber insulating washers are placed between body and frame. With this type of construction, one body can be used with different frames, fenders, hoods, and grilles. These changes, coupled with modifications in trim hardware, can result in a marked difference in appearance between two cars using the same body.

In an alternate body construction, known as unit or integral body-and-frame construction, the equivalent of a conventional chassis frame is incorporated as a component part of the underbody structure. The body and frame thus form one solid unit. In small cars this type of construction is somewhat lighter in weight than the separate body and frame. However, it is more prone to resonances and body vibrations that can cause objectionable noise levels. Another disadvantage is that it is not as adaptable for use with several car lines as is the separate body and frame. Since the body itself supplies the structural strength of the car, extra care is required to prevent body corrosion. Unit bodies employ a considerable amount of galvanized steel and often are dipped

Fig. 15. Steering linkage. Pitman arm causes turning.

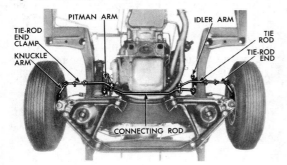

NEW BODY STYLE begins with sketches and drawings; then, on a wooden framework, a full-size clay model is hand-molded, painted, and trimmed.

into huge paint vats to minimize corrosion.

There is no general agreement as to the over-all preference of the two body types. In the United States in the 1960's, most cars less than 200 inches (508 cm) in length and several larger ones were using integral construction.

Fiber-glass bodies, used on some low-volume sports models, are made by building up layers of glass fiber mats and resin on die forms and then using a heated die to shape and cure the piece. Thickness averages about $\frac{1}{10}$ inch (0.25 cm). The individual body sections are bonded together, using aluminum rivets and an adhesive, then sanded and painted. Both the materials and direct labor costs are more expensive than in the case of steel bodies. However, tooling costs are much lower, and the system is economical for low volumes—perhaps up to 50,000 units per model.

OPTIONAL EQUIPMENT AND ACCESSORIES

While none of the optional equipment and accessories available to the American motorist are essential to the operation of his automobile, they nevertheless add materially to his driving comfort and safety. Factory-installed items include automatic transmission, power brakes, power steering, power seat, power windows, power radio antennas, tinted glass, limited-slip differential, air conditioning, radio, heater, windshield washers, backup lamps, stereo tape players, and seat belts.

In addition, the motorist has a wide choice of accessory items offered for sale by automobile dealers, department stores, and mail-order houses, such as seat covers, electric clocks, special wheel disks, cigarette lighters, and record players.

NEW-MODEL DEVELOPMENT

Each manufacturer's engineering and styling departments maintain continuous development programs to experiment with new ideas and try out new concepts. Engineers, for example, run daily tests on experimental engines, transmissions, and suspensions. Some of them never will reach production; others may appear in models that will not reach the public for three or four years. From these advanced programs management selects the mechanical and styling features to be blended into a new model.

With basic ground rules as to styling character, general size, and engineering aspects established, the stylists make dozens of sketches showing different designs incorporating the desired features. The best elements of these sketches ultimately are combined into full-scale drawings both of the exterior and of the interior. Seating arrangements, legroom, headroom, visibility, and engine and chassis requirements all are taken into consideration in developing these drawings.

Next, a full-scale clay model is built to establish exterior styling details in three dimensions.

CLAY MODEL is made in "modeling bridge" where symmetry can be assured and measurement is precisely according to design requirements.

AUTOMOBILE FRAME is immovable in body-holding fixture while various welding operations are performed.

The refined clay model subsequently leads to a fiber-glass model that is painted, fitted with glass, and trimmed inside and out to duplicate the appearance of the final product. Final model dimensions, including window openings, door openings, and seating arrangements, are transferred to drawings that guide the body engineers in developing such features as body structure and window mechanisms.

Simultaneously, other engineers are completing engine, suspension, transmission, electric-circuit, and related chassis designs. Each new design is tested, modified, and retested until it gives just the kind of performance desired. At the same time, it is undergoing durability tests, both in test cars and in the laboratory, where specially designed test machines telescope a lifetime of normal use into a few weeks or months. As a final check, several prototype cars are built and given exhaustive road tests. This permits an appraisal of the over-all character of the car that is impossible to obtain any other way.

Production specialists, who have the responsibility of actually building the cars, serve as consultants throughout the planning stages to ensure that production practicality is given consideration in the engineers' and stylists' proposals. These production experts become heavily involved when the engineering department turns over to them literally acres of blueprints and parts lists. The blueprints are reviewed carefully, and any changes required to improve producibility are worked out cooperatively with the engineering department. Tooling orders then are released. These cover the special machines and dies needed to build the new parts and must be ordered many months—in some cases more than a year—in advance of the scheduled start of production.

Another major task is planning necessary plant rearrangements. Each new machine must be properly integrated with existing equipment but cannot be installed until the current model run is completed. These plans are so carefully worked out that assembly plants usually are idle only three or four weeks of each year between model changes.

As the production tools become available, they are used to build a mock-up chassis. This serves as a check on both tools and inspection fixtures. During this stage, methods and standards engineers, who have followed the progress of the new car model for many months, are called in to make

their final studies to verify that manufacturing processes and facilities already planned are satisfactory. Those responsible for the assembly of the new model also disassemble and reassemble the mock-up to train supervisory personnel and to verify that the model can be assembled easily. At the same time, the service department studies the mock-up for service accessibility and gathers final information for service procedures.

PRODUCTION

Today, the manufacture of almost all items made up of many parts is done by using an assembly line. This technique was first developed by automobile manufacturers and still reaches its highest stage of refinement in this industry.

The parts to be assembled are first carried by conveyor from their raw or semifinished form through many stages of machining and finishing, almost all of which are done by automatic machinery. Each part is inspected closely, to make certain that its specifications are within the allowed tolerances, and stored in a "bank." Well-stocked parts-and-materials banks are necessary to ensure uninterrupted production. These banks then are used to supply an assembly line. In an engine-assembly line, for example, such items as pistons, bearings, crankshafts, and camshafts are supplied from the parts banks and assembled into the moving engine block. Once completely assembled, the engine is given a short operating test before being transferred to a storage area that constitutes the engine bank for the final car-assembly line.

This general assembly procedure is repeated for each built-up component of the car. Carburetors, alternators, transmissions, speedometers, windshield-wiper motors, starters—these and many other assemblies are put together and tested in the same general manner. Usually, these complicated subassemblies are built in specialized plants (either the car manufacturer's or a supplier's) and shipped, perhaps hundreds of miles, to the final-assembly plant.

Final assembly is a fascinating operation in which the car grows from a bare frame (if it uses this type of structure) to a finished vehicle in just a few hours. The frame is started down the assembly line, and various subassemblies—put together elsewhere and carried on a conveyor to the appropriate station—are progressively added: suspension- and axle-housing systems, fuel tank, brakes, engine-transmission assembly, radiator, wheels, and others. After the chassis items are installed, the body, completely upholstered and painted, arrives on an overhead conveyor and is lowered into place. Wiring harnesses and heater hoses are connected, front fenders and grille assembly installed, and soon, after some other additions and connections, the car reaches the end of the line. The gas tank is filled, the headlights are adjusted, and after final inspection the car is driven to a storage area to await shipment to the dealer who ordered it.

Perhaps the most amazing aspect of the assembly operation is the intricate scheduling involved. In a typical year just one line of cars (such as Chevrolet, Ford, or Plymouth) will offer 30 to 35 models representing a variety of body styles in two or three series. These series may differ in size and have different upholstery and trim. Taking into consideration the number of body styles, series, accessories, and equipment and color options available, it would be possible

RED BATH on the assembly line electrolytically applies a coat of red primer paint to the entire body of the automobile in order to prevent it from rusting or corroding if the surface paint is damaged.

FORD MOTOR COMPANY

for one manufacturer to build more than a million cars with no two identical. To give the purchaser this kind of individual choice requires a precise scheduling system so that the red body is dropped on the chassis with the red wheels equipped with the proper transmission, engine, equipment options, and accessories as specified by the eventual owner. See also MASS PRODUCTION.

ROAD TESTING

Customers expect each new model to incorporate engineering improvements, but at the same time, they expect these improvements to be thoroughly tested before being placed in production. Vast proving grounds, individually owned and operated by each manufacturer, provide standard roads of all types for conducting such tests. The larger American manufacturers support facilities of 4,000 to 8,000 acres (16–32 sq km), with up to 80 miles (129 km) of test roads. These roads duplicate potholed country roads, winding highways, hills of up to 60 percent grade, and high-speed tracks engineered to give no side thrust at car speeds of 140 miles (225 km) per hour. Surfaces similar to cobblestones (known as Belgian block roads), skid pads, simulated railroad crossings, and salt-bath, water, and mud pits also are included.

Highly accurate and frequently unique instruments are used for measuring such performance factors as maximum speeds, acceleration, hill-climbing ability, fuel consumption, riding qualities, and car-noise level. Desert proving grounds supplement the main facilities for extreme hot-weather tests; they also make it possible to run engineering tests during the winter without being hampered by ice and snow. The staggering total of 25 to 30 million test miles (40–48 million km) is accumulated on proving-ground roads each year.

WARRANTY

Each new-car purchaser receives a warranty guaranteeing replacement or repair of components that are shown to be defective during the warranty period.

Striking increases in warranty periods reflect the improved durability and quality control available through modern design and manufacturing methods, as well as the intense competitive pressures within the industry.

RALPH A. RICHARDSON
LEROY R. BUZAN
PHILIP A. LINCOLN
Technical Information Department
Research Laboratories, General Motors Corporation

6. Automobile Glossary

The following is a list of terms used in motoring and in the automotive industry. Cross references are to entries within this glossary unless specific reference is made to a separate article.

Acceleration.—Increase in the speed of a motor vehicle, or the rate of increase. A change from a higher to a lower speed is called *deceleration*.

Accelerator.—A pedal, actuated by the driver, for varying speed by changing the amount of fuel fed to the engine.

Air Brake.—A device providing a means to actuate the brake mechanism by air pressure.

Air Cleaner.—A filter at the carburetor air intake to keep out solid particles.

Air Conditioner.—A refrigeration system for cooling and controlling the air temperature in the passenger compartment.

Air-Cooled Engine.—An engine with fins on the cylinders for direct heat rejection from the engine to the air.

Air Suspension.—A system for supporting the frame of a vehicle, using air bellows or cylinders instead of springs.

Antifreeze.—A solution used in the cooling system to lower the freezing point below that of water.

Antiknock Gasoline.—A term for a gasoline with lead added to eliminate or reduce the noise of explosion. See also *Ethyl Gasoline; High-Octane Gasoline; Octane Number or Rating.*

Automatic Choke.—A temperature-controlled carburetor choke that automatically closes the choke valve for cold starting and opens it when the engine warms up.

Automatic Seat Adjuster.—An electrical or combination hydraulic and electrical arrangement for push-button adjustment of seat position.

Automatic Spark Advance.—A mechanism in the distributor employing centrifugal weights, vacuum control, or both, to control ignition timing as engine speed and load vary.

Automatic Transmission.—A device that automatically changes gear ratios between the engine and rear wheels without manual assist. It usually consists of a hydraulic torque converter or fluid coupling, plus servo-operated gear changes.

Axle.—A shaft upon which a wheel revolves.

Axle Housing.—The housing around the final-drive gears and differential on a rear-wheel-drive automobile.

Axle Shaft.—A shaft within an axle assembly for driving the wheels.

Ball Bearings.—Assemblies consisting of spheres of hardened steel rotating in a circular raceway enclosed in a case or housing for transferring the load.

Ball-Joint Suspension.—A method of supporting and locating the front wheels in which the hinge points are fitted with low-friction ball pivots.

Battery.—A 6- or 12-volt electrochemical storage unit for electricity received from the generator. It supplies power to operate various devices and accessories. It consists of 3 or 6 two-volt cells, each connected in series and containing a number of positive and negative plates, separators, and an electrolyte.

Battery Cables.—Heavy electric cables for grounding a battery to the vehicle frame and connecting the line side to the starting or cranking motor.

Battery Ignition.—An ignition system in which a low-voltage battery supplies electricity for the primary winding of an induction coil, whose secondary winding delivers the high voltage required for firing the spark plugs.

Bearing.—A mechanical part in or on which another turns.

Bevel Gear.—A gear designed to transmit power at an angle to its shaft.

Body.—The portion of the car enclosure that houses driver, passengers, and luggage.

Bore.—The diameter of the cylinder.

Bottom Dead Center.—The position of a piston at the extreme lower end of its travel.

Brake.—A device in the wheel assembly to halt motion. Brakes may be hydraulic or mechanical, disk or drum, direct-acting or power. See also *Power Brakes*.

Brake Drums.—Drums, mounted on the wheels, against which the brake shoes press to stop rotation.

Brake Fluid.—The fluid used in hydraulically powered brakes.

Brake Lining.—Replaceable friction material mounted on a brake shoe and bearing directly on the brake drum to stop rotation.

Breaker Arm.—A cam-actuated arm in the distributor that opens and closes the breaker points.

Breaker Plate.—The metal plate on which the distributor breaker points are mounted.

Breaker Points.—A pair of tungsten contacts, one fixed and one attached to a movable arm, mounted inside the distributor. They provide the necessary timed interruptions in the flow of primary current through the ignition coil.

Bumpers.—Steel members extending across the width of a car, front and rear, about 15 inches (38 cm) above the ground, approximately ⅛ inch (0.3 cm) thick, and usually chromium plated. They protect the car's grille, sheet metal, and lighting fixtures in minor collisions.

Bushing.—A cylindrical metal sleeve used as a bearing.

Cam.—A device for changing rotary motion to straight-line motion. In the engine the rotation of the cams opens and closes the valves.

Camber.—The vertical inclination, measured in degrees, by which a wheel is tilted sideways in or out.

Camshaft.—A shaft equipped with cams for lifting the intake and exhaust valves from their seats.

Carbon.—A by-product of combustion in the cylinders. Some of it is blown out through the exhaust, but some is deposited on spark plugs or other engine parts.

Carburetor.—A device for delivering gasoline and air, at proper ratio for every speed, to the cylinders.

Caster.—The amount, in degrees, by which the vertical axes of the ball-joint suspension steering knuckles (or, in older cars and some trucks, the kingpins) are tilted forward or backward.

Chassis.—The assembled parts of a car minus the body.

Choke.—A valve in the carburetor that provides a rich mixture to the engine for cold starting.

Chrome.—Bright or chromium-finished fittings, such as the radiator grille or bumpers. Some bearing surfaces in the engine also are chromium plated for high resistance to wear.

Classic.—An automobile of the "classic" age, chiefly the powerful, sleek, well-designed, and expensive cars of the 1920's.

Clutch.—A coupling by which rotating parts, such as the engine and transmission, may be engaged or disengaged; also the pedal operating the clutch.

Cold Plug.—A spark plug having a relatively short range of heat travel from the center electrode to the cylinder-head coolant.

Combustion Chamber.—The space inside the cylinder head and above the piston at top dead center in which combustion takes place.

Compression Pressure.—The pressure obtained in a cylinder on the compression stroke of the piston.

Compression Ratio.—The ratio of the volume in the cylinder above the piston when the piston is at the

bottom of its stroke to the volume when the piston is at the top of its stroke. In automobile engines this varies from 8.0:1 to 13.5:1.

Condenser.—An electrical device connected across the contact points in the distributor to prevent arcing.

Connecting Rod.—The rod connecting a piston with the crankshaft.

Convertible.—A body type designed for conversion from an open to a closed car and vice versa.

Cooling System.—A system for cooling the engine. In the water-cooled engine this includes the water jackets around the cylinders, radiator, water pump, fan, thermostat, and hose connections. In the air-cooled engine it includes the fan, pulleys, and cylinder fins.

Coupé.—A closed 2-door body having a bench seat to accommodate 2 or 3 persons, or sometimes 2 individual bucket seats. There also may be a rudimentary rear seat.

Crankcase.—The housing, usually cast as an integral part of the cylinder block, that carries the engine crankshaft and main bearings.

Crankcase Ventilation.—The removal of gases from the crankcase. In newer cars these gases are led back to the engine via the intake manifold and burned in the combustion chambers.

Crankpin.—A pin of the crankshaft on which a connecting rod operates.

Crankshaft.—The main shaft of the engine. It converts the reciprocating motion of the pistons to the rotary motion required to turn the drive shaft.

Cutout Relay.—An automatic switch that prevents battery current from flowing back through the generator when the generator voltage drops below that of the battery.

Cylinder.—The bore in the cylinder block in which a piston operates.

Cylinder Block.—Casting in which cylinders are bored.

Cylinder Head.—The casting that seals the cylinders at the top and contains the combustion chamber.

Dash.—The instrument panel.

Dead Center.—See *Bottom Dead Center; Top Dead Center.*

Defroster.—A part of the heating system that blows hot air on the windshield to melt ice and frost.

Diesel.—An internal combustion engine of the compression-ignition type used in some buses or trucks.

Differential.—A system of gears to transfer power from the engine to the axle shafts in such a way as to compensate the movement of the driving wheels when the car is on a curve.

Displacement.—The volume in cubic inches or cubic centimeters displaced by the piston in a single stroke. It may refer to a single cylinder or to all cylinders of a multicylinder engine.

Distributor.—A part of the ignition system that directs the high voltage from the ignition coil to the spark plugs.

Drive Shaft.—The main shaft connecting the transmission with the rear axle.

Electrolyte.—A sulfuric-acid solution for batteries.

Engine.—The power-producing unit in a motor vehicle: an internal combustion engine of either spark (gasoline) or compression-ignition (diesel) type. See also separate article INTERNAL COMBUSTION ENGINE.

Ethyl Gasoline.—A gasoline to which tetraethyl lead has been added to inhibit explosive combustion.

Exhaust Cam.—A cam that lifts an exhaust valve from its seat.

Exhaust Manifold.—A casting that collects the spent gases from the combustion chambers of the cylinders and delivers them to the exhaust pipe.

Exhaust Pipe.—The tube that carries the exhaust gases from the exhaust manifold to the muffler.

Exhaust Valve.—A valve that permits the discharge of spent gases from the combustion chamber.

Fan Belt.—A belt by which the fan, and in some cars other devices, are driven from the crankshaft.

Fire Wall.—A protective sheet-metal partition between the engine and passenger compartments.

Flywheel.—A heavy metal disk at the rear end of the crankshaft. Its inertia was used to smooth out speed fluctuations in the revolving crankshaft. In today's engines it serves mainly to carry a ring gear for engine starting.

Four-Barrel Carburetor.—A carburetor having four venturis, or throats, for the admission of the fuel-air mixture.

Four-Stroke Cycle, or Four-Cycle Engine.—The type of engine most commonly used in automobiles. The four strokes of the piston are intake, compression, power (expansion), and exhaust.

Front-Wheel Drive.—A motor-vehicle design in which the front axle is the driving axle. See also *Rear-Wheel Drive.*

Fuel Gauge.—An instrument for indicating the amount of gasoline in the tank.

Fuel-Injection Pump.—A mechanism to build up pressure for injecting fuel into the engine cylinder.

Fuel Line.—The tubular line through which fuel passes from the tank to the carburetor.

Fuel Pump.—A mechanically or electrically powered device for supplying fuel to the engine.

Fuel Tank.—A tank or compartment in a motor vehicle carrying fuel for use in its engine.

Gasket.—A packing for sealing the faces of a joint, as between the block and the cylinder head.

Gear Ratio.—The ratio of speeds obtained from a series of shafts and gears in a unit.

Gearbox.—The transmission. See *Transmission*.

Gearshift.—A mechanism by which the transmission gears are engaged or disengaged.

Generator.—A machine, often driven by the fan belt, for producing low-voltage current for the operation of a vehicle, including charging the battery.

Generator Regulator.—A device in the generator-battery circuit to regulate or control the rate of charge; also called *voltage regulator*.

Governor.—A control over engine speed, usually by means of an extra throttle valve in the carburetor.

Hardtop.—A coupé or sedan body type having a metal top that cannot be removed, but without a pillar between the side windows above the body belt line.

Headlight.—One of the lights at the front of a motor vehicle, consisting of a filament, reflector, and lens; also called a *head lamp*.

Helical Gear.—A gear having spiral teeth.

High-Compression Engine.—An engine with a high compression ratio requiring high-octane gasoline.

High Gear.—A gearshift position providing direct drive from the crankshaft to the differential and hence producing the highest road speed. It usually is equivalent to *third speed*.

High-Octane Gasoline.—A gasoline having a high octane rating for use in high-compression engines to prevent ping, or knock. See also *Octane Number or Rating*.

Hood.—The hinged cover for the engine compartment.

Horn.—An audible warning device, operated electrically.

Horsepower.—A unit measuring the ability of an engine to do work (1 hp = 550 foot-pounds per second).

Hot Plug.—A spark plug having a relatively long range of heat travel from the center electrode to the cylinder-head coolant.

Hot Rod.—A car souped up for rapid acceleration or sustained fast speed. See also *Souped Up*.

Hydraulic Drive.—A type of automatic transmission using oil in the coupling. See also *Automatic Transmission* and separate article HYDRAULIC DRIVE.

Hydraulic Valve Lifter.—An oil-operated device that maintains zero clearance in the valve train and, therefore, quiet valve operation.

Hydrometer.—A device for measuring battery charge by determining the specific gravity of the electrolyte.

Idle.—The running speed of an engine, without load and with the throttle closed.

Ignition Coil.—A set of windings in an ignition system that increases the voltage delivered from the battery to the spark plugs through the distributor.

Ignition Primary Circuit.—The low-voltage circuit, including the starter switch, ammeter, ignition switch, ignition coil, and spark plugs.

Ignition Secondary Circuit.—The high-voltage circuit, consisting of the coil, high-tension wires, rotor, distributor cap, and spark plugs.

Ignition Switch.—An electrical switch in the instrument panel, operated by a key that turns the ignition on and off.

Independent Wheel Suspension.—Wheels so mounted that they can deflect independently on road bumps. Each wheel has an individual spring and axle.

Instrument Panel.—The panel in the driver's compartment on which switches and instruments are mounted.

Insulator.—A material, such as the porcelain jacket of a spark plug, that prevents leakage of electric current.

Intake Cam.—A cam that lifts an intake valve from its seat.

Intake Manifold.—A casting that permits the distribution of a combustible mixture of fuel and air from the carburetor to the cylinders.

Intake Valve.—The valve that opens and closes the cylinder inlet.

Jack.—A device for lifting a vehicle to permit changing of a tire.

Jeep.—A small vehicle, originally designed for the United States Army, conforming to military requirements of road clearance, simplicity, and weight.

Journal.—The part of a shaft that rotates inside a bearing.

Kingpin.—A pin, also called a *pivot pin*, mounted on the front axle or spring suspension, on which the steering knuckle pivots.

Knock.—Detonation in the combustion chamber; also, the metallic sound caused by excessive clearance between running engine parts; also called *ping*.

Knock-off (or Knock-on) Spinner.—A spinner that holds the wheel on the axle. It is unscrewed by striking with a hammer or mallet, allowing fast wheel change.

Leaf Springs.—Lengths of flat spring steel assembled in stacks or singly between the frame and axles.

L-Head Engine.—An automotive engine having the valves mounted in the cylinder block at the side of the combustion chambers.

Lubricant.—A substance that reduces friction and heat in rubbing surfaces, such as oil or grease.

Lubricating System.—The parts that provide a flow of lubricating oil under pressure to all engine friction surfaces.

Lubrication Chart.—A schematic diagram of the chassis and engine, indicating at what points, how often, and with which lubricant the vehicle is to be lubricated.

Main Bearings.—The bearings in which the crankshaft rotates.

Manifold.—See *Exhaust Manifold; Intake Manifold*.

Muffler.—A device in the exhaust pipe consisting of a chamber usually equipped with baffle plates to deaden the sound of engine explosions.

Neon-Light Ignition Timing.—A method of setting or correcting spark timing by which spark-plug voltage is used to flash a neon light stroboscopically on a rotating timing mark.

Octane Number or Rating.—A measure of the antiknock qualities of a gasoline. Motor-vehicle gasolines have an antiknock number from 90 to over 100. The higher the octane value, the less fuel knock.

Odometer.—See *Speedometer*.

Oil.—A straight or compounded mineral oil for lubricating a motor vehicle.

Oil Consumption.—The amount of oil, expressed in miles per quart, used by an automotive engine.

Oil Control Rings.—Piston rings designed to limit the amount of oil passing the piston into the combustion chamber.

Oil Filter.—An auxiliary device mounted on an engine to remove impurities from the crankcase oil; also called an *oil cleaner*.

Oil Pan.—The lower part of the crankcase, in which oil is carried.

Oil Pump.—A pump for circulating oil. The engine oil pump circulates oil from a sump supply to the many bearings inside the engine.

Oil Strainer.—A wire-mesh sieve protecting the oil-pump intake.

Overdrive.—A semiautomatic two-speed planetary transmission, at the rear of a conventional transmission, that permits the engine to run more slowly than it would in direct drive for a comparable road speed.

Overhead-Valve Engine.—An engine having the valves mounted above the cylinders in the cylinder head.

Parking Lights.—Small front lights used at night to warn that a car is parked.

Performance.—The ability of a car to accelerate, attain high speeds, climb hills, and respond readily to the accelerator pedal.

Ping.—See *Knock*.

Pinion Gear.—The small gear driving the differential ring gear.

Piston.—A cylindrical device, closed at one end, that slides up and down in the cylinder.

Piston Pin.—See *Wrist Pin*.

Piston Ring.—A ring of roughly rectangular cross section held in a groove in the piston skirt to seal the combustion chamber gases.

Pitman Arm.—A lever on the cross shaft of the steering gear through which the steering arm is operated.

Planetary Gears.—Gears that rotate around a central, or "sun," gear in a manner similar to the solar planetary system. Planetary gears are used in many automatic transmissions.

Poppet Valve.—The device used for opening and closing the intake and exhaust passages to the combustion chamber in most automobile engines. It is made up of a cylindrical stem, which acts as a guide, and a circular head, which is the valve.

Power Brakes.—A vacuum-assist unit that operates in conjunction with the hydraulic brake system.

Power Plant.—The engine.

Power Steering.—A hydraulic-power mechanism to assist manual operation in order to reduce the turning effort at the steering wheel.

Propeller Shaft.—The drive shaft transmitting power between the transmission and differential.

Quarter Panel.—Rear fender area on modern cars.

Radiator.—An assembly of tubes, fins, and storage tanks for cooling water.

Rally (or Rallye).—A sports-car precision-driving contest in which the contestants must follow a prescribed route, keeping as close as possible to a prescribed speed for each leg of the trip.

Rear Axle.—Commonly, the driving axle of a motor vehicle.

Rear-Axle Coil-Spring Suspension.—A means of supporting the frame of a motor vehicle above the rear axle by means of coiled springs.

Rear-Wheel Drive.—The motor vehicle design in which the rear axle is the driving axle. It is customary on most American-made passenger cars, but some European makes use front-wheel drive.

Recap.—The method by which new treads are vulcanized on a worn tire casing; also a tire that has been treated in this fashion.

Recharge.—A charge given to a run-down or discharged battery in order to restore it to standard.

Regroove.—A tire in the worn tread of which new antiskid grooves have been cut.

Retread.—The method by which both new treads and new sidewalls are vulcanized on a worn tire casing; also a tire that has been treated in this fashion.

Ride Control.—The ability of shock absorbers, in connection with the spring suspension, to provide comfortable riding.

Rim.—The part of a wheel on which a tire is mounted.

Ring Gear.—A type of gear used in the differential and flywheel gear trains. The *differential ring gear* receives power from the pinion gear. The *flywheel ring gear,* on the periphery of the flywheel, engages the drive gear of the starter.

Road Clearance.—The minimum clearance between the road and the underbody of the automobile.

Rocker Panel.—The part of a car's body between the front and rear wheels and under the door or doors.

Roller Bearing.—An antifriction bearing in which cylindrical or conical rollers are held in a fixed cage.

Rotation.—A system of changing tires periodically, from wheel to wheel and including the spare, in order to distribute tire wear evenly.

Rotor.—Commonly, the plastic-insulated distributing arm under the distributor cap.

Running Board.—A step running all or partly along the side of a vehicle to facilitate the entrance and exit of driver and passengers. It no longer is placed on most cars.

Sealed Beam.—A type of headlight in which the reflector, bulb, and lens are a factory-sealed unit.

Sealed Bearings.—Bearings designed to operate throughout their life with no lubrication other than that provided at the time of manufacture.

Sealing Compound.—A pitchlike material used to seal the tops of storage-battery cells.

Sedan.—A closed 2- or 4-door body seating 4 or more passengers, including the driver. It provides more space between the front and rear seats than the coupé. See also *Hardtop.*

Shimmy.—Oscillation of the front wheels.

Shock Absorber.—A mechanism designed to control or limit spring action in order to prevent pitching.

Short Circuit.—A defect that shunts the electric current to ground without completing the desired circuit.

Slip Joint.—A splined (keyed) joint used to allow a shaft to become longer or shorter without causing misalignment of parts.

Souped Up.—The condition of an engine that, by fuel injection, supercharging, or other means, has been made to accelerate faster and attain higher speeds than it originally was designed to do.

Spare.—An extra tire carried for emergency.

Spark Advance.—The interval, in degrees of crankshaft travel, by which firing in the combustion chamber precedes the instant at which the piston reaches top dead center.

Spark Coil.—The electrical coil that transforms the low voltage from the battery to the high voltage required to make the current jump the spark-plug gap.

Spark Plug.—A threaded plug screwed into the combustion-chamber wall to supply the electric spark to ignite the air-fuel mixture.

Specific Gravity.—The ratio of the weight of battery electrolyte (acid) to the standard for distilled water.

Speedometer.—An instrument, usualy driven from the transmission, that indicates road speed. It usually includes an *odometer* to register the distance traveled.

Sports Car.—A streamlined, sometimes rakish, 2- or 4-seater, used more for fun than for transportation.

Spring.—An elastic device that recovers its original shape after being distorted. Many springs are used in an automobile, notably the suspension springs, valve springs, and clutch springs. The suspension springs support the frame and body from the axles. Valve springs return the valves to the closed position. Clutch springs hold the friction plates of a clutch in engagement.

Spring Shackles.—Devices for securing the ends of leaf springs to the frame.

Spring Suspension.—The manner in which the frame is supported by the springs.

Stabilizer Bar.—A steel bar designed to equalize spring compression in a pair of springs when they are under stress on uneven roads or in high-speed cornering.

Starting Motor.—An electric motor that cranks the engine for starting.

Starting Switch.—A switch that energizes the starting motor.

Station Wagon.—A closed-body vehicle suitable for carrying passengers and light freight, in which the freight is carried in the passenger enclosure instead of in a closed trunk; also known as a *suburban wagon* or *estate wagon.*

Steering Gear. The mechanism comprising the steering wheel, a steering column, gearbox, and the Pitman arm. It transmits motion to the drag link in order to turn the front wheels. The term also refers to the gearbox alone.

Steering Knuckle.—A fitting that supports a front wheel, pivoting on either a kingpin or ball joints and receiving steering effort from the steering arm that is connected to the Pitman arm.

Stock Car.—A racing car having a stock passenger-car body.

Streamlining.—The features of body design that reduce air resistance at high speed.

Stroke.—The travel of the pistons.

Supercharger.—An air compressor for forcing into each cylinder a greater charge of air than could be obtained by normal piston suction; also called *blower.*

Suspension.—See *Spring Suspension.*

Synchromesh Transmission.—A manually operated transmission with gears and synchronizing cones so designed that their speeds synchronize automatically prior to engagement in order to prevent gear clashing.

Synchronizer.—Any device for synchronizing the speed or timing of two operations, such as engaging gears.

Tappet.—A rod of adjustable length in a valve train.

Thermostat.—A thermal device controlling engine temperature by regulating the amount of water passing through the radiator.

Throttle.—A mechanism in the carburetor for controlling the amount of charge to the cylinders.

Throttle Linkage.—A series of controls actuating the throttle valve in the carburetor.

Timing.—The regulation of the intervals between series of events in the engine. *Valve timing* is the opening and closing of intake and exhaust valves in relation to piston travel and is controlled by the camshaft. *Ignition timing* is the firing of the charge at the proper point in piston travel and is controlled by adjustment of the distributor head.

Timing Gears.—The gears that drive the camshaft from the crankshaft.

Tire.—The pneumatic rubber casing around the rim of a wheel. Some tires have an *inner tube* to hold air, but most modern tires are *tubeless,* the outer casing being sealed so that it retains air under pressure.

Toe-in.—The amount, measured in inches, by which the front wheels are closer together in front than in back. *Toe-out* is the reverse of this.

Top Dead Center.—The position of a piston at the extreme upper end of its travel.

Torque.—The force delivered by the engine to the drive wheels, producing their rotation.

Torque Tube Drive.—A drive line in which the drive shaft is enclosed in a tube that prevents the rear-axle housing from rotating and transmits engine or braking thrusts to the frame.

Tractor.—A self-propelled unit for drawing another vehicle or such wheeled objects as farm implements; or, as a *truck tractor,* for hauling a cargo trailer or semi-trailer.

Trailer.—In private motoring, living quarters drawn by a passenger car, or a drawn 2-wheel unit for hauling a boat or light freight; in commercial usage, an over-the-road cargo carrier (often very large) drawn by a truck tractor.

Transmission.—A gearbox between the clutch and drive line for varying road speed and torque (rotary power).

Transverse Spring Mounting.—Springs mounted crosswise on a vehicle.

Tread.—The distance between right and left wheels; also, the antiskid grooves in that part of a tire casing that makes contact with the roadway.

Truck.—A motor vehicle for carrying cargo. See separate article Truck Transportation.

Tune-up.—An adjustment, usually of ignition and carburetion, to restore an engine to satisfactory performance.

Turn Signal.—A visual warning device, usually front and rear lamps, to signal in advance the direction of a turn; also called *directional.*

Universal Joint.—A joint in the drive shaft that takes care of the differences in the angle of the shaft as the axle moves up and down.

Upholstery.—The covering of the seats, including the padding.

Vacuum Brake.—A brake-actuating system in which vacuum or low pressure from the intake manifold operates the brakes.

Valve.—Any device for closing off or modifying the flow of gases or liquids through a pipe or orifice.

Valve Lash.—Clearance in a valve train.

Valve Lifter.—A push rod, riding on a cam of the camshaft, that raises a valve from its seat.

Valve Noise.—A clicking noise made by valves when they are not seating properly.

Valve Rocker Arm.—A type of walking beam used in overhead-valve engines to raise a valve from its seat. It is actuated by a push rod.

Valve Seat.—The metal face against which a poppet valve closes.

Valve Spring.—The coiled spring that holds a poppet valve closed.

Vaporization.—The act of converting a substance, such as gasoline, from a liquid to a gaseous state.

Vention Tube.—A tube having an internal circumferential constriction, or throat, for the purpose of increasing the speed of the gas flow at the point of constriction.

Voltage Regulator.—See *Generator Regulator*.

V-Type Engine.—An engine equipped with two banks of cylinders mounted in a V on one crankcase.

Vulcanizing.—The curing of raw rubber by means of heat and chemical action, used in the manufacture and repair of tires.

Water Jacket.—Integral passageways in the cylinder block and head through which the engine coolant is circulated.

Water Pump.—A pump that circulates water or some other coolant through the engine-cooling system.

Wheel.—One of the circular frames on which a vehicle rides or a spare tire is carried; often also the steering wheel.

Wheel Alignment.—The proper adjustment of all interrelated parts that affect steering.

Wheelbase.—The distance lengthwise between the centers of the front and rear wheels.

Windshield.—A sheet of shatterproof glass that extends across the front of the passenger compartment, providing good visibility and protection from the weather.

Windshield Wiper.—A device that clears the windshield of rain or snow by sweeping a rubber blade across the surface of the glass. The driving motor may be electric, vacuum, or hydraulic.

Wiring System.—The electrical wiring and components that make up the low- and high-tension circuitry required for the operation of a motor vehicle and its accessories.

Worm and Gear.—A form of gear set in which the worm shaft is at right angles to, and in another plane from, the gear shaft.

Wristpin.—The pin connecting the piston to the connecting rod, also called a *piston pin*.

FRANK DORR
Associate Editor of "Popular Science Monthly"
RALPH A. RICHARDSON

Bibliography

Allen, Frederick Lewis, *The Big Change* (New York 1952).

American Society of Tool and Manufacturing Engineers, *Tool Engineers' Handbook*, ed. by Frank W. Wilson, 2d ed. (New York 1959).

Anderson, Rudolph E., *The Story of the American Automobile* (Washington 1950).

Automobile Manufacturers Association, Detroit, *Automobile Facts and Figures* (annually); *Automobiles of America* (1962); *Motor Truck Facts* (annually).

Bailey, Thomas A., *The American Pageant*, 2d ed. (Boston 1961).

Barker, Ronald, *Automobiles and Automobiling* (New York 1965).

Chandler, Alfred Dupont, Jr., ed., *Giant Enterprise: Ford, General Motors, and the Automobile Industry* (New York 1964).

Crouse, William H., *Automotive Mechanics*, 4th ed. (New York 1960).

Donovan, Frank R., *Wheels for a Nation* (New York 1965).

Edwards, Charles E., *Dynamics of the United States Automobile Industry* (Columbia, S.C., 1965).

Greenleaf, William, *Monopoly on Wheels: Henry Ford and the Selden Automobile Patent* (Detroit 1961).

Miller, Eugene W., *A Geography of Manufacturing* (Englewood Cliffs, N.J., 1962).

Motor Service Magazine, *Automotive Encyclopedia* (Chicago, annually).

Nash, Frederick C., *Automotive Fundamentals* (New York 1966).

Nevins, Allan, and Hill, Frank Ernest, *Ford*, 3 vols. (New York 1954, 1957, 1963).

Oliver, Smith H., *Automobiles and Motorcycles in the United States National Museum*, U.S. National Museum Bulletin No. 213 (Washington 1957).

Rae, John Bell, *American Automobile: A Brief History* (Chicago 1965).

Society of Automotive Engineers, New York· *S.A.E. Handbook* (annually); *S.A.E. Journal* (monthly).

Stein, Ralph, *Treasury of the Automobile* (New York 1961).

AUTOMOBILE INSURANCE. See LIABILITY AND PROPERTY INSURANCE.

AUTOMOBILE RACING, ôt-ə-mō-bēl' rā'sing, includes local, national, and international competitions for individual and team speed and performance records in a variety of makes and models of cars. Racing events and championship tests include closed-circuit races—such as the Grand Prix and the Indianapolis 500-mile race—and sports car competitions, stock car races, rallying, drag racing, and measured-mile testing. Vehicles may be racing, sports, or stock cars.

INTERNATIONAL RACING

International racing began when arguments arose as to which manufacturer was making the most durable and fastest automobile. This led to the 732-mile race that was run in France in 1895, from Paris to Bordeaux and return. This race, one of the first in Europe, was won by a French Panhard, at an average speed of 15 mph.

Races in Europe were infrequent until 1900, when James Gordon Bennett, owner of the New York *Herald*, put up a trophy for a series of races, stipulating that competing cars had to be entirely the products of the country they represented. With this start, the contest for international motor supremacy was under way.

Grand Prix Racing. The Gordon Bennett races were run until 1906, when the Automobile-Club de France boycotted the event and ran its own race, called the Grand Prix. The cars in this contest took two days to complete 12 laps on a 64-mile course near Le Mans. Grand Prix racing grew rapidly until halted by World War I. It was resumed in 1921, and in September of that year the first Italian Grand Prix was held.

Grand Prix racing, supported by Italian and German automobile manufacturers, entered a new era in the 1930's, with the Alfa-Romeos, Maseratis, Mercedes-Benzes, and Auto-Unions providing superb competition. It was during this period that the Italian Tazio Nuvolari (1892–1953), the greatest race driver in history, won 64 major events in a 29-year racing career.

In 1950 the world drivers' championship for Formula I or "pure" racing machines was established by the Fédération Internationale de l'Automobile (FIA). A simple point system which took into account the driver's place of finish in the eight to ten Grand Prix events was adopted. Since then the Grand Prix circuit has included races in Monaco (the Monte Carlo), Belgium, Holland, France, England, Germany, Italy, Mexico, South Africa, and the United States.

WORLD CHAMPION DRIVERS

Year	Driver	Country	Car
1950	Giuseppe Farina	Italy	Alfa-Romeo
1951	Juan Fangio	Argentina	Alfa-Romeo
1952	Alberto Ascari	Italy	Ferrari
1953	Alberto Ascari	Italy	Ferrari
1954	Juan Fangio	Argentina	Maserati/Mercedes
1955	Juan Fangio	Argentina	Mercedes-Benz
1956	Juan Fangio	Argentina	Ferrari
1957	Juan Fangio	Argentina	Maserati
1958	Mike Hawthorne	England	Ferrari
1959	Jack Brabham	Australia	Cooper-Climax
1960	Jack Brabham	Australia	Cooper-Climax
1961	Phil Hill	United States	Ferrari
1962	Graham Hill	England	BRM
1963	Jim Clark	Scotland	Lotus-Climax
1964	John Surtees	England	Ferrari
1965	Jim Clark	Scotland	Lotus-Climax
1966	Jack Brabham	Australia	Brabham-Repco
1967	Denis Hulme	New Zealand	Brabham-Repco
1968	Graham Hill	England	Lotus-Ford
1969	Jackie Stewart	Scotland	Matra-Ford
1970	Jochen Rindt	Austria	Lotus-Ford
1971	Jackie Stewart	Scotland	Tyrrell-Ford
1972	Jackie Stewart	Scotland	Tyrrell-Ford

INDIANAPOLIS 500, held each Memorial Day at Speedway, Ind., is the best attended sporting event in the world.

In addition to the driving championship, there is a manufacturer's trophy. Competition for this trophy has not been dominated by any one factory because of frequent rules revisions designed to avoid such dominance.

Sports Car Competition. International sports car racing is also under FIA control. Generally, sports car classification is based either on the number of cars of a certain model in production or on engine displacement.

Two major championships are conducted for sports cars. The World's Constructors' Championship includes the 24-hour races at Daytona Beach, Fla., and Le Mans, France; a 12-hour race at Sebring, Fla.; a 1,000 kilometer race at the Nürburgring, Germany, and Monza, Italy; and the Targa Florio, a road race in Sicily. The other championship is the Challenge Mondial. This is an independent award based on the finishing order in all the above races except Daytona Beach.

International Rallying. Rallying is a very specialized form of racing. Under FIA rules rallying is a lengthy, arduous speed competition for production models. The object is to stay on a prescribed cross-country course and reach certain checkpoints, which may or may not be known to the drivers, within a prescribed time. Points are subtracted if a competitor arrives at the checkpoint either before or after his assigned time. The most significant international rallies are the Monte Carlo; the Shell 4,000 and the Winter Rally, both held in Canada; and the East African Safari.

RACING IN THE UNITED STATES

The first important automobile race in the United States was spurred by the success of the Paris-Bordeaux international run. It was held in Chicago on Nov. 28, 1895, under the auspices of the Chicago *Times Herald* and the object was to test both the speed and the stamina of American-made cars. J. Frank Duryea, one of America's leading auto manufacturing pioneers, won in a Duryea car at a speed of 7½ mph.

Automobile racing came of age with the Van-

derbilt Cup races, initiated by the millionaire William K. Vanderbilt in 1904. Races were run fairly regularly from 1904 through 1916 on road courses from Long Island, N.Y., to Savannah, Ga. Many accidents to cars and spectators accompanied the races, often won by a foreign car, and gradually they lost their appeal.

Closed-Circuit Speedway Racing. On Aug. 19, 1909, a group of automobile manufacturers headed by Carl G. Fisher opened a dirt track in Indianapolis, Ind. Their object was to test the endurance of the products of the infant automotive industry. The stock-car testing course soon was transformed into a speedway for racing cars. Its first official race, called the Indianapolis 500, was run on Memorial Day in 1911 and, with the exception of the war years, has been held on this day ever since.

The inaugural 500 was won by Ray Harroun, who drove a Marmon Wasp to an average speed of 74.59 miles per hour. Since then, racing technology has enabled speeds to increase almost yearly.

GRAND PRIX contestants at Le Mans, France, dash across the track to their cars at the start of the race.

WINNERS OF THE INDIANAPOLIS 500-MILE RACE

Year	Driver	Engine	Cylinder	Speed
1911	Ray Harroun	Marmon Wasp	6	74.59
1912	Joe Dawson	National	4	78.72
1913	Jules Goux	Peugeot	4	75.933
1914	Rene Thomas	Delage	4	82.47
1915	Ralph DePalma	Mercedes	4	89.84
1916	Dario Resta	Peugeot	4	84.00[2]
1919	Howard Wilcox	Peugeot	4	88.05
1920	Gaston Chevrolet	Monroe	4	88.62
1921	Tommy Milton	Frontenac	4	89.62
1922	Jimmy Murphy	Miller	8	94.48
1923	Tommy Milton	Miller	8	90.95
1924	L. L. Corum/Joe Boyer	Duesenberg	8	98.23
1925	Peter DePaolo	Duesenberg	8	101.13
1926	Frank Lockhart	Miller	8	95.904[3]
1927	George Souders	Duesenberg	8	97.545
1928	Louis Meyer	Miller	8	99.482
1929	Ray Keech	Miller	8	97.585
1930	Billy Arnold	Miller	8	100.448
1931	Louis Schneider	Miller	8	96.629
1932	Fred Frame	Miller	8	104.144
1933	Louis Meyer	Miller	8	104.162
1934	William Cummings	Offenhauser	4	104.863
1935	Kelly Petillo	Offenhauser	4	106.240
1936	Louis Meyer	Offenhauser	4	109.069
1937	Wilbur Shaw	Offenhauser	4	113.580
1938	Floyd Roberts	Offenhauser	4	117.200
1939	Wilbur Shaw	Maserati	8	115.035
1940	Wilbur Shaw	Maserati	8	114.277
1941	F. Davis/M. Rose	Offenhauser	4	115.117
1946	George Robson	Thorne/Sparks	6	114.820
1947	Mauri Rose	Offenhauser	4	116.338
1948	Mauri Rose	Offenhauser	4	119.814
1949	Bill Holland	Offenhauser	4	121.327
1950	Johnnie Parsons	Offenhauser	4	124.002[4]
1951	Lee Wallard	Offenhauser	4	126.244
1952	Troy Ruttman	Offenhauser	4	128.922
1953	Bill Vukovich	Offenhauser	4	128.740
1954	Bill Vukovich	Offenhauser	4	130.840
1955	Bob Sweikert	Offenhauser	4	128.209
1956	Pat Flaherty	Offenhauser	4	128.490
1957	Sam Hanks	Offenhauser	4	135.601
1958	Jim Bryan	Offenhauser	4	133.791
1959	Rodger Ward	Offenhauser	4	135.857
1960	Jim Rathmann	Offenhauser	4	138.767
1961	A. J. Foyt	Offenhauser	4	139.130
1962	Rodger Ward	Offenhauser	4	140.292
1963	Parnelli Jones	Offenhauser	4	143.137
1964	A. J. Foyt	Offenhauser	4	147.350
1965	Jimmy Clark	Ford	8	150.686
1966	Graham Hill	Ford	8	144.317
1967	A. J. Foyt	Ford	8	151.207
1968	Bobby Unser	Offenhauser	4	152.882
1969	Mario Andretti	Hawk-Ford	8	156.867
1970	Al Unser	Colt-Ford	8	155.749
1971	Al Unser	Colt-Ford	8	157.735
1972	Mark Donohue	Offenhauser	4	163.465
1973	Gordon Johncock	Offenhauser	4	159.014

[1] Average mph. For kilometers per hour, multiply mph by 1.61.
[2] 300 mi.   [3] 400 mi.   [4] 345 mi.

RAY HARROUN won the first "500" in a Marmon Wasp.

posed of earlier-model cars; nearly any engine modification is allowed for the modifieds, but the sportsmen's are restricted to one carburetor. Many of the Grand National Drivers have come from these lower classes.

In addition to NASCAR, USAC and several other independent associations conduct stock car races. More than 200 large tracks and several hundred small tracks throughout the United States are devoted to this popular form of racing.

Sports Car Racing. The Sport's Car Club of America (SCCA), established in Westport, Conn., in 1945, controls sports car racing. The best-known class is called informally "racing sports car," and cars are generally equipped with the American V-8 engine.

The SCCA holds two major championship series: (1) the United States Road Racing Championship, which consists of about 10 races over a six-month period in the spring and summer, and (2) the Canadian-American Challenge Cup, made up of a series of five races run in the fall.

Drag Racing. The National Hot Rod Association (NHRA), founded in 1951 at Los Angeles, Calif., sponsors drag racing. In this form of competition the object is to cover a prescribed straightaway distance, usually of one-quarter

The United States Auto Club (USAC), a member of the Fédération Internationale de l'Automobile, governs the Indianapolis 500. The USAC is an outgrowth of the Contest Board of the American Automobile Association (the board disbanded in 1955) and has its headquarters in Indianapolis. Its National Championship is determined on a point basis from driver placement in the 500; in races at Phoenix, Trenton (N.J.), Langhorne (Pa.), Milwaukee, and Atlanta; and in other select races at smaller tracks.

Stock Car Racing. The intense interest in stock car (production model) racing after World War II resulted in the founding of the National Association for Stock Car Auto Racing (NASCAR) in 1947 at Daytona Beach. By the mid-1960's, NASCAR was the world's largest professional organization devoted solely to automobile racing. Its major division, the Grand National, conducts races at approximately 30 tracks, including speedways at Daytona Beach; Atlanta; Charlotte and Rockingham, N.C.; and Darlington, S.C. Cars are three years old or less, resemble showroom models, and use stock production engines.

NASCAR's two other main divisions are the *modified* and *sportsmen's* classes. Both are com-

STOCK CAR races at the high-banked oval at Daytona Beach, Fla., draw the leading Grand National drivers.

DON E. BROWN. ASHLAND OIL AND REFINING COMPANY

DRAG RACING is a popular amateur sport. This 1,200-horsepower dragster can hit 206 mph in a quarter mile.

mile, as quickly as possible. This sport has over 75 classes, the difference among them being the amount of modification allowed.

The NHRA sponsors four major events—the Winternationals at Los Angeles, Calif.; the Springnationals at Bristol, Tenn.; a national meet at Indianapolis; and a World's Championship, bringing together the top competitors from seven regions in the United States for a final competition at Tulsa, Okla.

Rallying in the United States. American rallies differ from the high-speed European events in that the tours, acceleration runs, and hill climbs test a driver's mathematical ability as well as his skill at the wheel. Entrants are classified according to experience and the navigational aids used. For example, those with simple aids, such as a map and stopwatch, compete in the unequipped class. Those with elapsed-time clocks, calibrated speedometers, and average-speed calculators geared to the car's odometer compete in the equipped category.

A *gymkhana*, another kind of "obstacle" race, is run on an unused parking lot or open field. The driver must thread his stock car through a prescribed course set with obstacles and stop within marked boundaries. Winners are determined by the time required to run the course.

Rallies and gymkhanas are governed generally by the SCCA. Independent local groups, however, sponsor a variety of these programs.

Governing Organizations. Since World War II the controlling body of world racing has been the Fédération Internationale de l'Automobile (FIA), which exercises authority through the Commission Sportive Internationale (CSI), one of its several committees. The United States representative to the FIA is the Automobile Competition Committee of the United States (ACCUS).

Four widely diversified organizations in the United States belong to ACCUS: the United States Auto Club, the National Association for Stock Car Auto Racing, the Sports Car Club of America, and the National Hot Rod Association.

MEASURED MILE TESTING

The pursuit of the world's land speed record —in which the object is to travel, after a flying start, through a measured mile or kilometer course—has resulted in many momentous personal duels. The first—between Count Gaston de Chasseloup-Laubat of France and Camille Jenatzy of Belgium—was no exception. They raced electric cars in 1898 and 1899 at Achères, France, with Jenatzy timed in a 65.79 mph. On July 21, 1904, Louis Rigolly of France, driving a Gobron-Brillie at Ostend, Belgium, shattered the 100 mph barrier with a run of 103.56.

The record moved slowly but unspectacularly upward until the 1920's, when Capt. Malcolm Campbell, an English race driver, set a new record of 146.16 mph at Pendine, England, on Sept. 25, 1924. At Bonneville Salt Flats, Utah, on Sept. 3, 1935, Campbell pushed the ceiling to 301.13 mph in a Bluebird, and then retired. John Cobb, another Englishman, recorded 394.2 mph in a Railton-Mobil on Sept. 16, 1947. Cobb's record stood for six years.

The USAC certifies automotive tests and runs, operating within the rules of the FIA. In 1963 a controversy arose as to whether a land speed record of 407.45 mph made by the American Craig Breedlove in a 3-wheeled jet-propelled vehicle at Bonneville should stand. By the time the FIA ruled in 1964 that any vehicle that traveled on the ground and was controlled by the driver could legally seek the record, another American, Art Arfons, had driven his jet-propelled vehicle at 536.71 mph across the flats.

In 1965, Arfons and Breedlove set outstanding land speed marks at Bonneville. On November 7, Arfons drove his 21-foot, 17,500-horsepower jet racer, the "Green Monster," at 576.553 mph. On November 15, Breedlove raced his jet-propelled "Spirit of America" to a record 600.601 mph. All that was left to break was the sound barrier (738 mph at sea level).

KIM CHAPIN, *"Sports Illustrated"*

LAND SPEED RECORD of 600.601 mph was set by Craig Breedlove's "Spirit of America" on the Utah salt flats.

THE GOODYEAR TIRE AND RUBBER COMPANY

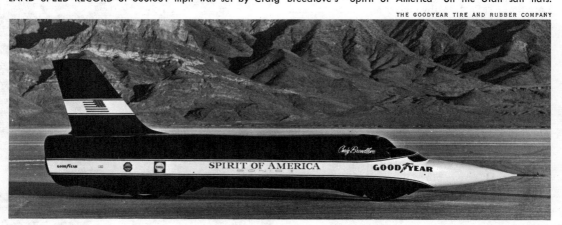

SPORTS CAR race at Bridgehampton, N.Y., an SCCA championship event, shows a Corvette leading a Ferrari.

IRV DOLIN

GLOSSARY OF AUTOMOBILE RACING TERMS

Championship Car.—A pure racing machine built specifically for the Indianapolis 500 and the other USAC championship races. It is similar to a Formula racer, except that the engine displacement is larger.

Closed Course.—A track designed solely for racing. It often has many characteristics of a road course.

Compact Sprint Car.—A racing car with an engine displacement limited to 110 cubic inches; also, a "midget" car.

Drag Race.—An acceleration race, generally ¼ mile, in which the object is low elapsed time rather than high terminal speed.

Dragster.—A vehicle of light tubular construction with the driver's seat behind the rear wheels.

Endurance Race.—A race over a defined period of time rather than over a prescribed length.

Engine Displacement.—The total volume of an engine's piston cylinders; a measure of engine size.

Factory Team.—A team of cars entered and subsidized by a manufacturer; also called a "works" team.

Flying Start.—A start in which the cars are moving at or near racing speed when the race officially begins.

Formula Car.—An FIA classification for a pure, single-seater racing car. Differences among the several Formula cars are determined by engine displacement.

Grand Touring Car.—A sports car that is a hybrid of a racing car and a passenger auto.

Grid Start.—A start in which the cars are lined up two or three abreast with engines running.

Jalopy.—An old car modified for racing.

Le Mans Start.—A start in which the drivers stand across the track from their cars while awaiting the starting signal.

Road Course.—A racing circuit laid out, wholly or in part, over public highways.

Sports Car.—A car built for highway driving. It may be modified for racing provided certain requirements are met, such as retaining the headlights and luggage space and carrying a spare tire.

Stock Car.—A car whose parts are essentially identical with those used in a standard production model.

Supercharger.—A compressor that provides the engine with more fuel-air mixture than can be supplied by normal atmospheric pressure.

Bibliography

Bloemker, Al, 500 Miles to Go, rev. ed. (New York 1966).

Clifton, Paul, The Fastest Men on Earth (New York 1966).

Frere, Paul, Sports Car and Competition Driving (Cambridge, Mass., 1963).

Hough, Richard, and Frostick, Michael, A History of the World's Racing Cars (New York 1965).

Moss, Stirling, and Purdy, Ken W., All but My Life (New York 1963).

Parks, Wally, Drag Racing Yesterday and Today (New York 1966).

Rudeen, Kenneth, The Swiftest (New York 1966).

Shaw, Wilbur, Gentlemen, Start Your Engines (New York 1955).

Stone, William S., A Guide to American Sports Car Racing, rev. ed. (Garden City, N.Y., 1963).

AUTOMOBILE SAFETY.

AUTOMOBILE SAFETY. As the motor vehicle has become essential in modern living, the problem of ensuring maximum safety for the driver, passengers, occupants of other vehicles, and pedestrians has become a grave concern. The problem is especially acute in the United States, where in the late 1960's more than 75 million passenger cars and more than 14 million trucks were registered; by 1980, according to estimates, the total number of vehicles might be 120 million. More than 64 percent of American workers drive or ride to work in cars, and most teen-agers begin to drive as soon as they reach the legal driving age. In a typical year, motor fatalities in the United States exceed 40,000, and disabling injuries total about 1.8 million. The total annual cost of traffic accidents, representing medical expenses, property damage, insurance payments, and loss of work time is estimated at $8.5 billion.

CAUSES OF ACCIDENTS

Research has indicated that there is no simple answer to the question of what causes traffic accidents. Each accident is a complex occurrence, involving more than one and sometimes many factors. Determination of the exact cause often is made difficult by inadequate reports from police at the scene, who in many cases are not equipped to collect and submit scientifically accurate information. In general, however, the causes lie in one of three areas—the driver, the car, or the road.

In the early 1960's, most traffic safety projects in the United States were centered on the driver. However, in 1965, interest shifted to the car. Mechanical defects and inadequate car safety design were the subject of congressional investigations, articles in the press, and programs on radio and television. For the first time, the federal government intervened in a major way in the traffic safety field. The General Services Administration, purchaser of all cars used by the U.S. government, drew up a list of many safety features which it required on cars it bought. Many of these features were later adopted as standard equipment by manufacturers.

Driver. Most safety authorities agree that driver error is involved in some 90 percent of traffic accidents. About four out of five drivers involved in fatal traffic accidents are violating some traffic law when the accident occurs. The commonest offense in the United States is "speed too fast for conditions" (37 percent), followed by "driving left of the center line" (14 percent).

As a guide to drivers, the American Automobile Association (AAA) has recommended the following basic rules of the road:

Be a sportsmanlike driver. Be courteous to every other driver and every pedestrian.

Keep speed reasonable for existing conditions.

Reduce speed at sundown. Drive so that you can stop within the visibility range of your headlights.

Stay behind the car ahead of you at least one car length for each 10 miles per hour of speed.

Stay in your line at hillcrests and curves.

Be extra alert at intersections.

Drive so as to protect pedestrians.

Do not drive so slowly that you impede traffic.

Always give yourself enough time. Don't hurry.

Get into the proper lane well in advance of turning. Always signal your intention to turn or stop.

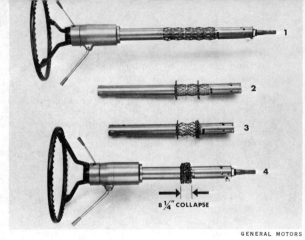

AUTOMOBILE SAFETY FEATURES include a steering column that collapses in a collision (four views show how a mesh section is compressed 8¼ inches) and a combination lap-and-shoulder harness.

Don't drive when angry or emotionally upset.

Yield your right-of-way to another driver if he is unsportsmanlike enough to try to bluff you.

Use the rearview mirror frequently.

Keep in the right lane except to pass. Don't weave.

Car. Mechanical failures, such as faulty brakes or tire blowouts, cause fewer accidents than formerly, as a result of improvements in automobile design and construction. Periodic motor-vehicle inspection, required by many states, is a valuable preventive of these failures.

Care of the car is a basic ingredient of driving safety. Cars should be checked regularly by competent mechanics. The AAA recommends these points for attention:

Steering. Are the front wheels aligned? Is the steering wheel free of excess play?

Windshield Wipers: Do they work properly and wipe clean?

Exhaust System: Is it tight, quiet, and leak free? Carbon monoxide leaks can be lethal.

Tires: Are they properly inflated? Do they have ample tread, and are they free from uneven wear and injury? Tires should be rotated every 5,000 miles.

Seat Belts: These should certainly be installed, and buckled on every time one gets in a car. Thousands of lives a year would be saved if every car were outfitted with seat belts and occupants used them.

Lights and Turn Signals: Do all lights operate properly? Are the headlights aimed to avoid glare?

Horn: Does it work properly?

Glass: Is all glass clean, and free from cracks, discoloration, and unauthorized stickers? Good vision is important to driving safety.

Rearview Mirrors: Are they adjusted for a clear view of the road behind?

Brakes: Have them tested regularly.

Road. Poorly engineered streets and highways contribute to traffic accidents. Well-engineered roads save lives. The U.S. Bureau of Public Roads estimates that 8,000 lives will be saved annually by construction of the national system of interstate and defense highways, all with controlled access, which is scheduled to be completed in the 1970's. Studies indicate that accident costs on highways where access is fully controlled are about 0.3 cent per vehicle-mile of travel compared to at least 1 cent per vehicle-mile on conventional highways. Annual travel on the new road system is expected to exceed 200 billion vehicle-miles each year. If the conservative estimate of a saving of 0.7 cent per vehicle-mile in accident costs is applied to this prediction, a yearly saving of $1.4 billion will result.

Signs, Signals, and Markings. A major contributing factor in highway accidents is the lack of uniformity in traffic-control devices among political subdivisions in the United States. Drivers in heavy traffic, often moving swiftly, have no time to consider the meaning of differing signs, signals, and markings as they cross municipal, county, or state lines. The AAA and other organizations believe that uniformity of guiding devices would help to lower the accident rate and that motorists have a right to expect this. Safety authorities in the United States are endeavoring to persuade all states and municipalities to conform to national standards outlined in the *Manual on Uniform Traffic Control Devices*, published by the National Committee on Uniform Traffic Control Devices.

Traffic Laws and Ordinances. A lack of uniformity is found also in traffic laws and ordinances. The motorist driving out of his home state in the United States, for example, is confronted with a bewildering array of regulations, some of which are arbitrarily enforced. In some states police apply crackdown methods to enforce safe driving. The AAA and most safety groups condemn these tactics as shortsighted and often more harmful than beneficial. The Uniform Vehicle Code, drafted by a committee of leading traffic and safety experts, offers the states a blue-print for modernizing their traffic laws.

PREVENTION OF ACCIDENTS

Efforts to prevent traffic accidents, with their rising toll of deaths and injuries, are being pushed by local, state, and federal agencies in the United States and by such organizations as the AAA, the National Safety Council, and the International Association of Chiefs of Police. Large sums are being spent and imaginative techniques employed in research. Since most studies assign major responsibility for accidents to the driver, the principal preventive moves are centered on him. These include improving the driving qualifications of motorists on the road and educating young people for their roles as drivers in the future.

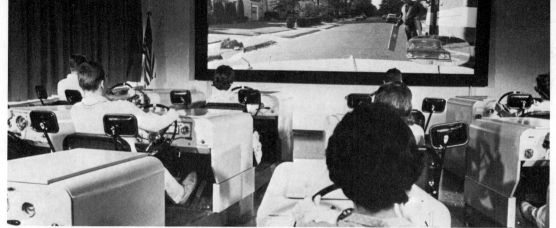

DRIVER TRAINING in the safety of a classroom teaches how to respond to a hazard. Students' reactions to situations in a training film are recorded automatically for an instructor to check.

License Tests. Increased attention is being devoted to driver-licensing procedures and how to strengthen them. Most states require only a simple test of vision, knowledge of driving regulations, and a behind-the-wheel test. These measures have proved inadequate to ensure highway safety. As a result, pressure has been exerted from many official quarters for more intensive screening methods to weed out accident-prone drivers. Such methods have been employed with varying degrees of success by commercial organizations and the armed services. Their validity usually has been so limited, however, that to eliminate even a small number of the accident prone a large proportion of safe drivers would also have to be rejected. To identify bad driving habits more accurately, research has been conducted by the Columbia University Teachers College Safety Research and Education Project, financed by the AAA Foundation for Traffic Safety, and a pilot test has been devised that requires only 10 minutes to give.

Licensed Drivers. Programs to improve performance of licensed drivers are helpful in promoting traffic safety. Many municipalities require accident repeaters to enroll in adult education classes in driving. The so-called point system used by many state motor-vehicle departments has also proved effective in reducing accidents. This system assigns a point value to each type of violation and accident, according to its gravity. When a driver incurs a certain number of points by involvement in violations or accidents, the department takes action through a warning, an interview, or revocation of the driver's license.

An Office of Highway Safety has been established in the U.S. Bureau of Public Roads to deal with the accident problem. One of its principal duties is to administer the federal driver-license register, a file of the names of drivers whose licenses have been withdrawn for driving while intoxicated or for conviction of a violation involving a traffic fatality.

Driver Education in the Schools. A vital weapon in the struggle to prevent traffic accidents is driver education in the schools. The program was organized by the AAA in the United States in the mid-1930's and by the late 1960's had trained more than 1.8 million high school students. Courses are offered in more than half of the nation's high schools. The AAA, emphasizing their value, urges that parents do not teach their children to drive, since they tend to pass along their own bad driving habits. Teaching is a job for a professional.

An accredited driver education course under AAA standards would include a minimum of 30 hours of classroom work, 6 hours of behind-the-wheel instruction, and 12 to 18 hours as an observer in a dual-control car while other students are taking instruction. An effective course requires a variety of equipment, including a dual-control car in good working order, well marked as a training vehicle. To measure reaction time and braking distance on the road, most courses use detonators attached to the car's front bumper. Stanchions and ropes are needed for practice in parking, turning, and backing.

In the classroom, instruments are used to test such vital factors as color vision, glare

CONTROLLED COLLISION STUDIES produce information on what happens when school buses crash as each is traveling at 30 mph, and when pedestrians are struck by a fast-moving automobile.

recovery rate, and reaction time. In many courses model traffic boards with tiny cars and mapped streets and intersections are used to set up traffic situations for students. Driving simulators that permit the student to become familiar with steering and braking also are employed in many high schools.

Since 1933, it has been estimated, driver education in the United States has saved some 11,000 lives and prevented 380,000 injuries and $1.6 billion in economic loss. Studies have shown that trained drivers have only half as many accidents and traffic violations as untrained drivers. Many states have passed legislation providing for state financial aid to high school driver education. Some major insurance companies offer special reduced premiums to youths who have successfully completed accredited driver education courses.

School Safety Patrols. School safety patrols were organized in the United States in the 1920's, when schoolchildren often were traffic-accident victims. By 1965 the rate of fatal motor accidents in the school-age group had dropped to 7 in 100,000, compared with 14.1 in the early 1920's. School safety patrols deserve a large measure of credit for this saving of lives.

School safety patrols are sponsored jointly by the schools, police, and AAA motor clubs. They consist of students from the upper elementary and junior high school grades, selected for leadership qualities and scholarship. The patrols guide and protect their classmates at school crossings. They are required to stay on the sidewalk in carrying out their responsibility and, under the patrol rules, are prohibited from directing traffic.

Pedestrian Safety. Impressive results have been obtained by campaigns to reduce traffic accidents involving pedestrians. In the United States the AAA conducts an annual pedestrian program appraisal, in which cities and states submit detailed reports of their records and activities in this field. Special awards are given to those with outstanding programs. Since 1937, when the appraisal plan was begun, pedestrian deaths have been cut almost in half. In that year they numbered 15,500; in 1965, 8,800.

Electronics Research. Research in electronics may hold the key to reducing traffic accidents in the future. Major automobile manufacturers are experimenting with prototype models of cars completely guided by electronic devices, and some engineers predict that principal highways in the future will be fitted with coaxial cables buried in the roadbed, while cars will be equipped with electronic controls that lock on to the cables to eliminate the need for steering. According to the AAA Foundation for Traffic Safety, by 1990 electronics will relieve the motorist of all but a few driving tasks, minimizing the human element in automobile operation. Since the driver is responsible for 90 percent of accidents, these advances should go far toward enhancing automobile safety. See also ACCIDENTS; TRAFFIC AND TRAFFIC CONTROL.

GENE B. DAVIS
American Automobile Association

Further Reading: American Automobile Association, *How to Drive* (Washington 1962); id., *Sportsmanlike Driving*, 5th ed. (New York 1965); Nader, Ralph, *Unsafe at Any Speed* (New York 1965); National Safety Council, *Accident Facts* (Chicago, annually).

AUTOMOBILES, Antique, early-model cars that are collected, restored, and exhibited as a hobby. These machines, of esthetic, historic, and financial value, are classified by date of production into five groups: (1) pioneer cars, (2) veteran cars, (3) vintage cars, (4) cars of the 1920's, and (5) cars of the 1930's. In addition, some cars are classified as "classic." Individuals, clubs, and museums preserve these automobiles, which were produced from the years of the horseless carriage in the late 1800's until about 1942. In the United States, more than 25,000 persons were actively engaged in this hobby in the mid-1960's.

Pioneer Cars. Any self-propelled vehicle built through 1905 is classified as a pioneer car. Probably the oldest gasoline vehicle in existence is a 2-cycle carriage built in 1875 by the Austrian Siegfried Marcus; it is preserved in a Vienna museum. Designers of the first practical gasoline-propelled machines were Karl Benz and Gottlieb Daimler of Germany, whose early products appeared in the 1880's. The French firm of Panhard and Levassor used the Daimler engine, and its early cars were successful in the first races.

American inventors whose first machines were designed and built during the pioneer car period were Charles E. and Frank J. Duryea, Elwood G. Haynes, Elmer Apperson, Alexander Winton, Henry Ford, Francis E. and Freelan O. Stanley, James W. Packard, Herbert H. Franklin, Ransom E. Olds, George N. Pierce, John D. Maxwell, and Henry M. Leland. The Duryeas completed their horseless buggy in Springfield, Mass., in 1893. Haynes and Apperson followed with a gasoline car which they demonstrated in Kokomo, Ind., in 1894. Both of these machines are preserved in the Smithsonian Institution, Washington, D.C.

Daimler's 1900 Mercedes, a car with a 35-horsepower 4-cylinder motor, introduced what became the conventional design of the modern automobile. Two years earlier, in Hartford, Conn., Hiram Percy Maxim had produced a 1-cylinder gasoline-driven Columbia (originally an electric car) along somewhat similar lines. Both cars are recognized today as milestones in automobile design.

Veteran Cars. Cars built between 1906 and

ANTIQUE CAR enthusiasts enjoy rallies and outings at which they display their prized possessions. Shown is a meet of the American Bugatti Club at Brookville, N.Y.

NOTABLE ANTIQUE AUTOMO-BILES include (top left) 1900 Mercedes, classified as "Pioneer"; (left) 1929 Lincoln Sport Phaeton, a "Classic" car; and (above) 1920 Ford Model T touring car.

1912 are classified as veteran automobiles. At this time American makers began producing machines equal to the top-quality European models. Entirely workable and generally very handsome, these machines are the most highly prized by collectors today.

Names such as Pierce-Arrow, Simplex, Packard, Mercer, Peerless, Lozier, White, Thomas Flyer, and Locomobile headed the American list. Other capable automobiles were the Ford, Buick, Cadillac, Oldsmobile, and Rambler. Among the popular European motorcars in this category were the Renault, Peugeot, and Panhard of France; Rolls-Royce and Napier of England; and the Italian Isotta-Fraschini and German Mercedes.

Vintage Cars. Machines that are classified as vintage cars are those manufactured between 1913 and 1919. In this period the self-starter and electric lights came into general use, styles became less quaint, and cars looked much more alike. Some models had high speed engines of 6, 8, and even 12 cylinders.

Cars of the 1920's and 1930's. The least interesting of all models to collectors are the machines of the 1920's. These cars, which were manufactured between 1920 and 1930 inclusive, introduced a smaller wheel, a fatter, lower-pressure tire, and the four-wheel or hydraulic brake. During these years some of the great European cars were developed, such as Vauxhall, Sunbeam, Bugatti, Alfa Romeo, and BMW. In the United States, the Chrysler made its debut (1923).

Classic Cars. The period of the classic car—the large custom-built car, with simple lines and luxurious details—encompassed the years 1925 to 1942. Outstanding among European quality cars was the Rolls-Royce of England. Other fashionable models included the Hispano-Suiza of Spain and of France; the Delage, Delahaye, Hotchkiss, Talbot (Darracq), and Voisin of France; the Horch, Maybach, and Mercedes-Benz of Germany; the Minerva of Belgium; and the Isotta-Fraschini of Italy. In the United States, the outstanding models included the Duesenberg, Packard, Pierce-Arrow, Cadillac, Cord, and Lincoln.

Classics were limited in luxury only by the purse of the buyer. Today they are scarce and very expensive. Final authority as to whether a car is considered a classic rests with the Classic Car Club of America, New York City.

1906 PIERCE GREAT ARROW, a "Veteran" car, won more reliability races than all other models combined.

1908 FRANKLIN touring car, classified as "Veteran," is a typical medium-sized American car of that period.

MAJOR AUTOMOTIVE MUSEUMS
United States
Arkansas—Museum of Automobiles, Morrilton.
California—Briggs Cunningham Automotive Museum, Costa Mesa.
Florida—Bellm's Cars of Yesterday, Sarasota; Early American Museum, Silver Springs.
Indiana—Indianapolis Motor Speedway Museum, Speedway.
Massachusetts—Museum of Antique Automobiles, Brookline.
Michigan—Henry Ford Museum, Greenfield Village, Dearborn.
Missouri—Ozark Auto Museum, Camdenton.
Nebraska—Harold Warp's Pioneer Village, Minden.
Nevada—Harrah's Automobile Collection, Reno.
New York—Long Island Automotive Museum, Southampton.
Ohio—Frederick C. Crawford Auto-Aviation Museum, Cleveland.
Pennsylvania—Gene Zimmerman's Antique Cars and Museum, Harrisburg; Swigart Museum, Huntingdon.
Virginia—Car and Carriage Caravan, Luray; Museum of Motoring Memories, Natural Bridge.
Europe
England—Montague Motor Museum, Beaulieu and Brighton.
France—Le Musée de l'Automobile de Rochetaillée, Lyon.
Germany—Daimler-Benz Museum, Stuttgart-Untertürkheim.
Italy—Museo dell'Automobile Carlo Biscaretti di Ruffia, Turin.
Switzerland—Swiss Transport Museum, Lucerne.

Clubs and Museums. In the United States, the four national organizations of interest to antique automobile enthusiasts are the Antique Automobile Club of America, Hershey, Pa.; the Horseless Carriage Club of America, Downey, Calif.; the Veteran Motor Car Club of America, Brookline, Mass.; and the Automotive Old Timers, Warrenton, Va. The oldest of the European clubs is the Veteran Car Club of Great Britain, London. See also the list above.

HENRY AUSTIN CLARK, JR.
Long Island Automotive Museum, Southampton, N.Y.

Bibliography
Bird, Anthony, *Antique Automobiles* (New York 1966).
Doyle, George Ralph, *The World's Automobiles, 1862–1962,* rev. by G.N. Georgano (London 1963).
Hebb, David, *Wheels on the Road: A History of the Automobile from the Steam Engine to the Car of Tomorrow* (New York 1966).
Maxim, Hiram Percy, *Horseless Carriage Days,* paperbound reprint (New York 1962).
Oliver, George A., *Early Motor Cars, 1894–1904* (Brattleboro, Vt., 1965).
Scott-Moncrieff, David, *Classic Cars: American, British and Continental Automobiles, 1930–1940* (Cambridge, Mass., 1964).
Scott-Moncrieff, David, *Veteran and Edwardian Motor Cars,* rev. ed., paperbound (New York 1962).

AUTONOMIC SYSTEM. See ANATOMY, COMPARATIVE—*Nervous System.*

AUTOPLASTY, ô'tō-plas-tē, is the repair of a diseased or injured part of the human body by an analogous part taken from another portion of the same body. The transferred part is called an autograft and may be bone, skin, muscle, or nerve.

Autografts are most frequently used in two types of cases. The first is a severe burn, when there is a transfer of a whole or a split-thickness skin graft from a donor area in the person burned. The graft hastens healing and seals in essential body proteins. The second most common autograft is the use of bone, either a sliver from the femur or tibia or chips from the iliac crest, to fuse a damaged spine or bridge an ununited fracture in a long bone. When suture material is required that will not react to the tissue to be transferred, fibrous bands are dissected from the tensor fascia lata (lateral portion of the thigh) and used as stitching. See also PLASTIC SURGERY.

AUTOPSY, ô'top-sē, is examination of the body after death. In autopsy an attempt to ascertain the cause of death is made by gross inspection of the organs, supplemented by microscopic and chemical studies of pieces of tissue removed from the body. Such examination is important because even detailed studies of the living patient may not have led to a correct diagnosis. Thus, autopsy may show an obscure prolonged fever to have been caused by an unsuspected cancer or abscess. In criminal cases a bullet may be removed for identification, or the possibility of poisoning may be explored by chemical tests. The correlation of clinical and pathological data that is made possible by autopsy has been the basis for many advances in medical knowledge.

Permission for an autopsy must be granted by the nearest of kin, who may or may not limit the examination to certain parts of the body. Frequently a family's religious or emotional scruples preclude performance of an autopsy. The medical examiner or coroner may order an autopsy in criminal cases or where suspicion of foul play exists.

IRVING SOLOMON, M.D.
Mount Sinai Hospital, New York

AUTOSUGGESTION is the process of influencing or attempting to influence one's own attitudes or behavior by other than rational means. In other words, it is suggestion that originates within the individual and is applied to the individual. In psychology, suggestion is a process of indirectly inducing someone to adopt an attitude or belief or to carry out an action. The process is indirect in the sense that it does not involve convincing a person by rational argument, commanding him, or forcing him. One example of suggestion is the advertising technique of frequently repeating the name of a product and stating—without supporting evidence—that the product should be bought. Suggestion is also illustrated by the behavior of hypnotized persons (see HYPNOSIS), and autosuggestion has been compared to an attempt at self-hypnosis.

Autosuggestion can be illustrated by a person's attempt to change his behavior or improve his health by repeating a form of words, for example, "Every day in every way I am getting better and better." The repetition is expected to make the person believe he is improving, and the belief is expected to produce improvement.

AUTRY, ô'trē, **Gene** (1908–   ), American actor and singer, who was the first and one of the most successful singing cowboys in motion pictures. With his horse Champion and his comic sidekick Smiley Burnette, he appeared in dozens of films during the 1930's and 1940's.

Orvon Gene Autry was born in Tioga, Texas, on Sept. 29, 1908. He worked as a railroad telegraph operator until 1931, when he wrote and recorded the song hit *That Silver-Haired Daddy of Mine,* which brought him a radio contract in Chicago. In 1934 he appeared in the motion picture *In Old Santa Fe,* the first of 82 musical western films in which he starred. Between 1939 and 1942, at the height of his career, he was one of the top 10 box-office attractions, had his own radio show, recorded many of his own and other western songs, and starred in national rodeos. After serving in the Air Force from 1942 to 1945, he resumed his motion picture career and managed his many business interests.

AUTUMN, ôt'əm, is the season of the year that follows summer and precedes winter. Astronomically, it is considered to extend from the autumnal equinox, September 22, in which the sun enters Libra, to the winter solstice, December 22, in which it enters Capricorn. In the United States, fall includes the months of September, October, and November; and in Britain, August, September, and October. In the Southern Hemisphere the seasons are reversed, the autumn extending from March 22 to June 22.

AUTUN, ō-tûn', is a town in France, in Saône-et-Loire department, 51 miles (82 km) northwest of Mâcon. It has extensive Roman remains, including an amphitheater and two well-preserved gates. The 12th century Cathedral of St. Lazare is known for its sculpture. The town manufactures cloth, carpets, and machinery.

Called *Augustodunum* by the Romans, it was the residence of the prefects of Roman Gaul and a center of commerce and learning. From the early 5th century A.D. to the 9th century it was often attacked by barbarians and gradually lost its importance. Population: (1962) 14,003.

AUTUNITE, ō-tun'īt, is a hydrated, or water-containing, phosphate of uranium and calcium. Under ultraviolet light its square, thin, yellow crystals exhibit a brilliant yellowish green fluorescence. Their bases have a glassy luster, but their edges appear somewhat pearly.

Autunite is widespread, with good deposits in France, Portugal, and Australia, and, in the United States, in North Carolina and Washington.

Composition: $Ca(UO_2)_2(PO_4)_2 \cdot 10 - 12H_2O$; hardness, 2.0 to 2.5; specific gravity, 3.1; crystal system, tetragonal.

AUVERGNE, ō-vern'yə, is a former province of south central France that is now divided into the departments of Puy-de-Dôme and Cantal. Much of this picturesque land is composed of high plateaus dotted with inactive volcanic peaks.

When Julius Caesar conquered Gaul, Auvergne was inhabited by a Celtic people, the *Arverni*. Their chief, Vercingetorix, united the tribes of Gaul in one last effort to defeat Caesar and free Gaul from Roman bondage. Like the rest of Gaul, Auvergne was Romanized and constituted part of *Prima Aquitania*. When Roman authority crumbled during the 4th and 5th centuries, Auvergne was successively occupied by various Germanic tribes until it came under the firm control of the Franks in the 6th century.

In the early Middle Ages, Auvergne was part of the Merovingian and Carolingian states. When the Carolingian empire fell apart in the 9th century, Auvergne became a separate county. William the Pious, who became the first hereditary count of Auvergne in 886, also acquired the duchy of Aquitaine. The marriage in 1152 of Eleanor of Aquitaine to Henry Plantagenet placed Auvergne under the English kings. In the early 13th century King Philip Augustus seized most of Auvergne and added it to the French royal domain. Later held in appanage, it became a duchy in 1360 and was forfeited to the crown in 1527.

BRYCE LYON, *Brown University*

AUXERRE, ô-sâr', a city in France, is the capital of the department of Yonne. It is 90 miles (145 km) southeast of Paris, on the Yonne River. It is built on the slope of a hill, and its streets are narrow. The city's 13th-century cathedral of St. Étienne is one of the most imposing Gothic structures in France. Other noteworthy churches are those of St. Germain and St. Pierre. The city also has a college, a museum of antiquities, and a botanic garden. A well-known light Burgundy wine is produced in Auxerre. Other products include textiles, leather goods, and earthenware.

Auxerre was a flourishing town before the Roman invasion of Gaul. Clovis expelled the Romans from the town. Later it formed part of the French duchy of Burgundy. It was united to France by Louis XI. Population: (1962) 28,949.

AUXIN, ôk'sən, is a chemical compound that in low concentrations affects plant growth. Natural auxins, such as indole-3-acetic acid, are present in plants. Synthetic auxins are manufactured and then applied to the plants. The main function of these plant hormones is to promote the elongation of cells and other growth effects. They are, however, involved in many aspects of plant culture, including prevention of preharvest drop of fruits, increase in fruit set, production of seedless fruits, weed control, stimulation of flower formation (pineapple), and prolongation of dormancy in nursery stock.

WALTER SINGER, *The New York Botanical Garden*

AV, äv, is the fifth month of the Jewish calendar, falling in July-August. The 9th of Av is a day of fasting to mourn the destruction of the first and second temples of Jerusalem, in 586 B.C. and 70 A.D. In the days of the Second Temple, a festival occurred on the 15th of Av in the vineyards of Judea, where young men would choose wives from among the dancing maidens.

RAPHAEL PATAI, *The Theodor Herzl Institute*

AVA, ä'və, was the ancient capital of Burma. It is now in ruins. It was situated on the left bank of the Irrawaddy River, just south of Mandalay, at the site where the only bridge across the Irrawaddy is located. The city was founded in 1364 as the capital of Upper Burma following the breakup of the empire of Pagan. It was built at the junction of the Myitnge and Irrawaddy rivers in order to control the rice supplies of the Kyaukse irrigated area.

The kingdom at Ava strove to restore Burmese control over the Mon kingdom of Lower Burma, but was itself threatened by the Shan states to its north and east. The Shans captured Ava in 1527 and destroyed much of its old Buddhist monastic culture. The Toungoo dynasty, which conquered the Mons and made Pegu its capital, recovered Ava from the Shans in 1555. After the failure of its attempts to conquer Siam the dynasty transferred the capital back to Ava in 1635. The capture of Ava in 1752 by the revised Mon kingdom of Pegu brought the Toungoo dynasty to an end but triggered a Burmese national movement that led to the final subjugation of the Mons and the reunification of the country under the Konbaung Dynasty.

The sites of subsequent capitals changed frequently but were mainly in the Ava region, and at Ava itself from 1765 to 1783 and again from 1823 to 1837. Europeans therefore came to call Burma the kingdom of Ava. After the capital was moved from Ava for the last time in 1837, the city was abandoned.

D.G.E. HALL, *University of London*

AVALANCHE, av′ə-lanch, a mass of snow or ice which slides down steep mountain slopes. Avalanches may occur at any season but are most frequent in early spring, after the snow has begun to melt. The water that collects beneath the snow bank loosens it, and the whole mass may then be precipitated to the base of the mountain. Such avalanches occur regularly in the Alps, where they are known as *grundlawinen*. Another type (*staublawinen*), occurring in the winter season, is characterized by the finely powdered condition of the snow, and results from the overloading of the snowfields. A third class is the ice avalanche, occurring along the course of glaciers.

AVALON, av′ə-lon, a resort city in California, is the main population center and port of Santa Catalina Island, in the Pacific Ocean, 27 miles (43 km) southwest of Long Beach. Steamship and airplane services provide connections with the mainland. Avalon is the starting point for tours of the island and surrounding waters. It is popular with sports fishermen, whose catches include tuna, swordfish, sea bass, barracuda, and mackerel. The annual Fiesta d'Oro takes place in May. Points of interest near the city are the Undersea Gardens, viewed from glass-bottomed boats, and Bird Park, an ornithological zoo. The city has a managerial form of government, adopted in 1961. Population: 1,520.

AVALON, av′ə-lon, a borough in Pennsylvania, is a residential suburb of Pittsburgh. It lies 6 miles (9.6 km) northwest of that city, on the north bank of the Ohio River, in Allegheny County. Avalon was settled in 1802 and was called *West Bellevue* until 1894. It adopted a council-manager form of government in 1928. Population: 7,065.

AVALON, av′ə-lon, in Celtic legend, was an island paradise to which King Arthur and other heroes were taken after their death. In medieval romantic poetry, Avalon was the name of the region where the fairy Fata Morgana (Morgan le Fay) held her court.

AVANT-GARDE, äv-än-gärd′, is a French military term meaning "vanguard," which has applied since the 19th century to advanced and experimental movements in the arts. Often associated with "modernism," the word "avant-garde" implies change in the form of art, as well as an effort on the part of the artist to release himself and his work from the bondage of established tastes. The avant-garde accepts a long struggle to sustain its existence before gaining recognition as a legitimate artistic expression.

The degree to which the avant-garde manifests opposition to established taste and academic practice often verges on scandal and violence, as in the Dada and surrealist public demonstrations of the 1920's. Artists and writers of the avant-garde usually form a loose community and rely on intellectual exchange and collaboration among the various arts. They often find inspiration in such disciplines outside the arts as science and revolutionary political movements, and their efforts tend to take shape around a publication or art gallery that is sympathetic to their work. It is often difficult to winnow the chaff of hoax and opportunism from their experiments and high-spirited behavior.

Origins. The origins of the avant-garde are primarily French, with roots in 19th century European romanticism. Its spirit emerges clearly in the antiacademic position of the impressionist and neoimpressionist painters, which coincided with the founding of the new theaters favoring extreme realism and with the symbolist movement in poetry. The pseudoscientific school of naturalism in the novel developed in the same period under the leadership of Zola. Out of this turmoil in the arts emerged the contradictory positions closely associated with the avant-garde: art for art's sake; the *poète maudit*, or "outcast poet," who defies society and traditional values; and Rimbaud's inflammatory dictum, "*changer la vie*" (change life). Contemporaneously, with Baudelaire as the key figure, the earlier traditions of the dandy and the starving Bohemian artist combined into the figure of the defiant, dedicated artist "on strike" against society but hard at work for his individual vision.

20th Century Avant-Garde. In the 20th century, Paris produced most of the highly organized movements that have come to represent the avant-garde to a wide segment of Western culture: fauvism, cubism, Dada, surrealism, and, after World War II, existentialism. Italy produced futurism, one of the earliest avant-garde schools of the 20th century, and England spawned vorticism in the years before World War II. In Germany the *Blaue Reiter* (Blue Rider) group of painters prepared the way for expressionism, a powerful movement that influenced and was influenced by all the arts, including motion pictures and architecture. Many of these movements had parallels in Russia after the Bolshevik Revolution—Miakovsky's poetry was oriented toward futurism, as were the films of Eisenstein.

The avant-garde spirit in the United States began with the historic Armory Show of 1913. However, among American avant-garde artists there was a tendency to avoid group activity except when in Europe. Generally, the American avant-garde organized its following abroad.

The enormous consumption of art and literature in the mid-20th century by new media of communication has exploited (some say eliminated) the avant-garde as an effective artistic minority. However, recent examples of experimentation in the arts, such as "happenings" (the combination of several arts in a single, semi-improvised performance) and "pop art," whose antiart attitude disavows Western art's entire esthetic heritage, suggest that a militantly progressive avant-garde element still exists among artists.

ROGER SHATTUCK, *University of Texas*

Further Reading: Ellman, Richard, and Fiedelson, Charles, eds., *The Modern Tradition: Backgrounds of Modern Literature* (New York and London 1965); Poggioli, Renato, *The Theory of the Avant-Garde* (Cambridge, Mass., 1967); Shattuck, Roger, *The Banquet Years: The Origins of the Avant-Garde in France, 1885–1918* (New York 1963).

AVARE, L', lä-vår′, a French comic drama in prose by Molière (q.v.), first produced in 1668. The play shows Molière's genius for combining satire, humor, and romantic interest.

L'avare (*The Miser*) is set in 17th-century Paris. Harpagon tries to prevent his daughter Élise and his son Cléante from marrying the humble lovers they have chosen. Instead, he hopes to marry Élise to a wealthy older man, and himself to wed Cléante's beloved, Mariane. However, Harpagon's plan is foiled because his fear of losing money makes him easy to manipulate.

AVARS, ä′värz, a nation of Mongolian or Turkish origin, who migrated to the regions around the Don River, the Caspian Sea, and the Volga River about the 5th century A.D. They served in Roman Emperor Justinian's army and later made themselves masters of areas from modern Yugoslavia to Germany. They extended their dominion over the Slavonians along the Danube, as well as over the Bulgarians on the Black Sea.

In 626 the Avars were driven back from Constantinople after a long siege, and subsequently lost control of many Slavic tribes. The Avars then shifted their center of activities north and made their main settlement on the Hungarian plain between the Danube and Tisza rivers. From Hungary they raided the eastern frontiers of the Franks until Charlemagne crushed them in 796. The last of the Avars submitted to Charlemagne in 805, and with their collapse many of the Slavic tribes in what is now eastern Germany recognized Charlemagne's suzerainty.

AVATAR, av′ə-tär, in Hindu mythology, an incarnation of the Deity. Ten avatars are particularly distinguished, and four of them are the subjects of puranas, or sacred poems. These ten are among the incarnations of Vishnu, the supreme god.

The Matsya avatar was the descent of the Deity in the form of a fish; Kachyapa or Kurma, in that of a tortoise; Varaha, as a boar; Narasinha, as a monster—half man, half lion; Vamana, as a dwarf; Parasurama, as the son of Jamadagni. All these incarnations took place in the Satya Yuga, or Golden Age. The seventh incarnation was in the form of the four sons of King Dasaratha, under the names of Rama, Lakshmana, Bharata, and Satrughna, in order to destroy demons that infested the earth. The achievements of Rama form the subject of the celebrated epic called the *Rāmāyaṅa.*

The eighth avatar of Vishnu, in the form of Krishna, is the best known of all, from the fact that it forms the subject of the great Sanskrit epic poem, the *Mahābhārata.* Its object was to relieve the earth of the Daityas and of the wicked men who oppressed it. The ninth was in the form of Buddha. The Kalki, or tenth avatar, is yet to come at the end of Kali Yuga, or the Iron Age. See also VISHNU.

AVE MARIA, ä′vä mə-rē′ə, is a Latin phrase meaning "Hail, Mary." In the Roman Catholic liturgy, the words *Ave Maria* begin a prayer to the Virgin Mary, and the prayer takes its name from this opening phrase. The first part of the prayer is based on the salutation to the Virgin by the angel Gabriel when he announced to her that she was to be the mother of the Saviour: "Hail, full of grace, the Lord is with thee" (Luke 1:28). Well-known musical settings for this prayer were composed by Schubert and Gounod. See also HAIL MARY.

AVEBURY, Baron. See LUBBOCK, JOHN.

AVEBURY, āv′bər-ē, is a village in Wiltshire, England, in the upper valley of the Kennet River, 75 miles (120 km) west of London. The village lies partly within the largest circle of standing stones in England, believed to have been erected about 2,000 B.C. The circle consists of stones 5 to 20 feet tall (1½ to 6 meters) and 3 to 12 feet wide (1 to 3½ meters). It encloses an area of more than 28 acres (11 hectares). Outside the circle is a broad ditch and a rampart, and within it are two smaller circles of stones. The stones are believed to have been used in religious rituals. Nearby are many barrows, or mounds marking ancient graves.

AVELLANEDA, ä-vä-lyä-nä′thä, **Alonso Fernández de,** the pen name of an unknown Spanish author who wrote a sequel to part 1 of Cervantes' *Don Quixote.* This sequel, published in 1614, was inspired by the great success of the first part of *Don Quixote,* which had appeared in 1605. Cervantes published his own part 2 in 1615. Avellaneda's work has been ascribed to several eminent Spanish authors.

AVELLANEDA, ä-vä-lyä-nä′thä, **Nicolás** (1836–1885), president of Argentina. He was born in Tucumán on Oct. 1, 1836. He was professor of political economy at the University of Buenos Aires and a well-known journalist. As minister of education (1868–1874) under President Domingo Sarmiento, Avellaneda effected a number of reforms. As Sarmiento's protégé he was elected president in 1874, after which he suppressed a revolt led by his rival, Bartolomé Mitre. During Avellaneda's six-year term, public finances were improved, troops were dispatched to subdue warring Indians in the south, and the city of Buenos Aires was detached from Buenos Aires province and federalized. The last measure became effective under Gen. Julio Roca, who succeeded Avellaneda in the presidency. Avellaneda died on Dec. 26, 1885.

AVELLANEDA, ä-vä-lyä-nä′thä, in Argentina, is a major industrial city and seaport in Buenos Aires province. A part of Greater Buenos Aires, it is separated from the city of Buenos Aires by the Riachuelo River.

The port section, at the river's mouth, is called Dock Sud. It ships hides, wool, and other animal products. Avellaneda has a large meatpacking plant, grain-processing plants, and oil refineries. It manufactures textiles, chemicals, plywood and other construction materials, and metal products.

The city, formerly called *Barracas al Sud,* was named in 1904 after Nicolás Avellaneda, president of Argentina from 1874 to 1880. A statue of him stands in the city. Population: (1960) 329,626.

AVELLANEDA Y ARTEAGA, ä-vä-lyä-nä′thä ē är-tā-ä′gä, **Gertrudis Gómez de** (1814–1873), Spanish writer, who is best known for the poems she published under the pseudonym *La Peregrina* (*the Pilgrim*). She also wrote novels and plays that were esteemed in her time, though their grandiose themes and piety now seem dated.

She was born in Camagüey, Cuba, on March 23, 1814. After 1836 she lived in Spain, except for a sojourn in Cuba from 1859 to 1863. She died in Madrid on Feb. 1, 1873.

Her sensitive lyrics, originally published in Spanish journals, recurrently use the themes of human and divine love. Her novels, including *El Mulato Sab* (1839), *Espatolino* (1844), and *Guatimozín* (1845), exemplify 19th century romanticism, as do her historical and biblical dramas, including *Alfonso Munio* (1844), *Saúl* (1850), and *Baltasar* (1858). She also wrote the comic play *Errores del corazón* (1852).

AVELLINO, ä-väl-lē'nō, is a town in Italy, in the Campania region, 29 miles (47 km) east of Naples. It is the capital of the province of the same name. Avellino is situated on a hill 1,150 feet (351 meters) above sea level and is the trade center for the surrounding agricultural region. Chestnuts and hazelnuts have been gathered in the vicinity since Pliny's time. The town has a theater and several fine monuments and schools. To the northwest is the famous 12th century convent of Monte Vergine, which is visited annually by thousands of pilgrims. Population: (1961) 31,744.

AVEMPACE (c. 1070–1138), ä-väm-pä'thä, was a Muslim philosopher. Avempace is the Latin form of his name, which in Arabic was *Abu Bakr Muhammad Ibn as-Sayigh Ibn Bajja.* He was born in the Muslim city of Saragossa, Spain, and lived there as a scholar and high government official until it fell to Aragon in 1118. Thereafter he lived in other parts of Muslim Spain and in Morocco. He died in Fez, Morocco.

Avempace was the foremost representative in western Islam of the Neoplatonic tradition of intellectual mysticism. His immediate Islamic philosophical lineage was from al-Farabi in the East and Ibn Masarra in Spain. His particular interest was in ethical and political philosophy. In his book *On the Union of the Intellect* he explains that the highest end of man is the uniting of his "acquired" or "passive" intellect, by means of abstracting universals, with the world's Active Intellect, which to Avempace is identical with God. This work was widely studied in Muslim Spain and Christian Europe. His *Regime of the Solitary Man* discusses the predicament of the philosopher in a worldly society.

GEORGE F. HOURANI, *University of Michigan*

AVENARIUS, ä-vä-nä'rē-ōōs, **Richard Heinrich Ludwig** (1843–1896), German philosopher, who founded a system of philosophy called empiriocriticism. This system, developed in his book *Kritik der reinen Erfahrung* (1888–90), is an idealistic dualism that attempts to relate pure experience to thought and action.

Avenarius was born on Nov. 19, 1843, in Paris, where his father was a bookseller. He was a nephew of the composer Richard Wagner and a brother of the poet and literary critic Ferdinand Avenarius (1856–1923). He studied philosophy at the universities of Zürich, Berlin, and Leipzig and received his Ph.D. at Leipzig in 1876. The same year he published his first major work, *Philosophie als Denken der Welt gemäss dem Prinzip des kleinsten Kraftmasses.*

Avenarius taught philosophy at Zürich from 1877 until his death. He was one of the founders of the Academic Philosophy Circle at Zürich and was the first editor of its quarterly journal. He died in Zürich on Aug. 19, 1896.

AVENCHES, à-väNSH', is a town in Switzerland, in the canton of Vaud, eight miles (12.8 km) northwest of Fribourg. Called *Aventicum* by the Romans, it was the capital of the Roman province of Helvetia and became a city of about 80,-000 people. Among the Roman remains are a ruined amphitheater, a Corinthian column, and parts of the town walls. A medieval tower stands at the entrance to the ampitheater. The Alamanni razed the city in 264 A.D., but it was rebuilt in the 11th century. Population: (1960) 4,940.

AVENTINE, av'ǝn-tīn, the southernmost of the seven hills of Rome, on the left bank of the Tiber, between the river and the Caelian hill. The Circus Maximus lay to the northeast of the Aventine, between it and the Palatine, and the baths of Caracalla were on the southeast. Ancus Marcius included it in the city and it was settled by the plebs in 455 B.C. The hills are all of volcanic origin.

AVENTINUS, ä-ven-tē'nōōs, **Johannes** (1477–1534), German historian. He was born *Johannes Turmair* (or *Thurmayr*), at Abensberg, Bavaria, on July 4, 1477. He studied at Ingolstadt, Vienna, Cracow, and Paris before being appointed tutor in 1509 to the two younger brothers of Duke William IV of Bavaria.

Encouraged by William, Aventinus began to write his masterpiece, the *Annales Boiorum*, about 1517. This work deals with the history of Bavaria as well as with general history from the earilest times to 1460. After finishing the Latin text of the book in 1521, he undertook a German version of it, which he completed some years later. The first printed edition of the *Annales* appeared in 1554.

Aventinus assisted in founding the Sodalitas Litteraria Angilostadensis. Under the auspices of this organization, several old manuscripts were brought to light.

He has been called the "Bavarian Herodotus" and was one of the foremost representatives of the humanistic approach to historical writing. This approach superseded that reflected in the medieval chronicles. He died at Regensburg, Bavaria, on Jan. 9, 1534.

AVERCAMP, a'vǝr-kàmp, **Hendrick** (1585–1634), Dutch painter, who is noted for his winter landscapes and skating scenes. Many of his paintings are crowded with small, moving figures of revelers or skaters. The figures, painted in both dark and bright colors, accent the pale, whitened color scheme that gives Avercamp's paintings their strong sense of winter atmosphere. He often incorporated suggestions of anecdotal incidents in the interplay of the moving figures.

Avercamp was born in Amsterdam, where he studied under the painter Pieter Isaaksz. Sometime before 1625 he moved to Kampen and lived there for the rest of his life.

Avercamp's early work shows the influence of the Flemish landscape painters, particularly Pieter Brueghel the Elder and Gillis van Coninxloo. This influence is noticeable in the high horizon, steep perspective, and circular composition of the paintings, including *Winter Scene with Skaters near a Castle* (National Gallery, London).

In his later work Avercamp moved away from the Flemish style and adopted the more realistic manner characteristic of 17th century Dutch landscape painting.

Among Avercamp's major works are *Scene on Ice* (National Gallery, London), *Winter Landscape* (Rijksmuseum, Amsterdam), *Pleasures on the Ice* (Leonard Koetser Gallery, London), and *Winter Landscape* (City Art Museum, St. Louis, Mo.). In addition to his oil paintings, he produced some delicate watercolors.

Barent Avercamp (1612–1670), a nephew, was his pupil and imitator.

Further Reading: Timmers, J.J.M., *History of Dutch Art and Life* (Camden, N.J., 1959).

AVERELL, ăʹvə-rəl, **William Woods** (1832–1900), American military officer. He was born in Cameron, N.Y., on Nov. 5, 1832, and graduated from West Point in 1855. He served on the frontier and in several Indian campaigns until the beginning of the Civil War, when he was appointed colonel of the 3d Pennsylvania Cavalry and assigned to the defenses of Washington.

During the war Averell distinguished himself on numerous occasions as a cavalry raider and commander, and at its close he was brevetted major general. In 1863–1864 he conducted raids and skirmishes which greatly hampered the Confederate forces and aided the Federal commands in carrying out their plans of campaign. He resigned from the Regular Army in 1865, and for the next three years was United States consul general at Montreal. He was the inventor of a system of asphalt paving and of the Averell insulating conduits for electric wires. He died at Bath, N.Y., on Feb. 3, 1900.

AVERNUS, Lake, ə-vûrʹnəs, a small lake about 10 miles west of Naples, Italy. Its modern name is *Lago d'Averno;* its Roman name was *Lacus Avernus.* In classical legend, the lake was the entrance to the lower world, or Hades. The surrounding land was covered by dense woods and, according to legend, the air was charged with such foul-smelling, unhealthful vapors that birds flying over Avernus were asphyxiated and fell into its waters.

Ancient writers believed that the Cimmerians lived along the banks of the Avernus and that the legendary Cumaean sibyl had a cave nearby. Under the Roman Emperor Augustus, a canal was built connecting the lake to the sea, and the lake became the site of a naval headquarters, known as *Portus Julius.*

AVERROËS (1126–1198), ə-verʹō-ēz, is the Latin name of the Muslim philosopher *Abu'l-Walid Muhammad Ibn Rushd.* He was born in Córdoba of a distinguished Spanish Arab family. Having received a broad education both in Islamic studies and in the secular, Hellenistic sciences in their Arabic form, he was able to write not only a standard digest of Islamic law but also a compendium of medicine, *al-Kulliyat* (in Latin, *Colliget*); the latter work was used in Europe for centuries. But his chief passion and talent were for philosophy.

While still in his 30's, Averroës published summaries (in Arabic, *Jami*) of Aristotle's works. In about 1168 he was commissioned by the Almohad ruler of Morocco and Spain to write detailed comments on the texts of Aristotle in their Arabic translations. The famous commentaries that resulted occupied most of Averroës' later years. Most of the works of Aristotle received a "Middle Commentary" (in Arabic, *Talkhis*). Some of the more important received, in addition, a more extensive "Great Commentary" (in Arabic, *Tafsir*). These summaries and commentaries are of interest not only for their patient and learned explanations of Aristotle's thought but for many of his own reflections. The same is true of his summary of Plato's *Republic.*

Averroës also wrote works expressing his thought more directly. Three are particularly important. In *Fasl al-Maqal* (The Decisive Treatise) he defends the right of Muslim scholars to practice philosophy. His *Al-Kashf an Manahij al-Adilla* . . . (Exposition of the Methods of Proof . . .) is a general treatise on Islamic theology. *Tahafut at-Tahafut* (The Collapse of the Collapse) is a lengthy point-by-point rebuttal of al-Ghazzali's attack on the philosophers (see GHAZZALI). For his pains he was tried as a heretic by the conservative religious community of Córdoba in 1195, condemned and exiled, but reprieved before his death in 1198.

His Philosophy. Averroës' philosophy is Aristotelian on the whole. There are inevitably developments of his own and accretions from the long heritage of Neoplatonism, although he tries to strip off the Neoplatonic ideas that had been merged with Aristotle's by the great synthesizer Avicenna (q.v.).

Averroës' metaphysics, like Aristotle's, starts from the concrete individual, composed of form and matter, as the primary reality. We know by sense and reason that such things exist. The task of philosophy is to classify their kinds and analyze the relations of form and matter in them. Forms and matter are eternal. Thus the world as a whole is eternal, while the composition of particular forms and matter is perishable. God's existence is proved by the necessity of a First Mover and by the signs of providence in the world. His creative activity is not to make the world from nothing, but to produce forms in a matter that would otherwise be mere potentiality, thus giving the world its actual character.

Just as the world contains a hierarchy of beings, from inanimate bodies to the souls of the celestial spheres, so man contains an order of functions, of which the highest is the understanding of forms by abstraction.

Averroës' complex doctrine of the intellect raises the problem of immortality in an acute manner (though he does not present it as a problem). Since the Active Intellect, which illuminates forms for human understanding, is one and comes from outside us, it cannot be an individual part of a man as he survives death. The passive intellect, on the other hand, on which forms are imprinted during our cognitive activity, depends for its individuality on our sensations and imagination, and these are closely connected with the mortal body. Thus it seems that the individual passive intellect too cannot survive death, and therefore nothing is left for personal immortality.

Averroës himself denied any real conflict between philosophy and Islam; both are true, and there is only one truth. But whereas philosophy expounds truth in scientific prose, for the restricted use of intellectuals, the Koran does so more imaginatively, sometimes by symbolic language. The Koran is thus more fitted for moral and religious education.

His works became known in Christian Europe in Latin and Hebrew translations after 1230. His doctrines of the intellect and the eternity of the world aroused fierce controversy after 1255, centering on Siger de Brabant. Aquinas criticized Averroës on these issues but learned much from him. For several centuries Averroës' commentaries on Aristotle were studied, and he had his devotees in the universities. But popular myth saw him as a vile atheist refuted by Aquinas. Modern scholarship has reappraised him as a courageous champion of philosophy with a sharp analytical mind.

GEORGE F. HOURANI, *University of Michigan*

Further Reading: Gauthier, L., *Ibn Rochd (Averroes)* (Paris 1948); Hourani, George F., *Averroës on the Harmony of Religion and Philosophy* (London 1961).

AVERY, ā′vər-ē, **Milton Clark** (1893–1965), American painter, who developed an independent style that often uses a subject primarily as a vehicle for lyrical color and flattened, decorative composition. Through stylized treatment, his subject matter—primarily figures and coastal landscapes—is given a quality of motionlessness and quiet. Thin washes of color, tuned to a sensitive pitch, characterize his mature work, including *Swimmers and Sunbathers* (1945; Museum of Modern Art, New York City) and *The Seine* (1953; Whitney Museum, New York City). The critic and painter Frederick S. Wight said that in Avery's painting there "is something not . . . widely present in our time: acceptance of the human condition and peace of mind."

Avery was born in Altmar, N.Y., on March 7, 1893. He took a life-drawing course at the Connecticut League of Art Students in 1913, but was primarily self-taught. In 1925 he moved to New York City, and the following year he married the commercial artist and illustrator Sally Michel. His first one-man show was at the Opportunity Gallery in New York in 1928. During the depression, Avery was one of the many artists who worked for the Works Progress Administration. Three New York galleries exhibited his work concurrently in 1945. He died in New York City on Jan. 3, 1965.

AVERY, ā′vər-ē, **Samuel Putnam** (1822–1904), American art expert. He was born in New York City on March 17, 1822. After studying engraving he became an art dealer. In 1867 he was appointed commissioner of the American art department at the International Exposition in Paris. One of the founders and for a long time a trustee of the Metropolitan Museum of Art in New York City, he persuaded William H. Vanderbilt to place his collection of paintings in that museum. He was the founder of the Avery Architectural Library at Columbia University, which he gave as a memorial to his son, Henry Ogden Avery. Samuel Avery died on Aug. 11, 1904.

AVES, ā′vēz, is a class of warm-blooded vertebrates with feathers, commonly known as *birds*. Their forelimbs are modified into wings that usually are capable of flight. The avian skeleton is fused in many places, and the bones have hollow spaces, making the skeleton rigid and lightweight. In addition, respiratory air sacs are present throughout the body. Their young are hatched from eggs incubated by the parents. There are about 8,600 species distributed over almost all regions. See also BIRD.

AVESTA. See ZEND-AVESTA.

AVEYRON, à-vā-rôN′, is a department of France, in the southern part of the country. The department, 3,385 square miles in area, is bounded on the north by the department of Cantal, on the east by the departments of Lozère and Gard, on the southeast by the department of Hérault, on the southwest by the department of Tarn, on the west by the department of Tarn-et-Garonne, and on the northwest by the department of Lot. It is extremely mountainous and is traversed by five rivers, the Aveyron, the Viaur, the Truyère, the Lot, and the Tarn. In the flat central region, rye, wheat, and potatoes are grown. Vegetables, fruits, and wine are produced along the rivers. The Causses region, in the southeast, raises sheep, and cattle are raised in the north. There is mining of coal. The village of Roquefort, famous for its cheese, is in the department.

The department corresponds to the ancient district of Rouergue, which was a dependency of the counts of Toulouse in the Middle Ages, came under the French crown in 1271, and was part of Guienne province from 1589 until the French Revolution. The capital of the department is Rodez. Population: (1962) 290,442.

AVEZZANA, ä-väd-dzä′nä, **Giuseppe** (1797–1879), Italian general and politician. He was born in Chieri, Piedmont, on Feb. 29, 1797. After participating in the unsuccessful uprising of 1821 on the side of the constitutionalists, he fled to Spain, where he joined the forces that favored constitutional government there. Meanwhile, the government of King Charles Felix of Sardinia condemned him to be hanged. Avezzana fled to the United States, where he stayed until he acquired an estate at Tampico, Mexico. In 1829 he won great military successes during the Mexican struggle for independence.

Taking advantage of a general amnesty, he returned to Italy in 1848 and served as minister of war in the Roman republic in 1849. After the collapse of the republic he returned to the United States for a few years. Back in Italy in the late 1850's, he participated in the struggle for unification of the country. After 1861 he was a deputy in the new Italian parliament and became one of the leaders of the Irredentists (q.v.). He died in Rome on Dec. 25, 1879.

AVIARY, ā′vē-er-ē, a house, enclosure, large cage, or other place for keeping birds confined. Usually it is placed out of doors, and every effort is made to keep the birds in a state of comparative freedom. Present-day aviaries generally are very large, wire-covered enclosures, with a birdhouse nearby for cold weather. Such aviaries afford the best means for the study of bird species, their habits of nesting, courtship, incubation, and molting.

There are several important aviaries in the United States and Europe. In New York City the birdhouse in the Zoological Park in the Bronx contains 152 indoor and outdoor cages that provide the birds with space to fly, pools of running water, shade trees, and rocky ledges. The large outdoor flying cage is a tall, arched enclosure of steel pipe and chain net and is the summer home of a mixed flock of water birds. There are individual aviaries for eagles and vultures, pheasants and pigeons, and many other specimens. The St. Louis Zoological Garden also contains an important aviary, one of the largest in the world.

Among the important European aviaries is the one in the Parc Zoologique de Clères in Rouen, France. This aviary contains 300 species and 1,700 specimens. The Leningrad Zoo in the USSR has an aviary with 108 species and 591 specimens. There are two noteworthy aviaries in the British Isles. One in the Zoological Society of London has 690 species and 1,352 specimens. The other, in Edinburgh, is the aviary in the Royal Zoological Society of Scotland, which contains over 1,000 specimens.

Aviaries have existed for a long time. The ancient Romans used an enclosed room with few windows as an aviary. In the 16th century Hernán Cortés found that peoples of Mexico had also built some aviaries.

AVIATION

COURTESY OF SMITHSONIAN INSTITUTION, NATIONAL AIR MUSEUM, WRIGHT BROTHERS COLLECTION

The age of aviation began with the successful powered flight of the Wright brothers' airplane in 1903.

AVIATION, ā-vē-ā'shən, is the science and art of operating powered aircraft. The term generally is restricted to the flight of heavier-than-air craft. In this article the history of aviation is reviewed; a list of other articles relating to the subject of aviation appears at the end of the article.

Early History. Man dreamed of flying for thousands of years before Orville Wright made the first successful powered flight in a heavier-than-air machine over the sand dunes of Kitty Hawk, N.C., on Dec. 17, 1903. Greek, Egyptian, Assyrian, and Oriental mythologies are filled with references to man's aspiration to conquer the air. Virtually all of these concepts of man's flight involved imitation of the soaring flight of birds.

Among the early scientific explorers who seriously studied the problem of manned flight were Roger Bacon, English philosopher and man of science, who about 1250 made the first recorded proposal for a gas-filled balloon, and Leonardo da Vinci, Florentine artist and scientist, who published a detailed treatise on human flight in 1505 and developed many detailed designs for flying machines, including the basic concept of what is now the helicopter.

Discovery of the lighter-than-air gas hydrogen in the 1760's turned aeronautical thinking back toward Bacon's balloon concept. The first successful balloons were built and flown by the French inventors Joseph and Étienne Montgolfier in 1783. The Montgolfier brothers used a large paper bag inflated with hot air for their early flights, which reached altitudes of 6,000 feet (1,800 meters). The knowledge of hydrogen combined with the development of soluble rubber soon led to the production of hydrogen-filled rubber envelopes. These continued as the basic lighter-than-air formula until the 1930's, when helium was substituted for hydrogen.

Development of the internal combustion engine provided a logical source of power for the gas-filled bags. The Brazilian Alberto Santos-Dumont first flew a powered lighter-than-air ship in Paris in 1898, and two years later the first of Count Ferdinand von Zeppelin's giant powered airships flew in Germany.

The century preceding the Wright brothers' successful flights was marked by an increasing interest in practical aeronautical science. Sir George Cayley in England, Clément Ader in France, Nicholas Mozhaisky in Russia, Samuel Pierpont Langley and Sir Hiram Stevens Maxim in the United States—all built heavier-than-air flying machines that failed to fly. By the end of the 19th century a promising approach to powered flight had been developed through the successful gliding flights of designs conceived by Otto Lilienthal in Germany and Octave Chanute in the United States. A variety of glider designs by these two men made over 4,000 successful flights before Lilienthal was killed while testing a new rudder design; and it was through the glider activities, first of Lilienthal and later of Chanute, that two of the four sons of Bishop Milton Wright of Dayton, Ohio, became interested in flying.

The Wright Brothers. Orville and Wilbur Wright were operating a successful bicycle manufacturing and repair shop in Dayton when they expressed their first formal interest in flight about 1899 by writing to the Smithsonian Institution in Washington, D.C., for suggested reading material on aeronautics. The Wrights eagerly read the articles by Lilienthal and Chanute recommended by the Smithsonian and entered into a correspondence with Chanute. This led to a significant personal and technical relationship between the two brothers and the famous structural engineer.

The Wright brothers' first ambition was to build a man-carrying kite. After making inquiries of Chanute and the United States Weath-

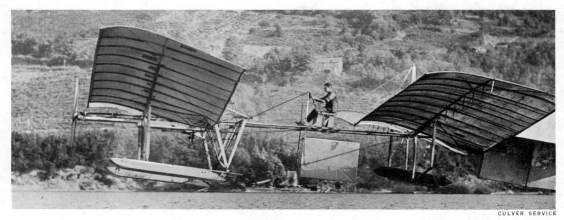

On its trial flight in 1896, Samuel Pierpont Langley's steam-powered plane fell into the Potomac River.

er Bureau for a suitable location, they settled on Kitty Hawk, N.C., where steady sea breezes and sand dunes combined to offer ideal conditions for gliding experiments. The Wrights built their first glider in the spring of 1900 and took it to Kitty Hawk in the fall. The glider, controlled by two ropes, was flown like a kite. It was built on the basis of data obtained from the writings of Lilienthal and Chanute and flew reasonably well on tether with a 50-pound (22-kg) payload of chains.

Encouraged by these efforts, the Wrights returned to Dayton determined to build a much larger, man-carrying glider. This new glider was flown at Kitty Hawk in the fall of 1901 in the presence of Chanute and proved to be a failure in the air. It was during these unsuccessful experiments in 1901 that the Wrights became convinced that the Chanute and Lilienthal data contained major flaws. They therefore started off on their own basic experimentation on airfoils—their first major step toward successful powered flight.

During the winter of 1902–1903 they built, in their bicycle shop, a crude wind tunnel from an old laundry starch box and obtained their first experimental confirmation that the data they had been using were wrong. Thereupon, they built a more efficient wind tunnel with an airstream propelled by a single cylinder gasoline engine, and they experimented with some 200 different airfoils. From these data they built a new glider that departed radically from earlier methods of achieving stability and control in the air. During the fall of 1902 they made a thousand flights with this glider at Kitty Hawk, surpassing all the previous performances of Chanute and Lilienthal. In the teeth of winds up to 36 miles (58 km) per hour they made successful gliding flights, and several glides went more than 600 feet (180 meters). Now sure they were on the right track and with confidence in their own data, the Wrights determined to build a powered machine for their 1903 experiments. The next nine months saw the bicycle business badly neglected as they wrestled with a variety of new problems posed by applying power to their 1902 glider design.

The first problem was the engine. The unsuccessful planes of Professor Langley and Hiram Maxim had been powered by steam engines much too heavy for their purpose. The Wrights' analy-

sis of the problem left them with specifications for an 8-horsepower engine that would deliver 1 hp for each 20 pounds (9 kg) of engine weight. None of the gasoline engine manufacturers of the day cared to take the order, so the brothers were forced back on their own resources.

They had designed and built the engine for their wind tunnel. Now, with the help of their mechanic, Charles Taylor, they designed and built an engine that embodied such modern concepts as direct fuel injection into the cylinders, use of aluminum to save weight, and water cooling. The Wright engine weighed only 170 pounds (76.5 kg) and delivered 16 hp for the first 15 seconds at 1,200 revolutions per minute but then dropped to an output of 12 hp. Even so, it weighed 6 pounds (2.7 kg) less per hp than the original specification, which the professional engine builders thought was impossible to achieve.

The Wrights turned again to their wind tunnel and books on marine engineering to develop a propeller design. Drawing on their bicycle experience, they rigged a chain drive to carry power from the engine to the two pusher propellers.

All these new tasks postponed their arrival at Kitty Hawk until late in September 1903. Then a combination of bad weather and vexing mechanical problems delayed the first attempt at powered flight until December 14. On that day, with Wilbur at the controls, the Wright plane climbed too steeply and crashed at the foot of a dune after having been aloft just 3½ seconds. It took two days to repair the damage and then, on December 17, Orville got his turn. He stayed in the air for 12 seconds and landed successfully some 120 feet (36 meters) from the takeoff point. The rest of the afternoon the brothers alternated at the controls and made three more flights, the longest of 59 seconds duration covering 852 feet (256 meters). Then another crash causing minor damage was followed by a gust of wind that tumbled the flying machine over and over and made further flying that year impossible.

That night Orville sent the following message to his father in Dayton: "Success four flights Thursday morning all against twenty-one-mile wind started from level with engine power alone average speed through air thirty-one miles longest 59 seconds inform press home Christmas. Orville Wright."

Although the press was informed, only three papers in the United States printed the story,

Louis Blériot's monoplane made the first flight across the English Channel on July 25, 1909.

and reports of the Wright brothers' flying achievements were greeted with press and scientific skepticism for several years after the first Kitty Hawk flights. The first complete account of the Wright flights was published in the March 1904 issue of the magazine *Gleanings in Bee Culture*.

The years immediately following the Wright brothers' flights saw an extremely slow growth in aviation, primarily because of the skepticism of the press and scientific leaders that powered flight by man was possible. During 1904 the Wrights designed a new model and logged only 45 minutes flying time. The next year, with the new model now flying out of Huffman's pasture near Dayton, the Wrights circled in banking and turning and stayed aloft for 38 minutes, covering 24 miles (39 km). They did no flying in 1906, concentrating on new engine design. In 1907 they made a triumphal tour of Europe during which they established subsidiary companies for the manufacture of their designs in England, France, and Germany.

Early Flight Records. Alberto Santos-Dumont became the first to fly in Europe in 1906, using a box-kite style biplane. In the United States a formidable rival to the Wrights developed from the Aerial Experiment Association financed by

Alexander Graham Bell, inventor of the telephone, and headed by Glenn Curtiss, who was already famous as a designer and racer of motorcycles.

The era from 1908 to the outbreak of World War I was dominated by the air meet in which aircraft designers and pilots competed in speed, endurance, altitude, and acrobatics for cash prizes put up by newspaper publishers, wealthy aviation enthusiasts, and a growing number of aero clubs that were being formed all over the world. Aircraft were built of wooden frameworks, covered with doped canvas and braced by wires and turnbuckles. They were relatively cheap to build and repair, the engines being the most expensive item. Pilots had no cockpits but sat, exposed to the wind, braced by rudder pedals and control wheel. For many years no safety belts were used, and a high percentage of fatalities in crashes resulted from the pilot being pitched out of his plane. Goggles, cap worn backwards, and checkered Norfolk style jacket became the uniform of the pilots during that era. Fierce competition at the air meets produced constantly improving performance that soon enabled the airplanes to race successfully against the automobiles of that vintage. Among the notable milestones of that era

The 1927 nonstop New York–Paris flight of Charles Lindbergh in the *Spirit of St. Louis* excited the world.

were Louis Blériot's first flight across the English Channel (1909); Walter R. Brookins' altitude record of 6,175 feet, or 1,852 meters (1910); Glenn Curtiss' flight of 152 miles (245 km) from Albany to New York in 2 hours 46 minutes flying time to win a $10,000 New York *World* prize (1910); and the first transcontinental crossing by an airplane—a Wright biplane piloted by Calbraith P. Rodgers (1911). It took Rodgers about 49 days, during which he survived 15 crashes, to fly from New York to Pasadena, Calif.

Both the Wright and the Curtiss organizations had teams of exhibition and racing pilots who competed for the big prize money. Air racing became the most exciting sport, and the names of the top pilots were as well known as those of baseball stars today. But crashes were frequent, and by the beginning of World War I few of the racing era pilots had survived.

Perhaps because Europe was drawing closer to a major war and its national leaders were more aware of the potential use of aircraft for military purposes, the development of aviation flourished more rapidly in Europe from 1910 onward than in the land of its inception.

The United States Army issued specifications for a military aircraft in 1907, specifying that it must be transportable by horse-drawn wagon. The Wrights were the successful bidders with their biplane model offered at $25,000 a plane. The first acceptance flights were made by Orville Wright at Fort Myer, Va., just outside Washington, D.C. It was here on Sept. 17, 1908, that the first fatal military accident occurred. Orville Wright was piloting Lt. Thomas Selfridge, who, ironically, had been a designer for the rival Curtiss group. At an altitude of 125 feet (37.5 meters) control trouble developed. Orville glided down to about 50 feet (15 meters) when the biplane fell completely out of control and crashed. Orville was thrown clear of the wreckage, suffering a broken thigh and ribs, but Selfridge was pinned in the wreckage of the aircraft and killed.

The Wright biplane sold to the Army had a length of 28 feet (8.5 meters), a wingspan of 36 feet 4 inches (11.1 meters), and weighed 1,200 pounds (540 kg). It could reach an altitude of 140 feet (43 meters) and had a top speed of 44 mph (71 kph) and a range of 125 miles (200 km). It had a 30 hp four-cylinder engine of the Wrights' own design and manufacture.

World War I. By the time war broke out in Europe, the U.S. Army had only one aero squadron, consisting of 8 aircraft and 16 officers. The Navy also had become interested in Glenn Curtiss' flying boat designs and Curtiss pusher designs with propellers at the rear of the wings, which proved their ability to take off from a specially planked surface on the deck of a battleship. In 1914, however, the Navy had only 9 planes and 21 engines for its aerial effort. A series of accidents with the Wright and Curtiss pusher designs put them into military disfavor, and the tractor design with the propeller in front became the standard just before the war.

By the end of 1915 only 100 aircraft, including both military and civil types, had been manufactured in the United States. However, in the 1913–1915 period many of the foundations were laid for the aeronautical development efforts of the next 30 years. The first aeronautical engineering course was established at the Massachusetts Institute of Technology about 1912 by Jerome C. Hunsaker, then a naval officer assigned to aircraft construction. The United States Weather Bureau began publication of a daily aviation weather map in 1914. The National Advisory Committee for Aeronautics, the spearhead of United States technical progress in aviation for the next 40 years, was created by an act of Congress in 1915.

At the beginning of World War I, France had the largest air force, with about 1,500 planes, followed by Germany, with 1,000 military aircraft. Britain lagged badly, with only a few hundred planes, including trainers. The outbreak of war plunged aviation into a forced-draft technical development that achieved more technical progress in three years than had been accomplished in the preceding decade. Aircraft speeds, which were about 60 mph (100 kph) at the beginning of the war, more than doubled to 145 mph (230 kph) for operational fighters in 1918. Altitude ceiling increased from about 14,000 feet (4,200 meters) in 1916 to over 30,000 feet (9,000 meters) by the end of the war. From the prewar aircraft, whose payload was usually only a pilot, a passenger, and gasoline, the useful load increased to more than 3,000 pounds (1,350 kg) in 1918 vintage bombers. Aircraft manufacturing plants and pilot training centers mushroomed in all the belligerent countries to provide a reservoir of facilities and trained personnel that gave the postwar growth of aviation much of its impetus.

From the beginning of World War I there was a bitter debate over the proper military function of the airplane. Most traditional military leaders felt the airplane was primarily a scouting weapon to extend the eyes and ears of the cavalry in locating enemy forces and positions, and it was in this role that the airplane operated during the first year of the war. German and French pilots flying unarmed reconnaissance planes waved to each other as they sped across opposing lines on their missions. Aircraft spotted enemy ground forces, took pictures of the terrain, and dropped propaganda leaflets. Gradually, as the character of the war changed into the bitter trench deadlock, the combative spirit of the airmen increased. Pistols and rifles were carried aloft to take potshots at enemy fliers. Small bombs and grenades were added to aerial equipment to toss at likely targets on the ground. Breaking through the restrictions artificially imposed by military leaders, the airmen added the airplane to the arsenal of deadly military weapons.

By 1915 the French were experimenting with a machine gun mounted to fire forward through the propeller arc. Heavy armor plate encased the blades. While firing a gun thus mounted, Lt. Roland Garros, a prewar aviation pioneer, shattered his propeller blades and was forced down behind German lines.

The Germans quickly sensed the importance of the French development and gave Anthony H.G. Fokker, a Dutchman whose services had been rejected by Britain and France before he settled in Germany, the job of developing a machine gun synchronized to fire through the propeller arc. Fokker solved the problem with a mechanical cam that stopped the machine gun from firing each time a propeller blade was in the line of fire.

German pilots flying planes equipped with the Fokker synchronized machine gun sallied out in force, driving Allied aircraft from the battle area. From this time onward the air in wartime would

Above left: Orville (1871–1948) and Wilbur (1867–1912) Wright made the first powered airplane flight in 1903. *Center:* Samuel Pierpont Langley (1834–1906), an American astronomer and physicist, also designed airplanes. *Right:* Glenn Curtiss (1878–1930) was a pioneer American aviator and inventor.

Above left: Richard E. Byrd (1888–1957), American explorer and scientist, was the first to reach both poles by air. *Center:* Alberto Santos-Dumont (1873–1932), a Brazilian flyer, experimented with the dirigible in France. *Right:* Charles A. Lindbergh (1902–   ) was the first to solo the Atlantic Ocean.

be a disputed area. Control of the air became a prize in itself and a necessary requisite for successful ground or sea operations. The French soon countered with a hydraulically operated machine gun synchronizer, and the air war flared into new fury.

Types of Military Planes. As the war dragged on, three primary types of battle planes emerged as the primary lines of technical development. First came the scout or fighter aircraft designed to drive enemy aircraft from the sky and maintain control of the air. These were single-seater aircraft with the best performance available—starting out at about 90 mph (140 kph) top speed in the early war years and pushing close to 150 mph (240 kph) before the war's end. They were armed with a pair of forward-firing machine guns. It was in this type of aircraft that the great aces of World War I fought and rolled up their record of kills. Baron Manfred von Richthofen of Germany topped the list of fighter pilots with 80 victims, followed by Maj. René Fonck of France with 75, British Maj. Edward "Mickey" Mannock with 73, Canadian Maj. William Avery Bishop with 72, and Capt. Ernst Udet of Germany with 62. The leading United States ace was Capt. Edward V. Rickenbacker, credited with destroying 21 aircraft and four balloons.

The fighter pilots preserved the last elements of the ancient chivalry of knights in combat during the bloody mass slaughter of trench war-

fare. When they were forced down behind enemy lines, the enemy air force entertained them as dinner guests before shipping them off to prison camps. When a fighter pilot was killed in enemy territory, the victors buried him with full military honors and dropped a note containing details of his demise and a photograph of his grave on his squadron aerodrome. Even in the swirling dogfights between squadrons of fighter planes, the combat usually consisted of individual duels.

However, a German schoolteacher named Oswald Boelcke, turned fighter pilot, changed this style of combat. Boelcke was the originator of fighter tactics that saw flights and squadrons deployed so that they fought as a group rather than as individuals. Boelcke was killed after 43 victories, in a mid-air collision with a wingman, before he could fully apply his tactics in combat over the western front. But his leading pupil, Baron Manfred von Richthofen, put them into practice with his wing of red-painted Fokker triplanes and dominated the air over northern France for months with Boelcke's tactics.

The continuing design series of Fokker dominated the German fighter planes. The most famous was his triplane, which was extremely maneuverable for dogfighting but short on range and level speed. The D-VII model, which used metal tubing instead of wood, was the first cantilever wing combat plane and had outstanding performance characteristics. The D-VIII Flying Razor was a high-wing monoplane with a tapered wing. Only a few reached combat, but they easily outclassed the other 1918 vintage fighters over the western front. On the Allied side, the British Sopwith Camel and SE-5 fighter planes, and the French Nieuport and Spad fighters, were the cream of their crop.

As the war settled down to the grim stalemate of the trenches, both sides sought means to surmount this obstacle and strike deeper at the roots of each other's war effort. This led to the development of bombers, the second primary type of battle plane. The Germans raided London and other key English towns in Zeppelins, but the giant airships soon succumbed to the double menaces of British fighters and North Sea weather. They were supplanted by the twin-engine Gotha bombers and later by the giant Siemens-Schuckert R-1 bombers with a wing span of 150 feet (45 meters) and engines located in the fuselage, where they could be repaired in flight.

The British retaliated with raids on the industrial towns of the Ruhr and Rhine valleys with Handley Page biplane bombers, which could deliver a 1,650-pound (750 kg) bomb load, and with the shorter-ranged de Havilland DH-4 bombers, which operated against supply dumps, artillery concentrations, and other rear line targets. The French developed the Farman and Bréquet bombers, while the Italians used the giant Caproni triplane bombers, which had a wingspan of 130 feet (39 meters) and could carry 3,000 pounds (1,350 kg) of bombs. They operated from Italian bases and penetrated deep into Austria and southern Germany on their raids.

The third specialized type of battle plane was the two-seater observation plane designed to photograph enemy terrain and observe troop movements, artillery concentrations, and supply dumps. Early in the war, captive balloons were used for this purpose, but they became too vulnerable to enemy fighter aircraft and were superseded by the observation plane protected by a covey of fighter aircraft. Many of the mass fighter combats over the western front were engaged in to control the sky for the operations of the observation planes.

United States in World War I. The first Americans to fight in the air over Europe were volunteers who enlisted in the French Foreign Legion and in 1915 formed the Lafayette Escadrille. Later, after the United States entered the war in April 1917, the first contingents of United States Army pilots were assigned to the Royal Flying Corps and flew under the command of British and Canadian officers.

The United States air effort was dominated by the personality and ideas of Brig. Gen. William (Billy) Mitchell, who was the first American aviator to reach the western front and who commanded the combat aviation units of the American Expeditionary Force during the final offensives of 1918. General Mitchell was an aerial strategist who saw far beyond the capabilities of the spruce and fabric planes he had to fly during World War I. Like the German Boelcke, he concentrated on developing tactics for using aircraft in large masses to achieve major strategic aims, rather than for aimless dogfighting. For the American offensives at St.-Mihiel and in the Argonne in 1918 he organized all the aviation under his command into a strategic offensive. His first effort was to sweep the Germans from the sky over the battlefield, thus denying them observation of American troop movements. He then turned his aerial offensive against the German rear areas to destroy their supplies and artillery and prevent reserves from moving into the battle line. These basic tactics of isolating the battlefield by aerial action were used effectively again in World War II and the Korean War. Mitchell also prepared to deliver a large-scale attack by paratroops and airborne infantry for an offensive planned in 1919 in much the same way that Allied troops hurdled the Rhine River barrier in 1945 by airborne assault.

Out of his experience in the brief but significant aerial action of 1918, General Mitchell developed the deep-seated convictions that were to lead to his postwar crusade for the development of adequate military airpower. They also would lead to his court-martial by the traditionalist element in the military leadership who, disputing the lessons of the western front, could

In 1920 this converted wartime de Havilland carried mail and was able to fly 100 miles (160 km) an hour.

The Ford Tri-Motor, employed in the transcontinental service begun in 1930, could carry 12 passengers.

not envision the airplane as anything more than a scouting force.

The United States entered World War I woefully weak in the air, with a strength of only 55 observation planes, 35 pilots, and 1,087 enlisted men. The performance of the aviation section of the Signal Corps on the Mexican border in support of Gen. John J. Pershing's punitive expedition in 1916 had proved it weak in maintenance and operational reliability, as well as in combat potential. Although the Allies soon swamped United States factories with orders for aircraft and engines, most of the combat planes had to be of foreign design because there were no modern American designs. The bulk of American design skill was concentrated on training planes and the engines for them. Among the foreign designs produced in the United States were the British de Havilland DH-4 bomber, the Lepère French fighter, the Italian Caproni triplane, and the French Hispano-Suiza engine. The only American-built combat planes to see use in Europe before the Armistice were a few Dayton-built DH-4S's. United States fighter squadrons flew French and British planes exclusively in combat until the war's end.

Stimulated by the huge wartime appropriations for aircraft that totaled $598,000,000 in 1917–1918, American manufacturers delivered 13,943 airplanes and 41,953 aircraft engines. United States designers produced some extremely good combat designs, but they were all too late to see service. These included the Curtiss-18 fighters and the Thomas Morse MB-3, both in the 150 mph class, and the Martin MB bomber, a twin-engine giant of its era.

The first practical guided missile—the Bug—also was developed in 1918 by Elmer A. Sperry and Charles F. Kettering. It was built of papier-mâché with wood framework and could carry a 300-pound (135-kg) bomb load automatically delivered on a target 40 miles (65 km) from takeoff. In concept and function it was the forerunner of the German V-1 flying bomb of 1944.

From 1919 to 1939. Aviation emerged from the war still continuing its rapid technical development, and with large quantities of war surplus aircraft, trained pilots, and technicians,

The Douglas DC-3, starting in 1936, was used heavily for many years in commercial and military transport.

but no immediate prospects of absorbing them into peaceful pursuits.

The rapid technical growth was evident in the spectacular performance of a series of planes developed during the final years of the war. The first transatlantic crossing by air was made in May 1919 by the U.S. Navy's NC-4 antisubmarine seaplane, with stops in Newfoundland and the Azores. The plane covered a distance of 3,396 nautical miles (6,289 km) from New York to Plymouth, England, in 53 hours 58 minutes. A month later a British Vickers-Vimy bomber flown by Capt. John Alcock and Lt. Arthur Whitten Brown of the Royal Air Force crossed from Newfoundland to Ireland in the first nonstop transatlantic flight, taking 15 hours 57 minutes for the flight from coast to coast. Another Vickers-Vimy flown by a Royal Air Force crew forged the first aerial link between England and Australia in the fall of 1919.

A new altitude record of 33,113 feet (9,934 meters) was set in 1920 by Maj. Rudolph W. Schroeder of the U.S. Army Air Service in a Lepère biplane with a supercharged Liberty engine. The world speed record was pushed up to 178 mph (286 kph) by a Verville Packard plane piloted by Lt. C.C. Moseley of the U.S. Army, winning the Pulitzer trophy race for 1920.

However, both military and civil aviation were headed for the doldrums during the early 1920's. Military pilots, stifled by the older leaders of the Army and Navy, were forced to fly obsolete war surplus types for many years. There was only a trickle of military funds to keep alive the continuity of technical development. Much of the aircraft airframe and engine industry evaporated after the war. Only a handful of dedicated men stuck to their trade of airplane building during the lean 1920's. Among these men were Glenn L. Martin and his aides Lawrence Bell, Donald Douglas, and J.D. Kindelberger (each of whom eventually was to head a giant aircraft firm of his own), William E. Boeing in Seattle, Frederick B. Rentschler at the Wright-Martin Company in New Jersey, Grover C. Loening, and a few others.

Civil aviation failed to grow significantly during the early 1920's. A generation of "barnstormers," equipped with war surplus Jennies powered by the Curtiss OX5 engine and the DH-4 powered by the Liberty engine, eked out a precarious living at county fairs by racing, stunting, hopping passengers, and dispensing flying lessons. The Post Office Department attempted to operate airmail routes, but many of these soon were abandoned because they offered little improvement in service. A few courageous groups ventured into the airline business, but passenger carrying was restricted by the small size of the planes available.

Court-Martial of General Mitchell. The major event during the early 1920's was the sensational climax to the career of Brig. Gen. William Mitchell and the seeds it sowed for the development of military airpower during the next two decades. General Mitchell returned from his wartime experience in France an ardent crusader for the large-scale development of airpower as the keystone of United States military policy. His first crusade was directed against the Navy, whose battleships he claimed were rendered obsolete by bomber aircraft. In 1921, with congressional approval, General Mitchell was given an opportunity to test his theories against a series of captured German vessels, including the superdreadnaught *Ostfriesland,* which had been unsinkable by British gunfire in the Battle of Jutland. General Mitchell's bombers sank the German warships, including the *Ostfriesland,* in a spectacular demonstration of aerial bombardment by land-based Martin bombers, making their attack on the ships at sea off the Virginia capes. Two years later the Army Air Service fliers sank the obsolete United States battleship *Virginia* in four minutes and the *New Jersey* in seven minutes. But it was not until eight battleships of the United States Navy were sunk by Japanese aircraft in Pearl Harbor on Dec. 7, 1941, that this lesson really was learned by the battleship admirals of the U.S. Navy.

Demoted from assistant chief of the Army Air Corps and exiled to a minor post in Texas, General Mitchell refused to abandon his crusade and deliberately invited court-martial by pointing out the technical fallacies in the Navy's ill-fated dirigible program. General Mitchell used his court-martial in 1925 as a sounding board to carry the case for airpower to the American public and to bring attention to the obsolete policies of the Army and Navy. Although Mitchell's military career was ended by his conviction, he stimulated public interest in the airpower situation. A series of congressional and presidential investigations eventually produced military and civil policies that revived aviation development during the 1930's.

Achievements of the 1920's. The military aviators still were primarily concerned with stretching the performance of their equipment and demonstrating its capabilities to an apathetic public. Among the outstanding military achievements of this period were: the first nonstop transcontinental flight in 1923 by Lts. John A. Macready and Oakley G. Kelly, who piloted a Fokker T-2 monoplane from New York to San Diego in 26 hours 50 minutes; the round-the-world flight of four Douglas World Cruisers in 1924, piloted by Air Service officers, covering 27,553 miles (44,339 km) in 175 days; the first aerial refueling operations by two Army pilots in 1923; and an endurance record without refueling of 28 hours 35 minutes, established in 1925 by U.S. Navy Lts. C.R. Schildhauer and J.R. Kyle in a PN-9 flying boat.

Among the other notable United States Navy achievements during this period were the first flight over the North Pole in 1926 by Lt. Comdr. Richard E. Byrd and his crew in a Fokker trimotor plane and the establishment of an altitude record of 37,995 feet (11,588 km) in 1927 by Lt. C.C. Champion, flying a Pratt & Whitney Wasp-powered Apache.

Out of the ferment of the early 1920's the technical and political developments emerged that were to pave the way for an undreamed-of expansion of commercial aviation and new combat potential for the military air services during the 1930's. On the technical side there were two major developments. One was the trend away from the biplane design, with its drag-creating mesh of struts and bracing wires, to the low-drag, cantilever wing monoplane design. The other was the development of the radial air-cooled engine. The latter proved to be so much more reliable and so much lighter than the water-cooled designs that it provided a significant performance margin for successful commercial operations and improved military performance. Charles

Lawrence developed the air-cooled radial engine in the United States, initially, with its significant development carried on by the Wright Aeronautical Corporation with its Whirlwind series and later by Pratt & Whitney Company with its Wasps and Hornets.

Politically, the sensations of the Mitchell court-martial, combined with growing public concern over airpower, produced a series of legislative acts that laid the foundation for sound military and commercial aviation development. The Air Corps Act of 1926 raised the Army's aviation to corps status and provided it with the nucleus of a professional officer corps of pilots and technicians. The Navy created the Bureau of Aeronautics under Rear Adm. William A. Moffett and under his guidance laid down a program to develop aircraft carriers as a challenge to the battleship. In the commercial field the Kelly Act of 1925 took the Post Office Department out of the airmail business and opened it to bids from private contractors. The Air Commerce Act of the following year established a uniform system of licensing, thus reducing the anarchy of commercial aviation. It also authorized creation of a federal airways system using light and radio beacons to mark highways of the air.

Lindbergh's Flight. These elements of the explosive aviation development of the 1920's were detonated by the spectacular nonstop flight of Charles A. Lindbergh from New York to Paris on May 20–21, 1927. Lindbergh's triumph was based on the combination of the Ryan monoplane (which Lindbergh named *Spirit of St. Louis*) and the Wright radial air-cooled engine—the two technical elements that were to dominate the postwar renaissance of aviation. The $25,000 prize for the first New York-Paris nonstop flight was offered in 1920 by the Orteig brothers, Frenchmen who had built a fortune from American hotels. But it was not until the combination of the efficient monoplane design and the reliable and light air-cooled engine was developed that even the most skillful and daring pilot could turn the trick. Lindbergh's solo flight to Paris in 33 hours 20 minutes touched off an aviation boom of such magnitude that even when its more ephemeral elements dissolved, the curve of civil and military aviation continued to rise.

The Lindbergh flight to Paris touched off a series of record-seeking flights that stretched over the next 10 years. Many of these were simple attempts to seek fame and glory for the participants, but others were solid efforts by technically skilled participants to push the parameter of aircraft performance to its maximum limits. For example, the transcontinental speed record, which stood at 21 hours 44 minutes in 1924 as a result of U.S. Army Lt. Russell L. Maughan's famous dawn-to-dusk flight across the United States in a Curtiss pursuit plane, was cut to 7 hours 28 minutes by Howard Hughes in 1937. In 1935, Hughes had pushed the world speed record to 352 mph (566.5 kph) in a plane of his own design and manufacture that set the transcontinental record. By 1933, Wiley Post had flown 15,596 miles (25,099 km) around the world solo in just 7 days 18 hours, piloting the Lockheed Vega monoplane *Winnie Mae*, which now hangs with its Wasp engine in the Smithsonian Institution.

But behind the spectacular façade of the record breakers, genuine and "phony," who filled the newspaper headlines of the late 1920's and early 1930's, the firm foundations of the United States bid for world leadership in both commercial and military airpower were being laid.

Commercial Developments. Commercial aviation in the United States was still in the cow pasture stage at the end of 1926, lagging far behind European airline developments which were spurred by strong government financial support. When Lester D. Gardner, editor of *Aviation Magazine*, made a 26,000-mile (41,840-km) air tour of Europe in 1926, he traveled a well-established commercial network that carried him through the busy airports of Croydon for London, Templehof for Berlin, Le Bourget for Paris, and to North Africa, Russia, and the Middle East. In contrast, the United States had only a trickle of airmail, carried in obsolete DH-4 planes. A single dimly lighted airway stretched from New York to Cheyenne, Wyo., and there was nothing that honestly could be called an American commercial airline. A few short-haul air express services and passenger charter operators were on the scene, but like the Post Office, they were plagued with inefficient and unreliable war surplus equipment. There was no air traffic control, no safety regulations, or aviation law.

Seven years later the United States boasted the busiest airport in the world. At Newark, N.J., the air terminal for New York City, airline traffic for 1933 surpassed the combined total of Croydon, Le Bourget, and Templehof for the same year. Commercial airports at Los Angeles, Chicago, and Camden, N.J. (serving Philadelphia), all were busier than any European airfield.

In 1933, United Air Lines was the largest United States air carrier, while the German Lufthansa dominated its field abroad. During 1933 the Lufthansa carried only 10 percent of the airmail tonnage and a little more than half the passenger volume of United, while the German transports flew only 40 percent of the route miles covered by United's planes. Pan American Airways operated more multiengine transports in 1933 than the combined total for all European airlines, and four years later, Pan American Airways Clippers became the first to span both the Pacific and Atlantic oceans in airline operations.

This surge carried United States commercial aviation to world leadership, which it has never relinquished. The surge was based on a favorable governmental climate that offered airline operators an opportunity to make a profit on airmail transport and on subsidized passenger service during their growth period. Another factor was the technical progress that made carriage of profitable payloads possible.

Technical Trends. The technical trends of this era still dominated commercial transport design until the advent of the gas turbine engine. It was in the early 1930's that aircraft construction switched from the spruce, fabric, and plywood of the 1920's to metal (mainly aluminum) as the dominant material. Propellers also were changed from wood to aluminum. The Ford all-metal trimotor design of the early 1930's started the trend, but the third motor soon was abandoned as engine reliability improved. The twin-engine Boeing 247 carrying 12 passengers, and the Douglas DC series with their low-wing monoplane designs became the new airliner standard. The DC-1 flown by Daniel W. Tomlinson set a new transcontinental speed record of 11 hours 5 minutes in 1935. By 1936 its successor, the 21-passenger DC-3, had given the airlines reliable

NORTH AMERICAN AVIATION, INC.

The P-51 (later F-51) Mustang (USA)

LOCKHEED AIRCRAFT CORP.

The P-38 Lightning (USA)

EWING GALLOWAY

The B-24 Liberator (USA)

NORTH AMERICAN AVIATION, INC.

The B-25H Mitchell (USA)

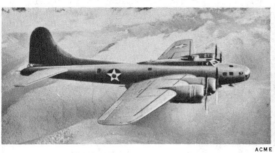

ACME

The B-17E Flying Fortress (USA)

EWING GALLOWAY

The RAF Mosquito (Great Britain)

BRITISH INFORMATION SERVICES

The Mark XII Spitfire (Great Britain)

SOVFOTO

The Stormavik (USSR)

UNITED PRESS

The Zero (Japan)

WIDE WORLD PHOTOS

The Stuka (Germany)

equipment with which they could begin to operate at a profit. The Douglas DC-3 was the workhorse of commercial and military transport operations for nearly 20 years.

During this same period burgeoning technical development was pushed primarily by the airline market with development of precise navigation instruments and radio navigation aids. Blind flying instruments that enabled airliners to operate through heavy clouds and bad weather, controllable pitch propellers for better takeoff and cruising performance, and air-to-ground radio communications all combined to increase the safety and reliability of airline operations during the 1930's. By 1939 the airlines of the United States were carrying close to 3 million passengers annually, and their service extended to every major city. Pan American World Airways had spanned both the Atlantic and Pacific and was operating extensively in Latin America—the forerunner of a large network of United States flag line international air services that blossomed after World War II.

Military Developments. Military airpower, however, was making less progress against the traditional advocates of sea and land power. In the Navy the aviators were fighting primarily against the advocates of the battleship for the development of aircraft carrier striking groups. In the Army Air Corps the battle was not only against the land-bound generals of the War Department but also against the battleship admirals of the Navy who fought successfully to limit the range of operations for land-based aircraft to within 300 miles (483 km) from the United States coasts until the eve of World War II.

During the early 1930's the foundations of the aircraft carrier striking forces were developed by naval aviators, although early carriers were simply converted cruisers. In the same period the Air Corps strategists pushed development of long-range heavy bombers.

In their concentration on long-range bomber development the Air Corps strategists neglected other fields, notably long-range fighter aircraft, that were to cause them considerable trouble in World War II. The Martin B-10 twin-engine bomber of the early 1930's was the first truly modern bomber, using all-metal construction, low-wing monoplane design, and carrying relatively heavy bomb loads and defensive armament. Its 250 mph (400 kph) speed was faster than that of the fighters of its day, adding further fuel to the arguments against building defensive fighter planes. By 1935 the first prototype Boeing B-17 bomber had been delivered to the Air Corps for flight testing.

Although the prototype crashed shortly after takeoff on its initial test flight at Wright Field near Dayton, Ohio, in July 1935, the Air Corps never lost its faith in the future of the big bomber. It continued to put most of its available procurement funds into pushing bomber development with the Boeing XB-15 and the Douglas XB-19, the latter being the largest aircraft in the world at the time of its flight testing in 1939. From this development emerged the production versions of the B-17 four-engine Flying Fortress, just going into operational service in small numbers by 1941, and the later B-29 long-range bomber, which proved decisive in the Pacific war.

While the Air Corps was concentrating on bomber development, it permitted fighter development to lag. One complicating factor was a policy decision to abandon reliance on the air-cooled radial engine and concentrate on a liquid-cooled design, because of lower frontal drag permitting more streamlined airframe designs. During the period of 1936–1941 the Air Corps turned its back on the air-cooled engine for fighter craft only. But continued support by the Navy kept this type in production and available for the widespread Army and Navy use necessitated by World War II. Another complicating factor was the concept that fighters were to function only as short-range interceptors. Consequently the long range needed later was neglected in fighter development.

The combination of a growing healthy commercial aviation and a military policy of continuous development of new types of aircraft put a solid floor under the aircraft manufacturing industry during the 1930's. This was to become the foundation for the enormous wartime expansion of 1940–1944. Such firms as Douglas, Boeing, Lockheed, and Consolidated stabilized on the West Coast on a mixed military-commercial market, while Grumman, Republic, Glenn L. Martin, Curtiss-Wright, and United Aircraft grew into substantial industrial enterprises along the Atlantic seaboard.

By the late 1930's the German Luftwaffe had again become a potent force in European skies. The Luftwaffe's Condor Legion performed impressively in combat during the Spanish Civil War of 1936–1939. In the spring of 1939 a Messerschmitt BF-109 fighter aircraft set a world speed record of 469 mph (754.8 kph). These events served notice that a new factor had entered the European airpower situation. Simultaneously, the Japanese were building a powerful naval air force, based on the U.S. concept of an aircraft carrier striking force.

World War II. When the European war began in 1939 the Germans had the strongest air force in Europe, although it was designed not for the exercise of independent airpower strategy but for close support of armored and infantry divisions of their army. The Luftwaffe was strong in fighters and dive bombers but weak in medium bombers and devoid of heavy bombers. German bombers lacked range, bomb load, and heavy defensive armament required for independent air strategy.

The French air force was large, but it consisted chiefly of obsolete planes. The Luftwaffe drove it from the skies by the spring of 1940.

The Royal Air Force (RAF) of Britain was developed primarily as a defensive weapon, although the doctrine of independent airpower was still strong among the British airmen who originated it. The eight-gun, high performance fighters of the RAF (the Hawker Hurricane and Supermarine Spitfire) were in the 350 mph (560 kph) class and had the edge over Luftwaffe formations operating near the edge of their range.

Both over Dunkerque and later, in the Battle of Britain, over the approaches to London, the RAF fighters scored decisive victories over the Luftwaffe in 1940. RAF Hurricanes and Spitfires inflicted such heavy losses on the Luftwaffe formations over England that daylight operations were abandoned, and the bombing attack on London switched to the cover of darkness. Never again did the Luftwaffe really threaten England from the air, and large scale offensive efforts were not renewed until the availability of the pilotless V-1 and V-2 missiles of 1944. If the Luftwaffe

The Boeing 727, introduced in 1964, was the first commercial three-engine jet. It seats 114 passengers.

The Douglas DC-8 is a jet-powered airliner that is employed by many of the world's airlines.

lacked the proper equipment for a sustained, successful air offensive against England, so did the RAF lack sufficient range and the right type of bomber equipment to carry the air battle deep into the German industrial complex.

Into this European air deadlock the U.S. Army Air Forces moved in 1943 with a new type of equipment and strategic concept. The equipment was the four-engined, high-altitude medium bomber symbolized by the Boeing B-17 Flying Fortress and the Convair B-24 Liberator, both designed to deliver five tons of bombs on precise enemy industrial targets in daylight in the face of enemy fighter and antiaircraft opposition. The doctrine was strategic airpower, carrying the war through the air to the heart of the enemy's war effort and wrecking his factories, transport system, and will to resist.

The U.S. Eighth and Fifteenth air forces, charged with executing this attack, ran into many difficulties during their early offensive against German-held Europe. Development of a sound strategic target system required a longer effort than anybody anticipated. It was not until the aircraft factories, synthetic oil refineries, and the transportation system were given top priority that the German war machine began to grind to a halt. Better navigation and bombing methods were needed. Bloody losses were inflicted by German flak and fighters until the defensive armament of the medium bombers was increased and long-range escort fighters entered the fray.

The appearance of the North American P-51 Mustang (after the war redesignated F-51—for "fighter"), with enough range to escort bomber formations to any target in Germany and sufficient performance to destroy enemy fighters encountered over these targets, was a decisive

turning point in the air battle for Europe. The combined Anglo-American air offensive, with the RAF carrying the burden at night and the Fortresses and Liberators bombing by day, finally crushed the German war effort.

In the Pacific a different but no less decisive pattern of airpower developed. Initial Japanese successes in the strikes on the United States battleships at Pearl Harbor, the British in Malaya, the Dutch in Indonesia, and the United States in the Philippines all were predicated on skillful use of naval airpower based on the aircraft carrier's long-range striking force. Fortunately United States Navy carriers were absent from Pearl Harbor during the Japanese surprise attack and were therefore available to blunt the enemy's advance through the Pacific in a series of extraordinary naval battles in the Coral Sea and off Midway in the spring of 1942. Both these battles were waged completely by both sides with naval carrier-based aircraft. Both sides suffered heavy losses in aircraft and carriers, but the Japanese were beaten decisively and lost the cream of their naval aviators.

Although the standard Japanese navy fighter, the Zero, was superior in performance to the Navy and Army fighters the United States used at the beginning of the Pacific war, the Japanese lacked the technical development effort to support a steady growth of new, improved aircraft types. By the middle of 1943, new United States types, such as the Grumman Hellcat, the Vought Corsair, and the Lockheed Lightning, had wrested air superiority from the Japanese. The airpower pattern during the first phase of the Pacific war saw the gigantic Navy carrier task forces spearheading the advance of amphibious landing forces to capture Japanese island strongholds. This de-

Vickers, in Great Britain, entered its jet-powered VC-10 in the field of intercontinental transport in 1965.

Above: The Soviet Union's AN-22 turboprop is a very large commercial transport plane that can carry 700 passengers. *Below:* The TU-114, another Soviet turboprop, provides intercontinental service.

veloped into a gigantic interdiction campaign whereby the sea and air communications of the Japanese empire were severed without assaulting major bastions of enemy strength, such as Truk and Rabaul. The climax of this campaign was reached in the capture of the Mariana Islands and the appearance of the Boeing B-29 Superfortress—the first heavy bomber to see combat.

Combination of the Mariana bases and the Superfortress' range put the Japanese home islands under the shadow of United States strategic airpower. As in the air over Europe, the strategic doctrine required considerable refinement before it was successful. High-altitude bombing proved unsuccessful because of the high winds. High explosive bombs also proved ineffective. To do this job properly, the B-29's had to use incendiary bombs that gutted the wooden cities of Japan, and they went down to 5,000-foot altitudes to confuse the enemy defense.

With the appearance of the atomic bomb that seared Hiroshima on Aug. 6, 1945, followed three days later by another dropped on Nagasaki, the Japanese war effort came to an end, and the Japanese empire surrendered without a single land battle in the homeland.

Commercial Aviation Since 1945. The years following World War II were marked by the expansion of commercial aviation on a scale never dreamed of by the most optimistic prophets of the prewar era; a fierce pace of technological development that pushed aircraft performance beyond all prewar predictions; and a bitter battle

for supremacy in nuclear airpower between the United States and the Soviet Union.

Initially, commercial operations were dominated by surplus war transports—the Douglas DC-3, the four-engine Douglas DC-4, the Lockheed four-engine Constellation, and the Curtiss twin-engine C-46. However, United States manufacturers were quick to convert their wartime engineering and manufacturing experience into design and production of a more modern series of airliners designed for maximum economy of operation.

Douglas produced a larger and faster version of its four-engine design, the DC-6, which proved to be the most successful of the transport designs in the decade following the war. This series was built in both passenger and cargo versions and later extended, by the addition of more powerful engines, into the DC-7, with cruising speed up to 365 mph (587 kph) and nonstop range of 5,000 miles (8,000 km). During this same period, Lockheed enlarged and refined its tripletailed Constellation design.

While the Americans continued to develop their tried and true line of piston-powered transports, the British struck boldly in the new direction of jet propulsion. The first fruits of this British effort came early in 1952, when British European Airways inaugurated the first commercial jet service with the Vickers Viscount powered by four Rolls Royce gas turbine engines driving propellers. The Viscount proved extremely successful in airliner service in Europe, Canada, and

The X-15 rocket-powered research plane drops from a Boeing B-52 as it begins its initial flight in 1959.

Australia and made the first penetration of the American transport market by a foreign product. The second British venture into the jet transport field was the de Havilland Comet, powered by four turbojets. The Comet was the first turbojet-powered aircraft to go into regularly scheduled airline service when it began operating on the British Overseas Airways Corporation routes to South Africa in 1952. The Comet program came to a temporary halt in 1954 as a result of two accidents over Italy in which the crew and passengers of two BOAC Comets were killed by what appeared to be mid-air explosions. Subsequent investigation by the Royal Aircraft Establishment disclosed that the pressurized cabins of the Comets had failed when metal fatigue occurred around the corners of the cabin windows. The resulting explosive decompression demolished the aircraft in the air. Corrections for these structural problems were made by de Havilland, and by the 1960's many Comet transports were operating on international air routes.

Russia was the second nation to have regular jet airliner service. The Tupolev-designed TU-104 began operating in 1956, and the TU-134, TU-154, and YAK-140 (all with rear-mounted turbofan engines) are medium- and short-range successors to the TU-104 series. The USSR has a large family of jet transports, from the long-range TU-114 to the Antonov AN-10, which can operate from grass and dirt fields. In the 1960's the Soviets unveiled the giant four-jet Ilyushin 62, designed to carry 180 passengers nonstop over intercontinental distances, and the even larger AN-22, which could carry more than 700 passengers. A Mach 2.2 supersonic transport, the TU-144, was also being developed.

The United States was late in entering the jet transport market; the Boeing 707 was not in regular service until 1959. By the 1960's, however, the United States dominated the international jet transport field and was expanding rapidly into air cargo service as well. The Boeing 737 and Douglas DC-9 extended transport operations to the short-haul field. Boeing and Lockheed were also building a "jumbo" jet capable of carrying 700 fully-equipped combat troops and military equipment such as tanks. A supersonic transport that could fly from New York to Paris in about three hours, at 1,800 mph (2,900 kph), was planned for service in the mid-1970's.

The French also were successful in the jet transport field, with their twin-jet Caravelle, introduced in the 1950's and designed for the short-haul market. The placing of engines at the rear of the fuselage on the Caravelle was widely copied in other jet transport designs. In the early 1960's the French and British formulated a joint development program for a supersonic transport named the Concorde. This giant delta-winged plane, built by a consortium of British and French firms with the financial support of both governments, is designed to carry 110 passengers on the transatlantic route at Mach 2.2, or 2.2 times the speed of sound—about 1,500 mph (2,400 kph).

Military and Research Craft Since 1945. Development of jet fighters in the late 1940's doomed the piston-powered bombers to obsolescence and made their replacement with jet bombers that could fly higher and faster a necessity. The jet bombers were forced to sacrifice range, due to high fuel consumption of jet engines, in return for the higher speed and altitudes offered. As a result, the technique of aerial refueling was revived and transformed from an occasional stunt into a routine operation.

During the immediate postwar period the United States concentrated its military airpower resources on the creation of a long-range striking force armed with atomic bombs. This organization, eventually known as Strategic Air Command (SAC), initially was equipped with Boeing B-50 bombers, an improved version of the wartime B-29. By 1948, SAC had in operation the first truly intercontinental aerial weapon system in the Convair B-36. This bomber was the largest military aircraft ever built, weighing some 400,000 pounds (180,000 kg) on a fully loaded takeoff. It was powered by six piston engines and four jet engines, which produced a total of more than 80,000 horsepower. The Convair B-36 could fly 10,000 miles (16,000 km) without refueling, dropping an atomic bomb load at the halfway point of its flight.

The Korean war stimulated military aircraft construction throughout the world, and the 1950's saw the development of the supersonic jet interceptor and the subsonic jet bomber. In the United States, the jet interceptors developed from the North American Mach 1.5 Super Sabre through the first generation of Mach 2 fighters included the Convair F-106 all-weather, delta-winged interceptor and the Lockheed F-104G Starfighter. Another Mach 2 interceptor and strike fighter, the McDonnell F4H, was powered by two afterburning turbojets and carried a radar operator as well as the pilot. Machine guns and cannon were superseded by radar and infrared-guided, air-to-air missiles on these fighters.

A basic new advance of the early 1960's was the variable-sweep wing, a hinge-mounted wing that enabled the pilot to alter the basic design of his aircraft while in flight. For low speeds the wing is fully extended; for supersonic performance the wing is swept back, a configuration capable of Mach 2.5 speeds. Convair built the Air Force's F-111 variable-sweep fighter-bomber.

United States bomber development was concentrated on the Boeing swept-wing B-47, powered by six turbojets and capable of only medium-range operations without refueling. About 1,500 B-47's were built for SAC by a production consortium of Boeing, Douglas, and Lockheed, and they formed the backbone of the U.S. nuclear striking force in the mid-1950's. They were joined in the latter half of the decade by the Boeing B-52, which eventually had a nonstop range of 12,000 miles (19,300 km) without refueling, and was armed with nuclear missiles. A total of 700 B-52's were manufactured, the B-47's being phased out of service beginning in 1961. The first supersonic bomber, the Convair B-58, entered operational service with SAC in 1960. The delta-winged craft could fly at Mach 2 for sustained periods. However, production of both the B-52 and the B-58 ceased in 1961 as intercontinental ballistic missiles began to take over the major role in the nuclear striking force.

The United States later became the first nation to fly military aircraft at Mach 3. This speed was attained in 1965 by the Lockheed A-11 reconnaissance aircraft and the North American XB-70A bomber. The A-11 went into service with SAC in 1966, but the XB-70 program was canceled after two prototypes were built. One XB-70A was destroyed in 1966 in a mid-air collision with a fighter aircraft.

In Britain, aircraft manufacturing also expanded as a result of the Korean conflict in the 1950's, and exports of British-manufactured jet engines, fighters, transports, and trainers became the largest single source of export income for the United Kingdom. In the field of jet interceptors the English Electric's Lightning P.1 joined the rank of Mach 2 interceptors. As for bombers, Britain developed its V-bomber force of Vickers Valiants, Handley Page Victors, and Avro Vulcans as its nuclear weapon delivery system and equipped the Vulcan with air-to-surface missiles to extend its striking range. All the V-bombers were subsonic and were scheduled to be superseded in the 1970's by supersonic aircraft.

NORTHROP CORP.

These Northrop F-5A supersonic tactical bombers are heavily armed with bombs, missiles, and cannon.

The appearance of the Russian swept-wing, jet-propelled MIG-15 fighter over Korea served surprising notice of the swift progress that the Soviet Union had made with its aircraft development in the jet field. The MIG-15 was an excellent high-altitude interceptor. The Soviet Union later produced several types of Mach 2 interceptors, including the Mikoyan-designed, delta-winged MIG-21 and MIG-23 and a Yakovlev all-weather craft—all of them carrying air-to-air missiles guided by radar or heat-seeking sensors. By 1965 the USSR was flight-testing a delta-winged fighter capable of Mach 3 speeds.

The USSR developed a large fleet of subsonic

The XB-70A, used for advanced testing by the U.S. Air Force, can fly three times faster than sound.

NORTH AMERICAN AVIATION, INC.

GENERAL DYNAMICS

The wings of the U.S. Air Force's F-111 supersonic fighter can pivot, providing a wide performance range.

bombers in the mid-1950's, consisting of the twin-jet Badger medium-range bomber and the four-jet Bison heavy bomber. The Badgers later were modified to carry long-range air-to-surface missiles instead of bombs and have been exported to a number of other nations. The Bison, however, was phased out of service after a limited production run, due to performance deficiencies.

Two types of supersonic bombers were displayed for the first time by the Soviets in their 1961 Tushino air show. They were the 200-foot-long Bounder with a thin delta wing, powered by four huge turbojets, and the smaller Blinder, powered by two aft-mounted jets and equipped with an air-to-ground missile. Both were in the Mach 2 speed range. Andrei Tupolev, dean of Soviet aircraft designers, also built a large turbo-prop-powered, long-range bomber known as the Bear, which is being used extensively for long-range reconnaissance beyond the Soviet borders.

In France the aircraft industry recovered from the effects of World War II and made rapid technical progress in the 1950's and 1960's. The French Dassault Mirage III joined the ranks of Mach 2 interceptors, and in the early 1960's the Mirage IV bomber became the basis of France's strategic retaliatory force and delivery system for its own nuclear weapons. The Mirage IV required refueling from a Boeing jet tanker force, purchased from the United States, in order to reach most of its required strategic targets. The German aircraft industry began its postwar resurgence in the early 1960's, largely by building United States and French designs under license, but also by starting to develop its own designs across a broad spectrum from jet transports to vertical-takeoff military planes.

Military aircraft thus reached the level of Mach 2 speeds in the early 1960's, while transport aircraft were flying in the 500–600 mph (800–1,000 kph) speed range. At the same time, however, research aircraft continued to push back the frontiers of flight by reaching speeds of Mach 5 and altitudes above 350,000 feet (106,000 meters). Spearheading this drive to expand man's range of flight was the United States–developed series of experimental research aircraft ranging from the X-1 to the X-15. It was just 50 years after the Wright brothers made their first faltering flights at Kitty Hawk that a young U.S. Air Force captain, Charles E. Yeager, flew the Bell X-1A rocket-powered research plane to

a maximum speed of 1,650 mph (2,650 kph), equivalent to 2½ times the speed of sound. (Yeager had been the first pilot to fly at the speed of sound in the original Bell X-1.) In the mid-1950's, later models in the series of research planes doubled the X-1's achievements.

But all these advances paled in the face of the assault on the frontiers of flight made by a group of United States military and NASA (National Aeronautics and Space Administration) pilots, who flew North American's X-15 to speeds beyond 4,000 mph (6,400 kph) and to altitudes above 350,000 feet (106,000 meters). The research explorations of the X-15 carried its pilots into the lower fringes of space, and the men were therefore awarded astronaut wings.

See also AEROSPACE INDUSTRY; AIR SAFETY; AIR TRANSPORTATION; AIRCRAFT; AIRPLANE; AIRPORT; AIRSHIP; GLIDING; LIGHTER-THAN-AIR CRAFT; MILITARY AERONAUTICS; NAVAL AVIATION.

ROBERT HOTZ
Editor of "Aviation Week & Space Technology"

Bibliography

American Heritage, eds., *American Heritage History of Flight* (New York 1962).
Balchen, Bernt, and Bergaust, Erik, *The Next Fifty Years of Flight* (New York 1960).
Byrd, Richard E., *Skyward* (New York 1928).
Caiden, Martin, *Barnstorming: The Great Years of Stunt Flying* (Des Moines, Iowa, 1965).
Caiden, Martin, *Flying* (New York 1963).
Caiden, Martin, *Wings into Space* (New York 1964).
Cochran, Jacqueline, *Stars at Noon* (Boston 1964).
Donovan, Frank, *Early Eagles* (New York 1962).
Ley, Willy, *Rockets, Missiles, and Space Travel* (New York 1961).
Lindbergh, Anne Morrow, *Listen! The Wind* (Chicago 1938).
Lindbergh, Anne Morrow, *North to the Orient* (Chicago 1935).
Lindbergh, Charles A., *The Spirit of St Louis* (New York 1953).
Lindbergh, Charles A., *We . . .* (New York 1927).
Macmillan, Norman, *Great Flights and Air Adventures* (New York 1965).
Nayler, J.L., and Ower, E., *Aviation: Its Technical Development* (Chester Springs, Pa., 1965).
Rickenbacker, Edward V., *Seven Came Through* (New York 1943).
Rolfe, Douglas, and Dawydoff, Alexis, *Airplanes of the World* (New York 1962).
Shippen, Katharine B., *A Bridle for Pegasus* (New York 1951).
Sikorsky, Igor I., *The Story of the Winged S* (New York 1958).
Wright, Orville, *How We Invented the Airplane*, ed. by Fred C. Kelly (New York 1953).

AVIATION INSURANCE. See LIABILITY INSURANCE.

AVIATION LAW, ā-vē-ā′shən lô, is a general term relating to various treaties, statutes, rules, regulations, and case-made laws that apply to airplanes, airline travel, liability resulting from damage caused by airplanes, and the right or power of governments or governmental agencies to tax airlines and aviation facilities.

International Agreements. The term "aviation law" frequently refers to aviation liability rules or, more colloquially, aviation accident law. The airplane flies great distances in a short time, and aircraft inevitably go from one country to another. In the early days of aviation, therefore, officials felt that there must be uniform rules, or international aviation would bring chaotic conditions. There was also a strong feeling that the liability of airlines must be limited if the fledgling industry was to prosper.

These basic attitudes underlay the international Paris Conference of 1925, which outlined the areas in which it believed uniformity was needed. These included airline liability, ticketing of passengers, and documentation for cargo and freight handling. The conference set up a committee of international air law experts, called the International Technical Committee of Aerial Legal Experts (CITEJA), with instructions to prepare a draft convention on airline liability and documentation and also to study nine broad areas with a view to the ultimate preparation of other draft conventions. The work of CITEJA continued up to World War II. After that it was continued by the Legal Committee of the International Civil Aviation Organization (ICAO).

CITEJA's initial work on airline liability and documentation produced its only convention of real importance, the Warsaw Convention of 1929. The United States was not a party to the 1925 Paris Conference or the 1929 Warsaw Convention, but it adhered to the latter in 1934.

The Warsaw Convention established some uniform rules for ticketing and documentation and imposed on airlines a limited liability to passengers in international transit. Under the terms of the convention an airline is presumed to be liable, but its liability is limited to $8,300 per passenger. The airline may upset the presumption and escape liability by proving it took all possible steps to avoid the damage. The passenger may recover more than $8,300 by proving the accident was caused by the carrier's "willful misconduct."

Considerable opposition arose in the United States to the Warsaw Convention and other proposed international treaties that would limit damages. Since the United States became the preeminent international air carrier, its antagonism to limitations of liability frustrated efforts of CITEJA and ICAO to enact additional conventions and develop a comprehensive code of international air law.

Other draft conventions were concluded and ratified by some countries, but none was widely adopted. These other conventions include several draft conventions on the charter and hire of aircraft; the Rome Convention of 1933 on damage to persons and property on the ground; the Hague Protocol of 1955, which modified the Warsaw Convention and doubled the $8,300 limitation; and the Guadalajara Convention of 1961, which extended the provisions of the Warsaw Convention to situations where the actual carrier was not the contracting carrier.

Opposition to the damages limitation of the Warsaw Convention led the United States to renounce the convention on Nov. 15, 1965. The renunciation was withdrawn prior to its effective date, however, when most airlines agreed to raise the $8,300 liability limit to $75,000.

Liability in the United States. Domestic aviation liability law in the United States is essentially the same as the law applicable to railroads or automobiles, except that the standards of conduct frequently come from the Federal Aviation Act or the Federal Aviation Regulations promulgated by the Federal Aviation Agency under the authority of the act. In determining negligence the court considers proven violations of a Federal Aviation Regulation, besides other evidence.

Since air flights usually cover greater distances than automobile travel, air liability cases raise more procedural questions than automobile cases do. An automobile accident in New York is likely to involve people from New York and a trial in that state, but an aviation accident in New York is likely to involve people from other states and trials in those states. Accordingly, aviation law has raised many "choice of law" questions and caused a revolution in choice of law principles. Until recently all states followed the rule that the law of the place of the accident would apply. Many states, largely moved by the aviation cases, now have abandoned that rule in favor of a more flexible approach in which the relative interests of the states are considered.

On the question of damages resulting from noise the Supreme Court has ruled that property owners may seek compensation from airport owners and operators. However, the right has been somewhat limited by later cases.

International Traffic Rules. The Paris Convention of 1919, which the United States did not sign or ratify, and the Pan American (Havana) Convention of 1928, which it did, declared that each country has complete and exclusive sovereignty over the air space above its territory. They also granted each country the privilege of flying over the land of the others. The Chicago Convention of 1944 reaffirmed the sovereignty principle and set up the International Civil Aviation Organization (ICAO) to advance international cooperation in aviation matters.

The same conference failed in an attempt to produce a second multilateral convention fixing the rights of countries to fly to, from, and over other countries. This failure left a gap in the international regulation of airline routes and in the control of rules and services. As a result, the Bermuda Air Conference of 1946, attended by the United States and the United Kingdom, achieved the first important bilateral agreement on routes. The International Air Transport Association, the airlines' trade association, was effectively given rate-making authority.

Air Tax Law. In the field of taxation the airlines continue to face the possibility of multiple taxation on their interstate facilities. There is still no clear standard governing the extent to which a state may levy taxes on an airline's property.

LEE S. KREINDLER
Chairman, Aviation Law Section
American Trial Lawyers Association

Further Reading: Billyou, De Forest, *Air Law*, 2d ed. (New York 1964); Kreindler, Lee S., *Aviation Accident Law*, 2 vols. (New York 1963); U.S. Government Printing Office, *Air Laws and Treaties of the World*, 3 vols. (Washington, D.C., 1965).

AVIATION MEDICINE. See under Space Medicine.

AVICENNA (980–1037), av-ə-sen'ə, was the most illustrious philosopher, scientist, and medical writer of medieval Islam. "Avicenna" is derived from the latter part of his Arabic name, *Abu Ali al-Husayn Ibn Abdallah Ibn Sina*, through the Hebrew, *Aven Sina*. He was born near Bukhara, then capital of the Samanid dynasty. By the time he was 10 years old Avicenna had learned the Koran as well as Arabic grammar and literature. While still in his teens, he knew enough about medicine to treat the ailing Samanid ruler Nuh Ibn Mansur. The successful treatment gained Avicenna access to the rich library of that prince. He soon emerged from it proficient in the Hellenic philosophical and mathematical sciences, including Aristotle's *Metaphysics*. After an unsettled life, in which he served as physician and man of affairs at various courts in eastern Persia, he died at Hamadan, leaving behind him an enormous number of writings.

His two most important books, the *Shifa* (*Healing of the Soul*) and the *Canon of Medicine*, exerted much influence on the development of thought in the East and, through Latin translations, in the West. The *Shifa* was nothing less than a comprehensive account of the whole of ancient knowledge, both theoretical and practical, which it set out to explain, scrutinize, and systematize. The work evidences the author's immense learning. It is divided into four principal parts, dealing with logic (including rhetoric and poetics), physics (including psychology, plants, and animals), mathematics, and metaphysics.

The part on logic covers the same ground as Aristotle's works on logic but includes material from later Greek writers. The sections on physics deal with such subjects as cosmology, meteorology, space, time, vacuum, and motion. The mathematical part comprises a condensed version of Euclid's *Elements*, an outline of Ptolemy's *Alma-gest*, and compendiums on arithmetic and music. In philosophy Avicenna's point of view combined Aristotelianism with Neo-Platonic elements and constituted an attempt to reconcile Greek ideas with Islamic beliefs. His later writings display a mystical tendency with a Gnostic and Hermetic influence.

Avicenna's voluminous encyclopedia of medicine, the *Canon*, is a systematic digest of all medical and pharmacological experience available to him. Because of its clear arrangement and rich material, it was often preferred in subsequent centuries to the works of Razi and Galen. The book deals with general principles, simple drugs, diseases affecting specific parts of the body, diseases spreading over large areas of the body (such as fevers), and compound medicines.

In basic conceptions the *Canon* follows Galen and the ancient tradition (theory of the four elements—air, water, fire, and earth; theory of the four humors—blood, phlegm, choler or yellow bile, and melancholy or black bile), but it incorporates many observations that are not to be found in Galen. The *Canon* enjoyed great prestige in Europe, where it continued to be used until the second half of the 17th century. Avicenna's medical writings included the *Poem on Medicine*, which was also widely read in Europe.

A.I. Sabra, *University of London*

Further Reading: Afnan, Soheil M., *Avicenna, His Life and Works* (London 1958); Browne, Edward G., *Arabian Medicine* (Cambridge, Eng., 1921); Gruner, Oskar Cameron, *A Treatise on the Canon of Medicine of Avicenna, Incorporating a Translation of the First Book* (London 1930).

AVIGNON, à-vē-nyôn', is a city in southeastern France and the capital of the department of Vaucluse. Magnificently situated on the left bank of the Rhône River, 40 miles (65 km) from the Mediterranean, Avignon has been a famous European city since the early 14th century. On the rail line between Paris and Marseille, it is an important commercial center for wine, grain, and leather. Because of its proud historical past, its architectural monuments (including the famous papal palace), and its superb site, Avignon is a major tourist center. Across the Rhône is the small village of Villeneuve-lès-Avignon, crowned by the impressive medieval fortress constructed by King Philip IV. Jutting out from Avignon is the famous 12th century bridge known as the Pont St.-Bénézet. Only 4 of the original 18 piers remain, on one of which stands the small Romanesque Chapel of St.-Bénézet. The song *Sur le Pont d'Avignon* is associated with this bridge.

History. When the Romans occupied southern Gaul, Avignon (from the Latin *Avenio*) was a chief town of the tribe of the Cavares. Under the Romans it became a thriving city, but with the Germanic invasions of the 5th and 6th centuries it declined. Never an integral part of the Merovingian or Carolingian states, Avignon belonged successively to the kingdoms of Burgundy and Arles and to the counties of Provence and Toulouse. In 1226 Louis VIII destroyed it for having supported the heretical Albigensians.

For almost a century Avignon remained an obscure town. It was rejuvenated when, in 1309, Pope Clement V decided to make it his residence. From then until 1377, a period known as the Babylonian Captivity, the popes resided at Avignon. During this time they constructed their famous palace, and Avignon was the center of Western Christendom. In 1348, Pope Clement VI pur-

PALACE OF THE POPES in Avignon housed the papal court during the 14th century "Babylonian Captivity."

FRITZ HENLE FROM MONKMEYER

chased Avignon from the countess of Provence. In 1377, Pope Gregory XI decided to return to Rome, but Avignon later became the residence of the two antipopes Clement VII and Benedict XIII during the Great Schism (1378–1417). The papacy continued to hold Avignon, which was governed by papal legates, until 1791. In that year it was annexed to France by the French National Assembly.

Papal Palace. On the high rocky plateau called Rocher des Doms are located the interesting 12th-century Romanesque Cathedral of Notre Dame des Doms with its exquisitely carved Gothic tomb of Pope John XXII, the papal gardens, and the massive Gothic palace of the popes erected between 1316 and 1370. The palace is an extremely impressive edifice, heavy and somber. Although it served as a residence and headquarters for the popes, it was essentially a stone fortress designed for their protection. It consists of two parts: the old palace, sober and severe, reflecting the austere temperament of Pope Benedict XII (reigned 1334–1342), who was a Cistercian monk, and the new palace, reflecting the cultivated artistic tastes of Pope Clement VI (reigned 1342–1352), which utilizes all the resources of architect and artist. The most striking feature of the palace is the magnificent great hall, with its incomparable acoustics. Population: (1962) 64,581.

BRYCE LYON, *Brown University*

ÁVILA, ä′vē-lä, **Blessed Juan de** (c. 1500–1569), Spanish missionary known as the Apostle of Andalusia. He was born in Almodóvar del Campo, Spain, about 1500, and won renown as a preacher and as the author of many spiritual works, notably *Epistolario espiritual* (1578). Ávila died in Montilla, Spain, on May 10, 1569, and was beatified in 1894. His feast day is May 10.

ÁVILA, ä′vē-lä, a city in Spain, is the capital of Ávila province. The city is officially called *Ávila de los Caballeros.* Situated 53 miles (85 km) northwest of Madrid, Ávila lies along the Adaja River. It serves a region that produces chick peas, cereals, and livestock. Industries within the city include woolens, flour milling, and tanning.

Ávila is chiefly noted for its medieval appearance. Many of its buildings date back to the 12th century and have remained unaltered. The city walls, built during the last years of the 11th century, are also intact. The churches of San Vicente and San Pedro are among the best examples of Romanesque architecture in Spain. The cathedral is noted for its sculptures of the period from the 13th century to the Renaissance. A church and convent mark the reputed birthplace of St. Teresa of Ávila, who was born here in 1515.

In ancient times the city was called *Avela* or *Abula.* It changed hands several times between the Moors and Christians until it finally was brought under Christian control by Alfonso VI of León and Castile in 1088. The city's industry and commerce declined drastically after Philip III expelled the Spanish Muslims (Moriscos) in 1607–1610. Population: (1960) 26,807.

ÁVILA CAMACHO, ä′vē-lä kä-mä′chō, **Manuel,** (1897–1955), Mexican political leader, who was president of Mexico during World War II. He gave his country an administration marked by moderation in internal affairs and by cooperation with the United States. This followed a long period of domestic social unrest and of friction with Mexico's northern neighbor.

Ávila Camacho was born at Teziutlán, Puebla, on April 24, 1897. After finishing a course in accounting in 1914, he joined the rebel army of Venustiano Carranza in an ultimately successful revolt against the regime of Victoriano Huerta. In joining the winning side, Ávila Camacho showed for the first time his remarkable ability to "guess right" in the stormy course of Mexican politics during the next two decades.

Rising in the army from 2d lieutenant to division general, Ávila Camacho early acquired the reputation of being a highly skilled administrator. His successful reform of the army, when he was chief of staff of the ministry of war and navy under President Abelardo Rodríguez, led to his appointment in 1937 as minister of national defense by his longtime friend President Lázaro Cárdenas.

In 1939, Ávila Camacho resigned from the cabinet to seek the nomination for president from the government party, the PRM (Party of the Mexican Revolution). He was elected on July 7, 1940, by an overwhelming majority.

As president, Ávila Camacho's campaign pledges to foster better relations with the United States were fulfilled in a number of ways. In 1941 a settlement of the oil expropriation controversy was negotiated, and in the early years of World War II, Mexico supplied much-needed raw materials to the United States. Mexico itself declared war on the Axis powers in 1942. As a further reflection of Ávila Camacho's international outlook, Mexico joined the Bretton Woods agreements and signed the United Nations Charter during his term of office. In domestic affairs, one of his early presidential acts was to inaugurate a strenuous program to reduce illiteracy. He also completed the land reforms inaugurated by his predecessor and fostered the expansion of Mexican industry.

On Dec. 1, 1946, Ávila Camacho was succeeded in the presidency by Miguel Alemán. He remained politically active as head of a strong political machine in his native province of Puebla. He died near Mexico City on Oct. 13, 1955.

AVITUS, ə-vī′təs, **Marcus Maecilius** (died 456), Roman emperor of the West. He was born at the end of the 4th century into a Gaulish family. He gained the favor of Emperor Constantius III, the colleague of Honorius, and of Theodoric II, king of the Visigoths. In 450 he served with distinction under Flavius Aëtius. He soon became prefect of Gaul and concluded a favorable treaty with the Goths. When Attila invaded the West, Avitus persuaded the Goths to join the Romans against the common enemy, the Huns. Through the influence of Theodoric, he was proclaimed emperor of the West in 455 at Arles; Marcian was emperor of the East. The following year the Roman general Ricimer deposed Avitus, who died shortly thereafter in Auvergne, Gaul.

AVIV, ä-vēv′, was the old Biblical name for the first month of the Hebrew year, falling in March-April. It is also spelled *Abib.* The word means *"spring"* in Hebrew. During the Babylonian Exile the Jews adopted Babylonian names for the months, and Aviv was renamed *Nisan.* The feast of Passover is celebrated on Nisan 15–22.

RAPHAEL PATAI, *The Theodor Herzl Institute*

AVOCADO, av-ə-k̇ä′dō, a tropical fruit and the tree that produces it. It is also called alligator pear. Native to Mexico, the West Indies, and parts of Central America, avocados now are cultivated in all tropical and most subtropical parts of the world. In the United States, California, Florida, and Hawaii produce a large quantity of avocados.

The avocado is a many-branched tree that grows to 60 feet (18 meters) or more. Its leaves, which are 5 to 10 inches (12 to 25 cm) long, are leathery and oval-shaped. Its flowers are small and greenish yellow and grow in terminal clusters. The avocado fruit is broadly pear-shaped. Its color varies from green to red or purple.

The avocado tree (*Persea gratissima* or *Persea americana*) belongs to the laurel family, Lauraceae. There are three varieties: the Mexican, the Guatemalan, and the West Indian. The Mexican variety has small, thin-skinned fruit; the Guatemalan has medium or large thick-skinned fruit; and the West Indian has large smooth-skinned fruit.

Avocados have several uses. The greenish yellow flesh or pulp of the fruit is used in salads (hence the name "salad fruit" sometimes given to the avocado). The oil extracted from the fruit is used as a salad oil and in soap and cosmetics.
WALTER SINGER, *The New York Botanical Garden*

AVOCET, av′ə-set, a wading bird with long legs and a slender upcurving bill. It is found in the warmer regions of the world. The avocet differs from most wading birds in having webbed front toes. There are four species—the North American, South American, European, and Australian.

The American avocet (*Recurvirostra americana*) is between 18 and 20 inches (45 to 50 cm) long. It is a showy bird, with black and white plumage (the black mainly on the wings), a chestnut head, and blue legs. Marshy areas and alkali lakes are its favorite habitats. It nests in western Canada, the northwestern United States, southern California, southern New Mexico, and western Texas. In the winter it may range from the southwestern parts of the United States

ROBERT C. HERMES FROM NATIONAL AUDUBON SOCIETY
Avocado fruit

to Guatemala. It rarely is found east of the Mississippi, where it once was hunted for game.

The avocet is frequently found in small flocks along with the stilt (another long-legged shore bird). It feeds on aquatic insects and shellfish near the surface of the water. The nests are simple, and the male and female takes turns incubating the eggs. Always rather noisy, avocets are especially so when guarding their nests from intruders.

ALFRED NOVAK, *Stephens College*

AVOGADRO, ä-vō-gä′dro, **Count Amedeo** (1776–1856), Italian physicist, who originated the hypothesis that equal volumes of all gases, under the same pressure and temperature conditions, contain the same number of molecules. He made this hypothesis in 1811. It has been fully proven since that time, and it is now known as *Avogadro's law*.

Avogadro was born in Turin, Italy, on Aug. 9, 1776. He practiced law and then studied physics and mathematics. He was appointed professor of physics at Vercelli in 1809. In 1811 he set forth his hypothesis in *Essai d'une manière de déterminer les masses relatives des molécules élémentaires des corps, et les proportions selon lesquelles elles entrent dans les combinaisons.* He also suggested that besides molecules that contained different elements there might be molecules that contained only one element. Although his work was disregarded until 1858, it led to the first accurate comparison of molecular weights.

In 1820, Avogadro became a professor of mathematical physics at the university of Turin. While at the university, he conducted research on the electrical, specific-heat, and thermal-expansion properties of substances. He died in Turin on July 9, 1856.

Avogadro's works in physics include *Fisica de' corpi ponderabili* (4 vols., 1837–41). A number is named in his honor. *Avogadro's number,* 6×10^{23}, is the number of molecules per gram molecular weight of a substance.

AVOIDANCE, ə-void′əns, in law, is a plea in which the defendant, without denying the plaintiff's allegation, introduces some new facts in the hope of evading its effect. In ecclesiastical law, avoidance signifies the vacancy of a benefice, or the fact of its being *void* of an incumbent.

American avocet (*Recurvirostra americana*)

ALLAN D. CRUICKSHANK

AVOIRDUPOIS, av-ər-də-poiz', is a system of weights and measures in which a pound contains 7,000 grains or 16 ounces, while a pound troy contains 5,760 grains or 12 ounces. All larger and coarser commodities are weighted by avoirdupois weight. The avoirdupois ounce is less than the troy ounce in the proportion of 72 to 79.

Avoirdupois is the weight used in the United States, where generally the hundredweight contains only 100 pounds and the ton contains 2,000 pounds.

AVON, 1st Earl of. See EDEN, ANTHONY.

AVON, ā'von, a town in Connecticut, is in Hartford County, on the Farmington River, 10 miles by road northwest of Hartford. It manufactures safety fuses and fungicide. Avon Old Farms School for boys, with 20 buildings, resembles an English village. The town was settled in 1640. Population: 8,352.

AVON, ā'von, a city in Ohio, is in Lorain County, about 20 miles (32.1 km) west of Cleveland and 5 miles (8 km) south of Lake Erie. Many of its residents commute to work in Cleveland, Lorain, and Elyria. The manufacture of aircraft products is among the industries. Avon is noted for its many greenhouses.

The site was settled in 1814. Avon became a village in 1917 and a city in 1960. Government is by mayor and council. Population: 7,214.

AVON LAKE, ā'von, is a residential and resort city in northern Ohio, on Lake Erie, 18 miles (28.9 km) west of Cleveland. There are bathing beaches on the lake front. Government is by mayor and council. Population: 12,261.

AVON PARK, ā'von, is a city in Florida, in Highlands County, 80 miles (128.7 km) south of Orlando and 125 miles (201.1 km) northwest of Miami, at almost the geographical center of the Florida peninsula. It is situated in the ridge section of the state, in the heart of a major citrus fruit-producing area; fruit packing is a leading industry. It is well known as a winter resort, and tourists contribute substantially to its economy.

Incorporated in 1923, the city has a mayor-council form of government. Pop. 6,712.

AVON RIVER, ā'vən, a tributary of the Severn River, in southwestern England. It is also called the *Upper Avon* to distinguish it from other English rivers named Avon. It rises in Northhamptonshire and flows 95 miles southwest to the Severn at Tewkesbury. Stratford-on-Avon, the birthplace of Shakespeare, is on this river.

The *Bristol Avon,* or *Lower Avon,* also in southwestern England, rises near Tetbury, in Gloucestershire. It flows 75 miles south and then northwest to the estuary of the Severn below the port of Bristol.

AVONDALE, av'ən-dāl, is a residential town in south central Arizona, in Maricopa County, 17 miles (27.3 km) west of Phoenix. Situated in the western part of the Salt River valley, it is a service and retail center of a rich irrigated agricultural region. Nearby at Litchfield Park is a United States naval air station.

Avondale became an incorporated place in 1946. Population: 6,304.

AVRANCHES, àv-ränsh', a coastal town in France is in western Normandy in the department of Manche. Situated on a rocky promontory overlooking the estuary of the Sée River, it is about eight miles (13 km) northeast of Mont-St.-Michel. The main occupations in the area are farming and livestock raising, and the town is a trade center for fruit, grain, and dairy produce. Fishing also is important.

The Jardin des Plantes, west of the town and on the edge of the promontory, presents a magnificent view of Mont-St.-Michel. In the center of town there is a stone slab marking the spot where Henry II of England made amends to papal representatives in 1172 for the murder of Thomas à Becket. Nearby, the library of the town hall contains a large collection of illuminated manuscripts.

The town had its origin as a Roman military station. It became important under the dukes of Normandy but was devastated during the Hundred Years' War. In the 17th century it was the center of a peasants' rebellion against the salt tax. During World War II, Avranches lay in the path of a major Allied offensive and was badly damaged, but the town has been rebuilt. Population: (1962) 8,828.

AVVAKUM (1620–1682), ä-vä-kōōm', a Russian priest, founded the Old Believer movement within the Russian Orthodox Church. His full name was *Avvakum Petrovich.* A rural priest from the village of Lopatitsa, Avvakum first became famous because of his oratorical and literary abilities. In 1647 in Moscow he joined a circle of Orthodox zealots who were concerned about the ecclesiastical reforms being introduced by Patriarch Nikon. Avvakum attracted many followers, including members of the nobility such as Theodocia Morozova, a relative of the czarina.

Because of his opposition to Nikon, Avvakum was exiled to Siberia in 1653. He returned to Moscow after Nikon's fall from power in 1662, but he was tried by an ecclesiastical court, unfrocked, and imprisoned in 1666. He and his closest followers were burned at the stake on April 14, 1682. The movement continued, and there are still Old Believers in the Russian Orthodox Church.

Avvakum's *Life,* written in 1672–1675, is the first Russian autobiography. Written in the vernacular, it is an outstanding example of 17th century Russian literature.

AVON RIVER at Stratford-on-Avon, England, flows past the Royal Shakespeare Theatre.

AWAJI, ä-wä-jē, an island of Japan, is situated between the larger islands of Honshu and Shikoku, at the eastern entrance of the Inland Sea. Roughly triangular in shape, it has an area of 229 square miles (593 sq km) and is one of the most densely populated islands in Japan.

Rice, wheat, and vegetables are the chief products, and fishing is an important industry. The principal city and administrative center is Sumoto, on the east coast of the island. Population: (1960) 198,808.

AWE, Loch, ô, a lake in Scotland, in Argyllshire. It is linked to Loch Etive by the Awe River. Loch Awe is 23 miles (37 km) long and of great depth. Its sloping shores are terminated by ranges of lofty mountains. Ben Cruachan, at its northern extremity, is the most conspicuous peak, rising to 3,670 feet (1,118.6 meters). A number of islets are scattered over the surface of the lake.

AWOLOWO, ä-wō′lō-wō, **Obafemi** (1909–   ), a leader of the independence movement in Nigeria. Born on March 6, 1909, at Ijebu-Remo in southwestern Nigeria, he was the son of a farmer. Awolowo was educated at mission schools in Ikenné and Abeokuta, and went to Wesley College in Ibadan for teacher's training. After working as a newspaper reporter he became a trade-union organizer and played an active role in the Nigerian Youth Movement.

In 1943 he helped found the Trade Union Congress in Nigeria. Studying part-time, he received a bachelor of commerce degree in 1944 and went to London to study law. While there he wrote a book entitled *Path to Nigerian Freedom,* published in 1947, and founded the Egbe Omo Oduduwa, a Yoruba cultural movement.

Returning to Ibadan in 1947, Awolowo established a successful law practice and remained active in the Egbe. He founded the Action Group in 1951 and that year his new party won the elections in the Western region. He became minister of local government, and after the institution of a new constitution in 1954 he was named prime minister of the Western region. His attempt to make the Action Group a nationwide party failed in the 1959 election, after which he became leader of the opposition in the Federal House of Representatives.

In 1962, following a split in the Action Group and the declaration of a state of emergency in the Western Region, Awolowo was tried for treason and was sentenced in September 1963 to ten years' imprisonment. He was released in August 1966 by the new Nigerian military government.

L. GRAY COWAN, *Columbia University*

AX, a tool for chopping wood or other material. It consists typically of an iron or steel head, with a sharpened edge, attached to a wooden handle. In ancient and medieval times the ax was an important weapon. The carpentry and logging trades use many kinds of axes and hatchets.

The ax was one of the first tools fashioned by man and one of the most important. Anthropologists and archaeologists trace the progress of human culture by the way in which particular groups of men produced axes and other tools at particular times.

The first axes were produced in the Old Stone Age. They were all-purpose tools to be held in the hand for chopping, pounding, digging, crushing, cutting, and slicing. Because they did not have handles, they are called "hand axes" or sometimes "fist hatchets."

As primitive man began to develop toolmaking skills, axes were formed by either of two methods: the *core,* by which a slab of flint or other stone was chipped along one side or end to produce a sharp cutting edge; and the *flake,* which ultilized a single piece of stone chipped from a large slab.

STONE AGE. A flint hand ax (A) of the Paleolithic with characteristic flaking scars. A Neolithic hand ax (B) ground to a high polish. A stone ax (C) made by Australian aborigines of the 20th century.

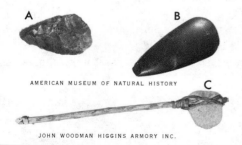

AMERICAN MUSEUM OF NATURAL HISTORY

JOHN WOODMAN HIGGINS ARMORY INC.

BRONZE AGE. A bronze battle ax (D) of Egypt, made sometime between the 12th and 18th dynasties (1991–1304 B.C.). The ax heads (E, F) are specimens of Roman craftsmanship of about the 3d century B.C.

THE METROPOLITAN MUSEUM OF ART

JOHN WOODMAN HIGGINS ARMORY INC.

IRON AGE. An ax (G) with perforated head and straight wooden handle, typical of Swiss La Tene culture. The battle ax (H) is of northern France (c. 700 A.D.), and (I) is the Viking tradition.

AMERICAN MUSEUM OF NATURAL HISTORY

JOHN WOODMAN HIGGINS ARMORY INC.   AMERICAN MUSEUM OF NATURAL HISTORY

A broad ax (J) of colonial America, which became the symbol of westward frontier expansion.

COLONIAL WILLIAMSBURG COLLECTION

A modern steel ax (K), double-edged, finely honed and polished.

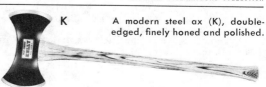

TRUE TEMPER CORP.

Stages of culture in the Stone Age have been classified according to the toolmaking traditions they adopted. Thus the Abbevillian was a core-tool culture, while the Acheulian was a blade-tool culture.

Stone Age man used the hand ax to skin the hides from game animals and to cut up the flesh. As he developed greater skills, he learned how to grind and polish the hand ax so that it would cut better. Later, he learned how to attach a wooden handle to the ax, by boring a hole either in the handle or in the stone head itself. By the time of the late Stone Age, axes were highly refined, durable tools. Grinding techniques superseded the older chipping and flaking methods and enabled man to make use of more durable stone materials, such as basalt.

For many hundreds of thousands of years the stone ax was man's principal tool. Excavated specimens of this ax indicate that early man, regardless of his geographical location, produced axes in much the same way. As certain cultures became more settled with the introduction of agriculture, they developed a division of labor, and skilled toolmakers in a factorylike system produced standardized axes and other tools.

Greater refinements in ax production occurred during the Bronze and Early Iron ages. Some of the earliest bronze axes were virtually copies in metal of traditional stone axes. However, as man improved his skills in working with metals, axes became elaborately decorated precision tools and weapons of war.

In addition to being a tool and weapon, the ax was a symbol of power and an emblem of divinity. Axes of bronze, jade, or polished stone were cult objects. The fasces carried by the Roman lictors included an ax as a symbol of authority. Through the Middle Ages the ax was a standard military weapon (see BATTLE AX).

The iron—later steel—ax became a basic tool of farmers, carpenters, and loggers. In fact, an ax was a household necessity where wood was used as fuel and building material. In colonial America the ax was the most valuable tool of the early settlers, and it became a symbol of the frontier. It was used to clear land for agriculture and to prepare building materials from raw timber. The typical American ax was vastly improved over the European type brought over by the first immigrants. The blade was made thinner, broader, and sharper, and the handle was set forward in the blade. Every community had at least one craftsman who specialized in making ax handles, the most favored wood being hickory.

With advances in metallurgy, ax heads by the late 19th century were made entirely of steel. In the 20th century, power tools tended to replace axes for timber cutting. The ax, however, remained an important tool.

Further Reading: Hawkes, Jacquetta, and Woolley, Sir Leonard, *History of Mankind*, vol. 1 (New York 1963); Oliver, John W., *History of American Technology* (New York 1956).

AXAYÁCATL, ä-shä-yä′kä-təl, was an Aztec emperor in Mexico in the 15th century. He was the father of Montezuma II, who was conquered by Cortes. Axayácatl's life dates are uncertain, although most historians believe that he reigned between 1469 and 1481.

After succeeding his father, Montezuma I, he led a number of successful military campaigns against Tehuántepec, Cotasta, and Tochtepec, and conquered the Matlatzinca territories in the Valley of Toluca. In addition, his victories over Tlaxcala and Tlaltelolco ensured for a time Aztec dominance over central Mexico. Axayácatl's attempt, however, to invade Michoacán, in Tarascan territory, was disastrous; after a crushing defeat, he never regained his ascendancy.

During his reign Axayácatl sponsored a number of cultural works. Notable among these was the Calendar Stone on which were carved details relating to the history of the Aztec world.

AXINITE, aks′ə-nīt, is a mineral silicate of aluminum and boron, containing also varying amounts of calcium, manganese, and iron. Axinite crystals are broad and have sharp edges and a characteristic axlike shape. They are transparent to translucent, have a glassy luster, and may be brown, violet, or yellow. Axinite is usually found in association with granite, often in cavities within the stone. There are good deposits in France, Switzerland, Japan, and the United States (in New Jersey and Nevada).

Composition: $HCa_2(Mn,Fe)Al_2B(SiO_4)_4$; hardness, 6.5 to 7.0; specific gravity, 3.3 to 3.4; crystal system, triclinic.

AXIOM, ak′sē-əm, a postulate or assumption, accepted as true without proof. Every deductive system of reasoning must have a set of axioms as initial premises. The axioms, undefined terms, and defined terms enable one to prove theorems.

A choice of axioms is arbitrary. One may choose many or few, but it is best to choose only a few simple ones to avoid misunderstandings and hidden contradictions. A set of axioms must be consistent—they must not be contradictory or lead to contradictory theorems. A set of axioms should also be independent; that is, no axiom should be deducible from the others.

Euclid structured his entire geometry on only 10 consistent and independent axioms. His concepts and axioms were well chosen. Many theorems in geometry could be deduced from them, and others could follow the same deductive steps.

In the 19th century, mathematicians gave much thought to the significance of axioms. Euclid's axiom on parallel lines was replaced by a different one, and logical non-Euclidean geometry was constructed. It was descriptive of space and did not conflict with man's experience or his measurements. This choice of axioms started a revolution in thought concerning the nature of mathematics.

In his study of infinite classes (1871–1874), Georg Cantor abandoned the Euclidean axiom that "the whole is greater than any of its parts." He showed that in the case of an infinite class, there may be as many members in part of the class as in the whole class. For example, there are as many even integers as there are odd and even integers.

The teaching of arithmetic now is oriented toward making structure explicit, and emphasis is placed on the conscious use of axioms. Children can easily see that bringing a set of two blocks to a set of three blocks $(3 + 2)$ results in the same set as bringing a set of three blocks to a set of two blocks $(2 + 3)$. This insight is generalized to the commutative axiom for addition. A similar explanation of other axioms helps give arithmetic a firm logical basis.

LEE E. BOYER
Harrisburg (Pa.) Area Community College

AXIS, ak′səs, the alliance of Nazi Germany and Fascist Italy against which the Allied Powers (notably France, Britain, the United States, and the USSR) fought in World War II. Mussolini coined the term on Nov. 1, 1936, in a speech occasioned by the signing of the secret "October Protocols" (Oct. 24, 1936), in which Italy and Germany agreed to cooperate in opposing communism in general and the republican forces in the Spanish Civil War in particular. He described the Rome-Berlin accord as an "axis around which can revolve all those European states with a will to collaboration and peace."

The aims of the Axis emerged clearly in the Italo-German Pact of Steel (May 22, 1939), in which each party agreed to support the other in case of war. The alliance was not untroubled. Hitler exploited it to Germany's advantage: for recognizing the Italian empire in Africa, he received a free hand to annex Austria and Czechoslovakia and to attack Poland in September 1939. Mussolini, for his part, mistrusted German expansionism, and the Italian people resented Nazi anti-Catholicism and the anti-Semitic legislation Italy had to adopt in 1938. The Axis collapsed on June 25, 1943, when Mussolini was taken captive by Italian anti-fascists.

C.M. KIMMICH, *Columbia University*

Further Reading: Wiskemann, Elizabeth, *The Rome-Berlin Axis*, new ed. (London 1966).

AXIS DEER, ak′səs, a white-spotted deer (*Axis axis*) of India and the East Indies, known locally among the Indians as *chitra* and among the English as *hog deer*. It resembles the European fallow deer in size and color. Easily domesticated, it is a favorite in European parks. The slender, sharp-pointed horns are not palmated and only a little branched. The female is hornless. The deer is timid and usually goes in small herds, in which females largely predominate. It lives in thick jungles near water and usually feeds at night.

AXMANSHIP, aks′mən-ship, is the practice of felling and cutting timber with an ax. It is also called *woodchopping*. A natural adjunct of frontier life, the activity expanded to an industry with the rise of the professional timber cutter. It acquired significance as a sport with the introduction of lumberjack competitions at fairs, carnivals, and agricultural shows.

Organized axmanship competitions originated in Tasmania about 1874 and led to the organization of the United Australian Axeman's Association in 1891. Since then, competitions have been held in Australia, New Zealand, Britain, Canada, and the United States (mostly in the Pacific Northwest). A championship timber carnival is held each year at Albany, Oreg., and a lumberjack championship is held annually at Hayward, Wis.

The principal axmanship contests are the *springboard chop* (tree felling), the *horizontal log chop*, and the *standing block chop*. For the springboard test a tall log secured on a false tree base is used. The contestant, climbing at full speed, must cut three notches in the trunk, each 3½ feet (1.07 meters) apart, and insert and balance a springboard in each notch. Standing on the top board he must cut halfway through the log, which is at least 12 inches (30 centimeters) in diameter. He then descends, removing the boards as he goes, and climbs the opposite side in the same manner, completing the cut from the top board. In the horizontal log chop the axman stands on a log secured at both ends and chops down between his feet. In the standing block chop he stands on the ground as he cuts a vertical log.

In all three events, axmen usually compete against the clock. They use several axes, each honed differently to deal with the texture of the wood to be chopped. Modern contests include such other lumberjack events as ax throwing, hand bucking (sawing), birling, and speed climbing, with ropes.

BILL BRADDOCK
New York "Times"

AXMINSTER, aks′min-stər, in England, is a rural district in Devonshire, on the Axe River, 24 miles east of Exeter. Axminster carpets were made here from 1755 until 1835, when the industry moved to Wilton, near Salisbury. It was reestablished in Axminster in 1936. The district lies in a dairy region. Population: (1961) 14,407.

AXOLOTL, ak′sə-lot-əl, a salamander that does not change (metamorphose) into an adult but remains permanently in the larval condition. It does, however, become sexually mature at about six months and breeds as an aquatic salamander.

The axolotl is a sturdily built amphibian with a broad head and bushy external gills. It is from 6 to 10 inches (15–25 cm) long and has

AXOLOTL (*left*), the larval form of the tiger salamander (*right*), does not metamorphose into an adult.

ZOOLOGICAL SOCIETY OF PHILADELPHIA   JOHN H. GERARD

teeth in both jaws. Found around Mexico City and in Colorado, it closely resembles the adult form.

The failure to metamorphose into an adult is called *neoteny*. Although the exact cause of neoteny is not known, it is probably environmental in the axolotl and is related to the sensitivity of its tissues to the thyroid hormone, thyroxine, which controls metamorphosis. It has been found that if dosages of thyroxine are administered to axolotls, they will metamorphose into the adult form. Also, after axolotls are moved to regions other than their native regions, they change into adults.

The axolotl belongs to the order Urodela, family Ambystomatidae. Its species is *Ambystoma tigrinum*, the tiger salamander. The adult tiger salamander is found throughout the United States and south to central Mexico.

Originally, the axolotl was considered as a separate species, *Siredon lichenoides*. It was discovered by accident to be the larval form of the tiger salamander in Paris in 1865 when some axolotls placed in the aquarium at the Jardin des Plantes lost their gills and changed into adults.

AXUM. See AKSUM.

AYACUCHO, ä-yä-kōō′chō, is a city in south central Peru, 200 miles (321 km) southeast of Lima. It is the capital of Ayacucho department. The city is situated at an altitude of 9,029 feet (2,752 meters) on the eastern slope of the Cordillera Occidental of the Andes mountains. Ayacucho trades in agricultural products of the region, notably grain and livestock. There are a cathedral and a number of other churches. The National University of San Cristóbal of Huamanga, founded in 1677, is situated in Ayacucho.

The city was founded in 1539 by Francisco Pizarro, the Spanish conqueror of Peru, and named Huamanga. The name was changed after the Battle of Ayacucho, fought Dec. 9, 1824, in the nearby valley of Ayacucho. This was a decisive engagement in the liberation of South America from the Spaniards. Peruvian and Colombian troops led by Gen. Antonio José de Sucre routed the army of the Spanish viceroy and took him prisoner. Population: (1961) 410,772.

AYALA, ä-yä′lä, **Eusebio** (1875–1942), president of Paraguay. He was born at Barrero Grande, Paraguay, on Aug. 14, 1875. Ayala was a prominent intellectual in the Liberal party. He served three terms in the Chamber of Deputies as a representative from Asunción and in 1910 became president of the chamber. Between 1910 and 1921 he held the portfolios of treasury, education, and foreign affairs. He was provisional president in 1921–1923 and ambassador to the United States in 1925–1927.

As president of Paraguay from 1932 to 1936 he pursued a moderate policy. He took a conciliatory position in the Chaco War with Bolivia, and although Paraguay's armies had the upper hand, he agreed to a truce. Overthrown by an army coup in 1936, he died in exile at Buenos Aires, Argentina, on June 4, 1942.

AYALA, López de. See LÓPEZ DE AYALA, PEDRO.

AYALA, Ramón Pérez de. See PÉREZ DE AYALA, RAMÓN.

AYALA Y HERRERA, ä-yä′lä ē er-re′rä, **Adelardo López de** (1828–1879), Spanish dramatist, whose realistic comedies satirize the vices of his time. He was born in Guadalcanal, Spain, in March 1828. After studying law in Seville, he went to Madrid and devoted himself to writing.

His early historical dramas, including *Un hombre de estado* (1851) and *Rioja* (1854), brought him national fame. His later plays were comedies in which he ridiculed such human vices as seduction, avarice, and materialism. These include *El tanto por ciento* (1861), *El nuevo don Juan* (1863), and *Consuelo* (1878). He died in Madrid on Dec. 30, 1879.

AYDELOTTE, ā′də-lot, **Frank** (1880–1956), American educator and scholar. Born in Sullivan, Ind., on Oct. 16, 1880, he graduated from the University of Indiana in 1900. He received a master of arts degree from Harvard University in 1903, and from 1905 to 1907 was a Rhodes Scholar at Oxford University, England.

As president of Swarthmore College from 1921 to 1940, he introduced the "Oxford plan" of teaching, involving an honors program for upperclassmen. This method was adopted by many colleges and universities in the United States.

Aydelotte was director of the Institute for Advanced Study at Princeton, N.J., from 1939 to 1947, and served as American secretary to the Rhodes trustees from 1918 to 1953. He died in Princeton, N.J., on Dec. 17, 1956.

His works include *Elizabethan Rogues and Vagabonds* (1913), *The Oxford Stamp* (1917), and *The American Rhodes Scholarships* (1946).

AYDIN, ī-din′, a town in Turkey, is the capital of Aydın vilayet. It is situated in the western part of Asiatic Turkey, on the Menderes River, about 55 miles southeast of İzmir. Aydm is a railroad center and trades in olives, figs, grapes, and cotton grown in the surrounding agricultural area. Tralles, whose ruins are nearby, was an important city in the ancient kingdom of Lydia. Population: (1965) 43,289.

AYE-AYE, ī′ī, is the common name of *Daubentonia madagascarensis*, a nocturnal, arboreal mammal found in Madagascar. It is about the size of a cat, is dusky brown in color, and has a long, bushy tail. It has a single pair of greatly enlarged chisel-like incisor teeth in both upper and lower jaws, closely resembling those of rodents, but its general anatomy proves it to be an aberrant lemur.

The aye-aye feeds on fruits, the succulent pith of bamboo and sugar cane, and insect grubs.

Aye-Aye

AYER, âr, **Alfred Jules** (1910–   ), British philosopher, who introduced the neopositivism of the Vienna Circle into the analytical movement in British philosophy. His *Language, Truth, and Logic,* published in 1936, when Ayer was only 26, is an uncompromising assertion of the neopositivist principle that statements that cannot be verified by experience must be recognized as "non-sense" statements. The book was a major factor in turning British and American philosophy from the construction of all-embracing philosophical systems to language analysis.

Ayer was born in London on Oct. 29, 1910. He attended Eton, graduated from Christ Church, Oxford, in 1932, and received his M.A. degree there in 1936. In 1932 he had spent some months in Vienna, where he attended the meetings of the Vienna Circle. This experience was the inspiration for *Language, Truth, and Logic,* which became the manifesto of the logical positivist, or logical empiricist, movement.

During World War II, Ayer served in the British army, returning to civilian life in 1945 with the rank of captain. His second book, *The Foundations of Empirical Knowledge* (1940), deals primarily with the problems of perception. In 1946 he went to London University as Grote professor of the philosophy of mind and logic. His appointment as Wykeham professor of logic at Oxford in 1959 symbolized the triumph of logical positivism in England. Ayer's later books include *The Problem of Knowledge* (1956), and *The Concept of a Person* (1963).

AYER, âr, **Francis Wayland** (1848–1923), American advertising executive, who originated many fundamental practices of modern advertising, including the agency-advertiser contract, marketing surveys, and copy preparation by an agency. He was born on Feb. 4, 1848, at Lee, Mass. As a youth he sold advertising space for publications. In 1869, with $250 of borrowed capital, he founded an advertising agency, N.W. Ayer & Son, Inc., in Philadelphia. Named for his father, it is one of the largest advertising agencies.

In 1875, Ayer devised the open-contract plan under which the agent was paid a commission by the advertiser for getting the lowest possible space rates from media. Although this method of compensation never became the industry standard, Ayer's plan helped to establish the agency as a representative of the advertiser rather than of the publisher, and this was an innovation. His plan also moved the agency into copy preparation and other functions besides space buying. In 1879, Ayer's agency became the first to run an advertising campaign based on a survey showing who were the best prospects for a client's product and what newspapers the prospects read. In 1892 the agency became the first to employ a full-time copywriter. Ayer died on March 3, 1923, in Meredith, N.Y.

JEROME H. WALKER, JR., *"Editor and Publisher"*

AYER, âr, a town in Massachusetts, in Middlesex County, is situated on the Nashua River, 28 miles (45 km) northwest of Boston. Ayer is a trading center in apple-growing country. Textile machinery is made in the town. Fort Devens, a large U.S. Army training center, is nearby. Ayer was settled before 1670 and was incorporated in 1871. Population: 7,393.

IDA K. NAPARSTEK
Ayer Junior-Senior High School

AYLESWORTH, ālz'wûrth, **Sir Allen Bristol** (1854–1952), Canadian lawyer and public official. He was born in Camden Township, Ontario, on Nov. 27, 1854, and was graduated from the University of Toronto in 1874. Named queen's counsel to Victoria in 1899, he served all subsequent British monarchs as counsel during his lifetime. He was a member of the Alaskan Boundary Commission in London in 1903 and represented British interests before the Hague Tribunal in the fisheries dispute of 1910. He was knighted in 1911. While in the Canadian House of Commons, he served as postmaster general (1905–1906) and as minister of justice (1906–1911). He was a Canadian senator from 1923 until his death in Toronto on Feb. 13, 1952.

AYLLÓN, ī-lyôn', **Lucas Vásquez de** (c. 1475–1526), Spanish explorer in America. In 1502, with Nicolás de Ovando, the new governor of Spain's American lands, he went to Santo Domingo, where he prospered and was appointed to public offices. He sent a vessel to explore the mainland coast beyond the Bahamas in 1521.

While in Spain in 1523, Ayllón secured a charter permitting him to explore 800 leagues of the coast north of Florida and to establish a colony under his governorship. He dispatched an exploring party in 1525, which marched up the coast some 250 leagues. The following year he himself set out with three ships and some 600 followers to found his colony. Sailing northward along the coast, Ayllón chose a landing site near a large river—possibly the Cape Fear in what is now North Carolina, although some have placed it near the future Jamestown, Va. The settlement of San Miguel de Guadalupe was ill-fated: the settlers were undisciplined and the Indians menacing, the land was swampy and pestilential, and Ayllón proved an inadequate leader. The weather turned very cold, and Ayllón died of a fever on Oct. 18, 1526. The colony then fell into disorder and soon was abandoned, the survivors returning to Santo Domingo.

AYLMER, āl'mər, **5th Baron** (1775–1850), British soldier and governor of Lower Canada. He was born *Matthew Aylmer,* in England, on May 24, 1775, and succeeded to his father's title in 1785. He entered the army in 1787 and served in the West Indies and Holland. He fought in the European wars following the French Revolution and served under the duke of Wellington in the Peninsular War in Spain and Portugal.

Aylmer, who was promoted full general in 1825, became governor-in-chief of Canada in 1831, but despite the title his administration covered only Lower Canada. Strong French-Canadian separatist feeling and his own lack of tact in dealing with it overwhelmed him. After a tumultuous and unpopular reign, he resigned in 1835. He died in London on Feb. 23, 1850.

AYLMER, āl'mər, a town in Ontario, Canada, is 25 miles (40 km) southeast of London. It is situated in a tobacco-growing and dairying district, and the town's principal industries are a tobacco-processing plant and a condensed-milk factory. There are also canneries and frozen-food plants. The town was named in 1837 for Lord Aylmer, governor-in-chief of Canada (1831–1835), and was incorporated in 1887. Population: 4,755.

AYLMER, āl'mər, a residential town in southwestern Quebec, Canada, is situated on Lake Deschênes, an expansion of the Ottawa River. It lies 8 miles (12.8 km) west of Hull, Quebec, and Ottawa, Ontario. There are greenhouses and a woodworking plant. The town was named for Lord Aylmer, governor-in-chief of Canada (1831–1835). Population: 7,198.

AYMARÁ INDIANS, ī-mä-rä', a group of South American Indian tribes living in the highlands around Lake Titicaca in southern Peru and northern Bolivia. Before they were conquered by the Incas and the Spaniards in the 15th and 16th centuries, the Aymará had attained a fairly advanced agriculture and technology. Many ethnologists believe that the great stone ruins at Tiahuanaco are of structures built by ancestors of the Aymará.

Aymará is also the name of an important subfamily of languages spoken by Indians of Peru and Bolivia. It is similar in vocabulary to Inca, but contains a number of Spanish words introduced since the time of the conquistadores.

AYMÉ, e-mä', **Marcel** (1902–1967), French novelist and playwright, known especially for his ability to deliver biting satire in a setting of cheerful, apparently harmless fantasy. He was born in Joigny, France, on March 28, 1902, and received irregular schooling in Dôle, where he lived with relatives after his mother's death. At his family's bidding, he went to medical school but dropped out after a year to settle in Paris. There he worked at various jobs until an illness forced him to return to Dôle for six months to recuperate. During this period he finished his first novel, *Brûlebois,* which was published in 1926, through the help of Jacques Reboul, editor of *Cahiers de France.*

Many of Aymé's early novels drew heavily on the simple peasant life he had observed around Dôle. In 1929 his fourth novel, *Table aux Crevés,* won the Théophraste Renaudot prize as the best novel of the year. *Jument verte* (1933), considered by many critics to be his masterpiece, established him as the heir to the tradition of Voltaire. Later novels, *Le chemin des écoliers* (1946) and *Uranus* (1948), reveal a deep but good-natured indifference toward a world ruled only by chance. Aymé's plays, which he began to write after World War II, have a Rabelaisian impiety and gusto, and his *Clérambard* was the hit of the 1950 theater season in Paris. Aymé also wrote several very successful children's books, of which the best known is *Contes du chat perché* (1934). He died in Paris on Oct. 14, 1967.

AYMON, ā-môN', a family of four brothers who were among the most illustrious heroes of the chivalric poetry of the Middle Ages. They were Alard, Renaut, Guichard, and Richard, the sons of Aymon, duke of Dordone. Their existence was doubted until 1879, when Auguste Honoré Longnon established that they lived in the first half of the 8th century. Fictionally, they are usually placed in the time of Charlemagne (742–814). Renaut and his horse, Bayard, play the major role in the brothers' exploits.

One of the earliest extant versions of their adventures is the chanson de geste *L'histoire des quatre fils Aymon,* also known as *Renaut de Montauban,* from the late 12th century. Renaut as Rinaldo, is the hero of Boiardo's *Orlando innamorato* (1499), Ariosto's *Orlando furioso* (1516), and Tasso's *Rinaldo* (1562). The adventures of the Aymon brothers were familiar to French children through the story *Les quatre fils Aymon.* This version of their life was included in the *Bibliothèque bleue* (1665), a collection of tales that was almost the sole reading matter in French country districts until the late 18th century.

AYORA, ä-yō'rä, **Isidro** (1879–   ), Ecuadorian physician and political leader. A distinguished physician and member of the Liberal party, he was installed as provisional president of Ecuador in 1925, following an army coup. He accepted the office reluctantly but undertook needed economic reforms energetically. He retained a group of United States economists to make a study of the country's economic problems and, on the basis of their findings, established a central bank and reformed the currency. Amid growing criticism caused by a deepening depression, he tendered his resignation in 1930, but the Congress refused to accept it. In 1932 he resigned, his resignation was accepted, and he resumed his medical practice.

AYR, âr, a county in Scotland, lies in an arc along the Firth of Clyde on the southwest coast. It is also known as *Ayrshire.* The shoreline is about 84 miles (135.2 km) long, and the land rises like an amphitheater from the coastal plain. The county contains 1,132 square miles (2,931.9 sq km), about half of which provides grazing land for the famous Ayrshire dairy cattle and sheep. Pigs and poultry are also raised, and potatoes, turnips, oats, and hay are grown.

Ayr is industrially important for its minerals and manufactures. There are an estimated billion tons of coal reserves under the central and southern portions, and many mines are in operation. Other minerals include bauxite, limestone, brick, and fire clay. The county is noted for its iron and steel mills and the manufacture of woolen products—chiefly carpets and hosiery—and lace. Other manufactures include agricultural machinery, aircraft, chemicals, and explosives. In the mid-1960's, one of Britain's major nuclear power stations became operative at Hunterston. There is an international airport at Prestwick, just north of Ayr.

The county town is Ayr, 31 miles (49.9 km) southwest of Glasgow, on the Ayr River. It has a population of 45,276 and is a trading center for the agricultural products of the county. There are also diversified industries, including metalworking, engineering, and manufacture of textiles, chemicals, and furniture.

The region has been inhabited since prehistoric times. There are traces of Roman occupation in the first century A.D. Ayr was ruled by the first Scottish king in the 11th century, and became a king's burgh (pronounced "borough") about 1200; since the 15th century it has been a royal burgh. At Largs, in northwest Ayr, a Norwegian invasion was repulsed in 1263. In the late 13th and 14th centuries much of the Scottish struggle for independence from England centered on Ayr. The county is known as "Burns Country" because the poet Robert Burns was born in 1759 at Alloway, a suburb of the town of Ayr. His cottage and a Burns museum are among the many tourist attractions of the county. Population: 342,822.

AYRER, ī′rər, **Jakob** (c. 1560–1605), German dramatist, whose work was very popular in his time but has little literary merit. He was born in Nürnberg, where he probably belonged to the Mastersinger guild, and where he died on March 26, 1605.

Ayrer wrote numerous comedies, tragedies, folk plays for Shrovetide, and musical vaudevilles. His work shows the influence of English comedy, brought to Germany by wandering actors, and formerly was believed to have been influenced by Shakespeare. However, the similarities in their plots are probably from the use of a common source. About 70 of Ayrer's plays were published in *Opus theatricum* (1618).

AYRES, ârz, **Leonard Porter** (1879–1946) American economist and statistician, who developed statistical methods for measuring results in education and became widely known for his accurate business forecasts. He was born in Niantic, Conn., on Sept. 15, 1879. In 1909, after several years in Puerto Rico as general superintendent of schools and a statistician, he became director of the department of education and statistics of the Russell Sage Foundation. There he designed an index-number method for measuring relative educational efficiency of state school systems and other methods for statistical measurement of the progress of students.

In World War I, Ayres served as head of the statistical section of the War Industries Board and later as chief of the statistical section of the American Expeditionary Forces. He assisted in writing the reparations and economic clauses of the Treaty of Versailles and in 1924 was chief economic adviser to the committee that formulated the Dawes Plan. He became vice president of the Cleveland Trust Co. in 1920. Ayres died in Cleveland on Oct. 29, 1946.

Ayres wrote extensively on economic conditions. He predicted the stock-market crash of 1929 and was one of the few economists who forecast that the business downturn that followed would develop into a severe depression. Among his writings were *Index Numbers for State School Systems* (1920); *Economics of Recovery* (1933); *The Chief Cause of This and Other Depressions* (1935); and *Turning Points in Business Cycles* (1939).

Ramon Knauerhase, *University of Connecticut*

AYSCUE, as′kū, **Sir George** (died 1671), English admiral who held important sea commands in the Anglo-Dutch wars of the 1600's. He was knighted by King Charles I and commanded his first ship in 1646. Two years later, when the Parliamentary party had defeated the royal forces in the Civil War, Ayscue persuaded a large part of the fleet to join the Parliamentary cause. As a reward, he was named an admiral and then led an expedition that took Barbados in the West Indies from the Royalists.

As second in command to Adm. Robert Blake, Ayscue fought severe but inconclusive battles with the Dutch led by Adm. Maarten Tromp in 1652 and by Adm. Michiel de Ruyter in 1653. The government was dissatisfied with his conduct in the second engagement and relieved him of command in 1664 after the Restoration. In a battle in 1666 he was captured by the Dutch and taken to Holland, but was returned to England in 1667.

AYTON, ā′tən, **Sir Robert** (1570–1638), Scottish poet and courtier, who was one of the first Scots to write verse in standard English. His name is sometimes spelled *Aytoun.*

Born in Cameron, Scotland, of an old Norman family, he received his M.A. degree at St. Andrews University in 1588 and then went to Paris to study civil law. When James VI of Scotland acceded to the English throne in 1603 as James I, Ayton addressed a long panegyric in Latin to the monarch. This brought him into favor at the English court, where he subsequently held such important posts as private secretary to James's wife, Anne of Denmark, and later to Henrietta Maria, wife of Charles I. He was knighted in 1612. At court and on diplomatic missions abroad he became acquainted with many of the most eminent of his time. He died in London on Feb. 28, 1638.

Ayton's English and Latin love songs, sonnets, and panegyrics were admired in his time but are now considered to have little literary value. Some of his Latin poems are included in *Delitiae poetarum Scotorum* (1637), edited by Sir John Scot. Ayton is also reputed to be the author of an early version of *Auld Lang Syne* (q.v.), but there is little evidence to substantiate this claim.

AYTOUN, ā′ten, **William Edmondstoune** (1813–1865), Scottish author, who is best known for his lyrical ballads and parodies of popular contemporary writers. A descendent of the poet Sir Robert Ayton, he was born in Edinburgh on June 21, 1813. He was educated at the University of Edinburgh and called to the bar in 1840.

Aytoun came to public attention with the publication of *Bon Gaultier Ballads* (1845), parodies of contemporary writers which he wrote in collaboration with Sir Theodore Martin. They also collaborated on humorous articles for *Blackwood's Magazine* and on translations of Goethe's poetry. From 1845, Aytoun was professor of rhetoric and English literature at the University of Edinburgh, and in 1854 he became editor of *Blackwood's.* He died at Blackhills, Scotland, on Aug. 4, 1865.

The *Lays of the Scottish Cavaliers* (1848), which achieved great popularity, established Aytoun as an original poet. His other major work is *Firmilian, a Spasmodic Tragedy* (1854), a mock-tragedy in verse that ridicules the poets of the "Spasmodic" school. He also published the collection *Ballads of Scotland* (1856) and an autobiographical novel, *Norman Sinclair* (1861).

AYUB KHAN (1855–1914), ä-ē-ōōb′ĸän′, Afghan prince, who defied both the British and the British-supported Afghan amir. After the death of his father, the exiled amir Sher Ali (died 1879), Ayub, a claimant to the throne, openly declared himself against the British. On July 27, 1880, he severely defeated troops led by Gen. George R. Burrows at Maiwand. He then laid siege to Kandahar. On September 1, Gen. Frederick Roberts, after making his famous forced march from Kabul, attacked Ayub's forces and scattered them, Ayub and the remnants of his army falling back on Herat. The following year Ayub succeeded in taking Kandahar, but the new amir, Abdur Rahman Khan, was finally able to overcome him. For a while Ayub was an exile in Persia, and in 1887 he organized an unsuccessful conspiracy to capture Herat. He finally gave himself up to the British.

AYUB KHAN, ī-o͞ob' кнän, **Mohammad** (1907–), president of Pakistan from 1958 to 1969. He was born in Abbottabad (in what is now West Pakistan) on May 14, 1907. Educated at Aligarh Muslim University and the Royal Military College at Sandhurst, England, he was commissioned in the British Indian army in 1928. He served in Burma during World War II, and when Pakistan became independent in 1947, he was one of its few experienced senior military officers.

Rise to Power. Rising rapidly in the Pakistani Army, Ayub Khan played a major role in its reorganization as commander in chief from 1951 and as defense minister in 1954–1955. He initiated and negotiated agreements with the United States that led to grants of military aid to Pakistan and its membership in the Baghdad Pact (later CENTO) and Southeast Asia Treaty Organization (SEATO).

When President Iskander Mirza abrogated the constitution on Oct. 7, 1958, Ayub Khan was appointed chief martial law administrator and supreme commander of the armed forces. On October 27 he seized the presidency, sending Mirza into exile.

Presidency. Under martial law powers, the new president instituted land reform in West Pakistan and appointed commissions to study reform in the educational, legal, social, and economic fields. Corrupt officials were dismissed, and tax evasion was reduced.

Ayub Khan became a field marshal in 1959. In the same year he established a system of "Basic Democracies," councils that acted in support of local administrators and as an electoral college. In 1960 he was confirmed as president by the councillors of the Basic Democracies and he appointed a commission to draft a new constitution, which was promulgated in 1962. He was reelected president in 1965.

Under Ayub Khan's regime the Pakistani economy experienced high but uneven rates of growth. His leadership in foreign affairs was marked by a diminishing reliance on the United States and a diplomacy that he likened to a "triangular tightrope" between the United States, the USSR, and Communist China. Relations with India worsened over Kashmir, and open warfare broke out in 1965. The fighting was brought to an end at the Russian-sponsored Tashkent Peace Conference in 1966.

Resignation. In the late 1960's, opposition to Ayub Khan's presidency became increasingly evident. The system of indirect election of the president and legislature was unpopular, and Pakistani opinion opposed the Tashkent peace settlement. In 1966, Foreign Minister Z. A. Bhutto left the cabinet and formed an opposition group. Poor harvests that year and the next put the government under further strain. An attempt on the president's life was reported in East Pakistan in December 1967, and shortly thereafter Ayub Khan fell victim to a pulmonary embolism. His recuperation was slow.

In February 1969, following student riots, industrial strikes, and continued attacks by Bhutto, Ayub Khan declared that he would not run for reelection in 1970 and that the presidential form of government he had introduced would be replaced by the parliamentary system. New disorders broke out, however, and on March 25, Ayub Khan resigned, transferring his powers to Gen. Mohammad Yahya Khan.

WAYNE WILCOX, *Columbia University*

AYUTTHAYA, ä-yo͞ot-tä-yä, is the name of a province in central Thailand, of its chief city, and of an early Siamese kingdom.

The city of Ayutthaya, at the junction of the Lopburi and Pa Sak rivers, about 40 miles (64 km) north of Bangkok, was founded in 1349 by Rama Tibodi (reigned 1350–1369), Siam's first king. Its foundation came shortly after Ramkhamhaeng (reigned c. 1270–c. 1317) established the territorial basis of the Siamese nation, and Rama Tibodi's state fell heir to this territory. Siamese civilization was largely formed in the Ayutthaya period on the basis of Sinhalese Buddhism and other cultural influences from China and northern India and from the Cambodian, Burmese, and Mon cultures. Despite constant conflict with surrounding states, Ayutthaya remained a major political and cultural center until it was destroyed by Burmese forces in 1767. The capital was then moved to Bangkok.

Ayutthaya today is an active trade center in agricultural products, linked by rail and highway with Bangkok. Nearby are the ruins of many early temples and monasteries—some of them restored—the Chao Sam Phraya Museum, and the remarkable old Royal Summer Palace, a popular tourist attraction. Population: (1969) 24,597.

JAMES R. SHIRLEY
Northern Illinois University

AYYUBID, ī-yo͞ob'id, was the name of a dynasty that governed Egypt from 1171 to 1250 and Syria-Palestine and Upper Mesopotamia from 1183 to 1260. It was founded in 1171 by Saladin (Salah ad-Din), a Kurdish emir from Syria.

Saladin defeated both the ruling Fatimid dynasty in Egypt and his Crusader competitors for the Fatimid lands. He and his successors recognized the overlordship of the Abbasid caliphs of Baghdad, thus returning Egypt to orthodoxy after two centuries of Fatimid adherence to the Ismaili branch of Islam. They abolished illegal taxes, endowed new schools, and generally patronized the orthodox religious community. Saladin proceeded to conquer the minor Muslim principalities of Syria and Upper Mesopotamia. Jerusalem and most of Palestine later fell to him, though the Christian principalities of Acre, Tyre, Tripoli, and Antioch withstood his assaults.

Saladin divided his kingdom into appanages for his heirs. The Ayyubid rulers of Egypt emerged as suzerains over the other Ayyubid princes. Despite wars between the family potentates, the Ayyubids maintained their solidarity and stimulated a brilliant period of religious and cultural activity. However, to avoid provoking further Crusades, to spare Egypt (which was nevertheless attacked in 1217 and 1249), and to protect the lucrative commerce with the West, the Ayyubids allowed the Crusaders to consolidate their coastal possessions.

After the death of Egypt's Ayyubid ruler al-Malik al-Kamil in 1238, ruthless fighting among the family princes tore apart the Ayyubid state, and in 1249 the dynasty in Egypt was snuffed out in a coup by recently recruited Turkish slaves (Mamluks), who then named their own generals to rule Egypt. The Ayyubid rulers in Syria, overwhelmed by the Mongol invasions, were displaced by the Mamluks in 1260, though a few minor princes retained their possessions.

IRA M. LAPIDUS
University of California at Berkeley

AZALEA

This species (*Azalea nudiflora*) is commonly known as pinxter flower.

ROCHE

AZALEA, ə-zăl′yə, is a group of flowering shrubs native to the Northern Hemisphere, especially eastern Asia and North America. Its fragrant flowers are in clusters and have five-parted floral envelopes with five to ten stamens. The leaves are located alternately on the plant stem and have short leaf stalks. Most azalea leaves are deciduous.

The genus *Azalea* is classified by most botanists with the genus *Rhododendron* in the heath family, Ericaceae. Azaleas commonly are divided into two groups: the Indian azaleas and the hardy deciduous azaleas, which include the Ghent hybrid forms. Most Indian azaleas are imported from Holland and forced in greenhouses. Propagation is by grafts or cuttings and rarely by seeds. The plants are grown in loose, moderately fertile soil and sheltered from the sun. They are watered freely during the summer, and then repotted in early autumn and brought into flower as desired from late autumn to early summer. Among the leading species of Indian azaleas is *A. indica* (two varieties, *amoena* and *alba*).

The members of the hardy deciduous azaleas need some protection in the north and in exposed situations to prevent injury to the flower buds caused by sudden variations of temperature. Their seedlings are sometimes grown for their own merits, but generally they are used for stocks upon which to graft choice varieties. The following are among the best known species of the hardy deciduous azaleas: *A. nudiflora*, pinxter flower, found from Canada to the Gulf of Mexico, which has pink, white, and sometimes purple flowers in midspring; *A. calendulacea*, found from New York to Georgia, which has large orange or flame-colored blossoms in late spring; *A. occidentalis*, or *A. californica*, a California species, which bears fragrant white-pinkish flowers in early summer; *A. arborescens*, found in the Allegheny Mountains, which has fragrant white or pink flowers in June; and *A. viscosa*, clammy azalea or white swamp honeysuckle, which is found in swamps from maritime Canada to Florida and westward to Arkansas and bears fragrant white or pink flowers in June or July. The best-known Asiatic members of this group are *A. mollis, A. rhombica,* and *A. pontica.*

AZAÑA, ä-thä′nyä, **Manuel** (1880–1940), Spanish statesman, who was premier and then president of the Spanish republic. He was born on Jan. 10, 1880, at Alcalá de Henares, and educated by the Augustinian Order at the Escorial. He emerged from this education with marked anticlerical sentiments. He later studied law in Paris and, until 1930, served as an official in the justice department of Spain. He first attracted attention as a literary critic and political essayist. His biography of Juan Valera won a national prize for literature in 1926.

In 1930, Azaña organized a liberal political group, the Acción Republicana, and worked actively for the overthrow of Alfonso XIII. When the Spanish republic was declared in 1931, he became minister of war in the provisional government. During the drafting of the constitution, he was the driving force behind the adoption of many of the articles dealing with the redistribution of land, restrictions on the clergy, establishment of secular education, and extension of the franchise to women. He became premier in December 1931, serving until November 1933.

During his two-year premiership, Azaña attempted to enforce many of the progressive provisions of the constitution, often dealing severely with opposition from the army and from clerical protests. He was imprisoned briefly in 1934 by the center-right coalition that followed his party to power.

He returned to political office as president of the republic in February 1936. The social unrest in Spain, however, fomented from the beginning of the republic by extremist groups, culminated in an uprising by the army in July 1936. Throughout the civil war that then engulfed Spain, Azaña failed to win enough support for the republic to crush the opposition. He remained in office until the victory of Gen. Francisco Franco's forces in 1939. He died in exile at Montauban, France, on Nov. 4, 1940.

AZANDE, ə-zän′dē, an African people referred to in some early writings as the *Niam-Niam.* Variations of the modern name include *Azandeh, Sande,* and *Zande.* They are one of the most famous of African peoples, having been described in popular books by a number of 19th century European travelers, Georg August Schweinfurth, Carlo Piaggia, Wilhelm Junker, and Gaetano Casati. The Azande occupy a territory in central Africa, in an area which is divided politically between Sudan, Congo (Kinshasa), and the Central African Republic. Their number has been estimated at about 1 million.

The Azande are essentially a political conglomerate, originating with the Ambomu people, who, under their Avongara aristocratic leaders, have conquered and brought within their political system a number of other peoples. The interest the Azande have for the student of African affairs lies very largely in the process by which this assimilation, both cultural and political, took place through a remarkable administrative service, headed by the Avongara aristocracy, who were the rulers in the several Zande kingdoms, each of which was autonomous. In the first instance the lower administrative posts were held by their Ambomu followers, but these were later supplemented by men of foreign origin as the process of assimilation continued. Peoples of different ethnic stocks and with different cultures were thus slowly made into a nation of mixed blood but with a common language, common institutions, and a common way of life.

In other respects the Azande are familiar to students of African societies. They have an agricultural economy, in which they show a sound and wide knowledge of food plants and their cultivation. Their staple food is the Ethiopian eleusine (a cultivated grass), but they also grow maize, fruits, and vegetables. They are famed for their abilities as craftsmen and musicians.

The Azande have aroused public interest because they have been regarded as cannibals. It appears to be certain that some of them practiced cannibalism, but it also is true that this was not a habit of the original Azande, the *Ambomu*, and their Avongara leaders. Of the ethnographic literature on the Azande relating to special topics, most has been written about their extensive beliefs and practices connected with witchcraft, which traditionally dominated their thought and to a large extent their activities.

E.E. Evans-Pritchard, *Oxford University*

Further Reading: Baxter, P.T.W., and Butt, A.J., *The Azande and Related Peoples of the Anglo-Egyptian Sudan and Belgian Congo* (London 1954); De Calonne-Beaufaict, A., *Azande* (Brussels 1921); Evans-Pritchard, Edward E., *Witchcraft, Oracles and Magic Among the Azande* (London and New York 1937).

AZAY-LE-RIDEAU, à-zā′lǝ-rē-dō′, is a château in France, situated 15 miles (35 km) southwest of Tours, on the Indre River. It derives its name from a lord called Rideau d'Azay, who once held the land on which the château was later built. Because of its great beauty, the château has been called the gem of the French Renaissance.

Early in the Middle Ages a strong feudal castle was constructed on the site of the present château, but in 1418 it was destroyed by King Charles VII. In the 16th century a French banker, Gilles Berthelot, acquired the site and between 1518 and 1529 had the Renaissance château constructed. Later, Francis I (reigned 1515–1547) seized Azay-le-Rideau, and it was subsequently owned by various proprietors. In 1905 the French government purchased the château.

Despite the Gothic symmetry of Azay-le-Rideau, such features as its machicolation are solely for ornamentation. The numerous windows and gracious rooms indicate that the château was designed for peaceful and ostentatious living. Probably the most remarkable part of the château is its grand gable, with double windows, that contains the main staircase.

Bryce Lyon, *Brown University*

THE AZAY-LE-RIDEAU château in the Loire country.

FRENCH GOVERNMENT TOURIST OFFICE

AZAZEL, ǝ-zā′zǝl, in the Old Testament, was a demon in the Wilderness of Judea (south of Jerusalem) to whom the scapegoat was sent on the Day of Atonement (Leviticus 16:1–28). The scapegoat was chosen by lot and symbolically laden with the sins of all Israel. Its death was believed to rid the people from impurity. This ceremony was deeply rooted in primitive folk religion. Vestiges of this belief persist in the modern observance of Yom Kippur.

The word "Azazel" occurs only three times in the Bible (Leviticus 16:8, 10, 26). In the Authorized Version of the Bible, the term was translated "scapegoat." The newer translation, however, makes Azazel the demon who was believed to destroy the goat. In the pseudepigraphic Book of Enoch, Azazel is the chief of the fallen angels. Similar characterizations persisted in later Jewish and Muslim traditions. See also Atonement; Yom Kippur.

AZEF, ǝ-zyef′, **Yevno Fishelevich** (1869–1918), Russian double agent. He was born in Lyskovo, Russia. From 1893 to 1908 he served both the czarist secret police (Okhrana) and the terrorist wing of the Socialist Revolutionary party. He organized the assassinations of Interior Minister V.K. Plehve (1904) and of an uncle of the czar (1905). At the same time he betrayed to the police certain activities of the party, causing the execution of several of its members. The secret police suspected him of playing a double role, but used him nevertheless. The discovery in 1908 that he was betraying party members severely crippled the political terrorist movement. He escaped to Berlin, where he engaged in stock-exchange speculation. He died there on April 24, 1918.

AZEGLIO, ä-dzā′lyō, **Marquess d'** (1798–1866), Italian author and statesman. He was born *Massimo Taparelli* in Turin, Italy, on Oct. 24, 1798. In 1833, following some early successes as an artist, he published his first novel, *Ettore Fieramosca*, based on an incident in southern Italy, in which 13 Italians challenged and overcame an equal number of Frenchmen. His second novel, *Niccolò de' Lapi* (1841), dramatized the siege of Florence in 1530. In both works he sought to imbue Italians with pride in their past and faith in their future.

Under the influence of his father-in-law, Alessandro Manzoni (q.v.), a leader of the *risorgimento*, d'Azeglio became identified with the romantic and political aspects of the movement. He took part in the revolution of 1848 and supported the house of Savoy in its eventually successful attempts to unite Italy. From 1849 to 1852 he was premier of Sardinia under Victor Emmanuel II, paving the way for Cavour. He died in Florence on Jan. 15, 1866.

D'Azeglio's polemical writings included *Degli ultimi casi di Romagna* (1846), an attack on the secular power of the popes, which he continued in *I lutti di Lombardia* (1846). His unfinished memoirs, *I miei ricordi*, were published posthumously in 1867. D'Azeglio expressed himself clearly and forcefully in his political writings. His novels, though heavy handed, are distinguished for vigorous style, good characterization, and inventiveness.

AZEOTROPIC MIXTURES. See Distillation—*Theory.*

AZERBAIDZHAN SOVIET SOCIALIST REPUBLIC,

ä-zər-bī-jän', a constituent republic of the USSR, located in eastern Transcaucasia on the Caspian Sea, on the border separating the Soviet Union from the Iranian province of Azerbaijan. The capital is Baku. The republic has a total area of about 33,000 square miles (75,500 sq km), including the Nagorno-Karabakh autonomous oblast and the Nakhichevan autonomous republic. Nagorno-Karabakh lies entirely within the borders of the Azerbaidzhan republic, whereas Nakhichevan is separated from Azerbaidzhan proper by a strip of the Armenian republic.

Azerbaidzhan's chief agricultural region and most populous district is the fertile Kura River valley. In the south, bordering the Caspian Sea, is the semitropical area of Lenkoran. There is an arid coastal plain north of Baku. The western end of the Greater Caucasus mountain range extends into northern Azerbaidzhan, and in the western part of the republic are extensions of the Lesser Caucasus range. Both Nagorno-Karabakh and Nakhichevan lie in the uplands of the Lesser Caucasus. The climate is dry, with hot summers and mild winters.

The majority of the republic's inhabitants are a Turkic people speaking the national language of the republic, Azeri Turkish, while 16 percent are Russians and 12 percent are Armenians; there are also some Georgians and other peoples of the Caucasus. The population of Nagorno-Karabakh is largely Armenian. Newspapers and books published in the Azeri language are written in the Cyrillic alphabet.

An important part of Soviet oil production is centered in Azerbaidzhan, where oil was discovered in the 19th century. Gasoline, kerosene, fuel oil, and other petroleum products are sent to many parts of the Soviet Union by rail, by boat across the Caspian Sea, or by pipeline to the Black Sea. Small amounts of iron ore are mined at Dashkesan. About 3 million acres are under cultivation, mostly in the Kura Valley; cotton, alfalfa, wheat, rice, fruit, silk, tobacco, and tea are the principal crops. Fishing and livestock are major industries.

History. The ancient name for the area of Soviet Azerbaidzhan was *Albania*, called *Arran* by the Arabs. It was long an important transit area for the migration of peoples and was the battleground of Arabs, Khazars, and Turks; it was dominated by the Turks after the 11th century. When Azerbaidzhan was conquered by the Russians at the beginning of the 19th century, they found it a stronghold of Islamic religion and culture (Shiite sect), in opposition to the Christianity of neighboring Georgia and Armenia. After the Bolshevik Revolution, Azerbaidzhan separated from Russia and declared its independence on May 28, 1918. A Soviet regime was proclaimed on April 28, 1920, following the reconquest of the area by the Red army. The region was part of the Transcaucasian Soviet republic until Dec. 5, 1936, when it attained its present status. Population: (1963) 4,232,000.

RICHARD N. FRYE, *Harvard University*

AZERBAIJAN, ä-zər-bī-jän', is a region in Iran, comprising the provinces of East Azerbaijan and West Azerbaijan, in the extreme northwest part of the country. The region, about 41,000 square miles (106,000 sq km) in area, is bounded on the north by the Aras (Araks) River and the Azerbaidzhan republic of the Soviet Union, on the west by Turkey, and on the east by the Caspian Sea.

Azerbaijan is a plateau with an average elevation of some 4,000 feet (1,200 meters), and it is the only large area in Iran where irrigation is not required for crops. Wheat, barley, cotton, and tobacco are grown, and the fruits of Azerbaijan are famous. The region's minerals have been little exploited, and its oil deposits are untouched. A variegated translucent marble known as Maragha or Tabriz marble is found in the region. Like Rizaiyeh (Urmia), shallow and salty, the largest lake in Iran, lies west of the city of Tabriz, capital of East Azerbaijan. Tabriz is joined by rail to Teheran, the capital of Iran, and to Dzhulfa in the USSR. The city of Rizaiyeh, capital of West Azerbaijan, lies just west of the lake.

In ancient times the region was called *Atropatene*, after Atropates, a general who established a small kingdom in the region of modern Azerbaijan during Alexander the Great's invasion of Persia in the 4th century B.C. After the Arab conquest in the 7th century A.D., first Ardebil and then Tabriz became the capital. In the 11th century, Turkish nomads overran the country, and Turkish became the regional language. After 1256, Azerbaijan was the center of a Mongol empire established by Hulagu, extending from the Oxus River to Syria. From 1514 the Ottoman Turks contested the area with the Iranians until the Turks were finally expelled by Nadir Shah in the first half of the 18th century.

Following the loss to Russia (1828) of the territory north of the Aras River, together with a strip of land along the Caspian Sea that is now part of Azerbaidzhan Soviet republic, the remainder of the region became a Persian province. In the early 20th century Azerbaijan was the center of a revolutionary movement that resulted in the Iranian constitution of 1906. In 1928 the region was reorganized into two provinces, East and West Azerbaijan, which were officially renamed 3d ostan and 4th ostan, respectively, in 1938. During World War II, Soviet troops occupied the two provinces of Azerbaijan, but they were withdrawn in May 1946 after an autonomous local government had been created with

Scale of Miles
0 — 50 — 100
Scale of Kilometers
0 — 50 — 100 — 150

RUSSIAN S F S R

AZERBAIDZHAN S S R

Caucasus

Black Sea

GEORGIAN S S R

Mountains

CASPIAN SEA

Kura River

BAKU

ARMENIAN S S R

TURKEY

NAKHICHEVAN A S S R

Lenkoran

Lake Van

IRAN

Lake Urmia

Soviet support. This government collapsed following the reoccupation of the region by Iranian troops in November 1946. See also IRAN—6. *History* (Iran and the Cold War).

Azerbaijan is inhabited chiefly by Turks, with a few Kurds and Armenians. Azeri Turkish (also spoken in Soviet Azerbaidzhan) is spoken throughout the region, except in a few isolated villages where archaic Iranian dialects are still heard. Population: (est.) 4,000,000.

RICHARD N. FRYE, *Harvard University*

AZHAR, Al-. See AL-AZHAR.

AZIKIWE, ȧ-zē′kē-wä, **Benjamin Nnamdi** (1904–), Nigerian statesman, who was the first president of independent Nigeria. Known to his friends and associates as *Zik*, he was born *Benjamin Azikiwe* on Nov. 16, 1904 in Zungeru, Northern Nigeria. He later changed his first name to *Nnamdi*. He was educated in mission schools in Onitsha, Calabar, and Lagos. In 1925 he became the first Nigerian to study in the United States, where he attended Storer College, Howard and Lincoln universities, and the University of Pennsylvania. From 1931 to 1934 he was an instructor in political science at Lincoln University.

Returning to Africa in 1934, Azikiwe became editor of the *African Morning Post* in Accra, Ghana. Three years later he founded the *West African Pilot* in Lagos and used it and other papers to spread the appeal of nationalism and to attack all forms of racial injustice. He became one of the most important leaders of the nationalist movement in Nigeria, and in 1944 he helped found the National Council of Nigeria and the Cameroons (NCNC), serving as its president from 1946 to 1960.

Azikiwe became a member of the legislative council in 1947 and pressed for rapid constitutional progress. In 1952–1953 he led the NCNC opposition in the house of assembly of the Western Region; he then resigned in 1953 and was elected to the Eastern Region assembly.

In 1954 Azikwe became the premier of the Eastern Region. Two years later, despite accusations of corrupt practices and growing criticism from other Nigerian leaders, Azikiwe called a new election in the Eastern Region and was triumphantly reelected. After the 1959 federal election, he allied his party to the Northern People's Congress and became president of the senate.

When Nigeria became independent in 1960 Azikiwe was named governor-general, and three years later he became president of the new republic. He was deposed following a military coup on Jan. 15, 1966.

L. GRAY COWAN, *Columbia University*

AZILIAN, ȧ-zēl′yȧn, in archaeology, was a Stone Age culture transitional between the Paleolithic and the Neolithic. The Azilians were food gatherers and lived principally in caves or on small islands. Their stone implements tended to be smaller than those of their Magdalenian predecessors, and their cave drawings were more abstract. A typical Azilian development was the flat harpoon of antler horn, hooked on both sides, and used more often in hunting land animals than in fishing.

The Azilian culture takes its name from the Mas d'Azil, a great cave about 40 miles (64 km) southwest of Toulouse in southern France where Azilian artifacts were first discovered.

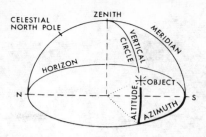

THE AZIMUTH of a celestial object is its angular horizontal distance, measured clockwise, from due south.

AZIMUTH, az′ə-məth, in astronomy, is a measurement that is used, together with altitude, to indicate the position of an object in the heavens. (The position depends on the location of the observer and the time of observation.) The azimuth of an object is its horizontal distance from true south. The distance is expressed as the angle, measured clockwise, from due south to the point on the horizon directly below the object. The altitude of the object is its angular distance above this point on the horizon. Azimuth and altitude constitute what is known as the horizon system of celestial coordinates.

In navigation and surveying, true north is generally used instead of true south as the reference direction to determine the azimuth of an object. See also HORIZON—*Celestial Horizon*; NAVIGATION—*Celestial Navigation*.

AZO, ä′dzō, Italian jurist. Also known as *Azzo* or (in Latin) *Azolinus Porcius*, he was born in Bologna, Italy. After about 1190, Azo was the leading professor of Roman law at Bologna, where he had studied under Johannes Bassianus, and where he in turn trained many famous jurists.

In Azo's work the medieval exegetic tradition, consisting of glosses on and dogmatic expositions of Justinian's *Corpus Juris Civilis*, reached perhaps its highest point. His *Summa codicis* and *Summa institutionum*, as well as other works, with additions by later jurists, served as standard texts of Roman law in Italy and elsewhere for centuries.

AZO DYES, ā′zō dīz, are a class of dyestuffs that have one or more azo groups (—N═N—) in the dye molecule. They have no analogues in natural coloring matter. Azo dyes are the most important group of dyestuffs; they account for about 31 percent of all dyes produced in the United States. Anthraquinone dyes account for about 27 percent of the total; the rest is divided among many smaller classes of dyes.

History. In England, Peter Griess discovered the diazotization process in 1860. In this process, aromatic amines are changed to diazonium salts. In 1864 he discovered the coupling process, which is the coupling of the diazonium salts with phenols and amines. The German dyestuff industry, which was just starting, was slow to recognize the great significance of Griess' discovery. In 1870, Friedrich Kekulé coupled diazotized aniline with phenol, making the first hydroxyazo dye. He also determined the structure of this azo dye. Thereafter the German dyestuff industry advanced quickly. The simplicity and versatility of the diazotization and coupling reactions resulted in the preparation of many new and important azo dyes. The German Heinrich Caro made Chrysoidine (1875), Z. Roussin made Orange II and Orange IV (1876), and Griess

THE AZORES ISLANDS are so hilly that many farms, like these on Santa Maria, must be terraced.

TOM HOLLYMAN, FROM PHOTO RESEARCHERS

made a number of dyes from diazotized sulfanilic acid. The Fast Yellows, the Ponceaus, and many more azo dyes were developed later.

Manufacture. All azo dyes are manufactured by the same basic two-step process. First, an aromatic amine, such as aniline, toluidine, or naphthylamine, is diazotized. Second, the resulting solution of the diazonium salt is coupled with a phenol or a naphthol or an aromatic amine to form the azo dye. In a typical diazotization, aniline is dissolved in water containing hydrochloric acid. The aniline hydrochloride solution is cooled to about 32° to 41° F (0° to 5° C) with ice, and an aqueous solution of sodium nitrite is added. The formation of the diazonium salt is instantaneous:

$$ArNH_2 + NaNO_2 + 2\ HCl \rightarrow ArN\equiv$$
$$NCl + NaCl + 2\ H_2O.$$

For a typical coupling reaction, 1 mole of beta-naphthol is dissolved in water containing caustic soda. Then the diazonium salt solution is added, and the yellow dye is formed almost instantaneously by coupling:

$$ArN\equiv NCl + C_{10}H_7ONa \rightarrow ArN\equiv$$
$$NC_{10}H_7OH + NaCl.$$

The azo dyes are highly versatile because they can be tailored to meet a large range of requirements. For instance, the chemist can make an azo dyestuff that will dye wool and silk, that is soluble in water, and that is insoluble in non-polar organic solvents simply by adding a sulfo group to the dyestuff molecule. He also can make a water-insoluble product (a pigment) by precipitating the aqueous solution of an azo dye with a reagent such as barium chloride.

Names for Azo Dyes. The *Colour Index*, the "bible" of all dyestuff chemists, manufacturers, and users, lists all commercial dyestuffs. It has brought order from chaos by allocating one C.I. number to all chemically identical dyes. Before its publication, dye nomenclature was confusing because companies used different trade names.

CURT BAMBERGER, *Patent Chems, Inc.*

AZORES, ā′zôrz, an archipelago in the Atlantic Ocean belonging to Portugal. It is located between latitudes 36° 56′ and 39° 43′ N and longitudes 24° 46′ and 31° 16′ W. The archipelago consists of nine small islands and the Formigas rocks, arranged in three distinct groups spaced widely across 390 miles (628 km) of ocean. The total area of the archipelago is 893 square miles (2,314 sq km).

Of the three groups, the southeastern portion, comprising São Miguel and Santa Maria, lies about 870 miles (1,400 km) west of Lisbon. The central group consists of Terceira, Graciosa, São Jorge, Pico, and Faial. The northwestern group includes Flores and Corvo, each about 2,300 miles (3,701 km) from New York City. The total population of the three island groups in 1960 was 327,480.

The Azores are divided into three political districts, which do not coincide with the islands' natural groupings. The districts send representatives to the Corporative Chamber at Lisbon. Each district is named after its capital, which, in each case, is also its chief seaport. The capitals, with their own and the district populations (1960), are: Ponta Delgada (city, 22,316; district, 181,924) on São Miguel; Angra do Heroísmo (city, 13,502; district, 96,174), on Terceira; and Horta (city, 7,109; district, 49,382), on the island of Faial.

Most of the inhabitants are Roman Catholics. Since 1534 the Azores have been a diocese of the archbishopric of Lisbon, with its seat at Angra. Most of the people are Portuguese. There are also some residents of Flemish and Breton stock.

Physical Features and Climate. Geologically the islands are typical volcanic formations, composed of basalts and trachytes. Volcanic outbursts and earthquakes have occurred at intervals since the archipelago was colonized, except on Santa Maria, Graciosa, Corvo, and Flores, which have remained practically undisturbed. On most of the islands the dying effects of recent vulcanism are seen in the hot springs and fumaroles. At times undersea eruptions off some of the larger eastern islands have built-up conical islets that are soon destroyed by waves.

The islands differ from one another in the details of their landforms. Pico consists mainly of the lofty 7,613-foot (2,320-meter) cone, after which it is named. São Jorge is a spear-shaped ridge and Corvo a vast crater. São Miguel, by far the largest and most populous island, is a tripartite structure with a tremendous crater on the west joined by a central hilly region to a high sharp ridge on the east. Santa Maria, different in its geology from the others, lacks cones and crater lakes, although it does have extensive calcareous deposits.

Climatically the Azores are warm, moist, and equable. In winter, strong westerly and southerly winds are common and bring rain on an average about one day in two. In summer the Azorean high-pressure area affects the islands more frequently; northerly and easterly winds become common, and normally rain falls about one day in four. The total annual rainfall decreases eastward from about 60 inches (152 cm) on Flores to 30 inches (76 cm) on Santa Maria. At sea level the mean monthly temperatures range from 57° F (14° C) in February to 72° F (22° C) in August. Maximum temperatures rarely exceed 84° F (29° C).

Economy. The islanders depend mainly on farming and fishing for their livelihood. The moist fertile soils yield abundantly, and subtropical and temperate crops flourish. Near sea level the numerous crops include pineapples, bananas, oranges, wine grapes, tobacco, and tea. From elevations of 1,600 to 3,000 feet (500 to 900 meters), cereal crops and pastures prevail, with luxuriant tree growth on a few islands. Above 3,000 feet, shrubs (including bay laurel and arborescent heath) are dominant. Only in Pico Island does the terrain exceed 3,700 feet (1,130 meters) in height. The most valuable marine products are tunny and the cachalot, or sperm whale. Canned tunny and whale oil, together with pineapples, butter, and cheese, are leading exports.

International communications provide some employment. Horta is the hub of transatlantic submarine cables, as well as an important radio center. The airport on Santa Maria serves numerous transatlantic commercial lines, while the extensive military airfield at Lajes on Terceira is the main Atlantic airbase for the North Atlantic Treaty Organization.

History. The Azores were probably known in the 14th century, but their effective discovery was due to Prince Henry the Navigator, of Portugal, who sent Gonçalo Velho Cabral in search of them. Velho found the Formigas in 1431 and reached and named Santa Maria in 1432. São Miguel was probably seen soon afterward, and by 1439 the central group, including Terceira (so named because it was the third to be seen) had been visited. The western group was reached by 1452. The first colonists were Portuguese, but between 1450 and 1466 many Flemish colonists arrived and, later, smaller numbers of Bretons and Moors. On Feb. 18, 1493, Santa Maria was Christopher Columbus' first stop on his return voyage from the West Indies. Vasco da Gama, when returning from India in 1499, landed at Terceira, where his brother died.

From 1580 to 1640 the Azores were under Spanish control. As the rendezvous of convoys from Latin America, they attracted raids by Elizabethan sea captains, including Sir Richard Grenville, of the *Revenge*, who was mortally wounded in a battle against a Spanish fleet off Flores in 1591.

The first airplane to cross the Atlantic, a U.S. Navy NC-4, landed at Horta on May 17, 1919, proceeding to Ponta Delgada on May 20 and to Lisbon on May 27. The civilian airport on Santa Maria and the military airfield on Terceira were established during World War II.

ROBERT P. BECKINSALE, *Oxford University*

Further Reading: Bryans, R., *The Azores* (London 1963); Dervenn, Claude, *The Azores* (London 1956).

AZORÍN. See MARTÍNEZ RUIZ, JOSÉ.

AZOV, ə-zôf', a city in the USSR, is in Rostov oblast, in the southern part of the Russian republic, 16 miles (26 km) southwest of Rostov-on-Don, with which it is connected by rail. A fishing port and minor industrial center, Azov is situated on the southernmost arm of the Don River delta.

The city was built near the site of the ancient Greek colony of Tanaïs (3d century B.C.) and is one of the oldest towns of the lower Don Valley. In the 10th century it was part of Kievan Russia. It was taken by the Turks in 1471, changed hands twice in the Russo-Turkish wars under Peter the Great (reigned 1682–1725), and was annexed by Russia in 1739. The annexation was confirmed by the Treaty of Kuchuk Kainarji in 1774. Population: (1959) 39,931.

THEODORE SHABAD
Author, "Geography of the USSR"

AZOV, Sea of, ə-zôf', an arm of the Black Sea, lying between the Crimean Peninsula, the east Ukrainian coast, and the north Caucasus. In Roman times it was known by the Latin name of *Palus Maeotis*. It is connected with the Black Sea by Kerch Strait. The Sea of Azov is about 210 miles (338 km) long and 85 miles (137 km) wide and has an area of 14,520 square miles (37,606 sq km). The sea narrows in its eastern part to form the Gulf of Taganrog, which receives the Don River. In the western part, the Arabat Tongue, a 70-mile- (113-km-) long peninsula, separates the Azov Sea from the Sivash (Putrid Sea), a 1,000-square mile (2,590-sq km) salty backwater along the northeast coast of the Crimea. The Sea of Azov is shallow and flat-bottomed, with a maximum depth of about 45 feet (14 meters); its water, constantly replenished by the Don and Kuban rivers, is almost fresh. The coastal waters are frozen from the end of December until the end of February. A counterclockwise current, impelled by the prevailing winds, parallels the coasts.

The sea is rich in fish, the principal food fish being anchovies, pike, perch, bream, carp, sturgeon, salmon, and herring. The principal ports on the sea are Rostov-on-Don, Zhdanov, Taganrog, Azov, Berdyansk, and Kerch. The chief shipping route is the one connecting Kerch and Zhdanov, used mostly for carrying Kerch iron ore to the Zhdanov steel plants. Other commodities shipped on the sea include coal from the Donets Basin, salt, fish, and grain.

THEODORE SHABAD
Author, "Geography of the USSR"

AZPEITIA, äth-pā'tyä, a town in the Basque region of Spain, is in Guipúzcoa province, 16 miles (26 km) southwest of San Sebastián. Marble, jasper, and limestone are quarried in the area. Manufactures include furniture, chocolate, and flour.

Near Azpeitia is the famous convent of St. Ignatius Loyola, started in the late 17th century. It includes a tower that marks his reputed birthplace. Population: (1960) 8,219.

AZTEC RUINS NATIONAL MONUMENT, az'-tek, is situated in the valley of the Animas River above its junction with the San Juan, close by the village of Aztec, in northwestern New Mexico. It was established in 1923 on land given by the American Museum of Natural History, which had conducted excavations, to preserve a group of prehistoric pueblos. The name "Aztec," however, is a misnomer. The pueblos, which are built chiefly on sandstone, were erected by an Indian people who irrigated their lands from the river. The largest pueblo, built about 1100 A.D. of masonry and wood, was three stories high and contained about 500 rooms. Much of the structure, covering 4.6 acres, is intact. A kiva room once used for ceremonials has been restored, and there is a museum containing jewelry, weapons, and implements of stone, wood, and bone excavated from the site.

THE PYRAMID OF TENAYUCA, near Mexico City, is an outstanding example of 12th century Aztec architecture. Its starkly severe units, rising one above the other, resulted from successive additions at 52-year intervals.

AZTECS, az′teks, one of the Indian tribes that invaded the Valley of Mexico during the 13th century A.D. The name *Azteca* is derived from Aztlán (Place of the Herons), the original, perhaps mythical, home of the tribe. The chronicles locate this place vaguely somewhere to the northwest of the Valley of Mexico. Chicomoztoc (Seven Caves) is another name for the Aztecs' place of origin. Before their arrival in the valley they discarded the name *Azteca* and substituted *Mexica,* supposedly at the inspiration of their tribal god, Huitzilopochtli. In the 16th century chronicles they are commonly referred to as Mexica, but in modern literature—especially in English—the term Aztecs is generally used.

Some archaeologists, however, prefer to call these people Mexica. When referring to Aztec culture, it is common to enlarge the frame of reference of the term to include closely related peoples of central Mexico at the time of the Spanish conquest. The speech of the Aztecs was Nahuatl, still spoken in central Mexico (see MEXICO—*The Indian Groups*). It belongs to the Uto-Aztecán linguistic stock, which includes languages once spoken over large areas from Oregon, Idaho, and Wyoming south to Nicaragua.

History. At first, after their arrival in the valley, the Aztecs settled in its northwestern section, in the region of the lakes of Zumpango and Xaltocán. There, for the first time, they made *chinampas,* artificial islands often called "floating gardens," built up in shallow water and intensively cultivated. It is probable that this horticultural technique, though new to the immigrant Mexica, was long known in the valley.

Later, the Aztecs moved to the Hill of Chapultepec, which they fortified with stone walls and where tradition records the establishment of a kingship, the first king being Huitzilihuitl, the elder. Then Culhuacán, at that time the leading city-state in the valley, and its allies attacked the Aztecs, inflicting a crushing defeat on them. Their king was taken as a prisoner to Culhuacán and sacrificed, and the tribe was confined to Tizapán, in the southern section of the valley.

Finally, they settled on an island in the western part of Lake Texcoco, where two sections of the tribe founded the twin towns of Mexico-Tenochtitlán and Mexico-Tlatelolco, from which are derived the tribal names *Tenochca* and *Tlatelolca.* The date traditionally accepted by most historians for the founding of Tenochtitlán is 1325, although various sources give dates ranging from 1194 (certainly much too early) to 1366. The dates for Tlatelolco range from 1325 to 1338. Research in the 1940's on the correlation between the several Indian calendars and our own led to discoveries that corrected these dates and indicated that 1345, 1349, or sometime between 1368 and 1371 are the most probable dates for the founding of both Tenochtitlán and Tlatelolco. Culhuacán gave Tenochtitlán its first king, Acamapichtli. The first king of Tlatelolco, Cuacuauhpitzahuac, was a son of the king of Azcapotzalco. The traditional date for the beginning of these reigns is 1375.

Until 1428 the Tenochca and Tlatelolca were vassals of Azcapotzalco, which from 1347 to 1428 held the political hegemony of the valley and was extending its dominion through wars of conquest in which the Mexica, as vassals, helped. In 1428, Chimalpopoca, king of Tenochtitlán, and Tlacateotl, king of Tlatelolco, were executed by order of the king of Azcapotzalco. Their killing was part of a series of executions of vassal lords suspected of disloyalty. However, a rebellion broke out in the same year. Its leaders were Itzcoatl, successor to Chimalpopoca, and Nezahualcoyotl, legitimate heir to the kingdom of Texcoco, whose father was one of the murdered vassal kings. The rebels had the help of the Tlaxcaltec. The war began with the storming of Azcapotzalco (1428) and ended with the enthroning of Nezahualcoyotl at Texcoco (1431). To fill the political vacuum left by the destruction of the power of Azcapotzalco, a triple alliance of Tenochtitlán, Texcoco, and Tlacopán was established. The people of Tlacopán and Azcapotzalco belonged to the same tribe, the Tepanec, but Tlacopán was included in the confederacy, probably for reasons of maintaining the balance of power between the victors. At first, the alliance was an instrument for the political consolidation of the valley, later for imperial expansion. The Tenochca became the

RELICS OF AZTEC CULTURE in the National Museum, Mexico City. The sculpture (*left*) is of a warrior wearing an eagle headdress. The Calendar Stone (*right*) dates from the 15th century. Carved of basalt rock, it is 12 feet in diameter and weighs about 20 tons. The face at the center represents the sun, and the figures within the concentric circles show details of Aztec history.

dominant power of the confederacy and were able to build an empire in central and southern Mexico that, by 1519, covered about 75,000 square miles (194,000 square kilometers) and had a population of 5 to 6 million people (see MEXICO—*Prehistory and Pre-Hispanic History*).

Relations between Tenochtitlán and Tlatelolco, which appear to have been strained from the start, came to a crisis in 1473. Axayacatl, king of Tenochtitlán, stormed the rival city and the Tlatelolcan king, Moquiuix, was killed or committed suicide. From this time on, Tlatelolco was administered through *cuauhtlahtoque,* governors under the control of Tenochtitlán.

In 1519, Hernán Cortés arrived. In 1521 the twin cities were stormed by the Spaniards and their Indian allies, the Aztecs making their last resistance in Tlatelolco. Subsequently, the conquistadores founded Mexico City on the debris of the twin cities.

Culture and Social Organization. When the primitive Aztecs first appeared in history, they were already undergoing a process of acculturation— that is, adaptation to the ways of life of the civilized peoples of central Mexico. We know much of the subsequent development of that culture, after the establishment of their twin city-states, Tenochtitlán and Tlatelolco. By the time of the Spanish conquest, these had become large urban communities. The first as a political center and the second as a commercial center concentrated, through tribute and trade respectively, the surpluses produced in large areas of central and southern Mexico. The size of the cities, their temples, palaces, and markets, and the causeways linking the island, on which the cities were situated, to the mainland excited the admiration of the Spaniards. Their joint urban population was probably between 50,000 and 75,000. Some estimates make it as high as 300,-000, certainly too high considering the extent of the urbanized area. A large part of the population were nobility and its retinue, the priesthood, merchants, and specialist craftsmen. It seems that the major part of the food supply for the urban population came from exterior sources, supplemented by the products of the garden plots and of the *chinampas* surrounding the island and by fishing.

Technologically, at the time of the conquest, the Aztecs, as all the other peoples in central Mexico, were in transition from the Neolithic to a metal stage, using mainly chipped and polished stone tools but also some metal (copper or bronze, and gold) for craftsmen's tools and for ornaments. Society was stratified, with an upper class composed of nobility and merchants; the lower classes were plebeians, *mayeques,* and slaves. The nobility had privately owned estates. The plebeians had communal lands owned by the *calpulli,* or clan, and allotted to individual members of the clan. The *mayeques* worked the estates of the nobility and had a position similar to serfs, being transferred with the land. Kingship was, in theory, elective among the members of the royal family. In practice, it seems to have been hereditary, with the succession from brother to brother in a generation and then to the sons of the eldest brother in like manner.

The major pyramids of Tenochtitlán and Tlatelolco had two sanctuaries each, one for Huitzilopochtli and the other for Tlaloc, the rain god. Human sacrifices were made to the gods, especially Huitzilopochtli, who besides being the tribal god was the war god and identified with the sun. In major ceremonies, thousands of war prisoners are said to have been sacrificed. The flesh of the sacrificed was eaten for religious motives, symbolizing form of communion with the deities.

PEDRO ARMILLAS, *Southern Illinois University*

Bibliography

Caso, Alfonso, *The Aztecs, People of the Sun* (Norman, Okla., 1959).
Duran, Diego, *Aztecs* (New York 1964).
León-Portilla, Miguel, *Aztec Thought and Culture* (Norman, Okla., 1963).
León-Portilla, Miguel, ed., *The Broken Spears; the Aztec Account of the Conquest of Mexico* (Boston 1962).
Soustelle, Jacques, *Daily Life Among the Aztecs* (New York 1962).
Vaillant, George C., *Aztecs of Mexico* (Garden City, N.Y., 1961).

AZUELA, ä-swā′lä, **Mariano** (1873–1952), Mexican novelist, whose work presents a powerful picture of the Mexican Revolution. He was born at Lagos de Moreno, in Jalisco state, on Jan. 1, 1873. After studying medicine in Guadalajara, he entered medical practice in Lagos in 1899, and in 1911 became mayor of the town. Meanwhile he had written several short stories and the novels *María Luisa* (1907), *Los fracasados* (1908), *Mala Yerba* (1909), and *Sin amor* (1912). After serving as director of public education of Jalisco (1914–1915), he joined the forces of Francisco (Pancho) Villa as a surgeon in 1915. After Villa's defeat, Azuela had to take refuge in El Paso, Texas, where he published his most successful work, *Los de abajo* (1915). This novel, translated into English as *The Underdogs* (1929), with illustrations by José Clemente Orozco, provides a vivid picture of the brutal, blind forces of the Mexican Revolution. Azuela later returned to Mexico City, where he pursued his medical practice and continued writing. He received the National Literary Prize in 1950. He died in Mexico City on March 1, 1952.

Besides *Los de abajo*, two other Azuela novels, *Los caciques* (1917) and *Las moscas* (1918), are based on the revolution. *La malhora* (1923), *El desquite* (1925), and *La luciérnaga* (1931) are novelettes depicting low life in the national capital. *Pedro Moreno* (1935) and *Pre-*

cursores (1935) are fictionalized biographies. Later novels, dealing with problems arising from the new social and political order of Mexico, include *El camarada Pantoja* (1937), *San Gabriel de Valdivias* (1938), *Regina Landa* (1939), *Avanzada* (1940), *La nueva burguesía* (1941), and *La marchanta* (1944).

AZURITE, azh′ə-rīt, is a common ore of copper. As its name implies, the mineral is a beautiful azure or Prussian blue. In the past it was used as a pigment in paints. The sharp crystals of azurite are transparent to translucent and have a brilliant glassy luster. They are often used in making jewelry. Larger crystals of azurite are darker in color and may appear nearly black.

Azurite occurs near the surface of copper deposits. It is almost always associated with the more abundant malachite (another copper carbonate mineral with a bright green color) and may alter to form that substance. For this reason azurite is sometimes referred to as *blue malachite*.

Azurite and malachite are occasionally found in stalactite form, with one mineral encircling the other. These stalactites may be cut and polished in cross sections and used ornamentally. The finest specimens of this sort come from Morenci, Ariz., which has also yielded very fine individual crystals of azurite. Good crystals have also been found in Bisbee, Ariz., in Siberia, and in Chessy, France. Because of the latter location, which has been famous for many years, azurite is often called *chessylite* in Europe and England. Large deposits of azurite occur in the copper mines of the western portion of the United States.

Composition: $Cu_3(CO_3)_2(OH)_2$; hardness, 3.5 to 4.0; specific gravity, 3.8; crystal system, monoclinic.

AZUSA, ə-zoo′sə, is a city in California, in Los Angeles County, 18 miles (29 km) northeast of Los Angeles and 2 miles (3.2 km) south of the entrance to San Gabriel Canyon. Formerly a shipping point for citrus fruits and avocados, it now manufactures chemicals, fabricated steel, rocket motors, bicycles, lawn mowers, and pipe casings. Its educational facilities include Azusa-Pacific College, a four-year liberal arts college and interdenominational school of religion, and nearby Citrus Junior College.

Azusa was founded by J.S. Slauson in 1887 during the real estate boom that swept southern California. Its name, taken from an Indian name for a hill just to the east, has been popularized as standing for "everything from A to Z in the USA." Azusa was incorporated in 1898. It has a city administrator-mayor-council form of government. Population: 25,217.